P9-ECY-089

Baptised – 26th Nov., 1966.

YOUR SECRET CHAIN REFERENCE INDEX

Subject	Code	First Text
The Scriptures	Sc	Luke 24:27
Prophecy of the Next World Empire	Pr	2 Pet 1:16-19
Second Coming of Christ	SCC	Heb 9:28
Signs of Christ's Coming	Sign	Luke 21:25-28
God's Plan to Save You from Sin	Save	1 Cor 1:18
Justification by Faith	Just	Rom 1:16,17
Bible Sanctification	San	Col 1:26,27
Home of the Saved	Hvn	2 Cor 12:1-4
Millennium	Mil	Rev 20:1-6
God's Rest	Sab	Gen 2:1-3
The Two Laws	TL	Exodus 20:3-17
The Origin of Evil	Evil	Luke 10:18
Ministry of Angels	Ang	Rev 5:11
Evil Angels	EA	Eph 6:12
Spiritualism	Sptsm	Lev 19:31
Truth about Death	Dth	1 Tim 1:17
What & Where is Hell	Hell	Job 30:23
God's Ownership	Tth	Ps 24:1
Bible Baptism	Bap	Eph 4:4-6
Nature of Christ	JW	Matt 3:3
Mysterious Little Horn	LH	Dan 7:1-7
Investigative Judgement	Jmnt	Rom 14:10
Seal of God and Mark of the Beast	S.M	Rev 14:6-20
The Body Temple	Body	3 Jn 2
The New Commandment	NC	John 14:15
The Sanctuary	Snty	Rom 15:4
Prophecy of 2300 Years	Dan	8:1-27
Church Unity	Unty	John 17:20,21
The Unpardonable Sin	Unsin	Matt 12:31,32

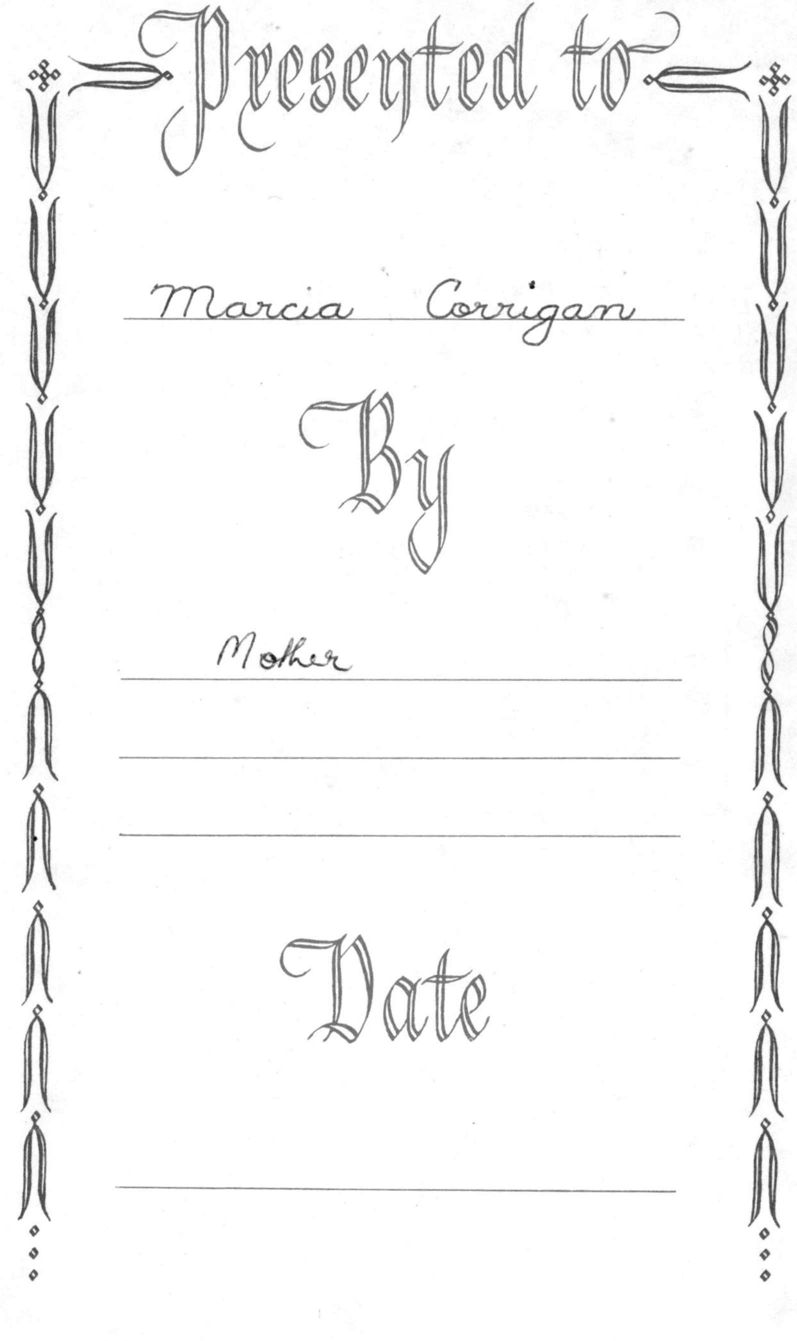
Presented to
Marcia Corrigan
By
Mother
Date

9 Steps to Hearing the Voice of God

Romans 3:23

Acts 2:36-38

Romans 10:9

1 Cor 7:23, 24

Eph 1:7

John 3:5,7

John 1:12-13

Matt 6:6

John 5:39

"If any man hear my voice, I will come into him"

Family Register

Parents' Names

Husband William Denis Brian Corrigan

Born 8th November, 1926

Wife Betty May Corrigan

Born 9th August, 1929

Married 10th April, 1950

Seventh Day Adventist

Church,

Bundaberg.

by

Pastor Potter

Births

Marcia Ruth Corrigan

Kenneth Ronald Corrigan

Annette Gaye Corrigan

Marriages

Deaths

Rebecca Corrigan

THE

HOLY BIBLE

CONTAINING

THE OLD AND NEW TESTAMENTS

*Translated out of the original tongues
and with the former translations
diligently compared and revised*

BY HIS MAJESTY'S SPECIAL COMMAND

Appointed to be read in Churches

*Authorized
King James Version*

Printed by Authority

LONDON AND NEW YORK
COLLINS' CLEAR-TYPE PRESS
GLASGOW . TORONTO . SYDNEY . AUCKLAND

Iona Clear Type Reference

LICENCE

In terms of the Letters Patent granted by Her late Majesty Queen Victoria to Her Printers for Scotland, and of the Instructions issued by Her said Majesty in Council, dated Eleventh July and Twenty-eighth December Eighteen Hundred and Thirty-nine, I hereby License and Authorise William Collins Sons and Company Limited, One Hundred and Forty Four Cathedral Street, Glasgow, to Print and Publish, as by the Authority of Her Majesty Queen Elizabeth the Second, *but so far as regards the Text only*, an Edition of the Holy Bible in Iona Clear Type, Octavo size, as proposed in their Declaration dated the Twentieth day of April Nineteen Hundred and Fifty Nine, the terms and conditions of the said Instructions being always and in all points fully complied with and observed by the said William Collins Sons and Company Limited.

Dated at Edinburgh the 27th day of August
Nineteen Hundred and Fifty Nine

W. R. MILLIGAN,
Lord Advocate.

Printed in Great Britain

TO THE
MOST HIGH AND MIGHTY PRINCE,

JAMES,

BY THE GRACE OF GOD,
KING OF GREAT BRITAIN, FRANCE AND IRELAND,
DEFENDER OF THE FAITH, Etc.

The Translators of the Bible wish Grace, Mercy, and Peace,
through JESUS CHRIST our Lord.

GREAT AND MANIFOLD were the blessings, most dread Sovereign, which Almighty God, the Father of all mercies, bestowed upon us the people of *England*, when first he sent Your Majesty's Royal Person to rule and reign over us. For whereas it was the expectation of many, who wished not well unto our *Sion*, that, upon the setting of that bright *Occidental Star*, Queen *Elizabeth*, of most happy memory, some thick and palpable clouds of darkness would so have overshadowed this land, that men should have been in doubt which way they were to walk, and that it should hardly be known who was to direct the unsettled State; the appearance of Your Majesty, as of the *Sun* in his strength, instantly dispelled those supposed and surmised mists, and gave unto all that were well affected exceeding cause of comfort; especially when we beheld the Government established in Your Highness, and Your hopeful Seed, by an undoubted Title; and this also accompanied with peace and tranquillity at home and abroad.

But among all our joys, there was no one that more filled our hearts than the blessed continuance of the preaching of God's sacred Word among us, which is that inestimable treasure which excelleth all the riches of the earth; because the fruit thereof extendeth itself, not only to the time spent in this transitory world, but directeth and disposeth men unto that eternal happiness which is above in heaven.

Then not to suffer this to fall to the ground, but rather to take it up, and to continue it in that state wherein the famous Predecessor of Your Highness did leave it; nay, to go forward with the confidence and resolution of a Man, in maintaining the truth of Christ, and propagating it far and near, is that which hath so bound and firmly knit the hearts of all Your Majesty's loyal and religious people unto You, that Your very name is precious among them: their eye doth behold You with comfort, and they bless You in their hearts, as that sanctified Person, who, under God, is the immediate Author of their true happiness. And this their contentment doth not diminish or decay, but every day increaseth and taketh strength, when they observe that the zeal of Your Majesty toward the house of God doth not slack or go backward, but is more and more kindled, manifesting itself abroad in the farthest parts of *Christendom*, by writing in defence of the Truth, (which hath given such a blow unto that man of sin as will not be healed,) and every day at home, by religious and learned discourse, by frequenting the house of God, by hearing the Word preached, by cherishing the Teachers thereof, by caring for the Church, as a most tender and loving nursing Father.

There are infinite arguments of this right Christian and religious affection in Your Majesty; but none is more forcible to declare it to others than the vehement and perpetuated desire of accomplishing and publishing of this work, which now, with all humility, we present unto Your Majesty. For when Your Highness had once, out of deep judgment, apprehended how convenient it was, that out of the Original Sacred Tongues, together with comparing of the labours, both in our own and other foreign Languages, of many worthy men who went before us, there should be one more exact Translation of the holy Scriptures into the *English Tongue*; Your Majesty did never desist to urge and to excite those to whom it was commended, that the Work might be hastened, and that the business might be expedited in so decent a manner, as a matter of such importance might justly require.

And now at last, by the mercy of God, and the continuance of our labours, it being brought unto such a conclusion, as that we have great hopes that the Church of *England* shall reap good fruit thereby, we hold it our duty to offer it to Your Majesty, not only as to our King and Sovereign, but as to the principal Mover and Author of the work; humbly craving of Your most Sacred Majesty, that, since things of this quality have ever been subject to the censures of ill-meaning and discontented persons, it may receive approbation and patronage from so learned and judicious a Prince as Your Highness is; whose allowance and acceptance of our labours shall more honour and encourage us, than all the calumniations and hard interpretations of other men shall dismay us. So that if, on the one side, we shall be traduced by Popish Persons at home or abroad, who therefore will malign us, because we are poor instruments to make God's holy Truth to be yet more and more known unto the people, whom they desire still to keep in ignorance and darkness; or, if, on the other side, we shall be maligned by self-conceited Brethren, who run their own ways, and give liking unto nothing but what is framed by themselves, and hammered on their anvil, we may rest secure, supported within by the truth and innocency of a good conscience, having walked the ways of simplicity and integrity, as before the Lord, and sustained without by the powerful protection of Your Majesty's grace and favour, which will ever give countenance to honest and Christian endeavours against bitter censures and uncharitable imputations.

The Lord of heaven and earth bless Your Majesty with many and happy days: that, as his heavenly hand hath enriched Your Highness with many singular and extraordinary graces, so You may be the wonder of the world in this latter age for happiness and true felicity, to the honour of that great God, and the good of his Church, through Jesus Christ our Lord and only Saviour.

THE NAMES OF

THE OLD AND NEW TESTAMENT BOOKS

Arranged in their order with page numbers and number of Chapters

THE BOOKS OF THE OLD TESTAMENT

THE BOOKS OF THE NEW TESTAMENT

THE NAMES OF

THE OLD AND NEW TESTAMENT BOOKS

Alphabetically Arranged

THE BOOKS OF THE OLD TESTAMENT

THE BOOKS OF THE NEW TESTAMENT

TABLE OF SIGNS USED IN THIS BOOK

Every effort has been made that the signs used in this book should be as few and simple as possible.

The words of which the pronunciation is marked are divided into syllables by short hyphens (-). The syllable on which most stress is to be laid in reading is marked (′). In compound names two accents are often introduced. The longer hyphen (–) indicates the division into parts of compound names so far as it is noted in the Authorized Version.

ä *as in* ah, arm, father.
ă ” abet, hat, dilemma.
ā ” tame.
â ” fare.
ạ ” call.
ĕ ” met, her, second.
ē ” mete.
ë = a *in* tame.
ī *as in* fine.
ĭ ” him, fir, plentiful.
î ” machine.
i̧ ” peculiar.
ō ” alone.
ŏ ” on, protect.
ô ” nor.
o̱ ” son.
ū ” tune.
û ” rude.
ŭ ” us.
u̇ ” turner.
ȳ ” lyre.

y̆ *as in* typical, fully.
a͞a = a *of* am.
a᷍a = a *of* fare.
ǣ } *as in* mediæval.
a͞e }
a᷍i ” aisle.
a̲i̲ ” hail.
a͞o = o *of* alone.
a᷍u *as in* maul.
e᷍e ” heed.
e᷍i = i *of* fine.
e᷍u *as in* neuter.
e͞w ” lewd.
o᷍i ” oil.
ç ” celestial.
c̲h̲ ” character.
c͞i ” delicious.
ġ ” giant.
ṡ ” his.
s͞i ” adhesion.
T͞h ” Thomas.
t̄i ” attraction.

H. A. REDPATH, M.A.

HOW TO USE A REFERENCE BIBLE

Between the columns of text on the page of many Bibles there runs a narrow column of explanations and references which are included to help the reader to understand and study the text.

In the narrow reference column two kinds of signs are used. Numbers are used when the original Hebrew or Greek can be translated in some other way, or when some further explanation is required. For instance in Isaiah 40.2 we read:

> Speak ye [1]comfortably to Jerusalem, and cry unto her, that her [2]warfare is accomplished,

Now in the reference column we see beside "1" the words "to the heart," and beside "2" the words "appointed time." That means that the translators wished to tell the reader that this verse could also be translated:

> Speak ye to the heart of Jerusalem, and cry unto her, that her appointed time is accomplished,

Sometimes these numbers stand before a word which required some explanation. In John 19.13 we read:

> When Pilate therefore heard that saying, he brought Jesus forth, and sat down in the judgement seat in a place that is called the Pavement, but in the Hebrew [1]Gabbatha.

In the reference column beside "1," we find the explanation, "That is, elevated." That means that the English equivalent of this Hebrew word "Gabbatha" is "elevated." The translators wished to keep the word "Gabbatha" in their translation but they also wished the reader to know what the word means in English.

Letters are used to introduce references to parallel passages in the Bible. In Acts 2.24 we read:

> Whom [s]God hath raised up.

We turn to the reference column and against the letter "s" we find eleven references to other passages of scripture. These passages are all passages in which reference is made to the Resurrection of Jesus. If we look them up and read them we will find an outline of what the New Testament has to say about the Resurrection of Jesus.

There are two specially interesting uses of these letters. First, when the Old Testament is quoted in the New Testament, there is a letter against the quotation, and in the reference column the Old Testament quotation is identified. For instance, in Luke 20.17 we read:

> And he beheld them, and said, What is this then that is written, The [l]stone which the builders rejected, the same is become the head of the corner?

We turn to the reference column and against the letter "l" we find the scripture reference Psalm 118.22. That tells us where the quotation comes from.

Secondly, the Gospels often tell the same story, each in its own way. We turn to John 6.5-14 which tells of the Feeding of the Five Thousand. Verse 5 reads thus:

> When [c]Jesus then lifted up *his* eyes, and saw a great company come unto him, he saith unto Philip, Whence shall we buy bread, that these may eat?

We turn to the reference column and against the letter "c" we find three references cited—Matthew 14.14: Mark 6.35: Luke 9.12. These are the passages in which the other Gospels tell the same story, and it is often of the greatest interest and value to read the different accounts in the other Gospels of the same incident.

THE FIRST BOOK OF MOSES, CALLED

GENESIS

CHAPTER 1

IN [a]the beginning [b]God created the
heaven and the earth.
2 And the earth was [c]without form,
and void; and darkness *was* upon the
face of the deep. [d]And the Spirit of God
moved upon the face of the waters.
3 [e]And God said, Let there be light:
and there was light.
4 And God saw the light, that *it was*
good: and God divided [1]the light from
the darkness.
5 And God called the light [f]Day, and
the darkness he called Night. [2]And the
evening and the morning were the first
day.
6 ¶ And God said, [g]Let there be a
[3]firmament in the midst of the waters,
and let it divide the waters from the
waters.
7 And God made the firmament, and
divided the waters which *were* under
the firmament from the waters which
were above the firmament: and it was
so.
8 And God called the firmament
Heaven. And the evening and the
morning were the second day.
9 ¶ And God said, [h]Let the waters
under the heaven be gathered together
unto one place, and let the dry *land*
appear: and it was so.
10 And God called the dry *land*
Earth; and the gathering together of
the waters called he Seas: and God
saw that *it was* good.
11 And God said, [i]Let the earth bring
forth [4]grass, the herb yielding seed,
and the fruit tree yielding fruit [j]after
his kind, whose seed *is* in itself, upon
the earth: and it was so.
12 And the earth brought forth grass,
and herb yielding seed after his kind,
and the tree yielding fruit, whose seed
was in itself, after his kind: and God
saw that *it was* good.
13 And the evening and the morning
were the third day.
14 ¶ And God said, [k]Let there be
lights in the firmament of the heaven
to divide [5]the day from the night; and
let them be for signs, and for seasons,
and for days, and years:
15 And let them be for lights in the
firmament of the heaven to give light
upon the earth: and it was so.
16 And God made two great lights;
the greater light [6]to rule the day, and
the lesser light to rule the night: *he
made* the stars also.
17 And God [l]set them in the firmament of the heaven to give light upon
the earth,
18 And to rule over the day and over
the night, and to divide the light from
the darkness: and God saw that *it was*
good.
19 And the evening and the morning
were the fourth day.
20 And God said, [m]Let the waters
bring forth abundantly the [7]moving
creature that hath [8]life, and [9]fowl *that*
may fly above the earth in the [10]open
firmament of heaven.
21 And God created great whales,
and every living creature that moveth,
which the waters brought forth abundantly, after their kind, and every
winged fowl after his kind: and God
saw that *it was* good.
22 And God blessed them, saying,
Be fruitful, and multiply, and fill the
waters in the seas, and let fowl multiply in the earth.
23 And the evening and the morning
were the fifth day.
24 ¶ And God said, [n]Let the earth
bring forth the living creature after his
kind, cattle, and creeping thing, and
beast of the earth after his kind: and
it was so.
25 And God made the beast of the
earth after his kind, and cattle after
their kind, and every thing that creepeth upon the earth after his kind: and
God saw that *it was* good.
26 ¶ And God said, [o]Let us make
man [p]in our image, after our likeness:
and let them have [q]dominion over the
fish of the sea, and over the fowl of the
air, and over the cattle, and over all
the earth, and over every creeping
thing that creepeth upon the earth.
27 So God created man in his *own*
image, in the [r]image of God created
he him; [s]male and female created he
them.
28 And [t]God blessed them, and God

CHAP. 1

a John 1.1,3. Heb. 1.10.
b Job 38.4. Isa. 44.24. Rom. 1.20. Col. 1.16. Heb. 11.3. Rev. 4.11.
c Jer. 4.23.
d Isa. 40.12.
e Ps. 33.9.
1 between the light and between the darkness.
f Ps. 74.16.
2 And the evening was, and the morning was.
g Job 37.18. Ps. 33.6. Ps. 136.5. Jer. 10.12.
3 expansion.
h Job 26.10. Job 38.8. Ps. 33.7. Ps. 95.5.
i Heb. 6.7.
4 tender grass.
j Luke 6.44.
k Deut. 4.19. Job 25.3,5. Ps. 74.16. Ps. 136.7.
5 between the day and between the night.
6 for the rule of the day, etc.
l Ps. 8.1.
m Ps. 104.24.
7 Or, creeping.
8 soul.
9 let fowl fly.
10 face of the firmament of heaven.
n Ps. 104.18-23.
o Ps. 100.3.
p Eph. 4.24. James 3.9.
q Ps. 8.6.
r 1 Cor. 11.7. Eph. 4.24. Col. 3.10.
s Mal. 2.15. Matt. 19.4. Mark 10.6.
t Ps. 127.3. 1 Tim. 4.3.

said unto them, Be [u]fruitful, and multiply, and replenish the earth, and subdue it: and have dominion over the fish of the sea, and over the fowl of the air, and over every living thing that [11]moveth upon the earth.

29 ¶ And God said, Behold, I have given you every herb [12] bearing seed, which *is* upon the face of all the earth, and every tree, in the which *is* the fruit of a tree yielding seed; [v]to you it shall be for meat.

30 And [w]to every beast of the earth, and [x]to every fowl of the air, and to every thing that creepeth upon the earth, wherein *there is* life, *I have given* every green herb for meat: and it was so.

31 And [y]God saw every thing that he had made, and, behold, *it was* very good. And the evening and the morning were the sixth day.

CHAPTER 2

THUS the heavens and the earth were finished, and all the host of them.

2 And [a]on the seventh day God ended his work which he had made; and he rested on the seventh day from all his work which he had made.

3 And God [b]blessed the seventh day, and sanctified it: because that in it he had rested from all his work which God [1]created and made.

4 ¶ These *are* the generations of the heavens and of the earth when they were created, in the day that the LORD God made the earth and the heavens,

5 And [c]every plant of the field before it was in the earth, and every herb of the field before it grew: for the [d]LORD God had not caused it to rain upon the earth, and *there was* not a man to till the ground.

6 But [2]there went up a mist from the earth, and watered the whole face of the ground.

7 And the LORD God formed man [3]*of* the dust of the ground, and breathed into his nostrils the breath of life; and man became a living soul.

8 ¶ And the LORD God planted a [e]garden eastward in Eden; and there he put the man whom he had formed.

9 And out of the ground made the LORD God to [f]grow every tree that is pleasant to the sight, and good for food; [g]the tree of life also in the midst of the garden, and the tree of knowledge of good and evil.

10 And [h]a river went out of Eden to water the garden; and from thence it was parted, and became into four heads.

11 The name of the first *is* Pī-sŏn: that *is* it which compasseth the whole land of [i]Hăv-ĭ-läh, where *there is* gold;

12 And the gold of that land *is* good: there *is* bdellium and the onyx stone.

13 And the name of the second river *is* Gī-hŏn: the same *is* it that compasseth the whole land of [4]Ē-thĭ-ō-pĭ-ă.

14 And the name of the third river *is* [j]Hĭd-dĕ-kĕl: that *is* it which goeth [5]toward the east of Assyria. And the fourth river *is* Eû-phrā-tēs.

15 And the LORD God took [6]the man, and put him into the garden of Eden to dress it and to keep it.

16 And the LORD God commanded the man, saying, Of every tree of the garden [7]thou mayest freely eat:

17 But of the tree of the knowledge of good and evil, thou shalt not eat of it: for in the day that thou eatest thereof [8]thou shalt surely die.

18 ¶ And the LORD God said, *It is* not good that the man should be alone; I will make him an help [9]meet for him.

19 And out of the ground the LORD God formed every beast of the field, and every fowl of the air; and [k]brought *them* unto Adam to see what he would call them: and whatsoever [10]Adam called every living creature, that *was* the name thereof.

20 And Adam [11]gave names to all cattle, and to the fowl of the air, and to every beast of the field; but for Adam there was not found an help meet for him.

21 And the LORD God caused a deep [l]sleep to fall upon Adam, and he slept: and he took one of his ribs, and closed up the flesh instead thereof;

22 And the rib, which the LORD God had taken from man, [12] made he a woman, and [m]brought her unto the man.

23 And Adam said, This *is* now bone [n]of my bones, and flesh of my flesh: she shall be called [13]Woman, because she was taken out of [14]Man.

24 Therefore [o]shall a man leave his father and his mother, and shall cleave unto his wife: and [p]they shall be one flesh.

25 And they were both naked, the man and his wife, and were not [q]ashamed.

CHAPTER 3

NOW the serpent was more subtil [a]than any beast of the field which the LORD God had made. And he said unto the woman, Yea, [1]hath

u ch. 9.1,7. Lev. 26.9. Ps. 128.3,4.
11 creepeth.
12 seeding seed.
v Job 36.31. Ps. 104.14, 15. Ps. 136.25. Ps. 146.7. Acts 14.17.
w Ps. 145.15, 16. Ps. 147.9.
x Job 38.41.
y Ps. 104.24. 1 Tim. 4.4.

CHAP. 2

a Ex. 31.17. Heb. 4.4.
b Ex. 16.22-30.
1 created to make.
c Ps. 104.14.
d Ps. 65.9.11.
2 Or, a mist which went up.
3 The dust of, etc.
e ch. 13.10.
f Eze. 31.8.
g ch. 3.22. Rev. 22.2, 14.
h Ps. 46.4.
i ch. 25.18.
4 Cush.
j Dan. 10.4.
5 Or, eastward to Assyria.
6 Or, Adam.
7 eating thou shalt eat.
8 dying thou shalt die.
9 as before him.
k Ps. 8.6.
10 Or, the man.
11 called.
l ch. 15.12.
12 builded.
m Pro. 18.22. Heb. 13.4.
n ch. 29.14. Judg. 9.2. 2 Sam. 5.1. Eph. 5.30.
13 Isha.
14 Ish. 1 Cor. 11.8.
o Ps. 45.10. Matt. 19.5. Mark 10.7. 1 Cor. 6.16.
p Eph. 5.28-31.
q Ex. 32.25. Isa. 47.3.

CHAP. 3

a Matt. 10. 16. Rev. 12.9. Rev. 20.2.
1 because, etc.

God said, Ye shall not eat of every
tree of the garden?
2 And the woman said unto the serpent, We may eat of the fruit of the
trees of the garden:
3 But [b]of the fruit of the tree which *is*
in the midst of the garden, God hath
said, Ye shall not eat of it, neither
shall ye touch it, lest ye die.
4 And the serpent said unto the woman, [c]Ye shall not surely die:
5 For God doth know that in the day
ye eat thereof, then your eyes shall be
opened, and ye shall be as gods, knowing good and evil.
6 And when the woman saw that the
tree *was* good for food, and that it *was*
[2]pleasant to the eyes, and a tree to be
desired to make *one* wise, she took of
the fruit thereof, and did eat, and gave
also unto her husband with her; [d]and
he did eat.
7 And the eyes of them both were
opened, and they knew that they *were*
naked; and they sewed fig leaves together, and made themselves [3]aprons.
8 And they heard the voice [e]of the
LORD God walking in the garden in
the [4]cool of the day: and Adam and
his wife [f]hid themselves from the
presence of the LORD God amongst
the trees of the garden.
9 And the LORD God called unto
Adam, and said unto him, [g]Where *art*
thou?
10 And he said, I heard thy voice in
the garden, and [h]I was afraid, because
I *was* naked; and I hid myself.
11 And he said, Who told thee that
thou *wast* naked? Hast thou eaten of
the tree, whereof I commanded thee
that thou shouldest not eat?
12 And the man said, [i]The woman
whom thou gavest *to be* with me, she
gave me of the tree, and I did eat.
13 And the LORD God said unto the
woman, What *is* this *that* thou hast
done? And the woman said, The serpent beguiled me, and I did eat.
14 And the LORD God said unto the
serpent, Because thou hast done this,
thou *art* cursed above all cattle, and
above every beast of the field; upon
thy belly shalt thou go, and [j]dust shalt
thou eat all the days of thy life:
15 And I will put [k]enmity between
thee and the woman, and between thy
seed and her seed; it [l]shall bruise thy
head, and thou shalt bruise his heel.
16 Unto the woman he said, I will
greatly multiply thy sorrow and thy
conception; in [m]sorrow thou shalt
bring forth children; and thy desire

b ch. 2.16,17.
c 2 Cor. 11.3. 1 Tim. 2.14.
2 a desire.
d Rom. 5.12-19.
3 Or, things to gird about.
e Job 38.1.
4 wind.
f Job 31.33. Ps. 139.1-12. Jer. 23.34. Amos 9.3.
g ch. 4.9.
h Job 23.15. 1 John 3.20.
i Pro. 28.13. Jas. 1.13.
j Isa. 65.25. Mic. 7.17.
k Num. 21.6, 7.
l Rom. 16.20. Heb. 2.14. 1 John 3.8.
m John 16.21. 1 Tim. 2.15.
5 Or, subject to thy husband.
n Job 5.7. Eccl. 2.23.
6 cause to bud.
o 1 Cor. 15. 21, 22.
7 Chavah, or, living.
p verse 5.
q ch. 2.9.
r ch. 2.8.
s Ps. 104.4. Heb. 1.7.
t John 14.6.

CHAP. 4

1 That is, gotten, or, acquired.
2 Hebel.
3 feeder.
4 at the end of days.
a Ex. 13.12. Ex. 34.19. Lev. 27.26. Num. 18.17. Pro. 3.9.
5 sheep, or, goats.
b Judg. 6.21.
c Heb. 11.4.
6 Or, have the excellency. Heb. 11.4.
7 Or, subject unto thee ch. 3.16.

shall be [5]to thy husband, and he shall
rule over thee.
17 And unto Adam he said, Because
thou hast hearkened unto the voice of
thy wife, and hast eaten of the tree, of
which I commanded thee, saying,
Thou shalt not eat of it: cursed *is* the
ground for thy sake; [n]in sorrow shalt
thou eat *of* it all the days of thy life;
18 Thorns also and thistles shall it
[6]bring forth to thee; and thou shalt
eat the herb of the field;
19 In the sweat of thy face shalt thou
eat bread, till thou return unto the
ground; for out of it wast thou taken:
for dust thou *art*, [o]and unto dust shalt
thou return.
20 And Adam called his wife's name
[7]Eve; because she was the mother of
all living.
21 Unto Adam also and to his wife
did the LORD God make coats of
skins, and clothed them.
22 ¶ And the LORD God said, Behold, [p]the man is become as one of us,
to know good and evil: and now, lest
he put forth his hand, [q]and take also
of the tree of life, and eat, and live for
ever:
23 Therefore the LORD God sent him
forth from the garden of Eden, to till
the ground from whence he was taken.
24 So he drove out the man; and he
placed at the [r]east of the garden of
Eden [s]Chĕr´-ū-bĭms, and a flaming
sword which turned every way, [t]to
keep the way of the tree of life.

CHAPTER 4

AND Adam knew Eve his wife; and
she conceived, and bare [1]Cain,
and said, I have gotten a man from
the LORD.
2 And she again bare his brother
[2]Abel. And Abel was a [3]keeper of
sheep, but Cain was a tiller of the
ground.
3 And [4]in process of time it came to
pass, that Cain brought of the fruit of
the ground an offering unto the LORD.
4 And Abel, he also brought of the
[a]firstlings of his [5]flock and of the fat
thereof. And the LORD had [b]respect
unto Abel and to his offering:
5 But [c]unto Cain and to his offering
he had not respect. And Cain was very
wroth, and his countenance fell.
6 And the LORD said unto Cain, Why
art thou wroth? and why is thy countenance fallen?
7 If thou doest well, shalt thou not
[6]be accepted? and if thou doest not
well, sin lieth at the door. And [7]unto

thee *shall be* his desire, and thou shalt rule over him.

8 And Cain talked with Abel his brother: and it came to pass, when they were in the field, that Cain rose up against Abel his brother, and [d]slew him.

9 ¶ And the LORD said unto Cain, Where *is* Abel thy brother? And he said, I know not: *Am* I my brother's keeper?

10 And he said, What hast thou done? the voice of thy brother's [8]blood [e]crieth unto me from the ground.

11 And now *art* thou [f]cursed from the earth, which hath opened her [g]mouth to receive thy brother's blood from thy hand;

12 When thou tillest the ground, it shall not henceforth yield unto thee her strength; a fugitive and a vagabond shalt thou be in the earth.

13 And Cain said unto the LORD, [9]My punishment *is* greater than I can bear.

14 Behold, thou hast driven me out this day from the face of the earth; and from thy face shall I be hid; and I shall be a fugitive and a vagabond in the earth; and it shall come to pass, *that* every one that findeth me shall slay me.

15 And the LORD said unto him, Therefore whosoever slayeth Cain, vengeance shall be taken on him sevenfold. And the LORD [h]set a mark upon Cain, lest any finding him should kill him.

16 ¶ And Cain went out from the presence [i]of the LORD, and dwelt in the land of Nod, on the east of Eden.

17 And Cain knew his wife; and she conceived, and bare [10]Ē´-nŏch: and he builded a city, and [j]called the name of the city, after the name of his son, Ē´-nŏch.

18 And unto Ē´-nŏch was born Ī´-răd: and Ī´-răd begat Mĕ-hū´-jā-ĕl: and Mĕ-hū´-jā-ĕl begat Mĕ-thū´-sā-ĕl: and Mĕ-thū´-sā-ĕl begat [11]Lā´-mĕch.

19 ¶ And Lā´-mĕch took unto him two wives: the name of the one *was* Ā´-dăh, and the name of the other Zillah.

20 And Ā´-dăh bare Jā´-băl: he was the father of such as dwell in tents, and *of such as have* cattle.

21 And his brother's name *was* Jū´-băl: he was the father of all such as handle the harp and organ.

22 And Zillah, she also bare Tū´-băl–cain, an [12]instructer of every artificer in brass and iron: and the sister of Tū´-băl–cain *was* Nā´-ă-măh.

23 And Lā´-mĕch said unto his wives, Ā´-dăh and Zillah, Hear my voice; ye wives of Lā´-mĕch, hearken unto my speech: for [13]I have slain a man to my wounding, and a young man [14] to my hurt.

24 If Cain shall be avenged sevenfold, truly Lā´-mĕch seventy and sevenfold.

25 ¶ And Adam knew his wife again; and she bare a son, and called his name [15]Seth: For God, *said she*, hath appointed me another seed instead of Abel, whom Cain slew.

26 And to Seth, to him also there was born a son; and he called his name [16]Ē´-nŏs: then began men to [17]call upon the name of the LORD.

CHAPTER 5

THIS *is* [a]the book of the generations of Adam. In the day that God created man, [b]in the likeness of God made he him;

2 Male and female created he them; and blessed them, and called their name Adam, in the day when they were created.

3 ¶ And Adam lived an hundred and thirty years, and begat *a son* in his own likeness, after his image; and called his name Seth:

4 And the days of Adam after he had begotten Seth were eight hundred years: and he begat sons and daughters:

5 And all the days that Adam lived were nine hundred and thirty years: [c]and he died.

6 And Seth lived an hundred and five years and begat Ē´-nŏs:

7 And Seth lived after he begat Ē´-nŏs eight hundred and seven years, and begat sons and daughters:

8 And all the days of Seth were nine hundred and twelve years: and he died.

9 ¶ And Ē´-nŏs lived ninety years, and begat [1]Cā-ī´-năn:

10 And Ē´-nŏs lived after he begat Cā-ī´-năn eight hundred and fifteen years, and begat sons and daughters:

11 And all the days of Ē´-nŏs were nine hundred and five years: and he died.

12 ¶ And Cā-ī´-năn lived seventy years, and begat [2]Mă-hăl´-ă-lēēl:

13 And Cā-ī´-năn lived after he begat Mă-hăl´-ă-lēēl eight hundred and forty years, and begat sons and daughters:

14 And all the days of Cā-ī´-năn were nine hundred and ten years: and he died.

d Matt. 23.35. 1 John 3. 12-15. Jude 11.

8 bloods.
e Heb. 12.14. Rev. 6.10.
f Deut. 28. 15-20. Gal. 3.10.
g Job 16.18.

9 Or, Mine iniquity is greater than that it may be forgiven.

h Eze. 9.4,6.
i 2 Ki. 13.23. 2 Ki. 24.20. Jer. 23.39. Jer. 52.3.
10 Chanoch.
j Ps. 49.11.
11 Lemech.
12 whetter.
13 Or, I would slay a man in my wound, etc.
14 Or, in my hurt.
15 Sheth, that is, appointed, or, put.
16 Enosh.
17 Or, call themselves by the name of the LORD. ch. 6.2. 1 Ki. 18.24. Ps. 116.17. Joel 2.32. Zeph. 3.9. John 1.12. Acts 15.17. 1 Cor. 1.2.

CHAP. 5
a 1 Chr. 1.1. Matt. 1.1. Luke 3.38.
b ch. 1.26,27. Eph. 4.24. Col. 3.10.
c ch. 3.19. Job 30.23. Ps. 49.7-9. Ps. 89.48. Rom. 5.12. 1 Cor. 15.21. Heb. 9.27.
1 Kenan.
2 Maleleel, that is, Praiser of God.

15 ¶ And Mă-hăl'-ă-lēel lived sixty
and five years, and begat Jâr'-ĕd:
16 And Mă-hăl'-ă-lēel lived after he
begat [3]Jâr'-ĕd eight hundred and thirty
years, and begat sons and daughters:
17 And all the days of Mă-hăl'-ă-lēel
were eight hundred ninety and five
years: and he died.
18 ¶ And Jâr'-ĕd lived an hundred
sixty and two years, and he [d]begat Ē'-
nŏch:
19 And Jâr'-ĕd lived after he begat Ē'-
nŏch eight hundred years, and begat
sons and daughters:
20 And all the days of Jâr'-ĕd were
nine hundred sixty and two years: and
he died.
21 ¶ And Ē'-nŏch lived sixty and five
years, and begat [4]Mĕ-thū'-sĕ-lăh:
22 And Ē'-nŏch [e]walked with God
after he begat Mĕ-thū'-sĕ-lăh three
hundred years, and begat sons and
daughters:
23 And all the days of Ē'-nŏch were
three hundred sixty and five years:
24 And Ē'-nŏch walked with God:
and he *was* not; [f]for God took him.
25 And Mĕ-thū'-sĕ-lăh lived an hundred eighty and seven years, and begat
[5]Lā'-mĕch:
26 And Mĕ-thū'-sĕ-lăh lived after he
begat Lā'-mĕch seven hundred eighty
and two years, and begat sons and
daughters:
27 And all the days of Mĕ-thū'-sĕ-lăh
were nine hundred sixty and nine
years: and he died.
28 ¶ And Lā'-mĕch lived an hundred
eighty and two years, and begat a son:
29 And he called his name [6]Noah,
saying, This *same* shall comfort us
concerning our work and toil of our
hands, because of the ground which
the LORD hath [g]cursed.
30 And Lā'-mĕch lived after he begat
Noah five hundred ninety and five
years, and begat sons and daughters:
31 And all the days of Lā'-mĕch were
seven hundred seventy and seven
years: and he died.
32 And Noah was five hundred years
old: and Noah begat Shĕm, Ham, and
Jā'-phĕth.

CHAPTER 6

AND it came to pass, when men began to multiply on the face of the
earth, and daughters were born unto
them,
2 That [a]the sons of God saw the
daughters of men that they *were* fair;
and they [b]took them wives of all which
they chose.
3 And the LORD said, [c]My spirit shall
not always strive with man, [d]for that
he also *is* flesh: yet his days shall be
an hundred and twenty years.
4 There were giants in the earth in
those days; and also after that, when
the sons of God came in unto the
daughters of men, and they bare *children* to them, the same *became* mighty
men which *were* of old, men of renown.
5 ¶ And [e]GOD saw that the wickedness of man *was* great in the earth,
and *that* [1]every [f]imagination of the
thoughts of his heart *was* only evil
[2]continually.
6 And it [g]repented the LORD that he
had made man on the earth, and it
[h]grieved him at his heart.
7 And the LORD said, I will destroy
man whom I have created from the
face of the earth; [3]both man, and
beast, and the creeping thing, and the
fowls of the air; for it repenteth me
that I have made them.
8 But Noah [i]found grace in the eyes of
the LORD.
9 ¶ These *are* the generations of
Noah: Noah was a just man *and* [4] perfect in his generations, *and* Noah
walked with God.
10 And Noah begat three sons, Shem,
Ham, and Jā'-phĕth.
11 The earth also was corrupt before
God, and the earth was filled with
violence.
12 And God looked [j]upon the earth,
and, behold, it was corrupt; for all
flesh had corrupted his way upon the
earth.
13 And God said unto Noah, The
[k]end of all flesh is come before me;
for the earth is filled with violence
through them; and, behold, I will destroy them [5]with the earth.
14 ¶ Make thee an ark of gō'-phĕr
wood; [6]rooms shalt thou make in the
ark, and shalt pitch it within and without with pitch.
15 And this *is the fashion* which thou
shalt make it *of:* The length of the ark
shall be three hundred cubits, the
breadth of it fifty cubits, and the
height of it thirty cubits.
16 A window shalt thou make to the
ark, and in a cubit shalt thou finish
it above; and the door of the ark shalt
thou set in the side thereof; *with* lower,
second, and third *stories* shalt thou
make it.
17 And, [l]behold, I, even I, do bring
a flood of waters upon the earth,
to destroy all flesh, wherein *is* the
breath of life, from under heaven;

3 Jered, that is, descending.
d 1 Chr. 1.3. Henoch. Jude. 14.15.
4 Or, Mathusala, that is, at his death the sending forth of waters.
e ch. 6.9. ch. 17.1. 2 Ki. 20.3. Ps. 16.8. Micah 6.8. Mal. 2.6. 1 Thes. 2.12.
f 2 Ki. 2.11. Heb. 11.5.
5 Lemech.
6 that is, rest, or, comfort.
g ch. 3.17. ch. 4.11.

CHAP. 6

a 2 Cor. 6.18.
b Deut. 7.3,4.
c Luke 19.42. Gal. 5.16, 17. 1 Pet. 3.20.
d Ps. 78. 39.
e Rom. 1.28-31.
1 the whole imagination, with the purposes and desires of the heart.
f ch. 8.21. Deut. 29.19. Pro. 6.18. Matt. 15.19.
2 every day.
g Num. 23. 19. 1 Sam. 15. 11.29.
h Isa. 63.10. Eph. 4.30.
3 from man unto beast.
i ch. 19.19. Ex. 33.12. Luke 1.30. Acts 7.46.
4 Or, upright.
j Ps. 14.2. Ps. 33.13.
k Eze. 7.2. Amos 8.2. 1 Pet. 4.7.
5 Or, from the earth.
6 nests.
l 2 Pet. 2.5.

and every thing that *is* in the earth [m]shall die.

18 But with thee will I establish my covenant; and thou shalt come into the ark, thou, and thy sons, and thy wife, and thy sons' wives with thee.

19 And of every living thing of all flesh, two of every *sort* shalt thou bring into the ark, to keep *them* alive with thee; they shall be male and female.

20 Of fowls after their kind, and of cattle after their kind, of every creeping thing of the earth after his kind, two of every *sort* shall come unto thee, to keep *them* alive.

21 And take thou unto thee of all [n]food that is eaten, and thou shalt gather *it* to thee; and it shall be for food for thee, and for them.

22 [o]Thus did Noah; [p]according to all that God commanded him, so did he.

CHAPTER 7

AND the LORD said unto Noah, Come [a]thou and all thy house into the ark; for thee have I seen righteous [b]before me in this generation.

2 Of every [c]clean beast thou shalt take to thee by [1]sevens, the male and his female: and of beasts that *are* not clean by two, the male and his female.

3 Of fowls also of the air by sevens, the male and the female; to keep seed alive upon the face of all the earth.

4 For yet seven days, and [d]I will cause it to rain upon the earth forty days and forty nights; and every living substance that I have made will I [2]destroy from off the face of the earth.

5 And Noah did according unto all [e]that the LORD commanded him.

6 And Noah *was* six hundred years old when the flood of waters was upon the earth.

7 ¶ And [f]Noah went in, and his sons, and his wife, and his sons' wives with him, into the ark, because of the waters of the flood.

8 Of clean beasts, and of beasts that *are* not clean, and of fowls, and of every thing that creepeth upon the earth,

9 There went in two and two unto Noah into the ark, the male and the female, as God had commanded Noah.

10 And it came to pass [3]after seven days, that the waters of the flood were upon the earth.

11 ¶ In the six hundredth year of Noah's life, in the second month, the seventeenth day of the month, the same day were all the [g]fountains of the great deep broken up, and [h]the [4]windows of heaven were opened.

12 And the rain was upon the earth forty days and forty nights.

13 In the selfsame day entered Noah, and Shem, and Ham, and Jā-phĕth, the sons of Noah, and Noah's wife, and the three wives of his sons with them, into the ark;

14 They, and every beast after his kind, and all the cattle after their kind, and every creeping thing that creepeth upon the earth after his kind, and every fowl after his kind, every bird of every [5]sort.

15 And they went in unto Noah into the ark, two and two of all flesh, wherein *is* the breath of life.

16 And they that went in, went in male and female of all flesh, as God had commanded him: and the LORD [i]shut him in.

17 And the flood was forty days upon the earth; and the waters increased, and bare up the ark, and it was lift up above the earth.

18 And the waters prevailed, and were increased greatly upon the earth; [j]and the ark went upon the face of the waters.

19 And the waters prevailed exceedingly upon the earth; [k]and all the high hills, that *were* under the whole heaven, were covered.

20 Fifteen cubits upward did the waters prevail; and the mountains were covered.

21 And [l]all flesh died that moved upon the earth, both of fowl, and of cattle, and of beast, and of every creeping thing that creepeth upon the earth, and every man:

22 All in whose [m]nostrils *was* [6]the breath of life, of all that *was* in the dry *land*, died.

23 And every living substance was destroyed which was upon the face of the ground, both man, and cattle, and the creeping things, and the fowl of the heaven; and they were destroyed from the earth: and [n]Noah only remained *alive*, and they that *were* with him in the ark.

24 And [o]the waters prevailed upon the earth an hundred and fifty days.

CHAPTER 8

AND [a]God remembered Noah, and every living thing, and all the cattle that *was* with him in the ark: and God [b]made a wind to pass over the earth, and the waters asswaged;

m Rom. 5. 12,14.
n ch. 1.29, 30.
o Heb. 11.7.
p ch. 7.5.

CHAP. 7
a Ps.91.1-10. Heb. 11.7. 1 Pet. 3.20. 2 Pet. 2.5.
b ch. 9.6. Ps. 33.18, 19. 2 Pet. 2.9.
c Lev. 11.
1 seven seven.
d Job 22.16. 2 Pet. 2.5.
2 blot out.
e ch. 6.22. Ps. 119.6.
f Heb. 6.18.
3 Or, on the seventh day.
g ch. 8.2. Pro. 8.28. Eze. 26.19.
h Ps. 78.23. Isa. 24.18. Mal. 3.10.
4 Or, floodgates.
5 wing.
i Ps. 91. Ps. 17.8. Ps. 145.20. 1 Pet. 1.5.
j Ps. 104.26.
k Ps. 104.6.
l ch. 6.13,17. Job 22.16. Matt. 24.39. Luke 17.27. 2 Pet. 3.6.
m ch. 2.7.
6 the breath of the spirit of life.
n Eze. 14. 14. Mal. 3.17, 18. Heb. 11.7. 1 Pet. 3.20. 2 Pet. 2.5.
o ch. 8.3,4. compared with verse 11 of this chapter.

CHAP. 8
a ch. 19.29. Ex. 2.24. 1 Sam. 1.19. Ps. 105.42. Ps. 136.23.
b Ex. 14.21. Ex. 15.10. Ps. 104.7.

2 The [c]fountains also of the deep and the windows of heaven were stopped, and the [d]rain from heaven was restrained;

3 And the waters returned from off the earth [1]continually: and after the end of [e]the hundred and fifty days the waters were abated.

4 And the ark rested in the seventh month, on the seventeenth day of the month, upon the mountains of Ăr′-ă-răt.

5 And the waters [2]decreased continually until the tenth month: in the tenth *month*, on the first *day* of the month, were the tops of the mountains seen.

6 ¶ And it came to pass at the end of forty days, that Noah opened the [f]window of the ark which he had made:

7 And he sent forth [g]a raven, which went forth [3]to and fro, until the waters were dried up from off the earth.

8 Also he sent forth a dove from him, to see if the waters were abated from off the face of the ground;

9 But the dove [h]found no rest for the sole of her foot, and she returned unto him into the ark, for the waters *were* on the face of the whole earth: then he put forth his hand, and took her, and [4]pulled her in unto him into the ark.

10 And he stayed yet other seven days; and again he sent forth the dove out of the ark;

11 And the dove came in to him in the evening; and, lo, in her mouth *was* an [i]olive leaf pluckt off: so Noah knew that the waters were abated from off the earth.

12 And he stayed yet other seven days; and sent forth the dove; which returned not again unto him any more.

13 ¶ And it came to pass in the six hundredth and first year, in the first *month*, the first *day* of the month, the waters were dried up from off the earth: and Noah removed the covering of the ark, and looked, and, behold, the face of the ground was dry.

14 And in the second month, on the seven and twentieth day of the month, was the earth dried.

15 ¶ And God spake unto Noah, saying,

16 Go [j]forth of the ark, thou, and thy wife, and thy sons, and thy sons' wives with thee.

17 Bring forth with thee every living thing that *is* with thee, of all flesh, *both* of fowl, and of cattle, and of every creeping thing that creepeth upon the earth; that they may breed abundantly in the earth, and [k]be fruitful, and multiply upon the earth.

18 And Noah went forth, and his sons, and his wife, and his sons' wives with him:

19 Every beast, every creeping thing, and every fowl, *and* whatsoever creepeth upon the earth, after their [5]kinds, went forth out of the ark.

20 ¶ And Noah builded an altar unto the LORD; and took of every clean [l]beast, and of every clean fowl, and offered burnt offerings on the altar.

21 And the LORD smelled a [6]sweet savour; and the LORD said in his heart, I will not again [m]curse the ground any more for man's sake; [7]for the [n]imagination of man's heart *is* evil from his youth; neither will I again [o]smite any more every thing living, as I have done.

22 [8]While the earth remaineth, seedtime and harvest, and cold and heat, and summer and winter, and [p]day and night shall not cease.

CHAPTER 9

AND [a]God blessed Noah and his sons, and said unto them, Be fruitful, and multiply, and replenish the earth.

2 And [b]the fear of you and the dread of you shall be upon every beast of the earth, and upon every fowl of the air, upon all that moveth *upon* the earth, and upon all the fishes of the sea; into your hand are they delivered.

3 Every moving thing that liveth shall be [c]meat for you; even as the green herb have I given you all things.

4 But flesh with the [d]life thereof, *which is* the blood thereof, shall ye not eat.

5 And surely your blood of your lives will I require; at the hand of [e]every beast will I require it, and at the hand of [f]man; at the hand of every man's [g]brother will I require the life of man.

6 Whoso [h]sheddeth man's blood, by man shall his blood be shed: for in the [i]image of God made he man.

7 And you, be ye fruitful, and multiply; bring forth abundantly in the earth, and multiply therein.

8 ¶ And God spake unto Noah, and to his sons with him, saying,

9 And I, behold, I establish my covenant with you, and with your seed after you;

10 And with [j]every living creature that *is* with you, of the fowl, of the cattle, and of every beast of the earth

c ch. 7.11.
d 1 Ki. 8.35. Job 38.37.
1 in going and returning.
e ch. 7.24.
2 were in going and decreasing.
f ch. 6.16.
g 1 Ki. 17.4.
3 in going forth and returning.
h Deut. 28. 65.
4 caused her to come.
i Luke 2.14.
j ch. 7.13. Ps. 121.8.
k ch. 1.22.
5 families.
l Lev. 11.
6 savour of rest. Lev. 1.9. Eze. 20.41. 2 Cor. 2.15. Eph. 5.2.
m ch. 3.17. ch. 6.17. Isa. 54.9.
7 Or, though.
n ch. 6.5. Ps. 51.5. Job 14.4. Job 15.14. Jer. 17.9. Rom. 1.21. Rom. 3.23. Eph. 2.1-3.
o ch. 9.15.
8 As yet all the days of the earth.
p Jer. 33.20, 25.
CHAP. 9
a ch. 1.28.
b Hos. 2.18. Jas. 3.7.
c Deut. 12.15. Deut. 14.3.
d Lev. 17.10. Lev. 19.26. Deut. 12.23. 1 Sam. 14. 34. Acts 15.20, 29.
e Ex. 21.28, 29.
f Num. 35.31.
g Acts 17.26.
h Ex. 21.12, 14. Lev. 24.17. Matt. 26.52. Rev. 13.10.
i ch. 1.27. 1 Cor. 11.7.
j ch. 8.1.

with you; from all that go out of the
ark, to every beast of the earth.
11 And I will establish my covenant
with you; neither shall all flesh be cut
off any more by the waters of a flood;
neither shall there any more be a
[k]flood to destroy the earth.
12 And God said, This *is* [l]the token
of the covenant which I make between
me and you and every living creature
that *is* with you, for perpetual generations:
13 I do set my bow in the cloud, and
it shall be for a token of a covenant
between me and the earth.
14 And it shall come to pass, when
I bring a cloud over the earth, that the
bow shall be seen in the cloud:
15 And I will remember my covenant, which *is* between me and you and
every living creature of all flesh; [m]and
the waters shall no more become a
flood to destroy all flesh.
16 And the bow shall be in the cloud;
and I will look upon it, that I may
remember the [n]everlasting covenant
between God and every living creature
of all flesh that *is* upon the earth.
17 And God said unto Noah, This *is*
the token of the covenant, which I
have established between me and all
flesh that *is* upon the earth.
18 ¶ And the sons of Noah, that went
forth of the ark, were Shem, and Ham,
and Jā-phĕth: and Ham *is* the [o]father
of [1]Canaan.
19 These *are* the three sons of Noah:
and [p]of them was the whole earth
overspread.
20 And Noah began *to be* [q]an husbandman, and he planted a vineyard:
21 And he drank of the wine, and
[r]was drunken; and he was uncovered
within his tent.
22 And Ham, the father of Canaan,
saw the nakedness of his father, and
told his two brethren without.
23 And [s]Shem and Jā-phĕth took a
garment, and laid *it* upon both their
shoulders, and went backward, and
covered the nakedness of their father;
and their faces *were* backward, and
they saw not their father's nakedness.
24 And Noah awoke from his wine,
and knew what his younger son had
done unto him.
25 And he said, [t]Cursed *be* Canaan;
a servant of [u]servants shall he be unto
his brethren.
26 And he said, [v]Blessed *be* the LORD
God of Shem; and Canaan shall be
[2]his servant.
27 God shall [3]enlarge Jā-phĕth, and

k 2 Pet. 3.5.
l Matt. 26. 26-28.
m Ex. 28.12. Lev. 26.42, 45. Isa. 54.9. Eze. 16.60.
n ch. 17.13, 19. 2 Sam. 23.5.
o ch. 10.6.
1 Chenaan.
p ch. 10.32. 1 Chr. 1.4.
q ch. 3.19. ch. 4.2. Eccl. 5.9.
r ch. 19.32, 36. Pro. 20.1. Eph. 5.18.
s Ex. 20.12. Gal. 6.1.
t Deut. 27.16. Matt. 25.41.
u Josh. 9.23. 1 Ki. 9.20.
v Ps. 144.15. Heb. 11.16.
2 Or, servant to them.
3 Or, persuade.
w Eph. 2.13, 14. Eph. 3.6.
x ch. 3.19. Job 30.23. Job 34. 15. Ps. 89.48.

CHAP. 10

a 1 Chr. 1. 5-7.
1 Or, Chittim.
2 Or, Rodanim.
b ch. 6.11.
c Mic. 5.6.
3 Or, Babylon.
4 Or, he went out into Assyria.
5 Or, the streets of the city.
d 1 Chr. 1.12.
6 Tzidon.
e ch. 13.12, 14,15. ch. 15.18-21. Num. 34.2, 12. Josh. 12.7.
7 Azzah.

he shall [w]dwell in the tents of Shem;
and Canaan shall be his servant.
28 ¶ And Noah lived after the flood
three hundred and fifty years.
29 And all the days of Noah were
nine hundred and fifty years: and he
[x]died.

CHAPTER 10

NOW these *are* the generations of
the sons of Noah, Shem, Ham,
and Jā-phĕth: and unto them were
sons born after the flood.
2 The [a]sons of Jā-phĕth; Gō-mĕr,
and Mā-gŏg, and Mā-dâi, and Jā-văn,
and Tū-băl, and Mē-shĕch, and Tī-răs.
3 And the sons of Gō-mĕr; Ăsh-kē-
năz, and Rī-phăth, and Tō-gär-măh.
4 And the sons of Jā-văn; Ē-lī-shăh,
and Tarshish, [1]Kittim, and [2]Dō-dā-
nĭm.
5 By these were the isles of the Gentiles divided in their lands; every one
after his tongue, after their families, in
their nations.
6 ¶ And the sons of Ham; Cŭsh, and
Mĭz-rā-ĭm, and Phŭt, and Canaan.
7 And the sons of Cŭsh; Sē-bă, and
Hăv-ĭ-lăh, and Săb-tăh, and Rā-ă-
măh, and Săb-tē-chă: and the sons of
Rā-ă-măh; Shē-bă, and Dē-dăn.
8 And Cŭsh begat Nimrod: he began
to be a mighty one in the earth.
9 He was a mighty hunter before the
LORD: wherefore it is said, Even as
Nimrod the mighty hunter before [b]the
LORD.
10 And the beginning of his kingdom
[c]was [3]Babel, and Ĕr-ĕch, and Ăc-căd,
and Căl-nĕh, in the land of Shī-när.
11 Out of that land [4]went forth Ăssh-
ûr, and builded Nĭn-ĕ-vĕh, and [5]the
city Rē-hō-bōth, and Cā-lăh,
12 And Rē-sĕn between Nĭn-ĕ-vĕh
and Cā-lăh: the same *is* a great city.
13 And Mĭz-rā-ĭm begat Lū-dĭm, and
Ăn-ă-mĭm, and Lĕ-hā-bĭm, and Năph-
tû-hĭm,
14 And Păth-rû-sĭm, and Căs-lû-
hĭm, ([d]out of whom came Philistim,)
and Căph-tō-rĭm.
15 ¶ And Canaan begat [6]Sī-dŏn his
firstborn, and Heth,
16 And the Jĕb-ū-sīte, and the Amorite, and the Gĭr-gă-sīte,
17 And the Hī-vīte, and the Är-kīte,
and the Sī-nīte,
18 And the Är-vă-dīte, and the Zĕm-
ă-rīte, and the Hā-măth-īte: and afterward were the families of the Canaanites spread abroad.
19 And [e]the border of the Canaanites
was from Sī-dŏn, as thou comest to
Gē-rär, unto [7]Gā-ză; as thou goest,

unto Sodom, and Gō-mŏr'-răh, and Ăd'-măh, and Zĕ-bō'-ĭm, even unto Lā'-shă.

20 These *are* the sons of Ham, after their families, after their tongues, in their countries, *and* in their nations.

21 ¶ Unto Shem also, the father of all the children of Ē'-bĕr, the brother of Jā'-phĕth the elder, even to him were *children* born.

22 The [f]children of Shem; Ē'-lăm, and Ăssh'-ŭr, and [8]Ăr-phăx'-ăd, and Lud, and Â'-ăm.

23 And the children of Â'-ăm; Uz, and Hul, and Gē'-thĕr, and Mash.

24 And Ăr-phăx'-ăd begat [9g]Sā'-lăh; and Sā'-lăh begat Ē'-bĕr.

25 And [h]unto Ē'-bĕr were born two sons: the name of one *was* [10]Pē'-lĕg; for in his days was the earth divided; and his brother's name *was* Jŏk'-tăn.

26 And Jŏk'-tăn begat Ăl-mō'-dăd, and Shē'-lĕph, and Hă-zär-mā'-vĕth, and Jē'-răh,

27 And Hă-dôr'-ăm, and Ū'-zăl, and Dĭk'-lăh,

28 And Ō'-băl, and Ă-bĭm'-ā-ĕl, and Shē'-bă,

29 And Ō'-phĭr, and Hăv'-ĭ-lăh, and Jō'-băb: all these *were* the sons of Jŏk'-tăn.

30 And their dwelling was from Mē'-shă, as thou goest unto Sē'-phär a mount of the east.

31 These *are* the sons of Shem, after their families, after their tongues, in their lands, after their nations.

32 These [i]*are* the families of the sons of Noah, after their generations, in their nations: [j]and by these were the nations divided in the earth after the flood.

CHAPTER 11

AND the whole earth [a]was of one [1]language, and of one [2]speech.

2 And it came to pass, as they journeyed [3]from the east, that they found a plain in the land of [b]Shī'-när; and they dwelt there.

3 And [4]they said one to another, Go to, let us make brick, and [5]burn them throughly. And they had brick for stone, and slime had they for morter.

4 And they said, Go to, let us build us a city and a tower, whose top [6]*may reach* [c]unto heaven; and let us make us [d]a name, lest we be [e]scattered abroad upon the face of the whole earth.

5 And [f]the LORD came down to see the city and the tower, which the children of men builded.

6 And the LORD said, Behold, the people *is* one, and they have all one language; and this they begin to do: and now nothing will be restrained from them, which they have [g]imagined to do.

7 Go to, [h]let us go down, and there confound their language, that they may [i]not understand one another's speech.

8 So the LORD scattered them abroad from thence [j]upon the face of all the earth: and they left off to build the city.

9 Therefore is the name of it called [7]Babel; [k]because the LORD did there confound the language of all the earth: and from thence did the LORD scatter them abroad upon the face of all the earth.

10 ¶ These *are* the generations of Shem: [l]Shem *was* an hundred years old, and begat Ăr-phăx'-ăd two years after the flood:

11 And Shem lived after he begat Ăr-phăx'-ăd five hundred years, and begat sons and daughters.

12 And Ăr-phăx'-ăd lived five and thirty years, and begat [m]Sā'-lăh:

13 And Ăr-phăx'-ăd lived after he begat Sā'-lăh four hundred and three years, and begat sons and daughters.

14 And Sā'-lăh lived thirty years, and begat Ē'-bĕr:

15 And Sā'-lăh lived after he begat Ē'-bĕr four hundred and three years, and begat sons and daughters.

16 And [n]Ē'-bĕr lived four and thirty years, and begat [8]Pē'-lĕg:

17 And Ē'-bĕr lived after he begat Pē'-lĕg four hundred and thirty years, and begat sons and daughters.

18 And Pē'-lĕg lived thirty years, and begat [9]Rē'-ū:

19 And Pē'-lĕg lived after he begat Rē'-ū two hundred and nine years, and begat sons and daughters.

20 And Rē'-ū lived two and thirty years, and begat [10]Sē'-rŭg:

21 And Rē'-ū lived after he begat Sē'-rŭg two hundred and seven years, and begat sons and daughters.

22 And Sē'-rŭg lived thirty years, and begat Nahor:

23 And Sē'-rŭg lived after he begat Nahor two hundred years, and begat sons and daughters.

24 And Nahor lived nine and twenty years, and begat [11]Tē'-răh:

25 And Nahor lived after he begat Tē'-răh an hundred and nineteen years, and begat sons and daughters.

26 And Tē'-răh lived seventy years,

---

f 1 Chr. 1.17.
8 Arpachshad.
9 Shelah.
g ch. 11.12.
h 1 Chr. 1.19.
10 That is, Division.
i 1 Chr. 1.4.
j ch. 9.19.

CHAP. 11

a Acts 2.6.
1 lip.
2 words.
3 Or, eastward, as ch. 13.11.
b Dan. 1.2.
4 a man said to his neighbour.
5 burn them to a burning.
6 may be very high.
c Deut. 1.28.
d John 5.44.
e Luke 1.51.
f ch. 18.21. Ps. 33.13. Ps. 53.2.
g Ps. 2.1,4.
h ch. 1.26.
i ch. 42.23. Deut. 28.49. Jer. 5.15. Acts 2.4-11. 1 Cor. 14.2, 11,23.
j ch. 10.25-32. Ps. 92.9. Pro. 19.29. Luke 1.51.
7 That is, Confusion.
k 1 Cor. 14. 23.
l 1 Chr. 1.17-27.
m Luke 3.35.
n 1 Chr. 1.19.
8 Or, Phalec, Luke 3.35.
9 Or, Ragau, Luke 3.35.
10 Or, Saruch. Luke 3.35.
11 Or, Thara, Luke 3.34.

and begat [o]Abram, Nahor, and Hâr´-ăn.

27 ¶ Now these *are* the generations of Tē´-răh: Tē´-răh begat Abram, Nahor, and Hâr´-ăn; and Hâr´-ăn begat [p]Lot.

28 And Hâr´-ăn died before his father Tē´-răh in the land of his nativity, in Ur of the Chăl´-dēēṡ.

29 And Abram and Nahor took them wives: the name of Abram's wife *was* [q]Sâr´-ā-ī; and the name of Nahor's wife, [r]Mĭl´-căh, the daughter of Hâr´-ăn, the father of Mĭl´-căh, and the father of Ĭs´-căh.

30 But Sâr´-ā-ī was [s]barren; she *had* no child.

31 And Tē´-răh took Abram his son, and Lot the son of Hâr´-ăn his son's son, and Sâr´-ā-ī his daughter in law, his son Abram's wife; and they [t]went forth with them from Ur of the Chăl´-dēēṡ, to go into the land of [u]Canaan; and they came unto [12]Hâr´-ăn, and dwelt there.

32 And the days of Tē´-răh were two hundred and five years: and Tē´-răh died in Hâr´-ăn.

CHAPTER 12

NOW the [a]LORD had said unto Abram, Get thee out of thy country, and from thy kindred, and from thy father's house, unto a land that I will shew thee:

2 And I will make of thee [b]a great nation, and I will bless thee, and make thy name great; and thou shalt be a blessing:

3 And I will [c]bless them that bless thee, and curse him that curseth thee: and [d]in thee shall all families of the earth be blessed.

4 So Abram departed, as the LORD had spoken unto him; and Lot went with him: and Abram *was* seventy and five years old when he departed out of Hâr´-ăn.

5 And Abram took Sâr´-ā-ī his wife, and Lot his brother's son, and all their substance that they had gathered, and the souls that they had gotten in [e]Hâr´-ăn; and they went forth to go [f]into the land of Canaan; and into the land of Canaan they came.

6 ¶ And Abram passed through the land unto the place of [1]Sī´-chĕm, unto the plain of [g]Mō´-rēh. And the Canaanite *was* then in the land.

7 And the LORD [h]appeared unto Abram, and said, [i]Unto thy seed will I give this land: and there builded he an [j]altar unto the LORD, who appeared unto him.

8 And he removed from thence unto a mountain on the east of Beth-el, and pitched his tent, *having* Beth-el on the west, and [2]Hā´-ī on the east: and there he builded an altar unto the LORD, and called upon the name of the LORD.

9 And Abram journeyed, [3]going on [k]still toward the south.

10 ¶ And there was [l]a famine in the land: and Abram [m]went down into Egypt to sojourn there; for the famine *was* [n]grievous in the land.

11 And it came to pass, when he was come near to enter into Egypt, that he said unto Sâr´-ā-ī his wife, Behold now, I know that thou *art* a [o]fair woman to look upon:

12 Therefore it shall come to pass when the Egyptians shall see thee, that they shall say, This *is* his wife: and they [p]will kill me, but they will save thee alive.

13 Say, [q]I pray thee, [r]thou *art* my sister: that it may be well with me for thy sake; and my soul shall live because of thee.

14 ¶ And it came to pass, that, when Abram was come into Egypt, the Egyptians beheld the woman that she *was* very fair.

15 The [s]princes also of Pharaoh saw her, and commended her before Pharaoh: and the woman was taken into Pharaoh's house.

16 And he entreated Abram well for her sake: and he had sheep, and oxen, and he asses, and menservants, and maidservants, and she asses, and camels.

17 And the LORD [t]plagued Pharaoh and his house with great plagues because of Sâr´-ā-ī Abram's wife.

18 And Pharaoh called Abram, and said, [u]What *is* this *that* thou hast done unto me? why didst thou not tell me that she *was* thy wife?

19 Why saidst thou, She *is* my sister? so I might have taken her to me to wife: now therefore behold thy wife, take *her*, and go thy way.

20 And Pharaoh commanded *his* men concerning him: and they sent him away, and his wife, and all that he had.

CHAPTER 13

AND Abram went up out of Egypt, he, and his wife, and all that he had, and Lot with him, into the south.

2 And Abram *was* [a]very rich in cattle, in silver, and in gold.

3 And he went on his journeys from the south even to Beth-el, unto the

o ch. 12.1. Josh. 24.2.
1 Chr. 1.26.
p ch. 12.4. ch. 13.10. ch. 14.12. ch. 19.1,29. 2 Pet. 2.7.
q ch. 17.15.
r ch.22.20.
s ch. 16.1.
t Neh. 9.7. Acts 7.4. Heb. 11.8.
u ch. 10.19.
12 Or, Charan.

CHAP. 12
a ch. 15.7. Acts 7.3.
b ch. 17.6. ch. 18.18. ch. 46.3. Num. 23.10. Deut. 26.5. 1 Ki. 3.8.
c ch.24.35. ch. 27.29. Ex. 23.22. Num. 24.9.
d ch. 22.18. ch. 26.4. ch. 28.14. Ps. 72.17. Acts 3.25. Gal. 3.8.
e ch. 11.31.
f Heb. 11.8.
1 Or, Sychar. John 4.5.
g Deut. 11. 30. Judg. 7.1.
h ch. 17.1.
i Deut. 34.4. Ps. 105. 9-12.
j ch. 13.4.
2 Or, Ai, or, Aija.
3 in going and journeying.
k ch. 13.3.
l ch. 26.1.
m. Ps. 105.13.
n ch. 43.1.
o ch. 26.7.
p ch. 20.11.
q Ps. 25.21. Eph. 4.25.
r ch. 20.5,13.
s Esth. 2.16.
t ch. 20.18. 1 Chr.16.21. Ps. 105.14. Heb. 13.4.
u ch.20.9. ch. 26.10. Pro. 21.1.

CHAP. 13
a ch. 24.35. Ps. 112.3. Pro. 10.22.

place where his tent had been at the beginning, between Beth-el and Hā-ī;

4 Unto the place of the [b]altar, which he had made there at the first: and there Abram called on the name of the LORD.

5 ¶ And Lot also, which went with Abram, had flocks, and herds, and tents.

6 And the land was [c]not able to bear them, that they might dwell together: for their substance was great, so that they could not dwell together.

7 And there was a [d]strife between the herdmen of Abram's cattle and the herdmen of Lot's cattle: and the Canaanite and the Pĕ-rĭz-zīte dwelled then in the land.

8 And Abram said unto Lot, [e]Let there be no strife, I pray thee, between me and thee, and between my herdmen and thy herdmen; for we *be* [1]brethren.

9 *Is* [f]not the whole land before thee? separate thyself, I pray thee, from me: [g]if *thou wilt take* the left hand, then I will go to the right; or if *thou depart* to the right hand, then I will go to the left.

10 And Lot lifted up his eyes, and [h]beheld all the [i]plain of Jordan, that it *was* well watered every where, before the LORD [j]destroyed Sodom and Gō-mŏr-răh, *even* as the garden of the LORD, like the land of Egypt, as thou comest [k]unto Zō-ăr.

11 Then Lot chose him all the plain of Jordan; and Lot journeyed east: and they separated themselves the one from the other.

12 Abram dwelled in the land of Canaan, and Lot dwelled in the cities [l]of the plain, and pitched *his* tent toward Sodom.

13 But [m]the men of Sodom *were* wicked and [n]sinners before the LORD exceedingly.

14 ¶ And the LORD said unto Abram, after that Lot was separated from him, [o]Lift up now thine eyes, and look from the place where thou art [p]northward, and southward, and eastward, and westward:

15 For all the land which thou seest, to thee will I give it, and to thy [q]seed for ever.

16 And I will make thy seed as the [r]dust of the earth: so that if a man can number the dust of the earth, *then* shall thy seed also be numbered.

17 Arise, walk through the land in the length of it and in the breadth of it; for I will give it unto thee.

b ch. 12.7,8.
c ch. 36.7. Luke 12.17, 18.
d ch. 26.20.
e Phil. 2.14, 15.
1 men brethren. Ex. 2.13. Ps. 133.1.
f ch. 20.15.
g Rom. 12.18. Heb. 12.14. Jas. 3.13-18.
h Num. 32.1.
i Deut. 34.3. Ps. 107.34.
j ch. 19.24. Ps. 107.34.
k ch. 14.2. ch. 19.22.
l ch. 19.29.
m ch. 18.20. Eze. 16.49. 2 Pet. 2.7.
n ch. 6.11.
o Isa. 49.18.
p ch. 28.14.
q 2 Chr. 20.7.
r ch. 26.4. Ex. 32.13. Num. 23.10. Deut. 1.10. 1 Chr. 27.23. Jer. 33.22. Rom. 4.16. Heb. 11.12.
2 plains.

CHAP. 14

a ch. 10.10.
b Isa. 11.11.
c Jas. 4.1.
d Deut. 29.23.
e ch. 19.22.
f Deut. 3.17. Num. 34.12. Josh. 3.16. Ps. 107.34.
1 Or, the plain of Kiriathaim.
2 Or, the plain of Paran.
g 2 Chr. 20.2.
h ch. 11.3.
i ch. 19.17,30.
j ch. 11.31.
k ch. 13.12. Jer. 2.17,19.

18 Then Abram removed *his* tent, and came and dwelt in the [2]plain of Măm-rē, which *is* in Hē-brŏn, and built there an altar unto the LORD.

CHAPTER 14

AND it came to pass in the days of Ăm-ră-phĕl king of [a]Shī-năr, Ăr-ī-ŏch king of Ĕl-lā-săr, Chĕd-ôr-lā-ō-mĕr king of [b]Ē-lăm, and Tī-dăl king of nations;

2 *That these* [c]made war with Bē-ră king of Sodom, and with Bĭr-shă king of Gō-mŏr-răh, Shī-năb king of [d]Ăd-măh, and Shĕm-ē-bĕr king of Zĕ-boi-ĭm, and the king of Bē-lă, which is [e]Zō-ăr.

3 All these were joined together in the vale of Sĭd-dĭm, [f]which is the salt sea.

4 Twelve years they served Chĕd-ôr-lā-ō-mĕr, and in the thirteenth year they rebelled.

5 And in the fourteenth year came Chĕd-ôr-lā-ō-mĕr, and the kings that *were* with him, and smote the Rĕph-ā-ĭms in Ăsh-tĕ-rōth Kăr-nā-ĭm, and the Zū-zĭms in Ham, and the Ē-mĭms in [1]Shā-vĕh Kĭr-ĭ-ă-thā-ĭm,

6 And the Hôr-ītes in their mount Sē-ĭr, unto [2]Ĕl-pâr-ăn, which *is* by the wilderness.

7 And they returned, and came to Ĕn-mĭsh-păt, which *is* Kā-dĕsh, and smote all the country of the Ă-măl-ĕk-ītes, and also the Amorites, that dwelt in [g]Hăz-ĕ-zŏn-tā-măr.

8 And there went out the king of Sodom, and the king of Gō-mŏr-răh, and the king of Ăd-măh, and the king of Zĕ-boi-ĭm, and the king of Bē-lă (the same *is* Zō-ăr;) and they joined battle with them in the vale of Sĭd-dĭm;

9 With Chĕd-ôr-lā-ō-mĕr the king of Ē-lăm, and with Tī-dăl king of nations and Ăm-ră-phĕl king of Shī-năr, and Ăr-ī-ŏch king of Ĕl-lā-săr; four kings with five.

10 And the vale of Sĭd-dĭm *was full of* [h]slimepits; and the kings of Sodom and Gō-mŏr-răh fled, and fell there; and they that remained fled to the [i]mountain.

11 And they took all the goods of Sodom and Gō-mŏr-răh, and all their victuals, and went their way.

12 And they took Lot, [j]Abram's brother's son, [k]who dwelt in Sodom, and his goods, and departed.

13 ¶ And there came one that had escaped, and told Abram the Hebrew; for he dwelt in the plain of Măm-rē the Amorite, brother of Ĕsh-

cŏl, and brother of Aner: and these [l]*were* confederate with Abram.

14 And when Abram heard that his [m]brother was taken captive, he [3]armed his [4]trained *servants*, born [n]in his own house, three hundred and eighteen, and pursued *them* [o]unto Dan.

15 And [p]he divided himself against them, he and his servants, by night, and smote them, and pursued them unto Hō-'bāh, which *is* on the left hand of Damascus.

16 And he brought back all the goods, and also brought again his brother Lot, and his goods, and the women also, and the people.

17 ¶ And the king of Sodom went out to meet him after his return from the slaughter of Chĕd-ôr-lā-ō-'mĕr, and of the kings that *were* with him, at the valley of Shā-'vēh, which *is* the [q]king's dale.

18 And [r]Mĕl-chĭz-'ĕd-ĕk king of Sā-'lĕm brought forth bread and wine: and he *was* the priest [s]of the most high God.

19 And he blessed him, and said, Blessed *be* Abram of the most high God, possessor of heaven and earth:

20 And blessed be the most high God, which hath delivered thine enemies into thy hand. And he gave him [t]tithes of all.

21 And the king of Sodom said unto Abram, Give me the [5]persons, and take the goods to thyself.

22 And Abram said to the king of Sodom, [u]I have lift up mine hand unto the LORD, the most high God, [v]the possessor of heaven and earth,

23 That I [w]will not *take* from a thread even to a shoelatchet, and that I will not take any thing that *is* thine, lest thou shouldest say, I have made Abram rich:

24 Save only that which the young men have eaten, and the portion of the men which went with me, Aner, Ĕsh-'cŏl, and Măm-'rē; let them take their portion.

CHAPTER 15

AFTER these things the word of the LORD came unto Abram in [a]a vision, saying, [b]Fear not, Abram: I *am* thy shield, *and* thy exceeding [c]great reward.

2 And Abram said, Lord GOD, what wilt thou give me, seeing I go childless, and the steward of my house *is* this Ĕl-ĭ-ē-'zĕr of Damascus?

3 And Abram said, Behold, to me thou hast given no seed: and, lo, one born in my house is mine heir.

4 And, behold, the word of the LORD *came* unto him, saying, This shall not be thine heir; but he that shall [d]come forth out of thine own bowels shall be thine heir.

5 And he brought him forth abroad, and said, Look now toward heaven, and [e]tell the stars, if thou be able to number them: and he said unto him, [f]So shall thy seed be.

6 And [g]he believed in the LORD; and he [h]counted it to him for righteousness.

7 And he said unto him, I *am* the LORD that [i]brought thee out of Ur of the Chăl-'dēēs, to give thee this land to inherit it.

8 And he said, Lord GOD, [j]whereby shall I know that I shall inherit it?

9 And he said unto him, Take me an heifer of three years old, and a she goat of three years old, and a ram of three years old, and a turtledove, and a young pigeon.

10 And he took unto him all these, and divided them in the midst, and laid each piece one against another: but the birds divided he not.

11 And when the fowls came down upon the carcases, Abram drove them away.

12 And when the sun was going down, a [k]deep sleep fell upon Abram; and, lo, an horror of great darkness fell upon him.

13 And he said unto Abram, Know of a surety that [l]thy seed shall be a stranger in a land *that is* not theirs, and shall serve them; and they shall [m]afflict them [n]four hundred years;

14 And also [o]that nation, whom they shall serve, will I judge: and afterward shall they come out with great substance.

15 And thou shalt go to thy fathers in peace; thou shalt be buried [p]in a good old age.

16 But in the fourth generation they shall come hither again: for the iniquity of the Amorites [q]*is* not yet full.

17 And it came to pass, that, when the sun went down, and it was dark, behold a smoking furnace, and [1]a burning lamp that passed between those pieces.

18 In the same day the LORD made a covenant with Abram, saying, Unto thy seed [r]have I given this land, from the river of Egypt unto the great river, the river Eû-phrā-'tēs:

l ver. 24.
m ch. 13.8.
3 Or, led forth.
4 Or, instructed.
n ch. 17.27. ch. 15.3. Eccl. 2.7.
o Deut. 34.1. Judg. 18.29. Isa. 41.2.
p 1 Sam. 30. 8,18,19.
q 2 Sam. 18. 18.
r Heb. 7.1,2.
s Ps. 110.4. Mic. 6.6. Acts 16.17. Heb. 7.10-22.
t Heb. 7.4.
5 souls.
u Dan. 12.7. Rev. 10.5.
v Ps. 24.1. Matt. 11.25.
w Esth. 9.15. 2 Cor. 11.9-12.

CHAP. 15

a ch. 46.2.
b Isa. 41.10.
c Ps. 58.11. Ps. 84.9,11. Heb. 11.6.
d ch. 17.16. 2 Sam. 7.12.
e Ps. 147.4.
f Ex. 32.13. Heb. 11.12.
g Rom. 4.3-6, 20-25.
h Ps. 106.31. Gal. 3.6.
i Acts 7.2.
j Judg. 6.36-40. 1 Sam. 14.9, 10. 2 Ki. 20.8. Luke 1.18.
k ch. 2.21.
l Ex. 1.1.
m Ex. 1.11.
n Ex. 12.40.
o Ex. 6.6. Ex. 7.14.
p ch. 25.8. Job 5.26. Heb. 11.13.
q Matt. 23. 32. 1 Thes. 2. 16. 2 Pet. 3.8,9.
1 a lamp of fire.
r ch. 17.8. Deut. 1.7. Num. 34.3. 2 Chr. 9.26. Neh. 9.8. Ps. 105.11.

19 The Kē-nītes, and the Kĕ-nĭz-
zītes, and the Kăd-mō-nītes,
20 And the Hittites, and the Pĕ-rĭz-
zītes, and the Rĕph-ā-ĭms,
21 And the Amorites, and the Canaanites, and the Gĭr-gă-shītes, and
the Jĕb-ū-sītes.

CHAPTER 16

NOW Sâr-ā-ī Abram's wife [a]bare
him no children: and she had an
handmaid, an Egyptian, whose name
was [1]Hā-gär.
2 And Sâr-ā-ī said unto Abram, Behold now, the LORD hath [b]restrained
me from bearing: I pray thee, go
in unto my maid; it may be that I
may [2]obtain children by her. And
Abram hearkened to the voice of
Sâr-ā-ī.
3 And Sâr-ā-ī Abram's wife took Hā-
gär her maid the Egyptian, after
Abram had dwelt ten years in the land
of Canaan, and gave her to her husband Abram to be his wife.
4 ¶ And he went in unto Hā-gär, and
she conceived: and when she saw that
she had conceived, her mistress was
[c]despised in her eyes.
5 And Sâr-ā-ī said unto Abram, My
wrong *be* upon thee: I have given my
maid into thy bosom; and when she
saw that she had conceived, I was despised in her eyes: the [d]LORD judge
between me and thee.
6 But Abram said unto Sâr-ā-ī, Behold, thy maid *is* in thy hand; do to
her [3]as it pleaseth thee. And when
Sâr-ā-ī [4]dealt hardly with her, she fled
from her face.
7 ¶ And the angel of the LORD found
her by a fountain of water in the wilderness, by the fountain in the way to
[e]Shur.
8 And he said, Hā-gär, Sâr-ā-ī's maid,
whence camest thou? and whither
wilt thou go? And she said, I flee from
the face of my mistress Sâr-ā-ī.
9 And the angel of the LORD said
unto her, Return to thy mistress, and
[f]submit thyself under her hands.
10 And the [g]angel of the LORD said
unto her, I will [h]multiply thy seed exceedingly, that it shall not be numbered for multitude.
11 And the angel of the LORD said
unto her, Behold, thou *art* with child,
and shalt bear a son, and shalt call
his name [5]Ĭsh-mā-ĕl; because [i]the
LORD hath heard thy affliction.
12 And he will be a wild man; his
hand *will be* against every man, and
every man's hand against him; and

CHAP. 16
a Judg. 13.2. Luke 1.7.
1 Or, Agar. Gal. 4.24.
b ch. 30.2.
2 be builded by her. Ruth 4.11.
c Pro. 30.23.
d Ex. 5.21.
3 that which is good in thine eyes.
4 afflicted her.
e ch. 25. 18.
f Eph. 6.5-9.
g ch. 22.15-18. Mal. 3.1.
h ch. 25.12.
5 That is, God shall hear.
i Ex. 2.23,24.
j ch. 25.18.
k Ps. 139. 1-12.
6 That is, The well of him that liveth and seeth me.

CHAP. 17
a ch. 5.22.
b Job 1.1.
1 Or, upright, or, sincere.
c Gal. 3.17, 18.
d Ex. 3.6.
2 multitude of nations.
3 That is, Father of a great multitude.
e ch. 26.24. ch. 28.13. Heb. 11.16. Rom. 9.7-9.
4 of thy sojournings. ch. 23.4. ch. 28.4.
f Ex. 6.7. Ex. 29. 45. Lev. 26.12. Deut. 4.37. Deut. 14.2. Deut. 26.18. Deut. 29.13. Ps. 48.14. Rev. 21.7.
g Ps. 25.10.
h Acts 7.8. Rom. 4.11. Gal. 6.15.
5 a son of eight days. Luke 2.21. John 7.22.

he [j]shall dwell in the presence of all
his brethren.
13 And she called the name of the
LORD that spake unto her, [k]Thou God
seest me: for she said, Have I also here
looked after him that seeth me?
14 Wherefore the well was called
[6]Bĕer-lă-hăi-rôi; behold, *it is* between
Kā-dĕsh and Bē-rĕd.
15 ¶ And Hā-gär bare Abram a son:
and Abram called his son's name,
which Hā-gär bare, Ĭsh-mā-ĕl.
16 And Abram *was* fourscore and
six years old, when Hā-gär bare Ĭsh-
mā-ĕl to Abram.

CHAPTER 17

AND when Abram was ninety years
old and nine, the LORD appeared
to Abram, and said unto him, I *am*
the Almighty God; [a]walk before me,
and be [b]thou [1]perfect.
2 And I will make my [c]covenant between me and thee, and will multiply
thee exceedingly.
3 And Abram [d]fell on his face: and
God talked with him, saying,
4 As for me, behold, my covenant *is*
with thee, and thou shalt be a father
of [2]many nations.
5 Neither shall thy name any more
be called Abram, but thy name shall
be [3]Abraham; for a father of many
nations have I made thee.
6 And I will make thee exceeding
fruitful, and I will make nations of
thee, and kings shall come out of thee.
7 And I will establish my covenant
between me and thee and thy seed
after thee in their generations for an
everlasting covenant, to be [e]a God
unto thee, and to thy seed after thee.
8 And I will give unto thee, and to
thy seed after thee, the land [4]wherein
thou art a stranger, all the land of Canaan, for an everlasting possession;
and [f]I will be their God.
9 ¶ And God said unto Abraham,
Thou [g]shalt keep my covenant therefore, thou, and thy seed after thee in
their generations.
10 This *is* my covenant, which ye
shall keep, between me and you and
thy seed after thee; Every man child
among you shall be circumcised.
11 And [h]ye shall circumcise the flesh
of your foreskin; and it shall be a
token of the covenant betwixt me and
you.
12 And [5]he that is eight days old shall
be circumcised among you, every man
child in your generations, he that is
born in the house, or bought with

money of any stranger, which *is* not
of thy seed.
13 He that is born in thy house, and
he that is bought with thy money,
must needs be circumcised: and my
covenant shall be in your flesh for an
everlasting covenant.
14 And the uncircumcised man child
whose flesh of his foreskin is not circumcised, that soul shall be [i]cut off
from this people; he hah broken my
covenant.
15 ¶ And God said unto Abraham,
As for Sâr-ā-ī thy wife, thou shalt not
call her name Sâr-ā-ī, but [6]Sarah *shall*
her name *be*.
16 And I will bless her, and [j]give thee
a son also of her: yea, I will bless her,
and [7]she shall be *a mother* of nations;
kings of people shall be of her.
17 Then Abraham fell upon his face,
and [k]laughed, and said in his heart,
Shall *a child* be born unto him that
is an hundred years old? and shall
[l]Sarah, that is ninety years old, bear?
18 And Abraham said unto God, O
that Ĭsh-mā-ĕl might live before thee!
19 And God said, [m]Sarah thy wife
shall bear thee a son indeed; and thou
shalt call his name Isaac: and I will
establish my covenant with him for an
everlasting covenant, *and* with his
seed after him.
20 And as for Ĭsh-mā-ĕl, I have heard
thee: Behold, I have blessed him, and
will make him fruitful, and will [n]mul-
tiply him exceedingly; [o]twelve princes
shall he beget, and I will make him
[p]a great nation.
21 But my covenant will I establish
with Isaac, which [q]Sarah shall bear
unto thee at this set time in the next
year.
22 And he left off [r]talking with him,
and God went up from Abraham.
23 ¶ And Abraham took Ĭsh-mā-ĕl
his son, and all that were born in his
house, and all that were bought with
his money, every male among the men
of Abraham's house; and circumcised
the flesh of their foreskin in the selfsame day, as [s]God had said unto
him.
24 And Abraham *was* ninety years
old and nine, when he was circumcised in the flesh of his foreskin.
25 And Ĭsh-mā-ĕl his son *was* thirteen years old, when he was circumcised in the flesh of his foreskin.
26 In [t]the selfsame day was Abraham
circumcised, and Ĭsh-mā-ĕl his son.
27 And all the men of [u]his house,
born [v]in the house, and bought with

i Ex. 4.24. Josh. 5.2-7.
6 That is, Princess.
j ch. 18.10. ch. 21.1.
7 she shall become nations.
k ch. 18.12. ch. 21.6.
l ch. 21.7.
m ch. 18.10. ch. 21.2. Gal. 4.28-31.
n ch. 16.10.
o ch. 25. 12-16.
p ch. 21.18.
q ch. 21.2.
r ch. 18.33. ch. 35.9-15.
s ver. 9.
t Ps. 119. 60.
u ch. 18.19.
v ch. 14.14.

CHAP. 18
a ch. 13.18. ch. 14.13. Acts 7.2.
b ver. 22. ch. 19.1.
c Heb. 13.2. 1 Pet. 4.9.
d ch. 24.32. ch. 43.24.
1 stay.
2 you have passed.
3 Hasten.
e ch. 24.67. Titus 2.5.
f ch. 21.2. Luke 1.13. Rom. 9.9.
g Rom. 4.19.
h Heb. 11.11.
i ch. 17.17. Luke 1.18.
j 1 Pet. 3.6.
k Ps. 115.3. Jer. 32.17. Zech. 8.6. Matt. 3.9. Matt. 19.26. Luke 1.37. Rom. 4.21. Heb. 11.19.

money of the stranger, were circumcised with him.

CHAPTER 18

AND the LORD [a]appeared unto him
in the plains of Măm-rē: and he
sat in the tent door in the heat of the
day;
2 And he lift up his eyes and looked,
and, lo, [b]three men stood by him: and
when he saw *them*, he [c]ran to meet
them from the tent door, and bowed
himself toward the ground,
3 And said, My Lord, if now I have
found favour in thy sight, pass not
away, I pray thee, from thy servant:
4 Let a little water, I pray you, be
fetched, and [d]wash your feet, and rest
yourselves under the tree:
5 And I will fetch a morsel of bread,
and [1]comfort ye your hearts; after
that ye shall pass on: for therefore
[2]are ye come to your servant. And
they said, So do, as thou hast said.
6 And Abraham hastened into the
tent unto Sarah, and said, [3]Make
ready quickly three measures of fine
meal, knead *it*, and make cakes upon
the hearth.
7 And Abraham ran unto the herd,
and fetcht a calf tender and good,
and gave *it* unto a young man; and he
hasted to dress it.
8 And he took butter, and milk, and
the calf which he had dressed, and
set *it* before them; and he stood by
them under the tree, and they did eat.
9 ¶ And they said unto him, Where
is Sarah thy wife? And he said, Behold, [e]in the tent.
10 And he said, I will certainly return
unto thee according to the time of life;
and, lo, Sarah thy wife shall have [f]a
son. And Sarah heard *it* in the tent
door, which *was* behind him.
11 Now Abraham and Sarah *were*
[g]old *and* well stricken in age; *and* it
ceased to be with Sarah after the
[h]manner of women.
12 Therefore Sarah laughed within
herself, saying, [i]After I am waxed old
shall I have pleasure, my [j]lord being
old also?
13 And the LORD said unto Abraham,
Wherefore did Sarah laugh, saying,
Shall I of a surety bear a child, which
am old?
14 Is any thing [k]too hard for the
LORD? At the time appointed I will
return unto thee, according to the
time of life, and Sarah shall have a
son.
15 Then Sarah denied, saying, I

laughed not; for she was afraid. And
he said, Nay; but thou didst laugh.
16 ¶ And the men rose up from
thence, and looked toward Sodom:
and Abraham went with them to bring
them on the way.
17 And the LORD said, [l]Shall I hide
from Abraham that thing which I do;
18 Seeing that Abraham shall surely
become a great and mighty nation,
and all the nations of the earth shall
[m]be blessed in him?
19 For I know him, that he [n]will command his children and his household
after him, and they shall keep the way
of the LORD, to do justice and judgment; that the LORD may bring upon
Abraham that which he hath spoken
of him.
20 And the LORD said, Because the
[o]cry of Sodom and Gō-mŏr´-răh is
great, and because their sin is very
grievous;
21 I will go down now, [p]and see
whether they have done altogether
according to the cry of it, which is
come unto me; and if not, I will know.
22 And the men turned their faces
from thence, and went toward Sodom:
but Abraham stood yet before the
[q]LORD.
23 ¶ And Abraham drew near, and
said, [r]Wilt thou also destroy the righteous with the wicked?
24 Peradventure there be [s]fifty righteous within the city: wilt thou also
destroy and not spare the place for
the fifty righteous that *are* therein?
25 That be far from thee to do after
this manner, to slay the righteous with
the wicked: and that the [t]righteous
should be as the wicked, that be far
from thee: Shall [u]not the Judge of all
the earth do right?
26 And the LORD said, [v]If I find in
Sodom fifty righteous within the city,
then I will spare all the place for their
sakes.
27 And Abraham answered and said,
[w]Behold now, I have taken upon me
to speak unto the Lord, which *am but*
[x]dust and ashes:
28 Peradventure there shall lack five
of the fifty righteous: wilt thou destroy all the city for *lack of* five? And
he said, If I find there forty and five,
I will not destroy *it*.
29 And he spake unto him [y]yet again,
and said, Peradventure there shall be
forty found there. And he said, I will
not do *it* for forty's sake.
30 And he said *unto him*, [z]Oh let not
the Lord be angry, and I will speak:

[l] Ps. 25.14. Amos 3.7. John 15.15
[m] ch. 12.3. ch. 22.18. Ps. 72.17. Acts 3.25. Gal. 3.8,9, 16,18.
[n] Deut. 6.6,7. Josh. 24.15. Eph. 6.4.
[o] ch. 4.10. ch. 19.13. James 5.4.
[p] ch. 11.5. Ex. 3.8. Ps. 14.2. Heb. 4.13.
[q] vers. 1,2.
[r] Num. 16. 22. 2 Sam. 24. 17. Ps. 11.4-7.
[s] Matt. 7.13, 14.
[t] Isa. 3.10,11.
[u] Job 8.3,20. Job 34.17. Ps. 58.11. Ps. 94.2. Rom. 3.5,6.
[v] Jer. 5.1. Eze. 22.30. Matt. 24.22.
[w] Luke 18.1.
[x] Ps. 8.4.
[y] 1 Thes. 5. 17.
[z] Isa. 55.8,9.
[a] Heb. 4.16.
[b] Judg. 6.39.
[c] Ex. 34.6,7. Ps. 34.15. Pro. 15.29. 1 John 3.22. Jas. 5.16.

CHAP. 19

[a] ch. 18.2,22.
[b] Heb. 13.2.
[c] Luke 24.28.
[d] ch. 18.8.
[e] Isa. 3.9.
[f] ch. 4.1. Judg. 19.22. Rom. 1.24. Jude 7.
[g] Judg. 19. 24.
[h] ch. 18.5.
[i] Ex. 2.14. Acts 7.26, 28. 2 Pet. 2.7,8.

Peradventure there shall thirty be
found there. And he said, I will not do
it, if I find thirty there.
31 And he said, Behold now, [a]I have
taken upon me to speak unto the
Lord: Peradventure there shall be
twenty found there. And he said, I
will not destroy *it* for twenty's sake.
32 And he said, [b]Oh let not the Lord
be angry, and I will speak yet but this
once: Peradventure ten shall be found
there. And he said, [c]I will not destroy
it for ten's sake.
33 And the LORD went his way, as
soon as he had left communing with
Abraham: and Abraham returned unto his place.

CHAPTER 19

AND there came [a]two angels to
Sodom at even; and Lot sat in the
gate of Sodom: and Lot seeing *them*
rose up to meet them; and he bowed
himself with his face toward the
ground;
2 And he said, Behold now, my lords,
[b]turn in, I pray you, into your servant's house, and tarry all night, and
wash your feet, and ye shall rise up
early, and go on your ways. And they
said, Nay; [c]but we will abide in the
street all night.
3 And he pressed upon them greatly;
and they turned in unto him, and
entered into his house; and [d]he made
them a feast, and did bake unleavened
bread, and they did eat.
4 ¶ But before they lay down, the
men of the city, *even* the men of Sodom, compassed the house round,
both old and young, all the people
from every quarter:
5 And [e]they called unto Lot, and said
unto him, [f]Where *are* the men which
came in to thee this night? bring them
out unto us, that we may know
them.
6 And [g]Lot went out at the door unto
them, and shut the door after him,
7 And said, I pray you, brethren, do
not so wickedly.
8 Behold now, I have two daughters
which have not known man; let me,
I pray you, bring them out unto you,
and do ye to them as *is* good in your
eyes: only unto these men do nothing;
for [h]therefore came they under the
shadow of my roof.
9 And they said, Stand back. And
they said *again*, [i]This one *fellow* came
in to sojourn, and he will needs be a
judge: now will we deal worse with
thee, than with them. And they press-

ed sore upon the man, *even* Lot, and
came near to break the door.
10 But the men put forth their hand,
and pulled Lot into the house to them,
and shut to the door.
11 And they smote the men that *were*
at the door of the house [j]with blindness, both small and great: so that
they wearied themselves to find the
door.
12 ¶ And the men said unto Lot, Hast
[k]thou here any besides? son in law,
and thy sons, and thy daughters, and
whatsoever thou hast in the city,
[l]bring *them* out of this place:
13 For we will destroy this place, because the cry of them is waxen great
before the face of the LORD; and the
LORD hath [m]sent us to destroy it.
14 And Lot went out, and spake unto
his sons in law, which married [n]his
daughters, and said, Up, [o]get you out
of this place; for the LORD will destroy
this city. But he seemed [p]as one that
mocked unto his sons in law.
15 ¶ And when the morning arose,
then the angels hastened Lot, saying,
Arise, take thy wife, and thy two
daughters, which [1]are here; lest thou
be consumed in [2]the iniquity of the
city.
16 And while he lingered, the men
laid hold upon his hand, and upon the
hand of his wife, and upon the hand of
his two daughters; [q]the LORD being
merciful unto him: and they brought
him forth, and set him without the
city.
17 ¶ And it came to pass, when they
had brought them forth abroad, that
he said, [r]Escape for thy life; [s]look not
behind thee, neither stay thou in all
the plain; escape to the mountain,
lest thou be consumed.
18 And Lot said unto them, Oh, not
so, my Lord:
19 Behold now, thy servant hath
found grace in thy sight, and [t]thou
hast magnified thy mercy, which thou
hast shewed unto me in saving my
life; and I cannot escape to the mountain, lest some evil take me, and I
die:
20 Behold now, this city *is* near to
flee unto, and it *is* a little one: Oh, let
me escape thither, (*is* it not a little
one?) and my soul shall live.
21 And he said unto him, See, I have
accepted [3]thee concerning this thing
also, that I will not overthrow this
city, for the which thou hast spoken.
22 Haste thee, escape thither; for I
cannot do any thing till thou be come
thither. Therefore the name of the
city was [u]called [4]Zō-ăr.
23 ¶ The sun was [5]risen upon the
earth when Lot entered into Zō-ăr.
24 Then [v]the LORD rained upon Sodom and upon Gō-mŏr-răh brimstone
and fire from the LORD out of heaven;
25 And he overthrew those cities,
and all [w]the plain, and all the inhabitants of the cities, and that which grew
upon the ground.
26 ¶ But his wife [x]looked back from
behind him, and she became a pillar
of salt.
27 ¶ And Abraham gat up early in the
morning to the place where he [y]stood
before the LORD:
28 And he looked toward Sodom and
Gō-mŏr-răh, and toward all the land
of the plain, and beheld, and, lo, [z]the
smoke of the country went up as the
smoke of a furnace.
29 ¶ And it came to pass, when God
destroyed the cities of the plain, that
God [a]remembered Abraham, and sent
Lot out of the midst of the overthrow,
when he overthrew the cities in the
which Lot dwelt.
30 ¶ And Lot went up out of Zō-ăr,
and [b]dwelt in the mountain, and his
two daughters with him; for he feared
to dwell in Zō-ăr: and he dwelt in a
cave, he and his two daughters.
31 And the firstborn said unto the
younger, Our father *is* old, and *there*
is not a man in the earth [c]to come in
unto us after the manner of all the
earth:
32 Come, [d]let us make our father
drink wine, and we will lie with him,
[e]that we may preserve seed of our
father.
33 And they made their father drink
wine that night: and the firstborn
went in, and lay with her father; and
he perceived not when she lay down,
nor when she arose.
34 And it came to pass on the morrow, that the firstborn said unto the
younger, Behold, I lay yesternight
with my father: let us make him
drink wine this night also; and go
thou in, *and* lie with him, that we may
preserve seed of our father.
35 And they made their father drink
wine that night also: and the younger
arose, and lay with him; and he perceived not when she lay down, nor
when she arose.
36 Thus were both the daughters of
Lot with child by their father.
37 And the firstborn bare a son, and
called his name Moab: the same [f]*is* the

j 2 Ki. 6.18. Acts 13.11.
k Josh. 6.22.
l ch. 7.1. 2 Pet. 2.9.
m 1 Chr. 21. 15.
n Jer. 51.6, 45.
o Num. 16. 21,45. Rev. 18.4.
p Ex. 9.21. Luke 17.28-30. Luke 24.11.
1 are found.
2 Or, punishment.
q Ex. 34.7. 1 Sam. 2.9. 1 Chr. 16.34. Ps. 25.10. Ps. 31.23. Ps. 32.10. Ps. 33. 18. Ps. 34.22. Ps. 97.10. Ps. 145.20. Pro. 2.8. Eph. 2.4,5.
r Heb. 2.3.
s ver. 26.
t 1 Tim. 1. 14-16.
3 thy face. Job 42.9. 1 Sam. 25. 35. Ps. 145.19.
u ch. 13.10. ch. 14.2.
4 That is, little.
5 gone forth.
v Deut. 29.23. Ps. 11.6. Isa. 13.19. Jer. 20.16. Jer. 50.40. Eze. 16. 49.50. Hosea 11.8. Amos 4.11. Zeph. 2.9. Luke 17.29. 2 Pet. 2.6. Jude 7.
w ch. 14.3. Ps. 107.34.
x Luke 17.31.
y ch. 18.22.
z Rev. 18.9.
a ch. 8.1. ch. 18.23.
b vers. 17,19.
c ch. 16.2,4. ch. 38.8. Deut. 25.5.
d Luke 21.34. 1 Cor. 15.33.
e Mark 12.19.
f Deut. 2.9.

father of the Moabites unto this day.
38 And the younger, she also bare
a son, and called his name Bĕn–ăm′-
mī: the [g]same *is* the father of the children of Ammon unto this day.

CHAPTER 20

AND Abraham journeyed from
thence [a]toward the south country,
and dwelled between Kā′-dĕsh and
Shur, and sojourned in [b]Gē′-rär.
2 And [c]Abraham said of Sarah his
wife, She *is* my sister: and Ă-bĭm′-ĕ-
lĕch king of Gē′-rär sent, and took
[d]Sarah.
3 But God [e]came to Ă-bĭm′-ĕ-lĕch in
[f]a dream by night, and said to him,
Behold, thou *art but* [g]a dead man, for
the woman which thou hast taken;
for she *is* [1]a man's wife.
4 But Ă-bĭm′-ĕ-lĕch had not come
near her: and he said, Lord, [h]wilt thou
slay also a righteous nation?
5 Said he not unto me, She *is* my
sister? and she, even she herself said,
He *is* my brother: in the [2]integrity of
my heart and innocency of my hands
have I done this.
6 And God said unto him in a dream,
Yea, I know that thou didst this in the
integrity of thy heart; for I also [i]with-
held thee from sinning against me:
therefore suffered I thee not to touch
her.
7 Now therefore restore the man *his*
wife; for he *is* a prophet, and he [j]shall
pray for thee, and thou shalt live:
and if thou restore *her* not, know
thou that thou shalt surely die, thou,
and all that *are* thine.
8 Therefore Ă-bĭm′-ĕ-lĕch rose early
in the morning, and called all his servants, and told all these things in their
ears: and the men were sore afraid.
9 Then Ă-bĭm′-ĕ-lĕch called Abraham, and said unto him, What hast
thou done unto us? and what have I
offended thee, that thou hast brought
on me and on my kingdom [k]a great
sin? thou hast done deeds unto me that
ought not to be done.
10 And Ă-bĭm′-ĕ-lĕch said unto Abraham, What sawest thou, that thou
hast done this thing?
11 And Abraham said, Because I
thought, [l]Surely the fear of God *is* not
in this place; and they will slay me for
my wife's sake.
12 And [m]yet indeed *she is* my sister;
she *is* the daughter of my father, but
not the daughter of my mother; and
she became my wife.
13 And it came to pass, when God
[n]caused me to wander from my father's house, that I said unto her, This *is*
thy kindness which thou shalt shew
unto me; at every place whither we
shall come, say of me, [o]He *is* my
brother.
14 And Ă-bĭm′-ĕ-lĕch took [p]sheep,
and oxen, and menservants, and
womenservants, and gave *them* unto
Abraham, and restored him Sarah his
wife.
15 And Ă-bĭm′-ĕ-lĕch said, [q]Behold,
my land *is* before thee: dwell [3]where
it pleaseth thee.
16 And unto Sarah he said, Behold,
I have given thy [r]brother a thousand
pieces of silver: behold, he *is* to thee
a covering of the eyes, unto all that
are with thee, and with all *other:* thus
she was reproved.
17 ¶ So Abraham [s]prayed unto God:
and God healed Ă-bĭm′-ĕ-lĕch, and his
wife, and his maidservants; and they
bare *children.*
18 For the LORD had [t]fast closed up
all the wombs of the house of Ă-bĭm′-
ĕ-lĕch, because of Sarah Abraham's
wife.

CHAPTER 21

AND the LORD [a]visited Sarah as he
had said, and the LORD did unto
Sarah [b]as he had spoken.
2 For Sarah conceived, [c]and bare
Abraham a son in his old age, at the
set time of which God had spoken to
him.
3 And Abraham [d]called the name of
his son that was born unto him, whom
Sarah bare to him, Isaac.
4 And Abraham [e]circumcised his son
Isaac being eight days old, as God had
commanded him.
5 And Abraham was an hundred
years old, when his son Isaac was born
unto him.
6 ¶ And Sarah said, [f]God hath made
me to laugh, *so that* all that hear will
laugh [g]with me.
7 And she said, Who would have
said unto Abraham, that Sarah should
have given children suck? for [h]I have
born *him* a son in his old age.
8 And the child grew, and was weaned: and Abraham made a great feast
the *same* day that Isaac was weaned.
9 ¶ And Sarah saw the [i]son of Hā′-
gär the Egyptian, which she had born
unto Abraham, [j]mocking.
10 Wherefore she said unto Abraham, [k]Cast out this bondwoman and
her son: for the son of this bondwoman shall not be heir with my son,
even with Isaac.

g Deut. 2.19.

CHAP. 20
a ch. 18.1.
b ch. 26.6.
c ch. 12.11-13. ch. 26.7.
d ch. 12.15.
e Ps. 105.14.
f Job 4.12. Job 33.15.
g ver. 7.
1 married to an husband.
h ch. 18.23-25.
2 Or, simplicity, or, sincerity.
i ch. 35.5. Ex. 34.4. 1 Sam. 25. 26,34.
j 1 Sam. 7.5. 2 Ki. 5.11. Job 42.8. Jas. 5.14-16. 1 John 5.16.
k ch. 39.9. Josh. 7.25.
l ch. 42.18. Neh. 5.15. Pro. 16.6.
m ch. 11.29.
n ch. 12.1,9, 11.
o ch. 12.13
p ch. 12.16.
q ch. 13.9. ch. 47.6.
3 as is good in thine eyes.
r ver. 5.
s Job 42.8. Jas. 5.16.
t ch. 12.17.

CHAP. 21
a 1 Sam. 2.21.
b ch. 17.19. ch. 18.10,14. Gal. 4.23.
c Acts 7.8. Heb. 11.11.
d ch. 17.19.
e ch. 17.10-12.
f Ps. 126.2. Isa. 54.1.
g Luke 1.14, 58.
h ch. 18.11.
i ch. 16.1,4, 15.
j Gal. 4.29.
k ch. 25.6. ch. 36.6,7. Gal. 4.30, 31.

11 And the thing was very [l]grievous in Abraham's sight because of his son.

12 ¶ And God said unto Abraham, Let it not be grievous in thy sight because of the lad, and because of thy bondwoman; in all that Sarah hath said unto thee, hearken unto her voice; for [m]in Isaac shall thy seed be called.

13 And also [n]of the son of the bondwoman will I make a nation, because he *is* thy seed.

14 And Abraham rose up early in the morning, and took bread, and a bottle of water, and gave *it* unto Hā'-gär, putting *it* on her shoulder, and the child, and [o]sent her away: and she departed, and wandered in the wilderness of Bē̂er–shē'-bă.

15 And [p]the water was spent in the bottle, and she cast the child under one of the shrubs.

16 And she went, and sat her down over against *him* a good way off, as it were a bowshot: for she said, [q]Let me not see the death of the child. And she sat over against *him*, and lift up her voice, and wept.

17 And [r]God heard the voice of the lad; and the angel of God called to Hā'-gär out of heaven, and said unto her, What aileth thee, Hā'-gär? fear not; for God hath heard the voice of the lad where he *is*.

18 Arise, lift up the lad, and hold him in thine hand; for [s]I will make him a great nation.

19 And God [t]opened her eyes, and she saw a well of water; and she went, and filled the bottle with water, and gave the lad drink.

20 And [u]God was with the lad; and he grew, and [v]dwelt in the wilderness, and became an archer.

21 And he dwelt in the wilderness of Pâr'-ăn: and his mother took him a wife out of the [w]land of Egypt.

22 ¶ And it came to pass at that time, that [x]Ă-bĭm'-ĕ-lĕch and Phī'-chŏl the chief captain of his host spake unto Abraham, saying, [y]God *is* with thee in all that thou doest:

23 Now therefore [z]swear unto me here by God [1]that thou wilt not deal falsely with me, nor with my son, nor with my son's son: *but* according to the kindness that I have done unto thee, thou shalt do unto me, and to the land wherein thou hast sojourned.

24 And Abraham said, I will swear.

25 And Abraham reproved Ă-bĭm'-ĕ-lĕch because of a well of water, which Ă-bĭm'-ĕ-lĕch's servants had violently [a]taken away.

l ch. 17.18.
m Rom. 9.7. Heb. 11.18.
n ch. 16.10. ch. 17.20. ch. 25.12.
o John 8.35.
p Num. 20.5. Ps. 63.1.
q ch. 44.34.
r Ex. 3.7. 2 Ki. 13.4, 23.
s ver. 13. ch. 25.12. Judg. 8.24.
t Num. 22.31. 2 Ki. 6.17. Luke 24.16.
u ch. 39.2, 3.
v ch. 16.12.
w ch. 24.4.
x ch. 20.2.
y ch. 26.28. Isa. 8.10.
z Josh. 2.12. 1 Sam. 24. 21.
1 if thou shalt lie unto me.
a ch. 26.15-22.
b ch. 26.28-31.
c ch. 33.8.
d ch. 31.48.
e ch. 26.33.
2 That is, the well of the oath.
f Josh. 13.2.
3 Or, tree.
g Deut. 33.27. Ps. 9.7. Ps. 29.10. Ps. 45.6. Ps. 90.2. Ps. 93.2. Isa. 9.6. Isa. 40.28. Isa. 63.16. Jer. 10.10. Lam. 5.19. Micah 5.2. Hab. 1.12. Rom. 16.26. Heb. 13.8. 1 Tim. 1.17. Rev. 10.6. Rev. 15.7.

CHAP. 22

a Heb. 11.17. Jas. 1.12-14.
1 Behold me.
b John 3.16.
c 2 Chr. 3.1.
d Heb. 11.17-19.
e John 19.17. 1 Pet. 2.24.

26 And Ă-bĭm'-ĕ-lĕch said, I wot not who hath done this thing: neither didst thou tell me, neither yet heard I *of it*, but to day.

27 And Abraham took sheep and oxen, and gave them unto Ă-bĭm'-ĕ-lĕch; and both of them [b]made a covenant.

28 And Abraham set seven ewe lambs of the flock by themselves.

29 And Ă-bĭm'-ĕ-lĕch said unto Abraham, [c]What *mean* these seven ewe lambs which thou hast set by themselves?

30 And he said, For *these* seven ewe lambs shalt thou take of my hand, that [d]they may be a witness unto me, that I have digged this well.

31 Wherefore he [e]called that place [2]Bē̂er–shē'-bă; because there they sware both of them.

32 Thus they made a covenant at Bē̂er–shē'-bă: then Ă-bĭm'-ĕ-lĕch rose up, and Phī'-chŏl the chief captain of his host, and they returned into the [f]land of the Philistines.

33 ¶ And *Abraham* planted a [3]grove in Bē̂er–shē'-bă, and called there on the name of the LORD, the [g]everlasting God.

34 And Abraham sojourned in the Philistines' land many days.

CHAPTER 22

AND it came to pass after these things, that [a]God did tempt Abraham, and said unto him, Abraham: and he said, [1]Behold, *here* I *am*.

2 And he said, [b]Take now thy son, thine only *son* Isaac, whom thou lovest, and get thee into the land [c]of Mō-rī'-ăh; and offer him there for a burnt offering upon one of the mountains which I will tell thee of.

3 ¶ And Abraham [d]rose up early in the morning, and saddled his ass, and took two of his young men with him, and Isaac his son, and clave the wood for the burnt offering, and rose up, and went unto the place of which God had told him.

4 Then on the third day Abraham lifted up his eyes, and saw the place afar off.

5 And Abraham said unto his young men, Abide ye here with the ass; and I and the lad will go yonder and worship, and come again to you.

6 And Abraham took the wood of the burnt offering, and [e]laid *it* upon Isaac his son; and he took the fire in his hand, and a knife; and they went both of them together.

7 And Isaac spake unto Abraham his

father, and said, My father: and he said, [2]Here *am* I, my son. And he said, Behold the fire and the wood: but where *is* the [3]lamb for a burnt offering?
8 And Abraham said, My son, God will provide himself [f]a lamb for a burnt offering: so they went both of them together.
9 And they came to the place which God had told him of; and Abraham built an altar there, and laid the wood in order, and [g]bound Isaac his son, and laid him on the altar upon the wood.
10 And Abraham [h]stretched forth his hand, and took the knife to slay his son.
11 And the angel of the LORD called unto him out of heaven, and said, Abraham, Abraham: and he said, Here *am* I.
12 And he said, [i]Lay not thine hand upon the lad, neither do thou any thing unto him: for now [j]I know that thou fearest God, seeing thou hast not withheld thy son, thine only *son* from me.
13 And Abraham lifted up his eyes, and looked, and behold behind *him* a ram caught in a thicket by his horns: and Abraham went and took the ram, and offered him up for a burnt offering [k]in the stead of his son.
14 And Abraham called the name of that place [4]Jĕ-hṓ-văh–jī́-rēh: as it is said *to* this day, In the mount of the LORD it shall be seen.
15 ¶ And the angel of the LORD called unto Abraham out of heaven the second time,
16 And said, [l]By myself have I sworn, saith the LORD, for because thou hast done this thing, and hast not withheld thy son, thine only *son:*
17 That in blessing I will bless thee, and in multiplying I will multiply thy seed as the [m]stars of the heaven, and as the [n]sand which *is* upon the sea [5]shore; and thy seed shall [o]possess the gate of his enemies;
18 And [p]in thy seed shall all the nations of the earth be blessed; because [q]thou hast obeyed my voice.
19 So Abraham returned unto his young men, and they rose up and went together to Bḗer–shḗ-bă; and Abraham dwelt at Bḗer–shḗ-bă.
20 ¶ And it came to pass after these things, that it was told Abraham, saying, Behold, [r]Mĭĺ-căh, she hath also born children unto thy brother Nahor;
21 Huz [s]his firstborn, and Buz his brother, and Kĕ-mū́-ĕl the father of [t]Ā́r-ăm,
22 And Chĕś-ĕd, and Hā́-zō, and Pĭĺ-dăsh, and Jĭd́-lăph, and Bĕ-thū́-ĕl.
23 And [u]Bĕ-thū́-ĕl begat Rebekah: these eight Mĭĺ-căh did bear to Nahor, Abraham's brother.
24 And his concubine, whose name *was* Rĕū́-măh, she bare also Tḗ-băh, and Gā́-hăm, and Thā́-hăsh, and Mā́-ă-chăh.

CHAPTER 23

AND Sarah was an hundred and seven and twenty years old: *these were* the years of the life of Sarah.
2 And Sarah died in Kĭŕ-jăth–ăŕ-bă; the same *is* Hḗ-brŏn in the land of Canaan: and Abraham came [a]to mourn for Sarah, and to weep for her.
3 ¶ And Abraham stood up from before his dead, and spake unto the sons of Heth, saying,
4 I *am* [b]a stranger and a sojourner with you: give me a possession of a [c]buryingplace with you, that I may bury my dead out of my sight.
5 And the children of Heth answered Abraham, saying unto him,
6 Hear us, my lord: thou *art* [1]a mighty [d]prince among us: in the choice of our sepulchres bury thy dead; none of us shall withhold from thee his sepulchre, but that thou mayest bury thy dead.
7 And Abraham stood up, and bowed [e]himself to the people of the land, *even* to the children of Heth.
8 And he communed with them, saying, If it be your mind that I should bury my dead out of my sight; hear me, and intreat for me to Ḗ-phrŏn the son of Zṓ-hăr,
9 That he may give me the cave of Măch-pḗ-lăh, which he hath, which *is* in the end of his field; for [2]as much money as it is worth he shall give it me for a possession of a buryingplace amongst you.
10 And Ḗ-phrŏn dwelt among the children of Heth: and Ḗ-phrŏn the Hittite answered Abraham in the [3]audience of the children of Heth, *even* of all that went in at the [f]gate of his city, saying,
11 Nay, [g]my lord, hear me: the field give I thee, and the cave that *is* therein, I give it thee; in the presence of the sons of my people give I it thee: bury thy dead.
12 And Abraham bowed down himself before the people of the land.
13 And he spake unto Ḗ-phrŏn in the audience of the people of the land,

2 Behold me.
3 Or, kid.
f 1 Pet. 1.19.
g John 10.17, 18. Heb. 11.17.
h Isa. 53.6-12.
i 1 Sam. 15. 22.
j ch. 26.5. Rom. 8.32. Jas. 2.22.
k 1 Cor. 5.7, 8.
4 That is, the Lord will see, or, provide.
l Ps. 105.9. Luke 1.73. Heb. 6.13, 14.
m ch. 15.5. Jer. 33.22.
n ch. 13.16.
5 lip.
Ps. 2.8.
o ch. 24.60. Micah 1.9.
p ch. 12.3. ch. 18.18. Gal. 3.8,9, 16,18.
q vers. 3.10. ch. 26.5.
r ch. 11.29.
s Job 1.1.
t Job 32.2.
u ch. 24.15.

CHAP. 23
a John 11. 31,35.
b ch. 17.8. 1 Chr. 29.15. Ps. 39.12. Ps. 105.12. Ps. 119.19. 2 Cor. 5.6,7. Heb. 11.9, 13. 1 Pet. 1.17. 1 Pet. 2.11.
c ch. 49.30.
1 a prince of God.
d ch. 13.2. ch. 14.14. ch. 24.35.
e Rom. 13.7.
2 full money.
3 ears.
f ch. 34.20, 24. Ruth 4.4.
g 2 Sam. 24. 20-24.

saying, But if thou *wilt give it*, I pray thee, hear me: [h]I will give thee money for the field; take *it* of me, and I will bury my dead there.

14 And Ē´phrŏn answered Abraham, saying unto him,

15 My lord, hearken unto me: the land *is worth* four hundred shekels [i]of silver; what *is* that betwixt me and thee? bury therefore thy dead.

16 And Abraham hearkened unto Ē´phrŏn; and Abraham [j]weighed to Ē´phrŏn the silver, which he had named in the audience of the sons of Heth, four hundred shekels of silver, current *money* with the merchant.

17 ¶ And [k]the field of Ē´phrŏn, which *was* in Măch-pē´lăh, which *was* before Măm´rē, the field, and the cave which *was* therein, and all the trees that *were* in the field, that *were* in all the borders round about, were made sure

18 Unto Abraham for a possession in the presence of the children of Heth, before all that went in at the gate of his city.

19 And after this, [l]Abraham buried Sarah his wife in the cave of the field of Măch-pē´lăh before Măm´rē: the same *is* Hē´brŏn in the land of Canaan.

20 And the field, and the cave that *is* therein, were [m]made sure unto Abraham for a possession of a buryingplace by the sons of Heth.

CHAPTER 24

AND Abraham [a]was old, *and* [1]well stricken in age: and the LORD had [b]blessed Abraham in all things.

2 And Abraham said [c]unto his eldest servant of his house, that ruled [d]over all that he had, [e]Put, I pray thee, thy hand under my thigh:

3 And I will make thee swear by the LORD, the God of heaven, and the God of the earth, that thou shalt [f]not take a wife unto my son of the daughters of the Canaanites, among whom I dwell:

4 But thou shalt go [g]unto my country, and to my kindred, and take a wife unto my son Isaac.

5 And the servant said unto him, Peradventure the woman will not be willing to follow me unto this land: must I needs bring thy son again unto the land from whence thou camest?

6 And Abraham said unto him, Beware [h]thou that thou bring not my son thither again.

7 ¶ The LORD God of heaven, which took [i]me from my father's house, and from the land of my kindred, and which spake unto me, and that sware unto me, saying, [j]Unto thy seed will I give this land; he shall send [k]his angel before thee, and thou shalt take a wife unto my son from thence.

8 And if the woman will not be willing to follow thee, then thou shalt [l]be clear from this my oath: only bring not my son thither again.

9 And the servant put his hand under the thigh of Abraham his master, and sware to him concerning that matter.

10 ¶ And the servant took ten camels of the camels of his master, and departed; [2]for all the goods of his master *were* in his hand: and he arose, and went to Mĕs-ŏ-pŏ-tā´mĭ-ă, unto [m]the city of Nahor.

11 And he made his camels to kneel down without the city by a well of water at the time of the evening, *even* the time that [3]women [n]go out to draw *water*.

12 And he said, [o]O LORD God of my master Abraham, [p]I pray thee, send me good speed this day, and shew kindness unto my master Abraham.

13 Behold, I stand *here* by the well of water; and the daughters of the men of the city come out to draw water:

14 And let it come to pass, that the damsel to whom I shall say, Let down thy pitcher, I pray thee, that I may drink; and she shall say, Drink, and I will give thy camels drink also: *let the same be* she [q]*that* thou hast appointed for thy servant Isaac; and [r]thereby shall I know that thou hast shewed kindness unto my master.

15 ¶ And it came to pass, [s]before he had done speaking, that, behold, Rebekah came out, who was born to Bĕ-thū´ĕl, son of [t]Mĭl´căh, the wife of Nahor, Abraham's brother, with her pitcher upon her shoulder.

16 And the damsel *was* [u]very [4]fair to look upon, a virgin, neither had any man known her: and she went down to the well, and filled her pitcher, and came up.

17 And the servant ran to meet her, and said, [v]Let me, I pray thee, drink a little water of thy pitcher.

18 And she said, [w]Drink, my lord: and she hasted, and let down her pitcher upon her hand, and gave him drink.

19 And when she had done giving him drink, she said, I will draw *water* for thy camels also, until they have done drinking.

20 And she hasted, and emptied her pitcher into the trough, and ran again

h Phil. 4.5-8.
i Ex. 30.13. Eze. 45.12.
j Jer. 32.9-12.
k ch. 25.9. ch. 49.30,31, 32. ch. 50.13. Acts 7.16.
l ch. 35.29.
m Ruth 4.7,8, 9,10. Jer. 32.10, 11.

CHAP. 24

a ch. 18.11.
1 gone into days.
b ch. 13.2. Gal. 3.9.
c ch. 15.2.
d ver. 10. ch. 39.4-6.
e ch. 47.29. Lam. 5.6.
f Ex. 34.16. Deut. 7.3. 2 Cor. 6.14-17.
g ch. 28.2.
h 2 Pet. 2.20-22.
i ch. 12.1,7.
j ch. 13.15. Ex. 32.13.
k Ex. 23.20. Ps. 34.7. Isa. 63.9.
l Josh. 2.17-20.
2 Or, and.
m ch. 27.43.
3 women which draw water go forth.
n Ex. 2.16. 1 Sam. 9.11.
o ver. 27. ch. 26.24. Ex. 3.6,15.
p Phil. 4.6.
q Pro. 19.14.
r Judg. 6.17-37. 1 Sam. 6.7.
s Ps. 34.15.
t ch. 11.29.
u ch. 26.7.
4 good of countenance.
v John 4.7.
w 1 Pet. 3.8. 1 Pet. 4.9.

unto the well to draw *water*, and drew for all his camels.

21 And the man [x]wondering at her held his peace, to wit whether the LORD had made his journey prosperous or not.

22 And it came to pass, as the camels had done drinking, that the man took a golden [5]earring of [y]half a shekel weight, and two bracelets for her hands of ten *shekels* weight of gold;

23 And said, Whose daughter *art* thou? tell me, I pray thee: is there room *in* thy father's house for us to lodge in?

24 And she said unto him, I *am* the daughter of Bĕ-thū'-ĕl the son of Mĭl'-cäh, which she bare unto Nahor.

25 She said moreover unto him, We have [z]both straw and provender enough, and room to lodge in.

26 And the man [a]bowed down his head, and worshipped the LORD.

27 And he said, [b]Blessed *be* the LORD God of my master Abraham, who hath not left destitute my master of [c]his mercy and his truth: I *being* in the way, [d]the LORD led me to the house of my master's brethren.

28 And the damsel ran, and told *them of* her mother's house these things.

29 ¶ And Rebekah had a brother, and his name *was* [e]Laban: and Laban ran out unto the man, unto the well.

30 And it came to pass, when he saw the earring and bracelets upon his sister's hands, and when he heard the words of Rebekah his sister, saying, Thus spake the man unto me; that he came unto the man; and, behold, he stood by the camels at the well.

31 And he said, Come in, [f]thou blessed of the LORD; wherefore standest thou without? for I have prepared the house, and room for the camels.

32 ¶ And the man came into the house: and he ungirded his camels, and [g]gave straw and provender for the camels, and water to wash his feet, and the men's feet that *were* with him.

33 And there was set *meat* before him to eat: but he said, [h]I will not eat, until I have told mine errand. And he said, Speak on.

34 And he said, I *am* Abraham's servant.

35 And the LORD hath [i]blessed my master greatly; and he is become great: and he hath given him [j]flocks, and herds, and silver, and gold, and menservants, and maidservants, and camels, and asses.

x Luke 2.19, 51.
5 Or, jewel for the forehead.
y Ex. 32.2,3. Isa. 3.19,20. 1 Pet. 3.3.
z 1 Pet. 4.9.
a ver. 52. Ex. 4.31.
b Ex. 18.10. Ruth 4.14. 1 Sam. 25. 32. 2 Sam. 18. 28. Luke 1.68.
c ch. 32.10. Ps. 98.3.
d ver. 48. Pro. 3.6.
e ch. 29.5.
f ch. 26.29. Judg. 17.2. Ruth 3.10. Ps. 115.15.
g ch. 43.24. Judg. 19.21.
h Job 23.12. John 4.34. Eph. 6.5-7.
i ver. 1. ch. 13.2.
j Job 1.3.
k ch. 21.2.
l ch. 21.10. ch. 25.5.
m ver. 3.
n ver. 7.
o ch. 5.22-24. ch. 17.1.
p Ex. 23.20.
q ver. 8.
r 1 Ki. 1.36. Acts 10.7,8, 22.
s Neh. 1.11. Ps. 90.17. Rom. 1.10.
t ver. 13.
u Heb. 13.2.
v ver. 15.
w 1 Sam. 1. 13. Isa. 65.24.
x Eze. 16. 11,12.
y ver. 26.
z Ps. 32.8. Ps. 48.14. Ps. 107.7. Isa. 48.17.
a ch. 47.29. Josh. 2.14.

36 And Sarah my master's wife bare [k]a son to my master when she was old: and [l]unto him hath he given all that he hath.

37 And my master [m]made me swear, saying, Thou shalt not take a wife to my son of the daughters of the Canaanites, in whose land I dwell:

38 But thou shalt go unto my father's house, and to my kindred, and take a wife unto my son.

39 And I said unto my master, Peradventure the woman will not follow me.

40 And [n]he said unto me, The LORD, before whom [o]I walk, will send his [p]angel with thee, and prosper thy way; and thou shalt take a wife for my son of my kindred, and of my father's house:

41 Then [q]shalt thou be clear from *this* my oath, when thou comest to my kindred; and if they give not thee *one*, thou shalt be clear from my oath.

42 And I came this day unto the well, and said, [r]O LORD God of my master Abraham, if now thou do [s]prosper my way which I go:

43 Behold, [t]I stand by the well of water; and it shall come to pass, that when the virgin cometh forth to draw *water*, and I say to her, Give me, I pray thee, a little water of thy pitcher to drink;

44 And she say to me, [u]Both drink thou, and I will also draw for thy camels: *let* the same *be* the woman whom the LORD hath appointed out for my master's son.

45 And [v]before I had [w]done speaking in mine heart, behold, Rebekah came forth with her pitcher on her shoulder; and she went down unto the well, and drew *water:* and I said unto her, Let me drink, I pray thee.

46 And she made haste, and let down her pitcher from her *shoulder*, and said, Drink, and I will give thy camels drink also: so I drank, and she made the camels drink also.

47 And I asked her, and said, Whose daughter *art* thou? And she said, The daughter of Bĕ-thū'-ĕl, Nahor's son, whom Mĭl'-cäh bare unto him: and I put the [x]earring upon her face, and the bracelets upon her hands.

48 And I [y]bowed down my head, and worshipped the LORD, and blessed the LORD God of my master Abraham, which had [z]led me in the right way to take my master's brother's daughter unto his son.

49 And now [a]if ye will deal kindly and truly with my master, tell me: and

if not, tell me; that I may turn to
the right hand, or to the left.
50 Then Laban and Bĕ-thū-ĕl answered and said, [b]The thing proceedeth from the LORD: we cannot speak
unto thee bad or good.
51 Behold, Rebekah *is* [c]before thee,
take *her*, and go, and let her be thy
master's son's wife, as the LORD hath
spoken.
52 And it came to pass, that, when
Abraham's servant heard their words,
he worshipped the LORD, *bowing him-*
self to the earth.
53 And the servant brought forth
jewels [d]of silver, and [6]jewels of gold,
and raiment, and gave *them* to Rebekah: he gave also to her brother and
to her mother [e]precious things.
54 And they did eat and drink, he
and the men that *were* with him, and
tarried all night; and they rose up in
the morning, and he said, [f]Send me
away unto my master.
55 And her brother and her mother
said, Let the damsel abide with us [7]*a*
few days, at the least ten; after that
she shall go.
56 And he said unto them, Hinder
me not, seeing the [g]LORD hath prospered my way; send me away that I
may go to my master.
57 And they said, We will call the
damsel, and inquire at her mouth.
58 And they called Rebekah, and
said unto her, Wilt thou go with this
man? And she said, I will go.
59 And they sent away Rebekah their
sister, and her [h]nurse, and Abraham's
servant, and his men.
60 And they blessed Rebekah, and
said unto her, Thou *art* our sister, be
thou [i]*the mother* of thousands of mil-
lions, and let thy [j]seed possess the gate
of those which hate them.
61 ¶ And Rebekah arose, and her
damsels, and they rode upon the camels, and followed the man: and the servant took Rebekah, and went his
way.
62 And Isaac came from the way of
the well [k]Lā-hâi-rôi; for he dwelt in
the south country.
63 And Isaac went out [8]to [l]meditate
in the field at the eventide: and he lifted up his eyes, and saw, and, behold,
the camels *were* coming.
64 And Rebekah lifted up her eyes,
and when she saw Isaac, she lighted
[m]off the camel.
65 For she *had* said unto the servant,
What man *is* this that walketh in the
field to meet us? And the servant *had*
said, It *is* my master: therefore she
took a [n]vail, and covered herself.
66 And the servant told Isaac all
things that he had done.
67 And Isaac brought her into his
mother Sarah's tent, and took Rebekah, and she became his wife; and he
loved her: and [o]Isaac was comforted
after his mother's *death*.

CHAPTER 25

THEN again Abraham took a wife,
and her name *was* Kĕ-tū-răh.
2 And she bare him [a]Zimran, and
Jŏk-shăn, and Mē-dăn, and Mĭd-ĭ-ăn,
and Ĭsh-băk, and Shû-ăh.
3 And Jŏk-shăn begat Shē-bă, and
Dē-dăn. And the sons of Dē-dăn were
Ăssh-û-rĭm, and Lĕ-tû-shĭm, and Lĕ-
ŭm-mĭm.
4 And the sons of Mĭd-ĭ-ăn; Ē-phăh,
and Ē-phĕr, and Hā-nŏch, and Ă-bī-
dă, and Ĕl-dā-ăh. All these *were* the
children of Kĕ-tū-răh.
5 ¶ And Abraham [b]gave all that he
had unto Isaac.
6 But unto the sons of the concubines, which Abraham had, Abraham
gave gifts, and [c]sent them away from
Isaac his son, while he yet lived, eastward, unto the [d]east country.
7 And these *are* the days of the years
of Abraham's life which he lived, an
hundred threescore and fifteen years.
8 Then Abraham gave up the ghost,
and died in [e]a good old age, an old
man, and full *of years;* and was [f]gath-
ered to his people.
9 And his sons [g]Isaac and Ĭsh-mā-ĕl
buried him [h]in the cave of Măch-pē-
lăh, in the field of Ē-phrŏn the son of
Zō-hăr the Hittite, which *is* before
Măm-rē;
10 The [i]field which Abraham purchased of the sons of Heth: there
was Abraham buried, and Sarah his
wife.
11 ¶ And it came to pass after the
death of Abraham, that God blessed
his son Isaac; and Isaac dwelt by the
well [j]Lā-hâi-rôi.
12 ¶ Now these *are* the [k]generations
of Ĭsh-mā-ĕl, Abraham's son, whom
Hā-găr the Egyptian, Sarah's handmaid, bare unto Abraham:
13 And these *are* the names of the
sons of Ĭsh-mā-ĕl, by their names,
according to their generations: the
firstborn of Ĭsh-mā-ĕl, Nĕ-bā-jōth;
and Kē-dăr, and Ăd-bēel, and Mĭb-
săm,
14 And Mĭsh-mă, and Dū-măh, and
Măs-să,

b Ps. 118.23. Matt. 21.42. Mark 12.11.
c ch. 20.15.
d Ex. 3.22. Ex. 11.2. Ex. 12.35.
6 vessels.
e 2 Chr. 21.3. Ezra 1.6.
f vers. 56,59.
7 Or, a full year, or, ten months.
g ver. 40.
h ch. 35.8.
i ch. 17.16. Ruth 4.11.
j ch. 22.17.
k ch. 16.14. ch. 25.11.
8 Or, to pray.
l Jos. 1.8. Ps. 1.2. Ps. 35.17. Ps. 77.12. Ps. 119.15. Ps. 143.5. Dan. 6.10. Matt. 6.5,6. Matt. 14.23. Mark 1.35. Mark 6.46. Luke 5.16. Luke 6.12. Acts 10.9.
m Josh. 15.18. 1 Sam. 25. 23.
n 1 Cor. 11. 3,6,7,10.
o 1 Thes. 4. 13.

CHAP. 25

a 1 Chr. 1.32.
b ch. 24.36.
c ch. 21.14.
d Judg. 6.3.
e ch. 15.15. ch. 47.8,9.
f ch. 35.29. ch. 49.33. Acts 13.36.
g ch. 50.13.
h ch. 49.29, 30.
i ch. 23.16.
j ch. 16.14. ch. 24.62.
k 1 Chr. 1.29.

15 [1]Hā´-där, and Tē´-mă, Jē´-tŭr, Nā´-phĭsh, and Kē´-dĕ-māh:

16 These *are* the sons of Ĭsh´-mā-ĕl, and these *are* their names, by their towns, and by their castles; [l]twelve princes according to their nations.

17 And these *are* the years of the life of Ĭsh´-mā-ĕl, an hundred and thirty and seven years: and he gave [m]up the ghost and died; and was gathered unto his people.

18 And they dwelt from [n]Hăv´-ĭ-lăh unto Shur, that *is* before Egypt, as thou goest toward Assyria: *and* he [2]died in the [o]presence of all his brethren.

19 ¶ And these *are* the generations of Isaac, Abraham's son: Abraham [p]begat Isaac:

20 And Isaac was forty years old when he took [q]Rebekah to wife, the [r]daughter of Bĕ-thū´-ĕl the Syrian of Pā´-dăn–âr´-ăm, the [s]sister to Laban the Syrian.

21 And Isaac [t]intreated the LORD for his wife, because she *was* barren: and the LORD was [u]intreated of him, and Rebekah his wife [v]conceived.

22 And the children struggled together within her; and she said, If *it be* so, why *am* I thus? And she went to [w]inquire of the LORD.

23 And the LORD said unto her, Two nations *are* in thy womb, and two [x]manner of people shall be separated from thy bowels; and *the one* people shall be stronger than *the other* people; and the elder shall serve the younger.

24 ¶ And when her days to be delivered were fulfilled, behold, *there were* twins in her womb.

25 And the first came out red, all [y]over like an hairy garment; and they called his name Esau.

26 And after that came his brother out, and [z]his hand took hold on Esau's heel; and his [a]name was called Jacob: and Isaac *was* threescore years old when she bare them.

27 And the boys grew: and Esau was a [b]cunning hunter, a man of the field; and Jacob *was* [c]a plain man, [d]dwelling in tents.

28 And Isaac loved Esau, because [3]he did [e]eat of *his* venison: [f]but Rebekah loved Jacob.

29 ¶ And Jacob sod pottage: and Esau came from the field, and he *was* faint:

30 And Esau said to Jacob, Feed me, I pray thee, [4]with that same red pottage; for I *am* faint: therefore was his name called [5]Ē´-dom.

31 And Jacob said, Sell me this day thy birthright.

32 And Esau said, Behold, I *am* [6]at the point to die: and what profit shall this birthright do to me?

33 And Jacob said, Swear to me this day; and he sware unto him: and he [g]sold his birthright unto Jacob.

34 Then Jacob gave Esau bread and pottage of lentiles; and [h]he did eat and drink, and rose up, and went his way: thus Esau despised *his* birthright.

CHAPTER 26

AND there was a famine in the land, beside [a]the first famine that was in the days of Abraham. And Isaac went unto [b]Ă-bĭm´-ĕ-lĕch king of the Philistines unto Gē´-rär.

2 And the LORD appeared unto him, and said, Go not down into Egypt; dwell in the [c]land which I shall tell thee of:

3 Sojourn [d]in this land, and [e]I will be with thee, and [f]will bless thee; for unto thee, and unto thy seed, [g]I will give all these countries, and I will perform [h]the oath which I sware unto Abraham thy father;

4 And [i]I will make thy seed to multiply as the stars of heaven, and will give unto thy seed all these countries; and [j]in thy seed shall all the nations of the earth be blessed;

5 Because [k]that Abraham obeyed my voice, and kept my charge, my commandments, my statutes, and my laws.

6 ¶ And Isaac dwelt in Gē´-rär:

7 And the men of the place asked *him* of his wife; and he said, [l]She *is* my sister: for [m]he feared to say, *She is* my wife; lest, *said he*, the men of the place should kill me for Rebekah; because she *was* [n]fair to look upon.

8 And it came to pass, when he had been there a long time, that Ă-bĭm´-ĕ-lĕch king of the Philistines looked out at a window, and saw, and, behold, Isaac *was* sporting with Rebekah his wife.

9 And Ă-bĭm´-ĕ-lĕch called Isaac, and said, Behold, of a surety she *is* thy wife: and how saidst thou, She *is* my sister? And Isaac said unto him, Because I said, Lest I die for her.

10 And Ă-bĭm´-ĕ-lĕch said, What *is* this thou hast done unto us? one of the people might lightly have lien with thy wife, and [o]thou shouldest have brought guiltiness upon us.

1 Or, Hadad. 1 Chr. 1.30.
l ch. 17.20.
m ver. 8. ch. 49.33. Mark 15.37.
n 1 Sam. 15.7.
2 fell.
o ch. 16.12.
p Matt. 1.2.
q ch. 24.67.
r ch. 22.23.
s ch. 24.29.
t 1 Sam. 1.11.
u 1 Chr. 5.20. 2 Chr. 33.13. Ezra 8.23.
v Rom. 9.10.
w 1 Sam. 9.9. 1 Sam. 10. 22.
x ch. 24.60.
y ch. 27.11.
z Hos. 12.3.
a ch. 27.36.
b ch. 27.3,5.
c Job 1.1,8. Job 2.3.
d Heb. 11.9.
3 venison was in his mouth.
e ch. 27.19.
f ch. 27.6.
4 with that red, with that red pottage.
5 That is, Red.
6 going to die.
g Heb. 12.16.
h 1 Cor. 15. 32.

CHAP. 26

a ch. 12.10.
b ch. 20.2.
c ch. 12.1. Ps. 37.3.
d ch. 20.1. Ps. 39.12. Heb. 11.9.
e ch. 28.15.
f ch. 12.2.
g ch. 13.15.
h Ps. 105.9.
i ch. 15.5.
j ch. 22.18. Ps. 72.17.
k ch. 22.16.
l ch. 12.13.
m Pro. 29.25.
n ch. 24.16.
o ch. 20.9.

11 And Ă-bĭm′-ĕ-lĕch charged all *his* people, saying, He that [p]toucheth this man or his wife shall surely be put to death.

12 Then Isaac sowed in that land, and [1]received in the same year an [q]hundredfold: and the LORD blessed [r]him.

13 And the man [s]waxed great, and [2]went forward, and grew until he became very great:

14 For he had possession of flocks, and possession of herds, and great store of [3]servants: and the Philistines [t]envied him.

15 For all the wells [u]which his father's servants had digged in the days of Abraham his father, the Philistines had stopped them, and filled them with earth.

16 And Ă-bĭm′-ĕ-lĕch said unto Isaac, Go from us; for [v]thou art much mightier than we.

17 ¶ And Isaac departed thence, and pitched his tent in the valley of Gē′-rär, and dwelt there.

18 And Isaac digged again the wells of water, which they had digged in the days of Abraham his father; for the Philistines had stopped them after the death of Abraham: [w]and he called their names after the names by which his father had called them.

19 And Isaac's servants digged in the valley, and found there a well of [4]springing water.

20 And the herdmen of Gē′-rär did [x]strive with Isaac's herdmen, saying, The water *is* ours: and he called the name of the well [5]Ē′-sĕk; because they strove with him.

21 And they digged another well, and strove for that also: and he called the name of it [6]Sĭt′-năh.

22 And he removed from thence, and digged another well; and for that they strove not: and he called the name of it [7]Rē-hō-bōth; and he said, For now the LORD hath made room for us, and we shall be [y]fruitful in the land.

23 And he went up from thence to Bē̆er–shē-bă.

24 And the LORD appeared unto him the same night, and said, [z]I *am* the God of Abraham thy father: [a]fear not, for [b]I *am* with thee, and will bless thee, and multiply thy seed for my servant Abraham's sake.

25 And he [c]builded an altar there, and [d]called upon the name of the LORD, and pitched his tent there: and there Isaac's servants digged a well.

26 ¶ Then Ă-bĭm′-ĕ-lĕch went to him from Gē′-rär, and Ă-hŭz′-zăth one of his friends, and Phī′-chŏl the chief captain of his army.

27 And Isaac said unto them, Wherefore come ye to me, seeing ye [e]hate me, and have sent me away from you?

28 And they said, [8]We saw certainly that the LORD [f]was with thee: and we said, Let there be now an oath betwixt us, *even* betwixt us and thee, and let us make a covenant with thee;

29 [9]That thou wilt do us no hurt, as we have not touched thee, and as we have done unto thee nothing but good, and have sent thee away in peace: [g]thou *art* now the blessed of the LORD.

30 And [h]he made them a feast, and they did eat and drink.

31 And they rose up betimes in the morning, and [i]sware one to another: and Isaac sent them away, and they departed from him in peace.

32 And it came to pass the same day, that Isaac's servants came, and told him concerning the well which they had digged, and said unto him, We have found water.

33 And he called it [10]Shē′-băh: therefore [j]the name of the city *is* [11]Bē̆er–shē′-bă unto this day.

34 ¶ And [k]Esau was forty years old when he took to wife Judith the daughter of Bē̆er′-ī the Hittite, and Băsh′-ĕ-măth the daughter of Ē′-lŏn the Hittite:

35 Which [l]were [12]a grief of mind unto Isaac and to Rebekah.

CHAPTER 27

AND it came to pass, that when Isaac was old, and [a]his eyes were dim, so that he could not see, he called Esau his eldest son, and said unto him, My son: and he said unto him, Behold, *here am* I.

2 And he said, Behold now, I am old, [b]I know not the day of my death:

3 Now [c]therefore take, I pray thee, thy weapons, thy quiver and thy bow, and go out to the field, and [1]take me *some* venison;

4 And make me savoury meat, such as I love, and bring *it* to me, that I may eat; that my soul [d]may bless thee before I die.

5 And Rebekah heard when Isaac spake to Esau his son. And Esau went to the field to hunt *for* venison, *and* to bring *it*.

6 ¶ And Rebekah spake unto Jacob her son, saying, Behold, I heard thy father speak unto Esau thy brother, saying,

7 Bring me venison, and make me

p Ps. 105.15.
1 found.
q Matt. 13.8. Mark 4.8.
r ch. 24.1. Job 42.12. Ps. 112.3. Pro. 3.16. Pro. 10.22. Matt. 6.33. Mark 10.30.
s Pro. 10.22.
2 went going.
3 Or, husbandry.
t ch. 37.11. Eccl. 4.4.
u ch. 21.30.
v Ex. 1.9.
w ch. 21.31.
4 living.
x ch. 21.25.
5 That is, Contention.
6 That is, Hatred.
7 That is, Room.
y ch. 17.6. Ex. 1.7.
z ch. 24.12. Ex. 3.6. Acts 7.32.
a ch. 15.1.
b ver. 3,4. Rom. 8.31.
c ch. 12.7. ch. 13.18.
d Ps. 116.17.
e Judg. 11.7.
8 Seeing we saw.
f ch. 21.22, 23.
9 If thou shalt, etc.
g ch. 24.31. Ps. 115.15.
h ch. 19.3.
i ch. 21.31.
10 That is, An oath.
j ch. 21.31.
11 That is, The well of the oath.
k ch. 36.2.
l ch. 27.46. ch. 28.1,8.
12 bitterness of spirit.

CHAP. 27

a ch. 48.10. 1 Sam. 3.2. Eccl. 12.3.
b Pro. 27.1. Jas. 4.14.
c ch. 25.27, 28.
1 hunt.
d ver. 27. ch. 48.9,15. ch. 49,28. Deut. 33.1. Heb. 11.20.

savoury meat, that I may eat, and bless thee before the LORD before my death.

8 Now therefore, my son, [e]obey my voice according to that which I command thee.

9 Go now to the flock, and fetch me from thence two good kids of the goats; and I will make them savoury [f]meat for thy father, such as he loveth:

10 And thou shalt bring *it* to thy father, that he may eat, and that he [g]may bless thee before his death.

11 And Jacob said to Rebekah his mother, Behold, [h]Esau my brother *is* a hairy man, and I *am* a smooth man:

12 My father peradventure [i]will feel me, and I shall seem to him as a deceiver; and I shall bring [j]a curse upon me, and not a blessing.

13 And his mother said unto him, Upon [k]me *be* thy curse, my son: only obey my voice, and go fetch me *them*.

14 And he went, and fetched, and brought *them* to his mother: and his mother [l]made savoury meat, such as his father loved.

15 And Rebekah took [2]goodly raiment [m]of her eldest son Esau, which *were* with her in the house, and put them upon Jacob her younger son:

16 And she put the skins of the kids of the goats upon his hands, and upon the smooth of his neck:

17 And she gave the savoury meat and the bread, which she had prepared, into the hand of her son Jacob.

18 ¶ And he came unto his father, and said, My father: and he said, Here *am* I; who *art* thou, my son?

19 And Jacob said unto his father, I *am* Esau thy firstborn; [n]I have done according as thou badest me: arise, I pray thee, sit and eat of my venison, [o]that thy soul may bless me.

20 And Isaac said unto his son, How *is it* that thou hast found *it* so quickly, my son? [p]And he said, Because the LORD thy God brought *it* [3]to me.

21 And Isaac said unto Jacob, Come near, I pray thee, that [q]I may feel thee, my son, whether thou *be* my very son Esau or not.

22 And Jacob went near unto Isaac his father; and he felt him, and said, The voice *is* Jacob's voice, but the hands *are* the hands of Esau.

23 And he discerned him not, because [r]his hands were hairy, as his brother Esau's hands: so he blessed him.

24 And he said, *Art* thou my very son Esau? And he said, [s]I *am*.

25 And he said, Bring *it* near to me, and I will eat of my son's venison, [t]that my soul may bless thee. And he brought *it* near to him, and he did eat: and he brought him wine, and he drank.

26 And his father Isaac said unto him, Come near now, and kiss me, my son.

27 And he came near, and kissed him: and he smelled the smell of his raiment, and blessed him, and said, See, [u]the smell of my son *is* as the smell of a field which the LORD hath blessed:

28 Therefore [v]God give thee of the [w]dew of heaven, and the [x]fatness of the earth, and [y]plenty of corn and wine:

29 Let [z]people serve thee, and nations bow down to thee: be lord over thy brethren, and [a]let thy mother's sons bow down to thee: cursed [b]*be* every one that curseth thee, and blessed *be* he that blesseth thee.

30 ¶ And it came to pass, as soon as Isaac had made an end of blessing Jacob, and Jacob was yet scarce gone out from the presence of Isaac his father, that Esau his brother came in from his hunting.

31 And he also had made savoury meat, and brought it unto his father, and said unto his father, Let my father arise, and [c]eat of his son's venison, that thy soul may bless me.

32 And Isaac his father said unto him, Who *art* thou? And he said, I *am* thy son, thy firstborn Esau.

33 And Isaac [4]trembled very exceedingly, and said, Who? where *is* he that hath [5]taken venison, and brought *it* me, and I have eaten of all before thou camest, and have blessed him? yea, [d]*and* he shall be blessed.

34 And when Esau heard the words of his father, [e]he cried with a great and exceeding bitter cry, and said unto his father, Bless me, *even* me also, O my father.

35 And he said, Thy brother came with [f]subtilty, and hath taken away thy blessing.

36 And he said, [g]Is not he rightly named [6]Jacob? for he hath supplanted me these two times: [h]he took away my birthright; and, behold, now he hath taken away my blessing. And he said, Hast thou not reserved a blessing for me?

37 And Isaac answered and said unto Esau, [i]Behold, I have made him thy lord, and all his brethren have I given to him for servants; and with [j]corn

e ver. 13.
f ver. 4.
g ch. 48.15.
h ch. 25.25.
i ver. 22.
j ch. 9.25. Deut. 27.18.
k ch. 43.9. 1 Sam. 25. 24. 2 Sam. 14.9. Matt. 27.25.
l vers. 4,9.
2 desirable.
m ver. 27.
n 1 Ki. 13.18. 1 Ki. 14.2. Isa. 28.15. Zech. 13.4.
o ver. 4.
p Ex. 20.7.
3 before me.
q ver. 12.
r ver. 16.
s Rom. 3.7,8. Eph. 4.25.
t ver. 4.
u Hosea 14.6. Song 2.13. Heb. 6.7.
v Heb. 11.20.
w Deut. 33. 13. 2 Sam. 1.21.
x Num. 18. 12.
y Deut. 33. 28. Ps. 65.9. Zech. 9.17.
z ch. 9.25. ch. 25.23.
a ch. 49.8.
b ch. 12.3. Num. 24.9.
c ver. 4.
4 tremble with a great trembling greatly.
5 hunted.
d ch. 28.3,4. Num. 23.20. Eph. 1.3. Rom. 11.29.
e Heb. 12.17.
f 1 Thes. 4.6.
g ch. 25.26.
6 That is, a supplanter.
h ch. 25.33.
i Fulfilled. 2 Sam. 8.14.
j ver. 28.

and wine have I [7]sustained him: and
what shall I do now unto thee, my
son?
38 And Esau said unto his father,
Hast thou but one blessing, my father? bless me, *even* me also, O my
father. And Esau lifted up his voice,
[k]and wept.
39 And Isaac his father answered
and said unto him, Behold, [l]thy dwelling shall be [8]the fatness of the earth,
and of the dew of heaven from above;
40 And by thy sword shalt thou live,
and [m]shalt serve thy brother; and [n]it
shall come to pass when thou shalt
have the dominion, that thou shalt
break his yoke from off thy neck.
41 ¶ And Esau [o]hated Jacob because
of the blessing wherewith his father
blessed him: and Esau said in his
heart, [p]The days of mourning for my
father are at hand; [q]then will I slay my
brother Jacob.
42 And these words of Esau her elder
son were told to Rebekah: and she
sent and called Jacob her younger
son, and said unto him, Behold, thy
brother Esau, as touching thee, doth
[r]comfort himself, *purposing* to kill
thee.
43 Now therefore, my son, obey my
voice; and arise, flee thou to Laban
my brother to [s]Hâr´ăn;
44 And tarry with him a few days,
until thy brother's fury turn away;
45 Until thy brother's anger turn
away from thee, and he forget *that*
which thou hast done to him: then
I will send, and fetch thee from thence:
why should I be deprived also of you
both in one day?
46 And Rebekah said to Isaac, [t]I am
weary of my life because of the daughters of Heth: [u]if Jacob take a wife of
the daughters of Heth, such as these
which are of the daughters of the land,
what good shall my life do me?

CHAPTER 28

AND Isaac called Jacob, and blessed
[a]him, and charged him, and said
unto him, Thou shalt not take a wife
of the daughters of Canaan.
2 Arise, go to Pā´dăn–âr´ăm, to the
house of Bĕ-thū´ĕl thy mother's father; and take thee a wife from thence
of the daughters of Laban thy mother's brother.
3 And [b]God Almighty bless thee, and
make thee fruitful, and multiply thee,
that thou mayest be [1]a multitude of
people;
4 And give thee [c]the blessing of
Abraham, to thee, and to thy seed
with thee; that thou mayest inherit
the land [2]wherein thou art a [d]stranger,
which God gave unto Abraham.
5 And Isaac sent away Jacob: and he
went to Pā´dăn–âr´ăm unto Laban,
son of Bĕ-thū´ĕl the Syrian, the brother of Rebekah, Jacob's and Esau's
mother.
6 ¶ When Esau saw that Isaac had
blessed Jacob, and sent him away to
Pā´dăn–âr´ăm, to take him a wife
from thence; and that as he blessed
him he gave him a charge, saying,
Thou shalt not take a wife of the
daughters of Canaan;
7 And that Jacob obeyed his father
and his mother, and was gone to Pā´-
dăn–âr´ăm;
8 And Esau seeing [e]that the daughters of Canaan [3]pleased not Isaac his
father;
9 Then went Esau unto Ĭsh´mā-ĕl,
and took unto the wives which he had
[f]Mā´hă-lăth the daughter of Ĭsh´mā-ĕl
Abraham's son, the [g]sister of Nĕ-bā´-
jōth, to be his wife.
10 ¶ And Jacob went out from Bē´er-
shē´bă, and went [h]toward Hâr´ăn.
11 And he lighted upon a certain
place, and tarried there all night, because the sun was set; and he took of
the stones of that place, and put *them*
for his pillows, and lay down in that
place to sleep.
12 And he [i]dreamed, and behold a
ladder set up on the earth, and the
top of it reached to heaven: and behold [j]the angels of God ascending
and descending on it.
13 And, [k]behold, the LORD stood
above it, and said, [l]I *am* the LORD
God of Abraham thy father, and the
God of Isaac: [m]the land whereon
thou liest, to thee will I give it, and to
thy seed;
14 And [n]thy seed shall be as the dust
of the earth, and thou shalt [4]spread
abroad to the [o]west, and to the east,
and to the north, and to the south:
and in thee and [p]in thy seed shall all
the families of the earth be blessed.
15 And, behold, [q]I *am* with thee, and
will [r]keep thee in all *places* whither
thou goest, and will [s]bring thee again
into this land; for [t]I will not leave
thee, [u]until I have done *that* which I
have spoken to thee of.
16 ¶ And Jacob awaked out of his
sleep, and he said, Surely the LORD is
in [v]this place; and I knew *it* not.
17 And he was afraid, and said, How
dreadful *is* this place! this *is* none

7 Or, supported.
k Heb. 12.17.
l Heb. 11.20.
8 Or, of the fatness.
m ch. 25.23. 2 Sam. 8.14. Obadiah 18, 19,20.
n Fulfilled. 2 Ki. 8.20.
o ch. 37.4,8.
p ch. 50.3,4, 10.
q Obadiah 10. 1 John 3.12.
r Ps. 64.5.
s ch. 11.31.
t ch. 26.35. ch. 28.8.
u ch. 24.3.

CHAP. 28

a ch. 27.33.
b ch. 17.1,6.
1 an assembly of people.
c ch. 12.2. ch. 22.17.
2 of thy sojournings.
d ch. 17.8. 1 Chr. 29.15. Ps. 39.12. Ps. 105.12. Ps. 119.19. 2 Cor. 5.6,7. Heb. 11.9, 13. 1 Pet. 1.17. 1 Pet. 2.11.
e ch. 24.3.
3 were evil in the eyes, etc.
f ch. 36.3. she is called Bashemath.
g ch. 25.13.
h Called, Acts 7.2. Charran.
i ch. 41.1. Job 33.15.
j John 1.51. Heb. 1.14.
k ch. 35.1. ch. 48.3.
l ch. 26.24.
m ch. 13.15.
n ch. 13.16.
4 break forth.
o ch. 13.14. Deut. 12.20.
p ch. 12.3.
q ch. 26.24. ch. 31.3.
r ch. 48.16. Ps. 121.5.
s ch. 35.6.
t Deut. 31.6.
u Num. 23. 19.
v Ex. 3.5. Josh. 5.15.

other but the house of God, and this *is* the gate of heaven.

18 And Jacob rose up early in the morning, and took the stone that he had put *for* his pillows, and set it up *for* a pillar, and poured oil upon the top of it.

19 And he called the name of that [w]place [5]Beth-el: but the name of that city *was called* Luz at the first.

20 And [x]Jacob vowed a vow, saying, If [y]God will be with me, and will keep me in this way that I go, and will give me [z]bread to eat, and raiment to put on,

21 So that [a]I come again to my father's house in peace; [b]then shall the LORD be my God:

22 And this stone, which I have set *for* a pillar, [c]shall be God's house: [d]and of all that thou shalt give me I will surely give the tenth unto thee.

CHAPTER 29

THEN Jacob [1]went on his journey, [a]and came into the land of the [2]people of the east.

2 And he looked, and behold a well in the field, and, lo, there *were* three flocks of sheep lying by it; for out of that well they watered the flocks: and a great stone *was* upon the well's mouth.

3 And thither were all the flocks gathered: and they rolled the stone from the well's mouth, and watered the sheep, and put the stone again upon the well's mouth in his place.

4 And Jacob said unto them, My brethren, whence *be* ye? And they said, Of Hâr'-ăn *are* we.

5 And he said unto them, Know ye Laban the son of Nahor? And they said, We know *him*.

6 And he said unto them, [3]*Is* [b]he well? And they said, *He is* well: and, behold, Rachel his daughter cometh with the sheep.

7 And he said, Lo, [4]*it is* yet high day, neither *is it* time that the cattle should be gathered together: water ye the sheep, and go *and* feed *them*.

8 And they said, We cannot, until all the flocks be gathered together, and *till* they roll the stone from the well's mouth; then we water the sheep.

9 ¶ And while he yet spake with them, Rachel came with her father's sheep: [c]for she kept them.

10 And it came to pass, when Jacob saw Rachel the daughter of Laban his mother's brother, and the sheep of Laban his mother's brother, that Jacob went near, and [d]rolled the stone from the well's mouth, and watered the flock of Laban his mother's brother.

11 And Jacob [e]kissed Rachel, and lifted up his voice, and wept.

12 And Jacob told Rachel that he *was* [f]her father's brother, and that he *was* Rebekah's son: [g]and she ran and told her father.

13 And it came to pass, when Laban heard the [5]tidings of Jacob his sister's son, that [h]he ran to meet him, and embraced him, and kissed him, and brought him to his house. And he told Laban all these things.

14 And Laban said to him, Surely [i]thou *art* my bone and my flesh. And he abode with him [6]the space of a month.

15 ¶ And Laban said unto Jacob, Because thou *art* my brother, shouldest thou therefore serve me for nought? tell me, what *shall* thy wages *be*?

16 And Laban had two daughters: the name of the elder *was* Leah, and the name of the younger *was* Rachel.

17 Leah *was* tender eyed; but Rachel was beautiful and well favoured.

18 And Jacob loved Rachel; and said, [j]I will serve thee seven years for Rachel thy younger daughter.

19 And Laban said, *It is* better that I give her to thee, than that I should give her to another man: abide with me.

20 And Jacob [k]served seven years for Rachel; and they seemed unto him *but* a few days, for [l]the love he had to her.

21 ¶ And Jacob said unto Laban, Give *me* my wife, for my days are fulfilled, that I may [m]go in unto her.

22 And Laban gathered together all the men of the place, and made a [n]feast.

23 And it came to pass in the evening, that he took Leah his daughter, and brought her to him; and he went in unto her.

24 And Laban gave unto his daughter Leah Zilpah his maid *for* an handmaid.

25 And it came to pass, that in the morning, behold, it *was* Leah: and he said to Laban, What *is* this thou hast done unto me? did not I serve with thee for Rachel? wherefore then hast thou beguiled me?

26 And Laban said, It must not be so done in our [7]country, to give the younger before the firstborn.

27 Fulfil [o]her week, and we will give

---

w Judg. 1.23. Hosea 4.15.
5 That is, The house of God.
x ch. 31.13. Judg. 11.30. 2 Sam. 15.8.
y ver. 15.
z 1 Tim. 6.8.
a Judg. 11.31. 2 Sam. 19. 24.
b Deut. 26. 17. 2 Sam. 15.8. 2 Ki. 5.17.
c ch. 35.7.
d Lev. 27.30.

CHAP. 29
1 lift up his feet.
a Num. 23.7. Hos. 12.12.
2 children.
3 Is there peace to him?
b ch. 43.27.
4 yet the day is great.
c Ex. 2.16.
d Ex. 2.17.
e ch. 33.4. ch. 45.14. Rom. 16.16. 1 Cor. 16.20. 2 Cor. 13.12. 1 Pet. 5.14.
f ch. 13.8. ch. 14.14.
g ch. 24.28.
5 hearing.
h ch. 24.29.
i ch. 2.23. Judg. 9.2. 2 Sam. 5.1. 2 Sam. 19. 12,13.
6 a month of days.
j ch. 31.41. 2 Sam. 3.14.
k ch. 30.26.
l Song 8.7.
m Judg. 15.1.
n Judg. 14.10. John 2.1.
7 place.
o Judg. 14. 12.

thee this also for the service which
thou shalt serve with me yet seven
other years.
28 And Jacob did so, and fulfilled her
week: and he gave him Rachel his
daughter to wife also.
29 And Laban gave to Rachel his
daughter Bĭl′-hăh his handmaid to be
her maid.
30 And he went in also unto Rachel,
and he loved also Rachel more than
Leah, and served with him yet [p]seven
other years.
31 ¶ And when the LORD [q]saw that
Leah *was* hated, he [r]opened her
womb: but Rachel *was* barren.
32 And Leah conceived, and bare a
son, and she called his name [8]Reuben:
for she said, Surely the LORD hath
[s]looked upon my affliction; now
therefore my husband will love me.
33 And she conceived again, and
bare a son; and said, Because the
LORD hath heard that I *was* hated, he
hath therefore given me this *son* also:
and she called his name [9]Simeon.
34 And she conceived again, and bare
a son; and said, Now this time will my
husband be joined unto me, because
I have born him three sons: therefore
was his name called [10]Levi.
35 And she conceived again, and bare
a son: and she said, Now will I praise
the LORD: therefore she called his
name [11]Judah; and [12]left bearing.

CHAPTER 30

AND when Rachel saw that [a]she
bare Jacob no children, Rachel
envied [b]her sister; and said unto
Jacob, Give me children, [c]or else I die.
2 And Jacob's anger was kindled
against Rachel: and he said, [d]*Am* I in
God's stead, who hath withheld from
thee the fruit of the womb?
3 And she said, Behold [e]my maid
Bĭl′-hăh, go in unto her; [f]and she shall
bear upon my knees, [g]that I may also
[1]have children by her.
4 And she gave him Bĭl′-hăh her
handmaid [h]to wife: and Jacob went
in unto her.
5 And Bĭl′-hăh conceived, and bare
Jacob a son.
6 And Rachel said, God hath judged
[i]me, and hath also heard my voice,
and hath given me a son: therefore
called she his name [2]Dan.
7 And Bĭl′-hăh Rachel's maid conceived again, and bare Jacob a second
son.
8 And Rachel said, With [3]great
wrestlings have I wrestled with my
sister, and I have prevailed: and she
called his [j]name [4]Năph′-tă-lī.
9 When Leah saw that she had left
bearing, she took Zilpah her maid,
and gave her Jacob to wife.
10 And Zilpah Leah's maid bare
Jacob a son.
11 And Leah said, A troop cometh:
and she called his name [5]Gad.
12 And Zilpah Leah's maid bare
Jacob a second son.
13 And Leah said, [6]Happy am I, for
the daughters [k]will call me blessed:
and she called his name [7]Asher.
14 ¶ And Reuben went in the days of
wheat harvest, and found mandrakes
[l]in the field, and brought them unto
his mother Leah. Then Rachel said to
Leah, Give [m]me, I pray thee, of thy
son's mandrakes.
15 And she said unto her, [n]*Is it* a
small matter that thou hast taken my
husband? and wouldest thou take
away my son's mandrakes also? And
Rachel said, Therefore he shall lie
with thee to night for thy son's mandrakes.
16 And Jacob came out of the field
in the evening, and Leah went out to
meet him, and said, Thou must come
in unto me; for surely I have hired
thee with my son's mandrakes. And
he lay with her that night.
17 And God hearkened unto Leah,
and she conceived, and bare Jacob the
fifth son.
18 And Leah said, God hath given
me my hire, because I have given my
maiden to my husband: and she called
his name [8]Ĭs′-să-chär.
19 And Leah conceived again, and
bare Jacob the sixth son.
20 And Leah said, God hath endued
me *with* a good dowry; now will my
husband dwell with me, because I
have born him six sons: and she called
his name [9]Zĕ-bū-lŭn.
21 And afterwards she bare a daughter, and called her name [10]Dinah.
22 ¶ And God [o]remembered Rachel,
and God hearkened to her, and [p]open-
ed her womb.
23 And she conceived, and bare a
son; and said, God hath taken away
[q]my reproach:
24 And she called his name [11]Joseph;
and said, [r]The LORD shall add to me
another son.
25 ¶ And it came to pass, when Rachel had born Joseph, that Jacob said
unto Laban, [s]Send me away, that I
may go unto [t]mine own place, and to
my country.

p ch. 30.26. ch. 31.41. Hos. 12.12.
q Ps. 127.3.
r ch. 30.1.
8 That is, See a son.
s Ex. 3.7. Ex. 4.31. Deut. 26.7. Ps. 25.18. Ps. 106.44.
9 That is, Hearing.
10 That is, Joined. Num. 18.2, 4.
11 That is, Praise.
12 stood from bearing.

CHAP. 30

a ch. 29.31.
b ch. 37.11.
c Job 5.2.
d ch. 16.2. 1 Sam. 1.5.
e ch. 16.2.
f ch. 50.23. Job 3.12.
g ch. 16.2.
1 be built by her.
h ch. 35.22.
i Ps. 35.24. Ps. 43.1. Lam. 3.59.
2 That is, Judging.
3 wrestlings of God.
j Called Nephthalim. Matt. 4.13.
4 That is, My wrestling.
5 That is, A troop, or, company. Isa. 65.11.
6 In my happiness.
k Pro. 31.28. Luke 1.48.
7 That is, Happy.
l Song 7.13.
Precious fruits, or sweet flowers.
m ch. 25.30.
n Num. 16.9.
8 That is, An hire.
9 That is, Dwelling.
10 That is, Judgment.
o ch. 8.1. 1 Sam. 1.19.
p ch. 29.31.
q 1 Sam. 1.6. Isa. 4.1. Luke 1.25.
11 That is, Adding.
r ch. 35.17.
s ch. 24.55.
t ch. 18.33. ch. 31.55.

26 Give *me* my wives and my children, [u]for whom I have served thee,
and let me go: for thou knowest my
service which I have done thee.
27 And Laban said unto him, I pray
thee, if I have found favour in thine
eyes, *tarry:* for [v]I have learned by experience that the LORD hath blessed
me [w]for thy sake.
28 And he said, [x]Appoint me thy
wages, and I will give *it*.
29 And he said unto him, [y]Thou
knowest how I have served thee, and
how thy cattle was with me.
30 For *it was* little which thou hadst
before I *came*, and it is *now* [12]increas-
ed unto a multitude; and the LORD
hath blessed thee [13] since my coming:
and now when shall I [z]provide for
mine own house also?
31 And he said, What shall I give
thee? And Jacob said, Thou shalt not
give me any thing: if thou wilt do this
thing for me, I will again feed *and*
keep thy flock:
32 I will pass through all thy flock
to day, removing from thence all the
speckled and spotted cattle, and all the
brown cattle among the sheep, and the
spotted and speckled among the
goats: and [a]*of such* shall be my hire.
33 So shall my [b]righteousness answer
for me [14]in time to come, when it shall
come for my hire before thy face:
every one that *is* not speckled and
spotted among the goats, and brown
among the sheep, that shall be counted
stolen with me.
34 And Laban said, Behold, I would
it might be according to thy word.
35 And he removed that day the he
goats that were ringstraked and spotted, and all the she goats that were
speckled and spotted, *and* every one
that had *some* white in it, and all the
brown among the sheep, and gave
them into the hand of his sons.
36 And he set three days' journey betwixt himself and Jacob: and Jacob
fed the rest of Laban's flocks.
37 ¶ And [c]Jacob took him rods of
green poplar, and of the hazel and
chesnut tree; and pilled white strakes
in them, and made the white appear
which *was* in the rods.
38 And he set the rods which he had
pilled before the flocks in the gutters
in the watering troughs when the
flocks came to drink, that they should
conceive when they came to drink.
39 And the flocks conceived before
the rods, and brought forth cattle
ringstraked, speckled, and spotted.

u ch. 29.20.
v ch. 39.3,5. Ps. 1.3. Isa. 61.9.
w ch. 26.24.
x ch. 29.15.
y ch. 31.6. Matt. 24.45. Titus 2.10.
12 broken forth.
13 at my foot.
z 1 Tim. 5.8.
a ch. 31.8.
b Ps. 37.6.
14 to-morrow.
c ch. 31.9.
d ver. 30. ch. 28.15. Job 1.3. Eccl. 2.7. Eze. 39.10.
e ch. 13.2. ch. 24.35. ch. 26.13.

CHAP. 31

a Job 5.2. Job 31.31. Ps. 57.4. Pro. 14.30. Eccles. 4.4. Rom. 13.13. Titus 3.3. James 3.8.
b Ps. 49.16.
c ch. 4.5.
d Deut. 28. 45.
1 as yesterday and the day before. 1 Sam. 19.7.
e ch. 28.15. ch. 32.9.
f ver. 2.
g ch. 21.22. Isa. 41.10. Heb. 13.5.
h ch. 30.29.
i ver. 41.
j Num. 14.22. Neh. 4.12. Job 19.3. Zech. 8.23.
k ch. 15.1. ch. 20.6. Job 22.25. Ps. 5.11. Ps. 7.10. Ps. 20.1. Ps. 62.2. Ps. 84.11. Ps. 105.14. Ps. 115.9. Pro. 30.5.
l ch. 30.32.
m vers. 1,16.
2 Or, he-goats.
n ch. 48.16.

40 And Jacob did separate the lambs,
and set the faces of the flocks toward
the ringstraked, and all the brown in
the flock of Laban; and he put his own
flocks by themselves, and put them
not unto Laban's cattle.
41 And it came to pass, whensoever
the stronger cattle did conceive, that
Jacob laid the rods before the eyes of
the cattle in the gutters, that they
might conceive among the rods.
42 But when the cattle were feeble,
he put *them* not in: so the feebler were
Laban's, and the stronger Jacob's.
43 And the man [d]increased exceedingly, and [e]had much cattle, and maidservants, and menservants, and camels, and asses.

CHAPTER 31

AND he [a]heard the words of Laban's
sons, saying, Jacob hath taken
away all that *was* our father's; and of
that which *was* our father's hath he
gotten all [b]this glory.
2 And Jacob beheld [c]the countenance
of Laban, and, behold, it *was* not [d]to-
ward him [1]as before.
3 And the LORD said unto Jacob, Return [e]unto the land of thy fathers, and
to thy kindred; and I will be with thee.
4 And Jacob sent and called Rachel
and Leah to the field unto his flock,
5 And said unto them, [f]I see your
father's countenance, that it *is* not toward me as before; but the God of my
father [g]hath been with me.
6 And [h]ye know that with all my
power I have served your father.
7 And your father hath deceived me,
and [i]changed my wages [j]ten times;
but God [k]suffered him not to hurt
me.
8 If he said thus, [l]The speckled shall
be thy wages; then all the cattle bare
speckled: and if he said thus, The ringstraked shall be thy hire; then bare all
the cattle ringstraked.
9 Thus God hath [m]taken away the
cattle of your father, and given *them*
to me.
10 And it came to pass at the time
that the cattle conceived, that I lifted
up mine eyes, and saw in a dream, and,
behold, the [2]rams which leaped upon
the cattle *were* ringstraked, speckled,
and grisled.
11 And [n]the angel of God spake unto
me in a dream, *saying*, Jacob: And I
said, Here *am* I.
12 And he said, Lift up now thine
eyes, and see, all the rams which leap
upon the cattle *are* ringstraked, speck-

led, and grisled: for [o]I have seen all
that Laban doeth unto thee.
13 I *am* the God of Beth-el, [p]where
thou anointedst the pillar, *and* where
thou vowedst a vow unto me: now
[q]arise, get thee out from this land, and
return unto the land of thy kindred.
14 And Rachel and Leah answered
and said unto him, [r]*Is there* yet any
portion or inheritance for us in our
father's house?
15 Are we not counted of him strangers? for [s]he hath sold us, and hath
quite devoured also our money.
16 For all the riches which God hath
taken from our father, that *is* ours,
and our children's: now then, whatsoever God hath said unto thee, do.
17 ¶ Then Jacob rose up, and set his
sons and his wives upon camels;
18 And he carried away all his cattle,
and all his goods which he had gotten,
the cattle of his getting, which he had
gotten in Pā´dăn–âr´ăm, for to go to
Isaac his father in the land of Canaan.
19 And Laban went to shear his
sheep: and Rachel had stolen the
[3]images [t]that *were* her father's.
20 And Jacob stole away [4]unawares
to Laban the Syrian, in that he told
him not that he fled.
21 So he fled with all that he had;
and he rose up, and passed over the
river, and [u]set his face *toward* the
mount Gilead.
22 And it was told Laban on the third
day that Jacob was fled.
23 And he took his [v]brethren with
him, and pursued after him seven
days' journey; and they overtook him
in the mount Gilead.
24 And God [w]came to Laban the
Syrian in a dream by night, and said
unto him, Take heed that thou [x]speak
not to Jacob [5]either good or bad.
25 ¶ Then Laban overtook Jacob.
Now Jacob had pitched his tent in
the mount: and Laban with his brethren pitched in the mount of Gilead.
26 And Laban said to Jacob, What
hast thou done, that thou hast stolen
away unawares to me, and [y]carried
away my daughters, as captives *taken*
with the sword?
27 Wherefore didst thou flee away
secretly, and [6]steal away from me;
and didst not tell me, that I might
have sent thee away with mirth, and
with songs, with tabret, and with
harp?
28 And hast not suffered me [z]to kiss
my sons and my daughters? thou
[a]hast now done foolishly in *so* doing.

[o] Ex. 3.7. Deut. 24.15. Ps. 12.5. Eph. 6.9.
[p] ch. 28.18.
[q] ver. 3. ch. 32.9.
[r] ch. 2.24.
[s] ch. 29.15.
3 teraphim. Judg. 17.5. 1 Sam. 19. 13. Ezek. 21.21. Hosea 3.4.
[t] ch. 35.2.
4 the heart of Laban.
[u] ch. 46.28. 2 Ki. 12.17. Luke 9.51.
[v] ch. 13.8.
[w] ch. 20.3. Job 33.15. Matt. 1.20.
[x] ch. 24.50.
5 from good to bad.
[y] 1 Sam. 30.2.
6 hast stolen me.
[z] Ruth 1.9. 1 Ki. 19.20. Acts 20.37.
[a] 1 Sam. 13. 13. 2 Chr. 16.9.
[b] ch. 28.13. Ps. 5.11,12. Ps. 84.11. Ps. 115.9.
[c] ver. 24.
[d] ver. 19. Josh. 24.2. Judg. 18.24. Ps. 115.4-9. Isa. 44.10-20. Jer. 10. 3-5. Acts 19.26.
[e] ch. 44. 9.
7 felt.
[f] Ex. 20.12. Lev. 19.32. Eph. 6.1.
[g] ver. 19.
[h] Eph. 4.26.
8 felt.
[i] 1 Sam. 12.3. 1 Cor. 6.5.
[j] Ex. 22.10.
[k] Ex. 22.12.
[l] ch. 29.27.
[m] ver. 7.
[n] Ps. 124.1.
[o] ver. 53. Isa. 8.13.

29 It is in the power of my hand to do
you hurt: but the [b]God of your father
spake unto me [c]yesternight, saying,
Take thou heed that thou speak not to
Jacob either good or bad.
30 And now, *though* thou wouldest
needs be gone, because thou sore
longedst after thy father's house, *yet*
wherefore hast thou stolen [d]my gods?
31 And Jacob answered and said to
Laban, Because I was afraid: for I
said, Peradventure thou wouldest take
by force thy daughters from me.
32 With whomsoever thou findest thy
gods, [e]let him not live: before our
brethren discern thou what *is* thine
with me, and take *it* to thee. For Jacob
knew not that Rachel had stolen them.
33 And Laban went into Jacob's
tent, and into Leah's tent, and into the
two maidservants' tents; but he found
them not. Then went he out of Leah's
tent, and entered into Rachel's tent.
34 Now Rachel had taken the images, and put them in the camel's
furniture, and sat upon them. And
Laban [7]searched all the tent, but found
them not.
35 And she said to her father, Let it
not displease my lord that I cannot
[f]rise up before thee; for the custom of
women *is* upon me. And he searched,
but found not the [g]images.
36 ¶ And Jacob [h]was wroth, and
chode with Laban: and Jacob answered and said to Laban, What *is* my
trespass? what *is* my sin, that thou
hast so hotly pursued after me?
37 Whereas thou hast [8]searched all
my stuff, what hast thou found of all
thy household stuff? [i]set *it* here before my brethren and thy brethren,
that they may judge betwixt us both.
38 This twenty years *have* I *been* with
thee; thy ewes and thy she goats have
not cast their young, and the rams of
thy flock have I not eaten.
39 That [j]which was torn *of beasts* I
brought not unto thee; I bare the loss
of it; of [k]my hand didst thou require
it, *whether* stolen by day, or stolen by
night.
40 *Thus* I was; in the day the drought
consumed me, and the frost by night;
and my sleep departed from mine
eyes.
41 Thus have I been twenty years in
thy house; I [l]served thee fourteen
years for thy two daughters, and six
years for thy cattle: and [m]thou hast
changed my wages ten times.
42 Except [n]the God of my father, the
God of Abraham, and the fear [o]of

Isaac, had been with me, surely thou
hadst sent me away now empty. [p]God
hath seen mine affliction and the
labour of my hands, and [q]rebuked
thee yesternight.
43 ¶ And Laban answered and said
unto Jacob, *These* daughters *are* my
daughters, and *these* children *are* my
children, and *these* cattle *are* my
cattle, and all that thou seest *is* mine:
and what can I do this day unto these
my daughters, or unto their children
which they have born?
44 Now therefore come thou, [r]let us
make a covenant, I and thou; and [s]let
it be for a witness between me and
thee.
45 And Jacob [t]took a stone, and set
it up *for* a pillar.
46 And Jacob said unto his brethren,
Gather stones; and they took stones,
and made an heap: and they did eat
there upon the heap.
47 And Laban called it [9]Jē-gär-sā-
hă-dū-thă: but Jacob called it [10]Gā-
leēd.
48 And Laban said, [u]This heap *is* a
witness between me and thee this day.
Therefore was the name of it called
Gā-leēd;
49 And [11]Mizpah; [v]for he said, The
LORD watch between me and thee,
when we are absent one from another.
50 If thou shalt afflict my daughters,
or if thou shalt take *other* wives beside my daughters, no man *is* with us;
see, God *is* witness betwixt me and
thee.
51 And Laban said to Jacob, Behold
this heap, and behold *this* pillar, which
I have cast betwixt me and thee;
52 This heap *be* witness, and *this* pillar *be* witness, that I will not pass over
this heap to thee, and that thou shalt
not pass over this heap and this pillar
unto me, for harm.
53 The God of Abraham, and the
God of Nahor, the God of their father, [w]judge betwixt us. And Jacob
[x]sware by the fear of his father Isaac.
54 Then Jacob [12]offered sacrifice upon the mount, and called his brethren
to eat bread: and they did eat bread,
and tarried all night in the mount.
55 And early in the morning Laban
rose up, and kissed his sons and his
daughters, and [y]blessed them: and
Laban departed, and returned unto
his place.

CHAPTER 32

AND Jacob went on his way, and
[a]the angels of God met him.
2 And when Jacob saw them, he said,

p ch. 29.32. Ex. 3.7.
q 1 Chr. 12. 17. Jude 9.
r ch. 26.28.
s Josh. 24.27.
t ch. 28.18.
9 That is, The heap of witness. Chald.
10 That is, The heap of witness. Heb.
u Josh. 24.27.
11 That is, A beacon, or, watch tower.
v Judg. 11.29. 1 Sam. 7.5.
w ch. 16.5.
x ch. 21.23.
12 Or, killed beasts.
y ch. 28.1. 2 Sam. 6.20.

CHAP. 32

a Ps. 91.11. Heb. 1.14.
b Josh. 5.14. 2 Ki. 6.16. Ps. 103.21. Ps. 148.2. Luke 2.13.
1 That is, Two hosts, or camps.
c ch. 33.14.
d ch. 36. 6-8. Deut. 2.5. Josh. 24.4.
2 field.
e Pro. 15.1.
f ch. 30.43.
g ch. 33.8.
h ch. 33.1.
i ch. 35.3.
j Pro. 2.11. Eph. 5.15.
k Ps. 50.15.
l ch. 28.13.
m ch. 31.3.
3 I am less than all, etc.
n 2 Sam. 9.8.
o ch. 24.27.
p Job 8.7.
q Ps. 59.1,2.
r Hos. 10.14.
4 upon.
s ch. 28.13-15.
t ch. 43.11.

This *is* God's [b]host: and he called the
name of that place [1]Mā-hă-nā-īm.
3 And Jacob sent messengers before
him to Esau his brother unto [c]the land
of Sē-īr, [d]the [2]country of Ē-dom.
4 And he commanded them, saying,
[e]Thus shall ye speak unto my lord
Esau; Thy servant Jacob saith thus,
I have sojourned with Laban, and
stayed there until now:
5 And [f]I have oxen, and asses, flocks,
and menservants, and womenservants: and I have sent to tell my lord,
that [g]I may find grace in thy sight.
6 ¶ And the messengers returned to
Jacob, saying, We came to thy brother Esau, and also [h]he cometh to
meet thee, and four hundred men with
him.
7 Then Jacob was greatly afraid and
[i]distressed: and he [j]divided the people
that *was* with him, and the flocks, and
herds, and the camels, into two
bands;
8 And said, If Esau come to the one
company, and smite it, then the other
company which is left shall escape.
9 ¶ And [k]Jacob said, [l]O God of my
father Abraham, and God of my father Isaac, the LORD [m]which saidst unto
me, Return unto thy country, and to
thy kindred, and I will deal well with
thee:
10 [3]I am not [n]worthy of the least of
all the [o]mercies, and of all the truth,
which thou hast shewed unto thy servant; for with my staff [p]I passed over
this Jordan; and now I am become
two bands.
11 Deliver [q]me, I pray thee, from the
hand of my brother, from the hand of
Esau: for I fear him, lest he will come
and smite me, *and* the [r]mother [4]with
the children.
12 And [s]thou saidst, I will surely do
thee good, and make thy seed as the
sand of the sea, which cannot be numbered for multitude.
13 ¶ And he lodged there that same
night; and took of that which came to
his hand a [t]present for Esau his brother;
14 Two hundred she goats, and twenty he goats, two hundred ewes, and
twenty rams,
15 Thirty milch camels with their
colts, forty kine, and ten bulls, twenty
she asses, and ten foals.
16 And he delivered *them* into the
hand of his servants, every drove by
themselves; and said unto his servants, Pass over before me, and put
a space betwixt drove and drove.

17 And he commanded the foremost, saying, When Esau my brother meeteth thee, and asketh thee, saying, Whose *art* thou? and whither goest thou? and whose *are* these before thee?

18 Then thou shalt say, *They be* thy servant Jacob's; it *is* a present sent unto my lord Esau: and, behold, also he *is* behind us.

19 And so commanded he the second, and the third, and all that followed the droves, saying, On this manner shall ye speak unto Esau, when ye find him.

20 And say ye moreover, Behold, thy servant Jacob *is* behind us. For he said, I will [u]appease him with the present that goeth before me, and afterward I will see his face; peradventure he will accept [5]of me.

21 So went the present over before him: and himself lodged that night in the company.

22 And he rose up that night, and took his two wives, and his two womenservants, and his eleven sons, and [v]passed over the ford Jăb-bo̱k.

23 And he took them, and [6]sent them over the brook, and sent over that he had.

24 ¶ And Jacob was left alone; and there wrestled a man with him until the [7]breaking of the day.

25 And when he saw that he prevailed not against him, he touched the hollow of his thigh; and the hollow [w]of Jacob's thigh was out of joint, as he wrestled with him.

26 And [x]he said, Let me go, for the day breaketh. And he said, I [y]will not let thee go, except thou bless me.

27 And he said unto him, What *is* thy name? And he said, Jacob.

28 And he said, Thy name shall be called no more Jacob, but [8]Israel: for as a prince hast thou power [z]with God and [a]with men, and hast prevailed.

29 And Jacob asked *him*, and said, Tell *me*, I pray thee, thy name. And he said, [b]Wherefore *is* it *that* thou dost ask after my name? And he blessed him there.

30 And Jacob called the name of the place [9]Pĕn-ĭ-ĕl: for [c]I have seen God face to face, and my life is preserved.

31 And as he passed over Pĕn-ū-ĕl the sun rose upon him, and he halted upon his thigh.

32 Therefore the children of Israel eat not *of* the sinew which shrank, which *is* upon the hollow of the thigh, unto this day: because he touched the hollow of Jacob's thigh in the sinew that shrank.

CHAPTER 33

AND Jacob lifted up his eyes, and looked, and, behold, [a]Esau came, and with him four hundred men. And he divided the children unto Leah, and unto Rachel, and unto the two handmaids.

2 And he put the handmaids and their children foremost, and Leah and her children after, and Rachel and Joseph hindermost.

3 And he passed over before them, and [b]bowed himself to the ground seven times, until he came near to his brother.

4 And [c]Esau ran to meet him, and embraced him, [d]and fell on his neck, and kissed him: and they wept.

5 And he lifted up his eyes, and saw the women and the children; and said, Who *are* those [1]with thee? And he said, The children which [e]God hath graciously given thy servant.

6 Then the handmaidens came near, they and their children, and they bowed themselves.

7 And Leah also with her children came near, and bowed themselves: and after came Joseph near and Rachel, and they bowed themselves.

8 And he said, [2]What *meanest* thou by [f]all this drove which I met? And he said, *These are* [g]to find grace in the sight of my lord.

9 And Esau said, I have enough, my brother; [3]keep that thou hast unto thyself.

10 And Jacob said, Nay, I pray thee, if now I have found grace in thy sight, then receive my present at my hand: for therefore I [h]have seen thy face, as though I had seen the face of God, and thou wast pleased with me.

11 Take, I pray thee, [i]my blessing that is brought to thee; because God hath dealt graciously with me, and because I have [4]enough. [j]And he urged him, and he took *it*.

12 And he said, Let us take our journey, and let us go, and I will go before thee.

13 And he said unto him, My lord knoweth that the children *are* tender, and the flocks and herds with young *are* with me: and if men should overdrive them one day, all the flock will die.

14 Let my lord, I pray thee, pass over before his servant: and I will lead on softly, [5]according as the cattle that go-

u Pro. 21.14.
5 my face.
v Deut. 3.16.
6 caused to pass.
7 ascending of the morning.
w Matt. 26. 41. 2 Cor. 12.7.
x Luke 24.28.
y Hos. 12.4.
8 That is, A prince of God. 2 Ki. 17.34.
z Hos. 12.3,4.
a ch. 25.31. ch. 27.33.
b Judg. 13.18.
9 That is, The face of God.
c ch. 16.13. Ex. 24.11. Ex. 33.20. Deut. 5.24. Judg. 6.22. Judg. 13.22. Isa. 6.5.

CHAP. 33
a ch. 32.6.
b ch. 18.2. ch. 42.6. ch. 43.26.
c ch. 32.28. Pro. 16.1. Pro. 21.1. Jer. 10.23.
d ch. 45.14.
1 to thee.
e ch. 48.9. Ps. 127.3. Isa. 8.18.
2 What is all this band to thee?
f ch. 32.16.
g ch. 32.5.
3 be that to thee that is thine.
h ch. 43.3. 2 Sam. 3.13. 2 Sam. 14. 24,28,32. Matt. 18.10.
i Judg. 1.15. 1 Sam. 25. 27. 2 Ki. 5.15.
4 all things, Phil. 4.18.
j 2 Ki. 5.23.
5 according to the foot of the work, etc., and according to the foot of the children.

eth before me and the children be able
to endure, until I come unto my lord
[k]unto Sē′-ïr.
15 And Esau said, Let me now [6]leave
with thee *some* of the folk that *are*
with me. And he said, [7]What needeth
it? [l]let me find grace in the sight of my
lord.
16 ¶ So Esau returned that day on his
way unto Sē′-ïr.
17 And Jacob journeyed to [m]Sŭc′-
cōth, and built him an house, and
made booths for his cattle: therefore
the name of the place is called [8]Sŭc′-
cōth.
18 ¶ And Jacob came to [n]Shā′-lĕm, a
city of [9]Shē′-chĕm, which *is* in the land
of Canaan, when he came from Pā′-
dăn–âr′-ăm; and pitched his tent before the city.
19 And [o]he bought a parcel of a field,
where he had spread his tent, at the
hand of the children of Hā′-môr, Shē′-
chĕm's father, for an hundred pieces
of money.
20 And he erected there an altar, and
[p]called it Ĕl–ĕl′-ō-hĕ–Ĭs′-rā-ĕl.

CHAPTER 34

AND [a]Dinah the daughter of Leah,
which she bare unto Jacob, [b]went
out to see the daughters of the land.
2 And when Shē′-chĕm the son of Hā′-
môr the Hī′-vīte, prince of the country,
[c]saw her, he [d]took her, and lay with
her, and [1]defiled her.
3 And his soul clave unto Dinah the
daughter of Jacob, and he loved the
damsel, and spake [2]kindly unto the
damsel.
4 And Shē′-chĕm [e]spake unto his
father Hā′-môr, saying, Get me this
damsel to wife.
5 And Jacob heard that he had defiled Dinah his daughter: now his sons
were with his cattle in the field: and
Jacob held his peace until they were
come.
6 ¶ And Hā′-môr the father of Shē′-
chĕm went out unto Jacob to commune with him.
7 And the sons of Jacob came out of
the field when they heard *it:* and the
men were grieved, and they were [f]very
wroth, because he had [g]wrought folly
in Israel in lying with Jacob's daughter; which [h]thing ought not to be
done.
8 And Hā′-môr communed with them,
saying, The soul of my son Shē′-chĕm
longeth for your daughter: I pray you
give her him to wife.
9 And [i]make ye marriages with us,
and give your daughters unto us, and
take our daughters unto you.
10 And ye shall dwell with us: and
[j]the land shall be before you; dwell
and [k]trade ye therein, and get [l]you
possessions therein.
11 And Shē′-chĕm said unto her father and unto her brethren, Let me find
grace in your eyes, and what ye shall
say unto me I will give.
12 Ask me never so much [m]dowry
and gift, and I will give according as
ye shall say unto me: but give me the
damsel to wife.
13 And the sons of Jacob answered
Shē′-chĕm and Hā′-môr his father [n]de-
ceitfully, and said, because he had defiled Dinah their sister:
14 And they said unto them, We cannot do this thing, to give our sister to
one that is uncircumcised; for [o]that
were a reproach unto us:
15 But in this will we consent unto
you: If ye will be as we *be*, that every
male of you be circumcised;
16 Then will we give our daughters
unto you, and we will take your
daughters to us, and we will dwell
with you, and we will become one
people.
17 But if ye will not hearken unto us,
to be circumcised; then will we take
our daughter, and we will be gone.
18 And their words pleased Hā′-môr,
and Shē′-chĕm Hā′-môr's son.
19 And the young man deferred not
to do the thing, because he had delight
in Jacob's daughter: and he *was* [p]more
honourable than all the house of his
father.
20 ¶ And Hā′-môr and Shē′-chĕm his
son came unto the [q]gate of their city,
and communed with the men of their
city, saying,
21 These men *are* peaceable with us;
therefore let them dwell in the land,
and trade therein; for the land, behold, *it is* large enough for them; let
us take their daughters to us for wives,
and let us give them our daughters.
22 Only herein will the men consent
unto us for to dwell with us, to be one
people, if every male among us be circumcised, as they *are* circumcised.
23 *Shall* not their cattle and their
substance and every beast of theirs *be*
ours? only let us consent unto them,
and they will dwell with us.
24 And unto Hā′-môr and unto Shē′-
chĕm his son hearkened all that [r]went
out of the gate of his city; and every
male was circumcised, all that went
out of the gate of his city.

k ch. 32.3.
6 set, or, place.
7 Wherefore is this?
l Ruth 2.13.
m Josh. 13.27. Judg. 8.5.
8 That is, booths.
n John 3.23.
9 Called Sychem. Acts 7.16. Josh. 24.1.
o Josh. 24.32. John 4.5.
p ch. 35.7.

CHAP. 34
a ch. 30.21.
b Titus 2.5.
c ch. 6.2. Judg. 14.1.
d ch. 20.2.
1 humbled her. Deut. 22.29.
2 to the heart of the damsel. Isa. 40.2. Hosea 2.14.
e Judg. 14.2.
f ch. 49.7. 2 Sam. 13. 21.
g Josh. 7.15. Judg. 20.6.
h Deut. 23.17. 2 Sam. 13. 12.
i Ex. 23.32.
j ch. 13.9. ch. 20.15.
k ch. 42.34.
l ch. 47.27.
m Ex. 22.16. Deut. 22.29. 1 Sam. 18. 25.
n 2 Sam. 13. 24.
o Josh. 5.9.
p 1 Chr. 4.9.
q 2 Sam. 15.2. Ruth 4.1.
r ch. 23.10.

25 ¶ And it came to pass on the third day, when they were sore, that two of the sons of Jacob, Simeon [s]and Levi, Dinah's brethren, took each man his sword, and came upon the city boldly, and slew all the males.

26 And they slew Hā-'môr and Shē-'chĕm his son with the [3]edge of the sword, and took Dinah out of Shē-'chĕm's house, and went out.

27 The sons of Jacob came upon the slain, and spoiled the city, because they had defiled their sister.

28 They took their sheep, and their oxen, and their asses, and that which *was* in the city, and that which *was* in the field,

29 And all their wealth, and all their little ones, and their wives took they captive, and spoiled even all that *was* in the house.

30 And Jacob said to Simeon and Levi, [t]Ye have [u]troubled me [v]to make me to stink among the inhabitants of the land, among the Canaanites and the Pĕ-rĭz-'zītes: and [w]I *being* few in number, they shall gather themselves together against me, and slay me; and I shall be destroyed, I and my house.

31 And they said, [x]Should he deal with our sister as with an harlot?

CHAPTER 35

AND God said unto Jacob, Arise, go up to [a]Beth-el, and dwell there: and make there an altar unto God, [b]that appeared unto thee [c]when thou fleddest from the face of Esau thy brother.

2 Then Jacob said unto his [d]household, and to all that *were* with him, Put away [e]the strange gods that *are* among you, and [f]be clean, and change your garments:

3 And let us arise, and go up to Beth-el; and I will make there an altar unto God, [g]who answered me in the day of my distress, [h]and was with me in the way which I went.

4 And they gave unto Jacob all the strange gods which *were* in their hand, and *all their* [i]earrings which *were* in their ears; and Jacob hid them under [j]the oak which *was* by Shē-'chĕm.

5 And they journeyed: and [k]the terror of God was upon the cities that *were* round about them, and they did not pursue after the sons of Jacob.

6 ¶ So Jacob came to [l]Luz, which *is* in the land of Canaan, that *is*, Beth-el, he and all the people that *were* with him.

7 And he [m]built there an altar, and called the place [1]Ĕl-bĕth'-ĕl: because [n]there God appeared unto him, when he fled from the face of his brother.

8 But [o]Dĕb-'ō-răh Rebekah's nurse died, and she was buried beneath Beth-el under an oak: and the name of it was called [2]Ăl-'lŏn-bā-'chûth.

9 ¶ And [p]God appeared unto Jacob again, when he came out of Pā-'dăn-âr-'ăm, and blessed him.

10 And God said unto him, Thy name *is* Jacob: [q]thy name shall not be called any more Jacob, but Israel [r]shall be thy name: and he called his name Israel.

11 And God said unto him, [s]I *am* God Almighty: be fruitful and multiply; a [t]nation and a company of nations shall be of thee, and kings shall come out of thy loins;

12 And the land [u]which I gave Abraham and Isaac, to thee I will give it, and to thy seed after thee will I give the land.

13 And God [v]went up from him in the place where he talked with him.

14 And Jacob [w]set up a pillar in the place where he talked with him, *even* a pillar of stone: and he poured a drink offering thereon, and he poured oil thereon.

15 And Jacob called the name of the place where God spake with him, [x]Beth-el.

16 ¶ And they journeyed from Beth-el; and there was but [3]a little way to come to Ē-'phrăth: and Rachel travailed, and she had hard labour.

17 And it came to pass, when she was in hard labour, that the midwife said unto her, Fear not; [y]thou shalt have this son also.

18 And it came to pass, as her soul was in departing, (for she died) that she called his name [4]Bĕn-ō-'nī: but his father called him [5]Benjamin.

19 And [z]Rachel died, and was buried in the way to [a]Ē-'phrăth, which *is* Beth-lehem.

20 And Jacob set a pillar upon her grave: that *is* the pillar of Rachel's grave [b]unto this day.

21 ¶ And Israel journeyed, and spread his tent beyond [c]the tower of Ē-'där.

22 And it came to pass, when Israel dwelt in that land, that Reuben went and [d]lay with Bĭl-'häh his father's concubine: and Israel heard *it*. Now the sons of Jacob were twelve:

23 The sons of Leah; [e]Reuben, Jacob's firstborn, and Simeon, and

s ch. 49.5-7.
3 mouth.
t ch. 49.6.
u Josh. 7.25.
v Ex. 5.21. 1 Sam. 13.4.
w Deut. 4.27. Ps. 105.12.
x Pro. 6.34.

CHAP. 35

a ch. 28.19.
b ch. 28.13.
c ch. 27.43.
d ch. 18.19 Josh. 24.15.
e ch. 31.19, 34. 1 Sam. 7.3.
f Ex. 19.10.
g ch. 32.7,24. Ps. 107.6.
h ch. 28.20. ch. 31.3,42.
i Hosea 2.13.
j Josh. 24.26.
k Ex. 15.16. Ex. 23.27. Ex. 34.24. Deut. 11.25. Josh. 2.9. Josh. 5.1. 1 Sam. 14. 15. 2 Chr. 14.14.
l ch. 28.19.
m Eccl. 5.4.
1 That is, The God of Beth-el.
n ch. 28.13.
o ch. 24.59.
2 That is, The oak of weeping.
p Hosea 12.4.
q ch. 17.5.
r ch. 32.28.
s ch. 17.1. ch. 48.3,4. Ex. 6.3.
t ch. 17.5,6. ch. 48.4.
u ch. 12.7. ch. 13.15. ch. 26.3,4. ch. 28.13. Ex. 32.13.
v ch. 17.22.
w ch. 28.18.
x ch. 28.19.
3 a little piece of ground.
y ch. 30.24.
4 That is, The son of my sorrow.
5 That is, The son of the right hand.
z ch. 48.7.
a Ruth 1.2. Ruth 4.11. Micah 5.2. Matt. 2.6.
b 1 Sam. 10.2.
c Micah 4.8.
d ch. 49.4. 1 Chr. 5.1.
e ch. 46.8. Ex. 1.2.

Levi, and Judah, and Ĭs´-să-chăr, and Zĕ-bū´-lŭn:

24 The sons of Rachel; Joseph, and Benjamin:

25 And the sons of Bĭl´-hăh, Rachel's handmaid; Dan, and Năph´-tă-lī:

26 And the sons of Zilpah, Leah's handmaid; Gad, and Asher: these *are* the sons of Jacob, which were born to him in Pā´-dăn–âr´-ăm.

27 ¶ And Jacob came unto Isaac his father unto [f]Măm´-rē, unto the city [g]of Âr´-băh, which *is* Hē´-brŏn, where Abraham and Isaac sojourned.

28 And the days of Isaac were an hundred and fourscore years.

29 And Isaac [h]gave up the ghost, and died, and [i]was gathered unto his people, *being* old and full of days: and [j]his sons Esau and Jacob buried him.

CHAPTER 36

NOW these *are* the generations of Esau, [a]who *is* Ē´-dŏm.

2 Esau [b]took his wives of the daughters of Canaan; Ā´-dăh the daughter of Ē´-lŏn the Hittite, [c]and Ă-hŏl´-ĭ-bä´-măh the daughter of Ā´-năh the daughter of Zĭb´-ĕ-ŏn the Hĭ´-vite;

3 And [d]Băsh´-ĕ-măth Ĭsh´-mā-ĕl's daughter, sister of Nĕ-bā´-jŏth.

4 And [e]Ā´-dăh bare to Esau Ĕ-lī´-phăz; and Băsh´-ĕ-măth bare Reū´-ĕl;

5 And Ă-hŏl-ĭ-bä´-măh bare Jē´-ŭsh, and Jā´-ă-lăm, and Kôr´-ăh: these *are* the sons of Esau, which were born unto him in the land of Canaan.

6 And Esau took his wives, and his sons, and his daughters, and all the [1]persons of his house, and his cattle, and all his beasts, and all his substance, which he had got in the land of Canaan; and went into the country from the face of his [f]brother Jacob.

7 For [g]their riches were more than that they might dwell together; and the land [h]wherein they were strangers could not bear them because of their cattle.

8 Thus dwelt Esau in [i]mount Sē´-ĭr: [j]Esau *is* Ē´-dŏm.

9 ¶ And these *are* the generations of Esau the father of [2]the Ē´-dŏm-ītes in mount Sē´-ĭr:

10 These *are* the names of Esau's sons; [k]Ĕ-lī´-phăz the son of Ā´-dăh the wife of Esau, Reū´-ĕl the son of Băsh´-ĕ-măth the wife of Esau.

11 And the sons of Ĕ-lī´-phăz were Tē´-măn, Omar, [3]Zē´-phō, and Gā´-tăm, and Kē´-năz.

12 And Tĭm´-nă was concubine to Ĕ-lī´-phăz Esau's son; and she bare to Ĕ-lī´-phăz [l]Ăm´-ă-lĕk: these *were* the sons of Ā´-dăh Esau's wife.

13 And these *are* the sons of Reū´-ĕl; Nahath, and Zē´-răh, Shăm´-măh, and Mĭz´-zăh: these were the sons of Băsh´-ĕ-măth Esau's wife.

14 ¶ And these were the sons of Ă-hŏl-ĭ-bä´-măh, the daughter of Ā´-năh the daughter of Zĭb´-ĕ-ŏn, Esau's wife: and she bare to Esau Jē´-ŭsh, and Jā´-ă-lăm, and Kôr´-ăh.

15 ¶ These *were* dukes of the sons of Esau: the sons of Ĕ-lī´-phăz the firstborn *son* of Esau; duke Tē´-măn, duke Omar, duke Zē´-phō, duke Kē´-năz,

16 Duke Kôr´-ăh, duke Gā´-tăm, *and* duke Ăm´-ă-lĕk: these *are* the dukes *that came* of Ĕ-lī´-phăz in the land of Ē´-dŏm; these *were* the sons of Ā´-dăh.

17 ¶ And these *are* the sons of Reū´-ĕl Esau's son; duke Nahath, duke Zē´-răh, duke Shăm´-măh, duke Mĭz´-zăh: these *are* the dukes *that came* of Reū´-ĕl in the land of Ē´-dŏm; these *are* the sons of Băsh´-ĕ-măth Esau's wife.

18 ¶ And these *are* the sons of Ă-hŏl-ĭ-bä´-măh Esau's wife; duke Jē´-ŭsh, duke Jā´-ă-lăm, duke Kôr´-ăh: these *were* the dukes *that came* of Ă-hŏl-ĭ-bä´-măh the daughter of Ā´-năh, Esau's wife.

19 These *are* the sons of Esau, who *is* Ē´-dŏm, and these *are* their dukes.

20 ¶ These [m]*are* the sons of Sē´-ĭr the [n]Hôr´-īte, who inhabited the land; Lō´-tăn, and Shō´-băl, and Zĭb´-ĕ-ŏn, and Ā´-năh,

21 And Dī´-shŏn, and Ē´-zĕr, and Dī´-shăn: these *are* the dukes of the Hôr´-ītes, the children of Sē´-ĭr in the land of Ē´-dŏm.

22 And the children of Lō´-tăn were Hôr´-ī and [4]Hē´-măm; and Lō´-tăn's sister *was* Tĭm´-nă.

23 And the children of Shō´-băl *were* these; [5]Ăl´-văn, and Măn´-ă-hăth, and Ē´-băl, [6]Shē´-phō, and Ō´-năm.

24 And these *are* the children of Zĭb´-ĕ-ŏn; both Ā´-jăh, and Ā´-năh: this *was that* Ā´-năh that found the mules [o]in the wilderness, as he fed the asses of Zĭb´-ĕ-ŏn his father.

25 And the children of Ā´-năh *were* these; Dī´-shŏn, and Ă-hŏl-ĭ-bä´-măh the daughter of Ā´-năh.

26 And these *are* the children of Dī´-shŏn; [7]Hĕm´-dăn, and Ĕsh´-băn, and Ĭth´-răn, and Chē´-răn.

27 The children of Ē´-zĕr *are* these; Bilhan, and Zā´-ă-văn, and [8]Ā´-kan.

28 The children of Dī´-shăn *are* these; Uz, and Ā´-răn.

f ch. 13.18.
g Josh. 14.15.
h Eccl. 12.7.
i ch. 15.15. ch. 25.8. ch. 49.33.
j ch. 25.9. ch. 49.31.

CHAP. 36
a ch. 25.30.
b ch. 26.34.
c ver. 25.
d ch. 28.9.
e 1 Chr. 1.35.
1 souls.
f Deut. 23.7.
g ch. 13.6,11.
h ch. 17.8. 1 Chr. 29.15. Ps. 39.12. Ps. 105.12. Ps. 119.19. 2 Cor. 5.6,7. Heb. 11.9. 1 Pet. 1.17. 1 Pet. 2.11.
i ch. 32.3.
j ver. 1.
2 Edom.
k 1 Chr. 1. 35, etc.
3 Or, Zephi.
l Ex. 17.8. Num. 24.20. Deut. 25. 17-19. 1 Sam. 15. 2,3.
m 1 Chr. 1. 38.
n ch. 14.6. Deut. 2.12, 22.
4 Or, Homam, 1 Chr. 1.39.
5 Or, Alian, 1 Chr. 1.40.
6 Or, Shephi, 1 Chr. 1.40.
o Lev. 19.19.
7 Or, Amram, 1 Chr. 1.41.
8 Or, Jakan. 1 Chr. 1.42.

29 These *are* the dukes *that came* of the Hôr'-ītes; duke Lō'-tăn, duke Shō'-băl, duke Zĭb'-ĕ-on, duke Ā'-năh,

30 Duke Dī'-shŏn, duke Ē'-zĕr, duke Dī'-shăn: these *are* the dukes *that came* of Hôr'-ī, among their dukes in the land of Sē'-ĭr.

31 ¶ And [p]these *are* the kings that reigned in the land of Ē'-dom, before there reigned any [q]king over the children of Israel.

32 And Bē'-lă the son of Bē'-ôr reigned in Ē'-dom: and the name of his city *was* Dĭn'-hă-băh.

33 And Bē'-lă died, and Jō'-băb the son of Zē'-răh of Bŏz'-răh reigned in his stead.

34 And Jō'-băb died, and Hū'-shăm of the land of Tē'-măn-ī reigned in his stead.

35 And Hū'-shăm died, and Hā'-dăd the son of Bē'-dăd, who smote Mĭd'-ī-ăn in the field of Moab, reigned in his stead: and the name of his city *was* Ā'-vĭth.

36 And Hā'-dăd died, and Săm'-lăh of Măs-rē'-kăh reigned in his stead.

37 And Săm'-lăh died, and Saul of Rē'-hō-bŏth *by* the river reigned in his stead.

38 And Saul died, and Bā'-ăl–hā'-năn the son of Ăch'-bôr reigned in his stead.

39 And Bā'-ăl–hā'-năn the son of Ăch'-bôr died, and [r]Hā'-dăr reigned in his stead: and the name of his city *was* Pā'-ū; and his wife's name *was* Mĕ-hĕt'-ă-bĕl, the daughter of Mā'-trĕd, the daughter of Mē'-ză-hăb.

40 And these *are* the names of the [s]dukes *that came* of Esau, according to their families, after their places, by their names; duke Tĭm'-năh, duke [9]Ăl'-văh, duke Jē'-thĕth,

41 Duke Ă-hŏl-ĭ-bā'-măh, duke Ē'-lăh, duke Pī'-nŏn,

42 Duke Kē'-năz, duke Tē'-măn, duke Mĭb'-zăr,

43 Duke Măg'-dĭ-ĕl, duke Ī'-răm: these *be* the dukes of Ē'-dom, according to their habitations in the land of their possession: he *is* Esau the father of [10]the Ē'-dom-ītes.

CHAPTER 37

AND Jacob dwelt in the land [1]wherein his father was a stranger, in the land of Canaan.

2 These *are* the generations of Jacob. Joseph, *being* seventeen years old, was feeding the flock with his brethren; and the lad *was* with the sons of Bĭl'-hăh, and with the sons of Zilpah, his father's wives: and Joseph brought unto his father [a]their evil report.

3 Now Israel loved Joseph more than all his children, because he *was* [b]the son of his old age: and he made him a coat of *many* [2]colours.

4 And when his brethren saw that their father loved him more than all his brethren, they [c]hated him, and could not speak peaceably unto him.

5 ¶ And Joseph dreamed a dream, and he told *it* his brethren: and they hated him yet the more.

6 And he said unto them, Hear, I pray you, this dream which I have dreamed:

7 For, [d]behold, we *were* binding sheaves in the field, and, lo, my sheaf arose, and also stood upright; and, behold, your sheaves stood round about, and made obeisance to my sheaf.

8 And his brethren said to him, Shalt thou indeed reign over us? or shalt thou indeed have dominion over us? And they hated him yet the more for his dreams, and for his words.

9 ¶ And he dreamed yet another dream, and told it his brethren, and said, Behold, I have dreamed a dream more; and, behold, [e]the sun and the moon and the eleven stars made obeisance to me.

10 And he told *it* to his father, and to his brethren: and his father rebuked him, and said unto him, What *is* this dream that thou hast dreamed? Shall I and thy mother and [f]thy brethren indeed come to bow down ourselves to thee to the earth?

11 And [g]his brethren envied him; but his father [h]observed the saying.

12 ¶ And his brethren went to feed their father's flock in Shē'-chĕm.

13 And Israel said unto Joseph, Do not thy brethren feed *the flock* in Shē'-chĕm? come, and I will send thee unto them. And he said to him, Here *am I*.

14 And he said to him, Go, I pray thee, [3] see whether it be well with thy brethren, and well with the flocks; and bring me word again. So he sent him out of the vale [i]of Hē'-brŏn, and he came to Shē'-chĕm.

15 ¶ And a certain man found him, and, behold, *he was* wandering in the field: and the man asked him, saying, What seekest thou?

16 And he said, I seek my brethren: [j]tell me, I pray thee, where they feed *their flocks*.

17 And the man said, They are departed hence; for I heard them say,

p 1 Chr. 1.43.
q 1 Sam. 10. 24.
r 1 Chr. 1.50. Hadad Pai. After his death was an Aristocracy. Ex. 15.15.
s 1 Chr. 1.51.
9 Or, Aliah.
10 Edom.
CHAP. 37
1 of his father's sojournings. ch. 17.8. ch. 23.4. ch. 28.4. ch. 36.7. ch. 47.9. 1 Chr. 29.15. Ps. 39.12. Ps. 105.12. Ps. 119.19. 2 Cor. 5.6,7. 1 Pet. 1.17. 1 Pet. 2.11. Heb. 11.9.
a 1 Sam. 2. 22-24.
b ch. 44.20.
2 Or, pieces. Judg. 5.30. 2 Sam. 13. 18. Ps. 45.14. Eze. 16.16.
c ch. 27.41. ch. 49.23. 1 Sam. 17. 28. John 7.3,5. 1 John 2.11. 1 John 3.10, 12.
d ch. 42.6,9. ch. 43.26. ch. 44.14.
e ch. 46.29.
f ch. 27.29.
g Acts 7.9.
h Dan. 7.28. Luke 2.19, 51.
3 see the peace of thy brethren, etc. ch. 29.6. 1 Sam. 17. 17.
i ch. 13.18. ch. 23.2,19. ch. 35.27. Josh. 14.14, 15. Judg. 1.10.
j Song 1.7.

Let us go to Dō-thăn. And Joseph went after his brethren, and found them in [k]Dō-thăn.

18 And when they saw him afar off, even before he came near unto them, they [l]conspired against him to slay him.

19 And they said one to another, Behold, this [4]dreamer cometh.

20 Come [m]now therefore, and let us slay him, and cast him into some pit, and we will say, Some evil beast hath devoured him: and we shall see what will become of his dreams.

21 And [n]Reuben heard *it*, and he delivered him out of their hands; and said, Let us not kill him.

22 And Reuben said unto them, Shed no blood, *but* cast him into this pit that *is* in the wilderness, and lay no hand upon him; that he might rid him out of their hands, to deliver him to his father again.

23 ¶ And it came to pass, when Joseph was come unto his brethren, that they stript Joseph out of his coat, *his* coat of *many* [5]colours that *was* on him;

24 And they took him, and cast him into a pit: and the pit *was* empty, *there was* no water in it.

25 And [o]they sat down to eat bread: and they lifted up their eyes and looked, and, behold, a company of [p]Ĭsh-mê̆e-lītes came from Gilead with their camels bearing spicery and [q]balm and myrrh, going to carry *it* down to Egypt.

26 And Judah said unto his brethren, What profit *is it* if we slay our brother, and [r]conceal his blood?

27 Come, and let us sell him to the Ĭsh-mê̆e-lītes, and [s]let not our hand be upon him; for he *is* [t]our brother *and* [u]our flesh. And his brethren [6]were content.

28 Then there passed by [v]Mĭd-ĭ-ă-nītes merchantmen; and they drew and lifted up Joseph out of the pit, and [w]sold Joseph to the Ĭsh-mê̆e-lītes for [x]twenty *pieces* of silver: and they brought Joseph into Egypt.

29 ¶ And Reuben returned unto the pit; and, behold, Joseph *was* not in the pit; and he [y]rent his clothes.

30 And he returned unto his brethren, and said, The [z]child *is* not; and I, whither shall I go?

31 And they took [a]Joseph's coat, and killed a kid of the goats, and dipped the coat in the blood;

32 And they sent the coat of *many* colours, and they brought *it* to their father; and said, This have we found: know now whether it *be* thy son's coat or no.

33 And he knew it, and said, *It is* my son's coat; an [b]evil beast hath devoured him; Joseph is without doubt rent in pieces.

34 And Jacob [c]rent his clothes, and put sackcloth upon his loins, and mourned for his son many days.

35 And all his sons and all his daughters [d]rose up to comfort him; but he refused to be comforted; and he said, [e]For I will go down into the grave unto my son mourning. Thus his father wept for him.

36 And [f]the Mĭd-ĭ-ă-nītes sold him into Egypt unto Pŏt-ĭ-phär, an [7]officer of Pharaoh's, *and* [8]captain of the guard.

CHAPTER 38

AND it came to pass at that time, that Judah went down from his brethren, and [a]turned in to a certain Adullamite, whose name *was* Hī-răh.

2 And Judah [b]saw there a daughter of a certain Canaanite, whose name *was* [c]Shû-äh; and he took her, and went in unto her.

3 And she conceived, and bare a son; and he called his name [d]Er.

4 And she conceived again, and bare a son; and she called his name [e]Ō-năn.

5 And she yet again conceived, and bare a son; and called his name [f]Shē-läh: and he was at Chē-zĭb, when she bare him.

6 And Judah [g]took a wife for Er his firstborn, whose name *was* Tā-mär.

7 And [h]Er, Judah's firstborn, was wicked in the sight of the LORD; [i]and the LORD slew him.

8 And Judah said unto Ō-năn, Go in unto [j]thy brother's wife, and marry her, and raise up seed to thy brother.

9 And Ō-năn knew that the seed should not be [k]his; and it came to pass, when he went in unto his brother's wife, that he spilled *it* on the ground, lest that he should give seed to his brother.

10 And the thing which he did [1]displeased the LORD: wherefore he slew [l]him also.

11 Then said Judah to Tāmär his daughter in law, [m]Remain a widow at thy father's house, till Shē-läh my son be grown: for he said, Lest peradventure he die also, as his brethren *did*. And Tā-mär went [n]and dwelt in her father's house.

12 ¶ And [2]in process of time the daughter of Shû-äh Judah's wife died;

k 2 Ki. 6.13.
l 1 Sam. 19.1. Ps. 31.13. Ps. 37.12,32. Ps. 94.21. Matt. 27.1. Mark 14.1. John 11.53. Acts 23.12.
4 master of dreams.
m Pro. 1.11. Pro. 6.17. 1 John 3. 12,13.
n ch. 42.22.
5 Or, pieces.
o Pro. 30.20. Amos 6.6.
p vers. 28,36.
q Jer. 8.22.
r ch. 4.10. Job 16.18.
s 1 Sam. 18. 17.
t ch. 42.21.
u ch. 29.14.
6 hearkened.
v ch. 39.1. Judg. 6.3.
w ch. 45.4,5. Ps. 105.17. Acts 7.9.
x Matt. 27.9.
y Job 1.20.
z ch. 42.13, 36. Jer. 31.15.
a ver. 23.
b ver. 20. ch. 44.28.
c ver. 29.
d 2 Sam. 12. 17.
e ch. 42.38.
f ch. 39.1.
7 eunuch: But the word doth signify not only eunuchs, but also chamberlains, courtiers, and officers.
8 chief of the slaughtermen, or, executioners.

CHAP. 38

a 2 Ki. 4.8.
b ch. 34.2.
c 1 Chr. 2.3.
d Num. 26. 19.
e ch. 46.12.
f Num. 26.20
g ch. 24.4.
h ch. 46.12.
i 1 Chr. 2.3.
j Matt. 22.24.
k Deut. 25.6.
1 was evil in the eyes of the LORD.
l Num. 26.19.
m Ruth 1.13.
n Lev. 22.13.
2 the days were multiplied.

and Judah was [o]comforted, and went up unto his sheepshearers to Tĭm´-năth, he and his friend Hī´-răh the Adullamite.

13 And it was told Tā´-mär, saying, Behold thy father in law goeth up [p]to Tĭm´-năth to shear his sheep.

14 And she put her widow's garments off from her, and covered her with a vail, and wrapped herself, and [q]sat in [3]an open place, which *is* by the way to Tĭm´-năth; for she saw [r]that Shē´-lăh was grown, and she was not given unto him to wife.

15 When Judah saw her, he thought her *to be* an harlot; because she had covered her face.

16 And he turned unto her by the way, and said, Go to, I pray thee, let me come in unto thee; (for he knew not that she *was* his daughter in law.) And she said, What wilt thou give me, that thou mayest come in unto me?

17 And he said, [s]I will send *thee* [4]a kid from the flock. And she said, Wilt [t]thou give *me* a pledge, till thou send *it?*

18 And he said, What pledge shall I give thee? And she said, Thy [u]signet, and thy bracelets, and thy staff that *is* in thine hand. And he gave *it* her, and came in unto her, and she conceived by him.

19 And she arose, and went away, and [v]laid by her vail from her, and put on the garments of her widowhood.

20 And Judah sent the kid by the hand of his friend the Adullamite, to receive *his* pledge from the woman's hand: but he found her not.

21 Then he asked the men of that place, saying, Where *is* the harlot, that *was* [5]openly by the way side? And they said, There was no harlot in this *place.*

22 And he returned to Judah, and said, I cannot find her; and also the men of the place said, *that* there was no harlot in this *place.*

23 And Judah said, Let her take *it* to her, lest we [6]be shamed: behold, I sent this kid, and thou hast not found her.

24 ¶ And it came to pass about three months after, that it was told Judah, saying, Tā´-mär thy daughter in law hath [w]played the harlot; and also, behold, she *is* with child by whoredom. And Judah said, Bring her forth, [x]and let her be burnt.

25 When she *was* brought forth, she sent to her father in law, saying, By the man, whose these *are, am* I with child: and she said, [y]Discern, I pray thee, whose *are* these, the signet, and bracelets, and staff.

26 And Judah [z]acknowledged *them*, and said, [a]She hath been more righteous than I; because that [b]I gave her not to Shē´-lăh my son. And he knew her again [c]no more.

27 ¶ And it came to pass in the time of her travail, that, behold, twins *were* in her womb.

28 And it came to pass, when she travailed, that *the one* put out *his* hand: and the midwife took and bound upon his hand a scarlet thread, saying, This came out first.

29 And it came to pass, as he drew back his hand, that, behold, his brother came out: and she said, [7]How hast thou broken forth? *this* breach *be* upon thee: therefore his name was called [8]Phâr´-ĕz.

30 And afterward came out his brother, that had the scarlet thread upon his hand: and his name was called [9]Zâr´-ăh.

CHAPTER 39

AND Joseph was brought down to Egypt; and [a]Pŏt´-ĭ-phär, an officer of Pharaoh, captain of the guard, an Egyptian, [b]bought him of the hands of the Ĭsh´-mēē-lītes, which had brought him down thither.

2 And [c]the LORD was with Joseph, and he was a prosperous man; and he was in the house of his master the Egyptian.

3 And his master saw that the LORD *was* with him, and that the LORD [d]made all that he did to prosper in his hand.

4 And Joseph [e]found grace in his sight, and he served him: and he made him [f]overseer over his house, and all *that* he had he put into his hand.

5 And it came to pass from the time *that* he had made him overseer in his house, and over all that he had, that [g]the LORD blessed the Egyptian's house for Joseph's sake; and the blessing of the LORD was upon all that he had in the house, and in the field.

6 And he left all that he had in Joseph's hand; and he knew not ought he had, save the bread which he did eat. And Joseph was [h]*a* goodly *person*, and well favoured.

7 ¶ And it came to pass after these things, that his master's wife cast her eyes upon Joseph; and she said, [i]Lie with me.

8 But he refused, and said unto his master's wife, Behold, my master wotteth not what *is* with me in the

o 2 Sam. 13. 39.
p Josh. 15. 10,57. Judg. 14.1.
q Pro. 7.12.
3 the door of eyes, or, of Enajim.
r vers. 11,26.
s Eze. 16.33.
4 a kid of the goats.
t ver. 20.
u ver. 25.
v ver. 14.
5 Or, in Enajim.
6 become a contempt.
w Judg. 19.2.
x Lev. 21.9. Deut. 22.21.
y ch. 37.32.
z ch. 37.33.
a 1 Sam. 24. 17.
b ver. 14.
c Job 34.31.
7 Or, wherefore hast thou made this breach against thee?
8 That is, a breach. ch. 46.12. Num. 26.20. 1 Chr. 2.4. Matt. 1.3.
9 That is, East, or, Brightness.

CHAP. 39

a ch. 37.36. Ps. 105.17.
b ch. 37.28.
c ch. 21.22. ch. 26.24,28. ch. 28.15. 1 Sam. 16. 18. 1 Sam. 18. 14,28. Job 17.9. Ps. 5.12. Pro. 3.7-10, 33. Pro. 30.5. Acts 7.9.
d Ps. 1.3. Pro. 10.6,22. Pro. 28.20.
e ch. 18.3. ch. 19.19.
f ch. 24.2.
g ch. 30.27.
h 1 Sam. 16. 12.
i 2 Sam. 13. 11.

house, and he hath committed all that
he hath to my hand;
9 *There is* none greater in this house
than I; neither hath he kept back any
thing from me but thee, because thou
art his wife: how [j]then can I do this
great wickedness, and [k]sin against
God?
10 And it came to pass, as she spake
to Joseph day by day, that he hearkened not unto her, to lie by her, *or* to
be with her.
11 And it came to pass about this
time, that *Joseph* went into the house
to do his business; and *there was* none
of the men of the house there within.
12 And [l]she caught him by his garment, saying, Lie with me: and he left
his garment in her hand, and fled, and
got him out.
13 And it came to pass, when she
saw that he had left his garment in her
hand, and was fled forth,
14 That she called unto the men of
her house, and spake unto them, saying, See, he hath brought in an Hebrew unto us to mock us; he came in
unto me to lie with me, and I cried
with a [1]loud voice:
15 And it came to pass, when he
heard that I lifted up my voice and
cried, that he left his garment with
me, and fled, and got him out.
16 And she laid up his garment by
her, until his lord came home.
17 And she [m]spake unto him according to these words, saying, The Hebrew servant, which thou hast brought
unto us, came in unto me to mock me:
18 And it came to pass, as I lifted
up my voice and cried, that he left his
garment with me, and fled out.
19 And it came to pass, when his
master heard the words of his wife,
which she spake unto him, saying,
After this manner did thy servant to
me; that his [n]wrath was kindled.
20 And Joseph's master took him,
and [o]put him into the [p]prison, a place
where the king's prisoners *were*
bound: and he was there in the prison.
21 ¶ But the LORD was with Joseph,
and [2]shewed him mercy, and [q]gave
him favour in the sight of the keeper
of the prison.
22 And the keeper of the prison committed [r]to Joseph's hand all the prisoners that *were* in the prison; and
whatsoever they did there, he was the
doer *of it*.
23 The keeper of the prison looked
not to any thing *that was* under his
hand; because [s]the LORD was with
him, and *that* which he did, the LORD
made *it* to prosper.

CHAPTER 40

AND it came to pass after these
things, *that* the [a]butler of the king
of Egypt and *his* baker had offended
their lord the king of Egypt.
2 And Pharaoh was [b]wroth against
two *of* his officers, against the chief of
the butlers, and against the chief of
the bakers.
3 And [c]he put them in ward in the
house of the captain of the guard, into
the prison, the place where Joseph *was*
bound.
4 And the captain of the guard charged Joseph with them, and he served
them: and they continued a season in
ward.
5 ¶ And they dreamed a dream both
of them, each man his dream in one
night, each man according to the interpretation of his dream, the butler
and the baker of the king of Egypt,
which *were* bound in the prison.
6 And Joseph came in unto them in
the morning, and looked upon them,
and, behold, they *were* sad.
7 And he asked Pharaoh's officers
that *were* with him in the ward of his
lord's house, saying, Wherefore [1]look
ye *so* sadly to day?
8 And they said unto him, [d]We have
dreamed a dream, and *there is* no interpreter of it. And Joseph said unto
them, [e]*Do* not interpretations *belong*
to God? tell me *them*, I pray you.
9 And the chief butler told his dream
to Joseph, and said to him, In my
dream, behold, a vine *was* before me;
10 And in the vine *were* three branches: and it *was* as though it budded,
and her blossoms shot forth; and the
clusters thereof brought forth ripe
grapes:
11 And Pharaoh's cup *was* in my
hand: and I took the grapes, and
pressed them into Pharaoh's cup,
and I gave the cup into Pharaoh's
hand.
12 And Joseph said unto him, This
[f]*is* the interpretation of it: The three
branches *are* three days:
13 Yet within three days shall Pharaoh [2]lift [g]up thine head, and restore
thee unto thy place: and thou shalt
deliver Pharaoh's cup into his hand,
after the former manner when thou
wast his butler.
14 But [3]think [h]on me when it shall be
well with thee, and [i]shew kindness, I
pray thee, unto me, and make men-

j Pro. 6.29, 32.
k ch. 20.6. Lev. 6.2. 2 Sam. 12. 13. Ps. 51.4.
l Pro. 7.13, etc.
1 great.
m Ex. 23.1. Ps. 120.3. Pro. 6.25. Pro. 23.27. Pro. 26.28. Pro. 30.23.
n Pro. 6.34.
o Ps. 105.18. 1 Pet. 2.19.
p ch. 40.3. ch. 41.14.
2 Extended kindness unto him.
q Ex. 3.21. Ex. 11.3. Ex. 12.36. Ps. 106.46. Pro. 16.7. Dan. 1.9. Acts 7.9.
r ch. 40. 3,4.
s vers. 2,3. Pro. 11.11.

CHAP. 40

a Neh. 1.11.
b Pro. 16.14.
c ch. 39.20.
1 are your faces evil? Neh. 2.2.
d ch. 41.15.
e ch. 41.16. Dan. 2.28.
f Judg. 7.14. Dan. 2.36. Dan. 4.19.
2 Or, reckon.
g Ps. 3.3. Jer. 52.31.
3 remember me with thee.
h Luke 23.42.
i Josh. 2.12. 1 Sam. 20. 14. 1 Ki. 2.7.

tion of me unto Pharaoh, and bring
me out of this house:
15 For indeed I was stolen away out
of the land of the Hebrews: and [j]here
also have I done nothing that they
should put me into the dungeon.
16 When the chief baker saw that
the interpretation was good, he said
unto Joseph, I also *was* in my dream,
and, behold, *I had* three [4]white baskets on my head:
17 And in the uppermost basket
there was of all manner of [5]bakemeats
for Pharaoh; and the birds did eat
them out of the basket upon my head.
18 And Joseph answered and said,
This *is* the interpretation thereof:
The three baskets *are* three days:
19 Yet within three days shall Pharaoh [6]lift up thy head from off thee, and
shall hang thee on a tree; and the
birds shall eat thy flesh from off
thee.
20 ¶ And it came to pass the third
day, *which was* [k]Pharaoh's birthday,
that he [l]made a feast unto all his servants: and he [7]lifted up [m]the head of
the chief butler and of the chief baker
among his servants.
21 And he [n]restored the chief butler
unto his butlership again; and [o]he
gave the cup into Pharaoh's hand:
22 But he [p]hanged the chief baker:
as Joseph had interpreted to them.
23 Yet did not the chief butler remember Joseph, but [q]forgat him.

CHAPTER 41

AND it came to pass at the end of
two full years, that Pharaoh
dreamed: and, behold, he stood by
the river.
2 And, behold, there came up out of
the river seven well favoured kine and
fatfleshed; and they fed in a meadow.
3 And, behold, seven other kine came
up after them out of the river, ill favoured and leanfleshed; and stood by
the *other* kine upon the brink of the
river.
4 And the ill favoured and leanfleshed kine did eat up the seven well
favoured and fat kine. So Pharaoh
awoke.
5 And he slept and dreamed the
second time: and, behold, seven ears
of corn came up upon one stalk, [1]rank
and good.
6 And, behold, seven thin ears and
blasted with the east wind sprung up
after them.
7 And the seven thin ears devoured
the seven rank and full ears. And

j ch. 39.20.
4 Or, full of holes.
5 meat of Pharaoh, the work of a baker, or, cook.
6 Or, reckon thee, and take thy office from thee.
k Matt. 14.6.
l Mark 6.21.
7 Or, reckoned.
m Matt. 25. 19.
n ver. 13.
o Neh. 2.1.
p Esth. 7.10.
q Job. 19.14. Ps. 31.12. Pro. 3.27. Eccl. 9.15. Amos 6.6. Heb. 13.16.

CHAP. 41

1 fat.
a Dan. 4.5.
b Ex. 7.11. Isa. 29.14. Dan. 1.20. Dan. 2.2.
c Matt. 2.1.
d ch. 40.2,3.
e ch. 39.20.
f ch. 40.5.
g 2 Ki. 5.4.
h ch. 37.36.
i ch. 40.12.
j ch. 40.22.
k Ps. 105.20.
l Dan. 2.25.
2 made him run.
m 1 Sam. 2.8. Ps. 113.7,8.
n Ps. 25. 14. Dan. 5.16.
3 Or, when thou hearest a dream thou canst interpret it.
o Ps. 25.14. Pro. 3.32. Dan. 2.30. Amos 3.7. John 15.15. Acts 3.12. 2 Cor. 3.5.
p ch. 40.8. Deut. 29.29. Dan 2. 22, 28,47. Dan. 4.2.
4 come to the inward parts of them.

Pharaoh awoke, and, behold, *it was*
a dream.
8 And it came to pass in the morning
[a]that his spirit was troubled; and he
sent and called for all [b]the magicians
of Egypt, and all the [c]wise men thereof: and Pharaoh told them his dream;
but *there was* none that could interpret them unto Pharaoh.
9 ¶ Then spake the chief butler unto
Pharaoh, saying, I do remember my
faults this day:
10 Pharaoh was [d]wroth with his servants, [e]and put me in ward in the captain of the guard's house, *both* me and
the chief baker:
11 And [f]we dreamed a dream in one
night, I and he; we dreamed each man
according to the interpretation of his
dream.
12 And [g]*there was* there with us a
young man, an Hebrew, [h]servant to
the captain of the guard; and we told
him, and he [i]interpreted to us our
dreams; to each man according to his
dream he did interpret.
13 And it came to pass, [j]as he interpreted to us, so it was; me he restored
unto mine office, and him he hanged.
14 ¶ Then [k]Pharaoh sent and called
Joseph, and [l]they [2]brought him hastily
[m]out of the dungeon: and he shaved
himself, and changed his raiment, and
came in unto Pharaoh.
15 And Pharaoh said unto Joseph,
I have dreamed a dream, and *there is*
none that can interpret it: [n]and I have
heard say of thee, *that* [3]thou canst understand a dream to interpret it.
16 And Joseph answered Pharaoh,
saying, [o]*It is* not in me: [p]God shall give
Pharaoh an answer of peace.
17 And Pharaoh said unto Joseph,
In my dream, behold, I stood upon the
bank of the river:
18 And, behold, there came up out
of the river seven kine, fatfleshed and
well favoured; and they fed in a
meadow:
19 And, behold, seven other kine
came up after them, poor and very
ill favoured and leanfleshed, such as
I never saw in all the land of Egypt for
badness:
20 And the lean and the ill favoured
kine did eat up the first seven fat
kine:
21 And when they had [4]eaten them
up, it could not be known that they
had eaten them; but they *were* still ill
favoured, as at the beginning. So I
awoke.
22 And I saw in my dream, and, be-

hold, seven ears came up in one stalk, full and good:

23 And, behold, seven ears, [5]withered, thin, *and* blasted with the east wind, sprung up after them:

24 And the thin ears devoured the seven good ears: and [q]I told *this* unto the magicians; but *there was* none that could declare *it* to me.

25 ¶ And Joseph said unto Pharaoh, The dream of Pharaoh *is* one: [r]God hath shewed Pharaoh what he *is* about to do.

26 The seven good kine *are* seven years; and the seven good ears *are* seven years: the dream *is* one.

27 And the seven thin and ill favoured kine that came up after them *are* seven years; and the seven empty ears blasted with the east wind shall be [s]seven years of famine.

28 This *is* the thing which I have spoken unto Pharaoh: What God *is* about to do he sheweth unto Pharaoh.

29 Behold, there come seven years of great plenty throughout all the land of Egypt:

30 And there shall arise after them seven years of famine; and all the plenty shall be forgotten in the land of Egypt; and the famine shall [t]consume the land;

31 And the plenty shall not be known in the land by reason of that famine following; for it *shall be* very [6]grievous.

32 And for that the dream was doubled unto Pharaoh twice; *it is* because the thing *is* [7]established by God, and God will shortly bring it to pass.

33 Now therefore let Pharaoh look out a man discreet and wise, and set him over the land of Egypt.

34 Let Pharaoh do *this*, and let him appoint [8]officers over the land, and take up the fifth part of the land of Egypt in the seven plenteous years.

35 And let them gather all the food of those good years that come, and lay up corn under the hand of Pharaoh, and let them keep food in the cities.

36 And that food shall be for store to the land against the seven years of famine, which shall be in the land of Egypt; that the land [9]perish not through the famine.

37 ¶ And the thing was good in the eyes of Pharaoh, and in the eyes of all his servants.

38 And Pharaoh said unto his servants, Can we find *such a one* as this *is*, a man [u]in whom the Spirit of God *is?*

5 Or, small.
q Ps. 60.11. Ps. 118.8. Ps. 146.3. Isa. 8.19. Dan. 4.7.
r Dan. 2.28, 29,45. Rev. 4.1.
s 2 Ki. 8.1.
t ch. 47.13. Ps. 105.16. 1 Ki. 17.1.
6 heavy.
7 Or, prepared of God.
8 Or, overseers.
9 be not cut off.
u Num. 27.18. Pro. 2.6. Job 32.8. Dan. 4.8. Dan. 5.11.
10 be armed, or, kiss.
v Ps. 105.21. Pro. 14.35. Eccl. 4.13, 14. Dan. 6.3. Acts 7.10.
w Esther 3. 10. Esther 8.2.
11 Or, silk.
x Dan. 5.29.
12 Abrech, or, Tender father.
13 Which in the Coptic, signifies, A revealer of secrets, or, The man to whom secrets are revealed.
14 Or, prince. Ex. 2.16. 2 Sam. 20. 26.
y 1 Sam. 16. 21. 1 Ki. 12.6,8. Dan. 1.19.
z ch. 22.17. Judg. 7.12. 1 Sam. 13.5. Ps. 78.27.
a ch. 46.20. ch. 48.5.
15 Or, prince.
16 That is, Forgetting.
17 That is, Fruitful.

39 And Pharaoh said unto Joseph, Forasmuch as God hath shewed thee all this, *there is* none so discreet and wise as thou *art:*

40 Thou shalt be over my house, and according unto thy word shall all my people [10]be ruled: only in the throne will I be greater than thou.

41 And Pharaoh said unto Joseph, See, I [v]have set thee over all the land of Egypt.

42 And Pharaoh [w]took off his ring from his hand, and put it upon Joseph's hand, and arrayed him in vestures of [11]fine linen, and [x]put a gold chain about his neck;

43 And he made him to ride in the second chariot which he had; and they cried before him, [12]Bow the knee: and he made him *ruler* over all the land of Egypt.

44 And Pharaoh said unto Joseph, I *am* Pharaoh, and without thee shall no man lift up his hand or foot in all the land of Egypt.

45 And Pharaoh called Joseph's name [13]Zăph´-năth–pā-ă-nē´-ăh; and he gave him to wife Ăs´-ĕ-năth the daughter of Pŏ-tĭ´–phĕr-ăh [14]priest of On. And Joseph went out over *all* the land of Egypt.

46 ¶ And Joseph *was* thirty years old when he [y]stood before Pharaoh king of Egypt. And Joseph went out from the presence of Pharaoh and went throughout all the land of Egypt.

47 And in the seven plenteous years the earth brought forth by handfuls.

48 And he gathered up all the food of the seven years, which were in the land of Egypt, and laid up the food in the cities: the food of the field, which *was* round about every city, laid he up in the same.

49 And Joseph gathered corn [z]as the sand of the sea, very much, until he left numbering; for *it was* without number.

50 And [a]unto Joseph were born two sons before the years of famine came, which Ăs´-ĕ-năth the daughter of Pŏ-tĭ´–phĕr-ăh [15]priest of On bare unto him.

51 And Joseph called the name of the firstborn [16]Mă-năs´-sēh: For God, *said he*, hath made me forget all my toil, and all my father's house.

52 And the name of the second called he [17]Ē´-phră-ĭm: For God hath caused me to be fruitful in the land of my affliction.

53 ¶ And the seven years of plente-

ousness, that was in the land of Egypt,
were ended.
54 And [b]the seven years of dearth
began to come, according as Joseph
had said: and the dearth was in all
lands; but in all the land of Egypt
there was bread.
55 And when all the land of Egypt
was famished, the people cried to
Pharaoh for bread: and Pharaoh said
unto all the Egyptians, Go unto
Joseph; what he saith to you, do.
56 And the famine was over all the
face of the earth: and Joseph opened
[18]all the storehouses, and sold [c]unto
the Egyptians; and the famine waxed
sore in the land of Egypt.
57 And [d]all countries came into
Egypt to Joseph for to buy *corn;* because that the famine was [e]*so* sore in
all lands.

CHAPTER 42

NOW when [a]Jacob saw that there
was corn in Egypt, Jacob said unto his sons, Why do ye look one upon
another?
2 And he said, Behold, I have heard
that there is corn in Egypt: get you
down thither, and buy for us from
thence; that we may [b]live, and not die.
3 ¶ And Joseph's ten brethren went
down to buy corn in Egypt.
4 But Benjamin, Joseph's brother,
Jacob sent not with his brethren; for
he said, [c]Lest peradventure mischief
befall him.
5 And the sons of Israel came to buy
corn among those that came: for the
famine was [d]in the land of Canaan.
6 And Joseph *was* [e]the governor over
the land, *and* he *it was* that sold to all
the people of the land: and Joseph's
brethren came, [f]and bowed down
themselves before him *with* their faces
to the earth.
7 And Joseph saw his brethren, and
he knew them, but made himself
strange unto them, and spake [1]rough-
ly unto them; and he said unto them,
Whence come ye? And they said,
From the land of Canaan to buy food.
8 And Joseph knew his brethren, but
they knew not him.
9 And Joseph [g]remembered the
dreams which he dreamed of them,
and said unto them, Ye *are* spies; to
see the nakedness of the land ye are
come.
10 And they said unto him, Nay, my
lord, but to buy food are thy servants
come.
11 We *are* all one man's sons; we *are*

b Ps. 105.16. Acts 7.11.
18 all wherein was.
c ch. 42.6. ch. 47.14,24. Pro. 11.26.
d Deut. 9.28.
e ch. 12.10. ch. 26.1. ch. 43.1. 2 Ki. 8.1.

CHAP. 42
a Acts 7.12.
b ch. 43.8. Ps. 33.18,19. Ps. 118.17. Isa. 38.1.
c ver. 38.
d ch. 12.10. ch. 26.1. Acts 7.11.
e ch. 41.41.
f ch. 27.29. ch. 33.6. ch. 37.7. Ruth 2.10. 1 Ki. 1.16. Isa. 60.14.
1 hard things with them.
g ch. 37.5,9.
h ch. 37.30. ch. 44.20. Lam. 5.7.
i 1 Sam. 1.26. 1 Sam. 17. 55.
2 bound.
3 gathered.
j Lev. 25.43. Neh. 5.15.
k ver. 34. ch. 43.5. ch. 44.23.
l Job 36.8,9. Hosea 5.15.
m Ps. 107.17. Pro. 5.22. Pro. 11.21. Pro. 21.13. Matt. 7.2.
n ch. 37.21.
o ch. 9.5. 1 Ki. 2.32. 2 Chr. 24.22. Ps. 9.12. Luke 11.50, 51.
4 an interpreter was between them.
p Matt. 5.44. Rom. 12.17, 20,21. 1 Pet. 3.9.
q ch. 43.21.

true *men,* thy servants are no spies.
12 And he said unto them, Nay, but
to see the nakedness of the land ye are
come.
13 And they said, Thy servants *are*
twelve brethren, the sons of one man
in the land of Canaan; and, behold,
the youngest *is* this day with our father, and one [h]*is* not.
14 And Joseph said unto them, That
is it that I spake unto you, saying, Ye
are spies:
15 Hereby ye shall be proved: [i]By
the life of Pharaoh ye shall not go
forth hence, except your youngest
brother come hither.
16 Send one of you, and let him fetch
your brother, and ye shall be [2]kept in
prison, that your words may be proved, whether *there be any* truth in you:
or else by the life of Pharaoh surely
ye *are* spies.
17 And he [3]put them all together into
ward three days.
18 And Joseph said unto them the
third day, This do, and live; *for* [j]I fear
God:
19 If ye *be* true *men,* let one of your
brethren be bound in the house of
your prison: go ye, carry corn for the
famine of your houses:
20 But [k]bring your youngest brother
unto me; so shall your words be verified, and ye shall not die. And they
did so.
21 ¶ And they said one to another,
We [l]*are* verily guilty concerning our
brother, in that we saw the anguish of
his soul, when he besought us, and we
would not hear; therefore [m]is this distress come upon us.
22 And Reuben answered them, saying, [n]Spake I not unto you, saying, Do
not sin against the child; and ye would
not hear? therefore, behold, also his
blood is [o]required.
23 And they knew not that Joseph
understood *them;* for [4]he spake unto
them by an interpreter.
24 And he turned himself about from
them, and wept; and returned to them
again, and communed with them, and
took from them Simeon, and bound
him before their eyes.
25 ¶ Then Joseph commanded to fill
their sacks with corn, and to restore
every man's money into his sack, and
to give them provision for the way:
and [p]thus did he unto them.
26 And they laded their asses with
the corn, and departed thence.
27 And as [q]one of them opened his
sack to give his ass provender in the

inn, he espied his money; for, behold, it *was* in his sack's mouth.

28 And he said unto his brethren, My money is restored; and, lo, *it is* even in my sack: and their heart [5]failed *them*, and they were afraid, saying one to another, What *is* this *that* God hath done unto us?

29 ¶ And they came unto Jacob their father unto the land of Canaan, and told him all that befell unto them; saying,

30 The man, *who is* the lord of the land, [r]spake [6]roughly to us, and took us for spies of the country.

31 And we said unto him, We *are* true *men;* we are no spies:

32 We *be* twelve brethren, sons of our father; one *is* not, and the youngest *is* this day with our father in the land of Canaan.

33 And the man, the lord of the country, said unto us, [s]Hereby shall I know that ye *are* true *men;* leave one of your brethren *here* with me, and take *food for* the famine of your households, and be gone:

34 And bring your youngest brother unto me: then shall I know that ye *are* no spies, but *that* ye *are* true *men: so* will I deliver you your brother, and ye shall [t]traffick in the land.

35 ¶ And it came to pass as they emptied their sacks, that, behold, every [u]man's bundle of money *was* in his sack: and when *both* they and their father saw the bundles of money, they were afraid.

36 And Jacob their father said unto them, Me have ye [v]bereaved *of my children:* Joseph *is* not, and Simeon *is* not, and ye will take Benjamin *away:* all these things are against me.

37 And Reuben spake unto his father, saying, Slay my two sons, if I bring him not to thee: deliver him into my hand, and I will bring him to thee again.

38 And he said, My son shall not go down with you; for his [w]brother is dead, and he is left alone: [x]if mischief befall him by the way in the which ye go, then shall ye bring [y]down my gray hairs with sorrow to the grave.

CHAPTER 43

AND the famine *was* [a]sore in the land.

2 And it came to pass, when they had eaten up the corn which they had brought out of Egypt, their father said unto them, Go again, buy us a little food.

5 went forth.
r ver. 7.
6 with us hard things.
s vers. 15,19, 20.
t ch. 34.10.
u ch. 43.21.
v ch. 43.14.
w ver. 13. ch. 37.33. ch. 44.28.
x ver. 4. ch. 44.29.
y ch. 37.35. ch. 44.31.

CHAP. 43

a ch. 12.10. ch. 26.1. ch. 41.57. 1 Ki. 18.2. 2 Ki. 8.1. Jer. 52.6. Lam. 5.10.
1 protesting protested.
b ch. 42.20. ch. 44.23.
2 asking asked us.
3 mouth.
4 knowing could we know.
c ch. 44.32. Phile. 18,19.
5 Or, twice by this.
d ch. 32.20. Pro. 18.16.
e ch. 37.25. Jer. 8.22. Eze. 27.17.
f ch. 42.25, 35.
g 1 Sam. 14. 6. 2 Sam. 22. 3,31. Job 13.15. Ps. 22.4. Ps. 34.8,22. Ps. 40.4. Ps. 52.8. Ps. 61.4. Ps. 71.5. Ps. 141.8. Pro. 28.5. Isa. 57.13. Nah. 1.7.
6 Or, and I, as I have been, etc. Esther 4.16.
h ch. 24.2. ch. 39.4. ch. 44.1.
7 kill a killing. 1 Sam. 25. 11.
8 eat.

3 And Judah spake unto him, saying, The man [1]did solemnly protest unto us, saying, Ye shall not see my face, except [b]your brother *be* with you.

4 If thou wilt send our brother with us, we will go down and buy thee food:

5 But if thou wilt not send *him,* we will not go down: for the man said unto us, Ye shall not see my face, except your brother *be* with you.

6 And Israel said, Wherefore dealt ye *so* ill with me, *as* to tell the man whether ye had yet a brother?

7 And they said, The man [2]asked us straitly of our state, and of our kindred, saying, *Is* your father yet alive? have ye *another* brother? and we told him according to the [3]tenor of these words: [4]could we certainly know that he would say, Bring your brother down?

8 And Judah said unto Israel his father, Send the lad with me, and we will arise and go; that we may live, and not die, both we, and thou, *and* also our little ones.

9 I will be surety for him; of my hand shalt thou require him: [c]if I bring him not unto thee, and set him before thee, then let me bear the blame for ever:

10 For except we had lingered, surely now we had returned [5]this second time.

11 And their father Israel said unto them, If *it must be* so now, do this; take of the best fruits in the land in your vessels, and [d]carry down the man a present, a [e]little balm, and a little honey, spices, and myrrh, nuts, and almonds:

12 And take double money in your hand; and the money [f]that was brought again in the mouth of your sacks, carry *it* again in your hand; peradventure it *was* an oversight:

13 Take also your brother, and arise, go again unto the man:

14 And [g]God Almighty give you mercy before the man, that he may send away your other brother, and Benjamin. [6]If I be bereaved *of my children,* I am bereaved.

15 ¶ And the men took that present, and they took double money in their hand, and Benjamin; and rose up, and went down to Egypt, and stood before Joseph.

16 And when Joseph saw Benjamin with them, he said to [h]the ruler of his house, Bring *these* men home, and [7]slay, and make ready; for *these* men shall [8]dine with me at noon.

17 And the man did as Joseph bade;

and the man brought the men into
Joseph's house.
18 And the men were afraid, because
they were brought into Joseph's
house; and they said, Because of the
money that was returned in our sacks
at the first time are we brought in;
that he may [9]seek occasion against us,
and fall upon us, and take us for bondmen, and our asses.
19 And they came near to the steward of Joseph's house, and they communed with him at the door of the
house,
20 And said, O sir, [10]we came indeed
down at the first time to buy food:
21 And [i]it came to pass, when we
came to the inn, that we opened our
sacks, and, behold, *every* man's money
was in the mouth of his sack, our
money in full weight: and we have
brought it again in our hand.
22 And other money have we brought
down in our hands to buy food: we
cannot tell who put our money in our
sacks.
23 And he said, Peace *be* to you, fear
not: your God, and the God of your
father, hath given you treasure in your
sacks: [11]I had your money. And he
brought Simeon out unto them.
24 And the man brought the men into
Joseph's house, [j]and gave *them* water,
and they washed their feet; and he
gave their asses provender.
25 And they made ready the present
against Joseph came at noon: for they
heard that they should eat bread there.
26 ¶ And when Joseph came home,
they brought him the present which
was in their hand into the house, and
[k]bowed themselves to him to the
earth.
27 And he asked them of *their* [12]wel-
fare, and said, [13]*Is* your father well,
the old man of [l]whom ye spake? *Is* he
yet alive?
28 And they answered, Thy servant
our father *is* in good health, he *is* yet
alive. [m]And they bowed down their
heads, and made obeisance.
29 And he lifted up his eyes, and saw
his brother Benjamin, [n]his mother's
son, and said, *Is* this your younger
brother, [o]of whom ye spake unto me?
And he said, God be gracious unto
thee, my son.
30 And Joseph made haste; [p]for his
bowels did yearn upon his brother:
and he sought *where* to weep; and he
entered into *his* chamber, and [q]wept
there.
31 And he washed his face, and went

9 roll himself upon us. Job 30.14.
10 coming down we came down. ch. 42.3,10.
i ch. 42.27,35.
11 your money came to me.
j ch. 18.4. ch. 24.32. Luke 7.44. John 13.5. 1 Tim. 5.10.
k ch. 27.29. ch. 33.6. ch. 37.7,10. Ruth 2.10.
12 peace. ch. 37.14.
13 Is there peace to your father?
l ch. 42.11,13.
m ch. 37.7,10. Pro. 14.19.
n ch. 35. 17, 18.
o ch. 42.13.
p 1 Ki. 3.26. Jer. 31.20.
q ch. 42.24. 2 Sam. 18. 33.
r ver. 25.
s ch. 46.34. Ex. 8.26.
t ch. 45.22.
14 drank largely. Hag. 1.6. John 2. 10.

CHAP 44

1 him that was over his house.
2 Or, maketh trial.
a ch. 43.21.
b ch. 31.32.

out, and refrained himself, and said,
Set on [r]bread.
32 And they set on for him by himself, and for them by themselves, and
for the Egyptians, which did eat with
him, by themselves: because the Egyptians might not eat bread with the Hebrews; for that *is* an [s]abomination
unto the Egyptians.
33 And they sat before him, the firstborn according to his birthright, and
the youngest according to his youth:
and the men marvelled one at another.
34 And he took *and sent* messes unto
them from before him: but Benjamin's
mess was [t]five times so much as any
of theirs. And they drank, and [14]were
merry with him.

CHAPTER 44

AND he commanded [1]the steward
of his house, saying, Fill the men's
sacks *with* food, as much as they can
carry, and put every man's money in
his sack's mouth.
2 And put my cup, the silver cup, in
the sack's mouth of the youngest, and
his corn money. And he did according
to the word that Joseph had spoken.
3 As soon as the morning was light,
the men were sent away, they and
their asses.
4 *And* when they were gone out of
the city, *and* not *yet* far off, Joseph said
unto his steward, Up, follow after the
men; and when thou dost overtake
them, say unto them, Wherefore have
ye rewarded evil for good?
5 *Is* not this *it* in which my lord
drinketh, and whereby indeed he [2]di-
vineth? ye have done evil in so doing.
6 ¶ And he overtook them, and he
spake unto them these same words.
7 And they said unto him, Wherefore
saith my lord these words? God forbid that thy servants should do according to this thing:
8 Behold, [a]the money, which we
found in our sacks' mouths, we
brought again unto thee out of the
land of Canaan: how then should we
steal out of thy lord's house silver or
gold?
9 With whomsoever of thy servants
it be found, [b]both let him die, and we
also will be my lord's bondmen.
10 And he said, Now also *let* it *be*
according unto your words: he with
whom it is found shall be my servant;
and ye shall be blameless.
11 Then they speedily took down
every man his sack to the ground, and
opened every man his sack.

12 And he searched, *and* began at
the eldest, and left at the youngest:
and the cup was found in Benjamin's
sack.
13 Then they [c]rent their clothes, and
laded every man his ass, and returned
to the city.
14 ¶ And Judah and his brethren
came to Joseph's house; for he *was*
yet there: and they [d]fell before him on
the ground.
15 And Joseph said unto them, What
deed *is* this that ye have done? wot
ye not that such a man as I can certainly [3]divine?
16 And Judah said, [e]What shall we
say unto my lord? what shall we
speak? or how shall we clear ourselves? God hath found out the iniquity of thy servants: behold, [f]we *are*
my lord's servants, both we, and *he*
also with whom the cup is found.
17 And he said, [g]God forbid that I
should do so: *but* the man in whose
hand the cup is found, he shall be my
servant; and as for you, get you up in
peace unto your father.
18 ¶ Then Judah came near unto
him, and said, Oh my lord, let thy
servant, I pray thee, speak a word in
my lord's ears, and [h]let not thine anger burn against thy servant: for thou
art [i]even as Pharaoh.
19 My lord asked his servants, saying, Have ye a father, or a brother?
20 And we said unto my lord, We
have a father, an old man, and [j]a child
of his old age, a little one; and his
brother is dead, and he alone is left of
his mother, and his father loveth
him.
21 And thou saidst unto thy servants,
[k]Bring him down unto me, that I may
set mine eyes upon him.
22 And we said unto my lord, The
lad cannot leave his father: for *if* he
should leave his father, *his father*
would die.
23 And thou saidst unto thy servants,
[l]Except your youngest brother come
down with you, ye shall see my face no
more.
24 And it came to pass when we
came up unto thy servant my father,
we told him the words of my lord.
25 And [m]our father said, Go again,
and buy us a little food.
26 And we said, We cannot go down:
if our youngest brother be with us,
then will we go down: for we may not
see the man's face, except our youngest brother *be* with us.
27 And thy servant my father said

c ch. 37.29, 34. Num. 14.6. 2 Sam. 1.11.
d ch. 37.7.
3 Or, make trial. ver. 5.
e Job 40.4.
f ver. 9.
g Josh. 22.29. Josh. 24.16. 1 Sam. 12. 23. 1 Sam. 14. 45. 1 Sam. 20.2. Job 27.5. Pro. 17.15. Luke 20.16. Rom. 3.4,6, 31. Rom. 6.2, 15. Rom. 7.7, 13. Rom. 9.14. Rom. 11.1, 11. 1 Cor. 6.15. Gal. 2.17. Gal. 3.21. Gal. 6.14.
h ch. 18.30, 32. Ex. 32.22.
i Pro. 19.12. ch. 41.40.
j ch. 37.3.
k ch. 42.15, 20.
l ch. 43.3,5.
m ch. 43.2.
n ch. 46.19.
o ch. 37.33.
p ch. 42.36, 38.
q 1 Sam. 18.1.
r ch. 43.9.
s Ex. 32.32.
4 find my father. Ex. 18.8. Job 31.29. Ps. 116.3. Ps. 119.143.

CHAP. 45

1 gave forth his voice in weeping. Num. 14.1.
a Acts 7.13.
2 Or, terrified. Job 4.5. Job 23.15. Ps. 77.4. Zech. 12.10. Matt. 14.26. Mark 6.50.
b ch. 37.28.
c Isa. 40.2. 2 Cor. 2.7.
3 neither let there be anger in your eyes.
d ch. 50.20. Deut. 23.14. 2 Sam. 16. 10,11. Job 5.19, 20, 21. Job 38.41. Ps. 33.18, 19. Ps. 37.18, 19. Ps. 62.11. Ps. 73.1. Ps. 105.16, 17. Acts 4.24. 2 Pet. 2.9.
4 to put for you a remnant.

unto us, Ye know that [n]my wife bare
me two *sons:*
28 And the one went out from me,
and I said, [o]Surely he is torn in pieces;
and I saw him not since:
29 And if ye [p]take this also from me,
and mischief befall him, ye shall bring
down my gray hairs with sorrow to
the grave.
30 Now therefore when I come to
thy servant my father, and the lad *be*
not with us; seeing [q]that his life is
bound up in the lad's life;
31 It shall come to pass, when he
seeth that the lad *is* not *with us*, that
he will die: and thy servants shall
bring down the gray hairs of thy servant our father with sorrow to the
grave.
32 For thy servant became surety for
the lad unto my father, saying, If [r]I
bring him not unto thee, then I shall
bear the blame to my father for ever.
33 Now therefore, I pray thee, let [s]thy
servant abide instead of the lad a
bondman to my lord; and let the lad
go up with his brethren.
34 For how shall I go up to my father, and the lad *be* not with me? lest
peradventure I see the evil that shall
[4]come on my father.

CHAPTER 45

THEN Joseph could not refrain
himself before all them that stood
by him; and he cried, Cause every
man to go out from me. And there
stood no man with him, while Joseph
made himself known unto his brethren.
2 And he [1]wept aloud: and the
Egyptians and the house of Pharaoh
heard.
3 And Joseph said unto his brethren,
[a]I *am* Joseph; doth my father yet live?
And his brethren could not answer
him; for they were [2]troubled at his
presence.
4 And Joseph said unto his brethren,
Come near to me, I pray you. And
they came near. And he said, I *am*
Joseph your brother, whom [b]ye sold
into Egypt.
5 Now therefore [c]be not grieved, [3]nor
angry with yourselves, that ye sold me
hither: for [d]God did send me before
you to preserve life.
6 For these two years *hath* the famine
been in the land: and yet *there are* five
years, in the which *there shall* neither
be earing nor harvest.
7 And God sent me before you [4]to
preserve you a posterity in the earth,

and to save your lives by a great deliverance.

8 So now *it was* not you *that* sent me hither, but God: and he hath made me a [e]father to Pharaoh, and lord of all his house, and a ruler throughout all the land of Egypt.

9 Haste ye, and go up to my father, and say unto him, Thus saith thy son Joseph, God hath made me lord of all Egypt: come down unto me, tarry not:

10 And [f]thou shalt dwell in the land of Gō'shĕn, and thou shalt be near unto me, thou, and thy children, and thy children's children, and thy flocks, and thy herds, and all that thou hast:

11 And there will I nourish thee; for [g]yet *there are* five years of famine; lest thou, and thy household, and all that thou hast, come to poverty.

12 And, behold, your eyes see, and the eyes of my brother Benjamin, that *it is* [h]my mouth that speaketh unto you.

13 And ye shall tell my father of all my glory in Egypt, and of all that ye have seen; and ye shall haste and [i]bring down my father hither.

14 And he fell upon his brother Benjamin's neck, and wept; and Benjamin wept upon his neck.

15 Moreover he kissed all his brethren, and wept upon them: and after that his brethren talked with him.

16 ¶ And the fame thereof was heard in Pharaoh's house, saying, Joseph's brethren are come: and it [5]pleased Pharaoh well, and his servants.

17 And Pharaoh said unto Joseph, Say unto thy brethren, This do ye; lade your beasts, and go, get you unto the land of Canaan;

18 And take your father and your households, and come unto me: and I will give you the good of the land of Egypt, and ye shall eat [j]the fat of the land.

19 Now thou art commanded, this do ye; take you wagons out of the land of Egypt for your little ones, and for your wives, and bring your father, and come.

20 Also [6]regard not your stuff; for the good of all the land of Egypt *is* yours.

21 And the children of Israel did so: and Joseph gave them wagons, according to the [7]commandment of Pharaoh, and gave them provision for the way.

22 To all of them he gave each man changes of raiment; but to Benjamin he gave three hundred *pieces* of silver, and five changes of raiment.

23 And to his father he sent after this *manner;* ten asses [8]laden with the good things of Egypt, and ten she asses laden with corn and bread and meat for his father by the way.

24 So he sent his brethren away, and they departed: and he said unto them, See that ye fall not out by the way.

25 ¶ And they went up out of Egypt, and came into the land of Canaan unto Jacob their father,

26 And told him, saying, Joseph *is* yet alive, and he *is* governor over all the land of Egypt. [k]And [9]Jacob's heart fainted, for he believed them not.

27 And they told him all the words of Joseph, which he had said unto them: and when he saw the wagons which Joseph had sent to carry him, the spirit of Jacob their father revived:

28 And Israel said, *It is* enough; Joseph my son *is* yet alive: I will go and see him before I die.

CHAPTER 46

AND Israel took his journey with all that he had, and came [a]to Bē̂er–shē'-bă, and offered sacrifices unto [b]the God of his father Isaac.

2 And God spake unto Israel [c] in the visions of the night, and said, Jacob, Jacob. And he said, Here *am* I.

3 And he said, I *am* God, [d]the God of thy father: fear not to go down into Egypt; for I will there make [e]of thee a great nation:

4 I [f]will go down with thee into Egypt; and I will also [g]surely bring thee up *again:* and [h]Joseph shall put his hand upon thine eyes.

5 And [i]Jacob rose up from Bē̂er–shē'-bă: and the sons of Israel carried Jacob their father, and their little ones, and their wives, in the wagons which Pharaoh had sent to carry him.

6 And they took their cattle, and their goods, which they had gotten in the land of Canaan, and came into Egypt, [j]Jacob, and all his seed with him:

7 His sons, and his sons' sons with him, his daughters, and his sons' daughters, and all his seed brought he with him into Egypt.

8 ¶ And [k]these *are* the names of the children of Israel, which came into Egypt, Jacob and his sons: Reuben, [l]Jacob's firstborn.

9 And the sons of Reuben; Hā'nŏch, and Phăl'lū, and Hĕz'rŏn, and Căr'mī.

10 ¶ And the [m]sons of Simeon; [1]Jĕ-mū'ĕl, and Jā'mĭn, and Ō'hăd, and

e ch. 41.43. Judg. 17.10. Job 29.16.
f ch. 47.1.
g 1 Tim. 5.4.
h ch. 42.23.
i Num. 18.12, 29. Acts 7.14.
5 was good in the eyes of Pharaoh. ch. 41.37.
j ch. 27.28.
6 let not your eye spare, etc.
7 mouth.
8 carrying.
k Job 29.24. Ps. 126.1. Luke 24.11, 41.
9 his.

CHAP. 46
a ch. 21.31.
b ch. 26.24. ch. 28.13. ch. 31.42.
c ch. 15.1. Job 33.14, 15.
d ch. 28.13.
e ch. 12.2. Deut. 26.5. Ex. 1.9.
f ch. 28.15. ch. 48.21.
g ch. 15.16. ch. 50.13. Ex. 3.8.
h ch. 50.1.
i ch. 15.13. Acts 7.15.
j Deut. 26.5. Josh. 24.4. Ps. 105.23. Isa. 52.4.
k Ex. 1.1. Ex. 6.14.
l Num. 26.5. 1 Chr. 5.1.
m Ex. 6.15. 1 Chr. 4.24.
1 Or, Nemuel.

[2]Jā´-chĭn, and [3]Zō´-hăr, and Shā´-ŭl the
son of a Canaanitish woman.
11 ¶ And the sons of Levi; [4]Gĕr´-
shŏn, Kō´-hăth, and Mĕ-rār´-ī.
12 ¶ And the sons of Judah; Er, and
Ō´-năn, and Shē´-lăh, and Phār´-ĕz, and
Zār´-ăh: but [n]Er and Ō´-năn died in the
land of Canaan. And the [o]sons of
Phār´-ĕz were Hĕz´-rŏn and Hă´-mŭl.
13 ¶ And the sons of Ĭs´-să-chār; Tō´-
lă, and [5]Phū´-văh, and Job, and Shĭm´-
rŏn.
14 ¶ And the sons of Zĕ-bū´-lŭn; Sē´-
rĕd, and Ē´-lŏn, and Jăh´-lēel.
15 These *be* the sons of Leah, which
she bare unto Jacob in Pā´-dăn–ār´-ăm,
with his daughter Dinah: all the souls
of his sons and his daughters *were*
thirty and three.
16 ¶ And the sons of Gad; [p]Zĭph´-ī-
on, and Hăg´-gī, Shū´-nī, and [6]Ĕz´-bŏn,
Ē´-rī, and [7]Ă-rō´-dī, and Ă-rē´-lī.
17 ¶ And [q]the sons of Asher; Jĭm´-
năh, and Ĭsh´-ū-ăh, and Ĭs´-ū-ī, and Bĕ-
rī´-ăh, and Sē´-răh their sister: and the
sons of Bĕ-rī´-ăh; Hē´-bĕr, and Măl´-
chī-ĕl.
18 These *are* [r]the sons of Zilpah,
whom Laban gave to Leah his daughter, and these she bare unto Jacob,
even sixteen souls.
19 The sons of Rachel Jacob's wife;
Joseph, and Benjamin.
20 ¶ And [s]unto Joseph in the land of
Egypt were born Mă-năs´-sēh and Ē´-
phră-ĭm, which Ăs´-ĕ-năth the daughter of Pŏ-tĭ-phĕr-ăh [8]priest of On
bare unto him.
21 ¶ And [t]the sons of Benjamin *were*
Bē´-lăh, and Bē´-chĕr, and Ăsh´-bĕl, Gē´-
ră, and Nā´-ă-măn, [u]Ē´-hī, and Rōsh,
[v]Mŭp´-pĭm, and [9]Hŭp´-pĭm, and Ărd.
22 These *are* the sons of Rachel,
which were born to Jacob: all the
souls *were* fourteen.
23 ¶ And [w]the sons of Dan; [10]Hū´-
shĭm.
24 ¶ And [x]the sons of Năph´-tă-lī;
Jăh´-zēel, and Gū´-nī, and Jē´-zĕr, and
Shĭl´-lĕm.
25 These [y]*are* the sons of Bĭl´-hăh,
which [z]Laban gave unto Rachel his
daughter, and she bare these unto
Jacob: all the souls *were* seven.
26 All [a]the souls that came with
Jacob into Egypt, which came out of
his [11]loins, besides Jacob's sons' wives,
all the souls *were* threescore and six;
27 And the sons of Joseph, which
were born him in Egypt, *were* two
souls: [b]all the souls of the house of
Jacob, which came into Egypt, *were*
threescore and ten.

2 Or, Jarib.
3 Or, Zerah. 1 Chr. 4.24.
4 Or, Gershom.
n ch. 38.3.
o ch. 38.29. 1 Chr. 2.5.
5 Or, Puah, and Jashub.
p Num. 26. 15. Zephon.
6 Or, Ozni.
7 Or, Arod.
q 1 Chr. 7.30.
r ch. 30.10.
s ch. 41.50.
8 Or, prince.
t 1 Chr. 7.6.
u Num. 26. 38. Ahiram.
v Num. 26. 39. Shupham. 1 Chr. 7.12. Shuppim.
9 Hupham.
w 1 Chr. 7.12.
10 Or, Shuham.
x 1 Chr. 7.13.
y ch. 30.5,7.
z ch. 29.29.
a Ex. 1.5.
11 thigh.
b Deut. 10. 22. Acts 7.14.
c ch. 31.21.
d Luke 2.29.
12 they are men of cattle.
e ch. 47.2,3.
f ch. 30.35. ch. 34.5. ch. 37.12.
g Ex. 8.26.

CHAP. 47.

a ch. 46.31.
b ch. 45.10. ch. 46.28.
c Acts 7.13.
d ch. 46.33.
e ch. 46.34.
f ch. 15.13. Deut. 26.5. Ps. 105.23. Isa. 52.4.
g ch. 43.1. Acts 7.11.
h ch. 46.34.
i ch. 20.15.
j ver. 4.

28 ¶ And he sent Judah before him
unto Joseph, [c]to direct his face unto
Gō´-shĕn; and they came into the land
of Gō´-shĕn.
29 And Joseph made ready his chariot, and went up to meet Israel his
father, to Gō´-shĕn, and presented
himself unto him; and he fell on his
neck, and wept on his neck a good
while.
30 And Israel said unto Joseph, Now
[d]let me die, since I have seen thy face,
because thou *art* yet alive.
31 And Joseph said unto his brethren, and unto his father's house, I will
go up, and shew Pharaoh, and say unto him, My brethren, and my father's
house, which *were* in the land of Canaan, are come unto me;
32 And the men *are* shepherds, for
[12]their trade hath been to feed cattle;
and they have brought their flocks,
and their herds, and all that they have.
33 And it shall come to pass, when
Pharaoh shall call you, and shall say,
[e]What *is* your occupation?
34 That ye shall say, Thy servants'
trade hath been about cattle [f]from our
youth even until now, both we, *and*
also our fathers: that ye may dwell in
the land of Gō´-shĕn; for every shepherd *is* [g]an abomination unto the
Egyptians.

CHAPTER 47

THEN Joseph [a]came and told Pharaoh, and said, My father and my
brethren, and their flocks, and their
herds, and all that they have, are come
out of the land of Canaan; and, behold, *they are* in the [b]land of Gō´-shĕn.
2 And he took some of his brethren,
even five men, and [c]presented them
unto Pharaoh.
3 And Pharaoh said unto his brethren, [d]What *is* your occupation? And
they said unto Pharaoh, [e]Thy servants
are shepherds, both we, *and* also our
fathers.
4 They said moreover unto Pharaoh,
[f]For to sojourn in the land are we
come; for thy servants have no pasture for their flocks; [g] for the famine
is sore in the land of Canaan: now
therefore, we pray thee, let thy servants [h]dwell in the land of Gō´-shĕn.
5 And Pharaoh spake unto Joseph,
saying, Thy father and thy brethren
are come unto thee:
6 The [i]land of Egypt *is* before thee;
in the best of the land make thy father
and brethren to dwell; in [j]the land of
Gō´-shĕn let them dwell: and if thou

knowest *any* men of activity among
them, then make them [k]rulers over my
cattle.
7 And Joseph brought in Jacob his
father, and set him before Pharaoh:
and Jacob blessed Pharaoh.
8 And Pharaoh said unto Jacob,
[1]How old *art* thou?
9 And Jacob said unto Pharaoh, The
[l]days of the years of my pilgrimage
are an hundred and thirty years: [m]few
and evil have the days of the years of
my life been, and have [n]not attained
unto the days of the years of the life
of my fathers in the days of their
pilgrimage.
10 And Jacob [o]blessed Pharaoh, and
went out from before Pharaoh.
11 ¶ And Joseph placed his father
and his brethren, and gave them a
possession in the land of Egypt, in the
best of the land, in the land of [p]Răm-
ĕ-sēs, as [q]Pharaoh had commanded.
12 And Joseph nourished his [r]father,
and his brethren, and all his father's
household, with bread, [2]according to
their families.
13 ¶ And *there was* no bread in all
the land; for the famine *was* very sore,
[s]so that the land of Egypt and *all* the
land of Canaan fainted by reason of
the famine.
14 And [t]Joseph gathered up all the
money that was found in the land of
Egypt, and in the land of Canaan, for
the corn which they bought: and
Joseph brought the money into Pharaoh's house.
15 And when money failed in the
land of Egypt, and in the land of Canaan, all the Egyptians came unto
Joseph, and said, Give us bread: for
[u]why should we die in thy presence?
for the money faileth.
16 And Joseph said, Give your cattle;
and I will give you for your cattle, if
money fail.
17 And they brought their cattle unto
Joseph: and Joseph gave them bread
in exchange for horses, and for the
flocks, and for the cattle of the herds,
and for the asses: and he [3]fed them
with bread for all their cattle for that
year.
18 When that year was ended, they
came unto him the second year, and
said unto him, We will not hide *it* from
my lord, how that our money is spent;
my lord also hath our herds of cattle;
there is not ought left in the sight of
my lord, but our bodies, and our
lands:
19 Wherefore shall we die before

k 1 Ki.11.28. Pro. 22.29. Pro. 12.24.
1 How many are the days of the years of thy life?
l Ps. 39.12. Ps. 119.19. 2 Cor. 5.6, 7. Heb. 11.9, 13. 1 Pet. 2.11.
m Job 7.7. Job 14.1. Ps. 102.3. Eccl. 2.23. Jas. 4.14. 1 Pet. 1.24.
n ch. 25.7. ch. 35.28.
o ver. 7.
p Ex. 1.11. Ex. 12.37.
q ver. 6.
r Pro. 10.1. Ex. 20.12.
2 Or, as a little child is nourished; according to the little ones. ch. 50.21.
s ch.41.30. Acts 7.11.
t ch. 41.56.
u ver. 19.
3 led them.
v Ezra 7.24.
4 Or, princes. ch. 41.45. 2 Sam. 8.18.
w ch. 33.15.
x ver. 22.
5 Or, princes.
y ver. 11.
z ch. 12.2. ch. 15.13,14. ch. 17.6. ch. 18.18. ch. 26.4. ch. 46.3. Ex. 1.7. Deut. 26.5. Ps. 105.24. Acts 7.17.
6 the days of the years of his life.
a Deut. 31. 14. 1 Ki. 2.1.
b ch. 24.2.
c ch. 24.49.
d ch. 50.25.
e 2 Sam. 19. 37.
f ch. 23.2, 17-20. ch. 25.9,10. ch.35.29. ch. 49.29. ch. 50.5,13. Acts 7.16. Heb. 11.22.

thine eyes, both we and our land? buy
us and our land for bread, and we and
our land will be servants unto Pharaoh: and give *us* seed, that we may
live, and not die, that the land be not
desolate.
20 And Joseph bought all the land of
Egypt for Pharaoh; for the Egyptians
sold every man his field, because the
famine prevailed over them: so the
land became Pharaoh's.
21 And as for the people, he removed
them to cities from *one* end of the
borders of Egypt even to the *other* end
thereof.
22 Only [v]the land of the [4]priests
bought he not; for the priests had a
portion *assigned them* of Pharaoh, and
did eat their portion which Pharaoh
gave them: wherefore they sold not
their lands.
23 Then Joseph said unto the people,
Behold, I have bought you this day
and your land for Pharaoh: lo, *here*
is seed for you, and ye shall sow the
land.
24 And it shall come to pass in the
increase, that ye shall give the fifth
part unto Pharaoh, and four parts
shall be your own, for seed of the field,
and for your food, and for them of
your households, and for food for
your little ones.
25 And they said, Thou hast saved
our lives: [w]let us find grace in the sight
of my lord, and we will be Pharaoh's
servants.
26 And Joseph made it a law over
the land of Egypt unto this day, *that*
Pharaoh should have the fifth *part;*
[x]except the land of the [5]priests only,
which became not Pharaoh's.
27 ¶ And Israel [y]dwelt in the land of
Egypt, in the country of Gō-shĕn; and
they had possessions therein, and
[z]grew, and multiplied exceedingly.
28 And Jacob lived in the land of
Egypt seventeen years: so [6]the whole
age of Jacob was an hundred forty
and seven years.
29 And the time [a]drew nigh that
Israel must die: and he called his son
Joseph, and said unto him, If now I
have found grace in thy sight, [b]put, I
pray thee, thy hand under my thigh,
and [c]deal kindly and truly with me;
[d]bury me not, I pray thee, in Egypt:
30 But [e]I will lie with my fathers, and
thou shalt carry me out of Egypt, and
[f]bury me in their buryingplace.
And he said, I will do as thou hast
said.
31 And he said, Swear unto me. And

he sware unto him. [g]And Israel bowed[g]
himself upon the bed's head.

CHAPTER 48

AND it came to pass after these
things, that *one* told Joseph, Behold, thy father *is* sick: and he took
with him his two sons, Mă-năs'-sēh
and Ē'-phră-ĭm.
2 And *one* told Jacob, and said, Behold, thy son Joseph cometh unto
thee: and Israel strengthened himself, and sat upon the bed.
3 And Jacob said unto Joseph, God
Almighty appeared unto me at [a]Luz in
the land of Canaan, and blessed me,
4 And said unto me, Behold, I will
make thee fruitful, and multiply thee,
and I will make of thee a multitude of
people; and will give this land to thy
seed after thee [b]*for* an everlasting
possession.
5 ¶ And now thy [c]two sons, Ē'-phră-
ĭm and Mă-năs'-sēh, which were born
unto thee in the land of Egypt before
I came unto thee into Egypt, *are* mine;
as Reuben and Simeon, they shall be
mine.
6 And thy issue, which thou begettest after them, shall be thine, *and*
shall be called after the name of their
brethren in their inheritance.
7 And as for me, when I came from
Pā'-dăn, [d]Rachel died by me in the
land of Canaan in the way, when yet
there was but a little way to come unto
Ē'-phrăth: and I buried her there in
the way of Ē'-phrăth; the same *is* Beth-
lehem.
8 And Israel beheld Joseph's sons,
and said, Who *are* these?
9 And Joseph said unto his father,
[e]They *are* my sons, whom God hath
given me in this *place*. And he said,
Bring them, I pray thee, unto me, and
[f]I will bless them.
10 Now [g]the eyes of Israel were [1]dim
for age, *so that* he could not see. And
he brought them near unto him; and
he [h]kissed them, and embraced them.
11 And Israel said unto Joseph, I
[i]had not thought to see thy face: and,
lo, God hath shewed me also thy seed.
12 And Joseph brought them out
from between his knees, and he bowed
himself with his face to the earth.
13 And Joseph took them both, Ē'-
phră-ĭm in his right hand toward
Israel's left hand, and Mă-năs'-sēh in
his left hand toward Israel's right
hand, and brought *them* near unto
him.
14 And Israel stretched out his right

ch. 48.2. 1 Ki. 1.47. Heb. 11.21.

CHAP. 48

a ch. 28.13, 19. ch. 35.6, 9, etc.
b ch. 17.8.
c ch. 41.50. ch. 46.20. Josh. 13.7. Josh. 14.4.
d ch. 35.19.
e ch. 33.5.
f ch. 27.4.
g ch. 27.1.
1 heavy. Isa. 6.10. Isa. 59.1.
h ch. 27.27.
i ch. 45.26.
j Heb. 11.21.
k ch. 28.15.
l Amos 9.12. Acts 15.17.
2 as fishes do increase.
m ver. 14.
3 was evil in his eyes.
n Num. 2.19. Deut. 33.17.
4 fulness.
o Ruth 4.11.
p ch. 50.24.
q Josh. 24.32. 1 Chr. 5.2. John 4.5.
r ch. 34.28. Josh. 17.14.

CHAP. 49

a Deut. 33.1. Amos 3.7.
b Deut. 4.30. Num. 24. 14.
c Ps. 34.11.
d Deut. 21.17.
1 do not thou excel.
e Deut. 27. 20. 1 Chr. 5.1.
2 Or, my couch is gone.

hand, and laid *it* upon Ē'-phră-ĭm's
head, who *was* the younger, and his
left hand upon Mă-năs'-sēh's head,
guiding his hands wittingly; for Mă-
năs'-sēh *was* the firstborn.
15 ¶ And [j]he blessed Joseph, and
said, God, before whom my fathers
Abraham and Isaac did walk, the
God which fed me all my life long
unto this day,
16 The Angel [k]which redeemed me
from all evil, bless the lads; and let
[l]my name be named on them, and the
name of my fathers Abraham and
Isaac; and let them [2]grow into a multitude in the midst of the earth.
17 And when Joseph saw that his
father [m]laid his right hand upon the
head of Ē'-phră-ĭm, it [3]displeased him:
and he held up his father's hand, to
remove it from Ē'-phră-ĭm's head unto
Mă-năs'-sēh's head.
18 And Joseph said unto his father,
Not so, my father: for this *is* the firstborn; put thy right hand upon his
head.
19 And his father refused, and said,
I know *it*, my son, I know *it:* he also
shall become a people, and he also
shall be great: but truly his [n]younger
brother shall be greater than he, and
his seed shall become a [4]multitude of
nations.
20 And he blessed them that day,
saying, [o]In thee shall Israel bless, saying, God make thee as Ē'-phră-ĭm and
as Mă-năs'-sēh: and he set Ē'-phră-ĭm
before Mă-năs'-sēh.
21 And Israel said unto Joseph, Behold, I die: but [p]God shall be with
you, and bring you again unto the
land of your fathers.
22 Moreover [q]I have given to thee
one portion above thy brethren, which
I took out of the hand of the [r]Amorite
with my sword and with my bow.

CHAPTER 49

AND Jacob called unto his sons,
and said, Gather yourselves together, that I may [a]tell you *that* which
shall befall you [b]in the last days.
2 Gather yourselves together, and
hear, ye sons of Jacob; and hearken
[c]unto Israel your father.
3 ¶ Reuben, thou *art* my firstborn,
my might, [d]and the beginning of my
strength, the excellency of dignity, and
the excellency of power:
4 Unstable as water, [1]thou [e]shalt not
excel; because thou wentest up to thy
father's bed; then defiledst thou *it:*
[2]he went up to my couch.

5 ¶ Simeon and Levi *are* [f]brethren; [3]instruments [g]of cruelty *are in* their habitations.

6 O my soul, [h]come not thou into their secret; [i]unto their assembly, mine honour, be not thou united: for in their anger they slew a man, and in their selfwill they [4]digged down a wall.

7 Cursed *be* their anger, for *it was* fierce; and their wrath, for it was cruel: [j]I will divide them in Jacob, and scatter them in Israel.

8 ¶ Judah, thou *art he* whom thy brethren shall praise: thy hand *shall be* in the neck of thine enemies; thy father's children shall bow down before thee.

9 Judah *is* a lion's whelp: from the prey, my son, thou art gone up: [k]he stooped down, he couched as a lion, and as an old lion; who shall rouse him up?

10 The [l]sceptre shall not depart from Judah, nor a [m]lawgiver from between his feet, [n]until Shī-lōh come; [o]and unto him *shall* the gathering of the people *be*.

11 Binding his foal unto the vine, and his ass's colt unto the choice vine; he washed his garments in wine, and his clothes in the blood of grapes:

12 His eyes *shall be* red with wine, and his teeth white with milk.

13 ¶ Zĕ-bū-lŭn [p]shall dwell at the haven of the sea; and he *shall be* for an haven of ships; and his border *shall be* unto Zī-dŏn.

14 ¶ Ĭs-să-chär *is* a strong ass couching between two burdens:

15 And he saw that rest *was* good, and the land that *it was* pleasant; and bowed his shoulder to bear, and became a servant unto tribute.

16 ¶ Dan [q]shall judge his people, as one of the tribes of Israel.

17 Dan [r]shall be a serpent by the way,[5] an adder in the path, that biteth the horse heels, so that his rider shall fall backward.

18 I [s]have waited for thy salvation, O LORD.

19 ¶ Gad, [t]a troop shall overcome him: but he shall overcome at the last.

20 ¶ Out of Asher his bread *shall be* fat, and he shall yield royal dainties.

21 ¶ Năph-tă-lī *is* a hind let loose: he giveth goodly words.

22 ¶ Joseph *is* a fruitful bough, *even* a fruitful bough by a well; *whose* [6]branches run over the wall:

23 The archers have [u]sorely grieved him, and shot *at him*, and hated him:

24 But his [v]bow abode in strength, and the arms of his hands were made strong by the hands of the [w]mighty *God* of Jacob; (from thence [x]*is* the shepherd, [y]the stone of Israel:)

25 *Even* by the God of thy father, who shall help thee; and by the Almighty, [z]who shall bless thee with blessings of heaven above, blessings of the deep that lieth under, blessings of the breasts and of the womb:

26 The blessings of thy father have prevailed above the blessings of my progenitors unto the utmost bound of the everlasting hills: they shall be on the head of Joseph, and on the crown of the head of him that was separate from his brethren.

27 ¶ Benjamin shall [a]ravin *as* a wolf: in the morning he shall devour the prey, [b]and at night he shall divide the spoil.

28 ¶ All these *are* the twelve tribes of Israel: and this *is it* that their father spake unto them, and blessed them; every one according to his blessing he blessed them.

29 And he charged them, and said unto them, I [c]am to be gathered unto my people: [d]bury me with my fathers [e]in the cave that *is* in the field of Ē-phrŏn the Hittite,

30 In the cave that *is* in the field of Măch-pē-lăh, which *is* before Măm-rē, in the land of Canaan, which [f]Abraham bought with the field of Ē-phrŏn the Hittite for a possession of a buryingplace.

31 There [g]they buried Abraham and Sarah his wife; [h]there they buried Isaac and Rebekah his wife; and there I buried Leah.

32 The purchase of the field and of the cave that *is* therein *was* from the children of Heth.

33 And when Jacob had made an end of commanding his sons, he gathered up his feet into the bed, and yielded up the ghost, and was gathered unto his people.

CHAPTER 50

AND Joseph [a]fell upon his father's face, and [b]wept upon him, and kissed him.

2 And Joseph commanded his servants the physicians to [c]embalm his father: and the physicians embalmed Israel.

3 And forty days were fulfilled for him; for so are fulfilled the days of those which are embalmed: and the Egyptians [1]mourned [d]for him threescore and ten days.

---

f Pro. 18.9.
3 Or, their swords are weapons of violence.
g ch. 34.25.
h Pro. 1.15.
i Ps. 26.9.
4 Or, houghed oxen.
j Josh. 21.1. 1 Chr. 4.24.
k Num. 24.9.
l Num. 24.17.
m Ps. 60.7.
n 1 Chr. 5.2. Isa. 11.1. Eze. 21.27. Dan. 9.25. Matt. 21.9. Luke 1.32.
o Isa. 2.2. Isa. 11.10. Isa. 42.1,4. Isa. 49.6. Isa. 55.4,5. Isa. 60.1-5. Hag. 2.7. Luke 2.30.
p Deut. 33. 18.
q Judg. 13.2. with Judg. 15.20.
r Judg. 18.27.
5 an arrow-snake.
s Ps. 25.3,5. Ps. 62.5. Ps. 119.166, 174. Ps. 130.5. Isa. 25.9. Isa. 40.31. Lam. 3.26. Rom. 2.7. 1 Cor. 1.7. Phil. 3.20. Titus 2.13.
t Deut. 33.20.
6 daughters.
u ch. 37.24.
v Job 29.20.
w Ps. 132.2,5.
x Ps. 80.1.
y Isa. 28.16.
z Deut. 33.13.
a Judg. 20. 21.25.
b Num. 23. 24. Esth. 8.11. Eze. 39.10. Zech. 14.1, 7.
c ch. 15.15. ch. 25.8.
d ch. 47.30. 2 Sam. 19. 37.
e ch. 50.13.
f ch. 23.16.
g ch. 23.19. ch. 25.9.
h ch. 35.29.

CHAP. 50

a ch. 46.4.
b 2 Ki. 13.14.
c 2 Chr. 16. 14. Matt. 26.12. Mark 14.8. Mark 16.1.
1 wept.
d Num. 20. 29. Deut. 34.8.

4 And when the days of his mourning
were past, Joseph spake unto [e]the
house of Pharaoh, saying, If now I
have found grace in your eyes, speak,
I pray you, in the ears of Pharaoh,
saying,
5 My father made me swear, saying,
Lo, I die: in my grave [f]which I have
digged for me in the land of Canaan,
there shalt thou bury me. Now therefore let me go up, I pray thee, and
bury my father, and I will come
again.
6 And Pharaoh said, Go up, and
bury thy father, according as he made
thee swear.
7 ¶ And Joseph went up to bury his
father: and with him went up all the
servants of Pharaoh, the elders of his
house, and all the elders of the land
of Egypt,
8 And all the house of Joseph, and
his brethren, and his father's house:
only their little ones, and their flocks,
and their herds, they left in the land of
Gō-shĕn.
9 And there went up with him both
chariots and horsemen: and it was
a very great company.
10 And they came to the threshingfloor of Ā-tăd, which *is* beyond Jordan, and there they [g]mourned with a
great and very sore lamentation: [h]and
he made a mourning for his father
seven days.
11 And when the inhabitants of the
land, the Canaanites, saw the mourning in the floor of Ā-tăd, they said,
This *is* a grievous mourning to the
Egyptians: wherefore the name of it
was called [2]Ā-bĕl–mĭz-rā-ĭm, which *is*
beyond Jordan.
12 And his sons did unto him according as he commanded them:
13 For [i]his sons carried him into the
land of Canaan, and buried him in the
cave of the field of Măch-pē-lāh,
which Abraham bought with the field
for a possession of a buryingplace of
Ē-phrŏn the Hittite, before Măm-rē.
14 ¶ And Joseph returned into Egypt,
he, and his brethren, and all that went
up with him to bury his father, after
he had buried his father.
15 ¶ And when Joseph's brethren
saw that their father was dead, they
[j]said, Joseph will peradventure hate
us, and will certainly requite us all
the evil which we did unto him.
16 And they [3]sent a messenger unto
Joseph, saying, Thy father did command before he died, saying,
17 So shall ye say unto Joseph, Forgive, I pray thee now, the trespass of
thy brethren, and their sin; for [k]they
did unto thee evil: and now, we pray
thee, forgive the trespass of the servants of [l]the God of thy father. And
Joseph wept when they spake unto
him.
18 And his brethren also went and
[m]fell down before his face; and they
said, Behold, we *be* thy servants.
19 And Joseph said unto them, Fear
not: [n]for *am* I in the place of God?
20 But [o]as for you, ye thought evil
against me; *but* [p]God meant it unto
good, to bring to pass, as *it is* this day,
to save much people alive.
21 Now therefore fear ye not: [q]I will
nourish you, and your little ones. And
he comforted them, and spake [4]kindly
unto them.
22 ¶ And Joseph dwelt in Egypt, he,
and his father's house: and Joseph
lived an hundred and ten years.
23 And Joseph saw Ē-phră-ĭm's children [r]of the third *generation:* the children also of Mā-chĭr the son of Mă-
năs-sēh [s]were [5]brought up upon
Joseph's knees.
24 And Joseph said unto his brethren, I die: and [t]God will surely visit
you, and bring you out of this [u]land
unto the land which he sware to Abraham, to Isaac, and to Jacob.
25 And [v]Joseph took an oath of the
children of Israel, saying, God will
surely visit you, and ye shall carry up
my bones from hence.
26 So Joseph died, *being* an hundred
and ten years old: and they embalmed
him, and he was put in a coffin in
Egypt.

e Esth. 4.2.
f 2 Chr. 16. 14. Isa. 22.16. Matt. 27.60.
g Acts 8.2.
h 1 Sam. 31. 13. Job 2.13.
2 That is, The mourning of the Egyptians.
i ch. 23.16. Acts 7.16.
j Job 15.21.
3 charged.
k Pro. 28.13.
l ch. 49.25.
m ch. 37.7, 10.
n Deut. 32. 35 Rom. 12.19. Heb. 10.30.
o Ps. 56.5. Isa. 10.7.
p ch. 45.5,7. Acts 3.13, 14,15.
q ch. 47.12. Matt. 5.44.
4 to their hearts.
r Job 42.16.
s ch. 30.3.
5 borne.
t Ex. 3.16,17. Heb. 11.22.
u ch. 26.3.
v ch. 47.29. Ex. 13.19. Josh. 24.32.

THE SECOND BOOK OF MOSES, CALLED

EXODUS

CHAPTER 1

NOW [a]these *are* the names of the children of Israel, which came into Egypt; Every man and his household came with Jacob.

2 Reuben, Simeon, Levi, and Judah,

3 Ĭs-sä-char, Zĕ-bū-lŭn, and Benjamin,

4 Dan, and Năph-tă-lī, Gad, and Asher.

5 And all the souls that came out of the [1]loins of Jacob were seventy [b]souls: for Joseph was in Egypt *already*.

6 And [c]Joseph died, and all his brethren, and [d]all that generation.

7 ¶ And [e]the children of Israel were fruitful, and increased abundantly, and multiplied, and waxed exceeding mighty; and the land was filled with them.

8 Now there arose up a new king over Egypt, which knew not Joseph.

9 And he said unto his people, Behold, [f]the people of the children of Israel *are* more and mightier than we:

10 Come [g]on, let us [h]deal wisely with them; lest they multiply, and it come to pass, that, when there falleth out any war, they join also unto our enemies, and fight against us, and *so* get them up out of the land.

11 Therefore they did set over them taskmasters [i]to afflict them with their [j]burdens. And they built for Pharaoh treasure cities, Pī-thŏm [k]and Rā-ăm-sēs.

12 [2]But the more they afflicted them, the more they multiplied and grew. And they were grieved because of the children of Israel.

13 And the Egyptians made the children of Israel to serve with rigour:

14 And they [l]made their lives bitter with hard bondage, [m]in morter, and in brick, and in all manner of service in the field: all their service, wherein they made them serve, *was* with rigour.

15 ¶ And the king of Egypt spake to the Hebrew midwives, of which the name of the one *was* Shĭph-răh, and the name of the other Pū-äh:

16 And he said, When ye do the office of a midwife to the Hebrew women, and see *them* upon the stools; if it *be* a son, then ye shall kill him: but if it *be* a daughter, then she shall live.

17 But the midwives [n]feared God, and did not [o]as the king of Egypt commanded them, but saved the men children alive.

18 And the king of Egypt called for the midwives, and said unto them, Why have ye done this thing, and have saved the men children alive?

19 And [p]the midwives said unto Pharaoh, Because the Hebrew women *are* not as the Egyptian women; for they *are* lively, and are delivered ere the midwives come in unto them.

20 Therefore [q]God dealt well with the midwives: and the people multiplied, and waxed very mighty.

21 And it came to pass, because the midwives feared God, [r]that he made them houses.

22 And Pharaoh charged all his people, saying, Every son that is born ye shall cast into the river, and every daughter ye shall save alive.

CHAPTER 2

AND there went [a]a man of the house of Levi, and took *to wife* a daughter of Levi.

2 And the woman conceived, and bare a son: and [b]when she saw him that he *was a* goodly *child*, she hid him three months.

3 And when she could not longer hide him, she took for him an ark of bulrushes, and daubed it with slime and with pitch, and put the child therein; and she laid *it* in the flags by the river's brink.

4 And [c]his sister stood afar off, to wit what would be done to him.

5 ¶ And the [d]daughter of Pharaoh came down to wash *herself* at the river; and her maidens walked along by the river's side; and when she saw the ark among the flags, she sent her maid to fetch it.

6 And when she had opened *it*, she saw the child: and, behold, the babe wept. And she had compassion on him, and said, This *is one* of the Hebrews' children.

7 Then said his sister to Pharaoh's

CHAP. 1

a Gen. 46.8. ch. 6.14.

1 thigh.

b Gen. 46.26. Deut. 10.22.

c Gen. 50.26. Acts 7.15.

d Eccl. 1.4.

e Gen. 46.3. Deut. 26.5. Ps. 105.24. Acts 7.17.

f Ps. 105.24.

g Ps. 10.2. Ps. 83.3.

h Job 5.13. Pro. 28.16. Acts 7.19.

i Gen. 15.13. ch. 3.7.

j ch. 2.11 ch. 5.4,5. Ps. 81.6. Pro. 27.3.

k Gen. 47.11.

2 And as they afflicted them, so they multiplied etc.

l ch. 2.23. ch. 22.21. Lev. 25.14, 17. Num. 20.15. Job. 20.19. Ps. 10.17,18. Pro. 14.31.

m Ps. 81.6.

n Pro. 16.6.

o Dan. 3.16, 18. Dan. 6.13. Acts 5.29.

p Josh. 2.4. 2 Sam. 17. 19,20.

q Pro. 11.18. Eccl. 8.12. Isa. 3.10. Heb. 6.10.

r 1 Sam. 2.35. 2 Sam. 7.11, 13,27,29. 1 Ki. 2.24. 1 Ki. 11.38. Ps. 127.1.

CHAP 2

a ch. 6.20. Num. 26.59. 1 Chr. 23.13, 14.

b Heb. 11.23.

c ch. 15.20. Num. 26.59.

d Acts 7.21.

daughter, Shall I go and call to thee a nurse of the Hebrew women, that she may nurse the child for thee?

8 And Pharaoh's daughter said to her, Go. And the maid went and called the child's mother.

9 And Pharaoh's daughter said unto her, Take this child away, and nurse it for me, and I will give *thee* thy wages. And the woman took the child, and nursed it.

10 And the child grew, and she brought him unto Pharaoh's daughter, and he became her son. And she called his name [1]Moses: and she said, Because I drew him out of the water.

11 ¶ And it came to pass in those days, [e]when Moses was grown, that he went out unto his brethren, and looked on their burdens: and he spied an Egyptian smiting an Hebrew, one of his brethren.

12 And he looked this way and that way, and when he saw that *there was* no man, he slew the Egyptian, and hid him in the sand.

13 And when he went out the second day, behold, two men of the Hebrews strove together: and he said to him that did the wrong, Wherefore smitest thou thy fellow?

14 And he said, Who made thee [2]a prince and a judge over us? intendest thou to kill me, as thou killedst the Egyptian? And Moses feared, and said, Surely this thing is known.

15 Now when Pharaoh heard this thing, he sought to slay Moses. But Moses fled from the face of Pharaoh, and dwelt in the land of Mĭd-ĭ-ăn: and he sat down by [f]a well.

16 Now [g]the [3]priest of Mĭd-ĭ-ăn had seven daughters: [h]and they came and drew *water*, and filled the troughs to water their father's flock.

17 And the shepherds came and drove them away: but Moses stood up and helped them, and watered their flock.

18 And when they came to [i]Reū-ĕl their father, he said, How *is it that* ye are come so soon to day?

19 And they said, An Egyptian delivered us out of the hand of the shepherds, and also drew *water* enough for us, and watered the flock.

20 And he said unto his daughters, And where *is* he? why *is* it *that* ye have left the man? call him, that he may [j]eat bread.

21 And Moses was content to dwell with the man: and he gave Moses Zĭp-pō-răh his daughter.

1 That is, Drawn out.
e Heb. 11.24-26.
2 a man, a prince. Gen. 13.8. Gen. 47.22, 26. 1 Sam. 8.18. 1 Sam. 20. 26.
f Gen. 24.11. Gen. 29.2.
g ch. 3.1.
3 Or, prince, as Gen. 41. 45.
h Gen. 29.10. 1 Sam. 9.11.
i Num. 10.29. Called also Jethro, or Jether.
j Gen. 31.54.
4 That is, A stranger here.
k ch. 18.3
l Heb. 11.13.
m ch. 7.7.
n Ps. 12.5.
o Gen. 18.20. Deut. 24.15. Jas. 5.4.
p ch. 6.5.
q Ps. 105.8.
r Gen. 15.14.
s 2 Sam. 16. 12. Luke 1.25.
5 knew.

CHAP. 3

a 1 Ki. 19.8.
b Deut. 33.16. Isa. 63.9. Acts 7.30.
c Ps. 111.2.
d Deut. 33.16.
e Josh. 5.15.
f Gen. 28.13. Mark 12.26.
g Isa. 6.1,5. Rev. 1.17
h Gen. 18.21.
i Gen. 11.5.
j ch. 12.51.
k Deut. 1.25.
l Num. 13.27.
m Gen. 15.18.

22 And she bare *him* a son, and he called his name [4]Gĕr-shŏm: [k]for he said, I have been [l]a stranger in a strange land.

23 ¶ And it came to pass [m]in process of time, that the king of Egypt died: and the children of Israel [n]sighed by reason of the bondage, and they cried, and their [o]cry came up unto God by reason of the bondage.

24 And God [p]heard their groaning, and God [q]remembered his covenant [r]with Abraham, with Isaac, and with Jacob.

25 And God [s]looked upon the children of Israel, and God [5]had respect unto *them*.

CHAPTER 3

NOW Moses kept the flock of Jĕth-rō his father in law, the priest of Mĭd-ĭ-ăn: and he led the flock to the backside of the desert, and came to [a]the mountain of God, *even* to Hôr-ĕb.

2 And [b]the angel of the LORD appeared unto him in a flame of fire out of the midst of a bush: and he looked, and, behold, the bush burned with fire, and the bush *was* not consumed.

3 And Moses said, I will now turn aside, and [c]see this great sight, why the bush is not burnt.

4 And when the LORD saw that he turned aside to see, God called unto [d]him out of the midst of the bush, and said, Moses, Moses. And he said, Here *am* I.

5 And he said, Draw not nigh hither: [e]put off thy shoes from off thy feet, for the place whereon thou standest *is* holy ground.

6 Moreover he said, [f]I *am* the God of thy father, the God of Abraham, the God of Isaac, and the God of Jacob. And Moses hid his face; for [g]he was afraid to look upon God.

7 ¶ And the LORD said, I have surely seen the affliction of my people which *are* in Egypt, and have heard their cry by reason of their taskmasters; for [h]I know their sorrows;

8 And [i]I am come down to [j]deliver them out of the hand of the Egyptians, and to bring them up out of that land [k]unto a good land and a large, unto a land [l]flowing with milk and honey; unto the place of the [m]Canaanites, and the Hittites, and the Amorites, and the Pĕ-rĭz-zītes, and the Hī-vītes, and the Jĕb-ū-sītes.

9 Now therefore, behold, the cry of the children of Israel is come unto me: and I have also seen the oppression

[n]wherewith the Egyptians oppress
them.
10 Come [o]now therefore, and I will
send thee unto Pharaoh, that thou
mayest bring forth my people the
children of Israel out of Egypt.
11 ¶ And Moses said unto God, Who
[p]*am* I, that I should go unto Pharaoh,
and that I should bring forth the children of Israel out of Egypt?
12 And he said, [q]Certainly I will be
with thee; and this *shall be* a token unto thee, that I have sent thee: When
thou hast brought forth the people out
of Egypt, ye shall serve God upon this
mountain.
13 And Moses said unto God, Behold, *when* I come unto the children of
Israel, and shall say unto them, The
God of your fathers hath sent me unto
you; and they shall say to me, [r]What
is his name? what shall I say unto
them?
14 And God said unto Moses, I AM
THAT I AM: and he said, Thus shalt
thou say unto the children of Israel,
[s]I AM hath sent me unto you.
15 And God said moreover unto
Moses, Thus shalt thou say unto the
children of Israel, The LORD God of
your fathers, the God of Abraham, the
God of Isaac, and the God of Jacob,
hath sent me unto you: this *is* [t]my
name for ever, and this *is* my memorial unto all generations.
16 Go, and gather the elders of
Israel together, and say unto them,
The [u]LORD God of your fathers, the
God of Abraham, of Isaac, and of
Jacob, appeared unto me, saying, [v]I
have surely visited you, and *seen* that
which is done to you in Egypt:
17 And I have said, [w]I will bring you
up out of the affliction of Egypt unto
the land of the Canaanites, and the
Hittites, and the Amorites, and the
Pĕ-rĭź-zītes, and the Hī́-vītes, and the
Jĕb́-ū-sītes, unto a land flowing with
milk and honey.
18 And they shall hearken to thy
voice: and thou shalt come, thou and
the elders of Israel, unto the king of
Egypt, and ye shall say unto him, The
LORD God of the Hebrews hath [x]met
with us: and now let us go, we beseech
thee, three days' journey into the wilderness, that we may sacrifice to the
LORD our God.
19 ¶ And I am sure that the king of
Egypt will not let you go, [1]no, not by
a mighty hand.
20 And I will stretch out my hand,
and smite Egypt with [y]all my wonders

n ch. 1.11.
o Ps. 105.26. Micah 6.4.
p 1 Sam. 18.18. 1 Ki. 3.7-9. Isa. 6.5,8. Jer. 1.6.
q Gen. 31.3. Deut. 31.23. Josh. 1.5. Isa. 43.2. Rom. 8.31.
r Gen. 32.29.
s ch. 6.3. John 8.58. Heb. 13.8. Rev. 1.4.
t Ps. 135.13. Hosea 12.5.
u Gen. 48.15.
v Gen. 50.24. ch. 2.25. ch. 4.31. Deut. 26.7. Ps. 80.14. Ps. 33.13,14. Luke 1.68.
w Gen. 15.14.
x Num. 23.3.
1 Or, but by strong hand.
y ch. 7.3. Deut. 6.22. Neh. 9.10. Ps. 105.27. Ps. 135.9. Jer. 32.20. Acts 7.36.
z ch. 12.31.
a ch. 11.3. ch. 12.36. Ps. 106.46. Pro. 16.7.
b Gen. 15.14. ch. 11.2.
c Job 27.17. Pro. 13.22. Eze. 39.10.
2 Or, Egypt.

CHAP. 4

a ch. 19.9.
b Num. 12.10. 2 Ki. 5.27.
c Num. 12.13,14. Deut. 32.39. 2 Ki. 5.14. Matt. 8.3.
d ch. 7.19.
1 shall be and shall be.
2 a man of words.
3 since yesterday, nor since the third day.
e ch. 6.12. Jer. 1.6.

which I will do in the midst thereof:
and [z]after that he will let you go.
21 And [a]I will give this people favour
in the sight of the Egyptians: and it
shall come to pass, that, when ye go,
ye shall not go empty:
22 But [b]every woman shall borrow
of her neighbour, and of her that sojourneth in her house, jewels of silver,
and jewels of gold, and raiment: and
ye shall put *them* upon your sons, and
upon your daughters; [c]and ye shall
spoil [2]the Egyptians.

CHAPTER 4

AND Moses answered and said,
But, behold, they will not believe
me, nor hearken unto my voice: for
they will say, The LORD hath not appeared unto thee.
2 And the LORD said unto him, What
is that in thine hand? And he said, A
rod.
3 And he said, Cast it on the ground.
And he cast it on the ground, and it became a serpent; and Moses fled from
before it.
4 And the LORD said unto Moses,
Put forth thine hand, and take it by
the tail. And he put forth his hand,
and caught it, and it became a rod in
his hand:
5 That they may [a]believe that the
LORD God of their fathers, the God of
Abraham, the God of Isaac, and the
God of Jacob, hath appeared unto
thee.
6 ¶ And the LORD said furthermore
unto him, Put now thine hand into thy
bosom. And he put his hand into his
bosom: and when he took it out, behold, his hand *was* leprous [b]as snow.
7 And he said, Put thine hand into
thy bosom again. And he put his hand
into his bosom again; and plucked it
out of his bosom, and, behold, [c]it was
turned again as his *other* flesh.
8 And it shall come to pass, if they
will not believe thee, neither hearken
to the voice of the first sign, that they
will believe the voice of the latter sign.
9 And it shall come to pass, if they
will not believe also these two signs,
neither hearken unto thy voice, that
thou shalt take of the water of the river, and pour *it* upon the dry *land:* and
[d]the water which thou takest out of
the river [1]shall become blood upon
the dry *land*.
10 ¶ And Moses said unto the LORD,
O my Lord, I *am* not [2]eloquent,
neither [3]heretofore, nor since thou
hast spoken unto thy servant: but [e]I

am slow of speech, and of a slow tongue.

11 And the LORD said unto him, Who [f]hath made man's mouth? or who maketh the dumb, or deaf, or the seeing, or the blind? have not I the LORD?

12 Now therefore go, and I will be [g]with thy mouth, and teach thee what thou shalt say.

13 And he said, O my Lord, send, [h]I pray thee, by the hand *of him whom* thou [4]wilt send.

14 And the anger of the LORD was kindled against Moses, and he said, *Is* not Aaron the Levite thy brother? I know that he can speak well. And also, behold, he cometh forth to meet thee: and when he seeth thee, he will be glad in his heart.

15 And thou shalt speak unto him, and [i]put words in his mouth: and I will be with thy mouth, and with his mouth, and [j]will teach you what ye shall do.

16 And he shall be thy spokesman unto the people: and he shall be, *even* he shall be to thee instead of a mouth, and [k]thou shalt be to him instead of God.

17 And thou shalt take this rod in thine hand, wherewith thou shalt do signs.

18 ¶ And Moses went and returned to [5]Jĕth-rō his father in law, and said unto him, Let me go, I pray thee, and return unto my brethren which *are* in Egypt, and see whether they be yet alive. And Jĕth-rō said to Moses, Go in peace.

19 And the LORD said unto Moses in Mĭd-ĭ-ăn, Go, return into Egypt: for [l]all the men are dead which sought thy life.

20 And Moses took his wife and his sons, and set them upon an ass, and he returned to the land of Egypt: and Moses took the [m]rod of God in his hand.

21 And the LORD said unto Moses, When thou goest to return into Egypt, see that thou do all those wonders before Pharaoh, which I have put in thine hand: but [n]I will harden his heart, that he shall not let the people go.

22 And thou shalt say unto Pharaoh, Thus saith the LORD, Israel [o]*is* my son, [p]*even* my firstborn:

23 And I say unto thee, Let my son go, that he may serve me: and if thou refuse to let him go, behold, I [q]will slay thy son, *even* thy firstborn.

24 ¶ And it came to pass by the way in the inn, that the [r]LORD met him, and sought to [s]kill him.

25 Then Zĭp-pō-răh took [t]a sharp [6]stone, and cut off the foreskin of her son, and [7]cast *it* at his feet, and said, Surely a bloody husband *art* thou to me.

26 So he let him go: then she said, A bloody husband *thou art*, because of the circumcision.

27 ¶ And the LORD said to Aaron, Go into the wilderness to meet Moses. And he went, and met him in [u]the mount of God, and kissed him.

28 And Moses told Aaron all the words of the LORD who had sent him, and all the signs which he had commanded him.

29 ¶ And Moses and Aaron went and [v]gathered together all the elders of the children of Israel:

30 And Aaron spake all the words which the LORD had spoken unto Moses, and did the signs in the sight of the people.

31 And the people [w]believed: and when they heard that the LORD had [x]visited the children of Israel, and that he had [y]looked upon their affliction, then [z]they bowed their heads and worshipped.

CHAPTER 5

AND afterward Moses and Aaron went in, and told Pharaoh, Thus saith the LORD God of Israel, Let my people go, that they may hold [a]a feast unto me in the wilderness.

2 And Pharaoh said, [b]Who *is* the LORD, that I should obey his voice to let Israel go? I know not the LORD, [c]neither will I let Israel go.

3 And they said, [d]The God of the Hebrews hath met with us: let us go, we pray thee, three days' journey into the desert, and sacrifice unto the LORD our God; lest he fall upon us with pestilence, or with the sword.

4 And the king of Egypt said unto them, [e]Wherefore do ye, Moses and Aaron, let the people from their works? get you unto your [f]burdens.

5 And Pharaoh said, Behold, the people of the land now *are* [g]many, and ye make them rest from their burdens.

6 And Pharaoh commanded the same day the [h]taskmasters of the people, and their officers, saying,

7 Ye shall no more give the people straw to make brick, as heretofore: let them go and gather straw for themselves.

f Ps. 94.9.
g Isa. 50.4. Jer. 1.9. Matt. 10.19. Mark 13.11. Luke 12.11, 12. Luke 21.14.
h Jonah 1.3.
4 Or, shouldest.
i Num. 23.12. Deut. 18.18. Isa. 51.16. Jer. 1.9.
j Deut. 5.31.
k ch. 7.1. ch. 18.19.
5 Jether.
l ch. 2.15,23. Matt. 2.20.
m ch. 17.9. Num. 20.8.
n Josh. 11.20. 1 Sam. 6.6. Dan. 5.20. Rom. 9.14-23. Jas. 1.13-17.
o Hosea 11.1. Rom. 9.4. 2 Cor. 6.18.
p Jer. 31.9. Jas. 1.18.
q ch. 11.5. ch. 12.29.
r Num. 22. 22.
s Gen. 17.14.
t Josh. 5.2,3.
6 Or, knife.
7 made it touch.
u ch. 3.1.
v ch. 3.16.
w ch. 3.18.
x ch. 3.16.
y ch. 2.25. ch. 3.7.
z Gen. 24.26. ch. 12.27. 1 Chr. 29.20.

CHAP. 5

a ch. 10.9.
b 2 Ki. 18.35. Job 21.15. Ps. 12.3-5. 2 Chr. 32.14.
c ch. 3.19.
d ch. 3.18.
e Pro. 28.15.
f ch. 1.11.
g ch. 1.7,9.
h ch. 1.11.

8 And the tale of the bricks, which
they did make heretofore, ye shall lay
upon them; ye shall not diminish
ought thereof: for they *be* idle; therefore they cry, saying, Let us go *and*
sacrifice to our God.
9 [1]Let there more work be laid upon
the men, that they may labour therein;
and let them not regard vain words.
10 ¶ And the [i]taskmasters of the people went out, and their officers, and
they spake to the people, saying,
Thus saith Pharaoh, I will not give
you straw.
11 Go ye, get you straw where ye can
find it: yet not ought of your work
shall be diminished.
12 So the people were scattered
abroad throughout all the land of
Egypt to gather stubble instead of
straw.
13 And the taskmasters hasted *them*,
saying, Fulfil your works, *your* [2]daily
tasks, as when there was straw.
14 And [j]the officers of the children of
Israel, which Pharaoh's taskmasters
had set over them, were beaten, *and*
demanded, Wherefore have ye not
fulfilled your task in making brick
both yesterday and to day, as heretofore?
15 ¶ Then the officers of the children
of Israel came and cried unto Pharaoh, saying, Wherefore dealest thou
thus with thy servants?
16 There is no straw given unto thy
servants, and they say to us, Make
brick: and, behold, thy servants *are*
beaten; but the fault *is* in thine own
people.
17 But he said, Ye *are* idle, *ye are*
idle: therefore ye say, Let us go *and*
do sacrifice to the LORD.
18 Go therefore now, *and* work; for
there shall no straw be given you, yet
shall ye deliver the tale of bricks.
19 And the officers of the children of
Israel did see *that* they *were* in evil
case, after it was said, Ye shall not
minish *ought* from your bricks of
your daily task.
20 ¶ And they met Moses and Aaron,
who stood in the way, as they came
forth from Pharaoh:
21 And [k]they said unto them, The
LORD look upon you, and judge; because ye have made our savour [3]to be
abhorred in the eyes of Pharaoh,
and in the eyes of his servants, to
put a sword in their hands to slay
us.
22 And Moses [l]returned unto the
LORD, and said, Lord, wherefore hast
thou *so* evil entreated this people?
why *is* it *that* thou hast sent me?
23 For since I came to Pharaoh to
speak in thy name, he hath done evil to
this people; [4]neither [m]hast thou delivered thy people at all.

CHAPTER 6

THEN the LORD said unto Moses,
Now shalt thou see what I will do
to Pharaoh: for with a strong hand
shall he let them go, and with a strong
hand [a]shall he drive them out of his
land.
2 And God spake unto Moses, and
said unto him, I *am* [1]the LORD:
3 And I appeared unto Abraham,
unto Isaac, and unto Jacob, by *the
name of* [b]God Almighty, but [c]by my
name JĔ-HŌ-VĂH was I not known
to them.
4 And [d]I have also established my
covenant with them, [e]to give them the
land of Canaan, the land of their pilgrimage, wherein they were strangers.
5 And [f]I have also heard the groaning of the children of Israel, whom the
Egyptians keep in bondage; and I
have remembered my covenant.
6 Wherefore say unto the children of
Israel, I *am* the LORD, and [g]I will bring
you out from under the burdens of the
Egyptians, and I will rid you out of
their bondage, and I will [h]redeem you
with a stretched out arm, and with
great judgments:
7 And I will [i]take you to me for a
people, and [j]I will be to you a God:
and ye shall know that I *am* the LORD
your God, which bringeth you out
[k]from under the burdens of the Egyptians.
8 And I will bring you in unto the
land, concerning the which I did
[2]swear [l]to give it to Abraham, to
Isaac, and to Jacob; and I will give it
you for an heritage: I *am* the LORD.
9 ¶ And Moses spake so unto the
children of Israel: but they hearkened
not unto Moses for [3]anguish of spirit,
and for cruel bondage.
10 And the LORD spake unto Moses,
saying,
11 Go in, speak unto Pharaoh king
of Egypt, that he let the children of
Israel go out of his land.
12 And Moses spake before the
LORD, saying, Behold, the children of
Israel have not hearkened unto me;
how then shall Pharaoh hear me,
[m]who *am* of uncircumcised lips?
13 And the LORD spake unto Moses
and unto Aaron, and gave them a

1 let the work be heavy upon the men.
i ch. 1.11. Pro. 29.12.
2 a matter of a day in his day.
j Gen. 15.13.
k ch. 6.9.
3 to stink. Gen. 34.30. 1 Sam. 13.4. 2 Sam. 10.6. 1 Chr. 19.6.
l Num. 11.11. 1 Sam. 30.6.
4 delivering thou hast not delivered.
m Matt. 14. 31. Heb. 10.23.

CHAP. 6

a ch. 11.1. ch. 12.31.
1 Or, JEHOVAH.
b Gen. 17.1. Gen. 35.11. Gen. 48.3.
c ch. 3.14. Ps. 68.4. John 8.58. Rev. 1.4.
d Gen. 15.18. Gen. 17.4,7.
e Gen. 17.8.
f ch. 2.24.
g ch. 3.17. ch. 7.4. Deut. 26.8. Ps 81.6. Ps. 136.11, 12.
h ch. 15.13. Deut. 7.8. 1 Chr. 17.21. Neh. 1.10.
i Deut. 7.6. 2 Sam. 7.24.
j Gen. 17.7,8. ch. 29.45,46. Deut. 29.13. Rev. 21.7.
k Ps. 81.6.
2 lift up my hand. Gen. 14.22.
l Gen. 15.18. Gen. 26.3.
3 shortness or straitness.
m Jer. 1.6.

charge unto the children of Israel, and unto Pharaoh king of Egypt, to bring the children of Israel out of the land of Egypt.

14 ¶ These *be* the heads of their fathers' houses: [n]The sons of Reuben the firstborn of Israel; Hā'nŏch, and Păl'lû, Hĕz'rŏn, and Cär'mī: these *be* the families of Reuben.

15 And [o]the sons of Simeon; Jĕ-mū'ĕl, and Jā'mĭn, and Ō'hăd, and Jā'chĭn, and Zō'hăr, and Shā'ŭl the son of a Canaanitish woman: these *are* the families of Simeon.

16 ¶ And these *are* the names [p]of the sons of Levi according to their generations; Gĕr'shŏn, and Kō'hăth, and Mĕ-râr'ī: and the years of the life of Levi *were* an hundred thirty and seven years.

17 The sons of Gĕr'shŏn; Lĭb'nī, and Shĭm'ī, according to their families.

18 And [q]the sons of Kō'hăth; Amram, and Ĭz'hăr, and Hē'brŏn, and Ŭz'zĭ-ĕl: and the years of the life of Kō'hăth *were* an hundred thirty and three years.

19 And the sons of Mĕ-râr'ī; Mā'hă-lī and Mū'shī: these *are* the families of Levi according to their generations.

20 And [r]Amram took him Jŏch'ĕ-bĕd his father's sister to wife; and she bare him Aaron and Moses: and the years of the life of Amram *were* an hundred and thirty and seven years.

21 ¶ And [s]the sons of Ĭz'hăr; Kôr'ăh, and Nĕph'ĕg, and Zĭch'rī.

22 And [t]the sons of Ŭz'zĭ-ĕl; Mī'shā-ĕl, and Ĕl-zā'phăn, and Zĭth'rī.

23 And Aaron took him Ē-lī'shĕ-bă, daughter of [u]Ăm-mĭn'ă-dăb, sister of Nā-ăsh'ŏn, to wife; and she bare him [v]Nadab, and Ă-bī'hū, Ĕl-ē-ā'zär, and Ĭth'ă-mär.

24 And the [w]sons of Kôr'ăh; Ăs'sĭr, and Ĕl-kā'năh, and Ă-bī'ă-săph: these *are* the families of the Kôr'hītes.

25 And Ĕl-ē-ā'zär Aaron's son took him *one* of the daughters of Pū'tī-ĕl to wife; and she [x]bare him Phĭn'ĕ-hăs: these *are* the heads of the fathers of the Levites according to their families.

26 These *are* that Aaron and Moses, to whom the LORD said, Bring out the children of Israel from the land of Egypt according to their [y]armies.

27 These *are* they which spake to Pharaoh king of Egypt, [z]to bring out the children of Israel from Egypt: these *are* that Moses and Aaron.

28 ¶ And it came to pass on the day *when* the LORD spake unto Moses in the land of Egypt,

29 That the LORD spake unto Moses, saying, I *am* the LORD: speak [a]thou unto Pharaoh king of Egypt all that I say unto thee.

30 And Moses said before the LORD, Behold, I *am* [b]of uncircumcised lips, and how shall Pharaoh hearken unto me?

CHAPTER 7

AND the LORD said unto Moses, See, I have made thee [a]a god to Pharaoh: and Aaron thy brother shall be thy prophet.

2 Thou shalt speak all that I command thee: and Aaron thy brother shall speak unto Pharaoh, that he send the children of Israel out of his land.

3 And I will harden Pharaoh's heart, and [b]multiply my [c]signs and my wonders in the land of Egypt.

4 But Pharaoh shall not hearken unto you, [d]that I may lay my hand upon Egypt, and bring forth mine armies, *and* my people the children of Israel, out of the land of Egypt [e]by great judgments.

5 And the Egyptians shall know that [f]I *am* the LORD, when [g]I stretch forth mine hand upon Egypt, and bring out the children of Israel from among them.

6 And Moses and Aaron did as the LORD commanded them, so did they.

7 And Moses *was* [h]fourscore years old, and Aaron fourscore and three years old, when they spake unto Pharaoh.

8 ¶ And the LORD spake unto Moses and unto Aaron, saying,

9 When Pharaoh shall speak unto you, saying, [i]Shew a miracle for you: then thou shalt say unto Aaron, [j]Take thy rod, and cast *it* before Pharaoh, *and* it shall become a serpent.

10 ¶ And Moses and Aaron went in unto Pharaoh, and they did so as the LORD had commanded: and Aaron cast down his rod before Pharaoh, and before his servants, and it [k]became a serpent.

11 Then Pharaoh also [l]called the wise men and [m]the sorcerers: now the magicians of Egypt, they also did [n]in like manner with their enchantments.

12 For they cast down every man his rod, and they became serpents: but Aaron's rod swallowed up their rods.

13 And he hardened Pharaoh's heart, that he hearkened not unto them; [o]as the LORD had said.

n Gen. 46.9. 1 Chr. 5.3.
o Gen. 46.10. 1 Chr. 4.24.
p Gen. 46.11. Num. 3.17. 1 Chr. 6.1.
q Num. 26. 57. 1 Chr. 6.18.
r ch. 2.1,2. Num. 26.59.
s Num. 16.1. 1 Chr. 6.37, 38.
t Lev. 10.4. Num. 3.30.
u Ruth 4.19, 20. 1 Chr. 2.10. Matt. 1.4.
v Lev. 10.1. Num. 3.2. Num. 26.60. 1 Chr. 6.3. 1 Chr. 24.1.
w Num. 26. 11.
x Num. 25.7, 11,12. Josh. 24.33.
y ch. 7.4. ch. 12.17,51. Num. 33.1.
z ch. 32.7. ch. 33.1. Ps. 77.20.
a ch. 7.2.
b ch. 4.10. Jer. 1.6.

CHAP. 7

a ch. 4.16. Jer. 1.10.
b ch. 11.9.
c ch. 4.7.
d ch. 10.1. ch. 11.9.
e ch. 6.6.
f ch. 8.22. ch. 14.4,18. Ps. 9.16. Ps. 59.13. Ps. 83.18.
g ch. 3.20.
h Deut. 29.5. Deut. 31.2. Deut. 34.7. Acts 7.23, 30.
i Isa. 7.11. John 2.18. John 6.30.
j ch. 4.2,17.
k ch. 4.3.
l Gen. 41.8. Dan. 2.2.
m 2 Tim. 3.8.
n ver. 22. ch. 8.7,18. Job 12.16. Pro. 12.5. Isa. 19.13. Zeph. 1.8,9. 2 Cor. 11.13. 2 Thes. 2.9, 11. 2 Tim. 3.13. 2 Pet. 2.13. Rev. 12.9. Rev. 13.14.
o ch. 4.21.

14 ¶ And the LORD said unto Moses,
[p]Pharaoh's heart *is* hardened, he refuseth to let the people go.
15 Get thee unto Pharaoh in the
morning; lo, he goeth out unto the
water; and thou shalt stand by
the river's brink against he come;
and [q]the rod which was turned to
a serpent shalt thou take in thine
hand.
16 And thou shalt say unto him, The
LORD God of the Hebrews hath sent
me unto thee, saying, Let my people
go, [r]that they may serve me in the wilderness: and, behold, hitherto thou
wouldest not hear.
17 Thus saith the LORD, In this thou
[s]shalt know that I *am* the LORD: behold, I will smite with the rod that *is*
in mine hand upon the waters which
are in the river, and [t]they shall be
turned [u]to blood.
18 And the fish that *is* in the river
shall die, and the river shall stink; and
the Egyptians shall lothe [v]to drink of
the water of the river.
19 ¶ And the LORD spake unto
Moses, Say unto Aaron, Take thy
rod, and [w]stretch out thine hand upon
the waters of Egypt, upon their
streams, upon their rivers, and upon
their ponds, and upon all their [1]pools
of water, that they may become
blood; and *that* there may be blood
throughout all the land of Egypt, both
in *vessels of* wood, and in *vessels of*
stone.
20 And Moses and Aaron did so, as
the LORD commanded; and [x]he lifted
up the rod, and smote the waters that
were in the river, in the sight of Pharaoh, and in the sight of his servants;
and all the waters that [y]*were* in the
river were turned to blood.
21 And the fish that *was* in the river
died; and the river stank, and the
Egyptians could not drink of the
water of the river; and there was
blood throughout all the land of
Egypt.
22 And the magicians of Egypt did so
with their enchantments: and Pharaoh's heart was hardened, neither
did he hearken unto them; as the
LORD had said.
23 And Pharaoh turned and went into his house, neither [z]did he set his
heart to this also.
24 And all the Egyptians digged
round about the river for water to
drink; for they could not drink of the
water of the river.
25 And seven days were fulfilled,
after that the LORD had smitten the
river.

CHAPTER 8

AND the LORD spake unto Moses,
Go unto Pharaoh, and say unto
him, Thus saith the LORD, Let my
people go, [a]that they may serve me.
2 And if thou [b]refuse to let *them* go,
behold, I will smite all thy borders
with [c]frogs:
3 And the river shall bring forth frogs
abundantly, which shall go up and
come into thine house, and into [d]thy
bedchamber, and upon thy bed, and
into the house of thy servants, and
upon thy people, and into thine ovens,
and into thy [1]kneadingtroughs:
4 And the frogs shall come up both
on thee, and upon thy people, and upon all thy servants.
5 ¶ And the LORD spake unto Moses,
Say unto Aaron, [e]Stretch forth thine
hand with thy rod over the streams,
over the rivers, and over the ponds,
and cause frogs to come up upon the
land of Egypt.
6 And Aaron stretched out his hand
over the waters of Egypt; and [f]the
frogs came up, and covered the land
of Egypt.
7 And [g]the magicians did so with
their enchantments, and brought up
frogs upon the land of Egypt.
8 ¶ Then Pharaoh called for Moses
and Aaron, and said, [h]Intreat the
Lord, that he may take away the frogs
from me, and from my people; and I
will let the people go, that they may
do sacrifice unto the LORD.
9 And Moses said unto Pharaoh,
[2]Glory over me: [3]when shall I intreat
for thee, and for thy servants, and for
thy people, [4]to destroy the frogs from
thee and thy houses, *that* they may
remain in the river only?
10 And he said, [5]To morrow. And he
said, *Be it* according to thy word: that
thou mayest know that [i]*there is* none
like unto the LORD our God.
11 And the frogs shall depart from
thee, and from thy houses, and from
thy servants, and from thy people;
they shall remain in the river only.
12 And Moses and Aaron went out
from Pharaoh: and Moses cried [j]unto
the LORD because of the frogs which
he had brought against Pharaoh.
13 And the LORD did according to
the word of Moses; and the frogs died
out of the houses, out of the villages,
and out of the fields.
14 And they gathered them together
upon heaps: and the land stank.

p ch. 8.15. ch. 10.1,20, 27.
q ch. 4.2,3.
r ch. 3.12,18. ch. 5.1,3.
s Ps. 9.16. Eze. 20.48. Eze. 25.17. Eze. 34.30. Joel 3.17.
t ch. 4.9.
u Rev. 16.4, 6.
v ver. 24.
w ch. 8.5. ch. 9.22. ch. 10.12,21. ch. 14.21,26.
1 gathering of their waters.
x ch. 17.5.
y Ps. 78.44. Ps. 105.29.
z Pro. 29.1.

CHAP. 8
a ch. 3.12.
b ch. 7.14. ch. 9.2.
c Rev. 16.13.
d Ps. 105.30.
1 Or, dough.
e ch. 7.19.
f Ps. 78.45. Ps. 105.30.
g ch. 7.11.
h ch. 9.28. ch. 10.17. Num. 21.7. 1 Ki. 13.6. Acts 8.24.
2 Or, Have this honour over me, etc.
3 Or, against when.
4 to cut off.
5 Or, against to-morrow.
i ch. 9.14. Deut. 33.26. 2 Sam. 7.22. 1 Chr. 17.20. Ps. 86.8. Isa. 46.9. Jer. 10.6,7.
j ch. 9.33. ch. 10.18. ch. 32.11. Jas. 5.16, 17,18.

15 But when Pharaoh saw that there was [k]respite, [l]he hardened his heart, and hearkened not unto them; as the LORD had said.

16 ¶ And the LORD said unto Moses, Say unto Aaron, Stretch out thy rod, and smite the dust of the land, that it may become lice throughout all the land of Egypt.

17 And they did so; for Aaron stretched out his hand with his rod, and smote the dust of the earth, and [m]it became lice in man, and in beast; all the dust of the land became lice throughout all the land of Egypt.

18 And [n]the magicians did so with their enchantments to bring forth lice, but they [o]could not: so there were lice upon man, and upon beast.

19 Then the magicians said unto Pharaoh, This *is* [p]the finger of God: and Pharaoh's heart was hardened, and he hearkened not unto them; as the LORD had said.

20 ¶ And the LORD said unto Moses, [q]Rise up early in the morning, and stand before Pharaoh; lo, he cometh forth to the water; and say unto him, Thus saith the LORD, Let my people go, that they may serve me.

21 Else, if thou wilt not let my people go, behold, I will send [6]swarms *of flies* upon thee, and upon thy servants, and upon thy people, and into thy houses: and the houses of the Egyptians shall be full of swarms *of flies*, and also the ground whereon they *are*.

22 And [r]I will sever in that day the land of Gō´shĕn, in which my people dwell, that no swarms *of flies* shall be there; to the end thou mayest know that I *am* the LORD in the midst of the earth.

23 And I will put [7]a division between my people and thy people: to [8]morrow shall this sign be.

24 And the LORD did so; [s]and there came a grievous swarm *of flies* into the house of Pharaoh, and *into* his servants' houses, and into all the land of Egypt: the land was [9]corrupted by reason of the swarm *of flies*.

25 ¶ And Pharaoh called for Moses and for Aaron, and said, Go ye, sacrifice to your God in the land.

26 And Moses said, It is not meet so to do; for we shall sacrifice the abomination of the Egyptians to the LORD our God: lo, shall we sacrifice the abomination [t]of the Egyptians before their eyes, and will they not stone us?

27 We will go [u]three days' journey into the wilderness, and sacrifice to the LORD our God, as [v]he shall command us.

28 And Pharaoh said, I will let you go, that ye may sacrifice to the LORD your God in the wilderness; only ye shall not go very far away: intreat [w]for me.

29 And Moses said, Behold, I go out from thee, and I will intreat the LORD that the swarms *of flies* may depart from Pharaoh, from his servants, and from his people, to morrow: but let not Pharaoh deal deceitfully any more in not letting the people go to sacrifice to the LORD.

30 And Moses went out from Pharaoh, and intreated the LORD.

31 And [x]the LORD did according to the word of Moses; and he removed the swarms *of flies* from Pharaoh, from his servants, and from his people; there remained not one.

32 And Pharaoh [y]hardened his heart at this time also, neither would he let the people go.

CHAPTER 9

THEN the LORD said unto Moses, Go [a]in unto Pharaoh, and tell him, Thus saith the LORD God of the Hebrews, Let my people go, that they may serve me.

2 For if thou [b]refuse to let *them* go, and wilt hold them still,

3 Behold, the [c]hand of the LORD is upon thy cattle which *is* in the field, upon the horses, upon the asses, upon the camels, upon the oxen, and upon the sheep: *there shall be* a very grievous murrain.

4 And [d]the LORD shall sever between the cattle of Israel and the cattle of Egypt: and there shall nothing die of all *that is* the children's of Israel.

5 And the LORD appointed a set time, saying, To morrow the LORD shall do this thing in the land.

6 And the LORD did that thing on the morrow, and [e]all the cattle of Egypt died: but of the cattle of the children of Israel died not one.

7 And Pharaoh sent, and, behold, there was not one of the cattle of the Israelites dead. And [f]the heart of Pharaoh was hardened, and he did not let the people go.

8 ¶ And the LORD said unto Moses and unto Aaron, Take to you handfuls of ashes of the furnace, and let Moses sprinkle it toward the heaven in the sight of Pharaoh.

9 And it shall become small dust in all the land of Egypt, and shall be a

k Eccl. 8.11.
l Pro. 21.29.
m Ps. 105.31.
n ch. 7.11.
o Luke 10.18. 2 Tim. 3.8,9.
p 1 Sam. 6.3, 9. Job 27.11. Ps. 8.3. Matt. 12.28. Luke 11.20. Acts 13.11.
q ch. 7.15.
6 Or, a mixture of noisome beasts, etc.
r ch. 9.4,6,26.
7 a redemption.
8 Or, by to-morrow.
s Ps. 78.45.
9 Or, destroyed.
t Gen. 46.34. Deut. 7.25, 26. Deut. 12.31.
u ch. 3.18.
v ch. 3.12.
w ch. 9.28. 1 Ki. 13.6. Ezra 6.10. Acts 8.24.
x Jas. 5.17.
y ch. 4.21. Pro. 28.14. Rom. 9.17-23. Jas. 1.13-17.

CHAP. 9

a ch. 8.1. Jer. 22.1.
b ch. 8.2. Rom. 2.5.
c ch. 7.4. 1 Sam. 5.6. 1 Sam. 6.3,5. Job 27.11. Ps. 39.10. Luke 11.20. Acts 13.11.
d ch. 8.22.
e Ps. 78.50.
f ch. 8.32.

[g]boil breaking forth *with* blains upon man, and upon beast, throughout all the land of Egypt.

10 And they took ashes of the furnace, and stood before Pharaoh; and Moses sprinkled it up toward heaven; and it became [h]a boil breaking forth *with* blains upon man, and upon beast.

11 And the [i]magicians could not stand before Moses because of the boils; for the boil was upon the magicians, and upon all the Egyptians.

12 And [j]the LORD hardened the heart of Pharaoh, and he hearkened not unto them; as [k]the LORD had spoken unto Moses.

13 ¶ And the LORD said unto Moses, [l]Rise up early in the morning, and stand before Pharaoh, and say unto him, Thus saith the LORD God of the Hebrews, Let my people go, that they may serve me.

14 For I will at this time send all my plagues upon thine heart, and upon thy servants, and upon thy people; [m]that thou mayest know that *there is* none like me in all the earth.

15 For now I will [n]stretch out my hand, that I may smite thee and thy people with pestilence; and thou shalt be cut off from the earth.

16 And in very deed for [o]this *cause* have I [1]raised thee up, for to shew *in* thee my power; and that my name may be declared throughout all the earth.

17 As yet exaltest thou thyself against my people, that thou wilt not let them go?

18 Behold, to morrow about this time I will cause it to rain a very grievous hail, such as hath not been in Egypt since the foundation thereof even until now.

19 Send therefore now, *and* gather thy cattle, and all that thou hast in the field; *for upon* every man and beast which shall be found in the field, and shall not be brought home, the hail shall come down upon them, and they shall die.

20 He that feared the word of the LORD among the servants of Pharaoh made his servants and his cattle flee into the houses:

21 And he that [2]regarded not the word of the LORD left his servants and his cattle in the field.

22 ¶ And the LORD said unto Moses, Stretch forth thine hand toward heaven, that there may be [p]hail in all the land of Egypt, upon man, and upon beast, and upon every herb of the field, throughout the land of Egypt.

23 And Moses stretched forth his rod toward heaven: and [q]the LORD sent thunder and hail, and the fire ran along upon the ground; and the LORD rained hail upon the land of Egypt.

24 So there was hail, and fire mingled with the hail, very grievous, such as there was none like it in all the land of Egypt since it became a nation.

25 And the hail smote throughout all the land of Egypt all that *was* in the field, both man and beast; and the hail [r]smote every herb of the field, and brake every tree of the field.

26 Only [s]in the land of Gō-shĕn, where the children of Israel *were*, was there no hail.

27 ¶ And Pharaoh sent, and called for Moses and Aaron, and said unto them, [t]I have sinned this time: [u]the LORD *is* righteous, and I and my people *are* wicked.

28 Intreat [v]the LORD (for *it is* enough) that there be no *more* [3]mighty thunderings and hail; and I will let you go, and ye shall stay no longer.

29 And Moses said unto him, As soon as I am gone out of the city, I [w]will spread abroad my hands unto the LORD; *and* the thunder shall cease, neither shall there be any more hail; that thou mayest know how that the [x]earth *is* the LORD'S.

30 But as for thee and thy servants, [y]I know that ye will not yet fear the LORD God.

31 And the flax and the barley was smitten: [z]for the barley *was* in the ear, and the flax *was* bolled.

32 But the wheat and the rie were not smitten: for they *were* [4]not grown up.

33 And Moses went out of the city from Pharaoh, and [a]spread abroad his hands unto the LORD: and the thunders and hail ceased, and the rain was not poured upon the earth.

34 And when Pharaoh saw that the rain and the hail and the thunders were ceased, he sinned yet more, and hardened his heart, he and his servants.

35 And the heart of Pharaoh was hardened, neither would he let the children of Israel go; as the LORD had spoken [5]by Moses.

CHAPTER 10

AND the LORD said unto Moses, Go in unto Pharaoh: [a]for I have hardened his heart, and the heart of

g Rev. 16.2.
h Deut. 28. 27.
i 2 Tim. 3.9.
j ch. 4.21. ch. 7.14. ch. 8.32. ch. 10.1,20. ch. 14.8. Deut. 2.30. Josh. 11.20. Isa. 63.17. John 12.40. Rom. 9.18. Jas. 1.13-16.
k ch. 4.21.
l ch. 8.20.
m Deut. 3.24. Deut. 33.26. 2 Sam. 7.22. 1 Chr. 17.20. Ps. 71.19. Ps. 86.8. Isa. 45.5-25. Isa. 46.9. Jer. 10.6,7.
n ch. 3.20.
o Pro. 16.4. Rom. 9.17. 1 Pet. 2.9.
1 made thee stand.
2 set not his heart unto.
p Rev. 16.21.
q Josh. 10.11. Ps. 18.13. Ps. 78.47. Ps. 105.32. Ps. 148.8. Isa. 30.30. Eze. 38.22. Rev. 8.7.
r Ps. 105.33.
s vers. 4,6. ch. 11.7. Isa. 32.18, 19.
t ch. 10.16.
u 2 Chr. 12.6. Ps. 129.4. Ps. 145.17. Lam. 1.18. Dan. 9.14.
v ch. 8.8,28. ch. 10.17. Acts 8.24.
3 voices of God. Ps. 29.3,4.
w 1 Ki. 8.22, 38. Ps. 143.6. Isa. 1.15.
x Ps. 24.1. 1 Cor. 10.26.
y Isa. 26.10.
z Ruth 1.22. Ruth 2.23.
4 hidden, or, dark.
a ch. 8.12.
5 by the hand of Moses. ch. 4.13.

CHAP. 10

a ch. 7.14. Deut. 2.30. Josh. 11.20. John 12.40. Rom. 9.18.

his servants, that [b]I might shew these
my signs before him:
2 And that [c]thou mayest tell in the
ears of thy son, and of thy son's son,
what things I have wrought in Egypt,
and my signs which I have done
among them; that ye may know how
that I *am* the LORD.
3 And Moses and Aaron came in unto Pharaoh, and said unto him, Thus
saith the LORD God of the Hebrews,
How long wilt thou refuse to [d]humble
thyself before me? let my people go,
that they may serve me.
4 Else, if thou refuse to let my people
go, behold, to morrow will I bring the
[e]locusts into thy coast:
5 And they shall cover the [1]face of
the earth, that one cannot be able to
see the earth: and [f]they shall eat the
residue of that which is escaped,
which remaineth unto you from the
hail, and shall eat every tree which
groweth for you out of the field:
6 And they [g]shall fill thy houses, and
the houses of all thy servants, and the
houses of all the Egyptians; which
neither thy fathers, nor thy fathers'
fathers have seen, since the day that
they were upon the earth unto this
day. And he turned himself, and went
out from Pharaoh.
7 And Pharaoh's servants said unto
him, How long shall this man be a
[h]snare unto us? let the men go, that
they may serve the LORD their God:
knowest thou not yet that Egypt is
destroyed?
8 And Moses and Aaron were
brought again unto Pharaoh: and he
said unto them, Go, serve the LORD
your God: [2]*but* who *are* they that
shall go?
9 And Moses said, [i]We will go with
our young and with our old, with our
sons and with our daughters, with our
flocks and with our herds will we go;
for [j]we *must hold* a feast unto the
LORD.
10 And he said unto them, Let the
LORD be so with you, as I will let you
go, and your little ones: look *to it:* for
evil *is* before you.
11 Not so: go now ye *that are* men,
and serve the LORD; for that ye did
desire. And they were driven out from
Pharaoh's presence.
12 ¶ And the LORD said unto Moses,
[k]Stretch out thine hand over the land
of Egypt for the locusts, that they
may come up upon the land of Egypt,
and [l]eat every herb of the land, *even*
all that the hail hath left.

b ch. 7.4.
c Deut. 4.9. Ps. 44.1. Ps. 71.18. Joel 1.3.
d 1 Ki. 21.29. 2 Chr. 34.27. Jas. 4.10. 1 Pet. 5.6.
e Pro. 30.27. Rev. 9.3.
1 eye.
f Joel 2.25.
g ch. 8.3,21.
h ch. 23.33. Josh. 23.13. 1 Sam. 18. 21. Eccl. 7.26. 1 Cor. 7.35.
2 who, and who, etc.
i Pro. 3.9.
j ch. 5.1.
k ch. 7.19.
l vers. 4,5.
m Deut. 28. 38. Ps. 78.46. Ps. 105.34. Rev. 9.2.
n Joel 2.2.
o ver. 5.
p Ps. 105.35.
3 hastened to call.
q ch. 9.27.
r ch. 9.28. 1 Ki. 13.6. Job 34.31.
s ch. 8.30.
4 fastened.
t Joel 2.20.
u ch. 4.21. ch. 11.10. Deut. 2.30. Josh. 11.20. 2 Chr. 28.22. Rom. 2.4, 5. Rom. 9.17-22. Jas. 1.13-17.
v ch. 9.22.
5 that one may feel darkness.
w Ps. 105.28.
x ch. 8.22.
y ver. 10.
6 into our hands.

13 And Moses stretched forth his rod
over the land of Egypt, and the LORD
brought an east wind upon the land
all that day, and all *that* night; *and*
when it was morning, the east wind
brought the locusts.
14 And [m]the locusts went up over all
the land of Egypt, and rested in all the
coasts of Egypt: very grievous *were*
they; [n]before them there were no such
locusts as they, neither after them
shall be such.
15 For they [o]covered the face of the
whole earth, so that the land was
darkened; and they [p]did eat every
herb of the land, and all the fruit of
the trees which the hail had left: and
there remained not any green thing
in the trees, or in the herbs of the field,
through all the land of Egypt.
16 ¶ Then Pharaoh [3]called for Moses
and Aaron in haste; and he said, [q]I
have sinned against the LORD your
God, and against you.
17 Now therefore forgive, I pray
thee, my sin only this once, [r]and intreat the LORD your God, that he may
take away from me this death only.
18 And he [s]went out from Pharaoh,
and intreated the LORD.
19 And the LORD turned a mighty
strong west wind, which took away
the locusts, and [4]cast them into [t]the
Red sea; there remained not one
locust in all the coasts of Egypt.
20 But the LORD [u]hardened Pharaoh's heart, so that he would not let
the children of Israel go.
21 ¶ And the LORD said unto Moses,
[v]Stretch out thine hand toward heav-
en, that there may be darkness over
the land of Egypt, [5]even darkness
which may be felt.
22 And Moses stretched forth his
hand toward heaven; and there was a
[w]thick darkness in all the land of
Egypt three days:
23 They saw not one another, neither
rose any from his place for three days:
[x]but all the children of Israel had
light in their dwellings.
24 ¶ And Pharaoh called unto Moses,
and said, Go ye, serve the LORD; only
let your flocks and your herds be stayed: let your little ones [y]also go with
you.
25 And Moses said, Thou must give
[6]us also sacrifices and burnt offerings,
that we may sacrifice unto the LORD
our God.
26 Our cattle also shall go with us;
there shall not an hoof be left behind;
for thereof must we take to serve the

LORD our God; and we know not with what we must serve the LORD, until we come thither.

27 ¶ But the LORD [z]hardened Pharaoh's heart, and he would not let them go.

28 And Pharaoh said unto him, Get thee from me, take heed to thyself, see my face no more; for in *that* day thou seest my face thou shalt die.

29 And Moses said, Thou hast spoken well, [a]I will see thy face again no more.

CHAPTER 11

AND the LORD said unto Moses, Yet will I bring one plague *more* upon Pharaoh, and upon Egypt; afterwards he will let you go hence: [a]when he shall let *you* go, he shall surely thrust you out hence altogether.

2 Speak now in the ears of the people, and let every man [1]borrow of his neighbour, and every woman of her neighbour, [b]jewels of silver, and jewels of gold.

3 And [c]the LORD gave the people favour in the sight of the Egyptians. Moreover the man [d]Moses *was* very great in the land of Egypt, in the sight of Pharaoh's servants, and in the sight of the people.

4 And Moses said, Thus saith the LORD, [e]About midnight will I go out into the midst of Egypt:

5 And [f]all the firstborn in the land of Egypt shall die, from the firstborn of Pharaoh that sitteth upon his throne, even unto the firstborn of the maidservant that *is* behind the mill; and all the firstborn of beasts.

6 And [g]there shall be a great cry throughout all the land of Egypt, such as there was none like it, nor shall be like it any more.

7 But against any of the children of Israel shall [h]not a dog move his tongue, against man or beast: that ye may know how that the LORD doth put [i]a difference between the Egyptians and Israel.

8 And all these thy servants shall come down unto me, and bow down themselves unto me, saying, Get thee out, and all the people [2]that follow thee: and after that I will go out. And he went out from Pharaoh in [3]a great anger.

9 And the LORD said unto Moses, Pharaoh shall not hearken unto you; that my wonders may be multiplied in the land of Egypt.

10 And Moses and Aaron did all these wonders before Pharaoh: and [j]the LORD hardened Pharaoh's heart, so that he would not let the children of Israel go out of his land.

z ver. 20. ch. 4.21. ch. 14.4,8.
a Heb. 11.27.

CHAP. 11

a ch. 12.31.
1 Or, demand.
b ch. 3.22. ch. 12.35.
c ch. 3.21. ch. 12.36. Ps. 106.46.
d 2 Sam. 7.9. Esther 9.4.
e ch. 12.12,23, 29. Amos 5.17.
f Amos 4.10.
g Amos 5.17.
h Josh. 10.21. Job 5.23. Hos. 2.18.
i Mal. 3.18.
2 that is at thy feet. Judg. 4.10. Judg. 8.5. 1 Ki. 20.10. 2 Ki. 3.9.
3 heat of anger.
j ch. 7.3,13. ch. 9.12,35. ch. 10.20,27. Deut. 2.30. Josh. 11.20. Isa. 63.17. John 12.40. Rom. 2.5. Rom. 9.22.

CHAP. 12

a ch. 13.4. Deut. 16.1.
1 Or, kid.
b Lev. 22.19. Mal. 1.8,14. Heb. 9.14. 1 Pet. 1.19.
2 son of a year. Lev. 23.12.
c Lev. 23.15. Num. 9.3. Num. 28.16. Deut. 16.1, 6.
3 between the two evenings. ch. 16.12.
d Num. 9.11. 1 Cor. 5.8.
e ch. 23.18.
f Deut. 16.5.
g ch. 11.4,5. Amos 5.17.
h Num. 33.4.
4 Or, princes. ch. 22.28. Ps. 82.1,6. John 10.34.
i Heb. 11.28.

CHAPTER 12

AND the LORD spake unto Moses and Aaron in the land of Egypt, saying,

2 This [a]month *shall be* unto you the beginning of months: it *shall be* the first month of the year to you.

3 ¶ Speak ye unto all the congregation of Israel, saying, In the tenth *day* of this month they shall take to them every man a [1]lamb, according to the house of *their* fathers, a lamb for an house:

4 And if the household be too little for the lamb, let him and his neighbour next unto his house take *it* according to the number of the souls; every man according to his eating shall make your count for the lamb.

5 Your lamb shall be [b]without blemish, a male [2]of the first year: ye shall take *it* out from the sheep, or from the goats:

6 And ye shall keep it up until the [c]fourteenth day of the same month: and the whole assembly of the congregation of Israel shall kill it [3]in the evening.

7 And they shall take of the blood, and strike *it* on the two side posts and on the upper door post of the houses, wherein they shall eat it.

8 And they shall eat the flesh in that night, roast with fire, [d]and unleavened bread; *and* with bitter *herbs* they shall eat it.

9 Eat not of it raw, nor sodden at all with water, but roast *with* fire; his head with his legs, and with the purtenance thereof.

10 And [e]ye shall let nothing of it remain until the morning; and that which remaineth of it until the morning ye shall burn with fire.

11 ¶ And thus shall ye eat it; *with* your loins girded, your shoes on your feet, and your staff in your hand; and ye shall eat it in haste: it [f]*is* the LORD's passover.

12 For I [g]will pass through the land of Egypt this night, and will smite all the firstborn in the land of Egypt, both man and beast; and [h]against all the [4]gods of Egypt I will execute judgment: I *am* the LORD.

13 And [i]the blood shall be to you for a token upon the houses where ye *are*: and when I see the blood, I will pass over you, and the plague shall not

be upon you [5]to destroy *you*, when I
smite the land of Egypt.
14 And this day shall be unto you for
a memorial; and ye shall keep it a
[j]feast to the LORD throughout your
generations; ye shall keep it a feast by
an ordinance for ever.
15 Seven [k]days shall ye eat unleavened bread; even the first day ye shall
put away leaven out of your houses:
for whosoever eateth leavened bread
from the first day until the seventh
day, that [l]soul shall be cut off from
Israel.
16 And in the first day *there shall be*
an holy convocation, and in the seventh day there shall be an holy convocation to you; no manner of work
shall be done in them, save *that* which
every [6]man must eat, that only may
be done of you.
17 And ye shall observe *the feast of*
unleavened bread; for [m]in this selfsame day have I brought your armies
out of the land of Egypt: therefore
shall ye observe this day in your generations by an ordinance for ever.
18 ¶ In [n]the first *month*, on the fourteenth day of the month at even, ye
shall eat unleavened bread, until the
one and twentieth day of the month
at even.
19 Seven [o]days shall there be no
leaven found in your houses: for whosoever eateth that which is leavened,
[p]even that soul shall be cut off from
the congregation of Israel, whether
he be a stranger, or born in the land.
20 Ye shall eat nothing leavened; in
all your habitations shall ye eat unleavened bread.
21 ¶ Then Moses called for all the
elders of Israel, and said unto them,
[q]Draw out and take you a [7]lamb according to your families, and kill the
passover.
22 And ye shall take a bunch of hyssop, and dip *it* in the blood that *is* in
the bason, and strike the lintel and
the two side posts with the blood that
is in the bason; and none of you shall
go out at the door of his house until
the morning.
23 For the LORD will pass through to
smite the Egyptians; and when he
seeth the blood upon the lintel, and on
the two side posts, the LORD will pass
over the door, and will [r]not suffer [s]the
destroyer to come in unto your houses
to smite *you*.
24 And ye shall observe this thing
for an ordinance to thee and to thy
sons for ever.

5 for a destruction.
j Lev. 23.4,5. 2 Ki. 23.21.
k Num. 28. 17. Deut. 16.3, 8. 1 Cor. 5.7.
l Gen. 17.14. Num. 9.13.
6 soul.
m ch. 13.3.
n Lev. 23.5.
o ch. 23.15. ch. 34.18.
p Num. 9.13.
q Num. 9.4. Josh. 5.10. Ezra 6.20. Luke 22.7.
7 Or, kid.
r Eze. 9.6. Rev. 7.3. Rev. 9.4.
s 2 Sam. 24. 16. 1 Cor. 10.10. Heb. 11.28.
t ch. 13.8,14. Deut. 32.7. Josh. 4.6. Ps. 78.6.
u Num. 8.17. Num. 33.4. Ps. 78.51. Ps. 105.36. Ps. 135.8. Ps. 136.10. Isa. 37.36.
8 house of the pit.
v ch. 11.6. Pro. 21.13. Eze. 7.27. Jas. 2.13.
w ch. 10.9.
x Gen. 27.34.
y ch. 11.8. Ps. 105.38.
z Gen. 20.3.
9 Or, dough. ch. 8.3.
10 Or, demanded.
a ch. 3.22. ch. 11.2.
b Gen. 15.14. ch. 3.22.
c Num. 33.3, 5.
d Gen. 47.11.
e Gen. 12.2. Gen. 46.3. ch. 38.26. Num. 1.46. Num. 11.21.
11 a great mixture. Num. 11.4.

25 And it shall come to pass, when
ye be come to the land which the
LORD will give you, according as he
hath promised, that ye shall keep this
service.
26 And [t]it shall come to pass, when
your children shall say unto you,
What mean ye by this service?
27 That ye shall say, It *is* the sacrifice
of the LORD's passover, who passed
over the houses of the children of
Israel in Egypt, when he smote the
Egyptians, and delivered our houses.
And the people bowed the head and
worshipped.
28 And the children of Israel went
away, and did as the LORD had commanded Moses and Aaron, so did
they.
29 ¶ And it came to pass, that at midnight the [u]LORD smote all the firstborn in the land of Egypt, from the
firstborn of Pharaoh that sat on his
throne unto the firstborn of the captive that *was* in the [8]dungeon; and all
the firstborn of cattle.
30 And Pharaoh rose up in the night,
he, and all his servants, and all the
Egyptians; and there was a great [v]cry
in Egypt; for *there was* not a house
where *there was* not one dead.
31 ¶ And he called for Moses and
Aaron by night, and said, Rise up,
and get you forth from among my
people, [w]both ye and the children of
Israel; and go, serve the LORD, as ye
have said.
32 Also take your flocks and your
herds, as ye have said, and be gone;
and [x]bless me also.
33 And [y]the Egyptians were urgent
upon the people, that they might send
them out of the land in haste; for they
said, [z]We *be* all dead *men*.
34 And the people took their dough
before it was leavened, their [9]knead-
ingtroughs being bound up in their
clothes upon their shoulders.
35 And the children of Israel did
according to the word of Moses; and
they [10]borrowed of the Egyptians
[a]jewels of silver, and jewels of gold,
and raiment:
36 And the LORD gave the people
favour in the sight of the Egyptians,
so that they lent unto them *such
things as they required*. [b]And they
spoiled the Egyptians.
37 ¶ And [c]the children of Israel
journeyed from [d]Răm-ĕ-sēs to Sŭc-
cōth, about [e]six hundred thousand on
foot *that were* men, beside children.
38 And [11]a mixed multitude went up

also with them; and flocks, and herds,
even very much cattle.
39 And they baked unleavened cakes
of the dough which they brought
forth out of Egypt, for it was not
leavened; because they were [f]thrust
out of Egypt, and could not tarry,
neither had they prepared for themselves any victual.
40 ¶ Now the sojourning of the children of Israel, who dwelt in Egypt,
was [g]four hundred and thirty years.
41 And it came to pass at the end of
the four hundred and thirty years,
even the selfsame day it came to pass,
that all [h]the hosts of the LORD went
out from the land of Egypt.
42 It *is* [12]a night to be much observed
unto the LORD for bringing them
out from the land of Egypt: this *is* that
night of the LORD to be observed of
all the children of Israel in their generations.
43 ¶ And the LORD said unto Moses
and Aaron, This *is* [i]the ordinance of
the passover: There shall no stranger
eat thereof:
44 But every man's servant that is
bought for money, when thou hast
[j]circumcised him, then shall he eat
thereof.
45 A [k]foreigner and an hired servant
shall not eat thereof.
46 In one house shall it be eaten;
thou shalt not carry forth ought of the
flesh abroad out of the house; neither
[l]shall ye break a bone thereof.
47 All the congregation of Israel
shall [13]keep it.
48 And when a stranger shall sojourn with thee, and will keep the
passover to the LORD, let all his males
be circumcised, and then let him come
near and keep it; and he shall be as
one that is born in the land: for no uncircumcised person shall eat thereof.
49 One [m]law shall be to him that is
homeborn, and unto the stranger that
sojourneth among you.
50 Thus did all the children of Israel;
as the LORD commanded Moses and
Aaron, so did they.
51 And it came to pass the selfsame
day, *that* the LORD did bring the children of Israel out of the land of Egypt
by [n]their armies.

CHAPTER 13

AND the LORD spake unto Moses,
saying,
2 Sanctify [a]unto me all the firstborn,
whatsoever openeth the womb among
the children of Israel, *both* of man and
of beast: it *is* mine.
3 ¶ And Moses said unto the people,
[b]Remember this day, in which ye
came out from Egypt, out of the
house of [1]bondage; for by [c]strength
of hand the LORD brought you out
from this *place:* there shall no leavened bread be eaten.
4 This [d]day came ye out in the month
Abib.
5 ¶ And it shall be when the LORD
shall bring thee into the land of the
Canaanites, and the Hittites, and the
Amorites, and the Hi'-vites, and the
Jĕb-ū-sites, which he sware unto thy
fathers to give thee, a land flowing
with milk and honey, that thou shalt
keep this service in this month.
6 Seven [e]days thou shalt eat unleavened bread, and in the seventh day
shall be a feast to the LORD.
7 Unleavened bread shall be eaten
seven days; and there shall no leavened bread be seen with thee, neither
shall there be leaven seen with thee in
all thy quarters.
8 ¶ And thou shalt [f]shew thy son in
that day, saying, *This is done* because
of that *which* the LORD did unto me
when I came forth out of Egypt.
9 And it shall be for a [g]sign unto thee
upon thine hand, and for a memorial
between thine eyes, that the LORD's
law may be in thy mouth: for with a
strong hand hath the LORD brought
thee out of Egypt.
10 Thou shalt therefore keep this
ordinance in his season from year to
year.
11 ¶ And it shall be when the LORD
shall bring thee into the land of the
Canaanites, as he [h]sware unto thee
and to thy fathers, and shall give it
thee,
12 That [i]thou shalt [2]set apart unto
the LORD all that openeth the matrix,
and every firstling that cometh of a
beast which thou hast; the males *shall
be* the LORD's.
13 And every firstling of an ass thou
shalt redeem with a [3]lamb; and if thou
wilt not redeem it, then thou shalt
break his neck: and all the firstborn
of man among thy children [j]shalt thou
redeem.
14 ¶ And [k]it shall be when thy son
asketh thee [4]in time to come, saying,
What *is* this? that thou shalt say unto
him, By strength of hand the LORD
brought us out from Egypt, from the
house of bondage:
15 And it came to pass, when Phar-

f ch. 6.1. ch. 11.1.
g Gen. 15.13. Acts 7.6. Gal. 3.17.
h ch. 7.4.
12 a night of observations.
i Num. 9.14.
j Gen. 17.12, 13.
k Lev. 22.10.
l Ps. 34.20. John 19.33.
13 do it.
m Num. 9.14. Num. 15.15. Gal. 3.28.
n Acts 7.36.
CHAP. 13
a ch. 22.29, 30. Lev. 27.26. Num. 3.13. Num. 8.16, 17. Num. 18.15. Deut. 15.19. Luke 2.23.
b ch. 12.42. Deut. 16.3.
1 servants.
c ch. 6.1.
d ch. 23.15. ch. 34.18. Deut. 16.1.
e ch. 12.15, 16.
f Ps. 44.1.
g ch. 12.14. Num. 15.39. Deut. 6.8. Deut. 11.18. Pro. 1.9. Isa. 49.16. Jer. 22.24. Matt. 23.5.
h Gen. 15.18. Gen. 17.8. Gen. 28.15. Ps. 105.42-45.
i ch. 22.29. ch. 34.19. Lev. 27.26. Num. 18.15. Eze. 44.30.
2 cause to pass over.
3 Or, kid.
j Num. 3.46.
k ch. 12.26. Deut. 6.20. Josh. 4.6, 21.
4 to morrow.

aoh would hardly let us go, that the
LORD slew all the firstborn in the land
of Egypt, both the firstborn of man,
and the firstborn of beast: therefore
I sacrifice to the LORD all that openeth the matrix, being males; but all
the firstborn of my children I redeem.
16 And it shall be for [l]a token upon
thine hand, and for frontlets between
thine eyes: for by strength of hand the
LORD brought us forth out of Egypt.
17 ¶ And it came to pass, when Pharaoh had let the people go, that God
led them not *through* the way of the
land of the Philistines, although that
was near; for God said, Lest peradventure the people repent [m]when they
see war, and they [n]return to Egypt:
18 But [o]God led the people about,
through the way of the wilderness of
the Red sea: and the children of Israel
went up [5]harnessed out of the land of
Egypt.
19 And Moses took the bones of
Joseph with him: for he had straitly
sworn the children of Israel, saying,
[p]God will surely visit you; and ye
shall carry up my bones away hence
with you.
20 ¶ And they took their journey
from Sŭc-cōth, and encamped in Ē-
thăm, [q]in the edge of the wilderness.
21 And [r]the LORD went before them
by day in a pillar of a cloud, to lead
them the way; and by night in a pillar
of fire, to give them light; to go by day
and night:
22 He [s]took not away the pillar of
the cloud by day, nor the pillar of
fire by night, *from* before the people.

CHAPTER 14

AND the LORD spake unto Moses,
saying,
2 Speak unto the children of Israel,
that they turn and encamp before [a]Pī-
hă-hī-rōth, between [b]Mĭg-dŏl and the
sea, over against Bā-ăl-zē-phŏn: before it shall ye encamp by the sea.
3 For Pharaoh will say of the children of Israel, [c]They *are* entangled in
the land, the wilderness hath shut
them in.
4 And [d]I will harden Pharaoh's
heart, that he shall follow after them;
and I [e]will be honoured upon Pharaoh, and upon all his host; that the
Egyptians may know that I *am* the
LORD. And they did so.
5 ¶ And it was told the king of Egypt
that the people fled: and the heart of
Pharaoh and of his servants was turned against the people, and they said,
Why have we done this, that we have
let Israel go from serving us?
6 And he made ready his chariot, and
took his people with him:
7 And he took six hundred chosen
chariots, and all the chariots of Egypt,
and captains over every one of them.
8 And the LORD hardened the heart
of Pharaoh king of Egypt, and he pursued after the children of Israel: and
the [f]children of Israel went out with
an high hand.
9 But the [g]Egyptians pursued after
them, all the horses *and* chariots of
Pharaoh, and his horsemen, and his
army, and overtook them encamping
by the sea, beside Pī-hă-hī-rōth, before Bā-ăl-zē-phŏn.
10 ¶ And when Pharaoh drew nigh,
the children of Israel lifted up their
eyes, and, behold, the Egyptians
marched after them; and they were
sore afraid: and the children of Israel
[h]cried out unto the LORD.
11 And [i]they said unto Moses, Because *there were* no graves in Egypt,
hast thou taken us away to die in the
wilderness? wherefore hast thou dealt
thus with us, to carry us forth out of
Egypt?
12 *Is* [j]not this the word that we did
tell thee in Egypt, saying, Let us alone,
that we may serve the Egyptians?
For *it had been* better for us to serve
the Egyptians, than that we should
die in the wilderness.
13 ¶ And Moses said unto the people,
Fear [k]ye not, stand still, and see the
salvation of the LORD, which he will
shew to you to day: [1]for the Egyptians
whom ye have seen to day, ye shall see
them again no more for ever.
14 The [l]LORD shall fight for you, and
ye shall [m]hold your peace.
15 ¶ And the LORD said unto Moses,
Wherefore criest thou unto me?
speak unto the children of Israel, that
they go forward:
16 But [n]lift thou up thy rod, and
stretch out thine hand over the sea,
and divide it: and the children of
Israel shall go on dry *ground* through
the midst of the sea.
17 And I, behold, I will [o]harden the
hearts of the Egyptians, and they shall
follow them: and I will get me honour
upon Pharaoh, and upon all his host,
upon his chariots, and upon his
horsemen.
18 And the Egyptians shall know that
I *am* the LORD, when I have gotten
me honour upon Pharaoh, upon his
chariots, and upon his horsemen.

l Deut. 6.8.
m ch. 14.11. Num. 14.1.
n Deut. 17. 16.
o ch. 14.2. Num. 33.6.
5 Or, by five in a rank.
p Gen. 50.25. Josh. 24.32. Acts 7.16.
q Num. 33.6.
r Deut. 1.33. Neh. 9.12, 19. Ps. 78.14. Isa. 4.5. 1 Cor. 10.1.
s Ps. 121.5-8.

CHAP. 14
a Num. 33.7.
b Jer. 44.1.
c Ps. 35.21. Ps. 71.11.
d Jas. 1.13-17.
e ch. 9.16. Rom. 9.17-23.
f ch. 6.1. ch. 13.9. Num. 33.3.
g ch. 15.9. Josh. 24.6.
h Josh. 24.7. Neh. 9.9. Ps. 34.17. Ps. 107.6.
i Ps. 106.7.
j ch. 6.9.
k 2 Chr. 20. 15,17. Isa. 41.10, 13,14.
1 Or, for whereas ye have seen the Egyptians to-day, etc.
l Deut. 20.4. Josh. 10.14, 42. Josh. 23.3. 2 Chr. 20.29. Neh. 4.20. Isa. 31.4.
m Isa. 30.15.
n ch. 7.19.
o Pro. 29.1.

19 ¶ And [p]the angel of God, which went before the camp of Israel, removed and went behind them; and the pillar of the cloud went from before their face, and stood behind them:

20 And it came between the camp of the Egyptians and the camp of Israel; and [q]it was a cloud and darkness *to them,* but it gave light by night *to these:* so that the one came not near the other all the night.

21 And Moses stretched out his hand over the sea; and the LORD caused the sea to go *back* by a strong east wind all that night, and made the sea dry *land,* and the waters were [r]divided.

22 And [s]the children of Israel went into the midst of the sea upon the dry *ground:* and the waters *were* [t]a wall unto them on their right hand, and on their left.

23 ¶ And the Egyptians pursued, and went in after them to the midst of the sea, *even* all Pharaoh's horses, his chariots, and his horsemen.

24 And it came to pass, that in the morning watch the LORD looked unto the host of the Egyptians through the pillar of fire and of the cloud, and troubled the host of the Egyptians,

25 And took off their chariot wheels, [2]that they drave them heavily: so that the Egyptians said, Let us flee from the face of Israel; for the LORD fighteth for them against the Egyptians.

26 ¶ And the LORD said unto Moses, Stretch out thine hand over the sea, that the waters may come again upon the Egyptians, upon their chariots, and upon their horsemen.

27 And Moses stretched forth his hand over the sea, and the sea returned [u]to his strength when the morning appeared; and the Egyptians fled against it; and the LORD [3]overthrew the Egyptians in the midst of the sea.

28 And [v]the waters returned, and covered the chariots, and the horsemen, *and* all the host of Pharaoh that came into the sea after them; there remained not so much as one of them.

29 But [w]the children of Israel walked upon dry *land* in the midst of the sea; and the waters *were* a wall unto them on their right hand, and on their left.

30 Thus the LORD [x]saved Israel that day out of the hand of the Egyptians; and Israel saw [y]the Egyptians dead upon the sea shore.

31 And Israel saw that great [4]work which the LORD did upon the Egyptians: and the people feared the LORD, and [z]believed the LORD, and his servant Moses.

p Gen. 48.16.
q Isa. 8.14. 2 Cor. 4.3.
r Josh. 3.16. Josh. 4.23. Neh. 9.11. Ps. 74.13. Ps. 106.9. Ps. 114.3.
s ch. 15.19. Num. 33.8. Ps. 66.6. Ps. 78.13. 1 Cor. 10.1. Heb. 11.29.
t Hab. 3.10.
2 Or, and made them to go heavily.
u Josh. 4.18.
3 shook off. Deut. 11.4. Neh. 9.11. Ps. 78.53.
v Hab. 3.8.
w Ps. 77.20. Ps. 78.52,53.
x Ps. 106.8, 10.
y Ps. 58.10. Ps. 59.10.
4 hand.
z ch. 19.9. John 2.11. John 11.45.

CHAP. 15
a Judg. 5.1. 2 Sam. 22.1.
b Isa. 12.2.
c 2 Sam. 22. 47. Ps. 99.5.
d Rev. 19.11.
e Ps. 83.18.
f Ps. 118.15.
g Deut. 4.24. Ps. 59.13. Heb. 12.29.
h Isa. 5.24.
i Job 4.9.
j Hab. 3.10.
k Isa. 53.12. Luke 11.22.
1 Or, repossess.
l 2 Sam. 7.22. 1 Ki. 8.23. Ps. 86.8. Jer. 49.19.
2 Or, mighty ones.
m Ps. 78.54.
n Josh. 2.9.
o Ps. 48.6.
p Hab. 3.7.

CHAPTER 15

THEN sang [a]Moses and the children of Israel this song unto the LORD, and spake, saying, I will sing unto the LORD, for he hath triumphed gloriously: the horse and his rider hath he thrown into the sea.

2 The LORD *is* my strength [b]and song, and he is become my salvation: he *is* my God, and I will prepare him an habitation; my father's God, and I [c]will exalt him.

3 The LORD *is* a man of [d]war: the LORD *is* [e]his name.

4 Pharaoh's chariots and his host hath he cast into the sea: his chosen captains also are drowned in the Red sea.

5 The depths have covered them: they sank into the bottom as a stone.

6 Thy [f]right hand, O LORD, is become glorious in power: thy right hand, O LORD, hath dashed in pieces the enemy.

7 And in the greatness of thine excellency thou hast overthrown them that rose up against thee: thou sentest forth thy wrath, *which* consumed [g]them [h]as stubble.

8 And [i]with the blast of thy nostrils the waters were gathered together, [j]the floods stood upright as an heap, *and* the depths were congealed in the heart of the sea.

9 The enemy said, I will pursue, I will overtake, I will [k]divide the spoil; my lust shall be satisfied upon them; I will draw my sword, my hand shall [1]destroy them.

10 Thou didst blow with thy wind, the sea covered them: they sank as lead in the mighty waters.

11 Who [l]*is* like unto thee, O LORD, among the [2]gods? who *is* like thee, glorious in holiness, fearful *in* praises, doing wonders?

12 Thou stretchedst out thy right hand, the earth swallowed them.

13 Thou in thy mercy hast led forth the people *which* thou hast redeemed: thou hast guided *them* in thy strength unto [m]thy holy habitation.

14 The [n]people shall hear, *and* be afraid: sorrow [o]shall take hold on the inhabitants of Palestina.

15 Then the dukes of Ē-dọm shall be amazed; [p]the mighty men of Moab, trembling shall take hold upon them; all the inhabitants of Canaan shall melt away.

16 Fear [q]and dread shall fall upon
them; by the greatness of thine arm
they shall be *as* still [r]as a stone; till
thy people pass over, O LORD, till the
people pass over, *which* [s]thou hast
purchased.
17 Thou shalt bring them in, and
plant [t]them in the mountain of thine
inheritance, *in* the place, O LORD,
which thou hast made for thee to
dwell in, *in* the Sanctuary, O Lord,
which thy hands have established.
18 The LORD shall reign for ever and
ever.
19 For the horse of Pharaoh went in
with his chariots and with his horsemen into the sea, and the LORD
brought again the waters of the sea
upon them; but the children of Israel
went on dry *land* in the midst of the
sea.
20 ¶ And Miriam the prophetess, the
sister of Aaron, [u]took a timbrel in her
hand; and all the women went out
after her with timbrels and with
dances.
21 And Miriam answered them, Sing
ye to the LORD, for he hath triumphed
gloriously; the horse and his rider
hath he thrown into the sea.
22 So Moses brought Israel from the
Red sea, and they went out into the
wilderness of Shur; and they went
three days in the wilderness, and
found no water.
23 ¶ And when they came [v]to Mâr-
ăh, they could not drink of the waters
of Mâr-ăh, for they *were* bitter:
therefore the name of it was called
[3]Mâr-ăh.
24 And the people murmured against
Moses, saying, What shall we drink?
25 And he [w]cried unto the LORD;
and the LORD shewed him a tree,
which [x]when he had cast into the
waters, the waters were made sweet:
there he [y]made for them a statute and
an ordinance, and there [z]he proved
them,
26 And said, [a]If thou wilt diligently
hearken to the voice of the LORD thy
God, and wilt do that which is right
in his sight, and wilt give ear to his
commandments, and keep all his
statutes, I will put none of these
[b]diseases upon thee, which I have
brought upon the Egyptians: for I *am*
the LORD [c]that healeth thee.
27 ¶ And [d]they came to Ē-lĭm,
where *were* twelve wells of water,
and threescore and ten palm trees:
and they encamped there by the
waters.

q Deut. 2.25.
r 1 Sam. 25. 37.
s Deut. 32.9. Isa. 43.1. Jer. 31.11. Titus 2.14. 1 Pet. 2.9. 2 Pet. 2.1.
t Ps. 44.2.
u Judg. 11.34. Judg. 21.21. 1 Sam. 18.6. 2 Sam. 6.16. 1 Chr. 15.16. Ps. 68.25. Ps. 81.2. Ps. 149.3. Jer. 31.4.
v Num. 33.8.
3 That is, Bitterness. Ruth 1.20.
w ch. 14.10. ch. 17.4. Ps. 50.15.
x 2 Ki. 2.21. 2 Ki. 4.41.
y Josh. 24.25.
z ch. 16.4. Deut. 8.2, 16. Judg. 2.22. Judg. 3.1,4. Ps. 66.10. Ps. 81.7.
a Deut. 7.12.
b Deut. 28. 27.
c ch. 23.25. Ps. 41.3,4. Ps. 103.3. Ps. 147.3.
d Num. 33.9.

CHAP. 16

a Eze. 30.15.
b ch. 15.24. Ps. 106.25. 1 Cor. 10.10.
c Num. 11.4.
d Ps. 78.24, 25. Ps. 105.40. John 6.31. 1 Cor. 10.3.
1 the portion of a day in his day. Pro. 30.8. Matt. 6.11.
e ch. 15.25. Deut. 8.2, 16.
f Lev. 25.21.
g ch. 6.7. Num. 16.28.
h Isa. 35.2. Isa. 40.5. John 11.4, 40.
i 1 Sam. 8.7. Luke 10.16. Rom. 13.2. 1 Thes. 4.8.
j 1 Ki. 8.10.
k Num. 14. 27.
l ver. 6.

CHAPTER 16

AND they took their journey from
Ē-lĭm, and all the congregation of
the children of Israel came unto the
wilderness of [a]Sin, which *is* between
Ē-lĭm and Sī-nâi, on the fifteenth day
of the second month after their departing out of the land of Egypt.
2 And the whole congregation of the
children of Israel [b]murmured against
Moses and Aaron in the wilderness:
3 And the children of Israel said unto them, Would to God we had died
by the hand of the LORD in the land of
Egypt, when [c]we sat by the flesh pots,
and when we did eat bread to the full;
for ye have brought us forth into this
wilderness, to kill this whole assembly
with hunger.
4 ¶ Then said the LORD unto Moses,
Behold, I will rain [d]bread from heaven
for you; and the people shall go out
and gather [1]a certain rate every day,
that I [e]may prove them, whether they
will walk in my law, or no.
5 And it shall come to pass, that on
the sixth day they shall prepare *that*
which they bring in; and [f]it shall be
twice as much as they gather daily.
6 And Moses and Aaron said unto
all the children of Israel, [g]At even,
then ye shall know that the LORD hath
brought you out from the land of
Egypt:
7 And in the morning, then ye shall
see the [h]glory of the LORD; for that he
heareth your murmurings against the
LORD: and what *are* we, that ye murmur against us?
8 And Moses said, *This shall be*,
when the LORD shall give you in the
evening flesh to eat, and in the morning bread to the full; for that the LORD
heareth your murmurings which ye
murmur against him: and what *are*
we? your murmurings *are* not against
us, but [i]against the LORD.
9 ¶ And Moses spake unto Aaron,
Say unto all the congregation of the
children of Israel, Come near before
the LORD: for he hath heard your
murmurings.
10 And it came to pass, as Aaron
spake unto the whole congregation of
the children of Israel, that they looked
toward the wilderness, and, behold,
the glory of the LORD appeared [j]in the
cloud.
11 ¶ And the LORD spake unto
Moses, saying,
12 I [k]have heard the murmurings of
the children of Israel: speak unto
them, saying, [l]At even ye shall eat

flesh, and [m]in the morning ye shall be
filled with bread; and [n]ye shall know
that I *am* the LORD your God.
13 And it came to pass, that at even
[o]the quails came up, and covered the
camp: and in the morning [p]the dew
lay round about the host.
14 And when the dew that lay was
gone up, behold, upon the face of the
wilderness *there lay* [q]a small round
thing, *as* small as the hoar frost on the
ground.
15 And when the children of Israel
saw *it*, they said one to another, [2]It *is*
măn-nă: for they wist not what it *was*.
And Moses said unto them, [r]This *is*
the bread which the LORD hath given
you to eat.
16 ¶ This *is* the thing which the LORD
hath commanded, Gather of it every
man according to his eating, [s]an ō-
mĕr [3]for every man, *according to* the
number of your [4]persons; take ye
every man for *them* which *are* in his
tents.
17 And the children of Israel did
so, and gathered, some more, some
less.
18 And when they did mete *it* with an
ō-mĕr, [t]he that gathered much had
nothing over, and he that gathered
little had no lack; they gathered every
man according to his eating.
19 And Moses said, Let no man
leave of it till the morning.
20 Notwithstanding they hearkened
not unto Moses; but some of them
left of it until the morning, and it bred
worms, and stank: and Moses was
wroth with them.
21 And they gathered it every morning, every man according to his eating:
and when the sun waxed hot, it
melted.
22 ¶ And it came to pass, *that* on the
sixth day they gathered twice as much
bread, two ō-mĕrs for one *man*: and
all the rulers of the congregation came
and told Moses.
23 And he said unto them, This *is*
that which the LORD hath said, To
morrow *is* [u]the rest of the holy sabbath unto the LORD: bake *that* which
ye will bake *to day*, and seethe
that ye will seethe; and that which remaineth over lay up for you to be
kept until the morning.
24 And they laid it up till the morning, as Moses bade: and it did not
[v]stink, neither was there any worm
therein.
25 And Moses said, Eat that to day;
for to day [w]*is* a sabbath unto the
LORD: to day ye shall not find it in the
field.
26 Six [x]days ye shall gather it; but on
the seventh day, *which is* the sabbath,
in it there shall be none.
27 ¶ And it came to pass, *that* there
went out *some* of the people on the
seventh day for to gather, and they
found none.
28 And the LORD said unto Moses,
How long [y]refuse ye to keep my commandments and my laws?
29 See, for that the LORD hath given
you the sabbath, therefore he giveth
you on the sixth day the bread of two
days; abide ye every man in his place,
let no man go out of his place on the
seventh day.
30 So the people rested on the seventh day.
31 And the house of Israel called the
name thereof Măn-nă: and [z]it *was*
like coriander seed, white; and the
taste of it *was* like wafers *made* with
honey.
32 ¶ And Moses said, This *is* the
thing which the LORD commandeth,
Fill an ō-mĕr of it to be kept for your
generations; that they may see the
bread wherewith I have fed you in the
wilderness, when I brought you forth
from the land of Egypt.
33 And Moses said unto Aaron,
Take [a]a pot, and put an ō-mĕr full of
măn-nă therein, and lay it up before
the LORD, to be kept for your generations.
34 As the LORD commanded Moses,
so Aaron laid it up [b]before the Testimony, to be kept.
35 And the children of Israel did eat
măn-nă [c]forty years, [d]until they came
to a land inhabited; they did eat
măn-nă, until they came unto the
borders of the land of Canaan.
36 Now an ō-mĕr *is* the tenth *part* of
an ē-phăh.

CHAPTER 17

AND [a]all the congregation of the
children of Israel journeyed from
the wilderness of Sin, after their journeys, according to the commandment
of the LORD, and pitched in Rĕph-ĭ-
dĭm: and *there was* no water for the
people to drink.
2 Wherefore [b]the people did chide
with Moses, and said, Give us water
that we may drink. And Moses said
unto them, Why chide ye with me?
wherefore do ye tempt [c]the LORD?
3 And the people thirsted there for
water; and the people [d]murmured

---

m ver. 7.
n ch. 6.7. 1 Ki. 20.28. Joel 3.17.
o Num. 11. 31. Ps. 78,27,28. Ps. 105,40.
p Num. 11. 9.
q Num. 11. 7. Deut. 8.3. Neh. 9.15. Ps. 78.24. Ps. 105.40.
2 Or, What is this? or, It is a portion.
r Isa. 25.6. John 6.31, 49, 58. 1 Cor. 10.3.
s ver. 36.
3 by the poll, or, head.
4 souls.
t 2 Cor. 8.15.
u Gen. 2.3. ch. 20.8. ch. 31.15. ch. 35.3. Lev. 23.3.
v ver. 20.
w Matt. 12. 12. Matt. 24.20. Heb. 4.4.
x ch. 20.9, 10.
y 2 Ki. 17.14. Ps. 78.10,22. Ps. 106.13. Jer. 4.14.
z Num. 11.7, 8.
a Heb. 9.4.
b ch. 25.16, 21. ch. 40.20. Num. 17.10. Deut. 10.5. 1 Ki. 8.9.
c Num. 33. 38. Deut. 8.2,3. Neh. 9.20, 21. John 6.31, 49.
d Josh. 5.12. Neh. 9.15.

CHAP. 17

a ch. 16.1. ch. 19.2. Num. 33.12, 14.
b Num. 20.3.
c Deut. 6.16. Ps. 78.18,41. Isa. 7.12. Matt. 4.7. 1 Cor. 10.9.
d ch. 16.2.

against Moses, and said, Wherefore *is* this *that* thou hast brought us up out of Egypt, to kill us and our children and our cattle with thirst?

4 And Moses cried unto the LORD, saying, What shall I do unto this people? they be almost ready to stone [e]me.

5 And the LORD said unto Moses, Go [f]on before the people, and take with thee of the elders of Israel; and thy rod, wherewith thou smotest [g]the river, take in thine hand, and go.

6 Behold, [h]I will stand before thee there upon the rock in Hôr´-ĕb; and thou shalt smite the rock, and there shall come water out of it, that the people may drink. And Moses did so in the sight of the elders of Israel.

7 And he called the name of the place [1]Măs´-săh, and [2]Mĕr´-ĭ-băh, because of the chiding of the children of Israel, and because they tempted the LORD, saying, Is the LORD among us, or not?

8 ¶ Then [i]came Ăm´-ă-lĕk, and fought with Israel in Rĕph´-ĭ-dĭm.

9 And Moses said unto [j]Joshua, Choose us out men, and go out, fight with Ăm´-ă-lĕk: to morrow I will stand on the top of the hill with the rod of God in mine hand.

10 So Joshua did as Moses had said to him, and fought with Ăm´-ă-lĕk: and Moses, Aaron, and Hur went up to the top of the hill.

11 And it came to pass, when Moses [k]held up his hand, that Israel prevailed: and when he let down his hand, Ăm´-ă-lĕk prevailed.

12 But Moses' hands *were* heavy; and they took a stone, and put *it* under him, and he sat thereon; and Aaron and Hur stayed up his hands, the one on the one side, and the other on the other side; and his hands were steady until the going down of the sun.

13 And Joshua discomfited Ăm´-ă-lĕk and his people with the edge of the sword.

14 And the LORD said unto Moses, Write [l]this *for* a memorial in a book, and rehearse *it* in the ears of Joshua: for [m]I will utterly put out the remembrance of Ăm´-ă-lĕk from under heaven.

15 And Moses built an altar, and called the name of it [3]Jĕ-hō´-văh–nĭs´-sī:

16 For he said, [4]Because [5]the LORD hath sworn *that* the LORD *will have* war with Ăm´-ă-lĕk from generation to generation.

CHAPTER 18

WHEN Jĕth´-rō, the priest of Mĭd´-ĭ-ăn, Moses' father in law, heard of all that God had done for Moses, and for Israel his people, *and* that the LORD had brought Israel out of Egypt;

2 Then Jĕth´-rō, Moses' father in law, took Zĭp´-pō-răh, Moses' wife, after he had sent her back,

3 And her two sons; of which the name of the one *was* [1]Gĕr´-shŏm; for he said, I have been an alien in a strange land:

4 And the name of the other *was* [2]Ĕl-ĭ-ē´-zĕr; for the God of my father, *said he, was* mine help, and delivered me from the sword of Pharaoh:

5 And Jĕth´-rō, Moses' father in law, came with his sons and his wife unto Moses into the wilderness, where he encamped at the mount of God:

6 And he said unto Moses, I thy father in law Jĕth´-rō am come unto thee, and thy wife, and her two sons with her.

7 ¶ And Moses went out to meet his father in law, and did obeisance, and kissed him; and they asked each other of *their* [3]welfare; and they came into the tent.

8 And Moses told his father in law all that the LORD had done unto Pharaoh and to the Egyptians for Israel's sake, *and* all the travail that had [4]come upon them by the way, and *how* the LORD delivered them.

9 And Jĕth´-rō rejoiced for all the goodness which the LORD had done to Israel, whom he had delivered out of the hand of the Egyptians.

10 And Jĕth´-rō said, Blessed *be* the LORD, who hath delivered you out of the hand of the Egyptians, and out of the hand of Pharaoh, who hath delivered the people from under the hand of the Egyptians.

11 Now I know that the LORD *is* greater [a]than all gods: [b]for in the thing wherein they dealt [c]proudly *he was* above them.

12 And Jĕth´-rō, Moses' father in law, took a burnt offering and sacrifices for God: and Aaron came, and all the elders of Israel, to eat bread with Moses' father in law before [d]God.

13 ¶ And it came to pass on the morrow, that Moses sat to judge the people: and the people stood by Moses from the morning unto the evening.

14 And when Moses' father in law saw all that he did to the people, he

e 1 Sam. 30.6. John 8.59. John 10.31.
f Eze. 2.6.
g Num. 20.8.
h Ps. 105.41. Ps. 114.8. 1 Cor. 10.4.
1 That is, Temptation. Ps. 95.8. Heb. 3.8.
2 That is, Chiding, or Strife.
i Gen. 36.12. Num. 24.20. Deut. 25.17. 1 Sam. 15.2.
j Called Jesus. Acts 7.45. Heb. 4.8.
k Jas. 5.16.
l ch. 34.27.
m Deut. 25. 19. 1 Sam. 30.1. 2 Sam. 8.12. Ezra. 9.14.
3 That is, the LORD my banner. Judg. 6.24.
4 Or, Because the hand of Amalek is against the throne of the LORD, therefore, etc.
5 the hand upon the throne of the LORD.

CHAP. 18

1 That is, A stranger there.
2 That is, My God is an help.
3 peace. Gen. 43.27. 2 Sam. 11.7.
4 found them.
a 2 Chr. 2. 5. Ps. 95.3. Ps. 97. 9. Ps. 135.5. Isa. 37.16-20. Dan. 2.47.
b ch. 1.10.
c Job 40.11. Ps. 119.21. Luke 1.51.
d Deut. 12.7. 1 Cor. 10.18, 21,31.

said, What *is* this thing that thou doest to the people? why sittest thou thyself alone, and all the people stand by
thee from morning unto even?
15 And Moses said unto his father
in law, Because the people come unto
me to inquire of God:
16 When they have [e]a matter, they
come unto me; and I judge between
[5]one and another, and I do [f]make
them know the statutes of God, and
his laws.
17 And Moses' father in law said unto him, The thing that thou doest *is*
not good.
18 [6]Thou wilt surely wear away,
both thou, and this people that *is* with
thee: for this thing *is* too heavy for
thee; [g]thou art not able to perform it
thyself alone.
19 Hearken now unto my voice, I
will give thee counsel, and God shall
be with thee: Be thou [h]for the people
to God-ward, that thou mayest [i]bring
the causes unto God:
20 And thou shalt [j]teach them ordinances and laws, and shalt shew
them [k]the way wherein they must
walk, and [l]the work that they must do.
21 Moreover thou shalt provide out
of all the people [m]able men, such as
[n]fear God, [o]men of truth, hating
covetousness; and place *such* over
them, *to be* rulers of thousands, *and*
rulers of hundreds, rulers of fifties,
and rulers of tens:
22 And let them judge the people at
all seasons: [p]and it shall be, *that* every
great matter they shall bring unto
thee, but every small matter they
shall judge: so shall it be easier for
thyself, and they shall bear *the burden*
with thee.
23 If thou shalt do this thing, and
God command thee *so*, then thou
shalt be able to endure, and all this
people shall also go to their place in
peace.
24 So Moses hearkened to the voice
of his father in law, and did all that he
had said.
25 And [q]Moses chose able men out
of all Israel, and made them heads
over the people, rulers of thousands,
rulers of hundreds, rulers of fifties,
and rulers of tens.
26 And they judged the people at all
seasons: the [r]hard causes they brought
unto Moses, but every small matter
they judged themselves.
27 ¶ And Moses let his father in law
depart; and [s]he went his way into his
own land.

e 2 Sam. 15.3. Job 31.13.
5 a man and his fellow.
f Num. 36.6.
6 Fading thou wilt fade.
g Num. 11. 14. Deut. 1.9, 12.
h Deut. 5.5.
i Num. 27.5.
j Deut. 4.1,5.
k Ps. 143.8.
l Deut. 1.18.
m Deut. 16. 18. Acts 6.3.
n Gen. 42.18. 2 Sam. 23.3.
o Eze. 18.8.
p Lev. 24.11. Num. 15.33. Deut. 17.8.
q Deut. 1.15. Acts 6.5.
r Job 29.16.
s Num. 10.29.

CHAP. 19

a Acts 7.38.
b Deut. 32. 11. Isa. 63.9. Rev. 12.14.
c Deut. 32.8. 1 Ki. 8.53. Ps. 135.4. Isa. 43.1. Titus 2.14.
d Deut. 10.14. Job. 41.11. Ps. 50.12. 1 Cor. 10.26.
e 1 Pet. 2.5,9. Rev. 20.6.
f Lev. 20.24. Deut. 7.6. Isa. 62.12. 1 Thes. 5.27.
g ch. 24.3,7. Deut. 26.17.
h Deut. 4.11. Ps. 97.2. Matt. 17.5.
i Deut. 4.12. John 12.29.
j Heb. 10.22.
k Lev. 15.5.
l ch. 34.5. Deut. 33.2.
m Heb. 12. 20.
1 Or, cornet.

CHAPTER 19

IN the third month, when the children of Israel were gone forth out
of the land of Egypt, the same day
came they *into* the wilderness of Sī-nāi.
2 For they were departed from Rĕph-
ĭ-dĭm, and were come *to* the desert of
Sī-nāi, and had pitched in the wilderness; and there Israel camped before
the mount.
3 And [a]Moses went up unto God,
and the LORD called unto him out of
the mountain, saying, Thus shalt
thou say to the house of Jacob, and
tell the children of Israel;
4 Ye have seen what I did unto the
Egyptians, and *how* [b]I bare you on
eagles' wings, and brought you unto
myself.
5 Now therefore, if ye will obey my
voice indeed, and keep my covenant,
then [c]ye shall be a peculiar treasure
unto me above all people: for [d]all the
earth *is* mine:
6 And ye shall be unto me [e]a kingdom of priests, and an [f]holy nation.
These *are* the words which thou shalt
speak unto the children of Israel.
7 ¶ And Moses came and called for
the elders of the people, and laid before their faces all these words which
the LORD commanded him.
8 And [g]all the people answered together, and said, All that the LORD
hath spoken we will do. And Moses
returned the words of the people unto
the LORD.
9 And the LORD said unto Moses,
Lo, I come unto thee [h]in a thick cloud,
[i]that the people may hear when I
speak with thee, and believe thee for
ever. And Moses told the words of
the people unto the LORD.
10 ¶ And the LORD said unto Moses,
Go unto the people, [j]and sanctify
them to day and to morrow, and let
them [k]wash their clothes,
11 And be ready against the third
day: for the third day the [l]LORD will
come down in the sight of all the
people upon mount Sī-nāi.
12 And thou shalt set bounds unto
the people round about, saying, Take
heed to yourselves, *that ye* go *not* up
into the mount, or touch the border of
it: [m]whosoever toucheth the mount
shall be surely put to death:
13 There shall not an hand touch it,
but he shall surely be stoned, or shot
through; whether *it be* beast or man,
it shall not live: when the [1]trumpet
soundeth long, they shall come up to
the mount.

14 ¶ And Moses went down from the
mount unto the people, and sanctified
the people; and they washed their
clothes.
15 And he said unto the people, Be
ready against the third day: come [n]not
at *your* wives.
16 ¶ And it came to pass on the third
day in the morning, that there were
thunders and lightnings, and a thick
cloud upon the mount, and the voice
of the trumpet exceeding loud; so that
all the people that *was* in the camp
trembled.
17 And [o]Moses brought forth the
people out of the camp to meet with
God; and they stood at the nether
part of the mount.
18 And [p]mount Sī'-nâi was altogether
on a smoke, because the LORD descended upon it [q]in fire: and the
[r]smoke thereof ascended as the smoke
of a furnace, and the whole [s]mount
quaked greatly.
19 And when the voice of the trumpet sounded long, and waxed louder
and louder, Moses spake, and God
[t]answered him by a voice.
20 And the LORD came down upon
mount Sī'-nâi, on the top of the mount:
and the LORD called Moses *up* to the
top of the mount; and Moses went up.
21 And the LORD said unto Moses,
Go down, [2]charge the people, lest
they break through unto the LORD to
[u]gaze, and many of them perish.
22 And let the priests also, which
come near to the LORD, [v]sanctify
themselves, lest the LORD [w]break
forth upon them.
23 And Moses said unto the LORD,
The people cannot come up to mount
Sī'-nâi: for thou chargedst us, saying,
Set bounds about the mount, and
sanctify it.
24 And the LORD said unto him,
Away, get thee down, and thou shalt
come up, thou, and Aaron with thee:
but let not the priests and the people
break through to come up unto the
LORD, lest he break forth upon them.
25 So Moses went down unto the
people, and spake unto them.

CHAPTER 20

AND God spake all these words,
[a]saying,
2 I [b]*am* the LORD thy God, which
have brought thee out of the land of
Egypt, [c]out of the house of [1]bondage.
3 Thou [d]shalt have no other gods
before me.
4 Thou [e]shalt not make unto thee
any graven image, or any likeness *of*
any thing that *is* in heaven above, or
that *is* in the earth beneath, or that *is*
in the water under the earth:
5 Thou [f]shalt not bow down thyself
to them, nor serve them: for I the
LORD thy God *am* [g]a jealous God,
[h]visiting the iniquity of the fathers
upon the children unto the third and
fourth *generation* of them that hate
me;
6 And [i]shewing mercy unto thousands of them that love me, and keep
my commandments.
7 Thou [j]shalt not take the name of
the LORD thy God in vain; for the
LORD [k]will not hold him guiltless that
taketh his name in vain.
8 Remember [l]the sabbath day, to
keep it holy.
9 Six [m]days shalt thou labour, and
do all thy work:
10 But the [n]seventh day *is* the sabbath of the LORD thy God: *in it* thou
shalt not do any work, thou, nor thy
son, nor thy daughter, thy manservant, nor thy maidservant, nor thy
cattle, [o]nor thy stranger that *is* within
thy gates:
11 For *in* six days the LORD made
heaven and earth, the sea, and all that
in them *is*, and rested the seventh
day: wherefore the LORD blessed the
sabbath day, and hallowed it.
12 ¶ Honour [p]thy father and thy
mother: that thy days may be long
upon the land which the LORD thy
God giveth thee.
13 Thou [q]shalt not kill.
14 Thou [r]shalt not commit adultery.
15 Thou [s]shalt not steal.
16 Thou shalt not bear false witness
against thy neighbour.
17 Thou [t]shalt not covet thy neighbour's house, thou [u]shalt not covet
thy neighbour's wife, nor his manservant, nor his maidservant, nor his
ox, nor his ass, nor any thing that *is*
thy neighbour's.
18 ¶ And [v]all the people saw the
thunderings, and the lightnings, and
the noise of the trumpet, and the
mountain smoking: and when the
people saw *it*, they removed, and
stood afar off.
19 And they said unto Moses,
Speak [w]thou with us, and we will hear:
but let not God speak with us, lest we
die.
20 And Moses said unto the people,
Fear not: [x]for God is come to prove
you, and [y]that his fear may be before
your faces, that ye sin not.

n 1 Cor. 7.5. Rev. 4.5.
o Deut 4.10.
p Judg. 5.5. Ps. 68. 7,8.
q 2 Chr. 7.1.
r Gen. 15.17. Ps. 144.5. Rev. 15.8.
s Ps. 68.8. Ps. 114.7. Jer. 4.24.
t Neh. 9.13. Ps. 81.7.
2 contest.
u 1 Sam. 6.19.
v Lev. 10.3.
w 2 Sam. 6.7.

CHAP. 20

a Deut. 5.22.
b Lev. 26.1. Deut. 5.6. Ps. 81.10. Hos. 13.4.
c ch. 13.3.
1 servants.
d Deut. 6.14. 2 Ki. 17.35. Jer. 25.6.
e Lev. 26.1. Deut. 4.16.
f Josh. 23.7. 2 Ki. 17.35. Isa. 44.15.
g Josh. 24.19. Neh. 1.2.
h Num. 14. 18. Job 5.4. Ps. 79.8. Isa. 14.20. Jer. 2.9. Eze. 18.19.
i Deut. 7.9. Ps. 89.34. Rom. 11.28.
j Ps. 15.4. Matt. 5.33.
k Micah 6.11.
l ch. 31.13. Deut. 5.12.
m Eze. 20.12. Luke 13.14.
n Gen. 2.2.
o Neh. 13.16.
p Lev. 19.3. Deut. 5.16. Jer. 35.7,18. Matt. 15.4. Mark 7.10. Luke 18.20. Eph. 6.2.
q Rom. 13.9.
r Matt. 5.27.
s Lev. 19.11. Matt. 19.18. 1 Thes. 4.6.
t Micah 2.2. Eph. 5.3.
u Pro. 6.29. Matt. 5.28.
v Heb. 12.18.
w Gal. 3.19.
x Gen. 22.1.
y Pro. 3.7.

21 And the people stood afar off,
and Moses drew near unto the thick
darkness where God *was*.
22 ¶ And the LORD said unto Moses,
Thus thou shalt say unto the children
of Israel, Ye have seen that I have
talked with you from heaven.
23 Ye shall not make with me gods
of silver, neither shall ye make unto
you gods of gold.
24 ¶ An altar of earth thou shalt
make unto me, and shalt sacrifice
thereon thy burnt offerings, and thy
peace offerings, thy sheep, and thine
oxen: in all [z]places where I record my
name I will come unto thee, and I will
[a]bless thee.
25 And [b]if thou wilt make me an
altar of stone, thou shalt not [2]build it
of hewn stone: for if thou lift up thy
tool upon it, thou hast polluted it.
26 Neither shalt thou go up by steps
unto mine altar, that thy nakedness
be not discovered thereon.

CHAPTER 21

NOW these *are* the judgments
which thou shalt [a]set before them.
2 If [b]thou buy an Hebrew servant,
six years he shall serve: and in the seventh he shall go out free for nothing.
3 If he came in [1]by himself, he shall
go out by himself: if he were married,
then his wife shall go out with him.
4 If his master have given him [c]a
wife, and she have born him sons or
daughters; the wife and her children
shall be her master's, and he shall go
out by himself.
5 And [d]if the servant [2]shall plainly
say, I love my master, my wife, and
my children; I will not go out free:
6 Then his master shall bring him
unto the [e]judges; he shall also bring
him to the door, or unto the door post;
and his master shall bore [f]his ear
through with an aul; and he shall
serve him for ever.
7 ¶ And if a man [g]sell his daughter to
be a maidservant, she shall not go out
as the menservants do.
8 If she [3]please not her master, who
hath betrothed her to himself, then
shall he let her be redeemed: to sell
her unto a strange nation he shall
have no power, seeing he hath dealt deceitfully with her.
9 And if he have betrothed her unto
his son, he shall deal with her after
the manner of daughters.
10 If he take him another *wife;* her
food, her raiment, [h]and her duty of
marriage, shall he not diminish.

z 2 Chr. 6.6.
a Gen. 12.2.
b Josh. 8.31.
2 build them with hewing.

CHAP. 21

a ch. 24.3,4. Deut. 4.14. Deut. 6.1.
b Lev. 25.39. Deut. 15.12. Jer. 34.14.
1 with his body.
c Lev. 25.44.
d Deut. 15. 16.
2 saying shall say.
e ch. 12.12. ch. 22.8,28. Deut. 16.18. Ps. 82.1.
f Ps. 40.6.
g Neh. 5.5.
3 be evil in the eyes of, etc.
h 1 Cor. 7.5.
i Gen. 9.6. Lev. 25.17. Num. 35.30. Matt. 26.52.
j Deut. 19.4, 5.
k 1 Sam. 24. 4,10,18.
l Num. 35.11. Josh. 20.2.
m Num. 15. 30. Deut. 19.11. Heb. 10.26.
n 1 Ki. 2.28-34. 2 Ki. 11.15
o Deut. 24.7.
p Gen. 37.28.
q ch. 22.4.
r Lev. 20.9. Pro. 20.20. Matt. 15.4. Mark 7.10.
4 Or, revileth.
5 Or, his neighbour.
s 2 Sam. 3.29.
6 his ceasing.
7 avenged. Gen. 4.15, 24. Lev. 25.43. Rom. 13.4. Eph. 6.9. 1 Tim. 3.3. Jas. 3.1.
t Lev. 25.45.
u Deut. 22. 18,19.
v Lev. 24.20. Deut. 19.21. Matt. 5.38. Matt. 7.2.
w Col. 4.1.
x Gen. 9.5.

11 And if he do not these three unto
her, then shall she go out free without
money.
12 ¶ He [i]that smiteth a man, so that
he die, shall be surely put to death.
13 And [j]if a man lie not in wait, but
God [k]deliver *him* into his hand; then
[l]I will appoint thee a place whither he
shall flee.
14 But if a man come [m]presumptu-
ously upon his neighbour, to slay him
with guile; thou [n]shalt take him from
mine altar, that he may die.
15 ¶ And he that smiteth his father,
or his mother, shall be surely put to
death.
16 ¶ And [o]he that stealeth a man,
and selleth [p]him, or if he be [q]found in
his hand, he shall surely be put to
death.
17 ¶ And [r]he that [4]curseth his father,
or his mother, shall surely be put to
death.
18 ¶ And if men strive together, and
one smite [5]another with a stone, or
with *his* fist, and he die not, but keepeth *his* bed:
19 If he rise again, and walk abroad
[s]upon his staff, then shall he that
smote *him* be quit: only he shall pay
for [6]the loss of his time, and shall
cause *him* to be thoroughly healed.
20 ¶ And if a man smite his servant,
or his maid, with a rod, and he die
under his hand; he shall be surely
[7]punished.
21 Notwithstanding, if he continue
a day or two, he shall not be punished:
for [t]he *is* his money.
22 ¶ If men strive, and hurt a woman
with child, so that her fruit depart
from her, and yet no mischief follow:
he shall be surely punished, according as the woman's husband will lay
upon him; and he shall [u]pay as the
judges *determine*.
23 And if *any* mischief follow, then
thou shalt give life for life,
24 Eye [v]for eye, tooth for tooth,
hand for hand, foot for foot,
25 Burning for burning, wound for
wound, stripe for stripe.
26 ¶ And [w]if a man smite the eye of
his servant, or the eye of his maid,
that it perish; he shall let him go free
for his eye's sake.
27 And if he smite out his manservant's tooth, or his maidservant's
tooth; he shall let him go free for his
tooth's sake.
28 ¶ If an ox gore a man or a woman,
that they die: then [x]the ox shall be
surely stoned, and his flesh shall not

be eaten; but the owner of the ox *shall*
be quit.
29 But if the ox were wont to push
with his horn in time past, and it hath
been testified to his owner, and he
hath not kept him in, but that he hath
killed a man or a woman; the ox shall
be stoned, and his owner also shall be
put to death.
30 If there be laid on him a sum of
money, then he shall give for the [y]ran-
som of his life whatsoever is laid upon
him.
31 Whether he have gored a son, or
have gored a daughter, according to
this judgment shall it be done unto
him.
32 If the ox shall push a manservant
or a maidservant; he shall give unto
their master [z]thirty shekels of silver,
and the ox shall be stoned.
33 ¶ And if a man shall open a pit,
or if a man shall dig a pit, and not
cover it, and an ox or an ass fall therein;
34 The owner of the pit shall make *it*
good, *and* give money unto the owner
of them; and the dead *beast* shall be
his.
35 ¶ And if one man's ox hurt another's, that he die; then they shall
sell the live ox, and divide the money
of it; and the dead *ox* also they shall
divide.
36 Or if it be known that the ox hath
used to push in time past, and his
owner hath not kept him in; he shall
surely pay ox for ox; and the dead
shall be his own.

CHAPTER 22

IF a man shall steal an ox, or a
[1]sheep, and kill it, or sell it; he shall
restore five oxen for an ox, and [a]four
sheep for a sheep.
2 ¶ If a [b]thief be found breaking up,
and be smitten that he die, *there*
shall [c]no blood *be shed* for him.
3 If the sun be risen upon him, *there*
shall be blood *shed* for him; *for* he
should make full restitution; if he
have nothing, then he shall [d]be sold
for his theft.
4 If the [2]theft be certainly [e]found in
his hand alive, whether it be ox, or
ass, or sheep; he shall [f]restore double.
5 ¶ If a man shall cause a field or
vineyard to be eaten, and shall put in
his beast, and shall feed in another
man's field; of the best of his own
field, and of the best of his own vineyard, shall he make restitution.
6 ¶ If fire break out, and catch in
thorns, so that the stacks of corn, or
the standing corn, or the field, be consumed *therewith;* he that kindled the
fire shall surely make restitution.
7 ¶ If a man shall deliver unto his
neighbour money or stuff to keep, and
it be stolen out of the man's house; if
the thief be found, let him pay double.
8 If the thief be not found, then the
master of the house shall be brought
unto the judges, *to see* whether he
have put his hand unto his neighbour's goods.
9 For all manner of trespass, *whether*
it be for ox, for ass, for sheep, for raiment, *or* for any manner of lost thing,
which *another* challengeth to be his,
the [g]cause of both parties shall come
before the judges; *and* whom the
judges shall condemn, he shall pay
double unto his neighbour.
10 If a man deliver unto his neighbour an ass, or an ox, or a sheep, or
any beast, to keep; and it die, or be
hurt, or driven away, no man seeing *it:*
11 *Then* shall an [h]oath of the LORD
be between them both, that he hath
not put his hand unto his neighbour's
goods; and the owner of it shall
accept *thereof*, and he shall not make
it good.
12 And [i]if it be stolen from him, he
shall make restitution unto the owner
thereof.
13 If it be torn in pieces, *then* let him
bring it *for* witness, *and* he shall not
make good that which was torn.
14 ¶ And if a man borrow *ought* of
his neighbour, and it be hurt, or die,
the owner thereof *being* not with it,
he shall surely make *it* good.
15 *But* if the owner thereof *be* with
it, he shall not make *it* good: if it *be*
an hired *thing*, it came for his hire.
16 ¶ And [j]if a man entice a maid that
is not betrothed, and lie with her,
he shall surely endow her to be his
wife.
17 If her father utterly refuse to give
her unto him, he shall [3]pay money
according to the [k]dowry of virgins.
18 ¶ Thou [l]shalt not suffer a witch to
live.
19 ¶ Whosoever lieth with a beast
shall surely be put to death.
20 ¶ He [m]that sacrificeth unto *any*
god, save unto the LORD only, he
shall be utterly destroyed.
21 ¶ Thou [n]shalt neither vex a
stranger, nor oppress him: for ye
were strangers in the land of Egypt.
22 ¶ Ye [o]shall not afflict any widow,
or fatherless child.

y Num. 35. 31.
z Zech. 11.12, 13. Matt. 26.15. Phil. 2.7.

CHAP. 22

1 Or, goat.
a 2 Sam. 12. 6. Luke 19.8. Pro. 6.31.
b Ex. 20.15. Lev. 19.11. Deut. 5.19. Matt. 10.19. Matt. 19.18. Matt. 24.43. Luke 18.20. Rom. 13.9. 1 Cor. 6.10. Eph. 4.28. 1 Pet. 4.15.
c Num. 35. 27.
d ch. 21.2. Matt. 18.25.
2 thing stolen.
e ch. 21.16.
f Pro. 6.31.
g Deut. 25.1. 2 Chr. 19.10.
h Heb. 6.16.
i Gen. 31.39.
j Deut. 22.28.
3 weigh. Gen. 23.16.
k 1 Sam. 18. 25.
l Deut. 18.10.
m Num. 25.2. Deut. 13.1. Deut. 17.2. Hosea 8.14. 1 Ki. 18.40. 1 Ki. 10.25.
n Lev. 19.33. Lev. 25.35. Deut. 10.19. Zech. 7.10. Mal. 3.5.
o Deut. 10. 18. Isa. 1.17. Eze. 22.7.

23 If thou afflict them in any wise,
and they [p]cry at all unto me, I will
surely hear [q]their cry;
24 And my [r]wrath shall wax hot, and
I will kill you with the sword; and
[s]your wives shall be widows, and your
children fatherless.
25 ¶ If [t]thou lend money to *any of*
my people *that is* poor by thee, thou
shalt not be to him as an usurer, neither shalt thou lay upon him usury.
26 If [u]thou at all take thy neighbour's raiment to pledge, thou shalt
deliver it unto him by that the sun
goeth down:
27 For that *is* his covering only, it *is*
his raiment for his skin: wherein shall
he sleep? and it shall come to pass,
when he crieth unto me, that I will
hear; for I *am* gracious.
28 ¶ Thou [v]shalt not revile the [4]gods,
nor curse the ruler of thy people.
29 ¶ Thou shalt not delay *to offer* [5]the
first [w]of thy ripe fruits, and of thy
[6]liquors: the firstborn of thy sons
shalt thou give unto me.
30 Likewise [x]shalt thou do with thine
oxen, *and* with thy sheep: seven [y]days
it shall be with his dam; on the eighth
day thou shalt give it me.
31 ¶ And ye shall be [z]holy men unto
me: neither [a]shall ye eat *any* flesh *that*
is torn of beasts in the field; ye shall
cast it to the dogs.

CHAPTER 23

THOU [a]shalt not [1]raise a false report: put not thine hand with the
wicked to be an [b]unrighteous witness.
2 ¶ Thou [c]shalt not follow a multitude to *do* evil; [d]neither shalt thou
[2]speak in a cause to decline after many
to wrest *judgment:*
3 ¶ Neither shalt thou [e]countenance
a poor man in his cause.
4 ¶ If [f]thou meet thine enemy's ox
or his ass going astray, thou shalt
surely bring it back to him again.
5 If thou see the ass of him that
hateth thee lying under his burden,
[3]and wouldest forbear to help him,
thou shalt surely help with him.
6 Thou [g]shalt not wrest the judgment of thy poor in his cause.
7 Keep [h]thee far from a false matter;
and the innocent and righteous slay
thou not: for [i]I will not justify the
wicked.
8 ¶ And [j]thou shalt take no gift: for
the gift blindeth [4]the wise, and perverteth the words of the righteous.
9 ¶ Also [k]thou shalt not oppress a
stranger: for ye know the [5]heart of a
stranger, seeing ye were strangers in
the land of Egypt.
10 And [l]six years thou shalt sow thy
land, and shalt gather in the fruits
thereof:
11 But the seventh *year* thou shalt
let it rest and lie still; that the poor of
thy people may eat: and what they
leave the beasts of the field shall eat.
In like manner thou shalt deal with
thy vineyard, *and* with thy [6]oliveyard.
12 Six [m]days thou shalt do thy work,
and on the seventh day thou shalt
rest: that thine ox and thine ass may
rest, and the son of thy handmaid,
and the stranger, may be refreshed.
13 And in all *things* that I have said
unto you be circumspect: and make
[n]no mention of the name of other
gods, neither let it be heard out of thy
mouth.
14 ¶ Three [o]times thou shalt keep a
feast unto me in the year.
15 Thou shalt keep the feast of unleavened bread: (thou shalt eat unleavened bread seven days, as I commanded thee, in the time appointed
of the month Abib; for in it thou camest out from Egypt: and none shall
appear before me empty:)
16 And [p]the feast of harvest, the
firstfruits of thy labours, which thou
hast sown in the field: and the feast of
ingathering, *which is* in the end of the
year, when thou hast gathered in thy
labours out of the field.
17 Three times in the year all thy
males shall appear before the Lord
GOD.
18 Thou shalt not offer the blood of
my sacrifice with leavened bread;
neither shall the fat of my [7]sacrifice
remain until the morning.
19 The [q]first of the firstfruits of thy
land thou shalt bring into the house
of the LORD thy God. Thou shalt not
seethe a kid in his mother's milk.
20 ¶ Behold, I send an Angel before
thee, to keep thee in the way, and to
bring thee into the place which I have
prepared.
21 Beware of him, and obey his voice,
provoke [r]him not; for he will [s]not
pardon your transgressions: for [t]my
name *is* in him.
22 But if thou shalt indeed obey his
voice, and do all that I speak; then [u]I
will be an enemy unto thine enemies,
and [8]an adversary unto thine adversaries.
23 For mine Angel shall go before
thee, and [v]bring thee in unto the
Amorites, and the Hittites, and the

p Deut. 15.9. Job 35.9.
q Job 34.28. Jas. 5.4.
r Job 31.23.
s Ps. 109.9.
t Lev. 25.35. Neh. 5.7. Eze. 18.8.
u Job 24.3. Pro. 20.16. Amos 2.8.
v Eccl. 10.20. 2 Pet. 2.10.
4 Or, judges. Ps. 82.6.
5 thy fulness.
w Pro. 3.9.
6 tear.
x Deut. 15. 19.
y Lev. 22.27.
z Lev. 19.2.
a Eze. 4.14.

CHAP. 23

a Pro. 10.18.
1 Or, receive.
b 1 Ki. 21.10. Pro. 19.5. Acts 6.11.
c 1 Ki. 19.10. Job 31.34. Luke 23.23.
d Ps. 72.2.
2 answer.
e Lev. 19.15.
f Pro. 25.21. 1 Thes. 5.15.
3 Or, wilt thou cease to help him? or, and wouldest cease to leave thy business for him: thou shalt surely leave it to join with him.
g Job 31.13.
h Eph. 4.25.
i Rom. 1.18.
j Pro. 17.8.
4 the seeing.
k Ps. 94.6.
5 soul.
l Lev. 25.3.
6 Or, olive trees.
m Luke 13. 14.
n Hosea 2.17.
o Deut. 16.16.
p Lev. 23.10.
7 Or, feast.
q Neh. 10.35. Pro. 3.9.
r Eph. 4.30.
s Josh. 24.19. 1 John 5.16.
t Isa. 9.6. Jer. 23.6. John 10. 38.
u Gen. 12.3.
8 Or, I will afflict them that afflict thee.
v Josh. 24.8.

Pĕ-rĭz-́zītes, and the Canaanites, *and*
the Hī-́vītes, and the Jĕb-́ū-šītes: and
I will cut them off.
24 Thou shalt not [w]bow down to
their gods, nor serve them, nor do
after their works: but thou shalt utterly overthrow them, and quite break
down their images.
25 And ye shall [x]serve the LORD your
God, and he [y]shall bless thy bread,
and thy water; and [z]I will take sickness away from the midst of thee.
26 ¶ There [a]shall nothing cast their
young, nor be barren, in thy land: the
number of thy days I will [b]fulfil.
27 I will send [c]my fear before thee,
and will destroy all the people to
whom thou shalt come, and I will
make all thine enemies turn their
[9]backs unto thee.
28 And [d]I will send hornets before
thee, which shall drive out the Hi
vite, the Canaanite, and the Hittit
from before thee.
29 I [e]will not drive them o
before thee in one year; lest th
become desolate, and the beast o
field multiply against thee.
30 By little and little I will drive them
out from before thee, until thou be increased, and inherit the land.
31 And [f]I will set thy bounds from
the Red sea even unto the sea of the
Philistines, and from the desert unto
the river: for I [g]will deliver the inhabitants of the land into your hand; and
thou shalt drive them out before
thee.
32 Thou shalt make no covenant
with them, nor with their gods.
33 They shall not dwell in thy land,
lest they make thee sin against me:
for if thou serve their gods, [h]it will
surely be a snare unto thee.

CHAPTER 24

AND he said unto Moses, Come up
unto the LORD, thou, and Aaron,
[a]Nadab, and Ă-bī-́hū, [b]and seventy of
the elders of Israel; and worship ye
afar off.
2 And Moses alone shall come near
the LORD: but they shall not come
nigh; neither shall the people go up
with him.
3 ¶ And Moses came and told the
people all the words of the LORD, and
all the judgments: and all the people
answered with one voice, and said, All
the words which the LORD hath said
will we do.
4 And Moses [c]wrote all the words of
the LORD, and rose up early in the
morning, and builded an altar under
the hill, and twelve [d]pillars, according
to the twelve tribes of Israel.
5 And he sent young men of the
children of Israel, which offered
burnt offerings, and sacrificed peace
offerings of oxen unto the LORD.
6 And Moses [e]took half of the blood,
and put *it* in basons; and half of the
blood he sprinkled on the altar.
7 And he took the book of the covenant, and read in the audience of the
people: and they said, All that the
LORD hath said will we do, and be
obedient.
8 And Moses took the blood, and
sprinkled *it* on the people, and said,
Behold [f]the blood of the covenant,
which the LORD hath made with you
concerning all these words.
9 ¶ Then went up Moses, and Aaron,
Nadab, and Ă-bī-́hū, and seventy of
the elders of Israel:
10 And they [g]saw the God of Israel:
there was under his feet as it were
work of [h]a sapphire stone, and
the body [i]of heaven in *his*

he nobles of the chil-
he [j]laid not his hand:
God, and did [l]eat and

12 the LORD said unto Moses,
Come to me into the mount, and
be there: and I will give thee [m]tables
of stone, and a law, and commandments which I have written; that thou
mayest teach them.
13 And Moses rose up, and [n]his
minister Joshua: and Moses went up
into the mount of God.
14 And he said unto the elders,
Tarry ye here for us, until we come
again unto you: and, behold, Aaron
and Hur *are* with you: if any man
have any matters to do, let him come
unto them.
15 And Moses went up into the
mount, and [o]a cloud covered the
mount.
16 And [p]the glory of the LORD abode
upon mount Sī-́nâi, and the cloud
covered it six days: and the seventh
day he called unto Moses out of the
midst of the cloud.
17 And the sight of the glory of the
LORD *was* like [q]devouring fire on the
top of the mount in the eyes of the
children of Israel.
18 And Moses went into the midst
of the cloud, and gat him up into the
mount: and Moses was [r]in the mount
forty days and forty nights.

w ch. 20.5.
x Deut. 10. 12. Josh 22.5. 1 Sam. 12. 20. Matt. 4.10.
y Deut. 28.5.
z Deut. 7.15.
a Job 21.10.
b Gen. 25.8.
c Gen. 35.5. Deut. 2.25. Josh. 2.9,11. 1 Sam. 14. 15.
9 neck. Ps. 18.40.
Deut. 7.20.
f 1 Ki. 4.
g Josh. 21.
h ch. 34.12, 15. Deut. 7.2. Deut. 12.30. Josh. 23.13. Judg. 2.3. 1 Sam. 18. 21. Ps. 106.36, 37.

CHAP. 24

a ch. 28.1. Lev. 10.1,2.
b Num. 11. 16.
c Deut. 31.9.
d Gen. 28.18. Gen. 31.45.
e Heb. 9.18.
f Heb. 9.20. Heb. 13.20. 1 Pet. 1.2.
g Gen. 32.30. ch. 3.6. ch. 33.20, 23. Judg. 13.22. Isa. 6.1,5. John 1.18. 1 Tim. 6.16. 1 John 4.12.
h Eze. 1.26. Eze. 10.1. Rev. 4.3.
i Matt. 17.2.
j ch. 19.21.
k Gen. 16.13. Deut. 4.33.
l Gen. 31.54. ch. 18.12. 1 Cor. 10.18.
m ch. 32.15. Deut. 5.22.
n ch. 33.11.
o ch. 19.9. Matt. 17.5.
p ch. 16.10. Num. 14.10.
q Heb. 12.18.
r Deut. 9.9.

CHAPTER 25

AND the LORD spake unto Moses,
saying,
2 Speak unto the children of Israel,
that they [1]bring me an [2]offering: [a]of
every man that giveth it willingly
with his heart ye shall take my offering.
3 And this *is* the offering which ye
shall take of them; gold, and silver,
and brass,
4 And blue, and purple, and scarlet,
and [3]fine linen, and goats' *hair*,
5 And rams' skins dyed red, and
badgers' skins, and shĭt'-tĭm wood,
6 Oil for the light, spices for anointing oil, and for sweet incense,
7 Onyx stones, and stones to be set
in the ē'-phŏd, and in the [b]breastplate.
8 And let them make me a [c]sanctu-
ary; that [d]I may dwell among them.
9 According to all that I shew thee,
after the pattern of the tabernacle,
and the pattern of all the instruments
thereof, even so shall ye make *it*.
10 ¶ And [e]they shall make an ark *of*
shĭt'-tĭm wood: two cubits and a half
shall be the length thereof, and a cubit
and a half the breadth thereof, and a
cubit and a half the height thereof.
11 And thou shalt overlay it with
pure gold, within and without shalt
thou overlay it, and shalt make upon
it a crown of gold round about.
12 And thou shalt cast four rings of
gold for it, and put *them* in the four
corners thereof; and two rings *shall*
be in the one side of it, and two rings
in the other side of it.
13 And thou shalt make staves *of*
shĭt'-tĭm wood, and overlay them with
gold.
14 And thou shalt put the staves into
the rings by the sides of the ark, that
the ark may be borne with them.
15 The [f]staves shall be in the rings of
the ark: they shall not be taken from
it.
16 And thou shalt put into the ark
[g]the testimony which I shall give thee.
17 And [h]thou shalt make a mercy
seat *of* pure gold: two cubits and a
half *shall be* the length thereof, and a
cubit and a half the breadth thereof.
18 And thou shalt make two chĕr'-ū-
bĭms *of* gold, *of* beaten work shalt
thou make them, in the two ends of
the mercy seat.
19 And make one cherub on the one
end, and the other cherub on the
other end: *even* [4]of the mercy seat
shall ye make the chĕr'-ū-bĭms on the
two ends thereof.

CHAP. 25
1 take for me.
2 Or, heave offering.
a 1 Chr. 29.3. 2 Cor. 9.7.
3 Or, silk. Gen. 41.42.
b ch. 28.15.
c Lev. 4.6.
d Heb. 3.6. Rev. 21.3.
e ch. 37.1. Deut. 10.3. Heb. 9.4.
f 1 Ki. 8.8.
g ch. 16.34. ch. 31.18. ch. 40.20. Num. 17.10. Deut. 10.2. Deut. 31.26. 1 Ki. 8.9. 2 Ki. 11.12.
h ch. 37.6. Rom. 3.25. Heb. 9.5.
4 Or, of the matter of the mercy seat.
i 1 Ki. 8.7. 1 Chr. 28.18.
j ch. 26.34. ch. 40.20.
k ch. 29.42, 43. ch. 30.6, 36. Lev. 16.2. Num. 17.4. Eze. 9.3. Jas. 2.13.
l Num. 7.89. 1 Sam. 4.4. 2 Sam. 6.2. 2 Ki. 19.15. Ps. 80.1. Ps. 90.1. Isa. 37.16.
m ch. 37.10. 1 Ki. 7.48. 2 Chr. 4.8. Heb. 9.2.
n ch. 37.16. Num. 4.7.
5 Or, to pour out withal.
o Lev. 24.5.
p ch. 37.17. 1 Ki. 7.49. Zech. 4.2. Heb. 9.2. Rev. 1.12. Rev. 4.5.
q ch. 37.18, 19. Num. 8.4.

20 And [i]the chĕr'-ū-bĭms shall stretch
forth *their* wings on high, covering the
mercy seat with their wings, and their
faces *shall look* one to another; toward the mercy seat shall the faces of
the chĕr'-ū-bĭms be.
21 And [j]thou shalt put the mercy
seat above upon the ark; and in the
ark thou shalt put the testimony that
I shall give thee.
22 And [k]there I will meet with thee,
and I will commune with thee from
above the mercy seat, from [l]between
the two chĕr'-ū-bĭms which *are* upon
the ark of the testimony, of all *things*
which I will give thee in commandment unto the children of Israel.
23 ¶ Thou [m]shalt also make a table
of shĭt'-tĭm wood: two cubits *shall be*
the length thereof, and a cubit the
breadth thereof, and a cubit and a
half the height thereof.
24 And thou shalt overlay it with
pure gold, and make thereto a crown
of gold round about.
25 And thou shalt make unto it a
border of an hand breadth round
about, and thou shalt make a golden
crown to the border thereof round
about.
26 And thou shalt make for it four
rings of gold, and put the rings in the
four corners that *are* on the four feet
thereof.
27 Over against the border shall the
rings be for places of the staves to
bear the table.
28 And thou shalt make the staves
of shĭt'-tĭm wood, and overlay them
with gold, that the table may be borne
with them.
29 And thou shalt make [n]the dishes
thereof, and spoons thereof, and covers thereof, and bowls thereof, [5]to
cover withal: *of* pure gold shalt thou
make them.
30 And thou shalt set upon the table
shewbread [o]before me alway.
31 ¶ And [p]thou shalt make a candlestick *of* pure gold: *of* beaten work
shall the candlestick be made: his
shaft, and his branches, his bowls, his
knops, and his flowers, shall be
of the same.
32 And [q]six branches shall come out
of the sides of it; three branches of
the candlestick out of the one side,
and three branches of the candlestick
out of the other side:
33 Three bowls made like unto
almonds, *with* a knop and a flower in
one branch; and three bowls made
like almonds in the other branch,

with a knop and a flower: so in the six branches that come out of the candlestick.

34 And in the candlestick *shall be* four bowls made like unto almonds, *with* their knops and their flowers.

35 And *there shall be* a knop under two branches of the same, and a knop under two branches of the same, and a knop under two branches of the same, according to the six branches that proceed out of the candlestick.

36 Their knops and their branches shall be of the same: all it *shall be* one beaten work *of* pure gold.

37 And thou shalt make the seven [r]lamps thereof: and [s]they shall [6]light the lamps thereof, that they may [t]give light over against [7]it.

38 And the tongs thereof, and the snuffdishes thereof, *shall be of* pure gold.

39 *Of* a talent of pure gold shall he make it, with all these vessels.

40 And [u]look that thou make *them* after their pattern, [8]which was shewed thee in the mount.

CHAPTER 26

MOREOVER thou shalt make the [a]tabernacle *with* ten curtains *of* fine twined linen, and blue, and purple, and scarlet: [b]*with* chĕr'-ū-bĭms of [1]cunning work shalt thou make them.

2 The length of one curtain *shall be* eight and twenty cubits, and the breadth of one curtain four cubits: and every one of the curtains shall have one measure.

3 The five curtains shall be coupled [c]together one to another; and *other* five curtains *shall be* coupled one to another.

4 And thou shalt make [d]loops of blue upon the edge of the one curtain from the selvedge in the coupling; and likewise shalt thou make in the uttermost edge of *another* curtain, in the coupling of the second.

5 Fifty loops shalt thou make in the one curtain, and fifty loops shalt thou make in the edge of the curtain that *is* in the coupling of the second; that the loops may take hold one of another.

6 And thou shalt make fifty taches of gold, and couple the curtains together with the taches: and it shall be one tabernacle.

7 ¶ And [e]thou shalt make curtains *of* goats' *hair* to be a covering upon the tabernacle: eleven curtains shalt thou make.

8 The length of one curtain *shall be* thirty cubits, and the breadth of one curtain four cubits: and the eleven curtains *shall be all* of one measure.

9 And thou shalt couple five curtains by themselves, and six curtains by themselves, and shalt double the sixth curtain in the forefront of the tabernacle.

10 And thou shalt make fifty loops on the edge of the one curtain *that is* outmost in the coupling, and fifty loops in the edge of the curtain which coupleth the second.

11 And thou shalt make fifty taches of brass, and put the taches into the loops, and couple the [2]tent together, that it may be one.

12 And the remnant that remaineth of the curtains of the tent, the half curtain that remaineth, shall hang over the backside of the tabernacle.

13 And a cubit on the one side, and a cubit on the other side [3]of that which remaineth in the length of the curtains of the tent, it shall hang over the sides of the tabernacle on this side and on that side, to cover it.

14 And [f]thou shalt make a covering for the tent *of* rams' skins dyed red, and a covering above *of* badgers' skins.

15 ¶ And thou shalt make boards for the tabernacle *of* shĭt'-tĭm wood standing up.

16 Ten cubits *shall be* the length of a board, and a cubit and a half *shall be* the breadth of one board.

17 Two [4]tenons *shall there be* in one board, set in order one against another: thus shalt thou make for all the boards of the tabernacle.

18 And thou shalt make the boards for the tabernacle, twenty boards on the south side southward.

19 And thou shalt make forty sockets [g]of silver under the twenty boards; two sockets under one board for his two tenons, and two sockets under another board for his two tenons.

20 And for the second side of the tabernacle on the north side *there shall be* twenty boards:

21 And their forty sockets *of* silver; two sockets under one board, and two sockets under another board.

22 And for the sides of the tabernacle [5]westward thou shalt make six boards.

23 And two boards shalt thou make for the corners of the tabernacle in the two sides.

24 And they shall be [6]coupled together beneath, and they shall be

r Rev. 1.12.
s ch. 27.21. ch. 30.8. Lev. 24.3,4. 2 Chr. 13.11.
6 Or, cause to ascend.
t Num. 8.2.
7 the face of it.
u ch. 26.30. Num. 8.4. 1 Chr. 28. 11, 19. Acts 7.44. Heb. 8.5.
8 which thou wast caused to see.

CHAP. 26

a ch. 25.9. ch. 29.42, 43. ch. 31.7. ch. 33.7. ch. 36.8. ch. 39.32-43. ch. 40.2,17. Acts 7.44, 45. Heb. 8.2-5. Heb. 9.2,11. Rev. 21.3.
b 1 Cor. 12. 28. Eph. 4.11, 12. Heb. 1.14.
1 the work of a cunning workman, or, embroiderer.
c 1 Cor. 12.4, 5,6,12.
d Eph. 4.13. Col. 2.2,19.
e ch. 36.14.
2 Or, covering.
3 in the remainder, or, surplusage.
f ch. 36.19. Num. 24.5.
4 hands.
g ch. 38.27.
5 seaward. Gen. 12.8.
6 twinned. Ps. 133.1. 1 Cor. 1.10. Col. 3.2,19.

coupled together above the head of it unto one ring: thus shall it be for them both; they shall be for the two corners.

25 And they shall be eight boards, and their sockets *of* silver, sixteen sockets; two sockets under one board, and two sockets under another board.

26 ¶ And thou shalt make [h]bars *of* shĭt´-tĭm wood; five for the boards of the one side of the tabernacle,

27 And five bars for the boards of the other side of the tabernacle, and five bars for the boards of the side of the tabernacle, for the two sides westward.

28 And the middle bar in the midst of the boards shall reach from end to end.

29 And thou shalt overlay the boards with gold, and make their rings *of* gold *for* places for the bars: and thou shalt overlay the bars with gold.

30 And thou shalt rear up the tabernacle according [i]to the fashion thereof which was shewed thee in the mount.

31 ¶ And [j]thou shalt make a vail *of* blue, and purple, and scarlet, and fine twined linen of cunning work: with chĕr´-ū-bĭms shall it be made:

32 And thou shalt hang it upon four pillars of shĭt´-tĭm *wood* overlaid with gold: their hooks *shall be of* gold, upon the four sockets of silver.

33 ¶ And thou shalt hang up the vail under the taches, that thou mayest bring in thither within the vail [k]the ark of the testimony: and [l]the vail shall divide unto you between [m]the holy *place* and the most holy.

34 And [n]thou shalt put the mercy seat upon the ark of the testimony in the most holy *place*.

35 And [o]thou shalt set the table without the vail, and the [p]candlestick over against the table on the side of the tabernacle toward the south: and thou shalt put the table on the north side.

36 And [q]thou shalt make an hanging for the door of the tent, *of* blue, and purple, and scarlet, and fine twined linen, wrought with needlework.

37 And thou shalt make for the hanging five [r]pillars *of* shĭt´-tĭm *wood*, and overlay them with gold, *and* their hooks *shall be of* gold: and thou shalt cast five sockets of brass for them.

CHAPTER 27

AND thou shalt make [a]an altar *of* shĭt´-tĭm wood, five cubits long, and five cubits broad; the altar shall be foursquare: and the height thereof *shall be* three cubits.

2 And thou shalt make [b]the horns of it upon the four corners thereof: his horns shall be of the same: and [c]thou shalt overlay it with brass.

3 And thou shalt make his pans to receive his ashes, and his shovels, [d]and his basons, and his fleshhooks, and his firepans: all the vessels thereof thou shalt make *of* brass.

4 And thou shalt make for it a [1]grate of network *of* brass; and upon the net shalt thou make four brasen rings in the four corners thereof.

5 And thou shalt put it under the compass of the altar beneath, that the net may be even to the midst of the altar.

6 And thou shalt make staves for the altar, staves *of* shĭt´-tĭm wood, and overlay them with brass.

7 And the staves shall be put into the rings, and the staves shall be upon the two sides of the altar, to bear [e]it.

8 Hollow with boards shalt thou make it: [f]as [2]it was shewed thee in the mount, so shall they make *it*.

9 ¶ And [g]thou shalt make the court of the tabernacle: for the south side southward *there shall be* hangings for the court *of* fine twined linen of an hundred cubits long for one side:

10 And the twenty pillars thereof and their twenty sockets *shall be of* brass; the hooks of the pillars and their fillets *shall be of* silver.

11 And likewise for the north side in length *there shall be* hangings of an hundred *cubits* long, and his twenty pillars and their twenty sockets *of* brass; the hooks of the pillars and their fillets *of* silver.

12 ¶ And *for* the breadth of the court on the west side *shall be* hangings of fifty cubits: their pillars ten, and their sockets ten.

13 And the breadth of the court on the east side eastward *shall be* fifty cubits.

14 The hangings of one side *of the gate shall be* fifteen cubits: their pillars three, and their sockets three.

15 And on the other side *shall be* hangings fifteen *cubits:* their pillars three, and their sockets three.

16 ¶ And for the gate of the court *shall be* an hanging of twenty cubits, *of* blue, and purple, and scarlet, and fine twined linen, wrought with needlework: *and* their pillars *shall be* four, and their sockets four.

17 All the pillars round about the

h ch. 36.31. Num. 3.36. Rom. 15.1. 1 Cor. 9.19. 2 Cor. 13.11. Gal. 6.2.
i ch. 25.9,40. ch. 27.8. Acts 7.44. Heb. 8.5.
j Lev. 16.2. 2 Chr. 3.14. Matt. 27.51. Mark 15.38. Luke 23.45. Heb. 9.3.
k ch. 25.16. ch. 37.1. ch. 40.21. Num. 3.31. Josh. 4.11. 1 Sam. 4.6. 1 Sam. 6.19. 1 Ki. 8.6. 1 Chr. 15.1. Ps. 132.8. Heb. 9.4. Rev. 11.19.
l 2 Chr. 3.14.
m Lev. 16.2. Matt. 24.15. Heb. 9.2,3.
n ch. 25.21. ch. 40.20. Lev. 16.2. Heb. 9.5.
o ch. 40.22. Heb. 9.2.
p ch. 40.24.
q ch. 36.37.
r ch. 36.38.

CHAP. 27

a ch. 38.1. Eze. 43.13.
b 1 Ki. 1.50. 1 Ki. 2.28. Ps. 118.27.
c Num. 16.38.
d 1 Sam. 2.13, 14.
1 Or, sieve, Amos 9.9.
e Num. 4.15. Isa. 52.11.
f ch. 25.40. ch. 26.30. Heb. 8.5. Acts 7.44.
2 he shewed.
g ch. 38.9. Ps. 100.4.

court *shall be* filleted with silver; their hooks *shall be of* silver, and their sockets *of* brass.

18 ¶ The length of the court *shall be* an hundred cubits, and the breadth [3]fifty every where, and the height five cubits *of* fine twined linen, and their sockets *of* brass.

19 All the vessels of the tabernacle in all the service thereof, and all the pins thereof, and all the [4]pins of the court, *shall be of* brass.

20 ¶ And [h]thou shalt command the children of Israel, that they bring thee pure oil olive beaten for the light, to cause the lamp [5]to burn always.

21 In the tabernacle of the congregation without [i]the vail, which *is* before the testimony, [j]Aaron and his sons shall order it from evening to morning before the LORD: *it* [k]*shall be* a statute for ever unto their generations on the behalf of the children of Israel.

CHAPTER 28

AND [a]take thou unto thee Aaron thy brother, and his sons with him, from among the children of Israel, that he may minister unto me in the priest's office, *even* Aaron, Nadab and Ă-bī-hū, Ĕl-ē-ā-zär and Ĭth-ă-mär, Aaron's sons.

2 And [b]thou shalt make holy garments for Aaron thy brother for glory and for beauty.

3 And [c]thou shalt speak unto all *that are* wise hearted, [d]whom I have filled with the spirit of wisdom, that they may make Aaron's garments to consecrate him, that he may minister unto me in the priest's office.

4 And these *are* the garments which they shall make; a breastplate, and an ē-phŏd, and a robe, and a broidered coat, a mitre, and a girdle: and they shall make holy garments for Aaron thy brother, and his sons, that he may minister unto me in the priest's office.

5 And they shall take gold, and blue, and purple, and scarlet, and fine linen.

6 ¶ And [e]they shall make the ē-phŏd *of* gold, *of* blue, and *of* purple, *of* scarlet, and fine twined linen, with cunning work.

7 It shall have the two shoulderpieces thereof joined at the two edges thereof; and *so* it shall be joined together.

8 And the [1]curious girdle of the ē-phŏd, which *is* upon it, shall be of the same, according to the work thereof; *even of* gold, *of* blue, and purple, and scarlet, and fine twined linen.

9 And thou shalt take two onyx stones, and grave on them the names of the children of Israel:

10 Six of their names on one stone, and *the other* six names of the rest on the other stone, according to their birth.

11 With the work of an engraver in stone, *like* the engravings of a signet, shalt thou engrave the two stones with the names of the children of Israel: thou shalt make them to be set in ouches of gold.

12 And thou shalt put the two stones upon the shoulders of the ē-phŏd *for* stones of memorial unto the children of Israel: and [f]Aaron shall bear their names before the LORD upon his two shoulders [g]for a memorial.

13 ¶ And thou shalt make ouches *of* gold;

14 And two chains *of* pure gold at the ends; *of* wreathen work shalt thou make them, and fasten the wreathen chains to the ouches.

15 ¶ And [h]thou shalt make the breastplate of judgment with cunning work; after the work of the ē-phŏd thou shalt make it; *of* gold, *of* blue, and *of* purple, and *of* scarlet, and *of* fine twined linen, shalt thou make it.

16 Foursquare it shall be *being* doubled; a span *shall be* the length thereof, and a span *shall be* the breadth thereof.

17 And [i]thou shalt [2]set in it settings of stones, *even* four rows of stones: *the first* row *shall be* a [3]sardius, a topaz, and a carbuncle: *this shall be* the first row.

18 And the second row *shall be* an emerald, a sapphire, and a diamond.

19 And the third row a ligure, an agate, and an amethyst.

20 And the fourth row a beryl, and an onyx, and a jasper: they shall be set in gold in their [4]inclosings.

21 And the stones shall be with the names of the children of Israel, twelve, according to their names, *like* the engravings of a signet; every one with his name shall they be [j]according to the twelve tribes.

22 ¶ And thou shalt make upon the breastplate chains at the ends *of* wreathen work *of* pure gold.

23 And thou shalt make upon the breastplate two rings of gold, and shalt put the two rings on the two ends of the breastplate.

24 And thou shalt put the two wreathen *chains* of gold in the two

3 fifty by fifty.
4 Or, nails, or, stakes. Ezra 9.8. Isa. 33.20. Zech. 10.4.
h Lev. 24.2.
5 to ascend up.
i ch. 26.31,33.
j ch. 30.8. 1 Sam. 3.3. 2 Chr. 13.11.
k ch. 28.43. ch. 29.9,28. Lev. 3.17. Lev. 16.34. Lev. 24.9. Num. 18.23. Num. 19.21. 1 Sam. 30. 25.

CHAP. 28

a Num. 16.1, 3. Num. 17.1, 3,8. Num. 18.7. Ps. 77.20. Ps. 99.6. Ps. 106.16. Ps. 115.10, 12. Ps. 118.3. Heb. 5.1,4.
b ch. 29.5,29. ch. 31.10. ch. 39.1,2. Lev. 8.7.30. Num. 20.26, 28.
c ch. 31.6. ch. 35.31-35. ch. 36.1. 1 Ki. 3.12. Isa. 28.26. Acts 6.3.
d ch. 35.30, 31. Deut. 34.9. Isa. 11.2. Isa. 28.24-26. 1 Cor. 12.7-11. Eph. 1.17.
e ch. 39.2. Lev. 8.7.
1 Or, embroidered.
f ch. 39.7. Zech. 6.13.
g Gen. 9.12-17. ch. 12.14. ch. 13.9. ch. 39.7. Lev. 24.7. Num. 16.40. Num. 31.54. Josh. 4.7. Ps. 135.13. Zech. 6.14. Mark 14.9. Acts 10.4. 1 Cor. 11.24, 25.
h ch. 39.8. Lev. 8.8. Isa. 59.17. 1 Thes. 5.7. Eph. 6.14.
i ch. 30.10. Mal. 3.17.
2 fill in it fillings of stone.
3 Or, ruby.
4 fillings. Jas. 1.3.
j Num. 1.5. Num. 2.3. Num. 10.14. Num. 26.5. Rev. 7.4-8. Rev. 21.12.

rings *which are* on the ends of the breastplate.

25 And *the other* two ends of the two wreathen *chains* thou shalt fasten in the two ouches, and put *them* on the shoulderpieces of the ē´phŏd before it.

26 ¶ And thou shalt make two rings of gold, and thou shalt put them upon the two ends of the breastplate in the border thereof, which *is* in the side of the ē´phŏd inward.

27 And two *other* rings of gold thou shalt make, and shalt put them on the two sides of the ē´phŏd underneath, toward the forepart thereof, over against the *other* coupling thereof, above the curious girdle of the ē´phŏd.

28 And they shall bind the breastplate by the rings thereof unto the rings of the ē´phŏd with a lace of blue, that *it* may be above the curious girdle of the ē´phŏd, and that the breastplate be not loosed from the ē´phŏd.

29 And Aaron shall [k]bear the names of the children of Israel in the breastplate of judgment upon his heart, when he goeth in unto the holy *place*, [l]for a memorial before the LORD continually.

30 ¶ And [m]thou shalt put in the breastplate of judgment the Ū´rĭm and the Thŭm´mĭm; and they shall be upon Aaron's heart, when he goeth in before the LORD: and Aaron shall bear the judgment of the children of Israel upon his heart before the LORD continually.

31 ¶ And [n]thou shalt make the robe of the ē´phŏd all *of* blue.

32 And there shall be an hole in the top of it, in the midst thereof: it shall have a binding of woven work round about the hole of it, as it were the hole of an habergeon, that it be not rent.

33 ¶ And *beneath* upon the [5]hem of it thou shalt make pomegranates *of* blue, and *of* purple, and *of* scarlet, round about the hem thereof; and bells of gold between them round about:

34 A golden bell and a pomegranate, a golden bell and a pomegranate, upon the hem of the robe round about.

35 And it shall be upon Aaron to minister: and his sound shall be heard when he goeth in unto the holy *place* before the LORD, and when he cometh out, that he die not.

36 ¶ And [o]thou shalt make a plate *of* pure gold, and grave upon it, *like* the engravings of a signet, HOLINESS TO THE LORD.

37 And thou shalt put it on a blue lace, that it may be upon the mitre; upon the forefront of the mitre it shall be.

38 And it shall be upon Aaron's forehead, that Aaron may [p]bear the iniquity of the holy things, which the children of Israel shall hallow in all their holy gifts; and it shall be always upon his forehead, that they may be [q]accepted before the LORD.

39 ¶ And thou shalt embroider the coat of fine linen, and thou shalt make the mitre *of* fine linen, and thou shalt make the girdle *of* needlework.

40 ¶ And [r]for Aaron's sons thou shalt make coats, and thou shalt make for them girdles, and bonnets shalt thou make for them, for glory and for beauty.

41 And thou shalt put them upon Aaron thy brother, and his sons with him; and shalt [s]anoint them, and [6]consecrate them, and sanctify them, that they may minister unto me in the priest's office.

42 And thou shalt make them linen [t]breeches to cover [7]their nakedness; from the loins even unto the thighs they shall [8]reach:

43 And they shall be upon Aaron, and upon his sons, when they come in unto the tabernacle of the congregation, or when they come near [u]unto the altar to minister in the holy *place*; that they [v]bear not iniquity, and die: [w]*it shall be* a statute for ever unto him and his seed after him.

CHAPTER 29

AND this *is* the thing that thou shalt do unto them to hallow them, to minister unto me in the priest's office: [a]Take one young bullock, and two rams without blemish,

2 And [b]unleavened bread, and cakes unleavened tempered with oil, and wafers unleavened anointed with oil: *of* wheaten flour shalt thou make them.

3 And thou shalt put them into one basket, and bring them in the basket, with the bullock and the two rams.

4 And Aaron and his sons thou shalt bring unto the door of the tabernacle of the congregation, and [c]shalt wash them with water.

5 And [d]thou shalt take the garments, and put upon Aaron the coat, and the robe of the ē´phŏd, and the ē´phŏd, and the breastplate, and gird him with the [e]curious girdle of the ē´phŏd:

6 And thou shalt put the mitre upon

k Song 8.6. Isa. 49.15, 16. Heb. 9.24.
l ver. 12.
m Lev. 8.8. Num. 27.21. Deut. 33.8. 1 Sam. 28.6. Ezra 2.63. Neh. 7.65.
n ch. 39.22. Lev. 8.7. 2 Sam. 6.14. Hosea 3.4.
5 Or, skirts.
o ch. 39.30. Lev. 8.9. 1 Chr. 16.29. Ps. 29.2. Ps. 93.5. Zech. 14.20. Heb. 4.15. Heb. 7.26. Heb. 12.14.
p Lev. 10.17. Lev. 22.9. Num. 18.1. Isa. 53.11. Eze. 4.4. John 1.29. Heb. 9.28. 1 Pet. 2.24.
q Lev. 1.4. Lev. 22.27. Lev. 23.11. Isa. 56.7.
r ch. 39.27. Eze. 44.17, 18.
s ch. 29.7. ch. 30.30. Lev. 10.7.
6 fill their hand. Lev. 8.1. Heb. 7.28.
t Lev. 6.10. Eze. 44.18.
7 flesh of their nakedness.
8 be.
u ch. 20.26.
v Lev. 20.19, 20. Num. 18.22.
w Lev. 17.7.

CHAP. 29

a Lev. 8.2.
b Lev. 6.20, 21, 22.
c ch. 40.12. Lev. 8.6. Heb. 10.22.
d Lev. 8.7.
e ch. 28.8.

his head, and put the holy crown upon
the mitre.
7 Then shalt thou take the anointing
[f]oil, and pour *it* upon his head, and
anoint him.
8 And thou shalt bring his sons, and
put coats upon them.
9 And thou shalt gird them with
girdles, Aaron and his sons, and [1]put
the bonnets on them: and the [g]priest's
office shall be theirs for a perpetual
statute: and thou shalt [2]consecrate
Aaron and his sons.
10 And thou shalt cause a bullock to
be brought before the tabernacle of
the congregation: and [h]Aaron and
his sons shall put their hands upon
the head of the bullock.
11 And thou shalt kill the bullock
before the LORD, *by* the door of the
tabernacle of the congregation.
12 And thou [i]shalt take of the blood
of the bullock, and put *it* upon [j]the
horns of the altar with thy finger, and
pour all the blood beside the bottom
of the altar.
13 And [k]thou shalt take all the fat
that covereth the inwards, and [3]the
caul *that is* above the liver, and the
two kidneys, and the fat that *is* upon
them, and burn *them* upon the altar.
14 But [l]the flesh of the bullock, and
his skin, and his dung, shalt thou burn
with fire without the camp: it *is* a sin
offering.
15 ¶ Thou [m]shalt also take one ram;
and Aaron and his sons shall put
[n]their hands upon the head of the ram.
16 And thou shalt slay the ram, and
thou shalt take his blood, and sprinkle
it round about upon the altar.
17 And thou shalt cut the ram in
pieces, and wash the inwards of him,
and his legs, and put *them* unto his
pieces, and [4]unto his head.
18 And thou shalt burn the whole
ram upon the altar: it *is* a burnt offering unto the LORD: it *is* [o]a sweet savour, an offering made by fire unto the
LORD.
19 ¶ And [p]thou shalt take the other
ram; and Aaron and his sons shall put
their hands upon the head of the ram.
20 Then shalt thou kill the ram, and
take of his blood, and put *it* upon the
tip of the right ear of Aaron, and upon
the tip of the right ear of his sons, and
upon the thumb of their right hand,
and upon the great toe of their right
foot, and sprinkle the blood upon the
altar round about.
21 And thou shalt take of the blood
that *is* upon the altar, and of [q]the

[f] ch. 30.25. Lev. 8.12. Lev. 10.7. Lev. 21.10. Num. 35.25. Ps. 133.1,2. Isa. 61.1.
1 bind.
[g] Num. 18.7.
2 fill the hand of.
[h] Lev. 1.4. Lev. 8.14.
[i] Lev. 8.15.
[j] ch. 27.2. ch. 30.2.
[k] Lev. 3.3.
3 It seemeth by anatomy and the Hebrew doctors to be the midriff.
[l] Lev. 4.11, 12,21. Heb. 13.11.
[m] Lev. 8.18.
[n] Lev. 1.4. Isa. 53.6. Gal. 4.3-5.
4 Or, upon.
[o] Gen. 8.21.
[p] Lev. 8.22.
[q] ch. 30.25. Lev. 8.30.
[r] Heb. 9.22.
[s] Lev. 8.26.
5 Or, shake to and fro.
[t] Lev. 8.28.
[u] Lev. 7.31, 34. Lev. 8.29. Num. 18.11, 18.
[v] Ps. 99.6.
[w] Deut. 18.3.
[x] Lev. 10.15.
[y] Lev. 7.34.
[z] Num. 20. 26.
[a] Num. 18.8. Num. 35.25.
6 he of his sons.
[b] Lev. 8.35.
[c] Lev. 8.31.
[d] Matt. 12.4.
[e] Lev. 10.14.

anointing oil, and sprinkle *it* upon
Aaron, and upon his garments, and
upon his sons, and upon the garments
of his sons with him: and [r]he shall be
hallowed, and his garments, and his
sons, and his sons' garments with him.
22 Also thou shalt take of the ram
the fat and the rump, and the fat that
covereth the inwards, and the caul
above the liver, and the two kidneys,
and the fat that *is* upon them, and the
right shoulder; for it *is* a ram of consecration:
23 And [s]one loaf of bread, and one
cake of oiled bread, and one wafer
out of the basket of the unleavened
bread that *is* before the LORD:
24 And thou shalt put all in the hands
of Aaron, and in the hands of his sons;
and shalt [5]wave them *for* a wave offering before the LORD.
25 And [t]thou shalt receive them of
their hands, and burn *them* upon the
altar for a burnt offering, for a sweet
savour before the LORD: it *is* an offering made by fire unto the LORD.
26 And thou shalt take [u]the breast of
the ram of Aaron's consecration, and
wave it *for* a wave offering before the
LORD: and it shall be [v]thy part.
27 And thou shalt sanctify [w]the
breast of the wave offering, and the
shoulder of the heave offering, which
is waved, and which is heaved up, of
the ram of the consecration, *even* of
that which *is* for Aaron, and of *that*
which is for his sons:
28 And it shall be Aaron's and his
sons' by [x]a statute for ever from the
children of Israel: for it *is* an heave
offering: and [y]it shall be an heave
offering from the children of Israel of
the sacrifice of their peace offerings,
even their heave offering unto the
LORD.
29 ¶ And the holy garments of
Aaron shall [z]be his sons' after him, to
be anointed therein, and [a]to be consecrated in them.
30 *And* [6]that son that is priest in his
stead shall put them on seven [b]days,
when he cometh into the tabernacle of
the congregation to minister in the
holy *place*.
31 ¶ And thou shalt take the ram of
the consecration, and [c]seethe his flesh
in the holy place.
32 And Aaron and his sons shall eat
the flesh of the ram, and the bread
[d]that *is* in the basket, *by* the door of
the tabernacle of the congregation.
33 And [e]they shall eat those things
wherewith the atonement was made,

to consecrate *and* to sanctify them: but [7]a stranger shall not eat *thereof*, because they *are* holy.

34 And if ought of the flesh of the consecrations, or of the bread, remain unto the morning, then thou shalt burn the remainder with fire: it shall not be eaten, because it *is* holy.

35 And thus shalt thou do unto Aaron, and to his sons, according to all *things* which I have commanded thee: [f]seven days shalt thou consecrate them.

36 And thou shalt [g]offer every day a bullock *for* a sin offering for atonement: and thou shalt cleanse the altar, when thou hast made an atonement for it, [h]and thou shalt anoint it, to sanctify it.

37 Seven days thou shalt make an atonement for the altar, and sanctify it; [i]and it shall be an altar most holy: [j]whatsoever toucheth the altar shall be holy.

38 ¶ Now this *is that* which thou shalt offer upon the altar; [k]two lambs of the first year day [l]by day continually.

39 The one lamb thou shalt offer in [m]the morning; and the other lamb thou shalt offer at even:

40 And with the one lamb a tenth deal of flour mingled with the fourth part of an hĭn of beaten oil; and the fourth part of an hĭn of wine *for* a drink offering.

41 And the other lamb thou shalt offer [n]at even, and shalt do thereto according to the meat offering of the morning, and according to the drink offering thereof, for a sweet savour, an offering made by fire unto the LORD.

42 *This shall be* [o]a continual burnt offering throughout your generations *at* the door of the tabernacle of the congregation before the LORD: [p]where I will meet you, to speak there unto thee.

43 And there I will meet with the children of Israel, and [8]*the tabernacle* [q]shall be sanctified by my glory.

44 And I will sanctify the tabernacle of the congregation, and the altar: I will [r]sanctify also both Aaron and his sons, to minister to me in the priest's office.

45 ¶ And [s]I will dwell among the children of Israel, and will be their God.

46 And they shall know that I *am* the LORD their God, that brought them forth out of the land of Egypt, that I may dwell among them: I *am* the LORD their God.

7 every one not a Levite. Num. 16.40.
f Lev. 8.33.
g Heb. 10.11.
h ch. 30.26.
i ch. 40.10.
j ch. 30.29. Matt. 23.19.
k Num. 28.3. 1 Chr. 16.40. 2 Chr. 2.4. 2 Chr. 13.11. 2 Chr. 31.3. Ezra 3.3.
l Dan. 9.27. Dan. 12.11.
m Eze. 46.13.
n 1 Ki. 18.29. 2 Ki. 16.15. Ezra 9.4,5. Ps. 141.2. Eze. 4.3,5. Dan. 9.21.
o Dan. 8.11.
p Num. 17.4.
8 Or, Israel.
q 1 Ki. 8.11. Hag. 2.7,9. Matt. 3.1.
r Lev. 21.15.
s Ex. 25.8. Lev. 26.12. Zech. 2.10. John 14.17. 2 Cor. 6.16. Rev. 21.3.

CHAP. 30

a ch. 37.25. ch. 40.5.
b Rev. 8.3.
1 roof.
2 walls.
3 ribs.
4 incense of spices. 1 Sam. 2.28. 1 Chr. 23.13. Luke 1.9.
5 causeth to ascend, or, setteth up.
6 between the two evens.
c Lev. 10.1.
d Lev. 23.27.
e ch. 38.25. Num. 1.2,5. Num. 26.2. 2 Sam. 24.2.
7 them that are to be numbered. Num. 31.50.
f Job 33.24. Job 36.18. Ps. 49.7. Matt. 20.28. Mark 10.45. 1 Tim. 2.6. 1 Pet. 1.18.
g 2 Sam. 24. 15.
h Matt. 17. 24.
i Lev. 27.25. Num. 3.47. Eze. 45.12.

CHAPTER 30

AND thou shalt make [a]an altar [b]to burn incense upon: *of* shĭt-tĭm wood shalt thou make it.

2 A cubit *shall be* the length thereof, and a cubit the breadth thereof; foursquare shall it be: and two cubits *shall be* the height thereof: the horns thereof *shall be* of the same.

3 And thou shalt overlay it with pure gold, the [1]top thereof, and the [2]sides thereof round about, and the horns thereof; and thou shalt make unto it a crown of gold round about.

4 And two golden rings shalt thou make to it under the crown of it, by the two [3]corners thereof, upon the two sides of it shalt thou make *it;* and they shall be for places for the staves to bear it withal.

5 And thou shalt make the staves *of* shĭt-tĭm wood, and overlay them with gold.

6 And thou shalt put it before the vail that *is* by the ark of the testimony, before the mercy seat that *is* over the testimony, where I will meet with thee.

7 And Aaron shall burn thereon [4]sweet incense every morning: when he dresseth the lamps, he shall burn incense upon it.

8 And when Aaron [5]lighteth the lamps [6]at even, he shall burn incense upon it, a perpetual incense before the LORD throughout your generations.

9 Ye shall offer no [c]strange incense thereon, nor burnt sacrifice, nor meat offering; neither shall ye pour drink offering thereon.

10 And [d]Aaron shall make an atonement upon the horns of it once in a year with the blood of the sin offering of atonements: once in the year shall he make atonement upon it throughout your generations: it *is* most holy unto the LORD.

11 ¶ And the LORD spake unto Moses, saying,

12 When [e]thou takest the sum of the children of Israel after [7]their number, then shall they give every man [f]a ransom for his soul unto the LORD, when thou numberest them; that there be no [g]plague among them, when *thou* numberest them.

13 This [h]they shall give, every one that passeth among them that are numbered, half a shekel after the shekel of the sanctuary: (a shekel [i]*is* twenty gē-rähs:) an half shekel *shall be* the offering of the LORD.

14 Every one that passeth among them that are numbered, from twenty

years old and above, shall give an offering unto the LORD.

15 The [j]rich shall not [8]give more, and the poor shall not [9]give less than half a shekel, when *they* give an offering unto the LORD, to make an atonement for your souls.

16 And thou shalt take the atonement money of the children of Israel, and shalt appoint it for the service of the tabernacle of the congregation; that it may be [k]a memorial unto the children of Israel before the LORD, to make an atonement for your souls.

17 ¶ And the LORD spake unto Moses, saying,

18 Thou [l]shalt also make a laver *of* brass, and his foot *also of* brass, to wash *withal* and thou shalt put it between the tabernacle of the congregation and the altar, and thou shalt put water therein.

19 For Aaron and his sons [m]shall wash their hands and their feet thereat:

20 When they go into the tabernacle of the congregation, they shall wash with water, that they die not; or when they come near to the altar to minister, to burn offering made by fire unto the LORD:

21 So they shall wash their hands and their feet, that they die not: and [n]it shall be a statute for ever to them, *even* to him and to his seed throughout their generations.

22 ¶ Moreover the LORD spake unto Moses, saying,

23 Take thou also unto [o]thee principal spices, of pure [p]myrrh five hundred *shekels*, and of sweet cinnamon half so much, *even* two hundred and fifty *shekels*, and of sweet [q]calamus two hundred and fifty *shekels*,

24 And of [r]cassia five hundred *shekels*, after the shekel of the sanctuary, and of oil olive an [s]hīn:

25 And thou shalt make it an oil of holy ointment, an ointment compound after the art of the [10]apothecary: it shall be [t]an holy anointing oil.

26 And [u]thou shalt anoint the tabernacle of the congregation therewith, and the ark of the testimony,

27 And the table and all his vessels, and the candlestick and his vessels, and the altar of incense,

28 And the altar of burnt offering with all his vessels, and the laver and his foot.

29 And thou shalt sanctify them, that they may be most holy: whatsoever toucheth them shall be holy.

30 And thou shalt anoint Aaron and his sons, and consecrate them, that *they* may minister unto me in the priest's office.

31 And thou shalt speak unto the children of Israel, saying, This shall be an holy anointing oil unto me throughout your generations.

32 Upon man's flesh shall it not be poured, neither shall ye make *any other* like it, after the composition of it: it *is* holy, *and* it shall be holy unto you.

33 Whosoever compoundeth *any* like it, or whosoever putteth *any* of it upon [11]a stranger, [v]shall even be cut off from his people.

34 ¶ And the LORD said unto Moses, Take [w]unto thee sweet spices, stăc'-tē, and ŏn'-ȳ-chă, and găl'-bă-nŭm; *these* sweet spices with pure frankincense: of each shall there be a like *weight:*

35 And thou shalt make it a perfume, a confection after the art of the apothecary, [12]tempered together, pure *and* holy:

36 And thou shalt beat *some* of it very small, and put of it before the testimony in the tabernacle of the congregation, [x]where I will meet with thee: [y]it shall be unto you most holy.

37 And *as for* the perfume which thou shalt make, ye shall not make to yourselves according to the composition thereof: it shall be unto thee holy for the LORD.

38 Whosoever shall make like unto that, to smell thereto, shall even be cut off from his people.

CHAPTER 31

AND the LORD spake unto Moses, saying,

2 See, [a]I have called by name Bĕz'-ă-lēel the [b]son of Ū'-rī, the son of Hur, of the tribe of Judah:

3 And I have [c]filled him with the spirit of God, in wisdom, and in understanding, and in knowledge, and in all manner of workmanship,

4 To devise cunning works, to work in gold, and in silver, and in brass,

5 And in cutting of stones, to set *them*, and in carving of timber, to work in all manner of workmanship.

6 And I, behold, I have given with him Ă-hō'-lĭ-ăb, [d]the son of Ă-hĭs'-ă-măch, of the tribe of Dan: and in the hearts of all that are [e]wise hearted I have put wisdom, that they may make all that I have commanded thee;

7 The [f]tabernacle of the congregation, and the ark of the testimony, and

j Job 34.19. Pro. 22.2. Acts 10.34. Rom. 2.11. Gal. 2.6. Eph. 6.9. Col. 3.25. 1 Pet. 1.17.
8 multiply.
9 diminish.
k Num. 16. 40.
l 1 Ki. 7.38.
m Isa. 52.11. Heb. 10.22.
n ch. 28.43.
o Song 4.14. Eze. 27.22.
p Ps. 45.8.
q Jer. 6.20.
r Ps. 45.8.
s ch. 29.40.
10 Or, perfumer.
t Num. 35.25. Ps. 89.20. Ps. 133.2.
u Lev. 8.10. Num. 7.1.
11 One not a priest. Lev. 22.10, 12, 13. Num. 1.51. Num. 3.10.
v Gen. 17.14. Lev. 7.20, 21.
w ch. 25.6. ch. 37.29.
12 salted. Lev. 2.13.
x ch. 29.42. Lev. 16.2.
y ch. 29.37. Lev. 2.3.

CHAP. 31

a ch. 35.30.
b 1 Chr. 2.20.
c ch. 35.31. 1 Ki. 7.14. Isa. 28.26. 1 Cor. 12.4-8.
d ch. 35.34.
e ch. 28.3. ch. 36.1.
f ch. 36.8.

the mercy seat that *is* thereupon, and
all the [1]furniture of the tabernacle,
8 And the table and his furniture,
and the pure candlestick with all his
furniture, and the altar of incense,
9 And the altar of burnt offering with
all his furniture, and the laver and his
foot,
10 And the cloths of service, and the
holy garments for Aaron the priest,
and the garments of his sons, to minister in the priest's office,
11 And the anointing oil, and sweet
incense for the holy *place:* according
to all that I have commanded thee
shall they do.
12¶ And the LORD spake unto Moses,
saying,
13 Speak thou also unto the children
of Israel, saying, [g]Verily my sabbaths
ye shall keep: for it *is* a sign between
me and you throughout your generations; that *ye* may know that I *am* the
LORD that doth sanctify you.
14 Ye [h]shall keep the sabbath therefore; for it *is* holy unto you: every one
that defileth it shall surely be put to
death: for whosoever [i]doeth *any* work
therein, that soul shall be cut off from
among his people.
15 Six days may work be done; but
in the seventh [j]*is* the sabbath of rest,
[2]holy to the LORD: whosoever doeth
any work in the sabbath day, he shall
surely be put to death.
16 Wherefore the children of Israel
shall keep the sabbath, to observe the
sabbath throughout their generations,
for a perpetual covenant.
17 It *is* [k]a sign between me and the
children of Israel for ever: for *in* [l]six
days the LORD made heaven and
earth, and on the seventh day he rested, and was refreshed.
18 ¶ And he gave unto Moses, when
he had made an end of communing
with him upon mount Sī-nâi, [m]two
tables of testimony, tables of stone,
written with the finger of God.

CHAPTER 32

AND when the people saw that
Moses [a]delayed to come down
out of the mount, the people gathered
themselves together unto Aaron, and
said unto him, [b]Up, make us gods,
which shall go before us; for *as for* this
Moses, the man that brought us up
out of the land of Egypt, we wot not
what is become of him.
2 And Aaron said unto them, Break
off the [c]golden earrings, which *are* in
the ears of your wives, of your sons,
and of your daughters, and bring
them unto me.
3 And all the people brake off the
golden earrings which *were* in their
ears, and brought *them* unto Aaron.
4 And [d]he received *them* at their
hand, and fashioned it with a graving
tool, after he had made it a molten
calf: and they said, These *be* thy gods,
O Israel, which brought thee up out of
the land of Egypt.
5 And when Aaron saw *it*, he built an
altar before it; and Aaron made
[e]proclamation, and said, To morrow
is a feast to the LORD.
6 And they rose up early on the morrow, and offered burnt offerings, and
brought peace offerings; and the [f]peo-
ple sat down to eat and to drink, and
rose up to play.
7 ¶ And the LORD said unto Moses,
[g]Go, get thee down; for thy people,
which thou broughtest out of the land
of Egypt, [h]have corrupted *themselves:*
8 They have turned aside quickly
out of the way which I [i]commanded
them: they have made them a molten
calf, and have worshipped it, and
have sacrificed thereunto, and said,
[j]These *be* thy gods, O Israel, which
have brought thee up out of the land
of Egypt.
9 And the LORD said unto Moses, I
[k]have seen this people, and, behold,
it *is* a stiffnecked people:
10 Now therefore [l]let me alone, that
my wrath may wax hot against them,
and that I may consume them: and [m]I
will make of thee a great nation.
11 And [n]Moses besought the [1]LORD
his God, and said, LORD, why doth
thy wrath wax hot against thy people,
which thou hast brought forth out of
the land of Egypt with great power,
and with a mighty hand?
12 Wherefore should the Egyptians
speak, and say, For mischief did he
bring them out, to slay them in the
mountains, and to consume them
from the face of the earth? Turn from
thy fierce wrath, and repent of this
evil against thy people.
13 Remember Abraham, Isaac, and
Israel, thy servants, to whom thou
[o]swarest by thine own self, and saidst
unto them, [p]I will multiply your seed
as the stars of heaven, and all this land
that I have spoken of will I give unto
your seed, and they shall inherit *it* for
ever.
14 And the LORD [q]repented of the
evil which he thought to do unto his
people.

1 vessels.
g Lev. 19.3. Lev. 26.2. Eze. 20.12. Eze. 44.24.
h Neh. 9.14. Deut. 5.15. Isa. 56.6. Isa. 58.13. Eze. 20.12.
i ch. 35.2. Num. 15.35.
j Gen. 2.2. ch. 16.23. ch. 20.10.
2 holiness. ch. 28.36.
k Eze. 20.12.
l Gen. 1.31.
m ch. 24.12. ch. 32.15. ch. 34.28,29. Deut. 4.13. Deut. 5.22. Deut. 9.10, 11. 2 Cor. 3.3.

CHAP. 32

a ch. 24.18. Deut. 9.9.
b Isa. 41.6,7. Acts 7.40.
c Judg. 8.24.
d ch. 20.23. Deut. 9.16. Judg. 7.3,4. 1 Ki. 12.28. Neh. 9.18. Ps. 106.19. Isa. 46.6. Acts 7.41. Rom. 1.23.
e Lev. 23.2. 2 Ki. 10.20.
f 1 Cor. 10.7.
g Deut. 9.12.
h Gen. 6.11. Deut. 4.16. Deut. 32.5. Judg. 2.19. Hosea 9.9.
i ch. 20.3,4, 23. Deut. 9.16.
j 1 Ki. 12.28.
k ch. 33.3,5. ch. 34.9. Deut. 9.6, 13. Deut. 31.27. 2 Chr. 30.8. Isa. 48.4. Acts 7.51.
l Deut. 9.14.
m Num. 14. 12.
n Deut. 9.18, 26-29. Ps. 74.1. Ps. 106.23.
1 the face of the LORD.
o Gen. 22.16. Heb. 6.13.
p Gen. 12.7. Gen. 13.15. Gen. 15.7, 18. Gen. 26.4. Gen. 28.13. Gen. 35.12.
q Num. 23. 19. Deut. 32.36. 2 Sam. 24. 16. 1 Chr. 21.15. Jer. 18.8. Hosea 11.8. Joel 2.13. Jonah 3.10.

15 ¶ And [r]Moses turned, and went
down from the mount, and the two
tables of the testimony *were* in his
hand: the tables *were* written on both
their sides; on the one side and on the
other *were* they written.
16 And the [s]tables *were* the work of
God, and the writing *was* the writing
of God, graven upon the tables.
17 And when Joshua heard the noise
of the people as they shouted, he said
unto Moses, *There is* a noise of war
in the camp.
18 And he said, *It is* not the voice of
them that shout for mastery, neither
is it the voice of *them that* cry for [2]be-
ing overcome: *but* the noise of *them
that* sing do I hear.
19 ¶ And it came to pass, as soon as
he came nigh unto the camp, that he
saw the calf, and the dancing: and
Moses' anger waxed hot, and he cast
the tables out of his hands, and brake
them beneath the mount.
20 And he took the calf which they
had made, and burnt *it* in the fire, and
ground *it* to powder, and strawed *it*
upon the water, and made the children
of Israel drink *of it*.
21 And Moses said unto Aaron,
What [t]did this people unto thee, that
thou hast brought so great a sin upon
them?
22 And Aaron said, Let not the anger
of my lord wax hot: [u]thou knowest
the people, that they *are set* on mischief.
23 For they said unto me, Make us
gods, which shall go before us: for *as
for* this Moses, the man that brought
us up out of the land of Egypt, we wot
not what is become of him.
24 And I said unto them, Whosoever
hath any gold, let them break *it* off.
So they gave *it* me: then I cast it into
the fire, and there came out this calf.
25 ¶ And when Moses saw that the
people *were* [v]naked; (for Aaron had
[w]made them naked unto *their* shame
among [3]their enemies:)
26 Then Moses stood in the gate of
the camp, and said, Who *is* on the
LORD's side? *let him come* unto me.
And all the sons of Levi gathered
themselves together unto him.
27 And he said unto them, Thus
saith the LORD God of Israel, Put
every man his sword by his side, *and*
go in and out from gate to gate
throughout the camp, and [x]slay every
man his brother, and every man his
companion, and every man his neighbour.

[r] Deut. 9.15.
[s] ch. 31.18.
2 weakness.
[t] Gen. 20.9.
[u] ch. 15.24.
[v] ch. 33.4,5.
[w] 2 Chr. 28. 19.
3 those that rose up against them.
[x] Deut. 33.9.
4 Or, And Moses said, Consecrate yourselves to day to the LORD, because every man hath been against his son, and against his brother, etc. Num. 25.11. Deut. 13.6. Deut. 33.9. Pro. 21.3. Zech. 13.3.
5 fill your hands.
[y] 1 Sam. 12. 20.
[z] 2 Sam. 16. 12. Amos 5.15.
[a] Deut. 9.14. Ps. 69.28. Rom. 9.3.
[b] Ps. 56.8. Ps. 139.16. Dan. 12.1. Phil. 4.3. Rev. 3.5. Rev. 20.12, 15. Rev. 22.19.
[c] Lev. 23.30. Eze. 18.4.
[d] Num. 20. 16.
[e] Amos 3.14. Rom. 2.5,6.
[f] 2 Sam. 12.9.

CHAP. 33

[a] Gen. 12.7.
[b] Deut. 7.22. Josh. 24.11.
[c] ch. 32.9. Deut. 9.6.
[d] 2 Sam. 19. 24.

28 And the children of Levi did according to the word of Moses: and
there fell of the people that day about
three thousand men.
29 For [4]Moses had said, [5]Consecrate
yourselves to day to the LORD, even
every man upon his son, and upon his
brother; that he may bestow upon
you a blessing this day.
30 ¶ And it came to pass on the morrow, that Moses said unto the people,
[y]Ye have sinned a great sin: and now
I will go up unto the LORD; [z]perad-
venture I shall make an atonement for
your sin.
31 And Moses returned unto the
LORD, and said, Oh, this people have
sinned a great sin, and have made
them gods of gold.
32 Yet now, if thou wilt forgive their
sin—; and if not, [a]blot me, I pray
thee, [b]out of thy book which thou hast
written.
33 And the LORD said unto Moses,
[c]Whosoever hath sinned against me,
him will I blot out of my book.
34 Therefore now go, lead the people
unto *the place* of which I have spoken
unto thee: behold, mine [d]Angel shall
go before thee: nevertheless [e]in the
day when I visit I will visit their sin
upon them.
35 And the LORD plagued the people,
because [f]they made the calf, which
Aaron made.

CHAPTER 33

AND the LORD said unto Moses,
Depart, *and* go up hence, thou and
the people which thou hast brought
up out of the land of Egypt, unto the
land which I sware unto Abraham, to
Isaac, and to Jacob, saying, Unto [a]thy
seed will I give it:
2 And I will send an angel before
thee; and [b]I will drive out the Canaanite, the Amorite, and the Hittite, and
the Pĕ-rĭz-zīte, the Hī-vīte, and the
Jĕb-ū-sīte:
3 Unto a land flowing with milk and
honey: for I will not go up in the
midst of thee; for thou *art* [c]a stiffnecked people: lest I consume thee
in the way.
4 ¶ And when the people heard these
evil tidings, they mourned: and [d]no
man did put on him his ornaments.
5 For the LORD had said unto Moses,
Say unto the children of Israel, Ye
are a stiffnecked people: I will come
up into the midst of thee in a moment,
and consume thee: therefore now
put off thy ornaments from thee,

that I [e]may know what to do unto
thee.
6 And the children of Israel stripped
themselves of their ornaments by the
mount Hôr'ĕb.
7 And Moses took the tabernacle,
and pitched it without the camp, afar
off from the camp, and called it the
Tabernacle of the congregation. And
it came to pass, *that* every one which
[f]sought the LORD went out unto the
tabernacle of the congregation, which
was without the camp.
8 And it came to pass, when Moses
went out unto the tabernacle, *that* all
the people rose up, and stood every
man [g]*at* his tent door, and looked
after Moses, until he was gone into
the tabernacle.
9 And it came to pass, as Moses entered into the tabernacle, the cloudy
pillar descended, and stood *at* the
door of the tabernacle, and *the LORD*
[h]talked with Moses.
10 And all the people saw the cloudy
pillar stand *at* the tabernacle door:
and all the people rose up and worshipped, every man *in* his tent door.
11 And [i]the LORD spake unto Moses
face to face, as a man speaketh unto
his friend. And he turned again into
the camp: but [j]his servant Joshua, the
son of Nun, a young man, departed
not out of the tabernacle.
12 ¶ And Moses said unto the LORD,
See, thou sayest unto me, Bring up
this people: and thou hast not let me
know whom thou wilt send with me.
Yet thou hast said, [k]I know thee by
name, and thou hast also found grace
in my sight.
13 Now therefore, I pray thee, [l]if I
have found grace in thy sight, shew
[m]me now thy way, that I may know
thee, that I may find grace in thy
sight: and consider that this nation *is*
[n]thy people.
14 And he said, [o]My presence shall
go *with thee*, and I will [p]give thee rest.
15 And he said unto him, [q]If thy
presence go not *with me*, carry us not
up hence.
16 For wherein shall it be known
here that I and thy people have found
grace in thy sight? [r]*is it* not in that
thou goest with us? so [s]shall we be
separated, I and thy people, from all
the people that *are* upon the face of
the earth.
17 And the LORD said unto Moses,
I [t]will do this thing also that thou hast
spoken: for thou hast found grace in
my sight, and I know thee by name.

Ps. 139.23.
f 2 Sam. 21. 1.
g Num. 16. 27.
h Ps. 99.7.
i Gen. 32.30. Deut. 5.24. Deut. 34.10.
j ch. 24.13.
k Ps. 1.6. Jer. 1.5. John 10.14. 2 Tim. 2.19.
l ch. 34.9.
m Ps. 25.4. Ps. 27.11. Ps. 86.11. Ps. 119.33.
n Deut. 9.26. Joel 2.17.
o ch. 40.34-38. Isa. 63.9.
p Deut. 3.20. Josh. 21.44. Josh. 22.4. Josh. 23.1. Ps. 95.11.
q ch. 34.9.
r Num. 14.14.
s Deut. 4.34. 2 Sam. 7.23. Ps. 147.20. Titus 2.14.
t Gen. 19.21. Jas. 5.16.
u 1 Tim. 6.16.
v Jer. 31.14.
w Rom. 4.4. Rom. 9.15.
x Gen. 32.30. Deut. 5.24. Judg. 13.22. Isa. 6.5. Rev. 1.16.
y Isa. 2.21.
z Ps. 91.1,4.
a John 1.18. 1 Tim. 6.16. 1 John 4.12.

CHAP. 34

a Deut. 10.1.
b Deut. 10.2, 4.
c Neh. 9.17. Joel 2.13.
d Rom. 2.4.
e Ps. 108.4.
f Jer. 32.18. Dan. 9.4.
g Eph. 4.32. 1 John 1.9.
h Josh. 24.19. Job 10.14.

18 And he said, I beseech thee, shew
me thy [u]glory.
19 And he said, [v]I will make all my
goodness pass before thee, and I will
proclaim the name of the LORD before
thee; [w]and will be gracious to whom I
will be gracious, and will shew mercy
on whom I will shew mercy.
20 And he said, Thou canst not see
my face: for [x]there shall no man see
me, and live.
21 And the LORD said, Behold, *there*
is a place by me, and thou shalt stand
upon a rock:
22 And it shall come to pass, while
my glory passeth by, that I will put
thee [y]in a clift of the rock, and will
[z]cover thee with my hand while I pass
by:
23 And I will take away mine hand,
and thou shalt see my back parts: but
my face shall [a]not be seen.

CHAPTER 34

AND the LORD said unto Moses,
Hew [a]thee two tables of stone like
unto the first: and [b]I will write upon
these tables the words that were in
the first tables, which thou brakest.
2 And be ready in the morning, and
come up in the morning unto mount
Sī-nâi, and present thyself there to me
in the top of the mount.
3 And no man shall come up with
thee, neither let any man be seen
throughout all the mount; neither let
the flocks nor herds feed before that
mount.
4 ¶ And he hewed two tables of
stone like unto the first; and Moses
rose up early in the morning, and
went up unto mount Sī'nâi, as the
LORD had commanded him, and took
in his hand the two tables of stone.
5 And the LORD descended in the
cloud, and stood with him there, and
proclaimed the name of the LORD.
6 And the LORD passed by before
him, and proclaimed, The LORD, The
LORD [c]God, merciful and gracious,
longsuffering, and abundant in [d]good-
ness and [e]truth,
7 Keeping [f]mercy for thousands, forgiving [g]iniquity and transgression and
sin, and that [h]will by no means clear
the guilty; visiting the iniquity of the
fathers upon the children, and upon
the children's children, unto the third
and to the fourth *generation*.
8 And Moses made haste, and bowed
his head toward the earth, and worshipped.
9 And he said, If now I have found

grace in thy sight, O Lord, let my
Lord, I pray thee, go among us; for
it *is* a stiffnecked people; and pardon
our iniquity and our sin, and take us
for [i]thine inheritance.
10 ¶ And he said, Behold, [j]I make a
covenant: before all thy people I will
[k]do marvels, such as have not been
done in all the earth, nor in any nation: and all the people among which
thou *art* shall see the work of the
LORD: for it *is* [l]a terrible thing that I
will do with thee.
11 Observe [m]thou that which I command thee this day: behold, I drive
out before thee the Amorite, and the
Canaanite, and the Hittite, and the
Pĕ-rĭz´-zīte, and the Hī´-vīte, and the
Jĕb´-ū-ṡīte.
12 Take [n]heed to thyself, lest thou
make a covenant with the inhabitants
of the land whither thou goest, lest it
be for a snare in the midst of thee:
13 But ye shall destroy their altars,
break their [1]images, and cut [o]down
their groves:
14 For thou shalt worship no other
god: for the LORD, whose name [p]*is*
Jealous, *is* a [q]jealous God:
15 Lest thou make a covenant with
the inhabitants of the land, and they
[r]go a whoring after their gods, and do
sacrifice unto their gods, and *one* [s]call
thee, and thou eat [t]of his sacrifice;
16 And thou take of their [u]daughters
unto thy sons, and their daughters
[v]go a whoring after their gods, and
make thy sons go a whoring after their
gods.
17 Thou [w]shalt make thee no molten
gods.
18 ¶ The feast of [x]unleavened bread
shalt thou keep. Seven days thou
shalt eat unleavened bread, as I commanded thee, in the time of the month
Abib: for in the month of Abib thou
camest out from Egypt.
19 All [y]that openeth the matrix *is*
mine; and every firstling among thy
cattle, *whether* ox or sheep, *that is*
male.
20 But [z]the firstling of an ass thou
shalt redeem with a [2]lamb: and if
thou redeem *him* not, then shalt thou
break his neck. All the firstborn of
thy sons thou shalt redeem. And none
shall appear before me [a]empty.
21 ¶ Six [b]days thou shalt work, but
on the seventh day thou shalt rest: in
earing time and harvest thou shalt
rest.
22 ¶ And [c]thou shalt observe the
feast of weeks, of the firstfruits of
wheat harvest, and the feast of ingathering at the [3]year's end.
23 ¶ Thrice [d]in the year shall all your
men children appear before the Lord
GOD, the God of Israel.
24 For I will [e]cast out the nations
before thee, and [f]enlarge thy borders:
[g]neither shall any man desire thy land,
when thou shalt go up to appear before the LORD thy God thrice in the
year.
25 Thou [h]shalt not offer the blood of
my sacrifice with leaven; neither [i]shall
the sacrifice of the feast of the passover be left unto the morning.
26 The [j]first of the firstfruits of thy
land thou shalt bring unto the house
of the LORD thy God. Thou shalt not
seethe a kid in his mother's milk.
27 And the LORD said unto Moses,
Write thou [k]these words: for after the
tenor of these words I have made a
covenant with thee and with Israel.
28 And [l]he was there with the LORD
forty days and forty nights; he did
neither eat bread, nor drink water.
And [m]he wrote upon the tables the
words of the covenant, the ten [4]com-
mandments.
29 ¶ And it came to pass, when
Moses came down from mount Sī´-
nâi with the two tables [n]of testimony
in Moses' hand, when he came down
from the mount, that Moses wist not
that [o]the skin of his face shone while
he talked with him.
30 And when Aaron and all the children of Israel saw Moses, behold, the
skin of his face shone; and they were
afraid to come nigh him.
31 And Moses called unto them; and
Aaron and all the rulers of the congregation returned unto him: and
Moses talked with them.
32 And afterward all the children of
Israel came nigh: [p]and he gave them
in commandment all that the LORD
had spoken with him in mount
Sī´-nâi.
33 And *till* Moses had done speaking with them, he put [q]a vail on his
face.
34 But when Moses went in before
the LORD to speak with him, he took
the vail off, until he came out. And he
came out, and spake unto the children
of Israel *that* which he was commanded.
35 And the children of Israel saw the
face of Moses, that the skin of Moses'
face shone: and Moses put the vail upon his face again, until he went in to
speak with him.

i Ps. 94.14. Zech. 2.12.
j Deut. 29.12.
k 2 Sam. 7. 23. Ps. 147.20.
l Isa. 64.3.
m Deut. 12. 28.
n Judg. 2.2.
1 statues.
o 2 Ki. 18.4.
p Isa. 57.15.
q ch. 20.5.
r Eze. 6.9.
s 1 Cor. 10. 27.
t 1 Cor. 8.4.
u Ezra 9.2.
v Num. 25.1, 2.
w Lev. 19.4.
x ch. 23.15.
y ch. 22.29. Eze 44.30. Luke 2.23.
z Num. 18. 15.
2 Or, kid.
a Deut. 16. 16. 2 Sam. 24. 24.
b Deut. 5.12. Luke 13.14.
c ch. 23.16.
3 revolution of the year.
d Deut. 16. 16.
e Lev. 18.24. Deut. 7.1. Josh. 24.8-13. Ps. 78.55. Ps. 80.8.
f Deut. 19.8.
g Gen. 35.5. 2 Chr. 17.10. Pro. 16.7.
h ch. 23.18.
i ch. 12.10.
j Deut. 26.2, 10. Neh. 10.35. Pro. 3.9.
k Deut. 31.9. Isa. 30.8.
l Deut. 9.9, 18.
m ch. 31.18. ch. 32.16. Deut. 10.2, 4.
4 words.
n ch. 32.15.
o Matt. 17.2.
p ch. 24.3.
q 2 Cor. 3.13.

CHAPTER 35

AND Moses gathered all the congregation of the children of Israel together, and said unto them, [a]These *are* the words which the LORD hath commanded, that *ye* should do them.

2 Six [b]days shall work be done, but on the seventh day there shall be to you [1]an holy day, a sabbath of rest to the LORD: whosoever doeth work therein shall be put to death.

3 Ye [c]shall kindle no fire throughout your habitations upon the sabbath day.

4 ¶ And Moses spake unto all the congregation of the children of Israel, saying, This [d]*is* the thing which the LORD commanded, saying,

5 Take ye from among you an offering unto the LORD: [e]whosoever *is* of a willing heart, let him bring it, an offering of the LORD; gold, and silver, and brass,

6 And blue, and purple, and scarlet, and fine linen, and goats' *hair*,

7 And rams' skins dyed red, and badgers' skins, and shĭt-tĭm wood,

8 And oil for the light, and spices for anointing oil, and for the sweet incense,

9 And onyx stones, and stones to be set for the ē-phŏd, and for the breastplate.

10 And [f]every wise hearted among you shall come, and make all that the LORD hath commanded;

11 The [g]tabernacle, his tent, and his covering, his taches, and his boards, his bars, his pillars, and his sockets,

12 The [h]ark, and the staves thereof, *with* the mercy seat, and the vail of the covering,

13 The [i]table, and his staves, and all his vessels, and the [j]shewbread,

14 The [k]candlestick also for the light, and his furniture, and his lamps, with the oil for the light,

15 And [l]the incense altar, and his staves, and [m]the anointing oil, and [n]the sweet incense, and the hanging for the door at the entering in of the tabernacle,

16 The [o]altar of burnt offering, with his brasen grate, his staves, and all his vessels, the laver and his foot,

17 The [p]hangings of the court, his pillars, and their sockets, and the hanging for the door of the court,

18 The pins of the tabernacle, and the pins of the court, and their cords,

19 The [q]cloths of service, to do service in the holy *place*, the holy garments for Aaron the priest, and the garments of his sons, to minister in the priest's office.

20 ¶ And all the congregation of the children of Israel departed from the presence of Moses.

21 And they came, every [r]one whose heart stirred him up, and every one whom his spirit made willing, *and* they brought the LORD's offering to the work of the tabernacle of the congregation, and for all his service, and for the holy garments.

22 And they came, both men and women, as many as were willing hearted, *and* brought bracelets, and earrings, and rings, and tablets, all jewels of gold: and every man that offered *offered* an offering of gold unto the LORD.

23 And [s]every man, with whom was found blue, and purple, and scarlet, and fine linen, and goats' *hair*, and red skins of rams, and badgers' skins, brought *them*.

24 Every one that did offer an offering of silver and brass brought the LORD's offering: and every man, with whom was found shĭt-tĭm wood for any work of the service, brought *it*.

25 And all the women that were wise hearted [t]did spin with their hands, and brought that which they had spun, *both* of blue, and of purple, *and* of scarlet, and of fine linen.

26 And all the women whose heart stirred them up in wisdom spun goats' *hair*.

27 And [u]the rulers brought onyx stones, and stones to be set, for the ē-phŏd, and for the breastplate;

28 And [v]spice, and oil for the light, and for the anointing oil, and for the sweet incense.

29 The children of Israel brought a [w]willing offering unto the LORD, every man and woman, whose heart made them willing to bring for all manner of work, which the LORD had commanded to be made by the hand of Moses.

30 ¶ And Moses said unto the children of Israel, See, [x]the LORD hath called by name Bĕz-ă-lēel the son of Ū-rī, the son of Hur, of the tribe of Judah;

31 And he hath filled him with the [y]spirit of God, in wisdom, in understanding, and in knowledge, and in all manner of workmanship;

32 And to devise curious works, to work in gold, and in silver, and in brass,

33 And in the cutting of stones, to set *them*, and in carving of wood, to

CHAP. 35
a ch. 34.32.
b ch. 31.14, 15. Lev. 23.3. Num. 15.32. Deut. 5.12. Luke 13.14.
1 holiness.
c ch. 16.23.
d ch. 25.1,2.
e ch. 25.2. 2 Cor. 9.7.
f ch. 31.6. 1 Ki. 7.14. Isa. 28.26.
g ch. 25.9. ch. 26.1,2. ch. 29.42,43. ch. 31.7. ch. 33.7. ch. 36.8. ch. 39.32-43. ch. 40.2. Acts 7.44, 45. Heb. 8.2,5. Heb. 9.2,11. Rev. 21.3.
h ch. 25.10.
i ch. 25.23.
j ch. 25.30. Lev. 24.5,6.
k ch. 25.31.
l ch. 30.1. ch. 37.25. ch. 40.5.
m ch. 30.23.
n ch. 30.34. 1 Sam. 2.28. 1 Chr. 23.13. 2 Chr. 29.11. Luke 1.9.
o ch. 27.1.
p ch. 27.9.
q ch. 31.10. ch. 39.1,41. Num. 4.5,6.
r ch. 25.2. ch. 36.2. 1 Chr. 28.2, 9. 1 Chr. 29.9. Ezra 7.27. 2 Cor. 8.12. 2 Cor. 9.7.
s 1 Chr. 29.8.
t ch. 28.3. ch. 31.6. ch. 36.1. 2 Ki. 23.7. Pro. 31.19, 22,24.
u 1 Chr. 29.6. Ezra 2.68.
v ch. 30.23.
w 1 Chr. 29. 9.
x ch. 31.2.
y Gen. 41.38. Job 32.8. Pro. 2.6.

nake any manner of cunning work.
34 And he hath put in his heart that
ıe may teach, *both* he, and Ă-hō-lĭ-
ıb, [z]the son of Ă-hĭs-ă-măch, of the
ribe of Dan.
35 Them hath he [a]filled with wisdom
of heart, to work all manner of work,
of the engraver, and of the cunning
vorkman, and of the embroiderer, in
ılue, and in purple, in scarlet, and in
ine linen, and of the weaver, *even* of
hem that do any work, and of those
hat devise cunning work.

CHAPTER 36

THEN wrought Bĕz-ă-lēel and Ă-
hō-lĭ-ăb, and every [a]wise hearted
nan, in whom the LORD put wisdom
ınd understanding to know how to
vork all manner of work for the ser-
ice of the [b]sanctuary, according to
ıll that the LORD had commanded.
2 And Moses called Bĕz-ă-lēel and
Ă-hō-lĭ-ăb, and every wise hearted
nan, in whose heart the LORD had put
visdom, *even* every one whose heart
stirred him up to come unto the work
o do it:
3 And they received of Moses all the
offering, which the children of Israel
had brought for the work of the service of the sanctuary, to make it *with-*
al. And they brought yet unto him free
offerings every morning.
4 And all the wise men, that wrought
ıll the work of the sanctuary, came
every man from his work which they
nade;
5 ¶ And they spake unto Moses, say-
ng, [e]The people bring much more
han enough for the service of the
vork, which the LORD commanded to
make.
6 And Moses gave commandment,
ınd they caused it to be proclaimed
hroughout the camp, saying, Let
neither man nor woman make any
more work for the offering of the
sanctuary. So the people were restrained from bringing.
7 For the stuff they had was sufficient
for all the work to make it, and too
much.
8 ¶ And every [f]wise hearted man
among them that wrought the work of
the tabernacle made ten curtains *of*
fine twined linen, and blue, and purple, and scarlet: *with* chĕr-ŭ-bĭms [g]of
cunning work made he them.
9 The length of one curtain *was*
twenty and eight cubits, and the
breadth of one curtain four cubits:
the curtains *were* all of one size.

z ch. 31.6.
a ver. 31. ch. 31.3,6. ch. 36.1,2. 1 Ki. 7.14. 2 Chr. 2.14. Isa. 28.26. Jas. 1.5.
CHAP. 36
a ch. 28.3. ch. 31.6. ch. 35.10,35. Job 32.8. Isa. 28.26. Pro. 2.6.
b ch. 25.8. Lev. 4.6. Lev. 19.30. Num. 18.5. Num. 30.8. 1 Ki. 6.16. Ps. 96.6. Ps. 134.2. Ps. 150.1. Isa. 63.18. Lam. 1.10. Lam. 2.20. Lam. 4.1. Eze. 5.11. Dan. 8.13, 14. Heb. 9.1,2.
c ch. 35.2,26. 1 Chr. 29.5.
d ch. 35.27.
e 2 Cor. 8.2,3.
f ch. 26.1. Job 32.8. Pro. 10.8. Pro. 15.14. Pro. 16.1. Pro. 18.15. Pro. 21.1.
g Gen. 3.24. 1 Ki. 6.23. 2 Chr. 3.10. Eze. 1.5-28. Eze. 10.1.
h ch. 26.5.
i ch. 26.7.
j ch. 26.14.
k ch. 26.15.
l ch. 25.5,10. Num. 25.1. Deut. 10.3. Josh. 2.1.
1 hands.

10 And he coupled the five curtains
one unto another: and *the other* five
curtains he coupled one unto another.
11 And he made loops of blue on the
edge of one curtain from the selvedge
in the coupling: likewise he made in
the uttermost side of *another* curtain,
in the coupling of the second.
12 Fifty [h]loops made he in one curtain, and fifty loops made he in the
edge of the curtain which *was* in the
coupling of the second: the loops held
one *curtain* to another.
13 And he made fifty taches of gold,
and coupled the curtains one unto
another with the taches: so it became
one tabernacle.
14 ¶ And [i]he made curtains *of* goats'
hair for the tent over the tabernacle:
eleven curtains he made them.
15 The length of one curtain *was*
thirty cubits, and four cubits *was* the
breadth of one curtain: the eleven
curtains *were* of one size.
16 And he coupled five curtains by
themselves, and six curtains by themselves.
17 And he made fifty loops upon the
uttermost edge of the curtain in the
coupling, and fifty loops made he upon the edge of the curtain which
coupleth the second.
18 And he made fifty taches *of* brass
to couple the tent together, that it
might be one.
19 And [j]he made a covering for the
tent *of* rams' skins dyed red, and a
covering *of* badgers' skins above
that.
20 ¶ And [k]he made boards for the
tabernacle *of* [l]shĭt-tĭm wood, standing
up.
21 The length of a board *was* ten cubits, and the breadth of a board one
cubit and a half.
22 One board had two [1]tenons,
equally distant one from another:
thus did he make for all the boards of
the tabernacle.
23 And he made boards for the tabernacle; twenty boards for the south
side southward:
24 And forty sockets of silver he
made under the twenty boards; two
sockets under one board for his two
tenons, and two sockets under another board for his two tenons.
25 And for the other side of the tabernacle, *which is* toward the north
corner, he made twenty boards,
26 And their forty sockets of silver;
two sockets under one board, and two
sockets under another board.

I.R. 3 D

27 And for the sides of the tabernacle
[2]westward he made six boards.
28 And two boards made he for the
corners of the tabernacle in the two
sides.
29 And they were [3]coupled beneath,
and coupled together at the head
thereof, to one ring: thus he did to
both of them in both the corners.
30 And there were eight boards; and
their sockets *were* sixteen sockets of
silver, [4]under every board two sockets.
31 ¶ And he made [m]bars of shĭt′-tĭm
wood; five for the boards of the one
side of the tabernacle,
32 And five bars for the boards of the
other side of the tabernacle, and five
bars for the boards of the tabernacle
for the sides westward.
33 And he made the middle bar to
shoot through the boards from the
one end to the other.
34 And he overlaid the boards with
gold, and made their rings *of* gold *to
be* places for the bars, and overlaid the
bars with gold.
35 ¶ And he made [n]a vail *of* blue, and
purple, and scarlet, and fine twined
linen: *with* chĕr′-ū-bĭms made he it of
cunning work.
36 And he made thereunto four pillars *of* shĭt′-tĭm *wood*, and overlaid
them with gold: their hooks *were of*
gold; and he cast for them four sockets of silver.
37 ¶ And he made an [o]hanging for
the tabernacle door *of* blue, and purple, and scarlet, and fine twined linen,
[5]of needlework;
38 And the five pillars of it with their
hooks: and he overlaid their chapiters [p]and their fillets with gold: but
their five sockets *were of* brass.

CHAPTER 37

AND [a]Bĕz′-ā-lēel made [b]the ark *of*
shĭt′-tĭm wood: two cubits and a
half *was* the length of it, and a cubit
and a half the breadth of it, and a cubit and a half the height of it:
2 And he overlaid it with pure gold
within and without, and made a
crown of gold to it round about.
3 And he cast for it four rings of gold,
to be set by the four corners of it; even
two rings upon the one side of it,
and two rings upon the other side
of it.
4 And he made [c]staves *of* shĭt′-tĭm
wood, and overlaid them with gold.
5 And he [d]put the staves into the
rings by the sides of the ark, to bear
the ark.

2 seaward.
chap. 26.22.

3 twinned.
ch. 26.24.
2 Sam. 5.6.
Ps. 133.1.
Acts 2.46.
1 Cor. 1.10.

4 two sockets, two sockets under one board.
m ch. 26.26.

n ch. 26.31.
Matt. 27.51.
Heb. 6.19.
Heb. 10.20.

o ch. 26.36.
5 the work of a needle-worker, or, embroiderer.
p 1 Ki. 7.16.
2 Chr. 4.12.
Jer. 52.22.

CHAP. 37

a ch. 35.30.
b ch. 25.10.
c Num. 4.6.
d Num. 1.50.
2 Sam. 6.3.
e ch. 25.17.
1 Or, out of, etc.
2 Or, out of, etc.
f Gen. 3.24.
ch. 25.22.
1 Ki. 6.23.
2 Chr. 3.10.
Ps. 80.1.
Eze. 1.5-28.
Eze. 10.1.
John 1.51.
Phil. 2.10.
1 Tim. 3.16.
Heb. 1.14.
1 Pet. 1.12.
g ch. 25.23.
Mal. 1.7,12.
h ch. 25.29.
3 Or, to pour out withal.
i ch. 25.31.
Lev. 24.4.
1 Chr. 28.15.
Zech. 4.2.
Matt. 5.15, 16.
John 5.35.
Phil. 2.15.
1 Pet. 2.9.
Rev. 1.20.

6 ¶ And he made the [e]mercy seat *of*
pure gold: two cubits and a half *was*
the length thereof, and one cubit and
a half the breadth thereof.
7 And he made two chĕr′-ū-bĭms *of*
gold, beaten out of one piece made he
them, on the two ends of the mercy
seat;
8 One cherub [1]on the end on this
side, and another cherub [2]on the *other*
end on that side: out of the mercy
seat made he the chĕr′-ū-bĭms on the
two ends thereof.
9 And the [f]chĕr′-ū-bĭms spread out
their wings on high, *and* covered with
their wings over the mercy seat, with
their faces one to another; *even* to
the mercy seatward were the faces of
the chĕr′-ū-bĭms.
10 ¶ And he made [g]the table *of* shĭt′-
tĭm wood: two cubits *was* the length
thereof, and a cubit the breadth thereof, and a cubit and a half the height
thereof:
11 And he overlaid it with pure gold,
and made thereunto a crown of gold
round about.
12 Also he made thereunto a border
of an handbreadth round about; and
made a crown of gold for the border
thereof round about.
13 And he cast for it four rings of
gold, and put the rings upon the four
corners that *were* in the four feet
thereof.
14 Over against the border were the
rings, the places for the staves to bear
the table.
15 And he made the staves *of* shĭt′-
tĭm wood, and overlaid them with
gold, to bear the table.
16 And he made the vessels which
were upon the table, his [h]dishes, and
his spoons, and his bowls, and his
covers [3]to cover withal, *of* pure gold.
17 ¶ And he made the [i]candlestick *of*
pure gold: *of* beaten work made he
the candlestick; his shaft, and his
branch, his bowls, his knops, and his
flowers, were of the same:
18 And six branches going out of the
sides thereof; three branches of the
candlestick out of the one side thereof, and three branches of the candlestick out of the other side thereof:
19 Three bowls made after the fashion of almonds in one branch, a knop
and a flower; and three bowls made
like almonds in another branch, a
knop and a flower: so throughout the
six branches going out of the candlestick.
20 And in the candlestick *were* four

bowls made like [j]almonds, his knops,
and his flowers:
21 And a knop under two branches
of the same, and a knop under two
branches of the same, and a knop under two branches of the same, according to the six branches going out of it.
22 Their knops and their branches
were of the same: all of it *was* one
beaten work *of* pure gold.
23 And he made his [k]seven lamps,
and his snuffers, and his snuffdishes,
of pure gold.
24 *Of* a talent of pure gold made he
it, and all the vessels thereof.
25 ¶ And [l]he made the incense altar
of shĭt-tĭm wood: the length of it *was*
a cubit, and the breadth of it a cubit;
it was foursquare; and two cubits *was*
the height of it; the horns thereof
were of the same.
26 And he overlaid it with pure gold,
both the top of it, and the sides thereof
round about, and the horns of it: also
he made unto it a crown of gold round
about.
27 And he made two rings of gold for
it under the crown thereof, by the two
corners of it, upon the two sides thereof, to be places for the staves to bear it
withal.
28 And he made the staves *of* shĭt-
tĭm wood, and overlaid them with
gold.
29 ¶ And he made [4]the holy anointing oil, and the pure [m]incense of sweet
spices, according to the work of the
apothecary.

CHAPTER 38

AND he made the altar [a]of burnt
offering *of* shĭt-tĭm wood: five cubits *was* the length thereof, and five
cubits the breadth thereof; *it was* foursquare; and three cubits the height
thereof.
2 And he made the horns thereof on
the four corners of it; the horns thereof were of the same: and he overlaid it
with brass.
3 And he made all the vessels of the
altar, the pots, and the shovels, and
the basons, *and* the fleshhooks, and
the firepans: all the vessels thereof
made he *of* [b]brass.
4 And he made for the altar a brasen
grate of network under the compass
thereof beneath unto the midst of it.
5 And he cast four rings for the four
ends of the grate of brass, *to be* places
for the staves.
6 And he made the staves *of* shĭt-tĭm
wood, and overlaid them with brass.
7 And he put the staves into the rings
on the sides of the altar, to bear it
withal; he made the altar hollow with
boards.
8 ¶ And he made [c]the laver *of* brass,
and the foot of it *of* brass, of the [1]look-
ingglasses of *the women* [2]assembling,
which assembled *at* the door of the
tabernacle of the congregation.
9 ¶ And he made [d]the court: on the
south side southward the hangings of
the court *were of* fine twined linen, an
hundred cubits:
10 Their pillars *were* twenty, and
their brasen sockets twenty; the hooks
of the pillars and their fillets *were of*
silver.
11 And for the north side *the hangings were* an hundred cubits, their
pillars *were* twenty, and their sockets
of brass twenty; the hooks of the pillars and their fillets *of* silver.
12 And for the west side *were* hangings of fifty cubits, their pillars ten,
and their sockets ten; the hooks of the
pillars and their fillets *of* silver.
13 And for the east side eastward
fifty cubits.
14 The hangings of the one side *of
the gate were* fifteen cubits; their pillars three, and their sockets three.
15 And for the other side of the court
gate, on this hand and that hand, *were*
hangings of fifteen cubits; their pillars
three, and their sockets three.
16 All the hangings of the court round
about *were* of fine twined linen.
17 And the sockets for the pillars
were of brass; the hooks of the pillars
and their fillets *of* silver; and the overlaying of their chapiters *of* silver; and
all the pillars of the court *were* filleted
with silver.
18 And the hanging for the gate of
the court *was* needlework, *of* blue,
[e]and purple, and scarlet, and fine
twined linen: and twenty cubits *was*
the length, and the height in the
breadth *was* five cubits, answerable to
the hangings of the court.
19 And their pillars *were* four, and
their sockets *of* brass four; their hooks
of silver, and the overlaying of their
chapiters and their fillets *of* silver.
20 And all the [f]pins of the tabernacle,
and of the court round about, *were of*
brass.
21 ¶ This is the sum of the tabernacle, *even* of [g]the tabernacle of testimony, as it was counted, according to
the commandment of Moses, *for* the
service of the Levites, by [h]the hand of
Ĭth-ă-mär, son to Aaron the priest.

j Num. 17.8. Jer. 1.11.
k Rev. 1.20. Rev. 4.5.
l ch. 30.1. ch. 40.26. 1 Ki. 9.25. 1 Chr. 29.6, 7. Isa. 60.6. Mal. 1.11. Heb. 7.25. 1 Pet. 2.5. Rev. 8.3.
4 unction of holiness. ch. 30.23, 34. Isa. 61.1. Isa. 11.2. Ps. 133.2. 1 John 2.20.
m Ps. 141.2. Song 4.14. Mal. 1.11. Heb. 5.7. Heb. 7.25. Rev. 5.8.

CHAP. 38

a ch. 27.1. 2 Chr. 29.23, 24. Ps. 51.15-19. Isa. 61.8. Eze. 44.11. Heb. 9.14. Heb. 13.10.
b 1 Ki. 7.45.
c ch. 30.18. 2 Ki. 16.17. 2 Chr. 4.2. Ps. 26.6. Eze. 36.25. Zech. 13.1. 2 Cor. 7.1. Heb. 10.22. 1 John 5.6.
1 Or, brasen glasses.
2 assembling by troops, as 1 Sam. 2.22.
d ch. 27.9. Ps. 84.2, 10. Ps. 92.13.
e 2 Chr. 3.14.
f ch. 27.19. 2 Chr. 3.9. Ezra 9.8. Isa. 22.23. Eph. 2.21, 22.
g Num. 1.50, 53. Num. 9.15. 2 Chr. 24.6. Acts 7.44.
h Num. 4.28, 33.

22 And [i]Bĕz-ă-lē̤el the son of Ū-rī, the son of Hur, of the tribe of Judah, made all that the LORD commanded Moses.

23 And with him *was* Ă-hō-lĭ-ăb, son of Ă-hĭs-ă-mă<u>ch</u>, of the tribe of Dan, an engraver, and a cunning workman, and an embroiderer in blue, and in purple, and in scarlet, and fine linen.

24 All the gold that was occupied for the work in all the work of the holy *place*, even the gold of the offering, was twenty and nine talents, and seven hundred and thirty shekels, after [j]the shekel of the sanctuary.

25 And the silver of them that were numbered of the congregation *was* an hundred talents, and a thousand seven hundred and threescore and fifteen shekels, after the shekel of the sanctuary:

26 A [k]bē-kăh for [3]every man, *that is*, half a shekel, after the shekel of the sanctuary, for every one that went to be numbered, from twenty years old and upward, for [l]six hundred thousand and three thousand and five hundred and fifty *men*.

27 And of the hundred talents of silver were cast [m]the sockets of the sanctuary, and the sockets of the vail; an hundred sockets of the hundred talents, a talent for a socket.

28 And of the thousand seven hundred seventy and five *shekels* he made hooks for the pillars, and overlaid their chapiters, and filleted them.

29 And the brass of the offering *was* seventy talents, and two thousand and four hundred shekels.

30 And therewith he made the sockets to the door of the tabernacle of the congregation, and the brasen altar, and the brasen grate for it, and all the vessels of the altar,

31 And the sockets of the court round about, and the sockets of the court gate, and all the pins of the tabernacle, and all the [n]pins of the court round about.

CHAPTER 39

AND of [a]the blue, and purple, and scarlet, they made [b]cloths of service, to do service in the holy *place*, and made the holy garments for Aaron; [c]as the LORD commanded Moses.

2 And [d]he made the ē-phŏd *of* gold, blue, and purple, and scarlet, and fine twined linen.

3 And they did beat the gold into thin plates, and cut *it into* wires, to work *it* in the blue, and in the purple, and in the scarlet, and in the fine linen, *with* cunning work.

4 They made shoulderpieces for it, to couple *it* together: by the two edges was it coupled together.

5 And the [e]curious girdle of his ē-phŏd, that *was* upon it, *was* of the same, according to the work thereof; *of* gold, blue, and purple, and scarlet, and fine twined linen; as the LORD commanded Moses.

6 ¶ And [f]they wrought [g]onyx stones inclosed in ouches of gold, graven, as signets are graven, with the [h]names of the children of Israel.

7 And he put them on the shoulders of the ē-phŏd, *that they should be* stones for a [i]memorial to the children of Israel; as the LORD commanded Moses.

8 ¶ And [j]he made the breastplate *of* cunning work, like the work of the ē-phŏd; *of* gold, blue, and purple, and scarlet, and fine twined linen.

9 It was foursquare; they made the breastplate double: a span *was* the length thereof, and a span the breadth thereof, *being* doubled.

10 And [k]they set in it four rows of stones: *the first* row *was* a [1]sardius, a [2]topaz, and a [3]carbuncle: this *was* the first row.

11 And the second row, an [4]emerald, a [5]sapphire, and a [6]diamond.

12 And the third row, a [7]ligure, an [8]agate, and an [9]amethyst.

13 And the fourth row, a [10]beryl, an [11]onyx, and a [12]jasper: *they were* inclosed in ouches of gold in their inclosings.

14 And the stones *were* according to the names of the children of Israel, twelve, according to their names, *like* the engravings of a signet, every one with his name, according to the twelve tribes.

15 And they made upon the breastplate chains at the ends, *of* wreathen work *of* pure gold.

16 And they made two ouches *of* gold, and two gold rings; and put the two rings in the two ends of the breastplate.

17 And they put the two wreathen chains of gold in the two rings on the ends of the breastplate.

18 And the two ends of the two wreathen chains they fastened in the two ouches, and put them on the shoulderpieces of the ē-phŏd, before it.

19 And they made two rings of gold,

i ch. 31.2,6.
j ch. 30.13. Lev. 5.15. Lev. 27.3, 25. Num. 3.47. Num. 18.16.
k ch. 30.13, 15.
3 a poll.
l Num. 1.46.
m ch. 26.19, 21,25,32.
n ch. 27.19. 2 Chr. 3.9. Ezra 9.8. Isa. 22.23. Eph. 2.21, 22.

CHAP. 39

a ch. 35.23.
b ch. 31.10. ch 35.19. Ps. 93.5. Eze. 43.12.
c ch. 28.4.
d ch. 28.6. Lev. 8.7.
e Isa. 11.5. Rev. 1.13.
f ch. 28.9.
g Job 28.16.
h Isa. 49.16. Rev. 2.17.
i ch. 28.12. Josh. 4.7. Neh. 2.20.
j ch. 28.15. Isa. 59.17.
k ch. 28.17.
1 Or, ruby. Reuben's stone.
2 Simeon's stone. Job 28.19. Eze. 28.13. Rev. 21.19, 20.
3 Levi's stone. Isa. 54.12.
4 Judah's stone. Eze. 27.16. Rev. 4.3.
5 Issachar's stone. Job 28.6. Song 5.14. Isa. 54.11.
6 Zebulum's stone. Jer. 17.1.
7 Dan's stone.
8 Naphtali's stone.
9 Gad's stone.
10 Asher's stone. Dan. 10.6.
11 Joseph's stone. Job 28.16.
12 Benjamin's stone. Rev. 21.11.

and put *them* on the two ends of the
breastplate, upon the border of it,
which *was* on the side of the ē-phŏd
inward.
20 And they made two *other* golden
rings, and put them on the two sides
of the ē-phŏd underneath, toward the
forepart of it, over against the *other*
coupling thereof, above the curious
girdle of the ē-phŏd.
21 And they did bind the breastplate
by his rings unto the rings of the ē-
phŏd with a lace of blue, that it might
be above the curious girdle of the ē-
phŏd, and that the breastplate might
not be loosed from the ē-phŏd; as the
LORD commanded Moses.
22 ¶ And [l]he made the robe of the
ē-phŏd *of* woven work, all *of* blue.
23 And *there was* an hole in the midst
of the robe, as the hole of an habergeon, *with* a band round about the
hole, that it should not rend.
24 And they made upon the hems of
the robe pomegranates *of* blue, and
purple, and scarlet, *and* twined *linen*.
25 And they made [m]bells *of* pure
gold, and put the bells between the
pomegranates upon the hem of the
robe, round about between the pomegranates;
26 A bell and a pomegranate, a bell
and a pomegranate, round about the
hem of the robe to minister *in;* as the
LORD commanded Moses.
27 ¶ And [n]they made coats *of* fine
linen *of* woven work for Aaron, and
for his sons,
28 And [o]a mitre *of* fine linen, and
goodly bonnets *of* fine linen, and[p] lin-
en breeches *of* fine twined linen,
29 And a girdle *of* fine twined linen,
and blue, and purple, and scarlet, *of*
needlework; as the LORD commanded
Moses.
30 ¶ And they made the plate of the
holy crown *of* pure gold, and wrote
upon it a writing, *like to* the engravings of a signet, [q]HOLINESS TO THE
LORD.
31 And they tied unto it a lace of
blue, to fasten *it* on high upon the
mitre; as the LORD commanded
Moses.
32 ¶ Thus was all the work of the
tabernacle of the tent of the congregation finished: and the children of
Israel did [r]according to all that the
LORD commanded Moses, so did they.
33 ¶ And they brought [s]the tabernacle unto Moses, the tent, and all his
furniture, his taches, his boards, his
bars, and his pillars, and his sockets,
34 And the covering of rams' skins
dyed red, and the covering of badgers' skins, and the vail of the covering,
35 The ark of the testimony, and the
staves thereof, and the mercy seat,
36 The table, *and* all the vessels
thereof, and the shewbread,
37 The [t]pure candlestick, *with* the
lamps thereof, *even with* the lamps
[u]to be set in order, and all the vessels
thereof, and the oil for light,
38 And the golden altar, and the
anointing oil, and [13]the sweet incense,
and the hanging for the tabernacle
door,
39 The [v]brasen altar, and his grate of
brass, his staves, and all his vessels,
the laver and his foot,
40 The hangings of the court, his
pillars, [w]and his sockets, and the hanging for the court gate, his cords, and
his pins, and all the vessels of the service of the tabernacle, for the tent of
the congregation,
41 The cloths of service to do service
in the holy *place*, and the holy garments for Aaron the priest, and his
sons' garments, to minister in the
priest's office.
42 According to all that the LORD
commanded Moses, so the children of
Israel made [x]all the work.
43 And Moses did look upon all the
work, and, behold, they had done it
as the LORD had commanded, even so
had they done it: and Moses [y]blessed
them.

CHAPTER 40

AND the LORD spake unto Moses,
saying,
2 On the first day of the [a]first month
shalt thou set up [b]the tabernacle of
the tent of the congregation.
3 And [c]thou shalt put therein the ark
of the testimony, and cover the ark
with the vail.
4 And [d]thou shalt bring in the table,
and set [e]in order [1]the things that are
to be set in order upon it; and thou
shalt bring in the candlestick, and light
the lamps thereof.
5 And thou shalt set the [f]altar of gold
for the incense before the ark of the
testimony, and put the hanging of the
door to the tabernacle.
6 And thou shalt set the altar of the
burnt offering before the door of the
tabernacle of the tent of the congregation.
7 And [g]thou shalt set the laver between the tent of the congregation and
the altar, and shalt put water therein.

l ch. 28.31. Lev. 8.7. 1 Sam. 2.18. 2 Sam. 6.14.
m ch. 28.33. The pomegranates prevented the bells from striking against each other.
n ch. 28.39, 40. Lev. 8.13. Isa. 61.10. Rom. 3.22. Gal. 3.27.
o ch. 28.4,39. Eze. 44.18.
p ch. 28.42. Lev. 6.10. Lev. 16.4. Eze. 44.17.
q Ps. 93.5. Zech. 14.20. Isa. 23.18.
r ch. 25.40.
s Heb. 9.1-28.
t Rev. 1.13-20.
u ch. 27.21. Matt. 5.14. Phil. 2.15.
13 the incense of sweet spices.
v ch. 38.30. 1 Ki. 8.64.
w Rev. 3.12.
x ch. 35.10.
y Gen. 14.19. Lev. 9.22. Num. 6.23. Josh. 22.6. 2 Sam. 6.18. 1 Ki. 8.14. 2 Chr. 30. 27.

CHAP. 40

a ch. 12.2. ch. 13.4.
b ch. 25.9. ch. 26.1,30. Num. 7.1. Acts 7.44, 45. Heb. 8.2-5. Heb. 9.2,11. Rev. 21.3.
c Num. 4.5.
d ch. 26.35.
e Lev. 24.5,6.
1 the order thereof.
f Heb. 9.24. Heb. 10.19-22.
g ch. 30.18.

8 And thou shalt set up the court round about, and hang up the hanging at the court gate.

9 And thou shalt take [h]the anointing oil, and anoint the tabernacle, and all that *is* therein, and shalt hallow it, and all the vessels thereof: and it shall be holy.

10 And thou shalt anoint the altar of the burnt offering, and all his vessels, and sanctify the altar: and [i]it shall be an altar [2]most holy.

11 And thou shalt anoint the laver and his foot, and sanctify it.

12 And [j]thou shalt bring Aaron and his sons unto the door of the tabernacle of the congregation, and wash them with water.

13 And thou shalt put upon Aaron the holy garments, [k]and anoint him, and sanctify him; that he may minister unto me in the priest's office.

14 And thou shalt bring [l]his sons, and clothe them with coats:

15 And thou shalt anoint them, as thou didst anoint their father, that they may minister unto me in the priest's office: for their anointing shall surely be [m]an everlasting priesthood throughout their generations.

16 Thus did Moses: according to all that the LORD commanded him, so did he.

17 ¶ And it came to pass in the first month in the second year, on the first *day* of the month, *that* the [n]tabernacle was reared up.

18 And Moses reared up the tabernacle, and fastened his sockets, and set up the boards thereof, and put in the bars thereof, and reared up his pillars.

19 And he spread abroad the tent over the tabernacle, and put the covering of the tent above upon it; as the LORD commanded Moses.

20 ¶ And he took and put the [3]testimony into the [o]ark, and set the staves on the ark, and put the mercy seat above upon the ark:

21 And he brought the ark into the tabernacle, and [p]set up the vail of the covering, and covered the ark of the testimony; as the LORD commanded Moses.

22 ¶ And [q]he put the table in the tent of the congregation, upon the side of the tabernacle northward, without the vail.

h ch. 30.23-26.
i ch. 29.36.
2 holiness of holinesses.
j Lev. 8.1-13.
k ch. 28.41. Ps. 133.2.
l Heb. 7.23.
m Num. 25.13. Heb. 7.11. 1 Pet. 2.5,9. Rev. 1.6.
n Num. 7.1.
3 tables of the law.
o ch. 25.16. Ps. 78.5. Isa. 8.20.
p ch. 35.12.
q ch. 26.35.
r ch. 26.35.
s ch. 25.37.
t ch. 30.6.
u ch. 30.7.
v ch. 26.36.
w ch. 29.38.
x ch. 30.18.
y ch. 30.19.
z ch. 27.9,16.
a Lev. 16.2. Num. 9.15. 1 Ki. 8.10. 2 Chr. 5.13. 2 Chr. 7.2. Isa. 6.4. Eze. 43.4. Hag. 2.7,9. Rev. 15.8.
b 1 Ki. 8.11. 2 Chr. 5.14. Ps. 78.14.
c Num. 10.11. Neh. 9.19.
4 journeyed.
d Num. 9.19-22.
e ch. 13.21. Num. 9.15.

23 And he set the bread in order upon it before the LORD; as the LORD had commanded Moses.

24 ¶ And [r]he put the candlestick in the tent of the congregation, over against the table, on the side of the tabernacle southward.

25 And [s]he lighted the lamps before the LORD; as the LORD commanded Moses.

26 ¶ And [t]he put the golden altar in the tent of the congregation before the vail:

27 And [u]he burnt sweet incense thereon; as the LORD commanded Moses.

28 ¶ And [v]he set up the hanging *at* the door of the tabernacle.

29 And he put the altar of burnt offering *by* the door of the tabernacle of the tent of the congregation, and [w]offered upon it the burnt offering and the meat offering; as the LORD commanded Moses.

30 ¶ And [x]he set the laver between the tent of the congregation and the altar, and put water there, to wash *withal*.

31 And Moses and Aaron and his sons washed their hands and their feet thereat:

32 When they went into the tent of the congregation, and when they came near unto the altar, they washed; [y]as the LORD commanded Moses.

33 And [z]he reared up the court round about the tabernacle and the altar, and set up the hanging of the court gate. So Moses finished the work.

34 ¶ Then [a]a cloud covered the tent of the congregation, and the glory of the LORD filled the tabernacle.

35 And Moses [b]was not able to enter into the tent of the congregation, because the cloud abode thereon, and the glory of the LORD filled the tabernacle.

36 And [c]when the cloud was taken up from over the tabernacle, the children of Israel [4]went onward in all their journeys:

37 But [d]if the cloud were not taken up, then they journeyed not till the day that it was taken up.

38 For [e]the cloud of the LORD *was* upon the tabernacle by day, and fire was on it by night, in the sight of all the house of Israel, throughout all their journeys.

THE THIRD BOOK OF MOSES, CALLED

LEVITICUS

CHAPTER 1

AND the LORD [a]called unto Moses,
and spake [b]unto him out of the
tabernacle of the congregation, saying,
2 Speak unto the children of Israel,
and say unto them, [c]If any man of you
bring an offering unto the LORD, ye
shall bring your offering of the cattle,
even of the herd, and of the flock.
3 If his offering *be* a burnt sacrifice of
the herd, let him offer a male without
[d]blemish: he shall offer it of his own
voluntary will at the door of the tabernacle of the congregation before the
LORD.
4 And [e]he shall put his hand upon
the head of the burnt offering; and it
shall be [f]accepted for him to [g]make
atonement for him.
5 And he shall kill the [h]bullock before the LORD: [i]and the priests,
Aaron's sons, shall bring the blood,
and [j]sprinkle the blood round about
upon the altar that *is by* the door of
the tabernacle of the congregation.
6 And he shall flay the burnt offering, and cut it into his pieces.
7 And the sons of Aaron the priest
shall put fire upon the altar, and [k]lay
the wood in order upon the fire:
8 And the priests, Aaron's sons,
shall lay the parts, the head, and the
fat, in order upon the wood that *is* on
the fire which *is* upon the altar:
9 But his inwards and his legs shall
he wash in water: and the priest shall
burn all on the altar, *to be* a burnt
sacrifice, an offering made by fire, of
a [l]sweet savour unto the LORD.
10 ¶ And if his offering *be* of the
flocks, *namely*, of the sheep, or of the
goats, for a burnt sacrifice; he shall
bring it a male without blemish.
11 And he shall kill it on the side of
the altar northward before the LORD:
and the priests, Aaron's sons, shall
sprinkle his blood round about upon
the altar.
12 And he shall cut it into his pieces,
with his head and his fat: and the
priest shall lay them in order on the
wood that *is* on the fire which *is* upon
the altar:

CHAP. 1
a Ex. 19.3.
b Num. 12.4, 5.
c ch. 22.18.
d Ex. 12.5. ch. 3.1. ch. 22.20,21. Deut. 15.21. Mal. 1.14. Eph. 5.27. Heb. 9.14. 1 Pet. 1.19.
e ch. 4.15. ch. 8.14. Ex. 29.10. Isa. 53.4. 2 Cor. 5.21. 1 Pet. 2.24.
f Isa. 56.7. Rom. 12.1. Phil. 4.18.
g Num. 15.25 Rom. 5.11.
h Micah 6.6.
i Heb. 10.11.
j Heb. 12.24. 1 Pet. 1.2.
k Gen. 22.9.
l Gen. 8.21. Eze. 20.28. 2 Cor. 2.15. Eph. 5.2. Phil. 4.18.
m ch. 5.7. Luke 2.24.
1 Or, pinch off the head with the nail.
2 Or, the filth thereof.
n Gen. 15.10.

CHAP. 2
a ch. 6.14. ch. 9.17. Num. 15.4.
b ch. 5.12. ch. 6.15. ch. 24.7. Isa. 66.3. Acts 10.4.
c ch. 7.9. ch. 10.12.13.
d Ex. 29.37. Num. 18.9.
e Ex. 29.2.
1 Or, on a flat plate, or, slice.

13 But he shall wash the inwards and
the legs with water: and the priest
shall bring *it* all, and burn *it* upon the
altar: it *is* a burnt sacrifice, an offering
made by fire, of a sweet savour unto
the LORD.
14 ¶ And if the burnt sacrifice for his
offering to the LORD *be* of fowls, then
he shall bring his offering of [m]turtle-
doves, or of young pigeons.
15 And the priest shall bring it unto
the altar, and [1] wring off his head, and
burn *it* on the altar; and the blood
thereof shall be wrung out at the side
of the altar:
16 And he shall pluck away his crop
with [2]his feathers, and cast it beside
the altar on the east part, by the place
of the ashes:
17 And he shall cleave it with the
wings thereof, *but* [n]shall not divide *it*
asunder: and the priest shall burn it
upon the altar, upon the wood that *is*
upon the fire: it *is* a burnt sacrifice, an
offering made by fire, of a sweet
savour unto the LORD.

CHAPTER 2

AND when any will offer [a]a meat
offering unto the LORD, his offering shall be *of* fine flour; and he shall
pour oil upon it, and put frankincense
thereon:
2 And he shall bring it to Aaron's
sons the priests: and he shall take
thereout his handful of the flour
thereof, and of the oil thereof, with all
the frankincense thereof; and the
priest shall burn [b]the memorial of it
upon the altar, *to be* an offering made
by fire, of a sweet savour unto the
LORD:
3 And [c]the remnant of the meat
offering *shall be* Aaron's and his
sons': [d]*it is* a thing most holy of
the offerings of the LORD made by
fire.
4 ¶ And if thou bring an oblation of
a meat offering baken in the oven, *it*
shall be unleavened cakes of fine flour
mingled with oil, or unleavened wafers
[e]anointed with oil.
5 ¶ And if thy oblation *be* a meat
offering *baken* [1]in a pan, it shall be *of*

fine flour unleavened, mingled with
oil.
6 Thou shalt part it in pieces, and
pour oil thereon: it *is* a meat offering.
7 ¶ And if thy oblation *be* a meat
offering *baken* in the fryingpan, it
shall be made *of* fine flour with oil.
8 And thou shalt bring the meat
offering that is made of these things
unto the LORD: and when it is presented unto the priest, he shall bring
it unto the altar.
9 And the priest shall take from the
meat offering a memorial thereof, and
shall burn *it* upon the altar: *it is* an
[f]offering made by fire, of a sweet
savour unto the LORD.
10 And that which is left of the meat
offering *shall be* Aaron's and his
sons': *it is* a thing most holy of the
offerings of the LORD [g]made by fire.
11 No meat offering, which ye shall
bring unto the LORD, shall be made
with [h]leaven: for ye shall burn no
leaven, nor any honey, in any offering
of the LORD made by fire.
12 ¶ As [i]for the oblation of the firstfruits, ye shall offer them unto the
LORD: but they shall not [2]be burnt on
the altar for a sweet savour.
13 And every oblation of thy meat
offering shalt [j]thou season with salt;
neither shalt thou suffer the [k]salt of
the covenant of thy God to be lacking
from thy meat offering: with [l]all thine
offerings thou shalt offer salt.
14 And if thou offer a meat offering
of thy firstfruits [m]unto the LORD,
thou [n]shalt offer for the meat offering
of thy firstfruits green ears of corn
dried by the fire, *even* corn beaten out
of [o]full ears.
15 And thou shalt put oil upon it,
and lay frankincense thereon: it *is* a
meat offering.
16 And the priest shall burn the
memorial of it, *part* of the beaten corn
thereof, and *part* of the oil thereof,
with all the frankincense thereof: *it is*
an offering made by fire unto the
LORD.

CHAPTER 3

AND if his oblation *be* a [a]sacrifice
of peace offering, if he offer *it* of
the herd; whether *it be* a male or female, he shall offer it without blemish
before the LORD.
2 And [b]he shall lay his hand upon
the head of his offering, and kill it *at*
the door of the tabernacle of the congregation: and Aaron's sons the
priests shall sprinkle the blood upon
the altar round about.

f Ex. 29.18. Rom. 12.1.
g Ex. 29.18, 37.
h ch. 6.17. Matt. 16.12. Mark 8.15. Luke 12.1. 1 Cor. 5.8. Gal. 5.9.
i Ex. 22.29. ch. 23.10,11. Deut. 26.10.
2 ascend.
j Mark 9.49. Col. 4.6.
k Num. 18. 19.
l Eze. 43.24.
m Ex. 23.19. Pro. 3.9.
n ch. 23.10. 14.
o 2 Ki. 4.42.

CHAP. 3
a ch. 22.21.
b Ex. 29.10. Isa. 53.4. Num. 8.12. 2 Cor. 5.21. Heb. 9.28. 1 Pet. 2.24. 1 Pet. 3.18.
1 Or, suet.
2 Or, midriff over the liver, and over the kidneys.
c Ex. 29.13. 1 Sam. 2.15, 16.
d 2 Cor. 5.21. Titus 2.11, 12. Heb. 7.26, 27. 1 Pet. 1.19.
e ch. 21.6,8, 17,21,22. ch. 22.25. Eze. 44.7. Mal. 1.7,12.
f ch. 7.23. 1 Sam. 2.15. 2 Chr. 7.7.
g ch. 6.18. ch. 7.36. ch. 17.7. ch. 23.14.

3 And he shall offer of the sacrifice
of the peace offering an offering made
by fire unto the LORD; the [1]fat that
covereth the inwards, and all the fat
that *is* upon the inwards,
4 And the two kidneys, and the fat
that *is* on them, which *is* by the flanks,
and the [2]caul above the liver, with the
kidneys, it shall he take away.
5 And Aaron's sons [c]shall burn it on
the altar upon the burnt sacrifice,
which *is* upon the wood that *is* on the
fire: *it is* an offering made by fire, of
a sweet savour unto the LORD.
6 ¶ And if his offering for a sacrifice
of peace offering unto the LORD *be* of
the flock; male or female, he shall
offer it [d]without blemish.
7 If he offer a lamb for his offering,
then shall he offer it before the LORD.
8 And he shall lay his hand upon the
head of his offering, and kill it before
the tabernacle of the congregation:
and Aaron's sons shall sprinkle the
blood thereof round about upon the
altar.
9 And he shall offer of the sacrifice
of the peace offering an offering made
by fire unto the LORD; the fat thereof,
and the whole rump, it shall he take off
hard by the backbone; and the fat
that covereth the inwards, and all the
fat that *is* upon the inwards,
10 And the two kidneys, and the fat
that *is* upon them, which *is* by the
flanks, and the caul above the liver,
with the kidneys, it shall he take away.
11 And the priest shall burn it upon
the altar: *it is* [e]the food of the offering
made by fire unto the LORD.
12 ¶ And if his offering *be* a goat,
then he shall offer it before the LORD.
13 And he shall lay his hand upon the
head of it, and kill it before the tabernacle of the congregation: and the
sons of Aaron shall sprinkle the blood
thereof upon the altar round about.
14 And he shall offer thereof his
offering, *even* an offering made by fire
unto the LORD; the fat that covereth
the inwards, and all the fat that *is* upon the inwards,
15 And the two kidneys, and the fat
that *is* upon them, which *is* by the
flanks, and the caul above the liver,
with the kidneys, it shall he take
away.
16 And the priest shall burn them
upon the altar: *it is* the food of the
offering made by fire for a sweet savour: [f]all the fat *is* the LORD's.
17 *It shall be* a [g]perpetual statute for
your generations throughout all your

dwellings, that ye eat neither [3]fat nor [h]blood.

CHAPTER 4

AND the LORD spake unto Moses, saying,

2 Speak unto the children of Israel, saying, [a]If a soul shall sin through ignorance against any of the commandments of the LORD *concerning things* which ought not to be done, and shall do against any of them:

3 If [b]the priest that is anointed do sin according to the sin of the people; then let him bring for his sin, which he hath sinned, a young [c]bullock without blemish unto the LORD for a sin offering.

4 And he shall bring the bullock unto [d]the door of the tabernacle of the congregation before the LORD; and shall lay his hand upon the bullock's head, and kill the bullock before the LORD.

5 And the priest that is anointed shall [e]take of the bullock's blood, and bring it to the tabernacle of the congregation:

6 And the priest shall dip his finger in the blood, and sprinkle of the blood seven times before the [f]LORD, before the vail of the sanctuary.

7 And the priest shall [g]put *some* of the blood upon the horns of the altar of sweet incense before the LORD, which *is* in the tabernacle of the congregation: and shall pour [h]all the blood of the bullock at the bottom of the altar of the burnt offering, which *is at* the door of the tabernacle of the congregation.

8 And he shall take off from it all the fat of the bullock for the sin offering; the fat that covereth the inwards, and all the fat that *is* upon the inwards,

9 And the two kidneys, and the fat that *is* upon them, which *is* by the flanks, and the caul above the liver, with the kidneys, it shall he take away,

10 As it was taken off from the bullock of the sacrifice of peace offerings: and the priest shall burn them upon the altar of the burnt offering.

11 And [i]the skin of the bullock, and all his flesh, with his head, and with his legs, and his inwards, and his dung,

12 Even the whole bullock shall he carry forth [1]without the camp unto a clean place, [j]where the ashes are poured out, and [k]burn him on the wood with fire: [2]where the ashes are poured out shall he be burnt.

13 ¶ And [l]if the whole congregation of Israel sin through ignorance, [m]and the thing be hid from the eyes of the assembly, and they have done *somewhat against* any of the commandments of the LORD *concerning things* which should not be done, and are guilty;

14 When the sin, which they have sinned against it, is known, then the congregation shall offer a young bullock for the sin, and bring him before the tabernacle of the congregation.

15 And the elders of the congregation shall [n]lay their hands upon the head of the bullock before the LORD: and the bullock shall be killed before the LORD.

16 And [o]the priest that is anointed shall bring of the bullock's blood to the tabernacle of the congregation:

17 And the priest shall dip his finger *in some* of the blood, and sprinkle *it* seven times before the LORD, *even* before the vail.

18 And he shall put *some* of the blood upon the horns of the altar which *is* before the LORD, that *is* in the tabernacle of the congregation, and shall pour out all the blood at the bottom of the altar of the burnt offering, which *is at* the door of the tabernacle of the congregation.

19 And he shall take all his fat from him, and burn *it* upon the altar.

20 And he shall do with the bullock as he did with the bullock for a sin offering, so shall he do with this: [p]and the priest shall make an atonement for them, and it shall be forgiven them.

21 And he shall carry forth the bullock without the camp, and burn him as he burned the first bullock: it *is* a sin offering for the congregation.

22 ¶ When a [q]ruler hath sinned, and done *somewhat* through ignorance *against* any of the commandments of the LORD his God *concerning things* which should not be done, and is guilty;

23 Or if his sin, wherein he hath sinned, come to his knowledge; he shall bring his offering, a kid of the goats, a male without blemish:

24 And he shall lay his hand upon the head of the goat, and kill it in the place where they kill the burnt offering before the LORD: it *is* a sin offering.

25 And the priest shall take of the blood of the sin offering with his finger, and put *it* upon the horns of the altar of burnt offering, and shall pour out his blood at the bottom of the altar of burnt offering.

26 And he shall burn all his fat upon the altar, as [r]the fat of the sacrifice of

3 Compare Deut. 32.14, with Neh. 8.10.
h Gen. 9.4. ch. 17.10. Deut. 12.16. 1 Sam. 14. 33. Eze. 44.7,15.

CHAP. 4

a ch. 5.15,17. Num. 15.22. 1 Sam. 14. 27. Ps. 19.12.
b ch. 8.12. ch. 21.10,12. Heb. 5.3.
c ch. 9.2.
d ch. 1.3,4.
e ch. 16.14. Num. 19.4. Heb. 9.13.
f Isa. 42.21. John 8.29. Rom. 3.24. 2 Cor. 5.19. Eph. 2.13. Rev. 5.9.
g ch. 9.9. ch. 16.18. ch. 8.15. Heb. 9.21-25.
h ch. 5.9.
i Ex. 29.14. Num. 19.5.
1 to without the camp.
j ch. 6.11.
k Heb. 13.11.
2 at the pouring out of the ashes.
l Num. 15.24. Josh. 7.11.
m ch. 5.2,3,4, 17.
n Ex. 29.10, 15,19. ch. 1.4. ch. 3.2,8,13. ch. 8.14,22. ch. 16.21. Isa. 53.6. Matt. 8.17. Heb. 9.28. 1 Pet. 2.24.
o Heb. 9.12, 13,14.
p Num. 15. 25. Dan. 9.24. Rom. 5.11. Heb. 2.17. Heb. 10.10, 11,12. 1 John 1.7. 1 John 2.2.
q Ex. 18.21. Num. 16.2. 2 Sam. 21. 1-3. 2 Sam. 24. 10-17. Ezra 9.2. Acts 3.17.
r ch. 3.5.

peace offerings: [s]and the priest shall make an atonement for him as concerning his sin, and it shall be forgiven him.

27 ¶ And [t]if [3]any one of the [4]common people sin through ignorance, while he doeth *somewhat against* any of the commandments of the LORD *concerning things* which ought not to be done, and be guilty;

28 Or [u]if his sin, which he hath sinned, come to his knowledge: then he shall bring his offering, a kid of the goats, a female without blemish, for his sin which he hath sinned.

29 And [v]he shall lay his hand upon the head of the sin offering, and slay the sin offering in the place of the burnt offering.

30 And the priest shall take of the blood thereof with his finger, and put *it* upon the horns of the altar of burnt offering, and shall pour out all the blood thereof at the bottom of the altar.

31 And [w]he shall take away all the fat thereof, [x]as the fat is taken away from off the sacrifice of peace offerings; and the priest shall burn *it* upon the altar for a sweet savour [y]unto the LORD; [z]and the priest shall make an atonement for him, and it shall be forgiven him.

32 And if he bring a [a]lamb for a sin offering, [b]he shall bring it a female without blemish.

33 And he shall lay his hand upon the head of the sin offering, and slay it for a sin offering in the place where they kill the burnt offering.

34 And the priest shall take of the blood of the sin offering with his finger, and put *it* upon the horns of the altar of burnt offering, and shall pour out all the blood thereof at the bottom of the altar:

35 And he shall take away all the fat thereof, as the fat of the lamb is taken away from the sacrifice of the peace offerings; and the priest shall burn them upon the altar, according to [c]the offerings made by fire unto the LORD: and the priest shall make an [d]atonement for his sin that he hath committed, and it shall be forgiven him.

CHAPTER 5

AND if a soul sin, [a]and hear the voice of swearing, and *is* a witness, whether he hath seen or known *of it;* if he do not utter *it*, then he shall [b]bear his iniquity.

2 Or [c]if a soul touch any unclean thing, whether *it be* a carcase of an unclean beast, or a carcase of unclean cattle, or the carcase of unclean creeping things, and *if* it be hidden from him; he also shall be unclean, and guilty.

3 Or if he touch the [d]uncleanness of man, whatsoever uncleanness *it be* that a man shall be defiled withal, and it be hid from him; when he knoweth *of it*, then he shall be guilty.

4 Or if a soul swear, [e]pronouncing with *his* lips [f]to do evil, or [g]to do good, whatsoever *it be* that a man shall pronounce with an oath, and it be hid from him; when he knoweth *of it*, then he shall be guilty in one of these.

5 And it shall be, when he shall be guilty in one of these *things*, that he shall [h]confess that he hath sinned in that *thing:*

6 And he shall bring his trespass offering unto the LORD for his sin which he hath sinned, a female from the flock, a lamb or a kid of the goats, for a sin offering; and the priest shall make an atonement for him concerning his sin.

7 And [i]if [1]he be not able to bring a lamb, then he shall bring for his trespass, which he hath committed, two turtledoves, or two young pigeons, unto the LORD; one for a sin offering, and the other for a burnt offering.

8 And he shall bring them unto the priest, who shall offer *that* which *is* for the sin offering first, and wring [2]off his head from his neck, but shall not divide *it* asunder:

9 And he shall sprinkle of the blood of the sin offering upon the side of the altar; and the rest of the blood shall be wrung out at the bottom of the altar: it *is* a sin offering.

10 And he shall offer the second *for* a burnt offering, [j]according to the [3]manner: and the priest shall make an atonement for him for his sin which he hath sinned, and it shall be forgiven him.

11 ¶ But if he be not able to bring two turtledoves, or two young pigeons, then he that sinned shall bring for his offering the tenth part of an ē-phäh of fine flour for a sin offering; [k]he shall put no oil upon it, neither shall he put *any* frankincense thereon: for it *is* a sin offering.

12 Then shall he bring it to the priest, and the priest shall take his handful of it, *even* a memorial thereof, and burn *it* on the altar, according [l]to the

s Num. 15.28
t Num. 15.27. Eccl. 7.20.
3 any soul.
4 people of the land.
u ver. 23.
v vers. 4,24.
w ch. 3.14.
x ch. 3.3.
y Ex. 29.18. ch. 1.9. Ezra 6.10.
z ver. 26.
a Isa. 53.7. John 1.29. Acts 8.32. 1 Pet. 1.19. Rev. 5.6-14. Rev. 13.8.
b ver. 28.
c ch. 3.5.
d Dan. 9.24. Rom. 5.11. Heb. 9.8-28. 1 John 1.7. 1 John 2.2.

CHAP. 5

a 1 Ki. 8.31. Pro. 29.24. Matt. 26.63.
b Gen. 17.14. ch. 7.18. ch. 17.16. ch. 19.8. ch. 20.17. Num. 9.13.
c ch. 11.24, 28,31,39. Num. 19.11, 13,16.
d ch. 12.1,2. ch. 13.1,2. ch. 15.1,2.
e That is, Rashly, as 1 Sam. 14. 24.
f 1 Sam. 25. 22. Mal. 3.5. Acts 23.12.
g Mark 6.23.
h ch. 26.40. Num. 5.7. Ezra 10.11.
i ch. 14.21.
1 his hand cannot reach to the sufficiency of a lamb.
2 Or, pinch off the head with the nail.
j ch. 1.14.
3 Or, ordinance.
k Num. 5.15.
l ch. 4.35.

offerings made by fire unto the LORD:
it *is* a sin offering.
13 And the priest shall make an
atonement for him as touching his sin
that he hath sinned in one of these,
and it shall be forgiven him: and *the
remnant* shall be the priest's, as a
meat offering.
14 ¶ And the LORD spake unto Moses,
saying,
15 If [m]a soul commit a trespass, and
sin through ignorance, in the holy
things of the LORD; then [n]he shall
bring for his trespass unto the LORD
a ram without blemish out of the
flocks, with thy estimation by shekels
of silver, after [o]the shekel of the sanctuary, for a trespass offering:
16 And he shall make amends for the
harm that he hath done in the holy
thing, and [p]shall add the fifth part
thereto, and give it unto the priest:
[q]and the priest shall make an atonement for him with the ram of the trespass offering, and it shall be forgiven
him.
17 ¶ And if a soul sin, and commit
any of these things which are forbidden to be done by the commandments
of the LORD; though he [r]wist *it* not,
yet is he guilty, and shall bear his iniquity.
18 And he shall bring a ram without
blemish out of the flock, with thy estimation, for a trespass offering, unto
the priest: and the priest shall make
an atonement for him concerning his
ignorance wherein he erred and wist
it not, and it shall be forgiven him.
19 It *is* a trespass [s]offering: [t]he hath
certainly trespassed against the LORD.

CHAPTER 6

AND the LORD spake unto Moses,
saying,
2 If a soul sin, and [a]commit a trespass against the LORD, and [b]lie unto
his neighbour in that [c]which was delivered him to keep, or in [1]fellowship,
or in a thing taken away by violence,
or hath [d]deceived his neighbour;
3 Or [e]have found that which was
lost, and lieth concerning it, and
sweareth [f]falsely; in any of all these
that a man doeth, sinning therein:
4 Then it shall be, because he hath
sinned, and is guilty, that he shall restore that which he took violently
away, or the thing which he hath deceitfully gotten, or that which was
delivered him to keep, or the lost thing
which he found,
5 Or all that about which he hath
sworn falsely; he shall even [g]restore it
in the principal, and shall add the fifth
part more thereto, *and* give it unto him
to whom it appertaineth, [2]in the day
of his trespass offering.
6 And he shall bring his trespass
offering unto the LORD, a ram without
[h]blemish out of the flock, with thy
estimation, for a trespass offering,
unto the priest:
7 And the priest shall make an atonement for him before the LORD: and it
shall be forgiven him for any thing of
all that he hath done in trespassing
therein.
8 ¶ And the LORD spake unto Moses,
saying,
9 Command Aaron and his sons,
saying, This *is* the law of the burnt
offering: It *is* the burnt offering, [3]be-
cause of the burning upon the altar
all night unto the morning, and the
fire of the altar shall be burning in it.
10 And [i]the priest shall put on his
linen garment, and his linen breeches
shall he put upon his flesh, and take
up the ashes which the fire hath consumed with the burnt offering on the
altar, and he shall put them beside the
altar.
11 And he shall put off his garments,
and put on other garments, and carry
forth the ashes without the camp unto
a clean place.
12 And the fire upon the altar shall
be burning in it; it shall not be put out:
and the priest shall burn wood on it
every morning, and lay the burnt
offering in order upon it; and he shall
burn thereon the fat of the peace
offerings.
13 The [j]fire shall ever be burning upon the altar; it shall never go out.
14 ¶ And [k]this *is* the law of the meat
offering: the sons of Aaron shall offer
it before the LORD, before the altar.
15 And he shall take of it his handful, of the flour of the meat offering,
and of the oil thereof, and all the
frankincense which *is* upon the meat
offering, and shall burn *it* upon the
altar *for* a sweet savour, *even* the
memorial of it, unto the LORD.
16 And the remainder thereof shall
Aaron and his sons eat: with unleavened [l]bread shall it be eaten in the holy
place; in the court of the tabernacle of
the congregation they shall eat it.
17 It [m]shall not be baken with leaven.
[n]I have given it *unto them for* their portion of my offerings made by fire; [o]it *is*
most holy, as *is* the sin offering, and as
the trespass offering.

m ch. 22.14.
n Ezra 10.19.
o Ex. 30.13. ch. 27.25.
p ch. 6.5. ch. 22.14. ch. 27.13,15, 27,31. Num. 5.7.
q ch. 4.26. Heb. 9.13, 14.
r Ps. 19.12. Luke 12.48. Heb. 5.2.
s Isa. 53.10.
t Ezra 10.2.

CHAP. 6

a Num. 5.6.
b ch. 19.11. Acts 5.4. Col. 3.9.
c Ex. 22.7,10.
1 putting of the hand, or, in dealing.
d Pro. 24.28. Pro. 26.19.
e Deut. 22.1.
f Ex. 22.11. ch. 19.12. Jer. 7.9. Zech. 5.4.
g ch. 5.16. Num. 5.7. 2 Sam. 12.6. Luke 19.8.
2 in the day of his trespass, or, in the day of his being found guilty.
h Ex. 12.5. ch. 3.1. ch. 22.20,21. Deut. 15.21. Eph. 5.27. 1 Tim. 2.5,6. Heb. 9.14.
3 Or, for the burning.
i Ex. 28.39-43. ch. 16.4. Eze. 44.17.
j Ps. 50.3. Isa. 33.14. Dan. 7.10.
k Num. 15.4.
l Num. 18.10.
m ch. 2.11.
n Num. 18.9, 10.
o Ex. 29.37.

18 All [p]the males among the children
of Aaron shall eat of it. *It* [q]*shall be*
a statute for ever in your generations
concerning the offerings of the LORD
made by fire: every [r]one that toucheth
them shall be holy.
19 ¶ And the LORD spake unto Moses,
saying,
20 This [s]*is* the offering of Aaron and
of his sons, which they shall offer unto
the LORD in the day when he is anointed; the tenth part of an [t]ē-phăh of fine
flour for a meat offering perpetual,
half of it in the morning, and half
thereof at night.
21 In a pan it shall be made with oil;
and when it is baken, thou shalt bring
it in: *and* the baken pieces of the meat
offering shalt thou offer *for* a sweet
savour unto the LORD.
22 And the priest of his sons that is
anointed in his stead shall offer it: *it is*
a statute for ever unto the LORD; [u]it
shall be wholly burnt.
23 For every meat offering for the
priest shall be wholly burnt: it shall
not be eaten.
24 ¶ And the LORD spake unto Moses,
saying,
25 Speak unto Aaron and to his sons,
saying, This *is* the law of the sin offering: [v]In the place where the burnt
offering is killed shall the sin offering
be killed before the LORD: [w]it *is* most
holy.
26 The [x]priest that offereth it for sin
shall eat it: in the holy place shall it be
eaten, in the court of the tabernacle
of the congregation.
27 Whatsoever [y]shall touch the flesh
thereof shall be holy: and when there
is sprinkled of the blood thereof upon
any garment, thou shalt wash that
whereon it was sprinkled in the holy
place.
28 But the earthen vessel wherein it
is sodden [z]shall be broken: and if it
be sodden in a brasen pot, it shall be
both scoured, and rinsed in water.
29 All [a]the males among the priests
shall eat thereof: it *is* most holy.
30 And [b]no sin offering, whereof *any*
of the blood is brought into the tabernacle of the congregation to reconcile
withal in the holy *place*, shall be eaten:
it shall be burnt in the fire.

CHAPTER 7

LIKEWISE [a]this *is* the law of the
trespass offering: [b]it *is* most holy.
2 In [c]the place where they kill the
burnt offering shall they kill the trespass offering: and the blood thereof
shall he sprinkle round about upon
the altar.
3 And he shall offer of it [d]all the fat
thereof; the rump, and the fat that
covereth the inwards,
4 And the two kidneys, and the fat
that *is* on them, which *is* by the flanks,
and the caul *that is* above the liver,
with the kidneys, it shall he take
away:
5 And the priest shall burn them upon the altar *for* an [e]offering made by
fire unto the LORD: it *is* a trespass
offering.
6 Every [f]male among the priests
shall eat thereof: it shall be eaten in
the holy place: it [g]*is* most holy.
7 As the sin offering *is*, so *is* [h]the trespass offering: *there is* one law for
them: the priest that maketh atonement therewith shall have *it*.
8 And the priest that offereth any
man's burnt offering, *even* the priest
shall have to himself the skin of the
burnt offering which he hath offered.
9 And [i]all the meat offering that is
baken in the oven, and all that is
dressed in the fryingpan, and in [1]the
pan, shall be the [j]priest's that offereth
it.
10 And every meat offering, mingled
with oil, and dry, shall all the sons of
Aaron have, one *as much* as another.
11 And [k]this *is* the law of the sacrifice of peace offerings, which he shall
offer unto the LORD.
12 If he offer it for a thanksgiving,
then he shall offer with the sacrifice
of thanksgiving unleavened cakes
mingled with oil, and unleavened
wafers [l]anointed with oil, and cakes
mingled with oil, of fine flour, fried.
13 Besides the cakes, he shall offer
for his offering [m]leavened bread with
the sacrifice of thanksgiving of his
peace offerings.
14 And of it he shall offer one out of
the whole oblation *for* an heave offering unto the LORD, [n]*and* it shall be the
priest's that sprinkleth the blood of
the peace offerings.
15 And [o]the flesh of the sacrifice of
his peace offerings for thanksgiving
shall be eaten the same day that it is
offered; he shall not leave any of it
until the morning.
16 But [p]if the sacrifice of his offering
be a vow, or a voluntary offering, it
shall be eaten the same day that he
offereth his sacrifice: and on the
morrow also the remainder of it shall
be eaten:
17 But the remainder of the flesh of

p Num. 18. 10.
q ch. 3.17.
r Ex. 29.37. ch. 22.3.
s Ex. 29.2.
t Ex. 16.36.
u Ex. 29.25. Isa. 53.10. Dan. 9.26. 1 Tim. 2.6.
v ch. 4.24,29.
w ch. 21.22. Ps. 93.5.
x Num. 18.9. Eze. 44.27, 28.
y Ex. 29.37. Ex. 30.29.
z ch. 11.33. ch. 15.12.
a Num. 18. 10.
b ch. 16.27. Heb. 13.11.

CHAP. 7

a ch. 5.1-6. ch. 6.1-7.
b Ex. 29.37. ch. 6.17. ch. 21.22.
c ch. 4.24,29, 33.
d Ex. 29.13. ch. 3.4,9,10, 14,15. ch. 4.8,9.
e Titus 2.14. Heb. 9.28.
f ch. 6.16. Num. 18.9.
g ch. 2.3. Ps. 93.5.
h ch. 6.25. ch. 14.13.
i ch. 2.3,10. Num. 18.9.
1 Or, on the flat plate, or, slice.
j ch. 2.3,10. ch. 5.13. Num. 5.9. 1 Cor. 9.7-14.
k ch. 3.1. ch. 22.18.
l ch. 2.4. Num. 6.15.
m Amos 4.5.
n Num. 18.8.
o ch. 22.30. Heb. 3.13-15.
p ch. 19.6.

the sacrifice on the third day shall be
burnt with fire.
18 And if *any* of the flesh of the sacrifice of his peace offerings be eaten at
all on the third day, it shall not be
accepted, neither shall it be [q]imputed
unto him that offereth it: it shall be an
[r]abomination, and the soul that eateth of it shall bear his iniquity.
19 And the flesh that toucheth any
unclean *thing* shall not be eaten; it
shall be burnt with fire: and as for the
flesh, all that be clean shall eat thereof.
20 But the soul that eateth *of* the
flesh of the sacrifice of peace offerings,
that *pertain* unto the LORD, having
[s]his uncleanness upon him, even that
soul [t]shall be cut off from his people.
21 Moreover the soul that shall touch
any unclean *thing*, *as* [u]the uncleanness of man, or *any* [v]unclean beast, or
any [w]abominable unclean *thing*, and
eat of the flesh of the sacrifice of peace
offerings, which *pertain* unto the
LORD, even that soul shall be cut off
from his people.
22 ¶ And the LORD spake unto Moses,
saying,
23 Speak unto the children of Israel,
saying, [x]Ye shall eat no manner of
fat, of ox, or of sheep, or of goat.
24 And the fat of the [2]beast that dieth
of itself, and the fat of that which is
torn with beasts, may be used in any
other use: but ye shall in no wise eat
of it.
25 For whosoever eateth the fat of
the beast, of which men offer an offering made by fire unto the LORD, even
the soul that eateth *it* shall be cut off
from his people.
26 Moreover [y]ye shall eat no manner
of blood, *whether it be* of fowl or of
beast, in any of your dwellings.
27 Whatsoever soul *it be* that eateth
any manner of blood, even that soul
shall be cut off from his people.
28 ¶ And the LORD spake unto
Moses, saying,
29 Speak unto the children of Israel,
saying, [z]He that offereth the sacrifice
of his peace offerings unto the LORD
shall bring his oblation unto the LORD
of the sacrifice of his peace offerings.
30 His own hands shall bring the
offerings of the LORD made by fire,
the fat with the breast, it shall he
bring, that [a]the breast may be waved
for a wave offering before the LORD.
31 And [b]the priest shall burn the fat
upon the altar: but the breast shall be
Aaron's and his sons'.
32 And [c]the right shoulder shall ye
give unto the priest *for* an heave offering of the sacrifices of your peace
offerings.
33 He among the sons of Aaron, that
offereth the blood of the peace offerings, and the fat, shall have the right
shoulder for *his* part.
34 For [d]the wave breast and the
heave shoulder have I taken of the
children of Israel from off the sacrifices of their peace offerings, and have
given them unto Aaron the priest and
unto his sons by a statute for ever
from among the children of Israel.
35 ¶ This *is the portion* of the anointing of Aaron, and of the anointing of
his sons, out of the offerings of the
LORD made by fire, in the day *when* he
presented them to minister unto the
LORD in the priest's office;
36 Which the LORD commanded to
be given them of the children of Israel, [e]in the day that he anointed them,
by a statute [f]for ever throughout their
generations.
37 This *is* the law [g]of the burnt offering, of the meat offering, [h]and of the
sin offering, and of the trespass offering, [i]and of the consecrations, and of
the sacrifice of the peace offerings;
38 Which the LORD commanded
Moses in mount Sī-nâi, in the day that
he commanded the children of Israel
to offer their oblations unto the LORD,
in the wilderness of Sī-nâi.

CHAPTER 8

AND the LORD spake unto Moses,
saying,
2 Take [a]Aaron and his sons with
him, and the garments, and [b]the
anointing oil, and a bullock for the
sin offering, and two rams, and a basket of unleavened bread;
3 And gather thou all the congregation together unto the door of the
tabernacle of the congregation.
4 And Moses did as the LORD commanded him; and the assembly was
gathered together unto the door of
the tabernacle of the congregation.
5 And Moses said unto the congregation, This *is* the thing which the
LORD commanded to be done.
6 And Moses brought Aaron and his
sons, and [c]washed them with water.
7 And he put upon him [d]the coat,
and girded him with the girdle, and
clothed him with the robe, and put the
ē-phŏd upon him, and he girded him
with the curious girdle of the ē-phŏd,
and bound *it* unto him therewith.
8 And he put the breastplate upon

q Gen. 4.4,5. Num. 18.27.
r ch. 11.10. Pro. 15.8. Eccl. 5.1. Jer. 6.20. Amos 5.22.
s ch. 15.3.
t Gen. 17.14.
u ch. 12.1. ch. 13.1. ch. 15.1. ch. 22.4.
v ch. 11.24, 28.
w ch. 11. 10-13,20,41,42. Deut. 14.3. Eze. 4.14.
x ch. 3.17. 1 Sam. 2.29.
2 carcase.
y Gen. 9.4. ch. 3.17. ch. 17.10-14. Deut. 12.16. 1 Sam. 14. 33. Eze. 44.15. Acts 15.20.
z ch. 3.1.
a Ex. 29.24, 27. ch. 8.27. Num. 6.20.
b ch. 3.5,11.
c ch. 9.21. Num. 6.20.
d Ex. 29.28. ch. 10.14,15. Num. 18.18. Deut. 18.3.
e Ex. 40.13, 15. ch. 8.12,30.
f Heb. 7.18-28. Heb. 8.1-13.
g ch. 6.9.
h ch. 6.25.
i Ex. 29.1. ch. 6.20.

CHAP. 8

a Ex. 29.1.
b Ex. 30.24, 25.
c Ex. 30.19. Ps. 26.6. Isa. 52.11. Eze. 36.25. 1 Cor. 6.11. Eph. 5.26. Heb. 9.9-14. Rev. 1.5,6.
d Ex. 28.4.

him: also he put in the breastplate [e]the Ū-rĭm and the Thŭm-mĭm.

9 And [f]he put the mitre upon his head; also upon the mitre, *even* upon his forefront, did he put the golden plate, the holy crown; as the LORD [g]commanded Moses.

10 And [h]Moses took the anointing oil, and anointed the tabernacle and all that *was* therein, and sanctified them.

11 And he sprinkled thereof upon the altar seven times, and anointed the altar and all his vessels, both the laver and his foot, to sanctify them.

12 And he [i]poured of the anointing oil upon Aaron's head, and anointed him, to sanctify him.

13 And [j]Moses brought Aaron's sons, and put coats upon them, and girded them with girdles, and [1]put bonnets upon them; as the LORD commanded Moses.

14 And [k]he brought the bullock for the sin offering: and Aaron and his sons [l]laid their hands upon the head of the bullock for the sin offering.

15 And he slew *it;* [m]and Moses took the blood, and put *it* upon the horns of the altar round about with his finger, and purified the altar, and poured the blood at the bottom of the altar, and sanctified it, to make reconciliation upon it.

16 And [n]he took all the fat that *was* upon the inwards, and the caul *above* the liver, and the two kidneys, and their fat, and Moses burned *it* upon the altar.

17 But the bullock, and his hide, his flesh, and his dung, he burnt with fire without the camp; as the LORD [o]commanded Moses.

18 ¶ And [p]he brought the ram for the burnt offering: and Aaron and his sons laid their hands upon the head of the ram.

19 And he killed *it;* and Moses sprinkled the blood upon the altar round about.

20 And he cut the ram into pieces; and Moses burnt the head, and the pieces, and the fat.

21 And he washed the inwards and the legs in water; and Moses burnt the whole ram upon the altar: it *was* a burnt sacrifice for a sweet savour, *and* an offering made by fire unto the LORD; [q]as the LORD commanded Moses.

22 ¶ And [r]he brought the other ram, the ram of consecration: and Aaron and his sons laid their hands upon the head of the ram.

23 And he slew *it;* and Moses took of the blood of it, and put *it* upon [s]the tip of Aaron's right ear, and upon the thumb of his right hand, and upon the great toe of his right foot.

24 And he brought Aaron's sons, and Moses put of the blood upon the tip of their right ear, and upon the thumbs of their right hands, and upon the great toes of their right feet: and Moses [t]sprinkled the blood upon the altar round about.

25 And [u]he took the fat, and the rump, and all the fat that *was* upon the inwards, and the caul *above* the liver, and the two kidneys, and their fat, and the right shoulder:

26 And [v]out of the basket of unleavened bread, that *was* before the LORD, he took one unleavened cake, and a cake of oiled bread, and one wafer, and put *them* on the fat, and upon the right shoulder:

27 And he put all [w]upon Aaron's hands, and upon his sons' hands, and waved them *for* a wave offering before the LORD.

28 And [x]Moses took them from off their hands, and burnt *them* on the altar upon the burnt offering: they *were* consecrations for [y]a sweet savour: it *is* an offering made by fire unto the LORD.

29 And Moses took the breast, and waved it *for* a wave offering before the LORD: *for* of the ram of consecration it was [z]Moses' part; as the LORD commanded Moses.

30 And [a]Moses took of the anointing oil, and of the blood which *was* upon the altar, and sprinkled *it* upon Aaron, *and* upon his garments, and upon his sons, and upon his sons' garments with him; and sanctified Aaron, *and* his garments, and his sons, and his sons' garments with him.

31 ¶ And Moses said unto Aaron and to his sons, [b]Boil the flesh *at* the door of the tabernacle of the congregation: and there eat it with the bread that *is* in the basket of consecrations, as I commanded, saying, Aaron and his sons shall eat it.

32 And [c]that which remaineth of the flesh and of the bread shall ye burn with fire.

33 And ye shall not go out of the door of the tabernacle of the congregation *in* seven days, until the days of your consecration be at an end: for [d]seven days shall he consecrate you.

e Num. 27. 21. Deut. 33.8. 1 Sam. 28.6. Ezra 2.63. Neh. 7.65.
f Ex. 29.6. Zech. 3.5.
g Ex. 28.37.
h Ex. 30.26, 27,28,29.
i Ex. 29.7. ch. 21.10,12. Ps. 133.2. Isa. 61.1.
j Ex. 29.8,9. Ps. 132.9. Isa. 61.10.
1 bound.
k Ex. 29.10. Ps. 51.19. Ps. 66.15. Eze. 43.19. Heb. 9.13, 14.
l ch. 4.4.
m Ex. 29.12, 36. ch. 4.7. Heb. 9.22.
n Ex. 29.13. ch. 4.8.
o Ex. 29.14. ch. 4.11,12.
p Ex. 29.15.
q Ex. 29.18.
r Ex. 29.19, 31. ch. 7.37. Rev. 1.5,6.
s Ex. 29.20. ch. 8.23. Rom. 12.1. 1 Cor. 6.20.
t Heb. 9.18-24.
u Ex. 29.22.
v Ex. 29.23.
w Ex. 29.24.
x Ex. 29.25.
y Gen. 8.21. Eph. 5.2.
z Ex. 29.26.
a Ex. 29.21. Ex. 30.30. Num. 3.3. 1 Pet. 1.2.
b Ex. 29.31. Eze. 46.20.
c Ex. 29.34.
d Ex. 29.30, 35. ch. 14.8. Num. 19.12. Eze. 43.25, 26.

34 As he [e]hath done this day, *so* the LORD hath commanded to do, to make an atonement for you.
35 Therefore shall ye abide *at* the door of the tabernacle of the congregation day and night seven days, and [f]keep the charge of the LORD, that ye die not: for so I am commanded.
36 So Aaron and his sons did all things which the LORD commanded by the hand of Moses.

CHAPTER 9

AND [a]it came to pass on the eighth day, *that* Moses called Aaron and his sons, and the elders of Israel;
2 And he said unto Aaron, [b]Take thee a young calf for a sin offering, and [c]a ram for a burnt offering, without blemish, and offer *them* before the LORD.
3 And unto the children of Israel thou shalt speak, saying, [d]Take ye a kid of the goats for a sin offering; and a calf and a lamb, *both* of the first year, without blemish, for a burnt offering;
4 Also a bullock and a ram for peace offerings, to sacrifice before the LORD; and a [e]meat offering mingled with oil: for [f]to day the LORD will appear unto you.
5 ¶ And they brought *that* which Moses commanded before the tabernacle of the congregation: and all the congregation drew near and stood before the LORD.
6 And Moses said, This *is* the thing which the LORD commanded that ye should do: and [g]the glory of the LORD shall appear unto you.
7 And Moses said unto Aaron, Go unto the altar, and [h]offer thy sin offering, and thy burnt offering, and make an atonement for thyself, and for the people: and [i]offer the offering of the people, and make an atonement for them; as the LORD commanded.
8 ¶ Aaron therefore went unto the altar, and slew the calf of the sin offering, which *was* for himself.
9 And [j]the sons of Aaron brought the blood unto him: and he dipped his finger in the blood, and [k]put *it* upon the horns of the altar, and poured out the blood at the bottom of the altar:
10 But [l]the fat, and the kidneys, and the caul above the liver of the sin offering, he burnt upon the altar; [m]as the LORD commanded Moses.
11 And [n]the flesh and the hide he burnt with fire without the camp.
12 And he slew the burnt offering; and Aaron's sons presented unto him the blood, which he sprinkled round about upon the altar.
13 And they presented the burnt offering unto him, with the pieces thereof, and the head: and he burnt *them* upon the altar.
14 And he did wash the inwards and the legs, and burnt *them* upon the burnt offering on the altar.
15 ¶ And [o]he brought the people's offering, and took the goat, which *was* the sin offering for the people, and slew it, and offered it for sin, as the first.
16 And he brought the burnt offering, and offered it according to the [1]manner.
17 And he brought the meat offering, and [2]took an handful thereof, and burnt *it* upon the altar, [p]beside the burnt sacrifice of the morning.
18 He slew also the bullock and the ram *for* a sacrifice of peace offerings, which *was* for the people: and Aaron's sons presented unto him the blood, which he sprinkled upon the altar round about,
19 And the fat of the bullock and of the ram, the rump, and that which covereth *the inwards*, and the kidneys, and the caul *above* the liver:
20 And they put the fat upon the breasts, and he burnt the fat upon the altar:
21 And the breasts and the right shoulder Aaron waved [q]*for* a wave offering before the LORD; as Moses commanded.
22 And Aaron lifted up his hand toward the people, and [r]blessed them, and came down from offering of the sin offering, and the burnt offering, and peace offerings.
23 And Moses and Aaron went into the tabernacle of the congregation, and came out, and [s]blessed the people: [t]and the glory of the LORD appeared unto all the people.
24 And [u]there came a fire out from [v]before the LORD, and consumed upon the altar the burnt offering and the fat: *which* when all the people saw, they [w]shouted, and fell on their faces.

CHAPTER 10

AND [a]Nadab and Ă-bī-hū, the sons of Aaron, took either of them his censer, and put fire therein, and put incense thereon, and offered [b]strange fire before the LORD, which he commanded them not.
2 And there [c]went out fire from the

e Heb. 7.16.
f Num. 3.7. Num. 9.19. Deut. 11.1. 1 Ki. 2.3. Eze. 48.11. 1 Tim. 1.18. 1 Tim. 5.21.

CHAP. 9

a ch. 14.10, 23. ch. 15.14. Eze. 43.27.
b Ex. 29.1. ch. 4.3.
c ch. 8.18.
d ch. 4.23. ch. 10.19. Ezra 6.17. Isa. 53.10. Rom. 8.3. 1 Pet. 2.24.
e ch. 2.4.
f Ex. 29.43.
g Ex. 24.16. Ex. 40.34, 35. 1 Ki. 8.10-12.
h 1 Sam. 3.14. Heb. 5.3. Heb. 7.27.
i ch. 4.16,20. Heb. 5.1.
j ch. 8.15.
k ch. 4.7.
l ch. 8.16.
m ch. 4.8.
n ch. 4.10,11. ch. 8.17.
o Isa. 53.10. John 1.29. 1 Cor. 15.3. 2 Cor. 5.21. Eph. 5.2. Gal. 1.4. Heb. 1.3. Heb. 2.17. 1 Pet. 2.24. 1 John 2.2. Rev. 1.5.
1 Or, ordinance.
2 filled his hand out of it.
p Ex. 29.38.
q Ex. 29.24.
r Deut. 21.5. Luke 24.50.
s 2 Sam. 6.18. 1 Chr. 16.2. 2 Chr. 6.3.
t Num. 16.19.
u Gen. 4.4. Gen. 15.17. 2 Chr. 7.1.
v Ex. 29.18.
w 1 Ki. 18.39. Ezra 3.11.

CHAP. 10

a Num. 26. 61.
b Ex. 30.9.
c Num. 16. 35. 2 Sam. 6.7.

LORD, and devoured them, and they
died before the LORD.
3 Then Moses said unto Aaron, This
is it that the LORD spake, saying, I will
be sanctified in them that [d]come nigh
me, and before all the people I will be
[e]glorified. And Aaron held his peace.
4 And Moses called Mī-shā-ĕl and
Ĕl-zā-phăn, the sons of [f]Ŭz-zī-ĕl the
uncle of Aaron, and said unto them,
Come near, [g]carry your brethren from
before the sanctuary out of the camp.
5 So they went near, and carried
them in their coats out of the camp;
as Moses had said.
6 And Moses said unto Aaron, and
unto Ĕl-ē-ā-zär and unto Ĭth-ă-mär,
his sons, [h]Uncover not your heads,
neither rend your clothes; lest ye die,
and lest [i]wrath come upon all the people: but let your brethren, the whole
house of Israel, bewail the burning
which the LORD hath kindled.
7 And [j]ye shall not go out from the
door of the tabernacle of the congregation, lest ye die: [k]for the anointing
oil of the LORD *is* upon you. And they
did according to the word of Moses.
8 ¶ And the LORD spake unto Aaron,
saying,
9 Do [l]not drink wine nor strong
drink, thou, nor thy sons with thee,
when ye go into the tabernacle of the
congregation, lest ye die: *it shall be* a
statute for ever throughout your generations:
10 And that ye may [m]put difference
between holy and unholy, and between unclean and clean;
11 And [n]that ye may teach the children of Israel all the statutes which
the LORD hath spoken unto them by
the hand of Moses.
12 ¶ And Moses spake unto Aaron,
and unto Ĕl-ē-ā-zär and unto Ĭth-ă-
mär, his sons that were left, Take the
[o]meat offering that remaineth of the
offerings of the LORD made by fire,
and eat it without leaven beside the
altar: for [p]it *is* most holy:
13 And ye shall eat it in the holy
place, because it *is* thy due, and thy
sons' due, of the sacrifices of the LORD
made by fire: for so I am commanded.
14 And [q]the wave breast and heave
shoulder shall ye eat in a clean place;
thou, and thy sons, and thy daughters
with thee: for *they be* thy due, and thy
sons' due, *which* are given out of the
sacrifices of peace offerings of the children of Israel.
15 The heave shoulder and the wave
breast shall they bring with the offerings made by fire of the fat, to wave *it*
for a wave offering before the LORD;
and it shall be thine, and thy sons'
with thee, by a statute for ever; as the
LORD hath commanded.
16 ¶ And Moses diligently sought
the [r]goat of the sin offering, and, behold, it was burnt: and he was angry
with Ĕl-ē-ā-zär and Ĭth-ă-mär, the
sons of Aaron *which were* left *alive*,
saying,
17 Wherefore [s]have ye not eaten the
sin offering in the holy place, seeing
it *is* most holy, and *God* hath given it
you to bear the iniquity of the congregation, to make atonement for
them before the LORD?
18 Behold, the blood of it was not
brought in within the holy *place*: ye
should indeed have eaten it in the holy
place, [t]as I commanded.
19 And Aaron said unto Moses, Behold, this [u]day have they offered their
sin offering and their burnt offering
before the LORD; and such things
have befallen me: and *if* I had eaten
the sin offering to day, should [v]it have
been accepted in the sight of the
LORD?
20 And when Moses heard *that*, he
was content.

CHAPTER 11

AND the LORD spake unto Moses
and to Aaron, saying unto them,
2 Speak unto the children of Israel,
saying, [a]These *are* the beasts which
ye shall eat among all the beasts that
are on the earth.
3 Whatsoever parteth the hoof, and
is clovenfooted, *and* cheweth the
cud, among the beasts, that shall ye
eat.
4 Nevertheless these shall ye not eat
of them that chew the cud, or of them
that divide the hoof: *as* the camel, because he cheweth the cud, but divideth
not the hoof; he *is* unclean unto you.
5 And the coney, because he cheweth the cud, but divideth not the hoof;
he *is* unclean unto you.
6 And the hare, because he cheweth
the cud, but divideth not the hoof;
he *is* [b]unclean unto you.
7 And the swine, though he divide
the hoof, and be clovenfooted, yet he
cheweth not the cud; [c]he *is* unclean to
you.
8 Of their flesh shall ye not eat, and
their carcase shall ye not touch; [d]they
are unclean to you.
9 ¶ These [e]shall ye eat of all that *are*
in the waters: whatsoever hath fins

d Ex. 19.22. Isa. 52.11. Eze. 20.41.
e Isa. 49.3. Eze. 28.22. John 13.31. 2 Thes. 1.10.
f Ex. 6.18. Num. 3.19.
g Acts 5.6.
h Num. 6.6,7.
i 2 Sam. 24.1.
j ch. 21.12.
k Ex. 28.41.
l Pro. 31.5. Isa. 28.7. Eze. 44.21. Hosea 4.11. Luke 1.15. Eph. 5.18. 1 Tim. 3.3. Titus 1.7.
m Jer. 15.19. Eze. 22.26.
n Deut. 24.8. Neh. 8.2,13. Jer. 18.18.
o Ex. 29.2. ch. 6.16. Num. 18.9, 10.
p ch. 21.21.
q Ex. 29.24. ch. 7.31,34. Num. 18.11.
r ch. 9.3,15.
s Eze. 44.29.
t ch. 6.26.
u ch. 9.8,12.
v Jer. 6.20. Jer. 14.12. Hosea 9.4.

CHAP. 11

a Deut. 14.4. Eze. 4.4. Dan. 1.8. Acts 10.12. Rom. 14.2. 1 Cor. 8.8. Col. 2.16.
b 1 Tim. 4.4, 5.
c Isa. 65.4. Isa. 66.3,17.
d Isa. 52.11. Acts 10.14, 15. Acts 15.29. Rom. 14.14, 17. 1 Cor. 8.8. Col. 2.16,21. Heb. 9.10.
e Deut. 14.9, 10.

and scales in the waters, in the seas,
and in the rivers, them shall ye eat.
10 And all that have not fins and
scales in the seas, and in the rivers, of
all that move in the waters, and of any
living thing which *is* in the waters, they
shall be an [f]abomination unto you:
11 They shall be even an abomination unto you; ye shall not eat of their
flesh, but ye shall have their carcases
in abomination.
12 Whatsoever hath no fins nor
scales in the waters, that *shall be* an
abomination unto you.
13 ¶ And [g]these *are they which* ye
shall have in abomination among the
fowls; they shall not be eaten, they *are*
an abomination: the eagle, and the
[1]ossifrage, and the [2]ospray,
14 And the vulture, and the kite after
his kind;
15 Every raven after his kind;
16 And the owl, and the night hawk,
and the cuckow, and the hawk after
his kind,
17 And the little owl, and the cormorant, and the great owl,
18 And the swan, and the [h]pelican,
and the [3]gier eagle,
19 And the stork, the heron after her
kind, and the lapwing, and the bat.
20 All [4]fowls that creep, going upon
all four, *shall be* an abomination unto
you.
21 Yet these may ye eat of every flying creeping thing that goeth upon *all*
four, which have legs above their feet,
to leap withal upon the earth;
22 *Even* these of them ye may eat;
the [i]locust after his kind, and the bald
locust after his kind, and the beetle
after his kind, and the grasshopper
[j]after his kind.
23 But all *other* flying creeping
things, which have four feet, *shall be*
an abomination unto you.
24 And for these ye shall be unclean:
whosoever toucheth the carcase of
them shall be unclean until the even.
25 And whosoever beareth *ought* of
the carcase of them [k]shall wash his
clothes, and be unclean until the even.
26 *The carcases* of every beast which
divideth the hoof, and *is* not clovenfooted, nor cheweth the cud, *are* unclean unto you: every one that toucheth them shall be unclean.
27 And [5]whatsoever goeth upon his
paws, among all manner of beasts
that go on *all* four, those *are* unclean
unto you: whoso toucheth their carcase shall be unclean until the even.
28 And he that beareth the carcase of
them shall wash his clothes, and be
unclean until the even: they *are* unclean unto you.
29 ¶ These also *shall be* [l]unclean unto you among the creeping things that
creep upon the earth; the weasel, and
[m]the mouse, and the [6]tortoise after his
kind,
30 And the ferret, and the chame-
leon, and the lizard, and the [n]snail,
and the [o]mole.
31 These *are* unclean to you among
all that creep: whosoever doth touch
them, when they be dead, shall be unclean until the even.
32 And upon whatsoever *any* of
them, when they are dead, doth fall, it
shall be unclean; whether *it be* any
vessel of wood, or raiment, or skin, or
sack, whatsoever vessel *it be*, wherein
any work is done, [p]it must be put into
water, and it shall be unclean until the
even; so it shall be cleansed.
33 And every earthen vessel, whereinto *any* of them falleth, whatsoever
is in it shall be unclean; and [q]ye shall
break it.
34 Of all meat which may be eaten,
that on which *such* water cometh shall
be unclean: and all drink that may be
drunk in every *such* vessel shall be
unclean.
35 And every *thing* whereupon *any*
part of their carcase falleth shall be
unclean; *whether it be* oven, or ranges
for pots, they shall be broken down:
for they *are* unclean, and shall be unclean unto you.
36 Nevertheless a fountain or pit,
[7]wherein *there is* plenty of water, shall
be clean: but that which toucheth
their carcase shall be unclean.
37 And if *any part* of their carcase
fall upon any sowing seed which is to
be sown, it *shall be* clean.
38 But if *any* water be put upon the
seed, and *any part* of their carcase fall
thereon, it *shall be* unclean unto you.
39 And if any beast, of which ye may
eat, die; he that toucheth the carcase
thereof shall be unclean until the even.
40 And [r]he that eateth of the carcase
of it shall wash his clothes, and be unclean until the even: he also that
beareth the carcase of it shall wash his
clothes, and be unclean until the even.
41 And every creeping thing that
creepeth upon the earth *shall be* an
abomination; it shall not be eaten.
42 Whatsoever goeth upon the belly,
and whatsoever goeth upon *all* four,
or whatsoever [8]hath more feet among
all creeping things that creep upon the

[f] ch. 7.18. Deut. 14.3.
[g] Deut. 14. 12. Rom. 14.1-23.
1 A species of eagle.
2 The black eagle.
[h] Ps. 102.6. Zeph. 2.14.
3 The golden vulture.
4 Supposed to mean all flying insects.
[i] Matt. 3. 4.
[j] Judg. 6.5. Jer. 46.23. Nah. 3.17.
[k] ch. 14. 8. ch. 15. 5. Num. 19.10, 22.
5 Supposed to mean monkeys, bears, frogs, etc.
[l] Heb. 9. 10.
[m] Isa. 66. 17.
6 Supposed to mean the frog.
[n] Ps. 58. 8.
[o] Isa. 2. 20.
[p] ch. 15. 12.
[q] ch. 6.28.
7 a gathering together of waters.
[r] ch. 17.15. ch. 22.8. Deut. 14.21. Eze. 4.14.
8 doth multiply feet.

earth, them ye shall not eat; for they
are an abomination.
43 Ye [s]shall not make [9]yourselves
abominable with any creeping thing
that creepeth, neither shall ye make
yourselves unclean with them, that ye
should be defiled thereby.
44 For [t]I *am* the LORD your God: ye
shall therefore sanctify yourselves,
and [u]ye shall be holy; for I *am* holy:
neither shall ye defile yourselves with
any manner of creeping thing that
creepeth upon the earth.
45 For [v]I *am* the LORD that bringeth
you up out of the land of Egypt, to be
your God: [w]ye shall therefore be holy,
for I *am* holy.
46 This *is* the law of the beasts, and
of the fowl, and of every living creature that moveth in the waters, and of
every creature that creepeth upon the
earth:
47 To [x]make a difference between
the unclean and the clean, and between the beast that may be eaten and
the beast that may not be eaten.

CHAPTER 12

AND the LORD spake unto Moses,
saying,
2 Speak unto the children of Israel,
saying, If a woman have conceived
seed, and born a man child: then [a]she
shall be unclean seven days; [b]accord-
ing to the days of the separation for
her infirmity shall she be unclean.
3 And in the [c]eighth day the flesh of
his foreskin shall be circumcised.
4 And she shall then continue in the
blood of her purifying three and thirty
days; she shall touch no hallowed
thing, nor come into the sanctuary,
until the days of her purifying be fulfilled.
5 But if she bear a maid child, then
she shall be unclean two weeks, as in
her separation: and she shall continue
in the blood of her purifying threescore and six days.
6 And [d]when the days of her purifying are fulfilled, for a son, or for a
daughter, she shall bring [e]a lamb [1]of
the first year for a burnt offering, and
a young pigeon, or a turtledove, for a
sin offering, unto the door of the tabernacle of the congregation, unto the
priest:
7 Who shall offer it before the LORD,
and make [f]an atonement for her; and
she shall be cleansed from the issue
of her blood. This *is* the law for her
that hath born a male or a female.
8 And [g]if [2]she be not able to bring a

s ch. 20.25.
9 your souls.
t Isa. 43.3. Isa. 51.15.
u Ex. 19.6. ch. 19.2. 1 Thes. 4.7. 1 Pet. 1.15.
v Gen. 35.1,2. Ex. 6.7. Rom. 14.17.
w Rom. 12.1. 1 Cor. 6.11.
x ch. 10.10. Jer. 15.19. Eze. 22.26.

CHAP. 12

a Luke 2.22.
b ch. 15.19.
c Gen. 17.12. Luke 1.59. John 7.22, 23.
d Luke 2.22.
e Isa. 53.7. Luke 24.26, 27. John 1.29, 36. 1 Pet. 1.18, 19. Rev. 5.6-8.
1 a son of his year.
f Heb. 9.9-28. Heb. 10.1-12.
g ch. 5.7. Luke 2.24. 2 Cor. 8.9.
2 her hand find not sufficiency of.
h ch. 4.26. ch. 13.

CHAP. 13

1 Or, swelling.
a Deut. 28. 27. Isa. 3.17.
b ch. 10.10, 11. Deut. 17.8, 9. Deut. 24.8. Eze. 22.26. Luke 17.11-16. John 13.8-10.
c ch. 11.25. ch. 14.8.
d 2 Sam. 3.29.
e 2 Ki. 5.3.
f Num. 12. 10,12. 2 Ki. 5.27. 2 Chr. 26.19, 20. Luke 5.14. Luke 17.14.
2 the quickening of living flesh.

lamb, then she shall bring two turtles,
or two young pigeons; the one for the
burnt offering, and the other for a sin
offering: and the [h]priest shall make
an atonement for her, and she shall be
clean.

CHAPTER 13

AND the LORD spake unto Moses
and Aaron, saying,
2 When a man shall have in the skin
of his flesh a [1]rising, [a]a scab, or bright
spot, and it be in the skin of his flesh
like the plague of leprosy; [b]then he
shall be brought unto Aaron the
priest, or unto one of his sons the
priests:
3 And the priest shall look on the
plague in the skin of the flesh: and
when the hair in the plague is turned
white, and the plague in sight *be* deeper than the skin of his flesh, it *is* a
plague of leprosy: and the priest shall
look on him, and pronounce him unclean.
4 If the bright spot *be* white in the
skin of his flesh, and in sight *be* not
deeper than the skin, and the hair
thereof be not turned white; then the
priest shall shut up *him that hath* the
plague seven days:
5 And the priest shall look on him
the seventh day: and, behold, *if* the
plague in his sight be at a stay, *and* the
plague spread not in the skin; then the
priest shall shut him up seven days
more:
6 And the priest shall look on him
again the seventh day: and, behold,
if the plague *be* somewhat dark, *and*
the plague spread not in the skin, the
priest shall pronounce him clean: it *is*
but a scab: and he shall [c]wash his
clothes, and be clean.
7 But if the scab spread much abroad
in the skin, after that he hath been
seen of the priest for his cleansing, he
shall be seen of the priest again:
8 And *if* the priest see that, behold,
the scab spreadeth in the skin, then
the priest shall pronounce him unclean: it *is* [d]a leprosy.
9 ¶ When the plague of leprosy is in
a man, then he shall [e]be brought unto
the priest;
10 And [f]the priest shall see *him:* and,
behold, *if* the rising *be* white in the
skin, and it have turned the hair white,
and *there be* [2]quick raw flesh in the
rising;
11 It *is* an old leprosy in the skin of
his flesh, and the priest shall pronounce him unclean, and shall not
shut him up: for he *is* unclean.

12 And if a leprosy break out abroad in the skin, and the leprosy cover all the skin of *him that hath* the plague from his head even to his foot, wheresoever the priest looketh;
13 Then the priest shall consider: and, behold, *if* the leprosy have covered all his flesh, he shall [3]pronounce *him* clean *that hath* the plague: it is all turned white: he *is* clean.
14 But when raw flesh appeareth in him, he shall be unclean.
15 And the [g]priest shall see the raw flesh, and pronounce him to be unclean: *for* the raw flesh *is* unclean: it *is* a leprosy.
16 Or if the raw flesh turn again, and be changed unto white, he shall [h]come unto the priest;
17 And the priest shall see him: and, behold, *if* the plague be turned into white; then the priest shall pronounce *him* clean *that hath* the plague: he [i]*is* clean.
18 ¶ The flesh also, in which, *even* in the skin thereof, was [j]a boil, and is healed,
19 And in the place of the boil there be a white rising, or a bright spot, white, and somewhat reddish, and it be shewed to the priest;
20 And if, when the priest seeth it, behold, it *be* in sight lower than the skin, and the hair thereof be turned white; the priest shall pronounce him unclean: it *is* a plague of leprosy broken out of the boil.
21 But if the priest look on it, and, behold, *there be* no white hairs therein, and *if* it *be* not lower than the skin, but *be* somewhat dark; then the priest shall shut him up seven days:
22 And if it spread much abroad in the skin, then the priest shall pronounce him unclean: it *is* a plague.
23 But if the bright spot stay in his place, *and* spread not, it *is* a burning boil; and the priest [k]shall pronounce him clean.
24 ¶ Or if there be *any* flesh, in the skin whereof *there is* [4]a hot burning, and the quick *flesh* that burneth have a white bright spot, somewhat reddish, or white;
25 Then the priest shall look upon it: and, behold, *if* the hair in the bright spot be turned white, and it *be in* sight deeper than the skin; it *is* a leprosy broken out of the burning: wherefore the priest shall pronounce him unclean: it *is* the [l]plague of leprosy.
26 But if the priest look on it, and, behold, *there be* no white hair in the bright spot, and it *be* no lower than the *other* skin, but *be* somewhat dark; then the priest shall shut him up seven days:
27 And the priest shall look upon him the seventh day: *and* if it be spread much abroad in the skin, then [m]the priest shall pronounce him unclean: it *is* the plague of leprosy.
28 And if the bright spot stay in his place, *and* spread not in the skin, but it *be* somewhat dark; it *is* a rising of the burning, and the priest shall pronounce him clean: for it *is* an inflammation of the burning.
29 ¶ If a man or woman have a plague upon the head or the beard;
30 Then [n]the priest shall see the plague: and, behold, if it *be* in sight deeper than the skin; *and there be* in it a yellow thin hair; then the priest shall pronounce him unclean: it *is* a dry [o]scall, *even* a leprosy upon the head or beard.
31 And if the priest look on the plague of the scall, and, behold, it *be* not in sight deeper than the skin, and *that there is* no black hair in it; then the priest shall shut up *him that hath* the plague of the scall seven days:
32 And in the seventh day the priest shall look on the plague: and, behold, *if* the scall spread not, and there be in it no yellow hair, and the scall *be* not in sight deeper than the skin;
33 He shall be [p]shaven, but the scall shall he not shave; and the priest shall shut up *him that hath* the scall seven days more:
34 And in the seventh day the priest shall look on the scall: and, behold, *if* the scall be not spread in the skin, nor *be* in sight deeper than the skin; then the priest shall pronounce him clean: and he shall wash his clothes, and be clean.
35 But if the scall spread much in the skin after his cleansing;
36 Then the priest shall look on him: and, behold, if the scall be spread in the skin, the priest shall not seek for yellow hair; he *is* unclean.
37 But if the scall be in his sight at a stay, and *that* there is black hair grown up therein; the scall is healed, he *is* clean: and the [q]priest shall pronounce him clean.
38 ¶ If a man also or a woman have in the skin of their flesh bright spots, *even* white bright spots;
39 Then the priest shall look: and, behold, *if* the bright spots in the skin

3 make clean the plague. Ex. 15.26. Ps. 103.2,3.
g Deut. 24.8.
h Luke 5.12-14.
i Deut. 32.39. Ps. 147.3.
j Ex. 9.9. Ex. 15.26. Deut. 28.27. 2 Ki. 20.7. Job 2.7. Ps. 38. 3-7. Isa. 38.21.
k Pro. 28.13. Luke 5.14. Luke 17.14. 1 Cor. 5.5. Gal. 6.1. 1 Pet. 4.2,3.
4 a burning of fire.
l Ex. 4.6,7. Num. 12.10. 2 Sam. 3.29. 2 Ki. 5.27. 2 Chr. 26.19. Luke 5.12-14.
m ch. 10.10. Jer. 15.19. Eze. 22.26.
n Deut. 24.8. Mal. 2.7 1 Cor. 12.9.
o Deut. 28. 27. Isa. 3.17.
p Job 1.20. Rom. 8.13.
q ch. 10.10. Jer. 15.19. Eze. 22.26. Eze. 44.23.

of their flesh *be* darkish white; it *is* a freckled spot *that* groweth in the skin; he *is* clean.

40 And the man whose [5]hair is fallen off his head, he *is* [r]bald; *yet is* he clean.

41 And he that hath his hair fallen off from the part of his head toward his face, he *is* forehead bald: *yet is* he clean.

42 And if there be in the bald head, or bald forehead, a white reddish sore; it *is* a leprosy sprung up in his bald head, or his bald forehead.

43 Then [s]the priest shall look upon it: and, behold, *if* the rising of the sore *be* white reddish in his bald head, or in his bald forehead, as the leprosy appeareth in the skin of the flesh;

44 He is a leprous man, he *is* unclean: the priest shall pronounce him utterly unclean; his plague *is* in his head.

45 And the leper in whom the plague *is*, his clothes shall be rent, and his head bare, and he shall put [t]a covering upon his upper lip, and shall cry, [u]Unclean, unclean.

46 All the days wherein the plague *shall be* in him he shall be defiled; he *is* unclean: he shall dwell alone; [v]without the camp *shall* his habitation *be*.

47 ¶ The [w]garment also that the plague of leprosy is in, *whether it be* a woollen garment, or a linen garment;

48 Whether *it be* in the warp, or woof; of linen, or of woollen; whether in a skin, or in any [6]thing made of skin;

49 And if the plague be greenish or reddish in the garment, or in the skin, either in the warp, or in the woof, or in any [7]thing of skin; it *is* a plague of leprosy, and shall be shewed unto the priest:

50 And [x]the priest shall look upon the plague, and shut up *it that hath* the plague seven days:

51 And he shall look on the plague on the seventh day: if the plague be spread in the garment, either in the warp, or in the woof, or in a skin, *or* in any work that is made of skin; the plague *is* [y]a fretting leprosy; it *is* unclean.

52 He shall therefore burn that garment, whether warp or woof, in woollen or in linen, or any thing of skin, wherein the plague is: for it *is* a fretting leprosy; it shall be burnt in the fire.

53 And if the priest shall look, and, behold, the plague be not spread in the garment, either in the warp, or in the woof, or in any thing of skin;

54 Then the priest shall command that they wash *the thing* wherein the plague *is*, and he shall shut it up seven days more:

55 And the priest shall look on the plague, after that it is washed: and, behold, *if* the plague have not changed his colour, and the plague be not spread; it *is* unclean; thou shalt burn it in the fire; it *is* fret inward, [8]*whether* it *be* bare within or without.

56 And if the priest look, and, behold, the plague *be* somewhat dark after the washing of it; then he shall rend it out of the garment, or out of the skin, or out of the warp, or out of the woof:

57 And if it appear still in the garment, either in the warp, or in the woof, or in any thing of skin; it *is* a spreading *plague:* thou shalt burn that wherein the plague *is* with fire.

58 And the garment, either warp, or woof, or whatsoever thing of skin *it be*, which thou shalt wash, if the plague be departed from them, then it shall be washed the second time, and shall be clean.

59 This *is* the law of the plague of leprosy in a garment of woollen or linen, either in the warp, or woof, or any thing of skins, to pronounce it clean, or to pronounce it unclean.

CHAPTER 14

AND the LORD spake unto Moses, saying,

2 This shall be the law of the leper in the day of his cleansing: He [a]shall be brought unto the priest:

3 And the priest shall go forth out of the camp; and the priest shall look, and, behold, *if* the plague of leprosy be healed in the leper;

4 Then shall the priest command to take for him that is to be cleansed two [1]birds alive *and* clean, and [b]cedar wood, [c]and scarlet, [d]and hyssop:

5 And the priest shall command that one of the birds be killed in an earthen vessel over running water:

6 As for the living bird, he shall take it, and the cedar wood, and the scarlet, and the hyssop, and shall dip them and the living bird in the blood of the bird *that was* killed over the running water:

7 And he shall [e]sprinkle upon him that is to be cleansed from the leprosy [f]seven times, and shall pronounce him clean, and shall let the living bird loose [2]into the open field.

8 And he that is to be cleansed shall [g]wash his clothes, and shave off all his

5 head is pilled.
r Isa. 15.2. Amos 8.10.
s ch. 10.10. Eze. 22.26.
t Eze. 24.17, 22. Micah 3.7.
u 1 Ki. 8.37. Job 40.4. Job 42.6. Ps. 61.1. Ps. 72.12. Isa. 6.5. Lam. 4.15. Luke 17.12, 13. Rev. 21.4.
v Num. 5.2. Num. 12.14. 2 Ki. 7.3. 2 Chr. 26.21. Luke 17.12. 1 Cor. 5.5. 2 Thes. 3.6. Heb. 12.15.
w Isa. 59.6. Eze. 16.16. Zech. 3.4. Rom. 1.21-31. Rom. 13.12. Jude 23.
6 work of.
7 vessel, or, instrument.
x Jer. 15.19. Eze. 44.23.
y ch. 14.44. Eze. 16.43.
8 whether it be bald in the head thereof, or in the forehead thereof.

CHAP. 14

a Jer. 15.19. Eze. 44.23. Luke 5.12, 14. Luke 17.14.
1 Or, sparrows.
b Num. 19.6.
c Heb. 9.19.
d Ex. 12.22. Num. 19.18. Ps. 51.7.
e Eze. 36.25. Heb. 9.13. Heb. 10.22.
f ch. 8.11. 2 Ki. 5.10, 14.
2 upon the face of the field.
g ch. 13.6.

hair, and [h]wash himself in water, that
he may be clean: and after that he
shall come into the camp, and [i]shall
tarry abroad out of his tent seven
days.
9 But it shall be on the seventh day,
that he shall shave all his hair off his
head and his beard and his eyebrows,
even all his hair he shall shave off: and
he shall wash his clothes, also he shall
wash his flesh in water, and he shall
be clean.
10 And on the eighth day [j]he shall
take two he lambs without blemish,
and one ewe lamb [3]of the first year
without blemish, and three tenth deals
of fine flour *for* [k]a meat offering,
mingled with oil, and one lŏg of oil.
11 And the priest that maketh *him*
clean shall present the man that is to
be made clean, and those things, before the LORD, *at* the door of the tabernacle of the congregation:
12 And the priest shall take one he
lamb, and [l]offer him for a trespass
offering, and the lŏg of oil, and [m]wave
them *for* a wave offering before the
LORD:
13 And he shall slay the [n]lamb in
[o]the place where he shall kill the sin
offering and the burnt offering, in the
holy place: for [p]as the sin offering *is*
the priest's, *so is* the trespass offering:
[q]it *is* most holy:
14 And the priest shall take *some* of
the blood [r]of the trespass offering,
and the priest shall put *it* upon [s]the
tip of the right ear of him that is to be
cleansed, and upon the thumb of his
right hand, and upon the great toe of
his right foot:
15 And the priest shall take *some* of
the lŏg of oil, and pour *it* into the palm
of his own left hand:
16 And the priest shall dip his right
finger in the oil that *is* in his left hand,
and shall sprinkle of the oil with his
finger seven times before the LORD:
17 And of the rest of the oil that *is* in
his hand shall the priest put upon the
tip of the right ear of him [t]that is to be
cleansed, and upon the thumb of his
right hand, and upon the great toe of
his right foot, upon the blood of the
trespass offering:
18 And the remnant of the oil that *is*
in the priest's hand he shall pour upon
the head of him that is to be cleansed:
and the priest shall make an [u]atone-
ment for him before the LORD.
19 And the priest shall offer the sin
offering, and make an atonement for
him that is to be cleansed from his un-

h ch. 11.25.
i Num. 5.2,3. Num. 12.15. 2 Chr. 26.20, 21.
j Luke 5.14.
3 the daughter of her year.
k ch. 2.1. Num. 15.4, 15.
l ch. 5.2,6,18. ch. 6.6,7.
m Ex. 29.24.
n Isa. 53.7. John 1.29. 1 Pet. 1.19. Rev. 5.6.
o Ex. 29.11. ch. 1.5,11.
p ch. 7.7.
q ch. 2.3. ch. 7.6.
r Eph. 1.7. Col. 1.14. Heb. 9.9-14. Rev. 12.11.
s Ex. 29.20. ch. 8.23. Rom. 12.1. 2 Cor. 7.1.
t Rom. 6.13-22. Rom. 12.1. 1 Cor. 6.20.
u ch. 4.26. Num. 15.28. Dan. 9.24. Rom. 5.11. 2 Cor. 5.18, 19. Eph. 2.12-22. Col. 1.19-22. Heb. 2.17. 1 John 1.7.
v ch. 5.7. ch. 12.8. Job 34.19. Pro. 17.5. Pro. 22.2. Luke 6.20. 1 John 5.3.
4 his hand reach not.
5 for a waving.
w ch. 12.8. ch. 15.14,15. Luke 2.24.
x 1 Thes. 5. 23. 1 John 1.7. Rev. 1.5.
y 1 Cor. 6.11.
z ch. 15.15. Rom. 8.3.

cleanness; and afterwards he shall
kill the burnt offering:
20 And the priest shall offer the
burnt offering and the meat offering
upon the altar: and the priest shall
make an atonement for him, and he
shall be clean.
21 And [v]if he *be* poor, and [4]cannot
get so much; then he shall take one
lamb *for* a trespass offering [5]to be
waved, to make an atonement for
him, and one tenth deal of fine flour
mingled with oil for a meat offering,
and a lŏg of oil;
22 And [w]two turtledoves, or two
young pigeons, such as he is able to
get; and the one shall be a sin offering,
and the other a burnt offering.
23 And he shall bring them on the
eighth day for his cleansing unto the
priest, unto the door of the tabernacle
of the congregation, before the LORD.
24 And the priest shall take the lamb
of the trespass offering, and the lŏg of
oil, and the priest shall wave them *for*
a wave offering before the LORD:
25 And he shall kill the lamb of the
trespass offering, and the priest shall
take *some* of the [x]blood of the trespass offering, and put *it* upon the tip
of the right ear of him that is to be
cleansed, and upon the thumb of his
right hand, and upon the great toe of
his right foot:
26 And the priest shall pour of the
oil into the palm of his own left hand:
27 And the priest shall sprinkle with
his right finger *some* of the oil that
is in his left hand seven times before
the LORD:
28 And the priest shall put of the oil
that *is* in his hand upon the tip of the
right ear of [y]him that is to be cleansed,
and upon the thumb of his right hand,
and upon the great toe of his right
foot, upon the place of the blood of
the trespass offering:
29 And the rest of the oil that *is* in
the priest's hand he shall put upon
the head of him that is to be cleansed,
to make an atonement for him before
the LORD.
30 And he shall offer the one of the
[z]turtledoves, or of the young pigeons,
such as he can get;
31 *Even* such as he is able to get, the
one *for* a sin offering, and the other
for a burnt offering, with the meat
offering: and the priest shall make an
atonement for him that is to be cleansed before the LORD.
32 This *is* the law *of him* in whom *is*
the plague of leprosy, whose hand is

not able to get *that which pertaineth* to his cleansing.

33 ¶ And the LORD spake unto Moses and unto Aaron, saying,

34 When [a]ye be come into the land of Canaan, which I give to you for a possession, and [b]I put the plague of leprosy in a house of the land of your possession;

35 And he that owneth the house shall come and tell the priest, saying, It seemeth to me *there is* as it were [c]a plague in the house:

36 Then the priest shall command that they [6]empty the house, before the priest go *into it* to see the plague, that [d]all that *is* in the house be not made unclean: and afterward the priest shall go in to see the house:

37 And he shall look on the plague and, behold, *if* the plague *be* in the walls of the house with hollow strakes, greenish or reddish, which in sight *are* lower than the wall;

38 Then the priest shall go out of the house to the door of the house, and shut up the house seven days:

39 And the priest shall come again the seventh day, and shall look: and, behold, *if* the plague be spread in the walls of the house;

40 Then [e]the priest shall command that they take away the stones in which the plague *is*, and they shall cast them into an unclean place without the city:

41 And he shall cause the house to be scraped within round about, and they shall pour out the dust that they scrape off without the city into an unclean place:

42 And they shall take other stones, and put *them* in the place of those stones; and he shall take other morter, and shall plaister the house.

43 And if the plague come again, and break out in the house, after that he hath taken away the stones, and after he hath scraped the house, and after it is plaistered;

44 Then the priest shall come and look, and, behold, *if* the plague be spread in the house, it *is* [f]a fretting leprosy in the house: it *is* unclean.

45 And he shall break down the house, the stones of it, and the timber thereof, and all the morter of the house; and he shall carry *them* forth out of the city into an unclean place.

46 Moreover he that goeth into the house all the while that it is shut up shall be unclean [g]until the even.

47 And he that lieth in the house shall wash his clothes; and he that eateth in the house shall wash his clothes.

48 And if the priest [7]shall come in, and look *upon it*, and, behold, the plague hath not spread in the house, after the house was plaistered: then the priest shall pronounce the house clean, because the plague is [h]healed.

49 And he shall take to cleanse the house two birds, and cedar wood, and scarlet, and hyssop:

50 And he shall kill the one of the birds in an earthen vessel over running water:

51 And he shall take the cedar wood, and the [i]hyssop, and the scarlet, and the living bird, and dip them in the blood of the slain bird, and in the running water, and sprinkle the house seven times:

52 And he shall cleanse the house with the blood of the bird, and with the running water, and with the living bird, and with the cedar wood, and with the hyssop, and with the scarlet:

53 But he shall let go the living bird out of the city into the open fields, and make an atonement for the house: and it shall be clean.

54 This *is* the law for all manner of plague of leprosy, and [j]scall,

55 And for the [k]leprosy of a garment, and of a house,

56 And [l]for a rising, and for a scab, and for a bright spot:

57 To [m]teach [8]when *it is* unclean, and when *it is* clean: this *is* the law of leprosy.

CHAPTER 15

AND the LORD spake unto Moses and to Aaron, saying,

2 Speak unto the children of Israel, and say unto them, [a]When any man hath a [1]running issue out of his flesh, *because of* his issue he *is* unclean.

3 And this shall be his uncleanness in his issue: whether his flesh run with his issue, or his flesh be stopped from his issue, it *is* his uncleanness.

4 Every bed, whereon he lieth that hath the issue, is unclean: and every [2]thing, whereon he sitteth, shall be unclean.

5 And whosoever toucheth his bed shall wash his clothes, [b]and bathe *himself* in water, and be unclean until the even.

6 And he that sitteth on *any* thing whereon he sat that hath the issue shall wash his clothes, and bathe *himself* in water, and be unclean until the even.

7 And he that toucheth the flesh of

a Gen. 17.8. Num. 32.22. Deut. 7.1. Deut. 19.1.
b Deut. 32. 39. Isa. 45.7. Amos 3.6.
c Ps. 91.10. Pro. 3.33. Zech. 5.4.
6 Or, prepare.
d Num. 19. 18. Ps. 51.7. Isa. 52.11. 1 Cor. 5.6,7. 2 Cor. 6.17. 2 Thes. 3.6. 1 Tim. 5.22. Rev. 18.4.
e Jer. 15.19. Eze. 22.26. Eze. 44.23.
f ch. 13.51. Zech. 5.4.
g ch. 17.15. ch. 22.6. Num. 19.7-10,21,22. 1 Cor. 15.33.
7 in coming in shall come in, etc.
h Deut. 32. 39. Job 5.18. Hosea 6.1. Luke 7.21.
i 1 Ki. 4.33. Ps. 51.7.
j ch. 13.30.
k ch. 13.47.
l ch. 13.2.
m Ex. 15.26. Deut. 4.6. Deut. 24.8. Ps. 78.5. Ps. 119.96. Pro. 6.23. Pro. 13.13. Eccl. 8.5. Eze. 44.23.
8 in the day of the unclean, and in the day of the clean.

CHAP. 15

a ch. 22.4. Num. 5.2. 2 Sam. 3.29. Matt. 9.20. Mark 5.25. Luke 8.43.
1 Or, running of the reins.
2 vessel.
b ch. 11.25. ch. 17.15. Heb. 9.10.

him that hath the issue shall wash his
clothes, and bathe *himself* in water,
and be unclean until the even.
8 And if he that hath the issue spit
[c]upon him that is clean; then he shall
wash his clothes, and bathe [d]*himself*
in water, and be unclean until the even.
9 And what saddle soever he rideth
upon that hath the issue shall be unclean.
10 And whosoever toucheth any
thing that was under him shall be unclean until the even: and he that
beareth *any of* those things shall wash
his clothes, and bathe *himself* in
water and be unclean until the even.
11 And whomsoever he [e]toucheth
that hath the issue, and hath not rinsed his hands in water, he shall wash
his clothes, and bathe *himself* in
water, and be unclean until the even.
12 And the [f]vessel of earth, that he
toucheth which hath the issue, shall
be broken: and every vessel of wood
shall be rinsed in water.
13 And when he that hath an issue is
cleansed of his issue; then he [g]shall
number to himself seven days for his
cleansing, and wash his clothes, and
bathe his flesh in running water, and
shall be clean.
14 And on the eighth day he shall
take to him [h]two turtledoves, or two
young pigeons, and come before the
LORD unto the door of the tabernacle
of the congregation, and give them
unto the priest:
15 And the priest shall offer them,
[i]the one *for* a sin offering, and the
other *for* a burnt offering; and [j]the
priest shall make an atonement for
him before the LORD for his issue.
16 And [k]if any man's seed of copulation go out from him, then he shall
wash all his flesh in water, and be unclean until the even.
17 And every garment, and every
skin, whereon is the seed of copulation, shall be washed with water, and
be unclean until the even.
18 The woman also with whom man
shall lie *with* seed of copulation, they
shall *both* bathe *themselves* in water,
and [l]be unclean until the even.
19 ¶ And [m]if a woman have an issue,
and her issue in her flesh be blood, she
shall be [3]put apart seven days: and
whosoever toucheth her shall be unclean until the even.
20 And every thing that she lieth upon in her separation shall be unclean:
every thing also that she sitteth upon
shall be unclean.
21 And whosoever toucheth her bed
shall wash his clothes, and bathe *himself* in water, and be unclean until the
even.
22 And whosoever toucheth any
thing that she sat upon shall wash his
clothes, and bathe [n]*himself* in water,
and be unclean until the even.
23 And if it *be* on *her* bed, or on any
thing whereon she sitteth, when he
toucheth it, he shall be unclean until
the even.
24 And [o]if any man lie with her at all,
and her flowers be upon him, he
shall be unclean seven days; and all
the bed whereon he lieth shall be
unclean.
25 And [p]if a woman have an issue of
her blood many days out of the time
of her separation, or if it run beyond
the time of her separation; all the
days of the issue of her uncleanness
shall be as the days of her separation:
she *shall be* unclean.
26 Every bed whereon she lieth all
the days of her issue shall be unto her
as the bed of her separation: and
whatsoever she sitteth upon shall be
unclean, as the uncleanness of her
separation.
27 And whosoever toucheth those
things shall be unclean, and shall
wash his clothes, and bathe *himself*
in water, and be unclean until the
even.
28 But if she be cleansed of her issue,
then she shall number to herself seven
days, and after that she shall be
clean.
29 And on the eighth day she shall
take unto her two turtles, or two
young pigeons, and bring them unto
the priest, to the door of the tabernacle of the congregation.
30 And the priest shall offer the one
for a sin offering, and the other *for* a
burnt offering; and the priest shall
make [q]an atonement for her before
the LORD for the issue of her uncleanness.
31 Thus shall ye [r]separate the children of Israel from their uncleanness;
that they die not in their uncleanness,
when they [s]defile my tabernacle that
is among them.
32 This *is* the law of him that hath an
issue, and *of him* whose seed goeth
from him, and is defiled therewith;
33 And of her that is sick of her
flowers, and of him that hath an issue,
of the man, and of the woman, and
of him that lieth with her that is unclean.

c Num. 12.8. Job 30.10.
d 2 Cor. 7.1.
e 1 Cor. 15. 33.
f ch. 6.28. ch. 11.32,33.
g ch. 14.8. Num. 12.14. Num. 19.11.
h ch. 14.22, 23. Num. 6.10. Heb. 10.10, 12,14.
i ch. 14.30,31.
j ch. 14.19, 31. Heb. 9.14. Heb. 10.1.
k ch. 22.4. Deut. 23.10.
l 1 Sam. 21.4.
m ch. 12.2. Eze. 36.17.
3 in her separation.
n 2 Cor. 7.1. Heb. 10.22.
o ch. 20.18.
p Matt. 9.20. Mark 5.25. Luke 8.43.
q Rom. 3.25. 2 Cor. 5.18-19. Eph. 1.7. Eph. 2.12-22. Col. 1.19-22. Heb. 2.17. Heb. 9.14. Heb. 10.1. Heb. 13.20. 1 John 1.2. 1 John 1.7. 1 John 2.1.
r ch. 11.47. Deut. 24.8. Eze. 22.26. Eze. 44.23.
s Num. 5.3. Num. 19.13, 20. Eze. 5.11. Eze. 23.38. 1 Cor. 3.17.

CHAPTER 16

AND the LORD spake unto Moses after the [a]death of the two sons of Aaron, when they offered before the LORD, and died;

2 And the LORD said unto Moses, Speak unto Aaron thy brother, that he [b]come not at all times into the holy *place* within the vail before the mercy seat, which *is* upon the ark; that he die not: for I [c]will appear in the cloud upon the mercy seat.

3 Thus shall Aaron [d]come into the holy *place*: [e]with a young bullock for a sin offering, and a ram for a burnt offering.

4 He shall put on [f]the holy linen coat, and he shall have the linen breeches upon his flesh, and shall be girded with a linen girdle, and with the linen mitre shall he be attired: these *are* [g]holy garments; therefore [h]shall he wash his flesh in water, and *so* put them on.

5 And he shall take of [i]the congregation of the children of Israel two kids of the goats for a sin offering, and one ram for a burnt offering.

6 And Aaron shall offer his bullock of the sin offering, which *is* for himself, and make [j]an atonement for himself, and for his house.

7 And he shall take the two goats, and present them before the LORD *at* the door of the tabernacle of the congregation.

8 And Aaron shall cast lots upon the two goats; one lot for the LORD, and the other lot for the [1]scapegoat.

9 And Aaron shall bring the goat upon which the LORD's [k]lot [2]fell, and offer him *for* a sin offering.

10 But the goat, on which the lot fell to be the scapegoat, shall be presented alive before the LORD, to make [l]an atonement with him, *and* to let him go for a scapegoat into the wilderness.

11 And Aaron shall bring the bullock of the sin offering, which *is* for himself, and shall make an atonement for himself, and for his house, and shall kill the bullock of the sin offering which *is* for himself:

12 And he shall take [m]a censer full of burning coals of fire from off the altar before the LORD, and his hands full of [n]sweet incense beaten small, and bring *it* within the vail:

13 And [o]he shall put the incense upon the fire before the LORD, that [p]the cloud of the incense may cover the [q]mercy seat that *is* upon the testimony, that he die not:

14 And [r]he shall take of the blood of the bullock, and sprinkle *it* with his finger upon the mercy seat eastward; and before the mercy seat shall he sprinkle of the blood with his finger seven times.

15 ¶ Then [s]shall he kill the goat of the sin offering, that *is* for the people, and bring his blood [t]within the vail, and do with that blood as he did with the blood of the bullock, and sprinkle it upon the mercy seat, and before the mercy seat:

16 And he shall [u]make an atonement for the holy *place*, because of the uncleanness of the children of Israel, and because of their transgressions in all their sins: and so shall he do for the tabernacle of the congregation, that [3]remaineth among them in the midst of their uncleanness.

17 And [v]there shall be no man in the tabernacle of the congregation when he goeth in to make an atonement in the holy *place*, until he come out, and have made an atonement for himself, and for his household, and for all the congregation of Israel.

18 And he shall go out unto the altar that *is* before the LORD, and make [w]an atonement for it; and shall take of the blood of the bullock, and of the blood of the goat, and put *it* upon the horns of the altar round about.

19 And he shall sprinkle of the blood upon it with his finger seven times, and cleanse it, and [x]hallow it from the uncleanness of the children of Israel.

20 ¶ And when he hath made an end [y]of reconciling the holy *place*, and the tabernacle of the congregation, and the altar, he shall bring the live goat:

21 And Aaron shall lay both his hands upon the head of the live goat, and confess over him all the iniquities of the children of Israel, and all their transgressions in all their sins, [z]putting them upon the head of the goat, and shall send *him* away by the hand of [4]a fit man into the wilderness:

22 And the goat shall [a]bear upon him all their iniquities unto a land [5]not inhabited: and he shall let go the goat in the wilderness.

23 And Aaron shall come into the tabernacle of the congregation, and [b]shall put off the linen garments, which he put on when he went into the holy *place*, and shall leave them there:

24 And he shall wash his flesh with water in the holy place, and put on his garments, and come forth, and offer his burnt offering, and the burnt

CHAP. 16
a ch. 10.1,2.
b Ex. 30.10. ch. 23.27,28. Heb. 9.7. Heb. 10.19.
c Ex. 25.22. Ex. 40.34. 1 Ki. 8.10, 11,12.
d Heb. 9.7-25.
e ch. 4.3.
f Ex. 28.39. ch. 6.10. Eze. 44.17. Phil. 2.7. Heb. 2.14.
g Ps. 93.5.
h Ex. 30.20. Heb. 10.22.
i ch. 4.14. Num. 29.11. 2 Chr. 29.21. Ezra 6.17. Eze. 45.22.
j ch. 9.7. Heb. 5.1,2. Heb. 7.27, 28.
1 Azazel.
k Pro. 16.33.
2 went up.
l Isa. 53.4-10. Rom. 3.25. 2 Cor. 5.21. Heb. 7.26. Heb. 9.23, 24. 1 John 2.2.
m ch. 10.1. Num. 16.18. Rev. 8.5.
n Ex. 30.34. Ex. 31.11. Ex. 37.29. Rev. 8.3,4.
o Ex. 31.1,7, 8. Num. 16.7, 18,46. Rev. 8.3,4.
p 1 Tim. 6.16.
q Ex. 25.21, 22.
r Heb. 10.4.
s Heb. 2.17.
t Heb. 6.19.
u Ex. 29.36.
3 dwelleth.
v Luke 1.10.
w Heb. 9.22.
x Eze. 43.20.
y Eze. 45.20.
z Isa. 53.6.
4 a man of opportunity.
a Ps. 103.1-13. Matt. 8.17. Heb. 9.28. 1 Pet. 2.24.
5 of separation.
b Eze. 42.14. Phil. 2.6-11.

offering of the people, and make an
atonement for himself, and for the
people.
25 And [c]the fat of the sin offering
shall he burn upon the altar.
26 And he that let go the goat for the
scapegoat shall wash his clothes, [d]and
bathe his flesh in water, and afterward
come into the camp.
27 And [e]the bullock *for* the sin offering, and the goat *for* the sin offering,
whose blood was brought in to make
atonement in the holy *place*, shall *one*
carry forth without the camp; and
they shall burn in the fire their skins,
and their flesh, and their dung.
28 And he that burneth them shall
wash his clothes, and bathe his flesh
in water, and afterward he shall come
into the camp.
29 ¶ And *this* shall be a statute for
ever unto you: *that* [f]in the seventh
month, on the tenth *day* of the month,
ye shall afflict your souls, and do no
work at all, *whether it be* one of your
own country, or a stranger that sojourneth among you:
30 For on that day shall *the priest*
make an atonement for you, to cleanse
[g]you, *that* ye may be clean from all
your sins before the LORD.
31 It [h]*shall be* a sabbath of rest unto
you, and ye shall afflict your souls, by
a statute for ever.
32 And the priest, whom he shall
anoint, and whom he [i]shall [6]conse-
crate to minister in the priest's office
in his father's stead, shall make the
atonement, and shall put on the linen
clothes, *even* the holy garments:
33 And he shall make an atonement
for the holy sanctuary, and he shall
make an atonement for the tabernacle of the congregation, and for the
altar, and he shall make an atonement for the priests, and for all the
people of the congregation.
34 And [j]this shall be an everlasting
statute unto you, to make an atonement for the children of Israel for all
their sins once [k]a year. And he did as
the LORD commanded Moses.

CHAPTER 17

AND the LORD spake unto Moses,
saying,
2 Speak unto Aaron, and unto his
sons, and unto all the children of Israel, and say unto them; This *is* the
thing which the LORD hath commanded, saying,
3 What man soever *there be* of the
house of Israel, that killeth an ox, or
lamb, or goat, in the camp, or that
killeth *it* out of the camp,
4 And [a]bringeth it not unto the door
of the tabernacle of the congregation,
to offer an offering unto the LORD before the tabernacle of the LORD; blood
shall be [b]imputed unto that man; he
hath shed blood; and that man [c]shall
be cut off from among his people:
5 To the end that the children of
Israel may bring their sacrifices, which
[d]they offer in the open field, even that
they may bring them unto the LORD,
unto the door of the tabernacle of the
congregation, unto the priest, and
offer them *for* peace offerings unto the
LORD.
6 And the priest shall sprinkle the
blood upon the altar of the LORD *at*
the door of the tabernacle of the
congregation, and burn [e]the fat for
a sweet savour unto the LORD.
7 And they shall no more offer their
sacrifices [f]unto devils, after whom
they [g]have gone a whoring. This shall
be a statute for ever unto them
throughout their generations.
8 ¶ And thou shalt say unto them,
Whatsoever man *there be* of the house
of Israel, or of the strangers which sojourn among you, that offereth a
burnt offering or sacrifice,
9 And bringeth it not unto the door
of the tabernacle of the congregation,
to offer it unto the LORD; even that
man shall be cut off from among his
people.
10 ¶ And [h]whatsoever man *there be*
of the house of Israel, or of the strangers that sojourn among you, that
eateth any manner of blood; I [i]will
even set my face against that soul that
eateth blood, and will cut him off
from among his people.
11 For the life of the flesh *is* in the
blood: and I have given it to you upon
the altar [j]to make an atonement for
your souls: for [k]it *is* the blood *that*
maketh an atonement for the soul.
12 Therefore I said unto the children
of Israel, No soul of you shall eat
blood, neither shall any stranger that
sojourneth among you eat blood.
13 And whatsoever man *there be* of
the children of Israel, or of the strangers that sojourn among you, [1]which
hunteth and catcheth any beast or
fowl that may be eaten; he shall even
[l]pour out the blood thereof, and [m]cov-
er it with dust.
14 For [n]*it is* the life of all flesh; the
blood of it *is* for the life thereof:
therefore I said unto the children of

c Ex. 29.13. ch. 4.10.
d ch. 15.5. Heb. 9.10.
e ch. 4.12,21. ch. 6.30. ch. 8.17. Heb. 13.11.
f Ex. 30.10. ch. 23.27. Num. 29.7. Isa. 58.3,5. Dan. 10.3, 12.
g Eze. 36.25. Jer. 33.8. Titus 2.14. Eph. 5.26. Heb. 9.13, 14.
h Ex. 31.15. Ex. 35.2. ch. 23.32.
i Ex. 29.29. Num. 20.26.
6 fill his hand.
j ch. 23.31. Num. 29.7.
k Ex. 30.10. Heb. 9.7,25.

CHAP. 17

a Deut. 12.5.
b Ps. 32.2. Rom. 4.6.
c Gen. 17.14.
d Gen. 21.33. Gen. 22.2. Deut. 12.2. 1 Ki. 14.22, 23. 2 Ki. 17.10. Eze. 20.28.
e Ex. 29.18. ch. 4.31. Num. 18.17.
f Deut. 32.17. 2 Chr. 11.15. Ps. 106.37. Acts 7.42, 43. 1 Cor. 10.20.
g Ex. 34.15. Deut. 31.16.
h Gen. 9.4. 1 Sam. 14. 33.
i ch. 26.17. Jer. 44.11. Eze. 15.7.
j Mark 14.24. Rom. 5.9. Eph. 1.7. Col. 1.14.
k Heb. 9.22.
1 that hunteth any hunting.
l Deut. 12.16. Deut. 15.23. 1 Sam. 14. 32-34.
m Eze. 24.7.
n Gen. 9.4.

Israel, Ye shall eat the blood of no manner of flesh: for the life of all flesh *is* the blood thereof: whosoever eateth it shall be cut off.

15 And [o]every soul that eateth [2]that which died *of itself*, or that which was torn *with beasts, whether it be* one of your own country, or a stranger, he shall both wash his clothes, and bathe *himself* in water, and be unclean until the even: then shall he be clean.

16 But if he wash *them* not, nor bathe his flesh; then [p]he shall bear his iniquity.

CHAPTER 18

AND the LORD spake unto Moses, saying,

2 Speak unto the children of Israel, and say unto them, [a]I am the LORD your God.

3 After [b]the doings of the land of Egypt, wherein ye dwelt, shall ye not do: and after [c]the doings of the land of Canaan, whither I bring you, shall ye not do: neither shall ye walk in their ordinances.

4 Ye shall do my judgments, and keep mine ordinances, to walk therein: I *am* the LORD your God.

5 Ye shall therefore keep my statutes, and my judgments: [d]which if a man do, he shall live in them: I [e]*am* the LORD.

6 ¶ None of you shall approach to any that is [1]near of kin to him, to uncover *their* nakedness: I *am* the LORD.

7 The nakedness of thy father, or the nakedness of thy mother, shalt thou not uncover: she *is* thy mother; thou shalt not uncover her nakedness.

8 The [f]nakedness of thy father's wife shalt thou not uncover: it *is* thy father's nakedness.

9 The [g]nakedness of thy sister, the daughter of thy father, or daughter of thy mother, *whether she be* born at home, or born abroad, *even* their nakedness thou shalt not uncover.

10 The nakedness of thy son's daughter, or of thy daughter's daughter, *even* their nakedness thou shalt not uncover: for theirs *is* thine own nakedness.

11 The nakedness of thy father's wife's daughter, begotten of thy father, she *is* thy sister, thou shalt not uncover her nakedness.

12 Thou shalt not uncover the nakedness of thy father's sister: she *is* thy father's near kinswoman.

13 Thou shalt not uncover the nakedness of thy mother's sister: for she *is* thy mother's near kinswoman.

o Ex. 22.31. Deut. 14.21.
2 a carcase.
p Num. 19. 20. Heb. 9.28.
CHAP. 18
a Ex. 6.7. Eze. 20.5.
b Eze. 20.7.
c Ex. 23.24.
d Luke 10.28. Rom. 10.5. Gal. 3.12.
e Isa. 44.6. Jer. 9.24. Mal. 3.6.
1 remainder of his flesh.
f Gen. 49.4. 1 Cor. 5.1.
g 2 Sam. 13. 12.
h Gen. 38.18. Eze. 22.11.
i Matt. 14.3, 4. Matt. 22.24.
2 Or, one wife to another. 1 Tim. 3.2.
j Gen. 30.15. Mal. 2.15.
k Eze. 18.6.
l Pro. 6.29. Mal. 3.5. Matt. 5.27, 28. 1 Cor. 6.9. Heb. 13.4.
m 2 Ki. 16.3. Jer. 19.5.
n 1 Ki. 11.7, 33.
o Eze. 36.20. Mal. 1.12.
p Isa. 42.8.
q Rom. 1.27. 1 Tim. 1.10.
r Matt. 15.18. 1 Cor. 3.17.
s Deut. 18.12.
t Num. 35.34. Isa. 24.5. Jer. 16.18.
u Isa. 26.21. Jer. 9.9.

14 Thou shalt not uncover the nakedness of thy father's brother, thou shalt not approach to his wife: she *is* thine aunt.

15 Thou [h]shalt not uncover the nakedness of thy daughter in law: she *is* thy son's wife; thou shalt not uncover her nakedness.

16 Thou [i]shalt not uncover the nakedness of thy brother's wife: it *is* thy brother's nakedness.

17 Thou shalt not uncover the nakedness of a woman and her daughter, neither shalt thou take her son's daughter, or her daughter's daughter, to uncover her nakedness; *for* they *are* her near kinswomen: it *is* wickedness.

18 Neither shalt thou take [2]a wife to her sister, [j]to vex *her*, to uncover her nakedness, beside the other in her life *time*.

19 Also [k]thou shalt not approach unto a woman to uncover her nakedness, as long as she is put apart for her uncleanness.

20 Moreover [l]thou shalt not lie carnally with thy neighbour's wife, to defile thyself with her.

21 And thou shalt not let any of thy seed pass [m]through *the* [n]*fire* to Molech, neither shalt thou [o]profane the name of thy God: I [p]*am* the LORD.

22 Thou [q]shalt not lie with mankind, as with womankind: it *is* abomination.

23 Neither shalt thou lie with any beast to defile thyself therewith: neither shall any woman stand before a beast to lie down thereto: it *is* confusion.

24 Defile [r]not ye yourselves in any of these things: [s]for in all these the nations are defiled which I cast out before you:

25 And [t]the land is defiled: therefore I do visit [u]the iniquity thereof upon it, and the land itself vomiteth out her inhabitants.

26 Ye shall therefore keep my statutes and my judgments, and shall not commit *any* of these abominations; *neither* any of your own nation, nor any stranger that sojourneth among you:

27 (For all these abominations have the men of the land done, which *were* before you, and the land is defiled;)

28 That the land spue not you out also, when ye defile it, as it spued out the nations that *were* before you.

29 For whosoever shall commit any of these abominations, even the souls that commit *them* shall be cut off from among their people.

30 Therefore shall ye keep mine ordinance, that *ye* commit not *any one* of these abominable customs, which were committed before you, and that ye defile not yourselves therein: I *am* the LORD your God.

CHAPTER 19

AND the LORD spake unto Moses, saying,
2 Speak unto all the congregation of the children of Israel, and say unto them, Ye [a]shall be holy: for I the LORD your God *am* holy.
3 ¶ Ye shall fear every man his mother, and his father, and [b]keep my sabbaths: I *am* the LORD your God.
4 ¶ Turn [c]ye not unto idols, nor make to yourselves molten gods: I *am* the LORD your God.
5 ¶ And if ye offer a sacrifice of peace offerings unto the LORD, ye shall offer it at your own will.
6 It shall be eaten the same day ye offer it, and on the morrow: and if ought remain until the third day, it shall be burnt in the fire.
7 And if it be eaten at all on the third day, it *is* abominable; it shall not be accepted.
8 Therefore *every one* that eateth it shall bear his iniquity, because he hath profaned the hallowed thing of the LORD: and that soul shall be cut off from among his people.
9 ¶ And [d]when ye reap the harvest of your land, thou shalt not wholly reap the corners of thy field, neither shalt thou gather the gleanings of thy harvest.
10 And thou shalt not glean thy vineyard, neither shalt thou gather *every* grape of thy vineyard; thou shalt leave them [e]for the poor and stranger: I *am* the LORD your God.
11 ¶ Ye shall not steal, neither deal falsely, neither [f]lie one to another.
12 ¶ And ye shall not swear by my name falsely, neither shalt thou profane the name of thy God: I *am* the LORD.
13 ¶ Thou shalt not defraud thy neighbour, neither rob *him:* [g]the wages of him that is hired shall not abide with thee all night until the morning.
14 ¶ Thou shalt not curse the deaf, [h]nor put a stumblingblock before the blind, but shalt [i]fear thy God: I *am* the LORD.
15 ¶ Ye [j]shall do no unrighteousness in judgment: thou shalt not respect the person of the poor, nor honour the person of the mighty: *but* in righteousness shalt thou judge thy neighbour.
16 ¶ Thou shalt not go up and down *as* a talebearer among thy people: neither shalt thou [k]stand against the blood of thy neighbour: I *am* the LORD.
17 ¶ Thou [l]shalt not hate thy brother in thine heart: [m]thou shalt in any wise rebuke thy neighbour, [1]and not suffer sin upon him.
18 ¶ Thou [n]shalt not avenge, nor bear any grudge against the children of thy people, [o]but thou shalt love thy neighbour as thyself: I *am* the LORD.
19 ¶ Ye shall keep my statutes. Thou shalt not let thy cattle gender with a diverse kind: thou shalt not sow thy field with mingled seed: neither shall a garment mingled of linen and woollen come upon thee.
20 ¶ And whosoever lieth carnally with a woman, that *is* a bondmaid, [2]betrothed to an husband, and not at all redeemed, nor freedom given her; [3]she shall be scourged; they shall not be put to death, because she was not free.
21 And he shall bring his trespass offering unto the LORD, unto the door of the tabernacle of the congregation, *even* a ram for a trespass offering.
22 And the priest shall make an atonement for him with the ram of the trespass offering before the LORD for his sin which he hath done: and the sin which he hath done shall be forgiven him.
23 ¶ And when ye shall come into the land, and shall have planted all manner of trees for food, then ye shall count the fruit thereof as uncircumcised: three years shall it be as uncircumcised unto you: it shall not be eaten of.
24 But in the fourth year all the fruit thereof shall be [4]holy [p]to praise the LORD *withal.*
25 And in the fifth year shall ye eat of the fruit thereof, that it may yield unto you the increase thereof: I *am* the LORD your God.
26 ¶ Ye shall not eat *any thing* with the blood: [q]neither shall ye use enchantment, nor observe times.
27 Ye [r]shall not round the corners of your heads, neither shalt thou mar the corners of thy beard.
28 Ye shall not [s]make any cuttings in your flesh for the dead, nor print any marks upon you: I *am* the LORD.
29 ¶ Do [t]not [5]prostitute thy daugh-

CHAP. 19

a Ex. 19.6. ch. 11.44. ch. 20.7,26. Eph. 1.4. 1 Thes. 4.7. 1 Pet. 1.16.
b Gen. 2.2. Ex. 20.8. Ex. 31.13. Neh. 9.14. Neh. 13.15-21. Isa. 56.2. Isa. 58.13. Mark 2.27. Heb. 4.9.
c Ex. 20.3-5. 1 Cor. 10.14.
d Ex. 23.11. ch. 23.22. Deut. 15.1-18. Deut. 24.19. Ruth 2.15.
e Ps. 41.1. Ps. 140.12. Pro. 14.31. Pro. 22.16. Pro. 29.7. Eccl. 5.8. Isa. 3.12-15. Jas. 2.1-9.
f 1 Ki. 13.18. Jer. 9.3-5. Acts 5.3,4. Eph. 4.25.
g Deut. 24.14. Mal. 3.5. Jas. 5.4.
h Rom. 14. 13.
i 1 Pet. 2.17.
j Ps. 82.2. Pro. 24.23. Jas. 2.9.
k 1 Ki. 21.13. Matt. 26.60.
l Gen. 27.41. 1 John 2.9, 11. 1 John 3.15.
m Luke 17.3.
1 Or, that thou bear not sin for him. 1 Cor. 5.2.
n Rom. 12.17.
o Matt. 5.43, 44.
2 reproached by, or, for man, or, abused by any.
3 there shall be a scourging, or, they shall be scourged.
4 holiness of praises to the LORD.
p Deut. 12. 17.18.
q 2 Ki. 17.17.
r Jer. 9.26.
s Deut. 14.1.
t Deut. 23.17.
5 profane.

ter, to cause her to be a whore; lest
the land fall to whoredom, and the
land become full of wickedness.
30 ¶ Ye [u]shall keep my sabbaths,
and reverence [v]my sanctuary: I *am* the
LORD.
31 ¶ Regard [w]not them that have
familiar spirits, neither seek after
wizards, to be defiled by them: I *am*
the LORD your God.
32 ¶ Thou [x]shalt rise up before the
hoary head, and honour the face of
the old man, and fear thy God: I *am*
the LORD.
33 ¶ And [y]if a stranger sojourn with
thee in your land, ye shall not [6]vex him.
34 *But* [z]the stranger that dwelleth
with you shall be unto you as one born
among you, and [a]thou shalt love him
as thyself; for ye were strangers in the
land of Egypt: I *am* the LORD your
God.
35 ¶ Ye shall do no unrighteousness
in judgment, in meteyard, in weight,
or in measure.
36 Just [b]balances, just [7]weights, a
just ē-phăh, and a just hĭn, shall ye
have: I *am* the LORD your God, which
brought you out of the land of Egypt.
37 Therefore [c]shall ye observe all my
statutes, and all my judgments, and
do them: I *am* the LORD.

CHAPTER 20

AND the LORD spake unto Moses,
saying,
2 Again, thou shalt say to the children of Israel, [a]Whosoever *he be* of
the children of Israel, or of the strangers that sojourn in Israel, that giveth
any of his seed unto Molech; he shall
surely be put to death: the people
of the land shall stone him with
stones.
3 And I will set my face against that
man, and will cut him off from among
his people; because he hath given of
his seed unto Molech, to defile [b]my
sanctuary, and to profane my holy
name.
4 And if the people of the land do
any ways hide their eyes from the
man, when he giveth of his seed unto
Molech, and kill him not:
5 Then I will set my face against that
man, and [c]against his family, and will
cut him off, and all that go [d]a whoring
after him, to commit whoredom with
Molech, from among their people.
6 ¶ And [e]the soul that turneth after
such as have familiar spirits, and after
wizards, to go a whoring after them,
I will even set my face against that

u ch. 26.2.
v Eccl. 5.1.
w 1 Sam. 28. 7. Isa. 8.19.
x 1 Ki. 2.19. Pro. 20.29. Pro. 23.22. 1 Tim. 5.1.
y Ex. 22.21.
6 Or, oppress.
z Ex. 12.48.
a Deut. 10. 19.
b Deut. 25. 13,15. Pro. 20.10.
7 stones.
c Deut. 6.25. Deut. 5.1. ch. 18.4,5.
CHAP. 20
a 2 Ki. 17.17. 2 Ki. 23.10. 2 Chr. 33.6.
b Eze. 5.11. Num. 19.20.
c Ex. 20.5.
d ch. 17.7.
e ch. 19.31. 2 Ki. 23.24.
f Ex. 22.31. Matt. 5.48. Eph. 1.4. Col. 3.12. 1 Thes. 5.23. 1 Pet. 1.16.
g Ex. 31.13.
h Ex. 21.17. Deut. 27.16. Pro. 20.20. Matt. 15.4.
i 2 Sam. 1.16. 1 Ki. 2.32.
j Deut. 22.22. Jer. 29.23. John 8.4,5. 1 Cor. 6.9. Heb. 13.4.
k ch. 18.8. Deut. 27.23.
l Gen. 19.5. ch. 18.22. Deut. 23.17. Judg. 19.22. Rom. 1.25, 32.
m ch. 18.17.
n Deut. 27. 21.
o Gen. 20. 12.
p ch. 15.24.
1 made naked.
q ch. 18.12.

soul, and will cut him off from among
his people.
7 ¶ Sanctify [f]yourselves therefore,
and be ye holy: for I *am* the LORD
your God.
8 And ye shall keep my statutes, and
do them: [g]I *am* the LORD which sanctify you.
9 ¶ For [h]every one that curseth his
father or his mother shall be surely
put to death: he hath cursed his father
or his mother; his [i]blood *shall be* upon
him.
10 ¶ [j]And the man that committeth
adultery with *another* man's wife, *even*
he that committeth adultery with his
neighbour's wife, the adulterer and
the adulteress shall surely be put to
death.
11 And [k]the man that lieth with his
father's wife hath uncovered his father's nakedness: both of them shall
surely be put to death; their blood
shall be upon them.
12 And if a man lie with his daughter
in law, both of them shall surely be
put to death: they have wrought confusion; their blood *shall be* upon them.
13 If [l]a man also lie with mankind,
as he lieth with a woman, both of
them have committed an abomination: they shall surely be put to death;
their blood *shall be* upon them.
14 And [m]if a man take a wife and her
mother, it *is* wickedness: they shall be
burnt with fire, both he and they;
that there be no wickedness among
you.
15 And [n]if a man lie with a beast, he
shall surely be put to death: and ye
shall slay the beast.
16 And if a woman approach unto
any beast, and lie down thereto, thou
shalt kill the woman, and the beast:
they shall surely be put to death;
their blood *shall be* upon them.
17 And [o]if a man shall take his sister,
his father's daughter, or his mother's
daughter, and see her nakedness, and
she see his nakedness; it *is* a wicked
thing; and they shall be cut off in the
sight of their people: he hath uncovered his sister's nakedness; he shall
bear his iniquity.
18 And [p]if a man shall lie with a
woman having her sickness, and shall
uncover her nakedness; he hath [1]dis-
covered her fountain, and she hath
uncovered the fountain of her blood:
and both of them shall be cut off from
among their people.
19 And [q]thou shalt not uncover the
nakedness of thy mother's sister, nor

of thy father's sister: for he uncovereth his near kin: they shall bear their iniquity.

20 And if a man shall lie with his uncle's wife, he hath uncovered his uncle's nakedness: they shall bear their sin; they shall die childless.

21 And [r]if a man shall take his brother's wife, it *is* [2]an unclean thing: he hath uncovered his brother's nakedness; they shall be childless.

22 ¶ Ye shall therefore keep all my [s]statutes, and all my judgments, and do them: that the land, whither I bring you to dwell therein, spue you not out.

23 And ye shall not walk in the manners of the nation, which I cast out before you: for they committed all these things, and therefore [t]I abhorred them.

24 But [u]I have said unto you, Ye shall inherit their land, and I will give it unto you to possess it, a land that floweth with milk and honey: I *am* the LORD your God, which have [v]separated you from *other* people.

25 Ye [w]shall therefore put difference between clean beasts and unclean, and between unclean fowls and clean: and ye shall not make your souls abominable by beast, or by fowl, or by any manner of living thing that [3]creepeth on the ground, which I have separated from you as unclean.

26 And ye shall be holy unto me: for [x]I the LORD *am* holy, and [y]have severed you from *other* people, that ye should be mine.

27 ¶ A [z]man also or woman that hath a familiar spirit, or that is a wizard, shall surely be put to death: they shall stone them with stones: their blood *shall be* upon them.

CHAPTER 21

AND the LORD said unto Moses, Speak unto the priests the sons of Aaron, and say unto them, There [a]shall none be defiled for the dead among his people:

2 But for his kin, that is near unto him, *that is*, for his mother, and for his father, and for his son, and for his daughter, and for his brother,

3 And for his sister a virgin, that is nigh unto him, which hath had no husband; for her may he be defiled.

4 *But* [1]he shall not defile himself, *being* a chief man among his people, to profane himself.

5 They [b]shall not make baldness upon their head, neither shall they shave off the corner of their beard, nor make any cuttings in their flesh.

6 They shall be holy unto their God, and not [c]profane the name of their God: for the offerings of the LORD made by fire, *and* the [d]bread of their God, they do offer: therefore they shall be holy.

7 They [e]shall not take a wife *that is* a whore, or profane; neither shall they take a woman [f] put away from her husband: for he *is* holy unto his God.

8 Thou shalt sanctify him therefore; for he offereth the bread of thy God: he shall be holy unto thee: [g]for I the LORD, which sanctify you, *am* holy.

9 ¶ And [h]the daughter of any priest, if she profane herself by playing the whore, she profaneth her father: she shall be burnt with fire.

10 And [i]*he that is* the high priest among his brethren, upon whose head the anointing oil was poured, and [j]that is consecrated to put on the garments, [k]shall not uncover his head, nor rend his clothes;

11 Neither shall he [l]go in to any dead body, nor defile himself for his father, or for his mother;

12 Neither [m]shall he go out of the sanctuary, nor profane the sanctuary of his God; for [n]the crown of the anointing oil of his God *is* upon him: I *am* the LORD.

13 And [o]he shall take a wife in her virginity.

14 A widow, or a divorced woman, or profane, *or* an harlot, these shall he not take: but he shall take a virgin of his own people to wife.

15 Neither shall he profane his seed among his people: for [p]I the LORD do sanctify him.

16 ¶ And the LORD spake unto Moses, saying,

17 Speak unto Aaron, saying, Whosoever *he be* of thy seed in their generations that hath *any* blemish, let him not [q]approach to offer the [2]bread of his God.

18 For whatsoever man *he be* that hath a blemish, he shall not approach: a blind man, or a lame, or he that hath a flat nose, or any thing [r]superfluous,

19 Or a man that is brokenfooted, or brokenhanded,

20 Or crookbackt, or a [3]dwarf, or that hath a blemish in his eye, or be scurvy, or scabbed, or [s]hath his stones broken;

21 No man that hath a blemish of the seed of Aaron the priest shall come nigh to offer the offerings of the

r ch. 18.16.
2 a separation.
s ch. 18.26. ch. 19.37.
t Deut. 9.5.
u Ex. 3.17. Ex. 6.8.
v Ex. 19.5. Ex. 33.16. Deut. 7.6. Deut. 14.2. 1 Ki. 8.53. Ps. 135.4. 1 Pet. 2.9.
w ch. 11.47. Deut. 14.4.
3 Or, moveth.
x ch. 19.2. Ps. 99.5. Isa. 6.3. Isa. 30.11. 1 Pet. 1.16. Rev. 3.7. Rev. 4.8.
y Titus 2.14.
z Ex. 22.18. Deut. 18.10. 1 Sam. 28.7.

CHAP. 21

a ch. 5.2. Eze. 44.25.
1 Or, being an husband among his people, he shall not defile himself for his wife, etc.
b ch. 19.27, 28. Deut. 14.1.
c Ex. 20.7. ch. 18.21. Deut. 5.11. Ps. 15.4. Matt. 5.33-37.
d ch. 3.11.
e Eze. 44.22.
f Deut. 24.1, 2.
g ch. 20.7, 8. Isa. 43.15.
h Gen. 38.24.
i Ex. 29.29. Num. 35.25.
j Ex. 28.2.
k ch. 10.6.
l Num. 19.14.
m ch. 10.7.
n Ex. 28.36. ch. 8.9, 12, 30.
o Eze. 44.22.
p Rom. 12.1. 1 Cor. 3.16, 17. Eph. 5.17.
q Num. 16.5. Ps. 65.4.
2 Or, food.
r ch. 22.23.
3 Or, too slender.
s Deut. 23.1.

LORD made by fire: he hath a blemish; he shall not come nigh to offer the bread of his God.

22 He shall eat the bread of his God, *both* of the [t]most holy, and of the [u]holy.

23 Only he shall not go in unto the vail, nor come nigh unto the altar, because he hath a blemish; that he profane not my sanctuaries: for I the LORD do sanctify them.

24 And Moses told *it* unto Aaron, and to his sons, and unto all the children of Israel.

CHAPTER 22

AND the LORD spake unto Moses, saying,

2 Speak unto Aaron and to his sons, that they [a]separate themselves from the holy things of the children of Israel, and that they profane not my holy name *in those things* which they [b]hallow unto me: I *am* the LORD.

3 Say unto them, Whosoever *he be* of all your seed among your generations, that goeth unto the holy things, which the children of Israel hallow unto the LORD, having his [c]uncleanness upon him, that soul shall be cut off from my presence: I *am* the LORD.

4 What man soever of the seed of Aaron *is* a leper, or hath [d]a [1]running issue; he shall not eat of the holy things, [e]until he be clean. And [f]whoso toucheth any thing *that is* unclean *by* the dead, or a man whose seed goeth from him;

5 Or [g]whosoever toucheth any creeping thing, whereby he may be made unclean, or [h]a man of whom he may take uncleanness, whatsoever uncleanness he hath;

6 The soul which hath touched any such shall be unclean until even, and shall not eat of the holy things, unless he [i]wash his flesh with water.

7 And when the sun is down, he shall be clean, and shall afterward eat of the holy things; because [j]it *is* his food.

8 That [k]which dieth of itself, or is torn *with beasts*, he shall not eat to defile himself therewith: I *am* the LORD.

9 They shall therefore keep mine ordinance, [l]lest they bear sin for it, and die therefore, if they profane it: I the LORD do sanctify them.

10 There shall no [m]stranger eat *of* the holy thing: a sojourner of the priest, or an hired servant, shall not eat *of* the holy thing.

11 But if the priest buy *any* soul [2]with his money, he shall eat of it, and he that is born in his house: they shall eat of his meat.

12 If the priest's daughter also be *married* unto [3]a stranger, she may not eat of an offering of the holy things.

13 But if the priest's daughter be a widow, or divorced, and have no child, and [n]is returned unto her father's house, [o]as in her youth, she shall eat of her father's meat: but there shall no stranger eat thereof.

14 ¶ And [p]if a man eat *of* the holy thing unwittingly, then he shall put the fifth *part* thereof unto it, and shall give *it* unto the priest with the holy thing.

15 And [q]they shall not profane the holy things of the children of Israel, which they offer unto the LORD;

16 Or [4]suffer them to bear the iniquity of trespass, when they eat their holy things: for I the LORD do sanctify them.

17¶ And the LORD spake unto Moses, saying,

18 Speak unto Aaron, and to his sons, and unto all the children of Israel, and say unto them, [r]Whatsoever *he be* of the house of Israel, or of the strangers in Israel, that will offer his oblation for all his vows, and for all his freewill offerings, which they will offer unto the LORD for a burnt offering;

19 *Ye shall offer* at your own will a male without blemish, of the beeves, of the sheep, or of the goats.

20 *But* [s]whatsoever hath a blemish, *that* shall ye not offer: for it shall not be acceptable for you.

21 And whosoever offereth a sacrifice of peace offerings unto the LORD to [t]accomplish *his* vow, or a freewill offering in beeves or [5]sheep, it shall be perfect to be accepted; there shall be no blemish therein.

22 Blind, or broken, or maimed, or having a wen, or scurvy, or scabbed, ye shall not offer these unto the LORD, nor make an offering by fire of them upon the altar unto the LORD.

23 Either a bullock or a [6]lamb that hath any thing [u]superfluous or lacking in his parts, that mayest thou offer *for* a freewill offering; but for a vow it shall not be accepted.

24 Ye shall not offer unto the LORD that which is bruised, or crushed, or broken, or cut; neither shall ye make *any offering thereof* in your land.

25 Neither [v]from a stranger's hand shall ye offer the bread of your God of any of these; because their [w]cor

t ch. 2.3,10. ch. 6.17,29. ch. 24.9. Num. 18.9.
u ch. 22.10. Num. 18.19.

CHAP. 22

a Num. 6.3.
b Ex. 13.12. Num. 18.32. Deut. 15.19.
c ch. 7.20.
d ch. 15.2.
1 running of the reins.
e ch. 15.13.
f Num. 19.11, 22.
g ch. 11.24.
h ch. 15.7,19.
i Heb. 10.22.
j Num. 18.11.
k Ex. 22.31. ch. 17.15.
l Ex. 28.43. Num. 18.22.
m One not a priest. Ex. 29.33. Num. 3.10. 1 Sam. 21.6.
2 with the purchase of his money.
3 a man a stranger.
n Gen. 38.11.
o Num. 18. 11.
p ch. 5.15,16.
q Num. 18. 32.
4 Or, lade themselves with the iniquity of trespass in their eating.
r Num. 15.14.
s Deut. 15.21. Deut. 17.1. Mal. 1.8,14. Eph. 5.27. Heb. 9.14.
t Num. 15.3, 8. Deut. 23.21. Ps. 61.8. Ps. 65.1.
5 Or, goats.
6 Or, kid.
u ch. 21.18.
v Num. 15. 15.
w Mal. 1.14.

ruption *is* in them, *and* blemishes *be*
in them: they shall not be accepted
for you.
26¶ And the LORD spake unto Moses,
saying,
27 When [x]a bullock, or a sheep, or a
goat, is brought forth, then it shall be
seven days under the dam; and from
the eighth day and thenceforth it shall
be accepted for an offering made by
fire unto the LORD.
28 And *whether it be* cow or [7]ewe, ye
shall not kill it [y]and her young both
in one day.
29 And when ye will [z]offer a sacrifice
of thanksgiving unto the LORD, offer
it at your own will.
30 On the same day it shall be eaten
up; ye shall leave none of it until the
morrow: I *am* the LORD.
31 Therefore [a]shall ye keep my commandments, and do them: I *am* the
LORD.
32 Neither shall ye profane my holy
name; but [b]I will be hallowed among
the children of Israel: I *am* the LORD
which hallow you,
33 That [c]brought you out of the land
of Egypt, to be your God: I *am* the
LORD.

CHAPTER 23

AND the LORD spake unto Moses,
saying,
2 Speak unto the children of Israel,
and say unto them, *Concerning* the
feasts of the LORD, which ye shall
[1]proclaim *to be* holy convocations,
even these *are* my feasts.
3 Six [b]days shall work be done: but
the seventh day *is* the sabbath of rest,
an holy convocation; ye shall do no
work *therein:* it *is* [c]the sabbath of the
LORD in all your dwellings.
4 ¶ These [d]*are* the feasts of the LORD,
even holy convocations, which ye
shall proclaim in their seasons.
5 In [e]the fourteenth *day* of the first
month at even *is* the LORD's passover.
6 And on the fifteenth day of the
same month *is* the feast of unleavened
bread unto the LORD: seven days ye
must eat unleavened bread.
7 In [f]the first day ye shall have an
holy convocation: ye shall do no servile work therein.
8 But ye shall offer an offering made
by fire unto the LORD seven days: in
the seventh day *is* an holy convocation: ye shall do no servile work
therein.
9 ¶ And the LORD spake unto Moses,
saying,
10 Speak unto the children of Israel,

x Ex. 22.30.
7 Or, she-goat.
y Deut. 22.6.
z Ps. 107.22. Ps. 116.17. Amos 4.5.
a ch. 19.37. Num. 15.40. Deut. 4.40.
b Isa. 6.3. Matt. 6.9. Luke 11.2.
c Ex. 6.7.

CHAP. 23
a Ex. 32.5. Joel 1.14. 2 Ki. 10.20. 2 Chr. 30.5. Ps. 81.3.
b Ex. 20.9. Deut. 5.13. Luke 13.14.
c Neh. 13.22. Isa. 56.2. Isa. 58.13.
d Ex. 23.14.
e Ex. 12.6. Num. 28.16. Deut. 16.1.
f Ex. 12.16. Num. 28.18.
g Ex. 23.16. Num. 15.2, 18. Deut. 16.9. Josh. 3.15.
1 omer, or, handful.
h Pro. 3.9. Rom. 11.16. 1 Cor. 15.20.
i Ex. 29.24. ch. 9.21.
j Ex. 34.22. ch. 25.8. Deut. 16.9.
k Acts 2.1.
l Ex. 23.16. Ex. 22.29. Num. 28.26. Deut. 26.1, 2.
m ch. 4.23, 28. Num. 28.30.
n Num. 18. 12. ch. 7.31-34. ch. 8.29. Deut. 18.4.
2 most holy.

and say unto them, [g]When ye be come
into the land which I give unto you,
and shall reap the harvest thereof,
then ye shall bring a [1]sheaf of [h]the
firstfruits of your harvest unto the
priest:
11 And he shall [i]wave the sheaf before the LORD, to be accepted for you:
on the morrow after the sabbath the
priest shall wave it.
12 And ye shall offer that day when
ye wave the sheaf an he lamb without
blemish of the first year for a burnt
offering unto the LORD.
13 And the meat offering thereof
shall be two tenth deals of fine flour
mingled with oil, an offering made by
fire unto the LORD *for* a sweet savour:
and the drink offering thereof *shall be*
of wine, the fourth *part* of an hin.
14 And ye shall eat neither bread,
nor parched corn, nor green ears, until
the selfsame day that ye have brought
an offering unto your God: *it shall be*
a statute for ever throughout your
generations in all your dwellings.
15 ¶ And [j]ye shall count unto you
from the morrow after the sabbath,
from the day that ye brought the sheaf
of the wave offering; seven sabbaths
shall be complete:
16 Even unto the morrow after the
seventh sabbath shall ye number [k]fifty
days; and ye shall offer a new meat
offering unto the LORD.
17 Ye shall bring out of your habitations two wave loaves of two tenth
deals: they shall be of fine flour; they
shall be baken with leaven; *they are*
[l]the firstfruits unto the LORD.
18 And ye shall offer with the bread
seven lambs without blemish of the
first year, and one young bullock, and
two rams: they shall be *for* a burnt
offering unto the LORD, with their
meat offering, and their drink offerings, *even* an offering made by fire, of
sweet savour unto the LORD.
19 Then ye shall sacrifice [m]one kid
of the goats for a sin offering, and two
lambs of the first year for a sacrifice
of peace offerings.
20 And the priest shall wave them
with the bread of the firstfruits *for* a
wave offering before the LORD, with
the two lambs: they [n]shall be [2]holy to
the LORD for the priest.
21 And ye shall proclaim on the selfsame day, *that* it may be an holy convocation unto you: ye shall do no servile work *therein: it shall be* a statute
for ever in all your dwellings throughout your generations.

22 ¶ And [o]when ye reap the harvest
of your land, thou shalt not make
clean riddance of the corners of thy
field when thou reapest, [p]neither shalt
thou gather any gleaning of thy harvest: thou shalt leave them unto the
poor, and to the stranger: I *am* the
LORD your God.
23 ¶ And the LORD spake unto Moses,
saying,
24 Speak unto the children of Israel,
saying, In the [q]seventh month, in the
first *day* of the month, shall ye have a
sabbath, a [r]memorial of blowing of
trumpets, an holy convocation.
25 Ye shall do no servile work *therein:* but ye shall offer an offering made
by fire unto the LORD.
26 ¶ And the LORD spake unto Moses,
saying,
27 Also on the tenth *day* of this seventh month [s]*there shall be* a day of
atonement: it shall be an holy convocation unto you; and ye shall
afflict your souls, and offer an offering
made by fire unto the LORD.
28 And ye shall do no work in that
same day: for it *is* a day of atonement, to make an atonement for you
before the LORD your God.
29 For whatsoever soul *it be* that
shall not be afflicted in that same day,
[t]he shall be cut off from among his
people.
30 And whatsoever soul *it be* that
doeth any work in that same day, the
same soul will I destroy from among
his people.
31 Ye shall do no manner of work:
it shall be a statute for ever throughout your generations in all your
dwellings.
32 It *shall be* unto you a sabbath of
rest, and ye shall afflict your souls:
in the ninth *day* of the month at even,
from even unto even, shall ye [3]cele-
brate your sabbath.
33 ¶ And the LORD spake unto Moses,
saying,
34 Speak unto the children of Israel,
saying, [u]The fifteenth day of this seventh month *shall be* the feast of tabernacles *for* seven days unto the LORD.
35 On the first day *shall be* an holy
convocation: ye shall do no servile
work *therein.*
36 Seven days ye shall offer an offering
made by fire unto the LORD: [v]on the
eighth day shall be an holy convocation unto you; and ye shall offer an
offering made by fire unto the LORD:
it *is* a [4]solemn assembly; *and* ye shall
do no servile work *therein.*

o Ex. 23.11. Deut. 15.1-18. Job 20.19. Ps. 112.9. Pro. 14.31. Pro. 29.7. Eccl. 5.8. Isa. 58.7,8. Jas. 2.1.
p ch. 19.9,10. Deut. 24.19. Ruth 2.15, 16.
q Num. 29.1. Num. 10.10.
r ch. 25.9.
s Ex. 30.10. ch. 16.30. Num. 29.7. Isa. 58.3,5. Dan. 10.3, 12.
t Gen. 17.14. ch. 13.46. Num. 5.2. 2 Chr. 26.21. 2 Thes. 3.6.
3 rest.
u Ex. 23.16. Num. 29.12. Deut. 16.13. Neh. 8.14. Zech. 14.16. John 7.2. Heb. 11.9.
v Num. 29.35. 2 Chr. 7.8,9. Neh. 8.18. John 7.37.
4 day of restraint.
w Ex. 23.16. Deut. 16.13. Matt. 21.8.
x Neh. 8.15.
5 fruit.
y Deut. 16. 14. Isa. 35.10. Isa. 66.10. Rom. 5.11.
z Deut. 31. 13. Ps. 78.5,6.

CHAP. 24

a Ex. 27.20. Ex. 39.37. Num. 8.2-4.
1 to cause to ascend.
b Ex. 31.8.
c Ex. 40.24.
d 1 Ki. 7.48. 2 Chr. 4.19. Heb. 9.2.

37 These *are* the feasts of the LORD,
which ye shall proclaim *to be* holy convocations, to offer an offering made by
fire unto the LORD, a burnt offering,
and a meat offering, a sacrifice, and
drink offerings, every thing upon his
day:
38 Beside the sabbaths of the LORD,
and beside your gifts, and beside all
your vows, and beside all your freewill offerings, which ye give unto the
LORD.
39 Also in the fifteenth day of the seventh month, when ye have gathered
[w]in the fruit of the land, ye shall keep
a feast unto the LORD seven days: on
the first day *shall be* a sabbath, and on
the eighth day *shall be* a sabbath.
40 And [x]ye shall take you on the first
day the [5]boughs of goodly trees, branches of palm trees, and the boughs of
thick trees, and willows of the brook;
[y]and ye shall rejoice before the LORD
your God seven days.
41 And ye shall keep it a feast unto
the LORD seven days in the year. *It
shall be* a statute for ever in your generations: ye shall celebrate it in the
seventh month.
42 Ye shall dwell in booths seven
days; all that are Israelites born shall
dwell in booths:
43 That [z]your generations may know
that I made the children of Israel to
dwell in booths, when I brought them
out of the land of Egypt: I *am* the
LORD your God.
44 And Moses declared unto the
children of Israel the feasts of the
LORD.

CHAPTER 24

AND the LORD spake unto Moses,
saying,
2 Command [a]the children of Israel,
that they bring unto thee pure oil
olive beaten for the light, [1]to cause the
lamps to burn continually.
3 Without the vail of the testimony,
in the tabernacle of the congregation,
shall Aaron order it from the evening
unto the morning before the LORD
continually: *it shall be* a statute for
ever in your generations.
4 He shall order the lamps upon the
[b]pure candlestick before the LORD
continually.
5 ¶ And thou shalt take fine flour,
and bake twelve [c]cakes thereof: two
tenth deals shall be in one cake.
6 And thou shalt set them in two
rows, six on a row, [d]upon the pure
table before the LORD.
7 And thou shalt put pure frankin-

cense upon *each* row, that it may be
on the bread for a memorial, *even* an
offering made by fire unto the LORD.
8 Every sabbath he shall [e]set it in
order before the LORD continually,
being taken from the children of Israel
by an everlasting covenant.
9 And [f]it shall be Aaron's and his
sons'; and [g]they shall eat it in the
holy place: for it *is* most holy unto
him of the offerings of the LORD made
by fire by a perpetual statute.
10 ¶ And the son of an Israelitish
woman, whose father *was* an Egyptian, went out among the children of
Israel: and this son of the Israelitish
woman and a man of Israel strove together in the camp;
11 And the Israelitish woman's son
blasphemed the name *of the LORD*,
[h]and cursed. And they [i]brought him
unto Moses: (and his mother's name
was Shĕ-lṓ-mĭth, the daughter of
Dĭb́-rī, of the tribe of Dan:)
12 And they [j]put him in ward, [2]that
the mind of the LORD might be shewed
them.
13 And the LORD spake unto Moses,
saying,
14 Bring forth him that hath cursed
without the camp; and let all that
heard *him* lay [k]their hands upon his
head, and let all the congregation
stone him.
15 And thou shalt speak unto the
children of Israel, saying, Whosoever
curseth his God [l]shall bear his sin.
16 And he that [m]blasphemeth the
name of the LORD, he shall surely be
put to death, *and* all the congregation
shall certainly stone him: as well the
stranger, as he that is born in the land,
when he blasphemeth the name *of the*
LORD, shall be put to death.
17 ¶ And [n]he that [3]killeth any man
shall surely be put to death.
18 And he that killeth a beast shall
make it good; [4]beast for beast.
19 And if a man cause a blemish in
his neighbour; as [o]he hath done, so
shall it be done to him;
20 Breach for breach, eye for eye,
tooth for tooth: as he hath caused a
blemish in a man, so shall it be done
to him *again*.
21 And [p]he that killeth a beast, he
shall restore it: and he that killeth a
man, he shall be put to death.
22 Ye shall have [q]one manner of law,
as well for the stranger, as for one of
your own country: for I *am* the LORD
your God.
23 ¶ And Moses spake to the chil-

e Num. 4.7. 1 Chr. 9.32. 2 Chr. 2.4.
f 1 Sam. 21.6. Matt. 12.4. Mark 2.26. Luke 6.4.
g Ex. 29.33. ch. 8.31.
h Job 1.5. Isa. 8.21.
i Ex. 18.22.
j Num. 15.34.
2 to expound unto them according to the mouth of the LORD.
k Deut. 17.7.
l ch. 5.1. Num. 9.13.
m 1 Ki. 21.10. Ps. 74.10,18. Matt. 12.31. Mark 3.28.
n Gen. 9.6. Deut. 19.11. Matt. 26.52. Rev. 13.10.
3 smiteth the life of a man.
4 life for life.
o Deut. 19.21. Matt. 5.38.
p Ex. 21.33.
q Ex. 12.49. ch. 19.34. Num. 15.16.
r Deut. 13.9.

CHAP. 25

1 rest.
a ch. 26.34, 35. 2 Chr. 36.21.
b 2 Ki. 19.29. Isa. 37.30.
2 of thy separation.
3 loud of sound.
c ch. 16.20, 30. ch. 23.24.
d Ex. 20.2. Isa. 49.24, 25. Isa. 61.2. Jer. 34.8,15, 17. Luke 4.19. Gal. 5.1.
e Num. 36.4.
f ch. 27.24. Num. 36.4.

dren of Israel, that they should bring
forth him that had cursed out of the
camp, [r]and stone him with stones.
And the children of Israel did as the
LORD commanded Moses.

CHAPTER 25

AND the LORD spake unto Moses in
mount Sī́-nâi, saying,
2 Speak unto the children of Israel,
and say unto them, When ye come
into the land which I give you, then
shall the land [1]keep a [a]sabbath unto
the LORD.
3 Six years thou shalt sow thy field,
and six years thou shalt prune thy
vineyard, and gather in the fruit thereof;
4 But in the seventh year shall be a
sabbath of rest unto the land, a sabbath for the LORD: thou shalt neither
sow thy field, nor prune thy vineyard.
5 That [b]which groweth of its own
accord of thy harvest thou shalt not
reap, neither gather the grapes [2]of thy
vine undressed: *for* it is a year of rest
unto the land.
6 And the sabbath of the land shall
be meat for you; for thee, and for thy
servant, and for thy maid, and for thy
hired servant, and for thy stranger
that sojourneth with thee,
7 And for thy cattle, and for the
beast that *are* in thy land, shall all the
increase thereof be meat.
8 ¶ And thou shalt number seven
sabbaths of years unto thee, seven
times seven years; and the space of
the seven sabbaths of years shall be
unto thee forty and nine years.
9 Then shalt thou cause the trumpet
[3]of the jû́-bĭ-lē to sound on the tenth
day of the seventh month, in [c]the day
of atonement shall ye make the trumpet sound throughout all your land.
10 And ye shall hallow the fiftieth
year, and [d]proclaim liberty throughout *all* the land unto all the inhabitants thereof: it shall be a jû́-bĭ-lē unto
you; and [e]ye shall return every man
unto his possession, and ye shall return every man unto his family.
11 A jû́-bĭ-lē shall that fiftieth year
be unto you: ye shall not sow, neither
reap that which groweth of itself in it,
nor gather *the grapes* in it of thy vine
undressed.
12 For it *is* the jû́-bĭ-lē; it shall be
holy unto you: ye shall eat the increase
thereof out of the field.
13 In [f]the year of this jû́-bĭ-lē ye shall
return every man unto his possession.
14 And if thou sell ought unto thy

neighbour, or buyest *ought* of thy neighbour's hand, ye [g]shall not oppress one another:

15 According to the number of years after the jû-bĭ-lē thou shalt buy of thy neighbour, *and* according unto the number of years of the fruits he shall sell unto thee:

16 According to the multitude of years thou shalt increase the price thereof, and according to the fewness of years thou shalt diminish the price of it: for *according* to the number *of the years* of the fruits doth he sell unto thee.

17 Ye [h]shall not therefore oppress one another; but thou shalt fear thy God: for I *am* the LORD your God.

18 ¶ Wherefore ye shall do my statutes, and keep my judgments, and do them; [i]and ye shall dwell in the land in safety.

19 And the land shall yield her fruit, and ye shall eat your fill, and dwell therein in safety.

20 And if ye shall say, [j]What shall we eat the seventh year? behold, we shall not sow, nor gather in our increase:

21 Then I will [k]command my blessing upon you in the sixth year, and it shall bring forth fruit for three years.

22 And [l]ye shall sow the eighth year, and eat *yet* of [m]old fruit until the ninth year; until her fruits come in ye shall eat *of* the old *store*.

23 ¶ The land shall not be sold for [4]ever: for [n]the land *is* mine; for ye *are* [o]strangers and sojourners with me.

24 And in all the land of your possession ye shall grant a redemption for the land.

25 ¶ If [p]thy brother be waxen poor, and hath sold away *some* of his possession, and if [q]any of his kin come to redeem it, then shall he redeem that which his brother sold.

26 And if the man have none to redeem it, and [5]himself be able to redeem it;

27 Then let him count the years of the sale thereof, and restore the overplus unto the man to whom he sold it; that he may return unto his possession.

28 But if he be not able to restore *it* to him, then that which is sold shall remain in the hand of him that hath bought it until the year of jû-bĭ-lē: and in the jû-bĭ-lē it shall go out, and he shall return unto his possession.

29 And if a man sell a dwelling house in a walled city, then he may redeem it within a whole year after it is sold; *within* a full year may he redeem it.

30 And if it be not redeemed within the space of a full year, then the house that *is* in the walled city shall be established for ever to him that bought it throughout his generations: it shall not go out in the jû-bĭ-lē.

31 But the houses of the villages which have no wall round about them shall be counted as the fields of the country: [6]they may be redeemed, and they shall go out in the jû-bĭ-lē.

32 Notwithstanding [r]the cities of the Levites, *and* the houses of the cities of their possession, may the Levites redeem at any time.

33 And if [7]a man purchase of the Levites, then the house that was sold, and the city of his possession, shall go out in *the year of* jû-bĭ-lē: for the houses of the cities of the Levites *are* their possession among the children of Israel.

34 But the [s]field of the suburbs of their cities may not be sold; for it *is* their perpetual possession.

35 ¶ And if thy brother be waxen poor, and [8]fallen in decay with thee; then thou shalt [9]relieve [t]him: *yea, though he be* a stranger, or a sojourner; that he may live with thee.

36 Take [u]thou no usury of him, or increase: but fear thy God; that thy brother may live with thee.

37 Thou shalt not give him thy money upon usury, nor lend him thy victuals for increase.

38 I *am* the LORD your God, which brought you forth out of the land of Egypt, to give you the land of Canaan, *and* to be your God.

39 ¶ And [v]if thy brother *that dwelleth* by thee be waxen poor, and be sold unto thee; thou shalt not [10]compel him to serve as a bondservant:

40 *But* as an hired servant, *and* as a sojourner, he shall be with thee, *and* shall serve thee unto the year of jû-bĭ-lē:

41 And *then* shall he depart from thee, *both* he and his children with him, and shall return unto his own family, and unto the possession of his fathers shall he return.

42 For they *are* [w]my servants, which I brought forth out of the land of Egypt: they shall not be sold [11]as bondmen.

43 Thou [x]shalt not rule over him with rigour; but [y]shalt fear thy God.

44 Both thy bondmen, and thy bondmaids, which thou shalt have, *shall be*

g ch. 19.13. 1 Sam. 12.3. Ps. 10.18. Micah 2.2.
h Pro. 14.31. Pro. 22.22. Jer. 7.6. 1 Thes. 4.6.
i ch. 26.5. Deut. 12.10. Ps. 4.8. Pro. 1.33.
j Num. 11.4-13. 2 Ki. 6.15. Matt. 6.25.
k Deut. 28.8. Ps. 33.12. Ps. 119.2. Pro. 3.33. Pro. 8.32. 1 Tim. 4.8.
l 2 Ki. 19.29.
m Josh. 5.11.
4 for cutting off, or, to be quite cut off.
n Deut. 32.43. 2 Chr. 7.20. Ps. 24.1. Ps. 85.1. Isa. 8.8.
o Ps. 119.19. 1 Pet. 2.11.
p Ruth 2.20.
q Ruth 3.2.
5 his hand hath attained and found sufficiency.
6 redemption belongeth unto it.
r Josh. 21.2.
7 Or, one of the Levites redeem them.
s Acts 4.36.
8 his hand faileth.
9 strengthen.
t Deut. 15.7. Ps. 37.26. Pro. 14.31. Luke 6.35. Acts 11.29. Rom. 12.10.
u Ex. 22.25. Deut. 23.19. Neh. 5.7. Ps. 15.5. Pro. 28.8.
v Ex. 21.2. Deut. 15.12. 1 Ki. 9.22. 2 Ki. 4.1. Jer. 34.14.
10 serve thyself with him with the service, etc.
w Rom. 6.22. 1 Cor. 7.23.
11 with the sale of a bondman.
x Ex. 1.13-14. Ex. 2.23. Ex. 3.7,9. Isa. 47.6. Eph. 6.9. Col. 4.1.
y Ex. 1.17,21. Deut. 25.18. Mal. 3.5.

of the heathen that are round about
you; of them shall ye buy bondmen
and bondmaids.
45 Moreover of the children of the
strangers that do sojourn among you,
of them shall ye buy, and of their
families that *are* with you, which they
begat in your land: and they shall be
your possession.
46 And ye shall take them as an inheritance for your children after you,
to inherit *them for* a possession; they
[12]shall be your bondmen for ever: but
over your brethren the children of
Israel, ye shall not rule one over another with rigour.
47 ¶ And if a sojourner or stranger
wax [13]rich by thee, and thy brother
that dwelleth by him wax poor, and
sell himself unto the stranger *or* sojourner by thee, or to the stock of the
stranger's family:
48 After that he is sold he may be redeemed again; one of his brethren
may redeem him:
49 Either his uncle, or his uncle's
son, may redeem him, or *any* that is
nigh of kin unto him of his family may
redeem him; or if he be able, he may
redeem himself.
50 And he shall reckon with him that
bought him from the year that he was
sold to him unto the year of jû-bĭ-lē:
and the price of his sale shall be according unto the number of years,
according to the time of an hired
servant shall it be with him.
51 If *there be* yet many years *behind*,
according unto them he shall give
again the price of his redemption out
of the money that he was bought for.
52 And if there remain but few years
unto the year of jû-bĭ-lē, then he shall
count with him, *and* according unto
his years shall he give him again the
price of his redemption.
53 *And* as a yearly hired servant shall
he be with him: *and the other* shall not
rule with rigour over him in thy sight.
54 And if he be not redeemed [14]in
these *years*, then he shall go out in the
year of jû-bĭ-lē, *both* he, and his children with him.
55 For unto me the children of Israel
are servants; they *are* my servants
whom I brought forth out of the land
of Egypt: I *am* the LORD your God.

CHAPTER 26

YE shall make you [a]no idols nor
graven image, neither rear you up
a [1]standing image, neither shall ye set
up *any* [2]image of stone in your land,
to bow down unto it: for I *am* the
LORD your God.
2 ¶ Ye shall keep my sabbaths, and
reverence my sanctuary: I *am* the
LORD.
3 ¶ If ye walk in my statutes, and
keep my commandments, and do
them;
4 Then [b]I will give you rain in due
season, and the land shall yield her increase, and the trees of the field shall
yield their fruit.
5 And your threshing shall reach unto the vintage, and the vintage shall
reach unto the sowing time: and [c]ye
shall eat your bread to the full, and
[d]dwell in your land safely.
6 And [e]I will give peace in the land,
and ye [f]shall lie down, and none shall
make *you* afraid: and I will [3]rid [g]evil
beasts out of the land, neither shall
[h]the sword go through your land.
7 And ye shall chase your enemies,
and they shall fall before you by the
sword.
8 And five of you shall chase an hundred, and an hundred of you shall put
ten thousand to flight: and your enemies shall fall before you by the
sword.
9 For I will [i]have respect unto you,
and make [j]you fruitful, and multiply
you, and establish my covenant with
you.
10 And ye shall eat old store, and
bring forth the old because of the new.
11 And [k]I will set my tabernacle
among you: and my soul shall not
abhor [l]you.
12 And [m]I will walk among you, and
[n]will be your God, and ye shall be my
people.
13 I *am* the LORD your God, which
brought you forth out of the land of
Egypt, that ye should not be their
bondmen; [o]and I have broken the
bands of your yoke, and made you go
upright.
14 ¶ But [p]if ye will not hearken unto
me, and will not do all these commandments;
15 And if ye shall [q]despise my statutes, or if your soul abhor my judgments, so that ye will not do all my
commandments, *but* that ye break my
covenant:
16 I also will do this unto you; I will
even appoint [4]over you terror, consumption, [r]and the burning ague, that
shall [s]consume the eyes, and cause
sorrow of heart: and ye shall [t]sow
your seed in vain, for your enemies
shall eat it.

12 ye shall serve yourselves with them.
13 his hand obtain, etc.
14 Or, by these means.

CHAP. 26

a Ex. 20.4,5. Deut. 5.8,9. Isa. 44.9-20. Ps. 97.7.
1 Or, pillar.
2 a stone of picture, or, figured stone.
b Deut. 28.12. Isa. 30.23.
c Deut. 11.15. Joel 2.19,26.
d Job 11.18.
e 1 Chr. 22.9. Isa. 45.7.
f Ps. 3.5. Jer. 30. 10.
3 cause to cease.
g 2 Ki. 17.25.
h Josh. 23.10.
i Ex. 2.25. 2 Ki. 13.23.
j Gen. 17.6,7.
k Eze. 37.26.
l Deut. 32.19.
m 2 Cor. 6.16. Eph. 2.21.
n Eze. 11.20.
o Eze. 34.27.
p Deut. 28. 15.
q 2 Ki. 17.15.
4 upon you.
r Deut. 28.22.
s 1 Sam. 2.33.
t Job 31.8.

17 And I will set my face against you,
and ye [u]shall be slain before your enemies: they [v]that hate you shall reign
over you; and [w]ye shall flee when none
pursueth you.
18 And if ye will not yet for all this
hearken unto me, then I will punish
you [x]seven times more for your sins.
19 And I will [y]break the pride of your
power; and I will make your heaven
as iron, and your earth as brass:
20 And your [z]strength shall be spent
in vain: for [a]your land shall not yield
her increase, neither shall the trees of
the land yield their fruits.
21 ¶ And if ye walk [5]contrary unto
me, and will not hearken unto me; I
will bring seven times more plagues
upon you according to your sins.
22 I [b]will also send wild beasts
among you, which shall rob you of
your children, and destroy your cattle,
and make you few in number; and
[c]your *high* ways shall be desolate.
23 And if [d]ye will not be reformed
by me by these things, but will walk
contrary unto me;
24 Then [e]will I also walk contrary
unto you, and will punish you yet sev-
en times for your sins.
25 And [f]I will bring a sword upon
you, that shall avenge the quarrel of
my covenant: and when ye are gathered together within your cities, I [g]will
send the pestilence among you; and
ye shall be delivered into the hand of
the enemy.
26 *And* [h]when I have broken the
staff of your bread, ten women shall
bake your bread in one oven, and they
shall deliver *you* your bread again by
weight: and [i]ye shall eat, and not be
satisfied.
27 And if ye will not for all this
hearken unto me, but walk contrary
unto me;
28 Then I will walk contrary unto
you also [j]in fury; and I, even I, will
chastise you seven times for your sins.
29 And [k]ye shall eat the flesh of your
sons, and the flesh of your daughters
shall ye eat.
30 And [l]I will destroy your high
places, and cut down your images, and
[m]cast your carcases upon the carcases
of your idols, and my soul shall [n]ab-
hor you.
31 And [o]I will make your cities waste,
and bring [p]your sanctuaries unto
desolation, and I will not smell the
savour of your sweet odours.
32 And [q]I will bring the land into
desolation: and your enemies which
dwell therein shall be astonished at it.
33 And [r]I will scatter you among the
heathen, and will draw out a sword
after you: and your land shall be desolate, and your cities waste.
34 Then [s]shall the land enjoy her
sabbaths, as long as it lieth desolate,
and ye *be* in your enemies' land; *even*
then shall the land rest, and enjoy her
sabbaths.
35 As long as it lieth desolate it shall
rest; because it did not rest in your
sabbaths, when ye dwelt upon it.
36 And upon them that are left *alive*
of you I [t]will send a faintness into their
hearts in the lands of their enemies;
and the [u]sound of a [6]shaken leaf shall
chase them; and they shall flee, as fleeing from a sword; and they shall fall
when none pursueth.
37 And [v]they shall fall one upon another, as it were before a sword, when
none pursueth: and [w]ye shall have no
power to stand before your enemies.
38 And ye shall perish among the
heathen, and the land of your enemies
shall eat you up.
39 And they that are left of you shall
[x]pine away in their iniquity in your
enemies' lands; and also in the iniquities of their fathers shall they pine
away with them.
40 If [y]they shall confess their iniquity, and the iniquity of their fathers,
with their trespass which they trespassed against me, and that also they
have walked contrary unto me;
41 And *that* I also have walked contrary unto them, and have brought
them into the land of their enemies;
if then their [z]uncircumcised hearts be
[a]humbled, and they then accept of the
punishment of their iniquity:
42 Then will I [b]remember my covenant with Jacob, and also my covenant
with Isaac, and also my covenant with
Abraham will I remember; and I will
[c]remember the land.
43 The land also shall be left of them,
and shall enjoy her sabbaths, while
she lieth desolate without them: and
they shall accept of the punishment of
their iniquity: because, even because
they despised my judgments, and because their soul abhorred my statutes.
44 And yet for all that, when they be
in the land of their enemies, I [d]will
not cast them away, neither will I abhor them, to destroy them utterly,
and to break my covenant with them:
for I *am* the LORD their God.
45 But I will [e]for their sakes remember the covenant of their ancestors,

u Judg. 2.14.
v Ps. 106.41.
w Ps. 53.5.
x 1 Sam. 2.5.
y 1 Sam. 4.10.
z Ps. 127.1.
a Deut. 28.18. Hag. 1. 10.
5 Or, at all adventures with me.
b Deut. 32. 24. 2 Ki. 17.25.
c Judg. 5.6. 2 Chr. 15.5.
d Jer. 5.3.
e 2 Sam. 22. 27.
f Eze. 6.3.
g Deut. 28.22. Num. 14.12. Amos 4.10.
h Isa. 3.1.
i Micah 6.14.
j Isa. 59.18.
k 2 Ki. 6.29.
l 2 Chr. 34.3.
m 2 Ki. 23.20.
n Ps. 78.59.
o Neh. 2.3.
p Ps. 74. 1-8. Jer. 22.5. Lam. 1.10.
q Jer. 9.11. Jer. 25.11.
r Deut. 4.27. Deut. 28.64. Ps. 44.11. Zech. 7.14.
s ch. 25.2-4. 2 Chr. 36.21.
t Gen. 35.5. Josh. 2.9-11.
u Pro. 28.1.
6 driven.
v Judg. 7.22. Isa. 10.4.
w Judg. 2.14.
x Neh. 1.9. Jer. 3.25.
y 1 Ki. 8.33. Job 34.31. Pro. 28.13. Jer. 3.12. Luke 15.18.
z Jer. 9.25. Acts 7.51. Rom. 2.29.
a 1 Ki. 21.29. 2 Chr. 12.6.
b Ex. 2.24. Ps. 106.45.
c Ps. 136.23.
d Deut. 4.31.
e Rom. 11.28.

whom I brought forth out of the land
of Egypt [f]in the sight of the heathen,
that I might be their God: I *am* the
LORD.
46 These [g]*are* the statutes and judgments and laws, which the LORD made
between him and the children of Israel
in mount Sī-nâi by the hand of Moses.

CHAPTER 27

AND the LORD spake unto Moses,
saying,
2 Speak unto the children of Israel,
and say unto them, [a]When a man
shall make a singular vow, the persons
shall be for the LORD by thy estimation.
3 And thy estimation shall be of the
male from twenty years old even unto
sixty years old, even thy estimation
shall be fifty shekels of silver, after
[b]the shekel of the sanctuary.
4 And if it *be* a female, then thy estimation shall be thirty shekels.
5 And if *it be* from five years old even
unto twenty years old, then thy estimation shall be of the male twenty
shekels, and for the female ten shekels.
6 And if *it be* from a month old even
unto five years old, then thy estimation shall be of the male five shekels
of silver, and for the female thy estimation *shall be* three shekels of silver.
7 And if *it be* from sixty years old and
above; if *it be* a male, then thy estimation shall be fifteen shekels, and
for the female ten shekels.
8 But [c]if he be poorer than thy estimation, then he shall present himself
before the priest, and the priest shall
value him; according to his ability
that vowed shall the priest value him.
9 And if *it be* a beast, whereof men
bring an offering unto the LORD, all
that *any man* giveth of such unto the
LORD [1]shall be holy.
10 He shall not alter it, nor change
it, a good for a bad, or a bad for a
good: and if he shall at all change
beast for beast, then it and the exchange thereof shall be holy.
11 And if *it be* any unclean beast, of
which they do not offer a sacrifice unto
the LORD, then he shall present the
beast before the priest:
12 And the priest shall value it,
whether it be good or bad: [2]as thou
valuest it, *who art* the priest, so shall it
be.
13 But if he will at all redeem it, then
he shall add a fifth *part* thereof unto
thy estimation.
14 ¶ And when a man shall [d]sanctify
his house *to be* holy unto the LORD,
then the priest shall estimate it, whether it be good or bad: as the priest shall
estimate it, so shall it stand.
15 And if he that sanctified it will redeem his house, then he shall add
the fifth *part* of the money of thy
estimation unto it, and it shall be
his.
16 And if a man shall sanctify unto
the LORD *some part* of a field of his
possession, then thy estimation shall
be according to the seed thereof: [3]an
hō-mĕr of barley seed *shall be valued*
at fifty shekels of silver.
17 If he sanctify his field from the
year of jû-bĭ-lē, according to thy estimation it shall stand.
18 But if he sanctify his field after
the jû-bĭ-lē, then the priest shall reckon [e]unto him the money according to
the years that remain, even unto the
year of the jû-bĭ-lē, and it shall be
abated from thy estimation.
19 And if he that sanctified the field
will in any wise redeem it, then he
shall add the fifth *part* of the money of
thy estimation unto it, and it shall be
assured to him.
20 And if he will not redeem the field,
or if he have sold the field to another
man, it shall not be redeemed any
more.
21 But the field, [f]when it goeth out
in the jû-bĭ-lē, shall be holy unto the
LORD, as a field devoted; [g]the possession thereof shall be the priest's.
22 And if *a man* sanctify unto the
LORD a field which he hath bought,
which *is* not of the fields of his possession;
23 Then the priest shall reckon unto
him the worth of thy estimation, *even*
unto the year of the jû-bĭ-lē: and he
shall give thine estimation in that day,
as a holy thing unto the LORD.
24 In [h]the year of the jû-bĭ-lē the field
shall return unto him of whom it was
bought, *even* to him to whom the
possession of the land *did belong*.
25 And all thy estimations shall be
according to the shekel of the sanctuary: twenty [i]gē-rähs shall be the
shekel.
26 ¶ Only the [4]firstling of the beasts,
which should be the LORD's firstling,
no man shall sanctify it; whether *it be*
ox, or sheep: it *is* the LORD's.
27 And if *it be* of an unclean beast,
then he shall redeem *it* according to
thine estimation, and shall add a fifth
part of it thereto: or if it be not re-

f Eze. 20.9.
g Deut. 33.4.
CHAP. 27
a Gen. 28.20-22. Num. 6.2. Deut. 23.21-23. 1 Sam. 1.11, 28. Job 22.27. Ps. 50.14,15. Eccl. 5.4-6. Jonah 1.16.
b Ex. 30.13. Num. 3.47. Num. 18.16.
c ch. 12.8. ch. 14.21,22. Luke 21.1. 2 Cor. 8.12.
1 shall be sacrificed.
2 according to thy estimation, O priest, etc.
d ch. 25.29-31. Num. 18.14. 2 Cor. 9.10.
3 Or, the land of an homer, etc.
e ch. 25.15, 16.
f ch. 25.10, 28,31.
g Num. 18. 14. Eze. 44.29.
h ch. 25.28. ch. 27.29. Isa. 35.9,10. Jer. 32.15.
i Ex. 30.13. Num. 3.47. Num. 18.16. Eze. 45.12.
4 firstborn, etc. Ex. 13.2,12. Ex. 22.30. Num. 18.17. Deut. 15.19.

deemed, then it shall be sold according to thy estimation.
28 Notwithstanding [j]no devoted
thing, that a man shall devote unto
the LORD of all that he hath, *both* of
man and beast, and of the field of his
possession, shall be sold or redeemed:
every devoted thing *is* most holy unto
the LORD.
29 None devoted, [5]which shall be devoted of men, shall be redeemed; *but*
shall surely be put to death.
30 And [k]all the tithe of the land,
whether of the seed of the land, *or* of
the fruit of the tree, *is* the LORD's: *it is*
holy unto the LORD.

j Josh. 6.17. Judg. 11.30, 31.
5 Persons. Ex. 22.20. Num. 21.2. Deut. 7.1. Deut. 20.16. Deut. 25.19. Josh. 6.17. 1 Sam. 15.3.
k Gen. 28.22. Num. 18.21. 2 Chr. 31.5. Neh. 13.12.
l Jer. 33.13 Eze. 20.37. Micah 7.14.

31 And if a man will at all redeem
ought of his tithes, he shall add thereto the fifth *part* thereof.
32 And concerning the tithe of the
herd, or of the flock, *even* of whatsoever [l]passeth under the rod, the tenth
shall be holy unto the LORD.
33 He shall not search whether it be
good or bad, neither shall he change
it: and if he change it at all, then both
it and the change thereof shall be holy;
it shall not be redeemed.
34 These *are* the commandments,
which the LORD commanded Moses
for the children of Israel in mount
Sī´nāi.

THE FOURTH BOOK OF MOSES, CALLED

NUMBERS

CHAPTER 1

AND the LORD spake unto Moses
in [a]the wilderness of Sī´nāi, [b]in
the tabernacle of the congregation, on
the first *day* of the second month, in
the second year after they were come
out of the land of Egypt, saying,
2 Take [c]ye the sum of all the congregation of the children of Israel,
after their families, by the house of
their fathers, with the number of
their names, every male by their
polls;
3 From twenty years old and upward, all that are able to go forth to
war in Israel: thou and Aaron shall
[1]number them by their armies.
4 And with you there shall be [d]a man
of every tribe; every one head of the
house of his fathers.
5 ¶ And these *are* the names of the
men that shall stand with you: of *the*
[e]*tribe of* Reuben; Ĕ-lī´-zûr the son of
Shĕd´-ē-ûr.
6 Of Simeon; Shĕ-lû´-mĭ-ĕl the son of
Zū-rĭ-shăd´-dāi.
7 Of Judah; [f]Näh´-shŏn the son of
Ăm-mĭn´-ă-dăb.
8 Of Ĭs´-să-char; Nĕth´-ă-nēel the son
of Zū´-ăr.
9 Of Zĕ-bū´-lŭn; Ē-lī´-ăb the son of
Hē´-lŏn.
10 Of the children of Joseph: of Ē´-
phră-ĭm; Ē-lī´-shă-mă the son of Ăm´-
mī-hŭd: of Mă-năs´-sĕh; Gă-mā´-lī-ĕl
the son of Pĕ-dăh´-zûr.
11 Of Benjamin; Ă-bī´-dăn the son of
[2]Gĭd-ĕ-ō´-nī.

CHAP. 1
a Ex. 19.1.
b Ex. 25.22.
c Ex. 30.12. 2 Sam. 24.2. 1 Chr. 21.2.
1 muster.
d ch. 2.2. 1 Chr. 27.1.
e Gen. 29.32. Deut. 33.6. Rev. 7.4.
f ch. 7.12. Ruth 4.20. 1 Chr. 2.10. Luke 3.32.
2 That is, a cutter down.
g ch. 2.14. he is called Reuel.
h Gen. 6.4. Ex. 18.21. ch. 7.2. Judg. 6.15. 1 Chr. 5.24. Micah 5.2.
i Ex. 18.21, 25. Deut. 1.15. 1 Sam. 22.7.
j Neh. 7.61. Heb. 7.3.
k ch. 26.1.2. 2 Sam. 24.1.

12 Of Dan; Ă-hī-ē´-zĕr the son of
Ăm-mĭ-shăd´-dāi.
13 Of Asher; Pā-ġĭ-ĕl the son of Ŏc´-
răn.
14 Of Gad; Ē-lī´-ă-săph the son [g]of
Deū´-ĕl.
15 Of Năph´-tă-lī; Ă-hī´-ră the son of
Ē´-năn.
16 These [h]*were* the renowned of the
congregation, princes of the tribes of
their fathers, heads [i]of thousands in
Israel.
17 ¶ And Moses and Aaron took
these men which are expressed by
their names:
18 And they assembled all the congregation together on the first *day* of
the second month, and they declared
their [j]pedigrees after their families, by
the house of their fathers, according
to the number of the names, from
twenty years old and upward, by their
polls.
19 As [k]the LORD commanded Moses,
so he numbered them in the wilderness of Sī´nāi.
20 And the children of Reuben, Israel's eldest son, by their generations,
after their families, by the house of
their fathers, according to the number
of the names, by their polls, every
male from twenty years old and upward, all that were able to go forth to
war;
21 Those that were numbered of
them, *even* of the tribe of Reuben,
were forty and six thousand and five
hundred.

22 ¶ Of the children of Simeon, by their generations, after their families, by the house of their fathers, those that were numbered of them, according to the number of the names, by their polls, every male from twenty years old and upward, all that were [l]able to go forth to war;

23 Those that were numbered of them, *even* of the tribe of Simeon, *were* fifty and nine thousand and three hundred.

24 ¶ Of the children of [m]Gad, by their generations, after their families, by the house of their fathers, according to the number of the names, from twenty years old and upward, all that were able to go forth to war;

25 Those that were numbered of them, *even* of the tribe of Gad, *were* forty and five thousand six hundred and fifty.

26 ¶ Of the [n]children of Judah, by their generations, after their families, by the house of their fathers, according to the number of the names, from twenty years old and upward, all that were able to go forth to war;

27 Those that were numbered of them, *even* of the tribe of Judah, *were* threescore and fourteen thousand and six hundred.

28 ¶ Of the children of Ĭs′-să-chär, by their generations, after their families, by the house of their fathers, according to the number of the names, from twenty years old and upward, all that were able to go forth to war;

29 Those that were numbered of them, *even* of the tribe of Ĭs′-să-chär, *were* fifty and four thousand and four hundred.

30 ¶ Of the children of Zĕ-bū′-lŭn, by their generations, after their families, by the house of their fathers, according to the number of the names, from twenty years old and upward, all that were able to go forth to war;

31 Those that were numbered of them, *even* of the tribe of Zĕ-bū′-lŭn, *were* fifty and seven thousand and four hundred.

32 ¶ Of the children of Joseph, *namely*, of the [o]children of Ē′-phră-ĭm, by their generations, after their families, by the house of their fathers, according to the number of the names, from twenty years old and upward, all that were able to go forth to war;

33 Those that were numbered of them, *even* of the tribe of Ē′-phră-ĭm, *were* forty thousand and five hundred.

34 ¶ Of the children of Mă-năs′-sēh, by their generations, after their families, by the house of their fathers, according to the number of the names, from twenty years old and upward, all that were able to go forth to war:

35 Those that were numbered of them, *even* of the tribe of Mă-năs′-sēh, *were* thirty and two thousand and two hundred.

36 ¶ Of the [p]children of Benjamin, by their generations, after their families, by the house of their fathers, according to the number of the names, from twenty years old and upward, all that were able to go forth to war;

37 Those that were numbered of them, *even* of the tribe of Benjamin, *were* thirty and five thousand and four hundred.

38 ¶ Of the [q]children of Dan, by their generations, after their families, by the house of their fathers, according to the number of the names, from twenty years old and upward, all that were able to go forth to war;

39 Those that were numbered of them, *even* of the tribe of Dan, *were* threescore, and two thousand and seven hundred.

40 ¶ Of the children of Asher, by their generations, after their families, by the house of their fathers, according to the number of the names, from twenty years old and upward, all that were able to go forth to war;

41 Those that were numbered of them, *even* of the tribe of Asher, *were* forty and one thousand and five hundred.

42 ¶ Of the children of Năph′-tă-lī, throughout their generations, after their families, by the house of their fathers, according to the number of the names, from twenty years old and upward, all that were able to go forth to war;

43 Those that were numbered of them, *even* of the tribe of Năph′-tă-lī, *were* fifty and three thousand and four hundred.

44 These [r]*are* those that were numbered, which Moses and Aaron numbered, and the princes of Israel, *being* twelve men: each one was for the house of his fathers.

45 So were all those that were numbered of the children of Israel, by the house of their fathers, from twenty years old and upward, all that were able to go forth to war in Israel;

46 Even all they that were numbered were [s]six hundred thousand and three thousand and five hundred and fifty.

l 2 Sam. 22. 35. Ps. 44.3. Ps. 60.12. Ps. 144.1. 1 Cor. 16.13. 2 Cor. 3.5. Eph. 6.12.
m Gen. 30.11. Gen. 49.19. Josh. 4.12. Jer. 49.1. Rev. 7.5.
n Gen. 29.35. Gen. 38.1-3. Gen. 49.8, with ch. 2.3,4. Deut. 33.7. 2 Sam. 24.9. 1 Chr. 5.2. Ps. 78.68. Matt. 1.2. Heb. 7.14. Rev. 5.5.
o Gen. 30.24. Gen. 48.19, 20, with ch. 2.18,19. Judg. 12.6. Ps. 60.7. Jer. 7.15. Obadiah 19.
p Gen. 35.16-18. Gen. 44.20. ch. 26.41. Judg. 20.44-46. 2 Chr. 17.17. Ps. 68.27. Rev. 7.8.
q Gen. 30.5,6. Gen. 46.23, with ch. 2.25.
r ch. 26.64.
s Gen. 13.16. Ex. 12.37. Deut. 10.22. ch. 26.51. 1 Ki. 4.20.

47 ¶ But [t]the Levites after the tribe of
their fathers were not numbered
among them.
48 For the LORD had spoken unto
Moses, saying,
49 Only [u]thou shalt not number the
tribe of Levi, neither take the sum of
them among the children of Israel:
50 But [v]thou shalt appoint the Levites
over the tabernacle of testimony,
and over all the vessels thereof, and
over all things that *belong* to it: they
shall bear the tabernacle, and all the
vessels thereof; and they shall minister unto it, [w]and shall encamp round
about the tabernacle.
51 And [x]when the tabernacle setteth
forward, the Levites shall take it
down: and when the tabernacle is to
be pitched, the Levites shall set it up:
and [3]the stranger that cometh nigh
shall be put to death.
52 And the children of Israel shall
pitch their tents, [y]every man by his
own camp, and every man by his own
standard, throughout their hosts.
53 But the Levites shall pitch round
about the tabernacle of testimony,
that there be [z]no wrath upon the congregation of the children of Israel:
[a]and the Levites shall keep the charge
of the tabernacle of testimony.
54 And the children of Israel did according to all that the LORD commanded Moses, so did they.

CHAPTER 2

AND the LORD spake unto Moses
and unto Aaron, saying,
2 Every [a]man of the children of Israel shall [b]pitch by his own standard,
with the ensign of their father's house:
[1]far off about the tabernacle of the
congregation shall they pitch.
3 And on the east side toward the
rising of the sun shall they of the
standard of the camp of Judah pitch
throughout their armies: and [c]Näh-
shŏn the son of Ăm-mĭn-ă-dăb *shall be*
captain of the children of Judah.
4 And his host, and those that were
numbered of them, *were* threescore
and fourteen thousand and six hundred.
5 And those that do pitch next unto
him *shall be* the tribe of Ĭs-să-chär:
[d]and Nĕth-ă-neel the son of Zū-är
shall be captain of the children of Ĭs-
să-chär.
6 And his host, and those that were
numbered thereof, *were* [e]fifty and four
thousand and four hundred.
7 *Then* the tribe of [f]Zĕ-bū-lŭn: and

[t] ch. 2.33. ch. 3.1. 1 Chr. 6.1. 1 Chr. 21.6.
[u] ch. 26.62.
[v] Ex. 31.18. ch. 3.7,8. ch. 4.15,25, 26,27,33.
[w] ch. 3.23,29, 35,38.
[x] ch. 10.17, 21.
3 every one not a Levite.
[y] ch. 2.2,34.
[z] Lev. 10.6. ch. 8.19. ch. 16.46. 1 Sam. 6.19.
[a] ch. 8.24. ch. 18.3,4. 1 Chr. 23,32. 2 Chr. 13.10.

CHAP. 2

[a] ch. 1.52.
[b] Num. 24. 2-9.
1 over against.
[c] ch. 10.14. Ruth 4.20. 1 Chr. 2.10. Matt. 1.4. Luke 3.32, 33.
[d] ch. 7.18,23.
[e] ch. 26.25.
[f] Gen. 49.13. Deut. 33.18.
[g] ch. 10.14. 1 Chr. 5.2. Ps. 78.52.
[h] Deut. 33.6. 1 Chr. 5.1.
2 Deuel.
[i] Gen. 49.3. ch. 10.18. 1 Chr. 5.1.
[j] Acts 7.44. Heb. 8.2.
[k] 1 Cor. 14. 40.
[l] Gen. 48.14-20. ch. 10.22. Deut. 33.17. Ps. 80.1. Jer. 31.9, 18-21. Hosea 11.3. Zech. 9.9-17.
[m] Ps. 68.27. Rev. 7.8.

Ē-lĭ-ăb the son of Hē-lŏn *shall be* captain of the children of Zĕ-bū-lŭn.
8 And his host, and those that were
numbered thereof, *were* fifty and sev-
en thousand and four hundred.
9 All that were numbered in the
camp of Judah *were* an hundred
thousand and fourscore thousand and
six thousand and four hundred,
throughout their armies. These [g]shall
first set forth.
10 ¶ On the south side *shall be* the
standard of the camp of Reuben [h]ac-
cording to their armies: and the captain of the children of Reuben *shall be*
Ĕ-lĭ-zûr the son of Shĕd-ē-ûr.
11 And his host, and those that were
numbered thereof, *were* forty and six
thousand and five hundred.
12 And those which pitch by him
shall be the tribe of Simeon: and the
captain of the children of Simeon
shall be Shĕ-lû-mĭ-ĕl the son of Zū-
rĭ-shăd-dâi.
13 And his host, and those that were
numbered of them, *were* fifty and nine
thousand and three hundred.
14 Then the tribe of Gad: and the
captain of the sons of Gad *shall be*
Ē-lĭ-ă-săph the son of [2]Reū-ĕl.
15 And his host, and those that were
numbered of them, *were* forty and five
thousand and six hundred and fifty.
16 All that were numbered in the
camp of Reuben *were* an hundred
thousand and fifty and one thousand
and four hundred and fifty, throughout their armies. [i]And they shall set
forth in the second rank.
17 ¶ Then [j]the tabernacle of the congregation shall set forward with the
camp of the Levites in the midst of
the camp: as they encamp, so shall
they set forward, every [k]man in his
place by their standards.
18 ¶ On the west side *shall be* the
standard of the camp of [l]Ē-phră-ĭm
according to their armies: and the
captain of the sons of Ē-phră-ĭm *shall*
be Ē-lĭ-shă-mă the son of Ăm-mĭ-
hŭd.
19 And his host, and those that were
numbered of them, *were* forty thousand and five hundred.
20 And by him *shall be* the tribe of
Mă-năs-sēh: and the captain of the
children of Mă-năs-sēh *shall be* Gă-
mā-lĭ-ĕl the son of Pĕ-dăh-zûr.
21 And his host, and those that were
numbered of them, *were* thirty and
two thousand and two hundred.
22 Then the tribe of [m]Benjamin: and
the captain of the sons of Benjamin

shall be Ă-bī´-dăn the son of [3]Gĭd-ĕ-
ō´-nī.
23 And his host, and those that were
numbered of them, *were* thirty and
five thousand and four hundred.
24 All that were numbered of the
camp of Ē´-phră-ĭm *were* an hundred
thousand and eight thousand and an
hundred, throughout their armies.
And [n]they shall go forward in the third
rank.
25 ¶ The standard of the camp of
[o]Dan *shall be* on the north side by their
armies: and the captain of the children
of Dan *shall be* Ă-hĭ-ē´-zĕr the son of
Ăm-mĭ´-shăd´-dâi.
26 And his host, and those that were
numbered of them, *were* threescore
and two thousand and seven hundred.
27 And those that encamp by him
shall be the tribe of Asher: and the
captain of the children of Asher *shall
be* Pā´-gĭ-ĕl the son of Ŏc´-răn.
28 And his host, and those that were
numbered of them, *were* forty and one
thousand and five hundred.
29 ¶ Then the tribe of [p]Năph´-tă-lī:
and the captain of the children of
Năph´-tă-lī *shall be* Ă-hī´-ră the son of
Ē´-năn.
30 And his host, and those that were
numbered of them, *were* fifty and
three thousand and four hundred.
31 All they that were numbered in
the camp of Dan *were* an hundred
thousand and fifty and seven thousand and six hundred. They [q]shall go
hindmost with their standards.
32 ¶ These *are* those which were
numbered of the children of Israel by
the house of their fathers: [r]all those
that were numbered of the camps
throughout their hosts *were* six hundred thousand and three thousand
and five hundred and fifty.
33 But [s]the Levites were not numbered among the children of Israel;
as the LORD commanded Moses.
34 And the children of Israel did according to all that [t]the LORD commanded Moses: [u]so they pitched by
their standards, and so they set forward, every one after their families,
according to the house of their
fathers.

CHAPTER 3

THESE also *are* the generations of
Aaron and Moses in the day *that*
the LORD spake with Moses in mount
Sī´-nâi.
2 And these *are* the names of the
sons of Aaron; Nadab [a]the firstborn,
and Ă-bī´-hū, Ĕl-ē-ā´-zär, and Ĭth´-ă-
mär.
3 These *are* the names of the sons of
Aaron, [b]the priests which were anointed, [1]whom he consecrated to minister
in the priest's office.
4 And [c]Nadab and Ă-bī´-hū died before the LORD, when they offered
strange fire before the LORD, in the
wilderness of Sī´-nâi, and they had no
children: and Ĕl-ē-ā´-zär and Ĭth´-ă-
mär ministered in the priest's office in
the sight of Aaron their father.
5 ¶ And the LORD spake unto Moses,
saying,
6 Bring [d]the tribe of Levi near, and
present them before Aaron the priest,
that they may minister unto him.
7 And they shall keep his charge, and
the charge of the whole congregation
before the tabernacle of the congregation, to do the service of the tabernacle.
8 And they shall keep all the instruments of the tabernacle of the congregation, and the charge of the children of Israel, to do the [e]service of
the tabernacle.
9 And [f]thou shalt give the Levites
unto Aaron and to his sons: they *are*
wholly given unto him out of the children of Israel.
10 And thou shalt appoint Aaron and
his sons, [g]and they shall wait on their
priest's office: and [h]the stranger that
cometh nigh shall be put to death.
11 And the LORD spake unto Moses,
saying,
12 And I, behold, [i]I have taken the
Levites from among the children of
Israel instead of all the firstborn that
openeth the matrix among the children of Israel: therefore the Levites
shall be mine;
13 Because [j]all the firstborn *are*
mine; *for* [k]on the day that I smote all
the firstborn in the land of Egypt I hallowed unto me all the firstborn in Israel, both man and beast: mine shall
they be: I *am* the LORD.
14 ¶ And the LORD spake unto Moses
in the wilderness of [l]Sī´-nâi, saying,
15 Number the children of Levi after
the house of their fathers, by their
families: every [m]male from a month
old and upward shalt thou number
them.
16 And Moses numbered them according to the [2]word of the LORD, as
he was commanded.
17 And [n]these were the sons of Levi
by their names; Gĕr´-shŏn, and Kō´-
hăth, and Mĕ-rär´-ī.
18 And these *are* the names of the

3 That is, A cutter down.
n ch. 10.22.
o Deut. 32.22.
p Gen. 30.8. Gen. 49.21. 2 Ki. 15.29. Rev. 7.6.
q ch. 10.25.
r Ex. 12.37. ch. 1.46. ch. 11.21.
s ch. 1.47. ch. 3.5-51. ch. 26.57-62. 1 Chr. 6.
t Ex. 39.42. ch. 24.2. Ps. 119.6. Isa. 45.12. Luke 1.6.
u Num. 24.2, 9. Song 6.10. 1 Cor. 14.40.

CHAP. 3

a Ex. 6.23. ch. 26.61. 1 Chr. 6.3.
b Ex. 28.41. Lev. 8.1.
1 whose hand he filled.
c Lev. 10.1. 1 Chr. 24.2. Isa. 66.15. 2 Thes. 1.8. Heb. 12.29.
d Ex. 32.26. ch. 8.6.
e ch. 1.50.
f ch. 8.19.
g ch. 18.7. 1 Chr. 6.49. Acts 6.3,4. Rom. 12.7.
h ch. 16.40. Every one not a Levite.
i ch. 8.16. ch. 18.6.
j Ex. 13.2. Lev. 27.26. ch. 8.16. Neh. 10.36. Luke 2.23.
k Ex. 13.12, 15.
l Ex. 19.1.
m ch. 26.62.
2 mouth.
n Gen. 46.11. Ex. 6.16. ch. 26.57. 1 Chr. 23.6.

sons of Gĕr´-shŏn by their families; Lĭb´-nī, [o]and Shĭm´-ĕ-ī.

19 And the sons of Kō´-hăth by their families; Amram, and Ī´-zĕ-hār, Hē´-brŏn, and Ŭz´-zĭ-ĕl.

20 And the sons of Mĕ-rār´-ī by their families; Māh´-lī, and Mū´-shī. These *are* the families of the Levites according to the house of their fathers.

21 Of Gĕr´-shŏn *was* the family of the Lĭb´-nītes, and the family of the Shĭm´-ītes: these *are* the families of the Gĕr´-shŏn-ītes.

22 Those that were numbered of them, according to the number of all the males, from a month old and upward, *even* those that were numbered of them *were* seven thousand and five hundred.

23 The [p]families of the Gĕr´-shŏn-ītes shall pitch behind the tabernacle westward.

24 And the chief of the house of the father of the Gĕr´-shŏn-ītes *shall be* Ē-lĭ´-ă-săph the son of Lā´-ĕl.

25 And [q]the charge of the sons of Gĕr´-shŏn in the tabernacle of the congregation *shall be* [r]the tabernacle, and [s]the tent, [t]the covering thereof, and [u]the hanging for the door of the tabernacle of the congregation,

26 And the [v]hangings of the court, and the [w]curtain for the door of the court, which *is* by the tabernacle, and by the altar round about, and [x]the cords of it for all the service thereof.

27 ¶ And [y]of Kō´-hăth *was* the family of the Amramites, and the family of the Ī´-zĕ-hār-ītes, and the family of the Hē´-brŏn-ītes, and the family of the Ŭz-zĭ-ē´-lītes: these *are* the families of the Kō´-hăth-ītes.

28 In the number of all the males, from a month old and upward, *were* eight thousand and six hundred, keeping the charge of the sanctuary.

29 The [z]families of the sons of Kō´-hăth shall pitch on the side of the tabernacle southward.

30 And the chief of the house of the father of the families of the Kō´-hăth-ītes *shall be* Ē-lĭ-zā´-phăn the son of Ŭz´-zĭ-ĕl.

31 And [a]their charge *shall be* [b]the ark, and [c]the table, and [d]the candlestick, and the [e]altars, and the vessels of the sanctuary wherewith they minister, and [f]the hanging, and all the service thereof.

32 And Ĕl-ē-ā´-zār the son of Aaron the priest *shall be* [g]chief over the chief of the Levites, *and have* the oversight of them that keep the charge of the sanctuary.

33 ¶ Of Mĕ-rār´-ī *was* the family of the Māh´-lītes, and the family of the Mū´-shītes: these *are* the families of Mĕ-rār´-ī.

34 And those that were numbered of them, according to the number of all the males, from a month old and upward, *were* six thousand and two hundred.

35 And the chief of the house of the father of the families of Mĕ-rār´-ī *was* Zū´-rĭ-ĕl the son of Ăb´-ĭ-hail: *these* [h]shall pitch on the side of the tabernacle northward.

36 And [3]*under* the custody and charge of the sons of Mĕ-rār´-ī *shall be* the boards of the tabernacle, and the bars thereof, and the pillars thereof, and the sockets thereof, and all the vessels thereof, and all that serveth thereto,

37 And the pillars of the court round about, and their sockets, and their pins, and their cords.

38 ¶ But [i]those that encamp before the tabernacle toward the east, *even* before the tabernacle of the congregation eastwards, *shall be* Moses, and Aaron and his sons, keeping [j]the charge of the sanctuary [k]for the charge of the children of Israel; and [4]the stranger that cometh nigh shall be put to death.

39 All [l]that were numbered of the Levites, which Moses and Aaron numbered at the commandment of the LORD, throughout their families, all the males from a month old and upward, *were* twenty and two thousand.

40 ¶ And the LORD said unto Moses, Number [m]all the firstborn of the males of the children of Israel from a month old and upward, and take the number of their names.

41 And [n]thou shalt take the Levites for me (I *am* the LORD) instead of all the firstborn among the children of Israel; and the cattle of the Levites instead of all the firstlings among the cattle of the children of Israel.

42 And Moses numbered, as the LORD commanded him, all the firstborn among the children of Israel.

43 And all the firstborn males by the number of names, from a month old and upward, of those that were numbered of them, were twenty and two thousand two hundred and threescore and thirteen.

o Ex. 6.17.
p ch. 1.53.
q ch. 4.24,25, 26. 1 Chr. 9.14, 33. 1 Chr. 23.32.
r Ex. 25.9.
s Ex. 26.1.
t Ex. 26.7,14.
u Ex. 26.36.
v Ex. 27.9.
w Ex. 27.16.
x Ex. 35.18.
y 1 Chr. 26. 23.
z ch. 1.53.
a ch. 4.15.
b Ex. 25.10.
c Ex. 25.23.
d Ex. 25.31.
e Ex. 27.1. Ex. 30.1.
f Ex. 26.32.
g ch. 20.25-28. 2 Ki. 25.18. 1 Chr. 9.20.
h ch. 1.53.
3 the office of the charge.
i ch. 1.53. ch. 2.3.
j ch. 18.5. 1 Chr. 6.48, 49.
k vers. 7,8.
4 Every one not a Levite.
l ch. 4.47,48. ch. 26.62.
m ver. 15.
n vers. 12,45.

44¶ And the LORD spake unto Moses,
saying,
45 Take the Levites instead of all the
firstborn among the children of Israel,
and the cattle of the Levites instead
of their cattle; and the Levites shall
be [o]mine: I *am* the LORD.
46 And for those that are to be redeemed [p]of the two hundred and
threescore and thirteen of the firstborn of the children of Israel, [q]which
are more than the Levites;
47 Thou shalt even take [r]five shekels
apiece by the poll, after the shekel of
the sanctuary shalt thou take *them:*
(the [s]shekel *is* twenty gē-rähs:)
48 And thou shalt give the money,
wherewith the odd number of them is
to be redeemed, unto Aaron and to
his sons.
49 And Moses took the [t]redemption
money of them that were over and
above them that were redeemed by
the Levites:
50 Of the firstborn of the children of
Israel took he the money; [u]a thousand three hundred and threescore
and five *shekels*, after the shekel of
the sanctuary:
51 And Moses gave the money of
them that were redeemed unto Aaron
and to his sons, according to the word
of the LORD, as the LORD commanded
Moses.

CHAPTER 4

AND the LORD spake unto Moses
and unto Aaron, saying,
2 Take the sum of the sons of Kō-
hăth from among the sons of Levi,
after their families, by the house of
their fathers,
3 From [a]thirty years old and upward
even until fifty years old, all that
enter into the [1]host, to do the work
in the tabernacle of the congregation.
4 This [b]*shall be* the service of the
sons of Kō-hăth in the tabernacle of
the congregation, *about* the most holy
things:
5 ¶ And when the camp setteth forward, Aaron shall come, and his sons,
and they shall take down [c]the covering vail, and cover the [d]ark of testimony with it:
6 And shall put thereon the covering
of badgers' skins, and shall spread
over *it* a cloth wholly of blue, and
shall put in [e]the staves thereof.
7 And upon the [f]table of shewbread
they shall spread a cloth of blue, and
put thereon the dishes, and the
spoons, and the bowls, and covers to

o vers. 12.41. 1 Sam. 1.28.
p ch. 18.15.
q vers. 39,43.
r Lev. 27.6. ch. 18.16.
s Lev. 27.25. ch. 18.16.
t 1 Tim. 2.6. Titus 2.14. Heb. 9.12. 1 Pet. 1.18. Gal. 4.4,5.
u vers. 46,47. Acts 20.33.

CHAP. 4

a Gen. 41.46. ch. 3.40. 1 Chr. 23.3, 24,27. Luke 3.23.
1 Or, warfare.
b ver. 15.
c Ex. 26.31. Lev. 16.2. 2 Chr. 3.14. Matt. 27.51. Heb. 9.3.
d Ex. 25.10, 16.
e Ex. 25.13.
f Lev. 24.6,8.
2 Or, pour out withal.
g Ex. 25.31.
h Ex. 25.37, 38.
i Ex. 30.1.
3 Or, bowls.
j ch. 7.9. Deut. 31.9. 2 Sam. 6.13.
k 2 Sam. 6.6, 7.
l ch. 3.31.
m Ex. 25.6. Lev. 24.2.
n Ps. 141.2. Mal. 1.11. Rev. 5.8.
o Ex. 29.40. ch. 28.3. Dan. 9.27.
p Ex. 30.23.
q ver. 4.

[2]cover withal: and the continual
bread shall be thereon:
8 And they shall spread upon them
a cloth of scarlet, and cover the same
with a covering of badgers' skins, and
shall put in the staves thereof.
9 And they shall take a cloth of blue,
and cover the [g]candlestick of the light,
[h]and his lamps, and his tongs, and his
snuffdishes, and all the oil vessels
thereof, wherewith they minister unto
it:
10 And they shall put it and all the
vessels thereof within a covering of
badgers' skins, and shall put *it* upon
a bar.
11 And upon [i]the golden altar they
shall spread a cloth of blue, and cover
it with a covering of badgers' skins,
and shall put to the staves thereof:
12 And they shall take all the instruments of ministry, wherewith they
minister in the sanctuary, and put
them in a cloth of blue, and cover
them with a covering of badgers'
skins, and shall put *them* on a bar:
13 And they shall take away the
ashes from the altar, and spread a
purple cloth thereon:
14 And they shall put upon it all the
vessels thereof, wherewith they minister about it, *even* the censers, the
fleshhooks, and the shovels, and the
[3]basons, all the vessels of the altar;
and they shall spread upon it a covering of badgers' skins, and put to the
staves of it.
15 And when Aaron and his sons
have made an end of covering the
sanctuary, and all the vessels of the
sanctuary, as the camp is to set forward; after that, the [j]sons of Kō-hăth
shall come to bear *it:* [k]but they shall
not touch *any* holy thing, lest they die.
These [l]*things are* the burden of the
sons of Kō-hăth in the tabernacle of
the congregation.
16 ¶ And to the office of Ĕl-ē-ā-zär
the son of Aaron the priest *pertaineth*
[m]the oil for the light, and the [n]sweet
incense, and the [o]daily meat offering,
and the [p]anointing oil, *and* the oversight of all the tabernacle, and of all
that therein *is*, in the sanctuary, and
in the vessels thereof.
17 ¶ And the LORD spake unto Moses
and unto Aaron, saying,
18 Cut ye not off the tribe of the
families of the Kō-hăth-ītes from
among the Levites:
19 But thus do unto them, that they
may live, and not die, when they
approach unto the [q]most holy things:

Aaron and his sons shall go in, and appoint them every one to his service and to his burden:

20 But [r]they shall not go in to see when the holy things are covered, lest they die.

21 ¶ And the LORD spake unto Moses, saying,

22 Take also the sum of the sons of Gĕr´-shŏn, throughout the houses of their fathers, by their families;

23 From [s]thirty years old and upward until fifty years old shalt thou number them; all that enter in [4]to perform the service, to do the work in the tabernacle of the congregation.

24 This *is* the service of the families of the Gĕr´-shŏn-ītes, to serve, and for [5]burdens:

25 And [t]they shall bear the curtains of the tabernacle, and the tabernacle of the congregation, his covering, and the covering of the badgers' skins that *is* above upon it, and the hanging for the door of the tabernacle of the congregation,

26 And the hangings of the court, and the hanging for the door of the gate of the court, which *is* by the tabernacle and by the altar round about, and their cords, and all the instruments of their service, and all that is made for them: so shall they serve.

27 At the [6]appointment of Aaron and his sons shall be all the service of the sons of the Gĕr´-shŏn-ītes, in all their burdens, and in all their service: and ye shall appoint unto them in charge all their burdens.

28 This *is* the service of the families of the sons of Gĕr´-shŏn in the tabernacle of the congregation: and their charge *shall be* under the hand of Ĭth´-ă-mär the son of Aaron the priest.

29 ¶ As for the sons of Mĕ-râr´-ī, thou shalt number them after their families, by the house of their fathers;

30 From [u]thirty years old and upward even unto fifty years old shalt thou number them, every one that entereth into the [7]service, to do the work of the tabernacle of the congregation.

31 And [v]this *is* the charge of their burden, according to all their service in the tabernacle of the congregation; the boards of the tabernacle, and the bars thereof, and the pillars thereof, and sockets thereof,

32 And the pillars of the court round about, and their sockets, and their pins, and their cords, with all their instruments, and with all their service: and by name ye shall reckon [w]the instruments of the charge of their burden.

33 This *is* the service of the families of the sons of Mĕ-râr´-ī, according to all their service, in the tabernacle of the congregation, under the hand of Ĭth´-ă-mär the son of Aaron the priest.

34 ¶ And [x]Moses and Aaron and the chief of the congregation numbered the sons of the Kō´-hăth-ītes after their families, and after the house of their fathers,

35 From [y]thirty years old and upward even unto fifty years old, every one that entereth into the service, for the work in the tabernacle of the congregation:

36 And those that were numbered of them by their families were two thousand seven hundred and fifty.

37 These *were* they that were numbered of the families of the Kō´-hăth-ītes, all that might do service in the tabernacle of the congregation, which Moses and Aaron did number according to the commandment of the LORD by the hand of Moses.

38 And those that were numbered of the sons of Gĕr´-shŏn, throughout their families, and by the house of their fathers,

39 From thirty years old and upward even unto fifty years old, every one that entereth into the service, for the work in the tabernacle of the congregation,

40 Even those that were numbered of them, throughout their families, by the house of their fathers, were two thousand and six hundred and thirty.

41 These *are* they that were numbered of the families of the sons of Gĕr´-shŏn, of all that might do service in the tabernacle of the congregation, whom Moses and Aaron did number according to the commandment of the LORD.

42 ¶ And those that were numbered of the families of the sons of Mĕ-râr´-ī, throughout their families, by the house of their fathers,

43 From [z]thirty years old and upward even unto fifty years old, every one that entereth into the service, for the work in the tabernacle of the congregation,

44 Even those that were numbered of them after their families, were three thousand and two hundred.

45 These *be* those that were numbered of the families of the sons of Mĕ-râr´-ī, whom Moses and Aaron

r 1 Sam 6.19.
s 1 Chr. 23.3, 24.27.
4 to war the warfare.
5 Or, carriage.
t Ex. 26.1-14. ch. 3.25,26.
6 mouth. Luke 1.70.
u vers. 3,23. Gen. 41.46. ch. 8.24,26. 1 Chr. 28.12, 13.
7 warfare. Ps. 110. 1-7. 1 Tim. 6.11. 2 Tim. 2.4. 2 Tim. 4.7.
v ch. 3.36,37.
w Ex. 25.9. ch. 3.8. ch. 7.1. 1 Chr. 9.29.
x ch. 3.19,27. ver. 2.
y ch. 8.24-26. 1 Chr. 23.24. Luke 3.23. 1 Tim. 3.6.
z vers. 35-40. Deut. 33.25. 2 Cor. 12.9.

numbered according to the word of
the LORD by the hand of Moses.
46 All those that were numbered of
the Levites, whom Moses and Aaron
and the chief of Israel numbered, after
their families, and after the house of
their fathers,
47 From [a]thirty years old and upward even unto fifty years old, every
one that came to do the service of the
ministry, and the service of the burden
in the tabernacle of the congregation,
48 Even those that were numbered
of them, were eight thousand and five
hundred and fourscore.
49 According to the commandment
of the LORD they were numbered by
the hand of Moses, [b]every one according to his service, and according to his
burden: thus were they numbered of
him, as the LORD commanded Moses.

CHAPTER 5

AND the LORD spake unto Moses,
saying,
2 Command the children of Israel,
that they put out of the camp every
[a]leper, and every one that hath an
[b]issue, and whosoever is defiled by
the [c]dead:
3 Both male and female shall ye put
out, without the camp shall ye put
them; that they defile not their camps,
[d]in the midst whereof I dwell.
4 And the children of Israel did so,
and put them out without the camp:
as the LORD spake unto Moses, so did
the children of Israel.
5 ¶ And the LORD spake unto Moses,
saying,
6 Speak unto the children of Israel,
When [e]a man or woman shall commit
any sin that men commit, to do a trespass against the LORD, and that person be guilty;
7 Then [f]they shall confess their sin
which they have done: and he shall
recompense his trespass [g]with the
principal thereof, and add unto it the
fifth *part* thereof, and give *it* unto *him*
against whom he hath trespassed.
8 But if the man have no kinsman to
recompense the trespass unto, let the
trespass be recompensed unto the
LORD, *even* to the priest; beside [h] the
ram of the atonement, whereby an
atonement shall be made for him.
9 And every [1]offering of all the holy
things of the children of Israel, which
they bring unto the priest, shall be his.
10 And every man's hallowed things
shall be his: whatsoever any man giveth the priest, it shall [i]be his.

11 ¶ And the LORD spake unto Moses,
saying,
12 Speak unto the children of Israel,
and say unto them, If any man's wife
[j]go aside, and commit a trespass
against him,
13 And a man [k]lie with her carnally,
and it be hid from the eyes of her
husband, and be kept close, and she
be defiled, and *there be* no witness
against her, neither she be taken *with
the manner;*
14 And [l]the spirit of jealousy come
upon him, and he be jealous of his
wife, and she be defiled: or if the
spirit of jealousy come upon him, and
he be jealous of his wife, and she be
not defiled:
15 Then shall the man bring his wife
unto the priest, and he shall bring her
[m]offering for her, the tenth *part* of an
ē-phăh of barley meal; he shall pour
no oil upon it, nor put frankincense
thereon; for it *is* an offering of
jealousy, an offering of memorial,
[n]bringing iniquity to remembrance.
16 And the priest shall bring her
near, and [o]set her before the LORD:
17 And the priest shall take holy
water in an earthen vessel; and of the
dust that is in the floor of the tabernacle the priest shall take, and put *it*
into the water:
18 And the priest shall set the woman
before the LORD, and uncover the woman's head, and put the offering of
memorial in her hands, which *is* the
jealousy offering: and the priest shall
have in his hand the bitter water that
causeth the curse:
19 And the priest shall charge her by
an oath, and say unto the woman, If
no man have lain with thee, and if thou
hast not gone aside to uncleanness
[2]*with another* instead of thy husband,
be thou free from this bitter water that
causeth the curse:
20 But if thou hast gone aside *to another* instead of thy husband, and if
thou be defiled, and some man have
lain with thee beside thine husband:
21 Then the priest shall [p]charge the
woman with an oath of cursing, and
the priest shall say unto the woman,
[q]The LORD make thee a curse and an
oath among thy people, when the
LORD doth make thy thigh to [3]rot, and
thy belly to swell;
22 And this water that causeth the
curse shall go [r]into thy bowels, to
make *thy* belly to swell, and *thy* thigh
to rot: [s]And the woman shall say,
Ā-mĕn, ā-mĕn.

a Rom. 12.6-8.
b 1 Cor. 12.4-28.

CHAP. 5
a Lev. 13.3, 46. ch. 12.14. Deut. 23.10. 2 Ki. 5.27. 2 Chr. 26.20. Isa. 52.11. Luke 17.12.
b Lev. 15.2.
c Lev. 21.1. ch. 9.6,10.
d Ex. 25.8. Lev. 26.11, 12. Deut. 32.19. Josh. 22.19. Ps. 76.2. Zech. 2.10. 2 Cor. 6.16. Rev. 21.3.
e Lev. 6.2,3.
f Lev. 5.5. Josh. 7.19.
g Lev. 6.5.
h Lev. 7.7.
1 Or, heave offering.
i Lev. 10.13.
j Pro. 2.16. Pro. 7.10-27. Hosea 4.13.
k Lev. 18.20. Pro. 30.20.
l Pro. 6.34. Song 8.6. Isa. 19.14.
m Lev. 5.11. Isa. 53.2.
n 1 Ki. 17.18.
o Lev. 1.3. Jer. 17.10. 1 Chr. 28.9. Mal. 3.5. Heb. 13.4.
2 under thy husband, or, being in the power of thy husband.
p Gen. 9.25. Josh. 6.26. Neh. 10.29. Mal. 4.6. Matt. 26.74.
q Isa. 65.15. Jer. 29.22.
3 fall.
r Ps. 109.18. Pro. 1.31.
s Deut. 27.15.

23 And the priest shall write these
curses in a book, and he shall blot
them out with the bitter water:
24 And he shall cause the woman to
drink the bitter water that causeth the
curse: and the water that causeth the
curse shall enter into her, *and become*
bitter.
25 Then the priest shall take the
jealousy offering out of the woman's
hand, and shall wave [t]the offering before the LORD, and offer it upon the
altar:
26 And [u]the priest shall take an
handful of the offering, *even* the
memorial thereof, and burn *it* upon
the altar, and afterward shall cause
the woman to drink the water.
27 And when he hath made her to
drink the water, then it shall come to
pass, *that*, if she be defiled, and have
done trespass against her husband,
that the water that causeth the curse
shall enter into her, *and become* bitter,
and her belly shall swell, and her
thigh shall rot: and the woman shall
[v]be a curse among her people.
28 And if the woman be not defiled,
but be clean; then she shall be [w]free,
and shall conceive seed.
29 This *is* the law of jealousies, when
a wife goeth aside *to another* instead
of her husband, and is defiled;
30 Or when the spirit of jealousy
cometh upon him, and he be jealous
over his wife, and shall set the woman
before the LORD, and the priest shall
execute upon her all this law.
31 Then shall the man be guiltless
from iniquity, and this woman shall
[x]bear her iniquity.

CHAPTER 6

AND the LORD spake unto Moses,
saying,
2 Speak unto the children of Israel,
and say unto them, When either man
or woman shall [1]separate *themselves*
to vow a vow of a Nazarite, to separate *themselves* unto the LORD:
3 He [a]shall separate *himself* from
wine and strong drink, and shall drink
no vinegar of wine, or vinegar of
strong drink, neither shall he drink
any liquor of grapes, nor eat moist
grapes, or dried.
4 All the days of his [2]separation shall
he eat nothing that is made of the
[3]vine tree, from the kernels even to
the husk.
5 All the days of the vow of his
separation there shall no [b]rasor come
upon his head: until the days be

t Lev. 8.27.
u Lev. 2.2,9.
v Deut. 28.37.
Ps. 83.9.
Eccl. 7.26.
Isa. 65.15.
Jer. 24.9.
Zech. 8.13.
w Job 17.8,9.
Ps. 37.5,6.
Rom. 5.3-5.
x Lev. 20.17.
Rom. 2.8,9.
CHAP. 6
1 Or, make
themselves
Nazarites.
a Lev. 10.9.
Judg. 13.4.
Amos 2.12.
Luke 1.15.
2 Or, Nazar-
iteship.
3 vine of the
wine.
b Judg. 13.5.
1 Sam. 1.11.
Lam. 4.7.
c Lev. 19.28.
Lev. 21.11.
Jer. 16.5,6.
Matt. 8.21,
22.
d ch. 9.6.
4 separation.
e Acts 18.18.
f Lev. 5.7.
5 fall.
g Acts 21.26.
h Lev. 4.2.
i Lev. 3.6.
j Lev. 2.4.
Lev. 8.2.
John 6.50-
53.
k Ex. 29.2.
l ch. 15.5,7.
Isa. 62.9.
Joel 1.9,13.
1 Cor. 10.3.
m Acts 21.24.

fulfilled, in the which he separateth
himself unto the LORD, he shall be
holy, *and* shall let the locks of the hair
of his head grow.
6 All the days that he separateth
himself unto the LORD [c]he shall come
at no dead body.
7 He [d]shall not make himself unclean for his father, or for his mother,
for his brother, or for his sister, when
they die: because the [4]consecration of
his God *is* upon his head.
8 All the days of his separation he
is holy unto the LORD.
9 And if any man die very suddenly
by him, and he hath defiled the head
of his consecration; then he [e]shall
shave his head in the day of his cleansing, on the seventh day shall he shave
it.
10 And [f]on the eighth day he shall
bring two turtles, or two young
pigeons, to the priest, to the door of
the tabernacle of the congregation:
11 And the priest shall offer the one
for a sin offering, and the other for a
burnt offering, and make an atonement for him, for that he sinned by the
dead, and shall hallow his head that
same day.
12 And he shall consecrate unto the
LORD the days of his separation, and
shall bring a lamb of the first year for
a trespass offering: but the days that
were before shall [5]be lost, because his
separation was defiled.
13 ¶ And this *is* the law of the Nazarite, when [g]the days of his separation
are fulfilled: he shall be brought unto
the door of the tabernacle of the congregation:
14 And he shall offer his offering unto the LORD, one he lamb of the first
year without blemish for a burnt offering, and one ewe lamb of the first year
without blemish for [h]a sin offering,
and one ram without blemish for
[i]peace offerings,
15 And a basket of unleavened
bread, cakes [j]of fine flour mingled
with oil, and wafers of unleavened
bread [k]anointed with oil, and their
meat offering, and their [l]drink offerings.
16 And the priest shall bring *them* before the LORD, and shall offer his sin
offering, and his burnt offering:
17 And he shall offer the ram *for* a
sacrifice of peace offerings unto the
LORD, with the basket of unleavened
bread: the priest shall offer also his
meat offering, and his drink offering.
18 And [m]the Nazarite shall shave the

head of his separation *at* the door of the tabernacle of the congregation, and shall take the hair of the head of his separation, and put [n]*it* in the fire which *is* under the sacrifice of the peace offerings.

19 And the priest shall take the sodden [o]shoulder of the ram, and one unleavened cake out of the basket, and one unleavened wafer, and [p]shall put *them* upon the hands of the Nazarite, after *the hair of* his separation is shaven:

20 And the priest shall wave [q]them *for* a wave offering before the LORD: this *is* holy for the priest, with the wave breast and heave shoulder: and [r]after that the Nazarite may drink wine.

21 This *is* the law of the Nazarite who hath vowed, *and of* his offering unto the LORD for his separation, beside *that* that his hand shall get: according to the vow which he vowed, so he must do after the law of his separation.

22 ¶ And the LORD spake unto Moses, saying,

23 Speak unto Aaron and unto his sons, saying, On this wise [s]ye shall bless the children of Israel, saying unto them,

24 The LORD [t]bless thee, and keep [u]thee:

25 The LORD [v]make his face shine upon thee, and [w]be gracious unto thee:

26 The LORD lift up his countenance upon thee, and give thee peace.

27 And they shall put my name upon the children of Israel; and I will bless them.

CHAPTER 7

AND it came to pass on the day that Moses had fully set up the tabernacle, and had anointed it, and sanctified it, and all the instruments thereof, both the altar and all the vessels thereof, and had anointed them, and [a]sanctified them;

2 That the princes of Israel, heads of the house of their fathers, who *were* the princes of the tribes, [1]and were over them that were numbered, [b]offered:

3 And they brought their offering before the LORD, six covered wagons, and twelve oxen; a wagon for two of the princes, and for each one an ox: and they brought them before the tabernacle.

4 And the LORD spake unto Moses, saying,

5 Take *it* of them, that they may be to do the service of the tabernacle of the congregation; and thou shalt give them unto the Levites, to every man according to his service.

6 And Moses took the wagons and the oxen, and gave them unto the Levites.

7 Two wagons and four oxen he gave unto the sons of Gĕr-shŏn, according to their service:

8 And four wagons and eight oxen he gave unto the sons of Mĕ-râr-ī, according unto their service, under the hand of Ĭth-ă-mär the son of Aaron the priest.

9 But unto the sons of Kō-hăth he gave none: because the service of the sanctuary belonging unto them [c]*was that* they should bear upon their shoulders.

10 ¶ And the princes offered [d]for dedicating of the altar in the day that it was anointed, even the princes offered their offering before the altar.

11 And the LORD said unto Moses, They shall offer their offering, each prince [e]on his day, for the dedicating of the altar.

12 ¶ And he that offered his offering the first day was Näh-shŏn the son of Ăm-mĭn-ă-dăb, of the tribe of Judah:

13 And his offering *was* one silver charger, the [f]weight thereof *was* an hundred and thirty *shekels*, one silver bowl of seventy shekels, after [2]the shekel of the sanctuary; both of them *were* full of fine flour mingled with oil for a meat offering:

14 One [g]spoon of ten *shekels* of gold, full of [h]incense:

15 One young bullock, one ram, one lamb of the first year, for a burnt offering:

16 One kid of the goats for [i]a sin offering:

17 And for a sacrifice of peace offerings, two oxen, five rams, five he goats, five lambs of the first year: this *was* the offering of Näh-shŏn [j]the son of Ăm-mĭn-ă-dăb.

18 ¶ On the second day Nĕth-ă-neel the son of Zū-är, prince of Ĭs-să-char, did offer:

19 He offered *for* his offering one silver charger, the weight thereof *was* an hundred and thirty *shekels*, one silver bowl of seventy shekels, after the shekel of the sanctuary; both of them full of fine flour mingled with oil for a meat offering:

20 One spoon of gold of ten *shekels*, full of incense:

21 One young bullock, one ram, one

n Luke 17.10. Rom. 6.6. Gal. 5.24. Eph. 4.23. Col. 3.9.
o Lev. 8.31.
p Ex. 29.23, 24.
q Lev. 9.21.
r Eccl. 9.7. Isa. 35.10. John 17.4, 5. Rev. 14.13.
s 1 Chr. 23. 13.
t Ps. 134.3.
u Ps. 121.7. John 17.11. 1 Pet. 1.5.
v Ps. 67.1. Ps. 80.3. Dan. 9.17.
w Gen. 43.29. John 1.17. Rom. 5.21.

CHAP. 7

a Gen. 32.26, 29. 1 Ki. 8.64. 1 Chr. 4.10. Matt. 23.19. Eph. 1.3.
1 who stood.
b Ex. 35.27. 1 Chr. 29.6-8. 2 Chr. 35.8. Neh. 7.70-72.
c 2 Sam. 6.13. 1 Chr. 23.26.
d Deut. 20.5. 1 Ki. 8.63. Ezra 6.16.
e 1 Cor. 14. 33.
f Ex. 25.29. Ezra 1.9,10. Jer. 52.19. Dan. 5.3.
2 There were three shekels: the royal shekel, value 1*s.* 3*d.*, the shekel of the sanctuary, value 2*s.* 6*d.*, and the common shekel, about 1*s.*
g 2 Ki. 25.14, 15.
h Ex. 30.34. Lev. 16.12, 13. ch. 16.46,47. Deut. 33.8, 10. Ps. 141.2. Isa. 60.6. Jer. 6.20. Jer. 41.5. Eze. 16.18. Mal. 1.11. Rev. 5.8.
i Lev. 4.23.
j Luke 3.32.

lamb of the first year, for [k]a burnt
offering:
22 One kid of the goats for a sin offering:
23 And for a sacrifice of [l]peace offerings, two oxen, five rams, five he
goats, five lambs of the first year: this
was the offering of Nĕth'-ă-nêel the
son of Zū'-ăr.
24 ¶ On the third day Ē-lī'-ăb the son
of Hē'-lŏn, prince of the children of
Zĕ-bū'-lŭn, *did offer:*
25 His offering *was* one silver charger, the weight whereof *was* an hundred
and thirty *shekels*, one silver bowl of
seventy shekels, after the shekel of
the sanctuary; both of them full of
fine flour mingled with oil for a meat
offering:
26 One golden spoon of ten *shekels*,
full of incense:
27 One young bullock, one ram, one
lamb [m]of the first year, for a burnt
offering:
28 One kid of the goats for a sin
offering:
29 And for a sacrifice of peace offerings, two oxen, five rams, five he
goats, five lambs of the first year: this
was the offering of Ē-lī'-ăb the son of
Hē'-lŏn.
30 ¶ On the fourth day Ĕ-lī'-zûr the
son of Shĕd'-ē-ûr, prince of the children of Reuben, *did offer:*
31 His offering *was* one silver charger
of the weight of an hundred and thirty
shekels, one silver bowl of seventy
shekels, after the shekel of the sanctuary; both of them full of fine
flour mingled with oil for a meat
offering:
32 One golden spoon of ten *shekels*,
full of incense:
33 One young bullock, one ram, one
lamb of the first year, for a burnt
offering:
34 One kid of the goats for a sin
offering:
35 And for a sacrifice of peace offerings, two oxen, five rams, five he
goats, five lambs of the first year: this
was the offering of Ĕ-lī'-zûr the son of
Shĕd'-ē-ûr.
36 ¶ On the fifth day Shĕ-lû'-mĭ-ĕl the
son of Zū-rĭ-shăd'-dâi, prince of the
children of Simeon, *did offer:*
37 His offering *was* one silver charger, the weight whereof *was* an hundred
and thirty *shekels*, one silver bowl of
seventy shekels, after the shekel of
the sanctuary; both of them full of
fine flour mingled with oil for a meat
offering:

k Gen. 8.20. Lev. 6.9. Ps. 20.1-3. Ps. 51.19. Eze. 45.17. Eph. 5.2. Heb. 9.13.
l Lev. 7.11, 13. 1 Ki. 8.63. Pro. 7.14. Col. 1.20.
m Isa. 53.7. John 1.29. Acts 8.32. Gal. 1.4. 1 Pet. 1.19. Rev. 5.6-14.
n Ex. 12.5. Isa. 53.7. John 1.29. Acts 8.32. Heb. 9.28. 1 Pet. 1.19. Rev. 5.6.
o ch. 1.14. ch. 2.14. ch. 10.20. Son of Reuel.
p Lev. 2.5. Lev. 14.10. Heb. 1.9. 1 John 2.27.
q Ps. 40.6. Ps. 50.8-14. Ps. 51.16. Isa. 1.11. Jer. 7.22. Amos 5.22. 2 Cor. 5.21.
3 A sacrifice of payment, or, of perfections.
r ch. 1.10. ch. 2.18. 1 Chr. 7.26.
s Deut. 33.10. Ps. 66.15. Ps. 141.2. Eze. 8.11. Mal. 1.11. Luke 1.10. Rev. 5.8. Rev. 8.3.
t Micah 6.6-8.
u ch. 1.10. ch. 2.20.

38 One golden spoon of ten *shekels*
full of incense:
39 One young bullock, one ram, one
[n]lamb of the first year, for a burnt
offering:
40 One kid of the goats for a sin offering:
41 And for a sacrifice of peace offerings, two oxen, five rams, five he
goats, five lambs of the first year: this
was the offering of Shĕ-lû'-mĭ-ĕl the
son of Zū-rĭ-shăd'-dâi.
42 ¶ On the sixth day [o]Ē-lĭ'-ă-săph
the son of Deû'-ĕl, prince of the children of Gad, *offered:*
43 His offering *was* one silver charger of the weight of an hundred and
thirty *shekels*, a silver bowl of seventy
shekels, after the shekel of the sanctuary; both of them full of fine flour
mingled with [p]oil for a meat offering:
44 One golden spoon of ten *shekels*,
full of incense:
45 One [q]young bullock, one ram,
one lamb of the first year, for a burnt
offering:
46 One kid of the goats for a sin offering:
47 And for a sacrifice of [3]peace offerings, two oxen, five rams, five he goats,
five lambs of the first year: this *was*
the offering of Ē-lĭ'-ă-săph the son of
Deû'-ĕl.
48 ¶ On the seventh day [r]Ē-lī'-shă-
mă the son of Ăm'-mĭ-hŭd, prince of
the children of Ē'-phră-ĭm, *offered:*
49 His offering *was* one silver charger, the weight whereof *was* an hundred
and thirty *shekels*, one silver bowl of
seventy shekels, after the shekel of
the sanctuary; both of them full of
fine flour mingled with oil for a meat
offering:
50 One golden spoon of ten *shekels*,
full of [s]incense:
51 One [t]young bullock, one ram, one
lamb of the first year, for a burnt offering:
52 One kid of the goats for a sin offering:
53 And for a sacrifice of peace offerings, two oxen, five rams, five he
goats, five lambs of the first year: this
was the offering of Ē-lī'-shă-mă the
son of Ăm'-mĭ-hŭd.
54 ¶ On the eighth day *offered* Gă-
mā-lī-ĕl [u]the son of Pĕ-dăh'-zûr,
prince of the children of Mă-năs'-sēh:
55 His offering *was* one silver charger
of the weight of an hundred and
thirty *shekels*, one silver bowl of seventy shekels, after the shekel of the
sanctuary; both of them full of fine

flour mingled with oil for a meat offering:

56 One golden spoon of ten *shekels*, full of [v]incense:

57 One young bullock, one ram, one [w]lamb of the first year, for a burnt offering:

58 One kid of the goats for a sin offering:

59 And for [x]a sacrifice of peace offerings, two oxen, five rams, five he goats, five lambs of the first year: this *was* the offering of Gă-mā́-lĭ-ĕl the son of Pĕ-dăh́-zŭr.

60 ¶ On the ninth day [y]Ă-bĭ́-dăn the son of Gĭd-ĕ-ṓ-nī, prince of the children of Benjamin, *offered:*

61 His offering *was* one silver charger, the weight whereof *was* an hundred and thirty *shekels*, one silver bowl of seventy shekels, after the shekel of the sanctuary; both of them full of fine flour mingled with oil for a meat offering:

62 One golden spoon of ten *shekels*, full of [z]incense:

63 One [a]young bullock, one ram, one lamb of the first year, for a burnt offering:

64 One kid of the goats for a sin offering:

65 And for a sacrifice of [b]peace offerings, two oxen, five rams, five he goats, five lambs of the first year: this *was* the offering of Ă-bĭ́-dăn the son of Gĭd-ĕ-ṓ-nī.

66 ¶ On the tenth day [c]Ā-hĭ-ḗ-zĕr the son of Ăm-mĭ-shăd́-dâi, prince of the children of Dan, *offered:*

67 His offering *was* one silver charger, the weight whereof *was* an hundred and thirty *shekels*, one silver bowl of seventy shekels, after the [d]shekel of the sanctuary; both of them full of fine flour mingled with oil for a meat offering:

68 One golden spoon of ten *shekels*, full of [e]incense:

69 One young bullock, one ram, one lamb of the first year, for a burnt offering:

70 One kid of the goats for a sin offering:

71 And for a sacrifice of peace offerings, two oxen, five rams, five he goats, five lambs of the first year: this *was* the offering of Ā-hĭ-ḗ-zĕr the son of Ăm-mĭ-shăd́-dâi.

72 ¶ On the eleventh day [f]Pā́-gĭ-ĕl the son of Ŏć-răn, prince of the children of Asher, *offered:*

73 His offering *was* one silver charger, the weight whereof *was* an hundred and thirty *shekels*, one silver bowl of seventy shekels, after the shekel of the sanctuary; both of them full of fine flour mingled with oil for a meat offering:

74 One golden spoon of ten *shekels*, full of [g]incense:

75 One young bullock, one ram, one lamb of the first year, for a burnt offering:

76 One kid of the goats for a sin offering:

77 And for a sacrifice of peace offerings, two oxen, five rams, five he goats, five lambs of the first year: this *was* the offering of Pā́-gĭ-ĕl the son of Ŏć-răn.

78 ¶ On the twelfth day [h]Ă-hī́-ră the son of Ḗ-năn, prince of the children of Năph́-tă-lī, *offered:*

79 His offering *was* one [i]silver charger, the weight whereof *was* an hundred and thirty *shekels*, one silver bowl of seventy shekels, after the shekel of the sanctuary; both of them full of fine flour mingled with oil for a meat offering:

80 One golden spoon of ten *shekels*, full of incense:

81 One young bullock, one ram, one lamb of the first year, for a burnt offering:

82 One kid of the goats for a sin offering:

83 And for a sacrifice of peace offerings, two oxen, five rams, five he goats, five lambs of the first year: this *was* the offering of Ă-hī́-ră the son of Ḗ-năn.

84 This *was* [j]the dedication of the altar, in the day when it was anointed, by [k]the princes of Israel: twelve chargers of silver, twelve silver bowls, twelve spoons of gold:

85 Each charger of silver *weighing* an hundred and thirty *shekels*, each bowl seventy: all the silver vessels *weighed* two thousand and four hundred *shekels*, after the shekel of the sanctuary:

86 The golden spoons *were* twelve, full of incense, *weighing* ten *shekels* apiece, after the [l]shekel of the sanctuary: all the gold of the spoons *was* an hundred and twenty *shekels*.

87 All the oxen for the [m]burnt offering *were* twelve bullocks, the rams twelve, the lambs of the first year twelve, with their [n]meat offering: and the kids of the goats for sin offering twelve.

88 And all the oxen for the sacrifice of the peace offerings *were* twenty and four bullocks, the rams sixty, the he

v Ex. 30.7.
w Ex. 12.5. John 1.29. Acts 8.32. 1 Pet. 1.19. Rev. 5.6.
x Lev. 3.1. Micah 5.5. 2 Cor. 5.19, 21. Eph. 2.14.
y ch. 1.11. ch. 2.22.
z Isa. 66.20. Ps. 141.2. Dan. 9.27. Rom. 15.16. Phil 4.18. Heb. 13. 15. Rev. 5.8.
a Ps. 40.6. Isa. 53.4. 2 Cor. 5.21.
b Lev. 3.1. 1 Ki. 8.63. Pro. 7.14. Col. 1.20.
c ch. 1 12. ch. 2.25.
d Lev. 27.25. ch. 3.47.
e Ex. 30.7-9. Ps. 141.2. Isa. 66.20. Dan. 9.27. Mal. 1.11. Luke 1.9. Rom. 15.16. Phil. 4.18. Heb. 13.15.
f ch. 1.13. ch. 2.27.
g Mal. 1.11. Luke 1.11.
h ch. 1.15. ch. 2.29.
i Ezra 1.9,10. Jer. 52.19. Dan. 5.2. Zech. 14.20. Matt. 14.8, 11.
j 1 Chr. 29.6. Ezra 2.68. Neh. 7.70. Isa. 60.6, 10. Heb. 13.10. Rev. 21.14.
k Judg. 5.9. Josh. 22.13, 14. Pro. 17.7. Hosea 13. 10.
l Ex. 30.13.
m Rom. 12.1.
n Lev. 2.1. Lev. 6.14-18. ch. 15.4.

goats sixty, the lambs of the first year
sixty. This *was* the dedication of the
altar, after that it was anointed.
89 And when Moses was gone into
the tabernacle of the congregation [o]to
speak with [4]him, then he heard [p]the
voice of one speaking unto him from
off the mercy seat that *was* upon the
ark of testimony, from between [q]the
two chĕr'-ū-bĭms: and he spake unto
him.

CHAPTER 8

AND the LORD spake unto Moses,
saying,
2 Speak unto Aaron, and say unto
him, When thou [a]lightest the lamps,
the seven lamps shall give light over
against the candlestick.
3 And Aaron did so; he lighted the
lamps thereof over against the candlestick, as the LORD commanded Moses.
4 And [b]this work of the candlestick
was of beaten gold, unto the shaft
thereof, unto the flowers thereof, *was*
[c]beaten work: according [d]unto the
pattern which the LORD had shewed
Moses, so he made the candlestick.
5¶ And the LORD spake unto Moses,
saying,
6 Take the Levites from among the
children of Israel, and [e]cleanse them.
7 And thus shalt thou do unto them,
to cleanse them: Sprinkle [1]water of
purifying upon them, and [2]let them
[f]shave all their flesh, and let them
wash their clothes, and *so* make themselves clean.
8 Then let them take a young bullock with [g]his meat offering, *even* fine
flour mingled with oil, and another
young bullock shalt thou take for a
sin offering.
9 And [h]thou shalt bring the Levites
before the tabernacle of the congregation: [i]and thou shalt gather the
whole assembly of the children of Israel together:
10 And thou shalt bring the Levites
before the LORD: and the children of
Israel [j]shall put their hands upon the
Levites:
11 And Aaron shall [3]offer the Levites
before the LORD *for* an [4]offering of
the children of Israel, that [5]they may
execute the service of the LORD.
12 And [k]the Levites shall lay their
hands upon the heads of the bullocks:
and thou shalt offer the one *for* a sin
offering, and the other *for* a burnt
offering, unto the LORD, to make an
atonement for the Levites.
13 And thou shalt set the Levites before Aaron, and before his sons, and
offer them *for* an offering unto the
LORD.
14 Thus shalt thou separate the Levites from among the children of Israel: and the Levites shall be [l]mine.
15 And after that shall the Levites go
in to do the service of the tabernacle of
the congregation: and thou shalt
cleanse them, [m]and offer them *for* an
offering.
16 For they *are* wholly given unto
me from among the children of Israel;
[n]instead of such as open every womb,
even instead of the firstborn of all the
children of Israel, have I taken them
unto me.
17 For [o]all the firstborn of the children of Israel *are* mine, *both* man and
beast: on the day that I smote every
firstborn in the land of Egypt I sanctified them for myself.
18 And I have taken the Levites for
all the firstborn of the children of
Israel.
19 And [p]I have given the Levites *as*
[6]a gift to Aaron and to his sons from
among the children of Israel, to do
the service of the children of Israel in
the tabernacle of the congregation,
and to make an atonement for the
children of Israel: [q]that there be no
plague among the children of Israel,
when the children of Israel come nigh
unto the sanctuary.
20 And Moses, and Aaron, and all
the congregation of the children of
Israel, did to the Levites according
unto all that the LORD commanded
Moses concerning the Levites, so did
the children of Israel unto them.
21 And the Levites were purified, and
they washed their clothes; and [r]Aaron
offered them *as* an offering before the
LORD; and Aaron made an atonement
for them to cleanse them.
22 And [s]after that went the Levites
in to do their service in the tabernacle
of the congregation before Aaron, and
before his sons: as the LORD had commanded Moses concerning the Levites, so did they unto them.
23¶ And the LORD spake unto Moses,
saying,
24 This *is it* that *belongeth* unto the
[t]Levites: from twenty and five years
old and upward they shall go in [7]to
wait upon the service of the tabernacle of the congregation:
25 And from the age of fifty years
they shall [8]cease waiting upon the service *thereof*, and shall serve no more:
26 But shall minister with their brethren in the tabernacle of the congrega-

o Ex. 31.18. ch. 11.17. ch. 12.8.
4 That is, God.
p Ex. 25.22. Lev. 1.1. Heb. 4.16.
q Gen. 3.24. 1 Ki. 6.23. Ps. 18.10. Ps. 99.1. Heb. 1.14.

CHAP. 8

a Ex. 40.25. Lev. 24.1,2. Ps. 119.105, 130. Isa. 8.20. Matt. 5.14. John 1.9.
b Ex. 25.31.
c Ex 25.18.
d Ex. 25.40.
e Ps. 26.6. Isa. 52. 11. Heb. 7.26.
1 sin water. ch. 19.9,17.
2 let them cause a rasor to pass over, etc.
f Lev. 14.8.9.
g Lev. 2.1.
h Ex. 29.4.
i Lev. 8.3.
j Lev. 1.4.
3 wave.
4 wave offering.
5 they may be to execute, etc.
k Ex. 29.10. Lev. 1.4. Lev. 8.14. Lev. 16.21.
l ch. 3.45. ch. 16.9. Mal. 3.17.
m Ex. 29.24.
n ch. 3.12,45.
o Ex. 13.2,12, 13,15. Luke 2.23.
p ch. 3.9.
6 given.
q ch. 1.53. ch. 16.46.
r Rom. 15.16.
s 2 Chr. 30. 15. 2 Chr. 31.2.
t ch. 4.3. 1 Chr. 23.3, 24,27.
7 to war the warfare of, etc.
8 return from the warfare of the service.

tion, [u]to keep the charge, and shall do no service. Thus shalt thou do unto the Levites touching their charge.

CHAPTER 9

AND the LORD spake unto Moses in the wilderness of Sī́-nâi, in the first month of the second year after they were come out of the land of Egypt, saying,

2 Let the children of Israel also keep [a]the passover at his appointed season.

3 In the fourteenth day of this month, [1]at even, ye shall keep it in his appointed season: according to all the rites of it, and according to all the ceremonies thereof, shall ye keep it.

4 And Moses spake unto the children of Israel, that they should keep the passover.

5 And [b]they kept the passover on the fourteenth day of the first month at even in the wilderness of Sī́-nâi: according to all that the LORD commanded Moses, so did the children of Israel.

6 ¶ And there were certain men, who were [c]defiled by the dead body of a man, that they could not keep the passover on that day: and [d]they came before Moses and before Aaron on that day:

7 And those men said unto him, We *are* defiled by the dead body of a man: wherefore are we kept back, that we may [e]not offer an offering of the LORD in his appointed season among the children of Israel?

8 And Moses said unto them, Stand still, and [f]I will hear what the LORD will command concerning you.

9 ¶ And the LORD spake unto Moses, saying,

10 Speak unto the children of Israel, saying, If any man of you or of your posterity shall be unclean by reason of a dead body, or *be* in a journey afar off, yet he shall keep the passover unto the LORD.

11 The [g]fourteenth day of the second month at even they shall keep it, *and* eat *it* with unleavened bread and bitter *herbs*.

12 They [i]shall leave none of it unto the morning, [j]nor break any bone of it: [k]according to all the ordinances of the passover they shall keep it.

13 But the man that *is* clean, and is not in a journey, and forbeareth to keep the passover, even the same soul [l]shall be cut off from among his people: because he brought not the offering of the LORD in his appointed season, that man shall [m]bear his sin.

14 And if a stranger shall sojourn among you, and will keep the passover unto the LORD; according to the ordinance of the passover, and according to the manner thereof, so shall he do: ye [n]shall have one ordinance, both for the [2]stranger, and for him that was born in the land.

15 ¶ And on the day that the tabernacle was reared up the cloud covered the tabernacle, *namely*, the tent of the testimony: and [o]at even there was upon the tabernacle as it were the appearance of fire, until the morning.

16 So it was alway: the [p]cloud covered it *by day*, and the appearance of fire by night.

17 And when the cloud [q]was taken up from the tabernacle, then after that the children of Israel journeyed: and in the place where the cloud abode, there the children of Israel pitched their tents.

18 At the commandment of the LORD the children of Israel journeyed, and at the commandment of the LORD they pitched: as [r]long as the cloud abode upon the tabernacle they rested in their tents.

19 And when the cloud [3]tarried long upon the tabernacle many days, then the children of Israel kept the charge of the LORD, and journeyed not.

20 And *so* it was, when the cloud was a few days upon the tabernacle; according to the commandment of the LORD they abode in their tents, and according to the commandment of the LORD [s]they journeyed.

21 And *so* it was, when the cloud [4]abode [t]from even unto the morning, and *that* the cloud was taken up in the morning, then they journeyed: whether *it was* by day or by night that the cloud was taken up, they journeyed.

22 Or *whether it were* two days, or a month, or a year, that the cloud tarried upon the tabernacle, remaining thereon, the children of Israel abode in their tents, and journeyed not: [u]but when it was taken up, they journeyed.

23 At the commandment of the LORD they rested in the tents, and [v]at the commandment of the LORD they journeyed: they kept the charge of the LORD, at the commandment of the LORD by the hand of Moses.

u ch. 1.53. 1 Chr. 23. 28-32. Eze. 44.8,11.

CHAP. 9

a Ex. 12.1. Lev. 23.5. ch. 28.16. Deut. 16.1, 2. Heb. 10.1.
1 between the two evenings.
b Josh. 5.10.
c ch. 5.2. ch. 6.6,7. John 18.28.
d Ex. 18.15.
e 1 Cor. 5.7,8.
f Ps. 25.14. Ps. 85.8. Pro. 3.5,6. John 7.17. Eph. 1.9,18. Heb. 3.5,6.
g 2 Chr. 30.2, 15.
h Ex. 12.8.
i Ex. 12.10.
j John 19.36.
k Ex. 12.43.
l Gen. 17.14. Ex. 12.15. Lev. 17.4, 10, 14-16. Heb. 6.6. Heb. 12.25.
m ch. 5.31. Gal. 3.10. Heb. 10.26.
n Ex. 12.49.
2 Proselyte.
o Ex. 13.21.
p Ex. 13.21, 22. Deut. 1.33. Neh. 9.12.
q Ex. 40.36, 37. ch. 10.11, 33,34. Ps. 78.14. Isa. 49.10. John 10.4.
r 1 Cor. 10.1.
3 prolonged.
s Ps. 48.14. Pro. 3.5,6.
4 was.
t Matt. 28.20.
u Ex. 40.36, 37. Ps. 73.24. Isa. 63.14.
v Ps. 73.24. Isa. 63.14.

CHAPTER 10

AND the LORD spake unto Moses, saying,

2 Make thee two trumpets of silver; of a whole piece shalt thou make them: that thou mayest use them for the [a]calling of the assembly, and for the journeying of the camps.

3 And when [b]they shall blow with them, all [c]the assembly shall assemble themselves to thee at the door of the tabernacle of the congregation.

4 And if they blow *but* with one *trumpet*, then the princes, *which are* [d]heads of the thousands of Israel, shall gather themselves unto thee.

5 When ye blow an alarm, then the [e]camps that lie on the east parts shall go forward.

6 When ye blow an alarm the second time, then the camps that lie on the south side shall take their journey: they shall blow an alarm for their journeys.

7 But when the congregation is to be gathered together, ye shall blow, but ye shall not [f]sound an alarm.

8 And [g]the sons of Aaron, the priests, shall blow with the trumpets; and they shall be to you for an ordinance for ever throughout your generations.

9 And if ye go to war in your land against the enemy that [h]oppresseth you, then ye shall blow an alarm with the trumpets; and ye shall be [i]remembered before the LORD your God, and ye shall be saved from your enemies.

10 Also [j]in the day of your gladness, and in your solemn days, and in the beginnings of your months, ye shall blow with the trumpets over your burnt offerings, and over the sacrifices of your peace offerings; that they may be to you [k]for a memorial before your God: I *am* the LORD your God.

11 ¶ And it came to pass on the twentieth *day* of the second month, in the second year, that the cloud was [l]taken up from off the tabernacle of the testimony.

12 And the children of Israel took [m]their journeys out of the wilderness [n]of Sī´-năi; and the cloud rested in the [o]wilderness of Pâr´-ăn.

13 And they first took their journey [p]according to the commandment of the LORD by the hand of Moses.

14 ¶ In the first *place* went the standard of the camp of the children of Judah according to their armies: and over his host *was* Näh´-shŏn the son of Ăm-mĭn´-ă-dăb.

15 And over the host of the tribe of the children of Ĭs´-să-chär *was* Nĕth-ă-nēel the son of Zū-är.

16 And over the host of the tribe of the children of Zĕ-bū´-lŭn *was* Ē-lī´-ăb the son of Hē-lŏn.

17 And [q]the tabernacle was taken down; and the sons of Gĕr´-shŏn and the sons of Mĕ-râr´-ī set forward, bearing [r]the tabernacle.

18 ¶ And the standard of the camp of Reuben set forward according to their armies: and over his host *was* Ĕlī´-zūr the son of Shĕd´-ē-ūr.

19 And over the host of the tribe of the children of Simeon *was* Shĕ-lū´-mī-ĕl the son of Zū-rī-shăd´-dāi.

20 And over the host of the tribe of the children of Gad *was* Ē-lī´-ă-săph the son of Dēū´-ĕl.

21 And the Kō´-hăth-ītes set forward, bearing the [1]sanctuary: and [2]*the other* did set up the tabernacle against they came.

22 ¶ And the standard of the camp of the children of Ē-phră-ĭm set forward according to their armies: and over his host *was* Ē-lī´-shă-mă the son of Ăm´-mī-hŭd.

23 And over the host of the tribe of the children of Mă-năs´-sĕh *was* Gă-mā´-lī-ĕl the son of Pĕ-däh´-zūr.

24 And over the host of the tribe of the children of Benjamin *was* Ă-bī´-dăn the son of Gĭd-ĕ-ō´-nī.

25 ¶ And [s]the standard of the camp of the children of Dan set forward, *which was* the rereward of all the camps throughout their hosts: and over his host *was* Ā-hī-ē´-zĕr the son of Ăm-mī-shăd´-dāi.

26 And over the host of the tribe of the children of Asher *was* Pā´-gī-ĕl the son of Ŏc´-răn.

27 And over the host of the tribe of the children of Năph´-tă-lī *was* Ă-hī-ră the son of Ē´-năn.

28 [3]Thus [t]*were* the journeyings of the children of Israel according to their armies, when they set forward.

29 ¶ And Moses said unto Hō´-băb the son of [u]Ră-gū´-ĕl the Mĭd´-ĭ-ă-nīte Moses' father in law, We are journeying unto the place of which the LORD said, [v]I will give it you: come thou with us, and [w]we will do thee good: for [x]the LORD hath spoken good concerning Israel.

30 And he said unto him, I will not go; but I will depart to mine own land, and to my kindred.

31 And he said, Leave us not, I pray thee; forasmuch as thou knowest how we are to encamp in the wilderness,

CHAP. 10

a Ps. 81.3. Ps. 89.15. Isa. 1.13. Hosea 8.1. Joel 1.14.
b Jer. 4.5. Joel 2.15.
c Ps. 22.22. Ps. 35.18. Ps. 36.7,8. Ps. 40.9,10. Isa. 55.1-4. Zech. 8.21-23. Rev. 22.17.
d Ex. 18.21. ch. 1.16.
e ch. 2.3.
f Joel 2.1.
g ch. 31.6. Josh. 6.4. 1 Chr. 15.24. 2 Chr. 13.12.
h Judg. 2.18. Judg. 3.27. Judg. 6.9. 1 Sam. 10. 18. Ps. 106.42.
i Gen. 8.1. 1 Ki. 8.44. Ps. 106.4.
j Lev. 23.24. 1 Chr. 15.24. 2 Chr. 7.6. Ezra 3.10. Neh. 12.35. Ps. 81.3.
k Ex. 28.29. Josh. 4.7. 1 Cor. 11. 24-26.
l ch. 9.17.
m Ex. 40.36.
n ch. 1.1.
o ch. 12.16. ch. 13.3,26. Deut. 1.1. Deut. 33.2. 1 Sam. 25.1. Hab. 3.3.
p ch. 2.34.
q ch. 1.51.
r ch. 4.24,31.
1 The most holy furniture.
2 That is, the Gershonites and the Merarites.
s Josh. 6.9.
3 These.
t Ps. 80.1. Song 6.10.
u Ex. 2.18.
v Gen. 12.7.
w Judg. 1.16.
x Gen. 32.12.

and thou mayest be to us [y]instead of eyes.

32 And it shall be, if thou go with us, yea, it shall be, that what goodness the LORD shall do unto us, the same will we do unto thee.

33 ¶ And they departed from [z]the mount of the LORD three days' journey: and the ark of the covenant of the LORD [a]went before them in the three days' journey, to search out a resting place for them.

34 And [b]the cloud of the LORD *was* upon them by day, when they went out of the camp.

35 And it came to pass, when the ark set forward, that Moses said, Rise [c]up, LORD, and let thine enemies be scattered; and let them that hate thee flee before thee.

36 And when it rested, he said, Return, [d]O LORD, unto the [4]many thousands of Israel.

CHAPTER 11

AND [a]*when* the people [1]complained, [2]it displeased the LORD: and the LORD heard *it;* and his anger was kindled; and the fire [b]of the LORD burnt among them, and consumed *them that were* in the uttermost parts of the camp.

2 And the people cried unto Moses; and when Moses [c]prayed unto the LORD, the fire [3]was quenched.

3 And he called the name of the place [4]Tăb'-ĕ-răh: because the fire of the LORD burnt among them.

4 ¶ And the [d]mixt multitude that *was* among them [5]fell a lusting: and the children of Israel also [6]wept again, and said, Who [e]shall give us flesh to eat?

5 We [f]remember the fish, which we did eat in Egypt freely; the cucumbers, and the melons, and the leeks, and the onions, and the garlick:

6 But now our soul *is* dried away: *there is* nothing at all, beside this măn'-nă, *before* our eyes.

7 And the măn'-nă *was* as coriander seed, and the [7]colour thereof as the colour [g]of bdellium.

8 *And* the people went about, and gathered *it*, and ground *it* in mills, or beat *it* in a mortar, and baked *it* in pans, and made cakes of it: and the taste of it was as the taste of fresh oil.

9 And when the dew fell upon the camp in the night, the măn'-nă fell upon it.

10 ¶ Then Moses heard the people weep throughout their families, every man in the door of his tent: and the anger of the LORD was kindled greatly; Moses also was displeased.

11 And [h]Moses said unto the LORD, Wherefore hast thou afflicted thy servant? and wherefore have I not found favour in thy sight, that thou layest the burden of all this people upon me?

12 Have I conceived all this people? have I begotten them, that thou shouldest say unto me, [i]Carry them in thy bosom, as a nursing [j]father beareth the sucking child, unto the land which thou [k]swarest unto their fathers?

13 Whence [l]should I have flesh to give unto all this people? for they weep unto me, saying, Give us flesh, that we may eat.

14 I [m]am not able to bear all this people alone, because *it is* too heavy for me.

15 And if thou deal thus with me, kill [n]me, I pray thee, out of hand, if I have found favour in thy sight; and let me not see [o]my wretchedness.

16 ¶ And the LORD said unto Moses, Gather unto me [p]seventy men of the elders of Israel, whom thou knowest to be the elders of the people, and officers over them; and bring them unto the tabernacle of the congregation, that they may stand there with thee.

17 And I will [q]come down and talk with thee there: and [r]I will take of the spirit which *is* upon thee, and will put *it* upon them; and they shall bear the burden of the people with thee, that thou bear *it* not thyself alone.

18 And say thou unto the people, Sanctify [s]yourselves against to morrow, and ye shall eat flesh: for ye have wept [t]in the ears of the LORD, saying, Who shall give us flesh to eat? for [u]*it was* well with us in Egypt: therefore the LORD will give you flesh, and ye shall eat.

19 Ye shall not eat one day, nor two days, nor five days, neither ten days, nor twenty days;

20 *But* even a [8]whole month, until it come out at your nostrils, and it be loathsome unto you: because that ye have despised the LORD which *is* among you, and have wept before him, saying, Why came we forth out of Egypt?

21 And Moses said, The people, among whom I *am, are* six hundred thousand footmen; and thou hast said, I will give them flesh, that they may eat a whole month.

y Job 29.15.
z Ex. 3.1.
a Deut. 1.33. Jer. 31.2.
b Neh. 9.12, 19. Ps. 105.39.
c Ps. 68.1,2. Isa. 51.9.
d Ps. 90.14-17. Ps. 132.8.
4 ten thousand thousands.

CHAP. 11

a Ex. 15.23, 24. Deut. 9.22. Lam. 3.39.
1 Or, were as it were complainers.
2 it was evil in the ears of, etc.
b Lev. 10.2. 2 Ki. 1.12.
c Jas. 5.16.
3 sunk.
4 That is, A burning.
d Ex. 12.38.
5 lusted a lust.
6 returned and wept.
e 1 Cor. 10.6.
f Ex. 16.3. Matt. 6.24-34. Rom. 8.7. Phil. 3.19.
7 eye of it as the eye of.
g Gen. 2.12.
h Ex. 17.4. Deut. 1.12. Jer. 15.10, 18. Mal. 3.14. 2 Cor. 11.28.
i Isa. 40.11. Eze. 34.23.
j Isa. 49.23. 1 Thes. 2.7.
k Gen. 22.16, 17. Gen. 26.3. Ex. 13.5.
l 2 Ki. 4.43. Matt. 15.33. Mark 8.4.
m Ex. 18.18.
n 1 Ki. 19.4. Job 6.8-10. Jonah 4.3.
o Zeph. 3.15.
p Ex. 24.1,9.
q Gen. 11.5.
r 1 Sam. 10.6. 2 Ki. 2.15. Job 32.8. Joel 2.28.
s Ex. 19.10.
t Ex. 16.7.
u Acts 7.39.
8 month of days.

22 Shall [v]the flocks and the herds be slain for them, to suffice them? or shall all the fish of the sea be gathered together for them, to suffice them?

23 And the LORD said unto Moses, Is [w]the LORD's hand waxed short? thou shalt see now whether [x]my word shall come to pass unto thee or not.

24 ¶ And Moses went out, and told the people the words of the LORD, and gathered the seventy men of the elders of the people, and set them round about the tabernacle.

25 And the LORD [y]came down in a cloud, and spake unto him, and took of the spirit that *was* upon him, and gave *it* unto the seventy elders: and it came to pass, [z]*that*, when the spirit rested upon them, they [a]prophesied, and did not cease.

26 But there remained two *of the* men in the camp, the name of the one *was* Ĕl'-dăd, and the name of the other Mē'-dăd: and the spirit rested upon them; and they *were* of them that were written, but [b]went not out unto the tabernacle: and they prophesied in the camp.

27 And there ran a young man, and told Moses, and said, Ĕl'-dăd and Mē'-dăd do prophesy in the camp.

28 And Joshua the son of Nun, the servant of Moses, *one* of his young men, answered and said, My lord Moses, [c]forbid them.

29 And Moses said unto him, Enviest thou for my sake? [d]would God that all the LORD's people were prophets, *and* that the LORD would put his spirit upon them!

30 And Moses gat him into the camp, he and the elders of Israel.

31 ¶ And there went forth a [e]wind from the LORD, and brought quails from the sea, and let *them* fall by the camp, as it were [9]a day's journey on this side, and as it were a day's journey on the other side, round about the camp, and as it were two cubits *high* upon the face of the earth.

32 And the people stood up all that day, and all *that* night, and all the next day, and they gathered the quails: he that gathered least gathered ten [f]hō'-mĕrs: and they spread *them* all abroad for themselves round about the camp.

33 And [g]while the flesh *was* yet between their teeth, ere it was chewed, the wrath of the LORD was kindled against the people, and the LORD smote the people with a very great plague.

[v] 2 Ki. 7.2. Matt. 15.33. Mark 6.37.
[w] Isa. 50.2.
[x] Eze. 12.25.
[y] Ex. 34.5. ch. 12.5.
[z] 2 Ki. 2.15.
[a] 1 Sam. 10. 5,6. Joel 2.28. Acts 2.17, 18. 1 Cor. 14.1.
[b] 1 Sam. 20. 26. Jer. 36.5.
[c] Mark 9.38. John 3.26.
[d] Acts 26.29. 1 Cor. 14.5.
[e] Ps. 78.26.
9 the way of a day.
[f] Ex. 16.36.
[g] Ps. 78.30.
10 That is, The graves of lust.
[h] ch. 33.17. Deut. 1.1.
11 they were in, etc.

CHAP. 12

1 Or, Cushite.
[a] Ex. 2.21.
2 taken.
[b] Ex. 15.20. Micah 6.4.
[c] Gen. 29.33. 2 Ki. 19.4. Ps. 94.9. Isa. 37.4.
[d] Ps. 147.6. Ps. 149.4. Matt. 5.5. 1 Tim. 6.11. 2 Tim. 2.25. 1 Pet. 3.4.
[e] Ps. 76.9.
[f] Ex. 34.5. ch. 16.19.
[g] Gen. 46.2. Job 33.15. Luke 1.11, 22.
[h] Matt. 1.20.
[i] Ps. 105.26.
[j] Heb. 3.2,5.
[k] Deut. 34. 10.
[l] 1 Cor. 13.12.
[m] Ex. 33.19.
[n] 2 Pet. 2.10.
[o] Deut. 24.9.
[p] 2 Ki. 5.27. 2 Chr. 26.19.
[q] 2 Sam. 19. 19.
[r] Ps. 88.4. Eph. 2.1-5. Col. 2.13. 1 Tim. 5.6.
[s] Jas. 5.16.

34 And he called the name of that place [10]Kĭb'-rōth–hăt-tā'-ă-văh: because there they buried the people that lusted.

35 *And* [h]the people journeyed from Kĭb'-rōth–hăt-tā'-ă-văh unto Hă-zē'-rōth; and [11]abode at Hă-zē'-rōth.

CHAPTER 12

AND Miriam and Aaron spake against Moses because of the [1]Ē-thĭ-ō'-pĭ-ăn woman whom he had married: for [a]he had [2]married an Ē-thĭ-ō'-pĭ-ăn woman.

2 And they said, Hath the LORD indeed spoken only by Moses? [b]hath he not spoken also by us? And the LORD [c]heard *it*.

3 (Now the man Moses *was* [d]very meek, above all the men which *were* upon the face of the earth.)

4 And [e]the LORD spake suddenly unto Moses, and unto Aaron, and unto Miriam, Come out ye three unto the tabernacle of the congregation. And they three came out.

5 And [f]the LORD came down in the pillar of the cloud, and stood *in* the door of the tabernacle, and called Aaron and Miriam: and they both came forth.

6 And he said, Hear now my words: If there be a prophet among you, *I* the LORD will make myself known unto him [g]in a vision, *and* will speak unto him [h]in a dream.

7 My [i]servant Moses *is* not so, who [j]*is* faithful in all mine house.

8 With him will I speak [k]mouth to mouth, even [l]apparently, and not in dark speeches; and [m]the similitude of the LORD shall he behold: wherefore then [n]were ye not afraid to speak against my servant Moses?

9 And the anger of the LORD was kindled against them; and he departed.

10 And the cloud departed from off the tabernacle; and, [o]behold, Miriam *became* [p]leprous, *white* as snow: and Aaron looked upon Miriam, and, behold, *she was* leprous.

11 And Aaron said unto Moses, Alas, my lord, I beseech thee, [q]lay not the sin upon us, wherein we have done foolishly, and wherein we have sinned.

12 Let her not be [r]as one dead, of whom the flesh is half consumed when he cometh out of his mother's womb.

13 And Moses [s]cried unto the LORD, saying, Heal her now, O God, I beseech thee.

14 ¶ And the LORD said unto Moses,

[t]If her father had but spit in her face, should she not be ashamed seven days? let her be shut [u]out from the camp seven days, and after that let her be received in *again*.

15 And [v]Miriam was shut out from the camp seven days: and the people journeyed not till Miriam was brought in *again*.

16 And afterward the people removed from Hă-zē-rōth, and pitched in the wilderness of Pâr-ăn.

CHAPTER 13

AND the LORD spake unto Moses, saying,

2 Send [a]thou men, that they may search the land of Canaan, which I give unto the children of Israel: of every tribe of their fathers shall ye send a man, every one a ruler among them.

3 And Moses by the commandment of the LORD sent them from the wilderness of Pâr-ăn: all those men *were* heads of the children of Israel.

4 And these *were* their names: of the tribe of Reuben, Shăm-mū-ă the son of Zăc-cŭr.

5 Of the tribe of Simeon, Shā-phăt the son of Hôr-ī.

6 Of the tribe of Judah, [b]Caleb the son of Jĕ-phŭn-nĕh.

7 Of the tribe of Ĭs-să-c͟hăr, Ī-găl the son of Joseph.

8 Of the tribe of Ē-phră-ĭm, Ō-shē-ă the son of Nun.

9 Of the tribe of Benjamin, Păl-tī the son of Rā-phû.

10 Of the tribe of Zĕ-bū-lŭn, Găd-dĭ-ĕl the son of Sō-dī.

11 Of the tribe of Joseph, *namely*, of the tribe of Mă-năs-sĕh, Găd-dī the son of Sū-sī.

12 Of the tribe of Dan, Ăm-mī-ĕl the son of Gĕ-măl-lī.

13 Of the tribe of Asher, Sē-thŭr the son of Michael.

14 Of the tribe of Năph-tă-lī, Năh-bī the son of Vŏph-sī.

15 Of the tribe of Gad, Geū-ĕl the son of Mā-c͟hī.

16 These *are* the names of the men which Moses sent to spy out the land. And Moses called [c]Ō-shē-ă the son of Nun [1]Jĕ-hŏsh-ū-ă.

17 ¶ And Moses sent them to spy out the land of Canaan, and said unto them, Get you up this *way* [2]southward, and go up into [d]the mountain:

18 And see the land, what it *is;* and the people that dwelleth therein, whether they *be* strong or weak, few or many;

19 And what the land *is* that they dwell in, whether it *be* good or bad; and what cities *they be* that they dwell in, whether in tents, or in strong holds;

20 And what the land *is*, whether it *be* fat [e]or lean, whether there be wood therein, or not. And [f]be ye of good courage, and bring of the fruit of the land. Now the time *was* the time of the firstripe grapes.

21 ¶ So they went up, and searched the land from the wilderness of Zin unto Rē-hŏb, as men come to Hā-măth.

22 And they ascended by the south, and came unto Hē-brŏn; where [g]Ă-hī-măn, Shē-shāī, and Tăl-māī, the children of Anak, *were*. (Now Hē-brŏn was built seven years [h]before Zō-ăn in Egypt.)

23 And they came unto the [3]brook of Ĕsh-cŏl, and cut down from thence a branch with one cluster of grapes, and they bare it between two upon a staff; and *they brought* of the pomegranates, and of the figs.

24 The place was called the [4]brook [5]Ĕsh-cŏl, because of the cluster of grapes which the children of Israel cut down from thence.

25 And they returned from searching of the land after forty days.

26 ¶ And they went and came to Moses, and to Aaron, and to all the congregation of the children of Israel, unto the wilderness of Pâr-ăn, to Kā-dĕsh; and brought back word unto them, and unto all the congregation, and shewed them the fruit of the land.

27 And they told him, and said, We came unto the land whither thou sentest us, and surely it floweth with [i]milk and honey; and this [j]*is* the fruit of it.

28 Nevertheless [k]the people *be* strong that dwell in the land, and the cities *are* walled, *and* very great: and moreover we saw the children of Anak there.

29 The [l]Ă-măl-ĕk-ītes dwell in the land of the south: and the Hittites, and the Jĕb-ū-sītes, and the Amorites, dwell in the mountains: and the Canaanites dwell by the sea, and by the coast of Jordan.

30 And [m]Caleb stilled the people before Moses, and said, Let us go up at once, and possess it; for we are well able to overcome it.

31 But the men that went up with him said, We be not able to go up against the people; for they *are* stronger than we.

---

t Heb. 12.9.
u Lev. 13.46. ch. 5.2,3.
v Deut. 24.9. 2 Chr. 26.20.

CHAP. 13

a ch. 32.8. Deut. 1.22.
b ch. 14.6,30. ch. 26.65. ch. 34.19. Josh. 14.6.
c Ex. 17.9.
1 He shall save.
2 Into the south country.
d Gen. 14.10. ch. 14.40. Deut. 1.19. Judg. 1.9,19.
e Deut. 8.7,8. Neh. 9.25-35. Eze. 20.6. Eze. 34.14.
f Deut. 31.6. Josh. 1.6,9. Heb. 13.6.
g Josh. 11.21, 22. Josh. 15.13, 14. Judg. 1.10.
h Ps. 78.12. Isa. 19.11. Isa. 30.4.
3 Or, valley.
4 Or, valley.
5 That is, A cluster of grapes.
i Ex. 3.8. Ex. 13.5. Ex. 33.3. Deut. 1.25.
j Deut. 1.25.
k Deut. 1.28. Deut. 9.1,2.
l Ex. 17.8. ch. 14.43. Judg. 6.3. 1 Sam. 14. 48. 1 Sam. 15.3.
m Josh. 14.7. Ps. 60.12. Ps. 118.10. Isa. 11.10. Rom. 8.31. Phil. 4.13. Heb. 11.33, 34.

32 And they [n]brought up an evil report of the land which they had
searched unto the children of Israel,
saying, The land, through which we
have gone to search it, *is* a land that
[6]eateth up the inhabitants thereof;
and [o]all the people that we saw in it
are [7]men of a great stature.
33 And there we saw the [p]giants, the
sons of Anak, *which come* of the giants:
and we were in our own sight [q]as grasshoppers, and so we were in their sight.

CHAPTER 14

AND all the congregation lifted up
their voice, and cried; and the
people wept that night.
2 And [a]all the children of Israel murmured against Moses and against
Aaron: and the whole congregation
said unto them, Would God [b]that we
had died in the land of Egypt! or
would God we had died in this wilderness!
3 And wherefore hath the LORD
brought us unto this land, to fall by
the sword, that our wives and our children should be a prey? were it not better for us to return into Egypt?
4 And they said one to another, Let
[c]us make a captain, and let us return
into Egypt.
5 Then Moses and Aaron fell on their
faces before all the assembly of the
congregation of the children of Israel.
6 ¶ And Joshua the son of Nun, and
Caleb the son of Jĕ-phŭn'-nĕh, *which*
were of them that searched the land,
rent their clothes:
7 And they spake unto all the company of the children of Israel, saying,
The land, which we passed through to
search it, *is* an exceeding good land.
8 If the LORD [d]delight in us, then he
will bring us into this land, and give
it us; [e]a land which floweth with milk
and honey.
9 Only [f]rebel not ye against the
LORD, neither [g]fear ye the people of
the land; for they [h]*are* bread for us:
their [1]defence is departed from them,
[i]and the LORD *is* with us: fear them
not.
10 But [j]all the congregation bade
stone them with stones. And [k]the
glory of the LORD appeared in the
tabernacle of the congregation before
all the children of Israel.
11 ¶ And the LORD said unto Moses,
How long will this people [l]provoke
me? and how long will it be ere they
[m]believe me, for all the signs which I
have shewed among them?

n Matt. 23.13.
6 Perhaps a plague was then in the country.
o Amos 2.9.
7 men of statures.
p 1 Sam. 17. 4-7.
q Isa. 40.22.
CHAP. 14
a Ps. 106.25.
b Deut. 28. 68.
c Neh. 9.17. Acts 7.39. Heb. 11.15.
d Deut. 10. 15. 2 Sam. 15. 25. 1 Ki. 10.9. Ps. 22.8. Ps. 147.10, 11. Isa. 62.4.
e ch. 13.27.
f Deut. 9.7, 23,24.
g Deut. 20.3.
h ch. 24.8.
1 shadow.
i Gen. 48.21. Ex. 33.16. Deut. 20.1. 2 Chr. 15.2. Isa. 41.10.
j Ex. 17.4.
k Ex. 16.10. Lev. 9.23.
l Heb. 3.8.
m Ps. 78.22. John 12.37.
n Ex. 32.10.
o Eze. 20.9.
p Ex. 15.14.
q Neh. 9.12.
r Josh. 7.9.
s Ps. 103.8. Ps. 145.8. Jonah 4.2.
t Ex. 34.7.
2 Or, hitherto.
u Jas. 5.16. 1 John 5.14.
v Ps. 72.19. Isa. 5.16. Isa. 11.9. Eze. 18.3. Hab. 2.14. Rev. 11.15.
w Deut. 1.31, 34. Ps. 95.11. Heb. 4.6,7.
x Gen. 31.7.
3 If they see the land.
y Deut. 1.35. Ps. 95.11. Ps. 106.26. Eze. 20.15. Heb. 3.18.
z Ps. 25.13. Ps. 37.11. Isa. 33.15. Matt. 5.5.

12 I will smite them with the pestilence, and disinherit them, and [n]will
make of thee a greater nation and
mightier than they.
13 ¶ And [o]Moses said unto the LORD,
Then the Egyptians shall hear *it*, (for
thou broughtest up this people in thy
might from among them;)
14 And they will tell *it* to the inhabitants of this land: [p]*for* they have heard
that thou LORD *art* among this people, that thou LORD art seen face to
face, and *that* thy [q]cloud standeth over
them, and *that* thou goest before them,
by day time in a pillar of a cloud, and
in a pillar of fire by night.
15 ¶ Now *if* thou shalt kill *all* this
people as one man, then the nations
which have heard the fame of thee
will speak, saying,
16 Because the LORD was not [r]able
to bring this people into the land
which he sware unto them, therefore
he hath slain them in the wilderness.
17 And now, I beseech thee, let the
power of my Lord be great, according
as thou hast spoken, saying,
18 The LORD *is* [s]longsuffering, and
of great mercy, forgiving iniquity and
transgression, and by no means clearing *the guilty*, [t]visiting the iniquity of
the fathers upon the children unto the
third and fourth *generation*.
19 Pardon, I beseech thee, the iniquity of this people according unto
the greatness of thy mercy, and as
thou hast forgiven this people, from
Egypt [2]even until now.
20 And the LORD said, I [u]have pardoned according to thy word:
21 But *as* truly *as* I live, [v]all the earth
shall be filled with the glory of the
LORD.
22 Because [w]all those men which
have seen my glory, and my miracles,
which I did in Egypt and in the wilderness, and have tempted me now [x]these
ten times, and have not hearkened to
my voice;
23 [3]Surely [y]they shall not see the land
which I sware unto their fathers,
neither shall any of them that provoked me see it:
24 But my servant Caleb, because he
had another spirit with him, and hath
followed me fully, him will I bring into
the land whereinto he went; and [z]his
seed shall possess it.
25 (Now the Ă-măl'-ĕk-ītes and the
Canaanites dwelt in the valley.) To
morrow turn you, and get you into the
wilderness by the way of the Red
sea.

26¶ And the LORD spake unto Moses
and unto Aaron, saying,
27 How [a]long *shall I bear with* this
evil congregation, which murmur
against me? I [b]have heard the murmurings of the children of Israel,
which they murmur against me.
28 Say unto them, [c]*As truly as* I live,
saith the LORD, as ye have spoken in
mine ears, so will I do to you:
29 Your carcases shall fall in this
wilderness; and [d]all that were numbered of you, according to your whole
number, from twenty years old and
upward, which have murmured
against me,
30 Doubtless ye shall not come into
the land, *concerning* which I [4]sware to
make you dwell therein, save [e]Caleb
the son of Jĕ-phŭn'-nĕh, and Joshua
the son of Nun.
31 But your little ones, which ye said
should be a prey, them will I bring in,
and they shall know the land which
[f]ye have despised.
32 But *as for* you, [g]your carcases,
they shall fall in this wilderness.
33 And your children shall [5]wander
[h]in the wilderness [i]forty years, and
bear your whoredoms, until your carcases be wasted in the wilderness.
34 After [j]the number of the days in
which ye searched the land, *even*
forty [k]days, each day for a year, shall
ye bear your iniquities, *even* forty
years, [l]and ye shall know my [6]breach
of promise.
35 I [m]the LORD have said, I will surely do it unto all this evil congregation,
that are gathered together against me:
in this wilderness they shall be consumed, and there they shall die.
36 And [n]the men, which Moses sent
to search the land, who returned, and
made all the congregation to murmur
against him, by bringing up a slander
upon the land,
37 Even those men that did bring
up the evil report upon the land, died
[o]by the plague before the LORD.
38 But [p]Joshua the son of Nun, and
Caleb the son of Jĕ-phŭn'-nĕh, *which*
were of the men that went to search
the land, lived *still*.
39 And Moses told these sayings unto all the children of Israel: and [q]the
people mourned greatly.
40 ¶ And they rose up early in the
morning, and gat them up into the top
of the mountain, saying, Lo, we [r]*be*
here, and will go up unto the place
which the LORD hath promised: for
we have sinned.

a Ex. 16.28. Matt. 17.17. Mark 9.19.
b Ex. 16.12. 1 Cor. 10.10.
c Heb. 3.17.
d ch. 26.64.
4 lifted up my hand.
e Deut. 1.36, 38.
f Ps. 106.24. Pro. 1.25,26. Heb. 12.16, 17.
g 1 Cor. 10.5.
5 Or, feed.
h Ps. 107.40.
i Deut. 2.14.
j ch. 13.25.
k Ps. 95.10.
l 1 Ki. 8.56. Ps. 77.8. Heb. 4.1.
6 Or, interruption.
m ch. 23.19.
n ch. 13.31.
o Jer. 28.16, 17. 1 Cor. 10.10. Heb. 3.17. Jude 5.
p Josh. 14.6.
q Pro. 19.3. Matt. 8.12. Heb. 12.17.
r Deut. 1.41. Eccl. 9.3. Matt. 7.21. Luke 13.25.
s 2 Chr. 24. 20.
t Job 9.4. Isa. 59.1,2. Jer. 2.37. 1 Cor. 10.22.
u Deut. 1.42. Ps. 44.1-3.
v Judg. 16.20.

CHAP. 15

a Lev. 23.10.
b Ex. 29.18, 25,41. Lev. 1.2,3.
c Lev. 7.16. Lev. 22.18, 21.
1 separating.
d Lev. 23.8, 12. ch. 28.19,27. ch. 29.2,8, 13. Deut. 16.10.
e Gen. 8.21. Lev. 1.9. Eze. 20.41. 2 Cor. 2.15. Eph. 5.2. Phil. 4.18.
f Lev. 2.1. Lev. 6.14. Lev. 7.9,10. Lev. 23.13. Isa. 66.20.
g Ex. 29.40.
h Lev. 14.10.
i ch. 28.7.
j Lev. 7.11.

41 And Moses said, Wherefore now
do ye transgress [s]the commandment
of [t]the LORD? but it shall not prosper.
42 Go [u]not up, for the LORD *is* not
among you; that ye be not smitten before your enemies.
43 For the Ă-măl'-ĕk-ītes and the Canaanites *are* there before you, and ye
shall fall by the sword: because [v]ye
are turned away from the LORD, therefore the LORD will not be with you.
44 But they presumed to go up unto
the hill top: nevertheless the ark of
the covenant of the LORD, and Moses,
departed not out of the camp.
45 Then the Ă-măl'-ĕk-ītes came
down, and the Canaanites which dwelt
in that hill, and smote them, and discomfited them, *even* unto Hôr'-măh.

CHAPTER 15

AND the LORD spake unto Moses,
saying,
2 Speak [a]unto the children of Israel,
and say unto them, When ye be come
into the land of your habitations,
which I give unto you,
3 And [b]will make an offering by fire
unto the LORD, a burnt offering, or a
sacrifice [c]in [1]performing a vow, or in
a freewill offering, [d]or in your solemn
feasts, to make a sweet [e]savour unto
the LORD, of the herd, or of the flock:
4 Then [f]shall he that offereth his
offering unto the LORD bring [g]a meat
offering of a tenth deal of flour
mingled with [h]the fourth *part* of an
hĭn of oil.
5 And [i]the fourth *part* of an hĭn of
wine for a drink offering shalt thou
prepare with the burnt offering or
sacrifice, for one lamb.
6 Or for a ram, thou shalt prepare
for a meat offering two tenth deals of
flour mingled with the third *part* of an
hĭn of oil.
7 And for a drink offering thou shalt
offer the third *part* of an hĭn of wine,
for a sweet savour unto the LORD.
8 And when thou preparest a bullock
for a burnt offering, or *for* a sacrifice
in performing a vow, or peace [j]offer-
ings unto the LORD:
9 Then shall he bring with a bullock
a meat offering of three tenth deals of
flour mingled with half an hĭn of oil.
10 And thou shalt bring for a drink
offering half an hĭn of wine, *for* an
offering made by fire, of a sweet savour unto the LORD.
11 Thus shall it be done for one bullock, or for one ram, or for a lamb, or
a kid.

12 According to the number that ye shall prepare, so shall ye do to every one according to their number.

13 All that are born of the country shall do these things after this manner, in offering an offering made by fire, of a sweet savour unto the LORD.

14 And if a stranger sojourn with you, or whosoever *be* among you in your generations, and will offer an offering made by fire, of a sweet savour unto the LORD; as ye do, so he shall do.

15 One [k]ordinance *shall be both* for you of the congregation, and also for the stranger that sojourneth *with you*, an ordinance for ever in your generations: as ye *are*, so shall the stranger be before the LORD.

16 One law and one manner shall be for you, and for the stranger that sojourneth with you.

17 ¶ And the LORD spake unto Moses, saying,

18 Speak unto the children of Israel, and say unto them, When ye come into the land whither I bring you,

19 Then it shall be, that, when ye eat of the [l]bread of the land, ye shall offer up an heave offering unto the LORD.

20 Ye [m]shall offer up a cake of the first of your dough *for* an heave offering: as *ye do* [n]the heave offering of the threshingfloor, so shall ye heave it.

21 Of the first of your dough ye shall give unto the LORD an heave offering in your generations.

22 ¶ And [o]if ye have erred, and not observed all these commandments, which the LORD hath spoken unto Moses,

23 *Even* all that the LORD hath commanded you by the hand of Moses, from the day that the LORD commanded *Moses*, and henceforward among your generations;

24 Then it shall be, [p]if *ought* be committed by ignorance [2]without the knowledge of the congregation, that all the congregation shall offer one young bullock for a burnt offering, for a sweet savour unto the LORD, with his meat offering, and his drink offering, according to the [3]manner, and one [q]kid of the goats for a sin offering.

25 And [r]the priest shall make an atonement for all the congregation of the children of Israel, and it shall be forgiven them; for it *is* ignorance: and they shall bring their offering, a sacrifice made by fire unto the LORD, and their sin offering before the LORD, for their ignorance:

26 And it shall be forgiven all the congregation of the children of Israel, and the stranger that sojourneth among them; seeing all the people *were* in ignorance.

27 ¶ And [s]if any soul sin through ignorance, then he shall bring a she goat of the first year for a sin offering.

28 And [t]the priest shall make an atonement for the soul that sinneth ignorantly, when he sinneth by ignorance before the LORD, to make an atonement for him; and it shall be forgiven him.

29 Ye shall have one law for him that [4]sinneth through ignorance, *both for* him that is born among the children of Israel, and for the stranger that sojourneth among them.

30 ¶ But [u]the soul that doeth *ought* [5]presumptuously, *whether he be* born in the land, or a stranger, the same reproached the LORD; and that soul shall be cut off from among his people.

31 Because he hath [v]despised the word of the LORD, and hath broken his commandment, that soul shall utterly be cut off; his [w]iniquity *shall be* upon him.

32 ¶ And while the children of Israel were in the wilderness, [x]they found a man that gathered sticks upon the sabbath day.

33 And they that found him gathering sticks brought him unto Moses and Aaron, and unto all the congregation.

34 And they puth im [y]in ward, because it was not declared what should be done to him.

35 And the LORD said unto Moses, The [z]man shall be surely put to death: all the congregation shall stone [a]him with stones without the camp.

36 And all the congregation brought him without the camp, and stoned him with stones, and he died; as the LORD commanded Moses.

37 ¶ And the LORD spake unto Moses, saying,

38 Speak unto the children of Israel, and bid [b]them that they make them fringes in the borders of their garments throughout their generations, and that they put upon the fringe of the borders a ribband of blue:

39 And it shall be unto you for a fringe, that ye may look upon it, and remember all the commandments of the LORD, and do them; and that ye [c]seek not after your own heart and your own eyes, after which ye use [d]to go a whoring:

k Lev. 24.22. ch. 9.14. Gal. 3.28. Col. 3.11.
l Josh. 5.11, 12.
m Ex. 23.19. Deut. 26.2, 10. Neh. 10.37. Pro. 3.9.
n Lev. 2.14. Lev. 23.10.
o Lev. 4.2. 1 John 2.1.
p Lev. 4.13.
2 from the eyes.
3 Or, ordinance.
q Lev. 4.23. ch. 28.15. Ezra 6.17.
r Lev. 4.20. Dan. 9.24. Rom. 5.11. Heb. 2.17. Heb. 10.10, 11, 12. 1 John 1.7.
s Lev. 4.27, 28. Ps. 19.13. Luke 12.48.
t Lev. 4.35.
4 doth.
u Deut. 17. 12. Ps. 19.13. Rom. 10.16. Heb. 10.26. 2 Pet. 2.10.
5 with an high hand.
v 2 Sam. 12.9. Pro. 13.13. Isa. 30.12. Heb. 10.28.
w Eze. 18.20.
x Ex. 35.2, 3.
y Lev. 24.12.
z Ex. 31.14, 15. Gal. 3.5.
a 1 Ki. 21.13. Acts 7.58.
b Deut. 22.12. Matt. 9.20. Matt. 23.5. Luke 8.43, 44.
c Deut. 29.19. Job 31.7. Jer. 9.14. Eze. 6.9.
d Lev. 34.15, 16. Ps. 73.27. Hosea 2.2. Jas. 4.4.

40 That ye may remember, and do
all my commandments, and be holy
[e]unto your God.
41 I *am* the LORD your God, which
brought you out of the land of Egypt,
to be your God: I *am* the LORD your
God.

CHAPTER 16

NOW [a]Kôr'-ăh, the son of Ĭz'-hār,
the son of Kō'-hăth, the son of
Levi, and Dā'-thăn and Ă-bī'-răm, the
sons of Ē-lī'-ăb, and On, the son of
Pē'-lĕth, sons of Reuben, took *men:*
2 And they rose up before Moses,
with certain of the children of Israel,
two hundred and fifty princes of the
assembly, famous in [b]the congregation, men of renown:
3 And [c]they gathered themselves together against Moses and against
Aaron, and said unto them, [1]*Ye take*
too much upon you, seeing [d]all the
congregation *are* holy, every one of
them, [e]and the LORD *is* among them:
wherefore then lift ye up yourselves
above the congregation of the LORD?
4 And when Moses heard *it*, [f]he fell
upon his face:
5 And he spake unto Kôr'-ăh and unto all his company, saying, Even to
morrow the LORD will shew who [g]*are*
his, and *who is* [h]holy; and will cause
him to come near unto him: even *him*
whom he hath [i]chosen will he cause to
come [j]near unto him.
6 This do; Take you censers, Kôr'-
ăh, and all his company;
7 And put fire therein, and put incense in them before the LORD to
morrow: and it shall be *that* the man
whom the LORD doth choose, he *shall*
be holy: *ye take* too much upon you,
ye sons of Levi.
8 And Moses said unto Kôr'-ăh,
Hear, I pray you, ye sons of Levi:
9 *Seemeth it but* [k]a small thing unto
you, that the God of Israel hath [l]sep-
arated you from the congregation of
Israel, to bring you near to himself
to do the service of the tabernacle of
the LORD, and to stand before the
congregation to minister unto them?
10 And he hath brought thee near *to*
him, and all thy brethren the sons of
Levi with thee: and seek ye the priesthood also?
11 For which cause *both* thou and all
thy company *are* gathered together
against the LORD: and [m]what *is*
Aaron, that ye murmur against him?
12 ¶ And Moses sent to call Dā'-thăn
and Ă-bī'-răm, the sons of Ē-lī'-ăb:
which said, We will not come up:

e Lev. 11.44, 45. Matt. 5.48. Rom. 12.1. Col. 1.22. 1 Thes. 5.8. 1 Pet. 1.15.
CHAP. 16
a Jude 11.
b ch. 26.9.
c Ps. 106.16.
1 It is much for you.
d Ex. 19.6.
e Ex. 29.45.
f ch. 20.6.
g 2 Tim. 2.19.
h Lev. 21.6-12.
i Ex. 28.1. 1 Sam. 2.28. Ps. 105.26.
j Lev. 10.3.
k 1 Sam. 18. 23. Isa. 7.13.
l Deut. 10.8.
m 1 Cor. 3.5.
n Acts 7.27, 35.
o Ex. 3.8. Lev. 20.24.
2 bore out, that is, blind with fair words.
p Gen. 4.4,5.
q 1 Sam. 12.3. Acts 20.33. 2 Cor. 7.2.
r Ex. 16.7,10. Lev. 9.6,23.
s Gen. 19.17. Jer. 51.6. Acts 2.40. Rev. 18.4.
t Ex. 32.10. Ps. 73.19. Isa. 37.36.
u Job 12.10. Eccl. 12.7. Isa. 57.16. Zech. 12.1. Heb. 12.9.
v 2 Sam. 24. 17. 1 Chr. 21.17. Eze. 18.20.
w Gen. 19.12. Isa. 52.11. Acts 2.40. 2 Cor. 6.17. Rev. 18.4.

13 *Is it* a small thing that thou hast
brought us up out of a land that floweth with milk and honey, to kill us in
the wilderness, except thou [n]make
thyself altogether a prince over us?
14 Moreover thou hast not brought
us into a [o]land that floweth with milk
and honey, or given us inheritance of
fields and vineyards: wilt thou [2]put
out the eyes of these men? we will not
come up.
15 And Moses was very wroth, and
said unto the LORD, [p]Respect not
thou their offering: [q]I have not taken
one ass from them, neither have I hurt
one of them.
16 And Moses said unto Kôr'-ăh, Be
thou and all thy company before the
LORD, thou, and they, and Aaron, to
morrow:
17 And take every man his censer,
and put incense in them, and bring ye
before the LORD every man his censer,
two hundred and fifty censers; thou
also, and Aaron, each *of you* his
censer.
18 And they took every man his censer, and put fire in them, and laid incense thereon, and stood in the door
of the tabernacle of the congregation
with Moses and Aaron.
19 And Kôr'-ăh gathered all the congregation against them unto the door
of the tabernacle of the congregation:
and [r]the glory of the LORD appeared
unto all the congregation.
20 And the LORD spake unto Moses
and unto Aaron, saying,
21 Separate [s]yourselves from among
this congregation, that I may [t]con-
sume them in a moment.
22 And they fell upon their faces,
and said, O God, [u]the God of the
spirits of all flesh, shall [v]one man sin,
and wilt thou be wroth with all the
congregation?
23 ¶ And the LORD spake unto Moses,
saying,
24 Speak unto the congregation,
saying, Get you up from about the
tabernacle of Kôr'-ăh, Dā'-thăn, and
Ă-bī'-răm.
25 And Moses rose up and went unto Dā'-thăn and Ă-bī'-răm; and the
elders of Israel followed him.
26 And he spake unto the congregation, saying, [w]Depart, I pray you,
from the tents of these wicked men,
and touch nothing of theirs, lest ye be
consumed in all their sins.
27 So they gat up from the tabernacle of Kôr'-ăh, Dā'-thăn, and Ă-bī'-
răm, on every side: and Dā'-thăn and

A-bī´-răm came out, and stood [x]in the
door of their tents, and their wives,
and their sons, and their little children.
28 And Moses said, [y]Hereby ye shall
know that the LORD hath sent me to
do all these works; for *I have* not *done*
them [z]of mine own mind.
29 If these men die [3]the common
death of all men, or if they be visited
[a]after the visitation of all men; *then*
the LORD hath not sent me.
30 But if the LORD [4]make [b]a new
thing, and the earth open her mouth,
and swallow them up, with all that
appertain unto them, and they [c]go
down quick into the pit; then ye shall
understand that these men have provoked the LORD.
31 ¶ And [d]it came to pass, as he had
made an end of speaking all these
words, that the ground clave asunder
that *was* under them:
32 And the earth opened her mouth,
and swallowed them up, and their
houses, and all [e]the men that *apper-*
tained unto Kôr´-ăh, and all *their*
goods.
33 They, and all that *appertained* to
them, went down alive into the pit,
and the earth closed upon them: and
they perished from among the congregation.
34 And all Israel that *were* round
about them fled at the cry of them:
for they said, Lest the earth swallow
us up *also*.
35 And there [f]came out a fire from
the LORD, and consumed the two hundred and fifty men that offered incense.
36 ¶ And the LORD spake unto Moses,
saying,
37 Speak unto Ĕl-ē-ā´-zär the son of
Aaron the priest, that he take up the
censers out of the burning, and scatter
thou the fire yonder; for they are
hallowed.
38 The censers of these [g]sinners
against their own souls, let them make
them broad plates *for* a covering of
the altar: for they offered them before
the LORD, therefore they are hallowed: [h]and they shall be a sign unto the
children of Israel.
39 And Ĕl-ē-ā´-zär the priest took the
brasen censers, wherewith they that
were burnt had offered; and they were
made broad *plates for* a covering of
the altar:
40 *To be* a memorial unto the children of Israel, [i]that no stranger,
which *is* not of the seed of Aaron,
come near to offer incense before the
LORD; that he be not as Kôr´-ăh, and
as his company: as the LORD said to
him by the hand of Moses.
41 ¶ But on the morrow [j]all the congregation of the children of Israel
murmured against Moses and against
Aaron, saying, Ye have killed the people of the LORD.
42 And it came to pass, when the
congregation was gathered against
Moses and against Aaron, that they
looked toward the tabernacle of the
congregation: and, behold, the [k]cloud
covered it, and the glory of the LORD
appeared.
43 And Moses and Aaron came before the tabernacle of the congregation.
44 ¶ And the LORD spake unto Moses,
saying,
45 Get you up from among this congregation, that I may consume them
as in a moment. And [l]they fell upon
their faces.
46 ¶ And Moses said unto Aaron,
Take a censer, and put fire therein
from off the altar, and put on incense,
and go quickly unto the congregation,
and make an atonement for them:
[m]for there is wrath gone out from the
LORD; the plague is begun.
47 And Aaron took as Moses commanded, and ran into the midst of
the congregation; and, behold, the
plague was begun among the people:
and he put on incense, and made an
atonement for the people.
48 And he [n]stood between the dead
and the living; and the plague was
stayed.
49 Now they that died in the plague
were fourteen thousand and seven
hundred, beside them that died about
the matter of Kôr´-ăh.
50 And Aaron returned unto Moses
unto the door of the tabernacle of the
congregation: and the plague was
stayed.

CHAPTER 17

AND the LORD spake unto Moses,
saying,
2 Speak unto the children of Israel,
and take of every one of them a rod
according to the house of *their* fathers,
of all their princes according to the
house of their fathers twelve rods:
write thou every man's name upon
his rod.
3 And thou shalt write Aaron's name
upon the rod of Levi: for one rod
shall be for the head of the house of
their fathers.
4 And thou shalt lay them up in the

x Job 9.4. Pro. 16.18.
y Deut. 18.22. Zech. 2.9.
z Jer. 23.16. Eze. 13.17.
3 as every man dieth.
a Ex. 20.5. Job 35.15. Isa. 10.3. Jer. 5.9. Lam. 4.22.
4 create a creature.
b Job 31.3. Isa. 28.21.
c Ps. 55.15. Rev. 9.2.
d ch. 26.10. ch. 27.3. Deut. 11.6. Ps. 106.17.
e 1 Chr. 6.22.
f ch. 11.1. Lev. 10.2. Ps. 106.18.
g Pro. 20.2. Hab. 2.10.
h ch. 17.10. ch. 26.10. Eze. 14.8. 1 Cor. 10.11. 2 Pet. 2.6.
i ch. 3.38. ch. 18. 4-7. 1 Ki. 13.1.
j ch. 14.2. Ps. 106.13, 26. Matt. 5.11. Acts 21.28. 2 Cor. 6.8.
k Ex. 16.7,10. Ex. 24.16. Ex. 40.34. Lev. 9.23. ch. 14.10.
l ch. 20.6. 1 Chr. 21.16. Matt. 26.39.
m Lev. 10.6. ch. 1.53. ch. 8.19. ch. 11.33. ch. 18.5. Josh. 7.1. Josh. 22.18, 20. 1 Sam. 6.19. 2 Sam. 24.1. 1 Chr. 27.24. Ps. 106.29.
n 2 Sam. 24. 16,17,25. Job 33.24. Ps. 106.30. Matt. 20.28. 1 Thes. 1.10. Heb. 7.24. Jas. 5.16.

tabernacle of the congregation before the testimony, [a]where I will meet with you.

5 And it shall come to pass, *that* the man's rod, [b]whom I shall choose, shall blossom: and I will make to cease from me the murmurings of the children of Israel, whereby they murmur against you.

6 ¶ And Moses spake unto the children of Israel, and every one of their princes gave him [1]a rod apiece, for each prince one, according to their fathers' houses, *even* twelve rods: and the rod of Aaron *was* among their rods.

7 And Moses laid up the rods before the LORD in [c]the tabernacle of witness.

8 And it came to pass, that on the morrow Moses went into the tabernacle of witness; and, behold, the rod of Aaron for the house of Levi was [d]budded, and brought forth buds, and bloomed blossoms, and yielded almonds.

9 And Moses brought out all the rods from before the LORD unto all the children of Israel: and they looked, and took every man his rod.

10 ¶ And the LORD said unto Moses, Bring Aaron's [e]rod again before the testimony, to be kept for [f]a token against the [2]rebels; and thou shalt quite take away their murmurings from me, that they die not.

11 And Moses did *so:* as the LORD commanded him, so did he.

12 And the children of Israel spake unto Moses, saying, Behold, we die, we perish, we all perish.

13 Whosoever [g]cometh any thing near unto the tabernacle of the LORD shall die: shall we be consumed with dying?

CHAPTER 18

AND the LORD said unto Aaron, Thou [a]and thy sons and thy father's house with thee shall [1]bear the iniquity of the sanctuary: and thou and thy sons with thee shall bear the iniquity of your priesthood.

2 And thy brethren also of the tribe of Levi, the tribe of thy father, bring thou with thee, that they may be [b]joined unto thee, and minister [c]unto thee: but thou and thy sons with thee *shall minister* before the tabernacle of witness.

3 And they shall keep thy charge, and the [d]charge of all the tabernacle: [e]only they shall not come nigh the vessels of the sanctuary and the altar, [f]that neither they, nor ye also, die.

4 And they shall be joined unto thee, and keep the charge of the tabernacle of the congregation, for all the service of the tabernacle: and a stranger shall not come nigh unto you.

5 And ye shall keep [g]the charge of the sanctuary, and the charge of the altar: that there be no wrath any more upon the children of Israel.

6 And I, behold, I have [h]taken your brethren the Levites from among the children of Israel: to you *they are* given *as* a gift for the LORD, to do the service of the tabernacle of the congregation.

7 Therefore thou and thy sons with thee shall keep your priest's office for every thing of the altar, and [i]within the vail; and ye shall serve: I have given your priest's office *unto you as* a service of gift: and [j]the stranger that cometh nigh shall be put to death.

8 ¶ And the LORD spake unto Aaron, Behold, [k]I also have given thee the charge of mine heave offerings of all the hallowed things of the children of Israel; unto thee have I given them [l]by reason of the anointing, and to thy sons, by an ordinance for ever.

9 This shall be thine of the most holy things, *reserved* from the fire: every oblation of theirs, every meat [m]offering of theirs, and every sin [n]offering of theirs, and every trespass offering of theirs, which they shall render unto me, *shall be* most holy for thee and for thy sons.

10 In the [2]most holy *place* shalt thou eat it; every male shall eat it: it shall be holy unto thee.

11 And this *is* thine; [o]the heave offering of their gift, with all the wave offerings of the children of Israel: I have given them unto thee, [p]and to thy sons and to thy daughters with thee, by a statute for ever: [q]every one that is clean in thy house shall eat of it.

12 All [r]the [3]best of the oil, and all the best of the wine, and of the wheat, the firstfruits of them which they shall offer unto the LORD, them have I given thee.

13 *And* whatsoever is first ripe in the land, which they shall bring unto the LORD, shall be thine; every one that is clean in thine house shall eat *of* it.

14 Every [s]thing devoted in Israel shall be thine.

15 Every thing that openeth [t]the matrix in all flesh, which they bring unto the LORD, *whether it be* of men or beasts, shall be thine: nevertheless [u]the firstborn of man shalt thou surely

CHAP. 17
a Ex. 25.22. Ex. 29.42, 43. Ex. 30.36. Lev. 16.2. 1 Ki. 8.10, 11,12.
b ch. 16.5.
1 a rod for one prince, a rod for one prince.
c Ex. 38.21. ch. 18.2. Acts 7.44.
d Gen. 40.10. Ps. 110.2. Song 2.3. Isa. 4.2. Isa. 9.7. Isa. 35.1,2.
e Heb. 9.4.
f Ex. 16.32. ch. 16.38. Deut. 31.19-26.
2 children of rebellion.
g ch. 18.4,7.

CHAP. 18
a ch. 17.13.
1 Be responsible for whatever is done about the sanctuary.
b Gen. 29.34.
c ch. 3.6-10.
d ch. 3.25,31.
e ch. 16.40.
f ch. 4.15.
g Ex. 27.21. Ex. 30.7. Lev. 24.3. 1 Chr. 9.19, 23,33. 1 Chr. 24.5.
h ch. 3.12,45.
i Heb. 9.3,6.
j 1 Sam. 6.19.
k Lev. 6.16, 18. Lev. 7.6,32. Lev. 10.14, 15. Deut. 6.11.
l Ex. 40.13, 15.
m Lev. 2.2,3. Lev. 10.12, 13.
n Lev. 4.22, 27. Lev. 6.25, 26.
2 Inner court.
o Ex. 29.27, 28. Lev. 7.30, 34.
p Lev. 10.14. Deut. 18.3.
q Lev. 22.2.
r Ex. 23.19. Deut. 18.4.
3 fat.
s Lev. 27.28.
t Ex. 13.2. Ex. 34.20. Lev. 27.26. ch. 3.13.
u Ex. 13.13. Lev. 27.27.

redeem, and the firstling of unclean
beasts shalt thou redeem.
16 And those that are to be redeemed
from a month old shalt thou redeem,
[v]according to thine estimation, for
the money of five shekels, after the
shekel of the sanctuary, which [w]*is*
twenty gē-rähs.
17 But [x]the firstling of a cow, or the
firstling of a sheep, or the firstling of
a goat, thou shalt not redeem; they
are holy: [y]thou shalt sprinkle their
blood upon the altar, and shalt burn
their fat *for* an offering made by fire,
for a sweet savour unto the LORD.
18 And the flesh of them shall be
thine, as the [z]wave breast and as the
right shoulder are thine.
19 All the heave offerings of the holy
things, which the children of Israel
offer unto the LORD, have I given thee,
and thy sons and thy daughters with
thee, by a statute for ever: it *is* [4]a covenant of salt for ever before the LORD
unto thee and to thy seed with thee.
20 ¶ And the LORD spake unto
Aaron, Thou shalt have no inheritance in their land, neither shalt thou
have any part among them: I [a]*am* thy
part and thine inheritance among the
children of Israel.
21 And, behold, [b]I have given the
children of Levi all the tenth in Israel
for an inheritance, for their service
which they serve, *even* the service of
the tabernacle of the congregation.
22 Neither must the children of Israel henceforth come nigh the tabernacle of the congregation, lest [c]they
bear sin, [5]and die.
23 But the Levites shall do the service of the tabernacle of the congregation, and they shall bear their iniquity: *it shall be* a statute for ever
throughout your generations, that
among the children of Israel they have
no inheritance.
24 But the tithes of the children of
Israel, which they offer *as* an heave
offering unto the LORD, I have given
to the Levites to inherit: therefore I
have said unto them, Among [d]the
children of Israel they shall have no
inheritance.
25¶ And the LORD spake unto Moses,
saying,
26 Thus speak unto the Levites, and
say unto them, When ye take of the
children of Israel the tithes which I
have given you from them for your
inheritance, then ye shall offer up an
heave offering of it for the LORD, *even*
[e]a tenth *part* of the tithe.

v Lev. 27.2,6. ch. 3.47.
w Ex. 30.13. Lev. 27.25. Eze. 45.12.
x Deut. 15. 19.
y Lev. 3.2,5.
z Ex. 29.26-28. Lev. 7.31.
4 A perpetual covenant.
a Deut. 10.9. Deut. 14.27. Deut. 18.1, 2. Josh. 13.14, 33. Josh. 18.7. Ps. 16.5. Ps. 73.26. Ps. 142.5. Eze. 44.28.
b Lev. 27.30, 32. Deut. 12.17-19. Neh. 10.37. Neh. 12.44. Heb. 7.5,8.
c Lev. 22.9.
5 to die.
d Deut. 10.9.
e Neh. 10.38.
6 fat.
f Matt. 10.10. Luke 10.7. 1 Cor. 9.13. 2 Cor. 12.13. Gal. 6.6. 1 Tim. 5.18. 1 Thes. 5.12, 13.
g Lev. 19.8. Lev. 22.16.

CHAP. 19

a Isa. 53.4-6. Gal. 4.4. Heb. 9.13, 14. Rev. 1.5.
b Deut. 21.3. 1 Sam. 6.7. John 10.17. Phil. 2.6,8.
c Lev. 4.12, 21. Lev. 13.46. Lev. 16.27. Lev. 24.14. Heb. 13.11.
d Lev. 4.6,17. Lev. 16.14. Isa. 52.15. Eze. 36.25. Heb. 9.13, 14. 1 Pet. 1.2.
e Ex. 29.14. Lev. 4.11,12. Isa. 53.10.
f Lev. 14.4,6.
g Lev. 11.25. Lev. 15.5.

27 And *this* your heave offering shall
be reckoned unto you, as though *it*
were the corn of the threshingfloor,
and as the fulness of the winepress.
28 Thus ye also shall offer an heave
offering unto the LORD of all your
tithes, which ye receive of the children
of Israel; and ye shall give thereof the
LORD's heave offering to Aaron the
priest.
29 Out of all your gifts ye shall offer
every heave offering of the LORD, of
all the [6]best thereof, *even* the hallowed
part thereof out of it.
30 Therefore thou shalt say unto
them, When ye have heaved the best
thereof from it, then it shall be counted unto the Levites as the increase of
the threshingfloor, and as the increase
of the winepress.
31 And ye shall eat it in every place,
ye and your households: for it *is* [f]your
reward for your service in the tabernacle of the congregation.
32 And ye shall [g]bear no sin by reason
of it, when ye have heaved from it the
best of it: neither shall ye pollute the
holy things of the children of Israel,
lest ye die.

CHAPTER 19

AND the LORD spake unto Moses
and unto Aaron, saying,
2 This *is* the ordinance of the law
which the LORD hath commanded,
saying, Speak unto the children of
Israel, that they bring thee [a]a red
heifer without spot, wherein *is* no
blemish, *and* [b]upon which never came
yoke:
3 And ye shall give her unto Ĕl-ē-ā-
zär the priest, that he may bring her
[c]forth without the camp, and *one* shall
slay her before his face:
4 And Ĕl-ē-ā-zär the priest shall take
of her blood with his finger, and
[d]sprinkle of her blood directly before
the tabernacle of the congregation
seven times:
5 And *one* shall burn the heifer in his
sight; her [e]skin, and her flesh, and her
blood, with her dung, shall he burn:
6 And the priest shall take [f]cedar
wood, and hyssop, and scarlet, and
cast *it* into the midst of the burning of
the heifer.
7 Then [g]the priest shall wash his
clothes, and he shall bathe his flesh in
water, and afterward he shall come
into the camp, and the priest shall be
unclean until the even.
8 And he that burneth her shall wash
his clothes in water, and bathe his flesh

in water, and shall be unclean until
the even.
9 And a man *that is* clean shall gather
up the [h]ashes of the heifer, and lay
them up without the camp in a clean
place, and it shall be kept for the congregation of the children of Israel [i]for
a water of separation: it *is* a purification for sin.
10 And he that gathereth the ashes of
the heifer shall wash his clothes, and
be unclean until the even: and it shall
be unto the children of Israel, and unto the stranger that sojourneth among
them, for a statute for ever.
11 ¶ He [j]that toucheth the dead body
of any [1]man shall be unclean seven
days.
12 He [k]shall purify himself with it on
the third day, and on the seventh day
he shall be clean: but if he purify not
himself the third day, then the seventh
day he shall not be clean.
13 Whosoever toucheth the dead
body of any man that is dead, and
purifieth not himself, defileth [l]the
tabernacle of the LORD; and that soul
shall be cut off from Israel: because
[m]the water of separation was not
sprinkled upon him, he shall be unclean; [n]his uncleanness *is* yet upon
him.
14 This *is* the law, when a man dieth
in a tent: all that come into the tent,
and all that *is* in the tent, shall be unclean seven days.
15 And every [o]open vessel, which
hath no covering bound upon it, *is*
unclean.
16 And whosoever toucheth one that
is slain with a sword in the open fields,
or a dead body, or a bone of a man,
or a grave, shall be unclean seven
days.
17 And for an unclean *person* they
shall take of the [2]ashes of the burnt
heifer of purification for sin, and [3]run-
ning water shall be put thereto in a
vessel:
18 And a clean person shall take hyssop, [p]and dip *it* in the water, and
sprinkle *it* upon the tent, and upon all
the vessels, and upon the persons that
were there, and upon him that touched
a bone, or one slain, or one dead, or a
grave:
19 And the clean *person* shall sprinkle
upon the unclean on the third day,
and on the seventh day: and [q]on the
seventh day he shall purify himself,
and wash his clothes, and bathe himself in water, and shall be clean at
even.

h Heb. 9.13.
i ch. 31.23. Zech. 13.1. 2 Cor. 7.1.
j Lev. 21.1. ch. 5.2. ch. 9.6,10. Isa. 52.11. Lam. 4.14. Hag. 2.13. Rom. 5.12. 2 Cor. 6.17. Eph. 2.1.
1 soul of man.
k ch. 31.19.
l Lev. 15.31.
m ch. 8.7.
n Lev. 7.20. Lev. 22.3.
o ch. 31.20. Lev. 11.32.
2 dust.
3 living waters shall be given.
p Ps. 51.7. John 15.2. John 17.19. 1 Cor. 1.30. Heb. 9.14.
q Lev. 14.9.
r Gen. 17.14. Mark 16.16. Acts 13. 39-41. Rom. 2.4,5. Gal. 3.10.
s Hag. 2.13.

CHAP. 20

a ch. 33.36.
b ch. 26.59.
c Ex. 17.1.
d Ex. 16.2, 7-12. ch. 16.19,42. ch. 21.5. 1 Cor. 10.10.
e Ex. 17.2. ch. 14.2.
f ch. 11.1,33. ch. 14.37. ch. 16.32,33, 49. Lam. 4.9.
g Ex. 5.21. ch. 11.5. Ps. 106.21. Acts 7.35, 40.
h ch. 14.5.
i Ex. 17.5.
j Neh. 9.15. Ps. 78.15,16. Isa. 43.20.
k ch. 17.10.

20 But the man that shall be unclean,
and shall not purify himself, that
[r]soul shall be cut off from among the
congregation, because he hath defiled
the sanctuary of the LORD: the water
of separation hath not been sprinkled
upon him; he *is* unclean.
21 And it shall be a perpetual statute
unto them, that he that sprinkleth the
water of separation shall wash his
clothes; and he that toucheth the
water of separation shall be unclean
until even.
22 And [s]whatsoever the unclean *person* toucheth shall be unclean; and the
soul that toucheth *it* shall be unclean
until even.

CHAPTER 20

THEN [a]came the children of Israel,
even the whole congregation, into
the desert of Zin in the first month:
and the people abode in Kā-dĕsh; and
[b]Miriam died there, and was buried
there.
2 And [c]there was no water for the
congregation: [d]and they gathered
themselves together against Moses
and against Aaron.
3 And the people [e]chode with Moses,
and spake, saying, Would God that
we had died when [f]our brethren died
before the LORD!
4 And [g]why have ye brought up the
congregation of the LORD into this
wilderness, that we and our cattle
should die there?
5 And wherefore have ye made us to
come up out of Egypt, to bring us in
unto this evil place? it *is* no place of
seed, or of figs, or of vines, or of pomegranates; neither *is* there any water
to drink.
6 And Moses and Aaron went from
the presence of the assembly unto the
door of the tabernacle of the congregation, and they [h]fell upon their faces:
and the glory of the LORD appeared
unto them.
7 ¶ And the LORD spake unto Moses,
saying,
8 Take [i]the rod, and gather thou the
assembly together, thou, and Aaron
thy brother, and speak ye unto the
rock before their eyes; and it shall
give forth his water, and [j]thou shalt
bring forth to them water out of the
rock: so thou shalt give the congregation and their beasts drink.
9 And Moses took the rod [k]from before the LORD, as he commanded
him.
10 And Moses and Aaron gathered

the congregation together before the
rock, and he said unto them, [l]Hear
now, ye rebels; must we fetch you
water out of this rock?
11 And Moses lifted up his hand,
and with his rod he smote the rock
[m]twice: and the [n]water came out
abundantly, and the congregation
drank, and their beasts *also*.
12 ¶ And the LORD spake unto Moses
and Aaron, Because [o]ye believed me
not, to sanctify [p]me in the eyes of the
children of Israel, therefore ye shall
not bring this congregation into the
land which I have given them.
13 This [q]*is* the water of [1]Mĕr´-ĭ-bäh;
because the children of Israel strove
with the LORD, and he was sanctified
in them.
14 ¶ And Moses [r]sent messengers
from Kā´-dĕsh unto the king of Ē´-dọm,
[s]Thus saith thy brother Israel, Thou
knowest all the travail that hath [2]be-
fallen us:
15 How our fathers went down into
Egypt, and we have dwelt in Egypt a
long time; and the Egyptians vexed
us, and our fathers:
16 And [t]when we cried unto the
LORD, he heard our voice, and sent
[u]an angel, and hath brought us forth
out of Egypt: and, behold, we *are* in
Kā´-dĕsh, a city in the uttermost of thy
border:
17 Let [v]us pass, I pray thee, through
thy country: we will not pass through
the fields, or through the vineyards,
neither will we drink *of* the water of
the wells: we will go by the king's *high*
way, we will not turn to the right hand
nor to the left, until we have passed
thy borders.
18 And Ē´-dọm said unto him, Thou
shalt not pass by me, lest I come out
against thee with the sword.
19 And the children of Israel said unto him, We will go by the high way:
and if I and my cattle drink of thy
water, [w]then I will pay for it: I will
only, without *doing* any thing *else*, go
through on my feet.
20 And he said, [x]Thou shalt not go
through. And Ē´-dọm came out against
him with much people, and with a
strong hand.
21 Thus Ē´-dọm refused to give Israel
passage through [y]his border: wherefore Israel [z]turned away from him.
22 ¶ And the children of Israel, *even*
the whole congregation, journeyed
from [a]Kā´-dĕsh, and [b]came unto
mount Hor.
23 And the LORD spake unto Moses
and Aaron in mount Hor, by the coast
of the land of Ē´-dọm, saying,
24 Aaron shall [c]be gathered unto his
people: for he shall not enter into the
land which I have given unto the children of Israel, because ye rebelled
against my [3]word at the water of Mĕr´-
ĭ-bäh.
25 Take [d]Aaron and Ĕl-ē-ā´-zär his
son, and bring them up unto mount
Hor:
26 And strip Aaron of his garments,
and put them upon Ĕl-ē-ā´-zär his son:
and Aaron shall be gathered *unto his
people*, and shall die there.
27 And Moses did as the LORD commanded: and they went up into mount
Hor in the sight of all the congregation.
28 And Moses [e]stripped Aaron of his
garments, and put them upon Ĕl-ē-ā´-
zär his son; and [f]Aaron died there in
the top of the mount: and Moses and
Ĕl-ē-ā´-zär came down from the
mount.
29 And when all the congregation
saw that Aaron was dead, they mourned for Aaron thirty [g]days, *even* all the
house of Israel.

CHAPTER 21

AND *when* [a]king Ā´-răd the Canaanite, which dwelt in the south,
heard tell that Israel came by the way
of the spies; then he fought against
Israel, and took *some* of them prisoners.
2 And [b]Israel vowed a vow unto the
LORD, and said, If thou wilt indeed
deliver this people into my hand, then
[c]I will utterly destroy their cities.
3 And the LORD hearkened to the
voice of Israel, and delivered up the
Canaanites; and they utterly destroyed them and their cities: and he called
the name of the place [1]Hôr´-măh.
4 ¶ And they journeyed from mount
Hor by the way of the Red sea, to
compass the land of Ē´-dọm: and the
soul of the people was much [2]dis-
couraged because of the way.
5 And the people [d]spake against
God, and against Moses, [e]Wherefore
have ye brought us up out of Egypt to
die in the wilderness? for *there is* no
bread, neither *is there any* water; and
[f]our soul loatheth this light bread.
6 And [g]the LORD sent [h]fiery serpents
among the people, and they bit the
people; and much people of Israel
died.
7 ¶ Therefore [i]the people came to
Moses, and said, We have sinned, for

l Ps. 106.33.
m Jas. 1.20.
n Ex. 17.6. Deut. 8.15. 1 Cor. 10.4.
o ch. 27.14. Deut. 3.26.
p Lev. 10.3. Eze. 20.41. 1 Pet. 3.15.
q Ps. 95.8.
1 That is, Strife.
r Judg. 11.16, 17.
s Deut. 23.7. Obad. 10. 12.
2 found us.
t Ex. 2.23. Ex. 3.7.
u Acts 7.35.
v ch. 21.22.
w Deut. 2.6, 28.
x Gen. 27.41. Gen. 32.6. Judg. 11.17. Ps. 120.7. Amos 1.11.
y Deut. 2.27, 29.
z Judg. 11.18. Rom. 12.18. Heb. 12.14.
a ch. 33.37.
b ch. 21.4.
c Gen. 25.8. ch. 27.13. Isa. 57.1,2. Heb. 12.23.
3 mouth.
d Deut. 32.50.
e Ex. 29.29, 30. ch. 23.10. Deut. 10.6. Job 30.23.
f ch. 23.10. Deut. 10.6. Job 14.12. Pro. 14.32. Hosea 13. 14. Rev. 14.13.
g Gen. 50.3, 10. Deut. 34.8.

CHAP. 21

a ch. 33.40. Judg. 1.16.
b Gen. 28.20. Judg. 11.30.
c Lev. 27.28.
1 That is, Utter destruction.
2 shortened, or, grieved.
d Ps. 78.19.
e Ex. 16.3.
f Pro. 27.7.
g Amos 9.3,4. 1 Cor. 10.9.
h Deut. 8.15.
i Ps. 78.34. Isa. 26.16. Hosea 5.15.

we have spoken against the LORD, and
against thee; [j]pray unto the LORD,
that he take away the serpents
from us. And Moses prayed for the
people.
8 And the LORD said unto Moses,
Make thee a fiery serpent, and set it
upon a pole: and it shall come to pass,
that every one that is bitten, when he
looketh upon it, shall live.
9 And [k]Moses made a serpent of
brass, and put it upon a pole, and it
came to pass, that if a serpent had bitten any man, when he beheld the serpent of brass, he lived.
10 ¶ And the children of Israel set
forward, and pitched in Ō-bŏth.
11 And they journeyed from Ō-bŏth,
and pitched at [3]Ī-jĕ-ăb-ă-rīm, in the
wilderness which *is* before Moab, toward the sunrising.
12 ¶ From thence they removed, and
pitched in the valley of Zâr-ĕd.
13 From thence they removed, and
pitched on the other side of Arnon,
which *is* in the wilderness that cometh out of the coasts of the Amorites:
for [l]Arnon *is* the border of Moab, between Moab and the Amorites.
14 Wherefore it is said in the book
of the wars of the LORD, [4]What he did
in the Red sea, and in the brooks of
Arnon,
15 And at the stream of the brooks
that goeth down to the dwelling of
Ar, and [5]lieth upon the border of
Moab.
16 And from thence *they went* to
[m]Bē-ĕr: that *is* the well whereof the
LORD spake unto Moses, Gather the
people together, and [n]I will give them
water.
17 ¶ Then [o]Israel sang this song,
[6]Spring up, O well; [7]sing ye unto it:
18 The princes digged the well, the
nobles of the people digged it, by *the
direction of* the [p]lawgiver, with their
staves. And from the wilderness *they
went* to Măt-tā-năh:
19 And from Măt-tā-năh to Nă-hăl-
ī-ĕl: and from Nă-hăl-ī-ĕl to Bā-
mŏth:
20 And from Bā-mŏth *in* the valley,
that *is* in the [8]country of Moab, to the
top of [9]Pĭs-găh, which looketh [q]to-
ward [10]Jĕ-shī-mon.
21 ¶ And [r]Israel sent messengers
unto Sī-hŏn king of the Amorites,
saying,
22 Let [s]me pass through thy land:
we will not turn into the fields, or into
the vineyards; we will not drink *of*
the waters of the well: *but* we will go
along by the king's *high* way, until we
be past thy borders.
23 And [t]Sī-hŏn would not suffer
Israel to pass through his border: but
Sī-hŏn gathered all his people together, and went out against Israel into
the wilderness: and [u]he came to Jā-
hăz, and fought against Israel.
24 And [v]Israel smote him with the
edge of the sword, and possessed his
land from Arnon unto Jăb-bok, even
unto the children of Ammon: for the
border of the children of Ammon *was*
strong.
25 And Israel took all these cities:
and Israel dwelt in all the cities of the
Amorites, in Hĕsh-bŏn, and in all the
[11]villages thereof.
26 For Hĕsh-bŏn *was* the city of Sī-
hŏn the king of the Amorites, who had
fought against the former king of Moab, and taken all his land out of his
hand, even unto Arnon.
27 Wherefore they that speak in
proverbs say, Come into Hĕsh-bŏn,
let the city of Sī-hŏn be built and prepared:
28 For there is [w]a fire gone out of
Hĕsh-bŏn, a flame from the city of Sī-
hŏn: it hath consumed [x]Ar of Moab,
and the lords of the high places of
Arnon.
29 Woe to thee, Moab! thou art undone, O people of [y]Chē-mŏsh: he hath
given his sons that escaped, and his
daughters, into captivity unto Sī-hŏn
king of the Amorites.
30 We have shot at them; Hĕsh-bŏn
is perished even [z]unto Dī-bŏn, and we
have laid them waste even unto Nō-
phăh, which *reacheth* unto Mē-dĕ-bă.
31 ¶ Thus Israel dwelt in the land of
the Amorites.
32 And Moses sent to spy [a]out Jā-
ă-zĕr, and they took the villages
thereof, and drove out the Amorites
that *were* there.
33 ¶ And they turned and went up
by the way of Bā-shăn: and Og the
king of Bā-shăn went out against
them, he, and all his people, to the
battle at [b]Ĕd-rĕ-ī.
34 And the LORD said unto Moses,
[c]Fear him not: for I have delivered
him into thy hand, and all his people,
and his land; and thou [d]shalt do to
him as thou didst unto Sī-hŏn king of
the Amorites, which dwelt at Hĕsh-
bŏn.
35 So [e]they smote him, and his sons,
and all his people, until there was
none left him alive: and they possessed his land.

j Ex. 8.8,28. 1 Sam. 12. 19. 1 Ki. 13.6. Acts 8.24.
k 2 Ki. 18.4. John 3.14, 15.
3 Or, Heaps of Abarim.
l ch. 22.36. Judg. 11.18.
4 Or, Vaheb in Suphah.
5 leaneth.
m Judg. 9.21.
n Rev. 7.17.
o Ex. 15.1. Ps. 105.2.
6 Ascend.
7 Or, answer.
p Deut. 33.4. Isa. 33.22.
8 field.
9 Or, the hill.
q ch. 23.28.
10 Or, the wilderness.
r Deut. 2.26. Judg. 11.19.
s ch. 20.17.
t Deut. 29.7.
u Deut. 2.32, 33.
v Deut. 29.7. Josh. 12.1, 2. Neh. 9.22. Ps. 135.10. Amos 2.9.
11 daughters.
w Isa. 15.4. Jer. 48.45, 46.
x Deut. 2.9. Isa. 15.1.
y Judg. 11.24. 1 Ki. 11.7, 33. 2 Ki. 23.13.
z Jer. 48.18, 22.
a Jer. 48.32.
b Josh. 13.12.
c Deut. 3.2.
d Ps. 135.10. Ps. 136.20.
e Deut. 3.3,4.

CHAPTER 22

AND [a]the children of Israel set forward, and pitched in the plains of
Moab on this side Jordan *by* Jericho.
2 ¶ And [b]Balak the son of Zĭṕ-pôr
saw all that Israel had done to the
Amorites.
3 And [c]Moab was sore afraid of the
people, because they *were* many: and
Moab was distressed because of the
children of Israel.
4 And Moab said unto the [d]elders of
Mĭd́-ĭ-ăn, Now shall this company
lick up all *that are* round about us, as
the ox licketh up the grass of the field.
And Balak the son of Zĭṕ-pôr *was*
king of the Moabites at that time.
5 He sent messengers therefore unto
[e]Bā́-lāam the son of Bḗ-ôr [f]to Pḗ-thôr,
which *is* by the river of the land of the
children of his people, to call him,
saying, Behold, there is a people come
out from Egypt: behold, they cover
the [1]face of the earth, and they abide
over against me:
6 Come now therefore, I pray thee,
[g]curse me this people; for they *are* too
mighty for me: peradventure I shall
prevail, *that* we may smite them, and
that I may drive them out of the land:
for I wot that he whom thou blessest
is blessed, and he whom thou cursest is
cursed.
7 And the elders of Moab and the
elders of Mĭd́-ĭ-ăn departed with the
[h]rewards of divination in their hand;
and they came unto Bā́-lāam, and
spake unto him the words of Balak.
8 And he said unto them, Lodge here
this night, and I will bring you word
again, as the LORD shall speak unto
me: and the princes of Moab abode
with Bā́-lāam.
9 And [i]God came unto Bā́-lāam, and
said, What men *are* these with thee?
10 And Bā́-lāam said unto God,
Balak the son of Zĭṕ-pôr, king of
Moab, hath sent unto me, *saying*,
11 Behold, *there is* a people come
out of Egypt, which covereth the face
of the earth: come now, curse me
them; peradventure [2]I shall be able to
overcome them, and drive them out.
12 And God said unto Bā́-lāam,
Thou shalt not go with them; thou
shalt not curse the people: for they [j]*are*
blessed.
13 And Bā́-lāam rose up in the morning, and said unto the princes of Balak, Get you into your land: for the
LORD refuseth to give me leave to go
with you.
14 And the princes of Moab rose up,
and they went unto Balak, and said,
Bā́-lāam refuseth to come with us.
15 ¶ And Balak sent yet again princes, more, and more honourable than
they.
16 And they came to Bā́-lāam, and
said to him, Thus saith Balak the son
of Zĭṕ-pôr, [3]Let nothing, I pray thee,
hinder thee from coming unto me:
17 For [k]I will promote thee unto very
great honour, and I will do whatsoever thou sayest unto me: come therefore, I pray thee, curse me this people.
18 And Bā́-lāam answered and said
unto the servants of Balak, If Balak
would give me his house full of silver
and gold, [l]I cannot go beyond the
word of the LORD my God, to do less
or more.
19 Now therefore, I pray you, tarry
ye also here this night, that I may
know what the LORD will say unto me
more.
20 And God came unto Bā́-lāam at
night, and said unto him, If the men
come to call thee, rise up, *and* go with
them; but yet [m]the word which I shall
say unto thee, that shalt thou do.
21 And Bā́-lāam rose up in the morning, and saddled his ass, and went
[n]with the princes of Moab.
22 ¶ And God's anger was kindled
because he went: [o]and the angel of the
the LORD stood in the way for an adversary against him. Now he was riding upon his ass, and his two servants
were with him.
23 And [p]the ass saw the angel of the
LORD standing in the way, and his
sword drawn in his hand: and the ass
turned aside out of the way, and went
into the field: and Bā́-lāam smote the
ass, to turn her into the way.
24 But the angel of the LORD stood
in a path of the vineyards, a wall *being*
on this side, and a wall on that side.
25 And when the ass saw the angel of
the LORD, she thrust herself unto the
wall, and crushed Bā́-lāam's [q]foot
against the wall: and he smote her
again.
26 And the angel of the LORD went
further, and stood in a narrow place,
[r]where *was* no way to turn either to
the right hand or to the left.
27 And when the ass saw the angel
of the LORD, she fell down under Bā́-
lāam: [s]and Bā́-lāam's anger was kindled, and he smote the ass with a staff.
28 And the LORD [t]opened the mouth
of the ass and she said unto Bā́-lāam,
What have I done unto thee, that thou
hast smitten me these three times?

CHAP. 22
a Gen. 35.5. ch. 33.48. Deut. 2.25. Josh. 2.9. Jer. 32.21.
b Judg. 11.25.
c Ex. 15.15.
d ch. 31.8. Josh. 13.21.
e Deut. 23.4. Josh. 13.22. Neh. 13.1, 2. Micah 6.5.
f Deut. 23.4.
1 eye.
g Gen. 12.3. ch. 23.7. Deut. 23.4. Josh. 24.9. 1 Sam. 17. 43. Neh. 13.2.
h Ex. 23.8. 1 Sam. 9.7,8. Pro. 17.23. Isa. 56.11. Micah 3.11.
i Gen. 20.3. Gen. 31.24.
2 I shall prevail in fighting against him.
j Gen. 12.2. Gen. 22.17. ch. 23.20. Deut. 23.5. Deut. 33.29. Ps. 144.15. Rom. 11.29.
3 Be not thou letted from, etc.
k Deut. 16. 19. Ps. 49.17. Matt. 4.8,9. Matt. 16.26.
l 1 Ki. 22.14. 2 Chr. 18.13.
m ch. 23.12, 26. ch. 24.13. Ps. 33.10,11. Isa. 37.29. Isa. 46.10.
n Pro. 15.27. 1 Tim. 6.9, 10. 2 Pet. 2.15. Jude 11.
o Ex. 4.24. Ex. 23.20.
p 2 Ki. 6.17.
q Isa. 47.12. 1 Cor. 3.19.
r Isa. 26.11. Hosea 2.6.
s Pro. 14.16. Pro. 27.3,4. Jas. 1.19.
t Matt. 19.26. 1 Cor. 1.19. 2 Pet. 2.16.

29 And Bā-lāam said unto the ass,
Because thou hast mocked me: I
would there were a sword in mine
hand, [u]for now would I kill thee.
30 And [v]the ass said unto Bā-lāam,
Am not I thine ass, [4]upon which thou
hast ridden [5]ever since *I was* thine unto
this day? was I ever wont to do so unto thee? And he said, Nay.
31 Then the LORD [w]opened the eyes
of Bā-lāam, and he saw the angel of
the LORD standing in the way, and his
sword drawn in his hand: and he
[x]bowed down his head, and [6]fell flat
on his face.
32 And the angel of the LORD said
unto him, Wherefore hast thou smitten thine ass these three times? behold, I went out [7]to withstand thee, because *thy* way is [y]perverse before me:
33 And the ass saw me, and turned
from me these three times: unless she
had turned from me, surely now
also I had slain thee, and saved her
alive.
34 And Bā-lāam said unto the angel
of the LORD, [z]I have sinned; for I
knew not that thou stoodest in the
way against me: now therefore, if it
[8]displease thee, I will get me back
again.
35 And the angel of the LORD said
unto Bā-lāam, Go with the men: but
only the word that I shall speak unto
thee, that thou shalt speak. So
Bā-lāam went with the princes of
Balak.
36 ¶ And when Balak heard that Bā-
lāam was come, [a]he went out to meet
him unto a city of Moab, which *is* in
the border of Arnon, which *is* in the
utmost coast.
37 And Balak said unto Bā-lāam,
Did I not earnestly send unto thee to
call thee? wherefore camest thou not
unto me? am I not able indeed to promote thee to honour?
38 And Bā-lāam said unto Balak,
Lo, I am come unto thee: have I now
any power at all to say any thing?
[b]the word that God putteth in my
mouth, that shall I speak.
39 And Bā-lāam went with Balak,
and they came unto [9]Kĭr-jăth-hū-
zōth.
40 And Balak offered oxen and
sheep, and sent to Bā-lāam, and to
the princes that *were* with him.
41 And it came to pass on the
morrow, that Balak took Bā-lāam,
and brought him up into the [c]high
places of Bā-ăl, that thence he might
see the utmost *part* of the people.

u Pro. 12.10. Eccl. 9.3. Jer. 17.9. Matt. 15.19.
v 1 Cor. 1.27.
4 who hast ridden upon me.
5 Or, ever since thou wast, etc.
w Gen. 21.19. 2 Ki. 6.17. 1 Chr. 21.16. Luke 24.16.
x Job 8.20. Pro. 11.2. Jer. 3.25.
6 Or, bowed himself.
7 to be an adversary unto thee.
y Deut. 23.4. Pro. 28.6. Micah 6.5. Acts 13.10. 2 Pet. 2.14, 15.
z 1 Sam. 26. 21. 2 Sam. 12. 13.
8 be evil in thine eyes.
a Gen. 14.17. Gen. 18.2. 1 Sam. 13. 10. Acts 28.15.
b 1 Ki. 22.14. 2 Chr. 18.13.
9 Or, A city of streets.
c Deut. 12.2. 2 Chr. 11.15. Jer. 48.35.

CHAP. 23

1 Or, he went solitary.
a Deut. 18.18. Jer. 1.9.
b Job 27.1. Ps. 78.2. Eze. 17.2. Micah 2.4. Hab. 2.6. Matt. 13.35.
c Gen. 10.22. Gen. 28.5.
d 1 Sam. 17. 10.
e Pro. 21.30. Isa. 47.12.
f Lev. 20.24. Deut. 33.28. 1 Ki. 8.53.
g Ezra 9.2. Eph. 2.14.
h Gen. 22.17.
2 my soul, or, my life.
i Ps. 116.15. Isa. 57.1, 2.
j Josh. 24.10. Neh. 13.2.
3 Or, The hill.
k Isa. 1.10, 11. Hosea 12. 11.

CHAPTER 23

AND Bā-lāam said unto Balak,
Build me here seven altars, and
prepare me here seven oxen and seven
rams.
2 And Balak did as Bā-lāam had
spoken; and Balak and Bā-lāam offered on *every* altar a bullock and a
ram.
3 And Bā-lāam said unto Balak,
Stand by thy burnt offering, and I will
go: peradventure the LORD will come
to meet me: and whatsoever he sheweth me I will tell thee. And [1]he went
to an high place.
4 And God met Bā-lāam: and he said
unto him, I have prepared seven altars, and I have offered upon *every*
altar a bullock and a ram.
5 And the LORD [a]put a word in Bā-
lāam's mouth, and said, Return unto
Balak, and thus thou shalt speak.
6 And he returned unto him, and,
lo, he stood by his burnt sacrifice, he,
and all the princes of Moab.
7 And [b]he took up his parable, and
said, Balak the king of Moab hath
brought me from [c]Ā̆r-ăm, out of the
mountains of the east, *saying*, Come,
curse me Jacob, and come, defy [d]Is-
rael.
8 How shall I curse, whom God hath
not cursed? or [e]how shall I defy,
whom the LORD hath not defied?
9 For from the top of the rocks I see
him, and from the hills I behold him:
lo, [f]the people shall dwell alone, and
[g]shall not be reckoned among the
nations.
10 Who [h]can count the dust of Jacob,
and the number of the fourth *part* of
Israel? Let [2]me die the [i]death of the
righteous, and let my last end be like
his!
11 And Balak said unto Bā-lāam,
What hast thou done unto me? [j]I
took thee to curse mine enemies, and,
behold, thou hast blessed *them* altogether.
12 And he answered and said, Must
I not take heed to speak that which
the LORD hath put in my mouth?
13 And Balak said unto him, Come,
I pray thee, with me unto another
place, from whence thou mayest see
them: thou shalt see but the utmost
part of them, and shalt not see them
all: and curse me them from thence.
14 ¶ And he brought him into the
field of Zō-phĭm, to the top of [3]Pĭs-găh,
[k]and built seven altars, and offered a
bullock and a ram on *every* altar.
15 And he said unto Balak, Stand

here by thy burnt offering, while I
meet *the LORD* yonder.
16 And the LORD met Bā-lāam, and
put a word in his mouth, and said, Go
again unto Balak, and say thus.
17 And when he came to him, behold, he stood by his burnt offering,
and the princes of Moab with him.
And Balak said unto him, What [l]hath
the LORD spoken?
18 And he took up his parable, and
said, Rise [m]up, Balak, and hear;
hearken unto me, thou son of Zĭp-pôr:
19 God [n]*is* not a man, that he should
lie; neither the son of man, that he
should repent: hath he said, and
shall he not do *it*? or hath he
spoken, and shall he not make it
good?
20 Behold, I have received *commandment* to bless: and [o]he hath blessed; and I cannot reverse it.
21 He [p]hath not beheld iniquity in
Jacob, neither hath he seen perverseness in Israel: the [q]LORD his God *is*
with him, [r]and the shout of a king *is*
among them.
22 God brought them out of Egypt;
he hath as it were [s]the strength of an
unicorn.
23 Surely *there is* no enchantment
[4]against Jacob, neither *is there* any
divination against Israel: according
to this time it shall be said of Jacob
and of Israel, [t]What hath God
wrought!
24 Behold, the people shall rise up as
a great lion, and lift up himself as a
young lion: he shall not lie down until he eat *of* the prey, and drink the
blood of the slain.
25 ¶ And Balak said unto Bā-lāam,
Neither curse them at all, nor bless
them at all.
26 But Bā-lāam answered and said
unto Balak, Told not I thee, saying,
All that the LORD speaketh, that I
must do?
27 ¶ And Balak said unto Bā-lāam,
Come, I pray thee, I will bring thee
unto another place; peradventure it
will please God that thou mayest
curse me them from thence.
28 And Balak brought Bā-lāam unto
the top of Pē-ôr, that looketh toward
[5]Jĕ-shī-mon.
29 And [u]Bā-lāam said unto Balak,
Build me here seven altars, and prepare me here seven bullocks and sev-
en rams.
30 And Balak did as Bā-lāam had
said, and offered a bullock and a ram
on *every* altar.

l 1 Sam. 3.17.
m Judg. 3.20.
n 1 Sam. 15. 29. Ps. 102.26, 27. Mal. 3.6. Rom. 11.29. Titus 1.2. Jas. 1.17.
o Gen. 12.2. Gen. 22.17. ch. 22.12.
p Jer. 50.20. Hos. 14. 2-4. Micah 7.18-20. Rom. 4.7. Rom. 6.14. 2 Cor. 5.19.
q Ex. 13.21.
r Ps. 89.15. Ps. 97.1. Ps. 98.6. Isa. 33.22. Luke 19.37, 38.
s Deut. 33.17.
4 Or, in.
t Ps. 31.19.
5 Or, the wilderness.
u 2 Pet. 2.16.

CHAP. 24
1 to the meeting of enchantments.
a ch. 11.25. 1 Sam. 19. 20. 2 Chr. 15.1. Matt. 7.21-23. 1 Cor. 12.8, 10.
b ch. 23.7.
2 who had his eyes shut, but now opened.
c 1 Sam. 19. 24. Eze. 1.28. Dan. 8.18. 2 Cor. 12.2. Rev. 1.10, 17.
d Ps. 1.3. Jer. 17.8.
e 1 Sam. 15. 32.
f 2 Sam. 5.12. 1 Ki. 4.21. 1 Chr. 14.2. Isa. 2.2.
g Gen. 12.3. Ex. 23.23. Ps. 122.6. Matt. 25.40, 45.

CHAPTER 24

AND when Bā-lāam saw that it
pleased the LORD to bless Israel,
he went not, as at other times, [1]to
seek for enchantments, but he set his
face toward the wilderness.
2 And Bā-lāam lifted up his eyes, and
he saw Israel abiding *in his tents* according to their tribes; and [a]the spirit
of God came upon him.
3 And [b]he took up his parable, and
said, Bā-lāam the son of Bē-ôr hath
said, and the man [2]whose eyes are
open hath said:
4 He hath said, which heard the
words of God, which saw the vision
of the Almighty, falling [c]*into a trance*,
but having his eyes open:
5 How goodly are thy tents, O Jacob,
and thy tabernacles, O Israel!
6 As the valleys are they spread forth,
as gardens by the river's side, as the
trees of lign aloes [d]which the LORD
hath planted, *and* as cedar trees beside the waters.
7 He shall pour the water out of his
buckets, and his seed *shall be* in many
waters, and his king shall be higher
than [e]Agag, and his kingdom [f]shall be
exalted.
8 God brought him forth out of
Egypt; he hath as it were the strength
of an unicorn: he shall eat up the nations his enemies, and shall break
their bones, and pierce *them* through
with his arrows.
9 He couched, he lay down as a lion,
and as a great lion: who shall stir him
up? Blessed [g]*is* he that blesseth thee,
and cursed *is* he that curseth thee.
10 ¶ And Balak's anger was kindled
against Bā-lāam, and he smote his
hands together: and Balak said unto
Bā-lāam, I called thee to curse mine
enemies, and, behold, thou hast altogether blessed *them* these three times.
11 Therefore now flee thou to thy
place: I thought to promote thee unto
great honour; but, lo, the LORD hath
kept thee back from honour.
12 And Bā-lāam said unto Balak,
Spake I not also to thy messengers
which thou sentest unto me, saying,
13 If Balak would give me his house
full of silver and gold, I cannot go beyond the commandment of the LORD,
to do *either* good or bad of mine own
mind; *but* what the LORD saith, that
will I speak?
14 And now, behold, I go unto my
people: come *therefore*, *and* I will advertise thee what this people shall do
to thy people in the latter days.

15 ¶ And he took up his parable, and
said, Bā-lāam the son of Bē-ôr hath
said, and the man whose eyes are open
hath said:
16 He hath said, which heard the
words of God, and knew the knowledge of the most High, *which* saw the
vision of the Almighty, falling *into a
trance*, but having his eyes open:
17 I [h]shall see him, but not now: I
shall behold him, but not nigh: there
shall come a [i]Star out of Jacob, and [j]a
Sceptre shall rise out of Israel, and
shall [3]smite the corners of Moab, and
destroy all the children of Sheth.
18 And [k]Ē-dom shall be a possession,
Sē-ïr also shall be a possession for his
enemies; and Israel shall do valiantly.
19 Out of Jacob shall come he that
shall have dominion, and shall destroy him that remaineth of the
city.
20 ¶ And when he looked on Ăm-ă-
lĕk, he took up his parable, and said,
Ăm-ă-lĕk *was* [4]the first of the nations;
but his latter end [5]*shall be* that he
perish for ever.
21 And he looked on the Kē-nītes,
and took up his parable, and said,
Strong is thy dwellingplace, and thou
puttest thy nest in a rock.
22 Nevertheless [6]the Kē-nīte shall be
wasted, [7]until Ăssh-ŭr shall carry thee
away captive.
23 And he took up his parable, and
said, Alas, who shall live when God
doeth this!
24 And ships *shall come* from the
coast of [l]Chĭt-tĭm, and shall afflict
Ăssh-ŭr, and shall afflict [m]Ē-bĕr, and
[n]he also shall perish for ever.
25 And Bā-lāam rose up, and went
and returned to his place: and Balak
also went his way.

CHAPTER 25

AND Israel abode in [a]Shĭt-tĭm, and
[b]the people began to commit
whoredom with the daughters of
Moab.
2 And [c]they called the people unto
the [d]sacrifices of their gods: and the
people did eat, and [e]bowed down to
their gods.
3 And Israel joined himself unto Bā-
ăl–pē-ôr: and [f]the anger of the LORD
was kindled against Israel.
4 And the LORD said unto Moses,
Take [g]all the heads of the people, and
hang them up before the LORD
against the sun, [h]that the fierce anger
of the LORD may be turned away from
Israel.
5 And Moses said unto the judges of
Israel, Slay [i]ye every one his men that
were joined unto Bā-ăl–pē-ôr.
6 ¶ And, behold, one of the children
of Israel came and brought unto his
brethren a Mĭd-ĭ-ă-nī-tĭsh woman in
the sight of Moses, and in the sight
of all the congregation of the children
of Israel, [j]who *were* weeping *before*
the door of the tabernacle of the congregation.
7 And when Phĭn-ĕ-hăs, [k]the son of
Ĕl-ē-ā-zär, the son of Aaron the
priest, saw *it*, he rose up from among
the congregation, and took [1]a javelin
in his hand;
8 And he went after the man of Israel into the tent, and thrust both of
them through, the man of Israel, and
the woman through her belly. So the
plague was stayed from the children
of Israel.
9 And [l]those that died in the plague
were twenty and four thousand.
10 ¶ And the LORD spake unto Moses,
saying,
11 Phĭn-ĕ-hăs, [m]the son of Ĕl-ē-ā-
zär, the son of Aaron the priest, hath
turned my wrath away from the children of Israel, while he was zealous
[2]for my sake among them, that I consumed not the children of Israel in my
[n]jealousy.
12 Wherefore say, [o]Behold, I give unto him my covenant of peace:
13 And he shall have it, and [p]his seed
after him, *even* the covenant of [q]an
everlasting priesthood; because he
was [r]zealous for his God, and made
an atonement for the children of
Israel.
14 Now the name of the Israelite
that was slain, *even* that was slain
with the Mĭd-ĭ-ă-nī-tĭsh woman, *was*
Zimri, the son of Sā-lû, a prince
of a [3]chief house among the Simeonites.
15 And the name of the Mĭd-ĭ-ă-nī-
tĭsh woman that was slain *was* Cŏz-bī,
the daughter of Zur; he *was* head over
a people, *and* of a chief house in Mĭd-
ĭ-ăn.
16 ¶ And the LORD spake unto Moses,
saying,
17 Vex the Mĭd-ĭ-ă-nītes, and smite
them:
18 For they vex you with their wiles,
wherewith they have beguiled you in
the matter of Pē-ôr, and in the matter
of Cŏz-bī, the daughter of a prince of
Mĭd-ĭ-ăn, their sister, which was slain
in the day of the plague for Pē-ôr's
sake.

h Job 19. 25-27.
i Jer. 23.5. Dan. 2.44. Luke 1.32, 33. Heb. 1.8. Rev. 22.16.
j Gen. 49.10. Ps. 110.2.
3 Or, smite through the princes of Moab.
k Gen. 27.37. 2 Sam. 8.14. Ps. 60.8-12. Isa. 34.5.
4 Or, the first of the nations that warred against Israel.
5 Or, shall be even to destruction.
6 Kain.
7 Or, how long shall it be ere Asshur carry thee away captive?
l Gen. 10.4. Isa. 23.1.
m Gen. 11.14.
n Lev. 26.28. Deut. 28.36. Matt. 23.27.

CHAP. 25

a ch. 33.49. Micah 6.5.
b ch. 31.16. Rev. 2.14.
c Josh. 22.17. Hosea 9.10.
d Ex. 34.15.
e Ex. 20.5.
f Ps. 106.29.
g Josh. 22.17.
h Deut. 13. 17.
i 1 Ki. 18.40.
j Joel 2.17.
k Ex. 6.25.
1 a spear, or, pike.
l 1 Cor. 10.8.
m Ps. 106.30.
2 with my zeal.
n Ex. 20.5. Ps. 78.53. Nah. 1.2. Zeph. 1.18.
o Mal. 3.1.
p 1 Chr. 6.4.
q Ex. 40.15.
r Acts 22.3.
3 house of a father.

CHAPTER 26

AND it came to pass after the plague, that the LORD spake unto Moses and unto Ĕl-ē-ā´-zär the son of Aaron the priest, saying,

2 Take [a]the sum of all the congregation of the children of Israel, from twenty years old and upward, throughout their fathers' house, all that are able to go to war in Israel.

3 And Moses and Ĕl-ē-ā´-zär the priest spake with them [b]in the plains of Moab by Jordan *near* Jericho, saying,

4 *Take the sum of the people*, from twenty years old and upward; as the LORD commanded Moses and the children of Israel, which went forth out of the land of Egypt.

5 ¶ Reuben, [c]the eldest son of Israel: the children of Reuben; Hā´-nŏch, *of whom cometh* the family of the Hā´-nŏch-ītes: of Păl´-lû, the family of the Păl´-lū-ītes:

6 Of Hĕz´-rŏn, the family of the Hĕz´-rŏn-ītes: of Cär´-mī, the family of the Cär´-mītes.

7 These *are* the families of the Reubenites: and they that were numbered of them were forty and three thousand and seven hundred and thirty.

8 And the sons of Păl´-lû; Ē-lī´-ăb.

9 And the sons of Ē-lī´-ăb; Nĕm´-ū-ĕl, and Dā´-thăn, and Ă-bī´-răm. This *is that* Dā´-thăn and Ă-bī´-răm, *which were* [d]famous in the congregation, who strove against Moses and against Aaron in the company of Kôr´-ăh, when they strove against the LORD:

10 And the earth opened her mouth, and swallowed them up together with Kôr´-ăh, when that company died, what time the fire devoured two hundred and fifty men: and they [e]became a sign.

11 Notwithstanding [f]the children of Kôr´-ăh died not.

12 ¶ The sons of Simeon after their families: of [g]Nĕm´-ū-ĕl, the family of the Nĕm-ū-ē´-lītes: of Jā´-mĭn, the family of the Jā´-mĭn-ītes: of Jā´-chĭn, [h]the family of the Jā´-chĭn-ītes:

13 Of [i]Zē´-răh, the family of the Zär´-hītes: of Shā´-ŭl, the family of the Shā-ū´-lītes.

14 These *are* the families of the Simeonites, twenty and two thousand and two hundred.

15 ¶ The children of Gad after their families: of [j]Zē´-phŏn, the family of the Zē´-phŏn-ītes: of Hăg´-gī, the family of the Hăg´-gītes: of Shû´-nī, the family of the Shû´-nītes:

16 Of [1]Ŏz´-nī, the family of the Ŏz´-nītes: of Ē´-rī, the family of the Ē´-rītes:

17 Of [k]Âr´-ŏd, the family of the Âr´-ō-dītes: of Ă-rē´-lī, the family of the Ă-rē´-lītes.

18 These *are* the families of the children of Gad according to those that were numbered of them, forty thousand and five hundred.

19 ¶ The [l]sons of Judah *were* Er and Ō´-năn: and Er and Ō´-năn died in the land of Canaan.

20 And [m]the sons of Judah after their families were; of Shē´-lăh, the family of the Shē-lā´-nītes: of Phâr´-ĕz, the family of the Phär´-zītes: of Zē´-răh, the family of the Zär´-hītes.

21 And the sons of Phâr´-ĕz were; of Hĕz´-rŏn, the family of the Hĕz´-rŏn-ītes: of Hăm´-ŭl, the family of the Hăm-ū´-lītes.

22 These *are* the families of Judah according to those that were numbered of them, threescore and sixteen thousand and five hundred.

23 ¶ *Of* [n]the sons of Ĭs´-să-chär after their families: *of* Tō´-lă, the family of the Tō´-lā-ītes: of [2]Pū´-ă, the family of the Pū´-nītes:

24 Of [3]Jăsh´-ŭb, the family of the Jăsh´-ū-bītes: of Shĭm´-rŏn, the family of the Shĭm´-rŏn-ītes.

25 These *are* the families of Ĭs´-să-chär according to those that were numbered of them, threescore and four thousand and three hundred.

26 ¶ *Of* [o]the sons of Zĕ-bū´-lŭn after their families: of Sē´-rĕd, the family of the Săr´-dītes: of Ē´-lŏn, the family of the Ē´-lŏn-ītes: of Jăh´-lēel, the family of the Jăh´-lēel-ītes.

27 These *are* the families of the Zĕ-bū´-lŭn-ītes according to those that were numbered of them, threescore thousand and five hundred.

28 ¶ The [p]sons of Joseph after their families *were* Mă-năs´-sēh and Ē´-phră-ĭm.

29 Of the sons of Mă-năs´-sēh: of Mā´-chĭr, [q]the family of the Mā´-chĭr-ītes: and Mā´-chĭr begat Gilead: of Gilead *come* the family of the Gileadites.

30 These *are* the sons of Gilead: *of* [r]Jē-ē´-zĕr, the family of the Jē-ē´-zĕr-ītes: of Hē´-lĕk, the family of the Hē´-lĕk-ītes:

31 And *of* Ăs´-rī-ĕl, the family of the Ăs´-rī-ē-lītes: and *of* Shē´-chĕm, the family of the Shē´-chĕm-ītes:

32 And *of* Shĕ-mī´-dă, the family of

CHAP. 26

a Ex. 30.12. ch. 1.2.
b ch. 22.1. ch. 31.12. ch. 33.48. ch. 35.1. Deut. 4.46-49. Deut. 34.1, 6-8.
c Gen. 29.32. Gen. 46.8. Gen. 49.2,3. Ex. 6.14. ch. 1.21. Deut. 33.6. 1 Chr. 5.1. Rev. 7.5.
d ch. 16.1,2. ch. 27.3. Deut. 11.6. Ps. 106.11. Isa. 65.16. Jude 11.
e ch. 16.38. 1 Sam. 2.34. Job 31.3. Ps. 145.20. Pro. 2.22. Pro. 10.29. Pro. 11.21. Jer. 29.22. Eze. 14.8. 1 Cor. 10.6. 2 Pet. 2.6. Jude 7.
f Ex. 6.24. 1 Chr. 6.22.
g Gen. 46.10. Ex. 6.15. Jemuel.
h 1 Chr. 4.24. Jarib.
i Gen. 46.10. Zohar.
j Gen. 46.16. Ziphion.
1 Or, Ezbon.
k Gen. 46.16. Arodi.
l Gen. 38.2. Gen. 46.12. 1 Chr. 2.3.
m Gen. 49.8. 1 Chr. 2.3. Rev. 7.5.
n Gen. 46.13. ch. 1.28,29. 1 Chr. 7.1.
2 Or, Phuvah.
3 Or, Job.
o Gen. 46.14. Gen. 49.13. ch. 1.30,31. Deut. 33.18.
p Gen. 41.51. Gen. 46.20. ch. 1.32-35. Deut. 33.17.
q ch. 32.39, 40. ch. 36.1. Deut. 3.15. Josh. 17.1. Judg. 5.14. 1 Chr. 7.14, 15.
r Called Abiezer. Josh. 17.2. Judg. 6.11, 24,34.

the Shĕ-mī´-dā-ītes: and *of* Hē´-phĕr,
the family of the Hē´-phĕr-ītes.
33 ¶ And [s]Zē-lŏph´-ĕ-hăd the son of
Hē´-phĕr had no sons, but daughters:
and the names of the daughters of Zē-
lŏph-ĕ-hăd *were* Mäh´-lăh, and Noah,
Hŏg´-lăh, Mĭl´-căh, and Tĭr´-zăh.
34 These *are* the families of Mă-năs´-
sĕh, and those that were numbered
of them, fifty and two thousand and
seven hundred.
35 ¶ These *are* the sons of Ē´-phră-ĭm
after their families: of Shû-thē-lăh,
the family of the Shû-thăl´-hītes: of
Bē´-chĕr, [t]the family of the Băch´-rītes:
of Tā´-hăn, the family of the Tā´-hăn-
ītes.
36 And these *are* the sons of Shû-
thē´-lăh: of Ē´-răn, the family of the Ē´-
răn-ītes.
37 These *are* the families of the sons
of Ē´-phră-ĭm according to those that
were numbered of them, thirty and
two thousand and five hundred.
These *are* the sons [u]of Joseph after
their families.
38 ¶ The [v]sons of Benjamin after
their families: of Bē´-lă, the family of
the Bē´-lā-ītes: of Ăsh´-bĕl, the family
of the Ăsh´-bĕl-ītes: of [w]Ă-hī´-răm, the
family of the Ă-hī´-răm-ītes:
39 Of [x]Shû´-phăm, the family of the
Shû´-phăm-ītes: of Hū´-phăm, the
family of the Hū´-phăm-ītes.
40 And the sons of Bē´-lă were [y]Ärd
and Nā´-ă-măn: *of Ard*, the family of
the Ärd-ītes: *and* of Nā´-ă-măn, the
family of the Nā´-ă-mītes.
41 These *are* the sons of Benjamin
after their families: and they that
were numbered of them *were* forty
and five thousand and six hundred.
42 ¶ These [z]*are* the sons of Dan after
their families: of [4]Shû´-hăm, the family
of the Shû´-hăm-ītes. These *are* the
families of Dan after their families.
43 All the families of the Shû´-hăm-
ītes, according to those that were numbered of them, *were* threescore and
four thousand and four hundred.
44 ¶ *Of* [a]the children of Asher after
their families: of Jĭm´-nă, the family
of the Jĭm´-nītes: of Jĕs´-ū-ī, the family
of the Jĕs´-ū-ītes: of Bĕ-rī´-ăh, the family of the Bĕ-rī´-ītes.
45 Of the sons of Bĕ-rī´-ăh: of Hē´-
bĕr, the family of the Hē´-bĕr-ītes: of
Măl´-chī-ĕl, the family of the Măl-chī-
ĕ´-lītes.
46 And the name of the daughter of
Asher *was* Sarah.
47 These *are* the families of the sons
of Asher according to those that were

s ch. 27.1. Josh. 17.3.
t 1 Chr. 7.20. Bered.
u Deut. 33. 13-17.
v Gen. 46.21. 1 Chr. 7.6. 1 Chr. 8.1.
w Gen. 46.21. Ehi. 1 Chr. 8.1. Aharah.
x Gen. 46.21. Muppim, and Huppim.
y 1 Chr. 8.3. Addar.
z Gen. 46.23. Gen. 49.16, 17. ch. 1.38,39. Deut.33.22.
4 Or, Hushim.
a Gen. 46.17. 1 Chr. 7.30.
b Gen. 46.24. 1 Chr. 7.13.
c 1 Chr. 7.13. Shallum.
d ch. 1.46. ch. 2.32.
5 Thus each man's portion would be fifteen acres.
e ch. 33.54.
6 multiply his inheritance.
7 diminish his inheritance.
f ch. 34.13. Josh. 11.23. Josh. 14.2. Josh. 17.14. Josh. 18.6, 10,11.
g Gen. 46.11. Ex. 6.16. 1 Chr. 6.1, 16.
h Ex. 2.1,2.
i Lev. 10.1,2. ch. 3.4. 1 Chr. 24.2.
j ch. 3.39.

numbered of them; *who were* fifty and
three thousand and four hundred.
48 ¶ *Of* [b]the sons of Năph´-tă-lī after
their families: of Jăh´-zēel, the family
of the Jăh´-zēel-ītes: of Gū´-nī, the family of the Gū´-nītes:
49 Of Jē´-zĕr, the family of the Jē´-zĕr-
ītes: of [c]Shĭl´-lĕm, the family of the
Shĭl´-lĕm-ītes.
50 These *are* the families of Năph´-
tă-lī according to their families: and
they that were numbered of them *were*
forty and five thousand and four
hundred.
51 These [d]*were* the numbered of the
children of Israel, six hundred thousand and a thousand seven hundred
and thirty.
52¶ And the LORD spake unto Moses,
saying,
53 Unto [5]these the land shall be
divided for an inheritance according
to the number of names.
54 To [e]many thou shalt [6]give the
more inheritance, and to few thou
shalt [7]give the less inheritance: to
every one shall his inheritance be giv-
en according to those that were numbered of him.
55 Notwithstanding the land shall be
divided [f]by lot: according to the
names of the tribes of their fathers
they shall inherit.
56 According to the lot shall the
possession thereof be divided between
many and few.
57 ¶ And [g]these *are* they that were
numbered of the Levites after their
families: of Gĕr´-shŏn, the family of
the Gĕr´-shŏn-ītes: of Kō´-hăth, the
family of the Kō´-hăth-ītes: of Mĕ-
rār´-ī, the family of the Mĕ-rār´-ītes.
58 These *are* the families of the Levites: the family of the Lĭb´-nītes, the
family of the Hē´-brŏn-ītes, the family
of the Măh´-lītes, the family of the
Mū´-shītes, the family of the Kôr´-ă-
thītes. And Kō´-hăth begat Amram.
59 And the name of Amram's wife
was [h]Jŏch´-ĕ-bĕd, the daughter of
Levi, whom *her mother* bare to Levi
in Egypt: and she bare unto Amram
Aaron and Moses, and Miriam their
sister.
60 And unto Aaron was born Nadab,
and Ă-bī-hū, Ĕl-ē-ā´-zăr, and Ĭth-ă-
mär.
61 And [i]Nadab and Ă-bī´-hū died,
when they offered strange fire before
the LORD.
62 And [j]those that were numbered
of them were twenty and three thousand, all males from a month old and

upward: [k]for they were not numbered among the children of Israel, because there was [l]no inheritance given them among the children of Israel.

63 ¶ These *are* they that were numbered by Moses and Ĕl-ē-ā-́zär the priest, who numbered the children of Israel in the plains of Moab by Jordan *near* Jericho.

64 But [m]among these there was not a man of them whom Moses and Aaron the priest numbered, when they numbered the children of Israel in the wilderness of Sī-́nâi.

65 For the LORD had said of them, They shall [n]surely die in the wilderness. And there was not left a man of them, [o]save Caleb the son of Jĕ-phŭn-́nēh, and Joshua the son of Nun.

CHAPTER 27

THEN came the daughters [a]of Zē-lŏph-́ĕ-hăd, the son of Hē-́phĕr, the son of Gilead, the son of Mā-́chĭr, the son of Mă-năs-́sēh, of the families of Mă-năs-́sēh the son of Joseph: and these *are* the names of his daughters; Māh-́lăh, Noah, and Hŏg-́lăh, and Mĭl-́căh, and Tĭr-́zăh.

2 And they stood before Moses, and before Ĕl-ē-ā-́zär the priest, and before the princes and all the congregation, *by* the door of the tabernacle of the congregation, saying,

3 Our father [b]died in the wilderness, and he was not in the company of them that gathered themselves together against the LORD [c]in the company of Kôr-́āh; but [d]died in his own sin, and had no sons.

4 Why should the name of our father be [1]done away from among his family, because he hath no son? Give unto us *therefore* a possession among the brethren of our father.

5 And Moses [e]brought their cause before the LORD.

6 ¶ And the LORD spake unto Moses, saying,

7 The daughters of Zē-lŏph-́ĕ-hăd speak right: thou [f]shalt surely give them a possession of an inheritance among their father's brethren; and thou shalt cause the inheritance of their father to pass unto them.

8 And thou shalt speak unto the children of Israel, saying, If a man die, and have no son, then ye shall cause his inheritance to pass unto his daughter.

9 And if he have no daughter, then ye shall give his inheritance unto his brethren.

k ch. 1.49.
l ch. 18.20,23, 24. ch. 35.2-8. Deut. 10.9. Deut. 14.27-29. Deut. 18.1, 2. Josh. 14.3, 23.
m ch. 1.1. Deut. 2.14, 15.
n ch. 14.28. Deut. 32.49, 50. Ps. 90.3-8. Rom. 11.22. 1 Cor. 10.5. Heb. 3.17, 18. Jude 5.
o ch. 14.30. ch. 32.12. Deut. 1.36, 38.

CHAP. 27

a ch. 14.35. ch. 26.33. ch. 36.1,11. 1 Chr. 7.15.
b ch. 26.64, 65.
c ch. 16.1,2.
d ch. 14.22-37. Rom. 5.12.
1 dimished.
e Ex. 18.15. Lev. 24.12, 13. Pro. 3.5,6.
f ch. 36.2.
g ch. 35.29.
h Deut. 3.27. Deut. 32.49.
i ch. 20.24,28. ch. 31.2. Deut. 10.6.
j Deut. 1.37. Ps. 106.32.
k Ex. 17.7. ch. 20.1,13, 24.
l ch. 16.22. Zech. 12.1. Heb. 12.9.
m Deut. 31.2. 1 Sam. 8.20. 2 Chr. 1.10.
n 1 Ki. 22.17. 2 Chr. 18.16. Matt. 9.36.
o Gen. 41.38.
p Deut. 31.7.
q ch. 11.17. 1 Sam. 10.6. 2 Ki. 2.15.
r Deut. 34.9. Josh. 1.15.
s Josh. 9.14. Judg. 1.1. 1 Sam. 23.9. 1 Sam. 30.7.
t Lev. 8.8. Deut. 33.8. 1 Sam. 28.6.
u Josh. 9.14. 1 Sam. 22. 10.
v Deut. 3.28. Isa. 55.4.

10 And if he have no brethren, then ye shall give his inheritance unto his father's brethren.

11 And if his father have no brethren, then ye shall give his inheritance unto his kinsman that is next to him of his family, and he shall possess it: and it shall be unto the children of Israel [g]a statute of judgment, as the LORD commanded Moses.

12 ¶ And the LORD said unto Moses, [h]Get thee up into this mount Ăb-́ă-rĭm, and see the land which I have given unto the children of Israel.

13 And when thou hast seen it, thou also shalt [i]be gathered unto thy people, as Aaron thy brother was gathered.

14 For ye [j]rebelled against my commandment in the desert of Zin, in the strife of the congregation, to sanctify me at the water before their eyes: that *is* [k]the water of Mĕr-́ĭ-băh in Kā-́dĕsh in the wilderness of Zin.

15 ¶ And Moses spake unto the LORD, saying,

16 Let the LORD, the [l]God of the spirits of all flesh, set a man over the congregation,

17 Which [m]may go out before them, and which may go in before them, and which may lead them out, and which may bring them in; that the congregation of the LORD be not [n]as sheep which have no shepherd.

18 ¶ And the LORD said unto Moses, Take thee Joshua the son of Nun, a man [o]in whom *is* the spirit, and lay thine hand upon him;

19 And set him before Ĕl-ē-ā-́zär the priest, and before all the congregation; and [p]give him a charge in their sight.

20 And [q]thou shalt put *some* of thine honour upon him, that all the congregation of the children of Israel [r]may be obedient.

21 And [s]he shall stand before Ĕl-ē-ā-́zär the priest, who shall ask *counsel* for him [t]after the judgment of Ū-́rĭm before the LORD: at [u]his word shall they go out, and at his word they shall come in, *both* he, and all the children of Israel with him, even all the congregation.

22 And Moses did as the LORD commanded him: and he took Joshua, and set him before Ĕl-ē-ā-́zär the priest, and before all the congregation:

23 And he laid his hands upon him, [v]and gave him a charge, as the LORD commanded by the hand of Moses.

CHAPTER 28

AND the LORD spake unto Moses,
saying,
2 Command the children of Israel,
and say unto them, My offering, *and*
[a]my bread for my sacrifices made by
fire, *for* [1]a sweet savour unto me, shall
ye observe to offer unto me in their
due season.
3 And thou shalt say unto them, This
[b]*is* the offering made by fire which ye
shall offer unto the LORD; two lambs
of the first year without spot [2]day
by day, *for* a continual burnt offering.
4 The one lamb shalt thou offer in
the morning, and the other lamb
shalt thou offer [3]at even;
5 And [c]a tenth *part* of an ē-phăh of
flour for a [d]meat offering, mingled
with the fourth *part* of an [e]hĭn of beat-
en oil.
6 *It is* a continual burnt offering,
which was ordained in mount Sī-nāi
for a sweet savour, a sacrifice made by
fire unto the LORD.
7 And the drink offering thereof *shall*
be the fourth *part* of an hĭn for the
one lamb: in [f]the holy *place* shalt thou
cause the strong wine to be poured unto the LORD *for* a drink offering.
8 And the other lamb shalt thou offer
at even: as the meat offering of the
morning, and as the drink offering
thereof, thou shalt offer *it*, a sacrifice
made by fire, of a sweet savour unto
the LORD.
9 ¶ And on the sabbath day two
lambs of the first year without spot,
and two tenth deals of flour *for* a meat
offering, mingled with oil, and the
drink offering thereof:
10 *This is* [g]the burnt offering of every
sabbath, beside the continual burnt
offering, and his drink offering.
11 ¶ And [h]in the beginnings of your
months ye shall offer a burnt offering
unto the LORD; two young bullocks,
and one ram, seven lambs of the first
year without spot;
12 And [i]three tenth deals of flour *for*
a meat offering, mingled with oil, for
one bullock; and two tenth deals of
flour *for* a meat offering, mingled with
oil, for one ram;
13 And a several tenth deal of flour
mingled with oil *for* a meat offering
unto one lamb; *for* a burnt offering of
a sweet savour, a sacrifice made by
fire unto the LORD.
14 And their drink offerings shall be
half an hĭn of wine unto a bullock, and
the third *part* of an hĭn unto a ram,

CHAP. 28
a Lev. 3.11. Mal. 1.7,12.
1 a savour of my rest.
b Ex. 29.38.
2 in a day.
3 between the two evenings.
c Ex. 16.36. Lev. 2.1. ch. 15.4.
d Lev. 2.1.
e Ex. 29.40.
f Ex. 29.42. Lev. 23.13. ch. 15.5,7, 10. Isa. 57.1.
g Eze. 46.4.
h ch. 10.10. 1 Sam. 20.5. 1 Chr. 23.31. 2 Chr. 2.4. Neh. 10.33. Isa. 1.13,14. Hosea 2.11. Col. 2.16.
i ch. 15.4. ch. 29.10.
j Ex. 12.6. Lev. 23.5. Eze. 45.21. Matt. 26.2, 17. Luke 22.7.
k Ex. 12.15-17. Lev. 23.6.
l Lev. 23.7.
m Lev. 22.20. ch. 29.8. Deut. 15.21.
n Lev. 16.18. Rom. 8.3. Gal. 4.4. Heb. 9.12.
o 2 Cor. 2.15. Eph. 5.2.
p Ex. 12.16. Lev. 23.8.
q Ex. 23.16. Lev. 23.10, 15. Deut. 16.10. Pro. 3.9. Acts 2.1.
r Lev. 23.18, 19.

and a fourth *part* of an hĭn unto a
lamb: this *is* the burnt offering of
every month throughout the months
of the year.
15 And one kid of the goats for a sin
offering unto the LORD shall be offered, beside the continual burnt offering, and his drink offering.
16 And [j]in the fourteenth day of the
first month *is* the passover of the
LORD.
17 And [k]in the fifteenth day of this
month *is* the feast: seven days shall unleavened bread be eaten.
18 In the [l]first day *shall be* an holy
convocation; ye shall do no manner
of servile work *therein:*
19 But ye shall offer a sacrifice made
by fire *for* a burnt offering unto the
LORD; two young bullocks, and one
ram, and seven lambs of the first year:
they [m]shall be unto you without
blemish:
20 And their meat offering *shall be of*
flour mingled with oil: three tenth
deals shall ye offer for a bullock, and
two tenth deals for a ram;
21 A several tenth deal shalt thou
offer for every lamb, throughout the
seven lambs:
22 And one [n]goat *for* a sin offering, to
make an atonement for you.
23 Ye shall offer these beside the
burnt offering in the morning, which
is for a continual burnt offering.
24 After this manner ye shall offer
daily, throughout the seven days, the
meat of the sacrifice made by fire, of
[o]a sweet savour unto the LORD: it shall
be offered beside the continual burnt
offering, and his drink offering.
25 And [p]on the seventh day ye shall
have an holy convocation; ye shall do
no servile work.
26 ¶ Also [q]in the day of the firstfruits,
when ye bring a new meat offering unto the LORD, after your weeks *be out*,
ye shall have an holy convocation; ye
shall do no servile work:
27 But ye shall offer the burnt offering for a sweet savour unto the LORD;
[r]two young bullocks, one ram, seven
lambs of the first year;
28 And their meat offering of flour
mingled with oil, three tenth deals
unto one bullock, two tenth deals unto one ram,
29 A several tenth deal unto one
lamb, throughout the seven lambs;
30 *And* one kid of the goats, to make
an atonement for you.
31 Ye shall offer *them* beside the continual burnt offering, and his meat

offering, (they shall be unto you without blemish) and their drink offerings.

CHAPTER 29

AND in the seventh month, on the
first *day* of the month, ye shall
have an holy convocation; ye shall do
no servile work: [a]it is a day of blowing
the trumpets unto you.
2 And ye shall offer a burnt offering
for a sweet savour unto the LORD; one
young bullock, one ram, *and* seven
lambs of the first year without blemish:
3 And their meat offering *shall be of*
flour mingled with oil, three tenth
deals for a bullock, *and* two tenth
deals for a ram,
4 And one tenth deal for one lamb,
throughout the seven lambs:
5 And one kid of the goats *for* a sin
offering, to make an atonement for
you:
6 Beside [b]the burnt offering of the
month, and his meat offering, and [c]the
daily burnt offering, and his meat
offering, and their drink offerings,
[d]according unto their manner, for [1]a
sweet savour, a sacrifice made by fire
unto the LORD.
7 ¶ And [e]ye shall have on the tenth
day of this seventh month an holy
convocation; and ye [f]shall afflict your
souls: ye shall not do any work *therein:*
8 But ye shall offer a burnt offering
unto the LORD *for* a sweet savour; one
young bullock, one ram, *and* seven
lambs of the first year; they [g]shall be
unto you without blemish:
9 And their meat offering *shall be of*
flour mingled with oil, three tenth
deals to a bullock, *and* two tenth deals
to one ram,
10 A several tenth deal for one lamb,
throughout the seven lambs:
11 One kid of the goats *for* a sin offering; beside [h]the sin offering of atonement, and the continual burnt offering, and the meat offering of it, and
their drink offerings.
12 ¶ And [i]on the fifteenth day of the
seventh month ye shall have an holy
convocation; ye shall do no servile
work, and ye shall keep a feast unto
the LORD seven days:
13 And [j]ye shall offer a burnt offering, a sacrifice made by fire, of a sweet
savour unto the LORD; thirteen young
bullocks, two rams, *and* fourteen
lambs of the first year; they shall be
without blemish:
14 And their meat offering *shall be of*

CHAP. 29

a Lev. 23.24. Ps. 89.15. Isa. 27.13. Zech. 9.14. Mark 16.15. 1 Cor. 15.52. Rev. 8.6-13.

b ch. 28.11.

c Ex. 29.38. Lev. 6.9. ch. 28.3. Dan. 12.11.

d ch. 15.11, 12.

1 a savour of rest.

e Lev. 16.29. Lev. 23.27.

f Ezra 8.21. Ps. 35.13. Isa. 58.5. Matt. 5.4. Luke 13.3,4. 1 Cor. 9.27. 2 Cor. 7.9. Jas. 4.9.

g Lev. 22.20. ch. 28.19. ch. 29.8. Deut. 15.21. Deut. 17.1.

h Lev. 16.3, 5.

i Ex. 23.16. Ex. 34.22. Lev. 23.33. Deut. 16.13. Eze. 45.25.

j Ezra 3.4. Dan. 9.24. Heb. 7.18, 19. Heb. 8.13. Heb. 10.1-18.

2 Perhaps the gradual decrease of the bullocks denoted the gradual abolition of the ceremonies.

k Lev. 2.1. ch. 15.12. ch. 28.7,14.

l Heb. 7.26. 1 Pet. 1.19. Rev. 5.6-14.

flour mingled with oil, three tenth
deals unto every bullock of the thirteen bullocks, two tenth deals to each
ram of the two rams,
15 And a several tenth deal to each
lamb of the fourteen lambs:
16 And one kid of the goats *for* a sin
offering; beside the continual burnt
offering, his meat offering, and his
drink offering.
17 ¶ And on the second day *ye shall
offer* twelve [2]young bullocks, two
rams, fourteen lambs of the first year
without spot:
18 And their meat offering and their
drink offerings for the bullocks, for
the rams, and for the lambs, *shall be*
according to their number, [k]after the
manner:
19 And one kid of the goats *for* a sin
offering; beside the continual burnt
offering, and the meat offering thereof, and their drink offerings.
20 ¶ And on the third day eleven
bullocks, two rams, fourteen lambs of
the first year without blemish;
21 And their meat offering and their
drink offerings for the bullocks, for
the rams, and for the lambs, *shall be*
according to their number, after the
manner:
22 And one goat *for* a sin offering;
beside the continual burnt offering,
and his meat offering, and his drink
offering.
23 ¶ And on the fourth day ten bullocks, two rams, *and* fourteen lambs
of the first year without blemish:
24 Their meat offering and their
drink offerings for the bullocks, for
the rams, and for the lambs, *shall be*
according to their number, after the
manner:
25 And one kid of the goats *for* a sin
offering; beside the continual burnt
offering, his meat offering, and his
drink offering.
26 ¶ And on the fifth day nine bullocks, two rams, *and* fourteen lambs
of the first year [l]without spot:
27 And their meat offering and their
drink offerings for the bullocks, for
the rams, and for the lambs, *shall be*
according to their number, after the
manner:
28 And one goat *for* a sin offering;
beside the continual burnt offering,
and his meat offering, and his drink
offering.
29 ¶ And on the sixth day eight bullocks, two rams, *and* fourteen lambs
of the first year without blemish:
30 And their meat offering and their

drink offerings for the bullocks, for the rams, and for the lambs, *shall be* according to their number, after the manner:

31 And one goat *for* a sin offering; beside the continual burnt offering, his meat offering, and his drink offering.

32 ¶ And on the seventh day seven bullocks, two rams, *and* fourteen lambs of the first year without blemish:

33 And their meat offering and their drink offerings for the bullocks, for the rams, and for the lambs, *shall be* according to their number, after the manner:

34 And one goat *for* a sin offering; beside the continual burnt offering, his meat offering, and his drink offering.

35 ¶ On the eighth day ye shall have a solemn [m]assembly: ye shall do no servile work *therein:*

36 But ye shall offer a burnt offering, a sacrifice made by fire, of a sweet savour unto the LORD: one bullock, one ram, seven lambs of the first year without blemish:

37 Their meat offering and their drink offerings for the bullock, for the ram, and for the lambs, *shall be* according to their number, after the manner:

38 And one goat *for* a sin offering; beside the continual burnt offering, and his meat offering, and his drink offering.

39 These *things* ye shall [3]do unto the LORD in your [n]set feasts, beside your [o]vows, and your freewill offerings, for your burnt offerings, and for your meat offerings, and for your drink offerings, and for your peace offerings.

40 And [p]Moses told the children of Israel according to all that the LORD commanded Moses.

CHAPTER 30

AND Moses spake unto [a]the heads of the tribes concerning the children of Israel, saying, This *is* the thing which the LORD hath commanded.

2 If [b]a man vow a vow unto the LORD, or swear [c]an oath to bind his soul with a bond; he shall not [1]break his word, he shall [d]do according to all that proceedeth out of his mouth.

3 If a woman also vow a vow unto the LORD, and bind *herself* by a bond, *being* in her father's house in her youth;

4 And her father hear her vow, and her bond wherewith she hath bound her soul, and her father shall hold his peace at her: then all her vows shall stand, and every bond wherewith she hath bound her soul shall stand.

5 But if her father disallow her in the day that he heareth; not any of her vows, or of her bonds wherewith she hath bound her soul, shall stand: and the LORD shall forgive her, because her father disallowed her.

6 And if she had at all an husband, when [2]she vowed, or uttered ought out of her lips, wherewith she bound her soul;

7 And her husband heard *it*, and held his peace at her in the day that he heard *it:* then her vows shall stand, and her bonds wherewith she bound her soul shall stand.

8 But if her husband [e]disallowed her on the day that he heard *it;* then he shall make her vow which she vowed, and that which she uttered with her lips, wherewith she bound her soul, of none effect: and the LORD shall forgive her.

9 But every vow of a widow, and of her that is [f]divorced, wherewith they have bound their souls, shall stand against her.

10 And if she vowed in her husband's house, or bound her soul by a bond with an oath;

11 And her husband heard *it*, and held his peace at her, *and* disallowed her not: then all her vows shall stand, and every bond wherewith she bound her soul shall stand.

12 But if her husband hath [3]utterly made them void on the day he heard *them; then* whatsoever proceeded out of her lips concerning her vows, or concerning the bond of her soul, shall not stand: her husband hath made them void; and the LORD shall forgive her.

13 Every vow, and every binding oath to afflict the soul, her husband may establish it, or her husband may make it void.

14 But if her husband altogether hold his peace at her from day to day; then he establisheth all her vows, or all her bonds, which *are* upon her: he confirmeth them, because he held his peace at her in the day that he heard *them*.

15 But if he shall any ways make them void after that he hath heard *them;* then he shall [4]bear her iniquity.

16 These *are* the statutes, which the

m Lev. 23.36. Ps. 47.5,6. Isa. 11.10. Isa. 54.1. Isa. 60.1. Matt. 28.1. John 7.37. Heb. 1.3. Heb. 4.9. Rev. 7.9-17. Rev. 11.15.
3 Or, offer.
n Lev. 23.2. 1 Chr. 23.31. Neh. 10.33. Isa. 1.14.
o Lev. 7.11, 16. Lev. 22.21, 23. Lev. 23.38. ch. 6.21. Deut. 12.6. 1 Cor. 10.31.
p Ex. 24.3. Deut. 5.27-31. John 1.17. Acts 7.37, 38.

CHAP. 30

a ch. 1.4,16. Deut. 1.13, 17.
b Gen. 28.20. Lev. 27.2. Judg. 11.30, 35. Ps. 56.12. Pro. 20.25. Eccl. 5.4.
c Lev. 5.4. Matt. 14.9. Acts 23.14.
1 profane.
d Job 22.27. Ps. 22.25. Ps. 50.14. Ps. 66.13,14. Nah. 1.15.
2 her vows were upon her.
e Gen. 3.16. 1 Cor. 7.4. Eph. 5.22-24. Col. 3.18. 1 Pet. 3.1.
f Lev. 21.7.
3 making void hath made them void.
4 Or, take away.

LORD commanded Moses, between a man and his wife, between the father and his daughter, *being yet* in her youth in her father's house.

CHAPTER 31

AND the LORD spake unto Moses, saying,
2 Avenge [a]the children of Israel of the Mĭd-ĭ-ă-nītes: afterward shalt thou [b]be gathered unto thy people.
3 And Moses spake unto the people, saying, Arm some of yourselves unto the war, and let them go against the Mĭd-ĭ-ă-nītes, and [c]avenge the LORD of Mĭd-ĭ-ăn.
4 [1]Of every tribe a thousand, throughout all the tribes of Israel, shall ye send to the war.
5 So there were delivered out of the thousands of Israel, a thousand of *every* tribe, twelve thousand armed for war.
6 And Moses sent them to the war, a thousand of *every* tribe, them and Phĭn-ĕ-hăs the son of Ĕl-ē-ā-zär the priest, to the war, with the holy instruments, and the [d]trumpets to blow in his hand.
7 And they warred against the Mĭd-ĭ-ă-nītes, as the LORD commanded Moses; [e]and they slew all the [f]males.
8 And they slew the kings of Mĭd-ĭ-ăn, beside the rest of them that were slain; *namely*, [g]Ē-vī, and Rē-kĕm, and Zur, and Hur, and Rē-bă, five kings of Mĭd-ĭ-ăn: [h]Bā-lāam also the son of Bē-ôr they slew with the sword.
9 And the children of Israel took *all* the women of Mĭd-ĭ-ăn captives, and their little ones, and took the spoil of all their cattle, and all their flocks, and all their goods.
10 And they burnt all their cities wherein they dwelt, and all their goodly castles, with fire.
11 And [i]they took all the spoil, and all the prey, *both* of men and of beasts.
12 And they brought the captives, and the prey, and the spoil, unto Moses, and Ĕl-ē-ā-zär the priest, and unto the congregation of the children of Israel, unto the camp at the plains of Moab, which *are* by Jordan *near* Jericho.
13 ¶ And Moses, and Ĕl-ē-ā-zär the priest, and all the princes of the congregation, went forth to meet them without the camp.
14 And Moses was wroth with the officers of the host, *with* the captains over thousands, and captains over hundreds, which came from the [2]battle.
15 And Moses said unto them, Have ye saved all [j]the women alive?
16 Behold, [k]these caused the children of Israel, through [l]the counsel of Bā-lāam, to commit trespass against the LORD in the matter of Pē-ôr, and there was a plague among the congregation of the LORD.
17 Now therefore [m]kill every male among the little ones, and kill every woman that hath known man by lying with [3]him.
18 But all the women children, that have not known a man by lying with him, keep alive for yourselves.
19 And [n]do ye abide without the camp seven days: whosoever hath killed any person, and whosoever [o]hath touched any slain, purify *both* yourselves and your captives on the third day, and on the seventh day.
20 And purify all *your* raiment, and all [4]that is made of skins, and all work of goats' *hair*, and all things made of wood.
21 ¶ And Ĕl-ē-ā-zär the priest said unto the men of war which went to the battle, This *is* the ordinance of the law which the LORD commanded Moses;
22 Only the gold, and the silver, the brass, the iron, the tin, and the lead,
23 Every thing that may abide the fire, ye shall make *it* go through the fire, and it shall be clean: nevertheless it shall be purified with [p]the water of separation: and all that abideth not the fire ye shall make go through the water.
24 And [q]ye shall wash your clothes on the seventh day, and ye shall be clean, and afterward ye shall come into the camp.
25 ¶ And the LORD spake unto Moses, saying,
26 Take the sum of the prey [5]that was taken, *both* of man and of beast, thou, and Ĕl-ē-ā-zär the priest, and the chief fathers of the congregation:
27 And [r]divide the prey into two parts; between them that took the war upon them, who went out to battle, and between all the congregation:
28 And levy a [s]tribute unto the LORD of the men of war which went out to battle: one [t]soul of five hundred, *both* of the persons, and of the beeves, and of the asses, and of the sheep:
29 Take *it* of their half, and give *it* unto Ĕl-ē-ā-zär the priest, *for* an heave offering of the LORD.

CHAP. 31
a ch. 25.17. Deut. 32.35, 43. Ps. 94.1.
b Gen. 15.15. Gen. 25.8. Gen. 35.29. Gen. 49.33. ch. 27.13. Acts 13.36.
c Deut. 32.35. Jer. 50.28. Ps. 94.1. Rom. 12.19. Heb. 10.30.
1 A thousand of a tribe, a thousand of a tribe.
d ch. 10.9.
e Deut. 20.13. Judg. 21.11. 1 Sam. 27.9. 1 Ki. 11.15, 16.
f Judg. 6.1, 2, 33.
g Josh. 13.21.
h ch. 22.10. ch. 24.25. Ps. 9.12. Pro. 16.5. Pro. 26.27. Matt. 7.22, 23. 1 Tim. 6.9, 10. 2 Pet. 2.14-22. Jude 11. Rev. 2.14.
i Deut. 20.14.
2 host of war.
j Deut. 2.34. Deut. 20.13. Josh. 6.21. Josh. 8.25. 1 Sam. 15.3.
k ch. 25.2.
l ch. 24.14. Deut. 4.3. Josh. 22.17. Ps. 106.28, 29. Hosea 9.10. Micah 6.5. 2 Pet. 2.15. Rev. 2.14.
m Judg. 21. 11.
3 a male.
n ch. 5.2. ch. 19.11.
o ch. 9.6, 10. ch. 19.11.
4 instrument, or, vessel of skins.
p ch. 8.7. ch. 19.9, 17.
q Lev. 11.25. Lev. 14.9. Lev. 15.13. ch. 19.10, 22. Ps. 51.2. Zech. 13.1. Eph. 5.26. Heb. 9.9, 10. Heb. 10.22. 1 John 1.7.
5 of the captivity.
r Josh. 22.8. 1 Sam. 30. 24. Ps. 68.12.
s 2 Sam. 8.11. 1 Chr. 18.11. 1 Chr. 26.27. Isa. 18.7. Isa. 23.18. Isa. 60.9. Matt. 22.21.
t ch. 18.26.

30 And of the children of Israel's
half, thou shalt take one portion of
fifty, of the persons, of the beeves, of
the asses, and of the [6]flocks, of all
manner of beasts, and give them unto
the Levites, which [u]keep the charge
of the tabernacle of the LORD.
31 And Moses and Ĕl-ē-ā-zär the
priest did as the LORD commanded
Moses.
32 And the booty, *being* the rest of
the prey which the men of war had
caught, was six hundred thousand and
seventy thousand and five thousand
sheep,
33 And threescore and twelve thousand beeves,
34 And threescore and one thousand
asses,
35 And thirty and two thousand persons in all, of women that had not
known man by lying with him.
36 And the half, *which was* the portion of them that went out to war, was
in number three hundred thousand
and seven and thirty thousand and
five hundred sheep:
37 And the LORD's [v]tribute of the
sheep was six hundred and threescore
and fifteen.
38 And the beeves *were* thirty and
six thousand; of which the LORD's
tribute *was* threescore and twelve.
39 And the asses *were* thirty thousand and five hundred; of which the
LORD's tribute *was* threescore and one.
40 And the persons *were* sixteen
thousand; of which the LORD's tribute *was* thirty and two persons.
41 And Moses gave the tribute,
which was the LORD's heave offering,
unto Ĕl-ē-ā-zär the priest, [w]as the
LORD commanded Moses.
42 And of the children of Israel's
half, which Moses divided from the
men that warred,
43 (Now the half *that pertained unto*
the congregation was three hundred
thousand and thirty thousand *and*
seven thousand and five hundred
sheep,
44 And thirty and six thousand
beeves,
45 And thirty thousand asses and
five hundred,
46 And sixteen thousand persons;)
47 Even of the children of Israel's
half, Moses took one portion of fifty,
both of man and of beast, and gave
them unto the Levites, which kept the
charge of the tabernacle of the LORD;
as the LORD commanded Moses.
48 ¶ And the officers which *were*
over thousands of the host, the captains of thousands, and captains of
hundreds, came near unto Moses:
49 And they said unto Moses, Thy
servants have taken the sum of the
men of war which *are* under our
[7]charge, and there lacketh not one
[x]man of us.
50 We have therefore brought an oblation for the LORD, what every man
hath [8]gotten, of jewels of gold, chains,
and bracelets, rings, earrings, and
tablets, [y]to make an atonement for
our souls before the LORD.
51 And Moses and Ĕl-ē-ā-zär the
priest took the gold of them, *even* all
wrought jewels.
52 And all the gold of the [9]offering
that they offered up to the LORD, of
the captains of thousands, and of the
captains of hundreds, was sixteen
thousand seven hundred and fifty
shekels.
53 (*For* [z]the men of war had taken
spoil, every man for himself.)
54 And Moses and Ĕl-ē-ā-zär the
priest took the gold of the captains of
thousands and of hundreds, and
brought it into the tabernacle of the
congregation, *for* [a]a memorial for
the children of Israel before the
LORD.

CHAPTER 32

NOW the children of Reuben and
the children of Gad had a very
great multitude of cattle: and when
they saw the land [a]of Jā-zĕr, and the
land of Gilead, that, behold, the place
was a place for cattle;
2 The children of Gad and the children of Reuben came and spake unto
Moses, and to Ĕl-ē-ā-zär the priest,
and unto the princes of the congregation, saying,
3 Ăt-ā-rōth, and Dī-bŏn, and Jā-zĕr,
and [b]Nimrah, and Hĕsh-bŏn, and Ĕl-
ĕ-ā-lēh, [c]and Shē-băm, and Nē-bō,
and [d]Bē-ŏn,
4 *Even* the country [e]which the LORD
smote before the congregation of Israel, *is* a land for cattle, and thy servants have cattle:
5 Wherefore, said they, if we have
found grace in thy sight, let this land
be given unto thy servants for a possession, *and* bring us not over Jordan.
6 ¶ And Moses said unto the children of Gad and to the children of
Reuben, Shall your brethren go to
war, and shall ye sit here?
7 And wherefore [1]discourage ye the
heart of the children of Israel from go-

6 Or, goats.
u ch. 3.7,8, 25, 31,36. ch. 18.3,4. 1 Chr. 9.27-29. 1 Chr. 23.32.
v Lev. 25.23. Deut. 10.14. Job 41.11. Ps. 24.1. Ps. 50.12. Pro. 3.9. Matt. 22.21. Mark 12.17.
w ch. 5.9,10. ch. 18.8,19.
7 hand.
x Ex. 23.7. Lev. 26.7-9. 1 Sam. 30. 19. Ps. 72.14. Ps. 116.15.
8 found.
y Ex. 30.12, 16. Lev. 17.11. Matt. 20.28. Rom. 3.25.
9 heave offering.
z Deut. 20.14.
a ch. 16.40. Ex. 30.16. Zech. 6.14. Luke 22.19. Acts 10.4.
CHAP. 32
a ch. 21.32. Josh. 13.25. 2 Sam. 24.5. Isa. 16.8,9.
b ver. 36. Beth-nimrah.
c ver. 38. Shibmah.
d ver. 38. Baal-meon.
e ch. 21.24, 34.
1 break.

ing over into the land which the LORD
hath given them?
8 Thus did your fathers, [f]when I sent
them from Kā-dĕsh–bär-nĕ-ă [g]to see
the land.
9 For [h]when they went up unto the
valley of Ĕsh-cŏl, and saw the land,
they discouraged the heart of the
children of Israel, that they should not
go into the land which the LORD had
given them.
10 And [i]the LORD's anger was kindled the same time, and he sware,
saying,
11 Surely none of the men that came
up out of Egypt, [j]from twenty years
old and upward, shall see the land
which I sware unto Abraham, unto
Isaac, and unto Jacob; because [k]they
have not [2]wholly followed me:
12 Save Caleb the son of Jĕ-phŭn-
nĕh the Kĕ-nĕz-īte, and Joshua the
son of Nun: [l]for they have wholly followed the LORD.
13 And the LORD's anger was kindled against Israel, and he made them
[m]wander in the wilderness forty years,
until [n]all the generation, that had done
evil in the sight of the LORD, was consumed.
14 And, behold, ye are risen up in
your fathers' stead, an increase of sinful men, to augment yet the fierce
[o]anger of the LORD toward Israel.
15 For if ye [p]turn away from after
him, he will yet again leave them in
the wilderness; and ye shall destroy
all this people.
16 ¶ And they came near unto him,
and said, We will build sheepfolds
here for our cattle, and cities for our
little ones:
17 But [q]we ourselves will go ready
armed before the children of Israel,
until we have brought them unto their
place: and our little ones shall dwell
in the fenced cities because of the inhabitants of the land.
18 We [r]will not return unto our
houses, until the children of Israel
have inherited every man his inheritance.
19 For we will not inherit with them
on yonder side Jordan, or forward;
[s]because our inheritance is fallen to
us on this side Jordan eastward.
20 ¶ And [t]Moses said unto them, If
ye will do this thing, if ye will go armed
before the LORD to war,
21 And will go all of you armed over
Jordan before the LORD, until he hath
driven out his enemies from before
him,

f ch. 13.3.
g Deut. 1.22.
h ch. 1.10. Deut. 1.24.
i ch. 14.11. Deut. 1.34. Ps. 95.11. Heb. 3.8-19.
j Deut. 1.35.
k ch. 14.24.
2 fulfilled after me.
l Deut. 1.36. Josh. 14.8,9. Job 4.7. Ps. 37.29. Pro. 11.31.
m ch. 14.33.
n ch. 26.64.
o Deut. 1.34.
p Deut. 30.17. 2 Chr. 7.19. 2 Chr. 15.2.
q Josh. 4.12, 13.
r Josh. 22.4.
s Josh. 12.1.
t Deut. 3.18. Josh. 1.14.
u Deut. 3.20. Josh. 11.23.
v Josh. 22.4.
w Deut. 3.12. Josh. 1.15. Josh. 13.8, 32.
x Gen. 4.7. Gen. 44.16. Ps. 140.11. Pro. 13.21. Isa. 3.11. Isa. 59.12. Rom. 2.9. 1 Cor. 4.5.
y vers. 16,34.
z Josh. 1.14.
a Josh. 4.12.
b Deut. 3.12. Josh. 12.6.
c ch. 21.24. Deut. 2.30-35. Deut. 3.1-8. Ps. 135.10, 11. Ps. 136.18-21.
d ch. 33.45.
e Deut. 2.36.
f vers. 1,3, Jazer.
g ver. 3. Nimrah.

22 And [u]the land be subdued before
the LORD: then afterward [v]ye shall return, and be guiltless before the LORD,
and before Israel; and this [w]land shall
be your possession before the LORD.
23 But if ye will not do so, behold,
ye have sinned against the LORD: and
be sure your [x]sin will find you out.
24 Build [y]you cities for your little
ones, and folds for your sheep; and do
that which hath proceeded out of your
mouth.
25 And the children of Gad and the
children of Reuben spake unto Moses,
saying, Thy servants will do as my
lord commandeth.
26 Our [z]little ones, our wives, our
flocks, and all our cattle, shall be there
in the cities of Gilead:
27 But [a]thy servants will pass over,
every man armed for war, before the
LORD to battle, as my lord saith.
28 So concerning them Moses commanded Ĕl-ē-ā-zär the priest, and
Joshua the son of Nun, and the chief
fathers of the tribes of the children
of Israel:
29 And Moses said unto them, If the
children of Gad and the children of
Reuben will pass with you over Jordan, every man armed to battle, before the LORD, and the land shall be
subdued before you; then ye shall give
them the land of Gilead for a possession:
30 But if they will not pass over with
you armed, they shall have possessions among you in the land of Canaan.
31 And the children of Gad and the
children of Reuben answered, saying,
As the LORD hath said unto thy servants, so will we do.
32 We will pass over armed before
the LORD into the land of Canaan,
that the possession of our inheritance
on this side Jordan *may be* ours.
33 And [b]Moses gave unto them, *even*
to the children of Gad, and to the children of Reuben, and unto half the
tribe of Mă-năs-sēh the son of Joseph,
[c]the kingdom of Sī-hŏn king of the
Amorites, and the kingdom of Og king
of Bā-shăn, the land, with the cities
thereof in the coasts, *even* the cities of
the country round about.
34 ¶ And the children of Gad built
[d]Dī-bŏn, and Ăt-ă-rōth, [e]and Ă-rō-ĕr,
35 And Ăt-rōth, Shō-phăn, and Jā-ā-
zĕr, [f]and Jŏg-bĕ-hăh,
36 And [g]Bĕth–nĭm-răh, and Bĕth–
hâr-ăn, fenced cities: and folds for
sheep.

37 And the children of Reuben built
Hĕsh-bŏn, and Ĕl-ĕ-ā-lĕh, and Kir-
jă-thā-im,
38 And [h]Nē-bō, and [i]Bā-ăl-mē-on,
(their [j]names being changed,) and
Shĭb-măh: and [3]gave other names unto the cities which they builded.
39 And the children of [k]Mā-chir the
son of Mă-năs-sēh went to Gilead,
and took it, and dispossessed the
Amorite which *was* in it.
40 And Moses gave [l]Gilead unto
Mā-chir the son of Mă-năs-sēh; and
he dwelt therein.
41 And [m]Jā-ir the son of Mă-năs-sēh
went and took the small towns thereof, and called them [n]Hā-vōth-jā-ir.
42 And Nō-băh went and took Kē-
năth, and the villages thereof, and
called it Nō-băh, after [o]his own name.

CHAPTER 33

THESE *are* the journeys of the children of Israel, which went forth
out of the land of Egypt with their
armies under the hand of Moses and
Aaron.
2 And Moses wrote their goings out
according to their journeys by the
commandment of the LORD: and
these *are* their journeys according to
their goings out.
3 And they [a]departed from Răm-ĕ-
sēs in the [b]first month, on the fifteenth
day of the first month; on the morrow
after the passover the children of Israel went out with an [c]high hand in
the sight of all the Egyptians.
4 For the Egyptians buried all *their*
firstborn, which the LORD had smitten among them: [d]upon their gods
also the LORD executed judgments.
5 And [e]the children of Israel removed from Răm-ĕ-sēs, and pitched
in Sŭc-cōth.
6 And they departed from [f]Sŭc-cōth,
and pitched in Ē-thăm, which *is* in the
edge of the wilderness.
7 And [g]they removed from Ē-thăm,
and turned again unto Pī-hă-hi-rōth,
which *is* before Bā-ăl-zē-phŏn: and
they pitched before Mĭg-dŏl.
8 And they departed from before Pī-
hă-hi-rōth, and [h]passed through the
midst of the sea into the wilderness,
and went three days' journey in the
wilderness of Ē-thăm, and pitched in
Mâr-ăh.
9 And they removed from Mâr-ăh,
and came unto Ē-lim: and in Ē-lim
were twelve fountains of water, and
threescore and ten palm trees; and
they pitched there.
10 And they removed from Ē-lim,
and encamped by the Red sea.
11 And they removed from the Red
sea, and encamped in the wilderness
[i]of Sin.
12 And they took their journey out
of the wilderness of Sin, and encamped in Dŏph-kăh.
13 And they departed from Dŏph-
kăh, and encamped in Ā-lŭsh.
14 And they removed from Ā-lŭsh,
and encamped at [j]Rĕph-ĭ-dĭm, where
was no water for the people to drink.
15 And they departed from Rĕph-ĭ-
dĭm, and pitched in the [k]wilderness of
Sī-nâi.
16 And they removed from the desert
of Sī-nâi, and pitched [l]at [1]Kĭb-rōth-
hăt-tā-ă-văh.
17 And they departed from Kĭb-
rōth-hăt-tā-ă-văh, and encamped at
Hă-zē-rōth.
18 And they departed from Hă-zē-
rōth, and pitched in [m]Rĭth-măh.
19 And they departed from Rĭth-
măh, and pitched at Rĭm-mŏn-pâr-ĕz.
20 And they departed from Rĭm-
mŏn-pâr-ĕz, and pitched in [n]Lĭb-
năh.
21 And they removed from Lĭb-năh,
and pitched at Rĭs-săh.
22 And they journeyed from Rĭs-săh,
and pitched in Kē-hĕ-lā-thăh.
23 And they went from Kē-hĕ-lā-
thăh, and pitched in mount Shā-phĕr.
24 And they removed from mount
Shā-phĕr, and encamped in Hă-rā-
dăh.
25 And they removed from Hă-rā-
dăh, and pitched in Măk-hē-lōth.
26 And they removed from Măk-hē-
lōth, and encamped at Tā-hăth.
27 And they departed from Tā-hăth,
and pitched at Târ-ăh.
28 And they removed from Târ-ăh,
and pitched in Mĭth-căh.
29 And they went from Mĭth-căh,
and pitched in Hăsh-mō-năh.
30 And they departed from Hăsh-
mō-năh, and [o]encamped at Mō-sē-
rōth.
31 And they departed from Mō-sē-
rōth, and pitched in Bĕn-ē-jā-ă-kăn.
32 And they removed [p]from Bĕn-ē-
jā-ă-kăn, and encamped [q]at Hôr-hă-
gĭd-găd.
33 And they went from Hôr-hă-gĭd-
găd, and pitched in Jŏt-bă-thăh.
34 And they removed from Jŏt-bă-
thăh, and encamped at Ĕb-rō-năh.
35 And they departed from Ĕb-rō-
năh, [r]and encamped at Ē-zī-ŏn-gā-
bĕr.

h Isa. 46.1.
i ch. 22.41.
j Ex. 23.13.
3 they called by names the names of the cities.
k Gen. 50.23. ch. 26.29. Josh. 17.1.
l Deut. 3.12. Josh. 17.1.
m Deut. 3.14. 1 Chr. 2.21.
n Judg. 10.4. 1 Ki. 4.13.
o 2 Sam. 18. 18. Ps. 49.11.

CHAP. 33

a Gen. 47.11. Ex. 1.11.
b Ex. 12.2. Ps. 105.38. Isa. 52.12. Micah 2.13.
c Ex. 14.8.
d Ex. 12.12. Isa. 19.1. Zeph. 2.11. Rev. 12.8.
e Ex. 12.37.
f Gen. 33.17. Ex. 13.20. Josh. 13.27. 1 Ki. 7.46. Ps. 60.6.
g Ex. 13.17, 18.
h Ex. 14.22.
i Ex. 16.1.
j Ex. 17.1.
k Ex. 16.1.
l ch. 11.34.
1 That is, The graves of lust.
m ch. 12.16. Deut. 1.1.
n Deut. 1.1. Laban.
o Deut. 10.6.
p Gen. 36.27. Deut. 10.6. 1 Chr. 1.42.
q Deut. 10.7. Gudgodah.
r Deut. 2.8. 1 Ki. 9.26. 1 Ki. 22.48.

36 And they removed from Ē-zi-ŏn-gā-bĕr, and pitched in the [s]wilderness of Zin, which *is* Kā-dĕsh.

37 And they removed from [t]Kā-dĕsh, and pitched in mount Hor, in the edge of the land of Ē-dọm.

38 And [u]Aaron the priest went up into mount Hor at the commandment of the LORD, and died there, in the fortieth year after the children of Israel were come out of the land of Egypt, in the first *day* of the fifth month.

39 And Aaron *was* an hundred and twenty and three years old when he died in mount Hor.

40 And [v]king Âr-ăd the Canaanite, which dwelt in the south in the land of Canaan, heard of the coming of the children of Israel.

41 And they departed from mount Hor, and pitched in Zăl-mō-năh.

42 And they departed from Zăl-mō-năh, and pitched in Pū-nŏn.

43 And they departed from Pū-nŏn, and pitched in Ō-bōth.

44 And they departed from Ō-bōth, and pitched in [2]Ī-jĕ–ăb-ă-rĭm, in the border of Moab.

45 And they departed from Ī-ĭm, and pitched in [w]Dī-bŏn–găd.

46 And they removed from Dī-bŏn–găd, and encamped in [x]Ăl-mŏn–dĭb-lă-thā-ĭm.

47 And they removed from Ăl-mŏn-dĭb-lă-thā-ĭm, [y]and pitched in the mountains of Ăb-ă-rĭm, before Nē-bō.

48 And they departed from the mountains of Ăb-ă-rĭm, [z]and pitched in the plains of Moab by Jordan *near* Jericho.

49 And they pitched by Jordan, from Bĕth–jĕs-ĭ-mōth *even* unto [3]Ā-bĕl–shĭt-tĭm in the plains of Moab.

50 ¶ And the LORD spake unto Moses in the plains of Moab by Jordan *near* Jericho, saying,

51 Speak unto the children of Israel, and say unto them, [a]When ye are passed over Jordan into the land of Canaan;

52 Then [b]ye shall drive out all the inhabitants of the land from before you, and destroy all their pictures, and destroy all their molten images, and quite pluck down all their high places:

53 And ye shall dispossess *the inhabitants of* the land, and dwell therein: for [c]I have given you the land to possess it.

54 And [d]ye shall divide the land by lot for an inheritance among your families: *and* to the more ye shall [4]give the more inheritance, and to the fewer ye shall [5]give the less inheritance: every man's *inheritance* shall be in the place where his lot falleth; according to the tribes of your fathers ye shall inherit.

55 But if ye will not drive out the inhabitants of the land from before you; then it shall come to pass, that those which ye let remain of them *shall be* [e]pricks in your eyes, and thorns in your sides, and shall vex you in the land wherein ye dwell.

56 Moreover it shall come to pass, *that* I shall do unto you, as I thought to do unto them.

CHAPTER 34

AND the LORD spake unto Moses, saying,

2 Command the children of Israel, and say unto them, When ye come into [a]the land of Canaan; (this *is* the land that shall fall unto you for an inheritance, *even* the land of Canaan with the coasts thereof:)

3 Then [b]your south quarter shall be from the wilderness of Zin along by the coast of Ē-dọm, and your south border shall be the outmost coast of the [c]salt sea eastward:

4 And your border shall turn from the south to the ascent of Ăk-răb-bĭm, and pass on to Zin: and the going forth thereof shall be from the south [d]to Kā-dĕsh–bär-nē-ă, and shall go on to Hā-zär–ăd-där, and pass on to Ăz-mŏn:

5 And the border shall fetch a compass from Ăz-mŏn [e]unto the river of Egypt, and the goings out of it shall be at the sea.

6 And *as for* the western border, ye shall even have [1]the great sea for a border: this shall be your west border.

7 And this shall be your north border: from the great sea ye shall point out for you mount [2]Hor:

8 From mount Hor ye shall point out *your border* [f]unto the entrance of Hā-măth; and the goings forth of the border shall be [g]to Zē-dăd:

9 ¶ And the border shall go on to Zĭph-rŏn, and the goings out of it shall be at [h]Hā-zär–ē-năn: this shall be your north border.

10 And ye shall point out your east border from Hā-zär–ē-năn to Shē-phăm:

11 And the coast shall go down from Shē-phăm [i]to Rĭb-lăh, on the east side

s ch. 13.21. ch. 20.1. ch. 27.14. ch. 34.3,4. Deut. 32.51. Josh. 15.1.
t ch. 20.22, 23. ch. 21.4.
u ch. 20.25, 28. Deut. 10.6. Deut. 32.50.
v ch. 21.1.
2 Or, Heaps of Abarim.
w ch. 32.34.
x Jer. 48.22.
y ch. 21.20.
z ch. 22.1.
3 Mournful Shittim, or, The plains of Shittim.
a Deut. 7.1. Deut. 9.1.
b Ex. 23.24. Ex. 34.12-17. Deut. 7.2-5, 25, 26. Deut. 12.2, 3,30,31. Deut. 20.16-18. Josh. 11.12. Judg. 2.2.
c Deut. 10. 14. Job 41.11. Ps. 24.1. Dan. 4.35.
d ch. 26.53.
4 multiply his inheritance.
5 diminish his inheritance.
e Josh. 23.13. Ps. 106.34.

CHAP. 34

a Gen. 17.8. Deut. 1.7. Ps. 78.55.
b Josh. 15.1.
c Gen. 14.3.
d ch. 32.8.
e Gen. 15.18. 1 Ki. 8.65. Isa. 27.12.
1 The Mediterranean.
2 Not the Mount Hor on the border of Edom where Aaron died, but Mount Hor north of Lebanon.
f ch. 13.21. Josh. 13.5,6. 2 Sam. 8.9. 2 Ki. 14.25. Isa. 10.9. Jer. 39.5.
g Eze. 47.15.
h Eze. 47.17.
i 2 Ki. 23.33.

of Ā-ĭn; and the border shall descend,
and shall reach unto the [3]side of the
sea of [j]Chĭn-nĕ-rĕth eastward:
12 And the border shall go down to
Jordan, and the goings out of it shall
be at the salt sea: this shall be your
land with the coasts thereof round
about.
13 And Moses commanded the children of Israel, saying, [k]This *is* the
land which ye shall inherit by lot,
which the LORD commanded to give
unto the nine tribes, and to the half
tribe:
14 For [l]the tribe of the children of
Reuben according to the house of
their fathers, and the tribe of the children of Gad according to the house of
their fathers, have received *their inheritance;* and half the tribe of Mă-
năs-sēh have received their inheritance:
15 The two tribes and the half tribe
have received their inheritance on this
side Jordan *near* Jericho eastward, toward the sunrising.
16 And the LORD spake unto Moses,
saying,
17 These *are* the names of the men
which shall divide the land unto you:
[m]Ĕl-ē-ā-zär the priest, and Joshua the
son of Nun.
18 And ye shall take one prince of
every tribe, to divide the land by inheritance.
19 And the names of the men *are*
these: Of the tribe of [n]Judah, Caleb
[o]the son of Jĕ-phŭn-nĕh.
20 And of the tribe of the children of
[p]Simeon, Shĕ-mū-ĕl the son of Ăm-
mĭ-hŭd.
21 Of the tribe of [q]Benjamin, Ē-lĭ-
dăd the son of Chĭs-lŏn.
22 And the prince of the tribe of the
children of Dan, Bŭk-kī the son of
Jŏg-lī.
23 The prince of [r]the children of
Joseph, for the tribe of the children of
Mă-năs-sēh, Hăn-nĭ-ĕl the son of
Ē-phŏd.
24 And the prince of the tribe of the
children of Ē-phră-ĭm, Kĕ-mū-ĕl the
son of Shĭph-tăn.
25 And the prince of the tribe of the
children of Zĕ-bū-lŭn, Ē-lĭ-zā-phăn
the son of Pär-năch.
26 And the prince of the tribe of the
children of Ĭs-să-chär, Păl-tī-ĕl the son
of Azzan.
27 And the prince of the tribe of the
children of Asher, Ă-hī-hŭd the son
of Shĕ-lō-mī.
28 And the prince of the tribe of the

3 shoulder.
j Deut. 3.17. Josh. 11.2.
k Josh. 14.1, 2.
l ch. 32.33.
m Ex. 6.23-25.
n Gen. 29.35. Deut. 33.7. Ps. 60.7.
o ch. 13.6,30. ch. 14.24,30. ch. 26.65. ch. 32.11,12. Deut. 1.36.
p Gen. 29.33. Gen. 49.5. Eze. 48.24.
q Gen. 35.18. Deut. 33.12. Ps. 68.27.
r Gen. 48.8-22. Deut. 33.13. Ps. 80.1.
s Deut. 32.8. Acts 17.26.

CHAP. 35

a Lev. 25.32, 33. ch. 18.20-24. Deut. 18.1, 2. Josh. 14.3,4. 1 Chr. 6.64. Eze. 45.1.
1 Six hundred and eight yards.
b Deut. 4.41. Josh. 20.2. Ps. 9.9. Ps. 62.7,8. Isa. 4.6.
2 above them ye shall give.
c 1 Chr. 6.54-81.
d Josh. 21.3.
e Ex. 16.18. ch. 26.54.
3 they inherit.
f Deut. 19.2.
g Ex. 21.13.
4 by error.
h Deut. 19.6.

children of Năph-tă-lī, Pĕ-däh-ĕl the
son of Ăm-mĭ-hŭd.
29 These *are they* whom the LORD
commanded to divide the [s]inheritance
unto the children of Israel in the land
of Canaan.

CHAPTER 35

AND the LORD spake unto Moses
in the plains of Moab by Jordan
near Jericho, saying,
2 Command [a]the children of Israel,
that they give unto the Levites of the
inheritance of their possession cities
to dwell in; and ye shall give *also* unto
the Levites suburbs for the cities
round about them.
3 And the cities shall they have to
dwell in; and the suburbs of them
shall be for their cattle, and for their
goods, and for all their beasts.
4 And the suburbs of the cities,
which ye shall give unto the Levites,
shall reach from the wall of the city
and outward [1]a thousand cubits round
about.
5 And ye shall measure from without
the city on the east side two thousand
cubits, and on the south side two
thousand cubits, and on the west side
two thousand cubits, and on the north
side two thousand cubits; and the city
shall be in the midst: this shall be to
them the suburbs of the cities.
6 And among the cities which ye
shall give unto the Levites *there shall
be* [b]six cities for refuge, which ye shall
appoint for the manslayer, that he
may flee thither: and [2]to them ye shall
add forty and two cities.
7 *So* all the cities which ye shall give
to the Levites *shall be* [c]forty and eight
cities: them *shall ye give* with their
suburbs.
8 And the cities which ye shall give
shall be [d]of the possession of the children of Israel: from [e]*them that have*
many ye shall give many; but from
them that have few ye shall give few:
every one shall give of his cities unto
the Levites according to his inheritance which [3]he inheriteth.
9 ¶ And the LORD spake unto Moses,
saying,
10 Speak unto the children of Israel,
and say unto them, [f]When ye be come
over Jordan into the land of Canaan;
11 Then [g]ye shall appoint you cities
to be cities of refuge for you; that the
slayer may flee thither, which killeth
any person [4]at unawares.
12 And [h]they shall be unto you cities
for refuge from the avenger; that the

manslayer die not, until he stand before the congregation in judgment.
13 And of these cities which ye shall
give six cities shall ye have for refuge.
14 Ye [i]shall give three cities on this
side Jordan, and three cities shall ye
give in the land of Canaan, *which* shall
be cities of refuge.
15 These six cities shall be a refuge,
both for the children of Israel, and [j]for
the stranger, and for the sojourner
among them: that every one that killeth any person unawares may flee
thither.
16 And [k]if he smite him with an instrument of iron, so that he die, he *is*
a murderer: the murderer shall surely
be put to death.
17 And if he smite him [5]with throwing a stone, wherewith he may die,
and he die, he *is* a murderer: the
murderer shall surely be put to death.
18 Or *if* he smite him with an hand
weapon of wood, wherewith he may
die, and he die, he *is* a murderer: the
murderer shall surely be put to death.
19 The [6]revenger of blood himself
shall slay the murderer: when he
meeteth him, he shall slay him.
20 But [l]if he thrust him of hatred,
or hurl at him [m]by laying of wait, that
he die;
21 Or in enmity smite him with his
hand, that he die: he that smote *him*
shall surely be put to death; *for* he *is*
a murderer: the revenger of blood
shall slay the murderer, when he
meeteth him.
22 But if he thrust him suddenly
without enmity, or have cast upon
him any thing without laying of wait,
23 Or with any stone, wherewith a
man may die, seeing *him* not, and
cast *it* upon him, that he die, and *was*
not his enemy, neither sought his
harm:
24 Then [n]the congregation shall
judge between the slayer and the revenger of blood according to these
judgments:
25 And the congregation shall deliver the slayer out of the hand of the
revenger of blood, and the congregation shall restore him to the city of his
refuge, whither he was fled: and he
[o]shall abide in it unto the death of the
high priest, which [p]was anointed with
the holy oil.
26 But if the slayer shall at any time
come without the border of the city
of his refuge, whither he was fled;
27 And the revenger of blood find
him without the borders of the city of
his refuge, and the revenger of blood
kill the slayer; [7]he shall not be guilty
of blood:
28 Because he should have remained
in the city of his refuge until the death
of the high priest: but after the death
of the high priest the slayer shall return into the land of his possession.
29 So these *things* shall be for [q]a
statute of judgment unto you throughout your generations in all your dwellings.
30 Whoso killeth any person, the
murderer shall be put to death by the
[r]mouth of witnesses: but one witness
shall not testify against any person
to cause him to die.
31 Moreover ye shall take no satisfaction for the life of a murderer,
which *is* [8]guilty of death: but he shall
be surely put to death.
32 And ye shall take [s]no satisfaction
for him that is fled to the city of his
refuge, that he should come again to
dwell in the land, until the death of
the priest.
33 So ye shall not pollute the land
wherein ye *are:* for blood [t]it defileth
the land: and [9]the land cannot be
cleansed of the blood that is shed
therein, but [u]by the blood of him that
shed it.
34 Defile [v]not therefore the land
which ye shall inhabit, wherein I
dwell: for [w]I the LORD dwell among
the children of Israel.

CHAPTER 36

AND the chief fathers of the families
of the children [a]of Gilead, the son
of Mā-chĭr, the son of Mă-năs-sēh, of
the families of the sons of Joseph,
came near, and spake before Moses,
and before the princes, the chief fathers of the children of Israel:
2 And they said, [b]The LORD commanded my lord to give the land for
an inheritance by lot to the children of
Israel: and [c]my lord was commanded
by the LORD to give the inheritance of
Zē-lŏph-ĕ-hăd our brother unto his
daughters.
3 And if they be married to any of the
sons of the *other* tribes of the children
of Israel, then shall their inheritance
be taken from the inheritance of our
fathers, and shall be put to the inheritance of the tribe [1]whereunto they are
received: so shall it be taken from the
lot of our inheritance.
4 And when [d]the jû-bĭ-lē of the children of Israel shall be, then shall their
inheritance be put unto the inherit-

i Deut. 4.41. 2 Cor. 8.13, 14.
j ch. 15.16.
k Ex. 21.12, 14. Lev. 24.17. Deut. 19.11, 12.
5 with a stone of the hand.
6 He was the nearest kinsman of the person slain.
l Gen. 4.8. 2 Sam. 3.27. 1 Ki. 2.31. Luke 4.29.
m Ex. 21.14. Deut. 19.11. 1 Sam. 18. 10, 11, 25. 1 Sam. 20.1. 1 Sam. 24. 11. Ps. 10.7-10.
n Josh. 20.6.
o Eph. 1.7.
p Ex. 29.7. Lev. 4.3. Lev. 21.10.
7 no blood shall be to him.
q ch. 27.11.
r Deut. 17.6. Matt. 18.16. 2 Cor. 13.1. 1 Tim. 5.19. Heb. 10.28. Rev. 11.3.
8 faulty to die.
s Acts 4.12. Gal. 2.21.
t Gen. 4.9-12. Lev. 18.25. Deut. 21.23. Ps. 106.38. Isa. 26.21. Hosea 4.2, 3. Micah 4.11.
9 there can be no expiation for the land.
u Gen. 9.6.
v Lev. 18.25. Deut. 21.23.
w ch. 5.3. Ps. 76.2. Isa. 8.18. Hosea 9.3. 2 Cor. 6.16.

CHAP. 36

a ch. 26.29.
b ch. 26.55. ch. 33.54.
c ch. 27.1, 7.
1 unto whom they shall be.
d Lev. 25.10.

ance of the tribe whereunto they are
received: so shall their inheritance be
taken away from the inheritance of
the tribe of our fathers.
5 And Moses commanded the children of Israel according to the word
of the LORD, saying, The tribe of the
sons of Joseph [e]hath said well.
6 This *is* the thing which the LORD
doth command concerning the daughters of Zē-lŏph-ĕ-hăd, saying, Let
them [2]marry to whom they think best;
only to the family of the tribe of their
father shall they marry.
7 So shall not the [f]inheritance of the
children of Israel remove from tribe
to tribe: for every one of the children of Israel shall [3]keep himself to
the inheritance of the tribe of his
fathers.
8 And [g]every daughter, that
possesseth an inheritance in any tribe
of the children of Israel, shall be wife
unto one of the family of the tribe
of her father, that the children of
Israel may enjoy every man the inheritance of his fathers.
9 Neither shall the inheritance remove from *one* tribe to another tribe;
but every one of the tribes of the children of Israel shall keep himself to his
own inheritance.
10 Even as the LORD commanded
Moses, so did the daughters of Zē-
lŏph-ĕ-hăd:
11 For [h]Măh-lăh, Tĭr-zăh, and Hŏg-
lăh, and Mĭl-căh, and Noah, the
daughters of Zē-lŏph-ĕ-hăd, were
married unto their father's brothers'
sons:
12 *And* they were married [4]into the
families of the sons of Mă-năs-sēh the
son of Joseph, and their inheritance
remained in the tribe of the family of
their father.
13 These *are* the commandments and
the judgments, [i]which the LORD commanded by the hand of Moses unto
the children of Israel in [j]the plains of
Moab by Jordan *near* Jericho.

e ch. 27.7.
2 be wives.
f 1 Ki. 21.3.
3 cleave to the, etc.
g 1 Chr. 23. 22.
h ch. 27.1.
4 to some that were of the families.
i ch. 22.1. ch. 26.3. ch. 31.12. Deut. 33.4. Neh. 9.12, 13, 14. John 1.17.
j ch. 26.3. ch. 33.50. ch. 22.1.

THE FIFTH BOOK OF MOSES, CALLED

DEUTERONOMY

CHAPTER 1

THESE *be* the words which Moses
spake unto all Israel [a]on this side
Jordan in the wilderness, in the plain
over against [1]the Red *sea*, between
Pâr-ăn, and Tō-phĕl, and Laban, and
Hă-zē-rōth, and Dī-ză-hăb.
2 (*There are* eleven days' *journey*
from Hôr-ĕb by the way of mount Sē-
ĭr [b]unto Kā-dĕsh–bär-nĕ-ă.)
3 And it came to pass [c]in the fortieth
year, in the eleventh month, on the
first *day* of the month, *that* Moses
spake unto the children of Israel, according unto all that the LORD had
given him in commandment unto
them;
4 After [d]he had slain Sī-hŏn the king
of the Amorites, which dwelt in Hĕsh-
bŏn, and Og the king of Bā-shăn,
which dwelt at Ăs-tă-rōth in [e]Ĕd-
rĕ-ī:
5 On this side Jordan, in the land of
Moab, began Moses to declare this
law, saying,
6 The LORD our God spake unto us
in Hôr-ĕb, saying, Ye have dwelt long
enough in this mount:
7 Turn you, and take your journey,
and go to the mount of the Amorites,
and unto [2]all *the places* nigh thereunto,
in the plain, in the hills, and in the
vale, and in the south, and by the sea
side, to the land of the Canaanites,
and unto Lĕb-ă-non, unto the great
river, the river Eû-phrā-tēs.
8 Behold, I have [3]set the land before
you: go in and possess the land which
the LORD sware unto your fathers,
[h]Abraham, Isaac, and Jacob, to give
unto them and to their seed after
them.
9 ¶ And [i]I spake unto you at that
time, saying, I am not able to bear you
myself alone:
10 The LORD your God hath multiplied you, and, behold, [j]ye *are* this
day as the stars of heaven for multitude.
11 (The LORD God of your fathers
make you a thousand times so many
more as ye *are*, and bless you, [k]as he
hath promised you!)
12 How [l]can I myself alone bear your
cumbrance, and your burden, and
your strife?
13 [4]Take you wise men, and understanding, and known among your

CHAP. 1
a Num. 32.6, 20, 29. Josh. 9.1.
1 Or, Zuph.
b Num. 13. 26. ch. 9.23.
c Num. 33. 38.
d Num. 21. 24. Neh. 9.22. Ps. 135.11.
e Josh. 13.12.
f Ex. 3.1.
g Ex. 19.1. Num. 10.11.
2 all his neighbours.
3 given.
h Gen. 12.7. Gen. 15.18.
i Ex. 18.18.
j Gen. 15.5. Gen. 22.17. Ex. 32.13. ch. 10.22. 1 Chr. 27.23.
k Gen. 22.17. Ex. 32.13.
l 1 Ki. 3.8. 2 Cor. 11.28.
4 Give.

tribes, and I will make them rulers
over you.
14 And ye answered me, and said,
The thing which thou hast spoken *is*
good *for us* to do.
15 So I took the chief of your tribes,
wise men, and known, and [5]made
them heads over you, captains over
thousands, and captains over hundreds, and captains over fifties, and
captains over tens, and officers among
your tribes.
16 And I charged your judges at that
time, saying, Hear *the causes* between
your brethren, and [m]judge righteously
between *every* man and his brother,
[n]and the stranger *that is* with him.
17 Ye [o]shall not [6]respect persons in
judgment; *but* ye shall hear the small
as well as the great; ye shall [p]not be
afraid of the face of man; for the
[q]judgment *is* God's: and the cause
that is too hard for you, [r]bring *it* unto
me, and I will hear it.
18 And I commanded you at that
time all the things which ye should do.
19 ¶ And when we departed from
Hôr-ĕb, we [s]went through all that
great and terrible wilderness, which ye
saw by the way of the mountain of the
Amorites, as the LORD our God commanded us; and [t]we came to Kā-
dĕsh–bär-nĕ-ă.
20 And I said unto you, Ye are come
unto the mountain of the Amorites,
which the LORD our God doth give
unto us.
21 Behold, the LORD thy God hath
set the land before thee: go up *and*
possess *it*, as the LORD God of thy
fathers hath said unto thee; fear [u]not,
neither be discouraged.
22 ¶ And ye came near unto me every
one of you, and said, We will send men
before us, and they shall search us out
the land, and bring us word again by
what way we must go up, and into
what cities we shall come.
23 And the saying pleased me well:
and [v]I took twelve men of you, one of
a tribe:
24 And they turned and went up into
the mountain, and came unto the valley of Ĕsh-cŏl, and searched it out.
25 And they took of the fruit of the
land in their hands, and brought *it*
down unto us, and brought us word
again, and said, *It is* a good land
which the LORD our God doth give us.
26 Notwithstanding [w]ye would not
go up, but rebelled against the commandment of the LORD your God:
27 And ye murmured in your tents,
and said, Because the LORD hated [x]us,
he hath brought us forth out of the
land of Egypt, to deliver us into the
hand of the Amorites, to destroy us.
28 Whither shall we go up? our
brethren have [7]discouraged our heart,
saying, [y]The people *is* greater and
taller than we; the cities *are* great and
walled up to heaven; and moreover
we have seen the sons of the [z]Anakims
there.
29 Then I said unto you, Dread not,
neither be afraid of them.
30 The [a]LORD your God which goeth
before you, he shall fight for you, according to all that he did for you in
Egypt before your eyes;
31 And in the wilderness, where thou
hast seen how that the LORD thy God
[b]bare thee, as a man doth bear his son,
in all the way that ye went, until ye
came into this place.
32 Yet in this thing [c]ye did not believe the LORD your God,
33 Who [d]went in the way before you,
to [e]search you out a place to pitch
your tents *in*, in fire by night, to shew
you by what way ye should go, and
in a cloud by day.
34 And the LORD heard the voice of
your words, and was wroth, [f]and
sware, saying,
35 Surely [g]there shall not one of
these men of this evil generation see
that good land, which I sware to give
unto your fathers,
36 Save Caleb the son of Jĕ-phŭn-
nĕh; he shall see it, and to him will I
give the land that he hath trodden
upon, and to his children, because he
hath [8]wholly followed the LORD.
37 Also [h]the LORD was angry with
me for your sakes, saying, Thou also
shalt not go in thither.
38 *But* Joshua the son of Nun, which
[i]standeth before thee, he shall go in
thither: [j]encourage him: for he shall
cause Israel to inherit it.
39 Moreover your little ones, which
ye said should be a prey, and your
children, which in that day had [k]no
knowledge between good and evil,
they shall go in thither, and unto them
will I give it, and they shall possess
it.
40 But *as for* you, turn you, and take
your journey into the wilderness by
the way of the Red sea.
41 Then ye answered and said unto
me, We have sinned against the LORD,
we will go up and fight, according to
all that the LORD our God commanded us. And when ye had girded on

5 gave.
m Ex. 23.2,3, 7,8. John 7.24.
n Lev. 24.22.
o 1 Sam. 16.7. Pro. 24.23. Jas. 2.1.
6 acknowledge faces.
p Pro. 28.21.
q 2 Chr. 19.6.
r Ex. 18.22, 26.
s Num. 10.12. ch. 8.15.
t Num. 13.26.
u Num. 13. 30. Josh. 1.9. Ps. 27.1-3. Ps. 46.1,7, 11. Isa. 41.10. Isa. 43.1,2. Luke 12.32. Heb. 13.6.
v Num. 13.3.
w Num. 14.1, 2,3,4. Ps. 106.24.
x ch. 9.28.
7 melted.
y Num. 13. 28,31,32,33. ch. 9.1,2.
z Num. 13.28.
a Ex. 14.14. Neh. 4.20.
b Ex. 19.4. ch. 32.11. Isa. 46.3,4. Hosea 11.3. Acts 13.18.
c Ps. 106.24. Jude 5.
d Ex. 13.21. Ps. 78.14.
e Num. 10. 33. Eze. 20.6.
f ch. 2.14.
g Num. 14. 22. Ps. 95.11.
8 fulfilled to go after.
h Num. 27. 14. ch. 3.26. ch. 4.21. Ps. 106.32.
i Ex. 24.13. Ex. 33.11. 1 Sam. 16. 22.
j ch. 31.7,23.
k Isa. 7.15, 16. Eze. 18.20.

every man his weapons of war, ye
were ready to go up into the hill.
42 And the LORD said unto me, Say
unto them, Go not up, neither fight;
for I *am* not among you; lest ye be
smitten before your enemies.
43 So I spake unto you; and ye would
not hear, but rebelled against the commandment of the LORD, [9]and went
presumptuously up into the hill.
44 And the Amorites which dwelt in
that mountain, came out against you,
and chased you, [l]as bees do, and destroyed you in Sē-ĭr, *even* unto Hôr-
măh.
45 And ye returned and wept before
the LORD; [m]but the LORD would not
hearken to your voice, nor give ear
unto you.
46 So ye abode in [n]Kā-dĕsh many
days, according unto the days that ye
abode *there.*

CHAPTER 2

THEN we turned, and took our
journey into the wilderness by the
way of the Red sea, as the LORD spake
unto me: and we compassed mount
Sē-ĭr many days.
2 And the LORD spake unto me, saying,
3 Ye have compassed this mountain
long enough: turn you northward.
4 And command thou the people,
saying, Ye *are* to pass through the
coast of your brethren the children of
Esau, which dwell in Sē-ĭr; and they
shall be afraid of you: take ye good
heed unto yourselves therefore:
5 Meddle not with them; for I will
not give you of their land, [1]no, not so
much as a foot breadth; because [a]I
have given mount Sē-ĭr unto Esau *for*
a possession.
6 Ye shall buy meat of them for
money, that ye may eat; and ye shall
also buy water of them for money,
that ye may drink.
7 For the LORD thy God hath blessed
thee in all the works of thy hand: he
knoweth thy walking through this
great wilderness: these forty years
the LORD thy God *hath been* with thee;
thou hast lacked nothing.
8 And when we passed by from our
brethren the children of Esau, which
dwelt in Sē-ĭr, through the way of the
plain [b]from Ē-lăth, and from Ē-zĭ-ŏn-
gā-bĕr, we turned and passed by the
way of the wilderness of Moab.
9 And the LORD said unto me, [2]Dis-
tress not the Moabites, neither contend with them in battle: for I will not
give thee of their land *for* a possession; because I have given [c]Ar unto
the children [d]of Lot *for* a possession.
10 The [e]Ē-mĭms dwelt therein in
times past, a people great, and many,
and tall, as [f]the Anakims;
11 Which also were accounted giants,
as the Anakims; but the Moabites
call them Ē-mĭms.
12 The [g]Hôr-ĭms also dwelt in Sē-ĭr
beforetime; but the children of Esau
[3]succeeded them, when they had destroyed them from before them, and
dwelt in their [4]stead; as Israel did unto
the land of his possession, which the
LORD gave unto them.
13 Now rise up, *said I,* and get you
over the [5]brook Zē-rĕd. And we went
over the brook Zē-rĕd.
14 And the space in which we came
from Kā-dĕsh-bär-nē-ă, until we
were come over the brook Zē-rĕd, *was*
thirty and eight years; until [h]all the
generation of the men of war were
wasted out from among the host, as
[i]the LORD sware unto them.
15 For indeed the [j]hand of the LORD
was against them, to destroy them
from among the host, until they were
consumed.
16 ¶ So it came to pass, when all the
men of war were consumed and dead
from among the people,
17 That the LORD spake unto me,
saying,
18 Thou art to pass over through Ar,
the coast of Moab, this day:
19 And *when* thou comest nigh over
against the children of Ammon, distress them not, nor meddle with them:
for I will not give thee of the land of
the children of Ammon *any* possession; because I have given it unto the
[k]children of Lot *for* a possession.
20 (That also was accounted a land
of giants: giants dwelt therein in old
time; and the Ammonites call them
[l]Zăm-zŭm-mĭms;
21 A people great, and many, and
tall, as the Anakims; but the LORD
destroyed them before them; and they
succeeded them, and dwelt in their
stead:
22 As he did to the children of Esau,
which [m]dwelt in Sē-ĭr, when he [n]de-
stroyed the Hôr-ĭms from before
them; and they succeeded them, and
dwelt in their stead even unto this day:
23 And [o]the Ā-vĭms which dwelt in
Hă-zē-rĭm, *even* unto [p]Azzah, [q]the
Căph-tō-rĭms, which came forth out
of Căph-tôr, destroyed them, and
dwelt in their stead.)

9 ye were presumptuous and went up.
l ch. 28.25. ch. 32.30. Ps. 118.12. Isa. 7.18.
m Job 27.9. Ps. 66.18. Pro. 1.24. Isa. 1.15. Jer. 11.7-14. Zech. 7.11.
n Num. 13. 25. Num. 20.1, 22.

CHAP. 2

1 even to the treading of the sole of the foot.
a Gen. 36.8. Deut. 32.8. Josh. 24.4. Ps. 115.3. Dan. 4.32, 35. Acts 17.26.
b 1 Ki. 9.26. 2 Ki. 14.22.
2 Or, use no hostility against Moab.
c Num. 21. 28.
d Gen. 19.36. Ps. 83.8.
e Gen. 14.5.
f Num. 13. 22. ch. 9.2.
g Gen. 14.6. Gen. 36.20.
3 inherited them.
4 Or, room.
5 Or, valley.
h Num. 14. 33. Num. 26.64. Ps. 78.33. Ps. 90.3-9.
i ch. 1.34,35.
j 1 Sam. 5.6, 9,11. 1 Sam. 7.13. Ps. 78. 33. Ps. 95.10, 11. Heb. 4.1-5.
k Gen. 19.38.
l Gen. 14.5. Zuzims.
m Gen. 36.8.
n Job 12.23.
o Josh. 13.3.
p Jer. 25.20. Zeph. 2.4.
q Gen. 10.14. Amos 9.7.

24 ¶ Rise ye up, take your journey,
and pass [r]over the river Arnon: behold,
I have given into thine hand Sī´hŏn the Amorite, king of Hĕsh´bŏn,
and his land: [6]begin to possess *it*, and
contend with him in battle.
25 This [s]day will I begin to put the
dread of thee and the fear of thee upon
the nations *that are* under the whole
heaven, who shall hear report of thee,
and shall tremble, and be in anguish
because of thee.
26 ¶ And I sent messengers out of
the wilderness of Kē´dĕ-mōth unto
Sī´hŏn king of Hĕsh´bŏn [t]with words
of peace, saying,
27 Let [u]me pass through thy land: I
will go along by the high way, I will
neither turn unto the right hand nor
to the left.
28 Thou shalt sell me meat for money,
that I may eat; and give me water
for money, that I may drink: [v]only I
will pass through on my feet;
29 (As [w]the children of Esau which
dwell in Sē´īr, and the Moabites
which dwell in Ar, did unto me;) until
I shall pass over Jordan into the land
which the LORD our God giveth us.
30 But [x]Sī´hŏn king of Hĕsh´bŏn
would not let us pass by him: for the
[y]LORD thy God hardened [z]his spirit,
and made his heart obstinate, that he
might deliver him into thy hand, as
appeareth this day.
31 And the LORD said unto me, Behold,
I have begun to give Sī´hŏn and
his land before thee: begin to possess,
that thou mayest inherit his land.
32 Then Sī´hŏn came out against us,
he and all his people, to fight at Jā´hăz.
33 And [a]the LORD our God delivered
him before us; and [b]we smote him,
and his sons, and all his people.
34 And we took all his cities at that
time, and [c]utterly destroyed [7]the men,
and the women, and the little ones, of
every city, we left none to remain:
35 Only the cattle we took for a prey
unto ourselves, and the spoil of the
cities which we took.
36 From [d]Ă-rō´ĕr, which *is* by the
brink of the river of Arnon, and *from*
the city that *is* by the river, even unto
Gilead, there was not one city too
strong for us: [e]the LORD our God delivered
all unto us:
37 Only unto the land of the children
of Ammon thou camest not, *nor* unto
any place of the river [f]Jăb´bok, nor
unto the cities in the mountains, nor
unto whatsoever the LORD our God
forbad us.

r Num. 21. 13,14.
6 begin, possess.
s Ex. 15.14. ch. 11.25.
t ch. 20.10. Esther 9.30.
u Num. 21. 21.
v Num. 20. 19.
w ch. 23.3.
x Num. 21. 23.
y Josh. 11.20.
z Ex. 4.21. Hosea 4.17.
a Ex. 23.31. ch. 7.2. Ps. 135.10, 11,12. Ps. 136.18, 19,20.
b ch. 29.7.
c Lev. 27.28. ch. 7.2,26. Josh. 7.11. Josh. 9.24. Josh. 11.14. 1 Sam. 15.3, 8,9.
7 every city of men, and women, and little ones.
d ch. 3,12. Josh. 13.9.
e Ps. 44.3.
f Gen. 32.22. Num. 21.24. ch. 3.16.

CHAP. 3

a Num. 21. 34.
b Deut. 29.8.
c ch. 2.24. Ps. 135.10, 11,12.
d Ps. 29.6. Ps. 89.12. Ps. 133.3.
e 1 Chr. 5.23.
f ch. 4.49.
g Josh. 12.5.
h Amos 2.9.
i Gen. 14.5, Rephaim.
j 2 Sam. 12. 26. Jer. 49.2. Amos 1.14.
k Num. 32. 33-38. ch. 2.36. Josh. 12.2. 2 Ki. 10.33.
l Num. 32.33.
m Num. 32. 39-42. 1 Chr. 5.33.
n 1 Chr. 2.22.

CHAPTER 3

THEN we turned, and went up the
way to Bā´shăn: and Og the king
of Bā´shăn came out against us, he
and all his people, to battle at Ĕd´rĕ-ī.
2 And the LORD said unto me, Fear
him not: for I will deliver him, and all
his people, and his land, into thy
hand; and thou shalt do unto him as
thou didst unto [a]Sī´hŏn king of the
Amorites, which dwelt at Hĕsh´bŏn.
3 So the LORD our God delivered into
our hands Og also, the king of Bā´shăn,
and all his people: and we smote
him until none was left to him remaining.
4 And we took all his cities at that
time, there was not a city which we
took not from them, threescore cities,
[b]all the region of Är´gŏb, the kingdom
of Og in Bā´shăn.
5 All these cities *were* fenced with
high walls, gates, and bars; beside unwalled
towns a great many.
6 And we utterly destroyed them, as
we did unto Sī´hŏn king [c]of Hĕsh´bŏn,
utterly destroying the men, women,
and children, of every city.
7 But all the cattle, and the spoil of
the cities, we took for a prey to ourselves.
8 And we took at that time out of the
hand of the two kings of the Amorites
the land that *was* on this side Jordan,
from the river of Arnon unto mount
Hermon;
9 (*Which* [d]Hermon the Sī-dō´nĭ-ăns
call Sĭ´rĭ-on; and the Amorites call it
[e]Shē´nĭr;)
10 All [f]the cities of the plain, and all
Gilead, and [g]all Bā´shăn, unto Săl´chăh
and Ĕd´rĕ-ī, cities of the kingdom
of Og in Bā´shăn.
11 For [h]only Og king of Bā´shăn remained
of the remnant [i]of giants; behold,
his bedstead *was* a bedstead of
iron; *is* it not [j]in Răb´băth of the children
of Ammon? nine cubits *was* the
length thereof, and four cubits the
breadth of it, after the cubit of a man.
12 And this land, *which* we possessed
at that time, [k]from Ă-rō´ĕr, which *is*
by the river Arnon, and half mount
Gilead, and the [l]cities thereof, gave I
unto the Reubenites and to the
Gadites.
13 And [m]the rest of Gilead, and all
Bā´shăn, *being* the kingdom of Og,
gave I unto the half tribe of Mă-năs´sĕh;
all the region of Är´gŏb, with all
Bā´shăn, which was called the land of
giants.
14 Jā´īr [n]the son of Mă-năs´sĕh took

all the country of Är-gŏb unto [o]the
coasts of Gĕ-shū-rī and Mā-ăch-ā-
thī; and called them after his own
name, Bā-shăn–hā-vōth–jā-īr, unto
this day.
15 And [p]I gave Gilead unto Mā-chīr.
16 And unto the Reubenites [q]and unto the Gadites I gave from Gilead
even unto the river Arnon half the
valley, and the border even unto the
river Jăb-bŏk, *which* [r]*is* the border of
the children of Ammon;
17 The plain also, and Jordan, and
the coast *thereof*, from [s]Chĭn-nĕ-rĕth
even unto the sea of the plain, [u]*even*
the salt sea, [1]under Ăsh-dōth–pĭs-găh
eastward.
18 ¶ And I commanded you at that
time, saying, The LORD your God
hath given you this land to possess it:
ye shall pass over armed before your
brethren the children of Israel, all
that are [2]meet for the war.
19 But your wives, and your little
ones, and your cattle, (*for* I know that
ye have much cattle,) shall abide in
your cities which I have given you;
20 Until the LORD have given rest
unto your brethren, as well as unto
you, and *until* they also possess the
land which the LORD your God hath
given them beyond Jordan: and *then*
shall ye [v]return every man unto his
possession, which I have given you.
21 ¶ And I commanded Joshua at
that time, saying, Thine eyes have seen
all that the LORD your God hath done
unto these two kings: so shall the
LORD do unto all the kingdoms
whither thou passest.
22 Ye shall not fear them: for the
[w]LORD your God he shall fight for
you.
23 And I besought the LORD at that
time, saying,
24 O Lord GOD, thou hast begun to
shew thy servant [x]thy greatness, and
thy mighty hand: for what [y]God *is*
there in heaven or in earth, that can
do according to thy works, and according to thy might?
25 I pray thee, let me go over, and
see the [z]good land that *is* beyond Jordan, that goodly mountain, and Lĕb-
ă-nŏn.
26 But the LORD was wroth with me
for your sakes, and would not hear
me: and the LORD said unto me, Let
it suffice thee; speak no more unto me
of this matter.
27 Get thee up into the top of [3]Pĭs-
găh, and lift up thine eyes westward,
and northward, and southward, and

o 2 Sam. 3.3. 2 Sam. 10.6.
p Num. 26. 29. Josh. 17.1.
q 2 Sam. 24.5.
r Num. 21.24.
s Num. 34.11.
t Gen. 13.10. Gen. 14.3. Josh. 12.3.
u Gen. 14.3. The sea of Sodom.
1 Or, under the springs of Pisgah, or, The hill.
2 sons of power.
v Josh. 22.4.
w Ex. 14.14. ch. 1.30.
x ch. 11.2. Neh. 9.32. Ps. 106.2. Ps. 145.3,6.
y Ex. 15.11. 2 Sam. 7.22. Ps. 71.19. Ps. 86.8.
z ch. 4.22.
3 Or, The hill.
a Num. 27. 18. ch. 1.38.
b ch. 4.46.

CHAP. 4

a Eze. 20.11. Rom. 10.5.
b ch. 12.32. Josh. 1.7. Pro. 30.6. Matt. 15.9. Rev. 22.18.
c Job 28.28. Ps. 19.7. Pro. 1.7. 2 Tim. 3.15.
d 1 Ki. 10.6,9. Dan. 1.20. Mal. 3.12. Acts 4.13.
e 2 Sam. 7.23.
f Ex. 25.8. Lev. 26.12. 1 Ki. 6.13. Ps. 46.1. Isa. 55.6. Zech. 2.10. Eph. 2.17. Jas. 4.8.
g Pro. 4.23.
h Pro. 3.1,3.
i Gen. 18.19. ch. 6.7. Ps. 78.5,6. Pro. 22.6. Eph. 6.4.
j Ex. 19.9,16. Heb. 12.18.

eastward, and behold *it* with thine
eyes: for thou shalt not go over this
Jordan.
28 But [a]charge Joshua, and encourage him, and strengthen him: for he
shall go over before this people, and
he shall cause them to inherit the land
which thou shalt see.
29 So we abode in [b]the valley over
against Bĕth–pē-ôr.

CHAPTER 4

NOW therefore hearken, O Israel,
unto the [a]statutes and unto the
judgments, which I teach you, for to
do *them*, that ye may live, and go in
and possess the land which the LORD
God of your fathers giveth you.
2 Ye [b]shall not add unto the word
which I command you, neither shall
ye diminish *ought* from it, that ye may
keep the commandments of the LORD
your God which I command you.
3 Your eyes have seen what the
LORD did because of Bā-ăl–pē-ôr: for
all the men that followed Bā-ăl–pē-ôr,
the LORD thy God hath destroyed
them from among you.
4 But ye that did cleave unto the
LORD your God *are* alive every one of
you this day.
5 Behold, I have taught you statutes
and judgments, even as the LORD my
God commanded me, that ye should
do so in the land whither ye go to
possess it.
6 Keep therefore and do *them;* for
this *is* your [c]wisdom and your understanding in the sight of the nations,
which shall hear all these statutes, and
say, [d]Surely this great nation *is* a wise
and understanding people.
7 For [e]what nation *is there so* great,
who *hath* [f]God *so* nigh unto them, as
the LORD our God *is* in all *things that*
we call upon him *for*?
8 And what nation *is there so* great,
that hath statutes and judgments *so*
righteous as all this law, which I set
before you this day?
9 Only take heed to thyself, and keep
[g]thy soul diligently, [h]lest thou forget
the things which thine eyes have seen,
and lest they depart from thy heart
all the days of thy life: but [i]teach them
thy sons, and thy sons' sons;
10 *Specially* [j]the day that thou stoodest before the LORD thy God in Hôr-
ĕb, when the LORD said unto me,
Gather me the people together, and I
will make them hear my words, that
they may learn to fear me all the days
that they shall live upon the earth,

and *that* they may teach their children.
11 And ye came near and stood under the mountain; and the mountain
burned with fire unto the [1]midst of
heaven, with darkness, clouds, and
thick darkness.
12 And the LORD spake unto you out
of the midst of the fire: ye heard the
voice of the words, but saw no similitude; [2]only *ye heard* a voice.
13 And he declared unto you his
covenant, which he commanded you
to perform, *even* ten commandments;
and he wrote them upon two tables of
stone.
14 ¶ And the LORD commanded me
at that time to teach you statutes and
judgments, that ye might do them in
the land whither ye go over to possess
it.
15 Take [k]ye therefore good heed unto yourselves; for ye saw no manner
of [l]similitude on the day *that* the LORD
spake unto you in Hôr'-ĕb out of the
midst of the fire:
16 Lest ye corrupt *yourselves*, and
make you a graven image, the similitude of any figure, [m]the likeness of
male or female,
17 The likeness of any beast that *is*
on the earth, the likeness of any
winged fowl that flieth in the air,
18 The likeness of any thing that
creepeth on the ground, the likeness
of any fish that *is* in the waters beneath
the earth:
19 And lest thou [n]lift up thine eyes
unto heaven, and when thou seest the
sun, and the moon, and the stars, *even*
[o]all the host of heaven, shouldest be
driven to worship them, and serve
them, which the LORD thy God hath
divided [3]unto all nations under the
whole heaven.
20 But the LORD hath taken you, and
brought you forth out of the iron
furnace, *even* out of Egypt, to be unto
him a people of inheritance, as *ye are*
this day.
21 Furthermore the LORD was angry
with me for your sakes, and sware
that I should not go over Jordan, and
that I should not go in unto that good
land, which the LORD thy God giveth
thee *for* an inheritance:
22 But [p]I must die in this land, I must
not go over Jordan: but ye shall go
over, and possess that good land.
23 Take heed unto yourselves, lest ye
forget the covenant of the LORD your
God, which he made with you, and
make you a graven image, *or* the like-

1 heart.
2 save a voice.
k Pro. 4.23, 27. Jer. 17.21. Mal. 2.15.
l Isa. 40.18. Acts 17.24-29.
m Rom. 1.23.
n ch. 17.3. Job 31.26.
o Gen. 2.1. 2 Ki. 17.16.
3 Or, imparted.
p 2 Pet. 1.13.
q Ex. 24.17. ch. 9.3. Isa. 33.14. Heb. 12.29.
r Ex. 20.5. ch. 6.15. Isa. 42.8.
s 2 Ki. 17.17.
t ch. 30.18, 19. Isa. 1.2. Micah 6.2.
u Lev. 26.33. ch. 28.62, 64. Neh. 1.8. Eze. 12.15.
v ch. 28.36, 64. 1 Sam. 26. 19. Jer. 16.13. Acts 7.42.
w 2 Chr. 15.4. Neh. 1.9. Isa. 55.6.
4 have found thee.
x Gen. 49.1. ch. 31.29. Jer. 23.20.
y Jer. 4.1, 2.
z Ex. 34.6. Num. 14.18. 2 Chr. 30.9. Neh. 9.31. Job 8.8. Ps. 86.5, 15. Ps. 103.8. Ps. 111.4. Ps. 116.5. Ps. 130.4, 7. Jonah 4.2.
a Job 8.8.
b Ex. 15.11. 1 Sam. 2.2. 2 Sam. 22. 31, 32. Isa. 44.6, 8. Matt. 24.31. Mark 12.29.
c ch. 32.39. 1 Sam. 2.2. 2 Sam. 22. 32. Isa. 45.5, 18. Mark 12.29.

ness of any *thing*, which the LORD thy
God hath forbidden thee.
24 For [q]the LORD thy God *is* a consuming fire, *even* [r]a jealous God.
25 ¶ When thou shalt beget children,
and children's children, and ye shall
have remained long in the land, and
shall corrupt *yourselves*, and make a
graven image, *or* the likeness of any
thing, and [s]shall do evil in the sight of
the LORD thy God, to provoke him to
anger:
26 I [t]call heaven and earth to witness
against you this day, that ye shall soon
utterly perish from off the land whereunto ye go over Jordan to possess it;
ye shall not prolong *your* days upon it,
but shall utterly be destroyed.
27 And the LORD [u]shall scatter you
among the nations, and ye shall be
left few in number among the heathen,
whither the LORD shall lead you.
28 And [v]there ye shall serve gods,
the work of men's hands, wood and
stone, which neither see, nor hear,
nor eat, nor smell.
29 But [w]if from thence thou shalt
seek the LORD thy God, thou shalt
find *him*, if thou seek him with all thy
heart and with all thy soul.
30 When thou art in tribulation, and
all these things [4]are come upon thee,
[x]*even* in the latter days, if thou [y]turn
to the LORD thy God, and shalt be
obedient unto his voice;
31 (For the LORD thy God *is* [z]a merciful God;) he will not forsake thee,
neither destroy thee, nor forget the
covenant of thy fathers which he
sware unto them.
32 For [a]ask now of the days that are
past, which were before thee, since
the day that God created man upon
the earth, and *ask* from [b]the one side
of heaven unto the other, whether
there hath been *any such thing* as this
great thing *is*, or hath been heard like
it?
33 Did *ever* people hear the voice of
God speaking out of the midst of the
fire, as thou hast heard, and live?
34 Or hath God assayed to go *and*
take him a nation from the midst of
another nation, by temptations, by
signs, and by wonders, and by war,
and by a mighty hand, and by a
stretched out arm, and by great terrors, according to all that the LORD
your God did for you in Egypt before
your eyes?
35 Unto thee it was shewed, that thou
mightest know that the LORD he *is*
God; *there* [c]*is* none else beside him.

36 Out [d]of heaven he made thee to
hear his voice, that he might instruct
thee: and upon earth he shewed thee
his great fire; and thou heardest his
words out of the midst of the fire.
37 And because he loved thy fathers,
therefore he chose their seed after
them, and brought thee out in his
sight with his mighty power out of
Egypt;
38 To drive out nations from before
thee greater and mightier than thou
art, to bring thee in, to give thee their
land *for* an inheritance, as *it is* this
day.
39 Know therefore this day, and
consider *it* in thine heart, [e]that the
LORD he *is* God in heaven above, and
upon the earth beneath: *there is* none
else.
40 Thou [f]shalt keep therefore his
statutes, and his commandments,
which I command thee this day, that
it may go well with thee, and with
thy children after thee, and that thou
mayest prolong *thy* days upon the
earth, which the LORD thy God giveth
thee, for ever.
41 ¶ Then Moses [h]severed three cities on this side Jordan toward the
sunrising;
42 That the slayer might flee thither,
which should kill his neighbour unawares, and hated him not in times
past; and that fleeing unto one of
these cities he might live:
43 *Namely*, [i]Bē´-zĕr in the wilderness,
in the plain country, of the Reubenites; and Rā´-mŏth in Gilead, of the
Gadites; and Gō´-lăn in Bā´-shăn, of
the Mă-năs´-sītes.
44 ¶ And this *is* the law which Moses
set before the children of Israel:
45 These *are* the testimonies, and the
statutes, and the judgments, which
Moses spake unto the children of
Israel, after they came forth out of
Egypt,
46 On this side Jordan, [j]in the valley
over against Bĕth–pē´-ôr, in the land
of Sī´-hŏn king of the Amorites, who
dwelt at Hĕsh´-bŏn, whom Moses and
the children of Israel smote, after they
were come forth out of Egypt:
47 And they possessed his land, and
the land [k]of Og king of Bā´-shăn, two
kings of the Amorites, which *were*
on this side Jordan toward the sunrising;
48 From [l]Ă-rō´-ĕr, which *is* by the
bank of the river Arnon, even unto
mount Sī´-ŏn, which *is* [m]Hermon,
49 And all the plain on this side Jordan eastward, even unto the sea of the
plain, under the springs of Pĭs´-găh.

CHAPTER 5

AND Moses called all Israel, and
said unto them, Hear, O Israel,
the statutes and judgments which I
speak in your ears this day, that ye
may learn them, and [1]keep, and do
them.
2 The [a]LORD our God made a covenant with us in Hôr´-ĕb.
3 The LORD [b]made not this covenant
with our fathers, but with us, *even* us,
who *are* all of us here alive this day.
4 The [c]LORD talked with you face to
face in the mount out of the midst of
the fire,
5 (I [d]stood between the LORD and you
at that time, to shew you the word of
the LORD: for [e]ye were afraid by
reason of the fire, and went not up into
the mount;) saying,
6 ¶ I [f]*am* the LORD thy God, which
brought thee out of the land of Egypt,
from the house of [2]bondage.
7 Thou [g]shalt have none other gods
before me.
8 Thou [h]shalt not make thee *any*
graven image, *or* any likeness *of any*
thing that *is* in heaven above, or that
is in the earth beneath, or that *is* in the
waters beneath the earth:
9 Thou shalt not bow down thyself
unto them, nor serve them: for I the
LORD thy God *am* a jealous God,
[i]visiting the iniquity of the fathers upon the children unto the third and
fourth *generation* of them that hate
me,
10 And [j]shewing mercy unto thousands of them that love me and keep
my commandments.
11 Thou [k]shalt not take the name of
the LORD thy God in vain: for the
LORD will not hold *him* guiltless that
taketh his name in vain.
12 Keep [l]the sabbath day to sanctify
it, as the LORD thy God hath commanded thee.
13 Six [m]days thou shalt labour, and
do all thy work:
14 But the seventh day *is* [n]the sabbath of the LORD thy God: *in it* thou
shalt not do any work, thou, nor thy
son, nor thy daughter, nor thy manservant, nor thy maidservant, nor
thine ox, nor thine ass, nor any of thy
cattle, nor thy stranger that *is* within
thy gates; that thy manservant and
thy maidservant may rest as well as
thou.
15 And remember that thou wast a

d Ex. 19.9,19. 1 Chr. 29.11. 2 Chr. 20.6. Heb. 12.18.
e Josh. 2.11. Isa. 42.8. Dan. 4.35.
f Lev. 22.31.
g ch. 5.16. ch. 6.3,18. ch. 22.7. Eph. 6.3.
h Num. 35.6.
i Josh. 20.8.
j ch. 3.29.
k Num. 21.35. ch. 3.3,4.
l ch. 2.36.
m Ps. 133.3.

CHAP. 5

1 keep to do them.
a Ex. 19.5. ch. 4.23. Heb. 8.6-13.
b Matt. 13.17. Heb. 8.9.
c Ex. 19.9,19. ch. 4.33,36. ch. 34.10.
d Ex. 19.16. Num. 16.48. Ps. 106.23. Jer. 30.21. Gal. 3.19. Heb. 12.18, 19.
e Ex. 19.16.
f Ex. 20.2. Lev. 26.1. ch. 6.4. Ps. 81.10.
2 servants.
g Ex. 20.3.
h Ex. 20.4. Ps. 97.7. Acts. 17.29.
i Ex. 34.7.
j Jer. 32.18. Dan. 9.4. 1 John 1.7.
k Ex. 20.7. Lev. 19.12. Matt. 5.33. Jas. 5.12.
l Ex. 20.8. Neh. 13.17.
m Ex. 23.12.
n Gen. 2.2. Heb. 4.4.

servant in the land of Egypt, and *that*
the LORD thy God brought thee out
thence through a mighty hand and by
a stretched out arm: therefore the
LORD thy God commanded thee to
keep the sabbath day.
16 ¶ Honour [o]thy father and thy
mother, as the LORD thy God hath
commanded thee; [p]that thy days may
be prolonged, and that it may go well
with thee, in the land which the LORD
thy God giveth thee.
17 Thou [q]shalt not kill.
18 Neither [r]shalt thou commit adultery.
19 Neither [s]shalt thou steal.
20 Neither [t]shalt thou bear false
witness against thy neighbour.
21 Neither [u]shalt thou desire thy
neighbour's wife, neither shalt thou
covet thy neighbour's house, his field,
or his manservant, or his maidservant,
his ox, or his ass, or any *thing* that *is*
thy neighbour's.
22 ¶ These words the LORD spake
unto all your assembly in the mount
out of the midst of the fire, of the
cloud, and of the thick darkness, with
a great voice: and he added no more.
And [v]he wrote them in two tables of
stone, and delivered them unto me.
23 And it came to pass, when ye
heard the voice out of the midst of the
darkness, (for the mountain did burn
with fire,) that ye came near unto me,
even all the heads of your tribes, and
your elders;
24 And ye said, Behold, the LORD
our God hath shewed us his glory and
his greatness, and we have heard his
voice out of the midst of the fire: we
have seen this day that God doth talk
with man, and he liveth.
25 Now therefore why should we
die? for this great fire will consume
us: if we [3]hear the voice of the LORD
our God any more, then we shall die.
26 For [w]who *is there of* all flesh, that
hath heard the voice of the living God
speaking out of the midst of the fire,
as we *have*, and lived?
27 Go thou near, and hear all that
the LORD our God shall say: and
[x]speak thou unto us all that the LORD
our God shall speak unto thee; and
we will hear *it*, and do *it*.
28 And the LORD heard the voice of
your words, when ye spake unto me;
and the LORD said unto me, I have
heard the voice of the words of this
people, which they have spoken unto
thee: they have well said all that they
have spoken.

o Lev. 19.3. ch. 27.16. Eph. 6.2,3. Col. 3.20.
p ch. 4.40.
q Matt. 5.21.
r Luke 18.20.
s Rom. 13.9.
t 1 Ki. 21.10.
u Micah 2.2. Hab. 2.9. Luke 12.15. Rom. 7.7. Gal. 5.14.
v Ex. 24.12.
3 add to hear.
w ch. 4.33.
x Heb. 12.19.
y ch. 32.29. Ps. 81.13. Isa. 48.18. Matt. 23.37. Luke 19.42. 2 Cor. 5.20. Heb. 12.25.
z ch. 11.1. Ps. 119.1-5. Luke 11.28. John 15.14. Rev. 22.14.
a Mal. 4.4. Gal. 3.19.
b ch. 17.20. Josh. 1.7. Pro. 4.27.
c ch. 10.12. Ps. 119.6. Eccl. 8.12. Luke 1.6. 1 Tim. 4.8.
d ch. 4.40. ch. 12.25,28. Eph. 6.3.

CHAP. 6

1 pass over.
a Ex. 20.20. Ps. 111.10. Ps. 128.1. Eccl. 12.13.
b Pro. 3.1.
c Isa. 9.6. Mark 12.29. John 1.1. 1 Cor. 8.4. Eph. 4.6. Phil. 2.5,6.
d ch. 30.6. Matt. 22.37. Mark 12.30-32.
e Isa. 51.7.
f Eph. 6.4.
2 whet, or, sharpen.
g Pro. 3.3. Pro. 7.3.
h ch. 11.20. Isa. 50.8. Isa. 57.8.

29 O [y]that there were such an hear
in them, that they would fear me, and
[z]keep all my commandments always
that it might be well with them, and
with their children for ever!
30 Go say to them, Get you into your
tents again.
31 But as for thee, stand thou here
by me, and [a]I will speak unto thee al
the commandments, and the statutes
and the judgments, which thou shal
teach them, that they may do *them* i
the land which I give them to posses
it.
32 Ye shall observe to do therefore
as the LORD your God hath command
ed you: [b]ye shall not turn aside to th
right hand or to the left.
33 Ye shall walk in [c]all the way
which the LORD your God hath com
manded you, that ye may live, and
that it may be [d]well with you, and *tha*
ye may prolong *your* days in the land
which ye shall possess.

CHAPTER 6

NOW these *are* the command
ments, the statutes, and th
judgments, which the LORD your Go
commanded to teach you, that y
might do *them* in the land whither y
[1]go to possess it:
2 That [a]thou mightest fear the LOR
thy God, to keep all his statutes and
his commandments, which I com
mand thee, thou, and thy son, and th
son's son, all the days of thy life; [b]and
that thy days may be prolonged.
3 ¶ Hear therefore, O Israel, and ob
serve to do *it;* that it may be well wit
thee, and that ye may increase might
ily, as the LORD God of thy father
hath promised thee, in the land tha
floweth with milk and honey.
4 Hear, O Israel: [c]The LORD our Go
is one LORD:
5 And [d]thou shalt love the LOR
thy God with all thine heart, an
with all thy soul, and with all th
might.
6 And [e]these words, which I com
mand thee this day, shall be in thin
heart:
7 And [f]thou shalt teach [2]them dil
gently unto thy children, and shal
talk of them when thou sittest in thin
house, and when thou walkest by th
way, and when thou liest down, an
when thou risest up.
8 And [g]thou shalt bind them for
sign upon thine hand, and they sha
be as frontlets between thine eyes.
9 And [h]thou shalt write them upo

the posts of thy house, and on thy
gates.
10 And it shall be, when the LORD
thy God shall have brought thee into
the land which he sware unto thy fathers, to Abraham, to Isaac, and to
Jacob, to give thee great and goodly
cities, [i]which thou buildedst not,
11 And houses full of all good *things*,
which thou filledst not, and wells digged, which thou diggedst not, vineyards and olive trees, which thou
plantedst not; when thou shalt have
eaten and be full;
12 *Then* beware lest thou forget the
LORD, which brought thee forth out
of the land of Egypt, from the house
of [3]bondage.
13 Thou shalt [j]fear the LORD thy
God, and serve him, and [k]shalt swear
by his name.
14 Ye shall not [l]go after other gods,
of the gods of the people which *are*
round about you;
15 (For the LORD thy God *is* a jealous
God among you) lest the anger of the
LORD thy God be kindled against
thee, and destroy thee from off the
face of the earth.
16 ¶ Ye [m]shall not tempt the LORD
your God, [n]as ye tempted *him* in
Măs-săh.
17 Ye shall [o]diligently keep the commandments of the LORD your God,
and his testimonies, and his statutes,
which he hath commanded thee.
18 And thou shalt do *that which is*
right and good in the sight of the
LORD: that it may be well with thee,
and that thou mayest go in and possess the good land which the LORD
sware unto thy fathers,
19 To cast out all thine enemies
from before thee, as the LORD hath
spoken.
20 *And* when thy son asketh thee [4]in
time to come, saying, What *mean* the
testimonies, and the statutes, and the
judgments, which the LORD our God
hath commanded you?
21 Then thou shalt say unto thy son,
We were Pharaoh's bondmen in
Egypt; and the LORD brought us out
of Egypt with a mighty hand:
22 And the LORD shewed signs and
wonders, great and [5]sore, upon Egypt,
upon Pharaoh, and upon all his household, before our eyes:
23 And he brought us out from
thence, that he might bring us in, to
give us the land which he sware unto
our fathers.
24 And the LORD commanded us to
do all these statutes, to fear the LORD
our God, for [p]our good always, that
[q]he might preserve us alive, as *it is* at
this day.
25 And [r]it shall be our righteousness,
if we observe to do all these commandments before the LORD our God,
as he hath commanded us.

CHAPTER 7

WHEN the LORD thy God shall
bring thee into the land whither
thou goest to possess it, and hath cast
out many nations before thee, the
Hittites, and the Gĭr-gă-shītes, and
the Amorites, and the Canaanites, and
the Pĕ-rĭz-zītes, and the Hī-vītes, and
the Jĕb-ū-sītes, seven nations greater
and mightier than thou;
2 And when the LORD thy God shall
deliver them before thee; thou shalt
smite them, *and* [a]utterly destroy
them; [b]thou shalt make no covenant
with them, nor shew mercy unto them:
3 Neither [c]shalt thou make marriages
with them; thy daughter thou shalt
not give unto his son, nor his daughter
shalt thou take unto thy son.
4 For they will turn away thy son
from following me, that they may
serve other gods: so will the anger of
the LORD be kindled against you, and
destroy thee suddenly.
5 But thus shall ye deal with them;
ye shall [d]destroy their altars, and
break down their [1]images, and cut
down their groves, and burn their
graven images with fire.
6 For [e]thou *art* an holy people unto
the LORD thy God: [f]the LORD thy God
hath chosen thee to be a special people unto himself, above all people
that *are* upon the face of the earth.
7 The LORD did not set his love upon
you, nor choose you, because ye were
more in number than any people; for
ye *were* the fewest of all people:
8 But because the LORD loved you,
and because he would keep the [g]oath
which he had sworn unto your fathers,
[h]hath the LORD brought you out
with a mighty hand, and redeemed
you out of the house of bondmen,
from the hand of Pharaoh king of
Egypt.
9 Know therefore that the LORD thy
God, he *is* God, [i]the faithful God,
[j]which keepeth covenant and mercy
with them that love him and keep his
commandments to a thousand generations;
10 And [k]repayeth them that hate
him to their face, to destroy them: he

i Josh. 24.13. Ps. 105.44.
3 bondmen, or, servants.
j ch. 13.4. Luke 4.8.
k Ps. 63.11.
l Jer. 25.6.
m Matt. 4.7.
n 1 Cor. 10.9.
o Ps. 119.4.
4 to-morrow.
5 evil.
p Job 35.7,8.
q Ps. 41.2. Luke 10.28.
r Rom. 10.3.

CHAP. 7

a Josh. 6.17.
b Ex. 23.32. Josh. 2.14. Judge 1.24.
c Josh. 23.12. 1 Ki. 11.2. Ezra 9.2.
d Ex. 23.24.
1 statues, or, pillars.
e Ps. 50.5. Jer. 2.3. Amos 3.2. Titus 2.14. 1 Pet. 2.5.
f Ps. 135.4. Amos 3.2. 1 Pet. 2.9.
g Ex. 32.13. Ps. 105.8. Luke 1.55.
h Ex. 13.3.
i Isa. 49.7. 1 Cor. 1.9. 2 Cor. 1.18. 1 Thes. 5.24. 2 Tim. 2.13. Heb. 11.11.
j Neh. 1.5. Dan. 9.4.
k Ps. 21.8. Pro. 11.31. Isa. 59.18. Nah. 1.2. Rom. 12.19.

will not be slack to him that hateth him, he will repay him to his face.

11 Thou shalt therefore keep the commandments, and the statutes, and the judgments, which I command thee this day, to do them.

12 ¶ Wherefore it shall come to pass, [2]if ye hearken to these judgments, and keep, and do them, that the LORD thy God shall keep unto thee the covenant and the mercy which he sware unto thy fathers:

13 And he will [l]love thee, and bless thee, and multiply thee: he will also bless the fruit of thy womb, and the fruit of thy land, thy corn, and thy wine, and thine oil, the increase of thy kine, and the flocks of thy sheep, in the land which he sware unto thy fathers to give thee.

14 Thou shalt be blessed above all people: there shall not be male or female barren among you, or among your cattle.

15 And the LORD will take away from thee all sickness, and will put none of the [m]evil diseases of Egypt, which thou knowest, upon thee; but will lay them upon all *them* that hate thee.

16 And thou shalt consume all the people which the LORD thy God shall deliver thee; thine eye shall have no pity upon them: neither shalt thou serve their gods; for that *will be* [n]a snare unto thee.

17 If thou shalt say in thine heart, These nations *are* more than I; how can I [o]dispossess them?

18 Thou shalt not be afraid of them: *but* shalt well [p]remember what the LORD thy God did unto Pharaoh, and unto all Egypt;

19 The great temptations which thine eyes saw, and the signs, and the wonders, and the mighty hand, and the stretched out arm, whereby the LORD thy God brought thee out: so shall the LORD thy God do unto all the people of whom thou art afraid.

20 Moreover [q]the LORD thy God will send the hornet among them, until they that are left, and hide themselves from thee, be destroyed.

21 Thou shalt not be affrighted at them: for the LORD thy God *is* among [r]you, [s]a mighty God and terrible.

22 And the LORD thy God will [3]put out those nations before thee by little and little: thou mayest not consume them at once, lest the beasts of the field increase upon thee.

23 But the LORD thy God shall deliver them [4]unto thee, and shall destroy them with a mighty destruction, until they be destroyed.

24 And [t]he shall deliver their kings into thine hand, and thou shalt destroy their name from under heaven: [u]there shall no man be able to stand before thee, until thou have destroyed them.

25 The graven images of their gods [v]shall ye burn with fire: thou shalt [w]not desire the silver or gold *that is* on them, nor take *it* unto thee, lest thou be [x]snared therein: for it *is* [y]an abomination to the LORD thy God.

26 Neither shalt thou bring an abomination into thine house, lest thou be a cursed thing like it: *but* thou shalt utterly detest it, and thou shalt utterly abhor it; [z]for it *is* a cursed thing.

CHAPTER 8

ALL the commandments which I command thee this day shall ye observe to do, that ye may live, and multiply, and go in and possess the land which the LORD sware unto your fathers.

2 And thou shalt remember all the way which the LORD thy God led [a]thee these forty years in the wilderness, to humble thee, *and* to prove thee, [b]to know what *was* in thine heart, whether thou wouldest keep his commandments, or no.

3 And he humbled thee, and suffered [c]thee to hunger, and fed thee with măn′-nă, which thou knewest not, neither did thy fathers know; that he might make thee know that man doth [d]not live by bread only, but by every *word* that proceedeth out of the mouth of the LORD doth man live.

4 Thy [e]raiment waxed not old upon thee, neither did thy foot swell, these forty years.

5 Thou [f]shalt also consider in thine heart, that, as a man chasteneth his son, *so* the LORD thy God chasteneth thee.

6 Therefore thou shalt keep the commandments of the LORD thy God, to walk in his ways, and to fear him.

7 For the LORD thy God bringeth thee into a good land, a land of brooks of water, of fountains and depths that spring out of valleys and hills;

8 A land of wheat, and barley, and vines, and fig trees, and pomegranates; a land [1]of oil olive, and honey;

9 A land wherein thou shalt eat bread without scarceness, thou shalt not lack any *thing* in it; a land whose

2 because.
l Ex. 23.25. Ps. 1.3. Ps. 11.7. Ps. 63.3. Ps. 146.8. Pro. 15.9. John 14.21.
m Ex. 9.14. ch. 28.27. Ps. 105.37.
n Judg. 8.27. Ps. 106.36.
o Num. 33. 53.
p Judg. 6.13. Ps. 77.11. Ps. 105.5. Ps. 135.8-10. Isa. 63.11-15.
q Ex. 23.28. Josh. 24. 12.
r Num. 14.9.
s ch. 10.17. Neh. 1.5.
3 pluck off.
4 before thy face.
t Josh. 10.24.
u ch. 11.25. Josh. 1.5.
v Ex. 32.20. ch. 12.3. 1 Chr. 14.12.
w Ex. 20.17. Josh. 7.1. Luke 12.15. Col. 3.5.
x Judg. 8.27. Zeph. 1.3.
y ch. 17.1.
z Lev. 27.28.
CHAP. 8
a Ps. 136.16. Amos 2.10.
b 2 Chr. 32. 31. John 2.25.
c Ex. 16.2. Ps. 78.23-25. 1 Cor. 10.3, 4.
d Ps. 104.29. Matt. 4.4. Heb. 13.5,6.
e ch. 29.5. Neh. 9.21.
f Ps. 89.32. Pro. 3.12. Heb. 12.5. Rev. 3.19.
1 of olive tree of oil.

stones *are* iron, and out of whose hills thou mayest dig brass.

10 When [g]thou hast eaten and art full, then thou shalt bless the LORD thy God for the good land which he hath given thee.

11 Beware that thou forget not the LORD thy God, in not keeping his commandments, and his judgments, and his statutes, which I command thee this day:

12 Lest [h]*when* thou hast eaten and art full, and hast built goodly houses, and dwelt *therein;*

13 And *when* thy herds and thy flocks multiply, and thy silver and thy gold is multiplied, and all that thou hast is multiplied;

14 Then [i]thine heart be lifted up, and thou [j]forget the LORD thy God, which brought thee forth out of the land of Egypt, from the house of bondage;

15 Who [k]led thee through that great and terrible [l]wilderness, *wherein were* fiery serpents, and scorpions, and drought, where *there was* no water; [m]who brought thee forth water out of the rock of flint;

16 Who fed thee in the wilderness [n]with măn-nă, which thy fathers knew not, that he might humble thee, and that he might prove thee, [o]to do thee good at thy latter end;

17 And [p]thou say in thine heart, My power and the might of *mine* hand hath gotten me this wealth.

18 But thou shalt remember the LORD thy God: [q]for *it is* he that giveth thee power to get wealth, that he may establish his covenant which he sware unto thy fathers, as *it is* this day.

19 And it shall be, if thou do at all forget the LORD thy God, and walk after other gods, and serve them, and worship them, I testify against you this day that ye shall surely perish.

20 As the nations which the LORD destroyeth before your face, [r]so shall ye perish; because ye would not be obedient unto the voice of the LORD your God.

g Ps. 103.2. 1 Cor. 10.31. 1 Tim. 4.3.
h Pro. 30.9.
i 1 Cor. 4.7.
j Ps. 106.21.
k Isa. 63.12.
l Num. 21.6. Hosea 13.5.
m Num. 20. 11.
n Ex. 16.15.
o Jer. 24.5,6. Rom. 8.28. 2 Cor. 4.17. Heb. 12.11. 1 Pet. 1.7.
p ch. 9.4.
q Pro. 10.22. Hosea 2.8.
r Lam. 1. Dan. 9.12. Zech. 1.6.

CHAPTER 9

HEAR, O Israel: Thou *art* to pass over Jordan this day, to go in to possess nations [a]greater and mightier than thyself, cities great and [b]fenced up to heaven,

2 A people great and tall, [c]the children of the Anakims, whom thou knowest, and *of whom* thou hast heard *say*, Who can stand before the children of Anak!

3 Understand therefore this day, that the LORD thy God *is* he which goeth [d]over before thee; *as* a [e]consuming fire he shall destroy them, and he shall bring them down before thy face: [f]so shalt thou drive them out, and destroy them quickly, as the LORD hath said unto thee.

4 Speak [g]not thou in thine heart, after that the LORD thy God hath cast them out from before thee, saying, For my righteousness the LORD hath brought me in to possess this land: but [h]for the wickedness of these nations the LORD doth drive them out from before thee.

5 Not [i]for thy righteousness, or for the uprightness of thine heart, dost thou go to possess their land: but for the wickedness of these nations the LORD thy God doth drive them out from before thee, and that he may perform [j]the word which the LORD sware unto thy fathers, Abraham, Isaac, and Jacob.

6 Understand therefore, that the LORD thy God giveth thee not this good land to possess it for thy righteousness; for thou *art* a stiffnecked people.

7 ¶ Remember, *and* forget not, how thou provokedst the LORD thy God to wrath in the wilderness: from [k]the day that thou didst depart out of the land of Egypt, until ye came unto this place, ye have been rebellious against the LORD.

8 Also [l]in Hôr-ĕb ye provoked the LORD to wrath, so that the LORD was angry with you to have destroyed you.

9 When I was gone up into the mount to receive the tables of stone, *even* the tables of the covenant which the LORD made with you, then I [m]abode in the mount forty days and forty nights, I neither did eat bread nor drink water:

10 And the LORD delivered unto me two tables of stone written with the finger of God; and on them *was written* according to all the words, which the LORD spake with you in the mount out of the midst of the fire in the day of the assembly.

11 And it came to pass at the end of forty days and forty nights, *that* the LORD gave me the two tables of stone, *even* the tables of the covenant.

12 And the LORD said unto me, Arise, [n]get thee down quickly from hence; for thy people which thou hast brought forth out of Egypt have corrupted *themselves;* they are [o]quickly turned aside out of the way which I

CHAP. 9
a ch. 4.38. ch. 7.1.
b ch. 1.28.
c Num. 13. 22.
d ch. 31.3. Micah 2.13. Rev. 19.11-15.
e ch. 4.24. Isa. 30.27. Nah. 1.5,6. 2 Thes. 1.8. Heb. 12.29.
f Ex. 23.31.
g ch. 8.11,17. Rom. 11.6. 1 Cor. 4.4.
h Gen. 15.16. Lev. 18.24. ch. 18.12.
i 2 Tim. 1.9. Titus 3.5.
j Gen. 12.7. Gen. 13.15. Gen. 15.7. Gen. 17.8. Gen. 26.4. Gen. 28.13. Ex. 32.13. Luke 1.54, 55. Acts 13.32, 33. Rom. 15.8.
k Ex. 14.11. Num. 11.4.
l Ex. 32.4. Ps. 106.19.
m Ex. 24.18. Luke 4.1.
n Ex. 32.7.
o ch. 31.29. Judg. 2.17.

commanded them; they have made them a molten image.

13 Furthermore [p]the LORD spake unto me, saying, I have seen this people, and, behold, [q]it *is* a stiffnecked people:

14 Let me alone, that I may destroy them, and [r]blot out their name from under heaven: and I will make of thee a nation mightier and greater than they.

15 So I turned and came down from the mount, and the mount burned with fire: and the two tables of the covenant *were* in my two hands.

16 And I looked, and, behold, ye had sinned against the LORD your God, *and* had made you a molten calf: ye had turned aside quickly out of the way which the LORD had commanded you.

17 And [s]I took the two tables, and cast them out of my two hands, and brake them before your eyes.

18 And I [t]fell down before the LORD, as at the first, forty days and forty nights: I did neither eat bread, nor drink water, because of all your sins which ye sinned, in doing wickedly in the sight of the LORD, to provoke him to anger.

19 For [u]I was afraid of the anger and hot displeasure, wherewith the LORD was wroth against you to destroy you. [v]But the LORD hearkened unto me at that time also.

20 And the LORD was very angry with Aaron to have destroyed him: and I prayed for Aaron also the same time.

21 And [w]I took your sin, the calf which ye had made, and burnt it with fire, and stamped it, *and* ground *it* very small, *even* until it was as small as dust: and I cast the dust thereof into the brook that descended out of the mount.

22 And at [x]Tăb´-ĕ-räh, and at Măs´-săh, and at [y]Kĭb´-rōth–hăt-tā´-ă-văh, ye provoked the LORD to wrath.

23 Likewise [z]when the LORD sent you from Kā´-dĕsh–bär´-nē-ă, saying, Go up and possess the land which I have given you; then ye rebelled against the commandment of the LORD your God, and ye [a]believed him not, nor hearkened to his voice.

24 Ye [b]have been rebellious against the LORD from the day that I knew you.

25 Thus I fell down before the LORD forty days and forty nights, as I fell down *at the first;* because the LORD had said he would destroy you.

p Ex. 32.9.
q ch. 10.16. ch. 31.27. 2 Ki. 17.14.
r ch. 29.20. Ps. 9.5. Ps. 109.13.
s Ps. 69.9. Ps. 119.139.
t Ex. 34.28. Ps. 106.23.
u Ex. 32.10, 11. Heb. 12.29.
v Ex. 32.14. ch. 10.10. Ps. 106.23. Amos 7.1-6. Jas. 5.15.
w Ex. 32.20. Isa. 2.18-21. Isa. 30.22. Isa. 31.7. Hosea 8.11.
x Num. 11.1.
y Num. 11.4.
z Num. 13.3.
a Ps. 78.22. Ps. 106.24. Heb. 3.18, 19. Heb. 4.2.
b ch. 31.27.
c 1 Sam. 7.9. Pro. 15.29. Jer. 15.1.
d Gen. 41.57. 1 Sam. 14. 25.
e Num. 14.16. ch. 32.26,27. Josh. 7.7-9. Ps. 115.1,2. Isa. 48.9-11.
f ch. 4.20. 1 Ki. 8.51. Neh. 1.10. Ps. 95.7.

CHAP. 10

a Ex. 34.1,2.
b Ex. 25.10.
c Ex. 25.5.
d Jer. 31.33.
1 words.
e Ex. 20.1.
f ch. 9.10. ch. 18.16.
g Ex. 34.29.
h Ex. 40.20.
i 1 Ki. 8.9.
j Num. 33.31.
k Num. 20. 28.
l Lev. 9.22. Num. 6.23. ch. 21.5.

26 I [c]prayed therefore unto the LORD, and said, O Lord GOD, destroy not thy people and thine inheritance, which thou hast redeemed through thy greatness, which thou hast brought forth out of Egypt with a mighty hand.

27 Remember thy servants, Abraham, Isaac, and Jacob; look not unto the stubbornness of this people, nor to their wickedness, nor to their sin:

28 Lest [d]the land whence thou broughtest us out say, [e]Because the LORD was not able to bring them into the land which he promised them, and because he hated them, he hath brought them out to slay them in the wilderness.

29 Yet they *are* thy people and thine [f]inheritance, which thou broughtest out by thy mighty power and by thy stretched out arm.

CHAPTER 10

AT that time the LORD said unto me, Hew [a]thee two tables of stone like unto the first, and come up unto me into the mount, and make [b]thee an ark of wood.

2 And I will write on the tables the words that were in the first tables which thou brakest, and thou shalt put them in the ark.

3 And I made an ark *of* [c]shĭt´-tĭm wood, and hewed two tables of stone like unto the first, and went up into the mount, having the two tables in mine hand.

4 And [d]he wrote on the tables, according to the first writing, the ten [1]commandments, [e]which the LORD spake unto you in the mount out of the midst of the fire in [f]the day of the assembly: and the LORD gave them unto me.

5 And I turned myself and [g]came down from the mount, and [h]put the tables in the ark which I had made; [i]and there they be, as the LORD commanded me.

6 ¶ And the children of Israel took their journey from Bē-ĕr´-ōth [j]of the children of Jā´-ă-kăn to Mō´-sē-ră: there [k]Aaron died, and there he was buried; and Ĕl-ē-ā´-zär his son ministered in the priest's office in his stead.

7 From thence they journeyed unto Gŭd-gō´-dăh; and from Gŭd-gō´-dăh to Jŏt´-băth, a land of rivers of waters.

8 ¶ At that time the LORD separated the tribe of Levi, to bear the ark of the covenant of the LORD, to stand before the LORD to minister unto him, and [l]to bless in his name, unto this day.

9 Wherefore [m]Levi hath no part nor inheritance with his brethren; the LORD *is* his inheritance, according as the LORD thy God promised him.

10 And I stayed in the mount, according to the [2]first time, forty days and forty nights; and the LORD hearkened unto me at that time also, *and* the LORD would not destroy thee.

11 And the LORD said unto me, Arise, [3]take *thy* journey before the people, that they may go in and possess the land, which I sware unto their fathers to give unto them.

12 ¶ And now, Israel, [n]what doth the LORD thy God require of thee, but to fear the LORD thy God, to walk in all his ways, and [o]to love him, and to serve the LORD thy God with all thy heart and with all thy soul,

13 To keep the commandments of the LORD, and his statutes, which I command thee this day for thy good?

14 Behold, [p]the heaven and the heaven of heavens *is* the LORD's thy God, [q]the earth *also*, with all that therein *is*.

15 Only the LORD had a delight in thy fathers to love them, and he chose their seed after them, *even* you above all people, as *it is* this day.

16 Circumcise therefore [r]the foreskin of your heart, and be no more stiffnecked.

17 For the LORD your God *is* [s]God of gods, and [t]Lord of lords, a great God, a mighty, and a terrible, which regardeth [u]not persons, nor taketh reward:

18 He [v]doth execute the judgment of the fatherless and widow, and loveth the stranger, in giving him food and raiment.

19 Love ye therefore the stranger: for ye were strangers in the land of Egypt.

20 Thou [w]shalt fear the LORD thy God; him shalt thou serve, and to him shalt thou cleave, [x]and swear by his name.

21 He [y]*is* thy praise, and he *is* thy God, that hath done for thee these great and terrible things, which thine eyes have seen.

22 Thy fathers went down into Egypt with threescore and ten persons; and now the LORD thy God hath made thee as the stars of heaven for multitude.

CHAPTER 11

THEREFORE thou shalt love the LORD thy God, and [a]keep his charge, and his statutes, and his judgments, and his commandments, alway.

2 And know ye this day: for *I speak* not with your children which have not known, and which have not seen the chastisement of the LORD your God, his greatness, his mighty hand, and his stretched out arm,

3 And his miracles, and his acts, which he did in the midst of Egypt unto Pharaoh the king of Egypt, and unto all his land;

4 And what he did unto the army of Egypt, unto their horses, and to their chariots; how he made the water of the Red sea to overflow them as they pursued after you, and *how* the LORD hath destroyed them unto this day;

5 And what he did unto you in the wilderness, until ye came into this place;

6 And [b]what he did unto Dā-thăn and Ă-bī-răm, the sons of Ē-lī-ăb, the son of Reuben: how the earth opened her mouth, and swallowed them up, and their households, and their tents, and all the [1]substance that [2]*was* in their possession, in the midst of all Israel:

7 But your eyes have seen all the great acts of the LORD which he did.

8 Therefore shall ye keep all the commandments which I command you this day, that ye may [c]be strong, and go in and possess the land, whither ye go to possess it;

9 And [d]that ye may prolong *your* days in the land, which the LORD sware unto your fathers to give unto them and to their seed, [e]a land that floweth with milk and honey.

10 ¶ For the land, whither thou goest in to possess it, *is* not as the land of Egypt, from whence ye came out, [f]where thou sowedst thy seed, and wateredst *it* with thy foot, as a garden of herbs:

11 But [g]the land, whither ye go to possess it, *is* a land of hills and valleys, *and* drinketh water of the rain of heaven:

12 A land which the LORD thy God [3]careth for: [h]the eyes of the LORD thy God *are* always upon it, from the beginning of the year even unto the end of the year.

13 ¶ And it shall come to pass, if ye shall hearken [i]diligently unto my commandments which I command you this day, to love [j]the LORD your God, and to serve him with all your heart and with all your soul,

14 That [k]I will give *you* the rain of your land in his due season, [l]the first

---

m Num. 18. 20,24. ch. 18.1,2. Eze. 44.28.
2 Or, former days.
3 go in journey.
n Micah 6.8.
o Matt. 22. 37. 1 Tim. 1.5.
p 1 Ki. 8.27. Ps. 115.16.
q Gen. 14.19. Ps. 24.1.
r Lev. 26.41. Rom. 2.28. Eph. 4.21. Col. 2.11.
s Ps. 136.2. Dan. 2.47.
t Rev. 17.14.
u 2 Chr. 19.7. Acts 10.34. Rom. 2.11. Gal. 2.6. Eph. 6.9. Col. 3.25. 1 Pet. 1.17.
v Ps. 68.5. Ps. 146.9.
w Matt. 4.10.
x Ps. 63.11.
y Ps. 22.3.

CHAP. 11

a Zech. 3.7.
b Num. 16.1. Ps. 106.17.
1 Or, living substance which followed them.
2 was at their feet.
c Josh. 1.6,7.
d ch. 4.40. ch. 5.16. Pro. 3.1,26. Pro. 10.27.
e Ex. 3.8.
f Zech. 14.18.
g ch. 8.7.
3 seeketh.
h 1 Ki. 9.3.
i ch. 6.17.
j 2 Thes. 3.5.
k Lev. 26.4. ch. 28.12.
l Joel 2.23. Jas. 5.7.

rain and the latter rain, that thou mayest gather in thy corn, and thy wine,
and thine oil.
15 And [m]I will [4]send grass in thy
fields for thy cattle, that thou mayest
[n]eat and be full.
16 Take heed to yourselves, [o]that
your heart be not deceived, and ye
turn aside, and serve other gods, and
worship them;
17 And *then* [p]the LORD's wrath be
kindled against you, and he [q]shut up
the heaven, that there be no rain, and
that the land yield not her fruit; and
lest ye perish quickly from off the
good land which the LORD giveth you.
18 ¶ Therefore shall ye lay up these
my words in your heart and in your
soul, and bind them for a sign upon
your hand, that they may be as frontlets between your eyes.
19 And ye shall [r]teach them your
children, speaking of them when thou
sittest in thine house, and when thou
walkest by the way, when thou liest
down, and when thou risest up.
20 And thou shalt write them upon
[s]the door posts of thine house, and
upon thy gates:
21 That [t]your days may be multiplied, and the days of your children,
in the land which the LORD sware unto
your fathers to give them, [u]as the days
of heaven upon the earth.
22 ¶ For if [v]ye shall diligently keep
all these commandments which I command you, to do them, to love the
LORD your God, to walk in all his
ways, and to cleave unto him;
23 Then will the LORD [w]drive out all
these nations from before you, and ye
shall [x]possess greater nations and
mightier than yourselves.
24 Every [y]place whereon the soles of
your feet shall tread shall be yours:
[z]from the wilderness and Lĕb-ă-non,
from the river, the river Eû-phrā-tēs,
even unto the uttermost sea shall your
coast be.
25 There [a]shall no man be able to
stand before you: *for* the LORD your
God shall lay the fear of you and the
dread of you upon all the land that ye
shall tread upon, as he [b]hath said unto
you.
26 ¶ Behold, [c]I set before you this
day a blessing and a curse;
27 A [d]blessing, if ye obey the commandments of the LORD your God,
which I command you this day:
28 And a [e]curse, if ye will not obey
the commandments of the LORD your
God, but turn aside out of the way

m Ps. 104.14.
4 give.
n Joel 2.19.
o Job 31.27.
p ch. 6.15.
q 1 Ki. 8.35. 2 Chr. 6.26. 2 Chr. 7.13.
r Pro. 22.6.
s Hab. 2.2.
t Pro. 3.2. Pro. 4.10. Pro. 9.11.
u Ps. 72.5. Ps. 89.29.
v ch. 6.17.
w ch. 4.38.
x ch. 9.1.
y Josh. 1.3. Josh. 14.9.
z Gen. 15.18. Num. 34.3.
a ch. 7.24.
b Ex. 23.27.
c ch. 30.1.
d ch. 28.2.
e ch. 28.15.
f ch. 27.12.

CHAP. 12

a ch. 4.10. 1 Ki. 8.40. Gal. 6.9.
b Ex. 34.33.
1 Or, inherit.
c 2 Ki. 16.4. 2 Ki. 17.10, 11. Jer. 3.6.
d Num. 33. 52. Judg. 2.2.
2 break down.
e Ps. 16.4. Zech. 13.2.
f ch. 26.2. 1 Ki. 8.29. 2 Chr. 7.12. Ps. 78.68.
g Lev. 17.3.
h ch. 14.22.
i ch. 14.26.
j Lev. 23.40. Eccl. 3.12. Eccl. 5.18.

which I command you this day, to go
after other gods, which ye have not
known.
29 And it shall come to pass, when
the LORD thy God hath brought thee
in unto the land whither thou goest to
possess it, that thou shalt put [f]the
blessing upon mount Gĕ-rī-zĭm, and
the curse upon mount Ē-băl.
30 *Are* they not on the other side
Jordan, by the way where the sun goeth down, in the land of the Canaanites, which dwell in the champaign
over against Gĭl-găl, beside the plains
of Mō-rĕh?
31 For ye shall pass over Jordan to
go in to possess the land which the
LORD your God giveth you, and ye
shall possess it, and dwell therein.
32 And ye shall observe to do all the
statutes and judgments which I set
before you this day.

CHAPTER 12

THESE *are* the statutes and judgments, which ye shall observe to
do in the land, which the LORD God
of thy fathers giveth thee to possess it,
[a]all the days that ye live upon the
earth.
2 Ye [b]shall utterly destroy all the
places, wherein the nations which ye
shall [1]possess served their gods, upon
the high mountains, and upon [c]the
hills, and under every green tree:
3 And [d]ye shall [2]overthrow their altars, and break their pillars, and burn
their groves with fire; and ye shall hew
down the graven images of their gods,
and destroy the [e]names of them out of
that place.
4 Ye shall not do so unto the LORD
your God.
5 But unto the place which the LORD
your God shall [f]choose out of all your
tribes to put his name there, *even* unto
his habitation shall ye seek, and thither thou shalt come:
6 And [g]thither ye shall bring your
burnt offerings, and your sacrifices,
[h]and your tithes, and heave offerings
of your hand, and your vows, and
your freewill offerings, and the firstlings of your herds and of your flocks:
7 And [i]there ye shall eat before the
LORD your God, and [j]ye shall rejoice
in all that ye put your hand unto, ye
and your households, wherein the
LORD thy God hath blessed thee.
8 Ye shall not do after all *the things*
that we do here this day, every man
whatsoever *is* right in his own eyes.
9 For ye are not as yet come to the

rest and to the inheritance, which the
LORD your God giveth you.
10 But *when* ye go over Jordan, and
dwell in the land which the LORD your
God giveth you to inherit, and *when*
he giveth you rest from all your enemies round about, so that ye dwell in
safety;
11 Then there shall be [k]a place which
the LORD your God shall choose to
cause his name to dwell there; thither
shall ye bring all that I command you;
your burnt offerings, and your sacrifices, your tithes, and the heave offering of your hand, and all [3]your choice
vows which ye vow unto the LORD:
12 And ye shall rejoice before the
LORD your God, ye, and your sons,
and your daughters, and your menservants, and your maidservants, and
the Levite that *is* within your gates;
forasmuch as [l]he hath no part nor
inheritance with you.
13 Take [m]heed to thyself that thou
offer not thy burnt offerings in every
place that thou seest:
14 But in the place which the LORD
shall choose in one of thy tribes, there
thou shalt offer thy burnt offerings,
and there thou shalt do all that I command thee.
15 Notwithstanding thou mayest kill
and eat flesh in all thy gates, whatsoever [n]thy soul lusteth after, according
to the blessing of the LORD thy God
which he hath given thee: the unclean
and the clean may eat thereof, [o]as of
the roebuck, and as of the hart.
16 Only [p]ye shall not eat the blood;
ye shall pour it upon the earth as
water.
17 ¶ Thou mayest not eat within thy
gates the tithe of thy corn, or of thy
wine, or of thy oil, or the firstlings of
thy herds or of thy flock, nor any of
thy vows which thou vowest, nor thy
freewill offerings, or heave offering of
thine hand:
18 But [q]thou must eat them before
the LORD thy God in the place which
the LORD thy God shall choose, thou,
and thy son, and thy daughter, and
thy manservant, and thy maidservant,
and the Levite that *is* within thy gates:
and thou shalt [r]rejoice before the
LORD thy God in all that thou puttest
thine hands unto.
19 Take [s]heed to thyself that thou
forsake not the Levite [4]as long as thou
livest upon the earth.
20 ¶ When the LORD thy God shall
enlarge thy border, [t]as he hath promised thee, and thou shalt say, I will eat

k ch. 14.23. ch. 15.20. ch. 16.2. ch. 17.8. ch. 18.6. ch. 26.2. ch. 31.11. Josh. 18.1. 1 Ki. 8.29. Ps. 78.68. Ps. 87. 2.
3 the choice of your vows.
l ch. 10.9. ch. 14.29.
m Lev. 17.4.
n Gen. 9.3.
o ch. 14.5. ch. 15.22.
p Gen. 9.4. Lev. 7.26. ch. 15.23. 1 Sam. 14. 33,34. Acts 15.20, 29.
q ch. 14.23.
r Eccl. 3.12, 13. Eccl. 5.18-20.
s ch. 14.27.
4 all thy days.
t Gen. 15.18. Gen. 28.14. ch. 11.24. ch. 19.8.
5 be strong.
u Gen. 9.4. Lev. 17.11, 14.
v ch. 4.40. Isa. 3.10.
w ch. 13.18. 1 Ki. 11.38.
x Num. 5.9, 10.
y 1 Sam. 21. 22,24.
z Lev. 1.5,9, 13. Lev. 17.11.
a Ps. 25.12, 13. Pro. 1.33. Pro. 3.1-4. Eccl. 8.12.
b Ex. 23.23. Ps. 78.55.
6 inheritest, or, possessest them.
7 after them.
c Lev. 18.3, 26-30. 2 Ki. 17.15. 2 Chr. 33.2.
8 abomination of the.
d Jer. 32.35.

flesh, because thy soul longeth to eat
flesh; thou mayest eat flesh, whatsoever thy soul lusteth after.
21 If the place which the LORD thy
God hath chosen to put his name
there be too far from thee, then thou
shalt kill of thy herd and of thy flock,
which the LORD hath given thee, as I
have commanded thee, and thou
shalt eat in thy gates whatsoever thy
soul lusteth after.
22 Even as the roebuck and the hart
is eaten, so thou shalt eat them: the
unclean and the clean shall eat *of*
them alike.
23 Only [5]be sure that thou eat not
the blood: [u]for the blood *is* the life;
and thou mayest not eat the life with
the flesh.
24 Thou shalt not eat it; thou shalt
pour it upon the earth as water.
25 Thou shalt not eat it; [v]that it may
go well with thee, and with thy children after thee, [w]when thou shalt do
that which is right in the sight of the
LORD.
26 Only thy [x]holy things which thou
hast, and [y]thy vows, thou shalt take,
and go unto the place which the LORD
shall choose:
27 And [z]thou shalt offer thy burnt
offerings, the flesh and the blood, upon the altar of the LORD thy God: and
the blood of thy sacrifices shall be
poured out upon the altar of the LORD
thy God, and thou shalt eat the
flesh.
28 Observe and hear all these words
which I command thee, that [a]it may
go well with thee, and with thy children after thee for ever, when thou
doest *that which is* good and right in
the sight of the LORD thy God.
29 ¶ When [b]the LORD thy God shall
cut off the nations from before
thee, whither thou goest to possess
them, and thou [6]succeedest them, and
dwellest in their land;
30 Take heed to thyself that thou be
not snared [7]by following them, after
that they be destroyed from before
thee; and that thou inquire not after
their gods, saying, How did these nations serve their gods? even so will I
do likewise.
31 Thou [c]shalt not do so unto the
LORD thy God: for every [8]abomina-
tion to the LORD, which he hateth,
have they done unto their gods; for
[d]even their sons and their daughters
they have burnt in the fire to their
gods.
32 What thing soever I command

you, observe to do it: [e]thou shalt not
add thereto, nor diminish from it.

CHAPTER 13

IF there arise among you a prophet,
or a dreamer of dreams, and [a]giveth
thee a sign or a wonder,
2 And [b]the sign or the wonder come
to pass, whereof he spake unto thee,
saying, Let us go after other gods,
which thou hast not known, and let
us serve them;
3 Thou shalt not hearken unto the
words of that prophet, or that dreamer
of dreams: for the LORD your God
[c]proveth you, to know whether ye love
the LORD your God with all your
heart and with all your soul.
4 Ye shall [d]walk after the LORD your
God, and fear him, and keep his commandments, and obey his voice, and
ye shall serve him, and cleave unto
him.
5 And [e]that prophet, or that dreamer
of dreams, shall [f]be put to death; because he hath [1]spoken to turn *you*
away from the LORD your God, which
brought you out of the land of Egypt,
and redeemed you out of the house of
bondage, to thrust thee out of the way
which the LORD thy God commanded
thee to walk in. [g]So shalt thou put the
evil away from the midst of thee.
6 ¶ If thy brother, the son of thy
mother, or thy son, or thy daughter,
or [h]the wife of thy bosom, or thy
friend, which *is* as thine own soul, entice thee secretly, saying, Let us go
and serve other gods, which thou hast
not known, thou, nor thy fathers;
7 *Namely*, of the gods of the people
which *are* round about you, nigh unto
thee, or far off from thee, from the *one*
end of the earth even unto the *other*
end of the earth;
8 Thou shalt [i]not consent unto him,
nor hearken unto him; neither shall
thine eye pity him, neither shalt thou
spare, neither shalt thou conceal him:
9 But thou shalt surely kill him;
thine [j]hand shall be first upon him to
put him to death, and afterwards the
hand of all the people.
10 And thou shalt stone him with
stones, that he die; because he hath
sought to thrust thee away from the
LORD thy God, which brought thee
out of the land of Egypt, from the
house of [2]bondage.
11 And [k]all Israel shall hear, and
fear, and shall do no more any such
wickedness as this is among you.
12 ¶ If [l]thou shalt hear *say* in one of
thy cities, which the LORD thy God
hath given thee to dwell there, saying,
13 *Certain* men, [3]the children of Bē-
lī-ăl, are [m]gone out from among you,
and have withdrawn [n]the inhabitants
of their city, saying, Let us go and
serve other gods, which ye have not
known;
14 Then shalt thou inquire, and
make search, and ask diligently; and,
behold, *if it be* truth, *and* the thing
certain, *that* such abomination is
wrought among you;
15 Thou shalt surely smite the inhabitants of that city with the edge of
the sword, [o]destroying it utterly, and
all that *is* therein, and the cattle thereof, with the edge of the sword.
16 And thou shalt gather all the
spoil of it into the midst of the street
thereof, and shalt burn with fire the
city, and all the spoil thereof every
whit, for the LORD thy God: and it
shall be [p]an heap for ever; it shall not
be built again.
17 And [q]there shall cleave nought of
the [4]cursed thing to thine hand: that
the LORD [r]may turn from the fierceness of his anger, and shew thee mercy,
and have compassion upon thee, and
multiply thee, [s]as he hath sworn unto
thy fathers;
18 When thou shalt hearken to the
voice of the LORD thy God, [t]to keep
all his commandments which I command thee this day, to do *that which is*
right in the eyes of the LORD thy God.

CHAPTER 14

YE *are* [a]the children of the LORD
your God: [b]ye shall not cut yourselves, nor make any baldness between
your eyes for the dead.
2 For [c]thou *art* an holy people unto
the LORD thy God, and the LORD hath
chosen thee to be a peculiar people
unto himself, above all the nations
that *are* upon the earth.
3 ¶ Thou [d]shalt not eat any abominable thing.
4 These [e]*are* the beasts which ye shall
eat: the ox, the sheep, and the goat,
5 The hart, and the roebuck, and the
fallow deer, and the wild goat, and the
[1]pygarg, and the wild ox, and the
chamois.
6 And every beast that parteth the
hoof, and cleaveth the cleft into two
claws, *and* cheweth the cud among the
beasts, that ye shall eat.
7 Nevertheless these ye shall not eat
of them that chew the cud, or of them
that divide the cloven hoof; *as* the

---

e Josh. 1.7. Pro. 30.6. Rev. 22.18.

CHAP. 13

a 2 Thes. 2.9.
b Jer. 28.9. Matt. 7.22.
c Matt. 24. 24. 1 Cor. 11.19. 2 Thes. 2.11.
d 2 Ki. 23.3. 2 Chr. 34.31. 1 John 1.7.
e 1 Ki. 18.40. Isa. 9.15,16. Zech. 13.3. Rev. 19.20.
f 1 Ki. 18.40. 2 Ki. 10.18-28.
1 spoken revolt against the LORD.
g 1 Cor. 5.13.
h Job 2.9. Micah 7.5.
i Pro. 1.10. Gal. 1.8,9.
j ch. 17.7. Acts 7.58.
2 bondmen.
k ch. 19.20.
l Josh. 22.11.
3 Or, naughty men.
m 1 John 2. 19.
n 2 Ki. 17.21.
o Josh. 6.17.
p Isa. 17.1. Isa. 25.2.
q ch. 7.26.
4 Or, devoted.
r Josh. 7.26.
s Gen. 22.17. Gen. 26.4, 24. Gen. 28.14.
t ch. 12.25.

CHAP. 14

a Gen. 6.2,4. Ps. 82.6,7. Jer. 3.19. Hosea 1.10. Rom. 1.10. Rom. 8.16. Gal. 3.26. 1 John 3.1.
b Lev. 19.28. Lev. 21.5. Jer. 16.6. 1 Thes. 4.13.
c Lev. 11.45. Lev. 19.2. Lev. 20.26. Isa. 62.12. Dan. 8.24. Rom. 12.1. 1 Pet. 2.9.
d Isa. 65.4. Eze. 4.14. Acts 10.13. Rom. 14.14.
e Lev. 11.2.
1 dishon, or, bison.

camel, and the hare, and the coney:
for they chew the cud, but divide not
the hoof; *therefore* they *are* unclean
unto you.
8 And the swine, because it divideth
the hoof, yet cheweth not the cud, it *is*
unclean unto you: ye shall not eat of
their flesh, nor touch their dead carcase.
9 ¶ These ye shall eat of all that *are*
in the waters: all that have fins and
scales shall ye eat:
10 And whatsoever hath not fins and
scales ye may not eat; it *is* unclean unto you.
11 ¶ *Of* all clean birds ye shall eat.
12 But [f]these *are they* of which ye
shall not eat: the eagle, and the ossi-
frage, and the ospray,
13 And the glede, and the kite, and
the vulture after his kind,
14 And every raven after his kind,
15 And the owl, and the night hawk,
and the cuckow, and the hawk after
his kind,
16 The little owl, and the great owl,
and the swan,
17 And the pelican, and the gier
eagle, and the cormorant,
18 And the stork, and the heron
after her kind, and the lapwing, and
the bat.
19 And every creeping thing that flieth *is* unclean unto you: they shall
not be eaten.
20 *But of* all clean fowls ye may eat.
21 ¶ Ye [g]shall not eat *of* any thing
that dieth of itself: thou shalt give it
unto the stranger that *is* in thy gates,
that he may eat it; or thou mayest sell
it unto an alien: for thou *art* an holy
people unto the LORD thy God. Thou
[h]shalt not seethe a kid in his mother's
milk.
22 Thou [i]shalt truly tithe all the increase of thy seed, that the field
bringeth forth year by year.
23 And thou shalt eat before the
LORD thy God, in the place which he
shall choose to place his name there,
the tithe of thy corn, of thy wine, and
of thine oil, and the firstlings of thy
herds and of thy flocks; that thou
[j]mayest learn to fear the LORD thy
God always.
24 And if the way be too long for
thee, so that thou art not able to carry
it; *or* [k]if the place be too far from thee,
which the LORD thy God shall choose
to set his name there, when the LORD
thy God hath blessed thee:
25 Then shalt thou turn *it* into
money, and bind up the money in
thine hand, and shalt go unto the
place which the LORD thy God shall
choose:
26 And thou shalt bestow that money for whatsoever thy soul lusteth
after, for oxen, or for sheep, or for
wine, or for strong drink, or for whatsoever thy soul [2]desireth: and thou
shalt eat there before the LORD thy
God, and thou shalt rejoice, thou, and
thine household,
27 And [l]the Levite that *is* within thy
gates; thou shalt nor forsake him; for
[m]he hath no part nor inheritance with
thee.
28 ¶ At [n]the end of three years thou
shalt bring forth all the tithe of thine
increase the same year, and shalt lay
it up within thy gates:
29 And the Levite, (because he hath
no part nor inheritance with thee,)
and [o]the stranger, and the fatherless,
and the widow, which *are* within thy
gates, shall come, and shall eat and be
satisfied; that the [p]LORD thy God may
bless thee in all the work of thine hand
which thou doest.

CHAPTER 15

AT the end of [a]*every* seven years
thou shalt make a release.
2 And this *is* the manner of the release: Every [1]creditor that lendeth
ought unto his neighbour shall release
it; he shall not exact *it* of his neighbour, or of his brother; because it is
called the LORD's release.
3 Of [b]a foreigner thou mayest exact
it again: but *that* which is thine with
thy brother thine hand shall release;
4 [2]Save when there shall be no poor
among you; [c]for the LORD shall
greatly bless thee in the land which
the LORD thy God giveth thee *for* an
inheritance to possess it:
5 Only if thou carefully hearken unto
the voice of the LORD thy God, to observe to do all these commandments
which I command thee this day.
6 For the LORD thy God blesseth
thee, as he promised thee: and thou
shalt lend unto many nations, but
thou shalt not borrow; and [d]thou
shalt reign over many nations, but
they shall not reign over thee.
7 ¶ If there be among you a poor
man of one of thy brethren within any
of thy gates in thy land which the
LORD thy God giveth thee, thou
[e]shalt not harden thine heart, nor shut
thine hand from thy poor brother:
8 But [f]thou shalt open thine hand
wide unto him, and shalt surely lend

f Lev. 11.13.
g Ex. 22.31. Lev. 17.15. Lev. 22.8. Eze. 4.14.
h Ex. 23.19.
i Lev. 27.30. ch. 12.6,17. Neh. 10.37.
j Ps. 2.11. Ps. 5.7. Ps. 111.10. Ps. 147.11. Pro. 3.13. Isa. 8.13. Jer. 32.38-41. Heb. 12.28.
k ch. 12.21.
2 asketh of thee.
l Rom. 13.4. Rom. 15.27. 1 Cor. 9.1-14.
m Num. 18.20. ch. 18.1,2.
n Amos 4.4.
o ch. 10.18. Ps. 94.6. Luke 14.12. Heb. 13.2.
p ch. 15.10. Ps. 41.1. Pro. 3.9,10. Pro. 11.24. Isa. 58.7-12. Mal. 3.10. Luke 11.41. 2 Cor. 9.6-11.

CHAP. 15

a Ex. 23.10. Jer. 34.14.
1 master of the lending of his hand.
b ch. 23.20.
2 Or, to the end that there be no poor among you.
c ch. 28.8.
d Pro. 22.7.
e Matt. 18.30. 1 John 3.17.
f Lev. 25.35. Matt. 5.42. Luke 6.34. Gal. 2.10.

him sufficient for his need, *in that*
which he wanteth.
9 Beware that there be not a [3]thought
in thy [4]wicked heart, saying, The seventh year, the year of release, is at
hand; and [g]thine eye be evil against
thy poor brother, and thou givest him
nought; and [h]he cry unto the LORD
against thee, and [i]it be sin unto
thee.
10 Thou shalt surely give him, and
[j]thine heart shall not be grieved when
thou givest unto him: because that
[k]for this thing the LORD thy God shall
bless thee in all thy works, and in all
that thou puttest thine hand unto.
11 For the poor shall never cease out
of the land: therefore I command
thee, saying, Thou shalt open thine
hand wide unto thy brother, to thy
poor, and to thy needy, in thy land.
12 ¶ *And* [l]if thy brother, an Hebrew
man, or an Hebrew woman, be sold
unto thee, and serve thee six years;
then in the seventh year thou shalt let
him go free from thee.
13 And when thou sendest him out
free from thee, thou shalt not let him
go away empty:
14 Thou shalt furnish him liberally
out of thy flock, and out of thy floor,
and out of thy winepress: *of that*
wherewith the LORD thy God hath
[m]blessed thee thou shalt give unto
him.
15 And thou shalt remember that
thou wast a bondman in the land of
Egypt, and the LORD thy God redeemed thee: therefore I command
thee this thing to day.
16 And it shall be, [n]if he say unto
thee, I will not go away from thee;
because he loveth thee and thine
house, because he is well with thee;
17 Then thou shalt take an aul, and
thrust *it* through his ear unto the door,
and he shall be thy servant for ever.
And also unto thy maidservant thou
shalt do likewise.
18 It shall not seem hard unto thee,
when thou sendest him away free from
thee; for he hath been worth a [o]double
hired servant *to thee*, in serving thee
six years: and the LORD thy God shall
bless thee in all that thou doest.
19 ¶ All [p]the firstling males that
come of thy herd and of thy flock thou
shalt sanctify unto the LORD thy God:
thou shalt do no work with the firstling of thy bullock, nor shear the firstling of thy sheep.
20 Thou [q]shalt eat *it* before the LORD
thy God year by year in the place
which the LORD shall choose, thou
and thy household.
21 And [r]if there be *any* blemish
therein, *as if it be* lame, or blind, *or*
have any ill blemish, thou shalt not
sacrifice it unto the LORD thy God.
22 Thou shalt eat it within thy gates:
the [s]unclean and the clean *person shall*
eat it alike, as the roebuck, and as the
hart.
23 Only thou shalt not eat [t]the blood
thereof; thou shalt pour it upon the
ground as water.

CHAPTER 16

OBSERVE the [a]month of Abib,
and keep the [b]passover unto the
LORD thy God: for in the month of
Abib the LORD thy God brought thee
forth out of Egypt by night.
2 Thou shalt therefore sacrifice the
passover unto the LORD thy God, of
the flock and the [c]herd, in the place
which the LORD shall choose to place
his name there.
3 Thou [d]shalt eat no leavened bread
with it; seven days shalt thou eat unleavened bread therewith, *even* the
bread of affliction; for thou camest
forth out of the land of Egypt in
haste: that thou mayest remember the
day when thou camest forth out of the
land of Egypt all the days of thy life.
4 And there shall be no leavened
bread seen with thee in all thy coast
seven days; neither [e]shall there *any*
thing of the flesh, which thou sacri-
ficedst the first day at even, remain all
night until the morning.
5 Thou mayest not [1]sacrifice the passover within any of thy gates, which
the LORD thy God giveth thee:
6 But at the place which the LORD
thy God shall choose to place his name
in, there thou shalt sacrifice the passover [f]at even, at the going down of the
sun, at the season that thou camest
forth out of Egypt.
7 And thou shalt [g]roast and eat *it* [h]in
the place which the LORD thy God
shall choose: and thou shalt turn in
the morning, and go unto thy tents.
8 Six days thou shalt eat unleavened
bread: and [i]on the seventh day *shall*
be a [2]solemn assembly to the LORD thy
God: thou shalt do no work *therein*.
9 ¶ Seven [j]weeks shalt thou number
unto thee: begin to number the seven
weeks from *such time as* thou begin-
nest *to put* the sickle to the corn.
10 And thou shalt keep the feast of
weeks unto the LORD thy God with [3]a
tribute of a freewill offering of thine

3 word.
4 Belial.
g ch. 28.54. Pro. 23.6. Matt. 20.15.
h ch. 24.15. Job 34.28. Ps. 12.5. Amos 5.11. Jas. 5.4.
i Matt. 25.41.
j Matt. 25.40. Acts 20.35. Rom. 12.8. 2 Cor. 9.5. 1 Tim. 6.18. 1 Pet. 4.11.
k ch. 14.29. Ps. 41.1. Pro. 14.21, 31. Pro. 22.9. Pro. 29.7.
l Ex. 21.2. Jer. 34.14.
m Pro. 10.22.
n Ex. 21.5,6.
o Isa. 16.14. Isa. 21.16.
p Ex. 13.2.
q ch. 12.5. ch. 14.23. ch. 16.11.
r Lev. 22.20. ch. 17.1.
s ch. 12.15, 22.
t Gen. 9.4. Lev. 7.26. ch. 12.16.

CHAP. 16

a Ex. 12.2. Lev. 23.5. Num. 9.2-5. John 18.28.
b 1 Cor. 5.7,8. Heb. 11.28.
c Ex. 12.5-7. 2 Chr. 35.7. Matt. 26.2. Mark 14.12. Luke 22.8, 15. 1 Cor. 5.7.
d Ex. 12.15, 19,39.
e Ex. 12.10.
1 Or, kill.
f Matt. 27.46.
g Ex. 12.8. 2 Chr. 35.13.
h 2 Ki. 23.23. John 2.13.
i Ex. 12.16. Lev. 23.8.
2 restraint.
j Ex. 23.16. Lev. 23.15. Num. 28.26. Acts 2.1.
3 Or, sufficiency.

hand, which thou shalt give *unto the*
LORD thy God, according [k]as the LORD
thy God hath blessed thee:
11 And thou shalt rejoice before the
LORD thy God, thou, and thy son, and
thy daughter, and thy manservant,
and thy maidservant, and the Levite
that *is* within thy gates, and [l]the
stranger, and the fatherless, and the
widow, that *are* among you, in the
place which the LORD thy God hath
chosen to place his name there.
12 And [m]thou shalt remember that
thou wast a bondman in Egypt: and
thou shalt observe and do these
statutes.
13 ¶ Thou [n]shalt observe the feast of
tabernacles seven days, after that thou
hast gathered in thy [4]corn and thy
wine:
14 And [o]thou shalt rejoice in thy
feast, thou, and thy son, and thy
daughter, and thy manservant, and
thy maidservant, and the Levite, the
stranger, and the fatherless, and the
widow, that *are* within thy gates.
15 Seven days shalt thou keep a
solemn feast unto the LORD thy God
in the place which the LORD shall
choose: because the LORD thy God
shall bless thee in all thine increase,
and in all the works of thine hands,
therefore thou shalt surely rejoice.
16 ¶ Three times in a year shall all
thy males appear before the LORD thy
God in the place which he shall
choose; in the feast of unleavened
bread, and in the feast of weeks, and
in the feast of tabernacles: and they
shall not appear before the LORD
empty:
17 Every man *shall give* [5]as he is able,
according to the blessing of the LORD
thy God which he hath given thee.
18 ¶ Judges and officers shalt thou
make thee in all thy gates, which the
LORD thy God giveth thee, throughout thy tribes: and they shall judge
the people with just judgment.
19 Thou [p]shalt not wrest judgment;
thou [q]shalt not respect persons, [r]neith-
er take a gift: for a gift doth blind the
eyes of the wise, and pervert the
[6]words of the righteous.
20 [7]That which is altogether just
shalt thou follow, that thou mayest
live, [8]and inherit the land which the
LORD thy God giveth thee.
21 ¶ Thou [t]shalt not plant thee a
grove of any trees near unto the altar
of the LORD thy God, which thou
shalt make thee.
22 Neither shalt thou set thee up *any*

k Pro. 10.22. Joel 2.14. 1 Cor. 16.2.
l Luke 14.12.
m Gen. 15.13. ch. 15.15. ch. 25.6. Ps. 105.23, 25.
n Lev. 23.24. Num. 29.12.
4 floor and thy wine-press.
o ch. 26.11. Neh. 8.9. Eccl. 9.7. Isa. 12.1-6. Isa. 25.6-8. Isa. 30.29.
5 according to the gift of his hand.
p Ex. 23.2. Lev. 19.15. 1 Sam. 8.3. Job 31.21, 22. Pro. 17.23. Eccl. 7.7. Isa. 1.17,23.
q Pro. 24.23. Acts 10.34.
r Ex. 23.8. Pro. 17.23. Eccl. 7.7.
6 Or, matters.
7 Justice, justice.
s ch. 4.1. Eze. 18.5.
t Ex. 34.13. Judg. 3.7. 1 Ki. 14.15. 2 Ki. 17.16. 2 Chr. 33.3.
8 Or, statue, or, pillar.

CHAP. 17

1 Or, goat.
a Job 31.26.
b Jer. 7.22.
c Lev. 24.14. Josh. 7.25.
d Num. 35. 30. Matt. 18.16. John 8.17. 2 Cor. 13.1. 1 Tim. 5.19. Heb. 10.28.
e 2 Chr. 19. 10. Hag. 2.11. Mal. 2.7.
f Ex. 21.13. Num. 35.11.
g ch. 12.5. Ps. 122.5.
h Jer. 18.18.
i ch. 19.17.
j Judg. 4.5. 1 Ki. 3.16.

[8]image; which the LORD thy God
hateth.

CHAPTER 17

THOU shalt not sacrifice unto the
LORD thy God *any* bullock, or
[1]sheep, wherein is blemish, *or* any evil-
favouredness: for that *is* an abomination unto the LORD thy God.
2 ¶ If there be found among you,
within any of thy gates which the
LORD thy God giveth thee, man or
woman, that hath wrought wickedness in the sight of the LORD thy God,
in transgressing his covenant,
3 And hath gone and served other
gods, and worshipped them, either
the [a]sun, or moon, or any of the host
of heaven, [b]which I have not commanded;
4 And it be told thee, and thou hast
heard *of it*, and inquired diligently,
and, behold, *it be* true, *and* the thing
certain, *that* such abomination is
wrought in Israel:
5 Then shalt thou bring forth that
man or that woman, which have committed that wicked thing, unto thy
gates, *even* that man or that woman,
and [c]shalt stone them with stones, till
they die.
6 At [d]the mouth of two witnesses, or
three witnesses, shall he that is worthy
of death be put to death; *but* at the
mouth of one witness he shall not be
put to death.
7 The hands of the witnesses shall be
first upon him to put him to death, and
afterward the hands of all the people.
So thou shalt put the evil away from
among you.
8 ¶ If [e]there arise a matter too hard
for thee in judgment, [f]between blood
and blood, between plea and plea, and
between stroke and stroke, *being*
matters of controversy within thy
gates: then shalt thou arise, [g]and get
thee up into the place which the LORD
thy God shall choose;
9 And [h]thou shalt come unto the
priests the Levites, and unto [i]the
judge that shall be in those days, and
inquire; [j]and they shall shew thee the
sentence of judgment:
10 And thou shalt do according to
the sentence, which they of that place
which the LORD shall choose shall
shew thee; and thou shalt observe to
do according to all that they inform
thee:
11 According to the sentence of the
law which they shall teach thee, and
according to the judgment which they
shall tell thee, thou shalt do: thou

shalt not decline from the sentence
which they shall shew thee, *to* the
right hand, nor *to* the left.
12 And [k]the man that will do presumptuously, and [2]will not hearken
unto the priest that standeth [l]to minister there before the LORD thy God,
or unto the judge, even that man shall
die: and thou shalt put away the evil
from Israel.
13 And all the people shall hear,
and fear, and do no more presumptuously.
14 ¶ When thou art come unto the
land which the LORD thy God giveth
thee, and shalt possess it, and shalt
dwell therein, and shalt say, [m]I will
set a king over me, [n]like as all the nations that *are* about me;
15 Thou shalt in any wise set *him*
king over thee, whom the LORD thy
God shall choose: *one* [o]from among
thy brethren shalt thou set king over
thee: thou mayest not set a stranger
over thee, which *is* not thy brother.
16 But he shall not multiply horses
[p]to himself, nor cause the people [q]to
return to Egypt, to the end that he
should multiply horses: forasmuch as
[r]the LORD hath said unto you, [s]Ye
shall henceforth return no more that
way.
17 Neither shall he multiply wives to
himself, that [t]his heart turn not away:
neither shall he greatly [u]multiply to
himself silver and gold.
18 And [v]it shall be, when he sitteth
upon the throne of his kingdom, that
he shall write him a copy of this law
in a book out of *that* [w]*which is* before
the priests the Levites:
19 And [x]it shall be with him, and he
shall read therein all the days of his
life: that he may learn to fear the
LORD his God, to keep all the words
of this law and these statutes, to do
them:
20 That his heart be not lifted up
above his brethren, and that he turn
[y]not aside from the commandment,
to the right hand, or *to* the left: to the
end that he may prolong *his* days in
his kingdom, he, and his children, in
the midst of Israel.

CHAPTER 18

THE priests the Levites, *and* all the
tribe of Levi, shall have no part
nor inheritance with Israel: they [a]shall
eat the offerings of the LORD made by
fire, and his inheritance.
2 Therefore shall they have no inheritance among their brethren: the

k Num. 15. 30. Ezra 10.8. Hosea 4.4.
2 not to hearken.
l ch. 18.5.
m 1 Sam. 10. 19. Hosea 13.9.
n 1 Sam. 8.5.
o Jer. 30.21.
p 1 Ki. 4.26. Ps. 20.7.
q Isa. 31.1.
r Ex. 13.17.
s Hosea 11.5.
t 1 Ki. 11.3.
u 1 Ki. 10.21.
v 2 Ki. 11.12.
w ch. 31.9. 2 Ki. 22.8.
x Josh. 1.8. Ps. 119.97.
y ch. 5.32. 1 Ki. 15.5.

CHAP. 18

a Num. 18.8, 9. 1 Cor. 9.13.
b Lev. 7.30.
c Ex. 22.29.
d ch. 10.8.
e Num. 35.2, 3.
f 2 Chr. 31.4.
1 his sales by the fathers.
g Lev. 18.26. ch. 12.29.
h Lev. 19.26.
i Lev. 18.24.
2 Or, upright, or sincere.
3 Or, inherit.
j 2 Ki. 21.6.
k Num. 24. 17. Isa. 11.1. Matt. 11.3. Matt. 21.11. Luke 2.25-34. Luke 4.16-22. Luke 7.16. Luke 24.19. John 4.19, 25,26. John 6.14. Acts 3.22. Acts 7.37.

LORD *is* their inheritance, as he hath
said unto them.
3 ¶ And this shall be the priest's due
from the people, from them that offer
a sacrifice, whether *it be* ox or sheep;
and [b]they shall give unto the priest
the shoulder, and the two cheeks, and
the maw.
4 The [c]firstfruit *also* of thy corn, of
thy wine, and of thine oil, and the first
of the fleece of thy sheep, shalt thou
give him.
5 For the LORD thy God hath chosen
him out of all thy tribes, to [d]stand to
minister in the name of the LORD, him
and his sons for ever.
6 ¶ And if a Levite come from any of
thy gates out of all Israel, where he
[e]sojourned, and come with all the desire of his mind unto the place which
the LORD shall choose;
7 Then he shall minister in the name
of the LORD his God, as all his brethren the Levites *do*, which stand there
before the LORD.
8 They shall have like [f]portions to
eat, beside [1]that which cometh of the
sale of his patrimony.
9 ¶ When thou art come into the
land which the LORD thy God giveth
thee, [g]thou shalt not learn to do after
the abominations of those nations.
10 There shall not be found among
you *any one* that maketh his son or
his daughter to pass through the fire,
[h]*or* that useth divination, *or* an observer of times, or an enchanter, or a
witch,
11 Or a charmer, or a consulter with
familiar spirits, or a wizard, or a
necromancer.
12 For all that do these things *are* an
abomination unto the LORD: and [i]be-
cause of these abominations the LORD
thy God doth drive them out from before thee.
13 Thou shalt be [2]perfect with the
LORD thy God.
14 For these nations, which thou
shalt [3]possess, hearkened unto observers [j]of times, and unto diviners:
but as for thee, the LORD thy God hath
not suffered thee so *to do*.
15 ¶ The LORD thy God will raise up
unto thee a [k]Prophet from the midst
of thee, of thy brethren, like unto me;
unto him ye shall hearken;
16 According to all that thou desiredst of the LORD thy God in Hôr-ĕb in
the day of the assembly, saying, Let
me not hear again the voice of the
LORD my God, neither let me see this
great fire any more, that I die not.

17 And the LORD said unto me, They have well *spoken that* which they have spoken.

18 I [l]will raise them up a Prophet from among their brethren, like unto thee, and will [m]put my words in his mouth; [n]and he shall speak unto them all that I shall command him.

19 And [o]it shall come to pass, *that* whosoever will not hearken unto my words which he shall speak in my name, I will require *it* of him.

20 But [p]the prophet, which shall presume to speak a word in my name, which I have not commanded him to speak, or [q]that shall speak in the name of other gods, even that prophet shall die.

21 And if thou say in thine heart, How shall we know the word which the LORD hath not spoken?

22 When [r]a prophet speaketh in the name of the LORD, if the thing follow not, nor come to pass, that *is* the thing which the LORD hath not spoken, *but* the prophet hath spoken it presumptuously: thou shalt not be afraid of him.

CHAPTER 19

WHEN the LORD thy God hath cut off the nations, whose land the LORD thy God giveth thee, and thou [1]succeedest them, and dwellest in their cities, and in their houses;

2 Thou [a]shalt separate three cities for thee in the midst of thy land, which the LORD thy God giveth thee to possess it.

3 Thou shalt prepare thee a way, and divide the coasts of thy land, which the LORD thy God giveth thee to inherit, into three parts, that every slayer may flee thither.

4 ¶ And this *is* the case of the slayer, which shall flee thither, that he may live: Whoso killeth his neighbour ignorantly, whom he hated not [2]in time past;

5 As when a man goeth into the wood with his neighbour to hew wood, and his hand fetcheth a stroke with the axe to cut down the tree, and the [3]head slippeth from the [4]helve, and [5]lighteth upon his neighbour, that he die; he shall flee unto one of those cities, and live:

6 Lest the avenger of the blood pursue the slayer, while his heart is hot, and overtake him, because the way is long, and [6]slay him; whereas he *was* not worthy of death, inasmuch as he hated him not [7]in time past.

7 Wherefore I command thee, saying, Thou shalt separate three cities for thee.

8 And if the LORD thy God [b]enlarge thy coast, as he hath sworn unto thy fathers, and give thee all the land which he promised to give unto thy fathers;

9 If thou shalt keep all these commandments to do them, which I command thee this day, to love the LORD thy God, and to walk ever in his ways; [c]then shalt thou add three cities more for thee, beside these three:

10 That innocent blood be not shed in thy land, which the LORD thy God giveth thee *for* an inheritance, and *so* blood be upon thee.

11 ¶ But if [d]any man [e]hate his neighbour, and lie in wait for him, and rise up against him, and smite him [8]mortally that he die, and fleeth into one of these cities:

12 Then the elders of his city shall send and fetch him thence, and deliver him into the hand of the avenger of blood, that he may die.

13 Thine eye shall not pity him, but [f]thou shalt put away *the guilt of* innocent blood from Israel, that it may go well with thee.

14 ¶ Thou [g]shalt not remove thy neighbour's landmark, which they of old time have set in thine inheritance, which thou shalt inherit in the land that the LORD thy God giveth thee to possess it.

15 ¶ One [h]witness shall not rise up against a man for any iniquity, or for any sin, in any sin that he sinneth: at the mouth of two witnesses, or at the mouth of three witnesses, shall the matter be established.

16 ¶ If a false witness [i]rise up against any man to testify against him [9]*that which is* wrong;

17 Then both the men, between whom the controversy *is*, shall stand before the LORD, before the priests and the judges, which shall be in those days;

18 And the judges shall make diligent inquisition: and, behold, *if* the witness *be* a false witness, *and* hath testified falsely against his brother;

19 Then [j]shall ye do unto him, as he had thought to have done unto his brother: so shalt thou put the evil away from among you.

20 And [k]those which remain shall hear, and fear, and shall henceforth commit no more any such evil among you.

l John 1.45.
m Isa. 51.16. John 17.8.
n John 4.25. John 8.28.
o Acts 3.23.
p ch. 13.5. Jer. 14.14. Zech. 13.3.
q Jer. 2.8.
r Jer. 28.9.

CHAP. 19

1 inheritest, or, possessest.
a Josh. 20.2.
2 from yesterday the third day.
3 iron.
4 wood.
5 findeth.
6 smite him in life.
7 from yesterday the third day.
b Gen. 15.18.
c Josh. 20.7.
d Ex. 21.12. Num. 35.16. Pro. 28.17.
e Pro. 29.10. 1 John 3.15.
8 in life.
f 1 Ki. 2.31.
g ch. 27.17. Job 24.2. Pro. 22.28. Hosea 5.10.
h Matt. 18.16. John 8.17. 2 Cor. 13.1. 1 Tim. 5.19. Heb. 10.28.
i Ps. 27.12. 1 Ki. 21.13.
9 Or, falling away.
j Pro. 19.5. Dan. 6.24.
k ch. 17.13. ch. 21.21.

21 And thine eye shall not pity; *but* [l]life *shall go* for life, eye for eye, tooth for tooth, hand for hand, foot for foot.

CHAPTER 20

WHEN thou goest out to battle against thine enemies, and seest [a]horses, and chariots, *and* a people more than thou, be not afraid of them: for the LORD thy God *is* [b]with thee, which brought thee up out of the land of Egypt.

2 And it shall be, when ye are come nigh unto the battle, that the priest shall approach and speak unto the people,

3 And shall say unto them, Hear, O Israel, ye approach this day unto battle against your enemies: let not your hearts [1]faint, fear not, and do not [2]tremble, neither be ye terrified because of them;

4 For the LORD your God *is* he that goeth with you, [c]to fight for you against your enemies, to save you.

5 ¶ And the officers shall speak unto the people, saying, What man *is there* that hath built a new house, and hath not [d]dedicated it? let him go and return to his house, lest he die in the battle, and another man dedicate it.

6 And what man *is he* that hath planted a vineyard, and hath not *yet* [3]eaten of it? let him *also* go and return unto his house, lest he die in the battle, and another man eat of it.

7 And [e]what man *is there* that hath betrothed a wife, and hath not taken her? let him go and return unto his house, lest he die in the battle, and another man take her.

8 And the officers shall speak further unto the people, and they shall say, [f]What man *is there that is* fearful and fainthearted? let him go and return unto his house, lest his brethren's heart [4]faint as well as his heart.

9 And it shall be, when the officers have made an end of speaking unto the people, that they shall make captains of the armies [5]to lead the people.

10 ¶ When thou comest nigh unto a city to fight against it, [g]then proclaim peace unto it.

11 And it shall be, if it make thee answer of peace, and open unto thee, then it shall be, *that* all the people *that is* found therein shall be [h]tributaries unto thee, and they shall serve thee.

12 And if it will make no peace with thee, but will make war against thee, then thou shalt besiege it:

13 And when the LORD thy God hath delivered it into thine hands, thou [i]shalt smite every male thereof with the edge of the sword:

14 But the women, and the little ones, and [j]the cattle, and all that is in the city, *even* all the spoil thereof, shalt thou [6]take unto thyself; and [k]thou shalt eat the spoil of thine enemies, which the LORD thy God hath given thee.

15 Thus shalt thou do unto all the cities *which are* very far off from thee, which *are* not of the cities of these nations.

16 But [l]of the cities of these people, which the LORD thy God doth give thee *for* an inheritance, thou shalt save alive nothing that breatheth:

17 But thou shalt utterly destroy them; *namely*, the Hittites, and the Amorites, the Canaanites, and the Pĕ-rĭz′-zītes, the Hī′-vītes, and the Jĕb′-ū-sītes; as the LORD thy God hath commanded thee:

18 That [m]they teach you not to do after all their abominations, which they have done unto their gods; so should ye [n]sin against the LORD your God.

19 ¶ When thou shalt besiege a city a long time, in making war against it to take it, thou shalt not destroy the trees thereof by forcing an axe against them: for thou mayest eat of them, and thou shalt not cut them down ([7]for the tree of the field *is* man's *life*) [8]to employ *them* in the siege:

20 Only the trees which thou knowest that they *be* not trees for meat, thou shalt destroy and cut them down; and thou shalt build bulwarks against the city that maketh war with thee, until [9]it be subdued.

CHAPTER 21

IF *one* be found [a]slain in the land which the LORD thy God giveth thee to possess it, lying in the field, *and* it be not known who hath slain him:

2 Then thy elders and thy judges shall come forth, and they shall measure unto the cities which *are* round about him that is slain:

3 And it shall be, *that* the city *which is* next unto the slain man, even the elders of that city shall take an heifer, which hath not been wrought with, *and* which hath not drawn in the yoke;

4 And the elders of that city shall bring down the heifer unto a rough valley, which is neither eared nor

l Ex. 21.23. Lev. 24.20.

CHAP. 20

a Ps. 20.7. Isa. 31.1.
b Num. 23. 21. ch. 31.6,8. 2 Chr. 13.12. 2 Chr. 32.7, 8. Ps. 23.4. Isa. 41.10.
1 be tender.
2 make haste.
c ch. 1.30. ch. 3.22. Josh. 23.10.
d Neh. 12.27. See title of Ps. 30.
3 made it common.
e ch. 24.5.
f Judg. 7.3.
4 melt.
5 to be in the head of the people.
g 2 Sam. 20. 18,20.
h 1 Ki. 9.21.
i Num. 31.7.
j Josh. 8.2.
6 spoil.
k Josh. 22.8.
l Num. 21.2, 3,35. Num. 33.52. ch. 7.1,2. Josh. 11.14.
m Ex. 34.12-17. ch. 7.4. ch. 12.30,31. ch. 18.9. Josh. 23.12, 13. 1 Cor. 15.33.
n Ex. 23.33. 2 Ki. 21.3-15. Ps. 106.34-41. Hosea 8.11.
7 Or, for, O man, the tree of the field is to be employed in the siege.
8 to go from before thee.
9 it come down.

CHAP. 21

a Ps. 9.12. Pro. 28.17.

sown, and shall strike off the heifer's
neck there in the valley:
5 And the priests the sons of Levi
shall come near; for [b]them the LORD
thy God hath chosen to minister unto
him, and to bless in the name of the
LORD; and [c]by their [1]word shall every
controversy and every stroke be *tried:*
6 And all the elders of that city, *that*
are next unto the slain *man,* shall
[d]wash their hands over the heifer that
is beheaded in the valley:
7 And they shall answer and say,
Our [e]hands have not shed this blood,
neither have our eyes seen *it.*
8 Be merciful, O LORD, unto thy people Israel, whom thou hast redeemed,
and [f]lay not innocent blood [2]unto thy
people of Israel's charge. And the
blood shall be forgiven them.
9 So [g]shalt thou put away the *guilt of*
innocent blood from among you,
when thou shalt do *that which is* right
in the sight of the LORD.
10 ¶ When thou goest forth to war
against thine enemies, and the [h]LORD
thy God hath delivered them into
thine hands, and thou hast taken them
captive,
11 And seest among the captives a
beautiful woman, and hast a desire
unto her, that thou wouldest have her
to thy wife;
12 Then thou shalt bring her home
to thine house; and she shall shave her
head, and [3]pare her nails;
13 And she shall put the raiment of
her captivity from off her, and shall
remain in thine house, [i]and bewail her
father and her mother a full month:
and after that thou shalt go in unto
her, and be her husband, and she shall
be thy wife.
14 And it shall be, if thou have no delight in her, then thou shalt let her go
whither she will; but thou shalt not
sell her at all for money, thou shalt
not make merchandise of her, because
thou [j]hast humbled her.
15 ¶ If a man have two wives, one beloved, and [k]another hated, and they
have born him children, *both* the beloved and the hated; and *if* the firstborn son be hers that was hated:
16 Then it shall be, [l]when he maketh
his sons to inherit *that* which he hath,
that he may not make the son of the
beloved firstborn before the son of
the hated, *which is indeed* the firstborn:
17 But he shall acknowledge the son
of the hated *for* the firstborn, by [m]giv-
ing him a double portion of all [4]that

b 1 Chr. 23.13.
c ch. 17.8,9.
1 mouth.
d Job 9.30. Ps. 19.12. Ps. 73.13. Jer. 2.22. Matt. 27.24. Heb. 9.10.
e 2 Sam. 3.28.
f Jer. 26.15. Eze. 22.3. Jonah 1.14. 1 Thes. 2.15, 16.
2 in the midst.
g ch. 19.13.
h 2 Chr. 32.8. Josh. 21.44.
3 make, or, dress, or, suffer to grow.
i Ps. 45.10.
j Gen. 34.2. Judg. 19.24.
k Gen. 29.33.
l 2 Chr. 11.19. 2 Chr. 21.3. Rom. 8.29.
m Gen. 25.5, 6. 1 Chr. 5.1.
4 that is found with him.
n Gen. 49.3.
o Gen. 25.31.
p Ex. 20.12. Lev. 19.3. Lev. 21.9. Pro. 1.8. Pro. 15.5. Eph. 6.1.
q ch. 19.19.
r ch. 13.11.
s ch. 22.26. 1 Sam. 26. 16. Matt. 26.66. Acts 23.29.
t Josh. 8.29. John 19.31.
u Gal. 3.13.
5 the curse of God.
v Lev. 18.25. Num. 35.34.

CHAP. 22

a Ex. 23.4. Rom. 12.10. 2 Pet. 1.7. 1 John 3.15. 1 John 4.21.
b Pro. 27.10. Zech. 7.9.
c 1 Cor. 14. 40.

he hath: for he *is* [n]the beginning of his
strength; [o]the right of the firstborn *is*
his.
18 ¶ If a man have a stubborn and
rebellious son, which will not obey the
voice of his [p]father, or the voice of his
mother, and *that,* when they have
chastened him, will not hearken unto
them:
19 Then shall his father and his
mother lay hold on him, and bring
him out unto the elders of his city,
and unto the gate of his place;
20 And they shall say unto the elders
of his city, This our son *is* stubborn
and rebellious, he will not obey our
voice; *he is* a glutton, and a drunkard.
21 And all the men of his city shall
stone him with stones, that he die: [q]so
shalt thou put evil away from among
you; [r]and all Israel shall hear, and
fear.
22 ¶ And if a man have committed a
sin worthy [s]of death, and he be to be
put to death, and thou hang him on a
tree:
23 His [t]body shall not remain all
night upon the tree, but thou shalt in
any wise bury him that day; (for [u]he
that is hanged *is* [5]accursed of God;)
that [v]thy land be not defiled, which the
LORD thy God giveth thee *for* an inheritance.

CHAPTER 22

THOU [a]shalt not see thy brother's
ox or his sheep go astray, [b]and
hide thyself from them: thou shalt in
any case bring them again unto thy
brother.
2 And if thy brother *be* not nigh unto
thee, or if thou know him not, then
thou shalt bring it unto thine own
house, and it shall be with thee until
thy brother seek after it, and thou
shalt restore it to him again.
3 In like manner shalt thou do with
his ass; and so shalt thou do with his
raiment; and with all lost thing of thy
brother's, which he hath lost, and thou
hast found, shalt thou do likewise:
thou mayest not hide thyself.
4 ¶ Thou shalt not see thy brother's
ass or his ox fall down by the way, and
hide thyself from them: thou shalt
surely help him to lift *them* up again.
5 ¶ The [c]woman shall not wear that
which pertaineth unto a man, neither
shall a man put on a woman's garment: for all that do so *are* abomination unto the LORD thy God.
6 ¶ If a bird's nest chance to be before thee in the way in any tree, or on

the ground, *whether they be* young
ones, or eggs, and the dam sitting upon the young, or upon the eggs, [d]thou
shalt not take the dam with the young:
7 *But* thou shalt in any wise let the
dam go, and take the young to thee;
[e]that it may be well with thee, and *that*
thou mayest prolong *thy* days.
8 ¶ When thou buildest a new house,
then thou shalt make a battlement for
thy roof, that thou bring not blood
upon thine house, if any man fall from
thence.
9 ¶ Thou [f]shalt not sow thy vineyard
with divers seeds: lest the [1]fruit of thy
seed which thou hast sown, and the
fruit of thy vineyard, be defiled.
10 ¶ Thou [g]shalt not plow with an ox
and an ass together.
11 ¶ Thou [h]shalt not wear a garment
of divers sorts, *as* of woollen and linen
together.
12 ¶ Thou shalt make thee [i]fringes
upon the four [2]quarters of thy vesture,
wherewith thou coverest *thyself*.
13 ¶ If any man take a wife, [j]and go
in unto her, and hate her,
14 And give occasions of speech
against her, and bring up an evil name
upon her, and say, I took this woman,
and when I came to her, I found her
not a maid:
15 Then shall the father of the
damsel, and her mother, take and
bring forth *the tokens of* the damsel's
virginity unto the elders of the city in
the gate:
16 And the damsel's father shall say
unto the elders, I gave my daughter
unto this man to wife, and he hateth
her;
17 And, lo, he hath given occasions
of speech *against her*, saying, I found
not thy daughter a maid; and yet
these *are the tokens of* my daughter's
virginity. And they shall spread the
cloth before the elders of the city.
18 And [k]the elders of that city shall
take that man and chastise him;
19 And they shall amerce him in an
hundred *shekels* of silver, and give
them unto the father of the damsel,
because he hath brought up an evil
name upon a virgin of Israel: and she
shall be his wife; he may not put her
away all his days.
20 But if this thing [l]be true, *and the
tokens of* virginity be not found for
the damsel:
21 Then they shall bring out the
damsel to the door of her father's
house, and the men of her city shall
stone her with stones that she die: be-

d Lev. 22.28. Neh. 9.6. Ps. 36.6. Ps. 145.9. Pro. 12.10. Matt. 10.29. Luke 12.6.
e ch. 4.40.
f Lev. 19.19. Matt. 6.24. Matt. 9.16. 2 Cor. 6.14-16. 2 Cor. 11.3.
1 fulness of thy seed.
g 2 Cor. 6.14, 15, 16.
h Lev. 19.19.
i Num. 15.38. Matt. 23.5.
2 wings.
j Gen. 29.21. Judg. 15.1.
k Ex. 18.21. ch. 1.9-18. Rom. 13.4.
l ch. 17.4.
m Gen. 34.7. Lev. 21.9. Judg. 20.6, 10.
n ch. 13.5. ch. 17.7.
o Lev. 20.10. Pro. 6.22. Mal. 3.5. Matt. 5.27, 28. John 8.5. 1 Cor. 6.9. Heb. 13.4.
p Matt. 1.18, 19.
q ch. 21.14. Matt. 1.20, 24.
3 Or, take strong hold of her.
r Ex. 22.16, 17.
s Lev. 18.8. Lev. 20.11. ch. 27.20. 1 Cor. 5.1.
t Gen. 9.22-27. Ruth 3.9.

CHAP. 23

a Ruth 4.5. Neh. 13.1, 2. Neh. 4.3-7.
b Gen. 14.18. ch. 2.29. 1 Sam. 25. 11. 1 Ki. 18.4. Isa. 63.9. Matt. 10.40, 42.
c Num. 22.5, 6. Josh. 24.9.

cause she hath [m]wrought folly in Israel, to play the whore in her father's
house: [n]so shalt thou put evil away
from among you.
22 ¶ If [o]a man be found lying with a
woman married to an husband, then
they shall both of them die, *both* the
man that lay with the woman, and the
woman: so shalt thou put away evil
from Israel.
23 ¶ If a damsel *that is* a virgin be [p]be-
trothed unto an husband, and a man
find her in the city, and lie with her;
24 Then ye shall bring them both out
unto the gate of that city, and ye shall
stone them with stones that they die;
the damsel, because she cried not, *being* in the city; and the man, because
he hath humbled [q]his neighbour's
wife: so thou shalt put away evil from
among you.
25 ¶ But if a man find a betrothed
damsel in the field, and the man [3]force
her, and lie with her: then the man
only that lay with her shall die:
26 But unto the damsel thou shalt do
nothing; *there is* in the damsel no sin
worthy of death: for as when a man
riseth against his neighbour, and slayeth him, even so *is* this matter:
27 For he found her in the field, *and*
the betrothed damsel cried, and *there
was* none to save her.
28 ¶ If [r]a man find a damsel *that is* a
virgin, which is not betrothed, and lay
hold on her, and lie with her, and they
be found;
29 Then the man that lay with her
shall give unto the damsel's father
fifty *shekels* of silver, and she shall be
his wife; because he hath humbled
her, he may not put her away all his
days.
30 ¶ A [s]man shall not take his father's
wife, nor [t]discover his father's skirt.

CHAPTER 23

HE that is wounded in the stones,
or hath his privy member cut off,
shall not enter into the congregation
of the LORD.
2 A bastard shall not enter into the
congregation of the LORD; even to his
tenth generation shall he not enter into the congregation of the LORD.
3 An [a]Ammonite or Moabite shall
not enter into the congregation of the
LORD; even to their tenth generation
shall they not enter into the congregation of the LORD for ever:
4 Because [b]they met you not with
bread and with water in the way, when
ye came forth out of Egypt; and [c]be-

cause they hired against thee Bā-lāam
the son of Bē-ôr of Pē-thôr of Mĕs-ŏ-
pŏ-tā-mĭ-ă, to curse thee.
5 Nevertheless the LORD thy God
would not hearken unto Bā-lāam; but
the LORD thy God turned [d]the curse
into a blessing unto thee, because the
LORD thy God loved thee.
6 Thou [e]shalt not seek their peace
nor their [1]prosperity all thy days for
ever.
7 ¶ Thou shalt not abhor an Ē-dŏm-
īte; [f]for he *is* thy brother: thou shalt
not abhor an Egyptian; because [g]thou
wast a stranger in his land.
8 The children that are begotten of
them shall enter into the congregation
of the LORD in their third generation.
9 ¶ When the host goeth forth against
thine enemies, then keep thee from
every wicked thing.
10 ¶ If [h]there be among you any
man, that is not clean by reason of uncleanness that chanceth him by night,
then shall he go abroad out of the
camp, he shall not come within the
camp:
11 But it shall be, when evening
[2]cometh on, he shall wash *himself*
with water: and when the sun is down,
he shall come into the camp *again*.
12 ¶ Thou shalt have a place also
without the camp, whither thou shalt
go forth abroad:
13 And thou shalt have a paddle upon thy weapon; and it shall be, when
thou [3]wilt ease thyself abroad, thou
shalt dig therewith, and shalt turn
back and cover that which cometh
from thee:
14 For the LORD thy God [i]walketh
in the midst of thy camp, to deliver
thee, and to give up thine enemies before thee; therefore shall thy camp be
[j]holy: that he see no [4]unclean thing in
thee, and turn away from thee.
15 ¶ Thou [k]shalt not deliver unto his
master the servant which is escaped
from his master unto thee:
16 He shall dwell with thee, *even*
among you, in that place which he
shall choose in one of thy gates, where
it [5]liketh him best: [l]thou shalt not
oppress him.
17 ¶ There shall be no [6]whore of [m]the
daughters of Israel, nor [n]a sodomite
of the sons of Israel.
18 Thou shalt not bring the hire of a
whore, or the price of a dog, into the
house of the LORD thy God for any
vow: for even both these *are* abomination unto the LORD thy God.
19 ¶ Thou [o]shalt not lend upon usury
to thy brother; usury of money, usury
of victuals, usury of any thing that is
lent upon usury:
20 Unto [p]a stranger thou mayest
lend upon usury; but unto thy brother
thou shalt not lend upon usury: [q]that
the LORD thy God may bless thee in
all that thou settest thine hand to in
the land whither thou goest to possess
it.
21 ¶ When [r]thou shalt vow a vow unto the LORD thy God, thou shalt not
slack to pay it: for the LORD thy God
will surely require it of thee; and it
would be sin in thee.
22 But if thou shalt forbear to vow,
it shall be no sin in thee.
23 That [s]which is gone out of thy lips
thou shalt keep and perform; *even* a
freewill offering, according as thou
hast vowed unto the LORD thy God,
which thou hast promised with thy
mouth.
24 ¶ When thou comest into thy
neighbour's vineyard, then thou mayest eat grapes thy fill at thine own
pleasure; but thou shalt not put *any*
in thy vessel.
25 When thou comest into the standing corn of thy neighbour, then [t]thou
mayest pluck the ears with thine hand;
but [u]thou shalt not move a sickle unto
thy neighbour's standing corn.

CHAPTER 24

WHEN a [a]man hath taken a wife,
and married her, and it come to
pass that she find no favour in his
eyes, because he hath found [1]some
uncleanness in her: then let him write
her a bill of [2]divorcement, and give *it*
in her hand, and send her out of his
house.
2 And when she is departed out of
his house, she may go and be another
man's *wife*.
3 And *if* the latter husband hate her,
and write her a bill of divorcement,
and giveth *it* in her hand, and sendeth
her out of his house; or if the latter
husband die, which took her *to be* his
wife;
4 Her [b]former husband, which sent
her away, may not take her again to
be his wife, after that she is defiled;
for that *is* abomination before the
LORD: and thou shalt not cause the
land to sin, which the LORD thy God
giveth thee *for* an inheritance.
5 ¶ When a man hath taken a new
wife, he shall not go out to war,
[3]neither shall he be charged with any
business: *but* he shall be free at home

d Pro. 26.2.
e Ezra 9.12.
1 good.
f Gen. 25.24, 25,26. Obad. 10,12.
g Ex. 22.21. Lev. 19.34. ch. 10.19.
h Lev. 15.16. Num. 5.2,3. 1 Cor. 5.11, 13.
2 turneth toward.
3 sittest down.
i Gen. 15.1. Lev. 26.12. Jer. 32.40. 2 Cor. 6.16.
j Ex. 3.5.
4 nakedness of any thing.
k 1 Sam. 30. 15.
5 is good for him.
l Ex. 22.21. Pro. 22.22. Jer. 7.6. Zech. 7.10. Mal. 3.5.
6 Or, sodomitess.
m Pro. 2.16.
n Gen. 19.5.
o Lev. 25.36. Neh. 5.2,7. Ps. 15.5. Luke 6.34.
p Lev. 19.34.
q ch. 15.10.
r Job 22.27. Ps. 61.8. Eccl. 5.4.5.
s Ps. 66.13.
t Matt. 12.1.
u Luke 12.15. 1 Cor. 6.10. Col. 3.5.

CHAP. 24

a Matt. 5.31. Mark 10.4.
1 matter of nakedness.
2 cutting off.
b Jer. 3.1.
3 not any thing shall pass upon him.

one year, and shall cheer [c]up his wife which he hath taken.

6 ¶ No man shall take the nether or the upper [d]millstone to pledge: for he taketh *a man's* life to pledge.

7 ¶ If [e]a man be found stealing any of his brethren of the children of Israel, and maketh merchandise of him, or selleth him; then that thief shall die; and thou shalt put evil away from among you.

8 ¶ Take heed in [f]the plague of leprosy, that thou observe diligently, and do according to all that the priests the Levites shall teach you: as I commanded them, *so* ye shall observe to do.

9 Remember [g]what the LORD thy God did [h]unto Miriam by the way, after that ye were come forth out of Egypt.

10 ¶ When thou dost [4]lend thy brother any thing, thou shalt not go into his house to fetch his pledge.

11 Thou shalt stand abroad, and the man to whom thou dost lend shall bring out the pledge abroad unto thee.

12 And if the man *be* poor, thou shalt not sleep with his pledge:

13 In [i]any case thou shalt deliver him the pledge again when the sun goeth down, that he may sleep in his own raiment, [j]and bless thee: and [k]it shall be righteousness unto thee before the LORD thy God.

14 ¶ Thou shalt not [l]oppress an hired servant *that is* poor and needy, *whether he be* of thy brethren, or of thy strangers that *are* in thy land within thy gates:

15 At his day [m]thou shalt give *him* his hire, neither shall the sun go down upon it; for he *is* poor, and [5]setteth his heart upon it: lest [n]he cry against thee unto the LORD, and it be sin unto thee.

16 The [o]fathers shall not be put to death for the children, neither shall the children be put to death for the fathers: every man shall be put to death for his own sin.

17 ¶ Thou [p]shalt not pervert the judgment of the stranger, *nor* of the fatherless; nor [q]take a widow's raiment to pledge:

18 But thou shalt remember that thou wast a bondman in Egypt, and the LORD thy God redeemed thee thence: therefore I command thee to do this thing.

19 ¶ When [r]thou cuttest down thine harvest in thy field, and hast forgot a sheaf in the field, thou shalt not go again to fetch it: it shall be for the stranger, for the fatherless, and for the widow: that the LORD thy God [s]may bless thee in all the work of thine hands.

20 When thou beatest thine olive tree, [6]thou shalt not go over the boughs again: it shall be for the stranger, for the fatherless, and for the widow.

21 When thou gatherest the grapes of thy vineyard, thou shalt not glean *it* [7]afterward: it shall be for the stranger, for the fatherless, and for the widow.

22 And thou shalt remember that thou wast a bondman in the land of Egypt: therefore I command thee to do this thing.

CHAPTER 25

IF there be a controversy between men, and they come unto judgment, that *the judges* may judge them; then they shall justify the righteous, and condemn the wicked.

2 And it shall be, if the wicked man *be* worthy [a]to be beaten, that the judge shall cause him to lie down, [b]and to be beaten before his face, according to his fault, by a certain number.

3 Forty [c]stripes he may give him, *and* not exceed: lest, *if* he should exceed, and beat him above these with many stripes, then thy brother should [d]seem vile unto thee.

4 ¶ Thou [e]shalt not muzzle the ox when he [1]treadeth out *the corn*.

5 ¶ If [f]brethren dwell together, and one of them die, and have no child, the wife of the dead shall not marry without unto a stranger: her [2]husband's brother shall go in unto her, and take her to him to wife, and perform the duty of an husband's brother unto her.

6 And it shall be, *that* the firstborn which she beareth [g]shall succeed in the name of his brother *which is* dead, that his name be not put out of Israel.

7 And if the man like not to take his [3]brother's wife, then let his brother's wife go up to the gate unto the elders, and say, My husband's brother refuseth to raise up unto his brother a name in Israel, he will not perform the duty of my husband's brother.

8 Then the elders of his city shall call him, and speak unto him: and *if* he stand *to it*, and say, I like not to take her;

9 Then shall his brother's wife come unto him in the presence of the elders,

c Pro. 5.18.
d Isa. 47.2.
e Ex. 21.16.
f Lev. 13.2. Matt. 8.4. Mark 1.44. Luke 5.14.
g Luke 17.32. 1 Cor. 10.6.
h Num. 12. 10.
4 lend the loan of any thing to, etc.
i Ex. 22.26. Job 24.7,8. Eze. 33.15. Amos 2.8.
j Job 29.11. 2 Cor. 9.13. 2 Tim. 1.18.
k ch. 6.25. Ps. 106.31. Dan. 4.27.
l Pro. 14.31. Amos 4.1. Mal. 3.5.
m Lev. 19.13.
5 lifteth his soul unto it.
n Job 27.13. Jas. 5.4.
o 2 Ki. 14.6. Eze. 18.20.
p Ex. 22.21, 22. Pro. 22.22. Isa. 1.23. Zech. 7.10. Mal. 3.5.
q Ex. 22.26.
r Lev. 23.22.
s Pro. 19.17.
6 thou shalt not bough it after thee.
7 after thee.

CHAP. 25

a Pro. 19.29. Luke 12.48.
b Matt. 10.17.
c 2 Cor. 11. 24.
d Job 18.3.
e Pro. 12.10. 1 Cor. 9.9. 1 Tim. 5.18.
1 thresheth.
f Luke 20.28.
2 Or, next kinsman.
g Gen. 38.9.
3 Or, next kinsman's wife.

[h]and loose his shoe from off his foot,
and spit in his face, and shall answer
and say, So shall it be done unto that
man that will not build up his brother's house.
10 And [i]his name shall be called in
Israel, The house of him that hath his
shoe loosed.
11 ¶ When men strive together one
with another, and the wife of the one
draweth near for to deliver her husband out of the hand of him that
smiteth him, and putteth forth her
hand, and taketh him by the secrets:
12 Then thou shalt cut off her hand,
thine [j]eye shall not pity *her*.
13 ¶ Thou [k]shalt not have in thy
bag [4]divers weights, a great and a
small.
14 Thou shalt not have in thine house
[5]divers measures, a great and a small.
15 *But* thou shalt have a perfect and
just weight, a perfect and just measure
shalt thou have: [l]that thy days may be
lengthened in the land which the LORD
thy God giveth thee.
16 For [m]all that do such things, *and*
all that do unrighteously, *are* an abomination unto the LORD thy God.
17 ¶ Remember [n]what Ăm'-ă-lĕk did
unto thee by the way, when ye were
come forth out of Egypt;
18 How he met thee by the way, and
smote the hindmost of thee, *even* all
that were feeble behind thee, when
thou *wast* faint and weary; and he
[o]feared not God.
19 Therefore it shall be, [p]when the
LORD thy God hath given thee rest
from all thine enemies round about,
in the land which the LORD thy God
giveth thee *for* an inheritance to
possess it, *that* thou shalt blot out the
remembrance of Ăm'-ă-lĕk from under
heaven; thou shalt not forget *it*.

CHAPTER 26

AND it shall be, when thou *art*
come in unto the land which the
LORD thy God giveth thee *for* an
inheritance, and possessest it, and
dwellest therein;
2 That [a]thou shalt take of the first of
all the fruit of the earth, which thou
shalt bring of thy land that the LORD
thy God giveth thee, and shalt put *it*
in a basket, and shalt [b]go unto the
place which the LORD thy God shall
choose to place his name there.
3 And thou shalt go unto the priest
that shall be in those days, and say
unto him, I profess this day unto the
LORD thy God, that I am come unto
the country which the LORD sware
unto our fathers for to give us.
4 And the priest shall take the basket out of thine hand, and set it down
before the altar of the LORD thy God.
5 And thou shalt speak and say before the LORD thy God, [c]A Syrian
[d]ready to perish *was* my father, and
he went down into Egypt, and sojourned there with a [e]few, and became
there a nation, great, mighty, and
populous:
6 And [f]the Egyptians evil entreated
us, and afflicted us, and laid upon us
hard bondage:
7 And [g]when we cried unto the LORD
God of our fathers, the LORD heard
our voice, and looked on our affliction, and our labour, and our oppression:
8 And the LORD brought us forth out
of Egypt with a mighty hand, and with
an outstretched arm, and [h]with great
terribleness, and with signs, and with
wonders:
9 And he hath brought us into this
place, and hath given us this land,
even [i]a land that floweth with milk
and honey.
10 And now, behold, I have brought
the firstfruits of the land, which [j]thou,
O LORD, hast given me. And thou
shalt set it before the LORD thy God,
and worship before the LORD thy
God:
11 And [k]thou shalt rejoice in every
good *thing* which the LORD thy God
hath given unto thee, and unto thine
house, thou, and the Levite, and the
stranger that *is* among you.
12 ¶ When thou hast made an end of
tithing all the [l]tithes of thine increase
the third year, *which is* [m]the year of
tithing, and hast given *it* unto the Levite, the stranger, the fatherless, and
the widow, that they may eat within
thy gates, and be filled;
13 Then thou shalt say before the
LORD thy God, I have brought away
the hallowed things out of *mine* house,
and also have given them unto the
Levite, and unto the stranger, to the
fatherless, and to the widow, according to all thy commandments which
thou hast commanded me: I have
not transgressed thy commandments,
[n]neither have I forgotten *them:*
14 I [o]have not eaten thereof in my
mourning, neither have I taken away
ought thereof for *any* unclean *use*, nor
given *ought* thereof for the dead: *but*
I have hearkened to the voice of the
LORD my God, *and* have done accord-

h Ruth 4.7. Isa. 20.2.
i Pro. 6.33. 1 Tim. 3.7.
j ch. 19.13.
k Lev. 19.35. Pro. 11.1. Eze. 45.10. Amos 8.5. Micah 6.11.
4 a stone and a stone.
5 an ephah and an ephah.
l Ex. 20.12.
m Pro. 11.1. Amos 8.5-7. 1 Cor. 8.9-11. 1 Thes. 4.6. Rev. 21.27.
n Ex. 17.8.
o Neh. 5.9, 15. Ps. 36.1. Pro. 16.6. Rom. 3.18.
p 1 Sam. 15.3.

CHAP. 26

a Ex. 23.19. Num. 18.13. Pro. 3.9. Rom. 8.23. 1 Cor. 15.20.
b ch. 12.5.
c Gen. 26.5. Hosea 12.12.
d Gen. 43.1,2.
e Gen. 46.27. ch. 10.22.
f Ex. 1.11.
g Ex. 3.9. Ex. 4.31.
h ch. 4.34. ch. 34.11,12.
i Ex. 3.8.
j ch. 8.18. Pro. 10.22.
k ch. 12.7, 12,18. ch. 16.11. Eccl. 3.12, 13. Isa. 65.14. Acts 2.46, 47. Phil. 4.4. 1 Tim. 6.17.
l Lev. 27.30. Num. 18.24.
m ch. 14.28, 29.
n Ps. 119.141, 153,176.
o Lev. 7.20. Hosea 9.4.

ing to all that thou hast commanded me.

15 Look [p]down from thy holy habitation, from heaven, and bless thy people Israel, and the land which thou hast given us, as thou swarest unto our fathers, a land that floweth with milk and honey.

16 ¶ This day the LORD thy God hath commanded thee to do these statutes and judgments: thou shalt therefore keep and do them with all thine heart, and with all thy soul.

17 Thou hast [q]avouched the LORD this day to be thy God, and to walk in his ways, and to keep his statutes, and his commandments, and his judgments, and to hearken unto his voice:

18 And [r]the LORD hath avouched thee this day to be his peculiar people, as he hath promised thee, and that *thou* shouldest keep all his commandments;

19 And to make thee [s]high above all nations which he hath made, in praise, and in name, and in honour; and that thou mayest be an [t]holy people unto the LORD thy God, as he hath spoken.

CHAPTER 27

AND Moses with the elders of Israel commanded the people, saying, Keep all the commandments which I command you this day.

2 And it shall be on the day when [a]ye shall pass over Jordan unto the land which the LORD thy God giveth thee, that [b]thou shalt set thee up great stones, and plaister them with plaister:

3 And thou shalt write upon them all the words of this law, when thou art passed over, that thou mayest go in unto the land which the LORD thy God giveth thee, a land that floweth with milk and honey; as the LORD God of thy fathers hath promised thee.

4 Therefore it shall be when ye be gone over Jordan, *that* ye shall set up these stones, which I command you this day, [c]in mount Ē´băl, and thou shalt plaister them with plaister.

5 And there shalt thou build an altar unto the LORD thy God, an altar of stones: thou [d]shalt not lift up *any* iron *tool* upon them.

6 Thou shalt build the altar of the LORD thy God of whole stones: and thou shalt offer burnt offerings thereon unto the LORD thy God:

7 And thou shalt offer peace offerings, and shalt eat there, and rejoice before the LORD thy God.

8 And thou shalt write upon the stones all the words of this law very [e]plainly.

9 ¶ And Moses and the priests the Levites spake unto all Israel, saying, Take heed, and hearken, O Israel; this day thou art become the people of the LORD thy God.

10 Thou shalt therefore obey the voice of the LORD thy God, and do his commandments and his statutes, which I command thee this day.

11 ¶ And Moses charged the people the same day, saying,

12 These shall stand [f]upon mount Gĕ-rī´zĭm to bless the people, when ye are come over Jordan; Simeon, and Levi, and Judah, and Ĭs´să-chär, and Joseph, and Benjamin:

13 And these shall stand upon mount Ē´băl [1]to curse; Reuben, Gad, and Asher, and Zĕ-bū´lŭn, Dan, and Năph´tă-lī.

14 ¶ And [g]the Levites shall speak, and say unto all the men of Israel with a loud voice,

15 Cursed [h]*be* the man that maketh *any* graven or molten image, an abomination unto the LORD, the work of the hands of the craftsman, and putteth *it* in *a* secret *place*. [i]And all the people shall answer and say, Ä´mĕn.

16 Cursed [j]*be* he that setteth light by his father or his mother. And all the people shall say, Ä´mĕn.

17 Cursed [k]*be* he that removeth his neighbour's landmark. And all the people shall say, Ä´mĕn.

18 Cursed [l]*be* he that maketh the blind to wander out of the way. And all the people shall say, Ä´mĕn.

19 Cursed [m]*be* he that perverteth the judgment of the stranger, fatherless, and widow. And all the people shall say, Ä´mĕn.

20 Cursed [n]*be* he that lieth with his father's wife; because he uncovereth his father's skirt. And all the people shall say, Ä´mĕn.

21 Cursed *be* he that lieth with any manner of beast. And all the people shall say, Ä´mĕn.

22 Cursed [o]*be* he that lieth with his sister, the daughter of his father, or the daughter of his mother. And all the people shall say, Ä´mĕn.

23 Cursed *be* he that lieth with his mother in law. And all the people shall say, Ä´mĕn.

24 Cursed [p]*be* he that smiteth his neighbour secretly. And all the people shall say, Ä´mĕn.

25 Cursed [q]*be* he that taketh reward

p 2 Chr. 6.26, 27. Ps. 80.14. Ps. 102.19, 20. Isa. 1.2. Isa. 63.15. Zech. 2.13. Acts 7.49.
q Ex. 20.19. Ps. 48.14.
r Ex. 6.7. ch. 7.6. ch. 14.2. ch. 28.9. ch. 29.13. 2 Sam. 7.23, 24.
s ch. 4.7, 8. ch. 28.1. Ps. 148.14.
t Ex. 19.6. Lev. 20.24, 26. ch. 7.6. Ps. 50.5. Isa. 62.12. 1 Cor. 3.17. 1 Thes. 5.27. 1 Pet. 2.9.

CHAP. 27

a Josh. 4.1.
b Josh. 8.32.
c ch. 11.29. Josh. 8.30.
d Ex. 20.25. Josh. 8.31.
e Hab. 2.2.
f ch. 11.29. Judg. 9.7.
1 for a cursing.
g ch. 33.10. Josh. 8.33. Neh. 8.7, 8. Dan. 9.11. Mal. 2.7-9.
h Ex. 20.4. Lev. 19.4. Lev. 26.1. ch. 4.16, 23. Isa. 44.9. Hosea 13.2.
i Num. 5.22. 1 Cor. 14.16.
j Ex. 20.12. Lev. 19.3.
k Pro. 22.28.
l Lev. 19.14. Job 29.15. Pro. 28.10. Matt. 15.14. Rev. 2.14.
m Ex. 22.21. ch. 10.18. Mal. 3.5.
n Lev. 18.8. 1 Cor. 5.1.
o 2 Sam. 13.1.
p Lev. 24.17. Num. 35.31.
q Ex. 23.7. ch. 10.17. Ps. 15.5.

to slay an innocent person. And all the people shall say, Ä-mĕn.

26 Cursed [r]*be* he that confirmeth not *all* the words of this law to do them. And all the people shall say, Ä-mĕn.

CHAPTER 28

AND it shall come to pass, [a]if thou shalt hearken diligently unto the voice of the LORD thy God, to observe *and* to do all his commandments which I command thee this day, that the LORD thy God will set thee [b]on high above all nations of the earth:

2 And all these blessings shall come on thee, and [c]overtake thee, if thou shalt hearken unto the voice of the LORD thy God.

3 Blessed [d]*shalt* thou *be* in the city, and blessed *shalt* thou *be* [e]in the field.

4 Blessed *shall be* [f]the fruit of thy body, and the fruit of thy ground, and the fruit of thy cattle, the increase of thy kine, and the flocks of thy sheep.

5 Blessed *shall be* thy basket and thy [1]store.

6 Blessed [g]*shalt* thou *be* when thou comest in, and blessed *shalt* thou *be* when thou goest out.

7 The LORD [h]shall cause thine enemies that rise up against thee to be smitten before thy face: they shall come out against thee one way, and flee before thee seven ways.

8 The LORD shall [i]command the blessing upon thee in thy [2]storehouses, and in all that thou [j]settest thine hand unto; and he shall bless thee in the land which the LORD thy God giveth thee.

9 The [k]LORD shall establish thee an holy people unto himself, as he hath sworn unto thee, if thou shalt keep the commandments of the LORD thy God, and walk in his ways.

10 And all people of the earth shall see that thou art [l]called by the name of the LORD; and they shall be afraid of thee.

11 And [m]the LORD shall make thee plenteous [3]in goods, in the fruit of thy [4]body, and in the fruit of thy cattle, and in the fruit of thy ground, in the land which the LORD sware unto thy fathers to give thee.

12 The LORD [n]shall open unto thee his good treasure, the heaven to give the rain unto thy land in his season, and to bless all the work of thine hand: and thou shalt lend unto many nations, and thou shalt not borrow.

13 And the LORD shall make thee the head, and not the tail; and thou shalt be above only, and thou shalt not be beneath; if that thou hearken unto the commandments of the LORD thy God, which I command thee this day, to observe and to do *them:*

14 And [o]thou shalt not go aside from any of the words which I command thee this day, *to* the right hand, or *to* the left, to go after other gods to serve them.

15 ¶ But it shall come to pass, [p]if thou wilt not hearken unto the voice of the LORD thy God, to observe to do all his commandments and his statutes which I command thee this day; that all these curses shall come upon thee, and overtake thee:

16 Cursed *shalt* thou *be* in the city, and cursed *shalt* thou *be* in the field.

17 Cursed *shall be* thy basket and thy store.

18 Cursed *shall be* the fruit of thy body, and the [q]fruit of thy land, the increase of thy kine, and the flocks of thy sheep.

19 Cursed *shalt* thou *be* when thou comest in, and cursed *shalt* thou *be* when thou goest out.

20 The LORD shall send upon thee cursing, [r]vexation, and [s]rebuke, in all that thou settest thine hand unto [5]for to do, until thou be destroyed, and until thou perish quickly; because of the wickedness of thy doings, whereby thou hast forsaken me.

21 The LORD shall make [t]the pestilence cleave unto thee, until he have consumed thee from off the land, whither thou goest to possess it.

22 The [u]LORD shall smite thee with a consumption, and with a fever, and with an inflammation, and with an extreme burning, and with the [6]sword, and with blasting, and with mildew; and they shall pursue thee until thou perish.

23 And thy heaven that *is* over thy head shall be brass, and the earth that *is* under thee *shall be* iron.

24 The LORD shall make the rain of thy land powder and dust: from heaven shall it come down upon thee, until thou be destroyed.

25 The [v]LORD shall cause thee to be smitten before thine enemies: thou shalt go out one way against them, and flee seven ways before them: and [w]shalt be [7]removed into all the kingdoms of the earth.

26 And thy carcase shall be meat unto all fowls of the air, and unto the beasts of the earth, and no man shall fray *them* away.

r Ps. 119.21. Jer. 11.3. Gal. 3.10.
CHAP. 28
a Ex. 15.26. Lev. 26.3. Ps. 106.3. Isa. 1.19. Isa. 3.10. Jer. 11.4.
b 1 Chr. 14.2. Rom. 2.10.
c Zech. 1.6.
d Ps. 128.1,4.
e Gen. 39.5.
f Gen. 22.17. 1 Tim. 4.8.
1 Or, dough, or, kneading trough.
g Ps. 121.8.
h 2 Sam. 22. 38.
i Lev. 25.21.
2 Or, barns.
j ch. 15.10.
k Gen. 17.7. Ex. 19.5. Isa. 1.26. Titus 2.14.
l 2 Chr. 7.14.
m Pro. 10.22.
3 Or, for good.
4 belly.
n Jas. 1.18.
o Josh. 1.7. 2 Ki. 22.2. Pro. 4.37.
p Lev. 26.14. Lam. 2.17. Dan. 9.11. Mal. 2.2. Rom. 2.8,9.
q Isa. 3.1. Hab. 3.17.
r Pro. 3.33. Zech. 5.3,4. Mal. 2.2.
s Ps. 80.16. Isa. 30.17. Isa. 51.20.
5 which thou wouldest do.
t Lev. 26.25. Num. 14.12. Jer. 16.4. Amos 4.10. Matt. 24.7.
u Lev. 26.16.
6 Or, drought.
v Lev. 26.17. ch. 32.30. Isa. 30.17.
w Jer. 15.4. Eze. 23.46.
7 for a removing.

27 The LORD will smite thee with the [x]botch of Egypt, and with the [y]emerods, and with the scab, and with the itch, whereof thou canst not be healed.

28 The LORD shall smite thee with madness, and blindness, and astonishment of heart:

29 And thou shalt grope at noonday, as the blind gropeth in darkness, and thou shalt not prosper in thy ways: and thou shalt be only oppressed and spoiled evermore, and no man shall save *thee.*

30 Thou [z]shalt betroth a wife, and another man shall lie with her: thou shalt build an house, and thou shalt not dwell therein: thou shalt plant a vineyard, and shalt not [8]gather the grapes thereof.

31 Thine ox *shall be* slain before thine eyes, and thou shalt not eat thereof: thine ass *shall be* violently taken away from before thy face, and [9]shall not be restored to thee: thy sheep *shall be* given unto thine enemies, and thou shalt have none to rescue *them.*

32 Thy sons and thy daughters *shall be* given unto another people, and thine eyes shall look, and fail *with longing* for them all the day long: and *there shall be* no might in thine hand.

33 The [a]fruit of thy land, and all thy labours, shall a nation which thou knowest not eat up; and thou shalt be only oppressed and crushed alway:

34 So that thou shalt be mad for the sight of thine eyes which thou shalt see.

35 The LORD shall smite thee in the knees, and in the legs, with a sore botch that cannot be healed, from the sole of thy foot unto the top of thy head.

36 The LORD shall [b]bring thee, and [c]thy king which thou shalt set over thee, unto a nation which neither thou nor thy fathers have known; and [d]there shalt thou serve other gods, wood and stone.

37 And thou shalt become [e]an astonishment, a proverb, [f]and a byword, among all nations whither the LORD shall lead thee.

38 Thou [g]shalt carry much seed out into the field, and shalt gather *but* little in; for the [h]locust shall consume it.

39 Thou shalt plant vineyards, and dress *them,* but shalt neither drink *of* the wine, nor gather *the grapes;* for the worms shall eat them.

40 Thou shalt have olive trees throughout all thy coasts, but thou shalt not anoint *thyself* with the oil; for thine olive shall cast *his fruit.*

41 Thou shalt beget sons and daughters, but [10]thou shalt not enjoy them; for [i]they shall go into captivity.

42 All thy trees and fruit of thy land shall the locust [11]consume.

43 The stranger that *is* within thee shall get up above thee very high; and thou shalt come down very low.

44 He shall lend to thee, and thou shalt not lend to him: [j]he shall be the head, and thou shalt be the tail.

45 Moreover all these curses shall come upon thee, and shall pursue thee, and overtake thee, till thou be destroyed; because thou hearkenedst not unto the voice of the LORD thy God, to keep his commandments and his statutes which he commanded thee:

46 And they shall be upon thee for [k]a sign and for a wonder, and upon thy seed for ever.

47 Because [l]thou servedst not the LORD thy God with joyfulness, and with gladness of heart, for the abundance of all *things;*

48 Therefore shalt thou serve thine enemies which the LORD shall send against thee, in hunger, and in thirst, and in nakedness, and in want of all *things:* and he shall [m]put a yoke of iron upon thy neck, until he have destroyed thee.

49 The [n]LORD shall bring a nation against thee from far, from the end of the earth, *as* [o]*swift* as the eagle flieth; a nation whose tongue thou shalt not [12]understand;

50 A nation [13]of fierce countenance, which [p]shall not regard the person of the old, nor shew favour to the young:

51 And he shall [q]eat the fruit of thy cattle, and the fruit of thy land, until thou be destroyed: which *also* shall not leave thee *either* corn, wine, or oil, *or* the increase of thy kine, or flocks of thy sheep, until he have destroyed thee.

52 And he shall [r]besiege thee in all thy gates, until thy high and fenced walls come down, wherein thou trustedst, throughout all thy land: and he shall besiege thee in all thy gates throughout all thy land, which the LORD thy God hath given thee.

53 And [s]thou shalt eat the fruit of thine own [14]body, the flesh of thy sons and of thy daughters, which the LORD thy God hath given thee, in the siege, and in the straitness, wherewith thine enemies shall distress thee:

x Ex. 9.9.
y 1 Sam. 5.6. Ps. 78.66.
z Job 31.10. Jer. 8.10.
8 profane, or, use it as common meat.
9 shall not return to thee.
a Lev. 26.16. Jer. 5.17.
b 2 Ki. 17.4. 2 Ki. 25.7, 11.
c Jer. 39.1. 2 Chr. 33.11.
d Jer. 16.13.
e 1 Ki. 9.7,8. Jer. 24.9. Zech. 8.13.
f Ps. 44.14.
g Micah 6.15. Hag. 1.6.
h Ex. 10.4. Joel 1.4.
10 they shall not be thine.
i Jer. 52.28.
11 Or, possess.
j Ezra 9.7. Lam. 1.5.
k Num. 26. 10. Isa. 8.18. Eze. 5.15. Eze. 14.8.
l Neh. 9.35, 36,37.
m Isa. 47.6. Jer. 27.12. Jer. 28.14. Matt. 11.29.
n Jer. 5.15. Jer. 6.22,23. Luke 19.43.
o Jer. 48.40. Jer. 49.22. Lam. 4.19. Eze. 17.3. Hosea 8.1.
12 hear.
13 strong of face. Pro. 7.13. Eccl. 8.1.
p 2 Chr. 36. 17. Isa. 47.6.
q Isa. 1.7. Isa. 62.8. Jer. 5.15-17.
r 2 Ki. 25.1. Jer. 37.8. Matt. 22.7.
s Lev. 26.29. 2 Ki. 6.28, 29. Jer. 19.9. Lam. 2.20. Lam. 4.10. Luke 21.23.
14 belly.

54 *So that* the man *that is* tender
among you, and very delicate, his eye
shall be evil toward his brother, and
toward the wife of his bosom, and toward the remnant of his children
which he shall leave:
55 So that he will not give to any of
them of the flesh of his children whom
he shall eat: because he hath nothing
left him in the siege, and in the straitness, wherewith thine enemies shall
distress thee in all thy gates.
56 The tender and delicate woman
among you, which would not adven-
ture to set the sole of her foot upon
the ground for delicateness and ten-
derness, her eye shall be evil toward
the husband of her bosom, and toward her son, and toward her daughter,
57 And [t]toward her [15]young one that
cometh out from between her feet,
and toward her children which she
shall bear: for she shall eat them for
want of all *things* secretly in the siege
and straitness, wherewith thine enemy shall distress thee in thy gates.
58 If thou wilt not observe to do all
the words of this law that are written
in this book, that thou mayest fear
[u]this glorious and fearful [v]name, THE
LORD THY GOD;
59 Then the LORD will make thy
plagues [w]wonderful, and the plagues
of thy seed, *even* great plagues, and of
long continuance, and sore sicknesses,
and of long continuance.
60 Moreover he will bring upon thee
all the diseases of Egypt, which thou
wast afraid of; and they shall cleave
unto thee.
61 Also every sickness, and every
plague, which *is* not written in the
book of this law, them will the LORD
[16]bring upon thee, until thou be
destroyed.
62 And ye shall be left few in number, whereas ye were [x]as the stars of
heaven for multitude; because thou
wouldest not obey the voice of the
LORD thy God.
63 And it shall come to pass, *that* as
the LORD [y]rejoiced over you to do you
good, and to multiply you; so the
LORD [z]will rejoice over you to destroy
you, and to bring you to nought; and
ye shall be plucked from off the
land whither thou goest to possess
it.
64 And the LORD [a]shall scatter thee
among all people, from the one end of
the earth even unto the other; and
there thou shalt serve other gods,
which neither thou nor thy fathers
have known, *even* wood and stone.
65 And [b]among these nations shalt
thou find no ease, neither shall the
sole of thy foot have rest: but [c]the
LORD shall give thee there a trembling heart, and failing of eyes, and
sorrow of mind:
66 And thy life shall hang in doubt
before thee; and thou shalt fear day
and night, and shalt have none assurance of thy life:
67 In [d]the morning thou shalt say,
Would God it were even! and at even
thou shalt say, Would God it were
morning! for the fear of thine heart
wherewith thou shalt fear, and for the
sight of thine eyes which thou shalt
see.
68 And the LORD [e]shall bring thee
into Egypt again with ships, by the
way whereof I spake unto thee, Thou
shalt see it no more again: and [17]there
ye shall be sold unto your enemies
for bondmen and bondwomen, and
no man shall buy *you*.

CHAPTER 29

THESE *are* the words of the covenant, which the LORD commanded
Moses to make with the children of
Israel in the land of Moab, beside the
covenant which he made with them in
Hôr-ĕb.
2 ¶ And Moses called unto all Israel,
and said unto them, Ye have seen all
that the LORD did before your eyes in
the land of Egypt unto Pharaoh, and
unto all his servants, and unto all his
land;
3 The [a]great temptations which
thine eyes have seen, the signs, and
those great miracles:
4 Yet [b]the LORD hath not given you
an heart to perceive, and eyes to see,
and ears to hear, unto this day.
5 And [c]I have led you forty years in
the wilderness: your clothes are not
waxen old upon you, and thy shoe is
not waxen old upon thy foot.
6 Ye [d]have not eaten bread, neither
have ye drunk wine or strong drink:
that ye might know that I *am* the LORD
your God.
7 And when ye came unto this place,
Sī-hŏn [e]the king of Hĕsh-bŏn, and Og
the king of Bā-shăn, came out against
us unto battle, and we smote them:
8 And we took their land, and gave
[f]it for an inheritance unto the Reubenites, and to the Gadites, and to the
half tribe of Mă-năs-sēh.
9 Keep [g]therefore the words of this

t Lam. 4.10.
15 afterbirth.
u Ex. 6.3. Ps. 99.3. Isa. 57.15. Isa. 29.23. Mal. 1.14.
v Ps. 20.1. Ps. 83.18. Ps. 113.3. Isa. 42.8. Mal. 2.3. Mal. 4.2. Phil. 2.10.
w 1 Ki. 9.7,9. 2 Chr. 21.12-15. Lam. 1.9,12. Lam. 4.12. Dan. 9.12.
16 cause to ascend.
x Neh. 9.23.
y Isa. 62.5. Jer. 32.41. Micah 7.18. Zeph. 3.17. Luke 15.6, 10.
z Pro. 1.26. Isa. 1.24.
a Lev. 26.33. Neh. 1.8.
b Gen. 8.9. Isa. 57.21. Amos 9.4.
c Lev. 26.36.
d Job 7.4.
e Jer. 43.7. Hosea 8.13.
17 Fulfilled at the destruction of Jerusalem by the Romans, A.D. 79.

CHAP. 29

a ch. 4.34. ch. 7.19.
b Ps. 13.3. Ps. 19.8. Ps. 146.8. Isa. 6.9. Isa. 63.17. Eze. 12.2. Matt. 13.14. John 8.43. Acts 28.26. Rom. 11.8. Eph. 4.18. 2 Thes. 2.11.
c ch. 1.3. ch. 8.2.
d Ex. 16.12. Neh. 9.15. Ps. 78.24.
e Num. 21. 23. ch. 2.32.
f Num. 32. 33.
g Josh. 1.7. 1 Ki. 2.3. Ps. 25.10. Isa. 56.1,2, 4,7. Jer. 1.5.

covenant, and do them, that ye may
prosper in all that ye do.
10 ¶ Ye stand this day all of you before the LORD your God; your captains of your tribes, your elders, and
your officers, *with* all the men of Israel,
11 Your little ones, your wives, and
thy stranger that *is* in thy camp, from
[h]the hewer of thy wood unto the
drawer of thy water:
12 That thou shouldest [1]enter into
covenant with the LORD thy God, and
into his oath, which the LORD thy God
maketh with thee this day:
13 That [i]he may establish thee to day
for a people unto himself, and *that* he
may be unto thee a God, as he hath
said unto thee, and as he hath sworn
unto thy fathers, to Abraham, to
Isaac, and to Jacob.
14 Neither with you only [j]do I make
this covenant and this oath;
15 But with *him* that standeth here
with us this day before the LORD our
God, [k]and also with *him* that *is* not
here with us this day:
16 (For ye know how we have dwelt
in the land of Egypt; and how we
came through the nations which ye
passed by;
17 And ye have seen their abominations, and their [2]idols, wood and
stone, silver and gold, which *were*
among them:)
18 Lest there should be among you
man, or woman, or family, or tribe,
whose heart turneth away this day
from the LORD our God, to go *and*
serve the gods of these nations; [l]lest
there should be among you a root that
beareth [3]gall and wormwood;
19 And it come to pass, when he
heareth the words of this curse, that
he bless himself in his heart, saying,
[m]I shall have peace, though I walk [n]in
the [4]imagination of mine heart, [o]to
add [5]drunkenness to thirst:
20 The [p]LORD will not spare him,
but then [q]the anger of the LORD and
[r]his jealousy shall smoke against that
man, and all the curses that are written in this book shall lie upon him,
and the LORD shall blot out his name
from under heaven.
21 And the LORD [s]shall separate him
unto evil out of all the tribes of Israel,
according to all the curses of the covenant that [6]are written in this book of
the law:
22 So that the generation to come of
your children that shall rise up after
you, and the stranger that shall come
from a far land, shall say, when they

h Josh. 9.21.
1 pass.
i Gen. 17.6,7.
j Jer. 31.31. Heb. 8.7,8.
k Acts 2.39. 1 Cor. 7.14.
2 dungy gods.
l Heb. 12.15.
3 rosh, or, a poisonful herb.
m Ps. 14.1.
n Num. 15. 39. Eccl. 11.9.
4 Or, stubbornness.
o Job 15.16. Isa. 30.1. Eph. 4.19.
5 the drunken to the thirsty.
p Eze. 14.7.
q Ps. 74.1.
r Ps. 79.5.
s Matt. 24.51.
6 is written.
7 wherewith the LORD, hath made it sick.
t Judg. 9.45. Ps. 107.34. Eze. 47.11. Zeph. 2.9. Luke 14.34, 35.
u Gen. 19.24.
v 1 Ki. 9.8.
8 Or, who had not given to them any portion.
9 divided.
w Ps. 11.6.
x 2 Chr. 7.20. Job 11.6,7. Ps. 52.5. Pro. 2.22.
y Job 11.6,7. Pro. 3.32. Jer. 23.18. Amos 3.7. Acts 1.7.
z Ps. 19.7. Luke 16.29. John 5.39. Acts 17.11. 2 Tim. 3.16.

CHAP. 30

a Lev. 26.40.
b ch. 28.
c 1 Ki. 8.47. Luke 15.17.
d Neh. 1.9.
e Ps. 106.45. Jer. 29.14. Lam. 3.22.
f Ps. 147.2. Eze. 34.13.
g ch. 28.64.

see the plagues of that land, and th
sicknesses [7]which the LORD hath lai
upon it;
23 *And that* the whole land thereo
is brimstone, [t]and salt, *and* burning
that it is not sown, nor beareth, no
any grass groweth therein, [u]like th
overthrow of Sodom, and Gō-mŏr
răh, Ăd-măh, and Zĕ-bō-ĭm, whic
the LORD overthrew in his anger, an
in his wrath:
24 Even all nations shall say, Where
fore [v]hath the LORD done thus unt
this land? what *meaneth* the heat o
this great anger?
25 Then men shall say, Because the
have forsaken the covenant of th
LORD God of their fathers, which h
made with them when he brough
them forth out of the land of Egypt:
26 For they went and served othe
gods, and worshipped them, god
whom they knew not, and [8]*whom* h
had not [9]given unto them:
27 And the anger of the LORD wa
kindled against this land, [w]to bring up
on it all the curses that are written i
this book:
28 And the LORD [x]rooted them ou
of their land in anger, and in wrath
and in great indignation, and cas
them into another land, as *it is* thi
day.
29 The [y]secret *things belong* unto th
LORD our God: but [z]those *thing*
which are revealed *belong* unto us an
to our children for ever, that *we* ma
do all the words of this law.

CHAPTER 30

AND [a]it shall come to pass, whe
[b]all these things are come upo
thee, the blessing and the curse, whic
I have set before thee, and [c]thou sha
call *them* to mind among all the na
tions, whither the LORD thy God hat
driven thee,
2 And shalt [d]return unto the LOR
thy God, and shalt obey his voice ac
cording to all that I command the
this day, thou and thy children, wit
all thine heart, and with all thy soul
3 That [e]then the LORD thy God wi
turn thy captivity, and have compas
sion upon thee, and will return an
[f]gather thee from all the nations
whither the LORD thy God hath scat
tered thee.
4 If [g]*any* of thine be driven out unt
the outmost *parts* of heaven, from
thence will the LORD thy God gathe
thee, and from thence will he fetch
thee:

5 And the LORD thy God will bring thee into the land which thy fathers possessed, and thou shalt possess it; and he will do thee good, and multiply thee above thy fathers.

6 And [h]the LORD thy God will circumcise thine heart, and the heart of thy seed, to love the LORD thy God with all thine heart, and with all thy soul, that thou mayest live.

7 And the LORD thy God will put all these curses upon thine enemies, and on them that hate thee, which persecuted thee.

8 And thou shalt return and obey the voice of the LORD, and do all his commandments which I command thee this day.

9 And the LORD thy God will make thee plenteous in every work of thine hand, in the fruit of thy body, and in the fruit of thy cattle, and in the fruit of [i]thy land, for good: for the LORD will again [j]rejoice over thee for good, as he rejoiced over thy fathers:

10 If thou shalt hearken unto the voice of the LORD thy God, to keep his commandments and his statutes which are written in this book of the law, *and* if thou turn unto the LORD thy God with all thine heart, and with all thy soul.

11 ¶ For this commandment which I command thee this day, it *is* not [k]hidden from thee, neither *is* it far off.

12 It [l]*is* not in heaven, that thou shouldest say, Who shall go up for us to heaven, and bring it unto us, that we may hear it, and do it?

13 Neither *is* it beyond the sea, that thou shouldest say, Who shall go over the sea for us, and bring it unto us, that we may hear it, and do it?

14 But the word *is* very nigh unto thee, in thy mouth, and in thy heart, that thou mayest do it.

15 ¶ See, [m]I have set before thee this day life and good, and death and evil;

16 In that I command thee this day to love the LORD thy God, to walk in his ways, and to keep his commandments and his statutes and his judgments, that thou mayest live and multiply: and the LORD thy God shall bless thee in the land whither thou goest to possess it.

17 But if thine heart turn away, so that thou wilt not hear, but shalt be drawn away, and worship other gods, and serve them,

18 ¶ I [n]denounce unto you this day, that ye shall surely perish, *and that* ye shall not prolong *your* days upon the land, whither thou passest over Jordan to go to possess it.

19 I call heaven and earth to record this day against you, *that* I have set before you life and death, blessing and cursing: therefore choose life, that both thou and thy seed may live:

20 That thou mayest love the LORD thy God, *and* that thou mayest obey his voice, and that thou mayest cleave unto him: for he *is* thy [o]life, and the length of thy days: that thou mayest dwell in the land which the LORD sware unto thy fathers, to Abraham, to Isaac, and to Jacob, [p]to give them.

h ch. 10.16.
i Eze. 34.27.
j Jer. 32.41. Zeph. 3.17. Luke 15.6, 10,32.
k Isa. 45.19.
l Pro. 30.4. John 3.13. Rom. 10.6.
m ch. 11.26. Mark 16.16. John 3.16. Gal. 3.13, 14.
n ch. 4.26. ch. 8.19. Isa. 63.17, 18.
o Job 12.10. Ps. 27.1. Ps. 66.9. Dan. 5.23. John 11.25. Acts 17.25, 28.
p Gen. 12.7. Gen. 13.15. Gen. 15.18. Gen. 17.1-8. Gen. 26.4. Gen. 28.13. Acts 7.5.

CHAP. 31

a Ex. 7.7. ch. 34.7.
b Num. 27. 17. 1 Ki. 3.7.
c Num. 20. 12. Num. 27.13. ch. 3.27.
d ch. 9.3.
e Num. 21. 24.
f ch. 7.2.
g 1 Chr. 22. 13.
h ch. 1.29. ch. 7.18.
i ch. 20.4. Ps. 118.6.
j Heb. 13.5.
k ch. 1.38.
l Ex. 13.21. Num. 14.9. Ps. 37.3. Rom. 8.31.
m 1 Chr. 28. 20.
n ch. 17.18.
o Num. 4.15. 1 Chr. 15.12.

CHAPTER 31

AND Moses went and spake these words unto all Israel.

2 And he said unto them, I [a]*am* an hundred and twenty years old this day; I can no more [b]go out and come in: also the LORD hath said unto me, [c]Thou shalt not go over this Jordan.

3 The LORD thy God, [d]he will go over before thee, *and* he will destroy these nations from before thee, and thou shalt possess them: *and* Joshua, he shall go over before thee, as the LORD hath said.

4 And the LORD shall do unto them [e]as he did to Si'hŏn and to Og, kings of the Amorites, and unto the land of them, whom he destroyed.

5 And [f]the LORD shall give them up before your face, that ye may do unto them according unto all the commandments which I have commanded you.

6 Be [g]strong and of a good courage, [h]fear not, nor be afraid of them: for the LORD thy God, he [i]*it is* that doth go with thee; he [j]will not fail thee, nor forsake thee.

7 ¶ And Moses called unto Joshua, and said unto him in the sight of all Israel, Be [k]strong and of a good courage: for thou must go with this people unto the land which the LORD hath sworn unto their fathers to give them; and thou shalt cause them to inherit it.

8 And the LORD, [l]he *it is* that doth go before thee; [m]he will be with thee, he will not fail thee, neither forsake thee: fear not, neither be dismayed.

9 ¶ And Moses wrote this law, and [n]delivered it unto the priests the sons of Levi, which [o]bare the ark of the covenant of the LORD, and unto all the elders of Israel.

10 And Moses commanded them,

saying, At the end of *every* seven years,
in the solemnity of [p]the year of release, [q]in the feast of tabernacles,
11 When all Israel is come [r]to appear
before the LORD thy God in the place
which he shall choose, thou [s]shalt
read this law before all Israel in their
hearing.
12 Gather [t]the people together, men,
and women, and children, and thy
stranger that *is* within thy gates, that
they may hear, and that they may
learn, and fear the LORD your God,
and observe to do all the words of this
law:
13 And *that* their children, which
have [u]not known *any thing*, [v]may hear,
and learn to fear the LORD your God,
as long as ye live in the land whither ye
go over Jordan to possess it.
14 ¶ And the LORD said unto Moses,
[w]Behold, thy days approach that thou
must die: call Joshua, and present
yourselves in the tabernacle of the
congregation, that I may give him a
charge. And Moses and Joshua went,
and presented themselves in the tabernacle of the congregation.
15 And [x]the LORD appeared in the
tabernacle in a pillar of a cloud: and
the pillar of the cloud stood over the
door of the tabernacle.
16 ¶ And the LORD said unto Moses,
Behold, thou shalt [1]sleep with thy
fathers; and this people will [y]rise up,
and [z]go a whoring after the gods of
the strangers of the land, whither they
go *to be* among them, and will [a]for-
sake me, and break my covenant
which I have made with them.
17 Then my anger shall be kindled
against them in that day, and [b]I will
forsake them, and I will [c]hide my face
from them, and they shall be devoured, and many evils and troubles shall
[2]befall them; so that they will say in
that day, [d]Are not these evils come upon us, because our God *is* [e]not among
us?
18 And I will surely hide my face in
that day for all the evils which they
shall have wrought, in that they are
turned unto other gods.
19 Now therefore write ye this song
for you, and teach it the children of
Israel: put it in their mouths, that this
song may be a witness for me against
the children of Israel.
20 For when I shall have brought
them into the land which I sware unto
their fathers, that floweth with milk
and honey; and they shall have eaten
and filled themselves, [f]and waxen fat;

p ch. 15.1.
q Lev. 23.34.
r ch. 16.16.
s Josh. 8.34. 2 Ki. 23.2.
t ch. 4.10.
u ch. 11.2. Pro. 22.6. Eph. 6.4.
v Ps. 78.6,7.
w Num. 27.13.
x Ex. 33.9. Ps. 99.7.
1 lie down.
y Ex. 32.6.
z Judg. 2.17.
a ch. 32.15. 1 Ki. 11.31-33. 2 Ki. 22.16,17. Isa. 1.4.
b 2 Chr. 15.2. 2 Chr. 24.20.
c ch. 32.20. Ps. 104.29. Isa. 8.17. Eze. 39.23.
2 find them.
d Num. 14.42. Isa. 63.17.
e Num. 14.42.
f ch. 32.15. Neh. 9.26. Ps. 17.10. Ps. 73.7. Ps. 119.70. Jer. 5.28. Hosea 13.6.
3 before.
g 1 Chr. 28.9. Hosea 5.3. Hosea 13.5. John 2.24. Rev. 2.23.
h Amos 5.25.
4 do.
i Josh. 1.6.
j 1 Ki. 8.9. 2 Ki. 22.8.
k ch. 9.24.
l ch. 9.6. 2 Chr. 30.8. Ps. 78.8.
m ch. 30.19.
n Judg. 2.19. Hosea 9.9.

CHAP. 32

a Ps. 50.4. Isa. 1.2.
b 2 Sam. 23.4. Isa. 55.10. Hosea 6.4. 1 Cor. 3.6-8.
c Ps. 72.6.

then will they turn unto other gods,
and serve them, and provoke me, and
break my covenant.
21 And it shall come to pass, when
many evils and troubles are befallen
them, that this song shall testify
[3]against them as a witness; for it shall
not be forgotten out of the mouths of
their seed: for [g]I know their imagination [h]which [4]they go about, even now,
before I have brought them into the
land which I sware.
22 ¶ Moses therefore wrote this song
the same day, and taught it the children of Israel.
23 And he gave Joshua the son of
Nun a charge, and said, [i]Be strong
and of a good courage: for thou shalt
bring the children of Israel into the
land which I sware unto them: and I
will be with thee.
24 ¶ And it came to pass, when
Moses had made an end of writing the
words of this law in a book, until they
were finished,
25 That Moses commanded the Levites, which bare the ark of the covenant of the LORD, saying,
26 Take this book of the law, and
[j]put it in the side of the ark of the covenant of the LORD your God, that it
may be there for a witness against
thee.
27 For [k]I know thy rebellion, and thy
[l]stiff neck: behold, while I am yet
alive with you this day, ye have been
rebellious against the LORD; and how
much more after my death?
28 ¶ Gather unto me all the elders
of your tribes, and your officers, that
I may speak these words in their ears,
[m]and call heaven and earth to record
against them.
29 For I know that after my death ye
will utterly [n]corrupt *yourselves*, and
turn aside from the way which I have
commanded you; and evil will befall
you in the latter days; because ye will
do evil in the sight of the LORD, to
provoke him to anger through the
work of your hands.
30 And Moses spake in the ears of
all the congregation of Israel the
words of this song, until they were
ended.

CHAPTER 32

GIVE [a]ear, O ye heavens, and I will
speak; and hear, O earth, the
words of my mouth.
2 My [b]doctrine shall drop as the rain,
my speech shall distil as the dew, [c]as
the small rain upon the tender herb,
and as the showers upon the grass:

3 Because I will publish the name of
he LORD: ascribe ye greatness unto
ur God.
4 *He is* the Rock, [d]his work *is* per-
ect: for [e]all his ways *are* judgment: [f]a
God of truth and without [g]iniquity,
ust and right *is* he.
5 [1]They have corrupted themselves,
heir spot *is* not *the spot* of his chil-
ren: *they are* a perverse and crooked
eneration.
6 Do ye thus [h]requite the LORD, O
oolish people and unwise? *is* not he
hy father *that* [j]hath bought thee?
ath he not made thee, and establish-
d thee?
7 ¶ Remember the days of old, con-
ider the years of [3]many generations:
sk thy father, and he will shew thee;
hy elders, and they will tell thee.
8 When the most High [k]divided to
he nations their inheritance, when he
separated the sons of Adam, he set
he bounds of the people according to
he number of the children of Israel.
9 For [m]the LORD's portion *is* his peo-
le; Jacob *is* the [4]lot of his inheritance.
10 He found him in a desert land,
nd in the waste howling wilderness;
e [5]led him about, he [n]instructed him,
e [o]kept him as the apple of his eye.
11 As an eagle stirreth up her nest,
uttereth over her young, spreadeth
broad her wings, taketh them, bear-
th them on her wings:
12 *So* the LORD alone did lead him,
nd *there was* no strange god with
im.
13 He [p]made him ride on the high
laces of the earth, that he might eat
he increase of the fields; and he made
im to suck honey out [q]of the rock,
nd oil out of the flinty rock;
14 Butter of kine, and milk of sheep,
vith fat of lambs, and rams of the
reed of Bā-shăn, and goats, with [r]the
at of kidneys of wheat; and thou
idst drink the [s]pure blood of the
rape.
15 ¶ But Jĕ-shū-rŭn waxed fat, and
icked: thou art waxen fat, thou art
rown thick, thou art covered *with*
atness; then he forsook [t]God *which*
nade him, and lightly esteemed the
Rock of his salvation.
16 They provoked him to jealousy
vith strange *gods*, with abominations
rovoked they him to anger.
17 They sacrificed unto devils, [6]not
o God; to gods whom they knew not,
o new *gods that* came newly up,
vhom your fathers feared not.
18 Of the Rock *that* begat thee thou
art unmindful, and hast forgotten
God that formed thee.
19 And when the LORD saw *it*, he [7]ab-
horred *them*, because of the provoking of his sons, and of his daughters.
20 And he said, I will hide my face
from them, I will see what their end
shall be: for they *are* a very froward
generation, children in [v]whom *is* no
faith.
21 They have moved me to jealousy
with *that which is* not God; they have
provoked me to anger [w]with their
vanities: and I [x]will move them to
jealousy with *those which are* not a
people; I will provoke them to anger
with a foolish nation.
22 For [y]a fire is kindled in mine anger, and [8]shall burn unto the lowest
hell, and [9]shall consume the earth
with her increase, and set on fire the
foundations of the mountains.
23 I will heap mischiefs upon them;
I will spend mine arrows upon them.
24 *They shall be* burnt with hunger,
and devoured with [10]burning heat, and
with bitter destruction: I will also
send the teeth of beasts upon them,
with the poison of serpents of the dust.
25 The [z]sword without, and terror
[11]within, shall [12]destroy both the
young man and the virgin, the suckling *also* with the man of gray hairs.
26 I said, I would scatter them into
corners, I would make the remembrance of them to cease from among
men:
27 Were it not that I feared the
wrath of the enemy, lest their adversaries should behave themselves
strangely, *and* lest they should [a]say,
[13]Our hand *is* high, and the LORD
hath not done all this.
28 For they *are* a nation void of
counsel, neither *is there any* understanding in them.
29 O [b]that they were wise, *that* they
understood this, *that* they would consider their latter end!
30 How should [c]one chase a thousand, and two put ten thousand to
flight, except their Rock [d]had sold
them, and the LORD had shut them
up?
31 For their rock *is* not as our Rock,
even [e]our enemies themselves *being*
judges.
32 For their vine [14]*is* of the vine of
Sodom, and of the fields of Gō-mŏr-
răh: their grapes *are* grapes of gall,
their clusters *are* bitter:
33 Their wine *is* the poison of dragons, and the cruel venom of asps.

d 2 Sam. 22. 31.
e Dan. 4.37.
f Jer. 10.10.
g Job 34.10.
1 He hath corrupted to himself.
2 Or, that they are not his children, that is their blot.
h Ps. 116.12.
i Isa. 63.16.
j 2 Sam. 7.23. Ps. 74.2.
3 generation and generation.
k Zech. 9.2.
l Gen. 11.8.
m 1 Sam. 10. 1.
4 cord.
5 Or, compassed him about.
n Deut. 4.26. Neh. 9.20. Ps. 32.7,10. Rom. 2.18.
o Ps. 17.8. Pro. 7.2.
p Isa. 58.14.
q Job 29.6.
r Ps. 147.14.
s Gen. 49.11. Matt. 26.28, 29.
t Isa. 1.4.
u Ps. 89.26.
6 Or, which were not God.
7 Or, despised.
v Matt. 17.17.
w 1 Sam. 12. 21.
x Rom. 10. 19.
y Lam. 4.11.
8 Or, hath burned.
9 Or, hath consumed.
10 burning coals.
z Lam. 1.20.
11 from the chambers.
12 bereave.
a Ps. 140.8.
13 Or, our high hand and not the LORD, hath done all this.
b Ps. 81.13.
c Josh. 23.10.
d Ps. 44.12.
e 1 Sam. 4.8.
14 Or, is worse than the vine of Sodom, etc.

34 *Is* not this [f]laid up in store with
me, *and* sealed up among my treasures?
35 To [g]me *belongeth* vengeance, and
recompence; their foot shall slide in
due time: for the day of their calamity
is at hand, and the things that shall
come upon them make haste.
36 For the LORD shall judge his people, and [h]repent himself for his servants, when he seeth that *their* [15]power
is gone, and *there is* none shut up, or
left.
37 And he shall say, [i]Where *are* their
gods, *their* rock in whom they trusted,
38 Which did eat the fat of their sacrifices, *and* drank the wine of their
drink offerings? let them rise up and
help you, *and* be [16]your protection.
39 See now that I, *even* I, *am* he, and
there [j]*is* no god with me: [k]I kill, and I
make alive; I wound, and I heal:
neither *is there any* that can deliver
out of my hand.
40 For I [l]lift up my hand to heaven,
and say, I live for ever.
41 If I whet my glittering sword, and
mine hand take hold on judgment; I
will render vengeance to mine enemies, and will reward them that hate me.
42 I will make mine arrows drunk
with blood, and my sword shall devour flesh; *and that* with the blood of
the slain and of the captives, from the
beginning of revenges [m]upon the enemy.
43 [17]Rejoice, [n]O ye nations, *with* his
people: for he will [o]avenge the blood
of his servants, and will render vengeance to his adversaries, and [p]will
be merciful unto his land, *and* to his
people.
44 ¶ And Moses came and spake all
the words of this song in the ears of
the people, he, and [18]Hō-shē-ă the son
of Nun.
45 And Moses made an end of speaking all these words to all Israel:
46 And he said unto them, Set your
hearts unto all the words which I testify among you this day, which ye shall
command your children to observe to
do, all the words of this law.
47 For it *is* not a vain thing for you;
[q]because it *is* your life: and through
this thing ye shall prolong *your* days
in the land, whither ye go over Jordan
to possess it.
48 And [r]the LORD spake unto Moses
that selfsame day, saying,
49 Get thee up into this mountain
Ăb-ă-rĭm, *unto* mount Nē-bō, which *is*
in the land of Moab, that *is* over

[f] Job 14.17.
[g] Ps. 94.1. Rom. 12.19. Heb. 10.30.
[h] Judg. 2.18. Ps. 90.13. Ps. 106.45.
15 hand.
[i] Judg. 10.14. 2 Ki. 3.13.
16 an hiding for you.
[j] Isa. 41.4. Isa. 45.5.
[k] 1 Sam. 2.6. Ps. 68.20. Isa. 43.13. Hosea 6.1.
[l] Ex. 6.8.
[m] Job 13.24.
17 Or, Praise his people, ye nations, or, Sing ye.
[n] Rom. 15.10.
[o] Rev. 6.10.
[p] Ps. 85.1.
18 Or, Joshua.
[q] Pro. 3.2. Rom. 10.5.
[r] Num. 27.12.
[s] Num. 20.11.
19 Or, strife at Kadesh.

CHAP. 33

[a] Gen. 49.28. Luke 24.50, 57.
[b] Ex. 19.18. Hab. 3.3.
[c] Dan. 7.10. Acts 7.53. Gal. 3.19. Heb. 2.2.
1 a fire of law.
[d] Hosea 11.1. Mal. 1.2.
[e] 1 Sam. 2.9. Ps. 50.5.
[f] Luke 10.39. Acts 22.3.
[g] John 7.19.
[h] Job 29.25.
[i] Gen. 49.8.
[j] Ex. 28.30. Lev. 8.8. Num. 27.21.
[k] ch. 13.6. Matt. 10.37. Mark 10.29. Luke 14.26.
[l] Ex. 32.26.
[m] Mal. 2.5.
2 Or, Let them teach, etc.
3 Or, let them put incense.
4 at thy nose.
[n] Ps. 51.19.

against Jericho; and behold the lan
of Canaan, which I give unto the chi
dren of Israel for a possession:
50 And die in the mount whith
thou goest up, and be gathered un
thy people; as Aaron thy brother die
in mount Hor, and was gathered unt
his people:
51 Because [s]ye trespassed against n
among the children of Israel at th
waters of [19]Mĕr-ĭ-bäh–Kā-dĕsh, in th
wilderness of Zin; because ye sanct
fied me not in the midst of the childre
of Israel.
52 Yet thou shalt see the land befo
thee; but thou shalt not go thither u
to the land which I give the childre
of Israel.

CHAPTER 33

AND [a]this *is* the blessing, wher
with Moses the man of God bles
ed the children of Israel before h
death.
2 And he said, [b]The LORD came fro
Sī-naī, and rose up from Sē-ĭr unt
them; he shined forth from mour
Pâr-ăn, and he came with [c]ten tho
sands of saints: from his right han
went [1]a fiery law for them.
3 Yea, he [d]loved the people; all [e]hi
saints *are* in thy hand: and they [f]sa
down at thy feet; *every one* shall re
ceive of thy words.
4 Moses [g]commanded us a law, *eve*
the inheritance of the congregation o
Jacob.
5 And he was [h]king in Jĕ-shū-rŭr
when the heads of the people *and* th
tribes of Israel were gathered togethe
6 ¶ Let Reuben live, and not die; an
let *not* his men be few.
7 ¶ And this *is the blessing* of Judah
and he said, Hear, LORD, the voice o
Judah, and bring him unto his people
[i]let his hands be sufficient for him
and be thou an help *to him* from hi
enemies.
8 ¶ And of Levi he said, [j]*Let* th
Thŭm-mĭm and thy Ū-rĭm *be* with th
holy one, whom thou didst prove a
Măs-săh, *and with* whom thou dids
strive at the waters of Mĕr-ĭ-bäh;
9 Who said unto his [k]father and t
his mother, I have not seen him
[l]neither did he acknowledge his breth
ren, nor knew his own children: fo
[m]they have observed thy words, an
kept thy covenant.
10 [2]They shall teach Jacob thy judg
ments, and Israel thy law: [3]they sha
put incense [4]before thee, [n]and whol
burnt sacrifice upon thine altar.
11 Bless, LORD, his substance, an

cept [o]the work of his hands: smite
rough the loins of them that rise
gainst him, and of them that hate
im, that they rise not again.
12 ¶ *And* of Benjamin he said, The
eloved of the LORD shall dwell in
fety by him; *and the LORD* shall
over him all the day long, and he
hall dwell between his shoulders.
13 ¶ And of Joseph he said, Blessed
of the LORD *be* his land, for the
recious things of heaven, for [q]the
ew, and for the deep that coucheth
eneath,
14 And for the precious fruits *brought*
orth by the sun, and for the precious
ings [5]put forth by the [6]moon,
15 And for the chief things of
e ancient mountains, and for the
recious things [r]of the lasting hills,
16 And for the precious things of the
arth and fulness thereof, and *for* the
ood will of [s]him that dwelt in the
ush: let *the blessing* come upon the
ead of Joseph, and upon the top of
e head of him *that was* separated
om his brethren.
17 His glory *is like* the firstling of his
ullock, and his horns *are like* the
orns of [7]unicorns: with them he shall
push the people together to the ends
f the earth: and they *are* the ten
housands of Ē´-phră-ĭm, and they *are*
he thousands of Mă-năs´-sēh.
18 ¶ And of Zĕ-bū´-lŭn he said, Re-
oice, Zĕ-bū´-lŭn, in thy going out;
nd, Ĭs´-să-chăr, in thy tents.
19 They shall [u]call the people unto
he mountain; there [v]they shall offer
acrifices of righteousness: for they
hall suck *of* the abundance of the
eas, and *of* treasures hid in the sand.
20 ¶ And of Gad he said, Blessed *be*
e that [w]enlargeth Gad: he dwelleth
s a lion, and teareth the arm with the
rown of the head.
21 And he [x]provided the first part for
imself, because there, *in* a portion of
he lawgiver, *was he* [8]seated; and [y]he
ame with the heads of the people, he
xecuted the justice of the LORD, and
is judgments with Israel.
22 ¶ And of Dan he said, Dan *is* a
ion's whelp: [z]he shall leap from Bā´-
shăn.
23 ¶ And of Năph´-tă-lī he said, O
Năph´-tă-lī, satisfied with favour, and
ull with the blessing of the LORD:
possess thou the west and the south.
24 ¶ And of Asher he said, *Let* Asher
be blessed with children; let him be
acceptable to his brethren, and let him
[a]dip his foot in oil.
25 [9]Thy shoes *shall be* iron and brass;
and as thy days, *so shall* thy strength
be.
26 ¶ *There is* [c]none like unto the God
of Jĕ-shŭ´-rŭn, [d]*who* rideth upon the
heaven in thy help, and in his excellency on the sky.
27 The eternal God *is thy* [e]refuge,
and underneath *are* the everlasting
arms: and he shall thrust out the enemy from before thee; and shall say,
Destroy *them*.
28 Israel [f]then shall dwell in safety
alone: the fountain of Jacob *shall be*
upon a land of corn and wine; also his
heavens shall drop down dew.
29 Happy [g]*art* thou, O Israel: who
[h]*is* like unto thee, O people saved by
the LORD, the shield of thy help, and
who *is* the sword of thy excellency!
and thine enemies [10]shall be found
liars unto thee; and thou shalt tread
upon their high places.

CHAPTER 34

AND Moses went up from the plains
of Moab unto the mountain of
Nē´-bō, to the top of [1]Pĭs´-găh, that *is*
over against Jericho. And the LORD
shewed him all the land of Gilead,
[a]unto Dan,
2 And all Năph´-tă-lī, and the land of
Ē´-phră-ĭm, and Mă-năs´-sēh, and all
the land of Judah, [b]unto the utmost
sea,
3 And the south, and the plain of the
valley of Jericho, [c]the city of palm
trees, unto Zō´-ăr.
4 And the LORD said unto him, This
is the land which I sware unto Abraham, unto Isaac, and unto Jacob, saying, I will give it unto thy seed: I have
caused thee to see *it* with thine eyes,
but thou shalt not go over thither.
5 ¶ So [d]Moses the servant of the
LORD died there in the land of Moab,
according to the word of the LORD.
6 And he buried him in a valley in
the land of Moab, over against Bĕth–
pē´-ôr: but [e]no man knoweth of his
sepulchre unto this day.
7 ¶ And [f]Moses *was* an hundred and
twenty years old when he died: his
[g]eye was not dim, nor [2]his natural
force abated.
8 ¶ And the children of Israel wept
for Moses in the plains of Moab
[h]thirty days: so the days of weeping
and mourning for Moses were ended.
9 ¶ And Joshua the son of Nun was
full of the [i]spirit of wisdom; for
[j]Moses had laid his hands upon him:
and the children of Israel hearkened

o Ps. 20.3.
p Gen. 49.25.
q Gen. 27.28.
5 thrust forth.
6 moons.
r Hab. 3.6.
s Ex. 3.2,4. Acts 7.30.
7 an unicorn.
t 1 Ki. 22.11.
u Isa. 2.3.
v Ps. 4.5.
w 1 Chr. 12.8.
x Num. 32. 16.
8 cieled.
y Num. 32. 16,21.
z Josh. 19.47.
a Josh. 19.32.
b Job 29.6.
9 Or, Under thy shoes shall be iron.
c Ps. 86.8. Jer. 10.6.
d Ps. 68.4,33, 34. Hab. 3.8.
e Ps. 90.1.
f Num. 23.9. Jer. 23.6.
g Ps. 144.15.
h 2 Sam. 7.23.
10 Or, shall be subdued.

CHAP. 34

1 Or, the hill.
a Judg. 18.28.
b Ex. 23.31. Num. 34.6. ch. 11.24.
c Judg. 1.16. 2 Chr. 28.15.
d ch. 32.50. Josh. 1.1,2. Mal. 4.4.
e Jude 9.
f ch. 31.2.
g Gen. 27.1.
2 moisture fled.
h Gen. 50.3. Num. 20.29. 1 Sam. 25.1. Isa. 57.1.
i Ex. 31.3. Num. 11.17. 1 Ki. 9.12. Isa. 11.2.
j Num. 27.18.

unto him, and did as the LORD commanded Moses.
10 ¶ And there [k]arose not a prophet
since in Israel like unto Moses, whom
[l]the LORD knew face to face,
11 In all the signs and the wonders,

k ch. 18.15, 18.
l Ex. 33.11. Num. 12.6. ch. 5.4.

which the LORD sent him to do in th
land of Egypt to Pharaoh, and to a
his servants, and to all his land,
12 And in all that mighty hand, an
in all the great terror which Mos
shewed in the sight of all Israel.

THE

BOOK OF JOSHUA

CHAPTER 1

NOW after the death of Moses the
servant of the LORD it came to
pass, that the LORD spake unto Joshua
the son of Nun, Moses' minister,
[a]saying,
2 Moses [b]my servant is dead; now
therefore arise, go over this Jordan,
thou, and all this people, unto the land
which I do give to them, *even* to the
children of Israel.
3 Every [c]place that the sole of your
foot shall tread upon, that have I given
unto you, as I said unto Moses.
4 From [d]the wilderness and this
Lĕb-ā-non even unto the great river,
the river Eû-phrā-tēs, all the land of
the Hittites, and unto the great sea
toward the going down of the sun,
shall be your coast.
5 There [e]shall not any man be able to
stand before thee all the days of thy
life: as [f]I was with Moses, *so* I will be
with thee: I will [g]not fail thee, nor forsake thee.
6 Be strong and of a good courage:
for [1]unto this people shalt thou divide
for an inheritance the land, which
I sware unto their fathers to give
them.
7 Only be thou strong and very
courageous, that thou mayest observe
to do according to all the law, [h]which
Moses my servant commanded thee:
turn not from it *to* the right hand or *to*
the left, that thou mayest [2]prosper
whithersoever thou goest.
8 This [i]book of the law shall not depart out of thy mouth; but [j]thou shalt
meditate therein day and night, that
thou mayest observe to do according
to all that is written therein: for [k]then
thou shalt make thy way prosperous,
and then thou shalt [3]have good success.
9 Have not I commanded thee? Be
strong and of a good courage; be [l]not
afraid, neither be thou dismayed: for

CHAP. 1
a Deut. 1.38.
b Deut. 34.5.
c Deut. 11.24.
d Gen. 15.18. Ex. 23.31. Num. 34.3. Deut. 1.7. 1 Chr. 5.9.
e Deut. 7.24. Ps. 46.11. Rom. 8.31, 37.
f Ex. 3.12.
g Deut. 31.6.
1 Or, thou shalt cause this people to inherit the land.
h Num. 27. 23. ch. 11.15.
2 Or, do wisely.
i Deut. 17.18, 19.
j Ps. 1.2.
k 1 Chr. 32. 13. Pro. 3.1.
3 Or, do wisely.
l Ps. 27.1. Jer. 1.8.
m Deut. 9.1. ch. 3.2.
n Num. 32. 20. ch. 22.2,3,4.
4 marshalled by five, as Ex. 13.18.
o ch. 22.4.
p Gen. 21.22. Gen. 26.24, 28. 1 Sam. 16. 18. 1 Ki. 1.37. Ps. 20.1-4,9. Rom. 8.31.

the LORD thy God *is* with thee whit
ersoever thou goest.
10 ¶ Then Joshua commanded th
officers of the people, saying,
11 Pass through the host, and com
mand the people, saying, Prepare yo
victuals; for [m]within three days y
shall pass over this Jordan, to go in t
possess the land, which the LOR
your God giveth you to posses
it.
12 ¶ And to the Reubenites, and t
the Gadites, and to half the tribe o
Mă-năs-sēh, spake Joshua, saying,
13 Remember [n]the word whic
Moses the servant of the LORD com
manded you, saying, The LORD you
God hath given you rest, and hat
given you this land.
14 Your wives, your little ones, an
your cattle, shall remain in the lan
which Moses gave you on this sid
Jordan; but ye shall pass before you
brethren [4]armed, all the mighty me
of valour, and help them;
15 Until the LORD have given you
brethren rest, as *he hath given* you, an
they also have possessed the lan
which the LORD your God giveth
them: [o]then ye shall return unto th
land of your possession, and enjoy it
which Moses the LORD's servant gav
you on this side Jordan toward th
sunrising.
16 ¶ And they answered Joshua
saying, All that thou commandest u
we will do, and whithersoever tho
sendest us, we will go.
17 According as we hearkened unto
Moses in all things, so will we hearken
unto thee: only the LORD thy God [p]be
with thee, as he was with Moses.
18 Whosoever *he be* that doth rebel
against thy commandment, and will
not hearken unto thy words in all that
thou commandest him, he shall be
put to death: only be strong and of a
good courage.

CHAPTER 2

AND Joshua the son of Nun [1]sent
[a]out of Shit-tim two men to spy
ecretly, saying, Go view the land,
ven Jericho. And they went, and
came into an harlot's house, named
Rahab, and [2]lodged there.
2 And [d]it was told the king of Jericho,
aying, Behold, there came men in
ither to night of the children of Israel
o search out the country.
3 And the king of Jericho sent unto
ahab, saying, Bring forth the men
hat are come to thee, which are en-
ered into thine house: for they be
ome to search out all the country.
4 And [e]the woman took the two men,
nd hid them, and said thus, There
ame men unto me, but I wist not
hence they *were:*
5 And it came to pass *about the time*
f shutting of the gate, when it was
ark, that the men went out: whither
he men went I wot not: pursue after
hem quickly; for ye shall overtake
hem.
6 But [f]she had brought them up to
he roof of the house, and hid them
ith the stalks of flax, which she had
aid in order upon the roof.
7 And the men pursued after them
he way to Jordan unto the fords: and
s soon as they which pursued after
hem were gone out, they shut the
ate.
8 ¶ And before they were laid down,
he came up unto them upon the roof;
9 And she said unto the men, I know
hat the LORD hath given you the land,
nd that your [g]terror is fallen upon
s, and that all the inhabitants of the
and [3]faint because of you.
10 For we have heard how the LORD
ried [h]up the water of the Red sea for
ou, when ye came out of Egypt; and
what ye did unto the two kings of
he Amorites, that *were* on the other
ide Jordan, Si-hŏn and Og, whom ye
tterly destroyed.
11 And as soon as we had [i]heard
hese things, [k]our hearts did melt,
either [4]did there remain any more
ourage in any man, because of you:
or [l]the LORD your God, he *is* God in
eaven above, and in earth beneath.
12 Now therefore, I pray you, swear
unto me by the LORD, since I have
hewed you kindness, that ye will also
hew kindness unto [n]my father's
ouse, and give me a true token:
13 And *that* ye will save alive my
ather, and my mother, and my breth-
en, and my sisters, and all that they
have, and deliver our lives from death.
14 And the men answered her, Our
life [5]for yours, if ye utter not this our
business. And it shall be, when the
LORD hath given us the land, that [o]we
will deal kindly and truly with thee.
15 Then she [p]let them down by a
cord through the window: for her
house *was* upon the town wall, and
she dwelt upon the wall.
16 And she said unto them, Get you
to the mountain, lest the pursuers
meet you; and hide yourselves there
three days, until the pursuers be returned: and afterward may ye go your
way.
17 And the men said unto her, We
will be blameless [q]of this thine oath
which thou hast made us swear.
18 Behold, *when* we come into the
land, thou shalt bind this line of scarlet thread in the window which thou
didst let us down by: [r]and thou shalt
[6]bring thy father, and thy mother, and
thy brethren, and all thy father's
household, home unto thee.
19 And it shall be, *that* whosoever
shall go [s]out of the doors of thy house
into the street, his blood *shall be* upon
his head, and we *will be* guiltless: and
whosoever shall be with thee in the
house, [t]his blood *shall be* on our head
if *any* hand be upon him.
20 And if thou utter this our business,
then we will be quit of thine oath
which thou hast made us to swear.
21 And she said, According unto
your words, so *be* it. And she sent
them away, and they departed: and
she bound the scarlet line in the window.
22 And they went, and came unto the
mountain, and abode there three days,
until the pursuers were returned: and
the pursuers sought *them* throughout
all the way, but found *them* not.
23 ¶ So the two men returned, and
descended from the mountain, and
passed over, and came to Joshua the
son of Nun, and told him all *things* that
befell them:
24 And they said unto Joshua, Truly
[u]the LORD hath delivered into our
hands all the land; for even all the inhabitants of the country do [7]faint because of us.

CHAPTER 3

AND Joshua rose early in the morning; and they removed from [a]Shit-
tim, and came to Jordan, he and all
the children of Israel, and lodged there
before they passed over.

CHAP. 2
1 Or, had sent.
a Num. 25.1.
b Heb. 11.31. Jas. 2.25.
c Matt. 1.5. But it is doubtful whether this is the same person.
2 lay.
d Ps. 127.1. Pro. 21.30.
e 2 Sam. 17. 19.
f Ex. 1.17.
g Gen. 35.5. Ex. 15.15. Deut. 2.25.
3 melt.
h ch. 4.23.
i Num. 21.24, 34,35.
j Ex. 15.14, 15.
k ch. 5.1. ch. 7.5. Isa. 13.7.
4 rose up.
l Deut. 4.39. 1 Ki. 8.60. Ps. 83.18. Dan. 4.34, 35. Zech. 8.20, 23.
m I Sam. 20. 14,15,17.
n Eph. 6.1,2. 1 Tim. 5.8.
5 instead of you to die.
o Matt. 5.7.
p Acts 9.25. Heb. 11.31.
q Ex. 20.7.
r Gen. 7.1. Gen. 19.12, 17. ch. 6.23. Esther 8.6. Acts 11.14. 2 Tim. 1.16.
6 gather.
s Num. 35. 26,27.
t Matt. 27.25.
u Ex. 23.31. ch. 6.2. ch. 21.44.
7 melt.

CHAP. 3
a Num. 25.1. ch. 2.1.

2 And it came to pass [b]after three days, that the officers went through the host;

3 And they commanded the people, saying, [c]When ye see the ark of the covenant of the LORD your God, [d]and the priests the Levites bearing it, then ye shall remove from your place, and go after it.

4 Yet [e]there shall be a space between you and it, about two thousand cubits by measure: come not near unto it, that ye may know the way by which ye must go: for ye have not passed *this* way [1]heretofore.

5 And Joshua said unto the people, Sanctify [f]yourselves: for to morrow the LORD will do wonders among you.

6 And Joshua spake unto the priests saying, [g]Take up the ark of the covenant, and pass over before the people. And they took up the ark of the covenant, and went before the people.

7 ¶ And the LORD said unto Joshua, This day will I begin to magnify [h]thee in the sight of all Israel, that they may know that, as I was with Moses, *so* I will be with thee.

8 And thou shalt command the priests that bear the ark of the covenant, saying, When ye are come to the brink of the water of Jordan, ye shall stand still in Jordan.

9 ¶ And Joshua said unto the children of Israel, Come hither, and hear the words of the LORD your God.

10 And Joshua said, Hereby ye shall know that the [i]living God *is* among you, and *that* he will without fail [j]drive out from before you the Canaanites, and the Hittites, and the Hī́-vītes, and the Pĕ-rĭź-zītes, and the Gĭŕ-gă-shītes, and the Amorites, and the Jĕb́-ū-sītes.

11 Behold, the ark of the covenant of [k]the Lord of all the earth passeth over before you into Jordan.

12 Now therefore [l]take you twelve men out of the tribes of Israel, out of every tribe a man.

13 And it shall come to pass, as soon as the soles of the feet of the priests that bear the ark of the LORD, the Lord of all the earth, shall rest in the waters of Jordan, *that* the waters of Jordan shall be cut off *from* the waters that come down from above; and they [m]shall stand upon an heap.

14 ¶ And it came to pass, when the people removed from their tents, to pass over Jordan, and the priests bearing the [n]ark of the covenant before the people;

b ch. 1.10,11.
c Num. 10.33.
d Deut. 31.9.
e Ex. 19.12. Deut. 28.58. 1 Chr. 16.30. Ps. 2.11. Heb. 12.28.
1 since yesterday and the third day.
f Lev. 20.7. Num. 11.18. ch. 7.13. 1 Sam. 16.5.
g Num. 4.15.
h ch. 4.14. 1 Chr. 29.25. 2 Chr. 1.1.
i Deut. 5.26. 1 Sam. 17. 26. 2 Ki. 19.4. Hosea 1.10. Matt. 16.16.
j Ex. 33.2. Deut. 7.1. Ps. 44.2.
k Ps. 24.1. Job 41.11. Micah 4.13. Zech. 4.14.
l ch. 4.2.
m Ex. 15.8. Ps. 78.13. Hab. 3.15.
n Ex 25.10. Num. 10.3. 2 Chr. 6.41. Ps. 132.8. Acts 7.45. Heb. 9.4.
o 1 Chr. 12. 15. Jer. 12.5.
2 Occasioned by melting of the snow on Lebanon.
p ch. 4.18. ch. 5.10,12.
q 1 Ki. 4.12. 1 Ki. 7.46.
r Deut. 3.17.
s Gen. 14.3. Num. 34.3. Deut. 3.17.
t Ex. 14.29. Heb. 11.29.

CHAP. 4

a Deut. 27.2. ch. 3.17.
b Num. 13.2. Num. 34.18. Deut. 1.23. ch. 1.4-15. ch. 3.12. 1 Ki. 18.31.
c Ex. 12.26. Deut. 6.20. Ps. 44.1. Ps. 48.13,14. Ps. 78.3,4,5, 6. Isa. 38.16.
1 to-morrow.
d ch. 3.13.
e Ex. 12.14. Num. 16.40. 1 Cor. 11.24.

15 And as they that bare the a
were come unto Jordan, and the fe
of the priests that bare the ark we
dipped in the brim of the water, (f
[o]Jordan overfloweth [2]all his banks [p]a
the time of harvest,)

16 That the waters which came dov
from above stood *and* rose up upc
an heap very far from the city Adar
that *is* beside [q]Zăŕ-ĕ-tăn: and tho
that came down toward [r]the sea of tl
plain, *even* the [s]salt sea, failed, *ar*
were cut off: and the people passe
over right against Jericho.

17 And the priests that bare the a
of the covenant of the LORD stoc
firm on dry ground in the midst
Jordan, [t]and all the Israelites passe
over on dry ground, until all the pe
ple were passed clean over Jordan.

CHAPTER 4

AND it came to pass, when all tl
people were clean passed ov
[a]Jordan, that the LORD spake un
Joshua, saying,

2 Take [b]you twelve men out of tl
people, out of every tribe a man,

3 And command ye them, sayin
Take you hence out of the midst
Jordan, out of the place where tl
priests' feet stood firm, twelve stone
and ye shall carry them over with yo
and leave them in the lodging plac
where ye shall lodge this night.

4 Then Joshua called the twelve me
whom he had prepared of the childre
of Israel, out of every tribe a man:

5 And Joshua said unto them, Pa
over before the ark of the LORD yo
God into the midst of Jordan, ar
take ye up every man of you a stor
upon his shoulder, according unto tl
number of the tribes of the children
Israel:

6 That this may be a sign among yo
that when [c]your children ask *the*
fathers [1]in time to come, sayin
What *mean* ye by these stones?

7 Then ye shall answer them, Th
[d]the waters of Jordan were cut off b
fore the ark of the covenant of tl
LORD; when it passed over Jorda
the waters of Jordan were cut off: ar
these stones shall be for a [e]memori
unto the children of Israel for ever.

8 And the children of Israel did so
Joshua commanded, and took u
twelve stones out of the midst of Jo
dan, as the LORD spake unto Joshu
according to the number of the trib
of the children of Israel, and carrie
them over with them unto the plac

here they lodged, and laid them
ɔwn there.
And Joshua [f]set up twelve stones
the midst of Jordan, in the place
here the feet of the priests which
re the ark of the covenant stood:
d they are there [2]unto this day.
0 ¶ For the priests which bare the
k stood in the midst of Jordan, until
ery thing was finished that the LORD
mmanded Joshua to speak unto the
ople, according to all that Moses
mmanded Joshua: and the people
sted and passed over.
1 And it came to pass, when all the
ople were clean passed over, that
e ark of the LORD passed over, and
e priests, in the presence of the
ople.
2 And [g]the children of Reuben, and
e children of Gad, and half the
ibe of Mă-năs-sēh, passed over arm-
 before the children of Israel, as
oses spake unto them:
3 About forty thousand [3]prepared
r war passed over before the LORD
to battle, to the plains of Jericho.
4 ¶ On that day the LORD magnified
oshua in the sight of all Israel; and
ey feared him, as they feared Moses,
 the days of his life.
5 And the LORD spake unto Joshua,
ying,
6 Command the priests that bear
he ark of the testimony, that they
me up out of Jordan.
7 Joshua therefore commanded the
iests, saying, Come ye up out of
rdan.
8 And it came to pass, when the
iests that bare the ark of the coven-
t of the LORD were come up out of
e midst of Jordan, *and* the soles of
e priests' feet were [4]lifted up unto
e dry land, that the waters of Jordan
turned unto their place, and [5]flowed
er all his banks, as *they did* be-
re.
9 ¶ And the people came up out of
rdan on the tenth *day* of the first
onth, and encamped [j]in Gĭl-găl, in
e east border of Jericho.
0 And those twelve stones, which
ey took out of Jordan, did Joshua
tch in Gĭl-găl.
1 And he spake unto the children of
rael, saying, When your children
all ask their fathers [6]in time to come,
ying, What *mean* these stones?
2 Then ye shall let your children
now, saying, Israel came over this
rdan on dry land.
3 For the LORD your God dried up

f Gen. 28.18. ch. 24.27. 1 Sam. 7.12.
2 B.C. 1427.
g Num. 32. 20.
3 Or, ready armed.
h ch. 3.7. 1 Sam. 2.30. 1 Chr. 29.12, 25. 2 Chr. 1.1.
i Ex. 25.16. Rev. 11.19.
4 plucked up.
5 went.
j ch. 5.9. 1 Sam. 11. 14,15. Amos. 4.4. Micah. 6.5.
6 to-morrow.
k Ex. 14.21. Neh. 9.11. Ps. 77.16,19. Isa. 43.16.
l Ex. 9.16. Deut. 28.10. 1 Sam. 17. 46. 1 Ki. 8.42. 2 Ki. 5.15. Ps. 89.7. Ps. 106.8. Dan. 3.26-29.
m 1 Chr. 29. 12. Ps. 89.13.
n Ex. 14.31. Ps. 76.6-8. Jer. 10.7.
7 all days.

CHAP. 5

a Num. 13. 29.
b Ex. 15.14. Ps. 48.6.
c 1 Ki. 10.5.
1 Or, knives of flints.
2 Or, Gibeah-haaraloth.
d Num. 14. 29. Num. 26.64.
e Deut. 1.3. Ps. 95.10.
f Heb. 3.11.
g Num. 14. 31.
3 when the people had made an end to be circumcised.
h Gen. 34.25.
i Lev. 18.3. ch. 24.14. 1 Sam. 14.6. Eze. 20.7.

the waters of Jordan from before you,
until ye were passed over, as the LORD
your God did to the Red sea, [k]which
he dried up from before us, until we
were gone over:
24 That [l]all the people of the earth
might know the hand of the LORD,
that it *is* [m]mighty: that ye might [n]fear
the LORD your God [7]for ever.

CHAPTER 5

AND it came to pass, when all the
kings of the Amorites, which *were*
on the side of Jordan westward, and
all the kings of the Canaanites, [a]which
were by the sea, heard [b]that the LORD
had dried up the waters of Jordan
from before the children of Israel, until we were passed over, that their
heart melted, [c]neither was there spirit
in them any more, because of the
children of Israel.
2 ¶ At that time the LORD said unto
Joshua, Make thee [1]sharp knives, and
circumcise again the children of Israel
the second time.
3 And Joshua made him sharp
knives, and circumcised the children
of Israel at [2]the hill of the foreskins.
4 And this *is* the cause why Joshua
did circumcise: [d]All the people that
came out of Egypt, *that were* males,
even all the men of war, died in the
wilderness by the way, after they
came out of Egypt.
5 Now all the people that came out
were circumcised: but all the people
that were born in the wilderness by the
way as they came forth out of Egypt,
them they had not circumcised.
6 For the children of Israel walked
[e]forty years in the wilderness, till all
the people *that were* men of war,
which came out of Egypt, were consumed, because they obeyed not the
voice of the LORD: unto whom the
LORD sware that [f]he would not shew
them the land, which the LORD sware
unto their fathers that he would give
us, a land that floweth with milk and
honey.
7 And [g]their children, *whom* he raised
up in their stead, them Joshua circumcised: for they were uncircumcised,
because they had not circumcised
them by the way.
8 And it came to pass, [3]when they
had done circumcising all the people,
that they abode in their places in the
camp, [h]till they were whole.
9 And the LORD said unto Joshua,
This day have I rolled away [i]the reproach of Egypt from off you. Where-

fore the name of the place is called
[4]Gĭl-găl unto this day.
10 ¶ And the children of Israel encamped in Gĭl-găl, and kept the passover [j]on the fourteenth day of the
month at even in the plains of Jericho.
11 And they did eat of the old corn
of the land on the morrow after the
passover, unleavened cakes, and
parched *corn* in the selfsame day.
12 ¶ And the măn-nă ceased on the
morrow after they had eaten of the
old corn of the land; neither had the
children of Israel măn-nă any more;
but they did eat of the fruit of the land
of Canaan that year.
13 ¶ And it came to pass, when
Joshua was by Jericho, that he lifted
up his eyes and looked, and, behold,
there stood [k]a man over against him
with his sword drawn in his hand: and
Joshua went unto him, and said unto
him, *Art* thou for us, or for our adversaries?
14 And he said, Nay; but *as* [5]captain
of the host of the LORD am I now
come. And Joshua fell [l]on his face to
the earth, and did worship, and said
unto him, What saith my lord unto his
servant?
15 And the captain of the LORD's
host said unto Joshua, [m]Loose thy
shoe from off thy foot; for the place
whereon thou standest *is* holy. And
Joshua did so.

CHAPTER 6

NOW Jericho [1]was straitly shut up
because of the children of Israel:
none went out, and none came in.
2 And the LORD said unto Joshua,
See, [a]I have given into thine hand
Jericho, and the king thereof, *and* the
mighty men of valour.
3 And ye shall compass the city, all
ye men of war, *and* go round about the
city once. Thus shalt thou do six days.
4 And seven priests shall bear before
the ark seven [b]trumpets of rams'
horns: and the seventh day ye shall
compass the city seven times, and [c]the
priests shall blow with the trumpets.
5 And it shall come to pass, that
when they make a long *blast* with the
ram's horn, *and* when ye hear the
sound of the trumpet, all the people
shall shout with a great shout; and the
wall of the city shall fall down [2]flat,
and the people shall ascend up every
man straight before him.
6 ¶ And Joshua the son of Nun called
the priests, and said unto them, Take up
the ark of the covenant, and let seven

4 That is, Rolling.
j Ex. 12.6. Num. 9.5.
k Gen. 18.2. Zech. 1.8. Acts 1.10.
5 Or, prince.
l Gen. 17.3. Lev. 9.24. Num. 16.22, 45.
m Ex. 3.5. Lev. 19.2. 1 Sam. 2.2. 1 Chr. 16.25, 29. Ps. 22.3. Ps. 29.2. Ps. 33.8. Ps. 76.7, 11. Ps. 89.7. Ps. 96.4, 9. Isa. 6.3. Acts 7.33. Rev. 4.8.

CHAP. 6

1 did shut up, and was shut up.
a ch. 2.9. 2 Sam. 5.19. Neh. 9.24. Dan. 5.18, 19.
b Judg. 7.16.
c Num. 10.8.
2 under it.
d ch. 4.13.
3 That is, before the ark.
e Num. 10. 25. Isa. 42.12, 13.
4 gathering host.
5 make your voice to be heard.
f Deut. 31.25.
g 1 Chr. 15. 26. Gal. 6.9.
h Judg. 7.20. 2 Chr. 13.14.
6 Or, devoted. Lev. 27.28. Micah 4.13.
i Gen. 12.3. ch. 2.4. 1 Sam. 15.6. Matt. 10.41. Heb. 6.10.
j Deut. 7.26. ch. 7.1, 11, 12. Isa. 52.11. Rom. 12.9. 2 Cor. 6.17. Eph. 5.11. 1 Thes. 5.22.

priests bear seven trumpets of ram
horns before the ark of the LORD.
7 And he said unto the people, Pa
on, and compass the city, and let hi
that is armed pass on before the ar
of the LORD.
8 ¶ And it came to pass, when Joshu
had spoken unto the people, that th
seven priests bearing the seven trum
pets of rams' horns [d]passed on [3]be
fore the LORD, and blew with th
trumpets: and the ark of the covenan
of the LORD followed them.
9 ¶ And the armed men went befor
the priests that blew with the trum
pets, [e]and the [4]rereward came afte
the ark, *the priests* going on, an
blowing with the trumpets.
10 And Joshua had commanded th
people, saying, Ye shall not shou
nor [5]make any noise with your voic
neither shall *any* word proceed out o
your mouth, until the day I bid yo
shout; then shall ye shout.
11 So the ark of the LORD compasse
the city, going about *it* once: and the
came into the camp, and lodged in th
camp.
12 ¶ And Joshua rose early in th
morning, [f]and the priests took up th
ark of the LORD.
13 And seven priests bearing seve
trumpets of rams' horns before th
ark of the LORD [g]went on continuall
and blew with the trumpets: and th
armed men went before them; but th
rereward came after the ark of th
LORD, *the priests* going on, and blov
ing with the trumpets.
14 And the second day they con
passed the city once, and returned ir
to the camp: so they did six days.
15 And it came to pass on the sevent
day, that they rose early about th
dawning of the day, and compasse
the city after the same manner seve
times: only on that day they compas
ed the city seven times.
16 And it came to pass at the sevent
time, when the priests blew with th
trumpets, Joshua said unto the pe
ple, [h]Shout; for the LORD hath give
you the city.
17 ¶ And the city shall be [6]accurse
even it, and all that *are* therein, to th
LORD: only Rahab the harlot sha
live, she and all that *are* with her in th
house, [i]because she hid the messe
gers that we sent.
18 And ye, [j]in any wise keep *you*
selves from the accursed thing, lest y
make *yourselves* accursed, when y
take of the accursed thing, and mak

he camp of Israel a curse, [k]and
rouble it.
19 But all the silver, and gold, and
vessels of brass and iron, *are* [7]conse-
crated unto the LORD: they shall come
nto the treasury of the LORD.
20 So the people shouted when *the*
priests blew with the trumpets: and it
ame to pass, when the people heard
he sound of the trumpet, and the
people shouted with a great shout,
hat [l]the wall fell down [8]flat, so that
he people went up into the city,
very man straight before him, and
hey took the city.
21 And they [m]utterly destroyed all
hat *was* in the city, both man and wo-
nan, young and old, and ox, and
heep, and ass, with the edge of the
word.
22 But Joshua had said unto the two
nen that had spied out the country,
Go into the harlot's house, and bring
out thence the woman, and all that
he hath, [n]as ye sware unto her.
23 And the young men that were
pies went in, and brought out Rahab,
and her father, and her mother, and
er brethren, and all that she had; and
hey brought out all her [9]kindred, and
eft them without the camp of Israel.
24 And they burnt the city with fire,
nd all that *was* therein: only the sil-
er, and the gold, and the vessels of
rass and of iron, they put into the
reasury of the house of the LORD.
25 And Joshua saved Rahab the har-
ot alive, and her father's household,
nd all that she had; and [p]she dwelleth
Israel *even* [10]unto this day; because
e hid the messengers, which Joshua
nt to spy out Jericho.
26 ¶ And Joshua adjured *them* at
at time, saying, [q]Cursed *be* the man
efore the LORD, that riseth up and
uildeth this city Jericho: he shall lay
e foundation thereof in his firstborn,
d in his youngest *son* shall he set up
e gates of it.
27 So [r]the LORD was with Joshua;
d his [s]fame was *noised* throughout
l the country.

CHAPTER 7

BUT the children of Israel committed a trespass in the accursed
ing: [a]for [1]Ā-chăn, the son of Cär-
ī, the son of [2]Zăb-dī, the son of Zē-
h, of the tribe of Judah, took of the
cursed thing: and the anger of the
ORD was kindled against the children
Israel.
And Joshua sent men from Jericho
to Ā-ī, which *is* beside Bĕth-ā-vĕn, on
the east side of Beth-el, and spake unto them, saying, Go up and view the
country. And the men went up and
viewed Ā-ī.
3 And they returned to Joshua, and
said unto him, Let not all the people
go up; but let [3]about two or three
thousand men go up and smite Ā-ī;
and make not all the people to labour
thither; for they *are but* few.
4 So there went up thither of the people about three thousand men: and
[b]they fled before the men of Ā-ī.
5 And the men of Ā-ī smote of them
about thirty and six men: for they
chased them *from* before the gate *even*
unto Shĕb-ă-rĭm, and smote them [4]in
the going down: wherefore [c]the hearts
of the people melted, and became as
water.
6 ¶ And Joshua [d]rent his clothes, and
fell to the earth upon his face before
the ark of the LORD until the eventide,
he and the elders of Israel, and [e]put
dust upon their heads.
7 And Joshua said, Alas, O Lord
GOD, wherefore [f]hast thou at all
brought this people over Jordan, to
deliver us into the hand of the Amorites, to destroy us? would to God we
had been content, and dwelt on the
other side Jordan!
8 O Lord, what shall I say, when
Israel turneth their [5]backs before their
enemies!
9 For the Canaanites and all the inhabitants of the land shall hear *of it*,
and shall environ us round, and [g]cut
off our name from the earth: and
[h]what wilt thou do unto thy great
name?
10 ¶ And the LORD said unto Joshua,
Get thee up; wherefore [6]liest thou
thus upon thy face?
11 Israel hath sinned, and they have
also transgressed my covenant which
I commanded them: for [i]they have
even taken of the accursed thing, and
have also stolen, and [j]dissembled also,
and they have put *it* even among their
own stuff.
12 Therefore [k]the children of Israel
could not stand before their enemies,
but turned *their* backs before their enemies, because they were [l]accursed:
neither will I be with you any more,
except ye destroy the accursed from
among you.
13 Up, [m]sanctify the people, and
say, Sanctify [n]yourselves against to
morrow: for thus saith the LORD God
of Israel, *There is* an accursed thing in

k ch. 7.25. Jonah 1.12.
7 holiness.
l Heb. 11.30.
8 under it.
m Deut. 7.2. 1 Sam. 15.3, 8,18,19. 1 Ki. 20.42. Jer. 48.18. Rev. 18.21.
n ch. 2.14. Heb. 11.31.
o ch. 2.13.
9 families.
p Matt. 1.5.
10 B.C. 1427.
q 1 Ki. 16.34. Mal. 1.4.
r Gen. 39.2. ch. 1.5. ch. 3.7. Judg. 1.19. 2 Sam. 7.9. Rom. 8.31.
s ch. 9.1,3. 1 Sam. 2.30.

CHAP. 7
a ch. 22.20.
1 1 Chr. 2.7. Achar.
2 Or, Zimri. 1 Chr. 2.6.
3 about two thousand men, or, about three thousand men.
b Lev. 26.17. Deut. 28.25. Isa. 30.17. Isa. 59.2.
4 Or, in Morad.
c Lev. 26.36. ch. 2.9,11. Ps. 22.14.
d Gen. 37.29. 2 Sam. 13. 31. Esther 4.1. Acts 14.14.
e 1 Sam. 4.12. 2 Sam. 1.2. Neh. 9.1. Job 2.12.
f Ex. 5.22.
5 necks.
g Ps. 83.4.
h Ex. 32.12.
6 fallest.
i ch. 6.17.
j Acts 5.1.
k Num. 14. 45.
l Deut. 7.26. ch. 6.18.
m Ex. 19.10.
n ch. 3.5.

the midst of thee, O Israel: thou canst
not stand before thine enemies, until
ye take away the accursed thing from
among you.
14 In the morning therefore ye shall
be brought according to your tribes:
and it shall be, *that* the tribe which
[o]the LORD taketh shall come according to the families *thereof;* and the
family which the LORD shall take shall
come by households; and the household which the LORD shall take shall
come man by man.
15 And [p]it shall be, *that* he that is
taken with the accursed thing shall be
burnt with fire, he and all that he hath:
because he hath transgressed the
covenant of the LORD, and because he
[q]hath wrought [7]folly in Israel.
16 ¶ So Joshua rose up early in the
morning, and brought Israel by their
tribes; and the tribe of Judah was
taken:
17 And he brought the family of Judah; and he took the family of the
Zär'-hītes: and he brought the family
of the Zär'-hītes man by man; and
Zăb'-dī was taken:
18 And he brought his household
man by man; and [r]Ā'-chăn, the son of
Cär'-mī, the son of Zăb'-dī, the son of
Zē'-räh, of the tribe of Judah, was
taken.
19 And Joshua said unto Ā'-chăn, My
son, give, [s]I pray thee, glory to the
LORD God of Israel, [t]and make confession unto him; and tell me now
what thou hast done; hide *it* not from
me.
20 And Ā'-chăn answered Joshua,
and said, Indeed I have sinned against
the LORD God of Israel, and thus and
thus have I done:
21 When I saw among the spoils a
goodly Babylonish garment, and two
hundred shekels of silver, and a
[8]wedge of gold of fifty shekels weight,
then I [u]coveted them, and took them;
and, behold, they *are* hid in the earth
in the midst of my tent, and the silver
under it.
22 ¶ So Joshua sent messengers, and
they ran unto the tent; and, behold, *it
was* hid in his tent, and the silver under
it.
23 And they took them out of the
midst of the tent, and brought them
unto Joshua, and unto all the children
of Israel, and [9]laid them out before the
LORD.
24 And Joshua, and all Israel with
him, took Ā'-chăn the son of Zē'-räh,
and the silver, and the garment, and

o 1 Sam. 10. 19-21. Pro. 16.33. Jonah 1.7. Acts 1.24-26.
p 1 Sam. 14. 38,39.
q Gen. 34.7.
7 Or, wickedness.
r Gen. 4.7. Num. 32.23. Pro. 13.21. Jer. 2.26. Acts 5.1-10.
s 1 Sam. 6.5. John 9.24.
t Num. 5.6,7. 2 Chr. 30.22. Ps. 51.3. Dan. 9.4.
8 tongue.
u Ex. 20.17. 1 Ki. 21.1. Pro. 15.27. Hab. 2.9. Luke 12.15. Rom. 7.7,8. Eph. 5.5. 1 Tim. 6.10.
9 poured.
v ch. 15.7.
w ch. 6.18. 1 Ki. 18.17. 1 Chr. 2.7. Gal. 5.12.
x Deut. 17.5.
y ch. 8.29. 2 Sam. 18. 17. Lam. 3.53.
z Deut. 13.17.
a Isa. 65.10.
10 That is, Trouble.

CHAP. 8

a Deut. 1.21. Deut. 7.18. ch. 1.9.
b ch. 2.11. ch. 6.2. Ps. 44.3.
c ch. 6.21.
d Deut. 20. 14.
e Judg. 20.29.
1 Or, in ambush.
f Judg. 20.32.
2 pulled.
g ch. 1.16. 2 Sam. 13. 28.

the wedge of gold, and his sons, an
his daughters, and his oxen, and hi
asses, and his sheep, and his tent, an
all that he had: and they brough
them unto [v]the valley of Ā'-chôr.
25 And Joshua said, [w]Why hast tho
troubled us? the LORD shall troubl
thee this day. [x]And all Israel stone
him with stones, and burned ther
with fire, after they had stoned ther
with stones.
26 And they [y]raised over him a grea
heap of stones unto this day. So [z]th
LORD turned from the fierceness of hi
anger. Wherefore the name of tha
place was called, [a]The valley of [10]Ā-
chôr, unto this day.

CHAPTER 8

AND the LORD said unto Joshua
Fear [a]not, neither be thou dismay
ed: take all the people of war wit
thee, and arise, go up to Ā'-ī: see, [b]
have given into thy hand the king o
Ā'-ī, and his people, and his city, an
his land:
2 And thou shalt do to Ā'-ī and he
king as thou didst unto [c]Jericho an
her king: only [d]the spoil thereof, an
the cattle thereof, shall ye take for
prey unto yourselves: lay thee an am
bush for the city behind it.
3 ¶ So Joshua arose, and all the peo
ple of war, to go up against Ā'-ī: an
Joshua chose out thirty thousan
mighty men of valour, and sent ther
away by night.
4 And he commanded them, sayin
Behold, [e]ye shall lie [1]in wait again
the city, *even* behind the city: go no
very far from the city, but be ye a
ready:
5 And I, and all the people that *ar*
with me, will approach unto the city
and it shall come to pass, when the
come out against us, as at the firs
that [f]we will flee before them,
6 (For they will come out after us
till we have [2]drawn them from th
city; for they will say, They flee befor
us, as at the first: therefore we will fle
before them.
7 Then ye shall rise up from the am
bush, and seize upon the city: for th
LORD your God will deliver it int
your hand.
8 And it shall be, when ye have take
the city, *that* ye shall set the city o
fire: according to the commandme
of the LORD shall ye do. [g]See, I hav
commanded you.
9 ¶ Joshua therefore sent them forth
and they went to lie in ambush, an

abode between Beth-el and Ā-ī, on
the west side of Ā-ī: but Joshua lodged
that night among the people.
10 And Joshua [h]rose up early in the
morning, and numbered the people,
and went up, he and the elders of Israel, before the people to Ā-ī.
11 And all the people, *even the people*
of war that *were* with him, went up,
and drew nigh, and came before the
city, and pitched on the north side of
Ā-ī: now *there was* a valley between
them and Ā-ī.
12 And he took about five thousand
men, and set them to lie in ambush
between Beth-el and Ā-ī, on the west
side [3]of the city.
13 And when they had set the people, *even* all the host that *was* on the
north of the city, and [4]their liers in
wait on the west of the city, Joshua
went that night into the midst of the
valley.
14 ¶ And it came to pass, when the
king of Ā-ī saw *it*, that they hasted and
rose up early, and the men of the city
went out against Israel to battle, he
and all his people, at a time appointed,
before the plain; but he wist [j]not that
there were liers in ambush against him
behind the city.
15 And Joshua and all Israel made
as if they were beaten before them,
and fled [l]by the way of the wilderness.
16 And all the people that *were* in
Ā-ī were called together to pursue
after them: and they pursued after
Joshua, and were drawn away [m]from
the city.
17 And there was not a man left in
Ā-ī or Beth-el, that went not out after
Israel: and they left the city open, and
pursued after Israel.
18 And the LORD said unto Joshua,
Stretch out the spear that *is* in thy
hand toward Ā-ī; for [n]I will give it into thine hand. And Joshua stretched
out the spear that *he had* in his hand
toward the city.
19 And the ambush arose quickly
out of their place, and they ran as
soon as he had stretched out his hand:
and they entered into the city, and
took it, and hasted and set the city on
fire.
20 And when the men of Ā-ī looked
behind them, they saw, and, behold,
the smoke of the city ascended up to
heaven, and they had no [5]power to
flee this way or that way: and the people that fled to the wilderness turned
back upon the pursuers.
21 And when Joshua and all Israel

h Gen. 22.3. ch. 3.1. ch. 6.12. ch. 7.16. Ps. 101.8. Ps. 119.60. Eccl. 9.10. Jer. 21.12.
i Gen. 12.8. Gen. 28.19. Judg. 1.22.
3 Or, of Ai.
4 their lying in wait.
j Judg. 20.34. Eccl. 9.12. Matt. 24.39, 50. 1 Thes. 5.1-3. 2 Pet. 2.3.
k Judg. 20. 36.
l ch. 15.61. ch. 16.1. ch. 18.12.
m Ex. 14.3,4. Ps. 9.16. Judg. 20.31
n Deut. 7.23, 24. Deut. 9.3. Deut. 31.5-8. ch. 1.5. Jer. 49.3.
5 hand.
o Lev. 27.29. Deut. 7.2. Job 20.5. Luke 17.26-30. 1 Thes. 5.3.
p Num. 31. 22,26. Matt. 20.15.
q Deut. 13. 16. 2 Ki. 19.25. Isa. 17.1. Jer. 9.11.
r B.C. 1427.
s ch. 10.26. Ps. 107.40.
t Deut. 21.23. ch. 10.27.
u ch. 7.26. 2 Sam. 18. 17.
v Gen. 8.20. Ex. 20.24.
w Deut. 27.4, 5.
x Deut. 27.5, 6.
y Ex. 20.24.
z Deut. 27.2, 8.

saw that the ambush had taken the
city, and that the smoke of the city
ascended, then they turned again, and
slew the men of Ā-ī.
22 And the other issued out of the
city against them; so they were in the
midst of Israel, some on this side, and
some on that side: and they smote
them, so that they let [o]none of them
remain or escape.
23 And the king of Ā-ī they took
alive, and brought him to Joshua.
24 And it came to pass, when Israel
had made an end of slaying all the
inhabitants of Ā-ī in the field, in the
wilderness wherein they chased them,
and when they were all fallen on the
edge of the sword, until they were
consumed, that all the Israelites returned unto Ā-ī, and smote it with the
edge of the sword.
25 And *so* it was, *that* all that fell
that day, both of men and women,
were twelve thousand, *even* all the
men of Ā-ī.
26 For Joshua drew not his hand
back, wherewith he stretched out the
spear, until he had utterly destroyed
all the inhabitants of Ā-ī.
27 Only [p]the cattle and the spoil of
that city Israel took for a prey unto
themselves, according unto the word
of the LORD which he commanded
Joshua.
28 And Joshua burnt Ā-ī, and made
it an [q]heap for ever, *even* a desolation
unto [r]this day.
29 And [s]the king of Ā-ī he hanged on
a tree until eventide: [t]and as soon as
the sun was down, Joshua commanded that they should take his carcase
down from the tree, and cast it at the
entering of the gate of the city, and
[u]raise thereon a great heap of stones,
that remaineth unto this day.
30 ¶ Then Joshua [v]built an altar unto
the LORD God of Israel [w]in mount
Ē-băl,
31 As Moses the servant of the LORD
commanded the children of Israel, as
it is written in the [x]book of the law of
Moses, an altar of whole stones, over
which no man hath lift up *any* iron:
and [y]they offered thereon burnt offerings unto the LORD, and sacrificed
peace offerings.
32 ¶ And [z]he wrote there upon the
stones a copy of the law of Moses,
which he wrote in the presence of the
children of Israel.
33 And all Israel, and their elders,
and officers, and their judges, stood
on this side the ark and on that side

before the priests the Levites, which
[a]bare the ark of the covenant of the
LORD, as well [b]the stranger, as he that
was born among them; half of them
over against mount Gĕ-rī-zĭm, and
half of them over against mount Ē-
băl; as [c]Moses the servant of the
LORD had commanded before, that
they should bless the people of Israel.
34 And afterward [d]he read all the
words of the law, [e]the blessings and
cursings, according to all that is written in the book of the law.
35 There was not a word of all that
Moses commanded, which Joshua
read not before all the congregation
of Israel, [f]with the women, and the
little ones, and the strangers [g]that
[6]were conversant among them.

CHAPTER 9

AND it came to pass, when all the
kings which *were* on this side Jordan, in the hills, and in the valleys,
and in all the coasts of the [a]great sea
over against Lĕb-ă-nŏn, [b]the Hittite,
and the Amorite, the Canaanite, the
Pĕ-rĭz-zīte, the Hī-vīte, and the Jĕb-
ū-şīte, heard *thereof;*
2 That they [c]gathered themselves together, to fight with Joshua and with
Israel, with one [1]accord.
3 ¶ And when the inhabitants of
Gibeon [d]heard [e]what Joshua had done
unto Jericho and to Ā-ī,
4 They did work wilily, and went and
made as if they had been ambassadors,
and took old sacks upon their asses,
and [f]wine bottles, old, and rent, and
bound up;
5 And old shoes and clouted upon
their feet, and old garments upon
them; and all the bread of their provision was dry *and* mouldy.
6 And they went to Joshua [g]unto the
camp at Gĭl-găl, and said unto him,
and to the men of Israel, We be come
from a far country: now therefore
make ye a league with us.
7 And the men of Israel said unto
[h]the Hī-vītes, Peradventure ye dwell
among us; and [i]how shall we make a
league with you?
8 And they said unto Joshua, We
[j]*are* thy servants. And Joshua said unto them, Who *are* ye? and from
whence come ye?
9 And they said unto him, [k]From a
very far country thy servants are come
because of the name of the LORD thy
God: for we [l]have heard the fame of
him, and all that he did in Egypt,
10 And [m]all that he did to the two

a Deut. 31.9, 25.
b Lev. 24.22. Num. 15.16.
c Deut. 11.29.
d Deut. 31. 11. Neh. 8.3.
e Deut. 29. 20,21.
f Deut. 31.12.
g Zech. 8.23.
6 walked.

CHAP. 9

a Num. 34.6.
b Gen. 15.18, 21. Ex. 3.17. Deut. 7.1.
c 1 Chr. 20.1. Ps. 2.1,2. Ps. 83.3,5. Pro. 11.21. Isa. 8.9,10, 12. Acts 4.26-28.
1 mouth.
d ch. 10.2. 2 Sam. 21.1, 2.
e ch. 6.27.
f Matt. 9.17. Luke 5.37, 38.
g ch. 5.10.
h ch. 11.19.
i Ex. 23.32. Deut. 7.2.
j Deut. 20.11.
k Deut. 20. 15.
l Ex. 15.14.
m Num. 21. 24,33.
2 in your hand.
3 Or, they received the men by reason of their victuals.
n Num. 27. 21. Judg. 1.1. 1 Sam. 22. 10. 1 Sam. 30.8. 2 Sam. 2.1. Isa. 30.1,2.
o 2 Sam. 21.2.
p ch. 18.25. Ezra 2.25.
q Ps. 15.4.
r 2 Sam. 21.1. Zech. 5.3,4. Mal. 3.5.
s Deut. 29.11.
t Gen. 9.25.

kings of the Amorites, that *were* be
yond Jordan, to Sī-hŏn king of Hĕsh
bŏn, and to Og king of Bā-shăn, whicl
was at Ăsh-tă-rōth.
11 Wherefore our elders and all th
inhabitants of our country spake to us
saying, Take victuals [2]with you for th
journey, and go to meet them, and sa
unto them, We *are* your servants
therefore now make ye a league wit
us.
12 This our bread we took hot *fo*
our provision out of our houses o
the day we came forth to go unto you
but now, behold, it is dry, and it i
mouldy:
13 And these bottles of wine, whicl
we filled, *were* new; and, behold, the
be rent: and these our garments an
our shoes are become old by reason c
the very long journey.
14 And [3]the men took of their vic
tuals, and [n]asked not *counsel* at th
mouth of the LORD.
15 And Joshua [o]made peace wit
them, and made a league with then
to let them live: and the princes of th
congregation sware unto them.
16 ¶ And it came to pass at the en
of three days after they had made
league with them, that they heard th
they *were* their neighbours, and *th*
they dwelt among them.
17 And the children of Israel journ
eyed, and came unto their cities o
the third day. Now their cities *we*
[p]Gibeon, and Chĕ-phī-răh, and Bĕe
ōth, and Kĭr-jăth-jē-ă-rĭm.
18 And the children of Israel smo
them not, [q]because the princes of tl
congregation had sworn unto them b
the LORD God of Israel. And all tl
congregation murmured against tl
princes.
19 But all the princes said unto a
the congregation, We have sworn unt
them by the LORD God of Israel: no
therefore we may not touch them.
20 This we will do to them; we wi
even let them live, lest [r]wrath be upo
us, because of the oath which v
sware unto them.
21 And the princes said unto then
Let them live; but let them be [s]hewe
of wood and drawers of water unto a
the congregation; as the princes ha
promised them.
22 ¶ And Joshua called for them, ar
he spake unto them, saying, Wher
fore have ye beguiled us, saying, W
are very far from you; when ye dw
among us?
23 Now therefore ye *are* [t]cursed, ar

there shall [4]none of you be freed from being bondmen, and hewers of wood and drawers of water for the house of my God.

24 And they answered Joshua, and said, Because it was certainly told thy servants, how that the LORD thy God [u]commanded his servant Moses to give you all the land, and to destroy all the inhabitants of the land from before you, therefore [v]we were sore afraid of our lives because of you, and have done this thing.

25 And now, behold, we *are* [w]in thine hand: as it seemeth good and right unto thee to do unto us, do.

26 And so did he unto them, and delivered them out of the hand of the children of Israel, that they slew them not.

27 And Joshua [5]made them that day hewers of wood and drawers of water for the congregation, and for the altar of the LORD, even unto this day, [x]in the place which he should choose.

CHAPTER 10

NOW it came to pass, when Ăd´-ō-nī-zē´-dĕk king of Jerusalem had heard how Joshua had taken Ā´-ī, and had utterly destroyed it; [a]as he had done to Jericho and her king, so he had done to [b]Ā´-ī and her king; and [c]how the inhabitants of Gibeon had made peace with Israel, and were among them;

2 That they [d]feared greatly, because Gibeon *was* a great city, as one of the [1]royal cities, and because it *was* greater than Ā´-ī, and all the men thereof *were* mighty.

3 Wherefore Ăd´-ō-nī-zē´-dĕk king of Jerusalem sent unto Hō´-hăm king of [e]Hē´-brŏn, and unto Pī´-răm king of Jär´-mûth, and unto Jă-phī´-ă king of Lā´-chīsh, and unto Dē´-bīr king of Ĕg´-lŏn, saying,

4 Come up unto me, and help me, that we may smite Gibeon: for [f]it hath made peace with Joshua and with the children of Israel.

5 Therefore the five kings of the Amorites, the king of Jerusalem, the king of Hē´-brŏn, the king of Jär´-mûth, the king of Lā´-chīsh, the king of Ĕg´-lŏn, [g]gathered themselves together, and went up, they and all their hosts, and encamped before Gibeon, and made war against it.

6 ¶ And the men of Gibeon sent unto Joshua [h]to the camp to Gĭl´-găl, saying, Slack not thy hand from thy servants; come up to us quickly, and save us, and help us: for all the kings of the Amorites that dwell in the mountains are gathered together against us.

7 So Joshua ascended from Gĭl´-găl, he, and [i]all the people of war with him, and all the mighty men of valour.

8 ¶ And the LORD said unto Joshua, [j]Fear them not: for I have delivered them into thine hand; [k]there shall not a man of them stand before thee.

9 Joshua therefore came unto them suddenly, *and* went up from Gĭl´-găl all night.

10 And the LORD [l]discomfited them before Israel, and slew them with a great slaughter at Gibeon, and chased them along the way that goeth up [m]to Bĕth–hôr´-ŏn, and smote them to [n]Ă-zē´-kăh, and unto Măk-kē´-däh.

11 And it came to pass, as they fled from before Israel, *and* were in the going down to Bĕth–hôr´-ŏn, that the [o]LORD cast down great stones from heaven upon them unto Ă-zē´-kăh, and they died: *they were* more which died with hailstones than *they* whom the children of Israel slew with the sword.

12 ¶ Then spake Joshua to the LORD in the day when the LORD delivered up the Amorites before the children of Israel, and he said in the sight of Israel, [p]Sun, [2]stand thou still upon Gibeon; and thou, Moon, in the valley of [q]Ăj´-ă-lŏn.

13 And the sun stood still, and the moon stayed, until the people had avenged themselves upon their enemies. [r]*Is* not this written in the book of [3]Jăsh´-ĕr? So the sun stood still in the midst of heaven, and hasted not to go down about a whole day.

14 And there was [s]no day like that before it or after it, that the LORD hearkened unto the voice of a man: for [t]the LORD fought for Israel.

15 ¶ And Joshua returned, and all Israel with him, unto the camp to Gĭl´-găl.

16 But these five kings fled, and hid themselves in a cave at Măk-kē´-däh.

17 And it was told Joshua, saying, The five kings are found hid in a cave at Măk-kē´-däh.

18 And Joshua said, Roll great stones upon the mouth of the cave, and set men by it for to keep them:

19 And stay ye not, *but* pursue after your enemies, and [4]smite the hindmost of them; suffer them not to enter into their cities: for the LORD your God hath delivered them into your hand.

20 And it came to pass, when Joshua

4 not be cut off from you.
u Ex. 23.32. Num. 33.51, 52,55,56. Deut. 7.1,2.
v Ex. 15.14.
w Gen. 16.6.
5 gave, or, delivered to be.
x Deut. 12.5. 1 Ki. 8.29. 1 Ki. 9.7. 2 Chr. 7.12, 20. Ps. 78.68.

CHAP. 10
a ch. 6.21.
b ch. 8.22.
c ch. 9.15.
d Ex. 15.14, 15,16. Deut. 11.25. Ps. 48.4-6. Pro. 1.26. Heb. 10.31. Rev. 6.15-17.
1 cities of the kingdom.
e Gen. 23.2.
f ch. 9.15.
g ch. 9.2.
h ch. 5.10.
i ch. 8.1.
j Deut. 7.24. ch. 11.6. ch. 23.9.
k ch. 1.5.
l Judg. 4.15. 1 Sam. 7.10. 2 Chr. 14.12. Ps. 18.14. Isa. 28.21.
m ch. 16.3,5.
n ch. 15.35.
o Ps. 18.13, 14. Ps. 77.17. Isa. 28.2. Isa. 30.30. Rev. 16.21.
p Deut. 4.19. Ps. 19.4. Isa. 28.21. Isa. 38.8. Isa. 60.20. Hab. 3.11.
2 be silent.
q Judg. 12.12.
r 2 Sam. 1.18.
3 Or, the upright?
s Isa. 38.8.
t Ex. 14.14. Deut. 1.30. Deut. 3.22. ch. 23.3,10. 2 Chr. 20.29. Neh. 4.20. Ps. 33.8,12-20. Isa. 31.4. Isa. 42.13. Isa. 52.10, 12. Zech. 14.3.
4 cut off the tail.

and the children of Israel had made an end of slaying them with a very great slaughter, till they were consumed, that the rest *which* remained of them entered into fenced cities.

21 And all the people returned to the camp to Joshua at Măk-kē′dăh in peace: [u]none moved his tongue against any of the children of Israel.

22 Then said Joshua, Open the mouth of the cave, and bring out those five kings unto me out of the cave.

23 And they did so, and brought forth those five kings unto him out of the cave, the king of Jerusalem, the king of Hē′brŏn, the king of Jär′mûth, the king of Lā′chĭsh, *and* the king of Ĕg′lŏn.

24 And it came to pass, when they brought out those kings unto Joshua, that Joshua called for all the men of Israel, and said unto the captains of the men of war which went with him, Come near, put [v]your feet upon the necks of these kings. And they came near, and put their feet upon the necks of them.

25 And Joshua said unto them, Fear not, [w]nor be dismayed, be strong and of good courage: [x]for thus shall the LORD do to all your enemies against whom ye fight.

26 And afterward Joshua smote them, and slew them, and hanged them on five trees: and [y]they were hanging upon the trees until the evening.

27 And it came to pass at the time of the going down of the sun, *that* Joshua commanded, and they took [z]them down off the trees, and cast them into the cave wherein they had been hid, and laid great stones in the cave's mouth, *which remain* until this very day.

28 ¶ And that day Joshua took Măk-kē′dăh, and smote it with the edge of the sword, and the king thereof he utterly destroyed, them, and all the souls that *were* therein; he let none remain: and he did to the king of Măk-kē′dăh [a]as he did unto the king of Jericho.

29 Then Joshua passed from Măk-kē′dăh, and all Israel with him, unto [b]Lĭb′năh, and fought against Lĭb′năh:

30 And the LORD delivered it also, and the king thereof, into the hand of Israel; and he smote it with the edge of the sword, and all the souls that *were* therein; he let none remain in it; but did unto the king thereof as he did unto the king of Jericho.

u Ex. 11.7. Isa. 54.17.
v Deut. 33. 29. Ps. 2.8-12. Ps. 91.13. Ps. 107.40. Ps. 110.5. Isa. 26.5,6. Mal. 4.3. Rev. 2.26, 27.
w ch. 1.9. 1 Sam. 17. 37. Ps. 63.9. 2 Cor. 1.10. 2 Tim. 4.17.
x Deut. 3.21.
y Num. 25.4. ch. 8.29. 2 Sam. 21.6, 9. Esther 2.23. Esther 7.9, 10. Ps. 149.7,9.
z Deut. 21.23. ch. 8.29.
a ch. 6.21.
b ch. 15.42. ch. 21.13. 2 Ki. 8.22. 2 Ki. 19.8.
c 2 Ki. 14.19. Micah 1.13.
d ch. 16.3,10. 1 Ki. 9.16, 17. 1 Chr. 20.4.
5 pulled down.
e Num. 13.22. ch. 14.13. ch. 15.13. Judg. 1.10. 2 Sam. 5.1,4.
f ch. 15.15. ch. 21.15.
g ch. 15.21-63. ch. 19.1-8.
h Ex. 23.31-33. Ex. 34.12. Deut. 7.2.
i Num. 13.17, 26.
j Gen. 10.19. Deut. 2.23. Amos 1.6. Zeph. 2.4. Zech. 9.5. Acts 8.26.
k ch. 11.16.
l Ps. 44.2. Ps. 80.8. Isa. 43.4.

31 ¶ And Joshua passed from Lĭb-năh, and all Israel with him, unto [c]Lā-chĭsh, and encamped against it, and fought against it:

32 And the LORD delivered Lā′chĭsh into the hand of Israel, which took it on the second day, and smote it with the edge of the sword, and all the souls that *were* therein, according to all that he had done to Lĭb′năh.

33 ¶ Then Hôr′ăm king of [d]Gē′zĕr came up to help Lā′chĭsh; and Joshua smote him and his people, until he had left him none remaining.

34 ¶ And from Lā′chĭsh Joshua passed unto Ĕg′lŏn, and all Israel with him; and they encamped against it, and fought against it:

35 And they took it on that day, and smote it with the edge of the sword, and all the souls that *were* therein he utterly [5]destroyed that day, according to all that he had done to Lā′chĭsh.

36 And Joshua went up from Ĕg-lŏn, and all Israel with him, unto [e]Hē′brŏn; and they fought against it:

37 And they took it, and smote it with the edge of the sword, and the king thereof, and all the cities thereof, and all the souls that *were* therein; he left none remaining, according to all that he had done to Ĕg′lŏn; but destroyed it utterly, and all the souls that *were* therein.

38 ¶ And Joshua returned, and all Israel with him, to [f]Dē′bĭr; and fought against it:

39 And he took it, and the king thereof, and all the cities thereof; and they smote them with the edge of the sword, and utterly destroyed all the souls that *were* therein; he left none remaining: as he had done to Hē′brŏn, so he did to Dē′bĭr, and to the king thereof; as he had done also to Lĭb′năh, and to her king.

40 ¶ So Joshua smote [g]all the country of the hills, and of the south, and of the vale, and of the springs, and all their kings: he left none remaining, but utterly destroyed all that breathed, as the LORD God of Israel [h]commanded.

41 And Joshua smote them from Kā′dĕsh-bär′nē-ă [i]even unto [j]Gā′ză, and [k]all the country of Gō′shĕn, even unto Gibeon.

42 And [l]all these kings and their land did Joshua take at one time, because the LORD God of Israel fought for Israel.

43 And Joshua returned, and all I

rael with him, unto the camp to Gĭl-
găl.

CHAPTER 11

AND it came to pass, when [a]Jā-bĭn
king of Hā-zôr had heard *those*
things, that he sent [b]to Jō-băb king of
Mā-dŏn, and to the king of Shĭm-rŏn,
and to the king of Ăch-shăph,
2 And to the kings that *were* on the
north of the mountains, and of the
plains south of [c]Chĭn-nĕ-rōth, and in
the valley, and in the borders [d]of Dor
on the west,
3 *And to* the Canaanite on the east
and on the west, and *to* the Amorite,
and the Hittite, and the Pĕ-rĭz-zīte,
and the Jĕb-ū-sīte in the mountains,
[e]and *to* the Hī-vīte under [f]Hermon [g]in
the land of Mĭz-pēh.
4 And they went out, they and all
their hosts with them, much people,
[h]even as the sand that *is* upon the sea
shore in multitude, with horses and
chariots very many.
5 And when all these kings were [1]met
together, they came and pitched together at the waters of Mē-rŏm, to
fight against Israel.
6 ¶ And the LORD said unto Joshua,
Be not afraid because of them: for to
morrow about this time will I deliver
them up all slain before Israel: thou
shalt hough [i]their horses, and burn
their chariots with fire.
7 So Joshua came, and all the people
of war with him, against them by the
waters of Mē-rŏm suddenly; and they
fell upon them.
8 And the LORD delivered them into
the hand of Israel, who smote them,
and chased them unto great [2]Zī-dŏn,
and unto [3]Mĭs-rē-phōth-mā-ĭm, and
unto the valley of Mĭz-pēh eastward;
and they smote them, until they left
them none remaining.
9 And Joshua did unto them as the
LORD bade him: he houghed their
horses, and burnt their chariots with
fire.
10 ¶ And Joshua at that time turned
back, and took Hā-zôr, and smote the
king thereof with the sword: for Hā-
zôr beforetime was the head of all
those kingdoms.
11 And they smote all the souls that
were therein with the edge of the
sword, utterly destroying *them:* there
was not [4]any left to breathe: and he
burnt Hā-zôr with fire.
12 And all the cities of those kings,
and all the kings of them, did Joshua
take, and smote them with the edge of
the sword, *and* he utterly destroyed
them, [j]as Moses the servant of the
LORD commanded.
13 But *as for* the cities that stood still
[5]in their strength, Israel burned none
of them, save Hā-zôr only; *that* did
Joshua burn.
14 And all the spoil of these cities,
and the cattle, the children of Israel
took for a prey unto themselves; but
every man they smote with the edge
of the sword, until they had destroyed
them, neither left they any to breathe.
15 ¶ As [k]the LORD commanded
Moses his servant, so [l]did Moses
command Joshua, and [m]so did Joshua; [6]he left nothing undone of all that
the LORD commanded Moses.
16 So Joshua took all that land, [n]the
hills, and all the south country, [o]and
all the land of Gō-shĕn, and the valley,
and the plain, and the mountain of Israel, and the valley of the same;
17 *Even* [p]from [7]the mount Hā-lăk,
that goeth up to Sē-ĭr, even unto Bā-
ăl–găd in the valley of Lĕb-ă-non under mount Hermon: and [q]all their
kings he took, and smote them, and
slew them.
18 [8]Joshua made war a long time
with all those kings.
19 There was not a city that made
peace with the children of Israel, save
[r]the Hī-vītes the inhabitants of Gibeon: all *other* they took in battle.
20 For [s]it was of the LORD to harden
their hearts, that they should come
against Israel in battle, that he might
destroy them utterly, *and* that they
might have no favour, but that he
might destroy them, [t]as the LORD
commanded Moses.
21 ¶ And at that time came Joshua,
and cut off [u]the Anakims from the
mountains, from Hē-brŏn, from Dē-
bĭr, from Anab, and from all the
mountains of Judah, and from all the
mountains of Israel: Joshua destroyed
them utterly with their cities.
22 There was none of the Anakims
left in the land of the children of Israel: only in Gā-ză, in [v]Gath, and in
[w]Ăsh-dŏd, there remained.
23 So Joshua took the whole land,
according [x]to all that the LORD said
unto Moses; and Joshua gave it for an
inheritance unto Israel according [y]to
their divisions by their tribes. [z]And
the land rested from war.

CHAPTER 12

NOW these *are* the kings of the
land, which the children of Israel
smote, and possessed their land on the

CHAP. 11
a Ps. 2.1,2. Ps. 83. 1-18.
b ch. 10.3. ch. 19.15.
c Num. 34. 11.
d ch. 17.11. 1 Ki. 4.11.
e Judg. 3.3.
f ch. 13.11.
g Gen. 31.49. Judg. 20.1. 1 Sam. 7.5-7. 1 Ki. 15.22.
h Gen. 22.17. Gen. 32.12. 1 Sam. 13.5.
1 assembled by appointment.
i 2 Sam. 8.4.
2 Or, Zidon-rabbah.
3 Burnings of waters, or, Salt pits.
4 any breath.
j Num. 33.52. Deut. 7.2.
5 on their heap.
k Ex. 34.11.
l Deut. 7.2.
m ch. 1.7.
6 he removed nothing.
n ch. 12.8.
o ch. 10.41.
p ch. 12.7.
7 Or, the smooth mountain.
q Deut. 7.24.
8 Till 1445. ver. 23.
r ch. 9.3,7.
s Ex. 4.21. 1 Sam. 2.25. 1 Ki. 12.15. Rom. 9.18. Jas. 1.13-17.
t Deut. 20.16.
u Num. 13. 22. Deut. 1.28. ch. 15.13,14. Judg. 1.10.
v 1 Sam. 17.4.
w ch. 15.46.
x Num. 34.2.
y Num. 26. 53.
z ch. 14.15. ch. 21.44. ch. 23.1.
B.C. 1445.

other side Jordan toward the rising of
the sun, [a]from the river Arnon [b]unto
mount Hermon, and all the plain on
the east:
2 Sī-hŏn king of the Amorites, who
dwelt in Hĕsh-bŏn, *and* ruled from Ă-
rō-ĕr, which *is* upon the bank of the
river Arnon, and from the middle
of the river, and from half Gilead,
even unto the river Jăb-bok, *which*
is the border of the children of
Ammon;
3 And [c]from the plain to the sea of
Chĭn-nĕ-rōth on the east, and unto the
sea of the plain, *even* the salt sea on the
east, [d]the way to Bĕth-jĕsh-ĭ-mōth;
and from [1]the south, under [2]Ăsh-
dōth-pĭs-găh:
4 ¶ And [e]the coast of Og king of Bā-
shăn, *which was* of [f]the remnant of the
giants, that dwelt at Ăsh-tă-rōth and
at Ĕd-rĕ-ī,
5 And reigned in mount Hermon,
and [g]in Săl-căh, and in all Bā-shăn,
unto [h]the border of the Gĕ-shū-rītes
and the Mā-ăch-ă-thītes, and half
Gilead, the border of Sī-hŏn king of
Hĕsh-bŏn.
6 Them did Moses the servant of the
LORD and the children of Israel
smite: and Moses the servant of the
LORD gave it *for* a possession unto the
Reubenites, and the Gadites, and the
half tribe of Mă-năs-sĕh.
7 ¶ And these *are* the kings of the
country which Joshua and the children of Israel smote on this side Jordan on the west, from Bā-ăl-găd in
the valley of Lĕb-ă-non even unto the
mount Hā-lăk, that goeth up [i]to Sē-ĭr;
which Joshua gave unto the tribes of
Israel *for* a possession according to
their divisions;
8 In [j]the mountains, and in the valleys, and in the plains, and in the
springs, and in the wilderness, and in
the south country; the Hittites, [k]the
Amorites, and the Canaanites, the
Pĕ-rĭz-zītes, the Hī-vītes, and the Jĕb-
ū-sītes:
9 ¶ The [l]king of Jericho, one; [m]the
king of Ā-ī, which *is* beside Beth-el,
one;
10 The [n]king of Jerusalem, one; the
king of Hē-brŏn, one;
11 The king of Jăr-mûth, one; the
king of Lā-chish, one;
12 The king of Ĕg-lŏn, one; the king
of Gē-zĕr, one;
13 The king of Dē-bĭr, one; the king
of Gē-dĕr, one;
14 The king of Hôr-măh, one; the
king of Âr-ăd, one;

CHAP. 12
a Num. 21. 24. Deut. 2.24. Isa. 16.2.
b Deut. 3.8,9.
c Deut. 3.17.
d ch. 13.20.
1 Or, Teman.
2 Or, The springs of Pisgah, or, The hill.
e Num. 21. 35.
f Deut. 3.11.
g ch. 13.11.
h Deut. 3.14. 1 Sam. 27.8. 2 Sam. 3.3. 2 Sam. 13. 37. 2 Ki. 25.23.
i Gen. 14.6. Gen. 32.3.
j ch. 10.40.
k Ex. 3.8.
l ch. 6.2.
m ch. 8.29.
n ch. 10.23.
o ch. 19.13. 1 Ki. 4.10.
3 Or, Sharon.
p ch. 11.1. ch. 19.15.
q ch. 19.37.
r Gen. 14.1,2.
CHAP. 13
a Gen. 18.11. ch. 14.10. ch. 23.1. 1 Ki. 1.1. Luke 1.7.
1 to possess it. Deut. 31.3.
b Ex. 23.29, 31. Deut. 11.23, 24.
c Gen. 10.14. Gen. 26.1.
d 1 Sam. 27.8. 2 Sam. 3.3. 2 Sam. 13. 37.
e Jer. 2.18.
f 1 Sam. 6.4, 16. Zeph. 2.5.
g Deut. 2.23.
2 Or, the cave.
h ch. 19.30.
i Judg. 1.34.
j 1 Ki. 5.18. Ps. 83.7.
k ch. 12.7.
l ch. 11.8.
m ch. 23.13.
n ch. 14.1,2.
o Num. 32. 33. ch. 22.4.

15 The king of Lĭb-năh, one; the king
of Adullam, one;
16 The king of Măk-kē-dăh, one;
the king of Beth-el, one;
17 The king of Tăp-pū-ăh, one; [o]the
king of Hē-phĕr, one;
18 The king of Ā-phĕk, one; the king
[3]of Lă-shâr-on, one;
19 The king of Mā-dŏn, one; the king
of Hā-zôr, one;
20 The king of [p]Shĭm-rŏn-mē-rŏn,
one; the king of Ăch-shăph, one;
21 The king of Tā-ă-năch, one; the
king of Mĕ-gĭd-dō, one;
22 The [q]king of Kē-dĕsh, one; the
king of Jŏk-nĕ-ăm of Carmel, one;
23 The king of Dor in the coast of
Dor, one; the king [r]of the nations of
Gĭl-găl, one;
24 The king of Tĭr-zăh, one: all the
kings thirty and one.

CHAPTER 13

NOW Joshua [a]was old *and* stricken
in years; and the LORD said unto
him, Thou art old *and* stricken in
years, and there remaineth yet very
much land [1]to be possessed.
2 This [b]*is* the land that yet remaineth:
all [c]the borders of the Philistines, and
[d]all Gĕ-shū-rī,
3 From [e]Sī-hôr, which *is* before
Egypt, even unto the borders of Ĕk-
rŏn northward, *which* is counted to
the Canaanite: [f]five lords of the Philistines; the Gā-ză-thītes, and the Ăsh-
dō-thītes, the Ĕsh-kă-lon-ītes, the
Gĭt-tītes, and the Ĕk-rŏn-ītes; also
[g]the Ā-vītes:
4 From the south, all the land of the
Canaanites, and [2]Mĕ-âr-ăh that *is* beside the Sī-dō-nĭ-ăns, [h]unto Ā-phĕk,
to the borders of the [i]Amorites:
5 And the land of [j]the Gĭb-lītes, and
all Lĕb-ă-non, toward the sunrising,
[k]from Bā-ăl-găd under mount Hermon unto the entering into Hā-
măth.
6 All the inhabitants of the hill country from Lĕb-ă-non unto [l]Mĭs-rĕ-
phōth-mā-ĭm, *and* all the Sī-dō-nĭ-
ăns, them [m]will I drive out from before the children of Israel: only divide
[n]thou it by lot unto the Israelites for
an inheritance, as I have commanded
thee.
7 Now therefore divide this land for
an inheritance unto the nine tribes,
and the half tribe of Mă-năs-sĕh,
8 With whom the Reubenites and
the Gadites have received their inheritance, which [o]Moses gave them,
beyond Jordan eastward, *even* as

Moses the servant of the LORD gave
them;
9 From Ă-rō-ĕr, that *is* upon the
bank of the river Arnon, and the city
that *is* in the midst of the river, [p]and
all the plain of Mē-dĕ-bă unto Dī-bŏn;
10 And all the cities of Sī-hŏn king of
the Amorites, which reigned in Hĕsh-
bŏn, unto the border of the children of
Ammon;
11 And [q]Gilead, and the border of
the Gĕ-shū-rītes and Mā-ăch-ā-thītes,
and all mount Hermon, and all Bā-
shăn unto Săl-căh;
12 All the kingdom of Og in Bā-shăn,
which reigned in Ăsh-tă-rōth and in
Ĕd-rĕ-ī, who remained of [r]the remnant
of the giants: [s]for these did Moses
smite, and cast them out.
13 Nevertheless the children of Israel
expelled not the Gĕ-shū-rītes, nor the
Mā-ăch-ā-thītes: but the Gĕ-shū-
rītes and the Mā-ăch-ā-thītes dwell
among the Israelites until this day.
14 Only [t]unto the tribe of Levi he
gave none inheritance; the sacrifices
of the LORD God of Israel made by
fire *are* their inheritance, as he said
unto them.
15 ¶ And Moses gave unto the tribe
of the children of Reuben *inheritance*
according to their families.
16 And their coast was [u]from Ă-rō-
ĕr, that *is* on the bank of the river Arnon, [v]and the city that *is* in the midst
of the river, and all the plain by Mē-
dĕ-bă;
17 Hĕsh-bŏn, and all her cities that
are in the plain; Dī-bŏn, and [3]Bā-
mōth–bā-ăl, and Bĕth–bā-ăl–mē-ŏn,
18 And [w]Jă-hā-zăh, and Kē-dĕ-
mōth, and Mĕph-ā-ăth,
19 And [x]Kīr-jă-thā-īm, and Sĭb-măh,
and Zâr-ĕth–shā-hăr in the mount of
the valley,
20 And Bĕth–pē-ôr, and [4]Ăsh-dōth–
pĭs-găh, and Bĕth–jĕsh-ĭ-mōth,
21 And [y]all the cities of the plain, and
all the kingdom of Sī-hŏn king of the
Amorites, which reigned in Hĕsh-bŏn,
[z]whom Moses smote with [a]the princes
of Mĭd-ĭ-ăn, Ē-vī, and Rē-kĕm, and
Zur, and Hur, and Rē-bă, *which were*
dukes of Sī-hŏn, dwelling in the
country.
22 ¶ Bā-lă-ăm [b]also the son of Bē-ôr,
the [5]soothsayer, did the children of
Israel slay with the sword among
them that were slain by them.
23 And the border of the children of
Reuben was Jordan, and the border
thereof. This *was* the inheritance of
the children of Reuben after their

[p] Num. 21. 30. Isa. 15.2.
[q] ch. 12.5.
[r] Deut. 3.11.
[s] Num. 21. 24.
[t] Num. 18.20. Deut. 10.9. Deut. 18.2. ch. 14.3,4.
[u] Num. 21. 28,30. Deut. 3.12. ch. 12.2.
[v] Num. 21. 28.
3 Or, the high places of Baal, and house of Baal-meon.
[w] Num. 21. 23.
[x] Num. 32. 37.
4 Or, Springs of Pisgah, or, The hill.
[y] Deut. 3.10.
[z] Num. 21. 24.
[a] Num. 31.8.
[b] Num. 22.5. 2 Pet. 2.15. Rev. 2.14.
5 Or, diviner.
[c] Num. 32. 35.
[d] Num. 21. 26,28,29. with Deut. 2.19. Judg. 11.13.
[e] 2 Sam. 11.1. 2 Sam. 12. 26.
[f] Gen. 33.17. 1 Ki. 7.46.
[g] ch. 11.2. Matt. 14.34. Luke 5.1.
[h] 1 Chr. 2.23.
[i] ch. 12.4.
[j] ch. 18.7.
[k] Num. 18. 20. Deut. 10.9. Deut. 12.12. ch. 18.7. Eze. 44.28.

CHAP. 14

[a] Num. 34. 17.
[b] Num. 26. 55. Ps. 16.5. Pro. 16.33. Pro. 18.18.
[c] Num. 32. 29. ch. 13.8.

families, the cities and the villages
thereof.
24 And Moses gave *inheritance* unto
the tribe of Gad, *even* unto the children of Gad according to their families.
25 And [c]their coast was Jā-zĕr, and
all the cities of Gilead, [d]and half the
land of the children of Ammon, unto
Ă-rō-ĕr that *is* before [e]Răb-băh;
26 And from Hĕsh-bŏn unto Rā-
măth–mĭz-pĕh, and Bĕt-ŏ-nĭm; and
from Mā-hă-nā-ĭm unto the border of
Dē-bĭr;
27 And in the valley, Bĕth–âr-ăm,
and Bĕth–nĭm-răh, [f]and Sŭc-cōth, and
Zā-phŏn, the rest of the kingdom of
Sī-hŏn king of Hĕsh-bŏn, Jordan and
his border, *even* unto the edge [g]of the
sea of Chĭn-nĕ-rĕth on the other side
Jordan eastward.
28 This *is* the inheritance of the children of Gad after their families, the
cities, and their villages.
29 ¶ And Moses gave *inheritance* unto the half tribe of Mă-năs-sĕh: and
this was *the possession* of the half tribe
of the children of Mă-năs-sĕh by their
families.
30 And their coast was from Mā-hă-
nā-ĭm, all Bā-shăn, all the kingdom of
Og king of Bā-shăn, and [h]all the towns
of Jā-ĭr, which *are* in Bā-shăn, threescore cities:
31 And half Gilead, and [i]Ăsh-tă-
rōth, and Ĕd-rĕ-ī, cities of the kingdom of Og in Bā-shăn, *were pertaining*
unto the children of Mā-chĭr the son
of Mă-năs-sĕh, *even* to the one half of
the children of Mā-chĭr by their
families.
32 These *are the countries* which
Moses did distribute for inheritance in
the plains of Moab, on the other side
Jordan, by Jericho, eastward.
33 But [j]unto the tribe of Levi Moses
gave not *any* inheritance: the [k]LORD
God of Israel *was* their inheritance, as
he said unto them.

CHAPTER 14

AND these *are the countries* which
the children of Israel inherited in
the land of Canaan, [a]which Ĕl-ē-ā-zăr
the priest, and Joshua the son of Nun,
and the heads of the fathers of the
tribes of the children of Israel, distributed for inheritance to them.
2 By [b]lot *was* their inheritance, as the
LORD commanded by the hand of
Moses, for the nine tribes, and *for* the
half tribe.
3 For [c]Moses had given the inherit-

ance of two tribes and an half tribe on the other side Jordan: but unto the Levites he gave none inheritance among them.

4 For [d]the children of Joseph were two tribes, Mă-năs´-sēh and Ē´-phră-ĭm: therefore they gave no part unto the Levites in the land, save cities to dwell *in*, with their suburbs for their cattle and for their substance.

5 As [e]the LORD commanded Moses, so the children of Israel did, and they divided the land.

6 ¶ Then the children of Judah came unto Joshua in Gĭl´-găl: and Caleb the son of Jĕ-phŭn´-nĕh [f]the Kĕ´-nĕz-īte said unto him, Thou knowest [g]the thing that the LORD said unto Moses the man of God concerning me and thee [h]in Kā´-dĕsh–bär´-nĕ-ă.

7 Forty years old *was* I when Moses the servant of the LORD sent me from Kā´-dĕsh–bär´-nĕ-ă to espy out the land; and I brought him word again as *it was* in mine heart.

8 Nevertheless my brethren that went up with me made the heart of the people melt: but [i]I wholly followed the LORD my God.

9 And Moses sware on that day, saying, Surely [j]the land [k]whereon thy feet have trodden shall be thine inheritance, and thy children's for ever, because thou hast wholly followed the LORD my God.

10 And now, behold, the LORD hath kept me alive, [l]as he said, these forty and five years, even since the LORD spake this word unto Moses, while *the children of* Israel [1]wandered in the wilderness: and now, lo, I *am* this day fourscore and five years old.

11 As [m]yet I *am as* strong this day as *I was* in the day that Moses sent me: as my strength *was* then, even so *is* my strength now, for war, both [n]to go out, and to come in.

12 Now therefore give me this mountain, whereof the LORD spake in that day; for thou heardest in that day how the Anakims *were* there, and *that* the cities *were* great *and* fenced: [o]if so be the LORD *will be* with me, then [p]I shall be able to drive them out, as the LORD said.

13 And Joshua [q]blessed him, and [r]gave unto Caleb the son of Jĕ-phŭn´-nĕh Hē´-brŏn for an inheritance.

14 Hē´-brŏn therefore became the inheritance of Caleb the son of Jĕ-phŭn´-nĕh the Kĕ´-nĕz-īte unto this day, because that he wholly followed the LORD God of Israel.

15 And [s]the name of Hē´-brŏn before *was* Kĭr´-jăth–är´-bă; *which Arba was* a great man among the Anakims. [t]And the land had rest from war.

CHAPTER 15

THIS then was the lot of the tribe of the children of Judah by their families; [a]*even* to the border of Ē´-dom the [b]wilderness of Zin southward *was* the uttermost part of the south coast.

2 And their south border was from the shore of the salt sea, from the [1]bay that looketh southward:

3 And it went out to the south side to [2]Mā´-ă-lĕh–ăc-răb´-bĭm, and passed along to Zin, and ascended up on the south side unto Kā´-dĕsh–bär´-nĕ-ă, and passed along to Hĕz´-rŏn, and went up to Ā´-där, and fetched a compass to Kär´-kă-ă:

4 *From thence* it passed [c]toward Ăz´-mŏn, and went out unto [d]the river of Egypt; and the goings out of that coast were at the sea: this shall be your south coast.

5 And the east border *was* the salt sea, *even* unto the end of Jordan. And *their* border in the north quarter *was* from the bay of the sea at the uttermost part of Jordan:

6 And the border went up to Bĕth–hŏg´-lă, and passed along by the north of Bĕth–ăr´-ă-băh; and the border went up [e]to the stone of Bō´-hăn the son of Reuben:

7 And the border went up toward Dē´-bĭr from [f]the valley of Ā´-chôr, and so northward, looking toward Gĭl´-găl, that *is* before the going up to Ă-dŭm´-mĭm, which *is* on the south side of the river: and the border passed toward the waters of Ĕn–shē´-mĕsh, and the goings out thereof were at [3]Ĕn–rō´-gĕl:

8 And the border went up [g]by the valley of the son of Hĭn´-nom unto the south side of the [h]Jĕb´-ū-sīte; the same *is* Jerusalem: and the border went up to the top of the mountain that *lieth* before the valley of Hĭn´-nom westward, which *is* at the end [i]of the valley of [4]the giants northward:

9 And the border was drawn from the top of the hill unto the fountain of the water of Nĕph-tō´-ăh, and went out to the cities of mount Ē´-phrŏn; and the border was drawn to [j]Bā´-ă-lăh, which [k]*is* Kĭr´-jăth–jē´-ă-rĭm:

10 And the border compassed from Bā´-ă-lăh westward unto mount Sē´-ĭr, and passed along unto the side of mount Jē´-ă-rĭm, which *is* Chĕs´-ă-lŏn,

d Gen. 48.5. 1 Chr. 5.1,2.
e Num. 35.2. ch. 21.2. Eze. 45.1-8.
f Num. 32. 12. ch. 15.17.
g Deut. 1.36.
h Num. 13. 26. Deut. 1.19.
i Deut. 1.36. Rev. 14.4.
j ch. 1.3.
k Num. 13. 22.
l Num. 14.30. Ps. 90.10.
1 walked.
m Deut. 34.7.
n Deut. 31.2.
o 1 Sam. 14.6. 2 Chr. 14.11, 12. Ps. 18.32. Ps. 44.3. Ps. 60.12. Ps. 118.10-12. Rom. 8.31. Phil. 4.13.
p ch. 15.14. Judg. 1.20.
q Gen. 47.7-10. ch. 22.6.
r ch. 10.37. ch. 21.11. 1 Chr. 6.55.
s Gen. 23.2. ch. 15.13.
t ch. 11.23.

CHAP. 15

a Num. 34.3.
b Num. 33. 36.
1 tongue.
2 Or, the going up to Acrabbim.
c Num. 34.5.
d Gen. 15.18. 1 Ki. 8.65.
e ch. 18.17.
f ch. 7.26. Isa. 65.10. Hosea 2.15.
3 Fuller's fountain.
g ch. 18.16. 2 Ki. 23.10. Jer. 19.2,6.
h ch. 18.28. Judg. 1.21. Judg. 19.10.
i ch. 18.16.
4 Or, Rephaim.
j 1 Chr. 13.6.
k Judg. 18.12.

on the north side, and went down to
Bĕth–shē´-mĕsh, and passed on [l]to
Tĭm´-năh:
11 And the border went out unto the
side of Ĕk´-rŏn [m]northward: and the
border was drawn to Shĭc´-rŏn, and
passed along to mount Bā´-ă-lăh, and
went out unto Jăb´-nē̂el; and the goings out of the border were at the sea.
12 And the west border *was* [n]to the
great sea, and the coast *thereof*. This
is the coast of the children of Judah
round about according to their families.
13 ¶ And [o]unto Caleb the son of Jĕ-
phŭn´-nĕh he gave a part among the
children of Judah, according to the
commandment of the LORD to Joshua,
even [5]the city of Är´-bă the father of
Anak, which *city is* Hē´-brŏn.
14 And Caleb drove thence [p]the
three sons of Anak, [q]Shē´-shâi, and Ă-
hī´-măn, and Tăl´-mâi, the children of
Anak.
15 And [r]he went up thence to the inhabitants of Dē´-bĭr: and the name of
Dē´-bĭr before *was* Kĭr´-jăth–sē´-phĕr.
16 ¶ And Caleb said, He that smiteth
Kĭr´-jăth–sē´-phĕr, and taketh it, to
him will I give Ăch´-săh my daughter
to wife.
17 And [s]Ŏth´-nĭ-ĕl the [t]son of Kē´-năz,
the brother of Caleb, took it: and he
gave him Ăch´-săh his daughter to wife.
18 And [u]it came to pass, as she came
unto him, that she moved him to ask
of her father a field: and [v]she lighted
off *her* ass; and Caleb said unto her,
What wouldest thou?
19 Who answered, Give me [w]a blessing; for thou hast given me a south
land; give me also springs of water.
And he gave her the upper springs,
and the nether springs.
20 This [x]*is* the inheritance of the
tribe of the children of Judah according to their families.
21 And the uttermost cities of the
tribe of the children of Judah toward
the coast of Ē´-dŏm southward were
[6]Kăb´-zēel, [y]and Ē´-dĕr, and Jā´-gŭr,
22 And Kī´-năh, and Dī-mō´-năh, and
Ă-dā´-dăh,
23 And Kē´-dĕsh, and Hā´-zôr, and
Ĭth´-năn,
24 Ziph, and [z]Tē´-lĕm, and Bĕ-ā´-lōth,
25 And Hā´-zôr, Hă-dăt´-tăh, and
Kĕr´-ĭ-ōth, *and* Hĕz´-rŏn, which *is* Hā´-
zôr,
26 Ā´-măm, and Shē´-mă, and Mō-lā´-
dăh,
27 And Hā´-zär–găd´-dăh, and Hĕsh´-
mŏn, and Bĕth–pā´-lĕt,
28 And Hā´-zär–shû´-ăl, and Bē̂er-
shē´-bă, and Bĭz-jŏth´-jăh,
29 Bā´-ă-lăh, and Ī´-ĭm, and Ā´-zĕm,
30 And Ĕl-tō´-lăd, and Chĕs´-ĭl, and
Hôr´-măh,
31 And [a]Ziklag, and Măd-măn´-năh,
and Săn-săn´-năh,
32 And Lĕ-bā´-ōth, and Shĭl´-hĭm, and
Ā´-ĭn, and [b]Rimmon: all the cities *are*
twenty and nine, with their villages:
33 *And* in the valley, [c]Ĕsh-tā-ŏl, and
Zôr´-ĕ-ăh, and Ăsh´-năh,
34 And Ză-nō´-ăh, and Ĕn–găn´-nĭm,
Tăp´-pū-ăh, and Ē´-năm,
35 [d]Jär´-mûth, and [e]Adullam, Sō´-cōh,
[f]and Ă-zē´-kăh,
36 And [g]Shă-rā´-ĭm, and Ăd-ī-thā´-ĭm,
and Gĕ-dē´-răh, [7]and Gĕ-dē-rō-thā´-
ĭm; fourteen cities with their villages:
37 Zē´-năn, and Hă-dăsh´-ăh, and
Mĭg´-dăl–găd,
38 And Dĭ´-lē-ăn, and [h]Mĭz´-pĕh, and
[i]Jŏk´-thē̂el,
39 [j]Lā´-chĭsh, and [k]Bŏz´-kăth, [l]and
Ĕg-lŏn,
40 And Căb´-bŏn, and Läh´-măm, and
Kĭth´-lĭsh,
41 And Gĕ-dē´-rŏth, Bĕth–dā´-gŏn,
and Nā´-ă-măh, and Măk-kē´-dăh; sixteen cities with their villages:
42 Lĭb´-năh, and Ē´-thĕr, and Ăsh´-ăn,
43 And Jĭph´-tăh, and Ăsh´-năh, and
Nĕz´-ĭb,
44 And Kē-ī´-lăh, and Ăch´-zĭb, and
Mă-rē´-shăh; nine cities with their villages:
45 Ĕk´-rŏn, with her towns and her
villages:
46 From Ĕk´-rŏn even unto the sea,
all that *lay* [8]near [m]Ăsh´-dŏd, with their
villages:
47 Ăsh´-dŏd with her towns and her
villages, Gā´-ză with her towns and her
villages, unto the [n]river of Egypt, and
[o]the great sea, and the border *thereof*:
48 ¶ And in the mountains, Shā´-mĭr,
and Jăt´-tĭr, and Sō´-cōh,
49 And Dăn´-năh, and Kĭr´-jăth–săn´-
năh, which *is* Dē´-bĭr,
50 And Anab, and Ĕsh´-tĕ-mōh, and
Ā´-nĭm,
51 And [p]Gō´-shĕn, and Hō´-lŏn, and
Gī´-lōh; eleven cities with their villages:
52 Arab, and Dū´-măh, and Ĕsh´-ĕ-ăn,
53 And [9]Janum, and Bĕth–tăp´-pū-ăh,
and Ă-phē´-kăh,
54 And Hŭm´-tăh, and [q]Kĭr´-jăth–är´-
bă, which *is* Hē´-brŏn, and Zī´-ôr; nine
cities with their villages:
55 Mā´-ŏn, Carmel, and Ziph, and
Jŭt´-tăh,

l Gen. 38.13.
m ch. 19.43.
n Deut. 11. 24. Eze. 47.20.
o ch. 14.13.
5 Or, Kirjath-arba.
p Judg. 1.10.
q Num. 13. 22.
r ch. 10.38.
s Judg. 3.9.
t ch. 14.6.
u Judg. 1.14.
v Gen. 24.64. 1 Sam. 25. 23.
w Gen. 33.11.
x Gen. 49.8-12.
6 Jekabzeel.
y Gen. 35.21.
z 1 Sam. 15.4.
a ch. 19.5. 1 Sam. 27.6. 1 Chr. 12.1.
b Neh. 11.29.
c ch. 19.41.
d ch. 10.3,5. 1 Sam. 17.1.
e ch. 12.15.
f ch. 10.10.
g 1 Sam. 17. 52.
7 Or, or.
h Not that in ch. 11.3, Gen. 31.49, or ch. 18.26.
i 2 Ki. 14.7.
j ch. 10.3. 2 Ki. 18.14. 2 Chr. 11.9.
k 2 Ki. 22.1.
l ch. 12.12.
8 by the place of.
m ch. 13.3.
n Gen. 15.18.
o Num. 34.6.
p ch. 10.41. ch. 11.16.
9 Or, Janus.
q Gen. 23.2. ch. 14.15.

56 And Jĕz′-rēel, and Jŏk′-dĕ-ăm, and Ză-nō′-ăh,
57 Cain, Gĭb′-ĕ-ăh, and Tĭm′-năh; ten cities with their villages:
58 Hăl′-hŭl, Bĕth′–zûr, and Gē′-dôr,
59 And Mā′-ă-răth, and Bĕth′–ă-nōth, and Ĕl′-tĕ-kŏn; six cities with their villages:
60 [r]Kĭr′-jăth–bā′-ăl, which *is* Kĭr′-jăth–jē′-ă-rĭm, and Răb′-băh; two cities with their villages:
61 In the wilderness, Bĕth–ăr′-ă-băh, Mĭd′-dĭn, and Sĕ-cā′-căh,
62 And Nĭb′-shăn, and the city of Salt, and [s]Ĕn–ġē′-dī; six cities with their villages.
63 ¶ As for the Jĕb′-ū-sītes the inhabitants of Jerusalem, [t]the children of Judah could not drive them out: [u]but the Jĕb′-ū-sītes dwell with the children of Judah at Jerusalem unto this day.

CHAPTER 16

AND the lot of the children of Joseph [1]fell from Jordan by Jericho, unto the water of Jericho on the east, to the wilderness that goeth up from Jericho throughout mount Beth-el,
2 And goeth out from Beth-el to Luz, [a]and passeth along unto the borders of Ăr′-chī to Ăt′-ă-rōth,
3 And goeth down westward to the coast of Jăph′-lē-tī, [b]unto the coast of Bĕth–hôr′-ŏn the nether, and to [c]Gē′-zĕr: and the goings out thereof are at the sea.
4 So [d]the children of Joseph, Mă-năs′-sĕh and Ē′-phră-ĭm, took their inheritance.
5 ¶ And the border of the children of Ē′-phră-ĭm according to their families was *thus:* even the border of their inheritance on the east side was [e]Ăt′-ă-rōth–ăd′-där, [f]unto Bĕth–hôr′-ŏn the upper;
6 And the border went out toward the sea to [g]Mĭch-mē′-thăh on the north side; and the border went about eastward unto Tā′-ă-năth–shī′-lōh, and passed by it on the east to Jă-nō′-hăh;
7 And it went down from Jă-nō′-hăh to Ăt′-ă-rōth, [h]and to Nā′-ă-răth, and came to Jericho, and went out at Jordan.
8 The border went out from Tăp′-pū-ăh westward unto the [i]river Kā′-năh; and the goings out thereof were at the sea. This *is* the inheritance of the tribe of the children of Ē′-phră-ĭm by their families.
9 And the separate cities for the children of Ē′-phră-ĭm *were* among the inheritance of the children of Mă-năs′-sĕh, all the cities with their villages.
10 And [j]they drave not out the Canaanites that dwelt in Gē′-zĕr: but the Canaanites dwell among the Ē′-phră-ĭm-ītes unto this day, and serve [k]under tribute.

CHAPTER 17

THERE was also a lot for the tribe of Mă-năs′-sĕh; for he *was* the [a]firstborn of Joseph; *to wit,* for [b]Mā′-chĭr the firstborn of Mă-năs′-sĕh, the father of Gilead: because he was a man of war, therefore he had [c]Gilead and Bā′-shăn.
2 There was also *a lot* for [d]the rest of the children of Mă-năs′-sĕh by their families; for [e]the children of [1]Ā-bĭ-ē′-zĕr, and for the children of Hē′-lĕk, and for the children of Ăs′-rĭ-ĕl, and for the children of Shē′-chĕm, and [f]for the children of Hē′-phĕr, and for the children of Shĕ-mĭ′-dă: these *were* the male children of Mă-năs′-sĕh the son of Joseph by their families.
3 ¶ But [g]Zē-lŏph′-ĕ-hăd, the son of Hē′-phĕr, the son of Gilead, the son of Mā′-chĭr, the son of Mă-năs′-sĕh, had no sons, but daughters: and these *are* the names of his daughters, Măh′-lăh, and Noah, Hŏg′-lăh, Mĭl′-căh, and Tĭr′-zăh.
4 And they came near before Ĕl-ē-ā′-zär [h]the priest, and before Joshua the son of Nun, and before the princes, saying, [i]The LORD commanded Moses to give us an inheritance among our brethren. Therefore according to the [2]commandment of the LORD he gave them an inheritance among the brethren of their father.
5 And there fell ten portions to Mă-năs′-sĕh, beside the land of Gilead and Bā′-shăn, which *were* on the other side Jordan;
6 Because the daughters of Mă-năs′-sĕh had an inheritance among his sons: and [j]the rest of Mă-năs′-sĕh's sons had the land of Gilead.
7 ¶ And the coast of Mă-năs′-sĕh was from Asher to Mĭch-mē′-thăh, that *lieth* before Shē′-chĕm; and the border went along on the right hand unto the inhabitants of Ĕn–tăp′-pū-ăh.
8 *Now* Mă-năs′-sĕh had the land of [3]Tăp′-pū-ăh: but [k]Tăp′-pū-ăh on the border of Mă-năs′-sĕh *belonged* to the children of Ē′-phră-ĭm;
9 And the coast descended [l]unto the [4]river Kā′-năh, southward of the river: these [m]cities of Ē′-phră-ĭm *are* among the cities of Mă-năs′-sĕh: the coast of Mă-năs′-sĕh also *was* on the north side

r ch. 18.14. 1 Sam. 7.1,2. 1 Chr. 13.6.
s 1 Sam. 23. 29.
t Judg. 1.8, 21.
u Judg. 1.21. 2 Sam. 24. 16,18. 2 Chr. 3.1. Zech. 9.7.

CHAP. 16
1 went forth.
a Gen. 28.19. ch. 18.13. Judg. 1.26.
b ch. 18.13. 2 Chr. 8.5.
c 1 Chr. 7.28.
d ch. 17.14.
e ch. 18.13.
f 2 Chr. 8.5.
g ch. 17.7.
h 1 Chr. 7.28.
i ch. 17.9. ch. 19.28.
j ch. 15.63. 1 Ki. 9.16.
k Gen. 9.25. ch. 17.12,13. 1 Ki. 9.20, 21.

CHAP. 17.
a Gen. 41.51. Gen. 46.20. Gen. 48.18.
b Gen. 50.23. 1 Chr. 7.14.
c Deut. 3.15.
d Num. 26. 29-32.
e 1 Chr. 7.18.
1 Jeezer.
f Num. 26. 32.
g Num. 26. 33.
h ch. 14.1.
i Num. 27.6, 7.
2 mouth.
j Num. 26.29.
3 Or, City of apples.
k ch. 12.17. ch. 15.34. ch. 16.8.
l ch. 16.8.
4 Or, Brook of reeds.
m ch. 16.9.

of the river, and the outgoings of it
were at the sea:
10 Southward *it was* Ē-phră-ĭm's,
and northward *it was* Mă-năs-sēh's,
and the sea is his border; and they met
together in Asher on the north, and
in Ĭs-să-char on the east.
11 And [n]Mă-năs-sēh had in Ĭs-să-
char and in Asher [o]Bĕth-shē-ăn and
her towns, and Ĭb-lĕ-ăm and her
towns, and the inhabitants of Dor and
her towns, and the inhabitants of En-
dor and her towns, and the inhabitants of Tā-ă-năch and her towns, and
the inhabitants of Mĕ-gĭd-dō and her
towns, *even* three countries.
12 Yet [p]the children of Mă-năs-sēh
could not drive out *the inhabitants of*
those cities; but the Canaanites would
dwell in that land.
13 Yet it came to pass, when the
children of Israel were waxen strong,
that they put the Canaanites to [q]trib-
ute; but [5]did not utterly drive them
out.
14 And [r]the children of Joseph spake
unto Joshua, saying, Why hast thou
given me *but* [s]one lot and one portion
to inherit, seeing I *am* [t]a great people,
forasmuch as the LORD hath blessed
me hitherto?
15 And Joshua answered them, If
thou *be* a great people, *then* get thee
up to the wood *country*, and cut down
for thyself there in the land of the Pĕ-
rĭz-zītes and of the [6]giants, if mount
Ē-phră-ĭm be too narrow for thee.
16 And the children of Joseph said,
The hill is not enough for us: and all
the Canaanites that dwell in the land
of the valley have chariots [u]of iron,
both they who *are* of Bĕth-shē-ăn and
her towns, and *they* who *are* [v]of the
valley of Jĕz-rē-el.
17 And Joshua spake unto the house
of Joseph, *even* to Ē-phră-ĭm and to
Mă-năs-sēh, saying, Thou *art* a great
people, and hast great power: thou
shalt not have one lot *only:*
18 But the mountain shall be thine;
for it *is* a wood, and thou shalt cut it
down: and the outgoings of it shall be
thine: for thou shalt drive out the Canaanites, though [w]they have iron
chariots, *and* though they *be* strong.

CHAPTER 18

AND the whole congregation of the
children of Israel assembled together [a]at Shī-lōh, and [b]set up the
tabernacle of the congregation [1]there.
And the land was subdued before
them.
2 And there remained among the
children of Israel seven tribes, which
had not yet received their inheritance.
3 And Joshua said unto the children
of Israel, [c]How long *are* ye slack to go
to possess the land, which the LORD
God of your fathers hath given you?
4 Give out from among you three
men for *each* tribe: and I will send
them, and they shall rise, and go
through the land, and describe it according to the inheritance of them;
and they shall come *again* to me.
5 And they shall divide it into seven
parts: Judah [d]shall abide in their coast
on the south, and [e]the house of Joseph
shall abide in their coasts on the
north.
6 Ye shall therefore describe the land
into seven parts, and bring *the descrip-
tion* hither to me, [f]that I may cast
lots for you here before the LORD our
God.
7 But [g]the Levites have no part
among you; for the priesthood of the
[h]LORD *is* their inheritance: and Gad,
[i]and Reuben, and half the tribe of
Mă-năs-sēh, have received their inheritance beyond Jordan on the east,
which Moses the servant of the LORD
gave them.
8 ¶ And the men arose, and went
away: and Joshua charged them that
went to describe the land, saying, Go
and walk through the land, and describe it, and come again to me, that
I may here cast lots for you before the
LORD in Shī-lōh.
9 And the men went and passed
through the land, and described it by
cities into seven parts in a book, and
came *again* to Joshua to the host at
Shī-lōh.
10 ¶ And Joshua cast [j]lots for them
in Shī-lōh before the LORD: and there
Joshua divided the land unto the children of Israel according to their divisions.
11 ¶ And the lot of the tribe of the
children of Benjamin came up according to their families: and the coast of
their lot came forth between the children of Judah and the children of
Joseph.
12 And [k]their border on the north
side was from Jordan; and the border
went up to the side of Jericho on the
north side, and went up through the
mountains westward; and the goings
out thereof were at the wilderness of
Bĕth-ā-vĕn.
13 And the border went over from
thence toward Luz, to the side of Luz,

n ch. 16.9. 1 Chr. 7.29.
o 1 Sam. 31. 10. 1 Ki. 4.12.
p Ex. 23.29-33.
q ch. 16.10.
5 driving they drove them not out.
r ch. 16.4.
s Gen. 48.22.
t Gen. 48.19.
6 Rephaim.
u Judg. 1.19.
v ch. 19.18. Judg. 6.33. 1 Ki. 4.12. 1 Ki. 18.46.
w ch. 11.4-6. ch. 13.6. Rom. 8.31. Heb. 13.6.
CHAP. 18
a ch. 19.51. ch. 21.2. ch. 22.9. Judg. 21.19. 1 Sam. 14.3. Ps. 78.58,59,60. Jer. 7.12.
b Judg. 18.31. 1 Sam. 1.3, 24. 1 Sam. 4.3,4.
1 Where it remained till taken by the Philistines at the death of Eli.
c Pro. 2.2-6. Pro. 10.4. Zeph. 3.16. Matt. 20.6. Phil. 3.13, 14.
d ch. 15.1.
e ch. 16.1,4.
f ch. 14.2.
g ch. 13.33.
h Deut. 10.9. Eze. 44.28.
i ch. 13.8.
j Pro. 16.33.
k ch. 16.1.

[l]which *is* Beth-el, southward; and the
border descended to Ăt-ă-rŏth–ā-dăr,
near the hill that *lieth* on the south
side of [m]the nether Bĕth–hôr-ŏn.
14 And the border was drawn *thence*,
and compassed the corner of [2]the sea
southward, from the hill that *lieth* before Bĕth–hôr-ŏn southward; and the
goings out thereof were at [n]Kĭr-jăth–
bā-ăl, which *is* Kĭr-jăth–jē-ă-rĭm, a
city of the children of Judah: this *was*
the west quarter.
15 And the south quarter *was* from
the end of Kĭr-jăth–jē-ă-rĭm, and the
border went out on the west, and went
out to [o]the well of waters of Nĕph-
tō-ăh:
16 And the border came down to the
end of the mountain that *lieth* before
[p]the valley of the son of Hĭn-nom, *and*
which *is* in the valley of [3]the giants on
the north, and descended to the valley
of Hĭn-nom, to the side of Jĕb-ū-sī on
the south, and descended to [4]Ĕn–rō-
gĕl,
17 And was drawn from the north,
and went forth to Ĕn–shē-mĕsh, and
went forth toward Gē-lī-lŏth, which *is*
over against the going up of Ă-dŭm-
mĭm, and descended to [q]the stone of
Bō-hăn the son of Reuben,
18 And passed along toward the side
over against [5]Ăr-ă-băh northward,
and went down unto Ăr-ă-băh:
19 And the border passed along to
the side of Bĕth–hŏg-lăh northward:
and the outgoings of the border were
at the north [6]bay of the salt sea at the
south end of Jordan: this *was* the
south coast.
20 And Jordan was the border of it
on the east side. This *was* the inheritance of the children of Benjamin, by
the coasts thereof round about, according to their families.
21 Now the cities of the tribe of the
children of Benjamin according to
their families were [r]Jericho, and
[s]Bĕth–hŏg-lăh, and the valley of Kē-
zĭz,
22 And Bĕth–ăr-ă-băh, and Zĕm-ă-
rā-ĭm, and Beth-el,
23 And Ā-vĭm, and Pâr-ăh, and Ŏph-
răh,
24 And Chē-phăr–hă-ăm-mō-nâi,
and Ŏph-nī, and [t]Gā-bă; twelve cities
with their villages:
25 Gibeon, and Rā-măh, and Bē-ēr-
ŏth,
26 And Mĭz-pēh, and Chĕ-phī-răh,
and Mō-zăh,
27 And Rē-kĕm, and Ĭr-pē-ēl, and
Tăr-ă-lăh,

l Gen. 28.19.
m ch. 16.3.
2 The pool of Gibeon.
n ch. 9.17. 1 Chr. 13.6.
o ch. 15.9.
p ch. 15.8. 2 Ki. 23.10. 2 Chr. 28.3. 2 Chr. 33.6. Isa. 30.33. Jer. 19.2.
3 Or, Rephaim.
4 Fuller's fountain.
q ch. 15.6.
5 Or, the plain. ch. 15.6.
6 tongue.
r ch. 2.1. ch. 6.26. 1 Ki. 16.34. Luke 10.30. Luke 19.1.
s ch. 15.6.
t ch. 21.17. 1 Sam. 15. 34. Ezra 2.26. Isa. 10.29.
u 2 Sam. 21. 14.
7 Which belonged partly to Benjamin, and partly to Judah. ch. 15.8.
v Gen. 46.21. 1 Chr. 7.6. 1 Chr. 8.1. Acts. 17.26.

CHAP. 19

a Gen. 49.7.
b 1 Chr. 4.28.
c Gen. 21.14, 31. Gen. 26.33. ch. 15.28.
d Neh. 11.26.
e 1 Chr. 4.29, 30.
f Gen. 49.13. Ex. 23.31. The Mediterranean.
g ch. 12.22. 1 Ki. 4.12. 1 Chr. 6.68.
1 Or, which is drawn.
h ch. 21.34.
i ch. 11.1. ch. 12.20.

28 And [u]Zē-lăh, Ē-lĕph, and [7]Jĕb-ū-
sī, which *is* Jerusalem, Gĭb-ē-ăth, *and*
Kĭr-jăth; fourteen cities with their
villages. This *is* the inheritance of the
children of Benjamin [v]according to
their families.

CHAPTER 19

AND the second lot came forth to
Simeon, *even* for the tribe of the
children of Simeon according to their
families: and their inheritance was
[a]within the inheritance of the children
of Judah.
2 And [b]they had in their inheritance
[c]Bē-ēr–shē-bă, or Shē-bă, and [d]Mō-lā-
dăh,
3 And Hā-zăr–shû-ăl, and Bā-lăh,
and Ā-zĕm,
4 And [e]Ĕl-tō-lăd, and Bĕth-ŭl, and
Hôr-măh,
5 And Ziklag, and Bĕth–măr-că-
bŏth, and Hā-zăr–sû-săh,
6 And Bĕth–lĕ-bā-ŏth, and Shă-rŭ-
hĕn; thirteen cities and their villages:
7 Ā-ĭn, Rĕm-mŏn, and Ē-thĕr, and
Ăsh-ăn; four cities and their villages:
8 And all the villages that *were* round
about these cities to Bā-ă-lăth–bē-ēr,
Rā-măth of the south. This *is* the inheritance of the tribe of the children
of Simeon according to their families.
9 Out of the portion of the children
of Judah *was* the inheritance of the
children of Simeon: for the part of the
children of Judah was too much for
them: therefore the children of
Simeon had their inheritance within
the inheritance of them.
10 ¶ And the third lot came up for
the children of Zĕ-bū-lŭn according to
their families: and the border of their
inheritance was unto Sâr-ĭd:
11 And their border went up toward
[f]the sea, and Măr-ă-lăh, and reached
to Dăb-bă-shĕth, and reached to the
river that *is* [g]before Jŏk-nē-ăm;
12 And turned from Sâr-ĭd eastward
toward the sunrising unto the border
of Chĭs-lŏth–tā-bôr, and then goeth
out to Dăb-ē-răth, and goeth up to
Jă-phī-ă,
13 And from thence passeth on along
on the east to Gĭt-tăh–hē-phĕr, to Ĭt-
tăh–kā-zĭn, and goeth out to Rĕm-
mŏn–[1]mē-thō-ăr to Nē-ăh;
14 And the border compasseth it on
the north side to Hăn-nă-thŏn: and
the outgoings thereof are in the valley
of Jĭph-thăh–ĕl:
15 And [h]Kăt-tăth, and Nă-hăl-lăl,
and [i]Shĭm-rŏn, and Ī-dă-lăh, and

Beth-lehem: twelve cities with their
villages.
16 This *is* [j]the inheritance of the children of Zĕ-bū´-lŭn according to their
families, these cities with their villages.
17 ¶ *And* the fourth lot came out to
Ĭs´-să-chär, for the children of Ĭs´-să-
chär according to their families.
18 And their border was toward Jĕz´-
rĕel, [k]and Chĕ-sŭl´-lōth, [l]and Shû´-
nĕm,
19 And Hăph´-ă-ră-ĭm, and Shī´-ŏn,
and Ă-nā´-hă-răth,
20 And Răb´-bĭth, and Kĭsh´-ĭ-ŏn, and
Abez,
21 And [m]Rĕm´-ĕth, and Ĕn–găn´-nĭm,
and Ĕn–hăd´-dăh, and Bĕth–păz´-zĕz;
22 And the coast reacheth [n]to Tā´-
bôr, and Shā-hă-zī´-măh, and Bĕth–
shē´-mĕsh; and the outgoings of their
border were at Jordan: sixteen cities
with their villages.
23 This *is* the inheritance of the tribe
of the children of Ĭs´-să-chär according
to their families, the cities and their
villages.
24 ¶ And the fifth lot came out for
the tribe of the children of Asher according to their families.
25 And their border was [o]Hĕl´-kăth,
and Hā´-lī, and Bē´-tĕn, and Ăch´-shăph.
26 And Ă-lăm´-mĕ-lĕch, and Ā´-măd,
and Mī´-shĕ-ăl; and reacheth to Carmel [p]westward, and to Shī´-hôr–lĭb´-
năth;
27 And turneth toward the sunrising
to Bĕth–dā´-gŏn, and reacheth to Zĕ-
bū´-lŭn, and to the valley of Jĭph´-thăh–
ĕl toward the north side of Bĕth–ē´-
mĕk, and Nēi´-ĕl, and goeth out to
[q]Cā´-bûl on the left hand,
28 And Hē´-brŏn, and Rē´-hŏb, and
Hăm´-mŏn, and [r]Kā´-năh, *even* unto
great [s]Zī´-dŏn;
29 And *then* the coast turneth to Rā´-
măh, and to the strong city [2]Tyre; and
the coast turneth to Hō´-săh; and the
outgoings thereof are at the sea from
the coast to [t]Ăch´-zĭb:
30 Ŭm´-măh also, and Ā´-phĕk, and
Rē´-hŏb: twenty and two cities with
their villages.
31 This *is* the inheritance of the tribe
of the children of Asher according to
their families, these cities with their
villages.
32 ¶ The sixth lot came out to the
children of Năph´-tă-lī, *even* for the
children of Năph´-tă-lī according to
their families.
33 And their coast was from Hē´-
lĕph, from Ăl´-lŏn to Zā-ă-năn´-nĭm,
and Ăd´-ă-mī, Nē´-kĕb, and Jăb´-nĕel,
unto Lakum; and the outgoings thereof were at Jordan:
34 And *then* [u]the coast turneth westward to Ăz´-nŏth–tā´-bôr, and goeth
out from thence to Hŭk´-kŏk, and
reacheth to Zĕ-bū´-lŭn on the south
side, and reacheth to Asher on the
west side, and to Judah upon Jordan
toward the sunrising.
35 And the fenced cities *are* Zĭd´-dĭm,
Zer, and [v]Hăm´-măth, Rakkath, and
[w]Chĭn´-nĕ-rĕth,
36 And Ăd´-ă-măh, and Rā´-măh, and
Hā´-zôr,
37 And Kē´-dĕsh, and Ĕd´-rĕ-ī, and
Ĕn–hā´-zôr,
38 And Ī´-rŏn, and Mĭg´-dăl–ĕl, Hôr´-
ĕm, and Bĕth´–ă-năth, and Bĕth–shē´-
mĕsh; nineteen cities with their villages.
39 This *is* the inheritance of the tribe
of the children of Năph´-tă-lī according to their families, the cities and
their villages.
40 ¶ *And* the seventh lot came out for
the tribe of the children of Dan according to their families.
41 And the coast of their inheritance
was [x]Zôr´-ăh, and Ĕsh´-tā-ŏl, and Ĭr–
shē´-mĕsh,
42 And [y]Shā-ă-lăb´-bĭn, and Ăj´-ă-
lŏn, and Jĕth´-lăh,
43 And Ē´-lŏn, and Thĭm´-nă-thăh,
and Ĕk´-rŏn,
44 And Ĕl´-tĕ-kĕh, and Gĭb´-bĕ-thŏn,
and Bā´-ă-lăth,
45 And Jehud, and Bĕn´-ē–bē´-răk,
and Găth–rĭm´-mŏn,
46 And Mē–jär´-kŏn, and Rakkon,
with the border [3]before [4]Jā´-phō.
47 And [z]the coast of the children of
Dan went out *too little* for them:
therefore the children of Dan went up
to fight against Lē´-shĕm, and took
it, and [a]smote it with the edge of the
sword, and possessed it, and dwelt
therein, and called Lē´-shĕm, [b]Dan,
after the name of Dan their father.
48 This [c]*is* the inheritance of the
tribe of the children of Dan according
to their families, these cities with their
villages.
49 ¶ When they had made an end of
dividing the land for inheritance by
their coasts, the children of Israel
gave an inheritance to Joshua the son
of Nun among them:
50 According to the word of the
LORD they gave him the city which he
asked, *even* [d]Tĭm´-năth–sē´-răh [e]in
mount Ē´-phră-ĭm: and he built the
city, and dwelt therein.

j Acts 17.26.
k ch. 15.16. Judg. 6.33. 1 Ki. 21.1, 23. 2 Ki. 8.29. Hosea 1.4,5.
l 1 Sam. 28.4. 2 Ki. 4.8.
m ch. 21.29. Jarmuth.
n Judg. 4.6. 1 Sam. 10.3. 1 Chr. 6.77. Ps. 89.12.
o 2 Sam. 2.16. 1 Chr. 6.75. Hukok.
p 1 Ki. 18.19. 2 Ki. 2.25. Isa. 35.2. Jer. 46.18. Amos 1.2. Amos 9.3. Micah 7.14.
q 1 Ki. 9.13.
r John 2.1. Cana.
s Gen. 10.15, 19. ch. 11.8. Judg. 1.31. Acts 27.3.
2 Tzor, that is, The rock.
t Gen. 38.5. Micah 1.14.
u Deut. 33. 23.
v Gen. 10.18.
w Deut. 3.17. ch. 11.2. ch. 12.3. Mark 6.53. Luke 5.1.
x Judg. 13.2.
y 1 Ki. 4.9.
3 Or, over against.
4 Or, Joppa.
z Judg. 18.1.
a Gen. 49.17.
b Judg. 18.29.
c Num. 26.54. Acts 17.26.
d ch. 24.30.
e 1 Chr. 7.24.

51 These [f]*are* the inheritances, which
Ĕl-ē-ā′-zär the priest, and Joshua the
son of Nun, and the heads of the fathers of the tribes of the children of Israel, divided for an inheritance by lot
[g]in Shī′-lōh before the LORD, at the
door of the tabernacle of the congregation. So they made an end of dividing the country.

CHAPTER 20

THE LORD also spake unto Joshua,
saying,
2 Speak to the children of Israel, saying, Appoint [a]out for you cities of
refuge, whereof I spake unto you by
the hand of Moses:
3 That the slayer that killeth *any*
person unawares *and* unwittingly
may flee thither: and they shall be
your refuge from the avenger of
blood.
4 And when he that doth flee unto
one of those cities shall stand at the
entering of the [b]gate of the city, and
shall declare his cause in the ears of
the elders of that city, they shall [1]take
him into the city unto them, and give
him a place, that he may dwell among
them.
5 And [c]if the avenger of blood pursue
after him, then they shall not deliver
the slayer up into his hand; because
he smote his neighbour unwittingly,
and hated him not beforetime.
6 And he shall dwell in that city, until
[d]he stand before the congregation for
judgment, *and* until the death of the
high priest that shall be in those days:
then shall the slayer return, and come
unto his own city, and unto his own
house, unto the city from whence he
fled.
7 ¶ And they [2]appointed [e]Kē′-dĕsh in
Galilee in mount Năph′-tă-lī, and Shē′-
chĕm [f]in mount Ē′-phră-ĭm, and [g]Kĭr′-
jăth-är′-bă, which *is* Hē′-brŏn, in [h]the
mountain of Judah.
8 And on the other side Jordan by
Jericho eastward, they assigned Bē′-
zĕr in [i]the wilderness upon the plain
out of the tribe of Reuben, and [j]Rā′-
mŏth in Gilead out of the tribe of Gad,
and [k]Gō′-lăn in Bā′-shăn out of the
tribe of Mă-năs′-sēh.
9 These [l]were the cities appointed for
all the children of Israel, and for the
stranger that sojourneth among them,
that whosoever killeth *any* person at
unawares might flee thither, and not
die by the hand of the avenger of
blood, until he stood before the congregation.

f Num. 34. 17. ch. 14.1.
g ch. 18.1,10. Ps. 78.58. Jer. 7.12.

CHAP. 20

a Ex. 21.13. Deut. 4.41-43. Rom. 8.1, 33,34. Heb. 6.18, 19.
b Ruth 4.1,2. Job 5.4. Jer. 38.7.
1 gather. Ps. 26.9.
c Num. 35. 12.
d Num. 35. 12,25.
2 sanctified.
e ch. 21.32. 1 Chr. 6.76.
f Gen. 33.18, 19. ch. 21.21. 2 Chr. 10.1.
g ch. 14.15. ch. 21.11,13.
h Luke 1.39.
i ch. 21.36. 1 Chr. 6.78.
j ch. 21.38. 1 Ki. 22.3.
k ch. 21.27.
l Num. 35.15.

CHAP. 21

a ch. 14.1. ch. 17.4.
b ch. 18.1.
c Num. 35.2. Matt. 10.10. Gal. 6.6. 1 Tim. 5.17, 18.
d ch. 24.33.
e Gen. 49.7. ch. 18.6. Pro. 16.33.
f Num. 35.2.
1 called.
g 1 Chr. 6.55.
2 Or, Kirjatharba.
h ch. 14.15. ch. 15.13.
i 2 Sam. 2.1-3. 2 Sam. 5.1-5. Luke 1.39.
j ch. 14.14.
k ch. 20.7-9. 1 Chr. 6.57.

CHAPTER 21

THEN came near the heads of the
fathers of the Levites unto Ĕl-ē-ā′-
zär [a]the priest, and unto Joshua the
son of Nun, and unto the heads of the
fathers of the tribes of the children of
Israel;
2 And they spake unto them at Shī′-
lōh [b]in the land of Canaan, saying,
[c]The LORD commanded by the hand
of Moses to give us cities to dwell in,
with the suburbs thereof for our
cattle.
3 And the children of Israel gave unto the Levites out of their inheritance,
at the commandment of the LORD,
these cities and their suburbs.
4 And the lot came out for the families of the Kō′-hăth-ītes: and the children of Aaron the priest, *which were*
of the Levites, [d]had by lot out of the
tribe of Judah, and out of the tribe of
Simeon, and out of the tribe of Benjamin, thirteen cities.
5 And the rest of the children of Kō′-
hăth *had* by lot out of the families of
the tribe of Ē′-phră-ĭm, and out of the
tribe of Dan, and out of the half tribe
of Mă-năs′-sēh, ten cities.
6 And the children of Gĕr′-shŏn *had*
by lot out of the families of the tribe
of Ĭs′-să-chär, and out of the tribe of
Asher, and out of the tribe of Năph′-
tă-lī, and out of the half tribe of Mă-
năs′-sēh in Bā′-shăn, thirteen cities.
7 The children of Mĕ-rār′-ī by their
families *had* out of the tribe of Reuben, and out of the tribe of Gad, and
out of the tribe of Zĕ-bū′-lŭn, twelve
cities.
8 And [e]the children of Israel gave by
lot unto the Levites these cities with
their suburbs, [f]as the LORD commanded by the hand of Moses.
9 ¶ And they gave out of the tribe of
the children of Judah, and out of the
tribe of the children of Simeon, these
cities which are *here* [1]mentioned by
name,
10 Which the children of Aaron, *being* of the families of the Kō′-hăth-
ītes, *who were* of the children of Levi,
had: for theirs was the first lot.
11 And [g]they gave them [2]the city of
Är′-bă the father of [h]Anak, which *city*
is Hē′-brŏn, [i]in the hill *country* of Judah, with the suburbs thereof round
about it.
12 But [j]the fields of the city, and the
villages thereof, gave they to Caleb
the son of Jĕ-phŭn′-nĕh for his possession.
13 ¶ Thus [k]they gave to the children

of Aaron the priest [l]Hē´brŏn with her suburbs, *to be* a city of refuge for the slayer; and [m]Lĭb´năh with her suburbs,

14 And [n]Jăt´tĭr with her suburbs, and [o]Ĕsh-tĕ-mō´ă with her suburbs,

15 And [p]Hō´lŏn with her suburbs, and [q]Dē´bĭr with her suburbs,

16 And [r]Ā´ĭn with her suburbs, and [s]Jŭt´tăh with her suburbs, *and* Bĕth–shē´mĕsh [t]with her suburbs; nine cities out of those two tribes.

17 And out of the tribe of Benjamin, Gibeon [u]with her suburbs, Gē´bă [v]with her suburbs,

18 Ăn´ă-thōth with her suburbs, and [w]Ăl´mŏn with her suburbs; four cities.

19 All the cities of the children of Aaron, the priests, *were* thirteen cities with their suburbs.

20 ¶ And [x]the families of the children of Kō´hăth, the Levites which remained of the children of Kō´hăth, even they had the cities of their lot out of the tribe of Ē´phră-ĭm.

21 For they gave them [y]Shē´chĕm with her suburbs in mount Ē´phră-ĭm, *to be* a city of refuge for the slayer; and Gē´zĕr with her suburbs,

22 And Kĭb´ză-ĭm with her suburbs, and Bĕth–hôr´ŏn with her suburbs; four cities.

23 And out of the tribe of Dan, Ĕl´tĕ-kēh with her suburbs, Gĭb´bĕ-thŏn with her suburbs,

24 Aî´jă-lŏn with her suburbs, Găth–rĭm´mŏn with her suburbs; four cities.

25 And out of the half tribe of Mă-năs´sēh, Tā´năch with her suburbs, and Găth–rĭm´mŏn with her suburbs; two cities.

26 All the cities *were* ten with their suburbs for the families of the children of Kō´hăth that remained.

27 ¶ And [z]unto the children of Gĕr´shŏn, of the families of the Levites, out of the *other* half tribe of Mă-năs´sēh *they gave* Gō´lăn [a]in Bā´shăn with her suburbs, *to be* a city of refuge for the slayer; and [3]Bĕ-ĕsh´–tĕ-răh with her suburbs; two cities.

28 And out of the tribe of Ĭs´să-chăr, Kĭ´shŏn with her suburbs, Dăb´ă-rēh with her suburbs,

29 Jär´mûth with her suburbs, Ĕn–găn´nĭm with her suburbs; four cities.

30 And out of the tribe of Asher, Mĭ´shăl with her suburbs, Abdon with her suburbs,

31 Hĕl´kăth with her suburbs, and Rē´hŏb with her suburbs; four cities.

l ch. 15.54.
m ch. 10.29. ch. 15.42. Isa. 37.8.
n ch. 15.48.
o ch. 15.50.
p 1 Chr. 6.58. Hilen.
q ch. 15.49.
r 1 Chr. 6.59. Ashan.
s ch. 15.55.
t ch. 15.10.
u ch. 18.25.
v ch. 18.24. Gaba.
w 1 Chr. 6.60. Alemeth.
x 1 Chr. 6.66.
y Gen. 33.19. ch. 20.7. 1 Ki. 12.1.
z 1 Chr. 6.71.
a Deut. 1.4. ch. 20.8. 1 Chr. 6.71.
3 Or, Ashtaroth.
b ch. 20.7.
c 1 Chr. 6.77.
d ch. 20.8.
e Deut. 4.43. 1 Ki. 4.13.
f Gen. 32.1. 2 Sam. 2.8.
g Gen. 49.7.
4 That is, 608 yards broad for barns, gardens, etc., and 1216 more for fields and vineyards.
h Gen. 13.15. Gen. 15.18. Gen. 26.3.
i ch. 11.23. ch. 22.4.
j Deut. 7.24.
k Ex. 3.7,8. ch. 23.14. 1 Ki. 8.56. Isa. 49.7,8, 15,16. Matt. 24.35. Luke 21.33.
CHAP. 22
a Num. 32. 20.
b ch. 1.16,17.

32 And out of the tribe of Năph´tă-lī, [b]Kē´dĕsh in Galilee with her suburbs, *to be* a city of refuge for the slayer; and Hăm´mōth–dôr with her suburbs, and Kär´tăn with her suburbs; three cities.

33 All the cities of the Gĕr´shŏn-ītes according to their families *were* thirteen cities with their suburbs.

34 ¶ And [c]unto the families of the children of Mĕ-rär´ī, the rest of the Levites, out of the tribe of Zĕ-bū´lŭn, Jŏk´nĕ-ăm with her suburbs, and Kär´tăh with her suburbs,

35 Dĭm´năh with her suburbs, Nā´hă-lăl with her suburbs; four cities.

36 And out of the tribe of Reuben, [d]Bē´zĕr with her suburbs, and Jă-hā´zăh with her suburbs,

37 Kē´dĕ-mōth with her suburbs, and Mĕph´ā-ăth with her suburbs; four cities.

38 And out of the tribe of Gad, Rā´mōth [e]in Gilead with her suburbs, *to be* a city of refuge for the slayer; and [f]Mā-hă-nā´ĭm with her suburbs,

39 Hĕsh´bŏn with her suburbs, Jā´zĕr with her suburbs; four cities in all.

40 So all the cities for the children of Mĕ-rär´ī by their families, which were remaining of the families of the Levites, were *by* their lot twelve cities.

41 All [g]the cities of the Levites within the possession of the children of Israel *were* forty and eight cities with their suburbs.

42 These cities were every one with [4]their suburbs round about them: thus *were* all these cities.

43 ¶ And the LORD gave unto Israel [h]all the land which he sware to give unto their fathers; and they possessed it, and dwelt therein.

44 And [i]the LORD gave them rest round about, according to all that he sware unto their fathers: and there [j]stood not a man of all their enemies before them; the LORD delivered all their enemies into their hand.

45 There [k]failed not ought of any good thing which the LORD had spoken unto the house of Israel; all came to pass.

CHAPTER 22

THEN Joshua called the Reubenites, and the Gadites, and the half tribe of Mă-năs´sēh,

2 And said unto them, Ye have kept [a]all that Moses the servant of the LORD commanded you, [b]and have obeyed my voice in all that I commanded you:

3 Ye have not left your brethren

these many days unto this day, but
have kept the charge of the commandment of the LORD your God.
4 And now the LORD your God hath
given rest unto your brethren, as he
promised them: therefore now return
ye, and get you unto your tents, *and* unto the land of your possession, [c]which
Moses the servant of the LORD gave
you on the other side Jordan.
5 But [d]take diligent heed to do the
commandment and the law, which
Moses the servant of the LORD charged you, [e]to love the LORD your God,
and to walk in all his ways, and to
keep his commandments, and to
cleave unto him, and to serve him with
all your heart and with all your soul.
6 So Joshua [f]blessed them, and sent
them away: and they went unto their
tents.
7 ¶ Now to the *one* half of the tribe
of Mă-năs´-sēh Moses had given
possession in Bā´-shăn: [g]but unto the
other half thereof gave Joshua among
their brethren on this side Jordan
westward. And when Joshua sent
them away also unto their tents, then
he blessed them,
8 And he spake unto them, saying,
Return with much riches unto your
tents, and with very much cattle, with
silver, and with gold, and with brass,
and with iron, and with very much
raiment: divide [h]the spoil of your enemies with your brethren.
9 ¶ And the children of Reuben and
the children of Gad and the half tribe
of Mă-năs´-sēh returned, and departed
from the children of Israel out of Shī´-lōh, which *is* in the land of Canaan, to
go unto the [i]country of Gilead, to the
land of their possession, whereof they
were possessed, according to the word
of the LORD by the hand of Moses.
10 ¶ And when they came unto the
borders of Jordan, that *are* in the land
of Canaan, the children of Reuben
and the children of Gad and the half
tribe of Mă-năs´-sēh built there an
altar by Jordan, a great altar to see to.
11 ¶ And the children of Israel heard
[j]say, Behold, the children of Reuben
and the children of Gad and the half
tribe of Mă-năs´-sēh have built an altar
over against the land of Canaan, in
the borders of Jordan, at the passage
of the children of Israel.
12 And when the children of Israel
heard *of it*, [k]the whole congregation
of the children of Israel gathered
themselves together at Shī´-lōh, to go
up to war against them.
13 And the children of Israel sent [l]unto the children of Reuben, and to the
children of Gad, and to the half tribe
of Mă-năs´-sēh, into the land of Gilead, [m]Phĭn´-ē-hăs the son of Ĕl-ē-ā´-zär the priest,
14 And with him ten princes, of each
[1]chief house a prince throughout all
the tribes of Israel; and [n]each one *was*
an head of the house of their fathers
among the thousands of Israel.
15 ¶ And they came unto the children
of Reuben, and to the children of Gad,
and to the half tribe of Mă-năs´-sēh,
unto the land of Gilead, and they
spake with them, saying,
16 Thus saith the whole congregation of the LORD, What trespass *is* this
that ye have committed against the
God of Israel, to turn away this day
from following the LORD, in that ye
have builded you an altar, [o]that
ye might rebel this day against the
LORD?
17 *Is* the iniquity [p]of Pē´-ôr too little
for us, from which we are not cleansed
until this day, although there was a
plague in the congregation of the
LORD,
18 But that ye must turn away this
day from following the LORD? and it
will be, *seeing* ye rebel to day against
the LORD, that to morrow [q]he will be
wroth with the whole congregation of
Israel.
19 Notwithstanding, if the land of
your possession *be* unclean, *then* pass
ye over unto the land of the possession
of the LORD, wherein the [r]LORD's tabernacle dwelleth, and take possession
among us: but rebel not against the
LORD, nor rebel against us, in building you an altar beside the altar of the
LORD our God.
20 Did [s]not Ā´-chăn the son of Zē´-răh
commit a trespass in the accursed
thing, and wrath fell on all the congregation of Israel? and that man
perished not alone in his iniquity.
21 ¶ Then [t]the children of Reuben
and the children of Gad and the half
tribe of Mă-năs´-sēh answered, and
said unto the heads of the thousands
of Israel,
22 The LORD [u]God of gods, the LORD
God of gods, he [v]knoweth, and Israel
he shall know; if *it be* in rebellion, or
if in transgression against the LORD,
(save us not this day,)
23 That we have built us an altar to
turn from following the LORD, or if to
offer thereon burnt offering or meat
offering, or if to offer peace offerings

c Deut. 29.8. ch. 13.8.
d Deut. 6.6, 17. 2 Ki. 10.31. Ps. 119.4. Matt. 22.36. Rom. 13.10. 1 Tim. 1.5.
e Deut. 10.12. Deut. 19.9. ch. 23.11. Luke 11.42. John 15.9, 10. 1 John 5.3. Jude 21.
f Gen. 47.7. ch. 14.13. 2 Sam. 6.18. Luke 24.50.
g ch. 17.5.
h 1 Sam. 30. 24.
i Num. 32.1, 26, 29.
j Lev. 17.8. Deut. 13.12.
k Judg. 20.1.
l Deut. 13.14.
m Ex. 6.25.
1 house of the father.
n Num. 1.4.
o Lev. 17.8, 9. 1 Sam. 15. 23.
p Deut. 4.3.
q Gen. 18.23, 25. ch. 7.1, 11, 12. 2 Sam. 1.17. 1 Chr. 21.1, 14.
r Lev. 17.8, 9. ch. 18.1.
s ch. 7.1, 5. 1 Chr. 2.6, 7.
t Pro. 15.1. Pro. 18.13. Pro. 24.26.
u Ex. 15.11. Deut. 10.17. Ps. 82.1. Ps. 86.8. Ps. 136.2. Dan. 2.47. Rev. 19.16.
v 1 Ki. 8.39. Job 10.7. Ps. 44.21. Ps. 139.1, 2. Jer. 12.3. John 2.25. 2 Cor. 11.11, 31. Heb. 4.13. Rev. 2.23.

thereon, let the LORD himself [w]require *it;*

24 And if we have not *rather* done it for fear of *this* thing, saying, [2]In time to come your children might speak unto our children, saying, What have ye to do with the LORD God of Israel?

25 For the LORD hath made Jordan a border between us and you, ye children of Reuben and children of Gad; ye have no part in the LORD: so shall your children make our children cease from fearing the LORD.

26 Therefore we said, Let us now prepare to build us an altar, not for burnt offering, nor for sacrifice:

27 But *that* it *may be* [x]a witness between us, and you, and our generations after us, that we might [y]do the service of the LORD before him with our burnt offerings, and with our sacrifices, and with our peace offerings; that your children may not say to our children in time to come, Ye have no part in the LORD.

28 Therefore said we, that it shall be, when they should *so* say to us or to our generations in time to come, that we may say *again*, Behold the pattern of the altar of the LORD, which our fathers made, not for burnt offerings, nor for sacrifices; but it *is* a witness between us and you.

29 God forbid that we should rebel against the LORD, and turn this day from following the LORD, to [z]build an altar for burnt offerings, for meat offerings, or for sacrifices, beside the altar of the LORD our God that *is* before his tabernacle.

30 ¶ And when Phĭn′-ĕ-hăs the priest, and the princes of the congregation and heads of the thousands of Israel which *were* with him, heard the words that the children of Reuben and the children of Gad and the children of Mă-năs′-sĕh spake, [3]it pleased them.

31 And Phĭn′-ĕ-hăs the son of Ĕl-ē-ā′-zär the priest said unto the children of Reuben, and to the children of Gad, and to the children of Mă-năs′-sĕh, This day we perceive that the LORD *is* [a]among us, because ye have not committed this trespass against the LORD: [4]now ye have delivered the children of Israel out of the hand of the LORD.

32 ¶ And Phĭn′-ĕ-hăs the son of Ĕl-ē-ā′-zär the priest, and the princes, returned from the children of Reuben, and from the children of Gad, out of the land of Gilead, unto the land of Canaan, to the children of Israel, and brought them word again.

33 And the thing pleased the children of Israel; and the children of Israel [b]blessed God, and did not intend to go up against them in battle, to destroy the land wherein the children of Reuben and Gad dwelt.

34 And the children of Reuben and the children of Gad called the altar [5]*Ed:* for it *shall be* a witness between us that the LORD *is* God.

CHAPTER 23

AND it came to pass a long time after that the LORD [a]had given rest unto Israel from all their enemies round about, that Joshua [b]waxed old *and* [1]stricken in age.

2 And Joshua [c]called for all Israel, *and* for their elders, and for their heads, and for their judges, and for their officers, and said unto them, I am old *and* stricken in age:

3 And ye have seen all that the LORD your God hath done unto all these nations because of you; for the LORD your God *is* he that hath fought for you.

4 Behold, I have divided unto you by lot these nations that remain, to be an inheritance for your tribes, from Jordan, with all the nations that I have cut off, even unto the great sea [2]westward.

5 And the LORD your God, [d]he shall expel them from before you, and drive them from out of your sight; and ye shall possess their land, [e]as the LORD your God hath promised unto you.

6 Be ye therefore very courageous to keep and to do all that is written in the book of the law of Moses, [f]that ye turn not aside therefrom *to* the right hand or *to* the left;

7 That ye [g]come not among these nations, these that remain among you; neither make [h]mention of the name of their gods, nor cause to swear *by them*, neither serve them, nor bow yourselves unto them:

8 [3]But cleave unto the LORD your God, as ye have done unto this day.

9 [4]For the LORD hath driven out from before you great nations and strong: but *as for* you, [i]no man hath been able to stand before you unto this day.

10 One [j]man of you shall chase a thousand: for the LORD your God, he *it is* that fighteth for you, as he hath promised you.

11 Take good heed therefore unto

w Deut. 18. 19. 1 Sam. 20. 16. Ps. 7.3,5. Ps. 10.13,14.
2 To-morrow.
x Gen. 31.48. ch. 24.27. 1 Sam. 7.12.
y Deut. 12.5, 6,11,12,17, 18,26,27.
z Deut. 12.13, 14.
3 it was good in their eyes.
a Ex. 25.8. Lev. 26.11, 12. 2 Chr. 15.2. Zech. 8.23. 1 Cor. 14.25. Rev. 21.3.
4 then.
b 1 Chr. 29. 20. Dan. 2.19. Luke 2.28.
5 That is, A witness.

CHAP. 23

a ch. 21.44.
b ch. 13.1.
1 come into days.
c Deut. 31.28. ch. 24.1.
2 at the sun-set.
d Ex. 23.30. Ex. 33.2. Deut. 11.23.
e Num. 33. 53.
f Deut. 5.32.
g Ex. 23.33. Deut. 7.2,3. Pro. 4.14. Eph. 5.11.
h Ex. 23.13. Ps. 16.4. Jer. 5.7. Zeph. 1.5.
3 Or, For if ye will cleave.
4 Or, Then the LORD will drive.
i ch. 1.5.
j Judg. 3.31. 2 Sam. 23.8.

[5]yourselves, that ye love the LORD
your God.
12 Else if ye do in any wise [k]go back,
and cleave unto the remnant of these
nations, *even* these that remain among
you, and shall make marriages with
them, and go in unto them, and they
to you:
13 Know for a certainty that the
[l]LORD your God will no more drive
out *any of* these nations from before
you; [m]but they shall be snares and
traps unto you, and scourges in your
sides, and thorns in your eyes, until
ye perish from off this good land which
the LORD your God hath given you.
14 And, behold, this day [n]I *am* going
the way of all the earth: and ye know
in all your hearts and in all your souls,
that [o]not one thing hath failed of all
the good things which the LORD your
God spake concerning you; all are
come to pass unto you, *and* not one
thing hath failed thereof.
15 Therefore [p]it shall come to pass,
that as all good things are come upon
you, which the LORD your God promised you; so shall the LORD bring upon you [q]all evil things, until he have
destroyed you from off this good land
which the LORD your God hath given
you.
16 When ye have transgressed the
covenant of the LORD your God,
which he commanded you, and have
gone and served other gods, and bowed yourselves to them; then shall the
anger of the LORD be kindled against
you, and ye shall perish quickly from
off the good land which he hath given
unto you.

CHAPTER 24

AND Joshua gathered all the tribes
of Israel to [a]Shē-chĕm, and [b]called
for the elders of Israel, and for their
heads, and for their judges, and for
their officers; and they [c]presented
themselves before God.
2 And Joshua said unto all the people, Thus saith the LORD God of Israel, [d]Your fathers dwelt on the other
side of the flood in old time, *even* Tē-
räh, the father of Abraham, and the
father of Nā-chôr: and they [e]served
other gods.
3 And [f]I took your father Abraham
from the other side of the flood, and
led him throughout all the land of
Canaan, and multiplied his seed, and
[g]gave him Isaac.
4 And I gave unto Isaac Jacob and
Esau: and I gave unto [h]Esau mount

5 your souls.
k Heb. 10.38. 2 Pet. 2.20.
l Judg. 2.3.
m 1 Ki. 11.4.
n Eccl. 12.3-7. Heb. 9.27.
o Luke 21.33.
p Deut. 28. 63.
q Lev. 26.16. Deut. 28.15, 16. Judg. 3.8,12. Luke 21.22.
CHAP. 24
a Gen. 12.6. Gen. 35.4. Judg. 9.1-3.
b Ex. 18.25. ch. 23.2.
c 1 Sam. 10. 19. Acts 10.33.
d Gen. 11.26. Deut. 26.5. Isa. 51.2.
e Gen. 31.53.
f Acts 7.2,3.
g Ps. 127.3.
h Gen. 36.8. Deut. 2.5. Acts 17.26.
i Ex. 3.10.
j Ex. 7.1. Ex. 8.1. Ex. 9.1.
k Ex. 12.37, 51. Micah 6.4.
l Ex. 14.9. Ps. 77.15-20. Ps. 78.13. Isa. 63.12, 13. Acts 7.36. Heb. 11.29.
m Num. 21. 21,33. Deut. 2.32.
n Judg. 11.25.
o Num. 22.5.
p Deut. 23.5.
q Num. 23. 11.
r Ex. 23.28. Deut. 7.20.
s Ps. 44.3,6.
t Deut. 6.10. ch. 11.13. Pro. 13.22.
u Deut. 10. 12. 1 Sam. 12. 24. Job 1.1. Acts 9.31.
v Gen. 17.1. Deut. 18.13. Ps. 119.1. 2 Cor. 1.12. Eph. 6.24.
w Lev. 17.7.
x Eze. 20.7.
y Ex. 23.24.

Sē-ïr, to possess it; but Jacob and his
children went down into Egypt.
5 I [i]sent Moses also and Aaron, and
[j]I plagued Egypt, according to that
which I did among them: and afterward I brought you out.
6 And I [k]brought your fathers out of
Egypt: and ye came unto the sea; [l]and
the Egyptians pursued after your fathers with chariots and horsemen unto
the Red sea.
7 And when they cried unto the
LORD, he put darkness between you
and the Egyptians, and brought the
sea upon them, and covered them;
and your eyes have seen what I have
done in Egypt: and ye dwelt in the
wilderness a long season.
8 And I brought you into the land of
the Amorites, which dwelt on the
other side Jordan; [m]and they fought
with you: and I gave them into your
hand, that ye might possess their land;
and I destroyed them from before
you.
9 Then [n]Balak the son of Zĭp-pôr,
king of Moab, arose and warred
against Israel, and [o]sent and called
Bā-lāam the son of Bē-ôr to curse you:
10 But [p]I would not hearken unto
Bā-lāam; therefore [q]he blessed you
still: so I delivered you out of his
hand.
11 And ye went over Jordan, and
came unto Jericho: and the men of
Jericho fought against you, the Amorites, and the Pĕ-rĭz-zītes, and the
Canaanites, and the Hittites, and the
Gĭr-gā-shītes, the Hī-vites, and the
Jĕb-ū-sītes; and I delivered them into
your hand.
12 And [r]I sent the hornet before you,
which drave them out from before
you, *even* the two kings of the Amorites; *but* not [s]with thy sword, nor with
thy bow.
13 And I have given you a land for
which ye did not labour, and cities
[t]which ye built not, and ye dwell in
them; of the vineyards and oliveyards
which ye planted not do ye eat.
14 ¶ Now [u]therefore fear the LORD,
and serve him in [v]sincerity and in
truth: and put [w]away the gods which
your fathers served on the other side of
the flood, and in [x]Egypt; and serve ye
the LORD.
15 And if it seem evil unto you to
serve the LORD, choose you this day
whom ye will serve; whether the gods
which your fathers served that *were*
on the other side of the flood, or [y]the
gods of the Amorites, in whose land

ye dwell: [z]but as for me and my house,
we will serve the LORD.
16 And the people answered and
said, God forbid that we should forsake the LORD, to serve other gods;
17 For the LORD our God, he *it is*
that brought us up and our fathers
out of the land of Egypt, from the
house of bondage, and which did
those great signs in our sight, and
preserved us in all the way wherein
we went, and among all the people
through whom we passed:
18 And the LORD drave out from before us all the people, even the Amorites which dwelt in the land: *therefore* will we also serve the LORD; for
he *is* our God.
19 And Joshua said unto the people,
[a]Ye cannot serve the LORD: for he *is*
an [b]holy God; he *is* a jealous God; [c]he
will not forgive your transgressions
nor your sins.
20 If [d]ye forsake the LORD, and serve
strange gods, [e]then he will turn and
do you hurt, and consume you, after
that he hath done you good.
21 And the people said unto Joshua,
Nay; but we will serve the LORD.
22 And Joshua said unto the people,
Ye *are* witnesses against yourselves
that [f]ye have chosen you the LORD, to
serve him. And they said, *We are* witnesses.
23 Now therefore [g]put away, *said he*,
the strange gods which *are* among
you, and incline your heart unto the
LORD God of Israel.
24 And the people said unto Joshua,
The LORD our God will we serve, and
his voice will we obey.

z Gen. 18.19.
a Ruth 1.15. Matt. 6.24. Luke 14.25-33.
b Lev. 19.2. 1 Sam. 6.20. Ps. 99.5,9. Isa. 5.16.
c Ex. 23.21. Isa. 27.11.
d ch. 23.12-15. 2 Chr. 15.2. Ezra 8.22. Isa. 1.28. Jer. 17.13. Heb. 10.26, 27,28.
e Isa. 63.10. Acts 7.42.
f Ps. 119.173.
g Gen. 35.2. 1 Sam. 7.3.
h Ex. 15.25.
i Deut. 31.24.
j Judg. 9.6.
k Gen. 28.18. ch. 4.3.
l Gen. 31.48.
m Deut. 32.1.
n ch. 19.50.
o Judg. 2.7.
1 prolonged their days after Joshua.
p Gen. 50.25. Ex. 13.19. Acts 7.16.
q Gen. 33.19.
2 Or, lambs.
r Ex. 6.25.

25 So Joshua [h]made a covenant with
the people that day, and set them a
statute and an ordinance in Shē-chĕm.
26 ¶ And Joshua [i]wrote these words
in the book of the law of God, and
took [j]a great stone, and [k]set it up there
under an oak, that *was* by the sanctuary of the LORD.
27 And Joshua said unto all the people, Behold, this stone shall be a
[l]witness unto us; for [m]it hath heard all
the words of the LORD which he spake
unto us: it shall be therefore a witness
unto you, lest ye deny your God.
28 So Joshua let the people depart,
every man unto his inheritance.
29 ¶ And it came to pass after these
things, that Joshua the son of Nun,
the servant of the LORD, died, *being*
an hundred and ten years old.
30 And they buried him in the border
of his inheritance in [n]Tĭm-năth-sē-
răh, which *is* in mount Ē-phră-ĭm, on
the north side of the hill of Gā-ăsh.
31 And [o]Israel served the LORD all
the days of Joshua, and all the days of
the elders that [1]overlived Joshua, and
which had known all the works of the
LORD, that he had done for Israel.
32 ¶ And [p]the bones of Joseph, which
the children of Israel brought up out
of Egypt, buried they in Shē-chĕm, in
a parcel of ground which [q]Jacob
bought of the sons of Hā-môr the
father of Shē-chĕm for an hundred
[2]pieces of silver: and it became the inheritance of the children of Joseph.
33 And Ĕl-ē-ā-zär the son of Aaron
died; and they buried him in a hill *that
pertained to* [r]Phĭn-ĕ-hăs his son, which
was given him in mount Ē-phră-ĭm.

THE

BOOK OF JUDGES

CHAPTER 1

NOW after the death of Joshua it
came to pass, that the children of
Israel asked [a]the LORD, saying, Who
shall go up for us against the Canaanites first, to fight against them?
2 And the LORD said, [b]Judah shall
go up: behold, I have delivered the
land into his hand.
3 And Judah said unto Simeon his
brother, Come up with me into my
lot, that we may fight against the Canaanites; and I likewise will go with

CHAP. 1
a Ex. 28.30. ch. 20.18. 1 Sam. 23.9.
b Gen. 49.8.
c Eccl. 4.9. Mark 6.7. 1 Cor. 12.26. Gal. 6.2.
d Deut. 9.1. Ps. 44.2.

thee into thy lot. [c]So Simeon went with
him.
4 And Judah went up; and [d]the
LORD delivered the Canaanites and
the Pĕ-rĭz-zītes into their hand:
and they slew of them in Bē-zĕk ten
thousand men.
5 And they found Ă-dō-nī-bē-zĕk in
Bē-zĕk: and they fought against him,
and they slew the Canaanites and the
Pĕ-rĭz-zītes.
6 But Ă-dō-nī-bē-zĕk fled; and they
pursued after him, and caught him,

and cut off his thumbs and his great
toes.
7 And Ăd'-ō-nī–bē'-zĕk said, Threescore and ten kings, having [1]their
thumbs and their great toes cut off,
[2]gathered *their meat* under my table:
[e]as I have done, so God hath requited
me. And they brought him to Jerusalem, and there he died.
8 Now [f]the children of Judah had
fought against Jerusalem, and had
taken it, and smitten it with the edge
of the sword, and set the city on fire.
9 ¶ And [g]afterward the children of
Judah went down to fight against the
Canaanites, that dwelt in the mountain, and in the south, and in the
[3]valley.
10 And Judah went against the Canaanites that dwelt in Hē'-brŏn: (now
the name of Hē'-brŏn before *was* [h]Kĭr'-
jăth–är'-bă:) and they slew Shē'-shăī,
and Ă-hī'-măn, and Tăl'-măī.
11 And [i]from thence he went against
the inhabitants of Dē'-bĭr: and the
name of Dē'-bĭr before *was* Kĭr'-jăth–
sē'-phĕr:
12 And Caleb said, He that smiteth
Kĭr'-jăth–sē'-phĕr, and taketh it, to him
will I give Ăch'-săh my daughter to
wife.
13 And Ŏth'-nĭ-ĕl the son of Kē'-năz,
Caleb's [j]younger brother, took it: and
he gave him Ăch'-săh his daughter to
wife.
14 And [k]it came to pass, when she
came *to him*, that she moved him to
ask of her father a field: and she lighted from off *her* ass; and Caleb said unto her, What wilt thou?
15 And she said unto him, [l]Give me
a [4]blessing: for thou hast given me a
south land; give me also springs of
water. And Caleb gave her the upper
springs and the nether springs.
16 ¶ And [m]the children of the Kē'-
nīte, Moses' father in law, went up
[n]out of the city of palm trees with the
children of Judah into the wilderness
of Judah, which *lieth* in the south of
[o]Âr'-ăd; [p]and they went and dwelt
among the people.
17 And Judah went with Simeon his
brother, and they slew the Canaanites that inhabited Zē'-phăth, and utterly destroyed it. And the name of
the city was called [q]Hôr'-măh.
18 Also Judah took [r]Gā'-ză with the
coast thereof, and Ăs'-kĕ-lŏn with the
coast thereof, and Ĕk'-rŏn with the
coast thereof.
19 And [s]the LORD was with Judah;
and [5]he drave out *the inhabitants of*
the mountain; but could not drive out
the inhabitants of the valley, because
they had chariots [t]of iron.
20 And [u]they gave Hē'-brŏn unto
Caleb, as Moses said: and he expelled
thence the three sons of Anak.
21 And [v]the children of Benjamin
did not drive out the Jĕb'-ū-sītes that
inhabited Jerusalem; but the Jĕb'-ū-
sītes dwell with the children of Benjamin in Jerusalem unto this day.
22 ¶ And the house of Joseph, they
also went up against Beth-el: and the
LORD *was* with them.
23 And the house of Joseph [w]sent to
descry Beth-el. (Now the name of the
city before *was* [x]Luz.)
24 And the spies saw a man come
forth out of the city, and they said unto him, Shew us, we pray thee, the entrance into the city, and [y]we will shew
thee mercy.
25 And when he shewed them the entrance into the city, they smote the
city with the edge of the sword; but
they let go the man and all his family.
26 And the man went into the land
of the Hittites, and built a city, and
called the name thereof Luz: which *is*
the name thereof unto this day.
27 ¶ Neither did [z]Mă-năs'-sĕh drive
out *the inhabitants of* Bĕth–shē'-ăn and
her towns, nor [a]Tā'-ă-năch and her
towns, nor the inhabitants of Dor and
her towns, nor the inhabitants of Ĭb'-
lĕ-ăm and her towns, nor the inhabitants of Mĕ-gĭd'-dō and her towns: but
the Canaanites would dwell in that
land.
28 And it came to pass, when Israel
was strong, that they put the Canaanites to tribute, and [6]did not utterly
drive them out.
29 ¶ Neither [b]did Ē'-phră-ĭm drive
out the Canaanites that dwelt in Gē'-
zĕr; but the Canaanites dwelt in Gē'-
zĕr among them.
30 ¶ Neither did Zĕ-bū'-lŭn drive out
the inhabitants of Kĭt'-rŏn, nor the inhabitants [c]of Nā'-hă-lŏl; but the Canaanites dwelt among them, and became tributaries.
31 ¶ Neither [d]did Asher drive out the
inhabitants of Ăc'-chō, nor the inhabitants of Zī'-dŏn, nor of Ăh'-lăb,
nor of Ăch'-zĭb, nor of Hĕl'-băh, nor of
Ā'-phĭk, nor of Rē'-hŏb:
32 But the Asherites [e]dwelt among
the Canaanites, the inhabitants of the
land: for they did not drive them out.
33 ¶ Neither [f]did Năph'-tă-lī drive
out the inhabitants of Bĕth–shē'-mĕsh,
nor the inhabitants of Bĕth'–ă-năth;

1 the thumbs of their hands and of their feet.
2 Or, gleaned.
e Lev. 24.19. Ps. 109.16. Pro. 1.31. Mark 4.24.
f Josh. 15.63.
g Josh. 10.12, 36.
3 Or, low country.
h Josh. 14.15.
i Josh. 15.15.
j ch. 3.9.
k Josh. 15.18.
l Gen. 33.11. 1 Sam. 25. 27. Heb. 6.7.
4 Or, present.
m Num. 10. 29-32. ch. 4.11. 1 Sam. 15.6. 1 Chr. 2.55. Jer. 35.2.
n Deut. 34.3. 2 Chr. 28.15.
o Num. 21.1.
p Num. 10. 32.
q Num. 21.3.
r Josh. 11.22. ch. 16.1. 1 Sam. 6.17.
s Gen. 39.2, 21. 2 Sam. 5.10. 2 Ki. 18.7. Rom. 8.31.
5 Or, he possessed the mountain.
t Josh. 17.16.
u Num. 14. 24. Deut. 1.36. Josh. 14.9, 13.
v Josh. 15.63. 2 Sam. 5.6.
w Josh. 2.1. ch. 18.2.
x Gen. 28.19.
y 1 Sam. 30. 15.
z Josh. 17.11.
a Josh. 21.25.
6 driving he drove them not out.
b 1 Ki. 9.16.
c Josh. 19.15.
d Josh. 19. 24-30.
e Ps. 106.34, 35.
f Josh. 19.38.

but he dwelt among the Canaanites, the inhabitants of the land: nevertheless the inhabitants of Bĕth–shē´mĕsh and of Bĕth´–ă-năth became tributaries unto them.

34 And the Amorites forced the children of Dan into the mountain: for they would not suffer them to come down to the valley:

35 But the Amorites would dwell in mount Hē´rĕs [g]in Aî´jă-lŏn, and in Shā-ăl´bĭm: yet the hand of the house of Joseph [7]prevailed, so that they became tributaries.

36 And the coast of the Amorites *was* [h]from [8]the going up to Ăk-răb´bĭm, from the rock, and upward.

CHAPTER 2

AND [a]an [1]angel of the LORD came up from Gĭl´găl to Bō´chĭm, and said, I made you to go up out of Egypt, and have brought you unto the land which I sware unto your fathers; and [b]I said, I will never break my covenant with you.

2 And ye shall make no league with the inhabitants of this land; ye shall throw down their altars: but ye have not obeyed my voice: why have ye done this?

3 Wherefore I also said, I will not drive them out from before you; but they shall be [c]*as thorns* in your sides, and [d]their gods shall be a snare unto you.

4 And it came to pass, when the angel of the LORD spake these words unto all the children of Israel, that the people lifted up their voice, and wept.

5 And they called the name of that place [2]Bō´chĭm: and they sacrificed there unto the LORD.

6 ¶ And when Joshua had let the people go, the children of Israel went every man unto his inheritance to possess the land.

7 And the people served the LORD all the days of Joshua, and all the days of the elders that [3]outlived Joshua, who had seen all the great works of the LORD, that he did for Israel.

8 And Joshua the son of Nun, the servant of the LORD, died, *being* an hundred and ten years old.

9 And they buried him in the border of his inheritance in Tĭm´năth–hē´rĕs, in the mount of Ē´phră-ĭm, on the north side of the hill Gā´ăsh.

10 And also all that generation were gathered unto their fathers: and there arose another generation after them, which [e]knew not the LORD, nor yet the works which he had done for Israel.

11 ¶ And the children of Israel did evil in the sight of the LORD, and served Bā´ă-lĭm:

12 And they [f]forsook the LORD God of their fathers, which brought them out of the land of Egypt, and followed [g]other gods, of the gods of the people that *were* round about them, and [h]bowed themselves unto them, and provoked the LORD to anger.

13 And they forsook the LORD, and served Bā´ăl and Ăsh´tă-rōth.

14 ¶ And [i]the anger of the LORD was hot against Israel, and [j]he delivered them into the hands of spoilers that spoiled them, and [k]he sold them into the hands of their enemies round about, so that [l]they could not any longer stand before their enemies.

15 Whithersoever they went out, the hand of the LORD was against them for evil, as the LORD had said, and [m]as the LORD had sworn unto them: and they were greatly distressed.

16 ¶ Nevertheless [n]the LORD raised up judges, which [4]delivered them out of the hand of those that spoiled them.

17 And yet they would not hearken unto their judges, but they [o]went a whoring after other gods, and bowed themselves unto them: they turned quickly out of the way which their fathers walked in, obeying the commandments of the LORD; *but* they did not so.

18 And when the LORD raised them up judges, then [p]the LORD was with the judge, and delivered them out of the hand of their enemies all the days of the judge: for [q]it repented the LORD because of their groanings by reason of them that oppressed them and vexed them.

19 And it came to pass, when the judge was dead, *that* they returned, and [5]corrupted *themselves* more than their fathers, in following other gods to serve them, and to bow down unto them; [6]they ceased not from their own doings, nor from their stubborn way.

20 ¶ And the anger of the LORD was hot against Israel; and he said, Because that this people hath [r]transgressed my covenant which I commanded their fathers, and have not hearkened unto my voice;

21 I also will not henceforth drive out any from before them of the nations which Joshua left when he died:

22 That through them I [s]may prove

g ch. 12.12.
7 was heavy.
h Num. 34.4.
8 Or, Maaleh-akrabbim.

CHAP. 2

a Gen. 16.7. Gen. 32.11. Ex. 3.1-6. John 1.1.
1 Or, messenger.
b Gen. 17.7. Ex. 6.4. Ps. 105.8-11. Micah 7.20. Luke 1.54, 55,72-75.
c Josh. 23.13.
d Ex. 23.33. Deut. 7.16. ch. 3.6. Ps. 106.36.
2 That is, Weepers.
3 prolonged days after Joshua.
e Ex. 5.2. 1 Sam. 2.12. 1 Chr. 28.9. Jer. 9.3. Gal. 4.8. 2 Thes. 1.8. Titus 1.16.
f Deut. 13.5. ch. 10.6,13. 1 Chr. 28.9.
g Deut. 6.14.
h Ex. 20.5.
i ch. 3.8. 2 Chr. 7.19. Ps. 78.58-62. Ps. 89.30. Isa. 1.28.
j 2 Ki. 17.20.
k ch. 3.8. Ps. 44.12. Isa. 50.1.
l Lev. 26.37. Josh. 7.12.
m Lev. 26. 14,34. Deut. 28.15-68.
n ch. 3.9. 1 Sam. 12. 11. Acts 13.20.
4 saved.
o Ex. 34.15, 16. Lev. 17.7. Rev. 17.1-5.
p Josh. 1.5.
q Gen. 6.6. Deut. 32.36. Ps. 106.44. Jer. 18.7-10.
5 Or, were corrupt.
6 they let nothing fall of their.
r Josh. 23.16.
s Deut. 8.2.

Israel, whether they will keep the way of the LORD to walk therein, as their fathers did keep *it*, or not.

23 Therefore the LORD [7]left those nations, without driving them out hastily; neither delivered he them into the hand of Joshua.

CHAPTER 3

NOW these *are* the nations which the LORD left, [a]to prove Israel by them, *even* as many *of Israel* as had not known all the wars of Canaan;

2 Only that the generations of the children of Israel might know, to teach them war, at the least such as before knew nothing thereof;

3 *Namely*, [b]five lords of the Philistines, and all the Canaanites, and the Sī-dō-nĭ-ăns, and the Hī-vites that dwelt in mount Lĕb-ă-non, from mount Bā-ăl-hĕr-mon unto the entering in of Hā-măth.

4 And they were to prove Israel by them, to know whether they would hearken unto the commandments of the LORD, which he commanded their fathers by the hand of Moses.

5 ¶ And [c]the children of Israel dwelt among the Canaanites, Hittites, and Amorites, and Pĕ-rĭz-zītes, and Hī-vites, and Jĕb-ū-sītes:

6 And [d]they took their daughters to be their wives, and gave their daughters to their sons, and served their gods.

7 And [e]the children of Israel did evil in the sight of the LORD, and forgat the LORD their God, and served Bā-ă-lĭm and [f]the groves.

8 ¶ Therefore the anger of the LORD was hot against Israel, and he sold them into the hand [g]of Chû-shăn–rĭsh-ă-thā-ĭm king of [1]Mĕs-ō-pō-tā-mĭ-ă: and the children of Israel served Chû-shăn–rĭsh-ă-thā-ĭm eight years.

9 And when the children of Israel [h]cried unto the LORD, the LORD [i]raised up a [2]deliverer to the children of Israel, who delivered them, *even* [j]Ŏth-nĭ-ĕl the son of Kē-năz, Caleb's younger brother.

10 And [k]the Spirit of the LORD [3]came upon him, and he judged Israel, and went out to war: and the LORD delivered Chû-shăn–rĭsh-ă-thā-ĭm king of [4]Mĕs-ō-pō-tā-mĭ-ă into his hand; and his hand prevailed against Chû-shăn–rĭsh-ă-thā-ĭm.

11 And the land had rest forty years. And Ŏth-nĭ-ĕl the son of Kē-năz died.

12 ¶ And [l]the children of Israel did evil again in the sight of the LORD: and the LORD strengthened Ĕg-lŏn [m]the king of Moab against Israel, because they had done evil in the sight of the LORD.

13 And he gathered unto him the children of Ammon [n]and Ăm-ă-lĕk, and went and smote Israel, and possessed [o]the city of palm trees.

14 So the children of Israel served [p]Ĕg-lŏn the king of Moab eighteen years.

15 But when the children of Israel [q]cried unto the LORD, the LORD raised them up a deliverer, Ē-hŭd the son of Gē-ră, [5]a Benjamite, a man [6]lefthanded: and by him the children of Israel sent a present unto Ĕg-lŏn the king of Moab.

16 But Ē-hŭd made him a dagger which had two edges, of a cubit length; and he did gird it under his raiment upon his right thigh.

17 And he brought the present unto Ĕg-lŏn king of Moab: and Ĕg-lŏn *was* a very fat man.

18 And when he had made an end to offer the present, he sent away the people that bare the present.

19 But he himself turned again from [r]the [7]quarries that *were* by Gĭl-găl, and said, I have a secret errand unto thee, O king: who said, Keep silence. And all that stood by him went out from him.

20 And Ē-hŭd came unto him; and he was sitting in [8]a summer parlour, which he had for himself alone. And Ē-hŭd said, I have a message from God unto thee. And he arose out of *his* seat.

21 And Ē-hŭd put forth his left hand, and took the dagger from his right thigh, and thrust it into his belly:

22 And the haft also went in after the blade; and the fat closed upon the blade, so that he could not draw the dagger out of his belly; and [9]the dirt came out.

23 Then Ē-hŭd went forth through the porch, and shut the doors of the parlour upon him, and locked them.

24 When he was gone out, his servants came; and when they saw that, behold, the doors of the parlour *were* locked, they said, Surely he [10]covereth his feet in his summer chamber.

25 And they tarried till they were ashamed: and, behold, he opened not the doors of the parlour; therefore they took a key, and opened *them*: and, behold, their lord *was* fallen down dead on the earth.

26 And Ē-hŭd escaped while they

7 Or, suffered.

CHAP. 3

a Gen. 22.1. Deut. 8.2, 16. John 2.24. 1 Cor. 11.19.
b Josh. 13.3.
c Ps. 106.35.
d Ex. 34.16. Deut. 7.3. Ezra 9.11.
e ch. 2.11.
f Ex. 34.13. Deut. 16.21. ch. 6.25.
g Hab. 3.7.
1 Aram-naharaim.
h ch. 6.7. ch. 10.10. 1 Sam. 12. 10. Neh. 9.27. Ps. 22.5. Ps. 106.44.
i ch. 2.16.
2 saviour.
j ch. 1.13.
k Num. 11. 29. 1 Sam. 10.6. 1 Sam. 11.6. 2 Chr. 15.1. Heb. 6.4.
3 was.
4 Aram.
l ch. 2.19. Jer. 16.12. Hosea 6.4. Matt. 23.32.
m 1 Sam. 12. 9.
n ch. 5.14.
o Deut. 34.3. ch. 1.16.
p Lev. 26.23-25. Deut. 28.48.
q Ps. 50.15. Ps. 78.34. Jer. 29.12, 13. Dan. 9.3.
5 Or, The son of Gemini.
6 shut of his right hand.
r Josh. 4.20.
7 Or, graven images.
8 a parlour of cooling.
9 Or, it came out at the fundament.
10 Or, easeth nature.

ırried, and passed beyond the quar-
ıes, and escaped unto Sē-ĭ-răth.
27 And it came to pass, when he was
ome, that [s]he blew a trumpet in [t]the
ıountain of Ē-phră-ĭm, and the chil-
ren of Israel went down with him
om the mount, and he before them.
28 And he said unto them, Follow
fter me: for [u]the LORD hath delivered
our enemies the Moabites into your
and. And they went down after him,
nd took the [v]fords of Jordan toward
Moab, and suffered not a man to pass
ver.
29 And they slew of Moab at that
ime about ten thousand men, [11]all
usty, and all men of valour; and there
scaped not a man.
30 So Moab was subdued that day
nder the hand of Israel. And the land
ad rest fourscore years.
31 ¶ And after him was [12]Shăm-gär
he son of Ā-năth, which slew of the
hilistines six hundred men with [w]an
x goad: [x]and he also delivered [13]Is-
ael.

CHAPTER 4

AND [a]the children of Israel again
did evil in the sight of the LORD,
when Ē-hŭd was dead.
2 And the LORD sold them into the
and of Jā-bĭn king of Canaan, that
eigned [b]in Hā-zôr; the captain of
whose host [c]*was* Sĭs-ĕ-ră, which dwelt
n Hă-rō-shĕth of the Gentiles.
3 And the children of Israel cried
nto the LORD: for he had nine hundred [d]chariots of iron; and twenty
ears [e]he mightily oppressed the children of Israel.
4 ¶ And [f]Dĕb-ŏ-răh, a prophetess,
he wife of Lăp-ĭ-dōth, she judged
srael at that time.
5 And [g]she dwelt under the palm
ree of Dĕb-ŏ-răh between Rā-măh
nd Beth-el in mount Ē-phră-ĭm: and
he children of Israel came up to her
or judgment.
6 And she sent and called [h]Bâr-ăk
he son of Ă-bĭn-ŏ-ăm out [i]of Kē-
dĕsh-năph-tă-lī, and said unto him,
Hath not the LORD God of Israel com-
nanded, *saying*, Go and draw toward
mount Tā-bôr, and take with thee ten
housand men of the children of
Năph-tă-lī and of the children of Zĕ-
bū-lŭn?
7 And [j]I will draw unto thee to the
[k]river Kī-shŏn Sĭs-ĕ-ră, the captain of
Jā-bĭn's army, with his chariots and
his multitude; and I will deliver him
into thine hand.
8 And Bâr-ăk said unto her, If thou
wilt go with me, then I will go: but if
thou wilt not go with me, *then* I will
not go.
9 And she said, I will surely go with
thee: notwithstanding the journey
that thou takest shall not be for thine
honour; for the LORD shall [l]sell Sĭs-
ĕ-ră into the hand of a woman. And
Dĕb-ŏ-răh arose, and went with Bâr-
ăk to Kē-dĕsh.
10 ¶ And Bâr-ăk called [m]Zĕ-bū-lŭn
and Năph-tă-lī to Kē-dĕsh; and he
went up with ten thousand men at [n]his
feet: and Dĕb-ŏ-răh went up with him.
11 Now Hē-bĕr [o]the Kē-nīte, *which*
was of the children of [p]Hō-băb the
father in law of Moses, had severed
himself from [q]the Kē-nītes, and pitched his tent unto the plain of Zā-ă-nā-
ĭm, which *is* by Kē-dĕsh.
12 And they shewed Sĭs-ĕ-ră that
Bâr-ăk the son of Ă-bĭn-ŏ-ăm was
gone up to mount Tā-bôr.
13 And Sĭs-ĕ-ră [1]gathered together
all his chariots, *even* nine hundred
chariots of iron, and all the people that
were with him, from Hă-rō-shĕth of
the Gentiles unto the river of Kī-shŏn.
14 And Dĕb-ŏ-răh said unto Bâr-ăk,
Up; for this *is* the day in which the
LORD hath delivered Sĭs-ĕ-ră into
thine hand: [r]is not the LORD gone out
before thee? So Bâr-ăk went down
from mount Tā-bôr, and ten thousand
men after him.
15 And [s]the LORD discomfited Sĭs-
ĕ-ră, and all *his* chariots, and all *his*
host, with the edge of the sword before Bâr-ăk; so that Sĭs-ĕ-ră lighted
down off *his* chariot, and fled away on
his feet.
16 But Bâr-ăk pursued after the
chariots, and after the host, unto Hă-
rō-shĕth of the Gentiles: and all the
host of Sĭs-ĕ-ră fell upon the edge of
the sword; *and* there was not [2]a man
left.
17 Howbeit [t]Sĭs-ĕ-ră fled away on his
feet to the tent of Jā-ĕl the wife of Hē-
bĕr the Kē-nīte: for *there was* peace
between Jā-bĭn the king of Hā-zôr and
the house of Hē-bĕr the Kē-nīte.
18 ¶ And Jā-ĕl went out to meet Sĭs-
ĕ-ră, and said unto him, Turn in, my
lord, turn in to me; fear not. And
when he had turned in unto her into
the tent, she covered him with a
[3]mantle.
19 And he said unto her, Give me, I
pray thee, a little water to drink; for
I am thirsty. And she opened [u]a
bottle of milk, and gave him drink,
and covered him.

s ch. 5.14. ch. 6.34. 1 Sam. 13.3.
t Josh. 17.15. ch. 7.24. ch. 17.1.
u ch. 7.9,15. 1 Sam. 17. 47.
v Josh. 2.7. ch. 12.5.
11 fat.
12 This seems to concern only the country next to the Philistines.
w 1 Sam. 17. 47,50.
x ch. 2.16.
13 So part is called Israel, ch. 4.1, and ch. 10.7.

CHAP. 4

a ch. 2.19.
b Josh. 11.1.
c 1 Sam. 12.9. Ps. 83.9.
d Josh. 17.19. ch. 1.19.
e Deut. 28.29, 33, 47,48. ch. 5.8. Ps. 106.42.
f 2 Ki. 22.14. 1 Cor. 1.27.
g Gen. 35.8.
h Heb. 11.32.
i Josh. 19.37.
j Ex. 14.4. Eze. 38.10-16. Joel 3.11-14.
k ch. 5.21. Ps. 83.9.
l ch. 2.14. Ps. 44.12. Isa. 50.1.
m ch. 5.18.
n Ex. 11.8.
o ch. 1.16.
p Ex. 3.1. Ex. 18.1.
q Num. 24. 21.
1 gathered by cry, or, proclamation.
r Deut. 9.3. 2 Sam. 5.24. Ps. 68.7. Isa. 52.12. Micah 2.13.
s Josh. 10.10. Ps. 83.9,10.
2 unto one.
t Job 12.21, 24. Ps. 18.14. Ps. 107.40. Pro. 29.23. Amos 5.19.
3 Or, rug, or, blanket.
u ch. 5.25.

20 Again he said unto her, Stand in
the door of the tent, and it shall be,
when any man doth come and inquire
of thee, and say, Is there any man
here? that thou shalt say, No.
21 Then Jā´-ĕl Hē´-bĕr's wife [v]took a
nail of the tent, and [4]took an hammer
in her hand, and went softly unto him,
and smote the nail into his temples,
and fastened it into the ground: for
he was fast asleep and weary. So he
died.
22 And, behold, as Bâr´-ăk pursued
Sĭs´-ĕ-ră, Jā´-ĕl came out to meet him,
and said unto him, Come, and I will
shew thee the man whom thou seekest. And when he came into her *tent*,
behold, Sĭs´-ĕ-ră lay dead, and the nail
was in his temples.
23 So [w]God subdued on that day Jā´-
bĭn the king of Canaan before the children of Israel.
24 And the hand of the children of Israel [5]prospered, and prevailed against
Jā´-bĭn the king of Canaan, until they
had destroyed Jā´-bĭn king of Canaan.

CHAPTER 5

THEN sang Dĕb´-ŏ-răh and Bâr´-ăk
the son of Ă-bĭn´-ŏ-ăm on that day,
saying,
2 Praise ye the LORD for the avenging
of Israel, when the people willingly
offered themselves.
3 Hear, O ye kings; give ear, O ye
princes; I, *even* I, will sing unto the
LORD; I will sing *praise* to the LORD
God of Israel.
4 LORD, [a]when thou wentest out of
Sē´-ĭr, when thou marchedst out of the
field of Ē´-dom, [b]the earth trembled,
and the heavens dropped, the clouds
also dropped water.
5 The [c]mountains [1]melted from before the LORD, *even* that Sī´-nâi from
before the LORD God of Israel.
6 In the days of [d]Shăm´-gär the son
of Anath, in the days of Jā´-ĕl, the
[e]highways were unoccupied, and the
[2]travellers walked through [3]byways.
7 *The inhabitants of* the villages ceased, they ceased in Israel, until that I
Dĕb´-ŏ-răh arose, that I arose a
[f]mother in Israel.
8 They [g]chose new gods; then *was*
war in the gates: [h]was there a shield
or spear seen among forty thousand in
Israel?
9 My heart *is* toward the governors
of Israel, that offered themselves willingly among the people. Bless ye the
LORD.
10 [4]Speak, ye [i]that ride on white

v ch. 5.26.
4 put.
w 1 Chr. 22. 18. Ps. 18.47.
5 going, went, and was hard.
CHAP. 5
a Deut. 33.2. Ps. 68.7,8.
b Isa. 64.3. Hab. 3.3.
c Deut. 4.11.
1 flowed.
d ch. 3.31.
e Lev. 26.22. Isa. 33.8. Lam. 1.4.
2 walkers of paths.
3 crooked ways.
f ch. 4.4-6. Isa. 49.23.
g Deut. 32. 16. ch. 2.12.
h ch. 4.3. 1 Sam. 13. 19,22.
4 Or, Meditate.
i ch. 12.14.
5 righteousnesses of the LORD.
j ch. 3.27.
k Num. 32. 39.
6 draw with the pen, etc.
7 his feet.
8 Or, In the divisions, etc.
9 impressions.
l Num. 32.1.
10 Or, In.
m Josh. 13. 25.
n Josh. 19.29.
11 Or, port.
12 Or, creeks.
o ch. 4.10.
13 exposed to reproach.
p ch. 4.16. Ps. 44.12.
q Josh. 10.11.
r ch. 4.15.
14 paths.
s ch. 4.7.
15 Or, tramplings, or plungings.
t ch. 21.9.
u 1 Sam. 17. 47.

asses, ye that sit in judgment, ar
walk by the way.
11 *They that are delivered* from th
noise of archers in the places of drav
ing water, there shall they rehear
the [5]righteous acts of the LORD, *eve*
the righteous acts *toward the inhabi*
ants of his villages in Israel: then sha
the people of the LORD go down to th
gates.
12 Awake, awake, Dĕb´-ŏ-răh: a
wake, awake, utter a song: aris
Bâr´-ăk, and lead thy captivity cap
tive, thou son of Ă-bĭn´-ŏ-ăm.
13 Then he made him that remainet
have dominion over the nobles amor
the people: the LORD made me hav
dominion over the mighty.
14 Out [j]of Ē´-phră-ĭm *was there* a ro
of them against Ăm´-ă-lĕk; after the
Benjamin, among thy people; out o
[k]Mā´-chĭr came down governors, an
out of Zĕ-bū´-lŭn they that [6]handle th
pen of the writer.
15 And the princes of Ĭs´-să-chär *we*
with Dĕb´-ŏ-răh; even Ĭs´-să-chär, an
also Bâr´-ăk: he was sent on [7]foot int
the valley. [8]For the divisions of Re
ben *there were* great [9]thoughts o
heart.
16 Why abodest thou [l]among th
sheepfolds, to hear the bleatings of th
flocks? [10]For the divisions of Reube
there were great searchings of heart
17 Gilead [m]abode beyond Jordar
and why did Dan remain in ships
Asher [n]continued on the sea [11]shor
and abode in his [12]breaches.
18 Zĕ-bū´-lŭn [o]and Năph´-tă-lī *were*
people *that* [13]jeoparded their lives ur
to the death in the high places of th
field.
19 The kings came *and* fought, the
fought the kings of Canaan in Tā´-ă
năch by the waters of Mĕ-gĭd´-dō
[p]they took no gain of money.
20 They [q]fought from heaven; th
[r]stars in their [14]courses fought agains
Sĭs´-ĕ-ră.
21 The [s]river of Kī´-shŏn swept ther
away, that ancient river, the river Kī
shŏn. O my soul, thou hast trodde
down strength.
22 Then were the horsehoofs broke
by the means of the [15]pransings, th
pransings of their mighty ones.
23 Curse ye Mē´-rŏz, said the angel o
the LORD, curse ye bitterly the inhabit
ants thereof; [t]because they came no
to the help of the LORD, to the help [u]o
the LORD against the mighty.
24 Blessed above women shall Jā´-ĕ
the wife of Hē´-bĕr the Kē´-nite be

lessed shall she be above women in
e tent.
5 He asked water, *and* she gave *him*
ılk; she brought forth butter in a
rdly dish.
5 She put her hand to the nail, and
r right hand to the workmen's
mmer; and [16]with the hammer she
ıote Sĭs-ĕ-ră, she smote off his head,
ıen she had pierced and stricken
rough his temples.
7 [17]At her feet he bowed, he fell,
lay down: at her feet he bowed, he
ll: where he bowed, there he fell
ɔwn [18]dead.
8 The mother of Sĭs-ĕ-ră looked out
a window, and cried through the
ttice, Why is his chariot *so* long in
ming? why tarry the wheels of his
ariots?
9 Her wise ladies answered her,
a, she returned [19]answer to herself,
0 Have [w]they not sped? have they
ot divided the prey; [20]to every man
damsel *or* two; to Sĭs-ĕ-ră a prey of
vers colours, a prey of divers colours
needlework, of divers colours of
eedlework on both sides, *meet* for
e necks of *them that take* the spoil?
1 So [x]let all thine enemies perish,
LORD: but *let* them that love him *be*
s the sun [z]when he goeth forth in his
ight. And the land had rest forty
ears.

CHAPTER 6

AND [a]the children of Israel did evil
in the sight of the LORD: and the
ORD delivered them into the hand [b]of
Iid-ĭ-ăn seven years.
2 And the hand of Mĭd-ĭ-ăn [1]pre-
ailed against Israel: *and* because of
e Mĭd-ĭ-ă-nītes the children of Israel
ade them [c]the dens which *are* in the
ountains, and caves, and strong
olds.
3 And *so* it was, when Israel had
own, that the Mĭd-ĭ-ă-nītes came up,
nd the Ă-măl-ĕk-ītes, [d]and the chil-
ren of the east, even they came up
gainst them;
4 And they encamped against them,
and destroyed the increase of the
arth, till thou come unto Gā-ză, and
eft no sustenance for Israel, neither
sheep, nor ox, nor ass.
5 For they came up with their cattle
nd their tents, and they came as
rasshoppers for multitude; *for* both
hey and their camels were without
umber: and they entered into the
and to destroy it.
6 And Israel was greatly impover-
shed because of the Mĭd-ĭ-ă-nītes;
and the children of Israel cried [f]unto
the LORD.
7 ¶ And it came to pass, when the
children of Israel cried unto the LORD
because of the Mĭd-ĭ-ă-nītes,
8 That the LORD sent [3]a prophet unto
the children of Israel, which said unto
them, Thus saith the LORD God of
Israel, I brought you up from Egypt,
and brought you forth out of the
house of bondage:
9 And I delivered you out of the hand
of the Egyptians, and out of the hand
of all that oppressed you, and drave
them out from before you, and gave
you their land;
10 And I said unto you, I *am* the
LORD your God; [g]fear not the gods of
the Amorites, in whose land ye dwell:
but ye have not obeyed my voice.
11 ¶ And there came an angel of the
LORD, and sat under an oak which
was in Ŏph-răh, that *pertained* unto
Jō-ăsh [h]the Ā-bi-ĕz-rīte: and his son
Gideon threshed wheat by the winepress, [4]to hide *it* from the Mĭd-ĭ-ă-
nītes.
12 And the [i]angel of the LORD appeared unto him, and said unto him,
The LORD *is* with thee, thou mighty
man of valour.
13 And Gideon said unto him, Oh
my Lord, if the LORD be with us, why
then is all this befallen us? and [j]where
be all his miracles which our fathers
told us of, saying, Did not the LORD
bring us up from Egypt? but now the
LORD hath [k]forsaken us, and delivered
us into the hands of the Mĭd-ĭ-ă-nītes.
14 And the LORD looked upon him,
and said, [l]Go in this thy might, and
thou shalt save Israel from the hand
of the Mĭd-ĭ-ă-nītes: have [m]not I sent
thee?
15 And he said unto him, Oh my
Lord, wherewith shall I save Israel?
behold, [5]my family *is* poor in Mă-năs-
sēh, and I *am* the least in my father's
house.
16 And the LORD said unto him,
Surely [n]I will be with thee, and thou
shalt smite the Mĭd-ĭ-ă-nītes as one
man.
17 And he said unto him, If now I
have found grace in thy sight, then
[o]shew me a sign that thou talkest with
me.
18 Depart [p]not hence, I pray thee,
until I come unto thee, and bring forth
my [6]present, and set *it* before thee.
And he said, I will tarry until thou
come again.
19 ¶ And Gideon went in, and made

v Pro. 31.31. Luke 1.28.
16 she hammered.
17 Between.
18 destroyed.
19 her words.
w Ex. 15.9.
20 to the head of a man.
x Ps. 48.4,5. Ps. 58.11. Ps. 68.1-3. Ps. 83.9. Rev. 6.10. Rev. 18.20.
y 2 Sam. 23.4. Ps. 37.6. Matt. 13.43.
z Ps. 19.5.

CHAP. 6

a Lev. 26.14. ch. 2.19.
b Gen. 25.2. Hab. 3.7.
1 was strong.
c 1 Sam. 13.6. Heb. 11.38.
d Gen. 29.1. ch. 7.12. 1 Ki. 4.30. Job. 1.3.
e Lev. 26.16. Deut. 28.30. Job 31.7,8. Jer. 5.17. Micah 6.15.
2 Or, goat.
f Ps. 50.15. Ps. 78.34. Hosea 5.15.
3 a man a prophet.
g 2 Ki. 17.35.
h Josh. 17.2. ch. 8.2.
4 to cause it to flee.
i Gen. 16.7-13. ch. 13.3. Luke 1.11, 28.
j Ps. 89.49. Isa. 59.1.
k 2 Chr. 15.2.
l 1 Sam. 12. 11. Heb. 11.32.
m Josh. 1.9.
5 my thousand is the meanest.
n Ex. 3.12.
o Ex. 4.1.
p Gen. 18.3.
6 Or, meat offering.

ready [7]a kid, and unleavened cakes of
an ē-´phäh of flour: the flesh he put in
a basket, and he put the broth in a pot,
and brought *it* out unto him under the
oak, and presented *it*.
20 And the angel of God said unto
him, Take the flesh and the unleavened cakes, and [q]lay *them* upon this
rock, and [r]pour out the broth. And
he did so.
21 ¶ Then the angel of the LORD put
forth the end of the staff that *was* in
his hand, and touched the flesh and
the unleavened cakes; and [s]there rose
up fire out of the rock, and consumed
the flesh and the unleavened cakes.
Then the angel of the LORD departed
out of his sight.
22 And when Gideon perceived that
he *was* an angel of the LORD, Gideon
said, Alas, O Lord GOD! for because
I have seen an angel of the LORD [t]face
to face.
23 And the LORD said unto him,
Peace [u]*be* unto thee; fear not: thou
shalt not die.
24 Then Gideon built an altar there
unto the LORD, and called it [8]Jĕ-hō-´
văh–shā-´lŏm: unto this day it *is* yet [v]in
Ŏph-´răh of the Ā-´bī–ĕz-´rītes.
25 ¶ And it came to pass the same
night, that the LORD said unto him,
Take thy father's young bullock, [9]even
the second bullock of seven years old,
and throw down the altar of Bā-´ăl
that thy father hath, and cut [w]down
the grove that *is* by it:
26 And build an altar unto the LORD
thy God upon the top of this [10]rock,
[11]in the ordered place, and take the
second bullock, and offer a burnt
sacrifice with the wood of the grove
which thou shalt cut down.
27 Then Gideon took ten men of his
servants, and did as the LORD had
said unto him: and *so* it was, because
he feared his father's household, and
the men of the city, that he could not
do *it* by day, that he did *it* [x]by night.
28 ¶ And when the men of the city
arose early in the morning, behold,
the altar of Bā-´ăl was cast down, and
the grove was cut down that *was* by it,
and the second bullock was offered
upon the altar *that was* built.
29 And they said one to another,
Who hath done this thing? And when
they inquired and asked, they said,
Gideon the son of Jō-´ăsh hath done
this thing.
30 Then the men of the city said unto
Jō-´ăsh, [y]Bring out thy son, that he
may die: because he hath cast down

7 a kid of the goats.
q ch. 13.19.
r 1 Ki. 18.33.
s Lev. 9.24. 2 Chr. 7.1.
t Gen. 16.13. Ex. 33.20. ch. 13.22.
u Dan. 10.19. Luke 24.36.
8 That is, The LORD send peace.
v ch. 8.32.
9 Or, and.
w Ex. 34.13. Deut. 7.5. ch. 3.7.
10 strong place.
11 Or, in an orderly manner.
x John 3.1.
y John 16.2. Acts 26.9.
12 That is, Let Baal plead. 1 Sam. 12. 11. Or, Jerub-besheth; that is, Let shame, or, confusion, plead. 2 Sam. 11. 21. Jer. 11.13. Hosea 9.10.
z Josh. 17.16. 1 Ki. 18.45.
a ch. 3.10. ch. 11.29. ch. 13.25. 1 Chr. 12.18. 2 Chr. 24.20. 1 Cor. 12.8-11.
13 clothed.
b ch. 3.27.
14 was called after him.
c Ex. 4.3,4,6, 7. Deut. 32.2. Ps. 72.6. Hosea 6.3,4.
d Gen 18.32.

CHAP. 7

a ch. 6.32. 1 Sam. 12. 11.
b Gen. 22.3. Josh. 3.1. Eccl. 9.10.
1 That is, Trembling.
c Gen. 12.6.

the altar of Bā-´ăl, and because he ha
cut down the grove that *was* by it
31 And Jō-´ăsh said unto all th
stood against him, Will ye plead f
Bā-´ăl? will ye save him? he that w
plead for him, let him be put to dea
whilst *it is yet* morning: if he *be* a go
let him plead for himself, because *o*
hath cast down his altar.
32 Therefore on that day he call
him [12]Jĕr-ŭb-bā-´ăl, saying, Let Bā-
plead against him, because he ha
thrown down his altar.
33 ¶ Then all the Mĭd-´ĭ-ă-nītes a
the Ă-măl-´ĕk-ītes and the children
the east were gathered together, a
went over, and pitched in [z]the vall
of Jĕz-´rē̆el.
34 But [a]the Spirit of the LORD [13]can
upon Gideon, and he blew a [b]trumpe
and Ā-´bī–ē-´zĕr [14]was gathered aft
him.
35 And he sent messengers throug
out all Mă-năs-´sēh; who also w
gathered after him: and he sent me
sengers unto Asher, and unto Zĕ-b
lŭn, and unto Năph-´tă-lī; and the
came up to meet them.
36 ¶ And Gideon said unto God,
thou wilt save Israel by mine hand,
thou hast said,
37 Behold, [c]I will put a fleece of wo
in the floor; *and* if the dew be on th
fleece only, and *it be* dry upon all th
earth *beside*, then shall I know tha
thou wilt save Israel by mine hand
as thou hast said.
38 And it was so: for he rose up earl
on the morrow, and thrust the flee
together, and wringed the dew out o
the fleece, a bowl full of water.
39 And Gideon said unto God, L
[d]not thine anger be hot against me
and I will speak but this once: let m
prove, I pray thee, but this once wit
the fleece; let it now be dry only upo
the fleece, and upon all the ground le
there be dew.
40 And God did so that night: for i
was dry upon the fleece only, and
there was dew on all the ground.

CHAPTER 7

THEN [a]Jĕr-ŭb-bā-´ăl, who *is* Gid
eon, and all the people that *wer*
with him, [b]rose up early, and pitche
beside the well of [1]Hâr-´ŏd: so that the
host of the Mĭd-´ĭ-ă-nītes were on the
north side of them, by the hill of Mō
rēh, in the [c]valley.
2 And the LORD said unto Gideon
The people that *are* with thee *are* too
many for me to give the Mĭd-´ĭ-ă-nītes

co their hands, lest Israel [d]vaunt
emselves against me, saying, Mine
vn hand hath saved me.
Now therefore go to, proclaim in
e ears of the people, saying, Whoso-
er [e]*is* fearful and afraid, let him re-
rn and depart early from mount
ilead. And there returned of the peo-
e twenty and two thousand; and
ere remained ten thousand.
And the LORD said unto Gideon,
e people *are* yet *too* many; bring
em down unto the water, and I will
y them for thee there: and it shall
, *that* of whom I say unto thee,
is shall go with thee, the same shall
with thee; and of whomsoever I
y unto thee, This shall not go with
ee, the same shall not go.
So he brought down the people un-
the water: and the LORD said unto
ideon, Every one that lappeth of
e water with his tongue, as a dog
ppeth, him shalt thou set by him-
lf; likewise every one that boweth
wn upon his knees to drink.
And the number of them that lap-
d, *putting* their hand to their mouth,
ere three hundred men: but all the
st of the people bowed down upon
eir knees to drink water.
And the LORD said unto Gideon,
y the three hundred men that lap-
d will I save you, and deliver the
id-ĭ-ă-nītes into thine hand: and let
the *other* people go every man unto
s place.
So the people took victuals in their
nd, and their trumpets: and he sent
the rest of Israel every man unto his
nt, and retained those three hundred
en: and the host of Mĭd-ĭ-ăn was be-
ath him in the valley.
¶ And it came to pass the same
ght, [g]that the LORD said unto him,
rise, get thee down unto the host;
r I have delivered it into thine hand.
0 But if thou fear to go down, go
ou with Phū-răh thy servant down
the host:
1 And thou shalt [h]hear what they
y; and afterward shall thine hands
strengthened to go down unto the
ost. Then went he down with Phū-
h his servant unto the outside of the
rmed men that *were* in the host.
2 And the Mĭd-ĭ-ă-nītes and the Ă-
ăl-ĕk-ites and [i]all the children of
e east lay along in the valley like
asshoppers for multitude; and their
mels *were* without number, as the
nd by the sea for multitude.
3 And when Gideon was come, be-

d Deut. 8.17. Deut. 9.4. 1 Sam. 17.47. Ps. 33.16,17,18. Ps. 44.6,7. Pro. 25.6. Eccl. 9.11. Isa. 10.13. Jer. 9.23,24. Zech. 4.6. Rom. 3.27. 1 Cor. 1.29. 2 Cor. 4.7. 2 Cor. 10.17. Eph. 2.9.
e Deut. 20.8.
2 separate, or, purify.
f 1 Sam. 14.6. Isa. 41.14-18.
g Gen. 46.2,3. Job 4.13. Matt. 1.20. Acts 18.9,10. Acts 27.23.
h Gen. 24.14. 1 Sam. 14.9,10.
3 Or, ranks by five.
i ch. 6.5,33. ch. 8.10.
j ch. 6.15. Isa. 41.14,15. 1 Cor. 1.27.
k Gen. 40.8.
4 the breaking thereof.
5 trumpets in the hand of all of them.
6 Or, firebrands, or, torches.
l Ex. 14.24. Luke 12.38. Rev. 16.15.
m Ex. 14.13,14. 2 Chr. 20.17. Isa. 30.7,15.
n Ex. 14.25. 2 Ki. 7.7. Job 15.21,22. Pro. 28.1.
o 2 Cor. 4.7.
p 1 Sam. 14.16-20. Ps. 83.9. Isa. 9.4.
q 1 Sam. 14.20. 2 Chr. 20.23.
7 Or, toward.
8 lip.

hold, *there was* a man that told a
dream unto his fellow, and said, Behold, I dreamed a dream, and, lo, [j]a
cake of barley bread tumbled into the
host of Mĭd-ĭ-ăn, and came unto a
tent, and smote it that it fell, and over-
turned it, that the tent lay along.
14 And [k]his fellow answered and
said, This *is* nothing else save the
sword of Gideon the son of Jō-ăsh, a
man of Israel: *for* into his hand hath
God delivered Mĭd-ĭ-ăn, and all the
host.
15 ¶ And it was *so*, when Gideon
heard the telling of the dream, and
[4]the interpretation thereof, that he
worshipped, and returned into the
host of Israel, and said, Arise; for the
LORD hath delivered into your hand
the host of Mĭd-ĭ-ăn.
16 And he divided the three hundred
men *into* three companies, and he put
[5]a trumpet in every man's hand, with
empty pitchers, and [6]lamps within the
pitchers.
17 And he said unto them, Look on
me, and do likewise: and, behold,
when I come to the outside of the
camp, it shall be *that*, as I do, so shall
ye do.
18 When I blow with a trumpet, I and
all that *are* with me, then blow ye the
trumpets also on every side of all the
camp, and say, *The sword* of the LORD,
and of Gideon.
19 ¶ So Gideon, and the hundred
men that *were* with him, came unto
the outside of the camp in the beginning of the [l]middle watch; and they
had but newly set the watch: and they
blew the trumpets, and brake the
pitchers that *were* in their hands.
20 And the three companies blew
the trumpets, and brake the pitchers,
and held the lamps in their left hands,
and the trumpets in their right hands
to blow *withal:* and they cried, The
sword of the LORD, and of Gideon.
21 And they [m]stood every man in his
place round about the camp: [n]and all
the host ran, and cried, and fled.
22 And the three hundred [o]blew the
trumpets, and [p]the LORD set every
[q]man's sword against his fellow, even
throughout all the host: and the host
fled to Bĕth-shĭt-tăh [7]in Zĕr-ĕ-răth,
and to the [8]border of Ā-bĕl-mĕ-hō-
lăh, unto Tăb-băth.
23 And the men of Israel gathered
themselves together out of Năph-tă-
lī, and out of Asher, and out of all Mă-
năs-sĕh, and pursued after the Mĭd-
ĭ-ă-nītes.

24 ¶ And Gideon sent messengers throughout all [r]mount Ē-phră-ĭm, saying, Come down against the Mĭd-ĭ-ă-nītes, and take before them the waters unto Bĕth–bâr-āh and Jordan. Then all the men of Ē-phră-ĭm gathered themselves together, and [s]took the waters unto Bĕth–bâr-āh [t]and Jordan.

25 And they took [u]two princes of the Mĭd-ĭ-ă-nītes, Ôr-ĕb and Zēeb; and they slew Ôr-ĕb upon the [v]rock Ôr-ĕb, and Zēeb they slew at the winepress of Zēeb, and pursued Mĭd-ĭ-ăn, and brought the heads of Ôr-ĕb and Zēeb to Gideon on the [w]other side Jordan.

CHAPTER 8

AND the [a]men of Ē-phră-ĭm said unto him, [1]Why hast thou served us thus, that thou calledst us not, when thou wentest to fight with the Mĭd-ĭ-ă-nītes? And they did chide with him [2]sharply.

2 And he said unto them, What have I done now in comparison of you? *Is* not the gleaning of the grapes of Ē-phră-ĭm better than the vintage of Ā-bĭ-ē-zĕr?

3 God [b]hath delivered into your hands the princes of Mĭd-ĭ-ăn, Ôr-ĕb and Zēeb: and what was I able to do in comparison of you? Then their [3]anger was abated toward him, when he had said that.

4 ¶ And Gideon came to Jordan, *and* passed over, he, and the three hundred men that *were* with him, faint, yet pursuing *them.*

5 And he said unto the men [c]of Sŭc-cōth, Give, I pray you, loaves of bread unto the people that follow me; for they *be* faint, and I am pursuing after Zē-bäh and Zăl-mŭn-nă, kings of Mĭd-ĭ-ăn.

6 ¶ And the princes of Sŭc-cōth said, [d]*Are* the hands of Zē-bäh and Zăl-mŭn-nă now in thine hand, that [e]we should give bread unto thine army?

7 And Gideon said, Therefore when the LORD hath delivered Zē-bäh and Zăl-mŭn-nă into mine hand, then I will [4]tear your flesh with the thorns of the wilderness and with briers.

8 ¶ And he went up thence [f]to Pĕn-ū-ĕl, and spake unto them likewise: and the men of Pĕn-ū-ĕl answered him as the men of Sŭc-cōth had answered *him.*

9 And he spake also unto the men of Pĕn-ū-ĕl, saying, When [g]I come again in peace, I will break down this tower.

10 ¶ Now Zē-bäh and Zăl-mŭn-nă *were* in Kär-kôr, and their hosts wi[th] them, about fifteen thousand *men,* [all] that were left of all [h]the hosts of [the] children of the east: for there fell [5][an] hundred and twenty thousand m[en] that drew sword.

11 ¶ And Gideon went up by the w[ay] of them that dwelt in tents on the ea[st] [i]of Nō-băh and Jŏg-bĕ-hăh, a[nd] smote the host: for the host w[as] [j]secure.

12 And when Zē-bäh and Zăl-mŭ[n-] nă fled, he pursued after them, a[nd] [k]took the two kings of Mĭd-ĭ-ăn, Z[ē-] bäh and Zăl-mŭn-nă, and [6]discomfit[ed] all the host.

13 ¶ And Gideon the son of Jō-ă[sh] returned from battle before the s[un] *was up,*

14 And caught a young man of t[he] men of Sŭc-cōth, and inquired [of] him: and he [7]described unto him t[he] princes of Sŭc-cōth, and the eld[ers] thereof, *even* threescore and seve[n]teen men.

15 And he came unto the men [of] Sŭc-cōth, and said, Behold Zē-b[äh] and Zăl-mŭn-nă, with whom ye d[id] upbraid me, saying, *Are* the hands [of] Zē-bäh and Zăl-mŭn-nă now in thi[ne] hand, that we should give bread un[to] thy men *that are* weary?

16 And he took the elders of the ci[ty,] and thorns of the wilderness and b[ri]ers, and with them he [8]taught the m[en] of Sŭc-cōth.

17 And he beat down the tower [of] [l]Pĕn-ū-ĕl, and slew the men of t[he] city.

18 ¶ Then said he unto Zē-bäh a[nd] Zăl-mŭn-nă, What manner of m[en] *were they* whom ye slew [m]at Tā-bô[r?] And they answered, As thou *art,* [so] *were* they; each one [9]resembled t[he] children of a king.

19 And he said, They *were* my bret[h]ren, *even* the sons of my mother: [as] the LORD liveth, if ye had saved the[m] alive, I would not slay you.

20 And he said unto Jē-thĕr his firs[t]born, Up, *and* slay them. But t[he] youth drew not his sword: for [he] feared, because he *was* yet a youth.

21 Then Zē-bäh and Zăl-mŭn-[nă] said, Rise thou, and fall upon us: f[or] as the man *is, so is* his strength. A[nd] Gideon arose, and [n]slew Zē-bäh a[nd] Zăl-mŭn-nă, and took away the [10]or[n]aments that *were* on their came[ls'] necks.

22 ¶ Then the men of Israel said un[to] Gideon, Rule thou over us, both tho[u,] and thy son and thy son's son als[o:]

---

r ch. 3.27. Rom. 15.30. Phil. 1.27.
s ch. 3.28.
t John 1.28.
u ch. 8.3. Ps. 83.11.
v Isa. 10.26.
w ch. 8.4.

CHAP. 8

a ch. 12.1. 2 Sam. 19. 41.
1 What thing is this thou hast done unto us?
2 strongly.
b ch. 7.24. Ps. 44.3. Pro. 15.1. Rom. 12.3, 6.
3 spirit.
c Gen. 33.17. Ps. 60.6.
d 1 Ki. 20.11.
e 1 Sam. 25. 11.
4 thresh.
f Gen. 32.30.
g 1 Ki. 22.27. Luke 12.45. 1 Thes. 5.2, 3.
h ch. 7.12.
5 Or, an hundred and twenty thousand, every one drawing a sword.
i Num. 32.35.
j ch. 18.27. Pro. 17.18. 1 Thes. 5.3.
k Ps. 83.11.
6 terrified.
7 writ.
8 made to know.
l 1 Ki. 12.25.
m ch. 4.6. Ps. 89.12.
9 according to the form, etc.
n Ps. 83.11.
10 Or, ornaments like the moon.

r thou hast delivered us from the
ınd of Mĭd-ĭ-ăn.
3 And Gideon said unto them, I will
ot rule over you, neither shall my son
le over you: [o]the LORD shall rule
er you.
4 ¶ And Gideon said unto them, I
ould desire a request of you, that ye
ould give me every man the earrings
his prey. (For they had golden ear-
ngs, [p]because they *were* Ĭsh-mā-ĕ-
es.)
5 And they answered, We will will-
gly give *them*. And they spread a
rment, and did cast therein every
an the earrings of his prey.
6 And the weight of the golden ear-
ngs that he requested was a thousand
d seven hundred *shekels* of gold;
side ornaments, and [11]collars, and
rple raiment that *was* on the
ngs of Mĭd-ĭ-ăn, and beside the
ains that *were* about their camels'
cks.
7 And Gideon [q]made an ē-phŏd
ereof, and put it in his city, *even* in
ph-răh: and all Israel [s]went thither
whoring after it: which thing be-
me [t]a snare unto Gideon, and to his
use.
8 ¶ Thus was Mĭd-ĭ-ăn subdued be-
re the children of Israel, so that they
ted up their heads no more. And
e country was in quietness forty
ars in the days of Gideon.
9 ¶ And Jĕr-ŭb-bā-ăl the son of Jō-
h went and dwelt in his own house.
0 And Gideon had [u]threescore and
n sons [12]of his body begotten: for he
d many wives.
1 And his concubine that *was* in
ē-chĕm, she also bare him a son,
hose name he [13]called [14]Ă-bĭm-ĕ-
ch.
2 ¶ And Gideon the son of Jō-ăsh
ed in a good old age, and was buried
the sepulchre of Jō-ăsh his father,
n Ŏph-răh of the Ā-bĭ-ĕz-rītes.
3 And it came to pass, [w]as soon as
ideon was dead, that the children
Israel turned again, and went a
horing after Bā-ă-lĭm, and [x]made
Bā-ăl–bē-rĭth their god.
4 And the children of Israel remem-
ered [y]not the LORD their God,
ho had delivered them out of the
ands of all their enemies on every
de:
5 Neither [z]shewed they kindness to
e house of Jĕr-ŭb-bā-ăl, *namely*,
ideon, according to all the good-
ess which he had shewed unto
rael.

o 1 Sam. 8.7. 1 Sam. 10. 19. Ps. 10.16. Ps. 29.10. Ps. 89.18. Isa. 26.13. Isa. 33.22. Isa. 43.15. Hosea 13. 10.
p Gen. 16.10. Gen. 25.13. Gen. 37.25.
11 Or, sweet jewels.
q ch. 17.5. ch. 18.14,17.
r ch. 6.24.
s Ex. 23.33. Ps. 73.27. Ps. 106.39.
t Deut. 7.16.
u ch. 9.2,5. ch. 10.4.
12 going out of his thigh.
13 set.
14 That is, My father the king.
v ch. 6.24.
w ch. 2.19.
x ch. 9.4.
15 That is, Idol of the covenant.
y Ps. 78.11, 42. Eccl. 12.1.
z ch. 9.16. Eccl. 9.14, 15.

CHAP. 9

a ch. 8.31.
1 What is good? whether, etc.
b ch. 8.30.
c Gen. 29.14. 2 Sam. 19. 13. 1 Chr. 11.1. Heb. 2.14.
2 after.
d Gen. 29.15.
e ch. 8.33.
f ch. 11.3. 1 Sam. 22.2. 2 Chr. 13.7. Pro. 12.11. Acts 17.5.
g ch. 6.24.
h 2 Ki. 10.17. Matt. 2.16, 20.
3 Or, by the oak of the pillar.
i Deut. 11.29. Josh. 8.33. John 4.20.
j 2 Ki. 14.9.
k ch. 8.22.
l Ps. 104.15.
4 go up and down for other trees.

CHAPTER 9

AND Ă-bĭm-ĕ-lĕch the son of Jĕr-
ŭb-bā-ăl went to Shē-chĕm unto
[a]his mother's brethren, and communed with them, and with all the family
of the house of his mother's father,
saying,
2 Speak, I pray you, in the ears of all
the men of Shē-chĕm, [1]Whether *is* better for you, either that all the sons of
Jĕr-ŭb-bā-ăl, *which are* [b]threescore
and ten persons, reign over you, or
that one reign over you? remember
also that I *am* [c]your bone and your
flesh.
3 And his mother's brethren spake
of him in the ears of all the men of
Shē-chĕm all these words: and their
hearts inclined [2]to follow Ă-bĭm-ĕ-
lĕch; for they said, He *is* [d]our brother.
4 And they gave him threescore and
ten *pieces* of silver out of the house of
[e]Bā-ăl–bē-rĭth, wherewith Ă-bĭm-ĕ-
lĕch hired [f]vain and light persons,
which followed him.
5 And he went unto his father's
house [g]at Ŏph-răh, and [h]slew his
brethren the sons of Jĕr-ŭb-bā-ăl, *being* threescore and ten persons, upon
one stone: notwithstanding yet Jō-
thăm the youngest son of Jĕr-ŭb-bā-
ăl was left; for he hid himself.
6 And all the men of Shē-chĕm gathered together, and all the house of
Mĭl-lō, and went, and made Ă-bĭm-
ĕ-lĕch king, [3]by the plain of the pillar
that *was* in Shē-chĕm.
7 ¶ And when they told *it* to Jō-thăm,
he went and stood in the top [i]of
mount Gĕ-rĭ-zĭm, and lifted up his
voice, and cried, and said unto them,
Hearken unto me, ye men of Shē-
chĕm, that God may hearken unto
you.
8 The [j]trees went forth *on a time* to
anoint a king over them; and [k]they
said unto the olive tree, Reign thou
over us.
9 But the olive tree said unto them,
Should I leave my fatness, wherewith
[l]by me they honour God and man,
and [4]go to be promoted over the
trees?
10 And the trees said to the fig tree,
Come thou, *and* reign over us.
11 But the fig tree said unto them,
Should I forsake my sweetness, and
my good fruit, and go to be promoted
over the trees?
12 Then said the trees unto the vine,
Come thou, *and* reign over us.
13 And the vine said unto them,
Should I leave my wine, which cheer-

eth God and man, and go to be promoted over the trees?
14 Then said all the trees unto the [5]bramble, Come thou, *and* reign over us.
15 And the bramble said unto the trees, If in truth ye anoint me king over you, *then* come *and* put your trust in [m]my shadow: and if not, [n]let fire come out of the bramble, and devour the [o]cedars of Lĕb-ă-non.
16 Now therefore, if ye have done truly and sincerely in that ye have made Ă-bĭm-ĕ-lĕch king, and if ye have dealt well with Jĕr-ŭb-bā-ăl and his house, and have done unto him [p]according to the deserving of his hands;
17 (For my father fought for you, and [6]adventured his life far, and delivered you out of the hand of Mĭd-ĭ-ăn:
18 And ye are risen up against my father's house this day, and have slain his sons, threescore and ten persons, upon one stone, and have made Ă-bĭm-ĕ-lĕch, the son of his maidservant, king over the men of Shē-chĕm, because he *is* your brother;)
19 If ye then have dealt truly and sincerely with Jĕr-ŭb-bā-ăl and with his house this day, *then* [q]rejoice ye in Ă-bĭm-ĕ-lĕch, and let him also rejoice in you:
20 But if not, let fire come out from Ă-bĭm-ĕ-lĕch, and devour the men of Shē-chĕm, and the house of Mĭl-lō; and let fire come out from the men of Shē-chĕm, and from the house of Mĭl-lō, and devour Ă-bĭm-ĕ-lĕch.
21 And Jō-thăm ran away, and fled, and went to [r]Bēer, and dwelt there, for fear of Ă-bĭm-ĕ-lĕch his brother.
22 ¶ When Ă-bĭm-ĕ-lĕch had reigned three years over Israel,
23 Then [s]God sent an evil spirit between Ă-bĭm-ĕ-lĕch and the men of Shē-chĕm; and the men of Shē-chĕm [t]dealt treacherously with Ă-bĭm-ĕ-lĕch:
24 That [u]the cruelty *done* to the threescore and ten sons of Jĕr-ŭb-bā-ăl might come, and their blood be laid upon Ă-bĭm-ĕ-lĕch their brother, which slew them; and upon the men of Shē-chĕm, which [7]aided him in the killing of his brethren.
25 And the men of Shē-chĕm set liers in wait for him in the top of the mountains, and they robbed all that came along that way by them: and it was told Ă-bĭm-ĕ-lĕch.
26 And Gā-ăl the son of Ē-bĕd came with his brethren, and went over to

5 Or, thistle.
m Isa. 30.2. Dan. 4.12. Hosea 14.7.
n Eze. 19.14.
o 2 Ki. 14.9. Ps. 104.16. Isa. 2.13.
p ch. 8.35.
6 cast his life.
q Isa. 8.6. Phil. 3.3. Jas. 4.16.
r Num. 21.16 Josh. 19.8. 2 Sam. 20. 14.
s 1 Sam. 16. 14. 1 Sam. 18.9. 10. 1 Ki. 12.15. 1 Ki. 22.22. 2 Chr. 18.19-22. Isa. 19.2,14. 2 Thes. 2.1, 11.
t Isa. 33.1. Matt. 7.2.
u 1 Sam. 15. 33. 1 Ki. 2.32. Esther 9.25. Ps. 7.16. Ps. 58.10,11. Matt. 23.35.
7 strengthened his hands to kill.
8 Or, songs.
v ch. 8.33.
w Ex. 5.2. 1 Sam. 25. 10.
x Gen. 34.2.
y 2 Sam. 15.4. 1 Ki. 20.11. Ps. 10.3.
9 Or, hot.
10 craftily, or, to Tormah.
11 as thine hand shall find.
z Mark 8.24.
12 navel.
13 Or, the regarders of the times, soothsayers.

Shē-chĕm: and the men of Shē-chĕ put their confidence in him.
27 And they went out into the field and gathered their vineyards, an trode *the grapes*, and made [8]merr and went into the house [v]of their go and did eat and drink, and curse Ă-bĭm-ĕ-lĕch.
28 And Gā-ăl the son of Ē-bĕd sai [w]Who *is* Ă-bĭm-ĕ-lĕch, and who Shē-chĕm, that we should serve him *is* not *he* the son of Jĕr-ŭb-bā-ăl? an Zē-bŭl his officer? serve the men [x]Hā-môr the father of Shē-chĕm: f why should we serve him?
29 And [y]would to God this peop were under my hand! then would I r move Ă-bĭm-ĕ-lĕch. And he said t Ă-bĭm-ĕ-lĕch, Increase thine arm and come out.
30 ¶ And when Zē-bŭl the ruler of t city heard the words of Gā-ăl the so of Ē-bĕd, his anger was [9]kindled.
31 And he sent messengers unto Ă bĭm-ĕ-lĕch [10]privily, saying, Behol Gā-ăl the son of Ē-bĕd and his bret ren be come to Shē-chĕm; and, b hold, they fortify the city again thee.
32 Now therefore up by night, tho and the people that *is* with thee, an lie in wait in the field:
33 And it shall be, *that* in the mor ing, as soon as the sun is up, tho shalt rise early, and set upon the cit and, behold, *when* he and the peop that *is* with him come out again thee, then mayest thou do to them [11] thou shalt find occasion.
34 ¶ And Ă-bĭm-ĕ-lĕch rose up, an all the people that *were* with him, b night, and they laid wait against Sh chĕm in four companies.
35 And Gā-ăl the son of Ē-bĕd we out, and stood in the entering of t gate of the city: and Ă-bĭm-ĕ-lĕch ro up, and the people that *were* with hi from lying in wait.
36 And when Gā-ăl saw the peopl he said to Zē-bŭl, Behold, there co people down from the top of t mountains. And Zē-bŭl said un him, [z]Thou seest the shadow of t mountains as *if they were* men.
37 And Gā-ăl spake again and sai See there come people down by t [12]middle of the land, and another co pany come along by the plain [13]of M ō-nĕ-nĭm.
38 Then said Zē-bŭl unto him, Whe *is* now thy mouth, wherewith tho saidst, Who *is* Ă-bĭm-ĕ-lĕch, that w should serve him? *is* not this the pe

le that thou hast despised? [a]go out,
pray now, and fight with them.
39 And Gā´-ăl went out before the
ıen of Shē´-chĕm, and fought with Ă-
ım´-ĕ-lĕch.
40 And Ă-bĭm´-ĕ-lĕch chased him,
nd he fled before him, and many were
verthrown *and* wounded, *even* unto
ıe entering of the gate.
41 And Ă-bĭm´-ĕ-lĕch dwelt at Ă-rû´-
ıăh: and Zē´-bŭl thrust out Gā´-ăl and
is brethren, that they should not
well in Shē´-chĕm.
42 And it came to pass on the mor-
ow, that the people went out into the
eld; and they told Ă-bĭm´-ĕ-lĕch.
43 And he took the people, and
ivided them into three companies,
nd laid wait in the field, and looked,
nd, behold, the people *were* come
rth out of the city; and he rose up
gainst them, and smote them.
44 And Ă-bĭm´-ĕ-lĕch, and the com-
any that *was* with him, rushed for-
ard, and stood in the entering of
ne gate of the city: and the two
ther companies ran upon all *the*
eople that *were* in the fields, and
lew them.
45 And Ă-bĭm´-ĕ-lĕch fought against
ne city all that day; and he took the
ity, and slew the people that *was*
herein, and [b]beat down the city, and
sowed it with salt.
46 ¶ And when all the men of the
ower of Shē´-chĕm heard *that*, they
ntered into an hold of the house [c]of
he god Bē´-rĭth.
47 And it was told Ă-bĭm´-ĕ-lĕch, that
ll the men of the tower of Shē´-chĕm
ere gathered together.
48 And Ă-bĭm´-ĕ-lĕch gat him up to
mount Zăl´-mŏn, he and all the peo-
le that *were* with him; and Ă-bĭm´-ĕ-
ĕch took an axe in his hand, and cut
own a bough from the trees, and took
, and laid *it* on his shoulder, and said
nto the people that *were* with him,
Vhat ye have seen [15]me do, make
aste, *and* do as I *have done*.
49 And all the people likewise cut
own every man his bough, and fol-
owed Ă-bĭm´-ĕ-lĕch, and put *them* to
he hold, and set the hold on fire upon
hem; so that all the men of the tower
f Shē´-chĕm died also, about a thou-
and men and women.
50 ¶ Then [e]went Ă-bĭm´-ĕ-lĕch to
hē´-bĕz, and encamped against Thē´-
ĕz, and took it.
51 But there was a strong tower
vithin the city, and thither fled all the
ıen and women, and all they of the

[a] 2 Sam. 2. 26,27. 2 Ki. 14.8. Jer. 2.28. Eze. 47.11. Zeph. 2.9.
[b] Deut. 29.23. See ver. 20. 1 Ki. 12.25. 2 Ki. 3.25. Job 8.22. Job 21.17, 30. Ps. 9.16. Ps. 11.6. Ps. 76.10. Ps. 119.119. Pro. 2.22. Eccl. 8.12, 13.
14 Thus marking it out for perpetual desolation and barrenness.
[c] ch. 8.33. 1 Ki. 18.26. 2 Ki. 1.2-4. Ps. 115.8. Isa. 28.15-18. Isa. 37.38.
[d] Ps. 68.14.
15 I have done.
[e] Ex. 14.4.
[f] ch. 4.17. 2 Sam. 11. 21. Job 31.3. Jer. 49.20. 1 Cor. 1.27.
[g] 1 Sam. 31.4.
[h] Gen. 9.5,6. Job 31.3. Ps. 9.12. Ps. 11.6. Ps. 58.10,11. Ps. 94.23. Pro. 5.22. Pro. 24.12. Acts 28.4. Rom. 2.6. Gal. 6.7. Rev. 19.20, 21.

CHAP. 10

[a] ch. 2.16. ch. 3.9.
1 save, or, deliver.
[b] ch. 5.10.
[c] Deut. 3.14.
2 Or, the villages of Jair.
[d] ch. 2.11. ch. 4.1. ch. 6.1.
[e] ch. 2.13. ch. 3.7. 2 Chr. 28. 23. Ps. 106.36.
[f] ch. 2.12.
[g] 1 Ki. 11.33. 1 Ki. 16.31. 2 Ki. 23.13. Ps. 106. 36.
[h] 1 Sam. 12.9.
3 crushed.

city, and shut *it* to them, and gat them
up to the top of the tower.
52 And Ă-bĭm´-ĕ-lĕch came unto the
tower, and fought against it, and went
hard unto the door of the tower to
burn it with fire.
53 And [f]a certain woman cast a piece
of a millstone upon Ă-bĭm´-ĕ-lĕch's
head, and all to brake his skull.
54 Then [g]he called hastily unto the
young man his armourbearer, and
said unto him, Draw thy sword, and
slay me, that men say not of me, A
woman slew him. And his young man
thrust him through, and he died.
55 And when the men of Israel saw
that Ă-bĭm´-ĕ-lĕch was dead, they departed every man unto his place.
56 ¶ Thus [h]God rendered the wickedness of Ă-bĭm´-ĕ-lĕch, which he did unto his father, in slaying his seventy
brethren:
57 And all the evil of the men of Shē´-
chĕm did God render upon their
heads: and upon them came the curse
of Jō´-thăm the son of Jĕr-ŭb-bā´-ăl.

CHAPTER 10

AND after Ă-bĭm´-ĕ-lĕch there arose
[a]to [1]defend Israel Tō´-lă the son of
Pū´-ăh, the son of Dodo, a man of Ĭs´-
să-chăr; and he dwelt in Shā´-mĭr in
mount Ē´-phră-ĭm.
2 And he judged Israel twenty and
three years, and died, and was buried
in Shā´-mĭr.
3 ¶ And after him arose Jā´-ĭr, a
Gileadite, and judged Israel twenty
and two years.
4 And he had thirty sons that rode
[b]on thirty ass colts, and they had
thirty cities, which [c]are called [2]Hā´-
vŏth–jā´-ĭr unto this day, which *are* in
the land of Gilead.
5 And Jā´-ĭr died, and was buried in
Cā´-mŏn.
6 ¶ And [d]the children of Israel did
evil again in the sight of the LORD,
and [e]served Bā´-ă-lĭm, and Ăsh´-tă-
rōth, and [f]the gods of Syria, and the
gods of [g]Zī´-dŏn, and the gods of Moab, and the gods of the children of
Ammon, and the gods of the Philistines, and forsook the LORD, and
served not him.
7 And the anger of the LORD was hot
against Israel, and he [h]sold them into
the hands of the Philistines, and into
the hands of the children of Ammon.
8 And that year they vexed and [3]op-
pressed the children of Israel: eighteen
years, all the children of Israel that
were on the other side Jordan in the

land of the Amorites, which *is* in
Gilead.
9 Moreover the children of Ammon
passed over Jordan to fight also
against Judah, and against Benjamin,
and against the house of Ḗ-phră-ĭm;
so that Israel was sore distressed.
10 ¶ And [i]the children of Israel cried
unto the LORD, saying, We have sinned against thee, both because we
have forsaken our God, and also served Bā́-ă-lĭm.
11 And the LORD said unto the children of Israel, *Did* not *I deliver you*
[j]from the Egyptians, and [k]from the
Amorites, [l]from the children of Ammon, [m]and from the Philistines?
12 [n]The Zī-dṓ-nĭ-ăns also, [o]and the
Ă-măĺ-ĕk-ītes, and the Mā́-ŏn-ītes,
did [p]oppress you; and ye cried to me,
and I delivered you out of their hand.
13 Yet [q]ye have forsaken me, and
served other gods: wherefore I will
deliver you no more.
14 Go and [r]cry unto the gods which
ye have chosen; let them deliver you
in the time of your tribulation.
15 ¶ And the children of Israel said
unto the LORD, We have sinned: do
[s]thou unto us whatsoever [4]seemeth
good unto thee; deliver us only, we
pray thee, this day.
16 And [t]they put away the [5]strange
gods from among them, and served
the LORD: and [u]his soul [6]was grieved
for the misery of Israel.
17 Then the children of Ammon were
[7]gathered together, and encamped in
Gilead. And the children of Israel
assembled themselves together, and
encamped in [v]Mĭź-pēh.
18 And the people *and* princes of
Gilead said one to another, What man
is he that will begin to fight against
the children of Ammon? he shall be
head over all the inhabitants of
Gilead.

CHAPTER 11

NOW Jĕph́-thăh the Gileadite was
[a]a mighty man of valour, and he
was the son of [1]an harlot: and Gilead
begat Jĕph́-thăh.
2 And Gilead's wife bare him sons;
and his wife's sons grew up, and they
thrust out Jĕph́-thăh, and said unto
him, Thou shalt not inherit in our
father's house; for thou *art* the son of
a strange woman.
3 Then Jĕph́-thăh fled [2]from his
brethren, and dwelt in the land of
Tŏb: and there were gathered vain
[b]men to Jĕph́-thăh, and went out with
him.

[i] 1 Sam. 12. 10.
[j] Ex. 14.30. 1 Sam. 12.8.
[k] Num. 21. 21.
[l] ch. 3.12.
[m] ch. 3.31.
[n] ch. 5.19.
[o] ch. 6.3.
[p] Ps. 106.42.
[q] Deut. 32.15. ch. 2.12. 1 Chr. 28.9.
[r] 2 Ki. 3.13.
[s] 1 Sam. 3.18.
4 is good in thine eyes.
[t] 2 Chr. 7.14.
5 gods of strangers.
[u] Ps. 106.44.
6 was shortened.
7 cried together.
[v] Gen. 31.49.

CHAP. 11

[a] ch. 6.12.
1 a woman an harlot.
2 from the face.
[b] ch. 9.4. 1 Sam. 22.2. Job 30.1-10. Acts 17.5.
3 after days.
[c] Gen. 26.27.
[d] Luke 17.4.
[e] ch. 10.18.
[f] Gen. 31.50. Jer. 29.23. Micah 1.2. Rom. 1.9. 1 Thes. 2.5.
4 be the hearer between us.
[g] ch. 10.17. ch. 20.1. 1 Sam. 10. 17. Pro. 16.3.
[h] Num. 21. 24.
[i] Gen. 32.22.
[j] Num. 22. 13-15. Deut. 2.9, 19. 2 Chr. 20.10.
[k] Num. 14. 25. Deut. 1.40. Josh. 5.6.
[l] Num. 13.26. Deut. 1.46.
[m] Num. 20. 14.

4 ¶ And it came to pass [3]in process o
time, that the children of Ammo
made war against Israel.
5 And it was so, that when the chil
dren of Ammon made war agains
Israel, the elders of Gilead went t
fetch Jĕph́-thăh out of the land o
Tŏb:
6 And they said unto Jĕph́-thăh
Come, and be our captain, that w
may fight with the children of Am
mon.
7 And Jĕph́-thăh said unto the elde
of Gilead, [c]Did not ye hate me, an
expel me out of my father's house
and why are ye come unto me nov
when ye are in distress?
8 And the elders of Gilead said unt
Jĕph́-thăh, Therefore [d]we turn agai
to thee now, that thou mayest go wit
us, and fight against the children o
Ammon, and be our [e]head over all th
inhabitants of Gilead.
9 And Jĕph́-thăh said unto the elder
of Gilead, If ye bring me home agai
to fight against the children of Ammon, and the LORD deliver them before me, shall I be your head?
10 And the elders of Gilead said unt
Jĕph́-thăh, [f]The LORD [4]be witness between us, if we do not so according t
thy words.
11 Then Jĕph́-thăh went with the
elders of Gilead, and the people
made him head and captain ove
them: and Jĕph́-thăh uttered all his
words [g]before the LORD in Mĭź-pēh.
12 ¶ And Jĕph́-thăh sent messengers
unto the king of the children of Ammon, saying, What hast thou to do
with me, that thou art come agains
me to fight in my land?
13 And the king of the children o
Ammon answered unto the messengers of Jĕph́-thăh, Because Israe
[h]took away my land, when they came
up out of Egypt, from Arnon even unto [i]Jăb́-bŏk, and unto Jordan: now
therefore restore those *lands* again
peaceably.
14 And Jĕph́-thăh sent messengers
again unto the king of the children o
Ammon:
15 And said unto him, Thus saith
Jĕph́-thăh, [j]Israel took not away the
land of Moab, nor the land of the children of Ammon:
16 But when Israel came up from
Egypt, and [k]walked through the wilderness unto the Red sea, and came
[l]to Kā́-dĕsh;
17 Then [m]Israel sent messengers unto the king of Ḗ-dŏm, saying, Let me,

I pray thee, pass through thy land:
but the king of Ē´-dọm would not
hearken *thereto.* And in like manner
they sent unto the king of Moab: but
he would not *consent:* and Israel
[n]abode in Kā´-dĕsh.
18 Then they went along through the
wilderness, and [o]compassed the land
of Ē´-dọm, and the land of Moab, and
[p]came by the east side of the land of
Moab, and pitched on the other side
of Arnon, but came not within the
border of Moab: for Arnon *was* the
border of Moab.
19 And [q]Israel sent messengers unto
Sī´-hŏn king of the Amorites, the king
of Hĕsh´-bŏn; and Israel said unto
him, Let us pass, we pray thee, through
thy land into my place.
20 But Sī´-hŏn trusted not Israel to
pass through his coast: but Sī´-hŏn
gathered all his people together, and
pitched in Jā´-hăz, and fought against
Israel.
21 And the LORD God of Israel delivered Sī´-hŏn and all his people into
the hand of Israel, and [r]they smote
them: so Israel possessed all the land
of the Amorites, the inhabitants of
that country.
22 And they possessed all the coasts
of the Amorites, from Arnon even unto Jăb´-bọk, and from the wilderness
even unto Jordan.
23 So now the LORD God of Israel
hath dispossessed the Amorites from
before his people Israel, and shouldest thou possess it?
24 Wilt not thou possess that which
Chē´-mŏsh [s]thy god giveth thee to
possess? So whomsoever the [t]LORD
our God shall drive out from before
us, them will we possess.
25 And now *art* thou any thing better
than [u]Balak the son of Zĭp´-pôr, king
of Moab? did he ever strive against
Israel, or did he ever fight against
them,
26 While Israel dwelt in Hĕsh´-bŏn
and her towns, and in [v]Ă-rō´-ĕr and
her towns, and in all the cities that
be along by the coasts of Arnon,
three hundred years? why therefore
did ye not recover *them* within that
time?
27 Wherefore I have not sinned
against thee, but thou doest me wrong
to war against me: the LORD [w]the
Judge be judge this day between the
children of Israel and the children of
Ammon.
28 Howbeit the king of the children
of Ammon hearkened not unto the

n Num. 20.1.
o Num. 21.4.
p Num. 21. 11.
q Num. 21. 21,35. Deut. 2.26. Josh. 13.8-12.
r Num. 21. 24. Deut. 2.33, 34.
s Num. 21. 29. 1 Ki. 11.7. Jer. 48.7.
t Ex. 23.28, 31. Ex. 34.11. Num. 33.50, 54. Deut. 7.16, 24. Deut. 9.3,6. Deut. 18.12. Josh. 3.10. Josh. 13.6. 2 Chr. 7.20. 2 Chr. 20.7. Ps. 44.2,3. Acts 13.19.
u Num. 22.2. Deut. 23.3, 4. Josh. 24.9. Micah 6.5.
v Deut. 2.36.
w Gen. 18.25. Job 9.15. John 5.22-23.
x ch. 3.10.
y Gen. 28.20. 1 Sam. 1.11. Eccl. 5.1,2.
5 that which cometh forth, which shall come forth.
z Lev. 27.2. 1 Sam. 1.11.
6 Or, or I will offer it, etc.
a Eze. 27.17.
7 Or, Abel.
b ch. 10.17.
c Ex. 15.20. 1 Sam. 18.6. Ps. 68.25. Jer. 31.4.
8 of himself, or, he had not of his own either son or daughter.
d Gen. 37.29. 2 Sam. 13. 30,31. Job 1.20.
e Eccl. 5.2.
f Ps. 15.4. Eccl. 5.4,5.
g Num. 30.2.
h 2 Sam. 18. 19.
9 go and go down.
i Gen. 30.23. Luke 1.25.
j 1 Sam. 1.22.

words of Jĕph´-thăh which he sent
him.
29 ¶ Then [x]the Spirit of the LORD
came upon Jĕph´-thăh, and he passed
over Gilead, and Mă-năs´-sĕh, and
passed over Mĭz´-pēh of Gilead, and
from Mĭz´-pēh of Gilead he passed
over *unto* the children of Ammon.
30 And Jĕph´-thăh [y]vowed a vow unto the LORD, and said, If thou shalt
without fail deliver the children of
Ammon into mine hands,
31 Then it shall be, that [5]whatsoever
cometh forth of the doors of my house
to meet me, when I return in peace
from the children of Ammon, [z]shall
surely be the LORD's, [6]and I will offer
it up for a burnt offering.
32 ¶ So Jĕph´-thăh passed over unto
the children of Ammon to fight against
them; and the LORD delivered them
into his hands.
33 And he smote them from Ă-rō´-ĕr,
even till thou come [a]to Mĭn´-nĭth, *even*
twenty cities, and unto [7]the plain of
the vineyards, with a very great
slaughter. Thus the children of Ammon were subdued before the children of Israel.
34 ¶ And Jĕph´-thăh came [b]to Mĭz´-
pēh unto his house, and, behold, [c]his
daughter came out to meet him with
timbrels and with dances: and she *was*
his only child; [8]beside her he had
neither son nor daughter.
35 And it came to pass, when he saw
her, that he [d]rent his clothes, and said,
Alas, my daughter! thou hast brought
me very low, and thou art one of them
that trouble me: for [e]I have opened my
mouth unto the LORD, and [f]I cannot
go back.
36 And she said unto him, My father,
if thou hast opened thy mouth unto
the LORD, do [g]to me according to that
which hath proceeded out of thy
mouth; forasmuch as the [h]LORD hath
taken vengeance for thee of thine
enemies, *even* of the children of
Ammon.
37 And she said unto her father, Let
this thing be done for me: let me alone
two months, that I may [9]go up and
down upon the mountains, and bewail [i]my virginity, I and my fellows.
38 And he said, Go. And he sent her
away *for* two months: and she went
with her companions, and bewailed
her virginity upon the mountains.
39 And it came to pass at the end of
two months, that she returned unto
her father, who [j]did with her *accord-*
ing to his vow which he had vowed:

and she knew no man. And it was a
[10]custom in Israel,
40 *That* the daughters of Israel went
[11]yearly to [12]lament the daughter of
Jĕph'-thăh the Gileadite four days in a
year.

CHAPTER 12

AND [a]the men of Ē'-phră-ĭm [1]gath-
ered themselves together, and
went northward, and said unto Jĕph'-
thăh, Wherefore passedst thou over
to fight against the children of Ammon, and didst not call us to go with
thee? we will burn thine house upon
thee with fire.
2 And Jĕph'-thăh said unto them, I
and my people were at great strife
with the children of Ammon; and
when I called you, ye delivered me not
out of their hands.
3 And when I saw that ye delivered
me not, I [b]put my life in my hands,
and passed over against the children
of Ammon, and the LORD delivered
them into my hand: wherefore then
are ye come up unto me this day, to
fight against me?
4 Then Jĕph'-thăh gathered together
all the men of Gilead, and fought with
Ē'-phră-ĭm: and the men of Gilead
smote Ē'-phră-ĭm, because they said,
Ye Gileadites *are* [c]fugitives of Ē'-
phră-ĭm among the Ē'-phră-ĭm-ītes,
and among the Mă-năs'-sītes.
5 And the Gileadites took [d]the passages of Jordan before the Ē'-phră-
ĭm-ītes: and it was *so*, that when those
Ē'-phră-ĭm-ītes which were escaped
said, Let me go over; that the men of
Gilead said unto him, *Art* thou an
Ē'-phră-ĭm-īte? If he said, Nay;
6 Then said they unto him, Say now
[2]Shĭb'-bō-lĕth: and he said Sĭb'-bō-
lĕth: for he could not frame to pronounce *it* right. Then they took him,
and slew him at the passages of Jordan: and there fell at that time of the
Ē'-phră-ĭm-ītes forty and two thousand.
7 And Jĕph'-thăh judged Israel six
years. Then died Jĕph'-thăh the Gileadite, and was buried in *one of* the
cities of Gilead.
8 ¶ And after him [3]Ĭb'-zăn of Beth-
lehem judged Israel.
9 And he had thirty sons, and thirty
daughters, *whom* he sent abroad, and
took in thirty daughters from abroad
for his sons. And he judged Israel
seven years.
10 Then died Ĭb'-zăn, and was buried
at Beth-lehem.
11 ¶ And after him [4]Ē'-lŏn, a Zĕ-bū'-
lon-īte, judged Israel; and he judged
Israel ten years.
12 And Ē'-lŏn the Zĕ-bū'-lon-īte died,
and was buried in Aî'-jă-lŏn in the
country of Zĕ-bū'-lŭn.
13 ¶ And after him [5]Abdon the son of
Hĭl'-lĕl, a Pī-rā'-thŏn-īte, judged Israel.
14 And he had forty sons and thirty
[6]nephews, that [e]rode on threescore and
ten ass colts: and he judged Israel
eight years.
15 And Abdon the son of Hĭl'-lĕl the
Pī-rā'-thŏn-īte died, and was buried in
Pī-rā'-thŏn in the land of Ē'-phră-ĭm,
[f]in the mount of the Ă-măl'-ĕk-ītes.

CHAPTER 13

AND the children of Israel [1]did evil
again in the sight of the LORD;
[2]and the LORD delivered them [a]into
the hand of the Philistines forty
years.
2 ¶ And there was a certain man of
[b]Zôr'-ăh, of the family of the Danites,
whose name *was* Mă-nō'-ăh; and his
wife *was* barren, and bare not.
3 And the [c]angel of the LORD appeared unto the woman, and said unto her, Behold now, thou *art* barren,
and bearest not: but thou shalt conceive, and bear a son.
4 Now therefore beware, I pray thee,
and [d]drink not wine nor strong drink,
and eat not any unclean *thing:*
5 For, lo, thou shalt conceive, and
bear a son; and no [e]rasor shall come
on his head: for the child shall be a
Nazarite unto God from the womb:
and he shall [f]begin to deliver Israel out
of the hand of the Philistines.
6 ¶ Then the woman came and told
her husband, saying, [g]A man of God
came unto me, and [h]his countenance
was like the countenance of an angel
of God, very terrible: but I asked him
not whence he *was*, neither told he
me his name:
7 But he said unto me, Behold, thou
shalt conceive, and bear a son; and
now drink no wine nor strong drink,
neither eat any unclean *thing:* for the
child shall be a Nazarite to God
from the womb to the day of his
death.
8 ¶ Then Mă-nō'-ăh intreated the
LORD, and said, O my Lord, let the
man of God which thou didst send
come again unto us, and teach us what
we shall do unto the child that shall be
born.
9 And God hearkened to the voice of
Mă-nō'-ăh; and the angel of God
came again unto the woman as she

10 Or, ordinance.
11 from year to year.
12 Or, talk with.

CHAP. 12

a ch. 8.1.
1 were called.
b 1 Sam. 19.5. Job 13.14. Ps. 119.109. Rom. 16.4. Rev. 12.11.
c 1 Sam. 25.10. Ps. 78.9.
d Josh. 22.11. ch. 3.28.
2 Which signifieth A burden, or, Ear of corn, or, Stream.
3 He seems to have been only a civil Judge to do justice in North-east Israel.
4 A civil Judge in North-east Israel.
5 A civil Judge also in North-east Israel.
6 sons' sons.
e ch. 5.10. ch. 10.4.
f Gen. 14.7. Ex. 17.8. ch. 3.13.

CHAP. 13

1 added to commit, etc.
2 This seems a partial captivity.
a 1 Sam. 12.9.
b Josh. 15.33.
c Gen. 16.7-13. Ex. 3.2-6. ch. 6.12. Hosea 12.3-5. Mal. 3.1. Luke 1.11, 13,28,31. Acts 7.30.
d Num. 6.2,3. Luke 1.15.
e Num. 6.5. 1 Sam. 1.11.
f 1 Sam. 7.13. 2 Sam. 8.1. 1 Chr. 18.1.
g Deut. 33.1. 1 Sam. 2.27. 1 Ki. 17.24.
h Matt. 28.3. Luke 9.29. Acts 6.15.

t in the field: but Mă-nō-ăh her hus-
and *was* not with her.
10 And the woman made haste, and
n, and shewed her husband, and
id unto him, Behold, the man hath
ppeared unto me, that came unto me
e *other* day.
11 And Mă-nō-ăh arose, and went
fter his wife, and came to the man,
nd said unto him, *Art* thou the man
at spakest unto the woman? And
e said, I *am*.
12 And Mă-nō-ăh said, Now let thy
ords come to pass. [3]How shall we
rder the child, and [4]*how* shall we do
nto him?
13 And the angel of the LORD said
nto Mă-nō-ăh, Of all that I said unto
e woman let her beware.
14 She may not eat of any *thing* that
ometh of the vine, neither let her
rink wine or strong drink, nor eat
ny unclean *thing:* all that I com-
anded her let her observe.
15 ¶ And Mă-nō-ăh said unto the
ngel of the LORD, I pray thee, let [i]us
etain thee, until we shall have made
ady a kid [5]for thee.
16 And the angel of the LORD said
nto Mă-nō-ăh, Though thou detain
e, I will not eat of thy bread: and if
ou wilt offer a burnt offering, thou
ust offer it unto the LORD. For Mă-
ō-ăh knew not that he *was* an angel
f the LORD.
17 And Mă-nō-ăh said unto the angel
f the LORD, What *is* thy name, that
hen thy sayings come to pass we
ay do thee honour?
18 And the angel of the LORD said
nto him, [j]Why askest thou thus after
y name, seeing it *is* [6]secret?
19 So Mă-nō-ăh took a kid with a
eat offering, [k]and offered *it* upon a
ock unto the LORD: and *the angel* did
ondrously; and Mă-nō-ăh and his
ife looked on.
20 For it came to pass, when the
ame went up toward heaven from
ff the altar, that the angel of the LORD
scended in the flame of the altar.
nd Mă-nō-ăh and his wife looked on
, and [l]fell on their faces to the
round.
21 But the angel of the LORD did no
ore appear to Mă-nō-ăh and to his
ife. [m]Then Mă-nō-ăh knew that he
vas an angel of the LORD.
22 And Mă-nō-ăh said unto his wife,
We shall surely die, because we have
een God.
23 But his wife said unto him, If the
ORD were pleased to kill us, he would
not have received a burnt offering and
a meat offering at our hands, neither
would he have shewed [o]us all these
things, nor would as at this time have
told us *such things* as these.
24 ¶ And the woman bare a son, and
called his name [7]Samson: and the
[p]child grew, and the LORD blessed
him.
25 And [q]the Spirit of the LORD began
to move him at times in [8]the camp
of Dan between [r]Zôr-ăh and Ĕsh-tā-
ŏl.

CHAPTER 14

AND Samson went down to [a]Tĭm-
năth, and [b]saw a woman in Tĭm-
năth of the daughters of the Philistines.
2 And he came up, and told his father
and his mother, and said, I have seen
a woman in Tĭm-năth of the daughters of the Philistines: now therefore
[c]get her for me to wife.
3 Then his father and his mother
said unto him, *Is there* never a woman
among the daughters of thy [d]breth-
ren, or among all my people, that thou
goest to take a wife of the [e]uncircum-
cised Philistines? And Samson said
unto his father, Get her for me; for
[1]she pleaseth me well.
4 But his father and his mother knew
not that it *was* [f]of the LORD, that he
sought an occasion against the Philistines: for at that time the Philistines
had dominion over Israel.
5 ¶ Then went Samson down, and his
father and his mother, to Tĭm-năth,
and came to the vineyards of Tĭm-
năth: and, behold, a young lion roared
[2]against him.
6 And [g]the Spirit of the LORD came
mightily upon him, and he rent him as
he would have rent a kid, and *he had*
nothing in his hand: but he told not
his father or his mother what he had
done.
7 And he went down, and talked with
the woman; and she pleased Samson
well.
8 ¶ And after a time he returned to
take her, and he turned aside to see
the carcase of the lion: and, behold,
there was a swarm of bees and honey
in the carcase of the lion.
9 And he took thereof in his hands,
and went on eating, and came to his
father and mother, and he gave them,
and they did eat: but he told not them
that he had taken the honey out of the
carcase of the lion.
10 ¶ So his father went down unto

3 What shall be the manner of the, etc.
4 What shall be his work? or, what shall he do?
i Gen. 18.5. ch. 6.18.
5 before thee.
j Gen. 32.29.
6 Or, wonderful.
k ch. 6.19,20. 1 Ki. 18.30-38.
l Lev. 9.24. 1 Chr. 21.16. Eze. 1.28. Dan. 10.9. Hosea 12.4, 5. Matt. 17.6.
m ch. 6.22.
n Gen. 32.30. Ex. 33.20. Deut. 4.3. ch. 6.22. Isa. 6.5.
o Ps. 25.14. Pro. 3.22. John 14.20-23.
7 That is, Serving like the sun.
p 1 Sam. 3.19. Luke 1.80. Luke 2.52.
q ch. 3.10. ch. 6.34. 1 Sam. 11.6. Matt. 4.1. John 3.34.
8 Mahaneh-dan.
r Josh. 15.33.

CHAP. 14

a Gen. 38.13. Josh. 15.10.
b Gen. 34.2. Ps. 119.37.
c Gen. 21.21. Gen. 24.2, 13.
d Gen. 24.3,4.
e Ex. 34.16. Deut. 7.3.
1 she is right in mine eyes.
f Josh. 11.20. 2 Chr. 10.15.
2 in meeting him.
g ch. 3.10. ch. 13.25. 1 Sam. 11.6.

the woman: and Samson made there
a feast; for so used the young men to
do.
11 And it came to pass, when they
saw him, that they brought thirty
companions to be with him.
12 ¶ And Samson said unto them,
I will now [h]put forth a riddle unto
you: if ye can certainly declare it me
[i]within the seven days of the feast, and
find *it* out, then I will give you thirty
[3]sheets and thirty change [j]of garments:
13 But if ye cannot declare *it* me,
then shall ye give me thirty sheets and
thirty change of garments. And they
said unto him, Put forth thy riddle,
that we may hear it.
14 And he said unto them, Out of the
eater came forth meat, and out of the
strong came forth sweetness. And
they could not in three days expound
the riddle.
15 And it came to pass on the seventh
day, that they said unto Samson's
wife, [k]Entice thy husband, that
he may declare unto us the riddle,
[l]lest we burn thee and thy father's
house with fire: have ye called
us [4]to take that we have? *is it* not
so?
16 And Samson's wife wept before
him, and said, [m]Thou dost but hate
me, and lovest me not: thou hast put
forth a riddle unto the children of my
people, and hast not told *it* me. And
he said unto her, Behold, I have not
told *it* my father nor my mother, and
shall I tell *it* thee?
17 And she wept before him [5]the
seven days, while their feast lasted:
and it came to pass on the seventh day,
that he told her, because she lay sore
upon him: and she told the riddle to
the children of her people.
18 And the men of the city said unto
him on the seventh day before the sun
went down, What *is* sweeter than
honey? and what *is* stronger than a
lion? And he said unto them, If ye had
not plowed with my heifer, ye had not
found out my riddle.
19 ¶ And [n]the Spirit of the LORD
came upon him, and he went down to
Ăsh-kĕ-lon, and slew thirty men of
them, and took their [6]spoil, and gave
change of garments unto them which
expounded the riddle. And his anger
was kindled, and he went up to his
father's house.
20 But Samson's wife was [o]*given* to
his companion, whom he had used as
his [p]friend.

h 1 Ki. 10. 1. Eze. 17.2. Luke 14.7.
i Gen. 29.27.
3 Or, shirts.
j Gen. 45.22.
k Gen. 3.6. ch. 16.5. Pro. 6.26. Micah 7.6.
l ch. 15.6.
4 to possess us, or, to impoverish us.
m ch. 16.15.
5 Or, the rest of the seven days, etc.
n Num. 11. 17. ch. 3.10. ch. 13.25. 1 Sam. 10.6. 1 Sam. 11.6. 1 Cor. 12.4, 11.
6 Or, apparel.
o ch. 15.2.
p John 3.29.

CHAP. 15

a Gen. 38.17. 1 Sam. 16. 20. Luke 15.29.
b ch. 14.20.
1 let her be thine.
2 Or, Now shall I be blameless from the Philistines, though, etc.
3 Or, Jackals, which were in great numbers in some parts of Palestine.
4 Or, torches.
c ch. 14.15.
5 That is, with great confusion.
d 1 Chr. 4.3. 2 Chr. 11.6.
6 went down.
e Lev. 26.25. Deut. 28.43, 44. ch. 2.13,14. ch. 14.4.

CHAPTER 15

BUT it came to pass within a whi
after, in the time of wheat harves
that Samson visited his wife with
kid; and he said, I will go in to n
wife into the chamber. But her fath
would not suffer him to go in.
2 And her father said, I verily thoug
that thou hadst utterly hated [b]he
therefore I gave her to thy companio
is not her younger sister fairer tha
she? [1]take her, I pray thee, instead
her.
3 ¶ And Samson said concernir
them, [2]Now shall I be more blamele
than the Philistines, though I do the
a displeasure.
4 And Samson went and caug
three hundred [3]foxes, and took [4]fir
brands, and turned tail to tail, and p
a firebrand in the midst between tw
tails.
5 And when he had set the brands
fire, he let *them* go into the standir
corn of the Philistines, and bur
up both the shocks, and also t
standing corn, with the vineyar
and olives.
6 ¶ Then the Philistines said, Wh
hath done this? And they answere
Samson, the son in law of the Tin
nīte, because he had taken his wif
and given her to his companion. [c]Ar
the Philistines came up, and burnt h
and her father with fire.
7 ¶ And Samson said unto then
Though ye have done this, yet will
be avenged of you, and after that
will cease.
8 And he smote them [5]hip and thig
with a great slaughter: and he we
down and dwelt in the top of the roc
[d]Ē-tăm.
9 ¶ Then the Philistines went up, an
pitched in Judah, and spread then
selves in Lē-hī.
10 And the men of Judah said, Wh
are ye come up against us? And the
answered, To bind Samson are w
come up, to do to him as he hath dor
to us.
11 Then three thousand men of Ju
dah [6]went to the top of the rock E
tăm, and said to Samson, Knowe
thou not that the Philistines *are* [e]rule
over us? what *is* this *that* thou ha
done unto us? And he said unto then
As they did unto me, so have I dor
unto them.
12 And they said unto him, We ar
come down to bind thee, that we ma
deliver thee into the hand of the Phili
tines. And Samson said unto then

swear unto me, that ye will not fall
upon me yourselves.
13 And they spake unto him, saying,
No; but we will bind thee fast, and deliver thee into their hand: but surely
we will not kill thee. And they bound
him with two new cords, and brought
him up from the rock.
14 ¶ *And* when he came unto Lē-hī,
the Philistines shouted against him:
and the Spirit of the LORD came
mightily upon him, and the cords that
were upon his arms became as flax that
was burnt with fire, and his bands
loosed from off his hands.
15 And he found [8]a new jawbone of
an ass, and put forth his hand, and
took it, and slew [f]a thousand men
therewith.
16 And Samson said, With the jawbone of an ass, [9]heaps upon heaps,
with the jaw of an ass have I slain a
thousand men.
17 And it came to pass, when he had
made an end of speaking, that he cast
away the jawbone out of his hand, and
called that place [10]Rā-măth–lē-hī.
18 ¶ And he was sore athirst, and
called on the LORD, and said, Thou
hast given this great deliverance into
the hand of thy servant: and now shall
I die for thirst, and fall into the hand
of the uncircumcised?
19 But God clave an hollow place
that *was* in [11]the jaw, and there came
water thereout; and when he had
drunk, [h]his spirit came again, and he
revived: wherefore he called the name
thereof [12]Ĕn–hăk-kôr-ē, which *is* in
Lē-hī unto this day.
20 And he judged Israel [i]in the days
of the Philistines [13]twenty years.

CHAPTER 16

THEN went Samson to Gā-ză, and
saw there [1]an harlot, and went in
unto her.
2 *And it was told* the Gā-zītes, saying,
Samson is come hither. And they
compassed *him* in, and laid wait for
him all night in the gate of the city,
and were [2]quiet all the night, saying,
In the morning, when it is day, we
shall kill him.
3 And Samson lay till midnight, and
arose at midnight, and took the doors
of the gate of the city, and the two
posts, and went away with them, [3]bar
and all, and put *them* upon his shoulders, and carried them up to the top
of an hill that *is* before Hē-brŏn.
4 ¶ And it came to pass afterward,
that he loved a woman [4]in the valley
of Sôr-ĕk, whose name *was* Dĕ-lī-lăh.
5 And the lords of the Philistines
came up unto her, and said unto her,
[b]Entice him, and see wherein his great
strength *lieth*, and by what *means* we
may prevail against him, that we may
bind him to [5]afflict him: and we will
give thee every one of us eleven hundred *pieces* of silver.
6 ¶ And Dĕ-lī-lăh said to Samson,
Tell me, I pray thee, wherein thy great
strength *lieth*, and wherewith thou
mightest be bound to afflict thee.
7 And Samson said unto her, If they
bind me with seven [6]green withs that
were never dried, then shall I be weak,
and be as [7]another man.
8 Then the lords of the Philistines
brought up to her seven green withs
which had not been dried, and she
[c]bound him with them.
9 Now *there were* men lying in wait,
abiding with her in the chamber. And
she said unto him, The Philistines *be*
upon thee, Samson. And he brake the
withs, as a thread of tow is broken
when it [8]toucheth the fire. [d]So his
strength was not known.
10 And Dĕ-lī-lăh said unto Samson,
Behold, thou hast mocked me, and
told me lies: now tell me, I pray thee,
wherewith thou mightest be bound.
11 And he said unto her, If they bind
me fast with new ropes [9]that never
were occupied, then shall I be weak,
and be as another man.
12 Dĕ-lī-lăh therefore took new
ropes, and bound [e]him therewith, and
said unto him, The Philistines *be* upon
thee, Samson. And *there were* liers in
wait abiding in the chamber. And he
brake them from off his arms like a
thread.
13 And Dĕ-lī-lăh said unto Samson,
Hitherto thou hast mocked me, and
told me lies: tell me wherewith thou
mightest be bound. And he said unto
her, If thou weavest the seven locks
of my head with the web.
14 And she fastened *it* with the pin,
and she said unto him, The Philistines
be upon thee, Samson. And he awaked
out of his sleep, and went away with
the pin of the beam, and with the
web.
15 ¶ And she said unto him, How
[f]canst thou say, I love thee, when thine
heart *is* not with me? thou hast mocked me these three times, and hast not
told me wherein thy great strength
lieth.
16 And it came to pass, when she
pressed him daily with her words, and

7 were melted.
8 moist.
f Lev. 26.8. Deut. 32.30. Josh. 23.10. ch. 3.31. 2 Sam. 23.8.
9 an heap, two heaps.
10 That is, The lifting up of the jawbone, or, casting away of the jawbone.
g Ps. 3.7.
11 Lehi, the name of the place.
h Gen. 45.27. Isa. 40.29.
12 That is, The well of him that called, or, cried.
i ch. 13.1.
13 He seems to have judged South-west Israel during twenty years of their servitude of the Philistines.

CHAP. 16

1 a woman an harlot.
a 1 Sam. 19. 11. 1 Sam. 23. 26. Ps. 118.10, 11,12. Acts 9.24. 2 Cor. 11.32, 33.
2 silent.
3 with the bar.
4 Or, by the brook.
b ch. 14.15. Pro. 2.16, 17,18,19. Pro. 5.3. Pro. 7.21.
5 Or, humble.
6 moist.
7 one.
c Pro. 6.26.
8 smelleth.
d John 5.14.
9 wherewith work hath not been done.
e Pro. 7.22.
f ch. 14.16. Pro. 2.16.

urged him, *so* that his soul was [10]vexed
unto death;
17 That he [g]told her all his heart, and
said unto her, [h]There hath not come a
rasor upon mine head: for I *have been*
a Nazarite unto God from my mother's
womb: if I be shaven, then my strength
will go from me, and I shall become
weak, and be like any *other* man.
18 And when Dĕ-lī-lăh saw that he
had told her all his heart, she sent and
called for the lords of the Philistines,
saying, Come up this once, for he
hath shewed me all his heart. Then the
lords of the Philistines came up unto
her, and brought money in their hand.
19 And [i]she made him sleep upon her
knees; and she called for a man, and
she caused him to shave off the seven
locks of his head; and she began to
afflict him, and his strength went
from him.
20 And she said, The Philistines *be*
upon thee, Samson. And he awoke
out of his sleep, and said, I will go out
as at other times before, and shake
myself. And he wist not that the LORD
[j]was departed from him.
21 ¶ But the Philistines took him,
and [11]put out his eyes, and brought
him down to Gā-ză, and bound him
with fetters of brass; and he did grind
in the prison house.
22 Howbeit the hair of his head began to grow again [12]after he was
shaven.
23 Then the lords of the Philistines
gathered them together for to offer a
great sacrifice unto [13]Dā-gŏn their
god, and to rejoice: for they said,
Our god hath delivered Samson our
enemy into our hand.
24 And when the people saw him,
they praised [k]their god: for they said,
Our god hath delivered into our hands
our enemy, and the destroyer of our
country, [14]which slew many of us.
25 And it came to pass, when their
hearts were [l]merry, that they said,
Call for Samson, that he may make us
sport. And they called for Samson out
of the prison house; and he made
[15]them sport: and they set him between
the pillars.
26 And Samson said unto the lad
that held him by the hand, Suffer me
that I may feel the pillars whereupon
the house standeth, that I may lean
upon them.
27 Now the house was full of men
and women; and all the lords of the
Philistines *were* there; and *there were*
upon the [m]roof about three thousand

10 shortened.
g 1 Chr. 28.9. 2 Chr. 15.2. Pro. 18.2. Micah 7.5.
h Num. 6.5. ch. 13.5. Acts 18.18.
i Pro. 5.3,4. Pro. 7.21. Eccl. 7.25, 26.
j Num. 14.9, 42,43. Josh. 7.12. 1 Sam. 16. 14. 1 Sam. 18. 12. 2 Chr. 15.2. Ps. 33.16. Pro. 22.14. Jer. 9.23, 24. Hosea 9.12.
11 bored out.
12 Or, as when he was shaven.
13 Signifies, A fish.
k 1 Sam. 31.9. 1 Chr. 10.9. Ps. 97.7. Ps. 115.3,8. Ps. 135.15, 18. Dan. 5.4,23. 1 Cor. 8.4. 1 Cor. 10.19, 20.
14 and who multiplied our slain.
l ch. 9.27. ch. 19.6-9. 2 Sam. 13. 28. 1 Ki. 20.12. Esther 3.15. Isa. 32.13. Dan. 5.2-4. Matt. 14.6, 7.
15 before them.
m Deut. 22.8.
n Jer. 15.15.
16 Or, he leaned on them.
17 my soul.
o ch. 13.25.

CHAP. 17

a Gen. 14.19. Ruth 2.20. 2 Sam. 2.5.
b Ex. 20.4,23. Lev. 19.4. Deut. 12.30. Ps. 115.4-8.
c Isa. 46.6.
d Ex. 28.4-15. ch. 8.27. 1 Sam. 23.6.
e Gen. 31.19. Hosea 3.4.
1 filled the hand.
f Deut. 33.5. ch. 18.1. ch. 19.1.
g Deut. 12.8.
h Josh. 19.15. ch. 19.1. Ruth 1.1,2. Micah 5.2. Matt. 2.1,5, 6.

men and women, that beheld whi
Samson made sport.
28 And Samson called unto th
LORD, and said, O Lord GOD, [n]re
member me, I pray thee, and strength
en me, I pray thee, only this once, O
God, that I may be at once avenged o
the Philistines for my two eyes.
29 And Samson took hold of the tw
middle pillars upon which the hous
stood, and [16]on which it was borne up
of the one with his right hand, and o
the other with his left.
30 And Samson said, Let [17]me di
with the Philistines. And he bowe
himself with *all his* might; and th
house fell upon the lords, and upo
all the people that *were* therein. So th
dead which he slew at his death wer
more than *they* which he slew in hi
life.
31 Then his brethren and all th
house of his father came down, an
took him, and brought *him* up, an
[o]buried him between Zŏr-ăh and Ĕsh-
tā-ŏl in the buryingplace of Mă-nō-ă
his father. And he judged Israel twen
ty years.

CHAPTER 17

AND there was a man of moun
Ē-phră-ĭm, whose name *was* Mi
căh.
2 And he said unto his mother, Th
eleven hundred *shekels* of silver tha
were taken from thee, about whic
thou cursedst, and spakest of also i
mine ears, behold, the silver *is* wit
me; I took it. And his mother said
[a]Blessed *be thou* of the LORD, m
son.
3 And when he had restored the elev
en hundred *shekels* of silver to hi
mother, his mother said, I had wholl
dedicated the silver unto the LOR
from my hand for my son, to [b]make
graven image and a molten image
now therefore I will restore it unt
thee.
4 Yet he restored the money unto hi
mother; and his mother [c]took tw
hundred *shekels* of silver, and gav
them to the founder, who made there
of a graven image and a molten image
and they were in the house of Mī-căh
5 And the man Mī-căh had an hous
of gods, and made [d]an ē-phŏd, an
[e]tĕr-ă-phĭm, and [1]consecrated one o
his sons, who became his priest.
6 In [f]those days *there was* no king i
Israel, [g]*but* every man did *that whic*
was right in his own eyes.
7 ¶ And there was a young man ou
[h]of Beth-lehem-judah of the family o

Judah, who *was* a Levite, and he sojourned there.
8 And the man departed out of the
city from Beth-lehem-judah to sojourn where he could find *a place:*
and he came to mount Ē-phră-ĭm to
the house of Mī-căh, [2]as he journeyed.
9 And Mī-căh said unto him, Whence
comest thou? And he said unto him,
I *am* a Levite of Beth-lehem-judah,
and I go to sojourn where I may find *a*
place.
10 And Mī-căh said unto him, Dwell
with me, [i]and be unto me a [j]father and
a priest, and I will give thee ten *she-*
kels of silver by the year, and [3]a suit of
apparel, and thy victuals. So the Levite went in.
11 And the Levite was content to
dwell with the man; and the young
man was unto him as one of his sons.
12 And Mī-căh consecrated the Levite; and the young man became his
priest, and was in the house of Mī-căh.
13 Then said Mī-căh, Now know I
that the LORD will do me good, seeing
I have a Levite to *my* priest.

CHAPTER 18

IN [a]those days *there was* no king in
Israel: and in those days the [b]tribe
of the Danites sought them an inheritance to dwell in; for unto that day *all*
their inheritance had not fallen unto
them among the tribes of Israel.
2 And the children of Dan sent of
their family five men from their coasts,
[1]men of valour, from [c]Zôr-ăh, and
from Ĕsh-tā-ŏl, to [d]spy out the land,
and to search it; and they said
unto them, Go, search the land: who
when they came to mount Ē-phră-ĭm,
to the [e]house of Mī-căh, they lodged
there.
3 When they *were* by the house of
Mī-căh, they knew the voice of the
young man the Levite: and they turned in thither, and said unto him, Who
brought thee hither? and what makest thou in this *place*? and what hast
thou here?
4 And he said unto them, Thus and
thus dealeth Mī-căh with me, and
hath [f]hired me, and I am his priest.
5 And they said unto him, [g]Ask
counsel, we pray thee, [h]of God, that
we may know whether our way which
we go shall be prosperous.
6 And the priest said unto them, Go
[i]in peace: before the LORD *is* your
way wherein ye go.
7 ¶ Then the five men departed, and
came to [j]Lā-ĭsh, and saw the people

2 in making his way.
i Gen. 45.8. ch. 18.19. Job 29.16. Isa. 22.21.
j Gen. 45.8. Job 29.16.
3 an order of garments, or, a double suit, etc.

CHAP. 18
a ch. 17.6. ch. 21.25.
b Josh. 19.47.
1 sons.
c ch. 13.25.
d Num. 13. 17.
e ch. 17.1.
f ch. 17.10. John 10.12, 13. Acts 20.33. 1 Tim. 3.3. Titus 1.11. 2 Pet. 2.3.
g 1 Ki. 22.5. Hosea 4.12.
h ch. 17.5.
i 1 Ki. 22.6.
j Josh. 19.47, called Leshem.
2 possessor, or, heir of restraint.
k Num. 13. 30. Num. 14.7-9. Josh. 2.23, 24. 1 Sam. 14. 48.
l 1 Ki. 22.3.
m Deut. 8.9.
3 girded.
n Josh. 15.60.
4 That is, Camp of Dan.
o 1 Sam. 14. 28.
p ch. 8.27. ch. 17.5. 1 Sam. 23.6.
5 asked him of peace.
q Gen. 31.19, 30. ch. 6.31. 2 Ki. 19.18. Isa. 41.29. Micah 5.13.

that *were* therein, how they dwelt
careless, after the manner of the Zi-
dō-nĭ-ăns, quiet and secure; and *there*
was no [2]magistrate in the land, that
might put *them* to shame in *any* thing;
and they *were* far from the Zi-dō-nĭ-
ăns, and had no business with *any*
man.
8 And they came unto their brethren
to Zôr-ăh and Ĕsh-tā-ŏl: and their
brethren said unto them, What *say* ye?
9 And they said, [k]Arise, that we may
go up against them: for we have seen
the land, and, behold, it *is* very good:
and *are* [l]ye still? be not slothful to go,
and to enter to possess the land.
10 When ye go, ye shall come unto a
people secure, and to a large land: for
God hath given it into your hands; [m]a
place where *there is* no want of any
thing that *is* in the earth.
11 ¶ And there went from thence of
the family of the Danites, out of Zôr-
ăh and out of Ĕsh-tā-ŏl, six hundred
men [3]appointed with weapons of war.
12 And they went up, and pitched in
[n]Kĭr-jăth–jē-ă-rĭm, in Judah: wherefore they called that place [4]Mā-hă-
nēh–dăn unto this day: behold, *it is*
behind Kĭr-jăth–jē-ă-rĭm.
13 And they passed thence unto
mount Ē-phră-ĭm, and came unto the
house of Mī-căh.
14 ¶ Then [o]answered the five men
that went to spy out the country of
Lā-ĭsh, and said unto their brethren,
Do ye know that there is in [p]these
houses an ē-phŏd, and tĕr-ă-phĭm,
and a graven image, and a molten image? now therefore consider what ye
have to do.
15 And they turned thitherward, and
came to the house of the young man
the Levite, *even* unto the house of Mī-
căh, and [5]saluted him.
16 And the six hundred men appointed with their weapons of war, which
were of the children of Dan, stood by
the entering of the gate.
17 And the five men that went to spy
out the land went up, *and* came in
thither, *and* took [q]the graven image,
and the ē-phŏd, and the tĕr-ă-phĭm,
and the molten image: and the priest
stood in the entering of the gate with
the six hundred men *that were* appointed with weapons of war.
18 And these went into Mī-căh's
house, and fetched the carved image,
the ē-phŏd, and the tĕr-ă-phĭm, and
the molten image. Then said the priest
unto them, What do ye?
19 And they said unto him, Hold thy

peace, [r]lay thine hand upon thy
mouth, and go with us, [s]and be to us a
father and a priest: *is it* better for thee
to be a priest unto the house of one
man, or that thou be a priest unto a
tribe and a family in Israel?
20 And the priest's heart was glad,
and he took the ē´-phŏd, and the tĕr´-
ă-phĭm, and the graven image, and
went in the midst of the people.
21 So they turned and departed, and
put the little ones and the cattle and
the carriage before them.
22 ¶ *And* when they were a good way
from the house of Mī´-căh, the men
that *were* in the houses near to Mī´-
căh's house were gathered together,
and overtook the children of Dan.
23 And they cried unto the children
of Dan. And they turned their faces,
and said unto Mī´-căh, What aileth
thee, [6]that thou comest with such a
company?
24 And he said, Ye have taken away
my gods which I made, and the priest,
and ye are gone away: and what have
I more? and what *is* this *that* ye say
unto me, What aileth thee?
25 And the children of Dan said unto
him, Let not thy voice be heard among
us, lest [7]angry fellows run upon thee,
and [8]thou lose thy life, with the lives of
thy household.
26 And the children of Dan went
their way: and when Mī´-căh saw
that they *were* too strong for him,
he turned and went back unto his
house.
27 And they took *the things* which
Mī´-căh had made, and the priest
which he had, and [t]came unto Lā´-ĭsh,
unto a people *that were* at quiet and
secure: [u]and they smote them with
the edge of the sword, and burnt the
city with fire.
28 And *there was* no deliverer, because it *was* far from [v]Zī´-dŏn, and
they had no business with *any* man;
and it was in the valley that *lieth* [w]by
Bĕth–rē´-hŏb. And they built a city,
and dwelt therein.
29 And [x]they called the name of the
city Dan, [y]after the name of Dan their
father, who was born unto Israel:
howbeit the name of the city *was* Lā´-
ĭsh at the first.
30 ¶ And the children of Dan set up
the graven image: and Jonathan, the
son of Gĕr´-shŏm, the son of Mă-năs´-
sēh, he and his sons were priests to
the tribe of Dan [z]until the day of the
captivity of the land.
31 And they set them up Mī´-căh's

r Job 21.5. Job 29.9. Pro. 30.32. Micah 7.16.
s Gen. 45.8. ch. 17.10. 2 Ki. 6.21. Job 29.16. Isa. 22.21. Matt. 23.9.
6 that thou art gathered together?
7 bitter of soul.
8 gather thy soul and the soul of thy household.
t Deut. 33.22.
u Josh. 19.47.
v ver. 7. Gen. 49.13. Josh. 8.11. ch. 10.12. Isa. 23.4-12. Eze. 27.8.
w Num. 13. 21. 2 Sam. 10.6.
x Josh. 19.47.
y Gen. 14.14. ch. 20.1. 1 Ki. 12.29.
z ch. 13.1. 1 Sam. 4.2. Ps. 78.60.
a Josh. 18.1. 1 Sam. 4.1.

CHAP. 19

a ch. 17.6.
1 a woman a concubine, or, a wife a concubine.
b ch. 17.7.
2 days four months, or, a year and four months.
3 to her heart.
4 strengthen.
5 till the day declined.
6 is weak.
7 it is the pitching time of the day.
8 to thy tent.
9 to over against.
c Josh. 18.28. 2 Sam. 5.6.

graven image, which he made, [a]all the
time that the house of God was in
Shī´-lōh.

CHAPTER 19

AND it came to pass in those days,
[a]when *there was* no king in Israel,
that there was a certain Levite sojourning on the side of mount Ē´-phră-
ĭm, who took to him a [1]concubine out
of [b]Beth-lehem-judah.
2 And his concubine played the
whore against him, and went away
from him unto her father's house to
Beth-lehem-judah, and was there
[2]four whole months.
3 And her husband arose, and went
after her, to speak [3]friendly unto her,
and to bring her again, having his servant with him, and a couple of asses:
and she brought him into her father's
house: and when the father of the
damsel saw him, he rejoiced to meet
him.
4 And his father in law, the damsel's
father, retained him; and he abode
with him three days: so they did eat
and drink, and lodged there.
5 ¶ And it came to pass on the fourth
day, when they arose early in the
morning, that he rose up to depart:
and the damsel's father said unto his
son in law, [4]Comfort thine heart with
a morsel of bread, and afterward go
your way.
6 And they sat down, and did eat and
drink both of them together: for the
damsel's father had said unto the
man, Be content, I pray thee, and
tarry all night, and let thine heart be
merry.
7 And when the man rose up to depart, his father in law urged him:
therefore he lodged there again.
8 And he arose early in the morning
on the fifth day to depart: and the
damsel's father said, Comfort thine
heart, I pray thee. And they tarried
[5]until afternoon, and they did eat
both of them.
9 And when the man rose up to depart, he, and his concubine, and his
servant, his father in law, the damsel's
father, said unto him, Behold, now
the day [6]draweth toward evening, I
pray you tarry all night: behold, [7]the
day groweth to an end, lodge here,
that thine heart may be merry; and
to morrow get you early on your way,
that thou mayest go [8]home.
10 But the man would not tarry that
night, but he rose up and departed,
and came [9]over against Jē´-bŭs, [c]which
is Jerusalem; and *there were* with him

two asses saddled, his concubine also
was with him.
11 *And* when they *were* by Jē-bŭs, the
day was far spent; and the servant
said unto his master, Come, I pray
thee, and let us turn in into this city
[d]of the Jĕb-ū-sītes, and lodge in it.
12 And his master said unto him,
We will not turn aside hither into the
city of a stranger, that *is* not of the
children of Israel; we will pass over
[e]to Gĭb-ĕ-ăh.
13 And he said unto his servant,
Come, and let us draw near to one of
these places to lodge all night, in Gĭb-
ĕ-ăh, or in Rā-măh.
14 And they passed on and went
their way; and the sun went down upon them *when they were* by Gĭb-ĕ-ăh,
which *belongeth* to Benjamin.
15 And they turned aside thither, to
go in *and* to lodge in Gĭb-ĕ-ăh: and
when he went in, he sat him down in
a street of the city: for *there was* no
man that [10]took them into his house to
lodging.
16 ¶ And, behold, there came an old
man from [f]his work out of the field at
even, which *was* also of mount Ē-
phră-ĭm; and he sojourned in Gĭb-ĕ-
ăh: but the men of the place *were*
[11]Benjamites.
17 And when he had lifted up his
eyes, he saw a wayfaring man in the
street of the city: and the old man
said, Whither goest thou? and whence
comest thou?
18 And he said unto him, We *are*
passing from Beth-lehem-judah toward the side of mount Ē-phră-ĭm;
from thence *am* I: and I went to Beth-
lehem-judah, but I *am now* going to
[g]the house of the LORD; and there *is*
no man that [12]receiveth me to house.
19 Yet there is both straw and provender for our asses; and there is bread
and wine also for me, and for thy
handmaid, and for the young man
which is with thy servants: *there is* no
want of any thing.
20 And the old man said, [h]Peace *be*
with thee; howsoever *let* all thy wants
lie upon me; [i]only lodge not in the
street.
21 So [j]he brought him into his house,
and gave provender unto the asses:
[k]and they washed their feet, and did
eat and drink.
22 ¶ *Now* as they were making their
hearts merry, behold, [l]the men of the
city, certain [m]sons of Bē-lĭ-ăl, beset the
house round about, *and* beat at the
door, and spake to the master of the
house, the old man, saying, [n]Bring
forth the man that came into thine
house, that we may know him.
23 And [o]the man, the master of the
house, went out unto them, and said
unto them, Nay, my brethren, *nay*, I
pray you, do not *so* wickedly; seeing
that this man is come into mine house,
[p]do not this folly.
24 Behold, [q]*here is* my daughter a
maiden, and his concubine; them I
will bring out now, and humble [r]ye
them, and do with them what seemeth
good unto you: but unto this man do
not [13]so vile a thing.
25 But the men would not hearken to
him: so the man took his concubine,
and brought her forth unto them; and
they [s]knew her, and abused her all the
night until the morning: and when the
day began to spring, they let her go.
26 Then came the woman in the
dawning of the day, and fell down at
the door of the man's house where her
lord *was*, till it was light.
27 And her lord rose up in the morning, and opened the doors of the
house, and went out to go his way:
and, behold, the woman his concubine
was fallen down *at* the door of the
house, and her hands *were* upon the
threshold.
28 And he said unto her, Up, and let
us be going. But [t]none answered. Then
the man took her *up* upon an ass, and
the man rose up, and gat him unto his
place.
29 ¶ And when he was come into his
house, he took a knife, and laid hold
on his concubine, [u]and divided her,
together with her bones, into twelve
pieces, and sent her into all the coasts
of Israel.
30 And it was so, that all that saw it
said, There was no such deed done
nor seen from the day that the children
of Israel came up out of the land of
Egypt unto this day: consider of it,
[v]take advice, and speak *your minds*.

CHAPTER 20

THEN [a]all the children of Israel
went out, and the congregation
was gathered together as one man,
from [1]Dan even to Bē-er-shē-bă, with
the land of Gilead, unto the LORD [b]in
Mĭz-pēh.
2 And the chief of all the people, *even*
of all the tribes of Israel, presented
themselves in the assembly of the people of God, four hundred thousand
footmen that [c]drew sword.
3 (Now the children of Benjamin

d Gen. 10.15, 16. Ex. 33.2. Num. 13.29. Josh. 15.8, 63. ch. 1.21. 2 Sam. 5.6. 2 Sam. 24. 16. 1 Chr. 1.13, 14.
e Josh. 18.28. 1 Sam. 10. 26. Isa. 10.29. Hosea 5.8.
10 gathered.
f Ps. 104.23.
11 sons of Jemini.
g Josh. 18.1. ch. 18.31. 1 Sam. 1.3, 7.
12 gathereth.
h Gen. 43.23. ch. 6.23.
i Gen. 19.2.
j Gen. 24.32. Gen. 43.24.
k Gen. 18.4. Gen. 24.32. Luke 7.38, 44. John 13.5. 1 Tim. 5.10.
l Gen. 19.4. ch. 20.5. Hosea 9.9. Hosea 10.9.
m Deut. 13. 13. 1 Sam. 2.12. 1 Ki. 21.10. 2 Chr. 13.7. 2 Cor. 6.15.
n Gen. 19.5. Rom. 1.26, 27.
o Gen. 19.6.
p 2 Sam. 13. 12.
q Gen. 19.8.
r Gen. 34.2. Deut. 21.14.
13 the matter of this folly.
s Gen. 4.1.
t ch. 20.5.
u ch. 20.6. 1 Sam. 11.7.
v ch. 20.7. Pro. 11.14. Pro. 13.10. Pro. 15.22. Pro. 20.18.

CHAP. 20

a Deut. 13.12. Josh. 22.12. ch. 21.5. 1 Sam. 11.7.
1 That is, The whole country.
b Judg. 10.17. Judg. 11.11. 1 Sam. 7.5. 1 Sam. 10. 17. 2 Ki. 25.23.
c ch. 8.10. 2 Sam. 24.9. 2 Ki. 3.26.

heard that the children of Israel were gone up to Mĭz´pĕh.) Then said the children of Israel, Tell *us*, how was this wickedness?

4 And [2]the Levite, the husband of the woman that was slain, answered and said, I [d]came into Gĭb´ĕ-ăh that *belongeth* to Benjamin, I and my concubine, to lodge.

5 And [e]the men of Gĭb´ĕ-ăh rose against me, and beset the house round about upon me by night, *and* thought to have slain me: and [f]my concubine have they [3]forced, that she is dead.

6 And [g]I took my concubine, and cut her in pieces, and sent her throughout all the country of the inheritance of Israel: for [h]they have committed lewdness and folly in Israel.

7 Behold, ye *are* all children of Israel; [i]give here your advice and counsel.

8 ¶ And all the people arose as one man, saying, We will not any *of us* go to his tent, neither will we any *of us* turn into his house.

9 But now this *shall be* the thing which we will do to Gĭb´ĕ-ăh; *we will go up* by lot against it;

10 And we will take ten men of an hundred throughout all the tribes of Israel, and an hundred of a thousand, and a thousand out of ten thousand, to fetch victual for the people, that they may do, when they come to Gĭb´ĕ-ăh of Benjamin, according to all the folly that they have wrought in Israel.

11 So all the men of Israel were gathered against the city, [4]knit together as one man.

12 ¶ And [j]the tribes of Israel sent men through all the tribe of Benjamin, saying, What wickedness *is* this that is done among you?

13 Now therefore deliver *us* the men, [k]the children of Bē´lĭ-ăl, which *are* in Gĭb´ĕ-ăh, that we may put them to death, and [l]put away evil from Israel. But the children of Benjamin would not [m]hearken to the voice of their brethren the children of Israel:

14 But the children of Benjamin gathered themselves together out of the cities unto Gĭb´ĕ-ăh, to go out to battle against the children of Israel.

15 And the children of Benjamin were numbered at that time out of the cities twenty and six thousand men that drew sword, beside the inhabitants of Gĭb´ĕ-ăh, which were numbered seven hundred chosen men.

16 Among all this people *there were* seven hundred chosen [n]men lefthanded; every one could sling stones at an hair *breadth*, and not miss.

17 And the men of Israel, beside Benjamin, were numbered four hundred thousand men that drew sword: all these *were* men of war.

18 ¶ And the children of Israel arose, and went up to the house of God, and [o]asked counsel of God, and said, Which of us shall go up first to the battle against the children of Benjamin? And the LORD said, Judah *shall go up* first.

19 And the children of Israel rose up in the morning, and encamped against Gĭb´ĕ-ăh.

20 And the men of Israel went out to battle against Benjamin; and the men of Israel put themselves in array to fight against them at Gĭb´ĕ-ăh.

21 And [p]the children of Benjamin came forth out of Gĭb´ĕ-ăh, and [q]destroyed down to the ground of the Israelites that day twenty and two thousand men.

22 And the people the men of Israel encouraged themselves, and set their battle again in array in the place where they put themselves in array the first day.

23 (And the children of Israel went up and wept [r]before the LORD until even, and asked counsel of the LORD, saying, Shall I go up again to battle against the children of Benjamin my brother? And the LORD said, Go up against him.)

24 And the children of Israel came near against the children of Benjamin the second day.

25 And Benjamin went forth against them out of Gĭb´ĕ-ăh the second day, and [s]destroyed down to the ground of the children of Israel again eighteen thousand men; all these drew the sword.

26 ¶ Then all the children of Israel, and all the people, went up, and came unto the house of God, and wept, and sat there before the LORD, and fasted that day until even, and offered burnt offerings and peace offerings before the LORD.

27 And the children of Israel inquired [t]of the LORD, (for [u]the ark of the covenant of God *was* there in those days,

28 And [v]Phĭn´ĕ-hăs, the son of Ĕl-ē-ā´zăr, the son of Aaron, [w]stood before it in those days,) saying, Shall I yet again go out to battle against the children of Benjamin my brother, or shall I cease? And the LORD said, Go

2 the man the Levite.
d ch. 19.15.
e ch. 19.22.
f ch. 19.25, 26.
3 humbled.
g ch. 19.29.
h Gen. 34.7. Josh. 7.15.
i Ex. 19.5,6. Josh. 9.14. ch. 19.30. Pro. 13.10.
4 fellows.
j Deut. 13.14. Josh. 22.13, 16. Matt. 18.15-18. Rom. 12.18.
k Deut. 13. 13. ch. 19.22. 1 Sam. 30. 22. 2 Sam. 20.1. 1 Ki. 21.13. 2 Chr. 13.7. 2 Cor. 6.15.
l Deut. 13.5. Deut. 17.12. 1 Cor. 5.13.
m 2 Chr. 25. 16. Rom. 1.32.
n ch. 3.15. 1 Chr. 12.2.
o Ex. 28.30. Num. 27.21. Josh. 9.14. ch. 1.1. 1 Sam. 22. 10,13.15. Ezra 8.21.
p Gen. 49.27.
q Deut. 23.9. Eccl. 9.1,11.
r Ps. 78.34-36. Hosea 5.15.
s Job 9.12. Ps. 66.18. Ps. 97.2. Hosea 10.9. Micah 3.4. John 9.31.
t Job 22.27. Ps. 50.15. Ps. 91.15. Pro. 3.6.
u Josh. 18.1. 1 Sam. 4.3,4. Ps. 78.60,61. Jer. 7.12.
v Ex. 6.25. Num. 25.7, 11. Josh. 22.13. Ps. 106.30, 31.
w Deut. 10.8.

up; for to morrow I will deliver them into thine hand.

29 And Israel [x]set liers in wait round about Gĭb'-ĕ-ăh.

30 And the children of Israel went up against the children of Benjamin on the third day, and put themselves in array against Gĭb'-ĕ-ăh, as at other times.

31 And the children of Benjamin went out against the people, *and* were drawn away from the city; and they began [5]to smite of the people, *and* kill, as at other times, in the highways, of which one goeth up to [6]the house of God, and the other to Gĭb'-ĕ-ăh in the field, about thirty men of Israel.

32 And the children of Benjamin said, They *are* smitten down before us, as at the first. But the children of Israel said, Let us flee, and draw them from the city unto the highways.

33 And all the men of Israel rose up out of their place, and put themselves in array at Bā'-ăl–tā'-mär: and the liers in wait of Israel came forth out of their places, *even* out of the meadows of Gĭb'-ĕ-ăh.

34 And there came against Gĭb'-ĕ-ăh ten thousand chosen men out of all Israel, and the battle was sore: [y]but they knew not that evil *was* near them.

35 And the LORD smote Benjamin before Israel: and the children of Israel destroyed of the Benjamites that day twenty and five thousand and an hundred men: all these drew the sword.

36 So the children of Benjamin saw that they were smitten: [z]for the men of Israel gave place to the Benjamites, because they trusted unto the liers in wait which they had set beside Gĭb'-ĕ-ăh.

37 And [a]the liers in wait hasted, and rushed upon Gĭb'-ĕ-ăh; and the liers in wait [7]drew *themselves* along, and smote all the city with the edge of the sword.

38 Now there was an appointed [8]sign between the men of Israel [9]and the liers in wait, that they should make a great [10]flame with smoke rise up out of the city.

39 And when the men of Israel retired in the battle, Benjamin began [11]to smite *and* kill of the men of Israel about thirty persons: for they said, Surely they are smitten down before us, as *in* the first battle.

40 But when the flame began to arise up out of the city with a pillar of smoke, the Benjamites looked [b]behind them, and, behold, [12]the flame of the city ascended up to heaven.

41 And when the men of Israel turned again, [c]the men of Benjamin were amazed: for they saw that evil [13]was come upon them.

42 Therefore they turned *their backs* before the men of Israel unto the way of the wilderness; but the battle overtook them; and them which *came* out of the cities they destroyed in the midst of them.

43 *Thus* they [d]inclosed the Benjamites round about, *and* chased them, *and* trode them down [14]with ease [15]over against Gĭb'-ĕ-ăh toward the sunrising.

44 And there fell of Benjamin eighteen thousand men; all these *were* men of valour.

45 And they turned and fled toward the wilderness unto [e]the rock of Rimmon: and they gleaned of them in the highways five thousand men; and pursued hard after them unto Gĭ'-dŏm, and slew two thousand men of them.

46 So that all which fell that day of Benjamin were twenty and five thousand men that drew the sword; all these *were* men of valour.

47 But [f]six hundred men turned and fled to the wilderness unto the rock Rimmon, and abode in the rock Rimmon four months.

48 And the men of Israel turned again upon the children of Benjamin, and smote them with the edge of the sword, as well the men of *every* city, as the beast, and all that [16]came to hand: also they set on fire all the cities that [17]they came to.

CHAPTER 21

NOW [a]the men of Israel had sworn in Mĭz'-pēh, saying, There shall not any of us give his daughter unto Benjamin to wife.

2 And the people came [b]to the house of God, and abode there till even before God, and lifted up their voices, and wept sore;

3 And said, O LORD God of Israel, why is this come to pass in Israel, that there should be to day one tribe lacking in Israel?

4 And it came to pass on the morrow, that the people rose early, and [c]built there an altar, and offered burnt offerings and peace offerings.

5 And the children of Israel said, Who *is there* among all the tribes of Israel that came not up with the congregation unto the LORD? For [d]they had made a great oath concerning him

x Josh. 8.4. 2 Sam. 5.23.
5 to smite of the people wounded as at, etc.
6 Or, Beth-el.
y Josh. 8.14. Job 21.13. Pro. 4.19. Eccl. 8.11. Isa. 3.10,11. Matt. 24.44. Luke 21.34. 1 Thes. 5.3.
z Josh. 8.15.
a Josh. 8.19.
7 Or, made a long sound with the trumpets.
8 Or, time.
9 with.
10 elevation.
11 to smite the wounded.
b Josh. 8.20.
12 the whole consumption.
c Ex. 15.9,10. Pro. 5.22. Pro. 11.5,6. Isa. 33.14. Luke 17.27, 28.
13 touched them.
d Hosea 9.9.
14 Or, from Menuchah, etc.
15 unto over against.
e Josh. 15.32.
f ch. 21.13. Isa. 1.9. Jer. 14.9,10. Lam. 3.32. Hab. 3.2.
16 was found.
17 were found.

CHAP. 21

a ch. 20.1. 1 Sam. 7.5,6.
b Josh. 18.1. ch. 20.18,26.
c Gen. 8.20. Ex. 20.24, 25. ch. 6.26. 1 Sam. 14. 35. 2 Sam. 24. 25. 1 Ki. 8.64. Heb. 13.10.
d Lev. 27.28, 29. ch. 5.23. 1 Sam. 11.7. Jer. 48.10.

that came not up to the LORD to Mĭz'-
pēh, saying, He shall surely be put to
death.
6 And the children of Israel repented
them for Benjamin their brother, and
said, There is one tribe cut off from
Israel this day.
7 How shall we do for wives for them
that remain, seeing we have sworn by
the LORD that we will not give them of
our daughters to wives?
8 ¶ And they said, What one *is there*
of the tribes of Israel that came not
up to Mĭz'-pēh to the LORD? And, behold, there came none to the camp
from [e]Jā'-bĕsh–gĭl'-ĕ-ăd to the assembly.
9 For the people were numbered,
and, behold, *there were* none of the
inhabitants of Jā'-bĕsh–gĭl'-ĕ-ăd there.
10 And the congregation sent thither
twelve thousand men of the valiant-
est, and commanded them, saying,
[f]Go and smite the inhabitants of Jā'-
bĕsh–gĭl'-ĕ-ăd with the edge of the
sword, with the women and the children.
11 And this *is* the thing that ye shall
do, Ye [g]shall utterly destroy every
male, and every woman that [1]hath
lain by man.
12 And they found among the inhabitants of Jā'-bĕsh–gĭl'-ĕ-ăd four
hundred [2]young virgins, that had
known no man by lying with any male:
and they brought them unto the camp
to [h]Shī'-lōh, which *is* in the land of
Canaan.
13 And the whole congregation sent
some [3]to speak to the children of Benjamin [i]that *were* in the rock Rimmon,
and to [4]call peaceably unto them.
14 And Benjamin came again at that
time; and they gave them wives which
they had saved alive of the women of
Jā'-bĕsh–gĭl'-ĕ-ăd: and yet so they sufficed them not.
15 And the people repented them for
Benjamin, because that the LORD had
made a breach in the tribes of Israel.
16 ¶ Then the elders of the congregation said, How shall we do for wives
for them that remain, seeing the women are destroyed out of Benjamin?
17 And they said, *There must be* an
inheritance for them that be escaped
of Benjamin, that a tribe be not destroyed out of Israel.
18 Howbeit we may not give them
wives of our daughters: [j]for the children of Israel have sworn, saying,
Cursed *be* he that giveth a wife to
Benjamin.
19 Then they said, Behold, *there is* a
feast of the LORD in Shī'-lōh [5]yearly *in
a place* which *is* on the north side of
Beth-el, [6]on the east side [7]of the highway that goeth up from Beth-el to
Shē'-chĕm, and on the south of Lĕ-
bō'-năh.
20 Therefore they commanded the
children of Benjamin, saying, Go and
lie in wait in the vineyards;
21 And see, and, behold, if the
daughters of Shī'-lōh come out [k]to
dance in dances, then come ye out of
the vineyards, and catch you every
man his wife of the daughters of Shī'-
lōh, and go to the land of Benjamin.
22 And it shall be, when their fathers
or their brethren come unto us to
complain, that we will say unto them,
[8]Be favourable unto them for our
sakes: because we reserved not to each
man his wife in the war: for ye did not
give unto them at this time, *that* ye
should be guilty.
23 And the children of Benjamin did
so, and took *them* wives, according to
their number, of them that danced,
whom they caught: and they went and
returned unto their inheritance,
and [l]repaired the cities, and dwelt in
them.
24 And the children of Israel departed thence at that time, every man
to his tribe and to his family, and
they went out from thence every man
to his inheritance.
25 In [m]those days *there was* no king
in Israel: [n]every man did *that which
was* right in his own eyes.

e 1 Sam. 11.1. 2 Sam. 2.5,6.
f Deut. 13.15. Josh. 7.24-26. ch. 5.23. 1 Sam. 11.7.
g Num. 31. 17.
1 knoweth the lying with man.
2 young women virgins.
h Josh. 18.1. Josh. 22.9. 1 Sam. 1.3. Ps. 78.59,60. Jer. 7.12,14.
3 and spake and called.
i ch. 20.47.
4 Or, proclaim peace.
j ch. 11.35.
5 from year to year.
6 Or, toward the sun-rising.
7 Or, on.
k Ex. 15.20. Ex. 32.6,19. ch. 11.34. 1 Sam. 18.6. 1 Sam. 21. 11. Jer. 31.4,13.
8 Or, Gratify us in them.
l ch. 20.48.
m ch. 17.6. ch. 18.1.
n Deut. 12.8. ch. 17.6. Lam. 5.14. Rom. 13.3, 4.5.

THE

BOOK OF RUTH

CHAPTER 1

NOW it came to pass in the days
when the [a]judges [1]ruled, that
there was [b]a famine in the land. And
a certain man [c]of Beth-lehem-judah
went to sojourn in the country of
Moab, he, and his wife, and his two
sons.
2 And the name of the man *was* Ē-
lim-ĕ-lĕch, and the name of his wife
Nā-ō-mī, and the name of his two sons
Māh-lŏn and Chi-lī-ŏn, Ĕph-ră-thītes
of Beth-lehem-judah. And they came
into the country of Moab, and [2]con-
tinued there.
3 And Ē-lim-ĕ-lĕch Nā-ō-mī's husband died; and she was left, and her
two sons.
4 And they took them wives of the
women of Moab; the name of the one
was Ôr-păh, and the name of the other
Ruth: and they dwelled there about
ten years.
5 And Māh-lŏn and Chi-lī-ŏn died
also both of them; and the woman was
left of her two sons and her husband.
6 ¶ Then she arose with her daughters in law, that she might return from
the country of Moab: for she had
heard in the country of Moab how
that the LORD had visited [f]his people
in [g]giving them bread.
7 Wherefore she went forth out of the
place where she was, and her two
daughters in law with her; and they
went on the way to return unto the
land of Judah.
8 And Nā-ō-mī said unto her two
daughters in law, [h]Go, return each to
her mother's house: [i]the LORD deal
kindly with you, as ye have dealt with
the dead, and with me.
9 The LORD grant you that ye may
find rest, each *of you* in the house of
her husband. Then she kissed them;
and they lifted up their voice, and
wept.
10 And they said unto her, Surely we
will return with thee unto thy people.
11 And Nā-ō-mī said, Turn again, my
daughters: why will ye go with me?
are there yet *any more* sons in my
womb, [k]that they may be your husbands?
12 Turn again, my daughters, go
your way; for I am too old to have an
husband. If I should say, I have hope,
[3]*if* I should have an husband also to
night, and should also bear sons;
13 Would ye [4]tarry for them till they
were grown? would ye stay for them
from having husbands? nay, my
daughters; for [5]it grieveth me much
for your sakes that [l]the hand of the
LORD is gone out against me.
14 And they lifted up their voice, and
wept again: and Ôr-păh kissed her
mother in law; but Ruth clave [m]unto
her.
15 And she said, Behold, thy sister
in law is gone back unto her people,
and unto her [n]gods: return thou after
thy sister in law.
16 And Ruth said, [6]Intreat me not to
leave thee, *or* to return from following
after thee: for whither thou goest, I
will go; and where thou lodgest, I will
lodge: thy people *shall be* my people,
and thy God my God:
17 Where thou diest, will I die, and
there will I be buried: [o]the LORD do so
to me, and more also, *if ought* but
death part thee and me.
18 When [p]she saw that she [7]was
stedfastly minded to go with her, then
she left speaking unto her.
19 ¶ So they two went until they
came to Beth-lehem. And it came to
pass, when they were come to Beth-
lehem, that [q]all the city was moved
about them, and they said, *Is* [r]this
Nā-ō-mī?
20 And she said unto them, Call me
not [8]Nā-ō-mī, call me [9]Mâr-ă: for the
Almighty hath dealt very bitterly with
me.
21 I went out full, [s]and the LORD
hath brought me home again empty:
why *then* call ye me Nā-ō-mī, seeing
the LORD hath testified against me,
and the Almighty hath afflicted
me?
22 So Nā-ō-mī returned, and Ruth
the Moabitess, her daughter in law,
with her, which returned out of the
country of Moab: and they came to
Beth-lehem [t]in the beginning of barley
harvest.

CHAP. 1

a Judg. 2.16.
1 judged.
b Gen. 12.10. Deut. 28.38. 1 Ki. 18.2.
c Judg. 17.8. Micah 5.2.
d Gen. 35.19.
e Judg. 3.30.
2 were.
f Ex. 4.31. Ps. 80.14. Jer. 29.10. Zeph. 2.7. Zech. 10.3. Luke 1.68.
g Gen. 28.20. Gen. 48.15. Ex. 16.4,6. Ps. 104.14, 16. Ps. 111.5. Ps. 132.15. Ps. 145.15. Pro. 30.8. Isa. 55.10. Matt. 6.11.
h Josh. 24.15.
i 2 Tim. 1.16.
j ch. 3.1.
k Gen. 38.11. Deut. 25.5.
3 Or, if I were with an husband.
4 hope.
5 I have much bitterness.
l Judg. 2.15. Job 19.21. Ps. 32.4. Ps. 38.2. Ps. 39.9,10.
m Deut. 4.4. Deut. 10.20. Pro. 17.17. John 6.66-69. Heb. 10.39.
n Josh. 24.15, 19,21. Judg. 11.24.
6 Or, Be not against me.
o 1 Sam. 3.17. 2 Ki. 6.31.
p Acts 21.14.
7 strengthened herself.
q Matt. 21.10.
r Isa. 23.7. Lam. 2.15.
8 That is, Pleasant.
9 That is, Bitter.
s 1 Sam. 2.7, 8.
t Ex. 9.31. 2 Sam. 21.9.

CHAPTER 2

AND Nā'-ō-mī had a [a]kinsman of her
husband's, a mighty man of
wealth, of the family of Ē-lĭm'-ĕ-lĕch;
and his name *was* [1]Bō'-ăz.
2 And Ruth the Moabitess said unto
Nā'-ō-mī, Let me now go to the field,
and glean [b]ears of corn after *him* in
whose sight I shall find grace. And she
said unto her, Go, my daughter.
3 And she went, and came, and gleaned in the field after the reapers: and
her [2]hap was to light on a part of the
field *belonging* unto Bō'-ăz, who *was*
of the kindred of Ē-lĭm'-ĕ-lĕch.
4 ¶ And, behold, Bō'-ăz came from
Beth-lehem, and said unto the reapers, [c]The LORD *be* with you. And they
answered him, [d]The LORD bless
thee.
5 Then said Bō'-ăz unto his servant
that was set over the reapers, Whose
damsel *is* this?
6 And the servant that was set over
the reapers answered and said, It *is*
the Moabitish damsel that [e]came back
with Nā'-ō-mī out of the country of
Moab:
7 And she said, I pray you, let me
glean and gather after the reapers
among the sheaves: so she came, and
hath continued even from the morning
until now, that she tarried a little in
the house.
8 Then said Bō'-ăz unto Ruth, Hearest thou not, my daughter? Go not to
glean in another field, neither go from
hence, but abide here fast by my
maidens:
9 *Let* thine eyes *be* on the field that
they do reap, and go thou after them:
have I not charged the young men that
they shall not touch thee? and when
thou art athirst, go unto the vessels,
and drink of *that* which the young men
have drawn.
10 Then she [f]fell on her face, and
bowed herself to the ground, and said
unto him, Why have I found grace in
thine eyes, that thou shouldest take
knowledge of me, seeing I *am* a
stranger?
11 And Bō'-ăz answered and said unto her, It [g]hath fully been shewed me,
[h]all that thou hast done unto thy
mother in law since the death of thine
husband: and *how* thou hast left thy
father and thy mother, and the land of
thy nativity, and art come unto a people which thou knewest not heretofore.
12 The [i]LORD recompense thy work,
and a full reward be given thee of the

CHAP. 2

a ch. 3.2,12.
1 That is, Strength is in him.
b Lev. 19.9. Deut. 24.19.
2 hap happened.
c Judg. 6.12. Ps. 118.26. Ps. 129.7,8. Luke 1.28. 2 Thes. 3.16. 2 Tim. 4.22.
d Col. 4.6.
e ch. 1.22.
f Gen. 18.2. 1 Sam. 25. 23.
g Pro. 31.31.
h ch. 1.14. Luke 5.11-28. Luke 14.33. Heb. 11.8,9, 24-26.
i 1 Sam. 24. 19. Ps. 19.11. Ps. 58.11. Pro. 11.18. Matt. 5.12. Matt. 6.1. Luke 6.35. 2 Tim. 1.18. Heb. 6.10.
j Ps. 17.8. Ps. 36.7. Ps. 57.1. Ps. 63.7.
3 Or, I find favour.
4 to the heart.
k 1 Sam. 25. 41. Phil. 2.3.
5 shame her not.
l Ps. 41.1.
m ch. 3.10. 2 Sam. 2.5. Job 29.13. 2 Tim. 1.16.
n Pro. 17.17.
6 Or, one that hath right to redeem.
7 Or, fall upon thee.

LORD God of Israel, under [j]whos
wings thou art come to trust.
13 Then she said, [3]Let me find favou
in thy sight, my lord; for that tho
hast comforted me, and for that tho
hast spoken [4]friendly unto thine hand
maid, [k]though I be not like unto on
of thine handmaidens.
14 And Bō'-ăz said unto her, At meal
time come thou hither, and eat of th
bread, and dip thy morsel in the vine
gar. And she sat beside the reapers
and he reached her parched *corn*, an
she did eat, and was sufficed, an
left.
15 And when she was risen up t
glean, Bō'-ăz commanded his youn
men, saying, Let her glean eve
among the sheaves, and [5]reproac
her not:
16 And let fall also *some* of the hand
fuls of purpose for her, and leave *them*
that she may glean *them*, and rebuk
her not.
17 So she gleaned in the field unti
even, and beat out that she had glean
ed: and it was about an ē'-phăh o
barley.
18 ¶ And she took *it* up, and went in
to the city: and her mother in la
saw what she had gleaned: an
she brought forth, and gave to he
that she had reserved after she wa
sufficed.
19 And her mother in law said unt
her, Where hast thou gleaned to day
and where wroughtest thou? blesse
be he that did [l]take knowledge of thee
And she shewed her mother in la
with whom she had wrought, an
said, The man's name with whom
wrought to day *is* Bō'-ăz.
20 And Nā'-ō-mī said unto her daugh
ter in law, [m]Blessed *be* he of the LORD
who [n]hath not left off his kindness t
the living and to the dead. And Nā'-ō
mī said unto her, The man *is* near o
kin unto us, [6]one of our next kins
men.
21 And Ruth the Moabitess said, H
said unto me also, Thou shalt kee
fast by my young men, until they hav
ended all my harvest.
22 And Nā'-ō-mī said unto Ruth he
daughter in law, *It is* good, my daugh
ter, that thou go out with his maidens
that they [7]meet thee not in any othe
field.
23 So she kept fast by the maiden
of Bō'-ăz to glean unto the end o
barley harvest and of wheat har
vest; and dwelt with her mother i
law.

CHAPTER 3

THEN Nā-ō-mī her mother in law
said unto her, My daughter, [a]shall
not seek [b]rest for thee, that it may be
'ell with thee?
2 And now *is* not Bō-ăz of our kin-
red, with [c]whose maidens thou wast?
ehold, he winnoweth barley to night
the threshingfloor.
3 Wash thyself therefore, [d]and anoint
ee, and put thy raiment upon thee,
nd get thee down to the floor: *but*
ake not thyself known unto the
an, until he shall have done eating
nd drinking.
4 And it shall be, when he lieth down,
hat thou shalt mark the place where
e shall lie, and thou shalt go in, and
ncover his feet, and lay thee down;
nd he will tell thee what thou shalt
o.
5 And she said unto her, [e]All that
hou sayest unto me I will do.
6 ¶ And she went down unto the
oor, and did according to all that her
other in law bade her.
7 And when Bō-ăz had eaten and
runk, and [f]his heart was merry, he
'ent to lie down at the end of the heap
f corn: and she came softly, and un-
overed his feet, and laid her down.
8 ¶ And it came to pass at midnight,
hat the man was afraid, and [2]turned
imself: and, behold, a woman lay at
is feet.
9 And he said, Who *art* thou? And
he answered, I *am* Ruth thine hand-
aid: spread [g]therefore thy skirt over
hine handmaid; for thou *art* [3]a near
insman.
10 And he said, [h]Blessed *be* thou of
he LORD, my daughter: *for* thou hast
hewed more kindness in the latter
nd than [i]at the beginning, inasmuch
s thou followedst not young men,
hether poor or rich.
11 And now, my daughter, fear not;
will do to thee all that thou requirest:
or all the [4]city of my people doth
now that thou [j]*art* a virtuous woman.
12 And now it is true that I *am thy*
ear kinsman: howbeit [k]there is a
insman nearer than I.
13 Tarry this night, and it shall be in
he morning, *that* if he [l]will perform
nto thee the part of a kinsman, well;
t him do the kinsman's part: but if
e will not do the part of a kinsman to
hee, then will I do the part of a kins-
an to thee, [m]*as* the LORD liveth: lie
own until the morning.
14 ¶ And she lay at his feet until the
orning: and she rose up before one

CHAP. 3
a 1 Cor. 7.36. 1 Tim. 5.8.
b Deut. 4.40. ch. 1.9. Ps. 128.2. Jer. 22.15, 16.
c ch. 2.8.
d 2 Sam. 14.2.
1 Or, lift up the clothes that are on his feet.
e Eph. 6.1. Col. 3.20.
f Judg. 19.6. 2 Sam. 13. 28. Esther 1.10.
2 Or, took hold on.
g Eze. 16.8.
3 Or, one that hath right to redeem.
h ch. 2.20.
i ch. 1.8.
4 gate.
j Pro. 12.4.
k ch. 4.1. 1 Thes. 4.6.
l Deut. 25.5. ch. 4.5. Matt. 22.24.
m Judg. 8.19. Jer. 4.2. Heb. 6.16.
n Rom. 12.17. 1 Cor. 10.32. 2 Cor. 8.21. 1 Thes. 5.22. 1 Pet. 2.12.

CHAP. 4
a ch. 3.12.
b Ex. 18.21, 22. Deut. 16.18. Deut. 17.9. 1 Ki. 21.8. Ps. 82.2. Pro. 31.23.
1 I said I will reveal in thine ear.
c Jer. 32.7, 8. Rom. 12.17. 2 Cor. 8.21. Phil. 4.8.
d Gen. 23.18.
e Lev. 25.25.
f Gen. 38.8. Deut. 25.5, 6. ch. 3.13. Matt. 22.24.
g ch. 3.12, 13.
h Deut. 25.7, 9.

could know another. And he said,
[n]Let it not be known that a woman
came into the floor.
15 Also he said, Bring the vail that
thou hast upon thee, and hold it. And
when she held it, he measured six
measures of barley, and laid *it* on her:
and she went into the city.
16 And when she came to her mother
in law, she said, Who *art* thou, my
daughter? And she told her all that
the man had done to her.
17 And she said, These six *measures*
of barley gave he me; for he said to
me, Go not empty unto thy mother in
law.
18 Then said she, Sit still, my daughter, until thou know how the matter
will fall: for the man will not be in
rest, until he have finished the thing
this day.

CHAPTER 4

THEN went Bō-ăz up to the gate,
and sat him down there: and, behold, [a]the kinsman of whom Bō-ăz
spake came by; unto whom he said,
Ho, such a one! turn aside, sit down
here. And he turned aside, and sat
down.
2 And he took ten men of [b]the elders
of the city, and said, Sit ye down here.
And they sat down.
3 And he said unto the kinsman, Nā-
ō-mī, that is come again out of the
country of Moab, selleth a parcel of
land, which *was* our brother Ē-lĭm-ĕ-
lĕch's:
4 And [1]I thought to advertise thee,
saying, [c]Buy *it* [d]before the inhabitants,
and before the elders of my people. If
thou wilt redeem *it*, redeem *it*: but if
thou wilt not redeem *it*, *then* tell me,
that I may know: [e]for *there is* none to
redeem *it* beside thee; and I *am* after
thee. And he said, I will redeem *it*.
5 Then said Bō-ăz, What day thou
buyest the field of the hand of Nā-ō-
mī, thou must buy *it* also of Ruth the
Moabitess, the wife of the dead, [f]to
raise up the name of the dead upon
his inheritance.
6 ¶ And [g]the kinsman said, I cannot
redeem *it* for myself, lest I mar mine
own inheritance: redeem thou my
right to thyself; for I cannot redeem
it.
7 Now [h]this *was the manner* in former
time in Israel concerning redeeming
and concerning changing, for to confirm all things; a man plucked off his
shoe, and gave *it* to his neighbour:
and this *was* a testimony in Israel.
8 Therefore the kinsman said unto

Bō´ăz, Buy *it* for thee. So he drew off
his shoe.
9 ¶ And Bō´ăz said unto the elders,
and *unto* all the people, Ye *are* witnesses this day, that I have bought all
that *was* Ē-lĭm´-ĕ-lĕch's, and all that
was Chĭ´-lĭ-ŏn's and Măh´-lŏn's, of the
hand of Nā´-ō-mī.
10 Moreover Ruth the Moabitess,
the wife of Măh´-lŏn, have I purchased
to be my wife, to raise up the name of
the dead upon his inheritance, [i]that
the name of the dead be not cut off
from among his brethren, and from
the gate of his place: ye *are* witnesses
this day.
11 And all the people that *were* in the
gate, and the elders, said, *We are* witnesses. [j]The LORD make the woman
that is come into thine house like
Rachel and like Leah, which two did
[k]build the house of Israel: and [2]do
thou worthily in [l]Ĕph´-ră-tăh, and [3]be
famous in Beth-lehem:
12 And let thy house be like the
house of Phâr´-ĕz, [m]whom Tā´-mär
bare unto Judah, of [n]the seed which
the LORD shall give thee of this young
woman.
13 ¶ So Bō´ăz took Ruth, and she
was his wife: and when he went in unto her, [o]the LORD gave her conception
and she bare a son.
14 And [p]the women said unto Nā´-ō
mī, Blessed *be* the LORD, which hat
not [4]left thee this day without a [5]kins
man, that his name may be famous i
Israel.
15 And he shall be unto thee a re
storer of *thy* life, and [6]a nourisher o
[7]thine old age: for thy daughter i
law, which loveth thee, which is [q]bette
to thee than seven sons, hath bor
him.
16 And Nā´-ō-mī took the child, an
laid it in her bosom, and became nurs
unto it.
17 And [r]the women her neighbour
gave it a name, saying, There is a so
born to Nā´-ō-mī; and they called hi
name Ō´-bĕd: he *is* the father of Jesse
the father of David.
18 ¶ Now these *are* the generation
of Phâr´-ĕz: [s]Phâr´-ĕz begat Hĕz´-rŏn,
19 And Hĕz´-rŏn begat Ram, an
Ram begat Ăm-mĭn´-ă-dăb,
20 And Ăm-mĭn´-ă-dăb begat Năh
shŏn, [t]and Năh´-shŏn begat [8]Săl´-mŏn
21 And Săl´-mŏn begat Bō´-ăz, an
Bō´-ăz begat Ō´-bĕd,
22 And Ō´-bĕd begat Jesse, and Jess
begat David.

[i] Deut. 25.6. [j] Gen. 1.28. Gen. 9.1. Gen. 17.16. Gen. 24.60. Gen. 28.3. Ps. 127.3. Ps. 128.3. [k] Deut. 25.9. 2 Or, get thee riches, or, power. [l] Gen. 35.16. Micah 5.2. 3 proclaim thy name. [m] Gen. 38.29. 1 Chr. 2.4. Matt. 1.3. [n] 1 Sam. 2.20. [o] Gen. 29.31. [p] Luke 1.58. Rom. 12.15. 4 caused to cease unto thee. 5 Or, redeemer. 6 to nourish. 7 thy gray hairs. [q] 1 Sam. 1.8. [r] Luke 1.58, 59. [s] 1 Chr. 2.4. Matt. 1.3. [t] Num. 1.7. 8 Or, Salmah.

THE FIRST

BOOK OF SAMUEL

otherwise called

THE FIRST BOOK OF THE KINGS

CHAPTER 1

NOW there was a certain man
of Rā-mă-thā´-ĭm-zō´-phĭm, of
mount Ē´-phră-ĭm, and his name *was*
[a]Ĕl-kā´-năh, the son of Jĕ-rō´-hăm, the
son of Ē-lī´-hū, the son of Tō´-hū, the
son of Zuph, [b]an Ĕph´-ră-thite:
2 And he had two wives; the name of
the one *was* Hannah, and the name of
the other Pĕ-nĭn´-năh: and Pĕ-nĭn´-năh
had children, but Hannah had no
children.
3 And this man went up out of his
city [1]yearly [c]to worship and to sacrifice unto the LORD of hosts in [d]Shĭ´-
lōh. And the two sons of Ē´-lī, Hŏph´-
nī and Phĭn´-ĕ-hăs, the priests of the
LORD, *were* there.
4 ¶ And when the time was that Ĕl-
kā´-năh offered, he gave to Pĕ-nĭn´-năl
his wife, and to all her sons and he
daughters, portions:
5 But unto Hannah he gave [2]
worthy portion; for he loved Hannah
[e]but the LORD had shut up her womb
6 And her adversary also [3]provoke
her sore, for to make her fret, becaus
the LORD had shut up her womb.
7 And *as* he did so [f]year by year
[4]when she went up to the house of th
LORD, so she provoked her; therefor
she wept, and did not eat.
8 Then said Ĕl-kā´-năh her husban
to her, Hannah, why weepest thou
and why eatest thou not? and why i
thy heart grieved? *am* not I [g]better t
thee than ten sons?
9 ¶ So Hannah rose up after they ha

CHAP. 1

[a] 1 Chr. 6.27. [b] Ruth 1.2. 1 from year to year. [c] Deut. 12.5. [d] Josh. 18.1. Judg. 18.31. 2 Or, a double portion. [e] Gen. 30.2. 3 angered her. [f] Ex. 23.14. Deut. 16.16. 4 from her going up, or, from the time that she, etc. [g] Ruth 4.15.

ten in Shī-lōh, and after they had
unk. Now Ē-lī the priest sat upon a
at by a post of the [h]temple of the
ORD.
0 And [i]she *was* [5]in bitterness of
ul, and prayed unto the LORD, and
ept sore.
1 And she [j]vowed a vow, and said,
LORD of hosts, if thou wilt indeed
ook on the affliction of thine hand-
aid, and [l]remember me, and not
rget thine handmaid, but wilt give
nto thine handmaid [6]a man child,
en I will give him unto the LORD all
e days of his life, and [m]there shall
rasor come upon his head.
2 And it came to pass, as she [7]con-
nued praying before the LORD, that
-lī marked her mouth.
3 Now Hannah, she spake in her
eart; only her lips moved, but her
ice was not heard: therefore Ē-lī
ought she had been drunken.
4 And Ē-lī said unto her, How long
ilt thou be drunken? put away thy
ine from thee.
5 And Hannah answered and said,
o, my lord, I *am* a woman [8]of a
rrowful spirit: I have drunk neither
ine nor strong drink, but have [n]pour-
d out my soul before the LORD.
6 Count not thine handmaid for a
aughter of [o]Bē-lī-ăl: for out of the
bundance of my [9]complaint and
rief have I spoken hitherto.
7 Then Ē-lī answered and said, Go
n peace: and [q]the God of Israel
rant *thee* thy petition that thou hast
sked of him.
8 And she said, [r]Let thine hand-
aid find grace in thy sight. So the
oman went [s]her way, and did eat,
nd her countenance was no more *sad*.
9 ¶ And they rose up in the morning
arly, and worshipped before the
ORD, and returned, and came to
eir house to Rā-măh: and Ĕl-kā-năh
new Hannah his wife; and the [t]LORD
emembered her.
20 Wherefore it came to pass, [10]when
he time was come about after Han-
ah had conceived, that she bare a
on, and called his name [11]Samuel,
aying, Because I have asked him of
he LORD.
21 And the man Ĕl-kā-năh, and all
is house, went up to offer unto the
ORD the yearly sacrifice, and his
ow.
22 But Hannah went not up; for she
aid unto her husband, *I will not go up*
ntil the child be weaned, and *then* I
ill [u]bring him, that he may appear
before the LORD, and there [v]abide for
ever.
23 And [w]Ĕl-kā-năh her husband said
unto her, Do what seemeth thee good;
tarry until thou have weaned him;
[x]only the LORD establish his word.
So the woman abode, and gave her
son suck until she weaned him.
24 ¶ And when she had weaned him,
she took [y]him up with her, with three
bullocks, and one ē-phăh of flour, and
a bottle of wine, and brought him unto the house of the LORD in Shī-lōh:
and the child *was* young.
25 And they slew a bullock, and
brought the child to Ē-lī.
26 And she said, Oh my lord, *as* thy
soul liveth, my lord, I *am* the woman
that stood by thee here, praying unto
the LORD.
27 For [z]this child I prayed; and the
LORD hath given me my petition
which I asked of him:
28 Therefore also I have [12]lent him
to the LORD; as long as he liveth [13]he
shall be lent to the LORD. And he
[a]worshipped the LORD there.

CHAPTER 2

AND Hannah [a]prayed, and said,
[b]My heart rejoiceth in the LORD,
mine horn is exalted in the LORD: my
mouth is enlarged over mine enemies;
because [c]I rejoice in thy salvation.
2 *There* [d]*is* none holy as the LORD:
for *there is* [e]none beside thee: neither
is there any rock like our God.
3 Talk no more so exceeding proudly; [f]let *not* [1]arrogancy come out of
your mouth: for the LORD *is* a God of
knowledge, and by him actions are
weighed.
4 The bows of the mighty men *are*
broken, and they that stumbled are
girded with strength.
5 *They* [g]*that were* full have hired out
themselves for bread; and *they that
were* hungry ceased: so that the [h]bar-
ren hath born seven; and she [i]that
hath many children is waxed feeble.
6 The [j]LORD killeth, and maketh
alive: he bringeth down to the grave,
and bringeth up.
7 The LORD [k]maketh poor, and maketh rich: he [l]bringeth low, and lifteth
up.
8 He [m]raiseth up the poor out of the
dust, *and* lifteth up the beggar from
the dunghill, [n]to set *them* among
princes, and to make them inherit the
throne of glory: for the [o]pillars of the
earth *are* the LORD's, and he hath set
the world upon them.

h ch. 3.3.
i Job 7.11.
5 bitter of soul.
j Gen. 28.20. Num. 21.2. Judg. 11.30.
k Gen. 29.32. Ex. 4.31. 2 Sam. 16. 12.
l Gen. 8.1. Ps. 132.1,2.
6 seed of men.
m Num. 6.5.
7 multiplied to pray.
8 hard of spirit.
n Ps. 62.8.
o 2 Cor 6.15.
9 Or, meditation.
p Judg. 18.6. ch. 25.35.
q Ps. 20.4,5.
r Gen. 33.15.
s Eccl. 9.7. John 16.24.
t Gen. 30.22.
10 in revolution of days.
11 That is, Asked of God.
u Luke 2.22.
v ch. 2.11.
w Num. 30.7.
x 2 Sam. 7.25.
y Deut. 12.5.
z Matt. 7.7.
12 Or, returned him, whom I have obtained by petition, to the LORD.
13 Or, he whom I have obtained by petition shall be returned.
a Gen. 24.26, 52.

CHAP. 2

a Phil. 4.6.
b Luke 1.46.
c Ps. 9.14. Ps. 13.5.
d Ex. 15.11. Isa. 6.3.
e Deut. 4.35. Ps. 73.25.
f Mal. 3.13.
1 hard.
g Luke 1.53.
h Ps. 113.9.
i Isa. 54.1. Gal. 4.27.
j Deut. 32.39. Job 5.18. Hosea 6.1. John 5.25-29. Rev. 1.18.
k Job 1.21. Ps. 102.10.
l Ps. 75.7.
m Dan. 4.17.
n Gen. 41.14. ch. 15.17. Job 36.7. Jas. 2.5. Rev. 1.6. Rev. 3.21.
o Heb. 1.3.

9 He [p]will keep the feet of his saints, and the wicked shall be silent in darkness; for by [q]strength shall no man prevail.

10 The adversaries of the LORD shall be broken to pieces; out of heaven shall he thunder upon them: [r]the LORD shall judge the ends of the earth; and he shall give strength unto his king, and exalt the horn of his anointed.

11 And Ĕl-kā´-năh went to Rā´-măh to his house. [s]And the child did minister unto the LORD before Ē´-lī the priest.

12 ¶ Now the sons of Ē´-lī *were* [t]sons of Bē´-lĭ-ăl; they [u]knew not the LORD.

13 And the priests' custom with the people *was, that,* when any man offered sacrifice, the priest's servant came, while the flesh was in seething, with a fleshhook of three teeth in his hand;

14 And he struck *it* into the pan, or kettle, or caldron, or pot; all that the fleshhook brought up the priest took for himself. So they did in Shī´-lōh unto all the Israelites that came thither.

15 Also before they burnt the fat, the priest's servant came, and said to the man that sacrificed, Give flesh to roast for the priest; for he will not have sodden flesh of thee, but raw.

16 And *if* any man said unto him, Let them not fail to burn the fat [2]presently, and *then* take *as much* as thy soul desireth; then he would answer him, *Nay;* but thou shalt give *it me* now: and if not, I will take *it* by force.

17 Wherefore the sin of the young men was very great [v]before the LORD: for men abhorred [w]the offering of the LORD.

18 ¶ But Samuel ministered before the LORD, *being* a child, girded [x]with a linen ē´-phŏd.

19 Moreover his mother made him a little coat, and brought *it* to him from year to year, when she came up with her husband to offer the yearly sacrifice.

20 ¶ And Ē´-lī blessed Ĕl-kā´-năh and his wife, and said, The LORD give thee seed of this woman for the [3]loan which is lent to the LORD. And they went unto their own home.

21 And the LORD [y]visited Hannah, so that she conceived, and bare three sons and two daughters. And the child Samuel [z]grew before the LORD.

22 ¶ Now Ē´-lī was very old, and heard all that his sons did unto all Israel; and how they lay with the women that [4]assembled *at* the door of the tabernacle of the congregation.

p Ps. 91.11.
q ch. 14.6.
r Ps. 96.13.
s ch. 3.1.
t Deut. 13.13.
u Rom. 1.28.
2 as on the day.
v Gen. 6.11.
w Mal. 2.8. Rom. 2.24.
x Ex. 28.4.
3 Or, petition which she asked, etc.
y Gen. 21.1.
z Luke 2.40.
4 assembled by troops.
5 Or, I hear evil words of you.
6 Or, to cry out.
a Num. 15. 30.
b Deut. 2.30. Pro. 15.10.
c Pro. 3.4. Luke 2.40. Acts 2.47. Rom. 14.18.
d 1 Ki. 13.1.
e Ex. 4.14.
f Ex. 28.1.
g Lev. 2.3.
h Deut. 32.15. Mal. 1.12.
i Deut. 12.5.
j 1 Chr. 15.2. Jer. 18.9.
k Ps. 18.20. Ps. 91.14.
l Num. 11.20. 2 Sam. 12.9, 10. Mal. 2.9.
m ch. 4.11.
7 Or, the affliction of the tabernacle, for all the wealth which God would have given Israel.
n Zech. 8.4.
8 men.
o ch. 4.11.
p 1 Ki. 2.35. 1 Chr. 29.22. Heb. 2.17.

23 And he said unto them, Why do
such things? for [5]I hear of your e
dealings by all this people.
24 Nay, my sons; for *it is* no good r
port that I hear: ye make the LORD
people [6]to transgress.
25 If one man sin against anothe
the judge shall judge him: but if a ma
[a]sin against the LORD, who shall i
treat for him? Notwithstanding th
hearkened not unto the voice of the
father, [b]because the LORD would sl
them.
26 And the child Samuel grew o
and was in [c]favour both with t
LORD, and also with men.
27 ¶ And [d]there came a man of G
unto Ē´-lī, and said unto him, Th
saith the LORD, [e]Did I plainly appe
unto the house of thy father, whe
they were in Egypt in Pharaoh
house?
28 And did I [f]choose him out of a
the tribes of Israel *to be* my priest,
offer upon mine altar, to burn incens
to wear an ē´-phŏd before me? an
[g]did I give unto the house of thy fath
all the offerings made by fire of t
children of Israel?
29 Wherefore [h]kick ye at my sac
fice and at mine offering, which I ha
commanded *in* [i]*my* habitation; an
honourest thy sons above me, to ma
yourselves fat with the chiefest of a
the offerings of Israel my people?
30 Wherefore the LORD God of Isra
saith, I said indeed *that* thy house, an
the house of thy father, should wa
before me for ever: but now the LOR
saith, [j]Be it far from me; for the
that honour me [k]I will honour, an
[l]they that despise me shall be light
esteemed.
31 Behold, [m]the days come, that
will cut off thine arm, and the arm
thy father's house, that there sha
not be an old man in thine house.
32 And thou shalt see [7]an enemy
my habitation, in all *the wealth* whic
God shall give Israel: and there sha
not be an [n]old man in thine house f
ever.
33 And the man of thine, *whom*
shall not cut off from mine altar, *sha*
be to consume thine eyes, and t
grieve thine heart: and all the i
crease of thine house shall die [8]in t
flower of their age.
34 And this *shall be* a sign unto the
that shall come upon thy two sons, o
Hŏph´-nī and Phĭn´-ĕ-hăs; [o]in one da
they shall die both of them.
35 And [p]I will raise me up a faithf

priest, *that* shall do according to *that*
which *is* in mine heart and in my mind:
and [q]I will build him a sure house; and
he shall walk before [r]mine anointed
for ever.
36 And [s]it shall come to pass, *that*
every one that is left in thine house
shall come *and* crouch to him for a
piece of silver and a morsel of bread,
and shall say, [9]Put me, I pray thee, into [10]one of the priests' offices, that I
may eat a piece of bread.

CHAPTER 3

AND the child Samuel ministered
unto the LORD before Ē-lī. And
[a]the word of the LORD was precious
in those days; *there was* no open
vision.
2 And it came to pass at that time,
when Ē-lī *was* laid down in his place,
and his eyes began to wax dim, *that* he
could not see;
3 And ere [b]the lamp of God went out
in the temple of the LORD, where the
ark of God *was*, and Samuel was laid
down *to sleep;*
4 That the LORD called Samuel: and
he answered, Here *am* I.
5 And he ran unto Ē-lī, and said,
Here *am* I; for thou calledst me. And
he said, I called not; lie down again.
And he went and lay down.
6 And the LORD called yet again,
Samuel. And Samuel arose and went
to Ē-lī, and said, Here *am* I; for
thou didst call me. And he answered,
I called not, my son; lie down
again.
7 [1]Now Samuel [c]did not yet know
the LORD, neither was the word of the
LORD yet revealed unto him.
8 And the LORD called Samuel again
the third time. And he arose and went
to Ē-lī, and said, Here *am* I; for thou
didst call me. And Ē-lī perceived that
the LORD had called the child.
9 Therefore Ē-lī said unto Samuel,
Go, lie down: and it shall be, if he call
thee, that thou shalt say, Speak,
LORD; for thy servant heareth. So
Samuel went and lay down in his
place.
10 And the LORD came, and stood,
and called as at other times, Samuel,
Samuel. Then Samuel answered,
[d]Speak; for thy servant heareth.
11 ¶ And the LORD said to Samuel,
Behold, I will do a thing in Israel, at
which both the ears of every one that
heareth it shall tingle.
12 In that day I will perform against
Ē-lī all [e]*things* which I have spoken
concerning his house: [2]when I begin,
I will also make an end.
13 [3]For I have told him that I will
judge his house for ever for the iniquity which he knoweth; because [f]his
sons made themselves [4]vile, and he
[5]restrained them not.
14 And therefore I have sworn unto
the house of Ē-lī, that the iniquity of
Ē-lī's house shall [g]not be purged with
sacrifice nor offering for ever.
15 ¶ And Samuel lay until the morning, and opened the doors of the house
of the LORD. And Samuel feared to
shew Ē-lī the vision.
16 Then Ē-lī called Samuel, and said,
Samuel, my son. And he answered,
Here *am* I.
17 And he said, What *is* the thing
that *the LORD* hath said unto thee? I
pray thee hide *it* not from me: [h]God
do so to thee, and [6]more also, if thou
hide *any* [7]thing from me of all the
things that he said unto thee.
18 And Samuel told him [8]every whit,
and hid nothing from him. And he
said, [i]It *is* the LORD: let him do what
seemeth him good.
19 ¶ And Samuel grew, and [j]the
LORD was with him, [k]and did let none
of his words fall to the ground.
20 And all Israel [l]from Dan even to
Bēer-shē-bă knew that Samuel *was*
[9]established *to be* a prophet of the
LORD.
21 And [m]the LORD appeared again in
Shī-lōh: for the LORD revealed himself to Samuel in Shī-lōh by the word
of the LORD.

CHAPTER 4

AND the word of Samuel [1]came to
all Israel. Now Israel went out
against the Philistines to battle, and
pitched [a]beside Ĕb-ĕn-ē-zĕr: and the
Philistines pitched in Ā-phĕk.
2 And the Philistines put themselves
in array against Israel: and when
[2]they joined battle, Israel was smitten
before the Philistines: and they slew
of [3]the army in the field about four
thousand men.
3 ¶ And when the people were come
into the camp, the elders of Israel
said, Wherefore hath the LORD smitten us to day before the Philistines?
Let us [4]fetch the ark of the covenant
of the LORD out of Shī-lōh unto us,
that, when it cometh among us, it may
save us out of the hand of our enemies.
4 So the people sent to Shī-lōh, that
they might bring from thence the ark
of the covenant of the LORD of hosts,

q 2 Sam. 7.11.
r Ps. 2.2.
s 1 Ki. 2.27.
9 Join.
10 Or, somewhat about the priesthood.

CHAP. 3
a Ps. 74.9. Amos 8.11.
b Ex. 27.21. Lev. 24.3.
1 Or, Thus did Samuel before he knew the LORD, and before the word of the LORD was revealed unto him.
c Jer. 9.24. Acts 19.2.
d Ps. 85.8. Acts 9.6.
e ch. 2.30.
2 beginning and ending.
3 Or, And I will tell him.
f ch. 2.12.
4 Or, accursed.
5 frowned not upon them.
g Num. 15.30. Isa. 22.14. Heb. 10.26-31.
h Ruth 1.17. Matt. 26.63.
6 so add.
7 Or, word.
8 all the things, or, words.
i Gen. 18.25. ch. 16.10-12. Job 1.21.
j Gen. 39.2. ch. 18.14. 2 Tim. 4.22.
k ch. 9.6.
l Judg. 20.1.
9 Or, faithful.
m Gen. 12.7. Num. 12.6.

CHAP. 4
1 was, or, came to pass.
a ch. 7.12.
2 the battle was spread.
3 the array.
4 take unto us.

[b]which dwelleth *between* [c]the chĕrʹ-ū-
bĭms: and the two sons of Ēʹ-lī, Hŏphʹ-
nī and Phĭnʹ-ĕ-hăs, *were* there with the
ark of the covenant of God.
5 And when the ark of the covenant
of the LORD came into the camp, all
Israel shouted with a great shout, so
that the earth rang again.
6 And when the Philistines heard the
noise of the shout, they said, What
meaneth the noise of this great shout
in the camp of the Hebrews? And they
understood that the ark of the LORD
was come into the camp.
7 And the Philistines were afraid, for
they said, God is come into the camp.
And they said, Woe unto us! for there
hath not been such a thing [5]heretofore.
8 Woe unto us! who shall deliver us
out of the hand of these mighty Gods?
these *are* the Gods that smote the
Egyptians with all the plagues in the
wilderness.
9 Be [d]strong, and quit yourselves like
men, O ye Philistines, that ye be not
servants unto the Hebrews, as [e]they
have been to you: [6]quit yourselves
like men, and fight.
10 ¶ And the Philistines fought, and
[f]Israel was smitten, and they fled
every man into his tent: and there
was a very great slaughter; for there
fell of Israel thirty thousand footmen.
11 And [g]the ark of God was taken;
[h]and the two sons of Ēʹ-lī, Hŏphʹ-nī and
Phĭnʹ-ĕ-hăs, [7]were slain.
12 ¶ And there ran a man of Benjamin out of the army, and came to Shīʹ-
lōh the same day with his clothes rent,
and [i]with earth upon his head.
13 And when he came, lo, Ēʹ-lī sat upon [j]a seat by the wayside watching:
for his heart trembled for the ark of
God. And when the man came into
the city, and told *it*, all the city cried
out.
14 And when Ēʹ-lī heard the noise of
the crying, he said, What *meaneth* the
noise of this tumult? And the man
came in hastily, and told Ēʹ-lī.
15 Now Ēʹ-lī was ninety and eight
years old; and his eyes [8]were dim,
that he could not see.
16 And the man said unto Ēʹ-lī, I *am*
he that came out of the army, and I
fled to day out of the army. And he
said, [k]What [9]is there done, my son?
17 And the messenger answered and
said, Israel is fled before the Philistines, and there hath been also a great
slaughter among the people, and thy
two sons also, Hŏphʹ-nī and Phĭnʹ-ĕ-
hăs, are dead, and the ark of God is
taken.
18 And it came to pass, when he
made mention of the ark of God, that
he fell from off the seat backward by
the side of the gate, and his neck
brake, and he died: for he was an old
man, and heavy. And he had judged
Israel forty years.
19 ¶ And his daughter in law, Phĭnʹ-
ĕ-hăs' wife, was with child, *near* [10]to
be delivered: and when she heard the
tidings that the ark of God was taken,
and that her father in law and her
husband were dead, she bowed herself and travailed; for her pains [11]came
upon her.
20 And about the time of her death
[l]the women that stood by her said unto her, Fear not; for thou hast born
a son. But she answered not, [12]neither
did she regard *it*.
21 And she named the child [13]Īʹ-chă-
bŏd, saying, [m]The glory is departed
from Israel: because the ark of God
was taken, and because of her father
in law and her husband.
22 And she said, The glory is departed from Israel: for the ark of God is
taken.

CHAPTER 5

AND the Philistines took the ark of
God, and brought it from Ĕbʹ-ĕn-
ēʹ-zĕr unto Ăshʹ-dŏd.
2 When the Philistines took the ark
of God, they brought it into the house
of Dāʹ-gŏn, and set it by Dāʹ-gŏn.
3 ¶ And when they of Ăshʹ-dŏd arose
early on the morrow, behold, Dāʹ-gŏn
[a]*was* fallen [b]upon his face to the earth
before the ark of the LORD. And they
took Dāʹ-gŏn, and set [c]him in his place
again.
4 And when they arose early on the
morrow morning, behold, Dāʹ-gŏn *was*
fallen upon his face to the ground before the ark of [d]the LORD; and [e]the
head of Dāʹ-gŏn and both the palms
of his hands *were* cut off upon the
threshold; only [1]*the stump of* Dāʹ-gŏn
was left to him.
5 Therefore neither the priests of Dāʹ-
gŏn, nor any that come into Dāʹ-gŏn's
house, tread [f]on the threshold of Dāʹ-
gŏn in Ăshʹ-dŏd unto this day.
6 But [g]the hand of the LORD was
heavy upon them of Ăshʹ-dŏd, and he
[h]destroyed them, and smote them
with [i]emerods, *even* Ăshʹ-dŏd and the
coasts thereof.
7 And when the men of Ăshʹ-dŏd saw
that *it was* so, they said, The ark of
the God of Israel shall not abide with

b 2 Sam. 6.2. Ps. 80.1.
c Ex. 25.18. Num. 7.89.
5 yesterday, or, the third day.
d 2 Sam. 10. 12. 1 Chr. 19.13. 1 Cor. 16.13. Eph. 6.10, 11.
e Judg. 13.1. ch. 12.9.
6 be men.
f Lev. 26.17. Deut. 28.25. Ps. 78.9,62.
g ch. 2.32. Ps. 78.61.
h Ps. 78.64.
7 died.
i Josh. 7.6. 2 Sam. 13. 19. Neh. 9.1. Job 2.12.
j ch. 1.9.
8 stood.
k 2 Sam. 1.4.
9 Is the thing.
10 Or, to cry out.
11 were turned.
l Gen. 35.17.
12 set not her heart.
13 That is, Where is the glory? or, There is no glory.
m Ps. 26.8. Ps. 78.61. Hosea 9.12.

CHAP. 5

a Ex. 12.12. Judg. 16.23.
b Ex. 18.11. 1 Chr. 16.24, 25,26. Ps. 95.3. Ps. 96.4,5. Isa. 19.1. Nah. 1.14.
c Isa. 46.7.
d Isa. 40.18.
e Jer. 50.2. Eze. 6.4,6. Micah 1.7.
1 Or, the fishy part. The upper part of Dagon resembled a man, and the lower a fish.
f Zeph. 1.9.
g Ex. 9.3. Ps. 7.11. Ps. 9.17. Ps. 32.4. Ps. 75.8. Ps. 139.19. Isa. 31.3. Dan. 4.35. Acts 13.11.
h ch. 6.5.
i Deut. 28.27. Ps. 78.66.

us: for his hand is sore upon us, and upon Dā-gŏn our god.

8 They sent therefore and gathered all the lords of the Philistines unto them, and said, What shall we do with the ark of the God of Israel? And they answered, Let the ark of the God of Israel be carried about unto Gath. And they carried the ark of the God of Israel about *thither*.

9 And it was *so*, that, after they had carried it about, [j]the hand of the LORD was against the city with a very great destruction: and [k]he smote the men of the city, both small and great, and they had emerods in their secret parts.

10 ¶ Therefore they sent the ark of God to Ĕk-rŏn. And it came to pass, as the ark of God came to Ĕk-rŏn, that the Ĕk-rŏn-ītes cried out, saying, They have brought about the ark of the God of Israel to [2]us, to slay us and our people.

11 So they sent and gathered together all the lords of the Philistines, and said, Send away the ark of the God of Israel, and let it go again to his own place, that it slay [3]us not, and our people: for there was a deadly destruction throughout all the city; the hand of God was very heavy there.

12 And the men that died not were smitten with the emerods: and [l]the cry of the city went up to heaven.

CHAPTER 6

AND the ark of the LORD was in the country of the Philistines seven months.

2 And the Philistines [a]called for the priests and the diviners, saying, What shall we do to the ark of the LORD? tell us wherewith we shall send it to his place.

3 And they said, If ye send away the ark of the God of Israel, send it not [b]empty; but in any wise return him [c]a trespass offering: then ye shall be healed, and it shall be known to you why his hand is not removed from you.

4 Then said they, What *shall be* the trespass offering which we shall return to him? They answered, Five golden emerods, and five golden mice, [d]*according to* the number of the lords of the Philistines: for one plague *was* on [1]you all, and on your lords.

5 Wherefore ye shall make images of your emerods, and images of your mice that [e]mar the land; and ye shall [f]give glory unto the God of Israel: peradventure he will [g]lighten his hand from off you, and from off your gods, and from off your land.

6 Wherefore then do ye harden your hearts, [h]as the Egyptians and Pharaoh hardened their hearts? when he had wrought [2]wonderfully among them, [i]did they not let [3]the people go, and they departed?

7 Now therefore make [j]a new cart, and take two milch kine, on [k]which there hath come no yoke, and tie the kine to the cart, and bring their calves home from them:

8 And take the ark of the LORD, and lay it upon the cart; and put the jewels of gold, which ye return him *for* a trespass offering, in a coffer by the side thereof; and send it away, that it may go.

9 And see, if it goeth up by the way of his own coast to [l]Bĕth–shē-mĕsh, *then* [4]he hath done us this great evil: but if not, then we shall know that *it is* not his hand *that* smote us; it *was* a chance *that* happened to us.

10 ¶ And the men did so; and took two milch kine, and tied them to the cart, and shut up their calves at home:

11 And they laid the ark of the LORD upon the cart, and the coffer with the mice of gold and the images of their emerods.

12 And the kine took the straight way to the way of Bĕth–shē-mĕsh, *and* [5]went along the highway, lowing as they went, and turned not aside *to* the right hand or *to* the left; and the lords of the Philistines went after them unto the border of Bĕth–shē-mĕsh.

13 And *they of* Bĕth–shē-mĕsh *were* reaping their wheat harvest in the valley: and they lifted up their eyes, and saw the ark, and rejoiced to see *it*.

14 And the cart came into the field of Joshua, a Bĕth–shē-mīte, and stood there, where *there was* a great stone: and they clave the wood of the cart, and offered the kine a burnt offering unto the LORD.

15 And the Levites took down the ark of the LORD, and the coffer that *was* with it, wherein the jewels of gold *were*, and put *them* on the great stone: and the men of Bĕth–shē-mĕsh offered burnt offerings and sacrificed sacrifices the same day unto the LORD.

16 And [m]when the five lords of the Philistines had seen *it*, they returned to Ĕk-rŏn the same day.

17 And these *are* the golden emerods which the Philistines returned *for* a trespass offering unto the LORD; for Ăsh-dŏd one, for Gā-ză one, for Ăs-

j Deut. 2.15. ch. 7.13.
k Ps. 78.66.
2 me, to slay me and my.
3 me not, and my.
l Ex. 11.6. Pro. 21.13. Isa. 15.3. Jer. 25.34. Amos 5.17.

CHAP. 6
a Gen. 41.8. Ex. 7.11. Dan. 2.2. Matt. 2.4.
b Ex. 23.15. Deut. 16.16.
c Lev. 5.15. Lev. 6.6.
d Josh. 13.3. Judg. 3.3.
1 them.
e ch. 5.6.
f Josh. 7.19. 1 Chr. 16.28. Isa. 42.12. Jer. 13.16. Mal. 2.2. John 9.24. Rev. 14.7.
g Ex. 9.3. ch. 5.6, 11. Ps. 39.10. Acts 13.11.
h Ex. 7.13. Ex. 8.15.
2 Or, reproachfully.
i Ex. 3.19, 20. Ex. 6.1. Ex. 11.1, 8. Ps. 105.38.
3 them.
j 2 Sam. 6.3.
k Num. 19.2.
l Josh. 15.10.
4 Or, it.
5 in a street they went.
m Josh. 13.3. Judg. 3.3. ch. 29.2. Zeph. 2.5.

kĕ-lon one, for Gath one, for Ĕk′-rŏn
one;
18 And the golden mice, *according to*
the number of all the cities of the
Philistines *belonging* to the five lords,
both of fenced cities, and of country
villages, even unto the [6]great *stone of*
Abel, whereon they set down the ark
of the LORD: *which stone remaineth*
unto this day in the field of Joshua,
the Bĕth–shē′-mīte.
19 ¶ And [n]he smote the men of Bĕth–
shē′-mĕsh, because they had looked
into the ark of the LORD, even he
smote of the people fifty thousand and
threescore and ten men: and the people lamented, because the LORD had
smitten *many* of the people with a
great slaughter.
20 And the men of Bĕth–shē′-mĕsh
said, Who [o]is able to stand before this
holy LORD God? and to whom shall
he go up from us?
21 ¶ And they sent messengers to the
inhabitants [p]of Kĭr′-jăth–jē′-ă-rĭm, saying, The Philistines have brought
again the ark of the LORD; come ye
down, *and* fetch it up to you.

CHAPTER 7

AND the men of [a]Kĭr′-jăth–jē′-ă-rĭm
came, and fetched up the ark of
the LORD, and brought it into the
house of [b]Ă-bĭn′-ă-dăb in the hill, and
sanctified Ĕl-ē-ā′-zär his son to keep
the ark of the LORD.
2 And it came to pass, while the ark
abode in Kĭr′-jăth–jē′-ă-rĭm, that the
time was long; for it was twenty years:
and all the house of Israel lamented
after the LORD.
3 ¶ And Samuel spake unto all the
house of Israel, saying, If ye do [c]return
unto the LORD with all your hearts,
then [d]put away the strange gods and
[e]Ăsh′-tă-rōth from among you, and
[f]prepare your hearts unto the LORD,
and [g]serve him only: and he will deliver you out of the hand of the Philistines.
4 Then the children of Israel did put
away Bā′-ă-lĭm [h]and Ăsh′-tă-rōth, and
served the LORD only.
5 And Samuel said, [i]Gather all Israel
to Mĭz′-pēh, and I will pray for you unto the LORD.
6 And they gathered together to Mĭz′-
pēh, and [j]drew water, and poured *it*
out before the LORD, and fasted [k]on
that day, and said there, [l]We have
sinned against the LORD. And Samuel
judged the children of Israel in Mĭz′-
pēh.
7 And when the Philistines heard that
the children of Israel were gathered
together to Mĭz′-pēh, the lords of the
Philistines went up against Israel. And
when the children of Israel heard *it*,
they were afraid of the Philistines.
8 And the children of Israel said to
Samuel, [1]Cease not to cry unto the
LORD our God for us, that he will save
us out of the hand of the Philistines.
9 ¶ And Samuel took a sucking lamb,
and offered *it for* a burnt offering
wholly unto the LORD: and [m]Samuel
cried unto the LORD for Israel; and the
LORD [2]heard him.
10 And as Samuel was offering up
the burnt offering, the Philistines drew
near to battle against Israel: [n]but the
LORD thundered with a great thunder
on that day upon the Philistines, and
discomfited them; and they were smitten before Israel.
11 And the men of Israel went out of
Mĭz′-pēh, and pursued the Philistines,
and smote them, until *they came* under
Bĕth′–cär.
12 Then Samuel took a stone, and
set *it* between Mĭz′-pēh and Shen, and
called the name of it [3]Ĕb-ĕn–ē′-zĕr,
saying, Hitherto hath the LORD helped
us.
13 ¶ So [o]the Philistines were subdued, and they [p]came no more into
the coast of Israel: and the hand of
the LORD was against the Philistines
all the days of Samuel.
14 And the cities which the Philistines had taken from Israel were restored to Israel, from Ĕk′-rŏn even unto Gath; and the coasts thereof did
Israel deliver out of the hands of the
Philistines. And there was peace between Israel and the Amorites.
15 And Samuel [q]judged Israel all the
days of his life.
16 And he went from year to year [4]in
circuit to Beth-el, and Gĭl′-găl, and
Mĭz′-pēh, and judged Israel in all those
places.
17 And his return *was* to Rā′-măh;
for there *was* his house; and there he
judged Israel; and there he built an
[r]altar unto the LORD.

CHAPTER 8

AND it came to pass, when Samuel
was old, that he [a]made his [b]sons
judges over Israel.
2 Now the name of his firstborn was
[1]Jō′-ĕl; and the name of his second,
Ă-bī′-ăh: *they were* judges in Bē′ĕr–
shē′-bă.
3 And his sons [c]walked not in his

6 Or, great Abel, that is, mourning.
n Ex. 19.21. Lev. 10.1-3. Num. 4.5, 15, 20. Deut. 29.29. 2 Sam. 6.7. Col. 2.18. 1 Pet. 4.17.
o 2 Sam. 6.9. Mal. 3.2. Rev. 6.17.
p Josh. 18.14. Judg. 18.12. 1 Chr. 13.5, 6.

CHAP. 7

a ch. 6.21. Ps. 132.6.
b 2 Sam. 6.4.
c Deut. 30.2. 1 Ki. 8.48. Isa. 55.7. Hosea 6.1. Joel 2,12.
d Gen. 35.2.
e Judg. 2.13.
f Deut. 30.6. 2 Chr. 30.19. Job 11.13. Pro. 16.1. Matt. 15.8.
g Deut. 6.13. Deut. 10.20. Josh. 24.14. Matt. 4.10. Luke 4.8.
h Judg. 2.11.
i Judg. 10.17. Judg. 11.11. ch. 10.17. 2 Ki. 25.23.
j 2 Sam. 14. 14.
k Neh. 9.1,2. Dan. 9.3. Joel 2.12.
l Lev. 26.40. Judg. 10.10. 1 Ki. 8.47. Job 33.27, 28. Ps. 106.6.
1 Be not silent from us from crying.
m Ps. 99.6.
2 Or, answered.
n Josh. 10.10. Judg. 4.15. ch. 2.10.
3 That is, the stone of help.
o Judg. 13.1.
p ch. 13.5.
q ch. 12.11.
4 and he circuited.
r Judg. 21.4.

CHAP. 8

a Deut. 16.18.
b Judg. 10.4. Judg. 12.14, compared with Judg. 5.10.
1 Vashni.
c Eccl. 2.19. Jer. 22.15.

ays, but turned aside after [d]lucre,
nd [e]took bribes, and perverted judg-
nent.
4 Then all the elders of Israel gather-
d themselves together, and came to
amuel unto Rā-măh,
5 And said unto him, Behold, thou
rt old, and thy sons walk not in thy
ays: now [f]make us a king to judge us
ke all the nations.
6 ¶ But the thing [2]displeased Samuel,
hen they said, Give us a king to
udge us. And Samuel prayed [g]unto
he LORD.
7 And the LORD said unto Samuel,
Iearken unto the voice of the people
n all that they say unto thee: for [h]they
ave not rejected thee, but [i]they have
ejected me, that I should not reign
ver them.
8 According to all the works which
hey have done since the day that I
rought them up out of Egypt even
nto this day, wherewith they have
orsaken me, and served other gods,
o do they also unto thee.
9 Now therefore [3]hearken unto their
oice: [4]howbeit yet protest solemnly
nto them, and shew them the man-
er of the king that shall reign over
hem.
10 ¶ And Samuel told all the words
f the LORD unto the people that
sked of him a king.
11 And he said, [j]This will be the
nanner of the king that shall reign
ver you: [k]He will take your sons, and
ppoint *them* for himself, for his chari-
ts, and *to be* his horsemen; and *some*
hall run before his chariots.
12 And he will appoint him captains
ver thousands, and captains over
fties; and *will set them* to ear his
round, and to reap his harvest, and
o make his instruments of war, and
nstruments of his chariots.
13 And he will take your daughters
o be confectionaries, and *to be* cooks,
nd *to be* bakers.
14 And [l]he will take your fields, and
our vineyards, and your oliveyards,
ven the best *of them*, and give *them*
o his servants.
15 And he will take the tenth of your
eed, and of your vineyards, and give
o his [5]officers, and to his servants.
16 And he will take your menser-
ants, and your maidservants, and
our goodliest young men, and your
sses, and put *them* to his work.
17 He will take the tenth of your
heep: and ye shall be his servants.
18 And ye shall cry out in that day

d Ex. 18.21. Deut. 16.19. 1 Tim. 3.3.
e Deut. 16.19. Ps. 15.5.
f ch. 12.13. Hosea 13. 10. Acts 13.21.
2 was evil in the eyes of Samuel.
g ch. 15.11. Pro. 3.5.
h Ex. 16.8. Matt. 10.24, 25. Luke 10.16.
i ch. 10.19.
3 Or, obey.
4 Or, notwithstanding when thou hast solemnly protested against them, then thou shalt shew, etc.
j Deut. 17.16.
k ch. 14.52. 2 Chr. 26. 10-15.
l 1 Ki. 21.7.
5 eunuchs.
m Job 27.9. Ps. 18.41. Pro. 1.25. Isa. 1.15. Micah 3.4. Luke 13.25.
n Isa. 66.4. Jer. 44.16.
o Hosea 13. 11.

CHAP. 9

a ch. 14.51. 1 Chr. 8.33. Acts 13.21.
1 Or, the son of a man of Jemini.
2 Or, substance.
b ch. 10.23.
c 2 Ki. 4.42.
d ch. 1.1.
e Deut. 33.1. ch. 2.27. 1 Ki. 13.1. 2 Ki. 6.6. 1 Tim. 6.11.
f ch. 3.19. Isa. 44.26. Matt. 24.35.
g Judg. 6.18. 1 Ki. 14.3. 2 Ki. 4.42.
3 is gone out of, etc.
4 is with us.

because of your king which ye shall
have chosen you; and the LORD [m]will
not hear you in that day.
19 ¶ Nevertheless the people [n]refused
to obey the voice of Samuel; and they
said, Nay; but we will have a king
over us;
20 That we also may be like all the
nations; and that our king may judge
us, and go out before us, and fight our
battles.
21 And Samuel heard all the words
of the people, and he rehearsed them
in the ears of the LORD.
22 And the LORD said to Samuel,
Hearken [o]unto their voice, and make
them a king. And Samuel said unto
the men of Israel, Go ye every man
unto his city.

CHAPTER 9

NOW there was a man of Benjamin, whose name *was* [a]Kish, the
son of Ă-bī-ĕl, the son of Zē-rôr, the
son of Bĕ-chō-răth, the son of Ă-phī-
ăh, [1]a Benjamite, a mighty man of
[2]power.
2 And he had a son, whose name *was*
Saul, a choice young man, and a goodly: and *there was* not among the children of Israel a goodlier person than
he: [b]from his shoulders and upward
he was higher than any of the people.
3 And the asses of Kish Saul's father
were lost. And Kish said to Saul his
son, Take now one of the servants
with thee, and arise, go seek the asses.
4 And he passed through mount Ē-
phră-ĭm, and passed through the land
of [c]Shăl-ĭ-shă, but they found *them*
not: then they passed through the
land of Shā-lĭm, and *there they were*
not: and he passed through the land
of the Benjamites, but they found
them not.
5 *And* when they were come to the
land of [d]Zuph, Saul said to his servant
that *was* with him, Come, and let us
return; lest my father leave *caring* for
the asses, and take thought for us.
6 And he said unto him, Behold now,
there is in this city [e]a man of God, and
he is an honourable man; all [f]that he
saith cometh surely to pass: now let
us go thither; peradventure he can
shew us our way that we should go.
7 Then said Saul to his servant, But,
behold, *if* we go, [g]what shall we bring
the man? for the bread [3]is spent in our
vessels, and *there is* not a present to
bring to the man of God: what [4]have
we?
8 And the servant answered Saul

again, and said, Behold, [5]I have here
at hand the fourth part of a shekel of
silver: *that* will I give to the man of
God, to tell us our way.
9 (Beforetime in Israel, when a man
[h]went to inquire of God, thus he
spake, Come, and let us go to the seer:
for *he that is* now *called* a Prophet was
beforetime called [i]a Seer.)
10 Then said Saul to his servant,
[6]Well said; come, let us go. So they
went unto the city where the man of
God *was*.
11 ¶ *And* as they went up [7]the hill to
the city, [j]they found young maidens
going out to draw water, and said unto
them, Is the seer here?
12 And they answered them, and
said, He is; behold, *he is* before you:
make haste now, for he came to day
to the city; for *there* [k]*is* a [8]sacrifice of
the people to day in the [l]high place:
13 As soon as ye be come into the
city, ye shall straightway find him, before he go up to the high place to eat:
for the people will not eat until he
come, because he doth bless the sacrifice; *and* afterwards they eat that be
bidden. Now therefore get you up;
for about [9]this time ye shall find
him.
14 And they went up into the city:
and when they were come into the
city, behold, Samuel came out against
them, for to go up to the high place.
15 ¶ Now [m]the LORD had [10]told
Samuel in his ear a day before Saul
came, saying,
16 To morrow about this time I will
send thee a man out of the land of
Benjamin, and [n]thou shalt anoint him
to be captain over my people Israel,
that he may save my people out of the
hand of the Philistines: for I have
[o]looked upon my people, because their
cry is come unto me.
17 And when Samuel saw Saul, the
LORD said unto him, [p]Behold the man
whom I spake to thee of! this same
shall [11]reign over my people.
18 Then Saul drew near to Samuel in
the gate, and said, Tell me, I pray
thee, where the seer's house *is*.
19 And Samuel answered Saul, and
said, I *am* the seer: go up before me
unto the high place; for ye shall eat
with me to day, and to morrow I will
let thee go, and will tell thee all that
is in thine heart.
20 And as for thine asses that were
lost [12]three days ago, set not thy mind
on them; for they are found. And on
whom *is* all the desire of Israel? *Is it*

5 there is found in my hand.
h Gen. 25.22. Ex. 28.30. Num. 27.21. Judg. 1.1.
i 2 Sam. 24. 11. 2 Ki. 17.13. 1 Chr. 29.29. Isa. 30.10. Amos 7.12.
6 Thy word is good.
7 in the ascent of the city.
j Gen. 24.11. Ex. 2.16.
k Gen. 31.54. ch. 16.2.
8 Or, feast.
l 1 Ki. 3.2.
9 to day.
m ch. 15.1. Ps. 25.14. Mark 11.2, 4. Acts 13.21.
10 revealed the ear of Samuel.
n ch. 10.1. ch. 15.1. ch. 16.3.
o Ex. 2.25. Ex. 3.7,9.
p ch. 16.12. Hosea 13. 11.
11 restrain in.
12 to day three days.
q Judg. 20.46. Ps. 68.27.
r Judg. 6.15.
13 according to this word.
s Lev. 7.32. Eze. 24.4. Acts 10.9.
14 Or, reserved.
t Deut. 22.8.
15 to day.
16 Or, cause thee to hear.
CHAP. 10
a ch. 16.13. 2 Ki. 9.3.
b Ex. 19.5,6. Deut. 32.9. Jer. 10.16.
c Gen. 35.19.
d Josh. 18.28.
1 the business.
e Josh. 19.22. Judg. 4.6,12. Ps. 89.12.
f Gen. 28.22. Gen. 35.1.

not on thee, and on all thy father
house?
21 And Saul answered and said, A
not I a Benjamite, of [q]the smallest
the tribes of Israel? and my [r]fami
the least of all the families of the tri
of Benjamin? wherefore then spea
est thou [13]so to me?
22 And Samuel took Saul and h
servant, and brought them into t
parlour, and made them sit in t
chiefest place among them that we
bidden, which *were* about thirty pe
sons.
23 And Samuel said unto the coo
Bring the portion which I gave the
of which I said unto thee, Set it b
thee.
24 And the cook took up [s]the sho
der, and *that* which *was* upon it, ar
set *it* before Saul. And *Samuel* sai
Behold that which is [14]left! set *it* b
fore thee, *and* eat: for unto this tin
hath it been kept for thee since I sai
I have invited the people. So Saul d
eat with Samuel that day.
25 ¶ And when they were come dov
from the high place into the cit
Samuel communed with Saul up
[t]the top of the house.
26 And they arose early: and it can
to pass about the spring of the da
that Samuel called Saul to the top
the house, saying, Up, that I ma
send thee away. And Saul arose, ar
they went out both of them, he ar
Samuel, abroad.
27 *And* as they were going down
the end of the city, Samuel said
Saul, Bid the servant pass on befo
us, (and he passed on,) but stand tho
still [15]a while, that I may [16]shew the
the word of God.

CHAPTER 10

THEN [a]Samuel took a vial of oi
and poured *it* upon his head, ar
kissed him, and said, *Is it* not becau
the LORD hath anointed thee *to b*
captain over his [b]inheritance?
2 When thou art departed from m
to day, then thou shalt find two me
by Rachel's [c]sepulchre in the bord
of Benjamin [d]at Zĕl'zăh; and they wi
say unto thee, The asses which tho
wentest to seek are found: and, l
thy father hath left [1]the care of th
asses, and sorroweth for you, sayin
What shall I do for my son?
3 Then shalt thou go on forward fro
thence, and thou shalt come to th
plain of [e]Tā'bôr, and there shall me
thee three men going up to God [f]

eth-el, one carrying three kids, and
nother carrying three loaves of bread,
nd another carrying a bottle of wine:
4 And they will [2]salute thee, and give
ee two *loaves* of bread; which thou
halt receive of their hands.
5 After that thou shalt come to the
ill of God, [g]where *is* the garrison of
e Philistines: and it shall come to
ass, when thou art come thither to
e city, that thou shalt meet a com-
any of prophets coming down from
the high place with a psaltery, and a
bret, and a pipe, and a harp, before
em: [i]and they shall prophesy:
6 And [j]the Spirit of the LORD will
ome upon thee, and [k]thou shalt pro-
hesy with them, and shalt be turned
nto another man.
7 And [3]let it be, when [l]these signs
re come unto thee, [4]*that* thou do as
ccasion serve thee; for God [m]*is* with
ee.
8 And thou shalt go down before me
o Gĭl'-găl; and, behold, I will come
own unto thee, to offer burnt offer-
ngs, *and* to sacrifice sacrifices of peace
fferings: [o]seven days shalt thou tarry,
ll I come to thee, and shew thee what
ou shalt do.
9 ¶ And it was *so*, that when he had
rned his [5]back to go from Samuel,
od [6]gave him another heart: and all
ose signs came to pass that day.
10 And when they came thither to
e hill, behold, [p]a company of pro-
hets met him; and the Spirit of God
ame upon him, and [q]he prophesied
mong them.
11 And it came to pass, when all that
new him beforetime saw that, beold, he prophesied among the pro-
hets, then the people said [7]one to
nother, What *is* this *that* is come unto
e son of Kish? [r]*Is* Saul also among
e prophets?
12 And one [8]of the same place an-
vered and said, But [s]who *is* their
ther? Therefore it became a prov-
rb, *Is* Saul also among the prophets?
13 And when he had made an end of
rophesying, he came to the high
lace.
14 ¶ And Saul's [t]uncle said unto him
nd to his servant, Whither went ye?
nd he said, To seek the asses: and
hen we saw that *they were* no where,
e came to Samuel.
15 And Saul's uncle said, Tell me, I
ray thee, what Samuel said unto you.
16 And Saul said unto his uncle, He
ld us plainly that the asses were
und. But of the matter of the king-

2 ask thee of peace.
g ch. 13.3.
h ch. 9.12.
i Ex. 15.20. 2 Ki. 3.15. 1 Cor. 14.1.
j Num. 11.25. Judg. 14.6. ch. 16.13. Matt. 7.22.
k ch. 19.23.
3 it shall come to pass, that when these signs, etc.
l Ex. 4.8.
4 do for thee as thine hand shall find.
m Gen. 21.20. Deut. 20.1. Judg. 6.12. Matt. 1.23.
n ch. 11.14.
o ch. 13.8.
5 shoulder.
6 turned.
p ch. 19.20.
q Matt. 7.21-23.
7 a man to his neighbour.
r Matt. 13.54. John 7.15. Acts 4.13.
8 from thence.
s Isa. 54.13.
t ch. 14.50.
u Judg. 11.11. ch. 11.15.
v ch. 7.5.
w Ex. 3.7,8. Ex. 14.11. Deut. 4.34. Judg. 6.8. Neh. 9.9-12, 27,28.
x ch. 8.7. ch. 12.12.
y Josh. 7.14. Acts 1.24.
z ch. 23.2.
9 Let the king live.
a Deut. 17.14. ch. 8.11.
b Deut. 13. 13. ch. 11.12. Acts 7.35, 51,52.
c 2 Sam. 8.2. 1 Ki. 4.21. 2 Chr. 17.5. Ps. 72.10. Matt. 2.11.
10 Or, he was as though he had been deaf.

CHAP. 11

a Judg. 21.8. ch. 31.11-13.
b Gen. 26.28. Ex. 23.32. 1 Ki. 20.34. Job 41.4. Eze. 17.13.

dom, whereof Samuel spake, he told
him not.
17 ¶ And Samuel called the people
together [u]unto the LORD to [v]Mĭz'-pēh;
18 And said unto the children of Israel, Thus [w]saith the LORD God of Israel, I brought up Israel out of Egypt,
and delivered you out of the hand of
the Egyptians, and out of the hand of
all kingdoms, *and* of them that oppressed you:
19 And [x]ye have this day rejected
your God, who himself saved you out
of all your adversities and your tribulations; and ye have said unto him,
Nay, but set a king over us. Now
therefore present yourselves before
the LORD by your tribes, and by your
thousands.
20 And when Samuel [y]had caused
all the tribes of Israel to come near,
the tribe of Benjamin was taken.
21 When he had caused the tribe of
Benjamin to come near by their families, the family of Mā'-trī was taken,
and Saul the son of Kish was taken:
and when they sought him, he could
not be found.
22 Therefore they [z]inquired of the
LORD further, if the man should yet
come thither. And the LORD answered, Behold, he hath hid himself among
the stuff.
23 And they ran and fetched him
thence: and when he stood among the
people, he was higher than any of the
people from his shoulders and upward.
24 And Samuel said to all the people,
See ye him whom the LORD hath
chosen, that *there is* none like him
among all the people? And all the
people shouted, and said, [9]God save
the king.
25 Then Samuel told the people the
[a]manner of the kingdom, and wrote *it*
in a book, and laid *it* up before the
LORD. And Samuel sent all the people
away, every man to his house.
26 ¶ And Saul also went home to
Gĭb'-ĕ-āh; and there went with him a
band of men, whose hearts God had
touched.
27 But [b]the children of Bē'-lĭ-ăl said,
How shall this man save us? And they
despised him, [c]and brought him no
presents. But [10]he held his peace.

CHAPTER 11

THEN Nahash the Ammonite came
up, and encamped against [a]Jā'-
bĕsh–gĭl'-ĕ-ăd: and all the men of Jā'-
bĕsh said unto Nahash, [b]Make a cov-

enant with us, and we will serve thee.
2 And Nahash the Ammonite answered them, On this *condition* will I
make *a covenant* with you, that I may
thrust out all your right eyes, and lay
it *for* [c]a reproach upon all Israel.
3 And the elders of Jā-bĕsh said unto
him, [1]Give us seven days' respite, that
we may send messengers unto all the
coasts of Israel: and then, if *there be*
no man to save us, we will come out
to thee.
4 ¶ Then came the messengers to
[d]Gĭb-ĕ-ăh of Saul, and told the tidings
in the ears of the people: and [e]all the
people lifted up their voices, and wept.
5 And, behold, Saul came after the
herd out of the field; and Saul said,
What *aileth* the people that they
weep? And they told him the tidings
of the men of Jā-bĕsh.
6 And [f]the Spirit of God came upon
Saul when he heard those tidings, and
his anger was kindled greatly.
7 And he took a yoke of oxen, and
[g]hewed them in pieces, and sent *them*
throughout all the coasts of Israel by
the hands of messengers, saying,
[h]Whosoever cometh not forth after
Saul and after Samuel, so shall it be
done unto his oxen. And [i]the fear of
the LORD fell on the people, and they
came out [2]with one consent.
8 And when he numbered them in
[j]Bē-zĕk, the children [k]of Israel were
three hundred thousand, and the men
of Judah thirty thousand.
9 And they said unto the messengers
that came, Thus shall ye say unto the
men of Jā-bĕsh-gĭl-ĕ-ăd, To morrow,
by *that time* the sun be hot, ye shall
have [3]help. And the messengers came
and shewed *it* to the men of Jā-bĕsh;
and they were glad.
10 Therefore the men of Jā-bĕsh
said, To morrow we will come out unto you, and ye shall do with us all that
seemeth good unto you.
11 And it was *so* on the morrow, that
[l]Saul put the people [m]in three companies; and they came into the midst
of the host in the morning watch, and
slew the Ammonites until the heat of
the day: and it came to pass, that they
which remained were scattered, so
[n]that two of them were not left together.
12 ¶ And the people said unto
Samuel, Who *is* he that said, Shall
[o]Saul reign over us? [p]bring the men,
that we may put them to death.
13 And Saul said, [q]There shall not a
man be put to death this day: for to
day [r]the LORD hath wrought salvatic
in Israel.
14 Then said Samuel to the peopl
Come, and let us go [s]to Gĭl-găl, an
renew the kingdom there.
15 And all the people went to Gi
găl; and there they made Saul kir
before the LORD in Gĭl-găl; and the
they sacrificed sacrifices of peace o
ferings before the LORD; and the
Saul and all the men of Israel rejoice
greatly.

CHAPTER 12

AND Samuel said unto all Israe
Behold, I have hearkened unt
[a]your voice in all that ye said unto m
and [b]have made a king over you.
2 And now, behold, the king [c]walket
before you: and I am old and gra
headed; and, behold, my sons *a*
with you: and I have walked befo
you from my childhood unto this da
3 Behold, here I *am:* witness again
me before the LORD, and before h
anointed: whose [d]ox have I taken?
whose ass have I taken? or who
have I defrauded? whom have I o
pressed? or of whose hand have I r
ceived *any* [1]bribe [2]to [e]blind mine ey
therewith? and I will restore it you.
4 And they said, Thou hast not d
frauded us, nor oppressed us, neith
hast thou taken ought of any man
hand.
5 And he said unto them, The LOR
is witness against you, and his anoin
ed *is* witness this day, that [f]ye hav
not found ought [g]in my hand. An
they answered, *He is* witness.
6 ¶ And Samuel said unto the pe
ple, *It* [h]*is* the LORD that [3]advance
Moses and Aaron, and that broug
your fathers up out of the land o
Egypt.
7 Now therefore stand still, that
may reason [i]with you before the LOR
of all the [4]righteous acts of the LOR
which he did [5]to you and to you
fathers.
8 When Jacob was come into Egyp
and your fathers cried unto the LOR
then the LORD sent Moses and Aaro
which brought forth your fathers ou
of Egypt, and made them dwell in th
place.
9 And when they forgat the LOR
their God, he sold them into the han
of Sĭs-ĕ-ră, captain of the host of Hā
zôr, and into the hand of the Phili
tines, and into the hand of the king
Moab, and they fought against them
10 And they cried unto the LOR
and said, We have sinned, because w

c Gen. 34.14. ch. 17.26.
1 Forbear us.
d ch. 10.26. ch. 14.2. 2 Sam. 21.6.
e Judg. 2.4. Judg. 21.2. Rom. 12.15.
f Judg. 3.10. Judg. 6.34. Judg. 11.29. ch. 10.10. ch. 16.13.
g Judg. 19.29.
h Judg. 21.5.
i Gen. 35.5. 2 Chr. 14.14. 2 Chr. 17.10. Pro. 14.26.
2 as one man.
j Judg. 1.5.
k 2 Sam. 24.9.
3 Or, deliverance.
l ch. 31.11.
m Judg. 7.16.
n Jas. 2.13.
o ch. 10.27. Ps. 21.8.
p Luke 19.27.
q 2 Sam. 19. 22.
r Ex. 14.13, 30. ch. 14.45. ch. 19.5.
s ch. 10.8.
CHAP. 12
a ch. 8.5.
b ch. 10.24.
c Num. 27. 17. ch. 8.20.
d Num. 16. 15. Acts 20.33. 1 Thes. 2.5.
1 ransom.
2 Or, that I should hide mine eyes at him.
e Deut. 16.19.
f John 18.38. Acts 23.9. 2 Cor. 1.12.
g Ex. 22.4. Ps. 17.3.
h Ex. 6.26. Neh. 9.9-14. Ps. 77.19, 20. Hosea 12. 13. Micah 6.4.
3 Or, made.
i Isa. 1.18. Isa. 5.3. Micah 6.2,3.
4 righteousnesses, or, benefits.
5 with.

ave forsaken the LORD, and have
erved Bā-ā-lim and Ăsh-tă-rōth: but
ow deliver us out of the hand of our
nemies, and we will serve thee.
11 And the LORD sent Jĕr-ŭb-bā-ăl,
nd Bē-dăn, and Jĕph-thăh, and
amuel, and delivered you out of the
and of your enemies on every side,
nd ye dwelled safe.
12 And when ye saw that Nahash
he king of the children of Ammon
ame against you, ye said unto me,
Nay; but a king shall reign over us:
hen [j]the LORD your God *was* your
ing.
13 Now therefore behold the king
hom ye have chosen, *and* whom ye
ave desired! and, behold, [k]the LORD
ath set a king over you.
14 If ye will [l]fear the LORD, and serve
im, and obey his voice, and not rebel
gainst the [6]commandment of the
ORD, then shall both ye and also the
ing that reigneth over you [7]continue
ollowing the LORD your God:
15 But if ye will [m]not obey the voice
f the LORD, but rebel against the
ommandment of the LORD, then
hall the hand of the LORD be against
ou, as *it was* against your fathers.
16 ¶ Now therefore stand and see
his great thing, which the LORD will
o before your eyes.
17 *Is it* not [n]wheat harvest to day?
will call unto the LORD, and he shall
end thunder and rain; that ye may
erceive and see that [p]your wicked-
ess *is* great, which ye have done in
e sight of the LORD, in asking you
king.
18 So Samuel called unto the LORD;
nd the LORD sent thunder and rain
at day: [q]and all the people greatly
ared the LORD and Samuel.
19 And all the people said unto
amuel, [r]Pray for thy servants unto
e LORD thy God, that we die not: for
e have added unto all our sins *this*
il, to ask us a king.
20 ¶ And Samuel said unto the peo-
le, Fear not: ye have done all this
ickedness: yet turn not aside from
ollowing the LORD, but serve the
ORD with all your heart;
21 And turn ye not aside: [s]for *then*
ould ye go after vain *things*, which
nnot profit nor deliver; for they *are*
in.
22 For the LORD will not forsake his
ople [t]for his great name's sake: be-
use [u]it hath pleased the LORD to
ake you his people.
23 Moreover as for me, [v]God forbid

j Gen. 17.7. Judg. 8.23. ch. 8.7.
k Hosea 13. 11.
l Deut. 6.13. Deut. 10.12. Deut. 13.4. Deut. 14.23. Deut. 17.19. Josh. 24.14. Ps. 81.13. Eccl. 8.12. Isa. 3.10.
6 mouth.
7 be after.
m Lev. 26.14. Deut. 28.15. Josh. 24.20.
n Pro. 26.1.
o Josh. 10.12. ch. 7.9. Jas. 5.16.
p ch. 8.7. Hosea 13. 10.
q Ex. 14.31. Ezra 10.9.
r Gen. 20.7. Ex. 9.28. Ps. 78.34,35. Acts 8.24. Jas. 5.15. 1 John 5.16.
s Jer. 16.19. Hab. 2.18. 1 Cor. 8.4.
t Ps. 106.8. Jer. 14.21.
u Mal. 1.2. Matt. 11.26. John 15.16.
v 1 Cor. 9.16.
8 from ceasing.
w 1 Ki. 8.36. 2 Chr. 6.27. Jer. 6.16.
x Ezra 9.13.
9 Or, what a great thing, etc.
y Josh. 24.20.
z Deut. 28.36.

CHAP. 13

1 the son of one year in his reigning.
a ch. 10.5.
2 Or, the hill.
3 did stink.
b Josh. 18.12.
c Judg. 6.2.
4 trembled after him.
d ch. 10.8.
e Deut. 12.5-14. ch. 15.22. 1 Ki. 3.4. 2 Chr. 26.16. Pro. 15.8. Pro. 21.3,27. Heb. 5.4.

that I should sin against the LORD [8]in
ceasing to pray for you: but I will
teach you the good [w]and the right way:
24 Only fear the LORD, and serve
him in truth with all your [x]heart: for
consider [9]how great *things* he hath
done for you.
25 But if ye shall still do wickedly,
[y]ye shall be consumed, [z]both ye and
your king.

CHAPTER 13

SAUL [1]reigned one year; and when
he had reigned two years over
Israel,
2 Saul chose him three thousand
men of Israel; *whereof* two thousand
were with Saul in Mĭch-măsh and in
mount Beth-el, and a thousand were
with Jonathan in Gĭb-ĕ-ăh of Benjamin: and the rest of the people he sent
every man to his tent.
3 And Jonathan smote [a]the garrison
of the Philistines that *was* in [2]Gē-bă,
and the Philistines heard *of it*. And
Saul blew the trumpet throughout all
the land, saying, Let the Hebrews
hear.
4 And all Israel heard say *that* Saul
had smitten a garrison of the Philistines, and *that* Israel also [3]was had
in abomination with the Philistines.
And the people were called together
after Saul to Gĭl-găl.
5 ¶ And the Philistines gathered
themselves together to fight with Israel, thirty thousand chariots, and
six thousand horsemen, and people
as the sand which *is* on the sea shore
in multitude: and they came up, and
[b]pitched in Mĭch-măsh, eastward
from Bĕth–ā-vĕn.
6 When the men of Israel saw that
they were in a strait, (for the people
were distressed,) then the people [c]did
hide themselves in caves, and in thickets, and in rocks, and in high places,
and in pits.
7 And *some of* the Hebrews went over
Jordan to the land of Gad and Gilead.
As for Saul, he *was* yet in Gĭl-găl, and
all the people [4]followed him trembling.
8 ¶ And [d]he tarried seven days, according to the set time that Samuel
had appointed: but Samuel came not
to Gĭl-găl; and the people were scattered from him.
9 And Saul said, Bring hither a burnt
offering to me, and peace offerings.
And he [e]offered the burnt offering.
10 And it came to pass, that as soon
as he had made an end of offering the
burnt offering, behold, Samuel came;

and Saul went out to meet him, that
he might [5]salute him.
11 ¶ And Samuel said, What hast
thou done? And Saul said, Because I
saw that the people were scattered
from me, and *that* thou camest not
within the days appointed, and *that*
the Philistines gathered themselves together at Mĭch-'măsh;
12 Therefore said I, The Philistines
will come down now upon me to Gĭl-'
găl, and I have not [6]made supplication unto the LORD: I forced myself
therefore, and offered a burnt offering.
13 And Samuel said to Saul, Thou
[f]hast done foolishly: [g]thou hast not
kept the commandment of the LORD
thy God, which he commanded thee:
for now would the LORD have established thy kingdom upon Israel for
ever.
14 But [h]now thy kingdom shall not
continue: [i]the LORD hath sought him
a man after his own heart, and the
LORD hath commanded him *to be*
captain over his people, because thou
hast not kept *that* which the LORD
commanded thee.
15 And Samuel arose, and gat him up
from Gĭl-'găl unto Gĭb-'ĕ-ăh of Benjamin. And Saul numbered the people
that were [7]present with him, [j]about
six hundred men.
16 And Saul, and Jonathan his son,
and the people *that were* present with
them, abode in [8]Gĭb-'ĕ-ăh of Benjamin: but the Philistines encamped in
Mĭch-'măsh.
17 ¶ And the spoilers came out of the
camp of the Philistines in three companies: one company turned unto the
way *that leadeth to* [k]Ŏph-'răh, unto the
land of Shû-'ăl:
18 And another company turned the
way *to* [l]Bĕth–hôr-'ŏn: and another
company turned *to* the way of the
border that looketh to the valley of
[9]Zĕ-bō-'ĭm toward the wilderness.
19 ¶ Now [m]there was no smith found
throughout all the land of Israel: for
the Philistines said, Lest the Hebrews
make *them* swords or spears:
20 But all the Israelites went down
to the Philistines, to sharpen every
man his share, and his coulter, and
his axe, and his mattock.
21 Yet they had [10]a file for the mat-
tocks, and for the coulters, and for the
forks, and for the axes, and [11]to sharp-
en the goads.
22 So it came to pass in the day of
battle, that [n]there was neither sword
nor spear found in the hand of any of

5 bless him.
6 entreated the face.
f 2 Sam. 12.7-9.
1 Ki. 18.18.
2 Chr. 16.9.
Job 34.18.
Pro. 19. 3.
Matt. 14.3,4.
g Lev. 17.1.
Num. 18.7.
ch. 15.11.
h ch. 2.30.
ch. 15.28.
i 2 Sam. 7.15.
Ps. 78.70.
Ps. 89.20.
Acts 13.22.
7 found.
j ch. 14.2.
8 Geba.
k Josh. 18.23.
l Josh. 18.13, 14.
1 Chr. 6.68.
2 Chr. 8.5.
9 Or, serpents.
m 2 Ki. 24.14.
Jer. 24.1.
10 a file with mouths.
11 to set.
n Judg. 3.31.
ch. 17.47,50.
Zech. 4.6.
1 Cor. 1.27, 29.
12 Or, standing camp.
o ch. 14.5.

CHAP. 14

1 Or, there was a day.
a ch. 13.15.
b ch. 22.9.
Ahimelech.
c ch. 4.21.
d Ex. 28.30.
ch. 2.28.
ch. 22.18.
e ch. 13.23.
2 tooth.
f Gen. 17.7-11.
Judg. 14.3.
ch. 17.36.
2 Sam. 1.20.
1 Chr. 10.4.
Eph. 2.11, 12.
Phil. 3.3.
g Deut. 32.30.
Josh. 14.12.
2 Chr. 14.11.
Ps. 115.1-3.
Zech. 4.6.
Matt. 19.26.
Rom. 8.31.
3 Be still.
h Gen. 24.14.
Judg. 7.11.
ch. 10.7.
2 Sam. 5.24.
Isa. 7.11,14.

the people that *were* with Saul a
Jonathan: but with Saul and wi
Jonathan his son was there found.
23 And the [12]garrison of the Phil
tines went out to the passage of [o]Mĭc
măsh.

CHAPTER 14

NOW [1]it came to pass upon a da
that Jonathan the son of Saul sa
unto the young man that bare
armour, Come, and let us go over
the Philistines' garrison, that *is* on t
other side. But he told not his fath
2 And Saul tarried in the utterm
part of Gĭb-'ĕ-ăh under a pomegran
tree which *is* in Mĭg-'rŏn: and the pe
ple that *were* with him *were* [a]about
hundred men;
3 And [b]Ă-hī-'ăh, the son of Ă-hī-'tŭ
Ī'–chă-bŏd's [c] brother, the son of Ph
ĕ-hăs, the son of Ē-'lī, [d]the LOR
priest in Shī-'lōh, wearing an ē-'phc
And the people knew not that Jon
than was gone.
4 ¶ And between the passages,
which Jonathan sought to go over u
to [e]the Philistines' garrison, *there w*
a sharp rock on the one side, and
sharp rock on the other side: and t
name of the one *was* Bō-'zĕz, and t
name of the other Sĕn-'ĕh.
5 The [2]forefront of the one *was* si
ate northward over against Mĭc
măsh, and the other southward ov
against Gĭb-'ĕ-ăh.
6 And Jonathan said to the you
man that bare his armour, Come, a
let us go over unto the garrison
these [f]uncircumcised: it may be th
the LORD will work for us: for *th*
is no restraint to the LORD to [g]sa
by many or by few.
7 And his armourbearer said ur
him, Do all that *is* in thine heart: tu
thee; behold, I *am* with thee acco
ing to thy heart.
8 Then said Jonathan, Behold,
will pass over unto *these* men, and
will discover ourselves unto them
9 If they say thus unto us, [3]Ta
until we come to you; then we v
stand still in our place, and will
go up unto them.
10 But if they say thus, Come up ur
us; then we will go up: for the Lo
hath delivered them into our ha
and [h]this *shall be* a sign unto us.
11 And both of them discove
themselves unto the garrison of
Philistines: and the Philistines sa
Behold, the Hebrews come forth
of the holes where they had hid the
selves.

2 And the men of the garrison an-
vered Jonathan and his armour-
earer, and said, Come up to us, and
e will shew you a thing. And Jona-
ıan said unto his armourbearer,
ome up after me: for the LORD hath
elivered them into the hand of Israel.
3 And Jonathan climbed up upon
's hands and upon his feet, and his
rmourbearer after him: and they fell
efore Jonathan; and his armour-
earer slew after him.
4 And that first slaughter, which
›nathan and his armourbearer made,
as about twenty men, within as it
ere [4]an half acre of land, *which* a yoke
oxen might plow.
5 And [i]there was trembling in the
›st, in the field, and among all the
eople: the garrison, and [j]the spoilers,
ey also trembled, and the earth
ıaked: so it was [5]a very great trem-
ing.
6 And the watchmen of Saul in Gĭb-
ăh of Benjamin looked; and, be-
›ld, the multitude melted away, and
ey went on beating down *one*
other.
7 Then said Saul unto the people
at *were* with him, Number now, and
e who is gone from us. And when
ey had numbered, behold, Jonathan
ıd his armourbearer *were* not *there*.
8 And Saul said unto Ă-hī-ăh, Bring
ther the ark of God. For the ark of
od was at that time with the children
Israel.
9 ¶ And it came to pass, while Saul
lked [k]unto the priest, that the [6]noise
at *was* in the host of the Philistines
ent on and increased: and [l]Saul said
ıto the priest, Withdraw thine hand.
0 And Saul and all the people that
re with him [7]assembled themselves,
ıd they came to the battle: and, be-
›ld, [m]every man's sword was against
s fellow, *and there was* a very great
scomfiture.
1 Moreover the Hebrews *that* were
th the Philistines before that time,
ıich went up with them into the
mp *from the country* round about,
en they also *turned* to be with the
raelites that *were* with Saul and
nathan.
2 Likewise all the men of Israel
ıich had [n]hid themselves in mount
phră-ĭm, *when* they heard that the
ilistines fled, even they also follow-
hard after them in the battle.
3 So [o]the LORD saved Israel that
y: and the battle passed over unto
ĕth–ā-vĕn.

4 Or, half a furrow of an acre of land.
i Josh. 2.9. Judg. 7.21. 2 Ki. 7.7. Job 18.11. Ps. 14.5.
j ch. 13.17.
5 a trembling of God.
k Num. 27. 21.
6 Or, tumult.
l Josh. 9.14. Ps. 106.13.
7 were cried together.
m Judg. 7.22. 2 Chr. 20.23. Isa. 9.19-21.
n ch. 13.6.
o Ex. 14.30. Deut. 33.29. ch. 10.19. 1 Chr. 11.14. Ps. 17.7. Ps. 44.6,7. Isa. 63.9. Hosea 1.7.
p ch. 13.5.
q Lev. 27.29. Num. 21.2. Deut. 27.15-26. Josh. 6.26. Judg. 11.30. Pro. 11.9.
r Deut. 9.28. Matt. 3.5.
s Ex. 3.8. Num. 13.27. Matt. 3.4.
8 Or, wood-honey.
9 adjuring adjured.
10 Or, weary.
t Gen. 9.4. Lev. 3.17. Lev. 7.26. Lev. 17.10. Deut. 12.16, 23,24. Acts 15.20, 29.
11 Or, dealt treacherously.
12 in his hand.
u Judg. 21.4. ch. 7.17. 2 Sam. 24. 25.
13 that altar he began to build unto the LORD.

24 ¶ And the men of Israel were distressed that day: for Saul had adjured
[q]the people, saying, Cursed *be* the
man that eateth *any* food until evening, that I may be avenged on mine
enemies. So none of the people tasted
any food.
25 And [r]all *they of* the land came to
a wood; and there was [s]honey upon
the ground.
26 And when the people were come
into the wood, behold, the honey
dropped; but no man put his hand to
his mouth: for the people feared the
oath.
27 But Jonathan heard not when his
father charged the people with the
oath: wherefore he put forth the end
of the rod that *was* in his hand, and
dipped it in [8]an honeycomb, and put
his hand to his mouth; and his eyes
were enlightened.
28 Then answered one of the people,
and said, Thy father [9]straitly charged
the people with an oath, saying, Cursed *be* the man that eateth *any* food this
day. And the people were [10]faint.
29 Then said Jonathan, My father
hath troubled the land: see, I pray
you, how mine eyes have been enlightened, because I tasted a little of
this honey.
30 How much more, if haply the people had eaten freely to day of the spoil
of their enemies which they found?
for had there not been now a much
greater slaughter among the Philistines?
31 And they smote the Philistines
that day from Mĭch-măsh to Aĭ-jă-
lŏn: and the people were very faint.
32 And the people flew upon the
spoil, and took sheep, and oxen, and
calves, and slew *them* on the ground:
and the people [t]did eat *them* with the
blood.
33 ¶ Then they told Saul, saying, Behold, the people sin against the LORD,
in that they eat with the blood. And
he said, Ye have [11]transgressed: roll a
great stone unto me this day.
34 And Saul said, Disperse yourselves among the people, and say unto
them, Bring me hither every man his
ox, and every man his sheep, and slay
them here, and eat; and sin not against
the LORD in eating with the blood.
And all the people brought every man
his ox [12]with him that night, and slew
them there.
35 And Saul [u]built an altar unto the
LORD: [13]the same was the first altar
that he built unto the LORD.

36 ¶ And Saul said, Let us go down
after the Philistines by night, and
spoil them until the morning light,
and let us not leave a man of them.
And they said, Do whatsoever seemeth good unto thee. Then said the
priest, [v]Let us draw near hither unto
God.
37 And Saul asked counsel of God,
Shall I go down after the Philistines?
wilt thou deliver them into the hand of
Israel? But he answered [w]him not that
day.
38 And Saul said, [x]Draw ye near
hither, all the [14]chief of the people:
and know and see wherein this sin
hath been this day.
39 For, [y]*as* the LORD liveth, which
saveth Israel, though it be in Jonathan
my son, he shall surely die. But *there*
was not a man among all the people
that answered him.
40 Then said he unto all Israel, Be ye
on one side, and I and Jonathan my
son will be on the other side. And the
people said unto Saul, Do what seemeth good unto thee.
41 Therefore Saul said unto the
LORD God of Israel, [15]Give a perfect
lot. [z]And Saul and Jonathan were
taken: but the people [16]escaped.
42 And Saul said, Cast *lots* between
me and Jonathan my son. And Jonathan was taken.
43 Then Saul said to Jonathan, Tell
[a]me what thou hast done. And Jonathan told him, and said, I did but taste
a little honey with the end of the rod
that *was* in mine hand, *and*, lo, I must
die.
44 And Saul answered, [b]God do so
and more also: for thou shalt surely
die, Jonathan.
45 And the people said unto Saul,
Shall Jonathan die, who hath wrought
this great salvation in Israel? God forbid: [c]*as* the LORD liveth, there shall
not one hair of his head fall to the
ground; for he [d]hath wrought with
God this day. So the people rescued
Jonathan, that he died not.
46 Then Saul went up from following
the Philistines: and the Philistines
went to their own place.
47 ¶ So Saul took the kingdom over
Israel, and fought against all his enemies on every side, against Moab, and
against the children [e]of Ammon, and
against Ē-dom, and against the kings
of [f]Zō-băh, and against the Philistines: and whithersoever he turned
himself, he [g]vexed *them*.
48 And he [17]gathered an host, and

v Mal. 2.7. Jas. 4.8.
w Ex. 14.3-5. ch. 28.6. Ps. 66.18. John 9.31.
x Josh. 7.14. ch. 10.19.
14 corners
y ch. 19.6. ch. 20.31. ch. 22.16. 2 Sam. 12.5. Eccl. 9.2.
15 Or, Shew the innocent.
z Josh. 7.16. ch. 10.20,21. John 1.7.
16 went forth.
a Josh. 7.19.
b ch. 25.22.
c 2 Sam. 14. 11. 1 Ki. 1.52. Luke 21.18.
d Isa. 13.3. Acts 15.12. 2 Cor. 6.1.
e ch. 11.11.
f 2 Sam. 10.6.
g Num. 25.17.
17 Or, wrought mightily.
h ch. 15.3,7. 1 Chr. 8.33.
i ch. 31.2.
18 Abiner.
j ch. 9.1.
k ch. 8.11.

CHAP. 15

a ch. 9.16.
b Ex. 17.8. Deut. 25.17.
c Lev. 27.28. Josh. 6.17.
d Ex. 20.5. Isa. 14.21.
e Gen. 3.17. Josh. 7.24.
f Josh. 15.24.
1 Or, fought.
g Num. 24. 21. Judg. 1.16.
h Gen. 18.25. Gen. 19.12. Acts 2.40. Rev. 18.4.
i Ex. 18.10. Num. 10.29.
j ch. 14.48.
k Gen. 2.11. Gen. 25.18.
l Gen. 16.7. ch. 27.8.
m 1 Ki. 20.34. Esther 3.1.
n ch. 30.1.
o Pro. 15.27. 1 Tim. 6.10.
2 Or, of the second sort.

[h]smote the Ă-măl-ĕk-ītes, and deli
ered Israel out of the hands of the
that spoiled them.
49 Now [i]the sons of Saul were Jon
than, and Ĭsh-ū-ī, and Mĕl-chī-shû-
and the names of his two daughte
were these; the name of the firstbo
Mē-răb, and the name of the young
Mī-chăl:
50 And the name of Saul's wife *w*
Ă-hĭn-ō-ăm, the daughter of Ă-hī-m
ăz: and the name of the captain of h
host *was* [18]Abner, the son of Ne
Saul's uncle.
51 And [j]Kish *was* the father of Sau
and Ner the father of Abner *was* t
son of Ă-bī-ĕl.
52 And there was sore war again
the Philistines all the days of Saul: an
when Saul saw any strong man,
any valiant man, [k]he took him un
him.

CHAPTER 15

SAMUEL also said unto Saul, T
[a]LORD sent me to anoint thee *to*
king over his people, over Isra
now therefore hearken thou unto t
voice of the words of the LORD.
2 Thus saith the LORD of hosts, I r
member *that* which Ăm-ă-lĕk did
Israel, [b]how he laid *wait* for him
the way, when he came up from Egy
3 Now go and smite Ăm-ă-lĕk, a
[c]utterly destroy all that they have, a
spare them not; but slay both m
and woman, [d]infant and suckling, [e]
and sheep, camel and ass.
4 And Saul gathered the people t
gether, and numbered them [f]in Tē-
ĭm, two hundred thousand footme
and ten thousand men of Judah.
5 And Saul came to a city of Ăm-
lĕk, and [1]laid wait in the valley.
6 ¶ And Saul said unto [g]the Kē-nīt
[h]Go, depart, get you down fro
among the Ă-măl-ĕk-ītes, lest I d
stroy you with them: [i]for ye shew
kindness to all the children of Isra
when they came up out of Egypt.
the Kē-nītes departed from among t
Ă-măl-ĕk-ītes.
7 And [j]Saul smote the Ă-măl-ĕk-īt
from Hăv-ĭ-lăh [k]*until* thou comest
[l]Shur, that *is* over against Egypt.
8 And [m]he took Agag the king of t
Ă-măl-ĕk-ītes alive, [n]and utterly d
stroyed all the people with the edge
the sword.
9 But Saul and the people spar
Agag, and [o]the best of the sheep, a
of the oxen, and [2]of the fatlings, a
the lambs, and all *that was* good, a
would not utterly destroy them: b

every thing *that was* vile and refuse,
that they destroyed utterly.
10 ¶ Then came the word of the
LORD unto Samuel, saying,
11 It [p]repenteth me that I have set up
Saul *to be* king: for he [q]is turned back
from following me, and [r]hath not
performed my commandments. And
it [s]grieved Samuel; and he cried unto
the LORD all night.
12 And when Samuel rose early to
meet Saul in the morning, it was told
Samuel, saying, Saul came to [t]Car-
mel, and, behold, he set him up a
place, and is gone about, and passed
on, and gone down to Gĭl′-găl.
13 And Samuel came to Saul: and
Saul said unto him, [u]Blessed *be* thou
of the LORD: [v]I have performed the
commandment of the LORD.
14 And Samuel said, What *meaneth*
then this bleating of the sheep in mine
ears, and the lowing of the oxen which
I hear?
15 And Saul said, They have brought
them from the Ă-măl′-ĕk-ītes: [w]for the
people spared the best of the sheep
and of the oxen, to sacrifice unto the
LORD thy God; and the rest we have
utterly destroyed.
16 Then Samuel said unto Saul, Stay,
and I will tell thee what the LORD hath
said to me this night. And he said unto
him, Say on.
17 And Samuel said, When thou *wast*
little in thine own sight, *wast* thou not
made the head of the tribes of Israel,
and the LORD anointed thee king over
Israel?
18 And the LORD sent thee on a
journey, and said, Go and utterly destroy the sinners the Ă-măl′-ĕk-ītes,
and fight against them until [3]they be
consumed.
19 Wherefore then didst thou not
obey the voice of the LORD, but didst
fly upon the spoil, and didst evil in the
sight of the LORD?
20 And Saul said unto Samuel, Yea,
I have obeyed the voice of the LORD,
and have gone the way which the
LORD sent me, and have brought Agag
the king of Ăm′-ă-lĕk, and have utterly
destroyed the Ă-măl′-ĕk-ītes.
21 But the people took of the spoil,
sheep and oxen, the chief of the things
which should have been utterly destroyed, to sacrifice unto the LORD
thy God in Gĭl′-găl.
22 And Samuel said, [x]Hath the LORD
as great delight in burnt offerings and
sacrifices, as in obeying the voice of
the LORD? Behold, [y]to obey *is* better
than sacrifice, *and* to hearken than the
fat of rams.
23 For rebellion *is as* the sin of
[4]witchcraft, and stubbornness *is as* iniquity and idolatry. Because thou hast
rejected the word of the LORD, he hath
also rejected thee from *being* king.
24 ¶ And [z]Saul said unto Samuel, I
[a]have sinned: for I have transgressed
the commandment of the LORD, and
thy words: because [b]I feared the people, and obeyed their voice.
25 Now therefore, I pray thee, pardon my sin, and turn again with me,
that I may worship the LORD.
26 And Samuel said unto Saul, I will
not return with thee: [c]for thou hast
rejected the word of the LORD, and
the LORD hath rejected thee from being king over Israel.
27 And as Samuel turned about to go
away, [d]he laid hold upon the skirt of
his mantle, and it rent.
28 And Samuel said unto him, The
[e]LORD hath rent the kingdom of Israel
from thee this day, and hath given it
to a neighbour of thine, *that is* better
than thou.
29 And also the [5]Strength of Israel
[f]will not lie nor repent: for he *is* not a
man, that he should repent.
30 Then he said, I have sinned: *yet*
[g]honour me now, I pray thee, before
the elders of my people, and before
Israel, and turn again with me, that I
may worship the LORD thy God.
31 So Samuel turned again after
Saul; and Saul worshipped the LORD.
32 ¶ Then said Samuel, Bring ye
hither to me Agag the king of the Ă-
măl′-ĕk-ītes. And Agag came unto him
delicately. And Agag said, Surely the
bitterness of death is past.
33 And Samuel said, [h]As thy sword
hath made women childless, so shall
thy mother be childless among women. And [i]Samuel hewed Agag in
pieces before the LORD in Gĭl′-găl.
34 ¶ Then Samuel went to Rā′-măh;
and Saul went up to his house to [j]Gĭb′-
ĕ-ăh of Saul.
35 And Samuel came no more to see
Saul until the day of his death: nevertheless Samuel mourned for Saul:
and the LORD repented that he had
made Saul king over Israel.

CHAPTER 16

AND the LORD said unto Samuel,
How long wilt thou mourn for
Saul, seeing I have rejected him from
reigning over Israel? [a]fill thine horn
with oil, and go, I will send thee to

p Gen. 6.6. 2 Sam. 24. 16.
q Josh. 22.16. 1 Ki. 9.6. Ps. 36.3. Zeph. 1.6. Matt. 24.13.
r ch. 13.13.
s ch. 16.1. Luke 19.41, 44. Rom. 9.1-3.
t Josh. 15.55.
u Gen. 14.19. Ruth 3.10.
v Luke 18.11.
w Gen. 3.12. Pro. 28.13.
3 they consume them.
x Ps. 50.8,9. Pro. 21.3. Isa. 1.11. Amos 5.21, 24. Micah 6.6. Matt. 9.13. Heb. 10.6.
y Ex. 19.5. Eccl. 5.1. Hosea 6.6. Matt. 5.24. Mark 12.33.
4 divination.
z 2 Sam. 12. 13.
a Ex. 9.27. Matt. 27.4.
b Ex. 23.2. Pro. 29.25. Isa. 51.12. Luke 23.20-25. Rev. 21.8.
c ch. 2.30.
d 1 Ki. 11.30.
e ch. 28.17.
5 Or, Eternity, or, Victory.
f Num. 23. 19. Eze. 24.14. 2 Tim. 2.13. Titus 1.2.
g ch. 2.30. Ps. 49.20. Pro. 4.8. Pro. 26.1. Rom. 2.28, 29.
h Gen. 9.6. Ex. 17.11. Judg. 1.7. Matt. 7.2. Rev. 16.6.
i 1 Ki. 18.40.
j ch. 11.4.

CHAP. 16
a 2 Ki. 9.1.

Jesse the Beth-lehemite: for I [b]have
provided me a king among his sons.
2 And Samuel said, How can I go?
if Saul hear *it*, he will kill me. And the
LORD said, Take an heifer [1]with thee,
and say, [c]I am come to sacrifice to the
LORD.
3 And call Jesse to the [2]sacrifice, and
[d]I will shew thee what thou shalt do:
and thou [e]shalt anoint unto me *him*
whom I name unto thee.
4 And Samuel did that which the
LORD spake, and came to Beth-lehem. And the elders of the town
[f]trembled at his [3]coming, and said,
[g]Comest thou peaceably?
5 And he said, Peaceably: I am come
to sacrifice unto the LORD: sanctify
[h]yourselves, and come with me to the
sacrifice. And he sanctified Jesse and
his sons, and called them to the sacrifice.
6 ¶ And it came to pass, when they
were come, that he looked [i]on Ē-lĭ'-ăb,
and [j]said, Surely the LORD's anointed
is before him.
7 But the LORD said unto Samuel,
Look not on [k]his countenance, or on
the height of his stature; because I
have refused him: for [l]*the LORD seeth*
not as man seeth; for man [m]looketh
on the [4]outward appearance, but the
LORD looketh [n]on the heart.
8 Then Jesse called Ă-bĭn'-ă-dăb, and
made him pass before Samuel. And
he said, Neither hath the LORD chosen
this.
9 Then Jesse made Shăm'-măh to
pass by. And he said, Neither hath the
LORD chosen this.
10 Again, Jesse made seven of his
sons to pass before Samuel. And
Samuel said unto Jesse, The LORD
hath not chosen these.
11 And Samuel said unto Jesse, Are
here all *thy* children? And he said,
[o]There remaineth yet the youngest,
and, behold, he keepeth the sheep.
And Samuel said unto Jesse, [p]Send
and fetch him: for we will not sit
[5]down till he come hither.
12 And he sent, and brought him in.
Now he *was* [q]ruddy, *and* withal [6]of a
beautiful countenance, and goodly to
look to. [r]And the LORD said, Arise,
anoint him: for this *is* he.
13 Then Samuel took the horn of oil,
and anointed [s]him in the midst of his
brethren: and [t]the Spirit of the LORD
came upon David from that day forward. So Samuel rose up, and went
to Rā'-măh.
14 ¶ But [u]the Spirit of the LORD de-

b Ps. 78.70. Acts 13.22.
1 In thine hand. c ch. 20.29.
2 Or, feast. d Ex. 4.15. e ch. 9.16.
f ch. 21.1. 2 Sam. 6.9. Hosea 6.5. Hosea 11. 10. Luke 5.8. Acts 24.25.
3 meeting. g 1 Ki. 2.13. h Ex. 19.10.
i Called Elihu, 1 Chr. 27.18. j 1 Ki. 12.26.
k Ps. 147.10.
l Isa. 55.8. m 2 Cor. 10.7.
4 eyes. n 1 Chr. 28.9. 2 Chr. 16.9. Ps. 7.9. Jer. 11.20. Acts 1.24. Rev. 2.23.
o ch. 17.12. p 2 Sam. 7.8. Ps. 78.70.
5 round. q Song 5.10.
6 fair of eyes. r ch. 9.17. s Ps. 89.20. t Num. 27.18. Judg. 11.29. u ch. 18.12. Ps. 51.11. v ch. 19.9.
7 Or, terrified.
8 Or, speech. w Gen. 41.46. 1 Ki. 10.8. Pro. 22.29.
CHAP. 17
a Josh. 15.35. 2 Chr. 28.18.
1 Or, The coast of bloods, called Pas-dammim.
2 ranged the battle.
3 a treader down.
b 2 Sam. 21. 19. 1 Chr. 20.5.
c Josh. 11.22. 2 Sam. 21. 22. 1 Chr. 8.13. 1 Chr. 18.1. 1 Chr. 20.8. 2 Chr. 26.6. Amos 6.2.
4 about eleven feet and a half.

parted from Saul, and [v]an evil spiri
from the LORD [7]troubled him.
15 And Saul's servants said unt
him, Behold now, an evil spirit fron
God troubleth thee.
16 Let our lord now command th
servants, *which are* before thee, to seel
out a man, *who is* a cunning player o
an harp: and it shall come to pass
when the evil spirit from God is upor
thee, that he shall play with his hand
and thou shalt be well.
17 And Saul said unto his servants
Provide me now a man that can pla
well, and bring *him* to me.
18 Then answered one of the ser
vants, and said, Behold, I have seen
son of Jesse the Beth-lehemite, *that i*
cunning in playing, and a mighty vali
ant man, and a man of war, and pru
dent in [8]matters, and a comely person
and the LORD *is* with him.
19 ¶ Wherefore Saul sent messen
gers unto Jesse, and said, Send m
David thy son, which *is* with the sheep
20 And Jesse took an ass *laden* wit
bread, and a bottle of wine, and a kid
and sent *them* by David his son unt
Saul.
21 And David came to Saul, an
stood [w]before him: and he loved hin
greatly; and he became his armour
bearer.
22 And Saul sent to Jesse, saying
Let David, I pray thee, stand befor
me; for he hath found favour in m
sight.
23 And it came to pass, when th
evil spirit from God was upon Saul
that David took an harp, and playe
with his hand: so Saul was refreshed
and was well, and the evil spirit de
parted from him.

CHAPTER 17

NOW the Philistines gathered to
gether their armies to battle, an
were gathered together [a]at Shō'-chōh
which *belongeth* to Judah, and pitch
ed between Shō'-chōh and Ă-zē'-kăh
in [1]Ē'-phĕs-dăm'-mĭm.
2 And Saul and the men of Israe
were gathered together, and pitche
by the valley of Ē'-lăh, and [2]set th
battle in array against the Philistines
3 And the Philistines stood on
mountain on the one side, and Israe
stood on a mountain on the other side
and *there was* a valley between them
4 ¶ And there went out [3]a champio
out of the camp of the Philistines
named [b]Gō-lī'-ăth, of [c]Gath, whos
height *was* [4]six cubits and a span.

5 And *he had* an helmet of brass upon
his head, and he *was* [5]armed with a
coat of mail; and the weight of the
coat *was* five thousand shekels of
brass.
6 And *he had* greaves of brass upon
his legs, and a [6]target of brass between his shoulders.
7 And [d]the staff of his spear *was* like
a weaver's beam; and his spear's head
weighed six hundred shekels of iron:
and one bearing a shield went before
him.
8 And he stood and cried unto the
armies of Israel, and said unto them,
Why are ye come out to set *your* battle
in array? *am* not I a Philistine, and ye
servants to Saul? choose you a man
for you, and let him come down to me.
9 If he be able to fight with me, and
to kill me, then will we be your servants: but if I prevail against him, and
kill him, then shall ye be our servants,
and [f]serve us.
10 And the Philistine said, I [g]defy
the armies of Israel this day; give me
a man, that we may fight together.
11 When Saul and all Israel heard
those words of the Philistine, they
were dismayed, and greatly afraid.
12 ¶ Now David *was* [h]the son of [i]that
Ĕph-ră-thīte of Beth-lehem-judah,
whose name *was* Jesse; and he had
eight sons: and the man went among
men *for* an old man in the days of
Saul.
13 And the three eldest sons of Jesse
went *and* followed Saul to the battle:
and [k]the names of his three sons that
went to the battle *were* Ē-lī-ăb the
firstborn, and next unto him Ă-bĭn-ă-
dăb, and the third Shăm-măh.
14 And David *was* the youngest: and
the three eldest followed Saul.
15 But David went and returned
from Saul to feed his father's sheep at
Beth-lehem.
16 And the Philistine drew near
morning and evening, and presented
himself forty days.
17 And Jesse said unto David his
son, Take now for thy brethren an
ē-phăh of this parched *corn*, and these
ten loaves, and run to the camp to thy
brethren;
18 And carry these ten [7]cheeses unto
the [8]captain of *their* thousand, and
look how thy brethren fare, and take
their pledge.
19 Now Saul, and they, and all the
men of Israel, *were* in the valley of Ē-
lăh, fighting with the Philistines.
20 ¶ And David rose up early in the
morning, and left the sheep with a
keeper, and took, and went, as Jesse
had commanded him; and he came to
the [9]trench, as the host was going
forth to the [10]fight, and shouted for
the battle.
21 For Israel and the Philistines had
put the battle in array, army against
army.
22 And David left [11]his carriage in
the hand of the keeper of the carriage,
and ran into the army, and came and
[12]saluted his brethren.
23 And as he talked with them, behold, there came up the champion,
the Philistine of Gath, Gō-lī-ăth by
name, out of the armies of the Philistines, and spake according to the
same words: and David heard *them*.
24 And all the men of Israel, when
they saw the man, fled [13]from him,
and were sore afraid.
25 And the men of Israel said, Have
ye seen this man that is come up?
surely to defy Israel is he come up:
and it shall be, *that* the man who killeth him, the king will enrich him with
great riches, and [m]will give him his
daughter, and make his father's house
free in Israel.
26 And David spake to the men that
stood by him, saying, What shall be
done to the man that killeth this Philistine, and taketh away [n]the reproach
from Israel? for who *is* this [o]uncir-
cumcised Philistine, that he should
defy the armies of [p]the living God?
27 And the people answered him
after this manner, saying, So shall
it be done to the man that killeth
him.
28 ¶ And Ē-lī-ăb his eldest brother
heard when he spake unto the men;
and [q]Ē-lī-ăb's anger was kindled
against David, and he said, Why camest thou down hither? and with whom
hast thou left those few sheep in the
wilderness? I know thy pride, and the
naughtiness of thine heart; for thou
art come down that thou mightest see
the battle.
29 And David said, What have I now
done? *Is* [r]*there* not a cause?
30 ¶ And he turned from him toward
another, and spake after the same
[14]manner: and the people answered
him again after the former manner.
31 And when the words were heard
which David spake, they rehearsed
them before Saul: and he [15]sent for
him.
32 ¶ And David said to Saul, [s]Let no
man's heart fail because of him; [t]thy

5 clothed.
6 Or, gorget.
d 2 Sam. 21. 19. 1 Chr. 11.23.
e ch. 8.17. 1 Chr. 21.3.
f ch. 11.1.
g Num. 23.7, 8. 2 Sam. 21. 21. Neh. 2.19.
h Ruth 4.22. ch. 16.1,18.
i Gen. 35.19.
j ch. 16.10, 11. 1 Chr. 2.13.
k ch. 16.6. 1 Chr. 2.13.
7 cheeses of milk.
8 captain of a thousand.
l Gen. 37.14.
9 Or, place of the carriage.
10 battle array, or, place of fight.
11 the vessels from upon him.
12 asked his brethren of peace, as Gen. 43.27. Judg. 18.15.
13 from his face.
m Josh. 15.16.
n ch. 11.2.
o ch. 14.6.
p Deut. 5.26. Jer. 10.10.
q Gen. 37.4. Pro. 18.19. Pro. 27.4. Eccl. 4.4. Matt. 10.36. Matt. 27.18. Mark 3.21.
r Pro. 15.1.
14 word.
15 took him.
s Num. 13.30. Num. 14.9. Deut. 20.1, 3. Isa. 30.3. Heb. 12.12.
t ch. 16.18.

servant will go and fight with this
Philistine.
33 And Saul said to David, [u]Thou
art not able to go against this Philistine to fight with him: for thou *art but*
a youth, and he a man of war from his
youth.
34 And David said unto Saul, Thy
servant kept his father's sheep, and
there came a lion, and a bear, and
took a [16]lamb out of the flock:
35 And I went out after him, and
smote him, and delivered *it* out of his
mouth: and when he arose against
me, I caught *him* by his beard, and
smote him, and slew him.
36 Thy servant slew both the lion and
the bear: and this uncircumcised Philistine shall be as one of them, seeing
he hath defied the armies of the living
God.
37 David said moreover, [v]The LORD
that delivered me out of the paw of the
lion, and out of the paw of the bear,
he will deliver me out of the hand of
this Philistine. And Saul said unto
David, Go, and [w]the LORD be with
thee.
38 ¶ And Saul [17]armed David with
his armour, and he put an helmet of
brass upon his head; also he armed
him with a coat of mail.
39 And David girded his sword upon
his armour, and he assayed to go; for
he had not proved *it*. And David said
unto Saul, I cannot go with these; for
I have not proved *them*. And David
put them off him.
40 And he took his staff in his hand,
and chose him five smooth stones out
of the [18]brook, and put them in a
shepherd's [19]bag which he had, even
in a scrip; and his sling *was* in his
hand: and he drew near to the Philistine.
41 And the Philistine came on and
drew near unto David; and the man
that bare the shield *went* before him.
42 And when the Philistine looked
about, and saw David, he [x]disdained
him: for he was *but* a youth, and
[y]ruddy, and of a fair countenance.
43 And the Philistine said unto
David, *Am* [z]I a dog, that thou comest
to me with staves? And the Philistine
cursed David by his gods.
44 And the Philistine [a]said to David,
Come to me, and I will give thy flesh
unto the fowls of the air, and to the
beasts of the field.
45 Then said David to the Philistine, Thou comest to me with a sword,
and with a spear, and with a shield:
[b]but I come to thee in the name of the
LORD of hosts, the God of the armies
of Israel, whom thou hast defied.
46 This day will the LORD [20]delive
thee into mine hand; and I will smite
thee, and take thine head from thee;
and I will give the [c]carcases of the host
of the Philistines this day unto the
fowls of the air, and to the wild beasts
of the earth; [d]that all the earth may
know that there is a God in Israel.
47 And all this assembly shall know
that the LORD [e]saveth not with sword
and spear: for [f]the battle *is* the
LORD's, and he will give you into our
hands.
48 And it came to pass, when the
Philistine arose, and came and drew
nigh to meet David, that David hasted, and ran toward the army to meet
the Philistine.
49 And David put his hand in his
bag, and took thence a stone, and
slang *it*, and smote the Philistine in
his forehead, that the stone [21]sunk into
his forehead; and he fell upon his face
to the earth.
50 So [g]David prevailed over the Philistine with a sling and with a stone,
and smote the Philistine, and slew
him; but *there was* no sword in the
hand of David.
51 Therefore David ran, and stood
upon the Philistine, and took his
sword, and drew it out of the sheath
thereof, and slew him, and cut off his
head therewith. And when the Philistines saw their champion was dead,
[h]they fled.
52 And the men of Israel and of Judah arose, and shouted, and pursued
the Philistines, until thou come to the
valley, and to the gates of Ĕk-rŏn. And
the wounded of the Philistines fell
down by the way [i]to Shā-ă-rā-ĭm, even
unto Gath, and unto Ĕk-rŏn.
53 And the children of Israel returned from chasing after the Philistines,
and they spoiled their tents.
54 And David took the head of the
Philistine, and brought it to Jerusalem; but he put his armour in his tent.
55 ¶ And when Saul saw David go
forth against the Philistine, he said
unto Abner, the captain of the host,
Abner, [j]whose son *is* this youth? And
Abner said, *As* thy soul liveth, O king,
I cannot tell.
56 And the king said, Inquire thou
whose son the stripling *is*.
57 And as David returned from the
slaughter of the Philistine, Abner
took him, and brought him befor

u Num. 13. 31. Deut. 9.2.
16 Or, kid.
v ch. 7.12. Ps. 18.16,17. Ps. 63.7. Ps. 77.11. Ps. 138.3. 2 Cor. 1.10. 2 Tim. 4.17, 18.
w ch. 20.13. 1 Chr. 22.11, 16.
17 clothed David with his clothes.
18 Or, valley.
19 vessel.
x Ps. 123.4. 1 Cor. 1.27, 28.
y ch. 16.12.
z ch. 24.14. 2 Sam. 3.8.
a 1 Ki. 20.10, 11. Jer. 9.23. Eze. 28.2,9, 10.
b 2 Sam. 22. 33,35. 2 Chr. 32.8. Ps. 124.8. Pro. 18.10. 2 Cor. 10.4. Phil. 4.13. Heb. 11.33, 34.
20 shut thee up.
c Deut. 28.26.
d Josh. 4.24. 1 Ki. 8.43. 2 Ki. 19.19. Isa. 52.10.
e Ps. 44.6,7. Hosea 1.7. Zech. 4.6.
f 2 Chr. 20. 15.
21 sunk as a stone in the water.
g Judg. 3.31. ch. 21.9. 2 Sam. 23. 21.
h Heb. 11.34.
i Josh. 15.36.
j ch. 16.21, 22.

ul with the head of the Philistine in
s hand.
8 And Saul said to him, Whose son
t thou, *thou* young man? And David
swered, *I am* the son of thy servant
esse the Beth-lehemite.

CHAPTER 18

AND it came to pass, when he had
made an end of speaking unto
ul, that the [a]soul of Jonathan was
it with the soul of David, [b]and
nathan loved him as his own soul.
And Saul took him that day, and
ould let him go no more home to
s father's house.
Then Jonathan and David made a
venant, because he loved him as his
vn soul.
And Jonathan stripped himself of
e robe that *was* upon him, and gave
to David, and his garments, even to
s sword, and to his bow, and to his
rdle.
¶ And David went out whitherso-
er Saul sent him, *and* [1]behaved him-
lf wisely: and Saul set him over the
en of war, and he was accepted in
e sight of all the people, and also in
e sight of Saul's servants.
And it came to pass as they came,
hen David was returned from the
ughter of the [2]Philistines, that [d]the
omen came out of all cities of Israel,
nging and dancing, to meet king
ul, with tabrets, with joy, and with
struments of musick.
And the women [e]answered *one an-
her* as they played, and said, Saul
th slain his thousands, and David
s ten thousands.
And Saul was very wroth, and the
ying [4]displeased him; and he said,
ey have ascribed unto David ten
ousands, and to me they have
cribed *but* thousands: and *what*
n he have more but the kingdom?
And Saul [f]eyed David from that
y and forward.
0 ¶ And it came to pass on the
orrow, that [g]the evil spirit from God
me upon Saul, [h]and he prophesied
the midst of the house: and David
ayed with his hand, as at other
nes: and *there was* a javelin in
ul's hand.
1 And Saul [i]cast the javelin; for he
id, I will smite David even to the
all *with it*. And David avoided out
his presence twice.
2 ¶ And Saul was afraid of David,
cause the [j]LORD was with him, and
as departed [k]from Saul.

k Ruth 4.22. 1 Chr. 2.13, 14,15. Isa. 11.1,10. Matt. 1.6. Acts 13.22. Rom. 15.12.

CHAP. 18

a Gen. 44.30. 2 Sam. 18. 33. Col. 2.2.
b Deut. 13.6. ch. 19.2. ch. 20.17. 2 Sam. 1.26. Pro. 18.24. John 15.17-19. 1 John 3.12-14.
c ch. 8.11. ch. 14.52.
1 Or, prospered.
2 Or, Philistines.
d Ex. 15.20. Judg. 5.1,2. Judg. 11.34. Ps. 68.25. Ps. 150.4. Jer. 31.4.
3 three-stringed instruments.
e Ex. 15.21. Judg. 5.3. 2 Chr. 5.13. Ps. 24.1-10. Isa. 5.1.
4 was evil in his eyes.
f Gen. 4.5. Matt. 20.15. Luke 15.28.
g ch. 16.14.
h ch. 19.24. Acts 16.16.
i ch. 19.10. ch. 20.33. Pro. 27.4.
j ch. 16.13.
k ch. 28.15.
l Num. 27.17. 2 Sam. 5.2.
5 Or, prospered.
m Gen. 39.2. Josh. 6.27. ch. 10.7. ch. 16.18. Acts 7.9.
n ch. 17.25.
6 a son of valour.
o Num. 32. 20. ch. 25.28.
p 2 Sam. 12.9.
q Ruth 2.10. ch. 9.21. 2 Sam. 7.18. Pro. 15.33.
r 2 Sam. 21.8.
s Judg. 7.22.
7 was right in his eyes.
t Ex. 10.7. Ps. 7.14-16. Pro. 26.24-26. Jer. 5.26.
8 According to these words.
u Gen. 34.12. Ex. 22.17.
v ch. 14.24.
9 was right in the eyes of.
10 fulfilled.

13 Therefore Saul removed him from
him, and made him his captain over a
thousand; and [l]he went out and came
in before the people.
14 And David [5]behaved himself
wisely in all his ways; and [m]the LORD
was with him.
15 Wherefore when Saul saw that he
behaved himself very wisely, he was
afraid of him.
16 But all Israel and Judah loved
David, because he went out and came
in before them.
17 ¶ And Saul said to David, Behold
my elder daughter Mē-răb, her [n]will
I give thee to wife: only be thou
[6]valiant for me, and fight the [o]LORD's
battles. For Saul said, [p]Let not mine
hand be upon him, but let the hand of
the Philistines be upon him.
18 And David said unto Saul, Who
[q]*am* I? and what *is* my life, *or* my
father's family in Israel, that I should
be son in law to the king?
19 But it came to pass at the time
when Mē-răb Saul's daughter should
have been given to David, that she
was given [r]unto Ā-drĭ-ĕl the [s]Mĕ-hō-
lă-thīte to wife.
20 And Mī-chăl Saul's daughter loved David: and they told Saul, and the
thing [7]pleased him.
21 And Saul said, I will give him her,
that she may be [t]a snare to him, and
that the hand of the Philistines may be
against him. Wherefore Saul said to
David, Thou shalt this day be my son
in law in *the one of* the twain.
22 ¶ And Saul commanded his servants, *saying*, Commune with David
secretly, and say, Behold, the king
hath delight in thee, and all his servants love thee: now therefore be the
king's son in law.
23 And Saul's servants spake those
words in the ears of David. And David
said, Seemeth it to you *a* light *thing*
to be a king's son in law, seeing that I
am a poor man, and lightly esteemed?
24 And the servants of Saul told him,
saying, [8]On this manner spake David.
25 And Saul said, Thus shall ye say
to David, The king desireth not any
[u]dowry, but an hundred foreskins of
the Philistines, [v]to be avenged of the
king's enemies. But Saul thought to
make David fall by the hand of the
Philistines.
26 And when his servants told David
these words, it [9]pleased David well to
be the king's son in law: and the days
were not [10]expired.
27 Wherefore David arose and went,

he and his men, and slew of the Philistines two hundred men; and [w]David
brought their foreskins, and they
gave them in full tale to the king, that
he might be the king's son in law. And
Saul gave him Mī-chăl his daughter
to wife.
28 ¶ And Saul saw and knew that
the LORD *was* with David, and *that*
Mī-chăl Saul's daughter loved him.
29 And [x]Saul was yet the more afraid
of David; and Saul became David's
enemy continually.
30 Then the princes of the Philistines
[y]went forth: and it came to pass, after
they went forth, *that* David behaved
himself [z]more wisely than all the servants of Saul; so that his name was
much [11]set by.

CHAPTER 19

AND Saul [a]spake to Jonathan his
son, and to all his servants, that
they should kill David.
2 But Jonathan Saul's son delighted
much in David: and Jonathan told
David, [b]saying, Saul my father seeketh to kill thee: now therefore, I pray
thee, take heed to thyself until the
morning, and abide in a secret *place*,
and hide thyself:
3 And I will go out and stand beside
my father in the field where thou *art*,
and I will commune with my father
of thee; and what I see, that I will tell
thee.
4 ¶ And Jonathan [c]spake good of
David unto Saul his father, and said
unto him, Let not the king sin [d]against
his servant, against David; because he
hath not sinned against thee, and because his works *have been* to thee-
ward very good:
5 For he did put his [e]life in his hand,
and slew [f]the Philistine, and [g]the
LORD wrought a great salvation for
all Israel: thou sawest *it*, and didst rejoice: [h]wherefore then wilt thou [i]sin
against innocent blood, to slay David
without a cause?
6 And Saul hearkened unto the voice
of Jonathan: and Saul sware, *As* the
LORD liveth, he shall not be slain.
7 And Jonathan called David, and
Jonathan shewed him all those things.
And Jonathan brought David to
Saul, and he was in his presence, as [1]in
times past.
8 ¶ And there was war again: and
David went out, and fought with the
Philistines, and slew them with a
great slaughter; and they fled from
[2]him.

w 2 Sam. 3. 14.
x ch. 12.15. Job 5.2,12, 13. Ps. 37.12,13. Eccl. 4.4. Jas. 2.13.
y 2 Sam. 11.1.
z Luke 21.15.
11 precious.
CHAP. 19
a Pro. 27.4.
b Acts 23.16.
c Pro. 31.8.
d Gen. 42.22. ch. 2.25. 2 Chr. 6.22. Ps. 35.12. Ps. 109.5. Pro. 17.13. Jer. 18.20. 1 Cor. 8.12. 1 John 3.15.
e Judg. 9.17. Judg. 12.3. ch. 28.21. Ps. 119.109.
f ch. 17.49.
g ch. 11.13. 1 Chr. 11.14.
h ch. 20.32.
i Matt. 27.4.
1 yesterday third day.
2 his face.
j ch. 16.14. ch. 18.10.
k Job 5.2. Ps. 5.6. Pro. 1.16. Pro. 29.10.
l Ps. 59, title.
m Josh. 2.15. Acts 9.24, 25.
3 teraphim.
n 2 Sam. 2.22.
o Pro. 17.17. Mal. 2.7.
p John 7.32, 45.
q ch. 10.5,6. 1 Cor. 14.3, 24,25.
r Num. 11.25. Joel 2.28.

9 And [j]the evil spirit from the LOR
was upon Saul, as he sat in his hou
with his javelin in his hand: an
David played with *his* hand.
10 And Saul [k]sought to smite Davi
even to the wall with the javelin; b
he slipped away out of Saul's presenc
and he smote the javelin into the wal
and David fled, and escaped th
night.
11 Saul [l]also sent messengers un
David's house, to watch him, and t
slay him in the morning: and Mī-ch
David's wife told him, saying, If the
save not thy life to night, to morro
thou shalt be slain.
12 ¶ So Mī-chăl [m]let David dow
through a window: and he went, an
fled, and escaped.
13 And Mī-chăl took an [3]image, an
laid *it* in the bed, and put a pillow
goats' *hair* for his bolster, and covere
it with a cloth.
14 And when Saul sent messenge
to take David, she said, He *is* sick.
15 And Saul sent the messenge
again to see David, saying, Bring hi
up to me in the bed, that I may sla
him.
16 And when the messengers we
come in, behold, *there was* an imag
in the bed, with a pillow of goats' *ha*
for his bolster.
17 And Saul said unto Mī-chăl, Wh
hast thou deceived me so, and se
away mine enemy, that he is escaped
And Mī-chăl answered Saul, He sai
unto me, Let me go; why [n]should
kill thee?
18 ¶ So David fled, and escaped, an
came to [o]Samuel to Rā-măh, and to
him all that Saul had done to hin
And he and Samuel went and dwelt i
Nāi-ōth.
19 And it was told Saul, saying, B
hold, David *is* at Nāi-ōth in Rā-mă
20 And [p]Saul sent messengers t
take David: [q]and when they saw th
company of the prophets prophesy
ing, and Samuel standing *as* appoin
ed over them, the Spirit of God wa
upon the messengers of Saul, and the
also [r]prophesied.
21 And when it was told Saul, h
sent other messengers, and they pr
phesied likewise. And Saul sent me
sengers again the third time, and the
prophesied also.
22 Then went he also to Rā-măh, an
came to a great well that *is* in Sē-chū
and he asked and said, Where *a*
Samuel and David? And *one* sai
Behold, *they be* at Nāi-ōth in Rā-mă

23 And he went thither to Nâi-ōth in
Rā-măh: and [s]the Spirit of God was
upon him also, and he went on, and
prophesied, until he came to Nâi-ōth
in Rā-măh.
24 And [t]he stripped off his clothes
also, and prophesied before Samuel
in like manner, and [4]lay down [u]naked
all that day and all that night. Wherefore they say, *Is* [v]Saul also among the
prophets?

CHAPTER 20

AND David fled from Nâi-ōth in
Rā-măh, and came and said before Jonathan, What have I done?
what *is* mine iniquity? and what *is* my
sin before thy father, that he seeketh
my life?
2 And he said unto him, [a]God forbid;
thou shalt not die: behold, my father
will do nothing either great or small,
but that he will [1]shew it me: and why
should my father hide this thing from
me? it *is* not *so*.
3 And David sware moreover, and
said, Thy father certainly knoweth
that I have found grace in thine eyes;
and he saith, Let not Jonathan know
this, lest he be grieved: but truly *as* the
LORD liveth, and *as* thy soul liveth,
there is but a step between me and
death.
4 Then said Jonathan unto David,
Whatsoever thy soul [3]desireth, I will
even do *it* for thee.
5 And David said unto Jonathan,
Behold, to morrow *is* the [b]new moon,
and I should not fail to sit with the
king at meat: but let me go, that I may
hide myself in the field unto the third
day at even.
6 If thy father at all miss me, then
say, David earnestly asked *leave* of me
that he might run [d]to Beth-lehem his
city: for *there is* a yearly [4]sacrifice
there for all the family.
7 If [e]he say thus, *It is* well; thy servant
shall have peace: but if he be very
wroth, *then* be sure that evil is determined by him.
8 Therefore thou shalt [f]deal kindly
with thy servant; for [g]thou hast
brought thy servant into a covenant
of the LORD with thee: notwithstanding, [h]if there be in me iniquity, slay
me thyself; for why shouldest thou
bring me to thy father?
9 And Jonathan said, Far be it from
thee: for if I knew certainly that evil
were determined by my father to come
upon thee, then would not I tell it
thee?

10 Then said David to Jonathan,
Who shall tell me? or what *if* thy father answer thee roughly?
11 ¶ And Jonathan said unto David,
Come, and let us go out into the field.
And they went out both of them into
the field.
12 And Jonathan said unto David,
O [i]LORD God of Israel, when I have
[5]sounded my father about to morrow
any time, *or* the third *day*, and, behold, *if there be* good toward David,
and I then send not unto thee, and
[6]shew it thee;
13 The [j]LORD do so and much more
to Jonathan: but if it please my father
to do thee evil, then I will shew it thee,
and send thee away, that thou mayest
go in peace: and [k]the LORD be with
thee, as he hath been with my father.
14 And thou shalt not only while yet
I live shew me the kindness of the
LORD, that I die not:
15 But *also* [l]thou shalt not cut off thy
kindness from my house for ever: no,
not when the LORD hath cut off the
enemies of David every one from the
face of the earth.
16 So Jonathan [7]made *a covenant*
with the house of David, *saying*, Let
[m]the LORD even require *it* at the hand
of David's enemies.
17 And Jonathan caused David to
swear again, [8]because he loved him:
for he loved him as he loved his own
soul.
18 Then Jonathan said to David, To
morrow *is* the new moon: and thou
shalt be missed, because thy seat will
be [9]empty.
19 And *when* thou hast stayed three
days, *then* thou shalt go down [10]quick-
ly, and come to [n]the place where thou
didst hide thyself [11]when the business
was *in hand*, and shalt remain by the
stone [12]Ē-zĕl.
20 And I will shoot three arrows on
the side *thereof*, as though I shot at a
mark.
21 And, behold, I will send a lad,
saying, Go, find out the arrows. If I
expressly say unto the lad, Behold,
the arrows *are* on this side of thee,
take them; then come thou: for *there
is* peace to thee, and [13]no hurt; [o]*as* the
LORD liveth.
22 But if I say thus unto the young
man, Behold, the arrows *are* beyond
thee; go thy way: for the LORD hath
sent thee away.
23 And *as touching* the matter which
thou and I have spoken of, behold, the
LORD *be* between thee and me for ever.

s Gen. 31.24. Num. 23.5. ch. 10.10. Pro. 21.1. Dan. 4.35. Matt. 7.22. John 11.51. 1 Cor. 13.2.
t Isa. 20.2.
4 fell.
u 2 Sam. 6. 14,20. Micah 1.8.
v ch. 10.11. Acts 9.21.

CHAP. 20

a Gen. 44.7. Josh. 22.29.
1 uncover mine ear.
2 Or, Say what is thy mind, and I will do, etc.
3 speaketh, or, thinketh.
b Num. 10. 10. Num. 28.11. 2 Ki. 4.23. 1 Chr. 23.31. 2 Chr. 2.4. Ezra 3.5. Neh. 10.33. Ps. 81.3. Isa. 1.13. Eze. 45.17.
c ch. 19.2. Ps. 55.12. John 8.59. Acts 17.14.
d ch. 16.4.
4 Or, feast.
e Deut. 1.23. 2 Sam. 17.4.
f Josh. 2.14. Ruth 1.8.
g ch. 18.3. ch. 23.18.
h 2 Sam. 14. 32.
i Josh. 22.22.
5 searched.
6 uncover thine ear.
j Ruth 1.17.
k Josh. 1.5. ch. 17.37. 1 Chr. 22.11, 16.
l Gen. 21.23. 2 Sam. 9.1,3, 7. 2 Sam. 21.7.
7 cut.
m ch. 25.22. ch. 31.2. 2 Sam. 4.7. 2 Sam. 21.8.
8 Or, by his love toward him.
9 missed.
10 greatly, or, diligently.
n ch. 19.2.
11 in the day of the business.
12 Or, that sheweth the way.
13 not any thing.
o Deut. 6.13. Deut. 10.20. Ps. 63.12. Isa. 65.16. Jer. 4.2.

24 ¶ So David [p]hid himself in the
field: and when the new moon was
come, the king sat him down to eat
meat.
25 And the king sat upon his seat, as
at other times, *even* upon a seat by the
wall: and Jonathan arose, and [q]Abner
sat by Saul's side, and David's place
was empty.
26 Nevertheless Saul spake not any
thing that day: for he thought, Something hath befallen him, he *is* [r]not
clean; surely he *is* not clean.
27 And it came to pass on the morrow, *which was* the second *day* of the
month, that David's place was empty:
and Saul said unto Jonathan his son,
Wherefore cometh not the son of
Jesse to meat, neither yesterday, nor
to day?
28 And Jonathan answered Saul,
David earnestly asked *leave* of me *to*
go to Beth-lehem:
29 And he said, Let me go, I pray
thee; for our family hath a sacrifice in
the city; and my brother, he hath
commanded me *to be there:* and now,
if I have found favour in thine eyes,
let me get away, I pray thee, and see
my brethren. Therefore he cometh not
unto the king's table.
30 Then Saul's anger was kindled
against Jonathan, and he said unto
him, [14]Thou son of the perverse rebellious *woman*, do not I know that thou
hast chosen the son of Jesse to thine
own confusion, and unto the confusion of thy mother's nakedness?
31 For as long as the son of Jesse liveth upon the ground, thou shalt not be
established, nor thy kingdom. Wherefore now send and fetch him unto me,
for he [15]shall surely die.
32 And Jonathan answered Saul his
father, and said unto him, Wherefore
[s]shall he be slain? what hath he done?
33 And Saul cast a javelin at him to
smite him: whereby Jonathan knew
that it was determined of his father to
slay David.
34 So Jonathan arose from the table
in fierce anger, and did eat no meat
the second day of the month: for he
was grieved for David, because his
father had done him shame.
35 ¶ And it came to pass in the morning, that Jonathan went out into the
field at the time appointed with David,
and a little lad with him.
36 And he said unto his lad, Run,
find out now the arrows which I shoot.
And as the lad ran, he shot an arrow
[16]beyond him.

p Pro. 27.12.
q ch. 14.50.
r Lev. 6.2,3. Lev. 7.21. Lev. 11.24, 27,31,40. Lev. 15.5. Num. 19.16. 1 Cor. 15.33. 2 Cor. 6.17. Eph. 2.1-3.
14 Son of perverse rebellion, or, Thou perverse rebel.
15 is the son of death.
s Gen. 31.36. ch. 19.5. Ps. 25.3. Ps. 69.4. Ps. 82.4. Pro. 14.25. Pro. 24.11. Pro. 31.9. Matt. 27.23. Luke 23.22. John 7.51. John 15.25.
16 to pass over him.
17 instruments.
18 that was his.
19 Or, the LORD be witness of that which, etc.
CHAP. 21
a ch. 22.19. Neh. 11.32. Isa. 10.32.
b ch. 14.3. called Ahiah. Called also Abiathar.
c Gen. 27.20-24. ch. 19.11. Ps. 119.29. Pro. 29.25. Gal. 2.12, 13. Col. 3.9.
1 found.
d Ex. 25.30. Lev. 24.5. Matt. 12.4.
e Ex. 19.15. Zech. 7.3.
f 1 Thes. 4.4.
2 Or, especially when this day there is other sanctified in the vessel.
g Lev. 8.26.
h Matt. 12.3. Mark 2.25. Luke 6.3.

37 And when the lad was come to the
place of the arrow which Jonathan
had shot, Jonathan cried after the lad,
and said, *Is* not the arrow beyond
thee?
38 And Jonathan cried after the lad,
Make speed, haste, stay not. And
Jonathan's lad gathered up the
arrows, and came to his master.
39 But the lad knew not any thing:
only Jonathan and David knew the
matter.
40 And Jonathan gave his [17]artillery
unto [18]his lad, and said unto him, Go,
carry *them* to the city.
41 ¶ *And* as soon as the lad was gone,
David arose out of *a place* toward the
south, and fell on his face to the
ground, and bowed himself three
times: and they kissed one another,
and wept one with another, until
David exceeded.
42 And Jonathan said to David, Go
in peace, [19]forasmuch as we have
sworn both of us in the name of the
LORD, saying, The LORD be between
me and thee, and between my seed
and thy seed for ever. And he arose
and departed: and Jonathan went in
to the city.

CHAPTER 21

THEN came David to [a]Nob to Ă-
hĭm-ĕ-lĕch [b]the priest: and Ă-him
ĕ-lĕch was afraid at the meeting o
David, and said unto him, Why ar
thou alone, and no man with thee?
2 And David said unto Ă-hĭm-ĕ-lĕcl
the priest, [c]The king hath commande
me a business, and hath said unto me
Let no man know any thing of th
business whereabout I send thee, an
what I have commanded thee: and
have appointed *my* servants to suc
and such a place.
3 Now therefore what is under thin
hand? give *me* five *loaves of* bread i
mine hand, or what there is [1]present.
4 And the priest answered Davic
and said, *There is* no common brea
under mine hand, but there is [d]hal
lowed bread; if [e]the young men hav
kept themselves at least from wome
5 And David answered the pries
and said unto him, Of a truth wome
have been kept from us about thes
three days, since I came out, and th
[f]vessels of the young men are hol
and *the bread is* in a manner commo
[2]yea, though it were sanctified this da
in [g]the vessel.
6 So the priest gave [h]him hallowe
bread: for there was no bread the

ut the shewbread, [i]that was taken
om before the LORD, to put hot
read in the day when it was taken
way.
Now a certain man of the servants
f Saul *was* there that day, detained
efore the LORD; and his name *was*
ō′-ĕg, an Ē′-dom-īte, the chiefest
f the herdmen that *belonged* to
aul.
¶ And David said unto Ă-hĭm′-ĕ-
ch, And is there not here under thine
and spear or sword? for I have
either brought my sword nor my
eapons with me, because the king's
usiness required haste.
And the priest said, The sword of
ō-lī-ăth the Philistine, whom thou
ewest in the valley of Ē′-lăh, behold,
is here wrapped in a cloth behind
e ē′-phŏd: if thou wilt take that, take
for *there is* no other save that here.
nd David said, *There is* none like
at; give it me.
0 ¶ And David arose, and fled that
y for fear of Saul, and went to [3]Ā′-
ish the king of Gath.
1 And [l]the servants of Ā′-chish said
nto him, *Is* not this David the king
the land? did they not sing one to
other of him in dances, saying,
Saul hath slain his thousands, and
avid his ten thousands?
2 And David laid up these words
his heart, and was sore afraid of
′chish the king of Gath.
3 And [n]he changed his behaviour
fore them, and feigned himself mad
their hands, and [4]scrabbled on the
ors of the gate, and let his spittle
l down upon his beard.
4 Then said Ā′-chish unto his ser-
nts, Lo, ye see the man [5]is mad:
herefore *then* have ye brought him
me?
5 Have I need of mad men, that ye
ve brought this *fellow* to play the
ad man in my presence? shall this
llow come into my house?

CHAPTER 22

DAVID therefore departed thence,
[a]and escaped [b]to the cave Adul-
m: and when his brethren and all
s father's house heard *it*, they went
wn thither to him.
And [c]every one *that was* in distress,
d every one that [1]*was* in debt, and
ery one *that was* [2]discontented,
thered themselves unto him; and
became a captain over them: and
ere were with him about four hun-
ed men.

i Lev. 24.8.
j ch. 22.9. Ps. 52. title.
k ch. 31.10.
3 Or, Abimelech.
l Ps. 56, title.
m ch. 18.7.
n Ps. 34, title.
4 Or, made marks.
5 Or, playeth the mad man.

CHAP. 22

a Ps. 57, title. Ps. 142, title.
b Josh. 12.15. 2 Sam. 23. 13. Micah 1.15. Heb. 11.38.
c Judg. 11.3.
1 had a creditor.
2 bitter of soul.
d Gen. 47.11. Ex. 20.12. Deut. 5.16. Pro. 10.1. Pro. 23.24. Matt. 19.19. Eph. 6.2. 1 Tim. 5.4.
e 2 Sam. 24. 11. 1 Chr. 21.9. 2 Chr. 29.25.
3 Or, grove in a high place.
f ch. 8.14.
4 uncovereth mine ear.
g ch. 18.3. ch. 20.30.
h ch. 21.7. Ps. 52. title.
i ch. 21.1.
j ch. 14.3.
k Num. 27. 21.
l ch. 21.6,9.
5 Behold me.
m ch. 19.4,5. ch. 20.32. ch. 24.11. Pro. 24.11, 12. Pro. 31.9.

3 ¶ And David went thence to Mĭz′-
pēh of Moab: and he said unto the
king of Moab, [d]Let my father and my
mother, I pray thee, come forth, *and*
be with you, till I know what God will
do for me.
4 And he brought them before the
king of Moab: and they dwelt with
him all the while that David was in the
hold.
5 ¶ And the prophet [e]Gad said unto
David, Abide not in the hold; depart,
and get thee into the land of Judah.
Then David departed, and came into
the forest of Hâr′-ĕth.
6 ¶ When Saul heard that David was
discovered, and the men that *were*
with him, (now Saul abode in Gĭb′-ĕ-
ăh under a [3]tree in Rā′-măh, having
his spear in his hand, and all his servants *were* standing about him;)
7 Then Saul said unto his servants
that stood about him, Hear now, ye
Benjamites; will the son of Jesse [f]give
every one of you fields and vineyards,
and make you all captains of thousands, and captains of hundreds;
8 That all of you have conspired
against me, and *there is* none that
[4]sheweth me that [g]my son hath made
a league with the son of Jesse, and
there is none of you that is sorry for
me, or sheweth unto me that my son
hath stirred up my servant against me,
to lie in wait, as at this day?
9 ¶ Then answered [h]Dō′-ĕg the Ē′-
dom-īte, which was set over the servants of Saul, and said, I saw the son
of Jesse coming to Nob, to Ă-hĭm′-ĕ-
lĕch [i]the son of [j]Ă-hī′-tŭb.
10 And [k]he inquired of the LORD for
him, and gave [l]him victuals, and gave
him the sword of Gō-lī′-ăth the Philistine.
11 Then the king sent to call Ă-hĭm′-
ĕ-lĕch the priest, the son of Ă-hī′-tŭb,
and all his father's house, the priests
that *were* in Nob: and they came all
of them to the king.
12 And Saul said, Hear now, thou
son of Ă-hī′-tŭb. And he answered,
[5]Here I *am*, my lord.
13 And Saul said unto him, Why
have ye conspired against me, thou
and the son of Jesse, in that thou hast
given him bread, and a sword, and
hast inquired of God for him, that he
should rise against me, to lie in wait,
as at this day?
14 Then Ă-hĭm′-ĕ-lĕch [m]answered
the king, and said, And who *is so* faithful among all thy servants as David,
which is the king's son in law, and go-

eth at thy bidding, and is honourable
in thine house?
15 Did I then begin to inquire of
God for him? be it far from me: let
not the king impute *any* thing unto
his servant, *nor* to all the house of my
father: for thy servant knew nothing
of all this, [6]less or more.
16 And the king said, Thou shalt
surely die, Ă-hĭm-ĕ-lĕch, thou, and all
thy father's house.
17 ¶ And the king said unto the [7]foot-
men that stood about him, Turn, and
slay the priests of the LORD; because
their hand also *is* with David, and because they knew when he fled, and did
not shew it to me. But the servants of
the king [n]would not put forth their
hand to fall upon the priests of the
LORD.
18 And [o]the king said to Dō-ĕg, Turn
thou, and fall upon the priests. And
Dō-ĕg the Ē-dom-īte turned, and he
fell upon the priests, and [p]slew on
that day fourscore and five persons
that did wear a [q]linen ē-phŏd.
19 And [r]Nob, the city of the priests,
smote [s]he with the edge of the sword,
both men and women, children and
sucklings, and oxen, and asses, and
sheep, with the edge of the sword.
20 ¶ And [t]one of the sons of Ă-hĭm-
ĕ-lĕch the son of Ă-hī-tŭb, named Ă-
bī-ă-thär, [u]escaped, and fled after
David.
21 And Ă-bī-ă-thär shewed David
that Saul had slain the LORD's priests.
22 And David said unto Ă-bī-ă-thär,
I knew *it* that day, when Dō-ĕg the
Ē-dom-īte *was* there, that he would
surely tell Saul: I have occasioned *the*
death of all the persons of thy father's
house.
23 Abide thou with me, fear not: for
[v]he that seeketh my life seeketh thy
life: but with me thou *shalt be* in safe-
guard.

CHAPTER 23

THEN they told David, saying, Behold, the Philistines fight against
[a]Kē-ī-lăh, and they rob the threshing-
floors.
2 Therefore David [b]inquired of the
LORD, saying, Shall I go and smite
these Philistines? And the LORD said
unto David, Go, and smite the Philistines, and save Kē-ī-lăh.
3 And David's men said unto him,
Behold, we be afraid here in Judah:
how much more then if we come to
Kē-ī-lăh against the armies of the
Philistines?
4 Then David inquired of the LORD
yet again. And the LORD answere
him and said, Arise, go down to K
ī-lăh; for I will deliver the Philistin
into thine hand.
5 So David and his men went to K
ī-lăh, and fought with the Philistine
and brought away their cattle, ar
smote them with a great slaughter. S
David saved the inhabitants of Kē-
lăh.
6 And it came to pass, when Ă-bī-
thär the son of Ă-hĭm-ĕ-lĕch fled [c]
David to Kē-ī-lăh, *that* he came dow
with an ē-phŏd in his hand.
7 ¶ And it was told Saul that Dav
was come to Kē-ī-lăh. And Saul sai
God [d]hath delivered him into mi
hand; for he is shut in, by entering i
to a town that hath gates and bars.
8 And Saul called all the people t
gether to war, to go down to Kē-ī-lă
to besiege David and his men.
9 ¶ And David knew that Saul secre
ly practised mischief against him; ar
[e]he said to Ă-bī-ă-thär the prie
Bring hither the ē-phŏd.
10 Then said David, O LORD God
Israel, thy servant hath certain
heard that Saul seeketh to come
Kē-ī-lăh, [f]to destroy the city for n
sake.
11 Will the men of Kē-ī-lăh deliv
me up into his hand? will Saul con
down as thy servant hath heard?
LORD God of Israel, I beseech the
tell thy servant. And the LORD sai
He will come down.
12 Then said David, Will the men
Kē-ī-lăh [1]deliver me and my men in
the hand of Saul? And the LORD sai
They will deliver *thee* up.
13 ¶ Then David and his men, *whi*
[g]*were* about six hundred, arose ar
departed out of Kē-ī-lăh, and we
whithersoever they could go. And
was told Saul that David was escap
from Kē-ī-lăh; and he forbare to g
forth.
14 And David abode in the wilde
ness in strong holds, and remained
[h]a mountain in the wilderness
[i]Ziph. And Saul sought [j]him eve
day, but [k]God delivered him not in
his hand.
15 And David saw that Saul w
come out to seek his life: and Dav
was in the wilderness of Ziph in
wood.
16 ¶ And Jonathan Saul's son aros
and went to David into the wood, ar
strengthened his hand in God.
17 And he said unto him, Fear nc
for the hand of Saul my father sh

6 little, or, great.
7 runners, or, guard.
n Ex. 1.17. Acts 4.19.
o Ps. 12.5. Pro. 28.15.
p ch. 2.31.
q Ex. 28.40.
r Neh. 11.32. Isa. 10.32.
s Ps. 10.1-18. Isa. 26.13.
t ch. 23.6.
u Judg. 9.5. ch. 2.33.
v 1 Ki. 2.26. Matt. 24.9. John 16.2. Heb. 12.1-3.

CHAP. 23

a Josh. 15.44.
b Num. 27. 21. ch. 28.6. ch. 30.8. 2 Sam. 5.19, 23. 1 Chr. 10.14. Ps. 37.5. Pro. 3.5,6.
c ch. 22.20.
d Ex. 15.9. ch. 24.4-6. ch. 26.8,9. Ps. 71.11.
e Num. 27. 21. ch. 30.7.
f ch. 22.19. 2 Sam. 20. 20. Esther 3.6. Ps. 44.22.
1 shut up.
g ch. 22.2.
h Ps. 11.1.
i Josh. 15.55.
j ch. 27.1. Ps. 54.3,4. Pro. 1.16.
k Deut. 33.3. 1 Sam. 2.9. Ps. 32.7. Ps. 33.18. Ps. 121.3,8. Pro. 2.8. Pro. 21.30. Rom. 8.31. 2 Tim. 3.11.

ıot find thee; and thou shalt be king
›ver Israel, and I shall be next unto
hee; [l]and that also Saul my father
:noweth.
18 And they two [m]made a covenant
•efore the LORD: and David abode in
he wood, and Jonathan went to his
ıouse.
19 ¶ Then [n]came up the Ziphites to
ˈaul to Gĭb-ˊĕ-ăh, saying, Doth not
)avid hide himself with us in strong
ıolds in the wood, in the hill of Hă-
hī-ˊlăh, which *is* [2]on the south of [3]Jĕ-
hī-ˊmon?
20 Now therefore, O king, come
lown according to all the desire of
hy soul to come down; and [4]our part
hall be to deliver him into the king's
ıand.
21 And Saul said, Blessed *be* ye of
he LORD; for ye have compassion on
ıe.
22 Go, I pray you, prepare yet, and
now and see his place where his
ıaunt is, *and* who hath seen him
here: for it is told me *that* he dealeth
ery subtilly.
23 See therefore, and take knowledge
f all the lurking places where he
ideth himself, and come ye again to
ıe with the certainty, and I will go
/ith you: and it shall come to pass,
ˈ he be in the land, that I will search
im out throughout all the thousands
f Judah.
24 And they arose, and went to Ziph
efore Saul: but David and his men
ere in the wilderness [o]of Mā-ˊŏn, in
ıe plain on the south of Jĕ-shī-ˊmon.
25 Saul also and his men went to seek
im. And they told David: wherefore
e came down [6]into a rock, and abode
ı the wilderness of Mā-ˊŏn. And when
aul heard *that*, he pursued after
)avid in the wilderness of Mā-ˊŏn.
26 And Saul went on this side of the
ıountain, and David and his men on
ıat side of the mountain: and [p]David
ıade haste to get away for fear of
aul; for Saul and his men [q]compassed
)avid and his men round about to
ıke them.
27 ¶ But [r]there came a messenger un-
› Saul, saying, Haste thee, and come;
›r the Philistines have [7]invaded the
nd.
28 Wherefore Saul returned from
ursuing after David, and went
gainst the Philistines: therefore they
ılled that place [8]Sē-lă-hăm-măh-ˊlĕ-
ŏth.
29 ¶ And David went up from thence,
ıd dwelt in strong holds at [s]Ĕn-ġē-ˊdī.

l ch. 24.20.
m ch. 18.3. 2 Sam. 21.7.
n ch. 26.1. Ps. 54, title.
2 on the right hand.
3 Or, the wilderness?
4 it becometh me.
5 foot shall be.
o Josh. 15.55. ch. 25.2.
6 Or, from the rock.
p ch. 19.12. ch. 20.38. 2 Sam. 15. 14. Ps. 31.22.
q 2 Chr. 20. 12. Ps. 17.9. 2 Cor. 1.8.
r Deut. 32.36. ch. 14.6. 2 Sam. 22. 1-51. 2 Ki. 19.9. Ps. 18.1-50. Isa. 37.6-9.
7 spread themselves upon, etc.
8 That is, The rock of divisions.
s 2 Chr. 20.2.

CHAP. 24

a ch. 23.28.
1 after.
b Ps. 38.12.
c Judg. 3.24.
d Ps. 57. title.
e ch. 26.8.
2 the robe which was Saul's.
f 2 Sam. 24. 10.
g ch. 26.11. 2 Sam. 1.14. Job 31.29, 30.
3 cut off.
h Ps. 141.6. Pro. 16.28. Pro. 17.9.
i Ps. 7.3. Ps. 35.7.
j ch. 26.20.
k Gen. 16.5. Judg. 11.27.

CHAPTER 24

AND it came to pass, [a]when Saul
was returned from [1]following the
Philistines, that it was told him, saying, Behold, David *is* in the wilderness
of Ĕn-ġē-ˊdī.
2 Then Saul took three thousand
chosen men out of all Israel, [b]and
went to seek David and his men upon
the rocks of the wild goats.
3 And he came to the sheepcotes by
the way, where *was* a cave; and Saul
went in to [c]cover his feet: and [d]David
and his men remained in the sides of
the cave.
4 And [e]the men of David said unto
him, Behold the day of which the
LORD said unto thee, Behold, I will
deliver thine enemy into thine hand,
that thou mayest do to him as it shall
seem good unto thee. Then David
arose, and cut off the skirt of [2]Saul's
robe privily.
5 And it came to pass afterward,
that David's [f]heart smote him, because he had cut off Saul's skirt.
6 And he said unto his men, The
[g]LORD forbid that I should do this
thing unto my master, the LORD's
anointed, to stretch forth mine hand
against him, seeing he *is* the anointed
of the LORD.
7 So David [3]stayed his servants with
these words, and suffered them not to
rise against Saul. But Saul rose up out
of the cave, and went on *his* way.
8 David also arose afterward, and
went out of the cave, and cried after
Saul, saying, My lord the king. And
when Saul looked behind him, David
stooped with his face to the earth, and
bowed himself.
9 ¶ And David said to Saul, Wherefore [h]hearest thou men's words, saying, Behold, David seeketh thy hurt?
10 Behold, this day thine eyes have
seen how that the LORD had delivered
thee to day into mine hand in the cave:
and *some* bade *me* kill thee: but *mine*
eye spared thee; and I said, I will not
put forth mine hand against my lord;
for he *is* the LORD's anointed.
11 Moreover, my father, see, yea,
see the skirt of thy robe in my hand:
for in that I cut off the skirt of thy
robe, and killed thee not, know thou
and see that *there is* neither [i]evil nor
transgression in mine hand, and I
have not sinned against thee; yet thou
[j]huntest my soul to take it.
12 The [k]LORD judge between me and
thee, and the LORD avenge me of thee:
but mine hand shall not be upon thee.

13 As saith the proverb of the ancients, Wickedness proceedeth from
the wicked: but mine hand shall not
be upon thee.
14 After whom is the [l]king of Israel
come out? after whom dost thou pursue? [m]after a dead dog, after [n]a flea.
15 The LORD therefore be judge, and
judge between me and thee, and [o]see,
and [p]plead my cause, and [4]deliver me
out of thine hand.
16 ¶ And it came to pass, when David
had made an end of speaking these
words unto Saul, that Saul said, [q]*Is*
this thy voice, my son David? And
Saul lifted up his voice, and wept.
17 And he said to David, Thou *art*
[r]more righteous than I: for thou [s]hast
rewarded me good, whereas I have rewarded thee evil.
18 And thou hast shewed this day
how that thou hast dealt well with me:
forasmuch as when the LORD had [5]de-
livered me into thine hand, thou killedst me not.
19 For if a man find his enemy, will
he let him go well away? wherefore
the LORD reward thee good for that
thou hast done unto me this day.
20 And now, behold, [t]I know well
that thou shalt surely be king, and
that the kingdom of Israel shall be
established in thine hand.
21 Swear now therefore unto me by
the LORD, that thou wilt not cut off
my seed after me, and that thou wilt
not destroy my name out of my father's house.
22 And David sware unto Saul. And
Saul went home; but David and his
men gat them up unto the hold.

CHAPTER 25

AND [a]Samuel died; and all the Israelites were gathered together,
and [b]lamented him, and buried him in
his house at Rā'-măh. And David
arose, and went down [c]to the wilderness of Pâr'-ăn.
2 And *there was* a man [d]in Mā'-ŏn,
whose [1]possessions *were* [e]in Carmel;
and the man *was* very great, and he
had three thousand sheep, and a thousand goats: and he was [f]shearing his
sheep in Carmel.
3 Now the name of the man *was* Nā'-
băl; and the name of his wife Ăb'-ĭ-
gail: and *she was* a [g]woman of good
understanding, and of a beautiful
countenance: but the man *was* [h]chur-
lish and evil in his doings; and he *was*
of the house of Caleb.
4 ¶ And David heard in the wilder-

[l] Pro. 5.23.
[m] ch. 17.43. 2 Sam. 9.8.
[n] ch. 26.20.
[o] 2 Chr. 24. 22.
[p] Ps. 35.1. Ps. 43.1. Micah 7.9.
4 judge.
[q] ch. 26.17.
[r] Gen. 38.26. Ex. 9.27.
[s] Matt. 5.44.
5 shut up.
[t] ch. 23.17. 2 Sam. 3.17. Matt. 2.3-6, 13,16.

CHAP. 25

[a] ch. 28.3. Isa. 57.1,2.
[b] Gen. 50.11. Deut. 34.8. Acts 8.2.
[c] Gen. 14.6. Num. 12.16. Ps. 120.5.
[d] ch. 23.24.
1 Or, business.
[e] Josh. 15.55.
[f] Gen. 38.13. 2 Sam. 13. 23.
[g] Ruth 4.11. Pro. 14.1. Pro. 24.3,4.
[h] Isa. 32.5,7.
[i] Gen. 38.13.
2 ask him in my name of peace.
[j] 2 Sam. 18. 28. 1 Chr. 12.18. Ps. 122.7. Matt. 10.12, 13. Luke 10.5.
3 shamed.
[k] Neh. 8.10. Esther 9.19.
4 rested.
[l] Judg. 9.28. Ps. 73.7,8.
[m] Judg. 8.6.
5 slaughter.
[n] ch. 30.24.
6 flew upon them.
7 shamed.
[o] Ex. 14.22. Job 1.10. Zech. 2.5.

ness that Nā'-băl did [i]shear his sheep.
5 And David sent out ten young men,
and David said unto the young men,
Get you up to Carmel, and go to Nā'-
băl, and [2]greet him in my name:
6 And thus shall ye say to him that
liveth *in prosperity*, [j]Peace *be* both to
thee, and peace *be* to thine house, and
peace *be* unto all that thou hast.
7 And now I have heard that thou
hast shearers: now thy shepherds
which were with us, we [3]hurt them not,
neither was there ought missing unto
them, all the while they were in
Carmel.
8 Ask thy young men, and they will
shew thee. Wherefore let the young
men find favour in thine eyes: for we
come in [k]a good day: give, I pray
thee, whatsoever cometh to thine
hand unto thy servants, and to thy
son David.
9 And when David's young men
came, they spake to Nā'-băl according
to all those words in the name of
David, and [4]ceased.
10 ¶ And Nā'-băl answered David's
servants, and said, [l]Who *is* David?
and who *is* the son of Jesse? there be
many servants now a days that break
away every man from his master.
11 Shall [m]I then take my bread, and
my water, and my [5]flesh that I have
killed for my shearers, and give *it* unto
men, whom I know not whence they
be?
12 So David's young men turned
their way, and went again, and came
and told him all those sayings.
13 And David said unto his men,
Gird ye on every man his sword. And
they girded on every man his sword;
and David also girded on his sword:
and there went up after David about
four hundred men; and two hundred
[n]abode by the stuff.
14 ¶ But one of the young men told
Ăb'-ĭ-gail, Nā'-băl's wife, saying, Behold, David sent messengers out of
the wilderness to salute our master;
and he [6]railed on them.
15 But the men *were* very good unto
us, and we were not [7]hurt, neither
missed we any thing, as long as we
were conversant with them, when we
were in the fields:
16 They were [o]a wall unto us both by
night and day, all the while we were
with them keeping the sheep.
17 Now therefore know and consider
what thou wilt do; for evil is determined against our master, and against
all his household: for he *is such* a son

of Bē-lī-ăl, that *a man* cannot speak to
him.
18 ¶ Then Ăb-ĭ-gail made haste, and
took [p]two hundred loaves, and two
bottles of wine, and five sheep ready
dressed, and five measures of parched *corn*, and an hundred [8]clusters of
raisins, and two hundred cakes of figs,
and laid *them* on asses.
19 And she said unto her servants,
[q]Go on before me; behold, I come
after you. But she told not her husband Nā-băl.
20 And it was *so*, *as* she rode on the
ass, that she came down by the covert
of the hill, and, behold, David and his
men came down against her, and she
met them.
21 Now David had said, Surely in
vain have I kept all that this *fellow*
hath in the wilderness, so that nothing
was missed of all that *pertained* unto
him: and he hath requited [r]me evil
for good.
22 So [s]and more also do God unto
the enemies of David, if I leave of all
that *pertain* to him by the morning
light any that pisseth against the wall.
23 And when Ăb-ĭ-gail saw David,
she hasted, and [t]lighted off the ass, and
fell before David on her face, and
bowed herself to the ground,
24 And fell at his feet, and said, Upon
me, my lord, *upon* me *let this* iniquity
be: and let thine handmaid, I pray
thee, speak in thine [9]audience, and
hear the words of thine handmaid.
25 Let not my lord, I pray thee, [10]re-
gard this man of Bē-lī-ăl, *even* Nā-băl:
for as his name *is*, so *is* he; [11]Nā-băl *is*
his name, and folly *is* with him: but I
thine handmaid saw not the young
men of my lord, whom thou didst
send.
26 Now therefore, my lord, [u]*as* the
LORD liveth, and *as* thy soul liveth,
seeing the LORD hath [v]withholden
thee from coming to *shed* blood, and
from [12]avenging thyself with thine
own hand, now [w]let thine enemies, and
they that seek evil to my lord, be as
Nā-băl.
27 And now [x]this [13]blessing which
thine handmaid hath brought unto
my lord, let it even be given unto the
young men that [14]follow my lord.
28 I pray thee, forgive the trespass
of thine handmaid: for [y]the LORD will
certainly make my lord a sure house;
because my lord fighteth the battles of
the LORD, and [z]evil hath not been
found in thee *all* thy days.
29 Yet a man is risen to pursue thee,
and to seek thy soul: but the soul of
my lord shall be [a]bound in the bundle
of life with the LORD thy God; and the
souls of thine enemies, them shall he
[b]sling out, [15]*as out* of the middle of a
sling.
30 And it shall come to pass, when
the LORD shall have done to my lord
according to all the good that he hath
spoken concerning thee, and shall
have appointed thee ruler over Israel;
31 That this shall be [16]no grief unto
thee, nor offence of heart unto my
lord, either that thou hast shed blood
causeless, or that my lord hath
avenged himself: but when the LORD
shall have dealt well with my lord,
then remember thine handmaid.
32 ¶ And David said to Ăb-ĭ-gail,
Blessed [c]*be* the LORD God of Israel,
which sent thee this day to meet
me:
33 And blessed *be* thy advice, and
blessed *be* thou, which hast kept me
this day from coming to *shed* blood,
and from avenging myself with mine
own hand.
34 For in very deed, *as* the LORD
God of Israel liveth, which hath kept
me back from hurting thee, except
thou hadst hasted and come to meet
me, surely there had not been left unto
Nā-băl by the morning light any that
pisseth against the wall.
35 So David received of her hand
that which she had brought him, and
said unto her, [d]Go up in peace to
thine house; see, I have hearkened to
thy voice, and have accepted [e]thy
person.
36 ¶ And Ăb-ĭ-gail came to Nā-băl;
and, behold, [f]he held a feast in his
house, like the feast of a king; and Nā-
băl's heart *was* merry within him, for
he *was* [g]very drunken: wherefore she
told him nothing, less or more, until
the morning light.
37 But it came to pass in the morning,
when the wine was gone out of Nā-
băl, and his wife had told him these
things, that his [h]heart died within
him, and he became *as* a stone.
38 And it came to pass about ten days
after, that [i]the LORD smote Nā-băl,
that he died.
39 ¶ And when David heard that Nā-
băl was dead, he said, Blessed *be* the
LORD, that hath [j]pleaded the cause of
my reproach from the hand of Nā-
băl, and hath kept his servant from
evil: for the LORD hath [k]returned the
wickedness of Nā-băl upon his own
head. And David sent and communed

p Gen. 32.13. 2 Sam. 17. 28,29. Pro. 18.16.
8 Or, lumps.
q Gen. 32.16.
r Gen. 44.4. Ps. 35.12. Pro. 17.13. 1 Pet. 2.20.
s Ruth 1.17. ch. 3.17. ch. 20.13,16.
t Josh. 15.18.
9 ears.
10 lay it to his heart.
11 That is, Fool.
u 2 Ki. 2.2.
v Gen. 20.6.
12 saving thyself.
w 2 Sam. 18. 32.
x Gen. 33.11.
13 Or, present.
14 walk at the feet of, etc.
y 2 Sam. 7.11. 1 Ki. 9.5. 1 Chr. 17.16.
z ch. 24.11.
a Deut. 33. 29. Ps. 66.9. Matt. 10.29, 30. Acts 17.28.
b Jer. 10.18.
15 in the midst of the bow of a sling.
16 no staggering, or, stumbling.
c Gen. 24.27. Ex. 18.10. Ezra 7.27. Ps. 41.12,13. Ps. 72.18. Luke 1.68.
d ch. 20.42. 2 Sam. 15.9. Luke 7.50.
e Gen. 19.21.
f 2 Sam. 13. 23.
g Pro. 20.1. Isa. 5.11. Hosea 4.11. Luke 21.34. Eph. 5.18.
h Deut. 28.28. Job 15.21.
i Ex. 12.29. 2 Sam. 6.7. Job 12.10. Ps. 104.29. Acts 12.23.
j Pro. 22.23.
k 2 Sam. 3. 28,29. Esther 7.10. Ps. 7.16.

with Ăb-ĭ-gail, to take her to him to
wife.
40 And when the servants of David
were come to Ăb-ĭ-gail to Carmel,
they spake unto her, saying, David
sent us unto thee, to take thee to him
to wife.
41 And she arose, and bowed herself
on *her* face to the earth, and said, Behold, *let* thine [l]handmaid *be* a servant
to wash the feet of the servants of my
lord.
42 And Ăb-ĭ-gail hasted, and arose,
and rode upon an ass, with five damsels of hers that went after her; and
she went [17]after the messengers of
David, and became his wife.
43 David also took Ă-hĭn-ŏ-ăm [m]of
Jĕz-rēel; and [n]they were also both of
them his wives.
44 ¶ But Saul had given [o]Mī-chăl his
daughter, David's wife, to [18]Phăl-tī
the son of Lā-ĭsh, which *was* of
[p]Gă-lĭm.

CHAPTER 26

AND the Ziphites came unto Saul to
Gĭb-ĕ-ăh, saying, [a]Doth not
David hide himself in the hill of Hă-
chī-lăh, *which is* before Jĕ-shī-mon?
2 Then Saul arose, and went down to
the wilderness of Ziph, having three
thousand chosen men of Israel with
him, to seek David in the wilderness
of Ziph.
3 And Saul pitched in the hill of Hă-
chī-lăh, which *is* before Jĕ-shī-mon,
by the way. But David abode in the
wilderness, and he saw that Saul came
after him into the wilderness.
4 David therefore sent out spies, and
understood that Saul was come in very
deed.
5 ¶ And David arose, and came to the
place where Saul had pitched: and
David beheld the place where Saul
lay, and Abner [b]the son of Ner, the
captain of his host: and Saul lay in
the [1]trench, and the people pitched
round about him.
6 Then answered David and said to
Ă-hĭm-ĕ-lĕch the Hittite, and to Ăb-
ĭ-shai [c]the son of Zĕr-ū-ĭ-ăh, brother
to Jō-ăb, saying, Who will go [d]down
with me to Saul to the camp? And
Ăb-ĭ-shai said, I will go down with
thee.
7 So David and Ăb-ĭ-shai came to the
people by night: and, behold, Saul
lay sleeping within the trench, and his
spear stuck in the ground at his bolster: but Abner and the people lay
round about him.
8 Then said Ăb-ĭ-shai to David, God

l Ruth 2.10, 13. Pro. 15.33.
17 at her feet.
m Josh. 15. 56. 2 Sam. 3.2.
n Gen. 2.24. ch. 27.3. Matt. 19.5, 8.
o 2 Sam. 3.14.
18 Phaltiel.
p Isa. 10.30.
CHAP. 26
a ch. 23.19. Ps. 54, title.
b ch. 14.50. ch. 17.55. 2 Sam. 2.8.
1 Or, midst of his carriages.
c 1 Chr. 2.16.
d Judg. 7.10.
2 shut up.
e ch. 25.38. Ps. 94.1,2, 23. Pro. 20.22. Luke 18.7. Rom. 12.19. Heb. 10.30. Rev. 18.8.
f Gen. 47.29. Deut. 31.14. Job 7.1. Ps. 37.13.
g ch. 31.6.
h Lev. 19.18. ch. 24.6,12. Pro. 24.29. Rom. 12.17, 19. 1 Pet. 3.9.
i Gen. 2.21. Esther 6.1. Isa. 29.10.
3 the sons of death.
j ch. 24.16.
k ch. 24.9,11.
l Ps. 7.3.
m ch. 16.14, 23. ch. 18.10. 2 Sam. 16. 11.
4 smell.

hath [2]delivered thine enemy into thi
hand this day: now therefore let m
smite him, I pray thee, with the spe
even to the earth at once, and I wi
not *smite* him the second time.
9 And David said to Ăb-ĭ-shai, D
stroy him not: for who can stretc
forth his hand against the LORD
anointed, and be guiltless?
10 David said furthermore, *As* th
LORD liveth, [e]the LORD shall smi
him; or [f]his day shall come to die;
he shall [g]descend into battle, an
perish.
11 The [h]LORD forbid that I shou
stretch forth mine hand against th
LORD's anointed: but, I pray the
take thou now the spear that *is* at h
bolster, and the cruse of water, an
let us go.
12 So David took the spear and th
cruse of water from Saul's bolster; an
they gat them away, and no man sa
it, nor knew *it*, neither awaked: fo
they *were* all asleep; because [i]a dee
sleep from the LORD was fallen upo
them.
13 ¶ Then David went over to th
other side, and stood on the top of a
hill afar off; a great space *being* be
tween them:
14 And David cried to the peopl
and to Abner the son of Ner, saying
Answerest thou not, Abner? The
Abner answered and said, Who *a*
thou *that* criest to the king?
15 And David said to Abner, *Art* no
thou a *valiant* man? and who *is* lik
to thee in Israel? wherefore then ha
thou not kept thy lord the king? fo
there came one of the people in to de
stroy the king thy lord.
16 This thing *is* not good that tho
hast done. *As* the LORD liveth, ye *a*
[3]worthy to die, because ye have no
kept your master, the LORD's anointe
And now see where the king's spear *i*
and the cruse of water that *was* a
his bolster.
17 And Saul knew David's voice, an
said, *Is* [j]this thy voice, my son David
And David said, *It is* my voice, m
lord, O king.
18 And he said, [k]Wherefore doth m
lord thus pursue after his servant
for what have I done? [l]or what evil
in mine hand?
19 Now therefore, I pray thee, le
my lord the king hear the words of hi
servant. If the LORD have stirre
[m]thee up against me, let him [4]accep
an offering: but if *they be* the childre
of men, cursed *be* they before th

,ORD; [n]for they have driven me out
nis day from [5]abiding in the [o]inherit-
nce of the LORD, saying, Go, serve
ther gods.
20 Now therefore, let not my blood
all to the earth before the face of the
,ORD: for the king of Israel is come
ut to seek [p]a flea, as when one
oth hunt a partridge in the moun-
ains.
21 ¶ Then said Saul, [q]I have sinned:
eturn, my son David: for I will no
nore do thee harm, because my soul
as [r]precious in thine eyes this day:
ehold, I have played the fool, and
ave erred exceedingly.
22 And David answered and said,
ehold the king's spear! and let one
f the young men come over and fetch
.
'3 The [s]LORD render to every man
is righteousness and his faithfulness:
or the LORD delivered thee into *my*
and to day, but I would not stretch
orth mine hand against the LORD's
nointed.
24 And, behold, as thy life was much
et by this day in mine eyes, so let my
fe be much set by in the eyes of the
ORD, and let him deliver me out of
l tribulation.
25 Then Saul said to David, Blessed
e thou, my son David: thou shalt
oth do great *things*, and also shalt
ill [t]prevail. So David went on his
ay, and Saul returned to his place.

CHAPTER 27

AND David said in his heart, I shall
now [1]perish one day by the hand
f Saul: *there is* nothing better for me
han that I should speedily escape into
e land of the Philistines; and Saul
hall despair of me, to seek me any
nore in any coast of Israel: so shall I
scape out of his hand.
And David arose, [a]and he passed
ver with the six hundred men that
ere with him [b]unto Ā-chīsh, the son
f Mā-ŏch, king of Gath.
And David dwelt with Ā-chīsh at
ath, he and his men, every man with
is household, *even* David with his
vo wives, Ă-hĭn-ŏ-ăm the Jĕz-reel-
ĕss, and Ăb-ĭ-gail the Carmelitess,
ā-băl's wife.
And it was told Saul that David was
ed to Gath: and he sought no more
gain for him.
¶ And David said unto Ā-chīsh, If
have now found grace in thine eyes,
t them give me a place in some town
the country, that I may dwell

n Deut. 4.28. Ps. 120.5.
5 cleaving.
o Ex. 15.17. Deut. 4.20. Deut. 9.26. 2 Sam. 14. 16. Ps. 106.4,5. Isa. 19.25.
p ch. 24.14.
q Ex. 9.27. Num. 22.34. ch. 15.24. Matt. 27.4.
r ch. 18.30.
s Ps. 7.8. Ps. 18.20. Ps. 28.4. Eccl. 8.12. Isa. 3.10,11.
t Gen. 32.28. Isa. 54.17.

CHAP. 27

1 be consumed.
a ch. 25.13.
b ch. 21.10.
c Josh. 15.31.
2 the number of days.
3 a year of days. ch. 29.3. Till 1056.
d Josh. 13.2.
e Judg. 1.29.
4 Or, Gerzites.
f Ex. 17.16. ch. 15.7,8.
g Gen. 25.18.
5 Or, Did you not make a road, etc.
h Ps. 141.3.
i 1 Chr. 2.9.
6 made himself to stink to his people Israel.

CHAP. 28

a ch. 29.1.
1 Knowing, know.
b Rom. 12.9.
c ch. 25.1. Isa. 57.1,2. Acts 16.16, 19.
d Ex. 22.18. Lev. 19.31. Deut. 18.10.
e Josh. 19.18.
f ch. 31.1.

there: for why should thy servant
dwell in the royal city with thee?
6 Then Ā-chīsh gave him Ziklag that
day: wherefore [c]Ziklag pertaineth unto the kings of Judah unto this day.
7 And [2]the time that David dwelt in
the country of the Philistines was [3]a
full year and four months.
8 ¶ And David and his men went up,
and invaded the [d]Gĕ-shū-rītes, and
[e]the [4]Gĕz-rītes, and [f]the Ă-măl-ĕk-
ītes: for those *nations were* of old
the inhabitants of the land, as [g]thou
goest to Shur, even unto the land of
Egypt.
9 And David smote the land, and left
neither man nor woman alive, and
took away the sheep, and the oxen,
and the asses, and the camels, and the
apparel, and returned, and came to
Ā-chīsh.
10 And Ā-chīsh said, [5]Whither have
ye made a road to day? And David
said, [h]Against the south of Judah, and
against the south of [i]the Jĕ-răh-
meel-ītes, and against the south of
the Kē-nītes.
11 And David saved neither man nor
woman alive, to bring *tidings* to Gath,
saying, Lest they should tell on us,
saying, So did David, and so *will be*
his manner all the while he dwelleth
in the country of the Philistines.
12 And Ā-chīsh believed David, saying, He hath [6]made his people Israel
utterly to abhor him; therefore he
shall be my servant for ever.

CHAPTER 28

AND [a]it came to pass in those days,
that the Philistines gathered their
armies together for warfare, to fight
with Israel. And Ā-chīsh said unto
David, [1]Know thou assuredly, that
thou shalt go out with me to battle,
thou and thy men.
2 And David said to Ā-chīsh, Surely
[b]thou shalt know what thy servant
can do. And Ā-chīsh said to David,
Therefore will I make thee keeper of
mine head for ever.
3 ¶ Now [c]Samuel was dead, and all
Israel had lamented him, and buried
him in Rā-măh, even in his own city.
And Saul had put away [d]those that
had familiar spirits, and the wizards,
out of the land.
4 And the Philistines gathered themselves together, and came and pitched
in [e]Shû-nĕm: and Saul gathered all
Israel together, and they pitched in
[f]Gĭl-bō-ă.
5 And when Saul saw the host of the

Philistines, he was [g]afraid, and his
heart greatly trembled.
6 And when Saul inquired of the
LORD, the [h]LORD answered him not,
neither [i]by dreams, nor [j]by Ū-rĭm, nor
by prophets.
7 ¶ Then said Saul unto his servants,
Seek me a woman that hath a familiar
spirit, that I may go to her, and inquire of her. And his servants said to
him, Behold, *there is* a woman that
hath a familiar spirit at En-dor.
8 And Saul disguised himself, and
put on other raiment, and he went,
and two men with him, and they came
to the woman by night: and he [k]said,
I pray thee, divine unto me by the
familiar spirit, and bring me *him* up,
whom I shall name unto thee.
9 And the woman said unto him, Behold, thou knowest what Saul hath
done, how he hath cut off those that
have familiar spirits, and the wizards,
out of the land: wherefore then layest
thou a snare for my life, to cause me
to die?
10 And Saul sware to her by the
LORD, saying, *As* the LORD liveth,
there shall no punishment happen to
thee for this thing.
11 Then said the woman, Whom
shall I bring up unto thee? And he
said, Bring me up Samuel.
12 And when the woman [l]saw
Samuel, she cried with a loud voice:
and the woman spake to Saul, saying,
Why hast thou deceived me? for thou
art Saul.
13 And the king said unto her, Be
not afraid: for what sawest thou?
And the woman said unto Saul, I saw
[m]gods ascending out of the earth.
14 And he said unto her, [2]What form
is he of? And she said, An old man
cometh up; and he *is* covered with [n]a
mantle. And Saul perceived that it *was*
Samuel, and he [o]stooped with *his* face
to the ground, and bowed himself.
15 ¶ And Samuel said to Saul, Why
hast thou disquieted me, to bring me
up? And Saul answered, [p]I am sore
distressed; for the Philistines make
war against me, and [q]God is departed
from me, and answereth me no more,
neither [3]by prophets, nor by dreams:
therefore I have called thee, that thou
mayest make known unto me what I
shall do.
16 Then said Samuel, Wherefore
then dost thou ask of me, seeing the
LORD is departed from thee, and is become thine enemy?
17 And the LORD hath done [4]to him,

g Job 15.21. Ps. 48.5,6. Isa. 57.20. Dan. 5.6.
h Pro. 1.28. Lam. 2.9.
i Num. 12.6.
j Ex. 28.30. Num. 27.21.
k Deut. 18. 11. 1 Chr. 10.13. Isa. 8.19.
l Isa. 57.2. Rev. 14.13.
m Ex. 22.28. Ps. 138.1.
2 What is his form?
n ch. 15.27.
o 2 Thes. 2. 10,11.
p Pro. 5.11. Pro. 14.14.
q ch. 18.12.
3 by the hand of prophets.
4 Or, for himself.
r ch. 15.28.
5 mine hand.
s ch. 15.9. 1 Ki. 20.42. 1 Chr. 10.13.
6 made haste and fell with the fulness of his stature.
t ch. 25.37. Job 15.20-24. Ps. 50.21.
u Judg. 12.3. ch. 19.5.
v Gen. 4.6. Pro. 25.20, 21.
w Gen. 18.7, 8. Luke 15.23, 27,30.

CHAP. 29

a ch. 28.1.
b ch. 4.1. 1 Ki. 20.30.
c ch. 28.1,2.

[r]as he spake by [5]me: for the LORD
hath rent the kingdom out of thin
hand, and given it to thy neighbour
even to David:
18 Because [s]thou obeyedst not th
voice of the LORD, nor executedst hi
fierce wrath upon Ăm-ă-lĕk, there
fore hath the LORD done this thing un
to thee this day.
19 Moreover the LORD will also de
liver Israel with thee into the hand o
the Philistines: and to morrow *sha*
thou and thy sons *be* with me: th
LORD also shall deliver the host o
Israel into the hand of the Philistine
20 Then Saul [6]fell straightway a
along on the earth, and [t]was sor
afraid, because of the words o
Samuel: and there was no strength i
him; for he had eaten no bread all th
day, nor all the night.
21 ¶ And the woman came unto Sau
and saw that he was sore troubled, an
said unto him, Behold, thine hand
maid hath obeyed thy voice, and
have put my life in my hand, and hav
hearkened unto thy words which tho
spakest unto me.
22 Now therefore, I pray thee, hearl
en thou also unto the voice of thir
handmaid, and let me set a morsel o
bread before thee; and eat, that tho
mayest have strength, when thou go
est on thy way.
23 But he refused, and said, [v]I wi
not eat. But his servants, togeth
with the woman, compelled him; ar
he hearkened unto their voice. So h
arose from the earth, and sat upon th
bed.
24 And the woman had [w]a fat calf
the house; and she hasted, and kille
it, and took flour, and kneaded *it*, a
did bake unleavened bread ther
of:
25 And she brought *it* before Sa
and before his servants; and they d
eat. Then they rose up, and went aw
that night.

CHAPTER 29

NOW [a]the Philistines gathered t
gether all their armies [b]to
phĕk: and the Israelites pitched by
fountain which *is* in Jĕz-reēl.
2 And the lords of the Philistin
passed on by hundreds, and by tho
sands: but David and his men pass
on in the rereward [c]with Ā-chĭsh.
3 Then said the princes of the Phil
tines, What *do* these Hebrews *her*
And Ā-chĭsh said unto the princes
the Philistines, *Is* not this David, t

servant of Saul the king of Israel,
which hath been with me these [d]days,
or these years, and I have found [e]no
fault in him since he fell *unto me* unto
this day?
4 And the princes of the Philistines
were wroth with him; and the princes
of the Philistines said unto him,
Make this fellow return, that he may
go again to his place which thou hast
appointed him, and let him not go
down with us to battle, lest in [g]the
battle he be an adversary to us: for
wherewith should he reconcile himself unto his master? *should it* not *be*
with the heads of these men?
5 *Is* not this David, of whom they
sang one to another in dances, saying,
Saul slew his thousands, and David
his ten thousands?
6 ¶ Then Ā-chish called David, and
said unto him, Surely, *as* the LORD
liveth, thou hast been upright, and
thy going out and thy coming in with
me in the host *is* good in my sight: for
I have not found evil in thee since the
day of thy coming unto me unto this
day: nevertheless [1]the lords favour
thee not.
7 Wherefore now return, and go in
peace, that thou [2]displease not the
lords of the Philistines.
8 ¶ And David said unto Ā-chish,
But what have I done? and what hast
thou found in thy servant so long as I
have been [3]with thee unto this day,
that I may not go fight against the enemies of my lord the king?
9 And Ā-chish answered and said to
David, I know that thou *art* good in
my sight, [j]as an angel of God: notwithstanding the princes of the Philistines have said, He shall not go up
with us to the battle.
10 Wherefore now rise up early in
the morning with thy master's servants that are come with thee: and as
soon as ye be up early in the morning,
and have light, depart.
11 So [k]David and his men rose up
early to depart in the morning, to return into the land of the Philistines.
And the Philistines went up to Jĕz-
rēel.

CHAPTER 30

AND it came to pass, when David
and his men were come to Ziklag
on the third day, that the [a]Ă-măl-ĕk-
ites had invaded the south, and Ziklag,
and smitten Ziklag, and burned it
with fire;
2 And had taken the women captives,
that *were* therein: [b]they slew not any,
either great or small, but carried *them*
away, and went on their way.
3 ¶ So David and his men came to
the city, and, behold, *it was* burned
with fire; and their wives, and their
sons, and their daughters, were taken
captives.
4 Then David and the people that
were with him [c]lifted up their voice
and wept, until they had no more
power to weep.
5 And David's two [d]wives were taken
captives, Ă-hĭn-ŏ-ăm the Jĕz-rēel-ī-
tĕss, and Ăb-ĭ-gail the wife of Nā-băl
the Carmelite.
6 And David was greatly distressed;
[e]for the people spake of stoning him,
because the soul of all the people was
[1]grieved, every man for his sons and
for his daughters: but [f]David encouraged himself in the LORD his God.
7 And [g]David said to Ă-bī-ă-thär the
priest, Ă-hĭm-ĕ-lĕch's son, I pray thee,
bring me hither the ē-phŏd. And Ă-
bī-ă-thär brought thither the ē-phŏd
to David.
8 And [h]David inquired at the LORD,
saying, Shall I pursue after this troop?
shall I overtake them? And he [i]an-
swered him, Pursue: for thou shalt
surely overtake *them*, and without
fail recover *all*.
9 So David went, he and the six hundred men that *were* with him, and
came to the brook Bē-sôr, where those
that were left behind stayed.
10 But David pursued, he and four
hundred men: for two hundred abode
behind, which were so faint that they
could not go over the brook Bē-sôr.
11 ¶ And [j]they found an Egyptian in
the field, and brought him to David,
and gave him bread, and he did eat;
and they made him drink water;
12 And they gave him a piece of a
cake of figs, and two clusters of raisins: [k]and when he had eaten, his
spirit came again to him: for he had
eaten no bread, nor drunk *any* water,
three days and three nights.
13 And David said unto him, To
whom *belongest* thou? and whence
art thou? And he said, I *am* a young
man of Egypt, servant to an Ă-măl-
ĕk-īte; and my master left me, because
three days agone I fell sick.
14 We made an invasion *upon* the
south of [l]the Chĕr-ĕ-thītes, and upon
the coast which *belongeth* to Judah,
and upon the south [m]of Caleb; and
we burned Ziklag with fire.
15 And David said to him, Canst
thou bring me down to this company?

d ch. 27.7.
e Dan. 6.5. John 19.6. 1 Pet. 3.16.
f 1 Chr. 12. 19.
g ch. 14.21.
h ch. 18.7. Pro. 27.14.
i Num. 27.17. 2 Sam. 3.25. Ps. 121.8. Isa. 37.28.
1 thou art not good in the eyes of the lords.
2 do not evil in the eyes of the lords.
3 before thee.
j 2 Sam. 14. 17.
k Ps. 37.23. Ps. 73.2. Ps. 91.11. Ps. 119.133. Pro. 16.9.
l 2 Sam. 4.4.

CHAP. 30
a Ex. 17.8, 14,16. Num. 24.20. Deut. 25.17, 19. ch. 15.7. ch. 27.8. 1 Chr. 4.43. Eze. 25.15.
b Job 38.11. Ps. 76.10. Isa. 27.8. Hab. 3.2.
c Num. 14.1.
d ch. 25.42.
e Ex. 17.4.
1 bitter.
f Ps. 31.24. Ps. 33.18. Ps. 39.7. Ps. 42.5. Ps. 43.5. Ps. 71.4,5. Ps. 119.81. Ps. 146.5. Lam. 3.24, 25. Joel 3.16. Hab. 3.17. Rom. 4.20.
g ch. 23.6,9.
h ch. 23.2,4.
i Ps. 22.4,5. Ps. 28.6. Ps. 50.15.
j Ps. 111.2.
k Judg. 15.19. ch. 14.27.
l 2 Sam. 8.18. Eze. 25.16. Zeph. 2.5.
m Josh. 14. 13.

And he said, Swear unto me by God,
that thou wilt neither kill me, nor deliver me into the hands of my master,
and I will bring thee down to this
company.
16 ¶ And when he had brought him
down, behold, *they were* spread
abroad upon all the earth, [n]eating and
drinking, and dancing, because of all
the great spoil that they had taken out
of the land of the Philistines, and out
of the land of Judah.
17 And David [o]smote them from the
twilight even unto the evening of [2]the
next day: and there escaped not a man
of them, save four hundred young
men, which rode upon camels, and
fled.
18 And David [p]recovered all that
the Ă-măl-ĕk-ītes had carried away:
and David rescued his two wives.
19 And there was nothing lacking to
them, neither small nor great, neither
sons nor daughters, neither spoil, nor
any *thing* that they had taken to
them: David recovered all.
20 And David took all the flocks and
the herds, *which* they drave before
those *other* cattle, and said, This *is*
David's spoil.
21 ¶ And David came to the two
hundred men, which were so faint that
they could not follow David, whom
they had made also to abide at the
brook Bē-sôr: and they went forth to
meet David, and to meet the people
that *were* with him: and when David
came near to the people, he [3]saluted
them.
22 Then answered all the wicked
men and *men* [q]of Bē-lĭ-ăl, of [4]those
that went with David, and said, Because they went not with us, we will
not give them *ought* of the spoil that
we have recovered, save to every man
his wife and his children, that they
may lead *them* away, and depart.
23 Then said David, Ye shall not do
so, my brethren, with that which the
LORD hath given us, who hath preserved us, and delivered the company
that came against us into our hand.
24 For who will hearken unto you in
this matter? but [r]as his part *is* that
goeth down to the battle, so *shall* his
part *be* that tarrieth by the stuff:
they shall part alike.
25 And it was *so* from that day [5]for-
ward, that he made it a statute and an
ordinance for Israel unto this day.
26 ¶ And when David came to Ziklag, he sent of the spoil unto the elders
of Judah, *even* to his friends, saying,
Behold a [6]present for you of the spo
of the enemies of the LORD;
27 To *them* which *were* in [s]Beth-e
and to *them* which *were* in [t]south Ră
mŏth, and to *them* which *were* i
[u]Jăt-tĭr,
28 And to *them* which *were* [v]in Ă-rō
ĕr, and to *them* which *were* in Sĭph
mōth, and to *them* which *were* i
[w]Ĕsh-tĕ-mō-ă,
29 And to *them* which *were* in Ră
chăl, and to *them* which *were* in th
cities of the [x]Jĕ-răh-meel-ītes, and t
them which *were* in the cities of th
[y]Kē-nītes,
30 And to *them* which *were* [z]in Hôr
măh, and to *them* which *were* in Chôr
ăsh-ăn, and to *them* which *were* i
Ă-thăch,
31 And to *them* which *were* in [a]Hē
brŏn, and to all the places wher
David himself and his men were won
to haunt.

CHAPTER 31

NOW [a]the Philistines fought a
gainst Israel: and the men o
Israel fled from before the Philistines
and fell down [1]slain in mount [b]Gĭl
bō-ă.
2 And the Philistines followed har
upon Saul and upon his sons; and th
Philistines slew [c]Jonathan, and Ă
bĭn-ă-dăb, and Măl-chĭ-shû-ă, Saul'
sons.
3 And [d]the battle went sore agains
Saul, and the [2]archers [3]hit him; an
he was sore wounded of the archers
4 Then [e]said Saul unto his armour
bearer, Draw thy sword, and thrus
me through therewith; lest [f]these un
circumcised come and thrust m
through, and [4]abuse me. But hi
armourbearer would not; for he wa
sore afraid. Therefore Saul took
sword, and [g]fell upon it.
5 And when his armourbearer sa
that Saul was dead, he fell likewis
upon his sword, and died with him.
6 So Saul [h]died, and his three sons
and his armourbearer, and all hi
men, that same day together.
7 ¶ And when the men of Israel tha
were on the other side of the valley
and *they* that *were* on the other sid
Jordan, saw that the men of Israe
fled, and that Saul and his sons wer
dead, they forsook the cities, and fled
and the Philistines came and dwelt i
them.
8 And it came to pass on the morrow
when the Philistines came to strip th
slain, that they found Saul and hi
three sons fallen in mount Gĭl-bō-ă.

n Ex. 32.6. ch. 25.36-38. 2 Sam. 13. 28. Dan. 5.1-4. Luke 12.19, 20. Luke 21.34. 1 Thes. 5.3. Rev. 11.10, 13.
o Job 20.5.
2 their morrow.
p Gen. 14.16.
3 Or, asked them how they did.
q Deut. 13.13. Judg. 19.22. ch. 25.17,25.
4 men.
r Num. 31.27. Ps. 68.12.
5 and forward.
6 blessing.
s Gen. 12.8.
t Josh. 19.8.
u Josh. 15.48.
v Josh. 13.16.
w Josh. 15.50.
x ch. 27.10.
y Judg. 1.16.
z Judg. 1.17.
a 2 Sam. 2.1.

CHAP. 31

a ch. 29.1. 1 Chr. 10.1.
1 Or, wounded.
b ch. 28.4.
c 1 Chr. 8.33.
d 2 Sam. 1.6.
2 shooters, men with bows.
3 found him.
e Judg. 9.54.
f ch. 14.6.
4 Or, mock me.
g 2 Sam. 1.10.
h ch. 12.25. Rom. 6.23.

• And they cut off his head, and
ripped off his armour, and sent into
e land of the Philistines round
oout, to [i]publish *it in* the house of
eir idols, and among the people.
0 And [j]they put his armour in
e house of [k]Ăsh-tă-rōth: and they
stened his body to the wall [l]of
ĕth′-shăn.
1 ¶ And when the inhabitants of Jā-
bĕsh–gĭl-ĕ-ăd heard [5]of that which the
Philistines had done to Saul;
12 All [m]the valiant men arose, and
went all night, and took the body of
Saul and the bodies of his sons from
the wall of Bĕth′–shăn, and came to
Jā-bĕsh, and [n]burnt them there.
13 And they took their bones, [o]and
buried *them* under a tree at Jā-bĕsh,
and fasted [p]seven days.

i 2 Sam. 1.20. *j* ch. 21.9. *k* Judg. 2.13. *l* Josh. 17.11. 5 Or, concerning him. *m* ch. 11.1-11. 2 Sam. 2.4-7. *n* 2 Chr. 16. 14. Amos 6.10. *o* 2 Sam. 21. 12,13,14. *p* Gen. 50.10.

THE SECOND

BOOK OF SAMUEL

otherwise called

THE SECOND BOOK OF THE KINGS

CHAPTER 1

NOW it came to pass after the
death of Saul, when David was
turned from the [a]slaughter of the
măl-ĕk-ītes, and David had abode
o days in Ziklag;
It came even to pass on the third
y, that, behold, [b]a man came out of
e camp from Saul with [c]his clothes
nt, and earth upon his head: and *so*
was, when he came to David, that
fell to the earth, and did obeis-
ce.
And David said unto him, From
ence comest thou? And he said
to him, Out of the camp of Israel
I escaped.
And David said unto him, [1]How
nt the matter? I pray thee, tell me.
d he answered, That the people are
d from the battle, and many of the
ople also are fallen and dead; and
ul and Jonathan his son are dead
o.
And David said unto the young
n that told him, How knowest thou
t Saul and Jonathan his son be
ad?
And the young man that told him
d, [2]As I happened by chance upon
ount Gĭl-bō-ă, behold, [e]Saul leaned
on his spear; and, lo, the chariots
d horsemen followed hard after
n.
And when he looked behind him,
saw me, and called unto me. And
nswered, [3]Here *am* I.
And he said unto me, Who *art*
ou? And I answered him, I *am* an
măl-ĕk-īte.
He said unto me again, Stand, I
pray thee, upon me, and slay me: for
[4]anguish is come upon me, because
my life *is* yet whole in me.
10 So I stood upon him, and slew
[f]him, because I was sure that he could
not live after that he was fallen: and
I took the crown that *was* upon his
head, and the bracelet that *was* on his
arm, and have brought them hither
unto my lord.
11 Then David took hold on his
clothes, and [g]rent them; and likewise
all the men that *were* with him:
12 And they mourned, and wept, and
fasted until even, for Saul, and for
Jonathan his son, and for the people
of the LORD, and for the house of
Israel; because they were fallen by
the sword.
13 ¶ And David said unto the young
man that told him, Whence *art* thou?
And he answered, I *am* the son of a
stranger, an Ă-măl-ĕk-īte.
14 And David said unto him, How
[h]wast thou not afraid to stretch forth
thine hand to destroy the LORD's
anointed?
15 And [i]David called one of the
young men, and said, Go near, *and*
fall upon him. And he smote him that
he died.
16 And David said unto him, Thy
[j]blood *be* upon thy head; [k]for thy
mouth hath testified against thee,
saying, I have slain the LORD's
anointed.
17 ¶ And David lamented with this
lamentation over Saul and over Jonathan his son:
18 (Also he bade them teach the
children of Judah [5]*the use of* the bow:

CHAP. 1
a 1 Sam. 11. 11. 1 Ki. 20.29, 30.
b ch. 4.10.
c Gen. 37.29. Num. 14.6. Josh. 7.6. 1 Sam. 4.12. Job 1.20. Acts 14.14.
1 What was, etc.
2 Meeting, I met.
d 1 Sam. 31.1.
e 1 Sam. 31.2-4.
3 Behold me.
4 Or, my coat of mail, or, my embroidered coat hindereth me, that my, etc.
f Judg. 9.54.
g ch. 3.31. 2 Chr. 34.27. Ezra 9.3.
h Num. 12.8. 1 Sam. 24.6. Ps. 105.15.
i 1 Sam. 22. 17,18. ch. 4.10.
j 1 Sam. 26.9.
k Luke 19.22.
5 Or, the ode of the bow.

behold, *it is* written [l]in the book [6]of
Jăsh-ĕr.)
19 The beauty of Israel is slain upon
thy high places: how are the mighty
fallen!
20 Tell [m]*it* not in Gath, publish *it* not
in the streets of Ăs-kĕ-lon; lest the
[n]daughters of the Philistines rejoice,
lest the daughters of [o]the uncircumcised triumph.
21 Ye mountains of Gĭl-bō-ă, [p]*let
there be* no dew, neither *let there be*
rain, upon you, nor fields of offerings:
for there the shield of the mighty is
vilely cast away, the shield of Saul, *as
though he had* not *been* [q]anointed with
oil.
22 From the blood of the slain, from
the fat of the mighty, [r]the bow of
Jonathan turned not back, and the
sword of Saul returned not empty.
23 Saul and Jonathan *were* lovely
and [7]pleasant in their lives, and in
their death they were not divided:
they were swifter than eagles, they
were [s]stronger than lions.
24 Ye daughters of Israel, weep over
Saul, who clothed you in scarlet, with
other delights, who put on ornaments
of gold upon your apparel.
25 How are the mighty fallen in the
midst of the battle! O Jonathan, *thou
wast* slain in thine high places.
26 I am distressed for thee, my brother Jonathan: very pleasant hast
thou been unto me: [t]thy love to me
was wonderful, passing the love of
women.
27 How are the mighty fallen, and
the weapons of war perished!

CHAPTER 2

AND it came to pass after this, that
David [a]inquired of the LORD, saying, Shall I go up into any of the cities
of Judah? And the LORD said unto
him, Go up. And David said, Whither
shall I go up? And he said, Unto [b]Hē-
brŏn.
2 So David went up thither, and his
two wives also, Ă-hĭn-ŏ-ăm the Jĕz-
reēl-ī-tĕss, and Ăb-ĭ-gail Nā-băl's
wife the Carmelite.
3 And [c]his men that *were* with him
did David bring up, every man with
his household: and they dwelt in the
[1]cities of Hē-brŏn.
4 And [d]the men of Judah came, and
there they anointed David king over
the house of Judah. And they told
David, saying, *That* [e]the men of Jā-
bĕsh-gĭl-ĕ-ăd *were they* that buried
Saul.

l Josh. 10.13. 6 Or, of the upright.
m 1 Sam. 31. 9. Micah 1.10.
n Ex. 15.20. 1 Sam. 18.6.
o 1 Sam. 31.4.
p Job 3.3,4.
q 1 Sam. 10.1.
r 1 Sam. 18.4.
7 Or, sweet.
s Judg. 14.18.
t 1 Sam. 18.1, 3. 1 Sam. 19.2.

CHAP. 2

a Num. 27. 21. 1 Sam. 23.2, 4,9.
b 1 Sam. 30. 31.
c 1 Sam. 27.2.
1 That is, suburbs.
d ch. 5.5.
e 1 Sam. 31. 11.
f Ps. 115.15.
g 2 Tim. 1.16.
h Matt. 5.44.
2 be ye the sons of valour.
i 1 Sam. 14. 50. 1 Sam. 17. 55.
3 the host which was Saul's.
4 Esh-baal.
j Gen. 32.2. ch. 17.27.
5 number of days.
k Josh. 9.3. Isa. 28.21.
6 them together.
l Jer. 41.12.
m Pro. 10.23. Pro. 13.10. Pro. 17.14. Pro. 20.3. Pro. 25.8. Pro. 26.18, 19.
7 That is, The field of strong men, or, of rocks.
n 1 Ki. 20.11.
o 1 Chr. 2.16.
p 1 Chr. 12.8.
8 of his feet.
9 as one of the roes that are in the field.

5 ¶ And David sent messengers u
the men of Jā-bĕsh-gĭl-ĕ-ăd, and s
unto them, Blessed [f]*be* ye of the Lo
that ye have shewed this kindness
to your lord, *even* unto Saul, a
have buried him.
6 And now [g]the LORD shew kindn
and truth unto you: and [h]I also
requite you this kindness, because
have done this thing.
7 Therefore now let your hands
strengthened, and [2]be ye valiant:
your master Saul is dead, and a
the house of Judah have anointed
king over them.
8 ¶ But [i]Abner the son of Ner, c
tain of [3]Saul's host, took [4]Ĭsh-bŏ
ĕth the son of Saul, and brought h
over to [j]Mā-hă-nā-ĭm;
9 And made him king over Gile
and over the Ăsh-ū-rītes, and o
Jĕz-reēl, and over Ē-phră-ĭm, a
over Benjamin, and over all Israel
10 Ĭsh-bŏsh-ĕth Saul's son *was* fo
years old when he began to reign o
Israel, and reigned two years. I
the house of Judah followed Davi
11 And the [5]time that David
king in Hē-brŏn over the house
Judah was seven years and six mont
12 ¶ And Abner the son of Ner, a
the servants of Ĭsh-bŏsh-ĕth the s
of Saul, went out from Mā-hă-nā
to [k]Gibeon.
13 And Jō-ăb the son of Zĕr-ū-ī-
and the servants of David, went o
and met [6]together by [l]the pool
Gibeon: and they sat down, the
on the one side of the pool, and
other on the other side of the pool
14 And Abner said to Jō-ăb, [m]
the young men now arise, and p
before us. And Jō-ăb said, Let th
arise.
15 Then there arose and went o
by number twelve of Benjamin, wh
pertained to Ĭsh-bŏsh-ĕth the son
Saul, and twelve of the servants
David.
16 And they caught every one
fellow by the head, and *thrust*
sword in his fellow's side; so they
down together: wherefore that pl
was called [7]Hĕl-kăth-hăz-zū-r
which *is* in Gibeon.
17 And there was a very sore ba
that day; [n]and Abner was beaten, a
the men of Israel, before the serva
of David.
18 ¶ And there were [o]three sons
Zĕr-ū-ī-ăh there, Jō-ăb, and Ă
shai, and Ăs-ă-hĕl: and Ăs-ă-hĕl
as [p]light [8]of foot [9]as a wild roe.

19 And Ăs-ă-hĕl pursued after Abner; and in going he turned not to the
right hand nor to the left [10]from following Abner.
20 Then Abner looked behind him,
and said, *Art* thou Ăs-ă-hĕl? And he
answered, I *am*.
21 And Abner said to him, Turn thee
aside to thy right hand or to thy left,
and lay thee hold on one of the [q]young
men, and take thee his [11]armour. But
Ăs-ă-hĕl would not turn aside from
following of him.
22 And Abner said again to Ăs-ă-hĕl,
Turn thee aside from following me:
wherefore should I smite thee to the
ground? how then should I hold up
my face to Jō-ăb thy brother?
23 Howbeit he refused to turn aside:
wherefore Abner with the hinder end
of the spear smote him under [r]the
fifth *rib*, that the spear came out behind him; and he fell down there, and
died in the same place: and it came to
pass, *that* as many as came to the
place where Ăs-ă-hĕl fell down and
died stood still.
24 Jō-ăb also and Ăb-ĭ-shâi pursued
after Abner: and the sun went down
when they were come to the hill of
Ăm-măh, that *lieth* before Gī-ăh by
the way of the wilderness of [s]Gibeon.
25 ¶ And the children of Benjamin
gathered themselves together after
Abner, and became one troop, and
stood on the top of an hill.
26 Then Abner called to Jō-ăb, and
said, Shall the sword devour for ever?
knowest thou not that it will be bitterness in the latter end? how long shall
it be then, ere thou bid the people return from following their [t]brethren?
27 And Jō-ăb said, *As* God liveth,
unless thou [u]hadst spoken, surely
then [12]in the morning the people had
[13]gone up every one from following
his brother.
28 So Jō-ăb blew a trumpet, and all
the people stood still, and pursued
after Israel no more, neither fought
they any more.
29 And Abner and his men walked
all that night through the plain, and
passed over Jordan, and went through
all [v]Bīth-rŏn, and they came to [w]Mā-
hă-nā-ĭm.
30 And Jō-ăb returned from following Abner: and when he had gathered
all the people together, there lacked
of David's servants nineteen men and
Ăs-ă-hĕl.
31 But the servants of David had
smitten of Benjamin, and of Abner's
men, *so that* three hundred and threescore men died.
32 ¶ And they took up Ăs-ă-hĕl, and
buried him in the sepulchre [x]of his
father, which *was in* Beth-lehem. And
Jō-ăb and his men went all night, and
they came to Hē-brŏn at break of day.

CHAPTER 3

NOW there was long [a]war between the house of Saul and the
house of David: but David waxed
stronger and stronger, and the house
of Saul waxed weaker and weaker.
2 ¶ And [b]unto David were sons born
in Hē-brŏn: and his firstborn was
Amnon, of [c]Ă-hĭn-ō-ăm the Jĕz-reēl-
ī-tĕss;
3 And his second, [1]Chī-lē-ăb, of Ăb-
ĭ-gail the wife of Nā-băl the Carmelite; and the third, Ăb-să-lom the son
of Mā-ă-căh the daughter of Tăl-mâi
king [d]of Gē-shûr;
4 And the fourth, [e]Ăd-ō-nī-jăh the
son of Hăg-gĭth; and the fifth, Shĕph-
ă-tī-ăh the son of Ă-bī-tăl;
5 And the sixth, Ĭth-rē-ăm, by Ĕg-
lăh David's wife. These were born to
David in Hē-brŏn.
6 ¶ And it came to pass, while there
was war between the house of Saul
and the house of David, that Abner
[f]made himself strong for the house of
Saul.
7 And Saul had a concubine, whose
name *was* [g]Rĭz-păh, the daughter of
Aî-ăh: and *Ish–bosh-eth* said to Abner, Wherefore hast thou [h]gone in
unto my father's concubine?
8 Then was Abner very wroth for the
words of Ĭsh–bŏsh-ĕth, and said, *Am*
I [i]a dog's head, which against Judah
do shew kindness this day unto the
house of Saul thy father, to his brethren, and to his friends, and have not
delivered thee into the hand of David,
that thou chargest me to day with a
fault concerning this woman?
9 So [j]do God to Abner, and more
also, except, [k]as the LORD hath
sworn to David, even so I do to him;
10 To translate the kingdom from
the house of Saul, and to set up the
throne of David over Israel and over
Judah, [l]from Dan even to Beēr–shē-
bă.
11 And he could not answer Abner
a word again, because he feared
him.
12 ¶ And Abner sent messengers to
David on his behalf, saying, Whose
is the land? saying *also*, Make thy
league with me, and, behold, my

10 from after Abner.
q 1 Sam. 17. 42.
11 garment, or, spoil.
r ch. 3.27. ch. 4.6. ch. 20.10.
s Josh. 9.3.
t Ps. 4.2. Acts 7.26.
u Pro. 17.14. Pro. 20.18. Pro. 25.8. Luke 14.31, 32.
12 from the morning.
13 Or, gone away.
v Song 2.17.
w Gen. 32.2. Josh. 21.38. ch. 17.24.
x Gen. 47.29, 30. Gen. 49.29. ch. 17.23. ch. 19.37.

CHAP. 3
a Ps. 46.9. Isa. 2.4. Micah 4.3. Matt. 10.35, 36. Gal. 5.17.
b 1 Chr. 3.1.
c 1 Sam. 25. 43.
1 Or, Daniel.
d 1 Sam. 27.8. ch. 13.37.
e 1 Ki. 1.5.
f ch. 2.8,9. 2 Chr. 25.8.
g ch. 21.8,10.
h ch. 16.21.
i Deut. 23.18. 1 Sam. 24. 15. ch. 16.9.
j Ruth 1.17.
k 1 Sam. 15. 28. 1 Chr. 12.23. Ps. 78.70. Ps. 89.19,20. Acts 13.22.
l Judg. 20.1. ch. 17.11.

hand *shall be* with thee, to bring about
all Israel unto thee.
13 ¶ And he said, Well; I will make
a league with thee: but one thing I require of thee, [2]that is, [m]Thou shalt not
see my face, except thou first bring
[n]Mī-chăl Saul's daughter, when thou
comest to see my face.
14 And David sent messengers to
Ĭsh–bŏsh-ĕth Saul's son, saying, Deliver *me* my wife Mī-chăl, which I
espoused to me for an [o]hundred foreskins of the Philistines.
15 And Ĭsh–bŏsh-ĕth sent, and took
her from *her* husband, *even* from
Phăl-tī-ĕl [p]the son of Lā-ĭsh.
16 And her husband went with her
[3]along weeping behind her to [q]Bă-hū-
rĭm. Then said Abner unto him, Go,
return. And he returned.
17 ¶ And Abner had communication
with the elders of Israel, saying, Ye
sought for David [4]in times past *to be*
king over you:
18 Now then do *it:* for the LORD
hath spoken of David, saying, By the
hand of my servant David I will save
my people Israel out of the hand of
the Philistines, and out of the hand
of all their enemies.
19 And Abner also spake in the ears
[r]of Benjamin: and Abner went also to
speak in the ears of David in Hē-brŏn
all that seemed good to Israel, and
that seemed good to the whole house
of Benjamin.
20 So Abner came to David to Hē-
brŏn, and twenty men with him. And
David made Abner and the men that
were with him a feast.
21 And Abner said unto David, I will
arise and go, and will gather all Israel
unto my lord the king, that they may
make a league with thee, and that thou
mayest reign over [s]all that thine heart
desireth. And David sent Abner
away; and he went in peace.
22 ¶ And, behold, the servants of
David and Jō-ăb came from *pursuing*
a troop, and brought in a great spoil
with them: but Abner *was* not with
David in Hē-brŏn; for he had sent
him away, and he was gone in peace.
23 When Jō-ăb and all the host that
was with him were come, they told
Jō-ăb, saying, Abner the son of Ner
came to the king, and he hath sent him
away, and he is gone in peace.
24 Then Jō-ăb came to the king, and
said, What hast thou done? behold,
Abner came unto thee; why *is* it *that*
thou hast sent him away, and he is
[5]quite gone?

25 Thou knowest Abner the son of
Ner, that he came to deceive thee, and
to know thy [t]going out and thy coming in, and to know all that thou
doest.
26 And when Jō-ăb was come out
from David, he sent messengers after
Abner, which brought him again from
the well of Sĭ-răh: but David knew *it*
not.
27 And when Abner was returned to
Hē-brŏn, Jō-ăb [u]took him aside in the
gate to speak with him [6]quietly, and
smote him there under the [v]fifth *rib*,
that he died, for the blood of [w]Ăs-ă-
hĕl his brother.
28 ¶ And afterward when David
heard *it*, he said, I and my kingdom
are guiltless before the LORD for ever
from the [7]blood of Abner the son of
Ner:
29 Let it [x]rest on the head of Jō-ăb,
and on all his father's house; and let
there not [8]fail from the house of Jō-
ăb one [y]that hath an issue, or that is
a leper, or that leaneth on a staff, or
that falleth on the sword, or that
lacketh bread.
30 So Jō-ăb and Ăb-ĭ-shaî his brother
slew Abner, because he had slain their
brother [z]Ăs-ă-hĕl at Gibeon in the
battle.
31 ¶ And David said to Jō-ăb, and to
all the people that *were* with him,
[a]Rend your clothes, and [b]gird you
with sackcloth, and mourn before
Abner. And king David *himself* followed the [9]bier.
32 And they buried Abner in Hē-
brŏn: and the king lifted up his voice,
and wept at [c]the grave of Abner; and
all the people wept.
33 And the king lamented over Abner, and said, Died Abner as a fool
[d]dieth?
34 Thy hands *were* not bound, nor
thy feet put into fetters: as a man
falleth before [10]wicked men, *so* fellest
thou. And all the people wept again
over him.
35 And when all the people came to
[e]cause David to eat meat while it was
yet day, David sware, saying, [f]So do
God to me, and more also, if I taste
bread, or ought else, till [g]the sun be
down.
36 And all the people took notice *of*
it, and it [11]pleased them: as whatsoever the king did pleased all the
people.
37 For all the people and all Israel
understood that day that it was not of
the king to slay Abner the son of Ner.

2 saying.
m Gen. 43.3. Gen. 44.23, 26.
n 1 Sam. 18. 20.
o 1 Sam. 18. 25,27.
p 1 Sam. 25. 44. Phalti.
3 going and weeping.
q ch. 19.16.
4 both yesterday and the third day.
r 1 Chr. 12. 29.
s Deut. 14.26.
5 going, gone.
t Num. 27.17. 1 Sam. 29.6. Ps. 121.8. Isa. 37.28.
u 1 Ki. 2.5. ch. 20.9,10.
6 Or, peaceably.
v Gen. 4.8. ch. 2.23. ch. 4.6.
w ch. 2.23.
7 bloods.
x Judg. 9.54, 56,57. 1 Ki. 2.32, 33. Ps. 7.11,16. Ps. 94.22,23. Pro. 2.22.
8 be cut off.
y Lev. 15.2.
z ch. 2.23.
a Josh. 7.6. ch. 1.2,11. 2 Ki. 19.1.
b Gen. 37.34. 2 Ki. 19.1. Job 16.15.
9 bed.
c 1 Sam. 31.4. ch. 1.12. Pro. 24.17.
d ch. 13.13. Eccl. 2.15, 16.
10 children of iniquity.
e ch. 12.17.
f Ruth 1.17.
g ch. 1.12.
11 was good in their eyes.

38 And the king said unto his ser-
ants, Know ye not that there is a
rince and a great man fallen this day
ı Israel?

39 And I *am* this day [12]weak, though
nointed king; and these men the sons
f Zĕr-ū-ī'-ăh [h]*be* too hard for me: [i]the
ORD shall reward the doer of evil
ccording to his wickedness.

CHAPTER 4

AND when Saul's son heard that
Abner was dead in Hē'-brŏn, his
ands were feeble, and all the Israel-
es were troubled.

2 And Saul's son had two men *that*
ere captains of bands: the name of
ne one *was* Bā'-ă-năh, and the name
f the [1]other Rē'-chăb, the sons of
immon a Bĕēr'-ō-thīte, of the chil-
ren of Benjamin: (for Bĕēr'-ōth [a]also
as reckoned to Benjamin:

3 And the Bĕēr'-ō-thītes fled [b]to Gĭt-
ī-ĭm, and were sojourners there until
ıis day.)

4 And [c]Jonathan, Saul's son, had a
on *that was* lame of *his* feet. He was
ve years old when the tidings came
f Saul and Jonathan [d]out of Jĕz'-rēĕl,
nd his nurse took him up, and fled:
nd it came to pass, as she made haste
o flee, that he fell, and became lame.
nd his name *was* [2]Mĕ-phĭb'-ō-shĕth.

5 And the sons of Rimmon the Bĕēr'-
-thīte, Rē'-chăb and Bā'-ă-năh, went,
nd came about the heat of the day to
he house of Ĭsh–bŏsh'-ĕth, who lay on
bed at noon.

6 And they came thither into the
nidst of the house, [e]*as though* they
vould have fetched wheat; and they
mote him [f]under the fifth *rib:* and
Rē'-chăb and Bā'-ă-năh his brother
scaped.

7 For when they came into the house,
e lay on his bed in his bedchamber,
nd they smote him, and slew him,
nd beheaded him, and took his head,
nd [g]gat them away through the plain
ll night.

8 And they brought the head of Ĭsh–
ŏsh'-ĕth unto David to Hē'-brŏn, and
aid to the king, Behold the head of
sh–bŏsh'-ĕth the son of Saul thine
nemy, [h]which sought thy life; and
he LORD hath avenged my lord the
ing this day of Saul, and of his seed.

9 ¶ And David answered Rē'-chăb
nd Bā'-ă-năh his brother, the sons of
Rimmon the Bĕēr'-ō-thīte, and said
nto them, *As* the LORD liveth, [i]who
ath redeemed my soul out of all
dversity,

10 When [j]one told me, saying, Behold, Saul is dead, [3]thinking to have
brought good tidings, I took hold of
him, and slew him in Ziklag, [4]who
thought that I would have given him
a reward for his tidings:

11 How much more, when wicked
men have slain a righteous person in
his own house upon his bed? shall I
not therefore now [k]require his blood
of your hand, and take you away
from the earth?

12 And David commanded his young
men, and they slew them, and cut off
their hands and their feet, and hanged
them up over the pool in Hē'-brŏn.
But they took the head of Ĭsh–bŏsh'-
ĕth, and buried *it* in the [l]sepulchre of
Abner in Hē'-brŏn.

CHAPTER 5

THEN [a]came all the tribes of Israel
to David unto Hē'-brŏn, and
spake, saying, Behold, [b]we *are* thy
bone and thy flesh.

2 Also in time past, when Saul was
king over us, [c]thou wast he that leddest out and broughtest in Israel: and
the LORD said to thee, [d]Thou shalt
feed my people Israel, and thou shalt
be a captain over Israel.

3 So [e]all the elders of Israel came to
the king to Hē'-brŏn; [f]and king David
made a league with them in Hē'-brŏn
[g]before the LORD: and they anointed
David king over Israel.

4 ¶ David *was* thirty years old when
he began to reign, [h]*and* he reigned
forty years.

5 In Hē'-brŏn he reigned over Judah
[i]seven years and six months: and in
Jerusalem he reigned thirty and three
years over all Israel and Judah.

6 ¶ And the king and his men went
[j]to Jerusalem unto [k]the Jĕb'-ū-sītes,
the inhabitants of the land: which
spake unto David, saying, Except
thou take away the blind and the
lame, thou shalt not come in hither:
[1]thinking, David cannot come in
hither.

7 Nevertheless David took the strong
hold of Zion: the same *is* the city of
David.

8 And David said on that day, Whosoever getteth up to the gutter, and
smiteth the Jĕb'-ū-sītes, and the lame
and the blind, *that are* hated of
David's soul, [l]*he shall be chief and*
captain. [2]Wherefore they said, The
blind and the lame shall not come into
the house.

9 So David dwelt in the fort, and

12 tender.
h ch. 19.7.
i ch. 19.13. Ps. 28.4. 2 Tim. 4.14.

CHAP. 4

1 second.
a Josh. 18.25.
b Neh. 11.33.
c ch. 9.3.
d 1 Sam. 29.1.
2 Or, Merib-baal.
e Judg. 5.25. Ps. 147.14.
f ch. 2.23. ch. 3.27.
g 1 Sam. 17. 54. Matt. 14.11.
h 1 Sam. 19.2. 1 Sam. 23. 15.
i Gen. 48.16. 1 Ki. 1.29. Ps. 31.7. Ps. 103.4.
j ch. 1.2.
3 he was in his own eyes as a bringer, etc.
4 Or, which was the reward I gave him for his tidings.
k Gen. 9.5,6.
l ch. 3.32.

CHAP. 5

a 1 Chr. 12. 23.
b Gen. 29.14.
c 1 Sam. 18. 13.
d 1 Sam. 16.1. ch. 7.7. Ps. 78.71.
e 1 Chr. 11.3.
f 2 Ki. 11.17.
g 1 Sam. 23. 18.
h 1 Chr. 26. 31.
i 1 Chr. 3.4.
j Judg. 1.21.
k Josh. 15.63.
1 Or, saying, David shall not, etc.
l 1 Chr. 11.6.
2 Or, Because they had said, even the blind and the lame, He shall not come into the house.

called it the city of David. And David
built round about [m]from Mĭl'-lō and
inward.
10 And David [3]went on, and grew
great, and the LORD God of hosts *was*
with him.
11 ¶ And [n]Hiram king of Tyre sent
messengers to David, and cedar trees,
and carpenters, and [4]masons: and
they built David an house.
12 And David perceived that the
LORD had established him king over
Israel, and that he had exalted his
kingdom [o]for his people Israel's sake.
13 ¶ And [p]David took *him* more concubines and wives out of Jerusalem,
after he was come from Hē'-brŏn: and
there were yet sons and daughters
born to David.
14 And these *be* the names of those
that were born unto him in Jerusalem;
Shăm'-mū-ă, and Shō'-băb, and Nathan, and Solomon,
15 Ĭb'-här also, and Ē-lĭ'-shû-ă, and
Nĕph'-ĕg, and Jă-phī'-ă,
16 And Ē-lĭ'-shă-mă, and Ē-lĭ'-ă-dă,
and Ē-lĭph'-ă-lĕt.
17 ¶ But [q]when the Philistines heard
that they had anointed David king
over Israel, all the Philistines came
up to seek David; and David heard
of it, [r]and went down to the hold.
18 The Philistines also came and
spread themselves in [s]the valley of
[5]Rĕph'-ā-ĭm.
19 And David [t]inquired of the LORD,
saying, Shall I go up to the Philistines? wilt thou deliver them into
mine hand? And the LORD said unto
David, Go up: for I will doubtless
deliver the Philistines into thine
hand.
20 And David came to [u]Bā'-ăl–pĕ-rā'-
zĭm, and David smote them there, and
said, The LORD hath broken forth
upon mine enemies before me, as the
breach of waters. Therefore he called
the name of that place [6]Bā'-ăl–pĕ-rā'-
zĭm.
21 And there they left their images,
and David and his men [7]burned them.
22 ¶ And the Philistines came up yet
again, and spread themselves in the
valley of Rĕph'-ā-ĭm.
23 And when David inquired of the
LORD, he said, Thou shalt not go up;
but fetch a compass behind them, and
come upon them over against the
mulberry trees.
24 And let it be, when thou hearest
the sound of a going in the tops of the
mulberry trees, that then thou shalt
bestir thyself: for then shall the LORD

m 1 Ki. 9.24. 2 Chr. 32.5.
3 went going and growing.
n 1 Ki. 5.2.
4 hewers of the stone of the wall.
o 2 Chr. 2.11. Esther 4.14. Isa. 45.4.
p Gen. 25.5, 6.
q 1 Chr. 11. 16.
r ch. 23.14.
s Isa. 17.5.
5 Or, Giants.
t Num. 27.21. 1 Sam. 23. 2,4. ch. 2.1.
u Isa. 28.21.
6 That is, The plain of breaches.
7 Or, took them away.

CHAP. 6

a 1 Chr. 13.5.
1 Or, Baalah, that is, Kirjath-jearim.
2 Or, at which the name, even the name of the LORD of hosts, was called upon.
b 1 Sam. 4.4. Ps. 80.1.
3 made to ride.
c Num. 7.9.
4 Or, The hill.
5 with.
6 Or, Chidon. 1 Chr. 13.9. That is, Destroying stroke.
d Num. 4.15.
7 Or, stumbled.
e 1 Sam. 6.19.
8 Or, rashness.
9 broken.
10 That is, The breach of Uzzah.
f Num. 17. 12,13. Ps. 119.120. Luke 5.8.
g Gen. 30.27. Pro. 3.9,10. Isa. 61.9.

go out before thee, to smite the ho
of the Philistines.
25 And David did so, as the LOR
had commanded him; and smote th
Philistines from Gē'-bă until tho
come to Gā'-zĕr.

CHAPTER 6

AGAIN, David gathered togeth
all *the* chosen *men* of Israel, thirt
thousand.
2 And [a]David arose, and went wi
all the people that *were* with him fro
[1]Bā'-ă-lē of Judah, to bring up fro
thence the ark of God, [2]whose nan
is called by the name of the LORD
hosts that [b]dwelleth *between* the chĕ
ū-bĭms.
3 And they [3]set the ark of God upo
a [c]new cart, and brought it out of th
house of Ă-bĭn'-ă-dăb that *was*
[4]Gĭb'-ē-ăh: and Ŭz'-zăh and Ă-hĭ'-
the sons of Ă-bĭn'-ă-dăb, drave th
new cart.
4 And they brought it out of th
house of Ă-bĭn'-ă-dăb which *was*
Gĭb'-ē-ăh, [5]accompanying the ark
God: and Ă-hĭ'-ō went before the ar
5 And David and all the house
Israel played before the LORD on a
manner of *instruments made of*
wood, even on harps, and on psalte
ies, and on timbrels, and on cornet
and on cymbals.
6 ¶ And when they came to [6]N
chŏn's threshingfloor, Ŭz'-zăh [d]p
forth *his hand* to the ark of God, an
took hold of it; for the oxen [7]shook
7 And the anger of the LORD w
kindled against Ŭz'-zăh; and [e]Go
smote him there for *his* [8]error; an
there he died by the ark of God.
8 And David was displeased, becau
the LORD had [9]made a breach upo
Ŭz'-zăh: and he called the name of th
place [10]Pē'-rĕz–ŭz'-zăh to this day.
9 And [f]David was afraid of the LOR
that day, and said, How shall the ar
of the LORD come to me?
10 So David would not remove th
ark of the LORD unto him into th
city of David: but David carried
aside into the house of Ō'-bĕd–ĕ'-do
the Gĭt'-tīte.
11 And the ark of the LORD continue
in the house of Ō'-bĕd–ĕ'-dom the Gi
tīte three months: and the LOR
[g]blessed Ō'-bĕd–ĕ'-dom, and all h
household.
12 ¶ And it was told king Davi
saying, The LORD hath blessed th
house of Ō'-bĕd–ĕ'-dom, and all tha
pertaineth unto him, because of th

rk of God. So David went and
rought up the ark of God from the
ouse of Ō-bĕd-ē-dom into the city
f David with gladness.
13 And it was *so*, that when [h]they that
are the ark of the LORD had gone
ix paces, he sacrificed [i]oxen and
atlings.
14 And David [j]danced before the
ORD with all *his* might; and David
vas girded with [k]a linen ē-phŏd.
15 So David and all the house of Is-
ael brought up the ark of the LORD
vith shouting, and with the sound of
he trumpet.
16 And as the ark of the LORD came
nto the city of David, Mī-chăl Saul's
aughter looked through a window,
nd saw king David leaping and dan-
ing before the LORD; and she despised
im in her heart.
17 ¶ And they brought in the ark of
he LORD, and set it in [l]his place, in
he midst of the tabernacle that David
ad [11]pitched for it: and David
offered burnt offerings and peace
fferings before the LORD.
18 And as soon as David had made
n end of offering burnt offerings
nd peace offerings, he blessed the
eople in the name of the LORD of
osts.
19 And he dealt among all the people,
ven among the whole multitude of
srael, as well to the women as men,
o every one a cake of bread, and a
good piece *of flesh*, and a flagon *of*
vine. So all the people departed
every one to his house.
20 ¶ Then [n]David returned to bless
his household. And Mī-chăl the
daughter of Saul came out to meet
David, and said, [o]How glorious was
the king of Israel to day, who [p]un-
covered himself to day in the eyes
of the handmaids of his servants, as
one of the [q]vain fellows [12]shamelessly
uncovereth himself!
21 And David said unto Mī-chăl, *It*
was [r]before the LORD, which chose me
before thy father, and before all his
house, to appoint me ruler over the
people of the LORD, over Israel:
therefore will I play before the
LORD.
22 And I will yet be more vile than
thus, and will be base in mine own
sight: and [13]of the maidservants which
thou hast spoken of, of them shall I
be had in honour.
23 Therefore Mī-chăl the daughter
of Saul [s]had no child unto the day of
her death.

h Num. 4.15. 1 Chr. 15.2, 15.
i 1 Ki. 8.5. 2 Chr. 5.6.
j Ex. 15.20. Judg. 11.34. Ps. 30.11.
k 1 Sam. 2.18.
l 1 Chr. 15.1.
11 stretched.
m 1 Ki. 8.5.
n Ps. 30. title.
o Eccl. 7.16.
p 1 Sam. 19. 24.
q Judg. 9.4.
12 Or, openly.
r 1 Sam. 13. 14.
13 Or, of the handmaids of my servants.
s 1 Sam. 15. 35. Isa. 22.14.

CHAP. 7

a 1 Chr. 17.1. Dan. 4.29, 30.
b ch. 5.11.
c Ex. 26.1.
d 1 Ki. 8.17. 1 Chr. 22.7.
1 to my servant, to David.
e 1 Ki. 8.16.
f Lev. 26.11.
2 1 Chr. 17.6. any of the judges.
g ch. 5.2. Ps. 78.71, 72. Eze. 34.2,15, 23. Matt. 2.6. Acts 20.28.
3 from after.
4 from thy face.
h Gen. 12.2. 1 Chr. 17.8. Luke 1.52.
i Ps. 44.2. Jer. 24.6. Amos 9.15.
j 1 Ki. 2.1.
k Deut. 31. 16. Acts 13.36.
l Ps. 132. 11. Isa. 11.1-3, 10.
m 1 Ki. 5.5.
n Ps. 89.4.
o Heb. 1.5.

CHAPTER 7

AND it came to pass, [a]when the king
sat in his house, and the LORD
had given him rest round about from
all his enemies;
2 That the king said unto Nathan the
prophet, See now, I dwell in [b]an house
of cedar, but the ark of God dwelleth
[c]within curtains.
3 And Nathan said to the king, Go,
do all that *is* [d]in thine heart; for the
LORD *is* with thee.
4 ¶ And it came to pass that night,
that the word of the LORD came unto
Nathan, saying,
5 Go and tell [1]my servant David,
Thus saith the LORD, Shalt thou build
me an house for me to dwell in?
6 Whereas I have not dwelt in *any*
house since [e]the time that I brought
up the children of Israel out of Egypt,
even to this day, but have walked in a
tent and in a tabernacle.
7 In all *the places* wherein I [f]have
walked with all the children of Israel
spake I a word with [2]any of the tribes
of Israel, whom I commanded [g]to
feed my people Israel, saying, Why
build ye not me an house of cedar?
8 Now therefore so shalt thou say
unto my servant David, Thus saith
the LORD of hosts, I took thee from
the sheepcote, [3]from following the
sheep, to be ruler over my people,
over Israel:
9 And I was with thee whithersoever
thou wentest, and have cut off all
thine enemies [4]out of thy sight, and
have made thee [h]a great name, like
unto the name of the great *men* that
are in the earth.
10 Moreover I will appoint a place
for my people Israel, and [i]will plant
them, that they may dwell in a place
of their own, and move no more;
neither shall the children of wickedness afflict them any more, as beforetime,
11 And as since the time that I commanded judges *to be* over my people
Israel, and have caused thee to rest
from all thine enemies. Also the LORD
telleth thee that he will make thee an
house.
12 ¶ And [j]when thy days be fulfilled,
and thou [k]shalt sleep with thy fathers,
[l]I will set up thy seed after thee,
which shall proceed out of thy bowels,
and I will establish his kingdom.
13 He [m]shall build an house for my
name, and I will [n]stablish the throne
of his kingdom for ever.
14 I [o]will be his father, and he shall

be my son. If [p]he commit iniquity, I
will chasten him with the rod of men,
and with the stripes of the children
of men:
15 But my mercy shall not depart
away from him, [q]as I took *it* from
Saul, whom I put away before thee.
16 And [r]thine house and thy kingdom shall be established for ever before thee: thy throne shall be established for ever.
17 According to all these words, and
according to all this vision, so did
Nathan speak unto David.
18 ¶ Then went king David in, and
sat before the LORD, and he said,
[s]Who *am* I, O Lord GOD? and what
is my house, that thou hast brought
me hitherto?
19 And this was yet a small thing
in thy sight, O Lord GOD; but thou
hast spoken also of thy servant's
house for a great while to come. And
[t]*is* this the [5]manner of man, O Lord
GOD?
20 And what can David say more
unto thee? for thou, Lord GOD, knowest [u]thy servant.
21 For thy [v]word's sake, and according to thine own heart, hast thou done
all these great things, to make thy
servants know *them*.
22 Wherefore [w]thou art great, O
LORD God: for [x]*there is* none like
thee, neither *is there any* God beside
thee, according to all that we have
heard with our ears.
23 And [y]what one nation in the earth
is like thy people, *even* like Israel,
whom God went to redeem for a people to himself, and to make him a
name, and to do for you great things
and terrible, for thy land, before [z]thy
people, which thou redeemedst to
thee from Egypt, *from* the nations and
their gods?
24 For [a]thou hast confirmed to thyself thy people Israel *to be* a people
unto thee for ever: and thou, LORD,
art become their God.
25 And now, O LORD God, the word
that thou hast spoken concerning thy
servant, and concerning his house,
establish *it* for ever, and do as thou
hast said.
26 And let [b]thy name be magnified
for ever, saying, The LORD of hosts *is*
the God over Israel: and let the house
of thy servant David be established
before thee.
27 For thou, O LORD of hosts, God
of Israel, hast [6]revealed to thy servant,
saying, I will build thee an house:

p Ps. 89.30.
q 1 Sam. 15. 23.
r Ps. 89.36, 37. John 12.34.
s Gen. 32.10.
t Isa. 55.8.
5 law.
u Gen. 18.19.
v Eph. 4.32.
w 1 Chr. 16. 25. 2 Chr. 2.5. Ps. 48.1. Ps. 86.10. Ps. 96.4. Ps. 135.5.
x Deut. 3.24. 1 Sam. 2.2. Ps. 86.8. Isa. 45.5.
y Deut. 4.7. Ps. 147.20.
z Neh. 1.10.
a Deut. 26.18.
b Ps. 72.19. Matt. 6.9.
6 opened the ear.
c John 17.17.
7 be thou pleased and bless.

CHAP. 8

a ch. 7.9. ch. 21.15-22. 1 Chr. 18.1.
1 Or, The bridle of Ammah.
b 1 Sam. 14. 47. Ps. 60.8.
c Ps. 72.10.
d ch. 10.6. Ps. 60, title.
e Gen. 15.18.
2 Or, of his.
3 Or, Tibhath.
4 Or, Chun.
5 ask him of peace.
6 was a man of wars with.
7 in his hand were.

therefore hath thy servant found in h
heart to pray this prayer unto thee
28 And now, O Lord GOD, thou a
that God, and [c]thy words be true, a
thou hast promised this goodness u
to thy servant:
29 Therefore now [7]let it please th
to bless the house of thy servant, th
it may continue for ever before the
for thou, O Lord GOD, hast spoken
and with thy blessing let the house
thy servant be blessed for ever.

CHAPTER 8

AND [a]after this it came to pass, th
David smote the Philistines, a
subdued them: and David to
[1]Mĕth-ĕg-ăm-măh out of the hand
the Philistines.
2 And [b]he smote Moab, and mea
ured them with a line, casting the
down to the ground; even with tw
lines measured he to put to death, a
with one full line to keep alive. An
so the Moabites became David's se
vants, *and* [c]brought gifts.
3 ¶ David smote also Hăd-ă-dē-zĕ
the son of Rē-hŏb, king of [d]Zō-băh,
he went to recover [e]his border at t
river Eû-phrā-tēs.
4 And David took [2]from him a thou
sand *chariots*, and seven hundre
horsemen, and twenty thousand foo
men: and David houghed all th
chariot *horses*, but reserved of the
for an hundred chariots.
5 And when the Syrians of Damasc
came to succour Hăd-ă-dē-zĕr king
Zō-băh, David slew of the Syria
two and twenty thousand men.
6 Then David put garrisons in Syri
of Damascus: and the Syrians be
came servants to David, *and* brough
gifts. And the LORD preserved Davi
whithersoever he went.
7 And David took the shields of gol
that were on the servants of Hăd-ă
dē-zĕr, and brought them to Jerusa
lem.
8 And from [3]Bē-tăh, and from [4]Bē
rō-thāi, cities of Hăd-ă-dē-zĕr, kin
David took exceeding much brass.
9 ¶ When Tō-ī king of Hā-măt
heard that David had smitten all th
host of Hăd-ă-dē-zĕr,
10 Then Tō-ī sent Joram his son unt
king David, to [5]salute him, and t
bless him, because he had fough
against Hăd-ă-dē-zĕr, and smitte
him: for Hăd-ă-dē-zĕr [6]had wars wit
Tō-ī. And *Joram* [7]brought with hi
vessels of silver, and vessels of gold
and vessels of brass:

1 Which also king David [f]did dedi-
te unto the LORD, with the silver
ıd gold that he had dedicated of all
ıtions which he subdued;
2 Of Syria, and of Moab, and of the
ildren of Ammon, and of the Philis-
nes, and of Ăm-ʹă-lĕk, and of the
oil of Hăd-ă-dēʹ-zĕr, son of Rēʹ-hŏb,
ng of Zōʹ-băh.
3 And David gat *him* a name when
returned from [8]smiting of the
rians in the [g]valley of salt, [9]*being*
ghteen thousand *men*.
4 ¶ And he put garrisons in Ēʹ-dom;
roughout all Ēʹ-dom put he garri-
ns, and [h]all they of Ēʹ-dom became
avid's servants. And the LORD [i]pre-
rved David whithersoever he went.
5 And David reigned over all Israel;
ıd David executed judgment and
stice unto all his people.
6 And [j]Jōʹ-ăb the son of Zĕr-ū-īʹ-ăh
ıs over the host; and [k]Jĕ-hŏshʹ-ă-
ăt the son of Ă-hīʹ-lŭd *was* [10]re-
rder;
7 And [l]Zāʹ-dŏk the son of Ă-hīʹ-tŭb,
ıd Ă-hĭmʹ-ĕ-lĕch the son of Ă-bīʹ-ă-
ăr, *were* the priests; and Sĕ-raîʹ-ăh
ıs the [11]scribe;
8 And [m]Bĕ-naîʹ-ăh the son of Jĕ-
ɔiʹ-ă-dă *was over* both the [n]Chĕrʹ-ē-
ites and the Pĕlʹ-ĕ-thites; and
avid's sons were [12]chief rulers.

CHAPTER 9

AND David said, Is there yet any
that is left of the house of Saul,
at I may shew [a]him kindness for
nathan's sake?
And *there was* of the house of
ıul a servant whose name [b]*was*
ʹ-bă. And when they had called
m unto David, the king said unto
m, *Art* thou Zīʹ-bă? And he said,
hy servant *is he*.
And the king said, *Is* there not yet
ıy of the house of Saul, that I may
ew [c]the kindness of God unto him?
nd Zīʹ-bă said unto the king, Jona-
an hath yet a son, *which is* [d]lame on
s feet.
And the king said unto him, Where
he? And Zīʹ-bă said unto the king,
ehold, he *is* in the house of [e]Māʹ-chĭr,
e son of Ăm-ʹmī-ĕl, in Lōʹ-dĕ-băr.
¶ Then king David sent, and fetch-
him out of the house of Māʹ-chĭr,
e son of Ăm-ʹmī-ĕl, from Lōʹ-dĕ-
ır.
Now when [1]Mĕ-phĭbʹ-ŏ-shĕth, the
n of Jonathan, the son of Saul, was
me unto David, he fell on his face,
ıd did reverence. And David said,

f 1 Ki. 7.51. 1 Chr. 18.11. 1 Chr. 22. 14-16. Micah 4.13. Rev. 21.24.
8 his smiting. g 2 Ki. 14.7. 9 Or, slaying.
h Gen. 27.29. i Ps. 37.28. Ps. 121.8.
j ch. 19.13. k 1 Ki. 4.3. 10 Or, remembrancer, or, writer of chronicles. l 1 Chr. 24.3.
11 Or, secretary. m 1 Chr. 18. 17. n 1 Sam. 30. 14. 12 Or, princes.
CHAP. 9
a 1 Sam. 18.3. Pro. 27.10.
b ch. 16.1. c Deut. 10. 15. 1 Sam. 20. 14. Luke 6.36. Titus 3.3,4. d ch. 4.4. e ch. 17.27. 1 Called Merib-baal. f Gen. 43.18, 23. 1 Sam. 12. 19,20,24. g Jer. 52.33. h 1 Sam. 24. 14. ch. 16.9. i ch. 16.4. ch. 19.29. Isa. 32.8. j ch. 19.17. k ch. 16.1-4. Pro. 12.17. l 1 Chr. 8.34. m ch. 19.33, 36. 2 Ki. 25.29.
CHAP. 10
a 1 Sam. 11.1. ch. 17.27. 1 Chr. 19.1. 1 In thine eyes doth David.

Mĕ-phĭbʹ-ŏ-shĕth. And he answered,
Behold thy servant!
7 ¶ And David said unto him, Fear
[f]not: for I will surely shew thee kindness for Jonathan thy father's sake,
and will restore thee all the land of
Saul thy father; and thou shalt [g]eat
bread at my table continually.
8 And he bowed himself, and said,
What *is* thy servant, that thou shouldest look upon such [h]a dead dog as I
am?
9 ¶ Then the king called to Zīʹ-bă,
Saul's servant, and said unto him, I
[i]have given unto thy master's son all
that pertained to Saul and to all his
house.
10 Thou therefore, and thy sons, and
thy servants, shall till the land for
him, and thou shalt bring in *the fruits*,
that thy master's son may have food
to eat: but Mĕ-phĭbʹ-ŏ-shĕth thy master's son shall eat bread alway at my
table. Now Zīʹ-bă [j]had fifteen sons
and twenty servants.
11 Then said Zīʹ-bă unto the king,
According [k]to all that my lord the king
hath commanded his servant, so shall
thy servant do. As for Mĕ-phĭbʹ-ŏ-
shĕth, *said the king*, he shall eat at my
table, as one of the king's sons.
12 And Mĕ-phĭbʹ-ŏ-shĕth had a
young son, whose [l]name *was* Mīʹ-chă.
And all that dwelt in the house of Zīʹ-
bă *were* servants unto Mĕ-phĭbʹ-ŏ-
shĕth.
13 So Mĕ-phĭbʹ-ŏ-shĕth dwelt in Jerusalem: for he did [m]eat continually at
the king's table; and was lame on
both his feet.

CHAPTER 10

AND it came to pass after this, that
the king [a]of the children of Ammon died, and Hāʹ-nŭn his son reigned
in his stead.
2 Then said David, I will shew kindness unto Hāʹ-nŭn the son of Nahash,
as his father shewed kindness unto
me. And David sent to comfort him
by the hand of his servants for his
father. And David's servants came into the land of the children of Ammon.
3 And the princes of the children of
Ammon said unto Hāʹ-nŭn their lord,
[1]Thinkest thou that David doth honour thy father, that he hath sent comforters unto thee? hath not David
rather sent his servants unto thee, to
search the city, and to spy it out, and
to overthrow it?
4 Wherefore Hāʹ-nŭn took David's
servants, and shaved off the one half

of their beards, and cut off their garments in the middle, *even* to [b]their
buttocks, and sent them away.
5 When they told *it* unto David, he
sent to meet them, because the men
were greatly ashamed: and the king
said, Tarry at [2]Jericho until your
beards be grown, and *then* return.
6 ¶ And when the children of Ammon saw that they [c]stank before
David, the children of Ammon sent
and hired [d]the Syrians of Bĕth–rē-
hōb, and the Syrians of Zō-bă, twenty
thousand footmen, and of king Mā-
ă-căh a thousand men, and of [3]Ĭsh'–
tōb twelve thousand men.
7 And when David heard of *it*, he
sent Jō-ăb, and all the host of the
[e]mighty men.
8 And the children of Ammon came
out, and put the battle in array at the
entering in of the gate: and the Syrians of Zō-bă, and of Rē-hōb, and
Ĭsh-tōb, and Mā-ă-căh, *were* by
themselves in the field.
9 When Jō-ăb saw that the front of
the battle was against him before and
behind, he chose of all the choice *men*
of Israel, and put *them* in array against
the Syrians:
10 And the rest of the people he delivered into the hand of Ăb-ĭ-shāī his
brother, that he might put *them* in
array against the children of Ammon.
11 And he said, If the Syrians be too
strong for me, then thou shalt help
me: but if the children of Ammon be
too strong for thee, then I will come
and help thee.
12 Be [f]of good courage, and let us
[g]play the men for our people, and for
the cities of our God: and the [h]LORD
do that which seemeth him good.
13 And Jō-ăb drew nigh, and the
people that *were* with him, unto the
battle against the Syrians: and they
fled before him.
14 And when the children of Ammon
saw that the Syrians were fled, then
fled they also before Ăb-ĭ-shāī, and
entered into the city. So Jō-ăb returned from the children of Ammon,
and came to Jerusalem.
15 ¶ And when the Syrians saw that
they were smitten before Israel, they
gathered themselves together.
16 And Hăd-ă-rē-zĕr sent, and
brought out the Syrians that *were* beyond [4]the river: and they came to Hē-
lăm; and [5]Shō-băch the captain of the
host of Hăd-ă-rē-zĕr *went* before
them.
17 And when it was told David, he

b Isa. 3.17. Isa. 20.4. Jer. 13.22, 26. Eze. 16.37. Micah 1.11. Nahum 3.5.
2 Probably some village near to it. Compare Josh. 6.24 with 1 Ki. 16.34.
c Gen. 34.30. Ex. 5.21. 1 Sam. 13.4.
d ch. 8.3,5.
3 Or, the men of Tob.
e ch. 23.8.
f Deut. 31.6.
g 1 Sam. 4.9.
h 1 Sam. 3.18. ch. 15.26. Ps. 20.7. Ps. 37.3,5, 40. Ps. 44.5,6. Ps. 118.8. Pro. 29.25.
4 That is, Euphrates.
5 Or, Shophach.
6 1 Chr. 19. 18. footmen.
i Gen. 14.4.
CHAP. 11
1 at the return of the year.
a 1 Chr. 20.1.
b Deut. 22.8.
c Gen. 34.2. Job 31.1. Ps. 119.37. Matt. 5.28.
2 Or, Bath-shuah.
3 Or, Ammiel.
d ch. 23.39.
e Ex. 20.17. Lev. 18.20. Heb. 13.4. Jas. 1.14.
4 Or, and when she had purified herself, etc., she returned.
f Lev. 15.19.
g Lev. 20.10.
5 of the peace of, etc.
h Ps. 44.21. Ps. 55.21.
i Gen. 18.4.
6 went out after him.
j Job 5.12-14.

gathered all Israel together, and p
ed over Jordan, and came to
lăm. And the Syrians set themse
in array against David, and fou
with him.
18 And the Syrians fled before
rael; and David slew *the men of* se
hundred chariots of the Syrians,
forty thousand [6]horsemen, and sm
Shō-băch the captain of their h
who died there.
19 And when all the kings *that* w
[i]servants to Hăd-ă-rē-zĕr saw t
they were smitten before Israel, t
made peace with Israel, and ser
them. So the Syrians feared to h
the children of Ammon any more

CHAPTER 11

AND it came to pass, [1]after the y
was expired, at the time w
kings go forth *to battle*, that Da
[a]sent Jō-ăb, and his servants w
him, and all Israel; and they destro
the children of Ammon, and besie
Răb-băh. But David tarried still
Jerusalem.
2 ¶ And it came to pass in an ev
ingtide, that David arose from off
bed, [b]and walked upon the roof of
king's house: and from the roof
[c]saw a woman washing herself; a
the woman *was* very beautiful to lo
upon.
3 And David sent and inquired a
the woman. And *one* said, *Is* not t
[2]Băth'–shĕ-bă, the daughter of [3]E
ăm, the wife [d]of Ū-rī-ăh the Hitti
4 And David sent messengers, a
took her; and she came in unto hi
and [e]he lay with her; [4]for she v
[f]purified from her uncleanness: a
she returned unto her house.
5 And the woman conceived, a
sent and told David, and said, [g]I
with child.
6 ¶ And David sent to Jō-ăb, *sayi*
Send me Ū-rī-ăh the Hittite. And J
ăb sent Ū-rī-ăh to David.
7 And when Ū-rī-ăh was come u
him, David demanded *of him* [5]how J
ăb did, and how the people did, a
how the war prospered.
8 And David said to Ū-rī-ăh, [h]G
down to thy house, and [i]wash thy fe
And Ū-rī-ăh departed out of the kin
house, and there [6]followed him
mess *of meat* from the king.
9 But [j]Ū-rī-ăh slept at the door of t
king's house with all the servants
his lord, and went not down to h
house.
10 And when they had told Davi

ying, Ū-rī-ăh went not down unto
s house, David said unto Ū-rī-ăh,
amest thou not from *thy* journey?
hy *then* didst thou not go down unto
ine house?
1 And Ū-rī-ăh said unto David, The
rk, and Israel, and Judah, abide in
nts; and [l]my lord Jō-ăb, and the
rvants of my lord, [m]are encamped
the open fields; shall I then go into
ine house, to eat and to drink, and
lie with my wife? *as* thou livest, and
thy soul liveth, I will not do this
ing.
2 And David said to Ū-rī-ăh, [n]Tarry
ere to day also, and to morrow I will
t thee depart. So Ū-rī-ăh abode in
rusalem that day, and the morrow.
3 And when David had called him,
e did eat and drink before him; and
e made him drunk: and at even he
ent out to lie on his bed with the ser-
ants of his lord, but went not down
his house.
4 ¶ And it came to pass in the
orning, that David [p]wrote a letter
Jō-ăb, and sent *it* by the hand of
-rī-ăh.
5 And he wrote in the letter, saying,
et ye Ū-rī-ăh in the forefront of the
ottest battle, and retire ye [8]from him,
at he may be [q]smitten, and die.
6 And it came to pass, when Jō-ăb
bserved the city, that he assigned
-rī-ăh unto a place where he knew
at valiant men *were*.
7 And the men of the city went out,
nd fought with Jō-ăb: and there fell
me of the people of the servants of
avid; and Ū-rī-ăh the Hittite died
lso.
8 ¶ Then Jō-ăb sent and told David
l the things concerning the war;
9 And charged the messenger, say-
g, When thou hast made an end of
lling the matters of the war unto the
ing,
20 And if so be that the king's wrath
rise, and he say unto thee, Wherefore
pproached ye so nigh unto the city
hen ye did fight? knew ye not that
hey would shoot from the wall?
21 Who smote [r]Ă-bĭm-ĕ-lĕch the son
f [s]Jĕ-rŭb-bĕ-shĕth? did not a woman
ast a piece of a millstone upon him
rom the wall, that he died in Thē-
ĕz? why went ye nigh the wall? then
ay thou, Thy servant Ū-rī-ăh the Hit-
ite is dead also.
22 ¶ So the messenger went, and
ame and shewed David all that Jō-ăb
ad sent him for.
23 And the messenger said unto
David, Surely the men prevailed
against us, and came out unto us into
the field, and we were upon them even
unto the entering of the gate.
24 And the shooters shot from off the
wall upon thy servants; and *some* of
the king's servants be dead, and thy
servant Ū-rī-ăh the Hittite is dead
also.
25 Then David said unto the messenger, Thus shalt thou say unto Jō-ăb,
Let not this thing [9]displease thee, for
the sword devoureth [10]one as well as
another: make thy battle more strong
against the city, and overthrow it: and
encourage thou him.
26 ¶ And when the wife of Ū-rī-ăh
heard that Ū-rī-ăh her husband was
dead, she mourned for her husband.
27 And when the mourning was past,
David sent and fetched her to his
house, and she [t]became his wife, and
bare him a son. But the thing that
David had done [11]displeased the LORD.

CHAPTER 12

AND the LORD sent Nathan unto
David. And [a]he came unto him,
and [b]said unto him, There were two
men in one city; the one rich, and the
other poor.
2 The rich *man* had exceeding many
flocks and herds:
3 But the poor *man* had nothing, save
one little ewe lamb, which he had
bought and nourished up: and it grew
up together with him, and with his
children; it did eat of his own [1]meat,
and drank of his own cup, and lay in
his bosom, and was unto him as a
daughter.
4 And there came a traveller unto
the rich man, and he spared to take of
his own flock and of his own herd, to
dress for the wayfaring man that was
come unto him; but took the poor
man's lamb, and dressed it for the man
that was come to him.
5 And David's anger was greatly
kindled against the man; and he said
to Nathan, *As* the LORD liveth, the
man that hath done this *thing* [2]shall
surely die:
6 And he shall restore the [c]lamb fourfold, because he did this thing, and
because he had no pity.
7 ¶ And Nathan said to David, Thou
art the man. Thus saith the LORD God
of Israel, [d]I anointed thee king over
Israel, and I delivered thee out of the
hand of Saul;
8 And I gave thee thy master's house,
and thy master's wives into thy bosom,

k 1 Sam. 4.4. ch. 7.2,6.
l ch. 20.6. Matt. 10.25.
m 2 Tim. 2.3.
n Job 20.12-14.
o Gen. 9.21, 22. Ex. 32.21. Pro. 20.1. Pro. 23.29-35. Hosea 4.11. Gal. 5.21.
p 1 Ki. 21.8. Ps. 19.13. Ps. 62.9. Eccl. 8.11. Jer. 9.1-4. Micah 7.3-5.
7 strong.
8 from after him.
q ch. 12.9.
r Judg. 9.53. ch. 20.21. Job 31.3.
s Judg. 6.32. Jerubbaal.
9 be evil in thine eyes.
10 so and such.
t ch. 12.9.
11 was evil in the eyes of. Job 10.14. Ps. 5.4. Ps. 45.7. Ps. 139.1-5. Pro. 15.9. Hab. 1.13.

CHAP. 12

a Ps. 51. title.
b ch. 14.5. 1 Ki. 20.35. Matt. 21.33, 45. Luke 15.11.
1 morsel.
2 is a child of death, or, is worthy to die.
c Ex. 22.1. Luke 19.8.
d 1 Sam. 16.13. ch. 7.8.

and gave thee the house of Israel and of Judah; and if *that had been* too little, I would moreover have given unto thee such and such things.

9 Wherefore [e]hast thou [f]despised the commandment of the LORD, to do evil in his sight? [g]thou hast killed Ū-rī-ăh the Hittite with the sword, and hast taken his wife *to be* thy wife, and hast slain him with the sword of the children of Ammon.

10 Now therefore [h]the sword shall never depart from thine house; because thou hast despised me, and hast taken the wife of Ū-rī-ăh the Hittite to be thy wife.

11 Thus saith the LORD, Behold, I will raise up evil against thee out of thine own house, and I will take [i]thy wives before thine eyes, and give *them* unto thy neighbour, and he shall lie with thy wives in the sight of this sun.

12 For thou didst *it* secretly: but [j]I will do this thing before all Israel, and before the sun.

13 And [k]David said unto Nathan, I [l]have sinned against the LORD. And Nathan said unto David, The LORD also hath put [m]away thy sin; thou shalt not die.

14 Howbeit, because by this deed thou hast given great occasion to the enemies of the LORD to [n]blaspheme, the child also *that is* born unto thee shall surely die.

15 ¶ And Nathan departed unto his house. And the LORD [o]struck the child that Ū-rī-ăh's wife bare unto David, and it was very sick.

16 David therefore [p]besought God for the child; and David [3]fasted, and went in, and lay [q]all night upon the earth.

17 And the elders of his house arose, *and went* to him, to raise him up from the earth: but he would not, neither did he eat bread with them.

18 And it came to pass on the seventh day, that the child died. And the servants of David feared to tell him that the child was dead: for they said, Behold, while the child was yet alive, we spake unto him, and he would not hearken unto our voice: how will he then [4]vex himself, if we tell him that the child is dead?

19 But when David saw that his servants whispered, David perceived that the child was dead: therefore David said unto his servants, Is the child dead? And they said, He is dead.

20 Then David arose from the earth, and washed, and [r]anointed *himself*, and changed his apparel, and cam into the house of the LORD, and [s]wor shipped: then he came to his ow house; and when he required, they se bread before him, and he did eat.

21 Then said his servants unto hir What thing *is* this that thou has done? thou didst fast and weep for th child, *while it was* alive; but when th child was dead, thou didst rise and ea bread.

22 And he said, While the child wa yet alive, I fasted and wept: for [t]I saic Who can tell *whether* GOD will b gracious to me, that the child ma live?

23 But now he is dead, wherefor should I fast? can I bring him bac again? [u]I shall go to him, but [v]he shal not return to me.

24 ¶ And David comforted Băth'shĕ-bă his wife, and went in unto he and lay with her: and [w]she bare a sor and [x]he called his name [5]Solomon and the LORD loved him.

25 And he sent by the hand of Na than the prophet; and he called hi name [6]Jĕd-ĭ-dī-ăh, because of th LORD.

26 ¶ And [y]Jō-ăb fought [z]against Răb băh of the children of Ammon, an took the royal city.

27 And Jō-ăb sent messengers t David, and said, I have fought agains Răb-băh, and have taken [7]the city o waters.

28 Now therefore gather the rest o the people together, and encam against the city, and take it: lest I tak the city, and [8]it be called after m name.

29 And David gathered all the peopl together, and went to Răb-băh, an fought against it, and took it.

30 And [a]he took their king's crow from off his head, the weight whereo *was* a talent of gold with the preciou stones: and it was *set* on David's head And he brought forth the spoil of th city [9]in great abundance.

31 And he brought forth the peopl that *were* therein, and [10]put *them* un der saws, and under harrows of iron and under axes of iron, and mad them pass through the brickkiln: an thus did he unto all the cities of th children of Ammon. So David and a the people returned unto Jerusalem.

CHAPTER 13

AND it came to pass after this, tha [a]Ăb-să-lom the son of David ha a fair sister, whose name *was* [b]Tā

---

e Gen. 9.5,6. 1 Sam. 15. 19.
f Lev. 26.15, 16. Num. 15.31. Pro. 13.13. Isa. 5.24.
g ch. 11.15.
h Amos 7.9.
i Deut. 28.30.
j ch. 16.22.
k 1 Sam. 15. 24.
l ch. 24.10. Job 7.20. Ps. 32.5. Pro. 28.13.
m Ps. 32.1. Micah 7.18. Zech. 3.4.
n Isa. 52.5. Eze. 36.20. Rom. 2.24.
o Gen. 4.7. Amos 3.2.
p Isa. 26.16. Jer. 18.8.
3 fasted a fast.
q ch. 13.31.
4 do hurt.
r Ruth 3.3.
s Ps. 95.6,7,8. Ps. 103.1,8-17. Pro. 3.7. Pro. 16.6.
t Isa. 38.1,5. Jonah 3.9.
u 2 Cor. 5.1-8. Heb. 11.10.
v Job 7.8,9.
w Matt. 1.6.
x 1 Chr. 22.9.
5 That is, Peaceable and perfect.
6 That is, Beloved of the LORD.
y 1 Chr. 20.1.
z Deut. 3.11.
7 That part where the cisterns were.
8 my name be called upon it.
a 1 Chr. 20.2.
9 very great.
10 Or, made them saw wood and stones, dig iron, and labour about furnaces.

CHAP. 13

a ch. 3.2,3.
b 1 Chr. 3.9.

när; and Amnon the son of David
oved her.
2 And Amnon was so vexed, that he
ell sick for his sister Tā´-mär; for she
vas a virgin; and [1]Amnon thought it
ard for him to do any thing to her.
3 But Amnon had a friend, whose
ame *was* Jŏn´-ă-dăb, [c]the son of
hĭm´-ĕ-ăh David's brother: and Jŏn´-
-dăb *was* a very subtil man.
4 And he said unto him, Why *art*
hou, *being* the king's son, [2]lean [3]from
ay to day? wilt thou not tell me? And
mnon said unto him, [d]I love Tā´-mär,
ny brother Ăb´-să-lo̱m's sister.
5 And Jŏn´-ă-dăb said unto him, Lay
hee down on thy bed, and make thy-
elf sick: and when thy father cometh
o see thee, say unto him, I pray thee,
et my sister Tā´-mär come, and give
ne meat, and dress the meat in my
ight, that I may see *it*, and eat *it* at
er hand.
6 ¶ So Amnon lay down, and made
imself sick: and when the king was
ome to see him, Amnon said unto the
ing, I pray thee, let Tā´-mär my sister
ome, and [e]make me a couple of cakes
n my sight, that I may eat at her hand.
7 Then David sent home to Tā´-mär,
aying, Go now to thy brother Amon's house, and dress him meat.
8 So Tā´-mär went to her brother Amon's house; and he was laid down.
nd she took [4]flour, and kneaded *it*,
nd made cakes in his sight, and did
ake the cakes.
9 And she took a pan, and poured
hem out before him; but he refused
o eat. And Amnon said, [f]Have out
ll men from me. And they went out
very man from him.
10 And Amnon said unto Tā´-mär,
ring the meat into the chamber, that
may eat of thine hand. And Tā´-mär
ook the cakes which she had made,
nd brought *them* into the chamber to
mnon her brother.
11 And when she had brought *them*
nto him to eat, he [g]took hold of her,
nd said unto her, Come lie with me,
ny sister.
12 And she answered him, Nay, my
rother, do not [5]force me; for [6]no such
hing ought to be done in Israel: do
ot thou this [h]folly.
13 And I, whither shall I cause my
hame to go? and as for thee, thou
halt be as one of the fools in Israel.
Now therefore, I pray thee, speak unto
he king; for he [i]will not withhold me
rom thee.
14 Howbeit he would not hearken

1 It was marvellous, or, hidden in the eyes of Amnon.
c 1 Chr. 2.13.
2 thin.
3 morning by morning.
d Isa. 3.9.
e Gen. 18.6.
4 Or, paste.
f Gen. 45.1. Judg. 3.19.
g Gen. 39.12. Pro. 7.13. Eccl. 7.26.
5 humble me.
6 It ought not so to be done.
h Gen. 34.7. Judg. 19.23. Pro. 7.7-23.
i Gen. 19.8. Lev. 18.9, 11. Judg. 19.24.
j Lev. 18.9. Deut. 22.25. Judg. 20.5. ch. 12.11. Esther 7.8.
7 with great hatred greatly.
k Gen. 37.3. Judg. 5.30. Ps. 45.14.
l Josh. 7.6. ch. 1.2. Job 2.12.
m Jer. 2.37.
8 Aminon.
9 set not thine heart.
10 and desolate.
n Lev. 19.17. Pro. 10.18. Eph. 4.26, 31. 1 John 2.9, 11.
o Gen. 38.12. 1 Sam. 25.4. 2 Ki. 3.4.
p Josh. 17.18.

unto her voice: but, being stronger
than she, [j]forced her, and lay with her.
15 ¶ Then Amnon hated her [7]ex-
ceedingly; so that the hatred wherewith he hated her *was* greater than the
love wherewith he had loved her. And
Amnon said unto her, Arise, be gone.
16 And she said unto him, *There is*
no cause: this evil in sending me away
is greater than the other that thou
didst unto me. But he would not
hearken unto her.
17 Then he called his servant that
ministered unto him, and said, Put
now this *woman* out from me, and
bolt the door after her.
18 And *she had* [k]a garment of divers
colours upon her: for with such robes
were the king's daughters *that were*
virgins apparelled. Then his servant
brought her out, and bolted the door
after her.
19 ¶ And Tā´-mär put [l]ashes on her
head, and rent her garment of divers
colours that *was* on her, and [m]laid her
hand on her head, and went on crying.
20 And Ăb´-să-lo̱m her brother said
unto her, Hath [8]Amnon thy brother
been with thee? but hold now thy
peace, my sister: he *is* thy brother;
[9]regard not this thing. So Tā´-mär remained [10]desolate in her brother Ăb´-
să-lo̱m's house.
21 ¶ But when king David heard of
all these things, he was very wroth.
22 And Ăb´-să-lo̱m spake unto his
brother Amnon neither good nor bad:
for Ăb´-să-lo̱m hated [n]Amnon, because he had forced his sister Tā´-mär.
23 ¶ And it came to pass after two
full years, [o]that Ăb´-să-lo̱m had sheepshearers in Bā´-ăl-hā´-zôr, which *is* beside [p]Ē´-phră-ĭm: and Ăb´-să-lo̱m invited all the king's sons.
24 And Ăb´-să-lo̱m came to the king,
and said, Behold now, thy servant
hath sheepshearers; let the king, I beseech thee, and his servants go with
thy servant.
25 And the king said to Ăb´-să-lo̱m,
Nay, my son, let us not all now go,
lest we be chargeable unto thee. And
he pressed him: howbeit he would not
go, but blessed him.
26 Then said Ăb´-să-lo̱m, If not, I
pray thee, let my brother Amnon go
with us. And the king said unto him,
Why should he go with thee?
27 But Ăb´-să-lo̱m pressed him, that
he let Amnon and all the king's sons
go with him.
28 ¶ Now Ăb´-să-lo̱m had commanded his servants, saying, Mark ye now

when Amnon's [q]heart is merry with
wine, and when I say unto you, Smite
Amnon; then kill him, fear not:
[11]have not I commanded you? be
courageous, and be [12]valiant.
29 And the servants of Ăb-́să-lom
did unto Amnon as Ăb-́să-lom had
commanded. Then all the king's sons
arose, and every man [13]gat him up
upon his mule, and fled.
30 ¶ And it came to pass, while they
were in the way, that tidings came to
David, saying, Ăb-́să-lom hath slain
all the king's sons, and there is not
one of them left.
31 Then the king arose, and tare [r]his
garments, and [s]lay on the earth; and
all his servants stood by with their
clothes rent.
32 And Jŏn-́ă-dăb, the son of Shĭm-́
ē-äh David's brother, answered and
said, Let not my lord suppose *that*
they have slain all the young men the
king's sons; for Amnon only is dead:
for by the [14]appointment of Ăb-́să-
lom this hath been [15]determined from
the day that he forced his sister Tā-́
mär.
33 Now therefore [t]let not my lord
the king take the thing to his heart, to
think that all the king's sons are dead:
for Amnon only is dead.
34 But Ăb-́să-lom fled. And the
young man that kept the watch lifted
up his eyes, and looked, and, behold,
there came much people by the way
of the hill side behind him.
35 And Jŏn-́ă-dăb said unto the king,
Behold, the king's sons come: [16]as thy
servant said, so it is.
36 And it came to pass, as soon as he
had made an end of speaking, that,
behold, the king's sons came, and
lifted up their voice and wept: and the
king also and all his servants wept
[17]very sore.
37 ¶ But Ăb-́să-lom fled, and went
to [u]Tăl-́maî, the son of [18]Ăm-́mĭ-hŭd,
king of Gē-́shŭr. And *David* mourned
for his son every day.
38 So Ăb-́să-lom fled, and went to
[v]Gē-́shŭr, and was there three years.
39 And *the soul of* king David [19]long-
ed to go forth unto Ăb-́să-lom: for he
was [w]comforted concerning Amnon,
seeing he was dead.

CHAPTER 14

NOW Jō-́ăb the son of Zĕr-ū-ī-́äh
perceived that the king's heart
was toward Ăb-́să-lom.
2 And Jō-́ăb sent to [a]Tĕ-kō-́äh, and
fetched thence a wise woman, and
said unto her, I pray thee, feign th
self to be a mourner, and put [b]on no
mourning apparel, and anoint not th
self with oil, but be as a woman th
had a long time mourned for the dea
3 And come to the king, and spe
on this manner unto him. So Jō-́
[c]put the words in her mouth.
4 ¶ And when the woman of Tĕ-k
äh spake to the king, [d]she fell on h
face to the ground, and did obeisanc
and said, [1]Help, O king.
5 And the king said unto her, Wh
aileth thee? And she answered, [e]I *a*
indeed a widow woman, and mi
husband is dead.
6 And thy handmaid had two sor
and they two strove together in t
field, and *there was* [2]none to pa
them, but the one smote the othe
and slew him.
7 And, behold, [f]the whole family
risen against thine handmaid, ar
they said, Deliver him that smote h
brother, that we may kill him, for t
life of his brother whom he slew; ar
we will destroy the heir also: and
they shall quench my coal which
left, and shall not leave to my husbar
neither name nor remainder [3]upon t
earth.
8 And the king said unto the woma
Go to thine house, and I will giv
charge concerning thee.
9 And the woman of Tĕ-kō-́äh sai
unto the king, My lord, O king, th
[g]iniquity *be* on me, and on my father
house: [h]and the king and his thror
be guiltless.
10 And the king said, Whosoeve
saith *ought* unto thee, bring him to m
and he shall not touch thee any mor
11 Then said she, I pray thee, let th
king remember the LORD thy Go
[4]that thou wouldest not suffer [i]the re
vengers of blood to destroy any mor
lest they destroy my son. And he sai
[j]*As* the LORD liveth, there shall nc
one hair of thy son fall to the earth.
12 Then the woman said, Let thin
handmaid, I pray thee, speak *on*
word unto my lord the king. And h
said, Say on.
13 And the woman said, Wherefor
then hast thou thought such a thin
against the [k]people of God? for th
king doth speak this thing as on
which is faulty, in that the king dot
not fetch home again his [l]banished.
14 For we [m]must needs die, and *ar*
as water spilt on the ground, whic
cannot be gathered up again; [5]neithe
doth God respect *any* person: ye

q Gen. 9.21. Ruth 3.7. 1 Sam. 25. 36. Esther 1.10. Ps. 104.15.
11 Or, will you not, since I have have commanded you?
12 sons of valour.
13 rode.
r Gen. 37.29, 34. ch. 1.11.
s ch. 12.16.
14 mouth.
15 Or, settled.
t ch. 19.19.
16 according to the word of thy servant.
17 with a great weeping greatly.
u ch. 3.3.
18 Ammihur.
v ch. 14.23.
19 Or, was consumed.
w Gen. 38.12.

CHAP. 14

a 2 Chr. 11.6. 2 Chr. 20.20. Neh. 3.5,27. Jer. 6.1. Amos 1.1.
b Ruth 3.3.
c Ex. 4.15.
d 1 Sam. 20. 41. ch. 1.2.
1 Save. Deut. 27.19. 2 Ki. 6.26.
e ch. 12.1.
2 no deliverer between them.
f Gen. 4.14. Num. 35.19. Deut. 19.12.
3 upon the face of the earth.
g Gen. 27.13. 1 Sam. 25. 24. Matt. 27.25.
h Num. 35. 33. ch. 3.28.
4 that the revenger of blood do not multiply to destroy.
i Num. 35.19. Josh. 20. 3-6.
j 1 Sam. 14. 45. Acts 27.34.
k Judg. 20.2.
l ch. 13.37.
m Job 30.23. Eccl. 3.19. Heb. 9.27.
5 Or, because God hath not taken away his life, he hath also devised means, etc.

oth he [n]devise means, that his ban-
;hed be not expelled from him.
15 Now therefore that I am come to
peak of this thing unto my lord the
ing, *it is* because the people have
nade me afraid: and thy handmaid
aid, I will now speak unto the king;
may be that the king will perform
he request of his handmaid.
16 For the king will hear, to deliver
is handmaid out of the hand of the
nan *that would* destroy me and my
on together out of the inheritance of
God.
17 Then thine handmaid said, The
vord of my lord the king shall now be
comfortable: for [o]as an angel of God,
o *is* my lord the king [7]to discern good
nd bad: therefore the LORD thy God
vill be with thee.
18 Then the king answered and said
nto the woman, Hide not from me, I
ray thee, the thing that I shall ask
hee. And the woman said, Let my
ord the king now speak.
19 And the king said, *Is not* the hand
f Jō´-ăb with thee in all this? And the
voman answered and said, *As* thy
oul liveth, my lord the king, none can
urn to the right hand or to the left
rom ought that my lord the king hath
poken: for thy servant Jō´-ăb, he bade
ne, and he put all these words in the
nouth of thine handmaid:
20 To fetch about this form of speech
ath thy servant Jō´-ăb done this thing:
nd my lord *is* wise, according [p]to the
visdom of an angel of God, to know
ll *things* that *are* in the earth.
21 ¶ And the king said unto Jō´-ăb,
Behold now, I have done this thing:
o therefore, bring the young man
Ăb´-să-lo̱m again.
22 And Jō´-ăb fell to the ground on
is face, and bowed himself, and
thanked the king: and Jō´-ăb said, To
ay thy servant knoweth that I have
ound grace in thy sight, my lord, O
ing, in that the king hath fulfilled the
equest of [9]his servant.
23 So Jō´-ăb arose [q]and went to Gē´-
hûr, and brought Ăb´-să-lo̱m to Jeru-
alem.
24 And the king said, Let him turn
o his own house, and let him not [r]see
ny face. So Ăb´-să-lo̱m returned to his
wn house, and saw not the king's
ace.
25 ¶ [10]But in all Israel there was none
o be so much praised as Ăb´-să-lo̱m
or his beauty: [s]from the sole of his
oot even to the crown of his head
here was no blemish in him.

[n] Num. 35. 15.
6 for rest.
[o] 1 Sam. 29.9.
7 to hear.
[p] ch. 19.27.
8 blessed.
9 Or, thy.
[q] Deut. 3.14. ch. 3.3.
[r] Gen. 43.3. ch. 3.13. Rev. 22.4.
10 And as Absalom there was not a beautiful man in all Israel to praise greatly.
[s] Deut. 28.35. Job 2.7. Isa. 1.6.
[t] ch. 18.9.
11 Six pounds and a quarter avoirdupois.
[u] ch. 18.18.
12 near my place.
[v] ch. 13.28. Pro. 29.12.
[w] Pro. 28.13.
[x] Gen. 33.4. Luke 15.20.

CHAP. 15

[a] ch. 12.11.
[b] 1 Ki. 1.5. Pro. 11.2.
[c] Pro. 1.16.
1 to come.
[d] Pro. 12.2.
2 Or, none will hear thee from the king downward.
[e] Judg. 9.29.

26 And when he polled his head, (for
it was at every year's end that he polled
it: because [t]*the hair* was heavy on him,
therefore he polled it:) he weighed
the hair of his head at [11]two hundred
shekels after the king's weight.
27 And [u]unto Ăb´-să-lo̱m there were
born three sons, and one daughter,
whose name *was* Tā´-mär: she was a
woman of a fair countenance.
28 ¶ So Ăb´-să-lo̱m dwelt two full
years in Jerusalem, and saw not the
king's face.
29 Therefore Ăb´-să-lo̱m sent for Jō´-
ăb, to have sent him to the king; but
he would not come to him: and when
he sent again the second time, he
would not come.
30 Therefore he said unto his servants, See, Jō´-ăb's field is [12]near mine,
and he hath barley there; go [v]and set
it on fire. And Ăb´-să-lo̱m's servants
set the field on fire.
31 Then Jō´-ăb arose, and came to
Ăb´-să-lo̱m unto *his* house, and said
unto him, Wherefore have thy servants set my field on fire?
32 And Ăb´-să-lo̱m answered Jō´-ăb,
Behold, I sent unto thee, saying, Come
hither, that I may send thee to the
king, to say, Wherefore am I come
from Gē´-shûr? *it had been* good for
me *to have been* there still: now therefore let me see the king's face; and if
[w]there be *any* iniquity in me, let him
kill me.
33 So Jō´-ăb came to the king, and
told him: and when he had called for
Ăb´-să-lo̱m, he came to the king, and
bowed himself on his face to the
ground before the king: and the king
[x]kissed Ăb´-să-lo̱m.

CHAPTER 15

AND [a]it came to pass after this, that
Ăb´-să-lo̱m [b]prepared him chariots and horses, and fifty men to run
before him.
2 And Ăb´-să-lo̱m [c]rose up early, and
stood beside the way of the gate: and
it was *so*, that when any man that had
a controversy [1]came to the king for
judgment, then Ăb´-să-lo̱m called unto
him, and said, Of what city *art* thou?
And he said, Thy servant *is* of one of
the tribes of Israel.
3 And Ăb´-să-lo̱m said unto him,
[d]See, thy matters *are* good and right;
but [2]*there is* no man *deputed* of the
king to hear thee.
4 Ăb´-să-lo̱m said moreover, [e]Oh that
I were made judge in the land, that
every man which hath any suit or

cause might come unto me, and I would do him justice!
5 And it was *so*, that when any man came nigh *to him* to do him obeisance, he put forth his hand, and [f]took him, and kissed him.
6 And on this manner did Ăb'-să-lo̤m to all Israel that came to the king for judgment: so [g]Ăb'-să-lo̤m stole the hearts of the men of Israel.
7 ¶ And it came to pass after [3]forty years, that Ăb'-să-lo̤m said unto the king, I pray thee, let me go and pay my vow, which I have vowed unto the LORD, in [h]Hē'-brŏn.
8 For [i]thy servant [j]vowed a vow while [k]I abode at Gē'-shu̇r in Syria, saying, If the LORD shall bring me again indeed to Jerusalem, then I will serve the LORD.
9 And the king said unto him, Go in peace. So he arose, and went to Hē'-brŏn.
10 ¶ But Ăb'-să-lo̤m sent spies throughout all the tribes of Israel, saying, As soon as ye hear the sound of the trumpet, then ye shall say, Ăb'-să-lo̤m reigneth in Hē'-brŏn.
11 And with Ăb'-să-lo̤m went two hundred men out of Jerusalem, *that were* [l]called; and they went [m]in their simplicity, and they knew not any thing.
12 And Ăb'-să-lo̤m sent for Ă-hĭth'-ō-phĕl the Gī'-lō-nite, [n]David's counseller, [o]from his city, *even* from Gī'-lōh, while he offered sacrifices. And the conspiracy was strong; for the people [p]increased continually with Ăb'-să-lo̤m.
13 ¶ And there came a messenger to David, saying, [q]The hearts of the men of Israel are after Ăb'-să-lo̤m.
14 And David said unto all his servants that *were* with him at Jerusalem, Arise, and let us [r]flee; for we shall not *else* escape from Ăb'-să-lo̤m: make speed to depart, lest he overtake us suddenly, and [4]bring evil upon us, and smite the city with the edge of the sword.
15 And the king's servants said unto the king, Behold, thy servants *are ready to do* whatsoever my lord the king shall [5]appoint.
16 And the [s]king went forth, and all his household [6]after him. And the king left [t]ten women, *which were* concubines, to keep the house.
17 And the king went forth, and all the people after him, and tarried in a place that was far off.
18 And all his servants passed on be-

[f] Ps. 12.2.
[g] Rom. 16.18.
3 Forty years from David's anointing as recorded in 1 Sam. 16.1. Or, four years from Absalom's return.
[h] ch. 2.1.
[i] 1 Sam. 16.2.
[j] Gen. 28.20. 1 Sam. 1.11. Ps. 56.12.
[k] ch. 13.38.
[l] 1 Sam. 9.13.
[m] Gen. 20.5. Pro. 14.15. Matt. 10.16. Rom. 16.18, 19.
[n] Ps. 41.9. Micah 7.5,6.
[o] Josh. 15.51.
[p] Ps. 3.1.
[q] Judg. 9.3.
[r] ch. 19.9. Ps. 3, title.
4 thrust.
5 choose.
[s] Ps. 3, title.
6 at his feet.
[t] ch. 12.11. ch. 16.21.
[u] ch. 8.18.
[v] ch. 18.2.
7 make thee wander in going.
[w] 1 Sam. 23. 13.
[x] Ruth 1.16. 1 Sam. 20.3. 2 Ki. 2.2,4,6.
[y] 1 Ki. 2.37. 2 Chr. 30.14.
[z] ch. 16.2. Matt. 3.1-3.
[a] Num. 4.15.
[b] Ps. 43.3.
[c] ch. 6.17.
[d] Num. 14.8. 1 Ki. 10.9. 2 Chr. 9.8.
[e] 1 Sam. 3.18.
[f] ch. 24.11.
[g] ch. 17.17.
[h] Zech. 14.4. Matt. 21.1. Luke 19.29. Acts 1.12.
8 going up, and weeping.
[i] Esther 6.12.
[j] Isa. 20.2.
[k] Jer. 14.3.

side him; [u]and all the Chĕr'-ĕ-thīt
and all the Pĕl'-ĕ-thītes, and all
Gĭt'-tītes, six hundred men which ca
after him from Gath, passed on
fore the king.
19 ¶ Then said the king to [v]Ĭt-tā'-ī t
Gĭt'-tīte, Wherefore goest thou a
with us? return to thy place, and abi
with the king: for thou *art* a strang
and also an exile.
20 Whereas thou camest *but* yest
day, should I this day [7]make thee
up and down with us? seeing I
[w]whither I may, return thou, and ta
back thy brethren: mercy and tru
be with thee.
21 And Ĭt-tā'-ī answered the king, a
said, *As* [x]the LORD liveth, and *as* r
lord the king liveth, surely in wh
place my lord the king shall be, whet
er in death or life, even there also w
thy servant be.
22 And David said to Ĭt-tā'-ī, Go a
pass over. And Ĭt-tā'-ī the Gĭt'-ti
passed over, and all his men, and
the little ones that *were* with him.
23 And all the country wept with
loud voice, and all the people pass
over: the king also himself pass
over the [y]brook Kī'-drŏn, and all t
people passed over, toward the wa
of the [z]wilderness.
24 ¶ And lo Zā'-dŏk also, and all t
Levites *were* with him, [a]bearing t
ark of the covenant of God: and the
set down the ark of God; and Ă-bī'-
thär went up, until all the people ha
done passing out of the city.
25 And the king said unto Zā'-dŏ
Carry back the ark of God into th
city: if I shall find favour in the eyes
the LORD, he [b]will bring me again, an
shew me *both* it, and his [c]habitation
26 But if he thus say, I have no d
light [d]in thee; behold, *here am* I, [e]l
him do to me as seemeth good unt
him.
27 The king said also unto Zā'-dŏ
the priest, *Art not* thou a [f]seer? retur
into [g]the city in peace, and your tw
sons with you, Ă-hī'-mă-ăz thy so
and Jonathan the son of Ă-bī'-ă-thä
28 See, I will tarry in the plain of th
wilderness, until there come wor
from you to certify me.
29 Zā'-dŏk therefore and Ă-bī'-ă-thä
carried the ark of God again to Jerusa
lem: and they tarried there.
30 ¶ And David went up by the as
cent of *mount* [h]Olivet, [8]and wept as h
went up, and [i]had his head covered
and he [j]went barefoot: and all th
people that *was* with him [k]covere

every man his head, and they went up, weeping as they went up.

31 ¶ And *one* told David, saying, Ă-hĭth-'ō-phĕl *is* [m]among the conspirators with Ăb-'să-lom. And David said, O LORD, I pray thee, turn [n]the counsel of Ă-hĭth-'ō-phĕl into foolishness.

32 ¶ And it came to pass, that *when* David was come to the top *of the mount*, where he worshipped God, behold, Hū-'shâi [o]the Är-'chīte came to meet him with [p]his coat rent, and earth upon his head:

33 Unto whom David said, If thou passest on with me, then thou shalt be a [q]burden unto me:

34 But if thou return to the city, and say unto Ăb-'să-lom, I will be thy servant, O king; *as* I *have been* thy father's servant hitherto, so *will* I now also *be* thy servant: then mayest thou for me defeat the counsel of Ă-hĭth-'ō-phĕl.

35 And *hast thou* not there with thee Zā-'dŏk and Ă-bī-'ă-thär the priests? therefore it shall be, *that* what thing soever thou shalt hear out of the king's house, thou shalt tell *it* to Zā-'dŏk and Ă-bī-'ă-thär the priests.

36 Behold, *they have* there with them their two sons, Ă-hī-'mă-ăz Zā-'dŏk's *son*, and Jonathan Ă-bī-'ă-thär's *son;* and by them ye shall send unto me every thing that ye can hear.

37 So Hū-'shâi [r]David's friend came into the city, and Ăb-'să-lom came into Jerusalem.

CHAPTER 16

AND [a]when David was a little past the top *of the hill*, behold, Zī-'bă the servant of Mĕ-phĭb-'ō-shĕth met him, with a couple of asses saddled, and upon them two hundred *loaves* of bread, and an hundred bunches of raisins, and an hundred of summer fruits, and a bottle of wine.

2 And the king said unto Zī-'bă, What meanest thou by these? And Zī-'bă said, The asses *be* for the king's household [c]to ride on; and the bread and summer fruit for the [d]young men to eat; and the wine, that [e]such as be faint in the wilderness may drink.

3 And the king said, And where *is* thy master's son? [f]And Zī-'bă said unto the king, Behold, he abideth at Jerusalem: for he said, To day shall the house of Israel restore me the kingdom of my father.

4 Then [g]said the king to Zī-'bă, Behold, thine *are* all that *pertained* unto Mĕ-phĭb-'ō-shĕth. And Zī-'bă said, I humbly beseech thee *that* [1]I may find grace in thy sight, my lord, O king.

5 ¶ And when king David came to Bă-hū-'rĭm, behold, thence came out a man of the family of the house of Saul, whose name [h]*was* Shĭm-'ĕ-ī, the son of Gē-'ră: [2]he came forth, and cursed still as he came.

6 And he cast stones at David, and at all the servants of king David: and all the people and all the mighty men *were* on his right hand and on his left.

7 And thus said Shĭm-'ĕ-ī when he cursed, Come out, come out, thou [3]bloody man, and thou man of Bē-'lĭ-ăl:

8 The LORD hath [i]returned upon thee all [j]the blood of the house of Saul, in whose stead thou hast reigned; and the LORD hath delivered the kingdom into the hand of Ăb-'să-lom thy son: and, [4]behold, thou *art taken* in thy mischief, because thou *art* a bloody man.

9 ¶ Then said Ăb-'ī-shâi the son of Zĕr-ū-ī-'ăh unto the king, Why should this dead dog curse [k]my lord the king? let me go over, I pray thee, and take off his head.

10 And the king said, [l]What have I to do with you, ye sons of Zĕr-ū-ī-'ăh? so let him curse, because the [m]LORD hath said unto him, Curse David. [n]Who shall then say, Wherefore hast thou done so?

11 And David said to Ăb-'ī-shâi, and to all his servants, Behold, my son, which came forth of my bowels, seeketh my life: how much more now *may this* Benjamite *do it?* let him alone, and let him curse; for the LORD hath bidden him.

12 It may be that the LORD will look on mine [5]affliction, and that the LORD will requite me [o]good for his cursing this day.

13 And as David and his men went by the way, Shĭm-'ĕ-ī went along on the hill's side over against him, and cursed as he went, and threw stones at him, and [6]cast dust.

14 And the king, and all the people that *were* with him, came weary, and refreshed themselves there.

15 ¶ And Ăb-'să-lom, and all the people the men of Israel, came to Jerusalem, and Ă-hĭth-'ō-phĕl with him.

16 And it came to pass, when Hū-'shâi the Är-'chīte, David's friend, was come unto Ăb-'să-lom, that Hū-'shâi said unto Ăb-'să-lom, [7]God save the king, God save the king.

l Ps. 126.6. Matt. 5.4. Rom. 12.15.
m Ps. 3.1. Ps. 55.12.
n ch. 16.23.
o Josh. 16.2.
p ch. 1.2.
q ch. 19.35.
r ch. 16.16. Pro. 17.17.
s ch. 16.15.

CHAP. 16

a ch. 15.30.
b ch. 9.2.
c Judg. 5.10. ch. 15.1.
d 1 Sam. 25. 27.
e ch. 15.23. Ps. 104.15. Pro. 31.6. 1 Tim. 5.23.
f ch. 19.27.
g Pro. 18.13.
1 I do obeisance.
h ch. 19.16.
2 Or, he still came forth and cursed.
3 man of blood.
i Judg. 9.24. Rev. 16.6.
j ch. 1.16. ch. 3.28,29.
4 behold thee in thy evil.
k Ex. 22.28.
l ch. 3.39. 1 Pet. 2.23.
m 2 Ki. 18.25. Lam. 3.38.
n Rom. 9.20.
5 eye, or, tears.
o Ps. 37.7. Lam. 3.22-26. Matt. 5.11, 12. Rom. 8.28. 2 Cor. 4.17.
6 dusted him with dust.
7 Let the king live.

17 And Ăb'-să-lo̱m said to Hū'-shâi, *Is* this thy kindness to thy friend? why [p]wentest thou not with thy friend?

18 And Hū'-shâi said unto Ăb'-să-lo̱m. Nay; but whom the LORD, and this people, and all the men of Israel, choose, his will I be, and with him will I abide.

19 And again, [q]whom should I serve? *should I* not *serve* in the presence of his son? as I have served in thy father's presence, so will I be in thy presence.

20 ¶ Then said Ăb'-să-lo̱m to Ă-hĭth'-ō-phĕl, Give [r]counsel among you what we shall do.

21 And Ă-hĭth'-ō-phĕl said unto Ăb'-să-lo̱m, Go in unto thy [s]father's concubines, which he hath left to keep the house; and all Israel shall hear that thou [t]art abhorred of thy father: then shall [u]the hands of all that *are* with thee be strong.

22 So they spread Ăb'-să-lo̱m a tent upon the top of the house; and Ăb'-să-lo̱m went in unto his father's concubines [v]in the sight of all Israel.

23 And the counsel of Ă-hĭth'-ō-phĕl, which he counselled in those days, *was* as if a man had inquired at the [8]oracle of God: so *was* all the counsel of Ă-hĭth'-ō-phĕl [w]both with David and with Ăb'-să-lo̱m.

CHAPTER 17

MOREOVER Ă-hĭth'-ō-phĕl said unto Ăb'-să-lo̱m, Let me now choose out twelve thousand men, and I will arise and pursue after David this night:

2 And I will come upon him while he *is* [a]weary and weak handed, and will make him afraid: and all the people that *are* with him shall flee; and I will [b]smite the king only:

3 And I will bring back all the people unto thee: the man whom thou seekest *is* as if all returned: *so* all the people shall be in [c]peace.

4 And the saying [1]pleased Ăb'-să-lo̱m well, and all the elders of Israel.

5 Then said Ăb'-să-lo̱m, Call now Hū'-shâi the Är'-chīte also, and let us hear likewise [2]what he saith.

6 And when Hū'-shâi was come to Ăb'-să-lo̱m, Ăb'-să-lo̱m spake unto him, saying, Ă-hĭth'-ō-phĕl hath spoken after this manner: shall we do *after* his [3]saying? if not; speak thou.

7 And Hū'-shâi said unto Ăb'-să-lo̱m, The counsel that Ă-hĭth'-ō-phĕl hath [4]given *is* not good at this time.

8 For, said Hū'-shâi, thou knowest thy father and his men, that they *be* mighty men, and they *be* [5]chafed in their minds, as [d]a bear robbed of h[er] whelps in the field: and thy father *is* a man of war, and will not lodge wi[th] the people.

9 Behold, he is hid now in some p[it,] or in some *other* place: and it w[ill] come to pass, when some of them [be] [6]overthrown at the first, that whos[o]ever heareth it will say, There is slaughter among the people that fo[l]low Ăb'-să-lo̱m.

10 And he also *that is* [7]valiant, who[se] heart *is* as the heart of a lion, sh[all] utterly melt: for all Israel knowe[th] that thy father *is* a mighty man, a[nd] *they* which *be* with him *are* valia[nt] men.

11 Therefore I counsel that all Isra[el] be generally gathered unto thee, fro[m] Dan even to Bē'er-shē'-bă, as the [e]sar[nd] that *is* by the sea for multitude; [8]a[nd] that thou go to battle in thine ow[n] person.

12 So shall we come upon him [in] some place where he shall be foun[d,] and we will light upon him as the de[w] falleth on the ground: and of him ar[d] of all the men that *are* with him the[re] shall not be left so much as one.

13 Moreover, if he be gotten into [a] city, then shall all Israel bring rop[es] to that city, and we will draw it in[to] the river, until there be not one sma[ll] stone found there.

14 And Ăb'-să-lo̱m and all the men [of] Israel said, The counsel of Hū'-sh[âi] the Är'-chīte *is* better than the couns[el] of Ă-hĭth'-ō-phĕl. For the [f]LORD ha[d] [9]appointed to defeat the good couns[el] of Ă-hĭth'-ō-phĕl, to the intent that th[e] LORD might bring evil upon Ăb'-să-lo̱m.

15 ¶ Then said Hū'-shâi unto Zā'-dō[k] and to Ă-bī'-ă-thär the priests, Thu[s] and thus did Ă-hĭth'-ō-phĕl couns[el] Ăb'-să-lo̱m and the elders of Israe[l;] and thus and thus have I counselled.

16 Now therefore send quickly, an[d] tell David, saying, Lodge not th[is] night in the plains of the wildernes[s,] but speedily pass over; lest the king b[e] swallowed up, and all the people tha[t] *are* with him.

17 Now [g]Jonathan and Ă-hī'-mă-ă[z] stayed [h]by [i]Ĕn-rō'-gĕl; for they migh[t] not be seen to come into the city: an[d] a wench went and told them; an[d] they went and told king David.

18 Nevertheless a lad saw them, an[d] told Ăb'-să-lo̱m: but they went both o[f] them away quickly, and came to

p ch. 15.32, 37. Pro. 17.17.
q 1 Sam. 28.2.
r Ex. 1.10. Ps. 2.2. Pro. 21.30. Matt. 27.1.
s Gen. 35.22. ch. 12.11. ch. 15.16.
t Gen. 34.30.
u ch. 2.7. Zech. 8.13.
v Lev. 18.8. Deut. 22.30. ch. 12.11. Pro. 28.7. Isa. 3.9. Micah 7.3,6.
8 word.
w ch. 15.12.
CHAP. 17
a Deut. 25.18. ch. 16.14. 1 Ki. 22.31. John 11.50.
b Zech. 13.7. Matt. 21.38.
c Jer. 6.14.
1 was right in the eyes of, etc.
2 what is in his mouth.
3 word?
4 counselled.
5 bitter of soul.
d Hosea 13.8.
6 fallen.
7 a son of valour.
e Gen. 22.17.
8 that thy face, or, presence go, etc.
f ch. 15.31, 34. Ps. 9.15.
9 commanded.
g ch. 15.27, 36.
h Josh. 2.4.
i Josh. 15.7. 1 Ki. 1.9. That is, The fuller's well.

ıan's house in [j]Bă-hū́-rĭm, which had
. well in his court; whither they went
lown.
19 And [k]the woman took and spread
. covering over the well's mouth, and
pread ground corn thereon; and the
hing was not known.
20 And when Ăb́-să-lom's servants
ame to the woman to the house, they
aid, Where *is* Ă-hī́-mă-ăz and Jona-
han? And [l]the woman said unto
hem, They be gone over the brook of
vater. And when they had sought and
ould not find *them*, they returned
ɔ Jerusalem.
21 And it came to pass, after they
'ere departed, that they came up out
f the well, and went and told king
)avid, and said unto David, Arise,
nd pass quickly over the water: for
ıus hath Ă-hĭth́-ō-phĕl counselled
gainst you.
22 Then David arose, and all the peo-
le that *were* with him, and they pass-
d over Jordan: by the morning light
ıere lacked not one of them that was
ot gone over Jordan.
23 ¶ And when Ă-hĭth́-ō-phĕl saw
ıat his counsel was not [10]followed, he
ıddled *his* ass, and arose, and gat
im home to his house, to his [m]city,
nd [11]put his household in order, and
ıanged himself, and died, and was
uried in the sepulchre of his father.
'4 Then David came to [o]Mā-hă-nā́-
n. And Ăb́-să-lom passed over Joran, he and all the men of Israel with
im.
25 ¶ And Ăb́-să-lom made Ă-mā́-să
ıptain of the host instead of Jṓ-ăb:
hich Ă-mā́-să *was* a man's son,
hose name *was* [12]Ĭth́-ră an Israelite,
ıat went in to [13]Ăb́-ĭ-gail the daugh-
r of Nahash, sister to Zĕr-ū-ī́-ăh Jṓ-
b's mother.
26 So Israel and Ăb́-să-lom pitched
ı the land of Gilead.
27 ¶ And it came to pass, when
avid was come to Mā-hă-nā́-ĭm, that
Shṓ-bī the son of Nahash of Răb́-
ăh, of the children of Ammon, and
Mā́-chir the son of Ăḿ-mī-ĕl of Lṓ-
ĕ-băr, and [r]Băr-zĭl-lā́-ī the Gileadite
f Rṓ-gĕ-lĭm,
28 Brought [s]beds, and [14]basons, and
ırthen vessels, and wheat, and
arley, and flour, and parched *corn*,
nd beans, and lentiles, and parched
ılse,
9 And honey, and butter, and sheep,
ıd cheese of kine, for David, and for
ıe people that *were* with him, [t]to eat:
r they said, The people *is* hungry,

j ch. 3.16. ch. 16.5. ch. 19.16.
k Josh. 2.6.
l Ex. 1.19. Josh. 2.4. 1 Sam. 19. 14-17. 1 Sam. 21.2. 1 Sam. 27. 11,12.
10 done.
m ch. 15.12.
11 gave charge concerning his house.
n 1 Sam. 31.4, 5. Ps. 55.23. Job 31.3. Matt. 27.5.
o Gen. 32.2. ch. 2.8.
12 Or, Jether an Ishmaelite.
13 Abigal.
p 1 Sam. 11.1. ch. 10.1. Ezra 2.61.
q ch. 9.4.
r ch. 19.31, 32.
s 1 Sam. 25. 18. Pro. 11.25. Matt. 5.7.
14 Or, cups.
t Deut. 15.7. Judg. 8.4-6. Ps. 34.8-10. Pro. 21.26. Eccl. 11.1. Isa. 58.7-12. Rom. 12.13.

CHAP. 18

a ch. 15.19.
b ch. 21.17.
1 set their heart on us.
2 as ten thousand of us.
3 be to succour.
c Josh. 17.15, 18. Josh. 20.7. Near to which Jephthah slew the Ephraimites. Judg. 12.5.
d Pro. 11.21.
4 multiplied to devour.
e ch. 14.26. Job 18.5-14. Matt. 27.5. 1 Cor. 11.14.

and weary, and thirsty, in the wilderness.

CHAPTER 18

AND David numbered the people
that *were* with him, and set captains of thousands and captains of
hundreds over them.
2 And David sent forth a third part
of the people under the hand of Jṓ-ăb,
and a third part under the hand of
Ăb́-ĭ-shai the son of Zĕr-ū-ī́-ăh, Jṓ-
ăb's brother, [a]and a third part under
the hand of Ĭt-tā́-ī the Gĭt́-tite. And
the king said unto the people, I will
surely go forth with you myself also.
3 But [b]the people answered, Thou
shalt not go forth: for if we flee away,
they will not [1]care for us; neither if
half of us die, will they care for us: but
now *thou art* [2]worth ten thousand of
us: therefore now *it is* better that thou
[3]succour us out of the city.
4 And the king said unto them, What
seemeth you best I will do. And the
king stood by the gate side, and all the
people came out by hundreds and by
thousands.
5 And the king commanded Jṓ-ăb
and Ăb́-ĭ-shai and Ĭt-tā́-ī, saying, *Deal*
gently for my sake with the young
man, *even* with Ăb́-să-lom. And all
the people heard when the king gave
all the captains charge concerning Ăb́-
să-lom.
6 ¶ So the people went out into the
field against Israel: and the battle was
in the wood [c]of Ḗ-phră-ĭm;
7 Where the people of Israel were
slain before the servants of David, and
there was there [d]a great slaughter that
day of twenty thousand *men*.
8 For the battle was there scattered
over the face of all the country: and
the wood [4]devoured more people that
day than the sword devoured.
9 ¶ And Ăb́-să-lom met the servants
of David. And Ăb́-să-lom rode upon
a mule, and the mule went under the
thick boughs of a great oak, and [e]his
head caught hold of the oak, and he
was taken up between the heaven and
the earth; and the mule that *was* under
him went away.
10 And a certain man saw *it*, and
told Jṓ-ăb, and said, Behold, I saw
Ăb́-să-lom hanged in an oak.
11 And Jṓ-ăb said unto the man that
told him, And, behold, thou sawest
him, and why didst thou not smite
him there to the ground? and I would
have given thee ten *shekels* of silver,
and a girdle.
12 And the man said unto Jṓ-ăb,

Though I should [5]receive a thousand
shekels of silver in mine hand, *yet*
would I not put forth mine hand
against the king's son: for in our hearing the king charged thee and Ăb-ī-
shâi and Ĭt-tā-ī, saying, [6]Beware that
none *touch* the young man Ăb-să-lom.
13 Otherwise I should have wrought
falsehood against mine own life: for
there is no matter hid from the king,
and thou thyself wouldest have set
thyself against *me*.
14 Then said Jō-ăb, I may not tarry
thus [7]with thee. And he took three
darts in his hand, and thrust them
through the heart of Ăb-să-lom, while
he *was* yet alive in the [8]midst of the
oak.
15 And ten young men that bare Jō-
ăb's armour compassed about and
smote Ăb-să-lom, and slew him.
16 And Jō-ăb blew the trumpet, and
the people returned from pursuing
after Israel: for Jō-ăb held back the
people.
17 And they took Ăb-să-lom, and
cast him into a great pit in the wood,
and [f]laid a very great heap of stones
upon him: and all Israel fled every
one to his tent.
18 ¶ Now Ăb-să-lom in his lifetime
had taken and reared up for himself a
pillar, which *is* in [g]the king's dale: for
he said, [h]I have no son to keep my
name in remembrance: and he [i]called
the pillar after his own name: and it is
called unto this day, Ăb-să-lom's
place.
19 ¶ Then said [j]Ă-hī-mă-ăz the son
of Zā-dŏk, Let me now run, and bear
the king tidings, how that the LORD
hath [9]avenged him of his enemies.
20 And Jō-ăb said unto him, Thou
shalt not [10]bear tidings this day, but
thou shalt bear tidings another day:
but this day thou shalt bear no tidings,
because the king's son is dead.
21 Then said Jō-ăb to [11]Cū-shī, Go
tell the king what thou hast seen. And
Cū-shī bowed himself unto Jō-ăb, and
ran.
22 Then said Ă-hī-mă-ăz the son of
Zā-dŏk yet again to Jō-ăb, But [12]how-
soever, let me, I pray thee, also run
after Cū-shī. And Jō-ăb said, Wherefore wilt thou run, my son, seeing that
thou hast no tidings [13]ready?
23 But howsoever, *said he*, let me run.
And he said unto him, Run. Then Ă-
hī-mă-ăz ran by the way of the plain,
and overran Cū-shī.
24 And David sat between the [k]two
gates: and [l]the watchman went up to
the roof over the gate unto the wa
and lifted up his eyes, and looked, a
behold a man running alone.
25 And the watchman cried, and to
the king. And the king said, If he
alone, *there is* tidings in his mout
And he came apace, and drew nea
26 And the watchman saw anoth
man running: and the watchman ca
ed unto the porter, and said, Beho
another man running alone. And t
king said, He also bringeth tidings.
27 And the watchman said, [14]M
thinketh the running of the foremo
is like the running of Ă-hī-mă-ăz t
son of Zā-dŏk. And the king said, [m]I
is a good man, and cometh with go
tidings.
28 And Ă-hī-mă-ăz called, and sa
unto the king. [15]All is well. And
fell down to the earth upon his fa
before the king, and said, Blessed
the LORD thy God, which hath [16]d
livered up the men that lifted up th
hand against my lord the king.
29 And the king said, [17]*Is* the you
man Ăb-să-lom safe? And Ă-hī-m
ăz answered, When Jō-ăb sent t
king's servant, and *me* thy servant
saw a great tumult, but I knew n
what *it was*.
30 And the king said *unto him*, Tu
aside, *and* stand here. And he turn
aside, and stood still.
31 And, behold, Cū-shī came; a
Cū-shī said, [18]Tidings, my lord t
king: for the LORD [n]hath aveng
thee this day of all them that rose
against thee.
32 And the king said unto Cū-shī,
the young man Ăb-să-lom safe? A
Cū-shī answered, The enemies of n
lord the king, and all that rise agair
thee to do *thee* hurt, be as *that* you
man *is*.
33 ¶ And the king was much move
and went up to the chamber over t
gate, and wept: and as he went, th
he said, [o]O my son Ăb-să-lom, n
son, my son Ăb-să-lom! would Go
had died for thee, O Ăb-să-lom, n
son, my son!

CHAPTER 19

AND it was told Jō-ăb, Behold, t
king weepeth and mourneth f
Ăb-să-lom.
2 And the [1]victory that day was *tu*
ed into mourning unto all the peopl
for the people heard say that day h
the king was grieved for his son.
3 And the people gat them by steal
that day into the city, as people bei

5 weigh upon mine hand.
6 Beware whosoever ye be of, etc.
7 before thee.
8 heart.
f Josh. 7.26. Jer. 22.18, 19. Lam. 3.53.
g Gen. 14.17.
h ch. 14.27. Job 13.12. Ps. 34.16. Ps. 109.13. Pro. 2.22.
i Ps. 49. 11.
j ch. 15.36. ch. 17.17.
9 judged him from the hand, etc.
10 be a man of tidings.
11 The Ethiopian.
12 be what may.
13 Or, convenient.
k 1 Sam. 1.9. 1 Sam. 4.13.
l ch. 13.34. 2 Ki. 9.17.
14 I see the running.
m 1 Ki. 1.42.
15 Peace, or, Peace be to thee.
16 shut up.
17 Is there peace?
18 Tidings is brought.
n Ps. 27.2. Ps. 55.18.
o ch. 19.4. Pro. 10.1. Pro. 19.13.
CHAP. 19
1 salvation, or, deliverance.

shamed steal away when they flee in
attle.
4 But the king [a]covered his face, and
he king cried with a loud voice, [b]O
ny son Ăb'-să-lom, O Ăb'-să-lom, my
on, my son!
5 And Jō'-ăb came into the house to
ne king, and said, Thou hast shamed
nis day the faces of all thy servants,
hich this day have saved thy life, and
ne lives of thy sons and of thy daugh-
rs, and the lives of thy wives, and the
ves of thy concubines;
6 [2]In that thou lovest thine enemies,
nd hatest thy friends. For thou hast
eclared this day, [3]that thou regardest
either princes nor servants: for this
ay I perceive, that if Ăb'-să-lom had
ved, and all we had died this day,
en it had pleased thee well.
7 Now therefore arise, go forth, and
peak [4]comfortably unto thy servants:
or I swear by the LORD, if thou go not
orth, there [c]will not tarry one with
ee this night: and that will be worse
nto thee than all the evil that befell
ee from thy youth until now.
8 Then the king arose, and sat in the
ate. And they told unto all the peo-
le, saying, Behold, the king doth sit
the gate. And all the people came
efore the king: for [e]Israel had fled
very man to his tent.
9 ¶ And all the people were at strife
roughout all the tribes of Israel, say-
g, The king [f]saved us out of the hand
f our enemies, and he delivered us
ut of the hand of the Philistines; and
ow he [g]is fled out of the land for Ăb'-
-lom.
10 And Ăb'-să-lom, whom we anoint-
d over us, is dead in battle. Now
erefore why [5]speak ye not a word
f bringing the king back?
11 ¶ And king David sent to Zā'-dŏk
nd to Ă-bī'-ă-thär the priests, saying,
peak unto the elders of Judah, say-
g, Why are ye the last to bring the
ng back to his house? seeing the
peech of all Israel is come to the king,
ven to his house.
12 Ye *are* my brethren, ye *are* my
ones and my flesh: wherefore then
e ye the last to bring back the
ng?
13 And [i]say ye to Ă-mā'-să, *Art* thou
ot of my bone, and of my flesh? [j]God
o so to me, and more also, if thou be
ot captain of the host before me con-
nually [k]in the room of Jō'-ăb.
14 And he bowed the heart of all the
en of Judah, [l]even as *the heart of*
ne man; so that they sent *this word*
unto the king, Return thou, and all
thy servants.
15 So the king returned, and came to
Jordan. And Judah came to [m]Gĭl'-găl,
to go to meet the king, to conduct the
king over Jordan.
16 ¶ And [n]Shĭm'-ĕ-ī the son of Gē'-ră,
a Benjamite, which *was* of Bă-hū'-rĭm,
hasted and came down with the men
of Judah to meet king David.
17 And *there were* a thousand men of
Benjamin with him, and [o]Zī'-bă the
servant of the house of Saul, and his
fifteen sons and his twenty servants
with him; and they went over Jordan
before the king.
18 And there went over a ferry boat
to carry over the king's household,
and to do [6]what he thought good. And
Shĭm'-ĕ-ī the son of Gē'-ră fell down
before the king, as he was come over
Jordan;
19 And said unto the king, Let [p]not
my lord impute iniquity unto me,
neither do thou remember [q]that which
thy servant did perversely the day that
my lord the king went out of Jerusalem, that the king should [r]take it to
his heart.
20 For thy servant doth know that I
have sinned: therefore, behold, I am
come the first this day of all [s]the house
of Joseph to go down to meet my lord
the king.
21 But Ă-bī'-shâi the son of Zĕr-ū-ī'-ăh
answered and said, Shall not Shĭm'-ĕ-ī
be put to death for this, because he
[t]cursed the LORD's anointed?
22 And David said, [u]What have I to
do with you, ye sons of Zĕr-ū-ī'-ăh,
that ye should this day be adversaries
unto me? [v]shall there any man be put
to death this day in Israel? for do not
I know that I *am* this day king over
Israel?
23 Therefore the [w]king said unto
Shĭm'-ĕ-ī, Thou shalt not die. And the
king sware unto him.
24 ¶ And [x]Mĕ-phĭb'-ŏ-shĕth the son
of Saul came down to meet the king,
and had neither dressed his feet, nor
trimmed his beard, nor washed his
clothes, from the day the king departed until the day he came *again* in
peace.
25 And it came to pass, when he was
come to Jerusalem to meet the king,
that the king said unto him, [y]Where-
fore wentest not thou with me, Mĕ-
phĭb'-ŏ-shĕth?
26 And he answered, My lord, O
king, my servant deceived me: for thy
servant said, I will saddle me an ass,

a ch. 15.30. 1 Sam. 4.12.
b ch. 18.33.
2 By loving, etc.
3 that princes or servants are not to thee.
4 to the heart of thy servants.
c Pro. 14.28.
d Ruth 4.1. ch. 18.4,24.
e 1 Ki. 12.16. 2 Ki. 14.12.
f 1 Sam. 17.1. ch. 5.18.
g ch. 15.14.
5 are ye silent?
h Gen. 2.23. Judg. 9.2. ch. 5.1.
i ch. 17.25. 1 Chr. 2.16, 17. 1 Chr. 12.18.
j Ruth 1.17. 1 Ki. 19.2.
k ch. 3.29,30. ch. 8.16.
l Judg. 20.1. Ps. 110.2,3. Acts 4.32.
m Josh. 5.9. 1 Sam. 11. 14,15.
n ch. 16.5.
o ch. 9.2,10. ch. 16.1,2.
6 the good in his eyes.
p Ps. 32.2. Rom. 4.6,8. 2 Cor. 5.19.
q ch. 16.5,6. Pro. 28.13. Matt. 5.25.
r ch. 13.33.
s ch. 16.5.
t Ex. 22.28. 1 Sam. 24.6. ch. 16.5,7, 13. Eccl. 10.20. Acts 23.5. 2 Pet. 2.10, 11.
u 1 Sam. 26.8. ch. 16.10. Matt. 8.29.
v 1 Sam. 11. 13.
w 1 Ki. 2.8,9, 37,46.
x ch. 9.6.
y ch. 16.17.

that I may ride thereon, and go to the
king; because thy servant *is* lame.
27 And [z]he hath slandered thy servant unto my lord the king; but [a]my
lord the king *is* as an angel of God: do
therefore *what is* good in thine eyes.
28 For all *of* my father's house were
but [7]dead men before my lord the
king: [b]yet didst thou set thy servant
among them that did eat at thine own
table. What right therefore have I yet
to cry any more unto the king?
29 And the king said unto him, Why
speakest thou any more of thy matters? I have said, [c]Thou and Zī´-bă
divide the land.
30 And Mĕ-phĭb´-ŏ-shĕth said unto
the king, Yea, let him take all, forasmuch as my lord the king is come
again in peace unto his own house.
31 ¶ And [d]Bär-zĭl-lā´-ī the Gileadite
came down from Rō´-gĕ-lĭm, and went
over Jordan with the king, to conduct
him over Jordan.
32 Now Bär-zĭl-lā´-ī was a very aged
man, *even* fourscore years old: and he
[e]had provided the king of sustenance
while he lay at Mā-hă-nā´-ĭm; for he
was a very great man.
33 And the king said unto Bär-zĭl-
lā´-ī, Come thou over with me, and I
will feed thee with me in Jerusalem.
34 And Bär-zĭl-lā´-ī said unto the
king, [8]How long have I to live, that I
should go up with the king unto Jerusalem?
35 I *am* this day [f]fourscore years old:
and can I discern between good and
evil? can thy servant taste what I eat
or what I drink? can I [g]hear any more
the voice of singing men and singing
women? wherefore then should thy
servant be yet a burden unto my lord
the king?
36 Thy servant will go a little way
over Jordan with the king: and why
should the king recompense it me
with such a reward?
37 Let thy servant, I pray thee, turn
back again, that I may die in mine
own city, *and be buried* by the grave
of my father and of my mother. But
behold thy [h]servant Chĭm´-hăm; let
him go over with my lord the king;
and do to him what shall seem good
unto thee.
38 And the king answered, Chĭm´-
hăm shall go over with me, and I will
do to him that which shall seem good
unto thee: and whatsoever thou shalt
[9]require of me, *that* will I do for thee.
39 And all the people went over
Jordan. And when the king was come

z ch. 16.3. Ps. 15.3. Ps. 63.11. Ps. 101.7. Pro. 6.16,17. Pro. 21.6.
a 1 Sam. 29.9. ch. 14.17,20.
7 men of death.
b ch. 9.7,10, 13.
c Deut. 19. 16-21. Ps. 82.2. Ps. 101.1-8. Pro. 29.4.
d 1 Ki. 2.7. Ezra 2.61. Neh. 7.63.
e ch. 17.27.
8 How many days are the years of my life?
f Ps. 90.10.
g Eccl. 12. 3-6.
h 1 Ki. 2.7. Jer. 41.17.
9 choose.
i Gen. 31.55.
j Gen. 14.19. Ex. 39.43. Josh. 22.6. 1 Sam. 2.20.
10 Chimhan.
k ver. 15.
l ver. 12. Ruth 4.12, 18-22. 1 Chr. 2.3-15. Ps. 78.68, 70. Matt. 1.1-6.
m 1 Ki. 11.30, 31.
11 set us at light.
n Judg. 8.1.
CHAP. 20
a ch. 12.10.
b Deut. 13.13. Judg. 19.22. 1 Sam. 2.12. ch. 23.6. 1 Ki. 21.10, 13. 2 Chr. 13.7.
c ch. 19.43.
d 1 Ki. 12.16. 2 Chr. 10.16.
e Pro. 17.14.
f ch. 15.16.
1 an house of ward.
2 bound.
3 in widowhood of life.
4 Call.
g 1 Sam. 26.6. ch. 2.18.

over, the king [i]kissed Bär-zĭl-lā´-ī, a
[j]blessed him; and he returned u
his own place.
40 Then the king went on to Gĭl´-g
and [10]Chĭm´-hăm went on with hi
and all the people of Judah conduct
the king, and also half the people
Israel.
41 ¶ And, behold, all the men of
rael came to the king, and said ur
the king, Why have our brethren t
men of Judah stolen thee away, a
have [k]brought the king, and his hou
hold, and all David's men with hi
over Jordan?
42 And all the men of Judah answe
ed the men of Israel, Because the ki
is [l]near of kin to us: wherefore th
be ye angry for this matter? have
eaten at all of the king's *cost?* or ha
he given us any gift?
43 And the men of Israel answer
the men of Judah, and said, We ha
ten [m]parts in the king, and we ha
also more *right* in David than ye: w
then did ye [11]despise us, that our a
vice should not be first had in bringi
back our king? [n]And the words of t
men of Judah were fiercer than t
words of the men of Israel.

CHAPTER 20

AND there [a]happened to be the
a man of [b]Bē´-lĭ-ăl, whose nar
was Shē´-bă, the son of Bĭch´-rī, a Be
jamite: and he blew a trumpet, a
said, [c]We have no part in David, neit
er have we inheritance in the son
Jesse: [d]every man to his tents,
Israel.
2 So [e]every man of Israel went u
from after David, *and* followed Sh
bă the son of Bĭch´-rī: but the men
Judah clave unto their king, fro
Jordan even to Jerusalem.
3 ¶ And David came to his house
Jerusalem; and the king took the te
women *his* [f]concubines, whom he ha
left to keep the house, and put the
in [1]ward, and fed them, but went n
in unto them. So they were [2]shut u
unto the day of their death, [3]living i
widowhood.
4 ¶ Then said the king to Ă-mā´-s
[4]Assemble me the men of Judah wit
in three days, and be thou here pre
ent.
5 So Ă-mā´-să went to assemble *th*
men of Judah: but he tarried long
than the set time which he ha
appointed him.
6 And David said to [g]Ăb´-ī-shai, No
shall Shē´-bă the son of Bĭch´-rī do

more harm than *did* Ăb´-să-lọm: take
thou [h]thy lord's servants, and pursue
after him, lest he get him fenced cities,
and [5]escape us.
7 And there went out after him Jō´-
ăb's men, and the [i]Chĕr´-ĕ-thītes, and
the Pĕl´-ĕ-thītes, and all the mighty
men: and they went out of Jerusalem,
to pursue after Shē´-bă the son of
Bĭch´-rī.
8 When they *were* at the great stone
which *is* in Gibeon, Ă-mā´-să went before them. And Jō´-ăb's garment that
he had put on was girded unto him,
and upon it a girdle *with* a sword
fastened upon his loins in the sheath
thereof; and as he went forth it fell
out.
9 And Jō´-ăb said to Ă-mā´-să, *Art*
thou in health, my brother? [j]And Jō´-
ăb took Ă-mā´-să by the beard with the
right hand to kiss him.
10 But Ă-mā´-să took no heed to the
sword that *was* in Jō´-ăb's hand: so [k]he
smote him therewith [l]in the fifth *rib*,
and shed out his bowels to the ground,
and [6]struck him not again; and he
died. So Jō´-ăb and Ăb´-ī-shāi his brother pursued after Shē´-bă the son of
Bĭch´-rī.
11 And one of Jō´-ăb's men stood by
him, and said, He that favoureth Jō´-
ăb, and he that *is* for David, *let him go*
after Jō´-ăb.
12 And Ă-mā´-să wallowed in blood
in the midst of the highway. And
when the man saw that all the people
stood still, he removed Ă-mā´-să out
of the highway into the field, and cast
a cloth upon him, when he saw that
every one that came by him stood still.
13 When he was removed out of the
highway, all the people went on after
Jō´-ăb, to pursue after Shē´-bă the son
of Bĭch´-rī.
14 ¶ And he went through all the
tribes of Israel unto [m]Abel, and to
Bĕth–mā´-ă-chăh, and all the Bē´-rītes:
and they were gathered together, and
went also after him.
15 And they came and besieged him
in Abel of Bĕth–mā´-ă-chăh, and they
cast up a bank against the city, and
it stood in the trench: and all the people that *were* with Jō´-ăb [8]battered the
wall, to throw it down.
16 ¶ Then cried a wise woman out of
the city, Hear, hear; say, I pray you,
unto Jō´-ăb, Come near hither, that I
may speak with thee.
17 And when he was come near unto
her, the woman said, *Art* thou Jō´-ăb?
And he answered, I *am he*. Then she
said unto him, Hear the words of thine
handmaid. And he answered, I do
hear.
18 Then she spake, saying, [9]They
were wont to speak in old time, saying, They shall surely ask *counsel* at
Abel: and so they ended *the matter*.
19 I *am one of them that are* peaceable *and* faithful in Israel: thou seekest to destroy a city and a [10]mother in
Israel: why wilt thou swallow up [o]the
inheritance of the LORD?
20 And Jō´-ăb answered and said, Far
be it, far be it from me, that I should
swallow up or destroy.
21 The matter *is* not so: but a man of
mount Ē´-phră-ĭm, Shē´-bă the son of
Bĭch´-rī [11]by name, hath lifted up his
hand against the king, *even* against
David: deliver him only, and I will depart from the city. And the woman
said unto Jō´-ăb, Behold, his head
shall be thrown to thee over the
wall.
22 Then the woman went unto all the
people [p]in her wisdom. And they cut
off the head of Shē´-bă the son of Bĭch´-
rī, and cast *it* out to Jō´-ăb. And he
blew a trumpet, and they [12]retired
from the city, every man to his tent.
And Jō´-ăb returned to Jerusalem unto
the king.
23 ¶ Now [q]Jō´-ăb *was* over all the
host of Israel: and Bĕ-nāi´-ăh the son
of Jĕ-hōi´-ă-dă *was* over the Chĕr´-ĕ-
thītes and over the Pĕl´-ĕ-thītes:
24 And Ă-dôr´-ăm *was* [r]over the tribute: and [s]Jĕ-hŏsh´-ă-phăt the son of
Ă-hī´-lŭd *was* [13]recorder:
25 And Shē´-vă *was* scribe: and Zā´-
dŏk [t]and Ă-bī´-ă-thăr *were* the priests:
26 And [u]Ī´-ră also the Jā´-īr-īte was [14]a
chief ruler about David.

CHAPTER 21

THEN there was a famine in the
days of David three years, year
after year; and David [1]inquired of
the LORD. And the LORD answered,
[a]*It is* for Saul, and for *his* bloody
house, because he slew the Gibeonites.
2 And the king called the Gibeonites,
and said unto them; (now the Gibeonites *were* not of the children of Israel,
but [b]of the remnant of the Amorites;
and the children of Israel had sworn
unto them: and Saul sought to slay
them in his zeal to the children of Israel and Judah.)
3 Wherefore David said unto the
Gibeonites, What shall I do for you?
and wherewith shall I make the atone-

h ch. 11.11. 1 Ki. 1.33.
5 deliver himself from our eyes.
i ch. 8.18. 1 Ki. 1.38.
j Matt. 26.49. Luke 22.47.
k Gen. 4.8. ch. 2.23.
l ch. 2.23.
6 doubled not his stroke.
m 1 Ki. 15.20. 2 Chr. 16.4.
n 2 Ki. 19.32. Jer. 32.24. Luke 19.43.
7 Or, it stood against the outmost wall.
8 marred to throw down.
9 Or, They plainly spake in the beginning, saying, Surely they will ask of Abel, and so make an end.
10 that is, A chief city.
o 1 Sam. 26. 19.
11 by his name.
p Eccl. 7.19.
12 were scattered.
q ch. 8.16.
r 1 Ki. 4.6.
s 1 Ki. 4.3.
13 Or, remembrancer.
t ch. 8.17.
u ch. 23.38.
14 Or, a prince.

CHAP. 21

1 sought the face, etc.
a Lev. 18.25. Num. 35.33. Isa. 26.21.
b Josh. 9.3.

ment, that ye may bless the [c]inheritance of the LORD?

4 And the Gibeonites said unto him, [2]We will have no silver nor gold of Saul, nor of his house; neither for us shalt thou kill any man in Israel. And he said, What ye shall say, *that* will I do for you.

5 And they answered the king, The man that consumed us, and that [3]devised against us *that* we should be destroyed from remaining in any of the coasts of Israel,

6 Let seven men of his sons be delivered unto us, and we will hang them up unto the LORD [d]in Gĭb´-ē-āh of Saul, [4]*whom* the LORD did choose. And the king said, I will give *them*.

7 But the king spared Mĕ-phĭb´-ŏ-shĕth, the son of Jonathan the son of Saul, because of the [e]LORD's oath that *was* between them, between David and Jonathan the son of Saul.

8 But the king took the two sons of [f]Rĭz´-păh the daughter of Aî´-ăh, whom she bare unto Saul, Är-mō´-nī and Mĕ-phĭb´-ŏ-shĕth; and the five sons of [5]Mī´-chăl the daughter of Saul, whom she [6]brought up for Ā´-drĭ-ĕl the son of Bär-zĭl-lā´-ī the Mĕ-hō´-lă-thīte:

9 And he delivered them into the hands of the Gibeonites, and they hanged them in the hill [g]before the LORD: and they fell *all* seven together, and were put to death in the days of harvest, in the first *days*, in the beginning of barley harvest.

10 ¶ And [h]Rĭz´-păh the daughter of Aî´-ăh took sackcloth, and spread it for her upon the rock, [i]from the beginning of harvest until water dropped upon them out of heaven, and suffered neither the birds of the air to rest on them by day, nor the beasts of the field by night.

11 And it was told David what Rĭz´-păh the daughter of Aî´-ăh, the concubine of Saul, had done.

12 ¶ And David went and took the bones of Saul and the bones of Jonathan his son from the men of [j]Jā´-bĕsh–gĭl´-ĕ-ăd, which had stolen them from the street of Bĕth´–shăn, where the Philistines had hanged them, when the Philistines had slain Saul in Gĭl-bō´-ă:

13 And he brought up from thence the bones of Saul and the bones of Jonathan his son; and they gathered the bones of them that were hanged.

14 And the bones of Saul and Jonathan his son buried they in the country of Benjamin in [k]Zē´-lăh, in the sepulchre of Kish his father: and they performed all that the king commanded. And after that God [l]was intreated for the land.

15 ¶ Moreover the Philistines had yet war again with Israel; and David went down, and his servants with him, and fought against the Philistines: and David waxed faint.

16 And Ĭsh´-bī–bē´-nŏb, which *was* of the sons of [7]the giant, the weight of whose [8]spear *weighed* [9]three hundred *shekels* of brass in weight, he being girded with a new *sword*, thought to have slain David.

17 But Ăb´-ĭ-shaî the son of Zĕr-ū-ī´-ăh succoured him, and smote the Philistine, and killed him. Then the men of David sware unto him, saying, Thou shalt go no more out with us to battle, that thou quench not the [10]light of Israel.

18 And it came to pass after this, that there was again a battle with the Philistines at Gob: then [m]Sĭb-bĕ-chaî the Hū´-shă-thīte slew [11]Săph, which *was* of the sons of [12]the giant.

19 And there was again a battle in Gob with the Philistines, where Ĕl-hā´-năn the son of [13]Jā´-ă-rĕ–ôr´-ĕ-gĭm, a Beth-lehemite, slew *the brother of* Gō-lī´-ăth the Gĭt´-tīte, the staff of whose spear *was* like a weaver's beam.

20 And [n]there was yet a battle in Gath, where was a man of *great* stature, that had on every hand six fingers, and on every foot six toes, four and twenty in number; and he also was born to [14]the giant.

21 And when he [15]defied Israel, Jonathan the son of Shĭm´-ĕ-ă the brother of David slew him.

22 These four were born to the giant in Gath, and fell by the hand of David, and by the hand of his servants.

CHAPTER 22

AND David [a]spake unto the LORD the words of this song in the day *that* the LORD had delivered him out of the hand of all his enemies, and out of the hand of Saul:

2 And he said, [b]The LORD *is* my rock, and my fortress, and my deliverer;

3 The God of my rock; [c]in him will I trust: *he is* my [d]shield, and the [e]horn of my salvation, my high [f]tower, and my [g]refuge, my saviour; thou savest me from violence.

4 I will call on the LORD, *who is* worthy to be praised: so shall I be saved from mine enemies.

5 When the [1]waves of death com-

---

c ch. 20.19.
2 Or, It is not silver nor gold that we have to do with Saul or his house, neither pertains it to us to kill, etc.
3 Or, cut us off.
d Judg. 20.4.
4 Or, chosen of the LORD.
e 1 Sam. 18.3. 1 Sam. 23. 18.
f ch. 3.7.
5 Or, Michal's sister.
6 bare to Adriel.
g ch. 6.17.
h ch. 3.7.
i Deut. 21.23.
j 1 Sam. 31. 11,12,13.
k Josh. 18.28.
l Josh. 7.26.
7 Or, Rapha.
8 the staff, or, the head.
9 Nine pounds and a half avoirdupois.
10 candle, or, lamp.
m 1 Chr. 11. 29.
11 Or, Sippai.
12 Or, Rapha.
13 Or, Jair.
n 1 Chr. 20.6.
14 Or, Rapha.
15 Or, reproached.

CHAP. 22

a Ex. 15.1.
b Gen. 15.1. Deut. 32.4. 1 Sam. 2.2. Ps. 18.2. Pro. 18.10. Matt. 18.11.
c Heb. 2.13.
d Gen. 15.1. Ps. 3.3.
e Luke 1.69.
f Pro. 18.10.
g Ps. 9.9. Ps. 18.2. Ps. 59.16. Isa. 32.2.
1 Or, pangs.

passed me, the floods of [2]ungodly men made me afraid;

6 The [3]sorrows of hell compassed me about; the snares of death prevented me;

7 In my distress [h]I called upon the LORD, and cried to my God: and he did [i]hear my voice out of his temple, and my cry *did enter* into his ears.

8 Then [j]the earth shook and trembled, the foundations of heaven moved and shook, because he was wroth.

9 There went up a smoke [4]out of his nostrils, and [k]fire out of his mouth devoured: coals were kindled by it.

10 He [l]bowed the heavens also, and came down; and darkness *was* under his feet.

11 And he rode upon a cherub, and did fly: and he was seen upon [m]the wings of the wind.

12 And he made darkness pavilions round about him, [5]dark waters, *and* thick clouds of the skies.

13 Through the brightness before him were coals of fire kindled.

14 The LORD [n]thundered from heaven, and the most High uttered his voice.

15 And he sent out [o]arrows, and scattered them; lightning, and discomfited them.

16 And the channels of the sea appeared, the foundations of the world were discovered, at the rebuking of the LORD, at the blast of the breath of his [6]nostrils.

17 He sent from above, he took me; he drew me out of [7]many waters;

18 He delivered me from my strong enemy, *and* from them that hated me: for they were too strong for me.

19 They prevented me in the day of my calamity: but the LORD was my stay.

20 He [p]brought me forth also into a large place: he delivered me, because he [q]delighted in me.

21 The LORD rewarded me according to my righteousness: according to the cleanness of my hands hath he recompensed me.

22 For I have kept the ways of the LORD, and have not wickedly departed from my God.

23 For all his [r]judgments *were* before me: and *as for* his statutes, I did not depart from them.

24 I was also [s]upright [8]before him, and have kept myself from mine iniquity.

25 Therefore the LORD hath recompensed me according to my righteousness; according to my cleanness [9]in his eye sight.

26 With the [t]merciful thou wilt shew thyself merciful, *and* with the upright man thou wilt shew thyself upright.

27 With the pure thou wilt shew thyself pure; and [u]with the froward thou wilt [10]shew thyself unsavoury.

28 And the [v]afflicted people thou wilt save: but thine eyes *are* upon the haughty, *that* thou mayest bring *them* down.

29 For thou *art* my [11]lamp, O LORD: and the LORD will lighten my darkness.

30 For by thee I have [12]run through a troop: by my God have I leaped over a wall.

31 *As for* God, [w]his way *is* perfect; [x]the word of the LORD *is* [13]tried: he *is* a buckler to all them that trust in him.

32 For [y]who *is* God, save the LORD? and who *is* a rock, save our God?

33 God *is* my [z]strength *and* power: and he [14]maketh my way [a]perfect.

34 He [15]maketh my feet like hinds' *feet:* and setteth me upon my high places.

35 He teacheth my hands [16]to war; so that a bow of steel is broken by mine arms.

36 Thou hast also given me the shield of thy salvation: and thy gentleness hath [17]made me great.

37 Thou hast enlarged my steps under me; so that my [18]feet did not slip.

38 I have pursued mine enemies, and destroyed them; and turned not again until I had consumed them.

39 And I have consumed them, and wounded them, that they could not arise: yea, they are fallen under my feet.

40 For thou hast girded me with strength to battle: them that rose up against me hast thou [19]subdued under me.

41 Thou hast also given me the necks of mine enemies, that I might destroy them that hate me.

42 They [b]looked, but *there was* none to save; *even* [c]unto the LORD, but he answered them not.

43 Then did I beat them as small as the dust of the earth, I did stamp them as the mire of the street, *and* did spread them abroad.

44 Thou also hast delivered me from the strivings of my people, thou hast kept me *to be* [d]head of the heathen: [e]a people *which* I knew not shall serve me.

45 [20]Strangers shall [21]submit them-

2 Belial.
3 Or, cords.
h Ps. 116.4.
i Ex. 3.7.
j Judg. 5.4. Ps. 18.7. Ps. 77.18.
4 by.
k Ps. 97.3. Hab. 3.5. Heb. 12.29.
l Isa. 64.1.
m Ps. 104.3.
5 binding of waters.
n Isa. 30.30.
o Deut. 32. 23. Ps. 7.13. Ps. 77.17. Ps. 144.6. Hab. 3.11.
6 Or, anger.
7 Or, great.
p Ps. 31.8.
q ch. 15.26.
r Deut. 7.12.
s Gen. 6.9. Job 1.1.
8 to him.
9 before his eyes.
t Matt. 5.7.
u Lev. 26.23.
10 Or, wrestle.
v Ps. 12.5. Matt. 5.3.
11 Or, candle.
12 Or, broken a troop.
w Dan. 4.37. Rev. 15.3.
x Ps. 12.6. Pro. 30.5.
13 Or, refined.
y Deut. 32. 31. 1 Sam. 2.2. Isa. 45.5,6.
z Ps. 27.1.
14 riddeth, or, looseth.
a Deut. 18. 13.
15 equalleth.
16 for the war.
17 multiplied me.
18 ankles.
19 caused to bow.
b 1 Sam. 28.6.
c Pro. 1.28.
d Deut. 28. 13.
e Isa. 55.5.
20 Sons of the stranger.
21 lie, or, yield feigned obedience.

selves unto me: as soon as they hear,
they shall be obedient unto me.
46 Strangers shall fade away, and
they shall be afraid [f]out of their close
places.
47 The LORD liveth; and blessed *be*
my rock; and exalted be the God of
the [g]rock of my salvation.
48 It *is* God that [22]avengeth me, and
that [h]bringeth down the people under
me,
49 And that bringeth me forth from
mine enemies: thou also hast lifted
me up on high above them that rose
up against me: thou hast delivered
me from the violent man.
50 Therefore I will give thanks unto
thee, O LORD, among [i]the heathen,
and I will sing praises unto thy name.
51 *He is* the tower of salvation for
his king: and sheweth mercy to his
anointed, unto David, and to his seed
for evermore.

CHAPTER 23

NOW these *be* the last words of
David. David the son of Jesse
said, and the man *who was* raised up
on high, the anointed of the God of
Jacob, and the sweet psalmist of Israel, said,
2 The [a]Spirit of the LORD spake by
me, and his word *was* in my tongue.
3 The God of Israel said, the Rock of
Israel spake to me, [1]He that ruleth
over men *must be* just, ruling [b]in the
fear of God.
4 And [c]*he shall be* as the light of the
morning, *when* the sun riseth, *even* a
morning without clouds; *as* the tender
grass *springing* out of the earth by
clear shining after rain.
5 Although my house *be* not so with
God; yet he hath made with me an
[d]everlasting covenant, ordered in all
things, and sure: for *this is* all my salvation, and all *my* desire, although he
make *it* not to grow.
6 ¶ But *the sons* of Bē-lī-ăl *shall be*
all of them as thorns thrust away, because they cannot be taken with
hands:
7 But the man *that* shall touch them
must be [2]fenced with iron and the staff
of a spear; and they shall be utterly
burned with fire in the *same* place.
8 ¶ These *be* the names of the mighty
men whom David had: [3]The Tăch-
mō-nīte that sat in the seat, chief
among the captains; the same *was*
Ăd-ĭ-nō the Ĕz-nīte: *he lift up his spear*
against eight hundred, [4]whom he slew
at one time.

f Micah 7.17.
g Ps. 89.26.
22 giveth avengement for me.
h Ps. 144.2.
i Rom. 15.9.
CHAP. 23
a 2 Pet. 1.21.
1 Or, Be thou ruler, etc.
b Ex. 18.21.
c Pro. 4.18.
d Isa. 55.3.
2 filled.
3 Or, Josheb-bassebet, the Tachmonite, head of the three.
4 slain.
e 1 Chr. 11. 12.
f 1 Chr. 11. 12.
5 Or, for foraging.
6 Or, the three captains over the thirty.
g Deut. 33. 29. 1 Sam. 22.1. 1 Chr. 29.11. 2 Chr. 14. 11-14. Ps. 3.8. Ps. 46.1. Ps. 98.1. Pro. 21.30, 31. Rom. 8.31.
h Or, giants.
i 1 Sam. 22.4. 1 Chr. 12.16.
j Lev. 17.10.
k ch. 2.18.
7 slain.
l Josh. 15.21.
8 great of acts.
m Ex. 15.15.
9 lions of God.

9 And after him *was* [e]Ĕl-ē-ā-zăr the
son of Dodo the Ă-hō-hīte, *one* of the
three mighty men with David, when
they defied the Philistines *that* were
there gathered together to battle,
and the men of Israel were gone
away:
10 He arose, and smote the Philistines until his hand was weary, and his
hand clave unto the sword: and the
LORD wrought a great victory that
day; and the people returned after
him only to spoil.
11 And after him *was* Shăm-măh the
son of Ā-gēe the Hâr-ă-rīte. [f]And the
Philistines were gathered together [5]in-
to a troop, where was a piece of
ground full of lentiles: and the people
fled from the Philistines.
12 But he stood in the midst of the
ground, and defended it, and slew the
Philistines: and the LORD wrought a
great victory.
13 And [6]three of the thirty chief went
down, and came to David in the harvest time unto [g]the cave of Adullam:
and the troop of the Philistines pitched in the valley of [h]Rĕph-ā-ĭm.
14 And David *was* then in [i]an hold,
and the garrison of the Philistines *was*
then *in* Beth-lehem.
15 And David longed, and said, Oh
that one would give me drink of the
water of the well of Beth-lehem, which
is by the gate!
16 And the three mighty men brake
through the host of the Philistines,
and drew water out of the well of
Beth-lehem, that *was* by the gate, and
took *it*, and brought *it* to David:
nevertheless he would not drink
thereof, but poured it out unto the
LORD.
17 And he said, Be it far from me, O
LORD, that I should do this: *is not this*
[j]the blood of the men that went in
jeopardy of their lives? therefore he
would not drink it. These things did
these three mighty men.
18 And [k]Ăb-ĭ-shāi, the brother of Jō-
ăb, the son of Zĕr-ū-ĭ-ăh, was chief
among three. And he lifted up his
spear against three hundred, [7]*and*
slew *them*, and had the name among
three.
19 Was he not most honourable of
three? therefore he was their captain:
howbeit he attained not unto the *first*
three.
20 And Bē-nāi-ăh the son of Jĕ-hoi-
ă-dă, the son of a valiant man, of
[l]Kăb-zēel, [8]who had done many acts,
[m]he slew two [9]lionlike men of Moab

he went down also and slew a lion in
the midst of a pit in time of snow:
21 And he slew an Egyptian, [10]a
goodly man: and the Egyptian had a
spear in his hand; but he went down
to him with a staff, and plucked the
spear out of the Egyptian's hand, and
slew him with his own spear.
22 These *things* did Bĕ-nā̂i-ăh the son
of Jĕ-hō̂i-ă-dă, and had the name
among three mighty men.
23 He was [11]more honourable than
the thirty, but he attained not to the
first three. And David set him [n]over
his [12]guard.
24 Ăs-ă-hĕl [o]the brother of Jō-ăb *was*
one of the thirty; Ĕl-hā-năn the son of
Dodo of Beth-lehem,
25 Shăm-măh [p]the Hâr-ŏd-īte, Ē-lī-
kă the Hâr-ŏd-īte,
26 Hē-lĕz the Păl-tīte, Ī-ră the son of
Ĭk-kĕsh the Tē-kō-īte,
27 Ă-bi-ē-zĕr the Ăn-ĕ-thō-thīte, Mĕ-
bŭn-nā̂i the Hū-shă-thīte,
28 Zăl-mŏn the Ă-hō-hīte, Mā-hă-
rā̂i the Nĕ-tŏph-ă-thīte,
29 Hē-lĕb the son of Bā-ă-năh, a Nĕ-
tŏph-ă-thīte, Ĭt-tā-ī the son of Rī-bā-ī
out of Gĭb-ē-ăh of the children of
Benjamin,
30 Bĕ-nā̂i-ăh the [q]Pī-rā-thŏn-īte,
Hĭd-dā-ī of the [13]brooks of [r]Gā-ăsh,
31 Ā-bi-ăl-bŏn the Är-bă-thīte, Ăz-
mā-vĕth the Bär-hū-mīte,
32 Ē-lī-ăh-bă the Shā-ăl-bō-nīte, of
the sons of Jăsh-ĕn, Jonathan,
33 Shăm-măh the Hâr-ă-rīte, Ā-hī-
ăm the son of Shâr-ăr the Hâr-ă-rīte,
34 Ē-lĭph-ē-lĕt the son of Ă-hăs-bā̂i,
the son of the Mā-ăch-ă-thīte, Ē-lī-
ăm the son of Ă-hĭth-ō-phĕl the Gī-
lō-nīte,
35 Hĕz-rā-ī the Carmelite, Pā-ă-rā̂i
the Är-bīte,
36 Ī-găl the son of Nathan of Zō-băh,
Bā-nī the Gadite,
37 Zē-lĕk the Ammonite, Nā-hă-rā̂i
the Bēer-ō-thīte, armourbearer to Jō-
ăb the son of Zĕr-ū-ī-ăh,
38 [s]Ī-ră an [t]Ĭth-rīte, Gâr-ĕb an Ĭth-
rīte,
39 [u]Ū-rī-ăh the Hittite: thirty and
seven in all.

CHAPTER 24

AND [a]again the anger of the LORD
was kindled against Israel, and
he moved David against them to say,
Go, number Israel and Judah.
2 For the king said to Jō-ăb the captain of the host, which *was* with him,
Go now through all the tribes of Israel, from Dan even to Bēer-shē-bă,

10 a man of countenance, or sight. 1 Chr. 11.23. a man of great stature.
11 Or, honourable among the thirty.
n ch. 8.18.
12 at his command, or, council.
o ch. 2.18.
p 1 Chr. 11. 27.
q Judg. 12.15.
13 Or, valleys.
r Judg. 2.9.
s ch. 20.26.
t Josh. 15.48.
u ch. 11.3,6.
CHAP. 24
a ch. 16.10. 1 Ki. 22.22.
1 Satan.
b 1 Chr. 27. 23.
2 Or, Compass.
c Gen. 26.4. Deut. 8.13, 14. 2 Chr. 32.25, 26. Pro. 18.12.
d 1 Chr. 21.4. Eccl. 8.4. Acts 5.29.
e Deut. 2.36.
3 Or, valley.
f Num. 32.1, 3.
4 Or, nether land newly inhabited.
g Josh. 19.47.
h Judg. 18.28.
i 1 Chr. 21.5.
j 1 Sam. 24.5. Pro. 18.4. 1 John 3.20.
k ch. 12.13. 1 Chr. 21.8.
l 1 Sam. 13. 13.
m 1 Sam. 22. 5.
n 1 Sam. 9.9.
o 1 Chr. 21. 12. That is, three years and the present added to those mentioned, ch. 21.1.

and number ye the people, that [c]I may
know the number of the people.
3 And Jō-ăb said unto the king, Now
the LORD thy God add unto the people, how many soever they be, an
hundredfold, and that the eyes of my
lord the king may see *it:* but why doth
my lord the king delight in this thing?
4 Notwithstanding [d]the king's word
prevailed against Jō-ăb, and against
the captains of the host. And Jō-ăb
and the captains of the host went out
from the presence of the king, to number the people of Israel.
5 ¶ And they passed over Jordan, and
pitched in [e]Ă-rō-ĕr, on the right side of
the city that *lieth* in the midst of the
[3]river of Gad, and toward [f]Jā-zĕr:
6 Then they came to Gilead, and to
the [4]land of Tăh-tĭm-hŏd-shī; and
they came [g]to Dăn-jā-ăn, and about
to [h]Zī-dŏn,
7 And came to the strong hold of
Tyre, and to all the cities of the Hī-
vītes, and of the Canaanites: and they
went out to the south of Judah, *even* to
Bēer-shē-bă.
8 So when they had gone through all
the land, they came to Jerusalem at
the end of nine months and twenty
days.
9 And Jō-ăb gave up the sum of the
number of the people unto the king:
[i]and there were in Israel eight hundred thousand valiant men that drew
the sword; and the men of Judah *were*
five hundred thousand men.
10 ¶ And [j]David's heart smote him
after that he had numbered the people. And David said unto the LORD,
[k]I have sinned greatly in that I have
done: and now, I beseech thee, O
LORD, take away the iniquity of thy
servant; for I have [l]done very foolishly.
11 For when David was up in the
morning, the word of the LORD came
unto the prophet [m]Gad, David's [n]seer,
saying,
12 Go and say unto David, Thus
saith the LORD, I offer thee three
things; choose thee one of them, that I
may *do it* unto thee.
13 So Gad came to David, and told
him, and said unto him, Shall [o]seven
years of famine come unto thee in thy
land? or wilt thou flee three months
before thine enemies, while they pursue thee? or that there be three days'
pestilence in thy land? now advise,
and see what answer I shall return to
him that sent me.
14 And David said unto Gad, I am in

a great strait: let us fall now into the hand of the LORD; [p]for his mercies *are* [5]great: and [q]let me not fall into the hand of man.

15 ¶ So the [r]LORD sent a pestilence upon Israel from the morning even to the time appointed: and there died of the people from Dan even to Bē-ēr-shē-bă seventy thousand men.

16 And when the [s]angel stretched out his hand upon Jerusalem to destroy it, [t]the LORD repented him of the evil, and said to the angel that destroyed the people, It is enough: stay now thine hand. And the angel of the LORD was by the threshingplace of [u]Ă-raû-năh the Jĕb-ū-site.

17 And David spake unto the LORD when he saw the angel that smote the people, and said, Lo, [v]I have sinned, and I have done wickedly: but these sheep, what have they done? let thine hand, I pray thee, be against me, and against my father's house.

18 ¶ And Gad came that day to David, and said unto him, [w]Go up, rear an altar unto the LORD in the threshingfloor of [6]Ă-raû-năh the Jĕb-ū-site.

19 And David, according to the saying of Gad, went up as the LORD commanded.

20 And Ă-raû-năh looked, and saw the king and his servants coming on toward him: and Ă-raû-năh went out, and bowed himself before the king on his face upon the ground.

21 And Ă-raû-năh said, Wherefore is my lord the king come to his servant? [x]And David said, To buy the threshingfloor of thee, to build an altar unto the LORD, that the [y]plague may be stayed from the people.

22 And Ă-raû-năh said unto David, Let my lord the king take and offer up what *seemeth* good unto him: [z]behold, *here be* oxen for burnt sacrifice, and threshing instruments and *other* instruments of the oxen for wood.

23 All these *things* did Ă-raû-năh, *as* a king, give unto the king. And Ă-raû-năh said unto the king, The LORD thy God accept [a]thee.

24 And the king said unto Ă-raû-năh, Nay; but I will surely buy *it* of thee at a price: neither will I offer burnt offerings unto the LORD my God of that which doth cost me nothing. So [b]David bought the threshingfloor and the oxen for fifty shekels of silver.

25 And David built [7]there an altar unto the LORD, and offered burnt offerings and peace offerings. So the LORD was [c]intreated for the land, and the plague was stayed from Israel.

p Ps. 103.8. Ps. 119.156.
5 Or, many.
q Isa. 47.6. Zech. 1.15.
r 1 Chr. 21. 14. 1 Chr. 27.24.
s Ex. 12.23. 1 Chr. 21.15. Ps. 104.4.
t Gen. 6.6. 1 Sam. 15. 11. Ps. 78.38. Joel 2.13. Jonah 3.10.
u 1 Chr. 21. 15. Ornan.
v 1 Chr. 21. 17.
w 1 Chr. 21. 18.
6 Araniah.
x Gen. 23.8.
y Num. 16. 48.
z 1 Ki. 19.21.
a Ps. 20.3. Eze. 20.40. 1 Pet. 2.5.
b 1 Chr. 21. 24.
7 Which became the site of the Temple.
c 2 Chr. 33. 13. Isa. 19.22.

THE FIRST

BOOK OF THE KINGS

commonly called

THE THIRD BOOK OF THE KINGS

CHAPTER 1

NOW king David was old *and* [1]stricken in years; and they covered him with clothes, but he gat no heat.

2 Wherefore his servants said unto him, [2]Let there be sought for my lord the king [3]a young virgin: and [a]let her stand before the king, and let her [4]cherish him, and let her lie in thy bosom, that my lord the king may get heat.

3 So they sought for a fair damsel throughout all the coasts of Israel, and found Ăb-ĭ-shăg a [b]Shû-năm-mite, and brought her to the king.

4 And the damsel *was* very fair, and cherished the king, and ministered to him: but the king [c]knew her not.

5 ¶ Then [d]Ăd-ō-nī-jăh the son of Hăg-gīth exalted himself, saying, I will [5]be king: and [e]he prepared him chariots and horsemen, and fifty men to run before him.

6 And his father had [f]not displeased him [6]at any time in saying, Why hast thou done so? and he also *was a* very goodly *man;* [g]and *his mother* bare him after Ăb-să-lom.

7 And he conferred with Jō-ăb the son of Zĕr-ū-ī-ăh, and [h]with Ā-bī-ă-thär the priest: and [i]they [7]following Ăd-ō-nī-jăh helped *him*.

8 But Zā-dŏk the priest, and Bĕ-nâi-

CHAP. 1
1 entered into days.
2 Let them seek.
3 a damsel, a virgin.
a 1 Sam. 16. 21.
4 be a cherisher unto him.
b Josh. 19.18.
c Gen. 4.1.
d 2 Sam. 3.4.
5 reign.
e Deut. 17.16.
f 1 Sam. 3.13.
6 from his days.
g 2 Sam. 3.3, 4.
h 2 Sam. 20. 25.
i ch. 2.22.
7 helped after Adonijah.

ăh the son of Jĕ-hôi′-ă-dă, and Nathan
the prophet, and [j]Shĭm′-ĕ-ī, and Rē′-ī,
and [k]the mighty men which *belonged*
to David, were not with Ăd-ō-nī′-jăh.
9 And Ăd-ō-nī′-jăh slew sheep and
oxen and fat cattle by the stone of Zō′-
hĕ-lĕth, which *is* by [8]Ĕn-rō′-gĕl, and
called all his brethren the king's sons,
and all the men of Judah the king's
servants:
10 But Nathan the prophet, and Bĕ-
nâi′-ăh, and the mighty men, and
Solomon his brother, he called not.
11 ¶ Wherefore Nathan spake unto
Băth′-shĕ-bă the mother of Solomon,
saying, Hast thou not heard that Ăd-
ō-nī′-jăh the son of Hăg′-gīth [l]doth
reign, and David our lord knoweth *it*
not?
12 Now therefore come, let me, I
pray thee, give [m]thee counsel, that
thou mayest save thine own life, and
the life of thy son Solomon.
13 Go and get thee in unto king
David, and say unto him, Didst not
thou, my lord, O king, swear unto
thine handmaid, saying, Assuredly
[n]Solomon thy son shall reign after me,
and he shall sit upon my throne? why
then doth Ăd-ō-nī′-jăh reign?
14 Behold, while thou yet talkest
there with the king, I also will come in
after thee, and [9]confirm thy words.
15 ¶ And Băth′-shĕ-bă went in unto
the king into the chamber: and the
king was very old: and Ăb′-ī-shăg the
Shû-năm′-mīte ministered unto the
king.
16 And Băth′-shĕ-bă bowed, and did
obeisance unto the king. And the king
said, [10]What wouldest thou?
17 And she said unto him, [o]My lord,
thou swarest by the LORD thy God
unto thine handmaid, *saying*, Assuredly Solomon thy son shall reign after
me, and he shall sit upon my throne.
18 And now, behold, Ăd-ō-nī′-jăh
reigneth; and now, my lord the king,
thou knowest *it* not:
19 And he hath slain oxen and fat
cattle and sheep in abundance, and
hath called all the sons of the king,
and Ă-bī′-ă-thăr the priest, and Jō′-ăb
the captain of the host: but Solomon
thy servant hath he not called.
20 And thou, my lord, O king, the
eyes of all Israel *are* upon thee, that
thou shouldest tell them who shall sit
on the throne of my lord the king after
him.
21 Otherwise it shall come to pass,
when my lord the king shall [11]sleep
with his fathers, that I and my son

j ch. 4.18.
k 2 Sam. 23.8.
8 Or, the fuller's well.
l 2 Sam. 3.4.
m Pro. 11.14.
n 1 Chr. 22.9.
9 fill up.
10 What to thee?
o Gen. 18.12. Eph. 5.33. 1 Pet. 6.3.
11 lie down.
12 sinners.
13 Let king Adonijah live.
14 before the king.
p Judg. 8.19. 1 Sam. 14. 39. 1 Sam. 25. 34. 2 Sam. 4.9. ch. 17.1. 2 Ki. 4.30.
q Gen. 48.16. 2 Sam. 4.9. Ps. 19.14. Ps. 31.5,7. Ps. 34.19,22. Ps. 71.23. Ps. 103.1,4. Lam. 3.58.
r Neh. 2.3. Dan. 2.4.
s 2 Sam. 20.6. Esther 6.8.
15 which belongeth to me.
t 2 Chr. 32. 30.
u 1 Sam. 10.1. 1 Sam. 16.3, 12. 2 Sam. 2.4. 2 Sam. 5.3. ch. 19.16. 2 Ki. 9.3.
v 2 Sam. 15. 10. 2 Ki. 9.13. Mark 11.9, 10.

Solomon shall be counted [12]offenders.
22 ¶ And, lo, while she yet talked
with the king, Nathan the prophet also
came in.
23 And they told the king, saying, Behold Nathan the prophet. And when
he was come in before the king, he
bowed himself before the king with
his face to the ground.
24 And Nathan said, My lord, O
king, hast thou said, Ăd-ō-nī′-jăh shall
reign after me, and he shall sit upon
my throne?
25 For he is gone down this day, and
hath slain oxen and fat cattle and
sheep in abundance, and hath called
all the king's sons, and the captains
of the host, and Ă-bī′-ă-thăr the priest;
and, behold, they eat and drink before
him, and say, [13]God save king Ăd-ō-
nī′-jăh.
26 But me, *even* me thy servant, and
Zā′-dŏk the priest, and Bĕ-nâi′-ăh the
son of Jĕ-hôi′-ă-dă, and thy servant
Solomon, hath he not called.
27 Is this thing done by my lord the
king, and thou hast not shewed *it* unto
thy servant, who should sit on the
throne of my lord the king after him?
28 ¶ Then king David answered and
said, Call me Băth′-shĕ-bă. And she
came [14]into the king's presence, and
stood before the king.
29 And the king sware, and said, *As*
[p]the LORD liveth, that [q]hath redeemed
my soul out of all distress,
30 Even as I sware unto thee by the
LORD God of Israel, saying, Assuredly
Solomon thy son shall reign after me,
and he shall sit upon my throne in my
stead; even so will I certainly do this
day.
31 Then Băth′-shĕ-bă bowed with
her face to the earth, and did reverence to the king, and said, Let [r]my
lord king David live for ever.
32 ¶ And king David said, Call me
Zā′-dŏk the priest, and Nathan the
prophet, and Bĕ-nâi′-ăh the son of Jĕ-
hôi′-ă-dă. And they came before the
king.
33 The king also said unto them,
Take [s]with you the servants of your
lord, and cause Solomon my son to
ride upon [15]mine own mule, and bring
him down [t]to Gī′-hŏn:
34 And let Zā′-dŏk the priest and Nathan the prophet [u]anoint him there
king over Israel: and [v]blow ye with the
trumpet, and say, God save king
Solomon.
35 Then ye shall come up after him,
that he may come and sit upon my

throne; for he shall be king in my
stead: and I have appointed him to be
ruler over Israel and over Judah.
36 And Bĕ-nâi´-ăh the son of Jĕ-hôi´-
ă-dă answered the king, and said, [w]Ā´-
mĕn: the LORD God of my lord the
king say so *too*.
37 As [x]the LORD hath been with my
lord the king, even so be he with Solomon, and make his throne greater
than the throne of my lord king David.
38 So Zā´-dŏk the priest, and Nathan
the prophet, and [y]Bĕ-nâi´-ăh the son
of Jĕ-hôi´-ă-dă, and the Chĕr´-ĕ-thītes,
and the Pĕl´-ĕ-thītes, went down, and
caused Solomon to ride upon king
David's mule, and brought him to
Gī´-hŏn.
39 And Zā´-dŏk the priest took an
horn of oil [z]out of the tabernacle, and
[a]anointed Solomon. And they blew
the trumpet; and [b]all the people said,
God save king Solomon.
40 And all the people came up after
him, and the people piped with
[16]pipes, and rejoiced with great joy, so
that the earth rent with the sound of
them.
41 ¶ And Ăd-ō-nī´-jăh and all the
guests that *were* with him heard *it* as
they had made an end of eating. And
when Jō´-ăb heard the sound of the
trumpet, he said, Wherefore *is this*
noise of the city being in an uproar?
42 And while he yet spake, behold,
Jonathan the son of Ā-bī´-ă-thăr the
priest came: and Ăd-ō-nī´-jăh said unto him, Come in; for [c]thou *art* a valiant man, and bringest good tidings.
43 And Jonathan answered and said
to Ăd-ō-nī´-jăh, Verily our lord king
David hath made Solomon king.
44 And the king hath sent with him
Zā´-dŏk the priest, and Nathan the
prophet, and Bĕ-nâi´-ăh the son of Jĕ-
hôi´-ă-dă, and the Chĕr´-ĕ-thītes, and
the Pĕl´-ĕ-thītes, and they have caused
him to ride upon the king's mule:
45 And Zā´-dŏk the priest and Nathan
the prophet have anointed him king in
Gī´-hŏn: and they are come up from
thence rejoicing, so that the city rang
again. This *is* the noise that ye have
heard.
46 And also Solomon [d]sitteth on the
throne of the kingdom.
47 And moreover the king's servants
came to bless our lord king David,
saying, God make the name of Solomon better than thy name, and make
his throne greater than thy throne.
[e]And the king bowed himself upon
the bed.

w Deut. 27. 15-26. Jer. 11.5. Matt. 6.13.
x Deut. 2.7. Josh. 1.5,17. 1 Sam. 20. 13. ch. 8.57. 2 Ki. 2.9. 1 Chr. 28.20.
y 2 Sam. 8.18.
z Ex. 30.23, 25,32. Ps. 89.20.
a 1 Sam. 10.1. 1 Chr. 29.22. Ps. 89.20.
b 1 Sam. 10. 24.
16 Or, flutes.
c 2 Sam. 18. 27.
d 1 Chr. 29. 23.
e Gen. 47.31.
f ch. 3.6. Ps. 132.11, 12.
g Ex. 21.14.
h 1 Sam. 14. 45. 2 Sam. 14. 11. Acts 27.34.
i Deut. 1.17.

CHAP. 2

a Gen. 3.19. Deut. 31.14. 2 Sam. 14. 14. Job 30.23. Ps. 89.48. Eccl. 12.7.
b Josh. 23.14. Heb. 9.27.
c Deut. 17.19. Josh. 1.7. 1 Sam. 18.5, 14,30. 1 Chr. 22.12, 13.
1 Or, do wisely.
d 2 Sam. 7.25.
e Ps. 132. 12.
f 2 Ki. 20.3.
g 2 Sam. 7.12.
2 be cut off from thee from the throne.
h 2 Sam. 3.39. 2 Sam. 19.5, 6,7.
i 2 Sam. 3.27.
j 2 Sam. 20. 10.
3 put.
k Pro. 20.26.

48 And also thus said the king, Blessed *be* the LORD God of Israel, which
hath [f]given *one* to sit on my throne
this day, mine eyes even seeing *it*.
49 And all the guests that *were* with
Ăd-ō-nī´-jăh were afraid, and rose up,
and went every man his way.
50 ¶ And Ăd-ō-nī´-jăh feared because
of Solomon, and arose, and went, and
[g]caught hold on the horns of the altar.
51 And it was told Solomon, saying,
Behold, Ăd-ō-nī´-jăh feareth king Solomon: for, lo, he hath caught hold on
the horns of the altar, saying, Let king
Solomon swear unto me to day that
he will not slay his servant with the
sword.
52 And Solomon said, If he will shew
himself a worthy man, [h]there shall not
an hair of him fall to the earth: [i]but if
wickedness shall be found in him, he
shall die.
53 So king Solomon sent, and they
brought him down from the altar.
And he came and bowed himself to
king Solomon: and Solomon said unto him, Go to thine house.

CHAPTER 2

NOW [a]the days of David drew
nigh that he should die; and he
charged Solomon his son, saying,
2 I [b]go the way of all the earth: be
thou strong therefore, and shew thyself a man;
3 And keep the charge of the LORD
thy God, [c]to walk in his ways, to keep
his statutes, and his commandments,
and his judgments, and his testimonies, as it is written in the law of Moses,
that thou mayest [1]prosper in all that
thou doest, and whithersoever thou
turnest thyself:
4 That the LORD may [d]continue his
word which he spake concerning me,
saying, [e]If thy children take heed to
their way, to walk before [f]me in truth
with all their heart and with all their
soul, there [g]shall not [2]fail thee (said he)
a man on the throne of Israel.
5 Moreover thou knowest also what
Jō´-ăb the son of Zĕr-ū-ī´-ăh [h]did to me,
and what he did to the two captains of
the hosts of Israel, unto Abner [i]the
son of Ner, and unto Ā-mā´-să [j]the son
of Jē´-thĕr, whom he slew, and [3]shed
the blood of war in peace, and put the
blood of war upon his girdle that *was*
about his loins, and in his shoes that
were on his feet.
6 Do therefore [k]according to thy wisdom, and let not his hoar head go
down to the grave in peace.

7 But shew kindness unto the sons of
Bär-zĭl-lā-ī [l]the Gileadite, and let
them be of those that [m]eat at thy
table: for so they [n]came to me when I
fled because of Ăb-´să-lom thy brother.
8 And, behold, *thou hast* with thee
Shĭm-´ĕ-ī [o]the son of Gē-´ră, a Benjamite of Bă-hū-´rĭm, which cursed me
with a [4]grievous curse in the day when
I went to Mā-hă-nā-´ĭm: but he came
down to meet me at Jordan, and I
sware to him by the LORD, saying, I
will not put thee to death with the
sword.
9 Now therefore [p]hold him not guiltless: for thou *art* a wise man, and
knowest what thou oughtest to do unto him; but his hoar head bring thou
down to the grave with blood.
10 So [q]David slept with his fathers,
and was buried in [r]the city of David.
11 And the days that David reigned
[s]over Israel *were* forty years: seven
years reigned he in Hē-´brŏn, and
thirty and three years reigned he in
Jerusalem.
12 ¶ Then [t]sat Solomon upon the
throne of David his father; and his
kingdom was established greatly.
13 ¶ And Ăd-ō-nī-´jăh the son of Hăg-´
gīth came to Băth´-shĕ-bă the mother
of Solomon. And she said, [u]Comest
thou peaceably? And he said, Peaceably.
14 He said moreover, I have somewhat to say unto thee. And she said,
Say on.
15 And he said, Thou knowest that
the kingdom was mine, and *that* all
Israel set their faces on me, that I
should reign: howbeit the kingdom is
turned about, and is become my brother's: for [v]it was his from the LORD.
16 And now I ask one petition of
thee, [5]deny me not. And she said unto
him, Say on.
17 And he said, Speak, I pray thee,
unto Solomon the king, (for he will
not say thee nay,) that he give me
[w]Ăb-´ĭ-shăg the Shû-năm-´mīte to wife.
18 And Băth´-shĕ-bă said, Well; I
will speak for thee unto the king.
19 ¶ Băth´-shĕ-bă therefore went unto king Solomon, to speak unto him
for Ăd-ō-nī-´jăh. And the king rose up
to meet her, and bowed himself [x]unto
her, and sat down on his throne, and
caused a seat to be set for the king's
mother; and [y]she sat on his right
hand.
20 Then she said, I desire one small
petition of thee; *I pray thee*, say me
not nay. And the king said unto her,

l 2 Sam. 19. 31.
m 2 Sam. 9.7.
n 2 Sam. 17. 27.
o 2 Sam. 16.5.
4 strong.
p Ex. 20.7.
q ch. 1.21. Job 14.1. Eccl. 12.5. Acts 2.29.
r 2 Sam. 5.7.
s 2 Sam. 5.4. 1 Chr. 29.26, 27.
t 1 Chr. 29. 23. 2 Chr. 1.1.
u 1 Sam. 16.4.
v 1 Chr. 22.9. 1 Chr. 28.5, 6,7. 2 Chr. 20.6. Job 9.12. Ps. 33.10,11. Ps. 115.3. Ps. 132.10. Pro. 19.21. Isa. 14.27. Isa. 43.13. Isa. 46.9,10. Dan. 2.21. Acts 5.39.
5 turn not away my face.
w ch. 1.3,4.
x Ex. 20.12. Lev. 19.32. Pro. 23.22.
y Ps. 45.9. Ps. 110.1. Matt. 20.21.
z ch. 1.7.
a Ruth 1.17. 1 Sam. 14. 44. 2 Sam. 3.9, 35. ch. 20.10.
b 2 Sam. 7.11.
c Josh. 21.18.
6 a man of death.
d 1 Sam. 23.6. 2 Sam. 15. 24,29.
e 1 Sam. 22. 20. 2 Sam. 15. 24.
f 1 Sam. 2.31.
g ch. 1.7.
h ch. 1.50. Ex. 21.14.
i Ex. 21.14.
j Num. 35.33. Deut. 19.13.

Ask on, my mother: for I will not say
thee nay.
21 And she said, Let Ăb-´ĭ-shăg the
Shû-năm-´mīte be given to Ăd-ō-nī-´
jăh thy brother to wife.
22 And king Solomon answered and
said unto his mother, And why dost
thou ask Ăb-´ĭ-shăg the Shû-năm-´mīte
for Ăd-ō-nī-´jăh? ask for him the kingdom also; for he *is* mine elder brother; even for him, and for Ă-bī-´ă-
thär [z]the priest, and for Jō-´ăb the son
of Zĕr-ū-ī-´ăh.
23 Then king Solomon sware by the
LORD, saying, [a]God do so to me, and
more also, if Ăd-ō-nī-´jăh have not
spoken this word against his own life.
24 Now therefore, *as* the LORD liveth, which hath established me, and
set me on the throne of David my
father, and who hath made me an
house, as he [b]promised, Ăd-ō-nī-´jăh
shall be put to death this day.
25 And king Solomon sent by the
hand of Bĕ-nāi-´ăh the son of Jĕ-hôi-´
ă-dă; and he fell upon him that he
died.
26 ¶ And unto Ă-bī-´ă-thär the priest
said the king, Get thee to [c]Ăn-´ă-thōth,
unto thine own fields; for thou *art*
[6]worthy of death: but I will not at this
time put thee to death, [d]because thou
barest the ark of the Lord GOD before
David my father, and because [e]thou
hast been afflicted in all wherein my
father was afflicted.
27 So Solomon thrust out Ă-bī-´ă-
thär from being priest unto the LORD;
that he might fulfil [f]the word of the
LORD, which he spake concerning the
house of Ē-´lī in Shī-´lōh.
28 ¶ Then tidings came to Jō-´ăb: for
Jō-´ăb [g]had turned after Ăd-ō-nī-´jăh,
though he turned not after Ăb-´să-lom.
And Jō-´ăb fled unto the tabernacle of
the LORD, and caught hold on the
horns of [h]the altar.
29 And it was told king Solomon that
Jō-´ăb was fled unto the tabernacle of
the LORD; and, behold, *he is* by the
altar. Then Solomon sent Bĕ-nāi-´ăh
the son of Jĕ-hôi-´ă-dă, saying, Go,
fall upon him.
30 And Bĕ-nāi-´ăh came to the tabernacle of the LORD, and said unto him,
Thus saith the king, Come forth. And
he said, Nay; but I will die here. And
Bĕ-nāi-´ăh brought the king word
again, saying, Thus said Jō-´ăb, and
thus he answered me.
31 And the king said unto him, Do
[i]as he hath said, and fall upon him,
and bury him; that [j]thou mayest take

away the innocent blood, which Jō´ăb shed, from me, and from the house of my father.

32 And the LORD [k]shall return his blood upon his own head, who fell upon two men more righteous and [l]better than he, and slew them with the sword, my father David not knowing *thereof, to wit,* Abner [m]the son of Ner, captain of the host of Israel, and [n]Ă-mā´să the son of Jē´thĕr, captain of the host of Judah.

33 Their blood shall therefore return upon the head of Jō´ăb, and upon [o]the head of his seed for ever: [p]but upon David, and upon his seed, and upon his house, and upon his throne, shall there be peace for ever from the LORD.

34 So Bĕ-nâi´ăh the son of Jĕ-hoi´ă-dă went up, and fell upon him, and slew him: and he was buried in his own house in [q]the wilderness.

35 ¶ And the king put Bĕ-nâi´ăh the son of Jĕ-hoi´ă-dă in his room over the host: and Zā´dŏk [r]the priest did the king put in the room of Ă-bī´ă-thär.

36 ¶ And the king sent and called for [s]Shĭm´ĕ-ī, and said unto him, Build [t]thee an house in Jerusalem, and dwell there, and go not forth thence any whither.

37 For it shall be, *that* on the day thou goest out, and passest over the [u]brook Kī´drŏn, thou shalt know for certain that thou shalt surely die: [v]thy blood shall be upon thine own head.

38 And Shĭm´ĕ-ī said unto the king, The saying *is* good: as my lord the king hath said, so will thy servant do. And Shĭm´ĕ-ī dwelt in Jerusalem many days.

39 And it came to pass at the end of three years, that two of the servants of Shĭm´ĕ-ī ran away unto Ā´chĭsh [w]son of Mā´ă-chăh king of Gath. And they told Shĭm´ĕ-ī, saying, Behold, thy servants *be* in Gath.

40 And Shĭm´ĕ-ī [x]arose, and saddled his ass, and went to Gath to Ā´chĭsh to seek his servants: and Shĭm´ĕ-ī went, and brought his servants from Gath.

41 And it was told Solomon that Shĭm´ĕ-ī had gone from Jerusalem to Gath, and was come again.

42 And the king sent and called for Shĭm´ĕ-ī, and said unto him, Did I not make thee to [y]swear by the LORD, and protested unto thee, saying, Know for a certain, on the day thou goest out, and walkest abroad any whither, that

k Gen. 4.11. Judg. 9.24. Ps. 7.16. Ps. 9.15,16.
l 2 Sam. 3.27. 2 Chr. 21.13. Esther 1.19.
m 2 Sam. 3. 27.
n 2 Sam. 20. 10.
o 2 Sam. 3.29.
p 2 Sam. 3.28. Pro. 16.7. Isa. 9.6,7. Phil. 4.7. Acts 7.45, 46.
q Josh. 15.61. Matt. 3.1.
r Num. 25. 11,13. 1 Sam. 2.35. 1 Chr. 6.53.
s 2 Sam. 16.5.
t Pro. 20.8, 26.
u 2 Sam. 15. 23. 2 Ki. 23.6.
v Lev. 20.9. 2 Sam. 1.16. Eze. 18.13.
w 1 Sam. 27. 2.
x Pro. 15.27.
y Ps. 15.4.
z Eze. 17.19.
a Ps. 7.16.
b Pro. 25.5.

CHAP. 3
a ch. 9.15.
b Lev. 17.3. Deut. 12.2. ch. 22.43.
c Deut. 6.5. Deut. 10.12. Ps. 31.23. Ps. 145.20. Matt. 22.37. Mark 12.30. Luke 10.27. Rom. 8.28. 1 Cor. 8.3. 1 John 5.3.
d 1 Chr. 16. 39.
e ch. 9.2. 2 Chr. 1.7.
f Num. 12.6. Matt. 1.20.
g John 15.7.
h 2 Chr. 1.8.
1 Or, bounty.
i 1 Chr. 29.1. Job 32.6-8. Eccl. 10.16. Jer. 1.6.
j Num. 27.17.
k Deut. 7.6.
l Gen. 13.16.
m 2 Chr. 1.10. Ps. 72.1. Pro. 2.3. Pro. 3.13-15. Jas. 1.5.
2 hearing.

thou shalt surely die? and thou said unto me, The word *that* I have hear *is* good.

43 Why then hast thou not kept th [z]oath of the LORD, and the comman ment that I have charged thee with

44 The king said moreover to Shĭn ĕ-ī, Thou knowest all the wickedne which thine heart is privy to, th thou didst to David my father: ther fore the LORD shall return [a]thy wicke ness upon thine own head;

45 And king Solomon *shall be* bless ed, and the [b]throne of David shall b established before the LORD for eve

46 So the king commanded Bĕ-nâ ăh the son of Jĕ-hoi´ă-dă; which wen out, and fell upon him, that he die And the kingdom was established i the hand of Solomon.

CHAPTER 3

AND Solomon made affinity wit Pharaoh king of Egypt, and too Pharaoh's daughter, and brought he into the city of David, until he ha made an end of building his ow house, and the house of the LORD, an [a]the wall of Jerusalem round about.

2 Only [b]the people sacrificed in hig places, because there was no hous built unto the name of the LORD, unti those days.

3 And Solomon [c]loved the LORD walking in the statutes of David hi father: only he sacrificed and burn incense in high places.

4 And the king went to Gibeon t sacrifice there; [d]for that *was* the grea high place: a thousand burnt offering did Solomon offer upon that altar.

5 ¶ In [e]Gibeon the LORD appeared t Solomon [f]in a dream by night: an God said, Ask [g]what I shall give thee

6 And [h]Solomon said, Thou has shewed unto thy servant David m father great [1]mercy, according as h walked before thee in truth, and i righteousness, and in uprightness o heart with thee; and thou hast kept fo him this great kindness, that thou hast given him a son to sit on hi throne, as *it is* this day.

7 And now, O LORD my God, thou hast made thy servant king instead o David my father: and [i]I *am but* a little child: I know not *how* [j]to go out o come in.

8 And thy servant *is* in the midst o thy people which thou [k]hast chosen a great people, [l]that cannot be numbered nor counted for multitude.

9 Give [m]therefore thy servant an [2]un-

lerstanding heart [n]to judge thy peo-
ɔle, that I may [o]discern between good
ınd bad: for who is able to judge this
hy so great a people?
10 And the speech pleased the Lord,
hat Solomon had asked this thing.
11 And God said unto him, Because
hou hast asked this thing, and hast
[p]not asked for thyself [3]long life; nei-
her hast asked riches for thyself, nor
ıast asked the life of thine enemies;
ɔut hast asked for thyself understand-
ng [4]to discern judgment;
12 Behold, [q]I have done according to
hy words: [r]lo, I have given thee a
vise and an understanding heart; so
hat there was none like thee before
hee, neither after thee shall any arise
ike unto thee.
13 And I have also [s]given thee that
which thou hast not asked, both
riches, and honour: so that there
shall not be any among the kings like
ınto thee all thy days.
14 And if thou wilt walk in my ways,
o keep my statutes and my com-
nandments, as thy father David did
walk, then I will lengthen [u]thy days.
15 And Solomon [v]awoke; and, be-
ıold, *it was* a dream. And he came to
erusalem, and stood before the ark
of the covenant of the LORD, and
offered up burnt offerings, and offered
peace offerings, and [w]made a feast to
ıll his servants.
16 ¶ Then came there two women,
that were [x]harlots, unto the king, and
[y]stood before him.
17 And the one woman said, O my
ord, I and this woman dwell in one
ıouse; and I was delivered of a child
with her in the house.
18 And it came to pass the third day
ıfter that I was delivered, that this
woman was delivered also: and we
were together; *there was* no stranger
with us in the house, save we two in
he house.
19 And this woman's child died in
he night; because she overlaid it.
20 And she arose at midnight, and
ook my son from beside me, while
thine handmaid slept, and laid it in
her bosom, and laid her dead child in
my bosom.
21 And when I rose in the morning
to give my child suck, behold, it was
dead: but when I had considered it in
the morning, behold, it was not my
son, which I did bear.
22 And the other woman said, Nay;
but the living *is* my son, and the dead
is thy son. And this said, No; but the
dead *is* thy son, and the living *is* my
son. Thus they spake before the king.
23 Then said the king, The one saith,
This *is* my son that liveth, and thy son
is the dead: and the other saith, Nay;
but thy son *is* the dead, and my son *is*
the living.
24 And the king said, Bring me a
sword. And they brought a sword before the king.
25 And the king said, Divide the living child in two, and give half to the
one, and half to the other.
26 Then spake the woman whose the
living child *was* unto the king, for [z]her
bowels [6]yearned upon her son, and
she said, O my lord, give her the living
child, and in no wise slay it. But the
other said, Let it be neither mine nor
thine, *but* divide *it*.
27 Then the king answered and said,
Give her the living child, and in no
wise slay it: she *is* the mother thereof.
28 And all Israel heard of the judgment which the king had judged; and
they feared the king: for they saw that
[a]the wisdom of God *was* [7]in him, to do
judgment.

CHAPTER 4

SO king Solomon was king over all
Israel.
2 And these *were* the princes which
he had; Ăz-ă-rī-ăh the son of Zā-dŏk
[1]the priest,
3 Ē-lĭ-hôr-ĕph and Ă-hī-ăh, the sons
of Shī-shă, [2]scribes; [a]Jĕ-hŏsh-ă-phăt
the son of Ă-hī-lŭd, the [3]recorder.
4 And [b]Bĕ-nâi-ăh the son of Jĕ-hôi-ă-
dă *was* over the host: and Zā-dŏk and
[c]Ă-bī-ă-thăr *were* the priests:
5 And Ăz-ă-rī-ăh the son of Nathan
was over the officers: and Zā-bŭd the
son of Nathan *was* [d]principal officer,
and [e]the king's friend:
6 And Ă-hī-shăr *was* over the household: and [f]Ăd-ō-nī-răm the son of Abda *was* over the [4]tribute.
7 ¶ And Solomon had twelve officers
over all Israel, which provided victuals for the king and his household:
each man his month in a year made
provision.
8 And these *are* their names: [5]The
son of Hur, in mount Ē-phră-ĭm:
9 [6]The son of Dē-kăr, in Mā-kăz, and
in Shā-ăl-bĭm, and Bĕth–shē-mĕsh,
and Ē-lŏn–bĕth–hā-năn:
10 [7]The son of Hē-sĕd, in Ă-rû-bŏth;
to him *pertained* Sō-chōh, and all the
land of Hē-phĕr:
11 [8]The son of Ă-bĭn-ă-dăb, in all the

n Ps. 72.1.
o Heb. 5.14.
p Jas. 4.3.
3 many days.
4 to hear.
q 1 John 5.14.
r ch. 4.29. ch. 5.12. Pro. 3.13-18. Eccl. 1.16.
s Matt. 6.33. Eph. 3.20.
t ch. 10.23. Pro. 3.16. 1 Cor. 3.21-23. 2 Cor. 6.10.
5 Or, hath not been.
u Ps. 91.16. Pro. 3.2.
v Gen. 41.7. Jer. 31.26.
w Gen. 31.54. ch. 8.65. Esther 1.3. Dan. 5.1. Mark 6.21.
x Lev. 19.29. Deut. 23.17.
y Num. 27.2.
z Gen. 43.30. Isa. 49.15. Jer. 31.20. Hosea 11.8.
6 were hot.
a Ezra 7.25. Isa. 11.3. Dan. 1.17. Col. 2.2.3.
7 in the midst of him.

CHAP. 4

1 Or, the chief officer.
2 Or, secretaries.
a 2 Sam. 8.16.
3 Or, remembrancer.
b ch. 2.35.
c ch. 2.27.
d 2 Sam. 8.18.
e 2 Sam. 15.37. 1 Chr. 27.33.
f ch. 5.14.
4 Or, levy.
5 Or, Benhur.
6 Or, Bendekar.
7 Or, Benhesed.
8 Or, Benabinadab.

region of Dor; which had Tā'-phăth
the daughter of Solomon to wife:
12 Bā'-ă-nă the son of Ă-hī'-lŭd; *to*
him pertained Tā'-ă-năch and Mĕ-gĭd'-
dō, and all Bĕth-shē'-ăn, which *is* by
Zär-tā'-năh beneath Jĕz-reel', from
Bĕth-shē'-ăn to Ā'-bĕl-mĕ-hō'-lăh, *even*
unto *the place that is* beyond Jŏk'-nĕ-
ăm:
13 [9]The son of Gē'-bĕr, in Rā'-mŏth-
gĭl'-ĕ-ăd; to him *pertained* [g]the towns
of Jā'-ĭr the son of Mă-năs'-sĕh, which
are in Gilead; to him *also pertained*
the [h]region of Är'-gŏb, which *is* in Bā'-
shăn, threescore great cities with
walls and brasen bars:
14 Ă-hĭn'-ă-dăb the son of Ĭd'-dō *had*
[10]Mā-hă-nā'-ĭm:
15 Ă-hī'-mă-ăz *was* in Năph'-tă-lī; he
also took Băs'-măth the daughter of
Solomon to wife:
16 Bā'-ă-năh the son of Hū'-shāi *was*
in Asher and in Ā'-lōth:
17 Jĕ-hŏsh'-ă-phăt the son of Pă-rū'-
ăh, in Ĭs'-să-chär:
18 Shĭm'-ĕ-ī the son of Ē'-lăh, in Benjamin:
19 Gē'-bĕr the son of Ū'-rī *was* in the
country of Gilead, *in* [i]the country of
Sī'-hŏn king of the Amorites, and of
Og king of Bā'-shăn; and *he was* the
only officer which *was* in the land.
20 ¶ Judah and Israel *were* many, as
[j]the sand which *is* by the sea in multitude, eating [k]and drinking, and making merry.
21 And Solomon reigned over all
kingdoms from [l]the river unto the land
of the Philistines, and unto the border
of Egypt: they brought presents, and
served Solomon all the days of his life.
22 ¶ And Solomon's [11]provision for
one day was thirty [12]measures of fine
flour, and threescore measures of
meal,
23 Ten fat oxen, and twenty oxen
out of the pastures, and an hundred
sheep, beside harts, and roebucks,
and fallowdeer, and fatted fowl.
24 For he had dominion over all *the*
region on this side the river, from
Tĭph'-săh even [m]to Azzah, over all the
kings on this side the river: and he had
peace on all sides round about him.
25 And Judah and Israel [n]dwelt
[13]safely, every man under his vine and
under his fig tree, from Dan even to
Bē'-ĕr-shē'-bă, all the days of Solomon.
26 ¶ And Solomon had forty thousand stalls of [o]horses for his chariots,
and twelve thousand horsemen.
27 And those officers provided victual for king Solomon, and for all that

9 Or, Ben-geber.
g Num. 32. 41.
h Deut. 3.4.
10 Or, to Mahanaim.
i Deut. 3.8.
j Gen. 22.17. ch. 3.8.
k 1 Sam. 30. 16. 1 Chr. 12.39. Ps. 72.3. Micah 4.4. Zech. 9.15. Acts 2.46.
l Gen. 15.18. Ex. 23.31. Deut. 11.24. 2 Chr. 9.26. Ps. 72.8.
11 bread.
12 cors. A cor is about 75 gallons.
m Gen. 10.19.
n Deut. 33. 28,29. Ps. 33.12. Jer. 23.6. Micah 4.4. Zech. 3.10.
13 confidently.
o Deut. 17.16. ch. 10.25,26. Ps. 20.7.
14 Or, mules, or, swift beasts.
p Gen. 25.6. Matt. 2.1.
q Acts 7.22.
r 1 Chr. 15. 19. Ps. 89, title.
s 1 Chr. 6.33. Ps. 88, title.
t Pro. 1.1. Eccl. 12.9.
u Song 1.1.
v ch. 10.1.

CHAP. 5

a Amos 1.9.
b 2 Chr. 2.3.
c 2 Sam. 7.5. 1 Chr. 22.8. 2 Chr. 6.6-8.
d 1 Chr. 22.8.
e 1 Chr. 22.9. Ps. 72.7. Isa. 9.7.
f 2 Chr. 2.4.
1 say.
g 2 Sam. 7.13. 1 Chr. 22.10.
h ch. 6.9,10, 16,20.

came unto king Solomon's table,
every man in his month: they lacked
nothing.
28 Barley also and straw for the
horses and [14]dromedaries brought
they unto the place where *the officers*
were, every man according to his
charge.
29 ¶ And God gave Solomon wisdom
and understanding exceeding much,
and largeness of heart, even as the
sand that *is* on the sea shore.
30 And Solomon's wisdom excelled
the wisdom of all the children [p]of the
east country, and all the [q]wisdom of
Egypt.
31 For he was wiser than all men;
than [r]Ē'-thăn the Ĕz'-ră-hīte, and [s]Hē'-
măn, and Chăl'-cŏl, and Där'-dă, the
sons of Mā'-hŏl: and his fame was in
all nations round about.
32 And [t]he spake three thousand
proverbs: and his [u]songs were a thousand and five.
33 And he spake of trees, from the
cedar tree that *is* in Lĕb'-ă-nŏn even
unto the hyssop that springeth out of
the wall: he spake also of beasts, and
of fowl, and of creeping things, and of
fishes.
34 And [v]there came of all people to
hear the wisdom of Solomon, from all
kings of the earth, which had heard
of his wisdom.

CHAPTER 5

AND Hiram king of Tyre sent his
servants unto Solomon; for he
had heard that they had anointed him
king in the room of his father: [a]for
Hiram was ever a lover of David.
2 And [b]Solomon sent to Hiram,
saying,
3 Thou knowest how that David my
father [c]could not build an house unto
the name of the LORD his God [d]for the
wars which were about him on every
side, until the LORD put them under
the soles of his feet.
4 But now the LORD my God hath
given me [e]rest on every side, *so that*
there is neither adversary nor evil
occurrent.
5 And, [f]behold, I [1]purpose to build
an house unto the name of the LORD
my God, as [g]the LORD spake unto
David my father, saying, Thy son,
whom I will set upon thy throne in thy
room, he shall build an house unto
my name.
6 Now therefore command thou that
they hew me [h]cedar trees out of Lĕb'-
ă-nŏn; and my servants shall be with

thy servants: and unto thee will I give
hire for thy servants according to all
that thou shalt [2]appoint: for thou
knowest that *there is* not among us
any that can skill to hew timber like
unto the [i]Sī-dō-nĭ-ăns.
7 ¶ And it came to pass, when Hiram
heard the words of Solomon, that he
rejoiced greatly, and said, Blessed *be*
the LORD this day, which hath given
unto David a wise son over this great
people.
8 And Hiram sent to Solomon, saying, I have [3]considered the things
which thou sentest to me for: *and* I
will do all thy desire concerning timber
of cedar, and concerning timber of fir.
9 My [j]servants shall bring *them* down
from Lĕb-ă-non unto the sea: [k]and I
will convey them by sea in floats unto
the place that thou shalt [4]appoint me,
and will cause them to be discharged
there, and thou shalt receive *them*:
and thou shalt accomplish my desire,
in [l]giving food for my household.
10 So Hiram gave Solomon cedar
trees and fir trees *according to* all his
desire.
11 And [m]Solomon gave Hiram twenty thousand [5]measures of wheat *for*
food to his household, and [6]twenty
measures of pure oil: thus gave Solomon to Hiram year by year.
12 And the LORD gave Solomon wisdom, as [n]he promised him: and there
was peace between Hiram and Solomon; and they two made a league
together.
13 ¶ And king Solomon raised a [7]levy
out of all Israel; and the levy was
thirty thousand men.
14 And he sent them to Lĕb-ă-non,
ten thousand a month by courses: a
month they were in Lĕb-ă-non, *and*
two months at home: [o]and Ăd-ō-nī-
răm *was* over the levy.
15 And Solomon had threescore and
ten thousand that bare burdens, and
fourscore thousand hewers in the
mountains;
16 Beside the chief of Solomon's
officers which *were* over the work,
three thousand and three hundred,
which ruled over the people that
wrought in the work.
17 And the king commanded, and
they brought great stones, costly
stones, *and* hewed stones, to lay the
foundation of the house.
18 And Solomon's builders and Hiram's builders did hew *them*, and the
stonesquarers: so they prepared
timber and stones to build the house.

CHAPTER 6

AND it came to pass in the four hundred and eightieth year after the
children of Israel were come out of the
land of Egypt, in the fourth year of
Solomon's reign over Israel, in the
month Zif, which *is* the second
[1]month, that he [2]began to build the
house of the LORD.
2 And [a]the house which king Solomon built for the LORD, the length
thereof *was* threescore cubits, and the
breadth thereof twenty *cubits*, and the
height thereof thirty cubits.
3 And the porch before the temple of
the house, twenty cubits *was* the length
thereof, according to the breadth of
the house; *and* ten cubits *was* the
breadth thereof before the house.
4 And for the house he made [3]win-
dows of narrow lights.
5 ¶ And [4]against the wall of the house
he built [5]chambers round about,
against the walls of the house round
about, *both* of the temple and of the
[6]oracle: and he made [7]chambers
round about:
6 The nethermost chamber *was* five
cubits broad, and the middle *was* six
cubits broad, and the third *was* seven
cubits broad: for without *in the wall*
of the house he made [8]narrowed rests
round about, that *the beams* should
not be fastened in the walls of the
house.
7 And the house, when it was in
building, was built of stone made
ready before it was brought thither:
so that there was neither hammer nor
axe *nor* any tool of iron heard in the
house, while it was in building.
8 The door for the middle chamber
was in the right [9]side of the house: and
they went up with winding stairs into
the middle *chamber*, and out of the
middle into the third.
9 So he built the house, and finished
it; and covered the house [10]with
beams and boards of cedar.
10 And *then* he built chambers
against all the house, five cubits high:
and they rested on the house with
timber of cedar.
11 ¶ And the word of the LORD came
to Solomon, saying,
12 *Concerning* this house which thou
art in building, if thou wilt walk in my
statutes, and execute my judgments,
and keep all my commandments to
walk in them; then will I perform my
word with thee, which I spake unto
David thy father:
13 And [b]I will dwell among the chil-

2 say.
i Eze. 27.5.
3 heard.
j ch. 9.20,21.
k 2 Chr. 2.16.
4 send.
l Ezra 3.7. Eze. 27.17. Acts 12.20.
m 2 Chr. 2.10.
5 cors. That is, about 42,500 boles.
6 About 1560 gallons, wine measure.
n ch. 3.12. 2 Chr. 1.12. Jas. 1.5.
7 tribute of men.
o ch. 12.18.
8 Or, Giblites.

CHAP. 6

1 Of the sacred year: about the end of April.
2 built.
a Eze. 41.1.
3 Or, windows broad within and narrow without: or, skewed and closed.
4 Or, upon, or, joining to.
5 floors.
6 Or, holy of holies.
7 ribs.
8 narrowings, or, rebatements.
9 shoulder.
10 Or, the vault-beams and the cielings with cedar.
b Ex. 25.8. Lev. 26.11. Ps. 132.13, 14. 2 Cor. 6.16. Heb. 3.6. Rev. 21.3.

dren of Israel, and [c]will not forsake my people Israel.

14 So Solomon built the house, and finished it.

15 And he built the walls of the house within with boards of cedar, [11]both the floor of the house, and the walls of the cieling: *and* he covered *them* on the inside with wood, and covered the floor of the house with planks of fir.

16 And he built twenty cubits on the sides of the house, both the floor and the walls with boards of cedar: he even built *them* for it within, *even* for the oracle, *even* for the [d]most holy *place*.

17 And the house, that *is*, the temple before it, was forty cubits *long*.

18 And the cedar of the house within *was* carved with [12]knops and [13]open flowers: all *was* cedar; there was no stone seen.

19 And the oracle he prepared in the house within, to [e]set there the ark of the covenant of the LORD.

20 And the oracle in the forepart *was* twenty cubits in length, and twenty cubits in breadth, and twenty cubits in the height thereof: and he overlaid it with [14]pure gold; and *so* covered the altar *which was of* cedar.

21 So Solomon overlaid the house within with pure gold: and he made a partition by the chains of gold before the oracle; and he overlaid it with gold.

22 And the whole house he overlaid with gold, until he had finished all the house: [f]also the whole altar that *was* by the oracle he overlaid with gold.

23 ¶ And within the oracle [g]he made two chĕr-ū-bĭms *of* [15]olive tree, *each* ten cubits high.

24 And five cubits *was* the one wing of the cherub, and five cubits the other wing of the cherub: from the uttermost part of the one wing unto the uttermost part of the other *were* ten cubits.

25 And the other cherub *was* ten cubits: both the chĕr-ū-bĭms *were* of one measure and one size.

26 The height of the one cherub *was* ten cubits, and so *was it* of the other cherub.

27 And he set the chĕr-ū-bĭms within the inner house: and [16]they stretched forth the wings of the chĕr-ū-bĭms, so that the wing of the one touched the *one* wall, and the wing of the other cherub touched the other wall; and their wings touched one another in the midst of the house.

[c] Deut. 31.6. Heb. 13.5.
11 Or, from the floor of the house unto the walls, etc., and so ver. 16.
[d] Ex. 26.33. Lev. 7.6. Num. 18.10. ch. 8.6. Heb. 9.3.
12 Or, gourds.
13 openings of flowers.
[e] Ex. 40.20. ch. 8.6-10.
14 shut up.
[f] Ex. 30.1.
[g] Ex. 25.20. 2 Chr. 3.10, 11,12. 2 Chr. 5.8.
15 trees of oil, or, oily trees.
16 Or, the cherubims stretched forth their wings.
17 openings of flowers.
[h] John 10.7.
18 Or, five-square.
19 Or, leaves of the doors.
20 openings of flowers.
21 Or, four-square.
[i] Eze. 41.23.
22 About the end of October.
23 Or, with all the appurtenances thereof, and with all the ordinances thereof.

CHAP. 7

[a] ch. 9.10. 2 Chr. 8.1.
1 ribs.
2 sight against sight.
3 Or, spaces and pillars were square in prospect.

28 And he overlaid the chĕr-ū-bĭms with gold.

29 And he carved all the walls of the house round about with carved figures of chĕr-ū-bĭms and palm trees and [17]open flowers, within and without.

30 And the floor of the house he overlaid with gold, within and without.

31 ¶ And for the [h]entering of the oracle he made doors *of* olive tree: the lintel *and* side posts *were* [18]a fifth part *of the wall*.

32 The [19]two doors also *were of* olive tree; and he carved upon them carvings of chĕr-ū-bĭms and palm trees and [20]open flowers, and overlaid *them* with gold, and spread gold upon the chĕr-ū-bĭms, and upon the palm trees.

33 So also made he for the door of the temple posts *of* olive tree, [21]a fourth part *of the wall*.

34 And the two doors *were of* fir tree: the two [i]leaves of the one door *were* folding, and the two leaves of the other door *were* folding.

35 And he carved *thereon* chĕr-ū-bĭms and palm trees and open flowers: and covered *them* with gold fitted upon the carved work.

36 ¶ And he built the inner court with three rows of hewed stone, and a row of cedar beams.

37 ¶ In the fourth year was the foundation of the house of the LORD laid, in the month Zif:

38 And in the eleventh year, in [22]the month Bul, which *is* the eighth month, was the house finished [23]throughout all the parts thereof, and according to all the fashion of it. So was he seven years in building it.

CHAPTER 7

BUT Solomon was building his own house [a]thirteen years, and he finished all his house.

2 ¶ He built also the house of the forest of Lĕb-ă-non; the length thereof *was* an hundred cubits, and the breadth thereof fifty cubits, and the height thereof thirty cubits, upon four rows of cedar pillars, with cedar beams upon the pillars.

3 And *it was* covered with cedar above upon the [1]beams, that *lay* on forty five pillars, fifteen *in* a row.

4 And *there were* windows *in* three rows, and [2]light *was* against light *in* three ranks.

5 And all the [3]doors and posts *were* square, with the windows: and light *was* against light *in* three ranks.

6 ¶ And he made a porch of pillars

the length thereof *was* fifty cubits, and
the breadth thereof thirty cubits: and
the porch *was* [4]before them: and the
other pillars and the thick beam *were*
[5]before them.
7 ¶ Then he made a porch for [b]the
throne where he might judge, *even* the
porch of judgment: and *it was* covered
with cedar [6]from one side of the floor
to the other.
8 ¶ And his house where he dwelt
had another court within the porch,
which was of the like work. Solomon
made also an house for Pharaoh's
daughter, [c]whom he had taken *to wife*,
like unto this porch.
9 All these *were of* costly stones,
according to the measures of hewed
stones, sawed with saws, within and
without, even from the foundation
unto the coping, and *so* on the outside
toward the great court.
10 And the foundation *was of* costly
stones, even great stones, stones of
ten cubits, and stones of eight cubits.
11 And above *were* costly stones,
after the measures of hewed stones,
and cedars.
12 And the great court round about
was with three rows of hewed stones,
and a row of cedar beams, both for
the inner court of the house of the
LORD, [d]and for the porch of the house.
13 ¶ And king Solomon sent and
fetched Hiram [e]out of Tyre.
14 He [f]*was* [7]a widow's son of the
tribe of Năph-tă-lī, and [g]his father *was*
a man of Tyre, a worker in brass: and
[h]he was filled with wisdom, and understanding, and cunning to work
all works in brass. And he came to
king Solomon, and wrought all his
work.
15 For he [8]cast [i]two pillars of brass,
of eighteen cubits high apiece: and
a line of twelve cubits did compass
either of them about.
16 And he made two chapiters *of*
molten brass, to set upon the tops of
the pillars: the height of the one chapiter *was* five cubits, and the height of
the other chapiter *was* five cubits:
17 *And* nets of checker work, and
wreaths of chain work, for the chapiters which *were* upon the top of the
pillars; seven for the one chapiter, and
seven for the other chapiter.
18 And he made the pillars, and two
rows round about upon the one network, to cover the chapiters that *were*
upon the top, with pomegranates: and
so did he for the other chapiter.
19 And the chapiters that *were* upon
the top of the pillars *were* of lily work
in the porch, four cubits.
20 And the chapiters upon the two
pillars *had pomegranates* also above,
over against the belly which *was* by
the network: and the pomegranates
were [j]two hundred in rows round
about upon the other chapiter.
21 And [k]he set up the pillars in the
[l]porch of the temple: and he set up the
right pillar, and called the name thereof [9]Jā-chĭn: and he set up the left
pillar, and called the name thereof
[10]Bō-ăz.
22 And upon the top of the pillars
was lily work: so was the work of the
pillars finished.
23 ¶ And he made [m]a molten sea, ten
cubits [11]from the one brim to the
other: *it was* round all about, and his
height *was* five cubits: and a line of
thirty cubits did compass it round
about.
24 And under the brim of it round
about *there were* knops compassing
it, ten in a cubit, [n]compassing the sea
round about: the knops *were* cast in
two rows, when it was cast.
25 It stood upon [o]twelve oxen, three
looking toward the north, and three
looking toward the west, and three
looking toward the south, and three
looking toward the east: and the sea
was set above upon them, and all their
hinder parts *were* inward.
26 And it *was* an hand breadth thick,
and the brim thereof was wrought like
the brim of a cup, with flowers of lilies:
it contained [12]two thousand bāths.
27 ¶ And he made ten bases of brass;
four cubits *was* the length of one base,
and four cubits the breadth thereof, and three cubits the height of
it.
28 And the work of the bases *was* on
this *manner:* they had [13]borders, and
the borders *were* between the ledges:
29 And on the borders that *were* between the ledges *were* [p]lions, oxen, and
chĕr-ū-bĭms: and upon the ledges
there was a base above: and beneath
the lions and oxen *were* certain additions made of thin work.
30 And every base had four brasen
wheels, and plates of brass: and the
four corners thereof had undersetters:
under the laver *were* undersetters
molten, at the side of every addition.
31 And the mouth of it within the
chapiter and above *was* a cubit: but
the mouth thereof *was* round *after* the
work of the base, a cubit and an half:
and also upon the mouth of it *were*

4 Or, according to them.
5 Or, according to them.
b ch. 10.18. Ps. 45.6. Ps. 110.1. Pro. 20.8. Isa. 9.7.
6 from floor to floor.
c ch. 3.1.
d John 10.23. Acts 3.11.
e 2 Chr. 4.11. Huram.
f 2 Chr. 2.14.
7 the son of a widow woman.
g 2 Chr. 4.16.
h Ex. 28.3. Ex. 31.3. Job 35.11. Isa. 28.26. Dan. 1.17. Luke 2.40.
8 fashioned.
i 2 Ki. 25.17. 2 Chr. 3.15. Jer. 52.21.
j 2 Ki. 25.17. 2 Chr. 3.16. Jer. 52.23.
k 2 Chr. 3.17. Song 3.10. Gal. 2.9. Rev. 3.12.
l ch. 6.3.
9 That is, He shall establish.
10 That is, In it is strength.
m 2 Ki. 25.13. 2 Chr. 4.2. Jer. 52.17.
11 from his brim to his brim.
n 2 Chr. 4.3.
o 2 Chr. 4.4,5. Jer. 52.20. Eze. 1.10. Rev. 4.6,7.
12 There were but 2000 bāths in it usually, but when quite filled it contained 3000, or 22,210 gallons, wine measure.
13 shootings.
p Gen. 3.24. ch. 6.27. Ps. 18.10. Eze. 1.10. Eze. 41.18, 19. Rev. 4.6-8.

gravings with their borders, foursquare, not round.
32 And under the borders *were* four
wheels; and the axletrees of the wheels
were [14]*joined* to the base: and the
height of a wheel *was* a cubit and
half a cubit.
33 And the work of the wheels *was*
like the work of a chariot wheel: their
axletrees, and their naves, and their
felloes, and their spokes, *were* all
molten.
34 And *there were* four undersetters
to the four corners of one base: *and*
the undersetters *were* of the very base
itself.
35 And in the top of the base *was*
there a round compass of half a cubit
high: and on the top of the base the
ledges thereof and the borders thereof *were* of the same.
36 For on the plates of the [15]ledges
thereof, and on the borders thereof,
he graved chĕr-ū-bĭms, lions, and
palm trees, according to the [16]pro-
portion of every one, and additions
round about.
37 After this *manner* he made the ten
bases: all of them had one casting,
one measure, *and* one size.
38 ¶ Then [q]made he ten lavers of
brass: one laver contained forty
bäths: *and* every laver was four cubits:
and upon every one of the ten bases
one laver.
39 And he put five bases on the right
[17]side of the house, and five on the
left side of the house: and he set the
sea on the right side of the house eastward over against the south.
40 ¶ And Hiram made the lavers, and
the shovels, and the basons. So Hiram
made an end of doing all the work
that he made king Solomon for the
house of the LORD:
41 The two pillars, and the *two* bowls
of the chapiters that *were* on the top
of the two pillars; and the two networks, to cover the two bowls of the
chapiters which *were* upon the top of
the pillars;
42 And four hundred pomegranates
for the two networks, *even* two rows
of pomegranates for one network, to
cover the two bowls of the chapiters
that *were* [18]upon the pillars;
43 And the ten bases, and ten lavers
on the bases;
44 And one sea, and twelve oxen under the sea;
45 And [r]the pots, and the shovels,
and the basons: and all these vessels,
which Hiram made to king Solomon
for the house of the LORD, *were of*
[19]bright brass.
46 In [s]the plain of Jordan did the
king cast them, [20]in the clay ground
[t]between Sŭc-cōth [u]and Zär-thăn.
47 And Solomon left all the vessels
unweighed, [21]because they were exceeding many: neither was the weight
of the brass [22]found out.
48 And Solomon made all the vessels
that *pertained* unto the house of the
LORD: the [v]altar of gold, and [w]the
table of gold, whereupon [x]the shewbread *was*,
49 And the candlesticks of pure gold,
five on the right *side*, and five on the
left, before the oracle, with the flowers,
and the lamps, and the tongs *of* gold,
50 And the bowls, and the snuffers,
and the basons, and the spoons, and
the [23]censers *of* pure gold; and the
hinges *of* gold, *both* for the doors of
the inner house, the most holy *place*,
and for the doors of the house, *to wit*,
of the temple.
51 So was ended all the work that
king Solomon made for the house of
the LORD. And Solomon brought in
the [24]things which David his father
had dedicated; *even* the silver, and the
gold, and the vessels, did he put
among the treasures of the house of
the LORD.

CHAPTER 8

THEN Solomon assembled the
elders of Israel, and all the heads of
the tribes, the [1]chief of the fathers of
the children of Israel, unto king Solomon in Jerusalem, that [a]they might
bring up the ark of the covenant of
the LORD out of [b]the city of David,
which *is* Zion.
2 And all the men of Israel assembled
themselves unto king Solomon at the
feast [c]in the month Ĕth-ă-nĭm, which
is the seventh month.
3 And all the elders of Israel came,
[d]and the priests took up the ark.
4 And they brought up the ark of the
LORD, [e]and the tabernacle of the congregation, and all the holy vessels that
were in the tabernacle, even those did
the priests and the Levites bring up.
5 And king Solomon, and all the congregation of Israel, that were assembled unto him, *were* with him before
the ark, sacrificing sheep and oxen,
that could not be told nor numbered
for multitude.
6 And the priests brought in the ark
of the covenant of the LORD unto [f]his
place, into the oracle of the house, t

14 in the base.
15 hands, or, handles.
16 nakedness.
q Ex. 30.17. 2 Chr. 4.6. Zech. 13.1. Titus 3.5.
17 shoulder.
18 upon the face of the pillars.
r Ex. 27.3. 2 Chr. 4.16. Zech. 14.20, 21.
19 made bright, or scoured.
s 2 Chr. 4.17.
20 in the thickness of the ground.
t Gen. 33.17. Josh. 3.16. 2 Chr. 4.17.
u Josh. 3.16.
21 for the exceeding multitude.
22 searched. 1 Chr. 22.14.
v Ex. 37.25.
w Ex. 37.10.
x Ex. 25.30. Lev. 24.5.
23 ash pans.
24 holy things of David.

CHAP. 8
1 princes.
a Num. 10. 33. 2 Sam. 6.17. ch. 3.15. 1 Chr. 13.3.
b 2 Sam. 5.7.
c Lev. 23.34. Deut. 16.13. 2 Chr. 7.8.
d Num. 4.15. Deut. 31.9. Josh. 3.3,6. 1 Chr. 15.14.
e ch. 3.4. 2 Chr. 1.3.
f Ex. 26.33.

e most holy *place*, *even* [g]under the
ings of the chĕr-ū-bĭms.
7 For the chĕr-ū-bĭms spread forth
eir two wings over the place of the
rk, and the chĕr-ū-bĭms covered the
rk and the staves thereof above.
8 And they [h]drew out the staves, that
e [2]ends of the staves were seen out
the [3]holy *place* before the oracle,
nd they were not seen without: and
ere they are unto this day.
9 *There* [i]*was* nothing in the ark save
he two tables of stone, which Moses
ut there at Hôr-ĕb, [4]when the LORD
ade *a covenant* with the children of
rael, when they came out of the land
f Egypt.
10 And it came to pass, when the
riests were come out of the holy
lace, that the cloud filled the house
f the LORD,
11 So that the priests could not stand
minister because of the cloud: for
e glory of the LORD had filled the
ouse of the LORD.
12 ¶ Then spake Solomon, The LORD
id that he would dwell [l]in the thick
arkness.
13 I have surely built thee an house
dwell in, [m]a settled place for thee
abide in for ever.
14 And the king turned his face
bout, and [n]blessed all the congrega-
on of Israel: (and all the congrega-
on of Israel stood;)
15 And he said, [o]Blessed *be* the LORD
od of Israel, which spake with
s mouth unto David my father,
nd hath with his hand fulfilled *it*,
ying,
16 Since [p]the day that I brought forth
y people Israel out of Egypt, I chose
o city out of all the tribes of Israel
build an house, that [q]my name
ight be therein; but I chose David
be over my people Israel.
17 And it was in the heart of David
y father to build an house for the
ame of the LORD God of Israel.
18 And the LORD said unto David
y father, Whereas it was in thine
eart to build an house unto my name,
ou didst well that it was in thine
eart.
19 Nevertheless thou shalt not build
e house; but thy son that shall come
rth out of thy loins, he shall build
e house unto my name.
20 And the LORD hath performed his
ord that he spake, and I am risen up
the room of David my father, and
t on the throne of Israel, as the LORD
romised, and have built an house

g ch. 6.27.
h Ex. 25.14.
2 heads.
3 Or, ark.
i Ex. 25.21. Deut. 10.2.
j Deut. 10.5. Heb. 9.4.
k Ex. 40.20.
4 Or, where.
l Lev. 16.2. Ps. 18.11. Ps. 97.2.
m Ps. 132.14. John 4.21-23. Acts 6.14.
n Josh. 22.6. 2 Sam. 6.18. 1 Chr. 16.2. 2 Chr. 6.3.
o Luke 1.68.
p 2 Chr. 6.5.
q Deut. 12.11.
r Deut. 31.26.
s 2 Ki. 23.3. 2 Chr. 6.12. Job 11.13. Ps. 63.4. Isa. 1.15. 1 Tim. 2.8.
t Ex. 15.11. 1 Chr. 29. 10-13. Ps. 35.10. Ps. 86.8-10. Jer. 10.6-16. Micah 7.18.
u Deut. 7.9. Neh. 1.5. Dan. 9.4.
v Gen. 17.1. 2 Ki. 20.3.
5 There shall not be cut off unto thee a man from my sight.
6 only if.
w 2 Sam. 7. 25.
x 2 Chr. 2.6. Ps. 113.4. Isa. 66.1. Jer. 23.24. Acts 7.49.
y 2 Cor. 12.2.
z Phil. 4.6.
a Dan. 6.10.
7 Or, in this place.
b 2 Chr. 20.9. Neh. 1.6.
8 Or, in this place.
c Ex. 34.6,7. Ps. 85.2. Ps. 103.2,3. Dan. 9.9. Matt. 6.12. 1 John 1.9.
9 and he require an oath of him.

for the name of the LORD God of
Israel.
21 And I have set there a place for
the ark, wherein *is* [r]the covenant of
the LORD, which he made with our
fathers, when he brought them out of
the land of Egypt.
22 ¶ And Solomon stood before the
[s]altar of the LORD in the presence of
all the congregation of Israel, and
spread forth his hands toward heaven:
23 And he said, LORD God of Israel,
[t]*there is* no God like thee, in heaven
above, or on earth beneath, [u]who
keepest covenant and mercy with thy
servants that walk [v]before thee with
all their heart:
24 Who hast kept with thy servant
David my father that thou promisedst
him: thou spakest also with thy
mouth, and hast fulfilled *it* with thine
hand, as *it is* this day.
25 Therefore now, LORD God of Israel, keep with thy servant David my
father that thou promisedst him, saying, [5]There shall not fail thee a man
in my sight to sit on the throne of
Israel; [6]so that thy children take heed
to their way, that they walk before me
as thou hast walked before me.
26 And [w]now, O God of Israel, let
thy word, I pray thee, be verified,
which thou spakest unto thy servant
David my father.
27 But [x]will God indeed dwell on
the earth? behold, the heaven and
[y]heaven of heavens cannot contain
thee; how much less this house that I
have builded?
28 Yet have thou respect unto the
[z]prayer of thy servant, and to his supplication, O LORD my God, to hearken
unto the cry and to the prayer, which
thy servant prayeth before thee to
day:
29 That thine eyes may be open toward this house night and day, *even*
toward the place of which thou hast
said, My name shall be there: that
thou mayest hearken unto the prayer
which thy servant shall [a]make [7]to-
ward this place.
30 And [b]hearken thou to the supplication of thy servant, and of thy people Israel, when they shall pray [8]to-
ward this place: and hear thou in
heaven thy dwelling place: and when
thou hearest, [c]forgive.
31 ¶ If any man trespass against his
neighbour, [9]and an oath be laid upon
him to cause him to swear, and the
oath come before thine altar in this
house:

32 Then hear thou in heaven, and do, and judge thy servants, condemning [d]the wicked, to bring his way upon his head; and justifying the righteous, to give him according to his righteousness.

33 ¶ When [e]thy people Israel be smitten down before the enemy, because they have sinned against thee, and [f]shall turn again to thee, and confess thy name, and pray, and make supplication unto thee [10]in this house:

34 Then hear thou in heaven, and forgive the sin of thy people Israel, and bring them again unto the land which thou gavest unto their fathers.

35 ¶ When heaven is shut up, and there is no rain, because they have sinned against thee; if they pray toward this place, and confess thy name, and turn from their sin, when thou afflictest them:

36 Then hear thou in heaven, and forgive the sin of thy servants, and of thy people Israel, that thou [g]teach them the [h]good way wherein they should walk, and give rain upon thy land, which thou hast given to thy people for an inheritance.

37 ¶ If [i]there be in the land famine, if there be pestilence, blasting, mildew, locust, *or* if there be caterpiller; if their enemy besiege them in the land of their [11]cities; whatsoever plague, whatsoever sickness *there be;*

38 What prayer and supplication soever be *made* by any man, *or* by all thy people Israel, which shall know every man the plague of his own heart, and spread forth his hands toward this house:

39 Then hear thou in heaven thy dwelling place, and forgive, and do, and give to every man according to his ways, whose heart thou knowest; (for thou, *even* thou only, knowest [j]the hearts of all the children of men;)

40 That they may fear thee all the days that they live in the land which thou gavest unto our fathers.

41 Moreover concerning a stranger, that *is* not of thy people Israel, but cometh out of a far country for thy name's sake;

42 (For they shall hear of thy great name, and of thy [k]strong hand, and of thy stretched out arm;) when he shall come and pray toward this house;

43 Hear thou in heaven thy dwelling place, and do according to all that the stranger calleth to thee for: [l]that all people of the earth may know thy name, to [m]fear thee, as *do* thy people Israel; and that they may know tl [12]this house, which I have builded, called by thy name.

44 ¶ If thy people go out to bat against their enemy, whithersoev thou shalt send them, and shall pr unto the LORD [13]toward the city whi thou hast chosen, and *toward* t house that I have built for thy nan

45 Then hear thou in heaven th prayer and their supplication, a maintain their [14]cause.

46 If they sin against thee, ([n]for *the is* no man that sinneth not,) and th be angry with them, and deliver the to the enemy, so that they carry the away captives unto the land of the e emy, far or near;

47 *Yet* [o]if they shall [15]bethink the selves in the land whither they we carried captives, and repent, a make supplication unto thee in t land of them that carried them ca tives, [p]saying, We have sinned, a have done perversely, we have co mitted wickedness;

48 And *so* [q]return unto thee with their heart, and with all their soul, the land of their enemies, which l them away captive, and pray [r]un thee toward their land, which th gavest unto their fathers, the ci which thou hast chosen, and the hou which I have built for thy name:

49 Then hear thou their prayer a their supplication in heaven thy dw ling place, and maintain their [16]caus

50 And forgive thy people that ha sinned against thee, and all the transgressions wherein they ha transgressed against thee, and [s]gi them compassion before them w carried them captive, that they m have compassion on them:

51 For they *be* thy people, and thi inheritance, which thou broughte forth out of Egypt, from the midst the furnace of iron:

52 That thine eyes may be open un the supplication of thy servant, a unto the supplication of thy peop Israel, to hearken unto them in that they call for unto thee.

53 For thou didst separate them fro among all the people of the earth, *be* thine inheritance, as thou spake by the hand of Moses thy servan when thou broughtest our fathers o of Egypt, O Lord GOD.

54 And it was *so*, that when Solomo had made an end of praying all th prayer and supplication unto t LORD, he arose from before the alt

d Deut. 25.1.
e Deut. 28. 25.
f Lev. 26.39. Jer. 20.12.
10 Or, toward.
g Ps. 5.8. Ps. 25.4,5. Ps. 27.11. Ps. 86.11. Ps. 94.12. Ps. 119.133. Isa. 35.8. Hosea 2.21.
h 1 Sam. 12. 23. Jer. 6.16.
i Lev. 26.16. Deut. 28.21-52.
11 Or, jurisdiction.
j 1 Chr. 28.9. Ps. 11.4. Jer. 17.10. Acts 1.24.
k Deut. 3.24.
l 1 Sam. 17. 46. Ps. 67.2.
m Ps. 102.15.
12 thy name is called upon this house.
13 the way of the city.
14 Or, right.
n 2 Chr. 6.36. Job 9.2. Ps. 130.3. Ps. 143.2. Pro. 20.9. Eccl. 7.20. Jas. 3.2. 1 John 1.8.
o Lev. 26.40.
15 bring back to their heart.
p Neh. 1.6. Ps. 106.6. Dan. 9.5.
q Deut. 4.29. Neh. 1.9. Pro. 23.26. Jer. 29.12. Dan. 6.10. Acts 8.37. Rom. 10.10.
r 2 Chr. 6.38. Ps. 5.7. Dan. 6.10.
16 Or, right.
s Ezra 7.6. Ps. 106.46.

f the LORD, from kneeling on his
nees with his hands spread up to
eaven.
55 And he stood, [t]and blessed all the
ongregation of Israel with a loud
oice, saying,
56 Blessed *be* the LORD, that hath
iven rest unto his people Israel, ac-
ording to all that he promised: there
hath not [17]failed one word of all his
ood promise, which he promised by
ie hand of Moses his servant.
57 The LORD our God be with us, as
e was with our fathers: [v]let him not
ave us, nor forsake us:
58 That he may [w]incline our hearts
nto him, to walk in all his ways, and
keep his commandments, and his
atutes, and his judgments, which he
ommanded our fathers.
59 And let these my words, where-
ith I have made supplication before
ie LORD, be nigh unto the LORD our
od day and night, that he maintain
e cause of his servant, and the cause
f his people Israel [18]at all times, as
ie matter shall require:
60 That [x]all the people of the earth
iay know that [y]the LORD *is* God, *and*
iat there is none else.
61 Let your [z]heart therefore be per-
ect with the LORD our God, to walk
his statutes, and to keep his com-
iandments, as at this day.
62 ¶ And the king, and all Israel with
im, offered sacrifice before the LORD.
63 And Solomon offered a sacrifice
f peace offerings, which he offered
nto the LORD, two and twenty thou-
and oxen, and an hundred and twen-
y thousand sheep. So the king and all
he children of Israel dedicated the
ouse of the LORD.
64 The same day did the king hallow
he middle of the court that *was* be-
ore the house of the LORD: for there
e offered burnt offerings, and meat
fferings, and the fat of the peace of-
erings: because the brasen altar that
as before the LORD *was* too little to
eceive the burnt offerings, and meat
fferings, and the fat of the peace
fferings.
65 And at that time Solomon held [a]a
east, and all Israel with him, a great
ongregation, from the [b]entering in of
Hā-măth unto the [c]river of Egypt,
efore the LORD our God, seven days
nd seven days, *even* fourteen days.
66 On the eighth day he sent the peo-
le away: and they [19]blessed the king,
nd went unto their tents joyful and
lad of heart for all the goodness that

t 2 Sam. 6.18.
u Deut. 12. 10. Josh. 21.45.
17 fallen.
v Deut. 31.6.
w Ps. 119.36. Jer. 10.23. 2 Cor. 3.5.
18 the thing of a day in his day.
x Josh. 4.24. 1 Sam. 17. 46. 2 Ki. 19.19.
y Deut. 4.35. ch. 18.39. Jer. 10.10-12.
z ch. 11.4.
a Lev. 23.34.
b Num. 34.8. Josh. 13.5. Judg. 3.3.
c Gen. 15.18. Ex. 23.31.
19 Or, thanked.

CHAP. 9

a 2 Chr. 7.11.
b ch. 7.1. 2 Chr. 8.1. Eccl. 2.4.
c 2 Chr. 8.6.
d ch. 3.5.
e 2 Ki. 20.5. Ps. 10.17. Dan. 9.23.
f ch. 8.29.
g Deut. 11. 12.
h Gen. 5.22. Gen. 6.9. Gen. 17.1. ch. 2.4. ch. 3.6. 2 Ki. 20.3. Ps. 16.8. Ps. 128.1. Micah 6.8. Mal. 2.6.
i 2 Sam. 7.12. ch. 2.4. 1 Chr. 22.10.
j 2 Sam. 7.14. 2 Chr. 7.19. Ps. 89.30.
k Deut. 4.26. 2 Ki. 17.23.
l Jer. 7.14.
m Deut. 28. 37. Ps. 44.14.
n Deut. 29. 24. 2 Chr. 7.21.
o Jer. 22.8.

the LORD had done for David his servant, and for Israel his people.

CHAPTER 9

AND [a]it came to pass, when Solomon had finished the building of
the house of the LORD, and [b]the king's
house, and [c]all Solomon's desire
which he was pleased to do,
2 That the LORD appeared to Solomon the second time, [d]as he had
appeared unto him at Gibeon.
3 And the LORD said unto him, I
[e]have heard thy prayer and thy supplication, that thou hast made before
me: I have hallowed this house, which
thou hast built, [f]to put my name there
for ever; and [g]mine eyes and mine
heart shall be there perpetually.
4 And if thou wilt [h]walk before me,
as David thy father walked, in integrity of heart, and in uprightness, to do
according to all that I have commanded thee, *and* wilt keep my statutes and
my judgments:
5 Then I will establish the throne of
thy kingdom upon Israel for ever, [i]as
I promised to David thy father, saying, There shall not fail thee a man
upon the throne of Israel.
6 *But* [j]if ye shall at all turn from following me, ye or your children, and
will not keep my commandments *and*
my statutes which I have set before
you, but go and serve other gods, and
worship them:
7 Then [k]will I cut off Israel out of the
land which I have given them; and
this house, which I have hallowed [l]for
my name, will I cast out of my sight;
[m]and Israel shall be a proverb and a
byword among all people:
8 And [n]at this house, *which* is high,
every one that passeth by it shall be
astonished, and shall hiss; and they
shall say, [o]Why hath the LORD done
thus unto this land, and to this house?
9 And they shall answer, Because
they forsook the LORD their God, who
brought forth their fathers out of the
land of Egypt, and have taken hold
upon other gods, and have worshipped them, and served them: therefore
hath the LORD brought upon them all
this evil.
10 ¶ And it came to pass at the end
of twenty years, when Solomon had
built the two houses, the house of the
LORD, and the king's house,
11 (*Now* Hiram the king of Tyre had
furnished Solomon with cedar trees
and fir trees, and with gold, according
to all his desire,) that then king Sol-

omon gave Hiram twenty cities [1]in the land of Galilee.

12 And Hiram came out from Tyre to see the cities which Solomon had given him; and they [2]pleased him not.

13 And he said, What cities *are* these which thou hast given me, my brother? And he called them the land of [3]Cā-bûl unto this day.

14 And Hiram sent to the king sixscore talents of gold.

15 ¶ And this *is* the reason of the [p]levy which king Solomon raised; for to build the house of the LORD, and his own house, and [q]Mĭl-lō, and the wall of Jerusalem, and [r]Hā-zôr, and [s]Mĕ-gĭd-dō, and [t]Gē-zĕr.

16 *For* Pharaoh king of Egypt had gone up, and taken Gē-zĕr, and burnt it with fire, and [u]slain the Canaanites that dwelt in the city, and given it *for* a present unto his daughter, Solomon's wife.

17 And Solomon built Gē-zĕr, and Bĕth–hôr-ŏn [v]the nether,

18 And [w]Bā-ă-lăth, and Tăd-môr in the wilderness, in the land,

19 And all the cities of store that Solomon had, and cities for his chariots, and cities for his horsemen, and [4]that which Solomon desired to build in Jerusalem, and in Lĕb-ă-non, and in all the land of his dominion.

20 *And* all the people *that were* left of the Amorites, Hittites, Pĕ-rĭz-zites, Hī-vites, and Jĕb-ū-sites, which *were* not of the children of Israel,

21 Their children [x]that were left after them in the land, whom the children of Israel also were not able utterly to destroy, upon those did Solomon levy a tribute of [y]bondservice unto this day.

22 But of the children of Israel did Solomon [z]make no bondmen: but they *were* men of war, and his servants, and his princes, and his captains, and rulers of his chariots, and his horsemen.

23 These *were* the chief of the officers that *were* over Solomon's work, five hundred and fifty, which bare rule over the people that wrought in the work.

24 ¶ But Pharaoh's daughter came up out of the city of David unto [a]her house which *Solomon* had built for her: then [b]did he build Mĭl-lō.

25 ¶ And three times in a year did Solomon offer burnt offerings and peace offerings upon the altar which he built unto the LORD, and he burnt incense [5]upon the altar that *was* befor the LORD. So he finished the house.

26 ¶ And king Solomon made a nav of ships in [c]Ē-zī-ŏn–gē-bĕr, which beside Ē-lōth, on the [6]shore of th Red sea, in the land of Ē-dom.

27 And [d]Hiram sent in the navy hi servants, shipmen that had knowledg of the sea, with the servants of Sol omon.

28 And they came to [e]Ō-phĭr, an fetched from thence gold, four hun dred and twenty talents, and brough *it* to king Solomon.

CHAPTER 10

AND when the [a]queen of Shē-b heard of the fame of Solomo concerning the name of the LORD, sh came [b]to prove him with hard ques tions.

2 And she came to Jerusalem wit a very great train, with camels tha bare spices, and very much gold, an precious stones: and when she wa come to Solomon, she commune with him of all that was in her heart.

3 And Solomon [c]told her all he [1]questions: there was not *any* thin hid from the king, which he told he not.

4 And when the queen of Shē-bă ha seen all Solomon's wisdom, and th house that he had built,

5 And the meat of his table, and th sitting of his servants, and the [2]attend ance of his ministers, and their appar el, and his [3]cupbearers, and [d]his ascen by which he went up unto the hous of the LORD; there was no more spiri in her.

6 And she said to the king, It was a true [4]report that I heard in mine own land of thy [5]acts and of thy wisdom.

7 Howbeit I believed not the words, until I came, and mine eyes had seen *it*: and, behold, the half was not told me: [6]thy wisdom and prosperity exceedeth the fame which I heard.

8 Happy [e]*are* thy men, happy *are* these thy servants, which stand continually before thee, *and* that hear thy wisdom.

9 Blessed [f]be the LORD thy God, which delighted in thee, to set thee on the throne of Israel: because the LORD loved Israel for ever, therefore [g]made he thee king, [h]to do judgment and justice.

10 And she gave the king an hundred and twenty talents of gold, and of spices very great store, and precious stones: there came no more such

1 which were inhabited by Canaanites.
2 were not right in his eyes.
3 That is, Displeasing, or, Dirty.
p ch. 5.13.
q 2 Sam. 5.9.
r Josh. 19.36.
s Josh. 17.11.
t Judg. 1.29.
u Josh. 16.10.
v Josh. 16.3. 2 Chr. 8.5.
w Josh. 19.44.
4 the desire of Solomon which he desired.
x Judg. 1.21.
y Gen. 9.25. Ezra 2.55. Neh. 7.57.
z Lev. 25.39. Jer. 34.14.
a ch. 3.1. 2 Chr. 8.11.
b ch. 11.27. 2 Chr. 32.5.
5 upon it.
c Num. 33.35. Deut. 2.8. ch. 22.48.
6 lip.
d ch. 5.6,7. ch. 10.11.
e Gen. 10.2. ch. 10.11. 2 Chr. 8.18. Ps. 45.9. Isa. 13.12.

CHAP. 10

a 2 Chr. 9.1. Ps. 72.10,15. Isa. 60.6. Jer. 6.20. Matt. 12.42. Luke 11.31.
b Judg. 14.12.
c Pro. 1.5.
1 words.
2 standing.
3 Or, butlers.
d 1 Chr. 26. 16.
4 word.
5 Or, sayings.
6 thou hast added wisdom and goodness to the fame.
e Pro. 8.34.
f ch. 5.7.
g Deut. 7.8. Dan. 2.21.
h 2 Sam. 8.15. Ps. 72.2. Pro. 8.15.

oundance of spices as these which
e queen of Shē-bă gave to king
olomon.
11 And [i]the navy also of Hiram, that
rought [j]gold from Ō-phĭr, brought in
om Ō-phĭr great plenty of [7]ăl-mŭg
ees, and precious stones.
12 And [k]the king made of the ăl-mŭg
ees [8]pillars for the house of the LORD,
d for the king's house, harps also
nd psalteries for singers: there came
o such ăl-mŭg trees, nor were seen
nto this day.
13 And king Solomon gave unto the
ueen of Shē-bă all her desire, what-
oever she asked, beside *that* which
olomon gave her [9]of his royal boun-
. So she turned and went to her own
ountry, she and her servants.
14 ¶ Now the weight of gold that
ame to Solomon in one year was six
undred threescore and six talents of
old,
15 Beside *that he had* of the mer-
hantmen, and of the traffick of the
pice merchants, and [l]of all the kings
f Arabia, and of the [10]governors of
e country.
16 ¶ And king Solomon made two
undred targets *of* beaten gold: six
undred *shekels* of gold went to one
rget.
17 And *he made* [m]three hundred
hields *of* beaten gold; three pound
f gold went to one shield: and the
ing put them in [n]the house of the
orest of Lĕb-ă-non.
18 ¶ Moreover [o]the king made a
reat throne of ivory, and overlaid it
ith the best gold.
19 The throne had six steps, and the
op of the throne *was* round [11]behind:
nd *there were* [12]stays on either side
n the place of the seat, and two lions
ood beside the stays.
20 And twelve lions stood there on
e one side and on the other upon
e six steps: there was not [13]the like
ade in any kingdom.
21 ¶ And all king Solomon's drink-
g vessels *were of* gold, and all the
essels of the house of the forest of
ĕb-ă-non *were of* pure gold; [14]none
ere of silver: it was nothing account-
d of in the days of Solomon.
22 For the king had at sea a navy of
hăr-shĭsh with the navy of Hiram:
nce in three years came the navy
f [p]Thăr-shĭsh, bringing gold, and
lver, [15]ivory, and apes, and peacocks.
23 So king Solomon exceeded all the
ings of the earth for riches and for
isdom.

i ch. 9.27.
j Job 22.24.
7 algum trees.
k 2 Chr. 9.11.
8 a prop, or rails.
9 according to the hand of king Solomon.
l Ps. 72.10. Isa. 21.13. Gal. 4.25.
10 Or, captains.
m ch. 14.26.
n ch. 7.2.
o 2 Chr. 9.17. Heb. 1.3,8. Rev. 20.11.
11 on the hinder part thereof.
12 hands.
13 so.
14 Or, there was no silver in them.
p Gen. 10.4. ch. 22.48. Ps. 48.7. Isa. 2.16.
15 Or, elephants' teeth.
16 sought the face of.
q Job 42.11. Ps. 68.29. Matt. 2.11.
r Deut. 17.16. ch. 4.26. 2 Chr. 1.14.
s 2 Chr. 1.15.
17 gave.
18 And the going forth of the horses which were Solomon's.
t Eze. 27.7.
u Josh. 1.4.
19 by their hand.

CHAP. 11

a Gen. 6.2.
1 Or, beside.
b Ex. 34.16.
c Deut. 17.17. Neh. 13.26.
d Judg. 2.13.
2 fulfilled not after.
e Num. 33.52.
f Num. 21. 29.
g 2 Ki. 23.13.

24 ¶ And all the earth [16]sought to
Solomon, to hear his wisdom, which
God had put in his heart.
25 And [q]they brought every man his
present, vessels of silver, and vessels
of gold, and garments, and armour,
and spices, horses, and mules, a rate
year by year.
26 ¶ And Solomon [r]gathered together chariots and horsemen: and he had
a thousand and four hundred chariots,
and twelve thousand horsemen, whom
he bestowed in the cities for chariots,
and with the king at Jerusalem.
27 And [s]the king [17]made silver *to be*
in Jerusalem as stones, and cedars
made he *to be* as the sycomore trees
that *are* in the vale, for abundance.
28 ¶ [18]And Solomon had horses
brought out of Egypt, and [t]linen yarn:
the king's merchants received the linen
yarn at a price.
29 And a chariot came up and went
out of Egypt for six hundred *shekels*
of silver, and an horse for an hundred
and fifty: and [u]so for all the kings of
the Hittites, and for the kings of Syria,
did they bring *them* out [19]by their
means.

CHAPTER 11

BUT king Solomon loved [a]many
strange women, [1]together with the
daughter of Pharaoh, women of the
Moabites, Ammonites, Ē-dom-ītes,
Zī-dō-nĭ-ăns, *and* Hittites;
2 Of the nations *concerning* which
the LORD said unto the children of Israel, [b]Ye shall not go in to them, neither shall they come in unto you: *for*
surely they will turn away your heart
after their gods: Solomon clave unto
these in love.
3 And he had seven hundred wives,
princesses, and three hundred concubines: and his wives turned away his
heart.
4 For it came to pass, when Solomon
was old, [c]*that* his wives turned away
his heart after other gods: and his
heart was not perfect with the LORD
his God, as *was* the heart of David his
father.
5 For Solomon went [d]after Ăsh-tō-
rĕth the goddess of the Zī-dō-nĭ-ăns,
and after Mĭl-cŏm the abomination of
the Ammonites.
6 And Solomon did evil in the sight
of the LORD, and [2]went not fully after
the LORD, as *did* David his father.
7 Then [e]did Solomon build an high
place for [f]Chē-mŏsh, the abomination
of Moab, in [g]the hill that *is* before
Jerusalem, and for Molech, the

abomination of the children of Ammon.

8 And likewise did he for all his strange wives, which burnt incense and sacrificed unto their gods.

9 ¶ And the LORD was [h]angry with Solomon, because his heart was turned from the LORD God of Israel, [i]which had appeared unto him twice,

10 And [j]had commanded him concerning this thing, that he should not go after other gods: but he kept not that which the LORD commanded.

11 Wherefore the LORD said unto Solomon, Forasmuch as this [3]is done of thee, and thou hast not kept my covenant and my statutes, which I have commanded thee, [k]I will surely rend the kingdom from thee, and will give it to thy servant.

12 Notwithstanding in thy days I will not do it for David thy father's sake: *but* I will rend it out of the hand of thy son.

13 Howbeit [l]I will not rend away all the kingdom; *but* will give one [m]tribe to thy son [n]for David my servant's sake, and for Jerusalem's sake [o]which I have chosen.

14 ¶ And the LORD [p]stirred up an adversary unto Solomon, Hā'dăd the Ē'dọm-īte: he *was* of the king's seed in Ē'dọm.

15 For [q]it came to pass, when David was in Ē'dọm, and Jō'ăb the captain of the host was gone up to bury the slain, [r]after he had smitten every male in Ē'dọm;

16 (For six months did Jō'ăb remain there with all Israel, until he had cut off every male in Ē'dọm:)

17 That Hā'dăd fled, he and certain Ē'dọm-ītes of his father's servants with him, to go into Egypt; Hā'dăd *being* yet a little child.

18 And they arose out of Mĭd'ĭ-ăn, and came to Pâr'ăn: and they took men with them out of Pâr'ăn, and they came to Egypt, unto Pharaoh king of Egypt; which gave him an house, and appointed him victuals, and gave him land.

19 And Hā'dăd found great favour in the sight of Pharaoh, so that he gave him to wife the sister of his own wife, the sister of Täh'pĕn-ēs the queen.

20 And the sister of Täh'pĕn-ēs bare him Gĕ-nū'băth his son, whom Täh'pĕn-ēs weaned in Pharaoh's house: and Gĕ-nū'băth was in Pharaoh's household among the sons of Pharaoh.

h Deut. 7.3. Ps. 90.7.
i ch. 3.5.
j ch. 6.12. 2 Chr. 7.17-22.
3 is with thee.
k ch. 12.15. 2 Ki. 17.15, 21.
l 2 Sam. 7.15. 1 Chr. 17.13, 14. Ps. 89.33.
m ch. 12.20.
n Ex. 32.13. 2 Ki. 13.23.
o Deut. 12.11. 2 Ki. 21.4. Ps. 132.13, 14. Isa. 14.32.
p Deut. 31. 16,17. 1 Chr. 5.26. Isa. 10.5,26. Nah. 1.2. Hosea 9.12.
q 1 Chr. 18. 12,13. Ps. 108.10.
r Num. 24.19. Deut. 20.13. Ps. 60, title. Mal. 1.2.3.
s ch. 2.10,34.
4 Send me away.
5 Not.
t 2 Sam. 8.3.
u 2 Sam. 10. 8,18.
v 2 Chr. 15.2.
w ch. 12.2. 2 Chr. 13.6.
x 2 Sam. 20. 21.
y ch. 9.24.
6 closed.
7 did work.
8 burden.
z Josh. 18.1. ch. 12.13. ch. 14.2.
a 1 Sam. 15. 27.
b ch. 12.1, 16-20.

21 And [s]when Hā'dăd heard Egypt that David slept with his fat ers, and that Jō'ăb the captain of th host was dead, Hā'dăd said to Pha aoh, [4]Let me depart, that I may go mine own country.

22 Then Pharaoh said unto him, B what hast thou lacked with me, tha behold, thou seekest to go to thi own country? And he answere [5]Nothing: howbeit let me go in an wise.

23 ¶ And God stirred him up *anoth* adversary, Rē'zŏn the son of Ē-lī' dăh, which fled from his lord [t]Hă ă-dē'zĕr king of Zō'băh:

24 And he gathered men unto hir and became captain over a ban [u]when David slew them *of Zo'ba* and they went to Damascus, and dwe therein, and reigned in Damascus.

25 And he was an adversary to Isra all the days [v]of Solomon, beside th mischief that Hā'dăd *did:* and he a horred Israel, and reigned over Syri

26 ¶ And [w]Jĕr-ŏ-bō'ăm the son Nē'băt, an Ĕph'ră-thīte of Zĕr'ē-d Solomon's servant, whose mother name *was* Zĕ-rû'ăh, a widow woma even he [x]lifted up *his* hand against th king.

27 And this *was* the cause that h lifted up *his* hand against the kin [y]Solomon built Mĭl'lō, *and* [6]repaire the breaches of the city of David h father.

28 And the man Jĕr-ŏ-bō'ăm *was* mighty man of valour: and Solomo seeing the young man that he [7]wa industrious, he made him ruler ov all the [8]charge of the house of Josep

29 And it came to pass at that tin when Jĕr-ŏ-bō'ăm went out of Jer salem, that the prophet [z]Ă-hī'jăh th Shī'lō-nīte found him in the way; ar he had clad himself with a new ga ment; and they two *were* alone in th field:

30 And Ă-hī'jăh caught the new ga ment that *was* on him, and rent [a]it twelve pieces:

31 And he said to Jĕr-ŏ-bō'ăm, Ta thee ten pieces: for thus saith th LORD, the God of Israel, Behold, [b]will rend the kingdom out of th hand of Solomon, and will give t tribes to thee:

32 (But he shall have one tribe f my servant David's sake, and f Jerusalem's sake, the city which have chosen out of all the tribes Israel:)

33 Because that they have forsak

e, and have worshipped Ăsh-´tō-rĕth
he goddess of the Zī-dō-´nĭ-ăns,
Chē-´mŏsh the god of the Moabites,
ıd [e]Mĭl-´cŏm the god of the children
Ammon, and have not walked in my
ays, to do *that which is* right in mine
ves, and *to keep* my statutes and my
dgments, as *did* David his father.
4 Howbeit I will not take the whole
ngdom out of his hand: but I will
ake him prince all the days of his
e for David my servant's sake,
hom I chose, because he kept my
ommandments and my statutes:
5 But I will take the kingdom out of
s son's hand, and will give it unto
ee, *even* ten tribes.
6 And unto his son will I give one
ibe, that [f]David my servant may
ave a [9]light alway before me in Jeru-
lem, the city which I have chosen
e to put my name there.
7 And I will take thee, and thou
alt reign according to all that thy
ul desireth, and shalt be king over
rael.
8 And it shall be, if thou wilt heark-
unto all that I command thee, and
ilt walk in my ways, and do *that is*
ght in my sight, to keep my statutes
ıd my commandments, as David my
rvant did; that I [g]will be with thee,
ıd build [h]thee a sure house, as I
uilt for David, and will give Israel
nto thee.
9 And I will for this afflict the seed
David, but not for ever.
0 Solomon sought therefore to kill
r-ŏ-bō-´ăm. And Jĕr-ŏ-bō-´ăm arose,
ıd fled into Egypt, unto Shĭ-´shăk
ng of Egypt, and was in Egypt until
e death of Solomon.
1 ¶ And [i]the rest of the [10]acts of
olomon, and all that he did, and his
isdom, *are* they not written in the
ook of the acts of Solomon?
2 And [j]the [11]time that Solomon
igned in Jerusalem over all Israel
as forty years.
3 And [k]Solomon slept with his
thers, and was buried in the city of
avid his father: and [l]Rē-hŏ-bō-´ăm
s son reigned in his stead.

CHAPTER 12

AND [a]Rē-hŏ-bō-´ăm went to Shē-´
chĕm: for all Israel were come to
hē-´chĕm to make him king.
2 And it came to pass, when [b]Jĕr-ŏ-
ō-´ăm the son of Nē-´băt, who was yet
n Egypt, heard *of it*, (for he was fled
om the presence of king Solomon,
ıd Jĕr-ŏ-bō-´ăm dwelt in Egypt;)

c Judg. 2.13.
d Num. 21. 29. Jer. 48.7,13.
e Acts 7.43.
f 2 Sam. 7.29. ch. 15.4. Ps. 132.17. Luke 1.69, 70,78,79. Acts 15.16, 17.
9 lamp, or, candle.
g Deut. 31.8. Josh. 1.5.
h 1 Chr. 17. 10, 24-27.
i 2 Chr. 9.29.
10 Or, words, or, things.
j 2 Chr. 9.30.
11 days.
k 2 Chr. 9.31.
l Matt. 1.7, called Roboam.

CHAP. 12

a 2 Chr. 10.1.
b ch. 11.26.
c ch. 11.40.
d 1 Sam. 8. 11-18. ch. 4.7,22. Job 20.19, 20,22,23. Pro. 3.31. Eccl. 5.8. Isa. 58.6. Eze. 45.8. Amos 4.1,2. Micah 2.1,3. Mal. 3.5. 1 Thes. 4.6.
e Job 12.12. Pro. 27.10. Eccl. 10.4. Jer. 42.2-5.
f 2 Chr. 10.7. Pro. 15.1.
g ch. 3.7. ch. 14.21. 2 Chr. 10.10, 11. Ps. 7.16. Ps. 140.11. Pro. 18.6,7. Isa. 47.6.
1 hardly.
h Judg. 14.4. ch. 22. 23. 2 Chr. 10.15. Ps. 5.10. Amos 3.6.

3 That they sent and called him. And
Jĕr-ŏ-bō-´ăm and all the congregation
of Israel came, and spake unto Rē-
hŏ-bō-´ăm, saying,
4 Thy father made our [d]yoke grievous: now therefore make thou the
grievous service of thy father, and his
heavy yoke which he put upon us,
lighter, and we will serve thee.
5 And he said unto them, Depart yet
for three days, then come again to me.
And the people departed.
6 ¶ And king Rē-hŏ-bō-´ăm [e]consult-
ed with the old men, that stood before
Solomon his father while he yet lived,
and said, How do ye advise that I may
answer this people?
7 And they spake unto him, saying,
[f]If thou wilt be a servant unto this
people this day, and wilt serve them,
and answer them, and speak good
words to them, then they will be thy
servants for ever.
8 But he forsook the counsel of the
old men, which they had given him,
and consulted with the young men
that were grown up with him, *and*
which stood before him:
9 And he said unto them, What
counsel give ye that we may answer
this people, who have spoken to me,
saying, Make the yoke which thy
father did put upon us lighter?
10 And the young men that were
grown up with him spake unto him,
saying, Thus shalt thou speak unto
this people that spake unto thee, saying, Thy father made our yoke heavy,
but make thou *it* lighter unto us; thus
shalt thou say unto them, My [g]little
finger shall be thicker than my father's
loins.
11 And now whereas my father did
lade you with a heavy yoke, I will add
to your yoke: my father hath chastised you with whips, but I will chastise
you with scorpions.
12 ¶ So Jĕr-ŏ-bō-´ăm and all the people came to Rē-hŏ-bō-´ăm the third
day, as the king had appointed, saying, Come to me again the third day.
13 And the king answered the people [1]roughly, and forsook the old
men's counsel that they gave him;
14 And spake to them after the counsel of the young men, saying, My father made your yoke heavy, and I will
add to your yoke: my father *also*
chastised you with whips, but I will
chastise you with scorpions.
15 Wherefore the king hearkened
not unto the people; for [h]the cause
was from the LORD, that he might

perform his saying, which the LORD spake [i]by Ă-hī'-jăh the Shī'-lō-nīte unto Jĕr-ŏ-bō'-ăm the son of Nē'-băt.

16 ¶ So when all Israel saw that the king hearkened not unto them, the people answered the king, saying, [j]What portion have we in David? neither *have we* inheritance in the son of Jesse: to your tents, O Israel: now see to thine own house, David. So Israel departed unto their tents.

17 But [k]*as for* the children of Israel which dwelt in the cities of Judah, Rē-hŏ-bō'-ăm reigned over them.

18 Then king Rē-hŏ-bō'-ăm [l]sent Ă-dôr'-ăm, who *was* over the tribute; and all Israel stoned him with stones, that he died. Therefore king Rē-hŏ-bō'-ăm [2]made speed to get him up to his chariot, to flee to Jerusalem.

19 So [m]Israel [3]rebelled against the house of David unto this day.

20 And it came to pass, when all Israel heard that Jĕr-ŏ-bō'-ăm was come again, that they sent and called him unto the congregation, and made him king over all Israel: there was none that followed the house of David, but the tribe of Judah [n]only.

21 ¶ And when [o]Rē-hŏ-bō'-ăm was come to Jerusalem, he assembled all the house of Judah, with the tribe of Benjamin, an hundred and fourscore thousand chosen men, which were warriors, to fight against the house of Israel, to bring the kingdom again to Rē-hŏ-bō'-ăm the son of Solomon.

22 But [p]the word of God came unto Shĕm-âi'-ăh the man of God, saying,

23 Speak unto Rē-hŏ-bō'-ăm, the son of Solomon, king of Judah, and unto all the house of Judah and Benjamin, and to the remnant of the people, saying,

24 Thus saith the LORD, Ye shall not go up, nor fight against your brethren the children of Israel: return every man to his house; for this thing is [q]from me. They hearkened therefore to the word of the LORD, and returned to depart, according to the word of the LORD.

25 ¶ Then Jĕr-ŏ-bō'-ăm built [r]Shē'-chĕm in mount Ē'-phră-ĭm, and dwelt therein; and went out from thence, and built [s]Pĕn-ū'-ĕl.

26 And Jĕr-ŏ-bō'-ăm said in [t]his heart, Now shall the kingdom return to the house of David:

27 If this people [u]go up to do sacrifice in the house of the LORD at Jerusalem, then shall the heart of this people turn again unto their lord, *eve*[n] unto Rē-hŏ-bō'-ăm king of Judah, an[d] they shall kill me, and go again to R[ē]-hŏ-bō'-ăm king of Judah.

28 Whereupon the king took counse[l], and made [v]two calves *of* gold, and sai[d] unto them, It is too much for you t[o] go up to Jerusalem: behold [w]thy god[s], O Israel, which brought thee up out o[f] the land of Egypt.

29 And he set the one in [x]Beth-e[l], and the other put he in [y]Dan.

30 And this thing became a [z]sin: f[or] the people went *to worship* before th[e] one, *even* unto Dan.

31 And he made an [a]house of hig[h] places, and [b]made priests of the lov[w]est of the people, which were not [of] the sons of Levi.

32 And Jĕr-ŏ-bō'-ăm ordained a fea[st] in the eighth month, on the fifteent[h] day of the month, like unto [c]the fea[st] that *is* in Judah, and he [4]offered upo[n] the altar. So did he in Beth-el, [5]sacri[-] ficing unto the calves that he ha[d] made: and [d]he placed in Beth-el th[e] priests of the high places which he ha[d] made.

33 So he [6]offered upon the alta[r] which he had made in Beth-el th[e] fifteenth day of the eighth month, *eve*[n] in the month which he [e]had devise[d] of his own heart; and ordained a fea[st] unto the children of Israel: and h[e] offered upon the altar, [7]and bur[nt] [f]incense.

CHAPTER 13

AND, behold, there [a]came a ma[n] of God out of Judah by the wor[d] of the LORD unto Beth-el: and [b]Jĕr-[ŏ-] bō'-ăm stood by the altar to [1]bur[n] incense.

2 And he cried against the altar i[n] the word of the LORD, and said, O altar, altar, thus saith the LORD; Be[-] hold, a child shall be born unto th[e] house of David, [c]Jō-sī'-ăh by name[;] and upon thee shall he offer th[e] priests of the high places that burn in[-] cense upon thee, and men's bone[s] shall be burnt upon thee.

3 And he gave [d]a sign the same da[y,] saying, This *is* the sign which th[e] LORD hath spoken; Behold, the alta[r] shall be rent, and the ashes that *ar*[e] upon it shall be poured out.

4 And it came to pass, when kin[g] Jĕr-ŏ-bō'-ăm heard the saying of th[e] man of God, which had cried agains[t] the altar in Beth-el, that he [e]put fort[h] his hand from the altar, saying, La[y] hold on him. And his hand, which h[e] put forth against him, [f]dried up, s[o]

i ch. 11.11.
j 2 Sam. 20.1.
k ch. 11.13. 2 Chr. 11. 13-17.
l 2 Sam. 20. 24. ch. 4.6. 2 Chr. 10.13.
2 strengthened himself.
m 1 Sam. 10. 19. 2 Ki. 17.21. 2 Chr. 10.19.
3 Or, fell away.
n ch. 11.13.
o 2 Chr. 11.1.
p 2 Chr. 11.2.
q Pro. 16.9.
r Gen. 12.6. Judg. 9.45.
s Gen. 32.30, 31. Judg. 8.17.
t Ps. 14.1. Rom. 8.7.
u Deut. 12.5.
v 2 Ki. 10.29. Hosea 8.4-7.
w Ex. 32.4.
x Gen. 28.19. Hosea 4.15.
y Judg. 18.29.
z ch. 13.34.
a ch. 13.32.
b Num. 3.10. ch. 13.33.
c Lev. 23.33. Num. 29.12.
4 Or, went up to the altar, etc.
5 Or, to sacrifice.
d Amos 7.13.
6 Or, went up to the altar, etc.
e Num. 15. 39.
7 to burn incense.
f ch. 13.1.

CHAP. 13

a 2 Ki. 23.17.
b ch. 12.32.
1 Or, to offer.
c 2 Ki. 23.15, 16.
d Ex. 4.8,9. Deut. 13.1-3. Isa. 7.14. John 2.18. 1 Cor. 1.22.
e Jer. 20.2. Acts 12.1.
f Pro. 21.30. Isa. 8.9,10. Acts 5.39. 2 Cor. 10.6.

that he could not pull it in again to him.

5 The altar also was rent, and the ashes poured out from the altar, according to the sign which the man of God had given by the word of the LORD.

6 And the king answered and said unto the man of God, [g]Intreat now the face of the LORD thy God, and pray for me, that my hand may be restored me again. And the man of God [h]besought [2]the LORD, and the king's hand was restored him again, and became as *it was* before.

7 And the king said unto the man of God, Come home with me, and refresh thyself, and [i]I will give thee a reward.

8 And the man of God said unto the king, [j]If thou wilt give me half thine house, I will not go in with thee, neither will I eat bread nor drink water in this place:

9 For so was it charged me by the word of the LORD, saying, [k]Eat no bread, nor drink water, nor turn again by the same way that thou camest.

10 So he went another way, and returned not by the way that he came to Beth-el.

11 ¶ Now there dwelt an old prophet in Beth-el; and his [3]sons came and told him all the works that the man of God had done that day in Beth-el: the words which he had spoken unto the king, them they told also to their father.

12 And their father said unto them, What way went he? For his sons had seen what way the man of God went, which came from Judah.

13 And he said unto his sons, Saddle me the ass. So they saddled him the ass: and he rode thereon,

14 And went after the man of God, and found him sitting under an oak: and he said unto him, *Art* thou the man of God that camest from Judah? And he said, I *am*.

15 Then he said unto him, Come home with me, and eat bread.

16 And he said, I may not return with thee, nor go in with thee: neither will I eat bread nor drink water with thee in this place:

17 For [4]it was said to me [l]by the word of the LORD, Thou shalt eat no bread nor drink water there, nor turn again to go by the way that thou camest.

18 He [m]said unto him, I *am* a prophet also as thou *art;* and [n]an angel spake unto me by the word of the LORD, saying, Bring him back with thee into thine house, that he may eat bread and drink water. *But* he [o]lied unto him.

19 So he went back with him, and did eat bread in his house, and drank water.

20 ¶ And it came to pass, as they sat at the table, that the [p]word of the LORD came unto the prophet that brought him back:

21 And he cried unto the man of God that came from Judah, saying, Thus saith the LORD, Forasmuch as thou hast disobeyed the mouth of the LORD, and hast not kept the commandment which the LORD thy God commanded thee,

22 But camest back, and hast eaten bread and drunk water in the place, of the which *the LORD* did say to thee, Eat no bread, and drink no water; thy carcase shall not come unto the sepulchre of thy fathers.

23 ¶ And it came to pass, after he had eaten bread, and after he had drunk, that he saddled for him the ass, *to wit*, for the prophet whom he had brought back.

24 And when he was gone, [q]a lion met him by the way, and slew him: and his carcase was cast in the way, and the ass stood by it, the lion also stood by the carcase.

25 And, behold, men passed by, and saw the carcase cast in the way, and the lion standing by the carcase: and they came and told *it* in the city where the old prophet dwelt.

26 And when the prophet that brought him back from the way heard *thereof*, he said, It *is* the man of God, who was disobedient unto the word of the LORD: therefore the LORD hath delivered him unto the lion, which hath [5]torn him, and slain him, according to the word of the LORD, which he spake unto him.

27 And he spake to his sons, saying, Saddle me the ass. And they saddled *him*.

28 And he went and found his carcase cast in the way, and the ass and the lion standing by the carcase: the lion had [r]not eaten the carcase, nor [6]torn the ass.

29 And the prophet took up the carcase of the man of God, and laid it upon the ass, and brought it back: and the old prophet came to the city, to mourn and to bury him.

g Ex. 8.8. Num. 21.7. Jer. 37.3. Acts 8.24. Jas. 5.16.
h Ex. 8.12. Matt. 5.44. Acts 7.60. Rom. 12.20.
2 the face of the LORD.
i 1 Sam. 9.7. 1 Cor. 2.14.
j Num. 22.18.
k 1 Cor. 5.11.
3 son.
4 a word was.
l ch. 20.35. 1 Thes. 4.15.
m Jer. 5.12. Matt. 7.15. 1 John 4.1.
n Gal. 1.8.
o Jer. 29.31, 32. Ps. 63.11. Pro. 6.16,17, 19. Eze. 13.8,9. 1 Tim. 4.1,2. 2 Pet. 2.18, 19.
p Num. 23.5. John 11.51.
q Deut. 4.24. 2 Sam. 6.7. ch. 20.36. 2 Ki. 2.24. Eccl. 12.13, 14. Nahum 1.2. 1 Pet. 4.17.
5 broken.
r Lev. 10.2,5. Job 5.22,23. Dan. 6.22.
6 broken.

30 And he laid his carcase in his own grave; and they mourned over him, *saying*, Alas, [s]my brother!

31 And it came to pass, after he had buried him, that he spake to his sons, saying, When I am dead, then bury me in the sepulchre wherein the man of God *is* buried; lay [t]my bones beside his bones:

32 For [u]the saying which he cried by the word of the LORD against the altar in Beth-el, and against all the [v]houses of the high places which *are* in the cities [w]of Să-mâr´-ī-ă, shall surely come to pass.

33 ¶ After [x]this thing Jĕr-ŏ-bō´-ăm returned not from his evil way, but [7]made again of the lowest of the people priests of the high places: whosoever would, he [8]consecrated him, and he became *one* of the priests of the high places.

34 And [y]this thing became sin unto the house of Jĕr-ŏ-bō´-ăm, even to [z]cut *it* off, and to destroy *it* from off the face of the earth.

CHAPTER 14

At that time Ă-bī´-jăh the son of Jĕr-ŏ-bō´-ăm fell sick.

2 And Jĕr-ŏ-bō´-ăm said to his wife, Arise, I pray thee, and disguise thyself, that thou be not known to be the wife of Jĕr-ŏ-bō´-ăm; and get thee to Shī´-lōh: behold, there *is* Ă-hī´-jăh the prophet, which told me that [a]*I should be* king over this people.

3 And [b]take [1]with thee ten loaves, and [2]cracknels, and a [3]cruse of honey, and go to him: he shall tell thee what shall become of the child.

4 And Jĕr-ŏ-bō´-ăm's wife did so, and arose, and [c]went to Shī´-lōh, and came to the house of Ă-hī´-jăh. But Ă-hī´-jăh could not see; for his eyes [4]were set by reason of his age.

5 ¶ And [d]the LORD said unto Ă-hī´-jăh, Behold, the wife of Jĕr-ŏ-bō´-ăm cometh to ask a thing of thee for her son; for he *is* sick: thus and thus shalt thou say unto her: for it shall be, when she cometh in, that she shall feign herself *to be* another *woman*.

6 And it was *so*, when Ă-hī´-jăh heard the sound of her feet, as she came in at the door, that he said, Come in, thou wife of Jĕr-ŏ-bō´-ăm; why feignest thou thyself *to be* another? for I *am* sent to thee *with* [5]heavy *tidings*.

7 Go, tell Jĕr-ŏ-bō´-ăm, Thus saith the LORD God of Israel, [e]Forasmuch as I exalted thee from among the people, and made thee prince over my people Israel,

8 And [f]rent the kingdom away from the house of David, and gave it thee: and *yet* thou hast not been as my servant David, who [g]kept my commandments, and who followed me with all his heart, to do *that* only *which was* right in mine eyes;

9 But hast done evil above all that were before thee: for [h]thou hast gone and made thee other gods, and molten images, to provoke me to anger, and [i]hast cast me behind thy back:

10 Therefore, behold, [j]I will bring evil upon the house of Jĕr-ŏ-bō´-ăm, and [k]will cut off from Jĕr-ŏ-bō´-ăm him that pisseth against the wall, *and* [l]him that is shut up and left in Israel, and will take away the remnant of the house of Jĕr-ŏ-bō´-ăm, as a man taketh away dung, till it be all gone.

11 Him [m]that dieth of Jĕr-ŏ-bō´-ăm in the city shall the dogs eat; and him that dieth in the field shall the fowls of the air eat: for the LORD hath spoken *it*.

12 Arise thou therefore, get thee to thine own house: *and* when thy feet enter into the city, the child shall die.

13 And all Israel shall mourn for him, and bury him: for he only of Jĕr-ŏ-bō´-ăm shall come to the grave, because in him [n]there is found *some* good thing toward the LORD God of Israel in the house of Jĕr-ŏ-bō´-ăm.

14 Moreover [o]the LORD shall raise him up a king over Israel, who shall cut off the house of Jĕr-ŏ-bō´-ăm that day: but what? even now.

15 For the LORD shall smite Israel, as a reed is shaken in the water, and he shall [p]root up Israel out of this [q]good land, which he gave to their fathers, and shall scatter them [r]beyond the river, because [s]they have made their groves, provoking the LORD to anger.

16 And [t]he shall give Israel up because of the sins of Jĕr-ŏ-bō´-ăm, who [u]did sin, and who made Israel to sin.

17 ¶ And Jĕr-ŏ-bō´-ăm's wife arose, and departed, and came [v]to Tĭr´-zăh: *and* when she came to the threshold of the door, the child died;

18 And they buried him; and all Israel mourned for him, according to the word of the LORD, which he spake by the hand of his servant Ă-hī´-jăh the prophet.

19 And the rest of the acts of Jĕr-ŏ-bō´-ăm, how he [w]warred, and how he

s ch. 14.13. Jer. 22.18. Acts 8.2.
t Ruth 1.17. Ps. 26.9. Eccl. 8.10.
u 2 Ki. 23. 16,19.
v Lev. 26.30. Hosea 12. 11.
w ch. 16.24. John 4.5. Acts 8.1,14.
x 2 Chr. 13.9. Jer. 3.8.
7 returned and made.
8 filled his hand.
y ch. 12.30. 2 Ki. 10.31.
z ch. 14.10. 2 Ki. 17.20-23.

CHAP. 14

a ch. 11.31.
b 1 Sam. 9.7.
1 in thine hand.
2 Or, cakes.
3 Or, bottle.
c ch. 11.29.
4 stood for his hoariness.
d Pro. 21.30.
5 hard.
e 2 Sam. 12.7. ch. 16.2.
f ch. 11.31.
g ch. 15.5.
h 2 Chr. 11. 15.
i Neh. 9.26. Ps. 50.17. Eze. 23.35.
j ch. 15.29.
k ch. 21.21. 2 Ki. 9.8.
l Deut. 32.36.
m ch. 21.24.
n 2 Chr. 12. 12. Philem. 6. 2 Pet. 2.8,9.
o ch. 15.27.
p Deut. 29. 28. Ps. 52.5. Amos 2.9. Zeph. 2.4. Matt. 15.13.
q Josh. 23.15.
r 2 Ki. 15.29.
s Ex. 34.13. Deut. 12.3.
t Isa. 13.24.
u ch. 12.30. ch. 13.4. ch. 16.2. Micah 6.16. Matt. 18.7.
v ch. 16.6. Song 6.4.
w 2 Chr. 13.2.

reigned, behold, they *are* written in the book of the chronicles of the kings of Israel.

20 And the days which Jĕr-ŏ-bō´-ăm reigned *were* two and twenty years: and he [6]slept with his fathers, and Nadab his son reigned in his stead.

21 ¶ And Rē-hŏ-bō´-ăm the son of Solomon reigned in Judah. Rē-hŏ-bō´-ăm *was* [x]forty and one years old when he began to reign, and he reigned seventeen years in Jerusalem, the city [y]which the LORD did choose out of all the tribes of Israel, to put his name there. And his mother's name *was* Nā´-ă-măh an Ammonitess.

22 And [z]Judah did evil in the sight of the LORD, and they [a]provoked him to jealousy with their sins which they had committed, above all that their fathers had done.

23 For they also built them [b]high places, and [7]images, [c]and groves, on every high hill, and [d]under every green tree.

24 And [e]there were also sodomites in the land: *and* they did according to all the abominations of the nations which the LORD cast out before the children of Israel.

25 ¶ And [f]it came to pass in the fifth year of king Rē-hŏ-bō´-ăm, *that* Shī´-shăk king of Egypt came up against Jerusalem:

26 And [g]he took away the treasures of the house of the LORD, and the treasures of the king's house; he even took away all: and he took away all the shields of gold which [h]Solomon had made.

27 And king Rē-hŏ-bō´-ăm made in their stead brasen shields, and committed *them* unto the hands of the chief of the [8]guard, which kept the door of the king's house.

28 And it was *so*, when the king went into the house of the LORD, that the guard bare them, and brought them back into the guard chamber.

29 ¶ Now the rest of the acts of Rē-hŏ-bō´-ăm, and all that he did, *are* they not written in the book of the chronicles of the kings of Judah?

30 And there was [i]war between Rē-hŏ-bō´-ăm and Jĕr-ŏ-bō´-ăm all *their* days.

31 And Rē-hŏ-bō´-ăm slept with his fathers, and was buried with his fathers in the city of David. And his mother's name *was* Nā´-ă-măh an Ammonitess. And Ă-bī´-jăm his son reigned in his stead.

6 lay down.
x Job 32.9. Eccl. 4.13.
y ch. 11.36.
z 2 Chr. 12.1.
a Ps. 78.58. Isa. 62.2,5. 1 Cor. 10.22.
b Deut. 12.2.
7 Or, standing images, or, statues.
c 2 Ki. 17.9.
d Isa. 57.5.
e Gen. 19.5. Deut. 23.17. ch. 15.12.
f ch. 11.40.
g ch. 7.51. 2 Chr. 12.9.
h ch. 10.17. 2 Chr. 9.15, 16. Pro. 23.5.
8 runners.
i ch. 12.24.

CHAP. 15

a 2 Chr. 13.2. Michaiah the daughter of Uriel.
b 2 Chr. 11. 21. Absalom.
c ch. 11.4. Ps. 119.80.
d Gen. 12.2. 2 Chr. 21.7. Isa. 37.35.
1 Or, candle.
e ch. 14.8. Luke 1.6.
f 2 Chr. 13.2, 3,22.
g 2 Chr. 14.1.
2 That is, grandmother's.
h 2 Chr. 14.2. 2 Chr. 15.17.
i ch. 14.24. ch. 22.46.
j Deut. 13.6. 2 Chr. 15.16. Matt. 10.37. Luke 12.51, 53.
3 cut off.
k Ex. 32.20.
l ch. 22.43.
4 holy.

CHAPTER 15

NOW in the eighteenth year of king Jĕr-ŏ-bō´-ăm the son of Nē´-băt reigned Ă-bī´-jăm over Judah.

2 Three years reigned he in Jerusalem. And his mother's name *was* [a]Mā´-ă-chăh, the daughter [b]of Ă-bī´-shā-lŏm.

3 And he walked in all the sins of his father, which he had done before him: and his [c]heart was not perfect with the LORD his God, as the heart of David his father.

4 Nevertheless [d]for David's sake did the LORD his God give him a [1]lamp in Jerusalem, to set up his son after him, and to establish Jerusalem:

5 Because David [e]did *that which was* right in the eyes of the LORD, and turned not aside from any *thing* that he commanded him all the days of his life, save only in the matter of Ū-rī´-ăh the Hittite.

6 And there was war between Rē-hŏ-bō´-ăm and Jĕr-ŏ-bō´-ăm all the days of his life.

7 Now [f]the rest of the acts of Ă-bī´-jăm, and all that he did, *are* they not written in the book of the chronicles of the kings of Judah? And there was war between Ă-bī´-jăm and Jĕr-ŏ-bō´-ăm.

8 And [g]Ă-bī´-jăm slept with his fathers; and they buried him in the city of David: and Ā´-să his son reigned in his stead.

9 ¶ And in the twentieth year of Jĕr-ŏ-bō´-ăm king of Israel reigned Ā´-să over Judah.

10 And forty and one years reigned he in Jerusalem. And his [2]mother's name *was* Mā´-ă-chăh, the daughter of Ă-bī´-shā-lŏm.

11 And [h]Ā´-să did *that which was* right in the eyes of the LORD, as *did* David his father.

12 And [i]he took away the sodomites out of the land, and removed all the idols that his fathers had made.

13 And also Mā´-ă-chăh his mother, even [j]her he removed from *being* queen, because she had made an idol in a grove; and Ā´-să [3]destroyed her idol, and [k]burnt *it* by the brook Kī´-drŏn.

14 But [l]the high places were not removed: nevertheless Ā´-să's heart was perfect with the LORD all his days.

15 And he brought in the [4]things which his father had dedicated, and the things which himself had dedicated, into the house of the LORD, silver, and gold, and vessels.

16 ¶ And there was war between Ā-
să and Bā-ăsh-ă king of Israel all their
days.
17 And [m]Bā-ăsh-ă king of Israel went
up against Judah, and [n]built Rā-măh,
[o]that he might not suffer any to go out
or come in to Ā-să king of Judah.
18 Then Ā-să took all the silver and
the gold *that were* left in the treasures
of the house of the LORD, and the
treasures of the king's house, and delivered them into the hand of his servants: and king Ā-să sent them to
[p]Běn-hā-dăd, the son of Tăb-rĭm-ọn,
the son of Hē-zĭ-ŏn, king of Syria, that
dwelt at [q]Damascus, saying,
19 *There is* a league between me and
thee, *and* between my father and thy
father: behold, I have sent unto thee
a present of silver and gold; come and
break thy league with Bā-ăsh-ă king of
Israel, that he may [5]depart from me.
20 So Běn-hā-dăd hearkened unto
king Ā-să, and sent the captains of the
hosts which he had against the cities
of Israel, and smote [r]Ī-jŏn, and [s]Dan,
[t]and Ā-běl-běth-mā-ă-chăh, and all
Cĭn-nĕ-rōth, with all the land of Năph-
tā-lī.
21 And it came to pass, when Bā-ăsh-
ă heard *thereof*, that he left off building of Rā-măh, and dwelt in Tĭr-zăh.
22 Then [u]king Ā-să made a proclamation throughout all Judah; none *was*
[6]exempted: and they took away the
stones of Rā-măh, and the timber
thereof, wherewith Bā-ăsh-ă had
builded; and king Ā-să built with
them Gē-bă [v]of Benjamin, and [w]Miz-
pah.
23 The rest of all the acts of Ā-să, and
all his might, and all that he did, and
the cities which he built, *are* they not
written in the book of the chronicles
of the kings of Judah? Nevertheless
in the time of [x]his old age he was
diseased in his feet.
24 And Ā-să slept with his fathers,
and was buried with his fathers in the
city of David his father: [y]and Jĕ-hŏsh-
ă-phăt [z]his son reigned in his stead.
25 ¶ And Nadab the son of Jĕr-ŏ-bō-
ăm [7]began to reign over Israel in the
second year of Ā-să king of Judah, and
reigned over Israel two years.
26 And he did evil in the sight of the
LORD, and walked in the way of his
father, and in [a]his sin wherewith he
made Israel to sin.
27 ¶ And [b]Bā-ăsh-ă the son of Ă-hī-
jăh, of the house of Ĭs-să-chăr, conspired against him; and Bā-ăsh-ă
smote him at [c]Gĭb-bĕ-thŏn, which *be-*

m 2 Chr. 16.1.
n Josh. 18.25. 1 Sam. 15. 34.
o ch. 12.27.
p ch. 20. 1-5, 33,34. 2 Ki. 8.7-15.
q Gen. 14.15. ch. 11.23.
5 go up.
r 2 Ki. 15.29.
s Judg. 18.29.
t 2 Sam. 20. 14.
u 2 Chr. 16.6.
6 free.
v Josh. 21 17.
w 1 Sam. 7.6. Jer. 40.6,10.
x 2 Chr. 16. 12. Ps. 90.10. Eccl. 12.1.
y ch. 22.41-43. Matt. 1.8.
z Matt. 1.8, called Josaphat.
7 reigned.
a ch. 12.30.
b ch. 14.14.
c Josh. 19.44. ch. 16.15.
d Deut. 32. 35.
e ch. 14.10, 14. Job 18.13-21. Ps. 21.10. Isa. 14.20.
f ch. 12.28, 29. ch. 13.33.

CHAP. 16
a ch. 21.20-24. 2 Chr. 19.2.
b 1 Sam. 2.8. ch. 14.7. Ps. 75.6,7. Jer. 27.5. Dan. 2.21.
c ch. 15.34.
d ch. 14.10. ch. 15.29. Isa. 66.24.
e ch. 14.11.
f 2 Chr. 16.1.
g ch. 14.17.

longed to the Philistines; for Nadab
and all Israel laid siege to Gĭb-bĕ-
thŏn.
28 Even in the third year of Ā-să king
of Judah did Bā-ăsh-ă [d]slay him, and
reigned in his stead.
29 And it came to pass, when he
reigned, *that* he smote all the house of
Jĕr-ŏ-bō-ăm; he left not to Jĕr-ŏ-bō-
ăm any that breathed, until he had [e]de-
stroyed him, according unto the saying of the LORD, which he spake by
his servant Ă-hī-jăh the Shī-lō-nīte:
30 Because of the sins of Jĕr-ŏ-bō-
ăm which he sinned, and which he
made Israel sin, by his provocation
wherewith he provoked the LORD God
of Israel to anger.
31 ¶ Now the rest of the acts of Nadab, and all that he did, *are* they not
written in the book of the chronicles
of the kings of Israel?
32 And there was war between Ā-să
and Bā-ăsh-ă king of Israel all their
days.
33 In the third year of Ā-să king of
Judah began Bā-ăsh-ă the son of Ă-
hī-jăh to reign over all Israel in Tĭr-
zăh, twenty and four years.
34 And he did evil in the sight of the
LORD, and walked in [f]the way of Jĕr-
ŏ-bō-ăm, and in his sin wherewith he
made Israel to sin.

CHAPTER 16

THEN the word of the LORD came to
Jehu [a]the son of Hă-nā-nī against
Bā-ăsh-ă, saying,
2 Forasmuch [b]as I exalted thee out of
the dust, and made thee prince over
my people Israel; and thou [c]hast
walked in the way of Jĕr-ŏ-bō-ăm, and
hast made my people Israel to sin, to
provoke me to anger with their sins;
3 Behold, I will take away the posterity of Bā-ăsh-ă, and the posterity
of his house; and will make thy house
like [d]the house of Jĕr-ŏ-bō-ăm the son
of Nē-băt.
4 Him [e]that dieth of Bā-ăsh-ă in the
city shall the dogs eat; and him that
dieth of his in the fields shall the fowls
of the air eat.
5 Now the rest of the acts of Bā-ăsh-ă,
and what he did, and his might, [f]*are*
they not written in the book of the
chronicles of the kings of Israel?
6 So Bā-ăsh-ă slept with his fathers,
and was buried in [g]Tĭr-zăh: and Ē-lăh
his son reigned in his stead.
7 And also by the hand of the prophet Jehu the son of Hă-nā-nī came the
word of the LORD against Bā-ăsh-ă,

nd against his house, even for all the
vil that he did in the sight of the
ORD, in provoking him to anger with
ie [h]work of his hands, in being like
ie house of Jĕr-ŏ-bō-ăm; and be-
ause [i]he killed him.
8 ¶ In the twenty and sixth year of
-să king of Judah began Ē-lăh the
on of Bā-ăsh-ă to reign over Israel in
ĭr-zăh, two years.
9 And [j]his servant Zimri, captain of
alf *his* chariots, conspired against
im, as he was in Tĭr-zăh, drinking
imself [k]drunk in the house of Arza
teward of *his* house in Tĭr-zăh.
10 And Zimri went in and smote him,
nd killed him, in the twenty and sev-
nth year of Ā-să king of Judah, and
eigned in his stead.
11 ¶ And it came to pass, when he
egan to reign, as soon as he sat on
is throne, *that* he slew all the house
f Bā-ăsh-ă: he left him not [l]one that
isseth against a wall, [2]neither of his
insfolks, nor of his friends.
12 Thus did Zimri destroy all the
ouse of Bā-ăsh-ă, according to the
ord of the LORD, which he spake
gainst Bā-ăsh-ă [3]by Jehu the pro-
het,
13 For [m]all the sins of Bā-ăsh-ă, and
ie sins of Ē-lăh his son, by which they
inned, and by which they made Is-
ael to sin, in provoking the LORD
God of Israel to anger with [n]their
anities.
14 Now the rest of the acts of Ē-lăh,
nd all that he did, *are* they not writ-
en in the book of the chronicles of
he kings of Israel?
15 ¶ In the twenty and seventh year
f Ā-să king of Judah did Zimri reign
seven days in Tĭr-zăh. And the peo-
le *were* encamped against [p]Gĭb-bĕ-
hŏn, which *belonged* to the Philis-
ines.
16 And the people *that were* encamp-
d heard say, Zimri hath conspired,
nd hath also slain the king: where-
ore all Israel made Omri, the captain
f the host, king over Israel that day
n the camp.
17 And Omri went up from Gĭb-bĕ-
hŏn, and all Israel with him, and they
esieged Tĭr-zăh.
18 And it came to pass, when Zimri
aw that the city was taken, that he
vent into the palace of the king's
ouse, and burnt the king's house
ver him with fire, and [q]died,
19 For his sins which he sinned in
oing evil [r]in the sight of the LORD, [s]in
valking in the way of Jĕr-ŏ-bō-ăm,

h Ps. 115.4. Isa. 2.8.
i ch. 14.14. 2 Ki. 10.30, 31. Hosea 1.4.
j ch. 15.27. 2 Ki. 9.31. 2 Ki. 12.20.
k 1 Sam. 25. 36-38. 2 Sam. 13. 28,29. ch. 20.16. Job 31.3. Pro. 20.1. Isa. 1.28.
1 which was over.
l 1 Sam. 25. 22.
2 Or, both his kinsmen and his friends.
3 by the hand of.
m Isa. 3.16.
n Deut. 32. 21. 1 Sam. 12. 21. Isa. 41.29. Jer. 10.8,15. Jonah 2.8. 1 Cor. 8.4.
o Job 20.5. Ps. 37.35.
p ch. 15.27.
q Judg. 9.54.
r Ps. 9.16.
s ch. 12.28.
t Isa. 9.18.
4 Shomeron.
u ch. 14.9. Micah 6.16.
v Jer. 16.19. Acts 14.15.
5 was it a light thing, etc.
w Gen. 6.2. Josh. 23.12. ch. 18.4-19.
x Judg. 18.7.
y ch. 21.25. 2 Ki. 10.18.
z 2 Ki. 10.21, 26,27.
a Ex. 34.13. Jer. 17.2.
b ch. 21.25.

and in his sin which he did, to make
Israel to sin.
20 Now the rest of the acts of Zimri,
and his treason that he wrought, *are*
they not written in the book of the
chronicles of the kings of Israel?
21 ¶ Then were the people of Israel
divided into [t]two parts: half of the
people followed Tĭb-nī the son of Gĭ-
năth, to make him king; and half followed Omri.
22 But the people that followed Omri prevailed against the people that
followed Tĭb-nī the son of Gĭ-năth:
so Tĭb-nī died, and Omri reigned.
23 ¶ In the thirty and first year of Ā-
să king of Judah began Omri to reign
over Israel, twelve years: six years
reigned he in Tĭr-zăh.
24 And he bought the hill Să-mâr-ĭ-ă
of Shē-mĕr for two talents of silver,
and built on the hill, and called the
name of the city which he built, after
the name of Shē-mĕr, owner of the
hill, [4]Să-mâr-ĭ-ă.
25 ¶ But [u]Omri wrought evil in the
eyes of the LORD, and did worse than
all that *were* before him.
26 For he walked in all the way of
Jĕr-ŏ-bō-ăm the son of Nē-băt, and in
his sin wherewith he made Israel to
sin, to provoke the LORD God of Israel to anger with [v]their vanities.
27 Now the rest of the acts of Omri
which he did, and his might that he
shewed, *are* they not written in the
book of the chronicles of the kings of
Israel?
28 So Omri slept with his fathers, and
was buried in Să-mâr-ĭ-ă: and Ahab
his son reigned in his stead.
29 ¶ And in the thirty and eighth
year of Ā-să king of Judah began
Ahab the son of Omri to reign over
Israel: and Ahab the son of Omri
reigned over Israel in Să-mâr-ĭ-ă
twenty and two years.
30 And Ahab the son of Omri did evil
in the sight of the LORD above all that
were before him.
31 And it came to pass, [5]as if it had
been a light thing for him to walk in
the sins of Jĕr-ŏ-bō-ăm the son of Nē-
băt, that he took to wife [w]Jĕz-ĕ-bĕl the
daughter of Ĕth-bā-ăl king of the [x]Zī-
dō-nĭ-ăns, [y]and went and served Bā-
ăl, and worshipped him.
32 And he reared up an altar for Bā-
ăl in the [z]house of Bā-ăl, which he had
built in Să-mâr-ĭ-ă.
33 And [a]Ahab made a grove; and
Ahab did [b]more to provoke the LORD
God of Israel to anger than all the

kings of Israel that were before him.
34 ¶ In his days did Hī´-ĕl the Beth-elite build Jericho: he laid the foundation thereof in Ă-bī´-răm his firstborn, and set up the gates thereof in his youngest *son* Sē´-gŭb, according [c]to the word of the LORD, which he spake by Joshua the son of Nun.

CHAPTER 17

AND [1]Ē-lī´-jăh the Tĭsh´-bīte, *who was* of the inhabitants of Gilead, said unto Ahab, [a]*As* the LORD God of Israel liveth, before whom [b]I stand, [c]there shall not be dew nor rain these [d]years, but according to my word.
2 And the word of the LORD came unto him, saying,
3 Get thee hence, and turn thee eastward, and hide thyself by the brook Chē´-rĭth, that *is* before Jordan.
4 And it shall be, *that* thou shalt drink of the brook; and [e]I have commanded the ravens to feed thee there.
5 So he went and did according unto the word of the LORD: for he went and dwelt by the brook Chē´-rĭth, that *is* before Jordan.
6 And the ravens brought him bread and flesh in the morning, and bread and flesh in the evening; and he drank of the brook.
7 And it came to pass [2]after a while, that the brook dried up, because there had been no rain in the land.
8 ¶ And the word of the LORD came unto him, saying,
9 Arise, get thee [f]to Zăr´-ĕ-phăth, which *belongeth* to Zī´-dŏn, and dwell there: behold, I have commanded a widow woman there to sustain thee.
10 So he arose and went to Zăr´-ĕ-phăth. And when he came to the gate of the city, behold, the widow woman *was* there gathering of sticks: and he called to her, and said, [g]Fetch me, I pray thee, a little water in a vessel, that I may drink.
11 And as she was going to fetch *it*, he called to her, and said, Bring me, I pray thee, a morsel of bread in thine hand.
12 And she said, *As* the LORD thy God liveth, I have not [h]a cake, but an handful of meal in a barrel, and a little oil in a cruse: and, behold, I *am* gathering two sticks, that I may go in and dress it for me and my son, that we may eat it, and [i]die.
13 And Ē-lī´-jăh said unto her, Fear not; go *and* do as thou hast said: but [j]make me thereof a little cake first, and

c Num. 15.30. Ps. 119.89, 126. Pro. 13.13. Isa. 40.8. Matt. 24.35. Luke 21.33. 1 Pet. 1.25.

CHAP. 17

1 Elijahu. Luke 1.17. Luke 4.25. Elias.
a 2 Ki. 3.14.
b Deut. 10.8.
c Jas. 5.17.
d Luke 4.25.
e Ps. 37.3.
2 at the end of days.
f Obad. 20. Luke 4.26. Sarepta.
g Gen. 24.7. Ps. 24.1. John 4.7. Heb. 11.37.
h Gen. 18.6.
i Gen. 21.15, 16.
j Gen. 22.1,2. 1 Pet. 1.7.
k Ps. 34.11. Phil. 4.19. 1 Tim. 4.8.
3 giveth.
l 2 Chr. 20. 20. Matt. 20.28. Heb. 11.8.
4 Or, a full year.
m Deut. 15. 10. Pro. 11.24.
5 by the hand of.
n 2 Sam. 16. 10. Luke 4.34. John 2.4.
o Ex. 15.25. Num. 11.11. 1 Sam. 7.8. ch. 18.36,37. Phil. 4.6. Jas. 5.13,16.
p 2 Ki. 4.34, 35.
6 measured.
7 into his inward parts.
q Ps. 65.2. Pro. 15.8, 29. Matt. 21.22. Luke 11.9, 10. 1 John 3.22.
r Deut. 32.39. Luke 7.14. Acts 20.10, 12. Heb. 11.35.
s John 3.2. John 16.30.

CHAP. 18

a Luke 4.25.
b Deut. 28. 12.
1 Obadiahu.
2 over his house.

bring *it* unto me, and after make fo
thee and for thy son.
14 For thus saith the LORD God o
Israel, [k]The barrel of meal shall no
waste, neither shall the cruse of oi
fail, until the day *that* the LORD [3]send
eth rain upon the earth.
15 And she went and [l]did accordin
to the saying of Ē-lī´-jăh: and she, an
he, and her house, did eat [4]*many* days
16 *And* [m]the barrel of meal waste
not, neither did the cruse of oil fai
according to the word of the LORI
which he spake [5]by Ē-lī´-jăh.
17 ¶ And it came to pass after thes
things, *that* the son of the woman, th
mistress of the house, fell sick; an
his sickness was so sore, that ther
was no breath left in him.
18 And she said unto Ē-lī´-jăh, Wha
[n]have I to do with thee, O thou man o
God? art thou come unto me to ca
my sin to remembrance, and to sla
my son?
19 And he said unto her, Give me th
son. And he took him out of he
bosom, and carried him up into a lof
where he abode, and laid him upo
his own bed.
20 And he [o]cried unto the LORD, an
said, O LORD my God, hast thou als
brought evil upon the widow wit
whom I sojourn, by slaying he
son?
21 And [p]he [6]stretched himself upo
the child three times, and cried unt
the LORD, and said, O LORD my Goc
I pray thee, let this child's soul com
[7]into him again.
22 And the LORD [q]heard the voice o
Ē-lī´-jăh; and the soul of the chil
came into him again, and he [r]revivec
23 And Ē-lī´-jăh took the child, an
brought him down out of the chambe
into the house, and delivered him unt
his mother: and Ē-lī´-jăh said, Se
thy son liveth.
24 ¶ And the woman said to Ē-lī´-jăh
Now by this [s]I know that thou *art*
man of God, *and* that the word of th
LORD in thy mouth *is* truth.

CHAPTER 18

AND it came to pass [a]*after* man
days, that the word of the LORI
came to Ē-lī´-jăh in the third year, say
ing, Go, shew thyself unto Ahab; an
[b]I will send rain upon the earth.
2 And Ē-lī´-jăh went to shew himsel
unto Ahab. And *there was* a sor
famine in Să-mâr´-ĭ-ă.
3 And Ahab called [1]Ō-bă-dī´-ăh
which *was* [2]the governor of *his* house

Now Ō-bă-dī´-ăh [c]feared the LORD
greatly:
4 For it was *so*, when [3]Jĕz´-ĕ-bĕl cut
ff the prophets of the LORD, that Ō-
ă-dī´-ăh took an hundred prophets,
nd hid them by fifty in a cave, and
fed them with bread and water.)
5 And Ahab said unto Ō-bă-dī´-ăh,
Go into the land, unto all fountains of
vater, and unto all brooks: peradven-
ure we may find grass to save the
orses and mules alive, [4]that we lose
ot all the beasts.
6 So they divided the land between
hem to pass throughout it: Ahab
vent one way by himself, and Ō-bă-
i´-ăh went another way by himself.
7 ¶ And as Ō-bă-dī´-ăh was in the
vay, behold, Ē-lī´-jăh met him: and he
new him, and fell on his face, and
aid, *Art* thou that my lord Ē-lī´-jăh?
8 And he answered him, I *am:* go,
ell thy lord, Behold, Ē-lī´-jăh *is here.*
9 And he said, What have I sinned,
hat thou wouldest deliver thy servant
nto the hand of Ahab, to slay me?
10 *As* the LORD thy God liveth, there
s no nation or kingdom, whither my
ord hath not sent to seek thee: and
vhen they said, *He is* not *there;* he
ook an oath of the kingdom and na-
ion, that they found thee not.
11 And now thou sayest, Go, tell thy
ord, Behold, Ē-lī´-jăh *is here.*
12 And it shall come to pass, *as soon*
s I am gone from thee, that the
Spirit of the LORD shall carry thee
vhither I know not; and *so* when I
ome and tell Ahab, and he cannot
nd thee, he shall slay me: but I
hy servant fear the LORD from my
outh.
13 Was it not told my lord what I did
vhen Jĕz´-ĕ-bĕl slew the prophets of
he LORD, how I hid an hundred men
f the LORD's prophets by fifty in a
ave, and fed them with bread and
vater?
14 And now thou sayest, Go, tell thy
ord, Behold, Ē-lī´-jăh *is here:* and he
hall slay me.
15 And Ē-lī´-jăh said, *As* the LORD of
osts liveth, before whom I stand, I
vill surely shew myself unto him to
ay.
16 So Ō-bă-dī´-ăh went to meet Ahab,
nd told him: and Ahab went to meet
-lī´-jăh.
17 ¶ And it came to pass, when Ahab
aw Ē-lī´-jăh, that Ahab said unto him,
Art thou he [g]that troubleth Israel?
18 And he answered, I have not
oubled Israel; but thou, and thy

c Neh. 7.2. Job 28.28.
3 Izebel.
d Matt. 10. 40-42.
4 that we cut not off ourselves from the beasts.
e Eze. 3.12, 14. Matt. 4.1. Acts 8.39.
f ch. 21.20.
g Josh. 7.25. Luke 23.2. Acts 16.20.
h ch. 9.9. 2 Chr. 15.2.
i Jer. 46.18.
j ch. 16.33.
k ch. 22.6.
l Matt. 6.24. 1 Cor. 10.21, 22. Rev. 3.15.
5 Or, thoughts?
m Josh. 24. 15. Ps. 100.3.
n ch. 19.10, 14.
o Lev. 9.24. 1 Chr. 21.26. 2 Chr. 7.1.
6 The word is good.
7 Or, answer.
p Ps. 115.5. Jer. 10.5. 1 Cor. 8.4.
8 Or, heard.
9 Or, leaped up and down at the altar.
10 with a great voice.
11 Or, he meditateth.
12 hath a pursuit.
q Lev. 19.28.
13 poured out blood upon them.
r 1 Cor. 11.4, 5.
14 ascending.

father's house, in [h]that ye have forsaken the commandments of the
LORD, and thou hast followed Bā´-ă-
lĭm.
19 Now therefore send, *and* gather to
me all Israel unto mount [i]Carmel, and
the prophets of Bā´-ăl four hundred
and fifty, and [j]the prophets of the
groves four hundred, which eat at
Jĕz´-ĕ-bĕl's table.
20 So Ahab sent unto all the children
of Israel, and [k]gathered the prophets
together unto mount Carmel.
21 And Ē-lī´-jăh came unto all the
people, and said, [l]How long halt ye
between two [5]opinions? if the LORD
be God, follow him: but if Bā´-ăl,
[m]*then* follow him. And the people
answered him not a word.
22 Then said Ē-lī´-jăh unto the people, [n]I, *even* I only, remain a prophet
of the LORD; but Bā´-ăl's prophets *are*
four hundred and fifty men.
23 Let them therefore give us two
bullocks; and let them choose one
bullock for themselves, and cut it in
pieces, and lay *it* on wood, and put no
fire *under:* and I will dress the other
bullock, and lay *it* on wood, and put no
fire *under:*
24 And call ye on the name of your
gods, and I will call on the name of
the LORD: and the God that [o]answer-
eth by fire, let him be God. And all the
people answered and said, [6]It is well
spoken.
25 And Ē-lī´-jăh said unto the prophets of Bā´-ăl, Choose you one bullock
for yourselves, and dress *it* first; for ye
are many; and call on the name of
your gods, but put no fire *under.*
26 And they took the bullock which
was given them, and they dressed *it*,
and called on the name of Bā´-ăl from
morning even until noon, saying, O
Bā´-ăl, [7]hear us. But *there was* [p]no
voice, nor any that [8]answered. And
they [9]leaped upon the altar which was
made.
27 And it came to pass at noon, that
Ē-lī´-jăh mocked them, and said, Cry
[10]aloud: for he *is* a god; either [11]he is
talking, or he [12]is pursuing, or he is in a
journey, *or* peradventure he sleepeth,
and must be awaked.
28 And they cried aloud, and [q]cut
themselves after their manner with
knives and lancets, till [13]the blood
gushed out upon them.
29 And it came to pass, when midday
was past, [r]and they prophesied until
the *time* of the [14]offering of the *evening*
sacrifice, that *there was* neither voice,

nor any to answer, nor any [15]that regarded.
30 And Ē-lī-jăh said unto all the people, Come near unto me. And all the
people came near unto him. And he
repaired the altar of the LORD *that was*
broken down.
31 And Ē-lī-jăh took twelve stones,
according to the number of the tribes
of the sons of Jacob, unto whom the
word of the LORD came, saying, [s]Is-
rael shall be thy name:
32 And with the stones he built an
altar in [t]the name of the LORD: and
he made a trench about the altar, as
great as would contain two measures
of seed.
33 And he [u]put the wood in order,
and cut the bullock in pieces, and laid
him on the wood, and said, Fill four
barrels with water, and [v]pour *it* on the
burnt sacrifice, and on the wood.
34 And he said, Do *it* the second
time. And they did *it* the second time.
And he said, Do *it* the third time. And
they did *it* the third time.
35 And the water [16]ran round about
the altar; and he filled the trench also
with water.
36 And it came to pass at [w]*the time of*
the offering of the *evening* sacrifice,
that Ē-lī-jăh the prophet came near,
and said, [x]LORD God of Abraham,
Isaac, and of Israel, let [y]it be known
this day that thou *art* God in Israel,
and *that* I *am* thy servant, and *that* [z]I
have done all these things at thy
word.
37 Hear me, O LORD, hear me, that
this people may know that thou *art*
the LORD God, and *that* thou hast
[a]turned their heart back again.
38 Then [b]the fire of the LORD fell,
and consumed the burnt sacrifice, and
the wood, and the stones, and the
dust, and licked up the water that *was*
in the trench.
39 And when all the people saw *it*,
they fell on their faces: and they said,
The LORD, he *is* the God; the LORD, he
is the God.
40 And Ē-lī-jăh said unto them,
[17]Take the prophets of Bā-ăl; let not
one of them escape. And they took
them: and Ē-lī-jăh brought them
down to the brook Kī-shŏn, and [c]slew
them there.
41 ¶ And Ē-lī-jăh said unto Ahab,
Get thee up, eat and drink; for *there is*
[18]a sound of abundance of rain.
42 So Ahab went up to eat and to
drink. And Ē-lī-jăh went up to the top
of Carmel; and he [d]cast himself down

15 attention.
s Gen. 32.28.
t Col. 3.17.
u Lev. 1.6.
v Judg. 6.20.
16 went.
w Ex. 29.39.
x Gen. 28.13. Ex. 3.6. Matt. 22.32. Heb. 11.16.
y ch. 8.43. 2 Ki. 19.19. Ps. 83.18.
z Num. 16. 28.
a Jer. 10.23.
b Lev. 9.24. Judg. 6.21. 2 Chr. 7.1.
17 Or, Apprehend.
c Deut. 13.5. Rev. 19.20.
18 Or, a sound of a noise of rain.
d Jas. 5.17.
e Hab. 2.3.
19 Tie, or, Bind.
f 2 Ki. 3.15. Eze. 1.3.
20 till thou come to Jezreel.
CHAP. 19
a ch. 18.40.
b Ruth 1.17. ch. 2.23.
c Pro. 27.1.
d Num. 11. 15. Jonah 4.3,8. Phil. 1.21-24.
1 for his life.
e Ps. 34.7. Acts 12.7. Heb. 1.14.
2 bolster.
f Ex. 24.18. Deut. 9.9, 18. Matt. 4.2. Luke 4.2.
g Ex. 3.1.
h Ex. 33.21.

upon the earth, and put his face between his knees,
43 And said to his servant, Go u
now, look toward the sea. And h
went up, and looked, and said, *Ther*
is nothing. And he said, Go [e]agai
seven times.
44 And it came to pass at the sevent
time, that he said, Behold, there aris
eth a little cloud out of the sea, like
man's hand. And he said, Go up, sa
unto Ahab, [19]Prepare *thy chariot*, an
get thee down, that the rain stop the
not.
45 And it came to pass in the mea
while, that the heaven was black wit
clouds and wind, and there was a grea
rain. And Ahab rode, and went t
Jĕz-rēēl.
46 And [f]the hand of the LORD wa
on Ē-lī-jăh; and he girded up his loins
and ran before Ahab [20]to the entranc
of Jĕz-rēēl.

CHAPTER 19

AND Ahab told Jĕz-ĕ-bĕl all tha
Ē-lī-jăh had done, and withal ho
he had slain [a]all the prophets with th
sword.
2 Then Jĕz-ĕ-bĕl sent a messenger un
to Ē-lī-jăh, saying, [b]So let the gods d
to me, and more also, if I make not th
life as the life of one of them by [c]t
morrow about this time.
3 And when he saw *that*, he arose
and went for his life, and came t
Bēēr-shē-bă, which *belongeth* to Ju
dah, and left his servant there.
4 ¶ But he himself went a day's journe
into the wilderness, and came and sa
down under a juniper tree: and he [d]re
quested [1]for himself that he might die
and said, It is enough; now, O LORD
take away my life; for I *am* not bette
than my fathers.
5 And as he lay and slept under
juniper tree, behold, then [e]an ange
touched him, and said unto him, Aris
and eat.
6 And he looked, and, behold, *ther*
was a cake baken on the coals, and
cruse of water at his [2]head. And he di
eat and drink, and laid him dow
again.
7 And the angel of the LORD cam
again the second time, and touche
him, and said, Arise *and* eat; becaus
the journey *is* too great for thee.
8 And he arose, and did eat an
drink, and went in the strength of tha
meat [f]forty days and forty nights unt
[g]Hôr-ĕb the mount of God.
9 ¶ And he came thither [h]unto a cav

and lodged there; and, behold, the
word of the LORD *came* to him, and he
said unto him, What dost thou here,
Ē-lī'-jăh?
10 And he said, [i]I have been very
[j]jealous for the LORD God of hosts:
for the children of Israel have forsaken thy covenant, thrown down
thine altars, [k]and slain thy prophets
with the sword; and [l]I, *even* I only,
am left; and they seek my life, to take
it away.
11 And he said, Go forth, and stand
[m]upon the mount before the LORD.
And, behold, the LORD passed by, and
[n]a great and strong wind rent the
mountains, and brake in pieces the
rocks before the LORD; *but* the LORD
was not in the wind: and after the
wind an earthquake; *but* the LORD
was not in the earthquake:
12 And after the earthquake a fire;
but the LORD *was* not in the fire: and
after the fire a [o]still small voice.
13 And it was *so*, when Ē-lī'-jăh
heard *it*, that [p]he wrapped his face in
his mantle, and went out, and stood in
the entering in of the cave. And, behold, *there came* a voice unto him, and
said, What doest thou here, Ē-lī'-jăh?
14 And he said, I have been very
jealous for the LORD God of hosts:
because the children of Israel have
forsaken thy covenant, thrown down
thine altars, and slain thy prophets
with the sword; and I, *even* I only, am
left; and they seek my life, to take it
away.
15 And the LORD said unto him, Go,
return on thy way to the wilderness of
Damascus: and [q]when thou comest,
anoint Hă-zā'-ĕl *to be* king over Syria:
16 And [r]Jehu the son of Nimshi shalt
thou anoint *to be* king over Israel: and
Ē-lī'-shă the son of Shā'-phăt of Ā'-
bĕl–mĕ-hō'-lăh shalt thou anoint *to be*
prophet in thy room.
17 And [t]it shall come to pass, *that*
him that escapeth the sword of Hă-
zā'-ĕl shall Jehu slay: and him that escapeth from the sword of Jehu [u]shall
Ē-lī'-shă slay.
18 Yet [3]I [v]have left *me* seven thous-
and in Israel, all the knees which have
not bowed unto Bā'-ăl, and [w]every
mouth which hath not kissed him.
19 ¶ So he departed thence, and
found Ē-lī'-shă the son of Shā'-phăt,
who *was* plowing *with* twelve yoke *of
oxen* before him, and he with the
twelfth: and Ē-lī'-jăh passed by him,
and cast his mantle upon him.
20 And he left the oxen, and ran after
Ē-lī'-jăh, and said, Let me, I pray thee,
kiss my father and my mother, and
then I will follow thee. And he said unto him, [4]Go back again: for what
have I done to thee?
21 And he returned back from him,
and took a yoke of oxen, and slew
them, and boiled [x]their flesh with the
instruments of the oxen, and gave unto the people, and they did eat. Then
[y]he arose, and went after Ē-lī'-jăh, and
[z]ministered unto him.

CHAPTER 20

AND Bĕn–hā'-dăd the king of Syria
gathered all his host together:
[a]and *there were* thirty and two kings
with him, and horses, and chariots:
and he went up and besieged Să-mâr'-
ĭ-ă, and warred against it.
2 And he sent messengers to Ahab
king of Israel into the city, and said
unto him, Thus saith Bĕn–hā'-dăd,
3 Thy silver and thy gold *is* mine; thy
wives also and thy children, *even* the
goodliest, *are* mine.
4 And the king of Israel answered
and said, My lord, O king, according
to thy saying, [b]I *am* thine, and all that
I have.
5 And the messengers came again,
and said, Thus speaketh Bĕn–hā'-dăd,
saying, Although I have sent unto
thee, saying, Thou shalt deliver me
thy silver, and thy gold, and thy wives,
and thy children;
6 Yet I will send my servants unto
thee to morrow about this time, and
they shall search thine house, and the
houses of thy servants; and it shall be,
that whatsoever is [1]pleasant in thine
eyes, they shall put *it* in their hand,
and take *it* away.
7 Then the king of Israel called [c]all
the elders of the land, and said, Mark,
I pray you, and see how this *man* seeketh mischief: for he sent unto me for
my wives, and for my children, and
for my silver, and for my gold; and [2]I
denied him not.
8 And all the elders and all the people
said unto him, Hearken not *unto him*,
nor consent.
9 Wherefore he said unto the messengers of Bĕn–hā'-dăd, Tell my lord
the king, All that thou didst send for
to thy servant at the first I will do: but
this thing I may not do. And the messengers departed, and brought him
word again.
10 And Bĕn–hā'-dăd sent unto him,
and said, [d]The gods do so unto me,
and more also, if the dust of Să-mâr'-

i Rom. 11.3.
j Ex. 20.5. Ps. 69.9.
k ch. 18.4.
l ch. 18.22. Rom. 11.3.
m Ex. 24.12.
n Eze. 1.4.
o Num. 14.18. Neh. 9.17. Job 4.16. Ps. 86.15. Ps. 103.8-18. Ps. 111.4. Jas. 5.11.
p Ex. 3.6. Isa. 6.2.
q 2 Ki. 8.12, 13.
r 2 Ki. 9.1.
s Luke 4.27, called Eliseus.
t 2 Ki. 8.12. 2 Ki. 9.14. Amos 2.14.
u 2 Ki. 2.23, 24. Isa. 11.4. Hosea 6.5. Rev. 19.21.
3 Or, I will leave.
v Isa. 1.9. Eze. 6.8. Joel 2.32. Rom. 11.4.
w Job 31.27. Hosea 13.2.
4 Go return.
x 2 Sam. 24. 22.
y Matt. 4.18-22. Luke 5.27, 28.
z Ex. 24.13.

CHAP. 20

a Gen. 14.1,2. 2 Ki. 8.7-15.
b Deut. 28.48.
1 desirable.
c Ex. 3.16. Lev. 4.15.
2 I kept not back from him.
d ch. 19.2. Acts 23.12.

ĭ-ă shall suffice for handfuls for all the
people that [3]follow me.
11 And the king of Israel answered
and said, Tell *him*, [e]Let not him that
girdeth on *his harness* boast himself
as he that putteth it off.
12 And it came to pass, when *Ben-*
ha-dad heard this [4]message, as he *was*
[f]drinking, he and the kings in the
[5]pavilions, that he said unto his servants, [6]Set *yourselves in array*. And
they set *themselves in array* against
the city.
13 ¶ And, behold, there [7]came a prophet unto Ahab king of Israel, saying,
Thus saith the LORD, Hast thou seen
all this great multitude? behold, I will
deliver it into thine hand this day; and
[g]thou shalt know that I *am* the LORD.
14 And Ahab said, By whom? And
he said, Thus saith the LORD, *Even* by
the [8]young men of the princes of the
provinces. Then he said, Who shall
[9]order the battle? And he answered,
Thou.
15 Then he numbered the young men
of the princes of the provinces, and
they were two hundred and thirty two:
and after them he numbered all the
people, *even* all the children of Israel,
being seven thousand.
16 And they went out at noon. But
Bĕn–hā-dăd *was* [h]drinking himself
drunk in the pavilions, he and the
kings, the thirty and two kings that
helped him.
17 And the young men of the princes
of the provinces went out first; and
Bĕn–hā-dăd sent out, and they told
him, saying, There are men come out
of Să-mâr-ĭ-ă.
18 And he said, [i]Whether they be
come out for peace, take them alive;
or whether they be come out for war,
take them alive.
19 So these young men of the princes
of the provinces came out of the city,
and the army which followed them.
20 And they slew every one his man:
and the Syrians [j]fled; and Israel pursued them: and [k]Bĕn–hā-dăd the king
of Syria escaped on an horse with the
horsemen.
21 And the king of Israel went out,
and smote the horses and chariots,
and slew the Syrians with a great
slaughter.
22 ¶ And the prophet came to the
king of Israel, and said unto him, Go,
strengthen thyself, and mark, and see
what thou doest: for [l]at the return of
the year the king of Syria will come up
against thee.

3 are at my feet.
e Pro. 27.1. Eccl. 7.8.
4 word.
f ch. 16.9. Pro. 31.4,5. Eccl. 10.16.
5 Or, tents.
6 Or, Place the engines. And they placed engines.
7 approached.
g Ex. 7.15. Ps. 9.16.
8 Or, servants.
9 bind, or, tie.
h ch. 16.9. Pro. 20.1. Hosea 4.11. Dan. 5.2,30. Eph. 5.18.
i 1 Sam. 2.3. 2 Ki. 14.8-12. Pro. 16.18. Luke 14.11.
j Lev. 26.8. Ps. 33.16.
k Job 40.11.
l 2 Sam. 11.1. 2 Chr. 36.10.
m 2 Chr. 32. 13-19. Isa. 42.8. Rom. 1.21-23.
n Job. 5.12, 13.
10 that was fallen.
o Josh. 13.4.
11 to the war with Israel.
12 Or, were victualled.
p Judg. 6.5.
q Ex. 20.5. Deut. 4.24. Josh. 24.19. Ps. 33.10. Ps. 47.8. Ps. 149.7. Isa. 30.27, 28. Nahum 1.2.
13 into a chamber within a chamber, or, from chamber to chamber.
r Gen. 37.34.

23 And the servants of the king of
Syria said unto him, [m]Their gods *are*
gods of the hills; therefore they
were stronger than we; but let us
fight against them in the plain, and
surely we shall be stronger than
they.
24 And do this thing, [n]Take the kings
away, every man out of his place, and
put captains in their rooms:
25 And number thee an army, like
the army [10]that thou hast lost, horse
for horse, and chariot for chariot: and
we will fight against them in the plain,
and surely we shall be stronger than
they. And he hearkened unto their
voice, and did so.
26 And it came to pass at the return
of the year, that Bĕn–hā-dăd numbered the Syrians, and went up to
[o]Ā-phĕk, [11]to fight against Israel.
27 And the children of Israel were
numbered, and [12]were all present, and
went against them: and the children
of Israel pitched before them like two
little flocks of kids; but the Syrians
[p]filled the country.
28 ¶ And there came a man of God,
and spake unto the king of Israel, and
said, Thus saith the LORD, [q]Because
the Syrians have said, The LORD *is*
God of the hills, but he *is* not God of
the valleys, therefore will I deliver all
this great multitude into thine hand
and ye shall know that I *am* the
LORD.
29 And they pitched one over against
the other seven days. And *so* it was
that in the seventh day the battle was
joined: and the children of Israel slew
of the Syrians an hundred thousand
footmen in one day.
30 But the rest fled to Ā-phĕk, into
the city; and *there* a wall fell upon
twenty and seven thousand of the men
that were left. And Bĕn–hā-dăd fled
and came into the city, [13]into an inner
chamber.
31 ¶ And his servants said unto him
Behold now, we have heard that the
kings of the house of Israel *are* merci
ful kings: let us, I pray thee, [r]pu
sackcloth on our loins, and ropes up
on our heads, and go out to the king o
Israel: peradventure he will save th
life.
32 So they girded sackcloth on thei
loins, and *put* ropes on their heads
and came to the king of Israel, and
said, Thy servant Bĕn–hā-dăd saith,
pray thee, let me live. And he said, *I*
he yet alive? he *is* my brother.
33 Now the men did diligently ob

serve whether *any thing would come* from him, and did hastily catch *it:* and they said, Thy brother Bĕn–hā-dăd. Then he said, Go ye, bring him. Then Bĕn–hā-dăd came forth to him; and he caused him to come up into the chariot.

34 And *Ben–ha-dad* said unto him, The [s]cities, which my father took from thy father, I will restore; and thou shalt make streets for thee in Damascus, as my father made in Să-mâr-ĭ-ă. Then *said Ahab*, I will send thee away with this covenant. So [t]he made a covenant with him, and sent him away.

35 ¶ And a certain man of [u]the sons of the prophets said unto his neighbour [v]in the word of the LORD, Smite me, I pray thee. And the man refused to smite him.

36 Then said he unto him, Because thou hast not obeyed the voice of the LORD, behold, as soon as thou art departed from me, a lion shall slay thee. And as soon as he was departed from him, [w]a lion found him, and slew him.

37 Then he found another man, and said, Smite me, I pray thee. And the man smote him, [14]so that in smiting he wounded *him*.

38 So the prophet departed, and waited for the king by the way, and disguised himself with ashes upon his face.

39 And [x]as the king passed by, he cried unto the king: and [y]he said, Thy servant went out into the midst of the battle; and, behold, a man turned aside, and brought a man unto me, and said, Keep this man: if by any means he be missing, then [z]shall thy life be for his life, or else thou shalt [15]pay a talent of silver.

40 And as thy servant was busy here and there, [16]he was gone. And the king of Israel said unto him, [a]So *shall* thy judgment *be;* thyself hast decided *it*.

41 And he hasted, and took the ashes away from his face; and the king of Israel discerned him that he *was* of the prophets.

42 And he said unto him, Thus saith the LORD, [b]Because thou hast let go out of *thy* hand a man [17]whom I appointed to utter destruction, therefore thy life shall go for his life, and thy people for his people.

43 And the king of Israel [c]went to his house heavy and displeased, and came to Să-mâr-ĭ-ă.

s ch. 15.20.
t Isa. 26.10. Isa. 28.15.
u 2 Ki. 2.3,5, 7,15.
v ch. 13.17, 18.
w ch. 13.24.
14 smiting and wounding.
x 2 Sam. 12.1.
y Judg. 9.7-20. 2 Sam. 14. 5-7.
z 2 Ki. 10.24.
15 weigh.
16 he was not.
a Job 15.6. Matt. 21.41. Luke 19.22.
b 1 Sam. 15.9. ch. 22.31-37.
17 of my curse.
c ch. 21.4. Esther 5.13. Job 5.2. Pro. 19.3.

CHAP. 21

a Judg. 6.33. 1 Sam. 29.1.
b Gen. 3.6. Ex. 20.17. Deut. 5.21. Hab. 2.9. Luke 12.15. 1 Tim. 6.9, 10. Jas. 1.14,15.
c 1 Sam. 8.14.
1 be good in thine eyes.
d Lev. 25.23. Num. 36.7. Eze. 46.18.
e 1 Sam. 8.14.
f Jer. 6.7. Micah 2.1.
2 Or, Call an assembly.
3 in the top of the people.
g Deut. 13.13. Judg. 19.22. 1 Sam. 2.12. 2 Sam. 20.1. 2 Cor. 6.15.
h Ex. 22.28. Lev. 24.15, 16. Acts 6.11.
i Lev. 24.14.
j Job 15.34. Pro. 11.9. Isa. 9.16,17. Isa. 58.4. 1 Tim. 4.2.

CHAPTER 21

AND it came to pass after these things, *that* Naboth the Jĕz-reēl-īte had a vineyard, which *was* in [a]Jĕz-reēl, hard by the palace of Ahab king of Să-mâr-ĭ-ă.

2 And Ahab spake unto Naboth, saying, [b]Give me thy [c]vineyard, that I may have it for a garden of herbs, because it *is* near unto my house: and I will give thee for it a better vineyard than it; *or*, if it [1]seem good to thee, I will give thee the worth of it in money.

3 And Naboth said to Ahab, The LORD forbid it me, [d]that I should give the inheritance of my fathers unto thee.

4 And Ahab came into his house heavy and displeased because of the word which Naboth the Jĕz-reēl-īte had spoken to him: for he had said, I will not give thee the inheritance of my fathers. And he laid him down upon his bed, and turned away his face, and would eat no bread.

5 ¶ But Jĕz-ĕ-bĕl his wife came to him, and said unto him, Why is thy spirit so sad, that thou eatest no bread?

6 And he said unto her, Because I spake unto Naboth the Jĕz-reēl-īte, and said unto him, Give me thy vineyard for money; or else, if it please thee, I will give thee *another* vineyard for it: and he answered, I will not give thee my vineyard.

7 And Jĕz-ĕ-bĕl his wife said unto him, Dost thou [e]now govern the kingdom of Israel? arise, *and* eat bread, and let thine heart be merry: I [f]will give thee the vineyard of Naboth the Jĕz-reēl-īte.

8 So she wrote letters in Ahab's name, and sealed *them* with his seal, and sent the letters unto the elders and to the nobles that *were* in his city, dwelling with Naboth.

9 And she wrote in the letters, saying, [2]Proclaim a fast, and set Naboth [3]on high among the people:

10 And set two men, [g]sons of Bē-lĭ-ăl, before him, to bear witness against him, saying, [h]Thou didst blaspheme God and the king. And *then* carry him out, and [i]stone him, that he may die.

11 And the men of his city, *even* the elders and the nobles who were the inhabitants in his city, did as Jĕz-ĕ-bĕl had sent unto them, *and* as it *was* written in the letters which she had sent unto them.

12 They [j]proclaimed a fast, and set Naboth on high among the people.

13 And there came in two men, children of Bē-lĭ-ăl, and sat before him: and the men of Bē-lĭ-ăl witnessed against him, *even* against Naboth, in the presence of the people, saying, Naboth did blaspheme God and the king. [k]Then they carried him forth out of the city, and stoned him with stones, that he died.

14 Then they sent to Jĕz'-ĕ-bĕl, saying, Naboth is stoned, and is dead.

15 ¶ And it came to pass, when Jĕz'-ĕ-bĕl heard that Naboth was stoned, and was dead, that Jĕz'-ĕ-bĕl said to Ahab, Arise, take possession of the vineyard of Naboth the Jĕz'-reēl-ite, which he refused to give thee for money: for Naboth is not alive, but dead.

16 And it came to pass, when Ahab heard that Naboth was dead, that Ahab rose up to go down to the vineyard of Naboth the Jĕz'-reēl-īte, to take possession of it.

17 ¶ And [l]the word of the LORD came to Ē-lī'-jăh the Tĭsh'-bīte, saying,

18 Arise, go down to meet Ahab king of Israel, [m]which *is* in Să-mâr'-ĭ-ă: behold, *he is* in the vineyard of Naboth, whither he is gone down to possess it.

19 And thou shalt speak unto him, saying, Thus saith the LORD, Hast [n]thou killed, and also taken possession? And thou shalt speak unto him, saying, Thus saith the LORD, [o]In the place where dogs licked the blood of Naboth shall dogs lick thy blood, even thine.

20 And Ahab said to Ē-lī'-jăh, Hast thou found me, [p]O mine enemy? And he answered, I have found *thee:* because [q]thou hast sold thyself to work evil in the sight of the LORD.

21 Behold, I [r]will bring evil upon thee, and will take away thy posterity, and will cut off from Ahab him [s]that pisseth against the wall, and [t]him that is shut up and left in Israel,

22 And will make thine house like the house of [u]Jĕr-ō-bō'-ăm the son of Nē'-băt, and like the house of [v]Bā-ăsh'-ă the son of Ă-hī'-jăh, for the provocation wherewith thou hast provoked *me* to anger, and made Israel to sin.

23 And [w]of Jĕz'-ĕ-bĕl also spake the LORD, saying, The dogs shall eat Jĕz'-ĕ-bĕl by the [4]wall of Jĕz'-reēl.

24 Him [x]that dieth of Ahab in the city the dogs shall eat; and him that dieth in the field shall the fowls of the air eat.

25 ¶ But [y]there was none like unto Ahab, which did sell himself to work wickedness in the sight of the LORD, [z]whom Jĕz'-ĕ-bĕl his wife [5]stirred up.

26 And he did very abominably in following idols, according to all *things* [a]as did the Amorites, whom the LORD cast out before the children of Israel.

27 And it came to pass, when Ahab heard those words, that he rent his clothes, and put [b]sackcloth upon his flesh, and fasted, and lay in sackcloth, and went softly.

28 And the word of the LORD came to Ē-lī'-jăh the Tĭsh'-bīte, saying,

29 Seest thou how Ahab [c]humbleth himself before me? because he humbleth himself before me, I will not bring the evil in his days: *but* [d]in his son's days will I bring the evil upon his house.

CHAPTER 22

AND they continued three years without war between Syria and Israel.

2 And it came to pass in the third year, that [a]Jĕ-hŏsh'-ă-phăt the king of Judah came down to the king of Israel.

3 And the king of Israel said unto his servants, Know ye [b]that Rā'-mŏth in Gilead *is* ours, and we *be* [1]still, *and* take it not out of the hand of the king of Syria?

4 And he said unto Jĕ-hŏsh'-ă-phăt, Wilt thou go with me to battle to Rā'-mŏth–gĭl'-ĕ-ăd? And Jĕ-hŏsh'-ă-phăt said to the king of Israel, [c]I *am* as thou *art*, my people as thy people, my horses as thy horses.

5 And Jĕ-hŏsh'-ă-phăt said unto the king of Israel, Inquire, I pray thee, at the word of the LORD to day.

6 Then the king of Israel [d]gathered the prophets together, about [2]four hundred men, and said unto them, Shall I go against Rā'-mŏth–gĭl'-ĕ-ăd to battle, or shall I forbear? And they said, Go up; for the Lord shall deliver *it* into the hand of the king.

7 And [e]Jĕ-hŏsh'-ă-phăt said, *Is there* not here a prophet of the LORD besides, that we might inquire of him?

8 And the king of Israel said unto Jĕ-hŏsh'-ă-phăt, [f]*There is* yet one man, Mī-cāi'-ăh the son of Ĭm'-lăh, by whom we may inquire of the LORD: but [g]I hate him; for he doth not prophesy good concerning me, but evil. And Jĕ-hŏsh'-ă-phăt said, Let not the king say so.

9 Then the king of Israel called an [3]officer, and said, Hasten *hither* Mī-cāi'-ăh the son of Ĭm'-lăh.

k Num. 15. 36. Josh. 7.24. Mark 15.20. Acts 7.58, 59. Heb. 11.37.
l Ps. 9.12.
m ch. 13.32.
n Gen. 4.9, 11.
o ch. 22.38.
p ch. 18.17. Isa. 29.21. Amos 5.10.
q 2 Ki. 17.17. Rom. 7.14.
r Deut. 32.35. ch. 14.10. Ps. 94. 1-23.
s 1 Sam. 25. 22.
t ch. 14.10.
u ch. 15.29.
v ch. 16.3,11.
w 2 Ki. 9.36. Ps. 7.16.
4 Or, ditch.
x ch. 14.11.
y ch. 16.30.
z Gen. 6.2-5. ch. 11.1,4.
5 Or, incited.
a Gen. 15.16. 2 Ki. 21.11.
b Gen. 37.34.
c Ps. 66.33. Ps. 78.34-37.
d 2 Ki. 9.25.

CHAP. 22

a 2 Chr. 18.2, 34.
b Deut. 4.43.
1 silent from taking it.
c 2 Ki. 3.7.
d ch. 18.19.
2 They were prophets of the groves, hirelings of Jezebel.
e 2 Ki. 3.11.
f ch. 19.10.
g ch. 20.43.
3 Or, eunuch.

10 And the king of Israel and Jĕ-
hŏsh-ā-phăt the king of Judah sat
each on his throne, having put on
their robes, in a [4]void place in the entrance of the gate of Să-mâr-ĭ-ă; and
all the prophets prophesied before
them.
11 And Zĕd-ē-kī-ăh the son of Chĕ-
nā-ă-năh made him horns of iron: and
he said, Thus saith the LORD, With
these shalt thou push the Syrians,
until thou have consumed them.
12 And all the prophets prophesied
so, saying, [h]Go up to Rā-mŏth–gĭl-ĕ-
ăd, and prosper: for the LORD shall
deliver *it* into the king's hand.
13 And the messenger that was gone
to call Mī-cāī-ăh spake unto him, saying, Behold now, the words of the prophets *declare* good unto the king with
one mouth: let thy word, I pray thee,
be like the word of one of them, and
speak *that which is* good.
14 And Mī-cāī-ăh said, *As* the LORD
liveth, what [i]the LORD saith unto me,
that will I speak.
15 ¶ So he came to the king. And the
king said unto him, Mī-cāī-ăh, shall
we go against Rā-mŏth–gĭl-ĕ-ăd to
battle, or shall we forbear? And he
answered him, Go, and prosper: for
the LORD shall deliver *it* into the hand
of the king.
16 And the king said unto him, How
many times shall I adjure thee that
thou tell me nothing but *that which is*
true in the name of the LORD?
17 And he said, I saw all Israel scattered upon [j]the hills, as sheep that
have not a shepherd: and the LORD
said, These have no master: let them
return every man to his house in peace.
18 And the king of Israel said unto
Jĕ-hŏsh-ā-phăt, Did I not tell thee
that he would prophesy no good concerning me, but evil?
19 And he said, Hear thou therefore
the word of the LORD: [k]I saw the
LORD sitting on his throne, and [l]all
the host of heaven standing by him on
his right hand and on his left.
20 And the LORD said, Who shall
[5]persuade Ahab, that he may go up
and fall at Rā-mŏth–gĭl-ĕ-ăd? And
one said on this manner, and another
said on that manner.
21 And there came forth a spirit, and
stood before the LORD, and said, I
will persuade him.
22 And the LORD said unto him,
Wherewith? And he said, I will go
forth, and I will be a lying spirit in the
mouth of all his prophets. And he
said, [m]Thou shalt persuade *him*, and
prevail also: go forth, and do so.
23 Now [n]therefore, behold, the LORD
hath put a lying spirit in the mouth of
all these thy prophets, and the LORD
hath spoken evil concerning thee.
24 But Zĕd-ē-kī-ăh the son of Chĕ-
nā-ă-năh went near, and [o]smote Mī-
cāī-ăh on the cheek, and said, Which
[p]way went the Spirit of the LORD from
me to speak unto thee?
25 And Mī-cāī-ăh said, Behold, thou
shalt see in that day, when thou shalt
go [6]into [7]an inner chamber to hide
thyself.
26 And the king of Israel said, Take
Mī-cāī-ăh, and carry him back unto
Amon the governor of the city, and to
Jō-ăsh the king's son;
27 And say, Thus saith the king, Put
this *fellow* in the prison, and feed him
with bread of affliction and with water
of affliction, until I come in peace.
28 And Mī-cāī-ăh said, If thou return
at all in peace, [q]the LORD hath not
spoken by me. And he said, Hearken,
O people, every one of you.
29 So the king of Israel and Jĕ-hŏsh-
ā-phăt the king of Judah went up to
Rā-mŏth–gĭl-ĕ-ăd.
30 And the king of Israel said unto
Jĕ-hŏsh-ā-phăt, [8]I will disguise myself, and enter into the battle; but put
thou on thy robes. And the king of
Israel [r]disguised himself, and went into the battle.
31 But the king of Syria commanded
his thirty and two captains that had
rule over his chariots, saying, Fight
neither with small nor great, save only
with the king of Israel.
32 And it came to pass, when the
captains of the chariots saw Jĕ-hŏsh-
ā-phăt, that they said, Surely it *is* the
king of Israel. And they turned aside
to fight against him: and Jĕ-hŏsh-ā-
phăt [s]cried out.
33 And it came to pass, when the
captains of the chariots perceived that
it *was* not the king of Israel, that they
turned back from pursuing him.
34 And a *certain* man drew a bow [9]at
a venture, and smote the king of Israel between the [10]joints of the harness: wherefore he said unto the
driver of his chariot, Turn thine hand,
and carry me out of the host; for I am
[11]wounded.
35 And the battle [12]increased that
day: and the king was stayed up in his
chariot against the Syrians, and died
at even: and the blood ran out of the
wound into the [13]midst of the chariot.

4 floor.
h Jer. 23.25-32.
i Num. 22.38. Ps. 27.1-14. Ps. 56.1-10. Pro. 28.1. Jer. 1.7,17-19. Eze. 2.3-8. Acts 4.13, 29,31. Acts 9.29. Rom. 8.31. 2 Cor. 3.12. Gal. 1.9,10. Eph. 6.19, 20. Phil. 1.20. 1 Thes. 2.2-6. 1 Tim. 3.13. 2 Tim. 4.1-5. Titus 1.9, 10. Heb. 13.5,6.
j Matt. 9.36.
k Isa. 6.1. Dan. 7.9.
l Job 1.6. Ps. 103.20. Dan. 7.10. Zech. 1.10. Matt. 18.10. Heb. 1.7,14.
5 Or, deceive.
m Job 12.16. Eze. 14.9. 2 Thes. 2.11.
n Eze. 14.9.
o Jer. 28.16.
p 2 Chr. 18. 23.
6 Or, from chamber to chamber.
7 a chamber in a chamber.
q Num. 16. 29. Deut. 18.20.
8 Or, when he was to disguise himself, and enter into the battle.
r 2 Chr. 35. 22.
s 2 Chr. 18. 31. Pro. 13.20.
9 in his simplicity.
10 joints and the breastplate.
11 made sick.
12 ascended.
13 bosom.

36 And there went a proclamation
throughout the host about the going
down of the sun, saying, Every man to
his city, and every man to his own
country.
37 ¶ So the king died, and [14]was
brought to Să-mâr´-ĭ-ă; and they
buried the king in Să-mâr´-ĭ-ă.
38 And *one* washed the chariot in the
pool of Să-mâr´-ĭ-ă; and the dogs licked up his blood; and they washed his
armour; [t]according unto the word of
the LORD which he spake.
39 Now the rest of the acts of Ahab,
and all that he did, and the [u]ivory
house which he made, and all the
cities that he built, *are* they not written in the book of the chronicles of the
kings of Israel?
40 So Ahab slept with his fathers;
and Ā-hă-zī´-ăh his son reigned in his
stead.
41 ¶ And [v]Jĕ-hŏsh´-ă-phăt the son
of Ā´-să began to reign over Judah
in the fourth year of Ahab king of
Israel.
42 Jĕ-hŏsh´-ă-phăt *was* thirty and five
years old when he began to reign; and
he reigned twenty and five years in
Jerusalem. And his mother's name
was Ă-zū´-băh the daughter of Shĭl´-
hī.
43 And [w]he walked in all the ways of
Ā´-să his father; he turned not aside
from it, doing *that which was* right in
the eyes of the LORD: nevertheless
[x]the high places were not taken away;
for the people offered and burnt incense yet in the high places.

14 came.

t Deut. 32.35. ch. 21.19. Ps. 33.11. Ps. 119.89. Isa. 14.27. Nahum 1.2. Matt. 24.35. 1 Pet. 1.25.
u Amos 3.15.
v 2 Chr. 20. 31.
w 2 Chr. 17.3.
x Deut. 12.5-14. ch. 14.23.
y 2 Chr. 19.2. 2 Cor. 6.14.
z Gen. 13.13. ch. 14.24. Jude 7.
a Gen. 25.23. 2 Sam. 8.14. 2 Ki. 3.9.
15 Or, had ten ships.
b 2 Chr. 20. 35.
c 2 Chr. 20. 37.
d ch. 9.26.
e 2 Chr. 21.1.
f ch. 15.26.
g Judg. 2.11. ch. 16.31.

44 And [y]Jĕ-hŏsh´-ă-phăt made peace
with the king of Israel.
45 Now the rest of the acts of Jĕ-
hŏsh´-ă-phăt, and his might that he
shewed, and how he warred, *are* they
not written in the book of the chronicles of the kings of Judah?
46 And [z]the remnant of the sodomites, which remained in the days of his
father Ā´-să, he took out of the land.
47 *There* [a]*was* then no king in Ē´-
dom: a deputy *was* king.
48 Jĕ-hŏsh´-ă-phăt [15]made [b]ships of
Thär´-shĭsh to go to Ō´-phĭr for gold:
but [c]they went not; for the ships were
broken [d]at Ē´-zĭ-ŏn-gē´-bĕr.
49 Then said Ā-hă-zī´-ăh the son of
Ahab unto Jĕ-hŏsh´-ă-phăt, Let my
servants go with thy servants in the
ships. But Jĕ-hŏsh´-ă-phăt would not.
50 ¶ And [e]Jĕ-hŏsh´-ă-phăt slept with
his fathers, and was buried with his
fathers in the city of David his father:
and Jĕ-hôr´-ăm his son reigned in his
stead.
51 ¶ Ā-hă-zī´-ăh the son of Ahab began to reign over Israel in Să-mâr´-ĭ-ă
the seventeenth year of Jĕ-hŏsh´-ă-
phăt king of Judah, and reigned two
years over Israel.
52 And he did evil in the sight of the
LORD, and [f]walked in the way of his
father, and in the way of his mother,
and in the way of Jĕr-ŏ-bō´-ăm the son
of Nē´-băt, who made Israel to sin:
53 For [g]he served Bā´-ăl, and worshipped him, and provoked to anger
the LORD God of Israel, according to
all that his father had done.

THE SECOND

BOOK OF THE KINGS

commonly called

THE FOURTH BOOK OF THE KINGS

II KINGS
CHAP. 1

CHAPTER 1

THEN Moab [a]rebelled against Israel after the [b]death of Ahab.
2 And Ā-hă-zī´-ăh fell down through
a lattice in his upper chamber that
was in Să-mâr´-ĭ-ă, and was sick: and
he sent messengers, and said unto
them, Go, inquire of [1]Bā´-ăl–zē´-bŭb
the god of [c]Ĕk´-rŏn whether I shall recover of this disease.
3 But the angel of the LORD said to

a 2 Sam. 8.2.
b ch. 3.5.
1 The master of flies.
c 1 Sam. 5. 10.
d Isa. 8.19. Jer. 2.10-13.
2 The bed whither thou art gone up, thou shalt not come down from it.
e Job 18.14-21. Pro. 11.19. Eccl. 8.13. Isa. 3.11. Rom. 6.23. Jas. 1.15.

Ē-lī´-jăh the Tĭsh´-bīte, Arise, go up to
meet the messengers of the king of
Să-mâr´-ĭ-ă, and say unto them, [d]*Is it*
not because *there is* not a God in Israel, *that* ye go to inquire of Bā´-ăl–zē´-
bŭb the god of Ĕk´-rŏn?
4 Now therefore thus saith the LORD,
[2]Thou shalt not come down from that
bed on which thou art gone up, [e]but
shalt surely die. And Ē-lī´-jăh departed.
5 ¶ And when the messengers turned

back unto him, he said unto them,
Why are ye now turned back?
6 And they said unto him, There
came a man up to meet us, and said
unto us, Go, turn again unto the king
that sent you, and say unto him, Thus
saith the LORD, *Is it* not because *there*
is not a God in Israel, *that* thou sendest to inquire of Bā́-ăl–zḗ-bŭb the god
of Ĕḱ-rŏn? therefore thou shalt not
come down from that bed on which
thou art gone up, but shalt [f]surely die.
7 And he said unto them, [3]What
manner of man *was he* which came up
to meet you, and told you these words?
8 And they answered him, *He was*
an [g]hairy man, and girt with a girdle
of leather about his loins. And he said,
It *is* Ē-lī́-jăh the Tĭsh́-bīte.
9 Then the king [h]sent unto him a
captain of fifty with his fifty. And he
went up to him: and, behold, he sat
on the top of an hill. And he spake unto him, Thou man [i]of God, the king
hath said, Come down.
10 And Ē-lī́-jăh answered and said to
the captain of fifty, If I *be* a man of
God, then let [j]fire come down from
heaven, and consume thee and thy
fifty. And there came down fire from
heaven, and consumed him and his
fifty.
11 Again [k]also he sent unto him another captain of fifty with his fifty.
And he answered and said unto him,
O man of God, thus hath the king
said, Come down quickly.
12 And Ē-lī́-jăh answered and said
unto them, If I *be* a man of God, let
fire come down from heaven, and consume thee and thy fifty. And the fire of
God came down from heaven, and
consumed him and his fifty.
13 ¶ And he sent [l]again a captain of
the third fifty with his fifty. And the
third captain of fifty went up, and
came and [4]fell on his knees before Ē-
lī́-jăh, and besought him, and said unto him, O man of God, I pray thee, let
my life, and the life of these fifty thy
servants, be [m]precious in thy sight.
14 Behold, there came fire down from
heaven, and burnt up the two captains
of the former fifties with their fifties:
therefore let my life now be precious
in thy sight.
15 And the angel of the LORD said
unto Ē-lī́-jăh, Go down with him: be
not [n]afraid of him. And he arose, and
went down with him unto the king.
16 And he said unto him, Thus saith
the LORD, Forasmuch as thou hast
sent messengers to inquire of Bā́-ăl–
zḗ-bŭb the god of Ĕḱ-rŏn, *is it* not because *there is* no God in Israel to inquire of his word? therefore thou
shalt not come down off that bed on
which thou art gone up, but shalt
surely die.
17 ¶ So he died according to the word
of the LORD which Ē-lī́-jăh had spok-
en. And [5]Jĕ-hôŕ-ăm reigned in his
stead in the second year of Jĕ-hôŕ-ăm
the son of Jĕ-hŏsh́-ă-phăt king of Judah; because he had no son.
18 Now the rest of the acts of Ā-hă-
zī́-ăh which he did, *are* they not written in the book of the chronicles of
the kings of Israel?

CHAPTER 2

AND it came to pass, when the
LORD would [a]take up Ē-lī́-jăh into
heaven by a whirlwind, that Ē-lī́-jăh
went with Ē-lī́-shă [b]from Gĭĺ-găl.
2 And Ē-lī́-jăh said unto Ē-lī́-shă,
Tarry [c]here, I pray thee; for the LORD
hath sent me to Beth-el. And Ē-lī́-shă
said *unto him*, *As* the LORD liveth, and
as [d]thy soul liveth, I will not leave
thee. So they went down to Beth-el.
3 And [e]the sons of the prophets that
were at Beth-el came forth to Ē-lī́-shă,
and said unto him, Knowest thou that
the LORD will take away thy master
from thy head to day? And he said,
Yea, I know *it;* hold ye your peace.
4 And Ē-lī́-jăh said unto him, Ē-lī́-
shă, tarry here, I pray thee; for the
LORD hath sent me to Jericho. And
he said, *As* the LORD liveth, and *as*
thy soul liveth, I will not leave thee.
So they came to Jericho.
5 And the sons of the prophets that
were at Jericho came to Ē-lī́-shă, and
said unto him, Knowest thou that the
LORD will take away thy master from
thy head to day? And he answered,
Yea, I know *it;* hold ye your peace.
6 And Ē-lī́-jăh said unto him, Tarry,
I pray thee, here; for the LORD hath
sent me to Jordan. And he said, *As* the
LORD liveth, and *as* thy soul liveth, I
will not leave thee. And they two went
on.
7 And fifty men of the sons of the
prophets went, and stood [1]to view afar
off: and they two stood by Jordan.
8 And Ē-lī́-jăh took his mantle, and
wrapped *it* together, and smote the
waters, and they [f]were divided hither
and thither, so that they two went
over on dry ground.
9 ¶ And it came to pass, when they
were gone over, that Ē-lī́-jăh said unto
Ē-lī́-shă, Ask what I shall do for thee,

f Pro. 14.32.
3 What was the manner of the man?
g Zech. 13.4. Matt. 3.4.
h ch. 6.13,14. Ps. 105.15.
i Amos 7.12. Matt. 27.29.
j Num. 11.1. Luke 9.54.
k Isa. 26.11.
l Pro. 27.22. Eccl. 9.3. Isa. 1.5. Jer. 5.3.
4 bowed.
m 1 Sam. 26. 21. Ps. 72.14.
n Isa. 51.12. Jer. 1.17. Eze. 2.6.
5 The second year that Jehoram was Prorex, and the eighteenth of Jehoshaphat.

CHAP. 2

a Gen. 5.24. Heb. 11.5.
b 1 Ki. 19.21.
c Ruth 1.15, 16.
d 1 Sam. 1.26. ch. 4.30.
e 1 Sam. 19. 20. 1 Ki. 20.35. ch. 4.1,38.
1 in sight, or, over against.
f Ex. 14.21. Josh. 3.16.

before I be taken away from thee. And
Ē-lī-shă said, I pray thee, let a [g]double
portion of thy spirit be upon me.
10 And he said, [2]Thou hast asked a
hard thing: *nevertheless*, if thou see
[h]me *when I am* taken from thee, it
shall be so unto thee; but if not, it
shall not be *so*.
11 And it came to pass, as they still
went on, and talked, that, behold,
there appeared [i]a chariot of fire, and
horses of fire, and parted them both
asunder; and Ē-lī-jăh went up by a
whirlwind into heaven.
12 ¶ And Ē-lī-shă saw *it*, and he cried,
[j]My father, my father, the chariot of
Israel, and the horsemen thereof.
And he [k]saw him no more: and he
took hold of his own clothes, and [l]rent
them in two pieces.
13 He took up also the mantle of Ē-
lī-jăh that fell from him, and went
back, and stood by the [3]bank of Jordan;
14 And he took the mantle of Ē-lī-
jăh that fell from him, and smote [m]the
waters, and said, Where *is* the LORD
God of Ē-lī-jăh? and when he also had
smitten the waters, they parted hither
and thither: and Ē-lī-shă went over.
15 And when the sons of the prophets
which *were* to view at Jericho saw him,
they said, The spirit of Ē-lī-jăh doth
rest on Ē-lī-shă. And they came to
meet him, and bowed themselves to
the ground before him.
16 ¶ And they said unto him, Behold
now, there be with thy servants fifty
[4]strong men; let them go, we pray
thee, and seek thy master: [n]lest peradventure the Spirit of the LORD hath
taken him up, and cast him upon
[5]some mountain, or into some valley.
And he said, Ye shall not send.
17 And when they urged him till he
was ashamed, he said, Send. They
sent therefore fifty men; and they
sought three days, but found him not.
18 And when they came again to him,
(for he tarried at Jericho,) he said unto
them, Did I not say unto you, Go not?
19 ¶ And the men of the city said unto
Ē-lī-shă, Behold, I pray thee, the situation of this city *is* pleasant, as my
lord seeth: but the water [o]*is* naught,
and the ground [6]barren.
20 And he said, Bring me a new
cruse, and put salt therein. And they
brought *it* to him.
21 And he went forth unto the spring
of the waters, and [p]cast the salt in
there, and said, Thus saith the LORD,
I have healed these waters; there shall
not be from thence any more death or
barren *land*.
22 So the waters were healed unto
this day, according to the saying of
Ē-lī-shă which he spake.
23 ¶ And he went up from thence unto Beth-el: and as he was going up by
the way, there came forth little children out of the city, and mocked [q]him,
and said unto him, Go up, thou bald
head; go up, thou bald head.
24 And he turned back, and looked
on them, and cursed them in the name
of the LORD. And there came forth two
she bears out of the wood, [r]and tare
forty and two children of them.
25 And he went from thence to mount
Carmel, and from thence he returned
to Să-mâr-ĭ-ă.

CHAPTER 3

NOW [a]Jĕ-hôr-ăm the son of Ahab
began to reign over Israel in Să-
mâr-ĭ-ă the eighteenth year of Jĕ-
hŏsh-ă-phăt king of Judah, and reigned twelve years.
2 And he wrought evil in the sight of
the LORD; but not like his father, and
like his mother: for he put away the
[1]image of Bā-ăl [b]that his father had
made.
3 Nevertheless he [c]cleaved unto the
[d]sins of Jĕr-ŏ-bō-ăm the son of Nē-
băt, which made Israel to sin; he departed not therefrom.
4 ¶ And Mē-shă king of Moab was [e]a
sheepmaster, and rendered unto the
king of Israel an hundred thousand
[f]lambs, and an hundred thousand
rams, with the wool.
5 But it came to pass, when [g]Ahab
was dead, that the king of Moab rebelled against the king of Israel.
6 ¶ And king Jĕ-hôr-ăm went out of
Să-mâr-ĭ-ă the same time, and numbered all Israel.
7 And he went and sent to Jĕ-hŏsh-
ă-phăt the king of Judah, saying, The
king of Moab hath rebelled against
me: wilt thou go with me against Moab to battle? And he said, I will go up:
[h]I *am* as thou *art*, my people as thy
people, *and* my horses as thy horses.
8 And he said, Which way shall we
go up? And he answered, The way
through the wilderness of Ē-dom.
9 So the king of Israel went, and the
king of Judah, and the king of Ē-dom:
and they fetched a compass of seven
days' journey: and there was no water
for the host, and for the cattle [2]that
followed them.
10 And the king of Israel said, Alas!

g Num. 11. 17-25.
2 Thou hast done hard in asking.
h Acts 1.10.
i ch. 6.17. Ps. 68. 17. Heb. 1.7,14.
j ch. 13.14.
k Acts 1.9.
l Gen. 37.29, 34. Josh. 7.6.
3 lip.
m John 14.12.
4 sons of strength.
n 1 Ki. 18.12. Eze. 8.3. Acts 8.39.
5 one of the mountains.
o Josh. 6.26.
6 causing to miscarry.
p Ex. 15.25. ch. 4.41. John 9.6.
q 2 Chr. 36. 16. Ps. 31.17,18. Ps. 94.4, 21-23. Pro. 13.13. Isa. 5.24. Isa. 28.22. Jer. 5.10-14. Luke 10.16. 1 Thes. 4.8. 2 Tim. 3.3. Jude 14.15, 18.
r Deut. 32.35, 41,43. Job 31.3. Nahum 1.2. Luke 12.5. Rom. 12.19. Heb. 10.30, 31.

CHAP. 3

a ch. 1.17.
1 statue.
b 1 Ki. 16.31, 32.
c ch. 10.28-31.
d 1 Ki. 12.28, 31,32.
e Gen. 13.2. Job 1.3.
f Isa. 16.1.
g ch. 1.1.
h 1 Ki. 22.4.
2 at their feet.

[i]that the LORD hath called these three
kings together, to deliver them into
the hand of Moab!
11 But [j]Jĕ-hŏsh'-ă-phăt said, *Is there*
not here a [k]prophet of the LORD, that
we may inquire [l]of the LORD by him?
And one of the king of Israel's servants answered and said, Here *is* Ē-lī'-
shă the son of Shā'-phăt, which poured
water on the hands of Ē-lī'-jăh.
12 And Jĕ-hŏsh'-ă-phăt said, The
word of the LORD is with him. So the
king of Israel and Jĕ-hŏsh'-ă-phăt and
the king of Ē'-dọm went [m]down to him.
13 And Ē-li'-shă said unto the king of
Israel, [n]What have I to do with thee?
[o]get thee to [p]the prophets of thy father,
and to the prophets of thy mother.
And the king of Israel said unto him,
Nay: for the LORD hath called these
three kings together, to deliver them
into the hand of Moab.
14 And Ē-lī'-shă said, [q]*As* the LORD
of hosts liveth, before whom I stand,
surely, were it not that I regard [r]the
presence of Jĕ-hŏsh'-ă-phăt the king of
Judah, I would not look toward thee,
nor see thee.
15 But now bring me [s]a minstrel.
And it came to pass, when the minstrel played, that [t]the hand of the
LORD came upon him.
16 And he said, Thus saith the LORD,
Make [u]this valley full of ditches.
17 For thus saith the LORD, Ye shall
not see wind, neither shall ye see rain;
yet that valley [v]shall be filled with
water, that ye may drink, both ye, and
your cattle, and your beasts.
18 And this is *but* a [w]light thing in the
sight of the LORD: [x]he will deliver the
Moabites also into your hand.
19 And [y]ye shall smite every fenced
city, and every choice city, and shall
fell every good tree, and stop all wells
of water, and [3]mar every good piece
of land with stones.
20 And it came to pass in the morning, when the [z]meat offering was offered, that, behold, there came water by
the way of Ē'-dọm, and the country
was filled with water.
21 ¶ And when all the Moabites
heard that the kings were come up to
fight against them, they [4]gathered all
that were able to [5]put on armour, and
upward, and stood in the border.
22 And they rose up early in the
morning, and the sun shone upon the
water, and the Moabites saw the
water on the other side *as* red as blood:
23 And they said, This *is* blood: the
kings are surely [6]slain, and they have
smitten one another: now therefore,
Moab, to the spoil.
24 And when they came to the camp
of Israel, the Israelites rose up and
smote the Moabites, so that they fled
before them: but [7]they went forward
smiting the Moabites, even in *their*
country.
25 And they beat down the cities, and
on every good piece of land cast every
man his stone, and filled it; and they
stopped all the wells of water, and
felled all the good trees: [8]only in [a]Kĭr-
hăr'-ă-sĕth left they the stones thereof; howbeit the slingers went about *it*,
and smote it.
26 ¶ And when the king of Moab saw
that the battle was too sore for him,
he took with him seven hundred men
that drew swords, to break through
even unto the king of Ē'-dọm: but they
could not.
27 Then he took his [9]eldest son that
should have reigned in his stead, and
offered [b]him *for* a burnt offering upon
the wall. And there was great indignation against Israel: and they departed
[10]from him, and returned to *their own*
land.

CHAPTER 4

NOW there cried a certain woman
of the wives of [a]the sons of the
prophets unto Ē-lī'-shă, saying, Thy
servant my husband is dead; and thou
knowest that thy servant did fear the
LORD: and the creditor is come [b]to
take unto him my two sons to be
bondmen.
2 And Ē-lī'-shă said unto her, What
shall I do for thee? tell me, what hast
thou in the house? And she said,
Thine handmaid hath not any thing
in the house, save [c]a pot of oil.
3 Then he said, Go, borrow thee vessels abroad of all thy neighbours,
even empty vessels; [1]borrow not a
few.
4 And when thou art come in, thou
shalt shut the door upon thee and upon thy sons, and shalt pour out into
all those vessels, and thou shalt set
aside that which is full.
5 So she went from him, and shut the
door upon her and upon her sons,
who brought *the vessels* to her; and
she poured out.
6 And it came to pass, when [d]the vessels were full, that she said unto her
son, Bring me yet a vessel. And he
said unto her, *There is* not a vessel
more. And the oil stayed.
7 Then she came and told the man of
God. And he said, Go, sell the oil, and

i Ps. 78.34. Pro. 19.3. Isa. 8.21.
j 1 Ki. 22.7.
k Amos 3.7.
l 1 Chr. 38.9. Ps. 55.22. Pro. 3.5,6.
m ch. 2.25.
n Eze. 14.3.
o Judg. 10.14. Ruth 1.15.
p 1 Ki. 18.19.
q 1 Ki. 17.1. ch. 5.16.
r Ps. 15.4.
s 1 Sam. 10.5.
t Eze. 1.3. Eze. 8.1.
u ch. 4.3.
v Ps. 107.35.
w Jer. 32.17, 27. Mark 10.27. Luke 1.37. Eph. 3.20.
x 1 Ki. 20.28.
y 1 Sam. 15.3.
3 grieve.
z Ex. 29.39, 40.
4 were cried together.
5 gird himself with a girdle.
6 destroyed.
7 Or, they smote in it even smiting.
8 until he left the stones thereof in Kir-hara-seth.
a Isa. 16.7,11.
9 Perhaps the king of Edom's son.
b Lev. 18.21. Deut. 12.31. ch. 17.17. 2 Chr. 28.3. Ps. 106.37, 38. Jer. 7.31. Eze. 16.20. Eze. 20.26, 31.
10 As they saw the Moabites so desperately resolute.

CHAP. 4

a 1 Ki. 20.35. ch. 2.3,5,7.
b Ex. 21.2. Lev. 25.39. Deut. 15. 12-15,18. Neh. 5.1-13. Jer. 34.8-18. Matt. 18.25.
c 1 Ki. 17.12.
1 Or, scant not.
d Matt. 14. 20.

pay thy [2]debt, and live thou and thy
children of the rest.
8 ¶ And [3]it fell on a day, that Ē-lī-́shă
passed to [e]Shû-́nĕm, where *was* a great
woman; and she [4]constrained him to
eat bread. And *so* it was, *that* as oft as
he passed by, he turned in thither to
eat bread.
9 And she said unto [f]her husband,
Behold now, I perceive that this *is* an
holy man of God, which passeth by us
continually.
10 Let us [g]make a little chamber, I
pray thee, on the wall; and let us set
for him there a bed, and a table, and a
stool, and a candlestick: and it shall
be, when he cometh to us, that he shall
turn in thither.
11 And it fell on a day, that he came
thither, and he turned into the chamber, and lay there.
12 And he said to Gĕ-hā-́zī his servant, Call this Shû-năm-́mīte. And
when he had called her, she stood before him.
13 And he said unto him, Say now
unto her, Behold, thou hast been careful for us with all this care; what *is* to
be done for thee? wouldest thou be
spoken for to the king, or to the captain of the host? And she answered, I
dwell among mine own people.
14 And he said, What then *is* to be
done for her? And Gĕ-hā-́zī answered,
Verily she hath no child, and her husband is old.
15 And he said, Call her. And when
he had called her, she stood in the
door.
16 And he said, [h]About this [5]season,
according to the time of life, thou shalt
embrace a son. And she said, Nay, my
lord, *thou* man of God, do not lie unto
thine handmaid.
17 And the woman conceived, and
bare a son at that season that Ē-lī-́shă
had said unto her, according to the
time of life.
18 ¶ And when the child was grown,
it fell on a day, that he went out to his
father to the reapers.
19 And he said unto his father, My
head, my head. And he said to a lad,
Carry him to his mother.
20 And when he had taken him, and
brought him to his mother, he sat on
her knees till noon, and *then* died.
21 And she went up, and laid him on
the bed of the man of God, and shut
the door upon him, and went out.
22 And she called unto her husband,
and said, Send me, I pray thee, one of
the young men, and one of the asses,

2 Or, creditor.
3 there was a day.
e Josh. 19.18. 1 Sam. 28.4.
4 laid hold on him.
f Pro. 31.10, 11.
g Matt. 10. 41,42. Matt. 25.40. Rom. 12.13. Heb. 13.1,2.
h Gen. 18.10, 14.
5 set time.
6 peace.
7 restrain not for me to ride.
i ch. 2.25.
8 by his feet.
j Matt. 15.23.
9 bitter.
k 1 Ki. 18.46. ch. 9.1.
l Luke 10.4.
m Ex. 7.19. Ex. 14.16. ch. 2.8,14. Acts 19.12.
n ch. 2.2.
10 attention.
o John 11.11.
p Matt. 6.6.
q 1 Ki. 17.20. Jas. 5.16.
r Acts 20.10.
11 once hither, and once thither.
s 1 Ki. 17.21.

that I may run to the man of God, an
come again.
23 And he said, Wherefore wilt tho
go to him to day? *it is* neither ne
moon, nor sabbath. And she said,
shall be [6]well.
24 Then she saddled an ass, and sai
to her servant, Drive, and go forward
[7]slack not *thy* riding for me, except
bid thee.
25 So she went and came unto th
man of God [i]to mount Carmel. And
came to pass, when the man of Go
saw her afar off, that he said to Gĕ
hā-́zī his servant, Behold, *yonder*
that Shû-năm-́mīte:
26 Run now, I pray thee, to meet he
and say unto her, *Is it* well with thee
is it well with thy husband? *is it* we
with the child? And she answered,
is well.
27 And when she came to the man o
God to the hill, she caught [8]him b
the feet: but Gĕ-hā-́zī [j]came near t
thrust her away. And the man of Go
said, Let her alone; for her soul
[9]vexed within her: and the LORD hat
hid *it* from me, and hath not told me
28 Then she said, Did I desire a so
of my lord? did I not say, Do not de
ceive me?
29 Then he said to Gĕ-hā-́zī, [k]Gir
up thy loins, and take my staff in thin
hand, and go thy way: if thou mee
any man, [l]salute him not; and if an
salute thee, answer him not again
and [m]lay my staff upon the face of th
child.
30 And the mother of the child said
[n]*As* the LORD liveth, and *as* thy sou
liveth, I will not leave thee. And h
arose, and followed her.
31 And Gĕ-hā-́zī passed on befor
them, and laid the staff upon the fac
of the child; but *there was* neithe
voice, nor [10]hearing. Wherefore h
went again to meet him, and told him
saying, The child is [o]not awaked.
32 And when Ē-lī-́shă was come int
the house, behold, the child was dead
and laid upon his bed.
33 He [p]went in therefore, and shu
the door upon them twain, and [q]pray
ed unto the LORD.
34 And he went up, and lay upon th
child, and put his mouth upon hi
mouth, and his eyes upon his eyes, an
his hands upon his hands: and [r]h
stretched himself upon the child; an
the flesh of the child waxed warm.
35 Then he returned, and walked i
the house [11]to and fro; and went up
[s]and stretched himself upon him: an

he child sneezed seven times, and the
hild opened his eyes.
36 And he called Gĕ-hā́-zī, and said,
all this Shû-năḿ-mīte. So he called
er. And when she was come in unto
im, he said, Take up thy son.
37 Then she went in, and fell at his
eet, and bowed herself to the ground,
nd [u]took up her son, and went out.
38 ¶ And Ē-lī́-shă came again [v]to
ĭĺ-găl: and *there was* a dearth in the
and; and the sons of the prophets
ere [w]sitting before him: and he said
nto his servant, Set on the great pot,
nd seethe pottage for the sons of the
rophets.
39 And one went out into the field to
ather herbs, and found a wild vine,
nd gathered thereof wild gourds his
ap full, and came and shred *them* into
he pot of pottage: for they [x]knew
hem not.
40 So they poured out for the men to
at. And it came to pass, as they were
ating of the pottage, that they cried
ut, and said, O *thou* man of God,
here is [y]death in the pot. And they
ould not eat *thereof*.
41 But he said, Then bring meal. And
he cast *it* into the pot; and he said,
our out for the people, that they may
at. And there was no [12]harm in the
ot.
42 ¶ And there came a man [a]from
ā́-ăl–shăĺ-ĭ-shă, [b]and brought the
nan of God bread of the firstfruits,
wenty loaves of barley, and full ears
of corn [13]in the husk thereof. And he
aid, Give unto the people, that they
nay eat.
43 And his servitor said, [c]What,
hould I set this before an hundred
nen? He said again, Give the people,
hat they may eat: for thus saith the
LORD, They shall eat, and shall leave
hereof.
44 So he set *it* before them, and they
lid eat, [d] and left *thereof*, according to
he [e]word of the LORD.

CHAPTER 5

NOW [a]Nā́-ă-măn, captain of the
host of the king of Syria, was a
[b]great man [1]with his master, and
honourable, because by him the
LORD had given [3]deliverance unto
Syria: he was also a mighty man in
valour, *but he was* a leper.
2 And the Syrians had gone out by
companies, and had brought away
captive out of the land of Israel a little
maid; and she [4]waited on Nā́-ă-măn's
wife.
3 And she said unto her mistress,
Would God my lord *were* [5]with the
prophet that *is* in Să-mâŕ-ĭ-ă! for he
would [6]recover him of his leprosy.
4 And *one* went in, and told his lord,
saying, Thus and thus said the maid
that *is* of the land of Israel.
5 And the king of Syria said, Go to,
go, and I will send a letter unto the
king of Israel. And he departed, and
[c]took [7]with him ten talents of silver,
and six thousand *pieces* of gold, and
ten changes of raiment.
6 And he brought the letter to the
king of Israel, saying, Now when this
letter is come unto thee, behold, I
have *therewith* sent Nā́-ă-măn my servant to thee, that thou mayest recover
him of his leprosy.
7 And it came to pass, when the king
of Israel had read the letter, that he
[d]rent his clothes, and said, *Am* I [e]God,
to kill and to make alive, that this man
doth send unto me to recover a man of
his leprosy? wherefore consider, I
pray you, and see how he seeketh a
quarrel against me.
8 ¶ And it was *so*, when Ē-lī́-shă the
man of God had heard that the king
of Israel had rent his clothes, that he
sent to the king, saying, Wherefore
hast thou rent thy clothes? let him
come now to me, and [f]he shall know
that there is a prophet in Israel.
9 So Nā́-ă-măn came with his horses
and with his chariot, and stood at the
door of the house of Ē-lī́-shă.
10 And Ē-lī́-shă sent a messenger
unto him, saying, Go and [g]wash in
Jordan seven times, and thy flesh shall
come again to thee, and thou shalt be
clean.
11 But Nā́-ă-măn was [h]wroth, and
went away, and said, Behold, [8]I
thought, He will surely come out to
me, and stand, and call on the name
of the LORD his God, and [9]strike his
hand over the place, and recover the
leper.
12 *Are* not [10]Ăb́-ă-nă and Phăŕ-păr,
rivers of Damascus, better than all the
waters of Israel? may I not wash in
them, and be clean? So he turned and
[i]went away in a rage.
13 And his servants came near, and
spake unto him, and said, My father,
if the prophet had bid thee *do some*
great thing, wouldest thou not have
done *it*? how much rather then, when
he saith to thee, Wash, and be clean?
14 Then went he down, and dipped
himself seven times in Jordan, according to the saying of the man of God:

t ch. 8.1.
u Heb. 11.35.
v ch. 2.1.
w Luke 10.39. Acts 22.3.
x Matt. 7.16.
y Ex. 10.17.
z Ex. 15.25. ch. 2.21. ch. 5.10. John 9.6.
12 evil thing.
a 1 Sam. 9.4.
b 1 Cor. 9.11. Gal. 6.6.
13 Or, in his scrip, or, garment.
c Luke 9.13. John 6.9.
d Matt. 14. 20. John 6.13.
e Gen. 18.14. Zech. 8.6. Matt. 19.26. Luke 1.37.

CHAP. 5

a Luke 4.27.
b Ex. 11.3. ch. 4.8. Esther 9.4.
1 before.
2 lifted up, or, accepted in countenance, or, gracious.
3 Or, victory.
4 was before.
5 before.
6 gather in.
c 1 Sam. 9.8.
7 in his hand.
d Gen. 37.29.
e Gen. 30.2. 1 Sam. 2.6.
f Ex. 4.30.
g ch. 4.41. John 9.7.
h 1 Cor. 2.14.
8 I said, or, I said with myself, He will surely come out, etc.
9 move up and down.
10 Or, Amana.
i Pro. 14.17. Eccl. 7.9. Eph. 4.31. Col. 3.8. Jas. 1.19.

and [j]his flesh came again like unto the flesh of a little child, and he [k]was clean.

15 ¶ And [l]he returned to the man of God, he and all his company, and came, and stood before him: and he said, Behold, now [m]I know that *there is* [n]no God in all the earth, but in Israel: now therefore, I pray thee, take [o]a blessing of thy servant.

16 But he said, [p]*As* the LORD liveth, before whom I stand, [q]I will receive none. And he urged him to take *it;* but he refused.

17 And Nā-ā-măn said, Shall there not then, I pray thee, be given to thy servant two mules' burden of earth? for thy servant will henceforth offer neither burnt offering nor sacrifice unto other gods, but unto the LORD.

18 In this thing the LORD pardon thy servant, *that* when my master goeth into the house of Rimmon to worship there, and he [r]leaneth on my hand, and I bow myself in the house of Rimmon: when I bow down myself in the house of Rimmon, the LORD pardon thy servant in this thing.

19 And he said unto him, Go in peace. So he departed from him [11]a little way.

20 ¶ But Gĕ-hā-zī, the servant of Ē-lī-shă the man of God, said, Behold, my master hath spared Nā-ā-măn this Syrian, in not receiving at his hands that which he brought: but, *as* the LORD liveth, I will run after [s]him, and take somewhat of him.

21 So Gĕ-hā-zī followed after Nā-ā-măn. And when Nā-ā-măn saw *him* running after him, he lighted down from the chariot to meet him, and said, [12]*Is* all well?

22 And he said, All *is* well. My master hath sent me, saying, Behold, even now there be come to me from mount Ē-phră-ĭm two young men of the sons of the prophets: give them, I pray thee, a talent of silver, and two changes of garments.

23 And Nā-ā-măn said, Be content, take two talents. And he urged him, and bound two talents of silver in two bags, with two changes of garments, and laid *them* upon two of his servants; and they bare *them* before him.

24 And when he came to the [13]tower, he took *them* from their hand, and bestowed *them* in the house: and he let the men go, and they departed.

25 But he went in, and [t]stood before his master. And Ē-lī-shă said unto him, Whence *comest thou,* Gĕ-hā-zī? And he said, Thy servant went [14]
whither.

26 And [u]he said unto him, Went n
mine heart *with thee,* when the m
turned again from his chariot to me
thee? *Is it* a time to receive money, a
to receive garments, and oliveyar
and vineyards, and sheep, and oxe
and menservants, and maidservants

27 The leprosy therefore of Nā-
măn [v]shall cleave unto thee, and un
thy seed for ever. And he went o
from his presence a leper [w]*as white*
snow.

CHAPTER 6

AND [a]the sons of the prophets sa
unto Ē-lī-shă, Behold now, t
place where we [1]dwell with thee is t
strait for us.

2 Let us go, we pray thee, unto Jo
dan, and take thence every man
beam, and let us make us a place the
where we may dwell. And he answe
ed, Go ye.

3 And one said, Be content, I pr
thee, and go with thy servants. A
he answered, I will go.

4 So he went with them. And wh
they came to Jordan, they cut dov
wood.

5 But as one was felling a beam, t
[2]axe head fell into the water: and
cried, and said, Alas, master! for
was borrowed.

6 And the man of God said, Whe
fell it? And he shewed him the plac
And [b]he cut down a stick and cast
in thither; and the iron did swim.

7 Therefore said he, Take *it* up
thee. And he put out his hand, a
took it.

8 ¶ Then the king of Syria warr
against Israel, and took counsel wi
his servants, saying, In such and su
a place *shall be* my [3]camp.

9 And the man of God sent unto t
king of Israel, saying, [c]Beware th
thou pass not such a place; for thith
the Syrians are come down.

10 And the king of Israel sent to t
place which the man of God told hi
and warned him of, and saved hi
self there, not once nor twice.

11 Therefore the heart of the king
Syria was sore troubled for this thin
and he called his servants, and sa
unto them, Will ye not shew me whi
of us *is* for the king of Israel?

12 And one of his servants sai
[4]None, my lord, O king: but Ē-lī-sh
the prophet that *is* in Israel, telleth t
king of Israel the words that th
speakest in thy bedchamber.

j Job 33.25.
k Luke 4.27.
l Luke 17.15.
m Isa. 43.10, 11. Rom. 10.10.
n Dan. 2.47.
o Gen. 33.11.
p ch. 3.14.
q Gen. 14.23. Matt. 10.8. Acts 8.18, 20.
r ch. 7.2,17.
11 a little piece of ground, as Gen. 35.16.
s Ex. 20.17. Josh. 6.18. 1 Sam. 8.3-5. Ps. 10.3. Pro. 1.19. Pro. 15.27. Luke 12.15. Col. 3.5. 1 Tim. 6.10.
12 Is there peace?
13 Or, secret place.
t Pro. 30.20. Eze. 33.31.
14 not hither or thither.
u Ps. 32.10. Ps. 63.11. Ps. 140.11. Pro. 13.21. Isa. 3.11. Isa. 57.21. Acts 13.9.
v 1 Tim. 6.10.
w Ex. 4.6. Lev. 12.2,3. Lev. 14.3, 35. Num. 12.10. ch. 15.5. 2 Chr. 26.19, 20.

CHAP. 6
a 1 Sam. 10. 12. ch. 2.3. ch. 4.1,38. ch. 9.1.
1 sit before.
2 iron.
b Ex. 15.25. ch. 2.21. ch. 4.41.
3 Or, encamping.
c ch. 13.14. Ps. 25.14. Pro. 3.32. Isa. 6.13. Amos 3.7. Matt. 5.13.
4 No.

13 ¶ And he said, Go and spy where he *is*, that I may send and fetch him. And it was told him, saying, Behold, *he is* in [d]Dō-thăn.

14 Therefore sent he thither horses, and chariots, and a [5]great host: and they came by night, and compassed the city about.

15 And when the [6]servant of the man of God was risen early, and gone forth, behold, an host compassed the city both with horses and chariots. And his servant said unto him, Alas, my master! how shall we do?

16 And he answered, Fear not: for [e]they that *be* with us *are* more than they that *be* with them.

17 And Ē-lī-shă prayed, and said, LORD, I pray thee, open his eyes, that he may see. And the LORD opened the eyes of the young man; and he saw: and, behold, the mountain *was* full of [f]horses and chariots of fire round about Ē-lī-shă.

18 And when they came down to him, Ē-lī-shă prayed unto the LORD, and said, Smite this people, I pray thee, with blindness. [g]And he smote them with blindness according to the word of Ē-lī-shă.

19 ¶ And Ē-lī-shă said unto them, This *is* not the way, neither *is* this the city: [7]follow me, and I will bring you to the man whom ye seek. But he led them to Să-mâr-ĭ-ă.

20 And it came to pass, when they were come into Să-mâr-ĭ-ă, that Ē-lī-shă said, LORD, open the eyes of these *men*, that they may see. And the LORD opened their eyes, and they saw; and, behold, *they were* in the midst of Să-mâr-ĭ-ă.

21 And the king of Israel said unto Ē-lī-shă, when he saw them, My [h]father, shall I smite *them*? shall I smite *them?*

22 And he answered, Thou shalt not smite *them:* wouldest thou smite those whom thou hast taken captive with thy sword and with thy bow? [i]set bread and water before them, that they may eat and drink, and go to their master.

23 And he prepared great provision for them: and when they had eaten and drunk, he sent them away, and they went to their master. So [j]the bands of Syria came no more into the land of Israel.

24 ¶ And it came to pass after this, that Bĕn–hā-dăd king of Syria gathered all his host, and went up, and besieged Să-mâr-ĭ-ă.

25 And there was a great [k]famine in Să-mâr-ĭ-ă: and, behold, they besieged it, until an ass's head was *sold* for fourscore *pieces* of silver, and the [8]fourth part of a căb of dove's dung for five *pieces* of silver.

26 And as the king of Israel was passing by upon the wall, there cried a woman unto him, saying, Help, my lord, O king.

27 And he said, [9]If the LORD do not help thee, whence shall I help thee? out of the barnfloor, or out of the winepress?

28 And the king said unto her, What [l]aileth thee? And she answered, This woman said unto me, Give thy son, that we may eat him to day, and we will eat my son to morrow.

29 So [m]we boiled my son, and did eat him: and I said unto her on the [10]next day, Give thy son, that we may eat him: and she hath hid her son.

30 ¶ And it came to pass, when the king heard the words of the woman, that he [n]rent his clothes; and he passed by upon the wall, and the people looked, and, behold, *he had* sackcloth within upon his flesh.

31 Then he said, [o]God do so and more also to me, if the head of Ē-lī-shă the son of Shā-phăt shall stand on him this day.

32 But Ē-lī-shă [p]sat in his house, and [q]the elders sat with him; and *the king* sent a man from before him: but ere the messenger came to him, he said to the elders, [r]See ye how this son of [s]a murderer hath sent to take away mine head? look, when the messenger cometh, shut the door, and hold him fast at the door: *is* not the sound of his master's feet behind him?

33 And while he yet talked with them, behold, the messenger came down unto him: and [11]he said, Behold, this evil *is* of the LORD; what [t]should I wait for the LORD any longer?

CHAPTER 7

THEN Ē-lī-shă said, Hear ye the word of the LORD; Thus saith the LORD, [a]To morrow about this time *shall* a measure of fine flour *be sold* for a shekel, and two measures of barley for a shekel, in the gate of Să-mâr-ĭ-ă.

2 Then [1]a lord on whose hand the king leaned answered the man of God, and said, Behold, [b]*if* the LORD would make windows in heaven, might this thing be? And he said, Behold, thou shalt see *it* with thine eyes, but [c]shalt not eat thereof.

d Gen. 37.17.
5 heavy.
6 Or, minister.
e 2 Sam. 22. 3,31. 2 Chr. 32.7. Ps. 3.3-8. Ps. 18.2. Ps. 27.1-3. Ps. 28.7,8. Ps. 34.22. Ps. 40.4. Ps. 55.18. Pro. 18.10. Isa. 43.1. Rom. 8.31.
f ch. 2.11. Ps. 34.7. Zech. 1.8. Heb. 1.14.
g Gen. 19.11. Acts 13.9.
7 Come ye after me.
h ch. 2.12.
i Pro. 25.21. Rom. 12.20.
j ch. 5.2.
k Lev. 26.26.
8 That is, about three gills, a cab being about three pints.
9 Or, Let not the LORD save thee.
l Judg. 18.23. Isa. 22.1.
m Lev. 26.29.
10 other.
n Gen. 37.29, 34. ch. 5.7.
o Ruth 1.17. 2 Sam. 3.9, 35. Acts 23.14.
p Ps. 118.6,9.
q Eze. 8.1. Mal. 3.16.
r Luke 13, 32.
s 1 Ki. 18.4.
11 That is, Jehoram.
t Job 21.15. Ps. 27.14. Pro. 30.9. Isa. 8.17. Hab. 2.3. Mal. 3.14. Rev. 16.9.

CHAP. 7

a Ex. 8.23. Josh. 3.5. Ps. 46.1.
1 a lord which belonged to the king leaning upon his hand.
b Gen. 7.11. Gen. 8.2. Mal. 3.10.
c Deut. 3.27. Heb. 3.17.

3 ¶ And there were four leprous men [d]at the entering in of the gate: and they said one to another, Why sit we here until we die?

4 If we say, We will enter into the city, then the famine *is* in the city, and we shall die there: and if we sit still here, we die also. Now therefore come, and let us fall unto the host of the Syrians: if they save us alive, we shall live; and if [e]they kill us, we shall but die.

5 And they rose up in the twilight, to go unto the camp of the Syrians: and when they were come to the uttermost part of the camp of Syria, behold, *there was* no man there.

6 For the LORD had made the host of the Syrians [f]to hear a noise of chariots, and a noise of horses, *even* the noise of a great host: and they said one to another, Lo, the king of Israel hath hired against us the kings of the Hittites, and [g]the kings of the Egyptians, to come upon us.

7 Wherefore they [h]arose and fled in the twilight, and left their tents, and their horses, and their asses, even the camp as it *was*, and fled for their life.

8 And when these lepers came to the uttermost part of the camp, they went into one tent, and did eat and drink, and carried thence silver, and gold, and raiment, and went and hid *it;* and came again, and entered into another tent, and carried thence *also*, and went and hid *it*.

9 Then they said one to another, We [i]do not well: this day *is* a day of [j]good tidings, and we hold our peace: if we tarry till the morning light, [2]some mischief will come upon us: now therefore come, that we may go and tell the king's household.

10 So they came and called unto the porter of the city: and they told them, saying, We came to the camp of the Syrians, and, behold, *there was* no man there, neither voice of man, but horses tied, and asses tied, and the tents as they *were*.

11 And he called the porters; and they told *it* to the king's house within.

12 ¶ And the king arose in the night, and said unto his servants, I will now shew you what the Syrians have done to us. They know that we *be* hungry; therefore are they gone out of the camp to hide themselves in the field, saying, When they come out of the city, we shall catch them alive, and get into the city.

13 And one of his servants answered and said, Let *some* take, I pray thee, five of the horses that remain, which are left [3]in the city, (behold, they *are* as all the multitude of Israel that are left in it: behold, *I say*, they *are* even as all the multitude of the Israelites that are consumed:) and let us send and see.

14 They took therefore two chariot horses; and the king sent after the host of the Syrians, saying, Go and see.

15 And they went after them unto Jordan: and, lo, all the way *was* full of garments and [4]vessels, which the Syrians had cast away in their haste. And the messengers returned, and told the king.

16 And the people went out, and spoiled the tents of the Syrians. So a measure of fine flour was *sold* for a shekel, and two measures of barley for a shekel, [k]according to the word of the LORD.

17 ¶ And the king appointed the lord on whose hand he leaned to have the charge of the gate: and the people trode upon him in the gate, and he died, [l]as the man of God had said, who spake when the king came down to him.

18 And it came to pass as the man of God had spoken to the king, saying, [m]Two measures of barley for a shekel, and a measure of fine flour for a shekel, shall be to morrow about this time in the gate of Să-mâr'ĭ-ă:

19 And that lord answered the man of God, and said, Now, behold, *if* the LORD should make windows in heaven, might such a thing be? And he said, Behold, thou shalt see it with thine eyes, but shalt not eat thereof.

20 And [n]so it fell out unto him: for the people trode upon him in the gate, and he died.

CHAPTER 8

THEN spake Ē-lī'-shă unto the woman, [a]whose son he had restored to life, saying, Arise, and go thou and thine household, and sojourn wheresoever thou canst sojourn: for the LORD [b]hath called for a famine; and it shall also come upon the land seven years.

2 And the woman arose, and did after the saying of the man of God: and she went with her household, and sojourned in the land of the Philistines seven years.

3 And it came to pass at the seven years' end, that the woman returned

d Lev. 13.46. Num. 5.2. Deut. 24.8, 9. ch. 5.27. Luke 17.12.
e Esther 4.16. Luke 15.17-19.
f Lev. 26.36. 2 Sam. 5.24. ch. 3.23. Job 15.21. Eze. 10.5. Rev. 6.15, 16.
g 1 Ki. 10.29.
h Job 18.11. Ps. 48.4,5,6. Pro. 28.1. Jer. 48.8,9.
i Phil. 2.14. 2 Pet. 1.19.
j Esther 9.17. Isa. 41.27. Nah. 1.15.
2 we shall find punishment.
3 in it.
4 Or, furniture.
k Num. 23. 19. Ps. 89.2. Isa. 40.8. Isa. 44.26. Matt. 24.35. Mark 13.31. 1 Cor. 1.9. 1 Thes. 5.24. 1 Pet. 1.25.
l Deut. 32.35, 39.40. ch. 6.32. 2 Chr. 36. 16. Job. 31.3. Ps. 94.4,21-23. Pro. 13.13. Isa. 5.24. Isa. 28.22. Jer. 5.11-14. Nah. 1.2. Luke 10.16. 1 Thes. 4.8. Heb. 10.30, 31. Jude 14,15.
m ver. 1.
n Num. 20. 12. Job 20.23. Jer. 17.6. Heb. 3.18.

CHAP. 8

a ch. 4.35.
b Lev. 26.19, 20, 26. 2 Sam. 24. 13. 1 Ki. 17.1. Ps. 105.16. Hag. 1.11.

out of the land of the Philistines: and she went forth to cry unto the king for her house and for her land.

4 And the king talked [c]with Gĕ-hā-́zī the servant of the man of God, saying, Tell me, I pray thee, all the great things that Ē-lī-́shă hath done.

5 And it came to pass, as he was telling the king how he had [d]restored a dead body to life, that, behold, the woman, whose son he had restored to life, cried to the king for her house and for her land. And Gĕ-hā-́zī said, My lord, O king, this *is* the woman, and this *is* her son, whom Ē-lī-́shă restored to life.

6 And when the king asked the woman, she told him. So the king appointed unto her a certain [1]officer, saying, Restore all that *was* hers, and all the fruits of the field since the day that she left the land, even until now.

7 ¶ And Ē-lī-́shă came to Damascus; and Bĕn–hā-́dăd the king of Syria was sick; and it was told him, saying, The man of God is come hither.

8 And the king said [e]unto Hă-zā-́ĕl, Take a present in thine hand, and go, meet the man of God, and [g]inquire of the LORD by him, saying, Shall I recover of this disease?

9 So Hă-zā-́ĕl went to meet him, and took a present [2]with him, even of every good thing of Damascus, forty camels' burden, and came and stood before him, and said, Thy son Bĕn–hā-́dăd king of Syria hath sent me to thee, saying, Shall I recover of this disease?

10 And Ē-lī-́shă said unto him, Go, say unto him, Thou mayest certainly recover: howbeit the LORD hath shewed me that he shall surely die.

11 And he settled his countenance stedfastly, until he was ashamed: and the man of God wept.

12 And Hă-zā-́ĕl said, Why weepeth my lord? And he answered, Because I know [i]the evil that thou wilt do unto the children of Israel: their strong holds wilt thou set on fire, and their young men wilt thou slay with the sword, and wilt [j]dash their children, and rip up their women with child.

13 And Hă-zā-́ĕl said, But what, *is* thy servant a dog, that he should do this great thing? And Ē-lī-́shă answered, [l]The LORD hath shewed me that thou *shalt be* king over Syria.

14 So he departed from Ē-lī-́shă, and came to his master; who said to him, What said Ē-lī-́shă to thee? And he answered, He told me *that* thou shouldest surely recover.

15 And it came to pass on the morrow, that he took a thick cloth, and dipped *it* in water, and spread *it* on his face, so that he died: and Hă-zā-́ĕl reigned in his stead.

16 ¶ And in the fifth year of Joram the son of Ahab king of Israel, Jĕ-hŏsh-́ă-phăt *being* then king of Judah, [m]Jĕ-hôr-́ăm the son of Jĕ-hŏsh-́ă-phăt king of Judah [4]began to reign.

17 Thirty [n]and two years old was he when he began to reign; and he reigned eight years in Jerusalem.

18 And he walked in the way of the kings of Israel, as did the house of Ahab: for the daughter of Ahab was his wife: and he did evil in the sight of the LORD.

19 Yet the LORD would not destroy Judah for David his servant's sake, [o]as he promised him to give him alway a [5]light, *and* to his children.

20 ¶ In his days [p]Ē-́dom revolted from under the hand of Judah, and [q]made a king over themselves.

21 So Joram went over to Zā-́ĭr, and all the chariots with him: and he rose by night, and smote the Ē-́dom-ītes which compassed him about, and the captains of the chariots: and the people fled into their tents.

22 [6]Yet Ē-́dom revolted from under the hand of Judah unto this day. [r]Then Lĭb-́năh revolted at the same time.

23 And the rest of the acts of Joram, and all that he did, *are* they not written in the book of the chronicles of the kings of Judah?

24 And Joram slept with his fathers, and was buried with his fathers in the city of David: and [7]Ā-hă-zī-́ăh his son reigned in his stead.

25 ¶ In the twelfth year of Joram the son of Ahab king of Israel did Ā-hă-zī-́ăh the son of Jĕ-hôr-́ăm king of Judah begin to reign.

26 [s]Two and twenty years old *was* Ā-hă-zī-́ăh when he began to reign; and he reigned one year in Jerusalem. And his mother's name *was* Ăth-ă-lī-́ăh, the [8]daughter of Omri king of Israel.

27 And [t]he walked in the way of the house of Ahab, and did evil in the sight of the LORD, as *did* the house of Ahab: for he *was* the son in law of the house of Ahab.

28 ¶ And he went with Joram the son of Ahab to the war against Hă-zā-́ĕl king of Syria in Rā-́mŏth–gĭl-́ĕ-ăd; and the Syrians wounded Joram.

29 And [u]king Joram went back to be healed in Jĕz-́rēel of the wounds

c ch. 5.27.
d ch. 4.35.
1 Or, eunuch.
e 1 Ki. 19.15.
f 1 Sam. 9.7. ch. 5.5.
g Josh. 9.14. 1 Sam. 9.9. ch. 1.2.
2 in his hand.
3 and set it.
h Gen. 45.2. Ps. 119.136. Jer. 9.1,18. Luke 19.41.
i ch. 10.32. ch. 12.17. Amos 1.3.
j ch. 15.16. Hos. 13.16. Amos 1.13.
k 1 Sam. 17. 43.
l 1 Ki. 19.15.
m 2 Chr. 21. 3,4.
4 reigned. Began to reign in consort with his father.
n 2 Chr. 21.5.
o 2 Sam. 7.13. 1 Ki. 11.36. 2 Chr. 21.7. Ps. 36.37.
5 candle, or, lamp.
p Gen. 27.40. ch. 3.27. 2 Chr. 21.8-10.
q 1 Ki. 22.47.
6 And so fulfilled, Gen. 27.40.
r Josh. 21.13. 2 Chr. 21.10.
7 called Azariah, 2 Chr. 22.6; and Jehoahaz, 2 Chr. 21.17. 2 Chr. 25.23.
s 2 Chr. 22.2.
8 Or, granddaughter.
t 2 Chr. 22.3, 4.
u ch. 9.15.

[9]which the Syrians had given him at
[10]Rā´măh, when he fought against Hă-
zā´ĕl king of Syria. And [v]Ā-hă-zī´ăh
the son of Jĕ-hôr´ăm king of Judah
went down to see Joram the son of
Ahab in Jĕz´rēel, because he was
[11]sick.

CHAPTER 9

AND Ē-lī´shă the prophet called
one of the [a]children of the prophets, and said unto him, [b]Gird up thy
loins, and take this box of oil in thine
hand, and [c]go to Rā´mŏth–gĭl´ĕ-ăd:
2 And when thou comest thither,
look out there Jehu the son of Jĕ-hŏsh´-
ă-phăt the son of Nimshi, and go in,
and make him arise up from among
his brethren, and carry him to an [1]in-
ner chamber;
3 Then [d]take the box of oil, and pour
it on his head, and say, Thus saith the
LORD, I have anointed thee king over
Israel. Then open the door, and flee,
and tarry not.
4 ¶ So the young man, *even* the
young man the prophet, went to Rā´-
mŏth–gĭl´ĕ-ăd.
5 And when he came, behold, the
captains of the host *were* sitting; and
he said, I have an errand to thee, O
captain. And Jehu said, Unto which
of all us? And he said, To thee, O
captain.
6 And he arose, and went into the
house; and he poured the oil on his
head, and said unto him, Thus [e]saith
the LORD God of Israel, I have anointed thee king over the people of the
LORD, *even* over Israel.
7 And thou shalt smite the house of
Ahab thy master, that [f]I may avenge
the blood of my servants the prophets, and the blood of all the servants
of the LORD, [g]at the hand of Jĕz´ĕ-bĕl.
8 For the whole house of Ahab shall
perish: and [h]I will cut off from Ahab
[i]him that pisseth against the wall, and
him [j]that is shut up and left in Israel:
9 And I will make the house of Ahab
like the house of [k]Jĕr-ŏ-bō´ăm the son
of Nē´băt, and like the house of [l]Bā-
ăsh´ă the son of Ă-hī´jăh:
10 And [m]the dogs shall eat Jĕz´ĕ-bĕl
in the portion of Jĕz´rēel, and *there
shall be* none to bury *her*. And he opened the door, and fled.
11 ¶ Then Jehu came forth to the
servants of his lord: and *one* said unto
him, *Is* all well? wherefore came [n]this
mad *fellow* to thee? And he said unto
them, Ye know the man, and his communication.
12 And they said, *It is* false; tell us

9 wherewith the Syrians had wounded.
10 Ramoth.
v ch. 9.16. 2 Chr. 22.6.
11 wounded.
CHAP. 9
a 1 Ki. 20.35. Jer. 1.9,10.
b ch. 4.29. Jer. 1.17.
c ch. 8.28.
1 chamber in a chamber.
d 1 Ki. 19.16.
e 1 Sam. 2.7, 8. 2 Chr. 22.7. Ps. 75.6,7. Ps. 83.18. Jer. 27.5. Dan. 2.21.
f Ps. 58.10, 11.
g 1 Ki. 18.4.
h 1 Ki. 14.10. Ps. 76. 8-10, 12. Ps. 110.5.
i 1 Sam. 25. 22.
j Deut. 32.36.
k 1 Ki. 14.10.
l 1 Ki. 16.3.
m vers. 35-37. 1 Ki. 14.10, 11. Jer. 15.3.
n Jer. 29.26. Hosea 9.7. Mark 3.21. John 10.20. Acts 17.18. 1 Cor. 4.10. 2 Cor. 5.13.
o Matt. 21.7. Mark 11.7, 8.
2 reigneth.
p ch. 8.29. 2 Chr. 22.6.
3 Jehoram.
4 smote.
5 let no escaper go, etc.
6 Or, marching.
7 in madness.
8 Bind.
q ch. 8.29. 2 Chr. 22.7.
9 found.
r 1 Ki. 14. 30-33. Isa. 47.9,11. Nah. 3.4. Rev. 2.20. Rev. 17.1-5.

now. And he said, Thus and thus
spake he to me, saying, Thus saith the
LORD, I have anointed thee king over
Israel.
13 Then they hasted, and [o]took every
man his garment, and put *it* under
him on the top of the stairs, and blew
with trumpets, saying, Jehu [2]is king
14 So Jehu the son of Jĕ-hŏsh´ă-phă
the son of Nimshi conspired agains
Joram. (Now Joram had kept Rā-
mŏth–gĭl´ĕ-ăd, he and all Israel, because of Hă-zā´ĕl king of Syria.
15 But [p]king [3]Joram was returned to
be healed in Jĕz´rēel of the wounds
which the Syrians [4]had given him
when he fought with Hă-zā´ĕl king o
Syria.) And Jehu said, If it be you
minds, *then* [5]let none go forth *nor* es
cape out of the city to go to tell *it* i
Jĕz´rēel.
16 So Jehu rode in a chariot, an
went to Jĕz´rēel; for Joram lay there
And Ā-hă-zī´ăh king of Judah wa
come down to see Joram.
17 And there stood a watchman o
the tower in Jĕz´rēel, and he spied th
company of Jehu as he came, an
said, I see a company. And Joran
said, Take an horseman, and send t
meet him, and let him say, *Is it* peace
18 So there went one on horseback
to meet him, and said, Thus saith th
king, *Is it* peace? And Jehu said, Wha
hast thou to do with peace? turn the
behind me. And the watchman told
saying, The messenger came to them
but he cometh not again.
19 Then he sent out a second o
horseback, which came to them, an
said, Thus saith the king, *Is it* peace
And Jehu answered, What hast tho
to do with peace? turn thee behin
me.
20 And the watchman told, saying
He came even unto them, and comet
not again: and the [6]driving *is* like th
driving of Jehu the son of Nimshi; fo
he driveth [7]furiously.
21 And Joram said, [8]Make ready
And his chariot was made ready. An
[q]Joram king of Israel and Ā-hă-zī´ă
king of Judah went out, each in hi
chariot, and they went out agains
Jehu, and [9]met him in the portion o
Naboth the Jĕz´rēel-īte.
22 And it came to pass, when Joran
saw Jehu, that he said, *Is it* peace
Jehu? And he answered, What peace
[r]so long as the whoredoms of th
mother Jĕz´ĕ-bĕl and her witchcraft
are so many?
23 And Joram turned his hands, an

led, and said to Ā-hă-zī-ăh, *There is*
reachery, O Ā-hă-zī-ăh.
24 And Jehu [10]drew a bow with his
ull strength, and smote Jĕ-hôr-âm
etween his arms, and the arrow went
ut at his heart, and he [11]sunk down
n his chariot.
25 Then said *Jehu* to Bĭd-kär his cap-
ain, Take up, *and* cast him in the por-
ion of the field of Naboth the Jĕz-
ēel-ite: for remember how that, when
and thou rode together after Ahab
is father, [s]the LORD laid this burden
pon him;
26 Surely I have seen yesterday the
[12]blood of Naboth, and the blood of
is sons, saith the LORD; and [t]I will
equite thee in this [13]plat, saith the
ORD. Now therefore take *and* cast
im into the plat *of ground*, according
o the word of the LORD.
27 ¶ But when Ā-hă-zī-ăh the king of
udah saw *this*, he fled by the way of
he garden house. And Jehu followed
fter him, and said, Smite him also in
he chariot. *And they did so* at the go-
ng up to Gur, which *is* by Ĭb-lĕ-ăm.
nd he fled to [u]Mĕ-gĭd-dō, and died
here.
28 And his servants carried him in a
hariot to Jerusalem, and buried him
n his sepulchre with his fathers in the
ity of David.
29 And in the eleventh year of Joram
e son of Ahab began Ā-hă-zī-ăh to
eign [14]over Judah.
30 ¶ And when Jehu was come to
ĕz-rēel, Jĕz-ĕ-bĕl heard *of it;* and [v]she
painted her face, and tired her head,
nd looked out at a window.
31 And as Jehu entered in at the
ate, she said, [w]*Had* Zimri peace, who
ew his master?
32 And he lifted up his face to the
indow, and said, Who *is* on my side?
ho? And there looked out to him
wo *or* three [16]eunuchs.
33 And he said, Throw her down. So
ey threw her down: and *some* of her
lood was sprinkled on the wall, and
n the horses: and he trode her under
oot.
34 And when he was come in, he did
at and drink, and said, Go, see now
this cursed *woman*, and bury her: for
she *is* a king's daughter.
35 And they went to bury her: but
ey found no more of her than the
ull, and the feet, and the palms of
er hands.
36 Wherefore they came again, and
old him. And he said, This *is* the word
f the LORD, which he spake [17]by his

10 filled his hand with a bow.
11 bowed.
s 1 Ki. 21.29. Jer. 23.33-38. Nah. 1.1. Matt. 11.30.
12 bloods.
t 1 Ki. 21.19. Esther 7.10.
13 Or, portion.
u Judg. 1.27. 1 Ki. 9.15. 2 Chr. 22.9. Zech. 12.11.
14 As viceroy to his father in his sickness, 2 Chr. 21.18. But in Joram's 12th year he began to reign alone, ch. 8.25.
v Eze. 23.40.
15 put her eyes in painting.
w 1 Ki. 16.9-20.
16 Or, chamberlains.
x Pro. 10.7. Isa. 65.15.
y 1 Ki. 16.31.
17 by the hand of.
z 1 Ki. 21.23.
a Ps. 83.10. Jer. 8.2.

CHAP. 10
a Deut. 16.18.
1 nourishers.
b ch. 5.6.
c ch. 9.24,27. Luke 14.31.
d Josh. 9.11, 24,25.
2 for me.
e Ex. 20.5. Job 21.19.
f 1 Ki. 21.21.
g ch. 9.14,24. Hosea 1.4.
h 1 Sam. 3.19. Ps. 33.11. Isa. 14.27. Matt. 24.35. 1 Pet. 1.25.

servant Ē-lī-jăh the Tĭsh-bīte, saying,
[z]In the portion of Jĕz-rēel shall dogs
eat the flesh of Jĕz-ĕ-bĕl:
37 And the carcase of Jĕz-ĕ-bĕl shall
be [a]as dung upon the face of the field
in the portion of Jĕz-rēel; *so* that they
shall not say, This *is* Jĕz-ĕ-bĕl.

CHAPTER 10

AND Ahab had seventy sons in Să-
mâr-ĭ-ă. And Jehu wrote letters,
and sent to Să-mâr-ĭ-ă, unto the [a]rul-
ers of Jĕz-rēel, to the elders, and to
[1]them that brought up Ahab's *children*, saying,
2 Now as [b]soon as this letter cometh
to you, seeing your master's sons *are*
with you, and *there are* with you chariots and horses, a fenced city also, and
armour;
3 Look even out the best and meetest
of your master's sons, and set *him* on
his father's throne, and fight for your
master's house.
4 But they were exceedingly afraid,
and said, Behold, [c]two kings stood
not before him: how then shall we
stand?
5 And he that *was* over the house,
and he that *was* over the city, the
elders also, and the bringers up *of the
children*, sent to Jehu, saying, We [d]*are*
thy servants, and will do all that thou
shalt bid us; we will not make any
king: do thou *that which is* good in
thine eyes.
6 Then he wrote a letter the second
time to them, saying, If ye *be* [2]mine,
and *if* ye will hearken unto my voice,
take ye the heads of the men your
master's [e]sons, and come to me to
Jĕz-rēel by to morrow this time. Now
the king's sons, *being* seventy persons,
were with the great men of the city,
which brought them up.
7 And it came to pass, when the letter came to them, that they took the
king's sons, and [f]slew seventy persons, and put their heads in baskets,
and sent him *them* to Jĕz-rēel.
8 ¶ And there came a messenger, and
told him, saying, They have brought
the heads of the king's sons. And he
said, Lay ye them in two heaps at the
entering in of the gate until the morning.
9 And it came to pass in the morning,
that he went out, and stood, and said
to all the people, Ye *be* righteous: behold, [g]I conspired against my master,
and slew him: but who slew all these?
10 Know now that there shall fall
[h]unto the earth nothing of the word of

the LORD, which the LORD spake concerning the house of Ahab: for the
LORD hath done *that* which he spake
[3]by his servant Ē-lī-jăh.
11 So Jehu slew all that remained of
the house of Ahab in Jĕz-rē-el, and all
his great men, and his [4]kinsfolks, and
his [i]priests, until he left him none remaining.
12 ¶ And he arose and departed, and
came to Să-mâr-ĭ-ă. *And* as he *was* at
the [5]shearing house in the way,
13 Jehu [6]met [j]with the brethren of
Ā-hă-zī-ăh king of Judah, and said,
Who *are* ye? And they answered, We
are the brethren of Ā-hă-zī-ăh; and
we go down [7]to salute the children of
the king and the children of the queen.
14 And he said, Take them alive. And
they took them alive, and slew them
at the pit of the shearing house, *even*
two and forty men; neither left he any
of them.
15 ¶ And when he was departed
thence, he [8]lighted on [k]Jĕ-hŏn-ă-dăb
the son of [l]Rē-chăb *coming* to meet
him: and he [9]saluted him, and said to
him, Is thine heart right, as my heart
is with thy heart? And Jĕ-hŏn-ă-dăb
answered, It is. If it be, [m]give *me* thine
hand. And he gave *him* his hand; and
he took him up to him into the chariot.
16 And he said, Come with me, and
see my [n]zeal for the LORD. So they
made him ride in his chariot.
17 And when he came to Să-mâr-ĭ-ă,
[o]he slew all that remained unto Ahab
in Să-mâr-ĭ-ă, till he had destroyed
[p]him, according to the saying of the
LORD, [q]which he spake to Ē-lī-jăh.
18 ¶ And Jehu gathered all the people together, and said unto them,
[r]Ahab served Bā-ăl a little; *but* Jehu
shall serve him much.
19 Now therefore call unto me all the
[s]prophets of Bā-ăl, all his servants,
and all his priests; let none be wanting: for I have a great sacrifice *to do*
to Bā-ăl; whosoever shall be wanting,
he shall not live. But Jehu did *it* in
subtilty, to the intent that he might
destroy the worshippers of Bā-ăl.
20 And Jehu said, [10]Proclaim a solemn assembly for Bā-ăl. And they
proclaimed it.
21 And Jehu sent through all Israel:
and all the worshippers of Bā-ăl came,
so that there was not a man left that
came not. And they came into the
[t]house of Bā-ăl; and the house of Bā-
ăl was [11]full from one end to another.
22 And he said unto him that *was*
over the vestry, Bring forth vestment
for all the worshippers of Bā-ăl. An
he brought them forth vestments.
23 And Jehu went, and Jĕ-hŏn-ă-dăb
the son of Rē-chăb, into the house o
Bā-ăl, and said unto the worshipper
of Bā-ăl, Search, and look that ther
be here with you none of the servant
of the LORD, but the worshippers o
Bā-ăl only.
24 And when they went in to offe
sacrifices and burnt offerings, Jeh
appointed fourscore men without, an
said, *If* any of the men whom I hav
brought into your hands escape, *h*
that letteth him go, [u]his life *shall b*
for the life of him.
25 And it came to pass, as soon as h
had made an end of offering the burn
offering, that Jehu said to the guar
and to the captains, Go in, *and* sla
them; let none come forth. And the
smote them with [12]the edge of th
sword; and the guard and the cap
tains cast *them* out, and went to th
city of the house of Bā-ăl.
26 And they brought forth the [13]im
ages out of the house of Bā-ăl, an
burned them.
27 And they brake down the imag
of Bā-ăl, and brake down the house o
Bā-ăl, and [v]made it a draught hous
unto this day.
28 Thus Jehu destroyed Bā-ăl out o
Israel.
29 ¶ Howbeit *from* the sins of Jĕr-ŏ
bō-ăm the son of Nē-băt, who mad
Israel to sin, Jehu departed not fror
after them, *to wit*, [w]the golden calve
that *were* in Beth-el, and that *were* i
Dan.
30 And the LORD said unto Jehu, Be
cause thou hast done well in executin
that which is right in mine eyes, *an*
hast done unto the house of Aha
according to all that *was* in mine hear
[x]thy children of the fourth *generatio*
shall sit on the throne of Israel.
31 But Jehu [14]took no [y]heed to wal
in the law of the LORD God of Isra
with all his heart: for he departed nc
from [z]the sins of Jĕr-ŏ-bō-ăm, whic
made Israel to sin.
32 ¶ In those days the LORD bega
[15]to cut Israel short: and Hă-ză-
[a]smote them in all the coasts of Israel
33 From Jordan [16]eastward, all th
land of Gilead, the Gadites, and th
Reubenites, and the Mă-năs-sītes
from Ă-rō-ĕr, which *is* by the rive
Arnon, [17]even [b]Gilead and Bā-shăn.
34 Now the rest of the acts of Jehu
and all that he did, and all his migh

3 by the hand of.
4 Or, acquaintance.
i 1 Ki. 18.19.
5 house of shepherds binding sheep.
6 found.
j ch. 8.29.
7 to the peace of, etc.
8 found.
k Jer. 35.6.
l 1 Chr. 2.55.
9 blessed.
m Ezra 10.19.
n Pro. 27.2. Matt. 6.2. Rom. 10.2.
o ch. 9.8. 2 Chr. 22.8.
p Job 18.5-21. Job 31.3. Ps. 34.16. Ps. 145.20. Pro. 2.22. Pro. 10.7,29. Mal. 4.1.
q 1 Ki. 21.21.
r 1 Ki. 16.31, 32.
s 1 Ki. 22.6.
10 Sanctify.
t 1 Ki. 16.32.
11 Or, so full, that they stood mouth to mouth.
u 1 Ki. 20.39.
12 the mouth.
13 statues.
v Ezra 6.11. Dan. 2.5.
w Ex. 32.4. 1 Ki. 12.28, 29. Hos. 8.5,6.
x ch. 13.1.
14 observed not.
y Pro. 4.23.
z Lev. 26. 14, 17. Deut. 28.15. 1 Ki. 12.30. 1 Ki. 13.34.
15 to cut off the ends.
a ch. 8.12. ch. 13.22.
16 toward the rising of the sun.
17 Or, even to Gilead and Bashan.
b Amos 1.3.

are they not written in the book of the
chronicles of the kings of Israel?
35 And Jehu slept with his fathers:
and they buried him in Să-mâr'-ĭ-ă.
And Jĕ-hō'-ă-hăz his son reigned in
his stead.
36 And [18]the time that Jehu reigned
over Israel in Să-mâr'-ĭ-ă *was* twenty
and eight years.

CHAPTER 11

AND when [a]Ăth-ă-lī'-ăh [b]the mother
of Ā-hă-zī'-ăh saw that her son was
dead, she arose and destroyed all the
seed royal.
2 But [2]Jĕ-hŏsh'-ĕ-bă, the daughter of
king Joram, sister of Ā-hă-zī'-ăh, took
Jō'-ăsh the son of Ā-hă-zī'-ăh, and
stole him from among the king's sons
which were slain; and they hid him,
even him and his nurse, in the bedchamber from Ăth-ă-lī'-ăh, so that he
was not slain.
3 And he was with her hid in the
house of the LORD six years. And Ăth-
ă-lī'-ăh did [c]reign over the land.
4 ¶ And [d]the seventh year Jĕ-hôi'-ă-
dă sent and fetched the rulers over
hundreds, with the captains and the
guard, and brought them to him into
the house of the LORD, and made a
covenant with them, and took an oath
of them in the house of the LORD, and
shewed them the king's son.
5 And he commanded them, saying,
This *is* the thing that ye shall do; A
third part of you that enter in [e]on the
sabbath shall even be keepers of the
watch of the king's house;
6 And a third part *shall be* at the gate
of Sur; and a third part at the gate behind the guard: so shall ye keep the
watch of the house, [4]that it be not
broken down.
7 And two [5]parts of all you that go
forth on the sabbath, even they shall
keep the watch of the house of the
LORD about the king.
8 And ye shall compass the king
round about, every man with his
weapons in his hand: and he that
cometh within the ranges, let him be
slain: and be ye with the king as he
goeth out and as he cometh in.
9 And [f]the captains over the hundreds did according to all *things* that
Jĕ-hôi'-ă-dă the priest commanded:
and they took every man his men that
were to come in on the sabbath, with
them that should go out on the sabbath, and came to Jĕ-hôi'-ă-dă the
priest.
10 And to the captains over hundreds
did the priest give king David's [g]spears
and shields, that *were* in the temple of
the LORD.
11 And the guard stood, every man
with his weapons in his hand, round
about the king, from the right [6]corner
of the temple to the left corner of the
temple, *along* by the altar and the
temple.
12 And he brought forth the king's
son, and put the crown upon him, and
gave him the [h]testimony; and they
made him king, and anointed him;
and they clapped their hands, and
said, [7]God save the king.
13 ¶ And [i]when Ăth-ă-lī'-ăh heard the
noise of the guard *and* of the people,
she came to the people into the temple
of the LORD.
14 And when she looked, behold, the
king stood by [j]a pillar, as the manner
was, and the princes and the trumpeters by the king, and all [k]the people of
the land rejoiced, and blew with trumpets: and Ăth-ă-lī'-ăh rent her clothes,
and cried, [l]Treason, Treason.
15 But Jĕ-hôi'-ă-dă the priest commanded the captains of the hundreds,
the officers of the host, and said unto
them, Have her forth without the
ranges: and him that followeth her kill
with the sword. For the priest had
said, Let her not be slain in the house
of the LORD.
16 And they laid hands on her; and
she went by the way by the which the
horses came into the king's house:
[m]and there was she slain.
17 ¶ And Jĕ-hôi'-ă-dă made [n]a covenant between the LORD and the king
and the people, that they should be
the LORD's people; [o]between the king
also and the people.
18 And all the people of the land
went into the [p]house of Bā'-ăl, and
brake it down; his altars and his images [q]brake they in pieces thoroughly,
and slew Măt'-tăn the priest of Bā'-ăl
before the altars. And [r]the priest appointed [8]officers over the house of the
LORD.
19 And he took the rulers over hundreds, and the captains, and the guard,
and all the people of the land; and they
brought down the king from the house
of the LORD, and came by the way of
the gate of the guard to the king's
house. And he sat on the throne of
the kings.
20 And all [s]the people of the land rejoiced, and the city was in quiet: and
they slew Ăth-ă-lī'-ăh with the sword
beside the king's house.

18 the days were.
CHAP. 11
a 2 Chr. 22. 10.
b ch. 8.26.
1 seed of the kingdom.
2 2 Chr. 22. 11. Jehoshabeath.
3 Or, Jehoash.
c 2 Chr. 22. 12. Ps. 12.8.
d 2 Chr. 23.1.
e 1 Chr. 9.25.
4 Or, from breaking up.
5 hands, or, companies.
f 2 Chr. 23.8.
g 1 Sam. 21.9. 2 Sam. 8.7. 1 Chr. 26.26, 27.
6 shoulder.
h Ex. 25.16. Deut. 17.14. Ps. 19.7. Isa. 8.16.
7 Let the king live.
i 2 Chr. 23. 12.
j ch. 23.3.
k Pro. 29.2. Matt. 21.9. Luke 19.37. Rev. 19.1-7.
l 1 Ki. 18.17, 18. ch. 9.23.
m Gen. 9.6. Ex. 21.12, 14. Lev. 24.17. Num. 35.30, 31. Pro. 11.31. Isa. 3.11. Matt. 26.52. Jas. 2.13. Rev. 13.10.
n Deut. 5.2,3. Jer. 11.3,6.
o 1 Sam. 10. 25.
p ch. 10.26. 2 Chr. 23.17.
q Ex. 32.20. Deut. 7.5. Judg. 6.25, 28. 2 Chr. 23.17.
r 2 Chr. 23. 18.
8 offices.
s Pro. 11.10.

21 Seven years old *was* Jĕ-hō-ăsh
when he began to reign.

CHAPTER 12

IN the seventh year of Jehu Jĕ-hō-
ăsh [a]began to reign; and forty years
reigned he in Jerusalem. And his
mother's name *was* Zĭ-bĭ-ăh of Bēer-
shē-bă.
2 And Jĕ-hō-ăsh did *that which was*
right in the sight of the LORD all his
days wherein Jĕ-hoi-ă-dă the priest instructed him.
3 But [b]the high places were not taken
away: the people still sacrificed and
burnt incense in the high places.
4 ¶ And Jĕ-hō-ăsh said to the priests,
[c]All the money of the [1]dedicated things
that is brought into the house of the
LORD, *even* the [d]money of every one
that passeth *the account*, [2]the money
that every man is set at, *and* all the
money that [3]cometh into any man's
heart to bring into the house of the
LORD,
5 Let the priests take *it* to them,
every man of his acquaintance: and
let them repair the breaches of the
house, wheresoever any breach shall
be found.
6 But it was *so, that* in the [4]three and
twentieth year of king Jĕ-hō-ăsh the
[e]priests had not repaired the breaches
of the house.
7 Then king Jĕ-hō-ăsh called for Jĕ-
hoi-ă-dă the priest, and the *other*
priests, and said unto them, Why repair ye not the breaches of the house?
now therefore receive no *more* money
of your acquaintance, but deliver it for
the breaches of the house.
8 And the priests consented to receive no *more* money of the people,
neither to repair the breaches of the
house.
9 But Jĕ-hoi-ă-dă the priest took [f]a
chest, and bored a hole in the lid of it,
and set it beside the altar, on the right
side as one cometh into the house of
the LORD: and the priests that kept
the [5]door put therein all the money
that was brought into the house of the
LORD.
10 And it was *so*, when they saw that
there was much money in the chest,
that the king's [6]scribe and the high
priest came up, and they [7]put up in
bags, and told the money that was
found in the house of the LORD.
11 And they gave the money, being
told, into the hands of them that did
the work, that had the oversight of the
house of the LORD: and they [8]laid it

CHAP. 12
a 2 Chr. 24.1.
b 1 Ki. 15.14. ch. 14.4.
c ch. 22.4.
1 holinesses, or, holy things.
d Ex. 30.13.
2 the money of the souls of his estimation.
3 ascendeth upon the heart of a man.
4 twentieth year and third year.
e 2 Chr. 24.5.
f Luke 21.1.
5 threshold.
6 Or, secretary.
7 bound up.
8 brought it forth.
9 went forth.
g 2 Chr. 34. 12. Matt. 24.45. 1 Cor. 4.2.
h Lev. 5.15. Num. 5.8-10.
i Lev. 7.7. Num. 18.9.
j ch. 8.12.
k 1 Ki. 15.18. ch. 16.8. 2 Chr. 16.2.
10 went up.
11 Or, Beth-millo.
l 2 Chr. 24.26, Zabad.
12 Or, Shimrith.
m 2 Chr. 24. 27.
CHAP. 13
1 the twentieth year and third year.
2 walked after.

out to the carpenters and builder
that wrought upon the house of th
LORD,
12 And to masons, and hewers o
stone, and to buy timber and hewe
stone to repair the breaches of th
house of the LORD, and for all tha
[9]was laid out for the house to repa
it.
13 Howbeit there were not made fo
the house of the LORD bowls of silve
snuffers, basons, trumpets, any ve
sels of gold, or vessels of silver, of th
money *that was* brought into th
house of the LORD:
14 But they gave that to the work
men, and repaired therewith the hou
of the LORD.
15 Moreover they reckoned not wit
the men, into whose hand they deli
ered the money to be bestowed o
workmen: for they dealt [g]faithfully
16 The [h]trespass money and sin mo
ey was not brought into the house o
the LORD: [i]it was the priests'.
17 ¶ Then [j]Hă-zā-ĕl king of Syr
went up, and fought against Gath, ar
took it: and Hă-zā-ĕl set his face to g
up to Jerusalem.
18 And Jĕ-hō-ăsh king of Judah too
[k]all the hallowed things that Jĕ-hŏsh
ă-phăt, and Jĕ-hôr-ăm, and Ā-hă-z
ăh, his fathers, kings of Judah, ha
dedicated, and his own hallowe
things, and all the gold *that was* foun
in the treasures of the house of th
LORD, and in the king's house, ar
sent *it* to Hă-zā-ĕl king of Syria: ar
he [10]went away from Jerusalem.
19 ¶ And the rest of the acts of Jo
ăsh, and all that he did, *are* they no
written in the book of the chronicle
of the kings of Judah?
20 And his servants arose, and mad
a conspiracy, and slew Jō-ăsh in [11]th
house of Mĭl-lō, which goeth down t
Sĭl-lă.
21 For [l]Jō-ză-chăr the son of Shĭm
ĕ-ăth, and Jĕ-hō-ză-băd the son o
[12]Shō-mĕr, his servants, smote hir
and he died; and they buried him wit
his fathers in the city of David: ar
[m]Ăm-ă-zī-ăh his son reigned in h
stead.

CHAPTER 13

IN [1]the three and twentieth year o
Jō-ăsh the son of Ā-hă-zī-ăh king o
Judah Jĕ-hō-ă-hăz the son of Jehu b
gan to reign over Israel in Să-măr-ĭ-
and reigned seventeen years.
2 And he did *that which was* evil i
the sight of the LORD, and [2]followe
the sins of Jĕr-ŏ-bō-ăm the son of N

ăt, which made Israel to sin; he de-
arted not therefrom.
3 ¶ And [a]the anger of the LORD was
indled against Israel, and he deliver-
d them into the hand of Hă-zā-ĕl
king of Syria, and into the hand of
ĕn–hā-dăd the son of Hă-zā-ĕl, all
heir days.
4 And Jĕ-hō-ă-hăz [c]besought the
ORD, and the LORD hearkened unto
im: for [d]he saw the oppression of
srael, because the king of Syria op-
ressed them.
5 (And [e]the LORD gave Israel a savour, so that they went out from under
he hand of the Syrians: and the chil-
ren of Israel dwelt in their tents, [3]as
eforetime.
6 Nevertheless they departed not
rom the sins of the house of Jĕr-ŏ-bō-
m, who made Israel sin, *but* [4]walked
herein: [f]and there [5]remained the
rove also in Să-mâr-ĭ-ă.)
7 Neither did he leave of the people
o Jĕ-hō-ă-hăz but fifty horsemen, and
en chariots, and ten thousand foot-
nen; for the king of Syria had de-
troyed them, [g]and had made them
ike the dust by threshing.
8 ¶ Now the rest of the acts of Jĕ-hō-
-hăz, and all that he did, and his
night, *are* they not written in the book
of the chronicles of the kings of Israel?
9 And Jĕ-hō-ă-hăz slept with his fath-
rs; and they buried him in Să-mâr-
-ă: and Jō-ăsh his son reigned in his
stead.
10 ¶ In the thirty and seventh year of
ō-ăsh king of Judah began [7]Jĕ-hō-
sh the son of Jĕ-hō-ă-hăz to reign
ver Israel in Să-mâr-ĭ-ă, *and reigned*
ixteen years.
11 And he did *that which was* evil in
he sight of the LORD; he departed not
rom all the sins of Jĕr-ŏ-bō-ăm the
on of Nē-băt, who made Israel sin:
ut he walked therein.
12 And [h]the rest of the acts of Jō-ăsh,
nd all that he did, and his [i]might
wherewith he fought against Ăm-ă-
ī-ăh king of Judah, *are* they not writ-
en in the book of the chronicles of the
ings of Israel?
13 And Jō-ăsh slept with his fathers;
nd Jĕr-ŏ-bō-ăm sat upon his throne:
nd Jō-ăsh was buried in Să-mâr-ĭ-ă
with the kings of Israel.
14 ¶ Now Ē-lī-shă was fallen sick of
is sickness whereof he died. And Jō-
ăsh the king of Israel came down unto
im, and wept over his face, and said,
O my father, my father, [j]the chariot
of Israel, and the horsemen thereof.

a Lev. 26.17. Deut. 4.23, 24. Deut. 6.13. Deut. 7.4. Judg. 2.14. Ps. 7.11. Isa. 10.5,6. Nah. 1.3-6.
b ch. 8.12.
c Num. 21.7. Judg. 6.6-8. Ps. 78.34. Jer. 2.27.
d Ex. 3.7. ch. 14.26. Pro. 15.3.
e ch. 14.25, 27. Luke 2.11.
3 as yesterday, and third day.
4 he walked.
f 1 Ki. 16.33.
5 stood.
g Amos 1.3.
6 Alone.
7 In consort with his father.
h ch. 14.15.
i ch. 14.9. 2 Chr. 25.17.
j ch. 2.12.
8 Make thine hand to ride.
k Gen. 49.24.
l 1 Ki. 20.26.
m Ex. 17.11.
9 He prophesied about sixty years.
n ch. 5.2.
10 went down.
o ch. 4.35. Matt. 27.52. John 5.25, 28,29.
p ch. 8.12.
q Ex. 33.19. ch. 14.27. Neh. 9.31. Isa. 30.18, 19. Jer. 12.15. Lam. 3.32.
r Ex. 2.24,25.
s Ex. 32.13. Micah 7.20. Luke 1.54, 55,72,73.
11 face.
12 returned and took.
t vers. 18,19.

CHAP. 14

a ch. 13.10.
b 2 Chr. 25.1.

15 And Ē-lī-shă said unto him, Take
bow and arrows. And he took unto
him bow and arrows.
16 And he said to the king of Israel,
[8]Put thine hand upon the bow. And he
put his hand *upon it:* and Ē-lī-shă put
his [k]hands upon the king's hands.
17 And he said, Open the window
eastward. And he opened *it*. Then Ē-
lī-shă said, Shoot. And he shot. And
he said, The arrow of the LORD's deliverance, and the arrow of deliverance from Syria: for thou shalt smite
the Syrians in [l]Ā-phĕk, till thou have
consumed *them.*
18 And he said, Take the arrows.
And he took *them*. And he said unto
the king of Israel, [m]Smite upon the
ground. And he smote thrice, and
stayed.
19 And the man of God was wroth
with him, and said, Thou shouldest
have smitten five or six times; then
hadst thou smitten Syria till thou
hadst consumed *it:* whereas now thou
shalt smite Syria *but* thrice.
20 ¶ And [9]Ē-lī-shă died, and they
buried him. And [n]the bands of the
Moabites invaded the land at the
coming in of the year.
21 And it came to pass, as they were
burying a man, that, behold, they
spied a band *of men;* and they cast the
man into the sepulchre of Ē-lī-shă:
and when the man [10]was let down, and
touched the bones of Ē-lī-shă, he [o]re-
vived, and stood up on his feet.
22 ¶ But [p]Hă-zā-ĕl king of Syria oppressed Israel all the days of Jĕ-hō-
ă-hăz.
23 And [q]the LORD was gracious unto
them, and had compassion on them,
and had [r]respect unto them, [s]because
of his covenant with Abraham, Isaac,
and Jacob, and would not destroy
them, neither cast he them from his
[11]presence as yet.
24 So Hă-zā-ĕl king of Syria died;
and Bĕn–hā-dăd his son reigned in his
stead.
25 And Jĕ-hō-ăsh the son of Jĕ-hō-
ă-hăz [12]took again out of the hand of
Bĕn–hā-dăd the son of Hă-zā-ĕl the
cities, which he had taken out of the
hand of Jĕ-hō-ă-hăz his father by war.
[t]Three times did Jō-ăsh beat him, and
recovered the cities of Israel.

CHAPTER 14

IN [a]the second year of Jō-ăsh son of
Jĕ-hō-ă-hăz king of Israel reigned
[b]Ăm-ă-zī-ăh the son of Jō-ăsh king of
Judah.

2 He was twenty and five years old when he began to reign, and reigned twenty and nine years in Jerusalem. And his mother's name *was* Jĕ-hō-ăd-dăn of Jerusalem.

3 And he did *that which was* right in the sight of the LORD, yet not like David his father: he did according to all things as Jō-ăsh his father did.

4 Howbeit [c]the high places were not taken away: as yet the people did sacrifice and burnt incense on the high places.

5 ¶ And it came to pass, as soon as the kingdom was confirmed in his hand, that he slew his servants which [d]had slain the king his father.

6 But the children of the murderers he slew not: according unto that which is written in the book of the law of Moses, wherein the LORD commanded, saying, The fathers [e]shall not be put to death for the children, nor the children be put to death for the fathers; but every man shall be put to death for his own sin.

7 He [f]slew of Ē-dom in [g]the valley of salt ten thousand, and took [1]Sē-lăh by war, and called the name of it [h]Jŏk-thĕ-ĕl unto this day.

8 ¶ Then [i]Ăm-ă-zī-ăh sent messengers to Jĕ-hō-ăsh, the son of Jĕ-hō-ă-hăz son of Jehu, king of Israel, saying, [j]Come, let us look one another in the face.

9 And Jĕ-hō-ăsh the king of Israel sent to Ăm-ă-zī-ăh king of Judah, saying, [k]The thistle that *was* in Lĕb-ă-non sent to the cedar [l]that *was* in Lĕb-ă-non, saying, Give thy daughter to my son to wife: and there passed by a wild beast that *was* in Lĕb-ă-non, and trode down the thistle.

10 Thou hast indeed smitten Ē-dom, and thine [m]heart hath lifted thee up: glory *of this*, and tarry [2]at home: for why shouldest thou [n]meddle to *thy* hurt, that thou shouldest fall, *even* thou, and Judah with thee?

11 But Ăm-ă-zī-ăh would not hear. Therefore Jĕ-hō-ăsh king of Israel went up; and he and Ăm-ă-zī-ăh king of Judah looked one another in the face at [o]Bĕth-shē-mĕsh, which *belongeth* to Judah.

12 And Judah [3]was put to the worse before Israel; and they fled every man to their tents.

13 And Jĕ-hō-ăsh king of Israel took Ăm-ă-zī-ăh king of Judah, the son of Jĕ-hō-ăsh the son of Ā-hă-zī-ăh, at Bĕth-shē-mĕsh, and came to Jerusalem, and brake down the wall of Jerusalem from the [p]gate of Ē-phră-ĭm un to [q]the corner gate, four hundre cubits.

c 1 Ki. 15.14. ch. 12.3.
d ch. 12.20.
e Deut. 24.16.
f 2 Chr. 25. 11.
g 2 Sam. 8.13. Ps. 60, title.
1 Or, The rock.
h Josh. 15.38.
i 2 Chr. 25. 17,18.
j Pro. 17.14.
k Judg. 9.8.
l 1 Ki. 4.33.
m 2 Chr. 32. 25. Eze. 28.2,17. Hab. 2.4.
2 at thy house.
n 2 Chr. 35. 21. Pro. 26.17.
o Josh. 21.16.
3 was smitten.
p 2 Chr. 25. 23. Neh. 8.16.
q Jer. 31.38. Zech. 14.10.
r ch. 24.13.
s ch. 13.12.
t 2 Chr. 25. 25.
u ch. 12.20, 21. 2 Chr. 25.27.
v Josh. 10.31.
w ch. 15.13. 2 Chr. 26.1. Uzziah.
x Deut. 2.8. 1 Ki. 9.26. ch. 16.6. It was a port on the Red sea.
4 Now he begins to reign alone.
y Num. 13. 21. Eze. 47.16-18. Amos 6.14.
z Deut. 3.17.
a Jonah 1.1. Matt. 12.39.
b Josh. 19.13.
c Ex. 3.7,9. ch. 13.4.
d Deut. 32. 36.
e ch. 13.5.
f 2 Sam. 8.6.

14 And he took all [r]the gold and sil ver, and all the vessels that were foun in the house of the LORD, and in th treasures of the king's house, an hostages, and returned to Să-mâr-ĭ-ă

15 ¶ Now [s]the rest of the acts of Jĕ hō-ăsh which he did, and his might and how he fought with Ăm-ă-zī-ăl king of Judah, *are* they not written i the book of the chronicles of the king of Israel?

16 And Jĕ-hō-ăsh slept with his fath ers, and was buried in Să-mâr-ĭ-ă wit the kings of Israel; and Jĕr-ŏ-bō-ăn his son reigned in his stead.

17 ¶ And [t]Ăm-ă-zī-ăh the son of Jō ăsh king of Judah lived after the deat of Jĕ-hō-ăsh son of Jĕ-hō-ă-hăz kin of Israel fifteen years.

18 And the rest of the acts of Ăm-ă zī-ăh, *are* they not written in the boo of the chronicles of the kings o Judah?

19 Now [u]they made a conspirac against him in Jerusalem: and he fle to [v]Lā-chĭsh; but they sent after hin to Lā-chĭsh, and slew him there.

20 And they brought him on horses and he was buried at Jerusalem wit his fathers in the city of David.

21 ¶ And all the people of Judah too [w]Ăz-ă-rī-ăh, which *was* sixteen year old, and made him king instead of hi father Ăm-ă-zī-ăh.

22 He built [x]Ē-lăth, and restored i to Judah, after that the king slep with his fathers.

23 ¶ In [4]the fifteenth year of Ăm-ă zī-ăh the son of Jō-ăsh king of Juda Jĕr-ŏ-bō-ăm the son of Jō-ăsh king o Israel began to reign in Să-mâr-ĭ-ă *and reigned* forty and one years.

24 And he did *that which was* evil i the sight of the LORD: he departed no from all the sins of Jĕr-ŏ-bō-ăm th son of Nē-băt, who made Israel to sin

25 He restored the coast of Israe from [y]the entering of Hā-măth unt [z]the sea of the plain, according to th word of the LORD God of Israel, whic he spake by the hand of his servan [a]Jonah, the son of Ā-mĭt-tāī, the pro phet, which *was* of [b]Găth-hē-phĕr.

26 For the LORD [c]saw the affliction o Israel, *that it was* very bitter: fo [d]*there was* not any shut up, nor an left, nor any helper for Israel.

27 And [e]the LORD said not that h would blot out the name of Israel fron under heaven: but he saved them b

he hand of Jĕr-ŏ-bō-ăm the son of
ō-ăsh.
28 ¶ Now the rest of the acts of Jĕr-
-bō-ăm, and all that he did, and his
night, how he warred, and how he re-
overed Damascus, and Hā-măth,
which belonged to Judah, for Israel,
re they not written in the book of the
hronicles of the kings of Israel?
29 And Jĕr-ŏ-bō-ăm slept with his
athers, *even* with the kings of Israel;
nd [5]Zăch-ă-rī-ăh his son reigned in
is stead.

CHAPTER 15

IN the [1]twenty and seventh year of
Jĕr-ŏ-bō-ăm king of Israel began
Ăz-ă-rī-ăh son of Ăm-ă-zī-ăh king of
udah to reign.
2 Sixteen years old was he when he
egan to reign, and he reigned two
nd fifty years in Jerusalem. And his
nother's name *was* Jĕch-ŏ-lī-ăh of
erusalem.
3 And he did *that which was* right in
he sight of the LORD, according to all
hat his father Ăm-ă-zī-ăh had done;
4 Save [b]that the high places were not
emoved: the people sacrificed and
urnt incense still on the high places.
5 ¶ And the LORD [c]smote the king,
o that he was a leper unto the day of
is death, and [d]dwelt in a several
ouse. And Jō-thăm the king's son
vas over the house, judging the
eople of the land.
6 And the rest of the acts of Ăz-ă-rī-
h, and all that he did, *are* they not
vritten in the book of the chronicles
f the kings of Judah?
7 So Ăz-ă-rī-ăh slept with his fathers;
nd [e]they buried him with his fathers
n the city of David: and Jō-thăm his
on reigned in his stead.
8 ¶ In the thirty and eighth year of
z-ă-rī-ăh king of Judah did Zăch-ă-
ī-ăh the son of Jĕr-ŏ-bō-ăm reign over
srael in Să-mâr-ĭ-ă six months.
9 And he did *that which was* evil in
he sight of the LORD, as his fathers
ad done: he departed not from the
ins of Jĕr-ŏ-bō-ăm the son of Nē-băt,
vho made Israel to sin.
10 And Shăl-lŭm the son of Jā-bĕsh
onspired against him, and [f]smote
im before the people, and slew him,
nd reigned in his stead.
11 And the rest of the acts of Zăch-
-rī-ăh, behold, they *are* written in the
ook of the chronicles of the kings of
srael.
12 This *was* [g]the word of the LORD
vhich he spake unto Jehu, saying,
Thy sons shall sit on the throne of Israel unto the fourth *generation*. And
so it came to pass.
13 ¶ Shăl-lŭm the son of Jā-bĕsh began to reign in the nine and thirtieth
year of Ŭz-zī-ăh [h]king of Judah; and
he reigned [2]a full month in Să-mâr-ĭ-ă.
14 For Mĕn-ă-hĕm the son of Gā-dī
went up from [i]Tĭr-zăh, and came to
Să-mâr-ĭ-ă, and smote Shăl-lŭm the
son of Jā-bĕsh in Să-mâr-ĭ-ă, and slew
him, and reigned in his stead.
15 And the rest of the acts of Shăl-
lŭm, and his conspiracy which he
made, behold, they *are* written in the
book of the chronicles of the kings of
Israel.
16 ¶ Then Mĕn-ă-hĕm smote [j]Tĭph-
săh, and all that *were* therein, and the
coasts thereof from Tĭr-zăh: because
they opened not *to him*, therefore he
smote *it; and* all [k]the women therein
that were with child he ripped up.
17 In the nine and thirtieth year of
Ăz-ă-rī-ăh king of Judah began Mĕn-
ă-hĕm the son of Gā-dī to reign over
Israel, *and reigned* ten years in Să-
mâr-ĭ-ă.
18 And he did *that which was* evil in
the sight of the LORD: he departed not
all his days from the sins of Jĕr-ŏ-bō-
ăm the son of Nē-băt, who made Israel
to sin.
19 *And* [l]Pŭl the king of Assyria came
against the land: and Mĕn-ă-hĕm
gave Pŭl a thousand talents of silver,
that his hand might be with him to
[m]confirm the kingdom in his hand.
20 And Mĕn-ă-hĕm [3]exacted the
money of Israel, *even* of all the mighty
men of wealth, of each man fifty shekels of silver, to give to the king of
Assyria. So the king of Assyria turned
back, and stayed not there in the land.
21 ¶ And the rest of the acts of Mĕn-
ă-hĕm, and all that he did, *are* they
not written in the book of the chronicles of the kings of Israel?
22 And Mĕn-ă-hĕm slept with his
fathers; and Pĕk-ă-hī-ăh his son reigned in his stead.
23 ¶ In the fiftieth year of Ăz-ă-rī-ăh
king of Judah Pĕk-ă-hī-ăh the son of
Mĕn-ă-hĕm began to reign over Israel in Să-mâr-ĭ-ă, *and reigned* [n]two
years.
24 And he did *that which was* evil in
the sight of the LORD: he departed not
from the sins of Jĕr-ŏ-bō-ăm the son
of Nē-băt, who made Israel to sin.
25 But Pē-kăh the son of Rĕm-ă-lī-
ăh, a captain of his, conspired against
him, and smote him in Să-mâr-ĭ-ă, in

5 After an interregnum of 11 years.

CHAP. 15

1 This is the 27th year of Jeroboam's partnership in the kingdom with his father, who made him consort at his going to the Syrian wars. It is the 16th year of Jeroboam's monarchy.
a ch. 14.21.
b ch. 12.3.
c 2 Chr. 26. 19.
d Lev. 13.46.
e 2 Chr. 26. 23.
f As prophesied. Hosea 1.4. Amos 7.9. Job 20.4-29. Job 27.13-23. Job 31.2,3. Ps. 1.4. Ps. 37.37. Ps. 52.3,5. Pro. 2.22.
g ch. 10.30. Job 23.13. Ps. 33.11. Ps. 119.89. Isa. 14.27. Matt. 24.35. 1 Pet. 1.25.
h 2 Chr. 26.1. Matt. 1.8. Ozias ver. 1. Azariah.
2 a month of days.
i Josh. 12.24. Song 6.4.
j 1 Ki. 4.24.
k ch. 8.12. 2 Chr. 36.17. Isa. 13.16, 18.
l 1 Chr. 5.26. Isa. 9.1.
m ch. 14.5.
3 caused to come forth.
n 1 Ki. 15.25. Job 20.5.

the palace of the king's house, with
Ăr´-gŏb and Ăr´-ĭ-ēh, and with him fifty
men of the Gileadites: and he killed
him, and reigned in his room.
26 And the rest of the acts of Pĕk-ă-
hī´-ăh, and all that he did, behold, they
are written in the book of the chronicles of the kings of Israel.
27 ¶ In the two and fiftieth year of
Ăz-ă-rī´-ăh king of Judah Pē´-kăh [o]the
son of Rĕm-ă-lī´-ăh began to reign over
Israel in Să-mâr´-ĭ-ă, *and reigned* twenty years.
28 And he did *that which was* evil in
the sight of the LORD: he departed
not from the sins of Jĕr-ŏ-bō´-ăm the
son of Nē´-băt, who made Israel to
sin.
29 In the days of Pē´-kăh king of Israel [p]came Tĭg´-lăth–pĭ-lē´-ṡĕr king of
Assyria, and took [q]Ī´-jŏn, and Ā´-bĕl–
bĕth–mā´-ă-chăh, and Jă-nō´-ăh, and
Kē´-dĕsh, and Hā´-zôr, and Gilead, and
Galilee, all the land of Năph´-tă-lī, and
carried them captive to Assyria.
30 And Hō-shē´-ă the son of Ē´-lăh
made a conspiracy against Pē´-kăh the
son of Rĕm-ă-lī´-ăh, and smote him,
and slew him, and reigned [4]in his
stead, [5]in the twentieth year of Jō´-
thăm the son of Ŭz-zī´-ăh.
31 And the rest of the acts of Pē´-kăh,
and all that he did, behold, they *are*
written in the book of the chronicles
of the kings of Israel.
32 ¶ In the second year of Pē´-kăh the
son of Rĕm-ă-lī´-ăh king of Israel began [r]Jō´-thăm the son of Ŭz-zī´-ăh king
of Judah to reign.
33 Five and twenty years old was he
when he began to reign, and he reigned sixteen years in Jerusalem. And
his mother's name *was* Jĕ-rû´-shă, the
daughter of Zā´-dŏk.
34 And he did *that which was* right
in the sight of the LORD: he did according to all that his father Ŭz-zī´-ăh
had done.
35 ¶ Howbeit [s]the high places were
not removed: the people sacrificed
and burned incense still in the high
places. [t]He built the higher gate of the
house of the LORD.
36 ¶ Now the rest of the acts of Jō´-
thăm, and all that he did, *are* they not
written in the book of the chronicles
of the kings of Judah?
37 In [u]those days the LORD began to
send against Judah Rē´-zĭn [v]the king
of Syria, and Pē´-kăh the son of Rĕm-
ă-lī´-ăh.
38 And Jō´-thăm slept with his fathers, and was buried with his fathers in

o 2 Chr. 28.6. Isa. 7.1.
p 1 Chr. 5.26. Isa. 9.1.
q 1 Ki. 15.20.
4 After an anarchy for some years.
5 In the fourth year of Ahaz, in the 20th year after Jotham, had begun to reign.
r 1 Chr. 3.12. Matt. 1.9.
s ver. 4.
t 2 Chr. 27.3.
u ch. 10.32. 2 Chr. 28.6. At the end of Jotham's reign.
v 2 Chr. 28.6. Isa. 7.1.

CHAP. 16

a 2 Chr. 28.1.
b Lev. 18.21. Deut. 18.10. ch. 17.17. 2 Chr. 28.3. Ps. 106.37. Jer. 7.31. Eze. 16.20.
c Deut. 12.31. ch. 21.2,11. 2 Chr. 33.2.
d Isa. 57.5-7. Jer. 17.2.
e Isa. 7.1.
f ch. 14.22.
1 Eloth.
g ch. 15.29.
2 Tilgath-pileser. 1 Chr. 5.26. 2 Chr. 28.20. Tilgath-pilneser.
h ch. 12.18.
3 Dammesek.
i Foretold, Amos 1.5.
4 That is, Media.

the city of David his father: and Aha
his son reigned in his stead.

CHAPTER 16

IN the seventeenth year of Pē´-kă
the son of Rĕm-ă-lī´-ăh [a]Ahaz th
son of Jō´-thăm king of Judah bega
to reign.
2 Twenty years old *was* Ahaz whe
he began to reign, and reigned sixtee
years in Jerusalem, and did not *tha*
which was right in the sight of th
LORD his God, like David his fathe
3 But he walked in the way of th
kings of Israel, yea, [b]and made his so
to pass through the fire, according t
the [c]abominations of the heathen
whom the LORD cast out from befor
the children of Israel.
4 And he sacrificed and burnt in
cense in the high places, and on [d]th
hills, and under every green tree.
5 ¶ Then [e]Rē´-zĭn king of Syria an
Pē´-kăh son of Rĕm-ă-lī´-ăh king of Is
rael came up to Jerusalem to war: an
they besieged Ahaz, but could no
overcome *him*.
6 At that time Rē´-zĭn king of Syri
[f]recovered Ē´-lăth to Syria, and drav
the Jews from [1]Ē´-lăth: and the Syrian
came to Ē´-lăth, and dwelt there unt
this day.
7 So Ahaz sent messengers [g]to [2]Tĭg
lăth–pĭ-lē´-ṡĕr king of Assyria, saying
I *am* thy servant and thy son: come up
and save me out of the hand of th
king of Syria, and out of the hand o
the king of Israel, which rise u
against me.
8 And Ahaz [h]took the silver and gol
that was found in the house of th
LORD, and in the treasures of th
king's house, and sent *it for* a presen
to the king of Assyria.
9 And the king of Assyria hearkene
unto him: for the king of Assyria wen
up against [3]Damascus, and [i]took it
and carried *the people of* it captive t
[4]Kīr, and slew Rē´-zĭn.
10 ¶ And king Ahaz went to Damas
cus to meet Tĭg-lăth–pĭ-lē´-ṡĕr king o
Assyria, and saw an altar that *was* a
Damascus: and king Ahaz sent to Ū
rī´-jăh the priest the fashion of th
altar, and the pattern of it, accordin
to all the workmanship thereof.
11 And Ū-rī´-jăh the priest built a
altar according to all that king Aha
had sent from Damascus: so Ū-rī´-jă
the priest made *it* against king Aha
came from Damascus.
12 And when the king was come fro
Damascus, the king saw the altar: an

the king approached to the altar, and
offered thereon.
13 And he burnt his burnt offering
and his meat offering, and poured his
drink offering, and sprinkled the
blood of [5]his peace offerings, upon
he altar.
14 And he brought also [k]the brasen
altar, which *was* before the LORD,
from the forefront of the house, from
between the altar and the house of the
LORD, and put it on the north side of
he altar.
15 And king Ahaz commanded Ū-rī-
āh the priest, saying, Upon the great
altar burn the [l]morning burnt offering, and the evening meat offering,
and the king's burnt sacrifice, and his
meat offering, with the burnt offering
of all the people of the land, and their
meat offering, and their drink offerings; and sprinkle upon it all the blood
of the burnt offering, and all the blood
of the sacrifice: and the brasen altar
shall be for me [m]to inquire *by*.
16 Thus did Ū-rī-jăh the priest, according to all that king Ahaz commanded.
17 ¶ And [n]king Ahaz cut off the [o]bor-
ders of the bases, and removed the
laver from off them; and took down
the sea from off the brasen oxen that
were under it, and put it upon a pavement of stones.
18 And the covert for the sabbath
that they had built in the house, and
the king's entry without, turned he
from the house of the LORD for the
king of Assyria.
19 ¶ Now the rest of the acts of Ahaz
which he did, *are* they not written in
the book of the chronicles of the kings
of Judah?
20 And Ahaz slept with his fathers,
and was [q]buried with his fathers in the
city of David: and Hĕz-ē-kī-āh his son
reigned in his stead.

CHAPTER 17

IN the twelfth year of Ahaz king of
Judah began [a]Hō-shē-ă the son of
Ē-lăh to reign in Să-mâr-ĭ-ă over Israel nine years.
2 And he did *that which was* evil in
the sight of the LORD, but not as the
kings of Israel that were before
him.
3 ¶ Against him came up [b]Shăl-măn-
ē-sĕr king of Assyria; and Hō-shē-ă
became his servant, and [1]gave him
presents.
4 And the king of Assyria found conspiracy in Hō-shē-ă: for he had sent

j 2 Chr. 26. 16,19.
5 which were his.
k Ex. 40.6,29. 2 Chr. 4.1.
l Ex. 29.39, 40,41.
m Gen. 44.5. 2 Chr. 33.6. Isa. 2.6. Hosea 4.12.
n 2 Chr. 28. 24.
o 1 Ki. 7.27.
p ch. 25.13-16. 2 Chr. 4.15.
q ch. 21.18-26. 2 Chr. 28.27.

CHAP. 17

a After an interregnum. ch. 15.30.
b ch. 18.9.
1 rendered.
2 Or, tribute.
c ch. 18.9.
d ch. 18.10. Hos. 13.16, foretold.
e Lev. 26.32. Deut. 28.36, 64.
f 1 Chr. 5.26.
g Lev. 18.3. Deut. 18.9. ch. 16.3.
h Deut. 13.6. Eze. 8.12.
i ch. 18.8.
j Isa. 57.5.
3 statues.
k Ex. 34.13. Deut. 16.21. Micah 5.14.
l Deut. 12.2. ch. 16.4.
m Ex. 20.3. Lev. 26.1. Deut. 5.7.
n Deut. 4.19.
4 by the hand of all.
o 1 Sam. 9.9.
p Isa. 1.16-20. Jer. 18.11.
q Deut. 31.27. Pro. 29.1.
r Deut. 29.25.
s Deut. 32.21. 1 Cor. 8.4.
t Ps. 115.8. Jer. 2.5. Rom. 1.21.

messengers to So king of Egypt, and
brought no present to the king of
Assyria, as *he had done* year by year:
therefore the king of Assyria shut him
up, and bound him in prison.
5 ¶ Then [c]the king of Assyria came
up throughout all the land, and went
up to Să-mâr-ĭ-ă, and besieged it
three years.
6 ¶ In [d]the ninth year of Hō-shē-ă the
king of Assyria took Să-mâr-ĭ-ă, and
[e]carried Israel away into Assyria, [f]and
placed them in Hā-lăh and in Hā-bôr
by the river of Gō-zăn, and in the cities
of the Mēdes.
7 For *so* it was, that the children of
Israel had sinned against the LORD
their God, which had brought them up
out of the land of Egypt, from under
the hand of Pharaoh king of Egypt,
and had feared other gods,
8 And [g]walked in the statutes of the
heathen, whom the LORD cast out
from before the children of Israel, and
of the kings of Israel, which they had
made.
9 And the children of Israel did secretly [h]*those* things that *were* not right
against the LORD their God, and they
built them high places in all their
cities, [i]from the tower of the watchmen to the fenced city.
10 And [j]they set them up [3]images
[k]and groves [l]in every high hill, and
under every green tree:
11 And there they burnt incense in
all the high places, as *did* the heathen
whom the LORD carried away before
them; and wrought wicked things to
provoke the LORD to anger:
12 For they served idols, [m]whereof
the LORD had said unto them, [n]Ye
shall not do this thing.
13 Yet the LORD testified against Israel, and against Judah, [4]by all the
prophets, *and by* all [o]the seers, saying,
[p]Turn ye from your evil ways, and
keep my commandments *and* my
statutes, according to all the law
which I commanded your fathers, and
which I sent to you by my servants the
prophets.
14 Notwithstanding they would not
hear, but [q]hardened their necks, like
to the neck of their fathers, that did
not believe in the LORD their God.
15 And they rejected his statutes,
and [r]his covenant that he made with
their fathers, and his testimonies
which he testified against them; and
they followed [s]vanity, and [t]became
vain, and went after the heathen that
were round about them, *concerning*

whom the LORD had charged them,
that they should [u]not do like them.
16 And they left all the commandments of the LORD their God, and
[v]made them molten images, *even* two
calves, [w]and made a grove, and worshipped all the host of heaven, [x]and
served Bā'-ăl.
17 And [y]they caused their sons and
their daughters to pass through the
fire, and used [z]divination and enchantments, and sold [a]themselves to
do evil in the sight of the LORD, to
provoke him to anger.
18 Therefore the LORD was very angry with Israel, and removed them out
of his sight: there was none left [b]but
the tribe of Judah only.
19 Also [c]Judah kept not the commandments of the LORD their God,
but walked in the statutes of Israel
which they made.
20 And the LORD rejected all the
seed of Israel, and afflicted them, and
[d]delivered them into the hand of
spoilers, until he had cast them out of
his sight.
21 For [e]he rent Israel from the house
of David; and [f]they made Jĕr-ŏ-bō'-
ăm the son of Nē'-băt king: and Jĕr-ŏ-
bō'-ăm drave Israel from following the
LORD, and made them sin a great sin.
22 For the children of Israel walked
in all the sins of Jĕr-ŏ-bō'-ăm which he
did; they departed not from them;
23 Until the LORD removed Israel
out of his sight, [g]as he had said by all
his servants the prophets. So was Israel carried away out of their own
land to Assyria unto this day.
24 ¶ And [h]the king of Assyria
brought *men* from Babylon, and from
Cū'-thăh, and from [i]Ā'-vă, and from
Hā'-măth, and from Sē-phăr-vā'-ĭm,
and placed *them* in the cities of Să-
mâr'-ĭ-ă instead of the children of Israel: and they possessed Să-mâr'-ĭ-ă,
and dwelt in the cities thereof.
25 And *so* it was at the beginning of
their dwelling there, *that* [j]they feared
not the LORD: therefore the LORD sent
lions among them, which slew *some* of
them.
26 Wherefore they spake to the king
of Assyria, saying, The nations which
thou hast removed, and placed in the
cities of Să-mâr'-ĭ-ă, know not the
manner of the God of the land: therefore he hath sent lions among them,
and, behold, they slay them, because
they know not the manner of the God
of the land.
27 Then the king of Assyria com-

u Deut. 12. 30,31.
v Ex. 32.8.
w 1 Ki. 14.15.
x 1 Ki. 16.31. ch. 11.18.
y Lev. 18.21. ch. 16.3. 2 Chr. 28.3. Ps. 106.37, 38. Isa. 57.5. Jer. 7.31. Eze. 16.20.
z Deut. 18.10. ch. 21.6. Isa. 2.6. Jer. 27.9. Micah 5.12. Acts 16.16. Gal. 5.20.
a Isa. 50.1.
b 1 Ki. 11.13, 32.
c Jer. 3.8.
d ch. 13.3.
e 1 Ki. 11.11, 31.
f 1 Ki. 12.20, 28.
g 1 Ki. 14.16.
h Ezra 4.2.
i ch. 18.34, Ivah.
j Eph. 2.12.
k Judg. 17.13.
l Lev. 18.21. Deut. 12.31.
m 1 Ki. 12.31.
n Isa. 29.13. Hosea 10.2. Zeph. 1.5. Matt. 6.24. Luke 16.13.
5 Or, who carried them away from thence.
o Gen. 32.28.
p Judg. 6.10.
q Ex. 20.5.
r Ex. 6.6.
s Deut. 10.20. Rev. 15.4.
t Deut. 5.32.
u Deut. 4.23.

manded, saying, Carry thither one
[k]the priests whom ye brought fro
thence; and let them go and dwe
there, and let him teach them th
manner of the God of the land.
28 Then one of the priests who
they had carried away from Să-mâ
ĭ-ă came and dwelt in Beth-el, an
taught them how they should fear th
LORD.
29 Howbeit every nation made god
of their own, and put *them* in th
houses of the high places which th
Să-măr'-ĭ-tăns had made, every na
tion in their cities wherein they dwel
30 And the men of Babylon mad
Sŭc'-cōth–bē'-nōth, and the men
Cŭth made Nĕr'-găl, and the men
Hā'-măth made Ă-shi'-mă,
31 And the Ā'-vites made Nĭb'-hă
and Tartak, and the Sē-phăr'-vite
burnt [l]their children in fire to Ă-drăn
mĕ-lĕch and Ă-năm'-mĕ-lĕch, the go
of Sē-phăr-vā'-ĭm.
32 So they feared the LORD, [m]an
made unto themselves of the lowe
of them priests of the high place
which sacrificed for them in the house
of the high places.
33 They [n]feared the LORD, and serv
ed their own gods, after the manner
the nations [5]whom they carried awa
from thence.
34 Unto this day they do after th
former manners: they fear not th
LORD, neither do they after their sta
utes, or after their ordinances, or afte
the law and commandment which th
LORD commanded the children
Jacob, [o]whom he named Israel;
35 With whom the LORD had made
covenant, and charged them, sayin
[p]Ye shall not fear other gods, nc
[q]bow yourselves to them, nor serv
them, nor sacrifice to them:
36 But the LORD, who brought yo
up out of the land of Egypt with grea
power and a [r]stretched out arm, [s]hi
shall ye fear, and him shall ye wo
ship, and to him shall ye do sacrific
37 And the statutes, and the ordi
ances, and the law, and the comman
ment, which he wrote for you, [t]y
shall observe to do for evermore; an
ye shall not fear other gods.
38 And the covenant that I hav
made with you [u]ye shall not forge
neither shall ye fear other gods.
39 But the LORD your God ye sha
fear; and he shall deliver you out
the hand of all your enemies.
40 Howbeit they did not hearke
but they did after their former manne

41 So these nations [v]feared the LORD,
and served their graven images, both
their children, and their children's
children: as did their fathers, so do
they unto this day.

CHAPTER 18

NOW it came to pass in the third
year of Hō-shē-ă son of Ē-lăh
king of Israel, *that* Hĕz-ē-kī-ăh the
[a]son of Ahaz king of Judah began to
reign.
2 Twenty and five years old was he
when he began to reign; and he reigned twenty and nine years in Jerusalem. His mother's name also *was* [b]Abi,
the daughter of Zăch-ă-rī-ăh.
3 And he did *that which was* right in
the sight of the LORD, according to all
that David his father did.
4 ¶ He [c]removed the high places, and
brake the [1]images, and cut down the
groves, and brake in pieces the [d]brasen
serpent that Moses had made: for unto those days the children of Israel
did burn incense to it: and he called
it [2]Nĕ-hŭsh-tăn.
5 He [e]trusted in the LORD God of Israel; so [f]that after him was none like
him among all the kings of Judah, nor
any that were before him.
6 For he [g]clave to the LORD, *and* departed not [3]from following him, but
kept his commandments, which the
LORD commanded Moses.
7 And the LORD [h]was with him; *and*
he prospered [i]whithersoever he went
forth: and he [j]rebelled against the
king of Assyria, and served him not.
8 He [k]smote the Philistines, *even* unto [4]Gaza, and the borders thereof,
from the tower of the watchmen to the
fenced city.
9 ¶ And [l]it came to pass in the fourth
year of king Hĕz-ē-kī-ăh, which *was*
the seventh year of Hō-shē-ă son of
Ē-lăh king of Israel, *that* Shăl-măn-ē-
sĕr king of Assyria came up against
Să-mâr-ī-ă, and besieged it.
10 And at the end of three years they
took it: *even* in the sixth year of Hĕz-
ē-kī-ăh, that *is* [m]the ninth year of Hō-
shē-ă king of Israel, Să-mâr-ī-ă was
taken.
11 And the king of Assyria did carry
away Israel unto Assyria, and put
them [n]in Hā-lăh and in Hā-bôr *by* the
river of Gō-zăn, and in the cities of the
Mēdes:
12 Because [o]they obeyed not the
voice of the LORD their God, but
transgressed his covenant, *and* all that
Moses the servant of the LORD com-

[v] Josh. 24.14. Zeph. 1.5. Luke 16.13. John 4.24. Rev. 3.15.
CHAP. 18
[a] 2 Chr. 28. 27.
[b] 2 Chr. 29.1, Abijah.
[c] 2 Chr. 31.1.
1 statues.
[d] Num. 21.9.
2 That is, A piece of brass.
[e] ch. 19.10. 2 Chr. 32.7, 8. Job 13.15. Ps. 13.5. Ps. 46.1,2. Matt. 27.43. Eph. 1.12.
[f] ch. 23.25.
[g] Deut. 10. 20. Josh. 23.8.
3 from after him.
[h] Gen. 39.2, 3. 2 Chr. 15.2. Ps. 46.11. Matt. 1.23.
[i] Ps. 60.12.
[j] ch. 16.7.
[k] 1 Chr. 4.41. Isa. 14.29.
4 Azzah.
[l] ch. 17.3.
[m] ch. 17.6.
[n] 1 Chr. 5.26.
[o] ch. 17.7. Dan. 9.6,10.
[p] 2 Chr. 32.1.
5 Sanherib.
[q] ch. 12.18. ch. 16.8. 2 Chr. 12.9.
6 them.
7 heavy.
[r] Isa. 7.3.
8 Or, secretary.
[s] 2 Chr. 32. 10.
9 Or, talkest.
10 word of the lips.
11 Or, But counsel and strength are for the war.
[t] Ezra 4.15.
[u] Isa. 36.6. Eze. 29.6,7.
12 trustest thee.
[v] 2 Chr. 31.1. Isa. 36.7.

manded, and would not hear *them*,
nor do *them*.
13 ¶ Now [p]in the fourteenth year of
king Hĕz-ē-kī-ăh did [5]Sĕn-năch-ĕr-ĭb
king of Assyria come up against all
the fenced cities of Judah, and took
them.
14 And Hĕz-ē-kī-ăh king of Judah
sent to the king of Assyria to Lā-chĭsh,
saying, I have offended; return from
me: that which thou puttest on me
will I bear. And the king of Assyria
appointed unto Hĕz-ē-kī-ăh king of
Judah three hundred talents of silver
and thirty talents of gold.
15 And Hĕz-ē-kī-ăh [q]gave *him* all the
silver that was found in the house of
the LORD, and in the treasures of the
king's house.
16 At that time did Hĕz-ē-kī-ăh cut
off *the gold from* the doors of the
temple of the LORD, and *from* the pillars which Hĕz-ē-kī-ăh king of Judah
had overlaid, and gave [6]it to the king
of Assyria.
17 ¶ And the king of Assyria sent
Tartan and Răb-să-rĭs and Răb′-shă-
kēh from Lā-chĭsh to king Hĕz-ē-kī-
ăh with a [7]great host against Jerusalem. And they went up and came to
Jerusalem. And when they were come
up, they came and stood by the conduit of the upper pool, [r]which *is* in
the highway of the fuller's field.
18 And when they had called to the
king, there came out to them Ē-lī-ă-
kĭm the son of Hĭl-kī-ăh, which *was*
over the household, and Shĕb-nă the
[8]scribe, and Jō-ăh the son of Ā-săph
the recorder.
19 And Răb′-shă-kēh said unto
them, Speak ye now to Hĕz-ē-kī-ăh,
Thus saith the great king, the king of
Assyria, [s]What confidence *is* this
wherein thou trustest?
20 Thou [9]sayest, (but *they are but*
[10]vain words,) [11]*I have* counsel and
strength for the war. Now on whom
dost thou trust, that thou rebellest
[t]against me?
21 Now, [u]behold, thou [12]trustest upon the staff of this bruised reed, *even*
upon Egypt, on which if a man lean,
it will go into his hand, and pierce it:
so *is* Pharaoh king of Egypt unto all
that trust on him.
22 But if ye say unto me, We trust in
the LORD our God: *is* not that he,
whose high [v]places and whose altars
Hĕz-ē-kī-ăh hath taken away, and
hath said to Judah and Jerusalem, Ye
shall worship before this altar in
Jerusalem?

23 Now therefore, I pray thee, give [13]pledges to my lord the king of Assyria, and I will deliver thee two thousand horses, if thou be able on thy part to set riders upon them.

24 How then wilt thou turn away the face of one captain of the least of my master's servants, and put thy trust on Egypt for chariots and for horsemen?

25 Am I now come up without the LORD against this place to destroy it? The LORD [w]said to me, Go up against this land, and destroy it.

26 Then said Ē-lī'-ă-kĭm the son of Hĭl-kī'-ăh, and Shĕb'-nă, and Jō'-ăh, unto Răb'-shă-kēh, Speak, I pray thee, to thy servants in the Syrian language; for we understand *it:* and talk not with us in the Jews' language in the ears of the people that *are* on the wall.

27 But Răb'-shă-kēh said unto them, Hath my master sent me to thy master, and to thee, to speak these words? *hath he* not *sent me* to the men which sit on the wall, that they may eat their own dung, and drink [14]their own piss with you?

28 Then Răb'-shă-kēh stood and cried with a loud voice in the Jews' language, and spake, saying, Hear the word of the great king, the king of Assyria:

29 Thus saith the king, [x]Let not Hĕz-ē-kī'-ăh deceive you: for he shall not be able to deliver you out of his hand:

30 Neither let Hĕz-ē-kī'-ăh make you trust in the LORD, saying, The LORD will surely deliver us, and this city shall not be delivered into the hand of the king of Assyria.

31 Hearken not to Hĕz-ē-kī'-ăh: for thus saith the king of Assyria, [15]Make *an agreement* with me by a present, and come out to me, and *then* eat ye every man of his own vine, and every one of his fig tree, and drink ye every one the waters of his [16]cistern:

32 Until I come and take you away to a land like your own land, [y]a land of corn and wine, a land of bread and vineyards, a land of oil olive and of honey, that ye may live, and not die: and hearken not unto Hĕz-ē-kī'-ăh, when he [17]persuadeth you, saying, The LORD will deliver us.

33 Hath [z]any of the gods of the nations delivered at all his land out of the hand of the king of Assyria?

34 Where [a]*are* the gods of Hā'-măth, and of Arpad? where *are* the gods of Sē-phăr-vā-'im, Hē'-nă, and [b]Ī'-văh? have they delivered Să-mâr'-ĭ-ă out of mine hand?

35 Who *are* they among all the gods of the countries, that have delivered their country out of mine hand, [c]that the LORD should deliver Jerusalem out of mine hand?

36 But the people held their peace, and answered him not a word: for the king's commandment was, saying, Answer him not.

37 Then came Ē-lī'-ă-kĭm the son of Hĭl-kī'-ăh, which *was* over the household, and Shĕb'-nă the scribe, and Jō-ăh the son of Ā'-săph the recorder, to Hĕz-ē-kī'-ăh [d]with *their* clothes rent and told him the words of Răb'-shă-kēh.

CHAPTER 19

AND it came to pass, when king Hĕz-ē-kī'-ăh heard *it,* that he rent his clothes, and covered himself with sackcloth, and went into the house of the [a]LORD.

2 And he sent Ē-lī'-ă-kĭm, which *was* over the household, and Shĕb'-nă the scribe, and the elders of the priests, covered with sackcloth, to Isaiah the prophet the son of Amoz.

3 And they said unto him, Thus saith Hĕz-ē-kī'-ăh, This day *is* a day of trouble, and of rebuke, and [1]blasphemy: for the children are come to the birth, and *there is* not strength to bring forth.

4 It [b]may be the LORD thy God will hear all the words of Răb'-shă-kēh [c]whom the king of Assyria his master hath sent to reproach the living God and [d]will reprove the words which the LORD thy God hath heard: wherefore [e]lift up *thy* prayer for the remnant that are [2]left.

5 So the servants of king Hĕz-ē-kī'-ăh came to Isaiah.

6 ¶ And [f]Isaiah said unto them, Thus shall ye say to your master, Thus saith the LORD, [g]Be not afraid of the words which thou hast heard, with which the servants of the king of Assyria have blasphemed me.

7 Behold, I will send [h]a blast upon him, and he shall hear a rumour, and shall return to his own land; and I will cause him to fall by the sword in his own land.

8 ¶ So Răb'-shă-kēh returned, and found the king of Assyria warring against Lĭb'-năh: for he had heard that he was departed from [i]Lā'-chĭsh.

9 And [j]when he heard say of Tĭr-hā-kăh king of Ē-thĭ-ō'-pĭ-ă, Behold, he is come out to fight against thee: he sent

13 Or, hostages.
w ch. 19.6,22. 2 Chr. 35.21. Isa. 7.17.
14 the water of their feet.
x 2 Chr. 32. 15. Job 5.19. Dan. 3.15-17.
15 Make with me a blessing, or, Seek my favour.
16 Or, pit.
y Deut. 8.7,8.
17 Or, deceiveth.
z ch. 19.12. 2 Chr. 32.14. Isa. 10.10, 11.
a ch. 19.13.
b ch. 17.24, Ava.
c Ps. 2.2,4. Ps. 50.21. Ps. 59.7,8. Isa. 10.5-15. Dan. 3.15. Rom. 1.21, 22,23.
d Job 1.20. Isa. 33.7. Jer. 36.24.
CHAP. 19
a Ps. 3.4,8. Ps. 27.14. Ps. 37.5-40. Ps. 55.16,22. Pro. 16.3. Isa. 37.1. Phil. 4.6. 1 Pet. 5.6,7.
1 Or, provocation.
b 2 Sam. 16. 12.
c ch. 18.35.
d Ps. 50.21.
e Jas. 5.16.
2 found.
f Isa. 37.6.
g Ex. 14.13. ch. 6.16.
h Job 4.9. Ps. 11.6.
i ch. 18.14.
j 1 Sam. 23. 27. Isa. 37.9.

essengers again unto Hĕz-ē-kī-ăh,
ying,
0 Thus shall ye speak to Hĕz-ē-kī-
ı king of Judah, saying, Let not thy
od [k]in whom thou trustest deceive
ee, saying, Jerusalem shall not be
livered into the hand of the king of
ssyria.
1 Behold, thou hast heard what the
ngs of Assyria have done to all
nds, by destroying them utterly:
d shalt thou be delivered?
2 Have the gods of the nations de-
ered them which my fathers have
stroyed; *as* Gō-zăn, [l]and Hâr-ăn,
d Rē-zĕph, and the children of
Eden which *were* in Thĕl-ă-sär?
3 Where [n]*is* the king of Hā-măth,
d the king of Arpad, and the king
the city of Sē-phăr-vā-ĭm, of Hē-nă,
d [o]Ī-văh?
4 ¶ And [p]Hĕz-ē-kī-ăh received the
tter of the hand of the messengers,
d read it: and Hĕz-ē-kī-ăh went up
to the house of the LORD, and
read it before the LORD.
5 And Hĕz-ē-kī-ăh prayed before
e LORD, and said, O LORD God of
rael, [q]which dwellest *between* the
ĕr-ū-bĭms, [r]thou art the God, *even*
ou alone, of all the kingdoms of the
rth; thou hast made heaven and
rth.
6 LORD, [s]bow down thine ear, and
ar: open, [t]LORD, thine eyes, and see:
d hear the words of Sĕn-năch-ĕr-ĭb,
hich hath sent him to reproach the
ing God.
7 Of a truth, LORD, the kings of
ssyria have destroyed the nations
d their lands,
8 And have [3]cast their gods into the
e: for they *were* no gods, but the
ork of men's hands, wood and
one: therefore they have destroyed
em.
9 Now therefore, O LORD our God,
beseech thee, save thou us out of his
nd, that [v]all the kingdoms of the
rth may know that thou *art* the
ORD God, *even* thou only.
0 ¶ Then Isaiah the son of Amoz
nt to Hĕz-ē-kī-ăh, saying, Thus
ith the LORD God of Israel, *That*
hich thou hast prayed to me against
ĕn-năch-ĕr-ĭb king of Assyria [w]I
ave heard.
1 This *is* the word that the LORD
ath spoken concerning him; The vir-
n [x]the daughter of Zion hath de-
ised thee, *and* laughed thee to
orn; the daughter of Jerusalem
ath [y]shaken her head at thee.

22 Whom hast thou reproached and
blasphemed? and against whom hast
thou exalted *thy* voice, and lifted up
thine eyes on high? *even* against the
[z]Holy *One* of Israel.
23 [4]By the messengers thou hast reproached the Lord, and hast said,
[a]With the multitude of my chariots I
am come up to the height of the mountains, to the sides of Lĕb-ă-nŏn, and
will cut down [5]the tall cedar trees
thereof, *and* the choice fir trees thereof: and I will enter into the lodgings of
his borders, *and into* [6]the forest of his
Carmel.
24 I have digged and drunk strange
waters, and with the sole of my feet
have I dried up all the rivers of [7]be-
sieged places.
25 [8]Hast thou not heard long ago *how*
[b]I have done it, *and* of ancient times
that I have formed it? now have I
brought it to pass, that thou [c]should-
est be to lay waste fenced cities *into*
ruinous heaps.
26 Therefore their inhabitants were
[9]of small power, they were dismayed
and confounded; they were *as* [d]the
grass of the field, and *as* the green
herb, *as* the grass on the housetops,
and *as corn* blasted before it be grown
up.
27 But [e]I know thy [10]abode, and thy
going out, and thy coming in, and thy
rage against me.
28 Because thy rage against me and
thy tumult is come up into mine ears,
therefore [f]I will put my hook in thy
nose, and my bridle in thy lips, and I
will turn thee back by the way by
which thou camest.
29 And this *shall be* [g]a sign unto
thee, Ye shall eat this year such things
as grow of themselves, and in the
second year that which springeth of
the same; and in the third year sow
ye, and reap, and plant vineyards, and
eat the fruits thereof.
30 And [11]the remnant that is escaped
of the house of Judah shall yet again
take root downward, and bear fruit
upward.
31 For out of Jerusalem shall go
forth a remnant, and [12]they that escape out of mount Zion: [h]the zeal of
the LORD *of hosts* shall do this.
32 Therefore thus saith the LORD
concerning the king of Assyria, He
shall not come into this city, nor shoot
an arrow there, nor come before it
with shield, nor cast a bank against
it.
33 By the way that he came, by the

k ch. 18.5. Isa. 37.10, 14.
l Gen. 11.31.
m Eze. 27.23.
n ch. 18.34.
o ch. 17.24.
p Isa. 37.14.
q Ex. 25.22. 1 Sam. 4.4. Ps. 80.1.
r Ps. 96.5. Isa. 44.6.
s Ps. 31.2.
t 2 Chr. 6.40.
3 given.
u Ps. 115.4.
v Ps. 83.18.
w Ps. 65.2.
x Lam. 2.13.
y Job 16.4. Ps. 22.7,8. Lam. 2.15.
z Ps. 71.22. Isa. 5.24.
4 By the hand of.
a Ps. 20.7.
5 the tallness.
6 Or, the forest and his fruitful field.
7 Or, fenced.
8 Or, Hast thou not heard how I have made it long ago, and formed it of ancient times? should I now bring it to be laid waste, and fenced cities to be ruinous heaps?
b Ps. 33.11. Isa. 45.7.
c Isa. 10.5.
9 short of hand.
d Ps. 129.6.
e Ps. 139.1.
10 Or, sitting.
f Job 41.2. Amos 4.2.
g ch. 20.8,9. Luke 2.12.
11 the escaping of the house of Judah that remaineth.
12 the escaping.
h Isa. 9.7.

same shall he return, and shall not
come into this city, saith the LORD.
34 For [i]I will defend this city, to save
it, for mine own sake, and for my servant [j]David's sake.
35 ¶ And [k]it came to pass that night,
that the angel of the LORD went out,
and smote in the camp of the Assyrians an hundred fourscore and five
thousand: and when they arose early
in the morning, behold, they *were* all
dead corpses.
36 So Sĕn-năch´-ĕr-ĭb king of Assyria
departed, and went and returned, and
dwelt at [l]Nĭn´-ĕ-vēh.
37 And it came to pass, as he was
worshipping in the house of Nĭs´-rŏch
his god, that Ă-drăm´-mĕ-lĕch and
Shă-rē´-zĕr his sons smote him with
the sword: and they escaped into the
land of [13]Är-mē´-nĭ-ă. And Ē-săr-hăd´-
don [m]his son reigned in his stead.

CHAPTER 20

IN [a]those days was Hĕz-ē-kī´-ăh sick
unto death. And the prophet Isaiah
the son of Amoz came to him, and
said unto him, Thus saith the LORD,
[1]Set thine house in order; for thou
shalt die, and not live.
2 Then he turned his face to the wall,
and prayed unto the LORD, saying,
3 I beseech thee, O LORD, [b]remem-
ber now how I have [c]walked before
thee in truth and with a perfect heart,
and have done *that which is* good in
thy sight. And Hĕz-ē-kī´-ăh wept [2]sore.
4 And it came to pass, afore Isaiah
was gone out into the middle [3]court,
that the word of the LORD came to
him, saying,
5 Turn again, and tell Hĕz-ē-kī´-ăh
the captain of my people, Thus saith
the LORD, the God of David thy father, [d]I have heard thy prayer, I have
seen [e]thy tears: behold, I will heal
thee: on the third day thou shalt go
up unto the house of the LORD.
6 And I will add unto thy days fifteen
years; and I will deliver thee and this
city out of the hand of the king of
Assyria; and I [f]will defend this city
for mine own sake, and for my servant David's sake.
7 And Isaiah said, Take a lump of
figs. And they took and laid *it* on the
boil, and he recovered.
8 ¶ And Hĕz-ē-kī´-ăh said unto Isaiah,
What *shall be* the sign that the LORD
will heal me, and that I shall go up
into the house of the LORD the third
day?
9 And Isaiah said, [g]This sign shalt

i ch. 20.6.
j 1 Ki. 11.12, 13.
k 2 Chr. 32. 21.
l Gen. 10.11. Jonah 1.2. Nahum 1.
13 Ararat.
m Ezra 4.2.
CHAP. 20
a 2 Chr. 32. 24. Isa. 38.1.
1 Give charge concerning thine house.
b Neh. 13.22. Ps. 132.1-5.
c Gen. 5.22, 24.
2 with a great weeping.
3 Or, city.
d 1 Ki. 18.37. ch. 19.20. 2 Chr. 32.20, 21. Ps. 65.2. Luke 11.9, 10. Acts 10.31.
e Job 16.20. Ps. 39.12.
f ch. 19.34. 2 Chr. 32.22.
g Isa. 38.7.
h Josh. 10.12-14. Isa. 38.8.
4 degrees.
i Isa. 39.1.
5 Or, Mero-dach-bala-dan.
j 2 Chr. 32. 27,31.
6 Or, spicery.
7 Or, jewels.
k Lev. 26.33. ch. 24.13. Jer. 27.21.
l ch. 24.12.
8 Fulfilled, Dan. 1.3.
m 1 Sam. 3. 18. Ps. 39.9. Lam. 3.22, 39.
9 Or, Shall there not be peace and truth?
n Neh. 3.16.

thou have of the LORD, that the Lo
will do the thing that he hath spoke
shall the shadow go forward ten
grees, or go back ten degrees?
10 And Hĕz-ē-kī´-ăh answered, It
a light thing for the shadow to
down ten degrees: nay, but let t
shadow return backward ten degre
11 And Isaiah the prophet cried ur
the LORD: and [h]he brought the shad
ten degrees backward, by which
had gone down in the [4]dial of Ah
12 ¶ At [i]that time [5]Bĕr-ō´-dăch–băl
dăn, the son of Băl´-ă-dăn, king
Babylon, sent letters and a present u
to Hĕz-ē-kī´-ăh: for he had hea
that Hĕz-ē-kī´-ăh had been sick.
13 And [j]Hĕz-ē-kī´-ăh hearkened un
them, and shewed them all the hou
of his [6]precious things, the silver, a
the gold, and the spices, and the pr
cious ointment, and *all* the house
his [7]armour, and all that was found
his treasures: there was nothing
his house, nor in all his dominic
that Hĕz-ē-kī´-ăh shewed them not.
14 ¶ Then came Isaiah the proph
unto king Hĕz-ē-kī´-ăh, and said un
him, What said these men? and fro
whence came they unto thee? A
Hĕz-ē-kī´-ăh said, They are come fro
a far country, *even* from Babylon.
15 And he said, What have they se
in thine house? And Hĕz-ē-kī´-ăh a
swered, All *the things* that *are* in mi
house have they seen: there is nothi
among my treasures that I have n
shewed them.
16 And Isaiah said unto Hĕz-ē-kī´-ă
Hear the word of the LORD.
17 Behold, the days come, that
that *is* in thine house, and that whi
thy fathers have laid up in store un
this day, [k]shall be carried into Bab
lon: nothing shall be left, saith t
LORD.
18 And of thy sons that shall iss
from thee, which thou shalt beg
[l]shall they take away; [8]and they sh
be eunuchs in the palace of the ki
of Babylon.
19 Then said Hĕz-ē-kī´-ăh unto Isaia
[m]Good *is* the word of the LORD whi
thou hast spoken. And he said, [9]*Is*
not *good*, if peace and truth be in n
days?
20 ¶ And the rest of the acts of Hĕ
ē-kī´-ăh, and all his might, and how
[n]made a pool, and a conduit, ar
brought water into the city, *are* th
not written in the book of the chro
icles of the kings of Judah?
21 And Hĕz-ē-kī´-ăh slept with h

hers: and Mă-năs-sēh his son reign-
in his stead.

CHAPTER 21

MĂ-NĂS-SĒH *was* twelve years
old when he began to reign, and
gned fifty and five years in Jerusa-
n. And his mother's name *was*
ph-zi–băh.
And he did *that which was* evil in
sight of the LORD, [a]after the
ominations of the heathen, whom
LORD cast out before the children
Israel.
For he built up again the high
ces which [b]Hĕz-ē-kī-ăh his father
d destroyed; and he reared up altars
Bā-ăl, and made a grove, as [c]did
ab king of Israel; and worshipped
l the host of heaven, and served
m.
And [e]he built altars in the house of
LORD, of which the LORD said, [f]In
usalem will I put my name.
And he built altars for all the host
heaven in the two courts of the
use of the LORD.
And [g]he made his son pass through
fire, and observed times, [h]and used
chantments, and dealt with familiar
rits and wizards: he wrought much
ckedness in the sight of the LORD,
provoke *him* to anger.
And he set a graven image of the
ove that he had made in the house,
which the LORD said to David, and
Solomon his son, In [i]this house,
d in Jerusalem, which I have chosen
t of all tribes of Israel, will I put my
me for ever:
Neither will I make the feet of Is-
el move any more out of the land
ich I gave their fathers; only if
ey will observe to do according to
that I have commanded them, and
cording to all the law that my ser-
nt Moses commanded them.
But they hearkened not: and Mă-
s-sēh seduced [j]them to do more evil
an did the nations whom the LORD
stroyed before the children of
ael.
¶ And the LORD spake by his ser-
nts the prophets, saying,
Because [k]Mă-năs-sēh king of Ju-
h hath done these abominations,
d hath done wickedly above all
t the Amorites did, which *were* be-
e him, and hath made Judah also
sin with his idols:
Therefore thus saith the LORD
od of Israel, Behold, I *am* bringing
h evil upon Jerusalem and Judah,

CHAP. 21
a ch. 16.3.
b ch. 18.4.
c 1 Ki. 16.32.
d Deut. 4.19. ch. 17.16.
e Jer. 32.34.
f 2 Sam. 7.13. 1 Ki. 8.29.
g Lev. 18.21. ch. 16.3. 2 Chr. 28.3.
h Lev. 19.26, 31. Deut. 18.10. ch. 17.17.
i 1 Ki. 8.29. ch. 23.27. Ps. 132.13, 14. Jer. 32.34.
j 1 Ki. 14.16. 2 Chr. 33.9. Pro. 29.12.
k ch. 23.26. Jer. 15.4.
l 1 Ki. 21.26. 1 Pet. 4.3. Rev. 21.8.
m 1 Sam. 3. 11. Jer. 19.3.
n Isa. 34.11. Lam. 2.8. Amos 7.7,8.
1 he wipeth and turneth it upon the face thereof.
o ch. 19.30.
p Gen. 9.6. ch. 24.4. Ps. 10.2,8. Ps. 106.38. Pro. 6.16,17. Isa. 59.3,7. Jer. 2.34. Lam. 4.13, 14. Eze. 9.9. Micah 3.9-12. Joel 3.19.
2 from mouth to mouth.
q 2 Chr. 33. 11-19
r 2 Chr. 33. 20. Jer. 22.19.
s 2 Chr. 33. 21-23.
t Deut. 32.15. Judg. 2.12.
u ch. 12.20. 2 Chr. 33. 24,25.

that whosoever heareth of it, both his
[m]ears shall tingle.
13 And I will stretch over Jerusalem
[n]the line of Să-mâr-ĭ-ă, and the plum-
met of the house of Ahab: and I will
wipe Jerusalem as *a man* wipeth a
dish, [1]wiping *it*, and turning *it* upside
down.
14 And I will forsake [o]the remnant
of mine inheritance, and deliver them
into the hand of their enemies; and
they shall become a prey and a spoil
to all their enemies;
15 Because they have done *that which
was* evil in my sight, and have provoked me to anger, since the day their
fathers came forth out of Egypt, even
unto this day.
16 Moreover Mă-năs-sēh [p]shed innocent blood very much, till he had
filled Jerusalem [2]from one end to another; beside his sin wherewith he
made Judah to sin, in doing *that which
was* evil in the sight of the LORD.
17 ¶ Now [q]the rest of the acts of Mă-
năs-sēh, and all that he did, and his
sin that he sinned, *are* they not written in the book of the chronicles of the
kings of Judah?
18 And [r]Mă-năs-sēh slept with his
fathers, and was buried in the garden
of his own house, in the garden of Ŭz-
ză: and Amon his son reigned in his
stead.
19 ¶ Amon [s]*was* twenty and two
years old when he began to reign, and
he reigned two years in Jerusalem.
And his mother's name *was* Mĕ-shŭl-
lĕ-mĕth, the daughter of Hâr-ŭz of
Jŏt-băh.
20 And he did *that which was* evil in
the sight of the LORD, as his father
Mă-năs-sēh did.
21 And he walked in all the way that
his father walked in, and served the
idols that his father served, and worshipped them:
22 And he [t]forsook the LORD God of
his fathers, and walked not in the way
of the LORD.
23 ¶ And [u]the servants of Amon conspired against him, and slew the king
in his own house.
24 And the people of the land slew
all them that had conspired against
king Amon; and the people of the land
made Jō-sī-ăh his son king in his
stead.
25 Now the rest of the acts of Amon
which he did, *are* they not written in
the book of the chronicles of the kings
of Judah?
26 And he was buried in his sepulchre

in the garden of Ŭz-ză: and Jō-sī-ăh
[v]his son reigned in his stead.

CHAPTER 22

JŌ-SĪ-ĂH [a]*was* eight years old when
he began to reign, and he reigned
thirty and one years in Jerusalem.
And his mother's name *was* Jĕ-dī-dăh,
the daughter of Ă-dâi-ăh of [b]Bŏs-căth.
2 And he did *that which was* right in
the sight of the LORD, and walked in
all the way of David his father, and
[c]turned not aside to the right hand or
to the left.
3 ¶ And [d]it came to pass in the
eighteenth year of king Jō-sī-ăh, *that*
the king sent Shā-phăn the son of
Ăz-ă-lī-ăh, the son of Mĕ-shŭl-lăm,
the scribe, to the house of the LORD,
saying,
4 Go up to Hĭl-kī-ăh the high priest,
that he may sum the silver which is
[e]brought into the house of the LORD,
which [f]the keepers of the [1]door have
gathered of the people:
5 And let them [g]deliver it into the
hand of the doers of the work, that
have the oversight of the house of the
LORD: and let them give it to the
doers of the work which *is* in the
house of the LORD, to repair the
breaches of the house,
6 Unto carpenters, and builders, and
masons, and to buy timber and hewn
stone to repair the house.
7 Howbeit [h]there was no reckoning
made with them of the money that
was delivered into their hand, because
they dealt [i]faithfully.
8 ¶ And Hĭl-kī-ăh the high priest
said unto Shā-phăn the scribe, [j]I have
found the book of the law in the house
of the LORD. And Hĭl-kī-ăh gave the
book to Shā-phăn, and he read it.
9 And Shā-phăn the scribe came to
the king, and brought the king word
again, and said, Thy servants have
[2]gathered the money that was found
in the house, and have delivered it into
the hand of them that do the work,
that have the oversight of the house
of the LORD.
10 And Shā-phăn the scribe shewed
the king, saying, Hĭl-kī-ăh the priest
hath delivered me a book. And Shā-
phăn [k]read it before the king.
11 And it came to pass, when the
king had heard the words of the book
of the law, that he rent his clothes.
12 And the king commanded Hĭl-kī-
ăh the priest, and Ă-hī-kăm the son of
Shā-phăn, and [l]Ăch-bôr the son of
[3]Mī-châi-ăh, and Shā-phân the scribe,

v Matt. 1.10, called Josias.

CHAP. 22
a 1 Chr. 3.14. 2 Chr. 34.1. Jer. 1.2. Zeph. 1.1. Matt. 1.10.
b Josh. 15.39.
c Deut. 5.32. Josh. 1.7. Pro. 4.27.
d 2 Chr. 34.8.
e ch. 12.4. 2 Chr. 24.8-12. Mark 12.41, 42.
f ch. 12.9. 1 Chr. 9.19. 2 Chr. 8.14. Neh. 11.19. Ps. 84.10.
1 threshold.
g ch. 12.11, 12,14.
h ch. 12.15.
i Neh. 7.2. 1 Cor. 4.2.
j Deut. 31.24.
2 melted.
k Jer. 36.21.
l Abdon, 2 Chr. 34.20.
3 Or, Micah.
m Ps. 25.14. Pro. 3.6.
n Deut. 29. 27.
o Ex. 15.20. Luke 2.36. 1 Cor. 11.5.
p Tikvath, 2 Chr. 34.22.
4 Or, Hasrah.
5 garments.
6 Or, in the second part.
q Dan. 9.11, 12-14.
r Ps. 115.4. Isa. 2.8,9. Isa. 44.17-20. Micah 5.13.
s 2 Chr. 34. 26.
t Eccl. 8.12.
u Ps. 51.17. Isa. 57.15.
v Ex. 10.3. Lev. 26.40, 41. 2 Chr. 33.12. Ps. 34.18. Ps. 51.17. Isa. 57.15. Luke 14.11. Jas. 4.6,7. 1 Pet. 5.5,6.
w Lev. 26.31, 32.
x Jer. 26.6.
y Ps. 37.37. Isa. 57.1,2.

CHAP. 23
a 2 Chr. 34. 29,30.

and Ăs-ă-hī-ăh a servant of the kin
saying,
13 Go ye, [m]inquire of the LORD
me, and for the people, and for
Judah, concerning the words of t
book that is found: for great *is* [n]
wrath of the LORD that is kind
against us, because our fathers h
not hearkened unto the words of t
book, to do according unto all t
which is written concerning us.
14 So Hĭl-kī-ăh the priest, and Ă-
kăm, and Ăch-bôr, and Shā-phăn, a
Ăs-ă-hī-ăh, went unto Hŭl-dăh
[o]prophetess, the wife of Shăl-lŭm
son of [p]Tĭk-văh, the son of [4]Hăr-h
keeper of the [5]wardrobe; (now
dwelt in Jerusalem [6]in the colleg
and they communed with her.
15 ¶ And she said unto them, T
saith the LORD God of Israel, Tell
man that sent you to me,
16 Thus saith the LORD, Behold
[q]will bring evil upon this place, a
upon the inhabitants thereof, *even*
the words of the book which the k
of Judah hath read:
17 Because they have forsaken
and have burned incense unto ot
gods, that they might provoke me
anger with all the works [r]of th
hands; therefore my wrath shall
kindled against this place, and sh
not be quenched.
18 But to [s]the king of Judah wh
sent you to inquire of the LORD, t
shall ye say to him, [t]Thus saith
LORD God of Israel, *As touching*
words which thou hast heard;
19 Because thine [u]heart was tend
and thou hast [v]humbled thyself
fore the LORD, when thou heard
what I spake against this place, a
against the inhabitants thereof, t
they should become [w]a desolation a
[x]a curse, and hast rent thy cloth
and wept before me; I also have hea
thee, saith the LORD.
20 Behold therefore, I will gat
thee unto thy fathers, and thou sh
[y]be gathered into thy grave in pea
and thine eyes shall not see all the e
which I will bring upon this pla
And they brought the king w
again.

CHAPTER 23

AND [a]the king sent, and they ga
ered unto him all the elders
Judah and of Jerusalem.
2 And the king went up into
house of the LORD, and all the me
Judah and all the inhabitants of Je
salem with him, and the priests, a

he prophets, and all the people, [1]both
mall and great: and he read in their
ars all the words of the book of the
ovenant [b]which was found in the
ouse of the LORD.
3 ¶ And the king [c]stood by a pillar,
nd made a covenant before the LORD,
o walk after the LORD, and to keep
is commandments and his testimon-
es and his statutes with all *their* heart
nd all *their* soul, to perform the
vords of this covenant that were
vritten in this book. And [d]all the peo-
le stood to the covenant.
4 And the king commanded Hĭl-kī-
h the high priest, and the priests of
he second order, and the keepers of
he door, to bring forth out of the
emple of the LORD all the vessels that
vere made for Bā-ăl, and for the
grove, and for all the host of heaven:
nd he burned them without Jerusa-
em in the fields of Kĭ-drŏn, and car-
ied the ashes of them unto Beth-el.
5 And he [2]put down [3]the idolatrous
riests, whom the kings of Judah had
rdained to burn incense in the high
laces in the cities of Judah, and in
he places round about Jerusalem;
hem also that burned incense unto
ā-ăl, to the sun, and to the moon,
nd to the [4]planets, and to all [f]the
ost of heaven.
6 And he brought out the grove from
he house of the LORD, without Jeru-
alem, unto the brook Kĭ-drŏn, and
urned it at the brook Kĭ-drŏn, and
tamped *it* small to powder, and cast
he powder thereof upon the [g]graves
f the children of the people.
7 And he brake down the houses of
the sodomites, that *were* by the house
f the LORD, [i]where the women wove
hangings for the grove.
8 And he brought all the priests out
f the cities of Judah, and defiled the
igh places where the priests had
urned incense, from Gē-bă [j]to Bē-er-
she-bă, and brake down the high
laces of the gates that *were* in the en-
ring in of the gate of Joshua the
overnor of the city, which *were* on a
an's left hand at the gate of the city.
9 Nevertheless [k]the priests of the
igh places came not up to the altar of
he LORD in Jerusalem, but [l]they did
at of the unleavened bread among
heir brethren.
10 And he defiled [m]Tō-phĕth, which
in the [n]valley of the children of Hĭn-
ŏm, that [o]no man might make his
on or his daughter to pass through
he fire to Molech.

1 from small even unto great.
b ch. 22.8.
c ch. 11.14.
d Jer. 4.2.
e ch. 21.3,7.
2 caused to cease.
3 Chemarim.
4 Or, twelve signs, or constellations.
f ch. 21.3.
g 2 Chr. 34.4.
h 1 Ki. 14.24.
i Eze. 16.16.
5 houses.
j 1 Ki. 15.22.
k Eze. 44.10. Mal. 2.8.
l 1 Sam. 2.36.
m Isa. 30.33.
n Josh. 15.8.
o Lev. 18.21.
p Deut. 4.19. 2 Chr. 14.5. Job 31.26.
6 Or, eunuch, or, officer.
q Jer. 19.13.
r ch. 21.5. 2 Chr. 33.3, 15.
7 Or, ran from thence.
8 That is, the mount of Olives.
s Neh. 13.26.
9 Or, Molech.
t Ex. 23.24. Ex. 32.20. Num. 33.52. Deut. 7.5, 25.
10 statues.
u 1 Ki. 12.28, 33. ch. 10.31.
v 1 Ki. 13.2.
11 to escape.
w 2 Chr. 34.6.

11 And he took away the horses that
the kings of Judah had given to [p]the
sun, at the entering in of the house of
the LORD, by the chamber of Nā-thăn–
mē-lĕch the [6]chamberlain, which *was*
in the suburbs, and burned the chariots of the sun with fire.
12 And the altars that *were* [q]on the
top of the upper chamber of Ahaz,
which the kings of Judah had made,
and the altars which Mă-năs-sēh [r]had
made in the two courts of the house
of the LORD, did the king beat down,
and [7]brake *them* down from thence,
and cast the dust of them into the
brook Kĭ-drŏn.
13 And the high places that *were* before Jerusalem, which *were* on the
right hand of [8]the mount of corruption, which [s]Solomon the king of Israel had builded for Ăsh-tō-rĕth the
abomination of the Zī-dō-nĭ-ăns, and
for Chē-mŏsh the abomination of the
Moabites, and for [9]Mĭl-cŏm the
abomination of the children of Ammon, did the king defile.
14 And [t]he brake in pieces the [10]im-
ages, and cut down the groves, and
filled their places with the bones of
men.
15 ¶ Moreover the altar that *was* at
Beth-el, *and* the high place which [u]Jĕr-
ŏ-bō-ăm the son of Nē-băt, who made
Israel to sin, had made, both that
altar and the high place he brake
down, and burned the high place, *and*
stamped *it* small to powder, and
burned the grove.
16 And as Jō-sī-ăh turned himself, he
spied the sepulchres that *were* there in
the mount, and sent, and took the
bones out of the sepulchres, and burned *them* upon the altar, and polluted
it, according to the word [v]of the LORD
which the man of God proclaimed,
who proclaimed these words.
17 Then he said, What title *is* that
that I see? And the men of the city told
him, *It is* the sepulchre of the man of
God, which came from Judah, and
proclaimed these things that thou
hast done against the altar of Beth-el.
18 And he said, Let him alone; let no
man move his bones. So they let his
bones [11]alone, with the bones of the
prophet that came out of Să-mâr-ĭ-ă.
19 And all the houses also of the high
places that *were* [w]in the cities of Să-
mâr-ĭ-ă, which the kings of Israel had
made to provoke *the LORD* to anger,
Jō-sī-ăh took away, and did to them
according to all the acts that he had
done in Beth-el.

20 And he [12]slew all the priests of the high places that *were* there upon the altars, and [x]burned men's bones upon them, and returned to Jerusalem.

21 ¶ And the king commanded all the people, saying, [y]Keep the passover unto the LORD your God, as [z]*it is* written in the book of this covenant.

22 Surely there was not holden such a passover from the days of the judges that judged Israel, nor in all the days of the kings of Israel, nor of the kings of Judah;

23 But in the eighteenth year of king Jō-sī́-ăh, *wherein* this passover was holden to the LORD in Jerusalem.

24 ¶ Moreover [a]the *workers with* familiar spirits, and the wizards, and the [13]images, and the idols, and all the abominations that were spied in the land of Judah and in Jerusalem, did Jō-sī́-ăh put away, that he might perform the words of [b]the law which were written in the book that Hĭl-kī́-ăh the priest found in the house of the LORD.

25 And [c]like unto him was there no king before him, that turned to the LORD with all his heart, and with all his soul, and with all his might, according to all the law of Moses; neither after him arose there *any* like him.

26 ¶ Notwithstanding the LORD turned not from the fierceness of his great wrath, wherewith his anger was kindled against Judah, because [d]of all the [14]provocations that Mă-năś-sēh had provoked him withal.

27 And the LORD said, I will remove Judah also out of my sight, as [e]I have removed Israel, and will cast off this city Jerusalem which I have chosen, and the house of which I said, [f]My name shall be there.

28 Now the rest of the acts of Jō-sī́-ăh, and all that he did, *are* they not written in the book of the chronicles of the kings of Judah?

29 ¶ In his days Phâŕ-ăōh–nḗ-c̲hōh king of Egypt went up against the king of Assyria to the river Eû-phrā́-tēs: and king Jō-sī́-ăh went against him; and he slew him [g]at Mĕ-gĭd́-dō, when he [h]had seen him.

30 And his servants carried him in a chariot dead from Mĕ-gĭd́-dō, and brought him to Jerusalem, and buried him in his own sepulchre. And the people of the land took [i]Jĕ-hṓ-ă-hăz the son of Jō-sī́-ăh, and anointed him, and made him king in his father's stead.

31 ¶ Jĕ-hṓ-ă-hăz *was* twenty and three years old when he began reign; and he reigned three months Jerusalem. And his mother's nar *was* [j]Hă-mū́-tăl, the daughter Jeremiah of Lĭb́-năh.

32 And he did *that which was* evil the sight of the LORD, according to that his fathers had done.

33 And Phâŕ-ăōh–nḗ-c̲hōh put him bands at [k]Rĭb́-lăh in the land of H măth, [15]that he might not reign Jerusalem; and [16]put the land to tribute of an hundred talents of silve and a talent of gold.

34 And Phâŕ-ăōh–nḗ-c̲hōh made Ē-ă-kĭm the son of Jō-sī́-ăh king in t room of Jō-sī́-ăh his father, and tur ed [l]his name to [m]Jĕ-hōi̇́-ă-kĭm, a took Jĕ-hṓ-ă-hăz away: and [n]he car to Egypt, and died there.

35 And Jĕ-hōi̇́-ă-kĭm gave the silv and the gold to Pharaoh; but he tax the land to give the money accordi to the commandment of Pharaoh: [o]exacted the silver and the gold of t people of the land, of every one a cording to his taxation, to give *it* un Phâŕ-ăōh–nḗ-c̲hōh.

36 ¶ Jĕ-hōi̇́-ă-kĭm *was* twenty a five years old when he began to reig and he reigned eleven years in Jerus lem. And his mother's name *was* Z bū́-dăh, the daughter of Pĕ-dāi̇́-ăh Rû́-măh.

37 And he did *that which was* evil the sight of the LORD, according to that his fathers had done.

CHAPTER 24

IN his [a]days Nĕb-ū-c̲hăd-nĕź-z king of Babylon came up, and J hōi̇́-ă-kĭm became his servant thr years: then he turned and rebell against him.

2 And [b]the LORD sent against hi bands of the C̲hăĺ-dēēṡ, and bands the Syrians, and bands of the Moa ites, and bands of the children of A mon, and sent them against Judah destroy it, [c]according to the word the LORD, which he spake [1]by his s vants the prophets.

3 Surely at the commandment of t LORD came *this* upon Judah, to move *them* out of his sight, for [d]t sins of Mă-năś-sēh, according to that he did;

4 And [e]also for the innocent blo that he shed: for he filled Jerusal with innocent blood; which [f]the Lo would not pardon.

5 ¶ Now the rest of the acts of hōi̇́-ă-kĭm, and all that he did,

12 Or, sacrificed.
x 2 Chr. 34.5.
y 2 Chr. 35.1.
z Ex. 12.3. Lev. 23.5. Num. 9 2. Deut. 16.2.
a ch. 21.6. 1 Chr. 10.13.
13 Or, teraphim.
b Lev. 19.31. Lev. 20.27. Deut. 18.11. ch. 22.8-13. 2 Chr. 34. 14-19.
c ch. 18.5.
d ch. 21.11. ch. 24.3. Jer. 15.4.
14 angers.
e ch. 17.18.
f 1 Ki. 8.29.
g Judg. 1.27. ch. 9.27. Zech. 12.11.
h ch. 14.8.
i ch. 14.21. 2 Chr. 36.1, 2. Jer. 22.11.
j ch. 24.18.
k Num. 34. 11. ch. 25.6.
15 Or, because he reigned.
16 set a mulct upon the land.
l ch. 24.17. Dan. 1.7.
m Matt. 1.11, Jakim.
n Jer. 22.11.
o Pro. 11.11.

CHAP. 24

a Lev. 26.25. ch. 17.5. 2 Chr. 36.6. Jer. 25.1,9. Dan. 1.1.
b Deut. 28. 49, 50. Jer. 25.9. Eze. 19.8.
c ch. 20.17. ch. 21.12.
1 by the hand of.
d ch. 21.2,11. ch. 23.26.
e ch. 21.16.
f Jer. 15.1. Lam. 3.42.

hey not written in the book of the
:hronicles of the kings of Judah?
6 So [g]Jĕ-hôi-ă-kĭm slept with his
athers: and Jĕ-hôi-ă-chĭn his son
eigned in his stead.
7 And [h]the king of Egypt came not
ıgain any more out of his land: for
the king of Babylon had taken from
he river of Egypt unto the river Eû-
hrā-tēs all that pertained to the king
f Egypt.
8 ¶ [2]Jĕ-hôi-ă-chĭn *was* eighteen years
ld when he began to reign, and he
eigned in Jerusalem three months.
nd his mother's name *was* Nĕ-hŭsh-
ă, the daughter of Ĕl-nā-thăn of Jeru-
alem.
9 And he did *that which was* evil in
he sight of the LORD, according to all
hat his father had done.
10 ¶ At [j]that time the servants of
Nĕb-ū-chăd-nĕz-zär king of Babylon
ame up against Jerusalem, and the
ity [3]was besieged.
11 And Nĕb-ū-chăd-nĕz-zär king of
Babylon came against the city, and his
ervants did besiege it.
12 And [k]Jĕ-hôi-ă-chĭn the king of
udah went out to the king of Bab-
lon, he, and his mother, and his ser-
ants, and his princes, and his [4]offic-
rs: [l]and the king of Babylon [m]took
im [n]in the eighth year of his reign.
13 And [o]he carried out thence all the
reasures of the house of the LORD,
nd the treasures of the king's house,
nd [p]cut in pieces all the vessels of
old which Solomon king of Israel had
nade in the temple of the LORD, [q]as
he LORD had said.
14 And [r]he carried away all Jerusa-
m, and all the princes, and all the
ighty men of valour, *even* ten thou-
and captives, and all [s]the craftsmen
nd smiths: none remained, save [t]the
oorest sort of the people of the land.
15 And [u]he carried away Jĕ-hôi-ă-
hĭn to Babylon, and the king's
nother, and the king's wives, and his
fficers, and the mighty of the land,
hose carried he into captivity from
rusalem to Babylon.
16 And [v]all the men of might, *even*
even thousand, and craftsmen and
miths a thousand, all *that were* strong
nd apt for war, even them the king of
abylon brought captive to Babylon.
17 ¶ And [w]the king of Babylon made
Măt-tă-nī-ăh his father's brother
ing in his stead, [y]and changed his
ame to Zĕd-ē-kī-ăh.
18 Zĕd-ē-kī-ăh [z]*was* twenty and one
ears old when he began to reign, and
he reigned eleven years in Jerusalem.
And [a]his mother's name *was* Hă-mū-
tăl, the daughter of Jeremiah of Lĭb-
năh.
19 And he did *that which was* evil in
the sight of the LORD, according to all
that Jĕ-hôi-ă-kĭm had done.
20 For [b]through the anger of the
LORD it came to pass in Jerusalem and
Judah, until he had cast them out from
his presence, that Zĕd-ē-kī-ăh [c]rebell-
ed against the king of Babylon.

CHAPTER 25

AND it came to pass [a]in the ninth
year of his reign, in the tenth
month, in the tenth *day* of the month,
that Nĕb-ū-chăd-nĕz-zär king of Babylon came, he, and all his host, against
Jerusalem, and pitched against it; and
they built forts against it round about.
2 And the city was besieged unto the
eleventh year of king Zĕd-ē-kī-ăh.
3 And on the ninth *day* of the *fourth*
month the famine prevailed in the
city, and there was no bread for the
people of the land.
4 ¶ And the city was broken up, and
all the men of war *fled* by night by the
way of the gate between two walls,
which *is* by the king's garden: (now
the Chăl-dēēs *were* against the city
round about:) and [b]*the king* went the
way toward the plain.
5 And the army of the Chăl-dēēs pursued after the king, and overtook him
in the plains of Jericho: and all his
army were scattered from him.
6 So they took the king, and brought
him up to the king of Babylon [c]to
Rĭb-lăh; and they [1]gave judgment upon him.
7 And they slew the sons of Zĕd-ē-
kī-ăh before his eyes, and [2]put out the
eyes of Zĕd-ē-kī-ăh, and bound him
with fetters of brass, and carried him
to Babylon.
8 ¶ And in the fifth month, on the
seventh *day* of the month, which *is*
[d]the nineteenth year of king Nĕb-ū-
chăd-nĕz-zär king of Babylon, came
Nĕb-ū-zär-ăd-ăn, [3]captain of the
guard, a servant of the king of Babylon, unto Jerusalem:
9 And [e]he burnt the house of the
LORD, and the [f]king's house, and all
the houses of Jerusalem, and every
great *man's* house burnt he with fire.
10 And all the army of the Chăl-dēēs,
that *were with* the captain of the
guard, [g]brake down the walls of Jerusalem round about.
11 Now [h]the rest of the people *that*

g 2 Chr. 36.6.
h Jer. 37.5.
i Jer. 46.2.
2 Jeconiah, 1 Chr. 3.16. Jer. 24.1. And Coniah, Jer. 22.24.
j Dan. 1.1.
3 came into siege.
k Jer. 24.1. Eze. 17.12.
4 Or, eunuchs.
l Jer. 25.1.
m ch. 25.27.
n Jer. 52.28.
o Isa. 39.6.
p Dan. 5.2.
q 1 Ki. 14.15.
r 2 Chr. 36.9, 10.
s 1 Sam. 13. 19,22.
t ch. 25.12. Jer. 39.10.
u 2 Chr. 36. 10. Esther 2.6.
5 Or, eunuchs.
v Jer. 52.28.
w Jer. 37.1.
x 1 Chr. 3.15. 2 Chr. 36.10, 11.
y ch. 23.34. 2 Chr. 36.4.
z 2 Chr. 36. 11. Jer. 37.1.
a ch. 23.31.
b Deut. 4.24. ch. 22.16,17. ch. 23.26,27.
c Eze. 17.15. 2 Chr. 36.13.

CHAP. 25

a 2 Chr. 36. 17. Jer. 34.2. Eze. 24.1.
b Jer. 39.4.
c ch. 23.33.
1 spake judgment with him.
2 made blind.
d ch. 24.12.
3 Or, chief marshal.
e 2 Chr. 36. 19. Ps. 74.3-7. Ps. 79.1. Isa. 64.11. Micah 3.12.
f Amos 2.5.
g Neh. 1.3.
h Jer. 39.9.

were left in the city, and the [4]fugitives
that fell away to the king of Babylon,
with the remnant of the multitude, did
Nĕb-ū-zär-ăd-ăn the captain of the
guard carry away.
12 But the captain of the guard left
[i]of the poor of the land *to be* vinedressers and husbandmen.
13 And [j]the pillars of [k]brass that
were in the house of the LORD, and the
bases, and the brasen sea that *was* in
the house of the LORD, did the Chăl-
dēeṡ break in pieces, and carried the
brass of them to Babylon.
14 And [l]the pots, and the shovels,
and the snuffers, and the spoons, and
all the vessels of brass wherewith they
ministered, took they away.
15 And the firepans, and the bowls,
and such [m]things as *were* of gold, *in*
gold, and of silver, *in* silver, the captain of the guard took away.
16 The two pillars, [5]one sea, and the
bases which Solomon had made
for the house of the LORD; the
brass of all these vessels was without weight.
17 The height of the one pillar *was*
eighteen cubits, and the chapiter upon
it *was* brass: and the height of the
chapiter three cubits; and the wreath-
en work, and pomegranates upon the
chapiter round about, all of brass:
and like unto these had the second
pillar with wreathen work.
18 ¶ And [n]the captain of the guard
took Sĕ-rāi-ăh [o]the chief priest, and
[p]Zĕph-ă-nī-ăh the second priest, and
the three keepers of the [6]door:
19 And out of the city he took an
[7]officer that was set over the men of
war, and [q]five men of them that [8]were
in the king's presence, which were
found in the city, and the [9]principal
scribe of the host, which mustered
the people of the land, and threescore
men of the people of the land *that*
were found in the city:
20 And Nĕb-ū-zär-ăd-ăn captain of
the guard took these, and brought
them to the king of Babylon to Rĭb-
lăh:
21 And the king of Babylon smote
them, and slew them at Rĭb-lăh in the

4 fallen away.
i ch. 24.14. Jer. 40.7.
j ch. 20.17.
k 1 Ki. 7.15.
l Ex. 27.3.
m Ex. 37.23. 2 Chr. 24.14. Esther 1.9-11. Dan. 5.2.
5 the one sea.
n Jer. 52.24.
o 1 Chr. 6.14. Ezra 7.1.
p Jer. 21.1.
6 threshold.
7 Or, eunuch.
q Jer. 52.25.
8 saw the king's face.
9 Or, scribe of the captain of the host.
r Lev. 26.33. Deut. 4.26. ch. 17.20. ch. 23.27. Jer. 24.9,10. Amos 5.27.
s Jer. 40.5.
t Jer. 27.12.
u Jer. 41.1,2. Zech. 7.5.
10 of the kingdom.
v Jer. 41.16-18.
w Deut. 28.68. Jer. 41.17.
x Gen. 40.13, 20.
11 good things with him.
y Esther 4.4. Jer. 27.6-11. Dan. 2.37.
z Gen. 41.14, 42.
a 2 Sam. 9.7.

land of Hā-măth. [r]So Judah w
carried away out of their land.
22 ¶ And [s]*as for* the people that r
mained in the land of Judah, who
Nĕb-ū-chăd-nĕz-zär king of Babyl
had left, even over them he ma
Gĕd-ă-lī-ăh the son of Ă-hī-kăm, t
son of Shā-phăn, ruler.
23 And when all the captains of t
armies, they and their men, heard th
the king of Babylon had made Gĕ
ă-lī-ăh governor, there came to Gĕ
ă-lī-ăh to Mizpah, even Ĭsh-mā-ĕl t
son of Nĕth-ă-nī-ăh, and Jō-hā-nă
the son of Că-rē-ăh, and Sĕ-rāi-ăh t
son of Tăn-hū-mĕth the Nĕ-tŏph-
thīte, and Jā-ăz-ă-nī-ăh the son of
Mā-ăch-ă-thīte, they and their men
24 And Gĕd-ă-lī-ăh sware to ther
and to their men, and said unto ther
[t]Fear not to be the servants of t
Chăl-dēeṡ: dwell in the land, and ser
the king of Babylon; and it shall
well with you.
25 But [u]it came to pass in the seven
month, that Ĭsh-mā-ĕl the son of Nĕt
ă-nī-ăh, the son of Ē-lī-shă-mă, of t
seed [10]royal, came, and ten men wi
him, and smote Gĕd-ă-lī-ăh, that
died, and the Jews and the Chăl-dē
that were with him at Mizpah.
26 And all the people, both small ar
great, and the captains of the armie
arose, and [v]came to Egypt: for the
were afraid of the Chăl-dēeṡ.
27 ¶ And [w]it came to pass in the se
en and thirtieth year of the captivi
of Jĕ-hōi-ă-chĭn king of Judah, in t
twelfth month, on the seven and twe
tieth *day* of the month, *that* Ē-vī
mĕr-ō-dăch king of Babylon in t
year that he began to reign did [x]lift u
the head of Jĕ-hōi-ă-chĭn king of J
dah out of prison;
28 And he spake [11]kindly to him, ar
set his throne above the throne of [y]t
kings that *were* with him in Babylo
29 And [z]changed his prison ga
ments: and he did [a]eat bread contin
ally before him all the days of his lif
30 And his allowance *was* a continu
allowance given him of the king,
daily rate for every day, all the days
his life.

THE FIRST

BOOK OF THE CHRONICLES

CHAPTER 1

ADAM, [a]Sheth, Ē´nŏsh,
2 Kē´năn, Mă-hăl´ă-leel, Jē´rĕd,
3 [b]Hē´nŏch, Mĕ-thū´sĕ-lăh, Lā´-
mĕch,
4 Noah, Shem, Ham, and Jā´phĕth.
5 ¶ The [c]sons of Jā´phĕth; Gō´mĕr,
and Mā´gŏg, and Mā´dāi, and Jā´văn,
and Tū´băl, and Mē´shĕch, and Tī´-
răs.
6 And the sons of Gō´mĕr; Ăsh-chē´-
năz, and [1]Rī´phăth, and Tō-gär´măh.
7 And the sons of Jā´văn; Ē-lī´shăh,
and Tarshish, Kittim, and [2]Dō´dă-
nĭm.
8 ¶ The [d]sons of Ham; Cŭsh, and
Mĭz´rā-ĭm, Pŭt, and Canaan.
9 And the sons of Cŭsh; Sē´bă, and
Hăv´ĭ-lăh, and Săb´tă, and Rā´ă-măh,
and Săb´tē-chă. And the sons of Rā´-
ă-măh; Shē´bă, and Dē´dăn.
10 And Cŭsh [e]begat Nimrod: he began to be mighty upon the earth.
11 And Mĭz´rā-ĭm begat Lū´dĭm, and
Ăn´ă-mĭm, and Lĕ-hā´bĭm, and Năph-
tû´hĭm,
12 And Păth-rû´sĭm, and Căs-lû´-
hĭm, (of whom came the Philistines,)
and [f]Căph´thō-rĭm.
13 And Canaan begat Zī´dŏn his
firstborn, and Heth,
14 The Jĕb´ū-sīte also, and the Amorite, and the Gĭr´gă-shīte,
15 And the Hī´vīte, and the Är´kīte,
and the Sī´nīte,
16 And the Är´vă-dīte, and the Zĕm´-
ă-rīte, and the Hā´măth-īte.
17 ¶ The sons of [g]Shem; Ē´lăm, and
Ăssh´ŭr, and Är-phăx´ăd, and Lud,
and Âr´ăm, and Uz, and Hul, and Gē´-
thĕr, and [3]Mē´shĕch.
18 And Är-phăx´ăd begat Shē´lăh,
and Shē´lăh begat Ē´bĕr.
19 And unto Ē´bĕr were born two
sons: the name of the one *was* [4]Pē´lĕg;
because in his days the earth was
divided: and his brother's name *was*
Jŏk´tăn.
20 And Jŏk´tăn begat Ăl-mō´dăd,
and Shē´lĕph, and Hă-zär-mā´vĕth,
and Jē´răh,

CHAP. 1
a Gen. 4.25.
b Jude 14.
c Gen. 10.2.
1 Or, Diphath, as it is in some copies.
2 Or, Rodanim, according to some copies.
d Gen. 10.6.
e Gen. 10.8, 13.
f Gen. 10.14. Deut. 2.23. Amos 9.7.
g Gen. 9.23, 26.
3 Or, Mash, Gen. 10.23.
4 That is, Division.
h Gen. 11.10. Luke 3.36.
i Num. 24.24. Luke 3.35.
j 2 Chr. 20.7. Neh. 9.7. Isa. 41.8. Rom. 4.16.
k Gen. 21.2, 3.
l Gen. 16.11, 15.
m Gen. 25. 13-16.
5 Or, Hadar, Gen. 25.15.
n Gen. 25.1, 2.
o Gen. 21.2, 3.
p Gen. 25.25.
q Deut. 2.22. Mal. 1.2,3. Rom. 9.13. Heb. 12.16.
6 Or, Zepho, Gen. 36.11.
r Gen. 36.20.
7 Or, Hemam. Gen. 36.22.
8 Or, Alvan, Gen. 36.23.
9 Or, Shepho, Gen. 36.23.

21 Hă-dôr´ăm also, and Ū´zăl, and
Dĭk´lăh,
22 And Ē´băl, and Ă-bĭm´ă-ĕl, and
Shē´bă,
23 And Ō´phĭr, and Hăv´ĭ-lăh, and
Jō´băb. All these *were* the sons of
Jŏk´tăn.
24 ¶ [h]Shem, Är-phăx´ăd, Shē´lăh,
25 [i]Ē´bĕr, Pē´lĕg, Rē´ū,
26 Sē´rŭg, Nahor, Tē´răh,
27 Abram; [j]the same *is* Abraham.
28 The sons of Abraham; [k]Isaac, and
[l]Ĭsh´mā-ĕl.
29 ¶ These *are* their generations:
The firstborn [m]of Ĭsh´mā-ĕl, Nĕ-bāi´-
ŏth; then Kē´där, and Ăd´beel, and
Mĭb´săm,
30 Mĭsh´mă, and Dū´măh, Măs´să,
[5]Hā´dăd, and Tē´mă,
31 Jē´tŭr, Nā´phĭsh, and Kē´dĕ-
măh. These are the sons of Ĭsh´mā-
ĕl.
32 ¶ Now [n]the sons of Kĕ-tū´răh,
Abraham's concubine: she bare Zim-
ran, and Jŏk´shăn, and Mē´dăn, and
Mĭd´ĭ-ăn, and Ĭsh´băk, and Shû´ăh.
And the sons of Jŏk´shăn; Shē´bă,
and Dē´dăn.
33 And the sons of Mĭd´ĭ-ăn; Ē´phăh,
and Ē´phĕr, and Hē´nŏch, and Ă-bī´-
dă, and Ĕl-dā´ăh. All these *are* the
sons of Kĕ-tū´răh.
34 And [o]Abraham begat Isaac. The
[p]sons of Isaac; Esau and Israel.
35 ¶ The sons of [q]Esau; Ĕ-lī´phăz,
Reū´ĕl, and Jē´ŭsh, and Jā´ă-lăm, and
Kôr´ăh.
36 The sons of Ĕ´lī-phăz; Tē´măn,
and Omar, [6]Zē´phī, and Gă´tăm, Kē´-
năz, and Tĭm´nă, and Ăm´ă-lĕk.
37 The sons of Reū´ĕl; Nahath, Zē´-
răh, Shăm´măh, and Mĭz´zăh.
38 And [r]the sons of Sē´ĭr; Lō´tăn,
and Shō´băl, and Zĭb´ĕ-on, and Ā´-
năh, and Dī´shŏn, and Ē´zĕr, and
Dī´shăn.
39 And the sons of Lō´tăn; Hôr´ī,
and [7]Hō´măm: and Tĭm´nă *was* Lō´-
tăn's sister.
40 The sons of Shō´băl; [8]Ăl´ĭ-ăn, and
Măn´ă-hăth, and Ē´băl, [9]Shē´phī, and

Ō´-năm. And the sons of Zĭb´-ĕ-o̱n;
Aî´-ăh, and Ā´-năh.
41 The sons of Ā´-năh; [s]Dī´-shŏn. And
the sons of Dī´-shŏn; [10]Amram, and
Ĕsh´-băn, and Ĭth´-răn, and Che̱´-răn.
42 The sons of Ē´-zĕr; Bĭl´-hăn, and
Zā´-văn, *and* [11]Jā´-kăn. The sons of Dī´-
shăn; Uz, and Âr´-ăn.
43 ¶ Now these *are* the [t]kings that
reigned in the land of Ē´-do̱m before
any king reigned over the children of
Israel; Bē´-lă the son of Bē´-ôr: and the
name of his city *was* Dĭn´-hă-băh.
44 And when Bē´-lă was dead, Jō´-băb
the son of Zē´-răh of Bŏz´-răh reigned
in his stead.
45 And when Jō´-băb was dead, Hū´-
shăm of the land of the Tē´-măn-ītes
reigned in his stead.
46 And when Hū´-shăm was dead,
Hā´-dăd [u]the son of Bē´-dăd, which
smote Mĭd´-ĭ-ăn in the field of Moab,
reigned in his stead: and the name of
his city *was* Ā´-vĭth.
47 And when Hā´-dăd was dead, Săm´-
lăh of Măs-rē´-kăh reigned in his stead.
48 And [v]when Săm´-lăh was dead,
Shā´-ŭl of Rē´-hŏ-bōth by the river
reigned in his stead.
49 And when Shā´-ŭl was dead, Bā´-
ăl–hā´-năn the son of Ăc̱h´-bôr reigned
in his stead.
50 And when Bā´-ăl–hā´-năn was
dead, [12]Hā´-dăd reigned in his stead:
and the name of his city *was* [13]Pā´-ī; and
his wife's name *was* Mĕ-hĕt´-ă-bĕl, the
daughter of Mā´-trĕd, the daughter of
Mē´-ză-hăb.
51 ¶ Hā´-dăd died also. And [w]the
dukes of Ē´-do̱m were; duke Tĭm´-năh,
duke [14]Ăl´-ĭ-ăh, duke Jē´-thĕth,
52 Duke Ă-hŏl-ĭ-bā´-măh, duke Ē´-
lăh, duke Pī´-nŏn,
53 Duke Kē´-năz, duke Tē´-măn, duke
Mĭb´-zăr,
54 Duke Măg´-dĭ-ĕl, duke Ī´-răm.
These *are* the dukes of Ē´-do̱m.

CHAPTER 2

THESE *are* the sons of [1]Israel;
[a]Reuben, Simeon, Levi, and Judah, Ĭs´-să-c̱hăr, and Zĕ-bū´-lŭn,
2 Dan, Joseph, and Benjamin,
Năph´-tă-lī, Gad, and Asher.
3 ¶ The sons of [b]Judah; Er, and Ō´-
năn, and Shē´-lăh: *which* three were
born unto him of the daughter of
[c]Shû´-ă the Canaanitess. And [d]Er, the
firstborn of Judah, was evil in the
sight of the LORD; and he slew him.
4 And [e]Tā´-mär his daughter in law
bare him Phăr´-ĕz and Zē´-răh. All the
sons of Judah *were* five.

s Gen. 36.25.
10 Or, Hemdan, Gen. 36.26.
11 Or, Akan, Gen. 36.27.
t Gen. 36.31.
u 1 Ki. 11.14.
v Gen. 36.37.
12 Or, Hadar, Gen. 36.39.
13 Or, Pau, Gen. 36.39.
w Ex. 15.15.
14 Or, Alvah.

CHAP. 2

1 Or, Jacob, Gen. 32.28. Ex. 32.13. Num. 13.4-15.
a Gen. 29.32. Gen. 30.5. Ex. 1.2.
b Gen. 29.35. Gen. 38.3. Num. 26.19. Deut. 33.7.
c Gen. 38.2.
d Gen. 38.7.
e Gen. 38.29, 30. Matt. 1.3.
f Gen. 46.12. Ruth 4.18.
2 Or, Zabdi, Josh. 7.1.
g 1 Ki. 4.31.
3 Or, Darda.
h ch. 4.1.
4 Or, Achan.
i Josh. 6.18.
5 Or, Aram, Matt. 1.3.4.
6 Or, Caleb.
j Ruth 4.19. Matt. 1.4.
k Num. 1.7. Num. 2.3.
7 Or, Salmon, Ruth 4.21. Matt. 1.4.
l 1 Sam. 16.6.
8 Or, Shammah, 1 Sam. 16.9.
m 2 Sam. 2. 18.
n 2 Sam. 17. 25.
9 Ithra an Israelite, 2 Sam. 17. 25.
o Ex. 31.2. 2 Chr. 1.5.
p Num. 27.1.
10 took.
q Num. 32. 41. Deut. 3.14.
r ch. 4.5.
s 2 Sam. 14.2. ch. 4.5. 2 Chr. 11.6. 2 Chr. 20.20. Neh. 3.5. Jer. 6.1. Amos 1.1.

5 The sons of [f]Phâr´-ĕz; Hĕz´-rŏn, and
Hăm´-ŭl.
6 And the sons of Zē´-răh; [2]Zimri, and
[g]Ē´-thăn, and Hē´-măn, and Căl´-cŏl,
and [3]Dâr´-ă: five of them in all.
7 And the sons of [h]Căr´-mī; [4]Ā´-c̱hăr
the troubler of Israel, who transgressed in the [i]thing accursed.
8 And the sons of Ē´-thăn; Ăz-ă-rī´-ăh.
9 The sons also of Hĕz´-rŏn, that
were born unto him; Jĕ-răh´-meēl, and
[5]Ram, and [6]C̱hĕ-lū´-baī.
10 And Ram [j]begat Ăm-mĭn´-ă-dăb;
and Ăm-mĭn´-ă-dăb begat Năh´-shŏn,
prince [k]of the children of Judah;
11 And Năh´-shŏn begat [7]Săl´-mă, and
Săl´-mă begat Bō´-ăz,
12 And Bō´-ăz begat Ō´-bĕd, and Ō´-
bĕd begat Jesse,
13 ¶ And [l]Jesse begat his firstborn
Ē-lī´-ăb, and Ă-bĭn´-ă-dăb the second,
and [8]Shĭm´-mă the third,
14 Nĕth´-ă-neēl the fourth, Răd´-dā-ī
the fifth,
15 Ō´-zĕm the sixth, David the seventh:
16 Whose sisters *were* Zĕr-ū-ĭ´-ăh
and Ăb´-ĭ-ga̱il. [m]And the sons of Zĕr-
ū-ĭ´-ăh; Ăb´-ĭ-shaī, and Jō´-ăb, and Ăs´-
ă-hĕl, three.
17 And [n]Ăb´-ĭ-ga̱il bare Ă-mā´-să: and
the father of Ă-mā´-să *was* [9]Jē´-thĕr the
Ĭsh´-meē-līte.
18 ¶ And Caleb the son of Hĕz´-
rŏn begat *children* of Ă-zū´-băh his
wife, and of Jĕr´-ĭ-ōth: her sons *are*
these; Jē´-shĕr, and Shō´-băb, and
Ardon.
19 And when Ă-zū´-băh was dead,
Caleb took unto him Ē´-phrăth, which
bare him Hur.
20 And Hur begat Ū´-rī, and Ū´-rī begat [o]Bĕz´-ă-leēl.
21 ¶ And afterward Hĕz´-rŏn went in
to the daughter of [p]Mā´-c̱hĭr the father
of Gilead, whom he [10]married when he
was threescore years old; and she bare
him Sē´-gŭb.
22 And Sē´-gŭb begat Jā´-ĭr, who had
three and twenty cities in the land of
Gilead.
23 And [q]he took Gē´-shŭr, and Ăr´-
ăm, with the towns of Jā´-ĭr, from
them, with Kē´-năth, and the towns
thereof, *even* threescore cities. All
these *belonged to* the sons of Mā´-c̱hĭr
the father of Gilead.
24 And after that Hĕz´-rŏn was dead
in Cā´-lĕb–ĕph´-ră-tăh, then Ă-bī´-ăh
Hĕz´-rŏn's wife bare him Ashur [r]the
father of [s]Tĕ-kō´-ă.
25 ¶ And the sons of Jĕ-răh´-meēl the
firstborn of Hĕz´-rŏn were, Ram the

rstborn, and Bū´-năh, and Ô´-rĕn, and
)´-zĕm, *and* Ă-hī´-jăh.
26 Jĕ-răh´-mē̆el had also another
ife, whose name *was* Ăt´-ă-răh; she
as the mother of Ō´-năm.
27 And the sons of Ram the firstborn
f Jĕ-răh´-mē̆el were, Mā´-ăz, and Jā´-
iīn, and Ē´-kĕr.
28 And the sons of Ō´-năm were,
hăm´-mā-ī, and Jā´-dă. And the sons
f Shăm´-mā-ī; Nadab, and Ă-bī´-
hûr.
29 And the name of the wife of Ă-bī´-
hûr *was* Ăb´-ĭ-hail, and she bare him
h´-băn, and Mō´-lĭd.
30 And the sons of Nadab; Sē´-lĕd,
nd Ăp´-pā-ĭm: but Sē´-lĕd died with-
ut children.
31 And the sons of Ăp´-pā-ĭm; Ĭsh´-ī.
nd the sons of Ĭsh´-ī; Shē´-shăn. And
he children of Shē´-shăn; Ăh´-lā-ī.
32 And the sons of Jā´-dă the brother
f Shăm´-mā-ī; Jē´-thĕr and Jonathan:
nd Jē´-thĕr died without children.
33 And the sons of Jonathan; Pē´-
ĕth, and Zā´-ză. These were the sons
f Jĕ-răh´-mē̆el.
34 ¶ Now Shē´-shăn had no sons, but
aughters. And Shē´-shăn had a ser-
ant, an Egyptian, whose name *was*
ăr´-hă.
35 And Shē´-shăn gave his daughter
o Jär´-hă his servant to wife; and she
are him Ăt´-tā-ī.
36 And Ăt´-tā-ī begat Nathan, and
Nathan begat [t]Zā´-băd,
37 And Zā´-băd begat Ĕph´-lăl, and
ph´-lăl begat Ō´-bĕd,
38 And Ō´-bĕd begat Jehu, and Jehu
egat Ăz-ă-rī´-ăh,
39 And Ăz-ă-rī´-ăh begat Hē´-lĕz, and
Iē´-lĕz begat Ĕl-ē-ā´-săh,
40 And Ĕl-ē-ā´-săh begat Sĭs´-ă-māi,
nd Sĭs´-ă-māi begat Shăl´-lŭm,
41 And Shăl´-lŭm begat Jĕk-ă-mī´-ăh,
nd Jĕk-ă-mī´-ăh begat Ē-lī´-shă-mă.
42 ¶ Now the sons of Caleb the bro-
her of Jĕ-răh´-mē̆el *were*, Mē´-shă his
irstborn, which *was* [11]the father of
Ziph; and the sons of Mă-rē´-shăh the
ather of Hē´-brŏn.
43 And the sons of Hē´-brŏn; Kôr´-ăh,
nd Tăp´-pū-ăh, and Rē´-kĕm, and Shē´-
nă.
44 And Shē´-mă begat Raham, the
ather of Jôr´-kō-ăm: and Rē´-kĕm beat Shăm´-mā-ī.
45 And the son of Shăm´-mā-ī *was*
Mā´-ŏn: and Mā´-ŏn *was* the father of
Bĕth´–zûr.
46 And Ē´-phăh, Caleb's concubine,
are Hâr´-ăn, and Mō´-ză, and Gā´-zĕz:
nd Hâr´-ăn begat Gā´-zĕz.

t ch. 11.41.
11 Called father, because his descendants peopled that city.
u Josh. 15.17.
12 Or, Reaiah, ch. 4.2.
13 Or, half of the Menuchites, or, Hatsiham-menuchoth.
14 Or, Atarites, or, crowns of the house of Joab.
v Gen. 15.19. Num. 24.21, 22. Judg. 1.16. 1 Sam. 15.6.
w Jer. 35.2.

CHAP. 3

a 1 Sam. 25. 43. 2 Sam. 3.2.
b Josh. 15.56.
1 Or, Chileab, 2 Sam. 3.3.
c 2 Sam. 3.5.
d 2 Sam. 2.11.
e 2 Sam. 5.5.
f ch. 14.4.
2 Or, Shammua.
g 2 Sam. 12. 24.
3 Or, Bathsheba.
4 Or, Eliam.
5 Or, Elishua.

47 And the sons of Jăh´-dā-ī; Rē´-
gĕm, and Jō´-thăm, and Gē´-shăn, and
Pē´-lĕt, and Ē´-phăh, and Shā´-ăph.
48 Mā´-ă-chăh, Caleb's concubine,
bare Shē´-bĕr, and Tĭr-hā´-năh.
49 She bare also Shā´-ăph the father
of Măd-măn´-năh, Shē´-vă the father of
Măch-bē´-năh, and the father of Gĭb´-
ē-ă: and the daughter of Caleb *was*
[u]Ăch´-săh.
50 ¶ These were the sons of Caleb
the son of Hur, the firstborn of Ĕph´-
ră-tăh; Shō´-băl the father of Kĭr´-
jăth–jē´-ă-rĭm,
51 Săl´-mă the father of Beth-lehem,
Hâr´-ĕph the father of Bĕth–gā´-dĕr.
52 And Shō´-băl the father of Kĭr´-
jăth–jē´-ă-rĭm had sons; [12]Hă-rō´-ĕh,
and [13]half of the Măn-ă-hē´-thītes.
53 And the families of Kĭr´-jăth–jē´-ă-
rĭm; the Ĭth´-rītes, and the Pū´-hītes,
and the Shû´-mă-thītes, and the Mĭsh´-
rā-ītes; of them came the Ză-rē´-ă-
thītes, and the Ĕsh-tā-ū´-lītes.
54 The sons of Săl´-mă; Beth-lehem,
and the Nĕ-tŏph´-ă-thītes, [14]Ăt´-ă-rŏth,
the house of Jō´-ăb, and half of the
Măn-ă-hē´-thītes, the Zôr´-ītes.
55 And the families of the scribes
which dwelt at Jā´-bĕz; the Tī´-ră-
thītes, the Shĭm´-ē-ă-thītes, *and* Sū´-
chă-thītes. These *are* the Kē´-nītes that
[v]came of Hē´-măth, the father of the
house of [w]Rē´-chăb.

CHAPTER 3

NOW these were the sons of David,
which were born unto him in Hē´-
brŏn; the firstborn Amnon, [a]of Ă-
hĭn´-ō-ăm the [b]Jĕz-rē̆el-ī´-tĕss; the second [1]Daniel, of Ăb´-ĭ-gail the Carmelitess:
2 The third, Ăb´-să-lom the son of
Mā´-ă-chăh the daughter of Tăl´-māi
king of Gē´-shûr: the fourth, Ăd-ō-nī´-
jăh the son of Hăg´-gĭth:
3 The fifth, Shĕph-ă-tī´-ăh of Ă-bĭ´-
tăl: the sixth, Ĭth´-rē-ăm by [c]Ĕg´-lăh
his wife.
4 *These* six were born unto him in Hē´-
brŏn; and [d]there he reigned seven
years and six months: and in [e]Jeru-
salem he reigned thirty and three
years.
5 And [f]these were born unto him in
Jerusalem; [2]Shĭm´-ē-ă, and Shō´-băb,
and Nathan, and [g]Solomon, four, of
[3]Băth´–shû-ă the daughter of [4]Ăm´-
mĭ-ĕl:
6 Ĭb´-hăr also, and [5]Ē-lĭ´-shă-mă, and
Ē-lĭph´-ē-lĕt,
7 And Nō´-găh, and Nĕph´-ĕg, and Jă-
phī´-ă,

8 And Ē-lī´-shă-mă, and [6]Ē-lī´-ă-dă, and Ē-lĭph´-ĕ-lĕt, [h]nine.

9 *These were* all the sons of David, beside the sons of the concubines, and [i]Tā´-mär their sister.

10 ¶ And Solomon's son [j]*was* Rē-hŏ-bō´-ăm, [7]Ă-bī´-ă his son, Ā´-să his son, Jĕ-hŏsh´-ă-phăt his son,

11 Joram his son, Ā-hă-zī´-ăh his son, Jō´-ăsh his son,

12 Ăm-ă-zī´-ăh his son, Ăz-ă-rī´-ăh his son, Jō´-thăm his son,

13 Ahaz his son, Hĕz-ē-kī´-ăh his son, Mă-năs´-sēh his son,

14 Amon his son, Jō-sī´-ăh his son.

15 And the sons of Jō-sī´-ăh *were*, the firstborn Jō-hā´-năn, the second Jĕ-hoi´-ă-kĭm, the third Zĕd-ē-kī´-ăh, the fourth Shăl´-lŭm.

16 And the sons of [k]Jĕ-hoi´-ă-kĭm: Jĕc-ō-nī´-ăh his son, Zĕd-ē-kī´-ăh [l]his son.

17 ¶ And the sons of Jĕc-ō-nī´-ăh; Ăs´-sĭr, [8]Să-lā´-thĭ-ĕl [m]his son,

18 Măl-chī´-răm also, and Pĕ-dai´-ăh, and Shĕn-ā´-zär, Jĕc-ă-mī´-ăh, Hō´-shă-mă, and Nĕd-ă-bī´-ăh.

19 And the sons of Pĕ-dai´-ăh [n]*were*, Zĕ-rŭb´-bă-bĕl, and Shĭm´-ĕ-ī: and the sons of Zĕ-rŭb´-bă-bĕl; Mĕ-shŭl´-lăm, and Hăn-ă-nī´-ăh, and Shĕ-lō´-mĭth their sister:

20 And Hă-shû´-băh, and Ō´-hĕl, and Bĕr-ē-chī´-ăh, and Hăs-ă-dī´-ăh, Jû´-shăb–hĕs´-ĕd, five.

21 And the sons of Hăn-ă-nī´-ăh; Pĕl-ă-tī´-ăh, and Jĕ-sai´-ăh: the sons of Rĕ-phai´-ăh, the sons of Arnan, the sons of Ō-bă-dī´-ăh, the son of Shĕch-ă-nī´-ăh.

22 And the sons of Shĕch-ă-nī´-ăh; Shĕm-ai´-ăh: and the sons of Shĕm-ai´-ăh; [o]Hăt´-tŭsh, and Ī-gĕ-ăl, and Bă-rī´-ăh, and Nē-ă-rī´-ăh, and Shā´-phăt, six.

23 And the sons of Nē-ă-rī´-ăh; Ĕl-ĭ-ō-ē´-nai, and [9]Hĕz-ē-kī´-ăh, and Ăz-rī´-kăm, three.

24 And the sons of Ĕl-ĭ-ō-ē´-nai *were*, Hō-dai´-ăh, and Ē-lī-ăsh´-ĭb, and Pĕ-lai´-ăh, and Ăk´-kŭb, and Jō-hā´-năn, and Dă-lai´-ăh, and Ă-nā´-nī, seven.

CHAPTER 4

THE sons of Judah; [a]Phăr´-ĕz, Hĕz´-rŏn, and [1]Căr´-mī, and Hur, and Shō´-băl.

2 And [2]Rē-ai´-ăh the son of Shō´-băl begat Jā´-hăth; and Jā´-hăth begat Ă-hū´-mai, and Lā´-hăd. These *are* the families of the Zôr´-ă-thītes.

3 And these *were of* the father of Ē´-tăm; Jĕz´-rēel, and Ĭsh´-mă, and Ĭd´-

6 Or, Beeliada, ch. 14.7.
h 2 Sam.5.14.
i 2 Sam.13.1.
j 1 Ki. 11.43.
7 Or, Abijam, 1 Ki. 15.1.
k Matt. 1.11.
l 2 Ki. 24.17. Being his successor.
8 Shealtiel.
m Matt. 1.12.
n Ezra 3.2.
o Ezra 8.2.
9 Hiskijahu.

CHAP. 4

a Gen. 38.29. Num. 26.20, 21. Ruth 4.18.
1 Or, Chelubai, ch. 2.9. or, Caleb, ch. 2.18.
2 Or, Haroeh, ch. 2.52.
b Gen. 34.19. Ps. 112.6.
3 That is, Sorrowful.
c Gen. 3.16.
d ch. 16.8. Job 12.4. Isa. 12.4.
4 If thou wilt, etc.
5 do me.
e Job 22.27, 28. Ps. 21.4. Ps. 66.19,20. Matt. 7.7-11.
6 Or, the city of Nahash.
f Josh. 15.17.
7 Or, Hathath, and Meonothai, who begat, etc.
g Neh. 11.35.
8 Or, inhabitants of the valley.
9 That is, craftsmen.
10 Or, Uknaz.
11 Or, the Jewess.
12 Or, Jehudijah, mentioned before.

băsh: and the name of their sister *wa*
Hăz-ĕl-ĕl-pō´-nī:
4 And Pĕn-ū´-ĕl the father of Gē-dôr
and Ē´-zĕr the father of Hū´-shăh
These *are* the sons of Hur, the first
born of Ĕph´-ră-tăh, the father o
Beth-lehem.
5 ¶ And Ashur the father of Tē-kō
ă had two wives, Hē´-lăh and Nā´-ă-răh
6 And Nā´-ă-răh bare him Ă-hū´-zăm
and Hē´-phĕr, and Tē´-mĕ-nī, and Hā
ă-hăsh´-tă-rī. These *were* the sons o
Nā´-ă-răh.
7 And the sons of Hē´-lăh *were*, Zē
rĕth, and Jĕ-zō´-är, and Ĕth´-năn.
8 And Cŏz begat Anub, and Zō-bē
băh, and the families of Ă-här´-hĕl th
son of Hâr´-ŭm.
9 ¶ And Jā´-bĕz was [b]more honour
able than his brethren: and his mothe
called his name [3]Jā´-bĕz, saying, Be
cause [c]I bare him with sorrow.
10 And Jā´-bĕz [d]called on the God o
Israel, saying, [4]Oh that thou wouldes
bless me indeed, and enlarge m
coast, and that thine hand might b
with me, and that thou wouldest [5]kee
me from evil, that it may not griev
me! And God [e]granted him that whic
he requested.
11 ¶ And Chē´-lŭb the brother o
Shû´-ăh begat Mē´-hĭr, which *was* th
father of Ĕsh´-tŏn.
12 And Ĕsh´-tŏn begat Bĕth–rā´-phă
and Pă-sē´-ăh, and Tē-hĭn´-năh th
father of [6]Ĭr–nā´-hăsh. These *are* th
men of Rē´-chăh.
13 And the sons of Kē´-năz; [f]Ŏth´-nī
ĕl, and Sĕ-rai´-ăh: and the sons of Ŏth
nī-ĕl; [7]Hā´-thăth.
14 And Mē-ō´-nō-thai begat Ŏph
răh: and Sĕ-rai´-ăh begat Jō´-ăb, th
father of [g]the [8]valley of [9]Chă-rā´-shĭm
for they were craftsmen.
15 And the sons of Caleb the son o
Jĕ-phŭn´-nĕh; Ī´-rû, Ē´-lăh, and Nā´-ăm
and the sons of Ē´-lăh, [10]even Kē´-năz
16 And the sons of Jĕ-hăl´-ĕ-lēel
Ziph, and Zī´-phăh, Tī´-rĭ-ă, and Ăs´-ă
rēel.
17 And the sons of Ezra *were*, Jē
thĕr, and Mē´-rĕd, and Ē´-phĕr, an
Jalon: and she bare Miriam, an
Shăm´-mă-ī, and Ĭsh´-băh the father c
Ĕsh-tĕ-mō´-ă.
18 And his wife [11]Jĕ-hū-dī´-jăh bar
Jē´-rĕd the father of Gē´-dôr, and Hē
bĕr the father of Sō´-chō, and Jĕ-kū
thĭ´-ĕl the father of Ză-nō´-ăh. An
these *are* the sons of Bĭth´-ĭ-ăh th
daughter of Pharaoh, which Mē´-rē
took.
19 And the sons of *his* wife [12]Hō-di

ɩ the sister of Naham, the father of
ē-ĭ-lăh the Gär-mīte, and Ĕsh-tĕ-
ō-ă the Mā-ăch-ă-thīte.
0 And the sons of Shī-mŏn *were*,
mnon, and Rĭn-năh, Bĕn–hā-năn,
d Tī-lŏn. And the sons of Ĭsh-ī
re, Zō-hĕth, and Bĕn–zō-hĕth.
1 ¶ The sons of Shē-lăh [h]the son of
dah *were*, Er the father of Lē-căh,
d Lā-ă-dăh the father of Mă-rē-
ăh, and the families of the house of
em that wrought fine linen, of the
use of Ăsh-bē-ă,
2 And Jō-kĭm, and the men of Chō-
bă, and Jō-ăsh, and Sâr-ăph, who
d the [i]dominion in Moab, and Jă-
ū-bī–lē-hĕm. And *these are* ancient
ings.
3 These *were* the potters, and those
at dwelt among plants and hedges:
ere they dwelt with the king for his
rk.
4 ¶ The sons of Simeon *were*,
Nĕm-ū-ĕl, and Jā-mĭn, [14]Jâr-ĭb, Zē-
h, *and* Shā-ŭl:
5 Shăl-lŭm his son, Mĭb-săm his
n, Mĭsh-mă his son.
6 And the sons of Mĭsh-mă; Hăm-
ĕl his son, Zăc-chŭr his son, Shĭm-
his son.
7 And Shĭm-ĕ-ī had sixteen sons and
daughters; but his brethren had
t many children, neither did all
eir family multiply, [15]like to the
ildren of Judah.
8 And they dwelt at Bē-er–shē-bă,
d Mō-lā-dăh, and Hā-zär–shû-ăl,
9 And at [16]Bĭl-hăh, and at Ē-zĕm,
d at [17]Tō-lăd,
0 And at Bĕ-thū-ĕl, and at Hôr-
ăh, and at Ziklag,
1 And at Beth-mär-că-bōth, and
Hā-zär–sû-sĭm, and at Bĕth-bĭr-ĕ-ī,
d at Shā-ă-rā-ĭm. These *were* their
ies unto the reign of David.
2 And their villages *were*, [19]Ē-tăm,
d Ā-ĭn, Rimmon, and Tō-chĕn, and
sh-ăn, five cities:
3 And all their villages that *were*
und about the same cities, unto
Bā-ăl. These *were* their habitations,
d [21]their genealogy.
4 And Mĕ-shō-băb, and Jăm-lĕch,
d Jō-shăh the son of Ăm-ă-zī-ăh,
5 And Jō-ĕl, and Jehu the son of
s-ĭ-bī-ăh, the son of Sĕ-râ-ī-ăh, the
n of Ăs-ĭ-ĕl,
6 And Ĕl-ĭ-ō-ē-nâ-ī, and Jā-ă-kō-
h, and Jĕsh-ō-hâ-ī-ăh, and Ă-sâ-ī-ăh,
d Ăd-ĭ-ĕl, and Jĕ-sĭm-ĭ-ĕl, and Bĕ-
ī-ăh,
7 And Zī-ză the son of Shĭ-phī, the
n of Ăl-lŏn, the son of Jĕ-dâ-ī-ăh, the

h Gen. 38.1.
i 2 Sam. 8.2.
13 Or, Jemuel, Gen. 46.10. Ex. 6.15. Num. 26.12.
14 Or, Jachin, Zohar.
15 unto.
16 Or, Balah, Josh. 19.3.
17 Or, Eltolad, Josh. 19.4.
18 Or, Hazar-susah, Josh. 19.5.
19 Or, Ether.
20 Or, Baalath-beer.
21 Or, as they divided themselves by nations among them.
22 coming.
j Gen. 9.22. Ps. 78.51.
k 2 Ki. 18.8.
l 1 Sam. 15.8. 2 Sam. 8.12.
CHAP. 5
a Gen. 29.32.
b Gen. 35.22.
c Gen. 48.15.
d Gen. 49.8. Num. 2.3. Ps. 60.7.
e Ps. 78.68-71. Jer. 23.5,6. Micah 5.2. Matt. 2.6.
1 Or, prince.
f Ex. 6.14. Num. 26.5.
2 Or, Tiglath-pileser, 2 Ki. 15.29.
g ver. 17.
3 Or, Shemaiah, ver. 4.
h Josh. 13.15.

son of Shĭm-rī, the son of Shĕm-â-ī-ăh;
38 These [22]mentioned by *their* names
were princes in their families: and the
house of their fathers increased
greatly.
39 ¶ And they went to the entrance
of Gē-dôr, *even* unto the east side of
the valley, to seek pasture for their
flocks.
40 And they found fat pasture and
good, and the land *was* wide, and
quiet, and peaceable; for *they* of
[j]Ham had dwelt there of old.
41 And these written by name came
in the days of Hĕz-ē-kī-ăh king of
Judah, and smote [k]their tents, and the
habitations that were found there,
and destroyed them utterly unto this
day, and dwelt in their rooms: because *there was* pasture there for their
flocks.
42 And *some* of them, *even* of the sons
of Simeon, five hundred men, went to
mount Sē-ĭr, having for their captains Pĕl-ă-tī-ăh, and Nē-ă-rī-ăh, and
Rĕ-phâ-ī-ăh, and Ŭz-zī-ĕl, the sons of
Ĭsh-ī.
43 And they smote [l]the rest of the Ă-
măl-ĕk-ītes that were escaped, and
dwelt there unto this day.

CHAPTER 5

NOW the sons of Reuben the firstborn of Israel, (for [a]he *was* the
firstborn; but, forasmuch as he [b]de-
filed his father's bed, [c]his birthright
was given unto the sons of Joseph the
son of Israel: and the genealogy is not
to be reckoned after the birthright.
2 For [d]Judah prevailed above his
brethren, and of him *came* [e]the chief
[1]ruler; but the birthright *was* Joseph's:)
3 The sons, *I say*, of [f]Reuben the
firstborn of Israel *were*, Hā-nŏch, and
Păl-lû, Hĕz-rŏn, and Cär-mī.
4 The sons of Jō-ĕl; Shĕm-â-ī-ăh his
son, Gog his son, Shĭm-ĕ-ī his son,
5 Mī-căh his son, Rĕ-â-ī-ă his son,
Bā-ăl his son,
6 Bē-er-ăh his son, whom [2]Tĭl-găth–
pĭl-nē-sĕr king of Assyria carried
away *captive*: he *was* prince of the
Reubenites.
7 And his brethren by their families,
when [g]the genealogy of their generations was reckoned, *were* the chief,
Jē-ĭ-ĕl, and Zĕch-ă-rī-ăh,
8 And Bē-lă the son of Ā-zăz, the son
of [3]Shē-mă, the son of Jō-ĕl, who
dwelt [h]in Ă-rō-ēr, even unto Nē-bō
and Bā-ăl–mē-ŏn:
9 And eastward he inhabited unto

the entering in of the wilderness from the river Eû-phrā′-tēṡ: because their cattle were multiplied [i]in the land of Gilead.

10 And in the days of Saul they made war with [j]the Hăg′-ă-rītes, who fell by their hand: and they dwelt in their tents [4]throughout all the east *land* of Gilead.

11 ¶ And the children of Gad dwelt over against them, in the land of [k]Bā′-shăn unto Săl′-c̱hăh:

12 Jō′-ĕl the chief, and Shā′-phăm the next, and Jā′-ă-nâi, and Shā′-phăt in Bā′-shăn.

13 And their brethren of the house of their fathers *were*, Michael, and Mĕ-shŭl′-lăm, and Shē′-bă, and Jō′-rā-ī, and Jā′-c̱hăn, and Zī′-ă, and Hē′-bĕr, seven.

14 These *are* the children of Ăb′-ĭ-ha̱il the son of Hū′-rī, the son of Jă-rō′-ăh, the son of Gilead, the son of Michael, the son of Jĕ-shĭsh′-âi, the son of Jăh′-dō, the son of Buz;

15 Ā′-hī the son of Ăb′-dĭ-ĕl, the son of Gū′-nī, chief of the house of their fathers.

16 And they dwelt in Gilead in Bā′-shăn, and in her towns, and in all the suburbs of [l]Shâr′-o̱n, upon [5]their borders.

17 All these were reckoned by genealogies in the days of [m]Jō′-thăm king of Judah, and in the days of Jĕr-ŏ-bō′-ăm [n]king of Israel.

18 ¶ The sons of Reuben, and the Gadites, and half the tribe of Mă-năs′-sēh, [6]of valiant men, men able to bear buckler and sword, and to shoot with bow, and skilful in war, *were* four and forty thousand seven hundred and threescore, that went out to the war.

19 And they made war with the Hăg′-ă-rītes, with [o]Jē′-tûr, and Nĕph′-ĭsh, and Nō′-dăb.

20 And they were helped against them, and the Hăg′-ă-rītes were delivered into their hand, and all that *were* with them: for they cried to God in the battle, and he was intreated of them; because they put [p]their trust in him.

21 And they [7]took away their cattle; of their camels fifty thousand, and of sheep two hundred and fifty thousand, and of asses two thousand, and of [8]men an hundred thousand.

22 For there fell down many slain, because the war *was* [q]of God. And they dwelt in their steads until [r]the captivity.

23 ¶ And the children of the half tribe of Mă-năs′-sēh dwelt in the lan they increased from Bā′-shăn un Bā′-ăl–hĕr′-mo̱n and Sē′-nĭr, and un mount Hĕr′-mo̱n.

24 And these *were* the heads of th house of their fathers, even Ē′-phĕ and Ĭsh′-ī, and Ē-lī′-ĕl, and Ăz′-rĭ-ĕ and Jeremiah, and Hō-dă-vī′-ăh, an Jăh′-dĭ-ĕl, mighty men of valour, [9]fam ous men, *and* heads of the house their fathers.

25 ¶ And they [s]transgressed again the God of their fathers, and went whoring after the gods of the peop of the land, whom God destroyed be fore them.

26 And the God of Israel stirred u the spirit of Pŭl king of Assyria, an the spirit of Tĭl′-găth–pĭl-nē′-ṡĕr kin of Assyria, and he carried them awa even the Reubenites, and the Gadite and the half tribe of Mă-năs′-sēh, an brought them unto Hā′-lăh, and Hā bôr, and Hâr′-ă, and to the river Gō zăn, unto this day.

CHAPTER 6

THE sons of Levi; [a]Gĕr′-shŏn, Kō hăth, and Mĕ-râr′-ī.

2 And the sons of Kō′-hăth; Amram Ĭz′-hăr, and Hē′-brŏn, and Ŭz′-zĭ-ĕl.

3 And the children of Amram Aaron, and Moses, and Miriam. Th sons also of Aaron; [b]Nadab, an Ă-bī′-hū, Ĕl-ē-ā′-zăr, and Ĭth′-ă-măr.

4 ¶ Ĕl-ē-ā′-zăr begat Phĭn′-ĕ-hăṡ, Phĭ ĕ-hăṡ begat Ă-bĭ′-shû-ă,

5 And Ă-bĭ′-shû-ă begat Bŭk′-kī, an Bŭk′-kī begat Ŭz′-zī,

6 And Ŭz′-zī begat Zĕr-ă-hī′-ăh, an Zĕr-ă-hī′-ăh begat Mĕ-râi′-ōth,

7 Mĕ-râi′-ōth begat Ăm-ă-rī′-ăh, an Ăm-ă-rī′-ăh begat Ă-hī′-tŭb,

8 And [c]Ă-hī′-tŭb begat Zā′-dŏk, an Zā′-dŏk [d]begat Ă-hĭ′-mă-ăz,

9 And Ă-hĭ′-mă-ăz begat Ăz-ă-rī′-ăl and Ăz-ă-rī′-ăh begat Jō-hā′-năn,

10 And Jō-hā′-năn begat Ăz-ă-rī′-ăl (he *it is* that [e]executed the priest office [1]in the temple that [f]Solomc built in Jerusalem:)

11 And [g]Ăz-ă-rī′-ăh begat Ăm-ă-ı ăh, and Ăm-ă-rī′-ăh begat Ă-hī′-tŭb,

12 And Ă-hī′-tŭb begat Zā′-dŏk, ar Zā′-dŏk begat [2]Shăl′-lŭm,

13 And Shăl′-lŭm begat Hĭl-kī′-ăl and Hĭl-kī′-ăh begat Ăz-ă-rī′-ăh,

14 And Ăz-ă-rī′-ăh begat [h]Sĕ-râi′-ăl and Sĕ-râi′-ăh begat Jĕ-hō′-ză-dăk,

15 And Jĕ-hō′-ză-dăk went *into ca tivity*, when [i]the LORD carried aw Judah and Jerusalem by the hand Nĕb-ū-c̱hăd-nĕz′-zăr.

i Josh. 22.9. Song 4.1. Micah 7.14.
j Gen. 25.12.
4 upon all the face of the east.
k Josh. 13.11. 24,25.
l ch. 27.29. Song 2.1. Isa. 35.2.
5 their goings forth.
m 2 Ki. 15.5.
n 2 Ki. 14.16. 28.
6 sons of valour.
o Gen. 25.15.
p Ps. 9.10. Ps. 20.7,8. Ps. 22.4,5.
7 led captive.
8 souls of men.
q Deut. 20.1, 4. Josh. 10.42. 2 Chr. 20.15. Rom. 8.31.
r 2 Ki. 15.29.
9 men of names.
s Deut. 32.15. Isa. 1.4.

CHAP. 6

a Gen. 46.11.
b Ex. 6.23. Lev. 10.1.
c 2 Sam. 8.17.
d 2 Sam. 15. 27.
e 2 Chr. 26. 17,18.
1 in the house.
f 2 Chr. 3.1.
g Ezra 7.3.
2 Or, Meshullam, ch. 9.11.
h Neh. 11.11.
i 2 Chr. 36. 17-21.

6 ¶ The sons of Levi; [j]Gĕr´-shŏm,
ō´-hăth, and Mĕ-râr´-ī.
7 And these *be* the names of the
ns of Gĕr´-shŏm; Lĭb´-nī, and Shĭm´-
ī.
8 And the sons of Kō´-hăth *were*,
mram, and Ĭz´-hār, and Hē´-brŏn,
d Ŭz´-zĭ-ĕl.
9 The sons of [k]Mĕ-râr´-ī; Măh´-lī,
d Mū´-shī. And these *are* the fami-
s of the Levites according to their
thers.
0 Of Gĕr´-shŏm; Lĭb´-nī his son, Jā´-
th his son, Zimmah his son,
1 Jō´-ăh [l]his son, [m]Ĭd´-dō his son,
-răh his son, [n]Jē-ăt´-ĕ-râi his son.
2 The sons of Kō´-hăth; [o]Ăm-mĭn´-
dăb his son, Kôr´-ăh his son, Ăs´-sĭr
s son,
3 Ĕl-kā´-năh his son, and Ē-bī´-ă-
ph his son, and Ăs´-sĭr his son,
4 Tā´-hăth his son, [p]Ū´-rĭ-ĕl his son,
z-zī´-ăh his son, and Shā´-ŭl his son.
5 And the sons of Ĕl-kā´-năh; Ă-
ā´-sâi, [q]and Ă-hī´-mōth.
6 *As for* Ĕl-kā´-năh: the sons of Ĕl-
-năh; Zō´-phâi [r]his son, and Na-
th [s]his son,
7 Ē-lĭ-ăb [t]his son, Jĕ-rō´-hăm his
n, Ĕl-kā´-năh his son.
8 And the sons of Samuel; the first-
rn [3]Văsh-nī, and Ă-bī´-ăh.
9 The sons of Mĕ-râr´-ī; Măh´-lī,
b-nī his son, Shĭm´-ĕ-ī his son, Ŭz-
his son,
0 Shĭm´-ĕ-ă his son, Hăg-gī´-ăh his
n, Ă-sâi´-ăh his son.
1 And these *are they* whom David
t over the service of song in the
use of the LORD, after that the ark
ad rest.
2 And they ministered before the
velling place of the tabernacle of the
ngregation with singing, until Sol-
non had built the house of the LORD
Jerusalem: and *then* they waited on
eir office according to their order.
3 And these *are* they that [4]waited
th their children. Of the sons of the
ō-hăth-ītes: Hē´-măn a singer, the
n of Jō´-ĕl, the son of Shĕ-mū´-ĕl,
4 The son of Ĕl-kā´-năh, the son of
-rō-hăm, the son of Ē-lī´-ĕl, the son
[5]Tō´-ăh,
5 The son of [6]Zuph, the son of Ĕl-
-năh, the son of Mā´-hăth, the son of
-mā´-sâi,
6 The son of Ĕl-kā´-năh, the son of
ō-ĕl, the son of Ăz-ă-rī´-ăh, the son
Zĕph-ă-nī´-ăh,
7 The son of Tā´-hăth, the son of Ăs´-
, the son of [w]Ē-bī´-ă-săph, the son of
ôr´-ăh,

j Ex. 6.16.
k Num. 3.33.
l ver. 42, Ethan.
m ver. 41, Adaiah.
n ver. 41, Ethni.
o vers. 2,18, Izhar.
p ver. 36, Zephaniah, Azariah, Joel.
q vers. 35,36.
r ver. 35, Zuph. 1 Sam. 1.1.
s ver. 34, Toah.
t ver. 34, Eliel.
3 Called also Joel, 1 Sam. 8.2.
u ch. 16.1. 2 Sam. 6.17.
4 stood.
5 ver. 26, Nahath.
6 Or, Zophai.
v ver. 24, Shaul, Uzziah, Uriel.
w Ex. 6.24.
x ver. 21, Jeaterai.
y ver. 21, Joah.
7 Called Jeduthun, ch. 9.16. 2 Chr. 35.15. Ps. 62. title.
8 Or, Kushaiah, ch. 15.17.
z Ex. 29.38. Lev. 10.21, 22. Num. 3.10. Heb. 5.1.
a Ex. 30.7. 1 Sam. 2.28. ch. 23.13. Luke 1.9.
b Ex. 6.23. Lev. 10.1. Num. 3.2. ch. 24.1. Ezra 7.2-5.
c Num. 35.1-9. Josh. 21.9-19. In this list Gibeon and Juttah are omitted.
d Josh. 21.11, 12.
e Josh. 14.13.
f Josh. 21.13.
g Josh. 21.15, Holon.

38 The son of Ĭz´-hār, the son of Kō´-
hăth, the son of Levi, the son of Israel.
39 And his brother Ā´-săph, who
stood on his right hand, *even* Ā´-săph
the son of Bĕr-ă-chī´-ăh, the son of
Shĭm´-ĕ-ă,
40 The son of Michael, the son of Bā-
ă-sēi´-ăh, the son of Măl-chī´-ăh,
41 The son of [x]Ĕth´-nī, the son of Zē´-
răh, the son of Ă-dâi´-ăh,
42 The son of [y]Ē´-thăn, the son of
Zimmah, the son of Shĭm´-ĕ-ī,
43 The son of Jā´-hăth, the son of
Gĕr´-shŏm, the son of Levi.
44 And their brethren the sons of
Mĕ-râr´-ī *stood* on the left hand: [7]Ē´-
thăn the son of [8]Kĭsh´-ī, the son of Ăb´-
dī, the son of Măl´-lŭch,
45 The son of Hăsh-ă-bī´-ăh, the son
of Ăm-ă-zī´-ăh, the son of Hĭl-kī´-ăh,
46 The son of Amzi, the son of Bā´-nī,
the son of Shā´-mĕr,
47 The son of Măh´-lī, the son of Mū´-
shī, the son of Mĕ-râr´-ī, the son of
Levi.
48 Their brethren also the Levites
were appointed unto all manner of
service of the tabernacle of the house
of God.
49 ¶ But Aaron and his sons offered
[z]upon the altar of the burnt offering,
and [a]on the altar of incense, *and were*
appointed for all the work of the *place*
most holy, and to make an atonement
for Israel, according to all that Moses
the servant of God had commanded.
50 And these *are* [b]the sons of Aaron;
Ĕl-ē-ā´-zăr his son, Phĭn´-ĕ-hăs his son,
Ă-bī´-shū-ă his son,
51 Bŭk-kī his son, Ŭz´-zī his son,
Zĕr-ă-hī´-ăh his son,
52 Mĕ-râi´-ōth his son, Ăm-ă-rī´-ăh
his son, Ă-hī´-tŭb his son,
53 Zā´-dŏk his son, Ă-hī´-mă-ăz his
son.
54 ¶ Now [c]these *are* their dwelling
places throughout their castles in their
coasts, of the sons of Aaron, of the
families of the Kō´-hăth-ītes: for
theirs was the lot.
55 And [d]they gave them Hē´-brŏn in
the land of Judah, and the suburbs
thereof round about it.
56 But [e]the fields of the city, and the
villages thereof, they gave to Caleb
the son of Jĕ-phŭn´-nĕh.
57 And [f]to the sons of Aaron they
gave the cities of Judah, *namely*, Hē´-
brŏn, *the city* of refuge, and Lĭb´-năh
with her suburbs, and Jăt´-tĭr, and Ĕsh-
tĕ-mō´-ă, with their suburbs,
58 And [g]Hī´-lĕn with her suburbs,
Dē´-bĭr with her suburbs,

59 And [h]Ăsh-ăn with her suburbs,
and Bĕth-shē-mĕsh with her suburbs:
60 And out of the tribe of Benjamin;
Gē-bă with her suburbs, and Ăl-ĕ-
mĕth [i]with her suburbs, and Ăn-ă-
thōth with her suburbs. All their
cities throughout their families *were*
thirteen cities.
61 And unto the sons of Kō-hăth,
which [j]*were* left of the family of that
tribe, *were cities given* out of the half
tribe, *namely, out of* the half *tribe* of
Mă-năs-sēh, [k]by lot, ten cities.
62 And to the sons of Gĕr-shŏm
throughout their families out of the
tribe of Ĭs-să-c̱hăr, and out of the tribe
of Asher, and out of the tribe of
Năph-tă-lī, and out of the tribe of Mă-
năs-sēh in Bā-shăn, thirteen cities.
63 Unto the sons of Mĕ-râr-ī *were
given* by lot, throughout their families, out of the tribe of Reuben, and
out of the tribe of Gad, and out of the
tribe of Zĕ-bū-lŭn, twelve [l]cities.
64 And the [m]children of Israel gave
to the Levites *these* cities with their
suburbs.
65 And they gave by lot out of the
tribe of the children of Judah, and out
of the tribe of the children of Simeon,
and out of the tribe of the children of
Benjamin, these cities, which are called by *their* names.
66 And [n]*the residue* of the families of
the sons of Kō-hăth had cities of their
coasts out of the tribe of Ē-phră-ĭm.
67 And [o]they gave unto them, *of* the
cities of refuge, Shē-c̱hĕm in mount
Ē-phră-ĭm with her suburbs; *they
gave* also Gē-zĕr with her suburbs,
68 And [9]Jŏk-mĕ-ăm with her suburbs, and Bĕth-hâr-ŏn with her suburbs,
69 And Aî-jă-lŏn with her suburbs,
and Găth-rĭm-mo̱n with her suburbs:
70 And out of the half tribe of Mă-
năs-sēh; Aner with her suburbs, and
Bĭ-lĕ-ăm with her suburbs, for the
family of the remnant of the sons of
Kō-hăth.
71 Unto the sons of Gĕr-shŏm *were
given* out of the family of the half
tribe of Mă-năs-sēh, Gō-lăn in Bā-
shăn with her suburbs, and [p]Ăsh-tă-
rōth with her suburbs:
72 And out of the tribe of Ĭs-să-c̱hăr;
[q]Kē-dĕsh with her suburbs, Dăb-ĕ-
răth with her suburbs,
73 And Rā-mŏth with her suburbs,
and Anem with her suburbs:
74 And out of the tribe of Asher;
Mā-shăl with her suburbs, and Abdon
with her suburbs,

[h] Josh. 21.16, Ain.
[i] Josh. 21.18, Almon.
[j] ver. 66.
[k] Josh. 21.5.
[l] Josh. 21.7, 34.
[m] Num. 35. 1-8.
[n] Josh. 21.4, 5, 20-26.
[o] Gen. 33.19.
9 See Josh. 21.22-35, where many of these cities have other names. Perhaps some of the cities were exchanged for others.
[p] Josh. 21.27, Beeshterah. Deut. 1.4.
[q] Josh. 21.28, Kishon.
[r] Num. 21.25. Deut. 2.24. Josh 12.2,5. Neh. 9.22. Song 7.4. Isa. 15.4.

CHAP. 7

[a] Gen. 30.17, 18. Num. 1.28, 29.
[b] Gen. 46.13. Num. 26.23.
[c] Gen. 46.13. Phuvah, Job.
[d] 2 Sam.24.1, 2. ch. 21. 1-5.
[e] ch. 5. 24.
[f] Gen. 46.21. Num. 26.38.

75 And Hū-kŏk with her subur
and Rē-hŏb with her suburbs:
76 And out of the tribe of Năph-tă
Kē-dĕsh in Galilee with her subur
and Hăm-mŏn with her suburbs, a
Kĭr-jă-thā-ĭm with her suburbs.
77 Unto the rest of the children
Mĕ-râr-ī *were given* out of the tribe
Zĕ-bū-lŭn, Rimmon with her s
urbs, Tā-bôr with her suburbs:
78 And on the other side Jordan
Jericho, on the east side of Jord
were given them out of the tribe
Reuben, Bē-zĕr in the wilderness w
her suburbs, and Jăh-zăh with h
suburbs,
79 Kē-dĕ-mōth also with her subur
and Mĕph-ă-ăth with her suburbs:
80 And out of the tribe of Gad; R
mŏth in Gilead with her suburbs, a
Mā-hă-nā-ĭm with her suburbs,
81 And [r]Hĕsh-bŏn with her suburb
and Jā-zĕr with her suburbs.

CHAPTER 7

NOW the sons of [a]Ĭs-să-c̱hăr we
[b]Tō-lă, and [c]Pū-ăh, Jăsh-ŭb, a
Shĭm-rŏn, four.
2 And the sons of Tō-lă; Ŭz-zī, a
Rē-phâi-ăh, and Jĕr-ĭ-ĕl, and Jă
mā-ī, and Jĭb-săm, and Shĕ-mū-
heads of their father's house, *to wit*,
Tō-lă: *they were* valiant men of mig
in their generations; [d]whose numb
was in the days of David two a
twenty thousand and six hundred.
3 And the sons of Ŭz-zī; Ĭz-ră-hī-ă
and the sons of Ĭz-ră-hī-ăh; Micha
and Ō-bă-dī-ăh, and Jō-ĕl, Ĭsh-ī-ă
five: all of them [e]chief men.
4 And with them, by their gene
tions, after the house of their fathe
were bands of soldiers for war, six a
thirty thousand *men*: for they h
many wives and sons.
5 And their brethren among all t
families of Ĭs-să-c̱hăr *were* valiant m
of might, reckoned in all by the
genealogies fourscore and seven tho
sand.
6 ¶ *The sons* of [f]Benjamin; Bē-lă, a
Bē-c̱hĕr, and Jĕd-ĭ-ă-ĕl, three.
7 And the sons of Bē-lă; Ĕz-bŏn, a
Ŭz-zī, and Ŭz-zī-ĕl, and Jĕr-ĭ-mōt
and Ī-rī, five; heads of the house
their fathers, mighty men of valou
and were reckoned by their gene
logies twenty and two thousand a
thirty and four.
8 And the sons of Bē-c̱hĕr; Zĕ-mī-
and Jō-ăsh, and Ĕl-ĭ-ĕ-zĕr, and Ĕl-
ō-ĕ-nāi, and Omri, and Jĕr-ĭ-mōt
and Ă-bī-ăh, and Ăn-ă-thōth, and Ă

ā-mĕth. All these *are* the sons of Bē-
chĕr.
9 And the number of them, after
their genealogy by their generations,
heads of the house of their fathers,
mighty men of valour, *was* twenty
thousand and two hundred.
10 The sons also of Jĕd-ĭ-ā-ĕl; Bilhan: and the sons of Bilhan; Jē-ŭsh
and Benjamin, and Ē-hŭd, and Chĕ-
nā-ă-năh, and Zē-thăn, and Thăr-
shĭsh, and Ă-hĭ-shā-hăr.
11 All these the sons of Jĕd-ĭ-ā-ĕl, by
the heads of their fathers, mighty men
of valour, *were* seventeen thousand
and two hundred *soldiers*, fit to go out
for war *and* battle.
12 Shŭp-pĭm [g]also, and Hŭp-pĭm, the
children of [h]Ir, *and* Hū-shĭm, the sons
of [i]Ā-hĕr.
13 ¶ The sons of Năph-tă-lī; Jăh-zĭ-
ĕl, and Gū-nī, and Jē-zĕr, and [j]Shăl-
lŭm, the sons of Bĭl-hăh.
14 ¶ The [k]sons of Mă-năs-sēh; Ăsh-
rĭ-ĕl, whom she bare: (*but* his concubine the Ăr-ăm-ĭ-tĕss bare Mā-chĭr
the father of Gĭl-ĕ-ăd:
15 And [1]Mā-chĭr took to wife *the*
sister of Hŭp-pĭm and Shŭp-pĭm,
whose sister's name *was* Mā-ă-chăh;)
and the name of the second *was* Zē-
lŏph-ĕ-hăd: and [l]Zē-lŏph-ĕ-hăd had
daughters.
16 And Mā-ă-chăh the wife of Mā-
chĭr bare a son, and she called his
name Pē-rĕsh; and the name of his
brother *was* Shē-rĕsh; and his sons
were Ū-lăm and Ră-kĕm.
17 And the sons of Ū-lăm; [m]Bē-dăn.
These *were* the sons of Gĭl-ĕ-ăd, the
son of Mā-chĭr, the son of Mă-năs-sēh.
18 And his sister Hăm-mō-lĕ-kĕth
bare Ī-shŏd, and [n]Ā-bĭ-ĕ-zĕr, and Mă-
hā-lăh.
19 And the sons of Shĕm-ī-dă were,
Ă-hĭ-ăn, and Shē-chĕm, and Lĭk-hĭ,
and Ă-nĭ-ăm.
20 ¶ And the sons of [o]Ē-phră-ĭm;
Shû-thē-lăh, and Bē-rĕd his son, and
Tā-hăth his son, and Ĕl-ă-dăh his son,
and Tā-hăth his son,
21 ¶ And Ză-băd his son, and Shû-
thē-lăh his son, and Ē-zĕr, and Ĕl-ē-
ăd, whom the men of Gath *that were*
born in *that* land slew, because they
came down to take away their cattle.
22 And Ē-phră-ĭm their father
mourned [p]many days, and his brethren came to comfort him.
23 ¶ And when he went in to his wife,
she conceived, and bare a son, and he
called his name [2]Bĕ-rī-ăh, because it
went evil with his house.

[g] Num. 26. 39, Shupham, and Hupham.
[h] ver. 7, Iri.
[i] Num. 26.38, Ahiram.
[j] Gen. 46.24, Shillem.
[k] Num. 27.1.

1 Herzon, a grandson of Judah, married Machir's daughter, and their child was reckoned to the tribe of Manasseh.
[l] Num. 27.1-11.
[m] 1 Sam. 12. 11.
[n] Num. 26. 30, Jeezer.
[o] Gen. 41.52. Num. 26.35, 36. Deut. 33.13, 17. Ps. 60.7.
[p] Gen. 37.34, 35. 2 Sam. 1.11. Job. 2.11. Ps. 69.11.
2 That is, In evil.
[q] Josh. 16.3. 1 Sam. 13. 18. 2 Chr. 8.5.
[r] Num. 13.8, 16, Nun.
[s] Josh. 16.7, Naarath.
3 daughters.
[t] Josh. 17.7.
[u] Josh. 17.11.
[v] Judg. 1.22-29.
[w] Gen. 46.17. Num. 26.44, 46. Deut. 33.24.
[x] ver. 34, Shamer.
[y] ver. 32.
[z] Deut. 2.14.

CHAP. 8

[a] Gen. 46.21. Num. 26.38. ch. 7.6.

24 (And his daughter *was* Shē-răh,
who built [q]Bĕth-hôr-ŏn the nether,
and the upper, and Ŭz-zĕn-shē-răh.)
25 And Rē-phăh *was* his son, also
Rē-shĕph, and Tē-lăh his son, and Tā-
hăn his son,
26 Lā-ă-dăn his son, Ăm-mĭ-hŭd his
son, Ē-lĭ-shă-mă his son,
27 Non [r]his son, Jĕ-hŏsh-ū-ă his son.
28 ¶ And their possessions and habitations *were*, Beth-el and the towns
thereof, and eastward [s]Nā-ă-răn, and
westward Gē-zĕr, with the [3]towns
thereof; Shē-chĕm also and the towns
thereof, unto Gā-ză and the towns
thereof:
29 And by the borders of the children
of [t]Mă-năs-sēh, Bĕth-shē-ăn and her
towns, Tā-ă-năch and her towns,
[u]Mĕ-gĭd-dō and her towns, Dor and
her towns. In these dwelt the [v]chil-
dren of Joseph the son of Israel.
30 ¶ The [w]sons of Asher; Ĭm-năh,
and Ĭs-ū-ăh, and Ĭsh-ū-āī, and Bĕ-rī-
ăh, and Sē-răh their sister.
31 And the sons of Bĕ-rī-ăh; Hē-bĕr,
and Măl-chĭ-ĕl, who *is* the father of
Bĭr-zā-vĭth.
32 And Hē-bĕr begat Jăph-lĕt, and
[x]Shō-mĕr, and Hō-thăm, and Shû-ă
their sister.
33 And the sons of Jăph-lĕt; Pā-săch,
and Bimhal, and Ăsh-văth. These *are*
the children of Jăph-lĕt.
34 And the sons of [y]Shā-mĕr; Ā-hī,
and Rōh-găh, Jĕ-hŭb-băh, and Âr-
ăm.
35 And the sons of his brother Hē-
lĕm; Zō-phăh, and Ĭm-nă, and Shē-
lĕsh, and Ā-măl.
36 The sons of Zō-phăh; Sū-ăh, and
Hăr-nĕ-phĕr, and Shû-ăl, and Bē-rī,
and Ĭm-răh,
37 Bē-zĕr, and Hod, and Shăm-mă
and Shĭl-shăh, and Ĭth-răn, and Bĕ-ĕr-ă.
38 And the sons of Jē-thĕr; Jĕ-phŭn-
nĕh, and Pĭs-păh, and Âr-ă.
39 And the sons of Ŭl-lă; Âr-ăh, and
Hăn-ĭ-ĕl, and Rē-zĭ-ă.
40 All these *were* the children of
Asher, heads of *their* father's house,
choice *and* mighty men of valour,
chief of the princes. And the number
throughout the genealogy of them
that were [z]apt to the war *and* to battle
was twenty and six thousand men.

CHAPTER 8

NOW Benjamin begat [a]Bē-lă his
firstborn, Ăsh-bĕl the second,
and Ă-hăr-ăh the third,
2 Nō-hăh the fourth, and Rā-phă the
fifth.

3 And the sons of Bē-lă were, [1]Ăd-
där, and Gē-ră, and Ă-bī-hŭd,
4 And Ă-bī-shû-ă, and Nā-ă-măn,
and Ă-hō-āh,
5 And Gē-ră, and [2]Shĕ-phū-phăn,
and Hū-răm.
6 And these *are* the sons of Ē-hŭd:
these are the heads of the fathers of
the inhabitants of Gē-bă, and they removed them to [b]Măn-ā-hăth:
7 And Nā-ă-măn, and Ă-hī-āh, and
Gē-ră, he removed them, and begat
Ŭz-ză, and Ă-hī-hŭd.
8 And Shā-hă-rā-īm begat *children* in
the [c]country of Moab, after he had
sent them away; Hū-shĭm and Bā-ă-
ră *were* his wives.
9 And he begat of Hō-dĕsh his wife,
Jō-băb, and Zĭ-bĭ-ă, and Mē-shă, and
Măl-chăm,
10 And Jē-ŭz, and Shă-chī-ă, and
Mĭr-mă. These *were* his sons, heads
of the fathers.
11 And of Hū-shĭm he begat Ă-bī-
tŭb, and Ĕl-pā-ăl.
12 The sons of Ĕl-pā-ăl; Ē-bĕr, and
Mĭ-shăm, and Shā-mĕd, who built Ō-
nō, [d]and Lod, with the towns thereof:
13 Bĕ-rī-āh also, and [e]Shē-mă, who
were heads of the fathers of the inhabitants of [f]Aī-jă-lŏn, who drove
away the inhabitants of Gath:
14 And Ă-hī-ō, Shā-shăk, and Jĕr-ĕ-
mōth,
15 And Zĕb-ă-dī-āh, and Âr-ăd, and
Ā-dĕr,
16 And Michael, and Ĭs-păh, and
Jō-hă, the sons of Bĕ-rī-āh;
17 And Zĕb-ă-dī-âh, and Mĕ-shŭl-
lăm, and Hĕz-ē-kī, and Hē-bĕr,
18 Ĭsh-mĕ-raî also, and Jĕz-lī-āh, and
Jō-băb, the sons of Ĕl-pā-ăl;
19 And Jakim, and Zĭch-rī, and Zăb-
dī,
20 And Ĕl-ī-ē-naî, and Zĭl-thaî, and
Ē-lī-ĕl,
21 And Ă-daî-āh, and Bĕ-raî-āh, and
Shĭm-răth, the sons of [3]Shĭm-hī;
22 And Ĭsh-păn, and Hē-bĕr, and
Ē-lī-ĕl,
23 And Abdon, and Zĭch-rī, and Hā-
năn,
24 And Hăn-ă-nī-āh, and Ē-lăm, and
Ăn-tō-thī-jăh,
25 And Ĭph-ĕ-deî-āh, and Pĕn-ū-ĕl,
the sons of Shā-shăk;
26 And Shăm-shĕ-raî, and Shĕ-hă-
rī-āh, and Ăth-ă-lī-āh,
27 And Jăr-ĕ-sī-āh, and Ē-lī-āh, and
Zĭch-rī, the sons of Jĕ-rō-hăm.
28 These *were* heads of the fathers,
by their generations, chief *men*. These
dwelt in Jerusalem.

1 Or, Ard, Gen. 46.21.
2 Or, Shupham, Num. 26.39. ch. 7.12, Shuppim.
b ch. 2.52.
c Ruth 1.1.
d Ezra 2.33. Neh. 6.2.
e ver. 21.
f Josh. 19.42.
3 Or, Shema, ver. 13.
4 Called, Jehiel, ch. 9.35.
g ch. 9.35.
h ch. 9.37, Zechariah.
i ch. 9.38, Shimeam.
j 1 Sam. 9.1. ch. 9.36,39. Acts 13.21.
k 1 Sam. 14. 49, Ishui.
l 2 Sam. 2.8, Ish-bosheth.
m 2 Sam. 9.6, 10. Mephibosheth.
n 2 Sam. 9.12. ch. 9.40.
o ch. 9.41, Tahrea.
p ch. 9.42, Jarah.
q ch. 9.43, Rephaiah.
r ch. 12.2. 2 Chr. 11.1. 2 Chr. 13.3. 2 Chr. 14.8. 2 Chr. 17. 14-19. Neh. 4.13. Song 3.7,8. Eph. 6.11-20.

CHAP. 9

a Ezra 2.59.
b Lev. 26.33. 2 Chr. 33.11.
c Ezra 2.70. Neh. 7.73.
d Josh. 9.27. Ezra 2.43.
e Neh. 11.1.
f Gen. 46.12. Num. 26.20.

29 And at Gibeon dwelt the [4]fathe
of Gibeon; whose [g]wife's name *wa*
Mā-ă-chāh:
30 And his firstborn son Abdon, an
Zur, and Kish, and Bā-ăl, and Nadab
31 And Gē-dôr, and Ă-hī-ō, [h]an
Zā-chĕr.
32 And Mĭk-lōth begat [i]Shĭm-ĕ-āh
And these also dwelt with their breth
ren in Jerusalem, over against them
33 ¶ And [j]Ner begat Kish, and Kis
begat Saul, and Saul begat Jonathan
and Măl-chī–shû-ă, and [k]Ă-bĭn-ă-dăb
and [l]Ĕsh–bā-ăl.
34 And the son of Jonathan [m]*wa*
Mĕr-ĭb–bā-ăl; and Mĕr-ĭb–bā-ăl [n]be
gat Mī-căh.
35 And the sons of Mī-căh *were*, Pī
thŏn, and Mē-lĕch, and [o]Târ-ĕ-ă, an
Ahaz.
36 And Ahaz begat [p]Jĕ-hō-ă-dăh
and Jĕ-hō-ă-dăh begat Ăl-ĕ-mĕth, an
Ăz-mā-vĕth, and Zimri; and Zimri be
gat Mō-ză,
37 And Mō-ză begat Bĭ-nĕ-ă: [q]Rā
phă *was* his son, Ĕl-ē-ā-săh his son
Ā-zĕl his son:
38 And Ā-zĕl had six sons, whos
names *are* these, Ăz-rī-kăm, Bō-chĕ
rû, and Ĭsh-mā-ĕl, and Shĕ-ă-rī-āh
and Ō-bă-dī-āh, and Hā-năn. All thes
were the sons of Ā-zĕl.
39 And the sons of Ē-shĕk his bro
ther *were*, Ū-lăm his firstborn, Jē
hŭsh the second, and Ē-lĭph-ĕ-lĕt th
third.
40 And the sons of Ū-lăm wer
mighty men of valour, [r]archers, an
had many sons, and sons' sons, a
hundred and fifty. All these *are* of th
sons of Benjamin.

CHAPTER 9

SO [a]all Israel were reckoned b
genealogies; and, behold, they *wer*
written in the book of the kings of Is
rael and Judah, *who* were [b]carrie
away to Babylon for their transgres
sion.
2 ¶ Now [c]the first inhabitants tha
dwelt in their possessions in thei
cities *were*, the Israelites, the priests
Levites, and the [d]Nĕth-ĭ-nĭmś.
3 And in [e]Jerusalem dwelt of the chi
dren of Judah, and of the childre
of Benjamin, and of the children o
Ē-phră-ĭm, and Mă-năs-sĕh;
4 Ū-thaî the son of Ăm-mī-hŭd, th
son of Omri, the son of Imri, the so
of Bā-nī, of the children of Phâr-ĕ
the [f]son of Judah.
5 And of the Shī-lō-nītes; Ă-saî-ā
the firstborn, and his sons.

6 And of the sons of Zĕ-răh; Jĕú-ĕl,
and their brethren, six hundred and
ninety.
7 And of the sons of Benjamin; Săl-
lû the son of Mĕ-shŭl-lăm, the son of
Hō-dă-vī-ăh, the son of Hăs-ĕ-nū-ăh,
8 And Ĭb-neī-ăh the son of Jĕ-rō-
hăm, and Ē-lăh the son of Ŭz-zī, the
son of Mĭch-rī, and Mĕ-shŭl-lăm the
son of Shĕph-ă-thī-ăh, the son of Rĕú-
ĕl, the son of Ĭb-nĭ-jăh;
9 And their brethren, according to
their generations, nine hundred and
fifty and six. All these men *were* chief
of the fathers in the house of their
fathers.
10 ¶ And [g]of the priests; Jĕ-dâĭ-ăh,
and Jĕ-hôĭ-ă-rĭb, and Jā-chĭn,
11 And [1]Ăz-ă-rī-ăh the son of Hĭl-kī-
ăh, the son of Mĕ-shŭl-lăm, the son of
Ză-dŏk, the son of Mĕ-râĭ-ōth, the son
of Ă-hī-tŭb, the ruler of the house of
God;
12 And Ă-dâĭ-ăh the son of Jĕ-rō-
hăm, the son of Păsh-ŭr, the son of
Măl-chī-jăh, and Mā-ăs-ī-ă-ī the son
of Ăd-ī-ĕl, the son of Jăh-zĕ-răh, the
son of Mĕ-shŭl-lăm, the son of Mĕ-
shĭl-lĕ-mĭth, the son of Ĭm-mĕr;
13 And their brethren, heads of the
house of their fathers, a thousand and
seven hundred and threescore; [2]very
able men for the work of the service of
the house of God.
14 And of [h]the Levites; Shĕm-âĭ-ăh
the son of Hăs-shŭb, the son of Ăz-rī-
kăm, the son of Hăsh-ă-bī-ăh, of the
sons of Mĕ-râr-ī;
15 And Băk-băk-kăr, Hē-rĕsh, and
Gā-lăl, and Măt-tă-nī-ăh the son of
Mī-căh, the son of Zĭch-rī, the son of
Ā-săph;
16 And Ō-bă-dī-ăh the son of Shĕm-
âĭ-ăh, the son of Gā-lăl, the son of Jĕ-
dū-thŭn, and Bĕr-ē-chī-ăh the son of
Ā-să, the son of Ĕl-kā-năh, that dwelt
in the villages of [i]the Nĕ-tŏph-ă-thītes.
17 And [j]the porters *were*, Shăl-lŭm,
and Ăk-kŭb, and Tăl-mŏn, and Ă-hī-
măn, and their brethren: Shăl-lŭm
was the chief;
18 Who hitherto *waited* in [k]the king's
gate eastward: they *were* porters in
the companies of the children of Levi.
19 And Shăl-lŭm the son of Kôr-ē,
the son of Ē-bī-ă-săph, the son of Kôr-
ăh, and his brethren, of the house
of his father, the [l]Kôr-ă-hītes, *were*
over the work of the service, keepers
of the [3]gates of the tabernacle: and
their fathers, *being* over the host of the
LORD, *were* keepers of the entry.
20 And [m]Phĭn-ĕ-hăs the son of Ĕl-ē-
ā-zăr was the ruler over them in time
past, *and* the LORD *was* with him.
21 *And* Zĕch-ă-rī-ăh the son of Mĕ-
shĕl-ĕ-mī-ăh *was* porter of the door of
the tabernacle of the congregation.
22 All these *which were* chosen to be
porters in the gates *were* two hundred
and twelve. These were reckoned by
their genealogy in their villages, whom
[n]David and Samuel [o]the seer [4]did ordain in their [5]set office.
23 So they and their children *had* the
oversight of the gates of the house of
the LORD, *namely*, the house of the
tabernacle, by wards.
24 In [p]four quarters were the porters,
toward the east, west, north, and
south.
25 And their brethren, *which were* in
their villages, *were* to come [q]after sev-
en days from time to time with them.
26 For these Levites, the four chief
porters, were in *their* [6]set office, and
were over the [7]chambers and treasuries of the house of God.
27 ¶ And they lodged round about
the house of God, because the charge
was upon them, and the opening
thereof every morning *pertained* to
them.
28 And *certain* of them had the
charge of the ministering vessels, that
they should [8]bring them in and out by
tale.
29 *Some* of them also *were* appointed
to oversee the vessels, and all the [9]in-
struments of the sanctuary, and the
fine flour, and the wine, and the
oil, and the frankincense, and the
spices.
30 And *some* of the sons of the priests
made [r]the ointment of the spices.
31 And Măt-tī-thī-ăh, *one* of the Levites, who *was* the firstborn of Shăl-
lŭm the Kôr-ă-hīte, had the [10]set
office [s]over the things that were made
[11]in the pans.
32 And *other* of their brethren, of the
sons of the Kō-hăth-ītes, *were* over
the [12]shewbread, to prepare *it* every
sabbath.
33 And these *are* [t]the singers, chief
of the fathers of the Levites, *who remaining* in the chambers *were* free:
for [13]they were employed in *that* work
day and night.
34 These chief fathers of the Levites
were chief throughout their generations; these dwelt at Jerusalem.
35 ¶ And in Gibeon dwelt the father
of Gibeon, Jĕ-hī-ĕl, whose wife's
name [u]*was* Mā-ă-chăh:
36 And his firstborn son Abdon, then

g Neh. 11.10.
1 Neh. 11.11. Seraiah.
2 mighty men of valour.
h ch. 6.19. Neh. 11.15-19.
i ch. 2.54. Neh. 7.26.
j ch. 23.5.
k 2 Ki. 11.19. Eze. 44.23.
l Num. 26.9, 11. ch. 6.33,38. Ps. 42, title.
3 thresholds.
m Ex. 6.25. Num. 3.32. Josh. 22.30, 31. Ps. 106.30.
n ch. 26.1,2.
o 1 Sam. 9.9.
4 founded.
5 Or, trust.
p ch. 26.13-19.
q 2 Chr. 23.8.
6 Or, trust.
7 Or, storehouses.
8 bring them in by tale, and carry them out by tale.
9 Or, vessels.
r Ex. 30.23. Song 1.3,13. Jer. 6.20. Eze. 27.19, 22. Mark 14.3.
10 Or, trust.
s Lev. 6.21.
11 Or, on flat plates, or, slices.
12 bread of ordering.
t ch. 6.31. ch. 13.8.
13 upon them.
u ch. 8.29.

Zur, and Kish, and Bā-ăl, and Ner,
and Nadab,
37 And Gē-dôr, and Ă-hi-ō, and
Zĕch-ă-rī-ăh, and Mĭk-lōth.
38 And Mĭk-lōth begat Shĭm-ĕ-ăm.
And they also dwelt with their brethren at Jerusalem, over against their
brethren.
39 And [v]Ner begat Kish; and Kish
begat Saul; and Saul begat Jonathan,
and Măl-chi-shû-ă, and Ă-bĭn-ă-dăb,
and Ĕsh-bā-ăl.
40 And the son of Jonathan *was* Mĕr-
ĭb-bā-ăl: and Mĕr-ĭb-bā-ăl begat Mī-
căh.
41 And the sons of [w]Mī-căh *were*, Pī-
thŏn, and Mē-lĕch, and [14]Tăh-rē-ă,
and [x]*Ahaz*.
42 And Ahaz begat [15]Jâr-ăh; and Jâr-
ăh begat Ăl-ĕ-mĕth, and Ăz-mā-vĕth,
and Zimri; and Zimri begat Mō-ză;
43 And Mō-ză begat Bĭ-nĕ-ă; and
[16]Rĕ-phâi-ăh his son, Ĕl-ē-ā-săh his
son, Ā-zĕl his son.
44 And Ā-zĕl had six sons, whose
names *are* these, Ăz-rī-kăm, Bō-chĕ-
rû, and Ĭsh-mā-ĕl, and Shē-ă-rī-ăh,
and Ō-bă-dī-ăh, and Hā-năn: these
were the sons of Ā-zĕl.

CHAPTER 10

NOW the [a]Philistines fought a-
gainst Israel; and the men of
Israel fled from before the Philistines,
and fell down [1]slain in mount Gĭl-bō-ă.
2 And the Philistines followed hard
after Saul, and after his sons; and the
Philistines slew Jonathan, and [2]Ă-bĭn-
ă-dăb, and Măl-chi-shû-ă, the sons of
Saul.
3 And the battle went sore against
Saul, and the [3]archers [4]hit him, and he
was wounded of the archers.
4 Then said Saul to his armourbearer, Draw thy sword, and thrust
me through therewith; lest these uncircumcised come and [5]abuse me. But
his armourbearer would not; for he
was sore afraid. So Saul took a
sword, and fell upon it.
5 And when his armourbearer saw
that Saul was dead, he fell likewise on
the sword, and died.
6 So Saul died, and his three sons,
and all his house died together.
7 And when all the men of Israel
that *were* in the valley saw that they
fled, and that Saul and his sons were
dead, then they forsook their cities,
and fled: and the Philistines came and
dwelt in them.
8 ¶ And it came to pass on the morrow, when the Philistines came to

v ch. 8.33.
w 2 Sam. 9. 12.
14 Or, Tarea, ch. 8.35.
x ch. 8.35.
15 Or, Jehoadah, ch. 8.36.
16 Or, Rapha, ch. 8.37.

CHAP. 10
a 1 Sam. 7.7. 1 Sam. 13.5.
1 thrust through, or, wounded.
2 Or, Ishui, 1 Sam. 14. 49.
3 shooters with bows.
4 found him.
5 Or, mock me.
b 1 Sam. 31. 10. Isa. 48.5.
6 transgessed.
c 1 Sam. 13. 13. 1 Ki. 18.18. 2 Chr. 16.9.
d Ex. 22.18. Lev. 19.31. Deut. 18.11. Isa. 8.19.
e 1 Sam. 28.7.
f 1 Sam. 13. 14.
7 Isai.

CHAP. 11
a 2 Sam. 5.1. ch. 12.23.
1 both yesterday and the third day.
2 Or, rule. Ps. 78.70, 71.
b 2 Sam. 5.3.
c Rom. 8.31.
3 by the hand of.
d 1 Sam. 16.1.
e 2 Sam. 5.6.
f Gen. 10.16. Ex. 3.17. Judg. 1.21.
4 head.
5 That is, Zion.

strip the slain, that they found Saul
and his sons fallen in mount Gĭl-bō-ă.
9 And when they had stripped him,
they took his head, and his armour,
and sent into the land of the Philistines round about, to carry tidings unto their idols, and to the people.
10 And [b]they put his armour in the
house of their gods, and fastened his
head in the temple of Dā-gŏn.
11 ¶ And when all Jā-bĕsh-gĭl-ĕ-ăd
heard all that the Philistines had done
to Saul,
12 They arose, all the valiant men,
and took away the body of Saul, and
the bodies of his sons, and brought
them to Jā-bĕsh, and buried their
bones under the oak in Jā-bĕsh, and
fasted seven days.
13 ¶ So Saul died for his transgression which he [6]committed against the
LORD, *even* [c]against the word of the
LORD, which he kept not, and also for
asking *counsel* of *one that had* a [d]famil-
iar spirit, [e]to inquire *of it;*
14 And inquired not of the LORD:
therefore he slew him, and [f]turned the
kingdom unto David the son of [7]Jesse.

CHAPTER 11

THEN [a]all Israel gathered themselves to David unto Hē-brŏn,
saying, Behold, we *are* thy bone and
thy flesh.
2 And moreover [1]in time past, even
when Saul was king, thou *wast* he that
leddest out and broughtest in Israel:
and the LORD thy God said unto thee,
Thou shalt [2]feed my people Israel, and
thou shalt be ruler over my people
Israel.
3 Therefore came all the elders of Israel to the king to Hē-brŏn; and David
made a covenant with them in Hē-
brŏn before the LORD; and they
[b]anointed David king over Israel, according to the word of the [c]LORD [3]by
[d]Samuel.
4 ¶ And David and all Israel went [e]to
Jerusalem, which *is* Jē-bŭs; [f]where the
Jĕb-ū-sites *were*, the inhabitants of the
land.
5 And the inhabitants of Jē-bŭs said
to David, Thou shalt not come hither.
Nevertheless David took the castle of
Zion, which *is* the city of David.
6 And David said, Whosoever smiteth the Jĕb-ū-sites first shall be [4]chief
and captain. So Jō-ăb the son of Zĕr-
ū-ī-ăh went first up, and was chief.
7 And David dwelt in the castle;
therefore they called [5]it the city of
David.

And he built the city round about,
en from Mĭl-lō round about: and
-ăb [6]repaired the rest of the city.
So David [7]waxed greater and
eater: for the LORD of hosts *was*
th him.
) ¶ These [g]also *are* the chief of the
ghty men whom David had, who
rengthened themselves with him in
s kingdom, *and* with all Israel, to
ake him king, according to [h]the
ord of the LORD concerning Israel.
1 And this *is* the number of the
ghty men whom David had; Jă-
ŏb-ĕ-ăm, [9]an Hăch-mō-nīte, the
ief of the captains: he lifted up his
ear against three hundred slain *by*
n at one time.
2 And after him *was* Ĕl-ē-ā-zär the
n of Dodo, the Ă-hō-hīte, who *was*
e of the three mighties.
3 He was with David at [10]Păs-dăm-
im, and there the Philistines were
thered together to battle, where was
parcel of ground full of barley; and
e people fled from before the Philis-
es.
4 And they [11]set themselves in the
idst of *that* parcel, and delivered it,
d slew the Philistines; and the LORD
ved *them* by a great [12]deliverance.
5 ¶ Now [13]three of the thirty cap-
ins went [i]down to the rock to David,
to the cave of Adullam; and the host
the Philistines encamped [j]in the
lley of [14]Rĕph-ā-ĭm.
6 And David *was* then in the hold,
d the Philistines' garrison *was* then
Beth-lehem.
7 And David longed, and said, Oh
at one would give me drink of the
ater of the well of Beth-lehem, that
at the gate!
8 And the three brake through the
ost of the Philistines, and drew
ater out of the well of Beth-lehem,
at *was* by the gate, and took *it*, and
ought *it* to David: but David would
t drink *of* it, but poured it out to the
RD,
9 And said, My God forbid it me,
at I should do this thing: shall I
ink the blood of these men [15]that
ve put their lives in jeopardy? for
ith *the jeopardy of* their lives they
ought it. Therefore he would not
ink it. These things did these three
ightiest.
0 ¶ And [k]Ăb-ī-shai the brother of
-ăb, he was chief of the three: for
ting up his spear against three hun-
ed, he slew *them*, and had a name
nong the three.

6 revived.
7 went in going and increasing.
g 2 Sam. 23.8.
8 Or, held strongly with him.
h 1 Sam. 16. 1,2.
9 Or, son of Hachmoni.
10 Or, Ephes-dammim, 1 Sam. 17.1.
11 Or, stood.
12 Or, salvation.
13 Or, three captains over the thirty.
i 2 Sam. 23. 13.
j ch. 14.9.
14 Or, giants, Isa. 17.5.
15 with their lives.
k 1 Sam. 26. 6-8. 2 Sam. 2.18. ch. 2.16.
l 2 Sam. 23. 19. 1 Cor. 15.41.
16 great of deeds.
m 2 Sam. 1. 23. ch. 12.8.
17 a man of measure.
n 2 Sam. 2. 18-23. ch. 27.7.
18 Or, Shammah.
19 Or, Harodite, 2 Sam. 32. 25.
20 Or, Paltite, 2 Sam. 23. 26.
21 Or, Mebunnai.
22 Or, Zalmon.
23 Or, Heleb.
24 Or, Hiddai.
25 Or, Abialbon.
6 Or, Jashen. See 2 Sam. 23.32.
27 Or, Sharar.
28 Or, Eliphelet.
29 Or, Ahasbai.
30 Or, Hezrai.
31 Or, Paarai the Arbite.
32 Or, the Haggerite.
o ch. 2.50,53.
p 2 Sam. 11.3.
33 Perhaps these last sixteen were of less note, and so are not added in 2 Sam. 23.

21 Of [l]the three, he was mor
ourable than the two; for he was
captain: howbeit he attained not
the *first* three.
22 Bĕ-nai-ăh the son of Jĕ-hoi-ā-dă,
the son of a valiant man of Kăb-zēel,
[16]who had done many acts; he [m]slew
two lionlike men of Moab: also he
went down and slew a lion in a pit in
a snowy day.
23 And he slew an Egyptian, [17]a man
of *great* stature, five cubits high; and
in the Egyptian's hand *was* a spear like
a weaver's beam; and he went down
to him with a staff, and plucked the
spear out of the Egyptian's hand, and
slew him with his own spear.
24 These *things* did Bĕ-nai-ăh the son
of Jĕ-hoi-ā-dă, and had the name
among the three mighties.
25 Behold, he was honourable among
the thirty, but attained not to the *first*
three: and David set him over his
guard.
26 ¶ Also the valiant men of the armies *were*, [n]Ăs-ā-hĕl the brother of Jō-
ăb, Ĕl-hā-năn the son of Dodo of
Beth-lehem,
27 [18]Shăm-mōth the [19]Hâr-ō-rīte, Hē-
lĕz the [20]Pē-lō-nīte,
28 Ī-ră the son of Ĭk-kĕsh the Tĕ-kō-
ite, Ā-bī-ē-zĕr the Ăn-tō-thīte,
29 [21]Sĭb-bĕ-cai the Hū-shă-thīte,
[22]I-lā-ī the Ă-hō-hīte,
30 Mā-hă-rai the Nĕ-tŏph-ă-thīte,
[23]Hē-lĕd the son of Bā-ă-năh the Nĕ-
tŏph-ă-thīte,
31 Ī-thā-ī the son of Rī-bā-ī of Gĭb-ē-
ăh, *that pertained* to the children of
Benjamin, Bĕ-nai-ăh the Pī-rā-thŏn-
ite,
32 [24]Hū-rā-ī of the brooks of Gā-
ăsh, [25]Ā-bī-ĕl the Är-bă-thīte,
33 Ăz-mā-vĕth the Bā-hă-rû-mīte,
Ē-lī-ăh-bă the Shā-ăl-bō-nīte,
34 The sons of [26]Hăsh-ĕm the Gī-
zŏn-ite, Jonathan the son of Shā-gē
the Hâr-ă-rīte,
35 Ă-hī-ăm the son of [27]Sā-căr the
Hâr-ă-rīte, [28]Ē-lī-phăl the son of [29]Ur,
36 Hē-phĕr the Mĕ-chē-ră-thīte, Ă-
hī-jăh the Pē-lō-nīte,
37 [30]Hĕz-rō the Carmelite, [31]Nā-ă-
rai the son of Ĕz-bai,
38 Jō-ĕl the brother of Nathan, Mĭb-
här the [32]son of Hăg-gē-rī,
39 Zē-lĕk the Ammonite, Nā-hă-rai
the Bē-rō-thīte, the armourbearer of
Jō-ăb the son of Zĕr-ū-ī-ăh,
40 Ī-ră the [o]Ĭth-rīte, Gâr-ĕb the Ĭth-
rīte,
41 Ū-rī-ăh [p]the Hittite, [33]Zā-băd the
son of Äh-lā-ī,

42 Ăd-ĭ-nă the son of Shī-ză the Reu-
benite, a captain of the Reubenites,
and thirty with him,
43 Hā-năn the son of Mā-ă-chăh, and
Jŏsh-ă-phăt the Mĭth-nīte,
44 Ŭz-zī-ă the Ăsh-tē-ră-thīte, Shā-
mă and Jĕ-hī-ĕl the sons of Hō-thăn
the Ă-rō-ĕr-īte,
45 Jĕd-ĭ-ā-ĕl the son of Shĭm-rī, and
Jō-hă his brother, the Tī-zīte,
46 Ē-lī-ĕl the Mă-hă-vīte, and Jĕr-ĭ-
bā-ī, and Jŏsh-ă-vī-ăh, the sons of Ĕl-
nā-ăm, and Ĭth-măh the Moabite,
47 Ē-lī-ĕl, and Ō-bĕd, and Jăs-ĭ-ĕl
the Mĕ-sŏb-ā-īte.

CHAPTER 12

NOW [a]these *are* they that came to
David to [b]Ziklag, [1]while he yet
kept himself close because of Saul the
son of Kish: and they *were* among the
mighty men, helpers of the war.
2 *They were* armed with bows, and
could use both the right hand and the
[c]left in *hurling* stones and *shooting*
arrows out of a bow, *even* of Saul's
brethren of Benjamin.
3 The chief *was* Ā-hī-ē-zĕr, then Jō-
ăsh, the sons of [2]Shĕm-ā-ăh the Gĭb-
ĕ-ă-thīte; and Jē-zī-ĕl, and Pē-lĕt, the
sons of Ăz-mā-vĕth; and Bĕ-rā-chăh,
and Jehu [d]the Ăn-tō-thīte,
4 And Ĭs-mā-ī-ăh the [e]Gibeonite, a
mighty man among the thirty, and
over the thirty; and Jeremiah, and Jă-
hā-zī-ĕl, and Jō-hā-năn, and Jŏs-ă-
băd the Gĕ-dē-ră-thīte,
5 Ē-lū-zā-ī, and Jĕr-ĭ-mōth, and Bē-ă-
lī-ăh, and Shĕm-ă-rī-ăh, and Shĕph-
ă-tī-ăh the Hă-rū-phīte,
6 Ĕl-kā-năh, and Jĕ-sī-ăh, and Ăz-ă-
rē-ĕl, and Jō-ē-zĕr, and Jă-shŏb-ē-ăm,
the Kôr-hītes,
7 And Jō-ē-lăh, and Zĕb-ă-dī-ăh, the
sons of Jĕ-rō-hăm of Gē-dôr.
8 And of the Gadites there separated
themselves unto David into the [f]hold
to the wilderness men of might, *and*
men [3]of war *fit* for the battle, that
could handle shield and buckler,
whose [g]faces *were like* the faces of
lions, and *were* [4]as swift as the roes
upon the mountains;
9 Ē-zĕr the first, Ō-bă-dī-ăh the second, Ē-lī-ăb the third,
10 Mĭsh-măn-năh the fourth, Jeremiah the fifth,
11 Ăt-tā-ī the sixth, Ē-lī-ĕl the seventh,
12 Jō-hā-năn the eighth, Ĕl-zā-băd
the ninth,
13 Jeremiah the tenth, Măch-bā-nā-ī
the eleventh.

CHAP. 12
a 1 Sam. 27.2.
b 1 Sam. 27.6.
1 being yet shut up.
c Judg. 20.16.
2 Or, Hasmaah.
d ch. 11.28.
e Josh. 10.2. 1 Ki. 3.4,5. Isa. 28.21.
f 1 Sam. 23. 14,29. ch. 11.16.
3 of the host.
g 2 Sam. 17. 10. ch. 11.22. Pro. 28.1.
4 as the roes upon the mountains to make haste.
5 Or, one that was least could resist an hundred, and the greatest a thousand.
6 filled over.
h Jer. 12.5.
7 before them.
8 be one.
9 Or, violence.
i Zech. 3.2.
10 the spirit clothed Amasai.
j 2 Sam. 17. 25.
k 1 Sam. 29. 2.
l 1 Sam. 29.4.
11 on our heads.
12 Or, with a band.
m 1 Sam. 30. 1.
13 heads, or, captains, or, men.
n 2 Sam. 2.3.
o ch. 10.14.
p 1 Sam. 16.1. ch. 11.10.
14 Or, prepared.

14 These *were* of the sons of Ga
captains of the host: [5]one of the lea
was over an hundred, and the greate
over a thousand.
15 These *are* they that went over Jo
dan in the first month, when it ha
[6]overflown all his [h]banks; and the
put to flight all *them* of the valley
both toward the east, and toward t
west.
16 And there came of the children
Benjamin and Judah to the hold un
David.
17 And David went out [7]to me
them, and answered and said un
them, If ye be come peaceably un
me to help me, mine heart shall [8]
knit unto you: but if *ye be come* to b
tray me to mine enemies, seeing *the*
is no [9]wrong in mine hands, the G
of our fathers look *thereon*, and [i]r
buke *it*.
18 Then [10]the spirit came [j]upon
mā-sā-ī, *who was* chief of the captain
and he said, Thine *are we*, David, an
on thy side, thou son of Jesse: peac
peace *be* unto thee, and peace *be*
thine helpers; for thy God helpe
thee. Then David received them, an
made them captains of the band.
19 And there fell *some* of Mă-nă
sēh to David, [k]when he came with t
Philistines against Saul to battle: b
they helped them not: for the lords
the Philistines upon advisement se
him away, saying, He [l]will fall
his master Saul [11]to *the jeopardy of* o
heads.
20 As he went to Ziklag, there fell
him of Mă-năs-sēh, Ăd-năh, and J
ză-băd, and Jĕd-ĭ-ā-ĕl, and Micha
and Jō-ză-băd, and Ē-lī-hū, and Z
thā-ī, captains of the thousands th
were of Mă-năs-sēh.
21 And they helped David [12]again
[m]the band *of the rovers:* for they *we*
all mighty men of valour, and we
captains in the host.
22 For at *that* time day by day the
came to David to help him, un
it was a great host, like the host
God.
23 ¶ And these *are* the numbers
the [13]bands *that were* ready armed
the war, *and* came [n]to David to H
brŏn, to [o]turn the kingdom of Saul
him, [p]according to the word of t
LORD.
24 The children of Judah that ba
shield and spear *were* six thousa
and eight hundred, ready [14]armed
the war.
25 Of the children of Simeon, migh

ıen of valour for the war, seven thou-
ınd and one hundred.
26 Of the children of Levi four thou-
ınd and six hundred.
27 And Jĕ-hoi'-ă-dă *was* the leader
f the Aaronites, and with him *were*
ıree thousand and seven hundred;
28 And [q]Zā'-dŏk, a young man mighty
f valour, and of his father's house
wenty and two captains.
29 And of the children of Benjamin,
ıe [15]kindred of Saul, three thousand:
ɔr hitherto [16]the greatest part of them
ad kept the ward of the house of
aul.
30 And of the children of Ē'-phră-ĭm
wenty thousand and eight hundred,
ıighty men of valour, [17]famous
ıroughout the house of their fathers.
31 And of the half tribe of Mă-năs'-
ēh eighteen thousand, which were
xpressed by name, to come and
ıake David king.
32 And of the children of Ĭs'-să-chăr,
hich were men [r]that had understand-
ıg of the times, to know what Israel
ught to do; the heads of them *were*
vo hundred; and all their brethren
ere at their commandment.
33 Of Zĕ-bŭ'-lŭn, such as went forth
) battle, [18]expert in war, with all in-
ruments of war, fifty thousand,
hich could [19]keep rank: *they were*
not of double heart.
34 And of Năph'-tă-lī a thousand cap-
ins, and with them with shield and
ear thirty and seven thousand.
35 And of the Danites expert in war
venty and eight thousand and six
undred.
36 And of Asher, such as went forth
battle, [21]expert in war, forty thou-
nd.
37 And on the other side of Jordan,
f the Reubenites, and the Gadites,
d of the half tribe of Mă-năs'-sēh,
ith all manner of instruments of war
r the battle, an hundred and twenty
ousand.
38 All these men of war, that could
ep rank, came with a perfect heart
Hē'-brōn, to make David king over
Israel: and all the rest also of Israel
ere of one heart to make David king.
39 And there they were with David
ree days, eating and drinking: for
eir brethren had prepared for them.
40 Moreover they that were nigh
em, *even* unto Ĭs'-să-chăr and Zĕ-
ŭ'-lŭn and Năph'-tă-lī, brought bread
n asses, and on camels, and on
ules, and on oxen, *and* [22]meat, meal,
kes of figs, and bunches of raisins,

q 2 Sam. 8.17. 1 Ki. 1.8. ch. 6.8. Eze. 44.15.
15 brethren, Gen. 31.23.
16 a multitude of them.
17 men of names.
r Esther 1.13.
18 Or, rangers of battle, or, ranged in battle.
19 Or, set the battle in array.
20 without a heart and a heart.
21 Or, keeping their rank.
22 Or, victual of meal.

CHAP. 13

a 2 Sam. 5.1. ch. 12.14. Ps. 132.1. Pro. 15.22.
1 let us break forth and send.
b ch. 10.7. Isa. 37.4.
2 in the cities of their suburbs.
3 bring about.
c 1 Sam. 7.1. 1 Sam. 14. 18.
d 2 Sam. 6.1.
e Josh. 13.3.
f 1 Sam. 6.21.
g Josh. 15.9, 60.
h Ex. 25.22. 1 Sam. 4.4.
4 made the ark to ride.
i Num. 4.15.
j 2 Sam. 6.5.
5 songs.
k 2 Sam. 6.6.
6 shook it.
l Num. 4.15. ch. 15.13, 15.
m Lev. 10.2.
7 That is, The breach of Uzza.
8 removed.
n 2 Sam. 6.11.

and wine, and oil, and oxen, and sheep
abundantly: for *there was* joy in Israel.

CHAPTER 13

AND David [a]consulted with the
captains of thousands and hundreds, *and* with every leader.
2 And David said unto all the congregation of Israel, If *it seem* good unto you, and *that it be* of the LORD our
God, [1]let us send abroad unto our
brethren every where, *that are* [b]left in
all the land of Israel, and with them
also to the priests and Levites *which*
are [2]in their cities *and* suburbs, that
they may gather themselves unto us:
3 And let us [3]bring again the ark of
our God to us: [c]for we inquired not at
it in the days of Saul.
4 And all the congregation said that
they would do so: for the thing was
right in the eyes of all the people.
5 So [d]David gathered all Israel together, from [e]Shī'-hôr of Egypt even
unto the entering of Hē'-măth, to bring
the ark of God [f]from Kĭr'-jăth–jē'-ă-
rĭm.
6 And David went up, and all Israel
to Bā'-ă-lăh, [g]*that is*, to Kĭr'-jăth–jē'-ă-
rĭm, which *belonged* to Judah, to bring
up thence the ark of God the LORD,
[h]that dwelleth *between* the chĕr'-ŭ-
bĭms, whose name is called *on it*.
7 And they [4]carried the ark of God
[i]in a new cart out of the house of Ă-
bĭn'-ă-dăb: and Ŭz'-ză and Ă-hī'-ō
drave the cart.
8 And David and all Israel [j]played
before God with all *their* might, and
with [5]singing, and with harps, and
with psalteries, and with timbrels, and
with cymbals, and with trumpets.
9 ¶ And when they came unto the
threshingfloor of [k]Chī'-dŏn, Ŭz'-ză put
forth his hand to hold the ark; for the
oxen [6]stumbled.
10 And the anger of the LORD was
kindled against Ŭz'-ză, and he smote
him, [l]because he put his hand to
the ark: and there he died before
[m]God.
11 And David was displeased, because the LORD had made a breach
upon Ŭz'-ză: wherefore that place is
called [7]Pē'-rĕz–ŭz'-ză to this day.
12 And David was afraid of God that
day, saying, How shall I bring the ark
of God *home* to me?
13 So David [8]brought not the ark
home to himself to the city of David,
but carried it aside into the house of
Ō'-bĕd–ē'-dŏm the Gĭt'-tīte.
14 And [n]the ark of God remained

with the family of Ō-bĕd–ē-dŏm in his house three months. And the LORD blessed [o]the house of Ō-bĕd–ē-dŏm, and all that he had.

CHAPTER 14

NOW [a]Hiram king of Tyre sent messengers to David, and timber of cedars, with masons and carpenters, to build him an house.

2 And David perceived that the LORD had confirmed him king over Israel, for his kingdom was lifted up on high, because of his people Israel.

3 ¶ And David took [1]more wives at Jerusalem: and David begat more sons and daughters.

4 Now [b]these *are* the names of *his* children which he had in Jerusalem; Shăm-mū-ă, and Shō-băb, Nathan, and Solomon,

5 And Ĭb-hār, and Ē-lĭ-shû-ă, and Ĕl-pā-lĕt,

6 And Nō-gāh, and Nĕph-ĕg, and Jă-phĭ-ă,

7 And Ē-lĭ-shā-mă, and [2]Bĕe-lĭ-ă-dă, and Ē-lĭph-ă-lĕt.

8 ¶ And when the Philistines heard that [c]David was anointed king over all Israel, all the Philistines went up to seek David. And David heard *of it*, and went out against them.

9 And the Philistines came and spread themselves in the valley of [3]Rĕph-ā-ĭm.

10 And David inquired of God, saying, Shall I go up against the Philistines? And wilt thou deliver them into mine hand? And the LORD said unto him, Go up; for I will deliver them into thine hand.

11 So they came up to Bā-ăl–pĕ-rā-zĭm; and David smote them there. Then David said, God hath broken in upon mine enemies by mine hand like the breaking forth of waters: therefore they called the name of that place [4]Bā-ăl–pĕ-rā-zĭm.

12 And when they had left their gods there, David gave a commandment, and they were burned with fire.

13 And [d]the Philistines yet again spread themselves abroad in the valley.

14 Therefore David inquired again of God; and God said unto him, Go not up after them; turn away from them, [e]and come upon them over against the mulberry trees.

15 And it shall be, when thou shalt hear a sound of going in the tops of the mulberry trees, *that* then thou shalt go out to battle: for God is gone forth before thee to smite the host o[f] the Philistines.

16 David therefore did as God com[manded] him: and they smote the ho[st] of the Philistines [f]from Gibeon eve[n] to Gā-zĕr.

17 And [g]the fame of David went o[ut] into all lands; and the LORD broug[ht] [h]the fear of him upon all nations.

CHAPTER 15

AND *David* made him houses in th[e] city of David, and prepared [a] place for the ark of God, and pitche[d] for it a tent.

2 Then David said, [1]None ought t[o] carry [b]the ark of God but the Levite[s]: for them hath the LORD chosen t[o] carry the ark of God, and to minist[er] unto him for ever.

3 And David [c]gathered all Israel t[o]gether to Jerusalem, to bring up th[e] ark of the LORD unto his place, whic[h] he had prepared for it.

4 And David assembled the childre[n] of Aaron, and the Levites:

5 Of the sons of [d]Kō-hăth; Ū-rĭ-[ĕl] the chief, and his [2]brethren an hu[n]dred and twenty:

6 Of the sons of Mĕ-rār-ī; Ă-sāi-ă[h] the chief, and his brethren two hu[n]dred and twenty:

7 Of the sons of Gĕr-shŏm; Jō-ĕl th[e] chief, and his brethren an hundr[ed] and thirty:

8 Of the sons of [e]Ē-lĭ-zā-phă[n]; Shĕm-â-ăh the chief, and his bret[h]ren two hundred:

9 Of the sons of [f]Hē-brŏn; Ē-lĭ-ĕl th[e] chief, and his brethren fourscore:

10 Of the sons of Ŭz-zĭ-ĕl; Ăm-mĭ-ă-dăb the chief, and his brethren a[n] hundred and twelve.

11 And David called for Zā-dŏk a[nd] Ă-bī-ă-thăr the priests, and for th[e] Levites, for Ū-rĭ-ĕl, Ă-sāi-ăh, and J[ō]-ĕl, Shĕm-â-ăh, and Ē-lĭ-ĕl, and Ăm-mĭn-ă-dăb,

12 And said unto them, Ye *are* th[e] chief of the fathers of the Levite[s]: [g]sanctify yourselves, *both* ye and yo[ur] brethren, that ye may bring up the a[rk] of the LORD God of Israel unto *th[e] place that* I have prepared for it.

13 For [h]because ye *did it* not at th[e] first, the [i]LORD our God made [a] breach upon us, for that we soug[ht] him not after the due order.

14 So the priests and the Levit[es] sanctified themselves to bring up t[he] ark of the LORD God of Israel.

15 And the children of the Levi[tes] bare the ark of God upon their sho[ulders]

---

o Gen. 30.27. ch. 26.5. Ps. 37.22. Pro. 3.9,10. Mal. 3.10.

CHAP. 14

a 2 Sam. 5.11.
1 yet. Deut. 17.14, 17.
b 2 Sam. 5.14. ch. 3.5.
2 Or, Eliada, 2 Sam. 5.16.
c 2 Sam. 5.17. ch. 11.3. Ps. 2.1-5.
3 Or, giants, ch. 11.15.
4 That is, A place of breaches, Isa. 28.21.
d 2 Sam. 5.22.
e 2 Sam. 5.23.
f 2 Sam. 5.25. Geba.
g 2 Chr. 26.8.
h Deut. 2.25.

CHAP. 15

a ch. 16.1. Ps. 132.2-5. Acts 7.46.
1 It is not to carry the ark of God, but for the Levites.
b Num. 4.2, 15. Deut. 10.8.
c 1 Ki. 8.1. ch. 13.5.
d Ex. 6.16, 18.
2 Or, kinsmen.
e Ex. 6.22.
f Num. 26. 58.
g Ex. 19.10, 22. Lev. 10.3. 1 Sam. 7.1. 2 Chr. 5.11. Eze. 48.11. John 17.17. Rom. 12.1, 2.
h 2 Sam. 6.3. ch. 13.7.
i ch. 13.10,11.

ers with the staves thereon, as [j]Moses
ommanded according to the word of
ıe LORD.
.6 And David spake to the chief of
ıe Levites to appoint their brethren
· *be* the singers with instruments [k]of
ıusick, psalteries and harps and
ymbals, sounding, by lifting up the
oice with joy.
17 So the Levites appointed [l]Hē-
ıăn the son of Jō-ĕl; and of his breth-
en, [m]Ā-săph the son of Bĕr-ē-chī-ăh;
ıd of the sons of Mĕ-râr-ī their breth-
en, [n]Ē-thăn the son of Kū-shâi-ăh;
18 And with them their brethren of
ıe second *degree*, Zĕch-ă-rī-ăh, Ben,
nd Jā-ā-zī-ĕl, and Shĕ-mī-ră-mōth,
nd Jĕ-hī-ĕl, and Ŭn-nī, Ē-lī-ăb, and
ĕ-nâi-ăh, and Mā-ă-sêi-ăh, and Măt-
-thī-ăh, and Ē-lĭph-ĕ-lēh, and Mĭk-
ĕi-ăh, and Ō-bĕd-ē-dom, and Jē-ī-ĕl,
ıe porters.
19 So the singers, Hē-măn, Ā-săph,
ıd Ē-thăn, *were appointed* to sound
ith cymbals of brass;
20 And Zĕch-ă-rī-ăh, and [3]Ā-zī-ĕl,
ıd Shĕ-mī-ră-mōth, and Jĕ-hī-ĕl, and
n-nī, and Ē-lī-ăb, and Mā-ă-sêi-ăh,
nd Bĕ-nâi-ăh, with psalteries on
Al-ă-mōth;
21 And Măt-tĭ-thī-ăh, and Ē-lĭph-ĕ-
h, and Mĭk-nêi-ăh, and Ō-bĕd-ē-
om, and Jē-ī-ĕl, and Ăz-ă-zī-ăh, with
arps [5]on the Shĕm-ĭn-ĭth to excel.
22 And Chĕn-ă-nī-ăh, chief of the
evites, [6]*was* for [7]song: he instructed
bout the song, because he *was* skilful.
23 And Bĕr-ē-chī-ăh and Ĕl-kā-năh
ere doorkeepers for the ark.
24 And Shĕb-ă-nī-ăh, and Jĕ-hŏsh-ă-
hăt, and Nĕth-ă-neel, and Ă-mā-sâi,
nd Zĕch-ă-rī-ăh, and Bĕ-nâi-ăh, and
-ī-ē-zĕr, the priests, [o]did blow with
ıe trumpets before the ark of God:
nd Ō-bĕd-ē-dom and Jĕ-hī-ăh *were*
oorkeepers for the ark.
25 ¶ So [p]David, and the elders of Is-
el, and the captains over thousands,
ent to bring up the ark of the coven-
nt of the LORD out of the house of
-bĕd-ē-dom with [q]joy.
26 And it came to pass, when God
elped the Levites that bare the ark of
ıe covenant of the LORD, that they
ffered seven bullocks and seven
ıms.
27 And David *was* clothed with a
obe of fine linen, and all the Levites
ıat bare the ark, and the singers, and
hĕn-ă-nī-ăh the master of the [8]song
ith the singers: David also *had* upon
m an ē-phŏd of linen.
28 Thus [s]all Israel brought up the

[j] Ex. 25.14. Num. 4.15.
[k] ch. 6.31. ch. 13.8. Ps. 33.2. Ps. 149.3.
[l] ch. 6.33.
[m] ch. 6.39.
[n] ch. 6.44.
3 Jaaziel, ver. 18.
4 That is, virginal, or, treble.
5 Or, on the eighth to oversee, Ps. 6, title.
6 Or, was for the carriage; he instructed about the carriage.
7 lifting up.
[o] Num. 10.8. Ps. 81.3.
[p] 2 Sam. 6.12, 13.
[q] Deut. 12.7, 18.
[r] Num. 23.1. Job 42.8.
8 Or, carriage.
[s] ch. 13.8.
[t] 2 Sam. 6.16.
[u] Acts 2.13.

CHAP. 16

[a] 2 Sam. 6. 17-19.
[b] Ps. 38. Ps. 70, title.
1 with instruments of psalteries and harps.
[c] 2 Sam. 23.1.
[d] Ps. 105.1.
[e] Ps. 95.1,2.
[f] Ps. 34.3. Isa. 45.25.
[g] Amos 5.6, 14.
[h] Ps. 103.2. Ps. 111.2.

ark of the covenant of the LORD with
shouting, and with sound of the cornet, and with trumpets, and with cymbals, making a noise with psalteries
and harps.
29 ¶ And it came to pass, [t]*as* the ark
of the covenant of the LORD came to
the city of David, that Mī-chăl the
daughter of Saul looking out at a window saw king David dancing and
playing: and she [u]despised him in her
heart.

CHAPTER 16

SO [a]they brought the ark of God,
and set it in the midst of the tent
that David had pitched for it: and
they offered burnt sacrifices and peace
offerings before God.
2 And when David had made an end
of offering the burnt offerings and the
peace offerings, he blessed the people
in the name of the LORD.
3 And he dealt to every one of Israel,
both man and woman, to every one a
loaf of bread, and a good piece of
flesh, and a flagon *of wine*.
4 ¶ And he appointed *certain* of the
Levites to minister before the ark of
the LORD, and to [b]record, and to thank
and praise the LORD God of Israel:
5 Ā-săph the chief, and next to him
Zĕch-ă-rī-ăh, Jē-ī-ĕl, and Shĕ-mī-ră-
mōth, and Jĕ-hī-ĕl, and Măt-tĭ-thī-ăh,
and Ē-lī-ăb, and Bĕ-nâi-ăh, and Ō-
bĕd-ē-dom: and Jē-ī-ĕl [1]with psalteries and with harps; but Ā-săph made
a sound with cymbals;
6 Bĕ-nâi-ăh also and Jă-hā-zī-ĕl the
priests with trumpets continually before the ark of the covenant of God.
7 ¶ Then on that day David delivered
first [c]*this psalm* to thank the LORD into
the hand of Ā-săph and his brethren.
8 Give [d]thanks unto the LORD, call
upon his name, make known his deeds
among the people.
9 Sing [e]unto him, sing psalms unto
him, talk ye of all his wondrous works.
10 Glory [f]ye in his holy name: let the
heart of them rejoice that seek the
LORD.
11 Seek [g]the LORD and his strength,
seek his face continually.
12 Remember his [h]marvellous works
that he hath done, his wonders, and
the judgments of his mouth;
13 O ye seed of Israel his servant, ye
children of Jacob, his chosen ones.
14 He *is* the LORD our God; his judgments *are* in all the earth.
15 Be ye mindful always of his covenant; the word *which* he commanded
to a thousand generations;

16 *Even of the* [i]covenant which he made with Abraham, and of his oath unto Isaac;

17 And hath confirmed the same to Jacob for a law, *and* to Israel *for* an everlasting covenant,

18 Saying, Unto thee will I give the land of Canaan, [2]the lot of your inheritance;

19 When ye were but [3]few, [j]even a few, and strangers in it.

20 And *when* they went from nation to nation, and from *one* kingdom to another people;

21 He suffered no man to do them wrong: yea, [k]he reproved kings for their sakes,

22 *Saying*, [l]Touch not mine anointed, and do my prophets no harm.

23 Sing [m]unto the LORD, all the earth; shew forth from day to day his salvation.

24 Declare [n]his glory among the heathen; his marvellous works among all nations.

25 For [o]great *is* the LORD, and greatly to be praised: he also *is* to be feared above all gods.

26 For all the gods [p]of the people *are* idols: but the LORD made the heavens.

27 Glory [q]and honour *are* in his presence; strength and gladness *are* in his place.

28 Give unto the LORD, ye kindreds of the people, give unto the LORD glory and strength.

29 Give unto the LORD the glory *due* unto his name: bring an offering, and come before him: worship the LORD in the beauty of holiness.

30 Fear before him, all the earth: the world also shall be stable, that it be not moved.

31 Let [r]the heavens be glad, and let the earth rejoice: and let *men* say among the nations, The LORD reigneth.

32 Let [s]the sea roar, and the fulness thereof: let the fields rejoice, and all that *is* therein.

33 Then shall the trees of the wood sing out at the presence of the LORD, because he cometh to judge the earth.

34 O [t]give thanks unto the LORD; for *he is* good; for his mercy *endureth* for ever.

35 And [u]say ye, Save us, O God of our salvation, and gather us together, and deliver us from the heathen, that we may give thanks to thy holy name, *and* glory in thy praise.

36 Blessed [v]*be* the LORD God of Israel for ever and ever. And [w]all t people said, Ā-mĕn, and praised t LORD.

37 ¶ So he left there before the ark the covenant of the LORD Ā-săph a his brethren, to minister before the a continually, as every day's work quired:

38 And Ō-bĕd-ē-dom with th brethren, threescore and eight; bĕd-ē-dom also the son of Jĕ-dū-th and Hō-săh *to be* porters:

39 And Zā-dŏk the priest, and brethren the priests, [x]before the ta ernacle of the LORD [y]in the high pla that *was* at Gibeon,

40 To offer burnt offerings unto t LORD upon the altar of the burnt offe ing continually [4]morning and evenir and *to do* according to all that is wr ten in the law of the LORD, which commanded Israel;

41 And with them Hē-măn and dū-thŭn, and the rest that were ch en, who were expressed by name, give thanks to the LORD, because [z] mercy *endureth* for ever;

42 And with them Hē-măn and dū-thŭn with trumpets and cymba for those that should make a soun and with musical instruments of Go And the sons of Jĕ-dū-thŭn we [5]porters.

43 And [a]all the people depart every man to his house: and Dav returned to bless [b]his house.

CHAPTER 17

NOW [a]it came to pass, as Dav sat in his house, that David sa to Nathan the prophet, Lo, I [b]dw in an house of cedars, but the ark the covenant of the LORD *remaine* under curtains.

2 Then Nathan said unto David, D all that *is* in thine heart; for God with thee.

3 ¶ And it came to pass the sa night, that the word of God came Nathan, saying,

4 Go and tell David my servan Thus saith the LORD, Thou shalt n build me an house to dwell in:

5 For I have not dwelt in an hou since the day that I brought up Isra unto this day; but [1]have gone fro [c]tent to tent, and from *one* tabernac *to another*.

6 Wheresoever I have walked with Israel, spake I a word to any of t judges of Israel, whom I command to feed my people, saying, Why ha ye not built me an house of cedar

[i] Gen. 15.18. Gen. 26.3. Gen. 28.13. Neh. 9.8. Heb. 6.13-18.
[2] the cord.
[3] men of number.
[j] Gen. 34.30. Heb. 11.13.
[k] Gen. 12.17. Ex. 7.15-18.
[l] Ps. 105.15. 1 John 2.27.
[m] Ps. 47.1. Ps. 96.1.
[n] Isa. 12.4.
[o] Ps. 24.8. Isa. 40.25,26.
[p] Lev. 19.4. Ps. 115.4-8. Isa. 45.20. 1 Cor. 8.4.
[q] Ps. 8.1.
[r] Isa. 35.10. Luke 2.13. Rev. 14.2.
[s] Ps. 96.10.
[t] Ps. 106.1. Ps. 107.1. Ps. 118.1.
[u] Ps. 106.47, 48.
[v] Ps. 72.18, 19.
[w] Deut. 27. 15. Neh. 8.6.
[x] ch. 21.29. 2 Chr. 1.3.
[y] 1 Ki. 3.4.
[4] in the morning, and in the evening.
[z] 2 Chr. 5.13. 2 Chr. 7.3. Ezra 3.11. Neh. 9.17. Ps. 25.10. Ps. 33.5. Ps. 86.5,15. Ps. 100.5. Ps. 103.17. Ps. 107.1. Ps. 118.1. Joel 2.13. Luke 6.36. Jas. 5.11.
[5] for the gate.
[a] 2 Sam. 6.19, 20.
[b] Gen. 18.19.

CHAP. 17

[a] 2 Sam. 7.1.
[b] ch. 14.1. Hag. 1.4. Acts 7.46.
[1] have been.
[c] Ex. 40.2. 2 Sam. 6.17.

Now therefore thus shalt thou say
ıto my servant David, Thus saith
e LORD of hosts, I took thee from
e sheepcote, *even* [2]from following
e sheep, that thou shouldest be ruler
'er my people Israel:
And I have been with thee whither-
ever thou hast walked, and have
.t off all thine enemies from before
ee, and have made thee a name like
e name of the great men that *are* in
e earth.
Also I [d]will ordain a place for my
ople Israel, and will plant them, and
ey shall dwell in their place, and
all be moved no more; neither shall
e children of wickedness waste
em [e]any more, as at the beginning,
0 And since the time that I com-
anded judges *to be* over my people
rael. Moreover I will subdue all
ine enemies. Furthermore I tell
ee that the LORD will build thee an
ouse.
1 ¶ And it shall come to pass, when
y days be expired that thou must go
be with thy fathers, that I will raise
thy seed after thee, which shall be
thy sons; and I will establish his
ngdom.
2 He shall build me an house, and
will stablish his throne for ever.
3 I [f]will be his father, and he shall
my son: and I will not take my
ercy away from him, as I took *it*
om *him* that was before thee:
4 But [g]I will settle him in mine
ouse and in my kingdom for ever:
d his throne shall be established for
ermore.
5 According to all these words, and
cording to all this vision, so did
athan speak unto David.
6 ¶ And [h]David the king came and
t before the LORD, and said, Who
m I, O LORD God, and what *is* mine
ouse, that thou hast brought me
therto?
7 And *yet* this was a small thing in
ine eyes, O God; for thou hast *also*
oken of thy servant's house for a
eat while to come, and hast regard-
me according to the estate of a
an of high degree, O LORD God.
8 What can David *speak* more to
ee for the honour of thy servant?
r [j]thou knowest thy servant.
9 O LORD, for thy servant's sake,
d according [k]to thine own heart,
st thou done all this greatness, in
aking known all *these* [3]great things.
0 O LORD, *there is* [l]none like thee,
ither *is there any* God beside thee,

2 from after.
d Jer. 31.12.
e 2 Chr. 15.2. Isa. 49.17.
f 2 Sam. 7.14, 15. ch. 22.10. Heb. 1.5.
g Ps. 2.6. Ps. 89.36. Isa. 9.7. Eze. 37.25. Dan. 2.44. Micah 4.1. Matt. 21.1-11. Luke 1.33. Heb. 1.8.
h 2 Sam. 7.18.
i Gen. 32.10. Ps. 144.3.
j Ps. 139.1. John 21.17.
k Matt. 11. 26. Eph. 1.11.
3 greatnesses.
l Ex. 15.11. Deut. 3.24. 1 Sam. 2.2. 2 Sam. 7.22. Ps. 86.8.
m 2 Chr. 6.33. Ps. 21.13. Matt. 6.9, 13. John 12.28.
4 hast revealed the ear of thy servant.
n Ex. 34.6. Titus 1.2. Heb. 6.18.
5 Or, it hath pleased thee.
o Ps. 72.17. Rom. 11.29.

CHAP. 18

a 2 Sam. 8.1.
b Num. 24. 17.
1 Or, Hadadezer, 2 Sam. 8.3.
c Gen. 15.18. Ps. 60, title.
d 2 Sam. 8.4, seven hundred.
2 Darmesek.

according to all that we have heard
with our ears.
21 And what one nation in the earth
is like thy people Israel, whom God
went to redeem *to be* his own people,
to make thee a name of greatness and
terribleness, by driving out nations
from before thy people, whom thou
hast redeemed out of Egypt?
22 For thy people Israel didst thou
make thine own people for ever; and
thou, LORD, becamest their God.
23 Therefore now, LORD, let the
thing that thou hast spoken concerning thy servant and concerning his
house be established for ever, and do
as thou hast said.
24 Let it even be established, that
[m]thy name may be magnified for ever,
saying, The LORD of hosts *is* the God
of Israel, *even* a God to Israel: and
let the house of David thy servant *be*
established before thee.
25 For thou, O my God, [4]hast told
thy servant that thou wilt build him
an house: therefore thy servant hath
found *in his heart* to pray before
thee.
26 And now, LORD, thou art God,
and hast [n]promised this goodness unto thy servant:
27 Now therefore [5]let it please thee
to bless the house of thy servant, that
it may be before thee for ever: for
[o]thou blessest, O LORD, and *it shall be*
blessed for ever.

CHAPTER 18

NOW after this [a]it came to pass,
that David smote the Philistines,
and subdued them, and took Gath
and her towns out of the hand of the
Philistines.
2 And he [b]smote Moab; and the
Moabites became David's servants,
and brought gifts.
3 ¶ And David smote [1]Hăd-ă-rē-zĕr
king of Zō-băh unto Hā-măth, as he
[c]went to stablish his dominion by the
river Eû-phrā-tēs.
4 And David took from him a thousand chariots, and [d]seven thousand
horsemen, and twenty thousand footmen: David also houghed all the
chariot *horses*, but reserved of them
an hundred chariots.
5 And when the Syrians of [2]Damas-
cus came to help Hăd-ă-rē-zĕr king of
Zō-băh, David slew of the Syrians two
and twenty thousand men.
6 Then David put *garrisons* in Syria-
damascus; and the Syrians became
David's servants, *and* brought gifts.

Thus the LORD preserved [e]David
whithersoever he went.
7 And David took the shields of gold
that were on the servants of Hăd-ă-rē-
zĕr, and brought them to Jerusalem.
8 Likewise from [3]Tĭb-hăth, and from
Chŭn, cities of Hăd-ă-rē-zĕr, brought
David very much brass, wherewith
[f]Solomon made the brasen sea, and
the pillars, and the vessels of brass.
9 ¶ Now when [g]Tō-ū king of Hā-
măth heard how David had smitten
all the host of Hăd-ă-rē-zĕr king of
Zō-băh;
10 He sent [h]Hă-dôr-ăm his son to
king David, [4]to inquire of his welfare,
and [5]to congratulate him, because he
had fought against Hăd-ă-rē-zĕr, and
smitten him; (for Hăd-ă-rē-zĕr [6]had
war with Tō-ū;) and *with him* all manner of vessels of gold and silver and
brass.
11 ¶ Them also king David dedicated
unto the LORD, with the silver and the
gold that he brought from all *these*
nations; from Ē-dom, and from Moab, and from the children of Ammon,
and from the Philistines, and from
Ăm-ă-lĕk.
12 Moreover [7]Ăb-ĭ-shāi the son of
Zĕr-ū-ī-ăh slew of the Ē-dom-ītes in
the valley of salt eighteen [i]thousand.
13 ¶ And [j]he put garrisons in Ē-dom;
and all the Ē-dom-ītes became David's
servants. Thus the LORD preserved
David whithersoever he went.
14 ¶ So David reigned over all Israel, and executed judgment and
justice among all his people.
15 And Jō-ăb the son of Zĕr-ū-ī-ăh
was over the host; and Jĕ-hŏsh-ă-phăt
the son of Ă-hī-lŭd, [8]recorder.
16 And Zā-dŏk the son of Ă-hī-tŭb,
and [9]Ă-bĭm-ĕ-lĕch the son of Ă-bī-ă-
thăr, *were* the priests; and [10]Shăv-shă
was scribe;
17 And [k]Bĕ-nāi-ăh the son of Jĕ-hōi-
ă-dă *was* over the Chĕr-ĕ-thītes and
the Pĕl-ĕ-thītes; and the sons of David
were chief [11]about the king.

CHAPTER 19

NOW [a]it came to pass after this,
that [b]Nahash the king of the children of Ammon died, and his son
reigned in his stead.
2 And David said, I will shew kindness unto Hā-nŭn the son of Nahash,
because his father shewed kindness to
me. And David sent messengers to
comfort him concerning his father. So
the servants of David came into the

e ch. 17.8. Ps. 91.14. Pro. 21.31.
3 Called in the book of Samuel Betah and Berothai.
f 2 Chr. 4.12, 15,16.
g 2 Sam. 8.9, Toi.
h 2 Sam. 8.10, Joram.
4 Or, to salute.
5 to bless.
6 was the man of wars.
7 Abshai.
i 2 Sam. 8.13.
j Gen. 27.29. Num. 24.18. 1 Sam. 10.5.
8 Or, remembrancer.
9 Called Ahimelech, 2 Sam. 8.17.
10 Called Seraiah, 2 Sam. 8.17, and Shisha, 1 Ki. 4.3.
k 2 Sam. 8. 18.
11 at the hand of the king.
CHAP. 19.
a 2 Sam. 10.1.
b 1 Sam. 11.1.
1 In thine eyes doth David, etc.
c Josh. 6.24, 26.
2 to stink.
d 1 Sam. 14. 47. 2 Sam. 8.3. 1 Ki. 11.23. ch. 18.5,9.
e Num. 21. 30. Isa. 15.2.
f 2 Sam. 11.1
3 the face of the battle was.
4 Or, young men.
5 Abshai.
g Ps. 20.7. Ps. 34.22. Ps. 40.4. Ps. 55.22. Pro. 28.25. Pro. 29.25. Isa. 30.18.

land of the children of Ammon
Hā-nŭn, to comfort him.
3 But the princes of the children
Ammon said to Hā-nŭn, [1]Thinke
thou that David doth honour t
father, that he hath sent comforte
unto thee? are not his servants co
unto thee for to search, and to ove
throw, and to spy out the land?
4 Wherefore Hā-nŭn took David
servants, and shaved them, and c
off their garments in the midst hard
their buttocks, and sent them away
5 Then there went *certain*, and to
David how the men were served. A
he sent to meet them: for the m
were greatly ashamed. And the ki
said, Tarry at Jericho [c]until yo
beards be grown, and *then* return.
6 ¶ And when the children of Am
mon saw that they had made ther
selves [2]odious to David, Hā-nŭn a
the children of Ammon sent a thou
and talents of silver to hire them cha
ots and horsemen out of Mĕs-ŏ-p
tā-mĭ-ă, and out of Sÿr-ĭ-ă-mā-
chăh, [d]and out of Zō-băh.
7 So they hired thirty and two thou
and chariots, and the king of Mā-
chăh and his people; who came a
pitched before [e]Mē-dĕ-bă. And t
children of Ammon gathered ther
selves together from their cities, a
came to battle.
8 And when David heard *of it*, he se
Jō-ăb, and all the host of the migh
men.
9 And the children of Ammon ca
out, and put the battle in array befo
the gate of [f]the city: and the kin
that were come *were* by themselves
the field.
10 Now when Jō-ăb saw that [3]t
battle was set against him before a
behind, he chose out of all the [4]choi
of Israel, and put *them* in array again
the Syrians.
11 And the rest of the people he d
livered unto the hand of [5]Ăb-ĭ-shāi h
brother, and they set *themselves*
array against the children of A
mon.
12 And he said, If the Syrians be t
strong for me, then thou shalt he
me: but if the children of Ammon
too strong for thee, then I will he
thee.
13 Be of good courage, and let us b
have ourselves valiantly for our pe
ple, and for the cities of our Go
[g]and let the LORD do *that which*
good in his sight.
14 So Jō-ăb and the people that *we*

vith him drew nigh before the Syrians
nto the battle; and they [h]fled before
im.
15 And when the children of Ammon
aw that the Syrians were fled, they
ikewise fled before Ăb-ī-shâi his bro-
her, and entered into the city. Then
ō-ăb came to Jerusalem.
16 ¶ And when the Syrians saw that
hey were put to the worse before Is-
ael, they sent messengers, and drew
orth the Syrians that *were* beyond the
river: and [i]Shō-phăch the captain of
he host of Hăd-ă-rē-zĕr *went* before
hem.
17 And it was told David; and he
athered all Israel, and passed over
ordan, and came upon them, and set
he battle in array against them. So
vhen David had put the battle in array
gainst the Syrians, they fought with
im.
18 But the Syrians [j]fled before Israel;
nd David slew of the Syrians seven
housand *men which fought in* chari-
ts, and forty thousand footmen, and
illed Shō-phăch the captain of the
ost.
19 And when the servants of Hăd-ă-
ē-zĕr saw that they were put to the
vorse before Israel, they made peace
vith David, and became his servants:
either would the Syrians help the
hildren of Ammon any more.

CHAPTER 20

AND [a]it came to pass, that [1]after
the year was expired, at the time
hat kings go out *to battle*, Jō-ăb led
orth the power of the army, and wast-
d the country of the children of Amnon, and came and besieged Răb-
ăh. But David tarried at Jerusalem.
And Jō-ăb [b]smote Răb-băh, and de-
troyed it.
2 And David [c]took the crown of their
ing from off his head, and found it
to weigh a talent of gold, and *there*
vere precious stones in it; and it
vas set upon David's head: and he
rought also exceeding much spoil
ut of the city.
3 And he brought out the people that
vere in it, and [3]cut *them* with saws,
nd with harrows of iron, and with
xes. Even so dealt David with all the
ities of the children of Ammon. And
David and all the people returned to
erusalem.
4 ¶ And it came to pass after this,
hat there [4]arose war at [5]Gē-zĕr with
he Philistines; at which time Sĭb-bĕ-
hâi the Hū-shă-thite slew [6]Sĭp-pā-ī,
that was of the children of [7]the giant:
and they were subdued.
5 And there was war again with the
Philistines; and Ĕl-hā-năn the son of
[8]Jā-īr slew Lăh-mī the brother of Gō-
lī-ăth the Gĭt-tīte, whose spear staff
was like a weaver's beam.
6 And yet again there was war at
Gath, where was [9]a man of *great* stature, whose fingers and toes *were* four
and twenty, six *on each hand*, and six
on each foot: and he also was [10]the son
of the giant.
7 But when he [11]defied Israel, Jonathan the son of [12]Shĭm-ĕ-ă David's
brother slew him.
8 These were born unto the giant in
Gath; and they fell by the hand of
David, and by the hand of his servants.

CHAPTER 21

AND [a]Satan stood up against Israel, and provoked David to number Israel.
2 And David said to Jō-ăb and to the
rulers of the people, Go, number Israel from Bē-ēr-shē-bă even to Dan;
[b]and bring the number of them to me,
that I may know *it*.
3 And Jō-ăb answered, The LORD
make his people an hundred times so
many more as they *be:* but, my lord
the king, *are* they not all my lord's
servants? why then doth my lord require this thing? why will he be a
cause of trespass to Israel?
4 Nevertheless [c]the king's word prevailed against Jō-ăb. Wherefore Jō-
ăb departed, and went throughout all
Israel, and came to Jerusalem.
5 ¶ And Jō-ăb gave the sum of the
number of the people unto David.
And all *they of* Israel were a thousand
thousand and an hundred thousand
men that drew sword: and Judah *was*
four hundred threescore and ten thousand men that drew sword.
6 But [d]Levi and Benjamin counted he
not among them: for the king's word
was abominable to Jō-ăb.
7 [1]And God was displeased with this
thing; therefore he smote Israel.
8 And David said unto God, [e]I have
sinned greatly, because I have done
this thing: but [f]now, I beseech thee,
do away the iniquity of thy servant;
for I have done very foolishly.
9 ¶ And the LORD spake unto Gad,
David's [g]seer, saying,
10 Go and tell David, saying, Thus
saith the LORD, I [2]offer thee three
things: choose thee one of them, that
I may do *it* unto thee.

h Lev. 26.7,8. Num. 14.9. Deut. 28.7.
6 That is, Euphrates.
i 2 Sam. 10. 16, Shobach.
j Ps. 33.16. Pro. 21.31.

CHAP. 20

a 2 Sam. 11.1. 2 Chr. 36.10. Eccl. 3.8.
1 at the return of the year.
b 2 Sam. 12. 26.
c 2 Sam. 12. 30,31.
2 the weight of.
3 Or, made them sawers of stone, diggers of iron, and cutters of wood.
4 stood, or, continued.
5 Or, Gob.
6 Or, Saph.
7 Or, Rapha, 2 Sam. 21. 18.
8 Jaare-oregim, 2 Sam. 21. 19.
9 a man of measure.
10 born to the giant, or, Rapha.
11 Or, reproached.
12 Called Shammah, 1 Sam. 16.9.

CHAP. 21

a 2 Sam. 24.1. Job 1.6. Zech. 3.1. Matt. 4.3. Luke 22.31. John 13.2. Acts 5.3. Rev. 12.9.
b ch. 27.23.
c Pro. 29.25. Eccl. 8.4. Acts 4.19.
d Num. 1.47-49. ch. 27.24.
1 And it was evil in the eyes of the LORD concerning this thing.
e 2 Sam. 12. 13. Ps. 25.11. Pro. 28.13, 14. 2 Cor. 7.10.
f 2 Sam. 12. 13. Ps. 51.1-3. Hosea 14.2.
g 1 Sam. 9.9.
2 stretch out.

11 So Gad came to David, and said
unto him, Thus saith the LORD,
[3]Choose thee
12 Either [h]three years' famine; or
three months to be destroyed before
thy foes, while that the sword of thine
enemies overtaketh *thee;* or else three
days the sword of the LORD, even the
pestilence, in the land, and the angel
of the LORD destroying throughout all
the coasts of Israel. Now therefore advise thyself what word I shall bring
again to him that sent me.
13 And David said unto Gad, I am in
a great strait: let me fall now into the
hand of the LORD; for very [4]great *are*
his mercies: but let me not fall into
the hand of man.
14 ¶ So the LORD sent pestilence upon Israel: and there fell of Israel seventy thousand men.
15 And God sent an [i]angel unto Jerusalem to destroy it: and as he was destroying, the LORD beheld, and [j]he repented him of the evil, and said to the
angel that destroyed, It is enough,
stay now thine hand. And the angel of
the LORD stood by the threshingfloor
of [5]Ŏr´-năn the Jĕb´-ū-şīte.
16 And David lifted up his eyes, and
[k]saw the angel of the LORD stand between the earth and the heaven, having a drawn sword in his hand stretched out over Jerusalem. Then David
and the elders *of Israel, who were*
clothed in sackcloth, fell upon their
faces.
17 And David said unto God, *Is it* not
I *that* commanded the people to be
numbered? even I it is that have
sinned and done evil indeed; but *as for*
these sheep, what have they done? let
thine hand, I pray thee, O LORD my
God, be on me, and on my father's
house; but not on thy people, that
they should be plagued.
18 ¶ Then the angel of the LORD
commanded Gad to say to David, that
David should go up, and set up an
altar unto the LORD in the threshingfloor of Ŏr´-năn the Jĕb´-ū-şīte.
19 And David went up at the saying
of Gad, which he spake in the name
of the LORD.
20 [6]And Ŏr´-năn turned back, and
saw the angel; and his four sons with
him hid themselves. Now Ŏr´-năn was
threshing wheat.
21 And as David came to Ŏr´-năn,
Ŏr´-năn looked and saw David, and
went out of the threshingfloor, and
bowed himself to David with *his* face
to the ground.

3 Take to thee.
h 2 Sam. 24. 13.
4 Or, many. Neh. 9.17. Ps. 100.5. Lam. 3.22.
i 2 Sam. 24. 16. Jer. 26.18. Matt. 23.37, 38.
j Gen. 6.6.
5 Araunah, 2 Sam. 24. 18.
k 2 Chr. 3.1.
6 Or, When Ornan turned back and saw the angel, then he and his four sons with him hid themselves.
7 Give.
l Num. 16.48.
m 2 Sam. 24. 24.
n Lev. 9.24. 2 Chr. 3.1.
o ch. 16.39.
p 1 Ki. 3.4. ch. 16.39.
q 2 Sam. 6.9. ch. 13.12. Job 13.21. Ps. 119.120.

CHAP. 22
a Deut. 12.5. 2 Sam. 24. 18. ch. 21.18,19, 26,28.
b 1 Ki. 9.21.
c 1 Ki. 7.47.
d 1 Ki. 5.6.
e ch. 29.1.

22 Then David said to Ŏr´-năr
[7]Grant me the place of *this* threshing
floor, that I may build an altar therei
unto the LORD: thou shalt grant it m
for the full price: that the plague ma
be [l]stayed from the people.
23 And Ŏr´-năn said unto David
Take *it* to thee, and let my lord th
king do *that which is* good in his eyes
lo, I give *thee* the oxen *also* for burn
offerings, and the threshing instru
ments for wood, and the wheat for th
meat offering; I give it all.
24 And king David said to Ŏr´-năn
Nay; but I will verily buy it for the ful
price: for I will not take *that* which *i*
thine for the LORD, nor offer burn
offerings without cost.
25 So [m]David gave to Ŏr´-năn for th
place six hundred shekels of gold b
weight.
26 And David built there an alta
unto the LORD, and offered burn
offerings and peace offerings, an
called upon the LORD; and [n]he an
swered him from heaven by fire upo
the altar of burnt offering.
27 And the LORD commanded th
angel; and he put up his sword agai
into the sheath thereof.
28 ¶ At that time when David sa
that the LORD had answered him i
the threshingfloor of Ŏr´-năn the Jĕb
ū-şīte, then he sacrificed there.
29 For [o]the tabernacle of the LORD
which Moses made in the wilderness
and the altar of the burnt offering
were at that season in the high place a
[p]Gibeon.
30 But David could not go before i
to inquire of God: for he [q]was afrai
because of the sword of the angel o
the LORD.

CHAPTER 22

THEN David said, [a]This *is* th
house of the LORD God, and thi
is the altar of the burnt offering fo
Israel.
2 And David commanded to gathe
together [b]the strangers that *were* i
the land of Israel; and he set mason
to hew wrought stones to build th
house of God.
3 And David prepared iron in abun
dance for the nails for the doors of th
gates, and for the joinings; and bras
in abundance without [c]weight;
4 Also cedar trees in abundance: fo
[d]the Zī-dō´-nĭ-ăns and they of Tyr
brought much cedar wood to David
5 And David said, [e]Solomon my so
is young and tender, and the house *tha*

s to be builded for the LORD *must be*
xceeding magnifical, of fame and of
lory throughout all countries: I
vill *therefore* now make preparation
or it. So David prepared abundantly
efore his death.
6 ¶ Then he called for Solomon his
on, and charged him to build an
ouse for the LORD God of Israel.
7 And David said to Solomon, My
on, as for me, [f]it was in my mind to
uild an house [g]unto the name of the
ORD my God:
8 But the word of the LORD came to
ne, saying, [h]Thou hast shed blood
bundantly, and hast made great
vars: thou shalt not build an house
nto my name, because thou hast
hed much blood upon the earth in
ny sight.
9 Behold, [i]a son shall be born to
hee, who shall be a man of rest; and
will give him [j]rest from all his enem-
es round about: for his name shall be
Solomon, and I will give peace and
uietness unto Israel in his days.
10 He [k]shall build an house for my
ame; and [l]he shall be my son, and I
vill be his father; and I will establish
he throne of his kingdom over Israel
or ever.
11 Now, my son, the [m]LORD be with
hee; and prosper thou, and build the
ouse of the LORD thy God, as he
ath said of thee.
12 Only the LORD [n]give thee wisdom
nd understanding, and give thee
harge concerning Israel, that thou
nayest keep the law of the LORD thy
God.
13 Then [o]shalt thou prosper, if thou
akest heed to fulfil the statutes and
udgments which the LORD charged
Moses with concerning Israel: [p]be
trong, and of good courage; dread
ot, nor be dismayed.
14 Now, behold, [2]in my trouble I
ave prepared for the house of the
ORD an hundred thousand talents of
old, and a thousand thousand tal-
nts of silver; and of brass and iron
vithout weight; for it is in abundance:
imber also and stone have I prepared;
nd thou mayest add thereto.
15 Moreover *there are* workmen
vith thee in abundance, hewers and
workers of stone and timber, and all
nanner of cunning men for every
nanner of work.
16 Of the gold, the silver, and the
rass, and the iron, *there is* no numer. Arise *therefore*, and be doing, and
he LORD be with thee.

f 2 Sam. 7.2. ch. 17.1. Acts 7.46.
g Deut. 12.5.
h 1 Ki. 5.3. ch. 28.3.
i ch. 28.5.
j 1 Ki. 4.25.
1 That is, Peaceable and perfect.
k 2 Sam. 7.13. 1 Ki. 5.5. ch. 17.12.
l Ps. 89.26,27. Heb. 1.5.
m Rom. 8. 31.
n Deut. 4.6. 1 Ki. 3.9. Ps. 72.1.
o Josh. 1.7. 1 Ki. 6. 12, 13. ch. 11.9,15. Isa. 3.10.
p ch. 28.20.
2 Or, in my poverty.
3 That is, masons and carpenters.
q Deut. 12.10. 2 Sam. 7.1. ch. 23.25.
r 2 Chr. 20.3.
s 1 Ki. 8.6. 2 Chr. 5.7.

CHAP. 23

a ch. 28.5. ch. 29.22-25.
b Num. 4.3.
1 Or, to oversee.
c Deut. 16.18. ch. 26.29.
d 2 Chr. 29. 25,26. Amos 6.5.
e Ex. 6.16. Num. 26.57. ch. 6.1. 2 Chr. 8.14.
2 divisions.
3 did not multiply sons.
f Ex. 6.18. ch. 6.2.
g Ex. 28.1. Num. 18.1, 7. Heb. 5.4.

17 ¶ David also commanded all the
princes of Israel to help Solomon his
son, *saying*,
18 *Is* not the LORD your God with
you? and [q]hath he *not* given you rest
on every side? for he hath given the
inhabitants of the land into mine
hand; and the land is subdued before
the LORD, and before his people.
19 Now [r]set your heart and your soul
to seek the LORD your God; arise
therefore, and build ye the sanctuary
of the LORD God, [s]to bring the ark of
the covenant of the LORD, and the
holy vessels of God, into the house
that is to be built to the name of the
LORD.

CHAPTER 23

SO when David was old and full of
days, he made [a]Solomon his son
king over Israel.
2 ¶ And he gathered together all the
princes of Israel, with the priests and
the Levites.
3 Now the Levites were numbered
from the age of [b]thirty years and upward: and their number by their polls,
man by man, was thirty and eight
thousand.
4 Of which, twenty and four thous-
and *were* [1]to set forward the work of
the house of the LORD; and six thous-
and *were* officers [c]and judges:
5 Moreover four thousand *were* porters; and four thousand praised the
LORD with the instruments which [d]I
made, *said David*, to praise *therewith*.
6 And [e]David divided them into
[2]courses among the sons of Levi,
namely, Gĕr-shŏn, Kō-hăth, and Mĕ-
râr-ī.
7 ¶ Of the Gĕr-shŏn-ītes *were*, Lā-ă-
dăn, and Shĭm-ĕ-ī.
8 The sons of Lā-ă-dăn; the chief *was*
Jĕ-hī-ĕl, and Zē-thăm, and Jō-ĕl,
three.
9 The sons of Shĭm-ĕ-ī; Shĕ-lō-mĭth,
and Hā-zī-ĕl, and Hâr-ăn, three.
These *were* the chief of the fathers of
Lā-ă-dăn.
10 And the sons of Shĭm-ĕ-ī *were*,
Jā-hăth, Zī-nă, and Jē-ŭsh, and Bĕ-
rī-ăh. These four *were* the sons of
Shĭm-ĕ-ī.
11 And Jā-hăth was the chief, and
Zī-zăh the second: but Jē-ŭsh and Bĕ-
rī-ăh [3]had not many sons; therefore
they were in one reckoning, according to *their* father's house.
12 ¶ The [f]sons of Kō-hăth; Amram,
Ĭz-hār, Hē-brŏn, and Ŭz-zī-ĕl, four.
13 The sons of Amram; Aaron and
Moses: and [g]Aaron was separated,

that he should sanctify the most holy
things, he and his sons for ever, [h]to
burn incense before the LORD, [i]to
minister unto him, and [j]to bless in his
name for ever.
14 Now *concerning* Moses the man
of God, his sons were named of the
tribe of Levi.
15 The [k]sons of Moses *were*, Gĕr-
shŏm, and Ĕl-ĭ-ē-zĕr.
16 Of the sons of Gĕr-shŏm, Shĕ-bū-
ĕl *was* the chief.
17 And the sons of Ĕl-ĭ-ē-zĕr *were*,
Rē-hă-bī-āh [4]the chief. And Ĕl-ĭ-ē-
zĕr had none other sons; but the sons
of Rē-hă-bī-āh [5]were very many.
18 Of the sons of Ĭz-hăr; Shĕ-lō-
mĭth the chief.
19 Of the sons of Hē-brŏn; Jĕ-rī-āh
the first, Ăm-ă-rī-āh the second, Jă-
hā-zī-ĕl the third, and Jĕ-kăm-ē-ăm
the fourth.
20 Of the sons of Ŭz-zī-ĕl; Mī-chăh
the first, and Jĕ-sī-āh the second.
21 ¶ The sons of Mĕ-rār-ī; Măh-lī,
and Mū-shī. The sons of Măh-lī; Ĕl-
ē-ā-zăr, and Kish.
22 And Ĕl-ē-ā-zăr died, and had no
sons, but daughters: and their [6]breth-
ren the sons of Kish [l]took them.
23 The [m]sons of Mū-shī; Măh-lī, and
Ē-dĕr, and Jĕr-ē-mŏth, three.
24 ¶ These *were* the sons of [n]Levi
after the house of their fathers; *even*
the chief of the fathers, as they were
counted by number of names by their
polls, that did the work for the service
of the house of the LORD, from the age
of [o]twenty years and upward.
25 For David said, The LORD God of
Israel hath given rest unto his people,
[7]that they may dwell in Jerusalem for
ever:
26 And also unto the Levites; they
shall no *more* [p]carry the tabernacle,
nor any vessels of it for the service
thereof.
27 For by the last words of David
the Levites *were* [8]numbered from
twenty years old and above:
28 Because [9]their office *was* to wait
on the sons of Aaron for the service of
the house of the LORD, in the courts,
and in the chambers, and in the purifying of all holy things, and the work
of the service of the house of God;
29 Both for [q]the shewbread, and for
[r]the fine flour for meat offering, and
for [s]the unleavened cakes, and for *that
which is baked in* the [10]pan, and for
that which is fried, and for all manner
of [t]measure and size;
30 And [u]to stand every morning to

h Ex. 30.7. Lev. 10.1,2. Num. 16.40. 1 Sam. 2.28.
i Deut. 21.5.
j Num. 6.23.
k Ex. 2.22.
4 Or, the first.
5 were highly multiplied.
6 Or, kinsmen. Gen. 13.8.
l Num. 36.6.
m ch. 24.30.
n Num. 10. 17.
o Num. 1.3.
7 Or, and he dwelleth in Jerusalem, etc.
p Num. 4.5.
8 number.
9 their station was at the hand of the sons of Aaron.
q Ex. 25.30. Lev. 24.5-9.
r Lev. 6.20.
s Lev. 2.4.
10 Or, flat plate.
t Lev. 19.35.
u ch. 6.31-33. ch. 9.33. 2 Chr. 31.2. Ps. 137.2-4. Rev. 5.8-14.
v Num. 10. 10. Ps. 81.3. Isa. 1.13,14.
w Lev. 23.4.
x Num. 1.53.
y Num. 3.6.

CHAP. 24

a Ex. 6.23. Lev. 10.1. Num. 3.2.
b Num. 3.4.
c Josh. 18.10. Pro. 16.33. Acts 1.26.
d Neh. 8.4.
1 house of the father.
e Neh. 7.39.
f Ezra 10.21.
g Neh. 12.4, 17. Luke 1.5.

thank and praise the LORD, and lik
wise at even;
31 And to offer all burnt sacrific
unto the LORD [v]in the sabbaths, in t
new moons, and on the [w]set feasts,
number, according to the order co
manded unto them, continually b
fore the LORD:
32 And that they should [x]keep t
charge of the tabernacle of the co
gregation, and the charge of the ho
place, and [y]the charge of the sons
Aaron their brethren, in the servi
of the house of the LORD.

CHAPTER 24

NOW *these are* the divisions of t
sons of Aaron. The sons
Aaron; [a]Nadab, and Ă-bī-hū, Ĕl-ē-
zăr, and Ĭth-ă-măr.
2 But [b]Nadab and Ă-bī-hū died b
fore their father, and had no childre
therefore Ĕl-ē-ā-zăr and Ĭth-ă-m
executed the priest's office.
3 And David distributed them, bo
Zā-dŏk of the sons of Ĕl-ē-ā-zăr, a
Ă-hĭm-ĕ-lĕch of the sons of Ĭth-ă-mă
according to their offices in their se
vice.
4 And there were more chief m
found of the sons of Ĕl-ē-ā-zăr than
the sons of Ĭth-ă-măr; and *thus* we
they divided. Among the sons of Ĕ
ē-ā-zăr *there were* sixteen chief m
of the house of *their* fathers, and eig
among the sons of Ĭth-ă-măr accor
ing to the house of their fathers.
5 Thus were they divided [c]by lot, o
sort with another; for the governo
of the sanctuary, and governors
the house of God, were of the sons
Ĕl-ē-ā-zăr, and of the sons of Ĭth-
măr.
6 And Shĕm-ā-ī-āh the son of Nĕt
ă-neel [d]the scribe, *one* of the Levit
wrote them before the king, and t
princes, and Zā-dŏk the priest, a
Ă-hĭm-ĕ-lĕch the son of Ă-bī-ă-thă
and *before* the chief of the fathers
the priests and Levites: one [1]princip
household being taken for Ĕl-ē-ā-ză
and *one* taken for Ĭth-ă-măr.
7 Now the first lot came forth
Jĕ-hoi-ă-rĭb, the second to [e]Jĕ-dă
ăh,
8 The third to [f]Hăr-ĭm, the fourth
Sē-ŏr-ĭm,
9 The fifth to Măl-chī-jăh, the six
to Mī-jă-mĭn,
10 The seventh to Hăk-kŏz, t
eighth [g]to Ă-bī-jăh,
11 The ninth to Jĕsh-ū-ă, the ten
to Shĕc-ă-nī-āh,

12 The eleventh to Ē-lī-ăsh-ĭb, the
velfth to Jakim,
13 The thirteenth to Hŭp-păh, the
ourteenth to Jĕ-shĕb-ĕ-ăb,
14 The fifteenth to Bĭl-găh, the six-
eenth to Ĭm-mĕr,
15 The seventeenth to Hē-zīr, the
ghteenth to Ăph-sēs,
16 The nineteenth to Pĕth-ă-hī-ăh,
e twentieth to Jĕ-hĕz-ĕk-ĕl,
17 The one and twentieth to Jā-chĭn,
e two and twentieth to Găm-ŭl,
18 The three and twentieth to Dĕl-
-ăh, the four and twentieth to Mā-
-zī-ăh.
19 These *were* the [h]orderings of
em in their service to come into the
ouse of the LORD, according to [i]their
anner, under Aaron their father, as
e LORD God of Israel had com-
anded him.
20 ¶ And the rest of the sons of Levi
ere these: Of the sons of Amram;
hû-bā-ĕl: of the sons of Shû-bā-ĕl;
h-dē-ăh.
21 Concerning [k]Rē-hă-bī-ăh: of the
ons of Rē-hă-bī-ăh, the first *was* Ĭs-
ī-ăh.
22 Of the Ĭz-hār-ītes; [l]Shĕ-lō-mŏth:
f the sons of Shĕ-lō-mŏth; Jā-
ăth.
23 And the sons *of* [m]*Hē-brŏn;* Jĕ-rī-
the first, Ăm-ă-rī-ăh the second, Jā-
ā-zī-ĕl the third, Jĕ-kăm-ĕ-ăm the
ourth.
24 *Of* the sons of Ŭz-zī-ĕl; Mī-
ăh: of the sons of Mī-chăh; Shā-
ĭr.
25 The brother of Mī-chăh *was* Ĭs-
ī-ăh: of the sons of Ĭs-shī-ăh; Zĕch-
rī-ăh.
26 The [n]sons of Mĕ-rār-ī *were* Măh-
and Mū-shī: the sons of Jā-ă-zī-ăh;
ē-nō.
27 ¶ The sons of Mĕ-rār-ī by Jā-ă-
-ăh; Bē-nō, and Shō-hăm, and Zăc-
r, and Ĭb-rī.
28 Of Măh-lī *came* Ĕl-ē-ā-zăr, [o]who
d no sons.
29 Concerning Kish: the son of Kish
as Jĕ-răh-mē-ĕl.
30 The [p]sons also of Mū-shī; Măh-lī,
d Ē-dĕr, and Jĕr-ī-mŏth. These
ere the sons of the Levites after the
ouse of their fathers.
31 These likewise cast lots over
ainst their brethren the sons of
aron in the presence of David the
ng, and Zā-dŏk, and Ă-hĭm-ĕ-lĕch,
d the chief of the fathers of the
iests and Levites, even the principal
thers over against their younger
ethren.

h Num. 4.49. ch. 9.25.
i ch. 9.25. Luke 1.8,23.
j ch. 23.16. Shebuel.
k ch. 23.17.
l ch. 23.18. Shelomith.
m ch. 15.9.
n Ex. 6.19. ch. 23.21.
o ch. 23.22.
p ch. 23.23.

CHAP. 25

a ch. 12.28. ch. 23.2.
b ch. 6.33. ch. 15.17.
c Ex. 15.20. Num. 11.25. 1 Sam. 10.5. ch. 15.16. ch. 16.4. Ps. 150.3-5. 1 Cor. 14.1. Rev. 15.2-4.
1 Otherwise called Jesharelah, ver. 14.
2 by the hands of the king: ver. 6.
d ver. 11, Izri.
3 With Shimei mentioned, ver. 17.
e ver. 18, Azareel.
f ver. 20, Shubael.
g 1 Sam. 9.9. 2 Sam. 24. 11. ch. 21.9. ch. 26.28. Amos 7.12.
4 Or, matters.
h Gen. 33.5. ch. 28.5. Ps. 127.3. Isa. 8.18.
5 by the hands of the king.
i Ps. 150.1. Eph. 5.19. Col. 3.16.
j 2 Chr. 23. 13.

CHAPTER 25

MOREOVER David and the captains [a]of the host separated to the
service of the sons [b]of Ā-săph, and of
Hē-măn, and of Jĕ-dū-thŭn, who
should [c]prophesy with harps, with
psalteries, and with cymbals: and the
number of the workmen according to
their service was:
2 Of the sons of Ā-săph; Zăc-cŭr, and
Joseph, and Nĕth-ă-nī-ăh, and [1]Ăs-ă-
rē-lăh, the sons of Ā-săph under the
hands of Ā-săph, which prophesied
[2]according to the order of the king.
3 Of Jĕ-dū-thŭn: the sons of Jĕ-dū-
thŭn; Gĕd-ă-lī-ăh, and [d]Zē-rī, and Jĕ-
shā-ăh, Hăsh-ă-bī-ăh, and Măt-tĭ-
thī-ăh, [3]six, under the hands of their
father Jĕ-dū-thŭn, who prophesied
with a harp, to give thanks and to
praise the LORD.
4 Of Hē-măn: the sons of Hē-măn;
Bŭk-kī-ăh, Măt-tă-nī-ăh, [e]Ŭz-zī-ĕl,
[f]Shĕ-bū-ĕl, and Jĕr-ī-mŏth, Hăn-ă-nī-
ăh, Hă-nā-nī, Ē-lī-ā-thăh, Gĭd-dăl-tī,
and Rō-măm-tī-ē-zĕr, Jŏsh-bĕ-kăsh-
ăh, Măl-lō-thī, Hō-thīr, *and* Mă-hā-
zī-ōth:
5 All these *were* the sons of Hē-măn
the king's [g]seer in the [4]words of God,
to lift up the horn. And [h]God gave to
Hē-măn fourteen sons and three
daughters.
6 All these *were* under the hands of
their father for song *in* the house of
the LORD, with cymbals, psalteries,
harps, for the service of the house
of God, [5]according to the king's
order to Ā-săph, Jĕ-dū-thŭn, and
Hē-măn.
7 So the number of them, with their
brethren that were instructed in the
[i]songs of the LORD, *even* all that were
cunning, was two hundred fourscore
and eight.
8 ¶ And they cast lots, ward against
ward, as well the small as the great,
[j]the teacher as the scholar.
9 Now the first lot came forth for
Ā-săph to Joseph: the second to Gĕd-
ă-lī-ăh, who with his brethren and
sons *were* twelve:
10 The third to Zăc-cŭr, *he,* his sons,
and his brethren, *were* twelve:
11 The fourth to Ĭz-rī, *he,* his sons,
and his brethren, *were* twelve:
12 The fifth to Nĕth-ă-nī-ăh, *he,* his
sons, and his brethren, *were* twelve:
13 The sixth to Bŭk-kī-ăh, *he,* his
sons, and his brethren, *were* twelve:
14 The seventh to Jĕsh-ă-rē-lăh, *he,*
his sons, and his brethren, *were*
twelve:

15 The eighth to Jĕ-shâi-ăh, *he*, his
sons, and his brethren, *were* twelve:
16 The ninth to Măt-tă-nī-ăh, *he*, his
sons, and his brethren, *were* twelve:
17 The tenth to Shĭm-ĕ-ī, *he*, his sons,
and his brethren, *were* twelve:
18 The eleventh to Ăz-ă-rēel, *he*, his
sons, and his brethren, *were* twelve:
19 The twelfth to Hăsh-ă-bī-ăh, *he*,
his sons, and his brethren, *were* twelve:
20 The thirteenth to Shû-bā-ĕl, *he*,
his sons, and his brethren, *were* twelve:
21 The fourteenth to Măt-tĭ-thī-ăh,
he, his sons, and his brethren, *were*
twelve:
22 The fifteenth to Jĕr-ĕ-mōth, *he*,
his sons, and his brethren, *were*
twelve:
23 The sixteenth to Hăn-ă-nī-ăh, *he*,
his sons, and his brethren, *were* twelve:
24 The seventeenth to Jŏsh-bĕ-kăsh-
ăh, *he*, his sons, and his brethren,
were twelve:
25 The eighteenth to Hă-nā-nī, *he*,
his sons, and his brethren, *were* twelve:
26 The nineteenth to Măl-lō-thī, *he*,
his sons, and his brethren, *were* twelve:
27 The twentieth to Ē-lī-ă-thăh, *he*,
his sons, and his brethren, *were* twelve:
28 The one and twentieth to Hō-thĭr,
he, his sons, and his brethren, *were*
twelve:
29 The two and twentieth to Gĭd-
dăl-tī, *he*, his sons, and his brethren,
were twelve:
30 The three and twentieth to Mă-
hā-zĭ-ōth, *he*, his sons, and his brethren, *were* twelve:
31 The [k]four and twentieth to Rō-
măm-tĭ-ē-zĕr, *he*, his sons, and his
brethren, *were* twelve.

CHAPTER 26

CONCERNING the divisions of
the porters: Of the [a]Kôr-hītes *was*
[b]Mĕ-shĕl-ĕ-mī-ăh the son of Kôr-ē, of
the sons of [c]Ā-săph.
2 And the sons of Mĕ-shĕl-ĕ-mī-ăh
were, Zĕch-ă-rī-ăh the firstborn, Jĕd-
ĭ-ă-ĕl the second, Zĕb-ă-dī-ăh the
third, Jăth-nī-ĕl the fourth,
3 Ē-lăm the fifth, Jē-hō-hā-năn the
sixth, Ĕl-ĭ-ō-ē-nâi the seventh.
4 Moreover the sons of Ō-bĕd–ē-dŏm
were, Shĕm-âi-ăh the firstborn, Jĕ-hō-
ză-băd the second, Jō-ăh the third,
and Sā-căr the fourth, and Nĕth-ă-
nēel the fifth,
5 Ăm-mĭ-ĕl the sixth, Ĭs-să-chăr the
seventh, Pē-ŭl-thâi the eighth: for
God blessed [1]him.
6 Also unto Shĕm-âi-ăh his son were
sons born, that ruled throughout the

[k] Rev. 4.4. Rev. 5.8. Rev. 11.16.

CHAP. 26

[a] Num. 16.1, 2. Num. 26.9-11. ch. 9.17. ch. 15.18. 2 Chr. 23.19. Jude 11.
[b] ver. 14, Shelemiah.
[c] ch. 6.23,37. ch. 9.19. Ebiasaph.
1 That is, Obed-edom, ch. 13.14. Gen. 33.5. Ps. 127.3.
[d] ch. 16.38.
[e] Gen. 4.7. Gen. 49.3. Deut. 21.17. ch. 5.1.
2 Or, as well for the small as for the great. Josh. 18.10. ch. 24.5. ch. 25.8. Pro. 18.18. Jonah 1.7. Acts 1.26. Acts 10.34. Gal. 3.28. Col. 3.11.
3 Meshelemiah, ver.1.
4 gatherings.
[f] 1 Ki. 10.5. ch. 24.31. ch. 25.8. 2 Chr. 9.4. Neh. 12.24.
5 Or, out part, 2 Ki. 23.11.
[g] Deut. 12.6. 1 Ki. 7.51. 1 Ki. 14.26. ch. 9.26-29. ch. 28.12. ch. 29.2-8. Mal. 3.10.
6 holy things. 2 Chr. 31.11, 12.
[h] ch. 6.17, Libni.
[i] ch. 29.8, Jehiel.
[j] Ex. 6.18. Num. 3.19. ch. 23.12.

house of their father: for they w
mighty men of valour.
7 The sons of Shĕm-âi-ăh; Ŏth-
and Rĕph-ā-ĕl, and Ō-bĕd, Ĕl-ză-b
whose brethren *were* strong men,
lī-hū, and Sĕm-ă-chī-ăh.
8 All these of the sons of Ō-bĕd
dŏm: they and their sons and th
brethren, able men for strength
the service, *were* threescore and t
of Ō-bĕd–ē-dŏm.
9 And Mĕ-shĕl-ĕ-mī-ăh had sons a
brethren, strong men, eighteen.
10 Also [d]Hō-săh, of the children
Mĕ-rār-ī, had sons; Simri the chi
(for *though* he was not [e]the firstbo
yet his father made him the chief;)
11 Hĭl-kī-ăh the second, Tĕb-ă-lī-
the third, Zĕch-ă-rī-ăh the fourth:
the sons and brethren of Hō-săh w
thirteen.
12 Among these *were* the divisions
the porters, *even* among the chief m
having wards one against another,
minister in the house of the LORD
13 ¶ And they cast lots, [2]as well t
small as the great, according to t
house of their fathers, for every ga
14 And the lot eastward fell to [3]Sh
ē-mī-ăh. Then for Zĕch-ă-rī-ăh
son, a wise counseller, they cast lo
and his lot came out northward.
15 To Ō-bĕd–ē-dŏm southward; a
to his sons the house of [4]Ă-s
pĭm.
16 To Shŭp-pĭm and Hō-săh *the*
came forth westward, with the g
Shăl-lĕ-chĕth, by the causeway of t
going [f]up, ward against ward.
17 Eastward *were* six Levites, nor
ward four a day, southward four
day, and toward Ă-sŭp-pĭm two *a*
two.
18 At [5]Pär-bär westward, four at t
causeway, *and* two at Pär-bär.
19 These *are* the divisions of t
porters among the sons of Kôr-ē, a
among the sons of Mĕ-rār-ī.
20 ¶ And of the Levites, Ă-hī-jăh w
over [g]the treasures of the house
God, and over the treasures of t
[6]dedicated things.
21 *As concerning* the sons of [h]Lā
dăn; the sons of the Gĕr-shŏn-īte L
ă-dăn, chief fathers, *even* of Lā-ă-d
the Gĕr-shŏn-īte, [i]*were* Jĕ-hī-ē-lī.
22 The sons of Jĕ-hī-ē-lī; Zē-thă
and Jō-ĕl his brother, *which were* o
the treasures of the house of t
LORD.
23 Of the [j]Amramites, *and* the
hār-ītes, the Hē-brŏn-ītes, *and* t
Ŭz-zī-ē-lītes:

24 And [k]Shĕ-bū́-ĕl the son of Gĕr-
hŏm, the son of Moses, *was* ruler of
he treasures.
25 And his brethren by Ĕl-ĭ-ē-́zĕr;
ĕ-hă-bī-́ăh his son, and Jĕ-shâi-́ăh
is son, and Joram his son, and Zĭch-
i his son, and [l]Shĕ-lō-́mĭth his son.
26 Which Shĕ-lō-́mĭth and his breth-
en *were* over all the treasures of the
edicated things, which David the
ing, and the chief fathers, the cap-
ains over thousands and hundreds,
nd the captains of the host, had
edicated.
27 [7]Out of the spoils won in battles
id they dedicate [m]to maintain the
ouse of the LORD.
28 And all that Samuel [n]the seer, and
aul the son of Kish, and Abner the
on of Ner, and Jō-́ăb the son of Zĕr-
-ĭ-́ăh, had dedicated; *and* whosoever
ad dedicated *any thing*, *it was* under
e hand of Shĕ-lō-́mĭth, and of his
rethren.
29 ¶ Of the Ĭz-hār-́ītes, Chĕn-ă-nī-́ăh
nd his sons *were* for the outward
usiness over Israel, for [o]officers and
dges.
30 *And* of the Hē-́brŏn-ītes, Hăsh-ă-
ī-́ăh and his brethren, men of valour,
thousand and seven hundred, *were*
fficers among them of Israel on this
de Jordan westward in all the busi-
ess of the LORD, and in the service of
e king.
31 Among the Hē-́brŏn-ītes *was* Jē-
-jăh [p]the chief, *even* among the Hē-
rŏn-ītes, according to the genera-
ons of his fathers. In the [q]fortieth
ar of the reign of David they were
ught for, and there were found
mong them mighty men of valour at
ă-́zĕr of Gilead.
32 And his brethren, men of valour,
ere two thousand and seven hundred
ief fathers, whom king David made
lers over the Reubenites, the Gad-
s, and the half tribe of Mă-năs-́sēh,
r every matter pertaining to God,
d [9]affairs of the king.

CHAPTER 27

NOW the children of Israel after
their number, *to wit*, the chief
thers and captains of thousands and
ndreds, and their officers that serv-
the king in any matter of the cours-
, which came in and went out month
month throughout all the months
the year, of every course *were* twen-
and four thousand.
Over the first course for the first
onth *was* [a]Jă-shŏb-́ē-ăm the son of
Zăb-́dĭ-ĕl: and in his course *were*
twenty and four thousand.
3 Of the children of [b]Pē-́rĕz *was* the
chief of all the captains of the host for
the first month.
4 And over the course of the second
month *was* [c]Dō-́dâi an Ā-hō-́hīte, and
of his course *was* Mĭk-́lōth also the
ruler: in his course likewise *were*
twenty and four thousand.
5 The third captain of the host for
the third month *was* Bĕ-nâi-́ăh the son
of Jĕ-hōi-́ă-dă, a [1]chief priest: and in
his course *were* twenty and four
thousand.
6 This *is that* Bĕ-nâi-́ăh, *who was*
mighty [d]*among* the thirty, and above
the thirty: and in his course *was* Ăm-
mī-́ză-băd his son.
7 The fourth *captain* for the fourth
month *was* [e]Ăs-́ă-hĕl the brother of
Jō-́ăb, and Zĕb-ă-dī-́ăh his son after
him: and in his course *were* twenty
and four thousand.
8 The fifth captain for the fifth month
was Shăm-́hŭth the Ĭz-́ră-hīte: and in
his course *were* twenty and four
thousand.
9 The sixth *captain* for the sixth
month *was* [f]Ī-́ră the son of Ĭk-́kĕsh the
Tĕ-kō-́īte: and in his course *were*
twenty and four thousand.
10 The seventh *captain* for the seventh month *was* [g]Hē-́lĕz the Pē-lō-
nīte, of the children of Ē-́phră-ĭm: and
in his course *were* twenty and four
thousand.
11 The eighth *captain* for the eighth
month *was* [h]Sĭb-́bĕ-câi the Hū-́shă-
thīte, of the Zăr-́hītes: and in his
course *were* twenty and four thousand.
12 The ninth *captain* for the ninth
month *was* [i]Ā-bī-ē-́zĕr the Ăn-ĕ-tō-
thīte, of the Benjamites: and in his
course *were* twenty and four thousand.
13 The tenth *captain* for the tenth
month *was* [j]Mā-́hă-râi the Nĕ-tŏph-
ă-thīte, of the Zăr-́hītes: and in his
course *were* twenty and four thousand.
14 The eleventh *captain* for the eleventh month *was* [k]Bĕ-nâi-́ăh the Pĭ-ră-
thŏn-īte, of the children of Ē-́phră-ĭm:
and in his course *were* twenty and four
thousand.
15 The twelfth *captain* for the twelfth
month *was* [l]Hĕl-́dâi the Nĕ-tŏph-́ă-
thīte, [m]of Ŏth-́nī-ĕl: and in his course
were twenty and four thousand.
16 ¶ Furthermore over the tribes of
Israel: the ruler of the Reubenites *was*
Ĕl-ĭ-ē-́zĕr the son of Zĭch-́rī: of the
Simeonites, Shĕph-ă-tī-́ăh the son of
Mā-́ă-chăh:

k ch. 23.16.
l ch. 23.18.
7 Out of the battles and spoils.
m 2 Ki. 12.14. Neh. 10.32.
n 1 Sam. 9.9.
o Deut. 1.16. Deut. 16.18. ch. 23.4. 2 Chr. 19.8-11.
8 over the charge.
p ch. 23.19.
q 2 Sam. 5.4. 1 Ki. 2.11. ch. 29.27.
r Num. 32.1, 3,35. Josh. 21.39. Isa. 16.9.
9 thing, 2 Chr. 19.11.

CHAP. 27

a 2 Sam. 23.8. ch. 11.11.
b Gen. 38.29, Pharez.
c 2 Sam. 23.9. Dodo.
1 Or, principal officer.
d 2 Sam. 23. 20,22,23.
e 2 Sam. 2.18, 23. ch. 11.26.
f 2 Sam. 23. 26.
g ch. 11.27.
h 2 Sam. 21. 18. ch. 11.29.
i ch. 11.28.
j 2 Sam. 23. 28. ch. 11.30.
k 2 Sam. 23. 30. ch. 11.31.
l ch. 11.30, Heled.
m Judg. 3.9.

17 Of the Levites, [n]Hăsh-ă-bī-ăh the son of Kĕ-mū-ĕl: of the Aaronites, Zā-dŏk:
18 Of Judah, [o]Ē-lĭ-hū, *one* of the brethren of David: of Ĭs-să-chăr, Omri the son of Michael:
19 Of Zĕ-bū-lŭn, Ĭsh-mâi-ăh the son of Ō-bă-dĭ-ăh: of Năph-tă-lī, Jĕr-ĭ-mōth the son of Ăz-rĭ-ĕl:
20 Of the children of Ē-phră-ĭm, Hō-shē-ă the son of Ăz-ă-zī-ăh: of the half tribe of Mă-năs-sĕh, Jō-ĕl the son of Pĕ-dâi-ăh:
21 Of the half *tribe* of Mă-năs-sĕh in Gilead, Ĭd-dō the son of Zĕch-ă-rī-ăh: of Benjamin, Jā-ăs-ĭ-ĕl the son of Abner:
22 Of Dan, Ăz-ă-rēel the son of Jĕ-rō-hăm. These *were* the princes of the tribes of Israel.
23 ¶ But David took not the number of them from twenty years old and under: because [p]the LORD had said he would increase Israel like to the stars of the heavens.
24 Jō-ăb the son of Zĕr-ū-ī-ăh began to number, but he finished not, because [q]there fell wrath for it against Israel; neither [2]was the number put in the account of the chronicles of king David.
25 ¶ And over the king's treasures *was* Ăz-mā-vĕth the son of Ăd-ĭ-ĕl: and over the storehouses in the fields, in the cities, and in the villages, and in the castles, *was* Jĕ-hŏn-ă-thăn the son of Ŭz-zī-ăh:
26 And over them that did the work of the field for tillage of the ground *was* Ĕz-rī the son of Chē-lŭb:
27 And over [r]the vineyards *was* Shĭm-ĕ-ī the Rā-mĕth-īte: [3]over the increase of the vineyards for the wine cellars *was* Zăb-dī the Shĭph-mīte:
28 And over the olive trees and the sycomore trees that *were* in the low plains *was* Bā-ăl-hā-năn the Gĕ-dē-rīte: and over the cellars of oil *was* Jō-ăsh:
29 And over the herds that fed in Shâr-on *was* Shĭt-rā-ī the Shâr-on-īte: and over the herds *that were* in the valleys *was* Shā-phăt the son of Ăd-lā-ī:
30 Over the camels also *was* Ō-bīl the Ĭsh-mā-ĕl-īte: and over the asses *was* Jĕh-dē-ī-ăh the Mĕ-rō-nō-thīte:
31 And over the flocks *was* Jā-zĭz the Hă-gē-rīte. All these *were* the rulers of the substance which *was* king David's.
32 Also Jonathan David's [4]uncle was a counseller, a wise man, and a [5]scribe:

n ch. 26.30.
o 1 Sam. 16.6, Eliab.
p Gen. 15.5. Ex. 32.13. Deut. 1.10. Deut. 10.22. Heb. 11.12.
q 2 Sam. 24. 15. ch. 21.7.
2 ascended.
r Song 8.11.
3 over that which was of the vineyards.
4 Or, nephew.
5 Or, secretary.
6 Or, Hachmonite.

CHAP. 28
a Josh. 23.2. ch. 23.2. ch. 27.16.
b Ex. 18.25. Deut. 1.15. ch. 27.1.
c ch. 27.25.
1 Or, cattle.
2 Or, and his sons.
3 Or, eunuchs.
d ch. 11.10.
e Deut. 17.20. ch. 11.1-3. Ps. 22.22. Heb. 2.11.
f 2 Sam. 7.2. 1 Ki. 8.17. ch. 17.2. Ps. 132.3.
g Ps. 99.5.
h 2 Sam. 7.5. 1 Ki. 5.3. ch. 17.4.
4 bloods.
i 1 Sam. 16.7.
j Gen. 49.8.
k 1 Sam. 16. 1.
l 1 Sam. 16. 12.
m ch. 3.1. ch. 14.4-7.
n ch. 22.9.
o 2 Chr. 1.9.
p 1 Ki. 9.4. 1 Ki. 11.11. ch. 22.13.
5 strong.
q Deut. 4.1.

and Jĕ-hī-ĕl the [6]son of Hăch-mō-n *was* with the king's sons:
33 And Ă-hĭth-ŏ-phĕl *was* the king' counseller: and Hū-shâi the Ăr-chīt *was* the king's companion:
34 And after Ă-hĭth-ŏ-phĕl *was* Jĕ hōi-ă-dă the son of Bĕ-nâi-ăh, an Ă-bī-ă-thăr: and the general of th king's army *was* Jō-ăb.

CHAPTER 28

AND David assembled all the prin ces of Israel, [a]the princes of th tribes, [b]and the captains of the com panies that ministered to the king b course, and the captains over th thousands, and captains over the hun dreds, and [c]the stewards over all th substance and [1]possession of the king [2]and of his sons, with the [3]officers, an with [d]the mighty men, and with a the valiant men, unto Jerusalem.
2 Then David the king stood up upo his feet, and said, Hear me, my [e]bret ren, and my people: *As for me*, [f]I *ha* in mine heart to build an house of re for the ark of the covenant of th LORD, and for [g]the footstool of ou God, and had made ready for th building:
3 But God said unto me, [h]Thou sha not build an house for my name, b cause thou *hast been* a man of wa and hast shed [4]blood.
4 Howbeit the LORD God of Isra chose [i]me before all the house of m father to be king over Israel for eve for he hath chosen [j]Judah *to be* t ruler; and of the house of Judah, t [k]house of my father; and [l]among t sons of my father he liked me to ma *me* king over all Israel:
5 And [m]of all my sons, (for the LO hath given me many sons,) he [n]ha chosen Solomon my son to sit upo the throne of the kingdom of the LO over Israel.
6 And he said unto me, [o]Solomon t son, he shall build my house and m courts: for I have chosen him *to* my son, and I will be his father.
7 Moreover I will establish his kin dom for ever, [p]if he be [5]constant to my commandments and my jud ments, as at this day.
8 Now therefore in the sight of Israel the congregation of the LOR and in the audience of our God, [q]ke and seek for all the commandme of the LORD your God: that ye m possess this good land, and leave for an inheritance for your childr after you for ever.

9 ¶ And thou, Solomon my son, know
thou the God of thy father, and serve
him with a [s]perfect heart and with a
willing mind: for [t]the LORD searcheth
all hearts, and understandeth all the
imaginations of the thoughts: [u]if thou
seek him, he will be found of thee;
but if thou forsake him, he will cast
thee off for ever.
10 Take [v]heed now; for the LORD
hath chosen thee to build an house
for the sanctuary: be strong, and do
it.
11 ¶ Then David gave to Solomon
his son the [w]pattern of the [x]porch, and
of the houses thereof, and of the treasuries thereof, and of the upper chambers thereof, and of the inner parlours
thereof, and of the place of the mercy
seat,
12 And the pattern [6]of all that he had
by the spirit, of the courts of the house
of the LORD, and of all the chambers
round about, of the [y]treasuries of the
house of God, and of the treasuries of
the dedicated things:
13 Also for the courses of the priests
and the Levites, and for all the work
of the service of the house of the LORD,
and for all the vessels of service in the
house of the LORD.
14 *He gave* of gold by weight for
things of gold, for all instruments of
all manner of service; *silver also* for
all instruments of silver by weight, for
all instruments of every kind of service:
15 Even the weight for the candlesticks of gold, and for their lamps of
gold, by weight for every candlestick,
and for the lamps thereof: and for the
candlesticks of silver by weight, *both*
for the candlestick, and *also* for the
lamps thereof, according to the use
of every candlestick.
16 And by weight *he gave* gold for
the tables of [z]shewbread, for every
table; and *likewise* silver for the
tables of silver:
17 Also pure gold for the fleshhooks,
and the bowls, and the cups: and for
the golden basons *he gave gold* by
weight for every bason; and *likewise*
silver by weight for every bason of
silver:
18 And for the altar of [a]incense refined gold by weight; and gold for the
pattern of the chariot of the [b]chĕr´-ū-
bims, that spread out *their wings*, and
covered the ark of the covenant of the
LORD.
19 All *this, said David*, [c]the LORD
made me understand in writing by
his hand upon me, *even* all the works
of this pattern.
20 And David said to Solomon his
son, [d]Be strong and of good courage,
and do *it:* fear not, nor be dismayed:
for the LORD God, *even* my God, *will*
be with thee; [e]he will not fail thee, nor
forsake thee, until thou hast finished
all the work for the service of the
house of the LORD.
21 And, behold, [f]the courses of the
priests and the Levites, *even they shall*
be with thee for all the service of the
house of God: and *there shall be* with
thee for all manner of workmanship
every willing skilful man, [g]for any
manner of service: also the princes
and all the people *will be* wholly at thy
commandment.

CHAPTER 29

FURTHERMORE David the king
said unto all the congregation,
Solomon my son, whom alone God
hath chosen, *is yet* young and [a]tender,
and the work *is* great: for the palace
is not for man, but for the LORD God.
2 Now I have prepared with all my
might for the house of my God the
gold for *things to be made* of gold,
and the silver for *things* of silver, and
the brass for *things* of brass, the iron
for *things* of iron, and wood for *things*
of wood; [b]onyx stones, and *stones* to
be set, glistering stones, and of divers
colours, and all manner of precious
stones, and marble stones in abundance.
3 Moreover, because I have [c]set my
affection to the house of my God, I
have of mine [d]own proper good, of
gold and silver, *which* I have given to
the house of my God, over and above
all that I have prepared for the holy
house,
4 *Even* three thousand talents of
gold, of the gold of [e]Ō´-phĭr, and seven
thousand talents of refined silver, to
overlay the walls of the houses *withal:*
5 The gold for *things* of gold, and the
silver for *things* of silver, and for all
manner of work *to be made* by the
hands of artificers. And who *then* is
willing [1]to consecrate his service this
day unto the LORD?
6 ¶ Then [f]the chief of the fathers and
princes of the tribes of Israel, and the
captains of thousands and of hundreds, with the [g]rulers of the king's
work, offered willingly,
7 And gave for the service of the
house of God of gold five thousand
talents and ten thousand drams, and

r Ps. 9.10. Jer. 9.24. Hosea 4.1.
s 2 Ki. 20.3. Ps. 101.2.
t 1 Sam. 16.7. 1 Ki. 8.39. ch. 29.17. Ps. 7.9. Pro. 17.3. Jer. 11.20. Rev. 2.23.
u 2 Chr. 15.2. Pro. 2.1-6. Matt. 7.7.
v ch. 22.16. Pro. 4.23.
w Ex. 25.40.
x 1 Ki. 6.2.
6 of all that was with him.
y ch. 26.20.
z Ex. 25.23. 1 Ki. 7.48. 2 Chr. 4.8.
a Ex. 30.1.
b Ex. 25.18. 1 Sam. 4.4. 1 Ki. 6.23. Ps. 18.10. Ps. 68.17. Ps. 80.1.
c Ex. 25.40.
d Deut. 31.7. Josh. 1.6,7. ch. 22.13.
e Josh. 1.5. Heb. 13.5.
f ch. 24.1. ch. 25.1.
g Ex. 35.25.

CHAP. 29

a 1 Ki. 3.7. ch. 22.5. Pro. 4.3.
b Ex. 28.9. Isa. 54.11, 12. Rev. 21.18.
c Ps. 26.8. Ps. 27.4. Ps. 84.1.
d Pro. 3.9.
e 1 Ki. 9.28. 2 Chr. 8.18.
1 to fill his hand.
f ch. 27.1.
g ch. 27.25.

of silver ten thousand talents, and of
brass eighteen thousand talents, and
one hundred thousand talents of iron.
8 And they with whom *precious*
stones were found gave *them* to the
treasure of the house of the LORD, by
the hand of [h]Jĕ-hi-ĕl the Gĕr-shŏn-īte.
9 Then the people rejoiced, for that
they [i]offered willingly, because with
perfect heart they offered willingly to
the LORD: and David the king also rejoiced with great joy.
10 ¶ Wherefore David blessed the
LORD before all the congregation: and
David said, [j]Blessed *be* thou, LORD
God of Israel our father, for ever
and ever.
11 Thine, [k]O LORD, *is* the greatness,
and the power, and the glory, and the
victory, and the majesty: for all *that*
is in the heaven and in the earth *is*
thine; thine *is* the kingdom, O LORD,
and thou art exalted as head above all.
12 Both [l]riches and honour *come* of
thee, and thou reignest over all; and
in thine hand *is* power and might; and
in thine hand *it is* to make great, and
to give strength unto all.
13 Now therefore, our God, we
thank thee, and praise thy glorious
name.
14 But who *am* I, and what *is* my
people, that we should [2]be able to offer
so willingly after this sort? for all
things *come* of thee, and [3]of thine own
have we given thee.
15 For [m]we *are* strangers before thee,
and sojourners, as *were* all our fathers:
our [n]days on the earth *are* as a shadow,
and *there is* none [4]abiding.
16 O LORD our God, all this store
that we have prepared to build thee
an house for thine holy name *cometh*
of thine hand, and *is* all thine own.
17 I know also, my God, that thou
[o]triest the heart, and [p]hast pleasure in
uprightness. As for me, in the uprightness of mine heart I have willingly offered all these things: and now
have I seen with joy thy people, which
are [5]present here, to offer willingly unto thee.
18 O LORD God of Abraham, Isaac,
and of Israel, our fathers, keep this
for ever in the imagination of the
thoughts of the heart of thy people,
and [6]prepare their heart unto thee:

h ch. 26.21.
i 1 Ki. 8.61. 2 Cor. 9.7.
j 1 Ki. 8.15, 16. 2 Chr. 6.4. Ps. 72.18.
k Dan. 4.34, 35. Matt. 6.13. 1 Tim. 1.17. Rev. 5.13.
l Deut. 8.18. 1 Sam. 2.7,8. Ps. 75.6. Pro. 10.22. Rom. 11.36.
2 retain, or, obtain strength.
3 of thine hand.
m Gen. 47.9. Ps. 39.12. Heb. 11.13. 1 Pet. 2.11.
n Job 14.2. Ps. 90.9. Ps. 102.11.
4 expectation.
o Deut. 8.2. 1 Sam. 16.7. ch. 28.9. Ps. 7.9. Pro. 16.2. Jer. 17.10. Heb. 4.13.
p Ps. 11.7. Pro. 11.20.
5 Or, found.
6 Or, stablish. Ps. 10.17. Jer. 10.23.
q Ps. 72.1.
r ch. 22.14.
7 gave the hand under Solomon. Gen. 24.2. Gen. 47.29. 2 Chr. 30.8. Eze. 17.18.
s 2 Chr. 1.12. Eccl. 2.9. Dan. 5.18, 19. Heb. 2.9.
t 2 Sam. 5.4. 1 Ki. 2.11.
u 2 Sam. 5.5.
v Gen. 15.15. Num. 23.10.
8 words, or, history.
w Dan. 2.21.

19 And [q]give unto Solomon my son
perfect heart, to keep thy command
ments, thy testimonies, and thy stat
utes, and to do all *these things*, and t
build the palace, *for* the which [r]I hav
made provision.
20 ¶ And David said to all the con
gregation, Now bless the LORD you
God. And all the congregation blesse
the LORD God of their fathers, an
bowed down their heads, and wor
shipped the LORD, and the king.
21 And they sacrificed sacrifices unt
the LORD, and offered burnt offering
unto the LORD, on the morrow afte
that day, *even* a thousand bullocks,
thousand rams, *and* a thousand lambs
with their drink offerings, and sacri
fices in abundance for all Israel:
22 And did eat and drink before th
LORD on that day with great gladnes
And they made Solomon the son o
David king the second time, an
anointed *him* unto the LORD *to be* th
chief governor, and Zā-dŏk *to b*
priest.
23 Then Solomon sat on the thron
of the LORD as king instead of Davi
his father, and prospered; and all Is
rael obeyed him.
24 And all the princes, and th
mighty men, and all the sons likewis
of king David, [7]submitted themselve
unto Solomon the king.
25 And the LORD magnified Solomo
exceedingly in the sight of all Israe
and bestowed [s]upon him *such* roy
majesty as had not been on any kin
before him in Israel.
26 ¶ Thus David the son of Jess
reigned over all Israel.
27 And [t]the time that he reigned ov
Israel *was* forty years; [u]seven yea
reigned he in Hē-brŏn, and thirty an
three *years* reigned he in Jerusalem.
28 And he [v]died in a good old ag
full of days, riches, and honour: an
Solomon his son reigned in his stea
29 Now the acts of David the kin
first and last, behold, they *are* writte
in the [8]book of Samuel the seer, and
the book of Nathan the prophet, ar
in the book of Gad the seer,
30 With all his reign and his migh
[w]and the times that went over hir
and over Israel, and over all the kin
doms of the countries.

THE SECOND

BOOK OF THE CHRONICLES

CHAPTER 1

AND [a]Solomon the son of David
was strengthened in his king-
ɔm, and [b]the LORD his God *was* with
m, and [c]magnified him exceedingly.
Then Solomon spake unto all Is-
el, to the [d]captains of thousands and
hundreds, and to the judges, and to
ery governor in all Israel, the chief
the fathers.
So Solomon, and all the congrega-
ɔn with him, went to the high place
at *was* at [e]Gibeon; for there was the
bernacle of the congregation of
od, which Moses the servant of the
ɔRD had made in the wilderness.
But [f]the ark of God had David
ought up from Kĭr-jăth–jē-ā-rĭm to
e place which David had prepared
r it: for he had pitched a tent for it
Jerusalem.
Moreover [g]the brasen altar, that
ĕz-ā-lēel the son of Ū-rī, the son of
ur, had made, [1]he put before the
bernacle of the LORD: and Solomon
d the congregation sought unto it.
And Solomon went up thither to
e brasen altar before the LORD,
ich *was* at the tabernacle of the con-
egation, and offered a [i]thousand
rnt offerings upon it.
¶ In [j]that night did God appear un-
Solomon, and said unto him, Ask
at I shall give thee.
And Solomon said unto God, Thou
st shewed great mercy unto David
y father, and hast made me [k]to
gn in his stead.
Now, O LORD God, let thy promise
to David my father be established:
r thou hast made me king over a
ople [2]like the dust of the earth in
ultitude.
0 Give [m]me now wisdom and know-
dge, that I may [n]go out and come in
fore this people: for who can judge
is thy people, *that is so* great?
1 And [o]God said to Solomon, Be-
use this was in thine heart, and thou
st not asked riches, wealth, or hon-
r, nor the life of thine enemies,
neither yet hast asked long life; but
hast asked wisdom and knowledge for
thyself, that thou mayest judge my
people, over whom I have made thee
king:
12 Wisdom and knowledge [p]*is* granted unto thee; and I will give thee riches, and wealth, and honour, such as
[q]none of the kings have had that *have*
been before thee, neither shall there
any after thee have the like.
13 ¶ Then Solomon came *from his*
journey to the high place that *was* at
Gibeon to Jerusalem, from before the
tabernacle of the congregation, and
reigned over Israel.
14 And [r]Solomon gathered chariots
and horsemen: and he had a thous-
and and four hundred chariots, and
twelve thousand horsemen, which he
placed in the chariot cities, and with
the king at Jerusalem.
15 And [s]the king [3]made silver and
gold at Jerusalem *as plenteous* as
stones, and cedar trees made he as
the sycomore trees that *are* in the vale
for abundance.
16 And [4]Solomon had horses brought
out of Egypt, and linen yarn: the
king's merchants received the linen
yarn at a price.
17 And they fetched up, and brought
forth out of Egypt a chariot for six
hundred *shekels* of silver, and an
horse for an hundred and fifty: and so
brought they out *horses* for all the
kings of the Hittites, and for the kings
of Syria, [5]by their means.

CHAPTER 2

AND Solomon [a]determined to build
an house for the name of the
LORD, and an house for his kingdom.
2 And [b]Solomon told out threescore
and ten thousand men to bear burdens, and fourscore thousand to hew
in the mountain, and three thousand
and six hundred to oversee them.
3 ¶ And Solomon sent to Hū-răm the
king of Tyre, saying, [c]As thou didst
deal with David my father, and didst

CHAP. 1

a 1 Ki. 2.46.
b Gen. 21.22. 1 Chr. 17.8. Matt. 28.20.
c 1 Chr. 29. 25. Phil. 2.9-11.
d 1 Chr. 27.1. ch. 29.20.
e 1 Ki. 3.4.
f 2 Sam. 6.2. 1 Chr. 15.1.
g Ex. 27.1.
h Ex. 31.2.
1 Or, was there.
i 1 Ki. 3.4.
j 1 Ki. 3.5. Isa. 58.9.
k 1 Chr. 28.5.
l 1 Ki. 3.7.
2 much as the dust of the earth.
m 1 Ki. 3.9. Ps. 119.34, 73. Pro. 3.13.
n Num. 27. 17. Deut. 31.2.
o 1 Sam. 16.7. 1 Ki. 3.11.
p Ps. 34.9,10. Matt. 6.33. Eph. 3.20.
q 1 Chr. 29. 25. ch. 9.22. Eccl. 2.9.
r 1 Ki. 4.26.
s Job 22.24.
3 gave.
4 the going forth of the horses which was Solomon's.
5 by their hand.

CHAP. 2

a 1 Ki. 5.5.
b 1 Ki. 5.15.
c 1 Chr. 14.1.

send him cedars to build him an house
to dwell therein, *even so deal with me.*
4 Behold, I build an house to the
name of the LORD my God, to dedicate *it* to him, *and* [d]to burn before
him [1]sweet incense, and for [e]the continual shewbread, and for the [f]burnt
offerings morning and evening, on the
sabbaths, and on the new moons, and
on the solemn feasts of the LORD our
God. This *is an ordinance* for ever to
Israel.
5 And the house which I build *is*
great: for [g]great *is* our God above all
gods.
6 But [h]who [2]is able to build him an
house, seeing the heaven and heaven
of heavens cannot contain him? who
am I then, that I should build him an
house, save only to burn sacrifice before him?
7 Send me now therefore a man cunning to work in gold, and in silver, and
in brass, and in iron, and in purple,
and crimson, and blue, and that can
skill [3]to grave with the cunning men
that *are* with me in Judah and in Jerusalem, [i]whom David my father did
provide.
8 Send [j]me also cedar trees, fir trees,
and [4]ăl´-gŭm trees, out of Lĕb´-ă-nŏn:
for I know that thy servants can skill
to cut timber in Lĕb´-ă-nŏn; and, behold, my servants *shall be* with thy
servants,
9 Even to prepare me timber in abundance: for the house which I am about
to build *shall be* [5]wonderful great.
10 And, [k]behold, I will give to thy
servants, the hewers that cut timber,
twenty thousand measures of beaten
wheat, and twenty thousand measures
of barley, and twenty thousand bāths
of wine, and twenty thousand bāths
of oil.
11 ¶ Then Hū´-răm the king of Tyre
answered in writing, which he sent to
Solomon, [l]Because the LORD hath
loved his people, he hath made thee
king over them.
12 Hū´-răm said moreover, [m]Blessed
be the LORD God of Israel, [n]that made
heaven and earth, who hath given to
David the king a wise son, [6]endued
with prudence and understanding,
that might build an house for the
LORD, and an house for his kingdom.
13 And now I have sent a cunning
man, endued with understanding, of
Hū´-răm my father's,
14 The [o]son of a woman of the daughters of Dan, and his father *was* a man
of Tyre, skilful to work in gold, and in

d Ex. 30.7.
1 incense of spices.
e Ex. 25.30. Lev. 24.8. Matt. 12.4.
f Ex. 29.38-42. Num. 28.3.
g Ex. 15.11. 1 Chr. 16.25. Ps. 86.8,9.
h ch. 6.18. Isa. 66.1.
2 hath retained, or, obtained strength.
3 to grave gravings.
i 1 Chr. 22.15.
j 1 Ki. 5.6.
4 Or, almuggim, 1 Ki. 10.11.
5 great and wonderful.
k 1 Ki. 5.11.
l Deut. 33.3.
m 1 Ki. 5.7.
n Gen. 1.1. Ps. 33.6. Ps. 102.25. Ps. 124.8. Acts 4.24. Rev. 10.6.
6 knowing prudence and understanding.
o 1 Ki. 7.13.
p 1 Ki. 5.8.
7 according to all thy need.
8 Japho, Josh. 19.46. Acts 9.36.
q 1 Ki. 5.13. ch. 8.7,8.
9 the men the strangers.
r 1 Chr. 22.2.

CHAP. 3

a 1 Ki. 6.1. 1 Chr. 29.19. John 2.19-21.
b Gen. 22.2.
1 Or, which was seen of David his father.
2 Or, Araunah, 2 Sam. 24.16.
c 1 Ki. 6.2.
3 founded.
d 1 Ki. 6.3.
e 1 Ki. 6.17.
4 covered.

silver, in brass, in iron, in stone, a
in timber, in purple, in blue, and
fine linen, and in crimson; also
grave any manner of graving, and
find out every device which shall
put to him, with thy cunning men, a
with the cunning men of my lo
David thy father.
15 Now therefore the wheat, and t
barley, the oil, and the wine, wh
my lord hath spoken of, let him se
unto his servants:
16 And [p]we will cut wood out of L
ă-nŏn, [7]as much as thou shalt ne
and we will bring it to thee in flo
by sea to [8]Joppa; and thou shalt ca
it up to Jerusalem.
17 ¶ And [q]Solomon numbered
[9]the strangers that *were* in the land
Israel, after the numbering whe
with [r]David his father had numbe
them; and they were found an hu
dred and fifty thousand and th
thousand and six hundred.
18 And he set threescore and
thousand of them *to be* bearers of bu
dens, and fourscore thousand *to*
hewers in the mountain, and th
thousand and six hundred overse
to set the people a work.

CHAPTER 3

THEN [a]Solomon began to bu
the house of the LORD at Jeru
lem in mount [b]Mō-rī´-ăh, [1]where
LORD appeared unto David his fa
er, in the place that David had prep
ed in the threshingfloor of [2]Ŏr´-năn t
Jĕb´-ū-şite.
2 And he began to build in the seco
day of the second month, in the fou
year of his reign.
3 ¶ Now these *are the things* [c]*whe*
in Solomon was [3]instructed for t
building of the house of God. T
length by cubits after the fi
measure *was* threescore cubits, a
the breadth twenty cubits.
4 And the [d]porch that *was* in t
front *of the house*, the length *of it* w
according to the breadth of the hou
twenty cubits, and the height *was*
hundred and twenty: and he overla
it within with pure gold.
5 And [e]the greater house he ceil
with fir tree, which he overlaid w
fine gold, and set thereon palm tre
and chains.
6 And he [4]garnished the house wi
precious stones for beauty: and t
gold *was* gold of Pär-vā´-ĭm.
7 He overlaid also the house, t
beams, the posts, and the walls the

f, and the doors thereof, with gold;
nd graved chĕr-ū-bĭms on the walls.
8 And he made the [5]most holy house,
ie length whereof *was* according to
ie breadth of the house, twenty cu-
its, and the breadth thereof twenty
ubits: and he overlaid it with fine
old, *amounting* to six hundred tal-
nts.
9 And the weight of the nails *was*
fty shekels of gold. And he overlaid
ie upper chambers with gold.
10 And [f]in the most holy house he
ade two chĕr-ū-bĭms [6]of image
ork, and overlaid them with gold.
11 ¶ And the wings of the chĕr-ū-
ĭms *were* twenty cubits long: one
ing *of the one cherub was* five cubits,
eaching to the wall of the house: and
ie other wing *was likewise* five cubits,
eaching to the wing of the other
nerub.
12 And *one* wing of the other cherub
as five cubits, reaching to the wall
f the house: and the other wing *was*
ve cubits *also*, joining to the wing of
ie other cherub.
13 The wings of these chĕr-ū-bĭms
pread themselves forth twenty cubits:
nd they stood on their feet, and their
ices *were* [7]inward.
14 ¶ And he made the [g]vail *of* blue,
nd purple, and crimson, and fine lin-
n, and [8]wrought chĕr-ū-bĭms thereon.
15 Also he made before the house
vo [h]pillars of thirty and five cubits
igh, and the chapiter that *was* on the
p of each of them *was* five cubits.
16 And he made chains, *as* in the
racle, and put *them* on the heads of
ie pillars; and made an hundred
omegranates, and put *them* on the
nains.
17 And he reared up the pillars be-
re the temple, one on the right hand,
nd the other on the left; and called
ie name of that on the right hand
Jā-chĭn, and the name of that on the
ft [11]Bō-ăz.

CHAPTER 4

MOREOVER he made [a]an altar
of brass, twenty cubits the length
iereof, and twenty cubits the breadth
iereof, and ten cubits the height
iereof.
2 ¶ Also [b]he made a molten sea of
n cubits [1]from brim to brim, round
compass, and five cubits the height
iereof; and a line of thirty cubits did
ompass it round about.
And [c]under it *was* the similitude of
xen, which did compass it round
about: ten in a cubit, compassing the
sea round about. Two rows of oxen
were cast, when it was cast.
4 It stood upon twelve oxen, three
looking toward the north, and three
looking toward the west, and three
looking toward the south, and three
looking toward the east: and the sea
was set above upon them, and all their
hinder parts *were* inward.
5 And the thickness of it *was* an handbreadth, and the brim of it like the
work of the brim of a cup, [2]with
flowers of lilies; *and* it received and
held [d]three thousand bāths.
6 ¶ He made also [e]ten lavers, and
put five on the right hand, and five on
the left, to wash in them: [3]such things
as they offered for the burnt offering
they washed in them; [f]but the sea *was*
for the priests to wash in.
7 And [g]he made ten candlesticks of
gold according [h]to their form, and set
them in the temple, five on the right
hand, and five on the left.
8 He [i]made also ten tables, and
placed *them* in the temple, five on the
right side, and five on the left. And he
made an hundred [4]basons of gold.
9 ¶ Furthermore [j]he made the court
of the priests, and the great court, and
doors for the court, and overlaid the
doors of them with brass.
10 And [k]he set the sea on the right
side of the east end, over against the
south.
11 And [l]Hū-răm made the pots, and
the shovels, and the [5]basons. And Hū-
răm [6]finished the work that he was to
make for king Solomon for the house
of God;
12 *To wit*, the two pillars, and the
[m]pommels, and the chapiters *which*
were on the top of the two pillars, and
the two wreaths to cover the two pommels of the chapiters which *were* on
the top of the pillars;
13 And [n]four hundred pomegranates
on the two wreaths; two rows of
pomegranates on each wreath, to
cover the two pommels of the chapiters which *were* [7]upon the pillars.
14 He made also [o]bases, and [8]lavers
made he upon the bases;
15 One sea, and twelve oxen under it.
16 The pots also, and the shovels, and
the fleshhooks, and all their instruments, did Hū-răm [p]his father make
to king Solomon for the house of the
LORD of [9]bright brass.
17 In [q]the plain of Jordan did the king
cast them, in the [10]clay ground between Sŭc-cōth and Zĕr-ĕ-dā-thăh.

5 house of holiness of holinesses, or, oracle.
f 1 Ki. 6.23.
6 Or, of moveable work.
7 Or, toward the house.
g Ex. 26.31. Matt. 27.51. Heb. 9.3.
8 caused to ascend.
h 1 Ki. 7.15.
9 long.
10 That is, He shall establish.
11 That is, In it is strength.

CHAP. 4

a Ex. 27.1. 1 Ki. 9.25. 2 Ki. 16.14.
b Ex. 30.18.
1 from his brim to his brim.
c 1 Ki. 7.24.
2 Or, like a lily flower.
d 1 Ki. 7.26.
e 1 Ki. 7.38.
3 the work of burnt offering.
f Heb. 9.9.
g 1 Ki. 7.49.
h Ex. 25.31.
i 1 Ki. 7.48.
4 Or, bowls.
j 1 Ki. 6.36.
k 1 Ki. 7.39.
l 1 Ki. 7.40.
5 Or, bowls.
6 finished to make.
m 1 Ki. 7.41.
n Ex. 28.33, 34. 1 Ki. 7.20. Song 4.13.
7 upon the face.
o 1 Ki. 7.27, 43.
8 Or, caldrons.
p 1 Ki. 7.14, 45.
9 made bright, or, scoured.
q 1 Ki. 7.46.
10 thicknesses of the ground.

18 Thus [r]Solomon made all these vessels in great abundance: for the weight of the brass could not be found out.

19 ¶ And [s]Solomon made all the vessels that *were for* the house of God, the golden altar also, and the tables [t]whereon the shewbread *was set;*

20 Moreover the candlesticks with their lamps, that they should burn after [u]the manner before the oracle, of pure gold;

21 And [v]the flowers, and the lamps, and the tongs, *made he of* gold, *and* that [11]perfect gold;

22 And the snuffers, and the [12]basons, and the spoons, and the censers, *of* pure gold: and the entry of the house, the inner doors thereof for the most holy *place*, and the doors of the house of the temple, *were of* [13]gold.

CHAPTER 5

THUS [a]all the work that Solomon made for the house of the LORD was finished: and Solomon brought in *all* the things that David his father had dedicated; and the silver, and the gold, and all the instruments, put he among the treasures of the house of God.

2 ¶ Then [b]Solomon assembled the elders of Israel, and all the heads of the tribes, the chief of the fathers of the children of Israel, unto Jerusalem, to bring up the ark of the covenant of the LORD [c]out of the city of David, which *is* Zion.

3 Wherefore [d]all the men of Israel assembled themselves unto the king [e]in the feast which *was* in the seventh month.

4 And all the elders of Israel came; and the [f]Levites took up the ark.

5 And they brought up the ark, and the tabernacle of the congregation, and all the holy vessels that *were* in the tabernacle, these did the priests *and* the Levites bring up.

6 Also king Solomon, and all the congregation of Israel that were assembled unto him before the ark, sacrificed sheep and oxen, which could not be told nor numbered for multitude.

7 And the priests brought in the ark of the covenant of the LORD unto his place, to the oracle of the house, into the most holy *place, even* under the wings of the chĕr-ū-bĭms:

8 For the chĕr-ū-bĭms spread forth *their* wings over the place of the ark, and the chĕr-ū-bĭms covered the ark and the staves thereof above.

r 1 Ki. 7.47.
s 1 Ki. 7.48-50. 2 Ki. 24.13. Jer. 28.3. Dan. 5.2,3.
t Ex. 25.30. 1 Chr. 28.16.
u Ex. 27.20, 21.
v Ex. 25.31.
11 perfections of gold.
12 Or, bowls.
13 That is, overlaid with gold.
CHAP. 5
a 1 Ki. 7.51. 1 Chr. 22.14.
b 1 Ki. 8.1. 1 Chr. 29.1. ch. 1.2.
c 2 Sam. 6.12.
d 1 Ki. 8.2.
e ch. 7.8,9,10.
f Josh. 3.6.
1 Or, they are there, as 1 Ki. 8.8.
g Deut. 10.2. ch. 6.11.
2 Or, where.
3 found.
h 1 Chr. 15. 16-22. ch. 29.25.
i 1 Chr. 15.24.
j 1 Chr. 16. 34,41. ch. 7.3. Ps. 136.1,26.
k Ex. 40.35. ch. 7.2. Isa. 6.4. Hag. 2.7. 2 Cor. 3.11. Rev. 15.8.
CHAP. 6
a 1 Ki. 8.12.
b Ex. 20.21. Lev. 16.2. Ps. 18.8-11. Heb. 12.18.
c ch. 12.13. Ps. 48.1.

9 And they drew out the staves *of* *ark*, that the ends of the staves w seen from the ark before the orac but they were not seen without. A [1]there it is unto this day.

10 *There was* nothing in the ark sa the two tables which Moses put [g]*the* *in* at Hôr-ĕb, [2]when the LORD mad *covenant* with the children of Isra when they came out of Egypt.

11 ¶ And it came to pass, when priests were come out of the h *place:* (for all the priests *that* w [3]present were sanctified, *and* did *then* wait by course:

12 Also [h]the Levites *which were* singers, all of them of Ā-săph, of H măn, of Jĕ-dū-thŭn, with their so and their brethren, *being* arrayed white linen, having cymbals and ps teries and harps, stood at the east e of the altar, and [i]with them an hu dred and twenty priests sounding w trumpets:)

13 It came even to pass, as the tru peters and singers *were* as one, make one sound to be heard in pra ing and thanking the LORD; and wh they lifted up *their* voice with trumpets and cymbals and instr ments of musick, and praised t LORD, *saying*, [j]For *he is* good; for h mercy *endureth* for ever: that *then* t house was filled with a cloud, *even* t house of the LORD;

14 So that the priests could not sta to minister by reason of the clou [k]for the glory of the LORD had fill the house of God.

CHAPTER 6

THEN [a]said Solomon, The LO hath said that he would dwell the [b]thick darkness.

2 But I have built an house of hab tation for thee, and a place for t dwelling for ever.

3 And the king turned his face, a blessed the whole congregation of rael: and all the congregation of Isr stood.

4 And he said, Blessed *be* the LO God of Israel, who hath with his han fulfilled *that* which he spake with h mouth to my father David, saying,

5 Since the day that I brought for my people out of the land of Egyp chose no city among all the tribes Israel to build an house in, that m name might be there; neither chos any man to be a ruler over my peo Israel:

6 But [c]I have chosen Jerusalem, th

y name might be there; and have
hosen David to be over my people
rael.
7 Now [e]it was in the heart of David
y father to build an house for the
ame of the LORD God of Israel.
8 But the LORD said to David my
ther, Forasmuch as it was in thine
eart to build an house for my name,
ou didst [f]well in that it was in thine
eart:
9 Notwithstanding thou shalt not
uild the house; but thy son which
all come forth out of thy loins, he
all build the house for my name.
10 The LORD therefore hath per-
rmed his word that he hath spoken:
r I am risen up in the room of David
y father, and am set on the throne
f Israel, as the LORD promised, and
ave built the house for the name of
e LORD God of Israel.
11 And in it have I put the ark,
herein [g]*is* the covenant of the LORD,
at he made with the children of
rael.
12 ¶ And [h]he stood before the altar
f the LORD in the presence of all the
ongregation of Israel, and [i]spread
rth his hands:
13 For Solomon had made a brasen
affold, of five cubits [1]long, and five
ibits broad, and three cubits high,
nd had set it in the midst of the court:
nd upon it he stood, and kneeled
own upon his knees before all the
ongregation of Israel, and spread
rth his hands toward heaven,
14 And said, O LORD God of Israel,
here is no God like thee in the heav-
, nor in the earth; which [k]keepest
ovenant, and *shewest* mercy unto thy
rvants, that [l]walk before thee with
l their hearts:
15 Thou [m]which hast kept with thy
rvant David my father that which
ou hast promised him; and spakest
ith thy mouth, and hast fulfilled *it*
ith thine hand, as *it is* this day.
16 Now therefore, O LORD God of
rael, keep with thy servant David
y father that which thou hast prom-
ed him, saying, [2]There shall not fail
ee a man in my sight to sit upon the
rone of Israel; [n]yet so that thy chil-
en take heed to their way to walk in
y law, as thou hast walked before
e.
17 Now then, O LORD God of Israel,
t thy word be verified, which thou
ast spoken unto thy servant David.
18 But [o]will God in very deed dwell
ith men on the earth? behold, [p]heav-

d 1 Sam. 16.1. 1 Chr. 28.4. Ps. 89.19,20.
e 2 Sam. 7.2. 1 Ki. 5.3. 1 Chr. 17.1.
f 1 Ki. 8.18-21. 2 Cor. 8.12.
g Ex. 40.20. ch. 5.10.
h 1 Ki. 8.22.
i Ezra 9.5. 1 Tim. 2.8.
1 the length thereof, etc.
j Ex. 15.11. Deut. 4.39. 2 Sam. 7.22. Ps. 86.8.
k Dan. 9.4.
l Gen. 5.24.
m 1 Chr. 22. 9,10.
2 There shall not a man be cut off.
n Ps. 132.12.
o Ps. 113.5,6.
p ch. 2.6. Isa. 66.1. Acts 7.49.
q Ps. 33.18. Ps. 34.15.
r Dan. 6.10.
3 Or, in this place.
4 pray.
s Isa. 43.25. Isa. 44.22.
5 and he require an oath of him.
t Pro. 1.31. Isa. 3.11. Rom. 2.8.
6 Or, be smitten.
u Deut. 32. 15. Judg. 2.11, 14,15. Ps. 51.4.
7 Or, toward.
v Lev. 26.19. Luke 4.25.
w Ps. 94.12. John 6.45.
x Zech. 10.1.
y ch. 20.9.
8 in the land of their gates.

en and the heaven of heavens cannot
contain thee; how much less this
house which I have built!
19 Have respect therefore to the
prayer of thy servant, and to his supplication, O LORD my God, to heark-
en unto the cry and the prayer which
thy servant prayeth before thee:
20 That thine [q]eyes may be open upon this house day and night, upon the
place whereof thou hast said that
thou wouldest put thy name there; to
hearken unto the prayer which thy
servant [r]prayeth [3]toward this place.
21 Hearken therefore unto the supplications of thy servant, and of thy
people Israel, which they shall [4]make
toward this place: hear thou from thy
dwelling place, *even* from heaven; and
when thou hearest, [s]forgive.
22 ¶ If a man sin against his neighbour, [5]and an oath be laid upon him to
make him swear, and the oath come
before thine altar in this house;
23 Then hear thou from heaven, and
do, and judge thy servants, by [t]requit-
ing the wicked, by recompensing his
way upon his own head; and by justifying the righteous, by giving him according to his righteousness.
24 ¶ And if thy people Israel [6]be put
to the worse before the enemy, because
[u]they have sinned against thee; and
shall return and confess thy name, and
pray and make supplication before
thee [7]in this house;
25 Then hear thou from the heavens,
and forgive the sin of thy people Israel, and [illegible] the
land which th[illegible]
to their fathers.
26 ¶ When the [v]heaven is shut up,
and there is no rain, because they have
sinned against thee; *yet* if they pray
toward this place, and confess thy
name, and turn from their sin, when
thou dost afflict them;
27 Then hear thou from heaven, and
forgive the sin of thy servants, and of
thy people Israel, [w]when thou hast
taught them the good way, wherein
they should walk; and [x]send rain upon thy land, which thou hast given unto thy people for an inheritance.
28 ¶ If there [y]be dearth in the land,
if there be pestilence, if there be blasting, or mildew, locusts, or caterpillers;
if their enemies besiege them [8]in the
cities of their land; whatsoever sore
or whatsoever sickness *there be:*
29 *Then* what prayer *or* what supplication soever shall be made of any
man, or of all thy people Israel, when

every one shall know his own sore and
his own grief, and shall spread forth
his hands [9]in this house:
30 Then hear thou from heaven thy
dwelling place, and forgive, and render unto every man according unto all
his ways, whose heart thou knowest;
(for thou only knowest [z]the hearts of
the children of men:)
31 That they may fear thee, to walk
in thy ways, [10]so long as they live [11]in
the land which thou gavest unto our
fathers.
32 ¶ Moreover concerning the stranger, which [a]is not of thy people Israel,
but is come from a far country for thy
great name's sake, and thy mighty
hand, and thy stretched out arm; if
they come and pray in this house;
33 Then hear thou from the heavens,
even from thy dwelling place, and do
according to all that the stranger calleth to thee for; that all people of the
earth may know thy name, and fear
thee, as *doth* thy people Israel, and
may know that [12]this house which I
have built is called by thy name.
34 If thy people go out to war against
their enemies by the way that thou
shalt send them, and they pray unto
thee toward this city which thou hast
chosen, and the house which I have
built for thy name;
35 Then hear thou from the heavens
their prayer and their supplication,
and maintain their [13]cause.
36 If they sin against thee, (for *there*
is no [b]man which sinneth not,) and
th[illegible]d deliver
[illegible]enemies, and
[illegible]ay captives unto
a [illegible]and far off or near;
37 Yet *if* they [15]bethink themselves
in the land whither they are carried
captive, and turn and pray unto thee
in the land of their captivity, saying,
We have sinned, we have done amiss,
and have dealt wickedly;
38 If they return to thee [c]with all
their heart and with all their soul in
the land of their captivity, whither
they have carried them captives, and
pray toward their land, which thou
gavest unto their fathers, and *toward*
the city which thou hast chosen, and
toward the house which I have built
for thy name:
39 Then hear thou from the heavens,
even from thy dwelling place, their
prayer and their supplications, and
maintain their [16]cause, and forgive
thy people which have sinned against
thee.

9 Or, toward this house.
z 1 Chr. 28.9. Ps. 11.4.
10 all the days which.
11 upon the face of the land.
a Deut. 4.6,7,8. Ps. 113.3. Isa. 56.3-8. Mal. 1.11. John 10.16. Acts 8.27.
12 thy name is called upon this house.
13 Or, right.
b Job 15.14-16. Pro. 20.9. Eccl. 7.20.
14 they that take them captives carry them away.
15 bring back to their heart.
c Jer. 29.12, 13.
16 Or, right.
17 to the prayer of this place.
d Ps. 132.8,9, 10,16.
e 1 Chr. 28.2.
f Isa. 61.10.
g Neh. 9.25.
h Ps. 89.20-28. Isa. 55.3.

CHAP. 7

a 1 Ki. 8.54. Isa. 65.24. Dan. 9.20. Acts 4.31.
b Gen. 15.17. Lev. 9.24. Judg. 6.21. 1 Ki. 18.38. 1 Chr. 21.26.
c Lev. 9.23. ch. 5.13. Eze. 10.3. Rev. 21.23.
d ch. 5.14.
e ch. 5.13. Ps. 103.17. Ps. 136.1.
f ch. 20.21.
g 1 Ki. 8.62.
h 1 Chr. 15.16.
1 by their hand.
i ch. 5.12.
j Num. 16.37. ch. 36.14. Heb. 13.10-12.
k 1 Ki. 8.65.
l Gen. 15.18.
2 a restraint.

40 Now, my God, let, I beseech thee
thine eyes be open, and *let* thine ear
be attent [17]unto the prayer *that is mad*
in this place.
41 Now [d]therefore arise, O LORI
God, into thy [e]resting place, thou, an
the ark of thy strength: let thy priests
O LORD God, be [f]clothed with salva
tion, and let thy saints rejoice [g]i
goodness.
42 O LORD God, turn not away th
face of thine anointed: [h]remembe
the mercies of David thy servant.

CHAPTER 7

NOW [a]when Solomon had mad
an end of praying, the [b]fire cam
down from heaven, and consumed th
burnt offering and the sacrifices; an
[c]the glory of the LORD filled the house
2 And [d]the priests could not enter in
to the house of the LORD, because th
glory of the LORD had filled the LORD'
house.
3 And when all the children of Israe
saw how the fire came down, and th
glory of the LORD upon the house
they bowed themselves with thei
faces to the ground upon the pave
ment, and worshipped, and praise
the LORD, [e]*saying*, For *he is* good; fo
[f]his mercy *endureth* for ever.
4 ¶ Then [g]the king and all the peopl
offered sacrifices before the LORD.
5 And king Solomon offered a sacri
fice of twenty and two thousand oxen
and an hundred and twenty thousan
sheep: so the king and all the peopl
dedicated the house of God.
6 And [h]the priests waited on thei
offices: the Levites also with instru
ments of musick of the LORD, whic
David the king had made to praise th
LORD, because his mercy *endureth* fo
ever, when David praised [1]by thei
ministry; and the [i]priests sounde
trumpets before them, and all Israe
stood.
7 Moreover [j]Solomon hallowed th
middle of the court that *was* befor
the house of the LORD: for there h
offered burnt offerings, and the fat o
the peace offerings, because the brase
altar which Solomon had made wa
not able to receive the burnt offerings
and the meat offerings, and the fat
8 ¶ Also [k]at the same time Solomo
kept the feast seven days, and all Is
rael with him, a very great congrega
tion, from the entering in of Hā-măt
unto [l]the river of Egypt.
9 And in the eighth day they mad
[2]a solemn assembly: for they kept th

edication of the altar seven days, and
he feast seven days.
10 And [m]on the three and twentieth
ay of the seventh month he sent the
eople away into their tents, glad and
nerry in heart for the goodness that
he LORD had shewed unto David, and
o Solomon, and to Israel his people.
11 Thus [n]Solomon finished the house
f the LORD, and the king's house: and
ll that came into Solomon's heart
o make in the house of the LORD, and
n his own house, he prosperously
ffected.
12 ¶ And the LORD [o]appeared to
olomon by night, and said unto him,
have heard thy prayer, [p]and have
hosen this place to myself for an
ouse of sacrifice.
13 If [q]I shut up heaven that there be
o rain, or if I command the locusts to
evour the land, or if I send pestilence
mong my people;
14 If my people, [3]which are called by
ny name, shall [r]humble themselves,
nd pray, and seek my face, and turn
rom their wicked ways; then [s]will I
ear from heaven, and will forgive
heir sin, and will heal their land.
15 Now [t]mine eyes shall be open,
nd mine ears attent [4]unto the prayer
hat is made in this place.
16 For now have [u]I chosen and sanc-
ified this house, that my name may
e there for ever: and mine eyes and
nine heart shall be there perpetually.
17 And [v]as for thee, if thou wilt
valk before me, as David thy father
valked, and do according to all that I
ave commanded thee, and shalt ob-
erve my statutes and my judgments;
18 Then will I stablish the throne of
hy kingdom, according as I have
ovenanted with David thy father,
aying, [5]There shall not fail thee a man
o be ruler in Israel.
19 But [w]if ye turn away, and forsake
ny statutes and my commandments,
vhich I have set before you, and shall
o and serve other gods, and worship
hem;
20 Then will I [x]pluck them up by the
oots out of my land which I have
iven them; and this house, which I
nave sanctified for my name, will I
ast out of my sight, and will make it
o be a proverb and a byword among
ll nations.
21 And [y]this house, which is high,
hall be an astonishment to every one
that passeth by it; so that he shall say,
Why hath the LORD done thus unto
this land, and unto this house?

m 1 Ki. 8.66.
n 1 Ki. 9.1.
o Gen. 12.7.
p Deut. 12.5. Ps. 78.68,69.
q ch. 6.26.
3 upon whom my name is called.
r Jas. 4.10.
s ch. 6.27.
t ch. 6.40.
4 to the prayer of this place.
u ch. 6.6.
v 1 Ki. 9.4.
5 There shall not be cut off to thee.
w Lev. 26.14. Deut. 28.15.
x Ps. 5.5.
y Jer. 7.14. Lam. 2.15.
z Deut. 29. 24.
a Judg. 2.13.
b 2 Ki. 17.18. ch. 36.16. Dan. 9.12.

CHAP. 8

a 1 Ki. 9.10.
b Num. 13. 31. 2 Sam. 8.3.
c 1 Ki. 9.17.
d Josh. 15.11.
1 all the desire of Solomon which he desired to build.
e 1 Ki. 9.20.
f Gen. 10.15. Deut. 7.1.
g Ex. 19.5. Deut. 23.19. Lev. 25.39. Gal. 4.28,31.
h 1 Ki. 5.16. ch. 2.18.
i 1 Ki. 3.1.
2 holiness.

22 And it shall be answered, Because
they forsook [a]the LORD God of
their fathers, which brought them
forth out of the land of Egypt,
and laid hold on other gods, and
worshipped them, and served them:
therefore [b]hath he brought all this
evil upon them.

CHAPTER 8

AND [a]it came to pass at the end of
twenty years, wherein Solomon
had built the house of the LORD, and
his own house,
2 That the cities which Hū-răm had
restored to Solomon, Solomon built
them, and caused the children of Israel to dwell there.
3 And Solomon went to [b]Hā-măth–
zō-băh, and prevailed against it.
4 And [c]he built Tăd-môr in the wilderness, and all the store cities, which
he built in Hā-măth.
5 Also he built Bĕth–hôr-ŏn the upper, and Bĕth–hôr-ŏn the nether,
fenced cities, with walls, gates, and
bars;
6 And [d]Bā-ā-lăth, and all the store
cities that Solomon had, and all the
chariot cities, and the cities of the
horsemen, and [1]all that Solomon desired to build in Jerusalem, and in
Lĕb-ā-non, and throughout all the
land of his dominion.
7 ¶ *As* [e]*for* all the people *that were*
left of the [f]Hittites, and the Amorites,
and the Pĕ-rĭz-zītes, and the Hī-vītes,
and the Jĕb-ū-sītes, which *were* not of
Israel,
8 *But* of their children, who were left
after them in the land, whom the children of Israel consumed not, them
did Solomon make to pay tribute until
this day.
9 But [g]of the children of Israel did
Solomon make no servants for his
work; but they *were* men of war, and
chief of his captains, and captains of
his chariots and horsemen.
10 And these *were* the chief of king
Solomon's officers, *even* [h]two hundred and fifty, that bare rule over the
people.
11 ¶ And Solomon [i]brought up the
daughter of Pharaoh out of the city of
David unto the house that he had
built for her: for he said, My wife
shall not dwell in the house of David
king of Israel, because *the places are*
[2]holy, whereunto the ark of the LORD
hath come.
12 ¶ Then Solomon offered burnt
offerings unto the LORD on the altar

of the LORD, which he had built before the porch,

13 Even after a certain [j]rate every day, offering according to the commandment of Moses, on the sabbaths, and on the new moons, and on the solemn feasts, three [k]times in the year, *even* in the feast of unleavened bread, and in the feast of weeks, and in the feast of tabernacles.

14 ¶ And he appointed, according to the order of David his father, the [l]courses of the priests to their service, and [m]the Levites to their charges, to praise and minister before the priests, as the duty of every day required: the [n]porters also by their courses at every gate: for [3]so had David the man of God commanded.

15 And they departed not from the commandment of the king unto the priests and Levites concerning any matter, or concerning the treasures.

16 Now all the work of Solomon was prepared unto the day of the foundation of the house of the LORD, and until it was finished. *So* the house of the LORD was perfected.

17 ¶ Then went Solomon to [o]Ē′zĭ-ŏn–gē′bĕr, and to [p]Ē′lōth, at the sea side in the land of Ē′dom.

18 And [q]Hū′răm sent him by the hands of his servants ships, and servants that had knowledge of the sea; and they went with the servants of Solomon to [r]Ō′phĭr, and took thence four hundred and fifty talents of gold, and brought *them* to king Solomon.

CHAPTER 9

AND [a]when the queen of Shē′bă heard of the fame of Solomon, she came to prove [b]Solomon with hard questions at Jerusalem, with a very great company, and camels that bare spices, and gold in abundance, and precious stones: and when she was come to Solomon, she communed with him of all that was in her heart.

2 And Solomon told her all her [1]questions: and there was nothing hid from Solomon which he told her not.

3 And when the queen of Shē′bă had seen the wisdom of Solomon, and the house that he had built,

4 And the meat of his table, and the sitting of his servants, and the attendance of his ministers, and their apparel; his [2]cupbearers also, and their apparel; and his ascent by which he went up into the house of the LORD; there was no more spirit in her.

5 And she said to the king, *It was* a
true [3]report which I heard in mine ow
land of thine [4]acts, and of thy wi
dom:
6 Howbeit I believed not their word
until I came, and mine eyes had see
it: and, behold, the one half of th
greatness of thy wisdom was not tol
me: *for* thou [5]exceedest the fame th
I heard.
7 Happy *are* thy men, and happy *a*
these thy servants, which stand co
tinually before thee, and hear th
wisdom.
8 Blessed [c]be the LORD thy Go
which delighted in thee to set thee o
his throne, *to be* king for the LORD th
God: because thy God loved Israe
to establish them for ever, therefo
made he thee king over them, to d
judgment and justice.
9 And she gave the king an hundre
and twenty talents of gold, and o
spices great abundance, and preciou
stones: neither was there any suc
spice as the queen of Shē′bă gave kin
Solomon.
10 And the servants also of Hū′răm
and the servants of Solomon, whic
[d]brought gold from Ō′phĭr, brough
[e]ăl′gŭm trees and precious stones.
11 And the king made *of* the ăl′gŭn
trees [6]terraces to the house of th
LORD, and to the king's palace, an
harps and psalteries for singers: an
there were none such seen before i
the land of Judah.
12 And king Solomon gave to th
queen of Shē′bă all her desire, what
soever she asked, beside *that* whic
she had brought unto the king. So sh
turned, and went away to her ow
land, she and her servants.
13 ¶ Now the weight of gold tha
came to Solomon in one year was si
hundred and threescore and six tal
ents of gold;
14 Beside *that which* chapmen and
merchants brought. And all [f]the kings
of Arabia and [7]governors of the coun
try brought gold and silver to Sol
omon.
15 ¶ And king Solomon made two
hundred targets *of* beaten gold: six
hundred *shekels* of beaten gold went
to one target.
16 And three hundred shields *made*
he of beaten gold: three hundred *she-*
kels of gold went to one shield. And
the king put them in the house of the
forest of Lĕb′ă-non.
17 Moreover the king made a great
throne of ivory, and overlaid it with
pure gold.

j Ex. 29.38. Num. 28.3, 9,11,26.
k Ex. 23.14. Deut. 16.16.
l 1 Chr. 24.1. ch. 5.11. Luke 1.5,8.
m 1 Chr. 25. 1.
n 1 Chr. 9.17.
3 so was the commandment of David the man of God.
o 1 Ki. 9.26.
p Deut. 2.8. 2 Ki. 14.22. Elath.
q 1 Ki. 9.27. ch. 9.10,13.
r Gen. 10.29. Job 22.24. Isa. 13.12.

CHAP. 9
a 1 Ki. 10.1. Matt. 12.42. Luke 11.31.
b Ps. 49.4. Ps. 78.2. Pro. 1.5. Eze. 20.49. Matt. 13.11, 35.
1 words.
2 Or, butlers.
3 word.
4 Or, sayings.
5 hast added to.
c Ps. 72.18, 19.
d 1 Ki. 5.2-6. 1 Ki. 9.27, 28. ch. 8.18. Ps. 72.10.
e 1 Ki. 10.11. almug trees.
6 highways, or, stairs.
f Ps. 68.29. Ps. 72.10. Isa. 45.14. Isa. 60.6. Jer. 25.24.
7 Or, captains.

18 And *there were* six steps to the
ırone, with a footstool of gold, *which*
ere fastened to the throne, and [8]stays
n each side of the sitting place, and
wo lions standing by the stays:
19 And twelve lions stood there on
ıe one side and on the other upon
ıe six steps. There was not the like
ıade in any kingdom.
20 ¶ And all the drinking vessels of
ing Solomon *were of* gold, and all
ıe vessels of the house of the forest
f Lĕb-ă-non *were of* [9]pure gold:
none *were of* silver; it was *not* any
hing accounted of in the days of Sol-
mon.
21 For the king's ships went [g]to Tar-
hish with the servants of Hū-răm:
very three years once came the
hips of Tarshish bringing gold, and
ilver, [11]ivory, and apes, and pea-
ocks.
22 And king Solomon [h]passed all the
ings of the earth in riches and wis-
om.
23 ¶ And all the kings of the earth
ought the presence of Solomon, to
ıear his wisdom, that God had put in
ıis heart.
24 And [i]they brought every man his
resent, vessels of silver, and vessels
f gold, and raiment, harness, and
pices, horses, and mules, a rate year
y year.
25 ¶ And Solomon [j]had four thous-
nd stalls for horses and chariots, and
welve thousand horsemen; whom he
estowed in the chariot cities, and
vith the king at Jerusalem.
26 ¶ And [k]he reigned over all the
ings from [l]the [12]river even unto the
and of the Philistines, and to the bor-
ler of Egypt.
27 And [m]the king [13]made silver in
erusalem as stones, and cedar trees
nade he as the sycomore trees that *are*
n the low plains in abundance.
28 And [n]they brought unto Solomon
ıorses out of Egypt, and out of all
ands.
29 ¶ Now [o]the rest of the acts of Solomon, first and last, *are* they not writ-
en in the [14]book of Nathan the prophet, and in the prophecy of [p]Ă-hī-jăh
he Shī-lō-nīte, and in the visions of
Id-dō the seer against Jĕr-ŏ-bō-ăm
he son of Nē-băt?
30 And [r]Solomon reigned in Jerusa-
em over all Israel forty years.
31 And Solomon slept with his fathers, and he was buried in the city of
David his father: and [15]Rē-hŏ-bō-ăm
his son reigned in his stead.

8 hands.
9 shut up.
10 Or, there was no silver in them.
g 1 Ki. 10.22. Ps. 48.7. Ps. 72.10. Isa. 2.16. Isa. 23.6, 14. Jonah 1.3.
11 Or, elephants' teeth.
h 1 Ki. 3.12, 13. Ps. 89.27. Matt. 12.42. Col. 2.2,3.
i Ps. 72.10,15.
j 1 Ki. 4.26. ch. 1.14.
k 1 Ki. 4.21.
l Gen. 15.18. Ps. 72.8.
12 That is, Euphrates.
m 1 Ki. 10. 27. ch. 1.15.
13 gave.
n Deut. 17. 16. 1 Ki. 4.26. ch. 1.16. Isa. 2.7. Isa. 31.1.
o 1 Ki. 11.41.
14 words.
p 1 Ki. 11.29.
q ch. 12.15.
r 1 Ki. 11.42, 43.
15 That is, Enlarger of the people.

CHAP. 10

a 1 Ki. 12.1.
b 1 Ki. 11.40.
c 1 Sam. 8.11-18. 1 Ki. 4.7. Matt. 23.4. 1 John 5.3.
d Job 8.8,9. Job 32.7.
1 for good.
e Pro. 15.1.
f 2 Sam. 17. 14. ch. 25.16. Pro. 1.25. Pro. 13.20. Eccl. 10.2.
2 laded.
g Pro. 12.13. Pro. 14.16.

CHAPTER 10

AND [a]Rē-hŏ-bō-ăm went to Shē-
chĕm: for to Shē-chĕm were all
Israel come to make him king.
2 And it came to pass, when Jĕr-ŏ-
bō-ăm the son of Nē-băt, who *was* in
Egypt, [b]whither he had fled from the
presence of Solomon the king, heard
it, that Jĕr-ŏ-bō-ăm returned out of
Egypt.
3 And they sent and called him. So
Jĕr-ŏ-bō-ăm and all Israel came and
spake to Rē-hŏ-bō-ăm, saying,
4 Thy father made our [c]yoke grievous: now therefore ease thou somewhat the grievous servitude of thy
father, and his heavy yoke that he put
upon us, and we will serve thee.
5 And he said unto them, Come
again unto me after three days. And
the people departed.
6 ¶ And king Rē-hŏ-bō-ăm took
counsel with the [d]old men that had
stood before Solomon his father while
he yet lived, saying, What counsel
give ye *me* to return answer to this
people?
7 And they spake unto him, saying,
If thou be [1]kind to this people, and
please them, [e]and speak good words
to them, they will be thy servants for
ever.
8 But he [f]forsook the counsel which
the old men gave him, and took counsel with the young men that were
brought up with him, that stood before him.
9 And he said unto them, What advice give ye that we may return answer to this people, which have spok-
ken to me, saying, Ease somewhat the
yoke that thy father did put upon us?
10 And the young men that were
brought up with him spake unto him,
saying, Thus shalt thou answer the
people that spake unto thee, saying,
Thy father made our yoke heavy, but
make thou *it* somewhat lighter for us;
thus shalt thou say unto them, My
little *finger* shall be thicker than my
father's loins.
11 For whereas my father [2]put a
heavy yoke upon you, I will put more
to your yoke: my father chastised you
with whips, but I *will chastise you* with
scorpions.
12 So Jĕr-ŏ-bō-ăm and all the people
came to Rē-hŏ-bō-ăm on the third
day, as the king bade, saying, Come
again to me on the third day.
13 And the king answered [g]them
roughly; and king Rē-hŏ-bō-ăm forsook the counsel of the old men,

14 And answered them after the advice of the young men, saying, My
father made your yoke heavy, but I
will add thereto: my father chastised
you with whips, but I *will chastise you*
with scorpions.
15 So the king hearkened not unto
the people: for the [3]cause was of God,
that the LORD might perform his
word, which he spake by the [h]hand of
Ă-hī´jăh the Shī´lō-nite to Jĕr-ŏ-bō´-
ăm the son of Nē´băt.
16 ¶ And when all Israel *saw* that the
king would not hearken unto them,
the people answered the king, saying,
What portion have we in David? and
we have none inheritance in the son of
Jesse: every man to your tents, O Israel: *and* now, David, see to thine
own house. So all Israel went to their
tents.
17 But *as for* the children of Israel
that dwelt in the cities of Judah, Rē-
hŏ-bō´ăm reigned over them.
18 Then king Rē-hŏ-bō´ăm sent Hă-
dôr´ăm that *was* over the tribute; and
the children of Israel stoned him with
stones, that he died. But king Rē-hŏ-
bō´ăm [4]made speed to get him up to
his chariot, to flee to Jerusalem.
19 And [i]Israel rebelled against the
house of David unto this day.

CHAPTER 11

AND [a]when Rē-hŏ-bō´ăm was come
to Jerusalem, he gathered of the
house of Judah and Benjamin an hundred and fourscore thousand chosen
men, which were warriors, to fight
against Israel, that he might bring the
kingdom again to Rē-hŏ-bō´ăm.
2 But the word of the LORD came
to [b]Shĕm-âi´ăh the man of God, saying,
3 Speak unto Rē-hŏ-bō´ăm the son
of Solomon, king of Judah, and to
all Israel in Judah and Benjamin, saying,
4 Thus saith the LORD, Ye shall not
go up, nor fight against your brethren:
return every man to his house: for this
thing is done of me. And they obeyed
the words of the LORD, and returned
from going against Jĕr-ŏ-bō´ăm.
5 ¶ And Rē-hŏ-bō´ăm dwelt in Jerusalem, and built cities for defence in
Judah.
6 He built even [c]Beth-lehem, and [d]Ē´-
tăm, and [e]Tĕ-kō´ă,
7 And Bĕth´-zûr, and Shō´cō, and
Adullam,
8 And Gath, and Mă-rē´shăh, and
Ziph,

3 wheeling about.
h 1 Ki. 11.29.
4 strengthened himself.
i 1 Ki. 12.19. 2 Ki. 17.21-23. ch. 13.5-7. Eccl. 2.19.

CHAP. 11

a 1 Ki. 12.21.
b Deut. 33.1. 1 Sam. 2.27. 1 Ki. 12.22-24. ch. 8.14. 1 Tim. 6.11.
c Gen. 35.19. 1 Sam. 17.12. Matt. 2.1.
d Judg. 15.8. 1 Chr. 4.31.
e 2 Sam. 14.2. ch. 20.20. Neh. 3.5. Jer. 6.1. Amos 1.1.
1 presented themselves to him.
f Num. 35.2. Josh. 21.20-42.
g 1 Ki. 12.28-33. ch. 13.9.
h 1 Ki. 12.31. Hos. 13.2.
i Lev. 17.7. Deut. 32.15, 16,17. 1 Cor. 10.20. Rev. 16.14.
j 1 Ki. 12.28.
k ch. 15.9. Ps. 69.32.
l ch. 12.1.
m Hosea 6.4. Matt. 13.18.
n 1 Ki. 15.2. See ch. 13.2, where she is called Michaiah the daughter of Uriel.
o Deut. 21. 15,16,17.
2 a multitude of wives.

9 And Ăd-ō-rā´ĭm, and Lā´chĭsh, an
Ă-zē´kăh,
10 And Zôr´ăh, and Aî´jă-lŏn, an
Hē´brŏn, which *are* in Judah and i
Benjamin fenced cities.
11 And he fortified the strong hold
and put captains in them, and store c
victual, and of oil and wine.
12 And in every several city *he pu*
shields and spears, and made ther
exceeding strong, having Judah an
Benjamin on his side.
13 ¶ And the priests and the Levite
that *were* in all Israel [1]resorted to hir
out of all their coasts.
14 For the Levites left [f]their suburb
and their possession, and came to Ju
dah and Jerusalem: for [g]Jĕr-ŏ-bō´ăr
and his sons had cast them off fron
executing the priest's office unto th
LORD:
15 And [h]he ordained him priests fo
the high places, and for [i]the devils
and [j]for the calves which he ha
made.
16 And [k]after them out of all th
tribes of Israel such as set their heart
to seek the LORD God of Israel cam
to Jerusalem, to sacrifice unto th
LORD God of their fathers.
17 So they [l]strengthened the king
dom of Judah, and made Rē-hŏ-bō
ăm the son of Solomon strong, thre
years: for [m]three years they walke
in the way of David and Solomon.
18 ¶ And Rē-hŏ-bō´ăm took hin
Mā´hă-lăth the daughter of Jĕr´ĭ-mōtl
the son of David to wife, *and* Ăb-ĭ-hai
the daughter of Ē-lĭ-ăb the son o
Jesse;
19 Which bare him children; Jē´ŭsh
and Shăm-ă-rĭ´ăh, and Ză´hăm.
20 And after her he took [n]Mā´ă-chăl
the daughter of Ăb´să-lom; which
bare him Ă-bī´jăh, and Ăt-tā´ī, and
Zī´ză, and Shĕ-lō´mĭth.
21 And Rē-hŏ-bō´ăm loved Mā´ă-
chăh the daughter of Ăb´să-lom above
all his wives and his concubines: (fo
he took eighteen wives, and threescore concubines; and begat twenty
and eight sons, and threescore daughters.)
22 And Rē-hŏ-bō´ăm [o]made Ă-bī´jăh
the son of Mā´ă-chăh the chief, *to be*
ruler among his brethren: for *he*
thought to make him king.
23 And he dealt wisely, and dispersed of all his children throughout all
the countries of Judah and Benjamin,
unto every fenced city: and he gave
them victual in abundance. And he
desired [2]many wives.

CHAPTER 12

ND [a]it came to pass, when Rē-hŏ-
bō-ăm had established the king-
m, and had strengthened himself,
e forsook the law of the LORD, and
Israel with him.
And [c]it came to pass, *that* in the
th year of king Rē-hŏ-bō-ăm Shī-
ăk king of Egypt came up against
rusalem, because they had trans-
essed against the LORD,
With twelve hundred chariots, and
reescore thousand horsemen: and
e people *were* without number that
me with him out of Egypt; [d]the Lū-
ms, the Sŭk-kĭ-ĭms, and the Ē-thĭ-
pĭ-ăns.
And he took the fenced cities which
rtained to Judah, and came to Jeru-
lem.
¶ Then came [e]Shĕm-âĭ-ăh the pro-
et to Rē-hŏ-bō-ăm, and *to* the prin-
s of Judah, that were gathered
gether to Jerusalem because of Shī-
ăk, and said unto them, Thus saith
e LORD, [f]Ye have forsaken me, and
erefore have I also left you in the
nd of Shī-shăk.
Whereupon the princes of Israel
d the king [g]humbled themselves;
d they said, [h]The LORD *is* righteous.
And when the LORD saw that they
mbled themselves, the word of [i]the
RD came to Shĕm-âĭ-ăh, saying,
ey have humbled themselves; *there-*
re I will not destroy them, but I will
ant them [1]some deliverance; and
y wrath shall not be poured out
on Jerusalem by the hand of Shī-
ăk.
Nevertheless [j]they shall be his ser-
nts; that they may know [k]my ser-
e, and the service of the kingdoms
the countries.
So [l]Shī-shăk king of Egypt came
against Jerusalem, and took away
e treasures of the house of the LORD,
d the treasures of the king's house;
took all: he carried away also the
ields of gold which Solomon had
ade.
0 Instead of which king Rē-hŏ-bō-
n made shields of brass, and com-
itted *them* [n]to the hands of the chief
the guard, that kept the entrance
the king's house.
1 And when the king entered into
e house of the LORD, the guard
me and fetched them, and brought
em again into the guard chamber.
2 And when he humbled himself,
e wrath of the LORD turned from
m, that he would not destroy *him*

CHAP. 12
a ch. 11.17.
b Deut. 8.14.
c 1 Ki. 14.24, 25.
d ch. 16.8.
e ch. 11.2.
f Deut. 28.25. ch. 15.2.
g Ex. 10.3. Lev. 26.40, 41, 42. ch. 33.12,19. ch. 34.27. Ps. 78.34. Jas. 4.10.
h Ex. 9.27.
i 1 Ki. 21.28, 29.
1 Or, a little while.
j Isa. 26.13.
k Deut. 28. 47,48.
l 1 Ki. 14.25, 26.
m 1 Ki. 10.16, 17. ch. 9.15,16.
n 2 Sam. 8.18. 1 Chr. 11.25.
2 Or, and yet in Judah there were good things.
o 1 Ki. 14.21. ch. 13.7.
p ch. 6.6. Ps. 48.1-3.
3 Or, fixed.
4 words.
q ch. 9.29.
r 1 Ki. 14.30.

CHAP. 13
a 1 Ki. 15.1.
b ch. 11.20.
1 bound together.
c Josh. 18.22.
d Judg. 11. 21-24. 1 Sam. 16. 12,13. 2 Sam. 7.12, 13,16. Ps. 89.20. Luke 1.31-33.
2 That is, A perpetual covenant of friendship.
e 1 Ki. 11.26. ch. 10.19.
f Judg. 9.4. Ps. 26.4. Pro. 12.11. Acts 17.5.

altogether: [2]and also in Judah things
went well.
13 ¶ So king Rē-hŏ-bō-ăm strengthened himself in Jerusalem, and reigned: for [o]Rē-hŏ-bō-ăm *was* one and
forty years old when he began to
reign, and he reigned seventeen years
in Jerusalem, [p]the city which the
LORD had chosen out of all the tribes
of Israel, to put his name there. And
his mother's name *was* Nā-ă-măh an
Ammonitess.
14 And he did evil, because he [3]pre-
pared not his heart to seek the LORD.
15 Now the acts of Rē-hŏ-bō-ăm,
first and last, *are* they not written in
the [4]book of Shĕm-âĭ-ăh the prophet,
[q]and of Ĭd-dō the seer concerning genealogies? [r]And *there were* wars between Rē-hŏ-bō-ăm and Jĕr-ŏ-bō-
ăm continually.
16 And Rē-hŏ-bō-ăm slept with his
fathers, and was buried in the city of
David: and Ă-bī-jăh his son reigned
in his stead.

CHAPTER 13

NOW [a]in the eighteenth year of
king Jĕr-ŏ-bō-ăm began Ă-bī-jăh
to reign over Judah.
2 He reigned three years in Jerusalem. His mother's name also *was* [b]Mī-
châĭ-ăh the daughter of Ū-rĭ-ĕl of Gĭb-
ē-ăh. And there was war between
Ă-bī-jăh and Jĕr-ŏ-bō-ăm.
3 And Ă-bī-jăh [1]set the battle in array
with an army of valiant men of war,
even four hundred thousand chosen
men: Jĕr-ŏ-bō-ăm also set the battle
in array against him with eight hundred thousand chosen men, *being*
mighty men of valour.
4 ¶ And Ă-bī-jăh stood up upon
mount Zĕm-ă-rā-ĭm, [c]which *is* in
mount Ē-phră-ĭm, and said, Hear me,
thou Jĕr-ŏ-bō-ăm, and all Israel;
5 Ought ye not to know that the
LORD God of Israel [d]gave the kingdom over Israel to David for ever,
even to him and to his sons by a [2]cov-
enant of salt?
6 Yet Jĕr-ŏ-bō-ăm the son of Nē-băt,
the servant of Solomon the son of
David, is risen up, and hath [e]rebelled
against his lord.
7 And there are gathered unto him
[f]vain men, the children of Bē-lĭ-ăl, and
have strengthened themselves against
Rē-hŏ-bō-ăm the son of Solomon,
when Rē-hŏ-bō-ăm was young and
tenderhearted, and could not withstand them.
8 And now ye think to withstand the

kingdom of the LORD in the hand of
the sons of David; and ye *be* a great
multitude, and *there are* with you
golden calves, which Jĕr-ŏ-bō-ăm
[g]made you for gods.
9 Have [h]ye not cast out the priests of
the LORD, the sons of Aaron, and the
Levites, and have made you priests
after the manner of the nations of
other lands? [i]so that whosoever cometh [3]to consecrate himself with a
young bullock and seven rams, *the
same* may be a priest of *them that are*
no gods.
10 But as for us, the LORD *is* our God,
and we have not forsaken him; and
the priests, which minister unto the
LORD, *are* the sons of Aaron, and the
Levites *wait* upon *their* business:
11 And they [j]burn unto the LORD
every morning and every evening
burnt sacrifices and sweet incense:
the [k]shewbread also *set they in order*
upon the pure table; and the candlestick of gold with the lamps thereof,
[l]to burn every evening: for we keep
the charge of the LORD our God: but
ye have forsaken him.
12 And, behold, [m]God himself *is* with
us for *our* captain, [n]and his priests
with sounding trumpets to cry alarm
against you. O children of Israel,
[o]fight ye not against the LORD God of
your fathers; for ye shall not prosper.
13 ¶ But Jĕr-ŏ-bō-ăm caused an ambushment to come about behind
them: so they were before Judah, and
the ambushment *was* behind them.
14 And when Judah looked back, behold, the battle *was* before and behind: and they cried unto the LORD,
and the priests sounded with the trumpets.
15 Then the men of Judah gave a
shout: and as the men of Judah shouted, it came to pass, that God smote
[p]Jĕr-ŏ-bō-ăm and all Israel before Ă-
bī-jăh and Judah.
16 And the children of Israel fled before Judah: and God delivered them
into their hand.
17 And Ă-bī-jăh and his people slew
them with a great slaughter: so there
fell down slain of Israel five hundred
thousand chosen men.
18 Thus the children of Israel were
[4]brought under at that time, and the
children of Judah prevailed, because
[q]they relied upon the LORD God of
their fathers.
19 And Ă-bī-jăh pursued after Jĕr-
ŏ-bō-ăm, and took cities from him,
Beth-el with the towns thereof, and

[g] Hosea 8.6.
[h] ch. 11.14, 15.
[i] Ex. 29.35.
[3] to fill his hand.
[j] ch. 2.4.
[k] Lev. 24.6.
[l] Ex. 27.20, 21. Lev. 24.2,3.
[m] Deut. 20.4. Josh. 5.14. Ps. 20.7.
[n] Num. 10.8.
[o] Job 15.25, 26. Acts 5.39.
[p] Num. 32.4. ch. 14.12.
[4] humbled.
[q] 1 Chr. 5.20. ch. 16.8,9. ch. 20.20. Ps. 22.5.
[r] Josh. 15.9. John 11.54.
[s] 1 Sam. 25. 38. Eze. 24.16. Acts 12.23.
[t] 1 Ki. 14.20.
[5] Or, commentary.
[u] ch. 9.29.

CHAP. 14

[a] 1 Ki. 15.8.
[b] ch. 15.17.
[c] Ex. 34.13.
[1] statues.
[d] 1 Ki. 11.7.
[2] sun images.
[e] ch. 16.8.
[f] Josh. 15.44. Micah 1.15.
[g] Ex. 14.10. 1 Chr. 5.20. ch. 13.14. Ps. 22.5. Acts 2.21.
[h] Judg. 7.7. 1 Sam. 14.6. 2 Cor. 12.9, 10.

Jĕ-shā-năh with the towns therec
and [r]Ē-phră-ĭn with the towns therec
20 Neither did Jĕr-ŏ-bō-ăm recov
strength again in the days of Ă-bī-jă
and the LORD struck [s]him, and [t]
died.
21 ¶ But Ă-bī-jăh waxed mighty, ar
married fourteen wives, and beg
twenty and two sons, and sixte
daughters.
22 And the rest of the acts of Ă-l
jăh, and his ways, and his sayings, *a*
written in the [5]story of the proph
[u]Ĭd-dō.

CHAPTER 14

SO Ă-bī-jăh slept with his father
and they buried him in the city
David: and Ā-să [a]his son reigned
his stead. In his days the land w
quiet ten years.
2 And Ā-să did *that which was* go
and right in the eyes of the LORD h
God:
3 For he took away the altars of t
strange *gods*, and [b]the high places, ar
brake [c]down the [1]images, [d]and c
down the groves:
4 And commanded Judah to seek t
LORD God of their fathers, and to c
the law and the commandment.
5 Also he took away out of all t
cities of Judah the high places and t
[2]images: and the kingdom was qui
before him.
6 ¶ And he built fenced cities in J
dah: for the land had rest, and he ha
no war in those years; because t
LORD had given him rest.
7 Therefore he said unto Judah, L
us build these cities, and make abo
them walls, and towers, gates, ar
bars, *while* the land *is* yet before u
because we have sought the LORD o
God, we have sought *him*, and he ha
given us rest on every side. So th
built and prospered.
8 And Ā-să had an army *of men* th
bare targets and spears, out of Jud
three hundred thousand; and out
Benjamin, that bare shields and dre
bows, two hundred and foursco
thousand: all these *were* mighty m
of valour.
9 ¶ And [e]there came out again
them Zē-răh the Ē-thĭ-ō-pĭ-ăn with
host of a thousand thousand, ar
three hundred chariots; and came u
to [f]Mă-rē-shăh.
10 Then Ā-să went out against hi
and they set the battle in array in t
valley of Zĕph-ă-thăh at Mă-rē-shă
11 And Ā-să [g]cried unto the LOR
his God, and said, LORD, *it is* [h]nothi

ith thee to help, whether with many,
r with them that have no power: help
s, O LORD our God; for we rest on
ee, and [i]in thy name we go against
is multitude. O LORD, thou *art* our
od; let not [3]man prevail against thee.
12 So the LORD [j]smote the Ē-thĭ-ō-
ĭ-ăns before Ā-să, and before Judah;
nd the Ē-thĭ-ō-pĭ-ăns fled.
13 And Ā-să and the people that *were*
ith him pursued them [k]unto Gē-rär:
nd the Ē-thĭ-ō-pĭ-ăns were over-
rown, that they could not recover
emselves; for they were [4]destroyed
efore the LORD, and before his host;
nd they carried away very much
oil.
14 And they smote all the cities
ound about Gē-rär; for [l]the fear of
e LORD came upon them: and they
oiled all the cities; for there was ex-
eding much spoil in them.
15 They smote also the tents of cattle,
d carried away sheep and camels in
undance, and returned to Jerusa-
m.

CHAPTER 15

AND [a]the Spirit of God came upon
Ăz-ă-rī-ăh the son of Ō-dĕd:
And he went out [1]to meet Ā-să, and
id unto him, Hear ye me, Ā-să, and
Judah and Benjamin; The [b]LORD
with you, while ye be with him; and
ye seek him, he will be found of
u; but [d]if ye forsake him, he will
rsake you.
Now [e]for a long season Israel *hath*
en without the true God, and with-
t [f]a teaching priest, and without
w.
But [g]when they in their trouble did
rn unto the LORD God of Israel, and
ught him, he was found of them.
And [h]in those times *there was* no
ace to him that went out, nor to
m that came in, but great vexations
re upon all the inhabitants of the
untries.
And [i]nation was [2]destroyed of na-
n, and city of city: for God did vex
em with all adversity.
Be ye strong therefore, and let not
ur hands be weak: for your work
all be [j]rewarded.
And when Ā-să heard these words,
d the prophecy of Ō-dĕd the proph-
he took courage, and put away the
ominable idols out of all the land
Judah and Benjamin, and out of
e [k]cities which he had taken from
ount Ē-phră-ĭm, and renewed the
tar of the LORD, that *was* before the
rch of the LORD.

9 And he gathered all Judah and
Benjamin, and [l]the strangers with
them out of Ē-phră-ĭm and Mă-năs-
sēh, and out of Simeon: for they fell to
him out of Israel in abundance, when
they saw that the LORD his God *was*
with him.
10 So they gathered themselves together at Jerusalem in the third month,
in the fifteenth year of the reign of
Ā-să.
11 And [m]they offered unto the LORD
[4]the same time, of the spoil *which* they
had brought, seven hundred oxen and
seven thousand sheep.
12 And they [n]entered into a covenant
to seek the LORD God of their fathers
with all their heart and with all their
soul;
13 That [o]whosoever would not seek
the LORD God of Israel should [p]be put
to death, whether small or great,
whether man or woman.
14 And they sware unto the LORD
with a loud voice, and with shouting,
and with trumpets, and with cornets.
15 And all Judah rejoiced at the oath:
for they had sworn with all their heart,
and sought him with their whole desire; and he was found of them: and
the LORD gave them rest round about.
16 ¶ And also *concerning* Mā-ă-chăh
the [5]mother of Ā-să the king, he removed her from *being* queen, because
she had made an [6]idol in a grove: and
Ā-să cut down her idol, and stamped
it, and burnt *it* at the brook Kĭ-drŏn.
17 But [q]the high places were not tak-
en away out of Israel: nevertheless
the heart of Ā-să was perfect all his
days.
18 ¶ And he brought into the house
of God the things that his father had
dedicated, and that he himself had
dedicated, silver, and gold, and vessels.
19 And there was no *more* war unto
the five and thirtieth year of the reign
of Ā-să.

CHAPTER 16

IN the [1]six and thirtieth year of the
reign of Ā-să [a]Bā-ăsh-ă king of Israel came up against Judah, and built
Rā-măh, [b]to the intent that he might
let none go out or come in to Ā-să
king of Judah.
2 Then Ā-să brought out silver and
gold out of the treasures of the house
of the LORD and of the king's house,
and sent to Bĕn-hā-dăd king of Syria,
that dwelt at [2]Damascus, saying,
3 *There is* a league between me and
thee, as *there was* between my father

i 1 Sam. 17. 45. Pro. 18.10. Nah. 1.7.
3 Or, mortal man.
j ch. 13.15.
k Gen. 10.19.
4 broken. Ps. 46.1-11.
l Gen. 35.5. Ex. 15.16. Deut. 11.25. ch. 17.10.

CHAP. 15

a Num. 24.2. Judg. 3.10. 2 Sam. 23.2. ch. 20.4. 2 Pet. 1.21.
1 before Asa.
b James 4.8.
c 1 Chr. 28.9. ch. 33.12,13. Isa. 55.7,8. Jer. 29.13. Matt. 7.7.
d 1 Chr. 28.9. ch. 12.1-3. Rom. 11.1, 2. Heb. 12.25.
e Hosea 3.4.
f Lev. 10.11.
g Deut. 4.29.
h Judg. 5.6.
i Matt. 24.7.
2 beaten in pieces.
j Gen. 15.1. Ruth 2.12. Ps. 58.11. Matt. 5.12-46. Luke 6.35. Col. 3.24.
3 abominations.
k ch. 13.19.
l ch. 11.16.
m ch. 14.15.
4 in that day.
n ch. 34.31. Neh. 10.29.
o Ex. 22.20.
p Deut. 13.5, 9,15.
5 That is, grandmother.
6 horror.
q Deut. 12.7. 1 Ki. 3.2-4. 2 Ki. 12.3. ch. 14.3,5.

CHAP. 16

1 That is, from the rending of the ten tribes from Judah, over which Asa was now king.
a 1 Ki. 15.17.
b ch. 15.9.
2 Darmesek.

and thy father: behold, I have sent
thee silver and gold; go, break thy
league with Bā-ăsh-ă king of Israel,
that he may depart from me.
4 And Bĕn–hā-dăd hearkened unto
king Ā-să, and sent the captains of
[3]his armies against the cities of Israel;
and they smote Ī-jŏn, and Dan, and
Ā-bĕl–mā-ĭm, and all the store cities
of Năph-tă-lī.
5 And it came to pass, when Bā-ăsh-ă
heard *it*, that he left off building of
Rā-măh, and let his work cease.
6 Then Ā-să the king took all Judah;
and they carried away the stones of
Rā-măh, and the timber thereof,
wherewith Bā-ăsh-ă was building; and
he built therewith Gē-bă and Mizpah.
7 ¶ And at that time [c]Hă-nā-nī the
seer came to Ā-să king of Judah, and
said unto him, [d]Because thou hast relied on the king of Syria, and not relied on the LORD thy God, therefore
is the host of the king of Syria escaped
out of thine hand.
8 Were not [e]the Ē-thĭ-ō-pĭ-ăns [f]and
the Lū-bĭms [4]a huge host, with very
many chariots and horsemen? yet,
because thou didst rely on the LORD,
he delivered them into thine hand.
9 For [g]the eyes of the LORD run to
and fro throughout the whole earth,
[5]to shew himself strong in the behalf
of *them* whose heart *is* perfect toward
him. Herein thou hast [h]done foolishly: therefore from henceforth [i]thou
shalt have wars.
10 Then Ā-să was wroth with the
seer, and put [j]him in a prison house;
for *he was* in a rage with him because
of this *thing*. And Ā-să [6]oppressed
some of the people the same time.
11 ¶ And, behold, the acts of Ā-să,
first and last, lo, they *are* written in
the book of the kings of Judah and
Israel.
12 And Ā-să in the thirty and ninth
year of his reign was [k]diseased in his
feet, until his disease *was* exceeding
great: yet in his disease he [l]sought not
to the LORD, but to the physicians.
13 ¶ And Ā-să slept with his fathers,
and died in the one and fortieth year
of his reign.
14 And they buried him in his own
sepulchres, which he had [7]made for
himself in the city of David, and laid
him in the bed which was filled [m]with
sweet odours and divers kinds *of spices*
prepared by the apothecaries' art: and
they made a very great burning for
him.

3 which were his.
c 1 Ki. 16.1. ch. 19.2.
d Ps. 146.3-6. Isa. 31.1. Jer. 17.5. Eph. 1.12-13.
e ch. 14.9.
f ch. 12.3.
4 in abundance.
g ch. 6.20. Job 34.21. Pro. 5.21. Jer. 16.17. Zech. 4.10. Heb. 4.13. 1 Pet. 3.12.
5 Or, strongly to hold with them, etc.
h 1 Sam. 13.13. 1 Chr. 21.8. Jer. 5.21. Matt. 5.22. 1 Cor. 15.36.
i 1 Ki. 15.32.
j ch. 18.26. Matt. 14.3.
6 crushed.
k Deut. 28.22.
l Jer. 17.5.
7 digged.
m Gen. 50.2. Mark 16.1.

CHAP. 17

a ch. 11.11.
b ch. 15.8.
c Rom. 8.31.
1 Or, of his father, and of David.
d Luke 1.6.
e 1 Ki. 12.28.
2 gave.
f 1 Ki. 10.27. ch. 18.1.
3 That is, was encouraged.
g 1 Ki. 22.43. ch. 14.3. ch. 15.17. ch. 19.3. ch. 20.33.
h ch. 15.3.
i Lev. 10.11. ch. 35.3. Neh. 8.7. Mal. 2.7.
j Gen. 35.5. Ex. 15.15. Deut. 11.25. ch. 14.14.
4 was.
k 2 Sam. 8.2.
5 Or, palaces.

CHAPTER 17

AND Jĕ-hŏsh-ă-phăt his son reign
in his stead, and strengthen
himself against Israel.
2 And he placed [a]forces in all t
fenced cities of Judah, and set gar
sons in the land of Judah, and in t
cities of Ē-phră-ĭm, which [b]Ā-să h
father had taken.
3 And the LORD was [c]with Jĕ-hŏs
ă-phăt, because he walked in the fir
ways [1]of his father David, and soug
not unto Bā-ă-lĭm;
4 But sought to the *LORD* God of h
father, and [d]walked in his comman
ments, and not [e]after the doings
Israel.
5 Therefore the LORD established t
kingdom in his hand; and all Jud
[2]brought to Jĕ-hŏsh-ă-phăt present
[f]and he had riches and honour
abundance.
6 And his heart [3]was lifted up in t
ways of the LORD: [g]moreover he to
away the high places and groves o
of Judah.
7 ¶ Also in the third year of his rei
he sent to his princes, *even* to Bĕn
hail, and to Ō-bă-dī-ăh, and to Zĕc
ă-rī-ăh, and to Nĕth-ă-neel, and
Mī-chāi-ăh, [h]to teach in the cities
Judah.
8 And with them *he sent* Levites, *ev*
Shĕm-āi-ăh, and Nĕth-ă-nī-ăh, a
Zĕb-ă-dī-ăh, and Ăs-ă-hĕl, and Sh
mī-ră-mōth, and Jĕ-hŏn-ă-thăn, a
Ăd-ō-nī-jăh, and Tō-bī-jăh, and Tō
ăd-ō-nī-jăh, Levites; and with the
Ē-lī-shă-mă and Jĕ-hôr-ăm, priests.
9 And [i]they taught in Judah, and *h*
the book of the law of the LORD wi
them, and went about throughout
the cities of Judah, and taught t
people.
10 ¶ And [j]the fear of the LORD [4]f
upon all the kingdoms of the lan
that *were* round about Judah, so th
they made no war against Jĕ-hŏsh-
phăt.
11 Also *some* of the Philistin
brought [k]Jĕ-hŏsh-ă-phăt presents, a
tribute silver; and the Arabia
brought him flocks, seven thousa
and seven hundred rams, and sev
thousand and seven hundred he goa
12 ¶ And Jĕ-hŏsh-ă-phăt waxed gre
exceedingly; and he built in Jud
[5]castles, and cities of store.
13 And he had much business in t
cities of Judah: and the men of w
mighty men of valour, *were* in Jer
salem.
14 And these *are* the numbers

em according to the house of their
thers: Of Judah, the captains of
ousands; Ăd-́năh the chief, and with
m mighty men of valour three hun-
ed thousand.
5 And [6]next to him *was* Jē-hō-hā-́
in the captain, and with him two
indred and fourscore thousand.
6 And next him *was* Ăm-ă-sī-́ăh the
n of Zĭch-́rī, [l]who willingly offered
mself unto the LORD; and with him
o hundred thousand mighty men of
lour.
7 And of Benjamin; Ē-lī-́ă-dă a
ighty man of valour, and with him
med men with bow and shield two
indred thousand.
8 And next him *was* Jĕ-hō-́ză-băd,
d with him an hundred and four-
ore thousand ready prepared for
e war.
9 These waited on the king, beside
ose whom the king put in the fenced
ies throughout all Judah.

CHAPTER 18

NOW Jĕ-hŏsh-́ă-phăt [a]had riches
and honour in abundance, and
ined affinity with Ahab.
And [1]after [c]*certain* years he went
wn to Ahab to Să-mâr-́ĭ-ă. And
hab killed sheep and oxen for him in
undance, and for the people that *he*
d with him, and persuaded him to
up *with him* to Rā-́mŏth–gĭl-́ĕ-ăd.
And Ahab king of Israel said unto
-hŏsh-́ă-phăt king of Judah, Wilt
ou go with me to Rā-́mŏth–gĭl-́ĕ-
? And he answered him, I *am* as
ou *art*, and my people as thy people;
d *we will be* with thee in the war.
¶ And Jĕ-hŏsh-́ă-phăt said unto the
ng of Israel, [d]Inquire, I pray thee, at
e word of the LORD to day.
Therefore the king of Israel gath-
ed together of prophets four hun-
ed men, and said unto them, Shall
go to Rā-́mŏth–gĭl-́ĕ-ăd to battle,
shall I forbear? And they said, [e]Go
; for God will deliver *it* into the
ng's hand.
But Jĕ-hŏsh-́ă-phăt said, *Is there*
t here a prophet of the LORD [2]be-
les, that we might inquire of him?
And the king of Israel said unto Jĕ-
sh-́ă-phăt, *There is* yet one man, by
om we may inquire of the LORD:
t I hate him; for he never prophe-
d good unto me, but always evil:
e same *is* Mī-căi-́ăh the son of Ĭm-́lă.
d Jĕ-hŏsh-́ă-phăt said, Let not the
ng say so.
And the king of Israel called for one

of his [3]officers, and said, [4]Fetch quickly Mī-căi-́ăh the son of Ĭm-́lă.
9 And the king of Israel and Jĕ-hŏsh-́
ă-phăt king of Judah sat either of
them on his throne, clothed in *their*
robes, and they sat in a [5]void place at
the entering in of the gate of Să-mâr-́
ĭ-ă; and all the prophets prophesied
before them.
10 And Zĕd-ē-kī-́ăh the son of Chĕ-
nā-́ă-năh had made him horns of
iron, and said, Thus saith the LORD,
With these thou shalt push Syria until
[6]they be consumed.
11 And all the prophets prophesied
so, saying, Go up to Rā-́mŏth–gĭl-́ĕ-
ăd, and prosper: for the LORD shall
deliver *it* into the hand of the king.
12 And the messenger that went to
call Mī-căi-́ăh spake to him, saying,
Behold, the words of the prophets *de-*
clare good to the king [7]with one assent;
let thy word therefore, I pray thee, be
like one of theirs, and speak thou
good.
13 And Mī-căi-́ăh said, *As* the LORD
liveth, [f]even what my God saith, that
will I speak.
14 And when he was come to the
king, the king said unto him, Mī-căi-́
ăh, shall we go to Rā-́mŏth–gĭl-́ĕ-ăd to
battle, or shall I forbear? And he said,
[g]Go ye up, and prosper, and they shall
be delivered into your hand.
15 And the king said to him, How
many times shall I adjure thee that
thou say nothing but the truth to me
in the name of the LORD?
16 Then he said, I did see all Israel
scattered upon the mountains, as
sheep that have no shepherd: and the
LORD said, These have no master; let
them return *therefore* every man to
his house in peace.
17 And the king of Israel said to Jĕ-
hŏsh-́ă-phăt, Did I not tell thee *that* he
would not prophesy good unto me,
[8]but evil?
18 Again he said, Therefore hear the
word of the LORD; I [h]saw the LORD
sitting upon his throne, and all the
host of heaven standing on his right
hand and *on* his left.
19 And the LORD said, Who shall entice Ahab king of Israel, that he may
go up and fall at Rā-́mŏth–gĭl-́ĕ-ăd?
And one spake saying after this manner, and another saying after that
manner.
20 Then there came out a [i]spirit, and
stood before the LORD, and said, I
will entice him. And the LORD said
unto him, Wherewith?

6 at his hand.
l Judg. 5.2,9. 1 Chr. 29.9, 14-17. Ps. 110.3. 2 Cor. 8.12.

CHAP. 18
a Deut. 8.10, 18. 1 Sam. 2.7, 30. 1 Chr. 29.11, 12. ch. 17.5. Ps. 112.2,3, 9. Pro. 4.5,6,7, 8. Pro. 10.22. Pro. 22.4. Eccl. 5.19. 1 Tim. 4.8.
b Gen. 6.2. 2 Cor. 6.14.
1 at the end of years.
c 1 Ki. 22.2. ch. 19.2.
d 1 Sam. 23.2, 4,9. 2 Sam. 2.1. ch. 34.26. Jer. 21.2.
e Jer. 23.17. Eze. 13.3. Matt. 23.16-19.
2 yet, or, more.
3 Or, eunuchs.
4 Hasten.
5 Or, floor.
6 thou consume them.
7 with one mouth.
f Num. 22. 18,20,35. Num. 24.13. 1 Ki. 22.14. Jer. 23.8. Eze. 2.7. Micah 2.6,7. Acts 20.27. 1 Cor. 11.23. 1 Thes. 2.4.
g 1 Ki. 18.27. Amos 4.4.
8 Or, but for evil?
h Ps. 103.20. Dan. 7.9.
i Job 1.6. 2 Thes. 2.9.

And he said, I will go out, and be
[j]a lying spirit in the mouth of all his
prophets. And *the LORD* said, Thou
shalt entice *him*, and thou shalt also
prevail: go out, and do *even* so.
22 Now therefore, behold, [k]the LORD
hath put a lying spirit in the mouth of
these thy prophets, and the LORD
hath spoken evil against thee.
23 Then Zĕd-ē-kī-ăh the son of Chĕ-
nā-ă-năh came near, and [l]smote Mī-
cā-ăh upon the cheek, and said,
Which way went the Spirit of the
LORD from me to speak unto thee?
24 And Mī-cā-ăh said, Behold, thou
shalt see on that day when thou shalt
go [9]into [10]an inner chamber to hide
thyself.
25 Then the king of Israel said, Take
ye Mī-cā-ăh, and carry him back to
Amon the governor of the city, and to
Jō-ăsh the king's son;
26 And say, Thus saith the king, Put
[m]this *fellow* in the prison, and feed
him with bread of affliction and with
water of affliction, until I return in
peace.
27 And Mī-cā-ăh said, If thou certainly return in peace, *then* hath not
the LORD spoken by me. And he said,
Hearken, all ye people.
28 So the king of Israel and Jĕ-hŏsh-
ă-phăt the king of Judah went up to
Rā-mŏth-gĭl-ĕ-ăd.
29 And the king of Israel said unto
Jĕ-hŏsh-ă-phăt, [n]I will disguise myself, and will go to the battle; but put
thou on thy robes. So the king of Israel disguised himself; and they went
to the battle.
30 Now the king of Syria had commanded the captains of the chariots
that *were* with him, saying, Fight ye
not with small or great, save only with
the king of Israel.
31 And it came to pass, when the
captains of the chariots saw Jĕ-hŏsh-
ă-phăt, that they said, It *is* the king of
Israel. Therefore they compassed
[o]about him to fight: but Jĕ-hŏsh-ă-
phăt cried out, and the LORD helped
him; and God moved [p]them *to depart*
from him.
32 For it came to pass, that, when
the captains of the chariots perceived
that it was not the king of Israel, they
turned back again [11]from pursuing
him.
33 And a *certain* man drew a bow [12]at
a venture, and smote the king of Israel [13]between the joints of the harness: therefore he said to his chariot
man, Turn thine hand, that thou mayest carry me out of the host; for I a
[14]wounded.
34 And the battle increased that da
howbeit the king of Israel stayed *hir*
self up in *his* chariot against the Sy
ans until the even: and about the tin
of the sun going down he died.

CHAPTER 19

AND Jĕ-hŏsh-ă-phăt the king of J
dah returned to his house in pea
to Jerusalem.
2 And Jehu the son of [a]Hă-nā-nī t
seer went out to meet him, and sa
to king Jĕ-hŏsh-ă-phăt, Shoulde
thou help the ungodly, and [b]love the
that hate the LORD? therefore
[c]wrath upon thee from before t
LORD.
3 Nevertheless there are [d]good thin
found in thee, in that thou hast tak
away the groves out of the land, a
hast prepared [e]thine heart to se
God.
4 And Jĕ-hŏsh-ă-phăt dwelt at Jer
salem: and [1]he went out again throu
the people from Bē-er-shē-bă to mou
Ē-phră-ĭm, and brought them ba
unto the LORD God of their fathers.
5 ¶ And he [f]set judges in the la
throughout all the fenced cities of J
dah, city by city,
6 And said to the judges, Take he
what ye do: for [g]ye judge not for ma
but for the LORD, [h]who *is* with you
the judgment.
7 Wherefore now let the fear of t
LORD be upon you; take heed and
it: for [i]*there is* no iniquity with t
LORD our God, nor [j]respect of p
sons, nor taking of gifts.
8 ¶ Moreover in Jerusalem did
hŏsh-ă-phăt set [k]of the Levites, and
the priests, and of the chief of the fa
ers of Israel, for the judgment of t
LORD, and for controversies, wh
they returned to Jerusalem.
9 And he charged them, saying, Th
shall ye do [l]in the fear of the LOR
faithfully, and with a perfect hear
10 And [m]what cause soever sh
come to you of your brethren t
dwell in their cities, between blo
and blood, between law and co
mandment, statutes and judgmen
ye shall even warn them that they tr
pass not against the LORD, and
[n]wrath come [o]upon you, and up
your brethren: this do, and ye sh
not trespass.
11 And, behold, Ăm-ă-rī-ăh the c
priest *is* over you in all matters of
LORD; and Zĕb-ă-dī-ăh the son

j Hos. 4.12. Zech. 13.2. John 8.44.
k Job 12.16. Isa. 19.14. Matt. 24.24, 25. Jas. 1.13.
l Mark 14.65. Acts 23.2.
9 Or, from chamber to chamber.
10 a chamber in a chamber.
m ch. 16.10. Luke 23.2.
n 1 Sam. 28.8. Pro. 10.24.
o Pro. 13.20.
p Ps. 46.1.
11 from after him.
12 in his simplicity.
13 between the joints and between the breastplate.
14 made sick.

CHAP. 19

a 1 Sam. 9.9.
b Ps. 15.4. Pro. 1.10.
c ch. 32.25.
d ch. 12.12.
e Ezra 7.10.
1 he returned and went out.
f Deut. 16.18.
g Deut. 1.17.
h Ps. 82.1. Eccl. 5.8.
2 in the matter of judgment.
i Deut. 32.4. Rom. 9.14.
j Deut. 10.17. Job 34.19. Acts 10.34. Rom. 2.11. Gal. 2.6. Eph. 6.9. Col. 3.25. 1 Pet. 1.17.
k Deut. 16. 18. 1 Chr. 23.4. ch. 17.8.
l 2 Sam. 23.3.
m Deut. 17.8.
n Num. 16. 46.
o Eze. 3.18.

:h-mā-ĕl, the ruler of the house of
ıdah, for all the king's matters: also
ıe Levites *shall be* officers before you.
)eal courageously, and the LORD
ıall be with the good.

CHAPTER 20

T came to pass after this also, *that*
the children of Moab, and the chil-
ren of Ammon, and with them *other*
eside the Ammonites, came against
ĕ-hŏsh-ă-phăt to battle.
2 Then there came some that told Jĕ-
ŏsh-ă-phăt, saying, There cometh a
reat multitude against thee from be-
ond the sea on this side Syria; and,
ehold, they *be* in [a]Hăz-ă-zŏn–tā-
ıär, which *is* [b]Ĕn–ġē-dī.
3 And Jĕ-hŏsh-ă-phăt feared, and
et [1]himself to seek the LORD, and
roclaimed [c]a fast throughout all
udah.
4 And [d]Judah gathered themselves
ogether, to ask *help* of the LORD: even
ut of all the cities of Judah they came
o seek the LORD.
5 ¶ And Jĕ-hŏsh-ă-phăt stood in the
ongregation of Judah and Jerusalem,
n the house of the LORD, before the
ıew court,
6 And said, O LORD God of our
athers, *art* not thou [e]God in heaven?
nd [f]rulest *not* thou over all the king-
loms of the heathen? and [g]in thine
ıand *is there not* power and might, so
hat none is able to withstand thee?
7 *Art* not thou [h]our God, [2]*who* didst
lrive out the inhabitants of this land
efore thy people Israel, and gavest it
o the seed of Abraham [i]thy friend for
ver?
8 And they dwelt therein, and have
uilt thee a sanctuary therein for thy
ıame, saying,
9 If, [j]*when* evil cometh upon us, *as*
he sword, judgment, or pestilence,
r famine, we stand before this house,
nd in thy presence, (for thy name *is*
n this house,) and cry unto thee in
ur affliction, then thou wilt hear and
ıelp.
10 And now, behold, the children of
Ammon and Moab and mount Sē-ĭr,
vhom thou wouldest [k]not let Israel
nvade, when they came out of the
and of Egypt, [l]but they turned from
hem, and destroyed them not;
11 Behold, *I say, how* they reward us,
o [m]come to cast us out of thy posses-
ion, which thou hast given us to in-
ıerit.
12 O our God, wilt thou not judge
[n]them? for [o]we have no might against

3 Take courage and do.

CHAP. 20

a Gen. 14.7.
b Josh. 15.62. 1 Sam. 23. 29. Song 1.14.
1 his face.
c Judg. 20.26. 1 Sam. 7.6. Ezra 8.21-23. Esther 4.16.
d Joel 1.14.
e Deut. 4.39. Josh. 2.11. Isa. 57.15. Matt. 6.9.
f 1 Chr. 29. 11,12. Ps. 47.2. Jer. 27.5. Dan. 4.17.
g Ps. 62.11. Matt. 6.13.
h Gen. 17.7. Ex. 6.7.
2 thou.
i Isa. 41.8. Jas. 2.23.
j ch. 6.28,29.
k Deut. 2.4.
l Num. 20.21.
m Ps. 83.12.
n 1 Sam. 3.13. Ps. 46.7-11. Rev. 19.11.
o 2 Cor. 3.5.
p Ps. 25.15. Ps. 121.1. Ps. 123.1.
q Num. 11. 25. ch. 15.1.
r Ex. 14.13. Deut. 1.29. ch. 32.7.
3 ascent.
4 Or, valley.
s Ex. 14.13.
t Num. 14.9. ch. 15.2. Ps. 46.7-11. Isa. 8.10. Amos 5.14.
u Ex. 4.31.
v Isa. 7.9. Isa. 26.3. John 11.40. Rom. 8.31.
w 1 Chr. 16. 29. Ps. 29.2. Ps. 50.2.
5 praisers.
x 1 Chr. 16. 34. ch. 7.36. Ezra 3.11. Ps. 106.1.
y ch. 5.13. ch. 7.3.
6 And in the time that they, etc.
7 in singing and praise.
z Judg. 7.22. 1 Sam. 14. 20.
8 Or, they smote one another.

this great company that cometh
against us; neither know we what to
do: but [p]our eyes *are* upon thee.
13 And all Judah stood before the
LORD, with their little ones, their
wives, and their children.
14 ¶ Then upon Jă-hā-zĭ-ĕl the son
of Zĕch-ă-rī-ăh, the son of Bĕ-nâi-ăh,
the son of Jē-ī-ĕl, the son of Măt-tă-
nī-ăh, a Levite of the sons of Ā-săph,
came [q]the Spirit of the LORD in the
midst of the congregation;
15 And he said, Hearken ye, all Judah, and ye inhabitants of Jerusalem,
and thou king Jĕ-hŏsh-ă-phăt, Thus
saith the LORD unto you, Be [r]not
afraid nor dismayed by reason of this
great multitude; for the battle *is* not
yours, but God's.
16 To morrow go ye down against
them: behold, they come up by the
[3]cliff of Zīz; and ye shall find them at
the end of the [4]brook, before the wilderness of Jĕ-rû-ĕl.
17 Ye [s]shall not *need* to fight in this
battle: set yourselves, stand ye *still,*
and see the salvation of the LORD with
you, O Judah and Jerusalem: fear not,
nor be dismayed; to morrow go out
against them: for [t]the LORD *will be*
with you.
18 And Jĕ-hŏsh-ă-phăt [u]bowed his
head with *his* face to the ground: and
all Judah and the inhabitants of Jerusalem fell before the LORD, worshipping the LORD.
19 And the Levites, of the children
of the Kō-hăth-ītes, and of the children of the Kôr-hītes, stood up to
praise the LORD God of Israel with a
loud voice on high.
20 ¶ And they rose early in the morning, and went forth into the wilderness of Tĕ-kō-ă: and as they went
forth, Jĕ-hŏsh-ă-phăt stood and said,
Hear me, O Judah, and ye inhabitants
of Jerusalem; [v]Believe in the LORD
your God, so shall ye be established;
believe his prophets, so shall ye prosper.
21 And when he had consulted with
the people, he appointed singers unto
the LORD, [w]and [5]that should praise
the beauty of holiness, as they went
out before the army, and to say,
[x]Praise the LORD; for [y]his mercy *en-*
dureth for ever.
22 ¶ [6]And when they began to [7]sing
and to praise, [z]the LORD set ambush-
ments against the children of Ammon, Moab, and mount Sē-ĭr, which
were come against Judah; and [8]they
were smitten.

23 For the children of Ammon and
Moab stood up against the inhabitants of mount Sē-ĭr, utterly to slay
and destroy *them:* and when they had
made an end of the inhabitants of Sē-
ĭr, every one helped [9]to destroy another.
24 And when Judah came toward the
watch tower in the wilderness, they
looked unto the multitude, and, behold, [a]they *were* dead bodies fallen to
the earth, and [10]none escaped.
25 And when Jĕ-hŏsh-ă-phăt and his
people came to take away the spoil
of them, they found among them in
abundance both riches with the dead
bodies, and [11]precious jewels, which
they stripped off for themselves, more
than they could carry away: and they
were three days in gathering of the
spoil, it was so much.
26 ¶ And on the fourth day they assembled themselves in the valley of
[12]Bĕ-rā-chăh; for there they blessed the
LORD: therefore the name of the same
place was called, The valley of Bĕ-rā-
chăh, unto this day.
27 Then they returned, every man of
Judah and Jerusalem, and Jĕ-hŏsh-ă-
phăt in the [13]forefront of them, to go
again to Jerusalem with joy; for the
LORD had [b]made them to rejoice over
their enemies.
28 And they came to Jerusalem with
psalteries and harps and trumpets unto the house of the LORD.
29 And [c]the fear of God was on all
the kingdoms of *those* countries, when
they had heard that the LORD fought
against the enemies of Israel.
30 So the realm of Jĕ-hŏsh-ă-phăt
was quiet: for his [d]God gave him rest
round about.
31 ¶ And [e]Jĕ-hŏsh-ă-phăt reigned
over Judah: *he was* thirty and five
years old when he began to reign, and
he reigned twenty and five years in
Jerusalem. And his mother's name
was Ă-zū-băh the daughter of Shĭl-hī.
32 And he walked in the way of Ā-să
his father, and departed not from it,
doing *that which was* right in the sight
of the LORD.
33 Howbeit the high places were not
taken away: for as yet the people had
not [f]prepared their hearts unto the
God of their fathers.
34 Now the rest of the acts of Jĕ-
hŏsh-ă-phăt, first and last, behold,
they *are* written in the [14]book of Jehu
the son of Hă-nā-nī, [g]who [15]*is* mentioned in the book of the kings of
Israel.

9 for the destruction.
a Ex. 14.13. Ps. 110.6. Isa. 37.36. Jer. 33.5.
10 there was not an escaping.
11 vessels of desire.
12 That is, Blessing.
13 head.
b Neh. 12.43.
c ch. 17.10.
d ch. 15.15. Job 34.29.
e 1 Ki. 22.41.
f ch. 12.14.
14 words.
g 1 Ki. 16. 1.
15 was made to ascend.
16 At first Jehoshaphat was unwilling, 1 Ki. 22.49.
h Gen. 10.4. 1 Ki. 10.22. ch. 9.21.

CHAP. 21

1 Alone.
2 Jehoram made partner of the kingdom with his father.
a Gen. 4.8. Judg. 9.5. 1 John 3.12.
b In consort, 2 Ki. 8.17.
c 2 Ki. 8.18. ch. 18.1. Neh. 13.26. Luke 1.69, 79.
3 lamp, or, candle.
d 2 Sam. 7.12, 13. 1 Ki. 11.36. 2 Ki. 8.19. Ps. 132.11.
e Gen. 27.40. 2 Ki. 8.20. Ps. 106.39. Rev. 17.1-5.
4 hand.
f Gen. 27.40.

35 ¶ And after this did Jĕ-hŏsh-ă
phăt king of Judah join himself wit
Ā-hă-zī-ăh king of Israel, who did ver
wickedly:
36 And he [16]joined himself with hir
to make ships to go to Tarshish: an
they made the ships in Ē-zi-ŏn-gĕ
bĕr.
37 Then Ĕl-ĭ-ē-zĕr the son of Dō-dă
văh of Mă-rē-shăh prophesied agains
Jĕ-hŏsh-ă-phăt, saying, Because tho
hast joined thyself with Ā-hă-zī-ăh
the LORD hath broken thy works. An
the ships were broken, that they wer
not able to go to [h]Tarshish.

CHAPTER 21

NOW Jĕ-hŏsh-ă-phăt slept with hi
fathers, and was buried with hi
fathers in the city of David. And Jĕ
hôr-ăm his son reigned in his [1]stead
2 And he had brethren the sons o
Jĕ-hŏsh-ă-phăt, Ăz-ă-rī-ăh, and Jĕ-hi
ĕl, and Zĕch-ă-rī-ăh, and Ăz-ă-rī-ăh
and Michael, and Shĕph-ă-tī-ăh: a
these *were* the sons of Jĕ-hŏsh-ă-phă
king of Israel.
3 And their father gave them grea
gifts of silver, and of gold, and of pre
cious things, with fenced cities in Ju
dah: but the kingdom gave he to [2]Jĕ
hôr-ăm; because he *was* the firstborn
4 Now when Jĕ-hôr-ăm was risen u
to the kingdom of his father, h
strengthened himself, and [a]slew all hi
brethren with the sword, and *diver*
also of the princes of Israel.
5 ¶ Jĕ-hôr-ăm [b]*was* thirty and tw
years old when he began to reign, an
he reigned eight years in Jerusalem.
6 And he walked in the way of th
kings of Israel, like as did the hous
of Ahab: for he had the daughter o
[c]Ahab to wife: and he wrought *tha*
which was evil in the eyes of the LORD
7 Howbeit the LORD would not de
stroy the house of David, because o
the covenant that he had made wit
David, and as he promised to give
[3]light to him and to his [d]sons for ever
8 ¶ In [e]his days the Ē-dŏm-ītes revolt
ed from under the [4]dominion of Ju
dah, and made themselves a king.
9 Then Jĕ-hôr-ăm went forth wit
his princes, and all his chariots wit
him: and he rose up by night, an
smote the Ē-dŏm-ītes which compass
ed him in, and the captains of th
chariots.
10 So the [f]Ē-dŏm-ītes revolted fron
under the hand of Judah unto thi
day. The same time *also* did Lĭb-năh
revolt from under his hand; becaus

he had forsaken the LORD God of his fathers.

11 Moreover he made high places in the mountains of Judah, and caused the inhabitants of Jerusalem to [g]commit fornication, and compelled Judah *thereto.*

12 ¶ And there came a [5]writing to him from Ē-lī-jăh the prophet, saying, Thus saith the LORD God of David thy father, Because thou hast not walked in the ways of Jĕ-hŏsh-ă-phăt thy father, nor in the ways of Ā-să king of Judah,

13 But hast walked in the way of the kings of Israel, and hast made Judah and the inhabitants of Jerusalem to [h]go a whoring, like to the [i]whoredoms of the house of Ahab, and also hast slain thy brethren of thy father's house, *which were* better than thyself:

14 Behold, with [6]a great plague will the LORD smite thy people, and thy children, and thy wives, and all thy goods:

15 And thou *shalt have* great sickness by disease of thy bowels, until thy bowels fall out by reason of the sickness day by day.

16 ¶ Moreover the LORD [j]stirred up against Jĕ-hôr-ăm the spirit of the Philistines, and of the Arabians, that *were* near the Ē-thĭ-ō-pĭ-ăns:

17 And they came up into Judah, and brake into it, and [7]carried away all the substance that was found in the king's house, [k]and his sons also, and his wives; so that there was never a son left him, save [8]Jĕ-hō-hăz, the youngest of his sons.

18 ¶ And after all this the LORD smote him in his bowels with an incurable disease.

19 And it came to pass, that in process of time, after the end of two years, his bowels fell out by reason of his sickness: so he died of sore diseases. And his people made no burning for him, like the burning of his fathers.

20 Thirty and two years old was he when he began to reign, and he reigned in Jerusalem eight years, and departed [9]without being desired. Howbeit they buried him in the city of David, but not in the sepulchres of the kings.

CHAPTER 22

AND the inhabitants of Jerusalem made [a]Ā-hă-zī-ăh his youngest son king in his stead: for the band of men that came with the Arabians to the camp had slain all [b]the eldest. So Ā-hă-zī-ăh the son of Jĕ-hôr-ăm king of Judah reigned.

2 Forty [c]and two years old *was* Ā-hă-zī-ăh when he began to reign, and he reigned one year in Jerusalem. His mother's name also *was* [d]Ăth-ă-lī-ăh the daughter of Omri.

3 He also walked in the ways of the house of Ahab: for his mother was his counseller to do wickedly.

4 Wherefore he did evil in the sight of the LORD like the house of Ahab: for they were his counsellers after the death of his father to [e]his destruction.

5 ¶ He walked also after their counsel, and went [f]with Jĕ-hôr-ăm the son of Ahab king of Israel to war against Hă-zā-ĕl king of Syria at Rā-mŏth-gĭl-ĕ-ăd: and the Syrians smote Joram.

6 And [g]he returned to be healed in Jĕz-rēel because of the wounds [1]which were given him at Rā-măh, when he fought with Hă-zā-ĕl king of Syria. And [2]Ăz-ă-rī-ăh the son of Jĕ-hôr-ăm king of Judah went down to see Jĕ-hôr-ăm the son of Ahab at Jĕz-rēel, because he was sick.

7 And the [3]destruction of Ā-hă-zī-ăh [h]was of God by coming to Joram: for when he was come, [i]he went out with Jĕ-hôr-ăm against Jehu the son of Nimshi, [j]whom the LORD had anointed to cut off the house of Ahab.

8 And it came to pass, that, when Jehu was [k]executing judgment upon the house of Ahab, and found the princes of Judah, and the sons of the brethren of Ā-hă-zī-ăh, that ministered to Ā-hă-zī-ăh, he slew them.

9 And [l]he sought Ā-hă-zī-ăh: and they caught him, (for he was hid in Să-mâr-ĭ-ă,) and brought him to Jehu: and when they had slain him, they buried him: Because, said they, he *is* the son of Jĕ-hŏsh-ă-phăt, who sought the LORD with all his heart. So the house of Ā-hă-zī-ăh had no power to keep still the kingdom.

10 ¶ But when Ăth-ă-lī-ăh the mother of Ā-hă-zī-ăh saw that her son was dead, she arose and destroyed all the seed royal of the house of Judah.

11 But [4]Jē-hō-shăb-ĕ-ăth, the daughter of the king, took Jō-ăsh the son of Ā-hă-zī-ăh, and stole him from among the king's sons that were slain, and put him and his nurse in a bedchamber. So Jē-hō-shăb-ĕ-ăth, the daughter of king Jĕ-hôr-ăm, the wife of Jĕ-hoi-ă-dă the priest, (for she was the sister of Ā-hă-zī-ăh,) hid him from Ăth-ă-lī-ăh, so that she slew him not.

---

g Lev. 17.7.
5 Which was writ before his death.
h Ex. 34.15.
i 2 Ki. 9.22.
6 a great stroke.
j 2 Sam. 24.1. 1 Ki. 11.14, 23. ch. 22.1.
7 carried captive.
k ch. 24.7.
8 Or, Ahaziah, ch. 22.1. or, Azariah, ch. 22.6. He became Prorex soon after, 2 Ki. 8.25.
9 without desire.

CHAP. 22

a 2 Ki. 8.24.
b ch. 21.17.
c 2 Ki. 8.26.
d ch. 21.6.
e ch. 24.17, 18. Pro. 1.10. Pro. 19.27.
f 2 Ki. 8.28.
g 2 Ki. 9.15.
1 wherewith they wounded him.
2 Otherwise called Ahaziah, ver. 1, and Jehoahaz, ch. 21.17.
3 treading down.
h Judg. 14.4. 1 Ki. 12.15. ch. 10.15. Ps. 5.10. Amos 3.6. Acts 2.23.
i 2 Ki. 9.21.
j 1 Ki. 19.16.
k 2 Ki. 10.10, 11.
l 2 Ki. 9.27. At Megiddo in the kingdom of Samaria.
4 Jehosheba, 2 Ki. 11.2.

12 And he was with them hid in the
house of God six years: and Ăth-ă-lī′-
ăh reigned over the land.

CHAPTER 23

AND [a]in the seventh year Jĕ-hôi′-ă-
dă strengthened himself, and took
the captains of hundreds, Ăz-ă-rī′-ăh
the son of Jĕ-rō′-hăm, and Ĭsh′-mā-ĕl
the son of Jē-hō-hā′-năn, and Ăz-ă-rī′-
ăh the son of Ō′-bĕd, and Mā-ă-sêi′-ăh
the son of Ă-dâi′-ăh, and Ē-lī-shā′-phăt
the son of Zĭch′-rī, into covenant with
him.
2 And they [b]went about in Judah,
and gathered the Levites out of all the
cities of Judah, and the chief of the
fathers of Israel, and they came to
Jerusalem.
3 And all the congregation made a
covenant with the king in the house of
God. And he said unto them, Behold,
the king's son shall reign, as the LORD
hath [c]said of the sons of David.
4 This *is* the thing that ye shall do; A
third part of you [d]entering on the
sabbath, of the priests and of the Levites, *shall be* porters of the [1]doors;
5 And a third part *shall be* at the
king's house; and a third part at
the gate [e]of the foundation: and all
the people *shall be* in the courts of the
house of the LORD.
6 But let none come into the house
of the LORD, save the priests, and [f]they
that minister of the Levites; they shall
go in, for they *are* [2]holy: but all the
people shall keep the watch of the
LORD.
7 And the Levites shall compass the
king round about, every man with his
weapons in his hand; and whosoever
else cometh into the house, he shall
be put to death: but be ye with the
king when he cometh in, and when he
goeth out.
8 So the Levites and all Judah did
according to all things that Jĕ-hôi′-ă-
dă the priest had commanded, and
took every man his men that were to
come in on the sabbath, with them
that were to go *out* on the sabbath:
for Jĕ-hôi′-ă-dă the priest dismissed
not the [g]courses.
9 Moreover Jĕ-hôi′-ă-dă the priest
delivered to the captains of hundreds
spears, and bucklers, and shields, that
had been king David's, which *were* in
the house of God.
10 And he set all the people, every
man having his weapon in his hand,
from the right [3]side of the [4]temple to
the left side of the temple, along by

CHAP. 23
a 2 Ki. 11.4.
b Ps. 112.5.
c 2 Sam. 7.12. 1 Ki. 2.4. ch. 6.16. ch. 7.18. Ps. 89.29,36.
d 1 Chr. 9.25. Luke 1.8,9.
1 thresholds.
e Acts 3.2.
f 1 Chr. 23. 28,29.
2 holiness.
g 1 Chr. 24.1.
3 shoulder.
4 house.
h Ex. 25.16. Deut. 17.18. Ps. 2.10,12. Isa. 8.16,20.
5 Let the king live.
i 1 Chr. 25.8.
6 Conspiracy.
j Num. 5.2. Num. 19.14.
k Neh. 3.28.
l Gen. 9.5. ch. 22.10. Matt. 7.2.
m Deut. 5.2, 3. 2 Ki. 11.17. ch. 15.12. ch. 29.10. Ezra 10.3. Neh. 9.38.
n 2 Ki. 10.23. ch. 34.4-7.
o Deut. 13.9. 2 Ki. 11.18, 19.
p 1 Chr. 23.6, 30,31. 1 Chr. 24.1.
q Ex. 29.38. Num. 28.2.
7 by the hands of David.
r 1 Chr. 26.1.
s 2 Ki. 11.19.

the altar and the temple, by the ki
round about.
11 Then they brought out the king
son, and put upon him the crown, ar
[h]*gave him* the testimony, and ma
him king. And Jĕ-hôi′-ă-dă and h
sons anointed him, and said, [5]Go
save the king.
12 ¶ Now when Ăth-ă-lī′-ăh hea
the noise of the people running an
praising the king, she came to the pe
ple into the house of the LORD:
13 And she looked, and, behold, th
king stood at his pillar at the enterir
in, and the princes and the trumpe
by the king: and all the people of th
land rejoiced, and sounded with trun
pets, also the singers with instrumen
of musick, and [i]such as taught to sir
praise. Then Ăth-ă-lī′-ăh rent h
clothes, and said, [6]Treason, Treaso
14 Then Jĕ-hôi′-ă-dă the prie
brought out the captains of hundre
that were set over the host, and sai
unto them, Have her forth of th
ranges: and whoso followeth her, l
him be slain with the sword. For th
priest said, [j]Slay her not in the hous
of the LORD.
15 So they laid hands on her; an
when she was come to the entering
[k]the horse gate by the king's hous
they [l]slew her there.
16 ¶ And Jĕ-hôi′-ă-dă made [m]a co
enant between him, and between a
the people, and between the king, tha
they should be the LORD's people.
17 Then all the people went [n]to th
house of Bā′-ăl, and brake it down, an
brake his altars and his images i
pieces, and [o]slew Măt′-tăn the pries
of Bā′-ăl before the altars.
18 Also Jĕ-hôi′-ă-dă appointed th
offices of the house of the LORD b
the hand of the priests the Levite
whom David had [p]distributed in th
house of the LORD, to offer the burn
offerings of the LORD, as *it is* writte
in the [q]law of Moses, with rejoicin
and with singing, *as it was ordaine*
[7]by David.
19 And he set the [r]porters at th
gates of the house of the LORD, tha
none *which was* unclean in any thin
should enter in.
20 And [s]he took the captains of hun
dreds, and the nobles, and the gover
nors of the people, and all the peopl
of the land, and brought down th
king from the house of the LORD: an
they came through the high gate int
the king's house, and set the king up
on the throne of the kingdom.

1 And [t]all the people of the land re-
iced: and the city was quiet, after
at they had slain Ăth-ă-lī-ăh with
e sword.

CHAPTER 24

Ō-ĂSH [a]*was* seven years old when
he began to reign, and he reigned
forty years in Jerusalem. His
other's name also *was* Zĭ-bĭ-ăh of
ēer–shē-bă.
And Jō-ăsh [b]did *that which was*
ght in the sight of the LORD all the
ys of Jĕ-hôi-ă-dă the priest.
And Jĕ-hôi-ă-dă took for him two
ives; and he begat sons and daugh-
rs.
¶ And it came to pass after this,
at Jō-ăsh was minded [1]to repair the
ouse of the LORD.
And he gathered together the
iests and the Levites, and said to
em, Go out unto the cities of Judah,
d [c]gather of all Israel money to re-
ir the house of your God from year
year, and see that ye hasten the
atter. Howbeit the Levites hastened
not.
And [d]the king called for Jĕ-hôi-ă-
ă the chief, and said unto him, Why
st thou not required of the Levites
bring in out of Judah and out of
rusalem the collection, *according to*
e commandment of [e]Moses the ser-
nt of the LORD, and of the congrega-
on of Israel, for the [f]tabernacle of
itness?
For [g]the sons of Ăth-ă-lī-ăh, that
icked woman, had broken up the
ouse of God; and also all the dedi-
ted [h]things of the house of the LORD
d they bestow upon Bā-ă-lĭm.
And at the king's commandment
hey made a chest, and set it with-
it at the gate of the house of the
ORD.
And they made [2]a proclamation
rough Judah and Jerusalem, to
ing in to the LORD the collection
at Moses the servant of God *laid*
oon Israel in the wilderness.
0 And all the princes and all the peo-
le rejoiced, and brought in, and cast
to the chest, until they had made an
d.
1 Now it came to pass, that at what
me the chest was brought unto the
ing's office by the hand of the Le-
tes, and when [j]they saw that *there*
as much money, the king's scribe
d the high priest's officer came and
nptied the chest, and took it, and
rried it to his place again. Thus they

t 1 Sam. 11. 15. 1 Ki. 1.40. Ps. 58.10. Pro. 11.10.
CHAP. 24
a 2 Ki. 11.21.
b ch. 25.2. ch. 26.5.
1 to renew.
c ch. 29.3. ch. 34.8.
d 2 Ki. 12.7.
e Ex. 30.12, 13,14,16.
f Num. 1.50. Num. 17.7, 8. Acts 7.44.
g ch. 21.17. ch. 22.3,4. Ps. 12.8.
h 2 Ki. 12.4.
i 2 Ki. 12.9.
2 a voice. Ex. 36.6.
j 2 Ki. 12.10.
3 the healing went up upon the work, or, by their hand.
k 1 Ki. 7.50.
4 Or, pestils.
l Ex. 29.38. Heb. 7.27. 1 Pet. 1.18, 19. Rev. 5.9.
m Job 5.26.
n 1 Ki. 2.10.
o Acts 20.29.
p 1 Ki. 14.23.
q Josh. 22.20. Judg. 5.8. 2 Sam. 24.1. ch. 19.2. Hosea 5.10.
r ch. 36.15. Neh. 9.26. Jer. 7.25,26. Luke 11.47-51.
s ch. 15.1.
5 clothed.
t Num. 14.41. 1 Sam. 13. 13,14.
u Deut. 29. 25,26. ch. 15.2. Jer. 2.19.
v Matt. 23. 35. Acts 7.58.
6 in the revolution of the year.

did day by day, and gathered money
in abundance.
12 And the king and Jĕ-hôi-ă-dă
gave it to such as did the work of the
service of the house of the LORD, and
hired masons and carpenters to repair
the house of the LORD, and also such
as wrought iron and brass to mend the
house of the LORD.
13 So the workmen wrought, and
[3]the work was perfected by them, and
they set the house of God in his state,
and strengthened it.
14 And when they had finished *it*,
they brought the rest of the money before the king and Jĕ-hôi-ă-dă, [k]where-
of were made vessels for the house of
the LORD, *even* vessels to minister, and
[4]to offer *withal*, and spoons, and vessels of gold and silver. And they [l]offer-
ed burnt offerings in the house of the
LORD continually all the days of Jĕ-
hôi-ă-dă.
15 ¶ But Jĕ-hôi-ă-dă waxed old, and
was [m]full of days when he died; an
hundred and thirty years old *was he*
when he died.
16 And they buried him in [n]the city
of David among the kings, because he
had done good in Israel, both toward
God, and toward his house.
17 Now after [o]the death of Jĕ-hôi-ă-
dă came the princes of Judah, and
made obeisance to the king. Then the
king hearkened unto them.
18 And they left the house of the
LORD God of their fathers, and served
[p]groves and idols: and wrath [q]came
upon Judah and Jerusalem for this
their trespass.
19 Yet he [r]sent prophets to them, to
bring them again unto the LORD; and
they testified against them: but they
would not give ear.
20 And [s]the Spirit of God [5]came upon Zĕch-ă-rī-ăh the son of Jĕ-hôi-ă-dă
the priest, which stood above the people, and said unto them, Thus saith
God, [t]Why transgress ye the commandments of the LORD, that ye cannot prosper? [u]because ye have forsak-
en the LORD, he hath also forsaken
you.
21 And they conspired against him,
and stoned [v]him with stones at the
commandment of the king in the
court of the house of the LORD.
22 Thus Jō-ăsh the king remembered
not the kindness which Jĕ-hôi-ă-dă his
father had done to him, but slew his
son. And when he died, he said, The
LORD look upon *it*, and require *it*.
23 ¶ And it came to pass [6]at the end

of the year, *that* [w]the host of Syria came up against him: and they came to Judah and Jerusalem, and destroyed all the princes of the people from among the people, and sent all the spoil of them unto the king of [7]Damascus.

24 For the army of the Syrians came [x]with a small company of men, and the LORD [y]delivered a very great host into their hand, because they had forsaken the LORD God of their fathers. So they executed [z]judgment against Jō-ăsh.

25 And when they were departed from him, (for they left him in great diseases,) [a]his own servants conspired against him for [b]the blood of the sons of Jĕ-hoi-ă-dă the priest, and slew him on his bed, and he died: and they buried him in the city of David, but they buried him not in the sepulchres of the kings.

26 And these are they that conspired against him; [8]Zā-băd the son of Shĭm-ĕ-ăth an Ammonitess, and Jĕ-hō-ză-băd the son of [9]Shĭm-rĭth a Moabitess.

27 ¶ Now *concerning* his sons, and the greatness of [c]the burdens *laid* upon him, and the [10]repairing of the house of God, behold, they *are* written in the [11]story of the book of the kings. And Ăm-ă-zī-ăh his son reigned in his stead.

CHAPTER 25

AM-Ă-ZĪ-ĂH [a]*was* twenty and five years old *when* he began to reign, and he reigned twenty and nine years in Jerusalem. And his mother's name *was* Jĕ-hō-ăd-dăn of Jerusalem.

2 And he did *that which was* right in the sight of the LORD, [b]but not with a perfect heart.

3 ¶ Now [c]it came to pass, when the kingdom was [1]established to him, that he slew his servants that had killed the king his father.

4 But he slew not their children, but *did* as *it is* written in the law in the book of Moses, where the LORD commanded, saying, [d]The fathers shall not die for the children, neither shall the children die for the fathers, but every man shall die for his own sin.

5 ¶ Moreover Ăm-ă-zī-ăh gathered Judah together, and made them captains over thousands, and captains over hundreds, according to the houses of *their* fathers, throughout all Judah and Benjamin: and he numbered them [e]from twenty years old and above, and found them three hundred thousand choice *men*, *able* to go fo
to war, that could handle spear a
shield.

6 He hired also an hundred thousa
mighty men of valour out of Israel f
an hundred talents of silver.

7 But there came a man of God
him, saying, O king, let not the ar
of Israel go with thee; for the [f]LORD
not with Israel, *to wit*, *with* all t
children of Ē-phră-ĭm.

8 But if thou wilt go, do *it*, be stro
for the battle: God shall make th
fall before the enemy: for God ha
[g]power to help, and to cast down.

9 And Ăm-ă-zī-ăh said to the man
God, But what shall we do for t
hundred talents which I have given
the [2]army of Israel? And the man
God answered, The LORD is [h]able
give thee much more than this.

10 Then Ăm-ă-zī-ăh separated the
to wit, the army that was come to hi
out of Ē-phră-ĭm, to go [3]home agai
wherefore their anger was great
kindled against Judah, and they r
turned home [4]in great anger.

11 ¶ And Ăm-ă-zī-ăh strengthen
himself, and led forth his people, a
went to [i]the valley of salt, and smo
of the children of Sē-ĭr ten tho
sand.

12 And *other* ten thousand *left* ali
did the children of Judah carry aw
captive, and brought them unto t
top of the rock, and cast them dov
from the top of the rock, that they
were broken in pieces.

13 ¶ But [5]the soldiers of the arn
which Ăm-ă-zī-ăh sent back, that th
should not go with him to battle, f
upon the cities of Judah, from S
mâr-ī-ă even unto Bĕth-hôr-ŏn, a
smote three thousand of them, a
took much spoil.

14 ¶ Now it came to pass, after th
Ăm-ă-zī-ăh was come from the slaug
ter of the Ē-dom-ītes, that he [j]broug
the gods of the children of Sē-ĭr, a
set them up *to be* his [k]gods, and bow
down himself before them, and bur
ed incense unto them.

15 Wherefore the anger of the LOR
was kindled against Ăm-ă-zī-ăh, a
he sent unto him a prophet, which sa
unto him, Why hast thou sought aft
[l]the gods of the people, which cou
not deliver their own people out
thine hand?

16 And it came to pass, as he talk
with him, that *the king* said unto hi
Art thou made of [m]the king's counse
forbear; why shouldest thou be smi

w 2 Ki. 12.17.
7 Darmesek.
x Lev. 26.8. Deut. 32.30. Isa. 30.17.
y Lev. 26.25. Deut. 28.25.
z Isa. 10.5.
a 2 Ki. 12.20.
b Ps. 10.14.
8 Or, Jozachar.
9 Or, Shomer.
c 2 Ki. 12.18.
10 founding.
11 Or, commentary.

CHAP. 25

a 2 Ki. 14.1.
b 2 Ki. 14.4. Isa. 29.13. Hosea 10.2.
c 2 Ki. 14.5.
1 confirmed upon him.
d Deut. 24.16. 2 Ki. 14.6. Jer. 31.30.
e Num. 1.3.
f 1 Ki. 12.28. ch. 15.2. Isa. 28.1-3. Hosea 4.6, 15-19. Hosea 5.6,7, 15.
g Gen. 18.14. Judg. 7.7. 1 Sam. 14.6. 1 Chr. 29.11. ch. 14.11. ch. 20.6. Job 5.18. Ps. 20.7. Ps. 118.6. Jer. 32.17. Matt. 19.26. Rom. 8.31.
2 band.
h Deut. 8.18. ch. 1.12. Pro. 10.22. Hag. 2.8.
3 to their place.
4 in heat of anger.
i 2 Ki. 14.7.
5 the sons of the band.
j ch. 28.23.
k Ex. 20.3,5.
l Ps. 96.5. Ps. 115.3-8. Isa. 46.1,2. Jer. 10.3-5. Acts 19.26. 1 Cor. 8.4.
m ch. 16.10. Pro. 9.7,8. 2 Tim. 4.3.

ı? Then the prophet forbare, and
ıd, I know that God hath [6]determin-
to destroy thee, because thou hast
ɪne this, and hast not hearkened un-
my counsel.
7 ¶ Then [n]Ăm-ă-zī-ăh king of Judah
ok advice, and sent to Jō-ăsh, the
n of Jĕ-hō-ă-hăz, the son of Jehu,
ng of Israel, saying, Come, let us see
e another in the face.
8 And Jō-ăsh king of Israel sent to
n-ă-zī-ăh king of Judah, saying,
ıe [7]thistle that *was* in Lĕb-ă-non
nt to the cedar that *was* in Lĕb-ă-
n, saying, Give thy daughter to my
n to wife: and there passed by [8]a
ld beast that *was* in Lĕb-ă-non, and
ɔde down the thistle.
9 Thou sayest, Lo, thou hast smit-
n the Ē-dom-ites; and thine heart
teth thee up to boast: abide now at
me; why shouldest thou [o]meddle
thine hurt, that thou shouldest
ll, *even* thou, and Judah with
ee?
0 But Ăm-ă-zī-ăh would not hear;
r [p]it *came* of God, that he might deer them into the hand *of their en-*
nies, because they sought after the
ɔds of Ē-dom.
1 So Jō-ăsh the king of Israel went
; and they saw one another in the
ce, *both* he and Ăm-ă-zī-ăh king of
ıdah, at Bĕth-shē-mĕsh, which *be-*
ngeth to Judah.
2 And Judah was [9]put to the worse
efore Israel, and they fled every man
his tent.
3 And Jō-ăsh the king of Israel took
m-ă-zī-ăh king of Judah, the son of
-ăsh, the son of [q]Jĕ-hō-ă-hăz, at
ĕth-shē-mĕsh, and brought him to
rusalem, and brake down the wall of
rusalem from the gate of Ē-phră-ĭm
[10]the corner gate, four hundred cu-
ts.
:4 And *he took* all the gold and the
lver, and all the vessels that were
und in the house of God with Ō-
ĕd-ē-dom, and the treasures of the
ng's house, the [11]hostages also, and
turned to Să-mâr-ĭ-ă.
:5 ¶ And [r]Ăm-ă-zī-ăh the son of Jō-
sh king of Judah lived after the death
Jō-ăsh son of Jĕ-hō-ă-hăz king of
rael fifteen years.
6 Now the rest of the acts of Ăm-ă-
-ăh, first and last, behold, *are* they
ot written in the book of the kings of
ıdah and Israel?
:7 ¶ Now after the time that Ăm-ă-
-ăh did turn away [12]from following
ıe LORD they [13]made a conspiracy

6 counselled.
n 2 Ki. 14.8,9.
7 Or, furze bush, or, thorn.
8 a beast of the field.
o ch. 35.21. Pro. 12.15.
p 1 Ki. 12.15. ch. 22.7.
9 smitten.
q ch. 21.17. ch. 22.1,6.
10 the gate of it that looketh.
11 sons of pledge, or, power.
r 2 Ki. 14.17.
12 from after.
13 conspired a conspiracy.
14 That is, The city of David, as it is, 2 Ki. 14.20.

CHAP. 26

1 Or, Azariah.
a ch. 24.2.
b Gen. 41.15. Dan. 1.17. Dan. 2.19.
2 in the seeing of God.
c ch. 21.16. Isa. 14.29.
3 Or, in the country of Ashdod.
d 1 Chr. 5.20. ch. 14.11. Acts 26.22.
e Gen. 19.38. 1 Sam. 11.1. 2 Sam. 8.2. ch. 17.11.
4 went.
f 2 Ki. 14.13. Zech. 14.10.
5 Or, repaired.
g ch. 21.16.
6 Or, cut out many cisterns.
7 Or, fruitful fields.
8 ground.

against him in Jerusalem; and he fled
to Lā-chĭsh: but they sent to Lā-chĭsh
after him, and slew him there.
28 And they brought him upon horses, and buried him with his fathers in
the city of [14]Judah.

CHAPTER 26

THEN all the people of Judah took
[1]Ŭz-zī-ăh, who *was* sixteen years
old, and made him king in the room of
his father Ăm-ă-zī-ăh.
2 He built Ē-lōth, and restored it to
Judah, after that the king slept with
his fathers.
3 Sixteen years old *was* Ŭz-zī-ăh
when he began to reign, and he reigned fifty and two years in Jerusalem.
His mother's name also *was* Jĕc-ō-lī-
ăh of Jerusalem.
4 And he did *that which was* right in
the sight of the LORD, according to all
that his father Ăm-ă-zī-ăh did.
5 And [a]he sought God in the days of
Zĕch-ă-rī-ăh, who [b]had understanding
[2]in the visions of God: and as long as
he sought the LORD, God made him
to prosper.
6 And he went forth and [c]warred
against the Philistines, and brake
down the wall of Gath, and the wall of
Jăb-nĕh, and the wall of Ăsh-dŏd, and
built cities [3]about Ăsh-dŏd, and
among the Philistines.
7 And God helped him [d]against the
Philistines, and against the Arabians
that dwelt in Gŭr-bā-ăl, and the Mĕ-
hū-nĭms.
8 And the Ammonites [e]gave gifts
to Ŭz-zī-ăh: and his name [4]spread
abroad *even* to the entering in of
Egypt; for he strengthened *himself* exceedingly.
9 Moreover Ŭz-zī-ăh built towers in
Jerusalem at the [f]corner gate, and at
the valley gate, and at the turning *of*
the wall, and [5]fortified them.
10 Also he built towers in [g]the desert,
and [6]digged many wells: for he had
much cattle, both in the low country,
and in the plains: husbandmen *also*,
and vine dressers in the mountains,
and in [7]Carmel: for he loved [8]hus-
bandry.
11 Moreover Ŭz-zī-ăh had an host of
fighting men, that went out to war by
bands, according to the number of
their account by the hand of Jē-ī-ĕl
the scribe and Mā-ă-sē-ăh the ruler,
under the hand of Hăn-ă-nī-ăh, *one* of
the king's captains.
12 The whole number of the chief of
the fathers of the mighty men of val-

our *were* two thousand and six hundred.

13 And under their hand *was* [9]an army, three hundred thousand and seven thousand and five hundred, that made war with mighty power, to help the king against the enemy.

14 And Ŭz-zī-ăh prepared for them throughout all the host shields, and spears, and helmets, and habergeons, and bows, and [10]slings *to cast* stones.

15 And he made in Jerusalem engines, invented by cunning men, to be on the towers and upon the bulwarks, to shoot arrows and great stones withal. And his name [11]spread far abroad; for he was marvellously helped, till he was strong.

16 ¶ But [h]when he was strong, his heart was [i]lifted up to *his* destruction: for he transgressed against the LORD his God, and went [j]into the temple of the LORD to burn incense upon the altar of incense.

17 And [k]Ăz-ă-rī-ăh the priest went in after him, and with him fourscore priests of the LORD, *that were* valiant men:

18 And they [l]withstood Ŭz-zī-ăh the king, and said unto him, [m]*It appertaineth* not unto thee, Ŭz-zī-ăh, to burn incense unto the LORD, but to the [n]priests the sons of Aaron, that are consecrated to burn incense: go out of the sanctuary; for thou hast trespassed; neither *shall it be* for thine honour from the LORD God.

19 Then Ŭz-zī-ăh was wroth, and *had* a censer in his hand to burn incense: and while he was wroth with the priests, [o]the leprosy even rose up in his forehead before the priests in the house of the LORD, from beside the incense altar.

20 And Ăz-ă-rī-ăh the chief priest, and all the priests, looked upon him, and, behold, he *was* leprous in his forehead, and they thrust him out from thence; yea, himself hasted [p]also to go out, because the LORD had smitten him.

21 And [q]Ŭz-zī-ăh the king was a leper unto the day of his death, and dwelt in a [12]several house, *being* a leper; for he was cut off from the house of the LORD: and Jō-thăm his son *was* over the king's house, judging the people of the land.

22 ¶ Now the rest of the acts of Ŭz-zī-ăh, first and last, did [r]Isaiah the prophet, the son of Amoz, write.

23 So [s]Ŭz-zī-ăh slept with his fathers, and they buried him with his fath-

9 the power of an army.
10 stones of slings.
11 went forth.
h Deut. 32. 15. ch. 25.19. Hab. 2.4. Col. 2.18.
i Deut. 8.14. ch. 25.19.
j 2 Ki. 16.12, 13.
k 1 Chr. 6.10.
l ch. 19.2. Jer. 13.18. Matt. 14.4.
m Num. 16. 40.
n Ex. 30.7.
o Num. 12. 10.
p Esther 6.12.
q 2 Ki. 15.5.
12 free.
r Isa. 1.1.
s Isa. 6.1.

CHAP. 27

a 2 Ki. 15.32. Isa. 1.1. Micah 1.1.
b ch. 26.16-21. Ps. 119.120.
c 2 Ki. 15.35.
1 Or, the tower. ch. 33.14.
d ch. 20.1. Jer. 49.1-6.
2 This.
3 Or, established. 1 Sam. 2.30. ch. 12.14. Ps. 34.8. Ps. 84.5.

CHAP. 28

a 2 Ki. 16.2.
b Ex. 34.17. Lev. 19.4.
c Judg. 2.11.
1 Or, offered sacrifice.
d 2 Ki. 23.10. Jer. 7.31.
e Lev. 18.21. ch. 33.6. Micah 6.7.

ers in the field of the burial which *b*
longed to the kings; for they said, I
is a leper: and Jō-thăm his son reign
in his stead.

CHAPTER 27

JŌ-THĂM [a]*was* twenty and fi
years old when he began to reig
and he reigned sixteen years
Jerusalem. His mother's name al
was Jĕ-rû-shăh, the daughter of Z
dŏk.

2 And he did *that which was* right
the sight of the LORD, according to
that his father Ŭz-zi-ăh did: howb
[b]he entered not into the temple of t
LORD. And [c]the people did yet co
ruptly.

3 He built the high gate of the hou
of the LORD, and on the wall of [1]
phĕl he built much.

4 Moreover he built cities in t
mountains of Judah, and in the fores
he built castles and towers.

5 ¶ He [d]fought also with the king
the Ammonites, and prevailed again
them. And the children of Ammo
gave him the same year an hundr
talents of silver, and ten thousar
measures of wheat, and ten thousar
of barley. [2]So much did the children
Ammon pay unto him, both the se
ond year, and the third.

6 So Jō-thăm became mighty, b
cause he [3]prepared his ways before t
LORD his God.

7 ¶ Now the rest of the acts of J
thăm, and all his wars, and his way
lo, they *are* written in the book of t
kings of Israel and Judah.

8 He was five and twenty years o
when he began to reign, and reigne
sixteen years in Jerusalem.

9 ¶ And Jō-thăm slept with his fat
ers, and they buried him in the city
David: and Ahaz his son reigned
his stead.

CHAPTER 28

AHAZ [a]*was* twenty years old whe
he began to reign, and he reigne
sixteen years in Jerusalem: but he di
not *that which was* right in the sight
the LORD, like David his father:

2 For he walked in the ways of th
kings of Israel, and made also molte
[b]images for [c]Bā-ă-lĭm.

3 Moreover he [1]burnt incense in th
[d]valley of the son of Hĭn-nŏm, an
burnt his [e]children in the fire, afte
the abominations of the heathe
whom the LORD had cast out befor
the children of Israel.

He sacrificed also and burnt in-
nse in the high places, and on the
lls, and under every green tree.
Wherefore [f]the LORD his God de-
ered him into the hand of the king
Syria; and they [g]smote him, and
rried away a great multitude of
em captives, and brought *them* to
)amascus. And he was also delivered
to the hand of the king of Israel, who
note him with a great slaughter.
¶ For [h]Pē-kăh the son of Rĕm-ă-lī-
slew in Judah an hundred and
enty thousand in one day, *which*
ere all [3]valiant men; because they
d [i]forsaken the LORD God of their
thers.
And Zĭch-rī, a mighty man of Ē-
hră-ĭm, slew Mā-ă-sēi-ăh the king's
n, and Ăz-rī-kăm the governor of
e house, and Ĕl-kā-năh *that was*
ext to the king.
And the children of Israel carried
way captive of their [j]brethren two
undred thousand, women, sons, and
aughters, and took also away much
oil from them, and brought the
oil to Să-mâr-ī-ă.
But a prophet of the LORD was
ere, whose name *was* Ō-dĕd: and he
ent out before the host that came to
ă-mâr-ī-ă, and said unto them, Beold, [k]because the LORD God of your
thers was wroth with Judah, he hath
elivered them into your hand, and ye
ave slain them in a rage *that* reach-
th [l]up unto heaven.
10 And now ye purpose to keep un-
er the children of Judah and Jerusa-
m for [m]bondmen and bondwomen
nto you: *but are there* not with you,
ven with [n]you, sins against the LORD
our God?
11 Now hear me therefore, and de-
ver the captives again, which ye have
ken captive of your brethren: [o]for
e fierce wrath of the LORD *is* upon
ou.
12 Then certain of the heads of the
hildren of Ē-phră-ĭm, Ăz-ă-rī-ăh the
on of Jō-hā-năn, Bĕr-ē-chī-ăh the son
f Mĕ-shĭl-lĕ-mōth, and Jĕ-hĭz-kī-ăh
he son of Shăl-lŭm, and Ă-mā-să the
on of Hăd-lā-ī, stood up against
hem that came from the war,
13 And said unto them, Ye shall not
ring in the captives hither: for where-
s we have offended against the LORD
lready, ye intend to [p]add *more* to our
ins and to our trespass: for our tres-
ass is great, and *there is* fierce wrath
gainst Israel.
14 So the armed men left the cap-

f Isa. 7.1
g 2 Ki. 16.5.
2 Darmesek.
h 2 Ki. 15.27. Isa. 9.21.
3 sons of valour.
i Josh. 23.16.
4 the second to the king.
j ch. 11.4.
k Judg. 3.8. Ps. 69.26. Eze. 26.2. Zech. 1.15.
l Gen. 4.10. Ezra 9.6. Rev. 18.5.
m Lev. 25.39.
n Jer. 25.29. 1 Pet. 4.17.
o Jas. 2.13.
p Num. 32. 14. Josh. 22.17.
q 2 Ki. 6.22. Rom. 12.20.
r Deut. 34.3.
s 2 Ki. 16.7.
t Lev. 26.18.
5 a captivity.
u Josh. 15.22.
v ch. 21.2.
w Ex. 32.25. Rev. 16.15.
x 2 Ki. 15.29. Isa. 7.20.
y ch. 33.12. Ps. 50.15. Rev. 16.11.
z ch. 25.14.
6 Darmesek.
a Jer. 44.17, 18.
b ch. 29.3,7.
7 Or, to offer.
c 2 Ki. 16.19, 20. ch. 27.7-9.

tives and the spoil before the princes
and all the congregation.
15 And the men which were expressed by name rose up, and took the
captives, and with the spoil clothed all
that were naked among them, and
arrayed them, and shod them, and
[q]gave them to eat and to drink, and
anointed them, and carried all the
feeble of them upon asses, and
brought them to Jericho, the [r]city of
palm trees, to their brethren: then they
returned to Să-mâr-ī-ă.
16 ¶ At [s]that time did king Ahaz send
unto the kings of Assyria to help him.
17 For [t]again the Ē-dom-ītes had
come and smitten Judah, and carried
away [5]captives.
18 The [u]Philistines also had invaded
the cities of the low country, and of
the south of Judah, and had taken
Bĕth-shē-mĕsh, and Ăj-ă-lŏn, and Gĕ-
dē-rōth, and Shō-chō with the villages
thereof, and Tĭm-năh with the villages
thereof, Gĭm-zō also and the villages
thereof: and they dwelt there.
19 For the LORD brought Judah low
because of Ahaz king of [v]Israel; for he
made [w]Judah naked, and transgressed
sore against the LORD.
20 And [x]Tĭl-găth-pĭl-nē-sĕr king of
Assyria came unto him, and distressed
him, but strengthened him not.
21 For Ahaz took away a portion *out*
of the house of the LORD, and *out* of
the house of the king, and of the princes, and gave *it* unto the king of
Assyria: but he helped him not.
22 ¶ And in the time [y]of his distress
did he trespass yet more against the
LORD: this *is that* king Ahaz.
23 For [z]he sacrificed unto the gods of
[6]Damascus, which smote him: and he
said, Because the gods of the kings of
Syria help them, *therefore* will I sacrifice to them, that [a]they may help me.
But they were the ruin of him, and of
all Israel.
24 And Ahaz gathered together the
vessels of the house of God, and cut in
pieces the vessels of the house of God,
and [b]shut up the doors of the house
of the LORD, and he made him altars
in every corner of Jerusalem.
25 And in every several city of Judah
he made high places [7]to burn incense
unto other gods, and provoked to anger the LORD God of his fathers.
26 ¶ Now [c]the rest of his acts and of
all his ways, first and last, behold, they
are written in the book of the kings of
Judah and Israel.
27 And Ahaz slept with his fathers,

and they buried him in the city, *even* in
Jerusalem: but they brought him not
into the sepulchres of the kings of
Israel: and Hĕz-ē-kī'-ăh his son reigned in his stead.

CHAPTER 29

HĔZ-Ē-KĪ'-ĂH [a]began to reign
when he was five and twenty years
old, and he reigned nine and twenty
years in Jerusalem. And his mother's
name *was* Ă-bī'-jăh, the daughter [b]of
Zĕc͟h-ă-rī'-ăh.
2 And he did *that which was* right in
the sight of the LORD, according to all
that David his father had done.
3 ¶ He in the [c]first year of his reign,
in the first month, [d]opened the doors
of the house of the LORD, and repaired
them.
4 And he brought in the priests and
the Levites, and gathered them together into the east street,
5 And said unto them, Hear me, ye
Levites, [e]sanctify now yourselves, and
sanctify the house of the LORD God
of your fathers, and carry forth [1]the
filthiness out of the holy *place*.
6 For our fathers have trespassed,
and done *that which was* evil in the
eyes of the LORD our God, and have
forsaken him, and have turned [f]away
their faces from the habitation of the
LORD, and [2]turned *their* backs.
7 Also [g]they have shut up the doors
of the porch, and put out the lamps,
and have not burned incense nor offered burnt offerings in the holy *place* unto the God of Israel.
8 Wherefore [h]the wrath of the LORD
was upon Judah and Jerusalem, and
he hath delivered them to [3]trouble, to
astonishment, and to [i]hissing, as ye
see with your eyes.
9 For, lo, [j]our fathers have fallen by
the sword, and our sons and our
daughters and our wives *are* in captivity for this.
10 Now *it is* in mine heart to make
a [k]covenant with the LORD God of
Israel, that his fierce wrath may turn
away from us.
11 My sons, [4]be not now negligent:
for the LORD hath [l]chosen you to
stand before him, to serve him, and
that ye should minister unto him, and
[5]burn incense.
12 ¶ Then the Levites arose, Mā-
hăth the son of Ă-mā-sâi, and Jō-ĕl
the son of Ăz-ă-rī'-ăh, of the sons of
the Kō'-hăth-ītes: and of the sons of
Mĕ-râr'-ī, Kish the son of Ăb'-dī, and
Ăz-ă-rī'-ăh the son of Jĕ-hăl'-ĕ-lĕl: and

CHAP. 29
a 2 Ki. 18.1. Hosea 1.1.
b ch. 26.5.
c Pro. 8.17.
d ch. 28.24.
e 1 Chr. 15. 12. ch. 35.6. Matt. 21.12, 13. 2 Cor. 6.16.
1 That is, Idols, etc.
f Jer. 2.27. Eze. 8.16.
2 given the neck.
g 2 Ki. 16.17, 18. ch. 28.24.
h Deut. 28. 15-20.
3 commotion, Deut. 28.25.
i 1 Ki. 9.8. Jer. 18.16.
j Lev. 26.17. ch. 28.5,6,8, 17.
k ch. 15.12. ch. 23.16. Neh. 9.38.
4 Or, be not now deceived, 1 Cor. 6.9.
l Num. 3.6.
5 Or, offer sacrifice.
6 Or, in the business of the LORD, ch. 30.12.
m 1 Chr. 23. 28.
n 1 Ki. 6.23. That is, the sanctuary, and holy of holies.
o 1 Ki. 6.3.
p ch. 28.24.
q Lev. 4.3,14.
r Lev. 8.14, 15,19,24.
7 near.
s Lev. 4.15, 24.

of the Gĕr'-shŏn-ītes; Jō-'ăh the son
Zimmah, and Eden the son of Jō-'ă
13 And of the sons of Ē-li-zā'-phā
Shĭm'-rī, and Jē-ī'-ĕl: and of the so
of Ā'-săph; Zĕc͟h-ă-rī'-ăh, and Măt-
nī'-ăh:
14 And of the sons of Hē'-măn; J
hī'-ĕl, and Shĭm'-ĕ-ī: and of the sons
Jĕ-dū'-thŭn; Shĕm-âi'-ăh, and U
zī'-ĕl.
15 And they gathered their brethre
and sanctified themselves, and car
according to the commandment of t
king, [6]by the words of the LORD, [m]
cleanse the house of the LORD.
16 And the priests went into [n]the i
ner part of the house of the LORD,
cleanse *it*, and brought out all the u
cleanness that they found in the ten
ple of the LORD into the court of t
house of the LORD. And the Levit
took *it*, to carry *it* out abroad into t
brook Kī'-drŏn.
17 Now they began on the first *d*
of the first month to sanctify, and
the eighth day of the month came th
to the [o]porch of the LORD: so th
sanctified the house of the LORD
eight days; and in the sixteenth day
the first month they made an end.
18 Then they went in to Hĕz-ē-kī'-ă
the king, and said, We have cleans
all the house of the LORD, and t
altar of burnt offering, with all the ve
sels thereof, and the shewbread tabl
with all the vessels thereof.
19 Moreover all the vessels, whic
king Ahaz in his reign did [p]cast aw
in his transgression, have we prepare
and sanctified, and, behold, they *a*
before the altar of the LORD.
20 ¶ Then Hĕz-ē-kī'-ăh the king ro
early, and gathered the rulers of t
city, and went up to the house of t
LORD.
21 And they brought seven bullock
and seven rams, and seven lambs, an
seven he goats, for a sin [q]offering f
the kingdom, and for the sanctuar
and for Judah. And he commande
the priests the sons of Aaron to offe
them on the altar of the LORD.
22 So they killed the bullocks, an
the priests received the blood, an
[r]sprinkled *it* on the altar: likewis
when they had killed the rams, the
sprinkled the blood upon the altar
they killed also the lambs, and the
sprinkled the blood upon the altar.
23 And they brought [7]forth the h
goats *for* the sin offering before th
king and the congregation; and the
laid their [s]hands upon them:

24 And the priests killed them, and
hey made reconciliation with their
lood upon the altar, [t]to make an
tonement for all Israel: for the king
ommanded *that* the burnt offering
nd the sin offering *should be made* for
ll Israel.
25 And [u]he set the Levites in the
ouse of the LORD with cymbals, with
salteries, and with harps, [v]according
the commandment of David, and of
Gad the king's seer, and Nathan the
rophet: [x]for *so was* the command-
ient [8]of the LORD [9]by his prophets.
26 And the Levites stood with the
nstruments [y]of David, and the
riests with [z]the trumpets.
27 And Hĕz-ē-kī-ăh commanded to
ffer the burnt offering upon the altar.
nd [10]when the burnt offering began,
the song of the LORD began *also* with
e trumpets, and with the [11]instru-
ents *ordained* by David king of
rael.
28 And all the congregation wor-
ipped, and the [12]singers sang, and
e trumpeters sounded: *and* all *this*
ontinued until the burnt offering was
nished.
29 And when they had made an end
f offering, [b]the king and all that were
present with him bowed themselves,
nd worshipped.
30 Moreover Hĕz-ē-kī-ăh the king
nd the princes commanded the Le-
ites to sing praise unto the LORD with
e words of David, and of Ā-săph the
er. And they sang [c]praises with
ladness, and they bowed their heads
nd worshipped.
31 Then Hĕz-ē-kī-ăh answered and
id, Now ye have [14]consecrated your-
lves unto the LORD, come near and
ring sacrifices and thank offerings
nto the house of the LORD. And the
ongregation brought in sacrifices and
ank offerings; and as many as were
f a free heart burnt offerings.
32 And the number of the burnt
fferings, which the congregation
rought, was threescore and ten
ullocks, an hundred rams, *and* two
undred lambs: all these *were* for a
urnt offering to the LORD.
33 And the consecrated things *were*
x hundred oxen and three thousand
eep.
34 But the priests were too few, so
at they could not flay all the burnt
ferings: wherefore [e]their brethren
e Levites [15]did help them, till the
ork was ended, and until the *other*
riests had sanctified themselves: [f]for

t Lev. 14.20. Col. 1.20.
u 1 Chr. 16.4.
v 1 Chr. 23.5. ch. 8.14.
w 2 Sam. 24. 11.
x ch. 30.12.
8 by the hand of the LORD.
9 by the hand of.
y Num. 10. 10. ch. 12.13. Amos 6.5.
z Num. 10.8, 10. 1 Chr. 15.24.
10 in the time.
a ch. 20.21.
11 hands of instruments.
12 song.
b ch. 20.18. Rom. 14.11.
13 found.
c Ps. 32.11. Phil. 4.4.
14 Or, filled your hand, ch. 13 9.
d Lev. 7.12.
e Num. 8.15. ch. 35.11.
15 strengthened them.
f ch. 30.3.
g 1 Chr. 29. 17. Ps. 7.10.
h Ex. 29.13. Lev. 3.16.
i Gen. 35.14.
j Ps. 118.23. Acts 2.41.

CHAP. 30

a Num. 9.10.
b Ex. 12.6.
c ch. 29.34.
1 was right in the eyes of the king.
2 from the hand.
d 1 Sam. 7.3, 4. Hosea 6.1. Joel 2.13. Mal. 3.7.
e 2 Ki. 15.19, 29.
f Eze. 20.18.
g ch. 29.8.
3 harden not your necks.
h Deut. 10.16.
4 give the hand.
i ch. 29.10.

the Levites *were* more [g]upright in
heart to sanctify themselves than the
priests.
35 And also the burnt offerings *were*
in abundance, with [h]the fat of the
peace offerings, and [i]the drink offerings for *every* burnt offering. So the
service of the house of the LORD was
set in order.
36 And Hĕz-ē-kī-ăh rejoiced, and all
the people, that God had prepared the
people: for [j]the thing was *done* suddenly.

CHAPTER 30

AND Hĕz-ē-kī-ăh sent to all Israel
and Judah, and wrote letters also
to Ē-phră-ĭm and Mă-năs-sēh, that
they should come to the house of the
LORD at Jerusalem, to keep the passover unto the LORD God of Israel.
2 For the king had taken counsel,
and his princes, and all the congregation in Jerusalem, to keep the passover
in the [a]second month.
3 For they could not keep it [b]at that
time, [c]because the priests had not
sanctified themselves sufficiently,
neither had the people gathered themselves together to Jerusalem.
4 And the thing [1]pleased the king and
all the congregation.
5 So they established a decree to
make proclamation throughout all
Israel, from Bē-er-shē-bă even to Dan,
that they should come to keep the
passover unto the LORD God of Israel
at Jerusalem: for they had not done *it*
of a long *time in such sort* as it was
written.
6 So the posts went with the letters
[2]from the king and his princes throughout all Israel and Judah, and according to the commandment of the king,
saying, Ye children of Israel, [d]turn
again unto the LORD God of Abraham, Isaac, and Israel, and he will return to the remnant of you, that are
escaped out of the hand of [e]the kings
of Assyria.
7 And be not ye [f]like your fathers,
and like your brethren, which trespassed against the LORD God of their
fathers, *who* therefore gave [g]them up
to desolation, as ye see.
8 Now [3]be ye not [h]stiffnecked, as
your fathers *were*, *but* [4]yield yourselves unto the LORD, and enter into
his sanctuary, which he hath sanctified for ever: and serve the LORD your
God, [i]that the fierceness of his wrath
may turn away from you.
9 For if ye turn again unto the LORD,

your brethren and your children *shall*
find [j]compassion before them that
lead them captive, so that they shall
come again into this land: for the
LORD your God *is* gracious [k]and merciful, and will not turn away *his* face
from you, if ye [l]return unto him.
10 So the posts passed from city to
city through the country of Ē-phră-ĭm
and Mă-năs-sēh even unto Zĕ-bŭ-lŭn:
but [m]they laughed them to scorn, and
mocked them.
11 Nevertheless [n]divers of Asher and
Mă-năs-sēh and of Zĕ-bŭ-lŭn humbled themselves, and came to Jerusalem.
12 Also in Judah [o]the hand of God
was to give them one heart to do the
commandment of the king and of the
princes, [p]by the word of the LORD.
13 ¶ And there assembled at Jerusalem much people to keep the feast
of unleavened bread in the second
month, a very great congregation.
14 And they arose and took away
[q]the altars that *were* in Jerusalem, and
all the altars for incense took they
away, and cast *them* into the brook
Kĭ-drŏn.
15 Then they killed the passover on
the fourteenth *day* of the second
month: and the priests and the Levites were [r]ashamed, and sanctified
themselves, and brought in the burnt
offerings into the house of the LORD.
16 And they stood in [5]their place after
their manner, according to the law of
Moses the man of God: the priests
sprinkled the blood, *which they re-*
ceived of the hand of the Levites.
17 For *there were* many in the congregation that were not sanctified:
[s]therefore the Levites had the charge
of the killing of the passovers for every
one *that was* not clean, to sanctify
them unto the LORD.
18 For a multitude of the people,
even many of Ē-phră-ĭm, and Mă-năs-
sēh, Ĭs-să-chăr, and Zĕ-bŭ-lŭn, had
not cleansed themselves, yet [t]did they
eat the passover otherwise than it was
written. But Hĕz-ē-kī-ăh prayed for
them, saying, The good LORD pardon
every one
19 *That* [u]prepareth his heart to seek
God, the LORD God of his fathers,
though *he be* not *cleansed* according
to the purification of the sanctuary.
20 And the LORD hearkened to Hĕz-
ē-kī-ăh, and [v]healed the people.
21 And the children of Israel that
were [6]present at Jerusalem kept [w]the
feast of unleavened bread seven days

j Lev. 26.40.
k Ex. 34.6. Micah 7.18.
l Isa. 55.7.
m ch. 36.16. Neh. 2.19. Matt. 21.35. Acts 17.32.
n ch. 11.16.
o ch. 29.36. Ps. 110.3. 2 Cor. 3.5. Heb. 13.21.
p ch. 29.25.
q ch. 28.24. Isa. 2.17-21.
r ch. 29.34.
5 their standing.
s ch. 29.34.
t Ex. 12.43.
u 1 Sam. 7.3. 1 Chr. 29.18. ch. 19.3. Job 11.13.
v Ex. 15.26. Jas. 5.16.
6 found.
w Ex. 12.15. Luke 22.1,7. 1 Cor. 5.7,8.
7 instruments of strength.
8 to the heart of all, etc. Isa. 40.2.
x Deut. 33. 10. ch. 17.9. 2 Tim. 4.2.
y Ezra 10.11.
z 1 Ki. 8.65.
9 lifted up, or, offered, ch. 35.7,8.
a ch. 29.34.
b vers. 11,18.
c Num. 6.23.
10 the habitation of his holiness, Ps. 68.5.

CHAP. 31

1 found.
a 2 Ki. 18.4.
2 statues, ch. 30.14.
3 until to make an end.
b 1 Chr. 23.6.
c 1 Chr. 23. 30,31.

with great gladness: and the Levite
and the priests praised the LORD da
by day, *singing* with [7]loud instru
ments unto the LORD.
22 And Hĕz-ē-kī-ăh spake [8]comfort
ably unto all the Levites [x]that taugh
the good knowledge of the LORD: an
they did eat throughout the feast sev
en days, offering peace offerings, an
[y]making confession to the LORD Go
of their fathers.
23 And the whole assembly too
counsel to keep [z]other seven days: an
they kept *other* seven days with glad
ness.
24 For Hĕz-ē-kī-ăh, king of Juda
[9]did give to the congregation a thou
and bullocks and seven thousan
sheep; and the princes gave to the con
gregation a thousand bullocks an
ten thousand sheep: and a great num
ber of priests sanctified [a]themselves
25 And all the congregation of Ju
dah, with the priests and the Levite
and all the congregation that [b]cam
out of Israel, and the strangers th
came out of the land of Israel, and th
dwelt in Judah, rejoiced.
26 So there was great joy in Jerus
lem: for since the time of Solomon th
son of David king of Israel *there w*
not the like in Jerusalem.
27 ¶ Then the priests the Levit
arose and [c]blessed the people: an
their voice was heard, and the
prayer came *up* to [10]his holy dwellin
place, *even* unto heaven.

CHAPTER 31

NOW when all this was finishe
all Israel that were [1]present we
out to the cities of Judah, and [a]brak
the [2]images in pieces, and cut dow
the groves, and threw down the hig
places and the altars out of all Juda
and Benjamin, in Ē-phră-ĭm also an
Mă-năs-sēh, [3]until they had utter
destroyed them all. Then all the chi
dren of Israel returned, every man t
his possession, into their own cities
2 ¶ And Hĕz-ē-kī-ăh appointed th
courses [b]of the priests and the Levit
after their courses, every man accor
ing to his service, the priests and L
vites [c]for burnt offerings and for pea
offerings, to minister, and to gi
thanks, and to praise in the gates
the tents of the LORD.
3 *He appointed* also the king's po
tion of his substance for the bur
offerings, *to wit*, for the morning an
evening burnt offerings, and the bur
offerings for the sabbaths, and for th

ew moons, and for the set feasts, as *it*
written in the [d]law of the LORD.
4 Moreover he commanded the peo-
le that dwelt in Jerusalem to give the
portion of the priests and the Levites,
hat they might be encouraged in [f]the
w of the LORD.
5 ¶ And as soon as the command-
nent [4]came abroad, the children of
srael brought in abundance the [g]first-
ruits of corn, wine, and oil, and
oney, and of all the increase of the
elds; and the tithe of all *things*
rought they in abundantly.
6 And *concerning* the children of Is-
ael and Judah, that dwelt in the cities
f Judah, they also brought in the
the of oxen and sheep, and the [h]tithe
f holy things which were consecrated
nto the LORD their God, and laid
hem [6]by heaps.
7 In the third month they began to
y the foundation of the heaps, and
nished *them* in the seventh month.
8 And when Hĕz-ē-kī´ăh and the
rinces came and saw the heaps, they
lessed the LORD, and [i]his people
srael.
9 Then Hĕz-ē-kī´ăh questioned with
he priests and the Levites concerning
he heaps.
10 And Ăz-ă-rī´ăh the chief priest of
he house of Zā´dŏk answered him,
nd said, Since [j]*the people* began to
ring the offerings into the house of
he LORD, we have had enough to eat,
nd have left plenty: for the LORD
ath blessed his people; and that
hich is left *is* this great store.
11 ¶ Then Hĕz-ē-kī´ăh commanded
o prepare [7]chambers in the house of
he LORD; and they prepared *them*,
12 And brought in the offerings and
he tithes and the dedicated *things*
ithfully: over [k]which Cō-nō-nī´ăh
he Levite *was* ruler, and Shĭm´ĕ-ī his
rother *was* the next.
13 And Jĕ-hī´ĕl, and Ăz-ă-zī´ăh, and
ahath, and Ăs´ă-hĕl, and Jĕr´ī-mōth,
nd Jō´ză-băd, and Ē-lī´ĕl, and Ĭs-mă-
hī´ăh, and Mā´hăth, and Bĕ-nāi´-
h, *were* overseers [8]under the hand of
ō-nō-nī´ăh and Shĭm´ĕ-ī his brother,
t the commandment of Hĕz-ē-kī´ăh
he king, and Ăz-ă-rī´ăh the ruler of
e house of God.
14 And Kôr´ē the son of Ĭm´năh the
evite, the porter toward the east, *was*
ver the freewill offerings of God, to
istribute the oblations of the LORD,
nd the [9]most holy things.
15 And [10]next him *were* Eden, and
Mĭn-ī-ă-mĭn, and Jĕsh´ū-ă, and Shĕm-
āī´ăh, Ăm-ă-rī´ăh, and Shĕc-ă-nī´ăh,
in [l]the cities of the priests, in *their* [11]set
office, to give to their brethren by
courses, as well to the great as to the
small:
16 Beside their genealogy of males,
from three years old and upward, *even*
unto every one that entereth into the
house of the LORD, his [12]daily portion
for their service in their charges according to their courses;
17 Both to the genealogy of the
priests by the house of their fathers,
and the Levites [m]from twenty years
old and upward, in their charges by
their courses;
18 And to the genealogy of all their
little ones, their wives, and their sons,
and their daughters, through all the
congregation: for in their [13]set office
they sanctified themselves in holiness:
19 Also of the sons of Aaron the
priests, *which were* in [n]the fields of the
suburbs of their cities, in every several
city, the men that [o]were expressed by
name, to give portions to all the males
among the priests, and to all that were
reckoned by genealogies among the
Levites.
20 ¶ And thus did Hĕz-ē-kī´ăh
throughout all Judah, [p]and wrought
that which was good and right and
truth before the LORD his God.
21 And in every work that he began
in the service of the house of God, and
in the law, and in the commandments,
to seek his God, he did *it* with all his
heart, [q]and prospered.

CHAPTER 32

AFTER [a]these things, and the establishment thereof, Sĕn-năch´-
ĕr-ĭb king of Assyria came, and entered into Judah, and encamped against
the fenced cities, and thought [1]to win
them for himself.
2 And when Hĕz-ē-kī´ăh saw that
Sĕn-năch´ĕr-ĭb was come, and that [2]he
was purposed to fight against Jerusalem,
3 He took counsel with his princes
and his mighty men to stop the waters
of the fountains which *were* without
the city: and they did help him.
4 So there was gathered much people together, who stopped all the
fountains, and the brook that [3]ran
through the midst of the land, saying,
Why should the kings of Assyria
come, and find much water?
5 Also [b]he strengthened himself, and
[c]built up all the wall that was broken,
and raised *it* up to the towers, and an-

d Num. 28.1.
e Num. 18.8. 1 Cor. 9.13.
f Mal. 2.7.
4 brake forth.
g Ex. 22.29. Num. 18.12. Pro. 3.9. Eze. 20.40. Jas. 1.18.
5 Or, dates.
h Lev. 27.30. Deut. 14.28.
6 heaps, heaps.
i Gen. 14.19. Deut. 33.29. 2 Sam. 6.18. Ps. 33.12.
j Hag. 2.19. Mal. 3.10.
7 Or, storehouses.
k Neh. 13.13.
8 at the hand.
9 holiness of holinesses.
10 at his hand.
l Josh. 21.9.
11 Or, trust, 1 Chr. 9.22.
12 for the things of the day upon his day.
m 1 Chr. 23. 24,27.
13 Or, trust.
n Lev. 25.34. Num. 35.2.
o vers. 12-15.
p 1 Ki. 15.5. John 1.47.
q Deut. 29.9. Josh. 4.7. 1 Tim. 4.8.

CHAP. 32

a 2 Ki. 18.13.
1 to break them up.
2 his face was to war.
3 overflowed.
b Isa. 22.9,10.
c ch. 25.23.

other wall without, and repaired [d]Mĭl-
lō *in* the city of David, and made
[4]darts and shields in abundance.
6 And he set captains of war over the
people, and gathered them together to
him in the street of the gate of the city,
and [5]spake comfortably to them, saying,
7 Be [e]strong and courageous, [f]be not
afraid nor dismayed for the king of
Assyria, nor for all the multitude that
is with him: [g]for *there be* more with
us than with him:
8 With him *is* an [h]arm of flesh; but
[i]with us *is* the LORD our God to help
us, and to fight our battles. And the
people [6]rested themselves upon the
words of Hĕz-ē-kī-ăh king of Judah.
9 ¶ After [j]this did Sĕn-năch-ĕr-ĭb
king of Assyria send his servants to
Jerusalem, (but he *himself laid siege*
against Lā-chĭsh, and all his [7]power
with him,) unto Hĕz-ē-kī-ăh king of
Judah, and unto all Judah that *were*
at Jerusalem, saying,
10 Thus saith Sĕn-năch-ĕr-ĭb king of
Assyria, Whereon do ye trust, that ye
abide [8]in the siege in Jerusalem?
11 Doth not Hĕz-ē-kī-ăh persuade
you to give over yourselves to die by
famine and by thirst, saying, The
LORD our God shall deliver us out of
the hand of the king of Assyria?
12 Hath not the same Hĕz-ē-kī-ăh
taken away his high places and his
altars, and commanded Judah and
Jerusalem, saying, Ye shall worship
before one altar, and burn incense
upon it?
13 Know ye not what I and my fathers have done unto all the people of
other lands? [k]were the gods of the nations of those lands any ways able to
deliver their lands out of mine hand?
14 Who *was there* among all the gods
of those nations that my fathers utterly destroyed, that could deliver his
people out of mine hand, that your
God should be able to deliver you out
of mine hand?
15 Now therefore let not Hĕz-ē-kī-
ăh deceive you, nor persuade you on
this manner, neither yet believe him:
for no god of any nation or kingdom
was able to deliver his people out of
mine hand, and out of the hand of my
fathers: [l]how much less shall your
God deliver you out of mine hand?
16 And his servants spake yet *more*
against the LORD God, and against
his servant Hĕz-ē-kī-ăh.
17 He [m]wrote also letters to rail on
the LORD God of Israel, and to speak
against him, saying, As the gods o
the nations of *other* lands have not de
livered their people out of mine hand
so shall not the God of Hĕz-ē-kī-ă
deliver his people out of mine hand.
18 Then [n]they cried with a loud voic
in the Jews' speech unto the people o
Jerusalem that *were* on the wall, t
affright them, and to trouble them
that they might take the city.
19 And [o]they spake against the Go
of Jerusalem, as against the gods o
the people of the earth, *which wer*
[p]the work of the hands of man.
20 And for this *cause* Hĕz-ē-kī-ăh th
king, and the prophet Isaiah the so
of Amoz, prayed and cried to heaven
21 ¶ And the LORD sent an ange
which cut off all the mighty men o
valour, and the leaders and captain
in the camp of the king of Assyria. S
he returned with shame of face to h
own land. And when he was come int
the house of his god, they that cam
forth of his own bowels [9]slew hi
there with the sword.
22 Thus the LORD [q]saved Hĕz-ē-k
ăh and the inhabitants of Jerusale
from the hand of Sĕn-năch-ĕr-ĭb th
king of Assyria, and from the hand o
all *other*, and guided them on ever
side.
23 And many brought gifts unto th
LORD to Jerusalem, and [10]presents t
Hĕz-ē-kī-ăh king of Judah: so that h
was [r]magnified in the sight of all na
tions from thenceforth.
24 ¶ In [s]those days Hĕz-ē-kī-ăh wa
sick to the death, and prayed unto th
LORD: and he spake unto him, and h
[11]gave him a sign.
25 But Hĕz-ē-kī-ăh [t]rendered n
again according to the benefit *don*
unto him; for his [u]heart was lifted up
therefore [v]there was wrath upon him
and upon Judah and Jerusalem.
26 Notwithstanding [w]Hĕz-ē-kī-ă
humbled himself for [12]the pride of h
heart, *both* he and the inhabitants o
Jerusalem, so that the wrath of th
LORD came not upon them in [x]th
days of Hĕz-ē-kī-ăh.
27 ¶ And Hĕz-ē-kī-ăh had exceedin
much riches and honour: and he mad
himself treasuries for silver, and fo
gold, and for precious stones, and fo
spices, and for shields, and for a
manner of [13]pleasant jewels;
28 Storehouses also for the increa
of corn, and wine, and oil; and stal
for all manner of beasts, and cotes fo
flocks.
29 Moreover he provided him citie

d 2 Sam. 5.9.
4 Or, swords, or weapons.
5 spake to their heart, ch. 30.22. Isa. 40.2.
e Deut. 31.6. Josh. 1.6,7.
f ch. 20.15.
g 2 Ki. 6.16.
h Jer. 17.5. 1 John 4.4.
i Num. 14.9. Deut. 20.1, 4. ch. 13.12. Ps. 18.2. Amos 5.14. Rom. 8.31.
6 leaned.
j 2 Ki. 18.17.
7 dominion.
8 Or, in the stronghold.
k 2 Ki. 18.33-35. Ps. 115.4-8.
l Ex. 5.2. John 19.10, 11.
m 2 Ki. 19.9.
n 2 Ki. 18.28.
o Isa. 10.10.
p Deut. 4.28. Ps. 115.4. Jer. 1.16. Hos. 8.5,6.
9 made him fall.
q Ps. 18.48-50.
10 precious things, ch. 17.5.
r 1 Chr. 29. 25. ch. 1.1.
s Isa. 38.1.
11 Or, wrought a miracle for him.
t Deut. 32.6. Luke 17.17.
u Deut. 8.12-14,17. ch. 25.19. 1 Pet. 5.5,6.
v ch. 24.18.
w Jer. 26.18.
12 the lifting up.
x 2 Ki. 20.19.
13 instruments of desire.

and possessions of flocks and herds in
abundance: for God had given him
[y]substance very much.
30 This [z]same Hĕz-ē-kī´-ăh also stopped the upper watercourse of Gī´-hŏn,
and brought it straight down to the
west side of the city of David. And
Hĕz-ē-kī´-ăh prospered in all his
works.
31 ¶ Howbeit in *the business of* the
[14]ambassadors of the princes of Babylon, who sent [a]unto him to inquire of
the wonder that was *done* in the land,
God left him, to try [b]him, that he
might know all *that was* in his
heart.
32 ¶ Now the rest of the acts of Hĕz-
ē-kī´-ăh, and his [15]goodness, behold,
they *are* written in [c]the vision of Isaiah
the prophet, the son of Amoz, *and* in
the [d]book of the kings of Judah and
Israel.
33 And Hĕz-ē-kī´-ăh slept with his
fathers, and they buried him in the
[16]chiefest of the sepulchres of the sons
of David: and all Judah and the inhabitants of Jerusalem did him [e]hon-
our at his death. And Mă-năs´-sēh his
son reigned in his stead.

CHAPTER 33

MĂ-NĂS´-SĒH [a]*was* twelve years
old when he began to reign, and
he reigned fifty and five years in Jerusalem:
2 But did *that which was* evil in the
sight of the LORD, like unto the [b]ab-
ominations of the heathen, whom the
LORD had cast out before the children
of Israel.
3 ¶ For [1]he built again the high
places which Hĕz-ē-kī´-ăh his father
had [c]broken down, and he reared up
altars for Bā´-ă-lĭm, and [d]made groves,
and worshipped [e]all the host of heav-
en, and served them.
4 Also he built altars in the house of
the LORD, whereof the LORD had said,
[f]In Jerusalem shall my name be for
ever.
5 And he built altars for all the host
of heaven [g]in the two courts of the
house of the LORD.
6 And [h]he caused his children to pass
through the fire in the valley of the
son of Hĭn´-nọm: [i]also he observed
times, and used enchantments, and
used witchcraft, and dealt [j]with a
familiar spirit, and with wizards: he
wrought much evil in the sight of the
LORD, to provoke him to anger.
7 And [k]he set a carved image, the
idol which he had made, in the house

y 1 Chr. 29. 12.
z Isa. 22.9.
14 interpreters.
a Isa. 39.1.
b Gen. 22.1. John 1.12.
15 kindnesses.
c Isa. 36.1.
d 2 Ki. 18.1.
16 Or, highest.
e 1 Sam. 2.30.
CHAP. 33
a 2 Ki. 21.1.
b Lev. 18.24-30. ch. 28.3.
1 he returned and built.
c 2 Ki. 18.4. ch. 31.1.
d Deut. 16. 21.
e Deut. 4.19. Zeph. 1.5.
f Deut. 12.11. 1 Ki. 8.29.
g ch. 4.9.
h Lev. 18.21. ch. 28.3.
i Deut. 18.10.
j 2 Ki. 21.6.
k 2 Ki. 21.7.
l Ps. 132.14.
m 2 Sam. 7. 10.
n Neh. 9.29.
o Deut. 28. 36. Job 36.8.
2 which were the king's.
p Ps. 107.10, 11.
3 Or, chains.
q Deut. 4.30, 31. Luke 15.16-18.
r Ex. 10.3. ch. 32.26. 1 Pet. 5.6.
s 1 Chr. 5.20. Ezra 8.23. Lam. 3.55, 56.
t Ps. 9.16. Dan. 4.25.
u 1 Ki. 1.33.
v ch. 27.3.
4 Or, the tower.
w Lev. 7.12.
x 1 Ki. 22.43. ch. 15.17. ch. 32.12.

of God, of which God had said to
David and to Solomon his son, In
[l]this house, and in Jerusalem, which
I have chosen before all the tribes of
Israel, will I put my name for ever:
8 Neither [m]will I any more remove
the foot of Israel from out of the land
which I have appointed for your fathers; so that they will take heed to do
all that I have commanded them, according to the whole law and the statutes and the ordinances by the hand
of Moses.
9 So Mă-năs´-sēh made Judah and
the inhabitants of Jerusalem to err,
and to do worse than the heathen,
whom the LORD had destroyed before the children of Israel.
10 And the [n]LORD spake to Mă-năs´-
sēh, and to his people: but they would
not hearken.
11 ¶ Wherefore [o]the LORD brought
upon them the captains of the host [2]of
the king of Assyria, which took Mă-
năs´-sēh among the thorns, and [p]bound
him with [3]fetters, and carried him to
Babylon.
12 And when [q]he was in affliction, he
besought the LORD his God, and
[r]humbled himself greatly before the
God of his fathers,
13 And prayed unto him: and he was
intreated [s]of him, and heard his supplication, and brought him again to
Jerusalem into his kingdom. Then
Mă-năs´-sēh [t]knew that the LORD he
was God.
14 Now after this he built a wall
without the city of David, on the west
side [u]of Gī´-hŏn, in the valley, even to
the entering in at the fish gate, and
compassed [v]about [4]Ō´-phĕl, and raised
it up a very great height, and put captains of war in all the fenced cities of
Judah.
15 And he took away the strange
gods, and the idol out of the house of
the LORD, and all the altars that he
had built in the mount of the house of
the LORD, and in Jerusalem, and cast
them out of the city.
16 And he repaired the altar of the
LORD, and sacrificed thereon peace
offerings and thank [w]offerings, and
commanded Judah to serve the LORD
God of Israel.
17 Nevertheless [x]the people did sacrifice still in the high places, *yet* unto
the LORD their God only.
18 ¶ Now the rest of the acts of Mă-
năs´-sēh, and his prayer unto his
God, and the words of the seers
that spake to him in the name of the

LORD God of Israel, behold, they *are written* in the book of the kings of Israel.

19 His prayer also, and *how God* was intreated of him, and all his sin, and his trespass, and the places wherein he built high places, and set up groves and graven images, before he was humbled: behold, they *are* written among the sayings of [5]the seers.

20 ¶ So Mă-năs´-sēh slept with his fathers, and they buried him in his own house: and Amon his son reigned in his stead.

21 ¶ Amon *was* two and twenty years old when he began to reign, and reigned two years in Jerusalem.

22 But he did *that which was* evil in the sight of the LORD, as did Mă-năs´-sēh his father: for Amon sacrificed unto all the carved images which Mă-năs´-sēh his father had made, and served them;

23 And humbled not himself before the LORD, as Mă-năs´-sēh his father had humbled himself; but Amon [6]trespassed more and more.

24 And [y]his servants conspired against him, and slew him in his own house.

25 ¶ But the people of the land slew all of them that had conspired against king Amon; and the people of the land made Jō-sī´-ăh his son king in his stead.

CHAPTER 34

JŌ-SĪ´-ĂH [a]*was* eight years old when he began to reign, and he reigned in Jerusalem one and thirty years.

2 And he did *that which was* right in the sight of the LORD, and walked in the ways of David his father, and declined *neither* to the right hand, nor to the left.

3 ¶ For in the eighth year of his reign, while he was yet [b]young, he began to seek [c]after the God of David his father: and in the twelfth year he began [d]to purge Judah and Jerusalem [e]from the high places, and the groves, and the carved images, and the molten images.

4 And [f]they brake down the altars of Bā´-ă-lĭm in his presence; and the [1]images, that *were* on high above them, he cut down; and the groves, and the carved images, and the molten images, he brake in pieces, and made dust *of them*, and [g]strowed *it* upon the [2]graves of them that had sacrificed unto them.

5 And he [h]burnt the bones of the priests upon their altars, and cleansed Judah and Jerusalem.

6 And *so did he* in the cities of Mă-năs´-sēh, and Ē´-phră-ĭm, and Simeon, even unto Năph´-tă-lī, with their [3]mattocks round about.

7 And when he had broken down the altars and the groves, and had beaten the [i]graven images [4]into powder, and cut down all the idols throughout all the land of Israel, he returned to Jerusalem.

8 ¶ Now [j]in the eighteenth year of his reign, when he had purged the land, and the house, he sent Shā´-phăn the son of Ăz-ă-lī´-ăh, and Mā-ă-sēi´-ăh the governor of the city, and Jō´-ăh the son of Jō´-ă-hăz the recorder, to repair the house of the LORD his God.

9 And when they came to Hĭl-kī´-ăh the high priest, they delivered [k]the money that was brought into the house of God, which the Levites that kept the doors had gathered of the hand of Mă-năs´-sēh and Ē´-phră-ĭm, and of all the remnant of Israel, and of all Judah and Benjamin; and they returned to Jerusalem.

10 And they put *it* in the hand of the workmen that had the oversight of the house of the LORD, and they gave it to the workmen that wrought in the house of the LORD, to repair and amend the house:

11 Even to the artificers and builders gave they *it*, to buy hewn stones, and timber for couplings, and [5]to floor the houses which the kings of Judah had destroyed.

12 And the men did the [l]work faithfully: and the overseers of them *were* Jā´-hăth and Ō-bă-dī´-ăh, the Levites, of the sons of Mĕ-rār´-ī; and Zĕch-ă-rī´-ăh and Mĕ-shŭl´-lăm, of the sons of the Kō´-hăth-ītes, to set *it* forward; and *other of* the Levites, all that could skill of instruments of musick.

13 Also *they were* over the bearers of burdens, and *were* overseers of all that wrought the work in any manner of service: [m]and of the Levites *there were* scribes, and officers, and porters.

14 ¶ And when they brought out the money that was brought into the house of the LORD, Hĭl-kī´-ăh the priest [n]found a book of the law of the LORD *given* [6]by Moses.

15 And Hĭl-kī´-ăh answered and said to Shā´-phăn the scribe, I have found the book of the law in the house of the LORD. And Hĭl-kī´-ăh delivered the book to Shā´-phăn.

5 Or, Hosai.
6 multiplied trespass, 2 Tim. 3.13.
y 2 Ki. 21.23, 24. ch. 24.25, 26. ch. 25.27, 28. Ps. 55.23.

CHAP. 34
a 1 Ki. 3.7-9. 1 Chr. 3.14, 15. ch. 35.25.
b 1 Sam. 1.24. Ps. 119.9. Pro. 8.17. Eccl. 12.1. 2 Tim. 3.15.
c ch. 15.2.
d 1 Ki. 13.2.
e ch. 33.17, 22.
f Lev. 26.30.
1 Or, sun images.
g Ex. 32.20.
2 face of the graves.
h 1 Ki. 13.2.
3 Or, mauls.
i Deut. 9.21.
4 to make powder.
j 2 Ki. 22.3.
k 2 Ki. 12.4.
5 Or, to rafter.
l 2 Ki. 12.15. Neh. 7.2. Pro. 28.20. 1 Cor. 4.2.
m 1 Chr. 23. 4, 5. Jer. 8.8. Matt. 26.3.
n Deut. 31. 24-26.
6 by the hand of.

16 And Shā-phăn carried the book to
the king, and brought the king word
back again, saying, All that was
committed [7]to thy servants, they
do *it*.
17 And they have [8]gathered together
the money that was found in the house
of the LORD, and have delivered it into
the hand of the overseers, and to the
hand of the workmen.
18 Then Shā-phăn the scribe told the
king, saying, Hĭl-kī-ăh the priest hath
given me a book. And Shā-phăn read
[9]it before the king.
19 And it came to pass, when the king
had heard the [o]words of the law, that
he [p]rent his clothes.
20 And the king commanded Hĭl-kī-
ăh, and Ă-hī-kăm the son of Shā-
phăn, and [10]Abdon the son of Mī-căh,
and Shā-phăn the scribe, and Ă-sāi-ăh
a servant of the king's, saying,
21 Go, inquire of the LORD for me,
and for them that are [q]left in Israel and
in Judah, concerning the words of the
book that is found: for great *is* the
wrath of the LORD that is poured
out upon us, because our fathers
have not kept the word of the LORD,
to do after all that is written in this
book.
22 And Hĭl-kī-ăh, and *they* that the
king *had appointed*, went to Hŭl-dăh
the [r]prophetess, the wife of Shăl-lŭm
the son of Tĭk-văth, [s]the son of [11]Hăš-
răh, keeper of the [12]wardrobe; (now
she dwelt in Jerusalem [13]in the col-
lege:) and they spake to her to that
effect.
23 ¶ And she answered them, Thus
saith the LORD God of Israel, Tell ye
the man that sent you to me,
24 Thus saith the LORD, Behold, I
[t]will bring evil upon this place, and
upon the inhabitants thereof, *even* all
the curses that are written in the book
which they have read before the king
of Judah:
25 Because they have forsaken me,
and have burned incense unto other
gods, that they might provoke me to
anger with all the works of their
hands; therefore my wrath shall be
poured out upon this place, and shall
not be quenched.
26 And as for the king of Judah, who
sent you to inquire of the LORD, so
shall ye say unto him, Thus saith the
LORD God of Israel *concerning* the
words which thou hast heard;
27 Because thine heart was [u]tender,
and thou didst humble thyself before
God, when thou heardest his words
against this place, and against the inhabitants thereof, and humbledst thyself before me, and didst rend thy
clothes, and weep before me; I have
even heard [v]*thee* also, saith the LORD.
28 Behold, I will gather thee to thy
fathers, and thou shalt be gathered to
thy grave in peace, neither shall thine
eyes see all the evil that I will bring
upon this place, and upon the inhabitants of the same. So they brought
the king word again.
29 ¶ Then [w]the king sent and gathered together all the elders of Judah and
Jerusalem.
30 And the king went up into the
house of the LORD, and all the men of
Judah, and the inhabitants of Jerusalem, and the priests, and the Levites,
and all the people, [14]great and small:
and he read in their ears all the words
of the book of the covenant that was
found in the house of the LORD.
31 And the king stood [x]in his place,
and made a covenant before the LORD,
to walk after the LORD, and to keep
his commandments, and his testimonies, and his statutes, with all his heart,
and with all his soul, to perform the
words of the covenant which are written in this book.
32 And he caused all that were [15]pre-
sent in Jerusalem and Benjamin to
stand *to it*. And the inhabitants of
Jerusalem did according to the covenant of God, the God of their
fathers.
33 And Jō-sī-ăh took away all the
abominations [y]out of all the countries
that *pertained* to the children of Israel, and made all that were present in
Israel to serve, *even* to serve the LORD
their God. [z]*And* all his days they departed not [16]from following the LORD,
the God of their fathers.

CHAPTER 35

MOREOVER [a]Jō-sī-ăh kept a
passover unto the LORD in Jerusalem: and they killed the passover on
the [b]fourteenth *day* of the first month.
2 And he set the priests in [c]their
charges, and [d]encouraged them to the
service of the house of the LORD,
3 And said unto the Levites [e]that
taught all Israel, which were holy unto
the LORD, [f]Put the holy ark in [g]the
house which Solomon the son of
David king of Israel did build; [h]*it shall*
not *be* a burden upon *your* shoulders:
serve now the LORD your God, and
his people Israel,
4 And prepare *yourselves* by [i]the

7 to the hand of.
8 poured out, or, melted.
9 in it.
Deut. 17.19. Josh. 1.8.
o Deut. 28.1-68. Rom. 7.7-14. Gal. 3.10-13.
p Gen. 39.34. Neh. 8.9. Ps. 119.120. Joel 2.13. Hab. 3.16.
10 Or, Achbor, 2 Ki. 22.12.
q 2 Ki. 17.6.
r Ex. 15.20. Judg. 4.4. Acts 21.9.
s 2 Ki. 22.14.
11 Or, Harhas.
12 garments.
13 Or, in the school, or, in the second part.
t Josh. 23.16. ch. 36.6,21. Jer. 25.9. Zech. 1.6.
u Ps. 51.17.
v Ps. 86.5.
w 2 Ki. 23.1.
14 from great even to small.
x 2 Ki. 11.14.
15 found.
y 1 Ki. 11.5.
z Jer. 3.10.
16 from after.

CHAP. 35

a 2 Ki. 23.21.
b Ex. 12.6.
c ch. 23.18. Ezra 6.18.
d 1 Chr. 22.19.
e Deut. 33.10.
f ch. 34.14.
g ch. 5.7.
h 1 Chr. 23.26.
i 1 Chr. 9.10.

houses of your fathers, after your courses, according to the [j]writing of David king of Israel, and according to the [k]writing of Solomon his son.

5 And [l]stand in the holy *place* according to the divisions of [1]the families of the fathers of your brethren [2]the people, and *after* the division of the families of the Levites.

6 So kill the passover, [m]and sanctify yourselves, and prepare your brethren, that *they* may do according to the word of the LORD by the hand of Moses.

7 And Jō-sī-ăh [3]gave to the people, of the flock, lambs and kids, all for the passover offerings, for all that were present, to the number of thirty thousand, and three thousand bullocks: these *were* of the king's substance.

8 And his princes [4]gave willingly unto the people, to the priests, and to the Levites: Hĭl-kī-ăh and Zĕch-ă-rī-ăh and Jĕ-hī-ĕl, rulers of the house of God, gave unto the priests for the passover offerings two thousand and six hundred *small cattle*, and three hundred oxen.

9 Cō-nă-nī-ăh also, and Shĕm-âi-ăh and Nĕth-ă-neel, his brethren, and Hăsh-ă-bī-ăh and Jē-ī-ĕl and Jō-ză-băd, chief of the Levites, [5]gave unto the Levites for passover offerings five thousand *small cattle*, and five hundred oxen.

10 So the service was prepared, and the priests [n]stood in their place, and the Levites in their courses, according to the king's commandment.

11 And they killed the passover, and the priests [o]sprinkled *the blood* from their hands, and the Levites flayed [p]*them*.

12 And they removed the burnt offerings, that they might give according to the divisions of the families of the people, to offer unto the LORD, as *it is* written [q]in the book of Moses. And so *did they* with the oxen.

13 And they [r]roasted the passover with fire accordingly to the ordinance: but the *other* holy *offerings* sod [s]they in pots, and in caldrons, and in pans, and [6]divided *them* speedily among all the people.

14 And afterward they made ready for themselves, and for the priests: because the priests the sons of Aaron *were busied* in offering of burnt offerings and the fat until night; therefore the Levites prepared for themselves, and for the priests the sons of Aaron.

15 And the singers the sons of Ā-săph *were* in their [7]place, according to the [t]commandment of David, and Ā-săph, and Hē-măn, and Jĕ-dū-thŭn the king's seer; and the porters [u]*waited* at every gate; they might not depart from their service; for their brethren the Levites prepared for them.

16 So all the service of the LORD was prepared the same day, to keep the passover, and to offer burnt offerings upon the altar of the LORD, according to the commandment of king Jō-sī-ăh.

17 And the children of Israel that were [8]present kept the passover at that time, and the feast [v]of unleavened bread seven days.

18 And [w]there was no passover like to that kept in Israel from the days of Samuel the prophet; neither did all the kings of Israel keep such a passover as Jō-sī-ăh kept, and the priests, and the Levites, and all Judah and Israel that were present, and the inhabitants of Jerusalem.

19 In the eighteenth year of the reign of Jō-sī-ăh was this passover kept.

20 ¶ After [x]all this, when Jō-sī-ăh had prepared the [9]temple, Nē-chō king of Egypt came up to fight against Cär-chē-mĭsh by Eû-phrā-tēs: and Jō-sī-ăh went out against him.

21 But he sent ambassadors to him, saying, What have I to do with thee, thou king of Judah? *I come* not against thee this day, but against [10]the house wherewith I have war: for [y]God commanded me to make haste: forbear thee from *meddling with* God, who *is* with me, that he destroy thee not.

22 Nevertheless Jō-sī-ăh would not turn his face from him, but [z]disguised himself, that he might fight with him, and hearkened not unto the words of Nē-chō from the mouth of God, and came to fight in the valley of Mĕ-gĭd-dō.

23 And the archers shot at king Jō-sī-ăh; and the king said to his servants, Have me away; for I am sore [11]wounded.

24 His [a]servants therefore took him out of that chariot, and put him in the second chariot that he had; and they brought him to Jerusalem, and he died, and was buried [12]in *one of* the sepulchres of his fathers. And [b]all Judah and Jerusalem mourned for Jō-sī-ăh.

25 ¶ And Jeremiah [c]lamented for Jō-sī-ăh: and [d]all the singing men and the

j 1 Chr. 23.1.
k ch. 8.14.
l Ps. 134.1.
1 the house of the fathers.
2 the sons of the people.
m Ex. 19.10. ch. 29.5. Job. 1.5. Ps. 51.7. Heb. 9.13, 14.
3 offered.
4 offered, 2 Cor. 9.7.
5 offered.
n Ezra 6.18.
o Lev. 1.5,6. ch. 29.22.
p ch. 29.34.
q Lev. 3.3.
r Ex. 12.8. Deut. 16.7.
s 1 Sam. 2.13, 14,15.
6 made them run.
7 station.
t 1 Chr. 25.1.
u 1 Chr. 9.17, 18. 1 Chr. 26.14.
8 found.
v Ex. 12.15. ch. 30.21. 1 Cor. 5.7,8.
w 2 Ki. 23.22, 23.
x 2 Ki. 23.29. Jer. 46.2.
9 house.
10 the house of my war.
y 2 Ki. 18.25. Dan. 4.35.
z 1 Ki. 14.2. ch. 18.29.
11 made sick, 1 Ki. 22.34.
a 2 Ki. 23.30.
12 Or, among the sepulchres.
b Zech. 12.11.
c Jer. 22.10. Lam. 4.20.
d Eccl. 12.5. Jer. 9.17. Matt. 9.23.

singing women spake of Jō-sī´-ăh in
their lamentations to this day, [e]and
made them an ordinance in Israel:
and, behold, they *are* written in the
lamentations.
26 Now the rest of the acts of Jō-sī´-
ăh, and his [13]goodness, according to
that which was written in the law of
the LORD,
27 And his deeds, first and last, behold, they *are* written in the book of
the kings of Israel and Judah.

CHAPTER 36

THEN [a]the people of the land took
Jĕ-hō´-ă-hăz the son of Jō-sī´-ăh,
and made him king in his father's
stead in Jerusalem.
2 Jĕ-hō´-ă-hăz *was* twenty and three
years old when he began to reign, and
he reigned three months in Jerusalem.
3 And the king of Egypt [1]put him
down at Jerusalem, and [2]condemned
the land in an hundred talents of silver and a talent of gold.
4 And the king of Egypt made Ē-lī´-ă-
kĭm his brother king over Judah and
Jerusalem, and turned his name to Jĕ-
hoi´-ă-kĭm. And Nē´-chō took [b]Jĕ-hō´-
ă-hăz his brother, and carried him to
Egypt.
5 ¶ Jĕ-hoi´-ă-kĭm [c]*was* twenty and
five years old when he began to reign,
and he reigned eleven years in Jerusalem: and he did *that which was* evil
in the sight of the LORD his God.
6 Against [d]him came up Nĕb-ū-chăd-
nĕz´-zär king of Babylon, and bound
him in [3]fetters, to [e]carry him to Babylon.
7 Nĕb-ū-chăd-nĕz´-zär [f]also carried
of the vessels of the house of the LORD
to Babylon, and put them in his temple
at Babylon.
8 Now the rest of the acts of Jĕ-hoi´-
ă-kĭm, and his abominations which he
did, and that which was found in him,
behold, they *are* written in the book
of the kings of Israel and Judah: and
[4]Jĕ-hoi´-ă-chĭn his son reigned in his
stead.
9 ¶ Jĕ-hoi´-ă-chĭn [g]*was* eight years old
when he began to reign, and he reigned three months and ten days in Jerusalem: and he did *that which was* evil
in the sight of the LORD.
10 And [5]when the year was expired,
king Nĕb-ū-chăd-nĕz´-zär sent, and
brought him to Babylon, with [h]the
goodly vessels of the house of the
LORD, and made Zĕd-ē-kī´-ăh his brother king over Judah and Jerusalem.

e Jer. 22.20.
13 kindnesses, Ps. 112.6. Pro. 22.1.
CHAP. 36
a 2 Ki. 23.30. ch. 33.25.
1 removed him.
2 mulcted.
b Eze. 19.3.
c 2 Ki. 23.36, 37.
d 2 Ki. 24.1. Dan. 1.1,2.
3 Or, chains. Foretold, Hab. 1.6,10.
e 2 Ki. 24.6.
f Dan. 1.1.
4 Jeconiah, 1 Chr. 3.16.
g 2 Ki. 24.8.
5 at the return of the year.
h Dan. 1.1.
6 vessels of desire.
i 2 Ki. 24.18. Jer. 52.1.
j Eze. 17.15.
k 2 Ki. 17.14. Neh. 8.16, 17.
l Jer. 25.3.
7 by the hand of his messengers.
8 That is, continually and carefully.
m Hosea 11. 8.
n ch. 30.10. Ps. 35.16.
o Pro. 1.25. Luke 16.14.
p Jer. 32.3.
q Ps. 74.1.
9 healing.
r Deut. 28.49. Ezra 9.7.
s 2 Ki. 25.13.
t 2 Ki. 25.9. Ps. 74.6,7.
10 the remainder from the sword.
u Jer. 27.7.
v Jer. 25.9.
w Lev. 26.34.
x Lev. 25.4,5.
y Jer. 29.10.

11 ¶ Zĕd-ē-kī´-ăh [i]*was* one and twenty years old when he began to reign,
and reigned eleven years in Jerusalem.
12 And he did *that which was* evil in
the sight of the LORD his God, *and*
humbled not himself before Jeremiah
the prophet *speaking* from the mouth
of the LORD.
13 And [j]he also rebelled against king
Nĕb-ū-chăd-nĕz´-zär, who had made
him swear by God: but he [k]stiffened
his neck, and hardened his heart
from turning unto the LORD God of
Israel.
14 ¶ Moreover all the chief of the
priests, and the people, transgressed
very much after all the abominations
of the heathen; and polluted the
house of the LORD which he had hallowed in Jerusalem.
15 And [l]the LORD God of their fathers sent to them [7]by his messengers,
rising up [8]betimes, and sending; because he had compassion [m]on his people, and on his dwelling place:
16 But [n]they mocked the messengers
of God, and [o]despised his words, and
[p]misused his prophets, until the [q]wrath
of the LORD arose against his people,
till *there was* no [9]remedy.
17 Therefore [r]he brought upon them
the king of the Chăl-dēēs, who slew
their young men with the sword in the
house of their sanctuary, and had no
compassion upon young man or maid-
en, old man, or him that stooped
for age: he gave *them* all into his
hand.
18 And [s]all the vessels of the house of
God, great and small, and the treasures of the house of the LORD, and the
treasures of the king, and of his princes; all *these* he brought to Babylon.
19 And [t]they burnt the house of God,
and brake down the wall of Jerusalem,
and burnt all the palaces thereof with
fire, and destroyed all the goodly vessels thereof.
20 And [10]them that had escaped from
the sword carried he away to Babylon;
[u]where they were servants to him and
his sons until the reign of the kingdom
of Persia:
21 To fulfil the word of the LORD by
the mouth of [v]Jeremiah, until the land
[w]had enjoyed her sabbaths: *for* as
long as she lay desolate [x]she kept
sabbath, to fulfil threescore and ten
years.
22 ¶ Now in the first year of Cyrus
king of Persia, that the word of the
LORD *spoken* by the mouth of Jeremiah [y]might be accomplished, the

LORD stirred up the spirit of Cyrus [z]king of Persia, that he made a proclamation throughout all his kingdom, and put it also in writing, saying,

23 Thus saith Cyrus king of Persia, All the kingdoms of the earth hath [a]the LORD God of heaven given me; and he hath charged me to build him an house in Jerusalem, which *is* in Judah. Who *is there* among you of all his people? The LORD his God *be* with him, and let him go up.

z Isa. 44.28.
a Dan. 2.21.

EZRA

CHAPTER 1

NOW in the first year of Cyrus king of Persia, that the word of the LORD [a]by the mouth of Jeremiah might be fulfilled, the LORD [b]stirred up the spirit of Cyrus king of Persia, [c]that he [1]made a proclamation throughout all his kingdom, and *put it* also in writing, saying,

2 Thus saith Cyrus king of Persia, The LORD God of heaven hath given me all the kingdoms of the earth; and he hath charged [d]me to build him an house at Jerusalem, which *is* in Judah.

3 Who *is there* among you of all his people? his God be with him, and let him go up to Jerusalem, which *is* in Judah, and build the house of the LORD God of Israel, (he [e]*is* the God,) which *is* in Jerusalem.

4 And whosoever remaineth in any place where he sojourneth, let the men of his place [2]help him with silver, and with gold, and with goods, and with beasts, beside the freewill offering for the house of God that *is* in Jerusalem.

5 ¶ Then rose up the chief of the fathers of Judah and Benjamin, and the priests, and the Levites, with all *them* whose spirit God had [f]raised, to go up to build the house of the LORD which *is* in Jerusalem.

6 And all they that *were* about them [3]strengthened their hands with vessels of silver, with gold, with goods, and with beasts, and with precious things, beside all *that* was willingly offered.

7 ¶ Also [g]Cyrus the king brought forth the vessels of the house of the LORD, [h]which Nĕb-ū-c̱hăd-nĕz´-zär had brought forth out of Jerusalem, and had put them in the house of his gods;

8 Even those did Cyrus king of Persia bring forth by the hand of Mĭth´-rĕ-dăth the treasurer, and numbered them unto [i]Shĕsh-băz´-zär, the prince of Judah.

9 And this *is* the number of them: thirty chargers of gold, a thousand chargers of silver, nine and twenty knives.

10 Thirty basons of gold, silver basons of a second *sort* four hundred and ten, *and* other vessels a thousand.

11 All the vessels of gold and of silver *were* five thousand and four hundred. All *these* did Shĕsh-băz´-zär bring up with *them of* [4]the captivity that were brought up from Babylon unto Jerusalem.

CHAPTER 2

NOW [a]these *are* the children of the [b]province that went up out of the captivity, of those which had been carried away, whom Nĕb-ū-c̱hăd-nĕz´-zär [c]the king of Babylon had carried away unto Babylon, and came again unto Jerusalem and Judah, every one unto his city;

2 Which came with Zĕ-rŭ´-bă-bĕl: Jĕsh´-ū-ă, Nē-hĕm-ī´-ăh, [1]Sĕ-rāi´-ăh, [2]Rē-ĕl-āi´-ăh, Môr-dĕ-cā´-ī, Bilshan, [3]Mispar, Bĭg-vā´-ī, [4]Rē´-hŭm, Bā´-ă-năh. The number of the men of the people of Israel:

3 The children of Pâr´-ŏsh, two thousand an hundred seventy and two.

4 The children of Shĕph-ă-tī´-ăh, three hundred seventy and two.

5 The children of Ā´-răh, [d]seven hundred seventy and five.

6 The children of [e]Pā´-hăth–mō´-ăb, of the children of Jĕsh´-ū-ă *and* Jō´-ăb, two thousand eight hundred and twelve.

7 The children of Ē´-lăm, a thousand two hundred fifty and four.

8 The children of Zăt´-tû, nine hundred forty and five.

9 The children of Zăc-cā´-ī, seven hundred and threescore.

10 The children of [5]Bā´-nī, six hundred forty and two.

11 The children of Bē-bā´-ī, six hundred twenty and three.

12 The children of Ăz´-găd, a thousand two hundred twenty and two.

CHAP. 1
a 2 Chr. 36. 22. Jer. 25.12.
b Lev. 26.42.
c ch. 5.13.
1 caused a voice to pass.
d Isa. 44.28.
e Deut. 3.24. 2 Sam. 22. 32. Ps. 86.10. Isa. 37.16. Dan. 6.26. Mark 12.32. 1 Cor. 8.6.
2 lift him up.
f Pro. 16.1. Phil. 2.13.
3 That is, helped them.
g ch. 5.14. ch. 6.5.
h 2 Ki. 24.13. 2 Chr. 36.7.
i ch. 5.14. Hag. 1.1.
4 the transportation.

CHAP. 2
a Neh. 7.6.
b ch. 5.8. ch. 6.2. Esther 1.1. Esther 8.9.
c 2 Ki. 24.14-16. 2 Chr. 36.20.
1 Or, Azariah, Neh. 7.7.
2 Or, Raamiah.
3 Or, Mispereth.
4 Or, Nehum.
d Neh. 6.18. Neh. 7.10.
e Neh. 7.11.
5 Or, Binnui, Neh. 7.15.

13 The children of [f]Ăd-ō-nī´-kăm, six
hundred sixty and six.
14 The children of Bĭg-vā´-ī, two
thousand fifty and six.
15 The children of Ā´-dĭn, four hundred fifty and four.
16 The children of Ā´-tĕr of Hĕz-ē-
kī´-ăh, ninety and eight.
17 The children of Bē-zā´-ī, three
hundred twenty and three.
18 The children of [6]Jôr´-ăh, an hundred and twelve.
19 The children of Hăsh´-ŭm, two
hundred twenty and three.
20 The children of [7]Gĭb´-băr, ninety
and five.
21 The children of [g]Beth-lehem, an
hundred twenty and three.
22 The men of Nĕ-tō´-phăh, fifty and
six.
23 The men of Ăn´-ă-thōth, an hundred twenty and eight.
24 The children of [8]Ăz-mā´-vĕth,
forty and two.
25 The children of Kĭr´-jăth–âr´-ĭm,
Chĕ-phī´-răh, and Bē̂er´-ōth, seven hundred and forty and three.
26 The children of [h]Rā´-măh and Gē´-
bă, six hundred twenty and one.
27 The men of Mĭch´-măs, an hundred twenty and two.
28 The men of Beth-el and Ā´-ī, two
hundred twenty and three.
29 The children of Nē´-bō, fifty and
two.
30 The children of Măg´-bĭsh, an
hundred fifty and six.
31 The children of the other [i]Ē´-lăm,
a thousand two hundred fifty and
four.
32 The children of Hâr´-ĭm, three
hundred and twenty.
33 The children of Lod, [9]Hā´-dĭd, and
Ō´-nō, seven hundred twenty and five.
34 The children of [j]Jericho, three
hundred forty and five.
35 The children of Sĕn´-ă-ăh, three
thousand and six hundred and thirty.
36 ¶ The priests: the children of [k]Jĕ-
dāi´-ăh, of the house of Jĕsh´-ū-ă, nine
hundred seventy and three.
37 The children of [l]Ĭm´-mĕr, a thous-
and fifty and two.
38 The children of [m]Păsh´-ŭr, a thous-
and two hundred forty and seven.
39 The children of [n]Hâr´-ĭm, a thous-
and and seventeen.
40 ¶ The Levites: the children of
Jĕsh´-ū-ă and Kăd´-mī-ĕl, of the children of [10]Hō-dă-vī´-ăh, seventy and
four.
41 ¶ The singers: the children of Ā´-
săph, an hundred twenty and eight.

f ch. 7.18. ch. 8.13.
6 Or, Hariph, Neh. 7.24.
7 Or, Gibeon, Josh. 9.17. 2 Sam. 21.2. Neh. 7.25.
g Gen. 35.19. 1 Chr. 2.51. Ruth 1.19. Matt. 2.6.
8 Or, Beth-azmaveth, Neh. 7.28.
h Josh. 18.25. 1 Sam. 7.17. 1 Sam. 15. 34. Neh. 7.30. Jer. 31.15.
i ver. 7. Neh. 7.34.
9 Or, Harid, as it is in some copies.
j Deut. 34.3. 2 Chr. 28.15. Neh. 7.36.
k 1 Chr. 9.10. 1 Chr. 24.7.
l 1 Chr. 24.14. ch. 10.20. Neh. 7.40.
m 1 Chr. 9.12. ch. 10.22. Neh. 7.41.
n 1 Chr. 24.8.
10 Or, Judah, ch. 3.9. Called also Hodevah, Neh. 7.43.
o 1 Chr. 9.2. Neh. 7.46.
11 Or, Sia.
12 Or, Shamlai.
13 Or, Nephishesim.
14 Or, Bazlith, Neh. 7.54.
p 1 Ki. 9.21.
15 Or, Perida, Neh. 7.57.
16 Or, Amon, Neh. 7.59.
q Josh. 9.21, 27. 1 Chr. 9.2. ch. 7.7.
r 1 Ki. 9.21.
17 Or, Addon, Neh. 7.61.
18 Or, pedigree.

42 ¶ The children of the porters: the
children of Shăl´-lŭm, the children of
Ā´-tĕr, the children of Tăl´-mŏn, the
children of Ăk´-kŭb, the children of
Hă-tī´-tă, the children of Shō-bā´-ī, *in*
all an hundred thirty and nine.
43 ¶ The [o]Nĕth´-ĭ-nĭmṡ: the children
of Zī´-hă, the children of Hă-sū´-phă,
the children of Tăb-bā´-ōth,
44 The children of Kē´-rŏs, the children of [11]Sī´-ă-hă, the children of Pā´-
dŏn,
45 The children of Lĕ-bā´-năh, the
children of Hăg´-ă-băh, the children of
Ăk´-kŭb,
46 The children of Hā´-găb, the children of [12]Shăl´-māi, the children of
Hā´-năn,
47 The children of Gĭd´-dĕl, the children of Gā´-hăr, the children of Rē-
āi´-ăh,
48 The children of Rē´-zĭn, the children of Nĕ-kō´-dă, the children of
Găz´-zăm,
49 The children of Ŭz´-ză, the children of Pă-sē´-ăh, the children of Bē´-
sāi,
50 The children of Ăs´-năh, the children of Mĕ-hū´-nĭm, the children of
[13]Nĕ-phū´-sĭm,
51 The children of Băk´-bŭk, the
children of Hă-kū´-phă, the children
of Hăr´-hŭr,
52 The children of [14]Băz´-lŭth, the
children of Mĕ-hī´-dă, the children of
Hăr´-shă,
53 The children of Băr´-kŏs, the children of Sĭs´-ĕ-ră, the children of Thā´-
măh,
54 The children of Nĕ-zī´-ăh, the children of Hă-tī´-phă.
55 ¶ The children of [p]Solomon's servants: the children of Sō-tā´-ī, the children of Sō´-phĕ-rĕth, the children of
[15]Pĕ-rū´-dă,
56 The children of Jā´-ă-lăh, the children of Dăr´-kŏn, the children of Gĭd´-
dĕl,
57 The children of Shĕph-ă-tī´-ăh, the
children of Hăt´-tĭl, the children of
Pō´-chĕ-rĕth of Zĕ-bā´-ĭm, the children
of [16]Ā´-mī.
58 All the [q]Nĕth´-ĭ-nĭmṡ, and the
children of [r]Solomon's servants, *were*
three hundred ninety and two.
59 And these *were* they which went
up from Tĕl–mē´-lăh, Tĕl–hăr´-să,
Cherub, [17]Ăd´-dăn, *and* Ĭm´-mĕr: but
they could not shew their father's
house, and their [18]seed, whether they
were of Israel:
60 The children of Dĕl-āi´-ăh, the
children of Tō-bī´-ăh, the children of

Nĕ-kō-́dă, six hundred fifty and two.
61 ¶ And of the children of the
priests: the children of Hă-bâi-́āh,
the children of Kŏz, the children of
Bär-zĭl-lā-́ī; which took a wife of the
daughters of [s]Bär-zĭl-lā-́ī the Gileadite, and was called after their name:
62 These sought their register *among*
those that were reckoned by genealogy, but they were not found:
[t]therefore [19]were they, as polluted,
put from the priesthood.
63 And the [20]Tĭr-́shă-thă said unto
them, that they [u]should not eat of the
most holy things, till there stood up a
priest with Ū-́rĭm [v]and with Thŭm-́
mĭm.
64 ¶ The [w]whole congregation together *was* forty and two thousand
three hundred *and* threescore,
65 Beside their servants and their
maids, of whom *there were* seven
thousand three hundred thirty and
seven: and *there were* among them
two hundred singing men and singing
women.
66 Their horses *were* seven hundred
thirty and six; their mules, two hundred forty and five;
67 Their camels, four hundred thirty
and five; *their* asses, six thousand sev-
en hundred and twenty.
68 ¶ And [x]*some* of the chief of the
fathers, when they came to the house
of the LORD which *is* at Jerusalem,
offered freely for the house of God to
set it up in his place:
69 They gave after their ability unto
the treasure of the work threescore
and one thousand drams of gold, and
five thousand pound of silver, and one
hundred priests' garments.
70 So the priests, and the Levites,
and *some* of the people, and the singers, and the porters, and the Nĕth-́ĭ-
nĭms, dwelt in their cities, and all Israel in their cities.

CHAPTER 3

AND when the seventh month was
come, and the children of Israel
were in the cities, the people gathered
themselves together as one man to
Jerusalem.
2 Then stood up [a]Jĕsh-́ū-ă the son of
Jō-́ză-dăk, and his brethren the
priests, and [b]Zĕ-rŭb-́bă-bĕl the son of
[c]Shē-ăl-́tĭ-ĕl, and his brethren, and
builded the altar of the God of Israel,
to offer burnt offerings thereon, as *it
is* [d]written in the law of Moses the
man of God.
3 And they set the altar upon his
bases; for fear *was* upon them because
of the people of those countries: and
they offered burnt offerings thereon
unto the LORD, *even* burnt [e]offerings
morning and evening.
4 They [f]kept also the feast of tabernacles, as [g]*it is* written, and *offered*[h]
the daily burnt offerings by number,
according to the custom, [1]as the duty
of every day required;
5 And afterward *offered* the [i]con-
tinual burnt offering, both of the new
moons, and of all the set feasts of the
LORD that were consecrated, and of
every one that willingly offered a freewill offering unto the LORD.
6 From the first day of the seventh
month began they to offer burnt offerings unto the LORD. But [2]the foundation of the temple of the LORD was not
yet laid.
7 They gave money also unto the
masons, and to the [3]carpenters; and
[j]meat, and drink, and oil, unto them
of Zī-́dŏn, and to them of Tyre, to
bring cedar trees from Lĕb-́ă-non to
the sea of [k]Jŏp-́pă, according [l]to the
grant that they had of Cyrus king of
Persia.
8 ¶ Now in the second year of their
coming unto the house of God at Jerusalem, in the second month, began
Zĕ-rŭb-́bă-bĕl the son of Shē-ăl-́tĭ-ĕl,
and Jĕsh-́ū-ă the son of Jō-́ză-dăk, and
the remnant of their brethren the
priests and the Levites, and all they
that were come out of the captivity
unto Jerusalem; [m]and appointed the
Levites, from twenty years old and upward, to set forward the work of the
house of the LORD.
9 Then stood [n]Jĕsh-́ū-ă *with* his sons
and his brethren, Kăd-́mĭ-ĕl and his
sons, the sons of [o]Judah, [4]together, to
set forward the workmen in the house
of God: the sons of Hĕn-ā-́dăd, *with*
their sons and their brethren the Levites.
10 And when the builders laid the
foundation [p]of the temple of the
LORD, [q]they set the priests in their apparel with trumpets, and the Levites
the sons of Ā-́săph with cymbals, to
praise the LORD, after the [r]ordinance
of David king of Israel.
11 And [s]they sang together by course
in praising and giving thanks unto the
LORD; because *he* [t]*is* good, [u]for his
mercy *endureth* for ever toward Israel.
And all the people shouted with a
great shout, when they praised the
LORD, because the foundation of the
house of the LORD was laid.

s 1 Ki. 2.7.
t Num. 3.10.
19 they were polluted from the priesthood.
20 Or, governor. See Neh. 8.9.
u Lev. 22.2, 10,15,16. Num. 18.9-11.
v Ex. 28.30.
w Isa. 10.22.
x Ex. 25.2.

CHAP. 3
a Hag. 1.1. Zech. 3.1, Joshua.
b ch. 2.2. Zech. 4.6-10. Matt. 1.12, Zorobabel.
c Luke 3.27, Salathiel.
d Ex. 20.24. Deut. 12.5.
e Ex. 29.38-42.
f Neh. 8.14. Zech. 14.16.
g Ex. 23.16.
h Num. 29. 12.
1 the matter of the day in his day.
i Ex. 29.38. Num. 28.3.
2 the temple of the LORD was not yet founded.
3 Or, workmen.
j 2 Chr. 2.10. Acts 12.20.
k Acts 9.36.
l ch. 6.3.
m 1 Chr. 23. 24,27.
n ch. 2.40.
o ch. 2.40. Hodaviah.
4 as one.
p Zech. 4.6-10.
q 1 Chr. 15. 27,28.
r 1 Chr. 6.31.
s Ex. 15.21. 2 Chr. 7.3. Jer. 33.11. Luke 1.50.
t Ps. 136.1.
u Jer. 33.11.

12 But many of the priests and Le-
ites and chief of the fathers, *who were*
ncient men, that had seen the first
ouse, when the foundation of this
ouse was laid before their eyes, wept
ith a loud voice; and many shouted
loud for joy:
13 So that the people could not dis-
ern the noise of the shout of joy from
e noise of the weeping of the people:
or the people shouted with a loud
hout, and the noise was heard afar
ff.

CHAPTER 4

NOW when the adversaries of Judah and Benjamin heard that [1]the
hildren of the captivity builded the
mple unto the LORD God of Israel;
2 Then they came to Zĕ-rŭb-′bā-bĕl,
nd to the chief of the fathers, and
aid unto them, Let [a]us build with
ou: for we seek your God, as ye *do;*
nd we do sacrifice unto [b]him since
e days of Ē-′sär–hăd-′dọn king of
ssur, which brought us up hither.
3 But Zĕ-rŭb-′bā-bĕl, and Jĕsh-′ū-ă,
nd the rest of the chief of the fathers
f Israel, said unto them, Ye [c]have
othing to do with us to build an
ouse unto our God; but we our-
lves together will build unto the
ORD God of Israel, [d]as king Cyrus the
ing of Persia hath commanded us.
4 Then [e]the people of the land weak-
ned the hands of the people of Judah,
d troubled them in building,
5 And hired counsellers against
em, to frustrate their purpose, all
e days of Cyrus king of Persia, even
ntil the reign of Dă-rī-′ŭs king of
ersia.
6 And in the reign of [2]Ă-hăs-ū-ē-′rŭs,
the beginning of his reign, wrote
ey *unto him* an accusation against
e inhabitants of Judah and Jerusa-
m.
7 ¶ And in the days of Är-tă-xĕrx-′ēs
rote [3]Bĭsh-′lăm, Mĭth-′rĕ-dăth, Tăb-′
l, and the rest of their [4]companions,
nto Är-tă-xĕrx-′ēs king of Persia; and
e writing of the letter *was* written in
e Syrian tongue, and interpreted in
e Syrian tongue.
8 Rē-′hŭm the chancellor and Shĭm-′
âi the [5]scribe wrote a letter against
erusalem to Är-tă-xĕrx-′ēs the king
this sort:
9 Then *wrote* Rē-′hŭm the chancellor,
d Shĭm-′shâi the scribe, and the rest
their [6]companions; [g]the Dī-′nā-ītes,
e Ă-phär-săth-′chĭtes, the Tär-′pĕ-
es, the Ă-phär-′sītes, the Är-′chĕ-
tes, the Babylonians, the Sû-săn-′
chītes, the Dĕ-hā-′vītes, *and* the Ē-′
lăm-ītes,
10 And the rest of the nations whom
the great and noble Ăs-năp-′păr
brought over, and set in the cities of
Să-mâr-′ĭ-ă, and the rest *that are* on
this side the river, [h]and [7]at such a time.
11 ¶ This *is* the copy of the letter that
they sent unto him, *even* unto Är-tă-
xĕrx-′ēs the king; Thy servants the
men on this side the river, and at such
a time.
12 Be it known unto the king, that
the Jews which came up from thee to
us are come unto Jerusalem, building
[i]the rebellious and the bad city, and
have [8]set up the walls *thereof*, and
[9]joined the foundations.
13 Be it known now unto the king,
that, if this city be builded, and the
walls set up *again*, *then* will they not
[10]pay [j]toll, tribute, and custom, and *so*
thou shalt endamage the [11]revenue of
the kings.
14 Now because [12]we have mainten-
ance from *the king's* palace, and it
was not meet for us to see the king's
dishonour, therefore have we sent and
certified the king;
15 That search may be made in the
book of the records of thy fathers: so
shalt thou find in the book of the records, and know that this city *is* a rebellious city, and [k]hurtful unto kings and
provinces, and that they have [13]moved
sedition [14]within the same of old time:
for which cause was this city destroyed.
16 We certify the king that, if this
city be builded *again*, and the walls
thereof set up, by this means thou
shalt have no portion on this side the
river.
17 ¶ *Then* sent the king an answer
unto Rē-′hŭm the chancellor, and *to*
Shĭm-′shâi the scribe, and *to* the rest
of their [15]companions that dwell in Să-
mâr-′ĭ-ă, and *unto* the rest beyond the
river, Peace, and at such a time.
18 The letter which ye sent unto us
hath been plainly read before me.
19 And [16]I commanded, and search
hath been made, and it is found that
this city of old time hath [17]made insurrection against kings, and *that* rebellion and sedition have been made
therein.
20 There have been mighty kings also
over Jerusalem, which have ruled
[l]over all *countries* [m]beyond the river;
and toll, tribute, and custom, was
paid unto them.
21 [18]Give ye now commandment to

CHAP. 4
1 the sons of the transportation.
a Esther 8.17.
b 2 Ki. 17.24, 32,33.
c John 4.9. Acts 8.21.
d 2 Chr. 36. 22,23. ch. 6.3. Isa. 44.28.
e ch. 3.3. Isa. 35.3,4. Jer. 38.4.
2 Ahashverosh.
3 Or, in peace.
4 societies.
5 Or, secretary.
f Ps. 112.6. Zech. 1.14. Rom. 8.28.
6 societies.
g 2 Ki. 17.30, 31.
h ch. 7.12.
7 Cheeneth.
i Amos 7.10. Luke 23.2. Acts 24.5.
8 Or, finished.
9 sewed together.
10 give.
j ch. 7.24. Matt. 9.9.
11 Or, strength.
12 we are salted with the salt of the palace.
k Esther 3.8. Acts 17.6,7.
13 made.
14 in the midst thereof.
15 societies.
16 by me a decree is set.
17 lifted up itself.
l 1 Chr. 18.3. Ps. 72.8.
m Gen. 15.18.
18 Make a decree.

cause these men to cease, and that this city be not builded, until *another* commandment shall be given from me.

22 Take heed now that ye fail not to do this: why should damage grow to the hurt of the kings?

23 ¶ Now when the copy of king Ăr-tă-xĕrx´-ēṡ' letter *was* read before Rē´-hŭm, and Shĭm´-shâi the scribe, and their companions, they went up in [n]haste to Jerusalem unto the Jews, and made them to cease [19]by force and power.

24 Then ceased the work of the house of God which *is* at Jerusalem. So it ceased unto [o]the second year of the reign of Dă-rī´-ŭs king of Persia.

CHAPTER 5

THEN the prophets, [a]Hăg´-gâi the prophet, and [b]Zĕch-ă-rī´-ăh the son of Ĭd´-dō, prophesied unto the Jews that *were* in Judah and Jerusalem in the name of the God of Israel, *even* unto them.

2 Then rose up [c]Zĕ-rŭb´-bă-bĕl the son of Shĕ-ăl´-tĭ-ĕl, and Jĕsh´-ū-ă the son of Jō´-ză-dăk, and began to build the house of God which *is* at Jerusalem: and with them *were* the prophets of God [d]helping them.

3 ¶ At the same time came to them [e]Tăt´-nâi, governor on [1]this side the river, and Shē´-thär–bŏz´-nâi, and their companions, and said thus unto them, Who hath commanded you to build this house, and to make up this wall?

4 Then said we unto them after this manner, What are the names of the men [2]that make this building?

5 But [f]the eye of their God was upon the elders of the Jews, that they could not cause them to cease, till the matter came to Dă-rī´-ŭs: and then they [g]returned answer by letter concerning this *matter*.

6 ¶ The copy of the letter that Tăt´-nâi, governor on this side the river, and Shē´-thär–bŏz´-nâi, [h]and his companions the Ă-phär´-să-chītes, which *were* on this side the river, sent unto Dă-rī´-ŭs the king:

7 They sent a letter unto him, [3]wherein was written thus; Unto Dă-rī´-ŭs the king, all peace.

8 Be it known unto the king, that we went into the province of Judea, to the house of the great God, which is builded with [4]great stones, and timber is laid in the walls, and this work goeth fast on, and prospereth in their hands.

9 Then asked we those elders, *and* said unto them thus, Who commanded you to build this house, and to make up these walls?

10 We asked their names also, to certify thee, that we might write the names of the men that *were* the chief of them.

11 And thus they returned us answer, saying, We are the [i]servants of the God of heaven and earth, and build the house that was builded these many years ago, which a great king of Israel builded and [j]set up.

12 But [k]after that our fathers had provoked the God of heaven unto wrath, he gave them into the hand of [l]Nĕb-ū-chăd-nĕz´-zär the king of Babylon, the Chăl-dē´-ăn, who destroyed this house, and carried the people away into Babylon.

13 But in the first year of [m]Cyrus the king of Babylon *the same* king Cyrus made a decree to build this house of God.

14 And [n]the vessels also of gold and silver of the house of God, which Nĕb-ū-chăd-nĕz´-zär took out of the temple that *was* in Jerusalem, and brought them into the temple of Babylon, those did Cyrus the king take out of the temple of Babylon, and they were delivered unto *one*, [o]whose name *was* Shĕsh-băz´-zär, whom he had made [5]governor;

15 And said unto him, Take these vessels, go, carry them into the temple that *is* in Jerusalem, and let the house of God be builded in his place.

16 Then came the same Shĕsh-băz´-zär, *and* laid [p]the foundation of the house of God which *is* in Jerusalem: and since that time even until now hath it been in building, and *yet* [q]it *is* not finished.

17 Now therefore, if *it seem* good to the king, [r]let there be search made in the king's treasure house, which *is* there at Babylon, whether it be *so*, that a decree was made of Cyrus the king to build this house of God at Jerusalem, and let the king send his pleasure to us concerning this matter.

CHAPTER 6

THEN Dă-rī´-ŭs the king made a decree, and [a]search was made in the house of the [1]rolls, where the treasures were [2]laid up in Babylon.

2 And there was found at [3]Ăch-mĕ-thă, in the palace that *is* in the province of the Mēdeṡ, a roll, and therein *was* a record thus written:

n Pro. 4.16.
19 by arm and power.
o Job 20.5.

CHAP. 5
a Hag. 1.1.
b Zech. 1.1.
c Hag. 1.12-15.
d ch. 6.14. Eccl. 12.11. Hag. 2.4-9.
e ch. 6.6.
1 Westward of Euphrates.
2 that build this building?
f 2 Chr. 16.9. ch. 7.6,28. Ps. 33.18. Isa. 41.10. 1 Pet. 3.12.
g ch. 6.6.
h ch. 4.9.
3 in the midst whereof.
4 stones of rolling.
i Josh. 24.15. Ps. 119.46. Jonah 1.9. Matt. 10.32. Luke 12.8. Acts 27.23.
j 1 Ki. 6.1.
k 2 Chr. 34. 24,25. 2 Chr. 36.16, 17.
l 2 Ki. 24.2. Jer. 39.1.
m ch. 1.1.
n ch. 1.7,8.
o Hag. 1.14.
5 Or, deputy.
p ch. 3.8,10.
q ch. 6.15.
r ch. 6.1,2. Pro. 25.2.

CHAP. 6
a ch. 5.17.
1 books.
2 made to descend.
3 Or, Ecbatana, the chief city of Media, or, in a coffer.

3 In the first year of Cyrus the king
e same Cyrus the king made a decree
oncerning the house of God at Jerusa-
m, Let the house be builded, the
lace where they offered sacrifices,
nd let the foundations thereof be
rongly laid; the height thereof
reescore cubits, *and* the breadth
ereof threescore cubits;
4 *With* [b]three rows of great stones,
nd a row of new timber: and [c]let the
xpences be given out of the king's
ouse:
5 And also let [d]the golden and silver
essels of the house of God, which
Něb-ū-chăd-něz'-zär took forth out of
e temple which *is* at Jerusalem, and
rought unto Babylon, be restored,
nd [4]brought again unto the temple
hich *is* at Jerusalem, *every one* to
is place, and place *them* in the house
f God.
6 Now [e]*therefore*, Tăt'-nāī, governor
eyond the river, Shē'-thär–bŏz'-nāī,
nd [5]your companions the Ă-phär'-să-
chites, which *are* beyond the river, be
e far from thence:
7 Let the work of this house of God
lone; let the governor of the Jews
nd the elders of the Jews build this
ouse of God in his place.
8 Moreover [6]I make a decree what
e shall do to the elders of these Jews
or the building of this house of God:
hat of the king's goods, *even* of the
ribute beyond the river, forthwith
xpences be given unto these men,
hat they be not [7]hindered.
9 And that which they have need of,
oth young bullocks, and rams, and
ambs, for the burnt offerings of the
God of heaven, wheat, salt, wine, and
oil, according to the appointment of
he priests which *are* at Jerusalem, let
t be given them day by day without
ail:
10 That [f]they may offer sacrifices [8]of
sweet savours unto the God of heaven,
and pray [g]for the life of the king, and
of his sons.
11 Also I have made a decree, that
whosoever shall alter this word, let
timber be pulled down from his house,
and being set up, [9]let him be hanged
thereon; [h]and let his house be made
a dunghill for this.
12 And the God that hath caused his
name [i]to dwell there destroy all kings
and people, that shall put to their
hand to alter *and* to destroy this house
of God which *is* at Jerusalem. I Dă-
rī'-ŭs have made a decree; let it be
done with speed.

13 ¶ Then Tăt'-nāī, governor on this
side the river, Shē'-thär–bŏz'-nāī, and
their companions, according to that
which Dă-rī'-ŭs the king had sent, so
they [j]did speedily.
14 And [k]the elders of the Jews builded, and they prospered through the
prophesying of Hăg'-gāī the prophet
and Zĕch-ă-rī'-ăh the son of Ĭd'-dō.
And they builded, and finished *it*, according to the commandment of the
God of Israel, and according to the
[10]commandment of [l]Cyrus, and [m]Dă-
rī'-ŭs, and Är-tă-xĕrx'-ēs [n]king of
Persia.
15 And this house was finished on
the third day of the month Ā'-där,
which was in the sixth year of the
reign of Dă-rī'-ŭs the king.
16 ¶ And the children of Israel, the
priests, and the Levites, and the rest
of [11]the children of the captivity, kept
[o]the dedication of this house of God
with joy,
17 And [p]offered at the dedication of
this house of God an hundred bullocks, two hundred rams, four hundred lambs; and for a sin offering for
all Israel, twelve he goats, according
to the number of the tribes of Israel.
18 And they set the priests in their
[q]divisions, and the Levites in their
[r]courses, for the service of God, which
is at Jerusalem; [12]as it is written in the
book of Moses.
19 And the children of the captivity
kept the passover [s]upon the fourteenth *day* of the first month.
20 For the priests and the Levites
were purified [t]together, all of them
were pure, and [u]killed the passover
for all the children of the captivity,
and for their brethren the priests, and
for themselves.
21 And the children of Israel, which
were come again out of captivity, and
all such as had separated [v]themselves
unto them from the filthiness of the
heathen of the land, to seek the LORD
God of Israel, did eat,
22 And kept the [w]feast of unleavened
bread seven days with joy: for the
LORD had made them joyful, and
[x]turned the heart of the king of Assyria unto them, to strengthen their
hands in the work of the house of
God, the God of Israel.

CHAPTER 7

NOW after these things, in the
reign of [1]Är-tă-xĕrx'-ēs king of
Persia, Ezra [a]the son of Sĕ-rāī'-ăh, the
son of Ăz-ă-rī'-ăh, the son of Hĭl-kī'-ăh,

b 1 Ki. 6.36.
c Ps. 68.29. Isa. 60.6.
d ch. 1.7,8. Jer. 27.16, 18-22. Dan. 1.2.
4 go.
e ch. 5.3.
5 their societies.
6 by me a decree is made.
7 made to cease.
f ch. 7.23. Jer. 29.7.
8 of rest. Gen. 8.21. Lev. 1.9.
g 1 Tim. 2.1, 2.
9 let him be destroyed.
h Dan. 2.5.
i Deut. 12.11. 2 Chr. 7.16. Ps. 132.13.
j Job 5.12. Ps. 9.16. 1 Cor. 3.19.
k ch. 5.1,2.
10 decree.
l ch. 1.1.
m ch. 4.24.
n ch. 7.1.
11 the sons of the transportation.
o 1 Ki. 8.63. 2 Chr. 7.5. John 10.22.
p Num. 7.2, 3. 1 Chr. 16.1-3. ch. 8.35.
q 1 Chr. 24.1.
r 1 Chr. 23.6.
12 according to the writing.
s Ex. 12.6.
t 2 Chr. 29. 34.
u Ex. 12.21. 2 Chr. 35.11.
v Ex. 12.48. Ps. 93.5.
w Ex. 12.15.
x Pro. 21.1.

CHAP. 7

1 Longimanus, Neh. 2.1.
a 1 Chr. 6.14.

2 The son of Shăl-lŭm, the son of Zā-dŏk, the son of Ă-hī-tŭb,

3 The son of Ăm-ă-rī-ăh, the son of Ăz-ă-rī-ăh, the son of Mĕ-raî-ōth,

4 The son of Zĕr-ă-hī-ăh, the son of Ŭz-zī, the son of Bŭk-kī,

5 The son of Ă-bī-shû-ă, the son of Phĭn-ĕ-hăs, the son of Ĕl-ē-ā-zăr, the son of Aaron the chief priest:

6 This Ezra went up from Babylon; and he *was* a ready scribe in the law of Moses, which the LORD God of Israel had given: and the king granted him all his request, according [b]to the hand of the LORD his God upon him.

7 And [c]there went up *some* of the children of Israel, and of the priests, and the Levites, and the singers, and the porters, and the Nĕth-ĭ-nĭms, [d]unto Jerusalem, in the seventh year of Är-tă-xĕrx-ēs the king.

8 And he came to Jerusalem in the fifth month, which *was* in the seventh year of the king.

9 For upon the first *day* of the first month [2]began he to go up from Babylon, and on the first *day* of the fifth month came he to Jerusalem, [e]according to the good hand of his God upon him.

10 For Ezra had prepared his heart to seek [f]the law of the LORD, and to do *it*, and to [g]teach in Israel statutes and judgments.

11 ¶ Now this *is* the copy of the letter that the king Är-tă-xĕrx-ēs gave unto Ezra the priest, the scribe, *even* a scribe of the words of the commandments of the LORD, and of his statutes to Israel.

12 Är-tă-xĕrx-ēs, [h]king of kings, [3]unto Ezra the priest, a scribe of the law of the God of heaven, perfect *peace*, [i]and at such a time.

13 I make a decree, that all they of the people of Israel, and *of* his priests and Levites, in my realm, which are minded of their own freewill to go up to Jerusalem, go with thee.

14 Forasmuch as thou art sent [4]of the king, and of his [j]seven counsellers, to inquire concerning Judah and Jerusalem, according to the law of thy God which *is* in thine hand;

15 And to carry the silver and gold, which the king and his counsellers have freely offered unto the God of Israel, [k]whose habitation *is* in Jerusalem,

16 And [l]all the silver and gold that thou canst find in all the province of Babylon, with the freewill offering of the people, and of the priests, [m]offering willingly for the house of th God which *is* in Jerusalem.

17 That thou mayest buy speedi with this money bullocks, ran lambs, with their [n]meat offerings a their drink offerings, and offer the [o]upon the altar of the house of yo God which *is* in Jerusalem.

18 And whatsoever shall seem go to thee, and to thy brethren, to with the rest of the silver and t gold, that do after the will of yo God.

19 The vessels also that are given th for the service of the house of t God, *those* deliver thou before t God of Jerusalem.

20 And [p]whatsoever more shall needful for the house of thy Go which thou shalt have occasion to b stow, bestow *it* out of the king's trea ure house.

21 And I, *even* I Är-tă-xĕrx-ēs t king, do make a decree to all [q]t treasurers which *are* beyond the rive that whatsoever Ezra the priest, t scribe of the law of the God of heave shall require of you, it be dor speedily,

22 Unto an hundred talents of silv and to an hundred [5]measures wheat, and to an hundred bāths wine, and to an hundred bāths of o and salt without prescribing *ho much.*

23 [6]Whatsoever is commanded b the God of heaven, let it be diligent done for the house of the God heaven: [r]for why should there b wrath against the realm of the kin and his sons?

24 Also we certify you, that touchin any of the priests and Levites, singers porters, Nĕth-ĭ-nĭms, or ministers this house of God, it shall not be law ful to impose toll, tribute, or custon upon them.

25 And thou, Ezra, after the wisdon of thy God, that *is* in thine hand, [s]se magistrates and judges, which ma judge all the people that *are* beyon the river, all such as know the laws o thy God; and teach [t]ye them that kno *them* not.

26 And whosoever will not do th law of thy God, and the law of th king, let judgment be executed speed ily upon him, whether *it be* unto death or [7]to banishment, or to confiscatio of goods, or to imprisonment.

27 ¶ Blessed [u]*be* the LORD God o our fathers, [v]which hath put *such thing* as this in the king's heart, t

b Gen. 32.28. ch. 6.22. Neh. 1.10, 11.
c ch. 8.1.
d ch. 2.43.
2 was the foundation of the going up.
e Neh. 2.8.
f 1 Sam. 7.3. 2 Chr. 12.14. Ps. 10.18. Ps. 119.45.
g Deut. 33. 10. Neh. 8.1. Mal. 2.7. 2 Tim. 4.2.
h Eze. 26.7. Dan. 2.37.
3 Or, to Ezra the priest, a perfect scribe of the law of the God of heaven, peace, etc.
i ch. 4.10.
4 from before the king.
j Esther 1.14.
k 2 Chr. 6.2. Ps. 135.21.
l ch. 8.26.
m 1 Chr. 29.6.
n Num. 15.4-13.
o Deut. 12.5.
p 1 Cor. 4.1,2.
q ch. 4.16,20. ch. 5.3,6.
5 cors.
6 Whatsoever is of the decree.
r ch. 6.10. Ps. 68.29. Isa. 60.12. Jer. 12.14. 1 Tim. 2.1,2.
s Ex. 18.21. Deut. 16.18. 1 Ki. 3.28. Ps. 19.7.
t 2 Chr. 17.7. Mal. 2.7. Matt. 13.52. Col. 1.28.
7 to rooting out.
u 1 Chr. 29. 10. ch. 6.22. Phil. 4.10.
v ch. 6.22. Neh. 2.12. Pro. 16.7. 2 Cor. 8.16.

eautify the house of the LORD which
: in Jerusalem:
28 And [w]hath extended mercy unto
ne before the king, and his counsel-
ers, and before all the king's mighty
rinces. And I was strengthened as
the hand of the LORD my God *was*
pon me, and I gathered together out
f Israel chief men to go up with me.

CHAPTER 8

THESE *are* now the chief of their
fathers, and *this is* the genealogy
f them that went up with me from
abylon, in the reign of Är-tă-xĕrx-ēs
ne king.
2 Of the sons of Phĭn-ĕ-hăs; Gĕr-
hŏm: of the sons of Ĭth-ă-mär; Dan-
l: of the sons of David; [a]Hăt-
ish.
3 Of the sons of Shĕch-ă-nī-ăh, of
ne sons of [b]Phâr-ŏsh; Zĕch-ă-rī-ăh:
nd with him were reckoned by genea-
gy of the males an hundred and
fty.
4 Of the sons of Pā-hăth–mō-ăb; Ĕl-
hō-ē-nâi the son of Zĕr-ă-hī-ăh, and
ith him two hundred males.
5 Of the sons of Shĕch-ă-nī-ăh; the
on of Jă-hă-zī-ĕl, and with him three
undred males.
6 Of the sons also of [c]Ā-dĭn; Ē-bĕd
ne son of Jonathan, and with him
fty males.
7 And of the sons of Ē-lăm; Jĕ-shâi-
h the son of Ăth-ă-lī-ăh, and with
im seventy males.
8 And of the sons of Shĕph-ă-tī-ăh;
ĕb-ă-dī-ăh the son of Michael, and
ith him fourscore males.
9 Of the sons of Jō-ăb; Ō-bă-dī-ăh
ne son of Jĕ-hī-ĕl, and with him two
undred and eighteen males.
10 And of the sons of Shĕ-lō-mĭth;
ne son of Jŏs-ĭ-phī-ăh, and with him
n hundred and threescore males.
11 And of the sons of Bē-bā-ī; Zĕch-
rī-ăh the son of Bē-bā-ī, and with
im twenty and eight males.
12 And of the sons of Ăz-găd; Jō-hā-
ăn [1]the son of Hăk-kă-tăn, and with
im an hundred and ten males.
13 And of the last sons of Ăd-ō-nī-
ăm, whose names *are* these, Ē-lĭph-
lĕt, Jē-ī-ĕl, and Shĕm-âi-ăh, and
ith them threescore males.
14 Of the sons also of Bĭg-vā-ī; Ū-
âi, and [2]Zăb-bŭd, and with them
venty males.
15 ¶ And I gathered them together
the river [d]that runneth to Ă-hā-vă;
nd there [3]abode we in tents three
ays: and I viewed the [e]people, and
the priests, and found there none of
the [f]sons of Levi.
16 Then sent I for Ĕl-ĭ-ē-zĕr, for Âr-
ĭ-ĕl, for Shĕm-âi-ăh, and for Ĕl-nā-
thăn, and for Jâr-ĭb, and for Ĕl-nā-
thăn, and for Nathan, and for Zĕch-ă-
rī-ăh, and for Mĕ-shŭl-lăm, chief men;
also for Jōi-ă-rĭb, and for Ĕl-nā-thăn,
men of understanding.
17 And I sent them with commandment unto Ĭd-dō the chief at the place
Căs-ĭ-phī-ă, and [4]I told them what
they should say unto Ĭd-dō, *and* to his
brethren the Nĕth-ĭ-nĭms, at the place
Căs-ĭ-phī-ă, that they should bring
unto us ministers for the house of our
God.
18 And by the [g]good hand of our God
upon us they [h]brought us a man of
understanding, of the sons of Măh-lī,
the son of Levi, the son of Israel; and
Shĕr-ē-bī-ăh, with his sons and his
brethren, eighteen;
19 And Hăsh-ă-bī-ăh, and with him
Jĕ-shâi-ăh of the sons of Mĕ-rär-ī, his
brethren and their sons, twenty;
20 Also [i]of the Nĕth-ĭ-nĭms, whom
David and the princes had appointed
for the service of the Levites, two
hundred and twenty Nĕth-ĭ-nĭms: all
of them were expressed by name.
21 ¶ Then I [j]proclaimed a fast there,
at the river of Ă-hā-vă, that we might
[k]afflict ourselves before our God, to
seek of him a right way [l]for us, and for
our little ones, and for all our substance.
22 For I [m]was ashamed to require of
the king a band of soldiers and horsemen to help us against the enemy in
the way: because we had spoken unto
the king, saying, The hand [n]of our
God *is* upon all them for [o]good that
seek him; but his power and his wrath
is [p]against all them that [q]forsake him.
23 So we fasted and besought our
God for this: and he was [r]intreated of
us.
24 ¶ Then I separated twelve of the
chief of the priests, Shĕr-ē-bī-ăh,
Hăsh-ă-bī-ăh, and ten of their brethren with them,
25 And weighed unto them [s]the silver, and the gold, and the vessels, *even*
the offering of the house of our God,
which the king, and his counsellers,
and his lords, and all Israel *there* present, had offered:
26 I even weighed unto their hand
six hundred and fifty talents of silver,
and silver vessels an hundred talents,
and of gold an hundred talents;
27 Also twenty basons of gold, of a

w ch. 9.9. Neh. 1.11.
x ch. 5.5.
CHAP. 8
a 1 Chr. 3.22.
b ch. 2.3.
c ch. 2.15. Neh. 7.20.
1 Or, the youngest son.
2 Or, Zaccur, as some read.
d Ps. 137.1. Acts 16.13.
3 Or, pitched.
e Pro. 27.23. Acts 20.28. Heb. 13.17.
f ch. 7.7. Num. 8.1.
4 I put words in their mouth.
g ch. 7.28. Pro. 3.6. Rom. 8.28.
h Lev. 10.10, 11. 2 Chr. 30.22. Neh. 8.7.
i ch. 2.43.
j 2 Chr. 20.3.
k Lev. 16.29. Isa. 58.3,5.
l Ps. 5.8.
m 1 Cor. 9. 15.
n 1 Chr. 28.9. ch. 7.6,9,28. Ps. 33.18,19. Isa. 3.10. Rom. 8.28. 1 Pet. 3.12.
o Ps. 33.18.
p Ps. 34.16.
q 2 Chr. 15.2.
r Deut. 4.29. 1 Chr. 5.20. 2 Chr. 33.13. Isa. 19.22. Jer. 29.12, 13.
s ch. 7.15,16.

thousand drams; and two vessels of
[5]fine copper, [6]precious as gold.
28 And I said unto them, Ye *are* holy
[t]unto the LORD; the vessels *are* [u]holy
also; and the silver and the gold *are* a
freewill offering unto the LORD God
of your fathers.
29 Watch [v]ye, and keep *them*, until
ye weigh *them* before the chief of the
priests and the Levites, and chief of
the fathers of Israel, at Jerusalem, in
the chambers of the house of the
LORD.
30 So took the priests and the Levites the weight of the silver, and the
gold, and the vessels, to bring *them*
to Jerusalem unto the house of our
God.
31 ¶ Then we departed from the river of Ă-hā-vă on the twelfth *day* of
the first month, to go unto Jerusalem:
and [w]the hand of our God was upon
us, and he delivered us from the hand
of the enemy, and of such as lay in
wait by the way.
32 And we [x]came to Jerusalem, and
abode there three days.
33 ¶ Now on the fourth day was the
silver and the gold and the vessels
weighed in the house of our God by
the hand of Mĕr-ĕ-mōth the son of
Ū-rī-āh the priest; and with him *was*
Ĕl-ē-ā-zär the son of Phĭn-ĕ-hăs; and
with them *was* Jō-ză-băd the son of
Jĕsh-ū-ă, and Nō-ă-dī-āh the son of
Bĭn-nū-ī, Levites;
34 By number *and* by weight of every
one: and all the weight was written at
that time.
35 *Also* the children of those that had
been carried away, which were come
out of the captivity, offered [y]burnt
offerings unto the God of Israel,
twelve bullocks for all Israel, ninety
and six rams, seventy and seven
lambs, twelve he goats *for* a sin offering: all *this was* a burnt offering unto
the LORD.
36 ¶ And they delivered the king's
commissions [z]unto the king's lieutenants, and to the governors on this side
the river: and they furthered [a]the people, and the house of God.

CHAPTER 9

NOW when these things were
done, the princes came to me,
saying, The people of Israel, and the
priests, and the Levites, have not
[a]separated themselves from the
people of the lands, [b]*doing* according
to their abominations, *even* of the
Canaanites, the Hittites, the Pĕ-rĭz-
zītes, the Jĕb-ū-sītes, the Ammonite
the Moabites, the Egyptians, an
the Amorites.
2 For they have [c]taken of the
daughters for themselves, and fo
their sons: so that the [d]holy seed hav
[e]mingled themselves with the peop
of *those* lands: yea, the hand of th
princes and rulers hath been chief i
this trespass.
3 And when I heard this thing, I [f]ren
my garment and my mantle, an
plucked off the hair of my head and c
my beard, and sat down [g]astonied.
4 Then were assembled unto m
every one that [h]trembled at the word
of the God of Israel, because of th
transgression of those that had bee
carried away; and I sat astonied unt
the [i]evening sacrifice.
5 ¶ And at the evening sacrifice
arose up from my [1]heaviness; an
having rent my garment and m
mantle, I fell upon my knees, an
spread [j]out my hands unto the LOR
my God,
6 And said, O my God, I [k]am asham
ed and blush to lift up my face to thee
my God: for our iniquities are in
creased over *our* head, and our [2]tres
pass is grown up unto the heavens.
7 Since the days of our fathers *hav*
we [l]*been* in a great trespass unto thi
day; and for our iniquities [m]have we
our kings, *and* our priests, been de
livered into the hand of the kings o
the lands, to the sword, to captivity
and to a spoil, and to confusion c
face, as *it is* this day.
8 And now for a [3]little space grac
hath been *shewed* from the LORD ou
God, to leave us a remnant to escape
and to give us [4]a nail in his holy place
that our God may [n]lighten our eyes
and give us a little reviving in ou
bondage.
9 For [o]we *were* bondmen; [p]yet ou
God hath not forsaken us in our bond
age, but hath [q]extended mercy unto u
in the sight of the kings of Persia, t
give us a reviving, to set up the hous
of our God, and [5]to repair the desola
tions thereof, and to give us [r]a wall i
Jerusalem.
10 And now, O our God, what sha
we say after this? for we have for
saken thy commandments,
11 Which thou hast commanded [6]b
thy servants the prophets, saying, Th
land, unto which ye go to possess i
is an unclean land with the filthines
of the people of the lands, with thei
abominations, which have filled

5 yellow, or, shining brass.
6 desirable.
t Deut. 33.8. Isa. 52.11.
u Lev. 22.2,3. Num. 4.4, 15,19,20. 1 Chr. 23.28. 2 Chr. 24.14.
v 1 Chr. 26. 20-26. Luke 12.37, 38.
w ch. 7.6,9, 28. Job 5.19-24. Isa. 41.10-14.
x Neh. 2.11.
y ch. 6.17.
z ch. 7.21.
a Isa. 56.6. Isa. 14.1. Zech. 8.1-23.

CHAP. 9

a Neh. 9.2.
b Deut. 12. 30.
c Deut. 7.3.
d Ex. 22.31.
e 2 Cor. 6.14.
f Isa. 15.2.
g Ps. 143.4.
h ch. 10.3. Isa. 66.2.
i Ex. 29.39.
1 Or, affliction.
j Ex. 9.29.
k Dan. 9.7.
2 Or, guiltiness.
l Ps. 106.6.
m Deut. 28. 36.
3 moment.
4 Or, a pin: that is, a constant and sure abode.
n Ps. 13.3.
o Neh. 9.36.
p Ps. 136.23.
q ch. 7.28.
5 to set up.
r Isa. 5.2.
6 by the hand of thy servants.

from one end to another with their
ncleanness.
12 Now therefore [s]give not your
laughters unto their sons, neither
ake their daughters unto your sons,
nor seek their peace or their wealth
or ever: that ye may be strong, and
at the good of the land, and [u]leave *it*
or an inheritance to your children for
ver.
13 And after all that is come upon us
or our evil deeds, and for our great
respass, seeing that thou our God
hast punished us less than our ini-
uities *deserve*, and hast given us *such*
leliverance as this;
14 Should we [v]again break thy com-
nandments, and [w]join in affinity with
he people of these abominations?
vouldest not thou be angry with us
ill thou hadst consumed *us*, so that
here should be no remnant nor escap-
ng?
15 O LORD God of Israel, [x]thou *art*
ighteous: for we remain yet escaped,
s *it is* this day: behold, we *are* [y]be-
ore thee in our trespasses: for we can-
ot [z]stand before thee because of this.

CHAPTER 10

NOW [a]when Ezra had prayed, and
when he had confessed, weeping
nd casting himself down before [b]the
ouse of God, there assembled unto
im out of Israel a very great congre-
ation of men and women and chil-
ren: for the people [1]wept very sore.
2 And Shĕch-ă-nī-ăh the son of Jĕ-
i-ĕl, *one* of the sons of Ē-lăm, an-
wered and said unto Ezra, We have
trespassed against our God, and have
aken strange wives of the people of
he land: yet now there is hope in Is-
ael concerning this thing.
3 Now therefore let us make a coven-
nt with our God [2]to put away all the
vives, and such as are born of them,
ccording to the counsel of my lord,
nd of those that [d]tremble [e]at the
ommandment of our God; and let
t be done according to the law.
4 Arise; for *this* matter *belongeth* un-
o thee: we also *will be* with thee: [f]be
of good courage, and do *it*.
5 Then arose Ezra, and made the
hief priests, the Levites, and all Is-
ael, [g]to swear that they should do
ccording to this word. And they
ware.
6 ¶ Then Ezra rose up from before
he house of God, and went into the
hamber of Jō-hā-năn the son of Ē-lī-
ish-ĭb: and *when* he came thither, he

7 from mouth to mouth.
s Ex. 23.32. Deut. 7.3. Josh. 23.12.
t Deut. 23.6. 2 Chr. 19.2.
u Gen. 18.19. Pro. 13.22.
8 hast withheld beneath our iniquities.
v Ex. 23.32, 33. Judg. 2.2. John 5.14. 2 Pet. 2.20.
w 2 Cor. 6.14.
x Neh. 9.33. Dan. 9.14.
y Rom. 3.19.
z Ps. 130.3.
CHAP. 10
a Dan. 9.20.
b 2 Chr. 20.9.
1 wept a great weeping.
c Ex. 34.13.
2 to bring forth.
d ch. 9.4. Ps. 119.53, 120. Isa. 66.2.
e Deut. 7.2,3.
f 1 Chr. 28. 10. Isa. 35.3,4.
g Neh. 5.12.
h Deut. 9.18.
3 devoted. Lev. 27.28. Josh. 6.19.
i 1 Sam. 12. 18.
4 the showers.
5 have caused to dwell, or, have brought back.
j Pro. 28.13. Jer. 3.13.
k Isa. 1.16, 17. Rom. 12.2.
6 Or, we have greatly offended in this thing.
l Num. 25.4. 2 Ki. 23.26. 2 Chr. 28. 11-13. 2 Chr. 29.10. 2 Chr. 30.8. Ps. 78.38. Isa. 12.1.
7 Or, till this matter be dispatched.
8 stood.

[h]did eat no bread, nor drink water:
for he mourned because of the transgression of them that had been carried
away.
7 And they made proclamation
throughout Judah and Jerusalem unto
all the children of the captivity, that
they should gather themselves together unto Jerusalem;
8 And that whosoever would not
come within three days, according to
the counsel of the princes and the elders, all his substance should be [3]for-
feited, and himself separated from the
congregation of those that had been
carried away.
9 ¶ Then all the men of Judah and
Benjamin gathered themselves together unto Jerusalem within three days.
It *was* the ninth month, on the twentieth *day* of the month; and [i]all the
people sat in the street of the house of
God, trembling because of *this* matter,
and for [4]the great rain.
10 And Ezra the priest stood up, and
said unto them, Ye have transgressed,
and [5]have taken strange wives, to increase the trespass of Israel.
11 Now therefore [j]make confession
unto the LORD God of your fathers,
and [k]do his pleasure: and separate
yourselves from the people of the
land, and from the strange wives.
12 Then all the congregation answered and said with a loud voice, As
thou hast said, so must we do.
13 But the people *are* many, and *it is*
a time of much rain, and we are not
able to stand without, neither *is this*
a work of one day or two: for [6]we are
many that have transgressed in this
thing.
14 Let now our rulers of all the congregation stand, and let all them which
have taken strange wives in our cities
come at appointed times, and with
them the elders of every city, and the
judges thereof, until the [l]fierce wrath
of our God [7]for this matter be turned
from us.
15 ¶ Only Jonathan the son of Ăs-ă-
hĕl and Jā-hă-zī-ăh the son of Tĭk-văh
[8]were employed about this *matter:* and
Mĕ-shŭl-lăm and Shăb-bĕ-thāi the
Levite helped them.
16 And the children of the captivity
did so. And Ezra the priest, *with* certain chief of the fathers, after the
house of their fathers, and all of them
by *their* names, were separated, and
sat down in the first day of the tenth
month to examine the matter.
17 And they made an end with all the

men that had taken strange wives by
the first day of the first month.
18 ¶ And among the sons of the
priests there were found that had tak-
en strange wives: *namely*, of the sons
of [m]Jĕsh´ū-ă the son of Jō´ză-dăk, and
his brethren; Mā-ă-sēi´āh, and Ĕl-ĭ-ē´-
zĕr, and Jâr´ĭb, and Gĕd-ă-lī´āh.
19 And they [n]gave their hands that
they would put away their wives; and
[o]*being* guilty, *they offered* a ram of the
flock for their trespass.
20 And of the sons of Ĭm´mĕr; Hă-
nā´nī, and Zĕb-ă-dī´āh.
21 And of the sons of Hâr´ĭm; Mā-
ă-sēi´āh, and Ē-lī´jāh, and Shĕm-âi´-
āh, and Jĕ-hī´ĕl, and Ŭz-zī´āh.
22 And of the sons of Păsh´ûr;
Ĕl-ĭ-ō-ē´nâi, Mā-ă-sēi´āh, Ĭsh´mā-ĕl,
Nĕth´ă-neel, Jō´ză-băd, and Ĕl-ā´sāh.
23 Also of the Levites; Jō´ză-băd,
and Shĭm´ĕ-ī, and Kĕ-lâi´āh, (the same
is Kĕ-lī´tă,) Pĕth-ă-hī´āh, Judah, and
Ĕl-ĭ-ē´zĕr.
24 Of the singers also; Ē-lī´ăsh-ĭb:
and of the porters; Shăl´lŭm, and Tē´-
lĕm, and Ū´rī.
25 Moreover of Israel: of the sons of
[p]Pâr´ŏsh; Ră-mī´āh, and Jĕ-zī´āh, and
Măl-chī´āh, and Mī´ă-mĭn, and Ĕl-ē-
ā´zär, and Măl-chī´jāh, and Bĕ-nâi´-
āh.
26 And of the sons of Ē´lăm; Măt-tă-
nī´āh, Zĕch-ă-rī´āh, and Jĕ-hī´ĕl, and
Ăb´dī, and Jĕr´ē-mŏth, and Ē-lī´āh.
27 And of the sons of [q]Zăt´tû; Ĕl-ĭ-
ō-ē´nâi, Ē-lī´ăsh-ĭb, Măt-tă-nī´āh, and
Jĕr´ē-mŏth, and Zā´băd, and Ă-zī´ză.
28 Of the sons also of Bē-bā´ī; Jĕ-hō-

m ch. 5.2. Hag. 1.1,12. Zech. 3.1. Zech. 6.11.
n 2 Ki. 10.15. 1 Chr. 29.24. 2 Chr. 30.8. Pro. 6.1. Pro. 22.26. Gal. 2.9.
o Lev. 5.15. Lev. 6.4,5,6.
p ch. 2.3. ch. 8.3. Neh. 7.8.
q ch. 2.8. Neh. 7.13.
r Neh. 3.11, Malchijah.
9 Or, Mabnadebai, according to some copies.
s Num. 32.38. ch. 2.29.
t Gen. 6.2-5. Ex. 23.2. Deut. 7.3.

hā´năn, Hăn-ă-nī´āh, Zăb-bā´ī, *an*
Ăth-lā´ī.
29 And of the sons of Bā´nī; Mĕ
shŭl´lăm, Măl´lŭch, and Ă-dâi´āh
Jăsh´ŭb, and Shē´ăl, and Rā´mŏth.
30 And of the sons of Pā´hăth–mō
ăb; Ăd´nă, and Chē´lăl, Bĕ-nâi´āh
Mā-ă-sēi´āh, Măt-tă-nī´āh, Bĕz´ă-leel
and Bĭn´nū-ī, and Mă-năs´sĕh.
31 And *of* the sons of Hâr´ĭm; Ĕl-ĭ
ē´zĕr, Ĭsh-ī´jāh, [r]Măl-chī´āh, Shĕm
âi´āh, Shĭm´ē-on,
32 Benjamin, Măl´lŭch, *and* Shĕm
ă-rī´āh.
33 Of the sons of Hăsh´ŭm; Măt-tē
nâi, Măt´tă-thăh, Zā´băd, Ē-lĭph´ĕ
lĕt, Jĕr-ē-mā´ī, Mă-năs´sĕh, *and* Shĭm
ĕ-ī.
34 Of the sons of Bā´nī; Mā-ă-dā´ī
Amram, and Ū´ĕl,
35 Bĕ-nâi´āh, Bĕ-dēi´āh, Chĕl´lûh,
36 Vă-nī´āh, Mĕr´ē-mŏth, Ē-lī´ăsh
ĭb,
37 Măt-tă-nī´āh, Măt-tē´nâi, and Jā
ă-sâu,
38 And Bā´nī, and Bĭn´nū-ī, Shĭm´ĕ-ī
39 And Shĕl-ē-mī´āh, and Nathan
and Ă-dâi´āh,
40 [9]Măch-năd´ĕ-bâi, Shā´shâi, Shâr
ā´ī,
41 Ăz´ă-reel, and Shĕl-ē-mī´āh
Shĕm-ă-rī´āh,
42 Shăl´lŭm, Ăm-ă-rī´āh, *and* Joseph
43 Of the sons of [s]Nē´bō; Jē-ī´ĕl
Măt-tĭ-thī´āh, Zā´băd, Zĕ-bī´nă, Jā
dâu, and Jō´ĕl, Bĕ-nâi´āh.
44 All [t]these had taken strang
wives: and *some* of them had wives b
whom they had children.

THE

BOOK OF NEHEMIAH

CHAPTER 1

THE words of [a]Nē-hĕm-ī´āh the
son of Hăch-ă-lī´āh. And it came
to pass in the month Chĭs´lēu, in the
[b]twentieth year, as I was in Shû´shăn
[c]the palace,
2 That Hă-nā´nī, one of my brethren,
came, he and *certain* men of Judah;
and I asked them concerning the Jews
that had escaped, which were left of
the captivity, and concerning Jerusalem.
3 And they said unto me, The remnant that are left of the captivity there
in the province *are* in great affliction

CHAP. 1
a ch. 10.1.
b Ezra 7.8. ch. 2.1.
c Esther 1.2. Dan. 8.2.
d ch. 2.17. Isa. 5.5. Jer. 5.10.
e 2 Ki. 25.10.
f Deut. 10.17. ch. 4.14. Job 37.22.
g Ex. 20.6. Deut. 7.9. Ps. 89.2. Heb. 6.13-18.
h 1 Ki. 8.28, 29. 2 Chr. 6.40.

and reproach: [d]the wall of Jerusalem
also [e]*is* broken down, and the gate
thereof are burned with fire.
4 ¶ And it came to pass, when
heard these words, that I sat dow
and wept, and mourned *certain* days
and fasted, and prayed before th
God of heaven,
5 And said, I beseech thee, [f]O LORD
God of heaven, the great and terribl
God, [g]that keepeth covenant an
mercy for them that love him and ob
serve his commandments:
6 Let thine ear now be attentive, an
thine [h]eyes open, that thou mayes

r the prayer of thy servant, which
ay before thee now, day and night,
the children of Israel thy servants,
I confess [i]the sins of the children of
ael, which we have sinned against
e: both I and my father's house
'e sinned.
We [j]have dealt very corruptly
inst thee, and have [k]not kept the
nmandments, nor the statutes, nor
judgments, which thou command-
t thy servant Moses.
Remember, I beseech thee, the
rd that thou commandedst thy ser-
t Moses, saying, *If* [l]ye transgress,
ill scatter you abroad among the
ions:
But [m]*if* ye turn unto me, and keep
commandments, and do them;
ough there were of you cast out un-
the uttermost part of the heaven,
will I gather them from thence, and
I bring them unto the place that I
e chosen to set my name there.
Now [o]these *are* thy servants and
people, whom thou hast redeemed
thy great power, and by thy strong
d.
O Lord, I beseech thee, let now
ne ear be attentive to the prayer of
servant, and to the prayer of thy
vants, who desire [p]to fear thy
ne: and prosper, I pray thee, thy
vant this day, and grant [q]him mercy
he sight of this man. For I was the
ng's cupbearer.

CHAPTER 2

ND it came to pass in the month
Ni´-săn, in the twentieth year of
-tă-xĕrx´-ēs the king, *that* wine *was*
ore him: and [b]I took up the wine,
I gave *it* unto the king. Now I had
been *beforetime* sad in his pres-
e.
Wherefore the king said unto me,
y *is* thy countenance sad, seeing
u *art* not sick? this *is* nothing *else*
[c]sorrow of heart. Then I was very
e afraid,
And said unto the king, [d]Let the
g live for ever: why should not my
ntenance be sad, when the [e]city,
place of my fathers' sepulchres,
h waste, and the gates thereof are
sumed with fire?
Then the king said unto me, For
at dost thou make request? So [f]I
yed to the God of heaven.
And I said unto the king, If it please
king, and if thy servant have found
our in thy sight, that thou wouldest
d me unto Judah, unto the city of
my fathers' sepulchres, that I may
build it.
6 And the king said unto me, (the
[1]queen also sitting by him,) For how
long shall thy journey be? and when
wilt thou return? So it pleased the
king to send me; and I set him [g]a time.
7 Moreover I said unto the king, If it
please the king, let letters be given me
to the governors beyond the river,
that they may convey me over till I
come into Judah;
8 And a letter unto Ā´-săph the keeper of the king's forest, that he may
give me timber to make beams for the
gates of the palace which *appertained*
[h]to the house, and for the wall of the
city, and for the house that I shall enter into. And the king granted me,
[i]according to the good hand of my
God upon me.
9 ¶ Then I came to the governors beyond the river, and gave them the
king's letters. Now the king had sent
captains of the army and horsemen
with me.
10 When Săn-băl´-lăt the [2]Hôr´-ŏn-īte,
and Tō-bī´-ăh the servant, the Ammonite, heard *of it*, it grieved them exceedingly that there was come a man
to seek the welfare of the children of
Israel.
11 So I [j]came to Jerusalem, and was
there three days.
12 ¶ And I arose in the night, I and
some few men with me; neither told
I *any* man what my God had put in
my heart to do at Jerusalem: neither
was there any beast with me, save the
beast that I rode upon.
13 And I went out by night [k]by the
gate of the valley, even before the
dragon well, and to the dung port, and
viewed the walls of Jerusalem, which
were [l]broken down, and the gates
thereof were consumed with fire.
14 Then I went on to the [m]gate of the
fountain, and to the king's pool: but
there was no place for the beast *that*
was under me to pass.
15 Then went I up in the night by [n]the
brook, and viewed the wall, and turned back, and entered by the gate of the
valley, and *so* returned.
16 And the rulers knew not whither
I went, or what I did; neither had I
as yet told *it* to the Jews, nor to the
priests, nor to the nobles, nor to the
rulers, nor to the rest that did the
work.
17 ¶ Then said I unto them, Ye see
the distress that we *are* in, how Jerusalem *lieth* waste, and the gates there-

i Dan. 9.20.
j Ps. 106.6.
k Deut. 28. 15.
l Lev. 26.33. Deut. 4.25.
m Lev. 26.39. Deut. 4.29.
n Deut. 30.4.
o Deut. 9.29. Dan. 9.15.
p Ps. 119.4. Isa. 26.8. Heb. 13.18.
q Gen. 32.11. Ps. 37.5. Pro. 16.3.
r ch. 2.1.

CHAP. 2

a Ezra 7.1. That is, of Artaxerxes Longimanus.
b ch. 1.11.
c Pro. 15.13.
d 1 Ki. 1.31. Dan. 2.4. Dan. 5.10.
e ch. 1.3. Ps. 137.5.
f 1 Sam. 1.13. ch. 1.11. Pro. 3.6.
1 wife. Probably Esther.
g ch. 5.14.
h Ezra 10.6, 9. ch. 3.7. That is, the temple.
i Ezra 5.5. Pro. 21.1. Isa. 66.14. Dan. 1.9. Acts 7.10.
2 Or, Moabite.
j Ezra 8.32.
k 2 Chr. 26.9. ch. 3.13.
l ch. 1.3. Jer. 5.10.
m 2 Ki. 20.20. 2 Chr. 32.30. ch. 3.15.
n 2 Sam. 15. 23. Jer. 31.40. John 18.1.

of are burned with fire: come, and let us build up the wall of Jerusalem, that we be no more [o]a reproach.

18 Then I told them of the hand of my God which was good upon me; as also the king's words that he had spoken unto me. And they said, Let us rise up and build. So they [p]strengthened their hands for *this* good *work*.

19 But when Săn-băl´-lăt the Hôr´-ŏn-īte, and Tō-bī´-ăh the servant, the Ammonite, and Gē´-shĕm the Arabian, heard *it*, they [q]laughed us to scorn, and despised us, and said, What *is* this thing that ye do? will ye rebel against the king?

20 Then answered I them, and said unto them, [r]The God of heaven, he will prosper us; therefore we his servants will arise and build: but [s]ye have no portion, nor right, nor memorial, in Jerusalem.

CHAPTER 3

THEN [a]Ē-lī-ăsh-ĭb the high priest rose up with his brethren the priests, [b]and they builded the sheep gate; they sanctified it, and set up the doors of it; [c]even unto the tower of Mē´-ăh they sanctified it, unto the tower of [d]Hăn´-ă-neel.

2 And [1]next unto him [e]builded the men of Jericho. And next to them builded Zăc´-cŭr the son of Imri.

3 But [f]the fish gate did the sons of Hăs-sĕ-nā´-ăh build, who *also* laid the beams thereof, and [g]set up the doors thereof, the locks thereof, and the bars thereof.

4 And next unto them repaired Mĕr´-ĕ-mōth the son of Ū-rī´-jăh, the son of Kŏz. And next unto them repaired Mĕ-shŭl´-lăm the son of Bĕr-ē-chī´-ăh, the son of Mĕ-shĕz´-ă-beel. And next unto them repaired Zā´-dŏk the son of Bā´-ă-nă.

5 And next unto them the Tĕ-kō´-ītes repaired; but their nobles put not their necks to [h]the work of their Lord.

6 Moreover [i]the old gate repaired Jĕ-hôi´-ă-dă the son of Pā-sē´-ăh, and Mĕ-shŭl´-lăm the son of Bĕs-ō-dêi´-ăh; they laid the beams thereof, and set up the doors thereof, and the locks thereof, and the bars thereof.

7 And next unto them repaired Mĕl-ă-tī´-ăh the Gibeonite, and Jā´-dŏn the Mĕ-rō´-nō-thīte, the men of Gibeon, [j]and of Mizpah, unto the throne [k]of the governor on this side the river.

8 Next unto him repaired Ŭz´-zī-ĕl the son of Här-hâi´-ăh, of the goldsmiths. Next unto him also repaired

o 1 Sam. 11.2. ch. 1.3. Ps. 44.13. Jer. 24.9. Lam. 3.45, 46. Eze. 5.14.
p 2 Sam. 2.7.
q Ps. 44.13. Ps. 79.4.
r Ps. 127.1. Rom. 8.31.
s Ezra 4.3. John 4.9. Acts 8.21.
CHAP. 3
a ch. 12.10.
b ch. 12.39. John 5.2.
c ch. 12.39.
d Jer. 31.38. Zech. 14.10.
1 at his hand.
e Ezra 2.34. ch. 7.36.
f 2 Chr. 33. 14. ch. 12.39. Zeph. 1.10.
g ch. 6.1.
h Judg. 5.23.
i ch. 12.39.
j Josh. 9.3.
k ch. 2.8.
2 Or, left Jerusalem unto the broad wall.
l ch. 12.38.
m Ezra 2.32.
3 second measure.
n ch. 12.38.
o Ex. 35.25. Luke 8.3. Phil. 4.3.
p ch. 2.13.
q Josh. 15.34.
r ch. 2.13.
s Jer. 6.1. Micah 1.11.
t ch. 2.14.
u Josh. 18.26. Judg. 20.1,3. Jer. 40.6.
v Isa. 8.6. Luke 13.4. John 9.7.
w 2 Ki. 20.20. Isa. 22.11.
x Song 3.7.
y Josh. 15.44. 1 Sam. 23.1.
z 2 Chr. 26.9.
4 Or, Zaccai.
a Eccl. 9.10. Rom. 12.11.

Hăn-ă-nī´-ăh the son of *one of* apothecaries, and they [2]fortified J salem unto the [l]broad wall.

9 And next unto them repaired phâi´-ăh the son of Hur, the rul the half part of Jerusalem.

10 And next unto them repaired dâi´-ăh the son of Hă-rû´-măph, over against his house. And next him repaired Hăt´-tŭsh the sor Hăsh-ăb-nī´-ăh.

11 Măl-chī´-jăh [m]the son of Hâr and Hăsh´-ŭb the son of Pā´-hăth-ăb, repaired the [3]other piece, and tower of the furnaces.

12 And next unto him repaired S lŭm the son of Hă-lō´-hĕsh, the rul the half part of Jerusalem, he and daughters.

13 The [p]valley gate repaired Hā´- and the inhabitants [q]of Ză-nō´ they built it, and set up the d thereof, the locks thereof, and the thereof, and a thousand cubits on wall unto the [r]dung gate.

14 But the dung gate repaired M chī´-ăh the son of Rē´-chăb, the rul part of [s]Bĕth–hăc´-cē-rĕm; he buil and set up the doors thereof, the lo thereof, and the bars thereof.

15 But [t]the gate of the fountain paired Shăl´-lŭn the son of Cŏl-hō´ the ruler of part of [u]Mizpah; he b it, and covered it, and set up the d thereof, the locks thereof, and the thereof, and the wall of the poo [v]Sĭ-lō´-ăh by the king's garden, and to the stairs that go down from city of David.

16 After him repaired Nē-hĕm-the son of Ăz-bŭk, the ruler of the part of Bĕth´-zŭr, unto *the place* c against the sepulchres of David, to the [w]pool that was made, and u the [x]house of the mighty.

17 After him repaired the Levi Rē-hŭm the son of Bā´-nī. Next u him repaired Hăsh-ă-bī´-ăh, the r of the half part [y]of Kē-ī´-lăh, in part.

18 After him repaired their brethr Bā-vā´-ī the son of Hĕn-ā´-dăd, the er of the half part of Kē-ī´-lăh.

19 And next to him repaired Ē- the son of Jĕsh´-ū-ă, the ruler of M pah, another piece over against going up to the armoury [z]at the tu ing *of the wall*.

20 After him Bâr´-ŭch the son [4]Zăb-bā´-ī earnestly [a]repaired the ot piece, from the turning *of the wall* u the door of the house of Ē-lī-ăsh the high priest.

1 After him repaired Mĕr-ĕ-mōth
e son of Ū-rī-jăh the son of Kŏz an-
her piece, from the door of the house
Ē-lī-ăsh-ĭb even to the end of the
use of Ē-lī-ăsh-ĭb.
2 And after him repaired the priests,
e men of the plain.
3 After him repaired Benjamin and
ăsh-ŭb over against their house. Af-
r him repaired Ăz-ă-rī-ăh the son of
ā-ă-seī-ăh the son of Ăn-ă-nī-ăh by
s house.
4 After him repaired Bĭn-nū-ī the
n of Hĕn-ā-dăd another piece, from
e house of Ăz-ă-rī-ăh unto the turn-
g *of the wall*, even unto the corner.
5 Pā-lăl the son of Ū-zāi, over
ainst the turning *of the wall*, and the
wer which lieth out from the king's
gh house, that *was* by the [b]court of
e prison. After him Pĕ-dāi-ăh the
n of Pâr-ŏsh.
6 Moreover [c]the Nĕth-ĭ-nĭmṡ [5]dwelt
[6]Ō-phĕl, unto *the place* over against
e water gate toward the east, and
e tower that lieth out.
7 After them the Tĕ-kō-ītes repaired
other piece, over against the great
wer that lieth out, even unto the
ll of Ō-phĕl.
8 From above the [e]horse gate re-
ired the priests, every one over
ainst his house.
9 After them repaired Zā-dŏk the
n of Ĭm-mĕr over against his house.
ter him repaired also Shĕm-āi-ăh
e son of Shĕch-ă-nī-ăh, the keeper
[7]the east gate.
0 After him repaired Hăn-ă-nī-ăh
e son of Shĕl-ē-mī-ăh, and Hā-nŭn
e sixth son of Zā-lăph, another
ece. After him repaired Mĕ-shŭl-
n the son of Bĕr-ē-chī-ăh over
ainst his chamber.
1 After him repaired Măl-chī-ăh the
ldsmith's son unto the place of the
ĕth-ĭ-nĭmṡ, and of the merchants,
er against the gate Mĭph-kăd, and
the [8]going up of the corner.
2 And between the going up of the
rner unto [f]the sheep gate repaired
e goldsmiths and the merchants.

CHAPTER 4

BUT it came to pass, [a]that when
Săn-băl-lăt heard that we builded
e wall, he was wroth, and took great
dignation, and mocked the Jews.
And he spake before his brethren
d the army of Să-mâr-ĭ-ă, and said,
hat do these feeble Jews? will they
rtify themselves? will they sacri-
e? will they make an end in a day?
will they revive the stones out of the
heaps of the rubbish which are
burned?
3 Now [b]Tō-bī-ăh the Ammonite *was*
by him, and he said, Even that which
they build, if a fox go up, he shall even
break down their stone wall.
4 Hear, [c]O our God; for we are [2]de-
spised: and [d]turn their reproach upon
their own head, and give them for a
prey in the land of captivity:
5 And [e]cover not their iniquity, and
let not their sin be blotted out from
before thee: for they have provoked
thee to anger before the builders.
6 So built we the wall; and all the
wall was joined together unto the half
thereof: for the people had a mind to
work.
7 ¶ But it came to pass, *that* when
Săn-băl-lăt, and Tō-bī-ăh, and the
Arabians, and the Ammonites, and
the Ăsh-dō-dītes, heard that the walls
of Jerusalem [3]were made up, *and* that
the breaches began to be stopped,
then they were very wroth,
8 And [f]conspired all of them together
to come *and* to fight against Jerusalem, and [4]to hinder it.
9 Nevertheless [g]we made our prayer
unto our God, and set a watch against
them day and night, because of them.
10 And Judah said, The strength of
the bearers of burdens is decayed,
and *there is* much rubbish; so that we
are not able to build the wall.
11 And our adversaries said, They
shall not know, neither see, till we
come in the midst among them, and
slay them, and cause the work to
cease.
12 And it came to pass, that when the
Jews which dwelt by them came, they
said unto us ten times, [5]From all
places whence ye shall return unto us
they will be upon you.
13 ¶ Therefore set I [6]in the lower
places behind the wall, *and* on the
higher places, I even set the people
after their families with their swords,
their spears, and their bows.
14 And I looked, and rose up, and
said unto the nobles, and to the rulers,
and to the rest of the people, [h]Be not
ye afraid of them: remember the
Lord, *which* [i]*is* great and terrible, and
[j]fight for your brethren, your sons,
and your daughters, your wives, and
your houses.
15 And it came to pass, when our enemies heard that it was known unto
us, [k]and God had brought their counsel to nought, that we returned all of

b ch. 12.39. Jer. 32.2.
c Ezra 2.43. ch. 7.46.
5 Or, which dwelt in Ophel, repaired unto.
6 Or, the tower.
d ch. 8.1,3.
e 2 Ki. 11.16. 2 Chr. 23.15. Jer. 31.40.
7 the sun gate, Jer. 19.2.
8 Or, corner chamber.
f ch. 12.39. John 5.2.

CHAP. 4

a Ezra 4.1-5. ch. 2.10. Ps. 2.1,4. Acts 5.17.
1 leave to themselves.
b ch. 2.10,19.
c Ps. 123. 3,4. Isa. 53.3. Luke 16.14.
2 despite.
d 1 Sam. 17. 26. Ps. 79.12. Pro. 3.34. Hos. 12.14.
e Ps. 59.5-13. Ps. 69.27. Jer. 18.23. 2 Tim. 4.14.
3 ascended.
f Ps. 2.1-3. Isa. 8.9,10. Acts 23.12, 13.
4 to make an error to it.
g Job 22.27. Ps. 50.15. Matt. 26.41.
5 Or, That from all places ye must return to us.
6 from the lower parts of the place, etc.
h Num. 14.9. Deut. 1.29.
i Deut. 10.17. Job 37.22. Heb. 12.20, 21,28,29.
j 2 Sam. 10. 12.
k Job 5.12. Ps. 33.10.

us to the wall, every one unto his
work.
16 And it came to pass from that
time forth, *that* the half of my servants
wrought in the work, and the other
half of them held both the spears, the
shields, and the bows, and the habergeons; and the rulers *were* behind all
the house of Judah.
17 They which builded on the wall,
and they that bare burdens, with those
that laded, *every one* with [l]one of his
hands wrought in the work, and with
the other *hand* held a weapon.
18 For the builders, every one had
his sword girded [7]by his side, and *so*
builded. And he that sounded the
trumpet *was* by me.
19 ¶ And I said unto the nobles, and
to the rulers, and to the rest of the people, The work *is* great and large, and
we are separated upon the wall, one
far from another.
20 In what place *therefore* ye hear
the sound of the trumpet, resort ye
thither unto us: [m]our God shall fight
for us.
21 So we laboured in the work: and
half of them held the spears from the
rising of the morning till the stars
appeared.
22 Likewise at the same time said I
unto the people, Let every one with
his servant lodge within Jerusalem,
that in the night they may be a guard
to us, and labour on the day.
23 So neither I, nor my brethren, nor
my servants, nor the men of the guard
which followed me, none of us put off
our clothes, [8]*saving that* every one
put them off for washing.

CHAPTER 5

AND there was a [a]great cry of the
people and of their wives against
[b]their brethren the Jews.
2 For there were that said, We, our
sons, and our daughters, *are* many:
therefore we [c]take up corn *for them*,
that we may eat, and live.
3 *Some* also there were that said, We
have mortgaged our lands, vineyards,
and houses, that we might buy corn,
because of the dearth.
4 There were also that said, We have
borrowed money for the king's tribute, *and that upon* our lands and vineyards.
5 Yet now [d]our flesh *is* as the flesh of
our brethren, our children as their
children: and, lo, [e]we bring into bondage our sons and our daughters to be
servants, and *some* of our daughters
are brought unto bondage *alrea*
neither *is it* in our power *to rede*
them; for other men have our la
and vineyards.
6 ¶ And I was very [f]angry whe
heard their cry and these words.
7 Then [1]I consulted with myself, a
[g]I rebuked the nobles, and the rule
and said unto them, Ye [h]exact usu
every one of his brother. And I set
great assembly against them.
8 And I said unto them, We after c
ability have [j]redeemed our brethr
the Jews, which were sold unto t
heathen; and will ye even sell yo
brethren? or shall they be sold ur
us? Then held they their peace, a
found nothing *to answer*.
9 Also I said, It *is* not good that
do: ought ye not to walk [k]in the fe
of our God [l]because of the reproa
of the heathen our enemies?
10 I likewise, *and* my brethren, a
my servants, might exact of the
money and corn: I pray you, let
leave off this usury.
11 Restore, I pray you, to them, ev
this day, their lands, their vineyar
their oliveyards, and their hous
also the hundredth *part* of the mone
and of the corn, the wine, and the o
that ye exact of them.
12 Then said they, We will resto
them, and will require nothing
them; so will we do as thou saye
Then I called the priests, [m]and to
an oath of them, that they should
according to this promise.
13 Also [n]I shook my lap, and sai
So God [o]shake out every man fro
his house, and from his labour, th
performeth not this promise, ev
thus be he shaken out, and [2]emptie
And all the congregation said, Ä-mĕ
and praised the LORD. [p]And the pe
ple did according to this promise.
14 ¶ Moreover from the time that
was appointed to be their governor
the land of Judah, from the twentie
year [q]even unto the two and thirtie
year of Är-tă-xĕrx-ēs the king, *that*
twelve years, I and my brethren hav
not eaten the [r]bread of the gove
nor.
15 But the former governors that *ha*
been before me were chargeable unt
the people, and had taken of the
bread and wine, beside forty sheke
of silver; yea, even their servants ba
rule over the people: but [s]so did not
because of the fear [t]of God.
16 Yea, also I continued in the wor
of this wall, neither bought we ar

l 1 Cor. 16.13. Eph. 6.10.
7 on his loins.
m Ex. 14.14. Deut. 1.30. Deut. 3.22. Josh. 23.10.
8 Or, every one went with his weapon for water.

CHAP. 5

a Isa. 5.7. Jas. 5.4.
b Lev. 25.35. Deut. 15.7.
c Gen. 41.57. Hag. 1.6.
d Gen. 37.27. Isa. 58.7. Acts 17.26.
e Ex. 21.7. Matt. 18.25.
f Ex. 11.8. ch. 13.8. Mark 3.5. Eph. 4.26.
1 my heart consulted in me.
g Lev. 19.17. 1 Tim. 5.20.
h Ex. 22.25. Deut. 23.19. Ps. 15.5.
i Pro. 27.5. Matt. 18.17.
j Lev. 25.48.
k Gen. 20.11. Lev. 25.36. Acts 9.31.
l Gen. 13.7,8. 2 Sam. 12. 14. Rom. 2.24. Titus 2.5. 1 Pet. 2.12.
m Ezra 10.5. Jer. 34.8,9.
n Matt. 10.14. Acts 13.51.
o Zech. 5.4.
2 empty, or, void.
p 2 Ki. 23.3.
q ch. 13.6.
r 1 Cor. 9.4.
s 2 Cor. 11.9.
t Gen. 42.18. Job 31.23. Ps. 112.1. Pro. 16.6. Eccl. 12.13, 14. Luke 18.2-4.

d: and all my servants *were* gather-
thither unto the work.
7 Moreover *there were* [u]at my table
hundred and fifty of the Jews and
ers, beside those that came unto us
m among the heathen that *are*
out us.
3 Now *that* [v]which was prepared *for*
daily *was* one ox *and* six choice
eep; also fowls were prepared for
, and once in ten days store of all
rts of wine: yet for all this required
t I the bread of the governor, be-
use the bondage was heavy upon
is people.
9 Think [w]upon me, my God, for
od, *according* to all that I have done
r this people.

CHAPTER 6

NOW it came to pass, [a]when Săn-
băl-lăt, and Tō-bī-ăh, and [1]Gē-
ĕm the Arabian, and the rest of our
emies, heard that I had builded the
ll, and *that* there was no breach
t therein; ([b]though at that time I
d not set up the doors upon the
tes;)
That Săn-băl-lăt and [c]Gē-shĕm sent
to me, saying, Come, let us meet to-
ther in *some one of* the villages in
e plain [d]of Ō-nō. But they [e]thought
do me mischief.
And I [f]sent messengers unto them,
ying, I *am* doing a great work, so
at I cannot come down: why should
e work cease, whilst I leave it, and
me down to you?
Yet they sent unto me [g]four times
ter this sort; and I answered them
ter the same manner.
Then sent Săn-băl-lăt his servant
to me in like manner the fifth time
th an open letter in his hand;
Wherein *was* written, It is [h]re-
rted among the heathen, and [2]Găsh-
û saith *it, that* [i]thou and the Jews
ink to rebel: for which cause thou
ildest the wall, that thou mayest be
eir king, according to these words.
And thou hast also appointed pro-
ets to preach of thee at Jerusalem,
ying, *There is* a king in Judah: and
w shall it be reported to the king
cording to these words. Come now
erefore, and let us take counsel to-
ther.
Then I sent unto him, saying, There
e no such things done as thou say-
, but thou [j]feignest them out of
ne own heart.
For they all made us afraid, saying,
eir hands shall be weakened from

u 2 Sam. 9.7.
v 1 Ki. 4.22.
w ch. 13.22.

CHAP. 6

a ch. 2.10.
1 Or, Gashmu, ver. 6.
b ch. 3.1,3.
c Pro. 26.24.
d 1 Chr. 8.12. ch. 11.25,35.
e Ps. 12.2. Pro. 26.24. Eccl. 4.4. Micah 7.4,5.
f Pro. 14.15.
g Pro. 1.10.
h Jer. 9.3. Rom. 3.8. 2 Cor. 6.8. 1 Pet. 2.12.
2 Or, Geshem, ver. 1.
i ch. 2.19. Ezra 4.13. Luke 23.2.
j Job 13.4. Ps. 36.3. Isa. 59.4. Dan. 11.27.
k Deut. 33. 25. Ps. 56.3. Isa. 41.10. 2 Cor. 12.9.
l Pro. 26.24.
m Pro. 28.1.
n Eze. 13.22.
o ch. 13.29.
p Eze. 13.17.
q ver. 1. ch. 2.10. ch. 4.1,7.
r Ps. 126.2.
3 multiplied their letters passing to Tobiah.
4 Or, matters.

CHAP. 7

a ch. 3.1-32.
b ch. 6.1.
c ch. 2.8.

the work, that it be not done. Now
therefore, *O* [k]*God*, strengthen my
hands.
10 Afterward I came unto the house
of Shĕm-âī-ăh the son of Dĕl-âī-ăh
the son of Mĕ-hĕt-ă-beel, who *was*
shut up; and he said, Let [l]us meet together in the house of God, within the
temple, and let us shut the doors of
the temple: for they will come to slay
thee; yea, in the night will they come
to slay thee.
11 And I said, Should [m]such a man
as I flee? and who *is there*, that, *being*
as I *am*, would go into the temple to
save his life? I will not go in.
12 And, lo, I perceived that God had
not sent him; but that [n]he pronounced
this prophecy against me: for Tō-bī-
ăh and Săn-băl-lăt had hired him.
13 Therefore *was* he hired, that I
should be afraid, and do so, and sin,
and *that* they might have *matter* for
an evil report, that they might reproach me.
14 My [o]God, think thou upon Tō-bī-
ăh and Săn-băl-lăt according to these
their works, and on the prophetess
[p]Nō-ă-dī-ăh, and the rest of the prophets, that would have put me in fear.
15 ¶ So the wall was finished in the
twenty and fifth *day* of *the month* Ē-lŭl,
in fifty and two days.
16 And it came to pass, that when
[q]all our enemies heard *thereof*, and all
the heathen that *were* about us saw
these things, they were much cast
down in their own eyes: for they [r]per-
ceived that this work was wrought of
our God.
17 ¶ Moreover in those days the
nobles of Judah [3]sent many letters unto Tō-bī-ăh, and *the letters* of Tō-bī-
ăh came unto them.
18 For *there were* many in Judah
sworn unto him, because he *was* the
son in law of Shĕch-ă-nī-ăh the son
of Âr-ăh; and his son Jō-hā-năn had
taken the daughter of Mĕ-shŭl-lăm
the son of Bĕr-ē-chī-ăh.
19 Also they reported his good deeds
before me, and uttered my [4]words to
him. *And* Tō-bī-ăh sent letters to put
me in fear.

CHAPTER 7

NOW it came to pass, when the
wall [a]was built, and I had set [b]up
the doors, and the porters and the
singers and the Levites were appointed,
2 That I gave my brother Hă-nā-nī,
and Hăn-ă-nī-ăh the ruler [c]of the

palace, charge over Jerusalem: for he
was [d]a faithful man, and feared [e]God
above many.
3 And I said unto them, Let not the
gates of Jerusalem be opened until the
sun be hot; and while they stand
by, let them shut the doors, and bar
them: and appoint watches of the inhabitants of Jerusalem, every one in
his watch, and every one *to be* over
against his house.
4 Now the city *was* [1]large and great:
but the people *were* few therein, and
the houses *were* not builded.
5 ¶ And my [f]God put into mine heart
to gather together the nobles, and the
rulers, and the people, that they might
be reckoned by genealogy. And I
found [2]a register of the genealogy of
them which came up at the first, and
found written therein,
6 These *are* the children of the province, that went up out of the captivity,
of those that had been carried away,
whom Nĕb-ū-c̲hăd-nĕz′-zăr the king of
Babylon had carried away, and came
again to Jerusalem and to Judah,
every one unto his city;
7 Who came with Zĕ-rŭb′-bă-bĕl,
Jĕsh′-ū-ă, Nē-hĕm-ī′-ăh, [3]Ăz-ă-rī′-ăh,
Rā-ă-mī′-ăh, Nā-hă-mā′-nī, Môr-dĕ-
cā′-ī, Bilshan, Mĭs′-pĕ-rĕth, Bĭg-vā′-ī,
Nē-hŭm, Bā′-ă-năh. The number, *I
say*, of the men of the people of Israel
was this;
8 The children of Pâr′-ŏsh, two thousand an hundred seventy and two.
9 The children of Shĕph-ă-tī′-ăh,
three hundred seventy and two.
10 The children of Âr′-ăh, six hundred fifty and two.
11 The children of Pā′-hăth–mō′-ăb,
of the children of Jĕsh′-ū-ă and Jō′-ăb,
two thousand and eight hundred *and*
eighteen.
12 The children of Ē′-lăm, a thousand
two hundred fifty and four.
13 The children of Zăt′-tû, eight hundred forty and five.
14 The children of Zăc-cā′-ī, seven
hundred and threescore.
15 The children of [4]Bĭn′-nū-ī, six hundred forty and eight.
16 The children of Bē-bā′-ī, six hundred twenty and eight.
17 The children of Ăz′-găd, two thousand three hundred twenty and two.
18 The children of Ăd-ō-nī′-kăm, six
hundred threescore and seven.
19 The children of Bĭg-vā′-ī, two
thousand threescore and seven.
20 The children of Ā′-dĭn, six hundred
fifty and five.

d Num. 12.7. ch. 13.13. Ps. 101.6. Matt. 24.45. 1 Cor. 4.2.
e Gen. 42.18. Ex. 18.21. ch. 5.15. Job 31.23. Pro. 16.6.
1 broad in spaces.
f Pro. 2.6. Rom. 11.36. 1 Cor. 4.7. 2 Cor. 8.16. Jas. 1.17.
2 Perhaps the one in Ezra 2.1 contained the number enrolled for the journey, and this only those who actually returned, as they are not exactly the same.
3 Or, Seraiah, Ezra 2.2.
4 Or, Bani, Ezra 2.10.
5 Or, Jorah, Ezra 2.18.
6 Or, Gibbar, Ezra 2.20.
g Gen. 35.6. Ruth 2.4. 1 Sam. 17. 12. 2 Chr. 11.6. Ezra 2.21. Micah 5.2. Matt. 2.1.
h Josh. 21.18. 1 Chr. 6.54, 60. Ezra 2.23. Jer. 1.1.
7 Or, Azmaveth, Ezra 2.24.
8 Or, Kirjath-arim, Ezra 2.25.
i 1 Sam. 13.2. Ezra 2.27. Isa. 10.28.
j 1 Chr. 24.7. Ezra 2.36.
k 1 Chr. 24. 14. Ezra 2.37.
l 1 Chr. 9.12. 1 Chr. 24.9.
m 1 Chr. 24. 8. Ezra 2.39. Ezra 10.31.
9 Or, Hodaviah, Ezra 2.40. or, Judah, Ezra 3.9.

21 The children of Ā′-tĕr of Hĕz
kī′-ăh, ninety and eight.
22 The children of Hăsh′-ŭm, th
hundred twenty and eight.
23 The children of Bē-zā′-ī, th
hundred twenty and four.
24 The children of [5]Hâr′-ĭph, an hu
dred and twelve.
25 The children of [6]Gibeon, nin
and five.
26 The men of [g]Beth-lehem and N
tō′-phăh, an hundred fourscore a
eight.
27 The men of [h]Ăn′-ă-thōth, an hu
dred twenty and eight.
28 The men of [7]Bĕth–ăz-mā′-vĕ
forty and two.
29 The men of [8]Kĭr′-jăth–jē′-ă-ri
C̲hĕ-phī′-răh, and Bē̂er′-ōth, sev
hundred forty and three.
30 The men of Rā′-măh and Gē′-
six hundred twenty and one.
31 The men of [i]Mĭc̲h′-măs, an hu
dred and twenty and two.
32 The men of Beth-el and Ā′-ī,
hundred twenty and three.
33 The men of the other Nē-bō, fi
and two.
34 The children of the other Ē′-lăm
thousand two hundred fifty and fo
35 The children of Hâr′-ĭm, th
hundred and twenty.
36 The children of Jericho, th
hundred forty and five.
37 The children of Lod, Hā′-dĭd, a
Ō′-nō, seven hundred twenty and o
38 The children of Sĕn′-ă-ăh, th
thousand nine hundred and thirty.
39 ¶ The priests: the children of [j]J
dâi′-ăh, of the house of Jĕsh′-ū-ă, ni
hundred seventy and three.
40 The children of [k]Ĭm′-mĕr, a tho
and fifty and two.
41 The children of [l]Păsh′-ŭr, a tho
and two hundred forty and seven.
42 The children of [m]Hâr′-ĭm, a tho
and and seventeen.
43 ¶ The Levites: the children
Jĕsh′-ū-ă, of Kăd′-mĭ-ĕl, *and* of t
children of [9]Hō′-dĕ-văh, seventy a
four.
44 ¶ The singers: the children of
săph, an hundred forty and eight.
45 ¶ The porters: the children
Shăl′-lŭm, the children of Ā′-tĕr, t
children of Tăl′-mŏn, the children
Ăk′-kŭb, the children of Hă-tī′-tă, t
children of Shō-bā′-ī, an hundr
thirty and eight.
46 ¶ The Nĕth′-ĭ-nĭms: the childr
of Zī′-hă, the children of Hă-shû′-p
the children of Tăb-bā′-ōth,
47 The children of Kē′-rŏs, the ch

n of [10]Sī´-ă, the children of Pā´-dŏn,
The children of Lĕ-bā´-nă, the
ldren of Hăg´-ă-bă, the children of
ăl´-mâî,
The children of Hā´-năn, the chil-
n of Gĭd´-dĕl, the children of Gā´-
,
The children of Rē-âî´-ăh, the
ldren of Rē´-zĭn, the children of
-kō´-dă,
The children of Găz´-zăm, the chil-
n of Ŭz´-ză, the children of Phă-
ăh,
The children of Bē´-sâî, the chil-
n of Mĕ-ū´-nĭm, the children of
ĕ-phĭsh´-ĕ-sĭm,
The children of Băk´-bŭk, the chil-
n of Hă-kū´-phă, the children of
r´-hûr,
The children of [13]Băz´-lĭth, the
ldren of Mĕ-hī´-dă, the children of
r´-shă,
The children of Bär´-kŏs, the chil-
n of Sĭs´-ĕ-ră, the children of Tā´-
h,
The children of Nĕ-zī´-ăh, the chil-
n of Hă-tī´-phă.
¶ The [n]children of Solomon's ser-
ts: the children of Sō-tā´-ī, the chil-
n of Sō´-phĕ-rĕth, the children of
ĕ-rī´-dă,
The children of Jā´-ă-lă, the chil-
n of Där´-kŏn, the children of Gĭd´-
,
The children of Shĕph-ă-tī´-ăh, the
ldren of Hăt´-tĭl, the children of
´chĕ-rĕth of Zĕ-bā´-ĭm, the children
[15]Amon.
All the Nĕth´-ĭ-nĭms, and the chil-
n of Solomon's servants, *were* three
ndred ninety and two.
And [o]these *were* they which went
also from Tĕl–mē´-lăh, Tĕl–hă-rē´-
, Cherub, [16]Ăd´-dŏn, and Ĭm´-mĕr:
t they could not shew their father's
use, nor their [17]seed, whether they
re of Israel.
The children of Dĕl-âî´-ăh, the
ldren of Tō-bī´-ăh, the children of
-kō´-dă, six hundred forty and two.
¶ And of the priests: the children
Hă-bâî´-ăh, the children of Kŏz, the
ldren of [p]Bär-zĭl-lā´-ī, which took
of the daughters of Bär-zĭl-lā´-ī
Gileadite to wife, and was called
er their name.
These sought their register *among*
se that were reckoned by gene-
gy, but it was not found: therefore
re they, as polluted, put from the
esthood.
And [18]the Tĭr´-shā-thă said unto
m, that they should not eat of the

10 Or, Siaha, Ezra 2.44.
11 Or, Shamlai.
12 Or, Nephusim, Ezra 2.50.
13 Or, Bazluth, Ezra 2.52.
n Gen. 9.25, 26. 1 Ki. 5.13, 14. 2 Chr. 2.17, 18.
14 Or, Peruda.
15 Or, Ami.
o Ezra 2.59.
16 Or, Addan.
17 Or, pedigree.
p 2 Sam. 17. 27. 2 Sam. 19. 31-34. 1 Ki. 2.7. Ezra 2.61.
18 Or, the governor.
q Ex. 28.30. Lev. 8.8. Num. 7.89. Num. 27.18-21. Deut. 33.8. Judg. 1.1.
19 part.
r ch. 8.9. ch. 10.1.
s Ezra 2.69.
t Job 34.19. Rom. 2.11. Gal. 3.28.
u ch. 11.20, 36.
v Ex. 23.14-17. Lev. 23.24-44. Ezra 3.1.

CHAP. 8

a Ezra 3.1.
b ch. 3.26. ch. 12.37.
c Ezra 7.6. Isa. 8.20. Jer. 8.8,9.
d 2 Chr. 34. 15. Isa. 8.20. Mal. 4.4.
e Deut. 31. 11,12.
f 1 Pet. 3.7.
1 that understood in hearing.
g Lev. 23.24.
2 from the light.
3 tower of wood.

most holy things, till there stood *up* a
priest with Ū´-rĭm [q]and Thŭm´-mĭm.
66 ¶ The whole congregation together *was* forty and two thousand three
hundred and threescore,
67 Beside their manservants and their
maidservants, of whom *there were*
seven thousand three hundred thirty
and seven: and they had two hundred
forty and five singing men and singing women.
68 Their horses, seven hundred
thirty and six: their mules, two hundred forty and five:
69 *Their* camels, four hundred thirty
and five: six thousand seven hundred
and twenty asses.
70 ¶ And [19]some of the chief of the
fathers gave unto the work. [r]The Tĭr´-
shā-thă gave to the treasure a thous-
and drams of gold, fifty basons, five
hundred and thirty priests' garments.
71 And *some* of the chief of the fathers gave to the treasure of the work
[s]twenty thousand drams of gold, and
two thousand and two hundred pound
of silver.
72 And *that* which [t]the rest of the
people gave *was* twenty thousand
drams of gold, and two thousand
pound of silver, and threescore and
seven priests' garments.
73 So the priests, and the Levites,
and the porters, and the singers, and
some of the people, and the Nĕth´-ĭ-
nĭms, and all Israel, dwelt in [u]their
cities; [v]and when the seventh month
came, the children of Israel *were* in
their cities.

CHAPTER 8

AND all [a]the people gathered themselves together as one man into
the street that *was* [b]before the water
gate; and they spake unto Ezra the
[c]scribe to bring the book [d]of the law
of Moses, which the LORD had commanded to Israel.
2 And Ezra the priest brought the
[e]law before the congregation both [f]of
men and women, and all [1]that could
hear with understanding, [g]upon the
first day of the seventh month.
3 And he read therein before the
street that *was* before the water gate
[2]from the morning until midday, before the men and the women, and
those that could understand; and the
ears of all the people *were attentive*
unto the book of the law.
4 And Ezra the scribe stood upon a
[3]pulpit of wood, which they had made
for the purpose; and beside him stood

Măt-tĭ-thī´ăh, and Shē´mă, and Ă-
nâi´ăh, and Ū-rī´jăh, and Hĭl-kī´ăh,
and Mā-ă-sêi´ăh, on his right hand;
and on his left hand, Pĕ-dâi´ăh, and
Mī´shā-ĕl, and Măl-chī´ăh, and Hăsh´-
ŭm, and Hăsh-bă-dā´nă, Zĕch-ă-rī´-
ăh, *and* Mĕ-shŭl´lăm.
5 And Ezra opened the book in the
[4]sight of all the people; (for he was
above all the people;) and when he
opened it, all the people stood [h]up:
6 And Ezra blessed the LORD, the
great God. And all the people answered, [i]Ā´mĕn, Ā´mĕn, with [j]lifting
up their hands: and [k]they bowed their
heads, and worshipped the LORD with
their faces to the ground.
7 Also Jĕsh´ū-ă, and Bā´nī, and
Shĕr-ē-bī´ăh, Jā´mĭn, Ăk´kŭb, Shăb´-
bĕ-thâi, Hō-dī´jăh, Mā-ă-sêi´ăh, Kĕ-
lī´tă, Ăz-ă-rī´ăh, Jō´ză-băd, Hā´năn,
Pĕ-lâi´ăh, and the Levites, [l]caused the
people to understand the law: and the
people *stood* in their place.
8 So they read in the book in the law
of God [m]distinctly, and gave the sense,
and caused *them* to understand the
reading.
9 ¶ And [n]Nē-hĕm-ī´ăh, which *is* [5]the
Tĭr´shā-thă, and Ezra the priest the
scribe, and [o]the Levites that taught
the people, said unto all the people,
[p]This day *is* holy unto the LORD your
God; [q]mourn not, nor weep. For all
the people wept, when they heard the
words of the law.
10 Then he said unto them, Go your
way, eat the fat, and drink the sweet,
[r]and send portions unto them for
whom nothing is prepared: for *this*
day *is* holy unto our Lord: neither be
ye sorry; for the joy of the LORD is
your strength.
11 So the Levites stilled all the people, saying, Hold your peace, for the
day *is* holy; neither be ye grieved.
12 And all the people went their way
to eat, and to drink, and to send portions, and to make great mirth, because they had understood the words
that were declared unto them.
13 ¶ And on the second day were
gathered together the chief of the
fathers of all the people, the priests,
and the Levites, unto Ezra the scribe,
even [6]to understand the words of the
law.
14 And they found written in the law
which the LORD had commanded [7]by
Moses, that the children of Israel
should dwell [8]in booths in the feast of
the seventh month:
15 And that they should publish and

4 eyes.
h Judg. 3.20.
i Num. 5.22. ch. 5.13. Matt. 6.13. 1 Cor. 14.16.
j Lam. 3.41.
k Ex. 4.31.
l Lev. 10.11.
m Hab. 2.2. Acts 8.30-35.
n Ezra 2.63. ch. 7.65.
5 Or, the governor.
o 2 Chr. 35.3. Hosea 4.6.
p Lev. 23.24.
q Deut. 16.14. Eccl. 3.4. Mal. 2.13.
r Esther 9.19. Luke 11.41. Rev. 11.10.
6 Or, that they might instruct in the words of the law.
7 by the hand of.
s Gen. 33.17. Lev. 23.34.
t Deut. 22.8.
u ch. 3.15.
v ch. 12.39.
w Deut. 31.10.
8 a restraint.
x Num. 29.35.

CHAP. 9

a ch. 8.2.
b Josh. 7.6. 1 Sam. 4.12. 2 Sam. 1.2. Job 2.12.
c Ezra 10.11. ch. 13.3.
1 strange children.
d Pro. 28.13. Jer. 3.13. 1 John 1.7-9.
e ch. 8.7.
2 Or, scaffold.
f Ex. 15.6,11. 1 Chr. 29.13. 2 Cor. 4.6.
g Deut. 6.4. Isa. 37.16. Mark 12.29.
h Rev. 14.7.
i Deut. 10.14.

proclaim in all their cities, and in Je
salem, saying, Go forth unto
mount, and fetch olive branches,
pine branches, and myrtle branc
and palm branches, and branches
thick trees, to make booths, as *i*
written.
16 ¶ So the people went forth,
brought *them*, and made themse
booths, every one upon the roof
his house, and in their courts, and
the courts of the house of God, an
the street of the [u]water gate, [v]and
the street of the gate of Ē´phră-ĭm
17 And all the congregation of th
that were come again out of the c
tivity made booths, and sat under
booths: for since the days of Jĕsh´
the son of Nun unto that day had
the children of Israel done so. A
there was very great gladness.
18 Also [w]day by day, from the f
day unto the last day, he read in
book of the law of God. And they k
the feast seven days; and on the eig
day *was* [8]a solemn assembly, [x]acco
ing unto the manner.

CHAPTER 9

NOW in the twenty and fourth
of this [a]month the children of
rael were assembled with fasting, a
with sackclothes, [b]and earth up
them.
2 And [c]the seed of Israel separa
themselves from all [1]strangers, a
stood [d]and confessed their sins, a
the iniquities of their fathers.
3 And they stood up in their pla
and read [e]in the book of the law of
LORD their God *one* fourth part of
day; and *another* fourth part they c
fessed, and worshipped the Lo
their God.
4 ¶ Then stood up upon the [2]sta
of the Levites, Jĕsh´ū-ă, and Bā´
Kăd´mĭ-ĕl, Shĕb-ă-nī´ăh, Bŭn´
Shĕr-ē-bī´ăh, Bā´nī, *and* Chĕ-nā´
and cried with a loud voice unto
LORD their God.
5 Then the Levites, Jĕsh´ū-ă, a
Kăd´mĭ-ĕl, Bā´nī, Hăsh-ăb-nī´ă
Shĕr-ē-bī´ăh, Hō-dī´jăh, Shĕb-ă-
ăh, *and* Pĕth-ă-hī´ăh, said, Stand
and bless the LORD your God for e
and ever: and blessed [f]be thy glorio
name, which is exalted above all ble
ing and praise.
6 Thou, [g]*even* thou, *art* LORD alo
[h]thou hast made heaven, the [i]heav
of heavens, with all their host,
earth, and all *things* that *are* there
the seas, and all that *is* therein, a

hou preservest them all; and the host
f heaven worshippeth thee.
7 Thou *art* the LORD the God, who
idst choose [k]Abram, and broughtest
im forth out of Ur of the Chăl-dēēṡ,
nd gavest him the name of Abraham;
8 And foundest his heart faithful be-
ore thee, and madest a covenant with
im to give the land of the Canaanites,
he Hittites, the Amorites, and the
ĕ-rĭz-zītes, and the Jĕb-ū-sītes, and
he Gĭr-gă-shītes, to give *it*, *I say*, to
is seed, and hast [l]performed thy
ords; for thou *art* righteous:
9 And didst see the affliction of our
athers in Egypt, and heardest their
ry by the Red sea;
10 And shewedst signs and wonders
pon Pharaoh, and on all his servants,
nd on all the people of his land: for
hou knewest that they dealt proudly
gainst them. So didst thou [m]get thee
name, as *it is* this day.
11 And thou didst divide the sea be-
ore them, so that they went through
he midst of the sea on the dry land;
nd their persecutors thou threwest
nto the deeps, as a stone into the
nighty waters.
12 Moreover thou [n]leddest them in
he day by a cloudy pillar; and in the
ight by a pillar of fire, to give them
ight in the way wherein they should
o.
13 Thou camest down also upon
nount Sī-nāi, and spakest with them
rom heaven, and gavest them [o]right
udgments, and [3]true laws, good stat-
tes and commandments:
14 And madest known unto them thy
oly [p]sabbath, and commandedst
hem precepts, statutes, and laws, by
he hand of Moses thy servant:
15 And [q]gavest them bread from
eaven for their hunger, and brought-
st forth water for them out of the
ock for their thirst, and promisedst
hem that they should [r]go in to possess
he land [4]which thou hadst sworn to
ive them.
16 But they and our fathers dealt
roudly, [s]and hardened their necks,
nd hearkened not to thy command-
nents,
17 And refused to obey, [t]neither
ere mindful of thy wonders that
hou didst among them; but hardened
heir necks, and in their rebellion ap-
ointed [u]a captain to return to their
ondage: but thou *art* [5]a God ready to
ardon, [v]gracious and merciful, slow
o anger, and of great kindness, and
orsookest them not.

j Ps. 36.6.
k Gen. 11.31.
l Josh. 23.14.
m Ex. 9. 16. Jer. 32.20. Dan. 9.15. Rom. 9.17.
n Ex. 13.21.
o Ps. 19.8,9. Rom. 7.12.
3 laws of truth.
p Gen. 2.3. Ex. 20.8. Isa. 56.2. Mark 2.27. Heb. 4.9.
q Ex. 16.14, 15. John 6.31.
r Deut. 1.8.
4 which thou hadst lift up thine hand to give them.
s Deut. 31.27. 2 Chr. 30.8. Ps. 106.6. Jer. 19.15.
t Ps. 78.11.
u Num. 14.4.
5 a God of pardons.
v Ex. 34.6. Num. 14.18. Ps. 86.5,15. Joel 2.13.
w Ps. 106.45.
x Ex. 13.21, 22. Num. 14.14.
y Num. 11. 17. Isa. 63.11.
z Deut. 8.4. Ps. 34.10.
a Gen. 15.5. 1 Chr. 27.23.
6 according to their will.
b Deut. 8.7-10. Eze. 20.6.
c Deut. 6.11.
7 Or, cisterns.
8 tree of food.
d Deut. 32. 15. Hosea 13.6.
e 1 Ki. 8.66. Rom. 2.4.
f Matt. 23.37. Acts 7.52.
9 they returned to do evil.

18 Yea, when they had made them
a molten calf, and said, This *is* thy
God that brought thee up out of
Egypt, and had wrought great provocations;
19 Yet thou in thy [w]manifold mercies
forsookest them not in the wilderness:
the [x]pillar of the cloud departed not
from them by day, to lead them in the
way; neither the pillar of fire by night,
to shew them light, and the way
wherein they should go.
20 Thou gavest also thy [y]good spirit
to instruct them, and withheldest not
thy măn-nă from their mouth, and
gavest them water for their thirst.
21 Yea, forty years didst thou sustain them in the wilderness, *so that*
they lacked nothing; [z]their clothes
waxed not old, and their feet swelled
not.
22 Moreover thou gavest them kingdoms and nations, and didst divide
them into corners: so they possessed
the land of Sī-hŏn, and the land of the
king of Hĕsh-bŏn, and the land of Og
king of Bā-shăn.
23 Their [a]children also multipliedst
thou as the stars of heaven, and
broughtest them into the land, concerning which thou hadst promised
to their fathers, that they should go in
to possess *it*.
24 So the children went in and possessed the land, and thou subduedst
before them the inhabitants of the
land, the Canaanites, and gavest them
into their hands, with their kings, and
the people of the land, that they
might do with them [6]as they would.
25 And they took strong cities, and
a [b]fat land, and possessed houses [c]full
of all goods, [7]wells digged, vineyards,
and oliveyards, and [8]fruit trees in
abundance: so they did eat, and were
filled, and became [d]fat, and delighted
themselves in thy [e]great goodness.
26 Nevertheless they were disobedient, and rebelled against thee, and
cast thy law behind their backs, and
slew thy [f]prophets which testified
against them to turn them to thee, and
they wrought great provocations.
27 Therefore thou deliveredst them
into the hand of their enemies, who
vexed them: and in the time of their
trouble, when they cried unto thee,
thou heardest *them* from heaven; and
according to thy manifold mercies
thou gavest them saviours, who saved
them out of the hand of their enemies.
28 But after they had rest, [9]they did
evil again before thee: therefore left-

est thou them in the hand of their enemies, so that they had the dominion
over them: yet when they returned,
and cried unto thee, thou heardest
them from heaven; and many times
didst thou deliver them according to
thy mercies;
29 And [g]testifiedst against them, that
thou mightest bring them again unto
thy law: yet they dealt proudly, and
hearkened not unto thy commandments, but sinned against thy judgments, ([h]which if a man do, he shall
live in them;) and [10]withdrew the
shoulder, and hardened their neck,
and would not hear.
30 ¶ Yet many years didst thou [11]for-
bear them, and [i]testifiedst against
them by thy spirit [12]in thy prophets:
yet would they not give ear: therefore
gavest thou them into the hand of the
people of the lands.
31 Nevertheless for thy great mercies' sake [j]thou didst not utterly consume them, nor forsake them; for
thou *art* a gracious and merciful God.
32 Now therefore, our God, the
great, the mighty, and the terrible
God, who keepest covenant and mercy, let not all the [13]trouble seem little
before thee, [14]that hath come upon us,
on our kings, on our princes, and on
our priests, and on our prophets, and
on our fathers, and on all thy people,
since [k]the time of the kings of Assyria
unto this day.
33 Howbeit [l]thou *art* just in all that
is brought upon us; for thou hast done
right, but we have done wickedly:
34 Neither have our kings, our princes, our priests, nor our fathers, kept
thy law, nor hearkened unto thy
commandments and thy testimonies,
wherewith thou didst testify against
them.
35 For they have not served thee in
their kingdom, and in thy great goodness that thou gavest them, and in the
large and fat land which thou gavest
before them, neither turned they from
their wicked works.
36 Behold, [m]we *are* servants this day,
and *for* the land that thou gavest unto
our fathers to eat the fruit thereof and
the good thereof, behold, we *are* servants in it:
37 And [n]it yieldeth much increase
unto the kings whom thou hast set
over us because of our sins: also they
have [o]dominion over our bodies, and
over our cattle, at their pleasure, and
we *are* in great distress.
38 And because of all this we make

g Deut. 4.26. Jer. 25.3-7. Hosea 6.5.
h Lev. 18.5. Matt. 19.17. Luke 10.28. Rom. 10.5. Gal. 3.12.
10 they gave a withdrawing shoulder.
11 protract over them.
i Ps. 78.8,40. Isa. 63.10. Jer. 7.25. Acts 7.51.
12 in the hand of thy prophets.
j Jer. 5.10.
13 weariness.
14 that hath found us.
k 2 Ki. 17.3. Isa. 7.17,18.
l Gen. 18.25. Ps. 119.137. Dan. 9.14.
m Deut. 28. 48.
n Deut. 28. 33.
o Deut. 28.48.
15 are at the sealing, or, sealed.

CHAP. 10

1 at the sealings.
a ch. 8.9.
2 Or, the governor.
b ch. 1.1.
c ch. 12.8.
d Ezra 2.36.
e Ezra 9.1. ch. 13.3.
f Deut. 29.12. ch. 5.12. Isa. 14.1. Rom. 12.9.
g 2 Ki. 23.3.
3 by the hand of.
h Gen. 6.2. Ex. 34.16. Deut. 7.3.

a sure *covenant*, and write *it;* and ou
princes, Levites, *and* priests, [15]seal *u*
to it.

CHAPTER 10

NOW [1]those that sealed [a]*were*, Nĕ
hĕm-ī-́ăh, [2]the Tĭr-́shā-thā, th
[b]son of Hăch-ă-lī-́ăh, and Zĭd-kī-́jă
2 Sĕ-raî-́ăh, Ăz-ă-rī-́ăh, Jeremiah,
3 Păsh-́ŭr, Ăm-ă-rī-́ăh, Măl-chī-́jă
4 Hăt-́tŭsh, Shĕb-ă-nī-́ăh, Măl-́lŭc
5 Hâr-́ĭm, Mĕr-́ē-mōth, Ō-bă-dī-́ăh,
6 Daniel, Gĭn-́nĕ-thŏn, Bâr-́ŭch,
7 Mĕ-shŭl-́lăm, Ă-bī-́jăh, Mī-́jă-mĭr
8 Mā-ă-zī-́ăh, Bĭl-gā-́ī, Shĕm-aî-́ăh
these *were* the priests.
9 And [c]the Levites: both Jĕsh-́ū-
the son of Ăz-ă-nī-́ăh, Bĭn-́nū-ī of th
sons of Hĕn-ā-́dăd, Kăd-́mī-ĕl;
10 And their brethren, Shĕb-ă-nī-́ă
Hō-dī-́jăh, Kĕ-lī-́tă, Pĕ-laî-́ăh, Hā
năn,
11 Mī-́chă, Rē-́hŏb, Hăsh-ă-bī-́ăh,
12 Zăc-́cŭr, Shĕr-ē-bī-́ăh, Shĕb-ă-nī
ăh,
13 Hō-dī-́jăh, Bā-́nī, Bĕ-nī-́nŭ.
14 The chief of the people; Pâr-́ŏsh
Pā-́hăth–mō-́ăb, Ē-́lăm, Zăt-́thŭ, Bā
nī,
15 Bŭn-́nī, Ăz-́găd, Bē-bā-́ī,
16 Ăd-ō-nī-́jăh, Bĭg-vā-́ī, Ā-́dĭn,
17 Ā-́tĕr, Hĭz-kī-́jăh, Ăz-́zŭr,
18 Hō-dī-́jăh, Hăsh-́ŭm, Bē-zā-́ī,
19 Hâr-́ĭph, Ăn-́ā-thōth, Nē-bā-́ī,
20 Măg-́pī-ăsh, Mĕ-shŭl-́lăm, Hē
zīr,
21 Mĕ-shĕz-́ă-bĕel, Zā-́dŏk, Jăd
dū-ă,
22 Pĕl-ă-tī-́ăh, Hā-́năn, Ă-naî-́ăh,
23 Hō-shē-́ă, Hăn-ă-nī-́ăh, Hăsh-́ŭ
24 Hăl-lō-́hĕsh, Pĭ-́lē-hă, Shō-́bĕk,
25 Rē-́hŭm, Hă-shăb-́năh, Mā-ă
seî-́ăh,
26 And Ă-hī-́jăh, Hā-́năn, Ā-́năn,
27 Măl-́lŭch, Hâr-́ĭm, Bā-́ă-năh.
28 ¶ And the rest of the people, th
[d]priests, the Levites, the porters, th
singers, the Nĕth-́ĭ-nĭms, and [e]all the
that had separated themselves fro
the people of the lands unto the la
of God, their wives, their sons, an
their daughters, every one havin
knowledge, and having understand
ing;
29 They clave to their brethren, the
nobles, [f]and entered into a curse, an
into an oath, [g]to walk in God's law
which was given [3]by Moses the ser
vant of God, and to observe and d
all the commandments of the LOR
our Lord, and his judgments and hi
statutes;
30 And that we would not give ou
[h]daughters unto the people of th

nd, nor take their daughters for our
ons:
31 And [i]*if* the people of the land
ring ware or any victuals on the sab-
ath day to sell, *that* we would not buy
of them on the sabbath, or on the
oly day: and *that* we would leave the
eventh year, and the [k]exaction of
very debt.
32 Also we made [l]ordinances for us,
o charge ourselves yearly with the
hird part of a shekel for the service
f the house of our God;
33 For [m]the shewbread, and for the
ontinual meat offering, and for the
ontinual burnt offering, of the sab-
aths, of the new moons, for the set
easts, and for the holy *things*, and for
he sin offerings to make an atone-
ent for Israel, and *for* all the work
f the house of our God.
34 And we cast the lots among the
riests, the Levites, and the people,
for the wood offering, to bring *it* into
he house of our God, after the houses
f our fathers, at times appointed
ear by year, to burn upon the altar
f the LORD our God, as [o]*it is* written
n the law:
35 And [p]to bring the firstfruits of our
round, and the firstfruits of all fruit
f all trees, year by year, unto the
ouse of the LORD:
36 Also the firstborn of our sons, and
f our cattle, as *it is* [q]written in the law,
nd the firstlings of our herds and of
ur flocks, to bring to the house of
ur God, unto the priests that minis-
er in the house of our God:
37 And [r]*that* we should bring the
rstfruits of our dough, and our offer-
ngs, and the fruit of all manner of
rees, of wine and of oil, unto the
riests, to the chambers of the house
f our God; and [s]the tithes of our
round unto the Levites, that the
ame Levites might have the tithes in
ll the cities of our tillage.
38 And the priest the son of Aaron
hall be with the Levites, when [t]the
evites take tithes: and the Levites
hall bring up the tithe of the tithes un-
o the house of our God, to [u]the cham-
ers, into the treasure house.
39 For the children of Israel and the
hildren of Levi [v]shall bring the offer-
ng of the corn, of the new wine, and
he oil, unto the chambers, where
re the vessels of the sanctuary,
nd the priests that minister, and
he porters, and the singers: [w]and we
vill not forsake the house of our
God.

i Ex. 20.10. Lev. 23.3. ch. 13.15. Jer. 17.21.
j Ex. 23.10. Lev. 25.4.
k Deut. 15.1. ch. 5.12.
4 every hand.
l Gen. 28.22.
m Lev. 24.5. 2 Chr. 2.4.
n ch. 13.31.
o Lev. 6.12.
p Ex. 23.19. Lev. 19.23. Num. 18.12. Deut. 26.2.
q Ex. 13.2,12, 13. Lev. 27.26, 27.
r Lev. 23.17. Num. 15.19. Deut. 18.4.
s Lev. 27.30, 32. 2 Chr. 31.6.
t Num. 18.26.
u 1 Chr. 9.26. 2 Chr. 31.11.
v Num. 18. 30. Deut. 12.6. ch. 13.12.
w ch. 13.10. Ps. 122.9. Matt. 18.20.

CHAP. 11

a Isa. 48.2. Matt. 4.5.
b Judg. 5.9.
c 1 Chr. 9.2. ch. 7.6.
d Ezra 2.43.
e Ezra 2.55.
f 1 Chr. 9.3.
g Gen. 38.29.
1 Or, men of activity.
h 1 Chr. 9.10.

CHAPTER 11

AND the rulers of the people dwelt
at Jerusalem: the rest of the people also cast lots, to bring one of ten
to dwell in Jerusalem the [a]holy city,
and nine parts *to dwell* in *other* cities.
2 And the people blessed all the men,
that willingly [b]offered themselves to
dwell at Jerusalem.
3 ¶ Now [c]these *are* the chief of the
province that dwelt in Jerusalem: but
in the cities of Judah dwelt every one
in his possession in their cities, *to wit*,
Israel, the priests, and the Levites, and
[d]the Nĕth-ĭ-nĭmṡ, and [e]the children of
Solomon's servants.
4 And [f]at Jerusalem dwelt *certain* of
the children of Judah, and of the children of Benjamin. Of the children of
Judah; Ă-thâiʹ-ăh the son of Ŭz-zīʹ-ăh,
the son of Zĕc̱h-ă-rīʹ-ăh, the son of
Ăm-ă-rīʹ-ăh, the son of Shĕph-ă-tīʹ-ăh,
the son of Mă-hălʹ-ă-lēēl, of the children of [g]Pēʹ-rĕz;
5 And Mā-ă-sēiʹ-ăh the son of Bârʹ-
ŭc̱h, the son of Cŏl–hōʹ-zĕh, the son of
Hă-zâiʹ-ăh, the son of Ă-dâiʹ-ăh, the
son of Jōiʹ-ă-rĭb, the son of Zĕc̱h-ă-rīʹ-
ăh, the son of Shī-lōʹ-nī.
6 All the sons of Pēʹ-rĕz that dwelt at
Jerusalem *were* four hundred threescore and eight [1]valiant men.
7 And these *are* the sons of Benjamin; Săl-lû the son of Mĕ-shŭlʹ-lăm,
the son of Jōʹ-ĕd, the son of Pĕ-dâiʹ-ăh,
the son of Kō-lâiʹ-ăh, the son of Mā-
ă-sēiʹ-ăh, the son of Īʹ-thī-ĕl, the son of
Jĕ-sâiʹ-ăh.
8 And after him Găb-bāʹ-ī, Săl-lāʹ-ī,
nine hundred twenty and eight.
9 And Jōʹ-ĕl the son of Zĭc̱hʹ-rī *was*
their overseer: and Judah the son of
Sĕnʹ-ū-ăh *was* second over the city.
10 Of [h]the priests: Jĕ-dâiʹ-ăh the son
of Jōiʹ-ă-rĭb, Jāʹ-c̱hĭn.
11 Sĕ-râiʹ-ăh the son of Hĭl-kīʹ-ăh, the
son of Mĕ-shŭlʹ-lăm, the son of Zāʹ-
dŏk, the son of Mĕ-râiʹ-ōth, the son of
Ă-hīʹ-tŭb, *was* the ruler of the house of
God.
12 And their brethren that did the
work of the house *were* eight hundred
twenty and two: and Ă-dâiʹ-ăh the son
of Jĕ-rōʹ-hăm, the son of Pĕl-ă-līʹ-ăh,
the son of Amzi, the son of Zĕc̱h-ă-rīʹ-
ăh, the son of Păshʹ-ŭr, the son of Măl-
c̱hīʹ-ăh,
13 And his brethren, chief of the
fathers, two hundred forty and two:
and Ă-măshʹ-âi the son of Ăzʹ-ă-rēēl,
the son of Ă-hāʹ-sâi, the son of Mĕ-
shĭlʹ-lĕ-mōth, the son of Ĭmʹ-mĕr,
14 And their brethren, mighty men

of valour, an hundred twenty and
eight: and their overseer *was* Zăb'-dĭ-
ĕl, [2]the son of *one of* the great men.
15 Also of the Levites: Shĕm-âi'-ăh
the son of Hăsh'-ŭb, the son of Ăz-rī'-
kăm, the son of Hăsh-ă-bī'-ăh, the son
of Bŭn'-nī;
16 And Shăb'-bĕ-thâi and Jō'-ză-băd,
of the chief of the Levites, [3]*had* the
oversight of [i]the outward business of
the house of God.
17 And Măt-tă-nī'-ăh the son of Mī'-
chă, the son of [j]Zăb'-dī, the son of Ā'-
săph, *was* the principal to begin the
thanksgiving in prayer: and Băk-bŭ-
kī'-ăh the second among his brethren,
and Abda the son of Shăm'-mū-ă, the
son of Gā'-lăl, the son of Jĕ-dū'-thŭn.
18 All the Levites in the [k]holy city
were two hundred fourscore and four.
19 Moreover [l]the porters, Ăk'-kŭb,
Tăl'-mŏn, and their brethren that kept
[4]the gates, *were* an hundred seventy
and two.
20 ¶ And the residue of Israel, of the
priests, *and* the Levites, *were* in all the
cities of Judah, every one in his inheritance.
21 But [m]the Nĕth'-ĭ-nĭmṡ dwelt in [5]Ō'-
phĕl: and Zī'-hă and Gĭs'-pă *were* over
the Nĕth'-ĭ-nĭmṡ.
22 The overseer also of the Levites at
Jerusalem *was* Ŭz'-zī the son of Bā'-nī,
the son of Hăsh-ă-bī'-ăh, the son of
Măt-tă-nī'-ăh, the son of Mī'-chă. Of
the sons of Ā'-săph, the singers *were*
over the business of the house of God.
23 For [n]*it was* the king's commandment concerning them, that [6] a certain
portion should be for the singers, due
for every day.
24 And Pĕth-ă-hī'-ăh the son of Mĕ-
shĕz'-ă-bĕel, of the children [o]of Zĕ'-răh
the son of Judah, *was* [p]at the king's
hand in all matters concerning the
people.
25 And for the villages, with their
fields, *some* of the children of Judah
dwelt [q]at Kĭr'-jăth-är'-bă, and *in* the
villages thereof, and at Dī'-bŏn, and *in*
the villages thereof, and [r]at Jĕ-kăb'-
zĕel, and *in* the villages thereof,
26 And at Jĕsh'-ū-ă, and at Mō-lā'-
dăh, and at Bĕth'-phĕ-lĕt,
27 And at Hā'-zär-shû'-ăl, and at
Bĕer-shē'-bă, and *in* the villages thereof,
28 And at Ziklag, and at Mĕ-kō'-năh,
and in the villages thereof,
29 And at Ĕn-rĭm'-mŏn, and at Ză-
rē'-ăh, and at Jär'-mûth,
30 Ză-nō'-ăh, Adullam, and *in* their
villages, at Lā'-chĭsh, and the fields
thereof, at Ā-zē'-kăh, and *in* the vi
lages thereof. And they dwelt fro
Bĕer-shē'-bă unto the valley of Hi
nom.
31 The children also of Benjami
[7]from Gē'-bă *dwelt* [8]at Mĭch'-măsh, an
Âi'-jă, and Beth-el, and *in* their vi
lages,
32 *And* at [s]Ăn'-ă-thōth, Nob, Ăn-ă
nī'-ăh,
33 Hā'-zôr, Rā'-măh, Gĭt-tā'-ĭm,
34 Hā'-dĭd, Zĕ-bō'-ĭm, Nĕ-băl'-lăt,
35 Lod, and Ō'-nō, [t]the valley o
craftsmen.
36 And of the [u]Levites *were* divi
sions *in* Judah, *and* in Benjamin.

CHAPTER 12

NOW these *are* the [a]priests and th
Levites that went up with Z
rŭb'-bă-bĕl the son of Shē-ăl'-tī-ĕ
and Jĕsh'-ū-ă: [b]Sĕ-râi'-ăh, Jeremia
Ezra,
2 Ăm-ă-rī'-ăh, [1]Măl'-lŭch, Hăt'-tŭsh,
3 [2]Shĕch-ă-nī'-ăh, [3]Rĕ-hŭm, [4]Mĕr'-ĕ
mōth,
4 Ĭd'-dō, [5]Gĭn'-nĕ-thō, [c]Ā-bī'-jăh,
5 [6]Mī'-ă-mĭn, [7]Mā-ă-dī'-ăh, Bĭl'-găh,
6 Shĕm-âi'-ăh, and Jōi'-ă-rĭb, Jĕ-dâi
ăh,
7 [8]Săl'-lû, Ā'-mŏk, Hĭl-kī'-ăh, Jĕ-dâi
ăh. These *were* the chief of the priest
and of their brethren in the days o
[d]Jĕsh'-ū-ă.
8 Moreover the Levites: Jĕsh'-ū-ă
Bĭn'-nū-ī, Kăd'-mĭ-ĕl, Shĕr-ē-bī'-ăh, Ju
dah, *and* Măt-tă-nī'-ăh, [e]*which wa*
over [9]the thanksgiving, he and hi
brethren.
9 Also Băk-bŭ-kī'-ăh and Ŭn'-nī, the
brethren, *were* over against them i
the watches.
10 ¶ And Jĕsh'-ū-ă begat Jōi'-ă-kĭm
Jōi'-ă-kĭm also begat Ē-lĭ-ăsh'-ĭb, an
Ē-lĭ-ăsh'-ĭb begat Jōi'-ă-dă,
11 And Jōi'-ă-dă begat Jonathan, an
Jonathan begat Jăd'-dū-ă.
12 And in the days of Jōi'-ă-kĭm wer
priests, the chief of the fathers: o
Sĕ-râi'-ăh, Mĕ-râi'-ăh; of Jeremiah
Hăn-ă-nī'-ăh;
13 Of Ezra, Mĕ-shŭl'-lăm; of Ăm-ă
rī'-ăh, Jĕ-hō-hā'-năn;
14 Of Mĕl'-ĭ-cû, Jonathan; of Shĕb
ă-nī'-ăh, Joseph;
15 Of Hăr'-ĭm, Ăd'-nă; of Mĕ-râi'-ōth
Hĕl-kā'-ī;
16 Of Ĭd'-dō, Zĕch-ă-rī'-ăh; of Gĭn
nĕ-thŏn, Mĕ-shŭl'-lăm;
17 Of Ā-bī'-jăh, Zĭch'-rī; of Mĭn-ĭ-ă
mĭn, of Mō-ă-dī'-ăh, Pĭl-tā'-ī;
18 Of Bĭl'-găh, Shăm'-mū-ă; of Shĕm
âi'-ăh, Jĕ-hŏn'-ă-thăn;

2 Or, the son of Haggedolim.
3 were over.
i 2 Ki. 12.15, 16. 1 Chr. 26.29. 2 Chr. 34.13. 1 Cor. 4.2.
j 1 Chr. 9.15, Zichri. ch. 7.44.
k 1 Ki. 11.13. Ezra 9.8. Matt. 24.15. Rev. 11.2. Rev. 21.2.
l 1 Chr. 9.17. ch. 7.45. ch. 12.25.
4 at the gates.
m 2 Chr. 27.3. Ezra 2.43, 58. ch. 3.26.
5 Or, the tower.
n Ezra 6.8,9.
6 Or, a sure ordinance.
o Gen. 38.30, Zarah.
p 1 Chr. 18. 17. 1 Chr. 23.28.
q Gen. 23.2. Josh. 14.15.
r Josh. 15.21, Kabzeel.
7 Or, of Geba.
8 Or, to Michmash.
s Jer. 1.1.
t 1 Chr. 4.14.
u Gen. 49.7.

CHAP. 12

a Ezra 2.1.
b ch. 10.2-8.
1 Or, Melicu, ver. 14.
2 Or, Shebaniah.
3 Or, Harim.
4 Or, Meraioth.
5 Or, Ginnethon.
c Luke 1.5.
6 Or, Miniamin.
7 Or, Moadiah.
8 Or, Sallai, ver. 20.
d Hag. 1.1. Zech. 3.1.
e 1 Chr. 16.8, 41. ch. 11.17.
9 That is, the psalms of thanksgiving.

9 And of Jŏi´-ă-rĭb, Măt-tē´-nâi; of
-dâi´-ăh, Ŭz´-zī;
0 Of Săl-lā´-ī, Kăl-lā´-ī; of Ā´-mŏk,
´bĕr;
1 Of Hĭl-kī´-ăh, Hăsh-ă-bī´-ăh; of
-dâi´-ăh, Nĕth´-ă-neel.
2 ¶ The Levites in the days of Ē-lī-
h-ĭb, Jŏi´-ă-dă, and Jō-hā´-năn, and
d´-dū-ă, *were* recorded chief of the
thers: also the priests, to the reign
Dă-rī´-ŭs the Persian.
3 The sons of Levi, the chief of the
thers, *were* written in the book of
he chronicles, even until the days of
)-hā´-năn the son of Ē-lī-ăsh´-ĭb.
4 And the chief of the Levites:
ăsh-ă-bī´-ăh, Shĕr-ē-bī´-ăh, and Jĕsh´-
-ă the son of Kăd´-mī-ĕl, with their
rethren over against them, to praise
nd to give thanks, [g]according to the
ommandment of David the man of
od, [h]ward over against ward.
5 Măt-tă-nī´-ăh, and Băk-bū-kī´-ăh,
-bă-dī´-ăh, Mĕ-shŭl´-lăm, Tăl´-mŏn,
k´-kŭb, *were* porters keeping the
ard at the [10]thresholds of the gates.
6 These *were* in the days of Jŏi´-ă-
im the son of Jĕsh´-ū-ă, the son of Jō´-
ı-dăk, and in the days of Nē-hĕm-ī´-
h [i]the governor, and of Ezra the
riest, [j]the scribe.
27 ¶ And at [k]the dedication of the
all of Jerusalem they sought the Le-
ites out of all their places, to bring
iem to Jerusalem, to keep the dedi-
ation with gladness, [l]both with
ıanksgivings, and with singing, *with*
ymbals, psalteries, and with harps.
28 And the sons of the singers gather-
d themselves together, both out of
ıe plain country round about Jeru-
ılem, and from the villages of Nĕ-
ph´-ă-thī;
29 Also from the house of Gĭl´-găl,
nd out of the fields of Gē´-bă and
z-mā´-vĕth: for the singers had build-
d them villages round about Jerusa-
m.
30 And the priests and the Levites
purified themselves, and purified the
eople, and the gates, and the wall.
31 Then I brought up the princes of
udah upon the wall, and appointed
wo great *companies of them that gave*
ıanks, *whereof one* went on the right
and upon the wall toward [n]the dung
ate:
32 And after them went Hō-shâi´-ăh,
nd half of the princes of Judah,
33 And Ăz-ă-rī´-ăh, Ezra, and Mĕ-
hŭl´-lăm,
34 Judah, and Benjamin, and Shĕm-
ı´-ăh, and Jeremiah,

35 And *certain* of the priests' sons
with [o]trumpets; *namely*, Zĕch-ă-rī´-ăh
the son of Jonathan, the son of Shĕm-
âi´-ăh, the son of Măt-tă-nī´-ăh, the son
of Mī-châi´-ăh, the son of Zăc´-cŭr, the
son of Ā´-săph:
36 And his brethren, Shĕm-âi´-ăh,
and Ăz-ă-rā´-ĕl, Mĭl´-ă-lâi, Gĭl´-ă-lâi,
Mā-ā´-ī, Nĕth´-ă-neel, and Judah, Hă-
nā´-nī, with [p]the musical instruments
of David the man of God, and Ezra
the scribe before them.
37 And [q]at the fountain gate, which
was over against them, they went up
by [r]the stairs of the city of David, at
the going up of the wall, above the
house of David, even unto [s]the water
gate eastward.
38 And the other *company of them*
that gave thanks went over against
them, and I after them, and the half
of the people upon the wall, from
beyond the [t]tower of the furnaces
even unto [u]the broad wall;
39 And [v]from above the gate of Ē´-
phră-ĭm, and above [w]the old gate, and
above the fish gate, and the tower of
Hăn´-ă-neel, and the tower of Mē´-ăh,
even unto the sheep gate: and they
stood still in the [x]prison gate.
40 So stood the two *companies of*
them that gave [y]thanks in the house
of God, and I, and the half of the rulers with me:
41 And the priests; Ē-lī´-ă-kĭm, Mā-
ă-sêi´-ăh, Mĭn-ĭ-ă-mĭn, Mī-châi´-ăh, Ĕl-
ī-ō-ē´-nâi, Zĕch-ă-rī´-ăh, *and* Hăn-ă-
nī´-ăh, with trumpets;
42 And Mā-ă-sêi´-ăh, and Shĕm-âi´-
ăh, and Ĕl-ē-ā´-zăr, and Ŭz´-zī, and Jē-
hō-hā´-năn, and Măl-chī´-jăh, and Ē´-
lăm, and Ē´-zĕr. And the singers [11]sang
loud, with Jĕz-ră-hī´-ăh *their* overseer.
43 Also that day they offered great
sacrifices, and rejoiced: [z]for God had
made them rejoice with great joy: the
wives also and the children rejoiced:
so that the joy of Jerusalem was heard
even afar off.
44 ¶ And [a]at that time were some
appointed over the chambers for the
treasures, for the offerings, for the
firstfruits, and for the tithes, to gather
into them out of the fields of the cities
the portions [12]of the law for the
priests and Levites: [13]for Judah rejoiced for the priests and for the Levites [14]that waited.
45 And both the singers and the porters kept the ward of their God, and
the ward of the purification, according [b]to the commandment of David,
and of Solomon his son.

f 1 Chr. 9.14.
g 1 Chr. 23.1. 1 Chr. 25.1.
h Ezra 3.11.
10 Or, treasuries. Or, assemblies.
i ch. 8.9.
j Ezra 7.6,11.
k Deut. 20.5. Ps. 30, title.
l 1 Chr. 25.6. 2 Chr. 5.13. Ps. 81.1-3. Rev. 5.8.
m Ex. 19.10.
n ch. 2.13.
o Num. 10.2. Josh. 6.4. 2 Chr. 5.12.
p 1 Chr. 23.5. 2 Chr. 8.14. Amos 6.5.
q ch. 2.14.
r 2 Sam. 5.7-9. ch. 3.15.
s ch. 3.26.
t ch. 3.11.
u ch. 3.8.
v 2 Ki. 14.13.
w ch. 3.6.
x Jer. 32.2.
y Ps. 42.4.
11 made their voice to be heard. 2 Chr. 29.30. Ps. 30.4. Ps. 81.1. Ps. 95.1. Ps. 96.1. Ps. 98.1. Eph. 5.19. Col. 3.16.
z Ps. 9.2. Ps. 92.4.
a 2 Chr. 31. 11,12. ch. 13.5.
12 That is, appointed by the law.
13 for the joy of Judah.
14 that stood.
b 1 Chr. 25.1.

46 For in the days of David and Ā-săph of old *there were* chief of the singers, and songs of praise and thanksgiving unto God.

47 And all Israel in the days of Zĕ-rŭb-bă-bĕl, and in the days of Nĕ-hĕm-ī-ăh, gave the portions of the singers and the porters, every day his portion: and they [15]sanctified *holy things* unto the Levites; and the Levites sanctified *them* unto the children of Aaron.

CHAPTER 13

On that day [1]they read in the book of Moses in the [2]audience of the people; and therein was found written, [a]that the Ammonite and the Moabite should not come into the congregation of God for ever;

2 Because they met not the children of Israel with bread and with water, but hired [b]Balaam against them, that he should curse them: howbeit [c]our God turned the curse into a blessing.

3 Now it came to pass, when they had heard the law, [d]that they separated from Israel all the mixed multitude.

4 ¶ And before this, Ē-lī-ăsh-ĭb the priest, [3]having the oversight of the chamber of the house of our God, *was* allied unto Tō-bī-ăh:

5 And he had prepared for him a great chamber, where aforetime they laid the meat offerings, the frankincense, and the vessels, and the tithes of the corn, the new wine, and the oil, [4]which was commanded *to be given* to the Levites, and the singers, and the porters; and the offerings of the priests.

6 But in all this *time* was not I at Jerusalem: [e]for in the two and thirtieth year of Är-tă-xĕrx-ēs king of Babylon came I unto the king, and [5]after certain days [6]obtained I leave of the king:

7 And I came to Jerusalem, and understood of the evil that Ē-lī-ăsh-ĭb did for Tō-bī-ăh, in preparing him a chamber in the courts of the house of God.

8 And it grieved me sore: therefore [f]I cast forth all the household stuff of Tō-bī-ăh out of the chamber.

9 Then I commanded, and they cleansed [g]the chambers: and thither brought I again the vessels of the house of God, with the meat offering and the frankincense.

10 ¶ And I perceived that the portions of the Levites had [h]not been

15 That is, set apart.

CHAP. 13

1 there was read.
2 ears.
a Deut. 23.3. Amos 2.1-3.
b Num. 22.5. Josh. 24.9.
c Num. 23.8-11. Deut. 23.5. Ps. 109.28. Micah 6.5.
d ch. 9.2. Jas. 1.27.
3 being set over.
4 the commandment of the Levites.
e ch. 5.14.
5 at the end of days.
6 Or, I earnestly requested.
f Ps. 69.9. Mark 11.15-17. John 2.13.
g 2 Chr. 29.5.
h ch. 10.37. Mal. 3.8. 1 Tim. 5.17, 18.
i Num. 35.2.
j Pro. 28.4.
k 1 Sam. 2.17.
7 standing.
l ch. 12.44.
8 Or, storehouses.
9 at their hand.
m 1 Cor. 4.2.
10 it was upon them.
n ch. 5.19.
11 kindnesses.
12 Or, observations.
o Ex. 20.10.
p Jer. 17.21.
13 add fierce wrath.
q Lev. 23.32.
r Ex. 31.14-17. ch. 7.3.
14 before the wall?

given *them:* for the Levites and t
singers, that did the work, were fl
every one to [i]his field.
11 Then [j]contended I with the rule
and said, [k]Why is the house of G
forsaken? And I gathered them t
gether, and set them in their [7]place.
12 Then [l]brought all Judah the tit
of the corn and the new wine and t
oil unto the [8]treasuries.
13 And I made treasurers over t
treasuries, Shĕl-ē-mī-ăh the prie
and Ză-dŏk the scribe, and of the L
vites, Pĕ-dāi-ăh: and [9]next to the
was Hā-năn the son of Zăc-cŭr, t
son of Măt-tă-nī-ăh: for they we
counted [m]faithful, and [10]their offi
was to distribute unto their brethre
14 Remember [n]me, O my God, co
cerning this, and wipe not out n
[11]good deeds that I have done for t
house of my God, and for the [12]offic
thereof.
15 ¶ In those days saw I in Juda
some treading wine presses on [o]t
sabbath, and bringing in sheaves, ar
lading asses; as also wine, grapes, ar
figs, and all *manner of* burdens, [p]whi
they brought into Jerusalem on t
sabbath day: and I testified *again*
them in the day wherein they sol
victuals.
16 There dwelt men of Tyre als
therein, which brought fish, and a
manner of ware, and sold on the sa
bath unto the children of Judah, an
in Jerusalem.
17 Then I contended with the nobl
of Judah, and said unto them, Wh
evil thing *is* this that ye do, an
profane the sabbath day?
18 Did not your fathers thus, and di
not our God bring all this evil upon u
and upon this city? yet ye [13]brin
more wrath upon Israel by profanir
the sabbath.
19 And it came to pass, that whe
the gates of Jerusalem [q]began to b
dark before the sabbath, I comman
ed that the gates should be shut, an
charged that they should not be ope
ed till after the sabbath: [r]and *some* o
my servants set I at the gates, *tha*
there should no burden be brought i
on the sabbath day.
20 So the merchants and sellers o
all kind of ware lodged without Jeru
salem once or twice.
21 Then I testified against them, an
said unto them, Why lodge ye [14]abou
the wall? if ye do *so* again, I will la
hands on you. From that time fort
came they no *more* on the sabbath.

22 And I commanded the Levites
nat [s]they should cleanse themselves,
nd *that* they should come *and* keep
he gates, to sanctify the sabbath day.
emember me, O my God, *concerning*
his also, and spare me according to
he [15]greatness of thy mercy.
23 ¶ In those days also saw I Jews
hat [16]had married wives of Ăsh-dŏd,
f Ammon, *and* of Moab:
24 And their children spake half in
he speech of Ăsh-dŏd, and [17]could
ot speak in the Jews' language, but
ccording to the language [18]of each
eople.
25 And I [t]contended with them, and
cursed them, and [u]smote certain of
hem, and plucked off their hair, and
nade them [v]swear by God, *saying*, Ye
hall not give your daughters unto
heir sons, nor take their daughters
nto your sons, or for yourselves.
26 Did [w]not Solomon king of Israel
in by these things? [x]yet among many
ations was there no king like him,
who was beloved of his God, and God
made him king over all Israel: nevertheless even him did outlandish women cause to sin.
27 Shall we then hearken unto you
to do all this great evil, to transgress
[y]against our God in marrying strange
wives?
28 And *one* of the sons of [z]Jŏi-ă-dă,
the son of Ē-lī-ăsh-ĭb the high priest,
was son in law to Săn-băl-lăt the Hôr-
ŏn-īte: therefore I chased him from
me.
29 Remember [a]them, O my God,
[20]because they have defiled the priesthood, and the [b]covenant of the
priesthood, and of the Levites.
30 Thus [c]cleansed I them from all
strangers, and [d]appointed the wards
of the priests and the Levites, every
one in his business;
31 And for the wood offering, at
times appointed, and for the firstfruits. Remember me, O my God, for
good.

s ch. 12.30.
15 Or, multitude.
16 had made to dwell with them.
17 they discerned not to speak.
18 of people and people.
t Pro. 28.4.
19 Or, reviled them.
u Deut. 25.2. Ezra 7.26.
v Ezra 10.5. ch. 10.29,30.
w 1 Ki. 11.1.
x 2 Sam. 12. 24,25.
y Ezra 10.2.
z ch. 12.10.
a ch. 6.14.
20 for the defilings.
b Mal. 2.4.
c ch. 10.30.
d ch. 12.1.

THE

BOOK OF ESTHER

CHAPTER 1

NOW it came to pass in the days of
Ă-hăs-ū-ē-rŭs, (this *is* Ă-hăs-ū-
rŭs which reigned, from India even
nto Ē-thĭ-ō-pĭ-ă, *over* [a]an hundred
nd seven and twenty provinces:)
2 *That* in those days, when the king
-hăs-ū-ē-rŭs [b]sat on the throne of
is kingdom, which *was* [c]in Shû-shăn
ne palace,
3 In the third year of his reign, he
made a feast unto all his princes and
is servants; the power of Persia and
lē-dĭ-ă, the nobles and princes of the
rovinces, *being* before him:
4 When he shewed the riches of his
lorious kingdom and the honour of
is excellent majesty many days, *even*
n hundred and fourscore days.
5 And when these days were expired,
he king made a feast unto all the peo-
le, that were [1]present in Shû-shăn
he palace, both unto great and small,
even days, in the court of the garden
f the king's palace;
6 *Where were* white, green, and [2]blue,
angings, fastened with cords of fine
nen and purple to silver rings and
illars of marble: the [e]beds *were* of
gold and silver, upon a pavement [3]of
red, and blue, and white, and black,
marble.
7 And they gave *them* drink in vessels of gold, (the vessels being diverse
one from another,) and [4]royal wine in
abundance, [5]according to the state of
the king.
8 And the drinking *was* according to
the law; none did [6]compel: for so the
king had appointed to all the officers
of his house, that they should do according to every man's pleasure.
9 Also Văsh-tī the queen made a
feast for the women *in* the royal house
which *belonged* to king Ă-hăs-ū-ē-rŭs.
10 ¶ On the seventh day, when the
heart of the king was merry with wine,
he commanded Mĕ-hū-măn, Bĭz-thă,
Här-bō-nă, Bĭg-thă, and Ă-băg-thă,
Zē-thär, and Cär-căs, the seven [7]cham-
berlains that served in the presence of
Ă-hăs-ū-ē-rŭs the king,
11 To [f]bring Văsh-tī the queen before the king with the crown royal, to
shew the people and the princes her
beauty: for she *was* [8]fair to look on.
12 But the queen Văsh-tī refused to
come at the king's commandment [9]by

CHAP. 1
a ch. 8.9. Dan. 6.1.
b 2 Sam. 7.1. Dan. 4.4.
c Neh. 1.1. Dan. 8.2.
d Gen. 40.20. ch. 2.18. Dan. 5.1. Mark 6.21.
1 found.
2 Or, violet.
e ch. 7.8. Amos 2.8.
3 Or, of porphyre, and marble, and alabaster, and stone of blue colour.
4 wine of the kingdom.
5 according to the hand of the king.
6 Or, trouble.
7 Or, eunuchs.
f Pro. 16.9.
8 good of countenance.
9 which was by the hand of his eunuchs.

his chamberlains: therefore was the king very wroth, and his anger burned in him.

13 ¶ Then the king said to [g]the wise men, which [h]knew the times, (for so *was* the king's manner toward all that knew law and judgment:

14 And the next unto him *was* Cär-shē-nă, Shē-thär, Ăd-mā-thă, Tar-shish, Mē-rĕś, Mär-sē-nă, *and* Mĕ-mū-căn, [i]the seven princes of Persia and Mē-dĭ-ă, which saw the king's face, *and* which sat the first in the kingdom;)

15 [10]What shall we do unto the queen Văsh-tī according to law, because she hath not performed the commandment of the king Ă-hăś-ū-ē-rŭs by the chamberlains?

16 And Mĕ-mū-căn answered before the king and the princes, Văsh-tī the queen hath not done wrong to the king only, but also to all the princes, and to all the people that *are* in all the provinces of the king Ă-hăś-ū-ē-rŭs.

17 For *this* deed of the queen shall come abroad unto all women, so that they shall despise their husbands in their eyes, when it shall be reported, The king Ă-hăś-ū-ē-rŭs commanded Văsh-tī the queen to be brought in before him, but she came not.

18 *Likewise* shall the ladies of Persia and Mē-dĭ-ă say this day unto all the king's princes, which have heard of the deed of the queen. Thus *shall there arise* too much contempt and wrath.

19 [11]If it please the king, let there go a royal commandment [12]from him, and let it be written among the laws of the Persians and the Mēdeś, [13]that it be not altered, That Văsh-tī come no more before king Ă-hăś-ū-ē-rŭs; and let the king give her royal estate [14]unto another that is better than she.

20 And when the king's decree which he shall make shall be published throughout all his empire, (for it is great,) all the wives shall give [j]to their husbands honour, both to great and small.

21 And the saying [15]pleased the king and the princes; and the king did according to the word of Mĕ-mū-căn:

22 For he sent letters into all the king's provinces, [k]into every province according to the writing thereof, and to every people after their language, that every man should bear [l]rule in his own house, and [16]that *it* should be published according to the language of every people.

g Jer. 10.7. Dan. 2.12.
h 1 Chr. 12. 32. Isa. 7.14. Dan. 9.24. Mal. 3.1. Matt. 16.3.
i Ezra 7.14.
10 What to do.
11 If it be good with the king.
12 from before him.
13 that it pass not away.
14 unto her companion.
j Eph. 5.22, 23. Col. 3.18. 1 Pet. 3.1.
15 was good in the eyes of the king.
k ch. 8.9.
l Eph. 5.22, 23,24.
16 that one should publish it according to the language of his people. ch. 3.12. Dan. 6.25.

CHAP. 2
a ch. 1.19.
b Gen. 12.14, 15. 1 Ki. 1.2.
1 unto the hand.
c 2 Ki. 24.14, 15. 2 Chr. 36.10, 20. Jer. 22.24.
2 Or, Jehoiachin.
3 nourished.
4 fair of form, and good of countenance.
5 her portions.
6 he changed her.
d ch. 3.8. Lev. 26.36. Deut. 28.65.

CHAPTER 2

AFTER these things, when the wrath of king Ă-hăś-ū-ē-rŭs was appeased, he remembered Văsh-tī, and what she had done, and [a]what was decreed against her.

2 Then said the king's servants that ministered unto him, [b]Let there be fair young virgins sought for the king:

3 And let the king appoint officers in all the provinces of his kingdom, that they may gather together all the fair young virgins unto Shû-shăn the palace, to the house of the women, [1]unto the custody of Hē-gē the king's chamberlain, keeper of the women; and let their things for purification be given *them:*

4 And let the maiden which pleaseth the king be queen instead of Văsh-tī. And the thing pleased the king; and he did so.

5 ¶ *Now* in Shû-shăn the palace there was a certain Jew, whose name *was* Môr-dĕ-cā-ī, the son of Jā-ïr, the son of Shĭm-ĕ-ī, the son of Kish, a Benjamite;

6 Who [c]had been carried away from Jerusalem with the captivity which had been carried away with [2]Jĕc-ō-nī-ăh king of Judah, whom Nĕb-ū-chăd-nĕz-zär the king of Babylon had carried away.

7 And he [3]brought up Hă-dăs-săh, that *is*, Esther, his uncle's daughter: for she had neither father nor mother, and the maid *was* [4]fair and beautiful; whom Môr-dĕ-cā-ī, when her father and mother were dead, took for his own daughter.

8 ¶ So it came to pass, when the king's commandment and his decree was heard, and when many maidens were gathered together unto Shû-shăn the palace, to the custody of Hē-gâi, that Esther was brought also unto the king's house, to the custody of Hē-gâi, keeper of the women.

9 And the maiden pleased him, and she obtained kindness of him; and he speedily gave her her things for purification, with [5]such things as belonged to her, and seven maidens, *which were* meet to be given her, out of the king's house: and [6]he preferred her and her maids unto the best *place* of the house of the women.

10 Esther had not shewed her people nor her kindred: for Môr-dĕ-cā-ī had charged her that she should not [d]shew *it.*

11 And Môr-dĕ-cā-ī walked every day before the court of the women's

house, [7]to know how Esther did, and
what should become of her.
12 ¶ Now when every maid's turn
was come to go in to king Ă-hăs-ū-ē-
rŭs, after that she had been twelve
months, according to the manner of
the women, (for so were the days of
their purifications accomplished, *to*
wit, six months with oil of myrrh, and
six months with sweet odours, and
with *other* things for the purifying of
the women;)
13 Then thus came *every* maiden unto the king; whatsoever she desired
was given her to go with her out of the
house of the women unto the king's
house.
14 In the evening she went, and on the
morrow she returned into the second
house of the women, to the custody of
Shā-ăsh-găz, the king's chamberlain,
which kept the concubines: she came
in unto the king no more, except the
king delighted in her, and that she
were called by name.
15 ¶ Now when the turn of Esther,
the daughter of Ăb-ĭ-hail the uncle of
Môr-dĕ-cā-ī, who had taken her for
his daughter, was come to go in unto
the king, she required nothing but
what Hē-gâi the king's chamberlain,
the keeper of the women, appointed.
And Esther obtained [e]favour in the
sight of all them that looked upon her.
16 So Esther was taken unto king
Ă-hăs-ū-ē-rŭs into his house royal in
the [f]tenth month, which *is* the month
Tē-bĕth, in the seventh year of his
reign.
17 And the king loved Esther above
all the women, and she obtained grace
and [8]favour [9]in his sight more than all
the virgins; so that he [g]set the royal
crown upon her head, and made her
queen instead of Văsh-tī.
18 Then the king [h]made a great feast
unto all his princes and his servants,
even Esther's feast; and he made a
[10]release to the provinces, and gave
gifts, according to the state of the
king.
19 And when the virgins were gathered together the second time, then
Môr-dĕ-cā-ī sat [i]in the king's gate.
20 Esther had not *yet* shewed her
kindred nor her people; as Môr-dĕ-
cā-ī had charged her: for Esther did
the commandment of Môr-dĕ-cā-ī,
like as when she was brought up with
him.
21 ¶ In those days, while Môr-dĕ-
cā-ī sat in the king's gate, two of the
king's chamberlains, [11]Bĭg-thăn and

7 to know the peace.
e Song 6.9. Acts 7.10. 2 Tim. 4.18.
f ch. 3.7.
8 Or, kindness.
9 before him.
g Gen. 41.40. 1 Sam. 2.8. ch. 3.14. Job 36.7. Ps. 75.5. Luke 1.48, 49. Jas. 2.5. Rev. 3.21.
h Gen. 29.22. Judg. 14.10. ch. 1.3. Matt. 25.1-10. Mark 6.21. Luke 14.8.
10 rest.
i ch. 3.2.
11 Or, Bigthana.
12 the threshold.
j ch. 6.2. Ps. 37.1,2, 7-10. Pro. 8.12. Pro. 14.17, 29. Eccl. 7.9. Eph. 4.26. Phil. 2.4. Jas. 1.19,20.
k Gen. 40.19. Deut. 21.22.
l ch. 6.1.

CHAP. 3

a Num. 24.7. 1 Sam. 15.8.
b ch. 2.19.
c Gen. 41.42. Deut. 25.19. Phil. 2.10.
d Ex. 1.17. Ps. 15.4.
e ch. 5.9.
f ch. 1.12. Job 5.2. Pro. 12.16. Dan. 3.19.
g Ps. 83.4.
h ch. 9.24. Matt. 27.35. Acts. 1.26.
i Ezra 4.13. Acts 16.20.
1 meet, or, equal.

Tē-rĕsh, of those which kept [12]the
door, were wroth, and sought to lay
hand on the king Ă-hăs-ū-ē-rŭs.
22 And the thing was known to Môr-
dĕ-cā-ī, who [j]told *it* unto Esther the
queen; and Esther certified the king
thereof in Môr-dĕ-cā-ī's name.
23 And when inquisition was made
of the matter, it was found out; therefore they were [k]both hanged on a
tree: and it was written in [l]the book of
the chronicles before the king.

CHAPTER 3

AFTER these things did king Ă-
hăs-ū-ē-rŭs promote Hā-măn the
son of Hăm-mĕ-dā-thă the [a]Ăg-ă-gīte,
and advanced him, and set his seat
above all the princes that *were* with
him.
2 And all the king's servants, that
were in [b]the king's gate, bowed, [c]and
reverenced Hā-măn: for the king had
so commanded concerning him. But
[d]Môr-dĕ-cā-ī bowed not, nor did *him*
reverence.
3 Then the king's servants, which
were in the king's gate, said unto Môr-
dĕ-cā-ī, Why transgressest thou the
king's commandment?
4 Now it came to pass, when they
spake daily unto him, and he hearkened not unto them, that they told Hā-
măn, to see whether Môr-dĕ-cā-ī's
matters would stand: for he had told
them that he *was* a Jew.
5 And when Hā-măn saw that Môr-
dĕ-cā-ī bowed [e]not, nor did him
reverence, then was Hā-măn [f]full
of wrath.
6 And he thought scorn to lay hands
on Môr-dĕ-cā-ī alone; for they had
shewed him the people of Môr-dĕ-
cā-ī: wherefore Hā-măn [g]sought to
destroy all the Jews that *were* throughout the whole kingdom of Ă-hăs-ū-
ē-rŭs, *even* the people of Môr-dĕ-cā-ī.
7 ¶ In the first month, that *is*, the
month Nī-săn, in the twelfth year of
king Ă-hăs-ū-ē-rŭs, [h]they cast Pur,
that *is*, the lot, before Hā-măn from
day to day, and from month to month,
to the twelfth *month*, that *is*, the
month Ā-dăr.
8 ¶ And Hā-măn said unto king Ă-
hăs-ū-ē-rŭs, There is a certain people
scattered abroad and dispersed among
the people in all the provinces of thy
kingdom; and [i]their laws *are* diverse
from all people; neither keep they the
king's laws: therefore it *is* not [1]for the
king's profit to suffer them.
9 If it please the king, let it be writ-

ten [2]that they may be destroyed: and
I will [3]pay ten thousand talents of silver to the hands of those that have
the charge of the business, to bring *it*
into the king's treasuries.
10 And [j]the king took his [k]ring from
his hand, and gave it unto Hā´-măn the
son of Hăm-mĕ-dā´-thă the Ăg´-ā-gīte,
the Jews' [4]enemy.
11 And the king said unto Hā´-măn,
The silver *is* given to thee, the people
also, to do with them as it seemeth
good to thee.
12 Then [l]were the king's [5]scribes
called on the thirteenth day of the first
month, and there was written according to all that Hā´-măn had commanded unto the king's lieutenants, and to
the governors that *were* over every
province, and to the rulers of every
people of every province according
[m]to the writing thereof, and *to* every
people after their language; [n]in the
name of king Ă-hăs-ū-ē´-rŭs was it
written, and sealed with the king's
ring.
13 And the letters were [o]sent by
posts into all the king's provinces, to
destroy, to kill, and to cause to perish,
all Jews, both young and old, little
children and women, in [p]one day, *even*
upon the thirteenth *day* of the twelfth
month, which *is* the month Ā´-där, and
[q]*to take* the spoil of them for a prey.
14 The [r]copy of the writing for a
commandment to be given in every
province was published unto all people, that they should be ready against
that day.
15 The posts went out, being hastened by the king's commandment, and
the decree was given in Shû´-shăn the
palace. And the king and Hā´-măn [s]sat
down to drink; but [t]the city Shû´-shăn
was perplexed.

CHAPTER 4

WHEN Môr-dĕ-cā´-ī perceived all
that was done, Môr-dĕ-cā´-ī rent
his [a]clothes, and put on sackcloth with
[b]ashes, and went out into the midst of
the city, and [c]cried with a loud and a
bitter cry;
2 And came even before the king's
gate: for none *might* enter into the
king's gate clothed with sackcloth.
3 And in every province, whithersoever the king's commandment and his
decree came, *there was* great mourning among the Jews, and fasting, and
weeping, and wailing; and [1]many lay
in sackcloth and ashes.
4 ¶ So Esther's maids and her [2]cham-
berlains came and told *it* her. Then
was the queen exceedingly grieved;
and she sent raiment to clothe Môr-
dĕ-cā´-ī, and to take away his sackcloth
from him: but he received *it* not.
5 Then called Esther for Hā´-tăch,
one of the king's chamberlains, [3]whom
he had appointed to attend upon her,
and gave him a commandment to
Môr-dĕ-cā´-ī, to know what it *was*, and
why it *was*.
6 So Hā´-tăch went forth to Môr-dĕ-
cā´-ī unto the street of the city, which
was before the king's gate.
7 And Môr-dĕ-cā´-ī told him of all
that had happened unto him, and of
the sum of [d]the money that Hā´-măn
had promised to pay to the king's
treasuries for the Jews, to destroy
them.
8 Also he gave him [e]the copy of the
writing of the decree that was given at
Shû´-shăn to destroy them, to shew *it*
unto Esther, and to declare *it* unto her,
and to charge her that she should go
in unto the king, to make [f]supplica-
tion unto him, and to make request
before him for her people.
9 And Hā´-tăch came and told Esther
the words of Môr-dĕ-cā´-ī.
10 ¶ Again Esther spake unto Hā´-
tăch, and gave him commandment
unto Môr-dĕ-cā´-ī;
11 All the king's servants, and the
people of the king's provinces, do
know, that whosoever, whether man
or woman, shall come unto the king
into [g]the inner court, who is not called,
[h]*there is* one law of his to put *him* to
death, [i]except such to whom the king
shall hold out the golden sceptre, that
he may live: but I have not been called
to come in unto the king these thirty
days.
12 And they told to Môr-dĕ-cā´-ī
Esther's words.
13 Then Môr-dĕ-cā´-ī commanded to
answer Esther, Think [j]not with thyself that thou shalt escape in the king's
house, more than all the Jews.
14 For if thou altogether holdest thy
peace at this time, *then* shall there [4]en-
largement and [k]deliverance arise to
the Jews from another place; but thou
and thy father's house shall be destroyed: and who knoweth whether
[l]thou art come to the kingdom for
such a time as this?
15 ¶ Then Esther bade *them* return
Môr-dĕ-cā´-ī *this answer*,
16 Go, gather together all the Jews
that are [5]present in Shû´-shăn, and
[m]fast ye for me, and neither eat nor

2 to destroy them.
3 weigh.
j Gen. 41.42.
k ch. 8.2,8.
4 Or, oppressor.
l ch. 8.9.
5 Or, secretaries.
m ch. 1.22. ch. 8.9.
n 1 Ki. 21.8. ch. 8.8,10. Dan. 6.8.
o ch. 8.10. Rom. 3.15.
p ch. 8.12.
q ch. 8.11. Isa. 10.6.
r ch. 8.13,14.
s Gen. 37.24, 25. Ps. 14.4. Pro. 30.20-22. Hosea 7.3. Amos 6.6. Matt. 14.6.
t ch. 8.15. Pro. 29.2.

CHAP. 4

a 2 Sam. 1.11. Job 1.20. Acts 14.14.
b Josh. 7.6. Eze. 27.30.
c Gen. 27.34.
1 sackcloth and ashes were laid under many.
2 eunuchs.
3 whom he had set before her.
d ch. 3.9.
e ch. 3.14,15.
f Job 9.15. Pro. 15.1. Acts 12.20.
g ch. 5.1.
h Dan. 2.9.
i ch. 5.2. ch. 8.4.
j Pro. 29.25.
4 respiration. Job 9.18.
k Lev. 26.42. Num. 23.22-24. Jer. 30.10. Amos 9.8.
l Ps. 75.5,6. Eccl. 3.1. Isa. 14.27. Isa. 54.17. Jer. 30.10, 24. Dan. 4.17, 35. Matt. 16.18.
5 found.
m Joel 1.14. Jonah 3.4.

drink [n]three days, night or day: I also
and my maidens will fast likewise;
and so will I go in unto the king, which
is not according to the law: and if I
perish, [o]I perish.
17 So Môr-dĕ-cā-ī [6]went his way, and
did according to all that Esther had
commanded him.

CHAPTER 5

NOW it came to pass [a]on the third
day, that Esther put on *her* royal
apparel, and stood in [b]the inner court
of the king's house, over against the
king's house: and the king sat upon
his royal throne in the royal house,
over against the gate of the house.
2 And it was so, when the king saw
Esther the queen standing in the
court, *that* [c]she obtained favour in his
sight: and the [d]king held out to Esther
the golden sceptre that *was* in his
hand. So Esther drew near, and touched the top of the sceptre.
3 Then said the king unto her, What
wilt thou, queen Esther? and what *is*
thy request? [e]it shall be even given
thee to the half of the kingdom.
4 And Esther answered, If *it seem*
good unto the king, let the king and
Hā-măn come this day unto the banquet that I have prepared for him.
5 Then the king said, Cause Hā-măn
to make haste, that he may do as
Esther hath said. So the king and Hā-
măn came to the banquet that Esther
had prepared.
6 ¶ And [f]the king said unto Esther
at the banquet of wine, What [g]*is* thy
petition? and it shall be granted thee:
and what *is* thy request? even to the
half of the kingdom it shall be performed.
7 Then answered Esther, and said,
My petition and my request *is;*
8 If I have found favour in the sight
of the king, and if it please the king to
grant my petition, and [1]to perform my
request, let the king and Hā-măn
come to the banquet that I shall prepare for them, and I will do to morrow
as the king hath said.
9 ¶ Then went Hā-măn forth that
day joyful [h]and with a glad heart: but
when Hā-măn saw Môr-dĕ-cā-ī in the
king's gate, that he [i]stood not up, nor
moved for him, he was full of indignation against Môr-dĕ-cā-ī.
10 Nevertheless Hā-măn [j]refrained
himself: and when he came home, he
sent and [2]called for his friends, and
Zē-rĕsh his wife.
11 And Hā-măn told them of [k]the
glory of his riches, and [l]the multitude
of his children, and all *the things*
wherein the king had promoted him,
and how he had [m]advanced him above
the princes and servants of the king.
12 Hā-măn said moreover, Yea,
Esther the queen did let no man
come in with the king unto the banquet that she had prepared but myself;
and [n]to morrow am I invited unto
her also with the king.
13 Yet [o]all this availeth me nothing,
so long as I see Môr-dĕ-cā-ī the Jew
sitting at the king's gate.
14 ¶ Then said Zē-rĕsh his wife and
all his friends unto him, Let a [3]gallows
be made of fifty cubits high, and to
morrow [p]speak thou unto the king
that Môr-dĕ-cā-ī may be hanged
thereon: then go thou in merrily with
the king unto the banquet. And the
thing pleased Hā-măn; and he caused
the [q]gallows to be made.

CHAPTER 6

ON that night [1]could not the king
sleep, and he commanded to
bring [a]the book of records of the
chronicles; and they were read before
the king.
2 And it was found written, that
Môr-dĕ-cā-ī had told of [2]Bĭg-thā-nă
and Tē-rĕsh, two of the king's chamberlains, the keepers of the [3]door,
who sought to lay hand on the king
Ă-hăș-ū-ē-rŭs.
3 And the king said, [b]What honour
and dignity hath been done to Môr-
dĕ-cā-ī for this? Then said the king's
servants that ministered unto him,
There is nothing done for him.
4 ¶ And the king said, Who *is* in the
court? Now Hā-măn was come into
[c]the outward court of the king's house,
[d]to speak unto the king to hang Môr-
dĕ-cā-ī on the gallows that he had prepared for him.
5 And the king's servants said unto
him, Behold, Hā-măn standeth in the
court. And the king said, Let him
come in.
6 So Hā-măn came in. And the king
said unto him, What shall be done unto the man [4]whom the king delighteth
to honour? Now Hā-măn thought in
his heart, To whom would the king
delight to do honour more than to
myself?
7 And Hā-măn answered the king,
For the man [5]whom the king delighteth to honour,
8 [6]Let the royal apparel be brought
[7]which the king *useth* to wear, and

n ch. 5.1.
o Ps. 34.15, 22. Ps. 37.3,5, 28-40. Ps. 55.22. Ps. 62.8. Ps. 115.9,10, 11. Pro. 29.25.
6 passed.

CHAP. 5
a ch. 4.16.
b ch. 6.4.
c Pro. 21.1.
d ch. 8.4.
e Mark 6.23.
f ch. 7.2.
g ch. 9.12.
1 to do.
h Job 20.5. John 16.20. Jas. 4.9.
i ch. 3.5. Ps. 15.4. Matt. 10.28.
j Gen. 43.30, 31.
2 caused to come.
k Gen. 31.1. Job 31.24, 25. Dan. 4.30. Mark 10.24.
l ch. 9.7.
m ch. 3.1.
n Pro. 27.1. 1 Thes. 5.3.
o 1 Ki. 21.4-6. Job 5.2.
3 tree.
p ch. 6.4.
q ch. 7.10. Ps. 59.7. Pro. 1.16.

CHAP. 6
1 the king's sleep fled away.
a ch. 2.23.
2 Or, Bigthan
3 threshold.
b Gal. 6.9.
c ch. 5.1.
d ch. 5.14. Job 5.13.
4 in whose honour the king delighteth.
5 in whose honour the king delighteth.
6 Let them bring the royal apparel.
7 wherewith the king clotheth himself.

[e]the horse that the king rideth upon,
and the crown royal which is set upon
his head:
9 And let this apparel and horse be
delivered to the hand of one of the
king's most noble princes, that they
may array the man *withal* whom the
king delighteth to honour, and [8]bring
him on horseback through the street
of the city, and [f]proclaim before him,
Thus shall it be done to the man whom
the king delighteth to honour.
10 Then the king said to Hā′măn,
Make [g]haste, *and* take the apparel and
the horse, as thou hast said, and
do even so to Môr-dĕ-cā′ī the Jew,
that sitteth at the king's gate: [9]let
nothing fail of all that thou hast spoken.
11 Then took Hā′măn the apparel
and the horse, and arrayed Môr-dĕ-
cā′ī, and brought him on horseback
through the street of the city, and proclaimed before him, Thus shall it be
done unto the man whom the king delighteth to honour.
12 ¶ And Môr-dĕ-cā′ī [h]came again
to the king's gate. But Hā′măn hasted
to his house mourning, and [i]having
his head covered.
13 And Hā′măn told Zē′rĕsh his wife
and all his friends every *thing* that had
befallen him. Then said his wise men
and Zē′rĕsh his wife unto him, If Môr-
dĕ-cā′ī *be* of the seed of the Jews, before whom thou hast begun to fall,
thou shalt not prevail against him,
but shalt surely fall before him.
14 And while they *were* yet talking
with him, came the king's chamberlains, and hasted to bring Hā′măn
unto the banquet that Esther had prepared.

CHAPTER 7

SO the king and Hā′măn came [1]to
banquet with Esther the queen.
2 And the king said again unto Esther
on the second day [a]at the banquet of
wine, What *is* thy petition, queen
Esther? and it shall be granted thee:
and what *is* thy request? and it shall
be performed, *even* to the half of the
kingdom.
3 Then Esther the queen answered
and said, If I have found favour in thy
sight, O king, and if it please the king,
let my life be given me at my petition,
and my people at my request:
4 For we are [b]sold, I and my people,
[2]to be destroyed, to be slain, and to
perish. But if we had been sold for
bondmen and bondwomen, I had
held my tongue, although the enemy
could not countervail the king's
damage.
5 ¶ Then the king Ă-hăṡ-ū-ē′rŭs
answered and said unto Esther the
queen, Who is he, and where is he,
[3]that durst presume in his heart to do
so?
6 And Esther said, [4]The adversary
and enemy *is* this wicked Hā′măn.
Then Hā′măn was afraid [5]before the
king and the queen.
7 ¶ And the king arising from the
banquet of wine in his wrath *went* into the palace garden: and Hā′măn
[c]stood up to make request for his life
to Esther the queen; for he saw that
there was evil determined against him
by the king.
8 Then the king returned out of the
palace garden into the place of the
banquet of wine; and Hā′măn was
fallen upon [d]the bed whereon Esther
was. Then said the king, Will he force
the queen also [6]before me in the
house? As the word went out of the
king's mouth, they covered [e]Hā-
măn's face.
9 And [f]Här-bō′năh, one of the chamberlains, said before the king, Behold
also, [g]the [7]gallows fifty cubits high,
which Hā′măn had made for Môr-dĕ-
cā′ī, who [h]had spoken good for the
king, standeth in the house of Hā-
măn. Then the king said, Hang him
thereon.
10 So [i]they hanged Hā′măn on the
gallows that he had prepared for Môr-
dĕ-cā′ī. Then was the king's wrath
pacified.

CHAPTER 8

ON that day did the king Ă-hăṡ-ū-ē-
rŭs give the house of Hā′măn the
Jews' enemy unto Esther the queen.
And Môr-dĕ-cā′ī came before the
king; for Esther had told what [a]he
was unto her.
2 And the king took off [b]his ring,
which he had taken from Hā′măn,
and gave it unto Môr-dĕ-cā′ī. And
Esther set Môr-dĕ-cā′ī over the house
of Hā′măn.
3 ¶ And Esther spake yet again before the king, and fell down at his
feet, [1]and besought him with tears to
put away the mischief of Hā′măn the
Ăg′ă-gīte, and his device that he had
devised against the Jews.
4 Then [c]the king held out the golden
sceptre toward Esther. So Esther
arose, and stood before the king,
5 And said, If it please the king, and
if I have found favour in his sight, and
the thing *seem* right before the king,

e 1 Ki. 1.33.
8 cause him to ride.
f Gen. 41.43.
g Job 5.11,13. Luke 14.11.
9 suffer not a whit to fall.
h ch. 2.19. Ps. 131.1.
i 2 Sam. 15. 30.

CHAP. 7

1 to drink.
a ch. 5.6.
b 1 Sam. 22. 23. ch. 3.9.
2 that they should destroy, and kill, and cause to perish.
3 whose heart hath filled him.
4 The man adversary.
5 Or, at the presence of.
c Pro. 14.19.
d ch. 1.6.
6 with me.
e Job 9.24.
f ch. 1.10. Job 9.24. Isa. 22.17.
g ch. 5.14. Ps. 7.16. Pro. 11.5,6.
7 tree.
h ch. 2.21-23. ch. 5.14. Job 27.20-23. Pro. 11.5,6.
i ch. 9.25. Ps. 7.15. Ps. 9.15,16. Dan. 6.24.

CHAP. 8

a ch. 2.7.
b Gen. 41.42. ch. 3.10. Dan. 5.29. Luke 15.22.
1 and she wept, and besought him.
c ch. 4.11.

and I *be* pleasing in his eyes, let it be
written to reverse [2]the letters devised
by Hā´-măn the son of Hăm-mĕ-dā´-
thă the Ăg-ă-gīte, [3]which he wrote to
destroy the Jews which *are* in all the
king's provinces:
6 For how can I [4]endure to [d]see the
evil that shall come unto my people?
or how can I endure to see the destruction of my kindred?
7 ¶ Then the king Ă-hăš-ū-ē´-rŭs said
unto Esther the queen and to Môr-dĕ-
cā´-ī the Jew, Behold, [e]I have given
Esther the house of Hā´-măn, and him
they have hanged upon the gallows,
because he laid his hand upon the
Jews.
8 Write ye also for the Jews, as it
liketh you, in the king's name, and
seal *it* with the king's ring: for the
writing which is written in the king's
name, and sealed with the king's ring,
[f]may no man reverse.
9 Then [g]were the king's scribes called at that time in the third month,
that *is*, the month Sī´-văn, on the three
and twentieth *day* thereof; and it was
written according to all that Môr-dĕ-
cā´-ī commanded unto the Jews, and
to the lieutenants, and the deputies
and rulers of the provinces which *are*
[h]from India unto Ē-thĭ-ō´-pĭ-ă, an
hundred twenty and seven provinces,
unto every province [i]according to the
writing thereof, and unto every people after their language, and to the
Jews according to their writing, and
according to their language.
10 And [j]he wrote in the king Ă-hăš-
ū-ē´-rŭs' name, and sealed *it* with the
king's ring, and sent letters by posts
on horseback, *and* riders on mules,
camels, *and* young dromedaries:
11 Wherein the king granted the
Jews which *were* in every city to gather themselves together, and to stand
for their life, to destroy, to slay, and
to cause to perish, all the power of
the people and province that would
assault them, *both* little ones and women, [k]and *to take* the spoil of them
for a prey,
12 Upon [l]one day in all the provinces
of king Ă-hăš-ū-ē´-rŭs, *namely*, upon
the thirteenth *day* of the twelfth
month, which *is* the month Ā´-där.
13 The [m]copy of the writing for a commandment to be given in every province *was* [5]published unto all people,
and that the Jews should be ready
against that day to avenge themselves
on their enemies.
14 *So* the posts that rode upon mules

2 the device.
3 Or, who wrote.
4 be able that I may see.
d Neh. 2.3. Ps. 137.6.
e Pro. 13.22.
f Dan. 6.8, 12-15. 2 Tim. 2.19.
g ch. 3.12.
h ch. 1.1.
i ch. 1.22.
j 1 Ki. 21.8.
k ch. 3.13. Isa. 10.6.
l Ex. 15.9,10. ch. 3.13.
m ch. 3.14,15.
5 revealed.
6 Or, violet.
n ch. 3.15. Pro. 28.12, 28.
o ch. 9.17. Job 11.17. Ps. 18.28. Pro. 4.18.
p 1 Sam. 25.8. Neh. 8.10. ch. 9.19,22.
q Ps. 18.43.
r Gen. 35.5. Ex. 15.16. Deut. 2.25. ch. 9.2.

CHAP. 9
a ch. 8.12.
b ch. 3.13.
c 2 Sam. 22. 41. Isa. 14.2.
d ch. 8.11.
e Ps. 71.13.
f Ex. 23.27. ch. 8.17.
1 those which did the business that belonged to the king.
g Pro. 16.7.
h 2 Sam. 3.1. 1 Chr. 11.9. Ps. 1.3. Pro. 4.18. Isa. 9.7.
2 according to their will.

and camels went out, being hastened
and pressed on by the king's commandment. And the decree was given
at Shû´-shăn the palace.
15 ¶ And Môr-dĕ-cā´-ī went out from
the presence of the king in royal apparel of [6]blue and white, and with a
great crown of gold, and with a garment of fine linen and purple: and
[n]the city of Shû´-shăn rejoiced and was
glad.
16 The Jews had [o]light, and gladness,
and joy, and honour.
17 And in every province, and in
every city, whithersoever the king's
commandment and his decree came,
the Jews had joy and gladness, a [p]feast
and a good day. And many of the
people of the land [q]became Jews; for
the [r]fear of the Jews fell upon them.

CHAPTER 9

NOW [a]in the twelfth month, that
is, the month Ā´-där, on the thirteenth day of the same, when [b]the
king's commandment and his decree
drew near to be put in execution, in
the day that the enemies of the Jews
hoped to have power over them,
(though it was turned to the contrary,
that the Jews had [c]rule over them that
hated them;)
2 The Jews [d]gathered themselves together in their cities throughout all
the provinces of the king Ă-hăš-ū-ē´-
rŭs, to lay hand on such as sought
[e]their hurt: and no man could withstand them; [f]for the fear of them fell
upon all people.
3 And all the rulers of the provinces,
and the lieutenants, and the deputies,
and [1]officers of the king, [g]helped the
Jews; because the fear of Môr-dĕ-cā´-ī
fell upon them.
4 For Môr-dĕ-cā´-ī *was* great in the
king's house, and his fame went out
throughout all the provinces: for this
man Môr-dĕ-cā´-ī [h]waxed greater and
greater.
5 Thus the Jews smote all their enemies with the stroke of the sword, and
slaughter, and destruction, and did
[2]what they would unto those that
hated them.
6 And in Shû´-shăn the palace the
Jews slew and destroyed five hundred
men.
7 And Pär-shăn-dā´-thă, and Dăl´-
phŏn, and Ăs-pā´-thă,
8 And Pôr-ā´-thă, and Ă-dā´-lĭ-ă, and
Ăr-ĭ-dā´-thă,
9 And Pär-măsh´-tă, and Ăr´-ĭ-sâī, and
Ăr´-ĭ-dâī, and Vă-jĕz´-ă-thă,

10 The [i]ten sons of Hā´-măn the son
of Hăm-mĕ-dā´-thă, the enemy of the
Jews, slew they; [j]but on the spoil laid
they not their hand.
11 On that day the number of those
that were slain in Shû´-shăn the palace
[3]was brought before the king.
12 ¶ And the king said unto Esther
the queen, The Jews have slain and
destroyed five hundred men in Shû´-
shăn the palace, and the ten sons of
Hā´-măn; what have they done in the
rest of the king's provinces? now
[k]what *is* thy petition? and it shall be
granted thee: or what *is* thy request
further? and it shall be done.
13 Then said Esther, If it please the
king, let it be granted to the Jews
which *are* in Shû´-shăn to do to morrow also [l]according unto this day's
decree, and [4]let Hā´-măn's ten [m]sons
be hanged upon the gallows.
14 And the king commanded it so to
be done: and the decree was given at
Shû´-shăn; and they hanged Hā´-măn's
ten sons.
15 For the Jews that *were* in Shû´-
shăn gathered [n]themselves together on
the fourteenth day also of the month
Ā´-där, and slew three hundred men
at Shû´-shăn; but on the prey they laid
not their hand.
16 But the other Jews that *were* in
the king's provinces [o]gathered themselves together, and stood for their
lives, and had rest from their enemies, and slew of their foes seventy
and five thousand, [p]but they laid not
their hands on the prey,
17 On the thirteenth day of the
month Ā´-där; and on the fourteenth
day [5]of the same rested they, and
made it a day of feasting and gladness.
18 But the Jews that *were* at Shû´-
shăn assembled together on the thirteenth *day* thereof, and on the fourteenth thereof; and on the fifteenth
day of the same they rested, and made
it a day of feasting and gladness.
19 Therefore the Jews of the villages,
that dwelt in the unwalled towns,
made the fourteenth day of the month
Ā´-där [q]*a day of* gladness and feasting,
[r]and a good day, and of [s]sending portions one to another.
20 ¶ And Môr-dĕ-cā´-ī wrote these
things, and sent letters unto all the
Jews that *were* in all the provinces of
the king Ā-hăs-ū-ē´-rŭs, *both* nigh and
far,
21 To stablish *this* among them, that
they should [t]keep the fourteenth day
of the month Ā´-där, and the fifteenth
day of the same, yearly,
22 As the days wherein the Jews rested from their enemies, and the month
which was [u]turned unto them from
sorrow to joy, and from mourning into a good day: that they should make
them days of feasting and joy, and of
[v]sending portions one to another, and
gifts to the poor.
23 And the Jews undertook to do as
they had begun, and as Môr-dĕ-cā´-ī
had written unto them;
24 Because Hā´-măn the son of Hăm-
mĕ-dā´-thă, the Ăg´-ă-gīte, the enemy
of all the Jews, [w]had devised against
the Jews to destroy them, and had
cast Pur, that *is*, the lot, to [6]consume
them, and to destroy them;
25 But [7]when *Esther* came before
the king, he commanded by letters
that his wicked device, which he devised against the Jews, should [x]re-
turn upon his own head, and that he
and his sons should be hanged on the
gallows.
26 Wherefore they called these days
Pū´-rĭm after the name of [8]Pur. Therefore for all the words of this letter, and
of that which they had seen concerning this matter, and which had come
unto them,
27 The Jews ordained, and took upon
them, and upon their seed, and upon
all such as [y]joined themselves unto
them, so as it should not [9]fail, that
they would keep these two days according to their writing, and according to their *appointed* time every year;
28 And *that* these days *should be* remembered and kept throughout every
generation, every family, every province, and every city; and *that* these
days of Pū´-rĭm should not [10] fail from
among the Jews, nor the memorial of
them [11]perish from their seed.
29 Then Esther the queen, [z]the
daughter of Ăb´-ī-hail, and Môr-dĕ-
cā´-ī the Jew, wrote with [12]all authority,
[a]to confirm this second letter of Pū´-
rĭm.
30 And he sent the letters unto all
the Jews, to [b]the hundred twenty and
seven provinces of the kingdom of Ā-
hăs-ū-ē´-rŭs, *with* words of peace and
truth,
31 To confirm these days of Pū´-rĭm
in their times *appointed*, according as
Môr-dĕ-cā´-ī the Jew and Esther the
queen had enjoined them, and as they
had decreed for themselves and for
their seed, the matters of the fastings
and their cry.

i Ex. 20.5. ch. 5.11. Job 18.19. Ps. 21.10.
j Gen. 14.23. ch. 8.11.
3 came.
k ch. 5.6.
l ch. 8.11.
4 let men hang.
m 2 Sam. 21. 6,9.
n ch. 8.11.
o Lev. 26.7,8. ch. 8.11.
p 1 Thes. 5. 22.
5 in it.
q Deut. 16. 11, 14. Neh. 8.10-12. ch. 8.17. Ps. 118.15. Rev. 11.10.
r 1 Sam. 25.8. Neh. 8.10-12. ch. 8.17.
s Neh. 8.10-12. Rev. 11.10.
t Ps. 145.4.
u Ps. 30.11. Matt. 5.4. John 16.20-22.
v Neh. 8.11. Acts 2.44-46.
w ch. 3.6,7.
6 crush.
7 when she came.
x 1 Sam. 24. 12,13. ch. 7.10. Ps. 7.16. Ps. 37.12,13.
8 That is, lot.
y ch. 8.17. Isa. 56.3,6. Zech. 2.11.
9 pass.
10 pass.
11 be ended.
z ch. 2.15.
12 all strength.
a ch. 8.10.
b ch. 1.1.

32 And the decree of Esther confirmed these matters of Pū-rĭm; and
it was written in the book.

CHAPTER 10

AND the king Ă-hăs-ū-ē-rŭs laid a
tribute upon the land, and *upon*
[a]the isles of the sea.
2 And all the acts of his power and of
his might, and the declaration of the
greatness of Môr-dĕ-cā-ī, whereunto
the king [1]advanced him, *are* they not
written in the book of the chronicles of
the kings of Mē-dĭ-ă and Persia?
3 For Môr-dĕ-cā-ī the Jew *was* [b]next
unto king Ă-hăs-ū-ē-rŭs, and great
among the Jews, and accepted of the
multitude of [c]his brethren, seeking the
wealth of his people, and speaking
[d]peace to all his seed.

CHAP. 10
a Gen. 10.5. Ps. 72.10. Isa. 24.15.
1 made him great.
b Gen. 41.40. 2 Chr. 28.7.
c Neh. 2.10. Ps. 122.8.
d Ps. 125.5. Pro. 12.20. Isa. 26.12.

THE

BOOK OF JOB

CHAPTER 1

THERE was a man [a]in the land of
Uz, whose name *was* [b]Job; and
that man was [c]perfect and upright,
and one that feared [d]God, and eschew-
ed evil.
2 And there were born unto him sev-
en sons and three daughters.
3 His [1]substance also was seven
thousand sheep, and three thousand
camels, and five hundred yoke of ox-
en, and five hundred she asses, and a
very great [2]household; so that this
man was the greatest of all the [3]men
of the east.
4 And his sons went and feasted *in*
their houses, every one his day; and
sent and called for their three sisters
to eat and to drink with them.
5 And it was so, when the days of
their feasting were gone about, that
Job sent and sanctified them, and
rose up early in the morning, [e]and
offered burnt offerings *according* to
the number of them all: for Job said,
[f]It may be that my sons have sinned,
and [g]cursed God in their hearts. Thus
did Job [4]continually.
6 ¶ Now [h]there was a day [i]when the
sons of God came to present themselves before the LORD, and [5]Satan
came also [6]among them.
7 And the LORD said unto Satan,
Whence comest thou? Then Satan
answered the LORD, and said, From
going [j]to and fro in the earth, and
from walking up and down in it.
8 And the LORD said unto Satan,
[7]Hast thou considered my servant
Job, that *there is* none like him in the
earth, a perfect and an upright man,
one that feareth God, and escheweth
evil?
9 Then Satan answered the LORD,
and said, Doth Job fear God for
nought?
10 Hast [k]not thou made an hedge
about him, and about his house, and
about all that he hath on every side?
[l]thou hast blessed the work of his
hands, and his [8]substance is increased
in the land.
11 But put forth thine hand now, and
touch all that he hath, [9]and he will
curse thee to thy face.
12 And the LORD said unto Satan,
Behold, all that he hath *is* in thy
[10]power; only upon himself put not
forth thine hand. So Satan went forth
from the presence of the LORD.
13 ¶ And there was a day [m]when his
sons and his daughters *were* eating
and drinking wine in their eldest brother's house:
14 And there came a messenger unto
Job, and said, The oxen were plowing, and the asses feeding beside them:
15 And the [n]Să-bē-ăns fell *upon them*,
and took them away; yea, they have
slain the servants with the edge of the
sword; and I only am escaped alone
to tell thee.
16 While he *was* yet speaking, there
came also another, and said, [11]The
fire of God is fallen from heaven, and
hath burned up the sheep, and the
servants, and consumed them; and I
only am escaped alone to tell thee.
17 While he *was* yet speaking, there
came also another, and said, The
Chăl-dē-ăns made out three bands,
and [12]fell upon the camels, and have
carried them away, yea, and slain the
servants with the edge of the sword;
and I only am escaped alone to tell
thee.
18 While he *was* yet speaking, there
came also another, and said, Thy sons

CHAP. 1
a Gen. 22.20.
b Jas. 5.11.
c Gen. 6.9.
d Pro. 8.13. 1 Pet. 3.11.
1 Or, cattle.
2 Or, husbandry.
3 sons of the east.
e Gen. 8.20. ch. 42.8.
f 2 Cor. 11.2.
g 1 Ki. 21.10, 13.
4 all the days.
h ch. 2.1.
i ch. 38.7. Dan. 7.10.
5 the adversary.
6 in the midst of them.
j Matt. 12.43. 1 Pet. 5.8.
7 Hast thou set thy heart on.
k Gen. 15.1. Ps. 34.7. Isa. 5.2.
l Ps. 128.1.
8 Or, cattle.
9 if he curse thee not to thy face.
10 hand.
m Eccl. 9.12. Luke 12.19, 20.
n Gen. 10.7.
11 Or, A great fire.
12 rushed.

and thy daughters *were* eating and
drinking wine in their eldest brother's
house:
19 And, behold, there came a great
wind [13]from the wilderness, and smote
the four corners of the house, and it
fell upon the young men, and they are
dead; and I only am escaped alone to
tell thee.
20 Then Job arose, and rent his
[14]mantle, and shaved his head, and
[o]fell down upon the ground, and worshipped,
21 And said, Naked came I out of
my mother's womb, and naked shall I
return thither: the [p]LORD gave, and
the LORD hath taken away; [q]blessed
be the name of the LORD.
22 In all this Job sinned not, nor
[15]charged God foolishly.

CHAPTER 2

AGAIN there was a day when the
sons of God came to present
themselves before the LORD, and
Satan came also among them to present himself before the LORD.
2 And the LORD said unto Satan,
From whence comest thou? And Satan answered the LORD, and said,
From going to and fro in the earth,
and from walking up and down in it.
3 And the LORD said unto Satan,
Hast thou considered my servant Job,
that *there is* none like him in the
earth, a perfect and an upright man,
one that feareth God, and escheweth
evil? and still he [a]holdeth fast his integrity, although thou movedst me
against him, [1]to destroy him [b]without
cause.
4 And Satan answered the LORD, and
said, Skin for skin, yea, all that a man
hath will he give for his life.
5 But put forth thine hand now, and
touch his [c]bone and his flesh, and he
will curse thee to thy face.
6 And the LORD said unto Satan,
Behold, he *is* in thine hand; [2]but save
his life.
7 ¶ So went Satan forth from the
presence of the LORD, and smote Job
with sore boils from the sole of his
foot unto his crown.
8 And he took him a potsherd to
scrape himself withal; [d]and he sat
down among the ashes.
9 ¶ Then said [e]his wife unto him,
Dost [f]thou still retain thine integrity?
curse God, and die.
10 But he said unto her, Thou speakest as one of the foolish women speaketh. What? [g]shall we receive good at
the hand of God, and shall we not re
ceive evil? In all this did not Job [h]si
with his lips.
11 ¶ Now when Job's three friend
heard of all this evil that was com
upon him, they came every one fron
his own place; Ĕ-lī'-phăz [i]the Tē'-măn
īte, and Bildad [j]the Shû'-hīte, and Zō
phär the Nā-ăm'-ă-thīte: for they ha
made an appointment together t
come [k]to mourn with him and t
comfort him.
12 And when they lifted up thei
eyes afar off, and knew him not, the
lifted up their voice, and wept; an
they rent every one his mantle, an
[l]sprinkled dust upon their heads to
ward heaven.
13 So they sat down with him upo
the ground [m]seven days and seve
nights, and none spake a word unt
him: for they saw that *his* grief wa
very great.

CHAPTER 3

AFTER this opened Job his mouth
and cursed his day.
2 And Job [1]spake, and said,
3 Let [a]the day perish wherein I wa
born, and the night *in which* it wa
said, There is a man child conceived
4 Let that day be darkness; let no
God regard it from above, neither le
the light shine upon it.
5 Let darkness and [b]the shadow o
death [2]stain it; let a cloud dwell upo
it; [3]let the blackness of the day terrif
it.
6 *As for* that night, let darkness
seize upon it; [4]let it not be joined unt
the days of the year, let it not come into the number of the months.
7 Lo, let that night be solitary, let no
joyful voice come therein.
8 Let them curse it that curse the
day, who [c]are ready to raise up [5]their
mourning.
9 Let the stars of the twilight thereof
be dark; let it look for light, but *have*
none; neither let it see [6]the dawning
of the day:
10 Because it shut not up the doors
of my *mother's* womb, nor hid sorrow
from mine eyes.
11 Why died I not from the womb?
why did I *not* give up the ghost when I
came out of the belly?
12 Why did the knees prevent me?
or why the breasts that I should suck?
13 For now should I have lain still
and been quiet, I should have slept:
then had I been at rest,
14 With kings and counsellers of the

13 from aside, etc.
14 Or, robe.
o Deut. 9.18. Matt. 26.39. 1 Pet. 5.6.
p Jas. 1.17.
q Gen. 45.5. Amos 3.6. Eph. 5.20.
15 Or, attributed folly to God.

CHAP. 2

a ch. 27.5,6. Jas. 1.12. 1 Pet. 1.7.
1 to swallow him up.
b Gen. 22.1. Matt. 7.11. John 9.2.
c ch. 19.20. Ps. 32.3,4.
2 Or, only.
d 2 Sam. 13. 19. ch. 42.6. Matt. 11.21.
e Gen. 3.6.
f 2 Ki. 6.33. ch. 21.15. Mal. 3.14.
g 2 Sam. 19. 28. ch. 1.21. Lam. 3.38-41. John 18.11. Rom. 12.12. Heb. 12.9-11.
h Ps. 39.1. Jas. 1.12.
i Gen. 36.11. Jer. 49.7.
j Gen. 25.2.
k ch. 42.11. Rom. 12.15.
l Neh. 9.1. Lam. 2.10.
m Gen. 50.10.

CHAP. 3

1 answered.
a ch. 10.18, 19. Jer. 15.10.
b ch. 16.16. Ps. 23.4. Isa. 9.2. Jer. 13.16. Matt. 4.16. Luke 1.79.
2 Or, challenge it.
3 Or, let them terrify it, as those who have a bitter day.
4 Or, let it not rejoice among the days.
c Jer. 9.17.
5 Or, a leviathan.
6 the eyelids of the morning.

arth, which built desolate places for
hemselves;
15 Or with princes that had gold,
vho filled their houses with silver:
16 Or as an hidden untimely birth I
ad not been; as infants *which* never
aw light.
17 There the wicked cease *from*
roubling; and there the [7]weary be at
est.
18 *There* the prisoners rest together;
hey hear not the voice of the oppres-
or.
19 The small and great are there; and
he servant *is* free from his master.
20 Wherefore [d]is light given to him
hat is in misery, and life unto the
itter *in* soul;
21 Which [8]long for death, but it *com-*
th not; and dig for it more than [e]for
id treasures;
22 Which rejoice exceedingly, *and*
re glad, when they can find the grave?
23 *Why is light given* to a man whose
vay is hid, [f]and whom God hath
edged in?
24 For my sighing cometh [9]before I
at, and my roarings are poured out
ke the waters.
25 For [10]the thing which I greatly
eared is come upon me, and that
vhich I was afraid of is come unto me.
26 I was not in safety, neither had I
est, neither was I quiet; yet trouble
ame.

CHAPTER 4

THEN Ĕ-lī-phăz the Tē-măn-īte
answered and said,
2 *If* we assay [1]to commune with thee,
vilt thou be grieved? but [2]who can
vithhold himself from speaking?
3 Behold, thou hast instructed many,
nd thou hast strengthened the weak
ands.
4 Thy words have upholden him that
vas falling, and thou hast strengthen-
d [3]the feeble knees.
5 But now it is come upon thee, and
ou [a]faintest; it toucheth thee, and
ou art troubled.
6 *Is* not *this* [b]thy fear, [c]thy confidence,
ny hope, and the uprightness of thy
ays?
7 Remember, I pray thee, who *ever*
erished, being innocent? or where
vere the righteous cut off?
8 Even as I have seen, [d]they that
low iniquity, and sow wickedness,
eap the same.
9 By the blast of God they perish,
nd [4]by the breath of his nostrils are
ey consumed.
10 The roaring of the lion, and the

7 wearied in strength.
d Jer. 20.18.
8 wait.
e Pro. 2.4.
f Lam. 3.7.
9 before my meat.
10 I feared a fear, and it came upon me.

CHAP. 4

1 a word.
2 who can refrain from words?
3 the bowing knees.
a Pro. 24.10. Luke 4.23.
b ch. 1.1.
c Pro. 3.26.
d Ps. 7.14.
4 That is, by his anger, Isa. 30.33.
e ch. 29.17. Ps. 3.7.
f Ps. 34.10.
5 by stealth.
g ch. 33.15.
6 met me.
7 the multitude of my bones.
h Ps. 104.4. Matt. 14.26. Heb. 1.14.
8 Or, I heard a still voice.
i 2 Pet. 2.4.
9 Or, nor in his angels, in whom he put light.
10 beaten in pieces.

CHAP. 5

1 Or, look?
2 Or, indignation.
3 Or, iniquity.
4 Or, labour.
5 the sons of the burning coal lift up to fly.
a Ps. 50.15.
6 and there is no search.
7 till there be no number.

voice of the fierce lion, and the [e]teeth
of the young lions, are broken.
11 The [f]old lion perisheth for lack of
prey, and the stout lion's whelps are
scattered abroad.
12 Now a thing was [5]secretly brought
to me, and mine ear received a little
thereof.
13 In [g]thoughts from the visions of
the night, when deep sleep falleth on
men,
14 Fear [6]came upon me, and trembling, which made [7]all my bones to
shake.
15 Then [h]a spirit passed before my
face; the hair of my flesh stood up:
16 It stood still, but I could not discern the form thereof: an image *was*
before mine eyes, [8]*there was* silence,
and I heard a voice, *saying*,
17 Shall mortal man be more just
than God? shall a man be more pure
than his maker?
18 Behold, he [i]put no trust in his
servants; [9]and his angels he charged
with folly:
19 How much less *in* them that dwell
in houses of clay, whose foundation
is in the dust, *which* are crushed before the moth?
20 They are [10]destroyed from morning to evening: they perish for ever
without any regarding *it*.
21 Doth not their excellency *which is*
in them go away? they die, even without wisdom.

CHAPTER 5

CALL now, if there be any that will
answer thee; and to which of the
saints wilt thou [1]turn?
2 For wrath killeth the foolish man,
and [2]envy slayeth the silly one.
3 I have seen the foolish taking root:
but suddenly I cursed his habitation.
4 His children are far from safety,
and they are crushed in the gate,
neither *is there* any to deliver *them*.
5 Whose harvest the hungry eateth
up, and taketh it even out of the
thorns, and the robber swalloweth up
their substance.
6 Although [3]affliction cometh not
forth of the dust, neither doth trouble
spring out of the ground;
7 Yet man is born unto [4]trouble, as
[5]the sparks fly upward.
8 I would [a]seek unto God, and unto
God would I commit my cause:
9 Which doeth great things [6]and
unsearchable; marvellous things
[7]without number:
10 Who giveth rain upon the earth,

and sendeth waters upon the [8]fields:
11 To set up on high those that be
low; that those which mourn may be
exalted to safety.
12 He disappointeth the devices of
the crafty, so that their hands [9]cannot
perform *their* enterprise.
13 He taketh the wise in their own
craftiness: and the counsel of the froward is carried headlong.
14 They [10]meet with darkness in the
daytime, and grope in the noonday
as in the night.
15 But he saveth the poor from the
sword, from their mouth, and from
the hand of the mighty.
16 So the poor hath hope, and iniquity stoppeth her mouth.
17 Behold, [b]happy *is* the man whom
God correcteth: therefore despise not
thou the chastening of the Almighty:
18 For he maketh sore, and bindeth
up: he woundeth, and his hands
make whole.
19 He [c]shall deliver thee in six
troubles: yea, in seven [d]there shall no
evil touch thee.
20 In famine he shall redeem thee
from death: and in war [11]from the
power of the sword.
21 Thou [e]shalt be hid [12]from the
scourge of the tongue: neither shalt
thou be afraid of destruction when it
cometh.
22 At destruction and famine thou
shalt laugh: neither shalt thou be
afraid of the beasts of the earth.
23 For [f]thou shalt be in league with
the stones of the field: and the beasts
of the field shall be at peace with thee.
24 And thou shalt know [13]that thy
tabernacle *shall be* in peace; and thou
shalt visit thy habitation, and shalt
not [14]sin.
25 Thou shalt know also that thy
seed *shall be* [15]great, and thine offspring as the grass of the earth.
26 Thou shalt come to *thy* grave in a
full age, like as a shock of corn [16]com-
eth in in his season.
27 Lo this, we have searched it, so
it *is;* hear it, and know thou *it* [17]for
thy good.

CHAPTER 6

BUT Job answered and said,
2 Oh that my grief were throughly
weighed, and my calamity [1]laid in the
balances together!
3 For now it would be heavier than
the sand of the sea: therefore [2]my
words are swallowed up.
4 For [a]the arrows of the Almighty
are within me, the poison whereof
drinketh up my spirit: the terrors
God do set themselves in array again
me.
5 Doth the wild ass bray [3]when
hath grass? or loweth the ox over h
fodder?
6 Can that which is unsavoury
eaten without salt? or is there *a*
taste in the white of an egg?
7 The things *that* my soul refused
touch *are* as my sorrowful meat.
8 Oh that I might have my reques
and that God would grant *me* [4]th
thing that I long for!
9 Even that it would please God
destroy me; that he would let loo
his hand, and cut me off!
10 Then should I yet have comfor
yea, [5]I would harden myself in so
row: let him not spare; for I have n
concealed the words of the Holy On
11 What *is* my strength, that I shou
hope? and what *is* mine end, that
should prolong my life?
12 *Is* my strength the strength
stones? or *is* my flesh [6]of brass?
13 *Is* not my help in me? and is wi
dom driven quite from me?
14 [7]To him that is afflicted pi
should be shewed from his friend; b
he forsaketh the fear of the Almight
15 My brethren have dealt decei
fully as a brook, *and* as the stream
brooks they pass away;
16 Which [8]are blackish by reason
the ice, *and* wherein the snow is hi
17 What time they wax warm, [9]th
vanish: [10]when it is hot, they are [11]co
sumed out of their place.
18 The paths of their way are turn
aside; they go to nothing, and pe
ish.
19 The troops of Tē-mă looked, t
companies of Shē-bă waited for the
20 They were confounded becau
they had hoped; they came thithe
and were ashamed.
21 [12]For now ye are [13]nothing; ye s
[b]*my* casting down, and are afraid.
22 Did I say, [c]Bring unto me? o
Give a reward for me of your su
stance?
23 Or, Deliver me from the enemy
hand? or, Redeem me from the ha
of the mighty?
24 Teach me, and I will [d]hold n
tongue: and cause me to understa
wherein I have erred.
25 How forcible are right words! b
what doth your arguing reprove?
26 Do ye imagine to reprove word
and the speeches of one that
desperate, *which are* as wind?

8 out-places.
9 Or, cannot perform any thing.
10 Or, run into.
b Ps. 94.12. Heb. 12.5. Jas. 1.12.
c Ex. 12.46. Ps. 34.19. John 19.36.
d Ps. 91.10. Pro. 1.33. 2 Thes. 3.3. 2 Pet. 2.9.
11 from the hands.
e Ps. 31.20.
12 Or, when the tongue scourgeth.
f Ps. 91.12.
13 Or, that peace is thy tabernacle.
14 Or, err.
15 Or, much.
16 ascendeth.
17 for thyself.

CHAP. 6

1 lifted up.
2 That is, I want words to express my grief.
a Deut. 32. 23,42. ch. 16.12-14. Ps. 7.13. Ps. 18.14. Ps. 21.12.
3 at grass.
4 my expectation.
5 Or, though I should be burned with pain.
6 brazen?
7 To him that melteth.
8 Or, mourn.
9 they are cut off.
10 in the heat thereof.
11 extinguished.
12 Or, For now ye are like to them.
13 not.
b Ps. 38.11.
c Acts 20.33.
d Ps. 39.1.

7 Yea, [14]ye overwhelm the father-
ss, and ye dig *a pit* for your friend.
8 Now therefore be content, look
›on me; for *it is* [15]evident unto you
I lie.
9 Return, I pray you, let it not be
iquity; yea, return again, my right-
›usness *is* [16]in it.
0 Is there iniquity [e]in my tongue?
.nnot [17]my taste discern perverse
.ings?

CHAPTER 7

'S there not [1]an [a]appointed time to
man upon earth? *are not* his days
so like the days of an hireling?
As a servant [2]earnestly desireth
.e shadow, and as an hireling look-
h for *the reward of* his work:
So am I made to possess months
›f vanity, and wearisome nights are
ɔpointed to me.
· When I lie down, I say, When shall
arise, and [3]the night be gone? and I
n full of tossings to and fro unto the
awning of the day.
· My flesh is clothed [c]with worms
ıd clods of dust; my skin is broken,
ıd become loathsome.
· My days are swifter than a weaver's
:uttle, and are spent without hope.
O remember that [d]my life *is* wind:
ine eye [4]shall no more [5]see good.
; The [e]eye of him that hath seen me
ıall see me no *more:* thine eyes *are*
pon me, and [6]I *am* not.
· *As* the cloud is consumed and van-
heth away: so [f]he that goeth down
› the grave shall come up no *more.*
.0 He shall return no more to his
ouse, neither shall his place know
im any more. 12SD Eccl 12:7
.1 Therefore I will [g]not refrain my
ıouth; I will speak in the anguish of
ıy spirit; I will complain in the bitter-
ess of my soul.
.2 *Am* I a sea, or a whale, that thou
:ttest a watch over me?
.3 When I say, My bed shall com-
ɔrt me, my couch shall ease my com-
laint;
.4 Then thou scarest me with dreams,
nd terrifiest me through visions:
.5 So that my soul chooseth strang-
ng, *and* death rather than my [7]life.
.6 I [h]loathe *it;* I would not live
lway: let me alone; for [i]my days *are*
anity.
.7 What [j]*is* man, that thou shouldest
ıagnify him? and that thou shouldest
:t thine heart upon him?
.8 And *that* thou shouldest visit him
very morning, *and* try him every mo-
ıent?

14 ye cause to fall upon.
15 before your face.
16 That is, in this matter.
e ch. 33.8-12. Jas. 3.13.
17 my palate.

CHAP. 7

1 Or, a warfare.
a ch. 14.5, 13,14. Ps. 39.4. Eccl. 3.1,2.
2 gapeth after.
b Ps. 39.5. Eccl. 1.14.
3 the evening be measured?
c ch. 17.14. Ps. 38.5-7. Isa. 1.6.
d Ps. 78.39. Jas. 4.14.
4 shall not return.
5 to see, that is, to enjoy.
e ch. 20.9.
6 That is, I can live no longer.
f 2 Sam. 12. 23. Ps. 39.13.
g Ps. 39.1,9.
7 bones.
h Gen. 27.46. ch. 10.1.
i Ps. 62.9. Eccl. 6.11.
j Ps. 8.4. Heb. 2.6.
k Ps. 36.6.
8 Or, observer.

CHAP. 8

a Gen. 18.25. Deut. 32.4. ch. 34.12. Dan. 9.14.
1 in the hand of their transgression.
b Deut. 4.32.
c Gen. 47.9. Ps. 39.5.
2 not.
d Ps. 129.6. Jer. 17.6. Jas. 1.10,11. 1 Pet. 1.24.
e ch. 11.20. ch. 18.14. Ps. 112.10. Pro. 10.28. Isa. 33.14. Matt. 24.51. Luke 12.1,2.
3 a spider's house.
f ch. 27.18. Ps. 112.10. Pro. 10.28.

19 How long wilt thou not depart
from me, nor let me alone till I swallow down my spittle?
20 I have sinned; what shall I do unto thee, [k]O thou [8]preserver of men?
why hast thou set me as a mark
against thee, so that I am a burden to
myself?
21 And why dost thou not pardon my
transgression, and take away mine iniquity? for now shall I sleep in the
dust; and thou shalt seek me in the
morning, but I *shall* not *be.*

CHAPTER 8

THEN answered Bildad the Shû-
hite, and said,
2 How long wilt thou speak these
things? and *how long shall* the words
of thy mouth *be like* a strong wind?
3 Doth [a]God pervert judgment? or
doth the Almighty pervert justice?
4 If thy children have sinned against
him, and he have cast them away [1]for
their transgression;
5 If thou wouldest seek unto God betimes, and make thy supplication to
the Almighty;
6 If thou *wert* pure and upright;
surely now he would awake for thee,
and make the habitation of thy righteousness prosperous.
7 Though thy beginning was small,
yet thy latter end should greatly increase.
8 For [b]inquire, I pray thee, of the
former age, and prepare thyself to the
search of their fathers:
9 (For [c]we *are but of* yesterday, and
know [2]nothing, because our days upon earth *are* a shadow:)
10 Shall not they teach thee, *and* tell
thee, and utter words out of their
heart?
11 Can the rush grow up without
mire? can the flag grow without
water?
12 Whilst [d]it *is* yet in his greenness,
and not cut down, it withereth before
any *other* herb.
13 So *are* the paths of all that forget
God; and the [e]hypocrite's hope shall
perish:
14 Whose hope shall be cut off, and
whose trust *shall be* [3]a spider's web.
15 He [f]shall lean upon his house,
but it shall not stand: he shall hold it
fast, but it shall not endure.
16 He *is* green before the sun, and
his branch shooteth forth in his garden.
17 His roots are wrapped about the
heap, *and* seeth the place of stones.

18 If [g]he destroy him from his place,
then *it* shall deny him, *saying*, I have
not seen thee.
19 Behold, this *is* the joy of his way,
and out [h]of the earth shall others
grow.
20 Behold, God will not [i]cast away
a perfect *man*, neither will he [4]help
the evil doers:
21 Till he fill thy mouth with laugh-
ing, and thy lips with [5]rejoicing.
22 They that hate thee shall be clothed with shame; and the dwelling place
of the wicked shall [6]come to nought.

CHAPTER 9

THEN Job answered and said,
2 I know *it is* so of a truth: but how
should [a]man be just [1]with God?
3 If he will contend with him, he cannot answer him one of a thousand.
4 *He is* wise in heart, and mighty in
strength: who hath hardened *himself*
against him, and hath prospered?
5 Which removeth the mountains,
and they know not: which overturneth
them in his anger.
6 Which [b]shaketh the earth out of her
place, and the pillars thereof tremble.
7 Which commandeth the sun, and
it riseth not; and sealeth up the stars.
8 Which alone spreadeth out the
heavens, and treadeth upon the
[2]waves of the sea.
9 Which [c]maketh [3]Ărc-tū́-rŭs, Ō-rī́-
on, and Plēí-ă-dēs, and the chambers
of the south.
10 Which doeth great things past
finding out; yea, and wonders without
number.
11 Lo, [d]he goeth by me, and I see *him*
not: he passeth on also, but I perceive him not.
12 Behold, [e]he taketh away, [4]who can
hinder him? who will say unto him,
What doest thou?
13 *If* God will not withdraw his anger, the [5]proud helpers do stoop under
him.
14 How much less shall I answer
him, *and* choose out my words *to reason* with him?
15 Whom, [f]though I were righteous,
yet would I not answer, *but* I would
make supplication to my judge.
16 If I had called, and he had answered me; *yet* would I not believe
that he had hearkened unto my voice.
17 For he breaketh me with a tempest, and multiplieth my [g]wounds
without cause.
18 He will not suffer me to take my
breath, but filleth me with bitterness.

g ch. 7.10. Ps. 37.36.
h Ps. 113.7.
i Ps. 37.24. 1 Thes. 5.23, 24.
4 take the ungodly by the hand.
5 shouting for joy.
6 not be.

CHAP. 9

a Ps. 143.2. Rom. 3.20.
1 Or, before God?
b Isa. 2.19, 21. Hag. 2.6,21. Heb. 12.26.
2 heights.
c Gen. 1.16. ch. 38. 31.
3 Ash, Cesil, and Cimah.
d ch. 23.8.
e Isa. 45.9. Jer. 18.6.
4 who can turn him away?
5 helpers of pride, or, strength.
f ch. 10.15.
g ch. 2.3. Ps. 25.3. John 9.3.
h Eccl. 9.1,2. Eze. 21.3. Luke 13.2-4.
i 2 Sam. 15. 30. Jer. 14.4.
6 ships of desire, or, ships of Ebeh.
7 Or, strengthen.
j Ex. 20.7. Ps. 130.3.
8 Or, make me to be abhorred.
k Eccl. 6.10. Isa. 45.9. Jer. 49.19.
l 1 Sam. 2.25.
9 one that should argue.
10 Or, umpire.
11 but I am not so with myself.

CHAP. 10

1 Or, cut off while I live.
2 the labour.
a 1 Sam. 16.7. Luke 16.15. Rev. 1.14.

19 If *I speak* of strength, lo, *he*
strong: and if of judgment, who sha
set me a time *to plead?*
20 If I justify myself, mine ow
mouth shall condemn me: *if I say,*
am perfect, it shall also prove me pe
verse.
21 *Though* I *were* perfect, *yet* wou
I not know my soul: I would despi
my life.
22 This *is* one *thing*, therefore I sa
it, He [h]destroyeth the perfect and t
wicked.
23 If the scourge slay suddenly,
will laugh at the trial of the innocer
24 The earth is given into the ha
of the wicked: he [i]covereth the fac
of the judges thereof; if not, wher
and who *is* he?
25 Now my days are swifter than
post: they flee away, they see no goo
26 They are passed away as the [6]sw
ships: as the eagle *that* hasteth to t
prey.
27 If I say, I will forget my con
plaint, I will leave off my heavines
and [7]comfort *myself:*
28 I am afraid of all my sorrows,
know that thou wilt [j]not hold me inn
cent.
29 *If* I be wicked, why then labour
in vain?
30 If I wash myself with snow wate
and make my hands never so clean,
31 Yet shalt thou plunge me in t
ditch, and mine own clothes shall [8]a
hor me.
32 For [k]*he is* not a man, as I *am*, *th*
I should answer him, *and* we shou
come together in judgment.
33 Neither [l]is there [9]any [10]daysma
betwixt us, *that* might lay his han
upon us both.
34 Let him take his rod away fro
me, and let not his fear terrify me:
35 *Then* would I speak, and not fea
him; [11]but *it is* not so with me.

CHAPTER 10

MY soul is [1]weary of my life; I wi
leave my complaint upon my
self; I will speak in the bitterness o
my soul.
2 I will say unto God, Do not con
demn me; shew me wherefore tho
contendest with me.
3 *Is it* good unto thee that tho
shouldest oppress, that thou should
est despise [2]the work of thine hands
and shine upon the counsel of th
wicked?
4 Hast thou eyes of flesh? or [a]sees
thou as man seeth?

5 *Are* thy days as the days of man? *are* thy years as man's days,

6 That thou inquirest after mine iniquity, and searchest after my sin?

7 [3]Thou knowest that I am not wicked; and *there is* none that can deliver out of thine hand.

8 Thine [b]hands [4]have made me and fashioned me together round about; yet thou dost destroy me.

9 Remember, I beseech thee, that thou [c]hast made me as the clay; and wilt thou bring me into dust again?

10 Hast [d]thou not poured me out as milk, and curdled me like cheese?

11 Thou hast clothed me with skin and flesh, and hast [5]fenced me with bones and sinews.

12 Thou hast granted me life and favour, and thy visitation hath preserved my spirit.

13 And these *things* hast thou hid in thine heart: I know that this *is* with thee.

14 If I sin, then thou markest me, and thou wilt not acquit me from mine iniquity.

15 If I be wicked, [e]woe unto me; and [f]*if* I be righteous, *yet* will I not lift up my head. *I am* full of confusion; therefore [g]see thou mine affliction;

16 For it increaseth. [h]Thou huntest me as a fierce lion: and again thou shewest thyself marvellous upon me.

17 Thou renewest [6]thy witnesses against me, and increasest thine indignation upon me; changes and war *are* against me.

18 Wherefore then hast thou brought me forth out of the womb? Oh that I had given up the ghost, and no eye had seen me!

19 I should have been as though I had not been; I should have been carried from the womb to the grave.

20 *Are* not my days few? [i]cease *then*, *and* let me [j]alone, that I may take comfort a little,

21 Before I go *whence* I shall not return, *even* [k]to the land of darkness [l]and the shadow of death;

22 A land of darkness, as darkness *itself; and* of the shadow of death, without any order, and *where* the light *is* as darkness.

CHAPTER 11

THEN answered Zō-phär the Nā-ăm-ă-thite, and said,

2 Should not the multitude of words be answered? and should [1]a man full of talk be justified?

3 Should thy [2]lies make men hold their peace? and when thou mockest, shall no man make thee ashamed?

4 For [a]thou hast said, My doctrine *is* pure, and I am clean in thine eyes.

5 But oh that God would speak, and open his lips against thee;

6 And that he would shew thee the secrets of wisdom, that *they are* double to that which is! Know therefore that [b]God exacteth of thee *less* than thine iniquity *deserveth*.

7 Canst [c]thou by searching find out God? canst thou find out the Almighty unto perfection?

8 *It is* [3]as high as heaven; what canst thou do? deeper than hell; what canst thou know?

9 The measure thereof *is* longer than the earth, and broader than the sea.

10 If he [4]cut off, and shut up, or gather together, then [5]who can hinder him?

11 For [d]he knoweth vain men: he seeth wickedness also; will he not then consider *it?*

12 For [6]vain man would be wise, though man be born *like* a wild ass's colt.

13 If thou [e]prepare thine heart, and stretch out [f]thine hands toward him;

14 If iniquity *be* in thine hand, put it far away, and let not wickedness dwell in thy tabernacles.

15 For [g]then shalt thou lift up thy face without spot; yea, thou shalt be stedfast, and shalt not fear:

16 Because thou shalt forget *thy* misery, *and* remember *it* as waters *that* pass away:

17 And *thine* age [7]shall be clearer than the noonday; thou shalt shine forth, thou shalt be as the morning.

18 And thou shalt be secure, because there is hope; yea, thou shalt dig *about thee, and* thou shalt take thy rest in safety.

19 Also thou shalt lie down, and none shall make *thee* afraid; yea, many shall [8]make suit unto thee.

20 But the eyes of the wicked shall fail, and [9]they shall not escape, and their hope *shall be as* [10]the giving up of the ghost.

CHAPTER 12

AND Job answered and said,

2 No doubt but ye *are* the people, and wisdom shall die with you.

3 But I have [1]understanding as well as you; [2]I *am* not inferior to you: yea, [3]who knoweth not such things as these?

4 I am *as* one mocked of his neigh-

---

3 It is upon thy knowledge.
b Ps. 119.73. Isa. 43.7.
4 took pains about me.
c Gen. 2.7. Isa. 45.9.
d Ps. 139.14.
5 hedged.
e Ps. 9.17. Isa. 3.11. Mal. 3.18.
f ch. 9.12.
g Ex. 3.7. Ps. 25.18. Lam. 1.20.
h Isa. 38.13. Lam. 3.10.
6 That is, thy plagues.
i Ps. 39.13.
j ch. 7.16.
k ch. 3.5. Ps. 88.12.
l Ps. 23.4.

CHAP. 11

1 a man of lips.
2 Or, devices.
a ch. 6.10. 1 Pet. 3.15.
b Lam. 3.22.
c ch. 5.9. Eccl. 3.11. Isa. 40.28. Matt. 11.27. Rom. 11.33. Eph. 3.8.
3 the heights of heaven.
4 Or, make a change.
5 who can turn him away?
d Ps. 10.11.
6 empty.
e 1 Sam. 7.3. Ps. 78.8.
f Ps. 143.6.
g Gen. 4.5. ch. 22.26. Ps. 119.6. 1 Tim. 2.8. 1 John 3. 21.
7 shall arise above the noonday.
8 intreat thy face.
9 flight shall perish from them.
10 Or, a puff of breath.
1 an heart.
2 I fall not lower than you.
3 with whom are not such as these?

bour, who [a]calleth upon God, and he
answereth him: the just upright *man*
is laughed to scorn.
5 He [b]that is ready to slip with *his*
feet *is as* a lamp despised in the
thought of him that is at ease.
6 The tabernacles of robbers prosper, and they that provoke God are
secure; into whose hand God bringeth
abundantly.
7 But ask now the beasts, and they
shall teach thee; and the fowls of the
air, and they shall tell thee:
8 Or speak to the earth, and it shall
teach thee: and the fishes of the sea
shall declare unto thee.
9 Who knoweth not in all these that
the hand of the LORD hath wrought
this?
10 In [c]whose hand *is* the [4]soul of
every living thing, and the breath of
[5]all mankind.
11 Doth not the ear try words? and
the [6]mouth taste his meat?
12 With the ancient *is* wisdom; and
in length of days understanding.
13 [7]With him *is* wisdom and strength,
he hath counsel and understanding.
14 Behold, he breaketh down, and
it cannot be built again: [d]he shutteth
[8]up a man, and there can be no opening.
15 Behold, he [e]withholdeth the
waters, and they dry up: also [f]he
sendeth them out, and they overturn
the earth.
16 With him *is* strength and wisdom:
the deceived and the deceiver *are* his.
17 He leadeth counsellers away spoiled, and maketh the judges fools.
18 He looseth the bond of kings, and
girdeth their loins with a girdle.
19 He leadeth princes away spoiled,
and overthroweth the mighty.
20 He removeth away [9]the speech of
the trusty, and taketh away the understanding of the aged.
21 He poureth contempt upon princes, and [10]weakeneth the strength of
the mighty.
22 He [g]discovereth deep things out
of darkness, and bringeth out to light
the shadow of death.
23 He increaseth the nations, and destroyeth them: he enlargeth the nations, and [11]straiteneth them *again*.
24 He taketh away the heart of the
chief of the people of the earth, and
causeth them to wander in a wilderness *where there is* no way.
25 They grope in the dark without
light, and he maketh them to [12]stagger
like *a* drunken *man*.

a ch. 16.20. Ps. 91.15. Jer. 33.3. Micah 7.7.
b Pro. 14.2.
c Num. 16. 22. Dan. 5.23. Acts 17.28.
4 Or, life.
5 all flesh of man.
6 palate.
7 That is, With God.
d Rev. 3.7.
8 upon.
e 1 Ki. 17.1.
f Gen. 7.11.
9 the lip of the faithful.
10 Or, looseth the girdle of the strong.
g Matt. 10. 26. 1 Cor. 4.5.
11 leadeth in.
12 wander.

CHAP. 13

a Pro. 17.28. Eccl. 5.3. Amos 5.13. Jas. 1.19.
b ch. 17.5. Rom. 3.5,8.
c Pro. 24.23.
1 Or, height of greatness.
2 Be silent from me.
d Ps. 119.109.
e Ps. 23.4. Pro. 14.32. Rom. 8.38, 39.
f ch. 27.5.
3 prove, or, argue.
g Isa. 12.1,2.
h ch. 33.6. Isa. 50.8.
i Ps. 10.1. Isa. 8.17.
j Lam. 2.5. 2 Thes.3.15.
k Isa. 17.13. Isa. 42.3.

CHAPTER 13

LO, mine eye hath seen all *this*, mine
ear hath heard and understood it.
2 What ye know, *the same* do I know
also: I *am* not inferior unto you.
3 Surely I would speak to the Almighty, and I desire to reason with
God.
4 But ye *are* forgers of lies, ye *are* all
physicians of no value.
5 O that ye would altogether hold
your peace! and [a]it should be your
wisdom.
6 Hear now my reasoning, and heark-
en to the pleadings of my lips.
7 Will [b]ye speak wickedly for God?
and talk deceitfully for him?
8 Will ye [c]accept his person? will ye
contend for God?
9 Is it good that he should search
you out? or as one man mocketh
another, do ye *so* mock him?
10 He will surely reprove you, if ye
do secretly accept persons.
11 Shall not his [1]excellency make
you afraid? and his dread fall upon
you?
12 Your remembrances *are* like unto
ashes, your bodies to bodies of clay.
13 [2]Hold your peace, let me alone,
that I may speak, and let come on me
what *will*.
14 Wherefore do I take my flesh in
my teeth, and [d]put my life in mine
hand?
15 Though [e]he slay me, yet will I
trust in him: [f]but I will [3]maintain
mine own ways before him.
16 He also *shall be* my [g]salvation:
for an hypocrite shall not come before
him.
17 Hear diligently my speech, and
my declaration with your ears.
18 Behold now, I have ordered *my*
cause; I know that I shall be justified.
19 Who [h]*is* he *that* will plead with
me? for now, if I hold my tongue, I
shall give up the ghost.
20 Only do not two *things* unto me:
then will I not hide myself from thee.
21 Withdraw thine hand far from
me: and let not thy dread make me
afraid.
22 Then call thou, and I will answer:
or let me speak, and answer thou me.
23 How many *are* mine iniquities and
sins? make me to know my transgression and my sin.
24 Wherefore [i]hidest thou thy face,
and holdest me [j]for thine enemy?
25 Wilt [k]thou break a leaf driven to
and fro? and wilt thou pursue the dry
stubble?

26 For thou writest bitter things
gainst me, and [l]makest me to possess
he iniquities of my youth.
27 Thou [m]puttest my feet also in the
tocks, and [4]lookest narrowly unto all
ny paths; thou settest a print upon
he [5]heels of my feet.
28 And he, as a rotten thing, con-
umeth, as a garment that is moth
aten.

CHAPTER 14

MAN *that is* born of a woman *is* [1]of
few days, and [a]full of trouble.
2 He [b]cometh forth like a flower, and
s cut down: he fleeth also as a sha-
low, and continueth not.
3 And [c]dost thou open thine eyes
ipon such an one, [d]and bringest me
nto judgment with thee?
4 [2]Who [e]can bring a clean *thing* out
of an unclean? not one.
5 Seeing his days *are* determined, the
umber of his months *are* with thee,
hou hast appointed his bounds that
ne cannot pass;
6 Turn [f]from him, that he may [3]rest,
ill he shall accomplish, as an hireling,
nis day.
7 For there is hope of a tree, if it be
cut down, that it will sprout again,
and that the tender branch thereof
will not cease.
8 Though the root thereof wax old
in the earth, and the stock thereof die
in the ground;
9 *Yet* through the scent of water it
will bud, and bring forth boughs like
a plant.
10 But man dieth, and [4]wasteth
away: yea, man giveth up the ghost,
and where *is* he?
11 *As* the waters fail from the sea,
and the flood decayeth and drieth
up:
12 So man lieth down, and riseth not:
[g]till the heavens *be* no more, they
shall not awake, nor be raised out of
their sleep.
13 O that thou wouldest hide me in
the grave, that thou wouldest keep
me secret, until thy wrath be past,
that thou wouldest appoint me a set
time, and remember me!
14 If a man die, shall he live *again?*
all the days of my appointed time
[h]will I wait, till [i]my change come.
15 Thou [j]shalt call, and I will answer
thee: thou wilt have a desire to the
work of thine hands.
16 For [k]now thou numberest my
steps: dost thou not watch over my
sin?
17 My transgression *is* sealed up in a

[l] Ps. 25.7.
[m] ch. 33.11.
4 observest.
5 roots.

CHAP. 14

1 short of days.
[a] ch. 15.14. Ps. 51.5. Eccl. 2.23.
[b] Isa. 40.6. Jas. 1.10. 1 Pet. 1.24.
[c] Ps. 144.3.
[d] Ps. 143.2.
2 Who will give?
[e] Gen. 5.3. Ps. 51.5. John 3.5. Rom. 5.12. Eph. 2.3.
[f] Ps. 39.13.
3 cease.
4 is weakened, or, cut off.
[g] Ps. 102.26. Isa. 51.6. Acts 3.21. Rom. 8.20. 2 Pet. 3.7. Rev. 20.11.
[h] ch. 13.15.
[i] Ps. 16.10. 1 Cor. 15. 42-58. Phil. 3.21.
[j] ch. 13.22. Ps. 50.4. John 5.28. 1 Thes. 4.16.
[k] Deut. 32. 34. ch. 10.6,14. ch. 13.27. Ps. 56.8. Pro. 5.21. Jer. 32.19. Hos. 13.12.
5 fadeth.
6 overflowest.
[l] 1 Sam. 4.20. Ps. 39.6. Eccl. 9.5. Isa. 63.16.
[m] Ps. 49.14.
[n] Pro. 14.32. Matt. 8.12.

CHAP. 15

1 knowledge of wind.
2 thou makest void.
3 Or, speech.
4 teacheth.
[a] Pro. 8.25.
[b] Matt. 11. 25. Rom. 11.34. 1 Cor. 2.11.
[c] ch. 13.2.
[d] Deut. 32.7. ch. 8.8-10. Pro. 16.31.
[e] ch. 14.4. Ps. 14.3. Pro. 20.9. Eccl. 7.20. Rom. 7.18. Eph. 2.2,3.
[f] ch. 25.5.
[g] Ps. 14.3.

bag, and thou sewest up mine iniquity.
18 And surely the mountain falling
[5]cometh to nought, and the rock is removed out of his place.
19 The waters wear the stones: thou
[6]washest away the things which grow
out of the dust of the earth; and thou
destroyest the hope of man.
20 Thou prevailest for ever against
him, and he passeth: thou changest
his countenance, and sendest him
away.
21 His sons come to honour, and he
[l]knoweth *it* not; and they are brought
low, but he perceiveth *it* not of them.
22 But [m]his flesh upon him shall have
pain, and [n]his soul within him shall
mourn.

CHAPTER 15

THEN answered Ĕ-lĭ-phăz the Tē-
măn-īte, and said,
2 Should a wise man utter [1]vain
knowledge, and fill his belly with the
east wind?
3 Should he reason with unprofitable
talk? or with speeches wherewith he
can do no good?
4 Yea, [2]thou castest off fear, and re-
strainest [3]prayer before God.
5 For thy mouth [4]uttereth thine iniquity, and thou choosest the tongue
of the crafty.
6 Thine own mouth condemneth
thee, and not I: yea, thine own lips
testify against thee.
7 *Art* thou the first man *that* was
born? or [a]wast thou made before the
hills?
8 Hast [b]thou heard the secret of
God? and dost thou restrain wisdom
to thyself?
9 What [c]knowest thou, that we know
not? *what* understandest thou, which
is not in us?
10 With [d]us *are* both the grayheaded
and very aged men, much elder than
thy father.
11 *Are* the consolations of God small
with thee? is there any secret thing
with thee?
12 Why doth thine heart carry thee
away? and what do thy eyes wink at,
13 That thou turnest thy spirit
against God, and lettest *such* words
go out of thy mouth?
14 What [e]*is* man, that he should be
clean? and *he which is* born of a woman, that he should be righteous?
15 Behold, [f]he putteth no trust in his
saints; yea, the heavens are not clean
in his sight.
16 How [g]much more abominable and

filthy *is* man, [h]which drinketh iniquity like water?

17 I will shew thee, hear me; and that *which* I have seen I will declare;

18 Which wise men have told from [i]their fathers, and have not hid *it:*

19 Unto whom alone the earth was given, and [j]no stranger passed among them.

20 The wicked man travaileth with pain all *his* days, and [k]the number of years is hidden to the oppressor.

21 [5]A dreadful sound *is* in his ears: [l]in prosperity the destroyer shall come upon him.

22 He believeth not that he shall return out of darkness, and he is waited for of the sword.

23 He [m]wandereth abroad for bread, *saying*, Where *is it?* he knoweth that [n]the day of darkness is ready at his hand.

24 Trouble and anguish shall make him afraid; they shall prevail against him, as a king ready to the battle.

25 For [o]he stretcheth out his hand against God, and strengtheneth himself against the Almighty.

26 He runneth upon him, *even* on *his* neck, upon the thick bosses of his bucklers:

27 Because [p]he covereth his face with his fatness, and maketh collops of fat on *his* flanks.

28 And he dwelleth in desolate cities *and* in houses which no man inhabiteth, which are ready to become heaps.

29 He shall not be rich, neither shall his substance continue, neither shall he prolong the perfection thereof upon the earth.

30 He shall not depart out of darkness; the flame shall dry up his branches, and by [q]the breath of his mouth shall he go away.

31 Let not him that is deceived trust [r]in vanity: for vanity shall be his recompence.

32 It shall be [6]accomplished [s]before his time, and his branch shall not be green.

33 He shall shake off his unripe grape as the vine, and shall cast off his flower as the olive.

34 For [t]the congregation of hypocrites *shall be* desolate, and fire shall consume the tabernacles of bribery.

35 They [u]conceive mischief, and bring forth [7]vanity, and their belly prepareth deceit.

h Pro. 19.28.
i Gen. 18.19.
j Joel 3.17.
k Ps. 90.12.
5 A sound of fears.
l 1 Thes. 5.3.
m Ps. 59.15.
n ch. 18.12.
o Mal. 3.13.
p Ps. 17.10.
q ch. 4.9. Isa. 11.4. Rev. 19.15.
r Ps. 62.10. Isa. 59.4.
6 Or, cut off.
s ch. 22.16. Ps. 55.23.
t Isa. 33.14.
u Ps. 7.14. Isa. 59.4.
7 Or, iniquity.

CHAP. 16

1 Or, troublesome.
2 words of wind.
a 2 Ki. 19.21. Ps. 22.7. Jer. 18.16. Lam. 2.15.
3 what goeth from me?
b Ps. 22.13.
c 1 Ki. 22.24. Lam. 3.30. Micah 5.1. Matt. 26.67. John 18.22. Acts 23.2.
d Ps. 35.15.
4 hath shut me up.
e Ps. 7.5.
f ch. 27.9.
g Rom. 1.9.
5 in the high places.
6 are my scorners.
h ch. 31.35.
7 Or, friend.
8 years of number.

CHAPTER 16

THEN Job answered and said,

2 I have heard many such things [1]miserable comforters *are* ye all.

3 Shall [2]vain words have an end? o what emboldeneth thee that tho answerest?

4 I also could speak as ye *do:* if you soul were in my soul's stead, I coul heap up words against you, an [a]shake mine head at you.

5 *But* I would strengthen you wit my mouth, and the moving of my lip should asswage *your grief.*

6 Though I speak, my grief is no aswaged: and *though* I forbear, [3]wha am I eased?

7 But now he hath made me weary thou hast made desolate all my com pany.

8 And thou hast filled me with wrin kles, *which* is a witness *against me:* an my leanness rising up in me beareth witness to my face.

9 He teareth *me* in his wrath, wh hateth me: he gnasheth upon me wit his teeth; mine enemy sharpeneth hi eyes upon me.

10 They have [b]gaped upon me wit their mouth; they have [c]smitten m upon the cheek reproachfully; the have [d]gathered themselves togethe against me.

11 God [4]hath delivered me to the ungodly, and turned me over into the hands of the wicked.

12 I was at ease, but he hath broken me asunder: he hath also taken *me* by my neck, and shaken me to pieces and set me up for his mark.

13 His archers compass me round about, he cleaveth my reins asunder and doth not spare; he poureth out my gall upon the ground.

14 He breaketh me with breach upon breach, he runneth upon me like a giant.

15 I have sewed sackcloth upon my skin, and [e]defiled my horn in the dust.

16 My face is foul with weeping, and on my eyelids *is* the shadow of death;

17 Not for *any* injustice in mine hands: also my prayer *is* pure.

18 O earth, cover not thou my blood, and let [f]my cry have no place.

19 Also now, behold, [g]my witness *is* in heaven, and my record *is* [5]on high.

20 My friends [6]scorn me: *but* mine eye poureth out *tears* unto God.

21 O [h]that one might plead for a man with God, as a man *pleadeth* for his [7]neighbour!

22 When [8]a few years are come, then

hall [i]go the way *whence* I shall not
turn.

CHAPTER 17

Y [1]breath is corrupt, my days are
extinct, [a]the graves *are ready* for
e.
Are there not mockers with me?
d doth not mine eye [2]continue in
eir [b]provocation?
Lay down now, put me in a surety
ith thee; who *is* he [c]*that* will strike
nds with me?
For thou hast hid their heart from
derstanding: therefore shalt thou
t exalt *them*.
He that speaketh flattery to *his*
iends, even the eyes of his children
all fail.
He hath made me also [d]a byword
the people; and [3]aforetime I was as
tabret.
Mine eye also is dim by reason of
rrow, and all [4]my members *are* as a
adow.
Upright *men* shall be astonied at
is, and the innocent shall stir up
mself against the hypocrite.
The [e]righteous also shall hold on
s way, and he that hath clean [f]hands
hall be stronger and stronger.
0 But as for you all, [g]do ye return,
d come now: for I cannot find *one*
ise *man* among you.
1 My [h]days are past, my purposes
e broken off, *even* [6]the thoughts of
y heart.
2 They change the night into day:
e light *is* [7]short because of dark-
ss.
3 If I wait, the grave *is* mine house:
have made my bed in the darkness.
4 I have [8]said to corruption, Thou
t my father: to the worm, *Thou art*
y mother, and my sister.
5 And where *is* now my hope? as
r my hope, who shall see it?
6 They [i]shall go down [j]to the bars
the pit, when *our* [k]rest together *is*
the dust.

CHAPTER 18

HEN answered Bildad the Shû-
hite, and said,
How long *will it be ere* ye make an
d of words? mark, and afterwards
e will speak.
Wherefore are we counted [a]as
easts, *and* reputed vile in your sight?
He [b]teareth [1]himself in his anger:
all the earth be forsaken for thee?
nd shall the rock be removed out of
is place?
[2]Yea, [c]the light of the wicked shall

[i] Eccl. 12.5.

CHAP. 17

1 Or, spirit is spent. *a* Ps. 88.3,4. 2 lodge. *b* 1 Sam. 1.6. *c* Pro. 6.1. *d* 1 Ki. 9.7. ch. 30.9. 3 Or, before them. 4 Or, my thoughts. *e* Pro. 4.18. *f* Ps. 24.4. 5 shall add strength. *g* ch. 6.29. *h* ch. 7.6. Isa. 38.10. 6 the possessions. 7 near. 8 cried, or, called. *i* 2 Cor. 1.9. *j* Ps. 88. 4-8. *k* ch. 3.17.

CHAP. 18

a ch. 12.7. Ps. 73.22. *b* ch. 13.14. 1 his soul. 2 Nevertheless. *c* Pro. 13.9. 3 Or, lamp. 4 hidden. *d* ch. 6.4. Ps. 73.19. Jer. 6.25. 2 Cor. 5.11. 5 scatter him. *e* ch. 15.23. 1 Thes. 5.3. 6 bars. *f* ch. 8.14. Ps. 112.10. Pro. 10.28. Matt. 7.26, 27. *g* Gen. 19.24. *h* Ps. 34.16. Pro. 2.22. 7 They shall drive him. *i* Isa. 14.22. Jer. 22.30. 8 Or, lived with him. 9 laid hold on horror. *j* Jer. 9.3. 1 Thes. 4.5. 2 Thes. 1.8. Titus 1.16.

CHAP. 19

a 1 Sam. 1.6. Ps. 6.2,3. 1 Or, harden yourselves against me. *b* Ps. 19.12. Eze. 18.4. *c* Ps. 38.16. Micah 7.8. *d* Lam. 1.13.

be put out, and the spark of his fire
shall not shine.
6 The light shall be dark in his tabernacle, and his [3]candle shall be put out
with him.
7 The steps of his strength shall be
straitened, and his own counsel shall
cast him down.
8 For he is cast into a net by his own
feet, and he walketh upon a snare.
9 The gin shall take *him* by the heel,
and the robber shall prevail against
him.
10 The snare *is* [4]laid for him in the
ground, and a trap for him in the way.
11 Terrors [d]shall make him afraid on
every side, and shall [5]drive him to his
feet.
12 His strength shall be hunger-
bitten, and [e]destruction *shall be* ready
at his side.
13 It shall devour the [6]strength of his
skin: *even* the firstborn of death shall
devour his strength.
14 His [f]confidence shall be rooted
out of his tabernacle, and it shall bring
him to the king of terrors.
15 It shall dwell in his tabernacle,
because *it is* none of his: [g]brimstone
shall be scattered upon his habitation.
16 His roots shall be dried up beneath, and above shall his branch be
cut off.
17 His [h]remembrance shall perish
from the earth, and he shall have no
name in the street.
18 [7]He shall be driven from light into
darkness, and chased out of the world.
19 He [i]shall neither have son nor
nephew among his people, nor any remaining in his dwellings.
20 They that come after *him* shall be
astonied at his day, as they that [8]went
before [9]were affrighted.
21 Surely such *are* the dwellings of
the wicked, and this *is* the place *of him*
that knoweth [j]not God.

CHAPTER 19

THEN Job answered and said,
2 How long will ye [a]vex my soul,
and break me in pieces with words?
3 These ten times have ye reproached
me: ye are not ashamed *that* ye [1]make
yourselves strange to me.
4 And be it indeed *that* I have erred,
[b]mine error remaineth with myself.
5 If indeed ye [c]will magnify *your-*
selves against me, and plead against
me my reproach:
6 Know now that [d]God hath overthrown me, and hath compassed me
with his net.

7 Behold, I cry out of [2]wrong, but I am not heard: I cry aloud, but *there is* no judgment.

8 He hath [e]fenced up my way that I cannot pass, and he hath set darkness in my paths.

9 He hath stripped me of my glory, and taken the crown *from* my head.

10 He hath destroyed me on every side, and I am gone: and mine hope hath he removed like a tree.

11 He hath also kindled [f]his wrath against me, and he counteth me unto him as *one of* his enemies.

12 His [g]troops come together, and raise up their way against me, and encamp round about my tabernacle.

13 He hath put [h]my brethren far from me, and mine acquaintance are verily estranged from me.

14 My kinsfolk have failed, and my familiar friends have forgotten me.

15 They that dwell in mine house, and my maids, count me for a stranger: I am an alien in their sight.

16 I called my servant, and he gave *me* no answer; I intreated him with my mouth.

17 My breath is strange to my wife, though I intreated for the children's *sake* of [3]mine own body.

18 Yea, [4]young children despised me; I arose, and they spake against me.

19 All [5]my inward friends abhorred me: and they whom I loved are turned against me.

20 My bone cleaveth to my skin [6]and to my flesh, and I am escaped with the skin of my teeth.

21 Have pity upon me, have pity upon me, O ye my friends; for the hand of God hath touched me.

22 Why do ye persecute me as God, and are not satisfied with my flesh?

23 [7]Oh that my words were now written! oh that they were printed in a book!

24 That they were graven with an iron pen and lead in the rock for ever!

25 For I know *that* my redeemer liveth, and *that* he shall stand at the latter *day* upon the earth:

26 [8]And *though* after my skin *worms* destroy this *body*, yet in my flesh shall I see God:

27 Whom I shall see for myself, and mine eyes shall behold, and not [9]another; [10]*though* my reins be consumed [11]within me.

28 But ye should say, Why persecute we him, [12]seeing the root of the matter is found in me?

2 Or, violence.
e Lam. 3.7,8.
f Deut. 32.22.
g Ps. 34.19.
h Ps. 31.11. Matt. 26.56. 2 Tim. 4.16.
3 my belly.
4 Or, the wicked.
5 the men of my secret.
6 Or, as.
7 Who will give, etc.
8 Or, After I shall awake, though this body be destroyed, yet out of my flesh shall I see God.
9 a stranger.
10 Or, my reins within me are consumed with earnest desire [for that day.]
11 in my bosom.
12 Or, and what root of matter is found in me?

CHAP. 20

1 my haste is in me.
a Ps. 37.35.
2 from near.
3 cloud.
4 Or, The poor shall oppress his children.
5 in the midst of his palate.
b Jer. 4.18.
c Matt. 27.3, 4.
d Jer. 17.6.
6 Or, streaming brooks.
7 according to the substance of his exchange.
8 crushed.
e Eccl. 5.13.
9 know.

29 Be ye afraid of the sword: f
wrath *bringeth* the punishments of t
sword, that ye may know *there is*
judgment.

CHAPTER 20

THEN answered Zō-phär the N
ăm-ā-thīte, and said,

2 Therefore do my thoughts ca
me to answer, and for *this* [1]I ma
haste.

3 I have heard the check of my r
proach, and the spirit of my und
standing causeth me to answer.

4 Knowest thou *not* this of old, sin
man was placed upon earth,

5 That [a]the triumphing of the wick
is [2]short, and the joy of the hypocr
but for a moment?

6 Though his excellency mount up
the heavens, and his head reach un
the [3]clouds;

7 *Yet* he shall perish for ever like h
own dung: they which have seen h
shall say, Where *is* he?

8 He shall fly away as a dream, a
shall not be found: yea, he shall
chased away as a vision of the nig

9 The eye also *which* saw him sh
see him no more; neither shall h
place any more behold him.

10 [4]His children shall seek to plea
the poor, and his hand shall resto
their goods.

11 His bones are full *of the sin* of h
youth, which shall lie down with hi
in the dust.

12 Though wickedness be sweet
his mouth, *though* he hide it under h
tongue;

13 *Though* he spare it, and forsake
not; but keep it still [5]within his mout

14 *Yet* his [b]meat in his bowels
turned, *it is* the gall of asps with
him.

15 He hath [c]swallowed down riche
and he shall vomit them up agai
God shall cast them out of his belly

16 He shall suck the poison of asp
the viper's tongue shall slay him.

17 He shall not see [d]the rivers, [6]t
floods, the brooks of honey a
butter.

18 That which he laboured for sh
he restore, and shall not swallow
down: [7]according to *his* substan
shall the restitution *be*, and he sha
not rejoice *therein*.

19 Because he hath [8]oppressed *a*
hath forsaken the poor; *because* h
hath violently taken away an hou
which he builded not;

20 Surely [e]he shall not [9]feel quietne

his belly, he shall not save of that
nich he desired.
1 [10]There shall none of his meat be
ft; therefore shall no man look for
s goods.
2 In the fulness of his sufficiency he
all be in straits: every hand of the
vicked shall come upon him.
3 *When* he is about to fill his belly,
od shall cast the fury of his wrath
pon him, and shall rain *it* upon him
hile he is eating.
4 He [g]shall flee from the iron
eapon, *and* the bow of steel shall
rike him through.
5 It is drawn, and cometh out of
e body; yea, the glittering sword
meth out of his gall: [h]terrors *are*
pon him.
6 All darkness *shall be* hid in his
cret places: [i]a fire not blown shall
nsume him; it shall go ill with him
at is left in his tabernacle.
7 The heaven [j]shall reveal his ini-
uity; and the earth shall rise up
gainst him.
8 The increase of his house shall
epart, *and his goods* shall flow away
the day of his wrath.
9 This [k]*is* the portion of a wicked
an from God, and the heritage
ppointed unto him by God.

CHAPTER 21

BUT Job answered and said,
2 Hear diligently my speech, and
t this be your consolations.
Suffer me that I may speak; and
ter that I have spoken, mock on.
As for me, *is* my [a]complaint to
an? and if *it were so*, why should
ot my spirit be [1]troubled?
[2]Mark me, and be astonished, and
y *your* hand upon *your* mouth.
Even when I remember I am afraid,
nd trembling taketh hold on my
esh.
Wherefore [b]do the wicked live,
ecome old, yea, are mighty in
ower?
Their seed is established in their
ght with them, and their offspring
efore their eyes.
Their houses [3]*are* safe from fear,
either *is* the rod of God upon them.
0 Their bull gendereth, and faileth
ot; their cow calveth, and casteth not
er calf.
1 They send forth their little ones
ke a flock, and their children dance.
2 They take the timbrel and harp,
nd rejoice at the sound of the organ.
3 They spend their days [4]in wealth,
and in a moment go down to the
grave.
14 Therefore they say unto God,
Depart from us; for we desire not the
knowledge of thy ways.
15 What *is* the Almighty, that we
should serve him? and what profit
should we have, if we pray unto him?
16 Lo, their good *is* not in their hand:
the counsel of the wicked is far from
me.
17 How oft is the [5]candle of the
wicked put out! and *how oft* cometh
their destruction upon them! *God* dis-
tributeth sorrows in his anger.
18 They are as stubble before the
wind, and as chaff that the storm
[6]carrieth away.
19 God layeth up [7]his iniquity for his
children: he rewardeth him, and he
shall know *it*.
20 His eyes shall see his destruction,
and he shall drink of the wrath of the
Almighty.
21 For what pleasure *hath* he in his
house after him, when the number of
his months is cut off in the midst?
22 Shall *any* teach God knowledge?
seeing he judgeth those that are high.
23 One dieth [8]in his full strength,
being wholly at ease and quiet.
24 His [9]breasts are full of milk, and
his bones are moistened with marrow.
25 And another dieth in the bitterness of his soul, and never eateth with
pleasure.
26 They shall lie [c]down alike in the
dust, and the worms [d]shall cover them.
27 Behold, I know your thoughts,
and the devices *which* ye wrongfully
imagine against me.
28 For ye say, Where *is* the house of
the prince? and where *are* [10]the dwelling places of the wicked?
29 Have ye not asked them that go
by the way? and do ye not know their
tokens,
30 That the [e]wicked is reserved to
the day of destruction? they shall be
brought forth to [11]the day of wrath.
31 Who shall declare his way to his
face? and who shall repay him *what* he
hath done?
32 Yet shall he be brought to the
[12]grave, and shall [13]remain in the
tomb.
33 The clods of the valley [f]shall be
sweet unto him, and every man shall
draw after him, as *there are* innumerable before him.
34 How then comfort ye me in vain,
seeing in your answers there remaineth [14]falsehood?

10 Or, There shall be none left for his meat.
11 Or, troublesome.
f Num. 11. 33. Ps. 78.30,31.
g Isa. 24.18. Jer. 48.43. Amos 5.19.
h ch. 18.11. Ps. 73.19.
i Ps. 21.9.
j Isa. 26.21.
k Deut. 29. 20,28. ch. 18.21. ch. 27.13. Ps. 11.5,6. Matt. 24.51.
12 of his decree from God.

CHAP. 21

a 1 Sam. 1.16. ch. 7.11,13. Ps. 22.1-3.
1 shortened?
2 Look unto me.
b ch. 12.6. Jer. 12.1-3.
3 are peace from fear.
4 Or, in mirth.
5 Or, lamp.
6 stealeth away.
7 That is, the punishment of his iniquity.
8 in his very perfection, or, in the strength of his perfection.
9 Or, milk pails.
c Eccl. 9.2.
d Isa. 14.11.
10 the tent of the tabernacles of the wicked.
e Pro. 16.4. Nahum 1.2.
11 the day of wraths.
12 graves.
13 watch in the heap.
f ch. 3.17,18.
14 transgression?

CHAPTER 22

THEN Ĕ-lī́-phăz the Tḗ-măn-īte
answered and said,
2 Can [a]a man be profitable unto God,
[1]as he that is wise may be profitable
unto himself?
3 *Is it* any pleasure to the Almighty,
that thou art righteous? or *is it* gain *to*
him, that thou makest thy ways perfect?
4 Will he reprove thee for fear of
thee? will he enter with thee into judgment?
5 *Is* not thy wickedness great? and
thine iniquities infinite?
6 For thou hast taken a pledge from
thy brother for nought, and [2]stripped
the naked of their clothing.
7 Thou hast not given water to the
weary to drink, and thou [b]hast withholden bread from the hungry.
8 But *as for* [3]the mighty man, he had
the earth; and the [4]honourable man
dwelt in it.
9 Thou hast sent widows away
empty, and the arms of the fatherless have been broken.
10 Therefore snares *are* round about
thee, and sudden fear troubleth
thee;
11 Or darkness, *that* thou canst not
see; and abundance of waters cover
thee.
12 *Is* not [c]God in the height of
heaven? and behold [5]the height of
the stars, how high they are!
13 And thou sayest, [6]How doth God
know? can he judge through the dark
cloud?
14 [d]Thick clouds *are* a covering to
him, that he seeth not; and he walketh
in the circuit of heaven.
15 Hast thou marked the [e]old way
which wicked men have trodden?
16 Which were cut down out of time,
[7]whose foundation was overflown
with a flood:
17 Which said unto God, Depart
from us: and what can the Almighty
do [8]for them?
18 Yet he filled [f]their houses with
good *things*: but the counsel of the
wicked is far from me.
19 The righteous [g]see *it*, and are
glad: and the innocent laugh them to
scorn.
20 Whereas our [9]substance is not
cut down, but [10]the remnant of them
the fire consumeth.
21 Acquaint now thyself [11]with him,
and be [h]at peace: thereby good shall
come unto thee.
22 Receive, I pray thee, the law from
his mouth, and lay up [i]his words
thine heart.
23 If thou return to the Almight
thou shalt be built up, thou shalt p
away iniquity far from thy tabe
nacles.
24 Then shalt thou lay up gold [12]
dust, and the *gold* of Ṓ-phĭr as t
stones of the brooks.
25 Yea, the Almighty shall be t
[13]defence, and thou shalt have [14]plen
of silver.
26 For then shalt thou have thy d
light in the Almighty, and shalt lift u
thy face unto God.
27 Thou shalt make thy prayer un
him, and he shall hear thee, and th
shalt pay thy vows.
28 Thou shalt [j]also decree a thin
and it shall be established unto the
and the light shall shine upon t
ways.
29 When *men* are cast down, the
thou shalt say, *There is* lifting u
and he shall save [15]the humble pe
son.
30 [16]He shall deliver the island of t
innocent: and it is delivered by t
pureness of thine hands.

CHAPTER 23

THEN Job answered and said,
2 Even to day *is* my complai
bitter: [1]my stroke is heavier than m
groaning.
3 Oh that I knew where I might fin
him! *that* I might come *even* to h
seat!
4 I would order *my* cause before hi
and fill my mouth with arguments.
5 I would know the words *which* h
would answer me, and understan
what he would say unto me.
6 Will [a]he plead against me with *h*
great power? No; but he would p
strength in me.
7 There the righteous might dispu
with him; so should I be delivered f
ever from my judge.
8 Behold, [b]I go forward, but he *is* n
there; and backward, but I cann
perceive him:
9 On the left hand, where he do
work, but I cannot behold *him:* h
hideth himself on the right hand, th
I cannot see *him:*
10 But he knoweth [2]the way that
take: *when* [c]he hath tried me, I sha
come forth as gold.
11 My [d]foot hath held his steps, h
way have I kept, and not declined.
12 Neither have I gone back fro
the commandment of his lips; [3]I ha

CHAP. 22

a Ps. 16.2.
1 Or, if he may be profitable, doth his good success depend thereon?
2 stripped the clothes of the naked.
b ch. 31.16, 17.
3 the man of arm.
4 eminent, or, accepted for countenance.
c Isa. 66.1.
5 the head of the stars.
6 Or, What.
d Ps. 139.12.
e Gen. 6.11-13.
7 a flood was poured upon their foundation.
8 Or, to them?
f Ps. 17.13, 14.
g Ps. 107.42.
9 Or, estate.
10 Or, their excellency.
11 That is, with God.
h Isa. 27.5.
i Ps. 119.11. Jer. 15.16.
12 Or, on the dust.
13 Or, gold.
14 silver of strength.
j Pro. 16.3.
15 him that hath low eyes.
16 Or, The innocent shall deliver the island.

CHAP. 23

1 my hand.
a ch. 9.19. Isa. 27.4.
b Ps. 10.1. 1 Tim. 6.16.
2 the way that is with me.
c Ps. 17.3. Jas. 1.12.
d Ps. 44.18.
3 I have hid, or, laid up.

teemed the words of his mouth
ore than [4]my necessary *food*.
3 But he *is* in one *mind*, [e]and who
n turn him? and *what* his soul de-
eth, even *that* he doeth.
4 For he performeth *the thing that*
[f]appointed for me: and many such
ings are with him.
5 Therefore am I [g]troubled at his
esence: when I consider, I am
raid of him.
6 For God maketh my heart soft,
id the Almighty troubleth me:
7 Because I was not cut [h]off before
e darkness, *neither* hath he covered
e darkness from my face.

CHAPTER 24

WHY, seeing [a]times are not hidden from the Almighty, do they
at know him not see his days?
Some remove the [b]landmarks; they
olently take away flocks, and [1]feed
ereof.
They drive away the ass of the
therless, they [c]take the widow's ox
r a pledge.
They turn the needy out of the
ay: [d]the poor of the earth hide
emselves together.
Behold, *as* wild asses in the desert,
o they forth to their work; rising be-
mes for a prey: the wilderness *yield-*
h food for them *and* for *their* chil-
ren.
They reap *every one* his [2]corn in the
eld: and [3]they gather the vintage of
e wicked.
They [e]cause the naked to lodge
ithout clothing, that *they have* no
overing in the cold.
They are wet with the showers of
e mountains, and [f]embrace the rock
r want of a shelter.
They pluck the fatherless from the
reast, and take a pledge of the poor.
0 They cause *him* to go naked
ithout clothing, and they take away
e sheaf *from* the hungry;
1 *Which* make oil within their walls,
nd tread *their* winepresses, and suffer
irst.
2 Men groan from out of the city,
nd the soul of the wounded crieth
ut: [g]yet God layeth not folly *to them*.
3 They are of those that rebel
gainst the light; they know not the
ays thereof, nor abide in the paths
ereof.
4 The murderer rising with the
ght killeth the poor and needy, and
the night is as a thief.
5 The eye also of the adulterer
waiteth for the twilight, saying, No
eye shall see me: and [4]disguiseth *his*
face.
16 In the dark they dig through
houses, *which* they had marked for
themselves in the daytime: [h]they
know not the light.
17 For the morning *is* to them even
as the shadow of death: if *one* know
them, they are in the terrors of the
shadow of death.
18 He *is* swift as the waters; their
portion is cursed in the earth: he beholdeth not the way of the vineyards.
19 Drought and heat [5]consume the
snow waters: *so doth* the grave *those*
which have sinned.
20 The womb shall forget him; the
worm shall feed sweetly on him; [i]he
shall be no more remembered; and
wickedness shall be broken as a tree.
21 He evil entreateth the barren *that*
beareth not: and doeth not good to
the widow.
22 He draweth also the mighty with
his power: he riseth up, [6]and no *man*
is sure of life.
23 *Though* it be given him *to be* in
safety, whereon he resteth; yet [7]his
eyes *are* upon their ways.
24 They are exalted [j]for a little while,
but [8]are gone and brought low; they
are [9]taken out of the way as all *other*,
and cut off as the tops of the ears of
corn.
25 And if *it be* not *so* now, who will
make me a liar, and make my speech
nothing worth?

CHAPTER 25

THEN answered Bildad the Shû-
hite, and said,
2 Dominion and fear *are* with him,
he maketh peace in his high places.
3 Is there any number of his armies?
and upon whom doth not his [a]light
arise?
4 How [b]then can man be justified
with God? or how can he be clean
that is born of a woman?
5 Behold even to the moon, and it
shineth not; yea, the stars are not pure
in his sight.
6 How much less man, *that is* [c]a
worm? and the son of man, *which is* a
worm?

CHAPTER 26

BUT Job answered and said,
2 How hast thou [a]helped *him that*,
is without power? *how* savest thou the
arm *that hath* no strength?
3 How hast thou counselled [b]*him*
that hath no wisdom? and *how* hast

4 Or, my appointed portion.
e ch. 34.29. Eccl. 3.14. Rom. 9.19. Jas. 1.17.
f 1 Thes. 3.3.
g Ps. 119.120.
h ch. 6.9.

CHAP. 24
a Acts 1.7.
b Deut. 19.14.
1 Or, feed them.
c Deut. 24.6, 10,12,17.
d Pro. 28.28.
2 mingled corn, or, dredge.
3 the wicked gather the vintage.
e Ex. 22.26. Deut. 24.12. Isa. 58.7.
f Lam. 4.5.
g Eccl. 8.11.
4 setteth his face in secret.
h John 3.20.
5 violently take.
i Pro. 10.7.
6 Or, he trusteth not his own life.
7 That is, God's.
j Ps. 37.35, 36.
8 are not.
9 closed up.

CHAP. 25
a Gen. 1.3-5, 14-16. Ps. 19.4-6. Ps. 139.8,11. Matt. 5.45. Jas. 1.17.
b ch. 4.17. ch. 9.2. Ps. 130.3. Ps. 143.2. Rom. 3.19, 20.
c Ps. 22.6.

CHAP. 26
a Pro. 25.11.
b 1 Cor. 2.4.

thou plentifully declared the thing as
it is?
4 To whom hast thou uttered words?
and whose spirit came from thee?
5 Dead *things* are formed from under the waters, [1]and the inhabitants
thereof.
6 Hell [c]*is* naked before him, and destruction hath no covering.
7 He [d]stretcheth out the north over
the empty place, *and* hangeth the
earth upon nothing.
8 He [e]bindeth up the waters in his
thick clouds; and the cloud is not
rent under them.
9 He holdeth back the face of his
throne, *and* spreadeth his cloud upon
it.
10 He [f]hath compassed the waters
with bounds, [2]until the day and night
come to an end.
11 The pillars of heaven tremble and
are astonished at his reproof.
12 He [g]divideth the sea with his
power, and by his understanding he
smiteth through [3]the proud.
13 By [h]his spirit he hath garnished
the heavens; his hand hath formed
the crooked serpent.
14 Lo, these *are* parts of his ways:
but how little a portion is heard of
him? but the thunder of his power
who can understand?

CHAPTER 27

MOREOVER Job [1]continued his
parable, and said,
2 *As* God liveth, [a]*who* hath taken
away my judgment; and the Almighty,
who hath [2]vexed my soul;
3 All the while my breath *is* in me,
and [3]the spirit of God *is* in my nostrils;
4 My lips shall not speak wickedness, nor my tongue utter deceit.
5 God forbid that I should justify
you: till I die [b]I will not remove mine
integrity from me.
6 My righteousness I [c]hold fast, and
will not let it go: [d]my heart shall not
reproach *me* [4]so long as I live.
7 Let mine enemy be as the wicked,
and he that riseth up against me as
the unrighteous.
8 For [e]what *is* the hope of the hypocrite, though he hath gained, when
God taketh away his soul?
9 Will [f]God hear his cry when trouble
cometh upon him?
10 Will [g]he delight himself in the Almighty? will he always call upon
God?
11 I will teach you [5]by the hand of

1 Or, with the inhabitants.
c Ps. 139.8. Pro. 15.11. Isa. 14.9. Amos 9.2. Heb. 4.13.
d Ps. 24. 1,2.
e Pro. 30.4.
f Jer. 5.22.
2 until the end of light with darkness.
g Ex. 14.21. Ps. 29.10. Ps. 74.13. Isa. 51.15.
3 pride, or, Rahab.
h Ps. 33.6.

CHAP. 27

1 added to take up.
a ch. 34.5.
2 made my soul bitter.
3 That is, the breath which God gave him.
b ch. 13.15.
c ch. 2.3.
d Acts 24.16.
4 from my days.
e Matt. 16.26.
f Pro. 1.28. Isa. 1.15. Micah 3.4. Zech. 7.13. Jas. 4.3.
g ch. 22.26.
5 Or, being in the hand, etc.
h Deut. 28. 32,41.
2 Ki. 10.6-10. Esther 9.10.
i Ps. 78.64.
j Pro. 28.8. Eccl. 2.26.
k Lam. 2.6.
l Num. 20.26.
6 in fleeing he would flee.

CHAP. 28

1 Or, a mine.
2 Or, dust.
a Pro. 2.4. Eccl. 1.13.
3 Or, gold ore.

God: *that* which *is* with the Almigh
will I not conceal.
12 Behold, all ye yourselves have se
it; why then are ye thus altogeth
vain?
13 This *is* the portion of a wick
man with God, and the heritage
oppressors, *which* they shall receive
the Almighty.
14 If [h]his children be multiplied,
is for the sword: and his offspri
shall not be satisfied with bread.
15 Those that remain of him shall
buried in death: and [i]his widows sh
not weep.
16 Though he heap up silver as t
dust, and prepare raiment as t
clay;
17 He may prepare *it*, but [j]the ju
shall put *it* on, and the innocent sh
divide the silver.
18 He buildeth his house as a mot
and as [k]a booth *that* the keeper ma
eth.
19 The rich man shall lie down, b
he shall not be [l]gathered: he opene
his eyes, and he *is* not.
20 Terrors take hold on him
waters, a tempest stealeth him aw
in the night.
21 The east wind carrieth him awa
and he departeth: and as a stor
hurleth him out of his place.
22 For *God* shall cast upon him, ar
not spare: [6]he would fain flee out
his hand.
23 *Men* shall clap their hands
him, and shall hiss him out of h
place.

CHAPTER 28

SURELY there is [1]a vein for t
silver, and a place for gold *whe*
they fine *it*.
2 Iron is taken out of the [2]earth, ar
brass *is* molten *out of* the stone.
3 He setteth an end to darkness, ar
[a]searcheth out all perfection: t
stones of darkness, and the shadow
death.
4 The flood breaketh out from t
inhabitant; *even the waters* forgotte
of the foot: they are dried up, the
are gone away from men.
5 *As for* the earth, out of it come
bread: and under it is turned up as
were fire.
6 The stones of it *are* the pla
of sapphires: and it hath [3]dust
gold.
7 *There is* a path which no fo
knoweth, and which the vulture's e
hath not seen:

The lion's whelps have not trodden
nor the fierce lion passed by it.
He putteth forth his hand upon the
ck; he overturneth the mountains
the roots.
He cutteth out rivers among the
ks; and his eye seeth every precious
ng.
He bindeth the floods [5]from over-
wing; and *the thing that is* hid
ngeth he forth to light.
But [b]where shall wisdom be
nd? and where *is* the place of
derstanding?
Man knoweth not the [c]price
reof; neither is it found in the land
the living.
The [d]depth saith, It *is* not in me:
d the sea saith, *It is* not with
.
[6]It [e]cannot be gotten for gold,
ther shall silver be weighed *for* the
ce thereof.
It cannot be valued with the gold
Ō-phĭr, with the precious onyx, or
sapphire.
The gold and the crystal cannot
ual it: and the exchange of it *shall*
be for [7]jewels of fine gold.
No mention shall be made of
ral, or of pearls: for the price of
sdom *is* above rubies.
The topaz of Ē-thĭ-ō-pĭ-ă shall
equal it, neither shall it be valued
h pure gold.
Whence then cometh wisdom?
d where *is* the place of understand-
?
Seeing it is hid from the eyes of all
ing, and kept close from the fowls
the [9]air.
Destruction and death say, We
ve heard the fame thereof with our
s.
God [f]understandeth the way
reof, and he knoweth the place
reof.
For he looketh to the ends of the
th, *and* [g]seeth under the whole
aven;
To [h]make the weight for the
nds; and he weigheth the waters by
asure.
When he [i]made a decree for the
n, and a way for the lightning of
thunder:
Then did he see it, and [10]declare
he prepared it, yea, and searched
out.
And [j]unto man he said, Behold,
e fear of the Lord, that *is* wisdom;
d to depart from evil *is* under-
nding.

4 Or, flint.
5 from weeping.
b ch. 11.7,8. Ps. 139.6. Eccl. 7.24.
c Pro. 3.15.
d Rom. 11. 33.
6 Fine gold shall not be given for it.
e Pro. 3.13, 14.
7 Or, vessels of fine gold.
8 Or, Ramoth.
9 Or, heaven.
f Acts 15.18. Heb. 4.13.
g Pro. 15.3.
h Ps. 135.7.
i ch. 38.25. Ps. 148.8. Jer. 14.22.
10 Or, number it.
j Deut. 29.29.
k Deut. 4.6. Ps. 111.10. Pro. 1.7.

CHAP. 29

1 added to take up.
a ch. 18.6. Ps. 18.28.
2 Or, lamp.
b Ps. 25.14. Pro. 3.32.
c Gen. 49.11. Deut. 32.13.
d Ps. 81.16.
3 with me.
4 The voice of the nobles was hid.
e Ps. 137.6.
f Ps. 72.12. Pro. 21.13.
g Ps. 132.9. Rom. 13.14. Eph. 6.14.
h Num. 10. 31.
i Pro. 29.7.
5 the jaw-teeth, or, the grinders.
6 cast.
j Ps. 30.6.
k Ps. 1.3. Jer. 17.8.
7 opened.
l Ps. 1.3.
8 new.
m Gen. 49. 24.
9 changed.

CHAPTER 29

MOREOVER Job [1]continued his
parable, and said,
2 Oh that I were as *in* months past,
as *in* the days *when* God preserved me;
3 When [a]his [2]candle shined upon my
head, *and when* by his light I walked
through darkness;
4 As I was in the days of my youth
when [b]the secret of God *was* upon
my tabernacle;
5 When the Almighty *was* yet with
me, *when* my children *were* about me;
6 When [c]I washed my steps with
butter, and [d]the rock poured [3]me out
rivers of oil;
7 When I went out to the gate through
the city, *when* I prepared my seat in
the street!
8 The young men saw me, and hid
themselves: and the aged arose, *and*
stood up.
9 The princes refrained talking, and
laid *their* hand on their mouth.
10 [4]The nobles held their peace, and
their [e]tongue cleaved to the roof of
their mouth.
11 When the ear heard *me*, then it
blessed me; and when the eye saw *me*,
it gave witness to me:
12 Because [f]I delivered the poor that
cried, and the fatherless, and *him that*
had none to help him.
13 The blessing of him that was ready
to perish came upon me: and I caused
the widow's heart to sing for joy.
14 I [g]put on righteousness, and it
clothed me: my judgment *was* as a
robe and a diadem.
15 I was [h]eyes to the blind, and feet
was I to the lame.
16 I *was* a father to the poor: and the
[i]cause *which* I knew not I searched out.
17 And I brake [5]the jaws of the
wicked, and [6]plucked the spoil out of
his teeth.
18 Then I said, [j]I shall die in my nest,
and I shall multiply *my* days as the
sand.
19 My [k]root *was* [7]spread out [l]by the
waters, and the dew lay all night upon
my branch.
20 My glory *was* [8]fresh in me, and
my [m]bow was [9]renewed in my hand.
21 Unto me *men* gave ear, and waited, and kept silence at my counsel.
22 After my words they spake not
again; and my speech dropped upon
them.
23 And they waited for me as for the
rain; and they opened their mouth
wide *as* for the latter rain.
24 *If* I laughed on them, they be-

lieved *it* not; and the light of my countenance they cast not down.
25 I chose out their way, and sat
chief, and dwelt as a king in the army,
as one *that* comforteth the mourners.

CHAPTER 30

BUT now *they that are* [1]younger
than I have me in derision, whose
fathers I would have disdained to
have set with the dogs of my flock.
2 Yea, whereto *might* the strength of
their hands *profit* me, in whom old
age was perished?
3 For want and famine *they were*
[2]solitary; fleeing into the wilderness
[3]in former time desolate and waste.
4 Who cut up mallows by the
bushes, and juniper roots *for* their
meat.
5 They were driven forth from among
men, (they cried after them as *after* a
thief;)
6 To dwell in the clifts of the valleys,
in [4]caves of the earth, and *in* the rocks.
7 Among the bushes they brayed;
under the nettles they were gathered
together.
8 *They were* children of fools, yea,
children of [5]base men: they were viler
than the earth.
9 And now am I their song, [a]yea, I
am their byword.
10 They abhor me, they flee far from
me, [6]and spare not to spit in my face.
11 Because he [b]hath loosed my cord,
and afflicted me, they have also let
loose the bridle before me.
12 Upon *my* right *hand* rise the
youth; they push away my feet, and
[c]they raise up against me the ways of
their destruction.
13 They [d]mar my path, they set
forward my calamity, they have
no helper.
14 They came *upon me* [e]as a wide
breaking in *of waters:* in the desolation they rolled themselves *upon me.*
15 Terrors are turned upon me: they
pursue [7]my soul as the wind: and my
welfare passeth away as a cloud.
16 And now my soul is [f]poured out
upon me; the days of affliction have
taken hold upon me.
17 My bones [g]are pierced in me in
the night season: and my sinews take
no rest.
18 By the great force *of my disease*
is my garment changed: it bindeth me
[h]about as the collar of my coat.
19 He hath cast me into the mire, and
I am become like dust and ashes.
20 I cry [i]unto thee, and thou dost not

CHAP. 30
1 of fewer days than I.
2 Or, dark as the night.
3 yesternight.
4 holes.
5 men of no name.
a ch. 17.6. Ps. 35.15. Ps. 69.11.
6 and withhold not spittle from my face.
b ch. 12.18.
c ch. 19.12.
d Ps. 69.26.
e Ps. 18.4. Ps. 69.14,15. Isa. 8.7,8.
7 my principal one.
f 1 Sam.1.15. Ps. 22.14. Ps. 42.4. Isa. 53.12.
g ch. 33.19-21. Ps. 6.2.
h ch.2.7.
i Ps. 22.2. Matt. 15.23.
8 turned to be cruel.
9 the strength of thy hand.
10 Or, wisdom.
11 heap.
j Luke 19.41. John 11.35. Rom. 12.15.
12 for him that was hard of day?
13 burned, 2 Cor. 11.29.
k Jer. 8.15.
l Lam. 3.1,2.
m Ps. 102.6.
14 Or, ostriches.

CHAP. 31
a Matt. 5.28.
b 2 Chr. 16.9. ch. 34.21. Pro. 5.21. Jer. 32.19.
1 Let him weigh me in balances of justice.
c Num. 15. 39. Eccl. 11.9. Eze. 6.9. Matt. 5.29.

hear me: I stand up, and thou regar
est me *not*.
21 Thou art [8]become cruel to m
with [9]thy strong hand thou oppos
thyself against me.
22 Thou liftest me up to the win
thou causest me to ride *upon it*, a
dissolvest my [10]substance.
23 For I know *that* thou wilt bri
me *to* death, and *to* the house appoi
ed for all living.
24 Howbeit he will not stretch o
his hand to the [11]grave, though th
cry in his destruction.
25 Did [j]not I weep [12]for him that w
in trouble? was *not* my soul [13]griev
for the poor?
26 When [k]I looked for good, th
evil came *unto me:* and when I wait
for light, there came darkness.
27 My bowels boiled, and rested n
the days of affliction prevented me.
28 I went mourning [l]without the su
I stood up, *and* I cried in the cong
gation.
29 I am a [m]brother to dragons, a
a companion to [14]owls.
30 My skin is black upon me, and m
bones are burned with heat.
31 My harp also is *turned* to mour
ing, and my organ into the voice
them that weep.

CHAPTER 31

I MADE a covenant with [a]mi
eyes; why then should I think up
a maid?
2 For what portion of God *is th*
from above? and *what* inheritance
the Almighty from on high?
3 *Is* not destruction to the wicke
and a strange *punishment* to the wor
ers of iniquity?
4 Doth [b]not he see my ways, a
count all my steps?
5 If I have walked with vanity, o
my foot hath hasted to deceit;
6 [1]Let me be weighed in an ev
balance, that God may know mi
integrity.
7 If my step hath turned out of t
way, and [c]mine heart walked af
mine eyes, and if any blot hath clea
ed to mine hands;
8 *Then* let me sow, and let anoth
eat; yea, let my offspring be root
out.
9 If mine heart have been deceiv
by a woman, or *if* I have laid wait
my neighbour's door;
10 *Then* let my wife grind unto a
other, and let others bow down up
her.

11 For this *is* an heinous crime; yea,
is an iniquity *to be punished by* the
ıdges.
12 For it *is* a fire *that* consumeth to
estruction, and would root out all
ıine increase.
13 If I did despise the cause of my
ıanservant or of my maidservant,
hen they contended with me;
14 What then shall I do when God
seth up? and when he visiteth, what
hall I answer him?
15 Did [d]not he that made me in the
omb make him? and [2]did not one
ıshion us in the womb?
16 If I have withheld the poor from
ıeir desire, or have caused the eyes
f the widow to fail;
17 Or have eaten my morsel myself
lone, and the fatherless hath not eat-
n thereof;
18 (For from my youth he was
rought up with me, as *with* a father,
ıd I have guided [3]her from my
ıother's womb;)
19 If I have seen any perish for want
f clothing, or any poor without cov-
ring;
20 If his loins have not blessed me,
nd *if* he were *not* warmed with the
eece of my sheep;
21 If I have lifted up my hand against
ıe fatherless, when I saw my help in
ıe gate:
22 *Then* let mine arm fall from my
ıoulder blade, and mine arm be
roken from [4]the bone.
23 For destruction *from* God *was* a
rror to me, and by reason of his
ighness I could not endure.
24 If I have made gold my hope, or
ave said to the fine gold, *Thou art* my
onfidence;
25 If I rejoiced because my wealth
as great, and because mine hand had
otten much;
26 If [e]I beheld [6]the sun when it shin-
l, or the moon walking [7]*in* bright-
ess;
27 And my heart hath been secretly
nticed, or [8]my mouth hath kissed my
and:
28 This also *were* an iniquity *to*
e punished by the judge: for [f]I
ıould have denied the God *that is*
bove.
29 If I rejoiced at the destruction of
im that hated me, or lifted up myself
hen evil found him:
30 Neither [g]have I suffered [9]my
ıouth to sin by wishing a curse to his
oul.
31 If the men of my tabernacle said
not, Oh that we had of his flesh! we
cannot be satisfied.
32 The [h]stranger did not lodge in the
street: *but* I opened my doors [10]to the
traveller.
33 If I covered my transgressions [11]as
Adam, by hiding mine iniquity in my
bosom:
34 Did I fear a [i]great multitude, or
did the contempt of families terrify
me, that I kept silence, *and* went not
out of the door?
35 Oh that one would hear me! [12]be-
hold, my desire *is, that* the Almighty
would answer me, and *that* mine adversary had written a book.
36 Surely I would take it upon my
shoulder, *and* bind it *as* a crown to
me.
37 I would declare unto him the number of my steps; as a prince would I go
near unto him.
38 If my land cry against me, or that
the furrows likewise thereof [13]com-
plain;
39 If I have eaten [14]the fruits thereof
without money, or have [15]caused the
owners thereof to lose their life:
40 Let thistles grow instead of wheat,
and [16]cockle instead of barley. The
words of Job are ended.

CHAPTER 32

SO these three men ceased [1]to answer
Job, because he *was* righteous in
his own eyes.
2 Then was kindled the wrath of Ĕ-
lī-hū the son of Bă-rā-chĕl [a]the Bū-
zīte, of the kindred of Ram: against
Job was his wrath kindled, because
he justified [2]himself rather than God.
3 Also against his three friends was
his wrath kindled, because they had
found no answer, and *yet* had condemned Job.
4 Now Ĕ-lī-hū had [3]waited till Job
had spoken, because they *were* [4]elder
than he.
5 When Ĕ-lī-hū saw that *there was* no
answer in the mouth of *these* three
men, then his wrath was kindled.
6 And Ĕ-lī-hū the son of Bă-rā-chĕl
the Bū-zīte answered and said, I *am*
[5]young, and ye *are* very old; wherefore I was afraid, and [6]durst not shew
you mine opinion.
7 I said, [b]Days should speak, and
multitude of years should teach wisdom.
8 But *there is* a spirit in man: and the
[c]inspiration of the Almighty giveth
them understanding.
9 Great men are [d]not *always* wise:

d ch. 34.19. Pro. 14.31. Mal. 2.10. Eph. 4.6.
2 Or, did he not fashion us in one womb?
3 That is, the widow.
4 Or, the chanel-bone.
5 found much.
e Deut. 4.19. Deut. 11.16. Jer. 8.2. Eze. 8.16.
6 the light.
7 bright.
8 my hand hath kissed my mouth.
f Josh. 24.23, 27. Pro. 30.9. Isa. 42.8. Titus 1.16. 2 Pet. 2.1. 1 John 2.23.
g Matt. 5.44. Rom. 12.14.
9 my palate.
h Gen. 19.2. Heb. 13.2. 1 Pet. 4.9.
10 Or, to the way.
11 Or, after the manner of men.
i Ex. 23.2. Pro. 29.25.
12 Or, behold, my sign is that the Almighty will answer me.
13 weep.
14 the strength thereof.
15 caused the soul of the owners thereof to expire, or, breathe out.
16 Or, noisome weeds.

CHAP. 32

1 from answering.
a Gen. 22.21.
2 his soul.
3 expected Job in words.
4 elder for days.
5 few of days.
6 feared.
b ch. 8.8,9.
c 1 Ki. 3.9.
d 1 Cor. 1.21.

neither do the aged understand judgment.
10 Therefore I said, Hearken to me;
I also will shew mine opinion.
11 Behold, I waited for your words;
I gave ear to your [7]reasons, whilst ye
searched out [8]what to say.
12 Yea, I attended [e]unto you, and,
behold, *there was* none of you that
convinced Job, *or* that answered his
words:
13 Lest [f]ye should say, We have
found out wisdom: God thrusteth him
down, not man.
14 Now he hath not [9]directed *his*
words against me: neither will I answer him with your speeches.
15 They were amazed, they answered
no more: [10]they left off speaking.
16 When I had waited, (for they
spake not, but stood still, *and* answered no more;)
17 *I said*, I will answer also my part,
I also will shew mine opinion.
18 For I am full of [11]matter, [12]the
spirit within me constraineth me.
19 Behold, my belly *is* as wine *which*
[13]hath no vent; it is ready to burst like
new bottles.
20 I will speak, that I may [14]be refreshed: I will open my lips and answer.
21 Let me not, I pray you, accept
any man's person, neither let me give
flattering titles unto man.
22 For I know not [g]to give flattering
titles; *in so doing* my maker would
soon [h]take me away.

CHAPTER 33

WHEREFORE, Job, I pray thee,
hear [a]my speeches, and hearken
to all my words.
2 Behold, now I have opened my
mouth, my tongue hath spoken [1]in my
mouth.
3 My words *shall be of* the [b]upright-
ness of my heart: and my lips shall
utter knowledge [2]clearly.
4 The Spirit of God hath [c]made me,
and the breath of the Almighty hath
given me life.
5 If thou canst answer me, set *thy*
words in order before me, stand up.
6 Behold, [d]I *am* [3]according to thy
wish in God's stead: I also am [4]formed
out of the clay.
7 Behold, my [e]terror shall not make
thee afraid, neither shall my hand be
heavy upon thee.
8 Surely thou hast spoken [5]in mine
hearing, and I have heard the voice
of *thy* words, *saying*,

7 understandings.
8 words.
e Pro. 18.13.
f Jer. 9.23.
9 Or, ordered his words.
10 they removed speeches from themselves.
11 words.
12 the spirit of my belly.
13 is not opened.
14 breathe.
g Acts 12.22.
h Acts 12. 23.
CHAP. 33
a ch. 13.6.
1 in my palate.
b 1 Thes. 1.3.
2 purely.
c Gen. 2.7.
d ch. 9.32.
3 according to thy mouth.
4 cut out of the clay.
e ch. 13.21.
5 in mine ears.
f ch. 10.7.
g ch. 13.24.
h ch. 13.27.
i Eccl. 7.20.
j Isa. 45.9.
6 he answereth not.
7 he revealeth, or, uncovereth.
8 work.
9 from passing by the sword.
k Deut. 8.5. Ps. 94.12, 13.
10 meat of desire.
l Ps. 102.5.
m 2 Chr. 36. 15,16. Mal. 2.7.
n Rom. 3.24.
11 Or, an atonement.
12 than childhood.
o 2 Ki.20.2-5. Ps. 6.1-9.
13 Or, He shall look upon men, and say, I have sinned.
14 Or, He hath delivered my soul, etc., and my life.
p Ps. 40.2. Zech. 9.11.

9 I am clean [f]without transgressior
I *am* innocent; neither *is there* iniquit
in me.
10 Behold, he [g]findeth occasion
against me, he counteth me for hi
enemy,
11 He putteth [h]my feet in the stocks
he marketh all my paths.
12 Behold, *in* this thou art [i]not just
I will answer thee, that God is greate
than man.
13 Why dost thou [j]strive agains
him? for [6]he giveth not account of an
of his matters.
14 For God speaketh once, ye
twice, *yet man* perceiveth it not.
15 In a dream, in a vision of th
night, when deep sleep falleth upo
men, in slumberings upon the bed;
16 Then [7]he openeth the ears of men
and sealeth their instruction,
17 That he may withdraw man *fron*
his [8]purpose, and hide pride fror
man.
18 He keepeth back his soul from th
pit, and his life [9]from perishing by th
sword.
19 He is [k]chastened also with pai
upon his bed, and the multitude of hi
bones with strong *pain*:
20 So that his life abhorreth bread
and his soul [10]dainty meat.
21 His flesh is consumed away, tha
it cannot be seen; and [l]his bones *tha*
were not seen stick out.
22 Yea, his soul draweth near unt
the grave, and his life to the destroy
ers.
23 If there be a [m]messenger with hir
an interpreter, one among a thous
and, to shew unto man his uprigh
ness:
24 Then he is [n]gracious unto hin
and saith, Deliver him from goin
down to the pit: I have found [11]a rar
som.
25 His flesh shall be fresher [12]than
child's: he shall return to the days c
his youth:
26 He shall pray [o]unto God, and h
will be favourable unto him: and h
shall see his face with joy: for he wi
render unto man his righteousness.
27 [13]He looketh upon men, and *if an*
say, I have sinned, and perverted *tha*
which was right, and it profited m
not;
28 [14]He will deliver his soul from gc
ing into the pit, and his life shall se
the light.
29 Lo, all these *things* worketh Go
oftentimes with man,
30 To bring back [p]his soul from th

pit, to be enlightened with the light
of the living.
31 Mark well, O Job, hearken unto
me: hold thy peace, and I will speak.
32 If thou hast any thing to say, answer [q]me: speak, for I desire to justify
thee.
33 If not, [r]hearken unto me: hold
thy peace, and I shall teach thee wisdom.

CHAPTER 34

FURTHERMORE Ē-lī-hū answered and said,
2 Hear my words, O ye wise *men;* and
give ear unto me, ye that have
knowledge.
3 For the ear trieth words, as the
mouth tasteth meat.
4 Let us choose to us judgment: let
us know among ourselves what *is*
good.
5 For Job hath said, [a]I am righteous:
and [b]God hath taken away my judgment.
6 Should [c]I lie against my right? [2]my
wound *is* incurable without transgression.
7 What man *is* like Job, *who* drinketh up scorning like water?
8 Which goeth in company with the
workers of iniquity, and walketh with
wicked men.
9 For [d]he hath said, It profiteth a
man nothing that he should delight
himself with God.
10 Therefore hearken unto me, ye
men of understanding: [e]far be it
from God, *that he should do* wickedness; and *from* the Almighty, *that he*
should commit iniquity.
11 For [f]the work of a man shall he
render unto him, and cause every
man to find according to *his* ways.
12 Yea, surely God will not do wickedly, neither will the Almighty pervert judgment.
13 Who hath given him a charge
over the earth? or who hath disposed
the whole world?
14 If he set his heart [5]upon man, *if*
he gather unto himself his spirit and
his breath;
15 All flesh shall perish together, and
man shall turn again unto dust.
16 If now *thou hast* understanding,
hear this: hearken to the voice of my
words.
17 Shall [h]even he that hateth right
govern? and wilt thou condemn him
that is most just?
18 *Is it fit* to say to a king, *Thou art*
wicked? *and* to princes, *Ye are* ungodly?
19 *How much less to him* that [i]ac-
cepteth not the persons of princes,
nor regardeth the rich more than the
poor? for they all *are* the work of his
hands.
20 In a moment shall they die, and
the people shall be troubled at
midnight, and pass away: and the
[7]mighty shall be taken away without
hand.
21 For his eyes *are* upon the ways of
man, and he seeth all his goings.
22 *There is* no darkness, nor shadow
of death, where the workers of iniquity may hide themselves.
23 For [j]he will not lay upon man
more *than right;* that he should [8]enter
into judgment with God.
24 He shall break in pieces mighty
men [9]without number, and set others
in their stead.
25 Therefore he knoweth their works,
and he overturneth *them* in the night,
so that they are [10]destroyed.
26 He striketh them as wicked men
[11]in the open sight of others;
27 Because they turned back [12]from
him, and would not consider any of
his ways:
28 So that they [k]cause the cry of the
poor to come unto him, and he heareth [l]the cry of the afflicted.
29 When he giveth quietness, who
then can make trouble? and when he
hideth *his* face, who then can behold
him? whether *it be done* against a
nation, or against a man only:
30 That the hypocrite [m]reign not,
[n]lest the people be ensnared.
31 Surely it is meet to be said unto
God, I have borne *chastisement,* I will
not offend *any more:*
32 *That which* I see not teach thou
me: if I have done iniquity, I will do
no more.
33 [13]*Should it be* according to thy
mind? he will recompense it, whether
thou refuse, or whether thou choose;
and not I: therefore speak what thou
knowest.
34 Let men [14]of understanding tell
me, and let a wise man hearken unto
me.
35 Job [o]hath spoken without knowledge, and his words *were* without
wisdom.
36 [15]My desire *is that* Job may be
tried unto the end because of *his* answers for wicked men.
37 For he addeth rebellion unto his
sin, he clappeth *his hands* among us,
and multiplieth his words against
God.

q 2 Cor. 1.24.
r Ps. 34.11.
CHAP. 34
1 palate.
a ch. 33.9.
b ch. 27.2.
c ch. 9.17.
2 mine arrow.
d ch. 9.22.
3 men of heart.
e Gen. 18.25. Deut. 32.4.
f Pro. 24.12. Matt. 16.27. Rev. 22.12.
4 all of it?
5 upon him.
g Eccl. 12.7.
h Gen. 18.25.
6 bind?
i Deut. 10.17.
7 they shall take away the mighty.
j Ezra 9.13.
8 go.
9 without searching out.
10 crushed.
11 in the place of beholders.
12 from after him.
k Eccl. 5.8. Jas. 5.4.
l Ex. 22.23. Ps. 34.17. Eccl. 3.16, 17.
m Pro. 29.2-12.
n 1 Ki. 12.28, 30.
13 Should it be from with thee?
14 of heart.
o ch. 38.2.
15 Or, My father, let Job be tried.

CHAPTER 35

ELIHU spake moreover, and said,
2 Thinkest thou this to be right, *that* thou saidst, My righteousness *is* more than God's?
3 For thou saidst, What advantage will it be unto thee? *and,* What profit shall I have, [1]*if I be cleansed* from my sin?
4 [2]I will answer thee, and thy companions with thee.
5 Look unto the heavens, and see; and behold the clouds *which* are higher than thou.
6 If thou sinnest, what doest thou against him? or *if* thy transgressions be multiplied, what doest thou unto him?
7 If [a]thou be righteous, what givest thou him? or what receiveth he of thine hand?
8 Thy wickedness *may hurt* a man as thou *art;* and thy righteousness *may profit* the son of man.
9 By [b]reason of the multitude of oppressions they make *the oppressed* to cry: they cry out by reason of the arm of the mighty.
10 But none saith, [c]Where *is* God my maker, [d]who giveth songs in the night;
11 Who [e]teacheth us more than the beasts of the earth, and maketh us wiser than the fowls of heaven?
12 There [f]they cry, but none giveth answer, because of the pride of evil men.
13 Surely God will not hear vanity, neither will the Almighty regard it.
14 Although thou sayest thou shalt not see him, *yet* judgment *is* before him; therefore trust thou in him.
15 But now, because *it is* not *so,* [3]he hath visited in his anger; yet [4]he knoweth *it* not in great extremity:
16 Therefore [g]doth Job open his mouth in vain; he multiplieth words without knowledge.

CHAPTER 36

ELIHU also proceeded, and said,
2 Suffer me a little, and I will shew thee [1]that *I have* yet to speak on God's behalf.
3 I will fetch my knowledge from afar, and will ascribe righteousness to my Maker.
4 For truly my words *shall* not *be* false: he that is perfect in knowledge *is* with thee.
5 Behold, God *is* mighty, and despiseth not *any: he is* mighty in strength *and* [2]wisdom.
6 He preserveth not the life of the wicked: but giveth right to the [3]poor.
7 He withdraweth not his eyes from the righteous: but [a]with kings *are they* on the throne; yea, he doth establish them for ever, and they are exalted.
8 And [b]if *they be* bound in fetters, *and* be holden in cords of affliction;
9 Then he sheweth them their work and their transgressions that they have exceeded.
10 He openeth also their ear to discipline, and commandeth that they return from iniquity.
11 If they obey and serve *him,* they shall spend [c]their days in prosperity, and their years in pleasures.
12 But if they obey not, [4]they shall perish by the sword, and they shall die without knowledge.
13 But the hypocrites in heart heap up wrath: they cry not when he bindeth them.
14 [5]They die in youth, and their life *is* among the [6]unclean.
15 He delivereth the [7]poor in his affliction, and openeth their ears in oppression.
16 Even so would he have removed thee out of the strait *into* a broad place, where *there is* no straitness; and [8]that which should be set on thy table *should be* full of fatness.
17 But thou hast fulfilled the judgment of the wicked: [9]judgment and justice take hold *on thee.*
18 Because *there is* wrath, *beware* lest he take thee away with *his* stroke: then a great ransom cannot [10]deliver thee.
19 Will he esteem thy riches? *no,* not gold, nor all the forces of strength.
20 Desire not the night, when people are cut off in their place.
21 Take heed, regard not iniquity: for this [d]hast thou chosen rather than affliction.
22 Behold, God exalteth by his power: who [e]teacheth like him?
23 Who hath enjoined him his way? or who [f]can say, Thou hast wrought iniquity?
24 Remember that thou [g]magnify his work, which men behold.
25 Every [h]man may see it; man may behold *it* afar off.
26 Behold, God *is* great, and [i]we know *him* not, [j]neither can the number of his years be searched out.
27 For he maketh small the drops of water: they pour down rain according to the vapour thereof:

CHAP. 35
1 Or, by it more than by my sin?
2 I will return to thee words.
a Pro. 9.12. Rom. 11.35.
b Ex. 2.23. Neh. 5.5. ch. 24.12. Ps. 12.5. Luke 18.3-7.
c Eccl. 12.1. Isa. 51.13. 1 Pet. 4.19.
d Ps. 42.8. Acts 16.25.
e ch. 32.8. Ps. 8.6. 1 John 5.20.
f Pro. 1.28.
3 That is, God.
4 That is, Job.
g ch. 34.35, 37.

CHAP. 36
1 that there are yet words for God.
2 heart.
3 Or, afflicted.
a Ps. 113.8.
b Ps. 107.10.
c ch. 11.13-19. Isa. 1.19. 1 Tim. 4.8. Jas. 5.5.
4 they shall pass away by the sword.
5 their soul dieth.
6 Or, sodomites, Deut. 23.17.
7 Or, afflicted.
8 the rest of thy table.
9 Or, judgment and justice should uphold thee.
10 turn thee aside.
d Heb. 11.25.
e Isa. 40.13. Rom. 11.34. 1 Cor. 2.16.
f Deut. 32.4.
g Ps. 33.4. Dan. 4.37. Jer. 9.24. 1 Cor. 1.31. 2 Cor. 10.17. Rev. 15.3.
h Rom. 1.19.
i 1 Cor. 13.12.
j Ps. 90.2. Heb. 1.12.

28 Which the clouds do drop *and* dis-
l upon man abundantly.
29 Also can *any* understand the
preadings of the clouds, *or* the noise
f his tabernacle?
30 Behold, he spreadeth his light up-
n it, and covereth [11]the bottom of
ie sea.
31 For by them judgeth he the peo-
le; he giveth meat in abundance.
32 With clouds he covereth the light;
nd commandeth it *not to shine* by *the*
loud that cometh betwixt.
33 The noise thereof sheweth con-
erning it, the cattle also concerning
the vapour.

CHAPTER 37

AT this also my heart trembleth,
and is moved out of his place.
2 [1]Hear attentively the noise of his
oice, and the sound *that* goeth out of
is mouth.
3 He directeth it under the whole
eaven, and his [2]lightning unto the
nds of the earth.
4 After it a voice roareth: he thun-
ereth with the voice of his excellency;
nd he will not stay them when his
oice is heard.
5 God thundereth marvellously with
is voice; great things doeth he, which
e cannot comprehend.
6 For he saith to the snow, Be thou
n the earth; [4]likewise to the small
in, and to the great rain of his
rength.
7 He sealeth up the hand of every
an; that [a]all men may know his
ork.
8 Then the beasts go into dens, and
main in their places.
9 [5]Out of the south cometh the
hirlwind: and cold out of the [6]north.
10 By the breath of God frost is giv-
n: and the breadth of the waters is
raitened.
11 Also by watering he wearieth the
ick cloud: he scattereth [7]his bright
loud:
12 And it is turned round about by
is counsels: that they may do what-
oever he commandeth them upon the
ce of the world in the earth.
13 He causeth it to come, whether
or [8]correction, or for his land, or for
ercy.
14 Hearken unto this, O Job: stand
ill, and consider the wondrous works
f God.
15 Dost thou know when God dis-
osed them, and caused the light of
is cloud to shine?

11 the roots.
12 that which goeth up.

CHAP. 37
1 Hear in hearing.
2 light.
3 wings of the earth.
4 and to the shower of rain, and to the showers of rain of his strength.
a Ps. 111.2.
5 Out of the chamber.
6 scattering winds.
7 the cloud of his light.
8 a rod.
b ch. 36.4.
c Gen. 1.6. ch. 37.11-18.
9 Gold.
d Ex. 33.20. Matt. 11.27. John 1.18.
e ch. 36.5. Ps. 99.4. Jer. 10.12.
f Lam. 3.33. Heb. 12.10.
g Matt. 10.28.
h Matt. 11. 25.

CHAP. 38
a Ex. 19.16, 18. 1 Ki. 19.11. 2 Ki. 2.1. Eze. 1.4.
b Ex. 11.12. 1 Ki. 18.46.
1 make me know.
c Ps. 104.5.
2 if thou knowest understanding.
3 sockets.
4 made to sink?
d ch. 1.6.
e Gen. 1.9. Ps. 33.7. Pro. 8.29.
5 Or, established my decree upon it.
6 the pride of thy waves.

16 Dost thou know the balancings of
the clouds, the wondrous works of
[b]him which is perfect in knowledge?
17 How thy garments *are* warm,
when he quieteth the earth by the
south *wind?*
18 Hast thou with him [c]spread out
the sky, *which is* strong, *and* as a
molten looking glass?
19 Teach us what we shall say unto
him; *for* we cannot order *our speech*
by reason of darkness.
20 Shall it be told him that I speak?
if a man speak, surely he shall be
swallowed up.
21 And now *men* see not the bright
light which *is* in the clouds: but the
wind passeth, and cleanseth them.
22 [9]Fair weather cometh out of the
north: with God *is* terrible majesty.
23 *Touching* the Almighty, [d]we cannot find him out: [e]*he is* excellent in
power, and in judgment, and in plenty
of justice: he will [f]not afflict.
24 Men do therefore [g]fear him: he
respecteth not any *that are* [h]wise of
heart.

CHAPTER 38

THEN the LORD answered [a]Job out
of the whirlwind, and said,
2 Who *is* this that darkeneth counsel
by words without knowledge?
3 Gird [b]up now thy loins like a man;
for I will demand of thee, and [1]answer
thou me.
4 Where [c]wast thou when I laid the
foundations of the earth? declare, [2]if
thou hast understanding.
5 Who hath laid the measures thereof, if thou knowest? or who hath
stretched the line upon it?
6 Whereupon are the [3]foundations
thereof [4]fastened? or who laid the
corner stone thereof;
7 When the morning stars sang together, and all [d]the sons of God shouted for joy?
8 Or [e]*who* shut up the sea with doors,
when it brake forth, *as if* it had issued
out of the womb?
9 When I made the cloud the garment
thereof, and thick darkness a swad-
dlingband for it,
10 And [5]brake up for it my decreed
place, and set bars and doors,
11 And said, Hitherto shalt thou
come, but no further: and here shall
[6]thy proud waves be stayed?
12 Hast thou commanded the morning since thy days; *and* caused the day-
spring to know his place;
13 That it might take hold of the

[7]ends of the earth, that the wicked
might be shaken out of it?
14 It is turned as clay *to* the seal; and
they stand as a garment.
15 And from the wicked their light
is withholden, and the high arm shall
be broken.
16 Hast thou entered into the springs
of the sea? or hast thou walked in the
search of the depth?
17 Have the gates of death been
opened unto thee? or hast thou seen
the doors of the shadow of death?
18 Hast thou perceived the breadth
of the earth? declare if thou knowest
it all.
19 Where *is* the way *where* light
dwelleth? and *as for* darkness, where
is the place thereof,
20 That thou shouldest take it [8]to the
bound thereof, and that thou shouldest know the paths *to* the house thereof?
21 Knowest thou *it*, because thou
wast then born? or *because* the number of thy days *is* great?
22 Hast thou entered into the treasures of the snow? or hast thou seen
the treasures of the hail,
23 Which [f]I have reserved against
the time of trouble, against the day of
battle and war?
24 By what way is the light parted,
which scattereth the east wind upon
the earth?
25 Who hath divided a watercourse
for the overflowing of waters, or a
way for the lightning of thunder;
26 To cause it to rain on the earth,
where no man *is; on* the wilderness,
wherein *there is* no man;
27 To [g]satisfy the desolate and waste
ground; and to cause the bud of the
tender herb to spring forth?
28 Hath [h]the rain a father? or who
hath begotten the drops of dew?
29 Out of whose womb came the
ice? and [i]the hoary frost of heaven,
who hath gendered it?
30 The waters are hid as *with* a stone,
and the face of the deep [9]is frozen.
31 Canst thou bind the sweet in-
fluences of [10]Plēi-ă-dēs, or loose
the bands of [11]Ō-rī-ọn?
32 Canst thou bring forth [12]Măzz-ă-
rōth in his season? or canst thou
[13]guide Ărc-tū-rŭs with his sons?
33 Knowest thou [j]the ordinances of
heaven? canst thou set the dominion
thereof in the earth?
34 Canst thou lift up thy voice to the
clouds, that abundance of waters may
cover thee?

7 wings.
8 Or, at.
f Ex. 9.18. Josh. 10.11. Ps. 9.13. Isa. 30.30.
g Ps. 107.35.
h 1 Sam. 12. 17,18. ch. 5.9,10. Ps. 147.8.
i ch. 6.16. Ps. 147.16.
9 is taken.
10 Cimah, or, the seven stars.
11 Cesil?
12 Or, the twelve signs.
13 guide them.
j Gen. 1.10. Ps. 119.90, 91. Jer. 31.35.
14 Behold us?
k ch. 32.8. Ps. 51.6. Eccl. 2.26.
15 who can cause to lie down.
16 Or, when the dust is turned into mire.
17 is poured.
18 the life.
l Ps. 147.9. Matt. 6.26. Luke 12.24.

CHAP. 39

a ch. 24.5. Jer. 2.24. Hosea 8.9.
1 salt places.
2 of the exactor.
3 Or, rhinoceros.
4 Or, the feathers of the stork and ostrich.

35 Canst thou send lightnings, tha
they may go, and say unto thee, [14]Her
we *are?*
36 Who [k]hath put wisdom in the in
ward parts? or who hath given under
standing to the heart?
37 Who can number the clouds i
wisdom? or [15]who can stay the bottle
of heaven.
38 [16]When the dust [17]groweth int
hardness, and the clods cleave fast to
gether?
39 Wilt thou hunt the prey for th
lion? or fill [18]the appetite of the youn
lions,
40 When they couch in *their* dens
and abide in the covert to lie in wait?
41 Who [l]provideth for the raven hi
food? when his young ones cry unt
God, they wander for lack of meat.

CHAPTER 39

KNOWEST thou the time when th
wild goats of the rock bring forth
or canst thou mark when the hinds d
calve?
2 Canst thou number the month
that they fulfil? or knowest thou th
time when they bring forth?
3 They bow themselves, they brin
forth their young ones, they cast ou
their sorrows.
4 Their young ones are in good lik
ing, they grow up with corn; they g
forth, and return not unto them.
5 Who hath sent out the wild as
free? or who hath loosed the bands o
the wild ass?
6 Whose [a]house I have made th
wilderness, and the [1]barren land hi
dwellings.
7 He scorneth the multitude of th
city, neither regardeth he the cryin
[2]of the driver.
8 The range of the mountains *is* hi
pasture, and he searcheth after ever
green thing.
9 Will the [3]unicorn be willing to serv
thee, or abide by thy crib?
10 Canst thou bind the unicorn wit
his band in the furrow? or will h
harrow the valleys after thee?
11 Wilt thou trust him, because hi
strength *is* great? or wilt thou leav
thy labour to him?
12 Wilt thou believe him, that he wi
bring home thy seed, and gather *it int*
thy barn?
13 *Gavest thou* the goodly wings unt
the peacocks? or [4]wings and feather
unto the ostrich?
14 Which leaveth her eggs in th
earth, and warmeth them in dust,

15 And forgetteth that the foot may
crush them, or that the wild beast may
break them.
16 She is [b]hardened against her
young ones, as though *they were* not
hers: her labour is in vain without
fear;
17 Because God hath deprived her
of wisdom, neither hath he [c]imparted
to her understanding.
18 What time she lifteth up herself
on high, she scorneth the horse and
his rider.
19 Hast thou given the horse
strength? hast thou clothed his neck
with thunder?
20 Canst thou make him afraid as a
grasshopper? the glory of his nostrils
is [5]terrible.
21 [6]He paweth in the valley, and rejoiceth in *his* strength: [d]he goeth on
to meet [7]the armed men.
22 He mocketh at fear, and is not
affrighted; neither turneth he back
from the sword.
23 The quiver rattleth against him,
the glittering spear and the shield.
24 He swalloweth the ground with
fierceness and rage: neither believeth
he that *it is* the sound of the trumpet.
25 He saith among the trumpets, Ha,
ha; and he smelleth the battle afar off,
the thunder of the captains, and the
shouting.
26 Doth the hawk fly by thy wisdom,
and stretch her wings toward the
south?
27 Doth the eagle mount up [8]at thy
command, and [e]make her nest on
high?
28 She dwelleth and abideth on the
rock, upon the [9]crag of the rock, and
the strong place.
29 From thence she seeketh the prey,
and her eyes behold afar off.
30 Her young ones also suck up
blood: and [f]where the slain *are*, there
is she.

CHAPTER 40

MOREOVER the LORD answered
Job, and said,
2 Shall he that [a]contendeth with the
Almighty instruct *him?* he that reproveth God, let him answer it.
3 ¶ Then Job answered the LORD,
and said,
4 Behold, [b]I am vile; what shall I
answer thee? [c]I will lay mine hand
upon my mouth.
5 Once have I spoken; but I will not
answer: yea, twice; but I will proceed
no further.

6 ¶ Then [d]answered the LORD unto
Job out of the whirlwind, and said,
7 Gird [e]up thy loins now like a man:
[f]I will demand of thee, and declare
thou unto me.
8 Wilt [g]thou also disannul my judgment? wilt thou condemn me, that
thou mayest be righteous?
9 Hast thou an arm like God? or
canst thou thunder with [h]a voice like
him?
10 Deck [i]thyself now *with* majesty
and excellency; and array thyself with
glory and beauty.
11 Cast abroad the rage of thy wrath:
and behold every one *that is* proud,
and abase him.
12 Look on every one *that* [j]*is* proud,
and bring him low; and tread down
the wicked in their place.
13 Hide them in the dust together;
and bind their faces in secret.
14 Then will I also confess unto thee
that thine own right hand can save
thee.
15 ¶ Behold now [1]bē-hē-mōth, which
I made with thee; he eateth grass as
an ox.
16 Lo now, his strength *is* in his loins,
and his force *is* in the navel of his belly.
17 [2]He moveth his tail like a cedar:
the sinews of his stones are wrapped
together.
18 His bones *are as* strong pieces of
brass; his bones *are* like bars of iron.
19 He *is* the chief of the ways of God:
he that made him can make his sword
to approach *unto him.*
20 Surely the mountains [k]bring him
forth food, where all the beasts of the
field play.
21 He lieth under the shady trees, in
the covert of the reed, and fens.
22 The shady trees cover him *with*
their shadow; the willows of the brook
compass him about.
23 Behold, [3]he drinketh up a river,
and hasteth not: he trusteth that he
can draw up [l]Jordan into his mouth.
24 [4]He taketh it with his eyes: *his*
nose pierceth through snares.

CHAPTER 41

CANST thou draw out [1]lē-vī-ā-
thăn with an hook? or his tongue
with a cord [2]*which* thou lettest down?
2 Canst thou [a]put an hook into his
nose? or bore his jaw through with a
thorn?
3 Will he make many supplications
unto thee? will he speak soft *words*
unto thee?
4 Will he make a covenant with thee?

b Lev. 26.29. Isa. 49.15. Jer. 19.9. Lam. 2.20. Eze. 5.10.
c ch. 35.11.
5 terror.
6 Or, His feet dig.
d Jer. 8.6.
7 the armour.
8 by thy mouth.
e Jer. 49.16.
9 tooth.
f Matt. 24.28. Luke 17.37.

CHAP. 40
a ch. 9.3. Isa. 45.9.
b Ezra 9.6. Ps. 51.4.
c ch. 29.9. Ps. 39.9. Zech. 2.13.
d ch. 38.1. Ps. 50.3.
e ch. 38.3.
f ch. 42.4.
g Ps. 51.4.
h ch. 37.4. Ps. 29.3.
i Ps. 93.1.
j Isa. 2.12. Dan. 4.37. Luke 18.14.
1 Supposed to be either the elephant or the hippopotamus.
2 Or, He setteth up.
k Ps. 104.14.
3 he oppresseth.
l Gen. 13.10. Jer. 12.5.
4 Or, Will any take him in his sight, or, bore his nose with a gin?

CHAP. 41
1 That is, a whale, or, crocodile.
2 which thou drownest?
a Ps. 32.9. Isa. 30.28. Isa. 37.29. Eze. 29.4.

wilt thou take him for a servant for ever?

5 Wilt thou play with him as *with* a bird? or wilt thou bind him for thy maidens?

6 Shall the companions make a banquet of him? shall they part him among the merchants?

7 Canst thou fill his skin with barbed irons? or his head with fish spears?

8 Lay thine hand upon him, remember the battle, do no more.

9 Behold, the hope of him is in vain: shall not *one* be cast down even at the sight of him?

10 None *is so* fierce that dare stir him up: who [b]then is able to stand before me?

11 Who [c]hath prevented me, that I should repay *him?* [d]*whatsoever is* under the whole heaven is mine.

12 I will not conceal his parts, nor his power, nor his comely proportion.

13 Who can discover the face of his garment? *or* who can come *to him* [3]with his double bridle?

14 Who can open the doors of his face? his teeth *are* terrible round about.

15 *His* [4]scales *are his* pride, shut up together *as with* a close seal.

16 One is so near to another, that no air can come between them.

17 They are joined one to another, they stick together, that they cannot be sundered.

18 By his neesings a light doth shine, and his eyes *are* like the eyelids of the morning.

19 Out of his mouth go burning lamps, *and* sparks of fire leap out.

20 Out of his nostrils goeth smoke, as *out* of a seething pot or caldron.

21 His breath kindleth coals, and a flame goeth out of his mouth.

22 In his neck remaineth strength, and [5]sorrow is turned into joy before him.

23 [6]The flakes of his flesh are joined together: they are firm in themselves; they cannot be moved.

24 His heart is as firm as a stone; yea, as hard as a piece of the nether *millstone.*

25 When he raiseth up himself, the mighty are afraid: by reason of breakings they purify themselves.

26 The sword of him that layeth at him cannot hold: the spear, the dart, nor the [7]habergeon.

27 He esteemeth iron as straw, *and* brass as rotten wood.

28 The arrow cannot make him flee: slingstones are turned with him into stubble.

29 Darts are counted as stubble: he laugheth at the shaking of a spear.

30 [8]Sharp stones *are* under him: he spreadeth sharp pointed things upon the mire.

31 He maketh the deep to boil like a pot: he maketh the sea like a pot of ointment.

32 He maketh a path to shine after him; *one* would think the deep *to be* hoary.

33 Upon earth there is not his like, [9]who is made without fear.

34 He beholdeth all high *things:* he *is* a king over all the children of pride.

CHAPTER 42

THEN Job answered the LORD, and said,

2 I know that thou [a]canst do every *thing*, and *that* [1]no thought can be withholden from thee.

3 Who [b]*is* he that hideth counsel without knowledge? therefore have I uttered that I understood not; [c]things too wonderful for me, which I knew not.

4 Hear, I beseech thee, and I will speak: I [d]will demand of thee, and declare thou unto me.

5 I have [e]heard of thee by the hearing of the ear: but [f]now mine eye seeth thee.

6 Wherefore I abhor *myself*, and repent in dust and ashes.

7 ¶ And it was *so*, that after the LORD had spoken these words unto Job, the LORD said to Ĕ-lī-phăz the Tē-măn-ite, My wrath is kindled against thee, and against thy two friends: for ye have not spoken of me *the thing that is* right, as my servant Job *hath.*

8 Therefore take unto you [g]now seven bullocks and seven rams, and [h]go to my servant Job, and offer up for yourselves a burnt offering; and my servant Job shall [i]pray for you: for [2]him will I accept: lest I deal with you *after your* folly, in that ye have not spoken of me *the thing which is* right, like my servant Job.

9 So Ĕ-lī-phăz the Tē-măn-ite and Bildad the Shū-hīte *and* Zō-phăr the Nā-ăm-ă-thīte went, and did according as the LORD commanded them: the LORD also accepted [3]Job.

10 And the LORD turned the captivity of Job, when he prayed for his friends: also the LORD [4]gave Job twice [j]as much as he had before.

11 Then came there unto him all his

b ch. 9.4. ch. 40.9-14. 1 Cor. 10.22.
c ch. 35.7. Rom. 11.35.
d Gen. 14.19. Ex. 9.29. Ex. 19.5. Deut. 10.14. Ps. 24.1. 1 Cor. 10.26.
3 Or, within.
4 strong pieces of shields.
5 sorrow rejoiceth.
6 The fallings.
7 Or, breastplate.
8 Sharp pieces of potsherd.
9 Or, who behave themselves without fear.

CHAP. 42

a Jer. 32.17. Matt. 3.9. Mark 14.36. Luke 1.37. Eph. 3.20.
1 Or, no thought of thine can be hindered.
b 1 Tim. 1.7.
c Ps. 40.5.
d ch. 38.3.
e Rom. 10.17.
f Num. 12.8, 9. Isa. 6.1.
g Num. 23.1. Heb. 10.4.
h Matt. 5.24.
i Gen. 20.17. Heb. 7.25. Jas. 5.16.
2 his face, or, person.
3 the face of Job.
4 added all that had been to Job unto the double.
j Isa. 40.2.

rethren, and all his sisters, and all
ey that had been of his acquaintance
fore, and did eat bread with him in
s house: and they bemoaned him,
d comforted him over all the evil
at the LORD had brought upon him:
ery man also gave him a piece of
oney, and every one an earring of
ld.
: So the LORD blessed [l]the latter
d of Job more than his beginning:
he had [m]fourteen thousand sheep,
d six thousand camels, and a thou-
nd yoke of oxen, and a thousand
e asses.

k ch. 19.13.
l ch. 8.7.
m ch. 1.3.
5 That is, Handsome as the day.
6 That is, Cassia.
7 That is, The horn, or, Child of beauty.
n ch. 5.26.
o Gen. 25.8.

13 He had also seven sons and three
daughters.
14 And he called the name of the
first, [5]Jĕ-mī́-mă; and the name of the
second, [6]Kĕ-zī́-ă; and the name of the
third, [7]Kĕŕ-ĕn-hăṕ-pŭch.
15 And in all the land were no women found *so* fair as the daughters of
Job: and their father gave them inheritance among their brethren.
16 After this [n]lived Job an hundred
and forty years, and saw his sons, and
his sons' sons, *even* four generations.
17 So Job died, *being* old and full of
[o]days.

THE

BOOK OF PSALMS

PSALM 1

LESSED [a]*is* the man that walketh
not in the counsel of the [1]ungodly,
r standeth in the way of sinners,
r sitteth in the seat of the scornful.
But his delight *is* in the law of the
RD; and in his law doth he medi-
e day and night.
And he shall be like a tree planted
the rivers of water, that bringeth
th his fruit in his season; his leaf
o shall not [2]wither; and whatso-
r he doeth shall [b]prosper.
The ungodly *are* not so: but *are* like
chaff which the wind driveth away.
Therefore the ungodly shall not
nd in the judgment, nor sinners in
congregation of the righteous.
For [c]the LORD knoweth the way of
righteous: but the way of the un-
lly shall perish.

PSALM 2

VHY do the heathen [1]rage, and
the people [2]imagine a vain thing?
The kings of the earth set them-
es, and the rulers take counsel to-
her, against the LORD, and against
[a]anointed, *saying*,
Let [b]us break their bands asunder,
cast away their cords from us.
He [c]that sitteth in the heavens
ll laugh: the Lord shall have them
erision.
hen shall he speak unto them in
wrath, and [3]vex them in his sore
leasure.
Yet have I [4]set my king [5]upon my
y hill of Zion.

PSALM 1
a Gen. 5.24. Job 31.5. Ps. 81.12. Pro. 4.14.
1 Or, wicked.
2 fade.
b Gen. 39.3. Ps. 128.2.
c Nah. 1.7. John 10.14.

PSALM 2
1 Or, tumultuously assemble.
2 meditate.
a Ps. 45.7. John 1.41.
b Luke 19.14.
c Ps. 11.4.
3 Or, trouble.
4 anointed.
5 upon Zion, the hill of my holiness.
6 Or, for a decree.
d Matt. 8.29. Acts 13.33. Heb. 1.5.
e Dan. 7.13, 14. John 17.4, 5.
f Matt. 21.44.
g John 5.22, 23.
h Jer. 17.7.

PSALM 3
a 2 Sam. 15. 12.
b 2 Sam. 16.8. Ps. 22.7,8.
1 Or, about.
c 2 Ki. 25.27. Ps. 27.6.
d Ps. 4.8. Pro. 3.24. Acts 12.6.

7 I will declare [6]the decree: the LORD
hath said unto me, [d]Thou *art* my Son:
this day have I begotten thee.
8 Ask [e]of me, and I shall give *thee*
the heathen *for* thine inheritance, and
the uttermost parts of the earth *for* thy
possession.
9 Thou [f]shalt break them with a rod
of iron; thou shalt dash them in
pieces like a potter's vessel.
10 Be wise now therefore, O ye
kings: be instructed, ye judges of the
earth.
11 Serve the LORD with fear, and rejoice with trembling.
12 Kiss [g]the Son, lest he be angry,
and ye perish *from* the way, when his
wrath is kindled but a little. Blessed
[h]*are* all they that put their trust in
him.

PSALM 3

A Psalm of David, when he fled from Absalom his son.

LORD, [a]how are they increased that
trouble me! many *are* they that rise
up against me.
2 Many *there be* which say of my
soul, [b]*There is* no help for him in God.
Sḗ-lăh.
3 But thou, O LORD, *art* a shield [1]for
me; my glory, and [c]the lifter up of
mine head.
4 I cried unto the LORD with my
voice, and he heard me out of his holy
hill. Sḗ-lăh.
5 I [d]laid me down and slept; I awaked; for the LORD sustained me.
6 I will not be afraid of ten thousands

of people, that have set *themselves*
against me round about.
7 Arise, O LORD; save me, O my
God: for thou hast smitten all mine
enemies *upon* the cheek bone; thou
hast broken the teeth of the ungodly.
8 Salvation [e]*belongeth* unto the
LORD: thy blessing *is* upon thy people. Sē-läh.

PSALM 4

To the [1]chief Musician on Neginoth,
A Psalm of David.

HEAR me when I call, O God of
my righteousness: thou hast enlarged me *when I was* in distress; [2]have
mercy upon me, and hear my prayer.
2 O ye sons of men, how long *will ye*
turn my glory into shame? *how long*
will ye love vanity, *and* seek after leasing? Sē-läh.
3 But know that [a]the LORD hath set
apart him that is godly for himself:
the LORD will hear when I call unto
him.
4 Stand [b]in awe, and sin not: commune with your own heart upon your
bed, and be still. Sē-läh.
5 Offer [c]the sacrifices of righteousness, and [d]put your trust in the LORD.
6 *There be* many that say, Who will
shew us *any* good? [e]LORD, lift thou up
the light of thy countenance upon us.
7 Thou hast put gladness in my
heart, more than in the time *that* their
corn and their wine increased.
8 I will both lay me down in peace,
and sleep: for [f]thou, LORD, only makest me dwell in safety.

PSALM 5

To the chief Musician upon Nehiloth,
A Psalm of David.

GIVE ear to my words, O LORD,
consider my meditation.
2 Hearken unto the voice of my cry,
my King, and my God: for unto thee
will I pray.
3 My [a]voice shalt thou hear in the
morning, O LORD; in the morning will
I direct *my prayer* unto thee, and will
look up.
4 For thou *art* not a God that hath
[b]pleasure in wickedness: neither shall
evil dwell with thee.
5 The [c]foolish shall not stand [1]in thy
sight: thou hatest all workers of iniquity.
6 Thou shalt destroy them that speak
leasing: the LORD will abhor [2]the
bloody and deceitful man.
7 But as for me, I will come *into* thy
house in the multitude of thy mercy:

e Ps. 37.39,40. Pro. 21.31. Hosea 13.4.

PSALM 4

1 Or, overseer.
2 Or, be gracious unto me.
a Ex. 33.16. 2 Pet. 2.9.
b Pro. 3.7. Eph. 4.26.
c Deut. 33. 19.
d Ps. 37.3.
e Ps. 80.3.
f Lev. 26.5. Deut. 12.10. John 14.27. Phil. 4.7.

PSALM 5

a Ps. 30.5.
b Mal. 2.17.
c Ps. 14.1. Hab. 1.13.
1 before thine eyes.
2 the man of bloods and deceit.
d 1 Ki. 8.29.
3 the temple of thy holiness.
4 those which observe me.
5 Or, stedfastness.
6 in his mouth, that is, in the mouth of any of them.
7 wickednesses.
8 Or, Make them guilty.
9 Or, from their counsels.
10 thou coverest over, or, protectest them.
e 1 Cor. 2.9.
11 crown him.

PSALM 6

1 Or, upon the eighth.
a Hosea 6.1.
b Pro. 18.14. Matt. 26.38.
c Ps. 30.9.
2 Or, every night.
d Ps. 3.4. Ps. 31.22. Ps. 40.1,2.

PSALM 7

a Hab. 3.1.
1 Or, business.
b 1 Pet. 5.8.

and in thy fear will I worship [d]tow
[3]thy holy temple.
8 Lead me, O LORD, in thy rig
eousness because of [4]mine enemi
make thy way straight before my fa
9 For *there is* no [5]faithfulness
their mouth; their inward part *is* [7]v
wickedness; their throat *is* an o
sepulchre; they flatter with th
tongue.
10 [8]Destroy thou them, O God;
them fall [9]by their own counsels; c
them out in the multitude of th
transgressions; for they have rebel
against thee.
11 But let all those that put th
trust in thee rejoice: let them e
shout for joy, because [10]thou defe
est them: let them also [e]that love
name be joyful in thee.
12 For thou, LORD, wilt bless
righteous; with favour wilt th
[11]compass him as *with* a shield.

PSALM 6

To the chief Musician on Neginoth [1]upor
Sheminith, A Psalm of David.

O LORD, rebuke me not in th
anger, neither chasten me in
hot displeasure.
2 Have mercy upon me, O LORD;
I *am* weak: O LORD, [a]heal me; for
bones are vexed.
3 My soul is also sore vexed:
thou, O LORD, [b]how long?
4 Return, O LORD, deliver my s
oh save me for thy mercies' sake.
5 For [c]in death *there is* no rem
brance of thee: in the grave who s
give thee thanks?
6 I am weary with my groaning;
the night make I my bed to swir
water my couch with my tears.
7 Mine eye is consumed becaus
grief; it waxeth old because of
mine enemies.
8 Depart from me, all ye worke
iniquity; for the LORD hath heard
voice of my weeping.
9 The LORD [d]hath heard my sup
cation; the LORD will receive
prayer.
10 Let all mine enemies be asha
and sore vexed: let them return
be ashamed suddenly.

PSALM 7

[a]Shiggaion of David, which he sang unto the
concerning the [1]words of Cush the Benja

O LORD my God, in thee do
my trust: save me from all t
that persecute me, and deliver m
2 Lest he tear my soul like [b]a

ıding *it* in pieces, while *there is*
one to deliver.
O LORD my God, [c]if I have done
is; if there be iniquity in my hands;
If I have rewarded evil unto him
at was at peace with me; (yea, [d]I
ve delivered him that without
use is mine enemy:)
Let the enemy persecute my soul,
d take *it;* yea, let him tread down
life upon the earth, and lay mine
nour in the dust. Sē-lāh.
Arise, O LORD, in thine anger, lift
thyself because of the rage of
ne enemies: and awake for me *to*
judgment *that* thou hast com-
ınded.
So shall the congregation of the
ople compass thee about: for their
es therefore return thou on high.
The LORD shall judge the people:
ge me, O LORD, according to my
hteousness, and according to mine
egrity *that is* in me.
Oh let the wickedness of the wicked
ne to an end; but establish the just:
r the righteous God trieth the
arts and reins.
[3]My defence *is* of God, which sav-
the upright in heart.
[4]God judgeth the righteous, and
d is angry *with the wicked* every
.
If he turn not, he will whet his
ord; he hath bent his bow, and
de it ready.
He hath also prepared for him the
truments of death; he ordaineth
arrows against the persecutors.
Behold, he travaileth with ini-
ty, and hath conceived mischief,
l brought forth falsehood.
[5]He made a pit, and digged it, and
allen into the ditch *which* he made.
His [h]mischief shall return upon
own head, and his violent dealing
ll come down upon his own pate.
I will praise the LORD according
his righteousness: and will sing
ise to the name of the LORD most
h.

PSALM 8

To the chief Musician [a]upon Gittith,
A Psalm of David.

LORD our Lord, how excellent
is thy name in all the earth! who
t set thy glory above the heavens.
Out [b]of the mouth of babes and
klings hast thou [1]ordained strength
ause of thine enemies, that thou
htest still the [c]enemy and the
nger.
When I [d]consider thy heavens, the

2 not a deliverer.
c 2 Sam. 16.7.
d 1 Sam. 24.7.
e Ps. 94.2.
f 1 Sam. 16.7.
3 My buckler is upon God.
4 Or, God is a righteous judge.
5 He hath digged a pit.
g Esther 7.10. Pro. 5.22.
h 1 Ki. 2.32.

PSALM 8
a Ps. 81, title.
b Matt. 11.25. 1 Cor. 1.27.
1 founded.
c Ps. 44.16.
d Job 22.12. Ps. 19.1. Rom. 1.20.
e Job 7.17. Ps. 144.3. Heb. 2.8.
f Gen. 1.26.
g 1 Cor. 15. 27. Heb. 2.6.
2 Flocks and oxen all of them.
h Job 11.7. Ps. 35.10.

PSALM 9
1 thou hast made my judgment.
2 in righteousness.
a Deut. 9.14.
3 Or, The destructions of the enemy are come to a perpetual end: and their cities hast thou destroyed, etc.
b Ps. 90.2. Micah 5.2. Hab. 1.12. Heb. 1.11.
4 an high place.
c Ps. 91.14. John 17.3. 2 Cor. 4.6. 2 Tim. 1.12. 1 John 2.3, 4.
5 Or, afflicted.

work of thy fingers, the moon and the
stars, which thou hast ordained;
4 What [e]is man, that thou art mindful of him? and the son of man, that
thou visitest him?
5 For thou hast made him a little
lower than the angels, and hast
crowned him with glory and honour.
6 Thou [f]madest him to have dominion over the works of thy hands; [g]thou
hast put all *things* under his feet:
7 [2]All sheep and oxen, yea, and the
beasts of the field;
8 The fowl of the air, and the fish of
the sea, *and whatsoever* passeth
through the paths of the seas.
9 O LORD our Lord, how [h]excellent
is thy name in all the earth!

PSALM 9

To the chief Musician upon Muthlabben,
A Psalm of David.

I WILL praise *thee*, O LORD, with
my whole heart; I will shew forth
all thy marvellous works.
2 I will be glad and rejoice in thee:
I will sing praise to thy name, O thou
most High.
3 When mine enemies are turned
back, they shall fall and perish at thy
presence.
4 For [1]thou hast maintained my right
and my cause; thou satest in the
throne judging [2]right.
5 Thou hast rebuked the heathen,
thou hast destroyed the wicked, thou
hast [a]put out their name for ever and
ever.
6 [3]O thou enemy, destructions are
come to a perpetual end: and thou
hast destroyed cities; their memorial
is perished with them.
7 But [b]the LORD shall endure for
ever: he hath prepared his throne for
judgment.
8 And he shall judge the world in
righteousness, he shall minister judgment to the people in uprightness.
9 The LORD also will be [4]a refuge for
the oppressed, a refuge in times of
trouble.
10 And they that know [c]thy name
will put their trust in thee: for thou,
LORD, hast not forsaken them that
seek thee.
11 Sing praises to the LORD, which
dwelleth in Zion: declare among the
people his doings.
12 When he maketh inquisition for
blood, he remembereth them: he forgetteth not the cry of the [5]humble.
13 Have mercy upon me, O LORD;
consider my trouble *which I suffer* of

them that hate me, thou that liftest
me up from the gates of death:
14 That I may shew forth all thy
praise in the gates of the daughter
of Zion: I will rejoice [d]in thy salvation.
15 The heathen are sunk down in
the pit *that* they made: in the net
which they hid is their own foot
taken.
16 The LORD is [e]known *by* the judgment *which* he executeth: the wicked
is snared in the work of his own hands.
[6]Hĭg-gâi-ŏn. Sē-läh.
17 The wicked shall be turned into
hell, *and* all the nations [f]that forget
God.
18 For [g]the needy shall not alway be
forgotten: the expectation of the poor
shall *not* perish for ever.
19 Arise, O LORD; let not man prevail: let the heathen be judged in thy
sight.
20 Put them in fear, O LORD: *that*
the nations may know themselves *to*
be but men. Sē-läh.

PSALM 10

WHY standest thou afar off, O
LORD? *why* hidest thou *thyself*
in times of trouble?
2 [1]The wicked in *his* pride doth persecute the poor: [a]let them be taken
in the devices that they have imagined.
3 For the wicked boasteth of his
[2]heart's desire, and [3]blesseth the covetous, *whom* the LORD abhorreth.
4 The wicked, [b]through the pride
of his countenance, will not seek
after God: [4]God *is* not in all his
thoughts.
5 His ways are always grievous; thy
judgments *are* far above out of his
sight: *as for* all his enemies, he puffeth
at them.
6 He hath said in his heart, I shall
not be moved: for *I shall* [5]never *be* in
adversity.
7 His mouth is full of cursing and
[6]deceit and fraud: under his tongue *is*
mischief and [7]vanity.
8 He sitteth in the lurking places of
the villages: in the secret places doth
he murder the innocent: his eyes [8]are
privily set against the poor.
9 He lieth in wait [9]secretly as a lion
in his den: he lieth in wait to catch the
poor: he doth catch the poor, when
he draweth him into his net.
10 [10]He croucheth, *and* humbleth
himself, that the poor may fall [11]by
his strong ones.
11 He hath said in his heart, G
hath forgotten: he hideth his fa
he will never see *it*.
12 Arise, O LORD; O God, lift
thine hand: forget not the [12]humbl
13 Wherefore doth the wicked co
temn God? he hath said in his hea
Thou wilt not require *it*.
14 Thou hast seen *it;* for thou
holdest mischief and spite, to requ
it with thy hand: the poor [13]comm
teth himself unto thee; thou art
helper of the fatherless.
15 Break thou the arm of the wick
and the evil *man:* seek out his wick
ness *till* thou find none.
16 The LORD *is* King for ever a
ever: the heathen are perished out
his land.
17 LORD, thou hast heard the des
of the humble: thou wilt [14]prep
their heart, thou wilt cause thine
to hear:
18 To judge the fatherless and
oppressed, that the man of the ea
may no more [15]oppress.

PSALM 11

To the chief Musician, *A Psalm* of David.

IN the LORD put I my trust: how
ye to my soul, Flee *as* a bird to y
mountain?
2 For, lo, the wicked bend *their* b
they make ready their arrow upon
string, that they may [1]privily shoo
the upright in heart.
3 If the foundations be destroy
what can the righteous do?
4 The [a]LORD *is* in his holy tem
the LORD's throne *is* in heaven:
eyes [b]behold, his eyelids try, the c
dren of men.
5 The LORD [c]trieth the righteo
but the wicked and him that lov
violence his soul hateth.
6 Upon the wicked he shall r
[2]snares, fire and brimstone, and
horrible tempest: *this shall be* the p
tion of their cup.
7 For the righteous LORD lov
righteousness; his countenance d
behold the upright.

PSALM 12

To the chief Musician [1]upon Sheminith,
A Psalm of David.

[2]HELP, LORD; for the [a]godly n
ceaseth; for the faithful fail fr
among the children of men.
2 They speak vanity every one w
his neighbour: *with* flattering
and with [3]a double heart do t
speak.

d Ps. 13.5.
e Ex. 7.5.
6 That is, Meditation.
f Job 8.13. Ps. 50.22. Jer. 2.32. Hosea 2.13.
g Ps. 12.5. Phil. 1.20.

PSALM 10

1 In the pride of the wicked he doth persecute.
a Pro. 5.22.
2 soul's.
3 Or, the covetous blesseth himself, he abhorreth the LORD.
b 2 Ki. 18.35. Job 21.15. Ps. 12.3-5.
4 Or, all his thoughts are, There is no God.
5 unto generation and generation.
6 deceits.
7 Or, iniquity.
8 hide themselves.
9 in the secret places.
10 He breaketh himself.
11 Or, into his strong parts.
12 Or, afflicted.
13 leaveth.
14 Or, establish.
15 Or, terrify.

PSALM 11

1 in darkness.
a Hab. 2.20.
b Eph. 5.13. Heb. 4.13.
c Job 5.17. Ps. 94.12.
2 Or, quick burning coals.
3 Or, a burning tempest.

PSALM 12

1 Or, upon the eighth.
2 Or, Save.
a Isa. 57.1.
3 an heart and an heart.

The LORD shall cut off all flattering
s, *and* the tongue that speaketh
oud things:
Who have said, With our tongue
ll we prevail; our lips [5]*are* our own:
o *is* lord over us?
For the oppression [b]of the poor, for
e sighing of the needy, now will I
se, saith the LORD; I will set *him*
safety *from him that* [6]puffeth at
n.
The words of the LORD [c]*are* pure
rds: *as* silver tried in a furnace of
th, purified seven times.
Thou shalt keep them, O LORD,
ou shalt preserve [7]them from this
neration for ever.
The wicked walk on every side,
en the vilest [8]men are exalted.

PSALM 13

To the [1]chief Musician, A Psalm of David.

HOW long wilt thou forget me, O
LORD? for ever? [a]how long wilt
ou hide thy face from me?
How long shall I take counsel in
y soul, *having* sorrow in my heart
ily? how long shall mine enemy be
alted over me?
Consider *and* hear me, O LORD my
od: lighten [b]mine eyes, [c]lest I sleep
e *sleep of* death;
Lest mine enemy say, I have
evailed against him; *and* those
at trouble me rejoice when I am
oved.
But [d]I have trusted in thy mercy;
y heart shall rejoice in thy salva-
n.
I will sing unto the LORD, be-
use he hath dealt bountifully with
e.

PSALM 14

To the chief Musician, *A Psalm* of David.

HE [a]fool hath said in his heart,
There is no God. [b]They are cor-
pt, they have done abominable
orks, *there is* none that doeth
od.
The LORD looked down from heav-
upon the children of men, to see if
ere were any that did understand,
d seek God.
They are all gone aside, they are
together become [1]filthy: *there*
none that doeth good, no, not
e.
Have all the workers of iniquity no
owledge? who eat up my people *as*
ey eat bread, and call not upon the
ORD.
There [2]were they in great fear: for
God *is* in the generation of the
righteous.
6 Ye have shamed the counsel of
the poor, because the LORD *is* his
refuge.
7 [3]Oh that the salvation of Israel *were*
come out of Zion! when the LORD
bringeth back the captivity of his people, Jacob shall rejoice, *and* Israel
shall be glad.

PSALM 15

A Psalm of David.

LORD, who shall [1]abide in thy tabernacle? who shall [a]dwell in thy
holy hill?
2 He [b]that walketh uprightly, and
worketh righteousness, and speaketh
the truth in his heart.
3 *He that* backbiteth not with his
tongue, nor doeth evil to his neighbour, nor [2]taketh up a reproach
against his neighbour.
4 In whose eyes a vile person is contemned; but he honoureth them
that fear the LORD. *He that* sweareth [c]to *his own* hurt, and changeth
not.
5 *He* [d]*that* putteth not out his money
to usury, nor taketh reward against
the innocent. He that doeth these
things shall never be moved.

PSALM 16

[1]Michtam of David.

PRESERVE me, O God: [a]for in
thee do I put my trust.
2 *O my soul,* thou hast said unto the
LORD, Thou *art* my Lord: my goodness *extendeth* not to thee;
3 *But* to the saints that *are* in the
earth, and *to* the excellent, in whom
is all my delight.
4 Their sorrows shall be multiplied
that [2]hasten *after* another *god:* their
drink offerings of blood will I not
offer, nor take up their names into my
lips.
5 The LORD *is* the portion [3]of mine
inheritance and of my cup: thou
maintainest my lot.
6 The lines are fallen unto me in
pleasant *places;* yea, I have a goodly
heritage.
7 I will bless the LORD, who hath
given me counsel: my reins also instruct me in the night seasons.
8 I have set the LORD always before
me: because *he is* at my right hand,
I shall not be moved.
9 Therefore my heart is glad, and my
glory rejoiceth: my flesh also shall
[4]rest in hope.

4 great things.
5 are with us.
b Ex. 3.7,8.
6 Or, would ensnare him.
c 2 Sam. 22. 31. Ps. 18.30. Pro. 30.5.
7 him: that is, every one of them.
8 of the sons of men.

PSALM 13
1 Or, overseer.
a Deut. 31.17. Job 13.24. Ps. 22.1. Isa. 59.2.
b Ezra 9.8. Ps. 18.28. Luke 2.32. Rev. 21.23.
c Ps. 76.5,6. Isa. 37.36. Jer. 51.39. Eph. 5.14.
d 2 Chr. 20. 12.

PSALM 14
a Ps. 10.4. Pro. 1.7,22.
b Gen. 6.12. Rom. 3.10.
1 stinking.
2 they feared a fear.
3 Who will give.

PSALM 15
1 sojourn.
a Ps. 2.6.
b Ps. 84.11. Isa. 33.15, 16.
2 Or, receiveth, or, endureth.
c Josh. 9.18-20.
d Eze. 18.8,9.

PSALM 16
1 Or, A golden Psalm.
a Ps. 25.20.
2 Or, give gifts to another.
3 of my part.
4 dwell confidently.

10 For [b]thou wilt not leave my soul
in hell; neither wilt thou suffer thine
[c]Holy One to see corruption.
11 Thou wilt shew me [d]the path of
life: in thy presence *is* fulness of joy;
at thy right hand *there are* pleasures
for evermore.

PSALM 17

A Prayer of David.

HEAR [1]the right, O LORD, attend
unto my cry, give ear unto my
prayer, *that goeth* [2]not out of feigned
lips.
2 Let my sentence come forth from
thy presence; let thine eyes behold
the things that are equal.
3 Thou hast proved [a]mine heart;
thou hast visited *me* in the night; thou
hast tried me, *and* shalt find nothing;
I am purposed *that* my mouth [b]shall
not transgress.
4 Concerning the works of men, by
[c]the word of thy lips I have kept *me*
from the paths of the destroyer.
5 Hold up my goings in thy paths,
that my footsteps [3]slip not.
6 I have called upon thee, for thou
wilt hear me, O God: incline thine
ear unto me, *and hear* my speech.
7 Shew thy marvellous lovingkindness, O thou [4]that savest by thy right
hand them which put their trust *in*
thee from those that rise up *against*
them.
8 Keep me [d]as the apple of the eye,
hide me under the shadow of thy
wings,
9 From the wicked [5]that oppress me,
from [6]my deadly enemies, *who* compass me about.
10 They are inclosed in their own
fat: with their mouth they speak
proudly.
11 They have now [e]compassed us in
our steps: they have set their eyes
bowing down to the earth;
12 [7]Like as a lion *that* is greedy of his
prey, and as it were a young lion
[8]lurking in secret places.
13 Arise, O LORD, [9]disappoint him,
cast him down: deliver my soul from
the wicked, [10]*which is* thy sword:
14 From men *which are* thy hand, O
LORD, from men of the world, *which*
have their portion in *this* life, and
whose belly thou fillest with thy hid
treasure: [11]they are full of children,
and leave the rest of their *substance* to
their babes.
15 As for me, [f]I will behold thy face
in righteousness: I shall be satisfied,
when I awake, with [g]thy likeness.

b Ps. 49.15. Acts 2.27.
c Dan. 9.24. Luke 1.35.
d Acts 2.28.

PSALM 17

1 justice.
2 without lips of deceit.
a Job 23.10.
b Jas. 3.2.
c Rom. 12.2.
3 be not moved.
4 Or, that savest them which trust in thee from those that rise up against thy right hand.
d Deut. 32. 10.
5 that waste me.
6 my enemies against the soul.
e 1 Sam. 23. 26.
7 The likeness of him [that is, of every one of them] is as a lion that desireth to ravin.
8 sitting.
9 prevent his face.
10 Or, by thy sword.
11 Or, their children are full.
f Job 19.26, 27.
g Col. 1.15.

PSALM 18

a 2 Sam. 22. 1-51.
b Deut. 32.4. 1 Sam. 2.2. Ps. 91.2.
1 my rock.
c Heb. 2.13.
d Ps. 76.4.
e Ps. 116.3.
2 Belial.
3 Or, cords.
f Acts 4.31.
4 by his.
g Isa. 64.1.
h Ps. 99.1.
i Ps. 104.3.
j Ps. 97.2.
k Ps. 29.3.
l Num. 24.8. Deut. 32.23. Job 6.4. Ps. 21.12.
m Ps. 144.7.
5 Or, great waters.

PSALM 18

To the chief Musician, *A Psalm* of David, the
vant of the LORD, who spake unto the LORI
words of [a]this song in the day *that* the LORI
livered him from the hand of all his enemies,
from the hand of Saul: And he said,

I [b]WILL love thee, O LORD,
strength.
2 The LORD *is* my rock, and my f
tress, and my deliverer; my God,
strength, in [c]whom I will trust;
buckler, and the horn of my sal
tion, *and* my high tower.
3 I will call upon the LORD, [d]*wh*
worthy to be praised: so shall I be s
ed from mine enemies.
4 The [e]sorrows of death compas
me, and the floods of [2]ungodly n
made me afraid.
5 The [3]sorrows of hell compassed
about: the snares of death preven
me.
6 In my distress I called upon
LORD, and cried unto my God:
heard my voice out of his temple, a
my cry came before him, *even* into
ears.
7 Then [f]the earth shook and tre
bled; the foundations also of the h
moved and were shaken, because
was wroth.
8 There went up a smoke [4]out of
nostrils, and fire out of his mouth
voured: coals were kindled by it.
9 He [g]bowed the heavens also, a
came down: and darkness *was* un
his feet.
10 And [h]he rode upon a cherub, a
did fly: [i]yea, he did fly upon the wi
of the wind.
11 He made darkness his sec
place; his [j]pavilion round about h
were dark waters *and* thick clouds
the skies.
12 At the brightness *that was* bef
him his thick clouds passed, h
stones and coals of fire.
13 The LORD also thundered in t
heavens, and the Highest gave
[k]voice; hail *stones* and coals of fire
14 Yea, [l]he sent out his arrows, a
scattered them; and he shot out lig
nings, and discomfited them.
15 Then the channels of waters w
seen, and the foundations of t
world were discovered at thy rebu
O LORD, at the blast of the breath
thy nostrils.
16 He [m]sent from above, he took n
he drew me out of [5]many waters.
17 He delivered me from my stro
enemy, and from them which hat
me: for they were too strong for me

8 They prevented me in the day of
y calamity: but the LORD was my
ıy.
9 He [n]brought me forth also into a
:ge place; he delivered me, because
delighted in me.
0 The [o]LORD rewarded me accord-
g to my righteousness; according to
e cleanness of my hands hath he
compensed me.
1 For I have kept the ways of the
)RD, and have not wickedly depart-
from my God.
2 For all his judgments *were* before
e, and I did not put away his states from me.
3 I was also upright [6]before him,
ıd I kept myself from mine iniquity.
4 Therefore [p]hath the LORD recom-
ensed me according to my righteous-
ss, according to the cleanness of my
ands [7]in his eyesight.
5 With [q]the merciful thou wilt shew
yself merciful; with an upright man
ou wilt shew thyself upright;
6 With the pure thou wilt shew thy
lf pure; and [r]with the froward thou
ilt [8]shew thyself froward.
7 For thou wilt save the afflicted
eople; but wilt bring down [s]high
ooks.
8 For [t]thou wilt light my [9]candle:
e LORD my God will enlighten my
arkness.
29 For by thee I have [10]run through
troop; and by my God have I leaped
ver a wall.
30 *As for* God, [u]his way *is* perfect:
he [v]word of the LORD is [11]tried: he *is*
buckler to all those that trust in him.
31 For [w]who *is* God save the LORD?
r who *is* a rock save our God?
32 *It is* God that girdeth me with
trength, and maketh my way perfect.
33 He maketh my feet like hinds'
eet, and setteth me upon my high
laces.
34 He teacheth my hands to war, so
hat a bow of steel is broken by mine
rms.
35 Thou hast also given me the shield
of thy salvation: and thy right hand
hath holden me up, and [12]thy gentleness hath made me great.
36 Thou hast enlarged my steps
under me, that [13]my feet did not
slip.
37 I have pursued mine enemies, and
overtaken them: neither did I turn
again till they were consumed.
38 I have wounded them that they
were not able to rise: they are fallen
under my feet.

39 For thou hast girded me with
strength unto the battle: thou hast
[14]subdued under me those that rose
up against me.
40 Thou hast also given me the necks
of mine enemies; that I might destroy
them that hate me.
41 They cried, but *there was* none to
save *them*: [x]*even* unto the LORD, but
he answered them not.
42 Then did I beat them small as the
dust before the wind: I did cast them
out as the dirt in the streets.
43 Thou hast delivered me from the
strivings of the people; *and* thou hast
made me the head of the heathen: a
people *whom* I have not known shall
serve me.
44 [15]As soon as they hear of me, they
shall obey me: [16]the strangers shall
[17]submit themselves unto me.
45 The [y]strangers shall fade away,
and be afraid out of their close places.
46 The [z]LORD liveth; and blessed *be*
my rock; and let the God of my salvation be exalted.
47 *It is* God that [18]avengeth me, and
[19]subdueth the people under me.
48 He delivereth me from mine enemies: yea, [a]thou liftest me up above
those that rise up against me: thou
hast delivered me from the [20]violent
man.
49 Therefore will I [21]give thanks unto
thee, O LORD, among the heathen,
and sing praises unto thy name.
50 Great deliverance [b]giveth he to
his king; and sheweth mercy to his
anointed, to David, and to his seed
for evermore.

PSALM 19

To the chief Musician, A Psalm of David.

THE [a]heavens declare the glory of
God; and the firmament sheweth
his handywork.
2 Day unto day uttereth speech, and
night unto night sheweth knowledge.
3 *There is* no speech nor language,
[1]*where* their voice is not heard.
4 [2]Their line is gone out through all
the earth, and their words to the end
of the world. In them hath he set a
tabernacle for the sun,
5 Which *is* [b]as a bridegroom coming
out of his chamber, *and* rejoiceth as
a strong man to run a race.
6 His going forth [c]*is* from the end of
the heaven, and his circuit unto the
ends of it: and there is nothing hid
from the heat thereof.
7 The [3]law of the LORD *is* perfect,
[4]converting the soul: the testimony of

n Ps. 118.5.
o 2 Sam. 22. 21. Pro. 18.10. Matt. 6.4. 1 Cor. 3.8.
6 with.
p Ruth 2.12. Matt. 10.41, 42.
7 before his eyes.
q Matt. 18. 32-35.
r Lev. 26.23.
8 Or, wrestle.
s Pro. 6.17.
t Job 18.6.
9 Or, lamp.
10 Or, broken.
u Deut. 32.4. Rom. 12.3. Rev. 15.3.
v Ps. 12.6.
11 Or, refined.
w Deut. 32. 31. 2 Sam. 22. 32.
12 Or, with thy meekness thou hast multiplied me.
13 mine ancles.
14 caused to bow.
x Pro. 1.28.
15 At the hearing of the ear.
16 the sons of the stranger.
17 lie, or, yield feigned obedience.
y Micah 7.17.
z Jer. 10.10.
18 giveth avengements for me.
19 Or, destroyeth.
a Ps. 59.1.
20 man of violence.
21 Or, confess.
b Ps. 144.10.

PSALM 19

a Isa. 40.22. Rom. 1.19.
1 without their voice heard, or, without these their voice is heard.
2 Or, Their rule, or, direction. Rom. 10.18.
b Eccl. 11.7.
c Eccl. 1.5.
3 Or, doctrine.
4 Or, restoring.

the LORD *is* sure, making wise the simple.

8 The statutes [d]of the LORD *are* right, rejoicing the heart: the commandment of the LORD *is* pure, enlightening the eyes.

9 The fear of the LORD *is* clean, enduring for ever: the judgments of the LORD *are* [5]true *and* righteous altogether.

10 More to be desired *are they* than gold, yea, than much fine gold: sweeter also than honey and the honeycomb.

11 Moreover by them is thy servant [e]warned: *and* in keeping of them *there is* great reward.

12 Who can understand *his* errors? cleanse thou me from secret *faults*.

13 Keep back thy servant also from presumptuous *sins;* let them not have dominion over me: then shall I be upright, and I shall be innocent from [6]the great transgression.

14 Let the words of my mouth, and the meditation of my heart, be acceptable in thy sight, O LORD, [7]my strength, and my [f]redeemer.

PSALM 20

To the chief Musician, A Psalm of David.

THE LORD hear thee in the day of trouble; the [a]name of the God of Jacob [1]defend thee;

2 Send [2]thee help from the sanctuary, and [3]strengthen thee out of Zion;

3 Remember all thy offerings, and [4]accept thy burnt sacrifice; Sē-lāh.

4 Grant thee [b]according to thine own heart, and fulfil all thy counsel.

5 We will rejoice [c]in thy salvation, and in the name of our God we [d]will set up *our* banners: the LORD fulfil all thy petitions.

6 Now know I that the LORD saveth his anointed; he will hear him [5]from his holy heaven [6]with the saving strength of his right hand.

7 Some *trust* in chariots, and some in horses: but we will [e]remember the name of the LORD our God.

8 They are brought down and fallen: but we are risen, and stand upright.

9 Save, LORD: let the king hear us when we call.

PSALM 21

To the chief Musician, A Psalm of David.

THE king shall joy in thy strength, O LORD; and in thy salvation how greatly shall he rejoice!

2 Thou hast given him [a]his heart's desire, and hast not withholden t request of his lips. Sē-lāh.

3 For thou preventest him with t blessings of goodness: thou settest crown of pure gold on his head.

4 He asked life of thee, [b]*and* tho gavest *it* him, *even* length of days f ever and ever.

5 His glory *is* great in thy salvatio honour and majesty hast thou laid u on him.

6 For thou hast [1]made him mo blessed for ever: thou hast [2]made hi exceeding glad with thy countenanc

7 For the king trusteth [c]in the LOR and through the mercy of the mo High he shall not be moved.

8 Thine hand shall find out all thin enemies: thy right hand shall find ou those that hate thee.

9 Thou shalt make them as [d]a fier oven in the time of thine anger: th LORD shall swallow them up in h wrath, and the fire shall devour them

10 Their fruit shalt thou destroy fro the earth, and their seed from amon the children of men.

11 For they intended evil agains thee: they imagined a mischievous de vice, *which* they are not able *to per form*.

12 Therefore [3]shalt thou make ther turn their [4]back, *when* thou sha make ready *thine arrows* upon th strings against the face of them.

13 Be thou exalted, LORD, in thin own strength: *so* will we sing [e]an praise thy power.

PSALM 22

To the chief Musician upon [1]Aijeleth Shahar, A Psalm of David.

MY [a]God, my God, why hast tho forsaken me? *why art thou so* fa [2]from helping me *and from* [b]the word of my roaring?

2 O my God, I cry in the daytime but thou hearest not; and in the nigh season, and [3]am not silent.

3 But thou *art* [c]holy, *O thou* that inhabitest the praises of Israel.

4 Our fathers trusted in thee: they trusted, and thou didst deliver them.

5 They cried unto thee, and were delivered: they trusted in thee, and were not confounded.

6 But I *am* a worm, and no man; a [d]reproach of men, and despised of the people.

7 All [e]they that see me laugh me to scorn: they [4]shoot out the lip, they shake the head, *saying*,

8 [5]He trusted on the LORD *that* he

---

d Neh. 9.13. Rom. 7.12.
5 truth.
e Pro. 6.22, 23.
6 Or, much.
7 my rock.
f Isa. 44.6.

PSALM 20
a Isa. 50.10.
1 set thee on an high place.
2 thy help.
3 support thee.
4 turn to ashes: or, make fat.
b 1 John 5. 14,15.
c Isa. 12.1,2.
d 1 Sam. 17. 45.
5 from the heaven of his holiness.
6 by the strength of the salvation of his right hand.
e Judg. 7.7.

PSALM 21
a John 11.42.
b 2 Sam. 7.19.
1 set him to be blessings.
2 gladded him with joy.
c Ps. 91.2.
d Deut. 32. 22.
3 Or, thou shalt set them as a butt.
4 shoulder.
e Rev. 15.3,4.

PSALM 22
1 Or, the hind of the morning.
a Matt. 27. 46.
2 from my salvation.
b Heb. 5.7.
3 there is no silence to me.
c Isa. 6.3. Rev. 4.8.
d Isa. 53.3.
e Matt. 9.24. Mark 15.20. Luke 16.14.
4 open.
5 He rolled himself on the LORD.

would deliver him: let him deliver
him, [6]seeing he delighted in him.
9 But thou *art* he that took me out of
the womb: thou [7]didst make me hope
when I was upon my mother's breasts.
10 I was cast upon thee from the
womb: thou *art* my God from my
mother's belly.
11 Be not far from me; for trouble *is*
near; for *there is* [8]none to help.
12 Many bulls have compassed me:
strong *bulls* of Bā-shăn have beset me
round.
13 They [9]gaped upon [f]me *with* their
mouths, *as* a ravening and a roaring
lion.
14 I am poured out like water, and
all my bones are [10]out of joint: my
heart is like wax; it is melted in the
midst of my bowels.
15 My [g]strength is dried up like a
potsherd; and my tongue cleaveth to
my jaws; and thou hast brought me
into the dust of death.
16 For dogs have compassed me:
the assembly of the wicked have inclosed me: they [h]pierced my hands
and my feet.
17 I may tell all my bones: they look
and stare upon me.
18 They [i]part my garments among
them, and cast lots upon my vesture.
19 But be not thou far from me, O
LORD: O my strength, haste thee to
help me.
20 Deliver my soul from the sword;
[11]my darling [12]from the power of the
dog.
21 Save [j]me from the lion's mouth
for thou hast heard me from the horns
of the unicorns.
22 I will declare thy name unto my
[k]brethren: in the midst of the congregation will I praise thee.
23 Ye that fear the LORD, praise him;
all ye the seed of Jacob, glorify him;
and fear him, all ye the seed of Israel.
24 For he hath not despised nor abhorred the affliction of the afflicted;
neither hath he hid his face from him;
but when he cried unto him, he heard.
25 My praise *shall be* of thee in the
great congregation: I will pay my
vows before them that fear him.
26 The [l]meek shall eat and be satisfied: they shall praise the LORD that
seek him: your [m]heart shall live for
ever.
27 All [n]the ends of the world shall remember and turn unto the LORD: and
all the kindreds of the nations shall
worship before thee.
28 For [o]the kingdom *is* the LORD's:
and he *is* the governor among the
nations.
29 All *they that be* fat upon earth
shall eat and worship: [p]all they that
go down to the dust shall bow before
him: and none can keep alive his own
soul.
30 A seed shall serve him; it shall be
accounted to the Lord for a generation.
31 They shall come, and shall declare his righteousness unto a people
that shall be born, that he hath done
this.

PSALM 23

A Psalm of David.

THE LORD *is* [a]my shepherd; I shall
not want.
2 He maketh me to lie down in [1]green
pastures: [b]he leadeth me beside the
[2]still waters.
3 He restoreth my soul: he leadeth
me in the paths of righteousness for
his name's sake.
4 Yea, though I walk through the
valley of the shadow of death, I will
fear no evil: for [c]thou *art* with me;
thy rod and thy staff they comfort me.
5 Thou preparest a table before me
in the presence of mine enemies: thou
[3]anointest my head with oil; my cup
runneth over.
6 Surely goodness and mercy shall
follow me all the days of my life: and
I will [d]dwell in the house of the LORD
[4]for ever.

PSALM 24

A Psalm of David.

THE [a]earth *is* the LORD's, and the
fulness thereof; the world, and
they that dwell therein.
2 For he hath founded it upon the
seas, and established it upon the
floods.
3 Who shall ascend into the hill of
the LORD? or who shall stand in his
holy place?
4 [1]He that hath clean hands, and a
[b]pure heart; who hath not lifted up
his soul unto vanity, nor sworn deceitfully.
5 He shall receive the blessing from
the LORD, and righteousness from the
God of his salvation.
6 This *is* the generation of them that
seek him, that seek thy face, [2]O Jacob.
Sē-lăh.
7 Lift up your heads, O ye gates; and
be ye lift up, ye everlasting doors;
[c]and the King of glory shall come in.
8 Who *is* this King of glory? The
LORD strong and mighty, the LORD
mighty in battle.

6 Or, if he delight in him.
7 Or, keptest me in safety.
8 not a helper.
9 opened their mouths against me.
f Ps. 35.21. 1 Pet. 5.8.
10 Or, sundered.
g Pro. 17.22.
h Zech. 12. 10. Luke 23.33. John 20.27.
i Matt. 27.35. Mark 15.24. Luke 23.34.
11 my only one.
12 from the hand.
j 2 Tim. 4.17.
k John 20.17.
l John 6.57.
m John 6.51.
n Ps. 2.8.
o Ps. 47.7-9. Zech. 14.9. Matt. 6.13.
p Isa. 26.19.

PSALM 23

a John 10.11. 1 Pet. 2.25.
1 pastures of tender grass.
b Eze. 34.14.
2 waters of quietness.
c Ps. 46.11. Isa. 8.10. Zech. 8.23. Matt. 1.23. Acts 18.9, 10.
3 makest fat.
d 2 Cor. 5.1.
4 to length of days.

PSALM 24

a Ex. 9.29. Job 41.11.
1 The clean of hands.
b Matt. 5.8.
2 Or, O God of Jacob.
c Hag. 2.7. Mal. 3.1. 1 Cor. 2.8.

9 Lift up your heads, O ye gates; even lift *them* up, ye everlasting doors; and the King of glory shall come in.

10 Who is this King of glory? The LORD of hosts, he *is* the King of glory. Sē'lāh.

PSALM 25

A Psalm of David.

UNTO [a]thee, O LORD, do I lift up my soul.

2 O my God, I [b]trust in thee: let me not be ashamed, let not mine enemies triumph over me.

3 Yea, let none that wait on thee be ashamed: let them be ashamed which transgress without cause.

4 Shew [c]me thy ways, O LORD; teach me thy paths.

5 Lead me in thy truth, and teach me: for thou *art* the God of my salvation; on thee do I wait all the day.

6 Remember, O LORD, [1]thy tender mercies and thy lovingkindnesses; for they *have been* ever of old.

7 Remember not the sins of my youth, nor my transgressions: [d]according to thy mercy remember thou me for thy goodness' sake, O LORD.

8 Good and upright *is* the LORD: therefore will he teach sinners in the way.

9 The meek will he guide in judgment: and the meek will he teach his way.

10 All the paths of the LORD *are* mercy and truth unto such as keep his covenant and his testimonies.

11 For [e]thy name's sake, O LORD, pardon mine iniquity; [f]for it *is* great.

12 What man *is* he that feareth the LORD? him [g]shall he teach in the way *that* he shall choose.

13 His soul [2]shall dwell at ease; and his [h]seed shall inherit the earth.

14 The [i]secret of the LORD *is* with them that fear him; [3]and he will shew them his covenant.

15 Mine [j]eyes *are* ever toward the LORD; for he shall [4]pluck my feet out of the net.

16 Turn [k]thee unto me, and have mercy upon me; for I *am* desolate and afflicted.

17 The troubles of my heart are enlarged: *O* bring thou me out of my distresses.

18 Look [l]upon mine affliction and my pain; and forgive all my sins.

19 Consider mine enemies; for they are many; and they hate me with [5]cruel hatred.

20 O keep my soul, and deliver me: let me not be ashamed; for I put my trust in thee.

21 Let integrity and uprightness preserve me; for I wait on thee.

22 Redeem [m]Israel, O God, out of all his troubles.

PSALM 25

a 1 Sam. 1.15. Ps. 86.4. Lam. 3.41.
b Ps. 7.1. Ps. 18.2. Rom. 10.11.
c Ex. 33.13. Ps. 143.8. Pro. 8.20.
1 thy bowels.
d Ps. 51.1.
e Ps. 31.3. Ps. 79.9.
f Rom. 5.20.
g Ps. 37.23.
2 shall lodge in goodness.
h Ps. 37.11, 22,29.
i Pro. 3.32. John 7.17. 2 Cor. 4.2-6.
3 Or, and his covenant to make them know it.
j Ps. 141.8.
4 bring forth.
k Ps. 69.16.
l 2 Sam. 16. 12.
5 hatred of violence.
m Ps. 130.8.

PSALM 26

a Ps. 7.8.
b Ps. 28.7. Pro. 29.25.
c Ps. 1.1. Jer. 15.17.
d Ps. 1.1. Ps. 5.5. Ps. 15.4. Ps. 31.6.
e Ex. 30.19. Ps. 73.13. 1 Tim. 2.8.
1 of the tabernacle of thy honour.
2 Or, Take not away.
3 men of blood.
4 filled with.

PSALM 27

1 approached against me.
2 Or, the delight.
a Pro. 18.10. Isa. 4.6. Col. 3.3.

PSALM 26

A Psalm of David.

JUDGE [a]me, O LORD; for I have walked in mine integrity: [b]I have trusted also in the LORD; *therefore* I shall not slide.

2 Examine me, O LORD, and prove me; try my reins and my heart.

3 For thy lovingkindness *is* before mine eyes: and I have walked in thy truth.

4 I [c]have not sat with vain persons, neither will I go in with dissemblers.

5 I have [d]hated the congregation of evil doers; and will not sit with the wicked.

6 I [e]will wash mine hands in innocency: so will I compass thine altar, O LORD:

7 That I may publish with the voice of thanksgiving, and tell of all thy wondrous works.

8 LORD, I have loved the habitation of thy house, and the place [1]where thine honour dwelleth.

9 [2]Gather not my soul with sinners, nor my life with [3]bloody men:

10 In whose hands *is* mischief, and their right hand is [4]full of bribes.

11 But as for me, I will walk in mine integrity: redeem me, and be merciful unto me.

12 My foot standeth in an even place: in the congregations will I bless the LORD.

PSALM 27

A Psalm of David.

THE LORD *is* my light and my salvation; whom shall I fear? the LORD *is* the strength of my life; of whom shall I be afraid?

2 When the wicked, *even* mine enemies and my foes, [1]came upon me to eat up my flesh, they stumbled and fell.

3 Though an host should encamp against me, my heart shall not fear: though war should rise against me, in this *will* I *be* confident.

4 One *thing* have I desired of the LORD, that will I seek after; that I may dwell in the house of the LORD all the days of my life, to behold [2]the beauty of the LORD, and to inquire in his temple.

5 For [a]in the time of trouble he shall

hide me in his pavilion: in the secret
of his tabernacle shall he hide me; he
shall set me up upon a rock.
6 And now shall mine head be lifted
up above mine enemies round about
me: therefore will I offer in his tabernacle sacrifices [3]of joy; I will sing, yea,
I will sing praises unto the LORD.
7 Hear, O LORD, *when* I cry with my
voice: have mercy also upon me, and
answer me.
8 [4]*When thou saidst*, Seek ye my face;
my heart said unto thee, Thy face,
LORD, will I seek.
9 Hide not thy face *far* from me; put
not thy servant away in anger: thou
hast been my help; leave me not,
neither forsake me, O God of my salvation.
10 When my father and [b]my mother
forsake me, then the LORD [5]will take
me up.
11 Teach me thy way, O LORD, and
lead me in [6]a plain path, because of
[7]mine enemies.
12 Deliver me not over unto the will
of mine enemies: for [c]false witnesses
are risen up against me, and such as
breathe out cruelty.
13 *I had fainted*, [d]unless I had believed to see the goodness of the LORD
in the land of the living.
14 Wait [e]on the LORD: be of good
courage, and he shall strengthen thine
heart: wait, I say, on the LORD.

PSALM 28

A Psalm of David.

UNTO thee will I cry, O LORD my
rock; be not silent [1]to me: lest, *if*
thou be silent to me, I become like
them that go down into the pit.
2 Hear the voice of my supplications, when I cry unto thee, when I
lift up my hands [2]toward thy holy
oracle.
3 Draw me not away with the wicked,
and with the workers of iniquity,
which speak peace to their neighbours, but mischief *is* in their hearts.
4 Give [a]them according to their
deeds, and according to the wickedness of their endeavours: give them
after the work of their hands; render
to them their desert.
5 Because they regard not the works
of the LORD, nor the operation of his
hands, he shall destroy them, and not
build them up.
6 Blessed *be* the LORD, because he
hath heard the voice of my supplications.
7 The LORD *is* [b]my strength and my
shield; my heart trusted in him, and
I am helped: therefore my heart
greatly rejoiceth; and with my song
will I praise him.
8 The LORD *is* [3]their strength, and he
is the [4]saving strength of his anointed.
9 Save thy people, and bless thine
inheritance: [5]feed them also, and lift
them up for ever.

PSALM 29

A Psalm of David.

GIVE [a]unto the LORD, O [1]ye
mighty, give unto the LORD glory
and strength.
2 Give unto the LORD [2]the glory due
unto his name; worship the LORD [3]in
the beauty of holiness.
3 The voice of the LORD *is* upon the
waters: the God of glory thundereth:
the LORD *is* upon [4]many waters.
4 The voice of the LORD *is* [5]powerful;
the voice of the LORD *is* [6]full of
majesty.
5 The voice of the LORD breaketh
the cedars; yea, the LORD breaketh
the cedars of Lĕb-ā-nọn.
6 He maketh them also to [b]skip like
a calf; Lĕb-ā-nọn and [c]Sĭr-ĭ-ọn like a
young unicorn.
7 The voice of the LORD [7]divideth
the flames of fire.
8 The voice of the LORD shaketh the
wilderness; the LORD shaketh the
wilderness of [d]Kā-dĕsh.
9 The voice of the LORD maketh the
hinds [8]to calve, and discovereth the
forests: and in his temple [9]doth every
one speak of *his* glory.
10 The LORD sitteth [e]upon the flood;
yea, the LORD sitteth King for
ever.
11 The LORD will [f]give strength unto
his people; the LORD will bless his
people with peace.

PSALM 30

A Psalm *and* Song *at* the dedication of
the house of David.

I WILL extol thee, O LORD; for thou
hast lifted me up, and hast not made
my foes to rejoice over me.
2 O LORD my God, I [a]cried unto
thee, and thou hast healed me.
3 O LORD, [b]thou hast brought up my
soul from the grave: thou hast kept
me alive, that I should not go down
to the pit.
4 Sing unto the LORD, O ye saints of
his, and give thanks [1]at the remembrance of his holiness.
5 For [2]his anger *endureth but* a moment; [c]in his favour *is* life: weeping

3 of shouting.
4 Or, My heart said unto thee, Let my face seek thy face.
b Isa. 49.15. John 16.32. 2 Tim. 4.16, 18.
5 will gather me.
6 a way of plainness.
7 those which observe me.
c 1 Sam. 22.9. Matt. 26.59, 60.
d Ps. 112.7,8.
e Ps. 62.1,5. Isa. 25.9. Hab. 2.3.

PSALM 28
1 from me.
2 Or, toward the oracle of thy sanctuary.
a 2 Tim. 4.14.
b Ps. 18.2.
3 Or, his strength.
4 strength of salvations.
5 Or, rule.

PSALM 29
a 1 Chr. 16. 28,29.
1 ye sons of the mighty.
2 the honour of his name.
3 Or, in his glorious sanctuary.
4 Or, great.
5 in power.
6 in majesty.
b Ps. 114.4.
c Deut. 3.9.
7 cutteth out.
d Num. 13. 26.
8 Or, to be in pain, and so bring forth.
9 Or, every whit of it uttereth, etc.
e Ps. 93.4.
f Isa. 40.29.

PSALM 30
a Ps. 6.2-4.
b Ps. 40.1,2.
1 Or, to the memorial.
2 there is but a moment in his anger.
c Ps. 16.11. Rev. 22.17.

may endure [3]for a night, but [4]joy *com-*
eth in the morning.
6 And in my [d]prosperity I said, I shall
never be moved.
7 LORD, by thy favour thou hast
[5]made my mountain to stand strong:
thou [e]didst hide thy face, *and* I was
troubled.
8 I cried to thee, O LORD; and unto
the LORD I made supplication.
9 What profit *is there* in my blood,
when I go down to the pit? [f]Shall the
dust praise thee? shall it declare thy
truth?
10 Hear, O LORD, [g]and have mercy
upon me: LORD, be thou my helper.
11 Thou hast turned for me my
mourning [h]into dancing: thou hast
put off my sackcloth, and girded me
with gladness;
12 To the end that [6]*my* glory may
sing praise to thee, and not be silent.
O LORD my God, I will give thanks
unto thee for ever.

PSALM 31

To the chief Musician, A Psalm of David.

IN thee, O LORD, do I put my trust;
let me never be ashamed: deliver me
in thy righteousness.
2 Bow [a]down thine ear to me; deliver
me speedily: be thou [1]my strong rock,
for an house of defence to save me.
3 For thou *art* my rock and my fortress; therefore [b]for thy name's sake
lead me, and guide me.
4 Pull me out of the net that they
have laid privily for me: for thou *art*
my strength.
5 Into [c]thine hand I commit my
spirit: thou hast redeemed me, O
LORD [d]God of truth.
6 I have hated them that regard lying
vanities: but I trust in the LORD.
7 I will be glad and rejoice in thy
mercy: for thou hast considered my
trouble; thou hast [e]known my soul in
adversities;
8 And hast not shut me up into the
hand of the enemy: [f]thou hast set my
feet in a large room.
9 Have mercy upon me, O LORD, for
I am in trouble: mine eye is consumed
with grief, *yea*, my soul and my belly.
10 For my life is spent with grief, and
my years with sighing: my strength
faileth because of mine iniquity, and
my bones are consumed.
11 I was a reproach among all mine
enemies, but [g]especially among my
neighbours, and a fear to mine acquaintance: they that did see me
without fled from me.

3 in the evening.
4 singing.
d Job 29.18.
5 settled strength for my mountain.
e Ps. 104.29.
f Ps. 115.17.
g Ps. 4.1.
h 2 Sam. 6.14.
6 That is, my tongue, or, my soul.

PSALM 31

a Ps. 71.2. Pro. 22.17.
1 to me for a rock of strength.
b Ps. 23.3. Jer. 14.7.
c Luke 23.46. Acts 7.59. 2 Tim. 1.12.
d Heb. 6.18.
e John 10.27.
f Ps. 18.19.
g Ps. 88.8.
2 a vessel that perisheth.
h Jer. 20.3. Lam. 2.22.
i Matt. 27.1.
j Num. 6.25. Ps. 4.6. Dan. 9.17.
k Ps. 25.2.
3 Or, let them be cut off for the grave.
l Ps. 12.3.
4 a hard thing.
m Isa. 64.4. 1 Cor. 2.9.
n Ps. 27.5.
o Job 5.21.
5 Or, fenced city.
p 1 Pet. 1.5.

PSALM 32

1 Or, giving instruction.
a Ps. 85.2. Rom. 4.6.
b Lev. 17.4. Rom. 5.13.
c John 1.47. 2 Cor. 1.12.
d Pro. 28.13. Isa. 65.24. Luke 15.18.

12 I am forgotten as a dead man out
of mind: I am like [2]a broken vessel.
13 For I have heard the slander of
many: fear [h]*was* on every side: while
they [i]took counsel together against
me, they devised to take away my life.
14 But I trusted in thee, O LORD: I
said, Thou *art* my God.
15 My times *are* in thy hand: deliver
me from the hand of mine enemies,
and from them that persecute me.
16 Make [j]thy face to shine upon thy
servant: save me for thy mercies' sake.
17 Let [k]me not be ashamed, O LORD;
for I have called upon thee: let the
wicked be ashamed, *and* [3]let them be
silent in the grave.
18 Let [l]the lying lips be put to silence;
which speak [4]grievous things proudly
and contemptuously against the righteous.
19 *Oh* [m]how great *is* thy goodness,
which thou hast laid up for them that
fear thee; *which* thou hast wrought
for them that trust in thee before the
sons of men!
20 Thou [n]shalt hide them in the secret of thy presence from the pride of
man: [o]thou shalt keep them secretly
in a pavilion from the strife of tongues.
21 Blessed *be* the LORD: for he hath
shewed me his marvellous kindness
in a [5]strong city.
22 For I said in my haste, I am cut
off from before thine eyes: nevertheless thou heardest the voice of my
supplications when I cried unto thee.
23 O love the LORD, all ye his saints:
for the LORD [p]preserveth the faithful,
and plentifully rewardeth the proud
doer.
24 Be of good courage, and he shall
strengthen your heart, all ye that hope
in the LORD.

PSALM 32

A Psalm of David, [1]Maschil.

BLESSED *is he whose* [a]transgres-
sion *is* forgiven, *whose* sin *is* covered.
2 Blessed *is* the man unto whom the
LORD [b]imputeth not iniquity, and [c]in
whose spirit *there is* no guile.
3 When I kept silence, my bones
waxed old through my roaring all the
day long.
4 For day and night thy hand was
heavy upon me: my moisture is turned into the drought of summer. Sē-lāh.
5 I acknowledged my sin unto thee,
and mine iniquity have I not hid. I
[d]said, I will confess my transgressions unto the LORD; and thou for-

vest the iniquity of my sin. Sē-läh.
For [e]this shall every one that is
dly pray [f]unto thee [2]in a time when
u mayest be found: surely in the
ods of great waters they shall not
ne nigh unto him.
Thou [g]*art* my hiding place; thou
lt preserve me from trouble; thou
lt compass me about with songs
deliverance. Sē-läh.
I will [h]instruct thee and teach thee
he way which thou shalt go: [3]I will
de thee with mine eye.
Be ye not as the horse, *or* as the
le, *which* have no understanding:
ose mouth must be held in with
and bridle, lest they come near un-
thee.
Many [i]sorrows *shall be* to the
ked: but [j]he that trusteth in the
RD, mercy shall compass him
out.
Be glad in the LORD, and rejoice,
righteous: and shout for joy, all *ye*
t are upright in heart.

PSALM 33

EJOICE in the LORD, O ye righteous: *for* praise is comely for the
right.
Praise the LORD with harp: sing
to him with the psaltery *and* an in-
ument of ten strings.
Sing [a]unto him a new song; play
fully with a loud noise.
For the word of the LORD *is* right;
d all his works *are done* in truth.
He loveth righteousness and judg-
nt: the earth is full of the [1]good-
ss of the LORD.
By the [b]word of the LORD were the
vens made; and all the host of
m by [c]the breath of his mouth.
He gathereth the waters of the sea
gether as an heap: he layeth up the
pth in storehouses.
Let all the earth fear the LORD: let
the inhabitants of the world stand
awe of him.
For [d]he spake, and it was *done;* he
mmanded, and it stood fast.
The LORD [2]bringeth the counsel
the heathen to nought: he maketh
devices of the people of none
ect.
The [e]counsel of the LORD stand-
for ever, the thoughts of his heart
all generations.
Blessed *is* the nation whose God
he LORD; *and* the people *whom* he
th chosen for his own inheritance.
The [f]LORD looketh from heaven;
beholdeth all the sons of men.

e 1 Tim. 1.16. *f* Isa. 55.6. John 7.34. 2 in a time of finding. *g* Ps. 9.9. Pro. 18.10. Isa. 4.6. Matt. 23.37. Col. 3.3. *h* Isa. 48.17. 3 I will counsel thee, mine eye shall be upon thee. *i* Pro. 13.21. *j* Ps. 34.8. Pro. 16.20. Jer. 17.7.

PSALM 33

a Isa. 42.10. 1 Or, mercy. *b* John 1.1-3. Heb. 11.3. *c* Job 26.13. *d* Gen. 1.3. 2 maketh frustrate. *e* Job 23.13. Pro. 19.21. Eze. 38.10. Acts 4.27, 28. 3 to generation and generation. *f* 2 Chr. 16.9. Job 28.24. Ps. 11.4. *g* Isa. 64.8. *h* Job 11.11. Ps. 44.21. Pro. 24.12. Jer. 32.19. Hosea 7.2. *i* Job 36.7. Ps. 34.15.

PSALM 34

1 Or, Achish, 1 Sam. 21. 13. *a* Jer. 9.24. 1 Cor. 1.31. *b* Ps. 18.6. Jonah 2.2. Matt. 7.7. Luke 11.9. 2 Or, They flowed. *c* Ps. 3.4. *d* 2 Sam. 22. 1. *e* Dan. 6.22. *f* Gen. 32.1. 2 Ki. 6.17. *g* Phil. 4.19. *h* 1 Pet. 3.10.

14 From the place of his habitation
he looketh upon all the inhabitants of
the earth.
15 He [g]fashioneth their hearts alike;
[h]he considereth all their works.
16 There is no king saved by the
multitude of an host: a mighty man
is not delivered by much strength.
17 An horse *is* a vain thing for safety:
neither shall he deliver *any* by his
great strength.
18 Behold, [i]the eye of the LORD *is*
upon them that fear him, upon them
that hope in his mercy;
19 To deliver their soul from death,
and to keep them alive in famine.
20 Our soul waiteth for the LORD:
he *is* our help and our shield.
21 For our heart shall rejoice in him,
because we have trusted in his holy
name.
22 Let thy mercy, O LORD, be upon
us, according as we hope in thee.

PSALM 34

A Psalm of David, when he changed his behaviour before [1]Abimelech; who drove him away, and he departed.

I WILL bless the LORD at all times:
his praise *shall* continually *be* in my
mouth.
2 My soul shall make her [a]boast in
the LORD: the humble shall hear
thereof, and be glad.
3 O magnify the LORD with me, and
let us exalt his name together.
4 I [b]sought the LORD, and he heard
me, and delivered me from all my
fears.
5 [2]They looked unto him, and were
lightened: and their faces were not
ashamed.
6 This [c]poor man cried, and the LORD
heard *him*, and [d]saved him out of all
his troubles.
7 The [e]angel of the LORD encampeth
[f]round about them that fear him, and
delivereth them.
8 O taste and see that the LORD *is*
good: blessed *is* the man *that* trusteth
in him.
9 O fear the LORD, ye his saints: for
there is [g]no want to them that fear
him.
10 The young lions do lack, and suffer hunger: but they that seek the
LORD shall not want any good *thing*.
11 Come, ye children, hearken unto
me: I will teach you the fear of the
LORD.
12 What [h]man *is he that* desireth
life, *and* loveth *many* days, that he
may see good?

13 Keep thy tongue from evil, and
thy lips from [i]speaking guile.
14 Depart from evil, and do good;
seek peace, and pursue it.
15 The [j]eyes of the LORD *are* upon
the righteous, and his ears *are open*
unto their cry.
16 The [k]face of the LORD *is* against
them that do evil, [l]to cut off the remembrance of them from the earth.
17 *The righteous* cry, and the LORD
heareth, and delivereth them out of
all their troubles.
18 The LORD *is* nigh [3]unto them that
are of a broken heart; and saveth such
as be [4]of a contrite spirit.
19 Many *are* the afflictions of the
righteous: but the LORD delivereth
him out of them all.
20 He keepeth all his bones: [m]not
one of them is broken.
21 Evil [n]shall slay the wicked: and
they that hate the righteous [5]shall be
desolate.
22 The LORD [o]redeemeth the soul of
his servants: and none of them that
trust in him shall be desolate.

PSALM 35

A Psalm of David.

PLEAD *my cause,* O LORD, with
them that strive with me: fight
against them that fight against me.
2 Take hold of shield and buckler,
and stand up for mine help.
3 Draw out also the spear, and stop
the way against them that persecute
me: say unto my soul, I *am* thy salvation.
4 Let them be confounded and put
to shame that seek after my soul: let
them be turned back and brought to
confusion that devise my hurt.
5 Let them be as chaff before the
wind: and let the angel of the LORD
chase *them.*
6 Let their way be [1]dark and slippery: and let the angel of the LORD
persecute them.
7 For without cause have they hid
for me their net *in* a pit, *which* without
cause they have digged for my soul.
8 Let [a]destruction come upon him
[2]at unawares; and [b]let his net that he
hath hid catch himself: into that very
destruction let him fall.
9 And my soul shall be joyful in the
LORD: it [c]shall rejoice in his salvation.
10 All my bones shall say, LORD,
who [d]*is* like unto thee, which deliverest the poor from him that is too
strong for him, yea, the poor and the
needy from him that spoileth him?

i 1 Pet. 2.22.
j Job 36.7.
k Lev. 17.10. Jer. 44.11.
l Pro. 10.7.
3 to the broken of heart.
4 contrite of spirit.
m John 19. 36.
n Ps. 94.23.
5 Or, shall be guilty.
o 2 Sam. 4.9. Ps. 103.4.

PSALM 35

1 darkness and slipperiness.
a 1 Thes. 5.3.
2 which he knoweth not of.
b Ps. 7.15. Pro. 5.22.
c 1 Sam. 2.1. Ps. 13.5. Isa. 61.10. Heb. 3.18.
d Ps. 71.19.
3 Witnesses of wrong.
4 they asked me.
5 depriving.
6 Or, afflicted.
7 walked.
8 as a friend, as a brother to me.
9 halting.
10 my only one.
11 strong.
12 falsely.
e Ex. 3.7.
f Ps. 7.8. Ps. 26.1. 2 Thes. 1.6.
13 Ah, ah, our soul.
14 my righteousness.

11 [3]False witnesses did rise up; [4]th
laid to my charge *things* that I kn
not.
12 They rewarded me evil for go
to the [5]spoiling of my soul.
13 But as for me, when they w
sick, my clothing *was* sackcloth
[6]humbled my soul with fasting; a
my prayer returned into mine o
bosom.
14 I [7]behaved myself [8]as though
had been my friend *or* brother: I bo
ed down heavily, as one that mou
eth *for his* mother.
15 But in mine [9]adversity they
joiced, and gathered themselves
gether: *yea,* the abjects gathered the
selves together against me, and
knew *it* not; they did tear *me,* a
ceased not:
16 With hypocritical mockers
feasts, they gnashed upon me w
their teeth.
17 Lord, how long wilt thou look o
rescue my soul from their destr
tions, [10]my darling from the lions.
18 I will give thee thanks in the gr
congregation: I will praise thee amo
[11]much people.
19 Let not them that are mine e
mies [12]wrongfully rejoice over m
neither let them wink with the e
that hate me without a cause.
20 For they speak not peace: b
they devise deceitful matters agai
them that are quiet in the land.
21 Yea, they opened their mo
wide against me, *and* said, Aha, a
our eye hath seen *it.*
22 *This* thou hast [e]seen, O LOR
keep not silence: O Lord, be not
from me.
23 Stir up thyself, and awake to
judgment, *even* unto my cause,
God and my Lord.
24 Judge me, O LORD my God,
cording [f]to thy righteousness; and
them not rejoice over me.
25 Let them not say in their hear
[13]Ah, so would we have it: let th
not say, We have swallowed him
26 Let them be ashamed and brou
to confusion together that rejoice
mine hurt: let them be clothed w
shame and dishonour that magn
themselves against me.
27 Let them shout for joy, and
glad, that favour [14]my righte
cause: yea, let them say continua
Let the LORD be magnified, wh
hath pleasure in the prosperity of
servant.
28 And my tongue shall speak of

hteousness *and* of thy praise all the
y long.

PSALM 36

To the chief Musician, *A Psalm* of David the servant of the LORD.

THE transgression of the wicked
saith within my heart, [a]*that there*
no fear of God before his eyes.
For he flattereth himself in his own
es, [1]until his iniquity be found to be
teful.
The words of his mouth *are* iniquity
d deceit: [b]he hath left off to be wise,
d to do good.
He [c]deviseth [2]mischief upon his
d; he setteth himself [d]in a way *that*
not good; he abhorreth not evil.
Thy [e]mercy, O LORD, *is* in the heav-
s; *and* thy faithfulness *reacheth* unto
e clouds.
Thy righteousness *is* like [3]the great
ountains; [f]thy judgments *are* a great
ep: O LORD, [g]thou preservest man
d beast.
How [4]excellent *is* thy lovingkind-
ss, O God! therefore the children
men [h]put their trust under the
adow of thy wings.
They shall be [5]abundantly satisfied
th the fatness of thy house; and
ou shalt make them drink [i]of the
er of thy pleasures.
For [j]with thee *is* the fountain of
e: in thy [k]light shall we see light.
) O [6]continue thy lovingkindness
to them that [l]know thee; and
y righteousness to the upright in
art.
Let not the foot of pride come
ainst me, and let not the hand of
e wicked remove me.
2 There are the workers of iniquity
len: they are cast down, and shall
t be able to rise.

PSALM 37

A Psalm of David.

RET not thyself because of evildoers, neither be thou envious
ainst the workers of iniquity.
For they shall soon be cut down
e the grass, and wither as the green
rb.
Trust in the LORD, and do good; *so*
alt thou dwell in the land, and [1]verily
ou shalt be fed.
Delight [a]thyself also in the LORD;
d he shall give thee the desires of
ine heart.
[2]Commit thy way unto the LORD;
ust also in him; and he shall bring *it*
pass.
And [b]he shall bring forth thy righteousness as the light, and thy judgment as the noonday.
7 [3]Rest in the LORD, and wait
patiently for him: fret not thyself because of him who prospereth in his
way, because of the man who bringeth
wicked devices to pass.
8 Cease from anger, and forsake
wrath: fret [c]not thyself in any wise to
do evil.
9 For evildoers shall be cut off: but
those that wait upon the LORD, they
shall inherit the earth.
10 For yet a little while, and the
wicked *shall* not *be:* yea, thou shalt
diligently consider his place, and it
shall not *be*.
11 But the meek shall inherit the
earth; and shall delight themselves
in the abundance of peace.
12 The wicked [4]plotteth against the
just, and gnasheth upon him with his
teeth.
13 The LORD shall laugh at him: for
he seeth that [d]his day is coming.
14 The wicked have drawn out the
sword, and have bent their bow, to
cast down the poor and needy, *and* to
slay [5]such as be of upright conversation.
15 Their sword shall enter into their
own heart, and their bows shall be
broken.
16 A [e]little that a righteous man hath
is better than the riches of many
wicked.
17 For the arms of the wicked shall
be broken: but the LORD upholdeth
the righteous.
18 The LORD [f]knoweth the days of
the upright: and their inheritance
shall be [g]for ever.
19 They shall not be ashamed in the
evil time: and [h]in the days of famine
they shall be satisfied.
20 But the wicked shall perish, and
the enemies of the LORD *shall be* as
[6]the fat of lambs: they shall consume;
into smoke shall they consume away.
21 The wicked borroweth, and pay-
eth not again: but the righteous
sheweth mercy, and giveth.
22 For [i]*such as be* blessed of him
shall inherit the earth; and *they that*
be cursed of him shall be cut off.
23 The [j]steps of a *good* man are
[7]ordered by the LORD: and he delighteth in his way.
24 Though [k]he fall, he shall not be
utterly cast down: for the LORD upholdeth *him with* his hand.
25 I have been young, and *now* am
old; yet have I not seen the right-

PSALM 36
a Gen. 20.11. Pro. 8.13. Eccl. 12.3.
1 to find his iniquity to hate.
b Jer. 4.22.
c Micah 2.1.
2 Or, vanity.
d Isa. 65.2.
e Ps. 57.10.
3 the mountains of God.
f Job 11.8. Rom. 11.33.
g Job 7.20. Ps. 145.9.
4 precious.
h Ruth 2.12.
5 watered.
i Job 20.17. Rev. 22.1.
j Isa. 12.3. Jer. 2.13. Zech. 13.1. John 4.10, 14. Rev. 21.6.
k Acts 26.18. Eph. 5.8. Col. 1.13. 1 Pet. 2.9.
6 draw out at length.
l Jer. 22.16.

PSALM 37
1 in truth, or, stableness.
a Job 27.10. Song 2.3. Isa. 58.14. 1 Pet. 1.8.
2 Roll thy way upon the LORD.
b Micah 7.9.
3 Be silent to the LORD.
c Job 5.2. Ps. 73.3. Pro. 14.29. Eph. 4.26. Jas. 1.19.
4 Or, practiseth.
d 1 Sam. 26. 10.
5 the upright of way.
e Pro. 15.16. 1 Tim. 6.6.
f Ps. 1.6.
g Isa. 60.21.
h Job 5.20.
6 the preciousness of lambs.
i Pro. 3.33.
j Ps. 121.3. Pro. 16.9.
7 Or, established.
k Micah 7.8. 2 Cor. 4.9.

eous forsaken, nor his seed begging
bread.
26 *He is* [8]ever merciful, and lendeth;
and his seed *is* blessed.
27 Depart from evil, and do good;
and dwell for evermore.
28 For the LORD [l]loveth judgment,
and forsaketh not his saints; they are
preserved for ever: but the seed of the
wicked shall be cut off.
29 The righteous shall inherit the
land, and dwell therein for ever.
30 The mouth of the righteous
speaketh wisdom, and his tongue
talketh of judgment.
31 The law of his God *is* in his heart;
none of his [9]steps shall slide.
32 The wicked watcheth the righteous, and seeketh to slay him.
33 The LORD will not leave him in
his hand, nor [m]condemn him when he
is judged.
34 Wait on the LORD, and keep his
way, and he shall exalt thee to inherit
the land: when the wicked are cut off,
thou shalt see *it*.
35 I have seen the wicked in great
power, and spreading himself like [10]a
green bay tree.
36 Yet he passed away, and, lo, he
was not: yea, I sought him, but he
could not be found.
37 Mark the perfect *man*, and behold the upright: for [n]the end of *that*
man *is* peace.
38 But the transgressors shall be destroyed together: the end of the
wicked shall be cut off.
39 But [o]the salvation of the righteous *is* of the LORD: *he is* their strength
in the time of trouble.
40 And the LORD shall help them,
and deliver them: he shall deliver
them from the wicked, and save them,
[p]because they trust in him.

PSALM 38

A Psalm of David, to bring to remembrance.

O LORD, rebuke me not in thy
wrath: neither chasten me in thy
hot displeasure.
2 For thine arrows stick fast in me,
and thy hand presseth me sore.
3 *There is* no soundness in my flesh
because of thine anger; neither *is there*
any [1]rest in my bones because of my
sin.
4 For mine iniquities are gone over
mine head: as an heavy burden they
are too heavy for me.
5 My wounds stink *and* are corrupt
because of my foolishness.
6 I am [2]troubled; I am bowed down

8 all the day.
l Ps. 11.7.
9 Or, goings.
m Ps. 109.31.
10 Or, a green tree that groweth in his own soil.
n Job 1.1. Isa. 32.17. Luke 2.25-30. Acts 7.59, 60. 1 Thes. 4.17. 2 Tim. 4.6-8. 2 Pet. 1.14.
o Ps. 3.8. Isa. 12.2. Jonah 2.8.
p 1 Chr. 5.20. Dan. 3.17.

PSALM 38

1 peace, or, health.
2 wried.
a Job 7.5.
3 is not with me.
b Luke 10.31.
4 stroke.
5 Or, my neighbours.
6 Or, thee do I wait for.
c Jer. 14.8.
7 Or, answer.
8 for halting.
d Job 31.33. Ps. 32.5. Pro. 28.13.
e 2 Cor. 7.9.
9 being living, are strong.
f 1 Pet. 3.13. 1 John 3.12.
g Ps. 22.1,11.
10 for my help.
h Ex. 15.2. Isa. 12.2.

PSALM 39

a 1 Chr. 16. 41.
b 1 Ki. 2.4. Pro. 4.26,27. Heb. 2.1.
1 a bridle, or, muzzle for my mouth.
c Col. 4.5.
2 troubled.
d Jer. 20.9.
3 Or, what time I have here.

greatly; I go mourning all the
long.
7 For my loins are filled with
loathsome *disease:* and *there is*
soundness in my flesh.
8 I am feeble and sore broken
have roared by reason of the disqui
ness of my heart.
9 Lord, all my desire *is* before th
and my groaning is not hid from th
10 My heart panteth, my stren
faileth me: as for the light of m
eyes, it also [3]is gone from me.
11 My lovers and my [b]friends sta
aloof from my [4]sore; and [5]my ki
men stand afar off.
12 They also that seek after my
lay snares *for me:* and they that s
my hurt speak mischievous thin
and imagine deceits all the day lon
13 But I, as a deaf *man*, heard n
and *I was* as a dumb man *that* open
not his mouth.
14 Thus I was as a man that hear
not, and in whose mouth *are* no
proofs.
15 For [6]in thee, O LORD, [c]do I ho
thou wilt [7]hear, O Lord my God.
16 For I said, *Hear me*, lest *otherw*
they should rejoice over me: when
foot slippeth, they magnify *themsel*
against me.
17 For I *am* ready [8]to halt, and
sorrow *is* continually before me.
18 For I will [d]declare mine iniqui
I will be [e]sorry for my sin.
19 But mine enemies [9]*are* lively,
they are strong: and they that h
me wrongfully are multiplied.
20 They also that render evil
good are mine adversaries; [f]beca
I follow *the thing that* good *is*.
21 Forsake [g]me not, O LORD: O
God, be not far from me.
22 Make haste [10]to help me, O L
[h]my salvation.

PSALM 39

To the chief Musician, *even* to [a]Jeduthun,
A Psalm of David.

I SAID, I will [b]take heed to my wa
that I sin not with my tongue: I
keep [1]my mouth with a bridle, [c]wh
the wicked is before me.
2 I was dumb with silence, I held
peace, *even* from good; and my s
row was [2]stirred.
3 My heart was hot within me, wh
I was musing [d]the fire burned: *t*
spake I with my tongue,
4 LORD, make me to know mine e
and the measure of my days, wha
is; that I may know [3]how frail I *a*

5 Behold, thou hast made my days
s an handbreadth; [e]and mine age *is*
s nothing before thee: verily every
nan [4]at his best state *is* altogether
anity. Sē-läh.
6 Surely every man walketh in [5]a
ain shew: surely they are disquieted
n vain: he heapeth up *riches*, and
noweth not who shall gather them.
7 And now, Lord, what wait I for?
ny hope *is* in thee.
8 Deliver me from all my transgres-
ions: make me not the reproach of
he foolish.
9 I was dumb, I opened not my
nouth; because thou didst *it*.
10 Remove thy stroke away from me:
am consumed by the [6]blow of thine
and.
11 When thou with rebukes dost cor-
ect man for iniquity, thou makest
his beauty to consume away like a
noth: surely every man *is* vanity.
ē-läh.
12 Hear my prayer, O LORD, and
ive ear unto my cry; hold not thy
eace at my tears: [f]for I *am* a stranger
vith thee, *and* a sojourner, as all my
athers *were*.
13 O spare [g]me, that I may recover
trength, before I go hence, and be no
nore.

PSALM 40

To the chief Musician, A Psalm of David.

I WAITED patiently for the LORD;
and he inclined unto me, and heard
ny cry.
2 He brought me up also out of [2]an
orrible pit, out of the miry clay, and
et my feet upon a rock, *and* estab-
ished my goings.
3 And he hath put a new song in my
nouth, *even* praise unto our God:
nany shall see *it*, and fear, and shall
rust in the LORD.
4 Blessed [a] *is* that man that maketh
he LORD his trust, and respecteth not
he proud, nor such as turn aside to
ies.
5 Many, O LORD my God, *are* thy
vonderful works *which* thou hast
lone, [b]and thy thoughts *which are* to
is-ward: [3]they cannot be reckoned up
n order unto thee: *if* I would declare
nd speak *of them*, they are more than
an be numbered.
6 Sacrifice [c]and offering thou didst
ot desire; mine ears hast thou [4]open-
d: burnt offering and sin offering
ast thou not required.
7 Then said I, Lo, I come: in the
olume of the book *it is* [d]written of
ne,

e Ps. 90.4.
4 settled.
5 an image.
6 conflict.
7 that which is to be desired in him to melt away.
f Lev. 25.23. 1 Chr. 29.15.
g Job 10.20, 21.

PSALM 40
1 In waiting I waited.
2 a pit of noise.
a Ps. 2.12.
b Isa. 55.8.
3 Or, none can order them unto thee.
c Hosea 6.6. Matt. 9.13.
4 digged.
d Luke 24.44. John 5.39. Acts 10.43. Heb. 10.7.
e Job 23.12. Jer. 15.16. John 4.34. Rom. 7.22.
5 in the midst of my bowels.
f Ps. 139.2.
g Acts 20.20. Rom. 1.16, 17. Phil. 3.9.
h Ps. 43.3.
i Ps. 38.4.
6 forsaketh.
j Neh. 5.19. Jonah 1.6.

PSALM 41
a Pro. 14.21. Mark 10.21.
1 Or, the weak, or, sick.
2 in the day of evil.
3 Or, do not thou deliver.
4 turn.
b Ps. 6.2.
c Ps. 12.2.

8 I [e]delight to do thy will, O my God:
yea, thy law *is* [5]within my heart.
9 I have preached righteousness in
the great congregation: lo, I have not
refrained my lips, O LORD, [f]thou
knowest.
10 I [g]have not hid thy righteousness
within my heart; I have declared thy
faithfulness and thy salvation: I have
not concealed thy lovingkindness and
thy truth from the great congregation.
11 Withhold not thou thy tender
mercies from me, O LORD: [h]let thy
lovingkindness and thy truth continually preserve me.
12 For innumerable evils have compassed me about: [i]mine iniquities
have taken hold upon me, so that I am
not able to look up; they are more
than the hairs of mine head: therefore
my heart [6]faileth me.
13 Be pleased, O LORD, to deliver
me: O LORD, make haste to help me.
14 Let them be ashamed and confounded together that seek after my
soul to destroy it; let them be driven
backward and put to shame that wish
me evil.
15 Let them be desolate for a reward
of their shame that say unto me, Aha,
aha.
16 Let all those that seek thee rejoice
and be glad in thee: let such as love
thy salvation say continually, The
LORD be magnified.
17 But I *am* poor and needy; [j]*yet* the
Lord thinketh upon me: thou *art* my
help and my deliverer; make no tarrying, O my God.

PSALM 41

To the chief Musician, A Psalm of David.

BLESSED [a]*is* he that considereth
[1]the poor: the LORD will deliver
him [2]in time of trouble.
2 The LORD will preserve him, and
keep him alive; *and* he shall be blessed
upon the earth: and [3]thou wilt not deliver him unto the will of his enemies.
3 The LORD will strengthen him upon the bed of languishing: thou wilt
[4]make all his bed in his sickness.
4 I said, LORD, be merciful unto me:
[b]heal my soul; for I have sinned
against thee.
5 Mine enemies speak evil of me,
When shall he die, and his name
perish?
6 And if he come to see *me*, [c]he
speaketh vanity: his heart gathereth
iniquity to itself; *when* he goeth
abroad, he telleth *it*.
7 All that hate me whisper together

against me: against me do they devise [5]my hurt.

8 [6]An evil disease, *say they*, cleaveth fast unto him: and *now* that he lieth he shall rise up no more.

9 Yea, [7]mine own familiar friend, in whom I trusted, [d]which did eat of my bread, hath [8]lifted up *his* heel against me.

10 But thou, O LORD, be merciful unto me, and raise me up, that I may requite them.

11 By this I know that thou favourest me, because mine enemy doth not triumph over me.

12 And as for me, thou upholdest me in mine integrity, and [e]settest me before thy face for ever.

13 Blessed *be* the LORD God of Israel from everlasting, and to everlasting. Ä-měn, and Ä-měn.

PSALM 42

To the chief Musician, [1]Maschil, for the sons of Korah.

AS the hart [2]panteth after the water brooks, so panteth my soul after thee, O God.

2 My [a]soul thirsteth for God, for the [b]living God: when shall I come and appear before God?

3 My tears have been my meat day and night, while they continually say unto me, Where *is* thy God?

4 When I remember these *things*, I pour out my soul in me: for I had gone with the multitude, [c]I went with them to the house of God, with the voice of joy and praise, with a multitude that kept holyday.

5 Why art thou [3]cast down, O my soul? and *why* art thou disquieted in me? [d]hope thou in God: for I shall yet [4]praise him [5]*for* the help of his countenance.

6 O my God, my soul is cast down within me: therefore will I remember thee from the land of Jordan, and of the Hěr-mō-nītes, from [6]the hill Mi-zär.

7 Deep [e]calleth unto deep at the noise of thy waterspouts: all thy waves and thy billows are gone over me.

8 *Yet* the LORD will [f]command his lovingkindness in the daytime, and in the night his song *shall be* with me, *and* my prayer unto the God of my life.

9 I will say unto God my rock, Why hast thou forgotten me? why go I mourning because of the oppression of the enemy?

10 *As* with a [7]sword in my bones, mine enemies reproach me; while they say daily unto me, Where *is* thy God?

11 Why art thou cast down, O my soul? and why art thou disquieted within me? hope thou in God: for I shall yet praise him, *who is* the health of my countenance, and my God.

PSALM 43

JUDGE [a]me, O God, and plead my cause against an [1]ungodly nation: O deliver me [2]from the deceitful and unjust man.

2 For thou *art* the God of [b]my strength: why dost thou cast me off? why go I mourning because of the oppression of the enemy?

3 O send out thy light and thy truth: let them lead me; let them bring me [c]unto thy holy hill, and to thy tabernacles.

4 Then will I go unto the altar of God, unto God [3]my exceeding joy: yea, upon the harp will I praise thee, O God my God.

5 Why art [d]thou cast down, O my soul? and why art thou disquieted within me? hope in God: for I shall yet praise him, *who is* the health of my countenance, and my God.

PSALM 44

To the chief Musician for the sons of Korah, Maschil.

WE have heard with our ears, O God, our fathers have told us *what* work thou didst in their days, in the times of old.

2 *How* [a]thou didst drive out the heathen with thy hand, and plantedst them; *how* thou didst afflict the people, and cast them out.

3 For [b]they got not the land in possession by their own sword, neither did their own arm save them: but thy right hand, and thine arm, and the light of thy countenance, because [c]thou hadst a favour unto them.

4 Thou [d]art my King, O God: command deliverances for Jacob.

5 Through thee [e]will we push down our enemies: through thy name will we tread them under that rise up against us.

6 For [f]I will not trust in my bow, neither shall my sword save me.

7 But thou hast saved us from our enemies, and hast put them to shame that hated us.

8 In [g]God we boast all the day long, and praise thy name for ever. Sē-läh.

9 But thou hast cast off, and put us

5 evil to me.
6 A thing of Belial.
7 the man of my peace.
d Obad. 7. John 13.18.
8 magnified.
e Ps. 34.15. Acts 2.28.

PSALM 42
1 Or, A Psalm giving instruction of the sons.
2 brayeth.
a John 7.37.
b 1 Thes. 1.9.
c Isa. 30.29.
3 bowed down.
d Ps. 56.3,11. Isa. 50.10. Lam. 3.24.
4 Or, give thanks.
5 Or, his presence is salvation.
6 Or, the little hill.
e Eze. 7.26.
f Deut. 28.8.
7 Or, killing.

PSALM 43
a Ps. 7.8.
1 Or, unmerciful.
2 from a man of deceit and iniquity.
b Ps. 28.7. Isa. 26.4.
c Ps. 2.6. Ps. 3.4.
3 the gladness of my joy.
d Ps. 42.5,11.

PSALM 44
a Ex. 15.17. Deut. 7.1. Josh. 10.42.
b Josh. 24.12.
c Deut. 4.37.
d Ps. 74.12.
e Dan. 8.4.
f Ps. 33.16.
g Ps. 34.2. Rom. 2.17. 1 Cor. 1.31.

to shame; and goest not forth with
our armies.
10 Thou makest us to [h]turn back
from the enemy: and they which hate
us spoil for themselves.
11 Thou hast given us [1]like sheep
appointed for meat; and hast [i]scatter-
ed us among the heathen.
12 Thou [j]sellest thy people [2]for
nought, and dost not increase *thy*
wealth by their price.
13 Thou makest us a reproach to our
neighbours, a scorn and a derision to
them that are round about us.
14 Thou makest us a byword among
the heathen, a shaking of the head
among the people.
15 My confusion *is* continually before me, and the shame of my face
hath covered me,
16 For the voice of him that reproacheth and blasphemeth; [k]by reason of the enemy and avenger.
17 All [l]this is come upon us; yet
have we not forgotten thee, neither
have we dealt falsely in thy covenant.
18 Our heart is not turned back,
neither have our [3]steps declined from
thy way;
19 Though thou hast sore broken us
in the [m]place of dragons, and covered
us with the shadow of death.
20 If we have forgotten the name of
our God, or stretched out our hands
to a strange god;
21 Shall [n]not God search this out?
for [o]he knoweth the secrets of the
heart.
22 Yea, for thy sake are we killed all
the day long; we are counted as sheep
for the slaughter.
23 Awake, why sleepest thou, O
Lord? arise, cast *us* not off for ever.
24 Wherefore hidest thou thy face,
and forgettest our affliction and our
oppression?
25 For our soul is bowed down to the
dust: our belly cleaveth unto the
earth.
26 Arise [4]for our help, and redeem us
for thy mercies' sake.

PSALM 45

To the chief Musician upon Shoshannim, for the sons of Korah, [1]Maschil, A Song of loves.

MY heart [2]is inditing a good matter: I speak of the things which I
have made touching the king: my
tongue *is* the pen of a ready writer.
2 Thou art fairer than the children of
men: grace is poured into thy lips:
therefore God hath blessed thee for
ever.

h Lev. 26.17. Deut. 28.25.
1 as sheep of meat.
i Deut. 4.27. 2 Ki. 17.6. Ps. 60.1. Jer. 32.37. Luke 21.24.
j Isa. 52.3,4.
2 without riches.
k Ps. 8.2.
l Dan. 9.13.
3 Or, goings.
m Isa. 34.13.
n Job 31.14. Ps. 139.1.
o 1 Sam. 16.7. Eccl. 12.14. John 2.25. Acts 1.24. Rom. 2.16. Heb. 4.12. Rev. 2.23.
4 a help for us.

PSALM 45

1 Or, of instruction.
2 boileth, or, bubbleth up.
3 prosper thou, ride thou.
a Ps. 93.2. Isa. 9.6,7. Heb. 1.8.
b Ps. 33.5. Matt. 3.15. Heb. 1.9.
4 Or, O God.
c Isa. 61.1. John 20.17.
d Deut. 21. 13.
e Ps. 95.6. Isa. 54.5.
5 thy face.
f Rev. 19.7,8.
g 1 Pet. 2.9. Rev. 1.6.
h Isa. 11.10. Mal. 1.11.

PSALM 46

1 Or, of.
a 1 Chr. 15. 20.
2 the heart of the seas.

3 Gird thy sword upon *thy* thigh, O
most mighty, with thy glory and thy
majesty.
4 And in thy majesty [3]ride prosperously because of truth and meekness
and righteousness; and thy right hand
shall teach thee terrible things.
5 Thine arrows *are* sharp in the heart
of the king's enemies; *whereby* the
people fall under thee.
6 Thy [a]throne, O God, *is* for ever and
ever: the sceptre of thy kingdom *is* a
right sceptre.
7 Thou [b]lovest righteousness, and
hatest wickedness: therefore [4]God,
[c]thy God, hath anointed thee with the
oil of gladness above thy fellows.
8 All thy garments *smell* of myrrh,
and aloes, *and* cassia, out of the ivory
palaces, whereby they have made thee
glad.
9 Kings' daughters *were* among thy
honourable women: upon thy right
hand did stand the queen in gold of
Ō-phĭr.
10 Hearken, O daughter, and consider, and incline thine ear; [d]forget
also thine own people, and thy father's house;
11 So shall the king greatly desire
thy beauty: [e]for he *is* thy Lord; and
worship thou him.
12 And the daughter of Tyre *shall be*
there with a gift; *even* the rich among
the people shall intreat [5]thy favour.
13 The [f]king's daughter *is* all glorious within: her clothing *is* of wrought
gold.
14 She shall be brought unto the
king in raiment of needlework: the
virgins her companions that follow
her shall be brought unto thee.
15 With gladness and rejoicing shall
they be brought: they shall enter into
the king's palace.
16 Instead of thy fathers shall be thy
children, [g]whom thou mayest make
princes in all the earth.
17 I [h]will make thy name to be remembered in all generations: therefore shall the people praise thee for
ever and ever.

PSALM 46

To the chief Musician [1]for the sons of Korah, A Song upon [a]Alamoth.

GOD *is* our refuge and strength, a
very present help in trouble.
2 Therefore will not we fear, though
the earth be removed, and though the
mountains be carried into [2]the midst
of the sea;
3 *Though* the waters thereof roar *and*

be troubled, *though* the mountains
shake with the swelling thereof. Sē´-
läh.
4 *There is* [b]a river, the streams whereof shall make glad [c]the city of God,
the holy *place* of the tabernacles of the
most High.
5 God *is* [d]in the midst of her; she
shall not be moved: God shall help
her, [3]*and that* right early.
6 The heathen raged, the kingdoms
were moved: he uttered his voice, the
earth melted.
7 The LORD of hosts *is* with us; the
God of Jacob *is* [4]our refuge. Sē´-läh.
8 Come, behold the works of the
LORD, what desolations he hath made
in the earth.
9 He maketh wars to cease unto the
end of the earth; he breaketh the bow,
and cutteth the spear in sunder; he
burneth the chariot in the fire.
10 Be still, and know that I *am* God:
I will be exalted among the heathen, I
will be exalted in the earth.
11 The LORD of hosts *is* with us; the
God of Jacob *is* our refuge. Sē´-läh.

PSALM 47

To the chief Musician, A Psalm [1]for the sons of Korah.

O CLAP your hands, all ye people;
shout unto God with the voice of
triumph.
2 For the LORD most high *is* [a]terrible;
he is [b]a great King over all the earth.
3 He [c]shall subdue the people under
us, and the nations under our feet.
4 He shall choose our [d]inheritance
for us, the excellency of Jacob whom
he loved. Sē´-läh.
5 God [e]is gone up with a shout, the
LORD with the sound of a trumpet.
6 Sing praises to God, sing praises:
sing praises unto our King, sing
praises.
7 For [f]God *is* the King of all the
earth: sing [g]ye praises [2]with understanding.
8 God reigneth over the heathen:
God sitteth upon the throne of his
holiness.
9 [3]The princes of the people are
gathered together, *even* the people of
the God of Abraham: for the shields
of the earth *belong* unto God: he is
greatly exalted.

PSALM 48

A Song *and* Psalm [1]for the sons of Korah.

GREAT *is* the LORD, and greatly
to be praised in the city of our
God, *in* the mountain [a]of his holiness.

b Isa. 8.7. Rev. 22.1.
c 2 Chr. 6.6. Ps. 48.1. Isa. 60.14. Heb. 12.22.
d Deut. 23.14. Isa. 12.6. Eze. 43.7.
3 when the morning appeareth.
4 an high place for us.

PSALM 47
1 Or, of.
a Deut. 7.21. Neh. 1.5.
b Mal. 1.14.
c Ps. 18.47.
d 1 Pet. 1.4.
e Ps. 24.7-10. Acts 1.9. Eph. 4.8-10. 1 Tim. 3.16.
f Zech. 14.9.
g 1 Cor. 14.15.
2 Or, every one that hath understanding.
3 Or, The voluntary of the people are gathered unto the people of the God of Abraham.

PSALM 48
1 Or, of.
a Isa. 2.2. Obad. 17. Micah 4.1.
b Jer. 3.19. Lam. 2.15.
c Eze. 20.6.
d Isa. 14.13.
e Matt. 5.35.
f 2 Sam. 10.6.
g Eze. 27.26.
h Isa. 2.2. Micah 4.1.
i Mal. 1.11.
2 Set your heart to her bulwarks.
3 Or, raise up.
j Isa. 25.9.

PSALM 49
1 Or, of.
a Ps. 78.2.
b Matt. 16.26.
c Job 36.18.
d Heb. 9.27.
e Ps. 89.48.

2 Beautiful [b]for situation, [c]the joy of
the whole earth, *is* mount Zion, [d]*on*
the sides of the north, the [e]city of the
great King.
3 God is known in her palaces for a
refuge.
4 For, lo, [f]the kings were assembled,
they passed by together.
5 They saw *it, and* so they marvelled;
they were troubled, *and* hasted away.
6 Fear took hold upon them there,
and pain, as of a woman in travail.
7 Thou [g]breakest the ships of Tarshish with an east wind.
8 As we have heard, so have we seen
in the city of the LORD of hosts, in the
city of our God: God will [h]establish
it for ever. Sē´-läh.
9 We have thought of thy lovingkindness, O God, in the midst of thy
temple.
10 According to [i]thy name, O God,
so *is* thy praise unto the ends of the
earth: thy right hand is full of righteousness.
11 Let mount Zion rejoice, let the
daughters of Judah be glad, because
of thy judgments.
12 Walk about Zion, and go round
about her: tell the towers thereof.
13 [2]Mark ye well her bulwarks, [3]con-
sider her palaces; that ye may tell *it*
to the generation following.
14 For [j]this God *is* our God for ever
and ever: he will be our guide *even* unto death.

PSALM 49

To the chief Musician, A Psalm [1]for the sons of Korah.

HEAR this, all *ye* people; give ear,
all *ye* inhabitants of the world:
2 Both low and high, rich and poor,
together.
3 My mouth shall speak of wisdom;
and the meditation of my heart *shall*
be of understanding.
4 I will [a]incline mine ear to a parable:
I will open my dark saying upon the
harp.
5 Wherefore should I fear in the
days of evil, *when* the iniquity of my
heels shall compass me about?
6 They that trust in their wealth, and
boast themselves in the multitude of
their riches;
7 None *of them* can by any means redeem his brother, nor [b]give to God a
ransom for him:
8 (For [c]the redemption of their soul
is precious, and it ceaseth for ever:)
9 That he should still [d]live for ever,
and not [e]see corruption.
10 For he seeth *that* wise men die,

likewise the fool and the brutish person perish, and leave their wealth to
others.
11 Their inward thought *is, that* their
houses *shall continue* for ever, *and*
their dwelling places [2]to all generations; they call *their* lands after their
own names.
12 Nevertheless man *being* in honour
abideth not: he is like the beasts *that*
perish.
13 This their way *is* their folly: yet
their posterity [3]approve their sayings.
Sē-lăh.
14 Like sheep they are laid in the
grave; death shall feed on them; and
[f]the upright shall have dominion over
them in the morning; and their
[4]beauty shall consume [5]in the grave
from their dwelling.
15 But God [g]will redeem my soul
[6]from the power of [7]the grave: for he
shall receive me. Sē-lăh.
16 Be not thou afraid when one is
made rich, when the glory of his house
is increased;
17 For when he dieth he shall carry
nothing away: his glory shall not descend after him.
18 Though [8]while he lived he blessed
his soul: and *men* will praise thee, when
thou doest well to thyself.
19 [9]He shall go to the generation of
his fathers; they shall never see light.
20 Man *that is* in honour, and understandeth not, is like [h]the beasts *that*
perish.

PSALM 50

A Psalm [1]of Asaph.

THE mighty God, *even* the LORD,
hath spoken, and called the earth
from the rising of the sun unto the
going down thereof.
2 Out of Zion, the perfection of
beauty, God hath shined.
3 Our God shall come, and shall not
keep silence: a fire shall devour before him, and it shall be very tempestuous round about him.
4 He [a]shall call to the heavens from
above, and to the earth, that he may
judge his people.
5 Gather [b]my saints together unto
me; those [c]that have made a covenant with me by sacrifice.
6 And the heavens shall declare his
righteousness: for God *is* judge himself. Sē-lăh.
7 Hear, O my people, and I will
speak; O Israel, and I will testify
against thee: I *am* God, *even* thy God.
8 I will not reprove thee for thy sacrifices or thy burnt offerings, *to have*
been continually before me.
9 I [d]will take no bullock out of thy
house, *nor* he goats out of thy folds.
10 For every beast of the forest *is*
mine, *and* the cattle upon a thousand
hills.
11 I know all the fowls of the mountains: and the wild beasts of the field
are [2]mine.
12 If I were hungry, I would not tell
thee: for the world *is* mine, and the
fulness thereof.
13 Will I eat the flesh of bulls, or
drink the blood of goats?
14 Offer [e]unto God thanksgiving;
and pay thy vows unto the most High:
15 And [f]call upon me in the day of
trouble: I will deliver thee, and thou
shalt glorify [g]me.
16 But unto the wicked God saith,
What hast thou to do to declare my
statutes, or *that* thou shouldest take
my covenant in thy mouth?
17 Seeing [h]thou hatest instruction,
and castest my words behind thee.
18 When thou sawest a thief, then
thou consentedst [i]with him, and [3]hast
been partaker with adulterers.
19 [4]Thou givest thy mouth to evil,
and thy tongue frameth deceit.
20 Thou sittest *and* speakest against
thy brother; thou slanderest thine
own mother's son.
21 These *things* hast thou done, and
[j]I kept silence; [k]thou thoughtest that
I was altogether *such an one* as thyself: *but* I will reprove thee, and set
them in order before thine eyes.
22 Now consider this, ye that forget
God, lest I tear *you* in pieces, and *there*
be none to deliver.
23 Whoso offereth praise glorifieth
me: and to him [5]that ordereth *his* conversation *aright* will I shew the salvation of God.

PSALM 51

To the chief Musician, [a]A Psalm of David, when Nathan the prophet came unto him, after he had gone in to Bath-sheba.

HAVE mercy upon me, O God, according to thy lovingkindness:
according unto the multitude of thy
tender mercies [b]blot out my transgressions.
2 Wash [c]me throughly from mine iniquity, and cleanse me from my sin.
3 For [d]I acknowledge my transgressions: and my sin *is* ever before me.
4 Against [e]thee, thee only, have I
sinned, and done *this* evil [f]in thy sight:
[g]that thou mightest be justified when

2 to generation and generation.
3 delight in their mouth.
f Dan. 7.22. Mal. 4.3. Luke 22.30. 1 Cor. 6.2. 2 Tim. 2.12. Rev. 2.26.
4 Or, strength.
5 Or, the grave being an habitation to every one of them.
g Hos. 13.14.
6 from the hand of the grave.
7 Or, hell.
8 in his life.
9 The soul shall go.
h Eccl. 3.19, 20,21.

PSALM 50

1 Or, for.
a Micah 6.1, 2.
b Isa. 13.3. 1 Cor. 6.2. 1 Thes. 3.13. Jude 14.
c Ex. 24.7. Isa. 59.20, 21. Heb. 8.6.
d Isa. 43.23. Micah 6.6. Acts 17.25.
2 with me.
e Hosea 14.2.
f Job 22.27.
g Ps. 22.23. Matt. 5.16. John 15.8.
h Pro. 1.7,28, 29. Pro. 5.12, 13. Rom. 2.21. 2 Thes. 2. 10-12.
i Rom. 1.32.
3 thy portion was with adulterers.
4 Thou sendest.
j Eccl. 8.11.
k Rom. 2.4.
5 that disposeth his way.

PSALM 51

a 2 Sam. 12.1.
b Col. 2.14.
c Eze. 36.25. Zech. 13.1. 1 Cor. 6.11. Heb. 9.14. 1 John 1.7. Rev. 1.5.
d Ps. 32.5.
e Gen. 39.9.
f Luke 15.21.
g Rom. 3.4.

thou speakest, *and* be clear when thou judgest.

5 Behold, [h]I was shapen in iniquity; and in sin did my mother [1]conceive me.

6 Behold, thou desirest truth in the inward parts: and in the hidden *part* thou shalt make me to know wisdom.

7 Purge me with hyssop, and I shall be clean: wash me, and I shall be whiter than snow.

8 Make me to hear joy and gladness; *that* the bones *which* thou hast broken may rejoice.

9 Hide thy face from my sins, and blot out all mine iniquities.

10 Create [i]in me a clean heart, O God; and renew [2]a right spirit within me.

11 Cast me not away [j]from thy presence; and take not thy [k]holy spirit from me.

12 Restore unto me the joy of thy salvation; and uphold me *with thy* free [l]spirit.

13 *Then* will I teach transgressors thy ways; and sinners shall be converted unto thee.

14 Deliver me from [3]bloodguiltiness, O God, thou God of my salvation: *and* my tongue shall sing aloud of thy righteousness.

15 O Lord, open thou my lips; and my mouth shall shew forth thy praise.

16 For thou desirest not sacrifice; [4]else would I give *it:* thou delightest not in burnt offering.

17 The sacrifices of God *are* a broken spirit: a broken and a contrite heart, O God, thou wilt not despise.

18 Do good in thy good pleasure unto Zion: build thou the walls of Jerusalem.

19 Then shalt thou be pleased with [m]the sacrifices of righteousness, with burnt offering and whole burnt offering: then shall they offer bullocks upon thine altar.

PSALM 52

To the chief Musician, Maschil, *A Psalm* of David, [a]when Doeg the Edomite came and told Saul, and said unto him, David is come to the house of Ahimelech.

WHY boastest thou thyself in mischief, O [b]mighty man? the goodness of God *endureth* continually.

2 Thy [c]tongue deviseth mischiefs; like [d]a sharp razor, working deceitfully.

3 Thou lovest evil more than good; *and* lying [e]rather than to speak righteousness. Sē-lāh.

4 Thou lovest all devouring words, [3]O *thou* deceitful tongue.

5 God shall likewise [2]destroy thee for ever, he shall take thee away, and pluck thee out of *thy* dwelling place, and [f]root thee out of the land of the living. Sē-lāh.

6 The [g]righteous also shall see, and fear, and [h]shall laugh at him:

7 Lo, *this is* the man *that* made not God his strength; but [i]trusted in the abundance of his riches, *and* strengthened himself in his [3]wickedness.

8 But I *am* [j]like a green olive tree in the house of God: I trust in the mercy of God for ever and ever.

9 I will praise thee for ever, because thou hast done *it:* and I will wait on thy name; for [k]*it is* good before thy saints.

PSALM 53

To the chief Musician upon Mahalath, Maschil, *A Psalm* of David.

THE [a]fool hath said in his heart, *There is* no God. Corrupt are they, and have done abominable iniquity: [b]*there is* none that doeth good.

2 God [c]looked down from heaven upon the children of men, to see if there were *any* that did understand, that did [d]seek God.

3 Every [e]one of them is gone back: they are altogether become filthy; *there is* none that doeth good, no, not one.

4 Have the workers of iniquity no [f]knowledge? who eat up my people *as* they eat bread: they have not called upon God.

5 There [1]were they in great fear, *where* no fear was: for God hath scattered the bones of him that encampeth *against* thee: thou hast put *them* to shame, because God hath despised them.

6 [2]Oh that the salvation of Israel *were come* out of Zion! When God bringeth back the captivity of his people, Jacob shall rejoice, *and* Israel shall be glad.

PSALM 54

To the chief Musician on Neginoth, Maschil, *A Psalm* of David, [a]when the Ziphims came and said to Saul, Doth not David hide himself with us?

SAVE me, O God, by thy name, and judge me by thy strength.

2 Hear my prayer, O God; give ear to the words of my mouth.

3 For strangers are risen up against me, and oppressors seek after my soul: they have not set God before them. Sē-lāh.

4 Behold, God *is* mine helper: the

---

h Job 14.4. John 3.6. Rom. 5.12.
1 warm me.
i Pro. 20.9. Jer. 13.27. Eze. 11.19. Acts 15.9. Eph. 2.10.
2 Or, a constant spirit.
j Gen. 4.14.
k Eze. 36.27. Rom. 8.9.
l Rom. 8.15. 2 Cor. 3.17.
3 bloods.
4 Or, that I should give it.
m Mal. 3.3.

PSALM 52
a 1 Sam. 22.9.
b 1 Sam. 21.7.
c Ps. 50.19. Pro. 12.18.
d Ps. 59.7.
e Jer. 9.4.
1 Or, and the deceitful tongue.
2 beat thee down.
f Pro. 2.22.
g Job 22.19.
h Ps. 58.10.
i Job 31.24, 25. Ps. 49.6.
3 Or, substance.
j Ps. 92.13.
k Ps. 54.6.

PSALM 53
a Ps. 10.4.
b Rom. 3.10.
c Ps. 33.13.
d 2 Chr. 15.2.
e Eccl. 7.29.
f Jer. 4.22.
1 they feared a fear.
2 Who will give salvations, etc.

PSALM 54
a 1 Sam. 23. 19. 1 Sam. 26.1.

[b]Lord *is* with them that uphold my
soul.
5 He shall reward evil unto [1]mine
enemies: cut them [c]off in thy truth.
6 I will freely sacrifice unto thee: I
will praise thy name, O LORD; for *it*
is good.
7 For he hath delivered me out of all
trouble: and mine eye hath seen *his*
desire upon mine enemies.

PSALM 55

To the chief Musician on Neginoth, Maschil,
A Psalm of David.

GIVE ear to my prayer, O God;
and hide not thyself from my
supplication.
2 Attend unto me, and hear me: I
mourn in my complaint, and make a
noise;
3 Because of the voice of the enemy,
because of the oppression of the
wicked: for they cast iniquity upon
me, and in wrath they hate me.
4 My [a]heart is sore pained within
me: and the terrors of death are fallen
upon me.
5 Fearfulness and trembling are come
upon me, and horror hath [1]over-
whelmed me.
6 And I said, Oh that I had wings
like a dove! *for then* would I fly away,
and be at rest.
7 Lo, *then* would I wander far off,
and remain in the wilderness. Sē-lāh.
8 I would hasten my escape from the
windy storm *and* tempest.
9 [2]Destroy, O Lord, *and* divide their
tongues: for I have seen violence and
strife in the city.
10 Day and night they go about it upon the walls thereof: mischief also and
sorrow *are* in the midst of it.
11 Wickedness *is* in the midst thereof: deceit and guile depart not from
her streets.
12 For *it was* not an enemy *that* reproached me; then I could have borne
it: neither *was it* he that hated me *that*
did magnify *himself* against me; then
I would have hid myself from him:
13 But *it was* thou, [3]a man mine
equal, my [b]guide, and mine acquaintance.
14 [4]We took sweet counsel together,
and walked unto the house of God in
company.
15 Let death seize upon them, *and* let
them [c]go down quick into [5]hell: for
wickedness *is* in their dwellings, *and*
among them.
16 As for me, I will call upon God;
and the LORD shall save me.

b Ps. 118.7. Isa. 41.10. Rom. 8.31, 32. Heb. 13.6.
1 those that observe me.
c Ps. 89.49.

PSALM 55

a Ps. 102.3-5. Matt. 26.37, 38. John 12.27. 2 Cor. 1.8-10.
1 covered me.
2 Swallow up.
3 a man according to my rank.
b 2 Sam. 15. 12.
4 Who sweetened counsel.
c Num. 16. 30.
5 Or, the grave.
d Dan. 6.10. Luke 18.1. Acts 3.1.
e 2 Chr. 32.7.
f Deut. 33.27.
6 Or, With whom also there be no changes, yet they fear not God.
7 he hath profaned.
8 Or, gift. Matt. 6.25. Luke 12.22.
g Ps. 37.24.
9 men of bloods and deceit.
10 shall not half their days.

PSALM 56

1 Or, A golden Psalm of David.
a 1 Sam. 21. 10,11.
b Ps. 31.9.
2 Mine observers.
c Ps. 57.3.
d 1 Sam. 30.6. 2 Chr. 20.3.
e Heb. 13.5,6.
f Acts 4.27, 28.
g Mal. 3.16.
h Isa. 8.9,10.
i Ps. 116.14-16.

17 Evening, [d]and morning, and at
noon, will I pray, and cry aloud: and
he shall hear my voice.
18 He hath delivered my soul in
peace from the battle *that was* against
me: for there [e]were many with me.
19 God shall hear, and afflict them,
[f]even he that abideth of old. Sē-lāh.
[6]Because they have no changes, therefore they fear not God.
20 He hath put forth his hands
against such as be at peace with him:
[7]he hath broken his covenant.
21 *The words* of his mouth were
smoother than butter, but war *was* in
his heart: his words were softer than
oil, yet *were* they drawn swords.
22 Cast thy [8]burden upon the LORD,
and he shall sustain thee: [g]he shall
never suffer the righteous to be moved.
23 But thou, O God, shalt bring them
down into the pit of destruction:
[9]bloody and deceitful men [10]shall not
live out half their days; but I will
trust in thee.

PSALM 56

To the chief Musician upon Jonath-elemrechokim,
[1]Michtam of David, when [a]the Philistines took
him in Gath.

BE [b]merciful unto me, O God: for
man would swallow me up; he
fighting daily oppresseth me.
2 [2]Mine enemies would daily swallow [c]*me* up: for *they be* many that fight
against me, O thou most High.
3 What [d]time I am afraid, I will trust
in thee.
4 In God I will praise his word, in
God I have put my trust; [e]I will not
fear what flesh can do unto me.
5 Every day they wrest my words: all
their thoughts *are* against me for evil.
6 They gather [f]themselves together,
they hide themselves, they mark my
steps, when they wait for my soul.
7 Shall they escape by iniquity? in
thine anger cast down the people, O
God.
8 Thou tellest my wanderings: put
thou my tears into thy bottle: *are*
[g]*they* not in thy book?
9 When I cry *unto thee*, then shall
mine enemies turn back: this I know;
for [h]God *is* for me.
10 In God will I praise *his* word: in
the LORD will I praise *his* word.
11 In God have I put my trust: I will
not be afraid what man can do unto
me.
12 Thy [i]vows *are* upon me, O God:
I will render praises unto thee.
13 For thou hast delivered my soul

from death: *wilt* not *thou deliver* my feet from falling, that I may walk before God in [j]the light of the living?

PSALM 57

To the chief Musician, [1]Al-taschith, Michtam of David, [a]when he fled from Saul in the cave.

BE merciful unto me, O God, be merciful unto me: for my soul trusteth in thee: yea, in the shadow of thy wings will I make my refuge, [b]until *these* calamities be overpast.

2 I will cry unto God most high; unto God [c]that performeth *all things* for me.

3 He [d]shall send from heaven, and save me [2]*from* the reproach of him that would swallow me up. Sē-lăh. God shall send [e]forth his mercy and his truth.

4 My soul *is* among lions: *and* I lie *even among* them that are set on fire, *even* the sons of men, [f]whose teeth *are* spears and arrows, and their [g]tongue a sharp sword.

5 Be [h]thou exalted, O God, above the heavens; *let* thy glory *be* above all the earth.

6 They [i]have prepared a net for my steps; my soul is bowed down: they have digged a pit before me, into the midst whereof they are fallen *themselves*. Sē-lăh.

7 My [j]heart is [3]fixed, O God, my heart is fixed: I will sing and give praise.

8 Awake [k]up, my glory; awake, psaltery and harp: I *myself* will awake early.

9 I will praise thee, O Lord, among the people: I will sing unto thee among the nations.

10 For [l]thy mercy *is* great unto the heavens, and thy truth unto the clouds.

11 Be thou exalted, O God, above the heavens: *let* thy glory *be* above all the earth.

PSALM 58

To the chief Musician, [1]Al-taschith, Michtam of David.

DO ye indeed speak righteousness, O congregation? do ye judge uprightly, O ye sons of men?

2 Yea, in heart ye work wickedness; [a]ye weigh the violence of your hands in the earth.

3 The wicked [b]are estranged from the womb: they go astray [2]as soon as they be born, speaking lies.

4 Their [c]poison *is* [3]like the poison of a serpent: *they are* like the deaf [4]adder *that* stoppeth her ear;

5 Which will not hearken to the voice of charmers, [5]charming never so wisely.

6 Break [d]their teeth, O God, in their mouth: break out the great teeth of the young lions, O LORD.

7 Let them melt away as waters *which* run continually: *when* he bendeth *his bow to shoot* his arrows, let them be as cut in pieces.

8 As a snail *which* melteth, let *every one of them* pass away: *like* the untimely birth of a woman, *that* they may not see the sun.

9 Before your pots can feel the thorns, he shall take them [e]away as with a whirlwind, [6]both living, and in *his* wrath.

10 The [f]righteous shall rejoice when he seeth the vengeance: he shall wash his feet in the blood of the wicked.

11 So that a man shall say, Verily [g]*there is* [7]a reward for the righteous: verily he is a God that judgeth [h]in the earth.

PSALM 59

To the chief Musician, [1]Al-taschith, Michtam of David; [a]when Saul sent, and they watched the house to kill him.

DELIVER me from mine enemies, O my God: [2]defend me from them that rise up against me.

2 Deliver me from the workers of iniquity, and save me from bloody men.

3 For, lo, they lie in wait for my soul: the mighty are gathered against me; not [b]*for* my transgression, nor *for* my sin, O LORD.

4 They run and prepare themselves without *my* fault: awake [3]to help me, and behold.

5 Thou therefore, O LORD God of hosts, the God of Israel, [c]awake to visit all the heathen: be not merciful to any wicked transgressors. Sē-lăh.

6 They return at evening: they make a noise like a dog, and go round about the city.

7 Behold, they belch out with their mouth: swords *are* in their lips: for who, *say they*, doth hear?

8 But thou, O LORD, [d]shalt laugh at them; thou shalt have all the heathen in derision.

9 *Because of* his strength will I wait upon thee: for God *is* [4]my defence.

10 The God of my mercy shall prevent me: God shall let me see *my desire* upon [5]mine enemies.

11 Slay [e]them not, lest my people forget: scatter them by thy power;

j Job 33.30.

PSALM 57

1 Or, Destroy not, A golden Psalm.
a 1 Sam. 22.1.
b Isa. 26.20.
c Ps. 138.8.
d Ps. 144.5.
2 Or, he reproacheth him that would swallow me up.
e Ps. 40.11. John 1.17.
f Pro. 30.14.
g Ps. 64.3.
h Ps. 108.5.
i Ps. 9.15.
j Ps. 108.1.
3 Or, prepared.
k Judg. 5.12.
l Ps. 108.4.

PSALM 58

1 Or, Destroy not, A golden Psalm of David.
a Ps. 94.20.
b Ps. 51.5.
2 from the belly.
c Ps. 140.4.
3 according to the likeness.
4 Or, asp.
5 Or, be the charmer never so cunning.
d Job 4.10.
e Pro. 10.25.
6 as living as wrath.
f Deut. 32.42. Job 22.19. Ps. 18.47. Pro. 10.11. Rev. 18.20.
g Rom. 2.6-11.
7 fruit of the, etc.
h Job 34.11. Eccl. 5.8. Jer. 32.19. Eze. 7.27. Rom. 14.12. Rev. 2.23.

PSALM 59

1 Or, Destroy not, A golden Psalm of David.
a 1 Sam. 19. 11.
2 set me on high.
b 1 Sam. 26. 18.
3 to meet me.
c Dan. 4.35.
d Ps. 2.4. Pro. 1.26.
4 my high place.
5 mine observers.
e Gen. 4.12, 13.

l bring them down, O Lord our
eld.
For the sin of their mouth *and* the
rds of their lips let them even be
en in their pride: and for cursing
d lying *which* they speak.
Consume *them* in wrath, con-
ne *them*, that they *may* not *be:* and
them know that God ruleth in
ob unto the ends of the earth. Sē-
.
And at evening let them return;
d let them make a noise like a dog,
d go round about the city.
Let them wander up and down
r meat, [7]and grudge if they be not
isfied.
But I will sing of thy power; yea,
vill sing aloud of thy mercy in the
orning: for thou hast been my de-
ce and refuge in the day of my
uble.
Unto thee, O my strength, will I
g: for God *is* my defence, *and* the
od of my mercy.

PSALM 60

the chief Musician upon Shushan-eduth, Michtam of David, to teach; [a]when he strove ith Aram-naharaim and with Aram-zobah, hen Joab returned, and smote of Edom in the alley of salt twelve thousand.

O GOD, thou hast cast us off,
thou hast [2]scattered us, thou hast
en displeased; O turn thyself to us
ain.
Thou hast made the earth to trem-
e; thou hast broken it: heal the
eaches thereof; for it shaketh.
Thou hast shewed thy people hard
ings: thou hast made us to drink
e wine of astonishment.
Thou [b]hast given a banner to them
at fear thee, that it may be displayed
cause of the truth. Sē-läh.
That [c]thy beloved may be deliver-
; save *with* thy right hand, and hear
e.
God hath [d]spoken in his holiness;
vill rejoice, I will [e]divide Shē-chĕm,
d mete out the [f]valley of Sŭc-cōth.
Gilead *is* mine, and Mă-năs-sēh *is*
ine; Ē-phră-ĭm [g]also *is* the strength
mine head; [h]Judah *is* my law-
ver;
Moab *is* my washpot; over Ē-dom
ll I cast out my shoe: Philistia,
iumph thou because of me.
Who will bring me *into* the [4]strong
y? who will lead me into Ē-dom?
0 *Wilt* not thou, O God, [i]*which*
dst cast us off? and *thou,* O God,
hich didst not go out with our
mies?

6 to eat.
7 Or, if they be not satisfied, then they will stay all night.

PSALM 60

1 Or, A golden Psalm.
a 2 Sam. 8.3.
2 broken.
b Isa. 11.10.
c Ps. 108.6.
d Ps. 89.35.
e Gen. 12.6.
f Josh. 13.27.
g Deut. 33.17.
h Gen. 49.10.
3 Or, triumph thou over me [ironically].
4 city of strength?
i Ps. 44.9.
5 salvation.
j 1 Chr. 19. 31.

PSALM 61

a 1 Tim. 2.8.
b Pro. 18.10.
c Ps. 15.1. Ps. 23.6. Rev. 3.12.
1 Or, make my refuge.
d 1 Cor. 3.21-23.
2 Thou shalt add days to the days of the king.
3 as generation and generation.
e Ps. 41.12. Luke 1.32.
f Ps. 56.12.

PSALM 62

1 Or, Only.
2 is silent.
3 high place.
a Isa. 30.13.
b Ps. 28.3.
4 in their inward parts.
c Micah 7.7, 10.
d Jer. 3.23.
e 1 Sam. 1.15. Ps. 42.4.
5 Or, alike.
f Isa. 26.4.

11 Give us help from trouble: for
vain *is* the [5]help of man.
12 Through God [j]we shall do valiantly: for he *it is that* shall tread down our
enemies.

PSALM 61

To the chief Musician upon Neginah, *A Psalm* of David.

HEAR my cry, O God; attend unto
my prayer.
2 From the [a]end of the earth will I
cry unto thee, when my heart is overwhelmed: lead me to the rock *that* is
higher than I.
3 For thou hast been a shelter for me,
and [b]a strong tower from the enemy.
4 I will abide in [c]thy tabernacle for
ever: I will [1]trust in the covert of thy
wings. Sē-läh.
5 For thou, O God, hast heard my
vows: thou hast given *me* [d]the heritage
of those that fear thy name.
6 [2]Thou wilt prolong the king's life:
and his years [3]as many generations.
7 He shall abide [e]before God for
ever: O prepare mercy and truth,
which may preserve him.
8 So will I [f]sing praise unto thy name
for ever, that I may daily perform my
vows.

PSALM 62

To the chief Musician, to Jeduthun, A Psalm of David.

[1]TRULY my soul [2]waiteth upon
God: from him *cometh* my salvation.
2 He only *is* my rock and my salvation; *he is* my [3]defence; I shall not be
greatly moved.
3 How long will ye imagine mischief
against a man? ye shall be slain all of
you: [a]as a bowing wall *shall ye be, and*
as a tottering fence.
4 They only consult to cast *him* down
from his excellency: they delight in
lies: [b]they bless with their mouth, but
they curse [4]inwardly. Sē-läh.
5 My soul, wait thou [c]only upon
God; for my expectation *is* from him.
6 He only *is* my rock and my salvation: *he is* my defence; I shall not be
moved.
7 In God *is* [d]my salvation and my
glory: the rock of my strength, *and* my
refuge, *is* in God.
8 Trust in him at all times; ye people,
pour [e]out your heart before him: God
is a refuge for us. Sē-läh.
9 Surely men of low degree *are* vanity, *and* men of high degree *are* a lie:
to be laid in the balance, they *are*
[5]altogether *lighter* than vanity.
10 Trust not in [f]oppression, and be-

come not vain in robbery: [g]if riches increase, set not your heart *upon them.*

11 God hath spoken once; twice have I heard this; that [6]power *belongeth* unto God.

12 Also unto thee, O Lord, *belongeth* mercy: for [h]thou renderest to every man according to his work.

PSALM 63

A Psalm of David, [a]when he was in the wilderness of Judah.

O GOD, thou *art* my God; early will I seek thee: my soul thirsteth for thee, my flesh longeth for thee in a dry and [1]thirsty land, where no water is;

2 To see thy [b]power and thy glory, so *as* I have seen thee in the sanctuary.

3 Because [c]thy lovingkindness *is* better than life, my lips shall praise thee.

4 Thus will I bless thee while I live: I will lift up my hands in thy name.

5 My soul [d]shall be satisfied as *with* [2]marrow and fatness; and my mouth shall praise *thee* with joyful lips:

6 When I remember thee [e]upon my bed, *and* meditate on thee in the *night* watches.

7 Because thou hast been [f]my help, therefore in the shadow of thy wings will I rejoice.

8 My soul followeth [g]hard after thee: thy right hand upholdeth me.

9 But those *that* seek my soul, to destroy *it*, shall go into the lower parts of the earth.

10 [3]They shall fall by the sword: they shall be a portion for foxes.

11 But the king shall rejoice in God; every one [h]that sweareth by him shall glory: but the mouth of them that speak lies shall be stopped.

PSALM 64

To the chief Musician, A Psalm of David.

HEAR my voice, O God, in my prayer: preserve my life from fear of the enemy.

2 Hide me [a]from the secret counsel of the wicked; from the insurrection of the workers of iniquity:

3 Who whet their tongue [b]like a sword, *and* bend *their bows to shoot* their arrows, *even* bitter words:

4 That they may shoot in secret at the perfect: suddenly do they shoot at him, and fear not.

5 They encourage themselves *in* an evil [1]matter: they commune [2]of laying snares privily; they say, Who shall see them?

g Mark 10.23. Luke 12.15.
6 Or, strength.
h 1 Pet. 1.17.
PSALM 63
a 1 Sam. 23. 14.
1 weary land without water.
b 1 Chr. 16. 11.
c John 3.16.
d Ps. 17.15. Isa. 25.6.
2 fatness.
e Ps. 149.5.
f 2 Cor. 1.10.
g Isa. 26.9.
3 They shall make him run out like water by the hands of the sword.
h Zeph. 1.5.
PSALM 64
a Ps. 143.9.
b Ps. 57.4.
1 Or, speech.
2 to hide snares.
3 Or, we are consumed by that which they have throughly searched.
4 a search searched.
5 their wound shall be.
c Pro. 12.13.
d Ps. 32.11. Phil. 4.4.
PSALM 65
1 is silent.
a Luke 11.9, 10.
b Isa. 66.23.
2 Words, or, Matters of iniquities.
c Heb. 9.14.
d Ps. 33.12.
e Matt. 8.26.
f Job 37.5.
3 Or, to sing.
4 Or, after thou hadst made it to desire rain.
5 Or, thou causest rain to descend into the furrows thereof.
6 thou dissolvest it.
7 the year of thy goodness.
g Ps. 104.3.

6 They search out iniquities; [3]th accomplish [4]a diligent search: bo the inward *thought* of every one *them*, and the heart, *is* deep.

7 But God shall shoot at them w an arrow; suddenly [5]shall they wounded.

8 So [c]they shall make their o tongue to fall upon themselves: that see them shall flee away.

9 And all men shall fear, and sh declare the work of God; for th shall wisely consider of his doing.

10 The righteous [d]shall be glad in t LORD, and shall trust in him; and the upright in heart shall glory.

PSALM 65

To the chief Musician, A Psalm *and* Song of David.

PRAISE [1]waiteth for thee, O Go in Si-on: and unto thee shall t vow be performed.

2 O thou [a]that hearest prayer, un [b]thee shall all flesh come.

3 [2]Iniquities prevail against me: *for* our transgressions, thou sh purge [c]them away.

4 Blessed [d]*is the man whom* th choosest, and causest to approach *u to thee, that* he may dwell in t courts: we shall be satisfied with t goodness of thy house, *even* of t holy temple.

5 *By* terrible things in righteousn wilt thou answer us, O God of o salvation; *who art* the confidence all the ends of the earth, and of th that are afar off *upon* the sea:

6 Which by his strength setteth f the mountains; *being* girded w power:

7 Which [e]stilleth the noise of t seas, the noise of their waves, and t tumult of the people.

8 They also that dwell in the utt most parts [f]are afraid at thy toke thou makest the outgoings of t morning and evening [3]to rejoice.

9 Thou visitest the earth, and [4]wat est it: thou greatly enrichest it wi the river of God, *which* is full of wat thou preparest them corn, when th hast so provided for it.

10 Thou waterest the ridges there abundantly: [5]thou settlest the furro thereof: [6]thou makest it soft wi showers: thou blessest the springi thereof.

11 Thou crownest [7]the year with t goodness; and thy [g]paths drop f ness.

12 They drop *upon* the pastures

wilderness: and the little hills [8]re-
:e on every side.
The pastures are clothed with
:ks; the valleys also are covered
:r with corn; they shout for joy,
y also sing.

PSALM 66

To the chief Musician, A Song *or* Psalm.

MAKE a joyful noise unto God,
[1]all ye lands:
Sing forth the honour of his name:
ke his praise glorious.
Say unto God, How terrible *art*
u in thy works! [a]through the great-
:s of thy power shall thine enemies
bmit themselves unto thee.
All [b]the earth shall worship thee,
d shall sing unto thee; they shall
g *to* thy name. Sē-läh.
Come [c]and see the works of God:
is terrible *in his* doing toward the
ldren of men.
He [d]turned the sea into dry *land:*
:y [e]went through the flood on foot:
:re did we rejoice in him.
He ruleth by his power for ever;
[f]eyes behold the nations: let not
: rebellious exalt themselves. Sē-läh.
O bless our God, ye people, and
ke the voice of his praise to be
ard:
Which [3]holdeth our soul in life, and
ffereth not our feet to be moved.
) For thou, O God, hast proved us:
ou hast tried us, as silver is tried.
1 Thou broughtest us into the net;
ou laidst affliction upon our loins.
2 Thou hast caused men to ride
er our heads; we went through fire
d through water: but thou brought-
: us out into a [4]wealthy *place.*
3 I will go into thy house with
rnt offerings: [h]I will pay thee my
ws,
4 Which my lips have [5]uttered, and
y mouth hath spoken, when I was in
ouble.
5 I will offer unto thee burnt sacri-
es of [6]fatlings, with the incense of
ms; I will offer bullocks with goats.
-läh.
6 Come *and* hear, all ye that fear
od, and I will declare what he hath
one for my soul.
7 I cried unto him with my mouth,
d he was extolled with my tongue.
8 If [i]I regard iniquity in my heart,
e Lord will not hear *me:*
9 *But* verily God hath heard *me;* he
th attended to the voice of my
ayer.
0 Blessed *be* God, which hath not

8 are girded with joy.

PSALM 66

1 all the earth.
a Ps. 18.44.
2 lie, or, yield feigned obedience.
b Ps. 67.3.
c Ps. 46.8.
d Ex. 14.21. Ps. 78.13. Isa. 63.13, 14.
e Josh. 3.14.
f Ps. 11.4.
3 putteth.
g Zech. 13.9.
4 moist.
h Ps. 116.14, 18. Eccl. 5.4. Jonah 2.9.
5 opened.
6 marrow.
i Job 11.14, 15. Pro. 15.29. Isa. 1.15.

PSALM 67

a Num. 6.25, 26. Ps. 4.6. Ps. 31.16. Ps. 119.135. 2 Cor. 4.6.
1 with us.
b Acts 13.10.
c Luke 2.30-32. Titus 2.11.
d Isa. 24.15, 16.
e Ps. 96.10.
2 lead.
f Lev. 26.4. Ps. 85.9-12. Isa. 1.19.
g Ps. 22.27.

PSALM 68

1 from his face.
2 rejoice with gladness.
3 Or, through the deserts; in JAH is his name.
a 1 Sam. 2.5.
4 in a house.
b Hab. 3.13.
5 shake out.
6 confirm it.
c Ps. 74.19.

turned away my prayer, nor his mercy
from me.

PSALM 67

To the chief Musician on Neginoth,
A Psalm *or* Song.

GOD be merciful unto us, and bless
us; *and* [a]cause his face to shine
[1]upon us; Sē-läh.
2 That [b]thy way may be known upon
earth, [c]thy saving health among all
nations.
3 Let [d]the people praise thee, O God;
let all the people praise thee.
4 O let the nations be glad and sing
for joy: for [e]thou shalt judge the people righteously, and [2]govern the nations upon earth. Sē-läh.
5 Let the people praise thee, O God;
let all the people praise thee.
6 *Then* [f]shall the earth yield her increase; *and* God, *even* our own God,
shall bless us.
7 God shall bless us; and [g]all the ends
of the earth shall fear him.

PSALM 68

To the chief Musician, A Psalm *or* Song
of David.

LET God arise, let his enemies be
scattered: let them also that hate
him flee [1]before him.
2 As smoke is driven away, *so* drive
them away: as wax melteth before the
fire, *so* let the wicked perish at the
presence of God.
3 But let the righteous be glad; let
them rejoice before God: yea, let
them [2]exceedingly rejoice.
4 Sing unto God, sing praises to his
name: extol him that rideth [3]upon the
heavens by his name JAH, and rejoice before him.
5 A father of the fatherless, and a
judge of the widows, *is* God in his holy
habitation.
6 God [a]setteth the solitary [4]in families: he bringeth out those which are
bound with chains: but the rebellious
dwell in a dry *land.*
7 O God, [b]when thou wentest forth
before thy people, when thou didst
march through the wilderness; Sē-
läh:
8 The earth shook, the heavens also
dropped at the presence of God: *even*
Sī-nâi itself *was moved* at the presence
of God, the God of Israel.
9 Thou, O God, didst [5]send a plentiful rain, whereby thou didst [6]confirm
thine inheritance, when it was weary.
10 Thy congregation hath dwelt
therein: thou, [c]O God, hast prepared
of thy goodness for the poor.

11 The Lord gave the word: great *was* the [7]company of those that published *it*.
12 Kings of armies [8]did flee apace: and she that tarried at home divided the spoil.
13 Though [d]ye have lien among the pots, [e]*yet shall ye be as* the wings of a dove covered with silver, and her feathers with yellow gold.
14 When the Almighty scattered kings [9]in it, it was *white* as snow in Săl´-mŏn.
15 The hill of God *is as* the hill of Bā´-shăn; an high hill *as* the hill of Bā´-shăn.
16 Why leap ye, ye high hills? *this is* the hill *which* God desireth to dwell in; yea, the LORD will dwell *in it* for ever.
17 The [f]chariots of God *are* twenty thousand, [10]*even* thousands of angels: the Lord *is* among them, *as in* Sī´-nâi, in the holy *place*.
18 Thou [g]hast ascended on high, thou [h]hast led captivity captive: thou [i]hast received gifts [11]for men; yea, *for* [j]the rebellious also, that [k]the LORD God might dwell *among them*.
19 Blessed *be* the Lord, *who* daily loadeth us *with benefits*, *even* the God of our salvation. Sē´-lăh.
20 *He that is* our God *is* the God of salvation; and [l]unto GOD the Lord *belong* the issues from death.
21 But God shall wound the head of his enemies, *and* the hairy scalp of such an one as goeth on still in his trespasses.
22 The Lord said, I will bring again from Bā´-shăn, I will bring *my people* again from the depths of the sea:
23 That thy foot may be [12]dipped in the blood of *thine* enemies, *and* the tongue of thy dogs in the same.
24 They have seen thy goings, O God; *even* the goings of my God, my King, in the sanctuary.
25 The singers went before, the players on instruments *followed* after; among *them were* the damsels playing with timbrels.
26 Bless ye God in the congregations, *even* the Lord, [13]from the fountain of Israel.
27 There *is* little Benjamin *with* their ruler, the princes of Judah [14]*and* their council, the princes of Zĕ-bū´-lŭn, *and* the princes of Năph´-tă-lī.
28 Thy God hath commanded thy strength: strengthen, O God, that which thou hast wrought for us.
29 Because of thy temple at Jerusalem shall [m]kings bring presents ur
thee.
30 Rebuke [15]the company of spe
men, the multitude of the bulls, wi
the calves of the people, *till every o*
submit himself with pieces of silv
[16]scatter thou the people *that* delig
in war.
31 Princes [n]shall come out of Egyp
[o]Ē-thĭ-ō´-pĭ-ă shall soon stretch out h
hands unto God.
32 Sing unto God, ye kingdoms
the earth; O sing praises unto t
Lord; Sē´-lăh:
33 To him that rideth upon the hea
ens of heavens, *which were* of old;
he doth [17]send out his voice, *and th*
a mighty voice.
34 Ascribe ye strength unto God:
excellency *is* over Israel, and
strength *is* in the [18]clouds.
35 O God, *thou art* terrible out of t
holy places: the God of Israel *is*
[p]that giveth strength and power un
his people. Blessed *be* God.

PSALM 69

To the chief Musician upon Shoshannim, *A Psalm* of David.

SAVE me, O God; for the wate
are come in unto *my* soul.
2 I sink in [1]deep mire, where *the*
is no standing: I am come into [2]de
waters, where the floods overfl
me.
3 I am weary of my crying: my thro
is dried: mine eyes fail while I wait f
my God.
4 They that [a]hate me without a cau
are more than the hairs of mine hea
they that would destroy me, *bei*
mine enemies wrongfully, are might
then I restored *that* which I took n
away.
5 O God, thou knowest my foolis
ness; and my [3]sins are not hid fro
thee.
6 Let not them that wait on thee,
Lord GOD of hosts, be ashamed f
my sake: let not those that seek th
be confounded for my sake, O God
Israel.
7 Because for thy sake I have bor
reproach; shame hath covered n
face.
8 I [b]am become a stranger unto n
brethren, and an alien unto n
mother's children.
9 For [c]the zeal of thine house ha
eaten me up; [d]and the reproaches
them that reproached thee are fall
upon me.
10 When I wept, *and chastened* m

7 army.
8 did flee, did flee.
d Ps. 81.6.
e Ps. 74.19. Eph. 5.26, 27.
9 Or, for her, she was.
f Deut. 33.2. 2 Ki. 6.17. Dan. 7.10.
10 Or, even many thousands.
g Acts 1.9. Eph. 4.8.
h Judg. 5.12.
i Acts 2.4.
11 in the man.
j 1 Tim. 1.13.
k Ps. 78.60.
l Deut. 32.39.
12 Or, red.
13 Or, ye that are of the fountain.
14 Or, with their company.
m 2 Chr. 32. 23. Isa. 60.16.
15 Or, the beasts of the reeds.
16 Or, he scattereth.
n Isa. 19.19.
o Isa. 45.14. Zeph. 3.10. Acts 8.27, 28.
17 give.
18 Or, heavens.
p Isa. 41.10. Zech. 10.12. John 15.5. Eph. 6.10. Phil. 4.13.

PSALM 69

1 the mire of depth.
2 depth of waters.
a John 15.25.
3 guiltiness.
b Isa. 53.3. John 1.11.
c 1 Ki. 19.10. Ps. 119.139. John 2.17.
d Rom. 15.3.

›ul with fasting, that was to my re-
roach.
'1 I made sackcloth also my gar-
ient; and I [e]became a proverb to
iem.
.2 They that sit in the gate speak
gainst me; and [f]I *was* the song of
ie [4]drunkards.
.3 But as for me, my prayer *is* unto
iee, O LORD, [g]*in* an acceptable time:
› God, in the multitude of thy mercy
ear me, in the truth of thy salvation.
.4 Deliver me out of the mire, and
t me not sink: let me be delivered
om them that hate me, and out of
ie deep waters.
5 Let not the waterflood overflow
ie, neither let the deep swallow me
p, and let not the pit shut her mouth
pon me.
.6 Hear me, O LORD; for thy loving-
indness *is* good: turn unto me ac-
ording to the multitude of thy tender
iercies.
7 And hide not thy face from thy
rvant; for I am in trouble: [5]hear me
peedily.
8 Draw nigh unto my soul, *and* re-
eem it: deliver me because of mine
iemies.
.9 Thou hast known [h]my reproach,
nd my shame, and my dishonour:
iine adversaries *are* all before thee.
'0 Reproach hath broken my heart;
nd I am full of heaviness: and I look-
l *for some* [6]to take pity, but *there was*
one; and for comforters, but I found
one.
.1 They gave me also gall for my
eat; and [i]in my thirst they gave me
negar to drink.
'2 Let their table become a snare be-
re them: and *that which should have*
een for *their* welfare, *let it become* a
ap.
:3 Let [j]their eyes be darkened, that
iey see not; and make their loins
ontinually to shake.
:4 Pour out thine indignation upon
iem, and let thy wrathful anger take
old of them.
5 Let [7]their habitation be desolate;
id [8]let none dwell in their tents.
6 For they persecute [k]*him* whom
iou hast smitten; and they talk to
ie grief of [9]those whom thou hast
ounded.
7 Add [10]iniquity unto their iniquity:
nd let them not come into thy right-
ousness.
8 Let them [m]be blotted out of the
ook of the living, [n]and not be writ-
n with the righteous.

e 1 Ki. 9.7. Ps. 44.13,14. Jer. 24.9.
f Job 17.6. Lam. 3.14.
4 drinkers of strong drink.
g Isa. 49.8. 2 Cor. 6.2.
5 make haste to hear me.
h Ps. 22.6. Isa. 53.3. Heb. 12.2.
6 to lament with me. Ps. 142.4,5.
i Matt. 27.34. Mark 15.36. John 19.29.
j 2 Cor. 3.14.
7 their palace.
8 let there not be a dweller.
k Isa. 53.4.
9 thy wounded.
10 Or, punishment of iniquity.
l Rom. 9.31.
m Ex. 32.32. Phil. 4.3. Rev. 3.5.
n Eze. 13.9. Luke 10.20. Heb. 12.23.
11 Or, meek, or, afflicted.
12 creepeth.
o Ps. 51.18. Ps. 102.13, 16. Isa. 14.32. Isa. 44.26.

PSALM 70

1 to my help.
a Ps. 109.29.
b Isa. 61.10. Hab. 3.17. Rom. 5.2. Phil. 3.1. 1 Pet. 1.2-9.
c Ps. 40.17.
d Judg. 5.28. Ps. 141.1. Heb. 10.37. Rev. 22.20.

PSALM 71

1 Be thou to me for a rock of habitation.
a Ps. 44.4.
b Jer. 17.7. Rom. 15.13.

29 But I *am* poor and sorrowful: let
thy salvation, O God, set me up on
high.
30 I will praise the name of God with
a song, and will magnify him with
thanksgiving.
31 *This* also shall please the LORD
better than an ox *or* bullock that hath
horns and hoofs.
32 The [11]humble shall see *this*, *and* be
glad: and your heart shall live that
seek God.
33 For the LORD heareth the poor,
and despiseth not his prisoners.
34 Let the heaven and earth praise
him, the seas, and every thing that
[12]moveth therein.
35 For [o]God will save Zion, and will
build the cities of Judah: that they
may dwell there, and have it in possession.
36 The seed also of his servants shall
inherit it: and they that love his name
shall dwell therein.

PSALM 70

To the chief Musician, *A Psalm* of David, to bring to remembrance.

MAKE *haste*, O God, to deliver
me; make haste [1]to help me, O
LORD.
2 Let them be [a]ashamed and confounded that seek after my soul:
let them be turned backward, and
put to confusion, that desire my
hurt.
3 Let them be turned back for a reward of their shame that say, Aha,
aha.
4 Let [b]all those that seek thee rejoice and be glad in thee: and let such
as love thy salvation say continually,
Let God be magnified.
5 But [c]I *am* poor and needy: make
haste unto me, O God: thou *art* my
help and my deliverer; O LORD, make
[d]no tarrying.

PSALM 71

IN thee, O LORD, do I put my trust:
let me never be put to confusion.
2 Deliver me in thy righteousness,
and cause me to escape: incline thine
ear unto me, and save me.
3 [1]Be thou my strong habitation,
whereunto I may continually resort:
thou hast given [a]commandment to
save me; for thou *art* my rock and my
fortress.
4 Deliver me, O my God, out of the
hand of the wicked, out of the hand
of the unrighteous and cruel man.
5 For thou [b]*art* my hope, O Lord

GOD: *thou art* my trust from my youth.

6 By [c]thee have I been holden up from the womb: thou art he that took me out of my mother's bowels: my praise *shall be* continually of thee.

7 I [d]am as a wonder unto many; but thou *art* my strong refuge.

8 Let my mouth be filled *with* thy praise *and with* thy honour all the day.

9 Cast me not off in the time of old age; forsake me not when my strength faileth.

10 For mine enemies speak against me; and they that [2]lay wait for my soul [e]take counsel together.

11 Saying, God hath forsaken him: persecute and take him; for *there is* none to deliver *him*.

12 O [f]God, be not far from me: O my God, [g]make haste for my help.

13 Let [h]them be confounded *and* consumed that are adversaries to my soul; let them be covered *with* reproach and dishonour that seek my hurt.

14 But I will hope continually, and will yet praise thee more and more.

15 My [i]mouth shall shew forth thy righteousness *and* thy salvation all the day; for I [j]know not the numbers *thereof*.

16 I will go in [k]the strength of the Lord GOD: I will make mention of thy righteousness, *even* of thine only.

17 O God, thou hast taught me from my youth: and hitherto have I declared thy wondrous works.

18 Now also [3]when I am old and grayheaded, O God, forsake me not; until I have shewed [4]thy strength unto *this* generation, *and* thy power to every one *that* is to come.

19 Thy [l]righteousness also, O God, *is* very high, who hast done great things: [m]O God, who *is* like unto thee!

20 *Thou*, [n]which hast shewed me great and sore troubles, [o]shalt quicken me again, and shalt bring me up again from the depths of the earth.

21 Thou shalt increase my greatness, and comfort me on every side.

22 I will also praise thee [5]with the psaltery, *even* thy truth, O my God: unto thee will I sing with the harp, O thou [p]Holy One of Israel.

23 My lips shall greatly rejoice when I sing unto thee; and [q]my soul, which thou hast redeemed.

24 My tongue also shall talk of thy righteousness all the day long: for they are confounded, for they are brought unto shame, that seek my hurt.

PSALM 72

A Psalm [1]for Solomon.

GIVE the king thy judgments, O God, and thy righteousness un the king's son.

2 He shall [a]judge thy people wi righteousness, and thy poor wi judgment.

3 The mountains shall bring peace the people, and the little hills, by righ eousness.

4 He shall judge the poor of the pe ple, he shall save the children of t needy, and shall break in pieces t oppressor.

5 They shall fear thee as long as t sun and moon endure, throughout a generations.

6 He [b]shall come down like rain up the mown grass: as showers *th* water the earth.

7 In his days shall the righteo flourish; and [c]abundance of peace [2] long as the moon endureth.

8 He [d]shall have dominion also fro sea to sea, and from the river unto t ends of the earth.

9 They that dwell in the wilderne shall bow before him; and his enemi shall lick the dust.

10 The [e]kings of Tarshish and of t isles shall bring presents: the kings Shē-bă and Sē-bă shall offer gifts.

11 Yea, all kings shall fall down b fore him: all nations shall serve hi

12 For he shall deliver the nee when he crieth; the poor also, a *him* that hath no helper.

13 He shall spare the poor and need and shall save the souls of the need

14 He shall redeem their soul fr deceit and violence: and precio shall their blood be in his sight.

15 And he shall live, and to hi [3]shall be given of the gold of Shē-b [f]prayer also shall be made for hi continually; *and* daily shall he praised.

16 There shall be an handful of co in the earth upon the top of t mountains; the fruit thereof sh shake like Lĕb-ă-non: [g]and *they* of t city shall flourish like grass of t earth.

17 His name [4]shall endure for eve [5]his name shall be continued as lo as the sun: and [h]*men* shall be bless in him: [i]all nations shall call h blessed.

18 Blessed *be* the LORD God, t God of Israel, who only doeth wo drous things.

19 And blessed *be* his glorious na

c Ps. 22.9. Isa. 46.3. Jer. 3.4.
d Isa. 8.18. Zech. 3.8. 1 Cor. 4.9.
2 watch, or, observe.
e 2 Sam. 17.1. Matt. 27.1.
f Ps. 22.11. Ps. 35.22.
g Ps. 70.1.
h Ps. 35.4. Ps. 40.14.
i Ps. 35.28.
j Ps. 40.5.
k Zech. 10.12. Eph. 3.16. Phil. 4.13. 2 Tim. 2.1.
3 unto old age and gray hairs.
4 thine arm.
l Ps. 57.10. Pro. 24.7. Isa. 5.16.
m Ex. 15.11. Ps. 35.10. Isa. 40.18, 25.
n Ps. 60.3.
o Hosea 6.1.
5 with the instrument of psaltery.
p 2 Ki. 19.22. Isa. 60.9.
q Ps. 103.4.

PSALM 72
1 Or, of.
a Isa. 11.2.
b 2 Sam. 23.4. Hosea 6.3.
c Isa. 2.4. Dan. 2.44. Luke 1.33.
2 till there be no moon.
d Ex. 23.31. 1 Ki. 4.21, 24. Ps. 2.8. Zech. 9.10.
e Isa. 49.7.
3 one shall give.
f Matt. 6.10. 1 Cor. 1.2,3.
g 1 Ki. 4.20.
4 shall be.
5 shall be as a son to continue his father's name for ever.
h Gen. 12.3. Jer. 4.2.
i Isa. 45.23, 24. Luke 1.48. Phil. 2.9-11.

r ever: and let the whole earth be
led *with* his glory; Ā-mĕn, and Ā-
ĕn.
0 The prayers of David the son of
sse are ended.

PSALM 73

A Psalm [1]of Asaph.

TRULY God *is* good to Israel, *even*
to such as are [3]of a clean heart.
But as for me, my feet were almost
ne; my steps had well nigh slipped.
For I was envious at the foolish,
en I saw the prosperity of the
cked.
For *there are* no bands in their
ath: but their strength *is* [4]firm.
They *are* not [5]in trouble *as other*
en; neither are they plagued [6]like
her men.
Therefore [a]pride compasseth them
out as a chain; violence covereth
em *as* a garment.
Their eyes stand out with fatness:
ey have more than heart could
sh.
They are corrupt, and speak wick-
ly *concerning* oppression: they
eak loftily.
They set their mouth [c]against the
avens, and their tongue walketh
rough the earth.
0 Therefore his people return hith-
: and waters of a full *cup* are wrung
t to them.
1 And they say, [d]How doth God
ow? and is there knowledge in the
ost High?
2 Behold, these *are* the ungodly,
ho prosper in the world; they in-
ease *in* riches.
3 Verily I have cleansed my heart *in*
in, [e]and washed my hands in inno-
ncy.
4 For all the day long have I been
agued, and [8]chastened every morn-
g.
5 If I say, I will speak thus; behold,
hould offend *against* the generation
thy children.
6 When [f]I thought to know this, [9]it
as too painful for me;
7 Until [g]I went into the sanctuary
God; *then* understood I their end.
8 Surely thou didst set them in slip-
ry places: thou castedst them down
to destruction.
9 How are they *brought* into deso-
tion, as in a moment! they are utter-
consumed with terrors.
0 As a dream when *one* awaketh;
, O Lord, when thou awakest, thou
alt despise their image.

PSALM 73
1 Or, for.
2 Or, Yet.
3 clean of heart.
4 fat.
5 in the trouble of other men.
6 with.
a Eccl. 8.11.
7 they pass the thoughts of the heart.
b 2 Pet. 2.18. Jude 16.
c Rev. 13.6.
d Job 22.13. Ps. 94.7.
e Job 21.15. Ps. 24.4. Mal. 3.14. Heb. 10.19-22.
8 my chastisement was.
f Eccl. 8.17.
9 it was labour in mine eyes.
g Ps. 77.13.
10 I knew not.
11 with thee.
h Isa. 58.8.
i John 14.3. 2 Cor. 5.1.
j Isa. 26.8,9. Hab. 3.17, 18.
k Ps. 84.2.
12 rock.
l Heb. 10.22.

PSALM 74
1 Or, A Psalm for Asaph to give instruction.
a Ps. 95.7. Jer. 23.1. Eze. 34.8, 31. Luke 12.32.
2 Or, tribe.
b Dan. 6.27.
3 They have sent thy sanctuary into the fire.
c Ps. 83.4.
4 break.
d 1 Sam. 3.1. Micah 3.6. Matt. 16.4.
e Ps. 44.4.

21 Thus my heart was grieved, and I
was pricked in my reins.
22 So foolish *was* I, and [10]ignorant:
I was *as* a beast [11]before thee.
23 Nevertheless I *am* continually
with thee: thou hast holden *me* by my
right hand.
24 Thou [h]shalt guide me with thy
counsel, and [i]afterward receive me *to*
glory.
25 Whom [j]have I in heaven *but thee?*
and *there is* none upon earth *that* I desire beside thee.
26 My [k]flesh and my heart faileth:
but God *is* the [12]strength of my heart,
and my portion for ever.
27 For, lo, they that are far from thee
shall perish: thou hast destroyed all
them that go a whoring from thee.
28 But *it is* good for me to [l]draw near
to God: I have put my trust in the
Lord GOD, that I may declare all thy
works.

PSALM 74

[1]Maschil of Asaph.

O GOD, why hast thou cast *us* off
for ever? *why* doth thine anger
smoke against [a]the sheep of thy pasture?
2 Remember thy congregation, *which*
thou hast purchased of old; the [2]rod
of thine inheritance, *which* thou hast
redeemed; this mount Zion, wherein
thou hast dwelt.
3 Lift up thy feet unto the perpetual
desolations; *even* all *that* the enemy
hath done wickedly in the sanctuary.
4 Thine enemies roar in the midst of
thy congregations; [b]they set up their
ensigns *for* signs.
5 *A man* was famous according as he
had lifted up axes upon the thick trees.
6 But now they break down the carved work thereof at once with axes and
hammers.
7 [3]They have cast fire into thy sanctuary, they have defiled *by casting*
down the dwelling place of thy name
to the ground.
8 They [c]said in their hearts, Let us
[4]destroy them together: they have
burned up all the synagogues of God
in the land.
9 We see not our signs: [d]*there is* no
more any prophet: neither *is there*
among us any that knoweth how long.
10 O God, how long shall the adversary reproach? shall the enemy blaspheme thy name for ever?
11 Why withdrawest thou thy hand,
even thy right hand? pluck *it* out of
thy bosom.
12 For [e]God *is* my King of old,

working salvation in the midst of the
earth.
13 Thou didst [5]divide the sea by thy
strength: [f]thou brakest the heads of
the [6]dragons in the waters.
14 Thou brakest the heads of lē-vī-
ă-thăn in pieces, *and* gavest him *to* [g]*be*
meat [h]to the people inhabiting the
wilderness.
15 Thou didst [i]cleave the fountain
and the flood: thou driedst up [7]mighty
rivers.
16 The day *is* thine, the night also *is*
thine: thou hast prepared the light
and the sun.
17 Thou hast [j]set all the borders of
the earth: thou hast [8]made summer
and winter.
18 Remember [k]this, *that* the enemy
hath reproached, O LORD, and *that*
the foolish people have blasphemed
thy name.
19 O deliver not the soul [l]of thy
turtledove unto the multitude *of the*
wicked: forget not the congregation
of thy poor for ever.
20 Have [m]respect unto the covenant:
for the dark places of the earth are
full of the habitations of cruelty.
21 O let not the [n]oppressed return
ashamed: let the poor and needy
praise thy name.
22 Arise, O God, plead thine own
cause: remember how the foolish
man [o]reproacheth thee daily.
23 Forget not the voice of thine enemies: the tumult of those that rise up
against thee [9]increaseth continually.

PSALM 75

To the chief Musician, [1]Al-taschith,
A Psalm *or* Song [2]of Asaph.

UNTO thee, O God, do we give
thanks, *unto thee* do we give
thanks: for *that* thy name is near thy
wondrous works declare.
2 When I shall [3]receive the congregation I will judge uprightly.
3 The earth and all the inhabitants
thereof are dissolved: I [a]bear up the
pillars of it. Sē-lăh.
4 I said unto the fools, Deal not foolishly: and to the wicked, Lift not up
the horn:
5 Lift not up your horn on high:
speak *not with* a stiff neck.
6 For promotion *cometh* neither
from the east, nor from the west, nor
from the [4]south.
7 But God *is* the judge: [b]he putteth
down one, and setteth up another.
8 For [c]in the hand of the LORD *there*
is a cup, and the wine is red; it is full

5 break.
f Isa. 51.9.
6 Or, whales.
g Num. 14.9.
h Ps. 72.9.
i Ex. 17.5,6. Num. 20.11. Josh. 3.13. Ps. 105.41. Isa. 11.16. Hab. 3.9. Rev. 16.12.
7 rivers of strength.
j Acts 17.26.
8 made them.
k Rev. 16.19.
l Song 2.14. Song 4.1.
m Gen. 17.7. Lev. 26.44. Jer. 33.21.
n Ps. 9.18.
o Isa. 37.23.
9 ascendeth.

PSALM 75
1 Or, Destroy not.
2 Or, for.
3 Or, take a set time.
a Heb. 1.3.
4 desert.
b 1 Sam. 2.7. 2 Sam. 5.2. Dan. 2.21. Luke 1.52.
c Job 21.20. Jer. 25.15. Rev. 14.10.

PSALM 76
1 Or, for.
a Ps. 46.9. Eze. 39.9.
b Eze. 38. 12.
c Isa. 46.12.
d Ps. 13.3. Jer. 51.39.
e Ex. 15.1. Nah. 2.13. Zech. 12.4.
f Job 41.10. Nah. 1.6.
g Ex. 9.16.
h Eccl. 5.4.
i Ps. 68.29.
2 to fear.
j Ps. 68.35.

PSALM 77
1 Or, for.
a Ps. 50.15.
b Isa. 26.9.
2 my hand.

of mixture; and he poureth out of t
same: but the dregs thereof, all t
wicked of the earth shall wring *th*
out, *and* drink *them.*
9 But I will declare for ever; I w
sing praises to the God of Jacob.
10 All the horns of the wicked a
will I cut off; *but* the horns of t
righteous shall be exalted.

PSALM 76

To the chief Musician on Neginoth,
A Psalm *or* Song [1]of Asaph.

IN Judah *is* God known: his nam
great in Israel.
2 In Sā-lĕm also is his tabernac
and his dwelling place in Zion.
3 There [a]brake he the arrows of t
bow, the shield, and the sword, a
the battle. Sē-lăh.
4 Thou *art* more glorious *and* exc
lent than [b]the mountains of prey.
5 The [c]stouthearted are spoiled, th
[d]have slept their sleep: and none
the men of might have found th
hands.
6 At [e]thy rebuke, O God of Jac
both the chariot and horse are c
into a dead sleep.
7 Thou, *even* thou, *art* to be feare
and who [f]may stand in thy sight wh
once thou art angry?
8 Thou didst cause judgment to
heard from heaven; the earth fear
and was still,
9 When God arose to judgme
to save all the meek of the ear
Sē-lăh.
10 Surely [g]the wrath of man sh
praise thee: the remainder of wra
shalt thou restrain.
11 Vow, [h]and pay unto the Lo
your God: [i]let all that be round ab
him bring presents [2]unto him t
ought to be feared.
12 He shall cut off the spirit of pr
ces: *he* [j]*is* terrible to the kings of t
earth.

PSALM 77

To the chief Musician, to Jeduthun,
A Psalm [1]of Asaph.

I CRIED unto God with my voi
even unto God with my voice; a
he gave ear unto me.
2 In [a]the day of my trouble [b]I sou
the Lord: [2]my sore ran in the nig
and ceased not: my soul refused to
comforted.
3 I remembered God, and w
troubled: I complained, and my spi
was overwhelmed. Sē-lăh.
4 Thou holdest mine eyes waking
am so troubled that I cannot speal

I [c]have considered the days of old,
e years of ancient times.
I call to remembrance my song in
e night: I commune with mine own
art: and my spirit made diligent
arch.
Will the LORD cast off for ever? and
ll he be favourable no more?
Is [d]his mercy clean gone for ever?
th *his* [e]promise fail [3]for evermore?
Hath God [f]forgotten to be gra-
ous? hath he in anger shut up his
nder mercies? Sē-läh.
0 And I said, This *is* [g]my infirmity:
t I will remember the years of the
ht hand of the most High.
1 I [h]will remember the works of the
RD: surely I will remember thy
nders of old.
2 I will meditate also of all thy work,
d talk of thy doings.
3 Thy [i]way, O God, *is* in the sanc-
ary: who *is so* great a God as *our*
od?
4 Thou *art* the God that doest
nders: thou hast declared thy
ength among the people.
5 Thou hast with *thine* arm redeem-
thy people, the sons of Jacob and
seph. Sē-läh.
6 The [j]waters saw thee, O God, the
ters saw thee; they were afraid: the
pths also were troubled.
7 [4]The clouds poured out water:
skies sent out a sound: thine
rows also went abroad.
8 The voice of thy thunder *was* in
heaven: the lightnings lightened
world: the earth trembled and
ook.
9 Thy [k]way *is* in the sea, and thy
th in the great waters, [l]and thy foot-
ps are not known.
0 Thou [m]leddest thy people like a
ck by the hand of Moses and Aaron.

PSALM 78

[1]Maschil of Asaph.

IVE [a]ear, O my people, *to* my
law: incline your ears to the words
my mouth.
I [b]will open my mouth in a parable:
ill utter dark sayings of old:
Which [c]we have heard and known,
d our fathers have told us.
We [d]will not hide *them* from their
ildren, [e]shewing to the generation
come the praises of the LORD, and
strength, and his wonderful works
t he hath done.
For he established a testimony in
cob, and appointed a law in Israel,
ich he commanded our fathers, that

c Deut. 32.7. Ps. 143.5. Isa. 51.9.
d Isa. 27.11. Jonah 2.4.
e Num. 23.19. Jer. 15.18. Rom. 9.6.
3 to generation and generation?
f Isa. 49.15.
g Job 42.3. Ps. 31.22. Jer. 10.19.
h 1 Chr. 16. 12. Ps. 28.5. Isa. 5.12.
i Ps. 73.17.
j Ex. 14.21. Josh. 3.15, 16.
4 The clouds were poured forth with water.
k Hab. 3.15.
l Ex. 14.28. Job 37.23.
m Isa. 63.11.

PSALM 78

1 Or, A Psalm for Asaph to give instruction.
a Ex. 19.5. Deut. 32.29.
b Ps. 49.4. Matt. 13.35.
c Ps. 44.1.
d Deut. 4.9.
e Ex. 12.26. Josh. 4.6,7.
f Ps. 102.18.
2 that prepared not their heart.
3 throwing forth.
g Isa. 17.10. Jer. 2.32.
h Gen. 32.3. Isa. 19.11.
i Ex. 17.6. Num. 20.11. Ps. 105.41. Isa. 41.18.
j Deut. 9.21.
k Heb. 3.16.
l Num. 11.4.
4 order.
m Ex. 17.6. Num. 20.11.
n Heb. 3.10.
o Gen. 7.11. Deut. 28.12.
p Neh. 9.15, 20. John 6.31. 1 Cor. 10.3.
5 Or, Every one did eat the bread of the mighty.

they should make them known to their
children:
6 That [f]the generation to come might
know *them, even* the children *which*
should be born; *who* should arise and
declare *them* to their children:
7 That they might set their hope in
God, and not forget the works of God,
but keep his commandments:
8 And might not be as their fathers,
a stubborn and rebellious generation;
a generation [2]*that* set not their heart
aright, and whose spirit was not stedfast with God.
9 The children of Ē-phră-ĭm, *being*
armed, *and* [3]carrying bows, turned
back in the day of battle.
10 They kept not the covenant of
God, and refused to walk in his law;
11 And [g]forgat his works, and his
wonders that he had shewed them.
12 Marvellous things did he in the
sight of their fathers, in the land of
Egypt, [h]*in* the field of Zō-ăn.
13 He divided the sea, and caused
them to pass through; and he made
the waters to stand as an heap.
14 In the daytime also he led them
with a cloud, and all the night with a
light of fire.
15 He [i]clave the rocks in the wilderness, and gave *them* drink as *out of*
the great depths.
16 He brought [j]streams also out of
the rock, and caused waters to run
down like rivers.
17 And they sinned yet more against
him by [k]provoking the most High in
the wilderness.
18 And they tempted God in their
heart by asking meat for their lust.
19 Yea, [l]they spake against God;
they said, Can God [4]furnish a table in
the wilderness?
20 Behold, [m]he smote the rock, that
the waters gushed out, and the
streams overflowed; can he give bread
also? can he provide flesh for his
people?
21 Therefore the LORD heard *this*,
and was wroth: so a fire was kindled
against Jacob, and anger also came up
against Israel;
22 Because they [n]believed not in
God, and trusted not in his salvation:
23 Though he had commanded the
clouds from above, [o]and opened the
doors of heaven,
24 And [p]had rained down măn-nă
upon them to eat, and had given them
of the corn of heaven.
25 [5]Man did eat angels' food: he sent
them meat to the full.

26 He caused an east wind [6]to blow
in the heaven: and by his power he
brought in the south wind.
27 He rained flesh also upon them
as dust, and [7]feathered fowls like as
the sand of the sea:
28 And he let *it* fall in the midst of
their camp, round about their habitations.
29 So they did eat, and were well
filled: for he gave them their own
desire;
30 They were not estranged from
their lust. But while their meat *was*
yet in their mouths,
31 The wrath of God came upon
them, and slew the fattest of them,
and [8]smote down the [9]chosen *men* of
Israel.
32 For all this they sinned still, and
believed not for his wondrous works.
33 Therefore their days did he consume in vanity, and their years in
trouble.
34 When [q]he slew them, then they
sought him: and they returned and inquired early after God.
35 And they remembered that God
was their rock, and the high God their
redeemer.
36 Nevertheless they did [r]flatter him
with their mouth, and they lied unto
him with their tongues.
37 For their heart was not right with
him, neither were they stedfast in his
covenant.
38 But he, *being* [s]full of compassion,
forgave *their* iniquity, and destroyed
them not: yea, many a time [t]turned
he his anger away, and did not stir up
all his wrath.
39 For he remembered [u]that they
were but flesh; [v]a wind that passeth
away, and cometh not again.
40 How oft did they [10]provoke him in
the wilderness, *and* grieve him in the
desert!
41 Yea, they turned back and tempted God, and limited the Holy One of
Israel.
42 They remembered not his hand,
nor the day when he delivered them
[11]from the enemy.
43 How he had [12]wrought his signs
in Egypt, and his wonders in the field
of Zō-ăn:
44 And had turned their rivers into
blood; and their floods, that they
could not drink.
45 He sent divers sorts of flies among
them, which devoured them; and
frogs, which destroyed them.
46 He gave also their increase unto

6 to go.
7 fowl of wing.
8 made to bow.
9 Or, young men.
q Hosea 5.15.
r Eze. 33.31.
s Ex. 34.6. Neh. 9.17. Ps. 86.15.
t 1 Ki. 21.29. Isa. 48.9. Micah 7.18. Rom. 2.4.
u Gen. 6.3. John 3.6. Jas. 4.14.
v Job 7.7,16.
10 Or, rebel against him.
11 Or, from affliction.
12 set.
13 killed.
14 Or, great hailstones.
15 He shut up.
16 Or, lightnings.
w Rom. 2.8.
17 He weighed a path.
18 Or, their beasts to the murrain.
x Gen. 9.22.
19 covered.
y Ex. 15.17.
z Eze. 20.27.
a Hosea 7.16.
b Lev. 26.30. Num. 33.52. Deut. 12.2.
c Heb. 4.13.
d 1 Sam. 4.11. Jer. 7.12.
e Judg. 18.30.
f 1 Sam. 4.12.
20 praised.
g Job 27.15.
h Isa. 42.13.

the caterpiller, and their labour unt
the locust.
47 He [13]destroyed their vines wit
hail, and their sycomore trees wit
[14]frost.
48 [15]He gave up their cattle also t
the hail, and their flocks to [16]hot thu
derbolts.
49 He cast upon them the [w]fierc
ness of his anger, wrath, and indign
tion, and trouble, by sending ev
angels *among them.*
50 [17]He made a way to his anger;
spared not their soul from death, b
gave [18]their life over to the pestilenc
51 And smote all the firstborn
Egypt; the chief of *their* strength
the tabernacles of [x]Ham:
52 But made his own people to g
forth like sheep, and guided them
the wilderness like a flock.
53 And he led them on safely, so th
they feared not: but the sea [19]ove
whelmed their enemies.
54 And he brought them to t
border of his [y]sanctuary, *even to* th
mountain, *which* his right hand h
purchased.
55 He cast out the heathen also b
fore them, and divided them an i
heritance by line, and made the trib
of Israel to dwell in their tents.
56 Yet they tempted and provok
the most high God, and kept not h
testimonies:
57 But [z]turned back, and dealt u
faithfully like their fathers: they we
turned aside [a]like a deceitful bow.
58 For they provoked him to ang
with their [b]high places, and mov
him to jealousy with their grav
images.
59 When God [c]heard *this*, he w
wroth, and greatly abhorred Israe
60 So [d]that he forsook the tabernac
of Shī-lōh, the tent *which* he plac
among men;
61 And [e]delivered his [f]strength in
captivity, and his glory into the e
emy's hand.
62 He gave his people over also un
the sword; and was wroth with his
heritance.
63 The fire consumed their you
men; and their maidens were n
[20]given to marriage.
64 Their priests fell by the swor
and their [g]widows made no lament
tion.
65 Then the Lord awaked as one o
of sleep, *and* [h]like a mighty man th
shouteth by reason of wine.
66 And he smote his enemies in t

nder parts: he put them to a perpet-
ıl reproach.
7 Moreover he refused the taber-
ıcle of Joseph, and chose not the
ibe of Ē-phră-ĭm:
8 But chose the tribe of Judah, the
ount Zion which he loved.
9 And [i]he built his sanctuary like
gh *palaces*, like the earth which he
ıth [21]established for ever.
0 He chose David also his servant,
ıd took him from the sheepfolds:
1 [22]From following the ewes great
ith young he brought him to [j]feed
cob his people, and Israel his in-
ritance.
2 So he fed them according to the
ntegrity of his heart; and guided
em by the skilfulness of his hands.

PSALM 79

A Psalm [1]of Asaph.

O GOD, the heathen are come into
thine inheritance; thy holy temple
ve they defiled; they [a]have laid Jeru-
lem on heaps.
The [b]dead bodies of thy servants
ve they given *to be* meat unto the
wls of the heaven, the flesh of thy
ints unto the beasts of the earth.
Their blood have they shed like
ter round about Jerusalem; and
ere was none to bury *them*.
We are become a reproach to our
ighbours, a scorn and derision to
em that are round about us.
How long, LORD? wilt thou be
gry for ever? shall thy [d]jealousy
rn like fire?
Pour out thy wrath upon the hea-
en that have [e]not known thee, and
on the kingdoms that have [f]not call-
upon thy name.
For they have devoured Jacob, and
d waste his dwelling place.
O [g]remember not against us [2]form-
iniquities: let thy tender mercies
eedily prevent us: for we are
ought very low.
Help us, O God of our salvation,
r the glory of thy name: and deliver
, and purge away our sins, [h]for thy
me's sake.
0 Wherefore should the heathen
y, Where *is* their God? let him be
own among the heathen in our
ht *by* the [3]revenging of the blood of
y servants *which is* shed.
1 Let the sighing of the prisoner
me before thee; [i]according to the
eatness of [4]thy power [5]preserve thou
ose that are appointed to die;
2 And render unto our neighbours
sevenfold into their bosom their reproach, wherewith they have reproached thee, O Lord.
13 So we thy people and sheep of thy
pasture will give thee thanks for ever:
[j]we will shew forth thy praise [6]to all
generations.

PSALM 80

To the chief Musician upon Shoshannim-Eduth, A Psalm [1]of Asaph.

GIVE ear, O Shepherd of Israel,
thou that leadest Joseph like a
flock; [a]thou that dwellest *between* the
chĕr-ū-bĭms, [b]shine forth.
2 Before Ē-phră-ĭm and Benjamin
and Mă-năs-sĕh stir up thy strength,
and [2]come *and* save us.
3 Turn [c]us again, O God, and cause
thy face to shine; and we shall be
saved.
4 O LORD God of hosts, how long
[3]wilt thou be angry against the prayer
of thy people?
5 Thou feedest them with the bread
of tears; and givest them tears to drink
in great measure.
6 Thou makest us a strife unto our
neighbours: and our enemies laugh
among themselves.
7 Turn [d]us again, O God of hosts,
and cause thy face to shine; and we
shall be saved.
8 Thou hast brought [e]a vine out of
Egypt: thou hast cast out the heathen,
and planted it.
9 Thou preparedst *room* before it,
and didst cause it to take deep root,
and it filled the land.
10 The hills were covered with the
shadow of it, and the boughs thereof
were like [4]the goodly cedars.
11 She sent out her boughs unto the
sea, and her branches [f]unto the river.
12 Why hast thou *then* [g]broken down
her hedges, so that all they which pass
by the way do pluck her?
13 The boar out of the wood doth
waste it, and the wild beast of the field
doth devour it.
14 Return, [h]we beseech thee, O God
of hosts: [i]look down from heaven, and
behold, and visit this vine;
15 And the vineyard which thy right
hand hath planted, and the branch
that thou madest strong for [j]thyself.
16 *It is* burned with fire, *it is* cut
down: they perish at the rebuke of
thy countenance.
17 Let [k]thy hand be upon the man
[l]of thy right hand, upon the son of
man *whom* thou madest strong for
thyself.

i 1 Ki. 6.1.
21 founded.
22 From after.
j 2 Sam. 5.2. 1 Chr. 11.2. Micah 5.2-4. Zech. 11.4.
k 1 Ki. 9.4.

PSALM 79
1 Or, for.
a 2 Ki. 25.9. Jer. 26.18.
b Jer. 7.33.
c Rev. 11.9.
d Deut. 29. 20. Eze. 36.5.
e Isa. 45.4.
f Ps. 53.4.
g Isa. 43.25.
2 Or, the iniquities of them that were before us.
h Josh. 7.9. Isa. 43.25. Jer. 14.7.
3 vengeance.
i Num. 14.17.
4 thine arm.
5 reserve the children of death.
j Isa. 43.21.
6 to generation and generation.

PSALM 80
1 Or, for.
a 1 Sam. 4.4. Ps. 99.1.
b Deut. 33.2.
2 come for salvation to us.
c 1 Ki. 18.37.
3 wilt thou smoke.
d 1 Ki. 18.37.
e Isa. 5.1,7. Jer. 2.21. Eze. 15.6.
4 the cedars of God.
f Ex. 23.31. Ps. 72.8.
g Isa. 5.5.
h Zech. 1.12, 16,17.
i Isa. 63.15.
j Isa. 49.5.
k Ps. 89.21.
l Ex. 4.22. Ps. 110.1. Dan. 7.13, 14. John 5.21-27.

18 So will not we go back from thee:
quicken us, and we will call upon thy
name.
19 Turn us again, O LORD God of
hosts, cause [m]thy face to shine; and
we shall be saved.

PSALM 81

To the chief Musician upon Gittith,
A Psalm [1]of Asaph.

SING aloud unto God our strength:
make a joyful noise unto the God
of Jacob.
2 Take a psalm, and bring hither the
timbrel, the pleasant harp with the
psaltery.
3 Blow up the trumpet in the new
moon, in the time appointed, on our
solemn feast day.
4 For [a]this *was* a statute for Israel,
and a law of the God of Jacob.
5 This he ordained in Joseph *for* a
testimony, when he went out [2]through
the land of Egypt: *where* I heard a
language *that* I understood not.
6 I removed his shoulder from the
burden: his hands [3]were delivered
from the [4]pots.
7 Thou calledst in trouble, and I delivered thee; I answered thee in the
secret place of thunder: I proved
thee at the waters of [5]Mĕr-ĭ-băh. Sē-
lăh.
8 Hear, O my people, and I will
testify unto thee: O Israel, if thou wilt
hearken unto me;
9 There shall no strange god be in
thee; neither shalt thou worship any
strange god.
10 I *am* the LORD thy God, which
brought thee out of the land of Egypt:
[b]open thy mouth wide, and I will fill
it.
11 But my people would not hearken
to my voice; and Israel would none of
me.
12 So [c]I gave them up [6]unto their
own hearts' lust: *and* they walked in
their own counsels.
13 Oh [d]that my people had hearkened unto me, *and* Israel had walked in
my ways!
14 I should soon have subdued their
enemies, and turned my hand against
their adversaries.
15 The haters of the LORD should
have [7]submitted themselves unto him:
but their time should have endured
for ever.
16 He should have fed them also
[8]with the finest of the wheat: and with
honey out of the rock should I have
satisfied thee.

m Num. 6.25. Ps. 27.4,9.

PSALM 81
1 Or, for.
a Lev. 23.24. Num. 10.10.
2 Or, against.
3 passed away.
4 Or, baskets.
5 Or, strife.
b Ps. 37.3. John 15.7.
c Acts 7.42. Rom. 1.24.
6 Or, to the hardness of their hearts, or, imaginations.
d Deut. 5.29. Isa. 48.18. Jer. 44.4,5. Matt. 23.37.
7 lied, or, yielded feigned obedience.
8 with the fat of wheat.

PSALM 82
1 Or, for.
a Eccl. 5.8.
b Ex. 21.6.
c Deut. 1.17. Ps. 58.1,2.
2 Judge.
d Ps. 11.3.
3 moved.
e Ex. 22.9. John 10.34.
f Job 21.32. Eze. 31.14.
g Ps. 2.8. Rev. 11.15.

PSALM 83
1 Or, for.
a Ps. 2.1.
b Ps. 27.5. Col. 3.3.
c 2 Sam. 10.6. 2 Chr. 20.1.
2 heart.
3 they have been an arm to the children of Lot.
d Num. 31.7, 8. Judg. 7.22. Isa. 9.4. Judg. 4.15.

PSALM 82

A Psalm [1]of Asaph.

GOD [a]standeth in the congregatio
of the mighty; he judgeth amon
[b]the gods.
2 How long will ye judge unjustl
and accept [c]the persons of the wic
ed? Sē-lăh.
3 [2]Defend the poor and fatherles
do justice to the afflicted and need
4 Deliver the poor and needy: r
them out of the hand of the wicked.
5 They know not, neither will th
understand; they walk on in dar
ness: [d]all the foundations of the ear
are [3]out of course.
6 I [e]have said, Ye *are* gods; and a
of you *are* children of the most Hig
7 But [f]ye shall die like men, and f
like one of the princes.
8 Arise, O God, judge the earth: f
[g]thou shalt inherit all nations.

PSALM 83

A Song *or* Psalm [1]of Asaph.

KEEP not thou silence, O Go
hold not thy peace, and be n
still, O God.
2 For, lo, [a]thine enemies make
tumult: and they that hate thee ha
lifted up the head.
3 They have taken crafty coun
against thy people, and consult
against [b]thy hidden ones.
4 They have said, Come, and [c]let
cut them off from *being* a nation; th
the name of Israel may be no more
remembrance.
5 For they have consulted togeth
with one [2]consent: they are confed
ate against thee:
6 The tabernacles of Ē-dom, and t
Ĭsh-mā-ĕ-lītes; of Moab, and t
Hăg-ă-rēnes;
7 Gē-băl, and Ammon, and Ăm-
lĕk; the Philistines with the inha
tants of Tyre;
8 Assur also is joined with the
[3]they have holpen the childen of L
Sē-lăh.
9 Do unto them as *unto* [d]the Mĭd
ă-nītes; as *to* [e]Sĭs-ĕ-ră, as *to* Jā-bĭn,
the brook of Kī-sŏn:
10 *Which* perished at En-dor: th
became *as* dung for the earth.
11 Make their nobles like Ôr-ĕb, a
like Zēeb: yea, all their princes as Z
băh, and as Zăl-mŭn-nă:
12 Who said, Let us take to o
selves the houses of God in possessi
13 O my God, make them like
wheel; as the stubble before the wi
14 As the fire burneth a wood, and

e flame setteth the mountains on
e;
5 So persecute them with thy tem-
st, and make them afraid with thy
orm.
6 Fill their faces with shame; that
ey may seek thy name, O LORD.
7 Let them be confounded and
oubled for ever; yea, let them be put
shame, and perish:
8 That *men* may know that thou,
iose name alone *is* JĔ-HŌ-VĂH *art*
e most high over all the earth.

PSALM 84

To the chief Musician upon Gittith, A Psalm [1]for the sons of Korah.

IOW [a]amiable *are* thy tabernacles,
O LORD of hosts!
My soul longeth, yea, even fainteth
r the courts of the LORD: my heart
id my flesh crieth out for the living
od.
[2]Yea, the sparrow hath found an
ouse, and the swallow a nest for her-
lf, where she may lay her young,
en thine altars, O LORD of hosts, my
ing, and my God.
Blessed *are* they that dwell in thy
ouse: they will be still praising thee.
-lăh.
Blessed *is* the man whose strength
in thee; in whose heart *are* the ways
them.
Who passing through the valley [3]of
ā-că make it a well; the rain also
lleth the pools.
They go [5]from strength to strength,
ery one of them in [b]Zion appeareth
fore God.
O LORD God of hosts, hear my
ayer: give ear, O God of Jacob.
-lăh.
Behold, [c]O God our shield, and
ok upon the face of thine anointed.
0 For a day in thy courts *is* better
ian a thousand. [6]I had rather be a
oorkeeper in the house of my God,
ian to dwell in the tents of wicked-
ss.
1 For the LORD God *is* a sun and
iield: the LORD will give grace and
ory: no good *thing* will he withhold
om them that walk uprightly.
2 O LORD of hosts, blessed *is* the
an that trusteth in thee.

PSALM 85

To the chief Musician, A Psalm [1]for the sons of Korah.

ORD, thou hast been [2]favourable
unto thy land: thou hast brought
ack the captivity of Jacob.
2 Thou hast forgiven the iniquity of
thy people, thou hast covered all their
sin. Sē-lăh.
3 Thou hast taken away all thy
wrath: [3]thou hast turned *thyself* from
the fierceness of thine anger.
4 Turn us, O God of our salvation,
and cause thine anger toward us to
cease.
5 Wilt thou be angry with us for
ever? wilt thou draw out thine anger
to all generations?
6 Wilt thou [b]not revive us again:
that thy people may rejoice in thee?
7 Shew us thy mercy, O LORD, and
grant us thy salvation.
8 I [c]will hear what God the LORD
will speak: for [d]he will speak peace
unto his people, and to his saints: but
let them not turn [e]again to folly.
9 Surely his salvation *is* nigh them
that fear him; that glory may dwell in
our land.
10 Mercy [f]and truth are met together; [g]righteousness and peace have
kissed *each other.*
11 Truth [h]shall spring out of the
earth; and righteousness shall look
down from heaven.
12 Yea, [i]the LORD shall give *that
which is* good; and our land shall
yield her increase.
13 Righteousness shall go before
him; and shall set *us* in the way of his
steps.

PSALM 86

[1]A Prayer of David.

BOW down thine ear, O LORD, hear
me: for I *am* poor and needy.
2 Preserve my soul; for I *am* [2]holy:
O thou my God, save thy servant that
trusteth in thee.
3 Be merciful unto me, O Lord: for
I cry unto thee [3]daily.
4 Rejoice the soul of thy servant: for
unto thee, O Lord, do I lift up my
soul.
5 For [a]thou, Lord, *art* good, and
ready to forgive; and plenteous in
mercy unto all them that call upon
thee.
6 Give ear, O LORD, unto my prayer;
and attend to the voice of my supplications.
7 In the day of my trouble I will
call upon thee: for thou wilt answer
me.
8 Among [b]the gods *there is* none like
unto thee, O Lord; neither *are there
any works* like unto thy works.
9 All [c]nations whom thou hast made
shall come and worship before thee,
O Lord; and shall glorify thy name.

PSALM 84
1 Or, of.
a Ps. 26.8. Ps. 27.4. Heb. 9.23, 24. Rev. 21.2,3.
2 Or, As the sparrow findeth a house, and the swallow a nest for herself, so findeth my soul thine altars.
3 Or, of mulberry trees make him a well, etc.
4 covereth.
5 Or, from company to company.
b Deut. 16.16.
c Gen. 15.1.
6 I would choose rather to sit at the threshold.

PSALM 85
1 Or, of.
2 Or, well pleased.
a Jer. 30.18. Eze. 39.25.
3 Or, thou hast turned thine anger from waxing hot.
b Hab. 3.2.
c Hab. 2.1.
d Zech. 9.10.
e 2 Pet. 2.20.
f Micah 7.20. John 1.17.
g Ps. 72.2,3. Isa. 32.17. Luke 2.14. John 14.27.
h Isa. 45.8. 2 Cor. 5.14-21.
i Jas. 1.17.

PSALM 86
1 Or, A Prayer, being a Psalm of David.
2 Or, one whom thou favourest.
3 Or, all the day.
a ver. 15. Ps. 130.7,8. Joel 2.13.
b Ex. 15.11. Deut. 3.24. 1 Sam. 2.2. 2 Sam. 7.22. 1 Ki. 8.23.
c Ps. 95.6,7. Isa. 43.7. Rev. 15.4.

10 For thou *art* great, and doest wondrous things: [d]thou *art* God alone.
11 Teach me thy way, O LORD; I
will walk in thy truth: unite my heart
to fear thy name.
12 I will praise thee, O Lord my God,
with all my heart: and I will glorify
thy name for evermore.
13 For great *is* thy mercy toward me:
and thou hast [e]delivered my soul from
the lowest [4]hell.
14 O God, the proud are risen
against me, and the assemblies of [5]vio-
lent *men* have sought after my soul;
and have not set thee before them.
15 But [f]thou, O Lord, *art* a God full
of compassion, and gracious, longsuffering, and plenteous in mercy and
truth.
16 O turn unto me, and have mercy
upon me; give thy strength unto thy
servant, and save the son of thine
handmaid.
17 Shew me a token for good; that
they which hate me may see *it*, and be
ashamed: because thou, LORD, hast
holpen me, and comforted me.

PSALM 87

A Psalm *or* Song [1]for the sons of Korah.

HIS foundation *is* in the holy
mountains.
2 The LORD loveth the gates of Zion
more than all the dwellings of Jacob.
3 Glorious [a]things are spoken of
thee, O city of God. Sē′läh.
4 I will make mention of [2]Rahab and
Babylon to them that know me: behold Philistia, and Tyre, with Ē-thĭ-
ō′pĭ-ă; this *man* was born there.
5 And of Zion it shall be said, This
and that man was born in her: and
[b]the highest himself shall establish her.
6 The [c]LORD shall count, when he
[d]writeth up the people, *that* this *man*
was born there. Sē′läh.
7 As well the singers as the players
on instruments *shall be there:* all my
springs *are* in thee.

PSALM 88

A Song *or* Psalm [1]for the sons of Korah, to the chief Musician upon Mahalath Leannoth, [2]Maschil of Heman the Ezrahite.

O LORD God of my salvation, I
have cried day *and* night before
thee:
2 Let my prayer come before thee:
incline thine ear unto my cry;
3 For my soul is full of troubles:
and my life [a]draweth nigh unto the
grave.
4 I am counted with them that go

d Deut. 6.4. Isa. 37.16. Mark 12.29. 1 Cor. 8.4. Eph. 4.6.
e Ps. 56.13.
4 Or, grave.
5 terrible.
f Ex. 34.6. Num. 14.18. Neh. 9.17. ver. 5. Ps. 103.8. Ps. 111.4. Joel 2.13.

PSALM 87
1 Or, of.
a Isa. 60.1.
2 Or, Egypt.
b Eze. 48.35. Matt. 16.18.
c Ps. 22.30.
d Isa. 4.3. Jer. 3.19. Eze. 13.9.

PSALM 88
1 Or, of.
2 Or, A Psalm of Heman the Ezrahite, giving instruction.
a Job 33.22. Ps. 107.18. Isa. 38.10.
3 Or, by thy hand.
b Job 10.21.
c Ps. 31.12. Eccl. 8.10.
d Job 6.4. Isa. 53.8. Dan. 9.26.
4 burnings.
5 Or, all the day.
e Job 19.13.

PSALM 89
1 Or, A Psalm for Ethan the Ezrahite, to give instruction.
a 1 Ki. 4.31.
2 to generation and generation.
b Eze. 34.23. Hosea 3.5. Acts 2.30. Heb. 7.21.
c 2 Sam. 7.16. 1 Ki. 9.5. Isa. 9.6,7. Luke 1.32. Rom. 1.3.

down into the pit: I am as a man *th*
hath no strength:
5 Free among the dead, like the sla
that lie in the grave, whom thou r
memberest no more: and they are c
off [3]from thy hand.
6 Thou hast laid me in the lowest p
in darkness, in the deeps.
7 Thy wrath lieth hard upon me, an
thou hast afflicted *me* with all th
waves. Sē′läh.
8 Thou hast put away mine acquain
ance far from me; thou hast made m
an abomination unto them: *I am* sh
up, and I cannot come forth.
9 Mine eye mourneth by reason
affliction: LORD, I have called dai
upon thee, I have stretched out m
hands unto thee.
10 Wilt thou shew wonders to th
dead? shall the dead arise *and* prai
thee? Sē′läh.
11 Shall thy lovingkindness be de
clared in the grave? *or* thy faithfu
ness in destruction?
12 Shall [b]thy wonders be known
the dark? [c]and thy righteousness
the land of forgetfulness?
13 But unto thee have I cried,
LORD; and in the morning shall m
prayer prevent thee.
14 LORD, why castest thou off m
soul? *why* hidest thou thy face fro
me?
15 I *am* afflicted and ready to d
from *my* youth up: *while* I [d]suffer th
terrors I am distracted.
16 Thy [4]fierce wrath goeth over m
thy terrors have cut me off.
17 They came round about me [5]dai
like water; they compassed me abo
together.
18 Lover [e]and friend hast thou p
far from me, *and* mine acquaintan
into darkness.

PSALM 89

[1]Maschil of [a]Ethan the Ezrahite.

I WILL sing of the mercies of th
LORD for ever: with my mouth wi
I make known thy faithfulness [2]t
all generations.
2 For I have said, Mercy shall b
built up for ever: thy faithfulne
shalt thou establish in the ve
heavens.
3 I have made a covenant with m
chosen, I have [b]sworn unto David m
servant,
4 Thy seed will I establish for eve
and build up thy throne [c]to all gener
tions. Sē′läh.
5 And the heavens shall praise th

ronders, O LORD: thy faithfulness
lso in the congregation of the saints.
5 For who in the heaven can be com-
ared unto the LORD? *who* among the
ons of the mighty can be likened un-
o the LORD?
7 God is greatly to be feared in the
ssembly of the saints, and to be had
n reverence of all *them that are* about
im.
8 O LORD God of hosts, who *is* a
trong LORD like unto thee? or to thy
aithfulness round about thee?
9 Thou [d]rulest the raging of the sea:
vhen the waves thereof arise, thou
tillest them.
10 Thou [e]hast broken [3]Rahab in
ieces, as one that is slain; thou hast
cattered thine enemies [4]with thy
trong arm.
11 The heavens *are* thine, the earth
lso *is* thine: *as for* the world and the
ulness thereof, thou hast founded
hem.
12 The north and the south thou hast
reated them: [f]Tā-bôr and Hĕr-mon
shall rejoice in thy name.
13 Thou hast [5]a mighty arm: strong
s thy hand, *and* high is thy right hand.
14 Justice and judgment *are* the
habitation of thy throne: mercy and
ruth shall go before thy face.
15 Blessed *is* the people that know
he joyful [h]sound: they shall walk, O
ORD, in the light of thy countenance.
16 In thy name shall they rejoice all
he day: and in thy righteousness
hall they be exalted.
17 For thou *art* the glory of their
trength: and in thy favour our horn
hall be exalted.
18 For [7]the LORD *is* our defence; and
the Holy One of Israel *is* our king.
19 Then thou spakest in vision to
hy holy one, and saidst, I have laid
elp upon *one that is* mighty; I have
xalted *one* chosen out of the people.
20 I have found David my servant;
vith my holy oil have I anointed him:
21 With whom my hand shall be
stablished: mine arm also shall
trengthen him.
22 The enemy shall not exact upon
im; nor the son of wickedness afflict
im.
23 And I will beat down his foes be-
ore his face, and plague them that
ate him.
24 But [j]my faithfulness and my
nercy *shall be* with him: and in my
ame shall his horn be exalted.
25 I will set his hand also in the sea,
nd his right hand in the rivers.

d Job 38.11. Nah. 1.4. Matt. 8.26.
e Isa. 30.7.
3 Or, Egypt.
4 with the arm of thy strength.
f Josh. 19.22. Judg. 4.6.
g Josh. 12.1.
5 an arm with might.
6 Or, establishment.
h Num. 10. 10.
7 Or, our shield is of the LORD, and our king is of the Holy One of Israel.
i Hosea 13. 10.
j Ps. 61.7.
k 2 Sam. 7.14. 1 Chr. 22.10. John 5.17.
l Ps. 2.7.
m Isa. 55.3.
n Isa. 9.7. Jer. 33.17. Dan. 7.14.
o Deut. 11. 21.
p 2 Sam. 7.14.
q Jer. 9.13.
8 profane my statutes.
9 I will not make void from him.
10 to lie.
r Ps. 110.4. Amos 4.2. Amos 8.7. Heb. 6.13, 17.
11 if I lie.
s 2 Sam. 7.16. Luke 1.33. John 12.34.
t Jer. 31.35.
u Lam. 5.16.
12 brightness.
v Job 7.7.

26 He shall cry unto me, Thou *art*
[k]my father, my God, and the rock of
my salvation.
27 Also I will make him [l]*my* firstborn, higher than the kings of the
earth.
28 My [m]mercy will I keep for him for
evermore, and my covenant shall
stand fast with him.
29 His seed also will I make *to endure* for ever, [n]and his throne as [o]the
days of heaven.
30 If [p]his children forsake [q]my law,
and walk not in my judgments;
31 If they [8]break my statutes, and
keep not my commandments;
32 Then will I visit their transgression with the rod, and their iniquity
with stripes.
33 Nevertheless my lovingkindness
[9]will I not utterly take from him, nor
suffer my faithfulness [10]to fail.
34 My covenant will I not break, nor
alter the thing that is gone out of my
lips.
35 Once have I sworn [r]by my holiness [11]that I will not lie unto David.
36 His [s]seed shall endure for ever,
and his throne as the sun before me.
37 It [t]shall be established for ever as
the moon, and *as* a faithful witness in
heaven. Sē-läh.
38 But thou hast cast off and abhorred, thou hast been wroth with
thine anointed.
39 Thou hast made void the covenant of thy servant: [u]thou hast profaned his crown *by casting it* to the
ground.
40 Thou hast broken down all his
hedges; thou hast brought his strong
holds to ruin.
41 All that pass by the way spoil him:
he is a reproach to his neighbours.
42 Thou hast set up the right hand
of his adversaries; thou hast made all
his enemies to rejoice.
43 Thou hast also turned the edge of
his sword, and hast not made him to
stand in the battle.
44 Thou hast made his [12]glory to
cease, and cast his throne down to the
ground.
45 The days of his youth hast thou
shortened: thou hast covered him with
shame. Sē-läh.
46 How long, LORD? wilt thou hide
thyself for ever? shall thy wrath burn
like fire?
47 Remember [v]how short my time is:
wherefore hast thou made all men in
vain?
48 What man *is he that* liveth, and

shall not [w]see death? shall he deliver his soul from the hand of the grave? Sē-lăh.

49 Lord, where *are* thy former lovingkindnesses, *which* thou [x]swarest unto David in thy truth?

50 Remember, Lord, the reproach of thy servants; *how* I do bear in my bosom *the reproach of* all the mighty people;

51 Wherewith thine enemies have reproached, O LORD; wherewith they have reproached the footsteps of thine anointed.

52 Blessed *be* the LORD for evermore. Ā-mĕn, and Ā-mĕn.

PSALM 90

[1]A Prayer of Moses the man of God.

LORD, thou hast been our dwelling place [2]in all generations.

2 Before the [a]mountains were brought forth, or ever thou hadst formed the earth and the world, even from everlasting to everlasting, thou *art* God.

3 Thou turnest man to destruction; and sayest, [b]Return, ye children of men.

4 For [c]a thousand years in thy sight *are but* as yesterday [3]when it is past, and *as* a watch in the night.

5 Thou carriest them away as with a flood; they are *as* a sleep: in the morning *they* [d]*are* like grass *which* [4]groweth up.

6 In [e]the morning it flourisheth, and groweth up; in the evening it is cut down, and withereth.

7 For we are consumed by thine anger, and by thy wrath are we troubled.

8 Thou [f]hast set our iniquities before thee, our [g]secret *sins* in the light of thy countenance.

9 For all our days are [5]passed away in thy wrath: we spend our years [6]as a tale *that is told*.

10 [7]The days of our years *are* threescore years and ten; and if by reason of strength *they be* fourscore years, yet *is* their strength labour and sorrow; for it is soon cut off, and we fly away.

11 Who knoweth the power of thine anger? even according to thy fear, *so is* thy wrath.

12 So [h]teach *us* to number our days, that we may [8]apply *our* hearts unto wisdom.

13 Return, O LORD, how long? and let it repent [i]thee concerning thy servants.

14 O satisfy us early with thy mercy;

w Heb. 11.5.
x 2 Sam. 7.15. Isa. 55.3.

PSALM 90
1 Or, A Prayer, being a Psalm of Moses.
2 in generation and generation.
a Job 38.4-6. Pro. 8.25.
b Gen. 3.19. Eccl. 12.7.
c Heb. 13.8. 2 Pet. 3.8.
3 Or, when he hath passed them.
d Isa. 40.6.
4 Or, is changed.
e Job 14.2. Ps. 92.7.
f Ps. 50.21. Jer. 16.17.
g Ps. 19.12. Pro. 5.21. Eccl. 12.14. Rom. 2.16. 1 Cor. 4.5. Heb. 4.12, 13.
5 turned away.
6 Or, as a meditation.
7 As for the days of our years, in them are seventy years.
h Ps. 39.4.
8 cause to come.
i Deut. 32.36.
j Ps. 44.1. Hab. 3.2.
k Isa. 26.12. 2 Thes. 2.16, 17.

PSALM 91
1 lodge.
a Ps. 61.4.
b Job 5.19. Pro. 3.23. Isa. 43.2.
c Mal. 1.5.
d Pro. 1.33. 2 Thes. 3.3. 2 Pet. 2.9.
e Ps. 34.7. Matt. 4.6. Luke 4.10. Heb. 1.14.
f Job 5.23. Ps. 37.24.
2 Or, asp.
g Job 22.27. Ps. 18.3. Jer. 33.3. Zech. 13.9. Heb. 5.7.
h Isa. 43.2.

that we may rejoice and be glad a
our days.
15 Make us glad according to th
days *wherein* thou hast afflicted u
and the years *wherein* we have see
evil.
16 Let [j]thy work appear unto th
servants, and thy glory unto their chi
dren.
17 And let the beauty of the LOR
our God be upon us: [k]and establis
thou the work of our hands upon u
yea, the work of our hands establis
thou it.

PSALM 91

HE that dwelleth in the secret plac
of the most High shall [1]abide ur
der the shadow of the Almighty.
2 I will say of the LORD, *He is* m
refuge and my fortress: my God; i
him will I trust.
3 Surely he shall deliver thee fro
the snare of the fowler, *and* from th
noisome pestilence.
4 He [a]shall cover thee with his feath
ers, and under his wings shalt tho
trust: his truth *shall be thy* shield an
buckler.
5 Thou [b]shalt not be afraid for th
terror by night; *nor* for the arrow *tha*
flieth by day;
6 *Nor* for the pestilence *that* walket
in darkness; *nor* for the destructio
that wasteth at noonday.
7 A thousand shall fall at thy sid
and ten thousand at thy right hand
but it shall not come nigh thee.
8 Only [c]with thine eyes shalt tho
behold and see the reward of th
wicked.
9 Because thou hast made the LOR
which is my refuge, *even* the mos
High, thy habitation;
10 There [d]shall no evil befall the
neither shall any plague come nig
thy dwelling.
11 For [e]he shall give his ange
charge over thee, to keep thee in a
thy ways.
12 They shall bear thee up in *thei*
hands, lest [f]thou dash thy foot agains
a stone.
13 Thou shalt tread upon the lio
and [2]adder: the young lion and th
dragon shalt thou trample unde
feet.
14 Because he hath set his love upo
me, therefore will I deliver him: I wi
set him on high, because he hat
known my name.
15 He [g]shall call upon me, and I wi
answer him: [h]I *will be* with him i

ouble; I will deliver him, and [i]hon-
ır him.
6 With [3]long life will I satisfy him,
ıd shew him my salvation.

PSALM 92

A Psalm *or* Song for the sabbath day.

'T *is a* good *thing* to give thanks unto the LORD, and to sing praises unto
y name, O most High:
To shew forth thy lovingkindness
the morning, and thy faithfulness
very night,
Upon an instrument of ten strings,
ıd upon the psaltery; [2]upon the harp
ith [3]a solemn sound.
For thou, LORD, hast made me
ad through thy work: I will triumph
the works of thy hands.
O LORD, how great are thy
orks! *and* thy [a]thoughts are very
eep.
A [b]brutish man knoweth not;
either doth a fool understand this.
When [c]the wicked spring as the
ass, and when all the workers of ini-
uity do flourish; *it is* that they shall
e destroyed for ever:
But thou, LORD, *art most* high for
vermore.
For, lo, thine enemies, O LORD,
r, lo, thine enemies shall perish; all
ıe workers of iniquity shall be scat-
ered.
0 But my horn shalt thou exalt like
ıe *horn of* an unicorn: I shall be
nointed with fresh oil.
1 Mine eye also shall see *my desire*
n mine enemies, *and* mine ears shall
ear *my desire* of the wicked that rise
p against me.
2 The [d]righteous shall flourish like
ıe palm tree: he shall grow like a
edar in Lĕb-ā-non.
3 Those that be [e]planted in the
ouse of the LORD shall flourish in
ıe courts of our God.
4 They shall still bring forth fruit
old age; they shall be fat and
lourishing;
5 To shew that the LORD *is* upright:
ıe *is* my rock, and [g]*there is* no un-
ghteousness in him.

PSALM 93

THE [a]LORD reigneth, [b]he is clothed
with majesty; the LORD is clothed
ith strength, *wherewith* he hath gird-
d himself: the world also is stablish-
d, that it cannot be moved.
Thy [c]throne *is* established [1]of old:
ıou *art* from everlasting.
The floods have lifted up, O LORD,
the floods have lifted up their voice;
the floods lift up their waves.
4 The LORD [d]on high *is* mightier than
the noise of many waters, *yea, than*
the mighty waves of the sea.
5 Thy testimonies are very sure:
holiness becometh thine house, O
LORD, [2]for ever.

PSALM 94

O LORD [1]God, to whom vengeance belongeth; O God, to
whom vengeance belongeth, [2]shew
thyself.
2 Lift up thyself, thou [a]judge of
the earth: render a reward to the
proud.
3 LORD, [b]how long shall the wicked,
how long shall the wicked triumph?
4 *How long* shall they [c]utter *and*
speak hard things? *and* all the workers
of iniquity boast themselves?
5 They break in pieces thy people,
O LORD, and afflict thine heritage.
6 They slay the widow and the stranger, and murder the fatherless.
7 Yet they say, The LORD shall not
see, neither shall the God of Jacob regard *it*.
8 Understand, ye brutish among the
people: and *ye* fools, when will ye be
wise?
9 He [d]that planted the ear, shall he
not hear? he that formed the eye, shall
he not see?
10 He that chastiseth the heathen,
shall not he correct? he [e]that teacheth
man knowledge, *shall not he know?*
11 The [f]LORD knoweth the thoughts
of man, that they *are* vanity.
12 Blessed [g]*is* the man whom thou
chastenest, O LORD, and teachest him
out of thy law;
13 That thou mayest give him rest
from the days of adversity, until the
pit be digged for the wicked.
14 For [h]the LORD will not cast off his
people, neither will he forsake his inheritance.
15 But judgment shall return unto
righteousness: and all the upright in
heart [3]shall follow it.
16 Who will rise up for me against
the evildoers? *or* who will stand up for
me against the workers of iniquity?
17 Unless the LORD *had been* my
help, my soul had [4]almost dwelt in
silence.
18 When I said, My foot slippeth;
thy mercy, O LORD, held me up.
19 In the multitude of my thoughts
within me thy comforts delight my
soul.

i 1 Sam. 2.30.
3 length of days.

PSALM 92
1 in the nights.
2 Or, upon the solemn sound with the harp.
3 Higgaion.
a Isa. 28.29. Rom. 11.33.
b Ps. 73.22.
c Job 21.7. Jer. 12.1. Mal. 3.15.
d Ps. 52.8. Song 7.7.
e Isa. 60.21. Matt. 15.13. John 15.2,5.
4 green.
f Deut. 32.4.
g Rom. 9.14.

PSALM 93
a Isa. 52.7. Rev. 19.6.
b Job 40.10. Ps. 104.1. Isa. 59.17.
c Pro. 8.22.
1 from then.
d Ps. 29.10.
2 to length of days.

PSALM 94
1 God of revenges.
2 shine forth.
a Gen. 18.25.
b Job 20.5.
c Jude 15.
d Ex. 4.11. Pro. 20.12.
e Job 35.11. Isa. 2.3. Isa. 28.26. John 6.45.
f 1 Cor. 3.20.
g Job 5.17. Pro. 3.11. 1 Cor. 11.32.
h Deut. 31.6. 1 Sam. 12. 22. 1 Ki. 6.13. Jer. 31.37.
3 shall be after it.
4 Or, quickly.

20 Shall [t]the throne of iniquity have
fellowship with thee, which [j]frameth
mischief by a law?
21 They [k]gather themselves together
against the soul of the righteous, and
[l]condemn the innocent blood.
22 But the LORD is my defence; and
my God *is* the rock of my refuge.
23 And [m]he shall bring upon them
their own iniquity, and shall cut them
off in their own wickedness; *yea*,
the LORD our God shall cut them
off.

PSALM 95

O COME, let us sing unto the
LORD: let us make a joyful noise
to the rock of our salvation.
2 Let us [1]come before his presence
with thanksgiving, and make a joyful
noise unto him with psalms.
3 For the LORD *is* a great God, and a
great King above all gods.
4 [2]In his hand *are* the deep places of
the earth: [3]the strength of the hills *is*
his also.
5 [4]The sea *is* his, and he made it: and
his hands formed the dry *land*.
6 O come, let us worship and bow
down: let [a]us kneel before the LORD
our [b]maker.
7 For he *is* our God; and we *are* the
people of his pasture, and the sheep
of his hand. [c]To day if ye will hear his
voice,
8 Harden not your heart, [d]as in the
[5]provocation, *and* as *in* the day of
temptation in the wilderness:
9 When your fathers tempted me,
proved me, and saw my work.
10 Forty [e]years long was I grieved
with *this* generation, and said, It *is* a
people that do err in their heart, and
they have not known my ways:
11 Unto whom [f]I sware in my wrath
[6]that they should not enter into my
rest.

PSALM 96

O SING unto the LORD a new
song: sing unto the LORD, all the
earth.
2 Sing unto the LORD, bless his
name; shew forth his salvation from
day to day.
3 Declare his glory among the heathen, his wonders among all people.
4 For the LORD *is* great, and greatly
to be praised: he *is* to be feared above
all gods.
5 For [a]all the gods of the nations *are*
idols: [b]but the LORD made the heavens.
6 Honour and majesty *are* before

t Amos 6.3. 2 Cor. 6.14.
j Ps. 58.2. Isa. 10.1.
k Matt. 27.1.
l Ex. 23.7. Pro. 17.15.
m Pro. 2.22.

PSALM 95
1 prevent his face.
2 In whose.
3 Or, the heights of the hills are his.
4 Whose the sea is.
a 1 Ki. 8.54. 1 Chr. 6.13. Ezra 9.5. Dan. 6.10. Luke 22.41. Acts 7.60. 1 Cor. 6.20. Eph. 3.14.
b Job 35.10. Isa. 54.5. John 1.3.
c Heb. 3.7.
d Num. 14. 22.
5 contention.
e Heb. 3.10.
f Num. 14. 23. Heb. 4.3.
6 if they enter.

PSALM 96
a Isa. 41.24. Jer. 10.11. Hab. 2.18, 19,20. Acts 19.26. 1 Cor. 8.4,5.
b Gen. 1.1. Isa. 42.5. Jer. 10.11.
c Ps. 29.1.
1 of his name.
2 Or, in the glorious sanctuary.
d Rev. 11.15.
e John 5.22.
f Rev. 19.11.

PSALM 97
1 many, or, great isles, Isa. 60.9.
2 Or, establishment.
a Dan. 7.10. Hab. 3.5.
b Ex. 20.4. Lev. 26.1. Isa. 37.18, 19. Jer. 10.14.
c Heb. 1.6.
d Eph. 1.21.
e Ps. 101.3. Amos 5.15. Rom. 7.15.
f 1 Sam. 2.9. Pro. 2.8.
g Dan. 3.28.
3 Or, to the memorial.

him: strength and beauty *are* in h
sanctuary.
7 Give [c]unto the LORD, O ye ki
dreds of the people, give unto t
LORD glory and strength.
8 Give unto the LORD the glory [1]d
unto his name: bring an offering, a
come into his courts.
9 O worship the LORD [2]in the beau
of holiness: fear before him, all t
earth.
10 Say among the heathen [d]*that* t
LORD reigneth: the world also sh
be established that it shall not
moved: he shall [e]judge the peop
righteously.
11 Let the heavens rejoice, and
the earth be glad; let the sea roar, a
the fulness thereof.
12 Let the field be joyful, and all th
is therein: then shall all the trees
the wood rejoice
13 Before the LORD: for he comet
for he cometh to judge the earth: [f]
shall judge the world with righteou
ness, and the people with his truth.

PSALM 97

THE LORD reigneth; let the ear
rejoice; let the [1]multitude of isl
be glad *thereof*.
2 Clouds and darkness *are* rou
about him: righteousness and jud
ment *are* the [2]habitation of h
throne.
3 A [a]fire goeth before him, and bur
eth up his enemies round about.
4 His lightnings enlightened t
world: the earth saw, and trembled
5 The hills melted like wax at t
presence of the LORD, at the presen
of the Lord of the whole earth.
6 The heavens declare his righteou
ness, and all the people see his glor
7 Confounded [b]be all they that ser
graven images, that boast ther
selves of idols: [c]worship him, all
gods.
8 Zion heard, and was glad; and t
daughters of Judah rejoiced becau
of thy judgments, O LORD.
9 For thou, LORD, *art* [d]high above
the earth: thou art exalted far abo
all gods.
10 Ye that love the LORD, [e]hate evi
he [f]preserveth the souls of his saint
[g]he delivereth them out of the hand
the wicked.
11 Light is sown for the righteou
and gladness for the upright in hea
12 Rejoice in the LORD, ye righteou
and give thanks [3]at the remembran
of his holiness.

PSALM 98

A Psalm.

) SING unto the LORD a new
song; for he hath done mar-
ellous things: [a]his right hand, and
is holy arm, hath gotten him the
ctory.
: The [b]LORD hath made known his
lvation: [c]his righteousness hath he
penly shewed in the sight of the
eathen.
3 He hath [d]remembered his mercy
nd his truth toward the house of
rael: [e]all the ends of the earth have
en the salvation of our God.
4 Make a joyful noise unto the LORD,
ll the earth: make a loud noise, and
joice, and sing praise.
5 Sing unto the LORD with the harp;
ith the harp, and the voice of a
salm.
6 With [f]trumpets and sound of cor-
et make a joyful noise before the
ORD, the King.
7 Let the sea roar, and the fulness
hereof; the world, and they that
well therein.
3 Let the floods clap *their* hands: let
he hills be joyful together
9 Before the LORD; for he cometh to
dge the earth: with righteousness
hall he judge the world, and the peo-
le with equity.

PSALM 99

THE LORD reigneth; let the people
tremble: he sitteth *between* the
hĕr-ū-bĭms; let the earth [1]be moved.
2 The LORD *is* great in Zion; and he
high above all the people.
3 Let them praise [a]thy great and
rrible name; *for* it *is* holy.
4 The [b]king's strength also loveth
dgment; thou dost [c]establish equity,
hou executest judgment and right-
ousness in Jacob.
5 Exalt ye the LORD our God, and
orship at [a]his footstool; *for* [2]he *is*
oly.
6 Moses and Aaron among his
riests, and Samuel among them that
all upon his name; they called upon
he LORD, and he answered them.
7 He [e]spake unto them in the cloudy
illar: they kept his testimonies, and
he ordinance *that* he gave them.
8 Thou answeredst them, O LORD
ur God: [f]thou wast a God that for-
avest them, though [g]thou tookest
engeance of their inventions.
9 Exalt the LORD our God, and wor-
hip at his holy hill; for the LORD our
God *is* holy.

PSALM 98

a Isa. 59.16.
b Isa. 52.10. Luke 2.30.
c Isa. 62.2. Rom. 3.25.
1 Or, revealed.
d Lev. 28.42. Deut. 4.31. Micah 7.20. Luke 1.54.
e Isa. 49.6. Luke 3.6. Acts 13.47.
f Num. 10. 10. 1 Chr. 15.28. 2 Chr. 29.27.

PSALM 99

1 stagger.
a Deut. 28.58. Isa. 6.3. Rev. 4.8.
b Deut. 32.3, 4. Job 36.5. Isa. 11.3-5. Jer. 23.5.
c Gen. 18.25. Deut. 32.4.
d 1 Chr. 28.2. Ps. 132.7. Isa. 66.1.
2 Or, it is holy. Lev. 19.2.
e Ex. 19.9. Num. 12.5.
f Num. 14. 20. Zeph. 3.7.
g Deut. 9.20.

PSALM 100

1 Or, thanksgiving.
2 all the earth.
a Job 10.8,9. Eccl. 12.1. Eph. 2.10.
3 Or, and his we are.
b Eze. 34.30.
4 to generation and generation.

PSALM 101

a 1 Sam. 18. 14.
b Gen. 18.19. Deut. 6.7. 1 Ki. 9.4.
1 thing of Belial.
c Josh. 23.6. 1 Sam. 12. 20.
d Matt. 7.23. 1 Cor. 5.11. 2 Tim. 2.19.
e Pro. 6.17. Luke 18.14.
f Rom. 13.4.
2 Or, perfect in the way.
3 shall not be established.
g Jer. 21.12.
h Hosea 9.3.

PSALM 102

a Jas. 4.14.
1 Or, into smoke.
b Lam. 1.13.

PSALM 100

A Psalm of [1]praise.

MAKE a joyful noise unto the
LORD, [2]all ye lands.
2 Serve the LORD with gladness:
come before his presence with singing.
3 Know ye that the LORD he *is* God:
it [a]*is* he *that* hath made us, [3]and not
we ourselves; [b]*we are* his people, and
the sheep of his pasture.
4 Enter into his gates with thanksgiving, *and* into his courts with praise:
be thankful unto him, *and* bless his
name.
5 For the LORD *is* good; his mercy *is*
everlasting; and his truth *endureth* [4]to
all generations.

PSALM 101

A Psalm of David.

I WILL sing of mercy and judgment: unto thee, O LORD, will I sing.
2 I will [a]behave myself wisely in a
perfect way. O when wilt thou come
unto me? I will [b]walk within my house
with a perfect heart.
3 I will set no [1]wicked thing before
mine eyes: I hate the work of them
[c]that turn aside; *it* shall not cleave to
me.
4 A froward heart shall depart from
me: I will not [d]know a wicked *person.*
5 Whoso privily slandereth his
neighbour, him will I cut off: [e]him
that hath an high look and a proud
heart will not I suffer.
6 Mine [f]eyes *shall be* upon the faithful of the land, that they may dwell
with me: he that walketh [2]in a perfect
way, he shall serve me.
7 He that worketh deceit shall not
dwell within my house: he that telleth
lies [3]shall not tarry in my sight.
8 I will [g]early destroy all the wicked
of the land; that I may cut off all
[h]wicked doers from the city of the
LORD.

PSALM 102

A Prayer of the afflicted, when he is overwhelmed, and poureth out his complaint before the LORD.

HEAR my prayer, O LORD, and let
my cry come unto thee.
2 Hide not thy face from me in the
day *when* I am in trouble; incline thine
ear unto me: in the day *when* I call
answer me speedily.
3 For [a]my days are consumed [1]like
smoke, and [b]my bones are burned as
an hearth.
4 My heart is smitten, and withered
like grass; so that I forget to eat my
bread.

5 By reason of the voice of my groaning my bones cleave to my [2]skin.
6 I am like a [c]pelican of the wilderness: I am like an owl of the desert.
7 I watch, and am as a sparrow alone
upon the house top.
8 Mine enemies reproach me all the
day; *and* they that are mad against me
[d]are sworn against me.
9 For I have eaten ashes like bread,
and mingled my drink with weeping,
10 Because of thine indignation and
thy wrath: for [e]thou hast lifted me up,
and cast me down.
11 My days *are* like a shadow that
declineth; and [f]I am withered like
grass.
12 But thou, O LORD, shalt [g]endure
for ever; and thy remembrance unto
all generations.
13 Thou shalt arise, *and* have mercy
upon Zion: for the time to favour her,
yea, the set [h]time, is come.
14 For thy [i]servants take pleasure in
her stones, and favour the dust thereof.
15 So the heathen shall [j]fear the
name of the LORD, and all the kings of
the earth thy glory.
16 When the LORD shall build up
Zion, he [k]shall appear in his glory.
17 He [l]will regard the prayer of the
destitute, and not despise their prayer.
18 This shall be [m]written for the
generation to come: and [n]the people
which shall be created shall praise the
LORD.
19 For he hath [o]looked down from
the height of his sanctuary; from heav-
en did the LORD behold the earth;
20 To hear the groaning of the prisoner; to loose [3]those that are appointed to death;
21 To declare the name of the LORD
in Zion, and his praise in Jerusalem;
22 When [p]the people are gathered
together, and the kingdoms, to serve
the LORD.
23 He [4]weakened my strength in the
way; he shortened my days.
24 I said, O my God, take me not
away in the midst of my days: thy
[q]years *are* throughout all generations.
25 Of [r]old hast thou laid the foundation of the earth: and the heavens *are*
the work of thy hands.
26 They [s]shall perish, but thou shalt
[5]endure: yea, all of them shall wax old
like a garment; as a vesture shalt thou
change them, and they shall be
changed:
27 But [t]thou *art* the same, and thy
years shall have no end.

2 Or, flesh.
c Isa. 34.11. Zeph. 2.14.
d Acts 23.12.
e Ps. 30.7.
f Jas. 1.10.
g 1 Tim. 6.16.
h Isa. 40.2.
i Dan. 9.2.
j 1 Ki. 8.43.
k Isa. 60.1.
l Neh. 2.8.
m Rom. 15.4. 1 Cor. 10.11.
n Ps. 22.31. Isa. 43.21
o Deut. 26.15. Ps. 14.2.
3 the children of death.
p Hosea 1.11.
4 afflicted.
q Ps. 90.2. Hab. 1.12. Rev. 1.4,8.
r Gen. 1.1. Ex. 20.11. Job 38.4-7. Heb. 1.10.
s Isa. 66.22. Rom. 8.20. 2 Pet. 3.7.
5 stand.
t Mal. 3.6.

PSALM 103

a Isa. 33.24. Matt. 9.2. Mark 2.5. Luke 7.47.
b Ex. 15.26. Jer. 17.14.
c Ex. 34.6. Num. 14.18. Deut. 5.10.
1 great of mercy.
d Isa. 57.16. Jer. 3.5. Micah 7.18.
e Ezra 9.13.
2 according to the height of the heaven.
f Isa. 43.25. Eph. 1.7.
g Deut. 8.5. Isa. 63.15, 16. Mal. 3.17.
3 it is not.
h Ex. 20.6.
i Deut. 7.9.
j Ps. 47.2.
4 mighty in strength.
k Matt. 6.10.

28 The children of thy servants sha
continue, and their seed shall be estab
lished before thee.

PSALM 103

A Psalm of David.

BLESS the LORD, O my soul: an
all that is within me, *bless* his hol
name.
2 Bless the LORD, O my soul, an
forget not all his benefits:
3 Who [a]forgiveth all thine iniquities
who healeth [b]all thy diseases;
4 Who redeemeth thy life from de
struction; who crowneth thee wit
lovingkindness and tender mercies
5 Who satisfieth thy mouth with goo
things; so that thy youth is renewe
like the eagle's.
6 The LORD executeth righteousnes
and judgment for all that are oppress
ed.
7 He made known his ways unt
Moses, his acts unto the children o
Israel.
8 The [c]LORD *is* merciful and gracious
slow to anger, and [1]plenteous i
mercy.
9 He [d]will not always chide: neithe
will he keep *his anger* for ever.
10 He [e]hath not dealt with us afte
our sins; nor rewarded us accordin
to our iniquities.
11 For [2]as the heaven is high abov
the earth, *so* great is his mercy towar
them that fear him.
12 As far as the east is from the west
so far hath he [f]removed our trans
gressions from us.
13 Like [g]as a father pitieth *his* chil
dren, *so* the LORD pitieth them tha
fear him.
14 For he knoweth our frame; he re
membereth that we *are* dust.
15 *As for* man, his days *are* as grass
as a flower of the field, so he flourish
eth.
16 For the wind passeth over it, an
[3]it is gone; and the place thereof sha
know it no more.
17 But the mercy of the LORD i
from everlasting to everlastin
upon them that fear him, and hi
righteousness [h]unto children's chil
dren;
18 To [i]such as keep his covenant, an
to those that remember his com
mandments to do them.
19 The LORD hath prepared hi
throne in the heavens; and [j]his king
dom ruleth over all.
20 Bless the LORD, ye his angels
[4]that excel in strength, that [k]do hi

ommandments, hearkening unto the
oice of his word.
21 Bless ye the LORD, all *ye* [l]his
osts; *ye* [m]ministers of his, that do his
leasure.
22 Bless the LORD, all his works in
ll places of his dominion: bless the
ORD, O my soul.

PSALM 104

BLESS the LORD, O my soul. O
LORD my God, thou art very great;
hou art clothed with honour and
najesty.
2 Who coverest *thyself* with light as
vith a garment: who stretchest out the
eavens like a curtain:
3 Who [a]layeth the beams of his cham-
ers in the waters: [b]who maketh the
louds his chariot: who walketh upon
he wings of the wind:
4 Who [c]maketh his angels spirits;
is ministers a flaming fire:
5 [1]*Who* laid the foundations of the
arth, *that* it should not be removed
or ever.
6 Thou coveredst it with the deep as
vith a garment: the waters stood
bove the mountains.
7 At thy rebuke they fled; at the voice
f thy thunder they hasted away.
8 [2]They go up by the mountains;
hey go down by the valleys [d]unto the
lace which thou hast founded for
hem.
9 Thou [e]hast set a bound that they
nay not pass over; that they turn not
gain to [f]cover the earth.
10 [3]He sendeth the springs into the
alleys, *which* [4]run among the hills.
11 They give drink to every beast of
he field: the wild asses [5]quench their
hirst.
12 By them shall the fowls of the
eaven have their habitation, *which*
sing among the branches.
13 He watereth the hills from his
hambers: the earth is satisfied with
he fruit of thy works.
14 He [g]causeth the grass to grow for
he cattle, and herb for the service of
nan: that he may bring forth [h]food
ut of the earth;
15 And [i]wine *that* maketh glad the
eart of man, *and* [7]oil to make *his* face
o shine, and bread *which* strengthen-
th man's heart.
16 The [8]trees of the LORD are full *of*
ap; the cedars of Lĕb-ă-non, which
he hath planted;
17 Where the birds make their nests:
s for the stork, the fir trees *are* her
ouse.
18 The high hills *are* a refuge for the
wild goats; *and* the rocks for the
[k]conies.
19 He [l]appointed the moon for
seasons: the sun [m]knoweth his going
down.
20 Thou [n]makest darkness, and it is
night: wherein [9]all the beasts of the
forest do creep *forth*.
21 The [o]young lions roar after their
prey, and seek their meat from God.
22 The sun ariseth, they gather themselves together, and lay them down in
their dens.
23 Man goeth forth unto [p]his work
and to his labour until the evening.
24 O [q]LORD, how manifold are thy
works! in wisdom hast thou made
them all: the earth is full of thy
riches.
25 *So is* this great and wide sea,
wherein *are* things creeping innumerable, both small and great beasts.
26 There go the ships: *there is* that
[r]lē-vī-ă-thăn, *whom* thou hast [10]made
to play therein.
27 These wait [s]all upon thee; that
thou mayest give *them* their meat in
due season.
28 *That* thou givest them they gather: thou openest thine hand, they are
filled with good.
29 Thou hidest thy face, they are
troubled: thou [t]takest away their
breath, they die, and return to their
dust.
30 Thou [u]sendest forth thy spirit,
they are created: and thou renewest
the face of the earth.
31 The glory of the LORD [11]shall endure for ever: the LORD shall rejoice
in his works.
32 He looketh on the earth, and it
[v]trembleth: he toucheth the hills, and
they smoke.
33 I will sing unto the LORD as long
as I live: I will sing praise to my God
while I have my being.
34 My meditation of him shall be
sweet: I will be glad in the LORD.
35 Let the [w]sinners be consumed out
of the earth, and let the wicked be no
more. Bless thou the LORD, O my
soul. [12]Praise ye the LORD.

PSALM 105

O [a]GIVE thanks unto the LORD;
call upon his name: make known
his deeds among the people.
2 Sing unto him, sing psalms unto
him: talk ye of all his wondrous
works.
3 Glory ye in his holy name: let the

l Gen. 32.2.
m Dan. 7.9.

PSALM 104

a Amos 9.6.
b Isa. 19.1.
c Heb. 1.7.
1 He hath founded the earth upon her bases.
2 Or, The mountains ascend, the valleys descend.
d Job 38.10.
e Job 26.10. Ps. 33.7. Jer. 5.22.
f Gen. 9.11.
3 Who sendeth.
4 walk.
5 break.
6 give a voice.
g Gen. 1.29, 30. Ps. 147.8.
h Ps. 136.25. Job 28.5.
i Judg. 9.13. Pro. 31.6,7. Eccl. 10.19. Jer. 31.12. Mark 14.23. John 2.9,10.
7 to make his face shine with oil, or, more than oil.
8 That is, large trees.
j Num. 24.6. Ps. 29.5.
k Pro. 30.26.
l Gen. 1.14.
m Job 38.12.
n Isa. 45.7.
9 all the beasts thereof do trample on the forest.
o Job 38.39.
p Gen. 3.19.
q Gen. 1.20-22.
r Job 41.1.
10 formed.
s Rom. 11.36.
t Eccl. 12.7.
u Isa. 32.15.
11 shall be.
v Hab. 3.10.
w Pro. 2.22.
12 Hallelujah.

PSALM 105

a Isa. 12.4.

heart of them rejoice that seek the LORD.

4 Seek the LORD, and his strength: seek [b]his face evermore.

5 Remember [c]his marvellous works that he hath done; his wonders, and the judgments of his mouth;

6 O ye seed of Abraham his servant, ye children of Jacob his chosen.

7 He *is* the LORD our God: [d]his judgments *are* in all the earth.

8 He hath [e]remembered his covenant for ever, the word *which* he commanded to a thousand generations.

9 Which [f]*covenant* he made with Abraham, and his oath unto Isaac;

10 And confirmed the same unto Jacob for a law, *and* to Israel *for* an everlasting covenant:

11 Saying, [g]Unto thee will I give the land of Canaan, [1]the lot of your inheritance:

12 When [h]they were *but* a few men in number; yea, very few, and [i]strangers in it.

13 When they went from one nation to another, from *one* kingdom to another people;

14 He [j]suffered no man to do them wrong: yea, [k]he reproved kings for their sakes;

15 *Saying*, Touch not mine anointed, and do my prophets no harm.

16 Moreover [l]he called for a famine upon the land: he brake the whole [m]staff of bread.

17 He [n]sent a man before them, *even* Joseph, *who* [o]was sold for a servant:

18 Whose [p]feet they hurt with fetters: [2]he was laid in iron:

19 Until the time that his word came: the word of the LORD tried him.

20 The king sent and loosed him; *even* the ruler of the people, and let him go free.

21 He made him lord of his house, and ruler of all his [3]substance:

22 To bind his princes at his pleasure; and teach his senators wisdom.

23 Israel [q]also came into Egypt; and Jacob sojourned in the land of Ham.

24 And [r]he increased his people greatly; and made them stronger than their enemies.

25 He turned their heart to hate his people, to deal subtilly with his servants.

26 He sent Moses his servant; *and* Aaron whom [s]he had chosen.

27 They shewed [4]his signs among them, and wonders in the land of Ham.

28 He sent darkness, and made it dark; and [t]they rebelled not agains his word.

29 He turned their waters into blood and slew their fish.

30 Their land brought forth frogs i abundance, in the chambers of thei kings.

31 He spake, and there came diver sorts of flies, *and* lice in all their coasts

32 [5]He gave them hail for rain, *an* flaming fire in their land.

33 He smote their vines also an their fig trees; and brake the trees o their coasts.

34 He spake, and the locusts came and caterpillers, and that withou number,

35 And did eat up all the herbs i their land, and devoured the fruit o their ground.

36 He smote also all the firstborn i their land, [u]the chief of all thei strength.

37 He brought them forth also wit silver and gold: and *there was* not on feeble *person* among their tribes.

38 Egypt was glad when they departed: for the fear of them fell upo them.

39 He [v]spread a cloud for a covering; and fire to give light in the night

40 *The* [w]*people* asked, and he brough quails, and satisfied them with th bread of heaven.

41 He [x]opened the rock, and th waters gushed out; they ran in the dr places *like* a river.

42 For he remembered [y]his hol promise, *and* Abraham his servant.

43 And he brought forth his peopl with joy, *and* his chosen with [6]glad ness:

44 And [z]gave them the lands of th heathen: and they inherited the labou of the people;

45 That [a]they might observe his statutes, and keep his laws. [7]Praise ye th LORD.

PSALM 106

[1]PRAISE ye the LORD. O giv thanks unto the LORD; for *he* i [a]good: for his mercy *endureth* for eve

2 Who [b]can utter the mighty acts o the LORD? *who* can shew forth all hi praise?

3 Blessed *are* they that [c]keep judgment, *and* he that [d]doeth righteousness at [e]all times.

4 Remember me, O LORD, with th favour *that thou bearest unto* thy people: O visit me with thy salvation;

5 That I may see the good of th chosen, that I may rejoice in the glad

b Ps. 27.8.
c Deut. 8.2.
d Isa. 26.9.
e Luke 1.72.
f Gen. 17.2. Gen. 22.16. Gen. 26.3. Ps. 111.5,9. Dan. 9.4. Luke 1.73. Heb. 6.17.
g Gen. 15.18.
1 the cord.
h Gen. 34.30. Deut. 7.7.
i Gen. 17.8. Heb. 11.9.
j Gen. 35.5.
k Gen. 12.17.
l Gen. 41.54. 2 Ki. 8.1.
m Lev. 26.26.
n Gen. 45.5.
o Gen. 37.28.
p Gen. 40.15.
2 his soul came into iron.
3 possession.
q Gen. 46.6.
r Ex. 1.7. Deut. 26.5. Acts 7.17.
s Ex. 3.10. Num. 16.5.
4 words of his signs.
t Ps. 99.7.
5 He gave their rain hail.
u Gen. 49.3.
v Ex. 13.21. Neh. 9.12.
w Ex. 16.12.
x Ex. 17.6. Neh. 9.15. Isa. 48.21. 1 Cor. 10.4.
y Gen. 15.14.
6 singing.
z Deut. 6.10. Josh. 13.7.
a Deut. 4.1.
7 Hallelujah.

PSALM 106

1 Hallelujah.
a Isa. 63.7. Matt. 19.17.
b Ps. 40.5.
c Jer. 22.15, 16. Matt. 22.37.
d Ps. 15.2.
e Acts 24.16. Gal. 6.9.

ess of thy nation, that I may glory
vith thine inheritance.
6 We have [f]sinned with our fathers,
ve have committed iniquity, we have
lone wickedly.
7 Our fathers understood not thy
vonders in Egypt; they remembered
not the multitude of thy mercies; but
rovoked *him* at the sea, *even* at the
Red sea.
8 Nevertheless he saved [g]them for
is name's sake, that he might make
is mighty power to be known.
9 He [h]rebuked the Red sea also, and it
was dried up: so [i]he led them through
he depths, as through the wilderness.
10 And he saved them from the hand
of him that hated *them*, and redeemed
hem from the hand of the enemy.
11 And the waters covered their enemies: there was not one of them left.
12 Then believed they his words;
hey sang his praise.
13 [2]They soon forgat his works; they
vaited not for his counsel:
14 But [3]lusted exceedingly in the
wilderness, and tempted God in the
desert.
15 And he gave them their request;
out sent [j]leanness into their soul.
16 They [k]envied Moses also in the
camp, *and* Aaron the saint of the
LORD.
17 The earth opened and swallowed
up Dā-thăn, and covered the company
of Ă-bī-răm.
18 And a fire was kindled in their
company; the flame burned up the
wicked.
19 They [l]made a calf in Hôr-ĕb, and
worshipped the molten image.
20 Thus [m]they changed their glory
into the similitude of an ox that eateth
grass.
21 They forgat God their saviour,
which had done great things in Egypt;
22 Wondrous works in the land of
Ham, *and* terrible things by the Red
sea.
23 Therefore [n]he said that he would
destroy them, had not Moses his
chosen stood [o]before him in the
breach, to turn away his wrath, lest
he should destroy *them*.
24 Yea, they despised [4]the pleasant
land, they [p]believed not his word:
25 But murmured in their tents, *and*
hearkened not unto the voice of the
LORD.
26 Therefore he lifted up his hand
against them, to overthrow them in
the wilderness:
27 [5]To overthrow their seed also

f Lev. 26.40. 1 Ki. 8.47. Dan. 9.5.
g Josh. 7.9. Ps. 143.11. Jer. 14.7,21.
h Ex. 14.21. Nah. 1.4.
i Isa. 63.11.
2 They made haste, they forgat.
3 lusted a lust.
j Isa. 10.16.
k Num. 16.1.
l Ex. 32.4.
m Jer. 2.11. Rom. 1.23.
n Ex. 32.10. Deut. 9.19. Eze. 20.13.
o Eze. 13.5.
4 a land of desire.
p Heb. 3.18.
5 To make them fall.
q Num. 25.2, 3. Deut. 4.3. Hosea 9.10. Rev. 2.14.
r Deut. 1.37.
s Num. 20. 10. Jas. 3.2.
t Judg. 1.21.
u Deut. 7.2. Judg. 2.2.
v Judg. 3.5. Isa. 2.6.
w Ex. 23.33. Deut. 7.10. Judg. 2.12. 2 Ki. 17.8-11. 2 Chr. 33.2-7.
x Deut. 12. 30,31. Isa. 57.5. Eze. 16.20.
y Num. 35. 33.
z Judg. 2.14. Neh. 9.27.
6 Or, impoverished, or, weakened.
a Judg. 10.10.
b Lev. 26.41.
c Lam. 3.32.
d Ezra 9.9. Jer. 42.12.
e Luke 1.74.
f 2 Cor. 5.15.

among the nations, and to scatter
them in the lands.
28 They [q]joined themselves also unto
Bā-ăl-pē-ôr, and ate the sacrifices of
the dead.
29 Thus they provoked *him* to anger
with their inventions: and the plague
brake in upon them.
30 Then stood up Phĭn-ĕ-hăs, and executed judgment: and *so* the plague
was stayed.
31 And that was counted unto him
for righteousness unto all generations for evermore.
32 They angered *him* also at the
waters of strife, [r]so that it went ill with
Moses for their sakes:
33 Because they provoked his spirit,
so that he [s]spake unadvisedly with his
lips.
34 They [t]did not destroy the nations,
concerning [u]whom the LORD commanded them:
35 But [v]were mingled among the
heathen, and learned their works.
36 And [w]they served their idols:
which were a snare unto them.
37 Yea, [x]they sacrificed their sons
and their daughters unto devils,
38 And shed innocent blood, *even* the
blood of their sons and of their daughters, whom they sacrificed unto the
idols of Canaan: and [y]the land was
polluted with blood.
39 Thus were they defiled with their
own works, and went a whoring with
their own inventions.
40 Therefore was the wrath of the
LORD kindled against his people, insomuch that he abhorred his own inheritance.
41 And [z]he gave them into the hand
of the heathen; and they that hated
them ruled over them.
42 Their enemies also oppressed
them, and they were [6]brought into
subjection under their hand.
43 Many times did he deliver them;
but they provoked *him* with their
counsel, and were brought low for
their iniquity.
44 Nevertheless he regarded their
affliction, when [a]he heard their cry:
45 And [b]he remembered for them his
covenant, and [c]repented according to
the multitude of his mercies.
46 He [d]made them also to be pitied
of all those that carried them captives.
47 Save us, O LORD our God, and
gather us [e]from among the heathen,
to give thanks [f]unto thy holy name,
and to triumph in thy praise.

48 Blessed *be* the LORD God of Israel from everlasting to everlasting: and let all the people say, Ä-mĕn. Praise ye the LORD.

PSALM 107

O GIVE thanks unto the LORD, for [a]*he is* good: for his mercy *endureth* for ever.

2 Let the redeemed of the LORD say *so*, whom he hath redeemed from the hand of the enemy;

3 And [b]gathered them out of the lands, from the east, and from the west, from the north, and [1]from the south.

4 They wandered in the wilderness in a solitary way; they found no city to dwell in.

5 Hungry and thirsty, their soul fainted in them.

6 Then [c]they cried unto the LORD in their trouble, *and* he delivered them out of their distresses.

7 And he led them forth by [d]the right way, that they might go to a city of habitation.

8 Oh that *men* would praise the LORD *for* his goodness, and *for* his wonderful works to the children of men!

9 For [e]he satisfieth the longing soul, and filleth the hungry soul with goodness.

10 Such as sit in darkness and in the shadow of death, *being* [f]bound in affliction and iron;

11 Because they [g]rebelled against the words of God, and contemned the [h]counsel of the most High:

12 Therefore he brought down their heart with labour; they fell down, and *there was* none [i]to help.

13 Then they cried unto the LORD in their trouble, *and* he saved them out of their distresses.

14 He [j]brought them out of darkness and the shadow of death, and brake their bands in sunder.

15 Oh that *men* would praise the LORD *for* his goodness, and *for* his wonderful works to the children of men!

16 For he hath [k]broken the gates of brass, and cut the bars of iron in sunder.

17 Fools [l]because of their transgression, and because of their iniquities, are afflicted.

18 Their soul abhorreth all manner of meat; and they draw near unto the gates of death.

19 Then they cry unto the LORD in their trouble, *and* he saveth them ou of their distresses.

20 He [m]sent his word, and heale them, and delivered *them* from thei destructions.

21 Oh that *men* would praise th LORD *for* his goodness, and *for* hi wonderful works to the children o men!

22 And [n]let them sacrifice the sacrifices of thanksgiving, and declare hi works with [2]rejoicing.

23 They that go down to the sea i ships, that do business in grea waters;

24 These see the works of the LORD and his wonders in the deep.

25 For he commandeth, and [3]raiset the stormy wind, which lifteth up th waves thereof.

26 They mount up to the heaven they go down again to the depths their [o]soul is melted because o trouble.

27 They reel to and fro, and stagge like a drunken man, and [4]are at thei wits' end.

28 Then they cry unto the LORD i their trouble, and he bringeth then out of their distresses.

29 He [p]maketh the storm a calm, so that the waves thereof are still.

30 Then are they glad because the be quiet; so he bringeth them unt their desired haven.

31 Oh that *men* would praise th LORD *for* his goodness, and *for* hi wonderful works to the children o men!

32 Let them exalt him also in th congregation of the people, and prais him in the assembly of the elders.

33 He [q]turneth rivers into a wilderness, and the watersprings into dr ground;

34 A [r]fruitful land into [5]barrenness for the wickedness of them that dwel therein.

35 He [s]turneth the wilderness into a standing water, and dry ground int watersprings.

36 And there he maketh the hungr [t]to dwell, that they may prepare a city for habitation;

37 And sow the fields, and plan vineyards, which may yield fruits o increase.

38 He [u]blesseth them also, so tha they are multiplied greatly; and suffereth not their cattle to decrease.

39 Again, they are [v]minished and brought low through oppression, affliction, and sorrow.

PSALM 107
a Matt. 19.17.
b Ps. 106.47. Isa. 49.12. Jer. 29.14. Eze. 39.27.
1 from the sea.
c Ps. 50.15. Isa. 41.17. Jer. 29.12-14. Hosea 5.15.
d Ezra 8.21. Isa. 63.12.
e Ps. 34.10. Isa. 55.1. Matt. 5.6. Luke 1.53.
f Job 36.8.
g Lam. 3.42.
h Ps. 73.24. Luke 7.30. Acts 20.27.
i Isa. 63.5.
j Ps. 146.7. Acts 12.7.
k Isa. 45.2.
l Ps. 14.1. Pro. 1.22. Lam. 3.39.
m Num. 21.8. 2 Ki. 20.4. Matt. 8.8.
n Lev. 7.12. Ps. 50.14. Heb. 13.15.
2 singing.
3 maketh to stand.
o Ps. 22.14. Isa. 13.7. Nah. 2.10.
4 all their wisdom is swallowed up.
p Ps. 65.7. Isa. 50.2. Matt. 8.26. Mark 4.39-41.
q 1 Ki. 17.1. Isa. 34.9,10. Eze. 30.12. Joel 1.20. Nah. 1.4.
r Gen. 13.10.
5 saltness.
s Isa. 41.18.
t Acts 17.26.
u Gen. 12.2.
v 2 Ki. 10.32.

) He [w]poureth contempt upon
inces, and causeth them to wander
the [6]wilderness, *where there is* no
ıy.
1 Yet [x]setteth he the poor on high
om affliction, and maketh *him*
milies like a flock.
2 The [y]righteous shall see *it*, and re-
ice: and all [z]iniquity shall stop her
outh.
3 Whoso [a]*is* wise, and will observe
ese *things*, even they shall under-
ınd the lovingkindness of the LORD.

PSALM 108

A Song *or* Psalm of David.

O GOD, my heart is fixed; I will
sing and give praise, even with
y glory.
Awake, psaltery and harp: I *my-*
lf will awake early.
I will praise thee, O LORD, among
e people: and I will sing praises unto
ee among the nations.
For thy [a]mercy *is* great above the
avens: and thy truth *reacheth* unto
e [1]clouds.
Be [b]thou exalted, O God, above the
avens: and thy glory above all the
rth;
That thy beloved may be delivered:
ve *with* thy right hand, and answer
e.
God hath spoken in his holiness; I
ill rejoice, I will divide Shē´chĕm,
ıd mete out the valley of Sŭc´cōth.
Gilead *is* mine; Mă-năs´sēh *is*
ine; Ē´phrā-ĭm also *is* the strength
mine head; Judah [c]*is* my lawgiver;
Moab *is* my washpot; over Ē´dŏm
ill I cast out my shoe; over Philistia
ill I triumph.
0 Who [d]will bring me into the
rong city? who will lead me into Ē´-
ŏm?
1 *Wilt* not *thou*, O God, *who* hast
ıst us off? and wilt not thou, O God,
forth with our hosts?
2 Give us help from trouble: for
in [e]*is* the help of man.
3 Through God we shall do valiant-
: for he [f]*it is that* shall tread down
ır enemies.

PSALM 109

To the chief Musician, A Psalm of David.

HOLD [a]not thy peace, O God of
my praise;
For the mouth of the wicked and
e [1]mouth of the deceitful [2]are open-
d against me: they have spoken
ainst me with a lying tongue.
They compassed me about also
with words of hatred; and fought
against me without [b]a cause.
4 For my love they are my adversaries: but I *give myself unto* prayer.
5 And [c]they have rewarded me evil
for good, and hatred for my love.
6 Set thou a wicked man over him:
and let [3]Satan stand at his right hand.
7 When he shall be judged, let him
[4]be condemned: and [d]let his prayer
become sin.
8 Let his days be few; *and* [e]let another take his [5]office.
9 Let [f]his children be fatherless, and
his wife a widow.
10 Let his children be continually
[g]vagabonds, and beg: let them seek
their bread also out of their desolate
places.
11 Let [h]the extortioner catch all that
he hath; and let the strangers spoil
his labour.
12 Let there be none to extend mercy
unto him: neither let there be any to
favour his fatherless children.
13 Let his [i]posterity be cut off; *and*
in the generation following let their
[j]name be blotted out.
14 Let [k]the iniquity of his fathers be
remembered with the LORD; and let
not the sin of his mother be [l]blotted
out.
15 Let them be before the LORD continually, that he may [m]cut off the
memory of them from the earth.
16 Because that he remembered not
to shew mercy, but persecuted the
poor and needy man, that he might
even slay the broken in heart.
17 As he loved cursing, so let it come
unto him: as he delighted not in blessing, so let it be far from him.
18 As he clothed himself with cursing
like as with his garment, so let it come
[6]into his bowels like water, and like
oil into his bones.
19 Let it be unto him as the garment
which covereth him, and for a girdle
wherewith he is girded continually.
20 *Let* this *be* the reward of mine adversaries from the LORD, and of them
that speak evil against my soul.
21 But do thou for me, O GOD the
Lord, for thy name's sake: because
thy mercy *is* good, deliver thou me.
22 For I *am* poor and needy, and my
heart is wounded within me.
23 I am gone like the shadow when it
declineth: I am tossed up and down
as the locust.
24 My [n]knees are weak through
fasting; and my flesh faileth of fatness.

w Josh. 10. 24-26. Job 12.21.
6 Or, void place.
x 1 Sam. 2.8. 2 Sam. 7.8. Job 8.7.
7 Or, after.
y Job 22.19.
z Job 5.16. Pro. 10.11.
a Jer. 9.12. Dan. 12.10.

PSALM 108

a Num. 14. 18. Deut. 7.9. Ps. 36.5. Mic. 7.18-20.
1 Or, skies.
b Ps. 57.5.
c Gen. 49.10.
d Ps. 60.9.
e Isa. 30.3.
f Isa. 25.10. Lam. 1.15. Mal. 4.3. Rev. 14.19, 20.

PSALM 109

a Ps. 83.1.
1 mouth of deceit.
2 have opened themselves.
b 1 Sam. 19. 4,5. Ps. 35.7,20. John 15.25.
c Ps. 38.20.
3 Or, an adversary.
4 go out guilty, or, wicked.
d Pro. 28.9.
e Acts 1.20.
5 Or, charge.
f Ex. 22.24. Jer. 18.21.
g Gen. 4.12.
h Job 18.9.
i Ps. 37.28.
j Pro. 10.7.
k Ex. 20.5.
l Neh. 4.5.
m Job 18.17.
6 within him.
n Heb. 12.12.

25 I became also a reproach unto them: *when* they looked upon me they [o]shaked their heads.

26 Help me, O LORD my God: O save me according to thy mercy:

27 That [p]they may know that this *is* thy hand; *that* thou, LORD, hast done it.

28 Let them curse, but bless thou: when they arise, let them be ashamed; but let thy [q]servant rejoice.

29 Let mine adversaries be clothed with shame, and let them cover themselves with their own confusion, as with a mantle.

30 I will greatly praise the LORD with my mouth; yea, I will praise him among the multitude.

31 For he shall stand at the right hand of the poor, to save *him* [7]from those that condemn his soul.

PSALM 110

A Psalm of David.

THE [a]LORD said unto my Lord, Sit thou at my right hand, until I make thine enemies thy footstool.

2 The LORD shall send the rod of thy strength out of Zion: rule thou in the midst of thine enemies.

3 Thy [b]people *shall be* willing in the day of thy power, [c]in the beauties of holiness [1]from the womb of the morning: thou hast the dew of thy youth.

4 The LORD hath sworn, [d]and will not repent, [e]Thou *art* a priest for ever after the order of Měl-chĭz'-ĕd-ĕk.

5 The Lord [f]at thy right hand shall strike through kings [g]in the day of his wrath.

6 He shall judge among the heathen, he shall fill *the places* with the dead bodies; [h]he shall wound the heads over [2]many countries.

7 He [i]shall drink of the brook in the way: therefore [j]shall he lift up the head.

PSALM 111

[1]PRAISE ye the LORD. I will praise the LORD with *my* whole heart, in the assembly of the upright, and *in* the congregation.

2 The [a]works of the LORD *are* great, sought out of all them that have pleasure therein.

3 His work *is* honourable and glorious: and his righteousness endureth for ever.

4 He hath made his wonderful works to be remembered: the LORD *is* gracious and full of compassion.

5 He hath given [2]meat unto them that fear him: he will ever be mind[ful] of his covenant.

6 He hath shewed his people t[he] power of his works, that he may gi[ve] them the heritage of the heathen.

7 The works of his hands *are* veri[ty] and judgment; [b]all his comman[d]ments *are* sure.

8 They [3]stand fast for ever and ev[er], *and are* [c]done in truth and uprightne[ss].

9 He sent redemption unto his pe[o]ple: he hath commanded his covena[nt] for ever: holy and reverend *is* h[is] name.

10 The [d]fear of the LORD *is* the b[e]ginning of wisdom: [4]a good unde[r]standing have all they [5]that do *h[is]* *commandments:* his praise endure[th] for ever.

PSALM 112

PRAISE ye the LORD. Blessed *is* t[he] the man *that* feareth the LORD, *th[at]* delighteth greatly in his comman[d]ments.

2 His seed shall be mighty up[on] earth: the generation of the uprig[ht] shall be blessed.

3 Wealth [a]and riches *shall be* in h[is] house: and his righteousness endu[r]eth for ever.

4 Unto the upright there arise[th] light in the darkness: *he is* graciou[s] and full of compassion, and righ[t]eous.

5 A [b]good man sheweth favour, an[d] lendeth: he will guide his affairs wi[th] [1]discretion.

6 Surely he shall not be moved f[or] ever: the righteous shall be in eve[r]lasting remembrance.

7 He shall not be afraid of evil ti[d]ings: his heart is fixed, trusting in th[e] LORD.

8 His heart *is* established, he sha[ll] not be afraid, until he see *his desi[re]* upon his enemies.

9 He [c]hath dispersed, he hath give[n] to the poor; his righteousness endu[r]eth for ever; his horn shall be exalte[d] with honour.

10 The [d]wicked shall see *it,* and b[e] grieved; he shall gnash with his teet[h] and melt away: the desire of th[e] wicked shall perish.

PSALM 113

[1]PRAISE ye the LORD. Praise, ye servants of the LORD, praise th[e] name of the LORD.

2 Blessed [a]be the name of the LOR[D] from this time forth and for eve[r]more.

3 From the [b]rising of the sun unto th[e]

---

o Isa. 37.22. Matt. 27.39.
p Job 37.7.
q Num. 22. 12. Isa. 65.14.
7 from the judges of his soul.

PSALM 110
a Ps. 45.6. Matt. 22.44. Mark 12.36. Luke 20.42. 1 Cor. 15.25. Heb. 1.13.
b Judg. 5.2.
c Ps. 96.9. Acts 2.41.
1 Or, more than the womb of the morning: thou shalt have, etc.
d Num. 23. 19.
e Zech. 6.13. Heb. 5.6.
f Ps. 16.8.
g Ps. 2.5. Rom. 2.5. Rev. 11.18.
h Hab. 3.13.
2 Or, great.
i Isa. 61.1. John 3.34.
j Isa. 53.12.

PSALM 111
1 Hallelujah.
a Job 38.1.
2 prey.
b Ps. 19.7.
3 are established.
c Rev. 15.3.
d Deut. 4.6. Job 28.28. Eccl. 12.13.
4 Or, good success.
5 that do them.

PSALM 112
a Pro. 3.16. Pro. 15.6. Isa. 33.6. Matt. 6.33. 2 Cor. 6.10.
b Luke 6.35.
1 judgment.
c Luke 11.41. Acts 4.35. Acts 20.35. Rom. 12.13. 2 Cor. 8.9. 2 Cor. 9.9. 1 Tim. 6.18.
d Luke 13.28.

PSALM 113
1 Hallelujah.
a Dan. 2.20.
b Isa. 59.19. Hab. 2.14. Mal. 1.11. Rev. 11.15.

›ing down of the same the LORD's
ıme *is* to be praised.
The LORD *is* high above all na-
›ns, *and* his glory above the heavens.
Who *is* like unto the LORD our
›od, who [2]dwelleth on high,
Who [c]humbleth *himself* to behold
e things that are in heaven, and in
e earth!
He [d]raiseth up the poor out of the
ıst, *and* lifteth the needy out of the
ınghill;
That he may [e]set *him* with princes,
en with the princes of his people.
He [f]maketh the barren woman [3]to
›ep house, *and to be* a joyful mother
children. Praise ye the LORD.

PSALM 114

WHEN Israel went out of Egypt,
the house of Jacob from a peo-
e of strange language;
Judah was his sanctuary, *and* Israel
s dominion.
The sea saw *it*, and fled: Jordan
as driven back.
The [a]mountains skipped like rams,
ıd the little hills like lambs.
What *ailed* thee, O thou sea, that
ıou fleddest? thou Jordan, *that* thou
ast driven back?
Ye mountains, *that* ye skipped like
ıms; *and* ye little hills, like lambs?
Tremble, thou earth, at the pres-
ıce of the Lord, at the presence of
ıe God of Jacob;
Which [b]turned the rock *into* a
anding water, the flint into a foun-
ın of waters.

PSALM 115

NOT [a]unto us, O LORD, not unto
us, but unto thy name give glory,
›r thy mercy, *and* for thy truth's sake.
2 Wherefore should the heathen say,
Where *is* now their God?
3 But [c]our God *is* in the heavens:
e hath done whatsoever he hath
leased.
4 Their [d]idols *are* silver and gold, the
ork of men's hands.
5 They have mouths, but they speak
ot: eyes have they, but they see
ot:
6 They have ears, but they hear not:
oses have they, but they smell not:
7 They have hands, but they handle
ot: feet have they, but they walk not:
either speak they through their
ıroat.
8 They [e]that make them are like unto
hem; *so is* every one that trusteth in
hem.

9 O Israel, trust thou in the LORD:
he [f]*is* their help and their shield.
10 O [g]house of Aaron, trust in the
LORD: he *is* their help and their shield.
11 Ye that fear the LORD, trust in the
LORD: he *is* their help and their shield.
12 The LORD hath been mindful of
us: he will [h]bless *us;* he will bless the
house of Israel; he will bless the house
of Aaron.
13 He [i]will bless them that fear the
LORD, *both* small [1]and great.
14 The LORD shall increase you more
and more, you and your children.
15 Ye *are* [j]blessed of the LORD which
[k]made heaven and earth.
16 The heaven, *even* the heavens, *are*
the LORD's: but the earth hath he giv-
en to the children of men.
17 The dead praise not the LORD,
neither any that go down into silence.
18 But [l]we will bless the LORD from
this time forth and for evermore.
Praise the LORD.

PSALM 116

I LOVE the LORD, because he hath
heard my voice *and* my supplications.
2 Because he hath inclined his ear
unto me, therefore will I call upon
him [1]as long as I live.
3 The sorrows of death compassed
me, and the pains of hell [2]gat hold
upon me: I found trouble and sorrow.
4 Then called I upon the name of the
LORD; O LORD, I beseech thee, deliver my soul.
5 Gracious *is* the LORD, [a]and righteous; yea, our God *is* merciful.
6 The LORD preserveth the simple:
I was brought low, and he helped me.
7 Return unto thy [b]rest, O my soul;
for the LORD hath dealt bountifully
with thee.
8 For thou hast delivered my soul
from death, mine eyes from tears, *and*
my feet from falling.
9 I will walk before the LORD in the
land of the living.
10 I [c]believed, therefore have I spok-
en: I was greatly afflicted:
11 I said in my haste, [d]All men *are*
liars.
12 What shall I render unto the
LORD *for* all his benefits toward me?
13 I will take the cup of salvation,
and call upon the name of the LORD.
14 I [e]will pay my vows unto the LORD
now in the presence of all his people.
15 Precious [f]in the sight of the LORD
is the death of his saints.
16 O LORD, truly I *am* thy servant;

2 exalteth himself to dwell.
c Isa. 57.15.
d 1 Sam. 2.8. Isa. 26.19. Dan. 12.2.
e Job 36.7.
f 1 Sam. 2.5. Gal. 4.27.
3 to dwell in an house.

PSALM 114
a Ps. 29.6. Ps. 68.16. Hab. 3.6.
b Ex. 17.6. Num. 20.11. Ps. 107.35.

PSALM 115
a Isa. 48.11. Eze. 36.32.
b Ps. 42.3,10. Ps. 79.10. Joel 2.17.
c 1 Chr. 16. 26. Ps. 135.6. Dan. 4.35.
d Deut. 4.28. Ps. 135.15, 16. Isa. 40.19. Jer. 10.3. Hosea 8.6. 1 Cor. 10.19, 20.
e Ps. 135.18. Isa. 44.9,10. Jonah 2.8. Hab. 2.18.
f Ps. 33.20. Pro. 30.5.
g Mal. 2.7.
h Eph. 1.3.
i Lev. 26.3. Deut. 11.27. Ps. 24.4. Pro. 10.6.
1 with.
j Gen. 14.19.
k Gen. 1.1. Ps. 96.5.
l Ps. 145.2. Dan. 2.20.

PSALM 116
1 in my days.
2 found me.
a Ezra 9.15. Neh. 9.8. Ps. 11.7. Jer. 12.1. Lam. 1.18. Rev. 16.5.
b Jer. 6.16. Matt. 11.29.
c 2 Cor. 4.13.
d 2 Ki. 4.16. Jer. 9.5. Rom. 3.4.
e Ps. 22.25. Jonah 2.9.
f Job 5.26. Ps. 72.14. Luke 16.22. Rev. 14.13.

I *am* thy servant, *and* the son of thine
handmaid: thou hast loosed my
bonds.
17 I will offer to thee the sacrifice of
thanksgiving, and will call upon the
name of the LORD.
18 I will pay my vows unto the LORD
now in the presence of all his people,
19 In the courts of the LORD's house,
in the midst of thee, O Jerusalem.
Praise ye the LORD.

PSALM 117

O PRAISE the LORD, all ye nations: praise him, all ye people.
2 For his merciful kindness is great
toward us: and the truth of the LORD
endureth for ever. Praise ye the LORD.

PSALM 118

O [a]GIVE thanks unto the LORD;
for *he is* good: because his mercy
endureth for ever.
2 Let [b]Israel now say, that his mercy
endureth for ever.
3 Let the house of Aaron now say,
that his mercy *endureth* for ever.
4 Let them now that fear the LORD
say, that his mercy *endureth* for ever.
5 I called upon the LORD [1]in distress: the LORD answered me, *and set*
[c]*me* in a large place.
6 The LORD *is* [2]on my side; I will not
fear: what can man do unto me?
7 The [d]LORD taketh my part with
them that help me: therefore shall I
see *my desire* upon them that hate
me.
8 *It* [e]*is* better to trust in the LORD
than to put confidence in man.
9 *It* [f]*is* better to trust in the LORD
than to put confidence in princes.
10 All nations compassed me about:
but in the name of the LORD will I [3]de-
stroy them.
11 They [g]compassed me about; yea,
they compassed me about: but in the
name of the LORD I will destroy them.
12 They compassed me [h]about like
bees; they are quenched [i]as the fire of
thorns: for in the name of the LORD I
will [4]destroy them.
13 Thou hast thrust sore at me that
I might fall: but the LORD helped me.
14 The [j]LORD *is* my strength and
song, and is become my salvation.
15 The voice of rejoicing and salvation *is* in the tabernacles of the righteous: the right hand of the LORD doeth valiantly.
16 The [k]right hand of the LORD is
exalted: the right hand of the LORD
doeth valiantly.

PSALM 118
a 1 Chr. 16.8.
b Ps. 115.9.
1 out of distress.
c Ps. 18.19.
2 for me.
d Ps. 54.4.
e Ps. 62.8. Isa. 2.22. Jer. 17.5,7.
f Ps. 146.3. Isa. 30.2,3.
3 cut them off.
g Ps. 88.17.
h Deut. 1.44.
i Eccl. 7.6.
4 cut down.
j Ex. 15.2.
k Ex. 15.6.
l Ps. 6.5.
m Ps. 73.28.
n Pro. 3.11, 12. 1 Cor. 11.32.
o Isa. 26.2.
p Ps. 24.7.
q Isa. 35.8.
r Matt. 21.42. Mark 12.10. Eph. 2.20. 1 Pet. 2.4,7.
5 This is from the LORD.
s Job 5.9.
t 2 Cor. 6.2.
u Zech. 4.7. Matt. 21.9. Mark 11.9. Luke 19.38.
v Esther 8.16. Micah 7.9. Mal. 4.2.
w Ex. 15.2. Isa. 25.1.

PSALM 119
1 Or, perfect, or, sincere.
a Ps. 128.1.
b Deut. 4.29.
c Rom. 7.16, 17. 1 John 3.9.
d Jer. 31.33. Rom. 7.22, 23. 2 Cor. 3.5.
e Job 22.26. 1 John 2.28.
2 judgments of thy righteousness.
f Pro. 1.4, 10.

17 I [l]shall not die, but live, and d
clare the [m]works of the LORD.
18 The LORD hath [n]chastened m
sore: but he hath not given me ov
unto death.
19 Open [o]to me the gates of righ
eousness: I will go into them, *and*
will praise the LORD:
20 This [p]gate of the LORD, [q]int
which the righteous shall enter.
21 I will praise thee: for thou ha
heard me, and art become my salva
tion.
22 The [r]stone *which* the builders r
fused is become the head *stone* of th
corner.
23 [5]This is the LORD's doing; [s]it
marvellous in our eyes.
24 This *is* [t]the day *which* the LOR
hath made; we will rejoice and b
glad in it.
25 Save now, I beseech thee,
LORD: O LORD, I beseech thee, sen
now prosperity.
26 Blessed [u]*be* he that cometh in th
name of the LORD: we have blesse
you out of the house of the LORD.
27 God *is* the LORD, which hat
shewed us [v]light: bind the sacrific
with cords, *even* unto the horns of th
altar.
28 Thou *art* my God, and I wi
praise thee: [w]*thou art* my God, I wi
exalt thee.
29 O give thanks unto the LORD; fo
he is good: for his mercy *endureth* fo
ever.

PSALM 119

ALEPH.

BLESSED *are* the [1]undefiled in th
way, who [a]walk in the law of th
LORD.
2 Blessed *are* they that keep hi
testimonies, *and that* [b]seek him wit
the whole heart.
3 They [c]also do no iniquity: the
walk in his ways.
4 Thou hast commanded *us* to kee
thy precepts diligently.
5 O [d]that my ways were directed t
keep thy statutes!
6 Then [e]shall I not be ashamed, whe
I have respect unto all thy command
ments.
7 I will praise thee with uprightnes
of heart, when I shall have learne
[2]thy righteous judgments.
8 I will keep thy statutes: O forsak
me not utterly.

BETH.

9 Wherewithal shall a [f]young ma
cleanse his way? by taking hee
thereto according to thy word.

0 With my whole heart have I
ought thee: O let me not wander
om thy commandments.
1 Thy [h]word have I hid in mine
eart, that I might not sin against
ee.
2 Blessed *art* thou, O LORD: [i]teach
e thy statutes.
3 With my lips have I declared all
e judgments of thy mouth.
4 I have rejoiced in the way of thy
stimonies, as *much as* in all riches.
5 I will [j]meditate in thy precepts,
nd have respect unto thy ways.
6 I will delight myself in thy stat-
tes: I will not forget thy word.

GIMEL.

17 Deal bountifully with thy servant,
at I may live, and keep thy word.
18 [3]Open thou mine eyes, that I may
ehold wondrous things out of thy
w.
19 I [k]*am* a stranger in the earth: hide
ot thy commandments from me.
20 My soul breaketh for the longing
at it hath unto thy judgments at all
mes.
21 Thou hast rebuked the proud *that
re* cursed, which do err from thy
ommandments.
22 Remove from me reproach and
ontempt; for I have kept thy testi-
onies.
23 Princes also did sit *and* speak
gainst me: *but* thy servant did medi-
ate in thy statutes.
24 Thy testimonies also *are* my de-
ght *and* [4]my counsellers.

DALETH.

25 My soul cleaveth unto the dust:
uicken thou me according to thy
ord.
26 I have declared my ways, and
hou heardest me: [m]teach me thy
tatutes.
27 Make me to understand the way
f thy precepts: so shall I talk of thy
ondrous works.
28 My soul [5]melteth for heaviness:
trengthen thou me according unto
hy word.
29 Remove [n]from me the way of ly-
ng: and [o]grant me thy law graciously.
30 I have chosen the way of truth:
hy judgments have I laid *before
ne.*
31 I have stuck unto thy testimonies:
) LORD, put me not to shame.
32 I will run the way of thy com-
nandments, when thou [p]shalt en-
arge my heart.

g 2 Chr. 15. 15.
h Luke 2.19.
i Ps. 25.4.
j Ps. 1.2.
3 Reveal. Eph. 1.17.
k Gen. 47.9. Heb. 11.13.
4 men of my counsel.
l Ps. 143.11.
m 1 Ki. 8.36. Ps. 27.11.
5 droppeth.
n Pro. 30.8.
o Heb. 8.10.
p 1 Ki. 4.29. Isa. 60.5. 2 Cor. 6.11.
q Matt. 10. 22. Rev. 2.26.
r Pro. 2.6. Jas. 1.5.
s Eze. 33.31. Mark 7.21. Luke 12.15. 1 Tim. 6.10. Heb. 13.5.
6 Make to pass. Isa. 33.15.
t Job 31.1.
u 2 Sam. 7.25.
7 Or, So shall I answer him that reproacheth me in a thing.
8 at large. John 8.32, 36. Rom. 8.2. 1 Cor. 7.22, 23. Gal. 5.1,13. Jas. 1.25. 1 Pet. 2.16.
v Matt. 10.18. Acts 26. 1,2.
w Ps. 27.13. Jer. 15.16. Rom. 15. 3-5. Heb. 6.17-19.
x Jer. 20.7.
y Job 23.11.
z Ezra 9.3.
a Ps. 63.6.

HE.

33 Teach me, O LORD, the way of
thy statutes; and I shall keep it *unto*
[q]the end.
34 Give [r]me understanding, and I
shall keep thy law; yea, I shall observe it with *my* whole heart.
35 Make me to go in the path of thy
commandments; for therein do I delight.
36 Incline my heart unto thy testimonies, and not to [s]covetousness.
37 [6]Turn away mine eyes [t]from beholding vanity; *and* quicken thou me
in thy way.
38 Stablish [u]thy word unto thy servant, who *is devoted* to thy fear.
39 Turn away my reproach which I
fear: for thy judgments *are* good.
40 Behold, I have longed after thy
precepts: quicken me in thy righteousness.

VAU.

41 Let thy mercies come also unto
me, O LORD, *even* thy salvation, according to thy word.
42 [7]So shall I have wherewith to
answer him that reproacheth me: for
I trust in thy word.
43 And take not the word of truth
utterly out of my mouth; for I have
hoped in thy judgments.
44 So shall I keep thy law continually
for ever and ever.
45 And I will walk [8]at liberty: for I
seek thy precepts.
46 I [v]will speak of thy testimonies
also before kings, and will not be
ashamed.
47 And I will delight myself in thy
commandments, which I have loved.
48 My hands also will I lift up unto
thy commandments, which I have
loved; and I will meditate in thy
statutes.

ZAIN.

49 Remember the word unto thy
servant, upon which thou hast caused
me to hope.
50 This *is* my [w]comfort in my affliction: for thy word hath quickened me.
51 The proud have had me greatly
[x]in derision: *yet* have I not [y]declined
from thy law.
52 I remembered thy judgments of
old, O LORD; and have comforted
myself.
53 Horror [z]hath taken hold upon me
because of the wicked that forsake
thy law.
54 Thy statutes have been my songs
in the house of my pilgrimage.
55 I [a]have remembered thy name, O

LORD, in the night, and have kept thy
law.
56 This I had, because I kept thy precepts.

CHETH.

57 *Thou* [b]*art* my portion, O LORD: I
have said that I would keep thy
words.
58 I intreated thy [9]favour with *my*
whole heart: be merciful unto me according to thy word.
59 I [c]thought on my ways, and turned
my feet unto thy testimonies.
60 I made haste, and delayed not to
keep thy commandments.
61 The [10]bands of the wicked have
robbed me: *but* I have not forgotten
thy law.
62 At [d]midnight I will rise to give
thanks unto thee because of thy righteous judgments.
63 I *am* a companion of all *them* that
fear thee, and of them that keep thy
precepts.
64 The [e]earth, O LORD, is full of thy
mercy: teach me thy statutes.

TETH.

[f]65 Thou hast dealt well with thy servant, O LORD, according unto thy
word.
66 Teach me good judgment and
knowledge: for I have believed thy
commandments.
67 Before [f]I was afflicted I went
astray: but now have I kept thy word.
68 Thou *art* [g]good, and doest good;
teach me thy statutes.
69 The proud have [h]forged a lie
against me: *but* I will keep thy precepts with *my* whole heart.
70 Their [i]heart is as fat as grease;
but I delight in thy law.
71 *It* [j]*is* good for me that I have been
afflicted; that I might learn thy statutes.
72 The [k]law of thy mouth *is* better
unto me than thousands of gold and
silver.

JOD.

73 Thy [l]hands have made me and
fashioned me: give me understanding,
that I may learn thy commandments.
74 They [m]that fear thee will be glad
when they see me; because I have
hoped in thy word.
75 I know, O LORD, that thy judgments *are* [11]right, and [n]*that* thou in
faithfulness hast afflicted me.
76 Let, I pray thee, thy merciful
kindness be [12]for my comfort, according to thy word unto thy servant.
77 Let thy tender mercies come unto

b Ps. 16.5. Jer. 10.16. Lam. 3.24.
9 face. Job 11.19.
c Lam. 3.40. Joel 2.13. Luke 15.17.
10 Or, companies.
d Acts 16.25.
e Ps. 33.5.
f Deut. 32.15. Jer. 31.18. Hosea 5.15. Heb. 12.11. Rev. 3.19.
g Ex. 34.6. Ps. 107.1. Matt. 19.17.
h Job 13.4.
i Acts 28.27.
j Heb. 12.10.
k Ps. 19.10. Pro. 8.10.
l Job 10.8. Ps. 100.3.
m Ps. 34.2.
11 righteousness.
n Ps. 89.30-33. Heb. 12.10.
12 to comfort me.
o Ps. 25.3.
p 2 Chr. 15.7. Pro. 4.23. John 1.47.
q Ps. 42.1,2. Ps. 73.26.
r Ps. 69.3.
s Job 30.30.
t Ps. 39.4.
u Ps. 7.6. Rev. 6.10.
v Ps. 35.7.
13 faithfulness.
w Ps. 7.1-5. Ps. 35.19.
x Matt. 5.18. 1 Pet. 1.25.
14 to generation and generation.
15 standeth.
y Gen. 8.22. Ps. 148.6. Jer. 33.25.
z Rom. 15.4.
a Hos. 2.7,16.
b Isa. 40.8. Matt. 5.18.
c Ps. 1.2.
d Deut. 4.6,8. Isa. 48.17.
16 it is ever with me.

me, that I may live: for thy law *is* m
delight.
78 Let the proud [o]be ashamed; f
they dealt perversely with me witho
a cause: *but* I will meditate in thy pr
cepts.
79 Let those that fear thee turn un
me, and those that have known th
testimonies.
80 Let my heart be [p]sound in th
statutes; that I be not ashamed.

CAPH.

81 My [q]soul fainteth for thy salva
tion: *but* I hope in thy word.
82 Mine [r]eyes fail for thy word, say
ing, When wilt thou comfort me?
83 For [s]I am become like a bottle i
the smoke; *yet* do I not forget th
statutes.
84 How [t]many *are* the days of th
servant? [u]when wilt thou execu
judgment on them that persecute me
85 The [v]proud have digged pits fo
me, which *are* not after thy law.
86 All thy commandments *are* [13]faith
ful: they persecute [w]me wrongfully
help thou me.
87 They had almost consumed m
upon earth; but I forsook not th
precepts.
88 Quicken me after thy lovingkind
ness; so shall I keep the testimon
of thy mouth.

LAMED.

89 For [x]ever, O LORD, thy word i
settled in heaven.
90 Thy faithfulness *is* [14]unto all gen
erations: thou hast established th
earth, and it [15]abideth.
91 They continue this day accordin
to thine [y]ordinances: for all *are* th
servants.
92 Unless [z]thy law *had been* my de
lights, I should then have perished i
mine affliction.
93 I will never forget thy precepts
for with them thou hast quickened me
94 I *am* [a]thine, save me; for I hav
sought thy precepts.
95 The wicked have waited for me t
destroy me: *but* I will consider th
testimonies.
96 I [b]have seen an end of all perfec
tion: *but* thy commandment *is* ex
ceeding broad.

MEM.

97 O how love I thy law! [c]it *is* m
meditation all the day.
98 Thou through thy commandment
hast made me [d]wiser than mine en
emies: for [16]they *are* ever with me.
99 I have more understanding tha

my teachers: [e]for thy testimonies
ɛ my meditation.
)0 I [f]understand more than the
cients, because I keep thy precepts.
)1 I have [g]refrained my feet from
ery evil way, that I might keep thy
ord.
)2 I have not departed from thy
dgments: for thou hast taught me.
)3 How [h]sweet are thy words unto
y [17]taste! *yea, sweeter* than honey to
y mouth!
)4 Through thy precepts I get un-
rstanding: therefore I hate every
se way.

NUN.

)5 Thy word *is* a [18]lamp unto my
et, and a light unto my path.
)6 I [i]have sworn, and I will per-
rm *it*, that I will keep thy righteous
dgments.
07 I am afflicted very much: quicken
e, O LORD, according unto thy word.
08 Accept, I beseech thee, [j]the free-
ll offerings of my mouth, O LORD,
d teach me thy judgments.
09 My [k]soul *is* continually in my
nd: yet do I not forget thy law.
10 The wicked have laid a snare for
e: yet I erred not from thy precepts.
11 Thy [l]testimonies have I taken as
heritage for ever: for they *are* the
joicing of my heart.
12 I have inclined mine heart [19]to
rform thy statutes alway, *even unto*
e end.

SAMECH.

13 I hate *vain* thoughts: but thy
w do I love.
14 Thou [m]*art* my hiding place and
y shield: I hope in thy word.
15 Depart [n]from me, ye evildoers:
r I will keep the commandments of
y God.
16 Uphold me according unto thy
ord, that I may live: and let me not
e ashamed of my hope.
17 Hold [p]thou me up, and I shall be
fe: and I will have respect unto thy
atutes continually.
18 Thou hast trodden down all
em that err from thy statutes: for
eir deceit *is* falsehood.
19 Thou [20]puttest away all the
icked of the earth [q]*like* dross: there-
ore I love thy testimonies.
20 My [r]flesh trembleth for fear of
ee; and I am afraid of thy judg-
ents.

AIN.

121 I have done judgment and jus-
ce: leave me not to mine oppres-
ors.

e 2 Tim. 3.15.
f Job 12.12. Job 32.7.
g 2 Cor. 7.1. Pro. 1.15.
h Ps. 19.10. Pro. 8.11.
17 palate.
18 Or, candle.
i Neh. 10.29.
j Hosea 14.2. Heb. 13.15.
k Judg. 12.3. Job 13.14.
l Deut. 33.4.
19 to do.
m Ps.32.7.
n Ps. 6.8. Matt. 7.23.
o Ps. 25.2. Rom. 5.5. Rom. 9.33.
p Ps. 71.6. John 10.28. Rom. 14.4.
20 causest to cease.
q Eze. 22.18.
r Hab. 3.16.
s Heb. 7.22.
t Ps. 19.10. Pro. 3.13,18. Pro. 8.11.
Eph. 3.8.
u Ps. 19.7. Pro. 1.4. 2 Pet. 1.19.
v Ex. 4.31. 1 Sam. 1.11. Ps. 106.4.
21 according to the custom towards those, etc.
w Rom. 6.12.
x Luke 1.74.
y Ps. 4.6.
z Jer. 9.1.
a Neh. 9.33. Jer. 12.1. Dan. 9.7.
22 righteousness.
23 faithfulness.
24 cut me off.
25 tried, or, refined.
b Pro. 15.16. Amos 7.2. Luke 6.20. 2 Cor. 8.9. Jas. 2.5.
c Ps. 19.9. John 17.17. Eph. 1.13.
26 found me.

122 Be [s]surety for thy servant for
good: let not the proud oppress me.
123 Mine eyes fail for thy salvation,
and for the word of thy righteousness.
124 Deal with thy servant according
unto thy mercy, and teach me thy
statutes.
125 I *am* thy servant; give me understanding, that I may know thy testimonies.
126 *It is* time for *thee*, LORD, to
work: *for* they have made void thy
law.
127 Therefore [t]I love thy commandments above gold; yea, above fine
gold.
128 Therefore I esteem all *thy* precepts *concerning* all *things to be* right;
and I hate every false way.

PE.

129 Thy testimonies *are* wonderful:
therefore doth my soul keep them.
130 The entrance of thy words giveth
light; [u]it giveth understanding unto
the simple.
131 I opened my mouth, and panted:
for I longed for thy commandments.
132 Look [v]thou upon me, and be
merciful unto me, [21]as thou usest to
do unto those that love thy name.
133 Order my steps in thy word: and
let not [w]any iniquity have dominion
over me.
134 Deliver [x]me from the oppression
of man: so will I keep thy precepts.
135 Make [y]thy face to shine upon
thy servant; and teach me thy statutes.
136 Rivers [z]of waters run down mine
eyes, because they keep not thy law.

TZADDI.

137 Righteous [a]*art* thou, O LORD,
and upright *are* thy judgments.
138 Thy testimonies *that* thou hast
commanded *are* [22]righteous and very
[23]faithful.
139 My zeal hath [24]consumed me,
because mine enemies have forgotten
thy words.
140 Thy word *is* very [25]pure: therefore thy servant loveth it.
141 I *am* [b]small and despised: *yet* do
not I forget thy precepts.
142 Thy righteousness *is* an everlasting righteousness, and thy law *is*
[c]the truth.
143 Trouble and anguish have [26]tak-
en hold on me: *yet* thy commandments *are* my delights.
144 The righteousness of thy testimonies *is* everlasting: give me understanding, and I shall live.

KOPH.

145 I cried with *my* whole heart; hear me, O LORD: I will keep thy statutes.

146 I cried unto thee; save me, [27]and I shall keep thy testimonies.

147 I prevented the dawning of the morning, and cried: I hoped in thy word.

148 Mine [d]eyes prevent the *night* watches, that I might meditate in thy word.

149 Hear my voice according unto thy lovingkindness: O LORD, quicken me according to thy judgment.

150 They draw nigh that follow after mischief: they are far from thy law.

151 Thou *art* [e]near, O LORD; and all thy commandments *are* truth.

152 Concerning thy testimonies, I have known of old that thou hast founded them [f]for ever.

RESH.

153 Consider [g]mine affliction, and deliver me: for I do not forget thy law.

154 Plead [h]my cause, and deliver me: quicken me according to thy word.

155 Salvation [i]*is* far from the wicked: for they seek not thy statutes.

156 [28]Great *are* thy tender mercies, O LORD: quicken me according to thy judgments.

157 Many *are* my persecutors and mine enemies; *yet* do I not decline from thy testimonies.

158 I beheld the transgressors, and was grieved; because they kept not thy word.

159 Consider how I love thy precepts: quicken me, O LORD, according to thy lovingkindness.

160 [29]Thy word *is* true *from* the beginning: and every one of thy righteous judgments *endureth* for ever.

SCHIN.

161 Princes [j]have persecuted me without a cause: but my heart standeth in awe of thy word.

162 I rejoice at thy word, as one that findeth great spoil.

163 I hate and abhor lying: *but* thy law do I love.

164 Seven times a day do I praise thee because of thy righteous judgments.

165 Great [k]peace have they which love thy law: and [30]nothing shall offend them.

166 LORD, I have hoped for thy salvation, and done thy commandments.

27 Or, that I may keep.
d Ps. 63.1,6.
e Ps. 145.18.
f Luke 21.33.
g Lam. 5.1.
h 1 Sam. 24. 15. Ps. 35.1. Micah 7.9.
i Job 5.4.
28 Or, Many.
29 The beginning of thy word is true.
j 1 Sam. 24. 11.
k Pro. 3.2. Isa. 32.17.
30 they shall have no stumbling-block.
l Job 34.21. Pro. 5.21.
m Josh. 24. 22. Pro. 1.29. Luke 10.42.
n Isa. 53.6. Matt. 10.6. Luke 15.4. 1 Pet. 2.25.
o Eze. 34.6. Matt. 18.11.

PSALM 120
1 Or, What shall the deceitful tongue give unto thee? or, what shall it profit thee?
2 added.
3 Or, It is as the sharp arrows of the mighty man, with coals of juniper.
a Gen. 10.2.
b 1 Sam. 25.1. Jer. 49.28.
4 Or, a man of peace.

PSALM 121
1 Or, Shall I lift up mine eyes to the hills? whence should my help come?
a 1 Sam. 2.9.
b Isa. 27.3.
c Isa. 49.10.

167 My soul hath kept thy testimc
ies; and I love them exceedingly.

168 I have kept thy precepts and t
testimonies: [l]for all my ways *are* t
fore thee.

TAU.

169 Let my cry come near befc
thee, O LORD: give me understandi
according to thy word.

170 Let my supplication come befc
thee: deliver me according to t
word.

171 My lips shall utter praise, wh
thou hast taught me thy statutes.

172 My tongue shall speak of t
word: for all thy commandments *a*
righteousness.

173 Let thine hand help me; for
[m]have chosen thy precepts.

174 I have longed for thy salvatio
O LORD; and thy law *is* my delight

175 Let my soul live, and it sh
praise thee; and let thy judgmen
help me.

176 I [n]have gone astray like a lo
sheep; seek [o]thy servant; for I do n
forget thy commandments.

PSALM 120

A Song of degrees.

IN my distress I cried unto t
LORD, and he heard me.

2 Deliver my soul, O LORD, from l
ing lips, *and* from a deceitful tongu

3 [1]What shall be given unto thee?
what shall be [2]done unto thee, thc
false tongue?

4 [3]Sharp arrows of the mighty, wi
coals of juniper.

5 Woe is me, that I sojourn [a]in M
sěch, *that* [b]I dwell in the tents of K
där!

6 My soul hath long dwelt with hi
that hateth peace.

7 I *am* [4]*for* peace: but when I spea
they *are* for war.

PSALM 121

A Song of degrees.

[1]I WILL lift up mine eyes unto th
hills, from whence cometh m
help.

2 My help *cometh* from the LORI
which made heaven and earth.

3 He [a]will not suffer thy foot to b
moved: he [b]that keepeth thee will nc
slumber.

4 Behold, he that keepeth Israel sha
neither slumber nor sleep.

5 The LORD *is* thy keeper: the LORI
is thy shade upon thy right hand.

6 The [c]sun shall not smite thee b
day, nor the moon by night.

7 The LORD shall [d]preserve thee from
ll evil: he shall preserve thy soul.
8 The LORD shall [e]preserve thy going
ut and thy coming in from this time
orth, and even for evermore.

d Job 5.19. Ps. 91.9,10. Pro. 12.21.
e Deut. 28.6. Pro. 2.8.

PSALM 122

A Song of degrees of David.

WAS glad when they said unto me,
[a]Let us go into the house of the
ORD.
2 Our feet shall stand within thy
ates, O Jerusalem.
3 Jerusalem is builded as a city that
s compact [b]together:
4 Whither [c]the tribes go up, the
ribes of the LORD, unto [d]the testi-
nony of Israel, to give thanks unto
he name of the LORD.
5 For there [1]are set thrones of judg-
nent, the thrones of the house of
David.
6 Pray [e]for the peace of Jerusalem:
hey shall prosper that love thee.
7 Peace be within thy walls, *and* prosperity within thy palaces.
8 For my brethren and companions'
sakes, I will now say, Peace *be* within
hee.
9 Because of the house of the LORD
our God I will seek thy good.

PSALM 122
a Isa. 2.3. Jer. 31.6. Zech. 8.21.
b 2 Sam. 5.9. Eph. 2.21.
c Deut. 16.16.
d Ex. 16.34.
1 do sit.
e Isa. 62.6. Jer. 51.50.

PSALM 123

A Song of degrees.

UNTO thee lift I up mine eyes, O
thou that dwellest in the heavens.
2 Behold, as the eyes of servants *look*
unto the hand of their masters, *and* as
the eyes of a maiden unto the hand of
her mistress; so our eyes *wait* upon
the LORD our God, until that he have
mercy upon us.
3 Have mercy upon us, O LORD,
have mercy upon us: for we are exceedingly filled with contempt.
4 Our soul is exceedingly filled with
the scorning of those that are at ease,
and with the contempt of the proud.

PSALM 124

A Song of degrees of David.

IF *it had* not *been* the LORD who was
[a]on our side, now may Israel say;
2 If *it had* not *been* the LORD who
was on our side, when men rose up
against us:
3 Then they had [b]swallowed us up
quick, when their wrath was kindled
against us:
4 Then the waters had overwhelmed
us, the stream had gone over our soul:
5 Then the proud waters had gone
over our soul.
6 Blessed *be* the LORD, who hath not
given us *as* a prey to their teeth.
7 Our soul is escaped as a bird out of
the snare of the fowlers: the snare is
broken, and we are escaped.
8 Our [c]help *is* in the name of the
LORD, who made heaven and earth.

PSALM 124
a Gen. 15.1. Num. 14.9. Josh. 1.5. Heb. 13.5. Rom. 8.31.
b Ps. 35.25. Pro. 1.12. Jer. 51.34.
c Ex. 18.4. Ps. 121.2. Pro. 18.10. Isa. 50.10. Heb. 13.6.

PSALM 125

A Song of degrees.

THEY that trust in the LORD *shall*
be as mount Zion, *which* cannot
be removed, *but* abideth for ever.
2 *As* the mountains *are* round about
Jerusalem, so the LORD *is* round about
his people from henceforth even for
ever.
3 For the rod of [1]the wicked shall not
rest upon the lot of the righteous; lest
the righteous put forth their hands
unto iniquity.
4 Do good, O LORD, unto *those that*
be good, and to *them that are* upright
in their hearts.
5 As for such as turn aside unto their
crooked [a]ways, the LORD shall lead
them forth with the workers of iniquity: *but* peace [b]*shall be* upon Israel.

PSALM 125
1 wickedness Pro. 22.8. Isa. 14.5.
a Pro. 2.15. Isa. 59.8. Phil. 2.15.
b Gal. 6.16.

PSALM 126

A Song of degrees.

WHEN the LORD [1]turned again
the captivity of Zion, [a]we were
like them that dream.
2 Then [b]was our mouth filled with
laughter, and our tongue with singing:
then said they among the heathen,
The LORD [2]hath done great things for
them.
3 The LORD hath done great things
for us; *whereof* we are glad.
4 Turn again our captivity, O LORD,
as the streams in the south.
5 They [c]that sow in tears shall reap
in [3]joy.
6 He that goeth forth and weepeth,
bearing [4]precious seed, shall doubtless come again with rejoicing, bringing his sheaves *with him*.

PSALM 126
1 returned the returning of Zion.
a Acts 12.9.
b Job 8.21.
2 hath magnified to do with them.
c Isa. 12.1-3. Jer. 31.9. Joel 2.17. Matt. 5.4. 2 Cor. 7.8-11.
3 Or, singing.
4 Or, seed basket.

PSALM 127

A Song of degrees [1]for Solomon.

EXCEPT the LORD build the house,
they labour in vain [2]that build it:
except the LORD keep the city, the
watchman waketh *but* in vain.
2 *It is* vain for you to rise up early, to
sit up late, to [a]eat the bread of sorrows: *for* so he giveth his beloved
sleep.
3 Lo, [b]children *are* an heritage of the
LORD: *and* [c]the fruit of the womb *is*
his reward.

PSALM 127
1 Or, of.
2 that are builders of it in it.
a Gen. 3.17.
b Gen. 33.5.
c Deut. 28.4.

4 As arrows *are* in the hand of a mighty man; so *are* children of the youth.

5 Happy *is* the man that [3]hath his quiver full of them: they shall not be ashamed, but they [4]shall speak with the enemies in the gate.

PSALM 128

A Song of degrees.

BLESSED *is* every one that feareth the LORD; that walketh in his ways.

2 For [a]thou shalt eat the labour of thine hands: happy *shalt* thou *be*, and *it shall be* well with thee.

3 Thy [b]wife *shall be* [c]as a fruitful vine by the sides of thine house: thy children [d]like olive plants round about thy table.

4 Behold, that thus shall the man be blessed that feareth the LORD.

5 The [e]LORD shall bless thee out of Zion: and thou shalt see the good of Jerusalem all the days of thy life.

6 Yea, thou shalt [f]see thy children's children, *and* peace upon Israel.

PSALM 129

A Song of degrees.

[1]MANY a time have they afflicted me from [a]my youth, may Israel now say:

2 Many a time have they afflicted me from my youth: yet they have not prevailed against me.

3 The [b]plowers plowed upon my back: they made long their furrows.

4 The LORD *is* [c]righteous: he hath cut asunder the cords of the wicked.

5 Let them all be confounded and turned back that hate Zion.

6 Let them be as [d]the grass *upon* the housetops, which withereth afore it groweth up:

7 Wherewith the mower filleth not his hand; nor he that bindeth sheaves his bosom.

8 Neither do they which go by say, [e]The blessing of the LORD *be* upon you: we bless you in the name of the LORD.

PSALM 130

A Song of degrees.

OUT [a]of the depths have I cried unto thee, O LORD.

2 Lord, hear my voice: let thine ears be attentive to the voice of my supplications.

3 If [b]thou, LORD, shouldest mark iniquities, O Lord, who shall stand?

4 But *there is* [c]forgiveness with thee, that thou mayest [d]be feared.

5 I [e]wait for the LORD, my soul doth wait, and in his word do I hope.

6 My soul *waiteth* for the Lord more than they that watch for the morning: [1]*I say, more than* they that watch for the morning.

7 Let Israel hope in the LORD: for with the LORD *there is* mercy, and [f]with him *is* plenteous redemption.

8 And [g]he shall redeem Israel from all his iniquities.

PSALM 131

A Song of degrees of David.

LORD, my heart is not haughty, nor mine eyes lofty: [a]neither do I [1]exercise myself in great matters, or in things too [2]high for me.

2 Surely I have behaved and quieted [3]myself, [b]as a child that is weaned of his mother: my soul *is* even as a weaned child.

3 Let Israel hope in the LORD [4]from henceforth and for ever.

PSALM 132

A Song of degrees.

LORD, remember David, *and* all his afflictions:

2 How he sware unto the LORD, *and* vowed unto the mighty *God* of Jacob;

3 Surely I will not come into the tabernacle of my house, nor go up into my bed;

4 I will [a]not give sleep to mine eyes, *or* slumber to mine eyelids,

5 Until I find out a place for the LORD, [1]an habitation for the mighty *God* of Jacob.

6 Lo, we heard of it [b]at Ĕph´-ră-tăh: [c]we found it [d]in the fields of the wood.

7 We will go into his tabernacles: we will worship at his footstool.

8 Arise, [e]O LORD, into thy rest; thou, and the ark of thy strength.

9 Let thy priests [f]be clothed with righteousness; and let thy saints shout for joy.

10 For thy servant David's sake turn not away the face of thine anointed.

11 The LORD hath sworn *in* truth unto David; he will not turn from it; [g]Of the fruit of [2]thy body will I set upon thy throne.

12 If thy children will keep my covenant and my testimony that I shall teach them, their children shall also sit upon thy throne for evermore.

13 For the LORD hath chosen Zion; he hath desired *it* for his habitation.

14 This *is* my rest for ever: here will I dwell; for I have desired it.

15 I will [3]abundantly bless her pro-

---

3 hath filled his quiver with them.
4 Or, shall subdue, or, destroy.

PSALM 128
a Isa. 3.10.
b Pro. 5.15.
c Eze. 19.10.
d Ps. 52.8.
e Ps. 134.3.
f Gen. 50.23.

PSALM 129
1 Or, Much.
a Eze. 23.3. Hosea 2.15.
b Heb. 11.36.
c 2 Thes. 1.6.
d Ps. 37.2. Jer. 17.5,6.
e Ruth 2.4. Ps. 118.26.

PSALM 130
a Lam. 3.55. Jonah 2.2.
b Ps. 143.2. John 8.7.9. Rom. 3.20.
c Ex. 34.7. Eph. 1.7.
d 1 Ki. 8.40. Jer. 33.8,9. Heb. 12.28.
e Isa. 26.8.
1 Or, which watch unto the morning.
f Isa. 55.7.
g Matt. 1.21.

PSALM 131
a Rom. 12.16.
1 walk.
2 wonderful.
3 my soul.
b Matt. 18.3.
4 from now.

PSALM 132
a Ruth 3.18.
1 habitations.
b Josh. 18.1. 1 Sam. 17. 12.
c 1 Sam. 7.1.
d 1 Chr. 13.5.
e Num. 10.35.
f Job 29.14. Isa. 61.10.
g 1 Ki. 8.25. 2 Chr. 6.16. Luke 1.69.
2 thy belly.
3 Or, surely.

ision: I will satisfy her poor with
read.
16 I [h]will also clothe her priests with
alvation: [i]and her saints shall shout
loud for joy.
17 There [j]will I make the horn of
David to bud: I have ordained a
lamp for mine anointed.
18 His enemies will I clothe with
hame: but upon himself shall his
rown flourish.

PSALM 133

A Song of degrees of David.

BEHOLD, how good and how
pleasant *it is* for [a]brethren to
dwell [1]together in unity!
2 *It is* like [b]the precious ointment upon the head, that ran down upon the
beard, *even* Aaron's beard: that went
down to the skirts of his garments;
3 As the dew of [c]Hĕr-mon, *and as the*
dew that descended upon the mountains of Zion: for [d]there the LORD
commanded the blessing, *even* [e]life
for evermore.

PSALM 134

A Song of degrees.

BEHOLD, bless ye the LORD, all *ye*
servants of the LORD, [a]which by
night stand in the house of the
LORD.
2 Lift [b]up your hands [1]*in* the sanctuary, and bless the LORD.
3 The [c]LORD that made heaven and
earth bless [d]thee out of Zion.

PSALM 135

PRAISE ye the LORD. Praise ye the
name of the LORD; praise *him*, O
ye servants of the LORD.
2 Ye [a]that stand in the house of the
LORD, in the courts of the house of
our God,
3 Praise the LORD; for the LORD *is*
good: sing praises unto his name; for
it is pleasant.
4 For [b]the LORD hath chosen Jacob
unto himself, *and* Israel for his peculiar treasure.
5 For I know that the LORD *is* great,
and *that* our Lord *is* above all gods.
6 Whatsoever the LORD pleased,
that did he in heaven, and in earth, in
the seas, and all deep places.
7 He [c]causeth the vapours to ascend
from the ends of the earth; he [d]mak-
eth lightnings for the rain; he bringeth
the wind out of his [e]treasuries.
8 Who smote the firstborn of Egypt,
[1]both of man and beast.
9 *Who* sent tokens and wonders into

h 2 Chr. 6.41. *i* Hosea 11. 12.
j Ps. 92.10. Eze. 29.21. Luke 1.69. 4 Or, candle.

PSALM 133

a Gen. 13.8. 1 Cor. 1.10. 1 even together. *b* Ex. 30.25.
c Deut. 4.48.
d Lev. 25.21. Deut. 28.8. *e* Dan. 12.2, 3. Matt. 25.34, 46. John 4.14. John 17.3. Heb. 7.25. 1 John 5.20.

PSALM 134

a Lev. 8.35. 1 Chr. 9.33. Ps. 130.6. Luke 2.37. *b* Ps. 28.2. 1 Tim. 2.8. 1 Or, in holiness. *c* Ps. 124.8. *d* Ps. 128.5.

PSALM 135

a Luke 2.37. *b* Ex. 19.5. Deut. 7.6,7. *c* Gen. 2.6. Job 5.10. Jer. 10.13. *d* Job 28.25. Zech. 10.1. *e* Job 38.22. 1 from man unto beast. *f* Num. 21. 24. *g* Josh. 12.7. *h* Gen. 17.8. *i* Ex. 3.15. 2 to generation and generation. *j* Deut. 32.36.

PSALM 136

a Ex. 18.11. Deut. 10.17. *b* 1 Tim. 6.15. Rev. 17.14. *c* Pro. 3.19. *d* Jer. 10.12. *e* Deut. 4.19. 1 for the rulings by day. *f* Ex. 12.51.

the midst of thee, O Egypt, upon
Pharaoh, and upon all his servants.
10 Who [f]smote great nations, and
slew mighty kings;
11 Sī-hŏn king of the Amorites, and
Og king of Bā-shăn, and [g]all the kingdoms of Canaan:
12 And gave their land *for* an heritage, an [h]heritage unto Israel his
people.
13 Thy [i]name, O LORD, *endureth* for
ever; *and* thy memorial, O LORD,
[2]throughout all generations.
14 For [j]the LORD will judge his people, and he will repent himself concerning his servants.
15 The idols of the heathen *are* silver
and gold, the work of men's hands.
16 They have mouths, but they
speak not; eyes have they, but they
see not;
17 They have ears, but they hear not;
neither is there *any* breath in their
mouths.
18 They that make them are like unto them: *so is* every one that trusteth
in them.
19 Bless the LORD, O house of Israel:
bless the LORD, O house of Aaron:
20 Bless the LORD, O house of Levi:
ye that fear the LORD, bless the LORD.
21 Blessed be the LORD out of Zion,
which dwelleth at Jerusalem. Praise
ye the LORD.

PSALM 136

O GIVE thanks unto the LORD; for
he is good: for his mercy *endur-*
eth for ever.
2 O give thanks unto [a]the God of
gods: for his mercy *endureth* for ever.
3 O give thanks to the [b]Lord of lords:
for his mercy *endureth* for ever.
4 To him who alone doeth great
wonders: for his mercy *endureth* for
ever.
5 To [c]him that by wisdom made the
heavens: for his mercy *endureth* for
ever.
6 To [d]him that stretched out the
earth above the waters: for his mercy
endureth for ever.
7 To [e]him that made great lights: for
his mercy *endureth* for ever:
8 The sun [1]to rule by day: for his
mercy *endureth* for ever:
9 The moon and stars to rule by
night: for his mercy *endureth* for
ever.
10 To him that smote Egypt in their
firstborn: for his mercy *endureth* for
ever:
11 And [f]brought out Israel from

among them: for his mercy *endureth* for ever:

12 With a strong hand, and with a stretched out arm: for his mercy *endureth* for ever.

13 To [g]him which divided the Red sea into parts: for his mercy *endureth* for ever:

14 And made Israel to pass through the midst of it: for his mercy *endureth* for ever:

15 But [2]overthrew Pharaoh and his host in the Red sea: for his mercy *endureth* for ever.

16 To [h]him which led his people through the wilderness: for his mercy *endureth* for ever.

17 To him which smote great kings: for his mercy *endureth* for ever:

18 And [i]slew famous kings: for his mercy *endureth* for ever:

19 Sī-hŏn [j]king of the Amorites: for his mercy *endureth* for ever:

20 And Og the king of Bā-shăn: for his mercy *endureth* for ever:

21 And [k]gave their land for an heritage: for his mercy *endureth* for ever:

22 *Even* an heritage unto Israel his servant: for his mercy *endureth* for ever.

23 Who [l]remembered us in our low estate: for his mercy *endureth* for ever:

24 And hath redeemed us from our enemies: for his mercy *endureth* for ever.

25 Who [m]giveth food to all flesh: for his mercy *endureth* for ever.

26 O give thanks unto the God of heaven: for his mercy *endureth* for ever.

PSALM 137

BY [a]the rivers of Babylon, there we sat down, yea, we wept, when we remembered Zion.

2 We hanged our [b]harps upon the willows in the midst thereof.

3 For there they that carried us away captive required of us [1]a song; and they that [2]wasted us *required of us* mirth, *saying*, Sing us *one* of the songs of Zion.

4 How shall we sing the LORD's song in a [3]strange land?

5 If I forget thee, O Jerusalem, let my right hand forget *her cunning*.

6 If I do not remember thee, let my [c]tongue cleave to the roof of my mouth; if I prefer not Jerusalem above [4]my chief joy.

7 Remember, O LORD, the [d]children of Ē-dom in the day of Jerusalem; who said, [5]Rase *it*, rase *it*, *even* to the foundation thereof.

8 O daughter of Babylon, [e]who ar to be [6]destroyed; happy *shall he be* [7]that rewardeth thee as thou hast served us.

9 Happy *shall he be*, that taketh and dasheth thy little ones against [8]the stones.

PSALM 138

A Psalm of David.

I WILL praise thee with my whol heart: before [a]the gods will I sing praise unto thee.

2 I will worship [b]toward thy holy temple, and praise thy name for thy lovingkindness and for thy truth: for thou hast magnified thy [c]word above all thy name.

3 In the day when I cried thou answeredst me, *and* [d]strengthenedst me *with* strength in my soul.

4 All the kings of the earth shall praise thee, O LORD, when they hear the words of thy mouth.

5 Yea, they shall sing in the ways of the LORD: for great *is* the glory of the LORD.

6 Though the LORD *be* high, yet hath he [e]respect unto the lowly: but the proud he knoweth afar off.

7 Though [f]I walk in the midst of trouble, thou wilt revive me: thou shalt stretch forth thine hand against the wrath of mine enemies, and thy right hand shall save me.

8 The [g]LORD will perfect *that which* concerneth me: thy mercy, O LORD, *endureth* for ever: forsake not the works of thine own hands.

PSALM 139

To the chief Musician, A Psalm of David.

O LORD, [a]thou hast searched me and known *me*.

2 Thou [b]knowest my downsitting and mine uprising, thou understandest [c]my thought afar off.

3 Thou [1]compassest my path and my lying down, and art acquainted *with* all my ways.

4 For *there is* not a word in my tongue, *but*, lo, O LORD, [d]thou knowest it altogether.

5 Thou hast beset me behind and before, and laid thine hand upon me.

6 *Such* knowledge *is* too wonderful for me; it is high, I cannot *attain* unto it.

7 Whither shall I go from thy spirit? or whither shall I flee from thy presence?

8 If I ascend up into heaven, thou *art* there: [e]if I make my bed in hell, behold, thou *art there*.

---

g Ps. 78.13.
2 shaked off.
h Deut. 8.15.
i Deut. 29.7.
j Num. 21.21.
k Josh. 12.1.
l Gen. 8.1. Deut. 32.36. Ps. 102.17. Isa. 63.9. Luke 1.48.
m Ps. 104.27.

PSALM 137

a Eze. 1.1. Dan. 8.2.
b Isa. 24.8. Lam. 5.15. Amos 8.10. Rev. 18.22.
1 the words of a song.
2 laid us on heaps.
3 land of a stranger?
c Eze. 3.26.
4 the head of my joy.
d Lam. 4.22. Obad. 10.
5 Make bare.
e Isa. 13.1.
6 wasted.
7 that recompenseth unto thee thy deed which thou didst to us.
8 the rock.

PSALM 138

a Ps. 119.46.
b 1 Ki. 8.29. Ps. 5.7. Dan. 6.10. Jonah 2.7.
c Isa. 42.21.
d Zech. 10.12. 2 Cor. 12.9.
e Pro. 3.34. Jas. 4.6.
f Ps. 23.3.
g Ps. 57.2. Phil. 1.6.

PSALM 139

a Jer. 12.3. Rev. 2.23.
b 2 Ki. 19.27.
c Matt. 9.4. John 2.24.
1 Or, winnowest.
d Heb. 4.13.
e Pro. 15.11.

9 If I take the wings of the morning,
and dwell in the uttermost parts of
the sea;
10 Even there shall thy hand lead me,
and thy right hand shall hold me.
11 If I say, Surely the darkness shall
cover me; even the night shall be
light about me.
12 Yea, the darkness [2]hideth not
from thee; but the night shineth as
the day: [3]the darkness and the light
are both alike *to thee*.
13 For thou hast possessed my reins:
thou hast covered me in my mother's
womb.
14 I will praise thee; for I am fear-
fully *and* wonderfully made: marvellous *are* thy works; and *that* my soul
knoweth [4]right well.
15 My [5]substance was not hid from
thee, when I was made in secret, *and*
curiously wrought in the lowest parts
of the earth.
16 Thine eyes did see my substance,
yet being unperfect; and in thy book
all *my members* were written, [7]*which*
in continuance were fashioned, when
as yet there was none of them.
17 How precious also are thy
thoughts unto me, O God! how great
is the sum of them!
18 *If* I should count them, they are
more in number than the sand: when
I awake, I am still with thee.
19 Surely thou wilt [f]slay the wicked,
O God: depart from me therefore, ye
bloody men.
20 For they [g]speak against thee
wickedly, *and* thine enemies take *thy*
name in vain.
21 Do not I hate them, O LORD, that
hate thee? and am not I grieved with
those that rise up against thee?
22 I hate them with perfect hatred:
I count them mine enemies.
23 Search [h]me, O God, and know my
heart: try me, and know my thoughts:
24 And see if *there be any* [8]wicked
way in me, and [i]lead me in the way
everlasting.

PSALM 140

To the chief Musician, A Psalm of David.

DELIVER me, O LORD, from the
evil man: preserve me from the
violent man;
2 Which imagine mischiefs in *their*
heart; continually are they gathered
together *for* war.
3 They have sharpened their tongues
like a serpent; adder's poison *is* under their lips. Sē-lăh.
4 Keep me, O LORD, from the hands
of the wicked; preserve me from the
violent man; who have purposed to
overthrow my goings.
5 The [a]proud have hid a snare for me,
and cords; they have spread a net by
the wayside; they have set gins for
me. Sē-lăh.
6 I said unto the LORD, [b]Thou *art* my
God: hear the voice of my supplications, O LORD.
7 O GOD the Lord, [c]the strength of
my salvation, thou hast covered my
head in the day of battle.
8 Grant not, O LORD, [d]the desires of
the wicked: further not his wicked
device; [2]*lest* they exalt themselves.
Sē-lăh.
9 *As for* the [e]head of those that compass me about, let the mischief of
their own lips cover them.
10 Let [f]burning coals fall upon
them: let them be cast into the fire;
into deep pits, that they rise not up
again.
11 Let not [3]an evil speaker be established in the earth: evil shall hunt the
violent man to overthrow *him*.
12 I know that the LORD [g]will maintain the cause of the afflicted, *and* the
right of the poor.
13 Surely the righteous shall give
thanks unto thy name: the upright
shall dwell in thy presence.

PSALM 141

A Psalm of David.

LORD, I cry unto thee: make haste
unto me; give ear unto my voice,
when I cry unto thee.
2 Let my prayer be [1]set forth before
thee *as* [a]incense; *and* [b]the lifting up of
my hands *as* the evening sacrifice.
3 Set a watch, O LORD, before my
mouth; keep the door of my lips.
4 Incline [c]not my heart to *any* evil
thing, to practise wicked works with
men that work iniquity: [d]and let me
not eat of their dainties.
5 [2]Let the righteous smite me; *it shall*
be a kindness: and let him reprove me;
it shall be an excellent oil, *which* shall
not break my head: for yet my prayer
also *shall be* in their calamities.
6 When their judges are overthrown
in stony places, they shall hear my
words; for they are sweet.
7 Our bones are scattered [e]at the
grave's mouth, as when one cutteth
and cleaveth *wood* upon the earth.
8 But [f]mine eyes *are* unto thee, O
GOD the Lord: in thee is my trust;
[3]leave not my soul destitute.
9 Keep me from the snares *which*

2 darkeneth not.
3 as is the darkness, so is the light.
4 greatly.
5 Or, strength, or, body.
6 all of them.
7 Or, what days they should be fashioned.
f Isa. 11.4.
g Job 21.14, 15. Jude 15.
h Job 31.6.
8 way of pain, or, grief.
i Matt. 7.14. John 14.6.

PSALM 140
1 man of violences.
a Ps. 10.9. Jer. 18.22. Luke 11.53, 54.
b Ps. 16.2.
c Deut. 33. 27-29. Ps. 18.32.
d Job 5.12, 13.
2 Or, let them not be exalted.
e Ps. 7.16.
f Ps. 11.6.
3 a man of tongue, or, an evil speaker, a wicked man of violence, be established in the earth: let him be hunted to his overthrow.
g Ps. 109.31.

PSALM 141
1 directed.
a Eph. 5.2.
b 1 Tim. 2.8.
c Matt. 6.13.
d Pro. 23.6. Matt. 20.15.
2 Or, Let the righteous smite me kindly, and reprove me; let not their precious oil break my head, etc.
e 2 Cor. 1.9.
f Ps. 25.15.
3 make not my soul bare.

they have laid for me, and the gins of
the workers of iniquity.
10 Let the [g]wicked fall into their own
nets, whilst that I withal [4]escape.

PSALM 142

[1]Maschil of David; A Prayer [a]when he
was in the cave.

I CRIED unto the LORD with my
voice; with my voice unto the LORD
did I make my supplication.
2 I poured out my complaint before
him; I shewed before him my trouble.
3 When my spirit was overwhelmed
within me, then thou knewest my
path. In the way wherein I walked
have they privily laid a snare for me.
4 [2]I looked on *my* right hand, and beheld, but *there was* no man that would
know me: refuge [3]failed me; [4]no man
cared for my soul.
5 I cried unto thee, O LORD: I said,
Thou *art* my refuge *and* [b]my portion
in the land of the living.
6 Attend unto my cry; for I [c]am
brought very low: deliver [d]me from
my persecutors; for they are stronger
than I.
7 Bring my soul out of prison, that I
may praise thy name: the righteous
[e]shall compass me about; for thou
shalt [f]deal bountifully with me.

PSALM 143

A Psalm of David.

HEAR my prayer, O LORD, give ear
to my supplications: in thy faithfulness answer me, *and* in thy righteousness.
2 And [a]enter not into judgment with
thy servant: for [b]in thy sight shall no
man living be justified.
3 For the [c]enemy hath persecuted
my soul; he hath smitten my life down
to the ground; he hath made me to
dwell in darkness, as those that have
been long dead.
4 Therefore is [d]my spirit overwhelmed within me; my heart within me is
desolate.
5 I remember [e]the days of old; I
meditate on all thy works; I muse on
the work of thy hands.
6 I stretch [f]forth my hands unto
thee: my soul *thirsteth* after thee, as a
thirsty land. Sē-lāh.
7 Hear me speedily, O LORD: my
spirit faileth: hide not thy face from
me, [1]lest I be like unto them that go
down into the pit.
8 Cause me to hear thy lovingkindness in the morning; for in thee do I
trust: cause me to know the way

g Esther 7.10. Ps. 7.15.
4 pass over.

PSALM 142
1 Or, A Psalm of David, giving instruction.
a 1 Sam. 22.1.
2 Or, Look on the right hand, and see.
3 perished from me.
4 no man sought after my soul.
b Lam. 3.24.
c Ps. 116.6.
d Ps. 7.1.
e Ps. 34.2.
f Ps. 119.17.

PSALM 143
a Job 14.3.
b Job 4.17. Eccl. 7.20. Gal. 2.16.
c Ps. 7.1,2.
d Ps. 61.2.
e Ps. 77.5,11.
f Ps. 28.2.
1 Or, for I am become like, etc.
2 hide me with thee.
g Ps. 25.4.
h John 14.26. Rom. 5.5. Gal. 5.22, 23. Eph. 4.30.

PSALM 144
1 my rock.
a 2 Sam. 22. 35.
2 to the war, etc.
3 Or, My mercy.
b Heb. 2.6.
c Isa. 64.1.
4 hands.
d Ps. 69.1.
e Mal. 2.11.
f Ps. 33.2.
5 Or, victory.
6 cut.
7 from kind to kind.
8 able to bear burdens, or, loaden with flesh.

wherein I should walk; for I lift up
soul unto thee.
9 Deliver me, O LORD, from m
enemies: I [2]flee unto thee to hide m
10 Teach [g]me to do thy will; for th
art my God: [h]thy spirit *is* good; le
me into the land of uprightness.
11 Quicken me, O LORD, for t
name's sake: for thy righteousne
sake bring my soul out of trouble.
12 And of thy mercy cut off mine e
emies, and destroy all them that aff
my soul: for I *am* thy servant.

PSALM 144

A Psalm of David.

BLESSED *be* the LORD [1]
strength, which [a]teacheth
hands [2]to war, *and* my fingers to fig
2 [3]My goodness, and my fortre
my high tower, and my deliverer;
shield, and *he* in whom I trust; w
subdueth my people under me.
3 LORD, [b]what *is* man, that thou ta
est knowledge of him! *or* the son
man, that thou makest account
him!
4 Man is like to vanity: his days *a*
as a shadow that passeth away.
5 Bow [c]thy heavens, O LORD, a
come down: touch the mountains, a
they shall smoke.
6 Cast forth lightning, and scat
them: shoot out thine arrows, and d
stroy them.
7 Send thine [4]hand from above;
[d]me, and deliver me out of gre
waters, from the hand [e]of stran
children;
8 Whose mouth speaketh vanity, a
their right hand *is* a right hand of fal
hood.
9 I will [f]sing a new song unto thee,
God: upon a psaltery *and* an instr
ment of ten strings will I sing prais
unto thee.
10 *It is he* that giveth [5]salvation un
kings: who delivereth David his s
vant from the hurtful sword.
11 Rid me, and deliver me from t
hand of strange children, who
mouth speaketh vanity, and th
right hand *is* a right hand of falsehoo
12 That our sons *may be* as plan
grown up in their youth; *that* o
daughters *may be* as corner ston
[6]polished *after* the similitude of
palace:
13 *That* our garners *may be* fu
affording [7]all manner of store: *th*
our sheep may bring forth thousan
and ten thousands in our streets:
14 *That* our oxen *may be* [8]strong

bour; *that there be* [g]no breaking in,
›r going out; that *there be* no com-
aining in our streets.
5 Happy [h]*is that* people, that is in
ch a case: *yea*, happy *is that* people,
ıose God *is* the LORD.

PSALM 145

David's *Psalm* of praise.

WILL extol thee, my God, O king;
and I will bless thy name for ever
ıd ever.
Every day will I bless thee; and I
ill praise thy name for ever and ever.
Great *is* the LORD, and greatly to
: praised; [1]and his greatness *is* un-
archable.
One generation shall praise thy
orks to another, and shall declare
y mighty acts.
I will speak of the glorious honour
' thy majesty, and of thy wondrous
'orks.
And *men* shall speak of the might
' thy terrible acts: and I will [3]de-
are thy greatness.
They shall abundantly [4]utter the
emory of thy great goodness, and
ıall sing of thy righteousness.
The [a]LORD *is* gracious, and full of
ɔmpassion; slow to anger, and [5]of
'eat mercy.
The [b]LORD *is* good to all: and his
nder mercies *are* over all his works.
0 All [c]thy works shall praise thee,
LORD; and thy saints shall bless
ıee.
1 They shall speak of the glory of
ıy kingdom, and talk of thy power;
2 To make known to the sons of
ıen his mighty acts, and the glorious
ıajesty of his kingdom.
3 Thy kingdom *is* [6]an everlasting
ıngdom, and thy dominion *endureth*
ıroughout all generations.
4 The LORD upholdeth all that fall,
ıd raiseth up all *those that be* bowed
ɔwn.
.5 The eyes of all [7]wait upon thee;
ıd thou givest them their meat in
ıe season.
.6 Thou openest thine hand, and
ıtisfiest the desire of every living
ıing.
.7 The LORD *is* righteous in all his
'ays, and [8]holy in all his works.
.8 The [d]LORD *is* nigh unto all them
ıat call upon him, to all that call upon
im [e]in truth.
.9 He will [f]fulfil the desire of them
ıat fear him: he also will hear their
'y, and will save them.
20 The LORD [g]preserveth all them

g Lev. 26.17.
h Deut. 33. 29.

PSALM 145

1 and of his greatness there is no search.
2 things, or, words.
3 declare it.
4 boil up. Ps. 45.1.
a Ex. 34.6. Num. 14.18. Ps. 57.10. Ps. 86.5,15. Lam. 3.22, 23. John 1.17.
5 great in mercy.
b Ps. 100.5. Nah. 1.7. Matt. 5.45. Acts 14.17.
c Ps. 19.1.
6 a kingdom of all ages. Isa. 9.7. Dan. 2.44. Micah 4.7. 1 Tim. 1.17. Rev. 11.15, 17.
7 Or, look unto thee.
8 Or, merciful, or, bountiful.
d Ps. 91.1. Isa. 61.10. John 14.23. Jas. 4.8. 1 John 2.24. Jude 23. Rev. 3.20.
e John 4.24.
f 1 John 5.14.
g 1 Pet. 1.5.

PSALM 146

1 Hallelujah.
a Isa. 2.22.
2 Or, salvation.
b Eccl. 12.7.
c 1 Cor. 2.6.
d Jer. 17.7.
e Rev. 14.7.
f Micah 7.20.

PSALM 147

a Deut. 30.3. Isa. 27.13. Jer. 32.37. Eze. 36.24.
b Isa. 61.1. Luke 4.18.
1 griefs.
c Gen. 15.5. Isa. 40.26.
d 1 Chr. 16. 25.
e Nah. 1.3.
2 of his understanding there is no number.
f Ps. 146.8.
g Eph. 5.20.
3 answer. Ex. 15.21.
h Job 38.26.

that love him: but all the wicked will
he destroy.
21 My mouth shall speak the praise
of the LORD: and let all flesh bless his
holy name for ever and ever.

PSALM 146

[1]PRAISE ye the LORD. Praise the
LORD, O my soul.
2 While I live will I praise the LORD:
I will sing praises unto my God while
I have any being.
3 Put [a]not your trust in princes, *nor*
in the son of man, in whom *there is*
no [2]help.
4 His [b]breath goeth forth, he returneth to his earth; in that very day [c]his
thoughts perish.
5 Happy [d]*is he* that *hath* the God of
Jacob for his help, whose hope *is* in
the LORD his God:
6 Which [e]made heaven, and earth,
the sea, and all that therein *is:* which
[f]keepeth truth for ever:
7 Which executeth judgment for the
oppressed: which giveth food to the
hungry. The LORD looseth the prisoners:
8 The LORD openeth *the eyes of* the
blind: the LORD raiseth them that are
bowed down: the LORD loveth the
righteous:
9 The LORD preserveth the strangers; he relieveth the fatherless and
widow: but the way of the wicked he
turneth upside down.
10 The LORD shall reign for ever,
even thy God, O Zion, unto all generations. Praise ye the LORD.

PSALM 147

PRAISE ye the LORD: for *it is* good
to sing praises unto our God; for
it is pleasant; *and* praise is comely.
2 The LORD doth build up Jerusalem: [a]he gathereth together the outcasts of Israel.
3 He [b]healeth the broken in heart,
and bindeth up their [1]wounds.
4 He [c]telleth the number of the stars;
he calleth them all by *their* names.
5 Great [d]*is* our Lord, and of great
[e]power: [2]his understanding *is* infinite.
6 The [f]LORD lifteth up the meek: he
casteth the wicked down to the
ground.
7 Sing unto the LORD [g]with thanksgiving; [3]sing praise upon the harp unto our God:
8 Who [h]covereth the heaven with
clouds, who prepareth rain for the
earth, who maketh grass to grow upon
the mountains.

9 He [i]giveth to the beast his food,
and to [j]the young ravens which cry.
10 He [k]delighteth not in the strength
of the horse: he taketh not pleasure in
the legs of a man.
11 The Lord taketh pleasure in them
that fear him, in those that hope in
his mercy.
12 Praise the LORD, O Jerusalem;
praise thy God, O Zion.
13 For he hath strengthened the bars
of thy gates; he hath blessed thy
children within thee.
14 [4]He maketh peace *in* thy borders,
and filleth thee with the [5]finest of the
wheat.
15 He [l]sendeth forth his commandment *upon* earth: his word runneth
very swiftly.
16 He giveth snow like wool: he
scattereth the hoarfrost like ashes.
17 He casteth forth his ice like mor-
sels: who can stand before his cold?
18 He sendeth out his word, and
melteth them: he causeth his wind to
blow, *and* the waters flow.
19 He sheweth [6]his word unto Jacob,
his [m]statutes and his judgments unto
Israel.
20 He [n]hath not dealt so with any nation: and *as for his* judgments, they
have not known them. Praise ye the
LORD.

PSALM 148

[1]PRAISE ye the LORD. Praise ye
the LORD from the heavens: praise
him in the heights.
2 Praise ye him, all his [a]angels:
praise ye him, all his hosts.
3 Praise ye him, sun and moon:
praise him, all ye stars of light.
4 Praise him, [b]ye heavens of heavens,
and ye waters that *be* above the heavens.
5 Let them praise the name of the
LORD: for [c]he commanded, and they
were created.
6 He [d]hath also stablished them for
ever and ever: he hath made a decree
which shall not pass.
7 Praise the LORD from the earth, ye
[e]dragons, and all deeps:
8 Fire, and hail; snow, and vapour;
stormy wind fulfilling his word:
9 Mountains, [f]and all hills; fruitful
trees, and all cedars:
10 Beasts, and all cattle; creeping
things, and [2]flying fowl:
11 Kings of the earth, and [g]all peo-

i Job 38.41. Matt. 6.26. Luke 12.24.
j Matt. 6.26.
k Hosea 1.7.
4 Who maketh thy border peace.
5 fat of wheat.
l Job 37.12.
6 his words.
m Deut. 33.4. Mal. 4.4. Rom. 3.2.
n Deut. 4.32. Acts 14.16. Rom. 3.1,2.

PSALM 148

1 Hallelujah.
a Dan. 7.10. Heb. 1.7.
b 1 Ki. 8.27.
c Heb. 11.3.
d Jer. 33.25.
e Isa. 43.20.
f Isa. 49.13.
2 birds of wing.
g Acts 17.28.
h Isa. 6.3. Phil. 2.9.
3 exalted.
i Eph. 2.17. 1 Pet. 2.9.

PSALM 149

1 Hallelujah.
a Isa. 42.10.
b Job 35.10.
c Zech. 9.9.
2 Or, with the pipe.
d Pro. 11.20.
3 throat.
e Deut. 7.1,2. Heb. 4.12. Rev. 1.16.
f Deut. 7.1,2. Rom. 16.20. Rev. 5.21.
g Rom. 16.20. 1 John 5.4.

PSALM 150

1 Hallelujah.
2 Or, cornet.
a Ex. 15.20.
3 Or, pipe.
b Isa. 38.20.
c Rev. 5.13.

ple; princes, and all judges of t
earth:
12 Both young men, and maider
old men, and children:
13 Let them praise the name of t
LORD: for [h]his name alone is [3]exc
lent; his glory *is* above the earth a
heaven.
14 He also exalteth the horn of
people, the praise of all his saint
even of the children of Israel, [i]a pe
ple near unto him. Praise ye t
LORD.

PSALM 149

[1]PRAISE ye the LORD. [a]Sing un
the LORD a new song, *and*
praise in the congregation of saints
2 Let Israel rejoice in [b]him that ma
him: let the children of Zion be joyf
in their [c]King.
3 Let them praise his name [2]in t
dance: let them sing praises unto hi
with the timbrel and harp.
4 For the LORD taketh [d]pleasure
his people: he will beautify the me
with salvation.
5 Let the saints be joyful in glory:
them sing aloud upon their beds.
6 *Let* the high *praises* of God *be*
their [3]mouth, and a [e]twoedged swo
in their hand;
7 To execute vengeance upon t
heathen, *and* punishments upon t
people;
8 To bind their kings with chain
and their nobles with fetters of iro
9 To [f]execute upon them the jud
ment written: this [g]honour have a
his saints. Praise ye the LORD.

PSALM 150

[1]PRAISE ye the LORD. Praise Go
in his sanctuary: praise him in t
firmament of his power.
2 Praise him for his mighty act
praise him according to his excelle
greatness.
3 Praise him with the sound of t
[2]trumpet: praise him with the psa
tery and harp.
4 Praise him [a]with the timbrel an
[3]dance: praise him [b]with stringed i
struments and organs.
5 Praise him upon the loud cymbal
praise him upon the high soundir
cymbals.
6 Let [c]every thing that hath breat
praise the LORD. Praise ye the LOR

THE PROVERBS

CHAPTER 1

THE [a]proverbs of Solomon the son
of David, king of Israel;
To know wisdom and instruction;
perceive the words of understand-
g;
To [b]receive the instruction of wis-
m, justice, and judgment, and
quity;
To give subtilty to the simple, to
e young man knowledge and [2]dis-
etion.
A wise *man* will hear, and will in-
ease learning; and a man of under-
anding shall attain unto wise coun-
ls:
To understand a proverb, and [3]the
terpretation; the words of the wise,
d their dark sayings.
¶ The fear of the LORD *is* [4]the be-
nning of knowledge: *but* fools de-
ise wisdom and instruction.
My son, hear the instruction of thy
ther, and forsake not the law of thy
other:
For they *shall be* [5]an ornament of
ace unto thy head, and chains about
y neck.
0 ¶ My son, if sinners entice thee,
onsent thou not.
1 If they say, Come with us, let [d]us
y wait for blood, let us lurk privily
r the innocent without cause:
2 Let us swallow them up alive as
e grave; and whole, [e]as those that
o down into the pit:
3 We shall find all precious sub-
ance, we shall fill our houses with
oil:
4 Cast in thy lot among us; let us
l have one purse:
5 My son, [f]walk not thou in the way
ith them; refrain thy foot from their
ath:
6 For [g]their feet run to evil, and
ake haste to shed blood.
7 Surely in vain the net is spread
n the sight of any bird.
8 And they lay wait for their *own*
ood; they lurk privily for their *own*
ves.
9 So [h]*are* the ways of every one that
greedy of gain; *which* taketh away
e life of the owners thereof.
0 ¶ [7]Wisdom crieth without; she
tereth her voice in the streets:
21 She crieth in the chief place of
concourse, in the openings of the
gates: in the city she uttereth her
words, *saying*,
22 How long, ye simple ones, will ye
love simplicity? and the scorners delight in their scorning, and fools hate
knowledge?
23 Turn you at my reproof: behold,
[i]I will pour out my spirit unto you, I
will make known my words unto you.
24 ¶ Because [j]I have called, and ye
refused; I have stretched out my hand,
and no man regarded;
25 But ye [k]have set at nought all my
counsel, and would none of my reproof:
26 I also will laugh at your calamity;
I will mock when your fear cometh;
27 When your fear cometh as desolation, and your destruction cometh
as a whirlwind; when distress and
anguish cometh upon you.
28 Then [l]shall they call upon me, but
I will not answer; they shall seek me
early, but they shall not find me:
29 For that they [m]hated knowledge,
and did not choose the fear of the
LORD:
30 They would none of my counsel:
they despised all my reproof.
31 Therefore [n]shall they eat of the
fruit of their own way, and be filled
with their own devices.
32 For the [8]turning away of the simple shall slay them, and the prosperity
of fools shall destroy them.
33 But whoso hearkeneth unto me
shall dwell safely, and shall be quiet
from fear of evil.

CHAPTER 2

MY son, if thou wilt receive my
words, and hide my commandments with thee;
2 So that thou incline thine ear unto
wisdom, *and* apply thine heart to understanding;
3 Yea, if thou criest after knowledge,
and [1]liftest up thy voice for understanding;
4 If [a]thou seekest her as silver, and
searchest for her as *for* hid treasures;
5 Then shalt thou understand the
fear of the LORD, and find the knowledge of God.

CHAP. 1
a 1 Ki. 4.32.
b ch. 2.1.
1 equities.
2 Or, advisement.
3 Or, an eloquent speech.
4 Or, the principal part.
5 an adding.
c Gen. 39.7. Judg. 16.16-21. Rom. 16.18. Eph. 5.11.
d ch. 12.6. Jer. 5.26. Micah 7.2.
e Ps. 28.1.
f ch. 4. 14.
g Isa. 59.7.
6 in the eyes of every thing that hath a wing.
h 2 Ki. 5.20-27. Micah 2.1-3. 1 Tim. 6.10.
7 Wisdoms, that is, excellent wisdom.
i Joel 2.28. John 7.37.
j Isa. 66.4. Jer. 7.13. Zech. 7.11.
k Luke 7.30.
l Isa. 1.15. Jer. 14.12. Micah 3.4. Jas. 4.3.
m Job 21.14. Ps. 50.16,17. Isa. 27.11. John 3.20. Acts 7.51.
n Isa. 3.11.
8 Or, ease of the simple.

CHAP. 2
1 givest thy voice.
a Ps. 19.10. ch. 3.14,15. Matt. 6.19-21.

6 For [b]the LORD giveth wisdom: out
of his mouth *cometh* knowledge and
understanding.
7 He layeth up sound wisdom for the
righteous: [c]*he is* a buckler to them
that walk uprightly.
8 He keepeth the paths of judgment,
and preserveth [d]the way of his saints.
9 Then shalt thou understand righteousness, and judgment, and equity;
yea, every good path.
10 ¶ When wisdom entereth into
thine heart, and knowledge is pleasant
unto thy soul;
11 Discretion shall preserve thee, understanding [e]shall keep thee:
12 To deliver thee from the way of
the evil *man*, from the man that speaketh froward things;
13 Who leave the paths of uprightness, to walk [f]in the ways of darkness;
14 Who rejoice to do evil, *and* delight in the frowardness of the wicked;
15 Whose ways *are* crooked, and
they froward in their paths:
16 To deliver thee from the strange
woman, *even* from the stranger *which*
flattereth with her words;
17 Which [g]forsaketh the guide of her
youth, and forgetteth [h]the covenant
of her God.
18 For her house inclineth unto
death, and her paths unto the dead.
19 None [i]that go unto her return
again, neither take they hold of the
paths of life.
20 That thou mayest [j]walk in the
way of good *men*, and keep the paths
of the righteous.
21 For the upright shall dwell in the
land, and the perfect shall remain
in it.
22 But the wicked shall be cut off
from the earth, and the transgressors
shall be [2]rooted out of it.

CHAPTER 3

MY son, forget not my law; [a]but
let thine heart keep my commandments:
2 For length of days, and [1]long life,
and peace, shall they add to thee.
3 Let not mercy and truth forsake
thee: bind [b]them about thy neck;
write [c]them upon the table of thine
heart:
4 So [d]shalt thou find favour and
[2]good understanding in the sight of
God and man.
5 ¶ Trust in the LORD with all thine
heart; and [e]lean not unto thine own
understanding.

b Luke 21.15. John 6.45. Jas. 1.5.
c Ps. 84.11.
d 1 Sam. 2.9. Ps. 37.23, 24,28,31. 1 Pet. 1.5.
e ch. 6.22.
f John 3.19. Eph. 4.18.
g Mal. 2.14.
h Gen. 2.24.
i Eccl. 7.26. Heb. 13.4.
j Heb. 6.12.
2 Or, plucked up.

CHAP. 3

a Deut. 30. 16.
1 years of life.
b Deut. 6.8.
c Jer. 17.1. 2 Cor. 3.3.
d 1 Sam. 2.26. Luke 2.52. Acts 2.47.
2 Or, good success.
e Jer. 9.23.
f 1 Chr. 28.9.
g Jer. 10.23.
h Rom. 12. 16.
3 medicine.
4 watering, or, moisten-ing.
i Ex. 23.19.
j Deut. 28.8.
k Job 5.17. Heb. 12.5.
l Deut. 8.5.
5 the man that draw-eth out under-standing.
m Job 28.13. ch. 2.4. ch. 8.11,19.
n Matt. 13.44.
o 1 Tim. 4.8.
p Matt. 11.29.
q Gen. 2.9.
r ch. 8.27. John 1.3. Heb. 1.2.
6 Or, pre-pared.
s Deut. 33.28. Job 36.28.
t Lev. 26.6.
u Rom. 13.7. Gal. 6.10.
7 the owners thereof.
v Lev. 19.13. Deut. 24.15.

6 In [f]all thy ways acknowledge hin
and he shall [g]direct thy paths.
7 ¶ Be [h]not wise in thine own eye
fear the LORD, and depart from ev
8 It shall be [3]health to thy navel, ar
[4]marrow to thy bones.
9 Honour [i]the LORD with thy sub
stance, and with the firstfruits of a
thine increase:
10 So [j]shall thy barns be filled wi
plenty, and thy presses shall burst o
with new wine.
11 ¶ My son, [k]despise not the cha
tening of the LORD; neither be wea
of his correction:
12 For whom the LORD loveth h
correcteth; [l]even as a father the sc
in whom he delighteth.
13 ¶ Happy *is* the man *that* finde
wisdom, and [5]the man *that* getteth u
derstanding.
14 For [m]the merchandise of it *is* be
ter than the merchandise of silver, ar
the gain thereof than fine gold.
15 She *is* more precious than rubie
and all [n]the things thou canst desi
are not to be compared unto her.
16 Length [o]of days *is* in her rig
hand; *and* in her left hand riches a
honour.
17 Her [p]ways *are* ways of pleasar
ness, and all her paths *are* peace.
18 She *is* [q]a tree of life to them th
lay hold upon her: and happy *is eve*
one that retaineth her.
19 The [r]LORD by wisdom ha
founded the earth; by understandi
hath he [6]established the heavens.
20 By his knowledge the depths a
broken up, and [s]the clouds drop dov
the dew.
21 ¶ My son, let not them depart fro
thine eyes: keep sound wisdom a
discretion:
22 So shall they be life unto thy sou
and grace to thy neck.
23 Then shalt thou walk in thy w
safely, and thy foot shall not stumb
24 When [t]thou liest down, thou sha
not be afraid: yea, thou shalt lie dow
and thy sleep shall be sweet.
25 Be not afraid of sudden fe
neither of the desolation of the wic
ed, when it cometh.
26 For the LORD shall be thy con
dence, and shall keep thy foot fro
being taken.
27 ¶ Withhold [u]not good from [7]the
to whom it is due, when it is in t
power of thine hand to do *it*.
28 Say [v]not unto thy neighbour, G
and come again, and to morrow I w
give; when thou hast it by thee.

9 [8]Devise not evil against thy neigh-
›ur, seeing he dwelleth securely by
ee.
0 ¶ Strive [w]not with a man without
use, if he have done thee no harm.
1 ¶ Envy thou not [9]the oppressor,
ıd choose none of his ways.
2 For the froward *is* abomination
the LORD: but his secret *is* with the
ghteous.
3 ¶ The [x]curse of the LORD *is* in the
ouse of the wicked: but [y]he blesseth
e habitation of the just.
4 Surely [z]he scorneth the scorners:
ıt he giveth grace unto the lowly.
5 The [a]wise shall inherit glory: but
ame [10]shall be the promotion of
ols.

CHAPTER 4

HEAR, [a]ye children, the instruction of a father, and attend to
ow understanding.
For I give you good doctrine, for-
ke ye not my law.
For I was my father's son, [b]tender
ıd only *beloved* in the sight of my
other.
He [c]taught me also, and said unto
e, Let thine heart retain my words:
ep my commandments, and live.
Get wisdom, get understanding:
rget *it* not; neither decline from the
ords of my mouth.
Forsake her not, and she shall pre-
rve thee: [d]love her, and she shall
ep thee.
Wisdom [e]*is* the principal thing;
erefore get wisdom: and with all thy
tting get understanding.
Exalt [f]her, and she shall promote
ee: she shall bring thee to honour,
hen thou dost embrace her.
She shall give to thine head an orn-
nent of grace: [1]a crown of glory shall
e deliver to thee.
0 Hear, O my son, and receive my
yings; and the years of thy life shall
many.
1 I have taught thee in the way of
isdom; I have led thee in right paths.
2 When thou goest, [g]thy steps shall
ot be straitened; [h]and when thou
nnest, thou shalt not stumble.
3 Take fast hold of instruction; let
er not go: keep her; for she *is* thy
fe.
4 ¶ Enter not into the path of the
icked, and go not in the way of evil
en.
5 Avoid it, pass not by it, turn from
, and pass away.
6 For they sleep not, except they
ave done mischief; and their sleep is
taken away, unless they cause *some* to
fall.
17 For they eat the bread of wickedness, and drink the wine of violence.
18 But [i]the path of the just [j]*is* as the
shining light, that shineth more and
more unto the perfect day.
19 The [k]way of the wicked *is* as darkness: they know not at what they
stumble.
20 ¶ My son, attend to my words;
incline thine ear unto my sayings.
21 Let them not depart from thine
eyes; keep them in the midst of thine
heart.
22 For they *are* life unto those that
find them, and [2]health to all their
flesh.
23 ¶ Keep thy heart [3]with all diligence; for out of it *are* the issues of
life.
24 Put away from thee [4]a froward
mouth, and perverse lips put far from
thee.
25 Let thine eyes look right on, and
let thine eyelids look straight before
thee.
26 Ponder the path of thy feet, and
[5]let all thy ways be established.
27 Turn not to the right hand nor
to the left: [l]remove thy foot from
evil.

CHAPTER 5

MY son, attend unto my wisdom,
and bow thine ear to my understanding:
2 That thou mayest regard discretion, and *that* thy lips may [a]keep
knowledge.
3 ¶ For the lips of a strange woman
drop *as* an honeycomb, and her
[1]mouth *is* smoother than oil:
4 But her end is [b]bitter as wormwood, sharp [c]as a twoedged sword.
5 Her feet go down [d]to death; her
steps take hold on hell.
6 Lest thou shouldest ponder the
path of life, her ways are moveable,
that thou canst not know *them*.
7 Hear me now therefore, O ye children, and depart not from the words
of my mouth.
8 Remove thy way far from her, and
come not nigh the door of her house:
9 Lest thou give thine honour unto
others, and thy years unto the cruel:
10 Lest strangers be filled with [2]thy
wealth; and thy labours *be* in the
house of a stranger;
11 And thou mourn at the last, when
thy flesh and thy body are consumed,
12 And say, How have I hated in-

8 Or, Practise no evil.
w Rom. 12. 18.
9 a man of violence.
x Zech. 5.4. Mal. 2.2.
y Ps. 1.3.
z Ps. 138.6. Matt. 23.12. Jas. 4.6.
a Dan. 12.2.
10 exalteth the fools.

CHAP. 4

a Ps. 34.11. ch. 1.8.
b 2 Sam. 12. 24. 1 Chr. 29.1.
c 1 Chr. 28.9. Eph. 6.4.
d 2 Thes. 2. 10.
e Matt. 13. 44. Luke 10.42.
f 1 Sam. 2.30. Dan. 12.3.
1 Or, she shall compass thee with a crown of glory.
g Ps. 18.36.
h Ps. 91.11. ch. 3.23.
i ch. 4.19. Jer. 13.16. John 11.9, 10.
i Matt. 5.14. Phil. 2.15.
j 2 Sam.23.4.
k 1 Sam. 2.9. Job 5.14. Isa. 59.9,10. Jer. 13.16. John 12.35.
2 medicine.
3 above all keeping.
4 frowardness of mouth, and perverseness of lips.
5 Or, all thy ways shall be ordered aright.
l Isa. 1.16.

CHAP. 5

a Mal. 2.7.
1 palate.
b Eccl. 7.26.
c Heb. 4.12.
d Heb. 13.4.
2 thy strength.

struction, and my heart despised reproof;
13 And have not obeyed the voice of
my teachers, nor inclined mine ear to
them that instructed me!
14 I was almost in all evil in the midst
of the congregation and assembly.
15 ¶ Drink waters out of thine own
cistern, and running waters out of
thine own well.
16 Let thy fountains be dispersed
abroad, *and* rivers of waters in the
streets.
17 Let them be only thine own, and
not strangers' with thee.
18 Let thy fountain be blessed: and
rejoice [e]with the wife of thy youth.
19 *Let [f]her be as* the loving hind and
pleasant roe; let her breasts [3]satisfy
thee at all times; and [4]be thou ravished
always with her love.
20 And why wilt thou, my son, be
ravished with a strange woman, and
embrace the bosom of a stranger?
21 For [g]the ways of man *are* before
the eyes of the LORD, and he pondereth all his goings.
22 ¶ His [h]own iniquities shall take
the wicked himself, and he shall be
holden with the cords of his [5]sins.
23 He [i]shall die without instruction;
and in the greatness of his folly he
shall go astray.

CHAPTER 6

MY son, [a]if thou be surety for thy
friend, *if* thou [b]hast stricken thy
hand with a stranger,
2 Thou art snared with the words of
thy mouth, thou art taken with the
words of thy mouth.
3 Do this now, my son, and deliver
thyself, when thou art come into the
hand of thy friend; go, humble thy
self, [1]and make sure thy friend.
4 Give [c]not sleep to thine eyes, nor
slumber to thine eyelids.
5 Deliver thyself as a roe from the
hand *of the hunter*, and as a bird from
the hand of the fowler.
6 ¶ Go [d]to the ant, thou sluggard;
consider her ways, and be wise:
7 Which having no guide, overseer,
or ruler,
8 Provideth her meat in the summer,
and gathereth her food in the harvest.
9 How long wilt thou sleep, O
sluggard? when wilt thou arise out of
thy sleep?
10 *Yet* a little sleep, a little slumber, a little folding of the hands to
sleep:
11 So shall thy poverty come as one

e Eccl. 9. 9. Mal. 2.14.
f Song 2.9.
3 water thee.
4 err thou always in her love.
g 2 Chr. 16.9. Job 31.4. Jer. 16.17. Hosea 7.2. Heb. 4.13.
h Ps. 9.15.
5 sin.
i Job 4.21. ch. 10.21.

CHAP. 6

a Gen. 43.9. ch. 27.13. Heb. 7.22.
b Ezra 10.19.
1 Or, so shalt thou prevail with thy friend.
c Ruth 3.18.
d Job 12.7.
e Ps. 35.19. ch. 10.10.
f Ps. 36.4. Isa. 32.7. Micah 2.1. Matt. 26.4.
2 casteth forth.
g Jer. 19.11.
3 of his soul.
4 Haughty eyes.
h Ps. 5.6. ch. 12.22. Hosea 4.1, 2. John 8.44.
i ch. 1.11. Isa. 1.15.
j Gen. 6.5.
k Isa. 59.7. Rom. 3.15.
l Ps. 27.12.
m Eph. 6.1.
n Ps. 19.8.
5 Or, candle.
6 Or, of the strange tongue.
o 2 Sam. 11. 2-5. Matt. 5.28.
p ch. 29.3.
7 the woman of a man. or, a man's wife.
q Eze. 13.18.
r Ex. 22.1,4.
8 heart.

that travelleth, and thy want as a
armed man.
12 ¶ A naughty person, a wick
man, walketh with a froward mout
13 He [e]winketh with his eyes, h
speaketh with his feet, he teache
with his fingers;
14 Frowardness *is* in his heart, h
[f]deviseth mischief continually; h
[2]soweth discord.
15 Therefore shall his calamity con
suddenly; suddenly shall he be [g]bro
en without remedy.
16 ¶ These six *things* doth the LOR
hate: yea, seven *are* an abominatic
[3]unto him:
17 [4]A proud look, [h]a lying tongu
and hands [i]that shed innocent bloo
18 An [j]heart that deviseth wick
imaginations, [k]feet that be swift
running to mischief,
19 A [l]false witness *that* speaketh lie
and he that soweth discord amor
brethren.
20 ¶ My [m]son, keep thy father's con
mandment, and forsake not the la
of thy mother:
21 Bind them continually upc
thine heart, *and* tie them about th
neck.
22 When thou goest, it shall lea
thee; when thou sleepest, it shall kee
thee; and *when* thou awakest, it sha
talk with thee.
23 For [n]the commandment *is*
[5]lamp; and the law *is* light; and r
proofs of instruction *are* the way o
life:
24 To keep thee from the evil wo
man, from the flattery [6]of the tongu
of a strange woman.
25 Lust [o]not after her beauty in thir
heart; neither let her take thee wit
her eyelids.
26 For [p]by means of a whorish wo
man *a man is brought* to a piece o
bread: and [7]the adulteress will hur
[q]for the precious life.
27 Can a man take fire in his bosom
and his clothes not be burned?
28 Can one go upon hot coals, an
his feet not be burned?
29 So he that goeth in to his neigh
bour's wife; whosoever toucheth h
shall not be innocent.
30 *Men* do not despise a thief, if h
steal to satisfy his soul when he
hungry;
31 But *if* he be found, [r]he shall re
store sevenfold; he shall give all th
substance of his house.
32 *But* whoso committeth adulter
with a woman lacketh [8]understand

g: he *that* doeth it destroyeth [s]his
vn soul.
3 A wound and dishonour shall he
t; and his reproach shall not be
iped away.
4 For jealousy *is* the rage of a man:
erefore he will not spare in the day
f vengeance.
5 [9]He will not regard any ransom;
either will he rest content, though
ou givest many gifts.

CHAPTER 7

MY son, keep my words, and lay
up my commandments with
ee.
2 Keep [a]my commandments, and
ve; and [b]my law as the apple of thine
ve.
3 Bind [c]them upon thy fingers, write
em upon the table of thine heart.
4 Say unto wisdom, Thou *art* my
ster; and call understanding *thy*
inswoman:
5 That they may keep thee from the
range woman, from the stranger
hich flattereth with her words.
6 ¶ For at the window of my house
looked through my casement,
7 And beheld among the simple
nes, I discerned among [1]the youths,
young man [d]void of understanding,
8 Passing through the street near her
orner; and he went the way to her
ouse,
9 In the [e]twilight, [2]in the evening,
n the black and dark night:
10 And, behold, there met him a wo-
nan *with* the [f]attire of an harlot, and
ubtil of heart.
11 (She *is* loud and stubborn; her
feet abide not in her house:
12 Now *is she* without, now in the
treets, and lieth in wait at every
orner.)
13 So she caught him, and kissed
im, *and* [3]with an impudent face said
nto him,
14 [4]*I have* peace offerings with me;
his day have I payed my vows.
15 Therefore came I forth to meet
hee, diligently to seek thy face, and
have found thee.
16 I have decked my bed with cover-
ngs of tapestry, with carved *works*,
vith [h]fine linen of Egypt.
17 I have perfumed my bed with
nyrrh, aloes, and cinnamon.
18 Come, let us take our fill of love
ntil the morning: let us solace our-
elves with loves.
19 For the goodman *is* not at home,
e is gone a long journey:
20 He hath taken a bag of money
[5]with him, *and* will come home at [6]the
day appointed.
21 With her much fair speech she
caused him to yield, with the flattering of her lips she forced him.
22 He goeth after her [7]straightway,
as an ox goeth to the slaughter, or as
a fool to the correction of the stocks;
23 Till a dart strike through his liver;
as a bird hasteth to the snare, and
knoweth not that it *is* for his life.
24 ¶ Hearken unto me now therefore, O ye children, and attend to the
words of my mouth.
25 Let not thine heart decline to her
ways, go not astray in her paths.
26 For she hath cast down many
wounded: yea, [i]many strong *men*
have been slain by her.
27 Her house *is* the way to [j]hell, going down to the chambers of death.

CHAPTER 8

DOTH not [a]wisdom cry? and understanding put forth her voice?
2 She standeth in the top of high
places, by the way in the places of the
paths.
3 She crieth at the gates, at the entry
of the city, at the coming in at the
doors.
4 Unto you, O men, I call; and my
voice *is* to the sons of man.
5 O ye simple, understand wisdom:
and, ye fools, be ye of an understanding heart.
6 Hear; for I will speak of [b]excellent
things; and the opening of my lips
shall be right things.
7 For my mouth shall [c]speak truth;
and wickedness *is* [1]an abomination
to my lips.
8 All the words of my mouth *are* in
righteousness; *there is* nothing [2]fro-
ward or perverse in them.
9 They *are* all plain to him that understandeth, and right to them that
find knowledge.
10 Receive my instruction, and not
silver; and knowledge rather than
choice gold.
11 For [d]wisdom *is* better than rubies;
and all the things that may be desired
are not to be compared to it.
12 I wisdom dwell with [3]prudence,
and find out knowledge of witty inventions.
13 The [e]fear of the LORD *is* to hate
evil: pride, [f]and arrogancy, and the
evil way, and the [g]froward mouth, do
I hate.
14 Counsel *is* mine, and sound wis-

s Job 31.12. Heb. 13.4.
9 He will not accept the face of any ransom.

CHAP. 7

a Lev. 18.5. ch. 4.4. Isa. 55.3.
b Deut. 32. 10.
c Deut. 6.8. ch. 3.3. Isa. 30.8. Jer. 17.1. 2 Cor. 3.3.
1 the sons.
d ch. 6.32.
e Job 24.15.
2 in the evening of the day.
f 1 Tim. 2.9.
g 1 Tim. 5.13. Titus 2.5.
3 she strengthened her face, and said.
4 Peace offerings are upon me.
h Isa. 19.9.
5 in his hand.
6 Or, the new moon.
7 suddenly.
i Neh. 13.26.
j ch. 2.18. 1 Cor. 6.9, 10. Heb. 13.4. Rev. 22.15.

CHAP. 8

a ch. 9.3. 1 Cor. 1.24.
b Ps. 49.3. ch. 2.6,7. Col. 1.26.
c John 8.14. Rom. 15.8.
1 the abomination of my lips.
2 wreathed.
d Job 28.15. Ps. 19.10.
3 Or, subtilty.
e ch. 16.6.
f Zech. 8.17. 1 Pet. 5.5.
g ch. 4.24.

dom: I *am* understanding; [h]I have
strength.
15 By [i]me kings reign, and princes
decree justice.
16 By me princes rule, and nobles,
even all the judges of the earth.
17 I [j]love them that love me; and
[k]those that seek me early shall find me.
18 Riches [l]and honour *are* with me;
yea, durable riches and righteousness.
19 My [m]fruit *is* better than gold, yea,
than fine gold; and my revenue than
choice silver.
20 I [4]lead in the way of righteousness, in the midst of the paths of judgment:
21 That I may cause those that love
me to inherit substance; and I will fill
their treasures.
22 The [n]LORD possessed me in the
beginning of his way, before his
works of old.
23 I [o]was set up from everlasting,
from the beginning, or ever the earth
was.
24 When *there were* no depths, I was
brought forth; when *there were* no
fountains abounding with water.
25 Before the [p]mountains were
settled, before the hills was I brought
forth:
26 While as yet he had not made the
earth, nor the [5]fields, nor [6]the highest
part of the dust of the world.
27 When he prepared the heavens, I
was there: when he set [7]a compass upon the face of the depth:
28 When he established the clouds
above: when he strengthened the
fountains of the deep:
29 When [q]he gave to the sea his decree, that the waters should not pass
his commandment: when [r]he appointed the foundations of the earth:
30 Then [s]I was by him, *as* one
brought up *with him:* [t]and I was daily
his delight, rejoicing always before
him;
31 Rejoicing [u]in the habitable part
of his earth; and [v]my delights *were*
with the sons of men.
32 Now therefore hearken unto me,
O ye children: for [w]blessed *are they*
that keep my ways.
33 Hear instruction, and be wise,
and refuse it not.
34 Blessed *is* the man that heareth
me, watching daily at my gates, waiting at the posts of my doors.
35 For [x]whoso findeth me findeth
life, and shall [8]obtain favour of the
LORD.

h Eccl. 7.19.
i Dan. 2.21. Matt. 28.18. Rom. 13.1.
j 1 Sam. 2.30.
k Jas. 1.5.
l Matt. 6.33.
m Job 28.15. ch. 3.14.
4 Or, walk.
n ch. 3.19. John 1.1.
o Gen. 1.26. Ps. 2.6. Micah 5.2. John 17.24.
p Job 15.7.
5 Or, open places.
6 Or, the chief part.
7 Or, a circle.
q Job 38.10.
r Job 38.4.
s John 1.1, 2, 18.
t Matt. 3.17. Col. 1.13.
u Isa. 4.2.
v Ps. 16.3.
w Luke 11.28.
x John 3.16, 36. Phil. 3.8, 9.
8 bring forth.
y Heb. 2.3.

CHAP. 9

a Matt. 16. 18. Eph. 2.20. 1 Tim. 3.15. Heb. 3.3-6.
1 her killing.
b Matt. 22.3, 4, 9. Luke 14.17, 21-23. Rom. 10.15.
c ch. 6.32. Matt. 11.25.
d Song 5.1. Isa. 55.1. Matt. 26.26-28.
e Matt. 7.6.
f Ps. 141.5.
g Matt. 13.12.
h Job 28.28.
i ch. 10.27.
j Job 35.6, 7.
k ch. 20.17.
2 of secrecies.

CHAP. 10

a Ps. 49.6. Luke 12.19.

36 But he that sinneth against m
[y]wrongeth his own soul: all they th
hate me love death.

CHAPTER 9

WISDOM hath [a]builded h
house, she hath hewn out h
seven pillars:
2 She hath killed [1]her beasts; sh
hath mingled her wine; she hath als
furnished her table.
3 She hath [b]sent forth her maidens
she crieth upon the highest places o
the city,
4 Whoso [c]*is* simple, let him turn i
hither: *as for* him that wanteth unde
standing, she saith to him,
5 Come, [d]eat of my bread, and drin
of the wine *which* I have mingled.
6 Forsake the foolish, and live; an
go in the way of understanding.
7 He that reproveth a scorner ge
teth to himself shame: and he that re
buketh a wicked *man getteth* himse
a blot.
8 Reprove [e]not a scorner, lest he hat
thee: [f]rebuke a wise man, and he wi
love thee.
9 Give *instruction* to a wise *man*
and he will be yet wiser: teach a jus
man, [g]and he will increase in learn
ing.
10 The [h]fear of the LORD *is* the be
ginning of wisdom: and the know
edge of the holy *is* understanding.
11 For [i]by me thy days shall be mul
tiplied, and the years of thy life sha
be increased.
12 If [j]thou be wise, thou shalt b
wise for thyself: but *if* thou scornest
thou alone shalt bear *it*.
13 ¶ A foolish woman *is* clamorous
she is simple, and knoweth nothing.
14 For she sitteth at the door of he
house, on a seat in the high places o
the city,
15 To call passengers who go righ
on their ways:
16 Whoso *is* simple, let him turn in
hither: and *as for* him that wanteth
understanding, she saith to him,
17 Stolen [k]waters are sweet, and
bread [2]*eaten* in secret is pleasant.
18 But he knoweth not that the dead
are there; *and that* her guests *are* in
the depths of hell.

CHAPTER 10

THE proverbs of Solomon. A wise
son maketh a glad father: but a
foolish son *is* the heaviness of his
mother.
2 Treasures [a]of wickedness profit

othing: [b]but righteousness deliver-
th from death.
3 The [c]LORD will not suffer the soul
f the righteous to famish: but he
asteth away [1]the substance of the
icked.
4 He becometh poor that dealeth
ith a slack hand: but [d]the hand of
he diligent maketh rich.
5 He that gathereth in summer *is* a
ise son: *but* he that sleepeth in harv-
st *is* a son that causeth shame.
6 Blessings *are* upon the head of the
ust: but [e]violence covereth the mouth
f the wicked.
7 The [f]memory of the just *is* blessed:
ut the name of the wicked shall rot.
8 The wise in heart will receive com-
nandments: but [2]a prating fool [3]shall
all.
9 He [g]that walketh uprightly walketh
urely: but he that perverteth his ways
hall be known.
10 He that winketh with the eye
auseth sorrow: but a prating fool
shall fall.
11 The [h]mouth of a righteous *man is*
well of life: but [i]violence covereth
he mouth of the wicked.
12 Hatred stirreth up strifes: but love
overeth all sins.
13 In the [k]lips of him that hath un-
erstanding wisdom is found: but a
od *is* for the back of him that is void
f [5]understanding.
14 Wise *men* lay up knowledge: but
he mouth of the foolish *is* near de-
truction.
15 The [l]rich man's wealth *is* his
trong city: the destruction of the
oor *is* their poverty.
16 The labour of the righteous *tend-
th* to life: the fruit of the wicked to
in.
17 He *is in* the way of life that keepeth
nstruction: but he that refuseth re-
roof [6]erreth.
18 He that hideth hatred *with* lying
ips, and he that uttereth a slander, *is*
fool.
19 In the [m]multitude of words there
vanteth not sin: but [n]he that refrain-
th his lips *is* wise.
20 The tongue of the just *is as* choice
ilver: the heart of the wicked *is* little
vorth.
21 The lips of the righteous feed
nany: but fools die for want [7]of wis-
lom.
22 The [o]blessing of the LORD, it mak-
th rich, and he addeth no sorrow
vith it.
23 *It is* as sport to a fool to do mis-

b Dan.4.27.
c Ps. 10.14.
1 Or, the wicked for their wickedness.
d ch. 13.4.
e Esther 7.8.
f Ps. 9.5,6. Eccl. 8.10.
2 a fool of lips.
3 Or, shall be beaten.
g Ps. 23.4. Isa. 33.15, 16.
4 Or, shall be beaten.
h Ps. 37.30.
i Ps. 107.42.
j 1 Cor. 13.4.
k Luke 4.22.
5 heart.
l Job 31.24. ch. 18.11. Luke 12.19. 1 Tim. 6.17.
6 Or, causeth to err.
m Eccl. 5.3.
n Ps. 39.1. ch. 17.27, 28. Jas. 1.19.
7 of heart.
o Gen. 12.2. Deut. 8.17, 18. 1 Sam. 2.7,8. 1 Tim. 4.8.
p Job 15.21.
q Matt. 5.6.
r Ps. 15.5. Matt. 7.24. 1 Tim. 6.19.
8 addeth.
s Eccl. 7.17.
t Ps. 16.9. Rom. 5.2.
u Job 8.13.
v Zech. 10.12. Phil. 4.13. Isa. 40.31.
w Ps. 1.6.
9 frowardnesses.

CHAP. 11

1 Balances of deceit.
2 a perfect stone.
a Dan. 4.30.
b Eze. 7.19. Zeph. 1.18.
c Gen. 7.1.
3 rectify.
d 1 Tim. 4.8.
e Eccl. 10.8.
f Job 8.13.
g Esther 8.15.

chief: but a man of understanding
hath wisdom.
24 The [p]fear of the wicked, it shall
come upon him: but the [q]desire of the
righteous shall be granted.
25 As the whirlwind passeth, so *is*
the wicked no *more:* but [r]the righteous *is* an everlasting foundation.
26 As vinegar to the teeth, and as
smoke to the eyes, so *is* the sluggard
to them that send him.
27 The fear of the LORD [8]prolongeth
days: but [s]the years of the wicked
shall be shortened.
28 The [t]hope of the righteous *shall
be* gladness: but the [u]expectation of
the wicked shall perish.
29 The way of the LORD [v]*is* strength
to the upright: [w]but destruction *shall
be* to the workers of iniquity.
30 The righteous shall never be removed: but the wicked shall not inhabit the earth.
31 The mouth of the just bringeth
forth wisdom: but the froward tongue
shall be cut out.
32 The lips of the righteous know
what is acceptable: but the mouth of
the wicked *speaketh* [9]frowardness.

CHAPTER 11

1 A FALSE balance *is* abomination
to the LORD: but [2]a just weight *is*
his delight.
2 *When* [a]pride cometh, then cometh
shame: but with the lowly *is* wisdom.
3 The integrity of the upright shall
guide them: but the perverseness of
transgressors shall destroy them.
4 Riches [b]profit not in the day of
wrath: but [c]righteousness delivereth
from death.
5 The righteousness of the perfect
shall [3]direct his way: but the wicked
shall fall by his own wickedness.
6 The [d]righteousness of the upright
shall deliver them: [e]but transgressors
shall be taken in *their own* naughtiness.
7 When a wicked man dieth, *his* expectation shall perish: and the hope
of unjust *men* perisheth.
8 The righteous is delivered out of
trouble, and the wicked cometh in his
stead.
9 An [f]hypocrite with *his* mouth destroyeth his neighbour: but through
knowledge shall the just be delivered.
10 When [g]it goeth well with the
righteous, the city rejoiceth: and when
the wicked perish, *there is* shouting.
11 By the blessing of the upright the

city is exalted: but it is overthrown by the mouth of the wicked.

12 He that is [4]void of wisdom despiseth his neighbour: but a man of understanding holdeth his peace.

13 [5]A talebearer revealeth secrets: but he that is of a faithful spirit concealeth the matter.

14 Where [h]no counsel *is*, the people fall: but in the multitude of counsellers *there is* safety.

15 He that is surety for a stranger [6]shall smart *for it:* and he that hateth [7]suretiship is sure.

16 A gracious woman retaineth honour: and strong *men* retain riches.

17 The [i]merciful man doeth good to his own soul: but *he that is* cruel troubleth his own flesh.

18 The wicked worketh a deceitful work: but [j]to him that soweth righteousness *shall be* a sure reward.

19 As righteousness *tendeth* to life: so he that pursueth evil *pursueth it* to his own death.

20 They that are of a froward heart *are* abomination to the LORD: but *such as are* upright in *their* way *are* his delight.

21 *Though* hand *join* in hand, the wicked shall not be unpunished: but the seed of the righteous shall be delivered.

22 *As* a jewel of gold in a swine's snout, *so is* a fair woman which [8]is without discretion.

23 The desire of the righteous *is* only good: *but* the expectation of the wicked *is* [k]wrath.

24 There is that scattereth, and yet increaseth; and *there is* that withholdeth more than is meet, but *it tendeth* to poverty.

25 [9]The liberal soul shall be made fat: and [l]he that watereth shall be watered also himself.

26 He [m]that withholdeth corn, the people shall curse him: [n]but blessing *shall be* upon the head of him that selleth *it*.

27 He that diligently seeketh good procureth favour: [o]but he that seeketh mischief, it shall come unto him.

28 He [p]that trusteth in his riches shall fall: but [q]the righteous shall flourish as a branch.

29 He that troubleth his own house [r]shall inherit the wind: and the fool *shall be* servant to the wise of heart.

30 The fruit of the righteous *is* a tree of life; and he that [10]winneth souls *is* wise.

31 Behold, [s]the righteous shall be recompensed in the earth: much mor the wicked and the sinner.

4 destitute of heart.
5 He that walketh, being a talebearer.
h 1 Ki. 12.1.
6 shall be sore broken.
7 those that strike hands.
i Matt. 25.31.
j Hos. 10.12. Gal. 6.8,9.
8 departeth from.
k Rom. 2.8.
9 The soul of blessing.
l Matt. 5.7.
m Amos 8.5.
n Job 29.13.
o Esther 7.10.
p Mark 10. 24. Luke 12.21. 1 Tim. 6.17.
q Jer. 17.8.
r Eccl. 5.16.
10 taketh.
s Jer. 25.29. 1 Pet. 4.17.

CHAP. 12

a ch. 31.23. 1 Cor. 11.7.
b ch. 14.30.
c Matt. 7.24.
d 1 Sam. 13. 13. ch. 1.25,26. ch. 3.35. Mal. 2.8,9. Matt. 27.4, 5.
1 perverse of heart.
e Deut. 25.4.
2 Or, bowels.
f Gen. 3.19. ch. 28.19. Eph. 4.28. 1 Thes. 4.11.
3 Or, the fortress.
g Ps. 1.3. Luke 8.15.
4 The snare of the wicked is in the transgression of lips.
h 2 Pet. 2.9.
i Isa. 3.10.
j Luke 18.11.
5 in that day.
k Zech. 1.5,6.

CHAPTER 12

WHOSO loveth instruction lov eth knowledge: but he that hat eth reproof *is* brutish.

2 A good *man* obtaineth favour o the LORD: but a man of wicked de vices will he condemn.

3 A man shall not be established by wickedness: but the root of the right eous shall not be moved.

4 A [a]virtuous woman *is* a crown t her husband: but she that maketh ashamed *is* as [b]rottenness in hi bones.

5 The thoughts of the righteous *are* right: *but* the counsels of the wicke *are* deceit.

6 The words of the wicked *are* to li in wait for blood: but the mouth o the upright shall deliver them.

7 The [c]wicked are overthrown, an *are* not: but the house of the right eous shall stand.

8 A man shall be commended ac cording to his wisdom: [d]but he tha is [1]of a perverse heart shall be de spised.

9 *He that is* despised, and hath a ser vant, *is* better than he that honour eth himself, and lacketh bread.

10 A [e]righteous *man* regardeth th life of his beast: but the [2]tender mer cies of the wicked *are* cruel.

11 He [f]that tilleth his land shall b satisfied with bread: but he that fol loweth vain *persons is* void of under standing.

12 The wicked desireth [3]the net o evil *men:* but [g]the root of the right eous yieldeth *fruit*.

13 [4]The wicked is snared by the trans gression of *his* lips: [h]but the just shal come out of trouble.

14 A man shall be satisfied with goo by the fruit of *his* mouth: and [i]th recompence of a man's hands shall b rendered unto him.

15 The [j]way of a fool *is* right in hi own eyes: but he that hearkeneth un to counsel *is* wise.

16 A fool's wrath is [5]presently known: but a prudent *man* covereth shame.

17 *He that* speaketh truth sheweth forth righteousness: but a fals witness deceit.

18 There is that speaketh like th piercings of a sword: but the tongu of the wise *is* health.

19 The [k]lip of truth shall be estab

shed for ever: but a lying tongue *is*
ut for a moment.
0 Deceit *is* in the heart of them that
nagine evil: but to the counsellers of
eace *is* joy.
1 There [l]shall no evil happen to the
st: but the wicked shall be filled
ith mischief.
2 Lying [m]lips *are* abomination to
e LORD: but they that deal truly *are*
is delight.
3 A prudent man concealeth knowl-
dge: but the heart of fools proclaim-
h foolishness.
4 The [n]hand of the diligent shall
ear rule: but the [6]slothful shall be
nder tribute.
5 Heaviness in the heart of man
aketh it stoop: but [o]a good word
aketh it glad.
6 The righteous *is* more [7]excellent
an his neighbour: but the way of
e wicked seduceth them.
7 The slothful *man* roasteth not
at which he took in hunting: but
e substance of a diligent man *is*
recious.
8 In the way of [p]righteousness *is*
fe; and *in* the pathway *thereof there*
no death.

CHAPTER 13

A WISE son *heareth* his father's
instruction: [a]but a scorner hear-
h not rebuke.
2 A man shall eat good by the fruit
f *his* mouth: but the soul of the
ansgressors *shall eat* violence.
3 He [b]that keepeth his mouth keep-
th his life: *but* he that openeth wide
is lips shall have destruction.
4 The soul of the sluggard desireth,
nd *hath* nothing: but the soul of the
iligent shall be made fat.
5 A righteous *man* hateth [c]lying: but
wicked *man* is loathsome, and com-
th to shame.
6 Righteousness [d]keepeth *him that is*
pright in the way: but wickedness
verthroweth [1]the sinner.
7 There is that maketh himself rich,
et *hath* nothing: *there is* that maketh
imself poor, yet *hath* great riches.
8 The ransom of a man's life *are* his
iches: but the poor heareth not re-
uke.
9 The light of the righteous rejoic-
th: but the [2]lamp of the wicked shall
e put out.
10 Only by pride cometh contention:
ut with the well advised *is* wis-
om.
11 Wealth [e]*gotten* by vanity shall be
diminished: but he that gathereth [3]by
labour shall increase.
12 Hope deferred maketh the heart
sick: but *when* the desire cometh, *it is*
a tree of life.
13 Whoso [f]despiseth the word shall
be destroyed: but he that feareth the
commandment [4]shall be rewarded.
14 The [g]law of the wise *is* a fountain
of life, to depart from [h]the snares of
death.
15 Good understanding giveth favour: but the way of transgressors *is*
hard.
16 Every [i]prudent *man* dealeth with
knowledge: but a fool [5]layeth open
his folly.
17 A wicked messenger falleth into
mischief: but [6]a faithful ambassador
is health.
18 Poverty and shame *shall be to* him
that refuseth instruction: but he that
[j]regardeth reproof shall be honoured.
19 The desire accomplished is sweet
to the soul: but *it is* abomination to
fools to depart from evil.
20 He that walketh with wise *men*
shall be wise: but a companion of
fools [7]shall be destroyed.
21 Evil [k]pursueth sinners: but to the
righteous good shall be repayed.
22 A good *man* leaveth an inheritance to his children's children: and
[l]the wealth of the sinner *is* laid up for
the just.
23 Much [m]food *is in* the tillage of the
poor: but there is *that is* destroyed for
want of judgment.
24 He [n]that spareth his rod hateth
his son: but he that loveth him chasteneth him betimes.
25 The righteous eateth to the satisfying of his soul: but the belly of the
wicked shall want.

CHAPTER 14

EVERY [a]wise woman buildeth her
house: but the foolish plucketh it
down with her hands.
2 He that walketh in his uprightness
feareth the LORD: [b]but *he that is* perverse in his ways despiseth him.
3 In the mouth of the foolish *is* a rod
of pride: [c]but the lips of the wise shall
preserve them.
4 Where no oxen *are*, the crib *is*
clean: but much increase *is* by the
strength of the ox.
5 A [d]faithful witness will not lie: but
a false witness will utter lies.
6 A scorner seeketh wisdom, and
findeth it not: but [e]knowledge *is* easy
unto him that understandeth.

l Rom. 8.28. 2 Thes. 1.6. 2 Pet. 2.9.
m Rev. 22.15.
n 1 Ki. 11.28. ch. 10.4.
6 Or, deceitful.
o Isa. 50.4.
7 Or, abundant.
p Deut. 30. 15. Matt. 19.17. Rom. 5.21. 2 Cor. 4.17. Rev. 2.7.

CHAP. 13
a 1 Sam. 2.25. ch. 9.7,8.
b Ps. 39.1.
c Col. 3.9. Rom. 12.9.
d ch. 11.3.
1 sin.
2 Or, candle.
e ch. 20.21.
3 with the hand.
f 2 Chr. 36. 16.
4 Or, shall be in peace.
g ch. 16.22.
h 2 Sam. 22.6. Ps. 116.3. ch. 15.24.
i ch. 12.23.
5 spreadeth.
6 an ambassador of faithfulness.
j ch. 15.5.
7 shall be broken.
k Ps. 32.10.
l Eccl. 2.26.
m ch. 12.11.
n ch. 19.18. ch. 22.15.

CHAP. 14
a Ruth 4.11. ch. 24.3,4.
b Job 12.4.
c ch. 12.6.
d Ex. 20.16.
e ch. 17.24.

7 Go from the presence of a foolish man, when thou perceivest not *in him* the lips of knowledge.

8 The wisdom of the prudent *is* to understand his way: but the [f]folly of fools *is* deceit.

9 Fools [g]make a mock at sin: but among the righteous *there is* favour.

10 The heart knoweth [1]his own bitterness; and a stranger doth not intermeddle with his joy.

11 The [h]house of the wicked shall be overthrown: but the tabernacle of the upright shall flourish.

12 There [i]is a way which seemeth right unto a man, but [j]the end thereof *are* the ways of death.

13 Even in laughter the heart is sorrowful; and [k]the end of that mirth *is* heaviness.

14 The backslider in heart shall be [l]filled with his own ways: and a [m]good man *shall be satisfied* from himself.

15 The simple believeth every word: but the prudent *man* looketh well to his going.

16 A [n]wise *man* feareth, and departeth from evil: but the fool rageth, and is confident.

17 *He that is* soon angry dealeth foolishly: and a man of wicked devices is hated.

18 The simple inherit folly: but the prudent are crowned with knowledge.

19 The evil bow before the good; and the wicked at the gates of the righteous.

20 The [o]poor is hated even of his own neighbour: but [2]the rich *hath* many friends.

21 He that despiseth his neighbour sinneth: [p]but he that hath mercy on the poor, happy *is* he.

22 Do they not err that devise evil? but mercy and truth *shall be* to them that devise good.

23 In all labour there is profit: but the talk of the lips *tendeth* only to penury.

24 The crown of the wise *is* their riches: *but* the foolishness of fools *is* folly.

25 A true witness delivereth souls: but a deceitful *witness* speaketh lies.

26 In the fear of the LORD *is* strong confidence: and his children shall have a place of refuge.

27 The [q]fear of the LORD *is* a fountain of life, to depart from the snares of death.

28 In the multitude of people *is* the king's honour: but in the want of

f Luke 12.20. 1 Cor. 3.19.
g ch. 1.22.
1 the bitterness of his soul.
h Job 8.15. ch. 3.33.
i ch. 16.25.
j Rom. 6.21.
k Eccl. 2.2.
l ch. 12.14.
m 2 Cor. 1.12. Phil. 4.7.
n ch. 22.3.
o ch. 19.7.
2 many are the lovers of the rich.
p Ps. 41.1.
q ch. 13.14.
r ch. 15.18. Matt. 11.29. 1 Cor. 13.4-5. Jas. 1.19.
3 short of spirit.
s Job 5.2. Ps. 112.10. Acts 7.9. Rom. 1.29. Jas. 4.5.
t Job 31.15, 16. ch. 17.5. Eccl. 5.8. Matt. 25.40. 1 John 3.17.
u Job 31.15. ch. 22.2.
v Job 13.15. Ps. 23.4. 2 Cor. 1.9. 2 Tim. 4. 18.
4 to nations.
w Matt. 24. 45,47.

CHAP. 15
1 belcheth, or, bubbleth.
a 2 Chr. 16.9. Job 34.21. ch. 5.21. Jer. 16.17. Zech. 4.10. Heb. 4.13.
2 The healing of the tongue.
b Isa. 61.8. Jer. 6.20. Amos 5.22.
c Luke 18.11.
d ch. 21.21. Isa. 51.1.7. 1 Tim. 6.11.
3 Or, Instruction.
e John 2.24. Acts 1.24.

people *is* the destruction of the princ

29 *He* [r]*that is* slow to wrath *is* great understanding: but *he that* [3]hasty of spirit exalteth folly.

30 A sound heart *is* the life of th flesh: but [s]envy the rottenness of th bones.

31 He [t]that oppresseth the poor r proacheth [u]his Maker: but he tha honoureth him hath mercy on th poor.

32 The wicked is driven away in h wickedness: but the [v]righteous hat hope in his death.

33 Wisdom resteth in the heart o him that hath understanding: bu *that which is* in the midst of fools made known.

34 Righteousness exalteth a natior but sin *is* a reproach [4]to any people.

35 The king's favour *is* toward wise [w]servant: but his wrath is *agains* him that causeth shame.

CHAPTER 15

A SOFT answer turneth awa wrath: but grievous words stir u anger.

2 The tongue of the wise uset knowledge aright: but the mouth o fools [1]poureth out foolishness.

3 The [a]eyes of the LORD *are* in ever place, beholding the evil and th good.

4 [2]A wholesome tongue *is* a tree o life: but perverseness therein *is* breach in the spirit.

5 A fool despiseth his father's in struction: but he that regardeth re proof is prudent.

6 In the house of the righteous *i* much treasure: but in the revenues o the wicked is trouble.

7 The lips of the wise disperse knowl edge: but the heart of the foolish *doet* not so.

8 The [b]sacrifice of the wicked *is* a abomination to the LORD: [c]but th prayer of the upright *is* his delight.

9 The way of the wicked *is* an abom ination unto the LORD: but he loveth him that [d]followeth after righteous ness.

10 [3]Correction *is* grievous unto hin that forsaketh the way: *and* he tha hateth reproof shall die.

11 Hell and destruction *are* before the LORD: how much more then the [e]hearts of the children of men?

12 A scorner loveth not one that re proveth him: neither will he go unto the wise.

13 A merry heart maketh a cheerfu

ıntenance: but by sorrow of the
ırt the spirit is broken.
The heart of him that hath under-
nding seeketh knowledge: but the
ɔuth of fools feedeth on foolishness.
All the days of the afflicted *are*
l: but he that is of a merry heart
th a continual feast.
Better [f]*is* little with the fear of the
RD than great treasure and trouble
erewith.
Better *is* a dinner of herbs where
ve is, than a stalled ox and hatred
erewith.
3 A wrathful man stirreth up strife:
t *he that is* slow to anger appeaseth
ife.
The way of the slothful *man is* as
hedge of thorns: but the way of
e righteous [4]*is* made plain.
A wise son maketh a glad father:
ıt a foolish man despiseth his
other.
1 Folly *is* joy to *him that is* [5]desti-
te of wisdom: [g]but a man of under-
nding walketh uprightly.
2 Without counsel purposes are dis-
pointed: but in the multitude of
unsellers they are established.
3 A man hath joy by the answer of
s mouth: and a word *spoken* [6]in due
ason, how good *is it*!
4 The [h]way of life *is* above to the
se, that he may depart from hell
neath.
5 The LORD will destroy the house
the proud: but he will establish the
order of the widow.
6 The thoughts of the wicked *are*
ı abomination to the LORD: but
e *words* of the pure *are* [7]pleasant
ords.
7 He [i]that is greedy of gain troub-
th his own house; but he that hateth
fts shall live.
8 The heart of the righteous studi-
h [j]to answer: but the mouth of the
icked poureth out evil things.
9 The LORD *is* [k]far from the wicked:
ıt he [l]heareth the prayer of the
ghteous.
0 The light of the eyes rejoiceth the
eart: *and* a good report maketh the
ones fat.
31 The ear that heareth the reproof
f life abideth among the wise.
32 He that refuseth [8]instruction de-
piseth his own soul: but he that
neareth reproof [10]getteth understand-
ng.
33 The fear of the LORD *is* the in-
truction of wisdom; and before
onour *is* humility.

CHAPTER 16

THE [1]preparations of the heart in
man, and [a]the answer of the
tongue, *is* from the LORD.
2 All the ways of a man *are* clean in
his own eyes; but the [b]LORD weigheth
the spirits.
3 [2]Commit thy works unto the LORD,
and thy thoughts shall be established.
4 The [c]LORD hath made all *things* for
himself: [d]yea, even the wicked for the
day of evil.
5 Every one *that is* proud in heart *is*
an abomination to the LORD: *though*
hand *join* in hand, he shall not be [3]un-
punished.
6 By [e]mercy and truth iniquity is
purged: and by the fear of the LORD
men depart from evil.
7 When a man's ways [f]please the
LORD, he maketh even his enemies to
be at peace with him.
8 Better *is* a little with righteousness
than great revenues without right.
9 A man's heart deviseth his way:
but [g]the LORD directeth his steps.
10 [4]A divine sentence *is* in the lips of
the king: his mouth transgresseth not
in judgment.
11 A [h]just weight and balance *are*
the LORD's: [5]all the weights of the bag
are his work.
12 *It is* an abomination to kings to
commit wickedness: for the throne is
established by righteousness.
13 Righteous lips *are* the delight of
kings; and they love him that speaketh right.
14 The wrath of a king *is as* messengers of death: but a wise man will
pacify it.
15 In the light of the king's countenance *is* life; and his favour *is* as a cloud
of the latter rain.
16 How much better *is it* to get wisdom than gold! and to get understanding rather to be chosen than
silver!
17 The [i]highway of the upright *is* to
depart from evil: he that keepeth his
way preserveth his soul.
18 Pride *goeth* before destruction,
and an haughty spirit before a fall.
19 Better *it is to be* of an humble
spirit with the lowly, than to divide
the spoil with the proud.
20 [6]He that handleth a matter wisely
shall find good: and whoso trusteth
[j]in the LORD, happy *is* he.
21 The wise in heart shall be called
prudent: and the sweetness of the lips
increaseth learning.
22 Understanding *is* a wellspring of

f ch. 16.8. Eccl. 4.6. 1 Tim. 6.6.

4 is raised up as a causey. Isa. 35.8.

5 void of heart.
g Eph. 5.15.

6 in his season.
h Phil. 3.20.
7 words of pleasantness.
i Josh. 6.18. 1 Sam. 8.3. ch. 1.19. Isa. 5.8. Zech. 5.3.
j 1 Pet. 3.15.
k Eph. 2.12.
l Ps. 34.15,16. John 9.31. Rom. 8.26.
8 Or, correction.
9 Or, obeyeth.
10 possesseth an heart.

CHAP. 16

1 Or, disposings. Jer. 10.23.
a Matt. 10.19.
b 1 Sam. 16.7. Dan. 5.27.
2 Roll.
c Isa. 43.7. Rom. 11.36.
d Job 21.30. Rom. 9.22.
3 held innocent.
e Dan. 4.27. Luke 11.41.
f Col. 1.10.
g Jer. 10.23.
4 Divination.
h Lev. 19.36.
5 all the stones.
i ch. 4.24-27. Isa. 35.8. Acts 24.16.
6 Or, He that understandeth a matter.
j Isa. 30.18.

life unto him that hath it: but the instruction of fools *is* folly.
23 The [k]heart of the wise [7]teacheth
his mouth, and addeth learning to his
lips.
24 Pleasant words *are as* an honeycomb, sweet to the soul, and health
to the bones.
25 There is a way that seemeth right
unto a man, but the end thereof *are*
the ways of death.
26 [8]He that laboureth laboureth for
himself; for his mouth [9]craveth it of
him.
27 [10]An ungodly man diggeth up
evil: and in his lips *there is* as a burning fire.
28 A froward man [11]soweth strife:
and a whisperer separateth chief
friends.
29 A violent man enticeth his neighbour, and leadeth him into the way
that is not good.
30 He shutteth his eyes to devise froward things: moving his lips he bringeth evil to pass.
31 The hoary head *is* a crown of
glory, *if* it be found in the way of
righteousness.
32 *He that is* slow to anger *is* better
than the mighty; and he that ruleth
his spirit than he that taketh a city.
33 The lot is cast into the lap; but
the whole disposing thereof *is* of the
LORD.

CHAPTER 17

BETTER *is* a dry morsel, and
quietness therewith, than an house
full of [1]sacrifices *with* strife.
2 A wise servant shall have rule over
a son that causeth shame, and shall
have part of the inheritance among
the brethren.
3 The [a]fining pot *is* for silver, and
the furnace for gold: but the LORD
trieth the hearts.
4 A wicked doer giveth heed to false
lips; *and* a liar giveth ear to a naughty
tongue.
5 Whoso mocketh the poor reproacheth his Maker: *and* [b]he that is
glad at calamities shall not be [2]un-
punished.
6 Children's children *are* the crown
of old men; and the glory of children
are their fathers.
7 [3]Excellent speech becometh not
a fool: much less do [4]lying lips a
prince.
8 A gift *is as* [5]a precious stone in the
eyes of him that hath it: whithersoever it turneth, it [c]prospereth.
9 He that covereth a transgression

k Matt. 12. 34.
7 maketh wise.
8 The soul of him that laboureth.
9 boweth unto him.
10 A man of Belial.
11 sendeth forth.

CHAP. 17

1 Or, good cheer.
a Ps. 26.2. ch. 27.21. Jer. 17.10. Mal. 3.3.
b Job 31.29. ch. 24.17. Obad. 12.
2 held innocent.
3 A lip of excellency.
4 a lip of lying.
5 a stone of grace. ch. 18.16.
c Gen. 39.21. Dan. 6.3.
6 Or, procureth.
7 Or, A reproof aweth more a wise man than to strike a fool an hundred times.
d Jer. 18.20. Rom. 12.17. 1 Thes. 5.15.
e ch. 20.3. Acts 6.1. Rom. 12.18. 1 Thes. 4.11.
f Ex. 23.7. Isa. 5.23.
8 heart.
9 The froward of heart.
10 Or, to a medicine.
g Ex. 23.8.
h Eccl. 2.14.
i Jas. 1.19.
11 Or, a cool spirit.

CHAP. 18

1 Or, He that separateth himself seeketh according to his desire, and intermeddleth in every business. Jude 19.

[6]seeketh love; but he that repeateth
matter separateth *very* friends.
10 [7]A reproof entereth more into
wise man than an hundred stripes in
a fool.
11 An evil *man* seeketh only reb
lion: therefore a cruel messenger sh
be sent against him.
12 Let a bear robbed of her whel
meet a man, rather than a fool in h
folly.
13 Whoso [d]rewardeth evil for goo
evil shall not depart from his house
14 The beginning of strife *is as* wh
one letteth out water: therefore [e]lea
off contention, before it be meddl
with.
15 He that [f]justifieth the wicked, an
he that condemneth the just, even th
both *are* abomination to the LORD.
16 Wherefore *is there* a price in t
hand of a fool to get wisdom, seei
he hath no heart *to it?*
17 A friend loveth at all times, and
brother is born for adversity.
18 A man void of [8]understandi
striketh hands, *and* becometh sure
in the presence of his friend.
19 He loveth transgression that lo
eth strife: *and* he that exalteth his ga
seeketh destruction.
20 [9]He that hath a froward hea
findeth no good: and he that hath
perverse tongue falleth into mischie
21 He that begetteth a fool *doeth*
to his sorrow: and the father of a fo
hath no joy.
22 A merry heart doeth good [10]*like*
medicine: but a broken spirit driet
the bones.
23 A wicked *man* taketh a gift out o
the bosom [g]to pervert the ways o
judgment.
24 Wisdom [h]*is* before him that hat
understanding; but the eyes of a foo
are in the ends of the earth.
25 A foolish son *is* a grief to hi
father, and bitterness to her that bar
him.
26 Also to punish the just *is* not good
nor to strike princes for equity.
27 He [i]that hath knowledge sparet
his words: *and* a man of understand
ing is of [11]an excellent spirit.
28 Even a fool, when he holdeth hi
peace, is counted wise: *and* he tha
shutteth his lips *is esteemed* a man o
understanding.

CHAPTER 18

[1]THROUGH desire a man, havin
separated himself, seeketh *an*
intermeddleth with all wisdom.

2 A fool hath no delight in understanding, but that his heart may discover itself.

3 When the wicked cometh, *then* cometh also contempt, and with ignominy reproach.

4 The words of a man's mouth *are as* deep waters, [a]*and* the wellspring of wisdom *as* a flowing brook.

5 *It* [b]*is* not good to accept the person of the wicked, to overthrow the righteous in judgment.

6 A fool's lips enter into contention, and his mouth calleth for strokes.

7 A fool's mouth *is* his destruction, and his lips *are* the snare of his soul.

8 The words of a [2]talebearer *are* [3]as wounds, and they go down into the [4]innermost parts of the belly.

9 He also that is slothful in his work is brother to him that is a great waster.

10 The [c]name of the LORD *is* a strong tower: the righteous runneth into it, and [5]is safe.

11 The rich man's wealth *is* his strong city, and as an high wall in his own conceit.

12 Before destruction the heart of man is haughty, and before honour *is* humility.

13 He that [6]answereth a matter before he heareth *it*, it *is* folly and shame unto him.

14 The spirit of a man will sustain his infirmity; but a wounded spirit who can bear?

15 The [d]heart of the prudent getteth knowledge; and the ear of the wise seeketh knowledge.

16 A [e]man's gift maketh room for him, and bringeth him before great men.

17 *He that is* first in his own cause *seemeth* just; but his neighbour cometh and searcheth him.

18 The lot causeth contentions to cease, and parteth between the mighty.

19 A brother offended *is harder to be won* than a strong city: and *their* contentions *are* like the bars of a castle.

20 A man's belly shall be satisfied with the fruit of his mouth; *and* with the increase of his lips shall he be filled.

21 Death [f]and life *are* in the power of the tongue: and they that love it shall eat the fruit thereof.

22 *Whoso* findeth a wife findeth a good *thing*, and obtaineth favour of the LORD.

23 The poor useth intreaties; but the rich answereth [g]roughly.

24 A man [h]*that hath* friends must shew himself friendly: and there is a friend *that* sticketh closer than a brother.

CHAPTER 19

BETTER [a]*is* the poor that walketh in his integrity, than *he that is* perverse in his lips, and is a fool.

2 Also, *that* the [b]soul *be* without knowledge, *it is* not good; and he that hasteth with *his* feet sinneth.

3 The foolishness of man perverteth his way: [c]and his heart fretteth against the LORD.

4 Wealth maketh many friends; but the poor is separated from his neighbour.

5 A [d]false witness shall not be [1]unpunished, and *he that* speaketh lies shall not escape.

6 Many will intreat the favour of the prince: and every man *is* a friend to [2]him that giveth gifts.

7 All the brethren of the poor do hate him: how much more do his friends go far from him? he pursueth *them with* words, *yet* they *are* wanting *to him.*

8 He that getteth [3]wisdom loveth his own soul: he that keepeth understanding shall find good.

9 A [e]false witness shall not be unpunished, and *he that* speaketh lies shall perish.

10 Delight is not seemly for a fool; much less [f]for a servant to have rule over princes.

11 The [4]discretion of a man deferreth his anger; [g]and *it is* his glory to pass over a transgression.

12 The king's wrath *is* as the roaring of a lion; but his favour *is* as dew upon the grass.

13 A foolish son *is* the calamity of his father: and the contentions of a wife *are* a continual dropping.

14 House [h]and riches *are* the inheritance of fathers: and a [i]prudent wife *is* from the LORD.

15 Slothfulness casteth into a deep sleep; and an idle soul shall suffer hunger.

16 He [j]that keepeth the commandment keepeth his own soul; *but* he that despiseth his ways shall die.

17 He [k]that hath pity upon the poor lendeth unto the LORD; and [5]that which he hath given will he pay him again.

18 Chasten thy son while there is hope, and let not thy soul spare [6]for his crying.

19 A man of great wrath shall suffer

a Ps. 78.2.
b Lev. 19.15. Deut. 1.17. Job 13.7,8. ch. 24.23.
2 Or, whisperer.
3 Or, like as when men are wounded.
4 chambers.
c 2 Sam. 22.3, 51. Ps. 18.2.
5 is set aloft.
6 returneth a word.
d Eph. 1.17.
e Gen. 39.2-6. Gen. 41.14, 38-44. Dan. 1.17, 19,20. Dan. 6.3.
f Matt. 12.37.
g Gen. 42.14-16. Jas. 2.3.
h John 15. 14-15.

CHAP. 19

a ch. 28.6.
b Hosea 4.6. John 16.3. Rom. 10.2.
c Ps. 37.7.
d Ex. 23.1.
1 held innocent.
2 a man of gifts.
3 an heart.
e Dan. 6.24.
f Eccl. 10.6.
4 Or, prudence. Jas. 1. 19.
g ch. 25.21. Matt. 5.44. Rom. 12.19. Eph. 4.32.
h 2 Cor. 12. 14.
i ch. 18.22.
j Luke 10.28. Rom. 2.7.
k ch. 14.21. Eccl. 11.1. 2 Cor. 9.6.
5 Or, his deed.
6 Or, to his destruction; or, to cause him to die.

punishment: for if thou deliver *him*, yet thou must [7]do it again.

20 Hear counsel, and receive instruction, that thou mayest be wise in thy latter end.

21 *There* [l]*are* many devices in a man's heart; nevertheless the counsel of the LORD, that shall stand.

22 The desire of a man *is* his kindness: and a poor man *is* better than a liar.

23 The [m]fear of the LORD *tendeth* to life: and *he that hath it* shall abide satisfied; he shall not be visited with evil.

24 A slothful *man* hideth his hand in *his* bosom, and will not so much as bring it to his mouth again.

25 Smite a scorner, and the simple [8]will beware: and reprove one that hath understanding, *and* he will understand knowledge.

26 He that wasteth *his* father, *and* chaseth away *his* mother, *is* a son that causeth shame, and bringeth reproach.

27 Cease, my son, to [n]hear the instruction *that causeth* to err from the words of knowledge.

28 [9]An ungodly witness scorneth judgment: and the mouth of the wicked devoureth iniquity.

29 Judgments are prepared for scorners, and stripes for the back of fools.

CHAPTER 20

WINE [a]*is* a mocker, strong drink *is* raging: and whosoever is deceived thereby is not wise.

2 The fear of a king *is* as the roaring of a lion: *whoso* provoketh him to anger sinneth *against* his own soul.

3 *It is* an [b]honour for a man to cease from strife: but every fool will be meddling.

4 The sluggard will not plow by reason of the [1]cold; *therefore* shall he beg in harvest, and *have* nothing.

5 Counsel in the heart of man *is like* deep water; but a man of understanding will draw it out.

6 Most [c]men will proclaim every one his own [2]goodness: but [d]a faithful man who can find?

7 The just *man* walketh in his integrity: his children *are* blessed after him.

8 A king that sitteth in the throne of judgment scattereth away all evil with his eyes.

9 Who [e]can say, I have made my heart clean, I am pure from my sin?

10 [3]Divers weights, *and* [4]divers measures, both of them *are* alike abomination to the LORD.

11 Even a child is [f]known by his doings, whether his work *be* pure, and whether *it be* right.

12 The [g]hearing ear, and the seeing eye, the LORD hath made even both of them.

13 Love [h]not sleep, lest thou come to poverty; open thine eyes, *and* thou shalt be satisfied with bread.

14 *It is* naught, *it is* naught, saith the buyer: but when he is gone his way, then he boasteth.

15 There is gold, and a multitude of rubies: but the lips of knowledge *are* a precious jewel.

16 Take his garment that is surety *for* a stranger: and take a pledge of him for a strange woman.

17 [5]Bread of deceit *is* sweet to a man; but afterwards his mouth shall be filled with gravel.

18 *Every* purpose is established by counsel: and with good advice make war.

19 He that goeth about *as* a talebearer revealeth secrets: therefore meddle not with him that [6]flattereth with his lips.

20 Whoso [i]curseth his father or his mother, his [7]lamp shall be put out in obscure darkness.

21 An inheritance *may be* gotten hastily at the beginning; [j]but the end thereof shall not be blessed.

22 Say [k]not thou, I will recompense evil; *but* wait on the LORD, and he shall save thee.

23 Divers weights *are* an abomination unto the LORD; and [8]a false balance *is* not good.

24 Man's [l]goings *are* of the LORD; how can a man then understand his own way?

25 *It is* a snare to the man *who* devoureth *that which is* holy, and after vows to make inquiry.

26 A wise king scattereth the wicked, and bringeth the wheel over them.

27 The spirit of man *is* the [9]candle of the LORD, searching all the inward parts of the belly.

28 Mercy and truth preserve the king: and his throne is upholden by mercy.

29 The glory of young men *is* their strength: and the beauty of old men *is* the gray head.

30 The blueness of a wound [10]cleanseth away evil: so *do* stripes the inward parts of the belly.

7 add.
l Gen. 37.19, 20. Esther 9.25. Eccl. 7.29. Isa. 14.26. Heb. 6.17.
m 1 Tim. 4.8.
8 will be cunning. Deut. 13.11.
n Matt. 7.15. Mark 4.24. John 10.5. Eph. 4.14. 1 Tim. 4.6.
9 A witness of Belial.
CHAP. 20
a Gen. 9.21. Isa. 28.7.
b Gen. 13.7.
1 Or, winter.
c Matt. 6.2.
2 Or, bounty.
d Ps. 12.1. Eccl. 7.28. Jer. 5.1. Luke 18.8.
e Job 14.4. Eccl. 7.20. 1 John 1.8.
3 A stone and a stone.
4 an ephah and an ephah.
f Matt. 7.16.
g Ex. 4.11. Rom. 11.36.
h Rom. 12.11.
5 Bread of lying, or, falsehood.
6 Or, enticeth.
i Ex. 21.17. Lev. 20.9. Matt. 15.4. Rom. 3.23.
7 Or, candle.
j ch. 28.8. Hab. 2.6.
k Deut. 32. 35. Rom. 12.17. 1 Pet. 3.9.
8 balances of deceit.
l Jer. 10.23. Rom. 8.26.
9 Or, lamp.
10 is a purging medicine against evil.

CHAPTER 21

THE king's heart *is* in the hand of
the LORD, *as* the rivers of water:
he turneth it whithersoever he will.
2 Every way of a man *is* right in his
own eyes: [a]but the LORD pondereth
the hearts.
3 To [b]do justice and judgment *is*
more acceptable to the LORD than
sacrifice.
4 [1]An high look, and a proud heart,
and [2]the plowing of the wicked, *is* sin.
5 The thoughts of the diligent *tend*
only to plenteousness; but of every
one *that is* hasty only to want.
6 The getting of treasures by a lying
tongue *is* a vanity tossed to and fro of
them that seek death.
7 The robbery of the wicked shall
destroy them; because they refuse to
do judgment.
8 The way of man *is* froward and
strange: but *as for* the pure, his work
is right.
9 *It is* better to dwell in a corner of
the housetop, than with [4]a brawling
woman in [5]a wide house.
10 The [c]soul of the wicked desireth
evil: his neighbour [6]findeth no favour
in his eyes.
11 When the scorner is punished, the
simple is made wise: and when the
wise is instructed, he receiveth knowledge.
12 The [d]righteous *man* wisely considereth the house of the wicked: *but
God* [e]overthroweth the wicked for
their wickedness.
13 Whoso [f]stoppeth his ears at the
cry of the poor, he also shall cry himself, but shall not be heard.
14 A gift in secret pacifieth anger:
and a reward in the bosom strong
wrath.
15 *It is* joy to the just to do judgment: but destruction *shall be* to the
workers of iniquity.
16 The man that wandereth out of
the way of understanding shall remain in the congregation of the dead.
17 He that loveth [7]pleasure *shall be*
a poor man: he that loveth wine and
oil shall not be rich.
18 The [g]wicked *shall be* a ransom for
the righteous, and the transgressor
for the upright.
19 *It is* better to dwell [8]in the wilderness, than with a contentious and an
angry woman.
20 *There* [h]*is* treasure to be desired
and oil in the dwelling of the wise; but
a foolish man spendeth it up.
21 He [i]that followeth after righteousness and mercy findeth life, righteousness, and honour.
22 A wise *man* scaleth the city of the
mighty, and casteth down the strength
of the confidence thereof.
23 Whoso keepeth his mouth and
his tongue keepeth his soul from
troubles.
24 Proud *and* haughty scorner *is* his
name, who dealeth [9]in proud wrath.
25 The desire of the slothful killeth
him; for his hands refuse to labour.
26 He coveteth greedily all the day
long: but the righteous giveth and
spareth not.
27 The sacrifice of the wicked *is*
abomination: how much more, *when*
he bringeth it [10]with a wicked mind?
28 [11]A false witness shall perish: but
the man that heareth speaketh constantly.
29 A wicked man hardeneth his face:
but *as for* the upright, he [12]directeth
his way.
30 *There is* no wisdom nor understanding nor counsel against the
LORD.
31 The horse *is* prepared against the
day of battle: but [13]safety *is* of the
LORD.

CHAPTER 22

A *GOOD* name *is* rather to be chos-
en than great riches, *and* [1]loving
favour rather than silver and gold.
2 The [a]rich and poor meet together:
the LORD *is* the maker of them all.
3 A prudent [b]*man* foreseeth the evil,
and hideth himself: but the simple
pass on, and are punished.
4 [2]By humility *and* the fear of the
LORD *are* riches, and honour, and
life.
5 Thorns *and* snares *are* in the way
of the froward: [c]he that doth keep his
soul shall be far from them.
6 [3]Train up a child [4]in the way he
should go: and when he is old, he will
not depart from it.
7 The rich ruleth over the poor, and
the borrower *is* servant [5]to the lender.
8 He that [d]soweth iniquity shall reap
vanity: [6]and the rod of his anger shall
fail.
9 [7]He that hath a bountiful eye shall
be blessed; for he giveth of his bread
to the poor.
10 Cast out the scorner, and contention shall go out; yea, strife and reproach shall cease.
11 He that loveth pureness of heart,
[8]*for* the grace of his lips the king *shall
be* his friend.
12 The eyes of the LORD preserve

CHAP. 21

a 1 Sam. 16.7. Jer. 17.10. John 2.24.
b Hosea 6.6.
1 Haughtiness of eyes.
2 Or, the light of the wicked.
3 saw them, or, dwell with them.
4 a woman of contentions.
5 an house of society.
c Jas. 4.5.
6 is not favoured.
d 1 Cor. 10. 10.
e Rom. 2.8.
f Ps. 58.4. Zech. 7.11. Acts 7.57. Matt. 7.2.
7 Or, sport.
g Isa. 43.3,4.
8 in the land of the desert.
h Ps. 112.3. ch. 10.22. Matt. 25.3.
i 1 Cor. 15.58.
9 in the wrath of pride.
10 in wickedness?
11 A witness of lies.
12 Or, considereth.
13 Or, victory.

CHAP. 22

1 Or, favour is better than, etc.
a Ps. 49.1,2.
b Isa. 26.20.
2 Or, The reward of humility, etc.
c 1 John 5.18.
3 Or, Catechise.
4 in his way.
5 to the man that lendeth.
d Job 4.8. Hosea 10. 13.
6 Or, and with the rod of his anger he shall be consumed.
7 Good of eye.
8 Or, and hath grace in his lips.

knowledge, and he overthroweth the [9]words of the transgressor.

13 The slothful *man* saith, *There is* a lion without, I shall be slain in the streets.

14 The mouth [e]of strange women *is* a deep pit: he that is abhorred of the LORD shall fall therein.

15 Foolishness *is* bound in the heart of a child; *but* the rod of correction shall drive it far from him.

16 He that [f]oppresseth the poor to increase his *riches, and* he that giveth to the rich, *shall* surely *come* to want.

17 Bow down thine ear, and hear the words of the wise, and apply thine heart unto my knowledge.

18 For *it is* a pleasant thing if thou keep them [10]within thee; they shall withal be fitted in thy lips.

19 That thy trust may be in the LORD, I have made known to thee this day, [11]even to thee.

20 Have not I written to thee excellent things in counsels and knowledge,

21 That I might make thee know the certainty of the words of truth; that [g]thou mightest answer the words of truth [12]to them that send unto thee?

22 Rob not the poor, because he *is* poor: neither [h]oppress the afflicted in the gate:

23 For the LORD will plead their cause, and spoil the soul of those that spoiled them.

24 Make no friendship with an angry man; and with a furious man thou shalt not go:

25 Lest thou learn his ways, and get a snare to thy soul.

26 Be not thou *one* of them that strike hands, *or* of them that are sureties for debts.

27 If thou hast nothing to pay, why should he take away thy bed from under thee?

28 Remove not the ancient [13]landmark, which thy fathers have set.

29 Seest thou a man [i]diligent in his business? he shall stand before kings; he shall not stand before [14]mean *men*.

CHAPTER 23

WHEN thou sittest to eat with a ruler, consider diligently what *is* before thee:

2 And put a knife to thy throat, if thou *be* a man given to appetite.

3 Be not desirous of his dainties: for they *are* deceitful meat.

4 Labour [a]not to be rich: [b]cease from thine own wisdom.

5 [1]Wilt thou set thine eyes upon that which is not? for *riches* certainly make themselves wings; they fly away as an eagle toward heaven.

6 Eat [c]thou not the bread of *him that hath* [d]an evil eye, neither desire thou his dainty meats:

7 For as he thinketh in his heart, so *is* he: Eat and drink, saith he to thee; but his heart *is* not with thee.

8 The morsel *which* thou hast eaten shalt thou vomit up, and lose thy sweet words.

9 Speak [e]not in the ears of a fool: for he will despise the wisdom of thy words.

10 Remove not the old [2]landmark; and enter not into the fields of the fatherless:

11 For [f]their redeemer *is* mighty; he shall plead their cause with thee.

12 Apply thine heart unto instruction, and thine ears to the words of knowledge.

13 Withhold not correction from the child: for *if* thou beatest him with the rod, he shall not die.

14 Thou shalt beat him with the rod, and shalt [g]deliver his soul from hell.

15 My son, if thine heart be wise, my heart shall rejoice, [3]even mine.

16 Yea, my reins shall rejoice, when thy lips speak right things.

17 Let not thine heart envy sinners: but *be thou* in the fear of the LORD all the day long.

18 For [h]surely there is an [4]end; and thine expectation shall not be cut off.

19 Hear thou, my son, and be wise, and guide thine heart in the way.

20 Be [i]not among winebibbers; among riotous eaters [5]of flesh:

21 For the drunkard and the glutton shall come to poverty: and drowsiness shall clothe *a man* with rags.

22 Hearken [j]unto thy father that begat thee, and despise not thy mother when she is old.

23 Buy [k]the truth, and sell *it* not; *also* wisdom, and instruction, and understanding.

24 The father of the righteous shall greatly rejoice: and he that begetteth a wise *child* shall have joy of him.

25 Thy father and thy mother shall be glad, and she that bare thee shall rejoice.

26 My son, give me thine heart, and let thine eyes observe my ways.

27 For a whore *is* a deep ditch; and a strange woman *is* a narrow pit.

28 She also lieth in wait [6]as *for* a prey, and increaseth the transgressors among men.

---

9 Or, the matters.
e ch. 2.16. Eccl. 7.26.
f Job 20.19, 20,23. Job 34.26, 27,28. Ps. 12.5. Eccl. 5.8. Isa. 3.14,15. Amos 2.6-8. Amos 5.11. Jas. 2.13.
10 in thy belly.
11 Or, trust thou also.
g 1 Pet. 3.15.
12 Or, to those that send thee?
h Mal. 3.5.
13 Or, bound. Deut. 19.14.
i 1 Ki. 11.28. ch. 10.4. Eccl. 9.10. Matt. 25.21. Rom. 12.11.
14 obscure men.

CHAP. 23

a ch. 28.20. John 6.27. 1 Tim. 6.9.
b ch. 3.5. Rom. 12.16.
1 Wilt thou cause thine eyes to fly upon.
c Ps. 141.4.
d Deut. 15.9. Matt. 20.15. Mark 7.22.
e Matt. 7.6.
2 Or, bound.
f Job 31.21. Jer. 50.34.
g 1 Cor. 5.5.
3 Or, even I will rejoice.
h Luke 16.25.
4 Or, reward.
i Isa. 5.22. Matt. 24.49. Luke 21.34. Rom. 13.13. Eph. 5.18.
5 of their flesh.
j Eph. 6.1.
k Matt. 13. 44.
6 Or, as a robber.

9 Who [l]hath woe? who hath sor-
w? who hath contentions? who
th babbling? who hath wounds
ithout cause? who hath redness of
es?
0 They that tarry long at the wine;
ey that go to seek mixed wine.
1 Look not thou upon the wine
hen it is red, when it giveth his colour
the cup, *when* it moveth itself aright.
2 At the last it biteth like a serpent,
d stingeth like [7]an adder.
3 Thine eyes shall behold strange
omen, and thine heart shall utter
erverse things.
4 Yea, thou shalt be as he that lieth
own [8]in the midst of the sea, or as he
at lieth upon the top of a mast.
5 They [m]have stricken me, *shalt*
ou say, *and* I was not sick; they
ave beaten me, *and* [9]I felt *it* not:
hen [n]shall I awake? I will seek it yet
gain.

CHAPTER 24

BE not thou envious against evil
men, neither desire to be with
em.
2 For their heart studieth destruc-
on, and their lips talk of mischief.
3 Through wisdom is an house build-
d; and by understanding it is estab-
shed:
4 And by knowledge shall the cham-
ers be filled with all precious and
leasant riches.
5 A wise man [1]*is* strong; yea, a man
f knowledge [2]increaseth strength.
6 For by wise counsel thou shalt
ake thy war: and in multitude of
ounsellers *there is* safety.
7 Wisdom *is* too high for a fool: he
peneth not his mouth in the gate.
8 He that deviseth to do evil shall be
alled a mischievous person.
9 The [a]thought of foolishness *is* sin:
nd the scorner *is* an abomination to
en.
10 *If* thou faint in the day of adver-
ity, thy strength *is* [3]small.
11 If [b]thou forbear to deliver *them*
at are drawn unto death, and *those*
at are ready to be slain;
12 If thou sayest, Behold, we knew
not; doth not he that pondereth the
eart consider *it?* and he that keepeth
y soul, doth *not* he know *it?* and
hall *not* he render to *every* man [c]ac-
ording to his works?
13 My son, eat thou honey, because
is good; and the honeycomb, *which*
sweet [4]to thy taste:
14 So *shall* the knowledge of wisdom
e unto thy soul: when thou hast
found *it*, then there shall be a reward,
and thy expectation shall not be cut
off.
15 Lay not wait, O wicked *man*,
against the dwelling of the righteous;
spoil not his resting place:
16 For [d]a just *man* falleth seven
times, and riseth up again: but the
wicked shall fall into mischief.
17 Rejoice not when thine enemy
falleth, and let not thine heart be glad
when he stumbleth:
18 Lest the LORD see *it*, and [5]it displease him, and he turn away his
wrath from him.
19 [6]Fret not thyself because of evil
men, neither be thou envious at the
wicked;
20 For [e]there shall be no reward to
the evil *man;* the [7]candle of the wicked
shall be put out.
21 My son, [f]fear thou the LORD and
the king: *and* meddle not with [8]them
that are given to change:
22 For their calamity shall rise suddenly; and who knoweth the ruin of
them both?
23 These *things* also *belong* to the
wise. [g]*It is* not good to have respect of
persons in judgment.
24 He [h]that saith unto the wicked,
Thou *art* righteous; him shall the
people curse, nations shall abhor
him:
25 But to them that rebuke *him* shall
be delight, and [9]a good blessing shall
come upon them.
26 *Every man* shall kiss *his* lips [10]that
giveth a right answer.
27 Prepare thy work without, and
make it fit for thyself in the field; and
afterwards build thine house.
28 Be [i]not a witness against thy
neighbour without cause; and deceive
not with thy lips.
29 Say [j]not, I will do so to him as he
hath done to me: I will render to the
man according to his work.
30 I went by the field of the slothful,
and by the vineyard of the man void
of understanding;
31 And, lo, [k]it was all grown over
with thorns, *and* nettles had covered
the face thereof, and the stone wall
thereof was broken down.
32 Then I saw, *and* [11]considered *it*
well: I looked upon *it, and* received
instruction.
33 *Yet* a little sleep, a little slumber,
a little folding of the hands to sleep:
34 So shall thy poverty come *as* one
that travelleth; and thy want as [12]an
armed man.

l 1 Ki. 20.16. ch. 20.1. Isa. 5.11. Nah. 1.10. Matt. 24.49, 50. Eph. 5.18.
7 Or, a cockatrice.
8 in the heart of the sea.
m ch. 27.22. Jer. 5.3.
9 I knew it not.
n Deut. 29. 19. Isa. 56.12. 2 Pet. 2.22.
CHAP. 24
1 is in strength.
2 strengtheneth might.
a Gen. 6.5. Ps. 119.113. Matt. 9.4. Acts 8.22. 2 Cor. 10.5.
3 narrow.
b Isa. 58.6,7. 1 John 3.16.
c Job 34.11. Jer. 32.19 Rom. 2.6. Rev. 2.23.
4 upon thy palate.
d Ps. 34.19. Micah 7.8.
5 it be evil in his eyes.
6 Or, Keep not company with the wicked.
e Ps. 11.6. Isa. 3.11.
7 Or, lamp.
f Rom. 13.7. 1 Pet. 2.17.
8 changers.
g Deut. 1.17. 2 Chr. 19.7. ch. 18.5. John 7.24.
h Isa. 5.23.
9 a blessing of good.
10 that answereth right words.
i Eph. 4.25.
j Matt. 5.39.
k Jer. 4.3. Matt. 13.7, 22. Heb. 6.8.
11 set my heart.
12 a man of shield.

CHAPTER 25

THESE *are* also proverbs of Solomon, which the men of Hĕz-ē-kī'-ăh king of Judah copied out.

2 *It* [a]*is* the glory of God to conceal a thing: but the honour of kings *is* [b]to search out a matter.

3 The heaven for height, and the earth for depth, and the heart of kings [1]*is* unsearchable.

4 Take away the dross from the silver, and there shall come forth a vessel for the finer.

5 Take away the wicked *from* before the king, and his throne shall be established in righteousness.

6 [2]Put not forth thyself in the presence of the king, and stand not in the place of great *men:*

7 For better *it is* that it be said unto thee, Come up hither; than that thou shouldest be put lower in the presence of the prince whom thine eyes have seen.

8 Go [c]not forth hastily to strive, lest *thou know not* what to do in the end thereof, when thy neighbour hath put thee to shame.

9 Debate [d]thy cause with thy neighbour *himself;* and [3]discover not a secret to another:

10 Lest he that heareth *it* put thee to shame, and thine infamy turn not away.

11 A word [4]fitly spoken *is like* apples of gold in pictures of silver.

12 *As* an earring of gold, and an ornament of fine gold, *so is* a wise reprover upon an obedient ear.

13 As the cold of snow in the time of harvest, *so is* a faithful messenger to them that send him: for he refresheth the soul of his masters.

14 Whoso boasteth himself [5]of a false gift *is like* [e]clouds and wind without rain.

15 By long forbearing is a prince persuaded, and a soft tongue breaketh the bone.

16 Hast thou found honey? eat so much as is sufficient for thee, lest thou be filled therewith, and vomit it.

17 [6]Withdraw thy foot from thy neighbour's house; lest he be [7]weary of thee, and *so* hate thee.

18 A man that beareth false witness against his neighbour [f]*is* a maul, and a sword, and a sharp arrow.

19 Confidence in an [g]unfaithful man in time of trouble *is like* a broken tooth, and a foot out of joint.

20 *As* he that taketh away a garment in cold weather, *and as* vinegar upon nitre, [h]so *is* he that singeth songs t an heavy heart.

21 If [i]thine enemy be hungry, giv him bread to eat; and if he be thirst give him water to drink:

22 For thou shalt heap coals of fir upon his head, [j]and the LORD shall re ward thee.

23 [8]The north wind driveth awa rain: so *doth* an angry countenance backbiting tongue.

24 *It is* better to dwell in the corne of the housetop, than with a brawlin woman and in a wide house.

25 *As* cold waters to a thirsty soul so *is* good news from a far country

26 A righteous [k]man falling dow before the wicked *is as* a trouble fountain, and a corrupt spring.

27 *It is* not good to eat much honey so [l]*for men* to search their own glor *is not* glory.

28 He that *hath* no rule over his ow spirit *is like* a city *that is* broken down *and* without walls.

CHAPTER 26

AS snow in summer, and as rain i harvest, so [a]honour is not seeml for a fool.

2 As the bird by wandering, as th swallow by flying, so the curse cause less [b]shall not come.

3 A whip for the horse, a bridle fo the ass, and a rod for the fool's back

4 Answer [c]not a fool according t his folly, lest thou also be like unt him.

5 Answer a fool according to hi folly, lest he be wise in [1]his own con ceit.

6 He that sendeth a message by th hand of a fool cutteth off the feet, *an* drinketh [2]damage.

7 The legs of the lame [3]are not equal so *is* a parable in the mouth of fools

8 [4]As he that bindeth a stone in sling, so *is* he that giveth honour to fool.

9 *As* a thorn goeth up into the han of a drunkard, so *is* a parable in th mouth of fools.

10 [5]The great *God* that formed al *things* both rewardeth the fool, and re wardeth transgressors.

11 As a dog returneth to his vomit *so* a fool [6]returneth to his folly.

12 Seest thou a man wise in his ow conceit? *there is* more hope of a foo than of him.

13 The slothful *man* saith, *There i* a lion in the way; a lion *is* in th streets.

CHAP. 25

a Rom. 11.33.
b Job 29.16.
1 there is no searching.
2 Set not out thy glory.
c Matt. 5.25.
d Matt. 18. 15.
3 Or, discover not the secret of another.
4 spoken upon his wheels.
5 in a gift of falsehood.
e Jude 12.
6 Or, Let thy foot be seldom in thy neighbour's house.
7 full of thee.
f Ps. 140.3.
g Job 6.14-20. 2 Tim. 4.16.
h Dan. 6.18.
i Matt. 5.44.
j 2 Sam. 16. 12.
8 Or, The north wind bringeth forth rain: so doth a backbiting tongue an angry countenance.
k Micah 7.8.
l Luke 14.11.

CHAP. 26

a Ps. 12.8.
b Num. 23.8.
c Isa. 36.21.
1 his own eyes.
2 Or, violence.
3 are lifted up.
4 Or, As he that putteth a precious stone in an heap of stones.
5 Or, A great man grieveth all, and he hireth the fool, he hireth also transgressors.
6 iterateth his folly.

14 *As* the door turneth upon his
inges, so *doth* the slothful upon his
ed.
15 The slothful hideth his hand in
is bosom; [7]it grieveth him to bring it
gain to his mouth.
16 The sluggard *is* wiser in his own
onceit than seven men that can ren-
er a reason.
17 He that passeth by, *and* [8]meddleth
ith strife *belonging* not to him, *is*
ke one that taketh a dog by the ears.
18 As a mad *man* who casteth [9]fire-
rands, arrows, and death,
19 So *is* the man *that* deceiveth his
eighbour, and saith, Am not I in
sport?
20 [10]Where no wood is, *there* the fire
oeth out: so where *there is* no [11]tale-
earer, the strife [12]ceaseth.
21 *As* coals *are* to burning coals, and
ood to fire; so *is* a [e]contentious man
kindle strife.
22 The [f]words of a talebearer *are* as
ounds, and they go down into the
innermost parts of the belly.
23 Burning lips [g]and a wicked heart
re like a potsherd covered with silver
ross.
24 He that hateth [14]dissembleth with
is lips, and layeth up deceit within
im;
25 When he [15]speaketh fair, believe
im not: for *there are* seven abomina-
ons in his heart.
26 *Whose* [16]hatred is covered by de-
eit, his wickedness shall be shewed
efore the *whole* congregation.
27 Whoso [h]diggeth a pit shall fall
herein: and he that rolleth a stone,
will return upon him.
28 A lying tongue [i]hateth *those that*
re afflicted by it; and a flattering
outh worketh ruin.

CHAPTER 27

BOAST [a]not thyself of [1]to morrow;
for thou knowest not what a day
ay bring forth.
2 Let another man praise thee, and
ot thine own mouth; a stranger, and
ot thine own lips.
3 A stone *is* [2]heavy, and the sand
eighty; but a [b]fool's wrath *is* heavier
han them both.
4 [3]Wrath *is* cruel, and anger *is* out-
ageous; but [c]who *is* able to stand be-
ore [4]envy?
5 Open [d]rebuke *is* better than secret
ove.
6 Faithful *are* the wounds of a friend;
ut the kisses of an enemy *are* [5]de-
eitful.
7 The full soul [6]loatheth an honeycomb; but to the hungry soul every
bitter thing is sweet.
8 As a bird that [e]wandereth from her
nest, so *is* a man that wandereth from
his place.
9 Ointment and perfume rejoice the
heart: so *doth* the sweetness of a man's
friend [7]by hearty counsel.
10 Thine own friend, and thy father's
friend, forsake not; neither go into
thy brother's house in the day of thy
calamity: *for* better *is* a neighbour *that*
is near than a brother far off.
11 My son, be wise, and make my
heart glad, [f]that I may answer him
that reproacheth me.
12 A prudent *man* [g]foreseeth the evil,
and hideth himself; *but* the simple pass
on, *and* are punished.
13 Take his garment that is surety
for a stranger, and take a pledge of
him for a strange woman.
14 He that [h]blesseth his friend with
a loud voice, rising early in the morning, it shall be counted a curse to him.
15 A continual dropping in a very
rainy day and a contentious woman
are alike.
16 Whosoever hideth her hideth the
wind, and the ointment of his right
hand, *which* bewrayeth *itself*.
17 Iron sharpeneth iron; so a man
sharpeneth the countenance of his
friend.
18 Whoso keepeth the fig tree shall
eat the fruit thereof: [i]so he that waiteth on his master shall be honoured.
19 As in water face *answereth* to face,
so the heart of man to man.
20 Hell [j]and destruction are [8]never
full; so the eyes of man are never
satisfied.
21 *As* the fining pot for silver, and
the furnace for gold; so *is* a man to
his praise.
22 Though thou shouldest bray a
fool in a mortar among wheat with a
pestle, *yet* will not his foolishness depart from him.
23 Be thou diligent to know the state
of thy flocks, *and* [9]look well to thy
herds.
24 For [10]riches *are* not for ever: and
doth the crown *endure* [11]to every generation?
25 The hay appeareth, and the tender
grass sheweth itself, and herbs of the
mountains are gathered.
26 The lambs *are* for thy clothing,
and the goats *are* the price of the field.
27 And *thou shalt have* goats' milk
enough for thy food, for the food of

7 Or, he is weary.
8 Or, is enraged.
9 flames, or, sparks.
d Eph. 5.4.
10 Without wood.
11 Or, whisperer.
12 is silent.
e 2 Sam. 20.1.
f Eze. 22.9.
13 chambers.
g Luke 22.48.
14 Or, is known.
15 maketh his voice gracious.
16 Or, hatred is covered in secret.
h Esther 7.10.
i Pro. 13.6.

CHAP. 27

a Luke 12.19.
1 to morrow day.
2 heaviness.
b Esther 1.12.
3 Wrath is cruelty, and anger an overflowing.
c 1 John 3.12.
4 Or, jealousy?
d Gal. 2.14.
5 Or, earnest, or, frequent.
6 treadeth under foot.
e Job 39.14.
7 from the counsel of the soul.
f Ps. 119.42.
g Isa. 32.2.
h Ps. 12.2.
i Deut. 20.6. 1 Ki. 11.8. ch. 12.24. 1 Cor. 3.8.
j ch. 30.15, 16. Hab. 2.5.
8 not.
9 set thy heart.
10 strength.
11 to generation and generation?

thy household, and *for* the [12]maintenance for thy maidens.

CHAPTER 28

THE wicked flee when no man pursueth: but the righteous are bold as a lion.

2 For the transgression of a land many *are* the princes thereof: but [1]by a man of understanding *and* knowledge the state *thereof* shall be prolonged.

3 A [a]poor man that oppresseth the poor *is like* a sweeping rain [2]which leaveth no food.

4 They that forsake the law praise the wicked : [b]but such as keep the law contend with them.

5 Evil men understand not judgment: but they [c]that seek the LORD understand all *things*.

6 Better *is* the poor that walketh in his uprightness, than *he that is* perverse *in his* ways, though he *be* rich.

7 Whoso keepeth the law *is* a wise son: but he that [3]is a companion of riotous *men* shameth his father.

8 He that by usury and [4]unjust gain increaseth his substance, he shall gather it for him that will pity the poor.

9 He [d]that turneth away his ear from hearing the law, [e]even his prayer *shall be* abomination.

10 Whoso causeth the righteous to go astray in an evil way, he shall fall himself into his own pit: but [f]the upright shall have good *things* in possession.

11 The rich man *is* wise [5]in his own conceit; but the poor that hath understanding searcheth him out.

12 When righteous *men* do rejoice, *there is* great glory: but when the wicked rise, a man is [6]hidden.

13 He that covereth his sins shall not prosper: but whoso confesseth and forsaketh *them* shall have mercy.

14 Happy *is* the man that feareth alway: but he that hardeneth his heart shall fall into mischief.

15 *As* a roaring lion, and a ranging bear; *so* [g]*is* a wicked ruler over the poor people.

16 The prince that wanteth understanding *is* also a great oppressor: *but* he that hateth covetousness shall prolong *his* days.

17 A man that doeth violence to the blood of *any* person shall flee to the pit; let no man stay him.

18 Whoso walketh uprightly shall be saved: but *he that is* perverse *in his* ways shall fall at once.

12 life.

CHAP. 28

1 Or, by men of understanding and wisdom shall they likewise be prolonged.
a Matt. 18.28.
2 without food.
b 1 Ki. 18.18. Matt. 3.7. Eph. 5.11. 1 Tim. 5.20.
c John 7.17.
3 Or, feedeth gluttons.
4 by increase.
d 2 Tim. 4.3.
e Ps. 66.18. Luke 13.25-27.
f Ps. 34.9,10. Matt. 6.33. Mark 10.30. Luke 18.29, 30. Rom. 8.32. 1 Cor. 3.22, 23.
5 in his eyes.
6 Or, sought for.
g Matt. 2.16.
7 Or, unpunished.
h Eze. 13.19.
8 Or, He that hath an evil eye hasteth to be rich.
9 a man destroying.
i 1 Tim. 6.6.

CHAP. 29

1 A man of reproofs.
2 Or, increased.
a 1 Ki. 1.48. ch. 10.1. ch. 15.20. Phil. 2.22.
3 a man of oblations.
b Job 29.16. Ps. 31.7. Isa. 35.3,4. Luke 22.32. Gal. 6.1.
4 Or, set a city on fire.

19 He that tilleth his land shall hav plenty of bread: but he that followet after vain *persons* shall have povert enough.

20 A faithful man shall abound wit blessings: but he that maketh haste t be rich shall not be [7]innocent.

21 To have respect of persons *is* nc good: for for a [h]piece of bread *tha* man will transgress.

22 [8]He that hasteth to be rich *hat* an evil eye, and considereth not tha poverty shall come upon him.

23 He that rebuketh a man after wards shall find more favour than h that flattereth with the tongue.

24 Whoso robbeth his father or hi mother, and saith, *It is* no transgres sion; the same *is* the companion of [9] destroyer.

25 He that is of a proud heart sti reth up strife: [i]but he that putteth hi trust in the LORD shall be made fat.

26 He that trusteth in his own hear is a fool: but whoso walketh wisely he shall be delivered.

27 He that giveth unto the poor sha not lack: but he that hideth his eye shall have many a curse.

28 When the wicked rise, men hid themselves: but when they perish, th righteous increase.

CHAPTER 29

[1]HE, that being often reprove hardeneth *his* neck, shall sud denly be destroyed, and that withou remedy.

2 When the righteous are [2]in auth ority, the people rejoice: but when th wicked beareth rule, the peopl mourn.

3 Whoso [a]loveth wisdom rejoicet his father: but he that keepeth com pany with harlots spendeth *his* sub stance.

4 The king by judgment establishet the land: but [3]he that receiveth gift overthroweth it.

5 A man that flattereth his neigh bour spreadeth a net for his feet.

6 In the transgression of an evil ma *there is* a snare: but the righteous dot sing and rejoice.

7 The [b]righteous considereth th cause of the poor: *but* the wicked re gardeth not to know *it*.

8 Scornful men [4]bring a city int a snare: but wise *men* turn awa wrath.

9 *If* a wise man contendeth with a foolish man, whether he rage o laugh, *there is* no rest.

0 [5]The bloodthirsty hate the up-
ght: but the just seek his soul.
1 A fool uttereth all his mind: but a
ise *man* keepeth it in till afterwards.
2 If a ruler hearken to lies, all his
ɪrvants *are* wicked.
.3 The poor and [6]the deceitful man
ɪeet together: [c]the LORD lighteneth
oth their eyes.
.4 The king that [d]faithfully judgeth
ɪe poor, his throne shall be estab-
shed for ever.
ɪ5 The rod and reproof give wisdom:
ut a child left *to himself* bringeth
is mother to shame.
ɪ6 When the wicked are multiplied,
ansgression increaseth: but [e]the
ghteous shall see their fall.
ɪ7 Correct [f]thy son, and he shall
ive thee rest; yea, he shall give de-
ght unto thy soul.
ɪ8 Where [g]*there is* no vision, the
eople [7]perish: but [h]he that keepeth
ɪe law, happy *is* he.
ɪ9 A servant will not be corrected by
ords: for though he understand he
ill not answer.
20 Seest thou a man *that is* hasty [8]in
is words? *there is* more hope of a
ool than of him.
21 He that delicately bringeth up his
ervant from a child shall have him
ecome *his* son at the length.
22 An angry man stirreth up strife,
nd a furious man aboundeth in trans-
ression.
23 A [i]man's pride shall bring him
ow: but honour shall uphold the
umble in spirit.
24 Whoso is partner with a thief
ateth his own soul: [j]he heareth curs-
ng, and bewrayeth *it* not.
25 The [k]fear of man bringeth a snare:
ut whoso putteth his trust in the
ORD [9]shall be safe.
26 Many seek [10]the ruler's favour;
ut *every* man's judgment *cometh*
rom the LORD.
27 An unjust man *is* an abomination
o the just: and *he that is* upright in
he way *is* abomination to the wicked.

CHAPTER 30

THE words of Ā-gŭr the son of Jā-
kĕh, *even* the prophecy: the man
pake unto Ī-thĭ-ĕl, even unto Ī-thĭ-ĕl
nd Ū-căl,
2 Surely [a]I *am* more brutish than *any*
nan, and have not the understanding
f a man.
3 I neither learned wisdom, nor
have the knowledge of the holy.
4 Who [b]hath ascended up into heav-
en, or descended? [c]who hath gathered
the wind in his fists? who hath bound
the waters in a garment? who hath
established all the ends of the earth?
what *is* his name, and what *is* his son's
name, if thou canst tell?
5 Every [d]word of God *is* [2]pure: he [e]*is*
a shield unto them that put their
trust in him.
6 Add [f]thou not unto his words, lest
he reprove thee, and thou be found a
liar.
7 Two *things* have I required of thee;
[3]deny me *them* not before I die:
8 Remove far from me vanity and
lies: give me neither poverty nor riches; [g]feed me with food [4]convenient for
me:
9 Lest [h]I be full, and [5]deny *thee*, and
say, Who *is* the LORD? or lest I be
poor, and steal, and take the name of
my God *in vain*.
10 [6]Accuse not a servant unto his
master, lest he curse thee, and thou be
found guilty.
11 *There is* a generation *that* curseth
their father, and doth not bless their
mother.
12 *There is* a generation [i]*that are* pure
in their own eyes, and *yet* is not washed from their filthiness.
13 *There is* a generation, O how lofty
are their eyes! and their eyelids are
lifted up.
14 *There is* [j]a generation, whose
teeth *are as* swords, and their jaw
teeth *as* knives, [k]to devour the poor
from off the earth, and the needy from
among men.
15 The horseleach hath two daughters, *crying*, Give, give. There are
three *things that* are never satisfied,
yea, four *things* say not, [7]*It is* enough:
16 The [l]grave; and the barren womb;
the earth *that* is not filled with water;
and the fire *that* saith not, *It is* enough.
17 The [m]eye *that* mocketh at *his*
father, and despiseth to obey *his*
mother, the ravens of [8]the valley shall
pick it out, and the young eagles shall
eat it.
18 There be three *things which* are
too wonderful for me, yea, four which
I know not:
19 The way of an eagle in the air; the
way of a serpent upon a rock; the way
of a ship in the [9]midst of the sea; and
the way of a man with a maid.
20 Such *is* the way of an adulterous
woman; she eateth, and wipeth her
mouth, and saith, I have done no
wickedness.
21 For three *things* the earth is dis-

5 Men of blood.
6 Or, the usurer.
c Matt. 5.45.
d Ps. 72.2.
e Ps. 37.36.
f ch. 13.24.
g 1 Sam. 3.1. Amos 8.11.
7 Or, is made naked.
h John 13.17. Jas. 1.25.
8 Or, in his matters?
i Isa. 2.11,12. Matt. 23.12. Luke 14.11.
j Lev. 5.1.
k Gen. 12.12.
9 shall be set on high.
10 the face of a ruler.

CHAP. 30

a Ps. 73.22.
1 know.
b John 3.13.
c Job 38.4.
d Ps. 12.6.
2 purified.
e Ps. 18.30. Ps. 84.11.
f Deut. 4.2. Rev. 22.18.
3 withhold not from me.
g Matt. 6.11.
4 of my allowance.
h Deut. 8.12. Neh. 9.25. Hosea 13.6.
5 belie thee.
6 Hurt not with thy tongue.
i Isa. 65.5. Luke 18.11. Titus 1.15, 16.
j Job 29.17.
k Ps. 14.4. Amos 8.4.
7 Wealth.
l ch. 27.20. Hab. 2.5.
m Gen. 9.22. Lev. 20.9.
8 Or, the brook.
9 heart.

quieted, and for four *which* it cannot
bear:
22 For [n]a servant when he reigneth;
and a fool when he is filled with meat;
23 For an odious *woman* when she is
married; and an handmaid that is
heir to her mistress.
24 There be four *things which are*
little upon the earth, but they *are* [10]ex-
ceeding wise:
25 The [o]ants *are* a people not strong,
yet they prepare their meat in the
summer;
26 The [p]conies *are but* a feeble folk,
yet make they their houses in the
rocks;
27 The locusts have no king, yet go
they forth all of them [11]by bands;
28 The spider taketh hold with her
hands, and is in kings' palaces.
29 There be three *things* which go
well, yea, four are comely in going:
30 A [12]lion *which is* strongest among
beasts, and turneth not away for any;
31 A [13]greyhound; an he goat also;
and a king, against whom *there is* no
rising up.
32 If thou hast done foolishly in lifting up thyself, or if thou hast thought
evil, [q]*lay* thine hand upon thy mouth.
33 Surely the churning of milk bringeth forth butter, and the wringing of
the nose bringeth forth blood: so the
forcing of wrath bringeth forth strife.

CHAPTER 31

THE words of king Lĕm-ū-ĕl, the
[1]prophecy that his mother taught
him.
2 What, my son? and what, the son
of my womb? and what, the son of
my vows?
3 Give not thy strength unto women,
nor thy ways [a]to that which destroyeth kings.
4 *It is* not for kings, [b]O Lĕm-ū-ĕl, *it*
is not for kings to drink wine; nor for
princes strong drink:
5 Lest [c]they drink, and forget the
law, and [2]pervert the judgment [3]of
any of the afflicted.
6 Give [d]strong drink unto him that
is ready to perish, and wine unto those
that be [4]of heavy hearts.
7 Let him drink, and forget his poverty, and remember his misery no
more.
8 Open thy mouth for the dumb in
the cause of all [5]such as are appointed
to destruction.
9 Open thy mouth, [e]judge righteously, and [f]plead the cause of the poo
and needy.
10 ¶ Who can find a virtuous wo
man? for her price *is* far above rubie
11 The heart of her husband dot
safely trust in her, so that he shall hav
no need of spoil.
12 She will do him good and not ev
all the days of her life.
13 She seeketh wool, and flax, an
worketh willingly with her hands.
14 She is like the merchants' ships
she bringeth her food from afar.
15 She [g]riseth also while it is ye
night, and [h]giveth meat to her house
hold, and a portion to her maidens.
16 She considereth a field, and [6]buy
eth it: with the fruit of her hands sh
planteth a vineyard.
17 She girdeth her loins wit
strength, and strengtheneth her arms
18 [7]She perceiveth that her mer
chandise *is* good: her candle goet
not out by night.
19 She layeth her hands to the spin
dle, and her hands hold the distaff.
20 [8]She stretcheth out her hand t
the poor; yea, she reacheth forth he
hands to the needy.
21 She is not afraid of the snow fo
her household: for all her househol
are clothed with [9]scarlet.
22 She maketh herself coverings o
tapestry; her clothing *is* silk an
purple.
23 Her husband is known [i]in th
gates, when he sitteth among the eld
ers of the land.
24 She maketh fine linen, and sellet
it; and delivereth girdles unto th
merchant.
25 Strength and [j]honour *are* he
clothing; and she shall rejoice in tim
to come.
26 She openeth her mouth with wis
dom; and in her tongue *is* the law o
kindness.
27 She [k]looketh well to the ways o
her household, and eateth not th
bread of idleness.
28 Her [l]children arise up, and cal
her blessed; her husband *also*, and h
praiseth her.
29 Many daughters [10]have done vir
tuously, but thou excellest them all.
30 Favour *is* deceitful, and beauty *is*
vain: *but* a woman *that* [m]feareth the
LORD, she shall be praised.
31 Give her of the fruit of her hands
and let her own works praise her in
the gates.

n ch. 19.10. Eccl. 10.7.
10 wise, made wise.
o ch. 6.6.
p Lev. 11.5. Ps. 104.18.
11 gathered together.
12 mighty old lion.
13 girt in the loins, or, horse.
q Eccl. 8.3. Micah 7.16. Rom. 3.19.

CHAP. 31

1 burden.
a Deut. 17.17. Neh. 13.26. ch. 7.26. Hosea 4.11.
b Eccl. 10.17.
c Hosea 4.11.
2 alter.
3 of all the sons of affliction.
d Ps. 104.15.
4 bitter of soul.
5 the sons of destruction.
e Lev. 19.15. Deut. 1.16. 2 Sam. 8.15. Isa. 1.17,23. Zech. 7.9. John 7.24. Heb. 1.9.
f ch. 21.13. Isa. 1.17. Jer. 22.16.
g Rom. 12.11.
h Matt. 24.45. Luke 12.42.
6 taketh.
7 She tasteth.
8 She spreadeth.
9 Or, double garments.
i Deut. 16.18. ch. 12.4. 1 Cor. 11.7.
j 1 Tim. 2.9, 10.
k ch. 14.1. 1 Tim. 5.14. 2 Tim. 3.15. Titus 2.4,5.
l 1 Ki. 2.19.
10 Or, have gotten riches.
m Ps. 112.1.

ECCLESIASTES

OR, THE PREACHER

CHAPTER 1

THE words of the Preacher, the son
of David, king in Jerusalem.
2 Vanity [a]of vanities, saith the
'reacher, vanity of vanities; [b]all *is*
anity.
3 What [c]profit hath a man of all his
abour which he taketh under the
un?
4 *One* generation passeth away, and
nother generation cometh: but [d]the
arth abideth for ever.
5 The [e]sun also ariseth, and the sun
;oeth down, and [1]hasteth to his place
vhere he arose.
6 The [f]wind goeth toward the south,
nd turneth about unto the north; it
vhirleth about continually, and the
vind returneth again according to his
ircuits.
7 All the [g]rivers run into the sea; yet
he sea *is* not full; unto the place from
vhence the rivers come, thither they
return again.
8 All [h]things *are* full of labour; man
:annot utter *it:* [i]the eye is not satisfied
vith seeing, nor the ear filled with
ıearing.
9 The [j]thing that hath been, it *is that*
vhich shall be; and that which is done
'*s* that which shall be done: and *there*
s no new *thing* under the sun.
10 Is there *any* thing whereof it may
›e said, See, this *is* new? it hath been
ılready of old time, which was before
ıs.
11 *There is* no remembrance of form-
:r *things;* neither shall there be *any*
·emembrance of *things* that are to
:ome with *those* that shall come after.
12 ¶ I the Preacher was king over
Israel in Jerusalem.
13 And I gave my heart to seek and
search out by wisdom concerning all
things that are done under heaven:
[k]this sore travail hath God given to
the sons of man [3]to be exercised therewith.
14 I have seen all the works that are
done under the sun; and, behold, all
is vanity and vexation of spirit.
15 *That* [l]*which is* crooked cannot be
made straight: and [4]that which is
wanting cannot be numbered.

CHAP. 1

a Ps. 39.5.
b Ps. 39.5,6. Ps. 62.9,10. ch. 4.4,6. Rom. 8.20.
c ch. 3.9.
d Ps. 104.5. 2 Pet. 3.10.
e Ps. 19.5.
1 panteth.
f John 3.8.
g Job 38.10. Ps. 104.8.
2 return to go.
h ch. 3.1.
i Pro. 27.20.
j Gen. 8.22. ch. 3.15.
k Gen. 3.19. ch. 3.10.
3 Or, to afflict them.
l ch. 7.13.
4 defect.
m 1 Ki. 3.12. ch. 2.9.
5 had seen much.
n ch. 2.3. 1 Thes. 5.21.
o Job 28.28. ch. 7.16. 1 Cor. 1.20.

CHAP. 2

a Ps. 10.6,11. Luke 12.19.
b Isa. 50.11.
c Pro. 14.13. ch. 7.6. Isa. 22.12, 13. Amos 6.5,6.
d ch. 1.17. Isa. 22.13. Amos 6.3-6. 1 Pet. 4.3.
1 to draw my flesh with wine.
2 the number of the days of their life.
3 sons of my house.
e 1 Ki. 9.28.
4 musical instrument and instruments.
f ch. 1.16.

16 I communed with mine own
heart, saying, Lo, I am come to great
estate, and have [m]gotten more wisdom than all *they* that have been before me in Jerusalem: yea, my heart
[5]had great experience of wisdom and
knowledge.
17 And [n]I gave my heart to know
wisdom, and to know madness and
folly: I perceived that this also is vexation of spirit.
18 For [o]in much wisdom *is* much
grief: and he that increaseth knowledge increaseth sorrow.

CHAPTER 2

I SAID [a]in mine heart, Go to now,
I will prove thee with mirth, therefore enjoy pleasure: and, behold,
[b]this also *is* vanity.
2 I said [c]of laughter, *It is* mad: and
of mirth, What doeth it?
3 I [d]sought in mine heart [1]to give myself unto wine, yet acquainting mine
heart with wisdom; and to lay hold
on folly, till I might see what *was* that
good for the sons of men, which they
should do under the heaven [2]all the
days of their life.
4 I made me great works; I builded
me houses; I planted me vineyards:
5 I made me gardens and orchards,
and I planted trees in them of all *kind*
of fruits:
6 I made me pools of water, to water
therewith the wood that bringeth
forth trees:
7 I got *me* servants and maidens, and
had [3]servants born in my house; also
I had great possessions of great and
small cattle above all that were in
Jerusalem before me:
8 I [e]gathered me also silver and gold,
and the peculiar treasure of kings and
of the provinces: I gat me men singers
and women singers, and the delights
of the sons of men, *as* [4]musical instruments, and that of all sorts.
9 So [f]I was great, and increased more
than all that were before me in Jerusalem: also my wisdom remained with
me.
10 And whatsoever mine eyes desired I kept not from them, I withheld

not my heart from any joy; for my
heart rejoiced in all my labour: and
[g]this was my portion of all my labour.
11 Then I looked on all the works
that my hands had wrought, and on
the labour that I had laboured to do:
and, behold, all *was* vanity and vexation of spirit, and *there was* no profit
under the sun.
12 ¶ And I turned myself to behold
wisdom, [h]and madness, and folly: for
what *can* the man *do* that cometh after
the king? [5]*even* that which hath been
already done.
13 Then I saw [6]that wisdom excelleth folly, as far as light excelleth
darkness.
14 The [i]wise man's eyes *are* in his
head; but the fool walketh in darkness; and I myself perceived also that
[j]one event happeneth to them all.
15 Then said I in my heart, As it
happeneth to the fool, so it [7]happen-
eth even to me; and why was I then
more wise? Then I said in my heart,
that this also *is* vanity.
16 For *there is* no remembrance of
the wise more than of the fool for
ever; seeing that which now *is* in the
days to come shall all be forgotten.
And how dieth the wise *man*? as the
fool.
17 Therefore I hated life; because
the work that is wrought under the
sun *is* grievous unto me: for all *is*
vanity and vexation of spirit.
18 ¶ Yea, I hated all my labour
which I had [8]taken under the sun: because [k]I should leave it unto the man
that shall be after me.
19 And who knoweth whether he
shall be a wise *man* or [l]a fool? yet
shall he have rule over all my labour
wherein I have laboured, and wherein
I have shewed myself wise under the
sun. This *is* [m]also vanity.
20 Therefore I went about to cause
my heart to despair of all the labour
which I took under the sun.
21 For there is a man whose labour
is in wisdom, and in knowledge, and
in equity; yet to a man that hath not
laboured therein shall he [9]leave it *for*
his portion. This also *is* vanity and a
great evil.
22 For [n]what hath man of all his
labour, and of the vexation of his
heart, wherein he hath laboured under
the sun?
23 For all his days *are* [o]sorrows, and
his travail grief; yea, his heart taketh
not rest in the night. This is also
vanity.

g ch. 3.22.
h ch. 1.17.
5 Or, in those things which have been already done.
6 that there is an excellency in wisdom more than in folly.
i ch. 8.1.
j ch. 9.2.
7 happeneth to me, even to me.
8 laboured.
k Ps. 49.10.
l 1 Ki. 12.13.
m 1 Tim. 6. 10.
9 give.
n ch. 1.3.
o Job 5.7.
10 Or, delight his senses.
11 before him.

CHAP. 3
a ch. 8.6.
1 to bear.
b Gen. 47.29. Job 7.1. Isa. 38.1. John 11.14. Heb. 9.27.
c Gen. 9.6. 1 Sam. 2.6. Hosea 6.1,2.
d Ex. 15.20. 2 Sam. 6.16. Ps. 149.3.
2 to be far from.
3 Or, seek.
e Amos 5.13.
f Luke 14.26.
g ch. 1.3.
h ch. 1.13.
i Deut. 32.4.
j 8.17. Rom. 11.33.
k ch. 2.24.
l Jas. 1.17.
m ch. 1.9.

24 ¶ *There is* nothing better for
man, *than* that he should eat a
drink, and *that* he [10]should make h
soul enjoy good in his labour. Th
also I saw, that it *was* from the ha
of God.
25 For who can eat, or who else ca
hasten *hereunto*, more than I?
26 For *God* giveth to a man that
good [11]in his sight wisdom, and know
edge, and joy: but to the sinner
giveth travail, to gather and to hea
up, that he may give to *him that*
good before God. This also *is* vani
and vexation of spirit.

CHAPTER 3

TO every *thing there is* a seaso
and a time [a]to every purpose u
der the heaven:
2 A time [1]to be born, and [b]a time t
die; a time to plant, and a time t
pluck up *that which is* planted;
3 A [c]time to kill, and a time to hea
a time to break down, and a time t
build up;
4 A time to weep, and a time t
laugh; a time to mourn, and a tim
[d]to dance;
5 A time to cast away stones, and
time to gather stones together;
time to embrace, and a time [2]to re
frain from embracing;
6 A time to [3]get, and a time to los
a time to keep, and a time to ca
away;
7 A time to rend, and a time to sew
[e]a time to keep silence, and a time t
speak;
8 A time to love, and a time [f]to hate
a time of war, and a time of peace.
9 What [g]profit hath he that worket
in that wherein he laboureth?
10 I [h]have seen the travail, whic
God hath given to the sons of men t
be exercised in it.
11 He [i]hath made every *thing* beauti
ful in his time: also he hath set th
world in their heart, so that [j]no ma
can find out the work that God mak
eth from the beginning to the end.
12 I know that *there is* no good i
them, but for *a man* to rejoice, and t
do good in his life.
13 And also [k]that every man shoul
eat and drink, and enjoy the good o
all his labour, it *is* the gift of God.
14 I know that, whatsoever God do
eth, it shall be for ever: [l]nothing ca
be put to it, nor any thing taken fron
it: and God doeth *it*, that *men* shoul
fear before him.
15 That [m]which hath been is now

and that which is to be hath already
been; and God requireth [4]that which
is past.
16 ¶ And moreover [n]I saw under the
sun the place of judgment, *that* wickedness *was* there; and the place of
righteousness, *that* iniquity *was* there.
17 I said in mine heart, [o]God shall
judge the righteous and the wicked:
for *there is* a time there for every purpose and for every work.
18 I said in mine heart concerning
the estate of the sons of men, [5]that
God might manifest them, and that
they might see that they themselves
are beasts.
19 For [p]that which befalleth the sons
of men befalleth beasts; even one
thing befalleth them: as the one dieth,
so dieth the other; yea, they have all
one breath; so that a man hath no
preeminence above a beast: for all *is*
vanity.
20 All go unto one place; [q]all are of
the dust, and all turn to dust again.
21 Who knoweth the spirit [6]of man
that [7]goeth upward, and the spirit of
the beast that goeth downward to the
earth?
22 Wherefore I perceive that *there is*
nothing better, than that a man should
rejoice in his own works; for that [r]*is*
his portion: for who shall bring him
to see what shall be after him?

CHAPTER 4

SO I returned, and considered all
the oppressions that are done under the sun: and behold the tears of
such as were oppressed, and they had
no comforter; and on the [1]side of their
oppressors *there was* power; but they
had no comforter.
2 Wherefore [a]I praised the dead
which are already dead more than the
living which are yet alive.
3 Yea, [b]better *is he* than both they,
which hath not yet been, who hath
not seen the evil work that is done under the sun.
4 ¶ Again, I considered all travail,
and [2]every right work, that [3]for this a
man is envied of his neighbour. This
is also vanity and vexation of spirit.
5 The [c]fool foldeth his hands together, and eateth his own flesh.
6 Better *is* an handful *with* quietness,
than both the hands full *with* travail
and vexation of spirit.
7 ¶ Then I returned, and I saw vanity under the sun.
8 There is one *alone*, and *there is* not
a second; yea, he hath neither child
nor brother: yet *is there* no end of all
his labour; neither is his eye [d]satisfied
with riches; [e]neither *saith he*, For
whom do I labour, and bereave my
soul of good? This *is* also vanity, yea,
it *is* a sore travail.
9 ¶ Two *are* better than one; because
they have a good reward for their
labour.
10 For if they fall, the one will lift up
his fellow: but woe to him *that is*
alone when he falleth; for *he hath* not
another to help him up.
11 Again, if two lie together, then
they have heat: but how can one be
warm *alone?*
12 And if one prevail against him,
two shall withstand him; and a three-
fold cord is not quickly broken.
13 ¶ Better *is* a poor and a wise child
than an old and foolish king, [4]who
will no more be admonished.
14 For out of prison he cometh to
reign; whereas also *he that is* born
in his kingdom becometh poor.
15 I considered all the living which
walk under the sun, with the second
child that shall stand up in his stead.
16 *There is* no end of all the people,
even of all that have been before them:
they also that come after shall not rejoice in him. Surely this also *is* vanity
and vexation of spirit.

CHAPTER 5

KEEP [a]thy foot when thou goest to
the house of God, and be more
ready to hear, [b]than to give the sacrifice of fools: for they consider not that
they do evil.
2 Be not rash with thy mouth, and
let not thine heart be hasty to utter
any [1]thing before God: for God *is* in
heaven, and thou upon earth: therefore let [c]thy words be few.
3 For a dream cometh through the
multitude of business; and a fool's
voice *is known* by multitude of words.
4 When [d]thou vowest a vow unto
God, defer not to pay it; for *he hath*
no pleasure in fools: [e]pay that which
thou hast vowed.
5 Better [f]*is it* that thou shouldest not
vow, than that thou shouldest vow
and not pay.
6 Suffer not thy mouth to cause thy
flesh to sin; [g]neither say thou before
the angel, that it *was* an error: wherefore should God be angry at thy voice,
and destroy the work of thine hands?
7 For in the multitude of dreams and
many words *there are* also *divers* vanities: but [h]fear thou God.

---

4 that which is driven away.
n ch. 5.8.
o Job 34.11. Matt. 16.27. Rom. 2.6. 2 Cor. 5.10. 2 Thes. 1.6.
5 Or, that they might clear God, and see, etc.
p Ps. 49.12.
q Gen. 3.19.
6 of the sons of man.
7 is ascending.
r ch. 2.10.

CHAP. 4

1 hand.
a Job 3.17. ch. 2.17.
b Job 3.11. ch. 6.3. Matt. 24.19. Luke 23.29.
2 all the rightness of work.
3 this is the envy of a man from his neighbour.
c Pro. 6.10.
d Pro. 27.20. ch. 1.8. Hab. 2.5,6. 1 John 2.16.
e Ps. 39.6. Luke 12.20.
4 who knoweth not to be admonished.

CHAP. 5

a Ex. 3.5. Josh. 5.15. Ps. 89.7. Isa. 1.12.
b 1 Sam. 15. 22. Ps. 50.8. Pro. 15.8. Hosea 6.6.
1 Or, word.
c Ps. 39.1. Pro. 10.19. Matt. 6.7.
d Gen. 28.20. Num. 30.2. Ps. 50.14. Isa. 19.21.
e Ps. 66.13, 14. Jonah 2.9.
f Pro. 20.25. Acts 5.4.
g 1 Cor. 11. 10. 1 Tim. 5.21.
h Deut. 10.12. Pro. 23.17. ch. 12.13. Heb. 12.28.

8 ¶ If thou [i]seest the oppression of the poor, and violent perverting of judgment and justice in a province, marvel not [2]at the matter: for [j]*he that is* higher than the highest regardeth; and *there be* higher than they.

9 ¶ Moreover the profit of the earth is for all: the king *himself* is served by the field.

10 He that loveth silver shall not be satisfied with silver; nor he that loveth abundance with increase: this *is* also vanity.

11 When goods increase, they are increased that eat them: and what good *is there* to the owners thereof, saving the beholding *of them* with their eyes?

12 The sleep of a labouring man *is* sweet, whether he eat little or much: but the abundance of the rich will not suffer him to sleep.

13 There [k]is a sore evil *which* I have seen under the sun, *namely*, riches kept for the owners thereof to their hurt.

14 But those riches perish by evil travail: and he begetteth a son, and *there is* nothing in his hand.

15 As [l]he came forth of his mother's womb, naked shall he return to go as he came, and shall take nothing of his labour, which he may carry away in his hand.

16 And this also *is* a sore evil, *that* in all points as he came, so shall he go: and [m]what profit hath he that [n]hath laboured for the wind?

17 All his days also he [o]eateth in darkness, and *he hath* much sorrow and wrath with his sickness.

18 ¶ Behold *that* which I have seen: [3]*it is* good and comely *for one* to eat and to drink, and to enjoy the good of all his labour that he taketh under the sun [4]all the days of his life, which God giveth him: for it *is* his portion.

19 Every man also to whom God hath given riches and wealth, and hath given him power to eat thereof, and to take his portion, and to rejoice in his labour; this *is* the gift of God.

20 [5]For he shall not much remember the days of his life; because [p]God answereth *him* in the joy of his heart.

CHAPTER 6

THERE is an evil which I have seen under the sun, and it *is* common among men:

2 A man to whom God hath given riches, wealth, and honour, so [a]that he wanteth nothing for his soul of all that he desireth, yet God [b]giveth him not power to eat thereof, but a stranger eateth it: this *is* vanity, and it *is* an evil disease.

3 ¶ If a man beget an hundred *children*, and live many years, so that the days of his years be many, and his soul be not filled with good, and [c]also *that* he have no burial; I say, [d]*that* an untimely birth *is* better than he.

4 For he cometh in with vanity, and departeth in darkness, and his name shall be covered with darkness.

5 Moreover he hath not seen the sun, nor known *any thing:* this hath more rest than the other.

6 ¶ Yea, though he live a thousand years twice *told*, yet hath he seen no good: do not all go to one place?

7 All [e]the labour of man *is* for his mouth, and yet the [1]appetite is not filled.

8 For what hath the wise more than the fool? what hath the poor, that knoweth to walk before the living?

9 ¶ Better *is* the sight of the eyes [2]than the wandering of the desire: this *is* also vanity and vexation of spirit.

10 That which hath been is named already, and it is known that it *is* man: neither [f]may he contend with him that is mightier than he.

11 ¶ Seeing there be many things that increase vanity, what *is* man the better?

12 For who knoweth what *is* good for man in *this* life, [3]all the days of his vain life which he spendeth as [g]a shadow? for [h]who can tell a man what shall be after him under the sun?

CHAPTER 7

A GOOD name *is* better than precious ointment; and [a]the day of death than the day of one's birth.

2 ¶ *It is* better to go to the [b]house of mourning, than to go to the house of feasting: for that *is* the end of all men; and the living will lay *it* to his heart.

3 [1]Sorrow *is* better than laughter: for [c]by the sadness of the countenance the heart is made better.

4 The heart of the wise *is* in the house of mourning; but the heart of fools *is* in the house of mirth.

5 *It is* better to hear the rebuke of the wise, than for a man to hear the song of fools.

6 For as the [2]crackling of thorns under a pot, so *is* the laughter of the fool: this also *is* vanity.

7 ¶ Surely oppression maketh a wise man mad; [d]and a gift destroyeth the heart.

i ch. 3.16.
2 at the will, or, purpose.
j Ps. 12.5. Isa. 57.15.
k ch. 6.1.
l Job 1.21. Ps. 49.17. 1 Tim. 6.7.
m ch. 1.3.
n Pro. 11.29.
o Ps. 127.2.
3 there is a good which is comely, etc.
4 the number of the days.
5 Or, Though he give not much, yet he remembereth, etc.
p Ex. 23.25.

CHAP. 6

a Deut. 8.7-10. Judg. 18.10. Job 21.10. Ps. 17.14. Luke 12.19.
b Luke 12.20.
c 2 Ki. 9.35. Esther 7.10. Isa. 14.19.
d Job 3.16. Ps. 58.8.
e Pro. 16.26. 1 Tim. 6.6-8.
1 soul.
2 than the walking of the soul.
f Job 9.32. Isa. 45.9. Rom. 9.19, 20.
3 the number of the days of the life of his vanity.
g Jas. 4.14.
h Ps. 39.6.

CHAP. 7

a Phil. 1.23. Rev. 14.13.
b Matt. 5.4.
1 Or, Anger.
c 2 Cor. 7.10.
2 sound.
d Ex. 23.8.

8 Better *is* the end of a thing than the
beginning thereof: [e]*and* the patient in
spirit *is* better than the proud in spirit.
9 Be [f]not hasty in thy spirit to be
angry: for anger resteth in the bosom
of fools.
10 Say not thou, What is *the cause*
that the former days were better than
these? for thou dost not inquire
[3]wisely concerning this.
11 ¶ Wisdom *is* [4]good with an inheritance: and *by it there is* profit to them
that see the sun.
12 For wisdom *is* a [5]defence, *and*
money *is* a defence: but the excellency
of knowledge *is*, *that* wisdom giveth
life to them that have it.
13 Consider the work of God: for
[g]who can make *that* straight, which
he hath made crooked?
14 In the day of prosperity be joyful,
but in the day of adversity consider:
God also hath [6]set the one over against
the other, to the end that man should
find nothing after him.
15 All *things* have I seen in the days
of my vanity: [h]there is a just *man* that
perisheth in his righteousness, and
there is a wicked *man* that prolongeth
his life in his wickedness.
16 Be [i]not righteous over much;
neither [j]make thyself over wise: why
shouldest thou [7]destroy thyself?
17 Be not over much wicked, neither
be thou foolish: [k]why shouldest thou
die [8]before thy time?
18 *It is* good that thou shouldest take
hold of this; yea, also from this withdraw not thine hand: for he that feareth God shall come forth of them all.
19 Wisdom strengtheneth the wise
more than ten mighty *men* which are
in the city.
20 For [l]*there is* not a just man upon
earth, that doeth good, and sinneth
not.
21 Also [9]take no heed unto all words
that are spoken; lest thou hear thy
servant curse thee:
22 For oftentimes also thine own
heart knoweth that thou thyself likewise hast cursed others.
23 ¶ All this have I proved by wisdom: I said, I will be wise; but it *was*
far from me.
24 That which is far off, [m]and exceeding deep, who can find it out?
25 [10]I applied mine heart to know,
and to search, and to seek out wisdom, and the reason *of things*, and to
know the wickedness of folly, even of
foolishness *and* madness:
26 And I find more bitter than death
the woman, whose heart *is* snares and
nets, *and* her hands *as* bands: [11]whoso
pleaseth God shall escape from her;
but the sinner shall be taken by her.
27 Behold, this have I found, saith
the preacher, [12]*counting* one by one,
to find out the account:
28 Which yet my soul seeketh, but I
find not: one man among a thousand
have I found; but a woman among all
those have I not found.
29 Lo, this only have I found, that
[n]God hath made man upright; but
they have sought out many inventions.

CHAPTER 8

WHO *is* as the wise *man?* and who
knoweth the interpretation of a
thing? a man's wisdom maketh his
face to shine, and [1]the boldness of his
face shall be changed.
2 I *counsel thee* to keep the king's
commandment, [a] and *that* in regard of
the oath of God.
3 Be not hasty to go out of his sight:
stand not in an evil thing; for he doeth
whatsoever pleaseth him.
4 Where the word of a king *is*, *there*
is power: [b]and who may say unto him,
What doest thou?
5 Whoso keepeth the command-
ment [2]shall feel no evil thing: and a
wise man's heart discerneth both time
and judgment.
6 ¶ Because [c]to every purpose there
is time and judgment, therefore the
misery of man *is* great upon him.
7 For [d]he knoweth not that which
shall be: for who can tell him [3]when
it shall be?
8 *There* [e]*is* no man that hath power
[f]over the spirit to retain the spirit;
neither *hath he* power in the day of
death: and *there is* no [4]discharge in
that war; neither shall wickedness deliver those that are given to it.
9 All this have I seen, and applied
my heart unto every work that is done
under the sun: *there is* a time wherein [g]one man ruleth over another to his
own hurt.
10 And so I saw the wicked buried,
who had come and gone from the
place of the holy, and they were forgotten in the city where they had so
done: this *is* also vanity.
11 Because [h]sentence against an evil
work is not executed speedily, therefore the heart of the sons of men is
fully set in them to do evil.
12 ¶ Though [i]a sinner do evil an hundred times, and his *days* be prolonged,
yet surely I know that [j]it shall be well

e Pro. 14.29.
f Pro. 16.32.
3 out of wisdom.
4 Or, as good as an inheritance, yea, better too.
5 shadow.
g Isa. 14.27.
6 made.
h ch. 8.14.
i Pro. 25.16. Phil. 3.6.
j Rom. 12.3.
7 be desolate?
k Job 15.32.
8 not in thy time?
l 1 Ki. 8.46. 2 Chr. 6.36. Pro. 20.9. Rom. 3.23. Gal. 3.22. 1 John 1.8.
9 give not thine heart.
m Deut. 30. 11-14. Job 11.12. Ps. 36.6. Isa. 55.8,9. Rom. 11.33. 1 Tim. 6.16.
10 I and my heart compassed.
11 he that is good before God.
12 Or, weighing one thing after another, to find out the reason.
n Gen. 1.27.

CHAP. 8

1 the strength.
a Rom. 13.5.
b Job 34.18.
2 shall know.
c ch. 3.1.
d Pro. 24.22. ch. 6.12.
3 Or, how it shall be?
e Ps. 49.6.
f Job 14.5.
4 Or, casting off weapons.
g 1 Sam. 18. 12.
h Job 21.14, 15. Ps. 10.6. Isa. 26.10. Rom. 2.4,5. 2 Pet. 3.4,10.
i Isa. 65.20. Rom. 2.5.
j Pro. 1.32. Isa. 3.10. Matt. 25.34.

with them that fear God, which fear before him:

13 But it shall not be well with the wicked, neither shall he prolong *his* days, *which are* as a shadow; because he feareth not before God.

14 There is a vanity which is done upon the earth; that there be just *men*, unto whom it happeneth according to the work of the wicked; again, there be wicked *men*, to whom it [k]happeneth according to the work of the righteous: I said that this also *is* vanity.

15 Then [l]I commended mirth, because a man hath no better thing under the sun, than to eat, and to drink, and to be merry: for that shall abide with him of his labour the days of his life, [m]which God giveth him under the sun.

16 ¶ When I applied mine heart to know wisdom, and to see the business that is done upon the earth: (for also *there is that* neither day nor night seeth sleep with his eyes:)

17 Then I beheld all the work of God, that a [n]man cannot find out the work that is done under the sun: because though a man labour to seek *it* out, yet he shall not find *it;* yea further; though a wise *man* think to know *it*, [o]yet shall he not be able to find *it*.

CHAPTER 9

FOR all this [1]I considered in my heart even to declare all this, that [a]the righteous, and the wise, and their works, *are* in the hand of God: no man knoweth either love or hatred *by* all *that is* before them.

2 All [b]*things come* alike to all: *there is* one event to the righteous, and to the wicked; to the good and to the clean, and to the unclean; to him that sacrificeth, and to him that sacrificeth not: as *is* the good, so *is* the sinner; *and* he that sweareth, as *he* that feareth an oath.

3 This *is* an evil among all *things* that are done under the sun, that *there is* one event unto all: yea, also the heart of the sons of men is full of evil, and madness *is* in their heart while they live, and after that *they go* to the dead.

4 ¶ For to him that is joined to all the living there is hope: for a living dog is better than a dead lion.

5 For the living know that they shall die: but [c]the dead know not any thing, neither have they any more a reward; for [d]the memory of them is forgotten.

6 Also their love, and their hatred, and their envy, is now perished; neither have they any more a portion for ever in any *thing* that is done under the sun.

7 ¶ Go thy way, [e]eat thy bread with joy, and drink thy wine with a merry heart; for God now accepteth thy works.

8 Let thy garments be always white; and let thy head lack no ointment.

9 [2]Live joyfully with the wife whom thou lovest all the days of the life of thy vanity, which he hath given thee under the sun, all the days of thy vanity: [f]for that *is* thy portion in *this* life, and in thy labour which thou takest under the sun.

10 Whatsoever thy hand findeth to do, do *it* with thy might; for *there is* no work, nor device, nor knowledge, nor wisdom, in the grave, whither thou goest.

11 ¶ I [g]returned, and saw under the sun, that the race *is* not to the swift, nor the battle to the strong, neither yet bread to the wise, nor yet riches to men of understanding, nor yet favour to men of skill; but time and chance happeneth to them all.

12 For [h]man also knoweth not his time: as the fishes that are taken in an evil net, and as the birds that are caught in the snare; so *are* the sons of men [i]snared in an evil time, when it falleth suddenly upon them.

13 ¶ This wisdom have I seen also under the sun, and it *seemed* great unto me:

14 *There* [j]*was* a little city, and few men within it; and there came a great king against it, and besieged it, and built great bulwarks against it:

15 Now there was found in it a poor wise man, and he by his wisdom delivered the city; yet no man remembered that same poor man.

16 Then [k]said I, Wisdom *is* better than strength: nevertheless [l]the poor man's wisdom *is* despised, and his words are not heard.

17 The [m]words of wise *men are* heard in quiet more than the cry of him that ruleth among fools.

18 Wisdom *is* better than weapons of war: but [n]one sinner destroyeth much good.

CHAPTER 10

[1]DEAD flies cause the ointment of the apothecary to send forth a stinking savour: *so doth* a little folly him that is in reputation for wisdom *and* honour.

k Ps. 73.14. ch. 2.14.
l ch. 3.12.
m Lev. 26.5.
n Job 5.9. ch. 3.11. Isa. 40.28. Rom. 11.33.
o Ps. 73.16.

CHAP. 9

1 I gave, or, set to my heart.
a 1 Sam. 2.9. Job 5.8. Pro. 16.3. ch. 8.14. Isa. 26.12. 2 Cor. 3.5. 1 Pet. 1.5.
b Ps. 73.3, 12,13,17. Mal. 3.15.
c Job 14,21. Ps. 6.5. Isa. 63.16.
d Job 7.8. Isa. 26.14.
e ch. 8.15.
2 See, or, Enjoy life.
f ch. 2.10,24.
g Amos 2.14. Jer. 9.23.
h ch. 8.7.
i Pro. 29.6. Luke 12.20. 1 Thes. 5.3.
j 2 Sam. 20. 16-22.
k Pro. 21.22. ch. 7.19.
l Mark 6.2.
m Gen. 41. 14. 2 Sam. 20. 17. Dan. 5.10.
n Josh. 7.1. 2 Ki. 17.21. Rom. 6.12, 16-23.

CHAP. 10

1 Flies of death.

A wise [a]man's heart *is* at his right
ınd; but a fool's heart at his left.
Yea also, when he that is a fool
alketh by the way, [2]his wisdom fail-
h *him*, [b]and he saith to every one
at he *is* a fool.
If the spirit of the ruler rise up
ainst thee, [c]leave not thy place; for
ielding pacifieth great offences.
There is an evil *which* I have seen
nder the sun, as an error *which* pro-
edeth [3]from the ruler:
Folly is set [4]in great dignity, and
e rich sit in low place.
I have seen servants [e]upon horses,
d princes walking as servants upon
e earth.
He that diggeth a pit shall fall into
; and whoso breaketh an hedge, a
rpent shall bite him.
Whoso removeth stones shall be
ırt therewith; *and* he that cleaveth
ood shall be endangered thereby.
0 If the iron be blunt, and he do not
het the edge, then must he put to
ore strength: but wisdom *is* profit-
le to direct.
1 Surely the serpent will [f]bite with-
ıt enchantment; and [5]a babbler is
better.
2 The words of a wise man's mouth
e [6]gracious; but the lips of a fool will
vallow up himself.
3 The beginning of the words of
s mouth *is* foolishness: and the
d of [7]his talk *is* mischievous mad-
ss.
4 A fool also [8]is full of words: a
an cannot tell what shall be; and
hat shall be [g]after him, who can
ll him?
5 The labour of the foolish wearieth
ery one of them, because he know-
h not how to go to the city.
6 ¶ Woe [h]to thee, O land, when thy
ng *is* a child, and thy princes eat in
e morning!
7 Blessed *art* thou, O land, when
y king *is* the son of nobles, and thy
rinces eat in due season, for strength,
d not for drunkenness!
8 ¶ By much slothfulness the build-
g decayeth; and through idleness
the hands the house droppeth
rough.
9 ¶ A feast is made for laughter,
d wine [9]maketh merry: but money
swereth all *things*.
0 ¶ Curse [j]not the king, no not in
y [10]thought; and curse not the rich
thy bedchamber: for a bird of the
r shall carry the voice, and that which
th wings shall tell the matter.

a Matt. 6.33. Col. 3.1.
2 his heart.
b Pro. 13.16.
c ch. 8.3.
d 1 Sam. 25. 24. Pro. 25.15.
3 from before.
4 in great heights.
e Pro. 19.10.
f Jer. 8.17.
5 the master of the tongue.
6 grace.
7 his mouth.
8 multiplieth words.
g Jas. 4.14.
h Isa. 3.4.
i Pro. 31.4.
9 maketh glad the life.
j Ex. 22.28.
10 Or, conscience.

CHAP. 11

1 upon the face of the waters.
a Deut. 15. 10. Pro. 11.18. Matt. 10.42. 2 Cor. 9.6.
b Ps. 112.9. Luke 6.30.
c Micah 5.5.
d Eph. 5.16.
e John 3.8.
2 shall be right.
f Deut. 29.19. Ps. 81.12. Acts 14.16. Eph. 2.2,3.
g ch. 12.14. Rom. 2.6.
3 Or, anger.
h 2 Cor. 7.1.

CHAP. 12

a Ps. 71.9. Zech. 8.4. 2 Cor. 5.1.
1 Or, the grinders fail, because they grind little.
b Gen. 27.1.
c Micah 7.1.
d 2 Sam. 19. 35.

CHAPTER 11

CAST thy bread [1]upon the waters:
[a]for thou shalt find it after many
days.
2 Give [b]a portion [c]to seven, and also
to eight; [d]for thou knowest not what
evil shall be upon the earth.
3 If the clouds be full of rain, they
empty *themselves* upon the earth: and
if the tree fall toward the south, or toward the north, in the place where the
tree falleth, there it shall be.
4 He that observeth the wind shall
not sow; and he that regardeth the
clouds shall not reap.
5 As [e]thou knowest not what *is* the
way of the spirit, *nor* how the bones
do grow in the womb of her that is
with child: even so thou knowest not
the works of God who maketh all.
6 In the morning sow thy seed, and
in the evening withhold not thine
hand: for thou knowest not whether
[2]shall prosper, either this or that, or
whether they both *shall be* alike
good.
7 ¶ Truly the light *is* sweet, and a
pleasant *thing it is* for the eyes to behold the sun:
8 But if a man live many years, *and*
rejoice in them all; yet let him remember the days of darkness; for they shall
be many. All that cometh *is* vanity.
9 ¶ Rejoice, O young man, in thy
youth; and let thy heart cheer thee in
the days of thy youth, [f]and walk in the
ways of thine heart, and in the sight
of thine eyes: but know thou, that for
all these *things* God [g]will bring thee
into judgment.
10 Therefore remove [3]sorrow from
thy heart, [h]and put away evil from thy
flesh: for childhood and youth *are*
vanity.

CHAPTER 12

REMEMBER now thy Creator in
the days of thy youth, while the
evil days come not, nor the years draw
nigh, when thou shalt say, I have no
pleasure in them;
2 While the sun, or the light, or the
moon, or the stars, be not darkened,
nor the clouds return after the rain:
3 In the days when the keepers of [a]the
house shall tremble, and the strong
men shall bow themselves, and [1]the
grinders cease because they are few,
and [b]those that look out of the windows be darkened,
4 And the [c]doors shall be shut in the
streets, when the sound of the grinding is low, and he shall rise up at the
voice of the bird, and all [d]the daugh-

ters of musick shall be brought
low;
5 Also *when* they shall be afraid of
that which is high, and fears *shall be* in
the way, and the [e]almond tree shall
flourish, and the grasshopper shall be
a burden, and desire shall fail: because man goeth to his long home, and
the mourners go about the streets:
6 Or ever the silver cord be loosed,
or the golden bowl be broken, or the
pitcher be broken at the fountain, or
the wheel broken at the cistern.
7 Then [f]shall the dust return to
the earth as it was: [g]and the spirit
shall return unto God [h]who gave
it.
8 ¶ Vanity of vanities, saith the
preacher; all *is* vanity.
9 And [2]moreover, because the preacher was wise, he still taught the people
knowledge; yea, he gave good heed,
and sought out, *and* set in order man
proverbs.
10 The preacher sought to find ou
[3]acceptable words: and *that which* wa
written *was* upright, *even* words c
truth.
11 The words of the wise *are* a
goads, and as nails fastened *by* th
masters of assemblies, *which* are give
from one shepherd.
12 And further, by these, my son, b
admonished: of making many book
there is no end; and much [4]study *is*
weariness of the flesh.
13 ¶ [5]Let us hear the conclusion o
the whole matter: Fear God, an
keep his commandments: for this
the whole *duty* of man.
14 For [i]God shall bring every wor
into judgment, with every secre
thing, whether *it be* good, or wheth
it be evil.

e Lev. 19.32.
f Gen. 3.19.
g ch. 3.21.
h Gen. 2.7. Num. 16.22.
2 Or, the more wise the preacher was, etc.
3 words of delight.
4 Or, reading.
5 Or, The end of the matter, even all that hath been heard, is.
i Matt. 12.36.

THE

SONG OF SOLOMON

CHAPTER 1

THE [a]song of songs, which *is*
Solomon's.
2 Let him kiss me with the kisses of
his mouth: for [1]thy love *is* better than
wine.
3 Because of the savour of thy good
ointments thy name *is as* ointment
poured forth, therefore do the [b]vir-
gins love thee.
4 Draw [c]me, we [d]will run after thee:
the king [e]hath brought me into his
chambers: we will be glad and rejoice
in thee, we will remember thy love
more than wine: [2]the upright love
thee.
5 I *am* black, but comely, O ye
daughters of Jerusalem, as the tents
of Kē-dār, as the curtains of Solomon.
6 Look not upon me, because I *am*
black, because the sun hath looked
upon me: my mother's children were
angry with me; they made me the
keeper of the vineyards; *but* mine own
vineyard have I not kept.
7 Tell me, O thou whom my soul
loveth, where thou feedest, where
thou [f]makest *thy flock* to rest at noon:
for why should I be [3]as one that turneth aside by the flocks of thy companions?
8 ¶ If thou know not, O thou fairest
among women, go thy way forth b
the footsteps of the flock, and fee
thy kids beside the shepherds' tents.
9 I have compared thee, [g]O my lov
[h]to a company of horses in Pharaoh
chariots.
10 Thy [i]cheeks are comely with row
of jewels, thy neck with chains *of gol*
11 We will make thee borders o
gold with studs of silver.
12 ¶ While the king *sitteth* at h
table, my spikenard sendeth forth th
smell thereof.
13 A bundle of myrrh *is* my wel
beloved unto me; he shall lie all nigl
betwixt my breasts.
14 My beloved *is* unto me *as* a clust
of [4]camphire in the vineyards of Ĕn
ġē-dī.
15 Behold, [j]thou *art* fair, [5]my love
behold, thou *art* fair; thou *hast* dove
eyes.
16 Behold, thou *art* fair, my belove
yea, pleasant: also our bed *is* green.
17 The beams of our house *are* ceda
and our [6]rafters of fir.

CHAP. 1
a 1 Ki. 4.32.
1 thy loves.
b ch. 6.8. Matt. 25.1. 2 Cor. 11.2.
c Jer. 31.3. Hos. 11.4. John 6.44.
d Phil. 3.12.
e Ps. 45.14. John 14.2. Eph. 2.6.
2 Or, they love thee uprightly.
f John 10.27.
3 Or, as one that is veiled.
g ch. 2.2.
h 2 Chr. 1.16.
i Eze. 16.11.
4 Or, cypress.
j ch. 4.1.
5 Or, my companion.
6 Or, galleries.

CHAPTER 2

I *AM* the rose of Shār-ŏn, *and* th
lily of the valleys.
2 As the lily among thorns, so *is* m
love among the daughters.

3 As the apple tree among the trees
f the wood, so *is* my beloved among
ie sons. [1]I sat down under his shadow
'ith great delight, and [a]his fruit *was*
weet to my [2]taste.
4 He brought me to the [3]banqueting
ouse, and his banner over me *was*
ove.
5 Stay me with flagons, [4]comfort me
'ith apples: for I *am* sick of love.
6 His [b]left hand *is* under my head,
nd his right hand doth embrace me.
7 [5]I charge you, O ye daughters of
erusalem, by the roes, and by the
inds of the field, that ye stir not up,
or awake *my* love, till he please.
8 ¶ The [c]voice of my beloved! beold, he cometh leaping upon the
ountains, skipping upon the hills.
9 My beloved is like a roe or a young
art: behold, he standeth behind our
all, he looketh forth at the windows,
hewing himself through the lattice.
10 My beloved spake, and said unto
ie, Rise up, my love, my fair one,
nd come away.
11 For, lo, the winter is past, the
in is over *and* gone;
12 The flowers appear on the earth;
ie time of the singing *of birds* is
ome, and the voice of the turtle is
eard in our land;
13 The fig tree putteth forth her
reen figs, and the vines *with* the ten-
er grape give a *good* smell. Arise, my
ove, my fair one, and come away.
14 ¶ O my dove, *that art* in the clefts
f the rock, in the secret *places* of the
tairs, [d]let me see thy countenance,
t me hear thy voice; for sweet *is* thy
oice, and thy countenance *is* comely.
15 Take us [e]the foxes, the little foxes,
iat spoil the vines: for our vines *have*
ender grapes.
16 ¶ My [f]beloved *is* mine, and I *am*
is: he feedeth among the lilies.
17 Until [g]the day break, and the
hadows flee away, turn, my beloved,
nd be thou [h]like a roe or a young
art upon the mountains [7]of Bē-thĕr.

CHAPTER 3

BY [a]night on my bed I sought him
whom my soul loveth: I sought
im, but I found him not.
2 I will rise now, and go about the
ty in the streets, and in the broad
ays I will seek him whom my soul
oveth: I sought him, but I found him
ot.
3 The [b]watchmen that go about the
ty found me: *to whom I said*, Saw
e him whom my soul loveth?

CHAP. 2
1 I delighted and sat down, etc.
a Gen. 3.6. Rev. 22.1.
2 palate.
3 house of wine.
4 straw me with apples.
b ch. 8.3.
5 I adjure you.
c John 10.4.
6 flourishing.
d ch. 8.13.
e Ps. 80.13. Eze. 13.4. Luke 13.32.
f ch. 6.3.
g ch. 4.6. Luke 1.78. Rom. 13.12. 2 Pet. 1.19.
h ch. 8.14.
7 Or, of division.

CHAP. 3
a Ps. 4.6. Ps. 6.6. Isa. 26.9.
b ch. 5.7. Isa. 21.6-8, 11,12.
c Pro. 8.17.
d Pro. 4.13. Rom. 8.35, 39.
e ch. 2.7.
f ch. 8.5. Jer. 2.2.
1 Or, a bed, or, throne.
g Matt. 22.37. John 13.1, 34. Rom. 5.8. Eph. 3.19. 1 Pet. 1.7,8.
h Ps. 110.3. Isa. 62.5. Rev. 11.15.

CHAP. 4
a ch. 1.15.
b ch. 6.5.
1 Or, that eat of, etc.
c ch. 6.6.
d 2 Sam. 22. 51. ch. 1.10.
e Neh. 3.19.
f Pro. 5.19. ch. 1.13. Isa. 66.10-12. 1 Pet. 2.2.
2 breathe.
g Eph. 5.27.

4 *It was* but [c]a little that I passed
from them, but I found him whom my
soul loveth: [d]I held him, and would
not let him go, until I had brought
him into my mother's house, and into
the chamber of her that conceived me.
5 I [e]charge you, O ye daughters of
Jerusalem, by the roes, and by the
hinds of the field, that ye stir not up,
nor awake *my* love, till he please.
6 ¶ Who [f]*is* this that cometh out of
the wilderness like pillars of smoke,
perfumed with myrrh and frankincense, with all powders of the merchant?
7 Behold his bed, which *is* Solomon's; threescore valiant men *are*
about it, of the valiant of Israel.
8 They all hold swords, *being* expert
in war: every man *hath* his sword upon his thigh because of fear in the
night.
9 King Solomon made himself [1]a
chariot of the wood of Lĕb-ā-nọn.
10 He made the pillars thereof *of*
silver, the bottom thereof *of* gold, the
covering of it *of* purple, the midst
thereof being paved [g]*with* love, for the
daughters of Jerusalem.
11 Go forth, O ye daughters of Zion,
and behold king Solomon with the
crown wherewith his mother crowned
him in the [h]day of his espousals, and
in the day of the gladness of his heart.

CHAPTER 4

BEHOLD, [a]thou *art* fair, my love;
behold, thou *art* fair; thou *hast*
doves' eyes within thy locks: thy hair
is as a [b]flock of goats, [1]that appear
from mount Gilead.
2 Thy [c]teeth *are* like a flock *of sheep*
that are even shorn, which came up
from the washing; whereof every one
bear twins, and none *is* barren among
them.
3 Thy lips *are* like a thread of scarlet,
and thy speech *is* comely: thy temples
are like a piece of a pomegranate within thy locks.
4 Thy [d]neck *is* like the tower of
David builded [e]for an armoury,
whereon there hang a thousand bucklers, all shields of mighty men.
5 Thy [f]two breasts *are* like two
young roes that are twins, which feed
among the lilies.
6 Until the day [2]break, and the
shadows flee away, I will get me to
the mountain of myrrh, and to the hill
of frankincense.
7 Thou [g]*art* all fair, my love; *there is*
no spot in thee.

8 ¶ Come with me from Lĕb-ā-non,
my spouse, with me from Lĕb-ā-non:
look from the top of Ă-mā-nă, from
the top of Shē-nĭr and [h]Hĕr-mon,
from the lions' dens, from the mountains of the leopards.
9 Thou hast [3]ravished my heart, my
sister, *my* [i]spouse; thou hast ravished
my heart with one of thine eyes, with
one chain of thy neck.
10 How fair is thy love, my sister,
my spouse! how much better is thy
love than wine! and the smell of thine
ointments than all spices!
11 Thy lips, O *my* spouse, drop *as*
the honeycomb: [j]honey and milk *are*
under thy tongue; and the smell of
thy garments *is* [k]like the smell of Lĕb-
ā-non.
12 A [l]garden [4]inclosed *is* my sister,
my spouse; a spring shut up, a fountain sealed.
13 Thy plants *are* an orchard of
pomegranates, with pleasant fruits;
[5]camphire, with spikenard,
14 Spikenard and saffron; calamus
and cinnamon, with all trees of
frankincense; myrrh and aloes, with
all the chief spices:
15 A fountain of gardens, a well of
[m]living waters, and streams from
Lĕb-ā-non.
16 ¶ Awake, O north wind; and
come, thou south; blow upon my garden, *that* the [n]spices thereof may flow
out. [o]Let my beloved come into his
garden, and eat his pleasant fruits.

CHAPTER 5

I AM [a]come into my garden, my
sister, *my* spouse: I have gathered
my myrrh with my spice; I have eaten
my honeycomb with my honey; I
have drunk my wine with my milk:
eat, O [b]friends; drink, [1]yea, drink
abundantly, O beloved.
2 ¶ I sleep, but my heart waketh: *it*
is the voice of my beloved [c]that knocketh, *saying*, Open to me, my sister, my
love, my dove, my undefiled: for my
head is filled with dew, *and* my locks
with the drops of the night.
3 I have put off my coat; how shall
I put it on? I have washed my feet;
how shall I defile them?
4 My beloved put in his hand by the
hole *of the door*, and my bowels were
moved [2]for him.
5 I rose up to open to my beloved;
and my hands dropped *with* myrrh,
and my fingers *with* [3]sweet smelling
myrrh, upon the handles of the lock.
6 I opened to my beloved; but my
beloved had [d]withdrawn himself, *a*
was gone: my soul failed when
spake: I sought him, but I could n
find him; I [e]called him, but he ga
me no answer.
7 The [f]watchmen that went abo
the city found me, they smote m
they wounded me; the keepers of t
walls took away my veil from me.
8 I charge you, O daughters of Jer
salem, if ye find my beloved, [4]that
tell him, that I *am* sick of love.
9 ¶ What *is* thy beloved more th
another beloved, O thou faire
among women? what *is* thy belove
more than *another* beloved, that th
dost so charge us?
10 My beloved *is* white and rudd
[5]the chiefest among ten thousand.
11 His head *is as* the most fine gol
his locks *are* [6]bushy, *and* black as
raven.
12 His [g]eyes *are* as *the eyes* of dov
by the rivers of waters, washed wi
milk, *and* [7]fitly set.
13 His cheeks *are* as a bed of spice
as [8]sweet flowers: his lips *like* lilie
dropping sweet smelling myrrh.
14 His hands *are as* gold rings s
with the beryl: his belly *is as* brig
ivory overlaid *with* sapphires.
15 His legs *are as* pillars of marb
set upon sockets of fine gold: h
countenance *is* as Lĕb-ā-non, exce
lent as the cedars.
16 [9]His mouth *is* most sweet: ye
[h]he *is* altogether lovely. This *is* my b
loved, and this *is* my friend, O daug
ters of Jerusalem.

CHAPTER 6

WHITHER is thy beloved gon
O [a]thou fairest among wome
whither is thy beloved turned aside
that we may seek him with thee.
2 My beloved is gone down in
his garden, to the beds of spices, t
[b]feed in the gardens, and to gath
[c]lilies.
3 I [d]*am* my beloved's, and my belo
ed *is* mine: he feedeth among th
lilies.
4 ¶ Thou *art* beautiful, O my lov
as Tĭr-zăh, comely as Jerusale
[e]terrible as *an army* with banners.
5 Turn away thine eyes from me, f
[1]they have overcome me: thy hair
[f]as a flock of goats that appear fro
Gilead.
6 Thy teeth *are* as a flock of shee
which go up from the washing, wher
of every one beareth twins, and *the*
is not one barren among them.

h Deut. 3.9.
3 Or, taken away my heart.
i Isa. 54.5. John 3.29. 2 Cor. 11.2. Rev. 19.7,8.
j Pro. 24.13, 14.
k Gen. 27.27. Hosea 14.6, 7.
l Isa. 58.11. Hosea 3.3.
4 barred.
5 Or, cypress.
m John 4.10.
n Gal. 5.22.
o ch. 5.1.

CHAP. 5
a ch. 4.16.
b Luke 15.7. John 3.29.
1 Or, and be drunken with loves.
c Pro. 8.4. Rev. 3.20.
2 Or (as some read), in me.
3 passing, or, running about.
d Hosea 5.15.
e Lam. 3.8.
f ch. 3.3. Acts 20.29, 30.
4 what.
5 a standard-bearer.
6 Or, curled.
g ch. 1.15.
7 sitting in fulness, that is, fitly placed, and set as a precious stone in the foil of a ring.
8 Or, towers of perfumes.
9 His palate.
h Ps. 45.2. Jer. 31.3. Rom. 8.35. Phil. 3.8.

CHAP. 6
a ch. 1.8.
b Isa. 40.11. Zeph. 3.17. Rev. 7.17.
c Isa. 56.8. John 10.16.
d ch. 2.16. Rev. 21.2.
e 2 Cor. 10.4.
1 Or, they have puffed me up.
f ch. 4.1.

7 As a piece of a pomegranate *are*
hy temples within thy locks.
8 There are threescore queens, and
ourscore concubines, and virgins
vithout number.
9 My dove, my undefiled is *but* one;
he *is* the *only* one of her mother, she
s the choice *one* of her that bare her.
The daughters saw her, and blessed
ier; *yea,* the queens and the concubines, and they praised her.
10 ¶ Who *is* she *that* looketh forth as
he morning, fair as the moon, clear
is the sun, *and* terrible as *an army*
vith banners?
11 I went down into the garden of
nuts to see the fruits of the valley, *and*
to see whether the vine flourished,
and the pomegranates budded.
12 [2]Or ever I was aware, my soul
made me *like* the chariots of Ăm-
mĭn-′ă-dĭb.
13 Return, return, O Shû-′lă-mīte;
eturn, return, that we may look upon
hee. What will ye see in the Shû-′lă-
mīte? As it were the company [4]of two
armies.

CHAPTER 7

HOW beautiful are thy feet with
shoes, [a]O prince's daughter! the
joints of thy thighs *are* like jewels, the
work of the hands of a cunning workman.
2 Thy navel *is like* a round goblet,
which wanteth not [1]liquor: thy belly
is like an heap of wheat set about with
lilies.
3 Thy [b]two breasts *are* like two
young roes *that are* twins.
4 Thy neck *is* as a tower of ivory;
thine eyes *like* the fishpools in Hĕsh′-
bŏn, by the gate of Băth–răb′-bĭm:
thy nose *is* as the tower of Lĕb′-
ă-non which looketh toward Damascus.
5 Thine head upon thee *is* like [2]Car-
mel, and the hair of thine head like
purple; the king *is* [3]held in the galleries.
6 How fair and how pleasant art
thou, O love, for delights!
7 This thy stature is like to a palm
tree, and thy breasts to clusters *of*
grapes.
8 I said, I will go up to the palm tree,
I will take hold of the boughs thereof:
now also thy breasts shall be as clusters of the vine, and the smell of thy
nose like apples;
9 And the roof of thy mouth like the
best wine for my beloved, that goeth
down [4]sweetly, causing the lips [5]of
those that are asleep to speak.

10 ¶ I [c]*am* my beloved's, and [d]his desire *is* toward me.
11 Come, my beloved, let us go forth
into the field; let us lodge in the villages.
12 Let us get up early to the vineyards; let us [e]see if the vine flourish,
whether the tender grape [6]appear, *and*
the pomegranates bud forth: there
will [f]I give thee my loves.
13 The [g]mandrakes give a smell,
and at our gates [h]*are* all manner of
pleasant *fruits,* new and old, *which* I
have laid up for thee, O my beloved.

CHAPTER 8

O THAT thou *wert* as my brother,
that sucked the breasts of my
mother! *when* I should find thee without, I would kiss thee; yea, [1]I should
not be despised.
2 I would lead thee, *and* bring thee
into my mother's house, *who* would
instruct me: I would cause thee to
drink of [a]spiced wine of the juice of
my pomegranate.
3 His [b]left hand *should be* under my
head, and his right hand should embrace me.
4 I charge you, O daughters of Jerusalem, [2]that ye stir not up, nor awake
my love, until he please.
5 Who *is* this that cometh up from
[c]the wilderness, leaning upon her beloved? I raised thee up under the
apple tree: there thy mother brought
thee forth: there she brought thee
forth *that* bare thee.
6 ¶ Set [d]me as a seal upon thine
heart, as a seal upon thine arm: for
[e]love *is* strong as death; jealousy *is*
[3]cruel as the grave: the coals thereof
are coals of fire, *which hath* a most
vehement flame.
7 Many waters cannot quench love,
neither can the floods drown it: [f]if a
man would give all the substance of
his house for love, it would utterly be
contemned.
8 ¶ We [g]have a little sister, and she
hath no breasts: what shall we do for
our sister in the day when she shall be
spoken for?
9 If she *be* a wall, we will build upon
her a palace of silver: and if she *be* [h]a
door, we will inclose her with boards
of cedar.
10 I [i]*am* a wall, and [j]my breasts like
towers: then was I in his eyes as one
that found [4]favour.
11 Solomon had a vineyard at Bā-′ăl-
hā-′mŏn; he [k]let out the vineyard unto
keepers; every one for the fruit there-

g ch. 7.12.
2 I knew not.
3 Or, set me on the chariots of my willing people.
4 Or, of Mahanaim.

CHAP. 7

a Ps. 45.13.
1 mixture.
b ch. 4.5.
2 Or, crimson.
3 bound.
4 straightly.
5 Or, of the ancient.
c ch. 2.16. Gal. 2.20.
d Ps. 45.11.
e ch. 6.11.
6 open.
f Ps. 63.3-8. Ps. 73.25. ch. 4.16.
g Gen. 30.14.
h ch. 5.1. Matt. 13.52. John 15.8.

CHAP. 8

1 they should not despise me.
a Pro. 9.2.
b ch. 2.6. Isa. 62.4,5. 2 Cor. 12.9.
2 why should ye stir up, or, why, etc.
c John 17.14.
d Isa. 49.16. Jer. 22.24. Hag. 2.23.
e Phil. 3.8.
3 hard.
f Pro. 6.35.
g Ps. 22.27.
h Rev. 3.20.
i Col. 2.7.
j Eze. 16.7.
4 peace.
k Matt. 21. 33.

of was to bring a thousand *pieces* of
silver.
12 My vineyard, which *is* mine, *is* before me: thou, O Solomon, *must have*
a thousand, and those that keep the
fruit thereof two hundred.

[l] ch. 2.14.
5 Flee away.
[m] ch. 2.17.

13 Thou that dwellest in the garden
the companions hearken to thy voice
[l]cause me to hear *it*.
14 ¶ [5]Make haste, my beloved, an
[m]be thou like to a roe or to a youn
hart upon the mountains of spices.

THE BOOK OF THE PROPHET

ISAIAH

CHAPTER 1

THE [a]vision of Isaiah the son of
Amoz, which he saw concerning
Judah and Jerusalem in the [b]days of
Ŭz-zī'-ăh, Jō'-thăm, Ahaz, *and* Hĕz-ē-
kī'-ăh, kings of Judah.
2 Hear, O heavens, and give ear, O
earth: for the LORD hath spoken, I
have nourished and brought up children, and they have rebelled against
me.
3 The ox knoweth his owner, and the
ass his master's crib: *but* Israel doth
[c]not know, my people doth not consider.
4 Ah sinful nation, a people [1]laden
with iniquity, a [d]seed of evildoers,
children that are corrupters: they
have forsaken the LORD, they have
provoked the Holy One of Israel unto
anger, they are [2]gone away backward.
5 ¶ Why [e]should ye be stricken any
more? ye will [3]revolt more and more:
the whole head is sick, and the whole
heart faint.
6 From the sole of the foot even unto
the head *there is* no soundness in it;
but wounds, and bruises, and putrify-
ing sores: they [f]have not been closed,
neither bound up, neither mollified
with [4]ointment.
7 Your [g]country *is* desolate, your
cities *are* burned with fire: your land,
strangers devour it in your presence,
and *it is* desolate, [5]as overthrown by
strangers.
8 And the daughter of Zion is left as
a cottage in a vineyard, as a lodge in a
garden of cucumbers, as a besieged
city.
9 Except [h]the LORD of hosts had left
unto us a very small remnant, we
should have been as Sodom, *and* we
should have been like unto Gō-mŏr'-
răh.
10 ¶ Hear the word of the LORD, ye
rulers of [i]Sodom; give ear unto the

CHAP. 1
[a] Num. 12.6.
[b] 2 Ki. 15.1.
[c] Jer. 9.3,6.
1 of heaviness.
[d] ch. 57.3,4.
2 alienated, or, separated.
[e] ch. 9.13. Jer. 2.30.
3 increase revolt.
[f] Jer. 8.22.
4 Or, oil.
[g] Deut. 28. 51.
5 as the overthrow of strangers.
[h] Rom. 9.29.
[i] Eze. 16.46.
[j] Ps. 50.8.
6 great he goats.
7 to be seen.
8 Or, grief.
[k] Job 27.9.
[l] 1 Tim. 2.8.
9 multiply prayer.
10 bloods.
[m] Jer. 4.14.
[n] Rom. 12.9.
[o] Micah 6.8.
11 Or, righten.
[p] 1 Sam. 12.7. ch. 41.21. Micah 6.2.
[q] Ps. 51.7. ch. 44.22. Micah 7.18. Eph. 1.6-8.
[r] Deut. 28.1.
[s] Titus 1.2.
[t] 2 Chr. 36.14. Jer. 5.5. Dan. 9.5. Hosea 9.15.

law of our God, ye people of Gō-mŏ
răh.
11 To what purpose *is* the multitud
of your [j]sacrifices unto me? saith th
LORD: I am full of the burnt offering
of rams, and the fat of fed beasts; an
I delight not in the blood of bullock
or of lambs, or of [6]he goats.
12 When ye come [7]to appear befo
me, who hath required this at you
hand, to tread my courts?
13 Bring no more vain oblations; in
cense is an abomination unto me; th
new moons and sabbaths, the callin
of assemblies, I cannot away with; *i*
is [8]iniquity, even the solemn meeting
14 Your new moons and your ap
pointed feasts my soul hateth: the
are a trouble unto me; I am weary t
bear *them*.
15 And [k]when ye spread forth you
hands, I will hide mine eyes from you
[l]yea, when ye [9]make many prayers,
will not hear: your hands are full o
[10]blood.
16 ¶ Wash [m]you, make you clean
put away the evil of your doings fron
before mine eyes; [n]cease to do evil;
17 Learn to do well; [o]seek judgment
[11]relieve the oppressed, judge the fath
erless, plead for the widow.
18 Come now, and [p]let us reason to
gether, saith the LORD: though you
sins be as scarlet, they [q]shall be a
white as snow; though they be red lik
crimson, they shall be as wool.
19 If [r]ye be willing and obedient, y
shall eat the good of the land:
20 But if ye refuse and rebel, ye sha
be devoured with the sword: for [s]th
mouth of the LORD hath spoken *it*.
21 ¶ How is the faithful city becom
an harlot! it was full of judgment
righteousness lodged in it; but no
murderers.
22 Thy silver is become dross, th
wine mixed with water:
23 Thy [t]princes *are* rebellious, and

companions of thieves: every one
loveth gifts, and followeth after rewards: they judge not the fatherless,
neither doth the cause of the widow
come unto them.
24 Therefore saith the Lord, the
LORD of hosts, the mighty One of Israel, Ah, [u]I will ease me of mine adversaries, and avenge me of mine enemies:
25 ¶ And I [v]will turn my hand upon
thee, and [12]purely purge away thy
dross, and take away all thy tin:
26 And I will restore thy judges as at
the first, and thy counsellers as at the
beginning: afterward thou shalt be
called, The city of righteousness, the
faithful city.
27 Zion shall be redeemed with judgment, and [13]her converts with righteousness.
28 ¶ And the [14]destruction of the
transgressors and of the sinners *shall*
be together, and they that forsake the
LORD shall be consumed.
29 For they shall be ashamed of the
[w]oaks which ye have desired, and [x]ye
shall be confounded for the gardens
that ye have chosen.
30 For ye shall be as an oak whose
leaf fadeth, and as a garden that hath
no water.
31 And the strong shall be as tow,
[15]and the maker of it as a spark, and
they shall both burn together, and
none shall quench *them*.

CHAPTER 2

THE word that Isaiah the son of
Amoz saw concerning Judah and
Jerusalem.
2 And [a]it shall come to pass in the
last days, [b]*that* the mountain of the
LORD's house shall [1]be established in
the top of the mountains, and shall be
exalted above the hills; and all nations shall flow unto it.
3 And many people shall go and say,
Come [c]ye, and let us go up to the
mountain of the LORD, to the house
of the God of Jacob; and he will teach
us of his ways, and we will walk in his
paths: [d]for out of Zion shall go forth
the law, and the word of the LORD
from Jerusalem.
4 And he [e]shall judge among the nations, and shall rebuke many people:
and [f]they shall beat their swords into
plowshares, and their spears into
[2]pruninghooks: nation shall not lift up
sword against nation, neither shall
they learn war any more.
5 O house of Jacob, come ye, and

u Deut. 28. 63.
v Rev. 3.19.
12 according to pureness.
13 Or, they that return of her.
14 breaking.
w ch. 57.5.
x ch. 65.3.
15 Or, and his work.

CHAP. 2

a Micah 4.1. Acts 2.17.
b Dan. 2.35. Rev. 14.1.
1 Or, be prepared.
c Zech. 8.21.
d Luke 24.47.
e John 5.22.
f Hosea 2.18.
2 Or, scythes.
g Acts 26.23.
3 Or, more than the east.
h Deut. 18. 14.
4 Or, abound with the children.
5 Or, nonentities.
i ch. 12.1,4. ch. 24.21,23. ch. 25.9. ch. 26.1. Jer. 30.7,8. Joel 3.18. Amos 9.11. Obad. 8. Micah 5.10.
6 pictures of desire.
7 Or, shall utterly pass away.
j Hosea 10.8. Luke 23.30. Rev. 6.16.
8 the dust.
k 2 Thes. 1.9.
l Ps. 7.6. Nah. 1.3-6. Hab. 3.6. Hag. 2.6. Heb. 12.26.
9 the idols of his silver, etc.
10 Or, which they made for him.
m Pro. 23.4.

let us [g]walk in the light of the
LORD.
6 ¶ Therefore thou hast forsaken thy
people the house of Jacob, because
they be replenished [3]from the east,
and [h]*are* soothsayers like the Philistines, and they [4]please themselves in
the children of strangers.
7 Their land also is full of silver and
gold, neither *is there any* end of their
treasures; their land is also full of
horses, neither *is there any* end of
their chariots:
8 Their land also is full of [5]idols; they
worship the work of their own hands,
that which their own fingers have
made:
9 And the mean man boweth down,
and the great man humbleth himself:
therefore forgive them not.
10 ¶ Enter into the rock, and hide
thee in the dust, for fear of the LORD,
and for the glory of his majesty.
11 The lofty looks of man shall be
humbled, and the haughtiness of men
shall be bowed down, and the LORD
alone shall be exalted in that [i]day.
12 For the day of the LORD of hosts
shall be upon every *one that is* proud
and lofty, and upon every *one that is*
lifted up; and he shall be brought low:
13 And upon all the cedars of Lĕb-ā-
non, *that are* high and lifted up, and
upon all the oaks of Bā-shăn,
14 And upon all the high mountains,
and upon all the hills *that are* lifted
up,
15 And upon every high tower, and
upon every fenced wall,
16 And upon all the ships of Tarshish, and upon all [6]pleasant pictures.
17 And the loftiness of man shall be
bowed down, and the haughtiness of
men shall be made low: and the LORD
alone shall be exalted in that day.
18 And the idols [7]he shall utterly
abolish.
19 And they shall go into [j]the holes
of the rocks, and into the caves of [8]the
earth, for [k]fear of the LORD, and for
the glory of his majesty, when he ariseth [l]to shake terribly the earth.
20 In that day a man shall cast [9]his
idols of silver, and his idols of gold,
[10]which they made *each one* for himself to worship, to the moles and to the
bats;
21 To go into the clefts of the rocks,
and into the tops of the ragged rocks,
for fear of the LORD, and for the glory
of his majesty, when he ariseth to
shake terribly the earth.
22 Cease [m]ye from man, whose

breath *is* in his nostrils: for wherein is he to be accounted of?

CHAPTER 3

FOR, behold, the Lord, the LORD of hosts, doth take away from Jerusalem and from Judah [a]the stay and the staff, the whole stay of bread, and the whole stay of water,

2 The mighty man, and the man of war, the judge, and the prophet, and the prudent, and the ancient,

3 The captain of fifty, and [1]the honourable man, and the counseller, and the cunning artificer, and the [2]eloquent orator.

4 And I will give [b]children *to be* their princes, and babes shall rule over them.

5 And the [c]people shall be oppressed, every one by another, and every one by his neighbour: the child shall behave himself proudly against [d]the ancient, and the base against the honourable.

6 When a man shall take hold of his brother of the house of his father, *saying*, Thou hast clothing, be thou our ruler, and *let* this ruin *be* under thy hand:

7 In that day shall he [3]swear, saying, I will not be an [4]healer; for in my house *is* neither bread nor clothing: make me not a ruler of the people.

8 For Jerusalem is ruined, and Judah is fallen: because their tongue and their doings *are* against the LORD, to provoke the eyes of his glory.

9 ¶ The shew of their countenance doth witness against them; and they declare their sin as Sodom, they hide *it* not. Woe unto their soul! for they have rewarded evil unto themselves.

10 Say ye to the righteous, that *it shall be* well *with him:* for they shall eat the fruit of their doings.

11 Woe unto the wicked! *it shall be* ill *with him:* for the reward of his hands shall be [5]given him.

12 ¶ *As for* my people, children *are* their oppressors, and women rule over them. O my people, [6]they which lead thee cause *thee* to err, and [7]destroy the way of thy paths.

13 The LORD standeth up to plead, and standeth to judge the people.

14 The LORD will enter into judgment with the ancients of his people, and the princes thereof: for ye have [8]eaten up the [e]vineyard; the spoil of the poor *is* in your houses.

15 What mean ye *that* ye beat my people to pieces, and grind the faces of the poor? saith the Lord GOD of hosts.

16 ¶ Moreover the LORD saith, Because the daughters of Zion are haughty, and walk with stretched forth necks and [9]wanton eyes, walking and [10]mincing *as* they go, and making a tinkling with their feet:

17 Therefore the Lord will smite with a scab the crown of the head of the daughters of Zion, and the LORD will [11]discover their secret parts.

18 In that day the Lord will take away the bravery of *their* tinkling ornaments *about their feet*, and *their* [12]cauls, and *their* round tires like the moon,

19 The [13]chains, and the bracelets, and the [14]mufflers,

20 The bonnets, and the ornaments of the legs, and the headbands, and the [15]tablets, and the earrings,

21 The rings, and nose jewels,

22 The changeable suits of apparel, and the mantles, and the wimples, and the crisping pins,

23 The glasses, and the fine linen, and the hoods, and the vails.

24 And it shall come to pass, *that* instead of sweet smell there shall be stink; and instead of a girdle a rent; and instead of well set hair baldness; and instead of a stomacher a girding of sackcloth; *and* burning instead of beauty.

25 Thy men shall fall by the sword, and thy [16]mighty in the war.

26 And [f]her gates shall lament and mourn; and she *being* [17]desolate shall sit upon the ground.

CHAPTER 4

AND in that day seven women shall take hold of one man, saying, We will eat our own bread, and wear our own apparel: only [1]let us be called by thy name, [2]to take away our [a]reproach.

2 In that day shall [b]the branch of the LORD be [3]beautiful and glorious, and [c]the fruit of the earth *shall be* excellent and comely [4]for them that are escaped of Israel.

3 And it shall come to pass, *that he that is* left in Zion, and *he that* remaineth in Jerusalem, shall be called holy, *even* every one that is written [5]among the living in Jerusalem:

4 When the Lord shall have washed away the filth of the daughters of Zion, and shall have purged the blood of Jerusalem from the midst thereof by the spirit of judgment, and by the spirit of burning.

CHAP. 3

a Lev. 26.26. Jer. 37.21. Eze. 14.13.
1 a man eminent in countenance.
2 Or, skilful of speech.
b Eccl. 10.16.
c Micah 3.1.
d Deut. 28.50. Lam. 4.16.
3 lift up the hand, Gen. 14.22; or, protest.
4 binder up.
5 done to him.
6 Or, they which call thee blessed.
7 swallow up.
8 Or, consumed.
e Matt. 21.33.
9 deceiving with their eyes.
10 Or, tripping nicely.
11 make naked.
12 Or, caps of net work.
13 Or, sweet balls.
14 Or, spangled ornaments.
15 houses of breath, or, perfume boxes.
16 might.
f Jer. 14.2. Lam. 1.4.
17 Or, cleansed, or, emptied.

CHAP. 4

1 let thy name be called upon us.
2 Or, take thou away.
a Luke 1.25.
b ch. 11.1. ch. 60.21. Jer. 23.5.
3 beauty and glory.
c Rom. 1.3,4.
4 for the escaping of Israel.
5 Or, to life.

5 And the LORD will create upon
every dwelling place of mount Zion,
and upon her assemblies, a [d]cloud and
smoke by day, and the shining of a
flaming fire by night: for [6]upon all the
glory *shall be* [7]a defence.
6 And there shall be a tabernacle for
a shadow in the daytime from the
heat, and for a place of refuge, and for
a covert from storm and from rain.

CHAPTER 5

NOW will I sing to my wellbeloved
a song of my beloved touching
[a]his vineyard. My wellbeloved hath a
vineyard in [1]a very fruitful hill:
2 And he [2]fenced it, and gathered
out the stones thereof, and planted it
with the choicest vine, and built a
tower in the midst of it, and also [3]made
a winepress therein: [b]and he looked
that it should bring forth grapes, and
it brought forth wild grapes.
3 And now, O inhabitants of Jerusalem, and men of Judah, judge, [c]I pray
you, betwixt me and my vineyard.
4 What could have been done more
to my vineyard, that I have not done
in it? wherefore, when I looked that
it should bring forth grapes, brought
it forth wild grapes?
5 And now go to; I will tell you what
I will do to my vineyard: I will take
away the hedge thereof, and it shall
be eaten up; *and* break down the wall
thereof, and it shall be [4]trodden down:
6 And I will lay it waste: it shall not
be pruned, nor digged; but there shall
come up briers and thorns: I will also
command the clouds that they rain no
rain upon it.
7 For the vineyard of the LORD of
hosts *is* the house of Israel, and the
men of Judah [5]his pleasant plant: and
he looked for judgment, but behold
[6]oppression; for righteousness, but
behold a cry.
8 ¶ Woe unto them that [d]join house
to house, *that* lay field to field, till
there be no place, that [7]they may be
placed alone in the midst of the earth!
9 [8]In mine ears *said* the LORD of
hosts, [9]Of a truth many houses shall
be desolate, *even* great and fair, without inhabitant.
10 Yea, ten acres of vineyard shall
yield one [e]bäth, and the seed of an hṓ-
mĕr shall yield an ḗ-phäh.
11 ¶ Woe [f]unto them that rise up
early in the morning, *that* they may
follow strong drink; that continue until night, *till* wine [10]inflame them!
12 And [g]the harp, and the viol, the
tabret, and pipe, and wine, are in their
feasts: but they [h]regard not the work
of the LORD, neither consider the
operation of his hands.
13 ¶ Therefore [i]my people are gone
into captivity, [j]because *they have* no
knowledge: and [11]their honourable
men *are* famished, and their multitude dried up with thirst.
14 Therefore hell hath enlarged herself, and opened her mouth without
measure: and their glory, and their
multitude, and their pomp, and he
that rejoiceth, shall descend into
it.
15 And the mean man shall be
brought down, and the mighty man
shall be humbled, and the eyes of the
lofty shall be humbled:
16 But the LORD of hosts shall be
exalted in judgment, and [12]God that
is holy shall be sanctified in righteousness.
17 Then shall the lambs feed after
their manner, and the waste places of
the fat ones shall strangers eat.
18 Woe unto them that draw iniquity
with cords of vanity, and sin as it
were with a cart rope:
19 That [k]say, Let him make speed,
and hasten his work, that we may see
it: and let the counsel of the Holy
One of Israel draw nigh and come,
that we may know *it*!
20 ¶ Woe unto them [13]that call evil
good, and good evil; that put darkness for light, and light for darkness;
that put bitter for sweet, and sweet for
bitter!
21 Woe unto *them that are* wise in
their own eyes, and prudent [14]in their
own sight!
22 Woe unto *them that are* mighty
to drink wine, and men of strength to
mingle strong drink:
23 Which justify the wicked for reward, and take away the righteousness of the righteous from him!
24 Therefore as [15]the fire devoureth
the stubble, and the flame consumeth
the chaff, *so* their root shall be as rottenness, and their blossom shall go up
as dust: because they have cast away
[l]the law of the LORD of hosts, and despised the word of the Holy One of
Israel.
25 Therefore is the anger of the
LORD kindled against his people, and
he hath stretched forth his hand
against them, and hath smitten them:
and the hills did tremble, and their
carcases *were* [16]torn in the midst of the
streets. For all this his anger is not

d Ex. 13.21, 22. Deut. 1.33.
6 Or, above.
7 a covering.

CHAP. 5

a Ps. 80.8.
1 the horn of the son of oil.
2 Or, made a wall about it.
3 hewed.
b Deut. 32.6.
c Rom. 3.4.
4 for a treading.
5 plant of his pleasures.
6 a scab.
d Micah 2.2.
7 ye.
8 Or, This is in mine ears, saith the LORD.
9 If not, etc.
e Lev. 27.16.
f Pro. 23.29, 30.
10 Or, pursue them!
g Amos 6.5.
h Job 34.27. Hosea 4.11.
i ch. 1.7. Hosea 4.6.
j ch. 1.3. Luke 19.44. Rom. 1.28. 2 Pet. 3.5.
11 their glory are men of famine.
12 the God the holy, or, the holy God.
k ch. 66.5. Jer. 17.15. Amos 5.18. 2 Pet. 3.3.
13 that say concerning evil, It is good, etc.
14 before their face!
15 the tongue of fire.
l 2 Ki. 17.14. Luke 7.30. John 12.48.
16 Or, as dung.

turned away, but his hand *is* stretched
out still.
26 ¶ And he will lift up an ensign to
the nations from far, and will hiss unto them from the end of the earth: and,
behold, they shall come with speed
swiftly:
27 None shall be weary nor stumble
among them; none shall slumber nor
sleep; neither shall the girdle of their
loins be loosed, nor the latchet of their
shoes be broken:
28 Whose arrows *are* sharp, and all
their bows bent, their horses' hoofs
shall be counted like flint, and their
wheels like a whirlwind:
29 Their roaring *shall be* like a lion,
they shall roar like young lions: yea,
they shall roar, and lay hold of the
prey, and shall carry *it* away safe, and
none shall deliver *it*.
30 And in that day they shall roar
against them like the roaring of the
sea: and if *one* look unto the land, behold darkness *and* [17]sorrow, [18]and the
light is darkened in the heavens
thereof.

CHAPTER 6

IN the year that [a]king Ŭz-zī-ăh died
I saw also [b]the Lord sitting upon a
throne, high and lifted up, and [1]his
train filled the temple.
2 Above it stood the sĕr-ă-phĭms:
each one had six wings; with twain
he covered his face, and with twain
he covered his feet, and with twain he
did fly.
3 And [2]one cried unto another, and
said, Holy, holy, holy, *is* the LORD of
hosts: [3]the whole earth *is* full of his
glory.
4 And the posts of the [4]door moved
at the voice of him that cried, and the
house was filled with smoke.
5 ¶ Then said I, Woe *is* me! for I am
[5]undone; because I *am* a man of unclean lips, and I dwell in the midst of
a people of unclean lips: for mine
eyes have seen the King, the LORD of
hosts.
6 Then flew one of the sĕr-ă-phĭms
unto me, [6]having a live coal in his
hand, *which* he had taken with the
tongs from off [c]the altar:
7 And he [7]laid *it* upon my mouth,
and said, Lo, this hath touched thy
lips; and thine iniquity is taken away,
and thy sin purged.
8 Also I heard the voice of the Lord,
saying, Whom shall I send, and who
will go for [d]us? Then said I, [8]Here *am*
I; send me.
9 ¶ And he said, Go, and tell this
people, [9]Hear ye indeed, but understand not; and see ye [10]indeed, but
perceive not.
10 Make the heart of this people fat,
and make their ears heavy, and shut
their eyes; lest they see with their eyes,
and hear with their ears, and understand with their heart, and convert,
and be healed.
11 Then said I, Lord, how long? And
he answered, Until the cities be wasted
without inhabitant, and the houses
without man, and the land [11]be utterly desolate,
12 And the Lord have [e]removed men
far away, and *there be* a great for-
saking in the midst of the land.
13 ¶ But yet in it *shall be* a tenth,
[12]and *it* shall return, and shall be eat-
en: as a teil tree, and as an oak, whose
[13]substance *is* in them, when they cast
their leaves: so the holy [f]seed *shall be*
the substance thereof.

CHAPTER 7

AND it came to pass in the days of
Ahaz [a]the son of Jō-thăm, the son
of Ŭz-zī-ăh, king of Judah, *that* Rē-
zĭn the king of Syria, and Pē-kăh the
son of Rĕm-ă-lī-ăh, king of Israel,
went up toward Jerusalem to war
against it, but could not prevail
against it.
2 And it was told the house of David,
saying, Syria [1]is confederate with Ē-
phră-ĭm. And his heart was moved,
and the heart of his people, as the
trees of the wood are moved with the
wind.
3 Then said the LORD unto Isaiah,
Go forth now to meet Ahaz, thou, and
[2]Shē-ăr–jăsh-ŭb thy son, at the end of
the [b]conduit of the upper pool in the
[3]highway of the fuller's field;
4 And say unto him, Take heed, and
be quiet; fear not, [4]neither be fainthearted for the two tails of these smoking firebrands, for the fierce anger of
Rē-zĭn with Syria, and of the son of
Rĕm-ă-lī-ăh.
5 Because Syria, Ē-phră-ĭm, and the
son of Rĕm-ă-lī-ăh, have taken evil
counsel against thee, saying,
6 Let us go up against Judah, and
[5]vex it, and let us make a breach therein for us, and set a king in the midst
of it, *even* the son of Tā-bē-ăl:
7 Thus saith the Lord GOD, It shall
not stand, neither shall it come to
pass.
8 For [c]the head of Syria *is* Damascus, and the head of Damascus *is* Rē-
zĭn; and within threescore and five

17 Or, distress.
18 Or, when it is light, it shall be dark in the destructions thereof.

CHAP. 6

a 2 Ki. 15.7.
b 1 Ki. 22.19. Eze. 10.1. John 12.41. Rev. 4.2.
1 Or, the skirts thereof.
2 this cried to this.
3 his glory is the fulness of the whole earth.
4 thresholds.
5 cut off.
6 and in his hand a live coal.
c Lev. 16.12. Heb. 13.10.
7 caused it to touch.
d Gen. 1.26.
8 Behold me.
9 Hear ye in hearing, or, without ceasing, etc.
10 in seeing.
11 desolate with desolation.
e Deut. 28. 64.
12 Or, when it is returned, and hath been broused.
13 Or, stock, or, stem.
f Rom. 11.5.

CHAP. 7

a 2 Ki. 16.5.
1 resteth on Ephraim.
2 That is, The remnant shall return.
b 2 Ki. 18.17. ch. 36.2.
3 Or, causey-way.
4 let not thy heart be tender.
5 Or, waken.
c 2 Sam. 8.6.

years shall Ē-phră-ĭm be broken, [6]that
it be not a people.
9 And the head of Ē-phră-ĭm *is* Să-
mâr-ĭ-ă, and the head of Să-mâr-ĭ-ă *is*
Rĕm-ă-lī-ăh's son. [7]If ye will not believe, surely ye shall not be established.
10 ¶ [8]Moreover the LORD spake
again unto Ahaz, saying,
11 Ask thee a sign of the LORD thy
God; [9]ask it either in the depth, or in
the height above.
12 But Ahaz said, I will not ask,
neither will I tempt the LORD.
13 And he said, Hear ye now, O
house of David; *Is it* a small thing for
you to weary men, but will ye weary
my God also?
14 Therefore the Lord himself shall
give you a sign; [d]Behold, a virgin shall
conceive, and bear [e]a son, and [10]shall
call his [f]name Ĭm-măn-ū-ĕl.
15 Butter and honey shall he eat,
that he may know to refuse the evil,
and choose the good.
16 For before the child shall know to
refuse the evil, and choose the good,
the land that thou abhorrest shall be
forsaken of [g]both her kings.
17 ¶ The [h]LORD shall bring upon
thee, and upon thy people, and upon
thy father's house, days that have not
come, from the day that Ē-phră-ĭm
[i]departed from Judah; *even* the king
of Assyria.
18 And it shall come to pass in that
day, *that* the LORD shall hiss for the
fly that *is* in the uttermost part of the
rivers of Egypt, and for the bee that
is in the land of Assyria.
19 And they shall come, and shall
rest all of them in the desolate valleys,
and in the holes of the rocks, and upon all thorns, and upon all [11]bushes.
20 In the same day shall the Lord
shave with [j]a rasor that is hired,
namely, by them beyond the river, by
the king of Assyria, the head, and the
hair of the feet: and it shall also consume the beard.
21 And it shall come to pass in that
day, *that* a man shall nourish a young
cow, and two sheep;
22 And it shall come to pass, for the
abundance of milk *that* they shall give
he shall eat butter: for butter and
honey shall every one eat that is left
[12]in the land.
23 And it shall come to pass in that
day, *that* every place shall be, where
there were a thousand vines at a thous-
and silverlings, it shall *even* be for
briers and thorns.

6 from a people.
7 Or, Do ye not believe? it is because ye are not stable.
8 And the LORD added to speak.
9 Or, make thy petition deep.
d Matt. 1.23. Luke 1.35.
e ch. 9.6.
10 Or, thou, O virgin, shalt call.
f 1 Tim. 3.16.
g 2 Ki. 15.30. ch. 8.4.
h 2 Chr. 28. 19. Neh. 9.32. ch. 8.7,8.
i 1 Ki. 12.16.
11 Or, commendable trees.
j 2 Ki. 16.7. ch. 10.5,6. Jer. 27.6,7.
12 in the midst of the land.

CHAP. 8

1 in making speed to the spoil he hasteneth the prey, or, make speed, etc.
a 2 Ki. 16.10.
2 approached unto.
b ch. 7.16.
3 Or, he that is before the king of Assyria shall take away the riches.
c Neh. 3.15. John 9.7.
4 the fulness of the breadth of thy land shall be the stretchings out of his wings.
d ch. 7.14. Matt. 1.23.
5 Or, yet.
e Job 5.12.
f Deut. 20.1. Josh. 1.5. Ps. 46.7,11. ch. 9.6. Matt. 1.23. Rom. 8.31.
6 in strength of hand.
g 1 Pet. 3.14.

24 With arrows and with bows shall
men come thither; because all the land
shall become briers and thorns.
25 And *on* all hills that shall be
digged with the mattock, there shall
not come thither the fear of briers and
thorns: but it shall be for the sending
forth of oxen, and for the treading of
lesser cattle.

CHAPTER 8

MOREOVER the LORD said unto
me, Take thee a great roll, and
write in it with a man's pen concerning [1]Mā-hĕr-shăl-ăl-hăsh-băz.
2 And I took unto me faithful witnesses to record, [a]Ū-rī-ăh the priest,
and Zĕch-ă-rī-ăh the son of Jĕ-bĕr-ĕ-
chī-ăh.
3 And I [2]went unto the prophetess;
and she conceived, and bare a son.
Then said the LORD to me, Call his
name Mā-hĕr-shăl-ăl-hăsh-băz.
4 For [b]before the child shall have
knowledge to cry, My father, and my
mother, [3]the riches of Damascus and
the spoil of Să-mâr-ĭ-ă shall be taken
away before the king of Assyria.
5 ¶ The LORD spake also unto me
again, saying,
6 Forasmuch as this people refuseth
the waters of [c]Shī-lō-ăh that go softly
and rejoice in Rē-zĭn and Rĕm-ă-lī-
ăh's son;
7 Now therefore, behold, the Lord
bringeth up upon them the waters of
the river, strong and many, *even* the
king of Assyria, and all his glory: and
he shall come up over all his channels,
and go over all his banks:
8 And he shall pass through Judah;
he shall overflow and go over, he shall
reach *even* to the neck; and [4]the
stretching out of his wings shall fill the
breadth of thy land, O [d]Ĭm-măn-ū-ĕl.
9 ¶ Associate yourselves, O ye people, [5]and ye shall be broken in pieces;
and give ear, all ye of far countries:
gird yourselves, and ye shall be
broken in pieces; gird yourselves, and
ye shall be broken in pieces.
10 Take [e]counsel together, and it
shall come to nought; speak the word,
and it shall not stand: [f]for God *is* with
us.
11 ¶ For the LORD spake thus to me
[6]with a strong hand, and instructed
me that I should not walk in the way
of this people, saying,
12 Say ye not, A confederacy, to all
them to whom this people shall say, A
confederacy; [g]neither fear ye their
fear, nor be afraid.

13 Sanctify [h]the LORD of hosts himself; and [i]*let* him *be* your fear, and *let* him *be* your dread.

14 And [j]he shall be for a sanctuary; but for [k]a stone of stumbling and for a rock of offence to both the houses of Israel, for a gin and for a snare to the inhabitants of Jerusalem.

15 And many among them [l]shall stumble, and fall, and be broken, and be snared, and be taken.

16 Bind [m]up the testimony, seal the law among my disciples.

17 And I will wait upon the LORD, that hideth his face from the house of Jacob, and [n]I will look for him.

18 Behold, [o]I and the children whom the LORD hath given me [p]*are* for signs and for wonders in Israel from the LORD of hosts, which dwelleth in mount Zion.

19 ¶ And when they shall say unto you, Seek unto them that have familiar spirits, and unto wizards that peep, and that mutter: should not a people seek unto their God? for the living [q]to the dead?

20 To the law and to the testimony: if they speak not according to this word, *it is* because *there is* [7]no light in them. Sc Luke 11:13

21 And they shall pass through it, hardly bestead and hungry: and it shall come to pass, that when they shall be hungry, they shall fret themselves, and curse their king and their God, and look upward.

22 And they shall look unto the earth; and behold trouble and darkness, dimness of anguish; and *they shall be* driven to darkness.

CHAPTER 9

NEVERTHELESS the dimness *shall* not *be* such as *was* in her vexation, when at the [a]first he lightly afflicted the land of Zĕ-bū-lŭn and the land of Năph-tă-lī, and afterward [b]did more grievously afflict *her by* the way of the sea, beyond Jordan, in Galilee [1]of the nations.

2 The [c]people that walked in darkness have seen a great light: they that dwell in the land of the shadow of death, upon them hath the light shined.

3 Thou hast multiplied the nation, *and* [2]not increased the joy: they joy before thee according to the joy in harvest, *and* as *men* rejoice when they divide the spoil.

4 [3]For thou hast broken the yoke of his burden, and the staff of his shoulder, the rod of his oppressor, as in the day [d]of Mĭd-ĭ-ăn.

5 [4]For every battle of the warrior *is* with confused noise, and garments rolled in blood; [5]but *this* shall be with burning *and* [6]fuel of fire.

6 For [e]unto us a child is born, unto us a son [f]is given: and [g]the government shall be upon his shoulder: and his name shall be called [h]Wonderful, Counseller, The [i]mighty God, The everlasting Father, [j]The Prince of Peace.

7 Of the increase of *his* government and peace [k]*there shall be* no end, upon the throne of David, and upon his kingdom, to order it, and to establish it with judgment and with justice from henceforth even for ever. The zeal of the LORD of hosts will perform this.

8 ¶ The Lord sent a word into Jacob, and it hath lighted upon Israel.

9 And all the people shall know, *even* Ē-phră-ĭm and the inhabitant of Să-mâr-ĭ-ă, that say in the pride and stoutness of heart,

10 The bricks are fallen down, but we will build with hewn stones: the sycomores are cut down, but we will change *them into* cedars.

11 Therefore the LORD shall set up the adversaries of Rē-zĭn against him, and [7]join his enemies together;

12 The Syrians before, and the Philistines behind; and they shall devour Israel [8]with open mouth. For all this his anger is not turned away, but his hand *is* stretched out still.

13 ¶ For [l]the people turneth not unto him that smiteth them, neither do they seek the LORD of hosts.

14 Therefore the LORD will cut off from Israel head and tail, branch and rush, in one day.

15 The ancient and honourable, he *is* the head; and the prophet that teacheth lies, he *is* the tail.

16 For [9]the leaders of this people cause *them* to err; and [10]*they that are* led of them *are* [11]destroyed.

17 Therefore the Lord shall have no joy in their young men, neither shall have mercy on their fatherless and widows: for every one *is* an hypocrite and an evildoer, and every mouth speaketh [12]folly. For all this his anger is not turned away, but his hand *is* stretched out still.

18 ¶ For wickedness burneth as the fire: it shall devour the briers and thorns, and shall kindle in the thickets of the forest, and they shall mount up *like* the lifting up of smoke.

h Num. 20. 12.
i Luke 12.5.
j Eze. 11.16.
k Luke 2.34. Rom. 9.33. 1 Pet. 2.8.
l Luke 20.18.
m Dan. 12.4.
n Hab. 2.3. Luke 2.25.
o Heb. 2.13.
p Zech. 3.8.
q Ps. 106.28.
7 no morning.

CHAP. 9

a 2 Ki. 15.29. 2 Chr. 16.4.
b Lev. 26.24. 1 Chr. 5.26. Matt. 4.15.
1 Or, populous.
c ch. 50.10. John 8.12. Eph. 5.8.
2 Or, to him.
3 Or, When thou brakest.
d Judg. 7.22. Ps. 83.9. ch. 10.26.
4 Or, When the whole battle of the warrior was, etc.
5 Or, and it was, etc.
6 meat.
e Luke 2.11.
f John 3.16.
g Matt. 28. 18. 1 Cor. 15.25.
h Judg. 13. 18.
i Ps. 45.3,6. Jer. 23.6. John 1.1. Titus 2.13.
j Eph. 2.14. Col. 1.20. Heb. 13.20.
k Dan. 2.44. Luke 1.32.
7 mingle.
8 with whole mouth.
l Jer. 5.3.
9 Or, they that call them blessed.
10 Or, they that are called blessed of them.
11 swallowed up.
12 Or, villany.

19 Through the wrath of the LORD
f hosts is the land darkened, and the
eople shall be as the [13]fuel of the fire:
o man shall spare his brother.
20 And he shall [14]snatch on the right
and, and be hungry; and he shall
at on the left hand, [m]and they shall
ot be satisfied: they shall eat every
ıan the flesh of his own arm:
21 Mă-năs′-sĕh, Ē′-phră-ĭm; and Ē′-
hră-ĭm, Mă-năs′-sĕh: *and* they to-
ether *shall be* against Judah. For all
nis his anger is not turned away, but
is hand *is* stretched out still.

13 meat.
14 cut.
m Lev. 26.26.

CHAPTER 10

WOE unto them that decree unrighteous decrees, and [1]that
vrite grievousness *which* they have
rescribed;
2 To turn aside the needy from judg-
nent, and to take away the right from
he poor of my people, that widows
nay be their prey, and *that* they may
ob the fatherless!
3 And what will ye do in [a]the day of
isitation, and in the desolation *which*
hall come from far? to whom will ye
lee for help? and where will ye leave
our glory?
4 Without me they shall bow down
ınder the prisoners, and they shall
all under the slain. For all this his
ınger is not turned away, but his hand
s stretched out still.
5 ¶ [2]O [3]Assyrian, the rod of mine
ınger, [4]and the staff in their hand is
nine indignation.
6 I will send him against an hypocritical nation, and against the people
of my wrath will I give him a charge,
to take the spoil, and to take the prey,
and [5]to tread them down like the mire
of the streets.
7 Howbeit [b]he meaneth not so, neither doth his heart think so; but *it is* in
his heart to destroy and cut off nations
not a few.
8 For [c]he saith, *Are* not my princes
altogether kings?
9 *Is* not [d]Căl-nō as [e]Cär-chē-mĭsh?
is not [f]Hā′-măth as Är′-păd? *is* not Să-
mâr′-ĭ-ă as [g]Damascus?
10 As my hand hath found the kingdoms of the idols, and whose graven
images did excel them of Jerusalem
and of Să-mâr′-ĭ-ă;
11 Shall I not, as I have done unto
Să-mâr′-ĭ-ă and her idols, so do to
Jerusalem and her idols?
12 Wherefore it shall come to pass,
that when the Lord hath performed
his whole work upon mount Zion and
on Jerusalem, I will [6]punish the fruit
[7]of the stout heart of the king of Assyria, and the glory of his high looks.
13 For [h]he saith, By the strength of
my hand I have done *it*, and by my
wisdom; for I am prudent: and I have
removed the bounds of the people,
and have robbed their treasures, and
I have put down the inhabitants [8]like
a valiant *man:*
14 And my hand hath found as a nest
the riches of the people: and as one
gathereth eggs *that are* left, have I
gathered all the earth; and there was
none that moved the wing, or opened
the mouth, or peeped.
15 Shall [i]the axe boast itself against
him that heweth therewith? *or* shall
the saw magnify itself against him
that shaketh it? [9]as if the rod should
shake *itself* against them that lift it
up, *or* as if the staff should lift up [10]*itself, as if it were* no wood.
16 Therefore shall the Lord, the
Lord of hosts, send among his fat ones
leanness; and under his glory he shall
kindle a burning like the burning of a
fire.
17 And the light of Israel shall be for
a fire, and his Holy One for a flame:
and it shall burn and devour his
thorns and his briers in one day;
18 And shall consume the glory of
his forest, and of his fruitful field,
[11]both soul and body: and they shall
be as when a standardbearer fainteth.
19 And the rest of the trees of his
forest shall be [12]few, that a child may
write them.
20 ¶ And it shall come to pass in that
day, *that* the remnant of Israel, and
such as are escaped of the house of
Jacob, shall no more again stay upon
him that smote them; but shall stay
upon the LORD, the Holy One of Israel, in truth.
21 The remnant shall return, *even*
the remnant of Jacob, unto the mighty
God.
22 For [j]though thy people Israel be
as the sand of the sea, *yet* a remnant
[13]of them shall return: the consumption decreed shall overflow [14]with
righteousness.
23 For [k]the Lord GOD of hosts shall
make a consumption, even determined, in the midst of all the land.
24 ¶ Therefore thus saith the Lord
GOD of hosts, O my people that dwellest in Zion, be not afraid of the Assyrian: he shall smite thee with a rod,
[15]and shall lift up his staff against thee,
after the manner of Egypt.

CHAP. 10
1 Or, to the writers that write grievousness.
a Hosea 9.7. Luke 19.44.
2 Or, Woe to the Assyrian.
3 Asshur.
4 Or, though.
5 to lay them a treading.
b Micah 4.12.
c 2 Ki. 18.24.
d Amos 6.2.
e 2 Chr. 35. 20. Jer. 46.2.
f Num. 13. 21. 2 Sam. 8.9. 2 Ki. 23.33. ch. 10.9.
g 2 Ki. 16.9.
6 visit upon.
7 of the greatness of the heart.
h Ex. 15.9. Ps. 20.7. ch. 37.24.
8 Or, like many people.
i Jer. 51.20. Rom. 9.20, 21.
9 Or, as if a rod should shake them that lift it up.
10 Or, that which is not wood.
11 from the soul, and even to the flesh.
12 number.
j Micah 5.3. Rom. 9.27.
13 in, or, among.
14 Or, in.
k ch. 28.22. Dan. 9.27.
15 Or, but he shall lift up his staff for thee.

25 For yet a very little while, [l]and the indignation shall cease, and mine anger in their destruction.

26 And the LORD of hosts shall stir up a scourge for him according to the slaughter of Mĭd'-ĭ-ăn at the rock of Ôr'-ĕb: and *as* his rod *was* upon the sea, so shall he lift it up after the manner of Egypt.

27 And it shall come to pass in that day, *that* his burden [16]shall be taken away from off thy shoulder, and his yoke from off thy neck, and the yoke shall be destroyed because of [m]the anointing.

28 He is come to [n]A-î'-ăth, he is passed to Mĭg'-rŏn; at Mĭch'-măsh he hath laid up his carriages:

29 They are gone over [o]the passage: they have taken up their lodging at Gē'-bă; Rā'-măh is afraid; Gĭb'-ĕ-ăh of Saul is fled.

30 [17]Lift up thy voice, O daughter of [p]Găl'-lĭm: cause it to be heard unto Lā'-ĭsh, O poor Ăn'-ă-thōth.

31 Măd-mē'-năh [q]is removed; the inhabitants of Gē'-bĭm gather themselves to flee.

32 As yet shall he remain [r]at Nob that day: he shall shake his hand *against* the mount of the daughter of Zion, the hill of Jerusalem.

33 Behold, the Lord, the LORD of hosts, shall lop the bough with terror: and the high ones of stature *shall be* hewn down, and the haughty shall be humbled.

34 And he shall cut down the thickets of the forest with iron, and Lĕb'-ă-non shall fall [18]by a mighty one.

CHAPTER 11

AND [a]there shall come forth a rod out of the [1]stem of [b]Jesse, and [c]a Branch shall grow out of his roots:

2 And [d]the spirit of the LORD shall rest upon him, the spirit of wisdom and understanding, the spirit of counsel and might, the spirit of knowledge and of the fear of the LORD;

3 And shall make him of [2]quick understanding in the fear of the LORD: and he shall not judge after the sight of his eyes, neither reprove after the hearing of his ears:

4 But [e]with righteousness shall he judge the poor, and [3]reprove with equity for the meek of the earth: and he shall [f]smite the earth with the rod of his mouth, and with the breath of his lips shall he slay the wicked.

5 And [g]righteousness shall be t girdle of his loins, and faithfulne the girdle of his reins.

6 The [h]wolf also shall dwell with t lamb, and the leopard shall lie dow with the kid; and the calf and t young lion and the fatling togethe and a little child shall lead them.

7 And the cow and the bear sha feed; their young ones shall lie dow together: and the lion shall eat stra like the ox.

8 And the sucking child shall pla on the hole of the asp, and the weane child shall put his hand on the [4]cocka trice' den.

9 They shall not hurt nor destroy i all my holy mountain: for [i]the eart shall be full of the knowledge c the LORD, as the waters cover th sea.

10 ¶ And in that day there shall be root of Jesse, which shall stand for a ensign of the people; to it shall th Gentiles [j]seek: and [k]his rest shall b [5]glorious.

11 And it shall come to pass in tha day, *that* the Lord shall set his han again the second time to recover th remnant of his people, which shall b left, [l]from Assyria, and from Egypt and from Păth'-rŏs, and from Cŭsh and from Ē'-lăm, and from Shĭ'-när and from Hā'-măth, and from th islands of the sea.

12 And he shall set up an ensign fo the nations, and shall assemble th outcasts of Israel, and gather togethe [m]the dispersed of Judah from the fou [6]corners of the earth.

13 The envy also of [n]Ē'-phră-ĭm shal depart, and the adversaries of Judah shall be cut off: Ē'-phră-ĭm shall no envy Judah, and Judah shall not ve Ē'-phră-ĭm.

14 But they shall fly upon the shoulders of the Philistines toward the west; they shall spoil [7]them of the east together; [8]they shall lay their hand upon Ē'-dom and Moab; [9]and the children of Ammon shall obey them.

15 And the LORD shall utterly destroy the tongue of the Egyptian sea; and with his mighty wind shall he shake his hand over the river, and shall smite it in the seven streams, [o]and make *men* go over [10]dryshod.

16 And there shall be an highway for the remnant of his people, which shall be left, from Assyria; like [p]as it was to Israel in the day that he came up out of the land of Egypt.

l Dan. 11.36.
16 shall remove.
m Ps. 105.15.
n Neh. 11.31.
o 1 Sam. 13. 23.
17 Cry shrill with thy voice.
p 1 Sam. 25. 44.
q Josh. 15.31.
r 1 Sam. 21.1.
18 Or, mightily.

CHAP. 11
a ch. 53.2. Zech. 6.12. Rev. 22.16.
1 Or, stump.
b Acts 13.23.
c Jer. 23.5. Zech. 3.8.
d ch. 42.1. Matt. 3.16. John 1.32. Acts 10.38.
2 scent, or, smell.
e Ps. 72.2,4. Rev. 19.11.
3 Or, decide.
f Mal. 4.6. 2 Thes. 2.8. Rev. 2.16.
g Eph. 6.14.
h Hosea 2.18.
4 Or, adder's.
i Hab. 2.14.
j Rom. 15.10.
k Heb. 4.1.
5 glory.
l Zech. 10.10.
m John 7.35.
6 wings.
n Gal. 3.28.
7 the children of the east.
8 Edom and Moab shall be the laying on of their hand.
9 the children of Ammon their obedience.
o Rev. 16.12.
10 in shoes.
p Ex. 14.29. ch. 51.10.

CHAPTER 12

ND [a]in that day thou shalt say, O
LORD, I will praise thee: though
ou wast angry with me, thine anger
turned away, and thou comfortedst
e.
Behold, God *is* my salvation; I will
ust, and not be afraid: for the LORD
-HŌ-VĂH *is* my strength and *my*
ng; he also is become my salvation.
Therefore with joy shall ye draw
ater [b]out of the wells of salvation.
And in that day shall ye say, Praise
e LORD, [1]call upon his name, de-
are his doings among the people,
ake mention that his name is ex-
ted.
Sing unto the LORD; for he hath
one excellent things: this *is* known
all the earth.
Cry [c]out and shout, thou [2]inhabit-
nt of Zion: for great *is* the Holy One
f Israel in the midst of thee.

CHAPTER 13

HE burden of Babylon, which
Isaiah the son of Amoz did see.
2 Lift [a]ye up a banner upon [b]the high
ountain, exalt the voice unto them,
hake the hand, that they may go into
e gates of the nobles.
3 I have commanded my sanctified
nes, I have also called [c]my mighty
nes for mine anger, *even* them that
ejoice in my highness.
4 The noise of a multitude in the
ountains, [1]like as of a great people;
tumultous noise of the kingdoms
f nations gathered together: the
ORD of hosts mustereth the host of
e battle.
5 They come from a far country,
rom the end of heaven, *even* the
ORD, and the weapons of his indig-
ation, to destroy the whole land.
6 ¶ Howl ye; [d]for the day of the
ORD *is* at hand; it shall come as a de-
truction from the Almighty.
7 Therefore shall all hands [2]be faint,
nd every man's heart shall melt:
8 And they shall be afraid: pangs
nd sorrows shall take hold of them;
hey shall be in pain as a woman that
ravaileth: they shall [3]be amazed [4]one
t another; their faces *shall be as*
flames.
9 Behold, [e]the day of the LORD com-
th, cruel both with wrath and fierce
nger, to lay the land desolate: and he
hall destroy the sinners thereof out
of it.
10 For the stars of heaven and the
constellations thereof shall not give
their light: the sun shall [f]be darkened
in his going forth, and the moon shall
not cause her light to shine.
11 And I will punish [6]the world for
their evil, and the wicked for their iniquity; and I will cause the arrogancy
of the proud to cease, and will lay low
the haughtiness of the terrible.
12 I will make a man more precious
than fine gold; even a man than the
golden wedge of Ō-phĭr.
13 Therefore [g]I will shake the heavens, and the earth shall remove out of
her place, in the wrath of the LORD
of hosts, and in [h]the day of his
fierce anger.
14 And it shall be as the chased roe,
and as a sheep that no man taketh up:
they shall every man turn to his own
people, and flee every one into his
own land.
15 Every one that is found shall be
thrust through; and every one that is
joined *unto them* shall fall by the
sword.
16 Their children also shall be dashed [i]to pieces before their eyes; their
houses shall be spoiled, and their
wives ravished.
17 Behold, [j]I will stir up the Mēdeṡ
against them, which shall not regard
silver; and *as for* gold, they shall not
delight in it.
18 *Their* bows also shall dash the
young men to pieces; and they shall
have no pity on the fruit of the womb;
their eye shall not spare children.
19 ¶ And Babylon, the glory of kingdoms, the beauty of the Chăl-dēeṡ'
excellency, shall be [7]as when God
overthrew Sodom and Gō-mŏr-
răh.
20 It [k]shall never be inhabited, neither shall it be dwelt in from generation
to generation: neither shall the Arabian pitch tent there; neither shall the
shepherds make their fold there.
21 But [8]wild beasts of the desert shall
lie there; and their houses shall be full
of [9]doleful creatures; and [10]owls shall
dwell there, and [11]satyrs shall dance
there.
22 And [12]the wild beasts of the islands
shall cry in their [13]desolate houses, and
[14]dragons in *their* pleasant palaces:
and her time *is* near to come, and her
days shall not be prolonged.

CHAPTER 14

FOR the LORD will have mercy on
Jacob, [a]and will yet choose Israel,
and set them in their own land: [b]and
the strangers shall be joined with

CHAP. 12
a ch. 2.11. Zech. 14.20, 21.
b Jer. 2.13. John 4.10, 14.
1 Or, proclaim his name.
c ch. 54.1. Zeph. 3.14. Luke 19.37-40.
2 inhabitress.

CHAP. 13
a Jer. 50.2.
b Jer. 51.25.
c Joel 3.11.
1 the likeness of.
d Amos 5.18. Zeph. 1.7. Rev. 6.17.
2 Or, fall down.
3 wonder.
4 every man at his neighbour.
5 faces of the flames.
e Mal. 4.1.
f Matt. 24.29.
6 That is, the Babylonian empire.
g Joel 3.16. Hag. 2.6. Matt. 24.29.
h Lam. 1.12.
i Nah. 3.10.
j Jer. 51.11.
7 as the overthrowing.
k ch. 14.23.
8 Ziim.
9 Ochim.
10 daughters of the owl, or, ostriches.
11 shaggy beasts, or, wild goats.
12 Iim.
13 Or, palaces.
14 Or, jackals.

CHAP. 14
a Ps. 102.13, 16. ch. 54.7,8. Jer. 31.3,4, 10,11. Zech. 1.17.
b ch. 60.4,5, 10.

them, and they shall cleave to the house of Jacob.

2 And the people shall take them, and bring them to their place: and the house of Israel shall possess them in the land of the LORD for servants and handmaids: and they shall take them captives, [1]whose captives they were; and they shall rule over their oppressors.

3 And it shall come to pass in the day that the LORD shall give thee rest from thy sorrow, and from thy fear, and from the hard bondage wherein thou wast made to serve,

4 ¶ That thou [c]shalt take up this [2]proverb against the king of Babylon, and say, How hath the oppressor ceased! the [3]golden city ceased!

5 The LORD hath broken the staff of the wicked, *and* the sceptre of the rulers.

6 He who smote the people in wrath with [4]a continual stroke, he that ruled the nations in anger, is persecuted, *and* none hindereth.

7 The whole earth is at rest, *and* is quiet: they break forth into singing.

8 Yea, [d]the fir trees rejoice at thee, *and* the cedars of Lĕb-ā-nọn, *saying*, Since thou art laid down, no feller is come up against us.

9 [5]Hell from beneath is moved for thee to meet *thee* at thy coming: it stirreth up the dead for thee, *even* all the [6]chief ones of the earth; it hath raised up from their thrones all the kings of the nations.

10 All they shall speak and say unto thee, Art thou also become weak as we? art thou become like unto us?

11 Thy pomp is brought down to the grave, *and* the noise of thy viols: the worm is spread under thee, and the worms cover thee.

12 How art thou fallen from heaven, [7]O Lucifer, son of the morning! *how* art thou cut down to the ground, which didst weaken the nations!

13 For thou hast said in thine heart, [e]I will ascend into heaven, [f]I will exalt my throne above the stars of God: I will sit also upon the mount of the congregation, in the sides [g]of the north:

14 I will ascend above the heights of the clouds; [h]I will be like the most High.

15 Yet thou [i]shalt be brought down to hell, to the sides of the pit.

16 They that see thee shall narrowly look upon thee, *and* consider thee, *saying, Is* this the man that made the

1 that had taken them captives.
c ch. 13.19. Hab. 2.6.
2 Or, taunting speech.
3 Or, exactress of gold!
4 a stroke without removing.
d ch. 55.12. Eze. 31.16.
5 Or, The grave.
6 leaders, or, great goats.
7 Or, O day star.
e Lam. 2.1. Matt. 11.23.
f Dan. 8.10. Rev. 12.4.
g Ps. 48.2.
h Zeph. 2.15. 2 Thes. 2.4.
i ch. 47.8. Eze. 28.8,9. Matt. 11.23. Acts 12.23.
8 Or, did not let his prisoners loose homewards?
j Ex. 20.5. Job 18.19. Matt. 23.35.
k 1 Ki. 14.10. Job 18.19. Pro. 10.7.
l 2 Chr. 20.6. Job 40.8. ch. 23.9. Jer. 4.28.
m 2 Ki. 16.20. 2 Chr. 28.27.
9 Or, adder.

earth to tremble, that did shak kingdoms;

17 *That* made the world as a wilde ness, and destroyed the cities thereo *that* [8]opened not the house of h prisoners?

18 All the kings of the nations, *eve* all of them, lie in glory, every one i his own house.

19 But thou art cast out of thy grav like an abominable branch, *and as* th raiment of those that are slain, thrus through with a sword, that go dow to the stones of the pit; as a carcas trodden under feet.

20 Thou shalt not be joined wit them in burial, because thou hast destroyed thy land, *and* slain thy people the seed of evildoers shall never be re nowned.

21 Prepare slaughter for his childre for the [j]iniquity of their fathers; tha they do not rise, nor possess the land nor fill the face of the world with cities

22 For I will rise up against them saith the LORD of hosts, and cut o from Babylon the name, and remnant [k]and son, and nephew, saith the LORD

23 I will also make it a possessio for the bittern, and pools of water and I will sweep it with the besom o destruction, saith the LORD of hosts

24 ¶ The LORD of hosts hath sworn saying, Surely as I have thought, s shall it come to pass; and as I hav purposed, *so* shall it stand:

25 That I will break the Assyrian i my land, and upon my mountain tread him under foot: then shall hi yoke depart from off them, and hi burden depart from off their shoulders.

26 This *is* the purpose that is purposed upon the whole earth: and thi *is* the hand that is stretched out upon all the nations.

27 For the LORD of hosts [l]hath purposed, and who shall disannul *it?* and his hand *is* stretched out, and who shall turn it back?

28 In the year that [m]king Ahaz died was this burden.

29 ¶ Rejoice not thou, whole Palestina, because the rod of him that smote thee is broken: for out of the serpent's root shall come forth a [9]cockatrice, and his fruit *shall be* a fiery flying serpent.

30 And the firstborn of the poor shall feed, and the needy shall lie down in safety: and I will kill thy root with famine, and he shall slay thy remnant.

31 Howl, O gate; cry, O city; thou,

whole Palestina, *art* dissolved: for there shall come from the north a smoke, and [10]none *shall be* alone in his [11]appointed times.

32 What shall *one* then answer the messengers of the nation? That the LORD hath founded Zion, and the poor of his people shall [12]trust in it.

CHAPTER 15

THE [a]burden of Moab. Because in the night [b]Ar of Moab is laid waste, *and* [1]brought to silence; because in the night Kĭr of Moab is laid waste, *and* brought to silence;

2 He is gone up to Bā′-jĭth, and to Dī′-bŏn, the high places, to weep: Moab shall howl over Nē′-bō, and over Mē′-dĕ-bă: on all their heads *shall be* baldness, *and* every beard cut off.

3 In their streets they shall gird themselves with sackcloth: on the tops of their houses, and in their streets, every one shall howl, [2]weeping abundantly.

4 And [c]Hĕsh′-bŏn shall cry, and Ĕl′-ē-ā′-lĕh: their voice shall be heard *even* unto Jā′-hăz: therefore the armed soldiers of Moab shall cry out; his life shall be grievous unto him.

5 My heart shall cry out for Moab; his fugitives *shall flee* unto Zō′-ăr, an heifer of three years old: for by [d]the mounting up of Lū′-hĭth with weeping shall they go it up; for in the way of Hŏr-ō-nā′-ĭm they shall raise up a cry of [4]destruction.

6 For the waters of Nĭm′-rĭm shall be desolate: for the hay is withered away, the grass faileth, there is no green thing.

7 Therefore the abundance they have gotten, and that which they have laid up, shall they carry away to the brook of the willows.

8 For the cry is gone round about the borders of Moab; the howling thereof unto Ĕg′-lā-ĭm, and the howling thereof unto Bē′ĕr–ē′-lĭm.

9 For the waters of Dī′-mŏn shall be full of blood: for I will bring [7]more upon Dī′-mŏn, lions upon him that escapeth of Moab, and upon the remnant of the land.

CHAPTER 16

SEND [a]ye the lamb to the ruler of the land from [1]Sē′-lă to the wilderness, unto the mount of the daughter of Zion.

2 For it shall be, *that*, as a wandering bird [2]cast out of the nest, *so* the daughters of Moab shall be at the fords of [b]Arnon.

3 [3]Take counsel, execute judgment; make thy shadow as the night in the midst of the noonday; hide the outcasts; bewray not him that wandereth.

4 Let mine outcasts dwell with thee, Moab; be thou a covert to them from the face of the spoiler: for the [4]extortioner is at an end, the spoiler ceaseth, [5]the oppressors are consumed out of the land.

5 And in mercy [c]shall the throne be [6]established: and he shall sit upon it in truth in the tabernacle of David, judging, and seeking judgment, and hasting righteousness.

6 ¶ We have heard of the [d]pride of Moab; *he is* very proud: *even* of his haughtiness, and his pride, and his wrath: [7]*but* his lies *shall* not *be* so.

7 Therefore shall Moab howl for Moab, every one shall howl: for the foundations of [e]Kĭr–hăr′-ĕ-sĕth shall ye [8]mourn; surely *they are* stricken.

8 For the fields of Hĕsh′-bŏn languish, *and* the vine of Sĭb′-măh: the lords of the heathen have broken down the principal plants thereof, they are come *even* unto Jā′-zĕr, they wandered *through* the wilderness: her branches are [9]stretched out, they are gone over the sea.

9 ¶ Therefore I will bewail with the weeping of Jā′-zĕr the vine of Sĭb′-măh: I will water thee with my tears, O Hĕsh′-bŏn, and Ĕl′-ē-ā′-lĕh: for [10]the shouting for thy summer fruits and for thy harvest is fallen.

10 And gladness is taken away, and joy out of the plentiful field; and in the vineyards there shall be no singing, neither shall there be shouting: the treaders shall tread out no wine in *their* presses; I have made *their vintage* shouting to cease.

11 Wherefore my bowels shall sound like an harp for Moab, and mine inward parts for Kĭr–hăr′-ĕsh.

12 ¶ And it shall come to pass, when it is seen that Moab is weary on the [f]high place, that he shall come to his sanctuary to pray; but he shall not prevail.

13 This *is* the word that the LORD hath spoken concerning Moab since that time.

14 But now the LORD hath spoken, saying, Within three years, [g]as the years of an hireling, and the glory of Moab shall be contemned, with all that great multitude; and the remnant *shall be* very small *and* [11]feeble.

10 Or, he shall not be alone.
11 Or, assemblies.
12 Or, betake themselves unto it.

CHAP. 15

a ch. 11.14. Jer. 9.26.
b Num. 21. 28.
1 Or, cut off.
2 descending into weeping, or, coming down with weeping.
c Num. 32.3.
3 Or, to the borders thereof, even to Zoar, as an heifer.
d Jer. 48.5.
4 breaking.
5 desolations.
6 Or, valley of the Arabians.
7 additions.

CHAP. 16

a 2 Ki. 3.4.
1 a rock, or, Petra.
2 Or, a nest forsaken.
b Num. 21. 13.
3 Bring.
4 wringer.
5 the treaders down.
c Ps. 89.14. Pro. 20.28. Dan. 7.14.
6 Or, prepared.
d Jer. 48.29.
7 Or, the falsehood of his pretensions.
e 2 Ki. 3.25.
8 Or, mutter.
9 Or, plucked up.
10 Or, the alarm is fallen upon, etc.
f Num. 22.4. ch. 15.2. Jer. 48.35.
g Deut. 15. 18. ch. 15.5.
11 Or, not many.

CHAPTER 17

THE [a]burden of Damascus. Behold,
Damascus is taken away from *being* a city, and it shall be a ruinous
heap.
2 The cities of Ă-rō-ĕr *are* forsaken:
they shall be for flocks, which shall
lie down, and [b]none shall make *them*
afraid.
3 The [c]fortress also shall cease from
Ē-phră-ĭm, and the kingdom from
Damascus, and the remnant of Syria:
they shall be as the glory of the children of Israel, saith the LORD of hosts.
4 And in that day it shall come to
pass, *that* the glory of Jacob shall be
made thin, and the [d]fatness of his
flesh shall wax lean.
5 And [e]it shall be as when the harvestman gathereth the corn, and
reapeth the ears with his arm; and it
shall be as he that gathereth ears in
the valley of Rĕph-ā-ĭm.
6 ¶ Yet gleaning grapes shall be left
in it, as the shaking of an olive tree,
two *or* three berries in the top of the
uppermost bough, four *or* five in the
outmost fruitful branches thereof,
saith the LORD God of Israel.
7 At that day shall a man [f]look to
his Maker, and his eyes shall have respect to the Holy One of Israel.
8 And he shall not look to the altars,
the work of his hands, neither shall
respect *that* which his fingers have
made, either the groves, or the [1]im-
ages.
9 ¶ In that day shall his strong cities
be as a forsaken bough, and an uppermost branch, which they left because
of the children of Israel: and there
shall be desolation.
10 Because [g]thou hast forgotten the
God of thy salvation, and hast not
been mindful of the rock of thy
strength, therefore shalt thou plant
pleasant plants, and shalt set it with
strange slips:
11 In the day shalt thou make thy
plant to grow, and in the morning
shalt thou make thy seed to flourish:
but the harvest *shall be* [2]a heap in the
day of grief and of desperate sorrow.
12 ¶ Woe to the [3]multitude of many
people, *which* make a noise like the
noise of the seas; and to the rushing
of nations, *that* make a rushing like
the rushing of [4]mighty waters!
13 The nations shall rush like the
rushing of many waters: but *God*
shall rebuke them, and they shall flee
far off, and shall be chased as the chaff
of the mountains before the wind, and
like [5]a rolling thing before the whirlwind.
14 And behold at eveningtide
trouble; *and* before the morning he
is not. This [h]*is* the portion of them
that spoil us, and the lot of them that
rob us.

CHAPTER 18

[1]WOE to the land shadowing with
wings, which *is* beyond the
rivers of Ē-thĭ-ō-pĭ-ă:
2 That sendeth ambassadors by the
sea, even in vessels of bulrushes upon
the waters, *saying*, Go, ye swift messengers, to a nation [2]scattered and
peeled, to a people terrible from their
beginning hitherto; [3]a nation meted
out and trodden down, [4]whose land
the rivers have spoiled!
3 All ye inhabitants of the world, and
dwellers on the earth, see ye, when
he lifteth up an ensign on the mountains; and when he bloweth a trumpet, hear ye.
4 For so the LORD said unto me, I
will take my rest, and I will [5]consider
in my dwelling place like a clear heat
[6]upon herbs, *and* like a cloud of dew
in the heat of harvest.
5 For afore the harvest, when the bud
is perfect, and the sour grape is ripen-
ing in the flower, he shall both cut off
the sprigs with pruning hooks, and
take away *and* cut down the branches.
6 They shall be left together unto the
fowls of the mountains, and to the
beasts of the earth: and the fowls shall
summer upon them, and all the beasts
of the earth shall winter upon them.
7 ¶ In that time [a]shall the present be
brought unto the LORD of hosts of a
people [7]scattered and peeled, and from
a people terrible from their beginning
hitherto; a nation meted out and
trodden under foot, whose land the
rivers have spoiled, to the place of the
name of the LORD of hosts, the mount
Zion.

CHAPTER 19

THE burden of Egypt. Behold, the
LORD rideth upon a swift cloud,
and shall come into Egypt: and the
idols of Egypt shall be moved at his
presence, and the heart of Egypt shall
melt in the midst of it.
2 And I will [1]set the Egyptians
against the [a]Egyptians: and they shall
fight every one against his brother,
and every one against his neighbour;
city against city, *and* kingdom against
kingdom.
3 And the spirit of Egypt [2]shall fail
in the midst thereof; and I will [3]de

CHAP. 17
a Jer. 49.23. Amos 1.3. Zech. 9.1. Fulfilled 740, 2 Ki. 16.9.
b Jer. 7.33.
c ch. 7.16.
d ch. 10.16.
e Jer. 51.33. Rev. 14.15-19.
f 2 Chr. 30. 11. Ps. 34.5. Hosea 5.15. Micah 7.7. Zech. 12.10.
1 Or, sun images.
g Ps. 106.13, 21.
2 Or, removed in the day of inheritance, and there shall be deadly sorrow.
3 Or, noise.
4 Or, many.
5 Or, thistle-down.
h Judg. 5.31. Ps. 8.3,9,18. Pro. 22.23.

CHAP. 18
1 Or, Ho.
2 Or, out-spread and polished.
3 a nation of line, line, and tread-ing under foot: or, a nation that meteth out, and tread-eth down.
4 Or, whose land the rivers de-spise!
5 Or, regard my set dwelling.
6 Or, after rain.
a Ps. 68.31. Zeph. 3.10. Mal. 1.11.
7 Or, out-spread and polished.

CHAP. 19
1 mingle.
a Judg. 7.22. 1 Sam. 14. 16. 2 Chr. 20.23.
2 shall be emptied.
3 swallow up.

roy the counsel thereof: and they
ıall seek to the idols, and to the
ıarmers, and to them that have
ımiliar spirits, and to the wizards.
4 And the Egyptians will I [4]give over
ıto the hand of a cruel lord; and a
erce king shall rule over them, saith
ıe Lord, the LORD of hosts.
5 And the [b]waters shall fail from the
ea, and the river shall be wasted and
ried up.
6 And they shall turn the rivers far
way; *and* the brooks [c]of defence shall
e emptied and dried up: the reeds
nd flags shall wither.
7 The paper reeds by the brooks, by
ıe mouth of the brooks, and every
ıing sown by the brooks, shall with-
r, be driven away, [5]and be no *more*.
8 The fishers also shall mourn, and
ll they that cast angle into the brooks
ıall lament, and they that spread
ets upon the waters shall languish.
9 Moreover they that work in fine
ax, and they that weave [6]networks,
ıall be confounded.
10 And they shall be broken in the
urposes thereof, all that make
uices *and* ponds [8]for fish.
11 ¶ Surely the princes of Zō-ăn *are*
ools, the counsel of the wise counsel-
rs of Pharaoh is become brutish:
ow say ye unto Pharaoh, I *am* the
on of the wise, the son of ancient
ings?
12 Where [d]*are* they? where *are* thy
ise *men?* and let them tell thee now,
nd let them know what the LORD of
osts hath purposed upon Egypt.
13 The princes of Zō-ăn are become
ools, the princes of [e]Nŏph are de-
eived; they have also seduced Egypt,
ven [9]*they that are* the stay of the
ibes thereof.
14 The LORD hath mingled [10]a per-
erse spirit in the midst thereof: and
ıey have caused Egypt to err in every
ork thereof, as a drunken *man* stag-
ereth in his vomit.
15 Neither shall there be *any* work
or Egypt, which the head or tail,
ranch or rush, may do.
16 In that day shall Egypt [f]be like
nto women: and it shall be afraid
nd fear because of the shaking of the
and of the LORD of hosts, which he
ıaketh over it.
17 And the land of Judah shall be a
rror unto Egypt, every one that
ıaketh mention thereof shall be
fraid in himself, because of the coun-
el of the LORD of hosts, which he
ath determined against it.

4 Or, shut up.
b Jer. 51.36. Eze. 30.12.
c 2 Ki. 19.24.
5 and shall not be.
6 Or, white works.
7 foundations.
8 of living things.
d ch. 41.22, 23. Acts. 7.22. 1 Cor. 1.20.
e Jer. 2.16. Hosea 9.6.
9 corners, or, governors.
10 a spirit of perverseness.
f Ps. 48.6. ch. 30.17. Jer. 30.5,7. Nah. 3.13.
11 the lip.
12 Or, of Heres, or, of the sun.
g Gen. 12.7. Ex. 24.4. Josh. 22.10. Heb. 13.10.
h Josh. 4.20. ch. 55.13.
i Mal. 1.11.
j ch. 11.15.
k Ps. 100.3. Hosea 2.23. Rom. 3.29. Eph. 2.10. Phil. 1.6.

CHAP. 20

a 2 Ki. 18.17.
1 by the hand of Isaiah.
b Zech. 13.4.
c 1 Sam. 19. 24.
d ch. 8.18.
2 the captivity of Egypt.
e 2 Sam. 10.4. Micah 1.11.
3 nakedness.

18 ¶ In that day shall five cities in the
land of Egypt speak [11]the language of
Canaan, and swear to the LORD of
hosts; one shall be called, The city [12]of
destruction.
19 In that [g]day shall there be an altar
to the LORD in the midst of the land of
Egypt, and a pillar at the border thereof to the LORD.
20 And [h]it shall be for a sign and for
a witness unto the LORD of hosts in
the land of Egypt: for they shall cry
unto the LORD because of the oppressors, and he shall send them a saviour,
and a great one, and he shall deliver
them.
21 And the LORD shall be known to
Egypt, and the Egyptians shall know
the LORD in that day, [i]and shall do
sacrifice and oblation; yea, they shall
vow a vow unto the LORD, and perform *it*.
22 And the LORD shall smite Egypt:
he shall smite and heal *it:* and they
shall return *even* to the LORD, and he
shall be intreated of them, and shall
heal them.
23 ¶ In that day [j]shall there be a
highway out of Egypt to Assyria, and
the Assyrian shall come into Egypt,
and the Egyptian into Assyria, and
the Egyptians shall serve with the
Assyrians.
24 In that day shall Israel be the
third with Egypt and with Assyria,
even a blessing in the midst of the land:
25 Whom the LORD of hosts shall
bless, saying, Blessed *be* Egypt my
people, and Assyria [k]the work of my
hands, and Israel mine inheritance.

CHAPTER 20

IN the year that [a]Tartan came unto
Ăsh-dŏd, (when Sär-gŏn the king
of Assyria sent him,) and fought
against Ăsh-dŏd, and took it;
2 At the same time spake the LORD
[1]by Isaiah the son of Amoz, saying,
Go and loose [b]the sackcloth from off
thy loins, and put off thy shoe from
thy foot. And he did so, [c]walking
naked and barefoot.
3 And the LORD said, Like as my
servant Isaiah hath walked naked and
barefoot three years [d]*for* a sign and
wonder upon Egypt and upon Ē-thĭ-
ō-pĭ-ă;
4 So shall the king of Assyria lead
away [2]the Egyptians prisoners, and
the Ē-thĭ-ō-pĭ-ăns captives, young and
old, naked and barefoot, [e]even with
their buttocks uncovered, to the
[3]shame of Egypt.

5 And [f]they shall be afraid and ashamed of Ē-thĭ-ṓ-pĭ-ă their expectation, and of Egypt their glory.

6 And the inhabitant of this [4]isle shall say in that day, Behold, such *is* our expectation, whither we flee for help to be delivered from the king of Assyria: and how shall we escape?

CHAPTER 21

THE burden of the desert of the sea. As [a]whirlwinds in the south pass through; *so* it cometh from the desert, from a terrible land.

2 A [1]grievous vision is declared unto me; the [b]treacherous dealer dealeth treacherously, and the spoiler spoileth. [c]Go up, O Ḗ-lăm: besiege, O Mḗ-dĭ-ă; all the sighing thereof have I made to cease.

3 Therefore are my loins filled with pain: pangs have taken hold upon me, as the pangs of a woman that travaileth: I was bowed down at the hearing *of it;* I was dismayed at the seeing *of it.*

4 [2]My heart panted, fearfulness affrighted me: [d]the night of my pleasure hath he [3]turned into fear unto me.

5 Prepare [e]the table, watch in the watchtower, eat, drink: arise, ye princes, *and* anoint the shield.

6 For thus hath the Lord said unto me, Go, set a watchman, let him declare what he seeth.

7 And he saw a chariot *with* a couple of horsemen, a chariot of asses, *and* a chariot of camels; and he hearkened diligently with much heed:

8 And [4]he cried, A lion: My lord, I stand continually upon [f]the watchtower in the daytime, and I am set in my ward [5]whole nights:

9 And, behold, here cometh a chariot of men, *with* a couple of horsemen. And he answered and said, [g]Babylon is fallen, is fallen; and all the graven images of her gods he hath broken unto the ground.

10 O [h]my threshing, and the [6]corn of my floor: that which I have heard of the LORD of hosts, the God of Israel, have I declared unto you.

11 ¶ The [i]burden of Dū́-măh. He calleth to me out of Sḗ-ĭr, Watchman, what of the night? Watchman, what of the night?

12 The watchman said, The morning cometh, and also the night: if ye will inquire, inquire ye: return, come.

13 ¶ The burden upon Arabia. In the forest in Arabia shall ye lodge, O ye travelling companies of [j]Dḗ-dă-nĭm.

f 2 Ki. 18.21. ch. 31.1-3.
4 Or, country.
CHAP. 21
a Zech. 9.14.
1 hard.
b 1 Sam. 24. 13. ch. 24.16.
c Jer. 49.34. ch. 13.17.
2 Or, My mind wandered.
d Deut. 28. 67.
3 put.
e Dan. 5.5.
4 Or, cried as a lion.
f Hab. 2.1.
5 Or, every night.
g ch. 13.19. Jer. 50.2. Rev. 14.8.
h Jer. 51.33. Micah 4.13. Hab. 3.12.
6 son.
i 1 Chr. 1.30. Eze. 35.2. Obad. 1.
j 1 Chr. 1.9.
k Job 6.19.
7 Or, bring ye.
8 from the face, or, for fear.
l Gen. 25.13. Ps. 120.5. Song 1.5. ch. 60.7.
9 bows.
m Num. 23. 19. 1 Sam. 15. 29. ch. 1.20. Matt. 24.35. Mark 13.31. Luke 21.33. 1 Pet. 1.25.
CHAP. 22
1 of the bow.
2 I will be bitter in weeping.
a Esther 3.15. Lam. 1.5.
b ch. 21.2. Jer. 49.35.
3 made naked.
4 the choice of thy valleys.
5 Or, toward.
c 1 Ki. 7.2.
d 2 Ki. 20.20. 2 Chr. 32.4. Song 4.4.
e Neh. 3.16.

14 The inhabitants of the land of [k]Tē-mă [7]brought water to him that wa thirsty, they prevented with thei bread him that fled.

15 For they fled [8]from the swords from the drawn sword, and from th bent bow, and from the grievousnes of war.

16 For thus hath the Lord said unt me, Within a year, according to th years of an hireling, and all the glor of [l]Kḗ-där shall fail:

17 And the residue of the number o [9]archers, the mighty men of the chil dren of Kḗ-där, shall be diminished for the LORD [m]God of Israel hat spoken *it.*

CHAPTER 22

THE burden of the valley of visior What aileth thee now, that tho art wholly gone up to the housetops

2 Thou that art full of stirs, a tumu tuous city, a joyous city: thy slai *men are* not slain with the sword, nc dead in battle.

3 All thy rulers are fled together, the are bound [1]by the archers: all that ai found in thee are bound togethei *which* have fled from far.

4 Therefore said I, Look away fror me; [2]I will weep bitterly, labour nc to comfort me, because of the spoilin of the daughter of my people.

5 For *it is* a day of trouble, and c treading down, and of perplexity [a]b the Lord GOD of hosts in the valley c vision, breaking down the walls, an of crying to the mountains.

6 And [b]Ḗ-lăm bare the quiver wit chariots of men *and* horsemen, an Kĭr [3]uncovered the shield.

7 And it shall come to pass, *that* [4]th choicest valleys shall be full of char ots, and the horsemen shall set them selves in array [5]at the gate.

8 ¶ And he discovered the coverir of Judah, and thou didst look in th day to the armour [c]of the house of tl forest.

9 Ye [d]have seen also the breaches c the city of David, that they are man and ye gathered together the wate of the lower pool.

10 And ye have numbered the hous of Jerusalem, and the houses have y broken down to fortify the wall.

11 Ye [e]made also a ditch betwee the two walls for the water of the ol pool: but ye have not looked unto tl maker thereof, neither had respe unto him that fashioned it long ago.

12 And in that day did the Lord Go

hosts call to weeping, and to mourn-
;, and to baldness, and to girding
h sackcloth:
And [f]behold joy and gladness,
ying oxen, and killing sheep, eat-
flesh, and drinking wine: let [g]us
and drink; for to morrow we shall
.
And it was revealed in mine ears
the LORD of hosts, Surely this ini-
ity shall [h]not be purged from you
ye die, saith the Lord GOD of hosts.
¶ Thus saith the Lord GOD of
sts, Go, get thee unto this treasurer,
n [i]unto Shĕb-nă, [j]which *is* over the
use, *and say*,
What hast thou here? and whom
st thou here, that thou hast hewed
e out a sepulchre here, [6]*as* he that
weth him out a sepulchre on high,
l that graveth an habitation for
nself in a rock?
Behold, [7]the LORD will carry thee
ay with [8]a mighty captivity, and
l surely cover thee.
He will surely violently turn and
s thee *like* a ball into a [9]large
intry: there shalt thou die, and
re the chariots of thy glory *shall be*
shame of thy lord's house.
And I will drive thee from thy
tion, and from thy state shall he
l thee down.
¶ And it shall come to pass in that
y, that I will call my servant [k]Ē-lī-
im the son of Hĭl-kī-ăh:
And I will clothe him with thy
be, and strengthen him with thy
dle, and I will commit thy govern-
nt into his hand: and he shall be [l]a
her to the inhabitants of Jerusalem,
d to the house of Judah.
And the key of the house of David
l I lay upon his shoulder; so he
all open, and none shall shut;
d he shall shut, and none shall
en.
And I will fasten him *as* a [m]nail
a sure place; and he shall be for
glorious throne to his father's
use.
And they shall hang upon him all
glory of his father's house, the off-
ing and the issue, all vessels of
all quantity, from the vessels of
s, even to all the [10]vessels of
gons.
In that day, saith the LORD of
sts, shall the nail that is fastened in
sure place be removed, and be cut
wn, and fall; and the burden that
s upon it shall be cut off: for the
RD hath spoken *it*.

f ch. 5.12. Amos 6.3. Luke 17.26-29.
g ch. 56.12. 1 Cor. 15.32.
h 1 Sam. 3.14. Eze. 24.13.
i 2 Ki. 18.37. ch. 36.3.
j 1 Ki. 4.6.
6 Or, O he.
7 Or, the LORD who covered thee with an excellent covering, and clothed thee gorgeously, shall surely, etc.
8 the captivity of a man.
9 large of spaces.
k 2 Ki. 18.18.
l Job 29.16.
m Ezra 9.8.
10 Or, instruments of viols.

CHAP. 23

a Jer. 25.22. Eze. 26.1-21. Amos 1.9. Zech. 9.2,4.
1 silent.
b Eze. 27.3.
c ch. 19.16.
d ch. 22.2.
2 from afar off.
e Isa. 2.12. Eze. 28.2. 1 Tim. 3.4.
3 to pollute. ch. 2.11,17. Luke 1.51, 52.
4 girdle.
5 Or, concerning a merchantman.
6 Canaan.
7 Or, strengths.
f Lam. 1.6. Hag. 2.22. Rev. 18.22.
g Ps. 71.3.
h ch. 2.16. Eze. 27.25. Rev. 18.22.
8 it shall be unto Tyre as the song of an harlot.

CHAPTER 23

THE [a]burden of Tyre. Howl, ye
ships of Tarshish; for it is laid
waste, so that there is no house, no
entering in: from the land of Chĭt-tĭm
it is revealed to them.
2 Be [1]still, ye inhabitants of the isle;
thou whom the merchants of Zī-dŏn,
that pass over the sea, have replenished.
3 And by great waters the seed of
Sī-hôr, the harvest of the river, *is* her
revenue; and [b]she is a mart of nations.
4 Be thou ashamed, O Zī-dŏn: for
the sea hath spoken, *even* the strength
of the sea, saying, I travail not, nor
bring forth children, neither do I
nourish up young men, *nor* bring up
virgins.
5 As [c]at the report concerning Egypt,
so shall they be sorely pained at the
report of Tyre.
6 Pass ye over to Tarshish; howl, ye
inhabitants of the isle.
7 *Is* this your [d]joyous *city*, whose
antiquity *is* of ancient days? her own
feet shall carry her [2]afar off to sojourn.
8 Who hath taken this counsel
against Tyre, [e]the crowning *city*,
whose merchants *are* princes, whose
traffickers *are* the honourable of the
earth?
9 The LORD of hosts hath purposed
it, [3]to stain the pride of all glory, *and*
to bring into contempt all the honourable of the earth.
10 Pass through thy land as a river,
O daughter of Tarshish: *there is* no
more [4]strength.
11 He stretched out his hand over the
sea, he shook the kingdoms: the
LORD hath given a commandment
[5]against [6]the merchant *city*, to destroy
the [7]strong holds thereof.
12 And he said, [f]Thou shalt no more
rejoice, O thou oppressed virgin,
daughter of Zī-dŏn: arise, pass over
to Chĭt-tĭm; there also shalt thou
have no rest.
13 Behold the land of the Chăl-dē-
ăns; this people was not, *till* the
Assyrian founded it for [g]them that
dwell in the wilderness: they set up
the towers thereof, they raised up the
palaces thereof; *and* he brought it to
ruin.
14 Howl, [h]ye ships of Tarshish: for
your strength is laid waste.
15 And it shall come to pass in that
day, that Tyre shall be forgotten seventy years, according to the days of
one king: after the end of seventy
years [8]shall Tyre sing as an harlot.

16 Take an harp, go about the city,
thou harlot that hast been forgotten;
make sweet melody, sing many songs,
that thou mayest be remembered.
17 ¶ And it shall come to pass after
the end of seventy years, that the
LORD will visit Tyre, and she shall
turn to her hire, and [i]shall commit
fornication with all the kingdoms of
the world upon the face of the earth.
18 And her merchandise and her
hire shall [j]be holiness to the LORD: it
shall not be treasured nor laid up;
for her merchandise shall be for them
that dwell before the LORD, to eat
sufficiently, and for [9]durable clothing.

CHAPTER 24

BEHOLD, the LORD maketh the
earth empty, and maketh it waste,
and [1]turneth it upside down, and
scattereth abroad the inhabitants
thereof.
2 And it shall be, as with the people,
so with the [2]priest; as with the servant, so with his master; as with the
maid, so with her mistress; [a]as with
the buyer, so with the seller; as with
the lender, so with the borrower; as
with the taker of usury, so with the
giver of usury to him.
3 The land shall be utterly emptied,
and utterly spoiled: for the LORD
hath spoken this word.
4 The earth mourneth *and* fadeth
away, the world languisheth *and*
fadeth away, [3]the haughty people of
the earth do languish.
5 The [b]earth also is defiled under the
inhabitants thereof; because they
have transgressed the laws, changed
the ordinance, broken the everlasting
covenant.
6 Therefore hath [c]the curse devoured
the earth, and they that dwell therein
are desolate: therefore the inhabitants
of the earth are burned, and few men
left.
7 The new wine mourneth, the vine
languisheth, all the merryhearted do
sigh.
8 The mirth of tabrets ceaseth, the
noise of them that rejoice endeth, the
joy of the harp ceaseth.
9 They shall not drink wine with a
song; strong drink shall be bitter to
them that drink it.
10 The city of confusion is broken
down: every house is shut up, that no
man may come in.
11 *There is* a crying for wine in the
streets; all joy is darkened, the mirth
of the land is gone.
12 In the city is left desolation, a
the gate is smitten with destructi
13 ¶ When thus it shall be in
midst of the land among the peo
there shall be as the shaking of
olive tree, *and* as the gleaning gra
when the vintage is done.
14 They shall lift up their voice, t
shall sing for the majesty of the Lo
they shall cry aloud from the sea.
15 Wherefore glorify ye the LORD
the [4]fires, *even* [d]the name of the Lo
God of Israel in the isles of the se
16 ¶ From the [5]uttermost part of
earth have we heard songs, *even* gl
to the righteous. But I said, [6]My le
ness, my leanness, woe unto me! [e]
treacherous dealers have dealt trea
erously; yea, the treacherous deal
have dealt very treacherously.
17 Fear, [f]and the pit, and the sna
are upon thee, O inhabitant of
earth.
18 And it shall come to pass, *that*
who fleeth from the noise of the f
shall fall into the pit; and he t
cometh up out of the midst of the
shall be taken in the snare: for
[g]windows from on high are open, a
[h]the foundations of the earth
shake.
19 The [i]earth is utterly broken do
the earth is clean dissolved, the ea
is moved exceedingly.
20 The earth shall reel to and
like a drunkard, and shall be remo
like a cottage; and the transgress
thereof shall be heavy upon it; an
shall fall, and not rise again.
21 And it shall come to pass in t
day, *that* the LORD shall [7]punish
host of the high ones *that are* on hi
[j]and the kings of the earth upon
earth.
22 And they shall be gathered
gether, [8]*as* prisoners are gathered
the [9]pit, and shall be shut up in
prison, and after many days shall t
be [10]visited.
23 Then the moon shall be confou
ed, and the sun ashamed, when
LORD of hosts [k]shall reign in mo
Zion, and in Jerusalem, and [11]bef
his ancients gloriously.

CHAPTER 25

O LORD, thou *art* my God; [a]I w
exalt thee, I will praise thy nan
for thou hast done wonderful *thin*
thy [b]counsels of old *are* faithfuln
and truth.
2 For thou hast made [c]of a city
heap; *of* a defenced city a ruin:

i Gen. 10.15, 19. Josh. 11.8. Rev. 17.2.
j Deut. 28.65, 66. Ps. 45.12. Lam. 1.3. Zech. 14.20, 21.
9 old.

CHAP. 24
1 perverteth the face thereof.
2 Or, prince.
a Eze. 7.12.
3 the height of the people.
b Gen. 3.17. Lev. 18.25. Num. 35.33.
c Lev. 26.15. Deut. 28.15. Dan. 9.11. Mal. 2.2.
4 Or, valleys.
d Mal. 1.11. Isa. 66.19.
5 wing.
6 Leanness to me, or, My secret to me.
e Jer. 3.20.
f Jer. 48.43, 44. Amos. 5.19.
g Gen. 7.11.
h Ps. 18.7.
i Jer. 4.23.
7 visit upon.
j Ps. 76.12.
8 with the gathering of prisoners.
9 Or, dungeon.
10 Or, found wanting.
k Heb. 12.22. Rev. 19.4.
11 Or, there shall be glory before his ancients.

CHAP. 25
a Ex. 15.2.
b Num. 23. 19.
c Jer. 51.37.

.lace of strangers to be no city; it
all never be built.
Therefore shall the strong people
lorify thee, the city of the terrible
ıtions shall fear thee.
For thou hast been a strength to
e poor, a strength to the needy in
s distress, [e]a refuge from the storm,
shadow from the heat, when the
ast of the terrible ones *is* as a storm
ainst the wall.
Thou shalt bring down the noise of
:angers, as the heat in a dry place;
en the heat with the shadow of a
ɔud: the branch of the terrible ones
all be brought low.
¶ And in this mountain shall [f]the
ɔRD of hosts make unto [g]all people
feast of fat things, a feast of wines
ı the lees, of fat things full of
arrow, of wines on the lees well re-
ıed.
And he will [1]destroy in this moun-
in the face of the covering [2]cast over
people, and [h]the vail that is spread
er all nations.
He will [i]swallow up death in vic-
ry; and the Lord GOD [j]will wipe
/ay tears from off all faces; and the
buke of his people shall he take
/ay from off all the earth: for the
ɔRD hath spoken *it*.
¶ And it shall be said in that day,
, this *is* our God; [k]we have waited
r him, and he will save us: this *is* the
ɔRD; we have waited for him, we
ll be glad and rejoice in his salva-
n.
) For in this mountain shall the
nd of the LORD rest, and Moab
all be [3]trodden down under him,
en as straw is [4]trodden down for
e dunghill.
1 And he shall spread forth his
nds in the midst of them, as he that
'immeth spreadeth forth *his hands*
swim: and he shall bring [l]down
eir pride together with the spoils of
eir hands.
2 And the [m]fortress of the high fort
thy walls shall he bring down, lay
w, *and* bring to the ground, *even* to
: dust.

CHAPTER 26

N that day shall this song be sung
n the land of Judah; We have a
'ong city; salvation will *God* ap-
ıint *for* walls and bulwarks.
Open [a]ye the gates, that the right-
us nation which keepeth the [1]truth
ay enter in.
Thou wilt keep *him* in [2]perfect
peace, *whose* [3]mind *is* stayed *on thee:*
because he trusteth in thee.
4 Trust ye in the LORD for ever: for
in the LORD JĔ-HŌ-VĂH *is* [4]ever-
lasting strength:
5 ¶ For he bringeth down them that
dwell on high; the lofty city, he layeth
it low; he layeth it low, *even* to the
ground; he bringeth it *even* to the
dust.
6 The foot shall tread it down, *even*
the feet of the poor, *and* the steps of
the needy.
7 The way of the just *is* uprightness:
thou, [b]most upright, dost weigh the
path of the just.
8 Yea, [c]in the way of thy judgments,
O LORD, have we waited for thee; the
desire of *our* soul *is* to thy name, and
to the remembrance of thee.
9 With [d]my soul have I desired thee
in the night; yea, with my spirit within me will I seek thee early: for [e]when
thy judgments *are* in the earth, the inhabitants of the world will learn
righteousness.
10 Let [f]favour be shewed to the
wicked, *yet* will he not learn righteousness: in [g]the land of uprightness
will he deal unjustly, and will not behold the majesty of the LORD.
11 LORD, *when* thy hand is lifted up,
[h]they will not see: *but* they shall see,
and be ashamed for *their* envy [5]at the
people; yea, the fire of thine enemies
shall devour them.
12 ¶ LORD, thou wilt ordain peace
for us: for thou also hast wrought all
our works [6]in us.
13 O LORD our God, [i]*other* lords beside thee have had dominion over us:
but by thee only will we make mention of thy name.
14 *They are* dead, they shall not live;
they are deceased, they shall not rise:
therefore hast thou visited and destroyed them, and made all their
memory to perish.
15 Thou hast increased the nation,
O LORD, thou hast increased the nation: thou art glorified: thou hadst
removed *it* far *unto* all the ends of the
earth.
16 LORD, [j]in trouble have they visited
thee, they poured out a [7]prayer *when*
thy chastening *was* upon them.
17 Like as a woman with child, *that*
draweth near the time of her delivery,
is in pain, *and* crieth out in her pangs;
so have we been in thy sight, O
LORD.
18 We have been with child, we have
been in pain, we have as it were

d Rev. 11.13.
e Ps. 46.1-11. Nah. 1.7.
f Pro. 9.2. Matt. 22.4.
g Dan. 7.14. Matt. 8.11.
1 swallow up.
2 covered.
h 2 Cor. 3.15. Eph. 1.17.
i Isa. 26.19. Hos. 13.14. 1 Cor. 15.54. 2 Cor. 5.4. Heb. 2.14.
j Rev. 7.17.
k Gen. 49.18. Titus 2.13.
3 Or, threshed.
4 Or, threshed in Madmenah.
l Job 40.11, 12. ch. 2.10-12, 15-17.
m ch. 26.5.

CHAP. 26

a Ps. 118.19. ch. 60.11. Rev. 21.13, 24-27.
1 truths.
2 peace, peace.
3 Or, thought, or, imagination.
4 the rock of ages.
b Deut. 32.4.
c Ps. 18.22. ch. 64.5. Mal. 4.4. Luke 1.6.
d Ps. 63.6. Song 3.1. Luke 6.12.
e Ps. 83.16.
f Eccl. 8.12. Rom. 2.4.
g Ps. 143.10.
h Job 34.27.
5 Or, toward thy people.
6 Or, for us.
i Ps. 66.12.
j 2 Chr. 33. 12. Hosea 5.15.
7 secret speech.

brought forth wind; we have not
wrought any deliverance in the earth;
neither have [k]the inhabitants of the
world fallen.
19 Thy [l]dead *men* shall live, *together*
with my dead body shall they arise.
[m]Awake and sing, ye that dwell in
dust: for thy dew *is as* the dew of
herbs, and the earth shall cast out the
dead.
20 ¶ Come, my people, [n]enter thou
into thy chambers, and shut thy doors
about thee: hide thyself as it were [o]for
a little moment, until the indignation
be overpast.
21 For, behold, the LORD [p]cometh
out of his place to punish the inhabitants of the earth for their iniquity: the
earth also shall disclose her [8]blood,
and shall no more cover her slain.

CHAPTER 27

IN that day the LORD with his sore
and great and strong sword shall
punish lē-vī-ă-thăn the [1]piercing serpent, [a]even lē-vī-ă-thăn that crooked
serpent; and he shall slay the [b]dragon
that *is* in the sea.
2 In that day sing ye unto her, A
vineyard of red wine.
3 I the LORD do keep it; I will water
it every moment: lest *any* hurt it, I will
keep it night and day.
4 Fury *is* not in me: who would set
[e]the briers *and* thorns against me in
battle? I would [2]go through them, I
would burn them together.
5 Or let him take hold of my strength,
that he may [d]make peace with me;
and he shall make peace with me.
6 He shall cause them that come of
Jacob to [e]take root: Israel shall blossom and bud, and fill the face of the
world with fruit.
7 ¶ Hath he smitten him, [3]as he
smote those that smote him? *or* is he
slain according to the slaughter of
them that are slain by him?
8 In [f]measure, [4]when it shooteth
forth, thou wilt debate with it: [5]he
stayeth his rough wind in the day of
the east wind.
9 By this therefore shall the iniquity
of Jacob be purged; and this *is* all the
fruit to take away his sin; when he
maketh all the stones of the altar as
chalkstones that are beaten in sunder,
the groves and [6]images shall not
stand up.
10 Yet the defenced city *shall be* desolate, *and* the habitation forsaken,
and left like a wilderness: there [g]shall
the calf feed, and there shall he lie

k Ps. 17.14.
l ch. 25.8. Hos. 13.14. John 5.28, 29.
m Dan. 12.2.
n Gen. 7.1.
o Ps. 30.5. 2 Cor. 4.17.
p Micah 1.3. Jude 14.
8 bloods.

CHAP. 27
1 Or, stiff, or, crossing like a bar.
a Ps. 74.13.
b Eze. 29.3.
c 2 Sam. 23.6.
2 Or, march against.
d Job 22.21. ch. 53.4,5. Eph. 2.12, 13,14.
e ch. 37.31. Hos. 14.5,6.
3 according to the stroke of those.
f Job 23.6. Ps. 6.1. Jer. 10.24. 1 Cor. 10.13.
4 Or, when thou sendest it forth.
5 Or, when he removeth it.
6 Or, sun images.
g ch. 17.2.
h Deut. 32. 28.
Ps. 28.5. ch. 1.3. Jer. 4.22. 2 Thes. 1.8.
i Deut. 32.18. ch. 44.2,21, 24.
j ch. 2.11.
k Num. 10.2. Ps. 81.3. Hosea 8.1. Matt. 24.31. Rev. 11.15.

CHAP. 28
1 broken.
a ch. 30.30. Eze. 13.11.
2 with feet.
3 swalloweth.
b Lev. 10.9. Deut. 29.6. Pro. 20.1. Hosea 4.11.
c ch. 56.10, 12.

down, and consume the branch
thereof.
11 When the boughs thereof a
withered, they shall be broken off: t
women come, *and* set them on fir
for [h]it *is* a people of no understandin
therefore he that made them will n
have mercy on them, and he [i]th
formed them will shew them
favour.
12 ¶ And it shall come to pass in th
day, *that* the LORD shall beat off fro
the channel of the river unto t
stream of Egypt, and ye shall be gat
ered one by one, O ye children of
rael.
13 And [j]it shall come to pass in th
day, *that* [k]the great trumpet shall
blown, and they shall come whi
were ready to perish in the land
Assyria, and the outcasts in the la
of Egypt, and shall worship the Lo
in the holy mount at Jerusalem.

CHAPTER 28

WOE to the crown of pride, to t
drunkards of Ē-phră-ĭm, who
glorious beauty *is* a fading flow
which *are* on the head of the fat v
leys of them that are [1]overcome wi
wine!
2 Behold, the Lord hath a migh
and strong one, [a]*which* as a tempest
hail *and* a destroying storm, as a flo
of mighty waters overflowing, sh
cast down to the earth with t
hand.
3 The crown of pride, the drunkar
of Ē-phră-ĭm, shall be trodden [2]und
feet:
4 And the glorious beauty, which
on the head of the fat valley, shall
a fading flower, *and* as the hasty fr
before the summer; which *when*
that looketh upon it seeth, while
is yet in his hand he [3]eateth it up.
5 ¶ In that day shall the LORD
hosts be for a crown of glory, and f
a diadem of beauty, unto the resid
of his people,
6 And for a spirit of judgment to hi
that sitteth in judgment, and f
strength to them that turn the bat
to the gate.
7 ¶ But they also [b]have erred throu
wine, and through strong drink a
out of the way; [c]the priest and t
prophet have erred through stro
drink, they are swallowed up of wi
they are out of the way through stro
drink; they err in vision, they stuml
in judgment.
8 For all tables are full of vomit a

thiness, *so that there is* no place
ean.
¶ Whom [d]shall he teach knowl-
lge? and whom shall he make to un-
erstand [4]doctrine? *them that are*
eaned from the milk, *and* drawn
om the breasts.
0 For precept [5]*must be* upon pre-
ept, precept upon precept; line upon
ne, line upon line; here a little, *and*
ere a little:
1 For with [6]stammering lips and
nother tongue [7]will he speak to this
eople.
12 To whom he said, This [e]*is* the
est *wherewith* ye may cause the
eary to rest; and this *is* the refresh-
ig: yet they would not hear.
13 But the word of the LORD was
nto them precept upon precept, pre-
ept upon precept; line upon line,
ne upon line; here a little, *and* there
little; that they might go, and fall
ackward, and be broken, and snar-
d, and taken.
14 ¶ Wherefore hear the word of the
ORD, ye scornful men, that rule this
eople which *is* in Jerusalem.
15 Because ye have said, We have
nade a covenant with death, and with
ell are we at agreement; when the
verflowing scourge shall pass
hrough, it shall not come unto us: for
ve have made lies our refuge, and
nder falsehood have we hid our-
elves:
16 ¶ Therefore thus saith the Lord
GOD, Behold, I lay in Zion for a
oundation a [f]stone, a tried stone, a
recious corner *stone*, a sure founda-
ion: he that believeth shall not make
aste.
17 Judgment also will I lay to the
ine, and righteousness to the plum-
net: and the hail shall sweep away
he refuge of lies, and the waters shall
overflow the hiding place.
18 ¶ And your covenant with death
shall be disannulled, and your agree-
nent with hell shall not stand; when
he overflowing scourge shall pass
through, then ye shall be [8]trodden
down by it.
19 From the time that it goeth forth
it shall take you: for morning by
morning shall it pass over, by day and
by night: and it shall be a vexation
only [9]*to* understand the report.
20 For the bed is shorter than that *a*
man can stretch himself *on it:* and the
covering narrower than that he can
wrap himself *in it*.
21 For the LORD shall rise up as *in*
[g]mount Pĕ-rā-zĭm, he shall be wroth,
as *in* the valley of [h]Gibeon, that he
may do [i]his work, his strange work;
and bring to pass his act, his strange
act.
22 Now therefore be ye not mockers,
lest your bands be made strong: for I
have heard from the Lord GOD of
hosts a consumption, even determined
upon the whole earth.
23 ¶ Give ye ear, and hear my voice;
hearken, and hear my speech.
24 Doth the plowman plow all day
to sow? doth he open and break the
clods of his ground?
25 When he hath made plain the face
thereof, doth he not cast abroad the
fitches, and scatter the cummin, and
cast in [10]the principal wheat and the
appointed barley and the [11]rie in their
[12]place?
26 [13]For his God doth instruct him
to discretion, *and* doth teach him.
27 For the fitches are not threshed
with a threshing instrument, neither
is a cart wheel turned about upon the
cummin; but the fitches are beaten
out with a staff, and the cummin with
a rod.
28 Bread *corn* is bruised; because he
will not ever be threshing it, nor
break *it with* the wheel of his cart, nor
bruise it *with* his horsemen.
29 This also cometh forth from the
LORD of hosts, [j]*which* is wonderful in
counsel, *and* excellent in working.

CHAPTER 29

1 WOE to [1]Âr-ĭ-ĕl, to Âr-ĭ-ĕl, [2]the
city *where* David dwelt! add ye
year to year; let them [3]kill sacrifices.
2 Yet I will distress Âr-ĭ-ĕl, and there
shall be heaviness and sorrow: and it
shall be unto me as Âr-ĭ-ĕl.
3 And I will camp against thee round
about, and will lay siege against thee
with a mount, and I will raise forts
against thee.
4 And thou shalt be brought down,
and shalt speak out of the ground,
and thy speech shall be low out of the
dust, and thy voice shall be, as of one
that hath a familiar spirit, [a]out of the
ground, and thy speech shall [4]whisper
out of the dust.
5 Moreover the multitude of thy
strangers shall be like small dust, and
the multitude of the terrible ones *shall*
be as chaff that passeth away: yea, it
shall be at an instant suddenly.
6 Thou shalt be visited of the LORD
of hosts with thunder, and with earthquake, and great noise, with storm

d Jer. 6.10.
4 the hearing?
5 Or, hath been.
6 stammerings of lip.
7 Or, he hath spoken.
e 2 Chr. 14.7.
f Gen. 49.24. Ps. 118.22. Matt. 21.42. Acts 4.11. Rom. 9.33. Eph. 2.20.
8 a treading down to it.
9 Or, when he shall make you to understand doctrine.
g 2 Sam. 5.20.
h Josh. 10.10.
i 1 Sam. 3.11. Jer. 30.14. Lam. 3.33. Eze. 5.16. Luke 19.27. Rom. 11.8.
10 Or, the wheat in the principal place, and barley in the appointed place.
11 Or, spelt.
12 border?
13 Or, And he bindeth it in such sort as his God doth teach him.
j Ps. 40.5. Jer. 32.19. Rom. 11.33.

CHAP. 29

1 Or, O Ariel, that is, The lion of God, or, hearth, or, fireplace of God.
2 Or, of the city.
3 cut off the heads.
a ch. 8.19.
4 peep, or, chirp.

and tempest, and the flame of devouring fire.

7 ¶ And the multitude of all the nations that fight against Âr-ĭ-ĕl, even all that fight against her and her munition, and that distress her, shall be as a dream of a night vision.

8 It shall even be as when an hungry *man* dreameth, and, behold, he eateth; but he awaketh, and his soul is empty: or as when a thirsty man dreameth, and, behold, he drinketh; but he awaketh, and, behold, *he is* faint, and his soul hath appetite: so shall the multitude of all the nations be, that fight against mount Zion.

9 ¶ Stay yourselves, and wonder; [5]cry ye out, and cry: they are drunken, but not with wine; they stagger, but not with strong drink.

10 For [b]the LORD hath poured out upon you the spirit of deep sleep, and hath closed [c]your eyes: the prophets and your [6]rulers, the seers hath he covered.

11 And the vision of all is become unto you as the words of a [7]book that is sealed, which *men* deliver to one that is learned, saying, Read this, I pray thee: [d]and he saith, I cannot; for it *is* sealed:

12 And the book is delivered to him that is not learned, saying, Read this, I pray thee: and he saith, I am not learned.

13 ¶ Wherefore the Lord said, Forasmuch [e]as this people draw near *me* with their mouth, and with their lips do honour me, but have removed their heart far from me, and their fear toward me is taught by the [f]precept of men:

14 Therefore, behold, [8]I will proceed to do a marvellous work among this people, *even* a marvellous work and a wonder: [g]for the wisdom of their wise *men* shall perish, and the understanding of their prudent *men* shall be hid.

15 Woe unto them that seek deep to hide their counsel from the LORD, and their works are in the dark, and [h]they say, Who seeth us? and who knoweth us?

16 Surely your turning of things upside down shall be esteemed as the potter's clay: for shall the work [i]say of him that made it, He made me not? or shall the thing framed say of him that framed it, He had no understanding?

17 *Is* it not yet a very little while, and Lĕb-ă-non shall be turned into a fruitful field, and the fruitful field shall b esteemed as a forest?

5 Or, take your pleasure, and riot.
b Micah 3.6. Rom. 11.8. 2 Thes. 2.10.
c Ps. 69.23. ch. 6.10.
6 heads.
7 Or, letter.
d Dan. 12.4. Matt. 11.25. Rev. 5.1.
e Ps. 17.1. ch. 48.1,2. Jer. 12.2. Eze. 33.31. Matt. 6.5. Mark 7.6.
f Col. 2.22.
8 I will add.
g Jer. 49.7. 1 Cor. 1.19.
h Job 22.13, 14. Ps. 10.11,13.
i Ps. 94.9. Rom. 9.20.
j John 15.11.
9 shall add.
k Jas. 2.5.
l Micah 2.1.
m Amos 5.10.
n Pro. 28.21.
o Josh. 24.3.
p ch. 19.25. Eph. 2.10.
q 1 Pet. 4.11.
r Hosea 3.5.
s ch. 28.7.
10 shall know understanding.

CHAP. 30
a Deut. 29.19. Rom. 2.5. 2 Tim. 3.13.
b Num. 27. 21. 1 Ki. 22.7. Jer. 21.2.
c Jer. 37.5,7.
d Jer. 2.36.
e Hosea 8.9.
f Jer. 37.7.

18 ¶ And in that day shall the de hear the words of the book, and th eyes of the blind shall see out of ol scurity, and out of darkness.

19 The [j]meek also [9]shall increa *their* joy in the LORD, and [k]the po among men shall rejoice in the Ho One of Israel.

20 For the terrible one is brought t nought, and the scorner is consume and all that [l]watch for iniquity are c off:

21 That make a man an offender fo a word, and [m]lay a snare for him th reproveth in the gate, and turn asid the just [n]for a thing of nought.

22 Therefore thus saith the LOR who [o]redeemed Abraham, concernin the house of Jacob, Jacob shall n now be ashamed, neither shall his fac now wax pale.

23 But when he seeth his childre [p]the work of mine hands, in the mids of him, they shall sanctify [q]my name and sanctify the Holy One of Jacob and shall [r]fear the God of Israel.

24 They also [s]that erred in spiri [10]shall come to understanding, an they that murmured shall learn doc trine.

CHAPTER 30

WOE to the rebellious children saith the LORD, that take coun sel, but not of me; and that cove with a covering, but not of my spirit [a]that they may add sin to sin:

2 That walk to go down into Egypt and have [b]not asked at my mouth; to strengthen themselves in the strength of Pharaoh, and to trust in th shadow of Egypt!

3 Therefore [c]shall the strength o Pharaoh be your shame, and the trus in the shadow of Egypt *your* con fusion.

4 For his princes were at Zō-ăn, an his ambassadors came to Hā-nĕs.

5 They [d]were all ashamed of a peo ple *that* could not profit them, nor b an help nor profit, but a shame, an also a reproach.

6 The [e]burden of the beasts of th south: into the land of trouble and anguish, from whence *come* the young and old lion, the viper and fiery flying serpent, they will carry their riches upon the shoulders of young asses, and their treasures upon the bunches of camels, to a people *that* shall not profit *them*.

7 For [f]the Egyptians shall help in

in, and to no purpose: therefore
ave I cried [1]concerning this, Their
rength *is* to sit still.
8 ¶ Now go, write it before them in
table, and note it in a book, that it
ay be for [2]the time to come for ever
nd ever:
9 That [g]this *is* a rebellious people, ly-
ng children, children *that* will not
ear the law of the LORD:
10 Which [h]say to the seers, See not;
nd to the prophets, Prophesy not
nto us right things, [i]speak unto us
mooth things, prophesy deceits:
11 Get [j]you out of the way, turn
side out of the path, cause the Holy
ne of Israel to cease from before us.
12 Wherefore thus saith the Holy
ne of Israel, Because ye despise this
ord, and trust in [3]oppression and
erverseness, and stay thereon:
13 Therefore this iniquity shall be to
ou as a breach ready to fall, swelling
ut in a high wall, whose breaking
ometh suddenly at an instant.
14 And he [k]shall break it as the
reaking of [4]the potters' vessel that is
roken in pieces; he shall not spare:
o that there shall not be found in the
ursting of it a sherd to take fire from
he hearth, or to take water *withal* out
f the pit.
15 For thus saith the Lord GOD, the
Holy One of Israel; [l]In returning and
est shall ye be saved; in quietness and
n confidence shall be your strength:
[m]and ye would not.
16 But ye said, No; for we will flee
upon horses; therefore shall ye flee:
nd, We will ride upon the swift;
herefore shall they that pursue you
e swift.
17 One [n]thousand *shall flee* at the
ebuke of one; at the rebuke of five
hall ye flee: till ye be left as [5]a beacon
upon the top of a mountain, and as an
nsign on an hill.
18 ¶ And therefore will the [o]LORD
wait, that he may be gracious unto
you, and therefore will he be exalted,
hat he may have mercy upon you:
or the LORD *is* a God of judgment:
[p]blessed *are* all they that wait for him.
19 For the people shall dwell in Zion
at Jerusalem: thou shalt weep no
more: he will be very gracious unto
thee at the voice of thy cry; when he
shall hear it, he will answer thee.
20 And *though* the Lord give you the
bread of adversity, and the water of
[6]affliction, yet shall not thy teachers
be removed into a corner any more,
but thine eyes shall see thy teachers:
21 And thine ears shall hear a word
behind thee, saying, This *is* the way,
walk ye in it, when ye turn [q]to the
right hand, and when ye turn to the
left.
22 Ye [r]shall defile also the covering
of [7]thy graven images of silver, and
the ornament of thy molten images
of gold: thou shalt [8]cast them away
as a menstruous cloth; thou shalt say
unto it, Get thee hence.
23 Then [s]shall he give the rain of thy
seed, that thou shalt sow the ground
withal; and bread of the increase of
the earth, and it shall be fat and plenteous: in that day shall thy cattle feed
in large pastures.
24 The oxen likewise and the young
asses that ear the ground shall eat
[9]clean provender, which hath been
winnowed with the shovel and with
the fan.
25 And there shall be upon every
high mountain, and upon every [10]high
hill, rivers *and* streams of waters in the
day of the great slaughter, when the
towers fall.
26 Moreover [t]the light of the moon
shall be as the light of the sun, and the
light of the sun shall be sevenfold, as
the light of seven days, in the day that
the LORD bindeth up the breach of
his people, and healeth the stroke of
their wound.
27 ¶ Behold, the name of the LORD
cometh from far, burning *with* his anger, and [11]the burden *thereof is* [12]heavy:
his lips are full of indignation, and his
tongue as a devouring fire:
28 And his [u]breath, as an overflowing stream, shall reach to the midst of
the neck, to sift the nations with the
sieve of vanity: and *there shall be* a
bridle in the jaws of the people, causing *them* to err.
29 Ye shall have a song, as in the
night *when* a holy solemnity is kept;
and gladness of heart, as when one goeth with a pipe to come into the mountain of the LORD, to the [13]mighty One
of Israel.
30 And the LORD shall cause [14]his
glorious voice to be heard, and shall
shew the lighting down of his arm,
with the indignation of *his* anger, and
with the flame of a devouring fire, *with*
scattering, and tempest, and hailstones.
31 For through the voice of the LORD
shall the Assyrian be beaten down,
which smote with a rod.
32 And [15]*in* every place where the
grounded staff shall pass, which the

1 Or, to her.
2 the latter day.
g Deut. 32. 20.
h Jer. 11.21.
i 1 Ki. 22.13.
j Acts 13.8.
3 Or, fraud.
k Ps. 2.9. 2 Pet. 2.4,5.
4 the bottle of potters.
l ch. 7.4.
m Ps. 81.11. Pro. 1.24. Jer. 44.16. Matt. 23.37.
n Lev. 26.8. Deut. 28.25. Josh. 23.10.
5 Or, a tree bereft of branches, or, boughs: or, a mast.
o 2 Pet. 3.9.
p Ps. 2.12. Pro. 16.20. Jer. 17.7.
6 Or, oppression.
q Deut. 5.32. Josh. 1.7. 2 Ki. 22.2. Pro. 4.27.
r 2 Chr. 31.1. ch. 2.20.
7 the graven images of thy silver.
8 scatter.
s Matt. 6.33. 1 Tim. 4.8.
9 leavened, or, savoury.
10 lifted up.
t ch. 60.19. Zech. 2.5. Rev. 21.23.
11 Or, and the grievousness of flame.
12 heaviness.
u 2 Thes. 2.8.
13 Rock.
14 the glory of his voice.
15 every passing of the rod founded.

LORD shall [16]lay upon him, *it* shall
be with tabrets and harps: and in
battles of shaking will he fight [17]with
it.
33 For [v]Tō-phĕt *is* ordained [18]of old;
yea, for the king it is prepared; he
hath made *it* deep *and* large: the pile
thereof *is* fire and much wood; the
breath of the LORD, like a stream of
brimstone, doth kindle it.

CHAPTER 31

WOE to them [a]that go down to
Egypt for help; and [b]stay on
horses, and trust in chariots, because
they are many; and in horsemen, because they are very strong; but they
look not unto the Holy One of Israel,
[c]neither seek the LORD!
2 Yet he also *is* wise, and will bring
evil, and will not [1]call back his words:
but will arise against the house of the
evildoers, and against the help of them
that work iniquity.
3 Now the Egyptians *are* [d]men, and
not God; and their horses flesh, and
not spirit. When the LORD shall
stretch out his hand, both he that helpeth shall fall, and he that is holpen
shall fall down, and they all shall fail
together.
4 For thus hath the LORD spoken unto me, Like as the lion and the young
lion roaring on his prey, when a multitude of shepherds is called forth
against him, *he* will not be afraid of
their voice, nor abase himself for the
[2]noise of them: so shall the LORD
of hosts come down to fight for
mount Zion, and for the hill thereof.
5 As [e]birds flying, so will the LORD of
hosts defend Jerusalem; defending
also he will deliver *it; and* passing over
he will preserve *it*.
6 ¶ Turn ye unto *him from* whom the
children of Israel have [f]deeply revolted.
7 For in that day every man shall
cast away his idols of silver, and [3]his
idols of gold, which your own hands
have made unto you *for* [g]a sin.
8 ¶ Then shall the Assyrian [h]fall
with the sword, not of a mighty man;
and the sword, not of a mean man,
shall devour him: but he shall flee
[4]from the sword, and his young men
shall be [5]discomfited.
9 And [6]he shall pass over to [7]his
strong hold for fear, and his princes
shall be afraid of the ensign, saith the
LORD, whose [i]fire *is* in Zion, and his
furnace in Jerusalem.

16 cause to rest upon him.
17 Or, against them.
v Jer. 7.31.
18 from yesterday.

CHAP. 31
a Deut. 28. 68. Eze. 17.15. Hosea 11.8.
b Ps. 20.7.
c Dan. 9.13. Hosea 7.7.
1 remove.
d Ps. 9.20. Eze. 28.9.
2 Or, multitude.
e Deut. 32. 11. Ps. 91.4.
f Hosea 9.9.
3 the idols of his gold.
g 1 Ki. 12.30.
h 2 Ki. 19.35.
4 Or, for fear of the sword.
5 for melting, or, tribute, or, tributary.
6 his rock shall pass away for fear.
7 Or, his strength.
i Lev. 6.13.

CHAP. 32
a 2 Chr. 31. 20. Ps. 7.1,2. Jer. 23.5. Zech. 9.9. Heb. 1.8,9. Rev. 19.11.
1 heavy.
b ch. 29.18.
2 hasty.
3 Or, elegantly.
4 Or, when he speaketh against the poor in judgment.
5 Or, be established.
c Amos 6.1.
6 Days above a year.
7 the fields of desire.
d Hosea 9.6.
8 Or, burning upon.
9 Or, clifts and watchtowers.
e Ps. 104.30.
f Zech. 8.3.
g Ps. 72.2,3. Micah 4.4,5. Luke 2.14.

CHAPTER 32

BEHOLD, [a]a king shall reign
righteousness, and princes sh
rule in judgment.
2 And a man shall be as an hidi
place from the wind, and a cove
from the tempest; as rivers of wat
in a dry place, as the shadow of
[1]great rock in a weary land.
3 And [b]the eyes of them that see sha
not be dim, and the ears of them th
hear shall hearken.
4 The heart also of the [2]rash shall u
derstand knowledge, and the tong
of the stammerers shall be ready
speak [3]plainly.
5 The vile person shall be no mo
called liberal, nor the churl said *to*
bountiful.
6 For the vile person will speak vi
lany, and his heart will work iniquit
to practise hypocrisy, and to utt
error against the LORD, to make em
ty the soul of the hungry, and he wi
cause the drink of the thirsty to fail.
7 The instruments also of the chu
are evil: he deviseth wicked devic
to destroy the poor with lying word
even [4]when the needy speaketh righ
8 But the liberal deviseth liber
things; and by liberal things shall h
[5]stand.
9 ¶ Rise up, ye women [c]that are
ease; hear my voice, ye careless daug
ters; give ear unto my speech.
10 [6]Many days and years shall ye b
troubled, ye careless women: for th
vintage shall fail, the gathering sha
not come.
11 Tremble, ye women that are
ease; be troubled, ye careless ones
strip you, and make you bare, an
gird *sackcloth* upon *your* loins.
12 They shall lament for the teats
for [7]the pleasant fields, for the fruit
ful vine.
13 Upon [d]the land of my people sha
come up thorns *and* briers; [8]yea, upo
all the houses of joy *in* the joyous city
14 Because the palaces shall be for
saken; the multitude of the city sha
be left; the [9]forts and towers shall b
for dens for ever, a joy of wild asses
a pasture of flocks;
15 Until [e]the spirit be poured upo
us from on high, and the wildernes
be a fruitful field, and the fruitful fiel
be counted for a forest.
16 Then [f]judgment shall dwell in th
wilderness, and righteousness remai
in the fruitful field.
17 And [g]the work of righteousnes
shall be peace; and the effect of right

ousness quietness and assurance for
ever.
18 And my people shall dwell in a
peaceable habitation, and in sure
dwellings, and in quiet resting places;
19 When it shall hail, coming down
[h]on the forest; [10]and the city shall be
low in a low place.
20 Blessed *are* ye that sow beside all
waters, that send forth *thither* the feet
of the [i]ox and the ass.

CHAPTER 33

WOE to thee [a]that spoilest, and
thou *wast* not spoiled; and dealest treacherously, and they dealt not
treacherously with thee! when [b]thou
shalt cease to spoil, thou shalt be
spoiled; *and* when thou shalt make an
end to deal treacherously, they shall
deal treacherously with thee.
2 O LORD, be gracious unto us; we
have waited for thee: be thou their
arm every morning, our salvation also
in the time of trouble.
3 At the noise of the tumult the people fled; at the lifting up of thyself the
nations were scattered.
4 And your spoil shall be gathered
like the gathering of the caterpiller:
as the running to and fro of locusts
shall he run upon them.
5 The [c]LORD is exalted; for he dwelleth on high: he hath filled Zion with
judgment and righteousness.
6 And [d]wisdom and knowledge shall
be the stability of thy times, *and*
strength of [1]salvation: the fear of the
LORD *is* his treasure.
7 Behold, their [2]valiant ones shall
cry without: [e]the ambassadors of
peace shall weep bitterly.
8 The [f]highways lie waste, the wayfaring man ceaseth: [g]he hath broken
the covenant, he hath despised the
cities, he regardeth no man.
9 The earth mourneth *and* languisheth: Lĕb-ā-nŏn is ashamed *and* [3]hewn
down: Shâr-ŏn is like a wilderness;
and Bā-shăn and Carmel shake off
their fruits.
10 Now [h]will I rise, saith the LORD;
now will I be exalted; now will I lift
up myself.
11 Ye shall conceive chaff, ye shall
bring forth stubble: your breath, *as*
fire, shall devour you.
12 And the people shall be *as* the
burnings of lime: *as* thorns cut up
shall they be burned in the fire.
13 ¶ Hear, ye *that are* far off, what
I have done; and, ye *that are* near,
acknowledge my might.
14 The sinners in Zion are afraid;
fearfulness hath surprised the hypocrites. Who among us shall dwell with
the devouring fire? who among us
shall dwell with everlasting burnings?
15 He that walketh [4]righteously, and
speaketh [5]uprightly; he that despiseth the gain of [6]oppressions, that
shaketh his hands from holding of
bribes, that stoppeth his ears from
hearing of [7]blood, and shutteth his
eyes from seeing evil;
16 He shall dwell on [8]high: his place
of defence *shall be* the munitions of
rocks: bread shall be given him; his
waters *shall be* sure.
17 Thine eyes shall see the king in
his beauty: they shall behold [9]the land
that is very far off.
18 Thine heart shall meditate terror.
Where [i]*is* the scribe? where *is* the
[10]receiver? where *is* he that counted
the towers?
19 Thou shalt not see a fierce people,
[j]a people of a deeper speech than thou
canst perceive; of a [11]stammering
tongue, *that thou canst* not understand.
20 Look upon Zion, the city of our
solemnities: thine eyes shall see Jerusalem a quiet habitation, a tabernacle
that shall not be taken down; not one
of the stakes thereof shall ever be removed, neither shall any of the cords
thereof be broken.
21 But [k]there the glorious LORD *will*
be unto us a place [12]of broad rivers *and*
streams; wherein shall go no galley
with oars, neither shall gallant ship
pass thereby.
22 For the LORD *is* our judge, the
LORD *is* our [13]lawgiver, [l]the LORD *is*
our king; he will save us.
23 [14]Thy tacklings are loosed; they
could not well strengthen their mast,
they could not spread the sail: then
is the prey of a great spoil divided;
the lame take the prey.
24 And the inhabitant shall not say,
I am sick: [m]the people that dwell
therein *shall be* forgiven *their* iniquity.

CHAPTER 34

COME near, ye nations, to hear;
and hearken, ye people: let the
earth hear, and [1]all that is therein;
the world, and all things that come
forth of it.
2 For the indignation of the LORD *is*
upon all nations, and *his* fury upon
all their armies: he hath utterly destroyed them, he hath delivered them
to the slaughter.

h Zech. 11.2.
10 Or, and the city shall be utterly abased.
i ch. 30.24.

CHAP. 33
a Hab. 2.8.
b Rev. 13.10.
c Ps. 97.9.
d Pro. 1.7. Matt. 6.33.
1 salvations.
2 Or, messengers.
e 2 Ki. 18.18.
f Judg. 5.6.
g 2 Ki. 18.14.
3 Or, withered away.
h Deut. 32. 36,43. Ps. 12.5. ch. 42.13,14. Zeph. 3.8.
4 in righteousnesses.
5 uprightnesses.
6 Or, deceits.
7 bloods.
8 heights, or, high places.
9 the land of far distances.
i 1 Cor. 1.20.
10 weigher?
j Jer. 5.15.
11 Or, ridiculous.
k Zech. 2.5.
12 broad of spaces, or, hands.
13 statute-maker.
l Ps. 44.4. Matt. 21.5. Rev. 19.16.
14 Or, They have forsaken thy tacklings.
m ch. 12.2. Rom. 11.27.

CHAP. 34
1 the fulness thereof.

3 Their slain also shall be cast out,
and their stink shall come up out of
their carcases, and the mountains
shall be melted with their blood.
4 And [a]all the host of heaven shall
be dissolved, and the heavens shall be
rolled together as a scroll: and all their
host shall fall down, as the leaf falleth off from the vine, and as a falling
fig from the fig tree.
5 For [b]my sword shall be bathed in
heaven: behold, it [c]shall come down
upon Ī-dū-mē'-ă, and upon the people
of my curse, to judgment.
6 The sword of the LORD is filled
with blood, it is made fat with fatness,
and with the blood of lambs and
goats, with the fat of the kidneys of
rams: [d]for the LORD hath a sacrifice in
Bŏz'-răh, and a great slaughter in the
land of Ī-dū-mē'-ă.
7 And the [2]unicorns shall come down
with them, and the bullocks with the
bulls; and their land shall be [3]soaked
with blood, and their dust made fat
with fatness.
8 For *it is* the day of the LORD's vengeance, *and* the year of recompences
for the controversy of Zion.
9 And the streams thereof shall be
turned into pitch, and the dust thereof
into brimstone, and the land thereof
shall become burning pitch.
10 It shall not be quenched night nor
day; the smoke thereof shall go up for
ever: [e]from generation to generation
it shall lie waste; none shall pass
through it for ever and ever.
11 ¶ But the [4]cormorant and the bittern shall possess it; the owl also and
the raven shall dwell in it: and he shall
stretch out upon it the line of confusion, and the stones of emptiness.
12 They shall call the nobles thereof
to the kingdom, but none *shall be*
there, and all her princes shall be
nothing.
13 And [f]thorns shall come up in her
palaces, nettles and brambles in the
fortresses thereof: and it shall be an
habitation of dragons, *and* a court for
[5]owls.
14 [6]The wild beasts of the desert
shall also meet with [7]the wild beasts
of the island, and the satyr shall cry
to his fellow; the [8]screech owl also
shall rest there, and find for herself
a place of rest.
15 There shall the great owl make
her nest, and lay, and hatch, and
gather under her shadow: there shall
the vultures also be gathered, every
one with her mate.

a Ps. 102.26. Eze. 32.7. Joel 2.31. Matt. 24.29. 2 Pet. 3.10.
b Jer. 46.10.
c Jer. 49.7. Mal. 1.4.
d ch. 63.1. Zeph. 1.7.
2 Or, rhinocerots.
3 Or, drunken.
e Mal. 1.4. Rev. 14.11. Rev. 18.18.
4 Or, pelican.
f ch. 32.13. Hosea 9.6.
5 daughters of the owl, or, ostriches.
6 Ziim.
7 Ijim.
8 Or, night monster.
g Ps. 56.8. Dan. 7.10. Mal. 3.16.
h Ps. 78.55. Pro. 16.33.

CHAP. 35

a Job 4.3,4. Heb. 12.12.
1 hasty.
b ch. 29.18. Matt. 9.27. John 9.6.
c ch. 29.18. Matt. 11.5. Mark 7.32.
d Matt. 11.5. Luke 7.22. John 5.8. Acts 3.2.
e Matt. 9.32.
f John 7.38.
2 Or, a court for reeds, etc.
g Joel 3.17. Rev. 21.27.
3 Or, for he shall be with them.
h Lev. 26.6. ch. 11.9.
i ch. 51.11. Eph. 1.7. Rev. 7.17.
j ch. 25.8. John 16.22. Rev. 7.17.

CHAP. 36

a 2 Chr. 32.1.

16 ¶ Seek ye out of the [g]book of the
LORD, and read: no one of these shall
fail, none shall want her mate: for my
mouth it hath commanded, and his
spirit it hath gathered them.
17 And he hath cast the [h]lot for them,
and his hand hath divided it unto
them by line: they shall possess it for
ever, from generation to generation
shall they dwell therein.

CHAPTER 35

THE wilderness and the solitary
place shall be glad for them; and
the desert shall rejoice, and blossom
as the rose.
2 It shall blossom abundantly, and
rejoice even with joy and singing: the
glory of Lĕb'-ă-nŏn shall be given unto it, the excellency of Carmel and
Shâr'-ŏn, they shall see the glory of the
LORD, *and* the excellency of our God.
3 ¶ Strengthen [a]ye the weak hands,
and confirm the feeble knees.
4 Say to them *that are* of a [1]fearful
heart, Be strong, fear not: behold,
your God will come *with* vengeance,
even God *with* a recompence; he will
come and save you.
5 Then the [b]eyes of the blind shall be
opened, and [c]the ears of the deaf shall
be unstopped.
6 Then shall the [d]lame *man* leap as
an hart, and the [e]tongue of the dumb
sing: for in the wilderness shall
[f]waters break out, and streams in the
desert.
7 And the parched ground shall become a pool, and the thirsty land
springs of water: in the habitation of
dragons, where each lay, *shall be*
[2]grass with reeds and rushes.
8 And an highway shall be there, and
a way, and it shall be called The way
of holiness; [g]the unclean shall not pass
over it; [3]but it *shall be* for those: the
wayfaring men, though fools, shall
not err *therein*.
9 No [h]lion shall be there, nor *any*
ravenous beast shall go up thereon,
it shall not be found there; but the redeemed shall walk *there:*
10 And the [i]ransomed of the LORD
shall return, and come to Zion with
songs and everlasting joy upon their
heads: they shall obtain joy and gladness, and [j]sorrow and sighing shall
flee away.

CHAPTER 36

NOW [a]it came to pass in the fourteenth year of king Hĕz-ē-kī'-ăh,
that Sĕn-năch'-ĕr-ĭb king of Assyria

came up against all the defenced cities
of Judah, and took them.
2 And the king of Assyria sent Răb-
shă-kēh from [b]Lā-chish to Jerusalem
unto king Hĕz-ē-kī-āh with a great
army. And he stood by the conduit of
the upper pool in the highway of the
fuller's field.
3 Then came forth unto him Ē-lī-ă-
kīm, Hĭl-kī-āh's son, which was over
the house, and Shĕb-nă the [1]scribe,
and Jō-āh, Ā-săph's son, the recorder.
4 ¶ And Răb-shă-kēh said unto
them, Say ye now to Hĕz-ē-kī-āh,
Thus saith the great king, the king of
Assyria, What confidence *is* this
wherein thou trustest?
5 I say, *sayest thou,* (but *they are but*
vain words) [3]*I have* counsel and
strength for war: now on whom dost
thou trust, that thou rebellest against
me?
6 Lo, thou trustest in the [4]staff of
this broken reed, on Egypt; whereon
if a man lean, it will go into his hand,
and pierce it: so *is* Pharaoh king of
Egypt to all that trust in him.
7 But if thou say to me, We trust in
the LORD our God: *is it* not he, whose
high places and [c]whose altars Hĕz-ē-
kī-āh hath taken away, and said to
Judah and to Jerusalem, Ye shall
worship before this altar?
8 Now therefore [5]give pledges, I
pray thee, to my master the king of
Assyria, and I will give thee two
thousand horses, if thou be able on
thy part to set riders upon them.
9 How then wilt thou turn away the
face of one [6]captain of the least of my
master's servants, and put thy trust
on Egypt for chariots and for horsemen?
10 And am I now come up without
the LORD against this land to destroy
it? the LORD said unto me, Go up
against this land, and destroy it.
11 ¶ Then said Ē-lī-ă-kīm and Shĕb-
nă and Jō-āh unto Răb-shă-kēh,
Speak, I pray thee, unto thy servants
in the [7]Syrian language; for we understand *it:* and speak not to us in the
Jews' language, in the ears of the people that *are* on the wall.
12 ¶ But Răb-shă-kēh said, Hath my
master sent me to thy master and to
thee to speak these words? *hath he*
not *sent me* to the men that sit upon
the wall, that they may eat their own
dung, and drink their own piss with
you?
13 Then Răb-shă-kēh stood, and
cried with a loud voice in the Jews'
language, and said, Hear ye the
words of the great king, the king of
Assyria.
14 Thus saith the king, Let not Hĕz-
ē-kī-āh deceive you: for he shall not
be able to deliver you.
15 Neither let Hĕz-ē-kī-āh make you
trust in the LORD, saying, The LORD
will surely deliver us: this city shall
not be delivered into the hand of the
king of Assyria.
16 Hearken not to Hĕz-ē-kī-āh: for
thus saith the king of Assyria, [8]Make
an agreement with me *by* a present,
and come out to me: [d]and eat ye every
one of his vine, and every one of his
fig tree, and drink ye every one the
waters of his own cistern;
17 Until I come and take you away
to a land like your own land, a land
of corn and wine, a land of bread and
vineyards.
18 *Beware* lest Hĕz-ē-kī-āh persuade
you, saying, The LORD will deliver us.
Hath any of the gods of the nations
delivered his land out of the hand of
the king of Assyria?
19 Where *are* the gods of [e]Hā-măth
and Ăr-phăd? where *are* the gods
of Sē-phăr-vā-īm? and have they
delivered Să-mâr-ĭ-ă out of my
hand?
20 Who *are they* among all the gods
of these lands, that have delivered
their land out of my hand, that [f]the
LORD should deliver Jerusalem out
of my hand?
21 But they held their peace, and answered [g]him not a word: for the
king's commandment was, saying,
Answer him not.
22 ¶ Then came Ē-lī-ă-kīm, the son
of Hĭl-kī-āh, that *was* over the household, and Shĕb-nă the scribe, and Jō-
āh, the son of Ā-săph, the recorder, to
Hĕz-ē-kī-āh with [h]*their* clothes rent,
and told him the words of Răb-shă-
kēh.

CHAPTER 37

AND [a]it came to pass, when king
Hĕz-ē-kī-āh heard *it,* that he rent
his clothes, and covered himself with
sackcloth, and went [b]into the house
of the LORD.
2 And he sent Ē-lī-ă-kīm, who *was*
over the household, and Shĕb-nă the
scribe, and the elders of the priests
covered with sackcloth, unto [c]Isaiah
the prophet the son of Amoz.
3 And they said unto him, Thus saith
Hĕz-ē-kī-āh, This day *is* a day of
trouble, and of [d]rebuke, and of [1]blas-
phemy: for the children are come to

b Josh. 10.3, 5.
2 Ki. 14.19. Micah 1.13.
1 Or, secretary.
2 a word of lips.
3 Or, but counsel and strength are for the war.
4 Or, support.
c 2 Ki. 18.4.
5 Or, engage, I pray thee, with.
6 governor (or, satrap) of the least of my master's servants? So thou hast reposed thyself on Egypt, etc.
7 Or, Aramean.
8 Make with me a blessing. Or, Seek my favour by a present.
d Micah 4.4. Zech. 3.10.
e Num. 34.8. Josh. 13.5.
f 2 Chr. 32. 15. Ps. 50.21. ch. 37.23. Dan. 3.15.
g Ps. 38.13. Pro. 9.7. Amos 5.13. Matt. 7.6.
h Gen. 37.34. 1 Sam. 4.12. 2 Sam. 1.11. 2 Ki. 18.18, 37. Job 1.20. ch. 33.7.

CHAP. 37

a 2 Ki. 19.1.
b 2 Chr. 6.24. Ps. 50.15. Zech. 13.9. Luke 18.1. Rom. 12.12. 1 Thes. 5.17.
c 2 Ki. 22.14.
d 2 Ki. 19.3. Ps. 39.11. Ps. 50.15. Hosea 5.9.
1 Or, provocation.

the birth, and *there is* not strength to
bring forth.
4 It may be the LORD thy God will
hear the words of Răb-shā-kēh,
whom the king of Assyria his master
hath sent to reproach the living God,
and will reprove the words which the
LORD thy God hath heard: wherefore
[e]lift up *thy* prayer for the remnant that
is [2]left.
5 So the servants of king Hĕz-ē-kī-
ăh came to Isaiah.
6 ¶ And Isaiah said unto them, Thus
shall ye say unto your master, Thus
saith the LORD, Be not afraid of the
words that thou hast heard, wherewith the servants of the king of
Assyria have blasphemed me.
7 Behold, I will [3]send a blast upon
him, and he shall hear a rumour, and
return to his own land; and I will
cause him to fall by the sword in his
own land.
8 ¶ So Răb-shā-kēh returned, and
found the king of Assyria warring
against [f]Lĭb-năh: for he had heard
that he was departed from Lā-chĭsh.
9 And he heard say concerning Tĭr-
hā-kăh king of Ē-thĭ-ō-pĭ-ă, He is
come forth to make war with thee.
And when he heard *it*, he sent messengers to Hĕz-ē-kī-ăh, saying,
10 Thus shall ye speak to Hĕz-ē-kī-
ăh king of Judah, saying, Let not thy
God, in whom thou trustest, deceive
thee, saying, Jerusalem shall not be
given into the hand of the king of
Assyria.
11 Behold, thou hast heard what the
kings of Assyria have done to all
lands by destroying them utterly; and
shalt thou be delivered?
12 Have the gods of the nations delivered them which my fathers have
destroyed, *as* Gō-zăn, [g]and Hâr-ăn,
and Rē-zĕph, and the children of
Eden which *were* in Tē-lăs-sär?
13 Where *is* the king of [h]Hā-măth,
and the king of Är-phăd, and the king
of the city of Sē-phär-vā-ĭm, Hē-nă,
and Ī-văh?
14 ¶ And Hĕz-ē-kī-ăh received the
letter from the hand of the messengers, and read it: and Hĕz-ē-kī-ăh
went up unto the house of the LORD,
and spread it before the LORD.
15 And Hĕz-ē-kī-ăh prayed unto the
LORD, saying,
16 O LORD of hosts, God of Israel,
that dwellest [i]*between* the chĕr-ū-bĭms,
thou *art* the God, *even* thou alone, of
all the kingdoms of the earth: thou
hast made heaven and earth.

e 1 Sam. 7.8. 2 Ki. 19.4. Jas. 5.14,18.
2 found.
3 Or, put a spirit into him.
f Josh. 15.39, 42. 2 Chr. 11.9. Neh. 11.30. Jer. 34.7.
g Gen. 11.31. Ex. 27.23.
h Jer. 49.23.
i Ex. 25.22.
j Dan. 9.18.
4 lands.
5 given.
6 By the hand of thy servants.
7 the tallness of the cedars thereof, and the choice of the fir trees thereof.
8 Or, the forest and his fruitful field.
9 Or, fenced and closed.
10 Or, Hast thou not heard how I have made it long ago, and formed it of ancient times? should I now bring it to be laid waste, and defenced cities to be ruinous heaps? as 2 Ki. 19.25.
11 short of hand.
12 Or, sitting.

17 Incline [j]thine ear, O LORD, an
hear; open thine eyes, O LORD, an
see: and hear all the words of Sĕn
năch-ĕr-ĭb, which hath sent to re
proach the living God.
18 Of a truth, LORD, the kings o
Assyria have laid waste all the [4]na
tions, and their countries,
19 And have [5]cast their gods into th
fire: for they *were* no gods, but th
work of men's hands, wood an
stone: therefore they have destroye
them.
20 Now therefore, O LORD our God
save us from his hand, that all th
kingdoms of the earth may know tha
thou *art* the LORD, *even* thou only.
21 ¶ Then Isaiah the son of Amo
sent unto Hĕz-ē-kī-ăh, saying, Thus
saith the LORD God of Israel, Whereas thou hast prayed to me against Sĕn-
năch-ĕr-ĭb king of Assyria:
22 This *is* the word which the LORD
hath spoken concerning him; The
virgin, the daughter of Zion, hath despised thee, *and* laughed thee to
scorn; the daughter of Jerusalem
hath shaken her head at thee.
23 Whom hast thou reproached and
blasphemed? and against whom hast
thou exalted *thy* voice, and lifted up
thine eyes on high? *even* against the
Holy One of Israel.
24 [6]By thy servants hast thou reproached the Lord, and hast said, By
the multitude of my chariots am I
come up to the height of the mountains, to the sides of Lĕb-ă-non; and
I will cut down [7]the tall cedars thereof,
and the choice fir trees thereof: and I
will enter into the height of his border,
and [8]the forest of his Carmel.
25 I have digged, and drunk water;
and with the sole of my feet have I
dried up all the rivers of the [9]besieged
places.
26 [10]Hast thou not heard long ago,
how I have done it; *and* of ancient
times, that I have formed it? now
have I brought it to pass, that thou
shouldest be to lay waste defenced
cities *into* ruinous heaps.
27 Therefore their inhabitants *were*
[11]of small power, they were dismayed
and confounded: they were *as* the
grass of the field, and *as* the green
herb, *as* the grass on the housetops,
and *as corn* blasted before it be grown
up.
28 But I know thy [12]abode, and thy
going out, and thy coming in, and thy
rage against me.
29 Because thy rage against me, and

hy tumult, is come up into mine ears,
herefore [k]will I put my hook in thy
ıose, and my bridle in thy lips, and I
vill turn thee back by the way by
vhich thou camest.
30 And this *shall be* a sign unto thee,
Ye shall eat *this* year such as groweth
of itself; and the second year that
vhich springeth of the same: and in
he third year sow ye, and reap, and
lant vineyards, and eat the fruit
hereof.
31 And [13]the remnant that is escaped
of the house of Judah shall again take
oot downward, and bear fruit up-
vard:
32 For out of Jerusalem shall go
orth a remnant, and [14]they that es-
ape out of mount Zion: [l]the zeal of
he LORD of hosts shall do this.
33 Therefore thus saith the LORD
oncerning the king of Assyria, He
hall not come into this city, nor shoot
n arrow there, nor come before it
vith [15]shields, nor cast a bank against
:.
34 By the way that he came, by the
ame shall he return, and shall
ot come into this city, saith the
LORD.
35 For I will [m]defend this city to save
: for mine own sake, and for my ser-
ant David's sake.
36 Then the [n]angel of the LORD went
orth, and smote in the camp of the
Assyrians a hundred and fourscore
nd five thousand: and when they
rose early in the morning, behold,
ıey *were* all dead corpses.
37 ¶ So Sĕn-năch-ĕr-ĭb king of As-
yria departed, and went and return-
d, and dwelt at Nĭn-ĕ-vēh.
38 And it came to pass, as he was
vorshipping in the house of Nĭs-rŏch
is god, that Ă-drăm-mĕ-lĕch and
hă-rē-zĕr his sons smote him with
ne sword; and they escaped into the
nd of [16]Ăr-mē-nĭ-ă: and Ē-săr-hăd-
on his son reigned in his stead.

CHAPTER 38

N [a]those days was Hĕz-ē-kī-ăh sick
unto death. And Isaiah the prophet
he son of Amoz came unto him, and
aid unto him, Thus saith the LORD,
Set thine house in order: for thou
halt die, and not live.
2 Then Hĕz-ē-kī-ăh turned his face
oward the wall, and prayed unto the
LORD,
3 And said, [b]Remember now, O
LORD, I beseech thee, how I have
valked before thee in truth and with
a perfect heart, and have done *that
which is* good in thy sight. And Hĕz-
ē-kī-ăh wept [2]sore.
4 ¶ Then came the word of the LORD
to Isaiah, saying,
5 Go, and say to Hĕz-ē-kī-ăh, Thus
saith the LORD, the God of David thy
father, I have heard thy prayer, I have
seen thy tears: behold, I will add unto
thy days fifteen years.
6 And I will deliver thee and this city
out of the hand of the king of Assyria:
and [c]I will defend this city.
7 And this *shall be* [d]a sign unto thee
from the LORD, that the LORD will do
this thing that he hath spoken;
8 Behold, I will bring again the shadow of the degrees, which is gone down
in the [3]sun dial of Ahaz, ten degrees
backward. So the sun returned ten degrees, by which degrees it was gone
down.
9 ¶ The writing of Hĕz-ē-kī-ăh king
of Judah, when he had been sick, and
was recovered of his sickness:
10 I said in the cutting off of my
days, I shall go to the gates of the
grave: [e]I am deprived of the residue
of my years.
11 I said, I shall not see the LORD,
even the LORD, [f]in the land of the living: I shall behold man no more with
the inhabitants of the world.
12 Mine [g]age is departed, and is removed from me as a shepherd's tent:
I have cut off like a weaver my life: he
will cut me off [4]with pining sickness:
from day *even* to night wilt thou
make an end of me.
13 I reckoned till morning, *that*, as
a lion, so will he break all my bones:
from day *even* to night wilt thou make
an end of me.
14 Like a crane *or* a swallow, so did
I chatter: [h]I did mourn as a dove:
mine eyes fail *with looking* upward: O
LORD, I am oppressed; [5]undertake
for me.
15 What shall I say? he hath both
spoken unto me, and himself hath
done *it:* I shall go softly all my years
[i]in the bitterness of my soul.
16 O Lord, by these *things men* live,
and in all these *things is* the life of my
spirit: so wilt thou recover me, and
make me to live.
17 Behold, [6]for peace I had great
bitterness: but [7]thou hast in love to
my soul *delivered it* from the pit of
corruption: for thou hast cast all my
sins behind thy back.
18 For [j]the grave cannot praise thee,
death can *not* celebrate thee: they

[k] Job 41.2. Ps. 32.9. ch. 30.28. Eze. 29.4. Amos 4.2. Jas. 3.3.
13 the escaping of the house of Judah that remaineth.
14 the escaping.
[l] 2 Ki. 19. 31.
15 shield.
[m] 2 Ki. 20.6. ch. 27.3.
[n] 2 Ki. 19.35.
16 Ararat.
CHAP. 38
[a] 2 Ki. 20.1. 2 Chr. 32.24.
1 Give charge concerning thy house.
[b] Neh. 5.19.
2 with great weeping.
[c] ch. 37.35.
[d] 2 Ki. 20.8. ch. 37.30.
3 degrees by, or, with the sun.
[e] Ps. 102.24.
[f] Job 35.14. Ps. 27.13. Ps. 31.22. Ps. 116.9.
[g] Job 7.6. Ps. 102.11, 23,24. 2 Cor. 5.4.
4 Or, from the thrum.
[h] ch. 59.11.
5 Or, ease me.
[i] Job 7.11.
6 Or, on my peace came great bitterness.
7 thou hast loved my soul from the pit.
[j] Ps. 6.5. Ps. 30.9. Eccl. 9. 10.

that go down into the pit cannot hope
for thy truth.
19 The living, the living, he shall
praise thee, as I *do* this day: [k]the father to the children shall make known
thy truth.
20 The LORD *was ready* to [l]save me:
therefore we will sing my songs to the
stringed instruments all the days of
our life in the house of the LORD.
21 For [m]Isaiah had said, Let them
take a lump of figs, and lay *it* for a
plaister upon the boil, and he shall
recover.
22 Hĕz-ē-kī'-ăh also had said, What
is the sign that I shall go up to the
house of the LORD?

CHAPTER 39

AT [a]that time Mĕr'-ō-dăch–băl'-ă-
dăn, the son of Băl'-ă-dăn, king of
Babylon, sent letters and a present to
Hĕz-ē-kī'-ăh: for he had heard that he
had been sick, and was recovered.
2 And [b]Hĕz-ē-kī'-ăh was glad of
them, and shewed them the house of
his [1]precious things, the silver, and
the gold, and the spices, and the
precious ointment, and all the house
of his [2]armour, and all that was found
in his treasures: there was nothing in
his house, nor in all his dominion,
that Hĕz-ē-kī'-ăh shewed them not.
3 ¶ Then came Isaiah the prophet
unto king Hĕz-ē-kī'-ăh, and said unto
him, What said these men? and from
whence came they unto thee? And
Hĕz-ē-kī'-ăh said, They are come from
a far country unto me, *even* from
Babylon.
4 Then said he, What have they seen
in thine house? And Hĕz-ē-kī'-ăh answered, All that *is* in mine house have
they seen: there is nothing among
my treasures that I have not shewed
them.
5 Then said Isaiah to Hĕz-ē-kī'-ăh,
Hear the word of the LORD of hosts:
6 Behold, the days come, [c]that all
that is in thine house, and *that* which
thy fathers have laid up in store until
this day, shall be carried to Babylon:
nothing shall be left, saith the LORD.
7 And of thy sons that shall issue
from thee, which thou shalt beget,
shall they take away; and [d]they shall
be eunuchs in the palace of the king
of Babylon.
8 Then said Hĕz-ē-kī'-ăh to Isaiah,
Good [e]*is* the word of the LORD which
thou hast spoken. He said moreover,
For there shall be peace and truth in
my days.

k Deut. 4.9. Ps. 78.3.
l Ps. 9.13,14. Ps. 46.1. Ps. 66.12.
m 2 Ki. 20.7.

CHAP. 39
a 2 Ki. 20.12.
b 2 Chr. 32. 31.
1 Or, spicery.
2 vessels, or, instruments, or, jewels.
c Lev. 26.33. Deut. 28.64. 1 Ki. 14.15. 2 Chr. 36.18. Amos 5.27.
d 2 Ki. 24.12. Dan. 1.2.
e 1 Sam. 3.18.

CHAP. 40
1 to the heart.
2 Or, appointed time.
a Matt. 3.3.
b Mal. 3.1. Mark 1.3. Luke 1.76. John 1.23.
3 Or, a straight place.
4 Or, a plain place.
c Ex. 16.7. Ps. 72.19. Eze. 36.23. Luke 2.10.
d 1 Pet. 1.25.
5 Or, O thou that tellest good tidings to Zion.
6 Or, O thou that tellest good tidings to Jerusalem.
7 Or, against the strong.
8 Or, recompence for his work.
e ch. 49.10. Eze. 34.23. John 10.11. Heb. 13.20. 1 Pet. 2.25. Rev. 7.17.
9 Or, that give suck.
10 a tierce.
11 a man of his counsel.
12 made him understand.
13 understandings?

CHAPTER 40

COMFORT ye, comfort ye my
people, saith your God.
2 Speak ye [1]comfortably to Jerusalem, and cry unto her, that her [2]war-
fare is accomplished, that her iniquity
is pardoned: for she hath received of
the LORD's hand double for all her
sins.
3 ¶ The [a]voice of him that crieth in
the wilderness, [b]Prepare ye the way
of the LORD, make straight in the
desert a highway for our God.
4 Every valley shall be exalted, and
every mountain and hill shall be made
low: and the crooked shall be made
[3]straight, and the rough places [4]plain:
5 And the [c]glory of the LORD shall be
revealed, and all flesh shall see *it* together: for the mouth of the LORD
hath spoken *it*.
6 The voice said, Cry. And he said,
What shall I cry? All flesh *is* grass,
and all the goodliness thereof *is* as the
flower of the field:
7 The grass withereth, the flower
fadeth: because the spirit of the LORD
bloweth upon it: surely the people *is*
grass.
8 The grass withereth, the flower
fadeth: but [d]the word of our God
shall stand for ever.
9 ¶ [5]O Zion, that bringest good tidings, get thee up into the high mountain; [6]O Jerusalem, that bringest good
tidings, lift up thy voice with strength;
lift *it* up, be not afraid; say unto the
cities of Judah, Behold your God!
10 Behold, the Lord GOD will come
[7]with strong *hand*, and his arm shall
rule for him: behold, his reward *is*
with him, and [8]his work before him.
11 He shall [e]feed his flock like a
shepherd: he shall gather the lambs
with his arm, and carry *them* in his
bosom, *and* shall gently lead those
[9]that are with young.
12 ¶ Who hath measured the waters
in the hollow of his hand, and meted
out heaven with the span, and comprehended the dust of the earth in
[10]a measure, and weighed the mountains in scales, and the hills in a
balance?
13 Who hath directed the Spirit of
the LORD, or *being* [11]his counseller
hath taught him?
14 With whom took he counsel, and
who [12]instructed him, and taught him in
the path of judgment, and taught him
knowledge, and shewed to him the
way of [13]understanding?
15 Behold, the nations *are* as a drop

f a bucket, and are counted as the mall dust of the balance: behold, he aketh up the isles as a very little hing.

16 And Lĕb-ă-non *is* not sufficient to urn, nor the beasts thereof sufficient or a burnt offering.

17 All nations before him *are* as othing; and they are counted to him ess than nothing, and vanity.

18 ¶ To whom then will ye [f]liken od? or what likeness will ye compare nto him?

19 The workman melteth a graven mage, and the goldsmith spreadeth over with gold, and casteth silver hains.

20 He that [14]*is* so impoverished that e hath no oblation chooseth a tree *hat* will not rot; he seeketh unto him cunning workman [g]to prepare a raven image, *that* shall not be noved.

21 Have [h]ye not known? have ye not eard? hath it not been told you from he beginning? have ye not understood from the foundations of the arth?

22 [15]*It is* he that sitteth upon the ircle of the earth, and the inhabitants hereof *are* as grasshoppers; that stretcheth out the heavens as a curain, and spreadeth them out as a ent to dwell in:

23 That bringeth the [j]princes to nohing; he maketh the judges of the arth as vanity.

24 Yea, they shall not be planted; ea, they shall not be sown: yea, their tock shall not take root in the earth: nd he shall also blow upon them, and hey shall wither, and the whirlwind hall take them away as stubble.

25 To [k]whom then will ye liken me, r shall I be equal? saith the Holy One.

26 Lift up your eyes on high, and beold who hath created these *things*, hat bringeth out their host by numer: [l]he calleth them all by names y the greatness of his might, for hat *he is* strong in power; not one aileth.

27 Why sayest thou, O Jacob, and peakest, O Israel, My way is hid from he LORD, and my judgment is passed ver from my God?

28 ¶ Hast thou not known? hast thou ot heard, *that* the everlasting God, he LORD, the Creator of the ends of he earth, fainteth not, neither is veary? [m]*there is* no searching of his nderstanding.

29 He giveth power to the faint; and

f Acts 17.29.
14 is poor of oblation.
g Jer. 10.4.
h Ps. 19.1. Acts 14.17. Rom. 1.19.
15 Or, Him that sitteth, etc.
i Gen. 1.1,6. Job 9.8. Ps. 104.2. Jer. 10.12.
j Job 12.21.
k ver. 18. Deut. 4.15. Acts 17.24-29.
l Ps. 147.4.
m Ps. 147.5. Rom. 11.33.
n Job 17.9. Ps. 25.3. ch. 8.17. Lam. 3.25. 2 Cor. 4.8-10,16.
16 change.

CHAP. 41

1 righteousness.
a ch. 46.11.
b ch. 45.1.
2 in peace.
c ch. 44.7. Acts 15.18.
d ch. 43.10. ch. 48.12. Rev. 1.11, 17.
3 Be strong.
4 Or, founder
5 Or, the smiting.
6 Or, saying of the soder, It is good.
e Gen. 18.19. 2 Chr. 20.7. Neh. 9.7.
f Deut. 31.6. Rom. 8.31.
g Ex. 23.22. Zech. 12.3.
7 the men of thy strife.
8 the men of thy contention.

to *them that have* no might he increaseth strength.

30 Even the youths shall faint and be weary, and the young men shall utterly fall:

31 But they that [n]wait upon the LORD shall [16]renew *their* strength; they shall mount up with wings as eagles; they shall run, and not be weary; *and* they shall walk, and not faint.

CHAPTER 41

KEEP silence before me, O islands; and let the people renew *their* strength: let them come near; then let them speak: let us come near together to judgment.

2 Who raised up [1]the righteous *man* [a]from the east, called him to his foot, gave the [b]nations before him, and made *him* rule over kings? he gave *them* as the dust to his sword, *and* as driven stubble to his bow.

3 He pursued them, *and* passed [2]safely; *even* by the way *that* he had not gone with his feet.

4 Who [c]hath wrought and done *it*, calling the generations from the beginning? I the LORD, the [d]first, and with the last; I *am* he.

5 The isles saw *it*, and feared; the ends of the earth were afraid, drew near, and came.

6 They helped every one his neighbour; and *every one* said to his brother, [3]Be of good courage.

7 So the carpenter encouraged the [4]goldsmith, *and* he that smootheth *with* the hammer [5]him that smote the anvil, [6]saying, It *is* ready for the sodering: and he fastened it with nails, *that* it should not be moved.

8 But thou, Israel, *art* my servant, Jacob whom I have chosen, the seed of Abraham my [e]friend.

9 *Thou* whom I have taken from the ends of the earth, and called thee from the chief men thereof, and said unto thee, Thou *art* my servant; I have chosen thee, and not cast thee away.

10 ¶ Fear thou not; [f]for I *am* with thee: be not dismayed; for I *am* thy God: I will strengthen thee; yea, I will help thee; yea, I will uphold thee with the right hand of my righteousness.

11 Behold, all they that were incensed against thee shall [g]be ashamed and confounded: they shall be as nothing; and [7]they that strive with thee shall perish.

12 Thou shalt seek them, and shalt not find them, *even* [8]them that con-

tended with thee: [9]they that war against thee shall be as nothing, and as a thing of nought.

13 For I the LORD thy God will hold thy right hand, saying unto thee, Fear not; I will help thee.

14 Fear not, thou worm Jacob, *and* ye [10]men of Israel; I will help thee, saith the LORD, [h]and thy redeemer, the Holy One of Israel.

15 Behold, [i]I will make thee a new sharp threshing instrument having [11]teeth: thou shalt thresh the mountains, and beat *them* small, and shalt make the hills as chaff.

16 Thou shalt [j]fan them, and the wind shall carry them away, and the whirlwind shall scatter them: and thou shalt rejoice in the LORD, *and* shalt glory in the Holy One of Israel.

17 *When* the poor and needy seek water, and *there is* none, *and* their tongue faileth for thirst, I the LORD will hear them, *I* the God of Israel will not forsake them.

18 I will open [k]rivers in high places, and fountains in the midst of the valleys: I will make [l]the wilderness a pool of water, and the dry land springs of water.

19 I will plant in the wilderness the cedar, the shĭt′-tăh tree, and the myrtle, and the oil tree; I will set in the desert the fir tree, *and* the pine, and the box tree together:

20 That [m]they may see, and know, and consider, and understand together, that the hand of the LORD hath done this, and the Holy One of Israel hath created it.

21 [12]Produce your cause, saith the LORD; bring forth your strong *reasons*, saith the King of Jacob.

22 Let them bring *them* forth, and shew us what shall happen: let them shew the former things, what they *be*, that we may [13]consider them, and know the latter end of them; or declare us things for to come.

23 Shew [n]the things that are to come hereafter, that we may know that ye *are* gods: yea, [o]do good, or do evil, that we may be dismayed, and behold *it* together.

24 Behold, ye *are* [14]of nothing, and your work [15]of nought: an abomination *is he that* chooseth you.

25 I have raised up *one* from the north, and he shall come: from the rising of the sun [p]shall he call upon my name: and he shall come upon princes as *upon* morter, and as the potter treadeth clay.

26 Who hath declared from the be ginning, that we may know? and be foretime, that we may say, *He i* righteous? yea, *there is* none tha sheweth, yea, *there is* none that de clareth, yea, *there is* none that heareth your words.

27 [16]The first *shall say* to Zion, Be hold, behold them: and I will give t Jerusalem one that bringeth good tidings.

28 For [q]I beheld, and *there was* n man; even among them, and *there was* no counseller, that, when I asked of them, could [17]answer a word.

29 Behold, they *are* all vanity; thei works *are* nothing: their molten im ages *are* wind and confusion.

CHAPTER 42

BEHOLD [a]my servant, whom I up hold; mine elect, *in whom* my sou [b]delighteth; I [c]have put my spirit up on him: he shall bring forth judgmen to the Gentiles.

2 He shall not cry, nor lift up, no cause his voice to be heard in th street.

3 A bruised reed shall he not break and the [1]smoking flax shall he no [2]quench: he shall bring forth judg ment unto truth.

4 He [d]shall not fail nor be [3]dis couraged, till he have set judgment i the earth: [e]and the isles shall wait fo his law.

5 ¶ Thus saith God the LORD, [f]h that created the heavens, and stretch ed them out; he that spread forth th earth, and that which cometh out c it; [g]he that giveth breath unto the peo ple upon it, and spirit to them tha walk therein:

6 I the LORD have called thee i righteousness, and will hold thin hand, and will keep thee, and giv thee for a covenant of the people, fo [h]a light of the Gentiles;

7 To open the blind eyes, [i]to brin out the prisoners from the prison, *an* them that sit in [j]darkness out of th prison house.

8 I [k]*am* the LORD: that *is* my name and my [l]glory will I not give to a other, neither my praise to graven im ages.

9 Behold, the former things are com to pass, and new things do I declare before they spring forth I tell you c them.

10 Sing [m]unto the LORD a new song *and* his praise from the end of th earth, ye [n]that go down to the sea, an

9 the men of thy war.
10 Or, few men.
h Job 19.25.
i Micah 4.13. 2 Cor. 10.4, 5.
11 mouths.
j Jer. 51.2.
k ch. 35.6,7.
l Ps. 107.35.
m Job 12.9.
12 Cause to come near.
13 set our heart upon them.
n Deut. 18. 22.
o Jer. 10.5.
14 Or, worse than nothing.
15 Or, worse than of a viper.
p Ezra 1.2.
16 Or, I the first say.
q ch. 63.5. Dan. 2.10.
17 return.

CHAP. 42
a ch. 49.3,6. ch. 52.13. Matt. 12.18. Phil. 2.7.
b Matt. 3.17. John 3.35. Eph. 1.6. Col. 1.12-14.
c ch. 11.2.
1 Or, dimly burning.
2 quench it.
d Heb. 12.2.
3 broken.
e Gen. 49.10.
f ch. 44.24. Zech. 12.1.
g Acts 17.25.
h Luke 2.32. Acts 13.47.
i Luke 4.18. 2 Tim. 2.26. Heb. 2.14.
j ch. 9.2.
k Ex. 3.14.
l ch. 48.11.
m Ps. 33.3. Ps. 40.3.
n Ps. 107.23.

l that is therein; the isles, and the
habitants thereof.
1 Let the wilderness and the cities
ereof lift up *their voice*, the villages
at Kē-dār doth inhabit: let the in-
bitants of the rock sing, let them
out from the top of the mountains.
2 Let them give glory unto the LORD,
d declare his praise in the islands.
3 The LORD shall go forth as a
ighty man, he shall stir up jealousy
e a man of war: he shall cry, yea,
ar; he shall [5]prevail against his en-
ies.
4 I have long time holden my peace;
have been still, *and* refrained my-
lf: *now* will I cry like a travailing
oman; I will destroy and [6]devour
once.
5 I will make waste mountains and
ls, and dry up all their herbs; and I
ll make the rivers islands, and I
ll dry up the pools.
6 And I will bring the blind by a
y *that* they knew not; I will lead
em in paths *that* they have not
own: I will make darkness light
fore them, and crooked things
raight. These things will I do unto
em, and not forsake them.
7 ¶ They shall be turned back, they
all be greatly ashamed, that trust in
aven images, that say to the molten
ages, Ye *are* our gods.
8 Hear, ye deaf; and look, ye blind,
at ye may see.
9 Who [o]*is* blind, but my servant? or
af, as my messenger *that* I sent?
o *is* blind as *he that is* perfect, and
nd as the LORD's servant?
Seeing many things, [p]but thou ob-
vest not; opening the ears, but he
areth not.
The LORD is well pleased for his
hteousness' sake; he will magnify
law, and make [8]*it* honourable.
But this *is* a people robbed and
iled; [9]*they are* all of them snared in
es, and they are hid in prison
uses: they are for a prey, and none
livereth; for [10]a spoil, and none
th, Restore.
Who among you will give ear to
s? *who* will hearken and hear [11]for
time to come?
Who gave Jacob for a spoil, and
ael to the robbers? did not the
RD, he against whom we have sin-
d? for they would not walk in his
ys, neither were they obedient unto
law.
Therefore he hath poured upon
n the fury of his anger, and the

4 the fulness thereof.
5 Or, behave himself mightily.
6 swallow, or, sup up.
7 into straightness.
o ch. 43.8. Eze. 12.2. John 9.39.
p Deut. 4.3. ch. 1.3. Rom. 2.21.
8 Or, him.
9 Or, in snaring all the young men of them.
10 a treading.
11 for the after time?
q 2 Ki. 25.9.
r Hosea 7.9.

CHAP. 43

a ch. 44.6.
b ch. 42.6. 1 Cor. 1.9. 2 Tim. 1.9.
c Ps. 66.12.
d Deut. 31.6, 8.
e Dan. 3.25.
f Pro. 21.18.
g Ex. 19.5,6.
1 Or, person.
h ch. 41.10, 14. ch. 44.2.
i ch. 63.19.
j Ps. 100.3. ch. 29.23. John 3.3. 2 Cor. 5.17. Eph. 2.10.
k ch. 6.9. ch. 42.19.
l ch. 44.8. John 1.7. Acts 1.8. Heb. 12.1. Rev. 1.5.
m ch. 41.8.
2 Or, nothing formed of God.
n Deut. 32. 16.
o Ps. 90.2. Pro. 8.23. Micah 5.2. Matt. 19.26.
3 turn it back?

strength of battle: [q]and it hath set him
on fire round about, [r]yet he knew not;
and it burned him, yet he laid *it* not to
heart.

CHAPTER 43

BUT now thus saith the LORD that
created thee, O Jacob, and he that
formed thee, O Israel, Fear not: [a]for
I have redeemed thee, [b]I have called
thee by thy name; thou *art* mine.
2 When [c]thou passest through the
waters, I [d]*will be* with thee; and
through the rivers, they shall not overflow thee: when thou walkest through
the fire, [e]thou shalt not be burned;
neither shall the flame kindle upon
thee.
3 For I *am* the LORD thy God, the
Holy One of Israel, thy Saviour: I
[f]gave Egypt *for* thy ransom, Ē-thĭ-ō-
pĭ-ă and Sē-bă for thee.
4 Since thou wast [g]precious in my
sight, thou hast been honourable, and
I have loved thee: therefore will I give
men for thee, and people for thy [1]life.
5 [h]Fear not: for I *am* with thee: I
will bring thy seed from the east, and
gather thee from the west;
6 I will say to the north, Give up;
and to the south, Keep not back:
bring my sons from far, and my
daughters from the ends of the earth;
7 *Even* every one that is [i]called by
my name: for [j]I have created him for
my glory, I have formed him; yea, I
have made him.
8 ¶ Bring [k]forth the blind people that
have eyes, and the deaf that have ears.
9 Let all the nations be gathered together, and let the people be assembled: who among them can declare
this, and shew us former things? let
them bring forth their witnesses, that
they may be justified: or let them
hear, and say, *It is* truth.
10 Ye *are* [l]my witnesses, saith the
LORD, and my [m]servant whom I have
chosen: that ye may know and believe
me, and understand that I *am* he: before me there was [2]no God formed,
neither shall there be after me.
11 I, *even* I, *am* the LORD; and beside
me *there is* no saviour.
12 I have declared, and have saved,
and I have shewed, when *there was* no
[n]strange *god* among you: therefore ye
are my witnesses, saith the LORD, that
I *am* God.
13 Yea, [o]before the day *was* I *am* he;
and *there is* none that can deliver out
of my hand: I will work, and who
shall [3]let it?
14 ¶ Thus saith the LORD, your re-

deemer, the Holy One of Israel; For
your sake I have sent to Babylon, and
have brought down all their [4]nobles,
and the Chăl-dē-ăns, whose cry *is* in
the ships.
15 I *am* the LORD, your Holy One,
the creator of Israel, your [p]King.
16 Thus saith the LORD, [q]which maketh a way in the sea, and a path in the
mighty waters;
17 Which [r]bringeth forth the chariot
and horse, the army and the power;
they shall lie down together, they shall
not rise: they are extinct, they are
quenched as tow.
18 ¶ Remember ye not the former
things, neither consider the things of
old.
19 Behold, I will do a [s]new thing;
now it shall spring forth; shall ye not
know it? I will even make a way in the
wilderness, *and* rivers in the desert.
20 The beast of the field shall honour
me, the dragons and the [5]owls: because [t]I give waters in the wilderness,
and rivers in the desert, to give drink
to my people, my chosen.
21 This [u]people have I formed for
myself; they shall shew forth my
praise.
22 ¶ But thou hast not called upon
me, O Jacob; but thou [v]hast been
weary of me, O Israel.
23 Thou hast not brought me the
[6]small cattle of thy burnt offerings;
neither hast thou honoured me with
thy sacrifices. I have not caused thee
to serve with an offering, nor wearied
thee with incense.
24 Thou hast bought me no sweet
cane with money, neither hast thou
[7]filled me with the fat of thy sacrifices:
but thou hast made me to serve with
thy sins, thou hast wearied [w]me with
thine iniquities.
25 I, *even* I, *am* he that [x]blotteth out
thy transgressions [y]for mine own
sake, and will not remember thy sins.
26 Put me in remembrance: let us
plead together: declare thou, that
thou mayest be justified.
27 [z]Thy first father hath sinned, and
thy [8]teachers have transgressed against
me.
28 Therefore [a]I have profaned the
[9]princes of the sanctuary, and have
[b]given Jacob to the curse, and Israel
to reproaches.

CHAPTER 44

YET now hear, [a]O Jacob my servant; and Israel, whom I have
chosen:

4 bars.
p Hos. 13.10.
q Ps. 77.19.
r Ex. 14.4.
s 2 Cor. 5.17. Rev. 21.5.
5 daughters of the owl, or, ostriches.
t ch. 48.21.
u Luke 1.74. Eph. 1.5.
v Mal. 1.13.
6 lambs, or, kids.
7 made me drunk, or abundantly moistened.
w ch. 1.14. Mal. 2.17. Jude 4.
x ch. 44.22. Jer. 31.34. Micah 7.18, 19.
y Eze. 36.22.
z Rom. 5.12.
8 interpreters, Mal. 2.7.
a ch. 47.6. Lam. 2.2.
9 Or, holy princes.
b Ps. 79.4. Jer. 24.9. Dan. 9.11. Zech. 8.13.

CHAP. 44

a ch. 41.8. Jer. 30.10.
b Deut. 32.15.
c Mal. 3.10. John 7.38.
d Ex. 13.9. Neh. 9.38.
e ch. 43.1.
f ch. 41.4. Rev. 1.8.
g Deut. 4.35. 1 Sam. 2.2. 2 Sam. 22. 32.
1 rock.
h ch. 41.24.
2 desirable.
i Deut. 4.28. Ps. 115.4. ch. 42.17-20.
j Jer. 10.5. Hab. 2.18.
k Ps. 97.7. ch. 42.17.
l ch. 40.19.
3 Or, with an axe.

2 Thus saith the LORD that ma
thee, and formed thee from the wom
which will help thee; Fear not,
Jacob my servant; and thou, [b]Jĕs-
rŭn, whom I have chosen.
3 For I will [c]pour water upon hi
that is thirsty, and floods upon the d
ground: I will pour my spirit upon t
seed, and my blessing upon thine o
spring:
4 And they shall spring up *as* amo
the grass, as willows by the wat
courses.
5 One shall say, I *am* the LORD's; a
another shall call *himself* by the nan
of Jacob; and another shall [d]su
scribe *with* his hand unto the LOR
and surname *himself* by the name
Israel.
6 Thus saith the LORD the King
Israel, and [e]his redeemer the LORD
hosts; [f]I *am* the first, and I *am* t
last; and beside me *there is* no Go
7 And who, as I, shall call, and sh
declare it, and set it in order for m
since I appointed the ancient peopl
and the things that are coming, a
shall come, let them shew unto then
8 Fear ye not, neither be afraid: ha
not I told thee from that time, a
have declared *it?* ye *are* even r
witnesses. Is there a God beside m
yea, [g]*there is* no [1]God; I know not *a*
9 ¶ They [h]that make a graven ima
are all of them vanity; and their [2]d
lectable things shall not profit; a
they *are* their own witnesses; [i]th
see not, nor know; that they may
ashamed.
10 Who hath formed a god, or m
ten a graven image [j]*that* is profital
for nothing?
11 Behold, all his fellows shall
[k]ashamed: and the workmen, they *a*
of men: let them all be gathered
gether, let them stand up; *yet* th
shall fear, *and* they shall be asham
together.
12 The [l]smith [3]with the tongs b
worketh in the coals, and fashion
it with hammers, and worketh it w
the strength of his arms: yea, he
hungry, and his strength faileth:
drinketh no water, and is faint.
13 The carpenter stretcheth out
rule; he marketh it out with a line;
fitteth it with planes, and he mark
it out with the compass, and mak
it after the figure of a man, accordi
to the beauty of a man; that it m
remain in the house.
14 He heweth him down cedars, a
taketh the cypress and the oak, wh

[4]strengtheneth for himself among
e trees of the forest: he planteth an
h, and the rain doth nourish *it*.
5 Then shall it be for a man to burn:
r he will take thereof, and warm
mself; yea, he kindleth *it*, and bak-
h bread; yea, he maketh a god, and
orshippeth *it;* he maketh it a graven
age, and falleth down thereto.
6 He burneth part thereof in the
e; with part thereof he eateth flesh;
roasteth roast, and is satisfied: yea,
warmeth *himself*, and saith, Aha, I
n warm, I have seen the fire:
7 And the residue thereof he mak-
n a god, *even* his graven image: he
lleth down unto it, and worshippeth
and prayeth unto it, and saith, Deer me; for thou *art* my god.
8 They [m]have not known nor un-
rstood: for [n]he hath [5]shut their eyes,
at they cannot see; *and* their hearts,
at they cannot understand.
9 And none [6]considereth in his
art, neither *is there* knowledge nor
derstanding to say, I have burned
rt of it in the fire; yea, also I have
ked bread upon the coals thereof;
ave roasted flesh, and eaten *it:* and
all I make the residue thereof an
omination? shall I fall down to the
ock of a tree?
) He feedeth on ashes: [o]a deceived
art hath turned him aside, that he
nnot deliver his soul, nor say, *Is*
ere not a lie in my right hand?
1 ¶ Remember these, O Jacob and
ael; for thou *art* my servant: I have
rmed thee; thou *art* my servant: O
ael, thou shalt not be forgotten of
.
2 I [p]have blotted out, as a thick
oud, thy transgressions, and, as a
oud, thy sins: return unto me; for I
ve [q]redeemed thee.
3 Sing, [r]O ye heavens; for the LORD
th done *it:* shout, ye lower parts of
e earth: break forth into singing,
mountains, O forest, and every
e therein: for the LORD hath re-
emed Jacob, and glorified himself
Israel.
4 Thus saith the LORD, [s]thy redeem-
and [t]he that formed thee from the
mb, I *am* the LORD that maketh all
ngs; that stretcheth [u]forth the heav-
s alone; that spreadeth abroad
e earth by myself;
5 That frustrateth the [v]tokens of the
rs, and maketh diviners mad; that
neth wise *men* backward, [w]and
keth their knowledge foolish;
6 That [x]confirmeth the word of his

4 Or, taketh courage.
m Ps. 81.12. ch. 45.20.
n Rom. 11.8, 10. 2 Thes. 2.11.
5 daubed.
6 setteth to his heart.
7 that which comes of a tree?
o Hosea 4.12. Rom. 1.21. 2 Thes. 2.11.
p ch. 1.18. ch. 43.25. ch. 53.11, 12. Jer. 33.8. Micah 7.18, 19. Col. 1.14.
q ch. 43.1. 1 Cor. 6.20. 1 Pet. 1.18, 19.
r Ps. 69.34. ch. 42.10. Rev. 18.20.
s Job 19.25. ch. 43.14.
t ch. 43.1.
u Job 9.8. Ps. 104.2. ch. 40.22.
v Jer. 50.36.
w 1 Cor. 1.20.
x Zech. 1.6. Matt. 5.18.
8 wastes.
y Jer. 50.38.
z 2 Chr. 36. 22,23.

CHAP. 45

a Ps. 73.23. ch. 41.13.
1 Or, strengthened.
b Ex. 33.12.
c ch. 44.1.
d Acts 17.23. Gal. 4.8,9. Eph. 2.12. 1 Thes. 4.5.
e Deut. 4.35.
f Ps. 18.32.
g Ps. 102.15. Mal. 1.11.
h Amos 3.6.
i Ps. 85.11.
j ch. 64.8.
k Jer. 18.6. Rom. 9.20.

servant, and performeth the counsel
of his messengers; that saith to Jerusalem, Thou shalt be inhabited; and
to the cities of Judah, Ye shall be built,
and I will raise up the [8]decayed places
thereof:
27 That [y]saith to the deep, Be dry,
and I will dry up thy rivers:
28 That saith of Cyrus, *He is* my
shepherd, and shall perform all my
pleasure: even saying to Jerusalem,
Thou [z]shalt be built; and to the temple, Thy foundation shall be laid.

CHAPTER 45

THUS saith the LORD to his anointed, to Cyrus, whose [a]right hand I
[1]have holden, to subdue nations before him; and I will loose the loins of
kings, to open before him the two
leaved gates; and the gates shall not
be shut;
2 I will go before thee, and make the
crooked places straight: I will break
in pieces the gates of brass, and cut in
sunder the bars of iron:
3 And I will give thee the treasures
of darkness, and hidden riches of secret places, that thou mayest know
that I, the LORD, which call [b]*thee* by
thy name, *am* the God of Israel.
4 For [c]Jacob my servant's sake, and
Israel mine elect, I have even called
thee by thy name: I have surnamed
thee, though thou hast not [d]known
me.
5 ¶ I [e]*am* the LORD, and *there is* none
else, *there is* no God beside me: [f]I
girded thee, though thou hast not
known me:
6 That [g]they may know from the rising of the sun, and from the west, that
there is none beside me. I *am* the LORD,
and *there is* none else.
7 I form the light, and create darkness: I make peace, [h]and create evil:
I the LORD do all these *things*.
8 Drop [i]down, ye heavens, from
above, and let the skies pour down
righteousness: let the earth open, and
let them bring forth salvation, and let
righteousness spring up together; I
the LORD have created it.
9 Woe unto him that striveth with
[j]his Maker! *Let* the potsherd *strive*
with the potsherds of the earth. [k]Shall
the clay say to him that fashioneth it,
What makest thou? or thy work, He
hath no hands?
10 Woe unto him that saith unto *his*
father, What begettest thou? or to the
woman, What hast thou brought
forth?

11 Thus saith the LORD, the Holy
One of Israel, and his Maker, Ask me
of things to come concerning [l]my
sons, and concerning [m]the work of my
hands command ye me.
12 I [n]have made the earth, and created man upon it: I, *even* my hands,
have stretched out the heavens, and all
their host have I commanded.
13 I have raised him up in righteousness, and I will [2]direct all his ways: he
shall build [o]my city, and he shall let
go my captives, [p]not for price nor reward, saith the LORD of hosts.
14 Thus saith the LORD, [q]The labour
of Egypt, and merchandise of Ē-thĭ-
ō'-pĭ-ă and of the Să-bē'-ăns, men of
stature, shall come over unto thee,
and they shall be thine: they shall
come after thee; in chains they shall
come over, and they shall fall down
unto thee, they shall make supplication unto thee, *saying*, [r]Surely God *is*
in thee; and *there is* none else, *there is*
no God.
15 Verily thou *art* a God [s]that hidest
thyself, O god of Israel, the Saviour.
16 They shall be ashamed, and also
confounded, all of them: they shall
go to confusion together *that are* mak-
ers of idols.
17 *But* [t]Israel shall be saved in the
LORD with an everlasting salvation:
ye shall not be ashamed nor confounded world without end.
18 For thus saith the LORD that created the heavens; God himself that
formed the earth and made it; he hath
established it, he created it not in
vain, he formed it to be inhabited: I
am the LORD; and *there is* none else.
19 I have not spoken in [u]secret, in a
dark place of the earth: I said not unto
the seed of Jacob, Seek ye me in vain:
[v]I the LORD speak righteousness, I declare things that are right.
20 ¶ Assemble yourselves and come;
draw near together, ye *that are* [w]escap-
ed of the nations: [x]they have no
knowledge that set up the wood of
their graven image, and pray unto a
god *that* cannot save.
21 Tell ye, and bring *them* near; yea,
let them take counsel together: who
hath declared this from ancient time?
who hath told it from that time? *have*
not I the LORD? and *there is* no God
else beside me; a just God and a Saviour; *there is* none beside me.
22 [3]Look unto me, and be ye saved,
all the ends of the earth: for I *am* God,
and *there is* none else.
23 I [y]have sworn by myself, the word

l Jer. 31.9.
m Isa. 29.23.
n Jer. 27.5.
2 Or, make straight.
o Ezra 1.1.
p Rom. 3.24.
q Ps. 68.31. ch. 49.23. Zech. 8.22.
r 1 Cor. 14. 25.
s Deut. 29.29. Ps. 36.6. ch. 8.17. Rom. 11.33, 34.
t 2 Sam. 23.5. Ps. 103.17. Hosea 1.7. Rom. 11.26.
u Deut. 30. 11.
v Neh. 9.13. Ps. 19.8. Rom. 7.12.
w Jer. 44.28.
x Rom. 1.22.
3 Or, Turn.
y Gen. 22.16. Jer. 22.5. Heb. 6.13.
z Rom. 14.11. Phil. 2.10.
a Gen. 31.53. Deut. 6.13. Ps. 63.11.
4 Or, Surely he shall say of me, In the LORD is all righteousness and strength.
5 righteousnesses.

CHAP. 46

a Jer. 51.44.
b Jer. 10.5.
1 their soul.
c Ex. 19.4. Deut. 1.31.
d Ps. 102.27. Mal. 3.6.
e Ps. 48.14.
f Jer. 10.5.
g Deut. 32.7.
h Ps. 33.11. Pro. 19.21. Acts 5.39. Heb. 6.17.
2 the man of my counsel.
i Num. 23.19. Titus 1.2.

is gone out of my mouth *in* righteo
ness, and shall not return, That un
me every [z]knee shall bow, [a]eve
tongue shall swear.
24 [4]Surely, shall *one* say, in the Lo
have I [5]righteousness and strengt
even to him shall *men* come; and
that are incensed against him shall
ashamed.
25 In the LORD shall all the seed
Israel be justified, and shall glory.

CHAPTER 46

BEL [a]boweth down, Nē'-bō stoo
eth, their idols were upon t
beasts, and upon the cattle: yo
carriages *were* heavy loaden; [b]*th*
are a burden to the weary *beast*.
2 They stoop, they bow down t
gether; they could not deliver t
burden, but [1]themselves are gone in
captivity.
3 ¶ Hearken unto me, O house
Jacob, and all the remnant of t
house of Israel, which [c]are borne
me from the belly, which are carri
from the womb:
4 And *even* to *your* old age [d]I *am* h
and *even* to hoar hairs [e]will I car
you: I have made, and I will bea
even I will carry, and will deliver *y*
5 ¶ To whom will ye liken me, a
make *me* equal, and compare m
that we may be like?
6 They lavish gold out of the ba
and weigh silver in the balance, *a*
hire a goldsmith; and he maketh i
god: they fall down, yea, they wo
ship.
7 They [f]bear him upon the should
they carry him, and set him in h
place, and he standeth; from his pla
shall he not remove: yea, *one* sh
cry unto him, yet can he not answ
nor save him out of his trouble.
8 Remember this, and shew you
selves men: bring *it* again to mind,
ye transgressors.
9 Remember [g]the former things
old: for I *am* God, and *there is* no
else; *I am* God, and *there is* no
like me,
10 Declaring the end from the beg
ning, and from ancient times *the thi*
that are not *yet* done, saying, [h]M
counsel shall stand, and I will do
my pleasure:
11 Calling a ravenous bird from t
east, [2]the man that executeth my cou
sel from a far country: yea, [i]I ha
spoken *it*, I will also bring it to pa
I have purposed *it*, I will also do it
12 ¶ Hearken unto me, ye sto

arted, that [j]*are* far from righteous-
ss:
3 I [k]bring near my righteousness;
shall not be far off, and my salva-
on [l]shall not tarry: and I will place
lvation [m]in Zion for Israel my glory.

CHAPTER 47

OME [a]down, and sit in the dust,
O virgin daughter of Babylon, sit
the ground: *there is* no throne, O
ughter of the Chăl-dē'ăns: for thou
alt no more be called tender and
licate.
Take [b]the millstones, and grind
eal: uncover thy locks, make bare
e leg, uncover the thigh, pass over
e rivers.
Thy [c]nakedness shall be uncovered,
a, thy shame shall be seen: [d]I will
ke vengeance, and I will not meet
ee as a man.
As for our redeemer, the LORD of
osts *is* his name, the Holy One of Is-
el.
Sit thou [e]silent, and get thee into
rkness, O daughter of the Chăl-dē'-
s: [f]for thou shalt no more be called,
e lady of kingdoms.
¶ I [g]was wroth with my people, I
ve polluted mine inheritance, and
ven them into thine hand: thou didst
ew them no mercy; upon [h]the
cient hast thou very heavily laid thy
ke.
¶ And thou saidst, I shall be [i]a lady
r ever: *so* that thou didst not lay
ese *things* to thy heart, neither didst
member the latter end of it.
Therefore hear now this, *thou that*
t given to pleasures, that dwellest
relessly, that sayest in thine heart,
am, and none else beside me; [k]I
all not sit *as* a widow, neither shall
now the loss of children:
But these two *things* shall come to
ee in [l]a moment in one day, the loss
children, and widowhood: they
all come upon thee in their perfec-
on [m]for the multitude of thy sorcer-
s, *and* for the great abundance of
ine enchantments.
0 ¶ For thou [n]hast trusted in thy
ickedness: [o]thou hast said, None
eth me. Thy wisdom and thy knowl-
dge, it hath [1]perverted thee; and thou
ast said in thine heart, I *am*, and none
se beside me.
1 ¶ Therefore shall evil come upon
ee; thou shalt not know [2]from
hence it riseth: and mischief shall
ll upon thee; thou shalt not be able
[3]put it off: and desolation [p]shall

j Rom. 10.3.
k Rom. 1.17.
l ch. 56.1. Hab. 2.3. Matt. 3.2. Luke 19.10. Acts 13.26. 1 Tim. 1.15.
m ch. 62.11. Zech. 9.9.

CHAP. 47

a Jer. 48.18. Lam. 2.10. Rev. 18.19.
b Ex. 11.5.
c Nah. 3.5.
d Matt. 7.2. Rom. 12.19.
e 1 Sam. 2.9.
f Dan. 2.37.
g 2 Chr. 28.9. ch. 10.6. Zech. 1.15.
h Deut. 28. 50.
i ver. 5. Rev. 18.7.
j Zeph. 2.15.
k Rev. 18.7.
l 1 Thes. 5.3.
m Dan. 2.2. Nah. 3.4. 2 Thes. 2.9, 10. Rev. 9.21.
n Ps. 52.7.
o Eze. 8.12.
1 Or, caused thee to turn away.
2 the morning thereof.
3 expiate.
p ch. 13.6. Dan. 5.30. Luke 17.27.
4 viewers of the heavens, Dan. 2.2.
5 that give knowledge concerning the months.
q Nah. 1.10. Mal. 4.1.
6 their souls.
r Rev. 18.11.

CHAP. 48

a Deut. 6.13. Jer. 7.9. Zeph. 1.5.
b Micah 3.11. Rom. 2.17.
c Josh. 21.45.
1 hard.
d Ex. 32.9. Deut. 31.27.

come upon thee suddenly, *which* thou
shalt not know.
12 Stand now with thine enchantments, and with the multitude of thy
sorceries, wherein thou hast laboured
from thy youth; if so be thou shalt be
able to profit, if so be thou mayest
prevail.
13 Thou art wearied in the multitude
of thy counsels. Let now the [4]astrolo-
gers, the stargazers, [5]the monthly
prognosticators, stand up, and save
thee from *these things* that shall come
upon thee.
14 Behold, they shall be as [q]stubble;
the fire shall burn them; they shall
not deliver [6]themselves from the power of the flame: *there shall* not *be* a
coal to warm at, *nor* fire to sit before it.
15 Thus shall they be unto thee with
whom thou hast laboured, *even* [r]thy
merchants, from thy youth: they shall
wander every one to his quarter; none
shall save thee.

CHAPTER 48

HEAR ye this, O house of Jacob,
which are called by the name of
Israel, and are come forth out of the
waters of Judah, [a]which swear by the
name of the LORD, and make mention of the God of Israel, *but* not in
truth, nor in righteousness.
2 For they call themselves of the holy
city, and [b]stay themselves upon the
God of Israel; The LORD of hosts *is*
his name.
3 I have declared the former things
from the beginning; and they went
forth out of my mouth, and I shewed
them; I did *them* suddenly, and [c]they
came to pass.
4 Because I knew that thou *art* [1]ob-
stinate, and [d]thy neck *is* an iron sinew,
and thy brow brass;
5 I have even from the beginning declared *it* to thee; before it came to pass
I shewed *it* thee: lest thou shouldest
say, Mine idol hath done them, and
my graven image, and my molten image, hath commanded them.
6 Thou hast heard, see all this; and
will not ye declare *it?* I have shewed
thee new things from this time, even
hidden things, and thou didst not
know them.
7 They are created now, and not from
the beginning; even before the day
when thou heardest them not; lest
thou shouldest say, Behold, I knew
them.
8 Yea, thou heardest not; yea, thou
knewest not; yea, from that time *that*

thine ear was not opened: for I knew
that thou wouldest deal very treacherously, and wast called a [e]transgressor
from the womb.
9 ¶ For [f]my name's sake will I defer mine anger, and for my praise will
I refrain for thee, that I cut thee not off.
10 Behold, [g]I have refined thee, but
not [2]with silver; I have chosen thee in
the furnace of affliction.
11 For mine own sake, *even* for mine
own sake, will I do *it*: [h]for how should
my name be polluted? and [i]I will not
give my glory unto another.
12 ¶ Hearken unto me, O Jacob and
Israel, my called; [j]I *am* he; I *am* [k]the
first, I also *am* the last.
13 Mine [l]hand also hath laid the
foundation of the earth, and [3]my right
hand hath spanned the heavens: *when*
I call unto them, they stand up together.
14 All ye, assemble yourselves, and
hear; which among them hath declared these *things?* The LORD hath
loved him: he will do his pleasure on
Babylon, and his arm *shall be on* the
Chăl-dē'-ăns.
15 I, *even* I, have spoken; yea, I have
called him: I have brought him, and
he shall make his way prosperous.
16 ¶ Come ye near unto me, hear ye
this; I have not spoken in secret from
the beginning; from the time that it
was, there *am* I: and now the [m]Lord
GOD, and his Spirit, hath sent me.
17 Thus saith the LORD, thy Redeemer, the Holy One of Israel; I *am*
the LORD thy God which teacheth
thee to profit, [n]which leadeth thee by
the way *that* thou shouldest go.
18 O [o]that thou hadst hearkened to
my commandments! then had thy
peace been as a river, and thy righteousness as the waves of the sea:
19 Thy [p]seed also had been as the
sand, and the offspring of thy bowels
like the gravel thereof; his name
should not have been cut off nor destroyed from before me.
20 ¶ Go [q]ye forth of Babylon, flee ye
from the Chăl-dē'-ăns, with a voice of
singing declare ye, tell this, utter it
even to the end of the earth; say ye,
The LORD hath [r]redeemed his servant
Jacob.
21 And they thirsted not *when* he led
them through the deserts: [s]he caused
the waters to flow out of the rock for
them: he clave the rock also, and the
waters gushed out.
22 *There is* no peace, saith the LORD,
unto the wicked.

e Ps. 58.3.
f Josh. 7.9. Ps. 106.8.
g Ps. 66.10. ch. 1.25. Mal. 3.3.
2 Or, for silver.
h Deut. 32. 26.
i ch. 42.8.
j Deut. 32.39.
k Rev. 1.17. Rev. 22.13.
l Ps. 102.25.
3 Or, the palm of my right hand hath spread out.
m Zech. 2.8, 9.
n Ps. 32.8.
o Deut. 5.29. Ps. 81.13.
p Gen. 22.17. Hosea 1.10.
q Zech. 2.6, 7. Rev. 18.4.
r Ex. 19.4.
s Num. 20. 11. Neh. 9.15. Ps. 105.41. 1 Cor. 10.4.

CHAP. 49

a Jer. 1.5. Matt. 1.20. Luke 1.15.
b Hosea 6.5.
c Zech. 3.8.
d Matt. 17.17. John 13.31.
e Eze. 3.19.
1 Or, my reward.
2 Or, That Israel may be gathered to him, and I may, etc.
3 Or, Art thou lighter than that thou shouldest, etc.
4 Or, desolations.
f Isa. 9.2. Luke 2.32.
5 Or, to him that is despised in soul.
g Ps. 69.13.
6 Or, raise up.
h ch. 42.7. Zech. 9.12.
i Ps. 22.26. John 6.35. Rev. 7.16.
j Ps. 121.6.
k Ps. 23.2.

CHAPTER 49

LISTEN, O isles, unto me; a
hearken, ye people, from far; T
[a]LORD hath called me from the wom
from the bowels of my mother ha
he made mention of my name.
2 And he hath made [b]my mouth li
a sharp sword; in the shadow of h
hand hath he hid me, and made me
polished shaft; in his quiver hath
hid me;
3 And said unto me, [c]Thou *art* n
servant, O Israel, [d]in whom I will
glorified.
4 Then [e]I said, I have laboured
vain, I have spent my strength f
nought, and in vain: *yet* surely n
judgment *is* with the LORD, and [1]n
work with my God.
5 ¶ And now, saith the LORD th
formed me from the womb *to be* h
servant, to bring Jacob again to hi
[2]Though Israel be not gathered, y
shall I be glorious in the eyes of t
LORD, and my God shall be n
strength.
6 And he said, [3]It is a light thing th
thou shouldest be my servant to rai
up the tribes of Jacob, and to resto
the [4]preserved of Israel: I will also gi
thee for a light [f]to the Gentiles, th
thou mayest be my salvation unto t
end of the earth.
7 Thus saith the LORD, the Redee
er of Israel, *and* his Holy One, [5]to hi
whom man despiseth, to him who
the nation abhorreth, to a servant
rulers, Kings shall see and aris
princes also shall worship, because
the LORD that is faithful, *and* the Ho
One of Israel, and he shall choo
thee.
8 Thus saith the LORD, [g]In an accep
able time have I heard thee, and in
day of salvation have I helped the
and I will preserve thee, and give th
for a covenant of the people, to [6]esta
lish the earth, to cause to inherit t
desolate heritages;
9 That thou mayest say [h]to the pri
oners, Go forth; to them that *are*
darkness, Shew yourselves. They sha
feed in the ways, and their pastu
shall be in all high places.
10 They shall not [i]hunger nor thirs
neither [j]shall the heat nor sun smi
them: for he that hath mercy on the
[k]shall lead them, even by the springs
water shall he guide them.
11 And I will make all my mountai
a way, and my highways shall be e
alted.
12 Behold, these shall come from fa

d, lo, these from the north and from
: west; and these from the land of
nim.
; ¶ Sing, O heavens; and be joyful,
earth; and break forth into singing,
nountains: for the LORD hath com-
ted his people, and will have mercy
on his afflicted.
. But Zion said, The LORD hath for-
ken me, and my Lord hath forgot-
1 me.
; Can [l]a woman forget her sucking
ld, [7]that she should not have com-
ssion on the son of her womb? yea,
y may forget, yet [m]will I not forget
e.
Behold, [n]I have graven thee upon
palms of *my* hands; thy walls *are*
ntinually before me.
' Thy children shall make haste;
destroyers and they that made
e waste shall go forth of thee.
3 ¶ Lift up thine eyes round about,
d behold: all these gather them-
ves together, *and* come to thee. *As*
ve, saith the LORD, thou shalt surely
the thee with them all, [o]as with an
nament, and bind them *on thee*, as a
de *doeth*.
) For thy waste and thy desolate
ces, and the land of thy destruc-
n, [p]shall even now be too narrow
reason of the inhabitants, and they
at swallowed thee up shall be far
ay.
) The children which thou shalt
ve, after [q]thou hast lost the other,
all say again in thine ears, The place
too strait for me: give place to me
at I may dwell.
l Then shalt thou say in thine
art, Who hath begotten me these,
eing [r]I have lost my children, and
n desolate, a captive, and removing
and fro? and who hath brought up
ese? Behold, I was left alone; these,
ere *had* they *been*?
2 Thus saith the Lord GOD, Behold,
will lift up mine hand to the Gen-
es, and set up my standard to the
ople: and they shall bring thy sons
their [8]arms, and thy daughters
all be carried upon *their* shoul-
rs.
3 And kings shall be thy [9]nursing
thers, and their [10]queens thy nursing
others: they shall bow down to
ee with *their* face toward the earth,
d [s]lick up the dust of thy feet; and
ou shalt know that I *am* the LORD:
r they shall not be ashamed that
ait for me.
4 ¶ Shall [u]the prey be taken from
the mighty, or [11]the lawful captive
delivered?
25 But thus saith the LORD, Even the
[12]captives of the mighty shall be taken
away, and the prey of the terrible shall
be delivered: for I will contend with
him that contendeth with thee, and I
will save thy children.
26 And I will feed them that oppress
thee with their own flesh; and they
shall be drunken with their own
[v]blood, as with [13]sweet wine: and all
flesh [w]shall know that I the LORD *am*
thy Saviour and thy Redeemer, the
mighty One of Jacob.

CHAPTER 50

THUS saith the LORD, Where *is* the
[a]bill of your mother's divorcement, whom I have put away? or
which of my [b]creditors *is it* to whom
I have sold you? Behold, for your iniquities have ye sold yourselves, and
for your transgressions is your mother
put away.
2 Wherefore, when I came, *was there*
no man? [c]when I called, *was there*
none to answer? [d]Is my hand shortened at all, that it cannot redeem? or
have I no power to deliver? behold, at
my rebuke I dry up the sea, I make the
rivers a wilderness: their fish stinketh,
because *there is* no water, and dieth
for thirst.
3 I clothe the heavens with blackness, and I make sackcloth their covering.
4 The [e]Lord GOD hath given me the
tongue of the learned, that I should
know how to speak a word in season
to *him that* [f]*is* weary: he wakeneth
morning by morning, he wakeneth
mine ear to hear as the learned.
5 ¶ The Lord GOD hath opened mine
ear, and I was not [g]rebellious, neither
turned away back.
6 I [h]gave my back to the smiters, and
my [i]cheeks to them that plucked off
the hair: I hid not my face from shame
and spitting.
7 ¶ For the Lord GOD will [j]help me;
therefore shall I not be confounded:
therefore have [k]I set my face like a
flint, and I know that I shall not be
ashamed.
8 *He is* near that justifieth me; who
will contend with me? let [l]us stand together: who *is* [1]mine adversary? let
him come near to me.
9 Behold, the Lord GOD will help me;
who *is* he *that* shall condemn me? [m]lo,
they all shall wax old as a garment; the
moth shall eat them up.

[l] Ps. 103.13. Matt. 7.11.
[7] from having compassion.
[m] Rom. 11. 29.
[n] Ex. 13.9. Song 8.6. Zech. 2.8.
[o] Pro. 17.6.
[p] ch. 54.1,2. Zech. 2.4.
[q] Matt. 3.9. Rom. 11.11.
[r] Gen. 42.13. Jer. 31.15.
[8] bosom.
[9] nourishers.
[10] princesses.
[s] Ps. 72.9. Micah 7.17.
[t] Ps. 34.22. Rom. 5.5.
[u] Matt. 12. 29. Luke 11.21.
[11] the captivity of the just.
[12] captivity.
[v] Rev. 14.20.
[13] Or, new wine.
[w] Ps. 9.16. ch. 43.3.

CHAP. 50.

[a] Deut. 24.1. Hosea 2.2.
[b] 2 Ki. 4.1. Matt. 18.25.
[c] Pro. 1.24. ch. 65.12. Jer. 7.13.
[d] Gen. 18.14. Num. 11.23. ch. 59.1.
[e] Ex. 4.11. Matt. 7.29. Mark 6.7. Luke 4.22, 32.
[f] Matt. 11.28.
[g] Matt. 26. 39. Phil. 2.8. Heb. 10.5.
[h] Matt. 26. 67.
[i] Lam. 3.30. Micah 5.1. Matt. 5.39.
[j] Rom. 8.31.
[k] Eze. 3.8,9.
[l] 1 Cor. 4.4.
[1] the master of my cause?
[m] Job 13.28. Ps. 39.11. Heb. 1.11, 12.

10 ¶ Who *is* among you that feareth the LORD, that obeyeth the voice of his servant, that walketh *in* darkness, and hath no light? let [n]him trust in the name of the LORD, and stay upon his God.

11 Behold, all ye that kindle a fire, that compass *yourselves* about with sparks: [o]walk in the light of your fire, and in the sparks *that* ye have kindled. [p]This shall ye have of mine hand; ye shall lie down in sorrow.

CHAPTER 51

HEARKEN to me, [a]ye that follow after righteousness, ye that seek the LORD: look unto the rock *whence* ye are hewn, and to the hole of the pit *whence* ye are digged.

2 Look [b]unto Abraham your father, and unto Sarah *that* bare you: for I called him alone, and blessed him, and increased him.

3 For the LORD [c]shall comfort Zion: he will comfort all her waste places; and he will make her wilderness like Eden, and her desert like [d]the garden of the LORD; joy and gladness shall be found therein, thanksgiving, and the voice of melody.

4 ¶ Hearken unto me, my people; and give ear unto me, O my nation: for a law shall proceed from me, and I will make my judgment to rest for a light of the people.

5 My [e]righteousness *is* near; my salvation is gone forth, and mine arms shall judge the people; the isles shall wait upon me, and [f]on mine arm shall they trust.

6 Lift up your eyes to the heavens, and look upon the earth beneath: for [g]the heavens shall vanish away like smoke, and the earth shall wax old like a garment, and they that dwell therein shall die in like manner: but my salvation shall be for ever, and my righteousness shall not be abolished.

7 ¶ Hearken unto me, ye that know righteousness, [h]the people in whose heart *is* my law; [i]fear ye not the reproach of men, neither be ye afraid of their revilings.

8 For the moth shall eat them up like a garment, and the worm shall eat them like wool: but my righteousness shall be for ever, and my salvation from generation to generation.

9 ¶ Awake, awake, [j]put on strength, O arm of the LORD; awake, as in the ancient days, in the generations of old. [k]*Art* thou not it that hath cut [l]Rahab, *and* wounded the [m]dragon?

n 2 Chr. 20. 20.
o Rom. 10.3.
p John 9.39.
CHAP. 51
a Pro. 15.9. Matt. 6.33. Rom. 9.30.
b Rom. 4.1. Heb. 11.11.
c Ps. 102.13. ch. 40.1.
d Gen. 13.10. Joel 2.3.
e ch. 46.13.
f Rom. 1.16.
g Matt. 24. 35. 2 Pet. 3.10.
h Ps. 37.31.
i Matt. 10.28. Luke 12.4. Acts 5.41.
j Rev. 11.17.
k Job 26.12.
l Ps. 87.4.
m Eze. 29.3.
n Ex. 14.21.
o 2 Cor. 1.3.
p Ps. 118.6.
q 1 Pet. 1.24.
r Job 9.8.
1 Or, made himself ready.
s Job 20.7.
t Zech. 9.11.
u Ex. 14.21. Ps. 74.13. Ps. 93.3,4. ch. 17.12. ch. 43.16.
v Deut. 18. 18. ch. 59.21. John 3.34.
w ch. 65.17. 2 Pet. 3.13.
x Deut. 28. 28, 34. Ps. 60.3. Rev. 14.10.
2 happened.
3 breaking.
y Amos 7.2.
z Lam. 2.11, 12.
a Jer. 50.34.

10 *Art* thou not it which [n]hath dr
the sea, the waters of the great de
that hath made the depths of the
a way for the ransomed to pass ov
11 Therefore the redeemed of
LORD shall return, and come with si
ing unto Zion; and everlasting j
shall be upon their head: they shall
tain gladness and joy; *and* sorrow a
mourning shall flee away.
12 I, *even* I, *am* he [o]that comfort
you: who *art* thou, that thou shou
est be afraid of [p]a man *that* shall d
and of the son of man *which* shall
made [q]*as* grass;
13 And forgettest the LORD t
maker, that [r]hath stretched forth t
heavens, and laid the foundations
the earth; and hast feared continua
every day because of the fury of t
oppressor, as if he [1]were ready to
stroy? [s]and where *is* the fury of t
oppressor?
14 The captive exile hasteneth th
he may be loosed, [t]and that he shou
not die in the pit, nor that his bre
should fail.
15 But I *am* the LORD thy God, th
divided the [u]sea, whose waves roare
The LORD of hosts *is* his name.
16 And [v]I have put my words in t
mouth, and I have covered thee in t
shadow of mine hand, that I [w]m
plant the heavens, and lay the found
tions of the earth, and say unto Zi
Thou *art* my people.
17 ¶ Awake, awake, stand up,
Jerusalem, which hast drunk at t
hand of the LORD the cup of his fu
[x]thou hast drunken the dregs of t
cup of trembling, *and* wrung *them* o
18 *There is* none to guide her amo
all the sons *whom* she hath broug
forth; neither *is there any* that take
her by the hand of all the sons *that* s
hath brought up.
19 These two *things* [2]are come un
thee; who shall be sorry for the
desolation, and [3]destruction, and t
famine, and the sword: [y]by wh
shall I comfort thee?
20 Thy [z]sons have fainted, they lie
the head of all the streets, as a wi
bull in a net: they are full of the fu
of the LORD, the rebuke of thy Go
21 ¶ Therefore hear now this, th
afflicted, and drunken, but not wi
wine:
22 Thus saith thy Lord the LOR
and thy God *that* [a]pleadeth the cau
of his people, Behold, I have tak
out of thine hand the cup of tre
bling, *even* the dregs of the cup of m

ury; thou shalt no more drink it
gain:
23 But I will [b]put it into the hand of
hem that afflict thee; [c]which have
aid to thy soul, Bow down, that we
nay go over: and thou hast laid thy
ody as the ground, and as the street,
o them that went over.

CHAPTER 52

AWAKE, awake; put on thy
strength, O Zion; put on thy
beautiful garments, O Jerusalem, the
holy city: for [b]henceforth there shall
no more come into thee the uncircumcised [c]and the unclean.
2 Shake thyself from the dust; arise,
and sit down, O Jerusalem: loose
thyself from the bands of thy neck,
O captive daughter of Zion.
3 For thus saith the LORD, [e]Ye have
sold yourselves for nought; and ye
shall be redeemed without money.
4 For thus saith the Lord GOD, My
people went down aforetime into
Egypt to sojourn there; and the Assyrian oppressed them without cause.
5 Now therefore, what have I here,
saith the LORD, that my people is tak-
en away for nought? they that rule
over them make them to howl, saith
the LORD; and my name continually
every day *is* [f]blasphemed.
6 Therefore my people shall know
my name: therefore *they shall know*
in that day that I *am* he that doth
speak: behold, *it is* I.
7 ¶ How [g]beautiful upon the mountains are the feet of him that bringeth
good tidings, that publisheth peace;
that bringeth good tidings of good,
that publisheth salvation; that saith
unto Zion, Thy God reigneth!
8 Thy watchmen shall lift up the
voice; with the voice together shall
they sing: for they shall see [h]eye to
eye, when the LORD shall bring again
Zion.
9 ¶ Break forth into joy, sing together, ye waste places of Jerusalem: for
the LORD hath comforted his people,
he hath redeemed Jerusalem.
10 The LORD hath made bare his
holy arm in the eyes of all the nations;
and [i]all the ends of the earth shall see
the salvation of our God.
11 ¶ Depart [j]ye, depart ye, go ye out
from thence, touch no unclean *thing;*
go ye out of the midst of her; be ye
clean, that bear the vessels of the
LORD.
12 For [k]ye shall not go out with haste,
nor go by flight: [l]for the LORD will go

b Zech. 12.2.
c Ps. 66.11, 12.

CHAP. 52

a Rev. 21.2.
b Nah. 1.15.
c ch. 26.2. Rev. 21.27.
d Zech. 2.7.
e Ps. 44.12. 1 Pet. 1.18.
f Rom. 2.24.
g Rom. 10.15.
h Zeph. 3.9.
i Luke 3.6.
j Jer. 50.8. 2 Cor. 6.17. Rev. 18.4.
k Ex. 12.33.
l Micah 2.13.
m Num. 10. 25. Ex. 14.19.
1 gather you up.
n ch. 42.1.
2 Or, prosper.
o Phil. 2.9.
p Ps. 22.6. ch. 53.3.
q Eze. 36.25. Acts 2.33. Heb. 9.13.
r Rom. 15.21. Eph. 3.5.

CHAP. 53

a John 12.38.
1 hearing? or, doctrine?
b 1 Cor. 1.18.
c Mark 9.12.
d Ps. 22.6.
e Heb. 4.15.
2 as an hiding of faces from him, or, from us. Or, he hid as it were his face from us.
f John 1.10.
g Matt. 8.17.
h Matt. 26. 66.
3 Or, tormented.
4 bruise.
5 hath made the iniquity of us all to meet on him.
i Acts 8.32.
j 1 Pet. 1.19.
6 Or, He was taken away by distress and judg-ment; but, etc.
k Dan. 9.26.
7 was the stroke upon him.
l Matt. 27.57.
8 deaths.
m 1 Pet. 2.22.
9 Or, when his soul shall make an offering.
n 2 Cor. 5.21. Gal. 3.13.

before you; [m]and the God of Israel
will [1]*be* your rereward.
13 ¶ Behold, [n]my servant shall [2]deal
prudently, [o]he shall be exalted and
extolled, and be very high.
14 As many were astonied at thee;
his visage [p]was so marred more than
any man, and his form more than the
sons of men:
15 So [q]shall he sprinkle many nations; the kings shall shut their
mouths at him: for *that* [r]which had
not been told them shall they see; and
that which they had not heard shall
they consider.

CHAPTER 53

WHO [a]hath believed our [1]report?
and to whom is [b]the arm of the
LORD revealed?
2 For he shall grow up before him as
a tender plant, and as a root out of a
dry ground: [c]he hath no form nor
comeliness; and when we shall see
him, *there is* no beauty that we should
desire him.
3 He [d]is despised and rejected of
men; a man of sorrows, [e]and acquainted with grief: and [2]we hid as it were
our faces from him; he was despised,
and [f]we esteemed him not.
4 ¶ Surely [g]he hath borne our griefs,
and carried our sorrows: yet we [h]did
esteem him stricken, smitten of God,
and afflicted.
5 But he *was* [3]wounded for our transgressions, *he was* bruised for our iniquities: the chastisement of our
peace *was* upon him; and with his
[4]stripes we are healed.
6 All we like sheep have gone astray;
we have turned every one to his own
way; and the LORD [5]hath laid on him
the iniquity of us all.
7 He was oppressed, and he was
afflicted, yet he opened not his mouth:
[i]he is brought as a [j]lamb to the
slaughter, and as a sheep before her
shearers is dumb, so he openeth not
his mouth.
8 [6]He was taken from prison and
from judgment: and who shall declare
his generation? for [k]he was cut off out
of the land of the living: for the transgression of my people [7]was he stricken.
9 And [l]he made his grave with the
wicked, and with the rich in his
[8]death; because he had done no violence, neither *was any* deceit in [m]his
mouth.
10 ¶ Yet it pleased the LORD to
bruise him; he hath put *him* to grief:
[9]when thou shalt make his soul [n]an

offering for sin, he shall see *his* seed, [o]he shall prolong *his* days, and [p]the pleasure of the LORD shall prosper in his hand.

11 He shall see of the travail of his soul, *and* shall be satisfied: by [q]his knowledge shall [r]my righteous servant [s]justify many; for he shall bear their iniquities.

12 Therefore [t]will I divide him *a portion* with the great, and he shall divide the spoil with [u]the strong; because he hath poured out his soul unto death: and he was [v]numbered with the transgressors; and he bare the sin of many, and [w]made intercession for the transgressors.

CHAPTER 54

SING, [a]O barren, thou *that* didst not bear; break forth into singing, and cry aloud, thou *that* didst not travail with child: for more *are* the children of the desolate than the children of the married wife, saith the LORD.

2 Enlarge the place of thy tent, and let them stretch forth the curtains of thine habitations: spare not, lengthen thy cords, and strengthen thy stakes;

3 For thou shalt break forth on the right hand and on the left; and thy seed shall inherit the Gentiles, and make the desolate cities to be inhabited.

4 Fear not; for thou shalt not be ashamed: neither be thou confounded; for thou shalt not be put to shame: for thou shalt forget the shame of thy youth, and shalt not remember the reproach of thy widowhood any more.

5 For thy Maker *is* thine husband; the LORD of hosts *is* his name; and thy Redeemer the Holy One of Israel; [b]The God of the whole earth shall he be called.

6 For the LORD hath called thee as a woman forsaken and grieved in spirit, and a wife of youth, when thou wast refused, saith thy God.

7 For [c]a small moment have I forsaken thee; but with great mercies will I gather thee.

8 In a little wrath I hid my face from thee for a moment; [d]but with everlasting kindness will I have mercy on thee, saith the LORD thy Redeemer.

9 For this *is as* the waters [e]of Noah unto me: for *as* I have sworn that the waters of Noah should no more go over the earth; so have I sworn that I would not be wroth with thee, nor rebuke thee.

10 For [f]the mountains shall depart, and the hills be removed; but [g]my kindness shall not depart from thee, neither shall the covenant of my peace be removed, saith the LORD that hath mercy on thee.

11 ¶ O thou afflicted, tossed with tempest, *and* not comforted, behold I will lay thy stones with fair colours, and lay thy foundations with sapphires.

12 And I will make thy windows of agates, and thy gates of carbuncles, and all thy borders of pleasant stones.

13 And all thy children *shall be* taught [h]of the LORD; and great *shall be* the [i]peace of thy children.

14 In righteousness shalt thou be established: thou shalt be far from oppression; for thou shalt not fear: and from terror; for it shall not come near thee.

15 Behold, they shall surely gather together, *but* not by me: whosoever shall gather together against thee shall fall for thy sake.

16 Behold, I have created the smith that bloweth the coals in the fire, and that bringeth forth an instrument for his work; and I have created the waster to destroy.

17 ¶ No [j]weapon that is formed against thee shall prosper; and every tongue *that* shall rise against thee in judgment thou shalt condemn. This *is* the heritage of the servants of the LORD, [k]and their righteousness *is* of me, saith the LORD.

CHAPTER 55

HO, [a]every one that thirsteth, come ye to the waters, and he that hath no money; [b]come ye, buy, and eat: yea, come, buy wine and milk without money and without price.

2 Wherefore do ye [1]spend money for *that which is* not bread? and your labour for *that which* satisfieth not? hearken diligently unto me, and eat ye *that which is* good, and let your soul delight itself in fatness.

3 Incline your ear, and [c]come unto me: hear, and your soul shall live; [d]and I will make an everlasting covenant with you, *even* the [e]sure mercies of David.

4 Behold, I have given him *for* a [f]witness to the people, [g]a leader and commander to the people.

5 Behold, [h]thou shalt call a nation *that* thou knowest not, and nations *that* knew not thee shall run unto thee because of the LORD thy God, and for the Holy One of Israel; [i]for he hath glorified thee.

o Rom. 6.9.
p Eph. 1.5.
q John 17.3.
r 1 John 2.1.
s Rom. 5.18.
t Phil. 2.9.
u Col. 2.15.
v Mark 15.28.
w Luke 23. 34.

CHAP. 54

a Gal. 4.27.
b Job 19.25. ch. 41.14. ch. 44.6. ch. 49.7. Rom. 3.29.
c 2 Cor. 4.17.
d Jer. 31.3.
e Jer. 31.35.
f Ps. 46.2.
g Ps. 89.33.
h ch. 11.9. 1 Cor. 2.10. 1 Thes. 4.9.
i John 14.27. Phil. 4.7.
j ch. 50.8,9. Acts 6.10. 2 Cor. 2.14. Rev. 12.10.
k ch. 45.24.

CHAP. 55

a John 4.14. 1 Cor. 1.22. Rev. 21.6.
b Matt. 13.44. John 7.37. Rev. 3.18.
1 weigh.
c Matt. 11. 28.
d ch. 54.8.
e 2 Sam. 7.8. Ps. 89.28. Acts 13.34.
f Mal. 3.5. 1 Tim. 6.13. Rev. 1.5.
g Eze. 34.23. Dan. 9.25. Heb. 2.10.
h ch. 52.15. Eph. 2.11, 12.
i Acts 3.13.

6 ¶ Seek [j]ye the LORD while he may
e found, call ye upon him while he is
ear:
7 Let the wicked forsake his way,
nd [2]the unrighteous man [k]his
ioughts: and let him return unto the
ORD, [l]and he will have mercy upon
im; and to our God, for [3]he will
bundantly pardon.
8 ¶ For my thoughts *are* not your
ioughts, neither *are* your ways my
ays, saith the LORD.
9 For *as* the heavens are higher than
ie earth, so are my ways higher than
our ways, and my thoughts than your
houghts.
10 For as the rain cometh down, and
he snow from heaven, and returneth
iot thither, but watereth the earth,
nd maketh it bring forth and bud,
hat it may give seed to the sower, and
read to the eater:
11 So shall my word be that goeth
orth out of my mouth: it shall not re-
urn unto me void, but it shall accomplish that which I please, and it
hall prosper *in the thing* whereto I
ent it.
12 For ye shall go out with joy, and
e led forth with peace: the moun-
ains and the hills shall break forth
efore you into singing, and all the
rees of the field shall clap *their* hands.
13 Instead of the thorn shall come
ip the fir tree, and instead of the brier
hall come up the myrtle tree: and it
shall be to the LORD for a name, for an
verlasting sign *that* shall not be cut
off.

CHAPTER 56

THUS saith the LORD, Keep [1]ye
judgment, and do justice: for [a]my
salvation *is* near to come, and my
righteousness to be revealed.
2 Blessed *is* the man *that* doeth this,
and the son of man *that* layeth hold
on it; that keepeth the sabbath from
polluting it, and [b]keepeth his hand
from doing any evil.
3 ¶ Neither let [c]the son of the stranger, that hath joined himself to the
LORD, speak, saying, The LORD hath
utterly separated me from his people:
neither let the eunuch say, Behold, I
am a dry tree.
4 For thus saith the LORD unto the
eunuchs that keep my sabbaths, and
choose *the things* that please me, and
take hold of my covenant;
5 Even unto them will I give in mine
[d]house and within my walls a place
[e]and a name better than of sons and of
daughters: I will give them an everlasting name, that shall not be cut off.
6 Also the sons of the stranger, that
join themselves to the LORD, to serve
him, and to love the name of the
LORD, to be his servants, every one
that keepeth the sabbath from polluting it, and taketh hold of my covenant;
7 Even them will I [f]bring to my holy
mountain, and make them joyful
in my house of prayer: their [g]burnt
offerings and their sacrifices *shall
be* accepted upon mine altar; for
[h]mine house shall be called an house
of prayer [i]for all people.
8 The Lord GOD which gathereth the
outcasts of Israel saith, [j]Yet will I
gather *others* to him, [2]beside those
that are gathered unto him.
9 ¶ All ye beasts of the field, come to
devour, *yea*, all ye beasts in the forest.
10 His watchmen *are* [k]blind: they
are all ignorant, [l]they *are* all dumb
dogs, they cannot bark; [3]sleeping,
lying down, loving to slumber.
11 Yea, *they are* [4]greedy dogs *which*
[5]can never have enough, and they *are*
shepherds *that* cannot understand:
they all look to their own way, every
one for his gain, from his quarter.
12 Come ye, *say they*, I will fetch
wine, and we will fill ourselves with
strong drink; and to morrow shall be
as this day, *and* much more abundant.

CHAPTER 57

THE righteous perisheth, and no
man layeth *it* to heart: and [1]merci-
ful men *are* taken away, none considering that the righteous is taken
away [2]from the evil *to come*.
2 He shall [3]enter into peace: they
shall rest in their beds, *each one* walking [4]*in* his uprightness.
3 ¶ But draw near hither, [a]ye sons of
the sorceress, the seed of the adulterer and the whore.
4 Against whom do ye sport yourselves? against whom make ye a wide
mouth, *and* draw out the tongue? *are*
ye not children of transgression, a seed
of falsehood,
5 Enflaming yourselves [5]with idols
under every green tree, slaying the
children in the valleys under the clifts
of the rocks?
6 Among the smooth *stones* of the
stream *is* thy portion; they, they *are*
thy lot: even to them hast thou poured
a drink offering, thou hast offered a
meat offering. Should I receive comfort in these?
7 Upon a lofty and high mountain

j Ps. 32.6. Amos 5.4, 14. Matt. 5.25. John 7.34. 2 Cor. 6.2. Heb. 3.13.
2 the man of iniquity.
k Zech. 8.17.
l Jer. 3.12.
3 he will multiply to pardon.

CHAP. 56

1 Or, equity.
a Matt. 3.2. Rom. 13.11.
b Ex. 20.11. ch. 58.13.
c Deut. 23.1. Acts 8.27. 1 Pet. 1.1.
d Eph. 2.22. 1 Tim. 3.15. Heb. 3.6.
e John 1.12. Rev. 3.12.
f 1 Pet. 1.1.
g Ps. 4.5. Mal. 1.11. Rom. 12.1. Heb. 13.15. 1 Pet. 2.5.
h Matt. 21. 13. Mark 11.17. Luke 19.46.
i Mal. 1.11.
j Gen. 49.10. ch. 43.6. Eph. 1.10.
2 to his gathered.
k Matt. 15. 14.
l Phil. 3.2.
3 Or, dreaming, or, talking in their sleep.
4 strong of appetite.
5 know not to be satisfied.

CHAP. 57

1 men of kindness, or, godliness.
2 Or, from that which is evil.
3 Or, go in peace.
4 Or, before him.
a Mal. 3.5.
5 Or, among the oaks.

hast thou set [b]thy bed: even thither wentest thou up to offer sacrifice.

8 Behind the doors also and the posts hast thou set up thy remembrance: for thou hast discovered *thyself to another* than me, and art gone up; thou hast enlarged thy bed, and [6]made thee *a covenant* with them; thou [c]lovedst their bed [7]where thou sawest *it*.

9 And [8]thou wentest to the king with ointment, and didst increase thy perfumes, and didst send thy messengers far off, and didst debase *thyself even* unto hell.

10 Thou art wearied in the greatness of thy way; *yet* saidst thou not, There is no hope: thou hast found the [9]life of thine hand; therefore thou wast not grieved.

11 And of whom hast thou been afraid or feared, that thou hast lied, and hast not remembered me, nor laid *it* to thy heart? have [d]not I held my peace even of old, and thou fearest me not?

12 I will declare thy righteousness, and thy works; for they shall not profit thee.

13 ¶ When thou criest, let thy companies deliver thee; but the wind shall carry them all away; vanity shall take *them*: but he that putteth his trust in me shall possess [e]the land, and shall inherit my holy mountain;

14 And shall say, Cast ye up, cast ye up, prepare the way, take up the stumblingblock out of the way of my people.

15 For thus saith the high and lofty One that inhabiteth eternity, whose [f]name *is* Holy; [g]I dwell in the high and holy *place*, with [h]him also *that is* of a contrite and humble spirit, to revive the spirit of the humble, and to revive the heart of the contrite ones.

16 For [i]I will not contend for ever, neither will I be always wroth: for the spirit should fail before me, and the souls [j]*which* I have made.

17 For the iniquity of his [k]covetousness was I wroth, and smote him: I hid me, and was wroth, and he went on [10]frowardly in the way of his heart.

18 I have seen his ways, and will heal him: I will [l]lead him also, and restore comforts unto him and to his mourners.

19 I create [m]the fruit of the lips; Peace, peace [n]to *him that is* far off, and to *him that is* near, saith the LORD; and I will heal him.

20 But the wicked *are* like the troubled sea, when it cannot rest, whose waters cast up mire and dirt.

21 *There is* no peace, saith my God, to the wicked.

CHAPTER 58

CRY [1]aloud, spare not, lift up thy voice like a trumpet, and shew my people their transgression, and the house of Jacob their sins.

2 Yet they seek me daily, and delight to know my ways, as a nation that did righteousness, and forsook not the ordinance of their God: they ask of me the ordinances of justice; they take delight in approaching to God.

3 ¶ Wherefore [a]have we fasted, *say they*, and thou seest not? *wherefore* have we afflicted our soul, and thou takest no knowledge? Behold, in the day of your fast ye find pleasure, and exact all your [2]labours.

4 Behold, ye fast for strife and debate, and to smite with the fist of wickedness: [3]ye shall not fast as *ye do this* day, to make your voice to be heard on high.

5 Is it [b]such a fast that I have chosen? [4]a day for a man to afflict his soul? *is it* to bow down his head as a bulrush, and to spread sackcloth and ashes *under him?* wilt thou call this a fast, and an acceptable day to the LORD?

6 *Is* not this the fast that I have chosen? to loose the bands of wickedness, to undo [5]the heavy burdens, and to let the [6]oppressed go free, and that ye break every yoke?

7 *Is it* not [c]to deal thy bread to the hungry, and that thou bring the poor that are [7]cast out to thy house? when thou seest the naked, that thou cover him; and that thou hide not thyself from [d]thine own flesh?

8 ¶ Then shall thy light break forth as the morning, and thine health shall spring forth speedily: and thy righteousness shall go before thee; the glory of the LORD [8]shall be thy rereward.

9 Then shalt thou call, and the LORD shall answer; thou shalt cry, and he shall say, Here I *am*. If thou take away from the midst of thee the yoke, the putting forth of the finger, and speaking vanity;

10 And *if* thou draw out thy soul to the hungry, and satisfy the afflicted soul; then shall [e]thy light rise in obscurity, and thy darkness *be* as the noonday:

11 And the LORD shall guide thee continually, and satisfy thy soul in

---

b Eze. 23.41.
6 Or, hewed it for thyself larger than theirs.
c Eze. 16.26.
7 Or, thou providedst room.
8 Or, thou respectedst the king.
9 Or, living.
d Ps. 50.21.
e Ps. 37.3,9. Matt. 5.5.
f Job 6.10. Luke 1.49.
g Ps. 68.4. Zech. 2.13.
h Ps. 34.18.
i Ps. 78.38,39. Micah 7.18.
j Heb. 12.9.
k Eze. 33.31.
10 turning away.
l Ps. 73.24.
m Heb. 13.15.
n Acts 2.39.

CHAP. 58

1 with the throat.
a Mal. 3.14.
2 griefs, or, things wherewith ye grieve others.
3 Or, ye fast not as this day.
b Zech. 7.5.
4 Or, to afflict his soul for a day?
5 the bundles of the yoke.
6 broken.
c Ps. 112.9. Pro. 22.9. Eccl. 11.1,2. Dan. 4.27. Matt. 25.35. Luke 11.41.
7 Or, afflicted.
d Gen. 29.14. Neh. 5.5. Matt. 15.5.
8 shall gather thee up.
e Job 11.17.

lrought, and make fat thy bones:
nd thou shalt be like a watered gard-
n, and like a spring of water, whose
/aters [10]fail not.
12 And *they that shall be* of thee
hall build the old waste places: thou
halt raise up the foundations of many
enerations; and thou shalt be called,
'he repairer of the breach, The re-
torer of paths to dwell in.
13 ¶ If [f]thou turn away thy foot from
he sabbath, *from* doing thy pleasure
n my holy day; and call the sabbath
delight, the holy of the LORD,
ıonourable; and shalt honour him,
ıot doing thine own ways, nor finding
hine own pleasure, nor speaking
thine own words:
14 Then [h]shalt thou delight thyself
n the LORD; and I will cause thee to
ide [i]upon the high places of the earth,
.nd feed thee with the heritage of
acob thy father: for [j]the mouth of the
.ORD hath spoken *it*.

CHAPTER 59

BEHOLD, the LORD's hand is not
[a]shortened, that it cannot save;
ıeither his ear heavy, that it cannot
ıear:
2 But your iniquities have separated
ıetween you and your God, and your
ins [1]have hid *his* face from you, that
ıe will not hear.
3 For your [b]hands are defiled with
ılood, and your fingers with iniquity;
our lips have spoken lies, your
ongue hath muttered perverseness.
4 None calleth for justice, nor *any*
ıleadeth for truth: they trust in vani-
y, and speak lies; [c]they conceive
nischief, and bring forth iniquity.
5 They hatch [2]cockatrice' eggs, and
weave the spider's web: he that eat-
th of their eggs dieth, and [3]that which
s crushed breaketh out into a viper.
6 Their webs shall not become gar-
nents, neither shall they cover them-
elves with their works: their works
ıre works of iniquity, and the act of
'iolence *is* in their hands.
7 Their [e]feet run to evil, and they
nake haste to shed innocent blood:
heir thoughts *are* thoughts of ini-
ıuity; wasting and [4]destruction *are* in
heir paths.
8 The way of peace they know not;
.nd *there is* no [5]judgment in their go-
ngs: they [f]have made them crooked
ıaths: whosoever goeth therein shall
ıot know peace.
9 ¶ Therefore is judgment far from
ıs, neither doth justice overtake us:
[g]we wait for light, but behold obscurity; for brightness, *but* we walk in
darkness.
10 We grope for the wall like the
blind, and we [h]grope as if *we had* no
eyes: we stumble at noonday as in the
night; *we are* in desolate places as dead
men.
11 We roar all like bears, and mourn
sore like doves: we look for judgment,
but *there is* none; for salvation, *but* it
is far off from us.
12 For our transgressions are multiplied before thee, and our sins testify
against us: for our transgressions *are*
with us; and *as for* our iniquities, we
know them;
13 In transgressing and lying against
the LORD, and departing away from
our God, speaking oppression and revolt, conceiving and uttering [i]from
the heart words of falsehood.
14 And judgment is turned away
backward, and justice standeth afar
off: for truth is fallen in [j]the street,
and equity cannot enter.
15 Yea, truth faileth; and he *that* departeth from evil [6]maketh himself a
prey: and the LORD saw *it*, and [7]it
displeased him that *there was* no
judgment.
16 ¶ And [k]he saw that *there was* no
man, and [l]wondered that *there was*
no intercessor: therefore his arm
brought salvation unto him; and his
righteousness, it sustained him.
17 For [m]he put on righteousness as
a breastplate, and an helmet of salvation upon his head; and he put on the
garments of vengeance *for* clothing,
and was clad with zeal as a cloke.
18 According to *their* [8]deeds, accordingly he will repay, fury to his adversaries, recompence to his enemies; to
the islands he will repay recompence.
19 So [n]shall they fear the name of the
LORD from the west, and his glory
from the rising of the sun. When the
enemy shall come in [o]like a flood, the
Spirit of the LORD shall [9]lift up a standard against him.
20 ¶ And [p]the Redeemer shall come
to Zion, and unto them that turn from
transgression in Jacob, saith the
LORD.
21 As [q]for me, this *is* my covenant
with them, saith the LORD; My [r]spirit
that *is* upon thee, and my words which
I have put in thy mouth, shall not depart out of thy mouth, nor out of the
mouth of thy seed, nor out of the
mouth of thy seed's seed, saith the
LORD, from henceforth and for ever.

9 droughts.
10 lie, or, deceive.
f Lev. 19.30. ch. 56.2.
g Matt. 12. 36.
h Job 22.26.
i Deut. 32.13.
j ch. 1.20. Micah 4.4. Matt. 24.3, 5.

CHAP. 59

a Num. 11. 23. ch. 50.2.
1 Or, have made him hide.
b ch. 1.15,21. Hosea 4.2. Micah 3.10. Rom. 3.15.
c Job 15.35. Ps. 7.14.
2 Or, adders'.
d Job 8.14.
3 Or, that which is sprinkled is as if there brake out a viper.
e Pro. 1.16.
4 breaking.
5 Or, right.
f Ps. 125.5. Pro. 2.15.
g Jer. 8.15.
h Deut. 28. 29. Amos 8.9. Zeph. 1.17.
i Matt. 12.34.
j Neh. 8.1.
6 Or, is accounted mad.
7 it was evil in his eyes.
k ch. 63.5. Jer. 5.1. Eze. 22.30.
l Mark 6.6.
m Ps. 35.2. 2 Cor. 6.7. 1 Thes. 5.8. Rev. 19.11.
8 recom- pences.
n Ps. 113.3. Mal. 1.11.
o Rev. 12.15.
9 Or, put him to flight.
p Rom. 11. 26.
q Heb. 8.10.
r ch. 61.1. Eze. 36.37.

CHAPTER 60

ARISE, [1]shine; for thy light is come,
and [a]the glory of the LORD is risen
upon thee.
2 For, behold, the darkness shall
cover the earth, and gross darkness
the people: but the LORD shall arise
upon thee, and his glory shall be seen
upon thee.
3 And the [b]Gentiles shall come to
thy light, and kings to the brightness
of thy rising.
4 Lift up thine eyes round about, and
see: all they gather themselves together, they come to thee: thy sons shall
come from far, and thy daughters
shall be nursed at *thy* side.
5 Then thou shalt see, and flow together, and thine heart shall fear, and
be enlarged; because the [2]abundance
of the sea shall be converted unto thee,
the [3]forces of the Gentiles shall come
unto thee.
6 The multitude of camels shall cover
thee, the dromedaries of Mĭd'-ĭ-ăn and
[c]Ē'-phăh; all they from Shē'-bă [d]shall
come: they shall bring [e]gold and incense; and they shall shew forth the
praises of the LORD.
7 All the flocks of [f]Kē'-dăr shall be
gathered together unto thee, the rams
of Nĕ-bâi'-ōth shall minister unto
thee: they shall come up with acceptance on mine altar, and I [g]will glorify
the house of my glory.
8 Who *are* these *that* fly as a cloud,
and as the doves to their windows?
9 Surely [h]the isles shall wait for me,
and the ships of Tarshish first, [i]to
bring thy sons from far, their [j]silver
and their gold with them, unto [k]the
name of the LORD thy God, and to the
Holy One of Israel, because [l]he hath
glorified thee.
10 And [m]the sons of strangers shall
build up thy walls, [n]and their kings
shall minister unto thee: for in my
wrath I smote thee, but in my favour
have I had mercy on thee.
11 Therefore thy gates shall be open
continually; they shall not be shut
day nor night; that *men* may bring unto thee the [4]forces of the Gentiles, and
that their kings *may be* brought.
12 For [o]the nation and kingdom that
will not serve thee shall perish; yea,
those nations shall be utterly wasted.
13 The [p]glory of Lĕb'-ă-nŏn shall
come unto thee, the fir tree, the pine
tree, and the box together, to beautify
the place of my sanctuary; and I will
make [q]the place of my feet glorious.
14 The sons also of them that afflicted thee shall come bending unto thee
and all they that despised thee sha
[r]bow themselves down at the soles
thy feet; and they shall call thee, Th
city of the LORD, The [s]Zion of th
Holy One of Israel.
15 Whereas thou hast been forsake
and hated, so that no man we
through *thee*, I will make thee a
eternal excellency, a joy of many ge
erations.
16 Thou shalt also suck the milk
the Gentiles, and shalt suck the brea
of kings: and thou shalt know that
the LORD *am* thy Saviour and thy Re
deemer, the mighty One of Jacob.
17 For brass I will bring gold, and fo
iron I will bring silver, and for woo
brass, and for stones iron: I will als
make thy officers peace, and thin
exactors righteousness.
18 Violence shall no more be hear
in thy land, wasting nor destructio
within thy borders; but thou shalt ca
[u]thy walls Salvation, and thy gate
Praise.
19 The [v]sun shall be no more th
light by day; neither for brightnes
shall the moon give light unto thee
but the LORD shall be unto thee a
everlasting light, and [w]thy God th
glory.
20 Thy [x]sun shall no more go down
neither shall thy moon withdraw it
self: for the LORD shall be thine eve
lasting light, and the days of th
mourning shall be ended.
21 Thy people also *shall be* all righ
eous: [y]they shall inherit the land fo
ever, [z]the branch of my planting, [a]th
work of my hands, that I may be glori
fied.
22 A [b]little one shall become a thous
and, and a small one a strong nation
I the LORD will hasten it in his time.

CHAPTER 61

THE [a]Spirit of the Lord GOD *is* up
on me; because the LORD hat
anointed me to preach good tiding
unto the meek; he hath sent me [b]t
bind up the brokenhearted, to pro
claim [c]liberty to the captives, and th
opening of the prison to *them that ar*
bound;
2 To [d]proclaim the acceptable yea
of the LORD, and [e]the day of ven
geance of our God; to [f]comfort a
that mourn;
3 To appoint unto them that mour
in Zion, [g]to give unto them beauty fo
ashes, the oil of joy for mourning
the garment of praise for the spirit o

CHAP. 60
1 Or, be enlightened: for thy light cometh.
a Mal. 4.2.
b Rev. 21.24.
2 Or, noise of the sea shall be turned toward thee.
3 Or, wealth.
c Gen. 25.4.
d Ps. 72.10.
e Matt. 2.11.
f Gen. 25.13.
g Hag. 2.7,9.
h Ps. 72.10.
i Gal. 4.26.
j Zech. 14.14.
k Jer. 3.17.
l ch. 55.5.
m Zech. 6.15.
n Rev. 21.24.
4 Or, wealth.
o Ps. 2.12. Zech. 14.17. Matt. 21.44. Luke 19.27. Rev. 2.26, 27.
p ch. 35.2.
q 1 Chr. 28.2. Heb. 12.22.
r Rev. 3.9.
s Heb. 12.22. Rev. 14.1.
t Ps. 98.2. ch. 43.3. Eze. 34.30. Rev. 5.9.
u ch. 26.1.
v Rev. 21.23.
w Zech. 2.5.
x Amos 8.9.
y Ps. 37.11. Matt. 5.5.
z Matt. 15.13.
a Eph. 2.10.
b Matt. 13.31. Hosea 1.10.

CHAP. 61
a ch. 11.2. Luke 4.18. John 1.32.
b Ps. 34.18. Hosea 6.1.
c Zech. 9.12. John 8.32-36.
d Lev. 25.9.
e Mal. 4.1,3.
f Matt. 5.4.
g Ps. 30.11.

aviness; that they might be called
ees of righteousness, the [h]planting
the LORD, [i]that he might be glori-
d.
¶ And they shall [j]build the old
astes, they shall raise up the former
solations, and they shall repair the
aste cities, the desolations of many
nerations.
And [k]strangers shall stand and feed
ur flocks, and the sons of the alien
all be your plowmen and your vine-
essers.
But [l]ye shall be named the Priests
the LORD: *men* shall call you the
inisters of our God: ye shall eat the
hes of the Gentiles, and in their
ory shall ye boast yourselves.
¶ For [m]your shame *ye shall have*
uble; and *for* confusion they shall
joice in their portion: therefore in
eir land they shall possess the
uble: everlasting joy shall be unto
em.
For I the LORD love judgment, I
te robbery for burnt offering; and
will direct their work in truth, [n]and
will make an everlasting covenant
th them.
And their seed shall be known
nong the Gentiles, and their off-
ring among the people: all that see
em shall acknowledge them, that
ey *are* the seed *which* the LORD hath
essed.
0 I will greatly rejoice in the LORD,
y soul shall be joyful in my God;
r he hath clothed me with the gar-
ents of salvation, he hath covered
e with the robe of righteousness, as
[o]bridegroom [1]decketh *himself* with
naments, and as a bride adorneth
rself with her jewels.
1 For as the earth bringeth forth
r bud, and as the garden causeth
e things that are sown in it to
ring forth; so the Lord GOD will
use [p]righteousness and [q]praise to
ring forth before all the nations.

CHAPTER 62

OR Zion's sake will I not hold my
peace, and for Jerusalem's sake I
ill not rest, until the righteousness
ereof go forth as brightness, and the
lvation thereof as a lamp *that*
rneth.
And the Gentiles shall see thy
ghteousness, and all kings thy glory:
nd thou shalt be called by a new
ame, which the mouth of the LORD
all name.
Thou shalt also be a [b]crown of

h ch. 60.21.
i John 15.8.
j Eze. 36.33.
k Eph. 2.12.
l Ex. 19.6.
m 2 Ki. 2.9. ch. 40.2. Zech. 9.12.
n ch. 55.3.
o Rev. 21.2.
1 decketh as a priest.
p Ps. 72.3.
q ch. 60.18.

CHAP. 62

a ch. 65.15. Rev. 3.12.
b Zech. 9.16.
c Hosea 1.10. 1 Pet. 2.10.
1 Azubah.
2 That is, My delight is in her.
3 That is, Married.
4 with the joy of the bridegroom.
d Song 3.3. ch. 52.8. Eze. 3.17. Heb. 13.17.
5 Or, ye that are the LORD's remembrancers.
6 silence.
e ch. 61.11. Zeph. 3.20.
7 If I give, etc.
f Deut. 28.31. Jer. 5.17.
g Deut. 12.12.
h Zech. 9.9. Matt. 21.5. John 12.15.
i ch. 40.10. ch. 49.4. Rev. 22.12.
8 Or, recompence.

CHAP. 63

1 decked.
a Rev. 19.13.
b Lam. 1.15. Mal. 4.3. Rev. 14.19, 20.

glory in the hand of the LORD, and a
royal diadem in the hand of thy God.
4 Thou [c]shalt no more be termed
Forsaken; neither shall thy land any
more be termed [1]Desolate: but thou
shalt be called [2]Hĕph-zĭ-băh, and thy
land [3]Bēū-lăh: for the LORD delighteth in thee, and thy land shall be
married.
5 ¶ For *as* a young man marrieth a
virgin, *so* shall thy sons marry thee:
and [4]*as* the bridegroom rejoiceth over
the bride, *so* shall thy God rejoice over
thee.
6 [d]I have set watchmen upon thy
walls, O Jerusalem, *which* shall never
hold their peace day nor night: [5]ye
that make mention of the LORD, keep
not silence,
7 And give him no [6]rest, till he establish, and till he make Jerusalem [e]a
praise in the earth.
8 The LORD hath sworn by his right
hand, and by the arm of his strength,
[7]Surely I will no more give [f]thy corn
to be meat for thine enemies; and the
sons of the stranger shall not drink
thy wine, for the which thou hast
laboured:
9 But they that have gathered it shall
eat it, and praise the LORD; and they
that have brought it together shall
drink it in [g]the courts of my holiness.
10 ¶ Go through, go through the
gates; prepare ye the way of the people; cast up, cast up the highway;
gather out the stones; lift up a standard for the people.
11 Behold, the LORD hath proclaimed unto the end of the world, [h]Say ye
to the daughter of Zion, Behold, thy
salvation cometh; behold, his [i]reward
is with him, and his [8]work before
him.
12 And they shall call them, The holy
people, The redeemed of the LORD:
and thou shalt be called, Sought out,
A city not forsaken.

CHAPTER 63

WHO *is* this that cometh from Ē-
dom, with dyed garments from
Bŏz-răh? this *that is* [1]glorious in his
apparel, travelling in the greatness of
his strength? I that speak in righteousness, mighty to save.
2 Wherefore [a]*art thou* red in thine
apparel, and thy garments like him
that treadeth in the winefat?
3 I have [b]trodden the winepress
alone; and of the people *there was*
none with me: for I will tread them in
mine anger, and trample them in my

fury; and their blood shall be sprinkled upon my garments, and I will stain
all my raiment.
4 For the day of vengeance *is* in mine
heart, and the year of my redeemed is
come.
5 And I looked, and [c]*there was* none
to help; and I wondered that *there was*
none to uphold: therefore mine own
[d]arm brought salvation unto me; and
my fury, it upheld me.
6 And I will tread down the people
in mine anger, and [e]make them drunk
in my fury, and I will bring down their
strength to the earth.
7 ¶ I will mention the lovingkindnesses of the LORD, *and* the praises of
the LORD, according to all that the
LORD hath bestowed on us, and the
great goodness toward the house of
Israel, which he hath bestowed on
them according to his mercies, and
according to the multitude of his lovingkindnesses.
8 For he said, Surely they *are* my
people, children *that* will not lie: [2]so
he was their Saviour.
9 In [f]all their affliction he was afflicted, and [g]the angel of his presence saved them: in [h]his love and in his pity he
redeemed them; and [i]he bare them,
and carried them all the days of
old.
10 ¶ But they rebelled, and [j]vexed
his holy Spirit: therefore he was turned to be their enemy, *and* he fought
against them.
11 Then he remembered the days of
old, Moses, *and* his people, *saying*,
Where *is* he that brought them up out
of the sea with the [3]shepherd of his
flock? where *is* he that put his holy
Spirit within him?
12 That led *them* by the right hand of
Moses with his glorious arm, dividing
the water before them, to make himself an everlasting name?
13 That led them through the deep,
as an horse in the wilderness, *that* they
should not stumble?
14 As a beast goeth down into the
valley, the Spirit of the LORD caused
him to rest: so didst thou lead thy
people, to make thyself a glorious
name.
15 ¶ Look down from heaven, and
behold from the habitation of thy
holiness and of thy glory: where *is*
thy zeal and thy strength, [4]the sounding of thy bowels and of thy mercies
toward me? are they restrained?
16 Doubtless thou *art* our father,
though [k]Abraham be ignorant of us,

c John 16.32.
d Ps. 44.3. Ps. 98.1. ch. 40.10. ch. 51.9.
e Rev. 16.6.
2 Or, and he became a Saviour for them.
f Acts 9.4.
g Ex. 14.19. Hosea 12.4, 5. Mal. 3.1. Acts 12.11.
h Deut. 7.7.
i Ex. 19.4.
j Ps. 78.8,40. Acts 7.51. Eph. 4.30. Heb. 10.29.
3 Or, shepherds.
4 Or, the multitude.
k Gal. 3.28.
5 Or, our redeemer, from everlasting is thy name.
l Ps. 119.10.
m ch. 6.10. Matt. 13.15.
n Dan. 8.24.
6 Or, thy name was not called upon them.

CHAP. 64

1 the fire of meltings.
a Ps. 31.19. 1 Cor. 2.9, 10. Col. 1.26,27. 1 Tim. 3.16. Rev. 21.1-4.
2 Or, seen a God beside thee, which doeth so for him, etc.
b Acts 10.35.
c Mal. 3.6.
d Phil. 3.9.
e Hosea 7.7.
3 melted.
4 by the hand.
f Jer. 18.6.
g Eph. 2.10.

and Israel acknowledge us not: tho
O LORD, *art* our father, [5]our redeeme
thy name *is* from everlasting.
17 ¶ O LORD, why hast [l]thou ma
us to err from thy ways, *and* harden
[m]our heart from thy fear? Return f
thy servants' sake, the tribes of thi
inheritance.
18 The [n]people of thy holiness ha
possessed *it* but a little while: o
adversaries have trodden down t
sanctuary.
19 We are *thine:* thou never bare
rule over them; [6]they were not call
by thy name.

CHAPTER 64

OH that thou wouldest rend t
heavens, that thou would
come down, that the mountai
might flow down at thy presence,
2 As *when* [1]the melting fire burnet
the fire causeth the waters to boil,
make thy name known to thine adve
saries, *that* the nations may tremb
at thy presence!
3 When thou didst terrible thin
which we looked not for, thou came
down, the mountains flowed down
thy presence.
4 For since the beginning of t
world *men* [a]have not heard, nor pe
ceived by the ear, neither hath the e
[2]seen, O God, beside thee, *what*
hath prepared for him that waite
for him.
5 Thou meetest him that rejoice
and [b]worketh righteousness, *those th*
remember thee in thy ways: behol
thou art wroth; for we have sinned:
[c]those is continuance, and we shall
saved.
6 But we are all as an unclean *thin*
and all our [d]righteousnesses *are*
filthy rags; and we all do fade as
leaf; and our iniquities, like the win
have taken us away.
7 And [e]*there is* none that calleth u
on thy name, that stirreth up himse
to take hold of thee: for thou hast h
thy face from us, and hast [3]consum
us, [4]because of our iniquities.
8 But now, O LORD, thou *art* o
father; we *are* the clay, [f]and thou o
potter; and we all *are* [g]the work
thy hand.
9 ¶ Be not wroth very sore, O LOR
neither remember iniquity for eve
behold, see, we beseech thee, we *a*
all thy people.
10 Thy holy cities are a wildernes
Zion is a wilderness, Jerusalem a des
lation.

1 Our [h]holy and our beautiful
ouse, where our fathers praised thee,
burned up with fire: and all our
leasant things are laid waste.
12 Wilt thou refrain thyself for
ese *things*, O LORD? wilt thou
old thy peace, and afflict us very
ore?

CHAPTER 65

[a]AM sought of *them that* asked not
for me; I am found of *them that*
ought me not: I said, Behold me, beold me, unto a nation *that* was [b]not
alled by my name.
2 I [c]have spread out my hands all
he day unto a rebellious people,
hich [d]walketh in a way *that was* not
ood, after their own thoughts;
3 A people that provoketh me to ang-
r continually to my face; [e]that sacri-
iceth in gardens, and burneth incense
upon altars of brick;
4 Which [f]remain among the graves,
nd lodge in the monuments, [g]which
at swine's flesh, and [2]broth of abom-
nable *things is in* their vessels;
5 Which [h]say, Stand by thyself, come
ot near to me; for I am holier than
hou. These *are* a smoke in my [3]nose,
fire that burneth all the day.
6 Behold, [i]*it is* written before me: I
vill not keep silence, but will recom-
ense, even recompense into their
osom,
7 Your iniquities, and [j]the iniquities
f your fathers together, saith the
ORD, which have burned incense up-
n the mountains, and blasphemed
ne upon the hills: therefore will I
neasure their former work into their
osom.
8 ¶ Thus saith the LORD, As the new
vine is found in the cluster, and *one*
aith, Destroy it not; [k]for a blessing
s in it: so will I do for my servants'
akes, that I may not destroy them
ll.
9 And I will bring forth a seed out of
acob, and out of Judah an inheritor
f my mountains: and mine [l]elect
hall inherit it, and my servants shall
lwell there.
10 And Shâr-on shall be a fold of
locks, and the [m]valley of Ā-chôr a
lace for the herds to lie down in, for
ny people that have sought me.
11 ¶ But ye *are* they that forsake the
ORD, that forget my holy mountain,
hat prepare [n]a table for [4]that troop,
nd that furnish the drink offering un-
o [5]that number.
12 Therefore will I number you to

h 2 Ki. 25.9. Ps. 74.7.
i Eze. 24.21.

CHAP. 65

a Ps. 22.27. ch. 2.2,3. Rom. 10.20. Eph. 2.12, 13.
b ch. 63.19.
c Rom. 10.21.
d Deut. 32.5. Ps. 36.4.
e Lev. 17.5. ch. 1.29.
1 upon bricks.
f Deut. 18.11.
g Lev. 11.7.
2 Or, pieces.
h Matt. 9.11. Luke 5.30. Jude 19.
3 Or, anger.
i Deut. 32.34. Mal. 3.16.
j Lev. 26.39. Ps. 106.6. Dan. 9.8. Matt. 23.32.
k Joel 2.14.
l Matt. 24.22.
m Hos. 2.15.
n Eze. 23.41. 1 Cor. 10.21.
4 Or, Fortune.
5 Or, Fate.
o Pro. 1.24. ch. 66.4. Jer. 7.13. Zech. 7.7.
6 breaking.
p Pro. 10.7.
q Acts 11.26.
r 2 Pet. 3.13.
7 come upon the heart.
s Rev. 7.17.
t Eccl. 8.12.
u Lev. 26.16.
8 shall make them continue long, or, shall wear out.
v Deut. 28. 41. Hosea 9.12.
w Ps. 32.5. Dan. 9.21. Matt. 6.8. Acts 4.31.

the sword, and ye shall all bow down
to the slaughter: [o]because when I called, ye did not answer; when I spake,
ye did not hear; but did evil before
mine eyes, and did choose *that* wherein I delighted not.
13 Therefore thus saith the Lord
GOD, Behold, my servants shall eat,
but ye shall be hungry: behold,
my servants shall drink, but ye
shall be thirsty: behold, my servants
shall rejoice, but ye shall be ashamed:
14 Behold, my servants shall sing for
joy of heart, but ye shall cry for
sorrow of heart, and shall howl for
[6]vexation of spirit.
15 And ye shall leave your name for
[p]a curse unto my chosen: for the Lord
GOD shall slay thee, and call [q]his servants by another name:
16 That he who blesseth himself in
the earth shall bless himself in the
God of truth; and he that sweareth in
the earth shall swear by the God of
truth; because the former troubles are
forgotten, and because they are hid
from mine eyes.
17 ¶ For, behold, I create [r]new heavens and a new earth: and the former
shall not be remembered, nor [7]come
into mind.
18 But be ye glad and rejoice for ever
in that which I create: for, behold, I
create Jerusalem a rejoicing, and her
people a joy.
19 And I will rejoice in Jerusalem,
and joy in my people: and the [s]voice
of weeping shall be no more heard in
her, nor the voice of crying.
20 There shall be no more thence
an infant of days, nor an old man that
hath not filled his days: for the child
shall die an hundred years old; [t]but
the sinner *being* an hundred years old
shall be accursed.
21 And [u]they shall build houses,
and inhabit *them;* and they shall
plant vineyards, and eat the fruit of
them.
22 They shall not build, and another
inhabit; they shall not plant, and another eat: for as the days of a tree *are*
the days of my people, and mine elect
[8]shall long enjoy the work of their
hands.
23 They shall not labour in vain,
nor [v]bring forth for trouble; for
they *are* the seed of the blessed of
the LORD, and their offspring with
them.
24 And it shall come to pass, that
before [w]they call, I will answer; and

while they are yet speaking, I will
hear.
25 The wolf and the lamb shall feed
together, and the lion shall eat straw
like the bullock: [x]and dust *shall be* the
serpent's meat. They shall not hurt
nor destroy in all my holy [y]mountain,
saith the LORD.

CHAPTER 66

THUS saith the LORD, [a]The heaven
is my throne, and the earth *is* my
footstool: where *is* the house that ye
build unto me? and where *is* the place
of my rest?
2 For all those *things* hath mine hand
made, and all those *things* have been,
saith the LORD: but to this *man* will I
look, *even* [b]to *him that is* poor and of
a contrite spirit, and [c]trembleth at my
word.
3 He that killeth an ox *is as if* he slew
a man; he that sacrificeth a [1]lamb, *as
if* he cut off a dog's neck; he that offereth an oblation, *as if he offered* swine's
blood; he that [2]burneth incense, *as if*
he blessed an idol. Yea, they have
chosen their own ways, and their
soul delighteth in their abominations.
4 I also will choose their [3]delusions,
and will bring their fears upon them;
[d]because when I called, none did answer; when I spake, they did not hear:
but they did evil before mine eyes,
and chose *that* in which I delighted
not.
5 ¶ Hear the word of the LORD, ye
that tremble at his word; Your brethren that [e]hated you, that cast you out
for [f]my name's sake, said, [g]Let the
LORD be glorified: but [h]he shall appear to your joy, and they shall be
ashamed.
6 A voice of noise from the city, a
voice from the temple, a voice of the
LORD that rendereth recompence to
his enemies.
7 Before she travailed, she brought
forth; before her pain came, she was
delivered of a man child.
8 Who hath heard such a thing? who
hath seen such things? Shall the earth
be made to bring forth in one day? *or*
shall a nation be born at once? for as
soon as Zion travailed, she brought
forth her children.
9 Shall I bring to the birth, and not
[4]cause to bring forth? saith the LORD:
shall I cause to bring forth, and shut
the womb? saith thy God.
10 Rejoice ye with Jerusalem, and be
glad with her, all ye that love her: re-

x Gen. 3.14. Rom. 16.20.
y ch. 2.2. Dan. 2.35. Rev. 14.1.
CHAP. 66
a 1 Chr. 28.2. 2 Chr. 6.18. Ps. 11.4. Matt. 5.34. Acts 7.48, 49.
b Ps. 34.18.
c Ezra 9.4. Ps. 119.120, 161. Pro. 28.14.
1 Or, kid.
2 maketh a memorial of.
3 Or, devices.
d Pro. 1.24.
e John 15.18.
f Matt. 24.9.
g ch. 5.19.
h 2 Thes. 1. 10. Titus 2.13.
4 Or, beget?
5 Or, brightness.
i ch. 48.18. ch. 60.5.
j ch. 60. 16.
k ch. 49.22. ch. 60.4.
l Eze. 37.1.
m ch. 9.5. 2 Thes. 1.8.
n ch. 27.1.
o ch. 65.3,4.
6 Or, one after another.
p Rev. 2.2. Heb. 4.13.
q Luke 2.34.
r Mal. 1.11.
s Rom. 12.1. Rom. 15.16.
7 Or, coaches.
t Ex. 19.6. ch. 61.6.

joice for joy with her, all ye th
mourn for her:
11 That ye may suck, and be sati
fied with the breasts of her consol
tions; that ye may milk out, and be d
lighted with the [5]abundance of h
glory.
12 For thus saith the LORD, Behol
[i]I will extend peace to her like a rive
and the glory of the Gentiles like
flowing stream: then shall ye [j]suck
ye shall be borne [k]upon *her* sides, an
be dandled upon *her* knees.
13 As one whom his mother con
forteth, so will I comfort you; an
ye shall be comforted in Jerusa
lem.
14 And when ye see *this*, your hea
shall rejoice, and [l]your bones sha
flourish like an herb: and the hand
the LORD shall be known toward hi
servants, and *his* indignation towar
his enemies.
15 For, [m]behold, the LORD will com
with fire, and with his chariots like
whirlwind, to render his anger wit
fury, and his rebuke with flames c
fire.
16 For by fire and by [n]his sword wi
the LORD plead with all flesh: and th
slain of the LORD shall be many.
17 They [o]that sanctify themselve
and purify themselves in the garden
[6]behind one *tree* in the midst, eatin
swine's flesh, and the abominatior
and the mouse, shall be consumed to
gether, saith the LORD.
18 For I [p]*know* their works and thei
thoughts: it shall come, that I wi
gather all nations and tongues
and they shall come, and see m
glory.
19 And [q]I will set a sign among them
and I will send those that escape o
them unto the nations, *to* Tarshish
Pŭl, and Lud, that draw the bow, *t*
Tū-băl, and Jā-văn, *to* the isles afa
off, that have not heard my fame
neither have seen my glory; [r]and the
shall declare my glory among th
Gentiles.
20 And they shall bring all you
brethren *for* [s]an offering unto th
LORD out of all nations upon horses
and in chariots, and in [7]litters, and up
on mules, and upon swift beasts, t
my holy mountain Jerusalem, saitl
the LORD, as the children of Israe
bring an offering in a clean vessel int
the house of the LORD.
21 And I will also take of them fo
[t]priests *and* for Levites, saith th
LORD.

2 For as [u]the new heavens and the
:w earth, which I will make, shall re-
ain before me, saith the LORD, so
all your seed and your name re-
ain.
3 And [v]it shall come to pass, *that*,
rom one new moon to another, and
om one sabbath to another, [w]shall
all flesh come to worship before me,
saith the LORD.
24 And they shall go forth, and look
upon the carcases of the men that
have transgressed against me: for
their worm shall not die, neither shall
their fire be quenched; and they shall
be an abhorring unto all flesh.

u 2 Pet. 3.13. Rev. 21.1.
v Zech. 14.16.
8 from new moon to his new moon, and from sabbath to his sabbath.
w Ps. 65.2.

THE BOOK OF THE PROPHET

JEREMIAH

CHAPTER 1

THE words of Jeremiah the son of
Hĭl-kī'-ăh, of the priests that *were*
n Ăn'-ă-thōth in the land of Ben-
.min:
2 To whom the [b]word of the LORD
ame in the days of Jō-sī'-ăh the son
f Amon king of Judah, in [c]the thir-
enth year of his reign.
3 It came also in the days of Jĕ-hoi'-
-kim the son of Jō-sī'-ăh king of Ju-
ah, [d]unto the end of the eleventh
ear of Zĕd-ē-kī'-ăh the son of Jō-sī'-
h king of Judah, [e]unto the carrying
way of Jerusalem captive [f]in the fifth
onth.
4 Then the word of the LORD came
nto me, saying,
5 Before I formed thee in the belly I
new thee; and before thou camest
orth out of the womb I [g]sanctified
ee, *and* I [1]ordained thee a prophet
nto the nations.
6 Then said I, [h]Ah, Lord GOD! beold, I cannot speak: for I *am* a child.
7 ¶ But the LORD said unto me, Say
ot, I *am* a child: for [i]thou shalt go to
l that I shall send thee, and [j]whatso-
ver I command thee thou shalt speak.
8 Be not afraid of their faces: for I
am with thee to deliver thee, saith the
ORD.
9 Then the LORD put forth his hand,
nd touched [l]my mouth. And the
ORD said unto me, Behold, I have
put my words in thy mouth.
10 See, [n]I have this day set thee over
he nations and over the kingdoms, to
oot out, and to pull down, and to de-
troy, and to throw down, to build,
nd to plant.
11 ¶ Moreover the word of the LORD
ame unto me, saying, Jeremiah,
what seest thou? And I said, I see a
od of an almond tree.
12 Then said the LORD unto me,
Thou hast well seen: for I will hasten
[p]my word to perform it.
13 And the word of the LORD came
unto me the second time, saying,
What seest thou? And I said, I see a
seething pot; and the face thereof *is*
[2]toward the north.
14 Then the LORD said unto me, Out
of the north an evil [3]shall break forth
upon all the inhabitants of the land.
15 For, lo, I will call the families of
the kingdoms of the north, saith the
LORD; and they shall come, and they
shall [q]set every one his throne at the
entering of the gates of Jerusalem, and
against all the walls thereof round
about, and against all the cities of
Judah.
16 And I will [r]utter my judgments
against them touching all their wickedness, [s]who have forsaken me, and
have burned incense unto other gods,
and worshipped the works of their
own hands.
17 ¶ Thou therefore [t]gird up thy
loins, and arise, and speak unto them
all that I command [u]thee: be not dismayed at their faces, lest I [4]confound
thee before them.
18 For, behold, I have made thee
this day a defenced city, and an iron
pillar, and brasen walls against the
whole land, against the kings of Judah, against the princes thereof,
against the priests thereof, and against
the people of the land.
19 And they shall fight against thee;
but they shall not prevail against thee;
for [v]I *am* with thee, saith the LORD, to
deliver thee.

CHAP. 1
a Josh. 21.18.
b 2 Pet. 1.21.
c ch. 25.3.
d ch. 39.2.
e ch. 52.12.
f 2 Ki. 25.8.
g Luke 1.15.
1 gave.
h Ex. 4.10.
i Ex. 7.1,2. Eze. 2.3,4. Matt. 28.20. Mark 16.15, 16.
j Num. 22.20. 1 Ki. 22.14.
k Ex. 3.12. Deut. 31.6. Acts 26.17.
l Isa. 6.7.
m Isa. 51.16.
n 1 Ki. 17.1. ch. 25.15. Rev. 11.3-6.
o 2 Cor. 10.4.
p Deut. 32. 35.
2 from the face of the north.
3 shall be opened.
q ch. 39.3.
r Lev. 26.15. ch. 4.12.
s Deut. 28.20.
t 1 Ki. 18.46.
u Ex. 3.12.
4 Or, break to pieces.
v Num. 14.9. Ps. 27.1. Rom. 8.31.

CHAPTER 2

MOREOVER the word of the
LORD came to me, saying,
2 Go and cry in the ears of Jerusalem, saying, Thus saith the LORD; I

remember [1]thee, the kindness of thy [a]youth, the love of thine espousals, when thou wentest after me in the wilderness, in a land *that was* not sown.

3 Israel *was* holiness unto the LORD, *and* the [b]firstfruits of his increase: all that devour him shall offend; evil shall come upon them, saith the LORD.

4 Hear ye the word of the LORD, O house of Jacob, and all the families of the house of Israel:

5 ¶ Thus saith the LORD, [c]What iniquity have your fathers found in me, that they are gone far from me, and have walked after vanity, and [d]are become vain?

6 Neither said they, Where *is* the LORD that brought us up out of the land of Egypt, that led us through the wilderness, through a land of deserts and of pits, through a land of drought, and of the shadow of death, through a land that no man passed through, and where no man dwelt?

7 And I brought you into [2]a plentiful country, to eat the fruit thereof and the goodness thereof; but when ye entered, ye defiled my land, and made mine heritage an abomination.

8 The priests said not, Where *is* the LORD? and they that handle the [e]law knew me not: the pastors also transgressed against me, and the prophets prophesied by Bā-ăl, and walked after *things that* do not profit.

9 ¶ Wherefore [f]I will yet plead with you, saith the LORD, and with your children's children will I plead.

10 For pass [3]over the isles of Chĭt-tĭm, and see; and send unto Kē-dăr, and consider diligently, and see if there be such a thing.

11 Hath [g]a nation changed *their* gods, which *are* yet no gods? [h]but my people have changed their glory for *that which* doth not profit.

12 Be astonished, O ye heavens, at this, and be horribly afraid, be ye very desolate, saith the LORD.

13 For my people have committed two evils; they have forsaken me the [i]fountain of living waters, *and* hewed them out cisterns, broken cisterns, that can hold no water.

14 ¶ *Is* Israel a servant? *is* he a homeborn *slave?* why is he [4]spoiled?

15 The young lions roared upon him, *and* [5]yelled, and they made his land waste: his cities are burned without inhabitant.

16 Also the children of Nŏph and Tă-hăp-ă-nēs [6]have broken the crown of thy head.

17 Hast thou not procured this unto thyself, in that thou hast forsaken the LORD thy God, when he led thee by the way?

18 And now what hast thou to do [j]in the way of Egypt, to drink the waters of [k]Sī-hôr? or what hast thou to do in the way of Assyria, to drink the waters of the river?

19 Thine own [l]wickedness shall correct thee, and thy backslidings shall reprove thee: know therefore and see that *it is* an evil *thing* and bitter, that thou hast forsaken the LORD thy God, and that my fear *is* not in thee, saith the Lord GOD of hosts.

20 ¶ For of old time I have broken thy yoke, *and* burst thy bands; and [m]thou saidst, I will not [7]transgress; when upon every high hill and under every green tree thou wanderest, playing the harlot.

21 Yet I had [n]planted thee a noble vine, wholly a right seed: how then art thou turned into the degenerate plant of a strange vine unto me?

22 For though thou wash thee with nitre, and take thee much soap, *yet* [o]thine iniquity is marked before me, saith the Lord GOD.

23 How [p]canst thou say, I am not polluted, I have not gone after Bā-ă-lĭm? see thy way [q]in the valley, know what thou hast done: [8]*thou art* a swift dromedary traversing her ways;

24 [9]A wild ass [10]used to the wilderness, *that* snuffeth up the wind at [11]her pleasure; in her occasion who can [12]turn her away? all they that seek her will not weary themselves; in her month they shall find her.

25 Withhold thy foot from being unshod, and thy throat from thirst: but thou saidst, [13]There is no hope: no; for I have loved strangers, and after them will I go.

26 As the thief is ashamed when he is found, so is the house of Israel ashamed; they, their kings, their princes, and their priests, and their prophets,

27 Saying to a stock, Thou *art* my father; and to a stone, Thou hast [14]brought me forth: for they have turned [15]*their* back unto me, and not *their* face: but in the time of their [r]trouble they will say, Arise, and save us.

28 But [s]where *are* thy gods that thou hast made thee? let them arise, if they [t]can save thee in the time of thy [16]trouble: for *according to* the number of thy cities are thy gods, O Judah.

CHAP. 2
1 Or, for thy sake.
a Eze. 16.8. Hosea 2.15.
b Jas. 1.18. Rev. 14.4.
c Isa. 5.4. Micah 6.3.
d Isa. 44.9. Rom. 1.21.
2 Or, the land of Carmel.
e Mal. 2.6. Rom. 2.20.
f Isa. 3.13. Hosea 2.2. Micah 6.2.
3 Or, over to.
g Micah 4.5.
h Ps. 106.20. Rom. 1.23.
i Ps. 36.9. ch. 17.13. Rev. 21.6.
4 become a spoil?
5 gave out their voice.
6 Or, feed on thy crown.
j Isa. 30. 1,2.
k Eze. 17.15.
l Isa. 3.9. Hosea 5.5.
m Ex. 19.8.
7 Or, serve.
n Ps. 80.8. Matt. 21.33. Mark 12.1.
o Deut. 32. 34. Ps. 90.8. Hos. 13.12.
p Gen. 3.12, 13. Pro. 30.12. Rom. 3.19.
q ch. 7.31.
8 Or, O swift dromedary.
9 Or, O wild ass.
10 taught.
11 the desire of her heart.
12 Or, reverse it?
13 Or, Is the case desperate?
14 Or, begotten me.
15 the hinder part of the neck.
r Judg. 10.10.
s Deut. 32.37.
t Isa. 45.20.
16 evil.

29 Wherefore will ye plead with me?
ye all have transgressed against me,
saith the LORD.
30 In vain have I smitten your children; they received no correction:
your own sword hath devoured [u]your
prophets, like a destroying lion.
31 ¶ O generation, see ye the word
of the LORD. Have I been a wilderness
unto Israel? a land of darkness?
wherefore say my people, [17]We are
lords; we will come no more unto
thee?
32 Can a maid forget her ornaments,
or a bride her attire? yet my people
have forgotten me days without number.
33 Why trimmest thou thy way to
seek love? therefore hast thou also
taught the wicked ones thy ways.
34 Also in thy skirts is found the
[w]blood of the souls of the poor innocents: I have not found it by [18]secret
search, but upon all these.
35 Yet thou sayest, Because I am innocent, surely his anger shall turn
from me. Behold, I will plead with
thee, [x]because thou sayest, I have not
sinned.
36 Why [y]gaddest thou about so
much to change thy way? [z]thou also
shalt be ashamed of Egypt, as [a]thou
wast ashamed of Assyria.
37 Yea, thou shalt go forth from him,
and thine [b]hands upon thine head:
for the LORD hath rejected thy con-
fidences, and thou shalt not prosper
in them.

CHAPTER 3

[1]THEY say, If a man put away his
wife, and she go from him, and become another man's, [a]shall he return
unto her again? shall not that land be
greatly polluted? but thou hast [b]play-
ed the harlot with many lovers; [c]yet
return again to me, saith the LORD.
2 Lift up thine eyes unto [d]the high
places, and see where thou hast not
been lien with. In [e]the ways hast thou
sat for them, as the Arabian in the
wilderness; and thou hast polluted the
land with thy whoredoms and with
thy wickedness.
3 Therefore [f]the showers have been
withholden, and there hath been no
latter rain; and thou hadst [g]a whore's
forehead, thou refusedst to be ashamed.
4 Wilt thou not from this time cry unto me, My father, thou *art* the [h]guide
of [i]my youth?
5 Will he reserve *his anger* for ever?
will he keep *it* to the end? Behold,
thou hast spoken and done evil things
as thou couldest.
6 ¶ The LORD said also unto me in
the days of Jō-sī-ăh the king, Hast
thou seen *that* which backsliding Israel hath done? she is gone up upon
every high mountain and under every
green tree, and there hath played the
harlot.
7 And [j]I said after she had done all
these *things*, Turn thou unto me. But
she returned not. And her treacherous sister Judah saw *it*.
8 And I saw, when for all the causes
whereby backsliding Israel committed adultery I had put her away, and
given her a bill of divorce; [k]yet her
treacherous sister Judah feared not,
but went and played the harlot also.
9 And it came to pass through the
[2]lightness of her whoredom, that she
defiled the land, and committed
adultery with stones and with stocks.
10 And yet for all this her treacherous sister Judah hath not turned unto
me with [l]her whole heart, but [3]feign-
edly, saith the LORD.
11 And the LORD said unto me, The
backsliding Israel hath justified herself more than treacherous Judah.
12 ¶ Go and proclaim these words
toward the north, and say, Return,
thou [m]backsliding Israel, saith the
LORD; *and* I will not cause mine anger
to fall upon you: for I *am* merciful,
saith the LORD, *and* I will not keep
anger for ever.
13 Only [n]acknowledge thine iniquity,
that thou hast transgressed against the
LORD thy God, and hast scattered
thy ways to the strangers under every
green tree, and ye have not obeyed my
voice, saith the LORD.
14 Turn, O backsliding children,
saith the LORD; for I am married unto
you: and I will take you one [o]of a city,
and two of a family, and I will bring
you to Zion:
15 And I will give you [p]pastors according to mine heart, which shall
[q]feed you with knowledge and understanding.
16 And it shall come to pass, when
ye be multiplied and increased in the
land, in those days, saith the LORD,
they [r]shall say no more, The ark of
the covenant of the LORD: neither
shall it [4]come to mind: neither shall
they remember it; neither shall they
visit *it;* neither shall [5]*that* be done any
more.
17 At that time they shall call Jerusalem the throne of the LORD; and all

u 2 Chr. 36. 16. Matt. 23.29. Luke 13.33, 34. Acts 7.52. 1 Thes. 2.15.
17 We have dominion.
v Ps. 106.21. ch. 13.25. Hosea 8.14.
w Ps. 106.38. ch. 19.4.
18 digging.
x Pro. 28.13.
y ch. 31.22. Hosea 5.13.
z Isa. 30.3. ch. 37.7.
a 2 Chr. 28. 16,21.
b 2 Sam. 13. 19.

CHAP. 3

1 Saying.
a Deut. 24.4.
b ch. 2.20.
c ch. 4.1. Hos. 14.1,2. Zech. 1.3. Luke 15.16, 24.
d Deut. 12.2.
e Gen. 38.14. Pro. 23.28.
f Lev. 26.19.
g Zeph. 3.5.
h Pro. 2.17. Mal. 2.14.
i ch. 2.2. Hos. 2.15.
j 2 Ki. 17.13.
k Eze. 23.11.
2 Or, fame.
l Hosea 7.14.
3 in falsehood.
m Isa. 44.22. ch. 4.1.
n Lev. 26.40, 42. Pro. 28.13. ch. 31.18-20. Luke 15.18-21.
o Rom. 11.5.
p ch. 23.4. Eph. 4.11.
q Acts 20.28.
r John 4.21-24.
4 come upon the heart.
5 Or, it be magnified.

the nations shall be gathered unto
it, to the name of the LORD, to Jerusalem: neither shall they walk any
more after the [6]imagination of their
evil heart.
18 In those days [s]the house of Judah
shall walk [7]with the house of Israel,
and they shall come together out of
[t]the land of the north to the land that
I have [8]given for an inheritance unto
your fathers.
19 But I said, How shall I put thee
among the children, and give thee a
[9]pleasant land, [10]a goodly heritage of
the hosts of nations? and I said, Thou
shalt call me, My [u]father; and shalt
not turn away [11]from me.
20 ¶ Surely *as* a wife treacherously
departeth from her [12]husband, so have
ye dealt treacherously with me, O
house of Israel, saith the LORD.
21 A voice was heard [v]upon the high
places, weeping *and* supplications of
the children of Israel: for they have
perverted their way, *and* they have forgotten the LORD their God.
22 Return, [w]ye backsliding children,
and I [x]will heal your backslidings.
Behold, we come unto thee; for thou
art the LORD our God.
23 Truly [y]in vain *is salvation hoped*
for from the hills, *and from* the multitude of mountains: [z]truly in the LORD
our God *is* the salvation of Israel.
24 For [a]shame hath devoured the
labour of our fathers from our youth;
their flocks and their herds, their sons
and their daughters.
25 We lie down in our shame, and our
confusion covereth us: for [b]we have
sinned against the LORD our God, we
and our fathers, from our youth even
unto this day, and have not obeyed
the voice of the LORD our God.

CHAPTER 4

IF thou wilt return, O Israel, saith
the LORD, [a]return unto me: and if
thou wilt put away thine abominations out of my sight, then shalt thou
not remove.
2 And [b]thou shalt swear, The LORD
liveth, in [c]truth, in judgment, and in
righteousness; [d]and the nations shall
bless themselves in him, and in him
[e]shall they glory.
3 ¶ For thus saith the LORD to the
men of Judah and Jerusalem, Break
[f]up your fallow ground, and [g]sow not
among thorns.
4 Circumcise [h]yourselves to the
LORD, and take away the foreskins of
your heart, ye men of Judah and in-

6 Or, stubbornness.
s Isa. 11.13. Hosea 1.11.
7 Or, to.
t Amos 9.15.
8 Or, caused your fathers to possess.
9 land of desire.
10 an heritage of glory, or, beauty.
u Isa. 63.16.
11 from after me.
12 friend.
v Isa. 15.2.
w Hosea 14. 1.
x Hosea 6.1.
y Ps. 121.1.
z Ps. 3.8. Isa. 12.2.
a Hosea 9.10.
b Ezra 9.7.

CHAP. 4

a Joel 2.12.
b Deut. 10. 20. Isa. 45.23.
c Isa. 48.1.
d Gal. 3.8.
e Isa. 45.25. 1 Cor. 1.31.
f Hos. 10.12.
g Matt. 13.7.
h Deut. 10. 16. Col. 2.11.
i Zeph. 2.2.
1 Or, strengthen.
j ch. 1.13.
2 breaking.
k Dan. 7.4.
l Isa. 22.12.
m Isa. 63.17. Eze. 14.9. 2 Thes. 2.11.
n Isa. 27.8. ch. 51.1. Eze. 17.10. Hosea 13.5.
3 Or, a fuller wind than those.
4 utter judgments.
o Isa. 5.28.
p Deut. 28. 49. Lam. 4.19. Hosea 8.1. Hab. 1.8.
q Isa. 1.16. Jas. 4.8.
r ch. 8.16.
s ch. 5.15.
t 2 Ki. 25.1.

habitants of Jerusalem: lest my [i]fur
come forth like fire, and burn tha
none can quench *it*, because of the evi
of your doings.
5 Declare ye in Judah, and publisl
in Jerusalem; and say, Blow ye th
trumpet in the land: cry, gather together, and say, Assemble yourselves
and let us go into the defenced cities
6 Set up the standard toward Zion
[1]retire, stay not: for I will bring evi
from the north, [j]and a great [2]destruc-
tion.
7 The [k]lion is come up from his thicket, and the destroyer of the Gentiles is
on his way; he is gone forth from his
place to make thy land desolate; *and*
thy cities shall be laid waste, withou
an inhabitant.
8 For this [l]gird you with sackcloth,
lament and howl: for the fierce anger
of the LORD is not turned back from
us.
9 And it shall come to pass at that
day, saith the LORD, *that* the heart of
the king shall perish, and the heart of
the princes; and the priests shall be
astonished, and the prophets shall
wonder.
10 Then said I, Ah, Lord GOD! surely
[m]thou hast greatly deceived this people and Jerusalem, saying, Ye shall
have peace; whereas the sword reacheth unto the soul.
11 At that time shall it be said to this
people and to Jerusalem, A [n]dry wind
of the high places in the wilderness toward the daughter of my people, not
to fan, nor to cleanse,
12 *Even* [3]a full wind from those *places*
shall come unto me: now also will I
[4]give sentence against them.
13 Behold, he shall come up as
clouds, and [o]his chariots *shall be* as a
whirlwind: his [p]horses are swifter
than eagles. Woe unto us! for we are
spoiled.
14 O Jerusalem, [q]wash thine heart
from wickedness, that thou mayest
be saved. How long shall thy vain
thoughts lodge within thee?
15 For a voice declareth [r]from Dan,
and publisheth affliction from mount
Ē-phră-ĭm.
16 Make ye mention to the nations;
behold, publish against Jerusalem,
that watchers come [s]from a far
country, and give out their voice
against the cities of Judah.
17 As [t]keepers of a field, are they
against her round about; because she
hath been rebellious against me, saith
the LORD.

18 Thy *u*way and thy doings have
rocured these *things* unto thee; this
: thy wickedness, because it is bitter,
ecause it reacheth unto thine heart.
19 ¶ My *v*bowels, my bowels! I am
ained at [5]my very heart; my heart
naketh a noise in me; I cannot hold
ny peace, because thou hast heard,
) my soul, the sound of the trumpet,
he alarm of war.
20 Destruction *w*upon destruction is
ried; for the whole land is spoiled:
uddenly are my *x*tents spoiled, *and*
ny curtains in a moment.
21 How long shall I see the standard,
nd hear the sound of the trumpet?
22 For my people *is* *y*fooiish, they
ave not known me; they *are* sottish
hildren, and they have none under-
tanding: *z*they *are* wise to do evil, but
o do good they have no knowledge.
23 I *a*beheld the earth, and, lo, *it was*
vithout *b*form, and void; and the
eavens, and they *had* no light.
24 I *c*beheld the mountains, and, lo,
hey trembled, and all the hills moved
ightly.
25 I beheld, and, lo, *there was* no
nan, and *d*all the birds of the heavens
vere fled.
26 I beheld, and, lo, the fruitful place
vas a wilderness, and all the cities
hereof were broken down at the pres-
nce of the LORD, *and* by his fierce
nger.
27 For thus hath the LORD said, The
whole land shall be desolate; yet *e*will
I not make a full end.
28 For *f*this shall the earth mourn,
and *g*the heavens above be black: because I have spoken *it*, I have purposed *it*, and will not *h*repent, neither will
I turn back from it.
29 The *i*whole city shall flee for the
noise of the horsemen and bowmen;
they shall go into thickets, and climb
up upon the rocks: every city *shall*
be forsaken, and not a man dwell
therein.
30 And *when* thou *art* spoiled, what
wilt thou do? Though thou clothest
thyself with crimson, though thou
deckest thee with ornaments of gold,
*j*though thou rentest thy [6]face with
painting, in vain shalt thou make thyself fair; *thy* *k*lovers will despise thee,
they will seek thy life.
31 For I have heard a voice as of a
woman in travail, *and* the anguish as
of her that bringeth forth her first
child, the voice of the daughter of
Zion, *that* bewaileth herself, *that*
*l*spreadeth her hands, *saying*, Woe *is*

u Job 20.6-11. Ps. 107.17. Pro. 1.31. Isa. 50.1. ch. 2.17.
v Isa. 16.11. Luke 19.41, 42.
5 the walls of my heart.
w Ps. 42.7.
x ch. 10.20.
y Rom. 1.22.
z Rom. 16.19. 1 Cor. 14.20.
a Isa. 24.19.
b Gen. 1.2.
c Eze. 38.20.
d Zeph. 1.3.
e ch. 5.10.
f Isa. 33.9. ch. 12.4. Hosea 4.3.
g Isa. 50.3.
h Num. 23. 19.
i 2 Ki. 25.4.
j 2 Ki. 9.30.
6 eyes.
k Lam. 1.2, 19.
l Isa. 1.15. Lam. 1.17.

CHAP. 5

a Eze. 22.30. Micah 7.2.
b Ps. 12.1.
c Titus 1.16.
d 2 Chr. 16.9.
e Isa. 1.5.
f ch. 7.28. Zeph. 3.2.
g ch. 8.7.
h Micah 3.1.
i Ps. 2.3.
j ch. 4.7.
k Hab. 1.8.
1 Or, deserts.
l Hosea 13.7.
2 are strong.
m Josh. 23.7. ch. 12.16. Amos 8.14.
n Gal. 4.8.
o Deut. 32. 15.
p Eze. 22.11.
q 2 Sam. 11. 2-4. ch. 13.27.
r Isa. 1.24. ch. 44.22. Eze. 7.9.
s ch. 39.8.
t ch. 3.20.
u 2 Chr. 36. 16.
v Isa. 28.15.
w ch. 14.13.

me now! for my soul is wearied because of murderers.

CHAPTER 5

RUN ye to and fro through the
streets of Jerusalem, and see now,
and know, and seek in the broad
places thereof, *a*if ye can find a man,
*b*if there be *any* that executeth judgment, that seeketh the truth; and I
will pardon it.
2 And *c*though they say, The LORD
liveth; surely they swear falsely.
3 O LORD, *are* not *d*thine eyes upon
the truth? thou hast *e*stricken them,
but they have not grieved; thou hast
consumed them, *f*but they have refused to receive correction: they have
made their faces harder than a rock;
they have refused to return.
4 Therefore I said, Surely these *are*
poor; they are foolish: for *g*they know
not the way of the LORD, *nor* the
judgment of their God.
5 I will get me unto the great men,
and will speak unto them; for *h*they
have known the way of the LORD, *and*
the judgment of their God: but these
have altogether broken *i*the yoke, *and*
burst the bonds.
6 Wherefore *j*a lion out of the forest
shall slay them, *k**and* a wolf of the
[1]evenings shall spoil them, a *l*leopard
shall watch over their cities: every one
that goeth out thence shall be torn in
pieces: because their transgressions
are many, *and* their backslidings [2]are
increased.
7 ¶ How shall I pardon thee for this?
thy children have forsaken me, and
*m*sworn by *them that* *n**are* no gods:
*o*when I had fed them to the full, they
then committed adultery, and assembled themselves by troops in the harlots' houses.
8 They *p*were *as* fed horses in the
morning: every one *q*neighed after his
neighbour's wife.
9 Shall I not visit for these *things?*
saith the LORD: *r*and shall not my soul
be avenged on such a nation as this?
10 ¶ Go *s*ye up upon her walls, and
destroy; but make not a full end: take
away her battlements; for they *are* not
the LORD's.
11 For *t*the house of Israel and the
house of Judah have dealt very treacherously against me, saith the LORD.
12 They *u*have belied the LORD, and
said, *v**It is* not he; neither shall evil
come upon us; *w*neither shall we see
sword nor famine:
13 And the prophets shall become

wind, and the word *is* not in them:
thus shall it be done unto them.
14 Wherefore thus saith the LORD
God of hosts, Because ye speak this
word, [x]behold, I will make my words
in thy mouth fire, and this people
wood, and it shall devour them.
15 Lo, I will bring a [y]nation upon
you from [z]far, O house of Israel, saith
the LORD: it *is* a mighty nation, it *is*
an ancient nation, a nation whose
language thou knowest not, neither
understandest what they say.
16 Their quiver *is* as an open sepulchre, they *are* all mighty men.
17 And they shall eat up [a]thine harvest, and thy bread, *which* thy sons
and thy daughters should eat: they
shall eat up thy flocks and thine herds:
they shall eat up thy vines and thy fig
trees: they shall impoverish thy fenced
cities, wherein thou trustedst, with the
sword.
18 Nevertheless in those days, saith
the LORD, I will not make a full end
with you.
19 ¶ And it shall come to pass, when
ye shall say, [b]Wherefore doeth the
LORD our God all these *things* unto
us? then shalt thou answer them, Like
as ye have forsaken me, and served
strange gods in your land, so [c]shall ye
serve strangers in a land *that is* not
yours.
20 Declare this in the house of Jacob,
and publish it in Judah, saying,
21 Hear now this, O [d]foolish people,
and without [3]understanding; which
have eyes, and see not; which have
ears, and hear not:
22 Fear [e]ye not me? saith the LORD:
will ye not tremble at my presence,
which have placed the sand *for* the
[f]bound of the sea by a perpetual decree, that it cannot pass it: and though
the waves thereof toss themselves,
yet can they not prevail; though
they roar, yet can they not pass over
it?
23 But this people hath a revolting
and a rebellious heart; they are revolted and gone.
24 Neither say they in their heart,
Let us now fear the LORD our God,
that [g]giveth rain, both the [h]former and
the latter, in his season: [i]he reserveth
unto us the appointed weeks of the
harvest.
25 ¶ Your iniquities have turned
away these *things*, and your sins have
withholden good *things* from you.
26 For among my people are found
wicked *men:* [4]they lay wait, as he that

x ch. 1.9. Hosea 6.5. Rev. 11.5.
y Deut. 28. 49. Isa. 5.26. ch. 1.15.
z Isa. 39.3.
a Lev. 26.16. Deut. 28.31. Judg. 6.3,4.
b Deut. 29. 24. 1 Ki. 9.8. ch. 13.22.
c Deut. 28. 48.
d Matt. 13.14. John 12.40. Acts 28.26.
3 heart.
e Rev. 15.4.
f Job 26.10. Pro. 8.29.
g Matt. 5.45.
h Joel 2.23.
i Gen. 8.22.
4 Or, they pry as fowlers lie in wait.
5 Or, coop.
j Ps. 73.12.
k Mal. 3.5.
6 Or, Astonishment and filthiness.
l Eze. 13.6.
7 Or, take into their hands.
m Isa. 30.10.

CHAP. 6

a Josh. 18.28. Judg. 1.21.
b Neh. 3.14.
1 Or, dwelling at home, or, pasture.
c 2 Ki. 25.1.
2 Or, pour out the engine of shot.
d 2 Ki. 21.16.
e Ps. 55.9-11. ch. 20.8. Eze. 7.11. Micah 7.2,3.
f Eze. 23.18. Hosea 9.12.
3 be loosed, or, disjointed.

setteth snares; they set a trap, the
catch men.
27 As a [5]cage is full of birds, so ar
their houses full of deceit: therefoı
they are become great, and waxe
rich.
28 They are waxen fat, they shine
yea, they overpass the deeds of th
wicked: they judge not the cause, th
cause of the fatherless, [j]yet they pros
per; and the right of the needy do the
not judge.
29 Shall [k]I not visit for these *things*
saith the LORD: shall not my soul b
avenged on such a nation as this?
30 ¶ [6]A wonderful and horrible thin
is committed in the land;
31 The prophets prophesy [l]falsely
and the priests [7]bear rule by thei
means; and my people [m]love *to hav*
it so: and what will ye do in the en
thereof?

CHAPTER 6

O YE children of [a]Benjamin, gath
er yourselves to flee out of th
midst of Jerusalem, and blow th
trumpet in Tĕ-kō'-ă, and set up a sig
of fire in [b]Bĕth-hăc'-cĕr-ĕm: for evi
appeareth out of the north, and grea
destruction.
2 I have likened the daughter of Zioı
to a [1]comely and delicate *woman*.
3 The shepherds with their flock
shall come unto her; [c]they shall pitch
their tents against her round about;
they shall feed every one in his place.
4 Prepare ye war against her; arise,
and let us go up at noon. Woe unto
us! for the day goeth away, for the
shadows of the evening are stretched
out.
5 Arise, and let us go by night, and
let us destroy her palaces.
6 ¶ For thus hath the LORD of hosts
said, Hew ye down trees, and [2]cast a
mount against Jerusalem: this *is* the
city to be visited; she *is* wholly [d]op-
pression in the midst of her.
7 As a fountain casteth out her waters, so she casteth out her wickedness:
violence and [e]spoil is heard in her;
before me continually *is* grief and
wounds.
8 Be thou instructed, O Jerusalem,
[f]lest my soul [3]depart from thee; lest
I make thee desolate, a land not inhabited.
9 ¶ Thus saith the LORD of hosts,
They shall throughly glean the remnant of Israel as a vine: turn back
thine hand as a grapegatherer into
the baskets.
10 To whom shall I speak, and give

arning, that they may hear? behold,
eir ear [g]*is* uncircumcised, and they
nnot hearken: behold, [h]the word
the LORD is unto them a reproach;
ey have no delight in it.
1 Therefore I am full of the fury of
e LORD; I am weary with holding
: I will pour it out upon the children
road, and upon the assembly of
ung men together: for even the hus-
nd with the wife shall be taken, the
ed with *him that is* full of days.
2 And [i]their houses shall be turned
to others, *with their* fields and
ives together: for I will stretch out
y hand upon the inhabitants of the
nd, saith the LORD.
3 For from the least of them even
to the greatest of them every one *is*
ven [j]to covetousness; and from the
ophet even unto the priest every one
aleth falsely.
4 They have [k]healed also the [4]hurt
the daughter of my people slightly,
ying, Peace, peace; when *there is* no
ace.
5 Were they [l]ashamed when they
d committed abomination? nay,
ey were not at all ashamed, neither
uld they blush: therefore they shall
ll among them that fall: at the time
at I visit them they shall be cast
own, saith the LORD.
6 Thus saith the LORD, Stand ye in
e ways, and see, and ask for the
old paths, where *is* the good way,
d walk therein, and ye shall find
est for your souls. But they said, We
ill not walk *therein*.
7 Also I set [o]watchmen over you,
ying, Hearken to the sound of the
umpet. But they said, We will not
earken.
8 ¶ Therefore hear, ye nations, and
now, O congregation, what *is* among
em.
9 Hear, O earth: behold, I will bring
vil upon this people, *even* the [p]fruit
f their thoughts, because they have
ot hearkened unto my words, nor to
y law, but rejected it.
20 To [q]what purpose cometh there to
e incense [r]from Shē-bă, and the
weet cane from a far country? your
urnt offerings *are* not acceptable,
or your sacrifices sweet unto me.
21 Therefore thus saith the LORD,
ehold, I [s]will lay stumblingblocks
efore this people, and the fathers and
e sons together shall fall upon them;
e neighbour and his friend shall
erish.
22 Thus saith the LORD, Behold, a

g Ex. 6.12. ch. 7.26. Acts 7.51.
h ch. 20.8. Luke 11.45. 2 Tim. 4.3,4.
i ch. 8.10. Zeph. 1.13.
j Isa. 56.11. Micah 3.5.
k Eze. 13.10.
4 bruise, or, breach.
l ch. 3.3.
m ch. 18.15. Mal. 4.4. Luke 16.29.
n Isa. 28.12. Matt. 11.29.
o Isa. 21.11. ch. 25.4. Hab. 2.1.
p Pro. 1.31.
q Isa. 66.3. Micah 6.6.
r Isa. 60.6.
s Job. 5.12. Isa. 8.14. ch. 13.16.
t Isa. 5.30.
u Ps. 48.6. Isa. 21.3. ch. 4.31. ch. 13.21. ch. 30.6. ch. 49.24.
v Judg. 5.6.
w Isa. 32.11. ch. 4.8. Micah 1.10.
x Zech. 12. 10.
5 Or, in.
y Eze. 22.18.
6 Or, Refuse silver.
z Hosea 9.17. Zech. 11.8.

CHAP. 7

a ch. 19.2,3. ch. 26.2.
b 1 Sam. 4.4. Micah 3.11.
c Deut. 6.14. Deut. 8.19. ch. 13.10.
d Deut. 4.40.

people cometh from the north country, and a great nation shall be raised
from the sides of the earth.
23 They shall lay hold on bow and
spear; they *are* cruel, and have no
mercy; their voice [t]roareth like the
sea; and they ride upon horses, set in
array as men for war against thee, O
daughter of Zion.
24 We have heard the fame thereof:
our hands wax feeble: anguish [u]hath
taken hold of us, *and* pain, as of a woman in travail.
25 Go not forth into the field, nor
[v]walk by the way; for the sword of the
enemy *and* fear *is* on every side.
26 ¶ O daughter of my people, gird
thee with sackcloth, [w]and wallow thyself in ashes: [x]make thee mourning,
as for an only son, most bitter lamentation: for the spoiler shall suddenly
come upon us.
27 I have set thee [5]*for* a tower *and* a
fortress among my people, that thou
mayest know and try their way.
28 They *are* all grievous revolters,
walking with slanders: *they* [y]*are* brass
and iron; they *are* all corrupters.
29 The bellows are burned, the lead
is consumed of the fire; the founder
melteth in vain: for the wicked are
not plucked away.
30 [6]Reprobate silver shall *men* call
them, because the LORD hath [z]rejected
them.

CHAPTER 7

THE word that came to Jeremiah
from the LORD, saying,
2 Stand [a]in the gate of the LORD's
house, and proclaim there this word,
and say, Hear the word of the LORD,
all *ye of* Judah, that enter in at these
gates to worship the LORD.
3 Thus saith the LORD of hosts, the
God of Israel, Amend your ways and
your doings, and I will cause you to
dwell in this place.
4 Trust ye not in lying words, saying,
The temple of the LORD, The temple
[b]of the LORD, The temple of the LORD,
are these.
5 For if ye throughly amend your
ways and your doings; if ye throughly
execute judgment between a man and
his neighbour;
6 *If* ye oppress not the stranger, the
fatherless, and the widow, and shed
not innocent blood in this place,
[c]neither walk after other gods to your
hurt:
7 Then [d]will I cause you to dwell in
this place, in the land that I gave to
your fathers, for ever and ever.

8 ¶ Behold, ye trust in lying words,
that cannot profit.
9 Will [e]ye steal, murder, and commit
adultery, and swear falsely, and burn
incense unto Bā-ăl, [f]and walk after
other gods whom ye know not;
10 And [g]come and stand before me
in this house, [1]which is called by my
name, and say, We are delivered to do
all these abominations?
11 Is [h]this house, which is called by
my name, become [i]a den of robbers in
your eyes? Behold, even [j]I have seen
it, saith the LORD.
12 But go ye now unto [k]my place
which *was* in Shī-lōh, [l]where I set my
name at the first, and [m]see what I did
to it for the wickedness of my people
Israel.
13 And now, because ye have done
all these works, saith the LORD, and I
spake unto you, rising [n]up early and
speaking, but ye heard not; and I
[o]called you, but ye answered not;
14 Therefore will I do unto *this*
house, which is called by my name,
wherein ye trust, and unto the place
which I gave to you and to your fathers, as I have done [p]to Shī-lōh.
15 And I will cast you out of my
sight, [q]as I have cast out all your brethren, *even* the whole seed of Ē-phră-ĭm.
16 Therefore [r]pray not thou for this
people, neither lift up cry nor prayer
for them, neither make intercession to
me: [s]for I will not hear thee.
17 ¶ Seest thou not what they do in
the cities of Judah and in the streets
of Jerusalem?
18 The children gather wood, and
the fathers kindle the fire, and the women knead *their* dough, to make cakes
to the [2]queen of heaven, and to pour
out drink offerings unto other gods,
that they may provoke me to anger.
19 Do [t]they provoke me to anger?
saith the LORD: *do they* not *provoke*
themselves to the confusion of their
own faces?
20 Therefore thus saith the Lord
GOD; Behold, mine anger and my fury
shall be poured out upon this place,
upon man, and upon beast, and upon
the trees of the field, and upon the
fruit of the ground; and it shall burn,
and shall not be quenched.
21 ¶ Thus saith the LORD of hosts,
the God of Israel; [u]Put your burnt
offerings unto your sacrifices, and eat
flesh.
22 For [v]I spake not unto your fathers,
nor commanded them in the day that
I brought them out of the land of

e 1 Ki. 18.21. Hosea 4.1.
f Ex. 20.3.
g Eze. 23.39.
1 whereupon my name is called.
h Isa. 56.7.
i Matt. 21.13. Mark 11.17.
j John 2.24.
k Josh. 18.1.
l Deut. 12.11.
m 1 Sam. 4. 10.
n 2 Chr. 36. 15.
o Pro. 1.24. Isa. 65.12.
p Ps. 78.60.
q 2 Ki. 17.23.
r Ex. 32.10.
s ch. 15.1.
2 Or, frame, or, workmanship of heaven.
t ch. 17.27. 1 Cor. 10.22.
u Isa. 1.11. ch. 6.20. Amos 5.21.
v 1 Sam. 15. 22. Ps. 51.16.
3 concerning the matter of.
w Ex. 15.26. Lev. 26.3, 12. Deut. 6.3. ch. 11.4,7.
x Ex. 19.5. Lev. 26.12.
y Deut. 29. 19.
4 Or, stubbornness.
5 were.
z Neh. 9.30. ch. 25.4.
a Neh. 9.17.
b Eze. 2.7.
6 Or, instruction.
c Job 1.20. Isa. 15.2. ch. 16.6.
d Eph. 2.3.
e 2 Ki. 21.4. 2 Chr. 33.4.
f 2 Ki. 23.10.
g Deut. 17.3.
7 came it upon my heart.
h 2 Ki. 23.10.
i Hosea 2.11.

Egypt, [3]concerning burnt offerings
sacrifices:
23 But this thing commanded I the
saying, [w]Obey my voice, and [x]I w
be your God, and ye shall be my pe
ple: and walk ye in all the ways tha
have commanded you, that it may
well unto you.
24 But they hearkened not, nor i
clined their ear, but [y]walked in t
counsels *and* in the [4]imagination
their evil heart, and [5]went backwar
and not forward.
25 Since the day that your fathe
came forth out of the land of Egy
unto this day I have [z]even sent un
you all my servants the prophe
daily rising up early and sendi
them:
26 Yet they hearkened not unto m
nor inclined their ear, [a]but harden
their neck: they did worse than the
fathers.
27 Therefore [b]thou shalt speak a
these words unto them; but they wi
not hearken to thee: thou shalt als
call unto them; but they will not a
swer thee.
28 But thou shalt say unto them, Th
is a nation that obeyeth not the voi
of the LORD their God, nor receive
[6]correction: truth is perished, and
cut off from their mouth.
29 ¶ Cut [c]off thine hair, *O Jerusalen*
and cast *it* away, and take up a lame
tation on high places; for the LOR
hath rejected and forsaken the [d]gene
ation of his wrath.
30 For the children of Judah hav
done evil in my sight, saith the LORI
[e]they have set their abominations i
the house which is called by my nam
to pollute it.
31 And they have built the [f]hig
places of Tō-phĕt, which *is* in the va
ley of the son of Hĭn-nŏm, to bu
their sons and their daughters in th
fire; [g]which I commanded *them* no
neither [7]came it into my heart.
32 ¶ Therefore, behold, the day
come, saith the LORD, that it shall n
more be called Tō-phĕt, nor the valle
of the son of Hĭn-nŏm, but the valle
of slaughter: [h]for they shall bury i
Tō-phĕt, till there be no place.
33 And the carcases of this peopl
shall be meat for the fowls of the hea
en, and for the beasts of the earth; an
none shall fray *them* away.
34 Then will I cause to [i]cease fro
the cities of Judah, and from the stree
of Jerusalem, the voice of mirth, an
the voice of gladness, the voice of th

degroom, and the voice of the
de: for [j]the land shall be desolate.

CHAPTER 8

T that time, saith the LORD, they
shall bring out the bones of the
gs of Judah, and the bones of his
nces, and the bones of the priests,
l the bones of the prophets, and the
nes of the inhabitants of Jerusalem,
of their graves:
And they shall spread them before
sun, and the moon, and all the host
heaven, whom they have loved, and
om they have served, and after
om they have walked, and whom
y have sought, and [a]whom they
ve worshipped: they shall not be
hered, nor be buried; [b]they shall be
dung upon the face of the earth.
And [c]death shall be chosen rather
n life by all the residue of them that
nain of this evil family, which
nain in all the places whither I
ve driven them, saith the LORD of
sts.
¶ Moreover thou shalt say unto
em, Thus saith the LORD; Shall they
l, and not arise? shall he turn away,
d not return?
Why *then* is this people of Jerusa-
n slidden back by a perpetual back-
ding? they hold fast deceit, they
fuse to return.
I [e]hearkened and heard, *but* they
ake not aright: no man repented
m of his wickedness, saying, What
ve I done? every one turned to his
urse, as the horse rusheth into the
ttle.
Yea, [f]the stork in the heaven know-
h her appointed times; and the
rtle and the crane and the swallow
serve the time of their coming; but
y people know not the judgment of
e LORD.
How do ye say, We *are* wise, and
he law of the LORD *is* with us? Lo,
rtainly [1]in vain made he *it;* the pen
the scribes *is* in vain.
[2]The wise *men* are ashamed, they
e dismayed and taken: lo, they have
jected the word of the LORD; and
hat wisdom *is* in them?
0 Therefore [i]will I give their wives
nto others, *and* their fields to them
at shall inherit *them:* for every one
om the least even unto the greatest
given to covetousness, [j]from the
rophet even unto the priest every one
ealeth falsely.
1 For they have [k]healed the hurt of
e daughter of my people slightly,

j Lev. 26.33.

CHAP. 8

a Deut. 4.19. 2 Ki. 23.5. ch. 44.19.
b 2 Ki. 9.36. Ps. 83.10.
c Job 3.21. Rev. 9.6.
d Isa. 1.20. ch. 5.3. Zech. 7.11.
e 2 Pet. 3.9.
f Isa. 1.3.
g Song 2.12.
h Ps. 147.19, 20. Hosea 8.12.
1 Or, the false pen of the scribes worketh for falsehood.
2 Or, Have they been ashamed, etc.
3 the wisdom of what thing.
i Deut. 28.30. ch. 6.12. Amos 5.11.
j Isa. 28.7. ch. 5.31. Lam. 4.13.
k ch. 6.14.
l Eze. 13.10.
m Isa. 3.9. ch. 3.3.
4 Or, In gathering I will consume.
n Isa. 5.1.
o Matt. 21. 19. Luke 13.6.
p ch. 23.15.
5 Or, poison.
q ch. 14.19.
6 the fulness thereof.
7 upon.
8 because of the country of them that are far off.
r Nah. 2.10.
s Gen. 37.25.
9 gone up?

CHAP. 9

1 Who will give my head, etc.

saying, [l]Peace, peace; when *there is* no
peace.
12 Were they [m]ashamed when they
had committed abomination? nay,
they were not at all ashamed, neither
could they blush: therefore shall they
fall among them that fall: in the time
of their visitation they shall be cast
down, saith the LORD.
13 ¶ [4]I will surely consume them,
saith the LORD: *there shall be* no
grapes [n]on the vine, nor figs on [o]the
fig tree, and the leaf shall fade; and
the things that I have given them shall
pass away from them.
14 Why do we sit still? assemble
yourselves, and let us enter into the
defenced cities, and let us be silent
there: for the LORD our God hath put
us to silence, and given us [p]water of
[5]gall to drink, because we have sinned
against the LORD.
15 We [q]looked for peace, but no good
came; and for a time of health, and behold trouble!
16 The snorting of his horses was
heard from Dan: the whole land
trembled at the sound of the neighing
of his strong ones; for they are come,
and have devoured the land, and [6]all
that is in it; the city, and those that
dwell therein.
17 For, behold, I will send serpents,
cockatrices, among you, which *will*
not *be* charmed, and they shall bite
you, saith the LORD.
18 ¶ *When* I would comfort myself
against sorrow, my heart *is* faint [7]in
me.
19 Behold the voice of the cry of the
daughter of my people [8]because of
them that dwell in a far country: *Is*
not the LORD in Zion? *is* not her king
in her? Why have they provoked me
to anger with their graven images, *and*
with strange vanities?
20 The harvest is past, the summer
is ended, and we are not saved.
21 For the hurt of the daughter of my
people am I hurt; I [r]am black; astonishment hath taken hold on me.
22 *Is there* no [s]balm in Gilead; *is*
there no physician there? why then is
not the health of the daughter of my
people [9]recovered?

CHAPTER 9

[1]OH that my head were waters, and
mine eyes a fountain of tears,
that I might weep day and night
for the slain of the daughter of my
people!
2 Oh that I had in the wilderness a

lodging place of wayfaring men; that
I might leave my people, and go from
them! for they *be* all adulterers, an
assembly of treacherous men.
3 And they bend their tongues *like*
their bow *for* lies: but they are not
valiant for the truth upon the earth;
for they proceed from evil to evil,
and they [a]know not me, saith the
LORD.
4 Take [b]ye heed every one of his
[2]neighbour, and trust ye not in any
brother: for every brother will utterly
supplant, and every neighbour will
walk with slanders.
5 And they will [3]deceive every one
his neighbour, and will not speak the
truth: they have taught their tongue
to speak lies, *and* weary themselves
to commit iniquity.
6 Thine habitation *is* in the midst of
deceit; through deceit [c]they refuse to
know me, saith the LORD.
7 Therefore thus saith the LORD of
hosts, Behold, [d]I will melt them, and
try them; for [e]how shall I do for the
daughter of my people?
8 Their tongue *is as* an arrow shot
out; it speaketh deceit: *one* speaketh
peaceably to his neighbour with his
mouth, but [4]in heart he layeth [5]his
wait.
9 ¶ Shall I not visit them for these
things? saith the LORD: shall not my
soul be avenged on such a nation as
this?
10 For the mountains will I take up
a weeping and wailing, and for the
[6]habitations of the wilderness a lamentation, because they are [7]burned up,
so that none can pass through *them;*
neither can *men* hear the voice of the
cattle; [8]both the fowl of the heavens
and the beast are fled; they are gone.
11 And I will make Jerusalem heaps,
and a den of dragons; and I will make
the cities of Judah [9]desolate, without
an inhabitant.
12 ¶ Who [f]*is* the wise man, that may
understand this? and *who is he* to
whom the mouth of the LORD hath
spoken, that he may declare it, for
what the land perisheth *and* is burned
up like a wilderness, that none passeth
through?
13 And the LORD saith, Because they
have forsaken my law which I set before them, and have not obeyed my
voice, neither walked therein;
14 But have walked after the [10]imag-
ination of their own heart, and after
Bā-ă-lĭm, which [g]their fathers taught
them:

[a] Judg. 2.10. 1 Sam. 2.12. Pro. 1.29. ch. 4.22. Rom. 1.28. 1 Cor. 15.34.
[b] Micah. 7.5, 6.
2 Or, friend.
3 Or, mock.
[c] Pro. 1.24.
[d] Isa. 1.25.
[e] Hosea 11.8.
4 in the midst of him.
5 Or, wait for him.
6 Or, pastures.
7 Or, desolate.
8 from the fowl even to, etc.
9 desolation.
[f] Ps. 107.43. Isa. 42.23. Hosea 14.9.
10 Or, stubbornness.
[g] Gal. 1.14.
[h] Ps. 80.5.
[i] Lam. 3.15.
11 Or, hemlock.
[j] Lev. 26.33. Deut. 28.64.
[k] Eze. 5.2.
[l] Eccl. 12.5. Amos 5.16. Matt. 9.23.
[m] ch. 14.17. Lam. 1.16.
[n] Lev. 18.28.
[o] Ps. 33.16. Eccl. 9.11. Isa. 5.21. Rom. 1.22.
[p] Ps. 20.7. 1 Cor. 1.31.
[q] Micah 3.2.
[r] Amos 3.2.
12 visit upon.
13 cut off into corners, or, having the corners of their hair polled.
[s] Lev. 26.41. Acts 7.51. Rom. 2.28.

15 Therefore thus saith the LORD
hosts, the God of Israel; Behold
will [h]feed them, *even* this people, w
[i]wormwood, and give them water
[11]gall to drink.
16 I will [j]scatter them also amo
the heathen, whom neither they n
their fathers have known: and [k]I w
send a sword after them, till I ha
consumed them.
17 ¶ Thus saith the LORD of hos
Consider ye, and call for the [l]mour
ing women, that they may come; a
send for cunning *women*, that th
may come:
18 And let them make haste, a
take up a wailing for us, that [m]o
eyes may run down with tears, a
our eyelids gush out with waters.
19 For a voice of wailing is heard o
of Zion, How are we spoiled! we a
greatly confounded, because we ha
forsaken the land, because our [n]dwe
ings have cast *us* out.
20 Yet hear the word of the LOR
O ye women, and let your ear recei
the word of his mouth, and teach yo
daughters wailing, and every one h
neighbour lamentation.
21 For death is come up into o
windows, *and* is entered into o
palaces, to cut off the children fro
without, *and* the young men from t
streets.
22 Speak, Thus saith the LORD, Ev
the carcases of men shall fall as du
upon the open field, and as the han
ful after the harvestman, and no
shall gather *them.*
23 ¶ Thus saith the LORD, [o]Let n
the wise *man* glory in his wisdo
neither let the mighty *man* glory in h
might, let not the rich *man* glory in h
riches:
24 But [p]let him that glorieth glory
this, that he understandeth and kno
eth me, that I *am* the LORD which exe
cise lovingkindness, judgment, a
righteousness, in the earth: [q]for
these *things* I delight, saith t
LORD.
25 ¶ Behold, the days come saith t
LORD, [r]that I will [12]punish all *the*
which are circumcised with the u
circumcised;
26 Egypt, and Judah, and Ē-do
and the children of Ammon, a
Moab, and all *that are* [13]in t
utmost corners, that dwell in t
wilderness: for all *these* nations *a*
uncircumcised, and all the hou
of Israel *are* [s]uncircumcised in t
heart.

CHAPTER 10

EAR ye the word which the LORD
speaketh unto you, O house of
ael:
Thus saith the LORD, [a]Learn not
way of the heathen, and be not dis-
yed at the signs of heaven; for the
athen are dismayed at them.
For the [1]customs of the people *are*
in: for *one* cutteth a tree out of the
est, the work of the hands of the
rkman, with the axe.
They deck it with silver and with
ld; they fasten it with nails and with
mmers, that it move not.
They *are* upright as the palm tree,
ut speak not: they must needs be
orne, because they cannot go. Be
t afraid of them; for they cannot
evil, neither also *is it* in them to do
od.
Forasmuch as *there is* none [d]like
to thee, O LORD; thou *art* great, and
name *is* great in might.
Who [e]would not fear thee, O King
nations? for [2]to thee doth it apper-
n: forasmuch as among all the wise
n of the nations, and in all their
ngdoms, *there is* none like unto
ee.
But they are [3]altogether brutish and
olish: the stock *is* a doctrine of van-
es.
Silver spread into plates is brought
om Tarshish, and [f]gold from U-
ăz, the work of the workman,
d of the hands of the founder:
ue and purple *is* their clothing:
ey *are* all the work of cunning
n.
0 But the LORD *is* the [4]true God, he
the [g]living God, and an [5]everlasting
ng: at his wrath the earth shall trem-
e, and the nations shall not be able
abide his indignation.
1 [6]Thus shall ye say unto them, The
ds that have not made the heavens
d the earth, *even* they shall perish
om the earth, and from under these
avens.
2 He [h]hath made the earth by his
wer, he hath established the world
his wisdom, and hath stretched out
e heavens by his discretion.
3 When he uttereth his voice, *there*
[7]multitude of waters in the heavens,
d he causeth the vapours to ascend
om the ends of the earth; he maketh
htnings [8]with rain, and bringeth
rth the wind out of his treasures.
4 Every man [9]is brutish in *his* know-
lge: every founder is confounded by
e graven image: for his molten im-

CHAP. 10
a Lev. 20.23.
1 statutes, or, ordinances are vanity.
b Ps. 115.5. Hab. 2.19.
c Ps. 115.7.
d Ex. 8.9. Ps. 86.8,10.
e Rev. 15.4.
2 Or, it liketh thee.
3 in one, or, at once.
f Dan. 10.5.
4 God of truth.
g 1 Tim. 6.17.
5 king of eternity, Isa. 57.15.
6 In the Chaldean language.
h Gen. 1.1,6. Job 38.4. Ps. 89.11. Ps. 136.5. Isa. 40.28. ch. 51.15. Acts 14.15.
7 Or, noise.
8 Or, for rain.
9 Or, is more brutish than to know.
i Ps. 16.5. Ps. 73.26. ch. 51.19. Lam. 3.24.
j Deut. 32.9. Ps. 74.2.
10 inhabitress.
k Eze. 6.10.
l Micah 7.9.
m Ps. 17.5. Ps. 119.116, 117. Pro. 16.1.
n Ps. 6.1. ch. 30.11. Hab. 3.2.
11 diminish me.
o Job 18.21. 1 Thes. 4.5. 2 Thes. 1.8.
CHAP. 11
a Deut. 27. 26. Deut. 28.15, etc. Gal. 3.10.
b Lev. 26.3.
c Deut. 7.12. Ps. 105.9.

age *is* falsehood, and *there is* no
breath in them.
15 They *are* vanity, *and* the work of
errors: in the time of their visitation
they shall perish.
16 The [i]portion of Jacob *is* not like
them: for he *is* the former of all *things;*
and [j]Israel *is* the rod of his inheritance: The LORD of hosts *is* his name.
17 ¶ Gather up thy wares out of the
land, O [10]inhabitant of the fortress.
18 For thus saith the LORD, Behold,
I will sling out the inhabitants of the
the land at this once, and will distress
them, [k]that they may find *it so*.
19 ¶ Woe is me for my hurt! my
wound is grievous: but I said, Truly
this *is* a grief, [l]and I must bear it.
20 My tabernacle is spoiled, and all
my cords are broken: my children are
gone forth of me, and they *are* not:
there is none to stretch forth my tent
any more, and to set up my curtains.
21 For the pastors are become brutish, and have not sought the LORD:
therefore they shall not prosper, and
all their flocks shall be scattered.
22 Behold, the noise of the bruit is
come, and a great commotion out of
the north country, to make the cities
of Judah desolate, *and* a den of dragons.
23 ¶ O LORD, I know that [m]the way
of man *is* not in himself: *it is* not in
man that walketh to direct his steps.
24 O LORD, [n]correct me, but with
judgment; not in thine anger, lest
thou [11]bring me to nothing.
25 Pour out thy fury upon the heathen
that [o]know thee not, and upon the
families that call not on thy name:
for they have eaten up Jacob, and devoured him, and consumed him, and
have made his habitation desolate.

CHAPTER 11

THE word that came to Jeremiah
from the LORD, saying,
2 Hear ye the words of this covenant,
and speak unto the men of Judah, and
to the inhabitants of Jerusalem;
3 And say thou unto them, Thus
saith the LORD God of Israel; Cursed
[a]*be* the man that obeyeth not the
words of this covenant,
4 Which I commanded your fathers
in the day *that* I brought them forth
out of the land of Egypt, from the iron
furnace, saying, [b]Obey my voice, and
do them, according to all which I
command you: so shall ye be my people, and I will be your God:
5 That I may perform the [c]oath

which I have sworn unto your fathers,
to give them a land flowing with milk
and honey, as *it is* this day. Then answered I, and said, [1]So be it, O LORD.
6 Then the LORD said unto me, Proclaim all these words in the cities of
Judah, and in the streets of Jerusalem, saying, Hear ye the words of this
covenant, [d]and do them.
7 For I earnestly protested unto your
fathers in the day *that* I brought them
up out of the land of Egypt, *even* unto
this day, rising early and protesting,
saying, Obey my voice.
8 Yet they obeyed not, nor inclined
their ear, but walked every one in the
[2]imagination of their evil heart: therefore I will bring upon them all the
words of this covenant, which I commanded *them* to do; but they did *them*
not.
9 And the LORD said unto me, A
[e]conspiracy is found among the men
of Judah, and among the inhabitants
of Jerusalem.
10 They are turned back to [f]the iniquities of their forefathers, which refused to hear my words; and they
went after other gods to serve them:
the house of Israel and the house of
Judah have broken my covenant
which I made with their fathers.
11 ¶ Therefore thus saith the LORD,
Behold, I will bring evil upon them,
which they shall not be able [3]to escape; and [g]though they shall cry unto
me, I will not hearken unto them.
12 Then shall the cities of Judah and
inhabitants of Jerusalem go, and [h]cry
unto the gods unto whom they offer
incense: but they shall not save them
at all in the time of their [4]trouble.
13 For *according to* the number of
thy cities were thy gods, O Judah; and
according to the number of the streets
of Jerusalem have ye set up altars to
that [5]shameful thing, *even* altars to
burn incense unto Bā-ăl.
14 Therefore [i]pray not thou for this
people, neither lift up a cry or prayer
for them: for I will not hear *them* in
the time that they cry unto me for
their [6]trouble.
15 [7]What hath my beloved to do in
mine house, *seeing* she hath wrought
[j]lewdness with many, and [k]the holy
flesh is passed from thee? [8]when thou
doest evil, then thou rejoicest.
16 The LORD called thy name, [l]A
green olive tree, fair, *and* of goodly
fruit: with the noise of a great tumult
he hath kindled fire upon it, and the
branches of it are broken.
17 For the LORD of hosts, [m]t
planted thee, hath pronounced
against thee, for the evil of the ho
of Israel and of the house of Jud
which they have done against the
selves to provoke me to anger in of
ing incense unto Bā-ăl.
18 ¶ And the LORD hath given
knowledge *of it*, and I know *it*: th
thou shewedst me their doings.
19 But I *was* like a lamb *or* an ox *t*
is brought to the slaughter; an
knew not that they had devised
vices against me, *saying*, Let us
stroy [9]the tree with the fruit there
[n]and let us cut him off from the land
the living, that his name may be
more remembered.
20 But, O LORD of hosts, [o]that j
gest righteously, that [p]triest the re
and the heart, let me see thy vengea
on them: for unto thee have I revea
my cause.
21 Therefore thus saith the LORD
the men of [q]Ăn-ă-thōth, that seek t
life, saying, [r]Prophesy not in the na
of the LORD, that thou die not by
hand:
22 Therefore thus saith the LORD
hosts, Behold, I will [10]punish the
the young men shall die by the swo
their sons and their daughters sh
die by famine:
23 And there shall be no remnant
them: for I will bring evil upon t
men of Ăn-ă-thōth, *even* [s]the year
their visitation.

CHAPTER 12

RIGHTEOUS [a]*art* thou, O LOR
when I plead with thee: yet [1]let
talk with thee of *thy* judgmen
[b]Wherefore doth the way of the wic
ed prosper? *wherefore* are all th
happy that deal very treacherousl
2 Thou hast planted them, yea, th
have taken root: [2]they grow, yea, th
bring forth fruit: [c]thou *art* near
their mouth, and far from their rei
3 But thou, O LORD, knowest m
thou hast seen me, and tried mi
heart [3]toward thee: pull them out li
sheep for the slaughter, and prepa
them for [d]the day of slaughter.
4 How long shall the land mour
and the herbs of every field wither, f
[e]the wickedness of them that dw
therein? the [f]beasts are consume
and the birds; because they said, I
shall not see our last end.
5 ¶ If thou hast run with the footme
and they have wearied thee, then h
canst thou contend with horses? a

1 Amen, Deut. 27.15.
d John 13.17. Rom. 2.13.
2 Or, stubbornness.
e Eze. 22.25. Hos. 6.9.
f Judg. 2.11. Eze. 20.18.
3 to go forth of.
g Ps. 18.41. Pro. 1.28. Isa. 1.15. ch. 14.12. Micah 3.4. Zech. 7.13.
h Deut. 32. 37. 2 Chr. 28.22, 23. Isa. 45.20.
4 evil.
5 shame.
i Ex. 32.10. ch. 7.16.
6 evil.
7 What is to my beloved in my house?
j Eze. 16.25.
k Hag. 2.12. Titus 1.15.
8 Or, when thy evil is.
l Ps. 52.8.
m Ps. 44.2. Isa. 5.2.
9 the stalk with his bread.
n Ps. 83.4.
o Ps. 7.8. Acts 17.31.
p 1 Sam. 16. 7. 1 Chr. 28.9. Ps. 7.9.
q ch. 1.1.
r Amos 2.12.
10 visit upon.
s Luke 19.44.

CHAP. 12

a Gen. 18.25.
1 Or, let me reason the case with thee.
b Job 12.6.
2 they go on.
c Isa. 29.13.
3 with thee.
d Jas. 5.5.
e Ps. 107.34.
f ch. 4.25. Hosea 4.3.

ı the land of peace, *wherein* thou
ıtedst, *they wearied thee*, then how
thou do in [g]the swelling of Jor-
?
'or even thy brethren, and the
ıse of thy father, even they have
lt treacherously with thee; yea,
y have called a multitude after
: believe them not, though they
ak [5]fair words unto thee.
I have forsaken mine house, I
e left mine heritage; I have given
dearly beloved of my soul into the
ıd of her enemies.
Mine heritage is unto me as a lion
he forest; it [7]crieth out against me:
refore [h]have I hated it.
Mine heritage *is* unto me *as* a
ckled bird, the birds round about
against her; come ye, assemble all
beasts of the field, [9]come to de-
r.
Many [i]pastors have destroyed my
eyard, they have [k]trodden my por-
under foot, they have made my
easant portion a desolate wilder-
s.
They have made it desolate, *and*
ıg desolate it mourneth unto me;
whole land is made desolate, be-
se [l]no man layeth *it* to heart.
The spoilers are come upon all
h places through the wilderness:
the sword of the LORD shall de-
r from the *one* end of the land even
he *other* end of the land: no flesh
ll have peace.
They [m]have sown wheat, but shall
p thorns: they have put them-
es to pain, *but* shall not profit: and
ey shall be ashamed of your reven-
because of the fierce anger of the
RD.
¶ Thus saith the LORD against all
ne evil neighbours, [n]that touch the
eritance which I have caused my
ple Israel to inherit; Behold, [o]I
l pluck them out of their land, and
ck out the house of Judah from
ong them.
And [p]it shall come to pass, after
t I have plucked them out I will re-
n, and have compassion on them,
d will bring them again, every man
his heritage, and every man to his
d.
And it shall come to pass, if they
l diligently learn the ways of my
ople, [r]to swear by my name, The
RD liveth; as they taught my people
[s]swear by Bā-ăl; then shall they be
ilt in the midst of my people.
7 But if they will not [u]obey, I will
utterly pluck up and destroy that nation, saith the LORD.

CHAPTER 13

THUS saith the LORD unto me, Go
and get thee a linen girdle, and put
it upon thy loins, and put it not in
water.
2 So I got a girdle according to the
word of the LORD, and put *it* on my
loins.
3 And the word of the LORD came
unto me the second time, saying,
4 Take the girdle that thou hast got,
which *is* upon thy loins, and arise, go
to [a]Eû-phrā-tēs, and hide it there in a
hole of the rock.
5 So I went, and hid it by Eû-phrā-
tēs, as the LORD commanded me.
6 And it came to pass after many
days, that the LORD said unto me,
Arise, go to Eû-phrā-tēs, and take the
girdle from thence, which I commanded thee to hide there.
7 Then I went to Eû-phrā-tēs, and
digged, and took the girdle from the
place where I had hid it: and, behold,
the girdle was marred, it was [b]profit-
able for nothing.
8 Then the word of the LORD came
unto me, saying,
9 Thus saith the LORD, After this
manner will [c]I mar the pride of Judah,
and the great pride of Jerusalem.
10 This evil people, which [d]refuse to
hear my words, which [e]walk in the
[1]imagination of their heart, and walk
after other gods, to serve them, and to
worship them, shall even be as this
girdle, which is good for nothing.
11 For as the girdle cleaveth to the
loins of a man, so have I caused to
cleave unto me the whole house of Israel and the whole house of Judah,
saith the LORD; that [f]they might be
unto me for a people, and [g]for a name,
and for a praise, and for a glory: but
they would not hear.
12 ¶ Therefore thou shalt speak unto
them this word; Thus saith the LORD
God of Israel, Every bottle shall be
filled with wine: and they shall say unto thee, Do we not certainly know
that every bottle shall be filled with
wine?
13 Then shalt thou say unto them,
Thus saith the LORD, Behold, I will
fill all the inhabitants of this land,
even the kings that sit upon David's
throne, and the priests, and the prophets, and all the inhabitants of Jerusalem, [h]with drunkennness.
14 And I will dash them [2]one against

g 1 Chr. 12. 15. ch. 49.19.
4 Or, they cried after thee fully.
5 good things.
6 the love.
7 giveth out his voice, or, yelleth.
h 2 Chr. 36. 16.
8 Or, taloned.
9 Or, cause them to come.
i ch. 6.3.
j Isa. 5.1,5.
k Isa. 63.18.
10 portion of desire.
l Isa. 42.25. Mal. 2.2.
m Lev. 26.16.
11 Or, ye.
n Zech. 2.8, 10.
o Deut. 30.3. ch. 32.37.
p Eze. 28.25.
q Amos 9.14.
r ch. 4.2.
s Josh. 23.7. Zeph. 1.5.
t 1 Cor. 3.9, 10. Eph. 2.20. 1 Pet. 2.5.
u Ps. 2.8,9. Isa. 60.12. Luke 19.27. 1 Pet. 2.8.

CHAP. 13

a Ps. 137.1. Micah 4.10.
b Isa. 64.6. ch. 24.8. Lam. 3.45.
c Lev. 26.19.
d 2 Chr. 36. 15,16.
e ch. 9.14. ch. 11.8.
1 Or, stubbornness.
f Gen. 17.7. Ex. 19.5.
g ch. 33.9.
h Ps. 60.3. Isa. 63.6. ch. 25.27. Eze. 23.32-34. Rev. 14.10.
2 a man against his brother.

another, even the fathers and the sons
together, saith the LORD: I will not
pity, nor spare, nor have mercy, [3]but
destroy them.
15 ¶ Hear [i]ye, and give ear; be not
proud: for the LORD hath spoken.
16 Give [j]glory to the LORD your God,
before he cause [k]darkness, and before
your feet stumble upon the dark
mountains, and, while ye look [l]for
light, he turn it [m]into the shadow
of death, *and* make *it* gross darkness.
17 But if ye will not hear it, my soul
shall weep in secret places for *your*
pride; and mine eye shall weep sore,
and run down with tears, because the
LORD's flock is carried away
captive.
18 Say unto [n]the king and to the
queen, Humble yourselves, sit down:
for your [4]principalities shall come
down, *even* the crown of your glory.
19 The cities of the south shall be
shut up, and none shall open *them*:
Judah shall be carried away captive
[o]all of it, it shall be wholly carried
away captive.
20 Lift up your eyes, and behold
them that [p]come from the north:
where *is* the flock *that* was given thee,
thy beautiful flock?
21 What wilt thou say when he shall
[5]punish thee? for thou hast taught
them *to be* captains, *and* as chief over
thee: shall not sorrows take thee, as a
woman in travail?
22 ¶ And if thou say in thine heart,
Wherefore [q]come these things upon
me? For the greatness of thine iniquity are [r]thy skirts discovered, *and*
thy heels [6]made bare.
23 Can the Ē-thĭ-ō-pĭ-ăn change his
skin, or the leopard his spots? *then*
may ye also do good, that are [7]accus-
tomed to do evil.
24 Therefore will I scatter them as
the stubble that passeth away by the
wind of the wilderness.
25 This [s]*is* thy lot, the portion of thy
measures from me, saith the LORD;
because thou hast forgotten me, and
trusted in [t]falsehood.
26 Therefore [u]will I discover thy
skirts upon thy face, that thy shame
may appear.
27 I have seen thine adulteries, and
[v]thy neighings, the lewdness of thy
whoredom, *and* thine abominations [w]on the hills in the fields. Woe
unto thee, O Jerusalem! wilt thou
not be made clean? [8]when *shall it*
once *be*?

3 from destroying them.
i Deut. 32.29.
j Josh. 7.19. 1 Sam. 6.5. Joel 2.12.
k Isa. 5.30. Amos 8.9.
l Isa. 59.9.
m Ps. 44.19.
n 2 Ki. 24.12.
4 Or, head tires.
o Lev. 26.31.
p ch. 6.22.
5 visit upon.
q ch. 16.10.
r Isa. 47.2. Nah. 3.5.
6 Or, shall be violently taken away.
7 taught.
s Job 20.29.
t ch. 10.14. Micah 3.11.
u Lam. 1.8. Hosea 2.10.
v ch. 5.8.
w Isa. 65.7. ch. 2.20.
8 after when yet?

CHAP. 14

1 the words of the dearths, or, restraints.
a Isa. 3.26.
b Ex. 11.6. Pro. 21.13. Isa. 15.3,4.
2 Or, cisterns.
c Ps. 40.14.
d 2 Sam. 15. 30.
e ch. 2.24.
f Ps. 25.11.
g ch. 17.13. Acts 28.20. 1 Tim. 1.1.
h Ps. 46.1.
i Isa. 59.1.
j Ex. 29.45.
3 thy name is called upon us.
k 1 Ki. 17.18. Ps. 109.14. Hosea 8.13. Heb. 8.12.
l Ex. 32.10. ch. 7.16.
m Pro. 1.28. Isa. 1.15. ch. 11.11. Micah 3.4.
4 peace of truth.
n Isa. 30.10. ch. 23.21. 2 Thes. 2.9-11.

CHAPTER 14

THE word of the LORD that ca
to Jeremiah concerning [1]
dearth.
2 Judah mourneth, and [a]the ga
thereof languish; they are black u
the ground; and [b]the cry of Jerusa
is gone up.
3 And their nobles have sent t
little ones to the waters: they cam
the [2]pits, *and* found no water; they
turned with their vessels empty; t
were [c]ashamed and confounded, [d]a
covered their heads.
4 Because the ground is chapt,
there was no rain in the earth,
plowmen were ashamed, they cove
their heads.
5 Yea, the hind also calved in
field, and forsook *it*, because th
was no grass.
6 And [e]the wild asses did stand
the high places, they snuffed up
wind like dragons; their eyes did f
because *there was* no grass.
7 ¶ O LORD, though our iniqui
testify against us, do thou *it* [f]for
name's sake: for our backslidings
many; we have sinned against the
8 O [g]the hope of Israel, [h]the savi
thereof in time of trouble, w
shouldest thou be as a stranger in
land, and as a wayfaring man *t*
turneth aside to tarry for a night?
9 Why shouldest thou be as a m
astonied, as a mighty man [i]*that* ca
not save? yet thou, [j]O LORD, *art*
the midst of us, and [3]we are called
thy name; leave us not.
10 ¶ Thus saith the LORD unto t
people, Thus have they loved to wa
der, they have not refrained their fe
therefore the LORD doth not acc
them; [k]he will now remember their
iquity, and visit their sins.
11 Then said the LORD unto m
Pray [l]not for this people for *th*
good.
12 When [m]they fast, I will not h
their cry; and when they offer bu
offering and an oblation, I will
accept them: but I will consume th
by the sword, and by the famine, a
by the pestilence.
13 ¶ Then said I, Ah, Lord G
behold, the prophets say unto the
Ye shall not see the sword, neit
shall ye have famine; but I will g
you [4]assured peace in this place.
14 Then the LORD said unto me, T
prophets prophesy lies in my nan
[n]I sent them not, neither have I co
manded them, neither spake u

em: they prophesy unto you a false
sion and divination, and a thing of
ought, and the deceit of their heart.
5 Therefore thus saith the LORD
ncerning the prophets that proph-
y in my name, and I sent them not,
t they say, Sword and famine shall
t be in this land; By sword and
mine shall [o]those prophets be con-
med.
6 And the people to whom they
ophesy shall be [p]cast out in the
reets of Jerusalem because of the
mine and the sword; and [q]they shall
ve none to bury them, them, their
ves, nor their sons, nor their daugh-
rs: for I will pour their wickedness
on them.
7 ¶ Therefore thou shalt say this
ord unto them; [r]Let mine eyes run
wn with tears night and day, and
t them not cease: [s]for the virgin
ughter of my people is broken with
great breach, with a very grievous
ow.
8 If I go forth into the [t]field, then
hold the slain with the sword! and
I enter into the city, then behold
em that are sick with famine! yea,
th the prophet and the priest [5]go
out into a land that they know not.
9 Hast [u]thou utterly rejected Judah?
th thy soul lothed Zion? why hast
ou smitten us, and *there is* no heal-
g for us? we looked for peace, and
ere is no good; and for the time of
aling, and behold trouble!
0 We [v]acknowledge, O LORD, our
ickedness, *and* the iniquity of our
thers: for we [w]have sinned against
ee.
1 Do not abhor *us*, for thy name's
ke, do not disgrace the [x]throne of
y glory: remember, break not thy
venant with us.
2 Are there *any* among the vanities
the Gentiles that can cause rain?
can the heavens give showers? [y]*art*
t thou he, O LORD our God? there-
re we will wait upon thee: for thou
st made all these *things*.

CHAPTER 15

HEN said the LORD unto me,
Though [a]Moses and [b]Samuel
ood before me, *yet* my mind *could*
t *be* toward this people: cast *them*
t of my sight, and let them go forth.
And it shall come to pass, if they
y unto thee, Whither shall we go
rth? then thou shalt tell them, Thus
ith the LORD; [c]Such as *are* for
ath, to death; and such as *are* for

o ch. 23.15.
p Matt. 15. 14.
q Ps. 79.3.
r Lam. 1.16.
s ch. 8.21.
t Eze. 7.15.
5 Or, make merchandise against a land, and men acknowledge it not.
u 2 Ki. 17.20. Ps. 78.59. Lam. 5.22.
v Ezra 9.5. 1 John 1.9.
w Dan. 9.8.
x ch. 17.12.
y Isa. 30.23.

CHAP. 15

a Ex. 32.11.
b 1 Sam. 7.9.
c Zech. 11.9.
d Lev. 26.16.
1 families.
e Deut. 28.26.
2 I will give them for a removing.
f Eze. 23.46.
g 2 Ki. 21.11.
h Isa. 51.19.
3 to ask of thy peace?
i Hos. 13.14.
4 Or, whatsoever is dear.
j Isa. 9.13. ch. 5.3.
5 Or, against the mother city a young man spoiling, etc., or, against the mother and the young men.
k 1 Sam. 2.5. Isa. 47.9.
l Amos 8.9.
m Job 3.1.
6 Or, I will entreat the enemy for thee.
n Ps. 44.12. Isa. 52.3. ch. 17.3.
o Deut. 32.22.

the sword, to the sword; and such as
are for the famine, to the famine; and
such as *are* for the captivity, to the
captivity.
3 And I will [d]appoint over them four
[1]kinds, saith the LORD: the sword to
slay, and the dogs to tear, and [e]the
fowls of the heaven, and the beasts of
the earth, to devour and destroy.
4 And [2]I will cause them to [f]be removed into all kingdoms of the earth,
because of Mă-năs´-sēh [g]the son of
Hĕz-ē-kī´-ăh king of Judah, for *that*
which he did in Jerusalem.
5 For [h]who shall have pity upon thee,
O Jerusalem? or who shall bemoan
thee? or who shall go aside [3]to ask
how thou doest?
6 Thou hast forsaken me, saith the
LORD, thou art gone backward:
therefore will I stretch out my hand
against thee, and destroy thee; [i]I am
weary with repenting.
7 And I will fan them with a fan in
the gates of the land; I will bereave
them of [4]children, I will destroy my
people, *since* [j]they return not from
their ways.
8 Their widows are increased to me
above the sand of the seas: I have
brought upon them [5]against the
mother of the young men a spoiler at
noonday: I have caused *him* to fall
upon it suddenly, and terrors upon
the city.
9 She [k]that hath borne seven languisheth: she hath given up the ghost;
[l]her sun is gone down while *it was* yet
day: she hath been ashamed and confounded: and the residue of them will
I deliver to the sword before their enemies, saith the LORD.
10 ¶ Woe [m]is me, my mother, that
thou hast borne me a man of strife
and a man of contention to the whole
earth! I have neither lent on usury,
nor men have lent to me on usury;
yet every one of them doth curse
me.
11 The LORD said, Verily it shall be
well with thy remnant; verily [6]I will
cause the enemy to entreat thee *well*
in the time of evil and in the time of
affliction.
12 Shall iron break the northern iron
and the steel?
13 Thy substance and thy treasures
will I give to the [n]spoil without price,
and *that* for all thy sins, even in all
thy borders.
14 And I will make *thee* to pass with
thine enemies into a land *which* thou
knowest not: for [o]a fire is kindled in

mine anger, *which* shall burn upon
you.
15 ¶ O LORD, [p]thou knowest: remember me, and visit me, [q]and revenge me of my persecutors; take
me not away in thy longsuffering:
know that [r]for thy sake I have suffered
rebuke.
16 Thy words were found, and I did
[s]eat them; and [t]thy word was unto me
the joy and rejoicing of mine heart:
for [7]I am called by thy name, O LORD
God of hosts.
17 I [u]sat not in the assembly of the
mockers, nor rejoiced; I sat alone because of thy hand: for thou hast filled
me with indignation.
18 Why is my pain [v]perpetual, and
my wound incurable, *which* refuseth
to be healed? wilt thou be altogether
unto me as a liar, *and* [w]*as* waters *that*
[8]fail?
19 ¶ Therefore thus saith the LORD,
[x]If thou return, then will I bring thee
again, *and* thou shalt stand before me:
and if thou [y]take forth the precious
from the vile, thou shalt be as my
mouth: let them return unto thee; but
return not thou unto them.
20 And I will make thee unto this
people a fenced brasen wall: and they
shall fight against thee, but they shall
not prevail against thee: for I *am*
with thee to save thee and to deliver
thee, saith the LORD.
21 And I will [z]deliver thee out of the
hand of the wicked, and I will redeem
thee out of the hand of the terrible.

CHAPTER 16

THE word of the LORD came also
unto me, saying,
2 Thou [a]shalt not take thee a wife,
neither shalt thou have sons or daughters in this place.
3 For thus saith the LORD concerning the sons and concerning the
daughters that are born in this place,
and concerning their mothers that
bare them, and concerning their fathers that begat them in this land;
4 They shall die of grievous deaths;
they shall not be lamented; neither
shall they be buried; *but* they shall be
as dung upon the face of the earth:
and they shall be consumed by the
sword, and by famine; and their carcases shall be meat for the fowls of
heaven, and for the beasts of the earth.
5 For thus saith the LORD, [b]Enter
not into the house of [1]mourning,
neither go to lament nor bemoan
them: for I have taken away my peace

p Job 10.7. Ps. 17.3. ch. 12.3. John 21.15, 17.
q ch. 11.20.
r Ps. 69.7. Matt. 5.10-12. 1 Pet. 4.14-16.
s Eze. 3.1.
t Job 23.12.
7 thy name is called upon me.
u Ps. 1.1.
v ch. 30.15.
w Job 6.15.
8 be not sure?
x Zech. 3.7.
y Eze. 22.26.
z Isa. 49.25.

CHAP. 16

a Gen. 19.14.
b Ps. 78.64. Eze. 24.17.
1 Or, mourning feast.
c Deut. 14.1.
d Isa. 22.12.
2 Or, break bread for them.
e Pro. 31.6.
f Isa. 24.7. ch. 7.34. Hosea 2.11. Rev. 18.23.
g Deut. 29. 24. ch. 5.19. ch. 13.22.
h Judg. 2.12, 13. 1 Ki. 9.9. 2 Chr. 7.22. Neh. 9.26-29. Ps. 106.35-41. ch. 5.7,9. Dan. 9.10-12.
i ch. 7.26. 2 Tim. 3.13.
3 Or, stubbornness.
j Lev. 18.27, 28. Deut. 4.26. 2 Chr. 7.20.
k ch. 15.14.
4 Or, Nevertheless.
l Amos 4.2. Hab. 1.15.

from this people, saith the LORD, *eve*
lovingkindness and mercies.
6 Both the great and the small sha
die in this land: they shall not b
buried, neither shall *men* lament fo
them, nor [c]cut themselves, nor [d]mak
themselves bald for them:
7 Neither shall *men* [2]tear *themselve*
for them in mourning, to comfo
them for the dead; neither shall *me*
give them the cup [e]of consolation t
drink for their father or for the
mother.
8 Thou shalt not also go into th
house of feasting, to sit with them t
eat and to drink.
9 For thus saith the LORD of host
the God of Israel; Behold, [f]I wi
cause to cease out of this place in you
eyes, and in your days, the voice o
mirth, and the voice of gladness, th
voice of the bridegroom, and th
voice of the bride.
10 ¶ And it shall come to pass, whe
thou shalt shew this people all thes
words, and they shall say unto the
[g]Wherefore hath the LORD pronoun
ed all this great evil against us? o
what *is* our iniquity? or what *is* ou
sin that we have committed again
the LORD our God?
11 Then shalt thou say unto then
[h]Because your fathers have forsake
me, saith the LORD, and have walke
after other gods, and have serve
them, and have worshipped then
and have forsaken me, and have n
kept my law;
12 And ye have done [i]worse tha
your fathers; for, behold, ye wal
every one after the [3]imagination o
his evil heart, that they may not heark
en unto me:
13 Therefore [j]will I cast you out o
this land [k]into a land that ye kno
not, *neither* ye nor your fathers; an
there shall ye serve other gods da
and night; where I will not shew yo
favour.
14 ¶ [4]Therefore, behold, the day
come, saith the LORD, that it shall n
more be said, The LORD liveth, th
brought up the children of Israel o
of the land of Egypt;
15 But, The LORD liveth, th
brought up the children of Israel fro
the land of the north, and from all t
lands whither he had driven then
and I will bring them again into the
land that I gave unto their fathers.
16 ¶ Behold, I will send for ma
[l]fishers, saith the LORD, and they sha
fish them; and after will I send f

any hunters, and they shall hunt
em from every mountain, and from
ery hill, and out of the holes of the
cks.
7 For mine [m]eyes *are* upon all their
ays: they are not hid from my face,
ither is their iniquity hid from mine
es.
8 And [n]first I will recompense their
iquity and their sin double; because
ey [o]have defiled my land, they have
ed mine inheritance with the car-
ses of their detestable and abomin-
le things.
9 O LORD, [p]my strength, and my
rtress, and my refuge in the day of
fliction, the [q]Gentiles shall come un-
thee from the ends of the earth, and
all say, Surely our fathers have in-
rited lies, vanity, and *things* [r]where-
there is no profit.
0 Shall a man make gods unto him-
lf, and [s]they *are* no gods?
1 Therefore, behold, I will this once
use them to know, I will cause them
know mine hand and my might;
d they shall know that my name *is*
he LORD.

CHAPTER 17

HE sin of Judah *is* written with [a]a
pen of iron, *and* with the [1]point of
diamond: *it* [b]*is* graven upon the
ble of their heart, and upon the
rns of your altars;
Whilst their children remember
eir altars and their [c]groves by the
een trees upon the high hills.
O my mountain in the field, [d]I will
ve thy substance *and* all thy treasures
the spoil, *and* thy high places for
, throughout all thy borders.
And thou, even [2]thyself, shalt dis-
ntinue from thine heritage that I
ve thee; and I will cause thee to
rve thine enemies in the land [e]which
ou knowest not: for ye have kindled
fire in mine anger, *which* shall burn
r ever.
¶ Thus saith the LORD; [f]Cursed
the man that trusteth in man, and
aketh flesh his arm, and whose heart
parteth from the LORD.
For he shall be like the heath in the
sert, and [g]shall not see when good
meth; but shall inhabit the parched
aces in the wilderness, *in* a salt land
d not inhabited.
Blessed [h]*is* the man that trusteth
the LORD, and whose hope the
RD is.
For he shall be as a tree planted by
e waters, and *that* spreadeth out her

m Job 34.21. Pro. 5.21. ch. 32.19.
n Micah 4.10.
o Eze. 43.7.
p Ps. 18.2.
q Ps. 22.27. Isa. 2.2.
r Isa. 44.10.
s Isa. 37.19. Gal. 4.8.
5 Or, JEHOVAH. Ex. 15.3. Ps. 83.18. Amos 5.8.

CHAP. 17

a Job 19.24.
1 nail.
b Pro. 3.3. 2 Cor. 3.3.
c 2 Ki. 16.4. 2 Chr. 24.18. Isa. 1.29.
d ch. 15.13.
2 in thyself.
e ch. 16.13.
f Isa. 30.1.
g Job 20.17.
h Ps. 2.12. Pro. 16.20.
3 Or, restraint.
i Gen. 6.5.
j 1 Sam. 16.7. 1 Chr. 28.9. Ps. 7.9. Ps. 139.23, 24. Pro. 17.3. ch. 11.20. ch. 20.12. Rom. 8.27. Rev. 2.23.
k Ps. 62.12. ch. 32.19. Rom. 2.6.
4 Or, gathereth young which she hath not brought forth.
l Luke 12.20.
m Ps. 73.27. Isa. 1.28. Isa. 65.13. ch. 2.26. Eze. 16.63. Eze. 36.32. Dan. 12.2.
n Luke 10.20.
o Isa. 5.19. Eze. 12.22. Amos 5.18. 2 Pet. 3.4.
5 after thee.
6 break them with a double breach.
p Ps. 49.1. ch. 19.3. ch. 22.2. Eze. 2.7. Eze. 3.17. Hosea 5.1. Micah 3.1.
q Num. 15. 32. Neh. 13.19.

roots by the river, and shall not see
when heat cometh, but her leaf shall
be green; and shall not be careful in
the year of [3]drought, neither shall
cease from yielding fruit.
9 ¶ The [i]heart *is* deceitful above all
things, and desperately wicked: who
can know it?
10 I the LORD [j]search the heart, *I* try
the reins, [k]even to give every man according to his ways, *and* according to
the fruit of his doings.
11 *As* the partridge [4]sitteth *on eggs*,
and hatcheth *them* not; *so* he that getteth riches, and not by right, shall
leave them in the midst of his days,
and at his end shall be [l]a fool.
12 ¶ A glorious high throne from the
beginning *is* the place of our sanctuary.
13 O LORD, the hope of Israel, all
that [m]forsake thee shall be ashamed,
and they that depart from me shall be
[n]written in the earth, because they
have forsaken the LORD, the fountain
of living waters.
14 Heal me, O LORD, and I shall be
healed; save me, and I shall be saved:
for thou *art* my praise.
15 ¶ Behold, they say unto me,
Where [o]*is* the word of the LORD? let
it come now.
16 As for me, I have not hastened
from *being* a pastor [5]to follow thee:
neither have I desired the woeful day;
thou knowest: that which came out
of my lips was *right* before thee.
17 Be not a terror unto me: thou *art*
my hope in the day of evil.
18 Let them be confounded that persecute me, but let not me be confounded: let them be dismayed, but let not
me be dismayed: bring upon them the
day of evil, and [6]destroy them with
double destruction.
19 ¶ Thus said the LORD unto me;
Go and stand in the gate of the children of the people, whereby the kings
of Judah come in, and by the which
they go out, and in all the gates of
Jerusalem;
20 And say unto them, [p]Hear ye the
word of the LORD, ye kings of Judah,
and all Judah, and all the inhabitants
of Jerusalem, that enter in by these
gates:
21 Thus saith the LORD; [q]Take heed
to yourselves, and bear no burden on
the sabbath day, nor bring *it* in by the
gates of Jerusalem;
22 Neither carry forth a burden out
of your houses on the sabbath day,
neither do ye any work, but hallow ye

the sabbath day, as [r]I commanded your fathers.

23 But they obeyed not, neither inclined their ear, but made their neck stiff, that they might not hear, nor receive instruction.

24 And it shall come to pass, if ye diligently hearken unto me, saith the LORD, to bring in no burden through the gates of this city on the sabbath day, but hallow the sabbath day, to do no work therein;

25 Then [s]shall there enter into the gates of this city kings and princes sitting upon the throne of David, riding in chariots and on horses, they, and their princes, the men of Judah, and the inhabitants of Jerusalem: and this city shall remain for ever.

26 And they shall come from the cities of Judah, and from the places about Jerusalem, and from the land of Benjamin, and from the [t]plain, and from the mountains, and from the south, bringing burnt offerings, and sacrifices, and meat offerings, and incense, and bringing [u]sacrifices of praise, unto the house of the LORD.

27 But if ye will not hearken unto me to hallow the sabbath day, and not to bear a burden, even entering in at the gates of Jerusalem on the sabbath day; then [v]will I kindle a fire in the gates thereof, [w]and it shall devour the palaces of Jerusalem, and it shall not be quenched.

CHAPTER 18

THE word which came to Jeremiah from the LORD, saying,

2 Arise, and go down to the potter's house, and there I will cause thee to hear my words.

3 Then I went down to the potter's house, and, behold, he wrought a work on the [1]wheels.

4 And the vessel [2]that he made of clay was [a]marred in the hand of the potter: so he [3]made it again another vessel, as seemed good to the potter to make *it*.

5 Then the word of the LORD came to me, saying,

6 O house of Israel, [b]cannot I do with you as this potter? saith the LORD. Behold, [c]as the clay *is* in the potter's hand, so *are* ye in mine hand, O house of Israel.

7 *At what* instant I shall speak concerning a nation, and concerning a kingdom, to [d]pluck up, and to pull down, and to destroy *it;*

8 If [e]that nation, against whom I have pronounced, turn from th evil, [f]I will repent of the evil tha thought to do unto them.

9 And *at what* instant I shall spe concerning a nation, and concerni a kingdom, to build and to plant *it*

10 If it do evil in my sight, that obey not my voice, then I will repe of the good, wherewith I said I wou benefit them.

11 ¶ Now therefore go to, speak the men of Judah, and to the inhab ants of Jerusalem, saying, Thus sai the LORD; Behold, I frame evil agai you, and devise a device against yo [g]return ye now every one from his e way, and make your ways and yo doings good.

12 And they said, There is no hop but we will walk after our own devic and we will every one do the imagin tion of his evil heart.

13 Therefore thus saith the LOR Ask [h]ye now among the heathen, w hath heard such things: the virgin Israel hath done a very horrible thi

14 Will *a man* leave [4]the snow Lĕb-ă-nŏn *which cometh* from t rock of the field? *or* shall the co flowing waters that come from a other place be forsaken?

15 Because my people [i]hath forg ten me, they have burned incense [j]vanity, and they have caused them stumble in their ways *from* the [k]ancie paths, to walk in [l]paths, *in* a way n cast up;

16 To make their land [m]desolate, *a* a perpetual [n]hissing; every one th passeth thereby shall be astonishe and wag his head.

17 I [o]will scatter them [p]as with east wind before the enemy; I w shew them the back, and not the fa in the day of their calamity.

18 ¶ Then said they, [q]Come, and us devise devices against Jeremia [r]for the law shall not perish from t priest, nor counsel from the wise, n the word from the prophet. Com and let us smite him [5]with the tongu and let us not give heed to any of h words.

19 Give heed to me, O LORD, a hearken to the voice of them that co tend with me.

20 Shall [s]evil be recompensed f good? for [t]they have digged a pit f my soul. Remember that I stood b fore thee to speak good for them, *a* to turn away thy wrath from them

21 Therefore deliver up their childr to the famine, and [6]pour out the

r Ex. 20.8. Ex. 23.12. Ex. 31.13. Eze. 20.12.
s Deut. 4.40.
t Zech. 7.7.
u Ps. 107.22.
v Lam. 4.11. Amos 1.4.
w 2 Ki. 25.9.

CHAP. 18

1 Or, frames, or, seats.
2 Or, that he made was marred, as clay in the hand of the potter.
a Rom. 11.15.
3 returned and made.
b Isa. 45.9.
c Isa. 64.8.
d ch. 1.10.
e Judg. 10.15, 16. 2 Chr. 12.6, 7. Isa. 1.16-19. Eze. 18.21. Luke 13.3-5.
f Jonah 3.10.
g 2 Ki. 17.13. Isa. 1.16-19.
h ch. 2.10. 1 Cor. 5.1.
4 Or, my fields for a rock, or, for the snow of Lebanon? shall the running waters be forsaken for the strange cold waters?
i ch. 2.13.
j Deut. 32.21. ch. 10.15.
k ch. 6.16.
l Isa. 53.6.
m ch. 49.13.
n Deut. 29. 24. 1 Ki. 9.8. Lam. 2.15. Micah 6.16.
o ch. 13.24.
p Ps. 48.7.
q ch. 11.19. Acts 7.51. 2 Tim. 4.3.
r Lev. 10.11. Mal. 2.7.
5 Or, for the tongue.
s Ps. 109.4.
t Ps. 35.7.
6 pour them out.

ood by the force of the sword; and
: their wives be bereaved of their
ildren, and *be* widows; and let their
en be put to death; *let* their young
en *be* slain by the sword in battle.
2 Let a cry be heard from their
ouses, when thou shalt bring a troop
ddenly upon them: for they have
gged a pit to take me, and hid
ares for my feet.
3 Yet, LORD, thou knowest all their
unsel against me [7]to slay *me:* [u]for-
ve not their iniquity, neither blot
it their sin from thy sight, but let
em be overthrown before thee; deal
us with them in the time of thine
ger.

CHAPTER 19

THUS saith the LORD, Go and get
a potter's earthen bottle, and *take*
the ancients of the people, and of
he ancients of the priests;
And go forth unto [b]the valley of the
n of Hĭn-nŏm, which *is* by the entry
[1]the east gate, [c]and proclaim there
e words that I shall tell thee,
And say, Hear ye the word of the
ORD, O kings of Judah, and inhabit-
nts of Jerusalem; Thus saith the
ORD of hosts, the God of Israel; Beold, I will bring evil upon this place,
e which whosoever heareth, his ears
all tingle.
Because they [d]have forsaken me,
d have estranged this place, and
ave burned incense in it unto other
ods, whom neither they nor their
thers have known, nor the kings of
udah, and have filled this place with
he blood of innocents;
They have built also the high places
f Bā-ăl, to burn their sons with
re *for* burnt offerings unto Bā-ăl,
which I commanded not, nor spake
, neither came *it* into my mind:
Therefore, behold, the days come,
ith the LORD, that this place shall no
ore be called Tō-phĕt, nor [g]The val-
y of the son of Hĭn-nŏm, but The
alley of slaughter.
7 And I will make void the counsel
f Judah and Jerusalem in this place;
and I will cause them to fall by the
word before their enemies, and by
e hands of them that seek their lives:
nd their [i]carcases will I give to be
eat for the fowls of the heaven, and
or the beasts of the earth.
8 And I will make this [j]city desolate,
nd an hissing; every one that passeth
ereby shall be astonished and hiss
ecause of all the plagues thereof.
9 And I will cause them to eat [k]the

7 for death.
u Neh. 4.5.

CHAP. 19

a Eze. 8.11.
b Josh. 15.8. 2 Ki. 23.10. 2 Chr. 28.3.
1 the sun gate.
c Pro. 1.20.
d Deut. 28. 20. Isa. 65.11. ch. 17.13.
e 2 Ki. 21.16.
f Lev. 18.21.
g Josh. 15.8.
h Lev. 26.17. Deut. 28.25. ch. 9.21.
i Deut. 28.26. Ps. 79.2. ch. 7.33. Rev. 19.18.
j Lev. 26.22. 1 Ki. 9.8. ch. 18.16. Lam. 2.15, 16. Zeph. 2.15.
k Lev. 26.29. Deut. 28.53. Isa. 9.20. Lam. 4.10.
l ch. 51.63.
m Ps. 2.9. Isa. 30.14. Lam. 4.2.
2 be healed.
n ch. 7.32.
o 2 Ki. 23.10.
p ch. 32.29. Zeph. 1.5.
q ch. 7.18.
r 2 Chr. 20.5.
s 2 Chr. 36. 16,17. ch. 7.26. Zech. 7.11-14. Acts 7.51, 52.

CHAP. 20

a 1 Chr. 24. 14.
1 That is, Fear round about.
b Job 18.11. ch. 6.25. ch. 46.5.

flesh of their sons and the flesh of their
daughters, and they shall eat every
one the flesh of his friend in the siege
and straitness, wherewith their enemies, and they that seek their lives,
shall straiten them.
10 Then [l]shalt thou break the bottle
in the sight of the men that go with
thee,
11 And shalt say unto them, Thus
saith the LORD of hosts; Even [m]so
will I break this people and this city,
as *one* breaketh a potter's vessel, that
cannot [2]be made whole again: and
they shall bury [n]*them* in Tō-phĕt, till
there be no place to bury.
12 Thus will I do unto this place,
saith the LORD, and to the inhabitants thereof, and *even* make this city
as Tō-phĕt:
13 And the houses of Jerusalem, and
the houses of the kings of Judah, shall
be defiled [o]as the place of Tō-phĕt, because of all the houses upon whose
[p]roofs they have burned incense unto
all the host of heaven, and have [q]pour-
ed out drink offerings unto other
gods.
14 Then came Jeremiah from Tō-
phĕt, whither the LORD had sent him
to prophesy; and he stood in [r]the
court of the LORD's house; and said
to all the people,
15 Thus saith the LORD of hosts, the
God of Israel; Behold, I will bring upon this city and upon all her towns all
the evil that I have pronounced
against it, because they [s]have hardened their necks, that they might not
hear my words.

CHAPTER 20

NOW Păsh-ŭr the son of [a]Ĭm-mĕr
the priest, who *was* also chief
governor in the house of the LORD,
heard that Jeremiah prophesied these
things.
2 Then Păsh-ŭr smote Jeremiah the
prophet, and put him in the stocks
that *were* in the high gate of Benjamin, which *was* by the house of the
LORD.
3 And it came to pass on the morrow,
that Păsh-ŭr brought forth Jeremiah
out of the stocks. Then said Jeremiah
unto him, The LORD hath not called
thy name Păsh-ŭr, but [1]Mā-gôr-mĭs-
sā-bĭb.
4 For thus saith the LORD, Behold,
I will make thee [b]a terror to thyself,
and to all thy friends: and they shall
fall by the sword of their enemies, and
thine eyes shall behold *it:* and I will

give all Judah into the hand of the king of Babylon, and he shall carry them captive into Babylon, and shall slay them with the sword.

5 Moreover I [c]will deliver all the [2]strength of this city, and all the labours thereof, and all the precious things thereof, and all the treasures of the kings of Judah will I give into the hand of their enemies, which shall spoil them, and take them, and carry them to Babylon.

6 And thou, Păsh-´ûr, and all that dwell in thine house shall go into captivity: and thou shalt come to Babylon, and there thou shalt die, and shalt be buried there, thou, and all thy friends, to whom thou hast [d]prophesied lies.

7 ¶ O LORD, thou hast deceived me, and I was [3]deceived: [e]thou art stronger than I, and hast prevailed: [f]I am in derision daily, every one mocketh me.

8 For since I spake, I cried out, I [g]cried violence and spoil; because the word of the LORD was made a reproach unto me, and a derision, daily.

9 Then I said, I will not make mention of him, nor speak any more in his name. But *his word* was in mine heart as a [h]burning fire shut up in my bones, and I was weary with forbearing, and [i]I could not *stay*.

10 ¶ For [j]I heard the defaming of many, fear on every side. Report, *say they*, and we will report it. [4]All my familiars watched for my halting, *saying*, Peradventure he will be enticed, and we shall prevail against him, and we shall take our revenge on him.

11 But the [k]LORD *is* with me as a mighty terrible one: therefore my persecutors shall stumble, and they shall not [l]prevail: they shall be greatly ashamed; for they shall not prosper: *their* everlasting confusion shall never be forgotten.

12 But, O LORD of hosts, [m]that triest the righteous, *and* seest the reins and the heart, [n]let me see thy vengeance on them: for unto thee have I opened my cause.

13 Sing unto the LORD, praise ye the LORD: for [o]he hath delivered the soul of the poor from the hand of evildoers.

14 ¶ Cursed [p]*be* the day wherein I was born: let not the day wherein my mother bare me be blessed.

15 Cursed *be* the man who brought tidings to my father, saying, A man child is born unto thee; making him very glad.

16 And let that man be as the cities

c 2 Ki. 20.17. ch. 3.24.
2 Or, wealth.
d ch. 14.13, 14. ch. 28.15.
3 Or, enticed.
e ch. 1.6,7.
f Job 12.4. Lam. 3.14.
g ch. 6.7.
h 1 Ki. 19.10. Ps. 39.3.
i Job 32.18, 19,20. Acts 18.5.
j Ps. 31.13.
4 Every man of my peace.
k Isa. 41.13. ch. 1.8. Rom. 8.31.
l ch. 15.20. ch. 17.18.
m ch. 11.20. ch. 17.10.
n Ps. 54.7. Ps. 59.10. Ps. 109.6-20. ch. 11.20. ch. 12.3. ch. 17.18.
o Ps. 35.9. Jas. 2.5,6.
p Job 3.3. ch. 15.10.
q Gen. 19.25.
r ch. 18.22.
s Job 3.10.
t Job 3.20.
u Lam. 3.1.

CHAP. 21

a ch. 38.1.
b 2 Ki. 25.18. ch. 29.25.
c Ex. 9.28.
d Isa. 13.4.
e Ex. 6.6.
f ch. 37.17. ch. 39.5.
g Deut. 28. 50. 2 Chr. 36.17.
h Deut. 30. 19. Isa. 1.19.
i ch. 38.2.

which the LORD [q]overthrew, and
pented not: and let [r]him hear the
in the morning, and the shouting
noontide;

17 Because [s]he slew me not from t
womb; or that my mother might ha
been my grave, and her womb *to*
always great *with me*.

18 Wherefore [t]came I forth out
the womb to [u]see labour and sorro
that my days should be consum
with shame?

CHAPTER 21

THE word which came unto Je
miah from the LORD, when ki
Zĕd-ē-kī´-ăh sent unto him [a]Păsh-
the son of Mĕl-chī´-ăh, and [b]Zĕph-
nī´-ăh the son of Mā-ă-sē̂ī´-ăh t
priest, saying,

2 Inquire, [c]I pray thee, of the Lo
for us; for Nĕb-ū-chăd-rĕz´-zär ki
of Babylon maketh war against us;
so be that the LORD will deal with
according to all his wondrous work
that he may go up from us.

3 ¶ Then said Jeremiah unto the
Thus shall ye say to Zĕd-ē-kī´-ăh:

4 Thus saith the LORD God of Israe
Behold, I will turn back the weapo
of war that *are* in your hands, wher
with ye fight against the king of Ba
ylon, and *against* the Chăl-dē´-ăn
which besiege you without the wall
and [d]I will assemble them into t
midst of this city.

5 And I myself will fight against yo
with an [e]outstretched hand and wi
a strong arm, even in anger, and
fury, and in great wrath.

6 And I will smite the inhabitants
this city, both man and beast: the
shall die of a great pestilence.

7 And afterward, saith the LORD,
[f]will deliver Zĕd-ē-kī´-ăh king of J
dah, and his servants, and the peopl
and such as are left in this city fro
the pestilence, from the sword, an
from the famine, into the hand
Nĕb-ū-chăd-rĕz´-zär king of Babylo
and into the hand of their enemie
and into the hand of those that see
their life: and he shall smite them wit
the edge of the sword; [g]he shall n
spare them, neither have pity, nc
have mercy.

8 ¶ And unto this people thou sha
say, Thus saith the LORD; Behold,
set before you the way of life, and th
way of death.

9 He that [i]abideth in this city sha
die by the sword, and by the famin
and by the pestilence: but he that g

h out, and falleth to the Chăl-dē′-ăns
at besiege you, he shall live, and [j]his
fe shall be unto him for a prey.
0 For I have [k]set my face against
is city for evil, and not for good,
aith the LORD: [l]it shall be given into
e hand of the king of Babylon, and
e shall [m]burn it with fire.
1 ¶ And touching the house of the
ing of Judah, *say*, Hear ye the word
f the LORD;
2 O house of David, thus saith the
ORD; [1]Execute judgment [n]in the
orning, and deliver *him that is* spoil-
d out of the hand of the oppressor,
st my fury go out like fire, and burn
at none can quench *it*, because of
e evil of your doings.
3 Behold, [o]I *am* against thee, O [2]in-
abitant of the valley, *and* rock of the
lain, saith the LORD; which say,
Who shall come down against us? or
ho shall enter into our habitations?
4 But I will [3]punish you according
o the fruit [q]of your doings, saith the
ORD: and I will kindle a fire in the
orest thereof, and [r]it shall devour all
hings round about it.

CHAPTER 22

THUS saith the LORD; Go down to
the house of the king of Judah,
nd speak there this word,
2 And say, Hear the word of the
ORD, O king of Judah, that sittest
pon the throne of David, thou, and
hy servants, and thy people that en-
er in by these gates:
3 Thus saith the LORD; [a]Execute ye
udgment and righteousness, and de-
iver the spoiled out of the hand of the
ppressor: and do no wrong, do no
iolence to the stranger, the father-
ess, nor the widow, neither shed inno-
ent blood in this place.
4 For if ye do this thing indeed, then
shall there enter in by the gates of
his house kings sitting [1]upon the
hrone of David, riding in chariots
nd on horses, he, and his servants,
nd his people.
5 But if ye will not hear these words,
[c]swear by myself, saith the LORD,
hat this house shall become a desola-
ion.
6 For thus saith the LORD unto the
king's house of Judah; Thou *art*
Gilead unto me, *and* the head of Lĕb′-
ă-non: *yet* surely I will make thee [d]a
wilderness, *and* cities *which* are not
inhabited.
7 And I will prepare destroyers
against thee, every one with his

j ch. 39.18.
k Lev. 17.10. ch. 44.11,27. Amos 9.4.
l ch. 38.3.
m ch. 34.2. ch. 37.10.
1 Judge.
n Ps. 101.8.
o Eze. 13.8.
2 inhabitress.
p ch. 49.4. Lam. 4.12. Obad. 3.4.
3 visit upon.
q Pro. 1.31. Isa. 3.10.
r 2 Chr. 36. 19. ch. 52.13.

CHAP. 22

a Isa. 58.6,7. ch. 7.23. Micah 6.8. Zech. 7.9. Matt. 23.23.
b ch. 17.25.
1 for David upon his throne.
c Num. 23. 19. 1 Sam. 15. 29. Ps. 95.11. Amos 6.8. Heb. 3.18.
d Micah 3.12.
e Isa. 37.24.
f ch. 21.14.
g Deut. 29. 24. 1 Ki. 9.8.
h 2 Ki. 22.17. 2 Chr. 34.25.
i 2 Ki. 22.20. Isa. 57.1,21.
j 1 Chr. 3.15. 2 Ki. 23.30.
k Lev. 19.13. Micah 3.10. Hab. 2.9. Jas. 5.4.
2 through-aired.
3 Or, my windows.
l Ps. 128.2. Isa. 3.10.
m 1 Chr. 28.9. Ps. 9.10. John 8.19. Titus 1.16. Jas. 1.22. 1 John 2.3.
n Eze. 19.6.
4 Or, incursion.
o 1 Ki. 13.30.
p 2 Chr. 36.6.
5 prosperities.

weapons: and they shall cut down thy
[e]choice cedars, and [f]cast *them* into the
fire.
8 And many nations shall pass by
this city, and they shall say every man
to his neighbour, [g]Wherefore hath the
LORD done thus unto this great city?
9 Then they shall answer, [h]Because
they have forsaken the covenant of
the LORD their God, and worshipped
other gods, and served them.
10 ¶ Weep ye not for [i]the dead,
neither bemoan him: *but* weep sore
for him that goeth away: for he shall
return no more, nor see his native
country.
11 For thus saith the LORD touching
Shăl′-lŭm [j]the son of Jō-sī′-ăh king of
Judah, which reigned instead of Jō-
sī′-ăh his father, which went forth out
of this place; He shall not return
thither any more:
12 But he shall die in the place whither they have led him captive, and shall
see this land no more.
13 ¶ Woe unto him that buildeth his
house by unrighteousness, and his
chambers by wrong; [k]*that* useth his
neighbour's service without wages,
and giveth him not for his work;
14 That saith, I will build me a wide
house and [2]large chambers, and cutteth him out [3]windows; and *it is* cieled
with cedar, and painted with ver-
milion.
15 Shalt thou reign, because thou
closest *thyself* in cedar? did not thy
father eat and drink, and do judgment
and justice, *and* [l]then *it was* well with
him?
16 He judged the cause of the poor
and needy; then *it was* well *with him*:
[m]*was* not this to know me? saith the
LORD.
17 But [n]thine eyes and thine heart
are not but for thy covetousness, and
for to shed innocent blood, and for
oppression, and for [4]violence, to do *it*.
18 Therefore thus saith the LORD
concerning Jĕ-hoi′-ă-kĭm the son of
Jō-sī′-ăh king of Judah; They shall not
lament for him, *saying*, [o]Ah my brother! or, Ah sister! they shall not
lament for him, *saying*, Ah lord! or,
Ah his glory!
19 He [p]shall be buried with the
burial of an ass, drawn and cast forth
beyond the gates of Jerusalem.
20 ¶ Go up to Lĕb′-ă-non, and cry;
and lift up thy voice in Bā′-shăn, and
cry from the passages: for all thy lovers are destroyed.
21 I spake unto thee in thy [5]prosper-

ity; *but* thou saidst, I will not hear.
[q]This *hath been* thy manner from thy
youth, that thou obeyedst not my
voice.
22 The wind shall eat up all [r]thy
pastors, and thy lovers shall go into
captivity: surely then shalt thou be
ashamed and confounded for all thy
wickedness.
23 O [6]inhabitant of Lĕb-ā-nŏn, that
makest thy nest in the cedars, how
gracious shalt thou be when pangs
come upon thee, [s]the pain as of a
woman in travail!
24 *As* I live, saith the LORD, though
[t]Cō-nī-āh the son of Jĕ-hoi-ā-kĭm king
of Judah were [u]the signet upon my
right hand, yet would I pluck thee
thence;
25 And [v]I will give thee into the hand
of them that seek thy life, and into the
hand *of them* whose face thou fearest,
even into the hand of Nĕb-ū-chăd-
rĕz-zär king of Babylon, and into the
hand of the Chăl-dē-āns.
26 And [w]I will cast thee out, and thy
mother that bare thee, into another
country, where ye were not born; and
there shall ye die.
27 But to the land whereunto they
[7]desire to return, thither shall they not
return.
28 *Is* this man Cō-nī-āh a despised
broken idol? *is he* [x]a vessel wherein *is*
no pleasure? wherefore are they cast
out, he and his seed, and are cast into
a land which they know not?
29 O earth, earth, earth, hear the word
of the LORD.
30 Thus saith the LORD, Write ye
this man [y]childless, a man *that* shall
not prosper in his days: for no man of
his seed shall prosper, sitting upon
the throne of David, and ruling any
more in Judah.

CHAPTER 23

WOE [a]be unto the pastors that
destroy and scatter the sheep of
my pasture! saith the LORD.
2 Therefore thus saith the LORD God
of Israel against the pastors that feed
my people; Ye have scattered my
flock, and driven them away, and
have not visited them: [b]behold, I will
visit upon you the evil of your doings,
saith the LORD.
3 And [c]I will gather the remnant of
my flock out of all countries whither
I have driven them, and will bring
them again to their folds; and they
shall be fruitful and increase.
4 And I will set up shepherds over
them which shall feed them: and the
shall fear no more, nor be dismaye
neither shall they be lacking, saith th
LORD.
5 ¶ Behold, [d]the days come, saith th
LORD, that I will raise unto David
righteous Branch, and a King sha
reign and prosper, [e]and shall execut
judgment and justice in the earth.
6 In [f]his days Judah shall be saved
and Israel shall dwell safely: and [g]thi
is his name whereby he shall be called
[1]THE LORD OUR RIGHTEOUSNESS.
7 Therefore, behold, the days come
saith the LORD, that they shall n
more say, The LORD liveth, whic
brought up the children of Israel ou
of the land of Egypt;
8 But, The LORD liveth, whic
brought up and which led the seed c
the house of Israel out of the nort
country, [h]and from all countrie
whither I had driven them; and the
shall dwell in their own land.
9 ¶ Mine heart within me is broke
because of the prophets; all [i]my bone
shake; I am like a drunken man, an
like a man whom wine hath overcome
because of the LORD, and because o
the words of his holiness.
10 For the land is full of adulterers
for because [j]of [2]swearing the lan
mourneth; the pleasant places of th
wilderness are dried up, and thei
[3]course is evil, and their force *is* no
right.
11 For [k]both prophet and priest ar
profane; yea, [l]in my house have I
found their wickedness, saith the
LORD.
12 Wherefore [m]their way shall be unto them as slippery *ways* in the darkness: they shall be driven on, and fall
therein: for I will bring evil upon
them, *even* the year of their visitation,
saith the LORD.
13 And I have seen [4]folly in the prophets of Să-mâr-ĭ-ă; they [n]prophesied
in Bā-ăl, and [o]caused my people Israel
to err.
14 I have seen also in the prophets
of Jerusalem [5]an horrible thing: they
commit adultery, and walk in lies:
they strengthen [p]also the hands of
evildoers, that none doth return from
his wickedness: they are all of them
unto me as [q]Sodom, and the inhabitants thereof as Gō-mŏr-răh.
15 Therefore thus saith the LORD of
hosts concerning the prophets; Behold, I will feed them with wormwood, and make them drink the water
of gall: for from the prophets of Jeru-

q ch. 3.25.
r ch. 23.1.
6 inhabitress.
s ch. 6.24.
t 2 Ki. 24.6. 1 Chr. 3.16.
u Song 8.6. Hag. 2.23.
v ch. 34.20.
w 2 Ki. 24.15.
7 lift up their mind.
x Ps. 31.12. ch. 48.38.
y 1 Chr. 3.16. Matt. 1.12.

CHAP. 23

a Eze. 34.2. Zech. 11.5-7, 15-17. John 10.10-12.
b Ex. 32.34.
c ch. 32.37.
d Isa. 4.2. Isa. 11.1. ch. 33.14. Dan. 9.24.
e Ps. 72.2. Isa. 32.1.
f Deut. 33.28. Zech. 14.11.
g ch. 33.16. 1 Cor. 1.30.
1 Jehovah-tsidkenu.
h Isa. 43.5.
i Hab. 3.16.
j Hosea 4.2.
2 Or, cursing.
3 Or, violence.
k Zeph. 3.4.
l Eze. 8.11.
m Pro. 4.19.
4 unsavoury, or, an absurd thing.
n 1 Ki. 18.18.
o Isa. 9.16.
5 Or, filthiness.
p Eze. 13.22.
q Isa. 1.9.

em is [6]profaneness gone forth into
the land.
Thus saith the LORD of hosts,
earken not unto the words of the
ophets that prophesy unto you:
y make you vain: they speak a
ion of their own heart, *and* not out
the mouth of the LORD.
They say still unto them that de-
se me, The LORD hath said, Ye
all have peace; and they say unto
ry one that walketh after the [7]im-
ination of his own heart, [t]No evil
all come upon you.
3 For [u]who hath stood in the [8]coun-
of the LORD, and hath perceived
d heard his word? who hath mark-
his word, and heard *it?*
) Behold, a [v]whirlwind of the LORD
gone forth in fury, even a grievous
irlwind: it shall fall grievously up-
the head of the wicked.
) The [w]anger of the LORD shall not
urn, until he have executed, and till
have performed the thoughts of his
art: in the [x]latter days ye shall con-
ler it perfectly.
I have not sent these prophets,
they ran: I have not spoken to
em, yet they prophesied.
2 But if they had stood in my coun-
, and had caused my people to hear
words, then they should have
rned them from their evil way, and
om the evil of their doings.
3 *Am* [y]I a God at hand, saith the
ORD, and not a God afar off?
4 Can any [z]hide himself in secret
aces that I shall not see him? saith
e LORD. Do [a]not I fill heaven and
rth? saith the LORD.
5 I have [b]heard what the prophets
id, that prophesy lies in my name,
ying, I have dreamed, I have
eamed.
5 How long shall *this* be in the
art of the prophets that prophesy
s? yea, *they are* prophets of the de-
it of their own heart;
7 Which think to [c]cause my people
forget my name by their dreams
hich they tell every man to his neigh-
our, [d]as their fathers have forgotten
y name for Bā-ăl.
8 The prophet [9]that hath a dream,
him tell a dream; and he that hath
y word, let him speak my word
ithfully. What *is* the chaff to the
heat? saith the LORD.
9 *Is* not my word like as a fire? saith
e LORD; and like a hammer *that*
eaketh the rock in pieces?
0 Therefore, behold, [f]I *am* against
the prophets, saith the LORD, that
steal my words every one from his
neighbour.
31 Behold, I *am* against the prophets, saith the LORD, [10]that use their
tongues, and say, He saith.
32 Behold, I *am* against them that
prophesy false dreams, saith the
LORD, and do tell them, and cause my
people to err by their lies, and by their
[g]lightness; yet I sent them not, nor
commanded them: therefore they
shall not profit this people at all, saith
the LORD.
33 ¶ And when this people, or the
prophet, or a priest, shall ask thee,
saying, What *is* the [h]burden of the
LORD? thou shalt then say unto them,
What burden? I will even forsake you,
saith the LORD.
34 And *as for* the prophet, and the
priest, and the people, that shall say,
The burden of the LORD, I will even
[11]punish that man and his house.
35 Thus shall ye say every one to his
neighbour, and every one to his brother, What hath the LORD answered?
and, What hath the LORD spoken?
36 And the burden of the LORD shall
ye mention no more: for every [i]man's
word shall be his burden; for ye [j]have
perverted the words of the living God,
of the LORD of hosts our God.
37 Thus shalt thou say to the prophet, What hath the LORD answered
thee? and, What hath the LORD
spoken?
38 But since ye say, The burden of
the LORD; therefore thus saith the
LORD; Because ye say this word, The
burden of the LORD, and I have sent
unto you, saying, Ye shall not say,
The burden of the LORD;
39 Therefore, behold, I, even I, will
[k]utterly forget you, and I will forsake
you, and the city that I gave you and
your fathers, *and cast you* out of my
presence:
40 And I will bring [l]an everlasting
reproach upon you, and a perpetual
shame, which shall not be forgotten.

CHAPTER 24

THE [a]LORD shewed me, and, behold, two baskets of figs *were* set
before the temple of the LORD, after
that Nĕb-ū-chăd-rĕz-zär [b]king of
Babylon had carried away captive
[c]Jĕc-ō-nī-ăh the son of Jĕ-hoi-ă-kĭm
king of Judah, and the princes of Judah, with the carpenters and smiths,
from Jerusalem, and had brought
them to Babylon.

6 Or, hypocrisy.
r Pro. 19.27. Matt. 7.15.
s Zech. 10.2.
7 Or, stubbornness.
t Micah 3.11.
u Job 15.8. 1 Cor. 2.16.
8 Or, secret.
v ch. 25.32.
w 2 Ki. 23.26, 27.
x Gen. 49.1.
y 1 Ki. 20.23, 28. Ps. 113.6.
z Ps. 139.7. Amos 9.2. Heb. 4.13.
a 1 Ki. 8.27. 2 Chr. 2.6. Ps. 11.4. Isa. 66.1.
b Heb. 4.13.
c Deut. 13.1. Acts 13.8. 2 Tim. 3.6-8.
d Judg. 3.7.
9 with whom is.
e 2 Cor. 2.17. 1 Pet. 4.10.
f Deut. 18.20. ch. 14.14,15.
10 Or, that smooth their tongues.
g Zeph. 3.4.
h Isa. 13.1. ch. 17.15. Mal. 1.1.
11 visit upon.
i Matt. 12.36.
j Acts 13.10, 11. Gal. 1.7,8.
k Deut. 31. 17,18. Hosea 4.6.
l ch. 20.11. Dan. 9.16.

CHAP. 24
a Amos 7.1.
b 2 Ki. 24.12. 2 Chr. 36.10.
c ch. 22.24.

2 One basket *had* very good figs, *even* like the figs *that are* first ripe: and the other basket *had* very naughty figs, which could not be eaten, [1]they were so bad.

3 Then said the LORD unto me, What seest thou, Jeremiah? And I said, Figs; the good figs, very good; and the evil, very evil, that cannot be eaten, they are so evil.

4 ¶ Again the word of the LORD came unto me, saying,

5 Thus saith the LORD, the God of Israel: Like these good figs, so [d]will I acknowledge [2]them that are carried away captive of Judah, whom I have sent out of this place into the land of the Chăl-dḗ-ăns for *their* good.

6 For I will set mine eyes upon them for good, and [e]I will bring them again to this land: and [f]I will build them, and not pull *them* down; and I will plant them, and not pluck *them* up.

7 And I will give them an [g]heart to know me, that I *am* the LORD: and they shall be my [h]people, and I will be their God: for they shall return unto me [i]with their whole heart.

8 ¶ And as the evil [j]figs, which cannot be eaten, they are so evil; surely thus saith the LORD, So will I give Zĕd-ē-kī́-ăh the king of Judah, and his princes, and the residue of Jerusalem, that remain in this land, and them [k]that dwell in the land of Egypt:

9 And I will deliver them [3]to be removed into all the kingdoms of the earth for *their* hurt, [l]*to be* a reproach and a proverb, a taunt and a curse, in all places whither I shall drive them.

10 And I will send the sword, the famine, and the pestilence, among them, till they be consumed from off the land that I gave unto them and to their fathers.

CHAPTER 25

THE word that came to Jeremiah concerning all the people of Judah [a]in the fourth year of Jĕ-hoi̇́-ă-kĭm the son of Jō-sī́-ăh king of Judah, that *was* the first year of Nĕb-ū-chăd-rĕź-zär king of Babylon;

2 The which Jeremiah the prophet spake unto all the people of Judah, and to all the inhabitants of Jerusalem, saying,

3 From the [b]thirteenth year of Jō-sī́-ăh the son of Amon king of Judah, even unto this day, that *is* the three and twentieth year, the word of the LORD hath come unto me, and I have spoken unto you, rising early and speaking; but ye have not hearken

4 And the LORD hath sent unto y all his [c]servants the prophets, risi early and sending *them;* but ye h not hearkened, nor inclined your to hear.

5 They said, [d]Turn ye again n every one from his evil way, and fr the evil of your doings, and dwell the land that the LORD hath given u you and to your fathers for ever a ever:

6 And go not after other gods serve them, and to worship them, a provoke me not to anger with works of your hands; and I will you no hurt.

7 Yet ye have not hearkened u me, saith the LORD; that ye mi [e]provoke me to anger with the wo of your hands to your own hurt.

8 ¶ Therefore thus saith the LORD hosts; Because ye have not heard words,

9 Behold, I will send and [f]take all families of the north, saith the Lo and Nĕb-ū-chăd-rĕź-zär the king Babylon, [g]my servant, and will br them against this land, and agai the inhabitants thereof, and agai all these nations round about, a will utterly destroy them, and [h]ma them an astonishment, and an hissi and perpetual desolations.

10 Moreover [1]I will take from th the voice [i]of mirth, and the voice gladness, the voice of the bridegroo and the voice of the bride, the sou of the millstones, and the light of t candle.

11 And this whole land shall be desolation, *and* an astonishment; a these nations shall serve the king Babylon seventy years.

12 ¶ And [j]it shall come to pass, wh [2]seventy years are accomplished, *th* I will [3]punish the king of Babylon, a that nation, saith the LORD, for th iniquity, and the land of the Chăl-d ăns, [k]and will make it perpetual des lations.

13 And I will bring upon that land my words which I have pronounc against it, *even* all that is written in t book, which Jeremiah hath proph sied against all the nations.

14 For many nations [l]and great kin shall [m]serve themselves of them als and [n]I will recompense them acco ing to their deeds, and according the works of their own hands.

15 ¶ For thus saith the LORD God Israel unto me; Take the [o]wine cup

1 for badness.
d Zech. 13.9. Heb. 2.11.
2 the captivity.
e ch. 12.15. ch. 23.3. Eze. 36.24.
f ch. 32.41. ch. 33.7.
g Deut. 30.6. Eze. 11.19.
h Isa. 51.16. ch. 7.23. ch. 30.22. Eze. 14.11. Zech. 8.8.
i Ps. 119.2. ch. 29.13.
j ch. 29.17.
k ch. 43.1.
3 for removing, or, vexation.
l Ps. 44.13.

CHAP. 25

a 2 Ki. 24.1,2. ch. 36.1. ch. 46.2. Dan. 1.1.
b ch. 1.2.
c 2 Chr. 36. 15. ch. 7.13,25. ch. 11.7. ch. 26.5. ch. 29.19.
d 2 Ki. 17.13. Eze. 18.30. Luke 13.3-5.
e ch. 7.19. ch. 32.30.
f ch. 1.15.
g ch. 40.2.
h ch. 18.16.
1 I will cause to perish from them.
i Rev. 18.23.
j ch. 29.10. Dan. 9.2.
2 Beginning cir. 606, 2 Ki. 24.1. Ending cir. 536, Ezra 1.1.
3 visit upon.
k Isa. 13.19.
l ch. 50.41.
m ch. 27.7.
n ch. 50.29. ch. 51.6,24.
o Job 21.20. Ps. 11.6. Ps. 75.8. Isa. 51.17, 22. Rev. 14.10.

s fury at my hand, and cause all the
tions, to whom I send thee, to drink
t.
5 And [p]they shall drink, and be
oved, and be mad, because of the
ord that I will send among them.
7 Then took I the cup at the LORD's
nd, and made all the nations to
ink, unto whom the LORD had sent
e:
8 *To wit*, [q]Jerusalem, and the cities
Judah, and the kings thereof, and
e princes thereof, to make them a
solation, an astonishment, an hiss-
g, and a curse; as *it is* this day;
9 Pharaoh [r]king of Egypt, and his
rvants, and his princes, and all his
ople;
0 And all the mingled people, and
l the kings of [s]the land of Uz, and
l the kings of the land of the Phili-
ines, and Ăsh-kĕ-lon, and Azzah,
d Ĕk-rŏn, and [t]the remnant of Ăsh-
od,
1 Ē-dom, and Moab, and the chil-
en of Ammon,
2 And all the kings of Tȳ-rŭs, and all
e kings of Zī-dŏn, and the kings of
e [4]isles which *are* beyond the sea,
3 Dē-dăn, and Tē-mă, and Buz, and
l [5]*that are* in the utmost corners,
4 And [u]all the kings of Arabia, and
l the kings of the [v]mingled people
at dwell in the desert,
5 And all the kings of Zimri, and
l the kings of Ē-lăm, and all the
ings of the Mēdes,
6 And all the kings of the north, far
nd near, one with another, and all
e kingdoms of the world, which *are*
pon the face of the earth: [w]and the
ing of Shē-shăch shall drink after
em.
27 Therefore thou shalt say unto
em, Thus saith the LORD of hosts,
e God of Israel; [x]Drink ye, and be
runken, and spue, and fall, and rise
o more, because of the sword which
will send among you.
28 And it shall be, if they refuse to
ake the cup at thine hand to drink,
hen shalt thou say unto them, Thus
aith the LORD of hosts; Ye shall cer-
ainly drink.
29 For, lo, [y]I begin to bring evil on
he city [6]which is called by my name,
nd should ye be utterly unpunished?
Ye shall not be unpunished: for [z]I
will call for a sword upon all the in-
abitants of the earth, saith the LORD
of hosts.
30 Therefore prophesy thou against
hem all these words, and say unto
them, The LORD [a]shall roar from on
high, and utter his voice from his holy
habitation; he shall mightily roar upon his [b]habitation; he shall give a
shout, as they that tread *the grapes*,
against all the inhabitants of the earth.
31 A noise shall come *even* to the
ends of the earth; for the LORD hath
[c]a controversy with the nations, [d]he
will plead with all flesh; he will give
them *that are* wicked to the sword,
saith the LORD.
32 Thus saith the LORD of hosts, Behold, evil shall go forth from nation
to nation, and a great whirlwind shall
be raised up from the coasts of the
earth.
33 And [e]the slain of the LORD shall
be at that day from *one* end of the
earth even unto the *other* end of the
earth: they shall not be lamented,
neither gathered, nor buried; they
shall be dung upon the ground.
34 ¶ Howl, ye shepherds, and cry;
and wallow yourselves *in the ashes*, ye
principal of the flock: for [7]the days of
your slaughter and of your disper-
sions are accomplished; and ye shall
fall like [8]a pleasant vessel.
35 And [9]the shepherds shall have no
way to flee, nor the principal of the
flock to escape.
36 A voice of the cry of the shepherds, and an howling of the principal
of the flock, *shall be heard:* for the
LORD hath spoiled their pasture.
37 And the peaceable habitations are
cut down because of the fierce anger
of [f]the LORD.
38 He hath forsaken his covert, as
the lion: for their land is [10]desolate because of the fierceness of the oppress-
or, and because of his fierce anger.

CHAPTER 26

IN the beginning of the reign of Jĕ-
hôi-ă-kĭm the son of Jō-sī-ăh king of
Judah came this word from the LORD,
saying,
2 Thus saith the LORD; Stand in the
[a]court of the LORD's house, and speak
unto all the cities of Judah, which
[b]come to worship in the LORD's
house, [c]all the words that I command
thee to speak unto them; diminish
[d]not a word:
3 If [e]so be they will hearken, and
turn every man from his evil way,
that I may [f]repent me of the evil,
which I purpose to do unto them because of the evil of their doings.
4 And thou shalt say unto them,
Thus saith the LORD; [g]If ye will not

p Nah. 3.11.
q Ps. 60.3. Eze. 9.8. Dan. 9.12. Amos 2.5.
r ch. 46.2.
s Job 1.1.
t Isa. 20.1.
4 Or, region by the sea side.
5 cut off into corners, or, having the corners of the hair polled.
u 2 Chr. 9.14.
v ch. 50.37.
w ch. 51.41.
x Hab. 2.16.
y Pro. 11.31. ch. 49.12. Obad. 16. Luke 23.31. 1 Pet. 4.17.
6 upon which my name is called.
z Eze. 38.21.
a Isa. 42.13. Joel 3.16. Amos 1.2.
b Ps. 68.16.
c Hosea 4.1. Micah 6.2.
d Joel 3.2.
e Isa. 34.2-8. ch. 12.12. Rev. 19.17-21.
7 your days for slaughter.
8 a vessel of desire.
9 flight shall perish from the shepherds, and escaping from, etc.
f Ps. 97.1-3. Isa. 66.15. Heb. 12.29.
10 a desolation.

CHAP. 26
a ch. 7.2. ch. 19.14. Luke 19.47, 48. John 8.2.
b Ex. 23.14. Deut. 12.5.
c Matt. 28. 20.
d Acts 20.27.
e ch. 36.3.
f ch. 18.8.
g Lev. 26.14. Deut. 28.15.

hearken to me, to walk in my law, which I have set before you,

5 To hearken to the words of my servants the prophets, [h]whom I sent unto you, both rising up early, and sending *them*, but ye have not hearkened;

6 Then will I make this house like [i]Shī'lōh, and will make this city [j]a curse to all the nations of the earth.

7 So the priests and the prophets and all the people heard Jeremiah speaking these words in the house of the LORD.

8 ¶ Now it came to pass, when Jeremiah had made an end of speaking all that the LORD had commanded *him* to speak unto all the people, that [k]the priests and the prophets and all the people took him, saying, Thou shalt surely die.

9 Why hast thou prophesied in the name of the LORD, saying, This house shall be like Shī'lōh, and this city shall be desolate without an inhabitant? And all the people were gathered against Jeremiah in the house of the LORD.

10 ¶ When the princes of Judah heard these things, then they came up from the king's house unto the house of the LORD, and sat down [1]in the entry of [l]the new gate of the LORD'S *house*.

11 Then spake the priests and the prophets unto the princes and to all the people, saying, [2]This man *is* worthy to die; [m]for he hath prophesied against this city, as ye have heard with your ears.

12 ¶ Then spake Jeremiah unto all the princes and to all the people, saying, The LORD sent me to prophesy against this house and against this city all the words that ye have heard.

13 Therefore now [n]amend your ways and your doings, and obey the voice of the LORD your God; and the LORD will repent him of the evil that he hath pronounced against you.

14 As for me, behold, [o]I *am* in your hand: do with me [3]as seemeth good and meet unto you.

15 But know ye for certain, that if ye put me to death, ye shall surely bring innocent blood upon yourselves, and upon this city, and upon the inhabitants thereof: for of a truth the LORD hath sent me unto you to speak all these words in your ears.

16 ¶ Then said the princes and all the people unto the priests and to the prophets; This man *is* not worthy to

h ch. 7.13.
i 1 Sam. 4.10. Ps. 78.60. ch. 7.12.
j Isa. 65.15.
k Amos 5.10. Matt. 27.20.
1 Or, at the door.
l 2 Ki. 15.35.
2 The judgment of death is for this man.
m ch. 38.4. Matt. 26.61.
n Isa. 1.19. Isa. 55.7. ch. 7.3. ch. 35.15. ch. 36.3. Hosea 14.1, 2.
o ch. 38.5.
3 as it is good and right in your eyes.
p Acts 5.34.
q Micah 1.1.
r Micah 3.12.
s 2 Chr. 32. 26.
4 the face of the LORD.
t Ex. 32.14. 2 Sam. 24. 16.
u Acts 5.39.
v 2 Chr. 16. 10. 2 Chr. 24.21.
w 1 Ki. 19.3.
x Ps. 12.8. Pro. 29.12.
y Matt. 23. 31.
5 sons of the people.
z 2 Ki. 22.12, 14. ch. 39.14.

CHAP. 27

a ch. 28.1.
1 Or, hath the LORD said.
b ch. 28.10. Eze. 4.1.

die: for he hath spoken to us in t
name of the LORD our God.

17 Then [p]rose up certain of the elde
of the land, and spake to all the asse
bly of the people, saying,

18 Mī'căh [q]the Mō-răs'-thīte proph
sied in the days of Hĕz-ē-kī'ăh king
Judah, and spake to all the people
Judah, saying, Thus saith the LORD
hosts; [r]Zion shall be plowed *like*
field, and Jerusalem shall becon
heaps, and the mountain of the hou
as the high places of a forest.

19 Did Hĕz-ē-kī-ăh king of Juda
and all Judah put him at all to death
[s]did he not fear the LORD, and b
sought [4]the LORD, and the LORD [t]r
pented him of the evil which he ha
pronounced against them? [u]Th
might we procure great evil again
our souls.

20 And there was also a man th
prophesied in the name of the LOR
Ū-rī'jăh the son of Shĕm-āi'ăh
Kir-jăth–jē'ā-rim, who prophesie
against this city and against this lan
according to all the words of Jer
miah:

21 And when Jĕ-hoi'ā-kim the kin
with all his mighty men, and all th
princes, heard his words, [v]the kin
sought to put him to death: but whe
Ū-rī'jăh heard it, he was afraid, an
[w]fled, and went into Egypt;

22 And Jĕ-hoi'ā-kim the [x]king sen
men into Egypt, *namely*, Ĕl-nā'thă
the son of Ăch'bôr, and *certain* me
with him into Egypt.

23 And they fetched forth Ū-rī'jă
out of Egypt, and brought him unt
Jĕ-hoi'ā-kim the king; [y]who slew hin
with the sword, and cast his dea
body into the graves of the [5]commo
people.

24 Nevertheless [z]the hand of Ă-hi
kăm the son of Shā'phăn was wit
Jeremiah, that they should not giv
him into the hand of the people to pu
him to death.

CHAPTER 27

IN the beginning of the reign of Jĕhoi'ā-kim the son of Jō-sī'ăh king [a]of Judah came this word unto Jeremiah from the LORD, saying,

2 Thus [1]saith the LORD to me; Make thee bonds and yokes, [b]and put them upon thy neck,

3 And send them to the king of Ĕdom, and to the king of Moab, and to the king of the Ammonites, and to the king of Tŷ'rŭs, and to the king of Zī'dŏn, by the hand of the messengers

which come to Jerusalem unto Zĕd-ē-
kī-´ăh king of Judah;
4 And command them [2]to say unto
their masters, Thus saith the LORD of
hosts, the God of Israel; Thus shall ye
say unto your masters;
5 I [c]have made the earth, the man
and the beast that *are* upon the
ground, by my great power and by my
outstretched arm, and [d]have given it
unto whom it seemed meet unto me.
6 And [e]now have I given all these
lands into the hand of Nĕb-ū-chăd-
nĕz-´zär the king of Babylon, my [f]ser-
vant; and [g]the beasts of the field have
I given him also to serve him.
7 And [h]all nations shall serve him,
and his son, and his son's son, [i]until
the very time of his land come: and
then many nations and great kings
shall serve themselves of him.
8 And it shall come to pass, *that* the
nation and kingdom which will not
serve the same Nĕb-ū-chăd-nĕz-´zär
the king of Babylon, and that will not
put their neck under the yoke of the
king of Babylon, that nation will I
[3]punish, saith the LORD, with the
sword, and with the famine, and with
the pestilence, until I have consumed
them by his hand.
9 Therefore [j]hearken not ye to your
prophets, nor to your diviners, nor to
your [4]dreamers, nor to your enchant-
ers, nor to your sorcerers, which speak
unto you, saying, Ye shall not serve
the king of Babylon:
10 For they prophesy a lie unto you,
to remove you far from your land;
and that I should drive you out, and
ye should perish.
11 But the nations that bring their
neck under the yoke of the king of
Babylon, and serve him, those will I
let remain still in their own land, saith
the LORD; and they shall till it, and
dwell therein.
12 ¶ I spake also to [k]Zĕd-ē-kī-´ăh
king of Judah according to all these
words, saying, Bring your necks under
the yoke of the king of Babylon, and
serve him and his people, and live.
13 Why [l]will ye die, thou and thy
people, by the sword, by the famine,
and by the pestilence, as the LORD
hath spoken against the nation that
will not serve the king of Babylon?
14 Therefore hearken not unto the
words of the prophets that speak unto
you, saying, Ye shall not serve the
king of Babylon: for they prophesy a
[m]lie unto you.
15 For I have not sent them, saith

2 Or, concerning their masters, saying.
c Ps. 96.5. Ps. 115.15. Isa. 42.5. Isa. 45.12.
d Gen. 1.29, 30. Deut. 2.5. Josh. 1.2,3. Ps. 115.16. Dan. 4.17.
e ch. 28.14. Dan. 2.37, 38.
f ch. 25.9. ch. 43.10.
g Ps. 50.10-12. Dan. 2.38.
h 2 Chr. 36. 20.
i ch. 25.12. ch. 50.27. Dan. 5.26.
3 visit upon.
j Pro. 19.27. ch. 14.14. Micah 3.7. Eph. 5.6.
4 dreams.
k ch. 28.1. ch. 38.17.
l Pro. 8.36. Eze. 18.31.
m ch. 14.14. ch. 23.21.
5 in a lie, or, lyingly.
n 2 Ki. 24.13. ch. 28.3. Dan. 1.2.
o Eze. 18.31.
p Gen. 20.7. Job 42.8. Isa. 37.4. Jas. 5.16.
q 2 Ki. 25.13. ch. 52.17.
r 2 Ki. 24.14, 15. ch. 24.1.
6 white ones.
s Lev. 26.24. Isa. 5.25.
t 2 Chr. 36. 21. ch. 29.10. ch. 32.5. Dan. 9.2.
u Ezra 1.7.

CHAP. 28
a ch. 27.1.
b ch. 36.12. 2 Tim. 3.8. 2 Pet. 2.1.
c ch. 27.12.
1 two years of days.
d 2 Ki. 24.13. 2 Chr. 36.10. ch. 27.16-22.

the LORD, yet they prophesy [5]a lie in
my name; that I might drive you out,
and that ye might perish, ye, and the
prophets that prophesy unto you.
16 Also I spake to the priests and to
all this people, saying, Thus saith the
LORD; Hearken not to the words of
your prophets that prophesy unto
you, saying, Behold, the [n]vessels of
the LORD's house shall now shortly be
brought again from Babylon: for they
prophesy a lie unto you.
17 Hearken not unto them; serve the
king of Babylon, and live: [o]wherefore
should this city be laid waste?
18 But if they *be* prophets, and if the
word of the LORD be with them, let
them now [p]make intercession to the
LORD of hosts, that the vessels which
are left in the house of the LORD, and
in the house of the king of Judah, and
at Jerusalem, go not to Babylon.
19 ¶ For thus saith the LORD of hosts
concerning [q]the pillars, and concerning the sea, and concerning the bases,
and concerning the residue of the vessels that remain in this city,
20 Which Nĕb-ū-chăd-nĕz-´zär king
of Babylon took not, when he carried
away [r]captive Jĕc-ō-nī-´ăh the son of
Jĕ-hôi-´ă-kĭm king of Judah from Jerusalem to Babylon, and all the [6]nobles
of Judah and Jerusalem;
21 Yea, thus saith the LORD of hosts,
the God of Israel, concerning the vessels that remain [s]*in* the house of the
LORD, and *in* the house of the king of
Judah and of Jerusalem;
22 They shall be carried to Babylon,
and there shall they be until the day
that I visit [t]them, saith the LORD; then
[u]will I bring them up, and restore
them to this place.

CHAPTER 28

AND [a]it came to pass the same year,
in the beginning of the reign of
Zĕd-ē-kī-´ăh king of Judah, in the
fourth year, *and* in the fifth month, *that*
[b]Hăn-ă-nī-´ăh the son of Ā-´zûr the
prophet, which *was* of Gibeon, spake
unto me in the house of the LORD, in
the presence of the priests and of all
the people, saying,
2 Thus speaketh the LORD of hosts,
the God of Israel, saying, I have brok-
en [c]the yoke of the king of Babylon.
3 Within [1]two full years will I bring
again into this place [d]all the vessels of
the LORD's house, that Nĕb-ū-chăd-
nĕz-´zär king of Babylon took away
from this place, and carried them to
Babylon:

4 And I will bring again to this place
Jĕc-ō-nī´-ăh the son of [2]Jĕ-hôi´-ă-kĭm
king of Judah, with all the [3]captives of
Judah, that went into Babylon, saith
the LORD: for I will break the yoke of
the king of Babylon.
5 ¶ Then the prophet Jeremiah said
unto the prophet Hăn-ă-nī´-ăh in the
presence of the priests, and in the
presence of all the people that stood
in the house of the LORD,
6 Even the prophet Jeremiah said,
[e]Ā´-mĕn: the LORD do so: the LORD
perform thy words which thou hast
prophesied, to bring again the vessels
of the LORD's house, and all that is
carried away captive, from Babylon
into this place.
7 Nevertheless hear thou now this
word that I speak in thine ears, and in
the ears of all the people;
8 The prophets that have been before
me and before thee of old prophesied
both against many countries, and
against great kingdoms, of war, and of
evil, and of pestilence.
9 The [f]prophet which prophesieth of
peace, when the word of the prophet
shall come to pass, *then* shall the
prophet be known, that the LORD
hath truly sent him.
10 ¶ Then Hăn-ă-nī´-ăh the prophet
took the yoke [g]from off the prophet
Jeremiah's neck, and brake it.
11 And Hăn-ă-nī´-ăh spake in the
presence of all the people, saying,
Thus saith the LORD; Even so will I
break the yoke of Nĕb-ū-c̲hăd-nĕz´-
zär king of Babylon [h]from the neck of
all nations within the space of two full
years. And the prophet Jeremiah went
[i]his way.
12 ¶ Then the word of the LORD came
unto Jeremiah *the prophet*, after that
Hăn-ă-nī´-ăh the prophet had broken
the yoke from off the neck of the
prophet Jeremiah, saying,
13 Go and tell Hăn-ă-nī´-ăh, saying,
Thus saith the LORD; Thou hast brok-
en the yokes of wood; but thou shalt
make for them yokes of iron.
14 For thus saith the LORD of hosts,
the God of Israel; [j]I have put a yoke
of iron upon the neck of all these nations, that they may serve Nĕb-ū-
c̲hăd-nĕz´-zär king of Babylon; and
they shall serve him: and I [k]have given
him the beasts of the field also.
15 ¶ Then said the prophet Jeremiah
unto Hăn-ă-nī´-ăh the prophet, Hear
now, Hăn-ă-nī´-ăh; The LORD hath not
sent thee; but [l]thou makest this people
to trust in a lie.

2 Or, Jehoiachin. 2 Ki. 24.12.
3 captivity.
e 1 Ki. 1.36. 1 Chr. 16.36. Ps. 41.13. Ps. 72.19. Ps. 89.52. Matt. 6.13. 1 Cor. 14.16. 2 Cor. 1.20. Rev. 1.18.
f Deut. 18.22. Isa. 8.20.
g 1 Ki. 22.24. Ps. 10.13.
h ch. 27.7.
i Pro. 26.4.
j Deut. 28.48. ch. 27.4,7.
k ch. 27.6.
l ch. 20.6. ch. 29.31.
4 revolt.
m Deut. 32. 35. 1 Sam. 2.9. Job 21.30. Ps. 9.16. Ps. 34.21. Pro. 11.21. Nah. 1.2,3. Rom. 2.2,3. Heb. 9.27. Heb. 12.29.
CHAP. 29
1 Or, Jehoiachin, 2 Ki. 24.12. 2 Chr. 36.10. ch. 22.26.
2 Or, chamberlains.
a Dan. 6.4. Rom. 13.1. 5. 1 Tim. 2.1.
b 1 Tim. 2.2.
c ch. 14.14. ch. 23.21. Eph. 5.6.
3 in a lie.
d 2 Chr. 36. 21.22. ch. 25.12. Dan. 9.2.

16 Therefore thus saith the LORD;
Behold, I will cast thee from off the
face of the earth: this year thou shalt
die, because thou hast taught [4]rebel-
lion against the LORD.
17 So Hăn-ă-nī´-ăh the prophet died
the [m]same year in the seventh month.

CHAPTER 29

NOW these *are* the words of the
letter that Jeremiah the prophet
sent from Jerusalem unto the residue
of the elders which were carried away
captives, and to the priests, and to the
prophets, and to all the people whom
Nĕb-ū-c̲hăd-nĕz´-zär had carried away
captive from Jerusalem to Babylon;
2 (After that [1]Jĕc-ō-nī´-ăh the king,
and the queen, and the [2]eunuchs, the
princes of Judah and Jerusalem, and
the carpenters, and the smiths, were
departed from Jerusalem;)
3 By the hand of Ĕl-ā´-săh the son of
Shā´-phăn, and Gĕm-ă-rī´-ăh the son of
Hĭl-kī´-ăh, (whom Zĕd-ē-kī´-ăh king of
Judah sent unto Babylon to Nĕb-
ū-c̲hăd-nĕz´-zär king of Babylon)
saying,
4 Thus saith the LORD of hosts, the
God of Israel, unto all that are carried
away captives, whom I have caused to
be carried away from Jerusalem unto
Babylon;
5 Build ye houses, and dwell *in them;*
and plant gardens, and eat the fruit
of them;
6 Take ye wives, and beget sons and
daughters: and take wives for your
sons, and give your daughters to husbands, that they may bear sons and
daughters; that ye may be increased
there, and not diminished.
7 And [a]seek the peace of the city
whither I have caused you to be carried
away captives, [b]and pray unto the
LORD for it: for in the peace thereof
shall ye have peace.
8 ¶ For thus saith the LORD of hosts,
the God of Israel; Let not your prophets and your diviners, that *be* in the
midst of you, [c]deceive you, neither
hearken to your dreams which ye
cause to be dreamed.
9 For they prophesy [3]falsely unto you
in my name: I have not sent them,
saith the LORD.
10 ¶ For thus saith the LORD, That
after seventy [d]years be accomplished
at Babylon I will visit you, and perform my good word toward you, in
causing you to return to this place.
11 For I know the thoughts that I
think toward you, saith the LORD,

thoughts of peace, and not of evil, to give you an [4]expected end.

12 Then shall ye [e]call upon me, and ye shall go and pray unto me, and I will hearken unto you.

13 And [f]ye shall seek me, and find *me*, when ye shall search for me [g]with all your heart.

14 And [h]I will be found of you, saith the LORD: and I will turn away your captivity, and [i]I will gather you from all the nations, and from all the places whither I have driven you, saith the LORD; and I will bring you again into the place whence I caused you to be carried away captive.

15 ¶ Because ye have said, The LORD hath raised us up prophets in Babylon;

16 *Know* that thus saith the LORD of the king that sitteth upon the throne of David, and of all the people that dwelleth in this city, *and* of your brethren that are not gone forth with you into captivity;

17 Thus saith the LORD of hosts; Behold, I will send upon them [j]the sword, the famine, and the pestilence, and will make them [k]like vile figs, that cannot be eaten, they are so evil.

18 And I will persecute them with the sword, with the famine, and with the pestilence, and [l]will deliver them to be removed to all the kingdoms of the earth, [5]to be a curse, and an astonishment, and an hissing, and a reproach, among all the nations whither I have driven them:

19 Because they have not hearkened to my words, saith the LORD, which [m]I sent unto them by my servants the prophets, rising up early and sending *them;* but ye would not hear, saith the LORD.

20 ¶ Hear ye therefore the word of the LORD, all ye of the captivity, whom [n]I have sent from Jerusalem to Babylon:

21 Thus saith the LORD of hosts, the God of Israel, of Ahab the son of Kō-lâi-́ăh, and of Zĕd-ē-kī-́ăh the son of Mā-ă-sêi-́ăh, which prophesy a [o]lie unto you in my name; Behold, I will deliver them into the hand of Nĕb-ū-chăd-rĕz-́zăr king of Babylon; and he shall slay them before your eyes;

22 And [p]of them shall be taken up a curse by all the captivity of Judah which *are* in Babylon, saying, The LORD make thee like Zĕd-ē-kī-́ăh and like Ahab, [q]whom the king of Babylon roasted in the fire;

23 Because [r]they have committed villany in Israel, and have committed adultery with their neighbours' wives, and have spoken lying words in my name, which I have not commanded them; even I know, and *am* [s]a witness, saith the LORD.

24 ¶ *Thus* shalt thou also speak to Shĕm-âi-́ăh the [6]Nĕ-hĕl-́ă-mīte, saying,

25 Thus speaketh the LORD of hosts, the God of Israel, saying, Because thou hast sent letters in thy name unto all the people that *are* at Jerusalem, [t]and to Zĕph-ă-nī-́ăh the son of Mā-ă-sêi-́ăh the priest, and to all the priests, saying,

26 The LORD hath made thee priest in the stead of Jĕ-hôi-́ă-dă the priest, that ye should be [u]officers in the house of the LORD, for every man *that is* [v]mad, and maketh himself a prophet, that thou shouldest [w]put him in prison, and in the stocks.

27 Now therefore why hast thou not [x]reproved Jeremiah of Ăn-́ă-thōth, which maketh himself a prophet to you?

28 For therefore he sent unto us *in* Babylon, saying, This *captivity is* long: build ye houses, and dwell *in them;* and plant gardens, and eat the fruit of them.

29 And Zĕph-ă-nī-́ăh the priest read this letter in the ears of Jeremiah the prophet.

30 ¶ Then came the word of the LORD unto Jeremiah, saying,

31 Send to all them of the captivity, saying, Thus saith the LORD concerning Shĕm-âi-́ăh the Nĕ-hĕl-́ă-mīte; Because that Shĕm-âi-́ăh hath prophesied unto you, [y]and I sent him not, and he caused you to trust in a lie:

32 Therefore thus saith the LORD; Behold, I will punish [z]Shĕm-âi-́ăh the Nĕ-hĕl-́ă-mīte, and his seed: he shall not have a man to dwell among this people; neither shall he behold the good that I will do for my people, saith the LORD; because [a]he hath taught [7]rebellion against the LORD.

CHAPTER 30

THE word that came to Jeremiah from the LORD, saying,

2 Thus speaketh the LORD God of Israel, saying, [a]Write thee all the words that I have spoken unto thee in a book.

3 For, lo, the days come, saith the LORD, that [b]I will bring again the captivity of my people Israel and Judah, saith the LORD: and [c]I will cause them to return to the land that I gave to

4 end and expectation.
e Dan. 9.3.
f Lev. 26.39, 40. Deut. 30.1. Ps. 32.6. Matt. 7.7.
g ch. 24.7.
h Deut. 4.7. Ps. 32.6. Isa. 55.6. Rom. 10.20.
i ch. 23.3,8. ch. 30.3.
j ch. 24.10.
k ch. 24.8.
l Deut. 28.21-28. 1 Ki. 9.7,8. 2 Chr. 29.8. ch. 15.4. ch. 24.9. Lam. 2.15, 16.
5 for a curse.
m ch. 25.4. ch. 32.33.
n Amos 3.6. Micah 4.10.
o 2 Pet. 2.1.
p Gen. 48.20. Isa. 65.15.
q Dan. 3.6.
r Zeph. 3.4.
s Pro. 5.21. ch. 13.27. ch. 16.17. Mal. 3.5. Heb. 4.13.
6 Or, dreamer.
t 2 Ki. 25.18. ch. 21.1.
u ch. 20.1. Acts 4.1.
v Deut. 13.1-5. 2 Ki. 9.11. Zech. 13.3-6.
w 2 Chr. 16. 10. ch. 20.2. Acts 16.24.
x Num. 16.3. Acts 4.17.
y ch. 28.15.
z Ex. 20.5. Rom. 2.8.
a ch. 28.16.
7 revolt.

CHAP. 30

a Isa. 30.8.
b Deut. 30.3. ch.27.22. ch. 29.14. ch. 31.23. Amos 9.14.
c ch. 16.15.

their fathers, and they shall possess it.

4 ¶ And these *are* the words that the LORD spake concerning Israel and concerning Judah.

5 For thus saith the LORD; We have heard a voice of trembling, [1]of fear, and not of peace.

6 Ask ye now, and see whether [2]a man doth travail with child? wherefore do I see every man with his hands on his loins, as a woman in travail, and all faces are turned into paleness?

7 Alas! [d]for that day *is* great, [e]so that none *is* like it: it *is* even the time of Jacob's trouble; but he shall be saved out of it.

8 For it shall come to pass in that day, saith the LORD of hosts, *that* I will break his yoke from off thy neck, and will burst thy bonds, and strangers shall no more serve themselves of him:

9 But they shall serve the LORD their God, and [f]David their king, whom I will [g]raise up unto them.

10 ¶ Therefore [h]fear thou not, O my servant Jacob, saith the LORD; neither be dismayed, O Israel: for, lo, I will save thee from afar, and thy seed from the land of their captivity; and Jacob shall return, and shall be in rest, and be quiet, and none shall make *him* afraid.

11 For I *am* with thee, saith the LORD, to save thee: [i]though I make a full end of all nations whither I have scattered thee, yet will [j]I not make a full end of thee: but I will correct thee in [k]measure, and will not leave thee altogether unpunished.

12 For thus saith the LORD, [l]Thy bruise *is* incurable, *and* thy wound *is* grievous.

13 *There is* none to plead thy cause, [3]that thou mayest be bound up: thou hast no healing medicines.

14 All [m]thy lovers have forgotten thee; they seek thee not; for I have wounded thee with the wound [n]of an enemy, with the [o]chastisement of a cruel one, for the multitude of thine iniquity; [p]*because* thy sins were increased.

15 Why criest thou for thine affliction? thy sorrow *is* incurable for the multitude of thine iniquity: *because* thy sins were increased, I have done these things unto thee.

16 [4]Therefore all they that devour thee shall [q]be devoured; and all thine adversaries, every one of them, shall go into captivity; and they that spoil thee shall be a spoil, and all that prey upon thee will I give for a prey.

17 For I will restore [r]health unto thee, and I will heal thee of thy wounds, saith the LORD; because they called thee an Outcast, *saying*, This *is* Zion, whom no man seeketh after.

18 ¶ Thus saith the LORD; Behold, I will bring again the captivity of Jacob's tents, and [s]have mercy on his dwellingplaces; and the city shall be builded upon her own [5]heap, and the palace shall remain after the manner thereof.

19 And [t]out of them shall proceed thanksgiving and the voice of them that make merry: and [u]I will multiply them, and they shall not be few; I will also glorify them, and they shall not be small.

20 Their children also shall [v]be as aforetime, and their congregation shall be established before me, and I will punish all that oppress them.

21 And [6]their nobles shall be of themselves, [w]and their governor shall proceed from the midst of them; and I will [x]cause him to draw near, and he shall approach unto me: for who *is* this that engaged his heart to approach unto me? saith the LORD.

22 And ye shall be [y]my people, and I will be your God.

23 Behold, the [z]whirlwind of the LORD goeth forth with fury, a [7]continuing whirlwind: it shall [8]fall with pain upon the head of the wicked.

24 The fierce anger of the LORD shall not return, until he have done *it*, and until he have performed the intents of his heart: in the latter days ye shall consider it.

CHAPTER 31

AT the same time, saith the LORD, will I be the God of all the families of Israel, and they shall be my people.

2 Thus saith the LORD, The people *which were* left of the sword found grace in the wilderness; *even* Israel, when [a]I went to cause him to rest.

3 The LORD hath appeared [1]of old unto me, *saying*, Yea, [b]I have loved thee with an [c]everlasting love: therefore [2]with lovingkindness have I drawn thee.

4 Again I will build thee, and thou shalt be built, O virgin of Israel: thou shalt again be adorned with thy [3]tabrets, and shalt go forth in the dances of them that make merry.

5 Thou [d]shalt yet plant vines upon the mountains of Să-mâr-ĭ-ă: the planters shall plant, and shall [4]eat *them* as common things.

---

1 Or, there is fear, and not peace.
2 a male.
d Isa. 22.4,5. Joel 2.11. Amos 5.18. Zeph. 1.14. 1 Thes. 4.16.
e Dan. 12.1.
f Isa. 55.3,4. Hosea 3.5.
g Luke 1.69. Acts 2.30.
h Isa. 41.13.
i Amos 9.8.
j ch. 4.27.
k Ps. 6.1. Isa. 27.8.
l 2 Chr. 36. 16. ch. 15.18.
3 for binding up, or, pressing.
m Lam. 1.2.
n Job 13.24.
o Job 30.21.
p ch. 5.6.
4 Or, Nevertheless.
q Ex. 23.22. Isa. 41.11.
r Ex. 15.26. Isa. 30.26. Hosea 6.2. Mal. 4.2. 1 Pet. 2.24.
s Ps. 102.13.
5 Or, little hill.
t Ezra 3.10, 11. Neh. 8.12. Isa. 35.10.
u Zech. 10.8.
v Isa. 1.26.
6 his glorious ones.
w Gen. 49.10.
x Num. 16.5.
y Eze. 36.28.
z ch. 25.32.
7 cutting.
8 Or, remain.

CHAP. 31

a Num. 10. 33.
1 from afar.
b Mal. 1.2.
c Rom. 11.28.
2 Or, have I extended lovingkindness unto thee.
3 Or, timbrels.
d Isa. 65.21. Amos 9.14.
4 profane them.

For there shall be a day, *that* the
atchmen upon the mount Ē-phră-ĭm
all cry, Arise [e]ye, and let us go up to
ion unto the LORD our God.
For thus saith the LORD; [f]Sing with
adness for Jacob, and shout among
e chief of the nations: publish ye,
raise ye, and say, O LORD, save thy
eople, the remnant of Israel.
Behold, I will bring them from the
orth country, and [g]gather them from
e coasts of the earth, *and* with them
e blind and the lame, the woman
ith child and her that travaileth with
ild together: a great company shall
turn thither.
They [h]shall come with weeping,
nd with [5]supplications will I lead
em: I will cause them to [i]walk by the
vers of waters in a straight way,
herein they shall not stumble: for I
n a father to Israel, and Ē-phră-ĭm
my [j]firstborn.
0 ¶ Hear the word of the LORD, O
nations, and declare *it* in the isles
ar off, and say, He that scattered
rael [k]will gather him, and keep him,
a shepherd *doth* his flock.
1 For [l]the LORD hath redeemed
cob, and ransomed him [m]from the
nd of *him that was* stronger than he.
2 Therefore they shall come and
ng in the height of Zion, and shall
ow together to [n]the goodness of the
ORD, for wheat, and for wine, and
r oil, and for the young of the flock
nd of the herd: and their soul shall
as a [o]watered garden; [p]and they
all not sorrow any more at all.
3 Then shall the virgin rejoice in the
ance, both young men and old to-
ther: for I will turn their mourning
to joy, and will comfort them, and
ake them rejoice from their sorrow.
4 And I will satiate the soul of the
iests with fatness, and my people
all be satisfied with my goodness,
ith the LORD.
5 ¶ Thus saith the LORD; [q]A voice
as heard in [r]Rā-măh, lamentation,
nd bitter weeping; Rahel weeping for
r children refused to be comforted
r her children, [s]because they *were*
ot.
6 Thus saith the LORD; Refrain thy
oice from weeping, and thine eyes
om tears: for thy work shall be re-
arded, saith the LORD; [t]and they
all come again from the land of the
emy.
7 And there is hope in thine end,
ith the LORD, that thy children shall
ome again to their own border.

[e] Isa. 2.3. Micah 4.2.
[f] Isa. 12.5.
[g] Eze. 34.13.
[h] Ps. 126.5. ch. 50.4.
5 Or, favours.
[i] Isa. 49.10.
[j] Ex. 4.22. Deut. 32.6. 1 Chr. 29.10. Isa. 63.16. ch. 3.4,19.
[k] Isa. 40.11.
[l] Isa. 44.23.
[m] Isa. 49.24.
[n] Hosea 3.5. Rev. 7.17.
[o] Isa. 58.11.
[p] Isa. 35.10. Rev. 21.4.
[q] Matt. 2.17.
[r] Josh. 18.25.
[s] Gen. 42.13. Job 7.21. Lam. 5.7. Matt. 2.18.
[t] Eze. 11.17, 18. Hosea 1.11.
[u] Ps. 85.4. ch. 17.14. Lam. 5.21.
[v] Deut. 30.2.
[w] Isa. 63.15. Hosea 11.8.
6 sound.
[x] Isa. 57.18. Hosea 14.4. Micah 7.18.
[y] ch. 50.5.
[z] ch. 2.18.
[a] ch. 3.6. Hosea 4.16.
[b] Ps. 122.5. Isa. 1.26.
[c] Zech. 8.3.
[d] ch. 33.12.
[e] Hosea 2.23.
[f] ch. 44.27. Dan. 9.14.
[g] ch. 1.10.
[h] ch. 24.6.
[i] Eze. 18.2.
[j] Gal. 6.5.
[k] ch. 32.40. ch. 33.14. Heb. 8.8.

18 ¶ I have surely heard Ē-phră-ĭm
bemoaning himself *thus;* Thou hast
chastised me, and I was chastised, as
a bullock unaccustomed *to the yoke:*
[u]turn thou me, and I shall be turned;
for thou *art* the LORD my God.
19 Surely [v]after that I was turned,
I repented; and after that I was instructed, I smote upon *my* thigh: I was
ashamed, yea, even confounded, because I did bear the reproach of my
youth.
20 *Is* Ē-phră-ĭm my dear son? *is he* a
pleasant child? for since I spake
against him, I do earnestly remember
him still: [w]therefore my bowels [6]are
troubled for him; [x]I will surely have
mercy upon him, saith the LORD.
21 Set thee up waymarks, make thee
high heaps: [y]set thine heart toward
the highway, *even* the way *which* thou
wentest: turn again, O virgin of Israel,
turn again to these thy cities.
22 ¶ How long wilt [z]thou go about,
O thou backsliding [a]daughter? for the
LORD hath created a new thing in the
earth, A woman shall compass a man.
23 Thus saith the LORD of hosts, the
God of Israel; As yet they shall use
this speech in the land of Judah and in
the cities thereof, when I shall bring
again their captivity; The [b]LORD bless
thee, O habitation of justice, *and*
[c]mountain of holiness.
24 And there shall dwell in Judah itself, and [d]in all the cities thereof together, husbandmen, and they *that* go
forth with flocks.
25 For I have satiated the weary
soul, and I have replenished every
sorrowful soul.
26 Upon this I awaked, and beheld;
and my sleep was sweet unto me.
27 ¶ Behold, the days come, saith
the LORD, that [e]I will sow the house
of Israel and the house of Judah with
the seed of man, and with the seed of
beast.
28 And it shall come to pass, *that*
like as I have [f]watched over them, to
[g]pluck up, and to break down, and to
throw down, and to destroy, and to
afflict; so will I watch over them, [h]to
build, and to plant, saith the LORD.
29 In [i]those days they shall say no
more, The fathers have eaten a sour
grape, and the children's teeth are set
on edge.
30 But [j]every one shall die for his
own iniquity: every man that eateth
the sour grape, his teeth shall be set
on edge.
31 ¶ Behold, [k]the days come, saith

the LORD, that I will make a new covenant with the house of Israel, and with the house of Judah:

32 Not [l]according to the covenant that I made with their fathers in the day *that* I [m]took them by the hand to bring them out of the land of Egypt; which my covenant they brake, [7]although I was an husband unto them, saith the LORD:

33 But [n]this *shall be* the covenant that I will make with the house of Israel; After those days, saith the LORD, [o]I will put my law in their inward parts, and write it in their hearts; [p]and will be their God, and they shall be my people.

34 And they shall teach no more every man his neighbour, and every man his brother, saying, Know the LORD: for [q]they shall all know me, from the least of them unto the greatest of them, saith the LORD: for [r]I will forgive their iniquity, and I will remember their sin no more.

35 ¶ Thus saith the LORD, [s]which giveth the sun for a light by day, *and* the ordinances of the moon and of the stars for a light by night, which divideth [t]the sea when the waves thereof roar; [u]The LORD of hosts *is* his name:

36 If [v]those ordinances depart from before me, saith the LORD, *then* the seed of Israel also shall cease from being a nation before me for ever.

37 Thus saith the LORD; [w]If heaven above can be measured, and the foundations of the earth searched out beneath, I will also cast off all the seed of Israel for all that they have done, saith the LORD.

38 ¶ Behold, the days come, saith the LORD, that the city shall be built to the LORD [x]from the tower of Hăn-ă-nēel unto the gate of the corner.

39 And the [y]measuring line shall yet go forth over against it upon the hill Gâr-ĕb, and shall compass about to Gō-ăth.

40 And the whole valley of the dead bodies, and of the ashes, and all the fields unto the brook of Kĭ-drŏn, [z]unto the corner of the horse gate toward the east, [a]*shall be* holy unto the LORD; it shall not be plucked up, nor thrown down any more for ever.

CHAPTER 32

THE word that came to Jeremiah from the LORD [a]in the tenth year of Zĕd-ē-kī-ăh king of Judah, which *was* the eighteenth year of Nĕb-ū-chăd-rĕz-zăr.

l John 1.17.
m Deut. 1.31.
7 Or, should I have continued an husband unto them?
n ch. 32.40.
o Ps. 40.8. 2 Cor. 3.3.
p ch. 24.7. ch. 30.22.
q Isa. 54.13. John 6.45. 1 Cor. 2.10.
r ch. 33.8. Rom. 11.27.
s Gen. 1.16.
t Isa. 51.15.
u ch. 10.16.
v Ps. 148.6.
w ch. 33.22.
x Neh. 3.1. Ps. 69.35. ch. 24.6. Dan. 9.25.
y Zech. 2.1.
z 2 Chr. 23.15. Neh. 3.28.
a Joel 3.17.

CHAP. 32

a 2 Ki. 25.1. ch. 39.1.
b Neh. 3.25. ch. 33.1. ch. 37.21. Matt. 5.12.
c ch. 21.4-7.
d 2 Ki. 25.4-7. ch. 39.5. ch. 52.9.
e ch. 27.22.
f Pro. 21.30. ch. 21.4.
g Lev. 25.24, 25,32. Ruth 4.4.
h ch. 1.1.
i Lev. 25.24.
j Gen. 23.16.
1 Or, seven shekels and ten pieces of silver.
2 wrote in the book.
k Isa. 8.2.
l ch. 36.4.
m Isa. 8.2.

2 For then the king of Babylor
army besieged Jerusalem: and Jer
miah the prophet was shut up in [b]th
court of the prison, which *was* in th
king of Judah's house.
3 For Zĕd-ē-kī-ăh king of Judah ha
shut him up, saying, Wherefore do
thou prophesy, and say, Thus saith th
LORD, [c]Behold, I will give this city in
the hand of the king of Babylon, an
he shall take it;
4 And Zĕd-ē-kī-ăh king of Juda
shall [d]not escape out of the hand
the Chăl-dē-ăns, but shall surely b
delivered into the hand of the king
Babylon, and shall speak with hi
mouth to mouth, and his eyes shall b
hold his eyes;
5 And he shall lead Zĕd-ē-kī-ăh
Babylon, and there shall he be un
[e]I visit him, saith the LORD: thoug
[f]ye fight with the Chăl-dē-ăns, ye sha
not prosper?
6 ¶ And Jeremiah said, The word
the LORD came unto me, saying,
7 Behold, Hăn-ă-mēel the son
Shăl-lŭm thine uncle shall come un
thee, saying, Buy thee my field that
in Ăn-ă-thōth: for [g]the right of r
demption *is* thine to buy *it*.
8 So Hăn-ă-mēel mine uncle's so
came to me in the court of the prisc
according to the word of the LOR
and said unto me, Buy my field, I pra
thee, that *is* [h]in Ăn-ă-thōth, which *is* i
the country of Benjamin: for the rig
of inheritance *is* thine, and [i]the r
demption *is* thine; buy *it* for thysel
Then I knew that this *was* the word
the LORD.
9 And I bought the field of Hăn-ă
mēel my uncle's son, that *was* in Ăn-ă
thōth, and weighed [j]him the mone
even [1]seventeen shekels of silver.
10 And I [2]subscribed the evidenc
and sealed *it*, and [k]took witnesses, an
weighed *him* the money in the ba
ances.
11 So I took the evidence of the pu
chase, *both* that which was seale
according to the law and custom, an
that which was open:
12 And I gave the evidence of th
purchase unto [l]Bâr-ŭch the son of Nē
rī-ăh, the son of Mā-ă-sēi-ăh, in th
sight of Hăn-ă-mēel mine uncle's *so*
and in the presence of the [m]witnesse
that subscribed the book of the pu
chase, before all the Jews that sat i
the court of the prison.
13 ¶ And I charged Bâr-ŭch befor
them, saying,
14 Thus saith the LORD of hosts, th

God of Israel; Take these evidences,
this evidence of the purchase, both
which is sealed, and this evidence
which is open; and put them in an
earthen vessel, that they may continue
many days.
15 For thus saith the LORD of hosts,
the God of Israel; Houses and fields
and vineyards shall be possessed
again in this land.
16 ¶ Now when I had delivered the
evidence of the purchase unto Bâr-ŭch
the son of Nē-rī-ăh, [n]I prayed unto
the LORD, saying,
17 Ah Lord GOD! behold, [o]thou hast
made the heaven and the earth by thy
great power and stretched out arm,
and there [p]is nothing [3]too hard for
thee:
18 Thou shewest [q]lovingkindness unto thousands, and recompensest the
iniquity of the fathers into the bosom
of their children after them: the
Great, the [r]Mighty God, [s]the LORD of
hosts, *is* his name,
19 Great [t]in counsel, and mighty in
work: for thine [u]eyes *are* open upon
all the ways of the sons of men: [v]to
give every one according to his ways,
and according to the fruit of his doings:
20 Which hast set signs and wonders
in the land of Egypt, *even* unto this
day, and in Israel, and among *other*
men; and hast made thee [w]a name,
as at this day;
21 And [x]hast brought forth thy people Israel out of the land of Egypt with
signs, and with wonders, and with a
strong hand, and with a stretched out
arm, and with great terror;
22 And hast given them this land,
which thou didst swear to their fathers
to give them, [y]a land flowing with
milk and honey;
23 And they came in, and possessed
it; but [z]they obeyed not thy voice,
neither walked in thy law; they have
done nothing of all that thou commandedst them to do: therefore thou
hast caused all this evil to come upon
them:
24 Behold the [5]mounts, they are
come unto the city to take it; and the
city is given into the hand of the Chăl-
dē-ăns, that fight against it, because
of [a]the sword, and of the famine, and
of the pestilence: and what thou hast
spoken [b]is come to pass; and, behold,
thou seest *it*.
25 And thou hast said unto me, O
Lord GOD, Buy thee the field for
money, and take witnesses; [6]for the
city is given into the hand of the Chăl-
dē-ăns.
26 ¶ Then came the word of the
LORD unto Jeremiah, saying,
27 Behold, I *am* the LORD, [c]the God
of all flesh: is [d]there any thing too
hard for me?
28 Therefore thus saith the LORD;
Behold, I will give this city into the
hand of the Chăl-dē-ăns, and into the
hand of Nĕb-ū-chăd-rĕz-zär king of
Babylon, and he shall take it:
29 And the Chăl-dē-ăns, that fight
against this city, shall come and [e]set
fire on this city, and burn it with the
houses, [f]upon whose roofs they have
offered incense unto Bā-ăl, and poured out drink offerings unto other gods,
to provoke me to anger.
30 For the children of Israel and the
children of Judah [g]have only done evil
before me from their youth: for the
children of Israel have only provoked
me to anger with the work of their
hands, saith the LORD.
31 For [h]this city hath been to me *as*
[7]a provocation of mine anger and of
my fury from the day that they built it
even unto this day; [i]that I should remove it from before my face,
32 Because of all the evil of the children of Israel and of the children of
Judah, which they have done to provoke me to anger, they, [j]their kings,
their princes, their priests, and their
prophets, and the men of Judah, and
the inhabitants of Jerusalem.
33 And they have turned unto me
the [8]back, and not the face: though I
taught them, [k]rising up early and
teaching *them*, yet they have not
hearkened to receive instruction.
34 But they [l]set their abominations
in the house, which is called by my
name, to defile it.
35 And they built the high places of
Bā-ăl, which *are* in the valley of the
son of Hĭn-nŏm, to [m]cause their sons
and their daughters to pass through
the fire [n]unto Molech; which I commanded them not, neither came it into
my mind, that they should do this
abomination, to cause Judah to
sin.
36 ¶ And now therefore thus saith
the LORD, the God of Israel, concerning this city, whereof ye say, It shall
be delivered into the hand of the king
of Babylon by the sword, and by the
famine, and by the pestilence;
37 Behold, I will [o]gather them out of
all countries, whither I have driven
them in mine anger, and in my fury,

n Gen. 32.9-12. Dan. 9.1. Phil. 4.6,7.
o 2 Ki. 19.15.
p Gen. 18.14. Zech. 8.6. Matt. 19.26. Mark 10.27. Luke 1.37. Rom. 4.21.
3 Or, hid from thee.
q Ex. 20.6. Deut. 5.9, 10.
r Ps. 45.3-6. Isa. 9.6. Titus 2.13.
s ch. 10.16.
t Isa. 28.29.
4 doing.
u Job 34.21. Ps. 33.13-15. Pro. 5.21. ch. 16.17.
v Ps. 62.12. Eccl. 12.14. ch. 17.10. Matt. 16.27. John 5.29.
w Ex. 9.16. 1 Chr. 17.21. Isa. 63.12.
x Ex. 6.6. 2 Sam. 7.23. 1 Chr. 17.21.
y Ex. 3.8. ch. 11.5.
z Neh. 9.26. Dan. 9.10.
5 Or, engines of shot.
a ch. 14.12.
b Josh. 23.15.
6 Or, though.
c Isa. 64.8.
d Ps. 115.3.
e ch. 21.10.
f ch. 19.13.
g Eze. 20.28.
h Zeph. 3.1.
7 for my anger.
i 2 Ki. 23.27.
j Isa. 1.4,6. Dan. 9.8.
8 neck.
k ch. 7.13.
l 2 Chr. 33.4, 5. ch. 7.30. Eze. 8.5.
m 2 Ki. 23.10. ch. 19.5.
n Lev. 18.21.
o Deut. 30.3.

and in great wrath; and I will bring
them again unto this place, and I will
cause them [p]to dwell safely:
38 And they shall be [q]my people, and
I will be their God:
39 And I will [r]give them one heart,
and one way, that they may fear me
[9]for ever, for the good of them, and
of their children after them:
40 And [s]I will make an everlasting
covenant with them, that I will not
turn away [10]from them, to do them
good; but [t]I will put my fear in their
hearts, that they shall not depart
from me.
41 Yea, [u]I will rejoice over them to
do them good, and [v]I will plant them
in this land [11]assuredly with my whole
heart and with my whole soul.
42 For thus saith the LORD; [w]Like as
I have brought all this great evil upon
this people, so will I bring upon them
all the good that I have promised
them.
43 And fields shall be bought in this
land, whereof [x]ye say, *It is* desolate
without man or beast; it is given into
the hand of the Chăl-dē-ăns.
44 Men shall buy fields for money,
and subscribe evidences, and seal
them, and take witnesses in [y]the land
of Benjamin, and in the places about
Jerusalem, and in the cities of Judah,
and in the cities of the mountains, and
in the cities of the valley, and in the
cities of the south: for [z]I will cause
their captivity to return, saith the
LORD.

CHAPTER 33

MOREOVER the word of the
LORD came unto Jeremiah the
second time, while he was yet shut [a]up
in the court of the prison, saying,
2 Thus saith the LORD [b]the maker
thereof, the LORD that formed it, to
establish it; [1]the LORD *is* his name;
3 Call [c]unto me, and I will answer
thee, and shew thee great and [2]mighty
things, which thou knowest not.
4 For thus saith the LORD, the God
of Israel, concerning the houses of this
city, and concerning the houses of the
kings of Judah, which are thrown
down by [d]the mounts, and by the
sword;
5 They come to fight with the Chăl-
dē-ăns, but *it is* to fill them with the
dead bodies of men, whom I have
slain in mine anger and in my fury,
and for all whose wickedness I have
hid my face from this city.
6 Behold, [e]I will bring it health and
cure, and I will cure them, and will re-

p ch. 23.6.
q ch. 24.7.
r Eze. 11.19.
9 all days.
s Isa. 55.3.
10 from after them.
t ch. 31.33.
u Deut. 30.9.
v ch. 24.6.
11 in truth, or, stability.
w ch. 31.28.
x ch. 33.10.
y ch. 17.26.
z ch. 33.7.

CHAP. 33

a ch. 32.2. ch. 37.21.
b Isa. 37.26.
1 Or, JEHOVAH. Ex. 15.3. Amos 5.8.
c Gen. 18.17. Deut. 4.7, 29. Ps. 50.15. Isa. 55.6,7. ch. 29.12. Acts 2.21.
2 Or, hidden.
d ch. 32.24.
e ch. 30.17.
f ch. 32.44.
g Isa. 1.26.
h Ps. 85.2,3. Isa. 40.2. ch. 31.34. Zech. 13.1. Heb. 9.13.
i Micah 7.18. 1 John 1.7-9.
j Ezra 1.2. Isa. 62.7.
k Isa. 60.5.
l Rev. 18.23.
m 1 Chr. 16.8. 2 Chr. 5.13.
n Lev. 7.12. 2 Chr. 29.31. Ps. 107.22. Jonah 2.9. Heb. 13.15.
o Isa. 65.10.
p ch. 17.26.
q Lev. 27.32.
r ch. 23.5.
s ch. 29.10.
t Isa. 4.2.
u Deut. 33. 28. Isa. 45.17.

veal unto them the abundance of
peace and truth.
7 And [f]I will cause the captivity of
Judah and the captivity of Israel to return, and will build them, [g]as at the
first.
8 And I will [h]cleanse them from all
their iniquity, whereby they have
sinned against me; and I will pardon
[i]all their iniquities, whereby they
have sinned, and whereby they have
transgressed against me.
9 ¶ And [j]it shall be to me a name of
joy, a praise and an honour before all
the nations of the earth, which shall
hear all the good that I do unto them:
and they [k]shall fear and tremble for
all the goodness and for all the prosperity that I procure unto it.
10 Thus saith the LORD; Again there
shall be heard in this place, which ye
say *shall be* desolate without man and
without beast, *even* in the cities of
Judah, and in the streets of Jerusalem, that are desolate, without man
and without inhabitant, and without
beast,
11 The [l]voice of joy, and the voice of
gladness, the voice of the bridegroom,
and the voice of the bride, the voice of
them that shall say, [m]Praise the LORD
of hosts: for the LORD *is* good; for his
mercy *endureth* for ever: *and* of them
that shall bring [n]the sacrifice of praise
into the house of the LORD. For I will
cause to return the captivity of the
land, as at the first, saith the LORD.
12 Thus saith the LORD of hosts;
Again [o]in this place, which is desolate
without man and without beast, and
in all the cities thereof, shall be an
habitation of shepherds causing *their*
flocks to lie down.
13 In [p]the cities of the mountains, in
the cities of the vale, and in the cities
of the south, and in the land of Benjamin, and in the places about Jerusalem, and in the cities of Judah, shall
the [q]flocks pass again under the hands
of him that telleth *them*, saith the
LORD.
14 Behold, [r]the days come, saith the
LORD, that [s]I will perform that good
thing which I have promised unto the
house of Israel and to the house of
Judah.
15 ¶ In those days, and at that time,
will I cause the [t]Branch of righteousness to grow up unto David; and he
shall execute judgment and righteousness in the land.
16 In [u]those days shall Judah be saved, and Jerusalem shall dwell safely:

nd [3]this *is the name* wherewith she
nall be called, The LORD our right-
ousness.
17 ¶ For thus saith the LORD; [4]David
hall never want a man to sit upon
he throne of the house of Israel;
18 Neither shall the priests the Le-
ites want a man before me to offer
burnt offerings, and to kindle meat
fferings, and to do sacrifice con-
nually.
19 ¶ And the word of the LORD came
nto Jeremiah, saying,
20 Thus saith the LORD; [w]If ye can
reak my covenant of the day, and my
ovenant of the night, and that there
hould not be day and night in their
eason;
21 *Then* may also my covenant be
roken with David my servant, that
e should not have a son to reign upon
is throne; and with the Levites the
riests, my ministers.
22 As the [x]host of heaven cannot be
umbered, neither the sand of the sea
neasured: so will I multiply the seed
f David my servant, and the Levites
hat minister unto me.
23 Moreover the word of the LORD
ame to Jeremiah, saying,
24 Considerest thou not what this
eople have spoken, saying, The two
amilies which the LORD hath chosen,
e hath even cast them off? thus they
ave despised my people, that they
hould be no more a nation before
hem.
25 Thus saith the LORD; If [y]my cov-
nant *be* not with day and night, *and if*
have not [z]appointed the ordinances
f heaven and earth;
26 Then will I cast away the seed of
acob, and David my servant, *so* that
will not take *any* of his seed *to be* rul-
rs over the seed of Abraham, Isaac,
nd Jacob: [a]for I will cause their
aptivity to return, and have mercy on
hem.

CHAPTER 34

THE word which came unto Jeremiah from the LORD, when [a]Něb-
-chăd-něz-zär king of Babylon, and
ll his army, and all the [b]kingdoms of
he earth [1]of his dominion, and all the
eople, fought against Jerusalem, and
gainst all the cities thereof, saying,
2 Thus saith the LORD, the God of
srael; Go and speak to Zěd-ē-kī-ăh
ing of Judah, and tell him, Thus saith
he LORD; Behold, [c]I will give this city
nto the hand of the king of Babylon,
nd [d]he shall burn it with fire:
3 And [e]thou shalt not escape out of
his hand, but shalt surely be taken,
and delivered into his hand; and thine
eyes shall behold the eyes of the king
of Babylon, and [2]he shall speak with
thee mouth to mouth, and thou shalt
go to Babylon.
4 Yet hear the word of the LORD, O
Zěd-ē-kī-ăh king of Judah; Thus saith
the LORD of thee, Thou shalt not die
by the sword:
5 *But* thou shalt die in peace: and
with the [f]burnings of thy fathers, the
former kings which were before thee,
so [g]shall they burn *odours* for thee;
and [h]they will lament thee, *saying*, Ah
lord! for I have pronounced the word,
saith the LORD.
6 Then Jeremiah the [i]prophet spake
all these words unto Zěd-ē-kī-ăh king
of Judah in Jerusalem,
7 When the king of Babylon's army
fought against Jerusalem, and against
all the cities of Judah that were left,
against Lā-chĭsh, and against Ă-zē-
kăh: for [j]these defenced cities remained of the cities of Judah.
8 ¶ *This is* the word that came unto
Jeremiah from the LORD, after that
the king Zěd-ē-kī-ăh had made a
covenant with all the people which
were at Jerusalem, to proclaim [k]lib-
erty unto them;
9 That [l]every man should let his
manservant, and every man his maidservant, *being* an Hebrew or an He-
brewess, go free; [m]that none should
serve himself of them, *to wit*, of a Jew
his brother.
10 Now when all the princes, and all
the people, which had entered into the
covenant, heard that every one should
let his manservant, and every one his
maidservant, go free, that none should
serve themselves of them any more,
then they obeyed, and let *them* go.
11 But [n]afterward they turned, and
caused the servants and the handmaids, whom they had let go free, to
return, and brought them into subjection for servants and for handmaids.
12 ¶ Therefore the word of the LORD
came to Jeremiah from the LORD, saying,
13 Thus saith the LORD, the God of
Israel; I made a covenant with your
fathers in the day that I brought them
forth out of the land of Egypt, out of
the house of bondmen, saying,
14 At the end of [o]seven years let ye
go every man his brother an Hebrew,
which [3]hath been sold unto thee; and
when he hath served thee six years,
thou shalt let him go free from thee:

3 he who shall call her is Jehovah-tsidkenu.
4 There shall not be cut off from David.
v Mal. 1.11. Rom. 12.1. 1 Pet. 2.5,9. Rev. 1.6.
w Gen. 8.22. Ps. 89.37. Isa. 54.9. ch. 31.36.
x Gen. 13.16. Gen. 15.5. ch. 31.37.
y Gen. 8.22.
z Ps. 74.16. Ps. 104.19. ch. 31.35.
a Isa. 14.1. ch. 31.20. Zech. 10.6.

CHAP. 34

a 2 Ki. 25.1. ch. 32.2.
b ch. 1.15. Dan. 2.37.
1 the dominion of his hand.
c ch. 21.10.
d ch. 32.29.
e ch. 32.4.
2 his mouth shall speak to thy mouth.
f 2 Chr. 16. 14.
g Dan. 2.46.
h ch. 22.18.
i 1 Ki. 21.19. Eze. 2.7. Matt. 14.4.
j 2 Ki. 18.13. 2 Chr. 11.5, 9.
k Ex. 21.2. Lev. 25.10. Deut. 15.12. Isa. 1.17. Micah 2.1-3, 7-13.
l Neh. 5.11.
m Lev. 25.39.
n ch. 37.5. Hosea 6.4.
o Ex. 21.2. Lev. 25.39. Deut. 15.12.
3 Or, hath sold himself.

but your fathers hearkened not unto me, neither inclined their ear.

15 And ye were [4]now turned, and had done right in my sight, in proclaiming liberty every man to his neighbour; and ye [p]had made a covenant before me [q]in the house [5]which is called by my name:

16 But ye turned and [r]polluted my name, and caused every man his servant, and every man his handmaid, whom ye had set at liberty at their pleasure, to return, and brought them into subjection, to be unto you for servants and for handmaids.

17 Therefore thus saith the LORD; Ye have not [s]hearkened unto me, in proclaiming liberty, every one to his brother, and every man to his neighbour: [t]behold, I proclaim a liberty for you, saith the LORD, to the sword, to the pestilence, and to [u]the famine; and I will make you [6]to be removed into all the kingdoms of the earth.

18 And I will give the men that have [v]transgressed my covenant, which have not performed the words of the covenant which they had made before me, when they cut [w]the calf in twain, and passed between the parts thereof,

19 The princes of Judah, and the princes of Jerusalem, the eunuchs, and the priests, and all the people of the land, which passed between the parts of the calf;

20 I will even give them into the hand of their enemies, and into the hand of them that seek their life: and their [x]dead bodies shall be for meat unto the fowls of the heaven, and to the beasts of the earth.

21 And Zĕd-ē-kī´-ăh king of Judah and his princes will I give into the hand of their enemies, and into the hand of them that seek their life, and into the hand of the king of Babylon's army, [y]which are gone up from you.

22 Behold, [z]I will command, saith the LORD, and cause them to return to this city; [a]and they shall fight against it, and take it, and burn it with fire: and [b]I will make the cities of Judah a desolation without an inhabitant.

CHAPTER 35

THE word which came unto Jeremiah from the LORD in the days of [a]Jĕ-hoi´-ă-kĭm the son of Jō-sī´-ăh king of Judah, saying,

2 Go unto the house of [b]the Rē´-chăb-ītes, and speak unto them, and bring them into the house of the LORD, into one of [c]the chambers, and give the wine to drink.

3 Then I took Jā-ăz-ă-nī´-ăh the so of Jeremiah, the son of Hă-băz-ĭ-n ăh, and his brethren, and all his son and the whole house of the Rē´-chăb ites;

4 And I brought them into the hous of the LORD, into the chamber of th sons of Hā´-năn, the son of Ĭg-dă-lī´-ăh a man of God, which *was* by the chan ber of the princes, which *was* above th chamber of Mā-ă-sē´-ăh the son Shăl´-lŭm, [d]the keeper of the [1]door:

5 And I set before the sons of th house of the Rē´-chăb-ītes pots full wine, and cups, and I said unto then Drink ye wine.

6 But they said, We will drink n wine: for [e]Jŏn´-ă-dăb the son of Rē chăb our father commanded us, say ing, Ye shall drink no wine, *neither* y nor your sons for ever:

7 Neither shall ye build house, nc sow seed, nor plant vineyard, nor hav *any:* but all your days ye shall dwe in tents; [f]that ye may live many day in the land where ye *be* strangers.

8 Thus have we [g]obeyed the voice c Jŏn´-ă-dăb the son of Rē´-chăb ou father in all that he hath charged us to drink no wine all our days, we, ou wives, our sons, nor our daughters;

9 Nor to build houses for us to dwel in: neither have we vineyard, no field, nor seed:

10 But we have dwelt in tents, an have obeyed, and done according t all that Jŏn´-ă-dăb our father com manded us.

11 But it came to pass, [h]when Nĕb ū-chăd-rĕz´-zăr king of Babylon cam up into the land, that we said, Come and let us go to Jerusalem for fear c the army of the Chăl-dē´-ăns, and fc fear of the army of the Syrians: so w dwell at Jerusalem.

12 ¶ Then came the word of the LOR unto Jeremiah, saying,

13 Thus saith the LORD of hosts, th God of Israel; Go and tell the men Judah and the inhabitants of Jerusa lem, Will ye not [i]receive instruction t hearken to my words? saith the LORI

14 The words of Jŏn´-ă-dăb the so of Rē´-chăb, that he commanded hi sons not to drink wine, are performed for unto this day they drink none, bu obey their father's commandment [j]notwithstanding I have spoken unt you, [k]rising early and speaking; bu [l]ye hearkened not unto me.

15 I [m]have sent also unto you all m

4 to-day.
p 2 Ki. 23.3. Neh. 10.29.
q ch. 7.10.
5 whereupon my name is called.
r Ex. 20.7. Lev. 19.12.
s Neh. 9.30.
t Matt. 7.2. Gal. 6.7. 1 Thes. 4.6.
u ch. 32.24, 36.
6 for a removing.
v Rom. 2.8.
w Gen. 15.10. Ps. 50.5.
x Deut. 28. 26. Ps. 79.2. ch. 7.33. ch. 16.4. Rev. 19.17-21.
y ch. 37.5.
z ch. 37.8. Amos 3.6.
a ch. 38.3. ch. 39.1,2,8.
b ch. 9.11. ch. 33.10. Micah 7.13. Zech. 1.12.

CHAP. 35
a 2 Ki. 23.34, 35. ch. 22.18. Dan. 1.1.
b 2 Ki. 10.15. 1 Chr. 2.55.
c 1 Ki. 6.5.
d 2 Ki. 12.9. 1 Chr. 9.18, 19.
1 threshold, or, vessel.
e 2 Ki. 10.15. 1 Chr. 2.55.
f Ex. 20.12. Deut. 4.40. Pro. 3.16. Eph. 6.2,3.
g Pro. 1.8. Col. 3.20.
h 2 Ki. 24.1.
i ch. 32.33.
j 2 Chr. 36. 15.
k ch. 7.13.
l Isa. 30.9.
m ch. 7.25.

vants the prophets, rising up early
d sending *them*, saying, Return [n]ye
w every man from his evil way, and
nend your doings, and go not after
her gods to serve them, and ye shall
vell in the land which I have given to
u and to your fathers: but ye have
t inclined your ear, nor hearkened
ito me.
6 Because the sons of Jŏn-ā-dăb the
n of Rē-chăb have performed the
mmandment of their father, which
commanded them; but this people
th not hearkened unto me:
7 Therefore thus saith the LORD
od of hosts, the God of Israel; Beold, I [o]will bring upon Judah and up-
n all the inhabitants of Jerusalem all
e evil that I have pronounced
ainst them: [p]because I have spoken
nto them, but they have not heard;
d I have called unto them, but they
ve not answered.
8 ¶ And Jeremiah said unto the
ouse of the Rē-chăb-ītes, Thus saith
e LORD of hosts, the God of Israel;
Because ye have obeyed the com-
andment of Jŏn-ā-dăb your father,
d kept all his precepts, and done
cording unto all that he hath com-
anded you:
9 Therefore thus saith the LORD of
osts, the God of Israel; [2]Jŏn-ā-dăb
e son of Rē-chăb shall not want a
an [r]to stand before me for ever.

CHAPTER 36

AND it came to pass in the fourth
year of Jĕ-hoi-ā-kĭm the son of
Jō-sī-ăh king of Judah, *that* this word
ame unto Jeremiah from the LORD,
ying,
2 Take thee a [a]roll of a book, and
rite [b]therein all the words that I have
oken unto thee against Israel, and
gainst Judah, and against [c]all the na-
ons, from the day I spake unto thee,
om the days of [d]Jō-sī-ăh, even unto
is day.
3 It [e]may be that the house of Judah
ill hear all the evil which I purpose
do unto them; that they may [f]return
very man from his evil way; that I
ay forgive their iniquity and their sin.
4 Then Jeremiah [g]called Bâr-ŭch the
on of Nē-rī-ăh: and [h]Bâr-ŭch wrote
om the mouth of Jeremiah all the
ords of the LORD, which he had
oken unto him, upon a roll of a
ook.
5 And Jeremiah commanded Bâr-
ch, saying, I *am* shut up; I cannot go
nto the house of the LORD:

n Isa. 1.16-19. ch. 3.14. ch. 18.11. ch. 25.5,6. Hosea 14.1-4. Acts 26.20.
o Lev. 26.14. Josh. 23.15. ch. 15.3,4. Micah 3.12.
p Pro. 1.24. Isa. 65.12. ch. 7.13.
q Ex. 20.12.
2 There shall not a man be cut off from Jonadab the son of Rechab to stand, etc.
r ch. 15.19.

CHAP. 36

a Isa. 8.1.
b ch. 30.2. Hab. 2.2.
c ch. 25.15.
d ch. 25.3.
e ch. 18.8. Eze. 12.3. Zeph. 2.3.
f Isa. 55.7. ch. 18.8. Jonah 3.8. Acts 26.20.
g ch. 32.12.
h ch. 45.1.
i Lev. 16.29.
j Lev. 23.4. Neh. 8.14, 15.
1 their supplication shall fall.
k Deut. 28. 15. Deut. 29.18.
l Judg. 20.26. 1 Sam. 7.6. 2 Chr. 20.3.
2 Or, secretary of state.
3 Or, door.
m Eze. 2.6.
n 1 Sam. 3.11. Acts 24.25.

6 Therefore go thou, and read in the
roll, which thou hast written from my
mouth, the words of the LORD in the
ears of the people in the LORD's house
upon the [i]fasting day: and also thou
shalt read them in the ears of all
Judah [j]that come out of their cities.
7 It may be [1]they will present their
supplication before the LORD, and
will return every one from his evil
way: for [k]great *is* the anger and the
fury that the LORD hath pronounced
against this people.
8 And Bâr-ŭch the son of Nē-rī-ăh
did according to all that Jeremiah the
prophet commanded him, reading in
the book the words of the LORD in the
LORD's house.
9 And it came to pass in the fifth year
of Jĕ-hoi-ā-kĭm the son of Jō-sī-ăh
king of Judah, in the ninth month,
that [l]they proclaimed a fast before the
LORD to all the people in Jerusalem,
and to all the people that came from
the cities of Judah unto Jerusalem.
10 Then read Bâr-ŭch in the book
the words of Jeremiah in the house of
the LORD, in the chamber of Gĕm-ă-
rī-ăh the son of Shā-phăn the [2]scribe,
in the higher court, at the [3]entry of
the new gate of the LORD's house, in
the ears of all the people.
11 ¶ When Mī-chai-ăh the son of
Gĕm-ă-rī-ăh, the son of Shā-phăn,
had heard out of the book all the
words of the LORD,
12 Then he went down into the king's
house, into the scribe's chamber: and,
lo, all the princes sat there, *even* Ē-lī-
shă-mă the scribe, and Dĕl-ai-ăh the
son of Shĕm-ai-ăh, and Ĕl-nā-thăn
the son of Ăch-bôr, and Gĕm-ă-rī-ăh
the son of Shā-phăn, and Zĕd-ē-kī-ăh
the son of Hăn-ă-nī-ăh, and all the
princes.
13 Then Mī-chai-ăh declared unto
them all the words that he had heard,
when Bâr-ŭch read the book in the
ears of the people.
14 Therefore all the princes sent Jĕ-
hū-dī the son of Nĕth-ă-nī-ăh, the son
of Shĕl-ē-mī-ăh, the son of Cū-shī, unto Bâr-ŭch, saying, Take in thine hand
the roll wherein thou hast read in the
ears of the people, and come. So Bâr-
ŭch the son of Nē-rī-ăh took the roll
in his hand, and came unto [m]them.
15 And they said unto him, Sit down
now, and read it in our ears. So Bâr-
ŭch read *it* in their ears.
16 Now it came to pass, when they
had heard all the words, they were
[n]afraid both one and other, and said

unto Bâr´-ŭch, We will surely tell the
king of all these words.
17 And they asked Bâr´-ŭch, saying,
Tell us now, How didst thou write all
these words at his mouth?
18 Then Bâr´-ŭch answered them, He
[o]pronounced all these words unto me
with his mouth, and I wrote *them* with
ink in the book.
19 Then said the princes unto Bâr-
ŭch, Go, hide thee, thou and Jeremiah; and let no man know where ye
be.
20 ¶ And they went in to the king
into the court, but they laid up the roll
in the chamber of Ē-lĭ´-shă-mă the
scribe, and told all the words in the
ears of the king.
21 So the king sent Jĕ-hū´-dī to fetch
the roll: and he took it out of Ē-lĭ´-shă-
mă the scribe's chamber. And Jĕ-hū´-
dī read it in the ears of the king, and in
the ears of all the princes which stood
beside the king.
22 Now the king sat in the [p]winter-
house in the ninth month: and *there
was a fire* on the hearth burning before
him.
23 And it came to pass, *that* when
Jĕ-hū´-dī had read three or four leaves,
[q]he cut it with the penknife, and cast
it into the fire that *was* on the hearth,
until all the roll was consumed in the
fire that *was* on the hearth.
24 Yet they were not afraid, nor rent
[r]their garments, *neither* the king, nor
any of his servants that heard all these
words.
25 Nevertheless Ĕl-nā´-thăn and Dĕl-
âi´-ăh and Gĕm-ă-rī´-ăh [s]had made intercession to the king that he would
not burn the roll: but he would not
hear them.
26 But the king commanded Jĕ-răh´-
mēel the son [4]of Hăm´-mĕ-lĕch, and
Sĕ-râi´-ăh the son of Ăz´-rĭ-ĕl, and Shĕl-
ē-mī´-ăh the son of Ăb´-dēel, to take
[t]Bâr´-ŭch the scribe and Jeremiah the
prophet: but [u]the LORD hid them.
27 ¶ Then the word of the LORD
came to Jeremiah, after [v]that the king
had burned the roll, and the words
which Bâr´-ŭch wrote at the mouth of
Jeremiah, saying,
28 Take thee again another roll, and
write in it all the former words that
were in the first roll, which Jĕ-hôi´-ă-
kĭm the king of Judah hath burned.
29 And thou shalt say to Jĕ-hôi´-ă-
kĭm king of Judah, Thus saith the
LORD; Thou hast burned this roll,
[w]saying, Why hast thou written therein, saying, The king of Babylon shall
certainly come and destroy this lar
and shall cause to cease from then
man and beast?
30 Therefore thus saith the LO
of Jĕ-hôi´-ă-kĭm king of Judah; [x]H
shall have none to sit upon the thro
of David: and his dead body shall
[y]cast out in the day to the heat, and
the night to the frost.
31 And I will [5]punish him and h
seed and his servants for their in
quity; and I will bring upon them, an
upon the inhabitants of Jerusaler
and upon the men of Judah, all th
evil that I have pronounced again
them; but they hearkened not.
32 ¶ Then took Jeremiah anoth
roll, and gave it to Bâr´-ŭch the scrib
the son of Nē-rī´-ăh; [z]who wrote ther
in from the mouth of Jeremiah all th
words of the book which Jĕ-hôi´-ă-ki
king of Judah had burned in the fire
and there were added besides unt
them many [6]like words.

CHAPTER 37

AND king [a]Zĕd-ē-kī´-ăh the son o
Jō-sī´-ăh reigned instead of Cō-n
ăh the son of Jĕ-hôi´-ă-kĭm, whor
Nĕb-ū-chăd-rĕz´-zăr king of Babylo
made king in the land of Judah.
2 But [b]neither he, nor his servants
nor the people of the land, did hearke
unto the words of the LORD, which h
spake [1]by the prophet Jeremiah.
3 And Zĕd-ē-kī´-ăh the king sent Jĕ
hū´-căl the son of Shĕl-ē-mī´-ăh an
Zĕph-ă-nī´-ăh [c]the son of Mā-ă-sēi´-ă
the priest to the prophet Jeremiah
saying, Pray now unto the LORD ou
God for us.
4 Now Jeremiah came in and wen
out among the people: for they ha
not put him into prison.
5 Then [d]Pharaoh's army was com
forth out of Egypt: [e]and when th
Chăl-dē´-ăns that besieged Jerusalen
heard tidings of them, they departe
from Jerusalem.
6 ¶ Then came the word of the LOR
unto the prophet Jeremiah, saying,
7 Thus saith the LORD, the God o
Israel; Thus shall ye say to the kin
of Judah, that [f]sent you unto me t
inquire of me; Behold, Pharaoh'
army, which is come forth to help you
shall return to Egypt into their ow
land.
8 And the [g]Chăl-dē´-ăns shall com
again, and fight against this city, an
take it, and burn it with fire.
9 Thus saith the LORD; Deceive no
[2]yourselves, saying, The Chăl-dē´-ăn

o Isa. 8.12. ch. 1.8. Matt. 10.16-32. Rom. 1.16. 1 Pet. 3.14, 15.
p Judg. 3.20. Amos 3.15.
q 1 Ki. 22.8. Isa. 29.21. 2 Tim. 4.3.
r Gen. 37.29, 34. 2 Sam. 1.11. 2 Ki. 22.11. Isa. 36.22.
s Gen. 37.26. Isa. 53.12. Matt. 27.24. Rom. 8.34. Eph. 5.7,11. Heb. 7.25.
4 Or, of the king.
t 1 Ki. 19.14. Matt. 23.34, 37.
u Ps. 34.19, 20. Ps. 46.1. ch. 1.19. 2 Pet. 2.9.
v Pro. 21.30.
w Amos 5.10.
x 2 Ki. 24.8, 12. ch. 22.30.
y ch. 22.19.
5 visit upon. Isa. 3.11. ch. 21.7.
z Ex. 4.15. Rom. 16.22.
6 as they.

CHAP. 37

a 1 Chr. 3.16. 2 Chr. 36.10. Dan. 1.1.
b 2 Ki. 24. 19,20. Pro. 29.12.
1 by the hand of the prophet.
c ch. 21.1,2.
d 2 Ki. 24.7.
e ch. 34.21.
f ch. 21.2.
g Ps. 33.10. Pro. 21.30. Isa. 30.1-7. ch. 34.22.
2 your souls.

shall surely depart from us: for they shall not depart.

10 For [h]though ye had smitten the whole army of the Chăl-dē-ănş that fight against you, and there remained but [3]wounded men among them, *yet* should they rise up every man in his tent, and burn this city with fire.

11 ¶ And it came to pass, that when the army of the Chăl-dē-ănş was broken up from Jerusalem for fear of Pharaoh's army,

12 Then Jeremiah went forth out of Jerusalem to go into the land of Benjamin, [5]to separate himself thence in the midst of the people.

13 And when he was in the gate of Benjamin, a captain of the ward *was* there, whose name *was* Ī-rī-jăh, the son of Shĕl-ē-mī-ăh, the son of Hăn-ă-nī-ăh; and he took Jeremiah the prophet, saying, Thou fallest away to the Chăl-dē-ănş.

14 Then said Jeremiah, *It is* [6]false; I fall not away to the Chăl-dē-ănş. But he hearkened not to him: so Ī-rī-jăh took Jeremiah, and brought him to the princes.

15 Wherefore the princes [i]were wroth with Jeremiah, and smote him, [j]and put him in prison in the house of Jonathan the scribe: for they had made that the prison.

16 ¶ When Jeremiah was entered into the [k]dungeon, and into the [7]cabins, and Jeremiah had remained there many days;

17 Then Zĕd-ē-kī-ăh the king sent, and took him out: and the king asked him secretly in his house, and said, [l]Is there *any* word from the LORD? And Jeremiah said, There is: for, said he, thou shalt be delivered into the hand of the king of Babylon.

18 Moreover Jeremiah said unto king Zĕd-ē-kī-ăh, What have I offended against thee, or against thy servants, or against this people, that ye have put me in prison?

19 Where *are* now your prophets which prophesied unto you, saying, The king of Babylon shall not come against you, nor against this land?

20 Therefore hear now, I pray thee, O my lord the king: [8]let my supplication, I pray thee, be accepted before thee; that thou cause me not to return to the house of Jonathan the scribe, lest I die there.

21 Then Zĕd-ē-kī-ăh the king commanded that they should commit Jeremiah [m]into the court of the prison, and [n]that they should give him daily a piece of bread out of the bakers' street, [o]until all the bread in the city were spent. Thus Jeremiah remained [p]in the court of the prison.

CHAPTER 38

THEN Shĕph-ă-tī-ăh the son of Măt-tăn, and Gĕd-ă-lī-ăh the son of Păsh-ŭr, and Jû-căl [a]the son of Shĕl-ē-mī-ăh, and [b]Păsh-ŭr the son of Măl-chī-ăh, [c]heard the words that Jeremiah had spoken unto all the people, saying,

2 Thus saith the LORD, [d]He that remaineth in this city shall die by the sword, by the famine, and by the pestilence: but he that goeth forth to the Chăl-dē-ănş shall live; for he shall have his life for a prey, and shall live.

3 Thus saith the LORD, [e]This city shall surely be given into the hand of the king of Babylon's army, which shall take it.

4 Therefore the princes said unto the king, We beseech thee, [f]let this man be put to death: for thus he weakeneth the hands of the men of war that remain in this city, and the hands of all the people, in speaking such words unto them: for this man seeketh not the [1]welfare of this people, but the hurt.

5 Then Zĕd-ē-kī-ăh the king said, Behold, he *is* [g]in your hand: for the king *is* not *he that* can do *any* thing against you.

6 Then [h]took they Jeremiah, and cast him into [i]the dungeon of Măl-chī-ăh the son [2]of Hăm-mĕ-lĕch, that *was* in the court of the prison: and they let down Jeremiah with cords. And in the dungeon *there was* no water, but mire: so Jeremiah sunk in the mire.

7 ¶ Now [j]when Ē-bĕd–mĕl-ĕch the Ē-thĭ-ō-pĭ-ăn, one of the eunuchs which was in the king's house, heard that they had put Jeremiah in the dungeon; the king then sitting [k]in the gate of Benjamin;

8 Ē-bĕd–mĕl-ĕch went forth out of the king's house, and [l]spake to the king, saying,

9 My lord the king, these men have done evil in all that they have done to Jeremiah the prophet, whom they have cast into the dungeon; and he is like to die for hunger in the place where [3]he is: for *there is* no more bread in the city.

10 Then the king commanded Ē-bĕd–mĕl-ĕch the Ē-thĭ-ō-pĭ-ăn, saying, Take from hence thirty men [4]with

h Lev. 26.36-38. Isa. 30.17. ch. 21.4,5.
3 thrust through.
4 made to ascend.
5 Or, to slip away from thence in the midst of the people.
6 falsehood, or, a lie.
i ch. 20.1-3. Matt. 21.35. John 18.22. Acts 5.40.
j Gen. 30.20. ch. 38.26. Acts 12.6. Rev. 2.10.
k ch. 38.6.
7 Or, cells.
l Mark 6.20.
8 let my supplication fall.
m ch. 32.2.
n 1 Ki. 17.6,9.
o 2 Ki. 25.3. ch. 38.9.
p 2 Cor. 6.4.

CHAP. 38

a ch. 37.3.
b ch. 21.1.
c ch. 21.8. Acts 4.2.
d ch. 21.9. Matt. 24.7, 8.
e ch. 21.10.
f Ps. 37.12-40. Pro. 29.10. ch. 26.11. Amos 7.10. Hab. 1.4. John 17.14. 2 Tim. 4.3. 1 John 3.12, 13.
1 peace.
g Eccl. 10.16.
h ch. 37.21.
i ch. 37.16. Lam. 3.53. Matt. 25.40. Mark 9.42.
2 Or, of the king.
j Ps. 68.31. ch. 39.16.
k Deut. 21. 19.
l Ps. 82.4. Pro. 14.25. Isa. 58.6.
3 he will die.
4 in thine hand.

thee, and take up Jeremiah the prophet out of the dungeon, before he
die.
11 So [m]Ē-bĕd–mĕl-ĕch took the men
with him, and went into the house of
the king under the treasury, and took
thence old cast clouts and old rotten
rags, and let them down by cords into
the dungeon to Jeremiah.
12 And Ē-bĕd–mĕl-ĕch the Ē-thĭ-ō-
pĭ-ăn said unto Jeremiah, Put now
these old cast clouts and rotten rags
under thine armholes under the cords.
And Jeremiah did so.
13 So they drew up Jeremiah with
cords, and took him up out of the
dungeon: and Jeremiah remained [n]in
the court of the prison.
14 ¶ Then Zĕd-ē-kī-ăh the king sent,
and took Jeremiah the prophet unto
him into the [5]third entry that *is* in the
house of the LORD: and the king said
unto Jeremiah, I will ask thee a thing;
hide nothing from me.
15 Then Jeremiah said unto Zĕd-ē-
kī-ăh, If I declare *it* unto thee, wilt
thou not surely put me to death? and
if I give thee counsel, wilt thou not
hearken unto me?
16 So Zĕd-ē-kī-ăh the king sware
secretly unto Jeremiah, saying, *As* the
LORD liveth, [o]that made us this soul, I
will not put thee to death, neither will
I give thee into the hand of these men
that seek thy life.
17 Then said Jeremiah unto Zĕd-ē-
kī-ăh, Thus saith the LORD, the God
of hosts, the God of Israel; If thou
wilt assuredly [p]go forth unto the king
of Babylon's princes, then thy soul
shall live, and this city shall not be
burned with fire; and thou shalt live,
and thine house:
18 But if thou wilt not go forth to the
king of Babylon's princes, then shall
this city be given into the hand of the
Chăl-dē-ăns, and they shall burn it
with fire, and thou [q]shalt not escape
out of their hand.
19 And Zĕd-ē-kī-ăh the king said unto Jeremiah, I [r]am afraid of the Jews
that are fallen to the Chăl-dē-ăns, lest
they deliver me into their hand, and
they [s]mock me.
20 But Jeremiah said, They shall not
deliver *thee*. Obey, I [t]beseech thee, the
voice of the LORD, which I speak unto
thee: so it shall be well unto thee, and
thy soul shall live.
21 But if thou refuse to go forth, this
is the word that the LORD hath shewed
me:
22 And, behold, all the women that
are left in the king of Judah's house
shall be brought forth to the king of
Babylon's princes, and those *women*
shall say, [6]Thy friends have set thee
on, and have prevailed against thee:
thy feet are sunk in the mire, *and* they
are turned away back.
23 So they shall bring out all thy
wives and thy [u]children to the Chăl-
dē-ăns: and thou shalt not escape out
of their hand, but shalt be taken by
the hand of the king of Babylon: and
[7]thou shalt cause this city to be burned
with fire.
24 ¶ Then said Zĕd-ē-kī-ăh unto
Jeremiah, Let no man know of these
words, and thou shalt not die.
25 But if the princes hear that I have
talked with thee, and they come unto
thee, and say unto thee, Declare unto
us now what thou hast said unto the
king, hide it not from us, and we will
not put thee to death; also what the
king said unto thee:
26 Then thou shalt say unto them, [v]I
presented my supplication before the
king, that he would not cause me to
return [w]to Jonathan's house, to die
there.
27 Then came all the princes unto
Jeremiah, and asked him: and he told
them according to all these words that
the king had commanded. So [8]they left
off speaking with him; for the matter
was not perceived.
28 So [x]Jeremiah abode in the court
of the prison until the day that Jerusalem was taken: and he was *there*
when Jerusalem was taken.

CHAPTER 39

IN the [a]ninth year of Zĕd-ē-kī-ăh
king of Judah, in the tenth month,
came Nĕb-ū-chăd-rĕz-zär king of
Babylon and all his army against Jerusalem, and they besieged it.
2 *And* in the eleventh year of Zĕd-ē-
kī-ăh, in the fourth month, the ninth
day of the month, the city was broken
up.
3 And [b]all the princes of the king
of Babylon came in, and sat in the
middle gate, *even* Nĕr-găl–shă-rē-zĕr,
Săm-găr–nē-bō, Sär-sĕ-chĭm, Răb-
să-rĭs, Nĕr-găl–shă-rē-zĕr, Rab-mag,
with all the residue of the princes of
the king of Babylon.
4 ¶ And [c]it came to pass, *that* when
Zĕd-ē-kī-ăh the king of Judah saw
them, and all the men of war, then
they fled, and went forth out of the
city by night, by the way of the king's
garden, by the gate betwixt the two

m Matt. 10. 41. Mark 9.41. 1 Cor. 1.27. Eph. 4.32.
n ch. 37.21. 2 Cor. 6.4,5.
5 Or, principal.
o Num. 16. 22. Isa. 42.5. Zech. 12.1. Acts 17.25, 28. Heb. 12.9.
p ch. 7.6,7. ch. 21.8,10.
q ch. 32.4.
r Pro. 29.25.
s 1 Sam. 31.4.
t Dan. 9.27. 2 Cor. 5.20.
6 Men of thy peace.
u ch. 39.6.
7 thou shalt burn, etc.
v ch. 37.20.
w ch. 37.15.
8 they were silent from him.
x ch. 15.20, 21. 2 Tim. 3.11.

CHAP. 39

a 2 Ki. 25.1-4. ch. 52.4-7.
b ch. 1.15. ch. 21.4.
c 2 Ki. 25.4. ch. 52.7.

valls: and he went out the way of the
lain.
5 But the Chăl-dē-ănsʼ army pursued
fter them, and [d]overtook Zĕd-ē-kī-ăh
n the plains of Jericho: and when they
ad taken him, they brought him up
o Nĕb-ū-chăd-nĕz-zär king of Ba-
ylon to [e]Rĭb-lăh in the land of Hă-
năth, where he [1]gave judgment upon
im.
6 Then the king of Babylon slew the
ons of Zĕd-ē-kī-ăh in Rĭb-lăh before
is eyes: also the king of Babylon
lew all the nobles of Judah.
7 Moreover [f]he put out Zĕd-ē-kī-ăh's
yes, and bound him [2]with chains, to
arry him to Babylon.
8 ¶ And [g]the Chăl-dē-ăns burned the
ing's house, and the houses of the
eople, with fire, and brake down the
valls of Jerusalem.
9 Then [h]Nĕb-ū-zär-ăd-ăn the [3]cap-
ain of the guard carried away captive
nto Babylon the remnant of the peo-
le that remained in the city, and
hose that fell away, that fell to him,
vith the rest of the people that re-
nained.
10 But Nĕb-ū-zär-ăd-ăn the captain
of the guard [i]left of the poor of the
eople, which had nothing, in the land
of Judah, and gave them vineyards
nd fields [4]at the same time.
11 ¶ Now Nĕb-ū-chăd-rĕz-zär king
of Babylon gave charge concerning
eremiah [5]to Nĕb-ū-zär-ăd-ăn the
aptain of the guard, saying,
12 Take him, and [6]look well to him,
nd do him no harm; but do unto him
ven as he shall say unto thee.
13 So Nĕb-ū-zär-ăd-ăn the captain
of the guard sent, and Nĕb-ū-shăs-
ăn, Răb-să-rĭs, and Nĕr-găl-shă-
ē-zĕr, Rab-mag, and all the king of
Babylon's princes;
14 Even they sent, [j]and took Jeremiah out of the court of the prison,
nd committed him [k]unto Gĕd-ă-lī-ăh
the son of Ă-hī-kăm the son of Shā-
phăn, that he should carry him home:
o he dwelt among the people.
15 ¶ Now the word of the LORD came
nto Jeremiah, while he was shut up
n the court of the prison, saying,
16 Go and speak to [m]Ē-bĕd-mĕl-ĕch
he Ē-thĭ-ō-pĭ-ăn, saying, Thus saith
the LORD of hosts, the God of Israel;
Behold, [n]I will bring my words upon
his city for evil, and not for good; and
they shall be *accomplished* in that day
before thee.
17 But I will deliver thee in that day,
saith the LORD: and thou shalt not be

d Josh. 5.10. ch. 32.4. ch. 38.18.
e 2 Ki. 23.33. ch. 52.9,26, 27.
1 spake with him judgments.
f 2 Ki. 25.7. Eze. 12.13. compared with ch. 32.4. ch. 52.11.
2 with two brasen chains, or, fetters.
g 2 Ki. 25.9. 2 Chr. 36.19. Isa. 5.9. ch. 38.18.
h 2 Ki. 25.11. ch. 52.15.
3 chief of the executioners, or, slaughtermen, or, chief marshal.
i 2 Ki. 25.11.
4 in that day.
5 by the hand of.
6 set thine eyes upon him.
j ch. 38.28.
k ch. 40.5.
l ch. 26.24.
m Matt. 10. 42.
n Dan. 9.12.
o ch. 21.9.
p Ruth 2.12. 1 Chr. 5.20. Ps. 32.7.

CHAP. 40

a ch. 39.14.
1 Or, manicles.
b Lev. 26.14-38. Deut. 28.15-68. Deut. 32.19-25. ch. 50.7. Lam. 2.17.
c Deut. 29. 24,25.
2 Or, are upon thine hand.
d ch. 39.12.
3 I will set mine eye upon thee.
e Gen. 13.9. Gen. 20.15.
f 2 Ki. 25.22.
g Gen. 39.1. Josh. 15.38. 1 Sam. 2.30. Pro. 15.16. Matt. 6.33. Acts 22.24, 27,28.
h ch. 39.14.
i Judg. 20.1. 1 Sam. 7.5, 6.
j 2 Ki. 25.23.
k ch. 39.10.
l 2 Ki. 25.23. ch. 41.1.

given into the hand of the men of
whom thou *art* afraid.
18 For I will surely deliver thee, and
thou shalt not fall by the sword, but
[o]thy life shall be for a prey unto thee:
[p]because thou hast put thy trust in
me, saith the LORD.

CHAPTER 40

THE word that came to Jeremiah
from the LORD, [a]after that Nĕb-
ū-zär-ăd-ăn the captain of the guard
had let him go from Rā-măh, when he
had taken him being bound in [1]chains
among all that were carried away
captive of Jerusalem and Judah,
which were carried away captive unto
Babylon.
2 And the captain of the guard took
Jeremiah, and said unto him, [b]The
LORD thy God hath pronounced this
evil upon this place.
3 Now the LORD hath brought *it*, and
done according as he hath said: [c]be-
cause ye have sinned against the LORD,
and have not obeyed his voice, therefore this thing is come upon you.
4 And now, behold, I loose thee this
day from the chains which [2]*were* upon
thine hand. [d]If it seem good unto thee
to come with me into Babylon, come;
and [3]I will look well unto thee: but if
it seem ill unto thee to come with me
into Babylon, forbear: behold, all [e]the
land *is* before thee: whither it seemeth
good and convenient for thee to go,
thither go.
5 Now while he was not yet gone
back, *he said*, Go back also to Gĕd-ă-
lī-ăh the son of Ă-hī-kăm the son of
Shā-phăn, [f]whom the king of Babylon
hath made governor over the cities of
Judah, and dwell with him among the
people: or go wheresoever it seemeth
convenient unto thee to go. So the
captain of the guard [g]gave him victuals and a reward, and let him go.
6 Then [h]went Jeremiah unto Gĕd-ă-
lī-ăh the son of Ă-hī-kăm [i]to Mizpah;
and dwelt with him among the people
that were left in the land.
7 ¶ Now [j]when all the captains of the
forces which *were* in the fields, *even*
they and their men, heard that the
king of Babylon had made Gĕd-ă-lī-
ăh the son of Ă-hī-kăm governor in
the land, and had committed unto him
men, and women, and children, and of
the [k]poor of the land, of them that
were not carried away captive to
Babylon;
8 Then they came to Gĕd-ă-lī-ăh to
Mizpah, even [l]Ĭsh-mā-ĕl the son of

Nĕth-ă-nī´ăh, and Jō-hā´năn and Jonathan the sons of Kă-rē´ăh, and Sĕ-rāī´ăh the son of Tăn-hū´mĕth, and the sons of Ē´phāī the Nĕ-tŏph´ă-thīte, and Jĕz-ă-nī´ăh the son of a Mā-ăch´ă-thīte, they and their men.

9 And Gĕd-ă-lī´ăh the son of Ă-hī´kăm the son of Shā´phăn sware unto them and to their men, saying, Fear not [4]to serve the Chăl-dē´ăns: dwell in the land, and serve the king of Babylon, and it shall be well with you.

10 As for me, behold, I will dwell at Mizpah to serve the Chăl-dē´ăns, which will come unto us: but ye, gather [m]ye wine, and summer fruits, and oil, and put *them* in your vessels, and dwell in your cities that ye have taken.

11 Likewise when all [n]the Jews that *were* in Moab, and among the Ammonites, and in Ē´dŏm, and that *were* in all the countries, heard that the king of Babylon had left a remnant of Judah, and that he had set over them Gĕd-ă-lī´ăh the son of Ă-hī´kăm the son of Shā´phăn;

12 Even all the Jews returned out of all places whither they were driven, and came to the land of Judah, to Gĕd-ă-lī´ăh, unto Mizpah, and gathered wine and summer fruits very much.

13 ¶ Moreover Jō-hā´năn the son of Kă-rē´ăh, and all the captains of the forces that *were* in the fields, came to Gĕd-ă-lī´ăh to Mizpah,

14 And said unto him, Dost thou certainly know that [o]Bā´ă-lĭs the king of the Ammonites hath sent Ĭsh´mā-ĕl the son of Nĕth-ă-nī´ăh [5]to slay thee? But Gĕd-ă-lī´ăh the son of Ă-hī´kăm believed them not.

15 Then Jō-hā´năn the son of Kă-rē´ăh spake to Gĕd-ă-lī´ăh in Mizpah secretly, saying, Let me go, I pray thee, and I will slay Ĭsh´mā-ĕl the son of Nĕth-ă-nī´ăh, and no man shall know *it:* wherefore should he slay thee, that all the Jews which are gathered unto thee should be scattered, and the remnant in Judah perish?

16 But Gĕd-ă-lī´ăh the son of Ă-hī´kăm said unto Jō-hā´năn the son of Kă-rē´ăh, Thou shalt [p]not do this thing: for thou speakest falsely of Ĭsh´mā-ĕl.

CHAPTER 41

NOW it came to pass in the seventh month, [a]*that* Ĭsh´mā-ĕl the son of Nĕth-ă-nī´ăh the son of Ē-lī´shā-mă, of the seed royal, and the princes of the king, even ten men with him, came unto Gĕd-ă-lī´ăh the son of Ă-hī´kăm to Mizpah; and there they [b]did eat bread together in Mizpah.

2 Then arose Ĭsh´mā-ĕl the son of Nĕth-ă-nī´ăh, and the ten men that were with him, and [c]smote Gĕd-ă-lī´ăh the son of Ă-hī´kăm the son of Shā´phăn with the sword, and slew him, whom the king of Babylon had made governor over the land.

3 Ĭsh´mā-ĕl also [d]slew all the Jews that were with him, *even* with Gĕd-ă-lī´ăh, at Mizpah, and the Chăl-dē´ăns that were found there, *and* the men of war.

4 And it came to pass the second day after he had slain Gĕd-ă-lī´ăh, and no man knew *it,*

5 That there came certain [e]from Shē´chĕm, from [f]Shī´lōh, and from Să-mâr´ĭ-ă, *even* fourscore men, [g]having their beards shaven, and their clothes rent, and having cut themselves, with offerings and incense in their hand, to bring *them* to the [h]house of the LORD.

6 And Ĭsh´mā-ĕl the son of Nĕth-ă-nī´ăh went forth from Mizpah to meet them, [1]weeping all along as he went: and it came to pass, as he met them, he said unto them, Come to Gĕd-ă-lī´ăh the son of Ă-hī´kăm.

7 And it was *so,* when they came into the midst of the city, that Ĭsh´mā-ĕl the son of Nĕth-ă-nī´ăh slew them, *and cast them* into the midst of the pit, he, and the men that *were* with him.

8 But ten men were found among them that said unto Ĭsh´mā-ĕl, Slay us not: for we have treasures in the field, of wheat, and of barley, and of oil, and of honey. So he forbare, and slew them not among their brethren.

9 Now the pit wherein Ĭsh´mā-ĕl had cast all the dead bodies of the men whom he had slain [2]because of Gĕd-ă-lī´ăh, *was* it which [i]Ā´să the king had made for fear of Bā-ăsh´ă king of Israel: *and* Ĭsh´mā-ĕl the son of Nĕth-ă-nī´ăh filled it with *them that were* slain.

10 Then Ĭsh´mā-ĕl carried away captive all the residue of the people that *were* in Mizpah, [j]*even* the king's daughters, and all the people that remained in Mizpah, whom Nĕb-ū-zăr-ăd´ăn the [k]captain of the guard had committed to Gĕd-ă-lī´ăh the son of Ă-hī´kăm: and Ĭsh´mā-ĕl the son of Nĕth-ă-nī´ăh carried them away captive, and departed to go over to [l]the Ammonites.

11 ¶ But when Jō-hā´năn the son of Kă-rē´ăh, and all [m]the captains of the

4 to stand before. And so ver. 10. Deut. 1.38.
m Deut. 16. 13. ch. 39.10.
n Isa. 16.4. ch. 24.9. Obad. 14.
o ch. 25.21. ch. 41.10. Amos 1.13. Zech. 1.15.
5 to strike thee in soul?
p 1 Cor. 13.5.

CHAP. 41
a 2 Ki. 25.25. ch. 40.6,8.
b Ps. 41.9. Luke 22.21.
c 2 Sam. 3.27. 2 Ki. 25.25. Ps. 41.9.
d Ps. 52.1. Pro. 1.16. Rom. 3.15.
e Gen. 33.18. Josh. 24.32.
f Josh. 18.1. ch. 7.12,14.
g Lev. 19.27, 28. Deut. 14.1. Isa. 15.2.
h 1 Sam. 1.7. 2 Ki. 25.9. ch. 50.4. Probably an altar built by Gedaliah.
1 in going and weeping.
2 by the hand, or, by the side of Gedaliah, or, near Gedaliah.
i Josh. 10.16-18.
j ch. 43.6.
k ch. 40.7.
l Neh. 2.10, 19.
m ch. 40.7, 8.13.

rces that *were* with him, heard of all
e evil that Ĭsh-´mā-ĕl the son of Nĕth-
ni-´ăh had done,
2 Then they took all the men, and
ent to fight with Ĭsh-´mā-ĕl the son of
ĕth-ă-nī-´ăh, and found him by [n]the
eat waters that *are* in Gibeon.
3 Now it came to pass, *that* when
the people which *were* with Ĭsh-´
ā-ĕl saw Jō-hā-´năn the son of Kă-
-´ăh, and all the captains of the
rces that *were* with him, then they
ere glad.
4 So all the people that Ĭsh-´mā-ĕl
d carried away captive from Miz-
h cast about and returned, and went
to Jō-hā-´năn the son of Kă-rē-´ăh.
5 But Ĭsh-´mā-ĕl the son of Nĕth-ă-
-´ăh escaped [o]from Jō-hā-´năn with
ght men, and went to the Ammon-
s.
6 Then took Jō-hā-´năn the son of
ă-rē-´ăh, and all the captains of the
rces that *were* with him, all the rem-
nt of the people whom he had re-
vered from Ĭsh-´mā-ĕl the son of
ĕth-ă-nī-´ăh, from Mizpah, after *that*
had slain Gĕd-ă-lī-´ăh the son of
-hī-´kăm, *even* mighty men of war,
d the women, and the children, and
e eunuchs, whom he had brought
ain from Gibeon:
7 And they departed, and dwelt in
e habitation of [p]Chĭm-´hăm, which
by Beth-lehem, to go to enter into
gypt,
8 [3]Because of the Chăl-dē-´ăns: for
ey were afraid of them, because Ĭsh-´
ā-ĕl the son of Nĕth-ă-nī-´ăh had
ain Gĕd-ă-lī-´ăh the son of Ă-hī-´kăm,
hom [q]the king of Babylon made gov-
nor in the land.

CHAPTER 42

HEN all the captains of the forces,
[a]and Jō-hā-´năn the son of Kă-rē-´
, and Jĕz-ă-nī-´ăh the son of Hō-
ā-´ăh, and all the people from the
st even unto the greatest, came
ar,
And said unto Jeremiah the pro-
et, [1]Let, we beseech thee, our suppli-
tion be accepted before thee, and
ray for us unto the LORD thy God,
en for all this remnant; (for we are
t *but* [c]a few of many, as thine eyes
behold us:)
That the LORD thy God may shew
the [d]way wherein we may walk, and
e thing that we may do.
Then Jeremiah the prophet said un-
them, I have heard *you;* behold, I
ll pray unto the LORD your God

n 2 Sam. 2.13.
o 1 Sam. 30. 17. 1 Ki. 20.20.
p 2 Sam. 19. 37,38.
3 From the face of.
q ch. 40.5.
CHAP. 42
a ch. 40.8,13. ch. 41.11.
1 Or, Let our supplication fall before thee.
b Ex. 8.28. 1 Sam. 7.8. 1 Ki. 13.6. Isa. 37.4. ch. 21.2. Acts 8.24. Jas. 5.16.
c Lev. 26.22.
d Ezra 8.21. Ps. 27.11. Pro. 3.5,6.
e 1 Ki. 22.14.
f 1 Sam. 3.18. Acts 20.20.
g Gen. 31.50.
h Deut. 6.3. ch. 7.23.
i ch. 24.6. ch. 31.28.
j Deut. 32.36. ch. 18.8.
k Num. 14.9. Deut. 20.4. Ps. 46.7. Isa. 43.5. Rom. 8.31.
l Ps. 106.45, 46.
m ch. 44.16.
n Deut. 17. 16. Luke 9.51.
o Eze. 11.8.
2 shall cleave after you.

according to your words; and it shall
come to pass, *that* whatsoever [e]thing
the LORD shall answer you, I will declare *it* unto you; I will [f]keep nothing
back from you.
5 Then they said to Jeremiah, [g]The
LORD be a true and faithful witness
between us, if we do not even according to all things for the which the
LORD thy God shall send thee to us.
6 Whether *it be* good, or whether *it be*
evil, we will obey the voice of the
LORD our God, to whom we send
thee; [h]that it may be well with us,
when we obey the voice of the LORD
our God.
7 ¶ And it came to pass after ten
days, that the word of the LORD came
unto Jeremiah.
8 Then called he Jō-hā-´năn the son
of Kă-rē-´ăh, and all the captains of
the forces which *were* with him, and
all the people from the least even to
the greatest,
9 And said unto them, Thus saith the
LORD, the God of Israel, unto whom
ye sent me to present your supplication before him;
10 If ye will still abide in this land,
then will [i]I build you, and not pull *you*
down, and I will plant you, and not
pluck *you* up: for I [j]repent me of the
evil that I have done unto you.
11 Be not afraid of the king of Babylon, of whom ye are afraid; be not
afraid of him, saith the LORD: [k]for I
am with you to save you, and to deliver you from his hand.
12 And [l]I will shew mercies unto
you, that he may have mercy upon
you, and cause you to return to your
own land.
13 ¶ But if [m]ye say, We will not dwell
in this land, neither obey the voice of
the LORD your God,
14 Saying, No; but we will go into
the land of Egypt, where we shall see
no war, nor hear the sound of the
trumpet, nor have hunger of bread;
and there will we dwell:
15 And now therefore hear the word
of the LORD, ye remnant of Judah;
Thus saith the LORD of hosts, the God
of Israel; If [n]ye wholly set your faces
to enter into Egypt, and go to sojourn
there;
16 Then it shall come to pass, *that*
the sword, [o]which ye feared, shall
overtake you there in the land of
Egypt, and the famine, whereof ye
were afraid, [2]shall follow close after
you there in Egypt; and there ye shall
die.

17 [3]So shall it be with all the men that set their faces to go into Egypt to sojourn there; they shall die [p]by the sword, by the famine, and by the pestilence: and [q]none of them shall remain or escape from the evil that I will bring upon them.

18 For thus saith the LORD of hosts, the God of Israel; As mine anger and my fury hath [r]been poured forth upon the inhabitants of Jerusalem; so shall my fury be poured forth upon you, when ye shall enter into Egypt: and [s]ye shall be an execration, and an astonishment, and a curse, and a reproach; and ye shall see this place no more.

19 ¶ The LORD hath said concerning you, O [t]ye remnant of Judah; Go ye not into Egypt: know certainly that I have [4]admonished you this day.

20 For [5]ye dissembled in your hearts, when ye sent me unto the LORD your God, saying, Pray for us unto the LORD our God; and according unto all that the LORD our God shall say, so declare unto us, and we will do *it*.

21 And *now* I have this day declared *it* to you; but [u]ye have not obeyed the voice of the LORD your God, nor any *thing* for the which he hath sent me unto you.

22 Now therefore know certainly that [v]ye shall die by the sword, by the famine, and by the pestilence, in the place whither ye desire [6]to go *and* to sojourn.

CHAPTER 43

AND it came to pass, *that* when Jeremiah had made an end of speaking unto all the people all the words of the LORD their God, for which the LORD their God had sent him to them, *even* all these words,

2 Then [a]spake Ăz-ă-rī'-ăh the son of Hō-shâi'-ăh, and Jō-hā'-năn the son of Kă-rē'-ăh, [b]and all the proud men, saying unto Jeremiah, Thou speakest falsely: the LORD our God hath not sent thee to say, Go not into Egypt to sojourn there:

3 But Bâr'-ŭch the son of Nē-rī'-ăh setteth thee on against us, for to deliver us into the hand of the Chăl-dē'-ăns, that they might put us to death, and carry us away captives into Babylon.

4 So Jō-hā'-năn the son of Kă-rē'-ăh, and all the captains of the forces, and all the people, obeyed not the voice of the LORD, to dwell in the land of Judah.

3 So shall all the men be.
p ch. 24.10.
q ch. 44.14, 28.
r 2 Chr. 34. 25. ch. 6.11. Eze. 22.22.
s ch. 18.16. ch. 24.9. ch. 26.6.
t Deut. 17.16.
4 testified against you.
5 Or, ye have used deceit against your souls.
u Zech. 7.11.
v Eze. 6.11.
6 Or, to go to sojourn.

CHAP. 43
a ch. 42.1.
b Ps. 12.4. ch. 42.1,2. Mal. 3.13. 2 Thes. 2.10, 11,12.
c ch. 40.11, 12.
d ch. 39.10.
e ch. 2.16. ch. 44.1. Called Hanes, Isa. 30.4.
f Dan. 2.21.
g ch. 25.9. Eze. 29.18, 20.
h ch. 44.13.
i ch. 15.2. Zech. 11.9.
j Ex. 12.12. Isa. 19.1. ch. 46.25.
1 statues, or, standing images.
2 Or, The house of the sun.

CHAP. 44
a Ex. 14.2. ch. 46.14.
b ch. 43.7.
c Isa. 19.13. Hosea 9.6.
d Isa. 11.11.

5 But Jō-hā'-năn the son of Kă-rē-
and all the captains of the forc
[c]took all the remnant of Judah, t
were returned from all nations, whi
er they had been driven, to dwell
the land of Judah;

6 *Even* men, and women, and ch
dren, and the king's daughters, a
[d]every person that Něb-ū-'zär-ăd-
the captain of the guard had left w
Gĕd-ă-lī'-ăh the son of Ă-hī-kăm t
son of Shā'-phăn, and Jeremiah t
prophet, and Bâr'-ŭch the son of N
rī'-ăh.

7 So they came into the land
Egypt: for they obeyed not the vo
of the LORD: thus came they *even*
[e]Täh'-păn-hēs.

8 ¶ Then came the word of the Lo
unto Jeremiah in Täh'-păn-hēs, sa
ing,

9 Take great stones in thine ha
and hide them in the clay in the bric
kiln, which *is* at the entry of Ph
aoh's house in Täh'-păn-hēs, in t
sight of the men of Judah;

10 And say unto them, Thus sa
the LORD of hosts, the God of Isra
Behold, [f]I will send and take Něb
chăd-rĕz'-zär the king of Babylon, [g]
servant, and will set his throne up
these stones that I have hid; and
shall spread his royal pavilion o
them.

11 And [h]when he cometh, he sh
smite the land of Egypt, *and deli*
[i]such *as are* for death to death; a
such *as are* for captivity to captivi
and such *as are* for the sword to t
sword.

12 And I will kindle a fire in t
houses of the [j]gods of Egypt; and
shall burn them, and carry them aw
captives: and he shall array hims
with the land of Egypt, as a shephe
putteth on his garment; and he sh
go forth from thence in peace.

13 He shall break also the [1]images
[2]Běth-shē'-měsh, that *is* in the land
Egypt; and the houses of the gods
the Egyptians shall he burn with fi

CHAPTER 44

THE word that came to Jeremi
concerning all the Jews whi
dwell in the land of Egypt, whi
dwell at [a]Mĭg'-dŏl, and at [b]Täh'-pă
hēs, and at [c]Nŏph, and in the count
of [d]Păth'-rŏs, saying,

2 Thus saith the LORD of hosts, t
God of Israel; Ye have seen all t
evil that I have brought upon Jerus
lem, and upon all the cities of Juda

d, behold, this day they *are* [e]a deso-
ion, and no man dwelleth therein,
Because of their wickedness which
ey have committed to provoke me
anger, in that they went [f]to burn in-
nse, *and* to serve [g]other gods, whom
ey knew not, *neither* they, ye, nor
ur fathers.
Howbeit [h]I sent unto you all my
rvants the prophets, rising early
d sending *them*, saying, Oh, do not
is abominable thing that I hate.
But they hearkened not, nor inned their ear to turn from their
ckedness, to burn no incense unto
her gods.
Wherefore [i]my fury and mine ang-
was poured forth, and was kindled
the cities of Judah and in the streets
Jerusalem; and they are wasted *and*
solate, as at this day.
Therefore now thus saith the
ORD, the God of hosts, the God of
rael; Wherefore commit ye *this*
eat evil [j]against your souls, to cut
f from you man and woman, child
d suckling, [1]out of Judah, to leave
u none to remain;
In that ye [k]provoke me unto wrath
ith the works of your hands, burn-
g incense unto other gods in the land
Egypt, whither ye be gone to dwell,
at ye might cut yourselves off, and
at ye might be a [l]curse and a re-
oach among all the nations of the
rth?
Have ye forgotten the [2]wickedness
your fathers, and the wickedness
the kings of Judah, and the wicked-
ss of their wives, and your own
ickedness, and the wickedness of
ur wives, which they have com-
itted in the land of Judah, and in
e streets of Jerusalem?
0 They are not [3]humbled *even* unto
is day, neither have [m]they feared,
or walked in my law, nor in my
atutes, that I set before you and be-
re your fathers.
1 ¶ Therefore thus saith the LORD
hosts, the God of Israel; Behold,
will set my face against you for evil,
d to cut off all Judah.
2 And I will take the remnant of
udah, that have set their faces to go
to the land of Egypt to sojourn
ere, and [o]they shall all be consumed,
d fall in the land of Egypt; they
all *even* be consumed by the sword
d by the famine: they shall die, from
e least even unto the greatest, by
e sword and by the famine: and
ey [p]shall be an execration, *and* an

e Lev. 26.32-34. Isa. 6.11. ch. 9.11. Micah 3.12. Luke 13.35.
f ch. 19.4.
g Deut. 13.6.
h 2 Chr. 36.15. ch. 7.25.
i ch. 42.18. 1 Cor. 10.11.
j Num. 16.38. ch. 7.19.
1 out of the midst of Judah.
k ch. 25.6,7.
l ch. 42.18.
2 wickednesses, or, punishments, etc.
3 contrite. Ps. 34.18. Isa. 57.15.
m Pro. 28.14.
n Lev. 17.10. ch. 21.10. Amos 9.4.
o Deut. 17.16. Isa. 30.1-3. ch. 2.18. Matt. 2.13, 14.
p ch. 18.16. ch. 24.9. Zech. 8.13.
4 visit.
5 lift up their soul.
q Ex. 5.2. Ps. 2.3. Pro. 1.24-27. ch. 6.16. Luke 19.14. Rom. 2.3-9.
r Num. 30.12. Deut. 23.23. Judg. 11.36.
6 Or, frame of heaven.
7 bread. Hosea 2.5.
s ch. 7.18.
8 Or, husbands?
t Gen. 6.3. Isa. 7.13. Isa. 43.24. Amos 2.13.
u Gen. 19.13. Gen. 24.25. Ps. 107.33, 34. ch. 25.11,18, 38.

astonishment, and a curse, and a reproach.
13 For I will [4]punish them that dwell
in the land of Egypt, as I have punished Jerusalem, by the sword, by the
famine, and by the pestilence:
14 So that none of the remnant of
Judah, which are gone into the land of
Egypt to sojourn there, shall escape
or remain, that they should return
into the land of Judah, to the which
they [5]have a desire to return to dwell
there: for none shall return but such
as shall escape.
15 ¶ Then all the men which knew
that their wives had burned incense
unto other gods, and all the women
that stood by, a great multitude, even
all the people that dwelt in the land of
Egypt, in Păth-rōs, answered Jeremiah, saying,
16 *As for* the word that thou hast
spoken unto us in the name of the
LORD, [q]we will not hearken unto
thee.
17 But we will certainly [r]do whatsoever thing goeth forth out of our own
mouth, to burn incense unto the
[6]queen of heaven, and to pour out
drink offerings unto her, as we have
done, we, and our fathers, our kings,
and our princes, in the cities of Judah,
and in the streets of Jerusalem: for
then had we plenty of [7]victuals, and
were well, and saw no evil.
18 But since we left off to burn incense to the queen of heaven, and to
pour out drink offerings unto her, we
have wanted all *things*, and have been
consumed by the sword and by the
famine.
19 And [s]when we burned incense to
the queen of heaven, and poured out
drink offerings unto her, did we make
her cakes to worship her, and pour
out drink offerings unto her, without
our [8]men?
20 ¶ Then Jeremiah said unto all the
people, to the men, and to the women,
and to all the people which had given
him *that* answer, saying,
21 The incense that ye burned in the
cities of Judah, and in the streets of
Jerusalem, ye, and your fathers, your
kings, and your princes, and the people of the land, did not the LORD remember them, and came it *not* into
his mind?
22 So that the LORD could [t]no longer
bear, because of the evil of your doings, *and* because of the abominations
which ye have committed; therefore is
your land [u]a desolation, and an

astonishment, and a curse, without an
inhabitant, as at this day.
23 Because ye have burned incense,
and because ye have sinned against
the LORD, and have not obeyed the
voice of the LORD, nor walked in his
law, nor in his statutes, nor in his
testimonies; therefore [v]this evil is
happened unto you, as at this day.
24 Moreover Jeremiah said unto all
the people, and to all the women,
Hear the word of the LORD, all Judah
[w]that *are* in the land of Egypt:
25 Thus saith the LORD of hosts, the
God of Israel, saying; Ye and your
wives have both spoken with your
mouths, and fulfilled with your hand,
saying, We will surely perform our
vows that we have vowed, to burn incense to the queen of heaven, and to
pour out drink offerings unto her: ye
will surely accomplish your vows, and
surely perform your vows.
26 Therefore hear ye the word of the
LORD, all Judah that dwell in the land
of Egypt; Behold, [x]I have sworn by
[y]my great name, saith the LORD, that
my name shall no more be named in
the mouth of any man of Judah in all
the land of Egypt, saying, The Lord
GOD liveth.
27 Behold, [z]I will watch over them
for evil, and not for good: and all the
men of Judah that *are* in the land of
Egypt shall be consumed by the sword
and by the famine, until there be an
end of them.
28 Yet [a]a small number that escape
the sword shall return out of the land
of Egypt into the land of Judah, and
all the remnant of Judah, that are
gone into the land of Egypt to sojourn
there, shall know whose words shall
stand, [9]mine, or theirs.
29 ¶ And this *shall be* a sign unto
you, saith the LORD, that I will punish
you in this place, that ye may know
that my words shall surely [b]stand
against you for evil:
30 Thus saith the LORD; Behold, I
[c]will give Phâr-ā-ōh–hŏph-ră king of
Egypt into the hand of his enemies,
and into the hand of them that seek
his life; as I gave Zĕd-ē-kī-āh [d]king
of Judah into the hand of Nĕb-ū-
chăd-rĕz-zär king of Babylon, his enemy, and that sought his life.

CHAPTER 45

THE [a]word that Jeremiah the prophet spake unto Bâr-ŭch the son
of Nē-rī-āh, when he had written these
words in a book at the mouth of Jere-

v Dan. 9.11, 12.
w ch. 43.7. ch. 46.14.
x Gen. 22.16.
y Ps. 50.16. Eze 20.39.
z ch. 1.10. ch. 2.17,19. ch. 4.18. ch. 5.19,29. ch. 11.17. ch. 31.28. Eze. 7.6.
a Lev. 26.44. Isa. 27.13. Hab. 3.2.
9 from me, or, from them.
b Ps. 33.11.
c ch. 46.25, 26. Eze. 29.3. Dan. 4.35.
d ch. 39.5.

CHAP. 45
a Isa. 50.4. ch. 36.1,4, 32.
b Isa. 5.5.
c Ps. 4.6. Matt. 6.34.
d Gen. 6.12. Isa. 66.16.
e ch. 21.9. ch. 38.2.

CHAP. 46
a ch. 25.15.
b 2 Ki. 23.29. 2 Chr. 35.20. ch. 25.9,19. Fulfilled presently.
c Isa. 8.9,10. ch. 51.11,12. Joel 3.9,10. Nah. 2.1.
1 broken in pieces.
2 fled a flight.
d ch. 6.25. ch. 20.4. Rev. 6.15-17.
e Dan. 11.19.
f Dan. 11.22.
3 Cush.
4 Put.
g Joel. 1.15.

miah, in the fourth year of Jĕ-hôi-
kĭm the son of Jō-sī-āh king of Juda
saying,
2 Thus saith the LORD, the God
Israel, unto thee, O Bâr-ŭch;
3 Thou didst say, Woe is me no
for the LORD hath added grief to n
sorrow; I fainted in my sighing, an
find no rest.
4 ¶ Thus shalt thou say unto hi
The LORD saith thus; Behold, [b]*th*
which I have built will I break dow
and that which I have planted I w
pluck up, even this whole land.
5 And [c]seekest thou great things f
thyself? seek *them* not: for, behol
[d]I will bring evil upon all flesh, sa
the LORD: but thy life will I give un
thee [e]for a prey in all places whith
thou goest.

CHAPTER 46

THE word of the LORD which can
to Jeremiah the prophet again
[a]the Gentiles;
2 Against Egypt, [b]against the army
Phâr-ā-ōh–nē-chō king of Egypt, whic
was by the river Eû-phrā-tēs in Că
chē-mish, which Nĕb-ū-chăd-rĕz-z
king of Babylon smote in the fourt
year of Jĕ-hôi-ă-kĭm the son of Jō-s
āh king of Judah.
3 Order [c]ye the buckler and shiel
and draw near to battle.
4 Harness the horses; and get up, y
horsemen, and stand forth with *yo*
helmets; furbish the spears, *and* pu
on the brigandines.
5 Wherefore have I seen them di
mayed *and* turned away back? an
their mighty ones are [1]beaten dow
and are [2]fled apace, and look n
back: *for* [d]fear *was* round about, sai
the LORD.
6 Let not the swift flee away, nor th
mighty man escape; [e]they shall stum
ble, and fall toward the north by th
river Eû-phrā-tēs.
7 Who *is* this *that* cometh up [f]as
flood, whose waters are moved as th
rivers?
8 Egypt riseth up like a flood, and *h*
waters are moved like the rivers; an
he saith, I will go up, *and* will cove
the earth; I will destroy the city an
the inhabitants thereof.
9 Come up, ye horses; and rage, y
chariots; and let the mighty men com
forth; [3]the Ē-thĭ-ō-pĭ-ăns and [4]th
Lĭb-y̆-ăns, that handle the shield; an
the Lȳd-ĭ-ăns, that handle *and* ben
the bow.
10 For this *is* [g]the day of the Lor

ɨOD of hosts, a day of vengeance,
ɑat he may avenge him of his adver-
ɑries: and [h]the sword shall devour,
ɑd it shall be satiate and made drunk
ith their blood: for the Lord GOD of
osts [i]hath a sacrifice in the north
ountry by the river Eû-phrā-tēs.
11 Go [j]up into Gilead, and take
alm, [k]O virgin, the daughter of
gypt: in vain shalt thou use many
ıedicines; *for* [5]thou shalt not be
ɹred.
12 The nations have heard of thy
ıame, and thy cry hath filled the land:
ɔr the mighty man hath stumbled
gainst the mighty, *and* they are fallen
oth together.
13 ¶ The word that the LORD spake
ɔ Jeremiah the prophet, how Nĕb-ū-
hăd-rĕz-zär king of Babylon should
ome *and* [l]smite the land of Egypt.
14 Declare ye in Egypt, and publish
ı Mĭg-dŏl, and publish in Nŏph and
ı Täh-păn-hēs: say ye, Stand fast,
nd prepare thee; for the sword shall
evour round about thee.
15 Why are thy valiant *men* swept
way? they stood not, because the
ORD did drive them.
16 He [6]made many to fall, yea, one
fell upon another: and they said,
ɹrise, and let us go again to our own
eople, and to the land of our nativity,
rom the oppressing sword.
17 They did cry there, Pharaoh king
f Egypt *is but* a noise; he hath passed
he time appointed.
18 *As* I live, saith the [n]King, whose
ıame *is* the LORD of hosts, Surely as
ā-bôr *is* among the mountains, and
s Carmel by the sea, *so* [o]shall he
ome.
19 O [p]thou daughter dwelling in
gypt, [7]furnish thyself to go into cap-
ivity: for Nŏph shall be waste and
lesolate without an inhabitant.
20 Egypt *is like* a very fair [q]heifer,
ut destruction cometh; it cometh
ɔut [r]of the north.
21 Also her hired men *are* in the
nidst of her like [8]fatted bullocks; for
hey also are turned back, *and* are
led away together: they did not stand,
ɔecause the day of their calamity was
ome upon them, *and* the time of their
visitation.
22 The [s]voice thereof shall go like a
erpent; for they shall march with an
ɹrmy, and come against her with axes,
ıs hewers of wood.
23 They shall cut down her forest,
aith the LORD, though it cannot be
earched; because they are more than
the grasshoppers, and *are* innumerable.
24 The daughter of Egypt shall be
confounded; she shall be delivered into the hand of the people of the north.
25 The LORD of hosts, the God of Israel, saith; Behold, I will punish the
[9]multitude of No, and Pharaoh, and
Egypt, [t]with their gods, and their
kings; even Pharaoh, and *all* them
that trust in him:
26 And [u]I will deliver them into the
hand of those that seek their lives, and
into the hand of Nĕb-ū-chăd-rĕz-zär
king of Babylon, and into the hand of
his servants: and afterward [v]it shall
be inhabited, as in the days of old,
saith the LORD.
27 ¶ But [w]fear not thou, O my servant Jacob, and be not dismayed, O
Israel: for, behold, I will save thee
from afar off, and thy seed from the
land of their captivity; and Jacob shall
return, and be in rest and at ease, and
none shall make *him* afraid.
28 Fear thou not, O Jacob my servant, saith the LORD: for I *am* with
thee; for I will make a full end of all
the nations whither I have driven
thee: but I will not make a full end of
thee, but correct thee in measure; yet
will I [10]not leave thee wholly unpunished.

CHAPTER 47

THE word of the LORD that came
to Jeremiah the [a]prophet against
the Philistines, [b]before that Pharaoh
smote [1]Gā-ză.
2 Thus saith the LORD; Behold,
[c]waters rise up [d]out of the north, and
shall be an overflowing flood, and
shall overflow the land, and [2]all that
is therein; the city, and them that
dwell therein: then the men shall cry,
and all the inhabitants of the land
shall howl.
3 At the [e]noise of the stamping of the
hoofs of his strong *horses*, at the rushing of his chariots, *and at* the rumbling
of his wheels, the fathers shall not look
back to *their* children for feebleness of
hands;
4 Because of the day that cometh to
spoil all the Philistines, *and* to cut off
from [f]Tȳ-rŭs and Zī-dŏn every helper
that remaineth: for the LORD will
spoil the Philistines, the [g]remnant of
[3]the country [h]of Căph-tôr.
5 Baldness [i]is come upon Gā-ză;
Ăsh-kĕ-lon is cut off *with* the remnant
of their valley: how long wilt thou cut
thyself?

h Deut. 32. 42.
i Isa. 34.6.
j ch. 8.22.
k Isa. 47.1.
5 no cure shall be unto thee.
l Isa. 19.1. ch. 43.10. Eze. 29. Fulfilled 571 B.C.
6 multiplied the faller.
m Lev. 26.37.
n Isa. 48.2. ch. 10.10. ch. 44.26. Mal. 1.14. 1 Tim. 1.17.
o Num. 23. 19.
p ch. 48.18.
7 make thee instruments of captivity.
q Hos. 10.11.
r ch. 1.14.
8 bullocks of the stall.
s Isa. 29.4.
9 Amon, or, nourisher.
t Eze. 30.13.
u ch. 44.30.
v ch. 48.47. ch. 49.39.
w Isa. 44.2.
10 Or, not utterly cut thee off.

CHAP. 47

a ch. 25.20. Zeph. 2.4,5.
b Amos 1.6. Zech. 9.56.
1 Azzah.
c Isa. 8.7.
d ch. 1.14.
2 the fulness thereof.
e Nah. 3.2.
f ch. 25.22. Amos 1.9, 10. Joel 3.4.
g Amos 9.7.
3 the isle.
h Gen. 10.14.
i Zeph. 2.4.

6 O thou [j]sword of the LORD, how
long *will it be* ere thou be quiet? [4]put
up thyself into thy scabbard, rest, and
be still.
7 [5]How can it be quiet, seeing the
LORD hath given [k]it a charge against
Ăsh-kĕ-lo̤n, and against the sea
shore? there hath [l]he appointed it.

CHAPTER 48

AGAINST [a]Moab thus saith the
LORD of hosts, the God of Israel;
Woe unto [b]Nē-bō! for it is spoiled:
Kĭr-ĭ-ă-thā-ĭm is confounded *and* tak-
ken: [1]Mĭs-găb is confounded and dismayed.
2 *There shall be* no more praise of
Moab: in Hĕsh-bŏn they have devised
evil against it; come, and let us cut it
off from *being* a nation. Also thou
shalt [2]be cut down, O Măd-mĕn; the
sword shall [3]pursue thee.
3 A voice of crying *shall be* from
Hŏr-ō-nā-ĭm, spoiling and great destruction.
4 Moab is destroyed; her little ones
have caused a cry to be heard.
5 For in the going up of Lū-hĭth [4]con-
tinual weeping shall go up; for in the
going down of Hŏr-ō-nā-ĭm the enemies have heard a cry of destruction.
6 Flee, save your lives, and be like
[5]the heath in the wilderness.
7 ¶ For [c]because thou hast trusted in
thy works and in thy treasures, thou
shalt also be taken: [d]and Chē-mŏsh
shall go forth into captivity *with* his
priests and his princes together.
8 And the spoiler shall come upon
every city, and no city shall escape:
the valley also shall perish, and the
plain shall be destroyed, as the LORD
hath spoken.
9 Give wings unto Moab, that it may
flee and get away: for the cities thereof shall be desolate, without any to
dwell therein.
10 Cursed [e]*be* he that doeth the work
of the LORD [6]deceitfully, and cursed
be he that keepeth back his sword
from blood.
11 ¶ Moab hath been at ease from
his youth, and [f]he hath settled on his
lees, and hath not been emptied from
vessel to vessel, neither hath he gone
into captivity: therefore his taste [7]re-
mained in him, and his scent is not
changed.
12 Therefore, behold, the days come,
saith the LORD, that I will send unto
him wanderers, that shall cause him
to wander, and shall empty his vessels, and break their bottles.

j Eze. 21.3.
4 gather thyself.
5 How canst thou?
k 1 Sam. 3.12.
l Micah 6.9.
CHAP. 48
a Isa. 15.1.
b Num. 32. 38.
1 Or, The high place.
2 Or, be brought to silence.
3 go after thee.
4 weeping with weeping.
5 Or, a naked tree, or, destitute.
c Ps. 49.6,7. Ps. 52.7. ch. 9.23. 1 Tim. 6.17. Rev. 18.17.
d Num. 21. 29.
e 1 Sam. 15.3.
6 Or, negligently.
f Zeph. 1.12.
7 stood.
g Judg. 11.24.
h Hosea 10.6.
i 1 Ki. 12.29. Amos 5.5,6.
j Ps. 33.6. Eccl. 9.11. Isa. 16.6. ch. 9.23.
8 the choice of.
k ch. 50.27.
l ch. 51.57. Mal. 1.14.
m Isa. 9.4. Isa. 14.4.
n Isa. 47.1. ch. 46.19.
o Num. 21. 30. Isa. 15.2.
9 inhabitress.
p Deut. 2.36.
q 1 Sam. 4.13, 16.
r Num. 21. 13.
s Amos 2.2.
t ch. 25.15.
u Pro. 24.17. Zeph. 2.8.
v ch. 2.26.
10 Or, movedst thyself.
w Ps. 55.6,7.
x Song 2.14.
y Isa. 16.6.
11 his bars, or, those on whom he stayeth, do not right.
z Isa. 15.5.

13 And Moab shall be ashamed c
[g]Chē-mŏsh, as the house of Israel wa
[h]ashamed of [i]Beth-el their confidenc
14 ¶ How say ye, [j]We *are* mighty an
strong men for the war?
15 Moab is spoiled, and gone up *ou*
of her cities, and [8]his chosen youn
men are gone [k]down to the slaughte
saith [l]the King, whose name *is* th
LORD of hosts.
16 The calamity of Moab *is* near t
come, and his affliction hasteth fast.
17 All ye that are about him, bemoa
him; and all ye that know his name
say, [m]How is the strong staff broker
and the beautiful rod!
18 Thou [n]daughter that dost inhabi
[o]Dī-bŏn, come down from *thy* glory
and sit in thirst; for the spoiler o
Moab shall come upon thee, *and* h
shall destroy thy strong holds.
19 O [9]inhabitant of [p]Ă-rō-ĕr, stan
[q]by the way, and espy; ask him tha
fleeth, and her that escapeth, *and* say
What is done?
20 Moab is confounded; for it i
broken down: howl and cry; tell ye i
in [r]Arnon, that Moab is spoiled,
21 And judgment is come upon th
plain country; upon Hō-lŏn, and up
on Jā-hā-zăh, and upon Mĕph-ā-ăth
22 And upon Dī-bŏn, and upon Nē
bō, and upon Bĕth–dĭb-lă-thā-ĭm,
23 And upon Kĭr-ĭ-ă-thā-ĭm, and up
on Bĕth–găm-ŭl, and upon Bĕth–mē
ŏn,
24 And upon [s]Kĕr-ĭ-ōth, and upo
Bŏz-răh, and upon all the cities of th
land of Moab, far or near.
25 The horn of Moab is cut off, an
his arm is broken, saith the LORD.
26 ¶ Make [t]ye him drunken: for h
magnified *himself* against the LORD
Moab also shall wallow in his vomit
and he also shall be in derision.
27 For [u]was not Israel a derisio
unto thee? [v]was he found amon
thieves? for since thou spakest of him
thou [10]skippedst for joy.
28 O ye that dwell in Moab, leav
the cities, and [w]dwell in the rock, an
be like the [x]dove *that* maketh her nes
in the sides of the hole's mouth.
29 We have heard the [y]pride of Mo
ab, (he is exceeding proud) his lofti
ness, and his arrogancy, and hi
pride, and the haughtiness of hi
heart.
30 I know his wrath, saith the LORD
but *it shall* not *be* so; [11]his lies sha
not so effect *it*.
31 Therefore [z]will I howl for Moab
and I will cry out for all Moab; *min*

eart shall mourn for the men of Kĭr–
ē-rĕs.
32 O vine of Sĭb-măh, I will weep for
hee with the weeping of Jā-zĕr: thy
lants are gone over the sea, they
each *even* to [a]the sea of Jā-zĕr: the
poiler is fallen upon thy summer
ruits and upon thy vintage.
33 And joy [b]and gladness is taken
rom the plentiful field, and from the
and of Moab; and I have caused wine
o fail from the winepresses: none
hall tread with shouting; *their* shout-
ng *shall be* no shouting.
34 From [c]the cry of Hĕsh-bŏn *even*
nto Ĕl-ĕ-ā-lĕh, *and even* unto Jā-hăz,
ave they uttered their voice, [d]from
ō-ăr *even* unto Hŏr-ō-nā-ĭm, *as* an
eifer of three years old: for the
vaters also of Nimrim shall be [12]deso-
ate.
35 Moreover I will cause to cease in
Moab, saith the LORD, [e]him that offer-
th in the high places, and him that
urneth incense to his gods.
36 Therefore [f]mine heart shall sound
or Moab like pipes, and mine heart
hall sound like pipes for the men of
ĭr–hē-rĕs: because the [g]riches *that* he
ath gotten are perished.
37 For [h]every head *shall be* bald, and
very beard [13]clipped: upon all the
ands *shall be* cuttings, and upon [i]the
oins sackcloth.
38 *There shall be* lamentation gener-
lly upon all the housetops of Moab,
nd in the streets thereof: for I have
roken Moab like [j]a vessel wherein *is*
o pleasure, saith the LORD.
39 They shall howl, *saying*, How is it
roken down! how hath Moab turned
he [14]back with shame! so shall Moab
e a derision and a dismaying to all
hem about him.
40 For thus saith the LORD; Behold,
he shall fly as an eagle, and shall
spread his wings over Moab.
41 [15]Kĕr-ĭ-ōth is taken, and the
trong holds are surprised, [m]and the
nighty men's hearts in Moab at that
ay shall be as the heart of a woman in
er pangs.
42 And Moab shall be destroyed
rom [n]*being* a people, because he
ath [o]magnified *himself* against the
ORD.
43 Fear, [p]and the pit, and the snare,
hall be upon thee, O inhabitant of
Moab, saith the LORD.
44 He that fleeth from the fear shall
all into the pit; and he that getteth up
ut of the pit shall be taken in the
nare: for [q]I will bring upon it, *even*

a Num. 21. 13.
b Isa. 16.9,10. Joel 1.12.
c Isa. 15.4,5, 6.
d Isa. 15.5,6.
12 desolations.
e Isa. 15.2.
f Isa. 15.5.
g Pro. 11.4. Eccl. 5.13, 14. Isa. 15.7. Luke 12.20, 21.
h Isa. 15.2,3. ch. 47.5.
13 diminished.
i Gen. 37.34.
j ch. 22.28.
14 neck.
k ch. 49.22. Dan. 7.4. Hosea 8.1. Hab. 1.8.
l Isa. 8.8.
15 Or, The cities.
m Isa. 13.8. ch. 30.6. Micah 4.9.
n Ps. 83.4. Isa. 16.13, 14.
o Pro. 16.18.
p Isa. 24.17, 18.
q ch. 11.23.
r Num. 21. 28.
s Num. 24.17.
16 children of noise.
t Num. 21.29. Judg. 11.24.
17 in captivity.
u ch. 49.6,39.

CHAP. 49

1 Or, Against.
2 Or, Melcom.
a Amos 1.13.
b Amos 1.14.
c Isa. 32.11.
3 Or, Melcom.
d ch. 48.7.
4 Or, thy valley floweth away.
e ch. 21.13.
f ch. 48.47.
g Amos 1.11.
h Job 5.12-14. Obad. 8.
i Isa. 19.11.
5 Or, they are turned back.
j Isa. 2.19.
k ch. 25.23.
l Mal. 1.3,4.
m Isa. 17.6.

upon Moab, the year of their visitation, saith the LORD.
45 They that fled stood under the
shadow of Hĕsh-bŏn because of the
force: but [r]a fire shall come forth out
of Hĕsh-bŏn, and a flame from the
midst of Sī-hŏn, [s]and shall devour the
corner of Moab, and the crown of the
head of the [16]tumultuous ones.
46 Woe [t]be unto thee, O Moab! the
people of Chē-mŏsh perisheth: for
thy sons are taken [17]captives, and thy
daughters captives.
47 ¶ Yet will I bring again the captivity of Moab [u]in the latter days,
saith the LORD. Thus far *is* the judgment of Moab.

CHAPTER 49

1 CONCERNING the Ammonites,
thus saith the LORD; Hath Israel
no sons? hath he no heir? why *then*
doth [2]their king [a]inherit Gad, and his
people dwell in his cities?
2 Therefore, behold, the days come,
saith the LORD, that I will cause an
alarm of war to be heard in [b]Răb-băh
of the Ammonites; and it shall be a
desolate heap, and her daughters
shall be burned with fire: then shall
Israel be heir unto them that were his
heirs, saith the LORD.
3 Howl, O Hĕsh-bŏn, for Ā-ī is spoiled: cry, ye daughters of Răb-băh,
[c]gird you with sackcloth; lament, and
run to and fro by the hedges; for
[3]their king shall go into captivity,
and his [d]priests and his princes together.
4 Wherefore gloriest thou in the valleys, [4]thy flowing valley, O backsliding
daughter? that trusted in her treasures, [e]*saying*, Who shall come unto
me?
5 Behold, I will bring a fear upon
thee, saith the Lord GOD of hosts,
from all those that be about thee; and
ye shall be driven out every man right
forth; and none shall gather up him
that wandereth.
6 And [f]afterward I will bring again
the captivity of the children of Ammon, saith the LORD.
7 ¶ Concerning [g]Ē-dom, thus saith
the LORD of hosts; [h]*Is* wisdom no
more in Tē-măn? [i]is counsel perished
from the prudent? is their wisdom
vanished?
8 Flee ye, [5]turn back, [j]dwell deep, O
inhabitants of [k]Dē-dăn; for I will
[l]bring the calamity of Esau upon him,
the time *that* I will visit him.
9 If [m]grapegatherers come to thee,

would they not leave *some* gleaning grapes? if thieves by night, they will destroy [6]till they have enough.

10 But I have made Esau bare, I have uncovered his secret places, and he shall not be able to hide himself: his seed is spoiled, and his brethren, and his neighbours, and [n]he *is* not.

11 Leave thy [o]fatherless children, I will preserve *them* alive; and let thy widows trust in me.

12 For thus saith the LORD; Behold, they [p]whose judgment *was* not to drink of the cup have assuredly drunken; and *art* thou he *that* shall altogether go unpunished? thou shalt not go unpunished, but thou shalt surely drink *of it*.

13 For [q]I have sworn by myself, saith the LORD, that [r]Bŏz-răh shall become a desolation, a reproach, a waste, and a curse; and all the cities thereof shall be perpetual wastes.

14 I have heard a [s]rumour from the LORD, and an ambassador is sent unto the heathen, *saying*, Gather ye together, and come against her, and rise up to the battle.

15 For, lo, I will make thee small among the heathen, *and* despised among men.

16 Thy terribleness hath deceived thee, *and* the pride of thine heart, O thou that dwellest in the clefts of the rock, that holdest the height of the hill: though thou shouldest make thy [t]nest as high as the eagle, [u]I will bring thee down from thence, saith the LORD.

17 Also Ē-dom shall be a desolation: every [v]one that goeth by it shall be astonished, and shall hiss at all the plagues thereof.

18 As [w]in the overthrow of Sodom and Gō-mŏr-răh and the neighbour *cities* thereof, saith the LORD, no man shall abide there, neither shall a son of man dwell in it.

19 Behold, [x]he shall come up like a lion from [y]the swelling of Jordan against the habitation of the strong: but I will suddenly make him run away from her: and who *is* a chosen *man*, *that* I may appoint over her? for [z]who *is* like me? and who will [7]appoint me the time? and [a]who *is* that shepherd that will stand before me?

20 Therefore [b]hear the counsel of the LORD, that he hath taken against Ē-dom; and his purposes, that he hath purposed against the inhabitants of Tē-măn: Surely the least of the flock shall draw them out: surely he shall make their habitations desolate wit[h] them.

21 The earth is moved at the noise o[f] their fall, at the cry the noise thereo[f] was heard in the [8]Red sea.

22 Behold, [c]he shall come up and fl[y] as the eagle, and spread his wing[s] over Bŏz-răh: and at that day sha[ll] the heart of the mighty men of Ē-dom be as the heart of a woman in he[r] pangs.

23 ¶ Concerning [d]Damascus. Hā-măth is confounded, and Arpad: fo[r] they have heard evil tidings: they ar[e] [9]fainthearted; [e]*there is* sorrow [10]o[n] the sea; it cannot be quiet.

24 Damascus is waxed feeble, *an[d]* turneth herself to flee, and fear hat[h] seized on *her*: anguish [f]and sorrow have taken her, as a woman in travail.

25 How is [g]the city of praise not left, the city of my joy!

26 Therefore her young men sha[ll] fall in her streets, and all the men o[f] war shall be cut off in that day, sait[h] the LORD of hosts.

27 And I will kindle [h]a fire in the wa[ll] of Damascus, and it shall consum[e] the palaces of [i]Bĕn-hā-dăd.

28 ¶ Concerning [j]Kē-där, and con-cerning the kingdoms of Hā-zôr, which Nĕb-ū-chăd-rĕz-zär king o[f] Babylon shall smite, thus saith th[e] LORD; Arise ye, go up to Kē-där, an[d] spoil [k]the men of the east.

29 Their [l]tents and their flocks sha[ll] they take away: they shall take t[o] themselves their curtains, and all thei[r] vessels, and their camels; and the[y] shall cry unto them, Fear *is* on ever[y] side.

30 ¶ Flee, [11]get you far off, dwe[ll] deep, O ye inhabitants of Hā-zôr, saith the LORD; for Nĕb-ū-chăd-rĕz-zär king of Babylon hath taken coun-sel against you, and hath conceived [a] purpose against you.

31 Arise, get you up unto th[e] wealthy nation, [12]that dwelleth with-out care, saith the LORD, which hav[e] neither gates nor bars, *which* dwe[ll] [m]alone.

32 And their camels shall be a booty, and the multitude of their cattle [a] spoil: and I will [n]scatter into all wind[s] them [o]*that are* [13]in the utmost corners; and I will bring their calamity fro[m] all sides thereof, saith the LORD.

33 And Hā-zôr [p]shall be a dwellin[g] for dragons, *and* a desolation for ever: there shall no man abide there, no[r] *any* son of man dwell in it.

34 ¶ The word of the LORD that cam[e]

6 their sufficiency.
n Isa. 17.14.
o Deut. 10. 18. Ps. 10.14, 18. Pro. 23.10, 11. Hosea 14.3. Mal. 3.5. Jas. 1.27.
p ch. 25.29. Obad. 16.
q Gen. 22.16. Isa. 45.23. Amos 6.8.
r Isa. 34.6. Amos 1.12.
s Obad. 1,2.
t Job 39.27.
u Pro. 15.25. Amos 9.2.
v ch. 18.16. ch. 50.13.
w Deut. 29. 23. ch. 50.40. Amos 4.11.
x ch. 4.7. Zech. 11.3.
y ch. 12.5.
z Ex. 15.11. Ps. 89.6,8.
7 Or, convent me in judgment.
a Job 41.10.
b ch. 50.45.
8 Weedy sea.
c ch. 4.13.
d Isa. 17.1. Amos 1.3.
9 melted.
e Isa. 57.20.
10 Or, as on the sea.
f Isa. 13.8.
g ch. 51.41.
h Amos 1.4.
i 2 Ki. 13.3.
j Isa. 21.13.
k Job 1.3.
l Ps. 120.5.
11 flit greatly.
12 Or, that is at ease.
m Num. 23.9. Deut. 33.28. Judg. 18.28. Micah 7.14.
n Deut. 28. 64. Eze. 5.10.
o ch. 25.23.
13 cut off into corners, or, that have the corners of their hair polled.
p ch. 9.11. Mal. 1.3.

to Jeremiah the prophet against [q]Ē-
lăm in the beginning of the reign of
Zĕd-ē-kī-ăh king of Judah, saying,
35 Thus saith the LORD of hosts; Behold, I will break [r]the bow of Ē-lăm,
the chief of their might.
36 And upon Ē-lăm will I bring the
four winds from the four quarters of
heaven, and will scatter them toward
all those winds; and there shall be no
nation whither the outcasts of Ē-lăm
shall not come.
37 For I will cause Ē-lăm to be dismayed before their enemies, and before them that seek their life: and I
will bring evil upon them, *even* my
fierce anger, saith the LORD; [s]and I
will send the sword after them, till I
have consumed them:
38 And I will [t]set my throne in Ē-lăm,
and will destroy from thence the king
and the princes, saith the LORD.
39 ¶ But it shall come to pass in the
latter days, *that* I will bring again the
captivity of Ē-lăm, saith the LORD.

CHAPTER 50

THE word that the LORD spake
against [a]Babylon *and* against the
land of the Chăl-dē-ăns [1]by Jeremiah
the prophet.
2 Declare ye among the nations, and
publish, and [2]set up a standard; publish, *and* conceal not: say, Babylon is
taken, [b]Bel is confounded, Mĕr-ō-
dăch is broken in pieces; [c]her idols are
confounded, her images are broken in
pieces.
3 For out of the north there cometh
up a [d]nation against her, which shall
make her land desolate, and none
shall dwell therein: they shall remove,
they shall depart, both man and beast.
4 ¶ In those days, and in that time,
saith the LORD, the children of Israel
shall come, [e]they and the children of
Judah together, [f]going and weeping:
they shall go, [g]and seek the LORD their
God.
5 They shall ask the way to Zion with
their faces thitherward, *saying*, Come,
and let us join ourselves to the LORD
in a [h]perpetual covenant *that* shall not
be forgotten.
6 My people hath been lost sheep:
their shepherds have caused them to
go astray, they have turned them away
on the mountains: they have gone
from mountain to hill, they have forgotten their [3]restingplace.
7 All that found them have devoured
them: and their [i]adversaries said, [j]We
offend not, because they have sinned

q Gen. 10.22. ch. 25.25.
r Gen. 14.1. Ezra 4.9. Isa. 21.2. ch. 25.25. Dan. 8.2.
s ch. 48.2.
t ch. 43.10. Dan. 7.9.

CHAP. 50
a Isa. 13.1. Isa. 21.1.
1 by the hand of Jeremiah.
2 lift up.
b Isa. 46.1.
c ch. 43.12.
d Isa. 13.17.
e Hosea 1.11.
f Ps. 126.5. Zech. 12.10.
g Ps. 105.4. Isa. 45.19. Hosea 3.5. Zech. 8.21, 22.
h ch. 31.31. 1 Pet. 2.25.
3 place to lie down in.
i Zech. 11.5.
j ch. 2.3. Dan. 9.16.
k Ps. 22.4.
l Isa. 48.20. ch. 51.6. Zech. 2.6. Rev. 18.4.
4 Or, destroyer.
m Rev. 17.16.
n Isa. 47.6.
5 big, or, corpulent.
6 Or, neigh as steeds.
o 1 Chr. 29. 24. 2 Chr. 30.8. Lam. 5.6.
p ch. 51.58.
q Ps. 137.8. Jas. 2.13. Rev. 16.6.
7 Or, scythe.
r Isa. 13.14.
s Joel 3.2. ch. 23.2. Matt. 9.36. 1 Pet. 2.25.
t ch. 2.15.
u 2 Ki. 17.6. 2 Chr. 28. 20. Isa. 7.17, 20. Isa. 8.7,8.
v 2 Ki. 24.10, 14.
w Isa. 65.10.

against the LORD, the habitation of
justice, even the LORD, [k]the hope of
their fathers.
8 Remove [l]out of the midst of Babylon, and go forth out of the land of
the Chăl-dē-ăns, and be as the he
goats before the flocks.
9 ¶ For, lo, I will raise and cause to
come up against Babylon an assembly
of great nations from the north country: and they shall set themselves in
array against her; from thence she
shall be taken: their arrows *shall be* as
of a mighty [4]expert man; none shall
return in vain.
10 And Chăl-dē-ă shall be a spoil:
all [m]that spoil her shall be satisfied,
saith the LORD.
11 Because [n]ye were glad, because ye
rejoiced, O ye destroyers of mine
heritage, because ye are grown [5]fat as
the heifer at grass, and [6]bellow as
bulls;
12 Your mother shall be sore confounded; she that bare you shall be
ashamed: behold, the hindermost of
the nations *shall be* a wilderness, a dry
land, and a desert.
13 Because of the wrath of the LORD
it shall not be inhabited, but it shall be
wholly desolate: every one that goeth
by Babylon shall be astonished, and
hiss at all her plagues.
14 Put yourselves in array against
Babylon round about: all ye that bend
the bow, shoot at her, spare no
arrows: for she hath sinned against
the LORD.
15 Shout against her round about:
she hath [o]given her hand: her foundations are fallen, [p]her walls are thrown
down: for it *is* the vengeance of the
LORD: take vengeance upon her;
[q]as she hath done, do unto her.
16 Cut off the sower from Babylon,
and him that handleth the [7]sickle in
the time of harvest: for fear of the
oppressing sword [r]they shall turn
every one to his people, and they shall
flee every one to his own land.
17 ¶ Israel *is* a [s]scattered sheep; the
[t]lions have driven *him* away: first [u]the
king of Assyria hath devoured him;
and last this [v]Nĕb-ū-chăd-rĕz-zăr king
of Babylon hath broken his bones.
18 Therefore thus saith the LORD of
hosts, the God of Israel; Behold, I
will punish the king of Babylon and
his land, as I have punished the king
of Assyria.
19 And [w]I will bring Israel again to
his habitation, and he shall feed on
Carmel and Bā-shăn, and his soul

shall be satisfied upon mount Ē-phrā-
ĭm and Gilead.
20 In those days, and in that time,
saith the LORD, [x]the iniquity of Israel
shall be sought for, and *there shall be*
none; and the sins of Judah, and they
shall not be found: for I will pardon
[y]them whom I reserve.
21 ¶ Go up against the land [8]of Mĕr-
ă-thā-ĭm, *even* against it, and against
the inhabitants of [9]Pē-kŏd: waste and
utterly destroy after them, saith the
LORD, and do [z]according to all that I
have commanded thee.
22 A sound of battle *is* in the land,
and of great destruction.
23 How is [a]the hammer of the whole
earth cut asunder and broken! how
is Babylon become a desolation
among the nations!
24 I have laid a snare for thee, and
thou art also taken, O Babylon, [b]and
thou wast not aware: thou art found,
and also caught, because thou hast
striven against the LORD.
25 The LORD hath opened his armoury, and hath brought forth the
[c]weapons of his indignation: for this
is the work of the Lord GOD of hosts
in the land of the Chăl-dē-ăns.
26 Come against her [10]from the utmost border, open her storehouses:
[11]cast her up as heaps, and destroy
her utterly: let nothing of her be
left.
27 Slay all her [d]bullocks; let them go
down to the slaughter: woe unto
them! for their day is come, the time
of [e]their visitation.
28 The voice of them that flee and
escape out of the land of Babylon, [f]to
declare in Zion the vengeance of the
LORD our God, the vengeance of his
temple.
29 Call together the archers against
Babylon: all ye that bend the bow,
camp against it round about; let none
thereof escape: recompense her [g]ac-
cording to her work; according to all
that she hath done, do unto her: [h]for
she hath been proud against the
LORD, against the Holy One of Israel.
30 Therefore [i]shall her young men
fall in the streets, and all her men of
war shall be cut off in that day, saith
the LORD.
31 Behold, I *am* against thee, *O thou*
[12]most proud, saith the Lord GOD of
hosts: for thy day is come, the time
that I will visit thee.
32 And [13]the most proud shall stumble and fall, and none shall raise him
up: and I [j]will kindle a fire in his

x ch. 31.34.
y Isa. 1.9.
8 Or, of the rebels.
9 Or, Visitation.
z Isa. 10.6.
a Isa. 14.6. ch. 51.20.
b Dan. 5.30.
c Isa. 13.5.
10 from the end.
11 Or, tread her.
d Ps. 22.12. Isa. 34.7.
e ch. 48.44.
f ch. 51.10.
g Lam. 3.64. 2 Thes. 1.6.
h Isa. 47.10.
i ch. 49.26. ch. 51.4.
12 pride.
13 pride. Hab. 2.5.
j ch. 21.14.
k Rev. 18.8.
l Pro. 23.11. Isa. 47.4.
m Dan. 5.30.
n Isa. 47.13.
14 bars, or, chief stays.
o ch. 25.20.
p ch. 51.30. Nah. 3.13.
q Isa. 44.27. ch. 51.32,36. Rev. 16.12.
r Isa. 13.21. ch. 51.37. Rev. 18.2.
s Isa. 13.20. ch. 25.12.
t Gen. 19.25. Deut. 29.23. Isa. 1.9. ch. 49.18. Amos 4.11. Zeph. 2.9. 2 Pet. 2.6. Jude 7.
u ch. 6.22. Rev. 17.16.
v ch. 6.23.
w Isa. 13.18.
x Isa. 5.30.
y ch. 49.24.

cities, and it shall devour all round
about him.
33 ¶ Thus saith the LORD of hosts
The children of Israel and the children
of Judah *were* oppressed together
and all that took them captives held
them fast; they refused to let them go.
34 Their [k]Redeemer *is* strong; the
[l]LORD of hosts *is* his name: he shall
throughly plead their cause, that he
may give rest to the land, and disquiet
the inhabitants of Babylon.
35 ¶ A sword *is* upon the Chăl-dē-
ăns, saith the LORD, and upon the inhabitants of Babylon, [m]and upon her
princes, and upon her wise [n]*men*.
36 A sword *is* upon the [14]liars; and
they shall dote: a sword *is* upon her
mighty men; and they shall be dismayed.
37 A sword *is* upon their horses, and
upon their chariots, and upon all the
[o]mingled people that *are* in the midst
of her; and they [p]shall become as
women: a sword *is* upon her treasures; and they shall be robbed.
38 A [q]drought *is* upon her waters;
and they shall be dried up: for it *is* the
land of graven images, and they are
mad upon *their* idols.
39 Therefore [r]the wild beasts of the
desert with the wild beasts of the
islands shall dwell *there*, [s]and the owls
shall dwell therein: and it shall be no
more inhabited for ever; neither shall
it be dwelt in from generation to generation.
40 As [t]God overthrew Sodom and
Gō-mŏr-răh and the neighbour *cities*
thereof, saith the LORD; *so* shall no
man abide there, neither shall any
son of man dwell therein.
41 Behold, [u]a people shall come from
the north, and a great nation, and
many kings shall be raised up from
the coasts of the earth.
42 They [v]shall hold the bow and the
lance: [w]they *are* cruel, and will not
shew mercy: their [x]voice shall roar
like the sea, and they shall ride upon
horses, *every one* put in array, like a
man to the battle, against thee, O
daughter of Babylon.
43 The king of Babylon hath heard
the report of them, and his hands waxed feeble: [y]anguish took hold of him,
and pangs as of a woman in travail.
44 Behold, he shall come up like a
lion from the swelling of Jordan unto
the habitation of the strong: but I will
make them suddenly run away from
her: and who *is* a chosen *man*, *that* I
may appoint over her? for who *is* like

e? and who will [15]appoint me the
me? and [z]who *is* that shepherd that
ill stand before me?
5 Therefore hear ye [a]the counsel of
e LORD, that he hath taken against
abylon; and his purposes, that he
ath purposed against the land of the
hăl-dē-ăns: Surely [b]the least of the
ock shall draw them out: surely he
nall make *their* habitation desolate
ith them.
46 At [c]the noise of the taking of
abylon the earth is moved, and the
ry is heard among the nations.

CHAPTER 51

THUS saith the LORD; Behold, I
will raise up against Babylon, and
gainst them that dwell in the [1]midst
f them that rise up against me, [a]a de-
troying wind;
2 And will send unto [b]Babylon fan-
ers, that shall fan her, and shall
mpty her land: [c]for in the day of
rouble they shall be against her round
bout.
3 Against *him that* bendeth let the
rcher bend his bow, and against *him*
hat lifteth himself up in his brigan-
line: and spare ye not her young men;
lestroy ye utterly all her host.
4 Thus the slain shall fall in the land
of the Chăl-dē-ăns, [d]and *they that are*
hrust through in her streets.
5 For [e]Israel *hath* not *been* forsaken,
nor Judah of his God, of the LORD of
hosts; though their land was filled
with sin against the Holy One of
Israel.
6 Flee [f]out of the midst of Babylon,
and deliver every man his soul: be not
cut off in her iniquity; for this *is* the
time of the LORD's vengeance; [g]he will
render unto her a recompence.
7 Babylon [h]*hath been* a golden cup
in the LORD's hand, that made all the
earth drunken: the [i]nations have
drunken of her wine; therefore the
nations [j]are mad.
8 Babylon is suddenly [k]fallen and
destroyed: [l]howl for her; [m]take balm
for her pain, if so be she may be healed.
9 We would have healed Babylon,
but she is not healed: forsake her, and
[n]let us go every one into his own
country: for her judgment reacheth
unto heaven, and is lifted up *even* to
the skies.
10 The LORD [o]hath brought forth our
righteousness: come, and let us declare in Zion the work of the LORD
our God.
11 Make [2]bright the arrows; gather
the shields: [p]the LORD hath raised up
the spirit of the kings of the Mēdes:
for his device *is* against Babylon, to
destroy it; because it *is* the vengeance
of the LORD, the vengeance of his
temple.
12 Set up [q]the standard upon the
walls of Babylon, make the watch
strong, set up the watchmen, prepare
the [3]ambushes: for the LORD hath
both devised and done that which he
spake against the inhabitants of
Babylon.
13 O [r]thou that dwellest upon many
waters, abundant in treasures, thine
end is come, *and* the measure of thy
covetousness.
14 The [s]LORD of hosts hath sworn
[4]by himself, *saying*, Surely I will fill
thee with men, as [t]with caterpillers;
and they shall [5]lift up a shout against
thee.
15 He [u]hath made the earth by his
power, he hath established the world
by his wisdom, and hath stretched
[v]out the heaven by his understanding.
16 When he uttereth *his* voice, *there*
is a [6]multitude of waters in the heavens; and he [w]causeth the vapours to
ascend from the ends of the earth: he
maketh lightnings with rain, and
bringeth forth the wind out of his
treasures.
17 Every man [7]is brutish by *his*
knowledge; every founder is confounded by the graven image: [x]for his
molten image *is* falsehood, and *there*
is no breath in them.
18 They [y]*are* vanity, the work of
errors: in the time of their visitation
they shall perish.
19 The [z]portion of Jacob *is* not like
them; for he *is* the former of all
things: and *Israel is* the rod of his inheritance: the LORD of hosts *is* his
name.
20 Thou [a]*art* my battle axe *and*
weapons of war: for [8]with thee will I
break in pieces the nations, and with
thee will I destroy kingdoms;
21 And with thee will I break in
pieces the horse and his rider; and
with thee will I break in pieces the
chariot and his rider;
22 With thee also will I break in
pieces man and woman; and with
thee will I break in pieces [b]old and
young; and with thee will I break in
pieces the young man and the maid;
23 I will also break in pieces with
thee the shepherd and his flock; and
with thee will I break in pieces the
husbandman and his yoke of oxen;

15 Or, convent me to plead? z Job 41.10. Dan. 5.2,20. a Ps. 33.11. Isa. 14.24. ch. 51.11. Acts 4.28. Eph. 1.11. b 1 Cor. 1.27. c Rev. 18.9.

CHAP. 51

1 heart. a 2 Ki. 19.7. ch. 4.11. b ch. 15.7. c ch. 50.14. d ch. 49.26. e Ps. 94.14. Zech. 1.15. f Rev. 18.4. g ch. 25.14. h Rev. 17.4. i Rev. 14.8. j ch. 25.16. k Isa. 21.9. 1 Thes. 5.2. Rev. 14.8. l Rev. 18.9. m ch. 46.11. n Isa. 13.14. ch. 46.16. o Ps. 37.6. 2 pure. p Isa. 13.17. q Nah. 2.1. 3 liers in wait. r Rev. 17.1. s ch. 49.13. 4 by his soul. t Nah. 3.15. 5 utter. u Gen. 1.1. Ps. 146.5,6. Isa. 40.26. Acts 14.15. Col. 1.16, 17. Heb. 1.2,3. v Job 9.8. 6 Or, noise. w Ps. 135.7. 7 Or, is more brutish than to know. x ch. 50.2. y Jonah 2.8. z Ps. 16.5. Ps. 73.26. ch. 10.16. Lam. 3.24. a Isa. 10.5. ch. 50.23. 8 Or, in thee, or, by thee. b 2 Chr. 36. 17.

and with thee will I break in pieces
captains and rulers.
24 And [c]I will render unto Babylon
and to all the inhabitants of Chăl-dē-ă
all their evil that they have done in
Zion in your sight, saith the LORD.
25 Behold, I *am* against thee, [d]O destroying mountain, saith the LORD,
which destroyest all the earth: and
I will stretch out mine hand upon
thee, and roll thee down from the
rocks, [e]and will make thee a burnt
mountain.
26 And they shall not take of thee a
stone for a corner, nor a stone for
foundations; but thou shalt be [9]deso-
late for ever, saith the LORD.
27 Set [f]ye up a standard in the land,
blow the trumpet among the nations,
[g]prepare the nations against her, call
together against her the [h]kingdoms
of Ăr-ă-răt, Mĭn-nī, and Ăsh-chē-năz;
appoint a captain against her; cause
the horses to come up as the rough
caterpillers.
28 Prepare against her the nations
with the kings of the Mēdes, the captains thereof, and all the rulers thereof, and all the land of his dominion.
29 And the land shall tremble and
sorrow: for every purpose of the LORD
shall be performed against Babylon,
[i]to make the land of Babylon a desolation without an inhabitant.
30 The mighty men of Babylon have
forborn to fight, they have remained
in *their* holds: their might hath failed;
[j]they became as women: they have
burned her dwellingplaces; [k]her bars
are broken.
31 One [l]post shall run to meet another, and one messenger to meet
another, to shew the king of
Babylon that his city is taken at *one*
end,
32 And that the passages are stopped,
and the reeds they have burned
with fire, and the men of war are
affrighted.
33 For thus saith the LORD of hosts,
the God of Israel; The daughter of
Babylon *is* like [m]a threshingfloor, [10]*it*
is time to thresh her: yet a little while,
and the [n]time of her harvest shall
come.
34 Nĕb-ū-chăd-rĕz-zär the king of
Babylon hath [o]devoured me, he hath
crushed me, he hath made me an
empty vessel, he hath swallowed me
up like a dragon, he hath filled his
belly with my delicates, he hath cast
me out.
35 [11]The violence done to me and to

c ch. 50.15, 16.
d Isa. 13.2. Zech. 4.7.
e Rev. 8.8.
9 everlasting desolations.
f Isa. 13.2.
g ch. 25.14.
h ch. 50.41.
i ch. 50.13.
j Isa. 19.16.
k Lam. 2.9. Amos 1.5.
l ch. 50.24.
m Isa. 21.10.
10 Or, in the time that he thresheth her.
n Joel 3.13. Matt. 13.30.
o 2 Chr. 36.9, 10. ch. 24.1.
11 My violence.
12 Or, remainder.
13 inhabitress.
p Zech. 1.15.
q ch. 50.38.
r Isa. 13.22.
s 2 Chr. 29.8. ch. 18.16.
14 Or, shake themselves.
t Dan. 5.1, 30.
u ch. 25.26.
v Isa. 13.19. ch. 49.25. Dan. 4.30.
w Isa. 8.7, 8.
x ch. 50.2.
y Rev. 18.4.
15 Or, let not.
z 2 Ki. 19.7.
16 visit upon.
a Isa. 44.23.
b ch. 50.3.
17 Or, Both Babylon is to fall, O ye slain of Israel, and with Babylon, etc.

my [12]flesh *be* upon Babylon, shall th
[13]inhabitant of Zion say; and m
blood upon the inhabitants of Chă
dē-ă, shall Jerusalem say.
36 Therefore thus saith the LORD
Behold, I [p]will plead thy cause, an
take vengeance for thee; [q]and I wi
dry up her sea, and make her spring
dry.
37 And [r]Babylon shall become heap
a dwellingplace for dragons, a
[s]astonishment, and an hissing, with
out an inhabitant.
38 They shall roar together like lions
they shall [14]yell as lions' whelps.
39 In their [t]heat I will make thei
feasts, and I will make them drunken
that they may rejoice, and sleep a per
petual sleep, and not wake, saith th
LORD.
40 I will bring them down like lamb
to the slaughter, like rams with he
goats.
41 How is [u]Shē-shăch taken! and
how is the [v]praise of the whole earth
surprised! how is Babylon become an
astonishment among the nations!
42 The [w]sea is come up upon Babylon: she is covered with the multitude of the waves thereof.
43 Her cities are a desolation, a dry
land, and a wilderness, a land wherein
no man dwelleth, neither doth *any* son
of man pass thereby.
44 And [x]I will punish Bel in Babylon,
and I will bring forth out of his mouth
that which he hath swallowed up: and
the nations shall not flow together any
more unto him: yea, the wall of Babylon shall fall.
45 My [y]people, go ye out of the
midst of her, and deliver ye every man
his soul from the fierce anger of the
LORD.
46 And [15]lest your heart faint, and ye
fear [z]for the rumour that shall be
heard in the land; a rumour shall both
come *one* year, and after that in *an-*
other year *shall come* a rumour, and
violence in the land, ruler against
ruler.
47 Therefore, behold, the days come,
that I will [16]do judgment upon the
graven images of Babylon: and her
whole land shall be confounded, and
all her slain shall fall in the midst of
her.
48 Then [a]the heaven and the earth,
and all that *is* therein, shall sing for
Babylon: for [b]the spoilers shall come
unto her from the north, saith the
LORD.
49 [17]As Babylon *hath caused* the slain

Israel to fall, so at Babylon shall fall
e slain of all [18]the earth.
0 Ye [c]that have escaped the sword,
away, stand not still: remember
e LORD afar off, and let Jerusalem
me into your mind.
1 We [d]are confounded, because we
ve heard reproach: shame hath
vered our faces: for strangers are
me into the sanctuaries of the
ORD's house.
2 Wherefore, behold, the days
me, saith the LORD, that I will do
dgment upon her graven images:
d through all her land the wounded
all groan.
3 Though [e]Babylon should mount
to heaven, and though she should
rtify the height of her strength, *yet*
om me shall spoilers come unto her,
ith the LORD.
4 A [f]sound of a cry *cometh* from
abylon, and great destruction from
e land of the Chăl-dē-ăns:
5 Because the LORD hath spoiled
abylon, and destroyed out of her
e great voice; when her waves do
ar like great waters, a noise of their
ice is uttered:
6 Because the spoiler is come upon
r, *even* upon Babylon, and her
ighty men are taken, every one of
eir bows is broken: [g]for the LORD
od of recompences shall surely re-
uite.
7 And I will make drunk her prin-
s, and her wise *men*, her captains,
d her rulers, and her mighty men:
d they shall sleep a perpetual sleep,
d not wake, saith [h]the King, whose
ame *is* the LORD of hosts.
8 Thus saith the LORD of hosts;
The broad walls of Babylon shall be
terly [20]broken, and her high gates
all be burned with fire; and the peo-
e [i]shall labour in vain, and the
lk in the fire, and they shall be
eary.
9 ¶ The word which Jeremiah the
ophet commanded Sĕ-rāi-ăh the son
Nē-rī-ăh, the son of Mā-ă-sēi-ăh,
hen he went [21]with Zĕd-ē-kī-ăh the
ng of Judah into Babylon in the
urth year of his reign. And *this* Sĕ-
ī-ăh *was* a [22]quiet prince.
0 So Jeremiah wrote in a book all
e evil that should come upon Bab-
on, *even* all these words that are writ-
n against Babylon.
1 And Jeremiah said to Sĕ-rāi-ăh,
hen thou comest to Babylon, and
alt see, and shalt read all these
ords;

62 Then shalt thou say, O LORD, thou
hast spoken against this place, to cut
it off, that none [j]shall remain in it,
neither man nor beast, but that it shall
be [23]desolate for ever.
63 And it shall be, when thou hast
made an end of reading this book,
[k]*that* thou shalt bind a stone to it, and
cast it into the midst of Eû-phrā-
tēṡ:
64 And thou shalt say, Thus shall
Babylon sink, and shall not rise from
the evil that I will bring upon her: and
they shall be weary. Thus far *are* the
words of Jeremiah.

CHAPTER 52

ZĔD-Ē-KĪ-ĂH *was* [a]one and twenty years old when he [1]began to
reign, and he reigned eleven years in
Jerusalem. And his mother's name
was Hă-mū-tăl the daughter of Jeremiah of Lĭb-năh.
2 And he did *that which was* evil in
the eyes of the LORD, according to all
that Jĕ-hôi-ă-kĭm had done.
3 For through the anger of the LORD
it came to pass in Jerusalem and Judah, till he had cast them out from his
presence, that Zĕd-ē-kī-ăh [b]rebelled
against the king of Babylon.
4 ¶ And it came to pass in [c]the ninth
year of his reign, in the tenth month,
in the tenth *day* of the month, *that*
Nĕb-ū-chăd-rĕz-zär king of Babylon
came, he and all his army, against
Jerusalem, and pitched [d]against it,
and built forts against it round
about.
5 So the city was besieged unto
the eleventh year of king Zĕd-ē-kī-
ăh.
6 And in the fourth month, in the
ninth *day* of the month, [e]the famine
was sore in the city, so that there
was no bread for the people of the
land.
7 Then the city was broken up, and
all the men of war fled, and went forth
out of the city by night by the way of
the gate between the two walls, which
was by the king's garden; (now the
Chăl-dē-ăns *were* by the city round
about:) and they went by the way of
the plain.
8 ¶ But the army of the Chăl-dē-ăns
pursued after the king, and overtook
Zĕd-ē-kī-ăh in the plains of Jericho;
and all his army was scattered from
him.
9 Then [f]they took the king, and
carried him up unto the king of Babylon to Rĭb-lăh in the land of Hā-

18 Or, the country.
c ch. 44.28.
d Ps. 44.15.
e ch. 49.16. Amos 9.2.
f Isa. 13.6-9. Isa. 15.5. ch. 50.22. Zeph. 1.10.
g Deut. 32.35. Ps. 94.1. Isa. 34.8.
h ch. 46.18. ch. 48.15.
19 Or, The walls of broad Babylon.
20 Or, made naked.
i Hab. 2.13.
21 Or, on the behalf of.
22 Or, prince of Menucha, or, chief chamberlain.
j ch. 50.3,39.
23 desolations.
k Rev. 18.21.

CHAP. 52

a 2 Ki. 24.18. 2 Chr. 36.11.
1 reigned.
b Eze. 17.12-16.
c 2 Ki. 25.1. ch. 39.1. Zech. 8.19.
d Deut. 28. 52-57. Isa. 42.24, 25. ch. 6.3-6.
e Lev. 26.14, 26. Isa. 3.1. Eze. 4.16.
f ch. 32.4.

măth; where he gave judgment upon him.

10 And [g]the king of Babylon slew the sons of Zĕd-ē-kī-ăh before his eyes: he slew also all the princes of Judah in Rĭb-lăh.

11 Then he [2]put out the eyes of Zĕd-ē-kī-ăh; and the king of Babylon bound him in [3]chains, and carried him to Babylon, and put him in [4]prison till the day of his death.

12 ¶ Now [h]in the fifth month, in the tenth *day* of the month, which *was* the nineteenth year of Nĕb-ū-chăd-rĕz-zăr king of Babylon, came [i]Nĕb-ū-zăr–ăd-ăn, [5]captain of the guard, *which* [6]served the king of Babylon, into Jerusalem,

13 And [j]burned the house of the LORD, and the king's house; and all the houses of Jerusalem, and all the houses of the great *men*, burned he with fire:

14 And all the army of the Chăl-dē-ăns, that *were* with the captain of the guard, brake down all the walls of Jerusalem round about.

15 Then Nĕb-ū-zăr–ăd-ăn the captain of the guard carried away captive *certain* of the poor of the people, and the residue of the people that remained in the city, and those that fell away, that fell to the king of Babylon, and the rest of the multitude.

16 But Nĕb-ū-zăr–ăd-ăn the captain of the guard left *certain* of the poor of the land for vinedressers and for husbandmen.

17 Also [k]the pillars of brass that *were* in the house of the LORD, and the bases, and the brasen sea that *was* in the house of the LORD, the Chăl-dē-ăns brake, and carried all the brass of them to Babylon.

18 The [l]caldrons also, and the [7]shovels, and the snuffers, and the [8]bowls, and the spoons, and all the vessels of brass wherewith they ministered, took they away.

19 And the basons, and the [9]firepans, and the bowls, and the caldrons, and the candlesticks, and the spoons, and the cups; *that* which *was* of gold *in* gold, and *that* which *was* of silver *in* silver, took the captain of the guard away.

20 The two pillars, one sea, and twelve brasen bulls that *were* under the bases, which king Solomon had made in the house of the LORD: [10]the brass of all these vessels was without weight.

g ch. 39.6,7.
2 blinded, Judg. 16.21.
3 Or, fetters.
4 house of the wards.
h 2 Ki. 25.8. Zech. 7.5.
i ch. 39.9.
5 chief of the executioners, or, slaughtermen, or, chief marshal. And so ver. 14.
6 stood before.
j 2 Ki. 25.9. Ps. 74.6,8. Isa. 64.10, 11. ch. 26.18. Matt. 24.1, 2.
k ch. 27.19.
l Ex. 27.3.
7 Or, instruments to remove the ashes.
8 Or, basons.
9 Or, censers.
10 their brass.
m 1 Ki. 7.15, 21,22. 2 Chr. 3.15.
11 thread.
n 1 Ki. 7.20. 2 Chr. 3.16.
o 1 Chr. 6.14.
p 2 Ki. 25.18. ch. 21.1.
12 threshold.
13 saw the face of the king.
14 Or, scribe of the captain of the host.
q Lev. 26.33.
r 2 Ki. 24.2.
s 2 Chr. 36. 20.
t ch. 39.9.
15 souls.
u 2 Ki. 25.27-30.
v Gen. 40.13-20.

21 And *concerning* the [m]pillars, t height of one pillar *was* eighte cubits; and a [11]fillet of twelve c bits did compass it; and the thic ness thereof *was* four fingers: *it* w hollow.

22 And a chapiter of brass *was* up it; and the height of one chapiter w five cubits, with network and pom granates upon the chapiters rou about, all *of* brass. The second pill also and the pomegranates *were* li unto these.

23 And there were ninety and s pomegranates on a side; [n]*and* all t pomegranates upon the network *we* an hundred round about.

24 ¶ And the captain of the gua took Sĕ-răī-ăh [o]the chief priest, [p]a Zĕph-ă-nī-ăh the second priest, a the three keepers of the [12]door:

25 He took also out of the city eunuch, which had the charge of t men of war; and seven men of the that [13]were near the king's perso which were found in the city; and t [14]principal scribe of the host, w mustered the people of the land; a threescore men of the people of t land, that were found in the midst the city.

26 So Nĕb-ū-zăr–ăd-ăn the capta of the guard took them, and broug them to the king of Babylon to Rĭ lăh.

27 And the king of Babylon smo them, and put them to death in Rĭ lăh in the land of Hā-măth. Thus [q]J dah was carried away captive out his own land.

28 This [r]*is* the people whom Nĕb-chăd-rĕz-zăr carried away captive: [s]the seventh year three thousa Jews and three and twenty:

29 In [t]the eighteenth year of Nĕb-chăd-rĕz-zăr he carried away capti from Jerusalem eight hundred thir and two [15]persons:

30 In the three and twentieth year Nĕb-ū-chăd-rĕz-zăr Nĕb-ū-zăr–ăd-ă the captain of the guard carried aw captive of the Jews seven hundr forty and five persons: all the perso *were* four thousand and six hu dred.

31 ¶ And [u]it came to pass in the sev and thirtieth year of the captivity Jĕ-hōī-ă-chĭn king of Judah, in t twelfth month, in the five and twe tieth *day* of the month, *that* Ē-vi mĕr-ō-dăch king of Babylon in t *first* year of his reign lifted [v] the head of Jĕ-hōī-ă-chĭn king

dah, and brought him forth out
prison,
2 And spake [16]kindly unto him, and
his throne above the throne of the
ngs that *were* with him in Baby-
n,
3 And changed his prison garments:
and [w]he did continually eat bread before him all the days of his life.
34 And *for* his diet, there was a continual diet given him of the king of
Babylon, [17]every day a portion until
the day of his death, all the days of his
life.

16 good things with him.
w 2 Sam. 9. 13.
17 the matter of the day in his day.

THE

LAMENTATIONS OF JEREMIAH

CHAPTER 1

HOW doth the city sit solitary, *that*
was full of people! [a]*how* is she be-
me as a widow! she *that was* great
nong the nations, *and* princess
mong the provinces, *how* is she be-
me tributary!
She [c]weepeth sore in [d]the night,
d her tears *are* on her cheeks:
mong all her lovers she hath none to
mfort *her;* all her friends have dealt
eacherously with her, they are be-
me her enemies.
Judah [f]is gone into captivity be-
use of affliction, and [1]because of
eat servitude: she [g]dwelleth among
e heathen, she finds no rest: all her
rsecutors overtook her between the
raits.
The ways of Zion do mourn, be-
use none come to the solemn feasts:
her gates are desolate: her priests
gh, her virgins are afflicted, and she
in bitterness.
Her adversaries are the chief, her
emies prosper; for the LORD hath
flicted her [h]for the multitude of her
ansgressions: her children are gone
to captivity before the enemy.
And from the daughter of Zion all
r beauty is departed: her princes
e become like harts *that* find no pas-
re, and they are gone without
rength before the pursuer.
Jerusalem remembered in the days
her affliction and of her miseries
l her [2]pleasant things that she had in
e days of old, when her people fell
to the hand of the enemy, and none
d help her: the adversaries [i]saw her,
d did mock at her sabbaths.
Jerusalem hath grievously sinned;
erefore she [3]is removed: all that
onoured her despise her, because
[j]they have seen her nakedness: yea,
she sigheth, and turneth backward.
9 Her filthiness *is* in her skirts; she
[k]remembereth not her last end; therefore she came down wonderfully: she
had no comforter. O LORD, behold
my affliction: for the enemy hath
magnified *himself.*
10 The adversary hath spread out
his hand upon all her [4]pleasant things:
for she hath seen *that* the heathen entered into her sanctuary, whom thou
didst command *that* [l]they should not
enter into thy congregation.
11 All her people sigh, they seek
bread; [m]they have given their pleasant
things for meat [5]to relieve the soul:
see, O LORD, and consider; for I am
become vile.
12 ¶ [6]*Is it* nothing to you, all ye that
[7]pass by? behold, and see [n]if there be
any sorrow like unto my sorrow,
which is done unto me, wherewith the
LORD hath afflicted *me* in the day of
his fierce anger.
13 From above hath he sent fire into
my bones, and it prevaileth against
them: he hath [o]spread a net for my
feet, he hath turned me back: he hath
made me desolate *and* faint all the day.
14 The [p]yoke of my transgressions is
bound by his hand: they are wreathed,
and come up upon my neck: he hath
made my strength to fall, the Lord
hath delivered me into *their* hands,
from whom I am not able to rise up.
15 The Lord hath trodden under foot
all my mighty *men* in the midst of me:
he hath called an assembly against me
to crush my young men: [q]the Lord
hath trodden [8]the virgin, the daughter
of Judah, *as* in a winepress.
16 For these *things* I weep; mine eye,
mine eye runneth down with water,

CHAP. 1
a Isa. 47.7. ch. 1.9.
b Ezra 4.20.
c Jer. 13.17. ch. 1.16.
d Job 7.3. Ps. 6.6.
e Jer. 4.30.
f Lev. 26.14, 32,33.
1 for the greatness of servitude.
g Deut. 28. 64.
h Jer. 30.14. ch. 3.39.
2 Or, desirable.
i Micah 4.11.
3 is become a removing, or, wandering.
j Jer. 13.22.
k Deut. 32. 29.
4 Or, desirable.
l Deut. 23.3. Neh. 13.1.
m Jer. 38.9.
5 Or, to make the soul to come again.
6 Or, It is nothing.
7 pass by the way?
n Dan. 9.12. Matt. 24.21. Luke 21.22.
o Job 18.8. Ps. 66.11. Eze. 12.13. Hosea 7.12.
p Deut. 28. 48. Pro. 5.22. Isa. 14.25. Matt. 11.29, 30.
q Isa. 63.3. Rev. 14.19.
8 Or, the winepress of the virgin, etc.

because the comforter that should [9]re-
lieve my soul is far from me: my children are desolate, because the enemy
prevailed.
17 Zion spreadeth forth her hands,
and there is none to comfort her: the
LORD hath commanded concerning
Jacob, *that* his adversaries *should be*
round about him: Jerusalem is as a
menstruous woman among them.
18 ¶ The LORD is [r]righteous; for I
have rebelled [s]against his [10]command-
ment: hear, I pray you, all people, and
behold my sorrow: my virgins and my
young men are gone into captivity.
19 I called for my lovers, *but* they deceived me: my priests and mine elders
gave up the ghost in the city, while
they sought their meat to relieve their
souls.
20 Behold, O LORD; for I *am* in distress: my [t]bowels are troubled; mine
heart is turned within me; for I have
grievously rebelled: abroad [u]the
sword bereaveth, at home *there is* as
death.
21 They have heard that I sigh:
there is none to comfort me: all mine
enemies have heard of my trouble;
they are glad that thou hast done *it:*
thou wilt bring [v]the day *that* thou hast
[11]called, and they shall be like unto
me.
22 Let all their wickedness come before thee; and do unto them, as thou
hast done unto me for all my transgressions: for my sighs *are* many, and
my heart *is* faint.

CHAPTER 2

HOW hath the Lord covered the
daughter of Zion with a cloud in
his anger, *and* [a]cast down from heaven
unto the earth [b]the beauty of Israel,
and remembered not [c]his footstool in
the day of his anger!
2 The Lord hath swallowed up all the
habitations of Jacob, and hath not
pitied: he hath thrown down in his
wrath the strong holds of the daughter
of Judah; he hath [1]brought *them* down
to the ground: he [d]hath polluted the
kingdom and the princes thereof.
3 He hath cut off in *his* fierce anger
all [e]the horn of Israel: [f]he hath drawn
back his right hand from before the
enemy, and he burned against Jacob
like a flaming fire, *which* devoureth
round about.
4 He [g]hath bent his bow like an enemy: he stood with his right hand as
an adversary, and slew [2]all *that were*
pleasant to the eye in the tabernacle
of the daughter of Zion: he pour
out his fury like fire.
5 The Lord was as an enemy: he ha
swallowed up Israel, [h]he hath sw
lowed up all her palaces: he hath d
stroyed his strong holds, and hath i
creased in the daughter of Jud
mourning and lamentation.
6 And he hath violently [i]taken aw
his [3]tabernacle, as [j]*if it were of* a ga
den: he hath destroyed his places
the assembly: the [k]LORD hath caus
the solemn feasts and sabbaths to b
forgotten in Zion, and hath despise
in the indignation of his anger th
king and the priest.
7 The Lord hath [l]cast off his altar, h
hath abhorred his sanctuary, he ha
[4]given up into the hand of the enem
the walls of her palaces; [m]they ha
made a noise in the house of the LOR
as in the day of a solemn feast.
8 The LORD hath purposed to d
stroy the wall of the daughter of Zio
[n]he hath stretched out a line, he ha
not withdrawn his hand from [5]d
stroying: therefore he made the ram
part and the wall to lament; the
languished together.
9 Her gates are sunk into the groun
he hath destroyed and broken h
bars: [o]her king and her princes *a*
among the Gentiles: [p]the law *is* n
more; [q]her prophets also find n
vision from the LORD.
10 The elders of the daughter of Zio
sit [r]upon the ground, *and* keep silenc
they have cast up dust upon the
heads; they have girded themselv
with sackcloth: the virgins of Jerus
lem hang down their heads to th
ground.
11 Mine [s]eyes do fail with tears, m
bowels are troubled, [t]my liver is pou
ed upon the earth, for the destructio
of the daughter of my people; becau
the children and the sucklings [6]swoo
in the streets of the city.
12 They say to their mothers, Whe
is corn and wine? when they swoone
as the wounded in the streets of th
city, when their soul was poured ou
into their mothers' bosom.
13 What thing shall I take to witne
for thee? [u]what thing shall I liken t
thee, O daughter of Jerusalem? wh
shall I equal to thee, that I may com
fort thee, O virgin daughter of Zion
for thy breach *is* great like the sea
who can heal thee?
14 Thy prophets have seen vain an
foolish things for thee: and they hav
not discovered [v]thine iniquity, to tur

9 bring back.
r Neh. 9.33. Dan. 9.7.
s 1 Sam. 12. 14.
10 mouth.
t Isa. 16.11. Jer. 4.19. Hosea 11.8.
u Deut. 32. 25.
v Jer. 46.1.
11 Or, proclaimed.

CHAP. 2

a Matt. 11. 23.
b 2 Sam. 1.19.
c 1 Chr. 28.2.
1 made to touch.
d Ps. 89.39.
e Job 16.15.
f Ps. 74.11.
g Isa. 63.10.
2 all the desirable of the eye.
h Jer. 52.13.
i Ps. 80.12. Isa. 5.5.
3 Or, hedge.
j Isa. 1.8.
k Zeph. 3.18.
l Ps. 78.59-61. Isa. 64.10, 11. Jer. 7.12-14. Eze. 7.20. Micah 3.12. Matt. 24.2.
4 shut up.
m Ps. 74.4.
n Isa. 34.11. Amos 7.7.
5 swallowing up.
o Deut. 28. 36. 2 Ki. 25.7.
p 2 Chr. 15.3.
q Ps. 74.9. Amos 8.11, 12. Micah 3.6, 7.
r Job 2.13. Isa. 47.1-5. ch. 4.5.
s Ps. 6.7.
t Job 16.13.
6 Or, faint.
u Job 5.1. Dan. 9.12.
v Isa. 58.1.

away thy captivity; but have seen for
hee false burdens and causes of
banishment.
15 All [w]that pass [7]by clap *their* hands
at thee; they hiss and wag their head
at the daughter of Jerusalem, *saying*,
's this the city that *men* call [x]The per-
ection of beauty, The joy of the whole
arth?
16 All thine enemies have opened
heir mouth against thee: they hiss
and gnash the teeth: they say, We
[y]have swallowed *her* up: certainly
his *is* the day that we looked for;
ve have found, [z]we have seen
t.
17 The LORD hath done *that* which
he had [a]devised; he hath fulfilled his
word that he had commanded in the
days of old: he hath thrown down,
and hath not pitied: and he hath caused *thine* enemy to [b]rejoice over thee,
he hath set up the horn of thine adversaries.
18 Their heart cried unto the Lord,
O wall of the daughter of Zion, [c]let
tears run down like a river day and
night: give thyself no rest; let not the
apple of thine eye cease.
19 Arise, cry out in the night: in the
beginning of [d]the watches pour [e]out
thine heart like water before the face
of the Lord: lift up thy hands toward
him for the life of thy young children,
that faint for hunger [f]in the top of
every street.
20 ¶ Behold, O LORD, and consider
to [g]whom thou hast done this. Shall
[h]the women eat their fruit, *and* children [8]of a span long? shall [i]the priest
and the prophet be slain in the sanctuary of the Lord?
21 The [j]young and the old lie on the
ground in the streets: my virgins and
my young men are fallen by the
sword; thou hast slain *them* in the day
of thine anger; thou hast killed, *and*
not pitied.
22 Thou hast called as in a solemn
day my [k]terrors round about, so that
in the day of the LORD's anger none
escaped nor remained: those [l]that I
have swaddled and brought up hath
mine enemy consumed.

CHAPTER 3

I AM the man *that* hath seen affliction by the rod of his wrath.
2 He hath led me, and brought *me into* darkness, but not *into* light.
3 Surely against me is he turned; he
turneth his hand *against me* all the
day.
4 My flesh and my skin hath he made
old; he hath broken my bones.
5 He hath builded against me, and
compassed *me* with gall and travail.
6 He [a]hath set me in dark places, as
they that be dead of old.
7 He hath hedged me about, that I
cannot get out: he hath made my
chain heavy.
8 Also [b]when I cry and shout, he
shutteth out my prayer.
9 He hath inclosed my ways with
hewn stone, he hath made my paths
crooked.
10 He [c]*was* unto me *as* a bear lying in
wait, *and as* a lion in secret places.
11 He hath turned aside my ways,
and pulled [d]me in pieces: he hath
made me desolate.
12 He hath bent his bow, and set [e]me
as a mark for the arrow.
13 He hath caused the [1]arrows of his
quiver to enter into my reins.
14 I was a derision [f]to all my people;
and their song all the day.
15 He hath [g]filled me with [2]bitter-
ness, he hath made me drunken with
wormwood.
16 He hath also broken my teeth with
[h]gravel stones, he hath [3]covered me
with ashes.
17 And thou hast removed my soul
far off from peace: I forgat [4]pros-
perity.
18 And [i]I said, My strength and my
hope is perished from the LORD:
19 [5]Remembering mine affliction and
my misery, the wormwood and the
gall.
20 My soul hath *them* still in remembrance, and is [6]humbled in me.
21 This I [7]recall to my mind, therefore have I hope.
22 ¶ *It* [j]*is of* the LORD's mercies that
we are not consumed, because his
compassions fail not.
23 *They are* new [k]every morning:
great *is* [l]thy faithfulness.
24 The LORD *is* my [m]portion, saith
my soul; therefore will I hope in him.
25 The LORD *is* good unto them that
[n]wait for him, to the soul *that* seeketh
him.
26 *It is* good that *a man* should both
hope and [o]quietly wait for the salvation of the LORD.
27 *It* [p]*is* good for a man that he bear
the yoke in his youth.
28 He [q]sitteth alone and keepeth
silence, because he hath borne *it* upon
him.
29 He [r]putteth his mouth in the dust;
if so be there may be hope.

w 1 Ki. 9.8.
7 by the way.
x Ps. 48.2.
y Ps. 56.2.
z Ps. 35.21.
a Lev. 26.16. Deut. 28.15.
b Deut. 28. 43,44. Ps. 38.16. ch. 1.5.
c Jer. 14.17. ch. 1.16.
d Mark 13. 35.
e Ps. 62.8.
f Isa. 51.20. ch. 4.1. Nah. 3.10.
g Ex. 32.11.
h Lev. 26.29. Deut. 28.53. Jer. 19.9. ch. 4.10.
8 Or, swaddled with their hands?
i ch. 4.13.
j 2 Chr. 36. 17.
k Ps. 31.13. Jer. 46.5.
l Hosea 9.12.

CHAP. 3

a Ps. 88.5.
b Job 30.20. Ps. 22.2.
c Hosea 5.14.
d Hosea 6.1.
e Job 6.4. Ps. 38.2.
1 sons.
f Neh. 4.2-4. Ps. 22.6,7. Jer. 20.7. Matt. 27.29- 31.
g Jer. 9.15.
2 bitter- nesses.
h Pro. 20.17.
3 Or, rolled me in the ashes.
4 good.
i Ps. 31.22.
5 Or, Remember.
6 bowed.
7 make to return to my heart.
j Neh. 9.31. Ps. 57.10. Mal. 3.6.
k Isa. 33.2.
l Heb. 10.23.
m Ps. 16.5.
n Ps. 130.6.
o Ps. 37.7.
p Ps. 94.12.
q Jer. 15.17.
r Job 42.6.

30 He [s]giveth *his* cheek to him that
smiteth him: he is filled full with reproach.
31 For [t]the Lord will not cast off for
ever:
32 But though he cause grief, yet will
he have compassion according to the
multitude of his mercies.
33 For [u]he doth not afflict [8]willingly
nor grieve the children of men.
34 To crush under his feet all the
prisoners of the earth,
35 To turn aside the right of a man
before the face of [9]the most High,
36 To subvert a man in his cause, the
[v]Lord [10]approveth not.
37 ¶ Who *is* he [w]*that* saith, and it
cometh to pass, *when* the Lord commandeth *it* not?
38 Out of the mouth of the most High
proceedeth not [x]evil and good?
39 Wherefore doth a living man
[11]complain, [y]a man for the punishment of his sins?
40 Let [z]us search and try our ways,
and turn again to the LORD.
41 Let [a]us lift up our heart with *our*
hands unto God in the heavens.
42 We [b]have transgressed and have
rebelled: thou hast not pardoned.
43 Thou hast covered with anger,
and persecuted us: thou hast slain,
thou hast not pitied.
44 Thou hast covered thyself with a
cloud, that *our* prayer should not pass
through.
45 Thou hast made us *as* [c]the offscouring and refuse in the midst of
the people.
46 All our enemies have opened their
mouths against us.
47 Fear and a snare is come upon
us, desolation and destruction.
48 Mine eye runneth down with rivers of water for the destruction of the
daughter of my people.
49 Mine eye trickleth down, and
ceaseth not, without any intermis-
sion,
50 Till the LORD [d]look down, and
behold from heaven.
51 Mine eye affecteth [12]mine heart
[13]because of all the daughters of my
city.
52 Mine enemies chased me sore, like
a bird, [e]without cause.
53 They have cut off my life [f]in the
dungeon, and [g]cast a stone upon me.
54 Waters [h]flowed over mine head;
then I said, I am cut off.
55 ¶ I [i]called upon thy name, O
LORD, out of the low dungeon.
56 Thou [j]hast heard my voice: hide

s Micah 5.1. Matt. 5.39.
t Ps. 94.14.
u Heb. 12.10.
8 from his heart.
9 Or, a superior.
v Hab. 1.13.
10 Or, seeth not.
w Ps. 33.9.
x Job 2.10.
11 Or, murmur.
y Micah 7.9.
z Ps. 119.59.
a Ps. 86.4.
b Dan. 9.5.
c 1 Cor. 4.13.
d Isa. 63.15.
12 my soul.
13 Or, more than all.
e Ps. 35.7. Ps. 69.4.
f Jer. 37.16.
g Dan. 6.17.
h Ps. 69.2.
i 2 Chr. 33. 12. Ps. 18.5,6. Jonah 2.2.
j Ps. 6.8. Rom. 8.26.
k Ps. 69.18. Isa. 58.9. Jas. 4.8.
l 1 Sam. 25. 39. Ps. 35.1. Jer. 51.36.
m Ps. 71.23.
n Jer. 11.19.
o Ps. 139.2.
p Ps. 28.4. Jer. 11.20. 2 Tim. 4.14. Rev. 6.10.
14 Or, obstinacy of heart.
q Ps. 8.3.

CHAP. 4

a 2 Cor. 4.7.
1 Or, sea calves.
b Job 39.14.
c Ps. 22.15.
d Job 24.8. Luke 15.16.
2 Or, iniquity.
e Gen. 19.25.
3 Or, distinguished ones.
4 darker than blackness.
f Ps. 102.5.

not thine ear at my breathing, at my
cry.
57 Thou [k]drewest near in the day
that I called upon thee: thou saidst,
Fear not.
58 O Lord, thou hast [l]pleaded the
causes of my soul; [m]thou hast redeemed my life.
59 O LORD, thou hast seen my
wrong: judge thou my cause.
60 Thou hast seen all their vengeance
and all their [n]imaginations against me.
61 Thou hast heard their reproach,
O LORD, *and* all their imaginations
against me;
62 The lips of those that rose up
against me, and their device against
me all the day.
63 Behold their [o]sitting down, and
their rising up; I *am* their musick.
64 ¶ Render [p]unto them a recompence, O LORD, according to the
work of their hands.
65 Give them [14]sorrow of heart, thy
curse unto them.
66 Persecute and destroy them in
anger from under the [q]heavens of the
LORD.

CHAPTER 4

HOW is the gold become dim! *how*
is the most fine gold changed! the
stones of the sanctuary are poured
out in the top of every street.
2 The precious sons of Zion, com-
parable to fine gold, how are they
esteemed [a]as earthen pitchers, the
work of the hands of the potter!
3 Even the [1]sea monsters draw out
the breast, they give suck to their
young ones: the daughter of my people *is become* cruel, like the ostriches
[b]in the wilderness.
4 The [c]tongue of the sucking child
cleaveth to the roof of his mouth for
thirst: the young children ask bread,
and no man breaketh *it* unto them.
5 They that did feed delicately are
desolate in the streets: they that were
brought up in scarlet [d]embrace dung-
hills.
6 For the [2]punishment of the iniquity
of the daughter of my people is greater
than the punishment of the sin of
Sodom, that was overthrown [e]as in a
moment, and no hands stayed on her.
7 Her [3]Nazarites were purer than
snow, they were whiter than milk,
they were more ruddy in body than
rubies, their polishing *was* of sapphire:
8 Their visage is [4]blacker than a coal;
they are not known in the streets:
[f]their skin cleaveth to their bones; it is
withered, it is become like a stick.

9 *They that be* slain with the sword
are better than *they that be* slain with
hunger: for these [5]pine away, stricken
through for *want of* the fruits of the
field.
10 The [g]hands of the pitiful women
have sodden their own children: they
were their meat in the destruction of
the daughter of my people.
11 The LORD hath accomplished his
fury; he hath poured out his fierce
anger, and hath [h]kindled a fire in
Zion, and it hath devoured the foundations thereof.
12 The kings of the earth, and all [i]the
inhabitants of the world, would not
have believed that the adversary and
the enemy should have entered into
the gates of Jerusalem.
13 ¶ For [j]the sins of her prophets,
and the iniquities of her priests, that
[k]have shed the blood of the just in the
midst of her,
14 They have wandered *as* blind *men*
in the streets, [l]they have polluted
themselves with blood, [6]so that men
could not touch their garments.
15 They cried unto them, Depart ye;
[7]*it is* unclean; depart, depart, touch
not: when they fled away and wandered, they said among the heathen,
They shall no more sojourn *there*.
16 The [8]anger of the LORD hath
divided them; he will no more regard
them: [m]they respected not the persons
of the priests, they favoured not the
elders.
17 As for us, [n]our eyes as yet failed
for our vain help: in our watching we
have watched for a nation *that* could
not save *us*.
18 They [o]hunt our steps, that we cannot go in our streets: our end is near,
our days are fulfilled; [p]for our end is
come.
19 Our persecutors are swifter than
the eagles of the heaven: they pursued
us upon the mountains, they laid wait
for us in [9]the wilderness.
20 The [q]breath of our nostrils, the
anointed of the LORD, [r]was taken in
their pits, of whom we said, Under his
shadow we shall live among the
heathen.
21 ¶ Rejoice and be glad, O daughter of Ē-dom, that dwellest in the
land of Uz; the cup also shall pass
through unto thee: thou shalt be
drunken, and shalt make thyself
naked.
22 ¶ [10]The punishment of thine iniquity is accomplished, O daughter of
Zion; he will no more carry thee away
into captivity: he will visit thine iniquity, O daughter of Ē-dom; he will
[11]discover thy sins.

5 flow out.
g ch. 2.20.
h Deut. 32. 22.
i Deut. 29.24.
j Jer. 5.31.
k Matt. 23. 31.
l Jer. 2.34.
6 Or, in that they could not but touch.
7 Or, ye polluted.
8 Or, face.
m ch. 5.12.
n 2 Ki. 24.7. Isa. 20.5,6.
o 2 Ki. 25.4.
p Jer. 51.33.
9 Or, the lower grounds.
q Gen. 2.7.
r Jer. 52.9.
10 Or, Thine iniquity.
11 Or, carry thee captive for thy sins.

CHAP. 5

1 cometh for price.
2 On our necks are we persecuted.
a Gen. 24.2. Jer. 50.15.
b Hosea 12.1.
c Jer. 16.12. Eze. 18.2. Matt. 23.32.
3 Or, terrors, or, storms.
d Isa. 13.16.
e Judg. 16.21.
f 2 Ki. 25.18.
4 The crown of our head is fallen.
g Job 17.7. Ps. 6.7.
5 for length of days?
6 Or, For wilt thou utterly reject us?

CHAPTER 5

REMEMBER, O LORD, what is
come upon us: consider, and behold our reproach.
2 Our inheritance is turned to strangers, our houses to aliens.
3 We are orphans and fatherless, our
mothers *are* as widows.
4 We have drunken our water for
money; our wood [1]is sold unto us.
5 [2]Our necks *are* under persecution:
we labour, *and* have no rest.
6 We [a]have given the hand [b]*to* the
Egyptians, *and to* the Assyrians, to be
satisfied with bread.
7 Our [c]fathers have sinned, *and are*
not; and we have borne their iniquities.
8 Servants have ruled over us: *there*
is none that doth deliver *us* out of their
hand.
9 We gat our bread with *the peril of*
our lives because of the sword of the
wilderness.
10 Our skin was black like an oven
because of the [3]terrible famine.
11 They [d]ravished the women in
Zion, *and* the maids in the cities of
Judah.
12 Princes are hanged up by their
hand: the faces of elders were not
honoured.
13 They took the young men [e]to
grind, and the children fell under the
wood.
14 The [f]elders have ceased from the
gate, the young men from their
musick.
15 The joy of our heart is ceased; our
dance is turned into mourning.
16 [4]The crown is fallen *from* our
head: woe unto us, that we have
sinned!
17 For this our heart is faint; [g]for
these *things* our eyes are dim.
18 Because of the mountain of Zion,
which is desolate, the foxes walk upon
it.
19 Thou, O LORD, remainest for ever;
thy throne from generation to generation.
20 Wherefore dost thou forget us
for ever, *and* forsake us [5]so long
time?
21 Turn thou us unto thee, O LORD,
and we shall be turned; renew our
days as of old.
22 [6]But thou hast utterly rejected us;
thou art very wroth against us.

THE BOOK OF THE PROPHET

EZEKIEL

CHAPTER 1

NOW it came to pass in [a]the thirtieth year, in the fourth *month*, in the fifth *day* of the month, as I *was* among the [1]captives by the river of Chē-bär, *that* [b]the heavens were opened, and I saw visions of God.

2 In the fifth *day* of the month, which *was* the fifth year of king Jĕ-hôi-ă-chĭn's captivity,

3 The [c]word of the LORD came expressly unto [2]Ē-zēk-ĭ-ĕl the priest, the son of Bū-zī, in the land of the Chăl-dē-ăns by the river Chē-bär; and [d]the hand of the LORD was there upon him.

4 ¶ And I looked, and, behold, a [e]whirlwind came [f]out of the north, a great cloud, and a fire [3]infolding itself, and a brightness *was* about it, and out of the midst thereof as the colour of amber, out of the midst of the fire.

5 Also [g]out of the midst thereof *came* the likeness of four living creatures. And this [h]*was* their appearance; they had the likeness of a man.

6 And every one had four faces, and every one had four wings.

7 And their feet *were* [4]straight feet; and the sole of their feet *was* like the sole of a calf's foot: and they sparkled [i]like the colour of burnished brass.

8 And [j]*they had* the hands of a man under their wings on their four sides; and they four had their faces and their wings.

9 Their wings *were* joined one to another; they turned not when they went; they went every one straight forward.

10 As for [k]the likeness of their faces, they four [l]had the face of a man, and the face of a lion, on the right side: and they four had the face of an ox on the left side; they four also had the face of an eagle.

11 Thus *were* their faces: and their wings *were* [5]stretched upward; two *wings* of every one *were* joined one to another, and [m]two covered their bodies.

12 And they went every one straight forward: whither the spirit was to go, they went; *and* they turned not when they went.

13 As for the likeness of the living creatures, their appearance *was* like burning coals of fire, [n]*and* like the appearance of lamps: it went up and down among the living creatures; and the fire was bright, and out of the fire went forth lightning.

14 And the living creatures [o]ran and returned as the appearance of a [p]flash of lightning.

15 ¶ Now as I beheld the living creatures, behold [q]one wheel upon the earth by the living creatures, with his four faces.

16 The [r]appearance of the wheels and their work *was* [s]like unto the colour of a beryl: and they four had one likeness: and their appearance and their work *was* as it were a wheel in the middle of a wheel.

17 When they went, they went upon their four sides: *and* they turned not when they went.

18 As for their rings, they were so high that they were dreadful; and their [6]rings *were* [t]full of eyes round about them four.

19 And [u]when the living creatures went, the wheels went by them: and when the living creatures were lifted up from the earth, the wheels were lifted up.

20 Whithersoever the spirit was to go, they went, thither *was their* spirit to go; and the wheels were lifted up over against them: for the spirit [7]of the living creature *was* in the wheels.

21 When those went, *these* went; and when those stood, *these* stood; and when those were lifted up from the earth, the wheels were lifted up over against them: for the spirit [8]of the living creature *was* in the wheels.

22 And [v]the likeness of the firmament upon the heads of the living creature *was* as the colour of the terrible crystal, stretched forth over their heads above.

23 And under the firmament *were* their wings straight, the one toward the other: every one had two, which covered on this side, and every one had two, which covered on that side, their bodies.

CHAP. 1
a 2 Ki. 23.3.
1 captivity.
b Matt. 3.16.
c 2 Pet. 1.21.
2 Jehezkel.
d 2 Ki. 3.15.
e Isa. 21.1. Jer. 23.19.
f Jer. 1.14. Jer. 4.6.
3 catching itself.
g Rev. 4.6.
h ch. 10.8.
4 a straight foot.
i Dan. 10.6. Rev. 1.15.
j Isa. 6.6. ch. 10.8. Rev. 4.8.
k Rev. 4.7.
l Num. 2.10.
5 Or, divided above.
m Isa. 6.2.
n Dan. 10.5, 6. Matt. 28.3. Rev. 4.5.
o Zech. 4.10.
p Ex. 3.2. Judg. 13.20. 2 Ki. 2.11. Ps. 104.4. Matt. 24.27.
q ch. 10.9.
r ch. 10.9,10.
s Dan. 10.6.
6 Or, strakes.
t Pro. 15.3. ch. 10.12. Rev. 5.6.
u ch. 10.16, 17.
7 Or, of life.
8 Or, of life.
v ch. 10.1.

4 And [w]when they went, I heard
e noise of their wings, like [x]the
ise of great waters, as the [y]voice of
e Almighty, the voice of speech, as
e noise of an host: when they stood,
ey let down their wings.
5 And there was a voice from the
mament that *was* over their heads,
ıen they stood, *and* had let down
eir wings.
6 ¶ And [z]above the firmament that
s over their heads *was* the likeness
a throne, [a]as the appearance of a
pphire stone: and upon the likeness
the throne *was* the likeness [b]as the
pearance of a man above upon

7 And [c]I saw as the colour of amber,
the appearance of fire round about
thin it, from the appearance of his
ins even upward, and from the
pearance of his loins even down-
rd, I saw as it were the appearance
fire, and it had brightness round
out.
8 As [d]the appearance of the bow
at is in the cloud in the day of rain,
was the appearance of the bright-
ss round about. This [e]*was* the
pearance of the likeness of the glory
the LORD. And when I saw *it*, [f]I fell
on my face, and I heard a voice of
e that spake.

CHAPTER 2

AND he said unto me, Son of man,
[a]stand upon thy feet, and I will
eak unto thee.
And [b]the spirit entered into me
hen he spake unto me, and set me
on my feet, that I heard him that
ake unto me.
And he said unto me, Son of man,
send thee to the children of Israel,
a rebellious [1]nation that hath re-
lled against me: they [c]and their
thers have transgressed against me,
en unto this very day.
For [d]*they are* [2]impudent children
d stiffhearted. I do send thee unto
em; and thou shalt say unto them,
hus saith the Lord GOD.
And [e]they, whether they will hear,
whether they will forbear, (for they
e a rebellious house,) yet [f]shall
now that there hath been a prophet
nong them.
¶ And thou, son of man, [g]be not
raid of them, neither be afraid of
eir words, though [3]briers and thorns
with thee, and thou dost dwell
mong scorpions: [h]be not afraid of
eir words, nor be dismayed at their

w ch. 10.5.
x Dan. 10.6. Rev. 1.15.
y Job 37.4,5. Ps. 18.13. ch. 10.5.
z ch. 10.1.
a Ex. 24.10.
b Isa. 6.1.
c ch. 8.2.
d Rev. 4.3.
e Ex. 33.20. Num. 12.8. ch. 8.4.
f ch. 43.3. Dan. 8.17. Acts 9.4. Rev. 1.17.

CHAP. 2

a Dan. 10.11.
b Num. 11. 25. Judg. 13.25. Neh. 9.30. ch. 3.24. Joel 2.28,29.
1 nations.
c Jer. 3.25.
d ch. 3.7.
2 hard of face.
e ch. 3.11.
f ch. 33.33.
g Matt. 10.28.
3 Or, rebels.
h Heb. 11.27. 1 Pet. 3.14.
i ch. 3.26,27.
j Jer. 1.7,17. Matt. 28.20.
4 rebellion.
k Rev. 10.9.
l Jer. 1.9.
m ch. 3.1.
n Isa. 3.11.

CHAP. 3

a ch. 2.8,9.
b Rev. 10.9.
1 deep of lip, and heavy of tongue.
2 deep of lip, and heavy of language.
3 Or, If I had sent thee, etc., would they not have hearkened unto thee?
c John 15.20.
4 stiff of forehead, and hard of heart.
d Jer. 1.18.

looks, [i]though they *be* a rebellious
house.
7 And [j]thou shalt speak my words
unto them, whether they will hear, or
whether they will forbear: for they *are*
[4]most rebellious.
8 But thou, son of man, hear what I
say unto thee; Be not thou rebellious
like that rebellious house: open thy
mouth, and [k]eat that I give thee.
9 ¶ And when I looked, behold, an
[l]hand *was* sent unto me; and, lo, [m]a
roll of a book *was* therein;
10 And he spread it before me; and
it *was* written within and without: and
there was written therein lamentations, and mourning, and [n]woe.

CHAPTER 3

MOREOVER he said unto me,
Son of man, eat that thou findest;
[a]eat this roll, and go speak unto the
house of Israel.
2 So I opened my mouth, and he
caused me to eat that roll.
3 And he said unto me, Son of man,
cause thy belly to eat, and fill thy
bowels with this roll that I give thee.
Then did I [b]eat *it;* and it was in my
mouth as honey for sweetness.
4 ¶ And he said unto me, Son of man,
go, get thee unto the house of Israel,
and speak with my words unto them.
5 For thou *art* not sent to a people
[1]of a strange speech and of an hard
language, *but* to the house of Israel;
6 Not to many people [2]of a strange
speech and of an hard language,
whose words thou canst not understand. [3]Surely, had I sent thee to them,
they would have hearkened unto
thee.
7 But the house of Israel will not
hearken unto thee; [c]for they will not
hearken unto me: for all the house of
Israel *are* [4]impudent and hard-
hearted.
8 Behold, I have made thy face strong
against their faces, and thy forehead
strong against their foreheads.
9 As [d]an adamant harder than flint
have I made thy forehead: fear them
not, neither be dismayed at their
looks, though they *be* a rebellious
house.
10 Moreover he said unto me, Son
of man, all my words that I shall speak
unto thee receive in thine heart, and
hear with thine ears.
11 And go, get thee to them of the
captivity, unto the children of thy people, and speak unto them, and tell
them, Thus saith the Lord GOD;

whether they will hear, or whether
they will forbear.
12 Then [e]the spirit took me up, and
I heard behind me a voice of a great
rushing, *saying*, Blessed *be* the glory
of the LORD from his place.
13 *I heard* also the noise of the wings
of the living creatures that [5]touched
one another, and the noise of the
wheels over against them, and a noise
of a great rushing.
14 So the spirit lifted me up, and
took me away, and I went [6]in bitterness, in the [7]heat of my spirit; but the
[f]hand of the LORD was strong upon
me.
15 ¶ Then I came to them of the captivity at Tĕl–ā-bīb, that dwelt by the
river of Chē-bär, and [g]I sat where they
sat, and remained there astonished
among them seven days.
16 And it came to pass at the end of
seven days, that the word of the LORD
came unto me, saying,
17 Son of man, I have made thee a
[h]watchman unto the house of Israel:
therefore hear the word at my mouth,
and give them warning from me.
18 When I say unto the wicked,
Thou shalt surely die; and thou givest
him not warning, nor speakest to
warn the wicked from his wicked way,
[i]to save his life; the same wicked *man*
[j]shall die in his iniquity; but his blood
will I require at thine hand.
19 Yet if thou warn the wicked, and
he turn not from his wickedness, nor
from his wicked way, he shall die in
his iniquity; but [k]thou hast delivered
thy soul.
20 Again, When a [l]righteous *man*
doth turn from his [8]righteousness, and
commit iniquity, and I lay a stumblingblock before him, he shall die:
because thou hast not given him
warning, he shall die in his sin, and his
righteousness which he hath done
shall not be remembered; but his
blood will I require at thine hand.
21 Nevertheless if thou warn the
righteous *man*, that the righteous sin
not, and he doth not sin, he shall surely [m]live, because he is warned; also
[n]thou hast delivered thy soul.
22 ¶ And the hand of the LORD was
there upon me; and he said unto me,
Arise, go forth into [o]the plain, and I
will there talk with thee.
23 Then I arose, and went forth into
the plain: and, behold, [p]the glory of
the LORD stood there, as the glory
which I [q]saw by the river of Chē-bär:
and I fell on my face.

e ch. 8.3. Acts 8.39.
5 kissed.
6 bitter.
7 hot anger.
f 2 Ki. 3.15.
g Job 2.13. Ps. 137.1.
h Song 3.3. Song 5.7. Isa. 21.6,8, 11,12. Isa. 52.8. Isa. 56.10. Jer. 6.17.
i Rom. 1.16. 1 Tim. 4.16.
j ch. 33.6.
k Acts 20.26.
l ch. 18.24. 2 Pet. 2.20.
8 righteousnesses.
m Rom. 2.7.
n Acts 18.6.
o ch. 8.4.
p ch. 1.28.
q ch. 1.1.
r ch. 2.2.
s ch. 4.8.
t ch. 24.27. Luke 1.20, 22.
9 a man reproving.
u ch. 2.5,6.
v ch. 24.27. ch. 33.22.
w ch. 12.2,3.

CHAP. 4

1 Or, chief leaders.
2 Or, a flat plate, or, slice.
a Isa. 8.18. ch. 12.6,11. Mark 14.22. Luke 2.34. John 4.48.
3 From the establishment of idolatry by Jeroboam. 1 Ki. 12.26, till 585 B.C.
b Num. 14. 34.
4 a day for a year, a day for a year.
c ch. 3.25.
5 from thy side to thy side.
6 Or, spelt.

24 Then [r]the spirit entered into m
and set me upon my feet, and spa
with me, and said unto me, Go, sh
thyself within thine house.
25 But thou, O son of man, beho
[s]they shall put bands upon thee, a
shall bind thee with them, and th
shalt not go out among them:
26 And [t]I will make thy tong
cleave to the roof of thy mouth, th
thou shalt be dumb, and shalt not
to them [9]a reprover: for [u]they *are* a r
bellious house.
27 But [v]when I speak with thee, I w
open thy mouth, and thou shalt s
unto them, Thus saith the Lord Go
He that heareth, let him hear; and
that forbeareth, let him forbear: [w]f
they *are* a rebellious house.

CHAPTER 4

THOU also, son of man, take th
a tile, and lay it before thee, a
pourtray upon it the city, *even* Jerus
lem:
2 And lay siege against it, and bu
a fort against it, and cast a mou
against it; set the camp also against
and set [1]*battering* rams against
round about.
3 Moreover take thou unto thee [2]a
iron pan, and set it *for* a wall of ir
between thee and the city: and set t
face against it, and it shall be besiege
and thou shalt lay siege against
[a]This *shall be* a sign to the house
Israel.
4 Lie thou also upon thy left side, a
lay the iniquity of the house of Isra
upon it: *according* to the number
the days that thou shalt lie upon
thou shalt bear their iniquity.
5 For I have laid upon thee the yea
of their iniquity, according to t
number of the days, [3]three hundr
and ninety days: [b]so shalt thou be
the iniquity of the house of Israel.
6 And when thou hast accomplish
them, lie again on thy right side, a
thou shalt bear the iniquity of t
house of Judah forty days: I have a
pointed thee [4]each day for a year.
7 Therefore thou shalt set thy fa
toward the siege of Jerusalem, a
thine arm *shall be* uncovered, and th
shalt prophesy against it.
8 And, [c]behold, I will lay bands up
thee, and thou shalt not turn th
[5]from one side to another, till th
hast ended the days of thy siege.
9 ¶ Take thou also unto thee whe
and barley, and beans, and lentil
and millet, and [6]fitches, and put the

one vessel, and make thee bread
ereof, *according* to the number of
e days that thou shalt lie upon thy
le, three hundred and ninety days
alt thou eat thereof.
0 And thy meat which thou shalt
t *shall be* by weight, twenty she-
ls a day: from time to time shalt
ou eat it.
1 Thou shalt drink also water by
easure, the sixth part of an hĭn:
om time to time shalt thou drink.
2 And thou shalt eat it *as* barley
kes, and thou shalt bake it with
ng that cometh out of man, in their
ht.
3 And the LORD said, Even thus
all [d]the children of Israel eat their
filed bread among the Gentiles,
hither I will drive them.
4 Then said I, [e]Ah Lord GOD! be-
ld, my soul hath not been polluted:
r from my youth up even till now
ve I [f]not eaten of that which dieth
itself, or is torn in pieces; neither
me there abominable [g]flesh into my
outh.
5 Then he said unto me, Lo, I have
ven thee cow's dung for man's dung,
d thou shalt prepare thy bread
erewith.
6 Moreover he said unto me, Son of
an, behold, I will break the [h]staff of
ead in Jerusalem: and they shall
at bread by weight, and with care;
d they shall drink water by measure,
d with astonishment:
7 That they may want bread and
ater, and be astonied one with an-
her, and consume [j]away for their
iquity.

CHAPTER 5

ND thou, son of man, take thee a
sharp knife, take thee a barber's
sor, [a]and cause *it* to pass upon thine
ead and upon thy beard: then take
ee balances to weigh, and divide the
ir.
Thou shalt burn with fire a third
art in the midst of [b]the city, when the
ays of the siege are fulfilled: and thou
alt take a third part, *and* smite about
with a knife: and a third part thou
alt scatter in the wind; and I will
raw out a sword after them.
3 Thou [c]shalt also take thereof a few
number, and bind them in thy
kirts.
Then take of them again, and cast
hem into the midst of the fire, and
urn them in the fire; *for* thereof shall
fire come forth into all the house of
srael.

d Dan. 1.8. Hosea 9.3.
e ch. 9.8. Acts 10.14.
f Ex. 22.31. Lev. 11.40.
g Lev. 19.7. Deut. 14.3. Isa. 65.4.
h Lev. 26.26. Ps. 105.16. Isa. 3.1. ch. 5.16.
i Lev. 26.26. Deut. 28.48. Ps. 68.3. Lam. 1.11. ch. 12.18,19.
j Lev. 26.39. ch. 24.23.

CHAP. 5

a Lev. 21.5. Isa. 7.20. ch. 44.20.
b ch. 4.1.
c Jer. 40.6.
1 wings.
d Jer. 41.1,2.
e Rom. 1.25. Jude 4.
f Jer. 2.10. ch. 11.12.
g Lam. 4.6. Dan. 9.12. Amos 3.2. Matt. 24.21.
h Deut. 28. 53. Jer. 19.9. Lam. 2.20.
i Lev. 26.33. ch. 12.14.
j 2 Chr. 36. 14. ch. 7.20.
k ch. 11.21.
l Jer. 15.2. ch. 6.12.
m Jer. 9.16. ch. 6.8.
n Lev. 26.33. ch. 12.14.
o Lam. 4.11. Dan. 9.2.
p Deut. 32. 36. Isa. 1.24.
q Lev. 26.31. Neh. 2.17.
r Deut. 28.37. Ps. 79.4. Jer. 24.9. Lam. 2.15.
s 1 Cor. 10. 11.

5 ¶ Thus saith the Lord GOD; This
is Jerusalem: I have set it in the midst
of the nations and countries *that are*
round about her.
6 And she hath [e]changed my judgments into wickedness more than the
nations, and my statutes more than
the countries that *are* round about
her: for they have refused my judgments and my statutes, they have not
walked in them.
7 Therefore thus saith the Lord GOD;
Because ye multiplied more than the
nations that *are* round about you, *and*
have not walked in my statutes, neither have kept my judgments, neither
have done according to the [f]judg-
ments of the nations that *are* round
about you;
8 Therefore thus saith the Lord GOD;
Behold, I, even I, *am* against thee, and
will execute judgments in the midst of
thee in the sight of the nations.
9 And [g]I will do in thee that which I
have not done, and whereunto I will
not do any more the like, because of
all thine abominations.
10 Therefore the fathers [h]shall eat
the sons in the midst of thee, and the
sons shall eat their fathers; and I will
execute judgments in thee, and the
whole remnant of thee will I [i]scatter
into all the winds.
11 Wherefore, *as* I live, saith the
Lord GOD; Surely, because thou hast
[j]defiled my sanctuary with all thy [k]de-
testable things, and with all thine
abominations, therefore will I also
diminish *thee;* neither shall mine eye
spare, neither will I have any pity.
12 ¶ A [l]third part of thee shall die
with the pestilence, and with famine
shall they be consumed in the midst
of thee: and a third part shall fall by
the sword round about thee; and [m]I
will scatter a third part into all the
winds, and [n]I will draw out a sword
after them.
13 Thus shall mine anger [o]be accomplished, and I will cause my fury to
rest upon them, [p]and I will be comforted: and they shall know that I the
LORD have spoken *it* in my zeal, when
I have accomplished my fury in them.
14 Moreover [q]I will make thee waste,
and a reproach among the nations
that *are* round about thee, in the sight
of all that pass by.
15 So it shall be a [r]reproach and a
taunt, an [s]instruction and an astonishment unto the nations that *are*
round about thee, when I shall execute
judgments in thee in anger and in fury

and in [t]furious rebukes. I the LORD
have spoken *it*.
16 When I shall [u]send upon them the
evil arrows of famine, which shall be
for *their* destruction, *and* which I will
send to destroy you: and I will increase the famine upon you, and will
break your staff of bread:
17 So will I send upon you famine
and evil [v]beasts, and they shall bereave
thee; and [w]pestilence and blood shall
pass through thee; and I will bring
the sword upon thee. I the LORD have
spoken *it*.

CHAPTER 6

AND the word of the LORD came
unto me, saying,
2 Son of man, set thy face toward the
mountains [a]of Israel, and prophesy
against them,
3 And say, Ye mountains of Israel,
hear the word of the Lord GOD; Thus
saith the Lord GOD to the mountains,
and to the hills, to the rivers, and to
the valleys; Behold, I, *even* I, will
bring a sword upon you, and [b]I will
destroy your high places.
4 And your altars shall be desolate,
and your [1]images shall be broken: and
[c]I will cast down your slain *men* before your [2]idols.
5 And I will [3]lay the dead carcases
of the children of Israel before their
idols; and I will scatter your bones
round about your altars.
6 In all your dwellingplaces the cities
shall be laid waste, and the high places
shall be desolate; that your altars
may be laid waste and made desolate,
and your idols may be broken and
cease, and your images may be cut
down, and your works may be
abolished.
7 And the slain shall fall in the midst
of you, and ye shall know that I *am*
the LORD.
8 ¶ Yet will [d]I leave a remnant, that
ye may have *some* that shall escape
the sword among the nations, when
ye shall be scattered through the
countries.
9 And they that escape of you shall
remember me among the nations
whither they shall be carried captives,
because [e]I am broken with their whorish heart, which hath departed from
me, and [f]with their eyes, which go a
whoring after their idols: [g]and they
shall lothe themselves for the evils
which they have committed in all their
abominations.
10 And they shall know that I *am* the

t ch. 25.17.
u Deut. 32. 23,24. ch. 14.21.
v Lev. 26.22.
w ch. 38.22.

CHAP. 6
a ch. 36.1.
b Lev. 26.30.
1 Or, sun images.
c Lev. 26.30.
2 dungy gods.
3 give.
d Jer. 44.28. ch. 5.2,12.
e Ps. 78.40. Isa. 7.13.
f Num. 15. 39. ch. 20.7.
g Lev. 26.39. Job 42.6. ch. 20.43.
h Lev. 26.36. ch. 12.16. ch. 5.12.
j Jer. 2.20. Jer. 15.2,3. ch. 5.12.
k Hos. 4.13.
l Isa. 57.5.
m Isa. 5.25.
4 Or, desolate from the wilderness.
n Num. 33. 46.

CHAP. 7
a Deut. 32. 20. Lam. 4.18. Amos 8.2. Matt. 24.6.
1 give.
b ch. 5.11.
c ch. 6.7.
2 awaketh against thee.
d Isa. 13.22. ch. 12.23-25. 1 Pet. 17.4.
3 Or, echo.
e Ps. 79.6. Isa. 42.25. Jer. 7.20. ch. 20.8.

LORD, *and that* I have not said in va
that I would do this evil unto them
11 ¶ Thus saith the Lord Go
Smite with [h]thine hand, and stan
with thy foot, and say, Alas for all t
evil abominations of the house
Israel! [i]for they shall fall by t
sword, by the famine, and by t
pestilence.
12 He that is far off shall die of t
pestilence; and he that is near sh
fall by the sword; and he that remai
eth and is besieged shall die by t
famine: thus will I accomplish n
fury upon them.
13 Then shall ye know that I *am* t
LORD, when their slain *men* shall
among their idols round about the
altars, [j]upon every high hill, [k]in a
the tops of the mountains, and und
every green tree, and [l]under eve
thick oak, the place where they d
offer sweet savour to all their idols.
14 So will I [m]stretch out my hand u
on them, and make the land desolat
yea, [4]more desolate than the wilde
ness toward [n]Dĭb-lăth, in all the
habitations: and they shall know th
I *am* the LORD.

CHAPTER 7

MOREOVER the word of t
LORD came unto me, saying,
2 Also, thou son of man, thus sai
the Lord GOD unto the land of Israe
[a]An end, the end is come upon t
four corners of the land.
3 Now *is* the end *come* upon thee, an
I will send mine anger upon thee, an
will judge thee according to thy way
and will [1]recompense upon thee a
thine abominations.
4 And [b]mine eye shall not spare the
neither will I have pity: but I wi
recompense thy ways upon thee, an
thine abominations shall be in t
midst of thee: and [c]ye shall know th
I *am* the LORD.
5 Thus saith the Lord GOD; An evi
an only evil, behold, is come.
6 An end is come, the end is com
it [2]watcheth for thee; behold, it
come.
7 The morning is come unto thee,
thou that dwellest in the land: t
[d]time is come, the day of trouble
near, and not the [3]sounding again
the mountains.
8 Now will I shortly [e]pour out m
fury upon thee, and accomplish mi
anger upon thee: and I will judge the
according to thy ways, and will reco
pense thee for all thine abomination

And mine eye shall not spare,
either will I have pity: I will recom-
ense [4]thee according to thy ways and
ine abominations *that* are in the
idst of thee; and ye shall know that
am the LORD that smiteth.
0 Behold the day, behold, it is come:
e morning is gone forth; the rod
ath blossomed, pride hath budded.
1 Violence [f]is risen up into a rod of
ickedness: none of them *shall re-*
ain, nor of their [5]multitude, nor of
ny of [6]theirs: neither *shall* [g]*there be*
ailing for them.
2 The time is come, the day draw-
h near: let not the buyer rejoice, nor
e seller mourn: for wrath *is* upon
l the multitude thereof.
3 For the seller shall not return to
at which is sold, [7]although they were
t alive: for the vision *is* touching
e whole multitude thereof, *which*
all not return; neither shall any
rengthen himself [8]in [9]the iniquity of
s life.
4 They have blown the trumpet,
ven to make all ready; but none go-
h to the battle: for my wrath *is* upon
l the multitude thereof.
5 The [h]sword *is* without, and the
estilence and the famine within: he
at *is* in the field shall die with the
word; and he that *is* in the city,
mine and pestilence shall devour
im.
16 ¶ But [i]they that escape of them
all escape, and shall be on the
ountains like doves of the valleys,
l of them mourning, every one for
is iniquity.
17 All [j]hands shall be feeble, and all
nees shall [10]be weak *as* water.
18 They shall also [k]gird *themselves*
ith sackcloth, and [l]horror shall
over them; and shame *shall be* upon
l faces, and baldness upon all their
eads.
19 They shall cast their silver in the
reets, and their gold shall be [11]re-
oved: their [m]silver and their gold
hall not be able to deliver them in
e day of the wrath of the LORD: they
hall not satisfy their souls, neither
ll their bowels: [12]because it is [n]the
tumblingblock of their iniquity.
20 ¶ As for the beauty of his orna-
ent, he set it in majesty: [o]but they
ade the images of their abomina-
ons *and* of their detestable things
erein: therefore have I [13]set it far
om them.
21 And I will give it into the hands
f the strangers for a prey, and to the
wicked of the earth for a spoil; and
they shall pollute it.
22 My face will I turn also from
them, and they shall pollute my secret
place: for the [14]robbers shall enter into
it, and defile it.
23 ¶ Make a chain: for the land is
full of bloody crimes, and [p]the city is
full of violence.
24 Wherefore I will bring [q]the worst
of the heathen, and they shall possess
their houses: I will also make the
pomp of the strong to cease; and
[15]their holy places shall be defiled.
25 [16]Destruction cometh; and they
shall seek peace, and *there shall be*
none.
26 Mischief [r]shall come upon mischief, and rumour shall be upon
rumour; [s]then shall they seek a vision
of the prophet; but the law shall
perish from [t]the priest, and counsel
from the ancients.
27 The king shall mourn, and the
prince shall be clothed with desolation, and the hands of the people of
the land shall be troubled: I will do
unto them after their way, and [17]ac-
cording to their deserts will I judge
them; and they shall know that I *am*
the LORD.

CHAPTER 8

AND it came to pass in the sixth
year, in the sixth *month*, in the
fifth *day* of the month, *as* I sat in mine
house, and the elders of Judah sat before me, that the hand of the Lord
GOD fell there upon me.
2 Then [a]I beheld, and lo a likeness as
the appearance of fire: from the
appearance of his loins even downward, fire; and from his loins even upward, as the appearance of brightness, as the colour of amber.
3 And he [b]put forth the form of an
hand, and took me by a lock of mine
head; and the spirit lifted me up between the earth and the heaven, and
[c]brought me in the visions of God to
Jerusalem, to the door [d]of the inner
gate that looketh toward the north;
where [e]*was* the seat of the image of
jealousy, which [f]provoketh to jealousy.
4 And, behold, the glory of the God
of Israel *was* there, according to the
vision that I [g]saw in the plain.
5 ¶ Then said he unto me, Son of
man, lift up thine eyes now the way
toward the north. So I lifted up mine
eyes the way toward the north, and
behold northward at the gate of the

4 upon thee.
f Jer. 6.7.
5 Or, tumult.
6 Or, their tumultuous persons.
g Jer. 16.5.
7 though their life were yet among the living.
8 Or, whose life is in his iniquity.
9 his iniquity.
h Deut. 32. 25.
i ch. 6.8.
j Isa. 13.7.
10 go into water.
k Jer. 6.26.
l Ps. 55.5.
11 for a separation, or, uncleanness.
m Pro. 11.4. Zeph. 1.18.
12 Or, because their iniquity is their stumbling block.
n ch. 44.12.
o Jer. 7.30.
13 Or, made it unto them an unclean thing.
14 Or, burglers.
p Gen. 9.6. 2 Ki.21.16. Ps. 10.8.
q Hab. 1.6.
15 Or, they shall inherit their holy places.
16 Cutting off.
r Deut. 32.23.
s Ps. 74.9. Lam.2.9.
t Mal. 2.7,8, 9.
17 with their judgments.

CHAP. 8

a ch. 1.26. Dan. 7.9.
b ch. 2.9. Dan. 5.5.
c ch. 11.1.
d 2 Ki. 16.14.
e Jer. 7.30.
f Ex. 20.4. Deut. 32.16.
g ch. 1.28.

altar this image of jealousy in the entry.
6 He said furthermore unto me, Son
of man, seest thou what they do? *even*
the great [h]abominations that the
house of Israel committeth here, that
I should go far off from my sanctuary?
but turn thee yet again, *and* thou
shalt see greater abominations.
7 ¶ And he brought me to the door of
the court; and when I looked, behold
a hole in the wall.
8 Then said he unto me, Son of man,
dig now in the wall: and when I had
digged in the wall, behold a door.
9 And he said unto me, Go in, and
behold the wicked abominations that
they do here.
10 So I went in and saw; and behold
every form of creeping things, and
abominable beasts, and all the idols
of the house of Israel, pourtrayed upon the wall round about.
11 And there stood before them seventy men of the ancients of the house
of Israel, and in the midst of them
stood Jā-ăz-ă-nī-ăh the [i]son of Shā-
phăn, with [j]every man his censer in
his hand; and a thick cloud of incense
went up.
12 Then said he unto me, Son of
man, hast thou seen what the ancients
of the house of Israel do in the dark,
every man in the chambers of his
imagery? for they say, [k]The LORD
seeth us not; the LORD hath [l]forsaken
the earth.
13 ¶ He said also unto me, Turn thee
yet again, *and* thou shalt see greater
abominations that they do.
14 Then he brought me to the door
of the gate of the LORD's house which
was toward the north; and, behold,
there sat [1]women weeping for Tăm-
mŭz.
15 ¶ Then said he unto me, Hast
thou seen *this*, O son of man? turn
thee yet again, *and* thou shalt see
greater abominations than these.
16 And he brought me into the inner
court of the LORD's house, and, behold, at the door of the temple of the
LORD, [m]between the porch and the
altar, [n]*were* about five and twenty
men, [o]with their backs toward the
temple of the LORD, and their faces
toward the east; and they worshipped
[p]the sun toward the east.
17 ¶ Then he said unto me, Hast
thou seen *this*, O son of man? [2]Is it a
light thing to the house of Judah that
they commit the abominations which
they commit here? for they have [q]filled
the land with violence, and have r
turned to provoke me to anger: an
lo, they put the branch to the
nose.
18 Therefore [r]will I also deal in fur
mine [s]eye shall not spare, neither w
I have pity: and though they [t]cry
mine ears with a loud voice, *yet* wil
not hear them.

CHAPTER 9

HE cried also in mine ears with
loud voice, saying, [a]Cause the
that have charge over the city to dra
near, even every man *with* his destro
ing weapon in his hand.
2 And, behold, six men came fro
the way of the higher gate, [1]which lie
toward the north, and every man
slaughter weapon in his hand; [b]an
one man among them *was* clothe
with linen, with a writer's inkhorn [3]b
his side: and they went in, and sto
beside the brasen altar.
3 And the glory of the God of Isra
was gone up from the cherub, wher
upon he was, to the threshold of t
house. And he called to the ma
clothed with linen, which *had* t
writer's inkhorn by his side;
4 And the LORD said unto him, G
through the midst of the city, throug
the midst of Jerusalem, and [4]set
mark upon the foreheads of the me
[c]that sigh and that cry for all t
abominations that be done in t
midst thereof.
5 ¶ And to the others he said i
[5]mine hearing, Go ye after hi
through the city, and smite: let n
your eye spare, neither have y
pity:
6 Slay [6]utterly old *and* young, bo
maids, and little children, and w
men: but come [d]not near any man u
on whom *is* the mark; and [e]begin
my sanctuary. Then they began at t
ancient men which *were* before t
house.
7 And he said unto them, Defile t
house, and fill the courts with t
slain: go ye forth. And they we
forth, and slew in the city.
8 ¶ And it came to pass, while the
were slaying them, and I was left, th
I [f]fell upon my face, and cried, an
said, Ah Lord GOD! wilt thou destro
all the residue of Israel in thy pourin
out of thy fury upon Jerusalem?
9 Then said he unto me, The iniqui
of the house of Israel and Judah *is* e
ceeding great, and the land [g]is [7]fu
of blood, and the city full of [8]pervers

h Deut. 31. 16. 2 Chr. 36.14.
i 2 Ki. 22.8. Jer. 26.24.
j Num. 16.17.
k Ps. 14.1. Isa. 29.15.
l Ps. 10.11.
1 women in a lewd and idolatrous manner, lamenting the death of Tammuz, or, Adonis, supposed also to be Baal-peor, Num. 25.3.
m Joel 2.17.
n ch. 11.1.
o Jer. 2.27.
p Deut. 4.19. Jer. 44.17.
2 Or, Is there any thing lighter than to commit.
q ch. 9.9.
r ch. 5.13.
s ch. 5.11.
t Pro. 1.28.

CHAP. 9

a Ps. 103.20.
1 which is turned.
2 a weapon of his breaking in pieces.
b Lev. 16.4.
3 upon his loins.
4 mark a mark.
c Ps. 119.53.
5 mine ears.
6 to destruction.
d Rev. 9.4.
e Jer. 25.29. Luke 12.47.
f Num. 14.5. Deut. 9.18. Josh. 7.6.
g 2 Ki. 21.16.
7 filled with.
8 Or, wresting of judgment.

ss: for they say, The LORD hath for-
ken the earth, and the [h]LORD seeth
t.
0 And as for me also, mine eye shall
t spare, neither will I have pity, *but*
will recompense their way upon
eir head.
1 And, behold, the man clothed
ith linen, which *had* the inkhorn by
s side, [9]reported the matter, saying,
nave done as thou hast commanded
e.

CHAPTER 10

THEN I looked, and, behold, in the
firmament [a]that was above the
ad of the chĕr-ū-bĭms there appear-
over them as it were a sapphire
one, as the appearance of the like-
ss of a throne.
2 And [b]he spake unto the man
othed with linen, and said, Go in
tween the wheels, *even* under the
erub, and fill [1]thine hand with [c]coals
fire from between the chĕr-ū-bĭms,
nd [d]scatter *them* over the city. And
went in in my sight.
3 Now the chĕr-ū-bĭms stood on the
ght side of the house, when the man
ent in; and the cloud filled the inner
ourt.
4 Then [e]the glory of the LORD [2]went
p from the cherub, *and stood* over
e threshold of the house; and [f]the
ouse was filled with the cloud, and
e court was full of the brightness of
e LORD's glory.
5 And the [g]sound of the chĕr-ū-bĭms'
ings was heard *even* to the outer
ourt, as the [h]voice of the Almighty
od when he speaketh.
6 And it came to pass, *that* when he
ad commanded the man clothed with
nen, saying, Take fire from between
e wheels, from between the chĕr-ū-
ims; then he went in, and stood be-
de the wheels.
7 And *one* cherub [3]stretched forth his
and from between the chĕr-ū-bĭms
nto the fire that *was* between the
hĕr-ū-bĭms, and took *thereof*, and
ut *it* into the hands of *him that was*
lothed with linen: who took *it*, and
ent out.
8 ¶ And [i]there appeared in the chĕr-
-bĭms the form of a man's hand un-
er their wings.
9 And [j]when I looked, behold the
our wheels by the chĕr-ū-bĭms, one
heel by one cherub, and another
heel by another cherub: and the
ppearance of the wheels *was* as the
olour of a beryl stone.
10 And *as for* their appearances, they

h Ps. 10.11. Isa. 29.15.
i Deut. 32.41.
9 returned the word.
CHAP. 10
a ch. 1.22. Rev. 4.3.
b ch. 9.2,3.
1 the hollow of thine hand.
c ch. 1.13.
d Rev. 8.5.
e ch. 1.28.
2 was lifted up.
f Ex. 40.35. ch. 43.5.
g ch. 1.24.
h Ps. 29.3.
3 sent forth.
i ch. 1.8.
j ch. 1.15.
4 flesh.
k ch. 1.18.
l Rev. 4.8.
5 Or, they were called in my hearing, Wheel, or, Galgal, that is, Move round.
m ch. 1.6,10.
n 2 Sam. 14. 17.
o 2 Sam. 24. 16.
p Dan. 9.21.
q ch. 1.5.
r ch. 1.19.
s ch. 1.12.
6 Or, of life.
t Ps. 78.60. ch. 7.20-22. Hosea 9.12.
u ch. 9.23. ch. 11.22.
v ch. 1.22.
w ch. 1.1.
x ch. 1.6. Rev. 4.7.
y ch. 1.8.
z ch. 1.10.
a ch. 1.12. Ps. 103.20.
CHAP. 11
a 1 Ki. 18.12. ch. 3.12,14. ch. 8.3.
b ch. 10.19.

four had one likeness, as if a wheel
had been in the midst of a wheel.
11 When they went, they went upon
their four sides; they turned not as
they went, but to the place whither the
head looked they followed it; they
turned not as they went.
12 And their whole [4]body, and their
backs, and their hands, and their
wings, and the [k]wheels, *were* full [l]of
eyes round about, *even* the wheels that
they four had.
13 As for the wheels, [5]it was cried
unto them in my hearing, O wheel.
14 And [m]every one had four faces:
the first face *was* the face of a cherub,
and the second [n]face *was* the face of a
man, and the third the face of [o]a lion,
and the fourth the face of [p]an eagle.
15 And the chĕr-ū-bĭms were lifted
up. This *is* [q]the living creature that I
saw by the river of Chē-bär.
16 And [r]when the chĕr-ū-bĭms went,
the wheels went by them: and when
the chĕr-ū-bĭms lifted up their wings
to mount up from the earth, the same
wheels also turned not from beside
them.
17 When [s]they stood, *these* stood;
and when they were lifted up, *these*
lifted up themselves *also:* for the
spirit [6]of the living creature *was* in
them.
18 Then the glory of the LORD departed [t]from off the threshold of the
house, and stood over the chĕr-ū-
bĭms.
19 And [u]the chĕr-ū-bĭms lifted up
their wings, and mounted up from the
earth in my sight: when they went out,
the wheels also *were* beside them, and
every one stood at the door of the east
gate of the LORD's house; and the
glory of the God of Israel *was* over
them above.
20 This [v]*is* the living creature that I
saw under the God of Israel by [w]the
river of Chē-bär; and I knew that they
were the chĕr-ū-bĭms.
21 Every [x]one had four faces apiece,
and every one four wings; and [y]the
likeness of the hands of a man *was* under their wings.
22 And [z]the likeness of their faces
was the same faces which I saw by the
river of Chē-bär, their appearances
and themselves: they went [a]every one
straight forward.

CHAPTER 11

MOREOVER [a]the spirit lifted me
up, and brought me unto the
[b]east gate of the LORD's house, which

looketh eastward: and behold [c]at the
door of the gate five and twenty men;
among whom I saw Jā-ăz-ă-nī-ăh the
son of Ā-zûr, and Pĕl-ă-tī-ăh the son
of Bĕ-nāi-ăh, princes of the people.
2 Then said he unto me, Son of man,
these *are* the men that devise mischief,
and give wicked counsel in this city:
3 Which say, [1]*It is* not near; let us
build houses: [d]this *city is* the caldron,
and we *be* the flesh.
4 ¶ Therefore prophesy against them,
prophesy, O son of man.
5 And the Spirit of the LORD fell upon me, and saith unto me, Speak;
Thus saith the LORD; Thus have ye
said, O house of Israel: for [e]I know
the things that come into your mind,
every one of them.
6 Ye have multiplied your slain in
this city, and ye have filled the streets
thereof with the slain.
7 Therefore thus saith the Lord GOD;
Your [f]slain whom ye have laid in the
midst of it, they *are* the flesh, and this
city is the caldron: but I will bring you
forth out of the midst of it.
8 Ye have [g]feared the sword; and I
will bring a sword upon you, saith the
Lord GOD.
9 And I will bring you out of the
midst thereof, and deliver you into
the hands of strangers, and [h]will execute judgments among you.
10 Ye [i]shall fall by the sword; I will
judge you in [j]the border of Israel;
[k]and ye shall know that I *am* the LORD.
11 This *city* shall not be your caldron,
neither shall ye be the flesh in the
midst thereof; *but* I will judge you in
[l]the border of Israel:
12 And ye shall know that I *am* the
LORD: [2]for ye have not walked in my
statutes, neither executed my judgments, but have [m]done after the
manners of the heathen that *are* round
about you.
13 ¶ And it came to pass, when I prophesied, that [n]Pĕl-ă-tī-ăh the son of
Bĕ-nāi-ăh died. Then [o]fell I down upon my face, and cried with a loud
voice, and said, Ah Lord GOD! wilt
thou make a full end of the remnant
of Israel?
14 Again the word of the LORD came
unto me, saying,
15 Son of man, thy brethren, *even*
thy brethren, the men of thy kindred,
and all the house of Israel wholly, *are*
they unto whom the inhabitants of
Jerusalem have said, Get you far from
the LORD: unto us is this land given
in possession.

c ch. 8.16.
1 Or, It is not for us to build houses near.
d Jer. 1.13.
e 1 Chr. 28.9. Ps. 7.9. Jer. 16.17. John 2.24. Heb. 4.11.
f Micah 3.3.
g Pro. 10.24.
h Ps. 106.30.
i Jer. 39.6.
j 2 Ki. 14.25.
k Ps. 9.16.
l Jer. 39.6.
2 Or, which have not walked.
m Deut. 12. 30. ch. 8.10.
n Acts 5.5.
o ch. 9.8.
p Ps. 31.20. Isa. 8.14.
q Jer. 24.5.
r ch. 37.23.
s Deut. 30.6. 2 Chr. 30.12. Jer. 24.7. Zeph. 3.9.
t Ps. 51.10. Jer. 31.33.
u Zech. 7.12.
v Jer. 11.4. ch. 14.11. ch. 36.28. Heb. 8.10.
w Heb. 3.12.
x ch. 1.19.
y ch. 8.4.
z Zech. 14.4.
a ch. 43.2.
b ch. 8.3. 2 Cor. 12.2.
c Acts 20.20.

CHAP. 12

a Isa. 6.9. Jer. 5.21. Matt. 13.13.
1 Or, instruments.

16 Therefore say, Thus saith th
Lord GOD; Although I have cast the
far off among the heathen, and a
though I have scattered them amo
the countries, [p]yet will I be to the
as a little sanctuary in the countri
where they shall come.
17 Therefore say, Thus saith th
Lord GOD; [q]I will even gather yo
from the people, and assemble yo
out of the countries where ye hav
been scattered, and I will give you th
land of Israel.
18 And they shall come thither, an
[r]they shall take away all the detestabl
things thereof and all the abomina
tions thereof from thence.
19 And [s]I will give them one hear
and I will put [t]a new spirit within you
and I will take [u]the stony heart out o
their flesh, and will give them a
heart of flesh:
20 That they may walk in my sta
utes, and keep mine ordinances, an
do them: and [v]they shall be my pe
ple, and I will be their God.
21 But *as for them* whose [w]hea
walketh after the heart of their detes
able things and their abominations,
will recompense their way upon the
own heads, saith the Lord GOD.
22 ¶ Then did the chĕr-ū-bĭms [x]lif
up their wings, and the wheels besid
them; and the glory of the God of Is
rael *was* over them above.
23 And [y]the glory of the LORD wen
up from the midst of the city, an
stood [z]upon the [a]mountain which
on the east side of the city.
24 ¶ Afterwards [b]the spirit took m
up, and brought me in a vision by th
Spirit of God into Chăl-dē-ă, to them
of the captivity. So the vision that
had seen went up from me.
25 Then I [c]spake unto them of th
captivity all the things that the LOR
had shewed me.

CHAPTER 12

THE word of the LORD also cam
unto me, saying,
2 Son of man, thou dwellest in th
midst of a rebellious house, which
[a]have eyes to see, and see not; the
have ears to hear, and hear not: fo
they *are* a rebellious house.
3 Therefore, thou son of man, pre
pare thee [1]stuff for removing, and re
move by day in their sight; and thou
shalt remove from thy place to an
other place in their sight: it may b
they will consider, though they *be*
rebellious house.

4 Then shalt thou bring forth thy
:uff by day in their sight, as stuff for
emoving: and thou shalt go forth at
ven in their sight, [2]as they that go
orth into captivity.
5 [3]Dig thou through the wall in their
ight, and carry out thereby.
6 In their sight shalt thou bear *it* up-
n *thy* shoulders, *and* carry *it* forth in
ie twilight: thou shalt cover thy face,
iat thou see not the ground: [b]for I
ave set thee *for* a sign unto the house
f Israel.
7 And I did so as I was commanded:
 brought forth my stuff by day, as
tuff for captivity, and in the even I
ligged through the wall with mine
and; I brought *it* forth in the twi-
ght, *and* I bare *it* upon *my* shoulder
i their sight.
8 ¶ And in the morning came the
'ord of the LORD unto me, saying,
9 Son of man, hath not the house of
srael, the rebellious house, said unto
iee, What [c]doest thou?
10 Say thou unto them, Thus saith
he Lord GOD; This [d]burden *concern-*
th the prince in Jerusalem, and all the
ouse of Israel that *are* among them.
11 Say, I *am* your sign: like as I have
one, so shall it be done unto them:
hey shall remove *and* go into cap-
vity.
12 And [e]the prince that *is* among
iem shall bear upon *his* shoulder in
ie twilight, and shall go forth: they
hall dig through the wall to carry out
hereby: he shall cover his face, that
e see not the ground with *his* eyes.
13 My [f]net also will I spread upon
im, and he shall be taken in my
nare: and [g]I will bring him to Bab-
lon *to* the land of the Chăl-dē'ăns;
et shall he not see it, though he shall
ie there.
14 And [h]I will scatter toward every
'ind all that *are* about him to help
im, and all his bands; and I will draw
ut the sword after them.
15 And [i]they shall know that I *am*
he LORD, when I shall scatter them
mong the nations, and disperse them
i the countries.
16 But [j]I will leave [6]a few men of
hem from the sword, from the famine,
nd from the pestilence; that they
iay declare all their abominations
mong the heathen whither they
ome; and they shall know that I *am*
he LORD.
17 ¶ Moreover the word of the LORD
ame to me, saying,
18 Son of man, [k]eat thy bread with
quaking, and drink thy water with
trembling and with carefulness;
19 And say unto the people of the
land, Thus saith the Lord GOD of the
inhabitants of Jerusalem, *and* of the
land of Israel; They shall eat their
bread with carefulness, and drink
their water with astonishment, that
her land may [l]be desolate from [7]all
that is therein, because [m]of the violence of all them that dwell therein.
20 And the cities that are inhabited
shall be laid waste, and the land shall
be desolate; and ye shall know that I
am the LORD.
21 ¶ And the word of the LORD came
unto me, saying,
22 Son of man, what *is* that proverb
that ye have in the land of Israel, saying, [n]The days are prolonged, and
every vision faileth?
23 Tell them therefore, Thus saith
the Lord GOD; I will make this
proverb to cease, and they shall no
more use it as a proverb in Israel; but
say unto them, [o]The days are at hand,
and the effect of every vision.
24 For [p]there shall be no more any
[q]vain vision nor flattering divination
within the house of Israel.
25 For I *am* the LORD: I will speak,
and the [r]word that I shall speak shall
come to pass; it shall be no more prolonged: for in your days, O rebellious
house, will I say the word, and will
perform it, saith the Lord GOD.
26 ¶ Again the word of the LORD
came to me, saying,
27 Son of man, behold, *they of* the
house of Israel say, The vision that he
seeth *is* for [s]many days *to come*, and
he prophesieth of the times *that are*
far off.
28 Therefore say unto them, Thus
saith the Lord GOD; [t]There shall none
of my words be prolonged any more,
but the word which I have spoken
shall be done, saith the Lord GOD.

CHAPTER 13

AND the word of the LORD came unto me, saying,
2 Son of man, prophesy against the
prophets of Israel that prophesy, and
say thou unto [1]them that prophesy out
of their [a]own hearts, Hear ye the
word of the LORD;
3 Thus saith the Lord GOD; Woe unto the foolish prophets, that [2]follow
their own spirit, [3]and have seen
nothing!
4 O Israel, thy prophets are [b]like the
foxes in the deserts.

2 as the goings forth of captivity.
3 Dig for thee.
b Isa. 8.18. ch. 4.3.
4 digged for me.
c ch. 24.19.
d Mal. 1.1.
5 by removing go into captivity.
e Jer. 39.4.
f Job 19.6. Jer. 52.9. Lam. 1.13.
g Jer. 52.11. ch. 17.16.
h ch. 5.10.
i Ps. 9.16. Isa. 26.9.
j Isa. 1.8. Jer. 4.27. ch. 6.8.
6 men of number.
k Lam. 5.9. ch. 4.16.
l Zech. 7.14.
7 the fulness thereof.
m Gen. 13.10. Ps. 107.34.
n Isa. 5.19. ch. 11.3. 2 Pet. 3.4.
o Joel 2.1. Obad. 15.
p ch. 13.23.
q Lam. 2.14.
r Isa. 55.11. Dan. 9.12. Zech. 1.6.
s Isa. 5.19. 2 Pet. 3.4.
t Jer. 4.7. Matt. 24.48-51. Rev. 3.3.

CHAP. 13

1 them that are prophets out of their own hearts.
a Jer. 14.14.
2 walk after.
3 Or, and things which they have not seen.
b Micah 3.5. Song 2.15. 2 Cor. 11.13.

5 Ye [c]have not gone up into the [4]gaps, neither [5]made up the hedge for the house of Israel to stand in the battle in the day of the LORD.

6 They [d]have seen vanity and lying divination, saying, The LORD saith: and the LORD hath not sent them: and they have made *others* to [e]hope that they would confirm the word.

7 Have ye not seen a vain vision, and have ye not spoken a lying divination, whereas ye say, The LORD saith *it;* albeit I have not spoken?

8 Therefore thus saith the Lord GOD; Because ye have spoken vanity, and seen lies, therefore, behold, I *am* against you, saith the Lord GOD.

9 And mine hand shall be upon the prophets that see vanity, and that divine lies: they shall not be in the [6]assembly of my people, neither [f]shall they be written in the writing of the house of Israel, [g]neither shall they enter into the land of Israel; and [h]ye shall know that I *am* the Lord GOD.

10 ¶ Because, even because they have [i]seduced my people, saying, Peace; [j]and *there was* no peace; and one built up [7]a wall, and, lo, others [k]daubed it with untempered *morter:*

11 Say unto them which daub *it* with untempered *morter*, that it shall fall: there [l]shall be an overflowing shower; and ye, O great hailstones, shall fall; and a stormy wind shall rend *it*.

12 Lo, when the wall is fallen, shall it not be said unto you, Where *is* the daubing wherewith ye have daubed *it?*

13 Therefore thus saith the Lord GOD; I will even rend *it* with a stormy wind in my fury; and there shall be an overflowing shower in mine anger, and great hailstones in *my* fury to consume *it*.

14 So will I break down the wall that ye have daubed with untempered *morter*, and bring it down to the ground, so that the foundation thereof shall be discovered, and it shall fall, and ye shall be consumed in the midst thereof: and [m]ye shall know that I *am* the LORD.

15 Thus will I accomplish my wrath upon the wall, and upon them that have daubed it with untempered *morter*, and will say unto you, The wall *is* no *more*, neither they that daubed it;

16 *To wit*, the prophets of Israel which prophesy concerning Jerusalem, and which see [n]visions of peace for her, and *there is* no peace, saith the Lord GOD.

17 ¶ Likewise, thou son of man, se [o]thy face against [p]the daughters of th people, which prophesy out of thei own heart; and prophesy thou agains them,

18 And say, Thus saith the Lor GOD; Woe to the *women* that sev pillows to all [8]armholes, and mak kerchiefs upon the head of ever stature to hunt souls! Will ye [q]hun the souls of my people, and will ye sav the souls alive *that come* unto you?

19 And will ye pollute me among m people [r]for handfuls of barley and fo pieces of bread, to slay the souls tha should not die, and to save the soul alive that should not live, by your lying to my people that hear *your* lies

20 Wherefore thus saith the Lor GOD; Behold, I *am* against your pil lows, wherewith ye there hunt th souls [9]to make *them* fly, and I will tea them from your arms, and will let th souls go, *even* the souls that ye hunt t make *them* fly.

21 Your kerchiefs also will I tear, an deliver my people out of your hand and they shall be no more in you hand to be hunted; and ye shall know that I *am* the LORD.

22 Because [s]with lies ye have mad the heart of the righteous sad, whom I have not made sad; and [t]strengthened the hands of the wicked, that h should not return from his wicke way, [10]by promising him life:

23 Therefore [u]ye shall see no mor vanity, nor divine divinations: for will deliver my people out of you hand: and [v]ye shall know that I *am* th LORD.

CHAPTER 14

THEN [a]came certain of the elder of Israel unto me, and sat befor me.

2 And the word of the LORD cam unto me, saying,

3 Son of man, these men have set u their idols in their heart, and put [b]th stumblingblock of their iniquity before their face: should [c]I be inquire of at all by them?

4 Therefore speak unto them, an say unto them, Thus saith the Lor GOD; Every man of the house of Israe that setteth up his idols in his heart and putteth the stumblingblock of hi iniquity before his face, and comet to the prophet; I the LORD will answe him that cometh according to th multitude of his idols;

5 That I may take the house of Israe in their own [d]heart, because they ar

c Ps. 106.23, 30. ch. 22.30.
4 Or, breaches.
5 hedged the hedge.
d ch. 12.24.
e Pro. 14.15. 2 Thes. 2.11.
6 Or, secret, or, council.
f Neh. 7.5. Luke 10.20. Heb. 12.23. Rev. 13.8.
g ch. 20.38.
h Ps. 9.16. ch. 11.10,12.
i 2 Tim. 3.13.
j Jer. 6.14.
7 Or, a slight wall.
k ch. 22.28.
l ch. 38.22.
m Jer. 6.14. ch. 14.8.
n Jer. 6.14. Jer. 8.11.
o ch. 4.3. ch. 20.46.
p Ex. 15.20. Isa. 3.16.
8 Or, elbows.
q ch. 22.25. Eph. 4.14. 2 Pet. 2.14.
r Pro. 28.21. Micah 3.5. Rom. 14.15.
9 Or, into gardens.
s Pro. 19.27.
t Jer. 23.14.
10 by quickening him, or, that I should save his life.
u ch. 12.24. Micah 3.6.
v ch. 14.8.

CHAP. 14

a ch. 8.1. ch. 20.1.
b ch. 3.20. ch. 7.19. 1 Pet. 2.8. Rev. 2.14.
c Pro. 15.8.
d Heb. 3.12-19.

ll estranged from me through their
dols.
6 ¶ Therefore say unto the house of
srael, Thus saith the Lord GOD; Re-
ent, and turn [1]*yourselves* from your
dols; and turn away your faces from
ll your abominations.
7 For every one of the house of Is-
ael, or of the stranger that sojourn-
th in Israel, which [e]separateth him-
elf from me, and setteth up his idols
n his heart, and putteth the stum-
lingblock of his iniquity before his
ace, and cometh to a prophet to in-
uire of him concerning me; I the
ORD will answer him by myself:
8 And [f]I will set my face against that
nan, and will make him [g]a sign and a
roverb, and I will cut him off from
he midst of my people; and ye shall
now that I *am* the LORD.
9 And if the prophet be deceived
hen he hath spoken a thing, I the
ORD [h]have deceived that prophet,
nd I will stretch out my hand upon
im, and will destroy him from the
nidst of my people Israel.
10 And they shall bear the punish-
nent of their iniquity: the punish-
nent of the prophet shall be even as
he punishment of him that seeketh
nto him;
11 That the house of Israel [i]may go
o more astray from me, neither be
olluted any more with all their trans-
ressions; [j]but that they may be my
eople, and I may be their God, saith
he Lord GOD.
12 ¶ The word of the LORD came
gain to me, saying,
13 Son of man, when the land sinneth
gainst me by trespassing grievously,
hen will I stretch out mine hand upon
t, and will break the [k]staff of the bread
hereof, and will send famine upon it,
nd will cut off man and beast from
t:
14 Though [l]these three men, Noah,
Daniel, and Job, were in it, they
hould deliver *but* their own souls [m]by
heir righteousness, saith the Lord
GOD.
15 ¶ If I cause [n]noisome beasts to
ass through the land, and they [2]spoil
t, so that it be desolate, that no man
nay pass through because of the
easts:
16 *Though* these three men *were* [3]in
t, *as* I live, saith the Lord GOD, they
hall deliver neither sons nor daugh-
ers; they only shall be delivered, but
he land shall be desolate.
17 ¶ Or *if* [o]I bring a sword upon that

1 Or, others.
e Jer. 2.13. Matt. 6.24. Jude 19.
f Lev. 17.10. Jer. 44.11. ch. 15.7.
g Num. 26. 10. Deut. 28.37. ch. 5.15.
h Job 12.16. Jer. 4.10. 2 Thes. 2.11.
i Ps. 119.67, 71. Jer. 31.18, 19. Heb. 12.11. 2 Pet. 2.15.
j Jer. 24.7. Jer. 30.22. Jer. 32.38. ch. 11.20. ch. 36.28.
k Lev. 26.26. Isa. 3.1. ch. 4.16.
l Jer. 7.16. Jer. 15.1.
m Pro. 11.4. 2 Pet. 2.9.
n Lev. 26.22. Num. 21.6.
2 Or, bereave.
3 in the midst of it.
o Lev. 26.25. ch. 5.12.
p Jer. 33.12. ch. 25.13. Hosea 4.3.
q 2 Sam. 24. 15.
r ch. 7.8. Rev. 16.3-6.
4 Or, Also when.
s Jer. 15.2,3. ch. 5.17. Amos 4.10. Rev. 6.4,8.
t ch. 6.8.
u ch. 20.43.
v Jer. 22.8,9.

CHAP. 15

a Ps. 80.8. Hosea 10.1.
b John 15.6.
1 Will it prosper?
2 made fit.
c Lev. 17.10. Ps. 34.16. Jer. 21.10.

land, and say, Sword, go through the
land; so that I [p]cut off man and beast
from it:
18 Though these three men *were* in
it, *as* I live, saith the Lord GOD, they
shall deliver neither sons nor daughters, but they only shall be delivered
themselves.
19 ¶ Or *if* I send [q]a pestilence into
that land, and [r]pour out my fury upon
it in blood, to cut off from it man and
beast:
20 Though Noah, Daniel, and Job,
were in it, *as* I live, saith the Lord
GOD, they shall deliver neither son
nor daughter; they shall *but* deliver
their own souls by their righteousness.
21 For thus saith the Lord GOD;
[4]How much more when [s]I send my
four sore judgments upon Jerusalem,
the sword, and the famine, and the
noisome beast, and the pestilence, to
cut off from it man and beast?
22 ¶ Yet, [t]behold, therein shall be
left a remnant that shall be brought
forth, *both* sons and daughters: behold, they shall come forth unto you,
and [u]ye shall see their way and their
doings: and ye shall be comforted
concerning the evil that I have brought
upon Jerusalem, *even* concerning all
that I have brought upon it.
23 And they shall comfort you, when
ye see their ways and their doings: and
ye shall know that I have not done
[v]without cause all that I have done in
it, saith the Lord GOD.

CHAPTER 15

AND the word of the LORD came
unto me, saying,
2 Son of man, What is the [a]vine tree
more than any tree, *or than* a branch
which is among the trees of the
forest?
3 Shall wood be taken thereof to do
any work? or will *men* take a pin of it
to hang any vessel thereon?
4 Behold, [b]it is cast into the fire for
fuel; the fire devoureth both the ends
of it, and the midst of it is burned. [1]Is
it meet for *any* work?
5 Behold, when it was whole, it was
[2]meet for no work: how much less
shall it be meet yet for *any* work, when
the fire hath devoured it, and it is
burned?
6 ¶ Therefore thus saith the Lord
GOD; As the vine tree among the
trees of the forest, which I have given
to the fire for fuel, so will I give the
inhabitants of Jerusalem.
7 And [c]I will set my face against

hem; they [d]shall go out from *one* fire,
and *another* fire shall devour them;
[e]and ye shall know that I *am* the LORD,
when I set my face against them.
8 And I will make the land desolate,
because they have [3]committed a trespass, saith the Lord GOD.

CHAPTER 16

AGAIN the word of the LORD came
unto me, saying,
2 Son of man, [a]cause Jerusalem to
know her abominations,
3 And say, Thus saith the Lord GOD
unto Jerusalem; Thy [1]birth and thy
nativity *is* of the land of Canaan; thy
father *was* an Amorite, and thy mother
an Hittite.
4 And *as for* thy nativity, [b]in the day
thou wast born thy navel was not cut,
neither wast thou washed in water [2]to
supple *thee;* thou wast not salted at
all, nor swaddled at all.
5 None eye pitied thee, to do any of
these unto thee, to have compassion
upon thee; but thou wast cast out in
the open field, to the lothing of thy
person, in the day that thou wast
born.
6 ¶ And when I passed by thee, and
saw thee [3]polluted in thine own blood,
I said unto thee *when thou wast* in thy
blood, Live; yea, I said unto thee
when thou wast in thy blood, Live.
7 I have [4]caused thee to multiply as
the bud of the field, and thou hast increased and waxen great, and thou art
come to [5]excellent ornaments: *thy*
breasts are fashioned, and thine hair
is grown, whereas thou *wast* naked
and bare.
8 Now when I passed by thee, and
looked upon thee, behold, thy time
was the time of love; [c]and I spread my
skirt over thee, and covered thy nakedness: yea, I sware unto thee, and
entered into a covenant with thee,
saith the Lord GOD, and [d]thou becamest mine.
9 Then washed I thee with water;
yea, I throughly washed away thy
[6]blood from thee, and I anointed thee
with oil.
10 I clothed thee also with broidered
work, and shod thee with badgers'
skin, and I girded thee about with fine
linen, and I covered thee with silk.
11 I decked thee also with ornaments, and I [e]put bracelets upon thy
hands, [f]and a chain on thy neck.
12 And I put a jewel on thy [7]fore-
head, and earrings in thine ears, and
a beautiful crown upon thine head.
13 Thus wast thou decked with gol
and silver; and thy raiment *was of* fin
linen, and silk, and broidered work
[g]thou didst eat fine flour, and hone
and oil: and thou wast exceedin
[h]beautiful, and thou didst prosper in
to a kingdom.
14 And thy [i]renown went fort
among the heathen for thy beauty
for it *was* perfect through my comeli
ness, which I had put upon thee, sait
the Lord GOD.
15 ¶ But [j]thou didst trust in thin
own beauty, [k]and playedst the harlo
because of thy renown, and poureds
out thy fornications on every one tha
passed by; his it was.
16 And [l]of thy garments thou dids
take, and deckedst thy high place
with divers colours, and playedst th
harlot thereupon: *the like things* sha
not come, neither shall it be *so*.
17 Thou hast also taken thy fai
jewels of my gold and of my silver
which I had given thee, and madest t
thyself images [8]of men, and dids
commit whoredom with them,
18 And tookest thy broidered gar
ments, and coveredst them: and tho
hast set mine oil and mine incense be
fore them.
19 My [m]meat also which I gave thee
fine flour, and oil, and honey, *where*
with I fed thee, thou hast even set i
before them for [9]a sweet savour: an
thus it was, saith the Lord GOD.
20 Moreover [n]thou hast taken th
sons and thy daughters, whom tho
hast borne unto me, and these has
thou sacrificed unto them [10]to be de
voured. *Is this* of thy whoredoms a
small matter,
21 That thou hast slain [o]my children
and delivered them to cause them t
pass through *the fire* for them?
22 And in all thine abominations an
thy whoredoms thou hast not remem
bered the days of [p]thy youth, whe
thou wast naked and bare, *and* was
polluted in thy blood.
23 And it came to pass after all th
wickedness, (woe, woe unto thee! sait
the Lord GOD;)
24 *That* thou hast also built unt
thee an [11]eminent place, [q]and has
made thee an high place in ever
street.
25 Thou hast built thy high place a
[r]every head of the way, and hast mad
thy beauty to be abhorred, and has
opened thy feet to every one that pass
ed by, and multiplied thy whoredoms
26 Thou hast also committed forni-

d Isa. 24.18. Jer. 48.43, 44. Amos 5.19.
e ch. 6.7. ch. 7.4.
3 trespassed a trespass.
CHAP. 16
a ch. 20.4.
1 cutting out, or, habitation.
b Hosea 2.3.
2 Or, when I looked upon thee.
3 Or, trodden under foot.
4 made thee a million.
5 ornament of ornaments.
c Ruth 3.9.
d Ex. 19.5.
6 bloods.
e Gen. 24.22.
f Gen. 41.42. Pro. 1.9. Song 1.10. Isa. 13.19. Dan. 5.7, 16,29.
7 nose.
g Deut. 32. 13.
h Ps. 48.2.
i Lam. 2.15.
j Deut. 32.15. Jer. 7.4. Micah 3.11.
k Isa. 1.21. Isa. 57.8. Jer. 2.20. Hosea 1.2.
l 2 Ki. 23.7. ch. 7.20. Hosea 2.8.
8 of a male.
m Deut. 32. 13. Hosea 2.8.
9 a savour of rest.
n 2 Ki. 16.3. Isa. 57.5. Jer. 7.31. ch. 20.26.
10 to devour.
o Gen. 17.7, 11. Ex. 13.2.
p Jer. 2.2. Hosea 2.3.
11 Or, brothel house.
q Lev. 26.30. Ps. 78.58. Isa. 57.5. Jer. 2.20.
r Pro. 9.14. Jer. 6.15.

ıtion with [s]the Egyptians thy neigh-
ours, great of flesh; and hast increas-
l thy whoredoms, to provoke me to
nger.
7 Behold, therefore I have stretched
ut my hand over thee, and have
iminished thine ordinary *food*, and
elivered thee unto the will of them
ıat hate thee, the [12]daughters of the
hilistines, which are ashamed of thy
wd way.
8 Thou [t]hast played the whore also
ith the Assyrians, because thou wast
nsatiable; yea, thou hast played the
arlot with them, and yet couldest not
e satisfied.
9 Thou hast moreover multiplied
ıy fornication in the land of Canaan
unto Chăl-dē´ă; and yet thou wast
ot satisfied herewith.
0 How weak is thine heart, saith the
ord GOD, seeing thou doest all these
ings, the work of an [v]imperious
horish woman;
1 [13]In that thou buildest thine emin-
nt place in the head of every way, and
ıakest thine high place in every
treet; and hast not been as an harlot,
ı that thou scornest hire;
2 *But as* a wife that committeth
dultery, *which* taketh strangers in-
tead of her husband!
3 They give gifts to all whores: but
thou givest thy gifts to all thy lovers,
nd [14]hirest them, that they may come
ınto thee on every side for thy whore-
om.
4 And the contrary is in thee from
ther women in thy whoredoms,
hereas none followed thee to com-
nit whoredoms: and in that thou giv-
st a reward, and no reward is given
ınto thee, therefore thou art con-
rary.
5 ¶ Wherefore, O harlot, hear the
ord of the LORD:
6 Thus saith the Lord GOD; Be-
ause thy filthiness was poured out,
nd thy nakedness discovered through
hy whoredoms with thy lovers, and
ith all the idols of thy abominations,
nd by [x]the blood of thy children,
hich thou didst give unto them;
7 Behold, therefore [y]I will gather
ll thy lovers, with whom thou hast
aken pleasure, and all *them* that thou
ıast loved, with all *them* that thou
ıast hated; I will even gather them
ound about against thee, and will dis-
over thy nakedness unto them, that
hey may see all thy nakedness.
8 And I will judge thee, [15]as women
hat break wedlock [z]and shed blood
are judged; and I will give thee blood
in fury and jealousy.
39 And I will also give thee into their
hand, and they shall throw down
thine eminent place, and shall break
down thy high places: they [a]shall strip
thee also of thy clothes, and shall
take [16]thy fair jewels, and leave thee
naked and bare.
40 They [b]shall also bring up a company against thee, [c]and they shall
stone thee with stones, and thrust thee
through with their swords.
41 And they shall [d]burn thine houses
with fire, and [e]execute judgments upon thee in the sight of many women:
and I will cause thee to [f]cease from
playing the harlot, and thou also shalt
give no hire any more.
42 So [g]will I make my fury toward
thee to rest, and my jealousy shall depart from thee, and I will be quiet, and
will be no more angry.
43 Because [h]thou hast not remembered the days of thy youth, but hast
fretted me in all these *things;* behold,
therefore [i]I also will recompense thy
way upon *thine* head, saith the Lord
GOD: and thou shalt not commit this
lewdness above all thine abominations.
44 ¶ Behold, every one that useth
proverbs shall use *this* proverb against
thee, saying, As *is* the mother, *so is*
her daughter.
45 Thou *art* thy mother's daughter,
that lotheth her husband and her children; and thou *art* the sister of thy
sisters, which lothed their husbands
and their children: your mother *was*
an Hittite, and your father an Amorite.
46 And thine elder sister *is* Să-mâr´-
ĭ-ă, she and her daughters that dwell
at thy left hand: and [17]thy younger
sister, that dwelleth at thy right hand,
is Sodom and her daughters.
47 Yet hast thou not walked after
their ways, nor done after their abominations: but, [18]as *if that were* a very
little *thing*, thou wast [j]corrupted more
than they in all thy ways.
48 *As* I live, saith the Lord GOD,
Sodom [k]thy sister hath not done, she
nor her daughters, as thou hast done,
thou and thy daughters.
49 Behold, this was the iniquity of
thy sister Sodom, pride, [l]fulness of
bread, and abundance of idleness was
in her and in her daughters, [m]neither
did she strengthen the hand of the
poor and needy.
50 And they were haughty, and com-

[s] ch. 8.10. ch. 20.7.
12 Or, cities.
[t] Judg. 10.6. 2 Ki. 16.7. Jer. 2.18.
[u] ch. 23.14.
[v] Pro. 30.20.
13 Or, In thy daughters is thine, etc.
[w] Isa. 30.6.
14 bribest.
[x] Ps. 106.38. Jer. 2.34.
[y] Isa. 47.2,3. Jer. 13.22. Lam. 1.8. ch. 23.9. Hosea 2.10. Nah. 3.5.
15 with judgments of.
[z] Gen. 9.6. Ex. 21.12. Lev. 24.17. Matt. 26.52. Rev. 13.10.
[a] ch. 23.26.
16 instruments of thine ornament.
[b] ch. 23.10.
[c] John 8.5.
[d] Deut. 13.16. 2 Ki. 25.9. Jer. 39.8.
[e] ch. 5.8. ch. 23.10. Rom. 2.8.
[f] ch. 23.27.
[g] ch. 5.13.
[h] Ps. 78.42.
[i] ch. 9.10. ch. 11.21.
17 lesser than thou.
18 Or, that was lothed as a small thing.
[j] 2 Ki. 21.9. ch. 5.6,7.
[k] Matt. 10.15. Mark 6.11. Luke 10.12.
[l] Gen. 13.10.
[m] Luke 16.20.

mitted [n]abomination before me:
therefore I [o]took them away as I saw
good.
51 Neither hath Să-mâr-ĭ-ă committed half of thy sins; but thou hast
multiplied thine abominations more
than they, and [p]hast justified thy sisters in all thine abominations which
thou hast done.
52 Thou also, which hast judged thy
sisters, bear thine own shame for thy
sins that thou hast committed more
abominable than they: they are more
righteous than thou: yea, be thou
confounded also, and bear thy shame,
in that thou hast justified thy sisters.
53 When [q]I shall bring again their
captivity, [r]the captivity of Sodom and
her daughters, and the captivity of
Să-mâr-ĭ-ă and her daughters, then
will I bring again the captivity of thy
captives in the midst of them:
54 That thou mayest bear thine own
shame, and mayest be confounded in
all that thou hast done, in that thou
art [s]a comfort unto them.
55 When thy sisters, Sodom and her
daughters, shall return to their former
estate, and Să-mâr-ĭ-ă and her daughters shall return to their former estate,
then thou and thy daughters shall return to your former estate.
56 For thy sister Sodom was not
[19]mentioned by thy mouth in the day
of thy [20]pride,
57 Before thy wickedness was discovered, as at the time of *thy* [t]reproach
of the daughters of [21]Syria, and all
that are round about her, the daughters of the Philistines, which [22]despise
thee round about.
58 Thou hast [23]borne thy lewdness
and thine abominations, saith the
LORD.
59 For thus saith the Lord GOD; I
will even deal with thee as thou hast
done, which hast [u]despised the oath in
breaking the covenant.
60 ¶ Nevertheless I will [v]remember
my covenant with thee in the days of
thy youth, and I will establish unto
thee [w]an everlasting covenant.
61 Then [x]thou shalt remember thy
ways, and be ashamed, when thou
shalt receive thy [y]sisters, thine elder
and thy younger: and I will give them
unto thee [z]for daughters, but [a]not by
thy covenant.
62 And [b]I will establish my covenant
with thee; and thou shalt know that
I *am* the LORD:
63 That thou mayest remember, and
be confounded, [c]and never open thy

[n] Gen. 13.13. Gen. 18.20.
[o] Job 18.18.
[p] Matt. 12.41.
[q] Isa. 1.9. Rom. 9.29.
[r] Jer. 20.16.
[s] ch. 14.22, 23.
19 for a report, or, hearing.
20 prides, or excellencies.
[t] 2 Ki. 16.5. 2 Chr. 28.18. Isa. 7.1.
21 Aram.
22 Or, spoil.
23 borne them.
[u] Deut. 29. 12,14. ch. 17.13,16.
[v] Ex. 2.24. Lev. 26.41, 42. Ps. 106.45. Hosea 2.15.
[w] Jer. 32.40.
[x] ch. 20.43.
[y] Song 8.8. Isa. 2.2.
[z] Isa. 54.1. Gal. 4.26.
[a] Jer. 31.31.
[b] Hosea 2.19, 20. Acts 7.8. Heb. 8.6-10, 13.
[c] Rom. 3.19.

CHAP. 17

1 embroidering.
[a] 2 Ki. 24.12.
2 put it in a field of seed.
[b] Deut. 8.7, 8,9.
[c] Isa. 15.7.
3 field.
[d] 2 Ki. 25.7.
[e] ch. 19.12. Hos. 13.15. Matt. 21.19. Mark 11.20. John 15.6. Jude 12.
[f] ch. 2.5.
[g] 2 Ki. 24.11-16.

mouth any more because of tl
shame, when I am pacified towa
thee for all that thou hast done, sai
the Lord GOD.

CHAPTER 17

AND the word of the LORD can
unto me, saying,
2 Son of man, put forth a riddle, a
speak a parable unto the house of I
rael;
3 And say, Thus saith the Lord Go
A great eagle with great wings, lon
winged, full of feathers, which ha
[1]divers colours, came unto Lĕb-ă-no
and [a]took the highest branch of tl
cedar:
4 He cropped off the top of his you
twigs, and carried it into a land
traffick; he set it in a city of me
chants.
5 He took also of the seed of tl
land, and [2]planted it in [b]a fruitf
field; he placed *it* by great waters, *a*
set it [c]*as* a willow tree.
6 And it grew, and became a sprea
ing vine of low stature, whose bra
ches turned toward him, and the roo
thereof were under him: so it becan
a vine, and brought forth branche
and shot forth sprigs.
7 There was also another great eag
with great wings and many feather
and, behold, this vine did bend h
roots toward him, and shot forth h
branches toward him, that he migl
water it by the furrows of her plant
tion.
8 It was planted in a good [3]soil l
great waters, that it might bring for
branches, and that it might bear frui
that it might be a goodly vine.
9 Say thou, Thus saith the Lo
GOD; Shall it prosper? [d]shall he n
pull up the roots thereof, and cut o
the fruit thereof, that it wither? it sha
wither in all the leaves of her sprin
even without great power or ma
people to pluck it up by the roo
thereof.
10 Yea, behold, *being* planted, sha
it prosper? [e]shall it not utterly withe
when the east wind toucheth it? it sha
wither in the furrows where it grew.
11 ¶ Moreover the word of the LOR
came unto me, saying,
12 Say now to [f]the rebellious hous
Know ye not what these *things mea*
tell *them*, Behold, [g]the king of Ba
ylon is come to Jerusalem, and ha
taken the king thereof, and the princ
thereof, and led them with him
Babylon;

13 And [h]hath taken of the king's
eed, and made a covenant with him,
nd hath [4]taken an oath of him: he
ath also taken the mighty of the land:
14 That the kingdom might [j]be base,
hat it might not lift itself up, [5]*but* that
y keeping of his covenant it might
tand.
15 But [k]he rebelled against him in
ending his ambassadors into Egypt,
hat they might give him horses and
nuch people. Shall he prosper? shall
e escape that doeth such *things?* or
hall he break the covenant, and be
elivered?
16 *As* I live, saith the Lord GOD,
urely in [m]the place *where* the king
welleth that made him king, whose
ath he despised, and whose covenant
e brake, *even* with him in the midst of
abylon he shall die.
17 Neither [n]shall Pharaoh with *his*
nighty army and great company make
or him in the war, by [o]casting up
nounts, and building forts, to cut off
nany persons:
18 Seeing he despised the oath by
reaking the covenant, when, lo, he
ad [p]given his hand, and hath done
ll these *things*, he shall not escape.
19 Therefore thus saith the Lord
GOD; *As* I live, surely mine oath that
e hath despised, and my covenant
hat he hath broken, even it will I
ecompense upon his own head.
20 And I will [q]spread my net upon
im, and he shall be taken in my snare,
nd I will bring him to Babylon, and
will plead with him there for his tres-
ass that he hath trespassed against
ne.
21 And [s]all his fugitives with all his
ands shall fall by the sword, and they
hat remain shall be scattered toward
ll winds: and ye shall know that I the
LORD have spoken *it*.
22 ¶ Thus saith the Lord GOD; I will
lso take of the [t]highest branch of the
igh cedar, and will set *it;* I will crop
ff from the top of his young twigs [u]a
ender one, and will [v]plant *it* upon an
igh mountain and eminent:
23 In [w]the mountain of the height of
srael will I plant it: and it shall bring
orth boughs, and bear fruit, and be a
oodly cedar: and under it shall dwell
ll fowl of every wing; in the shadow
of the branches thereof shall they
lwell.
24 And all the trees of the field shall
know that I the LORD have brought
down the high tree, have exalted the
low tree, have dried up the green tree,
and have made the dry tree to flourish:
I the LORD have spoken and have done
it.

CHAPTER 18

THE word of the LORD came unto
me again, saying,
2 What mean ye, that ye use this
proverb concerning the land of Israel,
saying, [a]The fathers have eaten sour
grapes, and the children's teeth are
set on edge?
3 *As* I live, saith the Lord GOD, ye
shall not have *occasion* any more to
use this proverb in Israel.
4 Behold, all [b]souls are mine; as the
soul of the father, so also the soul of
the son is mine: [c]the soul that sinneth,
it shall die.
5 ¶ But if a man be just, and do [1]that
which is lawful and right,
6 *And* [d]hath not eaten upon the
mountains, neither hath lifted up his
eyes to the idols of the house of Israel, neither hath defiled [e]his neighbour's wife, neither hath come near
to [f]a menstruous woman,
7 And hath not [g]oppressed any, *but*
have restored to the debtor [h]his
pledge, hath spoiled none by violence,
hath [i]given his bread to the hungry,
and hath covered the naked with a
garment;
8 He *that* hath not given [j]forth upon
usury, neither hath taken any increase, *that* hath withdrawn his hand
from iniquity, [k]hath executed true
judgment between man and man,
9 Hath walked in my statutes, and
hath kept my judgments, to deal truly;
he [l]*is* just, he shall surely [m]live, saith
the Lord GOD.
10 ¶ If he beget a son *that is* a [2]rob-
ber, [n]a shedder of blood, and [3]*that* doeth the like to *any* one of these *things*,
11 And that doeth not any of those
duties, but even hath eaten upon the
mountains, and [o]defiled his neighbour's wife,
12 Hath oppressed the poor and
needy, hath spoiled by violence, hath
not restored the pledge, and hath lifted
up his eyes to the idols, hath [p]com-
mitted abomination,
13 Hath [q]given forth upon usury, and
hath taken increase: shall he then
live? he shall not live: he hath done
all these abominations; he shall surely
die; his [4]blood shall be upon him.
14 ¶ Now, lo, *if* he beget a son, that
seeth all his father's sins which he
hath done, and considereth, and doeth not such like,
15 *That* hath not eaten upon the

h 2 Ki. 24.17.
i 2 Chr. 36.13.
4 brought him to an oath.
j ch. 29.14.
5 to keep his covenant, to stand to it.
k 2 Ki. 24.20. Jer. 52.3.
l Deut. 17.16. Isa. 30.1-4. Isa. 31.1,3. Jer. 37.5-7.
m Jer. 32.5. ch. 12.13.
n Jer. 37.7. Lam. 4.17. ch. 29.6,7.
o Jer. 52.4.
p 1 Chr. 29. 24.
q Josh. 10.16-18. 2 Chr. 33.11. Eccl. 9.12. Lam. 1.13. ch. 12.13.
r ch. 20.36.
s ch. 12.14.
t Isa. 11.1. Jer. 23.5.
u Isa. 53.2.
v Ps. 2.6.
w Isa. 2.2,3. Micah 4.1.

CHAP. 18

a Lam. 5.7.
b Zech. 12.1. Heb. 12.9.
c Rom. 6.23.
1 judgment and justice.
d ch. 22.9.
e Heb. 13.4.
f Lev. 18.19.
g Lev. 25.14.
h Deut. 24. 12.
i Isa. 58.7. Matt. 25.35.
j Lev. 25.36.
k Zech. 8.16.
l Hab. 2.4. Rom. 8.1.
m Amos 5.4.
2 Or, breaker up of an house.
n Ex. 21.12.
3 Or, that doeth to his brother besides any of these.
o 1 Cor. 6.9.
p 2 Ki. 21.11.
q Ex. 22.25.
4 bloods.

mountains, neither hath lifted up his
eyes to the idols of the house of Israel,
hath not defiled his neighbour's wife,
16 Neither hath oppressed any, [5]hath
not withholden the pledge, neither
hath spoiled by violence, *but* hath giv-
en [r]his bread to the hungry, and hath
covered the naked with a garment,
17 *That* hath taken off his hand from
the poor, *that* hath not received usury
nor increase, hath executed my judgments, hath walked in my statutes;
[s]he shall not die for the iniquity of his
father, he shall surely live.
18 *As for* his father, because he
cruelly oppressed, spoiled his brother
by violence, and did *that* which *is* not
good among his people, lo, even [t]he
shall die in his iniquity.
19 ¶ Yet say ye, Why? [u]doth not the
son bear the iniquity of the father?
When the son hath done that which
is lawful and right, *and* hath kept all
my statutes, and hath done them, he
shall surely live.
20 The soul that sinneth, it shall die.
The [v]son shall not bear the iniquity of
the father, neither shall the father bear
the iniquity of the son: [w]the righteousness of the righteous shall be upon
him, and [x]the wickedness of the
wicked shall be upon him.
21 But [y]if the wicked will turn from
all his sins that he hath committed,
and keep all my statutes, and do that
which is lawful and right, he shall
surely live, he shall not die.
22 All [z]his transgressions that he
hath committed, they shall not be
mentioned unto him: in [a]his righteousness that he hath done he shall
live.
23 Have [b]I any pleasure at all that
the wicked should die? saith the Lord
GOD: *and* not that he should return
from his ways, and live?
24 ¶ But [c]when the righteous turneth
away from his righteousness, and
committeth iniquity, *and* doeth according to all the abominations that
the wicked *man* doeth, shall he live?
[d]All his righteousness that he hath
done shall not be mentioned: in his
trespass that he hath trespassed, and
in his sin that he hath sinned, in them
shall he die.
25 ¶ Yet ye say, [e]The way of the
Lord is not equal. Hear now, O house
of Israel; Is not [f]my way equal? are
not your ways unequal?
26 When a righteous *man* turneth
away from his righteousness, and
committeth iniquity, and dieth in

5 hath not pledged the pledge, or, taken to pledge.
r Job 22.7. Pro. 22.9. Eccl. 11.1,2. Isa. 58.7-10. Matt. 25.35. Luke 11.41.
s ch. 20.18. Matt. 23.29-32. Rom. 2.7.
t ch. 3.18.
u Ex. 20.5. Deut. 5.9.
v Deut. 24.16. 2 Chr. 25.4.
w Isa. 3.10.
x Rom. 2.9.
y ch. 33.12.
z ch. 33.16.
a Rom. 8.13.
b 2 Pet. 3.9.
c ch. 33.12.
d Heb. 10.38. 2 John 8.
e Mal. 3.14.
f Gen. 18.25. Deut. 32.4. Ps. 145.17.
g Isa. 1.18.
h Eccl. 12.14. ch. 7.3.
i Matt. 3.2. Rev. 2.5.
6 Or, others.
j Eph. 4.22.
k Jer. 32.39. ch. 11.19.
l Lam. 3.33. ch. 33.11. 2 Pet. 3.9.
7 Or, others.

CHAP. 19

a ch. 26.17.
b 2 Ki. 23.31.
c 2 Ki. 23.33. 2 Chr. 36.4. Jer. 22.11.
d 2 Ki. 23.34.
e Jer. 22.13.
1 Or, their widows.
f 2 Ki. 24.2.
g 2 Chr. 36.6. Jer. 22.18, 19.
2 Or, in hooks.

them; for his iniquity that he hath
done shall he die.
27 Again, when the wicked man
turneth away [g]from his wickedness
that he hath committed, and doeth
that which is lawful and right, he shall
save his soul alive.
28 Because he considereth, and turneth away from all his transgressions
that he hath committed, he shall surely live, he shall not die.
29 Yet saith the house of Israel, The
way of the Lord is not equal. O house
of Israel, are not my ways equal? are
not your ways unequal?
30 Therefore [h]I will judge you, O
house of Israel, every one according
to his ways, saith the Lord GOD. [i]Re-
pent, and turn [6]*yourselves* from all
your transgressions; so iniquity shall
not be your ruin.
31 ¶ Cast [j]away from you all your
transgressions, whereby ye have transgressed; and make you a [k]new heart
and a new spirit: for why will ye die,
O house of Israel?
32 For [l]I have no pleasure in the
death of him that dieth, saith the Lord
GOD: wherefore turn [7]*yourselves*, and
live ye.

CHAPTER 19

MOREOVER [a]take thou up a lamentation for the princes of Israel,
2 And say, What *is* thy mother? A
lioness: she lay down among lions,
she nourished her whelps among
young lions.
3 And she brought up one of her
whelps: it [b]became a young lion, and
it learned to catch the prey; it devoured men.
4 The nations also heard of him; he
was taken in their pit, and they
brought him with chains unto the land
of [c]Egypt.
5 Now when she saw that she had
waited, *and* her hope was lost, then
she [d]took another of her whelps, *and*
made him a young lion.
6 And [e]he went up and down among
the lions, he became a young lion, and
learned to catch the prey, *and* devoured men.
7 And he knew [1]their desolate palaces, and he laid waste their cities; and
the land was desolate, and the fulness
thereof, by the noise of his roaring.
8 Then [f]the nations set against him
on every side from the provinces, and
spread their net over him: he was tak-
en in their pit.
9 And [g]they put him in ward [2]in
chains, and brought him to the king

f Babylon: they brought him into
iolds, that his voice should no more
e heard [h]upon the mountains of Is-
ael.
10 ¶ Thy mother *is* [i]like a vine [3]in
hy blood, planted by the waters: she
vas fruitful and [j]full of branches by
eason of many waters.
11 And she had strong rods for the
ceptres of them that bare rule, and
er stature [k]was exalted among the
hick branches, and she appeared in
er height with the multitude of her
ranches.
12 But she was plucked up in fury,
he was cast down to the ground, and
he [l]east wind dried up her fruit: her
trong rods were broken and wither-
d; the fire consumed them.
13 And now she *is* planted [m]in the
vilderness, in a dry and thirsty
round.
14 And [n]fire is gone out of a rod of
er branches, *which* hath devoured
er fruit, so that she hath no strong
od *to be* a sceptre to rule. This *is* a
amentation, and shall be for a
amentation.

CHAPTER 20

AND it came to pass in the seventh
year, in the fifth *month*, the tenth
ay of the month, *that* [a]certain of the
lders of Israel came to inquire of the
ORD, and sat before me.
2 Then came the word of the LORD
nto me, saying,
3 Son of man, speak unto the elders
f Israel, and say unto them, Thus
aith the Lord GOD; Are ye come to
nquire of me? *As* I live, saith the Lord
GOD, [b]I will not be inquired of by you.
4 Wilt thou [1]judge them, son of man,
vilt thou judge *them?* [c]cause them to
now the abominations of their
athers:
5 ¶ And say unto them, Thus saith
he Lord GOD; In the day when [d]I
hose Israel, and [2]lifted up mine hand
nto the seed of the house of Jacob,
nd made myself [e]known unto them
n the land of Egypt, when I lifted up
nine hand unto them, saying, [f]I *am*
he LORD your God;
6 In the day *that* I lifted up mine
and unto them, [g]to bring them forth
f the land of Egypt into a land that I
ad espied for them, flowing with
nilk and honey, which [h]*is* the glory
f all lands:
7 Then said I unto them, Cast ye
way every man [i]the abominations of
is eyes, and defile not yourselves
with the [j]idols of Egypt: I *am* the
LORD your God.
8 But they rebelled against me, and
would not hearken unto me: they did
not every man cast away the abominations of their eyes, neither did they
forsake the idols of Egypt: then I said,
I will pour out my fury upon them, to
accomplish my anger against them in
the midst of the land of Egypt.
9 But [k]I wrought for my name's sake,
that it should not be polluted before
the heathen, among whom they *were*,
in whose sight I made myself known
unto them, in bringing them forth out
of the land of Egypt.
10 ¶ Wherefore I caused them to go
forth out of the land of Egypt, and
brought them into the wilderness.
11 And [l]I gave them my statutes, and
[3]shewed them my judgments, which
[m]*if* a man do, he shall even live in
them.
12 Moreover also I gave them my
[n]sabbaths, to be a sign between me
and them, that they might know that
I *am* the LORD that sanctify them.
13 But the house of Israel rebelled
against me in the wilderness: they
walked not in my statutes, and they
[o]despised my judgments, which *if* a
man do, he shall even live in them;
and my sabbaths they greatly polluted: then I said, I would pour out
my fury upon them in the wilderness,
to consume them.
14 But I wrought for my name's
sake, that it should not be polluted before the heathen, in whose sight I
brought them out.
15 Yet also [p]I lifted up my hand unto
them in the wilderness, that I would
not bring them into the land which I
had given *them*, flowing with milk and
honey, which *is* the glory of all lands;
16 Because they despised my judgments, and walked not in my statutes,
but polluted my sabbaths: for [q]their
heart went after their idols.
17 Nevertheless [r]mine eye spared
them from destroying them, neither
did I make an end of them in the
wilderness.
18 But I said unto their children in
the wilderness, Walk ye not in the
statutes of your fathers, neither observe their judgments, nor defile
yourselves with their idols:
19 I *am* the LORD your God; [s]walk
in my statutes, and keep my judgments, and do them;
20 And [t]hallow my sabbaths; and
they shall be a sign between me and

h ch. 6.2.
i Ps. 80.8. ch. 15.2.
3 Or, in thy quietness, or, in thy likeness.
j Deut. 8.7.
k Dan. 4.11.
l Hos. 13.15.
m Deut. 28. 48.
n Judg. 9.15.

CHAP. 20

a ch. 8.1.
b 1 Sam. 28.6. Ps. 50.15. Pro. 15.8. Matt. 15.8.
1 Or, plead for them.
c ch. 16.2. Matt. 23.32.
d Ex. 6.7.
2 Or, sware.
e Ex. 3.8. Deut. 4.34.
f Gen. 17.7. Ex. 20.2.
g Ex. 3.8,17. Jer. 32.22.
h Ps. 48.2.
i 2 Chr. 15.8.
j Deut. 29.16. Josh. 24.14.
k Ex. 32.12. Num. 14.13.
l Deut. 4.8. Neh. 9.13.
3 made them to know.
m Rom. 10.5.
n Ex. 20.8. Deut. 5.12. Neh. 9.14.
o Pro. 1.25.
p Num. 14. 28. Ps. 95.11.
q Num. 15. 39. Ps. 78.37. ch. 14.3,4. Amos 5.25, 26. Acts 7.42, 43.
r 1 Sam. 24. 10. Neh. 9.19. Ps. 78.38.
s Deut. 5.32, 33. Deut. 6. Deut. 7. Deut. 8. Deut. 10. Deut. 11. Deut. 12.
t Ex. 20.11. Neh. 13.17-19. Isa. 58.13. Jer. 17.22.

you, that ye may know that I *am* the
LORD your God.
21 Notwithstanding [u]the children
rebelled against me: they walked not
in my statutes, neither kept my judgments to do them, which *if* a man do,
he shall even live in them; they polluted my sabbaths: then I said, I
would pour out my fury upon them,
to accomplish my anger against them
in the wilderness.
22 Nevertheless [v]I withdrew mine
hand, and wrought for my name's
sake, that it should not be polluted in
the sight of the heathen, in whose
sight I brought them forth.
23 I lifted up mine hand unto them
also in the wilderness, that I would
[w]scatter them among the heathen, and
disperse them through the countries;
24 Because they had not executed
my judgments, but had despised my
statutes, and had polluted my sabbaths, and [x]their eyes were after their
fathers' idols.
25 Wherefore [y]I gave them also
statutes *that were* not good, and judgments whereby they should not live;
26 And I polluted them in their own
gifts, in that they caused to pass
[z]through *the fire* all that openeth the
womb, that I might make them desolate, to the end that they might [a]know
that I *am* the LORD.
27 ¶ Therefore, son of man, speak
unto the house of Israel, and say unto
them, Thus saith the Lord GOD; Yet
in this your fathers have blasphemed
[b]me, in that they have [4]committed a
trespass against me.
28 *For* when I had brought them into
the land, *for* the which I lifted up mine
hand to give it to them, then [c]they saw
every high hill, and all the thick trees,
and they offered there their sacrifices,
and there they presented the provocation of their offering: there also they
made their [d]sweet savour, and poured
out there their drink offerings.
29 Then [5]I said unto them, What *is*
the high place whereunto ye go? And
the name thereof is called Bā-măh unto this day.
30 Wherefore say unto the house of
Israel, Thus saith the Lord GOD; Are
ye polluted after the manner of your
fathers? and commit ye whoredom
after their abominations?
31 For when ye offer your gifts, when
ye make your sons to pass through
the fire, ye pollute yourselves with all
your idols, even unto this day: and
[e]shall I be inquired of by you, O house

u Num. 25.1, 2. Deut. 9.23, 24.
v Ps. 78.38.
w Lev. 26.33. Deut. 28.64. Ps. 106.27.
x ch. 6.9. Mark 7.22.
y Ps. 81.12. Rom. 1.24.
z 2 Ki. 17.17. 2 Chr. 28.3. Jer. 32.35. ch. 16.20,21.
a ch. 6.7.
b Rom. 2.24.
4 trespassed a trespass.
c Isa. 57.5.
d ch. 16.19.
5 Or, I told them what the high place was, or, Bamah.
e Pro. 1.27, 28. Zech. 7.13. Matt. 25.11, 12.
f ch. 11.5.
g Jer. 21.5.
h ch. 17.20.
i Num. 14.21.
j Lev. 27.32. Jer. 33.13.
6 Or, a delivering.
k ch. 34.17. Matt. 3.12.
l Ps. 95.11. ch. 13.9. 1 Cor. 10.5. Heb. 4.6.
m Ps. 81.12. Amos 4.4.
n Pro. 21.27. Isa. 1.13. Jer. 7.9-11. ch. 23.38.
o Isa. 2.2. ch. 17.23.
p Isa. 56.7. Zech. 8.20. Mal. 3.4. Rom. 12.1.
7 Or, chief.
8 savour of rest.
q Jer. 24.7. ch. 36.23. John 17.3.
r ch. 11.17.
s ch. 16.61.
t Lev. 26.39. Hosea 5.15.

of Israel? *As* I live, saith the Lor
GOD, I will not be inquired of by you
32 And that [f]which cometh into you
mind shall not be at all, that ye say
We will be as the heathen, as the fami
lies of the countries, to serve wood an
stone.
33 ¶ *As* I live, saith the Lord GOD
surely with a mighty hand, [g]and wit
a stretched out arm, and with fur
poured out, will I rule over you:
34 And I will bring you out from th
people, and will gather you out of th
countries wherein ye are scattered
with a mighty hand, and with
stretched out arm, and with fury pour
ed out.
35 And I will bring you into the wil
derness of the people, and there will [h]
plead with you face to face.
36 Like [i]as I pleaded with your fath
ers in the wilderness of the land o
Egypt, so will I plead with you, saitl
the Lord GOD.
37 And I will cause you to [j]pass un
der the rod, and I will bring you int
[6]the bond of the covenant:
38 And [k]I will purge out from amon
you the rebels, and them that trans
gress against me: I will bring then
forth out of the country where the
sojourn, and [l]they shall not enter int
the land of Israel: and ye shall knov
that I *am* the LORD.
39 As for you, O house of Israel, thu
saith the Lord GOD; [m]Go ye, serve y
every one his idols, and hereafter *also*
if ye will not hearken unto me: [n]bu
pollute ye my holy name no more witl
your gifts, and with your idols.
40 For [o]in mine holy mountain, i
the mountain of the height of Israel
saith the Lord GOD, there shall all th
house of Israel, all of them in the land
serve me: there will [p]I accept them
and there will I require your offerings
and the [7]firstfruits of your oblations
with all your holy things.
41 I will accept you with your [8]swee
savour, when I bring you out from th
people, and gather you out of th
countries wherein ye have been scat
tered; and I will be sanctified in yo
before the heathen.
42 And [q]ye shall know that I *am* th
LORD, [r]when I shall bring you into th
land of Israel, into the country *fo*
the which I lifted up mine hand t
give it to your fathers.
43 And [s]there shall ye remembe
your ways, and all your doings, where
in ye have been defiled; and ye [t]shal
lothe yourselves in your own sight fo

ll your evils that ye have committed.
44 And [u]ye shall know that I *am* the
.ORD, when I have wrought with you
'or my name's sake, not according to
our wicked ways, nor according to
our corrupt doings, O ye house of
srael, saith the Lord GOD.
45 ¶ Moreover the word of the LORD
ame unto me, saying,
46 Son of man, set thy face toward
he south, and drop *thy word* toward
he south, and prophesy against the
orest of the south field;
47 And say to the forest of the south,
Iear the word of the LORD; Thus
aith the Lord GOD; Behold, I [w]will
indle a fire in thee, and it shall devour
every green tree in thee, and every
ry tree: the flaming flame shall not
e quenched, and all faces [y]from the
outh to the north shall be burned
herein.
48 And all flesh shall see that I the
.ORD have kindled it: it shall not be
uenched.
49 Then said I, Ah Lord GOD! they
ay of me, Doth he not speak para-
les?

CHAPTER 21

AND the word of the LORD came
unto me, saying,
2 Son [a]of man, set thy face toward
erusalem, and [b]drop *thy word* to-
ard the holy [c]places, and prophesy
gainst the land of Israel,
3 And say to the land of Israel, Thus
aith the LORD; Behold, I *am* against
hee, and will draw forth my sword
ut of his sheath, and will cut off from
hee [d]the righteous and the wicked.
4 Seeing then that I will cut off from
hee the righteous and the wicked,
herefore shall my sword go forth out
f his sheath against all flesh [e]from
he south to the north:
5 That all flesh may know that I the
.ORD have drawn forth my sword out
f his sheath: it [f]shall not return any
nore.
6 Sigh [g]therefore, thou son of man,
vith the breaking of *thy* loins; and
vith bitterness sigh before their eyes.
7 And it shall be, when they say unto
hee, Wherefore sighest thou? that
hou shalt answer, For the tidings;
ecause it cometh: and every heart
hall melt, and all hands shall be
eeble, and every spirit shall faint, and
ll knees [1]shall be weak *as* water: beold, it cometh, and shall be brought
o pass, saith the Lord GOD.
8 ¶ Again the word of the LORD came
nto me, saying,

u ch. 24.24.
v ch. 36.22.
w Jer. 21.14.
x Luke 23.31.
y ch. 21.4.

CHAP. 21
a ch. 20.46.
b Deut. 32.2. Amos 7.16.
c 1 Pet. 4.17.
d Job 9.22.
e ch. 20.47.
f Isa. 45.23.
g Isa. 22.4.
1 shall go into water.
h Deut. 32. 41.
2 Or, it is the rod of my son, it despiseth every tree.
3 Or, they are thrust down to the sword with my people.
i Jer. 31.19.
4 Or, When the trial hath been, what then? shall they not also belong to the despising rod?
j Job 9.23.
5 hand to hand.
k 1 Ki. 20.30. ch. 8.12.
6 Or, glittering, or, fear.
7 Or, sharpened.
l ch. 14.17.
8 set thyself, take the left hand.
m ch. 22.13.
n Deut. 28. 63. Isa. 1.24. ch. 16.42.
o Deut. 3.11. 2 Sam. 12. 26. Jer. 49.2.
9 mother of the way.
10 Or, knives.
11 teraphim.
12 rams, or, battering rams.
p Jer. 51.14.
q ch. 4.2.

9 Son of man, prophesy, and say,
Thus saith the LORD; Say, [h]A sword,
a sword is sharpened, and also furbished:
10 It is sharpened to make a sore
slaughter; it is furbished that it may
glitter: should we then make mirth?
[2]it contemneth the rod of my son, *as*
every tree.
11 And he hath given it to be furbished, that it may be handled: this
sword is sharpened, and it is furbished, to give it into the hand of the
slayer.
12 Cry and howl, son of man: for it
shall be upon my people, it *shall be*
upon all the princes of Israel: [3]terrors
by reason of the sword shall be upon
my people: [i]smite therefore upon *thy*
thigh.
13 [4]Because *it is* [j]a trial, and what if
the sword contemn even the rod? it
shall be no *more*, saith the Lord GOD.
14 Thou therefore, son of man, prophesy, and smite *thine* [5]hands together, and let the sword be doubled the
third time, the sword of the slain: it *is*
the sword of the great *men that are*
slain, which entereth into their [k]privy
chambers.
15 I have set the [6]point of the sword
against all their gates, that *their* heart
may faint, and *their* ruins be multiplied: ah! *it is* made bright, *it is*
[7]wrapped up for the slaughter.
16 Go [l]thee one way or other, *either*
on the right hand, [8]*or* on the left,
whithersoever thy face *is* set.
17 I will also [m]smite mine hands together, and [n]I will cause my fury to
rest: I the LORD have said *it*.
18 ¶ The word of the LORD came unto me again, saying,
19 Also, thou son of man, appoint
thee two ways, that the sword of the
king of Babylon may come: both
twain shall come forth out of one
land: and choose thou a place, choose
it at the head of the way to the city.
20 Appoint a way, that the sword
may come to [o]Răb′-băth of the Ammonites, and to Judah in Jerusalem
the defenced.
21 For the king of Babylon stood at
the [9]parting of the way, at the head of
the two ways, to use divination: he
made *his* [10]arrows bright, he consulted
with [11]images, he looked in the liver.
22 At his right hand was the divination for Jerusalem, to appoint [12]cap-
tains, to open the mouth in the slaughter, to [p]lift up the voice with shouting,
[q]to appoint *battering* rams against the

gates, to cast a mount, *and* to build a
fort.
23 And it shall be unto them as a
false divination in their sight, [13]to
them that have [r]sworn oaths: but he
will call to remembrance the iniquity,
that they may be taken.
24 Therefore thus saith the Lord
GOD; Because ye have made your iniquity to be remembered, in that your
transgressions are discovered, so that
in all your doings your sins do appear;
because, *I say*, that ye are come to
remembrance, ye shall be taken with
the hand.
25 ¶ And thou, [s]profane wicked
prince of Israel, whose day is come,
when iniquity *shall have* an end,
26 Thus saith the Lord GOD; Remove the diadem, and take off the
crown: this *shall* not *be* the same:
exalt [t]*him that is* low, and abase *him
that is* high.
27 [14]I will overturn, overturn, overturn, it: and it shall be no *more*, until
[u]he come whose right it is; and I will
give it *him*.
28 ¶ And thou, son of man, prophesy and say, Thus saith the Lord
GOD concerning the Ammonites, and
concerning their reproach; even say
thou, The sword, the sword *is* drawn:
for the slaughter *it is* furbished, to
consume because of the glittering:
29 Whiles they see vanity unto thee,
whiles they divine a lie unto thee, to
bring thee upon the necks of *them that
are* slain, of the wicked, whose day is
come, when their iniquity *shall have*
an end.
30 [15]Shall I cause *it* to return into his
sheath? I will judge thee in the place
where thou wast created, in the land
of thy nativity.
31 And I will pour out mine indignation upon thee, I will blow against
thee in the fire of my wrath, and deliver thee into the hand of [16]brutish
men, *and* skilful to destroy.
32 Thou shalt be for fuel to the fire;
thy blood shall be in the midst of the
land; thou shalt be no *more* remembered: for I the LORD have spoken *it*.

CHAPTER 22

MOREOVER the word of the
LORD came unto me, saying,
2 Now, thou son of man, wilt thou
[1]judge, wilt thou judge the [2]bloody
city? yea, thou shalt [3]shew her all her
abominations.
3 Then say thou, Thus saith the Lord
GOD, The city sheddeth blood in the
midst of it, that her time may come,
and maketh [a]idols against herself to
defile herself.
4 Thou art become guilty in thy
blood that thou hast [b]shed; and hast
defiled thyself in thine idols which
thou hast made; and thou hast caused
thy days to draw near, and art come
even unto thy years: therefore [c]have
I made thee a reproach unto the
heathen, and a mocking to all countries.
5 *Those that be* near, and *those that
be* far from thee, shall mock thee,
which art [4]infamous *and* much vexed.
6 Behold, [d]the princes of Israel, every
one were in thee to their [5]power to
shed blood.
7 In thee have they [e]set light by father
and mother: in the midst of thee have
they dealt by [6]oppression with the
stranger: in thee have they vexed the
fatherless and the widow.
8 Thou hast despised mine holy
things, and hast [f]profaned my sabbaths.
9 In thee are [7]men that carry tales to
shed blood: and in thee they eat upon
the mountains: in the midst of thee
they commit lewdness.
10 In thee have they [g]discovered their
fathers' nakedness: in thee have they
humbled her that was set [h]apart for
pollution.
11 And [8]one hath committed abomination with [i]his neighbour's wife;
and [9]another hath lewdly defiled his
daughter in law; and another in thee
hath humbled his sister, his father's
daughter.
12 In thee have [j]they taken gifts to
shed blood; [k]thou hast taken usury
and increase, and thou hast greedily
gained of thy neighbours by extortion, and [l]hast forgotten me, saith the
Lord GOD.
13 ¶ Behold, therefore I [m]have smitten mine hand at thy dishonest gain
which thou hast made, and at thy
blood which hath been in the midst of
thee.
14 Can [n]thine heart endure, or can
thine hands be strong, in the days that
I shall deal with thee? I [o]the LORD
have spoken *it*, and will do *it*.
15 And [p]I will scatter thee among
the heathen, and disperse thee in the
countries, and will consume thy
filthiness out of thee.
16 And thou [10]shalt take thine inheritance in thyself in the sight of the
heathen, and [q]thou shalt know that I
am the LORD.

13 Or, for the oaths made unto them.
r ch. 17.13.
s Gen. 13.13.
t Luke 1.52.
14 Perverted, perverted, perverted, will I make it.
u Gen. 49.10.
15 Or, Cause it to return.
16 Or, burning.

CHAP. 22

1 Or, plead for.
2 city of bloods?
3 make her know.
a Micah 6.16.
b Gen. 9.6. 2 Ki. 21.16. Ps. 106.38.
c Deut. 28. 37. 1 Ki. 9.7. 2 Chr. 7.20. Ps. 44.13,14. Jer. 18.16. Dan. 9.16.
4 polluted of name, much in vexation.
d Isa. 1.23. Zeph. 3.3.
5 arm.
e Deut. 27.16.
6 Or, deceit.
f Lev. 19.30.
7 men of slanders.
g Lev. 20.11. 1 Cor. 5.1.
h Lev. 18.19.
8 Or, every one.
i Jer. 5.8.
9 Or, every one hath by lewdness.
j Deut. 16.19.
k Ex. 22.25. Deut. 23.19.
l Deut. 32.18. Ps. 106.21. Jer. 2.32. ch. 23.35.
m ch. 21.17.
n Isa. 31.3. ch. 21.7. 1 Cor. 10.22.
o ch. 17.24.
p Deut. 4.27.
10 Or, shalt be profaned.
q Ex. 8.22. Ps. 9.16.

17 And the word of the LORD came
nto me, saying,
8 Son of man, [r]the house of Israel
to me become dross: all they *are*
rass, and tin, and iron, and lead, in
e midst of the furnace; they are *even*
e [11]dross of silver.
9 Therefore thus saith the Lord
OD; Because ye are all become
ross, behold, therefore I will gather
ou into the midst of Jerusalem.
0 [12]*As* they gather silver, and brass,
d iron, and lead, and tin, into the
idst of the furnace, to blow the fire
pon it, to melt *it;* so will I gather *you*
mine anger and in my fury, and I
ill leave *you there*, and melt you.
1 Yea, I will gather you, and blow
pon you in the fire of my wrath, and
shall be melted in the midst thereof.
2 As silver is melted in the midst of
e furnace, so shall ye be melted in
e midst thereof; and ye shall know
at I the LORD have poured out my
ry upon you.
3 ¶ And the word of the LORD came
to me, saying,
4 Son of man, say unto her, Thou
t the land that is not cleansed, nor
ined upon in the day of indigna-
on.
5 *There* [s]*is* a conspiracy of her pro-
hets in the midst thereof, like a roar-
g lion ravening the prey; they [t]have
voured souls; [u]they have taken the
easure and precious things; they
ve made her many widows in the
idst thereof.
6 Her [v]priests have [13]violated my
w, and have [w]profaned mine holy
ings: they have put [x]no difference
tween the holy and profane, neither
ve they shewed *difference* between
e unclean and the clean, and have
d their eyes from my sabbaths, and
am profaned among them.
7 Her [y]princes in the midst thereof
e like wolves ravening the prey, to
ed blood, *and* to destroy souls, to
t dishonest gain.
8 And [z]her prophets have daubed
em with untempered *morter*, seeing
nity, and divining lies unto them,
ying, Thus saith the Lord GOD,
hen the LORD hath not spoken.
9 The [a]people of the land have used
ppression, and exercised robbery,
d have vexed the poor and needy:
a, they have oppressed the stranger
wrongfully.
0 And [b]I sought for a man among
em, that should make up the hedge,
d stand in the [c]gap before me for

r Isa. 1.22.
11 drosses.
12 According to the gathering.
s Hosea 6.9. Jer. 6.13.
t Matt. 23.14. Acts 20.29.
u Micah 3.11. Zeph. 3.3.
v Mal. 2.8.
13 offered violence to.
w 1 Sam. 2. 29.
x Lev. 10.10.
y Isa. 1.23.
z ch. 13.10.
a Jer. 5.26.
14 Or, deceit.
15 without right.
b Jer. 5.1.
c Gen. 18.23.

CHAP. 23

a Jer. 3.7. ch. 16.46.
b Lev. 17.7. Josh. 24.14. ch. 20.8.
1 That is, His tent, or, tabernacle.
2 That is, My tabernacle in her.
c 2 Ki. 15.19. 2 Ki. 16.7. Hosea 5.13. Hosea 8.9. Hosea 10.6.
3 bestowed her whoredoms upon them.
4 The choice of the children of Asshur.
d 2 Ki. 17.3,4, 5,6,23.
e ch. 16.37, 41.
5 a name. Deut. 29.22.
6 she corrupted her inordinate love more than, etc.
7 more than the whoredoms of her sister.
f 2 Ki. 16.7.

the land, that I should not destroy it:
but I found none.
31 Therefore have I poured out mine
indignation upon them; I have consumed them with the fire of my wrath:
their own way have I recompensed
upon their heads, saith the Lord
GOD.

CHAPTER 23

THE word of the LORD came again
unto me, saying,
2 Son of man, there were two women,
the [a]daughters of one mother:
3 And [b]they committed whoredoms
in Egypt; they committed whoredoms
in their youth: there were their breasts
pressed, and there they bruised the
teats of their virginity.
4 And the names of them *were* Ă-hṓ-
lăh the elder, and Ă-hŏĺ-ĭ-băh her sister: and they were mine, and they bare
sons and daughters. Thus *were* their
names; Să-mâŕ-ĭ-ă *is* [1]Ă-hṓ-lăh, and
Jerusalem [2]Ă-hŏĺ-ĭ-băh.
5 And Ă-hṓ-lăh played the harlot
when she was mine; and she doted on
her lovers, on the [c]Assyrians *her*
neighbours,
6 *Which were* clothed with blue,
captains and rulers, all of them desirable young men, horsemen riding
upon horses.
7 Thus she [3]committed her whoredoms with them, with all them *that*
were [4]the chosen men of Assyria, and
with all on whom she doted: with all
their idols she defiled herself.
8 Neither left she her whoredoms
brought from Egypt: for in her youth
they lay with her, and they bruised
the breasts of her virginity, and poured their whoredoms upon her.
9 Wherefore I have delivered her
into the hand of her lovers, into the
hand of [d]the Assyrians, upon whom
she doted.
10 These [e]discovered her nakedness: they took her sons and her
daughters, and slew her with the
sword: and she became [5]famous
among women; for they had executed
judgment upon her.
11 And when her sister Ă-hŏĺ-ĭ-băh
saw *this*, [6]she was more corrupt in her
inordinate love than she, and in her
whoredoms [7]more than her sister in
her whoredoms.
12 She doted upon the [f]Assyrians
her neighbours, captains and rulers
clothed most gorgeously, horsemen
riding upon horses, all of them desirable young men.

13 Then I saw that she was defiled,
that they *took* both one way,
14 And *that* she increased her whoredoms: for when she saw men pourtrayed upon the wall, the [g]images of
the Chăl-dē-ăns pourtrayed with ver-
milion,
15 Girded with girdles upon their
loins, exceeding in dyed attire upon
their heads, all of them princes to look
to, after the manner of the Babylonians of Chăl-dē-ă, the land of their
nativity:
16 And [8]as soon as she saw them with
her eyes, she doted upon them, and
sent messengers unto them into Chăl-
dē-ă.
17 And the [9]Babylonians came to
her into the bed of love, and they defiled her with their whoredom, and
she was polluted with them, and her
mind was [10]alienated from them.
18 So she discovered her whoredoms, and discovered her nakedness:
then [h]my mind was alienated from
her, like as my mind was alienated
from her sister.
19 Yet she multiplied her whoredoms, in calling to remembrance the
days of her youth, wherein she had
played the harlot in the land of Egypt.
20 For she doted upon their para-
mours, whose [i]flesh *is as* the flesh of
asses, and whose issue *is like* the issue
of horses.
21 Thus thou calledst to remembrance the lewdness of thy youth, in
bruising thy teats by the Egyptians
for the paps of thy youth.
22 ¶ Therefore, O Ă-hŏl-ĭ-băh, thus
saith the Lord GOD; [j]Behold, I will
raise up thy lovers against thee, from
whom thy mind is alienated, and I will
bring them against thee on every side;
23 The Babylonians, and all the Chăl-
dē-ăns, Pē-kŏd, and Shō-ă, and Kō-ă,
and all the Assyrians with them: all of
them desirable young men, captains
and rulers, great lords and renowned,
all of them riding upon horses.
24 And they shall come against thee
[k]with chariots, wagons, and wheels,
and with an assembly of people, *which*
shall set against thee buckler and
shield and helmet round about: and I
will set judgment before them, and
they shall judge [l]thee according to
their judgments.
25 And I will set my jealousy against
thee, and they shall deal furiously
with thee: they shall take away thy
nose and thine ears; and thy remnant
shall fall by the sword: they shall take

g Jer. 50.2.

8 at the sight of her eyes.

9 children of Babel.

10 loosed, or, disjointed.

h Deut. 32. 19. Ps. 78.59. Jer. 12.8. Jer. 15.1. Lam. 2.7. Amos 6.8. Zech. 11.8.

i ch. 16.26.

j Isa. 10.5,6. ch.16.37.
k Jer. 47.3. Nah. 3.2.
l 2 Sam. 24. 14. Jer. 39.5. ch. 16.38.
m Jer. 13.22. ch. 16.39. Rev. 17.16.
11 instruments of thy decking.
n ch. 16.41. Micah 5.10.
o Jer. 21.7. ch. 16.37.
p ch. 16.39.
q ch. 6.9.
r Ps. 11.6. Jer. 25.15. Dan. 9.12.
s Deut. 28.37. ch. 22.4,5.
t Ps. 75.8. Isa. 51.17.
u Jer. 2.32. Jer. 3.21.
v 1 Ki. 14.9. Neh. 9.26.
12 Or, plead for.
w Isa. 58.1.
x ch. 16.38.
y ch. 16.20.
z ch. 22.8.

thy sons and thy daughters; and th
residue shall be devoured by the fire.
26 They [m]shall also strip thee out c
thy clothes, and take away thy [11]fa
jewels.
27 Thus [n]will I make thy lewdnes
to cease from thee, and thy whoredo
brought from the land of Egypt: s
that thou shalt not lift up thine eye
unto them, nor remember Egypt an
more.
28 For thus saith the Lord GOD; B
hold, I will deliver thee into the han
of them whom [o]thou hatest, into th
hand *of them* from whom thy mind
alienated:
29 And they shall deal with the
hatefully, and shall take away all th
labour, and shall [p]leave thee nake
and bare: and the nakedness of th
whoredoms shall be discovered, bot
thy lewdness and thy whoredoms.
30 I will do these *things* unto the
because thou hast gone [q]a whorin
after the heathen, *and* because tho
art polluted with their idols.
31 Thou hast walked in the way c
thy sister; therefore will I give h
[r]cup into thine hand.
32 Thus saith the Lord GOD; Tho
shalt drink of thy sister's cup dee
and large: thou [s]shalt be laughed t
scorn and had in derision; it co
taineth much.
33 Thou shalt be filled with drunke
ness and sorrow, with the cup
astonishment and desolation, with th
cup of thy sister Să-mâr-ĭ-ă.
34 Thou shalt [t]even drink it an
suck *it* out, and thou shalt break th
sherds thereof, and pluck off thi
own breasts: for I have spoken
saith the Lord GOD.
35 Therefore thus saith the Lo
GOD; Because [u]thou hast forgotte
me, and cast [v]me behind thy bac
therefore bear thou also thy lewdne
and thy whoredoms.
36 ¶ The LORD said moreover un
me; Son of man, wilt thou [12]judge
hō-lăh and Ă-hŏl-ĭ-băh? yea, [w]d
clare unto them their abominations
37 That they have committed adu
tery, and [x]blood *is* in their hands, ar
with their idols have they committ
adultery, and have also caused the
sons, [y]whom they bare unto me,
pass for them through *the fire*, to d
vour *them*.
38 Moreover this they have done u
to me: they have defiled my sanctua
in the same day, [z]and have profan
my sabbaths.

39 For when they had slain their
hildren to their idols, then they came
ne same day into my sanctuary to
rofane it; and, lo, [a]thus have they
one in the midst of mine house.
40 And furthermore, that ye have
ent for men [13]to come from far, unto
whom a messenger *was* sent; and, lo,
hey came: for whom thou didst
wash thyself, [d]paintedst thy eyes, and
eckedst thyself with ornaments,
41 And satest upon a [14]stately bed,
nd a table prepared before it, [e]where-
pon thou hast set mine incense and
nine oil.
42 And a voice of a multitude being
t ease *was* with her: and with the men
[15]of the common sort *were* brought
Să-bē-ăns from the wilderness, which
ut bracelets upon their hands, and
eautiful crowns upon their heads.
43 Then said I unto *her that was* old
n adulteries, Will they now commit
[17]whoredoms with her, and she *with*
hem?
44 Yet they went in unto her, as they
o in unto a woman that playeth the
arlot: so went they in unto Ă-hō-lăh
nd unto Ă-hŏl-ĭ-băh, the lewd wo-
nen.
45 ¶ And the righteous men, they
hall judge [f]them after the manner of
dulteresses, and after the manner of
vomen that shed blood; because they
re adulteresses, and blood *is* in their
ands.
46 For thus saith the Lord GOD; I
vill bring up a company upon them,
nd will give them [18]to be removed
nd spoiled.
47 And [g]the company shall stone
hem with stones, and [19]dispatch them
vith their swords; [h]they shall slay
heir sons and their daughters, and
urn up their houses with fire.
48 Thus will I cause lewdness to
ease out of the land, [i]that all women
nay be taught not to do after your
ewdness.
49 And they shall recompense your
ewdness upon you, and ye shall bear
he sins of your idols: and ye shall
now that I *am* the Lord GOD.

CHAPTER 24

AGAIN in the ninth year, in the
tenth month, in the tenth *day* of
he month, the word of the LORD
ame unto me, saying,
2 Son of man, write thee the name of
he day, *even* of this same day: the
ing of Babylon set himself against
erusalem this [a]same day.

a 2 Ki. 21.4. Jer. 23.11. ch. 44.7.
13 coming.
b Isa. 57.9.
c Ruth 3.3.
d 2 Ki. 9.30. Jer. 4.30.
14 honourable.
e Pro. 7.17. Jer. 44.17. ch. 16.18, 19. Hosea 2.8.
15 of the multitude of men.
16 Or, drunkards.
17 her whoredoms.
f ch. 16.38. John 8.4-7.
18 for a removing and spoil.
g ch. 16.40.
19 Or, single them out.
h 2 Chr. 36. 17. ch. 24.21.
i Deut. 13.11. 2 Pet. 2.6.

CHAP. 24

a 2 Ki. 25.1. Jer. 39.1.
b Ps. 78.2. ch. 17.12. Micah 2.4. Mark 12.12. Luke 8.10.
c Jer. 1.13. ch. 11.3.
1 Or, heap.
d 2 Ki. 21.16. ch. 22.3. Micah 7.2. Nah. 3.1.
e Joel 3.3. Obad. 11. Nah. 3.10.
f Lev. 17.13. Deut. 12.16.
g Jer. 16.17. Matt. 7.2.
h Nah. 3.1. Hab. 2.12.
i ch. 22.15.
2 Or, the Lord.
j Amos 4.6.
k ch. 5.13. ch. 8.18.
l Num. 23.19. 1 Sam. 15. 29. Ps. 33.9.
m ch. 5.11.
3 go.
4 Be silent.
n Num. 20. 29. Jer. 16.5.
o Lev. 10.6.
p 2 Sam. 15. 30.
q Micah 3.7.

3 And [b]utter a parable unto the rebellious house, and say unto them, Thus
saith the Lord GOD; Set [c]on a pot,
set *it* on, and also pour water into it:
4 Gather the pieces thereof into it,
even every good piece, the thigh, and
the shoulder; fill *it* with the choice
bones.
5 Take the choice of the flock, and
[1]burn also the bones under it, *and*
make it boil well, and let them seethe
the bones of it therein.
6 ¶ Wherefore thus saith the Lord
GOD; Woe to [d]the bloody city, to the
pot whose scum *is* therein, and whose
scum is not gone out of it! bring it out
piece by piece; let no [e]lot fall upon it.
7 For her blood is in the midst of
her; she set it upon the top of a rock;
[f]she poured it not upon the ground,
to cover it with dust;
8 That it might cause fury to come
up to take vengeance; [g]I have set her
blood upon the top of a rock, that it
should not be covered.
9 Therefore thus saith the Lord GOD;
[h]Woe to the bloody city! I will even
make the pile for fire great.
10 Heap on wood, kindle the fire,
consume the flesh, and spice it well,
and let the bones be burned.
11 Then set it empty upon the coals
thereof, that the brass of it may be
hot, and may burn, and *that* [i]the filthiness of it may be molten in it, *that*
the scum of it may be consumed.
12 She hath wearied [2]*herself* with
lies, and her great scum went not forth
out of her: her scum *shall be* in the
fire.
13 In thy filthiness *is* lewdness: because [j]I have purged thee, and thou
wast not purged, thou shalt not be
purged from thy filthiness any more,
[k]till I have caused my fury to rest upon
thee.
14 I [l]the LORD have spoken *it:* it
shall come to pass, and I will do *it;* I
will not go back, [m]neither will I spare,
neither will I repent; according to thy
ways, and according to thy doings,
shall they judge, saith the Lord GOD.
15 ¶ Also the word of the LORD came
unto me, saying,
16 Son of man, behold, I take away
from thee the desire of thine eyes with
a stroke: yet neither shalt thou mourn
nor weep, neither shall thy tears [3]run
down.
17 [4]Forbear to cry, [n]make no mourning for the dead, [o]bind the tire of thine
head upon thee, and put [p]on thy
shoes upon thy feet, and [q]cover not

thy [5]lips, and eat not the bread of men.

18 So I spake unto the people in the morning: and at even my wife died; and I did in the morning as I was commanded.

19 ¶ And the people said unto me, [r]Wilt thou not tell us what these *things are* to us, that thou doest *so?*

20 Then I answered them, The word of the LORD came unto me, saying,

21 Speak unto the house of Israel, Thus saith the Lord GOD; Behold, I [s]will profane my sanctuary, the excellency of your strength, [t]the desire of your eyes, and [6]that which your soul pitieth; and your sons and your daughters whom ye have left shall fall by the sword.

22 And ye shall do as I have done: [u]ye shall not cover *your* lips, nor eat the bread of men.

23 And your tires *shall be* upon your heads, and your shoes upon your feet: [v]ye shall not mourn nor weep; but [w]ye shall pine away for your iniquities, and mourn one toward another.

24 Thus [x]Ē-zēk'-ĭ-ĕl is unto you a sign: according to all that he hath done shall ye do: [y]and when this cometh, [z]ye shall know that I *am* the Lord GOD.

25 Also, thou son of man, *shall it* not *be* in the day when I take from them their strength, the joy of their glory, the desire of their eyes, and [7]that whereupon they set their minds, their sons and their daughters,

26 *That* he that escapeth in that day shall come unto thee, to cause *thee* to hear *it* with *thine* ears?

27 In [a]that day shall thy mouth be opened to him which is escaped, and thou shalt speak, and be no more dumb: and thou shalt be a sign unto them; and they shall know that I *am* the LORD.

CHAPTER 25

THE word of the LORD came again unto me, saying,

2 Son of man, set thy [a]face against the Ammonites, and prophesy against them;

3 And say unto the Ammonites, Hear the word of the Lord GOD; Thus saith the Lord GOD; [b]Because thou saidst, Aha, against my sanctuary, when it was profaned; and against the land of Israel, when it was desolate; and against the house of Judah, when they went into captivity;

4 Behold, therefore I will deliver thee to the [1]men of the east for a possession, and they shall set their palace in thee, and make their dwellings in thee: they shall eat thy fruit, and they shall [c]drink thy milk.

5 And I will make [d]Răb'-băh a stable for camels, and the Ammonites a couchingplace for flocks: and ye shall know that I *am* the LORD.

6 For thus saith the Lord GOD; Because thou hast clapped *thine* [2]hands, and stamped with the [3]feet, and rejoiced in [4]heart with all thy despite against the land of Israel;

7 Behold, therefore I will stretch out mine hand upon thee, and will deliver thee for [5]a spoil to the heathen; and I will cut thee off from the people, and I will cause thee to perish out of the countries: I will destroy thee; and thou shalt know that I *am* the LORD.

8 ¶ Thus saith the Lord GOD; Because that [e]Moab and Sē'-ïr do say, Behold, the house of Judah *is* like unto all the heathen;

9 Therefore, behold, I will open the [6]side of Moab from the cities, from his cities *which are* on his frontiers, the glory of the country, Bĕth–jĕsh-ĭ-mōth, Bā'-ăl–mē'-on, and Kĭr-ĭ-ă-thā'-ĭm,

10 Unto the men of the east [7]with the Ammonites, and will give them in possession, that the Ammonites may not be remembered among the nations.

11 And I will execute judgments upon Moab; and they shall know that I *am* the LORD.

12 ¶ Thus saith the Lord GOD; Because [f]that Ē'-dom hath dealt against the house of Judah [8]by taking vengeance, and hath greatly offended, and revenged himself upon them;

13 Therefore thus saith the Lord GOD; I will also stretch out mine hand upon Ē'-dom, and will cut off man and beast from it; and I will make it desolate from Tē'-măn; and [9]they of Dē'-dăn shall fall by the sword.

14 And [g]I will lay my vengeance upon Ē'-dom by the hand of my people Israel: and they shall do in Ē'-dom according to mine anger and according to my fury; and they shall know my vengeance, saith the Lord GOD.

15 ¶ Thus saith the Lord GOD; Because [h]the Philistines have dealt by revenge, and have taken vengeance with a despiteful heart, to destroy *it* [10]for the old hatred;

16 Therefore thus saith the Lord

---

5 upper lip.
r ch. 12.9.
s Jer. 7.14. ch. 7.20.
t Ps. 27.4.
6 the pity of your soul.
u Jer. 16.6.
v Job 27.15. Ps. 78.64.
w Lev. 26.39. ch. 33.10.
x Isa. 20.3. ch. 12.6.
y Jer. 17.15. John 13.19.
z ch. 25.5.
7 the lifting up of their soul.
a ch. 3.26.

CHAP. 25

a Jer. 49.1. Amos 1.13. Zeph. 2.9.
b Pro. 17.5.
1 children.
c Gen. 45.18.
d 2 Sam. 12. 26. Isa. 13.21. ch. 21.20. Zeph. 2.14.
2 hand.
3 foot.
4 soul.
5 Or, meat.
e Deut. 2.4,5. Isa. 15.1. Jer. 48.1.
6 shoulder of Moab.
7 Or, against the children of Ammon.
f 2 Chr. 28. 17. Ps. 137.7. Lam. 4.22. Amos 1.11. Obad. 10.
8 by revenging revengement.
9 Or, they shall fall by the sword unto Dedan.
g Isa. 11.14.
h Jer. 25.20. Joel 3.4. Amos 1.6.
10 Or, with perpetual hatred.

PROPHECY about Tyre.

OD; Behold, [i]I will stretch out mine
and upon the Philistines, and I will
it off [j]the Chĕr′-ĕ-thĭms, and destroy
e remnant of the [11]sea coast.
7 And I will execute great [12]ven-
eance upon them with furious re-
ukes; and they shall [k]know that I
n the LORD, when I shall lay my
engeance upon them.

CHAPTER 26

AND it came to pass in the eleventh
year, in the first *day* of the month,
at the word of the LORD came unto
e, saying,
2 Son of man, [a]because that Tȳ′-rŭs
ath said against Jerusalem, Aha,
he is broken *that was* [c]the gates of
e people: she is [d]turned unto me: I
hall be replenished, *now* she is laid
aste:
3 Therefore thus saith the Lord GOD;
ehold, I *am* against thee, O Tȳ′-rŭs,
nd will cause many nations to come
p against thee, as the sea causeth his
aves to come up.
4 And they shall destroy the walls of
ȳ′-rŭs, and break down her towers:
will also scrape her dust from
er, and make her like the top of a
ock.
5 It shall be *a place for* the spreading
f nets [e]in the midst of the sea: for I
ave spoken *it*, saith the Lord GOD:
nd it shall become a spoil to the na-
ions.
6 And her daughters which *are* in
he field shall be slain by the sword;
and they shall know that I *am* the
ORD.
7 ¶ For thus saith the Lord GOD;
Behold, I will bring upon Tȳ′-rŭs
Nĕb-ū-chăd-rĕz′-zär king of Babylon,
[g]king of kings, from the north, with
orses, and with chariots, and with
orsemen, and companies, and much
eople.
8 He shall slay with the sword thy
aughters in the field: and he shall
make a fort against thee, and [1]cast a
mount against thee, and lift up the
uckler against thee.
9 And he shall set engines of war
gainst thy walls, and with his axes he
hall break down thy towers.
10 By reason of the abundance of his
orses their dust shall cover thee: thy
walls shall shake at the noise of the
orsemen, and of the wheels, and of
he chariots, when he shall enter into
hy gates, [2]as men enter into a city
wherein is made a breach.
11 With the hoofs of his horses shall

i Zeph. 2.4.
j 1 Sam. 30. 14.
11 Or, haven of the sea.
12 vengeances.
k Ps. 9.16. Isa. 26.11. ch. 6.7.

CHAP. 26

a Isa. 23.1. Jer. 25.22. Amos. 1.9.
b ch. 25.3.
c Ps. 40.15. Lam. 1.1.
d Joel 3.4-6.

Hebrew: lo'...'od = duration i.e. time is undefined but to be derived from the context

e ch. 27.32. Matt. 4.19-21.
f Ps. 83.18. Isa. 37.20. ch. 25.5.
g Ezra 7.12. Dan. 2.37.
h 2 Sam. 20. 15. Jer. 52.4. ch. 21.22.
1 Or, pour out the engine of shot.
2 according to the enterings of a city broken up.
3 houses of thy desire.
i Isa. 14.11. Isa. 23.7,16. Jer. 7.34. Jer. 16.9. Hosea 2.11. Rev. 18.22.
j Isa. 23.16.
k Jer. 49.21.
l Isa. 23.8.
m Jonah 3.6.
4 tremblings.
n Job 2.13. Isa. 3.26.
o ch. 32.10.
p ch. 27.35.
q Rev. 18.9.
5 of the seas.
r Isa. 23.4.
s ch. 32.18. Luke 10.15.
t Isa. 4.5.
u ch. 27.36.
6 terrors.
v Ps. 37.36.
w Jer. 51.64.

he tread down all thy streets: he shall
slay thy people by the sword, and thy
strong garrisons shall go down to the
ground.
12 And they shall make a spoil of thy
riches, and make a prey of thy merchandise: and they shall break down
thy walls, and destroy [3]thy pleasant
houses: and they shall lay thy stones
and thy timber and thy dust in the
midst of the water.
13 And [i]I will cause the noise of thy
[j]songs to cease; and the sound of thy
harps shall be no more heard.
14 And I will make thee like the top
of a rock: thou shalt be *a place* to
spread nets upon; thou shalt be built
no more: for I the LORD have spoken
it, saith the Lord GOD.
15 ¶ Thus saith the Lord GOD to Tȳ′-
rŭs; Shall not the isles [k]shake at the
sound of thy fall, when the wounded
cry, when the slaughter is made in the
midst of thee?
16 Then all the [l]princes of the sea
shall come [m]down from their thrones,
and lay away their robes, and put off
their broidered garments: they shall
clothe themselves with [4]trembling;
[n]they shall sit upon the ground, and
[o]shall tremble at *every* moment, and
[p]be astonished at thee.
17 And they shall take up [q]a lamentation for thee, and say to thee, How
art thou destroyed, *that wast* inhabited [5]of seafaring men, the renowned
city, which wast strong [r]in the sea,
she and her inhabitants, which cause
their terror *to be* on all that haunt
it!
18 Now shall the isles tremble in the
day of thy fall; yea, the isles that *are*
in the sea shall be troubled at thy departure.
19 For thus saith the Lord GOD;
When I shall make thee a desolate
city, like the cities that are not inhabited; when I shall bring up the
deep upon thee, and great waters shall
cover thee;
20 When I shall bring thee down
with [s]them that descend into the pit,
with the people of old time, and shall
set thee in the low parts of the earth,
in places desolate of old, with them
that go down to the pit, that thou be
not inhabited; and I shall set [t]glory in
the land of the living;
21 I [u]will make thee [6]a terror, and
thou *shalt be* no *more*: [v]though thou
be sought for, yet [w]shalt thou never
be found again, saith the Lord
GOD.

CHAPTER 27

THE word of the LORD came again unto me, saying,

2 Now, thou son of man, [a]take up a lamentation for Tȳ-rŭs;

3 And say unto Tȳ-rŭs, [b]O thou that art situate at the entry of the sea, *which art* a [c]merchant of the people for many isles, Thus saith the Lord GOD; O Tȳ-rŭs, thou hast said, I *am* [1]of perfect beauty.

4 Thy borders *are* in the [2]midst of the seas, thy builders have perfected thy beauty.

5 They have [3]made all thy *ship* boards of fir trees of [d]Sē-nĭr: they have taken cedars from Lĕb-ă-non to make masts for thee.

6 *Of* the oaks of Bā-shăn have they made thine oars; [4]the company of the Ashurites have made thy benches *of* ivory, *brought* out [e]of the isles of Chĭt-tĭm.

7 Fine linen with broidered work from Egypt was that which thou spreadest forth to be thy sail; [5]blue and purple from the isles of [f]Ē-lī-shăh was that which covered thee.

8 The inhabitants of Zī-dŏn and Arvad were thy mariners: thy wise *men*, O Tȳ-rŭs, *that* were in thee, were thy pilots.

9 The ancients of [g]Gē-băl and the wise *men* thereof were in thee thy [6]calkers: all the ships of the sea with their mariners were in thee to occupy thy merchandise.

10 They of Persia and of Lud and of [h]Phŭt were in thine army, thy men of war: they hanged the shield and helmet in thee; they set forth thy comeliness.

11 The men of Arvad with thine army *were* upon thy walls round about, and the Găm-mă-dĭms were in thy towers: they hanged their shields upon thy walls round about; they have made thy beauty perfect.

12 Tarshish [i]*was* thy merchant by reason of the multitude of all *kind of* riches; with silver, iron, tin, and lead, they traded in thy fairs.

13 [j]Jā-văn, Tū-băl, and Mē-shĕch, they *were* thy merchants: [k]they traded the persons of men and vessels of brass in thy [7]market.

14 They of the house of [l]Tō-gär-măh traded in thy fairs with horses and horsemen and mules.

15 The men of [m]Dē-dăn *were* thy merchants; many isles *were* the merchandise of thine hand: they brought thee *for* a present horns of ivory an ebony.

16 Syria *was* thy merchant by reaso of the multitude of [8]the wares of th making: they occupied in thy fai with emeralds, purple, and broidere work, and fine linen, and coral, an [9]agate.

17 Judah, and the land of Israel, the *were* thy merchants: they traded i thy market [n]wheat of Mĭn-nĭth, an Păn-năg, and honey, and oil, an [10]balm.

18 Damascus *was* thy merchant i the multitude of the wares of th making, for the multitude of a riches; in the wine of Hĕl-bŏn, an white wool.

19 Dan also and Jā-văn [11]going t and fro occupied in thy fairs: brigh iron, cassia, and calamus, were in th market.

20 Dē-dăn [o]*was* thy merchant i [12]precious clothes for chariots.

21 Arabia, and all the princes of [p]Kē dăr, [13]they occupied with thee i lambs, and rams, and goats: in thes *were they* thy merchants.

22 The merchants of [q]Shē-bă an Rā-ă-măh, they *were* thy merchants they occupied in thy fairs with chie of all spices, and with all preciou stones, and gold.

23 [r]Hâr-ăn, and Căn-nēh, and Eder the merchants of [s]Shē-bă, Ăssh-ŭr *and* Chĭl-măd, *were* thy merchants.

24 These *were* thy merchants in [14]a sorts *of things*, in blue [15]clothes, an broidered work, and in chests of ric apparel, bound with cords, and mad of cedar, among thy merchandise.

25 The [t]ships of Tarshish did sing c thee in thy market: and thou wast re plenished, and made very glorious i the midst of the seas.

26 ¶ Thy rowers have brought the into great waters: [u]the east wind hat broken thee in the [16]midst of the seas

27 Thy [v]riches, and thy fairs, th merchandise, thy mariners, and th pilots, thy calkers, and the occupier of thy merchandise, and all thy me of war, that *are* in thee, [17]and in a thy company which *is* in the midst o thee, shall fall into the [18]midst of th seas in the day of thy ruin.

28 The [19]suburbs shall shake at th sound of the cry of thy pilots.

29 And [w]all that handle the oar, th mariners, *and* all the pilots of the sea shall come down from their ships they shall stand upon the land;

30 And shall cause their voice to b

CHAP. 27

a ch. 26.17.
b ch. 28.2.
c Isa. 23.3.
1 perfect of beauty.
2 heart.
3 built.
d Deut. 3.9.
4 the daughter, or, they have made thy hatches of ivory well trodden.
e Jer. 2.10.
5 Or, purple and scarlet.
f Gen. 10.4.
g Josh. 13.5.
6 strengtheners, or, stoppers of chinks.
h Jer. 46.9. ch. 30.5.
i 2 Chr. 20.36.
j 1 Chr. 1.5.
k Joel 3.6.
7 Or, merchandise.
l Gen. 10.3. 1 Chr. 1.6.
m Gen. 10.7. 1 Chr. 1.9.
8 thy works.
9 chrysoprase.
n 1 Ki. 5.9. Acts 12.20.
10 Or, rosin.
11 Or, Meuzal.
o Gen. 25.3.
12 clothes of freedom.
p Gen. 25.13. 1 Chr. 1.29.
13 they were the merchants of thy hand.
q Gen. 10.7. Ps. 72.10,15. Isa. 60.6.
r Gen. 11.31. 2 Ki. 19.12. Acts 17.4.
s Gen. 25.3.
14 Or, excellent things.
15 foldings.
t Isa. 2.16.
u Ps. 48.7.
16 heart.
v Pro. 11.4.
17 Or, even with all.
18 heart.
19 Or, waves.
w Rev. 18.17.

eard against thee, and shall cry bit-
rly, and shall [x]cast up dust upon
eir heads, they shall wallow [y]them-
elves in the ashes:
31 And they shall make themselves
tterly bald for thee, and gird them
ith sackcloth, and they shall weep
r thee with bitterness of heart *and*
itter wailing.
32 And in their wailing they shall
ake up a lamentation for thee, and
ment over thee, *saying*, What *city is*
ke Tȳ-rŭs, like the destroyed in the
idst of the sea?
33 When thy wares went forth out of
e seas, thou filledst many people;
ou didst enrich the kings of the
arth with the multitude of thy riches
nd of thy merchandise.
34 In the time *when* thou shalt be
roken by the seas in the depths of the
aters thy merchandise and all thy
ompany in the midst of thee shall fall.
35 All [z]the inhabitants of the isles
hall be astonished at thee, and their
ings shall be sore afraid, they shall
e troubled in *their* countenance.
36 The merchants among the people
shall hiss at thee; thou shalt be [20]a
error, and [21]never *shalt be* any more.

CHAPTER 28

THE word of the LORD came again
unto me, saying,
2 Son of man, say unto the prince of
Tȳ-rŭs, Thus saith the Lord GOD; Be-
ause [a]thine heart *is* lifted up, and
hou hast said, I *am* a God, I sit *in* the
eat of God, in the [1]midst of the seas;
yet thou *art* a man, and not God,
hough thou set thine heart as the
eart of God:
3 Behold, [c]thou *art* wiser than
Daniel; there is no secret that they
an hide from thee:
4 With thy wisdom and with thine
nderstanding thou hast gotten thee
iches, and hast gotten gold and sil-
er into thy treasures:
5 [2]By thy great wisdom *and* by thy
raffick hast thou increased thy
iches, and thine heart is lifted up be-
ause [d]of thy riches:
6 Therefore thus saith the Lord
GOD; Because thou hast set [e]thine
heart as the heart of God;
7 Behold, therefore I will bring
strangers upon thee, [f]the terrible of
the nations: and they shall draw their
swords against the beauty of thy wisdom, and they shall defile thy brightness.
8 They shall bring thee down to the
pit, and thou shalt die the deaths of
them that are slain in the midst of the
seas.
9 Wilt thou yet say before him that
slayeth thee, I *am* God? but thou *shalt*
be a man, and no God, in the hand of
him that [3]slayeth thee.
10 Thou shalt die the deaths of the
[g]uncircumcised by the hand of strangers: for I have spoken *it*, saith the
Lord GOD.
11 ¶ Moreover the word of the LORD
came unto me, saying,
12 Son of man, take up a lamentation upon the king of Tȳ-rŭs, and say
unto him, Thus saith the Lord GOD;
[h]Thou sealest up the sum, full of wisdom, and perfect in beauty.
13 Thou hast been in [i]Eden the garden of God; every precious stone *was*
thy covering, the [4]sardius, topaz, and
the diamond, the [5]beryl, the onyx, and
the jasper, the sapphire, the [6]emerald,
and the carbuncle, and gold: the
workmanship of [j]thy tabrets and of
thy pipes was prepared in thee in the
day that thou wast created.
14 Thou *art* the anointed [k]cherub
that covereth; and I have set thee *so*:
thou wast upon [l]the holy mountain
of God; thou hast walked up and
down in the midst of the stones of
fire.
15 Thou *wast* perfect in thy ways
from the day that thou wast created,
till iniquity was found in thee.
16 By the multitude of thy merchandise they have filled the midst of thee
with violence, and thou hast sinned:
therefore I will cast thee as profane
out of the mountain of God: and I
will destroy thee, O covering cherub,
from the midst of the stones of fire.
17 Thine heart was lifted up because
of thy beauty, thou hast corrupted thy
wisdom by reason of thy brightness:
I will cast thee to the ground, I [m]will
lay thee before kings, that they may
behold thee.
18 Thou hast defiled thy [7]sanctuaries
by the multitude of thine iniquities,
by the iniquity of thy traffic; therefore will I bring forth a [n]fire from the
midst of thee, it shall devour thee,
and I will bring thee to ashes upon
the earth in the sight of all them that
behold thee.
19 All they that know thee among
the people shall be astonished at
thee: thou shalt be [8]a terror, and never
shalt thou *be* any more.
20 ¶ Again the word of the LORD
came unto me, saying,

x Neh. 9.1. Lam. 2.10. Rev. 18.19.
y Esther 4.1.
z ch. 26.15.
a Jer. 18.16.
20 terrors.
21 shalt not be for ever.

CHAP. 28

a Deut. 8.14. 2 Chr. 26.16. Pro. 16.18. Isa. 2.12. Dan. 5.22, 23. 1 Tim. 3.6.
1 heart.
b Ps. 9.20. Isa. 31.3.
c Dan. 2.48. Zech. 9.2.
2 By the greatness of thy wisdom.
d Deut. 8.12, 13,14.
e Dan. 7.25, 26. Acts 12.22. 2 Thes. 2. 4.
f ch. 30.11.
3 Or, woundeth.
g ch. 31.18.
h ch. 27.3.
i Gen. 2.8. Gen. 3.23, 24. ch. 31.8,9. Joel 2.3.
4 Or, ruby.
5 Or, chrysolite.
6 Or, chrysoprase.
j ch. 26.13.
k Ex. 25.20.
l ch. 20.40.
m 2 Pet. 2.6. Jude 7.
7 palaces.
n Amos 1.10.
8 terrors.

21 Son of man, set thy face against Zī-dŏn, [o]and prophesy against it,

22 And say, Thus saith the Lord GOD; Behold, [p]I *am* against thee, O Zī-dŏn; and I will be glorified in the midst of thee: and they [q]shall know that I *am* the LORD, when I shall have executed judgments in her, and shall be [r]sanctified in her.

23 For [s]I will send into her pestilence, and blood into her streets; and the wounded shall be judged in the midst of her by the sword upon her on every side; and they shall know that I *am* the LORD.

24 ¶ And there shall be no more a [t]pricking brier unto the house of Israel, nor *any* grieving thorn of all *that are* round about them, that despised them; and they shall know that I *am* the Lord GOD.

25 Thus saith the Lord GOD; When I shall have [u]gathered the house of Israel from the people among whom they are scattered, and shall be sanctified in them in the sight of the heathen, then shall they dwell in their land that I have given to my servant Jacob.

26 And they shall dwell [9]safely therein, and shall [v]build houses, and [w]plant vineyards; yea, they shall dwell with confidence, when I have executed judgments upon all those that [10]despise them round about them; and they shall know that I *am* the LORD their God.

CHAPTER 29

IN the tenth year, in the tenth *month*, in the twelfth *day* of the month, the word of the LORD came unto me, saying,

2 Son of man, set thy face against Pharaoh king of Egypt, and prophesy against him, and [a]against all Egypt:

3 Speak, and say, Thus saith the Lord GOD; [b]Behold, I *am* against thee, Pharaoh king of Egypt, the great [c]dragon that lieth in the midst of his rivers, [d]which hath said, My river *is* mine own, and I have made *it* for myself.

4 But [e]I will put hooks in thy jaws, and I will cause the fish of thy rivers to stick unto thy scales, and I will bring thee up out of the midst of thy rivers, and all the fish of thy rivers shall stick unto thy scales.

5 And I will leave thee *thrown* into the wilderness, thee and all the fish of thy rivers: thou shalt fall upon the [1]open fields; [f]thou shalt not be brought together, nor gathered: [g]I have given thee for meat to the beast of the field and to the fowls of th heaven.

6 And all the inhabitants of Egyp shall know that I *am* the LORD, be cause they have been a [h]staff of ree to the house of Israel.

7 When [i]they took hold of thee b thy hand, thou didst break, and ren all their shoulder: and when the leaned upon thee, thou brakest, an madest all their loins to be at a stand

8 ¶ Therefore thus saith the Lor GOD; Behold, I will bring a sword up on thee, and cut off man and beas out of thee.

9 And the land of Egypt shall b desolate and waste; and they sha know that I *am* the LORD: [j]becaus he hath said, The river *is* mine, an I have made *it*.

10 Behold, therefore I *am* agains thee, and against thy rivers, [k]and I will make the land of Egypt [2]utterl waste *and* desolate, [3]from the towe of [4]Sȳ-ē-nē even unto the border o Ē-thĭ-ō-pĭ-ă.

11 No [l]foot of man shall pass throug it, nor foot of beast shall pass throug it, neither shall it be inhabited fort years.

12 And [m]I will make the land o Egypt desolate in the midst of th countries *that are* desolate, and he cities among the cities *that are* lai waste shall be desolate forty years and I will scatter the Egyptians among the nations, and will disperse them through the countries.

13 ¶ Yet thus saith the Lord GOD; At the end [n]of forty years will I gathe the Egyptians from the people whithe they were scattered:

14 And I will bring again the captivity of Egypt, and will cause them to return *into* the land of Păth-rŏs, into the land of their [5]habitation; and they shall be there a [6]base kingdom.

15 It shall be the basest of the kingdoms; neither shall it exalt itself any more above the nations: for I will diminish them, that they shall no more rule over the nations.

16 And it shall be no more [o]the confidence of the house of Israel, which bringeth *their* iniquity to remembrance, when they shall look afte them: but they shall know that I *am* the Lord GOD.

17 ¶ And it came to pass in the seven and twentieth year, in the first *month*, in the first *day* of the month, the word of the LORD came unto me, saying,

o Isa. 23.4,12. Jer. 25.22. ch. 32.30.
p Ex. 14.4. ch. 39.13.
q Ps. 9.16.
r ch. 20.41.
s ch. 38.22.
t Num. 33.55. Josh. 23.13.
u Isa. 11.12. Hosea 1.11. ch. 20.41.
9 Or, with confidence.
v Isa. 65.21. Amos 9.14.
w Jer. 31.5.
10 Or, spoil.

CHAP. 29
a Isa. 19.1. Jer. 25.19.
b Jer. 44.30. ch. 28.22.
c Ps. 74.13, 14. Isa. 27.1. ch. 32.2.
d ch. 28.2.
e 2 Ki. 19.28. Isa. 37.29. ch. 38.4.
1 face of the field.
f Jer. 8.2.
g Jer. 7.33.
h 2 Ki. 18.21. Isa. 36.6.
i Jer. 37.5.
j Pro. 16.18.
k ch. 30.12.
2 wastes of waste.
3 Or, from Migdol to Syene.
4 Seveneh.
l Jer. 43.11, 12. ch. 30.10-13.
m Jer. 25.17, 18. ch. 30.7.
n Isa. 19.23. Jer. 46.25, 26.
5 Or, birth.
6 low, that is, tributary.
o Isa. 30.2. Jer. 2.18,19. Lam. 4.17.

18 Son of man, [p]Něb-ū-chăd-rĕz-́zär king of Babylon caused his army to serve a great service against Tȳ-́rŭs: every head *was* made bald, and every shoulder *was* peeled: yet had he no wages, nor his army, for Tȳ-́rŭs, for the service that he had served against it:

19 Therefore thus saith the Lord GOD; Behold, I will give the land of Egypt unto Něb-ū-chăd-rĕz-́zär king of Babylon; and he shall take her multitude, and [7]take her spoil, and take her prey; and it shall be the wages for his army.

20 I have given him the land of Egypt [8]*for* his labour wherewith he [q]served against it, because they wrought for me, saith the Lord GOD.

21 ¶ In that day [r]will I cause the horn of the house of Israel to bud forth, and I will give thee [s]the opening of the mouth in the midst of them; and they shall know that I *am* the LORD.

CHAPTER 30

THE word of the LORD came again unto me, saying,

2 Son of man, prophesy and say, Thus saith the Lord GOD; [a]Howl ye, Woe worth the day!

3 For [b]the day *is* near, even the day of the LORD *is* near, a cloudy day; it shall be the time of the heathen.

4 And the sword shall come upon Egypt, and great [1]pain shall be in Ē-thĭ-ō-́pĭ-ă, when the slain shall fall in Egypt, and they shall [c]take away her multitude, and [d]her foundations shall be broken down.

5 Ē-thĭ-ō-́pĭ-ă, and [2]Lĭb-́ȳ-ă, and Lydia, and all [e]the mingled people, and Chŭb, and the [3]men of the land that is in league, shall fall with them by the sword.

6 Thus saith the LORD; They also that uphold Egypt shall fall; and the pride of her power shall come down: [4]from the tower of Sȳ-ē-́nē shall they fall in it by the sword, saith the Lord GOD.

7 And [f]they shall be desolate in the midst of the countries *that are* desolate, and her cities shall be in the midst of the cities *that are* wasted.

8 And they shall know that I *am* the LORD, when I have set a fire in Egypt, and *when* all her helpers shall be [5]destroyed.

9 In that day [g]shall messengers go forth from me in ships to make the careless Ē-thĭ-ō-́pĭ-ăns afraid, and great [h]pain shall come upon them, as in the day of Egypt: for, lo, it cometh.

10 Thus saith the Lord GOD; [i]I will also make the multitude of Egypt to cease by the hand of Něb-ū-chăd-rĕz-́zär king of Babylon.

11 He and his people with him, the [j]terrible of the nations, shall be brought to destroy the land: and they shall draw their swords against Egypt, and fill the land with the slain.

12 And I will make the rivers [6]dry, and sell [k]the land into the hand of the wicked: and I will make the land waste, and [7]all that is therein, by the hand of strangers: I the LORD have spoken *it*.

13 Thus saith the Lord GOD; I will also destroy [l]the idols, and I will cause *their* [8]images to cease out of [9]Nŏph; and [m]there shall be no more a prince of the land of Egypt: [n] and I will put a fear in the land of Egypt.

14 And I will make [o]Păth-́rŏs desolate, and will set fire in [10]Zō-́ăn, and will execute judgments in [11]No.

15 And I will pour my fury upon [12]Sin, the strength of Egypt; and I will cut off the multitude of No.

16 And I will set fire in Egypt: Sin shall have great pain, and No shall be rent asunder, and Nŏph *shall have* distresses daily.

17 The young men of [13]Ā-́vĕn and of [14]Pī–bē-́sĕth shall fall by the sword: and these *cities* shall go into captivity.

18 At [p]Tē-hăph-́nē-hēṡ also the day shall be [15]darkened, when I shall break there the yokes of Egypt: and the pomp of her strength shall cease in her: as for her, a cloud shall cover her, and her daughters shall go into captivity.

19 Thus will I execute judgments in Egypt: and they shall know that I *am* the LORD.

20 ¶ And it came to pass in the eleventh year, in the first *month*, in the seventh *day* of the month, *that* the word of the LORD came unto me, saying,

21 Son of man, I have [q]broken the arm of Pharaoh king of Egypt; and, lo, [r]it shall not be bound up to be healed, to put a roller to bind it, to make it strong to hold the sword.

22 Therefore thus saith the Lord GOD; Behold, I *am* against Pharaoh king of Egypt, and will [s]break his arms, the strong, and [t]that which was broken; and I will cause the sword to fall out of his hand.

23 And [u]I will scatter the Egyptians

p Jer. 27.6. ch. 26.7.
7 spoil her spoil, and prey her prey.
8 Or, for his hire.
q Jer. 25.9.
r 1 Sam. 2.10. Ps. 132.17.
s Gen. 18.17. ch. 3.26. Amos 3.7. Dan. 9.22-27.

CHAP. 30

a Isa. 13.6.
b ch. 7.7. Joel 2.1.
1 Or, fear.
c ch. 29.19.
d Jer. 50.15.
2 Phut.
e Jer. 25.20.
3 children.
4 Or, from Migdol to Syene.
f ch. 29.12.
5 broken.
g Isa. 18.1,2. Zeph. 2.12.
h Ps. 48.6. Isa. 19.17. ch. 26.16.
i ch. 29.19.
j ch. 28.7.
6 drought.
k Isa. 19.4.
7 the fulness thereof.
l Ex. 23.13. Zech. 13.2.
8 Or, nonentities.
9 Or, Memphis.
m Zech. 10. 11.
n Isa. 19.16.
o ch. 29.14.
10 Or, Tanis.
11 Or, Thebes.
12 Or, Pelusium.
13 Or, Heliopolis, or, On.
14 Or, Pubastum.
p Jer. 2.16.
15 Or, restrained.
q Jer. 48.25.
r Jer. 46.11.
s Ps. 37.17.
t 2 Ki. 24.7.
u ch. 29.12.

among the nations, and will disperse them through the countries.

24 And I will strengthen the arms of the king of Babylon, and put my sword in his hand: but I will break Pharaoh's arms, and he shall groan before him with the groanings of a deadly wounded *man*.

25 But I will strengthen the arms of the king of Babylon, and the arms of Pharaoh shall fall down; and [v]they shall know that I *am* the LORD, when I shall put my sword into the hand of the king of Babylon, and he shall stretch it out upon [w]the land of Egypt.

26 And I will scatter the Egyptians among the nations, and disperse them among the countries; and they shall know that I *am* the LORD.

CHAPTER 31

AND it came to pass in the eleventh year, in the third *month*, in the first *day* of the month, *that* the word of the LORD came unto me, saying,

2 Son of man, speak unto Pharaoh king of Egypt, and to his multitude; Whom art thou like in thy greatness?

3 ¶ Behold, [a]the Assyrian *was* a cedar in Lĕb-ă-non [1]with fair branches, and with a shadowing shroud, and of an high stature; and his top was among the thick boughs.

4 The waters [2]made him great, the deep [3]set him up on high with her rivers running round about his plants, and sent out her [4]little rivers unto all the trees of the field.

5 Therefore [b]his height was exalted above all the trees of the field, and his boughs were multiplied, and his branches became long because of the multitude of waters, [5]when he shot forth.

6 All the [c]fowls of heaven made their nests in his boughs, and under his branches did all the beasts of the field bring forth their young, and under his shadow dwelt all great nations.

7 Thus was he fair in his greatness, in the length of his branches: for his root was by great waters.

8 The cedars in the [d]garden of God could not hide him: the fir trees were not like his boughs, and the chesnut trees were not like his branches; nor any tree in the garden of God was like unto him in his beauty.

9 I [e]have made him fair by the multitude of his branches: so that all the trees of Eden, that *were* in the garden of God, envied him.

v Ex. 7.5. Ps. 9.16. Ps. 59.13.
w Jer. 44.30.

CHAP. 31

a Nah. 3.18. Zeph. 2.13.
1 fair of branches.
2 Or, nourished.
3 Or, brought him up.
4 Or, conduits.
b Ps. 37.35, 36. Isa. 10.7-11,13. Dan. 4.11.
5 Or, when it sent them forth.
c ch. 17.23. Dan. 4.12.
d Gen. 2.8.
e Ex. 9.16. Ps. 75.6. Dan. 4.22-24.
f 2 Chr. 25. 19. Job. 40.11, 12. Pro. 16.18. Isa. 14.13-15. ch. 28.17. Dan. 5.20. Jas. 4.6.
6 in doing he shall do unto him.
g ch. 28.7.
h ch. 32.5.
i Isa. 18.6.
7 Or, stand upon themselves for their height.
j Ps. 82.7.
k ch. 32.18.
8 to be black.
l ch. 26.15.
m Isa. 14.15.
n Isa. 14.8.
o ch. 32.31.
p Lam. 4.20.
q ch. 32.19.
r ch. 28.10.
9 That is, an emblem of Pharaoh.

10 ¶ Therefore thus saith the Lor GOD; Because thou hast lifted up thy self in height, and he hath shot u his top among the thick boughs and [f]his heart is lifted up in hi height;

11 I have therefore delivered him in to the hand of the mighty one of th heathen; [6]he shall surely deal wit him: I have driven him out for hi wickedness.

12 And strangers, [g]the terrible of th nations, have cut him off, and hav left him: [h]upon the mountains and i all the valleys his branches are fallen and his boughs are broken by all th rivers of the land; and all the peopl of the earth are gone down from his shadow, and have left him.

13 Upon [i]his ruin shall all the fowls of the heaven remain, and all the beasts of the field shall be upon his branches:

14 To the end that none of all the trees by the waters exalt themselves for their height, neither shoot up their top among the thick boughs, neither their trees [7]stand up in their height, all that drink water: for [j]they are all delivered unto death, [k]to the nether parts of the earth, in the midst of the children of men, with them that go down to the pit.

15 Thus saith the Lord GOD; In the day when he went down to the grave I caused a mourning: I covered the deep for him, and I restrained the floods thereof, and the great waters were stayed: and I caused Lĕb-ă-non [8]to mourn for him, and all the trees of the field fainted for him.

16 I made the nations [l]to shake at the sound of his fall, when [m]I cast him down to hell with them that descend into the pit: and [n]all the trees of Eden, the choice and best of Lĕb-ă-non, all that drink water, shall [o]be comforted in the nether parts of the earth.

17 They also went down into hell with him unto *them that be* slain with the sword; and *they that were* his arm, *that* [p]dwelt under his shadow in the midst of the heathen.

18 ¶ To [q]whom art thou thus like in glory and in greatness among the trees of Eden? yet shalt thou be brought down with the trees of Eden unto the nether parts of the earth: [r]thou shalt lie in the midst of the uncircumcised with *them that be* slain by the sword. This [9]*is* Pharaoh and all his multitude, saith the Lord GOD.

CHAPTER 32

AND it came to pass in the twelfth
year, in the twelfth month, in the
first *day* of the month, *that* the word
of the LORD came unto me, saying,
2 Son of man, [a]take up a lamentation
for Pharaoh king of Egypt, and say
unto him, Thou [b]art like a young lion
of the nations, and thou [c]*art* as a
whale in the seas: and thou camest
forth with thy rivers, and troubledst
the waters with thy feet, and fouledst
[d]their rivers.
3 Thus saith the Lord GOD; I will
therefore [e]spread out my net over
thee with a company of many people;
and they shall bring thee up in my net.
4 Then [f]will I leave thee upon the
land, I will cast thee forth upon the
open field, and [g]will cause all the
fowls of the heaven to remain upon
thee, and I will fill the beasts of the
whole earth with thee.
5 And I will lay thy flesh [h]upon the
mountains, and fill the valleys with
thy height.
6 I will also water with thy blood [2]the
land wherein thou swimmest, *even* to
the mountains; and the rivers shall be
full of thee.
7 And when I shall [3]put thee out, [i]I
will cover the heaven, and make the
stars thereof dark; I will cover the sun
with a cloud, and the moon shall not
give her light.
8 All the [4]bright lights of heaven will
I make [5]dark over thee, and set darkness upon thy land, saith the Lord
GOD.
9 I will also [6]vex the hearts of many
people, when I shall bring thy destruction among the nations, into
the countries which thou hast not
known.
10 Yea, I will make many people
amazed [j]at thee, and their kings shall
be horribly afraid for thee, when I
shall brandish my sword before them;
and [k]they shall tremble at *every* moment, every man for his own life, in
the day of thy fall.
11 ¶ For [l]thus saith the Lord GOD;
The sword of the king of Babylon
shall come upon thee.
12 By the swords of the mighty will I
cause thy multitude to fall, the [m]terri-
ble of the nations, all of them: and
[n]they shall spoil the pomp of Egypt,
and all the multitude thereof shall be
destroyed.
13 I will destroy also all the beasts
thereof from beside the great waters;
[o]neither shall the foot of man trouble
them any more, nor the hoofs of beasts
trouble them.
14 Then will I make their waters
deep, and cause their rivers to run
like oil, saith the Lord GOD.
15 When I shall make the land of
Egypt desolate, and the country shall
be [7]destitute of that whereof it was
full, when I shall smite all them that
dwell therein, [p]then shall they know
that I *am* the LORD.
16 This *is* the [q]lamentation wherewith they shall lament her: the daughters of the nations shall lament her:
they shall lament for her, *even* for
Egypt, and for all her multitude, saith
the Lord GOD.
17 ¶ It came to pass also in the
twelfth year, in the fifteenth *day* of
the month, *that* the word of the LORD
came unto me, saying,
18 Son of man, wail for the multitude
of Egypt, and [r]cast them down, *even*
her, and the daughters of the famous
nations, unto the nether parts of the
earth, with them that go down into
the pit.
19 Whom [s]dost thou pass in beauty?
[t]go down, and be thou laid with the
uncircumcised.
20 They shall fall in the midst of
them that are slain by the sword: [8]she
is delivered to the sword: draw her
and all her multitudes.
21 The [u]strong among the mighty
shall speak to him out of the midst of
hell with them that help him: they
are gone down, they lie uncircumcised, slain by the sword.
22 Ăssh-ŭr *is* there and all her company: his graves *are* about him: all of
them slain, fallen by the sword:
23 Whose [v]graves are set in the sides
of the pit, and her company is round
about her grave: all of them slain,
fallen by the sword, which caused
[9]terror in the land of the living.
24 There *is* [w]Ē-lăm and all her multitude round about her grave, all of
them slain, fallen by the sword, which
are gone down uncircumcised into
the nether parts of the earth, which
caused their terror in the land of
the living; yet have they borne their
shame with them that go down to
the pit.
25 They have set her a [10]bed in the
midst of the slain with all her multitude: her graves *are* round about
him: all of them uncircumcised, slain
by the sword: though their terror was
caused in the land of the living, yet
have they borne their shame with

CHAP. 32
a ch. 27.2.
b ch. 19.3,6.
c ch. 29.3.
1 Or, dragon.
d ch. 34.18.
e ch. 12.13.
f 1 Sam. 17. 44-46. Isa. 14.19. Jer. 8.2. ch. 29.5. ch. 39.4.
g 1 Sam. 17. 44.
h ch. 31.12.
2 Or, the land of thy swimming.
3 Or, extinguish.
i Isa. 13.10. Joel 2.31. Amos 8.9. Matt. 24.29. Rev. 6.12.
4 lights of the light in heaven.
5 them dark.
6 provoke to anger, or, grief.
j ch. 27.35.
k ch. 26.16.
l Jer. 46.26.
m ch. 28.7.
n ch. 29.19.
o ch. 29.11.
7 desolate from the fulness thereof.
p Ex. 7.5. Ps. 9.16. ch. 6.6,7.
q 2 Sam. 1.17. 2 Chr. 35.25. ch. 26.17.
r Jer. 1.10. ch. 26.20.
s ch. 31.2.
t ch. 28.10.
8 Or, the sword is laid.
u Isa. 1.31.
v Isa. 14.15.
9 Or, a dismaying.
w Jer. 49.34.
10 Or, bier.

them that go down to the pit: he is put
in the midst of *them that be* slain.
26 There *is* [x]Mē-shēch, Tū-băl, and
all her multitude: her graves *are* round
about him: all of them uncircumcised,
slain by the sword, though they caused
their terror in the land of the living.
27 And [y]they shall not lie with the
mighty *that are* fallen of the uncircumcised, which are gone down to
hell [11]with their weapons of war: and
they have laid their swords under their
heads, but their iniquities shall be upon their bones, though *they were* the
terror of the mighty in the land of the
living.
28 Yea, thou shalt be broken in the
midst of the uncircumcised, and shalt
lie with *them that are* slain with the
sword.
29 There *is* [z]Ē-dom, her kings, and
all her princes, which with their might
are [12]laid by *them that were* slain by
the sword: they shall lie with the uncircumcised, and with them that go
down to the pit.
30 There [a]*be* the princes of the north,
all of them, and all [b]the Zī-dō-nĭ-ăns,
which are gone down with the slain;
with their terror they are ashamed of
their might; and they lie uncircumcised with *them that be* slain by the
sword, and bear their shame with
them that go down to the pit.
31 Pharaoh shall see them, and shall
be comforted [c]over all his multitude,
even Pharaoh and all his army slain
by the sword, saith the Lord GOD.
32 For I have caused my terror in
the land of the living: and he shall be
laid in the midst of the uncircumcised
with *them that are* slain with the
sword, *even* Pharaoh and all his multitude, saith the Lord GOD.

CHAPTER 33

AGAIN the word of the LORD came
unto me, saying,
2 Son of man, speak to [a]the children
of thy people, and say unto them,
[1]When I bring the sword upon a land,
if the people of the land take a man
of their coasts, and set him for their
[b]watchman:
3 If when he seeth the sword come
upon the land, he blow the trumpet,
and warn the people;
4 Then [2]whosoever heareth the sound
of the trumpet, and taketh not warning; if the sword come, and take him
away, [c]his blood shall be upon his
own head.
5 He heard the sound of the trumpet,

x Gen. 10.2. ch. 27.13.
y Isa. 14.18.
11 with weapons of their war.
z ch. 25.12.
12 given, or, put.
a ch. 38.6,15.
b ch. 28.21.
c ch. 14.22.
CHAP. 33
a ch. 3.11.
1 A land when I bring a sword upon her.
b 2 Sam. 18. 24. Isa. 21.8. Hosea 9.8.
2 he that hearing heareth.
c Lev. 20.9, 11. 2 Sam. 1.16. ch. 18.13. Acts 18.6.
d Isa. 56.10.
e ch. 3.17. Hab. 2.1.
f Pro. 8.36. Isa. 3.11.
g Pro. 29.1. Luke 12.47. Acts 13.46. Heb. 2.2,3.
h ch. 24.23.
i Isa. 49.14.
j 2 Sam. 14. 14. Lam. 3.33. Hosea 11.9. 1 Tim. 2.4.
k Isa. 55.6,7. ch. 18.31.
l ch. 3.20.
m 2 Chr. 7. 14.
n ch. 3.20. Luke 18.9.
3 judgment and justice.
o ch. 18.7.
p Ex. 22.1. Num. 5.6,7. Luke 19.8.
q Lev. 18.5. ch. 20.11. Matt. 19.17.

and took not warning; his blood shal
be upon him. But he that taketh warn
ing shall deliver his soul.
6 But if the watchman see the swor
come, and [d]blow not the trumpet, an
the people be not warned; if th
sword come, and take *any* perso
from among them, he is taken awa
in his iniquity; but his blood will I re
quire at the watchman's hand.
7 ¶ So [e]thou, O son of man, I hav
set thee a watchman unto the house o
Israel; therefore thou shalt hear th
word at my mouth, and warn them
from me.
8 When I say unto the wicked, O
[f]wicked *man*, thou shalt surely die;
if thou dost not speak to warn the
wicked from his way, that wicked *man*
shall die in his iniquity; but his blood
will I require at thine hand.
9 Nevertheless, if thou warn the
wicked of his way to turn from it; if
[g]he do not turn from his way, he shall
die in his iniquity; but thou hast delivered thy soul.
10 Therefore, O thou son of man,
speak unto the house of Israel; Thus
ye speak, saying, If our transgressions and our sins *be* upon us, and we
[h]pine away in them, how should [i]we
then live?
11 Say unto them, *As* I live, saith the
Lord GOD, [j]I have no pleasure in the
death of the wicked; but that the
wicked turn from his way and live:
turn ye, turn ye from your evil ways;
for [k]why will ye die, O house of
Israel?
12 Therefore, thou son of man, say
unto the children of thy people, The
[l]righteousness of the righteous shall
not deliver him in the day of his transgression: as for the wickedness of the
wicked, [m]he shall not fall thereby in
the day that he turneth from his
wickedness; neither shall the righteous be able to live for his *righteousness* in the day that he sinneth.
13 When I shall say to the righteous,
that he shall surely live; [n]if he trust to
his own righteousness, and commit iniquity, all his righteousnesses shall not
be remembered; but for his iniquity
that he hath committed, he shall die
for it.
14 Again, when I say unto the
wicked, Thou shalt surely die; if he
turn from his sin, and do [3]that which
is lawful and right;
15 *If* the wicked [o]restore the pledge,
give [p]again that he had robbed, walk
in the [q]statutes of life, without com-

nitting iniquity; he shall surely live,
ıe shall not die.
16 None [r]of his sins that he hath
ommitted shall be mentioned unto
ım: he hath done that which is law-
ul and right; he shall surely live.
17 ¶ Yet the children of thy people
ay, The way of the Lord is not equal:
ut as for them, their way is not equal.
18 When the righteous turneth from
ıis righteousness, and committeth in-
quity, he shall even die thereby.
19 But if the wicked turn from his
vickedness, and do that which is law-
ul and right, he shall live thereby.
20 ¶ Yet ye say, [s]The way of the
ord is not equal. O ye house of Is-
ael, I will judge you every one after
ıis ways.
21 ¶ And it came to pass in the
welfth year [t]of our captivity, in the
enth *month*, in the fifth *day* of the
nonth, [u]*that* one that had escaped
ut of Jerusalem came unto me, say-
ng, [v]The city is smitten.
22 Now [w]the hand of the LORD was
ıpon me in the evening, afore he that
vas escaped came; and had opened
ny mouth, until he came to me in the
norning; and my mouth was opened,
nd I was no more dumb.
23 Then the word of the LORD came
nto me, saying,
24 Son of man, [x]they that inhabit
hose wastes [y]of the land of Israel
peak, saying, Abraham [z]was one,
nd he inherited the land: [a]but we *are*
nany; the land is given us for in-
eritance.
25 Wherefore say unto them, Thus
aith the Lord GOD; [b]Ye eat with the
lood, and [c]lift up your eyes toward
our idols, [d]and shed blood: and shall
e possess the land?
26 Ye stand upon your sword, ye
vork abomination, and ye defile every
ne his neighbour's wife: and shall ye
ossess the land?
27 Say thou thus unto them, Thus
aith the Lord GOD; *As* I live, surely
hey that *are* in the wastes shall fall by
he sword, and him that *is* in the open
ield [e]will I give to the beasts [4]to be de-
oured, and they that *be* in the forts
nd [f]in the caves shall die of the pesti-
ence.
28 For [g]I will lay the land [5]most deso-
ate, and the [h]pomp of her strength
hall cease; and [i]the mountains of
srael shall be desolate, that none
hall pass through.
29 Then shall they know that I *am*
he LORD, when I have laid the land
most desolate because of all their
abominations which they have committed.
30 ¶ Also, thou son of man, the children of thy people still are talking
[6]against thee by the walls and in the
doors of the houses, and speak [j]one
to another, every one to his brother,
saying, Come, I pray you, and hear
what is the word that cometh forth
from the LORD.
31 And [k]they come unto thee [7]as the
people cometh, and [8]they sit before
thee *as* my people, and they hear thy
words, but they will not do them: for
with their mouth [9]they shew much
love, *but* their heart goeth after their
covetousness.
32 And, lo, thou *art* unto them as [10]a
very lovely song of one that hath a
pleasant voice, and can play well on
an instrument: for [l]they hear thy
words, but they do them not.
33 And when this cometh to pass,
(lo, it will come,) then shall they know
that a prophet hath been among them.

CHAPTER 34

AND the word of the LORD came
unto me, saying,
2 Son of man, prophesy against the
[a]shepherds of Israel, prophesy, and
say unto them, Thus saith the Lord
GOD unto the shepherds; Woe [b]*be* to
the shepherds of Israel that do feed
themselves! should not the shepherds feed the flocks?
3 Ye [c]eat the fat, and ye clothe you
with the wool, [d]ye kill them that are
fed: *but* ye feed not the flock.
4 The [e]diseased have ye not strengthened, neither have ye healed that
which was sick, neither have ye bound
up *that which was* broken, neither
have ye brought again that which was
driven away, neither have ye sought
[f]that which was lost; but with force
[g]and with cruelty have ye ruled them.
5 And they [h]were scattered, [1]because
there is no shepherd: [i]and they became meat to all the beasts of the
field, when they were scattered.
6 My sheep wandered through all
the mountains, and upon every high
hill: yea, my flock was scattered upon
all the face of the earth, and none did
search or seek *after them*.
7 ¶ Therefore, ye shepherds, hear
the word of the LORD;
8 *As* I live, saith the Lord GOD, surely
because my flock became a prey, and
my flock became meat to every beast
of the field, because *there was* no

r ch. 18.22.
s ch. 18.25.
t ch. 1.2.
u ch. 24.26.
v 2 Ki. 25.4.
w ch. 1.3. ch. 3.22.
x ch. 34.2.
y ch. 36.4.
z Isa. 51.2. Acts 7.5.
a Micah 3.11. Matt. 3.9. John 8.39.
b Gen. 9.4.
c ch. 18.6.
d ch. 22.6.
e ch. 39.4.
4 to devour him.
f Judg. 6.2.
g 2 Chr. 36. 21. Isa. 6.11. Jer. 9.11. ch. 36.34.
5 desolation and desolation.
h ch. 24.21.
i ch. 6.2,3.
6 Or, of thee.
j Isa. 29.13.
k ch. 20.1.
7 according to the coming of the people.
8 Or, my people sit before thee.
9 they make loves, or, jests.
10 a song of loves.
l Jas. 1.22.

CHAP. 34

a ch. 33.24.
b Jer. 23.1.
c Isa. 56.11.
d Micah 3.3.
e Zech. 11.16. 2 Tim. 2.24.
f Luke 15.4.
g 1 Pet. 5.3.
h Matt. 9.36.
1 Or, without a shepherd.
i Isa. 56.9.

shepherd, neither did my shepherds
search for my flock, but the shepherds fed themselves, and fed not my
flock;
9 Therefore, O ye shepherds, hear
the word of the LORD;
10 Thus saith the Lord GOD; Behold, I *am* against the shepherds; and
[j]I will require my flock at their hand,
and cause them to cease from feeding
the flock; neither shall the shepherds
feed themselves any more; for I will
deliver my flock from their mouth,
that they may not be meat for them.
11 ¶ For thus saith the Lord GOD;
Behold, I, *even* I, will both search my
sheep, and seek them out.
12 [2]As a shepherd seeketh out his
flock in the day that he is among his
sheep *that are* scattered; so will I seek
out my sheep, and will deliver them
out of all places where they have been
scattered in [k]the cloudy and dark day.
13 And [l]I will bring them out from
the people, and gather them from the
countries, and will bring them to their
own land, and feed them upon the
mountains of Israel by the rivers, and
in all the inhabited places of the
country.
14 I [m]will feed them in a good pasture, and upon the high mountains of
Israel shall their fold be: there [n]shall
they lie in a good fold, and *in* a fat
pasture shall they feed upon the
mountains of Israel.
15 I will feed my flock, and I will
cause them to lie down, saith the
Lord GOD.
16 I [o]will seek that which was lost,
and bring again that which was driven
away, and will bind up *that which was*
broken, and will strengthen that
which was sick: but I will destroy the
fat and the strong; I will feed them
with judgment.
17 And *as for* you, O my flock, thus
saith the Lord GOD; [p]Behold, I judge
between [3]cattle and cattle, between
the rams and the [4]he goats.
18 *Seemeth it* a small thing unto you
to have eaten up the good pasture, but
[q]ye must tread down with your feet
the residue of your pastures? and to
have drunk of the deep waters, but ye
must foul the residue with your
feet?
19 And *as for* my flock, they eat that
which ye have trodden with your feet;
and they drink that which ye have
fouled with your feet.
20 ¶ Therefore thus saith the Lord
GOD unto them; Behold, I, *even* I,

j ch. 3.18. ch. 33.6-8. Heb. 13.17.
2 According to the seeking.
k Jer. 13.16. ch. 30.3. Joel 2.2. Zeph. 1.15. Acts 2.19-21.
l Isa. 65.9,10. Jer. 23.3. ch. 36.24.
m Ps. 23.2. Ps. 34.8,10. Isa. 25.6. Isa. 30.23, 24. Jer. 31.12-14,25. John 10.9.
n Jer. 33.12.
o Isa. 40.11. Isa. 61.1-3. Micah 4.6,7. Matt. 15.24. Mark 2.17.
p ch. 20.37. Zech. 10.3. Matt. 25.32.
3 small cattle of lambs and kids.
4 great he goats.
q Matt. 23. 13.
r Isa. 40.11. John 10.11. Heb. 13.20.
s Jer. 30.9. ch. 37.24.
t Gen. 17.7. Ex. 29.45.
u Luke 1.32.
v Lev. 26.6. Isa. 11.6.
w Jer. 23.6.
x Isa. 56.7.
y Gen. 12.2.
z Lev. 26.4.
a Ps. 68.9. Mal. 3.10.
b Ps. 85.12.
c Jer. 2.20.
d Jer. 25.14.
e ch. 36.4.
5 Or, for renown.
6 taken away.
f 2 Tim. 1.12.
g Ps. 100.3.

CHAP. 35

a Amos 1.11. Obad. 10.
1 desolation and desolation.

will judge between the fat cattle an
between the lean cattle.
21 Because ye have thrust with sid
and with shoulder, and pushed all th
diseased with your horns, till ye hav
scattered them abroad;
22 Therefore will I save my flock
and they shall no more be a prey; an
I will judge between cattle and cattle
23 And I will set up one [r]shepher
over them, and he shall feed them
[s]*even* my servant David; he shall fee
them, and he shall be their shepherd
24 And [t]I the LORD will be their God
and my servant David [u]a princ
among them; I the LORD have spoke
it.
25 And I will make with them a cov
enant of peace, and [v]will cause th
evil beasts to cease out of the land
and they [w]shall dwell safely in th
wilderness, and sleep in the woods.
26 And I will make them and th
places round about [x]my hill [y]a bless
ing; and I will [z]cause the shower t
come down in his season; there shal
be [a]showers of blessing.
27 And [b]the tree of the field shal
yield her fruit, and the earth shall yiel
her increase, and they shall be safe i
their land, and shall know that I *an*
the LORD, when I have [c]broken th
bands of their yoke, and delivere
them out of the hand of those tha
[d]served themselves of them.
28 And they shall no more [e]be a prey
to the heathen, neither shall the beas
of the land devour them; but the
shall dwell safely, and none shal
make *them* afraid.
29 And I will raise up for them a
plant [5]of renown, and they shall be n
more [6]consumed with hunger in th
land, neither bear the shame of th
heathen any more.
30 Thus shall they [f]know that I th
LORD their God *am* with them, an
that they, *even* the house of Israel, *ar*
my people, saith the Lord GOD.
31 And ye my [g]flock, the flock of m
pasture, *are* men, *and* I *am* your God
saith the Lord GOD.

CHAPTER 35

MOREOVER the word of th
LORD came unto me, saying,
2 Son of man, set thy face agains
mount Sē-īr, and [a]prophesy against it
3 And say unto it, Thus saith th
Lord GOD; Behold, O mount Sē-īr, I
am against thee, and I will stretch ou
mine hand against thee, and I wil
make thee [1]most desolate.

4 I will lay thy cities waste, and thou
halt be desolate, and thou shalt know
hat I *am* the LORD.
5 Because thou hast had a [2]perpetual
atred, and hast [3]shed *the blood of*
he children of Israel by the [4]force of
he sword in the time of their calamity,
in the time *that their* iniquity *had* an
nd:
6 Therefore, *as* I live, saith the Lord
GOD, I will prepare thee unto blood,
nd blood shall pursue thee: [c]sith
hou hast not hated blood, even blood
hall pursue thee.
7 Thus will I make mount Sē-ĭr
most desolate, and cut off from it him
hat passeth out and him that returneth.
8 And I will fill his mountains with
his slain *men:* in thy hills, and in thy
valleys, and in all thy rivers, shall they
fall that are slain with the sword.
9 I [d]will make thee perpetual desolations, and thy cities shall not return:
and ye shall know that I *am* the LORD.
10 Because thou hast said, [e]These
two nations and these two countries
shall be mine, and we will possess it;
[6]whereas the LORD was there:
11 Therefore, *as* I live, saith the
Lord GOD, I will even do [f]according
to thine anger, and according to thine
envy which thou hast used out of thy
hatred against them; and I will make
myself known [g]among them, when I
have judged thee.
12 And [h]thou shalt know that I *am*
the LORD, *and that* I have heard all thy
blasphemies which thou hast spoken
against the mountains of Israel, saying, They are laid desolate, they are
given us [7]to consume.
13 Thus with your mouth ye have
[8]boasted against me, and have multiplied your words against me: I have
heard *them*.
14 Thus saith the Lord GOD; When
[i]the whole earth rejoiceth, I will make
thee desolate.
15 As [j]thou didst rejoice at the inheritance of the house of Israel, because it was desolate, so will I do unto
thee: thou shalt be desolate, O mount
Sē-ĭr, and all Ī-dū-mē-ă, *even* all of it:
and they shall know that I *am* the
LORD.

CHAPTER 36

ALSO, thou son of man, prophesy
unto the mountains of Israel, and
say, Ye mountains of Israel, hear the
word of the LORD:
2 Thus saith the Lord GOD; Because
the enemy hath said against you, Aha,
[a]even the ancient high places are ours
in possession:
3 Therefore prophesy and say, Thus
saith the Lord GOD; [1]Because they
have made *you* desolate, and swallowed you up on every side, that ye
might be a possession unto the residue
of the heathen, and [2]ye are taken up in
the lips of talkers, and *are* an infamy
of the people:
4 Therefore, ye mountains of Israel,
hear the word of the Lord GOD; Thus
saith the Lord GOD to the mountains,
and to the hills, to the [3]rivers, and to
the valleys, to the desolate wastes, and
to the cities that are forsaken, which
became a prey [b]and derision to the
residue of the heathen that *are* round
about;
5 Therefore thus saith the Lord GOD;
Surely [c]in the fire of my jealousy have
I spoken against the residue of the
heathen, and against all Ī-dū-mē-ă,
[d]which have appointed my land into
their possession with the joy of all
their heart, with despiteful minds, to
cast it out for a prey.
6 Prophesy therefore concerning the
land of Israel, and say unto the mountains, and to the hills, to the rivers,
and to the valleys, Thus saith the Lord
GOD; Behold, I have spoken in my
jealousy and in my fury, because ye
have [e]borne the shame of the heathen:
7 Therefore thus saith the Lord GOD;
I have [f]lifted up mine hand, Surely the
heathen that *are* about you, they shall
bear their shame.
8 ¶ But ye, O mountains of Israel, ye
shall shoot forth your branches, and
yield your fruit to my people of Israel;
for they are at hand to come.
9 For, behold, I *am* for you, [g]and I
will turn unto you, and ye shall be tilled and sown:
10 And I will multiply men upon
you, all the house of Israel, *even* all of
it: and the cities shall be inhabited
and [h]the wastes shall be builded:
11 And [i]I will multiply upon you man
and beast; and they shall increase
and bring fruit: and I will settle you
after your old estates, and will do
better *unto you* than at your beginnings: [j]and ye shall know that I *am*
the LORD.
12 Yea, I will cause men to walk upon you, *even* my people Israel; and
[k]they shall possess thee, and thou
shalt be their inheritance, and thou
shalt no more henceforth [l]bereave
them *of men*.
13 Thus saith the Lord GOD; Be-

2 Or, hatred of old.
3 poured out the children.
4 hands.
b Ps. 137.7.
c Ps. 109. 17.
5 desolation and desolation.
d Jer. 49.17. Mal. 1.3,4.
e Ps. 83.4.
6 Or, though the LORD was there.
f Ps. 137.7. Matt. 7.2.
g Isa. 26.9.
h Ps. 9.16.
7 to devour.
8 magnified.
i Isa. 14.7,8.
j Pro. 17.5. Obad. 12.

CHAP. 36

a Deut. 32. 13. Ps. 78.69. Isa. 58.14. Hab. 3.19.
1 Because for because.
2 Or, ye are made to come upon the lip of the tongue.
3 Or, bottoms, or, dales.
b Ps. 79.4.
c Deut. 4.24. Isa. 66.15, 16. *ch.* 38.19. Zech. 1.15.
d ch. 35.10.
e Ps. 123.3,4. ch. 34.29.
f ch. 20.5.
g Hosea 2.21, 22,23. Hag. 2.19.
h Isa. 58.12. Isa. 61.4. Amos 9.14.
i Jer. 31.27. Jer. 33.12.
j ch. 35.9. Hosea 2.20. Joel 3.17. 1 John 5.20.
k Obad. 17.
l Jer. 15.7.

cause they say unto you, [m]Thou *land*
devourest up men, and hast bereaved
thy nations;
14 Therefore thou shalt devour men
no more, neither [4]bereave thy nations
any more, saith the Lord GOD.
15 Neither [n]will I cause *men* to hear
in thee the shame of the heathen any
more, neither shalt thou bear the reproach of the people any more, neither shalt thou cause thy nations to fall
any more, saith the Lord GOD.
16 ¶ Moreover the word of the LORD
came unto me, saying,
17 Son of man, when the house of
Israel dwelt in their own land, they
[o]defiled it by their own way and by
their doings: their way was before me
as [p]the uncleanness of a removed
woman.
18 Wherefore I poured my fury upon
them [q]for the blood that they had shed
upon the land, and for their [5]idols
wherewith they had polluted it:
19 And I [r]scattered them among the
heathen, and they were dispersed
through the countries: [s]according to
their way and according to their doings I judged them.
20 And when they entered unto the
heathen, whither they went, they [t]pro-
faned my holy name, when they said
to them, These *are* the people of the
LORD, and are gone forth out of his
land.
21 ¶ But I had pity [u]for mine holy
name, which the house of Israel had
profaned among the heathen, whither
they went.
22 Therefore say unto the house of
Israel, Thus saith the Lord GOD; I do
not *this* for your sakes, O house of Israel, [v]but for mine holy name's sake,
which ye have profaned among the
heathen, whither ye went.
23 And I will sanctify my great name,
which was profaned among the
heathen, which ye have profaned in
the midst of them; and the heathen
shall know that I *am* the LORD, saith
the Lord GOD, when I shall be [w]sancti-
fied in you before [6]their eyes.
24 For [x]I will take you from among
the heathen, and gather you out of all
countries, and will bring you into
your own land.
25 ¶ Then [y]will I sprinkle clean water
upon you, and ye shall be clean: [z]from
all your filthiness, and from all your
idols, will I cleanse you.
26 A [a]new heart also will I give you,
and a new spirit will I put within you:
and I will take away the stony heart
out of your flesh, and I will give you
an heart of flesh.
27 And I will put my [b]spirit within
you, and cause you to walk in my
statutes, and ye shall keep my judgments, and do *them*.
28 And [c]ye shall dwell in the land
that I gave to your fathers; and [d]ye
shall be my people, and I will be your
God.
29 I will also [e]save you from all your
uncleannesses: and [f]I will call for the
corn, and will increase it, and lay no
famine upon you.
30 And [g]I will multiply the fruit of
the tree, and the increase of the field,
that ye shall receive no more reproach
of famine among the heathen.
31 Then [h]shall ye remember your
own evil ways, and your doings that
were not good, and [i]shall lothe yourselves in your own sight for your iniquities and for your abominations.
32 Not [j]for your sakes do I *this*, saith
the Lord GOD, be it known unto you:
be ashamed and confounded for your
own ways, O house of Israel.
33 Thus saith the Lord GOD; In the
day that I shall have cleansed you
from all your iniquities I [k]will also
cause *you* to dwell in the cities, and
the wastes shall be builded.
34 And [l]the desolate land shall be
tilled, whereas it lay desolate in the
sight of all that passed by.
35 And they shall say, This land that
was desolate is become like the garden
[m]of Eden; and the waste and desolate
and ruined cities *are become* fenced,
and are inhabited.
36 Then the heathen that are left
round about you shall [n]know that I
the LORD build the ruined *places, and*
plant that that was desolate: [o]I the
LORD have spoken *it*, and I will do *it*.
37 Thus saith the Lord GOD; [p]I will
yet *for* this be inquired of by the
house of Israel, to do *it* for them; I
will increase them with men like a
flock.
38 As the [7]holy flock, as the flock of
Jerusalem in her solemn feasts; so
shall the waste cities be filled with
flocks of men: and they shall know
that I *am* the LORD.

CHAPTER 37

THE hand of the LORD was upon
me, and carried me out [a]in the
spirit of the LORD, and set me down
in the midst of the valley which *was*
full of bones,
2 And caused me to pass by them

m Num. 13. 32.
4 Or, cause to fall.
n Isa. 60.14. ch. 34.29. Zeph. 3.19, 20.
o Jer. 2.7.
p Lev. 15.19.
q ch. 16.36.
5 dung gods.
r ch. 22.15.
s ch. 7.3.
t Isa. 52.5. Rom. 2.24.
u ch. 20.9.
v Deut. 9.5. Ps. 106.8.
w ch. 20.41.
6 Or, your.
x ch. 34.13.
y Num. 19. 13. Isa. 52.15.
z Jer. 33.8. 1 John 1.7.
a Ps. 51.10. John 3.3-5. 2 Cor. 3.18.
b Isa. 44.3. ch. 37.14. Rom. 8.4,9. Gal. 5.5. Eph. 1.13.
c ch. 28.25.
d Jer. 30.22.
e Matt. 1.21.
f Ps. 105.16.
g ch. 34.27.
h ch. 6.9.
i Lev. 26.39. ch. 6.9.
j Deut. 9.5. Dan. 9.19.
k Rom. 8.30, 31,32.
l Jer. 25.9.
m Isa. 51.3.
n Ps. 58.11. ch. 17.24.
o ch. 17.24. ch. 22.14.
p Ps. 102.17. Isa. 45.11, 19. Jer. 29.11-13. ch. 14.3. Zech. 13.9. Matt. 7.7,8. Phil. 4.6. Jas. 4.3.
7 flock of holy things.

CHAP. 37

a ch. 3.14. Luke 4.1.

ound about: and, behold, *there were*
ery many in the open [1]valley; and,
o, *they were* very dry.
3 And he said unto me, Son of man,
an these bones live? And I answer-
d, O Lord GOD, [b]thou knowest.
4 Again he said unto me, [c]Prophesy
upon these bones, and say unto them,
) ye dry bones, hear the word of the
ORD.
5 Thus saith the Lord GOD unto
hese bones; Behold, I will [d]cause
reath to enter into you, and ye shall
ive:
6 And I will lay sinews upon you,
nd will bring up flesh upon you, and
over you with skin, and put breath
n you, and ye shall live; and [e]ye shall
now that I *am* the LORD.
7 So I prophesied as I was com-
nanded: and as I prophesied, there
vas a noise, and behold a shaking,
nd the bones came together, bone to
is bone.
8 And when I beheld, lo, the sinews
nd the flesh came up upon them, and
he skin covered them above: but
here was no breath in them.
9 Then said he unto me, Prophesy
unto the [2]wind, prophesy, son of man,
nd say to the wind, Thus saith the
Lord GOD; Come [f]from the four
winds, O breath, and breathe upon
hese slain, that they may live.
10 So I prophesied as he commanded
me, and [g]the breath came into them,
nd they lived, and stood up upon
heir feet, an exceeding great army.
11 ¶ Then he said unto me, Son of
man, these bones are the whole house
of Israel: behold, they say, Our [h]bones
are dried, and our hope is lost: we are
cut off for our parts.
12 Therefore prophesy and say unto
them, Thus saith the Lord GOD; Behold, [i]O my people, I will open your
graves, and cause you to come up out
of your graves, and bring [j]you into
the land of Israel.
13 And ye shall know that I *am* the
LORD, when I have opened your
graves, O my people, and brought
you up out of your graves,
14 And [k]shall put my spirit in you,
and ye shall live, and I shall place you
in your own land: then shall ye know
that I the LORD have spoken *it*, and
performed *it*, saith the LORD.
15 ¶ The word of the LORD came
again unto me, saying,
16 Moreover, thou son of man, take
[l]thee one stick, and write upon it,
For Judah, and for [m]the children of

1 champaign.
b 1 Sam. 2.6. Rom. 4.17. 2 Cor. 1.9.
c Isa. 55.11. Rom. 10.17.
d Ps. 104.30.
e ch. 6.7. Joel 2.27.
2 Or, breath.
f Ps. 104.30.
g Rev. 11.11.
h Ps. 141.7. Isa. 49.14.
i Isa. 26.19. Hosea 1.11.
j Ezra. 1.1. ch. 36.24. Amos 9.14.
k ch. 36.27.
l Num. 17.2.
m 2 Chr. 11. 12,13,16.
n ch. 12.9.
o Zech. 10.6.
p ch. 12.3.
q ch. 36.24.
r Isa. 11.13. Jer. 3.18. Hosea 1.11.
s Gen. 49.10. Jer. 23.5,6. ch. 34.23. John 10.16.
t Isa. 2.18. ch. 20.43. ch. 36.25. Hosea 14.8. Zech. 13.1, 2.
u ch. 36.28, 29.
v Isa. 40.11. Jer. 23.5. ch. 34.23, 24. Hosea 3.5. Luke 1.32.
w Ps. 78.71, 72. Zech. 13.7. John 10.16. 1 Pet. 5.4.
x Isa. 60.21. Amos 9.15.
y John 12.34.
z Ps. 89.3. Isa. 55.3. Jer. 32.40. ch. 34.25.
a 2 Cor. 6.16.
b Lev. 26.11. John 1.14.

Israel his companions: then take
another stick, and write upon it,
For Joseph, the stick of Ē'-phră-ĭm,
and *for* all the house of Israel his
companions:
17 And join them one to another into
one stick; and they shall become one
in thine hand.
18 ¶ And when the children of thy
people shall speak unto thee, saying,
[n]Wilt thou not shew us what thou
meanest by these?
19 Say [o]unto them, Thus saith the
Lord GOD; Behold, I will take the
stick of Joseph, which *is* in the hand
of Ē'-phră-ĭm, and the tribes of Israel
his fellows, and will put them with
him, *even* with the stick of Judah, and
make them one stick, and they shall
be one in mine hand.
20 ¶ And the sticks whereon thou
writest shall be in thine hand before
[p]their eyes.
21 And say unto them, Thus saith
the Lord GOD; Behold, [q]I will take the
children of Israel from among the
heathen, whither they be gone, and
will gather them on every side, and
bring them into their own land:
22 And [r]I will make them one nation
in the land upon the mountains of Israel; and one king shall [s]be king to
them all: and they shall be no more
two nations, neither shall they be
divided into two kingdoms any more
at all:
23 Neither [t]shall they defile themselves any more with their idols, nor
with their detestable things, nor with
any of their transgressions: but [u]I will
save them out of all their dwellingplaces, wherein they have sinned, and
will cleanse them: so shall they be my
people, and I will be their God.
24 And [v]David my servant *shall be*
king over them; and [w]they all shall
have one shepherd: they shall also
walk in my judgments, and observe
my statutes, and do them.
25 And they shall dwell in the land
that I have given unto Jacob my servant, wherein your fathers have dwelt;
and they shall dwell therein, *even* they,
and their children, and their children's
children [x]for ever: and [y]my servant
David *shall be* their prince for ever.
26 Moreover I will make a [z]covenant
of peace with them; it shall be an
everlasting covenant with them: and
I will place them, and multiply them,
and will set my sanctuary [a]in the midst
of them for evermore.
27 My [b]tabernacle also shall be with

them: yea, I will be their God, and
they shall be my people.
28 And the heathen shall know that
I the LORD do sanctify Israel, when
my sanctuary shall be in the midst of
them for evermore.

CHAPTER 38

AND the word of the LORD came
unto me, saying,
2 Son of man, set thy face against
[a]Gog, the land of Mā-gŏg, [1]the chief
prince of Mē-shĕch [b]and Tū-băl, and
prophesy against him,
3 And say, Thus saith the Lord GOD;
Behold, I *am* against thee, O Gog, the
chief prince of Mē-shĕch and Tū-băl:
4 And [c]I will turn thee back, and put
hooks into thy jaws, and I will bring
thee forth, and all thine army, horses
and horsemen, all [d]of them clothed
with all sorts *of armour*, *even* a great
company *with* bucklers and shields,
all of them handling swords:
5 Persia, Ē-thĭ-ō-pĭ-ă, and [2]Lĭb-ỹ-ă
with them; all of them with shield and
helmet:
6 Gō-mĕr, [e]and all his bands; the
house of Tō-gär-măh [f]of the north
quarters, and all his bands: *and* many
people with thee.
7 Be [g]thou prepared, and prepare for
thyself, thou, and all thy company
that are assembled unto thee, and be
thou a guard unto them.
8 ¶ After [h]many days [i]thou shalt be
visited: in the latter years thou shalt
come into the land *that is* brought
back from the sword, *and is* [j]gathered
out of many people, against [k]the
mountains of Israel, which have been
always waste: but it is brought forth
out of the nations, and they shall
[l]dwell safely all of them.
9 Thou shalt ascend and [m]come like
a storm, thou shalt be [n]like a cloud to
cover the land, thou, and all thy
bands, and many people with thee.
10 Thus saith the Lord GOD; It shall
also come to pass, *that* at the same
time shall things come into thy mind,
and thou shalt [3]think an evil thought:
11 And thou shalt say, I will go up
to the land of unwalled villages; I will
[o]go to them that are at rest, that dwell
[4]safely, all of them dwelling without
walls, and having neither bars nor
gates,
12 [5]To take a spoil, and to take a
prey; to turn thine hand upon the
desolate places *that are now* inhabited,
and upon the people *that are* gathered
out of the nations, which have gotten

CHAP. 38

a Rev. 20.8.
1 Or, prince of the chief.
b ch. 32.26.
c ch. 29.4.
d ch. 23.12.
2 Or, Phut.
e Gen. 10.2.
f ch. 27.14.
g Isa. 8.9.
h Deut. 4.30.
i Isa. 29.6.
j ch. 34.13.
k ch. 36.1.
l Jer. 23.6.
m Isa. 28.2.
n Jer. 4.13.
3 Or, conceive a mischievous purpose.
o Judg. 18.7-27.
4 Or, confidently.
5 To spoil the spoil, and to prey the prey.
6 navel.
p ch.27.22.
q ch. 19.3,5.
r Isa. 4.1.
s ch. 39.2.
t Ex. 14.4.
7 by the hands.
u Deut. 29.20. Isa. 42.13. ch. 36.5,6. Joel 2.18.
v Ps. 89.46.
w Hag. 2.6,7.
x Hosea 4.3.
y Jer. 4.24.
8 Or, towers, or, stairs.
z Ps. 105.16.
a Hosea 9.3.
b Judg. 7.22. 1 Sam. 14.20.

cattle and goods, that dwell in th
[6]midst of the land.
13 Shē-bă, [p]and Dē-dăn, and th
merchants of Tarshish, with [q]all th
young lions thereof, shall say unt
thee, Art thou come to take a spoil
hast thou gathered thy company t
take a prey? to carry away silver an
gold, to take away cattle and goods
to take a great spoil?
14 ¶ Therefore, son of man, prophes
and say unto Gog, Thus saith th
Lord GOD; In [r]that day when my peo
ple of Israel dwelleth safely, shalt tho
not know *it?*
15 And [s]thou shalt come from th
place out of the north parts, thou, an
many people with thee, all of then
riding upon horses, a great company
and a mighty army:
16 And thou shalt come up agains
my people of Israel, as a cloud to cov
er the land; it shall be in the latte
days, and I will bring thee against m
land, [t]that the heathen may know me
when I shall be sanctified in thee, O
Gog, before their eyes.
17 Thus saith the Lord GOD; *Ar*
thou he of whom I have spoken in ol
time [7]by my servants the prophets o
Israel, which prophesied in thos
days *many* years that I would brin
thee against them?
18 And it shall come to pass at th
same time when Gog shall com
against the land of Israel, saith th
Lord GOD, *that* my fury shall com
up in my face.
19 For [u]in my jealousy *and* [v]in the
fire of my wrath have I spoken,
Surely [w]in that day there shall be a
great shaking in the land of Israel;
20 So that [x]the fishes of the sea, and
the fowls of the heaven, and the beasts
of the field, and all creeping things
that creep upon the earth, and all the
men that *are* upon the face of the
earth, shall shake at my presence, and
[y]the mountains shall be thrown down,
and the [8]steep places shall fall, and
every wall shall fall to the ground.
21 And I will [z]call for a sword against
him throughout all [a]my mountains,
saith the Lord GOD: every [b]man's
sword shall be against his brother.
22 And I will plead against him with
pestilence and with blood; and I will
rain upon him, and upon his bands,
and upon the many people that *are*
with him, an overflowing rain, and
great hailstones, fire, and brimstone.
23 Thus will I magnify myself, and
sanctify myself; and I will be known

in the eyes of many nations, and they shall know that I *am* the LORD.

CHAPTER 39

THEREFORE, [a]thou son of man, prophesy against Gog, and say, Thus saith the Lord GOD; Behold, I *am* against thee, O Gog, the chief prince of Mē-shĕch and Tū-băl:

2 And I will turn thee back, and [1]leave but the sixth part of thee, [2]and will cause thee to come up from [3]the north parts, and will bring thee upon the mountains of Israel:

3 And I will smite thy bow out of thy left hand, and will cause thine arrows to fall out of thy right hand.

4 Thou shalt fall upon the mountains of Israel, thou, and all thy bands, and the people that *is* with thee: [b]I will give thee unto the ravenous birds of every [4]sort, and *to* the beasts of the field [5]to be devoured.

5 Thou shalt fall upon [6]the open field: for I have spoken *it*, saith the Lord GOD.

6 And [c]I will send a fire on Mā-gŏg, and among them that dwell [7]carelessly in [d]the isles: and they shall know that I *am* the LORD.

7 So will I make my holy name known in the midst of my people Israel; and I will not *let them* [e]pollute my holy name any more: [f]and the heathen shall know that I *am* the LORD, the Holy One in Israel.

8 ¶ Behold, [g]it is come, and it is done, saith the Lord GOD; this *is* the day whereof [h]I have spoken.

9 And they that dwell in the cities of Israel shall go forth, and shall set on fire and burn the weapons, both the shields and the bucklers, the bows and the arrows, and the [8]handstaves, and the spears, and they shall [9]burn them with fire seven years:

10 So that they shall take no wood out of the field, neither cut down *any* out of the forests; for they shall burn the weapons with fire: [i]and they shall spoil those that spoiled them, and rob those that robbed them, saith the Lord GOD.

11 ¶ And it shall come to pass in that day, *that* I will give unto Gog a place there of graves in Israel, the valley of the passengers on the east of the sea: and it shall stop the [10]*noses* of the passengers: and there shall they bury Gog and all his multitude: and they shall call *it* The valley of [11]Hā-mŏn–gŏg.

12 And seven months shall the house of Israel be burying of them, that [j]they may cleanse the land.

13 Yea, all the people of the land shall bury *them;* and it shall be to them [12]a renown the day that I [k]shall be glorified, saith the Lord GOD.

14 And they shall sever out [13]men of continual employment, passing through the land to bury with the passengers those that remain upon the face of the earth, to cleanse it: after the end of seven months shall they search.

15 And the passengers *that* pass through the land, when *any* seeth a man's bone, then shall he [14]set up a sign by it, till the buriers have buried it in the valley of Hā-mŏn–gŏg.

16 And also the name of the city *shall be* [15]Hă-mō-nāh. Thus shall they cleanse the land.

17 ¶ And, thou son of man, thus saith the Lord GOD; Speak [16]unto every feathered fowl, and to every beast of the field, Assemble [l]yourselves, and come; gather yourselves on every side to my [17]sacrifice that I do sacrifice for you, *even* a great sacrifice upon the mountains of Israel, that ye may eat flesh, and drink blood.

18 Ye [m]shall eat the flesh of the mighty, and drink the blood of the princes of the earth, of rams, of lambs, and of [18]goats, of bullocks, all of them [n]fatlings of Bā-shăn.

19 And ye shall eat fat till ye be full, and drink blood till ye be drunken, of my sacrifice which I have sacrificed for you.

20 Thus [o]ye shall be filled at my table with horses and chariots, with [p]mighty men, and with all [19]men of war, saith the Lord GOD.

21 And [q]I will set my glory among the heathen, and all the heathen shall see my judgment that I have executed, and [r]my hand that I have laid upon them.

22 So the house of Israel shall know that I *am* the LORD their God from that day and forward.

23 ¶ And the heathen shall know that the house of Israel went into captivity for their iniquity: because they trespassed against me, therefore [s]hid I my face from them, and [t]gave them into the hand of their enemies: so fell they all by the sword.

24 According [u]to their uncleanness and according to their transgressions have I done unto them, and hid my face from them.

25 Therefore thus saith the Lord

CHAP. 39
a ch. 38.2.
1 Or, strike thee with six plagues, or, draw thee back with an hook of six teeth.
2 Or, after I have caused and have brought.
3 the sides of the north.
b Isa. 34.2-8. Jer. 15.3. ch. 32.4,5. Rev. 19.17-21.
4 wing.
5 to devour.
6 the face of the field.
c Amos 1.4.
7 Or, confidently.
d Ps. 72.10.
e Lev. 18.21.
f ch. 38.16.
g ch. 7.3-8.
h ch. 38.17.
8 Or, javelins.
9 Or, make a fire of them, or, use them for fuel.
i Isa. 14.2.
10 Or, mouths.
11 That is, The multitude of Gog.
j Deut. 21.23.
12 Or, a day of renown.
k Ps. 126.2.
13 men of continuance.
14 build.
15 That is, The multitude.
16 to the fowl of every wing.
l Isa. 18.6.
17 Or, slaughter.
m ch. 29.4.
18 great goats.
n Deut. 32.14. Ps. 22.12.
o Ps. 76.6. ch. 38.4.
p Rev. 19.18.
19 champions of war.
q Ex. 9.16. Isa. 26.11. ch. 36.23. Mal. 1.11.
r Ex. 7.4.
s Deut. 31.17.
t Lev. 26.25.
u ch. 36.19.

GOD; Now [v]will I bring again the
captivity of Jacob, and have mercy upon the [w]whole house of Israel, and
will be jealous for my holy name;
26 After [x]that they have borne their
shame, and all their trespasses whereby they have trespassed against me,
when [y]they dwelt safely in their land,
and none made *them* afraid.
27 When [z]I have brought them again
from the people, and gathered them
out of their enemies' lands, and [a]am
sanctified in them in the sight of many
nations;
28 Then [b]shall they know that I *am*
the LORD their God, [20]which caused
them to be led into captivity among
the heathen: but I have gathered
them unto their own land, and have
left none of them any more there.
29 Neither [c]will I hide my face any
more from them: for I [d]have poured
out my spirit upon the house of Israel,
saith the Lord GOD.

CHAPTER 40

IN the five and twentieth year of our
captivity, in the beginning of the
year, in the tenth *day* of the month,
in the fourteenth year after that [a]the
city was smitten, in the selfsame day
[b]the hand of the LORD was upon me,
and brought me thither.
2 In [c]the visions of God brought he
me into the land of Israel, [d]and set me
upon a very high mountain, [1]by which
was as the frame of a city on the south.
3 And he brought me thither, and,
behold, *there was* a man, whose
appearance *was* like [e]the appearance
of brass, [f]with a line of flax in his
hand, [g]and a measuring reed; and he
stood in the gate.
4 And the man said unto me, Son [h]of
man, behold with thine eyes, and
hear with thine ears, and set thine
heart upon all that I shall shew thee;
for to the intent that I might shew *them*
unto thee *art* thou brought hither:
[i]declare all that thou seest to the
house of Israel.
5 And behold [j]a wall on the outside
of the house round about, and in the
man's hand a measuring reed of six
cubits *long* by the cubit and an hand
breadth: so he measured the breadth
of the building, one reed; and the
height, one reed.
6 ¶ Then came he unto the gate
[2]which looketh toward the east, and
went up the stairs thereof, and measured the threshold of the gate, *which*
was one reed broad; and the other

v Jer. 30.3.
w Hosea 1.11.
x Dan. 9.16.
y Lev. 26.5.
z ch. 28.25.
a ch. 36.23.
b ch. 34.30. Hosea 2.20.
20 by my causing of them, etc.
c Isa. 54.8.
d Joel 2.28.

CHAP. 40

a ch. 33.21.
b ch. 1.3.
c ch. 8.3.
d Rev. 21.10.
1 Or, upon which.
e Dan. 10.6.
f ch. 47.3.
g Rev. 11.1.
h ch. 2.7,8. ch. 3.17.
i ch. 43.10.
j Isa. 26.1.
2 whose face was the way toward the east.
k 1 Chr. 9.18.
l 1 Chr. 26.12, 13. Neh. 13.5,9, 12,13. Song 1.4. Isa. 26.20. Jer. 35.2.
3 Or, height.
4 limit, or, bound.
5 Or, pillars. Pro. 9.1. Rev. 3.12.
m Ex. 27.9. Lev. 6.16. Ps. 65.4. Ps. 84.2. Ps. 87.4. Ps. 100.4. Isa. 54.2. Isa. 60.8,9. Isa. 62.9. ch. 8.7. ch. 42.1.
6 closed.
7 Or, galleries, or, porches.
8 Or, within.
n Rev. 11.2.
9 Or, store houses.
o ch. 45.5.
10 Or, from without.
11 whose face was.

threshold *of the gate, which was* on
reed broad.
7 And *every* [k]little chamber *was* on
reed long, and one reed broad; an
between the little chambers *were* fiv
cubits; and the threshold of the gat
by the porch of the gate within *wa*
one reed.
8 He measured also the porch of th
gate within, one reed.
9 Then measured he the porch of th
gate, eight cubits; and the posts there
of, two cubits; and the porch of th
gate *was* inward.
10 And [l]the little chambers of th
gate eastward *were* three on this side
and three on that side; they three *wer*
of one measure: and the posts had on
measure on this side and on that side
11 And he measured the breadth o
the entry of the gate, ten cubits
and the [3]length of the gate, thirteen
cubits.
12 The [4]space also before the littl
chambers *was* one cubit *on this side*
and the space *was* one cubit on tha
side: and the little chambers *were* si
cubits on this side, and six cubits o
that side.
13 He measured then the gate from
the roof of *one* little chamber to th
roof of another: the breadth *was* fiv
and twenty cubits, door against door
14 He made also [5]posts of threescor
cubits, even unto the post of th
[m]court round about the gate.
15 And from the face of the gate o
the entrance unto the face of the porcl
of the inner gate *were* fifty cubits.
16 And *there were* [6]narrow window
to the little chambers, and to thei
posts within the gate round about
and likewise to the [7]arches: and win
dows *were* round about [8]inward: and
upon *each* post *were* palm trees.
17 Then brought he me into [n]the out
ward court, and, lo, *there were* [9]cham
bers, and a pavement made for th
court round about: [o]thirty chamber
were upon the pavement.
18 And the pavement by the side o
the gates over against the length o
the gates *was* the lower pavement.
19 Then he measured the breadth
from the forefront of the lower gate
unto the forefront of the inner cour
[10]without, an hundred cubits eastward
and northward.
20 ¶ And the gate of the outward
court [11]that looked toward the north,
he measured the length thereof, and
the breadth thereof.
21 And the little chambers thereo

re three on this side and three on
at side; and the posts thereof and
e [12]arches thereof were after the
easure of the first gate: the length
ereof *was* fifty cubits, and the
eadth five and twenty cubits.
2 And their windows, and their
ches, and their palm trees, *were* after
e measure of the gate that looketh
ward the east; and they went up un-
it by seven steps; and the arches
ereof *were* before them.
3 And the gate of the inner court
as over against the gate toward the
rth and toward the east; and he
easured from gate to gate an hun-
ed cubits.
4 ¶ After that he brought me toward
e south, and behold a gate toward
e south: and he measured the posts
ereof and the arches thereof ac-
rding to these measures.
5 And *there were* [p]windows in it
d in the arches thereof round about,
e those windows: the length *was*
ty cubits, and the breadth five and
enty cubits.
6 And *there were* seven steps to go
to it, and the arches thereof *were*
fore them: and it had palm trees,
e on this side, and another on that
de, upon the posts thereof.
7 And *there was* a gate in the inner
urt toward the south: and he meas-
ed from gate to gate toward the
uth an hundred cubits.
8 And he brought me to the inner
urt by the south gate: and he meas-
ed the south gate according to these
easures;
9 And the [q]little chambers thereof,
d the posts thereof, and the arches
ereof, according to these measures:
d *there were* windows in it and in
e arches thereof round about: *it*
as fifty cubits long, and five and
enty cubits broad.
0 And the arches round about *were*
e and twenty cubits long, and five
bits [13]broad.
1 And the arches thereof *were* to-
ard the utter court; and [r]palm trees
ere upon the posts thereof: and the
ing up to it *had* eight steps.
2 ¶ And he brought me into the
ner court toward the east: and he
easured the gate according to these
easures.
3 And the little chambers thereof,
nd the posts thereof, and the arches
ereof, *were* according to these
easures: and *there were* windows
erein and in the arches thereof round
about: *it was* fifty cubits long, and
five and twenty cubits broad.
34 And the arches thereof *were* toward the outward court; and palm
trees *were* upon the posts thereof, on
this side, and on that side: and the going up to it *had* eight steps.
35 ¶ And he brought me to the north
gate, and measured *it* according to
these measures;
36 The little chambers thereof, the
posts thereof, and the arches thereof,
and the windows to it round about:
the length *was* fifty cubits, and the
breadth five and twenty cubits.
37 And the posts thereof *were* toward the utter court; and palm trees
were upon the posts thereof, on this
side, and on that side: and the going
up to it *had* eight steps.
38 And the chambers and the entries
thereof *were* by the posts of the gates,
where they [s]washed the burnt offering.
39 ¶ And in the porch of the gate
were two tables on this side, and two
tables on that side, to slay thereon
the burnt offering and the [t]sin offering
and the [u]trespass offering.
40 And at the side without, [14]as one
goeth up to the entry of the north
gate, *were* two tables; and on the
other side, which *was* at the porch of
the gate, *were* two tables.
41 Four tables *were* on this side, and
four tables on that side, by the side
of the gate; eight tables, whereupon
they slew *their sacrifices*.
42 And the four tables *were* of hewn
stone for the burnt offering, of a cubit
and an half long, and a cubit and an
half broad, and one cubit high:
whereupon also they laid the instruments wherewith they slew the burnt
offering and the sacrifice.
43 And within *were* [15]hooks, an hand
broad, fastened round about: and
upon the tables *was* the flesh of the
offering.
44 ¶ And without the inner gate *were*
the chambers of [v]the singers in the inner court, which *was* at the side of the
north gate; and their prospect *was* toward the south: one at the side of the
east gate *having* the prospect toward
the north.
45 And he said unto me, This chamber, whose prospect *is* toward the
south, *is* for the priests, [w]the keepers
of the [16]charge of the house.
46 And the chamber whose prospect
is toward the north *is* for the priests,
[x]the keepers of the charge of the altar:

12 Or, galleries, or, porches.
p 1 Ki. 6.4. Isa. 54.12.
q 1 Ki. 6.5,6,10. 1 Chr. 28.11,12. 2 Chr. 3.9. 2 Chr. 31.11. Neh. 10.38,39. Neh. 12.44. Neh. 13.5,9,12,13. Jer. 35.2. Jer. 36.10.
13 breadth.
r Ps. 92.12. Song 7.7. Jer. 10.5.
s Lev. 1.9. Lev. 3.11. Heb. 9.14.
t Lev. 4.2,3. Isa. 53.5. 2 Cor. 5.21. Titus 2.14. Heb. 10.12,14. 1 Pet. 1.18,19. Rev. 5.9.
u Lev. 5.6. Lev. 6.6. Lev. 7.1. Lev. 14.12,13. Lev. 19.21,22. Num. 6.12. ch. 42.13. ch. 44.29.
14 Or, at the step.
15 Or, end irons, or, the two hearth-stones.
v 1 Chr. 6.31. Eph. 5.19. Col. 3.16.
w Lev. 8.35. Num. 3.7. Deut. 11.1. 1 Ki. 2.3. Rev. 1.6.
16 Or, ward, or, ordinance.
x Num. 18.5. ch. 44.15.

these *are* the sons of [y]Zā-dŏk among the sons of Levi, which [z]come near to the LORD to minister unto him.

47 So he measured the court, an hundred cubits long, and an hundred cubits broad, foursquare; and the altar *that was* before the house.

48 ¶ And he brought me to the porch of the house, and measured *each* post of the porch, five cubits on this side, and five cubits on that side: and the breadth of the gate *was* three cubits on this side, and three cubits on that side.

49 The [a]length of the porch *was* twenty cubits, and the breadth eleven cubits; and *he brought me* by the steps whereby they went up to it: and *there were* [b]pillars by the posts, one on this side, and another on that side.

CHAPTER 41

AFTERWARD he brought me to the [a]temple, and measured the posts, six cubits broad on the one side, and six cubits broad on the other side, *which was* the breadth of the tabernacle.

2 And the breadth of the [1]door *was* ten cubits; and the sides of the door *were* five cubits on the one side, and five cubits on the other side: and he measured the length thereof, forty cubits: and the breadth, twenty cubits.

3 Then went he inward, and measured the post of the door, two cubits; and the door, six cubits; and the breadth of the door, seven cubits.

4 So he [b]measured the length thereof, twenty cubits; and the breadth, twenty cubits, before the temple: and he said unto me, This *is* the most holy *place*.

5 After he measured the wall of the house, six cubits; and the breadth of *every* side chamber, four cubits, round about the house on every side.

6 And [c]the side chambers *were* three, [2]one over another, and [3]thirty in order; and they entered into the wall which *was* of the house for the side chambers round about, that they might [4]have hold, but they had not hold in the wall of the house.

7 And [5]*there was* an enlarging, and a winding about still upward to the side chambers: for the winding about of the house went still upward round about the house: therefore the breadth of the house *was still* upward, and so increased *from* the lowest *chamber* to the highest by the midst.

8 I saw also the height of the house

y 1 Ki. 2.35. ch. 43.19.
z Eph. 2.17. Col. 4.12.
a 1 Ki. 6.3.
b 1 Ki. 7.21.
CHAP. 41
a Zech. 6.12. Matt. 16.18. 1 Cor. 3.16. 2 Cor. 6.16. Eph. 2.21. Rev. 3.12.
1 Or, entrance.
b 1 Ki. 6.20. 2 Chr. 3.8. Rev. 21.2,3, 16,17.
c 1 Ki. 6.5,6.
2 side chamber over side chamber.
3 Or, three and thirty times, or, foot.
4 be holden.
5 it was made broader, and went round.
d Isa. 28.16. ch. 40.5.
6 Or, several walks, or, walks with pillars.
e 1 Ki. 7.4. Isa. 54.12. ch. 40.16. See ver. 26. 1 Cor. 13.12.
7 cieling of wood.
8 Or, and the ground unto the windows.
9 measures.
f Gen. 3.24. Ex. 25.22. 1 Sam. 4.4. 2 Sam. 22. 11. 1 Ki. 6.29. 2 Chr. 3.10. Ps. 80.1. Ps. 99.1. ch. 10.2.
g ch. 1.10. ch. 10.14. Rev. 4.7-9.
h ch. 1.10.
10 post.

round about: the [d]foundations of t
side chambers *were* a full reed of s
great cubits.
9 The thickness of the wall, whi
was for the side chamber without, *w*
five cubits: and *that* which *was* left *w*
the place of the side chambers th
were within.
10 And between the chambers *w*
the wideness of twenty cubits roun
about the house on every side.
11 And the doors of the side cham
bers *were* toward *the place that w*
left, one door toward the north, an
another door toward the south: an
the breadth of the place that was le
was five cubits round about.
12 Now the building that *was* befo
the separate place at the end towa
the west *was* seventy cubits broa
and the wall of the building *was* fi
cubits thick round about, and th
length thereof ninety cubits.
13 So he measured the house, a
hundred cubits long; and the separa
place, and the building, with th
walls thereof, an hundred cubits lon
14 Also the breadth of the face of th
house, and of the separate place to
ward the east, an hundred cubits.
15 And he measured the length
the building over against the separa
place which *was* behind it, and th
[6]galleries thereof on the one side an
on the other side, an hundred cubit
with the inner temple, and the porch
of the court;
16 The door posts, and [e]the narro
windows, and the galleries roun
about on their three stories, ov
against the door, [7]cieled with woo
round about, [8]and from the ground u
to the windows, and the windows *we*
covered;
17 To that above the door, even unt
the inner house, and without, and b
all the wall round about within an
without, by [9]measure.
18 And *it was* made [f]with chĕr-ū
bĭms and palm trees, so that a pal
tree *was* between a cherub and
cherub; and *every* cherub had [g]tw
faces;
19 [h]So that the face of a man *was* to
ward the palm tree on the one sid
and the face of a young lion towa
the palm tree on the other side: *it wa*
made through all the house roun
about.
20 From the ground unto above th
door *were* chĕr-ū-bĭms and palm tree
made, and *on* the wall of the templ
21 The [10]posts of the temple *wer*

quared, *and* the face of the sanctuary;
ıe appearance *of the one* as the ap-
earance *of the other*.
22 The [i]altar of wood *was* three cu-
its high, and the length thereof two
ubits; and the corners thereof, and
ıe length thereof, and the walls there-
f, *were* of wood: and he said unto
ıe, This *is* [j]the table that *is* before
the LORD.
23 And [l]the temple and the sanctu-
ry had two doors.
24 And the doors had two leaves
piece, two turning leaves; two *leaves*
or the one door, and two leaves for
he other *door*.
25 And *there were* made on them, on
he doors of the temple, chĕr-ū-bĭms
nd palm trees, like as *were* made up-
n the walls; and *there were* thick
lanks upon the face of the porch
vithout.
26 And *there were* [m]narrow windows
nd palm trees on the one side and on
he other side, on the sides of the
orch, and *upon* the side chambers of
he house, and thick planks.

CHAPTER 42

THEN [a]he brought me forth into
the [b]utter court, the way toward
he north: and he brought me into the
hamber that *was* over against the
eparate place, and which *was* before
he building toward the north.
2 Before the length of an hundred
ubits *was* the north door, and the
readth *was* fifty cubits.
3 Over against the twenty *cubits*
vhich *were* for the inner court, and
ver against the pavement which *was*
or the utter court, *was* gallery against
gallery in three *stories*.
4 And before the chambers *was* a
valk of ten cubits breadth inward, a
vay of one cubit; and their doors to-
vard the north.
5 Now the upper chambers *were*
horter: for the galleries [1]were higher
han these, [2]than the lower, and than
he middlemost of the building.
6 For they *were* in three *stories*, but
ad not pillars as the pillars of the
ourts: therefore *the building* was
traitened more than the lowest and
he middlemost from the ground.
7 And the wall that *was* without over
against the chambers, toward the ut-
er court on the forepart of the chambers, the length thereof *was* fifty
ubits.
8 For the length of the chambers that
vere in the utter court *was* fifty cubits:
and, lo, before the temple *were* an
hundred cubits.
9 And [3]from under these chambers
was [4]the entry on the east side, [5]as one
goeth into them from the utter court.
10 The chambers *were* in the thickness of the wall of the court toward
the east, over against the separate
place, and over against the building.
11 And the way before them *was* like
the appearance of the chambers
which *were* toward the north, as long
as they, *and* as broad as they: and all
their goings out *were* both according
to their fashions, and according to
their doors.
12 And according to the doors of the
chambers that *were* toward the south
was a door in the head of the way, *even*
the way directly before the wall toward the east, as one entereth into
them.
13 ¶ Then said he unto me, The
north chambers *and* the south chambers, which *are* before the separate
place, they *be* holy chambers, where
the priests [c]that approach unto the
LORD [d]shall eat the most holy things:
there shall they lay the most holy
things, and the [e]meat offering, and
the sin offering, and the trespass offering; for the place *is* holy.
14 When [f]the priests enter therein,
then shall they not go out of the holy
place into the utter court, but there
they shall lay their garments wherein
they minister; for they *are* holy; and
shall put on other garments, and shall
approach to *those things* which *are* for
the people.
15 Now when he had made an end
of measuring the inner house, he
brought me forth toward the gate
whose prospect *is* toward the east, and
measured it round about.
16 He measured the east [6]side with
the measuring reed, five hundred
reeds, with the measuring reed round
about.
17 He measured the north side, five
hundred reeds, with the measuring
reed round about.
18 He measured the south side, five
hundred reeds, with the measuring
reed.
19 ¶ He turned about to the west
side, *and* measured five hundred
reeds with the measuring reed.
20 He measured it by the four sides:
[g]it had a wall round about, five [h]hun-
dred *reeds* long, and five hundred
broad, to make [i]a separation between
the sanctuary and the profane place.

i Ex. 30.1. 1 Ki. 7.48. 2 Chr. 4.19. Rev. 8.3.
j Pro. 9.2. Song 1.12. ch. 44.16. Mal. 1.7,12.
k Ex. 30.8.
l 1 Ki. 6.31-35.
m 1 Ki. 6.4. ch. 40.16. See ver. 16.

CHAP. 42

a ch. 40.1. ch. 41.1. 2 Cor. 3.5.
b ch. 40.17-20. ch. 41.12,15. Rev. 11.2.
1 Or, did eat of these.
2 Or, and the building consisted of the lower and the middlemost.
3 Or, from the place.
4 Or, he that brought me.
5 Or, as he came.
c Ex. 30.20. Lev. 10.3. Num. 16.5, 40. Deut. 21.5. ch. 40.46.
d Lev. 6.16. Lev. 24.9.
e Lev. 2.3. Num. 18.9.
f Ex. 28.40-43. Ex. 29.4-9. Lev. 8.7,13. ch. 44.19.
6 wind.
g Isa. 5.2. ch. 40.5.
h ch. 45.2.
i 2 Cor. 6.17.

CHAPTER 43

AFTERWARD he brought me to
the gate, *even* the gate that [a]look-
eth toward the east:
2 And, [b]behold, the glory of the God
of Israel came from the way of the
east: and his [c]voice *was* like a noise of
many waters: [d]and the earth shined
with his glory.
3 And *it was* [e]according to the appearance of the vision which I saw,
even according to the vision that I
saw [1]when I came to [f]destroy the city:
and the visions *were* like the vision
that I saw [g]by the river Chē-bär; and I
fell upon my face.
4 And [h]the glory of the LORD came
into the house by the way of the gate
whose prospect *is* toward the east.
5 So [i]the spirit took me up, and
brought me into the inner court; and,
behold, [j]the glory of the LORD filled
the house.
6 And I heard *him* speaking unto me
out of the house; and [k]the man stood
by me.
7 ¶ And he said unto me, Son of man,
the [l]place of my throne, and the
[m]place of the soles of my feet, where
[n]I will dwell in the midst of the children of Israel for ever, and my holy
name, shall the house of Israel [o]no
more defile, *neither* they, nor their
kings, by their whoredom, nor by [p]the
carcases of their kings in their high
places.
8 In [q]their setting of their threshold
by my thresholds, and their post by
my posts, [2]and the wall between me
and them, they have even defiled my
holy name by their abominations that
they have committed: wherefore I
have consumed them in mine anger.
9 Now let them put away their
whoredom, and the carcases of their
kings, far from me, and I will dwell in
the midst of them for ever.
10 ¶ Thou son of man, [r]shew the
house to the house of Israel, that they
may be ashamed of their iniquities:
and let them measure the [3]pattern.
11 And if they be ashamed of all that
they have done, [s]shew them the form
of the house, and the fashion thereof,
and the goings out thereof, and the
comings in thereof, and all the forms
thereof, and all the ordinances thereof, and all the forms thereof, and all
the laws thereof: and write *it* in their
sight, that they may keep the whole
form thereof, and all the ordinances
thereof, and do them.
12 This *is* the law of the house; Upon
[t]the top of the mountain the whol
limit thereof round about *shall b*
most holy. Behold, this *is* the law c
the house.
13 ¶ And these *are* the measures c
the altar after the cubits: [u]The cub
is a cubit and an hand breadth; eve
the [4]bottom *shall be* a cubit, and th
breadth a cubit, and the border there
of by the [5]edge thereof round abo
shall be a span: and this *shall be* th
higher place of the altar.
14 And from the bottom *upon* th
ground *even* to the lower settle *sha*
be two cubits, and the breadth on
cubit; and from the lesser settle *eve*
to the greater settle *shall be* fou
cubits, and the breadth *one* cubit.
15 So [6]the altar *shall be* four cubits
and from [7]the altar and upward *sha*
be four horns.
16 And the altar *shall be* twelve *cu*
bits long, twelve broad, square in th
four squares thereof.
17 And the settle *shall be* fourtee
cubits long and fourteen broad in th
four squares thereof; and the borde
about it *shall be* half a cubit; and th
bottom thereof *shall be* a cubit about
and [v]his stairs shall look toward th
east.
18 ¶ And he said unto me, Son c
man, thus saith the Lord GOD; Thes
are the ordinances of the altar in th
day when they shall make it, to offe
burnt offerings thereon, and to [w]sprin
kle blood thereon.
19 And thou shalt give to [x]the priest
the Levites that be of the seed of Zā
dŏk, which approach unto me, t
minister unto me, saith the Lord GOD
[y]a young bullock for a sin offering.
20 And thou shalt take of the bloo
thereof, and put *it* on the four horn
of it, and on the four corners of th
settle, and upon the border roun
about: thus shalt thou cleanse an
purge it.
21 Thou shalt take the bullock als
of the sin offering, and he shall [z]bur
it in the appointed place of the house
[a]without the sanctuary.
22 And on the second day thou sha
offer a kid of the goats without blem
ish for a sin offering; and they sha
cleanse the altar, as they did cleanse
with the bullock.
23 When thou hast made an end o
cleansing *it*, thou shalt offer a youn
bullock without blemish, and a ra
out of the flock without blemish.
24 And thou shalt offer them befor
the LORD, [b]and the priests shall cas

CHAP. 43
a ch. 10.19.
b Isa. 6.3. ch. 3.23. ch. 9.3. ch. 10.18, 19.
c Rev. 1.15.
d Rev. 18.1.
e ch. 1.4.
1 Or, when I came to prophesy that the city should be destroyed.
f Jer. 1.10.
g ch. 3.23.
h ch. 10.19.
i ch. 3.12.
j 1 Ki. 8.10.
k ch. 40.3.
l Ps. 99.1.
m 1 Chr. 28. 2. Ps. 99.5.
n Ex. 25.8. Lev. 26.12. Ps. 68.16.
o ch. 39.7.
p Lev. 26.30. Jer. 16.18.
q 2 Ki. 16.14.
2 Or, for there was but a wall between me and them.
r ch. 40.4.
3 Or, sum, or, number.
s ch. 44.5,6. Matt. 28.20.
t Ps. 93.5. ch. 40.2. Rev. 21.27.
u ch. 40.5.
4 bosom.
5 lip.
6 Harel, that is, The mountain of God.
7 Ariel, that is, The lion of God.
v Ex. 20.26.
w Lev. 1.5. Heb. 9.18-22.
x 1 Ki. 2.27, 35. Isa. 61.5. Jer. 33.18. ch. 40.46.
y Ex. 29.10. Lev. 8.14, 15.
z Ex. 29.14.
a Heb. 13.11.
b Lev. 2.13.

t upon them, and they shall offer
m up *for* a burnt offering unto the
RD.
[c]Seven days shalt thou prepare
ry day a goat *for* a sin offering:
y shall also prepare a young bull-
, and a ram out of the flock, with-
blemish.
Seven days shall they purge the
ar and purify it; and they shall
nsecrate themselves.
And [d]when these days are expired,
hall be, *that* upon the eighth day,
l *so* forward, the priests shall make
ır burnt offerings upon the altar,
l your [9]peace offerings; and I will
cept you, saith the Lord GOD.

CHAPTER 44

HEN he brought me back the way
of the gate of the outward sanctu-
which [a]looketh toward the east;
d it *was* shut.
Then said the LORD unto me; This
e shall be shut, it shall not be open-
and no man shall enter in by it; be-
ıse the LORD, the God of Israel,
h entered in by it, therefore it shall
shut.
It is for [b]the prince; the prince, he
ıll sit in it to [c]eat bread before the
RD; he [d]shall enter by the way of
porch of *that* gate, and shall go out
the way of the same.
¶ Then brought he me the way of
north gate before the house: and
ooked, and, [e]behold, the glory of
LORD filled the house of the LORD:
d I fell upon my face.
And the LORD said unto me, Son
man, [1]mark well, and behold with
ne eyes, and hear with thine ears
that I say unto thee concerning all
ordinances of the house of the
RD, and all the laws thereof; and
rk well the entering in of the house,
h every going forth of the sanctu-
.
And thou shalt say to [h]the rebel-
us, *even* to the house of Israel, Thus
th the Lord GOD; O ye house of Is-
l, [i]let it suffice you of all your
ominations,
In [j]that ye have brought *into my*
ctuary [2]strangers, [k]uncircumcised
heart, and uncircumcised in flesh,
be in my sanctuary, to pollute it,
n my house, when ye offer [l]my
ead, the [m]fat and the blood, and
y have broken my covenant be-
ıse of all your abominations.
And ye have not [n]kept the charge
mine holy things: but ye have set

c Ex. 29.35.
8 fill their hands.
d Lev. 9.1.
9 Or, thank offerings.
e Job 42.8.
CHAP. 44
a ch. 43.1.
b Zech. 6.12. Phil. 2.8.
c Gen. 31.54.
d ch. 46.2,8.
e ch. 3.23.
f ch. 1.28.
g ch. 40.4.
1 set thine heart.
h ch. 2.5.
i 1 Pet. 4.3.
j Acts 21.28.
2 children of a stranger.
k Lev. 26.41. ch. 7.20.
l Lev. 21.6.
m Lev. 3.16.
n Lev. 22.2. Num. 18.3. 2 Tim. 4.1.
3 Or, ward, or, ordinance.
o Ps. 50.16.
p 2 Ki. 23.8. Neh. 9.34. Jer. 23.11. ch. 22.26.
q 1 Chr. 26.1.
r Num. 16.9.
4 were for a stumblingblock of iniquity unto, etc.
s Ps. 106.26.
t Num. 18.3.
5 the holy things of the holies.
u ch. 32.30.
v 1 Chr. 23. 28,32.
w ch. 40.46.
x 1 Sam. 2.35.
y Deut. 10.8.
z ch. 41.22.
a Mal. 2.7.
b Ex. 28.39.
6 in, or, with sweat, or, in sweating places.
c ch. 42.14.

keepers of my [3]charge in my sanctuary for yourselves.
9 ¶ Thus saith the Lord GOD; [o]No
stranger, uncircumcised in heart, nor
uncircumcised in flesh, shall enter into
my sanctuary, of any stranger that *is*
among the children of Israel.
10 And [p]the Levites that are gone
away far from me, when Israel went
astray, which went astray away from
me after their idols; they shall even
bear their iniquity.
11 Yet they shall be ministers in my
sanctuary, [q]*having* charge at the gates
of the house, and ministering to the
house: they shall slay the burnt offering and the sacrifice for the people,
and they [r]shall stand before them to
minister unto them.
12 Because they ministered unto
them before their idols, and [4]caused
the house of Israel to fall into iniquity;
therefore have I [s]lifted up mine hand
against them, saith the Lord GOD, and
they shall bear their iniquity.
13 And [t]they shall not come near unto me, to do the office of a priest unto
me, nor to come near to any of [5]my
holy things, in the most holy *place:*
but they shall [u]bear their shame, and
their abominations which they have
committed.
14 But I will make them [v]keepers of
the charge of the house, for all the
service thereof, and for all that shall
be done therein.
15 ¶ But [w]the priests the Levites, the
[x]sons of Zā-dŏk, that kept the charge
of my sanctuary when the children of
Israel went astray from me, they shall
come near to me to minister unto me,
and they [y]shall stand before me to
offer unto me the fat and the blood,
saith the Lord GOD:
16 They shall enter into my sanctuary, and they shall come near to my
[z]table, to minister unto me, and they
shall [a]keep my charge.
17 ¶ And it shall come to pass, *that*
when they enter in at the gates of the
inner court, [b]they shall be clothed
with linen garments; and no wool
shall come upon them, whiles they
minister in the gates of the inner
court, and within.
18 They shall have linen bonnets upon their heads, and shall have linen
breeches upon their loins; they shall
not gird *themselves* [6]with any thing
that causeth sweat.
19 And when they go forth into the
utter court, *even* into the utter court to
the people, [c]they shall put off their

garments wherein they ministered,
and lay them in the holy chambers,
and they shall put on other garments;
and they shall not [d]sanctify the people
with their garments.
20 Neither [e]shall they shave their
heads, nor suffer their locks to
grow long; they shall only poll their
heads.
21 Neither [f]shall any priest drink
wine, when they enter into the inner
court.
22 Neither shall they take for their
wives a widow, nor her that is [7]put
away: but they shall take maidens of
the seed of the house of Israel, or a
widow [8]that had a priest before.
23 And [g]they shall teach my people
the difference between the holy and
profane, and cause them to discern
between the unclean and the clean.
24 And [h]in controversy they shall
stand in judgment; *and* they shall
judge it according to my judgments:
and they shall keep my [i]laws and my
statutes in all mine assemblies; [j]and
they shall hallow my sabbaths.
25 And they shall come at no dead
person to defile themselves: but for
father, or for mother, or for son, or
for daughter, for brother, or for sister
that hath had no husband, they may
defile themselves.
26 And [k]after he is cleansed, they
shall reckon unto him seven days.
27 And in the day that he goeth into
the sanctuary, unto the inner court, to
minister in the sanctuary, he [l]shall
offer his sin offering, saith the Lord
GOD.
28 And it shall be unto them for an
inheritance: I [m]*am* their inheritance:
and ye shall give them no possession
in Israel: I *am* their possession.
29 They [n]shall eat the meat offering,
and the sin offering, and the trespass
offering; and every [9]dedicated thing in
Israel shall be theirs.
30 And the [10]first of all the firstfruits
of all *things*, and every oblation of all,
of every *sort* of your oblations, shall
be the priest's: ye shall [o]also give unto
the priest the first of your dough,
[p]that he may cause the blessing to rest
in thine house.
31 The priests shall not eat of any
thing that is [q]dead of itself, or torn,
whether it be fowl or beast.

CHAPTER 45

MOREOVER, [1]when ye shall divide by lot the land for inheritance, ye shall offer [a]an oblation unto

d Ex. 29.37.
e Isa. 28.7.
f Lev. 10.9. Luke 1.15. 1 Tim. 3.3.
7 thrust forth.
8 from a priest.
g Mal. 2.7.
h Deut. 17.8.
i 1 Tim. 4.12.
j ch. 22.26.
k Num. 6.10.
l Lev. 4.3.
m Num. 18. 20. Deut. 10.9. Josh. 13.14, 33. ch. 45.4.
n Lev. 6.18.
9 Or, devoted. Lev. 27.21, compared with Num. 18.14.
10 Or, chief.
o Num. 15. 20.
p Pro. 3.9.
q Ex. 22.31.

CHAP. 45

1 when ye cause the land to fall.
a Pro. 3.9, 10. ch. 48.8.
2 holiness.
b ch. 42.20.
3 Or, void places.
c ch. 44.15.
d ch. 48.13.
e ch. 40.17.
f Ps. 2.8. ch. 34.24. ch. 46.16-18. ch. 48.21.
g Jer. 22.17. ch. 22.27. ch. 46.18.
h ch. 44.6.
i Jer. 22.3.
4 expulsions.
j Lev. 19.35. Pro. 11.1.

the LORD, [2]an holy portion of
land: the length *shall be* the length
five and twenty thousand *reeds*, a
the breadth *shall be* ten thousa
This *shall be* holy in all the bord
thereof round about.
2 Of this there shall be for the sa
tuary five [b]hundred *in length*, w
five hundred *in breadth*, square rou
about; and fifty cubits round ab
for the [3]suburbs thereof.
3 And of this measure shalt th
measure the length of five and twe
thousand, and the breadth of
thousand: and in it shall be the sa
tuary *and* the most holy *place*.
4 The holy *portion* of the land sh
be for the [c]priests the ministers of
sanctuary, which shall come near
minister unto the LORD: and it sh
be a place for their houses, and
holy place for the sanctuary.
5 And [d]the five and twenty thousa
of length, and the ten thousand
breadth, shall also the Levites,
ministers of the house, have for the
selves, for a possession for [e]twe
chambers.
6 ¶ And ye shall appoint the poss
sion of the city five thousand bro
and five and twenty thousand lo
over against the oblation of the h
portion: it shall be for the whole ho
of Israel.
7 ¶ And [f]*a portion shall be* for
prince on the one side and on the ot
side of the oblation of the holy *p*
tion, and of the possession of the ci
before the oblation of the holy *p*
tion, and before the possession of
city, from the west side westward, a
from the east side eastward: and
length *shall be* over against one of
portions, from the west border u
the east border.
8 In the land shall be his possessi
in Israel: and [g]my princes shall
more oppress my people; and
rest of the land shall they give to
house of Israel according to th
tribes.
9 ¶ Thus saith the Lord GOD; Let
suffice you, O princes of Israel:
move violence and spoil, and exec
judgment and justice, take away yo
[4]exactions from my people, saith
Lord GOD.
10 Ye shall have just [j]balances, a
a just ē-phăh, and a just băth.
11 The ē-phăh and the băth shall
of one measure, that the băth n
contain the tenth part of an hō-m
and the ē-phăh the tenth part of an

ěr: the measure thereof shall be after
e hō-měr.
2 And the [k]shekel *shall be* twenty
-rähs: twenty shekels, five and
enty shekels, fifteen shekels, shall
your mā-nĕh.
3 This *is* the oblation that ye shall
fer; the sixth part of an ē-phäh of
hō-měr of wheat, and ye shall give
e sixth part of an ē-phäh of an hō-
ěr of barley:
4 Concerning the ordinance of oil,
e bäth of oil, *ye shall offer* the tenth
rt of a bäth out of the côr, *which is*
hō-měr of ten bäths; for ten bäths
e an hō-měr:
5 And one [5]lamb out of the flock,
t of two hundred, out of the fat pas-
es of Israel; for a meat offering,
d for a burnt offering, and for [6]peace
erings, to [l]make reconciliation for
em, saith the Lord GOD.
6 All the people of the land [7]shall
e this oblation [8]for the prince in
ael.
7 And it shall be the prince's part *to*
e burnt offerings, and meat offer-
s, and drink offerings, in the feasts,
d in the new moons, and in the sab-
ths, in all solemnities of the house
Israel: he [m]shall prepare the sin of-
ing, and the meat offering, and the
rnt offering, and the [9]peace offer-
s, to make reconciliation for the
use of Israel.
8 Thus saith the Lord GOD; In the
t *month*, in the first *day* of the
nth, thou shalt take a young bull-
k without blemish, [n]and cleanse
sanctuary:
9 And [o]the priest shall take of the
od of the sin offering, and put *it*
on the posts of the house, and upon
four corners of the settle of the
ar, and upon the posts of the gate
the inner court.
0 And so thou shalt do the seventh
of the month [p]for every one that
eth, and for *him that is* simple: so
ll ye reconcile the house.
In [q]the first *month*, in the four-
nth day of the month, ye shall
ve the passover, a feast of seven
ys; unleavened bread shall be
en.
2 And upon that day shall [r]the
nce prepare for himself and for all
people of the land [s]a bullock *for*
n offering.
3 And [t]seven days of the feast he
ll prepare a burnt offering to the
RD, seven bullocks and seven rams
hout blemish daily the seven days;
[u]and a kid of the goats daily *for* a sin
offering.
24 And [v]he shall prepare a meat offering of an ē-phäh for a bullock, and
an ē-phäh for a ram, and an hĭn of oil
for an ē-phäh.
25 In the seventh *month*, in the fifteenth day of the month, shall he do
the like in the [w]feast of the seven days,
according to the sin offering, according to the burnt offering, and according to the meat offering, and according
to the oil.

CHAPTER 46

THUS saith the Lord GOD; The
gate of the inner court that looketh toward the east shall be shut the
six working days; but on the [a]sabbath
it shall be opened, and in the day of the
new moon it shall be opened.
2 And [b]the prince shall enter by the
way of the porch of *that* gate without,
and shall stand by the post of the
gate, and the priests shall prepare his
burnt offering and his peace offerings,
and he shall worship at the threshold
of the gate: then he shall go forth; but
[c]the gate shall not be shut until the
evening.
3 Likewise [d]the people of the land
shall worship at the door of this gate
before the LORD in the sabbaths and
in the new moons.
4 And [e]the burnt offering that the
prince shall offer unto the LORD in the
sabbath day *shall be* six lambs without blemish, and a ram without
blemish.
5 And [f]the meat offering *shall be* an
ē-phäh for a ram, and the meat offering for the lambs [1]as he shall be able
to give, and an hĭn of oil to an ē-phäh.
6 And in the day of the new moon *it
shall be* a young bullock without
blemish, and six lambs, and a ram:
they shall be without blemish.
7 And he shall prepare a meat offering, an ē-phäh for a bullock, and an
ē-phäh for a ram, and for the lambs
according as his hand shall attain unto, and an hĭn of oil to an ē-phäh.
8 And when the prince shall enter,
he shall go in by the way of the porch
of *that* gate, and he shall go forth by
the way thereof.
9 ¶ But when the people of the land
[g]shall come before the LORD in the
solemn feasts, he that entereth in by
the way of the north gate to worship
shall go out by the way of the south
gate; and he that entereth by the way
of the south gate shall go forth by the

k Ex. 30.13. Lev. 27.25.
5 Or, kid.
6 Or, thank offerings.
l Lev. 1.4. Rom. 5.10. 2 Cor. 5.18, 19. Eph. 2.16. Col. 1.21. Titus 2.14.
7 shall be for.
8 Or, with.
m John 6.51. 2 Cor. 5.21. Gal. 3.13. Col. 1.20. 1 Pet. 2.24.
9 Or, thank offerings.
n Lev. 16.16. ch. 43.22,26. Heb. 9.22.
o ch. 43.20.
p Ps. 19.12. Lev. 4.27. Rom. 16.18. Heb. 5.2.
q Ex. 12.18. Lev. 23.5,6. Num. 9.2,3. Deut. 16.1.
r Matt. 20.28. 1 Pet. 2.24.
s Lev. 4.14.
t Lev. 23.8.
u Num. 28. 15.
v ch. 46.5,7.
w Lev. 23.34. Num. 29.12. Deut. 16.13.

CHAP. 46

a Isa. 66.23. ch. 45.17. Heb. 4.9,10.
b ch. 44.3.
c Matt. 25.10.
d Ps. 100.4. Luke 1.10.
e Num. 28.5, 9,11,12. ch. 45.17. There was no such oblation appointed by Moses.
f ver. 14. Num. 28.12. ch. 45.24.
1 the gift of his hand.
g Ex. 23.14, 17. Deut. 16.16. Ps. 84.7.

way of the north gate: he shall not return by the way of the gate whereby
he came in, but shall go forth over
against it.
10 And the prince in the midst of
them, when they go in, shall go in;
and when they go forth, shall go
forth.
11 And in the feasts and in the
solemnities the meat offering shall be
an ē-phăh to a bullock, and an ē-phăh
to a ram, and to the lambs as he is
able to give, and an hĭn of oil to an
ē-phăh.
12 Now when the prince shall prepare a voluntary [h]burnt offering or
peace offerings voluntarily unto the
LORD, [i]*one* shall then open him the
gate that looketh toward the east, and
he shall prepare his burnt offering and
his peace offerings, as he did on the
sabbath day: then he shall go forth;
and after his going forth *one* shall
shut the gate.
13 Thou [j]shalt daily prepare a burnt
offering unto the LORD *of* a lamb [2]of
the first year without blemish: thou
shalt prepare it [3]every morning.
14 And thou shalt prepare a meat
offering for it every morning, the
sixth part of an ē-phăh, and the third
part of an hĭn of oil, to temper with
the fine flour; a meat offering continually by a perpetual ordinance unto
the LORD.
15 Thus shall they prepare the lamb,
and the meat offering, and the oil,
every morning *for* a continual burnt
offering.
16 ¶ Thus saith the Lord GOD; If the
prince give a gift unto any of his sons,
the inheritance thereof shall be his
sons'; it *shall be* their possession by
inheritance.
17 But if he give a gift of his inheritance to one of his servants, then it
shall be his to [k]the year of liberty; after
it shall return to the prince: but his
inheritance shall be his sons' for
them.
18 Moreover [l]the prince shall not
take of the people's inheritance by
oppression, to thrust them out of their
possession; *but* he shall give his sons
inheritance out of his own possession:
that my people be not scattered every
man from his possession.
19 ¶ After he brought me through the
entry, which *was* at the side of the
gate, into the holy chambers of the
priests, which looked toward the
north: and, behold, there *was* a place
on the two sides westward.

h Lev. 1.3. Lev. 23.37. Num. 29.39. Matt. 20.28. John 10.18. Gal. 2.20. Titus 2.14.
i ch. 44.3.
j Ex. 29.38. Num. 28.3.
2 a son of his year.
3 morning by morning.
k Lev. 25.9, 10. Isa. 61.2.
l Ps. 78.72. Jer. 23.5,6. ch. 45.8.
m 2 Chr. 35. 13. ch. 44.29.
n Lev. 2.4,5, 7. ch. 43.23,24.
o Ex. 19.10. ch. 44.19. Heb. 10.22.
4 a court in a corner of a court, and a court in a corner of a court.
5 Or, made with chimneys.
6 cornered.
p Rom. 12.1. Rom. 15.16. Heb. 13.16.

CHAP. 47

a Ps. 46.4. Joel 3.18. Zech. 13.1. Zech. 14.8. Rev. 22.1.
b ch. 40.3. Zech. 2.1. Rev. 11.1.
1 waters of the ancles.
2 waters of swimming.

20 Then said he unto me, This *is* t
place where the priests [m]shall boil t
trespass offering and the sin offerin
where they [n]shall bake the meat offe
ing; that they bear *them* not o
into the utter court, to [o]sanctify t
people.
21 Then he brought me forth into t
utter court, and caused me to pass
the four corners of the court; and, b
hold, [4]in every corner of the cou
there was a court.
22 In the four corners of the cou
there were courts [5]joined of forty c
bits long and thirty broad: these fo
[6]corners *were* of one measure.
23 And *there was* a row *of buildi*
round about in them, round abo
them four, and *it was* made with bo
ing places under the rows rou
about.
24 Then said he unto me, These *a*
the places of them that boil, where t
ministers of the house shall boil [p]t
sacrifice of the people.

CHAPTER 47

AFTERWARD he brought
again unto the door of the hous
and, behold, [a]waters issued out fro
under the threshold of the house ea
ward: for the forefront of the hou
stood toward the east, and the wate
came down from under from the rig
side of the house, at the south *side*
the altar.
2 Then brought he me out of the w
of the gate northward, and led
about the way without unto the ut
gate by the way that looketh ea
ward; and, behold, there ran o
waters on the right side.
3 And when [b]the man that had t
line in his hand went forth eastwar
he measured a thousand cubits, a
he brought me through the wate
the [1]waters *were* to the ancles.
4 Again he measured a thousan
and brought me through the wate
the waters *were* to the knees. Aga
he measured a thousand, and broug
me through; the waters *were* to t
loins.
5 Afterward he measured a tho
sand; *and it was* a river that I cou
not pass over: for the waters we
risen, [2]waters to swim in, a river th
could not be passed over.
6 ¶ And he said unto me, Son of ma
hast thou seen *this?* Then he broug
me, and caused me to return to t
brink of the river.
7 Now when I had returned, behol

at the [3]bank of the river *were* very many trees [c]on the one side and on the other.

8 Then said he unto me, These waters issue out toward the east country, and go down into the [4]desert, and go into the sea: *which being* brought forth into the sea, the waters [d]shall be healed.

9 And it shall come to pass, *that* every thing that liveth, which moveth, whithersoever [5]the rivers shall come, [e]shall live: and there shall be a very great multitude of fish, because these waters shall come thither: for they shall be healed; and every thing shall live whither the river cometh.

10 And it shall come to pass, *that* the [f]fishers shall stand upon it from Ĕn–gē-́dī even unto Ĕn–ĕg-́lā-ĭm; they shall be a *place* to spread forth nets; their fish shall be according to their kinds, as the fish [g]of the great sea, exceeding many.

11 But the miry places thereof and the marishes thereof [6]shall not be healed; they shall be given to salt.

12 And by the river upon the bank thereof, on this side and on that side, [7]shall grow all trees for meat, [h]whose leaf shall not fade, neither shall the fruit thereof be consumed: it shall bring forth [8]new fruit according to his months, because their waters they issued out of the sanctuary: and the fruit thereof shall be for meat, and the leaf thereof [9]for medicine.

13 ¶ Thus saith the Lord GOD; This *shall be* the border, whereby ye shall inherit the land according to the twelve tribes of Israel: [i]Joseph *shall have two* portions.

14 And ye shall inherit it, one as well as another: *concerning* the which I [10]lifted up mine hand to give it unto your fathers: and this land shall [j]fall unto you for inheritance.

15 And this *shall be* the border of the land toward the north side, from the great sea, the [k]way of Hĕth-́lŏn, as men go to [l]Zē-́dăd;

16 [m]Hā-́măth, [n]Bĕ-rō-́thăh, Sĭb-́rā-ĭm, which *is* between the border of Damascus and the border of Hā-́măth; [11]Hā-́zär–hăt-́tī-cŏn, which *is* by the coast of Hau̇-́răn.

17 And the border from the sea shall be [o]Hā-́zär–ē-́năn, the border of Damascus, and the north northward, and the border of Hā-́măth. And *this is* the north side.

18 And the east side ye shall measure [12]from Hau̇-́răn, and from Damascus, and from Gilead, and from the land of Israel *by* Jordan, from the border unto the east sea. And *this is* the east side.

19 And the south side southward, from Tā-́mär *even* to the waters of [13]strife *in* Kā-́dĕsh, the [14]river to the great sea. And *this is* the south side [15]southward.

20 The west side also *shall be* the great sea from the border, till a man come over against Hā-́măth. This *is* the west side.

21 So shall ye divide this land unto you according to the tribes of Israel.

22 ¶ And it shall come to pass, *that* ye shall divide it by lot for an inheritance unto you, and [p]to the strangers that sojourn among you, which shall beget children among you: [q]and they shall be unto you as born in the country among the children of Israel; they shall have inheritance with you among the tribes of Israel.

23 And it shall come to pass, *that* in what tribe the stranger sojourneth, there shall ye give *him* his inheritance, saith the Lord GOD.

CHAPTER 48

NOW these *are* the names of the tribes. From [a]the north end to the coast of the way of Hĕth-́lŏn, as one goeth to Hā-́măth, Hā-́zär–ē-́năn, the border of Damascus northward, to the coast of Hā-́măth; for these are his sides east *and* west; [1]a *portion for* Dan.

2 And by the border of Dan, from the east side unto the west side, a *portion* for Asher.

3 And by the border of Asher, from the east side even unto the west side, a *portion for* Năph-́tă-lī.

4 And by the border of Năph-́tă-lī, from the east side unto the west side, a *portion for* Mă-năs-́sĕh.

5 And by the border of Mă-năs-́sĕh, from the east side unto the west side, a *portion for* Ē-́phră-ĭm.

6 And by the border of Ē-́phră-ĭm, from the east side even unto the west side, a *portion for* Reuben.

7 And by the border of Reuben, from the east side unto the west side, a *portion for* Judah.

8 ¶ And by the border of Judah, from the east side unto the west side, shall be [b]the offering which ye shall offer of five and twenty thousand *reeds in* breadth, and *in* length as one of the *other* parts, from the east side

3 lip.
c Ps. 1.3. Ps. 92.12. Isa. 41.19. Rev. 22.2.
4 Or, plain.
d Zech. 2.11. Mal. 1.11. Rev. 17.15.
5 two rivers.
e John 5.25. John 6.63. 1 Cor. 15.45.
f Matt. 4.19.
g ver. 15. Num. 34.6. Josh. 23.4.
6 Or, and that which shall not be healed.
7 shall come up.
h Job 8.16. Ps. 1.3. Isa. 61.3.
8 Or, principal.
9 Or, for bruises and sores.
i Gen. 48.5. 1 Chr. 5.1. Jer. 3.18. ch. 48.4,5.
10 Or, swore.
j Num. 34.2. ch. 48.29.
k ch. 48.1.
l Num. 34.8.
m Num. 34.8. 2 Ki. 14.25. Amos 6.2, 14.
n 2 Sam. 8.8.
11 Or, the middle village.
o Num. 34.9.
12 from between.
13 Or, Meribah.
14 Or, valley.
15 Or, toward Teman.
p Acts 2.5. Eph. 2.19-22.
q Rom. 10. 12.
CHAP. 48
a Num. 34.7-9. ch. 47.15.
1 one portion.
b ch. 45.1.

unto the west side: and the sanctuary shall be in the midst of it.

9 The oblation that ye shall offer unto the LORD *shall be* of five and twenty thousand in length, and of ten thousand in breadth.

10 And for them, *even* for the priests, shall be *this* holy oblation; toward the north five and twenty thousand in *length*, and toward the west ten thousand in breadth, and toward the east ten thousand in breadth, and toward the south five and twenty thousand in length: and the sanctuary of the LORD shall be in the midst thereof.

11 [2]*It shall be* for the priests that are sanctified of the sons of Zā-dŏk; which have kept my [3]charge, which went not astray when the children of Israel went astray, as the [c]Levites went astray.

12 And *this* oblation of the land that is offered shall be unto them [4]a thing most holy by the border of the Levites.

13 And over against the border of the priests the Levites *shall have* five and twenty thousand in length, and ten thousand in breadth: all the length *shall be* five and twenty thousand, and the breadth ten thousand.

14 And [d]they shall not sell of it, neither exchange, nor alienate the firstfruits of the land: for *it is* holy unto the LORD.

15 ¶ And [e]the five thousand, that are left in the breadth over against the five and twenty thousand, shall be [f]a profane *place* for the city, for dwelling, and for suburbs: and the city shall be in the midst thereof.

16 And these *shall be* the measures thereof; the north side four thousand and five hundred, and the south side four thousand and five hundred, and on the east side four thousand and five hundred, and the west side four thousand and five hundred.

17 And the suburbs of the city shall be toward the north two hundred and fifty, and toward the south two hundred and fifty, and toward the east two hundred and fifty, and toward the west two hundred and fifty.

18 And the residue in length over against the oblation of the holy *portion shall be* ten thousand eastward, and ten thousand westward: and it shall be over against the oblation of the holy *portion;* and the increase thereof shall be for food unto them that serve the city.

2 Or, The sanctified portion shall be for the priests.
3 Or, ward, or ordinance.
c 2 Chr. 29.4, 5. Neh. 9.34. Jer. 23.11. ch. 22.26. ch. 44.10. Zeph. 3.4. Mal. 2.7,8.
4 holiness of holinesses.
d Ex. 22.29. Lev. 27.10, 28,33.
e ch. 45.6.
f Deut. 20.5. ch. 42.20. ch. 44.23. ch. 45.6.
g Rev. 7.5.
h Num. 24.5. Isa. 33.20. Rev. 21.16.
i Josh. 18.1. Isa. 2.2. Isa. 11.10. Hosea 1.11. Hag. 2.7,9. Matt. 11.28. Matt. 13.16, 17. John 12.32. Rom. 15.9, 12. Rev. 2.1. Rev. 21.3.
5 one portion.
j 2 Chr. 20.2. ch. 47.19.
6 Meribah-kadesh. Num. 20.1, 13. Ps. 106.32. ch. 47.19.
k Gen. 15.18. Num. 34.15. Josh. 15.47. Isa. 27.12.
l ch. 47.14, 21,22.
m Isa. 60.18. Rev. 21.12.

19 And [g]they that serve the city shall serve it out of all the tribes of Israel.

20 All the oblation *shall be* five and twenty thousand by five and twenty thousand: ye shall offer the holy [h]oblation foursquare, with the possession of the city.

21 ¶ And the residue *shall be* for the prince, on the one side and on the other of the holy oblation, and of the possession of the city, over against the five and twenty thousand of the oblation toward the east border, and westward over against the five and twenty thousand toward the west border, over against the portions for the prince: and it shall be the holy oblation; and the sanctuary [i]of the house *shall be* in the midst thereof.

22 Moreover from the possession of the Levites, and from the possession of the city, *being* in the midst *of that* which is the prince's, between the border of Judah and the border of Benjamin, shall be for the prince.

23 As for the rest of the tribes, from the east side unto the west side, Benjamin *shall have* [5]a *portion.*

24 And by the border of Benjamin, from the east side unto the west side, Simeon *shall have* a *portion.*

25 And by the border of Simeon, from the east side unto the west side, Ĭs-să-c͟här a *portion.*

26 And by the border of Ĭs-să-c͟här, from the east side unto the west side, Zĕ-bū-lŭn a *portion.*

27 And by the border of Zĕ-bū-lŭn, from the east side unto the west side, Gad a *portion.*

28 And by the border of Gad, at the south side southward, the border shall be even from [j]Tā-mär *unto* the waters of [6]strife *in* Kā-dĕsh, *and* to [k]the river toward the great sea.

29 This [l]*is* the land which ye shall divide by lot unto the tribes of Israel for inheritance, and these *are* their portions, saith the Lord GOD.

30 ¶ And these *are* the goings out of the city on the north side, four thousand and five hundred measures.

31 And [m]the gates of the city *shall be* after the names of the tribes of Israel: three gates northward; one gate of Reuben, one gate of Judah, one gate of Levi.

32 And at the east side four thousand and five hundred: and three gates; and one gate of Joseph, one gate of Benjamin, one gate of Dan.

33 And at the south side four thou-

sand and five hundred measures: and
three gates; one gate of Simeon, one
gate of Ĭs´-să-char, one gate of Zĕ-bū´-
lŭn.
34 At the west side four thousand and
five hundred, *with* their three gates;
one gate of Gad, one gate of Asher,
one gate of Năph´-tă-lī.
35 *It was* round about [n]eighteen
thousand *measures:* and the name of
the city from *that* day *shall be*,[7] The
LORD *is* there.

n Ps. 72.8. Isa. 2.2. Mal. 1.11.
7 Jehovah-shammah. Ex. 17.15. Judg. 6.24. Ps. 132.14. Joel 3.21. Zech. 2.10.

THE BOOK OF

DANIEL

CHAPTER 1

IN the third year of the reign of Jĕ-
hôi´-ă-kĭm king of Judah [a]came
Nĕb-ū-chăd-nĕz´-zär king of Babylon
unto Jerusalem, and besieged it.
2 And the Lord gave Jĕ-hôi´-ă-kĭm
king of Judah into his hand, with part
[b]of the vessels of the house of God:
which he carried [c]into the land of Shi´-
när to the house of his god; and he
brought the vessels into the treasure
house of his god.
3 ¶ And the king spake unto Ăsh-pĕ-
năz the master of his eunuchs, that he
should bring [1]*certain* of the children
of Israel, and of the king's seed, and of
the princes;
4 Children [d]in whom *was* no blemish,
but well favoured, and skilful in all
wisdom, and cunning in knowledge,
and understanding science, and such
as *had* ability in them to stand in the
king's palace, and whom [e]they might
teach the learning and the tongue of
the Chăl-dē-ăns.
5 And the king appointed them a
daily provision of the king's meat, and
of [2]the wine which he drank: so
nourishing them three years, that at
the end thereof they might stand before the king.
6 Now among these were of the children of Judah, Daniel, Hăn-ă-nī´-ăh,
Mī´-shā-ĕl, and Ăz-ă-rī´-ăh:
7 Unto [f]whom the prince of the
eunuchs gave names: [g]for he gave unto Daniel *the name* of Bĕl-tē-shăz´-zär;
and to Hăn-ă-nī´-ăh, of Shā´-drăch;
and to Mī´-shā-ĕl, of Mē´-shăch; and
to Ăz-ă-rī´-ăh, of Ā-bĕd´-nĕ-gō.
8 ¶ But Daniel purposed in his heart
that he would not defile himself [h]with
the portion of the king's meat, nor
with the wine which he drank: therefore he requested of the prince of the
eunuchs that he might not defile himself.
9 Now [i]God had brought Daniel into
favour and tender love with the prince
of the eunuchs.
10 And the prince of the eunuchs
said unto Daniel, I fear my lord the
king, who hath appointed your meat
and your drink: for why should he
see your faces [3]worse liking than the
children which *are* of your [4]sort? then
shall ye make *me* endanger my head
to the king.
11 Then said Daniel to [5]Mĕl´-zär,
whom the prince of the eunuchs had
set over Daniel, Hăn-ă-nī´-ăh, Mī´-
shā-ĕl, and Ăz-ă-rī´-ăh,
12 Prove thy servants, I beseech thee,
ten days; and let them give us [6]pulse
[7]to eat, and water to drink.
13 Then let our countenances be
looked upon before thee, and the
countenance of the children that eat
of the portion of the king's meat: and
as thou seest, deal with thy servants.
14 So he consented to them in this
matter, and proved them ten days.
15 And at the end of ten days their
countenances appeared fairer and fat-
ter in flesh than all the children which
did eat the portion of the king's meat.
16 Thus Mĕl´-zär took away the portion of their meat, and the wine that
they should drink; and gave them
pulse.
17 ¶ As for these four children, God
[j]gave them [k]knowledge and skill in all
learning and wisdom: and [8]Daniel
had understanding in all visions and
dreams.
18 Now at the end of the days that
the king had said he should bring
them in, then the prince of the eunuchs
brought them in before Nĕb-ū-chăd-
nĕz´-zär.
19 And the king communed with
them; and among them all was found
none like Daniel, Hăn-ă-nī´-ăh, Mī´-
shā-ĕl, and Ăz-ă-rī´-ăh: therefore
stood they before the king.
20 And in all matters of [9]wisdom *and*

CHAP. 1
a 2 Ki. 24.1. 2 Chr. 36.6.
b Jer. 27.19.
c Gen. 10.10. Isa. 11.11. Zech. 5.11.
1 Foretold, 2 Ki. 20.17, 18.
d Lev. 21.18. Judg. 8.18. Acts 7.20.
e Acts 7.22.
2 the wine of his drink.
f Gen. 41.45.
g ch. 5.12.
h Deut. 32. 38. Ps. 141.4. Eze. 4.13. Hosea 9.3,4.
i Gen. 39.21. 1 Ki. 8.50.
3 sadder.
4 Or, term, or, continuance?
5 Or, The steward.
6 of pulse.
7 that we may eat, etc.
j 1 Ki. 3.12. Ps. 119.98-100. Pro. 2.6. Eccl. 2.26. Isa. 28.29.
k Acts 7.22.
8 Or, he made Daniel understand.
9 wisdom of understanding.

understanding, that the king inquired
of them, he found them ten times better than all the magicians *and* astrologers that *were* in all his realm.
21 And [l]Daniel continued *even* unto
the first year of king Cyrus.

CHAPTER 2

AND in the second year of the reign
of Nĕb-ū-chăd-nĕz´-zär Nĕb-ū-
chăd-nĕz´-zär dreamed dreams, wherewith [a]his spirit was troubled, and [b]his
sleep brake from him.
2 Then [c]the king commanded to call
the magicians, and the astrologers,
and the sorcerers, and the Chăl-dē´-
ăns, for to shew the king his dreams.
So they came and stood before the
king.
3 And the king said unto them, I
have dreamed a dream, and my spirit
was troubled to know the dream.
4 Then spake the Chăl-dē´-ăns to the
king in Sỹr´-ĭ-ăck, O king, live for ever:
tell thy servants the dream, and we
will shew the interpretation.
5 The king answered and said to the
Chăl-dē´-ăns, The thing is gone from
me: if ye will not make known unto
me the dream, with the interpretation
thereof, ye shall be [1]cut in pieces, and
your houses shall be made a dunghill.
6 But if ye shew the dream, and the
interpretation thereof, ye shall receive
of me gifts and [2]rewards and great
honour: therefore shew me the dream,
and the interpretation thereof.
7 They answered again and said, Let
the king tell his servants the dream,
and we will shew the interpretation of
it.
8 The king answered and said, I
know of certainty that ye would gain
[3]the time, because ye see the thing is
gone from me.
9 But if ye will not make known unto
me the dream, [d]*there is but* one decree
for you: for ye have prepared lying
and corrupt words to speak before me,
till the time be changed: therefore tell
me the dream, and I shall know that
ye can shew me the interpretation
thereof.
10 ¶ The Chăl-dē´-ăns answered before the king, and said, There is not a
man upon the earth that can shew the
king's matter: therefore *there is* no
king, lord, nor ruler, *that* asked such
things at any magician, or astrologer,
or Chăl-dē´-ăn.
11 And *it is* a rare thing that the king
requireth, and there is none other that
can shew it before the king, [e]except

l ch. 6.28. ch. 10.1. He lived to see that glorious time of the return of his people from the Babylonian captivity, but he did not die then. Until is so used, Ps. 112.8.

CHAP. 2

a Gen. 41.8.
b Esther 6.1.
c Gen. 41.8. Ex. 7.11.

1 made pieces.
2 Or, fee.
3 buy.
d Esther 4.11.
e Ex. 8.10. ch. 5.11. Matt. 19.26.
f Ps. 76.10. Ps. 94.20. Pro. 16.14. Pro. 19.12. Pro. 20.2. Pro. 28.15. Matt. 2.16.
4 returned.
5 chief of the execu-tioners, or, slaughter-men, or, chief marshal.
6 from before God.
7 Or, that they should not destroy Daniel, etc.
g Num. 12.6. Job 33.15, 16.
h Ps. 113.2.
i Job 12.13. Ps. 147.5. Jer. 32.19. Matt. 6.13.
j 1Chr.29.30. Esther 1.13. ch. 7.25.
k Job 12.18. Ps. 75.6,7. Jer. 27.5. ch. 4.17.
l Jas. 1.5.
m Job 12.22. Ps. 25.14.
n Ps. 139.11, 12. Heb. 4.13.
o ch. 5.11.
p Amos 3.7.
8 That I have found.

the gods, whose dwelling is not with
flesh.
12 For this cause the [f]king was angry
and very furious, and commanded to
destroy all the wise *men* of Babylon.
13 And the decree went forth that the
wise *men* should be slain; and they
sought Daniel and his fellows to be
slain.
14 ¶ Then Daniel [4]answered with
counsel and wisdom to Ăr´-ĭ-ŏch the
[5]captain of the king's guard, which
was gone forth to slay the wise *men* of
Babylon:
15 He answered and said to Ăr´-ĭ-ŏch
the king's captain, Why *is* the decree
so hasty from the king? Then Ăr´-ĭ-
ŏch made the thing known to Daniel.
16 Then Daniel went in, and desired
of the king that he would give him
time, and that he would shew the king
the interpretation.
17 Then Daniel went to his house,
and made the thing known to Hăn-ă-
nī´-ăh, Mī´-shā-ĕl, and Ăz-ă-rī´-ăh, his
companions:
18 That they would desire mercies
[6]of the God of heaven concerning this
secret; [7]that Daniel and his fellows
should not perish with the rest of the
wise *men* of Babylon.
19 ¶ Then was the secret revealed
unto Daniel [g]in a night vision. Then
Daniel blessed the God of heaven.
20 Daniel answered and said, Blessed [h]be the name of God for ever and
ever: [i]for wisdom and might are his:
21 And he changeth [j]the times and
the seasons: he [k]removeth kings, and
setteth up kings: [l]he giveth wisdom
unto the wise, and knowledge to them
that know understanding:
22 He [m]revealeth the deep and secret
things: [n]he knoweth what *is* in the
darkness, and [o]the light dwelleth with
him.
23 I thank thee, and praise thee, O
thou God of my fathers, who hast
given me wisdom and might, and hast
[p]made known unto me now what we
desired of thee: for thou hast *now*
made known unto us the king's
matter.
24 ¶ Therefore Daniel went in unto
Ăr´-ĭ-ŏch, whom the king had ordained to destroy the wise *men* of Babylon:
he went and said thus unto him; Destroy not the wise *men* of Babylon:
bring me in before the king, and I will
shew unto the king the interpretation.
25 Then Ăr´-ĭ-ŏch brought in Daniel
before the king in haste, and said thus
unto him, [8]I have found a man of the

[9]captives of Judah, that will make
known unto the king the interpretation.
26 The king answered and said to
Daniel, whose name *was* Bĕl-tē-shăz-
zär, Art thou able to make known unto me the dream which I have seen,
and the interpretation thereof?
27 Daniel answered in the presence
of the king, and said, The secret which
the king hath demanded cannot the
wise *men*, the astrologers, the magicians, the soothsayers, shew unto the
king;
28 But [q]there is a God in heaven that
revealeth secrets, [10]and maketh known
to the king Nĕb-ū-chăd-nĕz-zär what
shall be in the latter days. Thy dream,
and the visions of thy head upon thy
bed, are these;
29 As for thee, O king, thy thoughts
[11]came *into thy mind* upon thy bed,
what should come to pass hereafter:
and he that revealeth secrets maketh
known to thee what shall come to
pass.
30 But [r]as for me, this secret is not
revealed to me for *any* wisdom that I
have more than any living, [12]but for
their sakes that shall make known the
interpretation to the king, and that
thou mightest know the thoughts of
thy heart.
31 ¶ Thou, O king, [13]sawest, and behold a great image. This great image,
whose brightness *was* excellent, stood
before thee; and the form thereof *was*
terrible.
32 This image's head *was* of fine
gold, his breast and his arms of
silver, his belly and his [14]thighs of
brass,
33 His legs of iron, his feet part of
iron and part of clay.
34 Thou sawest till that a stone was
cut out [15]without hands, which smote
the image upon his feet *that were* of
iron and clay, and brake them to
pieces.
35 Then was the iron, the clay, the
brass, the silver, and the gold, broken
to pieces together, and became like
the chaff of the summer threshing-
floors; and the wind carried them
away, that no place was found for
them: and the stone that smote the
image [s]became a great mountain,
[t]and filled the whole earth.
36 ¶ This *is* the dream; and we will
tell the interpretation thereof before
the king.
37 Thou, [u]O king, *art* a king of kings:
for [v]the God of heaven hath given
thee a kingdom, power, and strength,
and glory.
38 And [w]wheresoever the children of
men dwell, the beasts of the field and
the fowls of the heaven hath he given
into thine hand, and hath made thee
ruler over them all. Thou *art* this head
of gold.
39 And after thee shall arise another
[x]kingdom inferior to thee, and another third kingdom of brass, which
shall bear rule over all the earth.
40 And [y]the fourth kingdom shall be
strong as iron: forasmuch as iron
breaketh in pieces and subdueth all
things: and as iron that breaketh all
these, shall it break in pieces and
bruise.
41 And whereas thou sawest the feet
and toes, part of potters' clay, and
part of iron, the kingdom shall be
divided; but there shall be in it of the
strength of the iron, forasmuch as
thou sawest the iron mixed with miry
clay.
42 And *as* the toes of the feet *were*
part of iron, and part of clay, *so* the
kingdom shall be partly strong, and
partly [16]broken.
43 And whereas thou sawest iron
mixed with miry clay, they shall mingle themselves with the seed of men:
but they shall not cleave [17]one to another, even as iron is not mixed with
clay.
44 And in [18]the days of these kings
shall the God of heaven set up a kingdom, which [z]shall never be destroyed:
and the [19]kingdom shall not be left to
other people, [a]*but* it shall break in
pieces and consume all these kingdoms, and it shall stand for ever.
45 Forasmuch [b]as thou sawest that
the stone was cut out of the mountain
[20]without hands, and that it brake in
pieces the iron, the brass, the clay, the
silver, and the gold; the great God
hath made known to the king what
shall come to pass [21]hereafter: and the
dream *is* certain, and the interpretation thereof sure.
46 ¶ Then [c]the king Nĕb-ū-chăd-
nĕz-zär fell upon his face, and worshipped Daniel, and commanded that
they should offer an oblation and
[d]sweet odours unto him.
47 The king answered unto Daniel,
and said, Of a truth *it is*, that your
God *is* a God of gods, and a Lord of
kings, and a revealer of secrets, seeing
thou couldest reveal this secret.
48 Then the king made Daniel a
great man, and gave him many great

9 children of the captivity of Judah.
q Gen. 40.8. Ps. 115.2,3. Amos 4.13.
10 and hath made known.
11 came up.
r Gen. 41.16. Acts 3.12.
12 Or, but for the intent that the interpretation may be made known to the king.
13 wast seeing.
14 Or, sides.
15 Or, which was not in hands.
s Isa. 2.2,3. Micah 4.1,2.
t Ps. 22.27. Ps. 67.1,2. Isa. 11.9. Zech. 14.8, 9. Rev. 11.15.
u Ezra 7.12. Isa. 47.5.
v Ezra 1.2.
w ch. 4.21. Jer. 27.6.
x ch. 5.28.
y ch. 7.7,23. John 11.48.
16 Or, brittle.
17 this with this.
18 their days.
z Gen. 49.10. Ps. 2.6. ch. 4.3,34. Micah 4.7. Luke 1.32.
19 kingdom thereof.
a Ps. 2.9. Isa. 60.12. 1 Cor. 15.24, 25.
b Isa. 28.16.
20 Or, which was not in hands.
21 after this.
c Acts 10.25. Acts 14.13. Rev. 19.10.
d Ezra 6.10.

gifts, and made him ruler over the
whole province of Babylon, and [e]chief
of the governors over all the wise *men*
of Babylon.
49 Then Daniel requested of the king,
and [f]he set Shā′-drăch, Mē′-shăch, and
Ă-bĕd′-nĕ-gō, over the affairs of the
province of Babylon: but Daniel [g]*sat*
in the gate of the king.

CHAPTER 3

NĔB-Ū-CHĂD-NĔZ′-ZÄR the
king made [a]an image of gold,
whose height *was* threescore cubits,
and the breadth thereof six cubits: he
set it up in the plain of Dū′-ră, in the
province of Babylon.
2 Then Nĕb-ū-chăd-nĕz′-zär the king
sent to gather together the princes,
the governors, and the captains, the
judges, the treasurers, the counsellers,
the sheriffs, and all the rulers of the
provinces, to come to the dedication
of the image which Nĕb-ū-chăd-nĕz′-
zär the king had set up.
3 Then the [b]princes, the governors,
and captains, the judges, the treasurers, the counsellers, the sheriffs, and
all the rulers of the provinces, were
gathered together unto the dedication
of the image that Nĕb-ū-chăd-nĕz′-zär
the king had set up; and they stood before the image that Nĕb-ū-chăd-nĕz′-
zär had set up.
4 Then an herald cried [1]aloud, To
you [2]it is commanded, [c]O people, nations, and languages,
5 *That* at what time ye hear the sound
of the cornet, flute, harp, sackbut,
psaltery, [3]dulcimer, and all kinds of
musick, ye fall down and worship the
golden image that Nĕb-ū-chăd-nĕz′-
zär the king hath set up:
6 And whoso falleth not down and
worshippeth shall the same hour be
cast into the midst of [d]a burning fiery
furnace.
7 Therefore at that time, when all
the people heard the sound of the
cornet, flute, harp, sackbut, psaltery,
and all kinds of musick, all the people,
the nations, and the languages, fell
down *and* worshipped the golden
image that Nĕb-ū-chăd-nĕz′-zär the
king had set up.
8 ¶ Wherefore at that time certain
Chăl-dē′-ăns [e]came near, [f]and accused
the Jews.
9 They spake and said to the king
Nĕb-ū-chăd-nĕz′-zär, [g]O king, live for
ever.
10 Thou, O king, hast made a decree,
that every man that shall hear the
sound of the cornet, flute, harp,
sackbut, psaltery, and dulcimer, and
all kinds of musick, shall fall down
and worship the golden image:
11 And whoso falleth not down and
worshippeth, *that* he should be cast into the midst of a burning fiery furnace.
12 There [h]are certain Jews whom
thou hast set over the affairs of the
province of Babylon, Shā′-drăch, Mē′-
shăch, and Ă-bĕd′-nĕ-gō; these men,
O king, [4]have not regarded thee: they
serve not thy gods, nor worship the
golden image which thou hast set up.
13 ¶ Then Nĕb-ū-chăd-nĕz′-zär in *his*
rage and fury commanded to bring
Shā′-drăch, Mē′-shăch, and Ă-bĕd′-
nĕ-gō. Then [i]they brought these men
before the king.
14 Nĕb-ū-chăd-nĕz′-zär spake and
said unto them, *Is it* [5]true, O Shā′-
drăch, Mē′-shăch, and Ă-bĕd′-nĕ-gō,
do not ye serve my [j]gods, nor worship
the golden image which I have set
up?
15 Now if ye be ready that at what
time ye hear the sound of the cornet,
flute, harp, sackbut, psaltery, and
dulcimer, and all kinds of musick, ye
fall down and worship the image
which I have made; [k]*well*: but if ye
worship not, ye shall be cast the
same hour into the midst of a burning fiery furnace; [l]and who *is* that
God that shall deliver you out of my
hands?
16 Shā′-drăch, Mē′-shăch, and Ă-
bĕd′-nĕ-gō, answered and said to the
king, O Nĕb-ū-chăd-nĕz′-zär, [m]we *are*
not careful to answer thee in this
matter.
17 If it be *so*, our God whom we serve
is able to deliver us from the burning
fiery furnace, and [n]he will deliver *us*
out of thine hand, O king.
18 But if not, [o]be it known unto thee,
O king, that we will not serve thy gods,
nor worship the golden image which
thou hast set up.
19 ¶ Then was Nĕb-ū-chăd-nĕz′-zär
[6]full of fury, and the form of his visage
was changed against Shā′-drăch, Mē′-
shăch, and Ă-bĕd′-nĕ-gō: *therefore*
he spake, and commanded that they
should heat the furnace one seven
times more than it was wont to be
heated.
20 And he commanded the [7]most
mighty men that *were* in his army to
bind Shā′-drăch, Mē′-shăch, and Ă-
bĕd′-nĕ-gō, *and* to cast *them* into the
burning fiery furnace.
21 Then these men were bound in

e Gen. 41.40. ch. 4.9.
f Pro. 28.12. ch. 1.17.
g Esther 2.19. Jer. 39.3. Amos 5.15.

CHAP. 3

a 1 Ki. 12.28. Ps. 96.5. Isa. 41.24. Hosea 2.8. 1 Cor. 8.4.
b Matt. 7.13. Acts 19.34, 35. Rom. 1.20, 23.
1 with might.
2 they command.
c ch. 4.1.
3 symphony, or, singing.
d Jer. 29.22. Rev. 13.15.
e ch. 6.12.
f Esther 3.6. Ezra 4.12-16.
g Neh. 2.3. ch. 2.4. ch. 5.10. Hosea 7.3.
h Esther 3.8. ch. 2.49.
4 have set no regard upon thee.
i Matt. 10.18. Mark 13.9. Acts 5.25-27.
5 Or, of purpose, as Ex. 21.13.
j Isa. 46.1.
k Ex. 32.32. Luke 13.9.
l Ex. 5.2. 2 Ki. 18.35.
m Matt. 10.19. Acts 26.24.
n 1 Sam. 17.37. Micah 7.7. 2 Cor. 1.10.
o Matt. 10.32. Heb. 11.25.
6 filled.
7 mighty of strength.

their [8]coats, their hosen, and their
[9]hats, and their *other* garments, and
were cast into the midst of the burning fiery furnace.
22 Therefore because the king's
[10]commandment was urgent, and the
furnace exceeding hot, the [11]flame of
the fire slew those men that took up
Shā-drăch, Mē-shăch, and Ă-bĕd'–
nĕ-gō.
23 And these three men, Shā-drăch,
Mē-shăch, and Ă-bĕd'–nĕ-gō, fell
down [p]bound into the midst of the
burning fiery furnace.
24 Then Nĕb-ū-chăd-nĕz-zär the
king was astonied, and rose up in
haste, *and* spake, and said unto [12]his
counsellers, Did not we cast three men
bound into the midst of the fire? They
answered and said unto the king,
True, O king.
25 He answered and said, Lo, I see
four men loose, [q]walking in the midst
of the fire, and [13]they have no hurt;
and the form of the fourth is like [r]the
Son of God.
26 ¶ Then Nĕb-ū-chăd-nĕz-zär came
near to the [14]mouth of the burning
fiery furnace, *and* spake, and said,
Shā-drăch, Mē-shăch, and Ă-bĕd'–
nĕ-gō, ye servants of the most high
God, come forth, and come *hither*.
Then Shā-drăch, Mē-shăch, and Ă-
bĕd'–nĕ-gō, came forth of the midst
of the fire.
27 And the princes, governors, and
captains, and the king's counsellers,
being gathered together, saw these
men, [s]upon whose bodies the fire had
no power, nor was an hair of their
head singed, neither were their coats
changed, nor the smell of fire had
passed on them.
28 *Then* Nĕb-ū-chăd-nĕz-zär spake,
and said, Blessed *be* the God of Shā-
drăch, Mē-shăch, and Ă-bĕd'–nĕ-gō,
who hath sent his angel, and delivered
his servants that [t]trusted in him, and
have changed the king's word, and
yielded their bodies, that they might
not serve nor worship any god, except
their own God.
29 Therefore [15]I make a decree, That
every people, nation, and language,
which speak [16]any thing amiss against
the God of Shā-drăch, Mē-shăch, and
Ă-bĕd'–nĕ-gō, shall be [17]cut in pieces,
and their houses shall be made a dunghill: [u]because there is no other God
that can deliver after this sort.
30 Then the king [18]promoted Shā-
drăch, Mē-shăch, and Ă-bĕd'–nĕ-gō,
in the province of Babylon.

8 Or, mantles.
9 Or, turbans.
10 word.
11 Or, spark.
p Ps. 33.18. Ps. 91.2. Isa. 43.2. 2 Cor. 1.8-10. 1 Pet. 4.12.
12 Or, his governors.
q Isa. 43.2.
13 there is no hurt in them.
r Job 1.6. Ps. 34.7. John 19.7. Heb. 1.14.
14 door.
s Mark 16.18. Heb. 11.34.
t 1 Chr. 5.20. Ps. 34.7,8. Eph. 1.12, 13. 1 Pet. 1.21.
15 a decree is made by me. ch. 6.26.
16 error.
17 made pieces.
u Deut. 32. 31. Ps. 3.8. ch. 6.27.
18 made to prosper.

CHAP. 4

a ch. 3.4.
1 It was seemly before me.
b Ps. 66.16. ch. 3.26.
c ch. 6.27.
d ch. 2.44.
e ch. 2.28.
f ch. 2.1.
g Gen. 41.8. Isa. 8.19.
h ch. 1.7.
i Ps. 25.14. Isa. 63.11. ch. 5.11-14.
j ch. 1.20. ch. 2.48.
2 I was seeing.
k Ps. 37.35, 36. Isa. 10.33, 34. Eze. 31.3.
l Eze. 17.23. Lam. 4.20.
m Ps. 103.20.
n Isa. 6.3,8. ch. 8.13. Matt. 18.10. Mark 1.24. Luke 4.34. Jude 14.
3 with might.
o ch. 5.20. Amos 3.6. Matt. 3.10. Luke 3.9.

CHAPTER 4

NĔB-Ū-CHĂD-NĔZ-ZÄR the
king, unto [a]all people, nations,
and languages, that dwell in all the
earth; Peace be multiplied unto you.
2 [1]I thought it good to shew the signs
and wonders [b]that the high God hath
wrought toward me.
3 How [c]great *are* his signs! and how
mighty *are* his wonders! his kingdom
is an [d]everlasting kingdom, and his
dominion *is* from generation to generation.
4 ¶ I Nĕb-ū-chăd-nĕz-zär was at rest
in mine house, and flourishing in my
palace:
5 I saw a dream which made me
afraid, and [e]the thoughts upon my
bed and the visions of my head
troubled [f]me.
6 Therefore made I a decree to bring
in all the wise *men* of Babylon before
me, that they might make known unto
me the interpretation of the dream.
7 Then [g]came in the magicians, the
astrologers, the Chăl-dē-ăns, and the
soothsayers: and I told the dream before them; but they did not make
known unto me the interpretation
thereof.
8 ¶ But at the last Daniel came in
before me, whose [h]name *was* Bĕl-tē-
shăz-zär, according to the name of
my god, [i]and in whom *is* the spirit of
the holy gods: and before him I told
the dream, *saying*,
9 O Bĕl-tē-shăz-zär, [j]master of the
magicians, because I know that the
spirit of the holy gods *is* in thee, and
no secret troubleth thee, tell me the
visions of my dream that I have seen,
and the interpretation thereof.
10 Thus *were* the visions of mine
head in my bed; [2]I saw, and behold a
[k]tree in the midst of the earth, and the
height thereof *was* great.
11 The tree grew, and was strong,
and the height thereof reached unto
heaven, and the sight thereof to the
end of all the earth:
12 The leaves thereof *were* fair, and
the fruit thereof much, and in it *was*
meat for all: [l]the beasts of the field
had shadow under it, and the fowls of
the heaven dwelt in the boughs thereof, and all flesh was fed of it.
13 I saw in the visions of my head
upon my bed, and, behold, [m]a watcher
and an holy [n]one came down from
heaven;
14 He cried [3]aloud, and said thus,
Hew [o]down the tree, and cut off his
branches, shake off his leaves, and

scatter his fruit: let [p]the beasts get away from under it, and the fowls from his branches:

15 Nevertheless leave the stump of his roots in the earth, even with a band of iron and brass, in the tender grass of the field; and let it be wet with the dew of heaven, and *let* his portion *be* with the beasts in the grass of the earth:

16 Let his heart be changed from man's, and let a beast's heart be given unto him; and let [q]seven times pass over him.

17 This matter *is* by the decree of the watchers, and the demand by the word of the holy ones: to the intent [r]that the living may know that [s]the most High ruleth in the kingdom of men, and giveth it to whomsoever he will, and setteth up over it the basest of men.

18 This dream I king Nĕb-ū-c̲hăd-nĕz′-zär have seen. Now thou, O Bĕl-tē-shăz′-zär, declare the interpretation thereof, [t]forasmuch as all the wise *men* of my kingdom are not able to make known unto me the interpretation: but thou *art* able; for the spirit of the holy gods *is* in thee.

19 ¶ Then Daniel, whose name *was* Bĕl-tē-shăz′-zär, was astonied for one hour, and his thoughts troubled him. The king spake, and said, Bĕl-tē-shăz′-zär, let not the dream, or the interpretation thereof, trouble thee. Bĕl-tē-shăz′-zär answered and said, My lord, the [u]dream *be* to them that hate thee, and the interpretation thereof to thine enemies.

20 The tree that thou sawest, which grew, and was strong, whose height reached unto the heaven, and the sight thereof to all the earth;

21 Whose leaves *were* fair, and the fruit thereof much, and in it *was* meat for all; under which the beasts of the field dwelt, and upon whose branches the fowls of the heaven had their habitation:

22 It [v]*is* thou, O king, that art grown and become strong: for thy greatness is grown, and reacheth unto heaven, [w]and thy dominion to the end of the earth.

23 And whereas the king saw a watcher and an holy one coming down from heaven, and saying, Hew the tree down, and destroy it; yet leave the stump of the roots thereof in the earth, even with a band of iron and brass, in the tender grass of the field; and let it be wet with the dew of heaven, [x]and *let* his portion *be* with the beasts of the field, till seven times pass over him;

24 This *is* the interpretation, O king, and this *is* the decree of the most High, which is come upon my lord [y]the king:

25 That they shall drive thee from men, and thy dwelling shall be with the beasts of the field, and they shall make thee [z]to eat grass as oxen, and they shall wet thee with the dew of heaven, and seven times shall pass over thee, [a]till thou know that the most High ruleth in the kingdom of men, and giveth [b]it to whomsoever he will.

26 And whereas they commanded to leave the stump of the tree roots; thy kingdom shall be sure unto thee, after that thou shalt have known that the [c]heavens do rule.

27 Wherefore, O king, let my counsel be acceptable unto thee, and [d]break off thy sins by righteousness, and thine iniquities by shewing mercy to the poor; [e]if it may be [4]a lengthening of thy tranquillity.

28 ¶ All this came upon the king Nĕb-ū-c̲hăd-nĕz′-zär.

29 At the end of twelve months he walked [5]in the palace of the kingdom of Babylon.

30 The king [f]spake, and said, Is not this great Babylon, that I have built for the house of the kingdom by the might of my power, and for the honour of my majesty?

31 While [g]the word *was* in the king's mouth, there fell a voice from heaven, *saying*, O king Nĕb-ū-c̲hăd-nĕz′-zär, to thee it is spoken; The kingdom is departed from thee.

32 And they shall drive thee from men, and thy dwelling *shall be* with the beasts of the field: they shall make thee to eat grass as oxen, and seven times shall pass over thee, until thou know that the most High ruleth in the kingdom of men, and giveth it to whomsoever he will.

33 The [h]same hour was the thing fulfilled upon Nĕb-ū-c̲hăd-nĕz′-zär: and he was driven from men, and did eat grass as oxen, and his body was wet with the dew of heaven, till his hairs were grown like eagles' *feathers*, and his nails like birds' *claws*.

34 And at the end of the days I Nĕb-ū-c̲hăd-nĕz′-zär lifted up mine eyes unto heaven, and mine understanding returned unto me, and I blessed the most High, and I praised and honour-

p Eze. 31.12.
q ch. 7.25. ch. 11.13. ch. 12.7.
r Ps. 9.16. Ps. 83.18. Jer. 16.31.
s ch. 2.21. ch. 5.21.
t Gen. 41.8, 15. Isa. 47.12-14. ch. 5.8,15.
u 2 Sam. 18. 32. Jer. 29.7.
v Job 20.5. ch. 2.38.
w Jer. 27.6,7, 8.
x ch. 5.21.
y Job 34.19. Ps. 107.40. Isa. 46.10, 11.
z Ps. 106.20.
a Ps. 9.16. Ps. 58.11. Ps. 64.9. Ps. 83.18.
b Jer. 27.5.
c Matt. 21.25. Luke 15.18.
d Isa. 58.7. Eze. 18.7. Acts 8.22. 1 Pet. 4.8.
e Ps. 41.1.
4 Or, an healing of thine error.
5 Or, upon.
f Pro. 16.18. Isa. 26.10.
g ch. 5.5. Acts 12.23.
h Job 20.5. Ps. 37.35,36.

him [i]that liveth for ever, whose
ominion *is* [j]an everlasting dominion,
nd his kingdom *is* from generation
generation:
35 And [k]all the inhabitants of the
arth *are* reputed as nothing: and [l]he
oeth according to his will in the army
f heaven, and *among* the inhabitants
f the earth: and [m]none can stay his
and, or say unto him, [n]What doest
ou?
36 At the same time my reason re-
rned unto me; and for the glory of
y kingdom, mine honour and bright-
ess returned unto me; and my coun-
ellers and my lords sought unto me;
nd I was established in my kingdom,
nd excellent majesty was added [o]un-
o me.
37 Now I Nĕb-ū-chăd-nĕz'-zär praise
nd extol and honour the King of
eaven, all whose works *are* truth,
nd his ways judgment: and those
hat walk in pride he is able to abase.

CHAPTER 5

BĔL-SHĂZ'-ZÄR the king [a]made
a great feast to a thousand of his
ords, and drank wine before the
housand.
2 Bĕl-shăz'-zär, whiles he tasted the
wine, commanded to bring the golden
nd silver vessels which his [1]father
Nĕb-ū-chăd-nĕz'-zär had [2]taken out
of the temple which *was* in Jerusalem;
hat the king, and his princes, his
wives, and his concubines, might
[b]drink therein.
3 Then they brought the golden vessels that were taken out of the temple
of the house of God which *was* at
Jerusalem; and the king, and his princes, his wives, and his concubines,
drank in them.
4 They drank wine, and praised the
[c]gods of gold, and of silver, of brass,
of iron, of wood, and of stone.
5 ¶ In [d]the same hour came forth
fingers of a man's hand, and wrote
over against the candlestick upon the
plaister of the wall of the king's
palace: and the king saw the part of
the hand that wrote.
6 Then the king's [3]countenance [4]was
changed, and his [e]thoughts troubled
him, so that the [5]joints of his loins
were loosed, and his knees [f]smote
one against another.
7 The king cried [6]aloud to bring in
[g]the astrologers, the Chăl-dē'-ăns, and
the soothsayers. *And* the king spake,
and said to the wise *men* of Babylon,
Whosoever shall read this writing, and
shew me the interpretation thereof,
shall be clothed with [7]scarlet, and *have*
a chain of gold about his neck, [h]and
shall be the third ruler in the kingdom.
8 Then came in all the king's wise
men: but [i]they could not read the
writing, nor make known to the king
the interpretation thereof.
9 Then was king Bĕl-shăz'-zär greatly
troubled, and his [8]countenance was
changed in him, and his lords were
astonied.
10 ¶ *Now* the queen, by reason of the
words of the king and his lords, came
into the banquet house: *and* the queen
spake and said, [j]O king, live for ever:
let not thy thoughts trouble thee, nor
let thy countenance be changed:
11 There is a man in thy kingdom, in
whom *is* the spirit of the holy gods;
and in the days of thy [9]father light and
understanding and wisdom, like the
wisdom of the gods, was found in
him; whom the king Nĕb-ū-chăd-
nĕz'-zär thy [10]father, the king, *I say*,
thy father, made [k]master of the magicians, astrologers, Chăl-dē'-ăns, *and*
soothsayers;
12 Forasmuch [l]as an excellent spirit,
and knowledge, and understanding,
[11]interpreting of dreams, and shewing
of hard sentences, and [12]dissolving of
[13]doubts, were found in the same
Daniel, whom the king named Bĕl-tē-
shăz'-zär: now let Daniel be called,
and he will shew the interpretation.
13 Then was Daniel brought in before the king. *And* the king spake and
said unto Daniel, *Art* thou that
Daniel, which *art* of the children of
the captivity of Judah, whom the king
my [14]father brought out of Jewry?
14 I have even heard of thee, that the
spirit of the gods *is* in thee, and *that*
light and understanding and excellent
wisdom is found in thee.
15 And now the wise *men*, the astrologers, have been brought in before me,
that they should read this writing, and
make known unto me the interpretation thereof: but they could not shew
the interpretation of the thing:
16 And I have heard of thee, that
thou canst [15]make interpretations,
and dissolve doubts: now if thou canst
read the writing, and make known to
me the interpretation thereof, thou
shalt be clothed with scarlet, and *have*
a chain of gold about thy neck, and
shalt be the third ruler in the kingdom.
17 ¶ Then Daniel answered and said
before the king, Let thy gifts be to thyself, and give thy [16]rewards to another;

i ch. 12.7. Rev. 4.10.
j Ps. 10.16. Jer. 10.10. Micah 4.7. Luke 1.33. Rev. 11.15.
k Ps. 39.5. Isa. 40.15.
l 1 Sam. 3.18. Ps. 33.11. Isa. 46.10, 11.
m Job 34.29.
n Job 9.12. Isa. 45.9.
o Job 42.12.

CHAP. 5

a Esther 1.3. Isa. 21.5. Jer. 51.39, 57. Nah. 1.10. Mark 6.21.
1 Or, grandfather.
2 brought forth.
b Pro. 20.1.
c Ps. 115.4-8. Rev. 9.20.
d ch. 4.31.
3 brightnesses.
4 changed it.
e Job 18.11.
5 bindings, or, knots, or, girdles.
f Nah. 2.10.
6 with might.
g Isa. 47.13.
7 Or, purple.
h ch. 6.2.
i Gen. 41.8. Isa. 47.13.
8 brightnesses.
j ch. 3.9.
9 Or, grandfather.
10 Or, grandfather.
k ch. 4.9.
l ch. 6.3.
11 Or, of an interpreter, etc.
12 Or, of a dissolver.
13 knots.
14 Or, grandfather.
15 interpret.
16 Or, fee.

yet I will read the writing unto the
king, and make known to him the interpretation.
18 O thou king, [m]the most high God
gave Nĕb-ū-chăd-nĕz-zär thy father a
kingdom, and majesty, and glory, and
honour:
19 And for the majesty that he gave
him, all [n]people, nations, and languages, trembled and feared before
him: whom he would he slew; and
whom he would he kept alive; and
whom he would he set up; and whom
he would he put down.
20 But [o]when his heart was lifted up,
and his mind hardened [17]in pride,
he was [18]deposed from his kingly
throne, and they took his glory from
him:
21 And he was [p]driven from the sons
of men; and [19]his heart was made like
the beasts, and his dwelling *was* with
the wild asses: they fed him with grass
like oxen, and his body was wet with
the dew of heaven; [q]till he knew that
the most high God ruled in the kingdom of men, and *that* he appointeth
over it whomsoever he will.
22 And thou his son, O Bĕl-shăz-zär,
[r]hast not humbled thine heart, though
thou knewest all this;
23 But hast [s]lifted up thyself against
the Lord of heaven; and they have
brought the vessels of his house before thee, and thou, and thy lords, thy
wives, and thy concubines, have drunk
wine in them; and thou hast praised
the gods of silver, and gold, of brass,
iron, wood, and stone, which see not,
[t]nor hear, nor know: and the God in
whose hand thy breath *is*, and [u]whose
are all thy ways, hast thou not glorified:
24 Then was the part of the hand sent
from him; and this writing was written.
25 ¶ And this *is* the writing that was
written, MĒ-NĒ, MĒ-NĒ, TĒ-KĔL, Ū-
PHÄR-SĬN.
26 This *is* the interpretation of the
thing: MĒ-NĒ; God hath numbered
[v]thy kingdom, and finished it.
27 TĒ-KĔL; [w]Thou art weighed in
the balances, and art found wanting.
28 PĒ-RĒS; Thy kingdom is divided,
and given to the [x]Mēdes and [y]Per-
sians.
29 Then commanded Bĕl-shăz-zär,
and they clothed Daniel with scarlet,
and *put* a chain of gold about his neck,
and made a proclamation concerning
him, that he should be the third ruler
in the kingdom.

m ch. 2.37.
n Jer. 25.9. ch. 3.4.
o Ex. 9.17. Pro. 16.5. Isa. 14.12-17. ch. 4.30.
17 Or, to deal proudly.
18 made to come down.
p ch. 4.32.
19 Or, he made his heart equal, etc.
q Ex. 9.14-16. ch. 4.17.
r 2 Chr. 33. 23. Ps. 119.46.
s Isa. 37.23. Jer. 50.29. Rev. 13.6.
t Ps. 115.5. Isa. 46.6,7. Hab. 2.18.
u Job 31.4. Ps. 139.3. Pro. 20.24.
v Jer. 25.12.
w Ps. 62.9. Jer. 6.30.
x Foretold, Isa. 21.2. Ezra 1.1. ch. 9.1.
y ch. 6.28.
z Jer. 51.31, 39,57.
a ch. 9.1.
20 he as the son of, etc.
21 Or, now.

CHAP. 6

a Esther 1.1.
b 1 Sam. 2.30.
c Pro. 3.35. ch. 5.12.
d Eccl. 4.4.
e Phil. 2.15. 1 Pet. 2.12.
1 Or, came tumultuously.
f Neh. 2.3. ch. 2.4.
2 Or, interdict.
g Esther 1.19.
3 passeth not.
h Ps. 118.9.
i Matt. 10.32.
j Ps. 5.7. Jonah 2.4.
k 1 Ki. 18.36. Ps. 55.17. Ps. 95.6. Luke 22.41. Acts 2.1,2, 15. 1 Thes. 5.17, 18.
l ch. 3.8.

30 ¶ In [z]that night was Bĕl-shăz-z
the king of the Chăl-dē-ăns slain.
31 And [a]Dă-rī-ŭs the Mē-dĭ-ăn too
the kingdom, [20]*being* [21]about thre
score and two years old.

CHAPTER 6

IT pleased Dă-rī-ŭs to set [a]over th
kingdom an hundred and twent
princes, which should be over th
whole kingdom;
2 And over these three president
of whom [b]Daniel *was* first: that th
princes might give accounts unt
them, and the king should have n
damage.
3 Then this Daniel was preferre
above the presidents and princes, be
cause [c]an excellent spirit *was* in him
and the king thought to set him ove
the whole realm.
4 ¶ Then [d]the presidents and prince
sought to find occasion against Danie
concerning the kingdom; but [e]the
could find none occasion nor fault
forasmuch as he *was* faithful, neithe
was there any error or fault found i
him.
5 Then said these men, We shall no
find any occasion against this Danie
except we find *it* against him concern
ing the law of his God.
6 Then these presidents and prince
[1]assembled together to the king, an
said thus unto him, King Dă-rī-ŭs
[f]live for ever.
7 All the presidents of the kingdom
the governors, and the princes, th
counsellers, and the captains, hav
consulted together to establish a roya
statute, and to make a firm [2]decree
that whosoever shall ask a petition o
any God or man for thirty days, save
of thee, O king, he shall be cast into
the den of lions.
8 Now, O king, establish the decree,
and sign the writing, that it be not
changed, according to the law [g]of the
Mēdes and Persians, which [3]altereth
not.
9 Wherefore [h]king Dă-rī-ŭs signed
the writing and the decree.
10 ¶ Now when Daniel knew that the
writing was signed, he went into his
house; and [i]his windows being open
in his chamber [j]toward Jerusalem, he
kneeled upon his knees [k]three times a
day, and prayed, and gave thanks before his God, as he did aforetime.
11 Then these men assembled, and
found Daniel praying and making
supplication before his God.
12 Then [l]they came near, and spake

ˌfore the king concerning the king's
ˌcree; Hast thou not signed a decree,
at every man that shall ask *a petition*
'any God or man within thirty days,
.ve of thee, O king, shall be cast into
e den of lions? The king answered
id said, The thing *is* true, according
the law of the Mēdeṡ and Persians,
hich altereth not.
3 Then answered they and said be-
re the king, That Daniel, which [m]*is*
' the children of the captivity of Ju-
ih, [n]regardeth not thee, O king, nor
e decree that thou hast signed, but
aketh his petition three times a day.
4 Then the king, when he heard
ese words, [o]was sore displeased with
mself, and set *his* heart on Daniel to
eliver him: and he laboured till the
ing down of the sun to deliver him.
5 Then these men assembled unto
e king, and said unto the king,
now, O king, that the law of the
lēdeṡ and Persians *is*, That no de-
ee nor statute which the king estab-
sheth may be changed.
6 Then the king commanded, and
ey brought Daniel, and cast *him* in-
the den of lions. *Now* the king spake
nd said unto Daniel, [p]Thy God
hom thou servest continually, he
ill deliver thee.
17 And [q]a stone was brought, and
id upon the mouth of the den; and
he king sealed it with his own signet,
nd with the signet of his lords; that
ne purpose might not be changed
oncerning Daniel.
18 ¶ Then the king went to his palace,
nd passed the night fasting: neither
vere [4]instruments of musick brought
efore him: and his [s]sleep went from
im.
19 Then the king arose very early in
he morning, and went in haste unto
he den of lions.
20 And when he came to the den, he
ried with a lamentable voice unto
Daniel: *and* the king spake and said
o Daniel, O Daniel, servant of the
iving God, [t]is thy God, whom thou
ervest continually, able to deliver
hee from the lions?
21 Then said Daniel unto the king,
[u]O king, live for ever.
22 My [v]God hath sent [w]his angel,
and hath [x]shut the lions' mouths, that
they have not hurt me: forasmuch as
before him innocency was found in
me; and also before thee, O king, have
I done no hurt.
23 Then was the king exceeding glad
for him, and commanded that they
should take Daniel up out of the den.
So Daniel was taken up out of the
den, [y]and no manner of hurt was
found upon him, because he believed
in his God.
24 ¶ And the king commanded, and
[z]they brought those men which had
accused Daniel, and they cast *them* into
the den of lions, them, [a]their children,
and their wives; and the lions had the
mastery of them, and brake all their
bones in pieces or ever they came at
the bottom of the den.
25 ¶ Then [b]king Dă-rī-ŭs wrote unto
all people, nations, and languages,
that dwell in all the earth; Peace be
multiplied unto you.
26 I [c]make a decree, That in every
dominion of my kingdom men [d]trem-
ble and fear before the God of Daniel:
[e]for he *is* the living God, and stedfast
for ever, and his kingdom *that* which
shall not [f]be destroyed, and his dominion *shall be even* unto the end.
27 He delivereth and rescueth, and
[g]he worketh signs and wonders in
heaven and in earth, who hath delivered Daniel from the [5]power of the
lions.
28 So this Daniel prospered in the
reign of Dă-rī-ŭs, [h]and in the reign of
[i]Cyrus the Persian.

CHAPTER 7

IN the first year of Bĕl-shăz-zär king
of Babylon Daniel [1]had a dream and
visions [a]of his head upon his bed: then
he wrote the dream, *and* told the sum
of the [2]matters.
2 Daniel spake and said, I saw in my
vision by night, and, behold, the four
winds of the heaven strove upon the
great sea.
3 And four great beasts [b]came up
from the sea, diverse one from another.
4 The first *was* [c]like a lion, and had
eagle's wings: I beheld till the wings
thereof were plucked, [3]and it was lifted
up from the earth, and made stand upon the feet as a man, and a man's
heart was given to it.
5 And [d]behold another beast, a second, like to a bear, and [4]it raised up
itself on one side, and *it had* three ribs
in the mouth of it between the teeth
of it: and they said thus unto it, Arise,
devour much flesh.
6 After this I beheld, and lo another,
like a leopard, which had upon the
back of it four wings of a fowl; the
beast had also [e]four heads; and dominion was given to it.

m ch. 1.6.
n Esther 3.8. ch. 3.12. Acts 17.7.
o ch. 3.13. Matt. 27.17-24. Mark 6.26.
p Isa. 41.10. 2 Cor. 1.10.
q Lam. 3.53. Mark 15.46.
r Matt. 27.66.
4 Or, table.
s Esther 6.1. Ps. 77.4. ch. 2.1.
t Gen. 18.14. Jer. 32.17. Zech. 8.6. Matt. 19.26. Luke 1.37.
u ch. 2.4.
v ch. 3.28.
w Heb. 1.14.
x 1 Sam. 17. 37. 2 Tim. 4.17. Heb. 11.33.
y Mark 16.18.
z Deut. 19.19.
a Deut. 24. 16. Esther 9.10.
b ch. 4.1.
c ch. 3.29.
d Ps. 99.1.
e ch. 4.34.
f ch. 2.44. ch. 4.3,34. Luke 1.33.
g ch. 4.3.
5 hand.
h ch. 1.21.
i Ezra 1.1.

CHAP. 7

1 saw.
a ch. 2.28.
2 Or, words.
b Zech. 6.1-4. Rev. 13.1.
c Deut. 28.49. Jer. 4.7,13.
3 Or, wherewith.
d ch. 2.39.
4 Or, it raised up one dominion.
e ch. 8.8,22.

7 After this I saw in the night visions, and behold a fourth beast, dreadful and terrible, and strong exceedingly; and it had great iron teeth: it devoured and brake in pieces, and stamped the residue with the feet of it: and it *was* diverse from all the beasts that *were* before it; [f]and it had ten horns.

8 I considered the horns, and, behold, there [g]came up among them another little horn, before whom there were three of the first horns plucked up by the roots: and, behold, in this horn *were* eyes like the eyes of man, and a mouth speaking great things.

9 ¶ I [h]beheld till the thrones were cast down, and [i]the Ancient of days did sit, whose [j]garment *was* white as snow, and the hair of his head like the pure wool: his throne *was like* the fiery flame, [k]*and* his wheels *as* burning fire.

10 A fiery stream issued and came forth from before him: [l]thousand thousands ministered unto him, and ten thousand times ten thousand stood before him: the judgment was set, and the books were opened.

11 I beheld then because of the voice of the great words which the horn spake: [m]I beheld *even* till the beast was slain, and his body destroyed, and given to the burning flame.

12 As concerning the rest of the beasts, they had their dominion taken away: yet [5]their lives were prolonged for a season and time.

13 I saw in the night visions, and, behold, *one* [n]like the Son of man came with the clouds of heaven, and came to the Ancient of days, and they brought him near before him.

14 And [o]there was given him dominion, and glory, and a kingdom, that all people, nations, and languages, should serve him: his dominion *is* [p]an everlasting dominion, which shall not pass away, and his kingdom *that* which shall not be destroyed.

15 ¶ I Daniel was grieved in my spirit in the midst of *my* [6]body, and the visions of my head troubled me.

16 I came near unto one of them that stood by, and asked him the truth of all this. So he told me, and made me know the interpretation of the things.

17 These great beasts, which are four, *are* four kings, *which* shall arise out of the earth.

18 But [q]the saints of the [7]most High shall take the kingdom, and possess the kingdom for ever, even for ever and ever.

f Rev. 12.3.
g ch. 8.9.
h 1 Cor. 15. 24. Rev. 20.4.
i Ps. 90.2.
j Ps. 104.2. Rev. 1.14.
k Ps. 104.3,4.
l Deut. 33.2. Ps. 68.17. Matt. 25.31, 32. Rev. 5.11.
m Rev. 19.20.
5 a prolonging in life was given them.
n Isa. 9.6,7. Eze. 1.26. Matt. 24.30. Mark 13.26. Luke 21.27. Rev. 1.7.
o Ps. 2.6. Ps. 110.1. Matt. 11.27. John 3.35.
p Isa. 9.7. Obad. 21. Micah 4.7. Luke 1.33. Heb. 12.28.
6 sheath.
q Isa. 60.12.
7 high ones, that is, things, or, places.
8 from all those.
r Rev. 11.7.
s 2 Thes. 2.8.
t 1 Cor. 6.2. Rev. 1.6. Rev. 20.4.
u Rev. 17.12.
v Isa. 37.23.
w Rev. 17.6. Rev. 18.24.
x ch. 2.21.
y Rev. 13.7.
z ch. 12.7. Rev. 12.14.
a Ps. 146.10. Luke 1.33. Rev. 11.15.
9 Or, rulers. Isa. 60.12.
b Luke 2.19.

CHAP. 8

a Neh. 1.1. Esther 2.8. Esther 3.15. Esther 4.16. Esther 8.15. Esther 9.11, 15.

19 Then I would know the truth the fourth beast, which was diver [8]from all the others, exceeding drea ful, whose teeth *were of* iron, and h nails *of* brass; *which* devoured, bral in pieces, and stamped the resid with his feet;

20 And of the ten horns that *were* his head, and *of* the other which can up, and before whom three fell; eve *of* that horn that had eyes, and mouth that spake very great thing whose look *was* more stout than h fellows.

21 I beheld, [r]and the same hor made war with the saints, and pr vailed against them;

22 Until the Ancient of [s]days cam [t]and judgment was given to the sain of the most High; and the time cam that the saints possessed the kingdon

23 Thus he said, The fourth bea shall be the fourth kingdom upo earth, which shall be diverse from a kingdoms, and shall devour the whol earth, and shall tread it down, an break it in pieces.

24 And [u]the ten horns out of th kingdom *are* ten kings *that* sha arise: and another shall rise afte them; and he shall be diverse from th first, and he shall subdue three kings

25 And [v]he shall speak *great* word against the most High, and sha [w]wear out the saints of the most High and think [x]to change times and laws and they [y]shall be given into his han [z]until a time and times and the divid ing of time.

26 But the judgment shall sit, an they shall take away his dominion, t consume and to destroy *it* unto the end

27 And the kingdom and dominion and the greatness of the kingdom un der the whole heaven, shall be give to the people of the saints of the mos High, [a]whose kingdom *is* an everlast ing kingdom, and all [9]dominions sha serve and obey him.

28 Hitherto *is* the end of the matter As for me Daniel, my cogitation much troubled me, and my counten ance changed in me: but I [b]kept th matter in my heart.

CHAPTER 8

IN the third year of the reign of king Bĕl-shăz-zär a vision appeared unt me, *even unto* me Daniel, after tha which appeared unto me at the first

2 And I saw in a vision; and it cam to pass, when I saw, that I *was* a [a]Shû-shăn *in* the palace, which *is* in

the province [b]of Ē-lăm; and I saw in a
vision, and I was by the river of Ū-lâi.
3 Then I lifted up mine eyes, and
saw, and, behold, there stood before
the river a ram which had *two* horns:
and the *two* horns *were* high; but one
was higher than [1]the other, and the
higher came up last.
4 I saw the ram pushing westward,
and northward, and southward; so
that no beasts might stand before
him, neither *was there any* that could
deliver out of his hand; [c]but he did
according to his will, and became
great.
5 And as I was considering, behold,
an he goat came from the west on the
face of the whole earth, and [2]touched
not the ground: and the goat *had* [3]a
notable horn between his eyes.
6 And he came to the ram that had
two horns, which I had seen standing
before the river, and ran unto him in
the fury of his power.
7 And I saw him come close unto the
ram, and he was moved with choler
against him, and smote the ram, and
brake his two horns: and there was no
power in the ram to stand before him,
but he cast him down to the ground,
and stamped upon him: and there was
none that could deliver the ram out of
his hand.
8 Therefore the he goat waxed very
great: and when he was strong, the
great horn was broken; and for it
came up [d]four notable ones toward
the four winds of heaven.
9 And out of one of them came forth
a little horn, which waxed exceeding
great, toward [e]the south, and toward
the east, and toward the [f]pleasant
land.
10 And [g]it waxed great, *even* [4]to the
host of heaven; and [h]it cast down
some of the host and of the stars to the
ground, and stamped upon them.
11 Yea, [i]he magnified *himself* even
[5]to the prince of the host, and [6]by him
the daily *sacrifice* was taken away,
and the place of his sanctuary was
cast down.
12 And [7]an host was given *him*
against the daily *sacrifice* by reason of
transgression, and it cast down the
truth to the ground; and it practised,
and prospered.
13 ¶ Then I heard [j]one saint speaking, and another saint said unto [8]that
certain *saint* which spake, How long
shall be the vision *concerning* the daily
sacrifice, and the transgression [9]of
desolation, to give both the sanctuary and the host to be trodden under
foot?
14 And he said unto me, Unto two
thousand and three hundred [10]days;
then shall the sanctuary be [11]cleansed.
15 ¶ And it came to pass, when I,
even I Daniel, had seen the vision, and
sought for the meaning, then, behold,
there stood before me as the appearance of a man.
16 And I heard a man's voice between *the banks of* Ū-lâi, which called,
and said, [k]Gabriel, make this *man* to
understand the vision.
17 So he came near where I stood:
and when he came, I was afraid, and
[l]fell upon my face: but he said unto
me, Understand, O son of man: for at
the time of the end *shall be* the vision.
18 Now as he was speaking with me,
I was in a deep sleep on my face toward the ground: but he touched me,
and [12]set me upright.
19 And he said, Behold, I will make
thee know what shall be in the last end
of the indignation: for at the time
appointed the end *shall be*.
20 The ram which thou sawest having *two* horns *are* the kings of Mē-dĭ-ă
and Persia.
21 And the rough goat *is* the king of
Grecia: and the great horn that *is* between his eyes *is* the first king.
22 Now that being broken, whereas
four stood up for it, four kingdoms
shall stand up out of the nation, but
not in his power.
23 And in the latter time of their
kingdom, when the transgressors
[13]are come to the full, a king [m]of fierce
countenance, and understanding dark
sentences, shall stand up.
24 And his power shall be mighty,
but [n]not by his own power: and he
shall destroy wonderfully, and shall
prosper, and practise, and shall destroy the mighty and the [14]holy people.
25 And through his policy also he
shall cause craft to prosper in his
hand; and he shall magnify *himself*
in his heart, and by [15]peace shall destroy many: he shall also stand up
against the Prince of princes; but he
shall be [o]broken without hand.
26 And the vision of the evening and
the morning which was told *is* true:
[p]wherefore shut thou up the vision;
for it *shall be* for many days.
27 And I Daniel fainted, and was sick
certain days; afterward I rose up,
[q]and did the king's business; and I was
astonished at the vision, but none
understood *it*.

b Gen. 10.22.
1 the second.
c ch. 11.3.
2 Or, none touched him in the earth.
3 a horn of sight.
d ch. 7.6.
e ch. 11.25.
f Ps. 48.2.
g Isa. 14.13. ch. 11.28.
4 Or, against the host.
h Rev. 12.4.
i Jer. 48.26. ch. 5.23. 2 Thes. 2.4.
5 Or, against.
6 Or, from him.
7 Or, the host was given over for the transgression against the daily sacrifice.
j 1 Pet. 1.12.
8 Palmoni, or, the numberer of secrets, or, the wonderful numberer.
9 Or, making desolate.
10 evening morning.
11 justified.
k ch. 9.21.
l Rev. 1.17.
12 made me stand upon my standing.
13 are accomplished.
m Deut. 28. 50.
n Rev. 13.7.
14 people of the holy ones.
15 Or, prosperity.
o Job 34.20. Lam. 4.6.
p Eze. 12.27. ch. 10.14. Rev. 22.10.
q ch. 2.48,49.

CHAPTER 9

IN the first year [a]of Dă-rī'-ŭs the son of Ă-hăṡ-ū-ē'-rŭs, of the seed of the Mēdeṡ, [1]which was made king over the realm of the Chăl-dē'-ăns;

2 In the first year of his reign I Daniel understood by books the number of the years, whereof the word of the LORD came to [b]Jeremiah the prophet, that he would accomplish seventy years in the desolations of Jerusalem.

3 ¶ And I set my face unto the Lord God, to seek by prayer and supplications, with fasting, and sackcloth, and ashes:

4 And I prayed unto the LORD my God, and made my confession, and said, O Lord, the great and dreadful God, keeping the covenant and mercy to them that love him, and to them that keep his commandments;

5 We [c]have sinned, and have committed iniquity, and have done wickedly, and have rebelled, even by departing from thy precepts and from thy judgments:

6 Neither [d]have we hearkened unto thy servants the prophets, which spake in thy name to our kings, our princes, and our fathers, and to all the people of the land.

7 O Lord, righteousness [2]*belongeth* unto thee, but unto us confusion of faces, as at this day; to the men of Judah, and to the inhabitants of Jerusalem, and unto all Israel, *that are* near, and *that are* far off, through all the countries whither thou hast driven them, because of their trespass that they have trespassed against thee.

8 O Lord, to us *belongeth* confusion of face, to our kings, to our princes, and to our fathers, because we have sinned against thee.

9 To [e]the Lord our God *belong* mercies and forgivenesses, though we have rebelled against him;

10 Neither have we obeyed the voice of the LORD our God, to walk in his laws, which he set before us by his servants the prophets.

11 Yea, all [f]Israel have transgressed thy law, even by departing, that they might not obey thy voice; therefore the curse is poured [g]upon us, and the oath that *is* written in the law of Moses the servant of God, because we have sinned against him.

12 And he [h]hath confirmed his words, which he spake against us, and against our judges that judged us, by bringing upon us a great evil: for under the whole heaven hath not been done as hath been done upon Jerusalem.

13 As *it is* written in the law of Moses, all this evil is come upon us: yet [3]made we not our prayer before the LORD our God, that we might turn from our iniquities, and understand thy truth.

14 Therefore hath the LORD watched upon the evil, and brought it upon us: for the LORD our God *is* righteous in all his works which he doeth: for we obeyed not his voice.

15 And now, O Lord our God, that hast brought thy people forth out of the land of Egypt with a mighty hand, and hast [4]gotten thee renown, as at this day; we have sinned, we have done wickedly.

16 ¶ O Lord, according to all thy righteousness, I beseech thee, let thine anger and thy fury be turned away from thy city Jerusalem, thy holy mountain: because for our sins, and for the iniquities of our fathers, Jerusalem and thy people *are become* a reproach to all *that are* about us.

17 Now therefore, O our God, hear the prayer of thy servant, and his supplications, and cause thy face to shine upon thy sanctuary that is desolate, for the Lord's sake.

18 O my God, incline thine ear, and hear; open thine eyes, and behold our desolations, and the city [5]which is called by thy name: for we do not [6]present our supplications before thee for our righteousnesses, but for thy great mercies.

19 O Lord, hear; O Lord, forgive; O Lord, hearken and do; defer not, for thine own sake, O my God: for thy city and thy people are called by thy name.

20 ¶ And whiles I *was* speaking, and praying, and confessing my sin and the sin of my people Israel, and presenting my supplication before the LORD my God for the holy mountain of my God;

21 Yea, whiles I *was* speaking in prayer, even the man Gabriel, whom I had seen in the vision at the beginning, being caused to fly [7]swiftly, touched me about the time of the evening oblation.

22 And he informed *me*, and talked with me, and said, O Daniel, I am now come forth [8]to give thee skill and understanding.

23 At the beginning of thy supplications the [9]commandment came forth, and I am come to shew *thee;* for thou

CHAP. 9
a ch. 1.21. ch. 5.31.
1 Or, in which he, etc.
b 2 Chr. 36. 21. Ezra 1.1. Jer. 25.11, 12.
c 1 Ki. 8.47. Ezra 9.6. Neh. 1.6. Neh. 9.33, 34. Ps. 106.6. Isa. 64.5,6, 7. Jer. 3.25. Jer. 14.7.
d 2 Chr. 36. 15,16.
2 Or, thou hast, etc. Ezra 9.15. Neh. 9.33. Ps. 51.4. Ps. 119.137. Jer. 12.1.
e Ex. 34.6. Num. 14.18. Neh. 9.17. Joel 2.13.
f Isa. 1.5,6. Jer. 8.10.
g Deut. 27. 15-26.
h Lam. 2.17. Matt. 5.18.
3 intreated we not the face of the, etc.
4 made thee a name.
5 whereupon thy name is called.
6 cause to fall.
7 with weariness, or, flight.
8 to make thee skilful of understanding.
9 word.

art [10]greatly beloved: therefore understand the matter, and consider the vision.

24 [11]Seventy weeks are determined upon thy people and upon thy holy city, [12]to finish the transgression, and [13]to make an end of sins, and to make reconciliation for iniquity, and to bring in everlasting righteousness, and to seal up the vision and [14]prophecy, and to anoint the most Holy.

25 Know therefore and understand, *that* from the going forth of the commandment [15]to restore and to build Jerusalem unto the Messiah the Prince *shall be* seven weeks, and threescore and two weeks: the street [16]shall be built again, and the [17]wall, even [18]in troublous times.

26 And after threescore and two weeks shall [i]Messiah be cut off, [19]but not for himself: [20]and the people of the prince that shall come shall destroy the city and the sanctuary; and the end thereof *shall be* with a flood, and unto the end of the war [21]desolations are determined.

27 And he shall confirm [22]the covenant with many for one week: and in the midst of the week he shall cause the sacrifice and the oblation to cease, [23]and for the overspreading of abominations he shall make *it* desolate, even until the consummation, and that determined shall be poured [24]upon the desolate.

CHAPTER 10

IN the third year of Cyrus king of Persia a thing was revealed unto Daniel, whose name was called Bĕl-tē-shăz´-zär; and the thing *was* true, but the time appointed *was* [1]long: and he understood the thing, and had understanding of the vision.

2 In those days I Daniel was mourning three [2]full weeks.

3 I ate no [3]pleasant bread, neither came flesh nor wine in my mouth, neither did I anoint myself at all, till three whole weeks were fulfilled.

4 And in the four and twentieth day of the first month, as I was by the side of the great river, which *is* [4]Hĭd´-dĕ-kĕl;

5 Then I lifted up mine eyes, and looked, and behold [5]a certain man clothed in linen, whose loins *were* girded with fine gold of Ū´-phăz:

6 His body also *was* like the beryl, and [a]his face as the appearance of lightning, and his eyes as lamps of fire, and his arms and his feet like in colour to polished brass, and the voice of his words like the voice of a multitude.

7 And I Daniel alone saw the vision: for the men that were with me saw not the vision; but a great quaking fell upon them, so that they fled to hide themselves.

8 Therefore I was left alone, and saw [b]this great vision, and there remained no strength in me: for my [6]comeliness was turned in me into corruption, and I retained no strength.

9 Yet heard I the voice of his words: and when I heard the voice of his words, then was I in a deep sleep [c]on my face, and my face toward the ground.

10 ¶ And, behold, an hand touched me, which [7]set me upon my knees and *upon* the palms of my hands.

11 And he said unto me, O Daniel, [8]a man greatly beloved, understand the words that I speak unto thee, and [9]stand upright: for unto thee am I now sent. And when he had spoken this word unto me, I stood trembling.

12 Then said he unto me, [d]Fear not, Daniel: for from the first day that thou didst set thine heart to understand, and to chasten thyself before thy God, thy words were heard, and I am come for thy words.

13 But the prince of the kingdom of Persia withstood me one and twenty days: but, lo, [e]Michael, [10]one of the chief princes, came to help me; and I remained there with the kings of Persia.

14 Now I am come to make thee understand what shall befall thy people in the latter days: for yet the vision *is* for *many* days.

15 And when he had spoken such words unto me, [f]I set my face toward the ground, and I became dumb.

16 And, behold, *one* like the similitude of the sons of men touched [g]my lips: then I opened my mouth, and spake, and said unto him that stood before me, O my lord, by the vision my sorrows are turned upon me, and I have retained no strength.

17 For how can [11]the servant of this my lord talk with this my lord? for as for me, straightway there remained no strength in me, neither is there breath left in me.

18 Then there came again and touched me *one* like the appearance of a man, and he strengthened me,

19 And said, O man greatly beloved, [h]fear not: peace *be* unto thee, be strong, yea, be strong. And when he

10 a man of desires.
11 They begin from the 20th of Artaxerxes.
12 Or, to restrain.
13 Or, to seal up.
14 prophet.
15 Or, to build again Jerusalem.
16 shall return and be built.
17 Or, breach, or, ditch.
18 in strait of times.
i Isa. 53.8.
19 Or, and shall have nothing.
20 Or, and [the Jews] they shall be no more his people: or, and the prince's [Messiah's] future people.
21 Or, it shall be cut off by desolations.
22 Or, a.
23 Or, and upon the battlements shall be the idols of the desolator.
24 Or, upon the desolator.

CHAP. 10

1 great.
2 weeks of days.
3 bread of desires.
4 Or, Tigris.
5 one man.
a Eze. 1.7. Rev. 1.14, 15.
b Matt. 17.1, 2.
6 Or, vigour.
c Song 5.2.
7 moved. Rev. 1.17.
8 a man of desires.
9 stand upon thy standing.
d Luke 2.10.
e ch. 12.1. Jude 9.
10 Or, the first.
f ch. 8.18.
g Isa. 6.7. Jer. 1.9.
11 Or, this servant of my lord.
h Ex. 14.13. Deut. 31.6. Isa. 41.10. Isa. 43.1. Rom. 8.31.

had spoken unto me, I was strengthened, and said, Let my lord speak; for
thou hast strengthened me.
20 Then said he, Knowest thou
wherefore I come unto thee? and now
will I return to fight [i]with the prince
of Persia: and when I am gone forth,
lo, the prince of Grecia shall come.
21 But I will shew thee that which is
noted in the scripture of truth: and
there is none that [12]holdeth with me
in these things, but Michael your
prince.

CHAPTER 11

ALSO I [a]in the first year of Dă-rī-ŭs
[b]the Mēde, *even* I, stood to confirm and to strengthen him.
2 And now will I shew thee the truth.
Behold, there shall stand up yet three
kings in Persia; and the fourth shall be
far richer than *they* all: and by his
strength through his riches he shall
stir up all against the realm of Grecia.
3 And [c]a mighty king shall stand up,
that shall rule with great dominion,
and [d]do according to his will.
4 And when he shall stand up, his
[e]kingdom shall be broken, and shall
be divided toward the four winds of
heaven; and not to his posterity, [f]nor
according to his dominion which he
ruled: for his kingdom shall be plucked up, even for others beside those.
5 ¶ And the king of the south shall
be strong, and *one* of his princes; and
he shall be strong above him, and have
dominion; his dominion *shall be* a
great dominion.
6 And in the end of years they [1]shall
join themselves together; for the
king's daughter of the south shall
come to the king of the north to make
[2]an agreement: but she shall not retain the power of the arm; neither
shall he stand, nor his arm: but she
shall be given up, and they that
brought her, and [3]he that begat her,
and he that strengthened her in *these*
times.
7 But out of a branch of her roots
shall *one* stand up [4]in his estate, which
shall come with an army, and shall enter into the fortress of the king of the
north, and shall deal against them,
and shall prevail:
8 And shall also carry captives into
Egypt their gods, with their princes,
and with [5]their precious vessels of silver and of gold; and he shall continue
more years than the king of the north.
9 So the king of the south shall come
into *his* kingdom, and shall return into
his own land.

10 But his sons [6]shall be stirred up,
and shall assemble a multitude of
great forces: and *one* shall certainly
come, [g]and overflow, and pass
through: [7]then shall he return, and be
stirred up, *even* to his fortress.
11 And the king of the south shall be
moved with choler, and shall come
forth and fight with him, *even* with the
king of the north: and he shall set
forth a great multitude; but the multitude shall be given into his hand.
12 *And* when he hath taken away the
multitude, his [h]heart shall be lifted
up; and he shall cast down *many* ten
thousands: but he shall not be
strengthened *by it*.
13 For the king of the north shall return, and shall set forth a multitude
greater than the former, and shall certainly come [8]after certain years with a
great army and with much riches.
14 And in those times there shall
many stand up against the king of the
south: also [9]the robbers of thy people
shall exalt themselves to establish the
vision; but they shall fall.
15 So the king of the north shall
come, [i]and cast up a mount, and take
[10]the most fenced cities: and the arms
[j]of the south shall not withstand, neither [11]his chosen people, neither *shall*
there be any strength to withstand.
16 But he that cometh against him
shall do according to his own will, and
[k]none shall stand before him: and he
shall stand in the [12]glorious land,
which by his hand shall be consumed.
17 He shall also [l]set his face to enter
with the strength of his whole kingdom, and [13]upright ones with him;
thus shall he do: and he shall give him
the daughter of women, [14]corrupting
her: but she shall not stand *on his side*,
neither [m]be for him.
18 After this shall he turn his face unto the isles, and shall take many: but
a prince [15]for his own behalf shall
cause [16]the reproach offered by him to
cease; without his own reproach he
shall cause *it* to turn upon him.
19 Then he shall turn his face toward
the fort of his own land: but he
shall stumble and fall, [n]and not be
found.
20 Then shall stand up [17]in his estate
[18]a raiser of taxes *in* the glory of the
kingdom: but within few days he shall
be destroyed, neither in [19]anger, nor in
battle.
21 And [20]in his estate shall stand up
a [o]vile person, to whom they shall not
give the honour of the kingdom: but

i Isa. 37.36. Acts 12.23.
12 strengtheneth himself.

CHAP. 11
a ch. 9.1.
b ch. 5.31.
c ch. 7.6. ch. 8.5.
d ch. 8.4.
e ch. 7.8. ch. 8.8. Matt. 12.25.
f ch. 8.22.
1 shall associate themselves.
2 rights.
3 Or, whom she brought forth.
4 Or, in his place, or, office.
5 vessels of their desire.
6 Or, shall war.
g Isa. 8.8. Jer. 46.7,8. ch. 9.26.
7 Or, then shall he be stirred up again.
h 2 Chr. 25. 19. Pro. 16.18. Isa. 10.7-12. ch. 5.19,20, 23.
8 at the end of times, even years.
9 the children of robbers.
i Jer. 6.6.
10 the city of munitions.
j Ps. 33.16.
11 the people of his choices.
k Josh. 1.5.
12 the land of ornament, or, goodly land.
l 2 Chr. 20.3.
13 Or, much uprightness, or, equal conditions.
14 to corrupt.
m ch. 9.26.
15 for him.
16 his reproach.
n Ps. 37.36.
17 Or, in his place.
18 one that causeth an exacter to pass over.
19 angers.
20 Or, in his place.
o 1 Sam. 3.13.

e shall come in peaceably, and obtain
he kingdom by flatteries.
2 And with the arms of a flood shall
hey be overflown from before him,
nd shall be broken; yea, [r]also the
rince of the covenant.
3 And after the league *made* with
im he shall work deceitfully: for he
hall come up, and shall become
rong with a small people.
4 He shall enter [21]peaceably even
pon the fattest places of the pro-
nce; and he shall do *that* which his
thers have not done, nor his fathers'
thers; he shall scatter among them
e prey, and spoil, and riches: *yea*,
nd he shall [22]forecast his devices
gainst the strong holds, even for a
me.
5 And [23]he shall stir up his power
nd his courage against the king of
e south with a great army; and the
ing of the south shall be stirred up
battle with a very great and mighty
rmy; but he shall not stand: for they
hall forecast devices against him.
6 Yea, they that [s]feed of the portion
f his meat shall destroy him, and his
rmy shall overflow: and many shall
ll down slain.
7 And both these kings' [24]hearts
hall be to do mischief, and they shall
peak [t]lies at one table; but it shall not
rosper: for yet the end *shall be* at the
me appointed.
8 Then shall he return into his land
ith great riches; and his heart *shall*
against the holy covenant; and he
hall do *exploits*, and return to his
wn land.
9 At the [25]time appointed he shall
eturn, and come toward the south;
ut it shall not be as the former, or
s the latter.
0 ¶ For [u]the ships of Chĭt´tĭm shall
ome against him: therefore he shall
e grieved, and return, and have in-
ignation against the holy covenant:
shall he do; he shall even return,
nd have intelligence with them that
rsake the holy covenant.
1 And arms shall stand on his part,
nd they [v]shall pollute the sanctuary
f strength, and shall take away the
aily *sacrifice*, and they shall place
e abomination that [26]maketh deso-
te.
2 And such as do wickedly against
e covenant shall he [27]corrupt by
atteries: but the people that do
know their God shall be strong, and
o *exploits*.
3 And [x]they that understand among
the people shall instruct many: [y]yet
they shall fall by the sword, and by
flame, by captivity, and by spoil,
many days.
34 Now when they shall fall, they
shall be holpen with a little help: but
many shall cleave to them with flatteries.
35 And *some* of them of understanding shall fall, to try [28]them, and to
purge, and to make *them* white, *even*
to the time of the end: because *it is* yet
for a time appointed.
36 And the king shall do according
to his will; and he shall [z]exalt himself, and magnify himself above every
god, and shall speak marvellous
things against the God of gods, and
shall prosper till the indignation be
accomplished: for that that is determined shall be done.
37 Neither shall he regard the God
of his fathers, nor the desire of women, [a]nor regard any god: for he shall
magnify himself above all.
38 [29]But [30]in his estate shall he honour
the God of [31]forces: and a god whom
his fathers knew not shall he honour
with gold, and silver, and with precious stones, and [32]pleasant things.
39 Thus shall he do in the [33]most
strong holds with a strange god, whom
he shall acknowledge *and* increase
with glory: and he shall cause them
to rule over many, and shall divide
the land for [34]gain.
40 And at the time of the end shall
the king of the south push at him:
and the king of the north shall come
against him like a whirlwind, with
chariots, and with horsemen, and
with many ships; and he shall enter
into the countries, and shall overflow
and pass over.
41 He shall enter also into the [35]glori-
ous land, and many *countries* shall be
overthrown: but these shall escape
out of his hand, *even* Ē´dọm, and Moab, and the chief of the children of
Ammon.
42 He shall [36]stretch forth his hand
also upon the countries: and the land
of Egypt shall not escape.
43 But he shall have power over the
treasures of gold and of silver, and
over all the precious things of Egypt:
and the Lĭb´y̆-ăns and the Ē-thĭ-ō´pĭ-
ăns *shall be* at his steps.
44 But tidings out of the east and out
of the north shall trouble him: therefore he shall go forth with great fury
to destroy, and utterly to make away
many.

p 2 Sam. 15.6.
q ch. 8.24.
r ch. 8.10.
21 Or, into the peaceable and fat, etc.
22 think his thoughts.
23 Fulfilled 170 B.C.
s Micah 7.5.
24 their hearts.
t Ps. 12.2.
25 Fulfilled 169 B.C.
u Fulfilled 168 B.C. Num. 24.24. Jer. 2.10.
v ch. 8.11.
26 Or, astonisheth.
27 Or, cause to dissemble.
w 1 Chr. 28.9.
x Mal. 2.7.
y Heb. 11.35.
28 Or, by them.
z 2 Thes. 2.4.
a Isa. 14.13.
29 Or, But in his stead.
30 as for the Almighty God, in his seat he shall honour, yea, he shall honour a god, whom, etc.
31 Mauzzim, or, God's protectors, or, munitions.
32 things desired.
33 fortresses of munitions.
34 a price.
35 land of delight, or, ornament, or, goodly land.
36 send forth.

45 And he shall plant the tabernacles
of his palace between [b]the seas in the
[37]glorious holy mountain; yet he shall
come to his end, and none shall help
him.

CHAPTER 12

AND at that time shall Michael
stand up, the great prince which
standeth for the children of thy people: [a]and there shall be a time of
trouble, such as never was since there
was a nation *even* to that same time:
and at that time thy people [b]shall be
delivered, every one that shall be
[c]found written in the book.
2 And many of them that sleep in the
dust of the earth shall awake, [d]some
to everlasting life, and some to shame
and everlasting contempt.
3 And they that be [1]wise shall shine
as the brightness of the firmament;
and they that turn many to righteousness [e]as the stars for ever and
ever.
4 But thou, O Daniel, shut up the
words, and seal the book, *even* to the
time of the end: many shall run to and
fro, and knowledge shall be increased.
5 ¶ Then I Daniel looked, and, behold, there stood other two, the one
on this side of the [2]bank of the river,
and the other on that side of the bank
of the river.
6 And *one* said to the man clothed in
linen, which *was* [3]upon the waters o
the river, [f]How long *shall it be to* th
end of these wonders?
7 And I heard the man clothed i
linen, which *was* upon the waters o
the river, when he held up his righ
hand and his left hand unto heaver
and sware by him that liveth for eve
[g]that *it shall be* for a time, times, an
[4]an half; and [h]when he shall hav
accomplished to scatter the power o
the holy people, all these *things* sha
be finished.
8 And I heard, but I understood not
then said I, O my Lord, what *shall* b
the end of these *things?*
9 And he said, Go thy way, Daniel
for the words *are* closed up and seale
till the time of the end.
10 Many [i]shall be purified, and mad
white, and tried; but the wicked sha
do wickedly: and none of the wicke
shall understand; [j]but the wise sha
understand.
11 And from the time *that* the dail
sacrifice shall be taken away, [5]and th
abomination that [6]maketh desolat
set up, *there shall be* a thousand tw
hundred and ninety days.
12 Blessed *is* he that waiteth, an
cometh to the thousand three hundre
and five and thirty days.
13 But go thou thy way till the en
be: [7]for thou shalt [k]rest, and stand [l]i
thy lot at the end of the days.

b Ps. 48.2.
37 mountain of delight of holiness, or, goodly.
CHAP. 12
a Matt. 24.21. Rev. 16.18.
b Isa. 11.11. Jer. 30.7. Hosea 3.5. Joel 3.16. Rom. 11.26.
c Ex. 32.32. Isa. 4.3. Eze. 13.9. Luke 10.20.
d Matt. 25.46.
1 Or, teachers.
e 1 Cor. 15. 41.
2 lip.
3 Or, from above.
f Ps. 74.9. 1 Pet. 1.12. Rev. 6.10.
g ch. 7.25.
4 Or, part.
h Luke 21.24.
i Zech. 13.9.
j John 7.17.
5 to set up the abomination, etc.
6 Or, astonisheth.
7 Or, and, etc.
k Isa. 57.2.
l Ps. 1.5.

HOSEA

CHAPTER 1

THE [a]word of the LORD that came
unto Hō-ṡē-ă, the son of Bē̂er-ī,
in the days of Ŭz-zī-ăh, Jō-thăm,
Ahaz, *and* Hĕz-ē-kī-ăh, kings of Judah, and in the days of Jĕr-ŏ-bō-ăm
the son of Jō-ăsh, king of Israel.
2 The beginning of the word of the
LORD by Hō-ṡē-ă. And the LORD said
to Hō-ṡē-ă, Go, take unto thee a wife
of whoredoms and children of whoredoms: [b]for the land hath committed
great whoredom, *departing* from the
LORD.
3 So he went and took Gō-mĕr the
daughter of Dĭb-lā-ĭm; which conceived, and bare him a son.
4 And the LORD said unto him, Call
his name Jĕz-rē̂el; for yet a little
while, and I will [1]avenge the blood of
Jĕz-rē̂el upon the house of Jehu, and
will cause to cease the kingdom o
the house of Israel.
5 And it shall come to pass at tha
day, that I will break the bow of Israe
in the valley of Jĕz-rē̂el.
6 ¶ And she conceived again, an
bare a daughter. And *God* said unt
him, Call her name [2]Lō-rû-hä-măh
for [3]I will no more have mercy upon th
house of Israel; [4]but I will utterl
take them away.
7 But I will have mercy upon th
house of Judah, and will save them b
the LORD their God, and will not sav
them by bow, nor by sword, no
by battle, by horses, nor by horse
men.
8 ¶ Now when she had weaned Lō
rû-hä-măh, she conceived, and bar
a son.
9 Then said *God*, Call his name [5]Lō-

CHAP. 1
a 2 Pet. 1.21.
b Deut. 31.16. Judg. 2.17. Ps. 78.27.
1 visit.
2 That is, Not having obtained mercy.
3 I will not add any more to.
4 Or, that I should altogether pardon them.
5 That is, Not my people.

n-mi: for ye *are* not my people, and
will not be your *God.*
10 ¶ Yet [c]the number of the children
Israel shall be as the sand of the sea,
hich cannot be measured nor num-
ered; and it shall come to pass, *that*
the place where it was said unto
em, Ye *are* not my people, *there* it
all be said unto them, *Ye are* [d]the
ns of the living God.
11 Then shall the children of Judah
d the children of Israel be gathered
gether, and appoint themselves one
ead, and they shall come up out of
e land: for great *shall be* the day of
z-reel.

CHAPTER 2

SAY ye unto your brethren, [1]Ăm-
mi; and to your sisters, [2]Rû-hā-
ăh.
2 Plead with your mother, plead:
r [a]she *is* not my wife, neither *am* I
er husband: let her therefore put
way her [b]whoredoms out of her sight,
nd her adulteries from between her
reasts;
3 Lest [c]I strip her naked, and set her
s in the day that she was born, and
ake her as [d]a wilderness, and set her
ke a dry land, and slay her with
hirst.
4 And I will not have mercy upon
er children; for they *be* the children
f whoredoms.
5 For their mother hath played the
arlot: she that conceived them hath
one shamefully: for she said, I will
o after my lovers, [f]that give *me* my
read and my water, my wool and my
ax, mine oil and my [3]drink.
6 ¶ Therefore, behold, [g]I will hedge
p thy way with thorns, and [4]make a
all, that she shall not find her paths.
7 And she shall follow after her lov-
rs, but she shall not overtake them;
nd she shall seek them, but shall not
nd *them:* then shall she say, [h]I will
o and return to my first [i]husband;
or then *was it* better with me than
ow.
8 For she did not know that I gave
er corn, and [5]wine, and oil, and mul-
plied her silver and gold, [6]*which* they
repared for Bā-ăl.
9 Therefore will I return, and take
way my corn in the time thereof, and
ny wine in the season thereof, and
vill [7]recover my wool and my flax
iven to cover her nakedness.
10 And now will I discover her [8]lewd-
ess in the sight of her lovers, and
one shall deliver her out of mine
and.

c Gen. 26.4. Ex. 32.13. Num. 23.10. Deut. 1.10. 1 Ki. 3.8. 1 Chr. 27.23. Rom. 9.27.
6 Or, instead of that.
d John 1.12.

CHAP. 2

1 That is, My people.
2 That is, Having obtained mercy.
a Isa. 50.1.
b Jer. 3.1,9, 13. Eze. 16.25. ch. 1.2.
c Jer. 13.22.
d Eze. 19.13.
e Amos 8.11.
f Jer. 44.17.
3 drinks.
g Job 19.8.
4 wall a wall.
h Luke 15.18.
i Eze. 16.8.
5 new wine.
6 Or, wherewith they made Baal.
7 Or, take away.
8 folly, or, villany.
j Isa. 24.7. Jer. 7.34. Amos 8.10.
9 make desolate.
k Isa. 5.5.
l Judg. 3.7.
m Eze. 23.40.
n Eze. 20.35.
10 to her heart, or, friendly.
o Josh. 7.26. Isa. 65.10. Lam. 3.21. Zech. 9.12. 1 Cor. 13.13.
11 That is, My husband.
12 That is, My lord.
p Ex. 23.13.
q Job 5.23. Isa. 11.6.
r Isa. 2.4. Zech. 9.10.
s Lev. 26.5. Jer. 23.6.
t Isa. 54.13. Jer. 31.33.
u Zech. 8.12.
v Zech. 10.9.
w Zech. 13.9.

11 I [j]will also cause all her mirth to
cease, her feast days, her new moons,
and her sabbaths, and all her solemn
feasts.
12 And I will [9]destroy her vines and
her fig trees, whereof she hath said,
These *are* my rewards that my lovers
have given me: and [k]I will make them
a forest, and the beasts of the field
shall eat them.
13 And I will visit upon her [l]the days
of Bā-ă-lĭm, wherein she burned incense to them, and she [m]decked herself with her earrings and her jewels,
and she went after her lovers, and forgat me, saith the LORD.
14 ¶ Therefore, behold, I will allure
her, and [n]bring her into the wilderness, and speak [10]comfortably unto
her.
15 And I will give her her vineyards
from thence, and [o]the valley of Ā-chôr
for a door of hope: and she shall sing
there, as in the days of her youth, and
as in the day when she came up out of
the land of Egypt.
16 And it shall be at that day, saith
the LORD, *that* thou shalt call me
[11]Ĭsh-ī; and shalt call me no more
[12]Bā-ă-lī.
17 For [p]I will take away the names
of Bā-ă-lĭm out of her mouth, and they
shall no more be remembered by their
name.
18 And in that day will I make a
[q]covenant for them with the beasts of
the field, and with the fowls of heaven,
and *with* the creeping things of the
ground: and [r]I will break the bow and
the sword and the battle out of the
earth, and will make them to lie [s]down
safely.
19 And I will betroth thee unto me
for ever; yea, I will betroth thee unto
me in righteousness, and in judgment, and in lovingkindness, and in
mercies.
20 I will even betroth thee unto me
in faithfulness: and [t]thou shalt know
the LORD.
21 And it shall come to pass in that
day, I [u]will hear, saith the LORD, I
will hear the heavens, and they shall
hear the earth;
22 And the earth shall hear the corn,
and the wine, and the oil; and they
shall hear Jĕz-reel.
23 And I [v]will sow her unto me in the
earth; and I will have mercy upon her
that had not obtained mercy; and I
[w]will say to *them which were* not my
people, Thou *art* my people; and
they shall say, *Thou art* my God.

CHAPTER 3

THEN said the LORD unto me, Go yet, love a woman beloved of *her* friend, yet an adulteress, according to the love of the LORD toward the children of Israel, who look to other gods, and love flagons [1]of wine.

2 So I bought her to me for fifteen *pieces* of silver, and *for* an hṓ-mĕr of barley, and an [2]half hṓ-mĕr of barley:

3 And I said unto her, Thou shalt abide [a]for me many days; thou shalt not play the harlot, and thou shalt not be for *another* man: so *will* I also *be* for thee.

4 For the children of Israel shall abide many days without a king, and without a prince, and without a sacrifice, and without [3]an image, and without an [b]ē-phŏd, and *without* tĕŕ-ă-phĭm:

5 Afterward shall the children of Israel return, and [c]seek the LORD their God, and David [d]their king; and shall fear the LORD and his goodness in the [e]latter days.

CHAPTER 4

HEAR the word of the LORD, ye children of Israel: for the LORD hath a [a]controversy with the inhabitants of the land, because *there is* no truth, nor mercy, nor knowledge [b]of God in the land.

2 By swearing, and lying, and killing, and stealing, and committing adultery, they break out, and [1]blood toucheth blood.

3 Therefore [c]shall the land mourn, and every [d]one that dwelleth therein shall languish, with the beasts of the field, and with the fowls of heaven; yea, the fishes of the sea also shall be taken away.

4 Yet let no man strive, nor reprove another: for thy people *are* as they [e]that strive with the priest.

5 Therefore shalt thou fall [f]in the day, and the prophet also shall fall with thee in the night, and I will [2]destroy thy mother.

6 ¶ My people are [3]destroyed for lack of knowledge: because thou hast rejected knowledge, I will also reject thee, that thou shalt be no priest to me: seeing thou hast forgotten the law of thy God, I will also forget thy children.

7 As they were increased, so they sinned against me: *therefore* will I change their glory into shame.

8 They eat up the sin of my people,

CHAP. 3
1 of grapes.
2 lethech.
a Deut. 21. 13.
3 a standing, or, statue, or, pillar.
b Ex. 28.6.
c Isa. 27.12, 13. Jer. 3.22,23.
d 1 Ki. 12.16. Isa. 55.3,4. Jer. 30.9. Eze. 34.23.
e Micah 4.1.

CHAP. 4
a Micah 6.2.
b Jer. 4.22.
1 bloods.
c Amos 8.8.
d Zeph. 1.3.
e Deut. 17. 12.
f Jer. 6.4.
2 cut off.
3 cut off. Isa. 5.13.
4 lift up their soul to their iniquity.
5 visit upon.
6 cause to return.
g Micah 6.14. Hag. 1.6.
h Isa. 28.7.
i Jer. 2.27.
j Isa. 44.20. Rev. 17.2.
k Job 31.9, 10. Amos 7.17. Rom. 1.28.
7 Or, Shall I not, etc.
8 Or, be punished.
l ch. 9.15. Amos 4.4.
9 That is, House of idols.
m Amos. 8. 14.
n Matt. 15. 14.
10 is gone.
11 shields.

CHAP. 5
1 Or, and I have been a correction.
a Ps. 90.8. Amos 3.2.

and they [4]set their heart on their in
quity.
9 And there shall be, like peopl
like priest: and I will [5]punish them f
their ways, and [6]reward them the
doings.
10 For [g]they shall eat and not ha
enough: they shall commit whor
dom, and shall not increase: becau
they have left off to take heed to th
LORD.
11 Whoredom and wine and ne
wine [h]take away the heart.
12 ¶ My people ask counsel at the
[i]stocks, and their staff declareth unt
them: for [j]the spirit of whoredor
hath caused *them* to err, and they hav
gone a whoring from under the
God.
13 They sacrifice upon the tops
the mountains, and burn incense upo
the hills, under oaks and poplars an
elms, because the shadow thereof
good: [k]therefore your daughters sha
commit whoredom, and your spous
shall commit adultery.
14 [7]I will not punish your daughte
when they commit whoredom, n
your spouses when they commit adu
tery: for themselves are separate
with whores, and they sacrifice wit
harlots: therefore the people *that* dot
not understand shall [8]fall.
15 ¶ Though thou, Israel, play th
harlot, *yet* let not Judah offend; an
[l]come not ye unto Gĭĺ-găl, neither g
ye up to [9]Bĕth-ā́-vĕn, nor [m]swea
The LORD liveth.
16 For Israel slideth back as a back
sliding heifer: now the LORD will fee
them as a lamb in a large place.
17 Ḗ-phră-ĭm *is* joined to idols: l
[n]him alone.
18 Their drink [10]is sour: they hav
committed whoredom continuall
her [11]rulers *with* shame do love, Giv
ye.
19 The wind hath bound her up i
her wings, and they shall be ashame
because of their sacrifices.

CHAPTER 5

HEAR ye this, O priests; an
hearken, ye house of Israel; an
give ye ear, O house of the king; fo
judgment *is* toward you, because y
have been a snare on Mizpah, and
net spread upon Tā́-bôr.
2 And the revolters are profound t
make slaughter, [1]though I *have been*
rebuker of them all.
3 I [a]know Ḗ-phră-ĭm, and Israel
not hid from me: for now, O Ḗ-phră

, thou committest whoredom, *and*
rael is defiled.
[2]They will not frame their doings to
rn unto their God: for the spirit of
horedoms *is* in the midst of them,
d they have not known the LORD.
And the pride of Israel doth testify
his face: therefore shall Israel and
-phră-ĭm fall in their iniquity; Judah
so shall fall with them.
They shall go with their flocks and
ith their herds to seek the LORD;
ıt they shall not find *him;* he hath
ithdrawn himself from them.
They have dealt treacherously
ainst the LORD: for they have be-
otten strange children: now shall [b]a
onth devour them with their por-
ons.
Blow ye the cornet in Gĭb-ĕ-āh,
nd the trumpet in Rā-măh: cry aloud
[c]Bĕth-ā-vĕn, after thee, O Ben-
min.
Ē-phră-ĭm shall be desolate in the
ay of rebuke: among the tribes of
rael have I made known that which
all surely be.
0 The princes of Judah were like
em that [d]remove the bound: *there-*
re I will pour out my wrath upon
em like water.
1 Ē-phră-ĭm *is* oppressed *and* brok-
n in judgment, because he willingly
alked after [e]the commandment.
2 Therefore *will* I *be* unto Ē-phră-
n as a moth, and to the house of Ju-
ah as [3]rottenness.
3 When Ē-phră-ĭm saw his sick-
ess, and Judah *saw* his wound, then
ent Ē-phră-ĭm to the Assyrian, and
nt [4]to king Jâr-ĕb: yet could he not
eal you, nor cure you of your wound.
4 For I *will be* unto Ē-phră-ĭm as a
on, and as a young lion to the house
f Judah: I, *even* I, will tear and go
way; I will take away, and none shall
scue *him*.
15 ¶ I will go *and* return to my place,
ill they acknowledge their offence,
nd seek my face: in their affliction
ey will seek me early.

CHAPTER 6

COME, and let us return unto the
LORD: for [a]he hath torn, and [b]he
ill heal us; he hath smitten, and he
ill bind us up.
2 After two days will he revive us: in
he third day he will raise us up, and
e shall live in his sight.
3 Then [c]shall we know, *if* we follow
n to know the LORD: his going forth
s prepared as the morning; and he
shall come unto us [d]as the rain, as the
latter *and* former rain unto the earth.
4 ¶ O Ē-phră-ĭm, what shall I do unto thee? O Judah, what shall I do unto
thee? for your [1]goodness *is* as a morning cloud, and as the early dew it goeth away.
5 Therefore have I hewed *them* by the
[e]prophets; I have slain them by [f]the
words of my mouth: [2]and thy judgments *are as* the light *that* goeth forth.
6 For I desired [g]mercy, and [h]not sacrifice; and the [i]knowledge of God more
than burnt offerings.
7 But they [3]like men have transgressed the covenant: there have they
dealt treacherously against me.
8 Gilead *is* a city of them that work
iniquity, *and is* [4]polluted with blood.
9 And as troops of robbers wait for a
man, *so* the company of priests murder in the way [5]by consent: for they
commit [6]lewdness.
10 I have seen an horrible thing in
the house of Israel: there *is* the whoredom of Ē-phră-ĭm, Israel is defiled.
11 Also, O Judah, he hath set an
harvest for thee, [j]when I returned the
captivity of my people.

CHAPTER 7

WHEN I would have healed Israel, then the iniquity of Ē-phră-
ĭm was discovered, and the [1]wicked-
ness of Să-mâr-ĭ-ă: for they commit
falsehood; and the thief cometh in,
and the troop of robbers [2]spoileth
without.
2 And they [3]consider not in their
hearts *that* I remember all their wickedness: now their [a]own doings have
beset them about; they are [b]before my
face.
3 They make the king glad with their
wickedness, and the princes with
[c]their lies.
4 They *are* all adulterers, as an oven
heated by the baker, [4]*who* ceaseth
[5]from raising after he hath kneaded
the dough, until it be leavened.
5 In the day of our king the princes
have made *him* sick [6]with bottles of
wine; he stretched out his hand with
scorners.
6 For they have [7]made ready their
heart like an oven, whiles they lie in
wait: their baker sleepeth all the night;
in the morning it burneth as a flaming
fire.
7 They are all hot as an oven, and
have devoured their judges; all their
kings [d]are fallen: [e]*there is* none among
them that calleth unto me.

2 They will not give, or, Their doings will not suffer them.
b Eze. 12.28. Zech. 11.8.
c Josh. 7.2.
d Deut. 19.14.
e 1 Ki. 12.28.
3 Or, a worm.
4 Or, to the king of Jareb, or, to the king that should plead.
5 till they be guilty.

CHAP. 6

a Job 5.18.
b Ex. 15.26. Isa. 30.26. Jer. 30.17. Eze. 34.16.
c Pro. 2.1-9. Matt. 13.11.
d Job 29.23.
1 Or, mercy, or, kindness.
e Jer. 1.10.
f Heb. 4.12.
2 Or, that thy judgments might be, etc.
g Pro. 21.3. Matt. 12.7.
h Ps. 50.8.
i John 17.3.
3 Or, like Adam.
4 Or, cunning for blood.
5 with one shoulder, or, to Shechem.
6 Or, enormity.
j Ps. 126.1.

CHAP. 7

1 evils.
2 strippeth.
3 say not to.
a Pro. 5.22.
b Ps. 90.8.
c Rom. 1.32.
4 Or, the raiser will cease.
5 Or, from waking.
6 Or, with heat through wine.
7 Or, applied.
d 2 Ki. 15.10.
e Isa. 9.13.

8 Ē'phră-ĭm, he [f]hath mixed himself among the people; Ē'phră-ĭm is a cake not turned.

9 Strangers have devoured his strength, and he knoweth *it* not: yea, gray hairs are [8]here and there upon him, yet he knoweth not.

10 And the pride of Israel testifieth to his face: and they do not return to the LORD their God, nor seek him for all this.

11 ¶ Ē'phră-ĭm also is like a silly dove without heart: they call to Egypt, they go to Assyria.

12 When they shall go, I will spread my net upon them; I will bring them down as the fowls of the heaven; I will chastise them, as [g]their congregation hath heard.

13 Woe unto them! for they have fled from me: [9]destruction unto them! because they have transgressed against me: though I have redeemed them, yet they have spoken lies against me.

14 And they have not [h]cried unto me with their heart, when they howled upon their beds: they assemble themselves for corn and wine, *and* they rebel against me.

15 Though I [10]have bound *and* strengthened their arms, yet do they imagine mischief against me.

16 They return, *but* not to the most High: they are like a deceitful bow: their princes shall fall by the sword for the [i]rage of their tongue: this *shall be* their derision in the land of Egypt.

CHAPTER 8

SET the trumpet to [1]thy mouth. *He shall come* [a]as an eagle against the house of the LORD, because they have transgressed my covenant, and trespassed against my law.

2 Israel [b]shall cry unto me, My God, we know thee.

3 Israel hath cast off *the thing that is* good: the enemy shall pursue him.

4 They [c]have set up kings, but not by me: they have made princes, and I knew *it* not: of their silver and their gold have they made them idols, that they may be cut off.

5 ¶ Thy calf, O Să-mâr'ĭ-ă, hath cast *thee* off; mine anger is kindled against them: [d]how long *will it be* ere they attain to innocency?

6 For from Israel *was* it also: the workman made it; therefore it *is* not God: but the calf of Să-mâr'ĭ-ă shall be broken in pieces.

7 For they have sown the wind, and
they shall reap the whirlwind: it ha
no [2]stalk: the bud shall yield no mea
if so be it yield, the strangers sha
swallow it up.

8 Israel is swallowed up: now sha
they be among the Gentiles as a vess
wherein *is* no pleasure.

9 For [e]they are gone up to Assyri
a wild ass alone by himself: Ē'phr
ĭm hath hired [3]lovers.

10 Yea, though they have hir
among the nations, now will I gath
them, and they shall [4]sorrow [5]a litt
for the burden [f]of the king of prince

11 Because Ē'phră-ĭm hath ma
many altars to sin, altars shall be un
him to sin.

12 I have written to him [g] the gre
things of my law, *but* they were coun
ed as [h]a strange thing.

13 [6]They sacrifice flesh *for* the sacr
fices of mine offerings, and eat *it; b*
the LORD accepteth them not; no
will he remember their iniquity, an
visit their sins: they shall return
Egypt.

14 For Israel hath forgotten h
Maker, and [i]buildeth temples; an
Judah hath multiplied fenced citie
but I will send a fire upon his citie
and it shall devour the palaces thereo

CHAPTER 9

REJOICE not, O Israel, for joy, a
other people: for thou hast gon
a whoring from thy God, thou ha
loved a reward [1]upon every cornfloo

2 The floor and the [2]winepress sha
not feed them, and the new wine sha
fail in her.

3 They shall not dwell in [a]the LORD
land; [b]but Ē'phră-ĭm shall return t
Egypt, and [c]they shall eat uncle
things in Assyria.

4 They shall not offer wine *offering*
to the LORD, neither shall they b
pleasing unto him: their sacrifice
shall be unto them [d]as the bread o
mourners; all that eat thereof shall b
polluted: for their bread for their so
shall not come into the house of th
LORD.

5 What will ye do in the solemn da
and in the day of the feast of th
LORD?

6 For, lo, they are gone because o
[3]destruction: Egypt shall gather the
up, Mĕm'phĭs shall bury them: [4]th
pleasant *places* for their silver, nettle
shall possess them: thorns *shall be* i
their tabernacles.

7 The days of visitation are com
the days of recompence are come

---

f Ps. 106.35.
8 sprinkled.
g Lev. 26.14.
9 spoil.
h Job 35.9. Ps. 78.34-37. Isa. 29.13. Jer. 3.10.
10 Or, chastened.
i Ps. 73.9.

CHAP. 8

1 the roof of thy mouth.
a Jer. 4.13. Hab. 1.8.
b Ps. 78.34. Matt. 7.21.
c 1 Ki. 12.16-20. 2 Ki. 15.13, 17,25. Shallum, Menahem, Pekahiah.
d Jer. 13.27.
2 Or, standing corn.
e 2 Ki. 15.19.
3 loves.
4 Or, begin.
5 Or, in a little while.
f Isa. 10.8. Eze. 26.7. Dan. 2.37.
g Deut. 4.6. Neh. 9.13, 14. Pro. 22.20. Rom. 3.1,2.
h Job 21.14.
6 Or, In the sacrifices of mine offerings they, etc.
i 1 Ki. 12.31.

CHAP. 9

1 Or, in, etc.
2 Or, winefat.
a Lev. 18.25. Deut. 4.26, 27.
b ch. 11.5. Not into Egypt itself, but into another bondage as bad as that.
c Eze. 4.13.
d Deut. 26. 14.
3 spoil.
4 the desire, or, their silver shall be desired, the nettle, etc.

srael shall know *it:* the prophet *is* a
ɔol, the [5]spiritual man *is* mad, for the
ıultitude of thine iniquity, and the
reat hatred.
8 The watchman of Ē-́phră-ĭm *was*
ith my God: *but* the prophet *is* a
nare of a fowler in all his ways, *and*
atred [6]in the house of his God.
9 They have deeply corrupted *them-*
elves, as in the days of [e]Gĭb-́ĕ-ăh:
herefore he will remember their ini-
uity, he will visit their sins.
10 I found Israel [f]like grapes in the
ilderness; I saw your fathers as the
rstripe in the fig tree at her first time:
ut they [g]went to Bā-́ăl–pē-́ôr, and
eparated themselves unto *that* shame;
nd *their* abominations were accord-
ng as they loved.
11 *As for* Ē-́phră-ĭm, their glory shall
y away like a bird, from the birth,
nd from the womb, and from the
onception.
12 Though they bring up their chil-
ren, yet will I bereave them, *that*
here shall not *be* a man *left:* yea, woe
lso to them when I depart [h]from
hem!
13 Ē-́phră-ĭm, as I saw Tȳ-́rŭs, *is*
lanted in a pleasant place: but Ē-́
hră-ĭm shall bring forth his children
o the murderer.
14 Give [i]them, O LORD: what wilt
hou give? give them a [7]miscarrying
vomb and dry breasts.
15 All their wickedness *is* in Gĭl-́găl:
or there I hated them: for the wicked-
ess of their doings I will drive them
ut of mine house, I will love them
o more: all their princes *are* revolt-
rs.
16 Ē-́phră-ĭm is smitten, their root is
ried up, they shall bear no fruit: yea,
hough they bring forth, yet will I
lay *even* [8]the beloved *fruit* of their
vomb.
17 My God will [j]cast them away,
ecause they did not hearken unto
im: and they shall be wanderers
mong the nations.

CHAPTER 10

ISRAEL *is* [1]an empty vine, he bringeth forth fruit unto himself: accord-
ng to the multitude of his fruit he
ath increased the altars; according
o the goodness of his land they have
nade goodly [2]images.
2 [3]Their heart is divided; now shall
hey be found faulty: he shall [4]break
lown their altars, he shall spoil their
mages.
3 For now they shall say, We have
no king, because we feared not the
LORD; what then should a king do to
us?
4 They have spoken words, swearing
falsely in making a covenant: thus
judgment springeth up as hemlock in
the furrows of the field.
5 The inhabitants of Să-mâr-́ĭ-ă shall
fear because of [a]the calves of Bĕth–ā-́
vĕn: for the people thereof shall
mourn over it, and [5]the priests thereof *that* rejoiced on it, for the glory
thereof, because it is departed from
it.
6 It shall be also carried unto Assyria *for* a present to [b]king Jâr-́ĕb:
Ē-́phră-ĭm shall receive shame, and
Israel shall be ashamed of his own
counsel.
7 *As for* Să-mâr-́ĭ-ă, her king is cut
off as the foam upon [6]the water.
8 The high places also of Ā-́vĕn, the
[c]sin of Israel, shall be destroyed: the
thorn and the thistle shall come up on
their altars; and they [d]shall say to the
mountains, Cover us; and to the hills,
Fall on us.
9 O Israel, thou hast sinned from the
days of Gĭb-́ĕ-ăh: there they stood:
the battle in Gĭb-́ĕ-ăh against the children of iniquity did not overtake
them.
10 *It is* in [e]my desire that I should
chastise them; and the people shall
be gathered against them, [7]when they
shall bind themselves in their two
furrows.
11 And Ē-́phră-ĭm *is as* an heifer *that*
is taught, *and* loveth to tread out *the*
corn; but I passed over upon [8]her fair
neck: I will make Ē-́phră-ĭm to ride;
Judah shall plow, *and* Jacob shall
break his clods.
12 Sow [f]to yourselves in righteousness, reap in mercy; break up your
fallow ground: for *it is* time to seek
the LORD, till he come and rain righteousness upon you.
13 Ye [g]have plowed wickedness, ye
have reaped iniquity; ye have eaten
the fruit of lies: because thou didst
trust in thy way, in the multitude of
thy mighty men.
14 Therefore shall a tumult arise
among thy people, and all thy fortresses shall be spoiled, as Shăl-́măn
spoiled [h]Bĕth–ăr-́bĕl in the day of
battle: the mother was dashed in
pieces upon *her* children.
15 So shall Beth-el do unto you because of [9]your great wickedness: in a
morning shall the king of Israel utterly
be cut off.

5 man of the spirit.
6 Or, against.
e Judg. 19.22.
f Deut. 32.10.
g Num. 25.3.
h Deut. 31. 17. 1 Sam. 28. 15. ch. 5.6.
i Luke 23.29.
7 that casteth the fruit.
8 the desires.
j 2 Ki. 17.18.

CHAP. 10

1 Or, a vine emptying the fruit which it giveth.
2 statues, or, standing images.
3 Or, He hath divided their heart.
4 behead.
a 1 Ki. 12.28. 2 Ki. 10.29. 2 Chr. 11.15. ch. 8.5,6.
5 Or, Chemarim.
b ch. 5.13.
6 the face of the water.
c Deut. 9.21.
d Rev. 6.16.
e Deut. 28.63. 1 Ki. 14.16. Amos 8.14.
7 Or, when I shall bind them for their two transgressions, or, in their two habitations.
8 the beauty of her neck.
f Pro. 11.18. Eccl. 11.6. Isa. 32.20. Jas. 3.18.
g Job 4.8. Pro. 22.8. ch. 8.7.
h 2 Ki. 18.34.
9 the evil of your evil.

CHAPTER 11

WHEN Israel *was* a child, then I loved him, [a]and called my son [b]out of Egypt.

2 *As* they called them, so they went from them: [c]they sacrificed unto Bā-ă-lĭm, and burned incense to graven images.

3 I [d]taught Ē-phră-ĭm also to go, taking them by their arms; but they knew not that [e]I healed them.

4 I drew them with cords of a man, with bands of love: and I was to them as they that [1]take off the yoke on their jaws, and I [f]laid meat unto them.

5 ¶ He shall not return into the land of Egypt, but the Assyrian shall be his king, because they [g]refused to return.

6 And the sword shall abide on his cities, and shall consume his branches, and devour *them*, because of their own counsels.

7 And my people are bent to backsliding from me: though they called them to the most High, [2]none at all would exalt *him*.

8 How [h]shall I give thee up, Ē-phră-ĭm? *how* shall I deliver thee, Israel? how shall I make thee [i]as Ăd-māh? *how* shall I set thee as Zĕ-bō-ĭm? [j]mine heart is turned within me, my repentings are kindled together.

9 I will not execute the fierceness of mine anger, I will not return to destroy Ē-phră-ĭm: [k]for I *am* God, and not man; the Holy One in the midst of thee: and I will not enter into the city.

10 They shall walk after the LORD: he shall roar like a lion: when he shall roar, then the children shall tremble from the west.

11 They shall tremble as a bird out of Egypt, and as a dove out of the land of Assyria: and I will place them in their houses, saith the LORD.

12 Ē-phră-ĭm compasseth me about with lies, and the house of Israel with deceit: but Judah yet ruleth with God, and is faithful [3]with the saints.

CHAPTER 12

Ē-PHRĂ-ĬM feedeth on wind, and followeth after the east wind: he daily increaseth lies and desolation; [a]and they do make a covenant with the Assyrians, and oil is [b]carried into Egypt.

2 The LORD hath also a controversy with Judah, and will [1]punish Jacob according to his ways; according to his doings will he recompense him.

3 ¶ He took his brother by the heel in the womb, and by his strength h [2]had power with God:

4 Yea, he had power over the angel and prevailed: he wept, and mad supplication unto him: he found hir *in* [c]Beth-el, and there he spake wit us;

5 Even the LORD God of hosts; th LORD *is* his memorial.

6 Therefore turn thou to thy God keep mercy and judgment, and wai on thy God continually.

7 ¶ *He is* [3]a merchant, the balance of deceit *are* in his hand: he loveth t [4]oppress.

8 And Ē-phră-ĭm said, Yet I am be come rich, I have found me out sub stance: [5]*in* all my labours they shal find none iniquity in me [6]that *wer* sin.

9 And I *that am* the LORD thy Go from the land of Egypt will yet mak thee to dwell in tabernacles, as in th days of the solemn feast.

10 I have also spoken by the proph ets, and I have multiplied visions, an used similitudes, [7]by the ministry o the prophets.

11 *Is there* iniquity *in* Gilead? surel they are vanity: they sacrifice bull ocks in [d]Gĭl-găl; yea, their altars *ar* as heaps in the furrows of the fields.

12 And Jacob fled into the countr of Syria, and Israel served for a wife and for a wife he kept *sheep*.

13 And by a prophet the LORD brought Israel out of Egypt, and by prophet was he preserved.

14 Ē-phră-ĭm provoked *him* to ange [8]most bitterly: therefore shall he leav his [9]blood upon him, and his [e]re proach shall his Lord return unto him

CHAPTER 13

WHEN Ē-phră-ĭm spake [a]trem bling, he exalted himself in Is rael; but [b]when he offended in Bā-ăl he died.

2 And now [1]they sin more and more and have made them molten image of their silver, *and* idols according t their own understanding, all of it th work of the craftsmen: they say o them, Let [2]the men that sacrifice kis the calves.

3 Therefore they shall be as th morning cloud, and as the early de that passeth away, as the chaff *that* i driven with the whirlwind out of th floor, and as the smoke out of th chimney.

4 Yet I *am* the LORD thy God fron the land of Egypt, and thou shal

---

CHAP. 11

a Matt. 2.15.
b Ex. 4.22.
c 2 Ki. 17.16.
d Isa. 46.3.
e Ex. 15.26.
1 lift up.
f Ps. 78.25.
g 2 Ki. 17.13. Jer. 8.4-6. ch. 6.1. Amos 4.6. Zech. 1.4. 728 B.C. They became tributaries to Salmanasser.
2 together they exalted not.
h Jer. 9.7.
i Gen. 19.25.
j Jer. 31.20.
k Num. 23. 19. Isa. 55.8,9. Mal. 3.6. Rom. 11.29.
3 Or, with the most holy.

CHAP. 12

a 2 Ki. 17.4.
b Isa. 30.6.
1 visit upon.
2 was a prince, or, behaved himself princely.
c Gen. 28.12.
3 Or, Canaan.
4 Or, deceive.
5 Or, all my labours suffice me not: he shall have punishment of iniquity in whom is sin.
6 which.
7 by the hand.
d Amos 4.4.
8 with bitternesses.
9 bloods.
e Deut. 28.37. Dan. 11.18.

CHAP. 13

a Pro. 18.12.
b 2 Ki. 17.16.
1 they add to sin.
2 Or, the sacrificers of men.

know no god but me: for *there is* no saviour beside me.

5 ¶ I did know thee in the wilderness, in the land of [3]great drought.

6 According to their pasture, so were they filled; they were filled, and their heart was exalted; therefore have they forgotten me.

7 Therefore I will be unto them as a lion: as a leopard by the way will I observe *them:*

8 I will meet them as a bear *that is* bereaved *of her whelps,* and will rend the caul of their heart, and there will I devour them like a lion: [4]the wild beast shall tear them.

9 ¶ O Israel, thou hast destroyed thyself; but in me [5]*is* thine help.

10 [6]I will be thy king: where *is any other* that may save thee in all thy cities? and thy judges of whom thou saidst, Give me a king and princes?

11 I [c]gave thee a king in mine anger, and took *him* away in my wrath.

12 The [d]iniquity of Ē-phră-ĭm *is* bound up; his sin *is* hid.

13 The sorrows of a travailing woman shall come upon him: he *is* an unwise son; for he should not stay [7]long in *the place of* the breaking forth of children.

14 I [e]will ransom them from [8]the power of the grave; I will redeem them from death: [f]O death, I will be thy plagues; O grave, I will be thy destruction: [g]repentance shall be hid from mine eyes.

15 ¶ Though he be fruitful among *his* brethren, an east wind shall come, the wind of the LORD shall come up from the wilderness, and his spring shall become dry, and his fountain shall be dried up: he shall spoil the treasure of all [9]pleasant vessels.

16 [10]Să-mâr-ĭ-ă shall become desolate; [h]for she hath rebelled against her God: they shall fall by the sword: their infants shall be dashed in pieces, and their women with child shall be ripped up.

CHAPTER 14

O ISRAEL, [a]return unto the LORD thy God; for thou hast fallen by thine iniquity.

2 Take with you [b]words, and turn to the LORD: say unto him, Take away all iniquity, and [1]receive *us* graciously: so will we render the calves [c]of our lips.

3 Ăssh-ŭr shall not save us; we will not ride upon horses: neither will we say any more to the work of our hands, *Ye are* our gods: for in thee the fatherless findeth mercy.

4 ¶ I will heal their backsliding, I will love them freely: for mine anger is turned away from him.

5 I will be as the dew unto Israel: he shall [2]grow as the lily, and [3]cast forth his roots as Lĕb-ă-nŏn.

6 His branches [4]shall spread, and his beauty shall be as the olive tree, and his smell as Lĕb-ă-nŏn.

7 They that dwell under his shadow shall return; they shall revive *as* the corn, and [5]grow as the vine: the [6]scent thereof *shall be* as the wine of Lĕb-ă-nŏn.

8 Ē-phră-ĭm *shall say,* What have I to do any more with idols? [d]I have heard *him,* and observed him: I *am* like a green fir tree. [e]From me is thy fruit found.

9 Who [f]*is* wise, and he shall understand these *things?* prudent, and he shall know them? for [g]the ways of the LORD *are* right, and the just shall walk in them: but the transgressors shall fall therein.

3 droughts.
4 the beast of the field.
5 in thy help.
6 Rather, Where is thy king? King Hoshea being then in prison.
c 1 Sam. 8.7.
d Deut. 32. 34.
7 a time.
e Isa. 25.8.
8 the hand.
f Isa. 26.19. 1 Cor. 15.54. 1 Thes. 4.14-17. Rev. 21.4.
g Rom. 11.29.
9 vessels of desire.
10 Fulfilled. 2 Ki. 17.6.
h 2 Ki. 18.12.

CHAP. 14

a 1 Sam. 7.3, 4. Isa. 55.6, 7. ch. 12.6.
b Joel 2.17. Rom. 8.26.
1 Or, give good.
c Heb. 13.15.
2 Or, blossom.
3 strike.
4 shall go.
5 Or, blossom.
6 Or, memorial.
d Jer. 31.18.
e Jas. 1.17.
f John 18.37.
g Matt. 11.19.

JOEL

CHAPTER 1

THE [a]word of the LORD that came to Jō-ĕl the son of Pĕ-thū-ĕl.

2 Hear this, ye old men, and give ear, all ye inhabitants of the land. Hath [b]this been in your days, or even in the days of your fathers?

3 Tell [c]ye your children of it, and *let* your children *tell* their children, and their children another generation.

4 [1]That which the palmerworm hath left hath the locust eaten; and that which the locust hath left hath the cankerworm eaten; and that which the cankerworm hath left hath the caterpiller eaten.

5 Awake, ye drunkards, and weep; and howl, all ye drinkers of wine, because of the new wine; [d]for it is cut off from your mouth.

6 For [e]a nation is come up upon my land, strong, and without number,

CHAP. 1

a Heb. 1.1. 2 Pet. 1.21.
b Deut. 4.32. Isa. 7.17 Dan. 12.1. ch. 2.2. Matt. 24.21.
c Ps. 78.4.
1 The residue of the palmer-worm.
d Isa. 32.10.
e Pro. 30.25.

[f]whose teeth *are* the teeth of a lion,
and he hath the cheek teeth of a great
lion.
7 He hath [g]laid my vine waste, and
[2]barked my fig tree: he hath made it
clean bare, and cast *it* away; the branches thereof are made white.
8 ¶ Lament [h]like a virgin girded with
sackcloth for [i]the husband of her
youth.
9 The [j]meat offering and the drink
offering is cut off from the house of
the LORD: the priests, the LORD's
ministers, mourn.
10 The field is wasted, [k]the land
mourneth; for the corn is wasted:
the [l]new wine is [3]dried up, the oil
languisheth.
11 Be [m]ye ashamed, O ye husbandmen; howl, O ye vinedressers, for the
wheat and for the barley; because the
harvest of the field is perished.
12 The vine is dried up, and the fig
tree languisheth; the pomegranate
tree, the palm tree also, and the apple
tree, *even* all the trees of the field, are
withered: because joy [n]is withered
away from the sons of men.
13 Gird [o]yourselves, and lament, ye
priests: howl, ye ministers of the
altar: come, lie all night in sackcloth,
ye ministers of my God: for the meat
offering and the drink offering is
withholden from the house of your
God.
14 ¶ Sanctify [p]ye a fast, call a [4]solemn
assembly, gather the elders [q]*and* all the
inhabitants of the land *into* the house
of the LORD your God, and cry unto
the LORD,
15 Alas [r]for the day! for the day of
the LORD *is* at hand, and as a destruction from the Almighty shall it
come.
16 Is not the meat cut off before our
eyes, *yea*, [s]joy and gladness from the
house of our God?
17 The [5]seed is rotten under their
clods, the garners are laid desolate,
the barns are broken down; for the
corn is withered.
18 How do [t]the beasts groan! the
herds of cattle are perplexed, because
they have no pasture; yea, the flocks
of sheep are made desolate.
19 O LORD, to thee will I cry: for the
fire hath devoured the [6]pastures of the
wilderness, and the flame hath burned
all the trees of the field.
20 The beasts of the field [u]cry also
unto thee: for [v]the rivers of waters are
dried up, and the fire hath devoured
the pastures of the wilderness.

f Rev. 9. 8.
g Isa. 5.6.
2 laid my fig tree for a barking.
h Isa. 22.12.
i Pro. 2.17.
j ch. 2.14.
k Jer. 12.11.
l Isa. 24.7.
3 Or, ashamed.
m Jer. 14.3.
n Isa. 9.3. Jer. 48.33. Hosea 9.1, 2.
o Jer. 4.8.
p 2 Chr. 20.3.
4 Or, day of restraint.
q 2 Chr. 20. 13.
r Jer. 30.7. ch. 2.3. Amos 5.16-18.
s Deut. 12.7, 12. Deut. 16.11.
5 grains.
t 1 Ki. 18.5. Hosea 4.3.
6 Or, habitations.
u Job 38.41. Ps. 104.21.
v 1 Ki. 17.7.

CHAP. 2

1 Or, cornet.
a Num. 10.5. Ps. 87.1.
b Obad. 15. Zeph. 1.14.
c Amos 5.18.
d ch.1. 6.
e Ex. 10.14.
2 of generation and generation.
f Zech. 7.14.
g Jer. 8.21.
3 pot.
4 Or, dart.
h Jer. 50.34.
i Num. 24.23. Mal. 3.2.
j Jer. 4.1. Hosea 12.6.
k 2 Ki. 22.19. Ps. 34.18. Isa. 57.15. Matt. 5.3,4.
l Ex. 34.6. Jonah 4.2.

CHAPTER 2

BLOW ye the [1]trumpet in Zion, and
sound [a]an alarm in my holy mountain: let all the inhabitants of the land
tremble: for [b]the day of the LORD
cometh, for *it is* nigh at hand;
2 A [c]day of darkness and of gloominess, a day of clouds and of thick
darkness, as the morning spread upon
the mountains: [d]a great people and a
strong; [e]there hath not been ever the
like, neither shall be any more after it,
even to the years [2]of many generations.
3 A fire devoureth before them; and
behind them a flame burneth: the land
is as the garden of Eden before them,
[f]and behind them a desolate wilderness; yea, and nothing shall escape
them.
4 The appearance of them *is* as the
appearance of horses; and as horsemen, so shall they run.
5 Like the noise of chariots on the
tops of mountains shall they leap, like
the noise of a flame of fire that devoureth the stubble, as a strong people set
in battle array.
6 Before their face the people shall
be much pained: [g]all faces shall gather
[3]blackness.
7 They shall run like mighty men;
they shall climb the wall like men of
war; and they shall march every one
on his ways, and they shall not break
their ranks:
8 Neither shall one thrust another;
they shall walk every one in his path:
and *when* they fall upon the [4]sword,
they shall not be wounded.
9 They shall run to and fro in the
city; they shall run upon the wall,
they shall climb up upon the houses;
they shall enter in at the windows like
a thief.
10 The earth shall quake before
them; the heavens shall tremble: the
sun and the moon shall be dark, and
the stars shall withdraw their shining:
11 And the LORD shall utter his voice
before his army: for his camp *is* very
great: [h]for *he is* strong that executeth
his word: for the day of the LORD *is*
great and very terrible; and [i]who can
abide it?
12 ¶ Therefore also now, saith the
LORD, turn [j]ye *even* to me with all your
heart, and with fasting, and with
weeping, and with mourning:
13 And [k]rend your heart, and not
your garments, and turn unto the
LORD your God: for he [l]*is* gracious
and merciful, slow to anger, and of

great kindness, and repenteth him of the evil.

14 Who [m]knoweth *if* he will return and repent, and leave [n]a blessing behind him; *even* a meat offering and a drink offering unto the LORD your God?

15 ¶ Blow the trumpet in Zion, sanctify a fast, call a solemn assembly:

16 Gather the people, [o]sanctify the congregation, assemble the elders, [p]gather the children, and those that suck the breasts: let the [q]bridegroom go forth of his chamber, and the bride out of her closet.

17 Let the priests, the ministers of the LORD, weep [r]between the porch and the altar, and let them say, [s]Spare thy people, O LORD, and give not thine heritage to reproach, that the heathen should [5]rule over them: wherefore should they say among the people, Where *is* their God?

18 ¶ Then will the LORD [t]be jealous for his land, [u]and pity his people.

19 Yea, the LORD will answer and say unto his people, Behold, I will send you [v]corn, and wine, and oil, and ye shall be satisfied therewith: and I will no more make you a reproach among the heathen:

20 But [w]I will remove far off from you the northern *army*, and will drive him into a land barren and desolate, with his face toward the east sea, and his hinder part toward the [x]utmost sea, and his stink shall come up, and his ill savour shall come up, because [6]he hath done great things.

21 ¶ Fear [y]not, O land; be glad and rejoice: for the LORD will do great things.

22 Be not afraid, ye beasts of the field: for [z]the pastures of the wilderness do spring, for the tree beareth her fruit, the fig tree and the vine do yield their strength.

23 Be glad then, ye children of Zion, and rejoice [a]in the LORD your God: for he hath given you [7]the former rain [8]moderately, and he will [b]cause to come down for you [c]the rain, the former rain, and the latter rain in the first *month*.

24 And the floors shall be full of wheat, and the fats shall overflow with wine and oil.

25 And I will restore to you the years that the locust hath eaten, the cankerworm, and the caterpiller, and the palmerworm, my great army which I sent among you.

26 And ye shall [d]eat in plenty, and be satisfied, and praise the name of the LORD your God, that hath dealt wondrously with you: and my people shall never be ashamed.

27 And ye shall know that I *am* in [e]the midst of Israel, and *that* [f]I *am* the LORD your God, and none else: and my people shall never be ashamed.

28 ¶ And [g]it shall come to pass afterward, *that* I [h]will pour out my spirit upon all flesh; [i]and your sons and [j]your daughters shall prophesy, your old men shall dream dreams, your young men shall see visions:

29 And also upon [k]the servants and upon the handmaids in those days will I pour out my spirit.

30 And [l]I will shew wonders in the heavens and in the earth, blood, and fire, and pillars of smoke.

31 The sun shall be turned into darkness, and the moon into blood, before the great and the terrible day of the LORD come.

32 And it shall come to pass, *that* [m]whosoever shall call on the name of the LORD shall be delivered: for [n]in mount Zion and in Jerusalem shall be deliverance, as the LORD hath said, and in [o]the remnant whom the LORD shall call.

CHAPTER 3

FOR, behold, in those days, and in that time, when I shall bring again the captivity of Judah and Jerusalem,

2 I [a]will also gather all nations, and will bring them down into the [b]valley of Jĕ-hŏsh´-ă-phăt, and will [c]plead with them there for my people and *for* my heritage Israel, whom they have scattered among the nations, and parted my land.

3 And they have [d]cast lots for my people; and have given a boy for an harlot, and sold a girl for wine, that they might drink.

4 Yea, and what have ye to do with me, O [e]Tyre, and Zi´-dŏn, and all the coasts of Palestine? [f]will ye render me a recompence? and if ye recompense me, swiftly [g]*and* speedily will I return your recompence upon your own head;

5 Because ye have taken my silver and my gold, and have carried into your temples my goodly [1]pleasant things:

6 The children also of Judah and the children of Jerusalem have ye sold unto [2]the Grecians, that ye might remove them far from their border.

7 Behold, I will raise them out of the

m Josh. 14. 12. Zeph. 2.3.
n Isa. 65.8. Hag. 2.19.
o Ex. 19.10.
p 2 Chr. 20. 13.
q 1 Cor. 7.5.
r Matt. 23.35.
s Ex. 32.11. Isa. 37.20.
5 Or, use a by word against them.
t Isa. 42.13. Zech. 1.14.
u Deut. 32. 36. Ps. 103.13.
v Mal. 3.10.
w Ex. 10.19.
x Deut. 11. 24.
6 he hath magnified to do.
y 1 John 4.18.
z Zech. 8.12.
a Ps. 28.7. Isa. 12.2-6. Hab. 3.17-18. Zech. 10.7.
7 Or, a teacher of righteousness.
8 according to righteousness.
b Lev. 26.4.
c Jas. 5.7.
d Micah 6.14.
e Lev. 26.11.
f Isa. 45.5.
g Isa. 44.3.
h John 7.39.
i Isa. 54.13.
j Acts 21.9.
k 1 Cor. 12. 13. Gal. 3.28.
l Mark 13.24.
m Ps. 50.15. Jer. 33.3. Acts 2.21. Rom. 10.13. 1 Cor. 1.2.
n Isa. 46.13. Obad. 17.
o Isa. 11.11. Rom. 9.27.

CHAP. 3

a Zech. 14.2.
b 2 Chr. 20. 26.
c Isa. 66.16.
d Obad. 11.
e Amos 1.6, 9.
f Eze. 25.15.
g Deut. 32.35. Luke 18.7. Jas. 2.13.
1 desirable.
2 the sons of the Grecians.

place whither ye have sold them, and
will return your recompence upon
your own head:
8 And I will sell your sons and your
daughters into the hand of the children of Judah, and they shall sell
them to [h]the Să-bē'ăns, to a people
far off: for the LORD hath spoken *it*.
9 ¶ Proclaim ye this among the Gentiles; [3]Prepare war, wake up the
mighty men, let all the men of war
draw near; let them come up:
10 Beat [i]your plowshares into
swords, and your [4]pruninghooks into
spears: [j]let the weak say, I *am* strong.
11 Assemble yourselves, and come,
all ye heathen, and gather yourselves
together round about: thither [5]cause
thy mighty ones to come down, O
LORD.
12 Let the heathen be wakened, and
come up to [k]the valley of Jĕ-hŏsh'ă-
phăt: for there will I sit to [l]judge all
the heathen round about.
13 Put [m]ye in the sickle, for [n]the harvest is ripe: come, get you down; for
the press is full, the fats overflow; for
their wickedness *is* great.
14 Multitudes, multitudes in the valley of [6]decision: for the day of the
LORD *is* near in the valley of decision.
15 The sun and the moon shall be
darkened, and the stars shall withdraw their shining.
16 The LORD also shall roar out of
Zion, and utter his voice from Jerusalem; and the heavens and the earth
shall shake: but the LORD *will be* the
[7]hope of his people, and the strength
of the children of Israel.
17 So shall ye know that I *am* the
LORD your God dwelling in Zion, my
holy mountain: then shall Jerusalem
be [8]holy, and there shall no [o]strangers
pass through her any more.
18 ¶ And it shall come to pass in that
day, *that* the mountains shall drop
down new wine, and the hills shall
flow with milk, and all the rivers of
Judah shall [9]flow with waters, and [p]a
fountain shall come forth of the house
of the LORD, and shall water the valley of Shĭt'tim.
19 Egypt shall be a desolation, and
Ē'dom shall be a desolate wilderness,
for the violence *against* the children
of Judah, because they have shed innocent blood in their land.
20 But Judah shall [10]dwell for ever,
and Jerusalem from generation to
generation.
21 For I will cleanse their blood *that*
I have not cleansed: [11]for the LORD
dwelleth in Zion.

h Eze. 23.42.
3 Sanctify.
i Isa. 2.4.
4 Or, scythes.
j Zech. 12.8.
5 Or, the LORD shall bring down.
k 2 Chr. 20. 26.
l Ps. 96.13.
m Rev. 14.15.
n Jer. 51.33.
6 Or, concision, or, threshing.
7 place of repair, or, harbour.
8 holiness.
o Isa. 35.8. Nah. 1.15. Rev. 21.27.
9 go.
p Eze. 47.1. Zech. 13.1. Rev. 22.1.
10 Or, abide.
11 Or, even I the LORD that dwelleth in Zion.

AMOS

CHAPTER 1

THE words of Amos, who was
among the [a]herdmen of Tĕ-kō'ă,
which he saw concerning Israel in
[b]the days of Ŭz-zī'ăh king of Judah,
and in the days of Jĕr-ŏ-bō'ăm the son
of Jō'ăsh king of Israel, two years before the [c]earthquake.
2 And he said, The LORD will roar
from Zion, and utter his voice from
Jerusalem; and the habitations of the
shepherds shall mourn, and the top of
Carmel shall wither.
3 Thus saith the LORD; For three
transgressions of [d]Damascus, [1]and
for four, I will not [2]turn away *the
punishment* thereof; [e]because they
have threshed Gilead with threshing
instruments of iron:
4 But I will send a fire into the house
of Hă-ză'ĕl, which shall devour the
palaces of Bĕn–hă'dăd.
5 I will break also the bar of Damascus, and cut off the inhabitant from
[3]the plain of Ā'vĕn, and him that
holdeth the sceptre from [4]the house of
Eden: and [f]the people of Syria shall
go into captivity unto Kĭr, saith the
LORD.
6 ¶ Thus saith the LORD; For three
transgressions of Gā'ză, and for four,
I will not turn away *the punishment*
thereof; because they [5]carried away
captive the whole captivity, to deliver
them up to Ē'dom:
7 But I will send a fire on the wall [h]of
Gā'ză, which shall devour the palaces
thereof:
8 And I will cut off the inhabitant
from Ăsh'dŏd, and him that holdeth
the sceptre from Ăsh'kĕ-lon, and I
will turn mine hand against Ĕk'rŏn:
and the remnant of the Philistines
shall perish, saith the Lord GOD.
9 ¶ Thus saith the LORD; For three
transgressions of Tȳ'rŭs, and for four,
I will not turn away *the punishment*
thereof; because they delivered up the

CHAP. 1
a 2 Sam. 14.2. 2 Chr. 11.6. Ps. 78.70.
b Hosea 1.1.
c Zech. 14.5.
d Isa. 8.4.
1 Or, yea, for four.
2 Or, convert it, or, let it be quiet.
e 2 Ki. 10.33.
3 Or, Bikath-aven.
4 Or, Beth-eden.
f Isa. 7.1.
g 2 Chr. 28. 18.
5 Or, carried them away with an entire captivity.
h 2 Ki. 18.8.

whole captivity to Ē-dŏm, and remembered not [6]the brotherly covenant:
10 But I will send a fire on the wall
of Tȳ-rŭs, which shall devour the
palaces thereof.
11 ¶ Thus saith the LORD; For three
transgressions of [i]Ē-dŏm, and for
four, I will not turn away *the punishment* thereof; because he did pursue
his brother [j]with the sword, and [7]did
cast off all pity, and his anger did tear
perpetually, and he kept his wrath for
ever:
12 But I will send a fire upon Tē-
măn, which shall devour the palaces
of Bŏz-răh.
13 ¶ Thus saith the LORD; For three
transgressions of the children of Ammon, and for four, I will not turn
away *the punishment* thereof; because
they have [8]ripped up the women with
child of Gilead, that they might enlarge their border:
14 But I will kindle a fire in the wall
[k]of Răb-băh, and it shall devour the
palaces thereof, with shouting in the
day of battle, with a tempest in the
day of the whirlwind:
15 And [l]their king shall go into captivity, he and his princes together,
saith the LORD.

CHAPTER 2

THUS saith the LORD; For three
transgressions of [a]Moab, and for
four, I will not turn away *the punishment* thereof; because [b]he burned the
bones of the king of Ē-dŏm into lime:
2 But I will send a fire upon Moab,
and it shall devour the palaces of
[c]Kĕr-ĭ-ōth: and Moab shall die with
tumult, with shouting, *and* with the
sound of the trumpet:
3 And I will cut off [d]the judge from
the midst thereof, and will slay all the
princes thereof with him, saith the
LORD.
4 ¶ Thus saith the LORD; For three
transgressions of Judah, and for four,
I will not turn away *the punishment*
thereof; [e]because they have despised
the law of the LORD, and have not
kept his commandments, and [f]their
lies caused them to err, after [g]the
which their fathers have walked:
5 But [h]I will send a fire upon Judah,
and it shall devour the palaces of
Jerusalem.
6 ¶ Thus saith the LORD; For three
transgressions of Israel, and for four,
I will not turn away *the punishment*
thereof; because they sold [i]the righteous for silver, and the poor for a pair
of shoes;
7 That pant after the dust of the
earth on the head of the poor, and
turn [j]aside the way of the meek: and
[k]a man and his father will go in unto
the *same* [1]maid, to profane [l]my holy
name:
8 And they lay *themselves* down upon clothes [m]laid to pledge [n]by every
altar, and they drink the wine of [2]the
condemned *in* the house of their god.
9 ¶ Yet destroyed I the [o]Amorite before them, whose height *was* like the
height of the cedars, and he *was* strong
as the oaks; yet I destroyed his fruit
from above, and his roots from beneath.
10 Also I brought you up from the
land of Egypt, and led you forty years
through the wilderness, to possess the
land of the Amorite.
11 And I raised up of your sons for
prophets, and of your young men
for [p]Nazarites. *Is it* not even thus,
O ye children of Israel? saith the
LORD.
12 But ye gave the Nazarites wine to
drink; and commanded the prophets,
[q]saying, Prophesy not.
13 Behold, [3]I am pressed under you,
as a cart is pressed *that is* full of
sheaves.
14 Therefore the flight shall perish
from the swift, and the strong shall
not strengthen his force, neither shall
the mighty deliver [4]himself:
15 Neither shall he stand that handleth the bow; and *he that is* swift of
foot shall not deliver *himself:* neither
shall he that rideth the horse deliver
himself.
16 And *he that is* [5]courageous among
the mighty shall flee away naked in
that day, saith the LORD.

CHAPTER 3

HEAR this word that the LORD
hath spoken against you, O children of Israel, against the whole family which I brought up from the land of
Egypt, saying,
2 You only have I known of all the
families of the earth: [a]therefore I will
[1]punish you for all your iniquities.
3 Can two walk together, except they
be agreed?
4 Will a lion roar in the forest, when
he hath no prey? will a young lion
[2]cry out of his den, if he have taken
nothing?
5 Can a bird fall in a snare upon the
earth, where no gin *is* for him? shall

6 the covenant of brethren.
i Mal. 1.4.
j 2 Chr. 28. 17.
7 corrupted his compassions.
8 Or divided the mountains.
k Deut. 3.11. Eze. 25.5.
l Jer. 49.3.

CHAP. 2

a Eze. 25.8. Zeph. 2.8.
b 2 Ki. 3.27.
c Jer. 48.41.
d Num. 24. 17. Jer. 48.7.
e Lev. 26.14. 2 Sam. 12.9, 10. 2 Chr. 36. 14-17. Neh. 1.7. Isa. 5.24. Eze. 20.13, 16. Dan. 9.11.
f Isa. 28.15. Jer. 16.19.
g Eze. 20.13.
h Hosea 8.14.
i Isa. 29.21. ch. 5.11,12.
j Isa. 10.2.
k Eze. 22.11.
1 Or, young woman.
l Lev. 20.3. Eze. 36.20. Rom. 2.24.
m Ex. 22.26.
n 1 Cor. 10. 21.
2 Or, such as have fined, or, mulcted.
o Num. 21. 24.
p Judg. 13.5.
q Isa. 30.10. Acts 4.18.
3 Or, I will press your place, as a cart full of sheaves presseth.
4 his soul, or, life.
5 strong of his heart.

CHAP. 3

a Eze. 9.6. Dan. 9.12. Matt. 11.22. Luke 12.47. Rom. 2.9. 1 Pet. 4.17.
1 visit upon.
2 give forth his voice.

one take up a snare from the earth,
and have taken nothing at all?
6 Shall a [b]trumpet be blown in the
city, and the people [3]not be afraid?
shall there be evil in a city, [4]and the
LORD hath not done *it?*
7 Surely the Lord GOD will do nothing, but [c]he revealeth his secret unto
his servants the prophets.
8 The lion hath roared, who will not
fear? the Lord GOD hath spoken,
[d]who can but prophesy?
9 ¶ Publish in the palaces at Ăsh-
dŏd, and in the palaces in the land of
Egypt, and say, Assemble yourselves
upon the mountains of Să-mâr-ĭ-ă,
and behold the great tumults in the
midst thereof, and the [5]oppressed in
the midst thereof.
10 For they know not to do right,
saith the LORD, who store up violence
and [6]robbery in their palaces.
11 Therefore thus saith the Lord
GOD; An [e]adversary *there shall be*
even round about the land; and he
shall bring down thy strength from
thee, and thy palaces shall be spoiled.
12 Thus saith the LORD; As the shepherd [7]taketh out of the mouth of the
lion two legs, or a piece of an ear; so
shall the children of Israel be taken
out that dwell in Să-mâr-ĭ-ă in the
corner of a bed, and [8]in Damascus *in*
a couch.
13 Hear ye, and testify in the house
of Jacob, saith the Lord GOD, the
God of hosts.
14 That in the day that I shall [9]visit
the transgressions of Israel upon him
I will also visit the altars of Beth-el:
and the horns of the altar shall be cut
off, and fall to the ground.
15 And I will smite the winter house
with the summer house; and the
houses of ivory shall perish, and the
great houses shall have an end, saith
the LORD.

CHAPTER 4

HEAR this word, ye kine of Bā-
shăn, that *are* in the mountain of
Să-mâr-ĭ-ă, which oppress the poor,
which crush the needy, which say to
their masters, Bring, and let us drink.
2 The Lord GOD hath sworn by his
holiness, that, lo, the days shall come
upon you, that he will take you away
with hooks, and your posterity with
fishhooks.
3 And ye shall go out at the breaches,
every *cow at that which is* before her;
and [1]ye shall cast *them* into the palace,
saith the LORD.
4 ¶ Come [a]to Beth-el, and transgress; at Gĭl-găl [b]multiply transgression; and [c]bring your sacrifices every
morning, *and* your tithes after [2]three
years:
5 And [3]offer a sacrifice of thanksgiving with leaven, and proclaim *and*
publish the [d]free offerings: for [4]this
liketh you, O ye children of Israel,
saith the Lord GOD.
6 ¶ And I also have given [e]you cleanness of teeth in all your cities, and
want of bread in all your places: [f]yet
have ye not returned unto me, saith
the LORD.
7 And also I have withholden the
rain from you, when *there were* yet
three months to the harvest: and I
caused it to rain upon one city, and
caused it not to rain upon another
city: one piece was rained upon, and
the piece whereupon it rained not
withered.
8 So two *or* three cities wandered unto one city, to drink water; but they
were not satisfied: yet have ye not returned unto me, saith the LORD.
9 I [g]have smitten you with blasting
and mildew: [5]when your gardens and
your vineyards and your fig trees and
your olive trees increased, the palmer-
worm devoured *them:* yet have ye not
returned unto me, saith the LORD.
10 I have sent among you the pestilence [6]after the manner of Egypt:
your young men have I slain with the
sword, [7]and have taken away your
horses; and I have made the stink of
your camps to come up unto your
nostrils: yet have ye not returned unto me, saith the LORD.
11 I have overthrown *some* of you,
as God overthrew [h]Sodom and Gō-
mŏr-răh, [i]and ye were as a firebrand
plucked out of the burning: yet have
ye not returned unto me, saith the
LORD.
12 Therefore thus will I do unto thee,
O Israel: *and* because I will do this
unto thee, [j]prepare to meet thy God,
O Israel.
13 For, lo, he that formeth the mountains, and createth the [8]wind, [k]and declareth unto man what *is* his thought,
that maketh the morning darkness,
[l]and treadeth upon the high places of
the earth, [m]The LORD, The God of
hosts, *is* his name.

CHAPTER 5

HEAR ye this word which [a]I take
up against you, *even* a lamentation, O house of Israel.
2 The virgin of Israel is fallen; she

b Eze. 33.3.
3 Or, not run together?
4 Or, and shall not the LORD do somewhat?
c Gen. 6.13. Pro. 3.32. Dan. 9.22-27. John 15.15. Rev. 1.1,19.
d 1 Cor. 9.16.
5 Or, oppressions.
6 Or, spoil.
e 2 Ki. 17.6.
7 delivereth.
8 Or, on the bed's feet.
9 Or, punish Israel for.

CHAP. 4.

1 Or, ye shall cast away the things of the palace.
a Eze. 20.39.
b Hosea 4.15.
c Num. 28.3, 4.
2 three years of days.
3 offer by burning.
d Deut. 12.6.
4 so ye love.
e 1 Ki. 17.1.
f Isa. 9.13. Jer. 5.3. Hosea 5.15. Hag. 2.17.
g Deut. 28. 22.
5 Or, the multitude of your gardens, etc., did the palmer-worm, etc.
6 Or, in the way.
7 with the captivity of your horses.
h Isa. 13.19.
i Zech. 3.2.
j Eze. 13.5. Matt. 5.25, 26. 1 Thes. 5.2. Rev. 3.3.
8 Or, spirit.
k Ps. 139.2. Dan. 2.28. Matt. 9.4. John 2.25.
l Deut. 32.13.
m Isa. 47.4.

CHAP. 5

a Jer. 7.29.

hall no more rise: she is forsaken upon her land; *there is* none to raise her
ip.
3 For thus saith the Lord GOD; The
ity that went out *by* a thousand shall
eave an hundred, and that which
vent forth *by* an hundred shall leave
en, to the house of Israel.
4 ¶ For thus saith the LORD unto the
iouse of Israel, [b]Seek ye me, and [c]ye
hall live:
5 But seek not [d]Beth-el, nor enter
nto Gĭl-găl, and pass not to [e]Bē̂er-
hē-bă: for Gĭl-găl shall surely go into
aptivity, and Beth-el shall come to
iought.
6 Seek the LORD, and ye shall live;
est he break out like fire in the house
of Joseph, and devour *it*, and *there be*
ione to quench *it* in Beth-el.
7 Ye who turn judgment to worm-
vood, and leave off righteousness in
he earth,
8 *Seek him* that maketh the [f]seven
tars and Ō-rī-on, and turneth the
hadow of death into the morning,
ind maketh the day dark with night:
hat [g]calleth for the waters of the sea,
ind poureth them out upon the face
of the earth: [h]The LORD *is* his name:
9 That strengtheneth the [1]spoiled
gainst the strong, so that the spoiled
hall come against the fortress.
10 They [i]hate him that rebuketh in
he gate, and they [j]abhor him that
peaketh uprightly.
11 Forasmuch therefore as your
reading *is* upon the poor, and ye take
rom him burdens of wheat: ye [k]have
uilt houses of hewn stone, but ye
hall not dwell in them; ye have plant-
d [2]pleasant vineyards, but ye shall
iot drink wine of them.
12 For I know your manifold trans-
ressions and your mighty sins: they
fflict the just, they take [3]a bribe, and
hey [l]turn aside the poor in the gate
rom their right.
13 Therefore the prudent shall keep
ilence in that time; for it *is* an evil
ime.
14 Seek [m]good, and not evil, that ye
nay live: and so the LORD, the God of
iosts, shall be with you, as [n]ye have
poken.
15 Hate [o]the evil, and love the good,
nd establish judgment in the gate:
it may be that the LORD God of hosts
vill be gracious unto the remnant of
oseph.
16 Therefore the LORD, the God of
iosts, the Lord, saith thus; Wailing
hall be in all streets; and they shall
say in all the highways, Alas! alas! and
they shall call the husbandman to
mourning, [q]and such as are skilful
of lamentation to wailing.
17 And in all vineyards *shall be* wailing: for [r]I will pass through thee, saith
the LORD.
18 Woe [s]unto you that desire the day
of the LORD! to what end *is* it for you?
the day of the LORD *is* darkness, and
not light.
19 As if a man did flee from a lion,
and a bear met him; or went into the
house, and leaned his hand on the
wall, and a serpent bit him.
20 *Shall* not the day of the LORD *be*
darkness, and not light? even very
dark, and no brightness in it?
21 ¶ I [t]hate, I despise your feast days,
and I will not [4]smell in your solemn
assemblies.
22 Though ye offer me burnt offerings and your meat offerings, I will
not accept *them:* neither will I regard
the [5]peace offerings of your fat beasts.
23 Take thou away from me the
noise of thy songs; for I will not hear
the melody of thy viols.
24 But let judgment [6]run down as
waters, and righteousness as a mighty
stream.
25 Have [u]ye offered unto me sacrifices and offerings in the wilderness
forty years, O house of Israel?
26 But ye have borne [7]the tabernacle
of your Moloch and Chī-ŭn your
images, the star of your god, which
ye made to yourselves.
27 Therefore will I cause you to go
into captivity beyond Damascus,
saith the LORD, whose name *is* The
God of hosts.

CHAPTER 6

WOE to them *that* [1]*are* at ease in
Zion, and trust in the mountain of Să-mâr-ī-ă, *which are* named
[2]chief of the nations, to whom the
house of Israel came!
2 Pass ye unto [a]Căl-nēh, and see; and
from thence go ye to [b]Hā-măth the
great: then go down to Gath of the
Philistines: *be they* better than these
kingdoms? or their border greater
than your border?
3 Ye that [c]put far away the evil day,
and cause the [3]seat of violence to
come near;
4 That lie upon beds of ivory, and
[4]stretch themselves upon their couches, and eat the lambs out of the flock,
and the calves out of the midst of the
stall;

b 2 Chr. 15.2.
c Isa. 55.3.
d ch.4.4.
e ch. 8.14.
f Job 38.31.
g Job 38.34.
h ch. 4.13.
1 spoil.
i Isa. 29.21.
j 1 Ki. 22.8.
k Micah 6.15. Zeph. 1.13.
2 vineyards of desire.
3 Or, a ransom.
l Isa. 29.21.
m Ps. 34.12-16. Pro. 11.27. Isa. 1.16,17. Micah 6.8. Matt. 7.7. Rom. 2.7-9.
n Micah 3.11.
o Rom. 12.9.
p Ex. 32.30.
q Jer. 9.17.
r Ex. 12.12.
s Isa. 5.19. Eze. 12.22. Mal. 3.1. 2 Pet. 3.4.
t Isa. 1.11.
4 Or, smell your holy days.
5 Or, thank offerings.
6 roll.
u Acts 7.42.
7 Or, Siccuth your king.
1 Or, are secure, or, insolent.
2 Or, first-fruits.
a Gen. 10.10. Isa. 10.9. Taken 794 B.C.
b Num. 34.8. 2 Ki. 14.25.
c Eccl. 8.11. Isa. 47.7. Isa. 56.12. Eze. 12.27. ch. 5.18.
3 Or, habitation.
4 Or, abound with superfluities.

5 That [5]chant to the sound of the viol, *and* invent to themselves instruments of musick, like David;

6 That drink [6]wine in bowls, and anoint themselves with the chief ointments: but they are not grieved for the [7]affliction of Joseph.

7 ¶ Therefore now shall they go captive with the first that go captive, and the banquet of them that stretched themselves shall be removed.

8 The Lord GOD hath sworn by himself, saith the LORD the God of hosts, I abhor the excellency of Jacob, and hate his palaces: therefore will I deliver up the city with all [8]that is therein.

9 And it shall come to pass, if there remain ten men in one house, that they shall die.

10 And a man's uncle shall take him up, and he that burneth him, to bring out the bones out of the house, and shall say unto him that *is* by the sides of the house, *Is there* yet *any* with thee? and he shall say, No. Then shall he say, Hold thy tongue: for [9]we may not make mention of the name of the LORD.

11 For, behold, the LORD commandeth, and he will smite the great house with [10]breaches, and the little house with clefts.

12 ¶ Shall horses run upon the rock? will *one* plow *there* with oxen? for ye have turned judgment into gall, and the fruit of righteousness into hemlock:

13 Ye which rejoice in a thing of nought, which say, Have we not taken to us horns by our own strength?

14 But, behold, I will raise up against you a nation, O house of Israel, saith the LORD the God of hosts; and they shall afflict you from [d]the entering in of Hē-măth unto the [11]river of the wilderness.

CHAPTER 7

THUS hath the Lord GOD shewed unto me; and, behold, he formed [1]grasshoppers in the beginning of the shooting up of the latter growth; and, lo, *it was* the latter growth after the kings mowings.

2 And it came to pass, *that* when they had made an end of eating the grass of the land, then I said, O Lord GOD, forgive, I beseech thee: [2]by whom shall Jacob arise? for he *is* small.

3 The [a]LORD repented for this: It shall not be, saith the LORD.

4 ¶ Thus hath the Lord GOD shewed unto me: and, behold, the Lord GOD called to contend by fire, and it devoured the great deep, and did eat up a part.

5 Then said I, O Lord GOD, cease, I beseech thee: by whom shall Jacob arise? for he *is* small.

6 The LORD [b]repented for this: This also shall not be, saith the Lord GOD.

7 ¶ Thus he shewed me: and, behold, the Lord stood upon a wall *made* by a plumbline, with a plumbline in his hand.

8 And the LORD said unto me, Amos, what seest thou? And I said, A plumbline. Then said the Lord, Behold, [c]I will set a plumbline in the midst of my people Israel: [d]I will not again pass by them any more:

9 And [e]the high places of Isaac shall be desolate, and the sanctuaries of Israel shall be laid waste; and [f]I will rise against the house of Jĕr-ŏ-bō-ăm with the sword.

10 ¶ Then Ăm-ă-zī-ăh [g]the priest of Beth-el sent to [h]Jĕr-ŏ-bō-ăm king of Israel, saying, Amos hath conspired against thee in the midst of the house of Israel: the land is not able to bear all his words.

11 For thus Amos saith, Jĕr-ŏ-bō-ăm shall die by the sword, and Israel shall surely be led away captive out of their own land.

12 Also Ăm-ă-zī-ăh said unto Amos, O thou seer, go, flee thee away into the land of Judah, and there eat bread, and prophesy there:

13 But [i]prophesy not again any more at Beth-el: [j]for it *is* the king's [3]chapel, and it *is* the [4]king's court.

14 ¶ Then answered Amos, and said to Ăm-ă-zī-ăh, I *was* no prophet, neither *was* I a [k]prophet's son; but [l]I *was* an herdman, and a gatherer of [5]sycomore fruit:

15 And the LORD took me [6]as I followed the flock, and the LORD said unto me, Go, prophesy unto my people Israel.

16 ¶ Now therefore hear thou the word of the LORD: Thou sayest, Prophesy not against Israel, and drop [m]not *thy word* against the house of Isaac.

17 Therefore [n]thus saith the LORD; [o]Thy wife shall be an harlot in the city, and thy sons and thy daughters shall fall by the sword, and thy land shall be divided by line; and thou shalt die in a polluted land: and Israel shall surely go into captivity forth of his land.

5 Or, quaver.
6 Or, in bowls of wine.
7 breach.
8 the fulness thereof.
9 Or, they will not, or, have not.
10 Or, droppings.
d 1 Ki. 8.65.
11 Or, valley.

CHAP. 7

1 Or, green worms.
2 Or, who of [or, for] Jacob shall stand?
a Deut. 32.36. 1 Chr. 21.15. Ps. 106.45. Hosea 11.8. Joel 2.14. Jonah 3.10. Jas. 5.16.
b Ps. 102.17.
c 2 Ki. 21.13. Isa. 28.17.
d Micah 7.18.
e Beer-sheba, Gen. 26.23.
f Fulfilled, 2 Ki. 15.10.
g 1 Ki. 12.32.
h 2 Ki. 14.23.
i ch. 2.12.
j 1 Ki. 12.32.
3 Or, sanctuary.
4 house of the kingdom.
k 2 Ki. 2.5.
l Zech. 13.5.
5 Or, wild figs.
6 from behind.
m Isa. 30.10. Micah 2.6.
n Jer. 28.12. Jer. 29.21, 25,31,32.
o Lam. 5.11.

CHAPTER 8

THUS hath the Lord GOD shewed
unto me: and behold a basket of
ımmer fruit.
And he said, Amos, what seest
ıou? And I said, A basket of summer
uit. Then said the LORD unto me,
The end is come upon my people of
rael; I will not again pass by them
ıy more.
3 And the songs of the temple [1]shall
e howlings in that day, saith the
ord GOD: *there shall be* many dead
odies in every place; they shall cast
em forth [2]with silence.
4 ¶ Hear this, O ye that swallow up
ıe needy, even to make the poor of
ıe land to fail,
5 Saying, When will the [3]new moon
e gone, that we may sell corn? and
he sabbath, that we may [4]set forth
heat, making the ē-phăh [c]small, and
ıe shekel great, and [5]falsifying the
alances by deceit?
6 That we may buy the poor for sil-
er, and the needy for a pair of shoes;
ea, and sell the refuse of the wheat?
7 The LORD hath sworn by [d]the ex-
ellency of Jacob, Surely [e]I will never
orget any of their works.
8 Shall [f]not the land tremble for this,
nd every one mourn that dwelleth
ıerein? and it shall rise up wholly as
flood; and it shall be cast out and
rowned, [g]as *by* the flood of Egypt.
9 And it shall come to pass in that
ay, saith the Lord GOD, that [h]I will
ause the sun to go down at noon, and
will darken the earth in the clear day:
10 And I will turn your feasts into
ıourning, and all your songs into
ımentation; and I will bring up sack-
loth upon all loins, and baldness up-
n every head; [i]and I will make it as
he mourning of an only *son*, and the
nd thereof as a bitter day.
11 ¶ Behold, the days come, saith
he Lord GOD, that I will send a fam-
ıe in the land, not a famine of bread,
ıor a thirst for water, but of [j]hearing
he words of the LORD:
12 And they shall wander from sea
o sea, and from the north even to the
ast, they shall run to and fro to seek
he word of the LORD, and shall not
ınd *it*.
13 In that day shall the fair virgins
ınd young men faint for thirst.
14 They that swear [k]by the sin of Să-
mâr-ĭ-ă, and say, Thy god, O Dan,
iveth; and, The [6]manner of Bē-ēr-shē-
ă liveth; even they shall fall, and
ıever rise up again.

CHAP. 8

a Jer. 1.12. Lam. 4.18. Eze. 7.2.
1 shall howl.
2 be silent.
3 Or, month.
b Neh. 13.15.
4 open.
c Micah 6.10.
5 perverting the balances of deceit.
d Ps. 68.34.
e Hosea 8.13.
f Hosea 4.3.
g ch. 9.5.
h Job 5.14. Isa. 13.10. Jer. 15.9. ch. 4.13. Micah 3.6. 1 Thes. 5.2, 3.
i Jer. 6.26. Zech. 12.10. Luke 7.12, 13.
j 1 Sam. 3.1. Ps. 74.9. Eze. 7.26. Micah 3.6.
k Deut. 9.21. 1 Ki. 12.30. Hosea 8.5, 6. Hosea 10.5. Micah 1.5.
6 way.

CHAP. 9

1 Or, chapiter, or, knop.
2 Or, wound them.
a Ps. 139.8.
b Job 20.6. Obad.4.
c Jer. 23.24.
d Deut. 28. 65.
e Lev. 17.10.
f Micah 1.4.
3 ascensions, or, spheres.
4 Or, bundle.
g Deut. 2.23. Jer. 47.4.
h ch. 1.5.
i Ps. 11.4.
j Jer. 30.11.
5 cause to move.
6 stone.
k Acts 15.16.
7 hedge, or, wall.
l Obad. 19.
m Num. 24. 18.

CHAPTER 9

I SAW the Lord standing upon the
altar: and he said, Smite the [1]lintel
of the door, that the posts may shake:
and [2]cut them in the head, all of them;
and I will slay the last of them with the
sword: he that fleeth of them shall not
flee away, and he that escapeth of
them shall not be delivered.
2 Though [a]they dig into hell, thence
shall mine hand take them; [b]though
they climb up to heaven, thence will
I bring them down:
3 And though they [c]hide themselves
in the top of Carmel, I will search and
take them out thence; and though they
be hid from my sight in the bottom of
the sea, thence will I command the
serpent, and he shall bite them:
4 And though they go into captivity
before their enemies, [d]thence will I
command the sword, and it shall slay
them: and I [e]will set mine eyes upon
them for evil, and not for good.
5 And the Lord GOD of hosts *is* he
that toucheth the land, and it shall
[f]melt, and all that dwell therein shall
mourn: and it shall rise up wholly like
a flood; and shall be drowned, as *by*
the flood of Egypt.
6 *It is* he that buildeth his [3]stories in
the heaven, and hath founded his
[4]troop in the earth; he that calleth for
the waters of the sea, and poureth
them out upon the face of the earth:
The LORD *is* his name.
7 *Are* ye not as children of the Ē-thĭ-
ō-pĭ-ăns unto me, O children of Israel? saith the LORD. Have not I
brought up Israel out of the land of
Egypt? and the Philistines [g]from
Căph-tôr, and the Syrians [h]from Kĭr?
8 Behold, [i]the eyes of the Lord GOD
are upon the sinful kingdom, and I
[j]will destroy it from off the face of the
earth; saving that I will not utterly
destroy the house of Jacob, saith the
LORD.
9 For, lo, I will command, and I will
[5]sift the house of Israel among all nations, like as *corn* is sifted in a sieve,
yet shall not the least [6]grain fall upon
the earth.
10 All the sinners of my people shall
die by the sword, which say, The evil
shall not overtake nor prevent us.
11 ¶ In [k]that day will I raise up the
tabernacle of David that is fallen, and
[7]close up the breaches thereof; and I
will raise up his ruins, and I will build
it as in the days of old:
12 That [l]they may possess the remnant of [m]Ē-dom, and of all the hea-

then, [8]which are called by my name,
saith the LORD that doeth this.
13 Behold, [n]the days come, saith the
LORD, that the plowman shall overtake the reaper, and the treader of
grapes him that [9]soweth seed; and the
mountains shall drop [10]sweet wine,
and all the hills shall melt.
14 And I will bring again the captivity of my people of Israel, and they
shall [o]build the waste cities, and i
habit *them;* and they shall plant vin
yards, and drink the wine thereo
they shall also make gardens, and e
the fruit of them.
15 And I will plant them upon the
land, [p]and they shall no more be pul
ed up out of their land which
have given them, saith the LOR
thy God.

8 upon whom my name is called.
n Lev. 26.5.
9 draweth forth.
10 Or, new.
o Isa. 61.4.
p Isa. 60.21.

OBADIAH

THE vision of Ō-bă-dī-́ăh. Thus
saith the Lord GOD [a]concerning
Ē-́dom; We have heard a rumour
from the LORD, and an ambassador is
sent among the heathen, Arise ye, and
let us rise up against her in battle.
2 Behold, I have made thee small
among the heathen: thou art greatly
despised.
3 ¶ The pride of thine heart hath deceived thee, thou that dwellest in the
clefts [b]of the rock, whose habitation
is high; [c]that saith in his heart, Who
shall bring me down to the ground?
4 Though [d]thou exalt *thyself* as the
eagle, and though thou set thy nest
among the stars, thence will I bring
thee down, saith the LORD.
5 If thieves came to thee, if robbers
by night, (how art thou cut off!) would
they not have stolen till they had
enough? if the grapegatherers came
to thee, would they not leave [1]*some*
grapes?
6 How are *the things* of Esau searched out! *how* are his hidden things
sought up!
7 All the men of thy confederacy
have brought thee *even* to the border:
[2]the men that were at peace with thee
have deceived thee, *and* prevailed
against thee; [3]*they that eat* thy bread
have laid a wound under thee: *there*
is none understanding [4]in him.
8 Shall I not in that day, saith the
LORD, even destroy the wise *men* out
of Ē-́dom, and understanding out of
the mount of Esau?
9 And thy [e]mighty *men*, O Tē-́măn,
shall be dismayed, to the end that
every one of the mount of Esau may
be cut off by slaughter.
10 ¶ For *thy* [f]violence against thy
brother Jacob shame shall cover thee,
and [g]thou shalt be cut off for ever.
11 In the day that thou stoodest on
the other side, in the day that th
strangers [5]carried away captive h
forces, and foreigners entered into hi
gates, and [h]cast lots upon Jerusalem
even thou *wast* as one of them.
12 But [6]thou shouldest not hav
looked [i]on the day of thy brother i
the day that he became a stranger
neither shouldest thou have [j]rejoice
over the children of Judah in the da
of their destruction; neither should
est thou have [7]spoken proudly in th
day of distress.
13 Thou shouldest not have entere
into the gate of my people in the da
of their calamity; yea, thou shouldes
not have looked on their affliction i
the day of their calamity, nor hav
laid *hands* on their [8]substance in th
day of their calamity;
14 Neither shouldest thou have stoo
in the crossway, to cut off those of hi
that did escape; neither shouldes
thou have [9]delivered up those of hi
that did remain in the day of dis
tress.
15 For the day of the LORD *is* nea
upon all the heathen: [k]as thou has
done, it shall be done unto thee: thy
reward shall return upon thine ow
head.
16 For as ye have drunk upon my
holy mountain, *so* shall all the heathe
drink continually, yea, they shal
drink, and they shall [10]swallow down
and they shall be as though they ha
not been.
17 ¶ But upon mount Zion shall b
[11]deliverance, and [12]there shall b
holiness; and the house of Jacob shal
possess their possessions.
18 And the house of Jacob shall be a
fire, and the house of Joseph a flame
and the house of Esau for stubble
and they shall kindle in them, and devour them; and there shall not be *any*

a Isa. 21.11. Eze. 25.12, 13,14. Joel 3.19. Mal. 1.3.
b 2 Ki. 14.7. 2 Chr. 25.12.
c Isa. 14.13. Rev. 18.7.
d Job 20.6. Isa. 14.14, 15. Jer. 49.16. Amos 9.2. Hab. 2.9.
1 Or, gleanings?
2 the men of thy peace.
3 the men of thy bread.
4 Or, of it.
e Ps. 76.5. Jer. 49.22. Amos 2.16. Nah. 3.13.
f Gen. 27.41. Ps. 137.7. Eze. 35.5, 15. Amos 1.11.
g Mal. 1.4.
5 Or, carried away his substance.
h Nah. 3.10.
6 Or, do not behold, etc.
i Micah 4.11.
j Pro. 24.17.
7 magnified thy mouth.
8 Or, forces.
9 Or, shut up.
k Judg. 1.7. Ps. 137.8. Eze. 35.15. Joel 3.7,8.
10 Or, sup up.
11 Or, they that escape.
12 Or, it shall be holy.

maining of the house of Esau; for
e LORD hath spoken *it*.
9 And *they of* the south shall possess
e mount of Esau; [l]and *they of* the
ain the Philistines: and they shall
ossess the fields of Ē-phră-ĭm, and the
elds of Să-mâr-ĭ-ă: and Benjamin
all possess Gilead.
0 And the captivity of this host of
the children of Israel *shall possess* that
of the Canaanites, *even* [m]unto Zăr-ĕ-
phăth; and the captivity of Jerusalem,
[13]which *is* in Sĕ-phâr-ăd, shall possess
the cities of the south.
21 And [n]saviours shall come up on
mount Zion to judge the mount of
Esau; and the kingdom [o]shall be the
LORD's.

l Zeph. 2.7.
m 1 Ki. 17.9.
13 Or, shall possess that which is in Sepharad.
n Isa. 19.20.
o Dan. 2.24. Zech. 14.9. Rev. 11.15.

JONAH

CHAPTER 1

NOW the word of the LORD came
unto [a]Jonah the son of Ă-mĭt-tāi,
ying,
Arise, go to Nĭn-ĕ-vēh, [b]that great
ty, and cry against it; for their
ickedness is come up before me.
But Jonah rose up to flee unto Tar-
ish [d]from the presence of the LORD,
d went down to [e]Joppa; and he
und a ship going to Tarshish: so he
id the fare thereof, and went down
to it, to go with them unto Tarshish
om the presence of the LORD.
¶ But the LORD [1]sent out a great
ind into the sea, and there was a
ighty tempest in the sea, so that the
ip was [2]like to be broken.
Then the mariners were afraid, and
ied every man unto his god, and cast
rth the wares that *were* in the ship
to the sea, to lighten *it* of them. But
nah was gone down into the sides of
e ship; and he lay, and was fast
leep.
So the shipmaster came to him, and
id unto him, What meanest thou, O
eeper? arise, [g]call upon thy God, if
be that God will think upon us, that
e perish not.
And they said every one to his fel-
w, Come, and let us [h]cast lots, that
e may know for whose cause this
il *is* upon us. So they cast lots, and
e lot fell upon Jonah.
Then said they unto him, [i]Tell us,
e pray thee, for whose cause this evil
upon us; What *is* thine occupation?
d whence comest thou? what *is* thy
untry? and of what people *art* thou?
And he said unto them, I *am* an
ebrew; and I fear [3]the LORD, the
od of heaven, which hath made the
a and the dry *land*.
0 Then were the men [4]exceedingly
raid, and said unto him, Why hast
ou done this? For the men knew
that he fled from the presence of the
LORD, because he had told them.
11 ¶ Then said they unto him, What
shall we do unto thee, that the sea
[5]may be calm unto us? for the sea
[6]wrought, and was tempestuous.
12 And he said unto them, Take me
up, and cast me forth into the sea; so
shall the sea be calm unto you: for I
know that for [j]my sake this great tempest *is* upon you.
13 Nevertheless the men [7]rowed
hard to bring *it* to the land; [k]but they
could not: for the sea wrought, and
was tempestuous against them.
14 Wherefore they cried unto the
LORD, and said, We beseech thee, O
LORD, we beseech thee, let us not
perish for this man's life, and lay [l]not
upon us innocent blood: for thou, O
LORD, hast done as it pleased thee.
15 So they took up Jonah, and cast
him forth into the sea: and the sea
[8]ceased from her raging.
16 Then the men feared the LORD
exceedingly, and [9]offered a sacrifice
unto the LORD, and made vows.
17 ¶ Now the LORD had prepared a
great fish to swallow up Jonah. And
[m]Jonah was in the [10]belly of the fish
three days and three nights.

CHAPTER 2

THEN Jonah prayed unto the LORD
his God out of the fish's belly,
2 And said, I cried [1]by reason of
mine affliction unto the LORD, and he
heard me; out of the belly of [2]hell
cried I, *and* thou heardest my voice.
3 For [a]thou hadst cast me into the
deep, in the [3]midst of the seas; and the
floods compassed me about: all thy
billows and thy waves passed over me.
4 Then [b]I said, I am cast out of thy
sight; yet I will look again toward [c]thy
holy temple.
5 The waters compassed me about,

CHAP. 1
a 2 Ki. 14.25.
b Gen. 10.11. ch. 3.3. Nah. 2.8. Matt. 12.41.
c Gen. 18.20. Ezra 9.6. Jas. 5.4.
d Isa. 23.1.
e Josh. 19.46. 2 Chr. 2.16. Acts 9.36.
f Gen. 4.16.
1 cast forth.
2 thought to be broken.
g Ps. 78.34. Matt. 8.25.
h Josh. 7.14. 1 Sam. 10. 20. Pro. 16.33. Acts 1.26.
i Josh. 7.19.
3 Or, JEHOVAH.
4 with great fear.
5 may be silent from us.
6 went, or, grew more and more tempestuous.
j Eccl. 9.18.
7 digged.
k Pro. 21.30.
l Deut. 21.8.
8 stood.
9 sacrificed a sacrifice unto the LORD, and vowed vows.
m Matt. 12. 40.
10 bowels.
CHAP. 2
1 Or, out of mine affliction.
2 Or, the grave.
a Ps. 88.6.
3 heart.
b Ps. 31.22. Isa. 49.14.
c 1 Ki. 8.38.

even to the soul: the depth closed me
round about, the weeds were wrapped
about my head.
6 I went down to the [4]bottoms of the
mountains; the earth with her bars
was about me for ever: yet hast thou
brought up my life from [5]corruption,
O LORD my God.
7 When my soul fainted within me I
remembered the LORD: [d]and my
prayer came in unto thee, into thine
holy temple.
8 They that observe [e]lying vanities
forsake their own mercy.
9 But I will [f]sacrifice unto thee with
the voice of thanksgiving; I will pay
that that I have vowed. Salvation *is*
of the LORD.
10 ¶ And the LORD [g]spake unto the
fish, and it vomited out Jonah upon
the dry *land*.

CHAPTER 3

AND the word of the LORD came
unto Jonah the second time, saying,
2 Arise, go unto Nĭn´-ĕ-vēh, that
great city, and preach unto it the
preaching that I bid thee.
3 So Jonah arose, and went unto
Nĭn´-ĕ-vēh, according to the word of
the LORD. Now Nĭn´-ĕ-vēh was an
[1]exceeding great city of three days'
journey.
4 And Jonah began to enter into the
city a day's journey, and [a]he cried,
and said, Yet forty days, and Nĭn´-ĕ-
vēh shall be overthrown.
5 ¶ So the people of [b]Nĭn´-ĕ-vēh believed God, and proclaimed a fast,
and put on sackcloth, from the greatest of them even to the least of them.
6 For word came unto the king of
Nĭn´-ĕ-vēh, and he arose from his
throne, and he laid his robe from him,
and covered *him* with sackcloth, [c]and
sat in ashes.
7 And [d]he caused *it* to be proclaimed
and [2]published through Nĭn´-ĕ-vēh by
the decree of the king and his [3]nobles,
saying, Let neither man nor beast,
herd nor flock, taste any thing: let
them not feed, nor drink water:
8 But let man and beast be covered
with sackcloth, and cry mightily unto
God: yea, let them turn [e]every one
from his evil way, and from the violence that *is* in their hands.
9 Who can tell *if* God will turn and

4 cuttings off.
5 Or, the pit.
d Ps. 18.6. Ps. 34.6. Ps. 130.2. Jer. 2.13.
e 2 Ki. 17.15. Ps. 31.6. Jer. 10.8.
f Ps. 50.14. Ps. 66.13-15. Hosea 14.2. Heb. 13.15.
g ch. 1.17. Matt. 8.9.

CHAP. 3
1 of God.
a Deut. 18. 22.
b Matt. 12.41. Luke 11.32.
c Job 2.8. Jer. 6.26. Lam. 3.29. Micah 1.10.
d 2 Chr. 20.3. Joel 2.15.
2 said.
3 great men.
e Isa. 1.16. Eze. 33.11. Dan. 4.27.

CHAP. 4
a Matt. 20. 15.
b Ex. 34.6.
c 1 Ki. 19.4.
1 Or, Art thou greatly angry?
2 Kikajon, or, palm-crist.
3 rejoiced with great joy.
4 Or, silent.
d Ps. 121.6.
5 Or, Art thou greatly angry?
6 Or, I am greatly angry.
7 Or, spared.
8 was the son of the night.
e Eze. 33.11.
f Deut. 1.39.
g Ps. 36.6.

repent, and turn away from his fierc
anger, that we perish not?
10 ¶ And God saw their works, tha
they turned from their evil way; an
God repented of the evil, that he ha
said that he would do unto them; an
he did *it* not.

CHAPTER 4

BUT [a]it displeased Jonah exceed
ingly, and he was very angry.
2 And he prayed unto the LORD, an
said, I pray thee, O LORD, *was* not th
my saying, when I was yet in m
country? Therefore I fled before unt
Tarshish: for I knew that thou *art*
[b]gracious God, and merciful, slow t
anger, and of great kindness, and re
pentest thee of the evil.
3 Therefore [c]now, O LORD, take,
beseech thee, my life from me; for *it i*
better for me to die than to live.
4 ¶ Then said the LORD, [1]Doest tho
well to be angry?
5 So Jonah went out of the city, an
sat on the east side of the city, an
there made him a booth, and sat un
der it in the shadow, till he might se
what would become of the city.
6 And the LORD God prepared
[2]gourd, and made *it* to come up ove
Jonah, that it might be a shadow ove
his head, to deliver him from his grie
So Jonah [3]was exceeding glad of th
gourd.
7 But God prepared a worm whe
the morning rose the next day, and i
smote the gourd that it withered.
8 And it came to pass, when the su
did arise, that God prepared a [4]vehe
ment east wind; and [d]the sun beat up
on the head of Jonah, that he fainted
and wished in himself to die, and said
It is better for me to die than to live.
9 And God said to Jonah, [5]Does
thou well to be angry for the gourd
And he said, [6]I do well to be angry
even unto death.
10 Then said the LORD, Thou has
[7]had pity on the gourd, for the whic
thou hast not laboured, neithe
madest it grow; which [8]came up in
night, and perished in a night:
11 And should not I [e]spare Nĭn´-ĕ
vēh, that great city, wherein are mor
than sixscore thousand persons [f]tha
cannot discern between their righ
hand and their left hand; and *als*
much [g]cattle?

MICAH

CHAPTER 1

THE [a]word of the LORD that came
to [b]Mī-căh the Mō-răs-thīte in the
ays of Jō-thăm, Ahaz, *and* Hĕz-ē-kī-
h, kings of Judah, which he saw con-
erning Să-mâr-ĭ-ă and Jerusalem.
2 [1]Hear, all ye people; hearken, O
arth, and [2]all that therein is: and let
ie Lord GOD be witness against you,
ie Lord from his holy temple.
3 For, behold, [c]the LORD cometh
orth out of his place, and will come
own, and tread upon the high places
f the earth.
4 And the mountains shall be molten
nder him, and the valleys shall be
left, as wax before the fire, *and* as
ie waters *that are* poured down [3]a
teep place.
5 For the [d]transgression of Jacob *is*
ll this, and for the sins of the house
f Israel. What *is* the transgression
f Jacob? *is it* not Să-mâr-ĭ-ă? and
hat *are* the high places of Judah?
re they not Jerusalem?
6 Therefore I will make Să-mâr-ĭ-ă
s [e]an heap of the field, *and* as plant-
ngs of a vineyard: and I will pour
own the stones thereof into the val-
ey, and I will discover the founda-
ions thereof.
7 And all the graven images thereof
hall be beaten to pieces, and all the
ires thereof shall be burned with the
re, and all the idols thereof will I lay
esolate: for she gathered *it* of the
ire of an harlot, and they shall return
o the hire of an harlot.
8 Therefore I will wail and howl, I
vill go stripped and naked: I will
nake a wailing like the dragons, and
nourning as the [4]owls.
9 For [5]her wound *is* incurable; for [f]it
s come unto Judah; he is come unto
he gate of my people, *even* to Jerusa-
em.
10 ¶ Declare ye *it* not at Gath, weep
e not at all: in the house of [6]Ăph-răh
oll thyself in the dust.
11 Pass ye away, [7]thou inhabitant of
ă-phĭr, having thy shame naked: the
nhabitant of [8]Zā-ă-năn came not
orth in the mourning of [9]Bĕth-ē-zĕl;
e shall receive of you his standing.
12 For the inhabitant of Mâr-ŏth
[10]waited carefully for good: but evil
came down from the LORD unto the
gate of Jerusalem.
13 O thou inhabitant of Lā-chĭsh,
bind the chariot to the swift beast:
she *is* the beginning of the sin to the
daughter of Zion: for the transgressions of Israel were found in thee.
14 Therefore shalt thou give presents
[11]to Mō-rĕsh-ĕth-găth: the houses of
[12]Ăch-zĭb *shall be* a lie to the kings of
Israel.
15 Yet will I bring an heir unto thee,
O inhabitant of Mă-rē-shăh: [13]he shall
come unto Adullam the glory of
Israel.
16 Make thee bald, and poll thee for
thy delicate children; enlarge thy
baldness as the eagle; for they [g]are
gone into captivity from thee.

CHAPTER 2

WOE to them [a]that devise iniquity,
and [b]work evil upon their beds!
when the morning is light, they practise it, because [c]it is in the power of
their hand.
2 And they covet fields, and take
them by violence; and houses, and
take *them* away: so they [1]oppress a
man and his house, even a man and
his heritage.
3 Therefore thus saith the LORD; Behold, against [d]this family do I devise
an evil, from which ye shall not remove your necks; neither shall ye go
haughtily: for this time *is* evil.
4 ¶ In that day shall *one* take up a
parable against you, and lament [2]with
a doleful lamentation, *and* say, We be
utterly spoiled: he hath changed the
portion of my people: how hath he
removed *it* from me! [3]turning away he
hath divided our fields.
5 Therefore thou shalt have none
that shall [e]cast a cord by lot in the
congregation of the LORD.
6 [4]Prophesy ye not, *say they to them
that* prophesy: they shall not prophesy to them, *that* they shall not take
shame.
7 ¶ O *thou that art* named the house
of Jacob, is the spirit of the LORD
[5]straitened? *are* these his doings? do
not my words do good to him that
walketh [6]uprightly?
8 Even [7]of late my people is risen up

CHAP. 1

a 2 Pet. 1.21.
b Jer. 26.18.
1 Hear, ye people, all of them.
2 the fulness thereof.
c Isa. 26.21. Eze. 3.12. Heb. 12.1, 19.
3 a descent.
d Jer. 2.18,19. Hosea 5.5.
e 2 Ki. 19.25.
4 daughters of the owl.
5 Or, she is grievously sick of her wounds.
f 2 Ki. 18.13.
6 That is, Dust.
7 thou inhabitress, or, thou that dwellest fairly.
8 Or, the country of flocks.
9 Or, a place near.
10 Or, was grieved.
11 Or, for.
12 That is, A lie.
13 Or, the glory of Israel shall come, etc.
g 2 Ki. 17.6.

CHAP. 2

a Esther 3.8, 9. Ps. 7.11-14. Isa. 32.7. Hosea 7.6.
b Ps. 36.4.
c Gen. 31.29.
1 Or, defraud.
d Jer. 8.3.
2 with a lamentation of lamentations.
3 Or, instead of restoring.
e Deut. 32.8, 9.
4 Drop, etc., or, Prophesy not as they prophesy.
5 Or, shortened?
6 upright?
7 yesterday.

as an enemy: ye pull off the robe [8]with
the garment from them that pass by
securely as men averse from war.
9 The [9]women of my people have ye
cast out from their pleasant houses;
from their children have ye taken
away my glory for ever.
10 Arise ye, and depart; for this *is* not
your [f]rest: because it is polluted, it
shall destroy *you*, even with a sore destruction.
11 If a man [10]walking in the spirit and
falsehood do lie, *saying*, I will prophesy unto thee of wine and of strong
drink; he shall even be the prophet of
this people.
12 ¶ I will surely assemble, O Jacob,
all of thee; I will surely gather the
[g]remnant of Israel; I will put them together as the sheep of Bŏz-răh, as the
flock in the midst of their fold: they
shall make great noise by reason of
the multitude of men.
13 The breaker is come up before
them: they have broken up, and have
passed through the gate, and are gone
out by it: and their king shall pass before them, and the LORD on the head
of them.

CHAPTER 3

AND I said, Hear, I pray you, O
heads of Jacob, and ye princes of
the house of Israel; [a]*Is it* not for you
to know judgment?
2 Who hate the good, and love the
evil; who pluck off their skin from off
them, and their flesh from off their
bones;
3 Who also [b]eat the flesh of my people, and flay their skin from off them;
and they break their bones, and chop
them in pieces, as for the pot, and as
flesh within the caldron.
4 Then [c]shall they cry unto the LORD,
but he will not hear them: he will even
hide his face from them at that time,
as they have behaved themselves ill in
their doings.
5 ¶ Thus saith the LORD [d]concerning
the prophets that make my people
err, that [e]bite with their teeth, and
cry, Peace; and he that putteth not into their mouths, they even prepare
war against him.
6 Therefore [f]night *shall be* unto you,
[1]that ye shall not have a vision; and it
shall be dark unto you, [2]that ye shall
not divine; and the sun shall go down
over the prophets, and the day shall
be dark over them.
7 Then shall the seers be ashamed,
and the diviners confounded: yea,
they shall all cover their [3]lips; for *ther*
[g]*is* no answer of God.
8 ¶ But truly I am full of power b
the [h]spirit of the LORD, and of judg
ment, and of might, [i]to declare unt
Jacob his transgression, and to Israe
his sin.
9 Hear this, I pray you, ye heads c
the house of Jacob, and princes of th
house of Israel, that abhor judgmen
and pervert all equity.
10 They build up Zion with [4]bloo
and Jerusalem with iniquity.
11 The [j]heads thereof judge for re
ward, and [k]the priests thereof teac
for hire, and the prophets there
divine for money: yet [l]will they lea
upon the LORD, [5]and say, *Is* not th
LORD among us? none evil can com
upon us.
12 Therefore shall Zion for your sak
be [m]plowed *as* a field, [n]and Jerusale
shall become heaps, and the mountai
of the house as the high places of th
forest.

CHAPTER 4

BUT [a]in the last days it shall com
to pass, *that* the mountain of th
house of the LORD shall be establishe
in the top of the mountains, and
shall be exalted above the hills; an
people shall flow unto it.
2 And many nations shall come, an
say, Come, and let us go up to th
mountain of the LORD, and to th
house of the God of Jacob; and h
[b]will teach us of his ways, and we wi
walk in his paths: for the law shall g
forth of Zion, and the word of th
LORD from Jerusalem.
3 ¶ And he shall judge among man
people, and rebuke strong natio
afar off; and they shall beat the
swords [c]into plowshares, and the
spears into [1]pruninghooks: natio
shall not lift up a sword against n
tion, neither [d]shall they learn war a
more.
4 But [e]they shall sit every man und
his vine and under his fig tree; a
none shall make *them* afraid: for th
mouth of the LORD of hosts ha
spoken *it*.
5 For [f]all people will walk every o
in the name of his god, and we [g]w
walk in the name of the LORD o
God for ever and ever.
6 In that day, saith the LORD, will
assemble her that halteth, and [i]I w
gather her that is driven out, and h
that I have afflicted;
7 And I will make her that halted

8 over against a garment.
9 Or, wives.
f Deut. 12.9.
10 Or, walk with the wind, and lie falsely.
g Isa. 11.11. ch. 4.6,7. Zeph. 3.19.

CHAP. 3
a Jer. 5.4,5.
b Ps. 14.4.
c Pro. 1.28.
d Isa. 56.10.
e Matt. 7.15.
f Eze. 13.23.
1 from a vision.
2 from divining.
3 upper lip.
g Ps. 74.9. Amos 8.11.
h 1 Cor. 2.1,4.
i Isa. 58.1.
4 bloods.
j Isa. 1.23. Eze. 22.12. Hosea 4.18. ch. 7.3.
k Jer. 6.13. Titus 1.11.
l 1 Sam. 4.5, 6. Isa. 48.2.
5 saying.
m ch. 1.6.
n Ps. 79.1.

CHAP. 4
a Isa. 2.2. Eze. 17.22. Dan. 2.44.
b John 6.45.
c Isa. 2.4. Hosea 2.18. Joel 3.10.
1 Or, scythes.
d Ps. 72.7. Luke 1.33.
e 1 Ki. 4.25. Isa. 36.16. Jer. 31.10. Zech. 3.10.
f Jer. 2.11.
g Ex. 3.14,15.
h Isa. 56.8. Jer. 3.18. Eze. 34.16. Zeph. 3.19.
i Ps. 147.2. Eze. 34.13.

mnant, and her that was cast far off
strong nation: and the LORD shall
ign over them in mount Zion from
nceforth, even for ever.
¶ And thou, O tower of the [2]flock,
e strong hold of the daughter of
on, unto thee shall it come, even the
st dominion; the kingdom shall
me to the daughter of Jerusalem.
Now why dost thou cry out aloud?
there no king in thee? is thy coun-
ller perished? for pangs have taken
ee as a woman in travail.
0 Be in pain, and labour to bring
rth, O daughter of Zion, like a wo-
an in travail: for now shalt thou go
rth out of the city, and thou shalt
well in the field, and thou shalt go
en to Babylon; there shalt thou be
elivered; there the LORD shall re-
eem thee from the hand of thine en-
nies.
1 ¶ Now also many nations are
athered against thee, that say, Let
er be defiled, and let our eye look
pon Zion.
2 But they know not the thoughts
f the LORD, neither understand they
is counsel: for he shall gather them
s the sheaves into the floor.
3 Arise and thresh, O daughter of
ion: for I will make thine horn iron,
nd I will make thy hoofs brass: and
ou shalt beat in pieces many peo-
le: [k]and I will consecrate their gain
nto the LORD, and their substance
nto the Lord of the whole earth.

CHAPTER 5

NOW gather thyself in troops, O
daughter of troops: he hath laid
ege against us: they [a]shall smite the
dge of Israel with a rod upon the
heek.
2 But thou, [b]Beth-lehem Ĕph-ră-tăh,
hough thou be little among the thou-
ands of Judah, *yet* out of thee shall
e come forth unto me *that is* to be
uler in Israel; whose goings [d]forth
ave been from of old, from [1]ever-
sting.
3 Therefore will he give them up, un-
l the time *that* she which travaileth
ath brought forth: then the remnant
f his brethren shall return unto the
hildren of Israel.
4 ¶ And he shall stand and [2]feed in
he strength of the LORD, in the
ajesty of the name of the LORD his
od; and they shall abide: for now
shall he be great unto the ends of the
arth.
5 And this *man* [f]shall be the peace,

j Isa. 9.6. Dan. 7.14. Luke 1.33. Rev. 11.15.
2 Or, Edar.
k Rev. 21.24.

CHAP. 5

a Job 16.10. Lam. 3.30. Matt. 27.30
b Gen. 35.19. Ps. 132.6. Matt. 2.6. John 7.42.
c Gen. 49.10. Isa. 9.6.
d Ps. 90.2. Pro. 8.22. John 1.1.
1 the days of eternity.
2 Or, rule.
e Ps. 72.8. Isa. 52.13. Zech. 9.10. Luke 1.32.
f Isa. 9.6. Luke 2.14. Eph. 2.14. Col. 1.20.
3 princes of men.
4 eat up.
g Gen. 10.8.
5 Or, with her own naked swords.
h Luke 1.71.
i Ps. 110.3.
6 Or, goats.
j Zech. 9.10.
k Zech. 13.2.
7 Or, statues.
l Isa. 2.8.
8 Or, enemies.

CHAP. 6

1 Or, with.
a Hosea 12.2.
b Ps. 50.7. Isa. 5.3,4. Jer. 2.5,31.

when the Assyrian shall come into our
land: and when he shall tread in our
palaces, then shall we raise against
him seven shepherds, and eight [3]prin-
cipal men.
6 And they shall [4]waste the land of
Assyria with the sword, and the land
[g]of Nimrod [5]in the entrances thereof:
thus shall he [h]deliver *us* from the
Assyrian, when he cometh into our
land, and when he treadeth within
our borders.
7 And the remnant of Jacob shall be
in the midst of many [i]people as a dew
from the LORD, as the showers upon
the grass, that tarrieth not for man,
nor waiteth for the sons of men.
8 ¶ And the remnant of Jacob shall
be among the Gentiles in the midst of
many people as a lion among the
beasts of the forest, as a young lion
among the flocks of [6]sheep: who, if he
go through, both treadeth down, and
teareth in pieces, and none can deliver.
9 Thine hand shall be lifted up upon
thine adversaries, and all thine enemies shall be cut off.
10 And [j]it shall come to pass in that
day, saith the LORD, that I will cut off
thy horses out of the midst of thee,
and I will destroy thy chariots:
11 And I will cut off the cities of thy
land, and throw down all thy strong
holds:
12 And I will cut off witchcrafts out
of thine hand; and thou shalt have no
more soothsayers:
13 Thy [k]graven images also will I cut
off, and thy [7]standing images out of
the midst of thee; and thou shalt [l]no
more worship the work of thine
hands.
14 And I will pluck up thy groves
out of the midst of thee: so will I destroy thy [8]cities.
15 And I will execute vengeance in
anger and fury upon the heathen,
such as they have not heard.

CHAPTER 6

HEAR ye now what the LORD
saith; Arise, contend thou [1]before
the mountains, and let the hills hear
thy voice.
2 Hear ye, O mountains, [a]the LORD's
controversy, and ye strong foundations of the earth: for the LORD hath
a controversy with his people, and he
will plead with Israel.
3 O my people, [b]what have I done
unto thee? and wherein have I wearied
thee? testify against me.

4 For I brought thee up out of the
land of Egypt, and redeemed thee out
of the house of servants; and I sent
before thee Moses, Aaron, and
Miriam.
5 O my people, remember now what
Balak [c]king of Moab consulted, and
what Bā-lāam the son of Bē-ôr answered him from [d]Shĭt-tĭm unto Gĭl-
găl; that ye may know the [e]righteous-
ness of the LORD.
6 ¶ Wherewith [f]shall I come before
the LORD, *and* bow myself before the
high God? shall I come before him
with burnt offerings, with calves [2]of a
year old?
7 Will [g]the LORD be pleased with
thousands of rams, *or* with ten thousands of rivers of oil? [h]shall I give my
firstborn *for* my transgression, the
fruit of my [3]body *for* the sin of my
soul?
8 He hath shewed thee, O man, what
is good; and what doth the LORD require of thee, but to do justly, and to
love mercy, and to [4]walk humbly with
thy God?
9 The LORD's voice crieth unto the
city, and [5]*the man of* wisdom shall see
thy name: hear ye the rod, and who
hath appointed it.
10 ¶ [6]Are there yet the treasures of
wickedness in the house of the wicked,
and the [7]scant measure *that is* abominable?
11 [8]Shall I count *them* pure with the
[i]wicked balances, and with the bag of
deceitful weights?
12 For the rich men thereof are full
of violence, and the inhabitants thereof have spoken lies, and their tongue
is deceitful in their mouth.
13 Therefore also will I make *thee*
sick in smiting thee, in making *thee*
desolate because of thy sins.
14 Thou shalt eat, but not be satisfied; and thy casting down *shall be* in
the midst of thee; and thou shalt take
hold, but shalt not deliver; and *that*
which thou deliverest will I give up
to the sword.
15 Thou shalt sow, but thou shalt not
reap; thou shalt tread the olives, but
thou shalt not anoint thee with oil;
and sweet wine, but shalt not drink
wine.
16 ¶ For [9]the statutes of [j]Omri are
kept, and all the works of the house
of Ahab, and ye walk in their counsels; that I should make thee a [10]deso-
lation, and the inhabitants thereof an
hissing: therefore ye shall bear the reproach of my people.

c Num. 22.5. Rev. 2.14.
d Num. 25.1.
e Judg. 5.11.
f Ps. 15.1. John 6.28.
2 sons of a year?
g Ps. 50.9. Isa. 1.11.
h 2 Ki. 16.3.
3 belly.
4 humble thyself to walk.
5 Or, thy name shall see that which is.
6 Or, Is there yet unto every man an house of the wicked, etc.
7 measure of leanness.
8 Or, Shall I be pure with, etc.
i Hosea 12.7. Amos 3.10.
9 Or, he doth much keep the, etc.
j 1 Ki. 16.25.
10 Or, astonishment.

CHAP. 7

1 the gatherings of summer.
a Jer. 2.3. Hosea 9.10.
2 Or, godly, or, merciful.
b 1 Sam. 24. 11. Ps. 57.6. Hab. 1.15.
c Hosea 4.18.
d Isa. 1.23.
3 the mischief of his soul.
e Gen. 9.22, 24. Matt. 10.21.
f Ps. 37.5,6. Pro. 24.17. Lam. 4.21.
4 Or, And thou wilt see her that is mine enemy, and cover her with shame.
5 she shall be for a treading down.
6 Or, even to.
7 Or, After that it hath been.
8 Or, Rule.

CHAPTER 7

WOE is me! for I am as [1]whe
they have gathered the summ
fruits, as the grapegleanings of th
vintage: *there is* no cluster to eat: [a]m
soul desired the firstripe fruit.
2 The [2]good *man* is perished out o
the earth: and *there is* none uprig
among men: they all lie in wait fo
blood; [b]they hunt every man his br
ther with a net.
3 ¶ That they may do evil with bot
hands earnestly, [c]the prince asket
[d]and the judge *asketh* for a rewar
and the great *man*, he uttereth [3]h
mischievous desire: so they wrap it u
4 The best of them *is* as a brier: th
most upright *is sharper* than a thor
hedge: the day of thy watchmen *an*
thy visitation cometh; now shall b
their perplexity.
5 ¶ Trust ye not in a friend, put y
not confidence in a guide: keep th
doors of thy mouth from her tha
lieth in thy bosom.
6 For the [e]son dishonoureth th
father, the daughter riseth up again
her mother, the daughter in la
against her mother in law; a man's en
emies *are* the men of his own house.
7 Therefore I will look unto th
LORD; I will wait for the God of m
salvation: my God will hear me.
8 ¶ Rejoice [f]not against me, O min
enemy: when I fall, I shall arise; whe
I sit in darkness, the LORD *shall be*
light unto me.
9 I will bear the indignation of th
LORD, because I have sinned agains
him, until he plead my cause, and ex
ecute judgment for me: he will brin
me forth to the light, *and* I shall be
hold his righteousness.
10 Then [4]*she that is* mine enemy sha
see *it*, and shame shall cover her whic
said unto me, Where is the LORD th
God? mine eyes shall behold her
now [5]shall she be trodden down as th
mire of the streets.
11 *In* the day that thy walls are to b
built, *in* that day shall the decree b
far removed.
12 *In* that day *also* he shall come eve
to thee from Assyria, [6]and *from* th
fortified cities, and from the fortres
even to the river, and from sea t
sea, and *from* mountain to mountain
13 [7]Notwithstanding the land sha
be desolate because of them tha
dwell therein, for the fruit of their doings.
14 ¶ [8]Feed thy people with thy rod
the flock of thine heritage, which dwel

solitarily [g]*in* the wood, in the midst of Carmel: let them feed *in* Bā´-shăn and Gilead, as in the days of old.

15 According to the days of thy coming out of the land of Egypt will I shew unto him marvellous *things*.

16 ¶ The nations [h]shall see and be confounded at all their might: they shall lay *their* hand upon *their* mouth, their ears shall be deaf.

17 They shall lick the dust like a serpent, they shall move out of their holes like [9]worms of the earth: they shall be afraid of the LORD our God, and shall fear because of thee.

18 Who [i]*is* a God like unto thee, that pardoneth [j]iniquity, and passeth by the transgression of the remnant of his heritage? [k]he retaineth not his anger for ever, because he delighteth *in* mercy.

19 He will turn again, he will have compassion upon us; he will subdue [l]our iniquities; and thou wilt cast all their sins into the depths of the sea.

20 Thou [m]wilt perform the truth to Jacob, *and* the mercy to Abraham, which thou hast sworn unto our fathers from the days of old.

[g] Num. 23.9. Deut. 33.28.
[h] Isa. 26.11.
[9] Or, creeping things.
[i] Ex. 15.11. Ps. 89.6,8.
[j] Ex. 34.6,7.
[k] Ps. 103.9. Isa. 57.16.
[l] Rom. 6.6.
[m] Rom. 11. 29.

NAHUM

CHAPTER 1

THE burden of Nĭn´-ĕ-vĕh. The book of the vision of Nahum the Ĕl´-kō-shīte.

2 [1]God *is* jealous, and the LORD revengeth; the LORD revengeth, and [2]*is* furious; the LORD will take vengeance on his adversaries, and he reserveth *wrath* for his enemies.

3 The LORD *is* [a]slow to anger, and great in power, and will not at all acquit *the wicked:* the [b]LORD *hath* his way in the whirlwind and in the storm, and the clouds *are* the dust of his feet.

4 He [c]rebuketh the sea, and maketh it dry, and drieth up all the rivers: Bā´-shăn languisheth, and Carmel, and the flower of Lĕb´-ă-non languisheth.

5 The [d]mountains quake at him, and the hills melt, and the earth is burned at his presence, yea, the world, and all that dwell therein.

6 Who can stand before his indignation? and who can [3]abide in the fierceness of his anger? his fury is poured out like fire, and the rocks are thrown down by him.

7 The LORD *is* good, a [4]strong hold in the day of trouble; [e]and he knoweth them that trust in him.

8 But with an [f]overrunning flood he will make an utter end of the place thereof, and darkness shall pursue his enemies.

9 What do ye imagine against the LORD? he will make an utter end: affliction shall not rise up the second time.

10 For while *they be* folden together *as* thorns, and while they are drunken *as* drunkards, they shall be devoured as stubble fully dry.

11 There is *one* come out of thee, that imagineth evil against the LORD, a wicked counseller.

12 Thus saith the LORD; [5]Though *they be* quiet, and likewise many, yet thus shall they be [6]cut down, when he shall pass through. Though I have afflicted thee, I will afflict thee no more.

13 For now will I break his yoke from off thee, and will burst thy bonds in sunder.

14 And the LORD hath given a commandment concerning thee, *that* no more of thy name be sown: out of the house of thy gods will I cut off the graven image and the molten image: I will make thy grave; for thou art vile.

15 Behold upon the mountains the feet of him that bringeth good tidings, that publisheth peace! O Judah, [7]keep thy solemn feasts, perform thy vows: for [8]the wicked shall no more pass through thee; he is utterly cut off.

CHAPTER 2

[1]HE that dasheth in pieces is come up before thy face: keep the munition, watch the way, make *thy* loins strong, fortify *thy* power mightily.

2 For the LORD hath turned away [2]the excellency of Jacob, as the excellency of Israel: for the emptiers have emptied them out, and marred their vine branches.

3 The shield of his mighty men is made red, the valiant men *are* [3]in scarlet: the chariots *shall be* with [4]flaming

CHAP. 1
[1] Or, The LORD is a jealous God, and a revenger.
[2] that hath fury.
[a] Ex. 34.6,7. Ps. 103.8. Micah 7.18.
[b] Ex. 19.16.
[c] Josh. 3.15, 16.
[d] 2 Sam. 22.8.
[3] stand up.
[4] Or, strength.
[e] Ps. 1.6. 2 Tim. 2.19.
[f] Amos 8.8.
[5] Or, If they would have been at peace, so should they have been many, and so should they have been shorn, and he should have passed away.
[6] shorn.
[7] feast.
[8] Belial.

CHAP. 2
[1] Or, The disperser, or, hammer.
[2] Or, the pride of Jacob, as the pride of Israel.
[3] Or, dyed scarlet.
[4] Or, fiery torches.

torches in the day of his preparation,
and the fir trees shall be terribly
shaken.
4 The chariots shall rage in the
streets, they shall justle one against
another in the broad ways: [5]they shall
seem like torches, they shall run like
the lightnings.
5 He shall recount his [6]worthies:
they shall stumble in their walk;
they shall make haste to the wall
thereof, and the [7]defence shall be prepared.
6 The gates of the rivers shall be
opened, and the palace shall be [8]dis-
solved.
7 And [9]Hŭz-zăb shall be [10]led away
captive, she shall be brought up, and
her maids shall lead *her* as with the
voice of doves, tabering upon their
breasts.
8 But Nĭn-ĕ-vĕh *is* [11]of old like a pool
of water: yet they shall flee away.
Stand, stand, *shall they cry;* but none
shall [12]look back.
9 Take ye the spoil of silver, take the
spoil of gold: [13]for *there is* none end
of the store *and* glory out of all the
[14]pleasant furniture.
10 She is empty, and void, and waste:
and the heart melteth, and the knees
smite together, and much pain *is* in all
loins, and the faces of them all gather
blackness.
11 Where *is* [15]the dwelling of the
lions, and the feedingplace of the
young lions, where the lion, *even* the
old lion, walked, *and* the lion's whelp,
and none made *them* afraid?
12 The lion did tear in pieces enough
for his whelps, and strangled for his
lionesses, and filled his holes with
prey, and his dens with ravin.
13 Behold, I *am* against thee, saith
the LORD of hosts, and I will burn her
chariots in the smoke, and the sword
shall devour thy young lions: and I
will cut off thy prey from the earth,
and the voice of thy messengers shall
no more be heard.

CHAPTER 3

WOE to the [1]bloody city! it *is* all
full of lies *and* robbery; the prey
departeth not;
2 The noise of a whip, and the noise
of the rattling of the wheels, and of
the pransing horses, and of the jump-
ing chariots.
3 The horseman lifteth up both [2]the
bright sword and the glittering spear:
and *there is* a multitude of slain, and
a great number of carcases; and *there*
is none end of *their* corpses; they
stumble upon their corpses:
4 Because of the multitude of the
whoredoms of the wellfavoured harlot, the [a]mistress of witchcrafts, that
selleth nations through her whoredoms, and families through her witchcrafts.
5 Behold, I *am* against thee, saith the
LORD of hosts; and [b]I will discover
thy skirts upon thy face, and I will
shew the nations thy nakedness, and
the kingdoms thy shame.
6 And I will cast abominable filth upon thee, and make thee vile, and will
set thee as a gazingstock.
7 And it shall come to pass, *that* all
they that look upon thee shall flee
from thee, and say, Nĭn-ĕ-vĕh is laid
waste: who will bemoan her? whence
shall I seek comforters for thee?
8 Art thou better than [3]populous No,
that was situate among the rivers, *that*
had the waters round about it, whose
rampart *was* the sea, *and* her wall *was*
from the sea?
9 Ē-thĭ-ō-pĭ-ă [c]and Egypt *were* her
strength, and *it was* infinite; Pŭt and
Lū-bĭm were [4]thy helpers.
10 Yet *was* she carried away, she
went into captivity: her young children also were dashed in pieces at the
top of all the streets: and they [d]cast
lots for her honourable men, and all
her great men were bound in chains.
11 Thou also shalt be drunken: thou
shalt be hid, thou also shalt seek
strength because of the enemy.
12 All thy stong holds *shall be like*
[e]fig trees with the firstripe figs: if they
be shaken, they shall even fall into the
mouth of the eater.
13 Behold, [f]thy people in the midst
of thee *are* women: the gates of thy
land shall be set wide open unto thine
enemies: the fire shall devour thy
bars.
14 Draw thee waters for the siege,
fortify thy strong holds: go into clay,
and tread the morter, make strong
the brickkiln.
15 There shall the fire devour thee;
the sword shall cut thee off, it shall
eat thee up like [g]the cankerworm:
make thyself many as the cankerworm, make thyself many as the
locusts.
16 Thou hast multiplied [5]thy merchants above the stars of heaven: the
cankerworm [6]spoileth, and flieth
away.
17 Thy [h]crowned *are* as the locusts,
and thy captains as the great grass-

5 their shew.
6 Or, gallants.
7 covering, or, coverer.
8 Or, molten.
9 Or, that which was established, or, there was a stand made.
10 Or, discovered.
11 Or, from the days that she hath been.
12 Or, cause them to turn.
13 Or, and their infinite store.
14 vessels of desire.
15 [The rapacious character of the king of Assyria is here allegorically set forth.]

CHAP. 3
1 city of bloods.
2 the flame of the sword, and the lightning of the spear.
a Isa. 47.9. Dan. 2.2. 2 Thes. 2.9, 10. Rev. 9.20, 21.
b Isa. 47.2,3.
3 No Amon, or, nourishing.
c Eze. 30.5.
4 in thy help.
d Joel 3.3. Obad. 11.
e Rev. 6.13.
f Isa. 19.16. Jer. 50.37.
g Joel 1.4.
5 Or, thy hired soldiers.
6 Or, spreadeth himself.
h Rev. 9.7.

hoppers, which camp in the hedges in
the cold day, *but* when the sun ariseth
they flee away, and their place is not
known where they *are*.
18 Thy shepherds slumber, O king [i]of
Assyria: thy [7]nobles shall dwell *in the
dust:* thy people [j]is scattered upon the
mountains, and no man gathereth
them.
19 *There is* no [8]healing of thy bruise;
thy wound is grievous: all [k]that hear
the bruit of thee shall clap the hands
over thee: for upon whom hath not
thy wickedness passed continually?

i Jer. 50.18. Eze. 31.3.
7 Or, valiant ones.
j 1 Ki. 22.17.
8 wrinkling.
k Isa. 14.8. Lam. 2.15. Zeph. 2.15.

HABAKKUK

CHAPTER 1

THE burden which Hă-băk-kŭk
the prophet did see.
2 O LORD, how long [a]shall I cry, and
thou wilt not hear! *even* cry out unto
thee *of* violence, and thou wilt not
save!
3 Why dost thou shew me iniquity,
and cause *me* to behold grievance?
for spoiling and violence *are* before
me: and there are *that* raise up strife
and contention.
4 Therefore [b]the law is slacked, and
judgment doth never go forth: for
the wicked doth compass about the
righteous; therefore [1]wrong judgment proceedeth.
5 ¶ Behold ye among the heathen,
and regard, and wonder marvellously:
for *I* will work a work in your days,
which ye will not believe, though it be
told *you*.
6 For, lo, [2]I raise up the Chăl-dē-ăns,
that bitter and hasty nation, which
shall march through the [3]breadth of
the land, to possess the dwellingplaces *that are* not theirs.
7 They *are* terrible and dreadful:
[4]their judgment and their dignity shall
proceed of themselves.
8 Their horses [c]also are swifter than
the leopards, and are more [5]fierce than
the evening wolves: and their horsemen shall spread themselves, and
their horsemen shall come from far;
they shall fly as the eagle *that* hasteth
to eat.
9 They shall come all for violence:
[6]their faces shall sup up *as* the east
wind, and they shall gather the captivity as the sand.
10 And they shall scoff at the kings,
and the princes shall be a scorn unto
them: they shall deride every strong
hold; for they shall heap dust, and
take it.
11 Then shall *his* mind change, and
he shall pass over, and offend, *imputing* this his power unto his god.
12 ¶ *Art* thou not from everlasting,
O LORD my God, mine Holy One? we
shall not die. O LORD, thou hast ordained them for judgment; and, O
[7]mighty God, thou hast [8]established
them for correction.
13 *Thou art* of purer eyes than to behold evil, and canst not look on [9]in-
iquity: wherefore lookest thou upon
them that deal treacherously, *and*
holdest thy tongue when the wicked
devoureth *the man that is* more righteous than he?
14 And makest men as the fishes of
the sea, as the creeping things, *that
have* no ruler over them?
15 They take up all of them with the
angle, they catch them in their net,
and gather them in their [10]drag: therefore they rejoice and are glad.
16 Therefore they sacrifice unto their
net, and burn incense unto their drag;
because by them their portion *is* fat,
and their meat [11]plenteous.
17 Shall they therefore [12]empty their
net, and not spare continually to slay
the nations?

CHAPTER 2

I WILL stand upon [a]my watch, and
set me upon the [1]tower, and will
watch to see what he will say [2]unto
me, and what I shall answer [3]when I
am reproved.
2 And the LORD answered me, and
said, [b]Write the vision, and make *it*
plain upon tables, that he may run
that readeth it.
3 For [c]the vision *is* yet for an appointed time, but at the end it shall
speak, and not lie: though it tarry,
wait for it; because it will surely come,
it will not tarry.
4 Behold, his soul *which* is lifted up
is not upright in him: but [d]the just
shall live by his faith.
5 ¶ [4]Yea also, because he transgresseth by wine, *he is* a proud man,
neither keepeth at home, who en-

CHAP. 1
a Ps. 27.7. 2 Pet. 2.8.
b Job 12.6. Ps. 12.8. Ps. 58.1,2.
1 Or, wrested.
2 Fulfilled, 2 Chr. 36.6.
3 breadths.
4 Or, from them shall proceed the judgment of these, and the captivity of these.
c Deut. 28. 49,50.
5 sharp.
6 the opposition of their faces toward the east: or, the supping up of their faces, etc., or, their faces shall look toward the east.
7 rock.
8 founded.
9 Or, grievance.
10 Or, flue net.
11 fat, or, dainty.
12 Or, spread.

CHAP. 2
a Ps. 73.16, 17. Isa. 21.8.
1 fenced place.
2 Or, in me.
3 upon my reproof, or, arguing; or, when I am argued with.
b Deut. 27.8. Isa. 8.1. Rom. 15.4. Rev. 1.19.
c Dan. 10.14.
d John 3.36. Rom. 1.17. 2 Cor. 5.7. Gal. 3.11.
4 Or, How much more.

largeth his [e]desire as hell, and *is* as
death, and cannot be satisfied, but
gathereth unto him all nations, and
heapeth unto him all people:
6 Shall not all these take up a parable
against him, and a taunting proverb
against him, and say, [5]Woe to him
that increaseth *that which is* not his!
how long? and to him that ladeth
himself with thick clay!
7 Shall they not rise up suddenly that
shall bite thee, and awake that shall
vex thee, and thou shalt be for booties
unto them?
8 Because thou hast spoiled many
nations, all the remnant of the people
shall spoil thee; because of men's
[6]blood, and *for* the violence of the
land, of the city, and of all that dwell
therein.
9 ¶ Woe to him that [7]coveteth an evil
covetousness to his house, that he may
set his nest on high, that he may be
delivered from the [8]power of evil!
10 Thou hast consulted shame to thy
house by cutting off many people, and
hast sinned *against* thy soul.
11 For the stone shall cry out of the
wall, and the [9]beam out of the timber
shall [10]answer it.
12 ¶ Woe to him that buildeth a
town with [11]blood, and stablisheth a
city by iniquity!
13 Behold, *is it* not of the LORD of
hosts that the people shall labour [f]in
the very fire, and the people shall
weary themselves [12]for very vanity?
14 For the earth shall be filled [13]with
the knowledge of the glory of the
LORD, as the waters cover the sea.
15 ¶ Woe unto him that giveth his
neighbour drink, that puttest thy
bottle to *him*, and makest *him* drunken
also, that thou mayest look on their
nakedness!
16 Thou art filled [14]with shame for
glory: drink thou also, and let thy
foreskin be uncovered: the cup of the
LORD's right hand shall be turned unto thee, and shameful spewing *shall be*
on thy glory.
17 For the violence [g]of Lĕb-ă-non
shall cover thee, and the spoil of
beasts, *which* made them afraid, because of men's blood, and for the violence of the land, of the city, and of all
that dwell therein.
18 ¶ What profiteth the graven image
that the maker thereof hath graven it;
the molten image, and a teacher of
lies, that the [15]maker of his work trusteth therein, to make dumb idols?
19 Woe unto him that saith to the
wood, Awake; to the dumb stone
Arise, it shall teach! Behold, it *is* laid
over with gold and silver, and *there is*
no breath at all in the midst of it.
20 But the LORD *is* in his holy temple: [16]let all the earth keep silence before him.

CHAPTER 3

A PRAYER of Hă-băk-kŭk the
prophet [1]upon Shĭg-ĭ-ō-nōth.
2 O LORD, I have heard [2]thy speech
and was afraid: O LORD, [3]revive thy
work in the midst of the years, in the
midst of the years make known; in
wrath remember mercy.
3 God came from [4]Tē-măn, and the
Holy One from mount Pâr-ăn. Sē-lăh.
His glory covered the heavens, and
the earth was full of his praise.
4 And *his* brightness was as the
light; he had [5]horns *coming* out of his
hand: and there *was* the hiding of his
power.
5 Before him went the pestilence, and
[6]burning coals went forth at his feet.
6 He stood, and [a]measured the earth:
he beheld, and drove asunder [b]the nations; and the everlasting mountains
were scattered, the perpetual hills did
bow: his ways *are* everlasting.
7 I saw the tents of [7]Cū-shăn [8]in
affliction: *and* the curtains of the land
of Mĭd-ĭ-ăn did tremble.
8 Was the [c]LORD displeased against
the rivers? *was* thine anger against the
rivers? *was* thy wrath against the sea,
that thou didst ride upon thine horses
and thy chariots [9]of salvation?
9 Thy bow was made quite naked,
according to the oaths of the tribes,
even thy word. Sē-lăh. Thou didst
cleave the [10]earth with rivers.
10 The mountains saw thee, *and* they
trembled: the overflowing of the
water passed by: the deep uttered
his voice, *and* lifted up his hands on
high.
11 The sun *and* moon stood still in
their habitation: [11]at the light of thine
arrows they went, *and* at the shining
of thy glittering spear.
12 Thou didst march through the
land in indignation, thou didst thresh
[d]the heathen in anger.
13 Thou wentest forth [e]for the salvation of thy people, *even* for salvation
with thine anointed; thou woundedst
the head out of the house of the wicked, [12]by discovering the foundation
unto the neck. Sē-lăh.
14 Thou didst strike through with
his staves the head of his villages: they
[13]came out as a whirlwind to scatter

e Pro. 27.20.
5 Or, Ho, he.
6 bloods.
7 Or, gaineth an evil gain.
8 palm of the hand.
9 Or, piece, or, fastening.
10 Or, witness against it.
11 bloods.
f Isa. 50.11.
12 Or, in vain?
13 Or, by knowing the glory.
14 Or, more with shame than with glory.
g Jer. 50.33.
15 fashioner of his fashion.
16 be silent all the earth before him.

CHAP. 3

1 Or, according to variable songs, or, tunes.
2 thy report, or, thy hearing.
3 Or, preserve alive.
4 Or, the south.
5 Or, bright beams out of his side.
6 Or, burning diseases.
a Ex. 23.31. Deut. 32.8.
b Num. 21. 24,34.
7 Ethiopia.
8 Or, under affliction, or, vanity.
c Ex. 14.21, 22.
9 Or, were salvation?
10 Or, rivers of the earth.
11 Or, thine arrows walked in the light.
d Ps. 44.2,3. Micah 4.13.
e 2 Sam. 5.20.
12 making naked.
13 were tempestuous.

me: their rejoicing *was* as to devour
the poor secretly.
15 Thou didst walk through the sea
with thine horses, *through* the [14]heap
of great waters.
16 When I heard, my belly trembled;
my lips quivered at the voice: rottenness entered into my bones, and I
trembled in myself, that I might rest
in the day of trouble: when he cometh
up unto the people, he will [15]invade
them with his troops.
17 ¶ Although the [f]fig tree shall not
blossom, neither *shall* fruit *be* in the
vines; the labour of the olive shall
[16]fail, and the fields shall yield no
meat; the flock shall be cut off from
the fold, and *there shall be* no herd in
the stalls:
18 Yet [g]I will rejoice in the LORD, I
will joy in the God of my salvation.
19 The LORD God *is* [h]my strength,
and he will make my feet like hinds'
feet, and he will make me to walk upon mine high places. To the chief
singer on my [17]stringed instruments.

14 Or, mud.
15 Or, cut them in pieces.
f 2 Cor. 4.8,9.
16 lie.
g Ps. 42.5. Isa. 61.10. 2 Cor. 4.8,9.
h Ps. 27.1.
17 Neginoth.

ZEPHANIAH

CHAPTER 1

THE [a]word of the LORD which came
unto Zĕph-ă-nī-ăh the son of Cū-
shī, the son of Gĕd-ă-lī-ăh, the son of
Ăm-ă-rī-ăh, the son of Hĭz-kī-ăh, in
the days of Jō-sī-ăh the son of Amon,
king of Judah.
2 [1]I will utterly consume all *things*
from off [2]the land, saith the LORD.
3 I will consume man and beast; I
will consume the fowls of the heaven,
and the fishes of the sea, and the [3]stum-
blingblocks with the wicked; and I
will cut off man from off the land,
saith the LORD.
4 I will also stretch out mine hand
upon Judah, and upon all the inhabitants of Jerusalem; and [4]I will cut off
the remnant of Bā-ăl from this place,
and the name of the [b]Chĕm-ă-rĭms
with the priests;
5 And them that worship the host of
heaven upon the housetops; and them
that worship *and* that swear [5]by the
LORD, and that swear [c]by Măl-chăm;
6 And them that are turned back
from the LORD; and *those* that have
not sought the LORD, nor inquired for
him.
7 Hold thy peace at the presence of
the Lord GOD: for the day of the
LORD *is* at hand: for the LORD hath
prepared a sacrifice, he hath [6]bid his
guests.
8 And it shall come to pass in the day
of the LORD's sacrifice, that I will
punish the princes, and the king's
children, and all such as are clothed
with strange apparel.
9 In the same day also will I punish
all those that leap on the threshold,
which fill their masters' houses with
violence and deceit.
10 And it shall come to pass in that
day, saith the LORD, *that there shall be*
the noise of a cry from the [d]fish gate,
and an howling from the second, and
a great crashing from the hills.
11 Howl, [e]ye inhabitants of [8]Măk-
tĕsh, for all the merchant people are
cut down; all they that bear silver are
cut off.
12 And it shall come to pass at that
time, *that* I will search Jerusalem with
candles, and punish the men that are
[9]settled on their lees: [f]that say in their
heart, The LORD will not do good,
neither will he do evil.
13 Therefore their goods shall become a booty, and their houses a
desolation: they shall also build
houses, but [g]not inhabit *them;* and
they shall plant vineyards, but not
[h]drink the wine thereof.
14 The [i]great day of the LORD *is*
near, *it is* near, and hasteth greatly,
even the voice of the day of the LORD:
the mighty man shall cry there bitterly.
15 That day *is* a day of wrath, a day
of trouble and distress, a day of
wasteness and desolation, a day of
darkness and gloominess, a day of
clouds and thick darkness,
16 A day of [j]the trumpet and alarm
against the fenced cities, and against
the high towers.
17 And I will bring distress upon
men, that they shall walk like blind
men, because they have sinned against
the LORD: and their blood shall be
poured out as dust, and their flesh as
the dung.
18 Neither [k]their silver nor their
gold shall be able to deliver them in
the day of the LORD's wrath; but the
whole land shall be devoured [l]by the

CHAP. 1
a 2 Tim. 3.16. 2 Pet. 1.21.
1 By taking away I will make an end.
2 the face of the land.
3 Or, idols.
4 Fulfilled.
b Hosea 10.5.
5 Or, to the LORD.
c 1 Ki. 11.33.
6 sanctified, or, prepared.
7 visit upon.
Jer. 39.6.
d 2 Chr. 33. 14. Neh. 3.13.
e Jas. 5.1. Rev. 18.11, 12.
8 the merchant street.
9 curded, or, thickened.
f Job 21.15. Ps. 10.11,13.
g Deut. 28.30. Amos 5.11.
h Micah 6.15.
i Jer. 30.7. Joel 2.1. Mal. 4.5. Rev. 6.17.
j Jer. 4.19. Jer. 8.16. Hosea 5.8. Amos 3.6.
k Eze. 7.19.
l ch. 3.8.

fire of his jealousy: for he shall make even a speedy riddance of all them that dwell in the land.

CHAPTER 2

GATHER [a]yourselves together, yea, gather together, O nation [1]not desired;

2 Before the decree bring forth, *before* the day pass as the chaff, before [b]the fierce anger of the LORD come upon you, before the day of the LORD's anger come upon you.

3 Seek [c]ye the LORD, [d]all ye meek of the earth, which have wrought his judgment; seek righteousness, seek meekness: [e]it may be ye shall be hid in the day of the LORD's anger.

4 ¶ For Gā´-zā shall be forsaken, and Ăsh´-kĕ-lon a desolation: they shall drive out Ăsh´-dŏd [f]at the noon day, and Ĕk´-rŏn shall be rooted up.

5 Woe unto the inhabitants of the [g]sea coast, the nation of the Chĕr´-ĕ-thītes! the word of the LORD *is* against you; [h]O Canaan, the land of the Philistines, I will even destroy thee, that there shall be no inhabitant.

6 And the sea coast shall be dwellings *and* cottages for shepherds, [i]and folds for flocks.

7 And the coast shall be for the [j]remnant of the house of Judah; they shall feed thereupon: in the houses of Ăsh´-kĕ-lon shall they lie down in the evening: [2]for the LORD their God shall visit [k]them, and [l]turn away their captivity.

8 ¶ I [m]have heard the reproach of Moab, and the revilings of the children of Ammon, whereby they have reproached my people, and [n]magnified *themselves* against their border.

9 Therefore *as* I live, saith the LORD of hosts, the God of Israel, Surely [o]Moab shall be as Sodom, and [p]the children of Ammon as Gō-mŏr´-răh, *even* the breeding of nettles, and saltpits, and a perpetual desolation: the residue of my people shall spoil them, and the remnant of my people shall possess them.

10 This shall they have for their pride, because they have reproached and magnified *themselves* against the people of the LORD of hosts.

11 The LORD *will be* terrible unto them: for he will [3]famish all the gods of the earth; and [q]*men* shall worship him, every one from his place, *even* all [r]the isles of the heathen.

12 ¶ Ye [s]Ē-thĭ-ō´-pĭ-ăns also, ye *shall be* slain by my sword.

13 And he will stretch out his han against the north, and destroy As syria; and will make Nĭn´-ĕ-vēh a deso lation, *and* dry like a wilderness.

14 And flocks shall lie down in th midst of her, all [t]the beasts of the na tions: both the [4]cormorant and th bittern shall lodge in the [5]upper lin tels of it; *their* voice shall sing in th windows; desolation *shall be* in th thresholds: [6]for he shall uncover th cedar work.

15 This *is* the rejoicing city [u]tha dwelt carelessly, [v]that said in he heart, I *am*, and *there is* none besid me: how is she become a desolation a place for beasts to lie down in! ever one that passeth by her shall hiss, *an* wag his hand.

CHAPTER 3

WOE to [1]her that is filthy and pol luted, to the oppressing city!

2 She [a]obeyed not the voice; she re ceived [b]not [2]correction; she truste not in the LORD; she drew not near t her God.

3 Her princes within her *are* roarin lions; her judges *are* evening wolves they gnaw not the bones till th morrow.

4 Her [c]prophets *are* light *and* treach erous persons: her priests have pol luted the sanctuary, they have don [d]violence to the law.

5 The just LORD [e]*is* in the midst there of; he will not do iniquity: [3]ever morning doth he bring his judgmen to light, he faileth not; but the un just knoweth no shame.

6 I have cut off the nations: the [4]towers are desolate; I made the streets waste, that none passeth by their cities are destroyed, so tha there is no man, that there is non inhabitant. Mil Rev 20:11-15

7 I said, Surely thou wilt fear m thou wilt receive instruction; so the dwelling should not be cut off, howsc ever I punished them: but they ros early, *and* [f]corrupted all their doing

8 ¶ Therefore [g]wait ye upon me, sait the LORD, until the day that I rise u to the prey: for my determination to [h]gather the nations, that I ma assemble the kingdoms, to pour upo them mine indignation, *even* all m fierce anger: for all the earth shall b devoured with the fire of my jealous

9 For then will I turn to the peopl a pure [5]language, that they may a call upon the name of the LORD, t serve him with one [6]consent.

CHAP. 2

a Joel 2.16.
1 Or, not desirous.
b 2 Ki. 23.26.
c Amos 5.6.
d Ps. 76.9.
e Joel 2.14. Amos 5.15.
f Jer. 6.4.
g Eze. 25.16.
h Josh. 13.3.
i Isa. 17.2.
j Isa. 11.11. Micah 5.7. Hag. 1.12.
2 Or, when, etc.
k Ex. 4.31. Micah 4.10. Luke 1.68.
l Ps. 126.4. Jer. 23.3. Eze. 39.25. Micah 4.10.
m Jer. 48.27. Eze. 25.8.
n Jer. 49.1.
o Isa. 15.1. Amos 2.1.
p Amos 1.13.
3 make lean.
q Gen. 49.10. Ps. 2.8. Ps. 22.27. Isa. 2.2,3. Isa. 11.9, 10. Mal. 1.11. John 4.21. 1 Tim. 2.8.
r Gen. 10.5.
s Isa. 18.1.
t Isa. 13.21.
4 Or, pelican.
5 Or, knops, or, chapiters.
6 Or, when he hath uncovered.
u Isa. 47.8.
v Rev. 18.7.

CHAP. 3

1 craw, or, gluttonous.
a Jer. 22.21.
b Jer. 5.3.
2 Or, instruction.
c Jer. 23.11.
d Eze. 22.26.
e Deut. 32.4. Ps. 99.3,4.
3 morning by morning.
4 Or, corners.
f Gen. 6.12.
g Pro. 20.22.
h Joel 3.2.
5 lip.
6 shoulder.

10 From [i]beyond the rivers of Ē-thĭ-
ŏ-pĭ-ă my suppliants, *even* the daugh-
er of my dispersed, shall bring mine
offering.
11 In that day shalt thou not be
ashamed for all thy doings, wherein
thou hast transgressed against me:
for then I will take away out of the
midst of thee them that rejoice [j]in thy
pride, and thou shalt no more be
haughty [7]because of my holy mountain.
12 I will also leave in the midst of
thee an [k]afflicted and poor people, and
they shall trust in the name of the
LORD.
13 The remnant of Israel shall not
do iniquity, nor speak lies; neither
shall a deceitful tongue be found in
their mouth: for they shall feed and
lie down, and none shall make *them*
afraid.
14 ¶ Sing, O daughter of Zion; shout,
O Israel; be [l]glad and rejoice with all
the heart, O daughter of Jerusalem.
15 The LORD hath taken away thy
judgments, he hath cast out thine en-

[i] Ps. 68.31. Mal. 1.11. Acts 8.27.
[j] Matt. 3.9.
[7] in my holy.
[k] Isa. 14.32. Isa. 57.15. Matt. 5.3. Luke 6.20.
[l] Ps. 14.7.
[m] John 1.49.
[n] Eze. 48.35. Rev. 21.3.
[o] Isa. 35.3.
[8] Or, faint.
[9] he will be silent.
[p] Lam. 2.6.
[10] the burden upon it was reproach.
[11] I will set them for a praise.
[12] of their shame.
[q] Ps. 22.27.

emy: the king [m]of Israel, *even* the
LORD, [n]*is* in the midst of thee: thou
shalt not see evil any more.
16 In that day it shall be said to Jerusalem, Fear thou not: *and to* Zion,
[o]Let not thine hands be [8]slack.
17 The LORD thy God in the midst
of thee *is* mighty; he will save, he will
rejoice over thee with joy; [9]he will
rest in his love, he will joy over thee
with singing.
18 I will gather *them that* [p]*are* sorrowful for the solemn assembly, *who* are of
thee, *to whom* [10]the reproach of it *was*
a burden.
19 Behold, at that time I will undo
all that afflict thee: and I will save her
that halteth, and gather her that was
driven out; and [11]I will get them praise
and fame in every land [12]where they
have been put to shame.
20 At that time [q]will I bring you
again, even in the time that I gather
you: for I will make you a name and
a praise among all people of the earth,
when I turn back your captivity before your eyes, saith the LORD.

HAGGAI

CHAPTER 1

IN the second year of Dā-rī-ŭs the
king, in the sixth month, in the first
day of the month, came the word of
the LORD [1]by Hăg-gāi the prophet unto [a]Zĕ-rŭb-bă-bĕl the son of Shē-
ăl-tī-ĕl, [2]governor of Judah, and to
Joshua the son of Jŏs-ĕ-dĕch, [b]the
high priest, saying,
2 Thus speaketh the LORD of hosts,
saying, This people say, The time is
not come, the time that the LORD's
house should be built.
3 Then came the word of the LORD
by Hăg-gāi [c]the prophet, saying,
4 *Is it* time for you, O ye, to dwell in
your cieled houses, and this house
lie waste?
5 Now therefore thus saith the LORD
of hosts; [3]Consider your ways.
6 Ye have sown much, and bring in
little; ye eat, but ye have not enough;
ye drink, but ye are not filled with
drink; ye clothe you, but there is none
warm; and he that earneth wages
earneth wages *to put it* into a bag
[4]with holes.

CHAP. 1

[1] by the hand of Haggai.
[a] 1 Chr. 3.17.
[2] Or, captain.
[b] 1 Chr. 6.15.
[c] Ezra 5.1.
[3] Set your heart on your ways.
[4] pierced through.
[5] Or, blow it away.
[d] Deut. 28. 23. 2 Chr. 6.26. Jer. 3.3. Joel 1.18,19.
[e] 1 Ki. 17.1.
[f] ch. 2.17.
[g] Ezra 5.2. Isa. 55.11.

7 ¶ Thus saith the LORD of hosts;
Consider your ways.
8 Go up to the mountain, and bring
wood, and build the house; and I will
take pleasure in it, and I will be glorified, saith the LORD.
9 Ye looked for much, and, lo, *it*
came to little; and when ye brought
it home, I did [5]blow upon it. Why?
saith the LORD of hosts. Because of
mine house that *is* waste, and ye run
every man unto his own house.
10 Therefore [d]the heaven over you is
stayed from dew, and the earth is
stayed *from* her fruit.
11 And I [e]called for a drought upon
the land, and upon the mountains,
and upon the corn, and upon the new
wine, and upon the oil, and upon *that*
which the ground bringeth forth, and
upon men, and upon cattle, and [f]upon
all the labour of the hands.
12 ¶ Then [g]Zĕ-rŭb-bă-bĕl the son of
Shē-ăl-tī-ĕl, and Joshua the son of
Jŏs-ĕ-dĕch, the high priest, with all
the remnant of the people, obeyed the
voice of the LORD their God, and the

words of Hăg'-gâi the prophet, as the LORD their God had sent him, and the people did [h]fear before the LORD.

13 Then spake Hăg'-gâi the LORD's messenger in the LORD's message unto the people, saying, [i]I *am* with you, saith the LORD.

14 And [j]the LORD stirred up the spirit of Zĕ-rŭb'-bă-bĕl the son of Shē-ăl'-tĭ-ĕl, [k]governor of Judah, and the spirit of Joshua the son of Jŏs'-ĕ-dĕch, the high priest, and the spirit of all the remnant of the people; [l]and they came and did work in the house of the LORD of hosts, their God,

15 In the four and twentieth day of the sixth month, in the second year of Dă-rī'-ŭs the king.

CHAPTER 2

IN the seventh *month*, in the one and twentieth *day* of the month, came the word of the LORD [1]by the prophet Hăg'-gâi, saying,

2 Speak now to Zĕ-rŭb'-bă-bĕl the son of Shē-ăl'-tĭ-ĕl, governor of Judah, and to Joshua the son of Jŏs'-ĕ-dĕch, the high priest, and to the residue of the people, saying,

3 Who [a]*is* left among you that saw this house in her first glory? and how do ye see it now? [b]*is it* not in your eyes in comparison of it as nothing?

4 Yet now [c]be strong, O Zĕ-rŭb'-bă-bĕl, saith the LORD; and be strong, O Joshua, son of Jŏs'-ĕ-dĕch, the high priest; and be strong, all ye people of the land, saith the LORD, and work: for [d]I *am* with you, saith the LORD of hosts:

5 *According* [e]*to* the word that I covenanted with you when ye came out of Egypt, so [f]my spirit remaineth among you: fear ye not.

6 For thus saith the LORD of hosts; Yet [g]once, it *is* a little while, and I [h]will shake the heavens, and the earth, and the sea, and the dry *land;*

7 And I will shake all nations, and [i]the desire of all nations shall come: and I will fill [j]this house with glory, saith the LORD of hosts.

8 The silver *is* mine, and the gold *is* mine, saith the LORD of hosts.

9 The [k]glory of this latter house shall be greater than of the former, saith the LORD of hosts: and in this place will I [l]give peace, saith the LORD of hosts.

10 ¶ In the four and twentieth *day* of the ninth *month*, in the second year of Dă-rī'-ŭs, came the word of the LORD by Hăg'-gâi the prophet, saying,

11 Thus saith the LORD of hosts; Ask [m]now the priests *concerning* the law, saying,

12 If one bear holy flesh in the skirt of his garment, and with his skirt do touch bread, or pottage, or wine, or oil, or any meat, shall it be holy? And the priests answered and said, No.

13 Then said Hăg'-gâi, If *one that is* [n]unclean by a dead body touch any of these, shall it be unclean? And the priests answered and said, It shall be unclean.

14 Then answered Hăg'-gâi, and said, [o]So *is* this people, and so *is* this nation before me, saith the LORD; and so *is* every work of their hands; and that which they offer there *is* unclean.

15 And now, I pray you, [p]consider from this day and upward, from before a stone was laid upon a stone in the temple of the LORD:

16 Since those *days* were, when *one* came to an heap of twenty *measures*, there were *but* ten: when *one* came to the pressfat for to draw out fifty *vessels* out of the press, there were *but* twenty.

17 I [q]smote you with blasting and with mildew and with hail in all the labours of your hands; yet [r]ye *turned* not to me, saith the LORD.

18 Consider now from this day and upward, from the four and twentieth day of the ninth *month*, *even* from [s]the day that the foundation of the LORD's temple was laid, consider *it*.

19 Is the seed yet in the barn? yea, as yet the vine, and the fig tree, and the pomegranate, and the olive tree, hath not brought forth: from this day will I bless *you*.

20 ¶ And again the word of the LORD came unto Hăg'-gâi in the four and twentieth *day* of the month, saying,

21 Speak to Zĕ-rŭb'-bă-bĕl, governor of Judah, saying, [t]I will shake the heavens and the earth;

22 And [u]I will overthrow the throne of kingdoms, and I will destroy the strength of the kingdoms of the heathen; and [v]I will overthrow the chariots, and those that ride in them; and the horses and their riders shall come down, every one by the sword of his brother.

23 In that day, saith the LORD of hosts, will I take thee, O Zĕ-rŭb'-bă-bĕl, my servant, the son of Shē-ăl'-tĭ-ĕl, saith the LORD, [w]and will make thee as a signet: for [x]I have chosen thee, saith the LORD of hosts.

h Ps. 111.10. Pro. 1.7. Eccl. 12.13.
i 2 Chr. 15.2. Isa. 41.10. Matt. 28.20. Rom. 8.31.
j 2 Chr. 36. 22. Ps. 110.3.
k ch. 2.21.
l 1 Cor. 15.58.

CHAP. 2

1 by the hand of.
a Ezra 3.12.
b Zech. 4.10.
c Zech. 8.9.
d Ex. 3.12. 1 Sam. 16. 18. ch. 1.13. Mark 16.20. Rom. 8.31.
e Ex. 29.45, 46.
f Neh. 9.20. Isa. 63.11. Zech. 4.6.
g Heb. 12.26.
h Isa. 34.4. Jer. 4.26.
i Gen. 3.15. Deut. 18.15. Mal. 3.1.
j Ps. 24.7.
k Luke 11.31. John 1.14.
l Ps. 85.8,9. Isa. 9.6. Luke 2.14.
m Lev. 10.10. Deut. 33.10.
n Num. 19. 11.
o Titus 1.15.
p ch. 1.5.
q Deut. 28.22. 1 Ki. 8.37.
r Jer. 5.3. Amos 4.6, 8-11.
s Zech. 8.9.
t Eze. 21.27. Heb. 12.26.
u Dan. 2.44. Matt. 24.7.
v Micah 5.10.
w Song 8.6. Jer. 22.24.
x Isa. 42.1.

ZECHARIAH

CHAPTER 1

IN the eighth month, [a]in the second year of Dă-rī´-ŭs, came the word of the LORD unto [b]Zĕch-ă-rī´-ăh, the son of Bĕr-ē-chī´-ăh, the son of Ĭd´-dō the prophet, saying,

2 The LORD hath been [1]sore displeased with your fathers.

3 Therefore say thou unto them, Thus saith the LORD of hosts; Turn ye [c]unto me, saith the LORD of hosts, and I will turn unto you, saith the LORD of hosts.

4 Be ye not as your fathers, unto whom the former prophets have cried, saying, Thus saith the LORD of hosts; [d]Turn ye now from your evil ways, and *from* your evil doings: but they did not hear, nor hearken unto me, saith the LORD.

5 Your fathers, where *are* they? and the prophets, do they live for ever?

6 But [e]my words and my statutes, which I commanded my servants the prophets, did they not [2]take hold of your fathers? and they returned and said, [f]Like as the LORD of hosts thought to do unto us, according to our ways, and according to our doings, so hath he dealt with us.

7 ¶ Upon the four and twentieth day of the eleventh month, which *is* the month Sē´-băt, in the second year of Dă-rī´-ŭs, came the word of the LORD unto Zĕch-ă-rī´-ăh, the son of Bĕr-ē-chī´-ăh, the son of Ĭd´-dō the prophet, saying,

8 I saw by night, and behold [g]a man riding upon a red horse, and he stood among the myrtle trees that *were* in the bottom; and behind him *were there* [h]red horses, [3]speckled, and white.

9 Then said I, O my lord, what *are* these? And the angel that talked with me said unto me, I will shew thee what these *be*.

10 And the man that stood among the myrtle trees answered and said, [i]These *are they* whom the LORD hath sent to walk to and fro through the earth.

11 And [j]they answered the angel of the LORD that stood among the myrtle trees, and said, We have walked to and fro through the earth, and, behold, all the earth sitteth still, and is at rest.

12 ¶ Then the angel of the LORD answered and said, [k]O LORD of hosts, how long wilt thou not have mercy on Jerusalem and on the cities of Judah, against which thou hast had indignation [l]these threescore and ten years?

13 And the LORD answered the angel that talked with me [m]*with* good words *and* comfortable words.

14 So the angel that communed with me said unto me, Cry thou, saying, Thus saith the LORD of hosts; I am [n]jealous for Jerusalem and for Zion with a great jealousy.

15 And I am very sore displeased with the heathen *that are* at ease: for [o]I was but a little displeased, and they helped forward the affliction.

16 Therefore thus saith the LORD; I [p]am returned to Jerusalem with mercies: my house shall be built in it, saith the LORD of hosts, and a [q]line shall be stretched forth upon Jerusalem.

17 Cry yet, saying, Thus saith the LORD of hosts; My cities through [4]prosperity shall yet be spread abroad; [r]and the LORD shall yet comfort Zion, and [s]shall yet choose Jerusalem.

18 ¶ Then lifted I up mine eyes, and saw, and behold four horns.

19 And I said unto the angel that talked with me, What *be* these? And he answered me, These [t]*are* the horns which have scattered Judah, Israel, and Jerusalem.

20 And the LORD shewed me four carpenters.

21 Then said I, What come these to do? And he spake, saying, These *are* the horns which have scattered Judah, so that no man did lift up his head: but these are come to fray them, to cast out the horns of the Gentiles, which [u]lifted up *their* horn over the land of Judah to scatter it.

CHAPTER 2

I LIFTED up mine eyes again, and looked, and behold [a]a man with a measuring line in his hand.

2 Then said I, Whither goest thou? And he said unto me, [b]To measure Jerusalem, to see what *is* the breadth thereof, and what *is* the length thereof.

CHAP. 1

a Ezra 4.24. Hag. 1.1.
b Ezra 5.1.
1 with displeasure.
c Jer. 25.5. Micah 7.19. Mal. 3.7. Luke 15.20.
d Isa. 1.16, 17. Jer. 3.12. Eze. 33.11. Hosea 14.1. Matt. 3.8,9. Acts 3.19.
e Isa. 55.1.
2 Or, overtake.
f Lam. 1.18.
g Josh. 5.13. Rev. 6.4.
h ch. 6.2.
3 Or, bay.
i Ps. 91.11. Heb. 1.14.
j Ps. 103.20.
k Ps. 102.13. Rev. 6.10.
l Dan. 9.2. ch. 7.5.
m Isa. 40.1,2. Jer. 29.10.
n Joel 2.18. ch. 8.2.
o Isa. 47.6.
p Isa. 12.1.
q ch. 2.1,2.
4 good.
r Isa. 51.3.
s ch. 3.2.
t Ezra. 4.1. Hab. 3.14.
u Ps. 75.4,5.

CHAP. 2

a Eze. 40.3. ch. 1.16.
b Rev. 11.1.

3 And, behold, the angel that talked with me went forth, and another angel went out to meet him,

4 And said unto him, Run, speak to this young man, saying, [c]Jerusalem shall be inhabited *as* towns without walls for the multitude of men and cattle therein:

5 For I, saith the LORD, will be unto her a [d]wall of fire round about, [e]and will be the glory in the midst of her.

6 ¶ Ho, ho, *come forth*, and flee from the land of the north, saith the LORD: for I have [f]spread you abroad as the four winds of the heaven, saith the LORD.

7 Deliver thyself, O Zion, that dwellest *with* the daughter of Babylon.

8 For thus saith the LORD of hosts; After the glory hath he sent me unto the nations which spoiled you: for he that [g]toucheth you toucheth the apple of his eye.

9 For, behold, I will shake mine hand upon them, and they shall be a spoil to their servants: and ye shall know that the LORD of hosts hath sent me.

10 ¶ Sing and rejoice, O daughter of Zion: for, lo, I come, and I [h]will dwell in the midst of thee, saith the LORD.

11 And [i]many nations shall be joined to the LORD in that day, and shall be [j]my people: and I will dwell in the midst of thee, and thou [k]shalt know that the LORD of hosts hath sent me unto thee.

12 And the LORD shall [l]inherit Judah his portion in the holy land, and shall choose Jerusalem again.

13 Be [m]silent, O all flesh, before the LORD: for he is raised up out of [1]his holy habitation.

CHAPTER 3

AND he shewed me [a]Joshua the high priest standing before the angel of the LORD, and [1]Satan standing at his right hand [2]to resist him.

2 And [b]the LORD said unto Satan, [c]The LORD rebuke thee, O Satan; even the LORD that [d]hath chosen Jerusalem rebuke thee: [e]*is* not this a brand plucked out of the fire?

3 Now Joshua was clothed with filthy [f]garments, and stood before the angel.

4 And he answered and spake unto those that stood before him, saying, Take away the filthy garments from him. And unto him he said, Behold, I have caused thine iniquity to pass from thee, and [g]I will clothe thee with change of raiment.

5 And I said, Let them set a fair mitre [h]upon his head. So they set a fair mitre upon his head, and clothed him with garments. And the angel of the LORD stood by.

6 And the angel of the LORD protested unto Joshua, saying,

7 Thus saith the LORD of hosts; If thou wilt walk in my ways, and if thou wilt keep my [3]charge, then thou shalt also [i]judge my house, and shalt also keep my courts, and I will give thee [4]places to walk among these that stand by.

8 Hear now, O Joshua the high priest, thou, and thy fellows that sit before thee: for they *are* [5]men wondered at: for, behold, I will bring forth [j]my servant [k]the BRANCH.

9 For behold the stone that I have laid before Joshua; [l]upon one stone *shall* [m]*be* seven eyes: behold, I will engrave the graving thereof, saith the LORD of hosts, and [n]I will remove the iniquity of that land in one day.

10 In that day, saith the LORD of hosts, shall ye call every man his neighbour under [o]the vine and under the fig tree.

CHAPTER 4

AND the angel that talked with me came again, and waked me, [a]as a man that is wakened out of his sleep,

2 And said unto me, What seest thou? And I said, I have looked, and behold [b]a candlestick all *of* gold, [1]with a bowl upon the top of it, and [c]his seven lamps thereon, and [2]seven pipes to the seven lamps, which *are* upon the top thereof:

3 And [d]two olive trees by it, one upon the right *side* of the bowl, and the other upon the left *side* thereof.

4 So I answered and spake to the angel that talked with me, saying, What *are* these, my lord?

5 Then the angel that talked with me answered and said unto me, Knowest thou not what these be? And I said, No, my lord.

6 Then he answered and spake unto me, saying, This *is* the word of the LORD unto Zĕ-rŭb-bă-bĕl, saying, Not by [3]might, nor by power, but by my spirit, saith the LORD of hosts.

7 Who *art* thou, [e]O great mountain? before Zĕ-rŭb-bă-bĕl *thou shalt become* a plain: and he shall bring forth [f]the headstone *thereof* [g]*with* shoutings, *crying*, Grace, grace unto it.

c Eze. 36.10.
d Ps. 46.11. Isa. 4.5.
e Rev. 21.23.
f Deut. 28.64.
g 2 Thes. 1.6.
h Lev. 26.12. 2 Cor. 6.16.
i Isa. 2.2,3.
j Ex. 12.49.
k Eze. 33.33.
l Deut. 32.9.
m Ps. 46.10. Hab. 2.20. Rom. 3.19.
1 the habitation of his holiness.

CHAP. 3

a Hag. 1.1.
1 That is, an adversary.
2 to be his adversary.
b Ps. 109.31. Matt. 4.10. Luke 22.31. Rom. 16.20.
c Jude 9.
d Rom. 8.33.
e Rom. 11.5.
f Isa. 64.6.
g Rev. 19.8.
h Ex. 29.6.
3 Or, ordinance.
i Deut. 17.9.
4 walks.
5 men of wonder, or, sign.
j Isa. 42.1.
k Isa. 4.2.
l Isa. 28.16.
m Rev. 5.6.
n Isa. 53.4.
o 1 Ki. 4.25. Micah 4.4.

CHAP. 4

a Dan. 8.18.
b Ex. 25.31.
1 with her bowl.
c Ex. 25.37. Rev. 4.5.
2 Or, seven several pipes to the lamps, etc.
d Rev. 11.4.
3 Or, army.
e Isa. 40.3,4. Matt. 21.21.
f Ps. 118.22.
g Ezra 3.11.

8 Moreover the word of the LORD
came unto me, saying,
9 The hands of Zĕ-rŭb´-bă-bĕl have
laid the foundation of this house; his
hands shall [h]also finish it; and thou
[i]shalt know that the LORD of hosts
hath sent me unto you.
10 For who hath despised the day of
small [j]things? [4]for they shall rejoice,
and shall see the [5]plummet in the hand
of Zĕ-rŭb´-bă-bĕl *with* those seven;
[k]they *are* the eyes of the LORD, which
run to and fro through the whole
earth.
11 ¶ Then answered I, and said unto
him, What *are* these two olive trees
upon the right *side* of the candlestick
and upon the left *side* thereof?
12 And I answered again, and said
unto him, What *be these* two olive
branches which [6]through the two
golden pipes [7]empty [8]the golden *oil*
out of themselves?
13 And he answered me and said,
Knowest thou not what these *be?* And
I said, No, my lord.
14 Then said he, These *are* the two
[9]anointed ones, that stand by the
Lord of the whole earth.

CHAPTER 5

THEN I turned, and lifted up mine
eyes, and looked, and behold a
flying roll.
2 And he said unto me, What seest
thou? And I answered, I see a flying
roll; the length thereof *is* twenty cubits, and the breadth thereof ten
cubits.
3 Then said he unto me, This *is* the
[a]curse that goeth forth over the face
of the whole earth: for [1]every one that
stealeth shall be cut off *as* on this side
according to it; and every one that
sweareth shall be cut off *as* on that side
according to it.
4 I will bring it forth, saith the LORD
of hosts, and it shall enter into the
house of the thief, and into the house
[b]of him that sweareth falsely by my
name: and it shall remain in the
midst of his house, and [c]shall consume it with the timber thereof and
the stones thereof.
5 ¶ Then the angel that talked with
me went forth, and said unto me,
Lift up now thine eyes, and see what
is this that goeth forth.
6 And I said, What *is* it? And he
said, This *is* an ē´-phäh that goeth
forth. He said moreover, This *is* their
resemblance through all the earth.
7 And, behold, there was lifted up a
[2]talent of lead: and this *is* a woman
that sitteth in the midst of the ē´-phäh.
8 And he said, This *is* wickedness.
And he cast it into the midst of the
ē´-phäh; and he cast the weight of
lead upon the mouth thereof.
9 Then lifted I up mine eyes, and
looked, and, behold, there came out
two women, and the wind *was* in their
wings; for they had wings like the
wings of a stork: and they lifted up
the ē´-phäh between the earth and the
heaven.
10 Then said I to the angel that talked with me, Whither do these bear the
ē´-phäh?
11 And he said unto me, [d]To build it
an house in the land of Shī´-när: and
it shall be established, and set there
upon her own base.

CHAPTER 6

AND I turned, and lifted up mine
eyes, and looked, and, behold,
there came four chariots out from between two mountains; and the mountains *were* mountains of brass.
2 In the first chariot *were* [a]red horses;
and in the second chariot black
horses;
3 And in the third chariot [b]white
horses; and in the fourth chariot
grisled and [1]bay horses.
4 Then I answered [c]and said unto
the angel that talked with me, What
are these, my lord?
5 And the angel answered and said
unto me, [d]These *are* the four [2]spirits
of the heavens, which go forth from
[e]standing before the Lord of all the
earth.
6 The black horses which *are* therein
go forth into [f]the north country; and
the white go forth after them; and the
grisled go forth toward the south
country.
7 And the bay went forth, and sought
to go that they [g]might walk to and fro
through the earth: and he said, Get
you hence, walk to and fro through
the earth. So they walked to and fro
through the earth.
8 Then cried he upon me, and spake
unto me, saying, Behold, these that
go toward the north country have
quieted [h]my spirit in the north
country.
9 ¶ And the word of the LORD came
unto me, saying,
10 Take of *them of* the captivity,
even of Hĕl´-dāi, of Tō-bī´-jăh, and of
Jĕ-dāi´-ăh, which are [i]come from Babylon, and come thou the same day,

h Ezra 6.15.
i 1 Cor. 2.4.
j Hag. 2.3.
4 Or, since the seven eyes of the LORD shall rejoice.
5 stone of tin.
k 2 Chr. 16.9.
6 by the hand.
7 Or, empty out of themselves oil into the gold.
8 the gold.
9 sons of oil.

CHAP. 5

a Pro. 3.33. Isa. 24.6. Mal. 4.6. Gal. 3.10, 13. Heb. 6.8.
1 Or, every one of this people that stealeth holdeth himself guiltless, as it doth.
b Lev. 19.12. Matt. 5.33-36. Jas. 5.12.
c Lev. 14.45.
2 Or, weighty piece.
d Jer. 29.5.

CHAP. 6

a ch. 1.8. Rev. 6.4.
b Rev. 6.2.
1 Or, strong.
c ch. 5.10.
d Ps. 68.17. Heb. 1.7,14.
2 Or, winds.
e 1 Ki. 22.19. Job 1.6. Dan. 7.10. Luke 1.19.
f Jer. 1.14.
g Gen. 13.17.
h Eccl. 10.4.
i Ezra 8.1.

and go into the house of Jō-sī´-ăh the
son of Zĕph-ă-nī´-ăh;
11 Then take silver and gold, and
make [j]crowns, and set *them* upon the
head of Joshua the son of Jŏs´-ĕ-dĕch,
the high priest;
12 And speak unto him, saying,
Thus speaketh the LORD of hosts,
saying, Behold the [k]man whose name
is The [l]BRANCH; and he shall [3]grow
up out of his place, and he [m]shall
build the temple of the LORD:
13 Even he shall build the temple of
the LORD; and he [n]shall bear the glory,
and shall sit and rule upon his throne;
and [o]he shall be a priest upon his
throne: and the counsel of peace shall
be between them both.
14 And the crowns shall be to Hē´-
lĕm, and to Tō-bī´-jăh, and to Jĕ-dāi´-
ăh, and to Hen the son of Zĕph-ă-nī´-
ăh, [p]for a memorial in the temple of
the LORD.
15 And [q]they *that are* far off shall
come and build in the temple of the
LORD, and ye shall know that the
LORD of hosts hath sent me unto you.
And *this* shall come to pass, if ye will
diligently obey the voice of the LORD
your God.

CHAPTER 7

AND it came to pass in the fourth
year of king Dā-rī´-ŭs, *that* the
word of the LORD came unto Zĕch-ă-
rī´-ăh in the fourth *day* of the ninth
month, *even* in Chĭs´-lēū;
2 When they had sent unto the house
of God Shĕr-ē´-zĕr and Rē´-gĕm-mĕl´-
ĕch, and their men, [1]to pray before
the LORD,
3 *And* to [a]speak unto the priests
which *were* in the house of the LORD
of hosts, and to the prophets, saying,
Should I weep in the fifth month,
separating myself, as I have done
these so many years?
4 ¶ Then came the word of the LORD
of hosts unto me, saying,
5 Speak unto all the people of the
land, and to the priests, saying, When
ye fasted and mourned in the fifth and
seventh *month*, [b]even those seventy
years, did ye at all fast unto [c]me, *even*
to me?
6 And when ye did eat, and when ye
did drink, [2]did not ye eat *for yourselves*, and drink *for yourselves?*
7 [3]*Should ye* not *hear* the words
which the LORD hath cried [4]by the
former prophets, when Jerusalem
was inhabited and in prosperity, and
the cities thereof round about her,

[j] Ex. 28.36.
[k] Isa. 9.6. Micah 5.5. ch. 13.7. Mal. 3.1. Mark 15.39. Luke 1.78. John 1.45.
[l] Ps. 80.15-17. Isa. 4.2. ch. 3.8.
[3] Or, branch up from under him.
[m] Matt. 16.18. Eph. 2.20. Phil. 2.9. Heb. 2.9.
[n] Ps. 21.5. Isa. 22.24.
[o] Ps. 110.4. Heb. 3.1.
[p] Mark 14.9.
[q] Eph. 2.13.

CHAP. 7

[1] to entreat the face of the LORD.
[a] Deut. 17.9. Mal. 2.7.
[b] ch. 1.12.
[c] Isa. 58.4. Matt. 6.16. Rom. 14.6.
[2] Or, be not ye they that, etc.
[3] Or, Are not these the words.
[4] by the hand of, etc.
[d] Jer. 17.26.
[5] Judge judgment of truth.
[6] they gave a backsliding shoulder.
[7] made heavy.
[8] by the hand of.
[9] land of desire.

CHAP. 8

[a] Nah. 1.2.
[b] Isa. 1.21.
[c] Isa. 2.2,3.
[d] Ps. 48.1,2. Jer. 31.23.
[e] 1 Sam. 2.31. Isa. 65.20.
[1] for multitude of days.
[2] Or, hard, or, difficult.
[f] Num. 11.23. Job 42.2. Luke 1.37. Rom. 4.21.

when *men* [d]inhabited the south and
the plain?
8 ¶ And the word of the LORD came
unto Zĕch-ă-rī´-ăh, saying,
9 Thus speaketh the LORD of hosts,
saying, [5]Execute true judgment, and
shew mercy and compassions every
man to his brother:
10 And oppress not the widow, nor
the fatherless, the stranger, nor the
poor; and let none of you imagine evil against his brother in your
heart.
11 But they refused to hearken, and
[6]pulled away the shoulder, and [7]stop-
ped their ears, that they should not
hear.
12 Yea, they made their hearts *as* an
adamant stone, lest they should hear
the law, and the words which the
LORD of hosts hath sent in his spirit
[8]by the former prophets: therefore
came a great wrath from the LORD of
hosts.
13 Therefore it is come to pass, *that*
as he cried, and they would not hear;
so they cried, and I would not hear,
saith the LORD of hosts:
14 But I scattered them with a whirlwind among all the nations whom
they knew not. Thus the land was
desolate after them, that no man passed through nor returned: for they laid
the [9]pleasant land desolate.

CHAPTER 8

AGAIN the word of the LORD of
hosts came *to me*, saying,
2 Thus saith the LORD of hosts; I
[a]was jealous for Zion with great
jealousy, and I was jealous for her
with great fury.
3 Thus saith the LORD; I am returned
unto Zion, and will dwell in the midst
of Jerusalem: and Jerusalem [b]shall be
called a city of truth; and [c]the mountain of the LORD of hosts [d]the holy
mountain.
4 Thus saith the LORD of hosts;
There [e]shall yet old men and old women dwell in the streets of Jerusalem,
and every man with his staff in his
hand [1]for very age.
5 And the streets of the city shall be
full of boys and girls playing in the
streets thereof.
6 Thus saith the LORD of hosts; If it
be [2]marvellous in the eyes of the remnant of this people in these days,
[f]should it also be marvellous in mine
eyes? saith the LORD of hosts.
7 Thus saith the LORD of hosts; Behold, I will save my people from the

east country, and from [3]the west
country;
8 And I will bring them, and they
shall dwell in the midst of Jerusalem:
[g]and they shall be my people, and I
will be their God, in truth and in
righteousness.
9 ¶ Thus saith the LORD of hosts;
Let [h]your hands be strong, ye that
hear in these days these words by the
mouth of [i]the prophets, which *were* in
[j]the day *that* the foundation of the
house of the LORD of hosts was laid,
that the temple might be built.
10 For before these days [4]there was
no hire for man, nor any hire for
beast; neither *was there any* peace to
him that went out or came in because
of the affliction: for I set all men
every one against his neighbour.
11 But now I *will* not *be* unto the
residue of this people as in the former
days, saith the LORD of hosts.
12 For the seed *shall be* [5]prosperous;
the vine shall give her fruit, and the
ground shall give her increase, and
the heavens shall give their dew; and
I will cause the remnant of this people
to [k]possess all these *things*.
13 And it shall come to pass, *that* as
ye were [l]a curse among the heathen, O
house of Judah, and house of Israel;
so will I save you, and [m]ye shall be a
blessing: [n]fear not, *but* let your hands
be strong.
14 For thus saith the LORD of hosts;
[o]As I thought to punish you, when
your fathers provoked me to wrath,
saith the LORD of hosts, [p]and I repented not:
15 So again have I thought in these
days to do well unto Jerusalem and to
the house of Judah: fear ye not.
16 ¶ These *are* the things that ye shall
do; [q]Speak ye every man the truth to
his neighbour; [6]execute the judgment
of truth and peace in your gates:
17 And [r]let none of you imagine evil
in your hearts against his neighbour;
and love no false oath: for all these
are things that [s]I hate, saith the
LORD.
18 ¶ And the word of the LORD of
hosts came unto me, saying,
19 Thus saith the LORD of hosts;
[t]The fast of the fourth *month*, and the
fast of the fifth, [u]and the fast of the
seventh, and the fast of the tenth,
shall be to the house of Judah [v]joy and
gladness, and cheerful [7]feasts; therefore love the truth and peace.
20 Thus saith the LORD of hosts; *It
shall* yet *come to pass*, that there shall

3 the country of the going down of the sun.
g Lev. 25.17. Jer. 4.2. Eze. 11.20. ch. 13.9. Rev. 21.3.
h Hag. 2.4.
i Ezra 5.1,2.
j Hag. 2.18.
4 Or, the hire of man became nothing, etc.
5 of peace.
k Isa. 61.7. Matt. 6.33. 1 Tim. 4.8.
l Jer. 42.18.
m Gen. 12.2.
n Deut. 20.3, 4. Eph. 6.10.
o Jer. 31.28.
p 2 Chr. 36. 16.
q Pro. 12.19.
6 judge truth, and the judgment of peace.
r Pro. 3.29.
s Pro. 6.16.
t Jer. 52.6.
u Jer. 41.1.
v Isa. 35.10.
7 Or, solemn, or, set times.
8 going, or, continually to intreat the face of the LORD.

CHAP. 9

a Amos 1.3.
b Ps. 145.15.
c Jer. 49.23.
d Amos 1.9.
e Obad. 20.
f Eze. 28.3.
g Eze. 26.17.
h Zeph. 2.4.
i Acts 8.26.
1 bloods.
j Deut. 33.27. Ps. 34.7.
k Ex. 3.7.
l Matt. 21.5. John 12.15.
m Ps. 2.6. Matt. 21.5. Luke 19.38. John 1.49.
n Isa. 45.21. Acts 22.14. 1 Pet. 3.18.
2 Or, saving himself.

come people, and the inhabitants of
many cities:
21 And the inhabitants of one *city*
shall go to another, saying, Let us go
[8]speedily to pray before the LORD, and
to seek the LORD of hosts: I will go
also.
22 Yea, many people and strong nations shall come to seek the LORD of
hosts in Jerusalem, and to pray before
the LORD.
23 Thus saith the LORD of hosts; In
those days *it shall come to pass*, that
ten men shall take hold out of all languages of the nations, even shall take
hold of the skirt of him that is a Jew,
saying, We will go with you: for we
have heard *that* God *is* with you.

CHAPTER 9

THE burden of the word of the
LORD in the land of Hā-drăch, and
[a]Damascus *shall be* the rest thereof:
when [b]the eyes of man, as of all the
tribes of Israel, *shall be* toward the
LORD.
2 And [c]Hā-măth also shall border
thereby; [d]Tȳ-rŭs, and [e]Zī-dŏn, though
it be [f]very wise.
3 And Tȳ-rŭs did build herself a
strong hold, and heaped up silver as
the dust, and fine gold as the mire of
the streets.
4 Behold, the Lord will cast her out,
and he will smite [g]her power in the
sea; and she shall be devoured with
fire.
5 Ăsh-kĕ-lon [h]shall see *it*, and fear;
Gā-ză [i]also *shall see it*, and be very
sorrowful, and Ĕk-rŏn; for her expectation shall be ashamed; and the
king shall perish from Gā-ză, and
Ăsh-kĕ-lon shall not be inhabited.
6 And a bastard shall dwell in Ăsh-
dŏd, and I will cut off the pride of the
Philistines.
7 And I will take away his [1]blood out
of his mouth, and his abominations
from between his teeth: but he that
remaineth, even he, *shall be* for our
God, and he shall be as a governor in
Judah, and Ĕk-rŏn as a Jĕb-ū-site.
8 And [j]I will encamp about mine
house because of the army, because
of him that passeth by, and because
of him that returneth: and no oppress-
or shall pass through them any more:
for now [k]have I seen with mine
eyes.
9 ¶ Rejoice [l]greatly, O daughter of
Zion; shout, O daughter of Jerusalem: behold, thy [m]King cometh unto
thee: he *is* [n]just, and [2]having salva-

tion; lowly, and riding upon an ass,
and upon a colt the foal of an ass.
10 And I will cut off the chariot from
Ē´-phră-ĭm, and the horse from Jerusalem, and the battle bow shall be cut
off: and he shall speak peace [o]unto the
heathen: and his dominion *shall be*
[p]from sea *even* to sea, and from the
river *even* to the ends of the earth.
11 As for thee also, [3]by the blood of
thy covenant I have sent forth thy
[q]prisoners out of the pit wherein *is* no
water.
12 ¶ Turn you to the strong hold, ye
prisoners of hope: even to day do I
declare *that* I will render double unto
thee;
13 When I have bent Judah for me,
filled the bow with Ē´-phră-ĭm, and
raised up thy sons, O Zion, against
thy sons, O Greece, and made thee as
the sword of a mighty man.
14 And the LORD shall be seen over
them, and his arrow shall go forth as
the lightning: and the Lord GOD
shall blow the trumpet, and shall go
with whirlwinds of the south.
15 The LORD of hosts shall defend
them; and they shall devour, and
[4]subdue with sling stones; and they
shall drink, *and* make a noise as
through wine; and they [5]shall be filled
like bowls, *and* as [r]the corners of the
altar.
16 And [s]the LORD their God shall
save them in that day as the flock of
his people: for [t]*they shall be as* the
stones of a crown, lifted [u]up as an ensign upon his land.
17 For how great *is* his goodness,
and how great *is* his beauty! corn
shall make the young men [6]cheerful,
and new wine the maids.

CHAPTER 10

ASK ye [a]of the LORD rain [b]in the
time of the latter rain; *so* the
LORD shall make [1]bright clouds, and
give them showers of rain, to every
one grass in the field.
2 For the [2]idols have spoken vanity,
and the diviners have seen a lie, and
have told false dreams; they comfort
in vain: therefore they went their way
as a flock, they [3]were troubled, because *there was* no shepherd.
3 Mine anger was kindled against
the shepherds, and I [4]punished the
goats: for the LORD of hosts hath
[c]visited his flock the house of Judah,
and have made them as his goodly
horse in the battle.
4 Out of him came forth the corner,
out of him [d]the nail, out of him the
battle bow, out of him every oppressor
together.
5 ¶ And they shall be as mighty *men*,
which tread down *their enemies* in the
mire of the streets in the battle: and
they shall fight, because the LORD *is*
with them, and [5]the riders on horses
shall be confounded.
6 And I will strengthen the house of
Judah, and I will save the house of
Joseph, and I will bring them again
to place them; for I have mercy upon
them: and they shall be as though I
had not cast them off: for I *am* the
LORD their God, and will hear them.
7 And *they of* Ē´-phră-ĭm shall be like
a mighty *man*, and their heart shall rejoice as through wine: yea, their children shall see *it*, and be glad; their
heart shall rejoice in the LORD.
8 I will [e]hiss for them, and gather
them; for I have redeemed them: and
they shall increase as they have increased.
9 And I will sow them among the
people: and they shall remember me
in far countries; and they shall live
with their children, and turn again.
10 I will [f]bring them again also out
of the land of Egypt, and gather them
out of Assyria; and I will bring them
into the land of Gilead and Lĕb´-ā-
non; and [g]*place* shall not be found for
them.
11 And he shall pass through the sea
with affliction, and shall smite the
waves in the sea, and all the deeps of
the river shall dry up: and the pride of
Assyria shall be brought down, and
the [h]sceptre of Egypt shall depart
away.
12 And I will strengthen them in the
LORD; and they shall walk up and
down in his name, saith the LORD.

CHAPTER 11

OPEN thy doors, O Lĕb´-ā-non,
that the fire may devour thy
cedars.
2 Howl, fir tree; for the cedar is fall-
en; because the [1]mighty are spoiled:
howl, O ye oaks of Bā´-shăn; for [2]the
forest of the vintage is come down.
3 ¶ *There is* a voice of the howling of
the shepherds; for their glory is spoiled: a voice of the roaring of young
lions; for the pride of Jordan is
spoiled.
4 Thus saith the LORD my God;
Feed the flock of the slaughter;
5 Whose possessors slay them, and
[a]hold themselves not guilty: and they

o Ps. 72.3,7. Isa. 11.10. Eph. 2.14. Col. 1.20,21.
p Ps. 2.8. Ps. 72.8. Isa. 9.6,7. Micah 5.4. Rev. 11.15.
3 Or, whose covenant is by blood.
q Isa. 61.1.
4 Or, subdue the stones of the sling.
5 Or, shall fill both the bowls, etc.
r Lev. 4.25.
s Eze. 37.23.
t Mal. 3.17.
u Isa. 11.12.
6 Or, grow, or, speak.

CHAP. 10

a Jer. 14.22.
b Joel 2.23.
1 Or, lightnings.
2 teraphims.
3 Or, answered that, etc.
4 visited upon. Eze. 34. 17.
c Ex. 4.31. Ruth 1.6. Zeph. 2.7. Luke 1.68. 1 Pet. 2.12.
d Isa. 22.23.
5 Or, they shall make the riders on horses ashamed.
e Isa. 5.26.
f Rom. 11.25.
g Ex. 14.26, 27. Isa. 49.20.
h Eze. 30.13.

CHAP. 11

1 Or, gallants.
2 Or, the defenced forest.
a Deut. 29. 19. Jer. 2.3. Hosea 12.8. John 16.2.

that sell them [b]say, Blessed *be* the
LORD; for I am rich: and their own
shepherds pity them not.
6 For I will no more pity the inhabitants of the land, saith the LORD: but,
lo, I will [3]deliver the men every one
into his neighbour's hand, and into
the hand of his king: and they shall
smite the land, and out of their hand
I will not deliver *them*.
7 And I will feed the flock of slaughter, [4]*even* you, [c]O poor of the flock.
And I took unto me two staves;
the one I called Beauty, and the
other I called [5]Bands; and I fed the
flock.
8 Three shepherds also I cut off [d]in
one month; and my soul [6]lothed
them, and their soul also abhorred
me.
9 Then said I, I will not feed you:
that [e]that dieth, let it die; and that
that is to be cut off, let it be cut off;
and let the rest eat every one the flesh
[7]of another.
10 ¶ And I took my staff, *even* Beauty,
and cut it asunder, that I might break
my covenant which I had made with
all the people.
11 And it was broken in that day:
and [8]so the poor of the flock that waited upon me knew that it *was* the word
of the LORD.
12 And I said unto them, [9]If ye think
good, give *me* my price; and if not,
forbear. So they [f]weighed for my
price thirty *pieces* of silver.
13 And the LORD said unto me, Cast
it unto the [g]potter: a goodly price that
I was prised at of them. And I took
the thirty *pieces* of silver, and cast
them to the potter in the house of the
LORD.
14 Then I cut asunder mine other
staff, *even* [10]Bands, that I might break
the brotherhood between Judah and
Israel.
15 ¶ And the LORD said unto me,
Take [h]unto thee yet the instruments of
a foolish shepherd.
16 For, lo, I will raise up a shepherd
in the land, *which* shall not visit those
that be [11]cut off, neither shall seek the
young one, nor heal that that is brok-
en, nor [12]feed that that standeth still:
but he shall eat the flesh of the fat, and
tear their claws in pieces.
17 Woe [i]to the idol shepherd that
leaveth the flock! the sword *shall be*
upon his arm, and upon his right eye:
his arm shall be clean dried up,
and his right eye shall be utterly [j]dark-
ened.

b Deut. 29. 19. Hosea 12.8. 1 Tim. 6.9. 2 Pet. 2.3.
3 make to be found.
4 Or, verily the poor.
c Zeph. 3.12. Matt. 11.5.
5 Or, Binders.
d Hosea 5.7.
6 was straitened for them.
e Jer. 15.2.
7 of his fellow, or, neighbour.
8 Or, the poor of the flock, etc., certainly knew.
9 If it be good in your eyes.
f Ex. 21.32. Matt. 26.15.
g Matt. 27.9.
10 Or, Binders.
h Eze. 34.2.
11 Or, hidden.
12 Or, bear.
i Jer. 23.1. John 10.12.
j Micah 3.6.

CHAP. 12

a Heb. 12.9.
1 Or, slumber, or, poison.
2 Or, and also against Judah shall he be which shall be in siege against Jerusalem.
b Matt. 21.44.
c Ps. 76.6.
3 Or, There is strength to me and to the inhabitants, etc.
d 1 Cor. 1.27, 29,31.
e Joel 3.10.
4 fallen, or, abject.
f Joel 2.28.
g Ps. 22.16. Luke 2.35. John 19.34. Rev. 1.7.
h Acts 2.37.
i 2 Chr. 35. 24.

CHAPTER 12

THE burden of the word of the
LORD for Israel, saith the LORD,
which stretcheth forth the heavens,
and layeth the foundation of the
earth, and [a]formeth the spirit of man
within him.
2 Behold, I will make Jerusalem a
cup of [1]trembling unto all the people
round about, [2]when they shall be in
the siege both against Judah *and*
against Jerusalem.
3 ¶ And in that day will I make Jerusalem a [b]burdensome stone for all
people: all that burden themselves
with it shall be cut in pieces, though
all the people of the earth be gathered
together against it.
4 In that day, saith the LORD, [c]I will
smite every horse with astonishment,
and his rider with madness: and I will
open mine eyes upon the house of Judah, and will smite every horse of the
people with blindness.
5 And the governors of Judah shall
say in their heart, [3]The inhabitants of
Jerusalem *shall be* my strength in the
LORD of hosts their God.
6 ¶ In that day will I make the governors of Judah like an hearth of fire
among the wood, and like a torch of
fire in a sheaf; and they shall devour
all the people round about, on the
right hand and on the left: and Jerusalem shall be inhabited again in her
own place, *even* in Jerusalem.
7 The LORD also shall save [d]the tents
of Judah first, that the glory of the
house of David and the glory of the
inhabitants of Jerusalem do not magnify *themselves* against Judah.
8 In that day shall the LORD defend
the inhabitants of Jerusalem; and [e]he
that is [4]feeble among them at that day
shall be as David; and the house of
David *shall be* as God, as the angel of
the LORD before them.
9 ¶ And it shall come to pass in that
day, *that* I will seek to destroy all the
nations that come against Jerusalem.
10 And [f]I will pour upon the house
of David, and upon the inhabitants of
Jerusalem, the spirit of grace and of
supplications: and they shall [g]look
upon me whom they have pierced, and
they shall mourn for him, as one
mourneth for *his* only *son*, and shall
be in bitterness for him, as one that is
in bitterness for *his* firstborn.
11 In that day shall there be a great
[h]mourning in Jerusalem, [i]as the
mourning of Hā-dăd-rĭm-mon in the
valley of Mĕ-gĭd-don.

12 And the land shall mourn, [5]every family apart; the family of the house of David apart, and their wives apart; the family of the house of Nathan apart, and their wives apart;

13 The family of the house of Levi apart, and their wives apart; the family [6]of Shĭm'-ĕ-ī, and their wives apart;

14 All the families that remain, every family apart, and their wives apart.

CHAPTER 13

IN that day there shall be [a]a fountain opened to the house of David and to the inhabitants of Jerusalem for sin and for [1]uncleanness.

2 ¶ And it shall come to pass in that day, saith the LORD of hosts, *that* I will [b]cut off the names of the idols out of the land, and they shall no more be remembered: and also I will cause the [c]prophets and the unclean spirit to pass out of the land.

3 And it shall come to pass, *that* when any shall yet prophesy, then his [d]father and his mother that begat him shall say unto him, Thou shalt not live; for thou speakest lies in the name of the LORD: and his father and his mother that begat him shall thrust him through when he prophesieth.

4 And it shall come to pass in that day, *that* the prophets shall be ashamed every one of his vision, when he hath prophesied; neither shall they wear [2]a rough garment [3]to deceive:

5 But he shall say, I *am* no prophet, I *am* an husbandman; for man taught me to keep cattle from my youth.

6 And *one* shall say unto him, What *are* these wounds in thine hands? Then he shall answer, *Those* with which I was wounded *in* the house of my friends.

7 ¶ Awake, O sword, against my [e]shepherd, and against the man [f]*that is* my fellow, saith the LORD of hosts: [g]smite the shepherd, and the sheep shall be scattered: and I will turn mine hand upon [h]the little ones.

8 And it shall come to pass, *that* in all the land, saith the LORD, two parts therein shall be cut off *and* die; [i]but the third shall be left therein.

9 And I will bring the third part through [j]the fire, and will [k]refine them as silver is refined, and will try them as gold is tried: they shall call on my name, and I will hear them: I will say, It *is* my people: and they shall say, The LORD *is* my God.

5 families, families.

6 Or, of Simeon, as the LXX.

CHAP. 13

a Isa. 1.16,17. John 1.29. 1 Cor. 6.11. Heb. 9.14. 1 Pet. 1.19. 1 John 1.7. Rev. 1.5.
1 separation, for uncleanness.
b Ex. 23.13.
c 2 Pet. 2.1.
d Deut. 13.6.
2 a garment of hair.
3 to lie.
e Isa. 40.11. Heb. 13.20.
f John 10.30.
g Isa. 53.4,6. Mark 14.27. John 1.29.
h Luke 12.32.
i Rom. 11.5.
j Isa. 48.10.
k Ps. 66.10. Isa. 48.10. Mal. 3.4. 1 Pet. 1.6,7. Rev. 2.10.

CHAP. 14

a Joel 3.2.
b Eze. 11.23. Acts 1.11, 12.
c Joel 3.12.
1 Or, my mountains.
2 Or, when he shall touch the valley of the mountains to the place he separated.
d Amos 1.1.
e Matt. 24.30.
f Joel 3.11.
3 That is, it shall not be clear in some places, and dark in other places of the world.
4 precious.
5 thickness.
6 Or, the day shall be one.
g Rev. 21.23.
h Eze. 47.1.
7 Or, eastern.
i Ps. 2.8.
j Eph. 4.5,6.
8 Or, compassed.
9 Or, shall abide.
k Neh. 3.1.
l Jer. 31.40.
10 Or, shall abide.

CHAPTER 14

BEHOLD, the day of the LORD cometh, and thy spoil shall be divided in the midst of thee.

2 For [a]I will gather all nations against Jerusalem to battle; and the city shall be taken, and the houses rifled, and the women ravished; and half of the city shall go forth into captivity, and the residue of the people shall not be cut off from the city.

3 Then shall the LORD go forth, and fight against those nations, as when he fought in the day of battle.

4 ¶ And his feet shall stand in that day upon [b]the mount of Olives, which *is* before Jerusalem on the east, and the mount of Olives shall cleave in the midst thereof toward the east and toward the west, [c]*and there shall be* a very great valley; and half of the mountain shall remove toward the north, and half of it toward the south.

5 And ye shall flee *to* the valley of [1]the mountains; [2]for the valley of the mountains shall reach unto Ā'-zăl: yea, ye shall flee, like as ye fled from before the [d]earthquake in the days of Ŭz-zī'-ăh king of Judah; [e]and the LORD my God shall come, *and* [f]all the saints with thee.

6 And it shall come to pass in that day, [3]*that* the light shall not be [4]clear, *nor* [5]dark:

7 But [6]it shall be one day which shall be known to the LORD, not day, nor night: but it shall come to pass, *that* at [g]evening time it shall be light.

8 And it shall be in that day, *that* living waters [h]shall go out from Jerusalem; half of them toward the [7]former sea, and half of them toward the hinder sea: in summer and in winter shall it be.

9 And the LORD shall be [i]king over all the earth: in that day shall there be [j]one LORD, and his name one.

10 All the land shall be [8]turned as a plain from Gē'-bă to Rĭm'-mŏn south of Jerusalem: and it shall be lifted up, and [9]inhabited in her place, from Benjamin's gate unto the place of the first gate, unto the corner gate, [k]and *from* the tower of Hăn'-ă-nēel unto the king's winepresses.

11 And *men* shall dwell in it, and there shall be [l]no more utter destruction; but Jerusalem [10]shall be safely inhabited.

12 ¶ And this shall be the plague wherewith the LORD will smite all the people that have fought against Jerusalem; Their flesh shall consume

away while they stand upon their feet, and their eyes shall consume away in their holes, and their tongue shall consume away in their mouth.

13 And it shall come to pass in that day, *that* [m]a great tumult from the LORD shall be among them; and they shall lay hold every one on the hand of his neighbour, and his hand shall rise up against the hand of his neighbour.

14 And [11]Judah also shall fight [12]at Jerusalem; and the wealth of all the heathen round about shall be gathered together, gold, and silver, and apparel, in great abundance.

15 And so shall be the plague of the horse, of the mule, of the camel, and of the ass, and of all the beasts that shall be in these tents, as this plague.

16 ¶ And it shall come to pass, *that* every one that is left of all the nations which came against Jerusalem shall even [n]go up from year to year to worship [o]the King, the LORD of hosts, and to keep [p]the feast of tabernacles.

17 And [q]it shall be, *that* whoso will not come up of *all* the families of the earth unto Jerusalem to worship the King, the LORD of hosts, even upon them shall be no rain.

18 And if the family of Egypt go not up, and come not, [13]that *have* no *rain;* there shall be the plague, wherewith the LORD will smite the heathen that come not up to keep the feast of tabernacles.

19 This shall be the [14]punishment of Egypt, and the punishment of all nations that come not up to keep the feast of tabernacles.

20 ¶ In that day shall there be upon the [15]bells of the horses, HOLINESS UNTO THE LORD; and the pots in the LORD's house shall be like the bowls before the altar.

21 Yea, [r]every pot in Jerusalem and in Judah shall be holiness unto the LORD of hosts: and all they that sacrifice shall come and take of them, and seethe therein: and in that day there shall be no more [s]the Canaanite in the [t]house of the LORD of hosts.

m 1 Sam. 14. 15.
11 Or, thou also, O Judah, shalt.
12 Or, against.
n Isa. 66.23.
o 1 Tim. 6.15.
p Lev. 23.34. Neh. 8.14. Hosea 12.9.
q Isa. 60.12.
13 upon whom there is not.
14 Or, sin.
15 Or, bridles.
r Col. 3.17.
s Isa. 35.8. Rev. 21.27.
t Eph. 2.19.

MALACHI

CHAPTER 1

THE burden of the word of the LORD to Israel [1]by Măl'-ă-chī.

2 I have loved you, saith the LORD. Yet ye say, Wherein hast thou loved us? *Was* not Esau Jacob's brother? saith the LORD: yet I loved [a]Jacob.

3 And I hated Esau, and [b]laid his mountains and his heritage waste for the dragons of the wilderness.

4 Whereas Ē'-dŏm saith, We are impoverished, but we will return and build the desolate places; thus saith the LORD of hosts, They shall build, but I will throw down; and they shall call them, The border of wickedness, and, The people against whom the LORD hath indignation for ever.

5 And your eyes shall see, and ye shall say, [c]The LORD will be magnified [2]from the border of Israel.

6 ¶ A son [d]honoureth *his* father, and a servant his master: [e]if then I *be* a father, where *is* mine honour? and if I *be* a master, where *is* my fear? saith the LORD of hosts unto you, O priests, that despise my name. And ye say, Wherein have we despised thy name?

7 [3]Ye offer polluted bread upon mine altar; and ye say, Wherein have we polluted thee? In that ye say, [f]The table of the LORD *is* contemptible.

8 And if ye offer the blind [4]for sacrifice, *is it* not evil? and if ye offer the lame and sick, *is it* not evil? offer it now unto thy governor; will he be pleased with thee, or accept [g]thy person? saith the LORD of hosts.

9 And now, I pray you, beseech [5]God that he will be gracious unto us: [h]this hath been [6]by your means: will he regard your persons? saith the LORD of hosts.

10 Who *is there* even among you that would shut the doors *for nought?* [i]neither do ye kindle *fire* on mine altar for nought. I have no pleasure in you, saith the LORD of hosts, [j]neither will I accept an offering at your hand.

11 For [k]from the rising of the sun even unto the going down of the same my name *shall be* great among the Gentiles; [l]and in every place [m]incense *shall be* offered unto my name, and a pure offering: for [n]my name *shall be* great among the heathen, saith the LORD of hosts.

CHAP. 1
1 by the hand of Malachi.
a Gen. 25.23. Gen. 28.13. Rom. 9.13.
b Eze. 35.3.
c Ps. 35.27. Ps. 83.18.
2 from upon, or, upon.
d Ex. 20.12. Deut. 5.16. Matt. 15.4. Luke 18.20. Eph. 6.2.
e Luke 6.46.
3 Or, Bring unto, etc.
f Eze. 41.22.
4 to sacrifice.
g Job 42.8.
5 the face of God.
h Hosea 13.9.
6 from your hand.
i 1 Cor. 9.13. Phil. 3.18, 19.
j Isa. 1.11.
k Isa. 59.19.
l John 4.21. 1 Tim. 2.8.
m Rev. 8.3.
n Isa. 66.19.

12 ¶ But ye have profaned it, in that
ye say, The table of the LORD *is* polluted; and the fruit thereof, *even* his
meat, *is* contemptible.
13 Ye said also, Behold, what a
weariness *is it!* [7]and ye have snuffed
at it, saith the LORD of hosts; and ye
brought *that which was* torn, and the
lame, and the sick; thus ye brought an
offering: should [o]I accept this of your
hand? saith the LORD.
14 But [p]cursed *be* the deceiver,
[8]which hath in his flock a male, and
voweth, and sacrificeth unto the Lord
a corrupt thing: for I *am* a great King,
saith the LORD of hosts, and my name
is dreadful among the heathen.

CHAPTER 2

AND now, O ye priests, this commandment *is* for you.
2 If [a]ye will not hear, and if ye will
not lay *it* to heart, to give glory unto
my name, saith the LORD of hosts, I
will even send a curse upon you, and
I will curse your blessings: yea, I have
cursed them already, because ye do
not lay *it* to heart.
3 Behold, I will [1]corrupt your seed,
and [2]spread dung upon your faces,
even the dung of your solemn feasts;
and [3]*one* shall take you away with it.
4 And ye shall know that I have sent
this commandment unto you, that my
covenant might be with Levi, saith the
LORD of hosts.
5 My [b]covenant was with him of life
and peace; and I gave them to him
[c]*for* the fear wherewith he feared me,
and was afraid before my name.
6 The law of truth was in his mouth,
and iniquity was not found in his lips:
he walked with me in peace and
equity, and did [d]turn many away from
iniquity.
7 For [e]the priest's lips should keep
knowledge, and they should seek the
law at his mouth: [f]for he *is* the messenger of the LORD of hosts.
8 But ye are departed out of the way;
ye [g]have caused many to [4]stumble at
the law; ye have corrupted the covenant of Levi, saith the LORD of hosts.
9 Therefore have I also made you
contemptible and base before all the
people, according as ye have not kept
my ways, but [5]have been partial in
the law.
10 Have [h]we not all one father? hath
[i]not one God created us? why do we
deal treacherously every man against
his brother, by profaning the covenant of our fathers?

7 Or, whereas ye might have blown it away.
o Lev. 22.20. Isa. 1.12.
p Acts 5.1.
8 Or, in whose flock is.

CHAP. 2
a Deut. 28. 15.
1 Or, reprove.
2 scatter.
3 Or, it shall take you away to it.
b Num. 25. 12.
c Deut. 33.9.
d Dan. 12.3. Luke 1.16, 17. Jas. 5.20.
e Deut. 17.9.
f Isa. 42.19. Hag. 1.13. Gal. 4.14.
g 1 Sam. 2.17.
4 Or, fall in the law.
5 accepted faces, or, lifted up the face against.
h Isa. 51.2. Matt. 3.9. 1 Cor. 8.6. Heb. 12.9.
i Ps. 100.3.
6 Or, ought to love.
j Neh. 13.23.
7 Or, him that walketh, and him that answereth.
k Matt. 19.4, 5.
8 Or, excellency.
9 a seed of God.
10 Or, unfaithfully.
l Deut. 24.1.
11 Or, if he hate her, put her away.
12 to put away.

CHAP. 3
a Mark 1.2.
b Isa. 40.3.
c Acts 7.38.
d Isa. 63.9.
e Hag. 2.7.
f Rev. 6.17.
g Isa. 4.4.
h Isa. 1. 25. Zech. 13.9.
i Rom. 15.16. 1 Pet. 2.5.

11 ¶ Judah hath dealt treacherously
and an abomination is committed i
Israel and in Jerusalem; for Juda
hath profaned the holiness of th
LORD which he [6]loved, and [j]hat
married the daughter of a strange god
12 The LORD will cut off the man tha
doeth this, [7]the master and the scholar
out of the tabernacles of Jacob, an
him that offereth an offering unto th
LORD of hosts.
13 And this have ye done again
covering the altar of the LORD wit
tears, with weeping, and with crying
out, insomuch that he regardeth no
the offering any more, or receiveth *i*
with good will at your hand.
14 ¶ Yet ye say, Wherefore? Because
the LORD hath been witness between
thee and the wife of thy youth, against
whom thou hast dealt treacherously:
yet *is* she thy companion, and the
wife of thy covenant.
15 And [k]did not he make one? Yet
had he the [8]residue of the spirit. And
wherefore one? That he might seek [9]a
godly seed. Therefore take heed to
your spirit, and let none deal [10]treach-
erously against the wife of his youth.
16 For [l]the LORD, the God of Israel,
saith [11]that he hateth [12]putting away:
for *one* covereth violence with his garment, saith the LORD of hosts: therefore take heed to your spirit, that ye
deal not treacherously.
17 ¶ Ye have wearied the LORD with
your words. Yet ye say, Wherein have
we wearied *him?* When ye say, Every
one that doeth evil *is* good in the sight
of the LORD, and he delighteth in
them; or, Where *is* the God of judgment?

CHAPTER 3

BEHOLD, [a]I will send my messenger, and he shall [b]prepare the way
before me: and [c]the Lord, whom ye
seek, shall suddenly come to his temple, [d]even the messenger of the covenant, whom ye delight in: behold, [e]he
shall come, saith the LORD of hosts.
2 But who may abide the day of his
coming? and [f]who shall stand when
he appeareth? for [g]he *is* like a refiner's
fire, and like fullers' soap:
3 And [h]he shall sit *as* a refiner and
purifier of silver: and he shall purify
the sons of Levi, and purge them as
gold and silver, that they may offer
[i]unto the LORD an offering in righteousness.
4 Then shall the offering of Judah
and Jerusalem be pleasant unto the

.ORD, as in the days of old, and as in
'ormer years.
5 And I [j]will come near to you to
ıdgment; and I will be a swift witness
gainst the sorcerers, and against the
dulterers, [k]and against false swear-
rs, and against those that [2]oppress the
ıireling in *his* wages, the widow, and
he fatherless, and that turn aside the
tranger *from his right*, and fear not
ne, saith the LORD of hosts.
6 For I *am* the LORD, [l]I change not;
herefore [m]ye sons of Jacob are not
onsumed.
7 ¶ Even from the days of [n]your
athers ye are gone away from mine or-
linances, and have not kept *them*.
Return unto me, and I will return
ınto you, saith the LORD of hosts.
3ut ye said, Wherein shall we return?
8 ¶ Will a man rob God? Yet ye have
obbed me, But ye say, Wherein have
ve robbed thee? In [p]tithes and offer-
ngs.
9 Ye *are* cursed with a curse: for ye
ıave robbed me, *even* this whole
ıation.
10 Bring [q]ye all the tithes [r]into the
torehouse, that there may be meat in
nine house, and prove me now here-
vith, saith the LORD of hosts, if I will
ıot open you the windows [s]of heaven,
ınd [3]pour you out a blessing, that
here shall not *be room* enough *to re-
eive it*.
11 And I will rebuke [t]the devourer
or your sakes, and he shall not [4]de-
troy the fruits of your ground; neith-
r shall your vine cast her fruit before
he time in the field, saith the LORD of
ıosts.
12 And all nations shall call you
ɔlessed: for ye shall be [u]a delight-
ome land, saith the LORD of hosts.
13 ¶ Your words have been stout
ıgainst me, saith the LORD. Yet ye
ay, What have we spoken *so much*
ıgainst thee?
14 Ye [v]have said, It *is* vain to serve
God: and what profit *is it* that we
ıave kept [5]his ordinance, and that we
have walked [6]mournfully before the
LORD of hosts?
15 And now [w]we call the proud
happy; yea, they that work wickedness [7]are set up; *they that* tempt [x]God
are even delivered.
16 ¶ Then they [y]that feared the LORD
spake [z]often one to another: and the
LORD hearkened, and heard *it*, and a
book of remembrance was written before him for them that feared the
LORD, and that thought upon his
name.
17 And they shall be mine, saith the
LORD of hosts, in that day when I
make up my [8]jewels; and I will spare
them, as a man spareth his own son
that serveth him.
18 Then shall ye return, and discern
between the righteous and the wicked,
between him that serveth God and
him that serveth him not.

CHAPTER 4

FOR, behold, the day cometh, that
shall burn as an oven; and all the
proud, yea, and all that do wickedly,
shall be stubble: and the day that
cometh shall burn them up, saith the
LORD of hosts, that it shall leave them
neither root nor branch.
2 ¶ But unto you that fear my name
shall the [a]Sun of righteousness arise
with healing in his wings; and ye shall
go forth, and grow up as calves of the
stall. Mil Obadiah 15,16
3 And [b]ye shall tread down the
wicked; for they shall be ashes under
the soles of your feet in the day that I
shall do *this*, saith the LORD of hosts.
4 ¶ Remember ye the law of Moses
my servant, which I commanded unto
him [c]in Hôr-ĕb for all Israel, *with* the
statutes and judgments.
5 ¶ Behold, I will send you [d]Ē-lī-jăh
the prophet [e]before the coming of the
great and dreadful day of the LORD:
6 And he shall [f]turn the heart of the
fathers to the children, and the heart
of the children to their fathers, lest I
come and smite the earth with [g]a curse.

1 Or, ancient.
j 1 Thes. 1.7. Jas. 5.8,9.
k Jas. 5.4.
2 Or, defraud.
l Num. 23.19. Rom. 11.29.
m 1 Sam. 15. 29. Lam. 3.22.
n Acts 7.51.
o Deut. 30.1-4. Isa. 55.6,7. Zech. 1.3.
p Neh. 13.10.
q Pro. 3.9.
r 1 Chr. 26. 20.
s Gen. 7.11.
3 empty out.
t Amos 4.9.
4 corrupt.
u Dan. 8.9.
v Job 21.14. Ps. 73.11-13. Zeph. 1.12.
5 his observation.
6 in black.
w Ps. 73.12.
7 are built.
x Ps. 95.9.
y Gen. 22.12. 1 Ki. 18.3, 12. Job 28.28. Ps. 33.18. Ps. 111.10.
z Heb. 3.13.
8 Or, special treasure.

CHAP. 4

a Luke 1.78. Eph. 5.14. 2 Pet. 1.19.
b Micah 7.10.
c Deut. 4.10.
d Matt. 11. 14.
e Joel 2.31.
f Luke 1.17.
g Dan. 9.26. Mark 13.14. Luke 19.27, 43. Luke 21.20.

THE END OF THE OLD TESTAMENT

THE

NEW TESTAMENT

OF

OUR LORD AND SAVIOUR

JESUS CHRIST

Translated out of the original Greek
and with the former translations
diligently compared and revised

BY HIS MAJESTY'S SPECIAL COMMAND

PRINTED BY AUTHORITY

APPOINTED TO BE READ IN CHURCHES

THE GOSPEL ACCORDING TO

ST. MATTHEW

CHAPTER 1

THE book of the [a]generation of
Jesus Christ, [b]the son of David,
the son of Abraham.
2 Abraham begat Isaac; and Isaac
begat Jacob; and Jacob begat Judas
and his brethren;
3 And Judas begat Phâr´-ĕs and Zâr´-ă
of Thā´-mär; and [d]Phâr´-ĕs begat Ĕs´-
rōm; and Ĕs´-rōm begat Âr´-ăm;
4 And Âr´-ăm begat Ă-mĭn´-ă-dăb;
and Ă-mĭn´-ă-dăb begat [e]Nā-ăs´-sŏn;
and Nā-ăs´-sŏn begat Săl´-mŏn;
5 And Săl´-mŏn begat Bō´-ŏz [f]of Rā´-
chăb; and Bō´-ŏz begat Ō´-bĕd of Ruth;
and Ō´-bĕd begat Jesse;
6 And [g]Jesse begat David the king;
and David [h]the king begat Solomon
of her *that had been the wife* of Ū-rī´-ăs;
7 And [i]Solomon begat Rō-bō´-ăm;
and Rō-bō´-ăm begat Ă-bī´-ă; and Ă-
bī´-ă begat Ā´-să;
8 And Ā´-să begat Jŏs´-ă-phăt; and
Jŏs´-ă-phăt begat Joram; and Joram
begat Ō-zī´-ăs;
9 And Ō-zī´-ăs begat Jō´-ă-thăm; and
Jō´-ă-thăm begat Ā´-chăz; and Ā´-chăz
begat Ĕz-ē-kī´-ăs;
10 And [j]Ĕz-ē-kī´-ăs begat Mă-năs´-
sēs; and Mă-năs´-sēs begat Amon; and
Amon begat Jō-sī´-ăs;
11 And [1]Jō-sī´-ăs begat Jĕch-ō-nī´-ăs
and his brethren, about the time they
were [k]carried away to Babylon:
12 And after they were brought to
Babylon, Jĕch-ō-nī´-ăs begat Să-lā´-
thĭ-ĕl; and Să-lā´-thĭ-ĕl begat [l]Zō-rŏb´-
ă-bĕl;
13 And Zō-rŏb´-ă-bĕl begat Ă-bī´-ŭd;
and Ă-bī´-ŭd begat Ē-lī´-ă-kĭm; and Ē-
lī´-ă-kĭm begat Ā´-zôr;
14 And Ā´-zôr begat Sā´-dŏc; and Sā´-
dŏc begat Ā´-chĭm; and Ā´-chĭm begat
Ē-lī´-ŭd;
15 And Ē-lī´-ŭd begat Ĕl-ē-ā´-zär; and
Ĕl-ē-ā´-zär begat Măt´-thăn; and Măt´-
thăn begat Jacob;
16 And Jacob begat Joseph the husband of Mary, of whom was born
Jesus, who is called Christ.
17 So all the generations from Abraham to David *are* fourteen generations; and from David until the carrying away into Babylon *are* fourteen
generations; and from the carrying
away into Babylon unto Christ *are*
fourteen generations.
18 ¶ Now the [n]birth of Jesus Christ
was on this wise: When as his mother
Mary was espoused to Joseph, before
they came together, she was found
with child of the Holy Ghost.
19 Then Joseph her husband, being
a just *man*, [o]and not willing to make
her a publick example, was minded to
put her away privily.
20 But while he thought on these
things, behold, the angel of the Lord
appeared unto him in a dream, saying,
Joseph, thou son of David, fear not to
take unto thee Mary thy wife: [p]for
that which is [2]conceived in her is of
the Holy Ghost.
21 And she shall bring forth a son,
and thou shalt call his name [3]JESUS:
for [q]he shall save his people from their
sins.
22 Now all this was done, that it
might be fulfilled which was spoken
of the Lord by the prophet, saying,
23 Behold, [r]a virgin shall be with
child, and shall bring forth a son, and
[4]they shall call his name Ĕm-măn´-ū-
ĕl, which being interpreted is, [s]God
with us.
24 Then Joseph being raised from
sleep did as the angel of the Lord had
bidden him, and took unto him his
wife:
25 And knew her not till she had
brought forth her firstborn son: and
he called his name JESUS.

CHAPTER 2

NOW when [a]Jesus was born in
Bethlehem of Judæa in the days
of Herod the king, behold, there came
wise men [b]from the east to Jerusalem,
2 Saying, [c]Where is he that is born
King of the Jews? for we have seen
his [d]star in the east, and are come to
worship him.
3 When Herod the king had heard
these things, he was troubled, and all
Jerusalem with him.
4 And when he had gathered all the
[e]chief priests and [f]scribes of the peo-

CHAP. 1

a Luke 3.23.
b Ps. 132.11. Isa. 11.1. ch. 22.42. Acts 2.30. Rom. 1.3.
c Gal. 3.16.
d Ruth 4.18. 1 Chr. 2.5,9.
e Num. 1.7.
f Josh. 6.22. Heb. 11.31.
g 1 Sam. 16.1.
h 2 Sam. 12. 24.
i 1 Ki. 11.43. 1 Chr. 3.10. 2 Chr. 13.7.
j 2 Ki. 20.21.
1 Some read; Josias begat Jakim, and Jakim begat Jechonias. 1 Chr. 3.15.
k 2 Ki. 25.11. Jer. 27.20. Jer. 52.11. Dan. 1.2.
l Ezra 3.2. Ezra 5.2. Hag. 1.1.
m Gen. 3.15. Isa. 9.6. Isa. 53.2.
n Gal. 4.4. Heb. 10.15.
o Deut. 24.1.
p Luke 1.35.
2 begotten.
3 That is, Saviour.
q Gen. 49.10. Jer. 33.16. Dan. 9.24. Acts 5.31.
r Isa. 7.14.
4 Or, his name shall be called.
s Isa. 9.6. John 1.14. Rom. 1.3,4. 1 Tim. 3.16.

CHAP. 2

a Dan. 9.24. Luke 2.4.
b 1 Ki. 4.30. Isa. 11.10.
c Ps. 2.6. Isa. 9.6,7. Luke 2.11. John 1.49.
d Num. 24. 17. Isa. 60.3. Rev. 22.16.
e Ps. 2.1.
f 2 Chr. 34. 13. Jer. 8.8. Mark 8.31. Luke 20.19.

ple together, [g]he demanded of them
where Christ should be born.
5 And they said unto him, In Beth-
lehem of Judæa: for thus it is written
by the prophet,
6 And [h]thou Bethlehem, *in* the land
of Juda, art not the least among the
princes of Juda: for out of thee shall
come a Governor, that [i]shall [1]rule my
people Israel.
7 Then Herod, when he had privily
called the wise men, inquired of them
diligently what time the star appeared.
8 And he sent them to Bethlehem,
and said, Go and search diligently for
the young child; and when ye have
found *him*, bring me word again, that
I may come and worship him also.
9 When they had heard the king,
they departed; and, lo, the star, which
they saw in the east, went before
them, till it came and stood over
where the young child was.
10 When they saw the star, they rejoiced with exceeding great joy.
11 ¶ And when they were come into
the house, they saw the young child
with Mary his mother, and fell down,
and [j]worshipped him: and when they
had opened their treasures, they [2]pre-
sented unto him gifts; gold, and
frankincense, and myrrh.
12 And being warned of God [k]in a
dream that they should not return to
Herod, they departed into their own
country another way.
13 And when they were departed,
behold, the angel of the Lord appeareth to Joseph in a dream, saying,
Arise, and take the young child and
his mother, and flee into Egypt, and
be thou there until I bring thee word:
for Herod will seek the young child
to destroy him.
14 When he arose, he took the young
child and his mother by night, and departed into Egypt:
15 And was there until the death of
Herod: that it might be fulfilled which
was spoken of the Lord by the prophet, saying, [l]Out of Egypt have I called
my son.
16 ¶ Then Herod, when he saw that
he was mocked of the wise men, was
exceeding wroth, and sent forth, and
slew all the children that were in Beth-
lehem, and in all the coasts thereof,
from two years old and under, according to the time which he had diligently
inquired of the wise men.
17 Then was fulfilled that which was
spoken by [m]Jeremy the prophet, saying,

g Mal. 2.7.
h Micah 5.2. John 7.42.
i Gen. 49.10. Num. 24.19. Ps. 2.1-6.
1 Or, feed. Isa. 40.11.
j Ps. 2.12. John 5.23.
2 Or, offered. Ps. 22.29. Ps. 72.10. Isa. 49.7. Isa. 60.6.
k Job 33.15. ch. 1.20.
l Num. 24.8. Hos. 11.1.
m Jer. 31.15.
n ch. 3.13. Luke 2.39.
o Luke 2.4. John 1.45.
p Judg. 13.5. 1 Sam. 1.11.
3 That is, Branch, or, Separated one. Num. 6.2. Zech. 6.12.

CHAP. 3

a Mal. 3.1. Mark 1.4. Luke 3.2. John 1.28.
b Josh. 14.10.
c Dan. 2.44. ch. 4.17. ch. 10.7.
d Isa. 40.3. Luke 3.4.
e Luke 1.76.
f Mark. 1.6.
g 2 Ki. 1.8. Zech. 13.4.
h Lev. 11.22.
i Deut. 8.8. Deut. 32.13. 1 Sam. 14. 25. 2 Ki. 18.32. Ps. 81.16. Eze. 27.17. Luke 24.42.
j Acts 19.4.
k Rom. 5.9. 1 Thes. 1.10. 1 Thes. 5.9.
1 Or, answerable to amendment of life. 2 Cor. 7.1, 11.
l John 8.33. Acts 13. 26. Rom. 4.1.
m Ps. 80.15, 16. Isa. 5. 2-7. ch. 7.19. John 15.6. Heb. 6.8.

18 In Rā-mă was there a voice heard
lamentation, and weeping, and grea
mourning, Rachel weeping *for* he
children, and would not be comforted
because they are not.
19 ¶ But when Herod was dead, be
hold, an angel of the Lord appearet
in a dream to Joseph in Egypt,
20 Saying, Arise, and take the youn
child and his mother, and go into th
land of Israel: for they are dead whic
sought the young child's life.
21 And he arose, and took the youn
child and his mother, and came int
the land of Israel.
22 But when he heard that Är-chĕ
lā-ŭs did reign in Judæa in the roon
of his father Herod, he was afraid t
go thither: notwithstanding, bein
warned of God in a dream, he turne
aside [n]into the parts of Galilee:
23 And he came and dwelt in a cit
[o]called Nazareth: that it might be fu
filled [p]which was spoken by the pro
phets, He shall be called a [3]Nazarene

CHAPTER 3

IN those days came [a]John th
Baptist, preaching [b]in the wilder
ness of Judæa,
2 And saying, Repent ye: [c]for th
kingdom of heaven is at hand.
3 For this is he that was spoken o
by the prophet Ē-sāi-ăs, saying, Th
[d]voice of one crying in the wilderness
[e]Prepare ye the way of the Lord, mak
his paths straight.
4 And [f]the same John [g]had his ra
ment of camel's hair, and a leather
girdle about his loins; and his mea
was [h]locusts and wild [i]honey.
5 Then went out to him Jerusalen
and all Judæa, and all the regio
round about Jordan,
6 And [j]were baptized of him in Jo
dan, confessing their sins.
7 ¶ But when he saw many of th
Pharisees and Săd-dū-çēes come t
his baptism, he said unto them,
generation of vipers, who hath warne
you to flee from [k]the wrath to come
8 Bring forth therefore fruits [1]me
for repentance:
9 And think not to say within you
selves, [l]We have Abraham to *ou*
father: for I say unto you, that Go
is able of these stones to raise up chi
dren unto Abraham.
10 And now also the axe is laid unt
the root of the trees: [m]therefore ever
tree which bringeth not forth goo
fruit is hewn down, and cast into th
fire.

1 I [n]indeed baptize you with water
ıto repentance: but he that cometh
ter me is mightier than I, whose
oes I am not worthy to bear: [o]he
all baptize you with the Holy
host, and *with* fire:
2 Whose fan *is* in his hand, and he
ill throughly [p]purge his floor, and
ther his wheat into the garner; but
will [q]burn up the chaff with un-
enchable fire.
3 ¶ Then cometh Jesus [r]from Gali-
e to Jordan unto John, to be bap-
ed of him.
4 But John forbad him, saying, I
ve need to be baptized of thee, and
mest thou to me?
5 And Jesus answering said unto
m, Suffer *it to be so* now: for thus
becometh us to [s]fulfil all righteous-
ss. Then he suffered him.
6 And [t]Jesus, when he was baptized,
nt up straightway out of the water:
d, lo, the heavens were opened unto
m, and he saw [u]the Spirit of God
scending like a dove, and lighting
on him: 3CB Matt 28:19,20
7 And [v]lo a voice from heaven, say-
g, [w]This is my beloved Son, in whom
m well pleased.

CHAPTER 4

HEN was [a]Jesus led up of [b]the
Spirit into the wilderness to be
mpted of the devil.
And when he had [d]fasted forty
ys and forty nights, he was after-
rd an hungred.
And when the tempter came to
n, he said, If thou be the Son of
od, command that these stones be
de bread.
But he answered and said, [e]It is
itten, [f]Man shall not live by bread
ne, but by every word that pro-
edeth out of the mouth of God.
Then the devil taketh him up into
e holy city, and setteth him on a
nacle of the temple,
And saith unto him, If thou be the
n of God, cast thyself down: for it
written, [h]He shall give his angels
arge concerning thee: and in *their*
nds they shall bear thee up, lest at
y time thou dash thy foot against a
ne.
Jesus said unto him, It is written
ain, [i]Thou shalt not tempt the Lord
God.
Again, the devil taketh him up into
exceeding high mountain, and
weth him all the kingdoms of the
rld, and the glory of them;

n Mark 1.8. Luke 3.16. John 1.33. Acts 1.5. Acts 8.36, 38. Acts 10.47. Acts 11.16.
o Isa. 4.4. Mal. 3.2. Acts 2.3,4. Titus 3.5.
p Mal. 3.3.
q Mal. 4.1. ch. 13.30.
r ch. 2.22.
s Dan. 9.24.
t Mark. 1.10.
u Isa. 11.2. Luke 3.22. John 1.32.
v John 12.28.
w Ps. 2.7. Isa. 42.1. Luke 9.35. Col. 1.13.

CHAP. 4

a Mark 1.12. Luke 4.1.
b 1 Ki. 18.12. Ezek. 3.14. Acts 8.39.
c Heb. 4.15.
d Ex. 34.28.
e Eph. 6.17
f Deut. 8.3.
g Neh. 11.1.
h Ps. 91.11.
i Deut. 6.16.
j Deut. 6.13.
k James 4.7.
l Heb. 1.14.
m Luke 3.20.
1 Or, delivered up.
n Isa. 9.1,2.
o Isa. 42.7. Luke 2.32.
p Mark 1.14.
q ch. 10.7.
r Mark 1.16.
s ch. 16.18. John 1.42.
t Eze. 47.10. Luke 5.10.
u Mark 10. 28. Luke 18.28.
v Mark 1.19. Luke 5.10.
w ch. 9.35. Mark 1.21, 39. Luke 4.15.
x Isa. 52.13.

9 And saith unto him, All these
things will I give thee, if thou wilt fall
down and worship me.
10 Then saith Jesus unto him, Get
thee hence, Satan: for it is written,
[j]Thou shalt worship the Lord thy
God, and him only shalt thou
serve.
11 Then the devil [k]leaveth him, and,
behold, [l]angels came and ministered
unto him.
12 ¶ Now [m]when Jesus had heard
that John was [1]cast into prison, he departed into Galilee;
13 And leaving Nazareth, he came
and dwelt in Că-pĕr-′nă-ŭm, which is
upon the sea coast, in the borders of
Ză-bū-′lo̱n and Nĕph-′thă-lĭm:
14 That it might be fulfilled which
was spoken by Ē-ṡāi-′ăs the prophet,
saying,
15 The [n]land of Ză-bū-′lo̱n, and the
land of Nĕph-′thă-lĭm, *by* the way of
the sea, beyond Jordan, Galilee of the
Gentiles;
16 The [o]people which sat in darkness
saw great light; and to them which sat
in the region and shadow of death
light is sprung up.
17 ¶ From [p]that time Jesus began to
preach, and to say, [q]Repent: for the
kingdom of heaven is at hand.
18 ¶ And [r]Jesus, walking by the sea
of Galilee, saw two brethren, Simon
[s]called Peter, and Andrew his brother,
casting a net into the sea: for they
were fishers.
19 And he saith unto them, Follow
me, and I [t]will make you fishers of
men.
20 And [u]they straightway left *their*
nets, and followed him.
21 And [v]going on from thence, he
saw other two brethren, James *the son*
of Zĕb-′ĕ-dēē, and John his brother, in
a ship with Zĕb-′ĕ-dēē their father,
mending their nets; and he called
them.
22 And they immediately left the
ship and their father, and followed
him.
23 ¶ And Jesus went about all Galilee, teaching [w]in their synagogues, and
preaching the gospel of the kingdom,
and healing all manner of sickness
and all manner of disease among the
people.
24 And his [x]fame went throughout
all Syria: and they brought unto him
all sick people that were taken with
divers diseases and torments, and
those which were possessed with devils, and those which were lunatick,

and those that had the palsy; and he
healed them.
25 And there followed him great
multitudes of people from Galilee,
and *from* Dĕ-căp´-ŏ-lĭs, and *from* Jerusalem, and *from* Judæa, and *from* beyond Jordan.

CHAPTER 5

AND seeing the multitudes, [a]he
went up into a mountain: and
when he was set, his disciples came
unto him:
2 And he opened his mouth, and
taught them, saying,
3 Blessed [b]*are* the poor in spirit: for
theirs is the kingdom of heaven.
4 Blessed [c]*are* they that mourn: for
they shall be comforted.
5 Blessed [d]*are* the meek: [e]for they
shall inherit the earth.
6 Blessed *are* they which do hunger
and thirst after righteousness: [f]for
they shall be filled.
7 Blessed *are* the merciful: [g]for they
shall obtain mercy.
8 Blessed [h]*are* the pure in heart: for
[i]they shall see God.
9 Blessed *are* [j]the peacemakers: for
they shall be called the children of
God.
10 Blessed [k]*are* they which are persecuted for righteousness' sake: for
theirs is the kingdom of heaven.
11 Blessed are ye, when *men* shall revile you, and persecute *you*, and shall
say all manner of evil against you
[1]falsely, for my sake.
12 Rejoice, and be exceeding glad:
for great *is* your reward in heaven: for
so persecuted they the prophets which
were before you.
13 ¶ Ye are the salt of the earth: but
if the salt have lost his savour, wherewith shall it be salted? it is thenceforth
good for nothing, but to be cast out,
and to be trodden under foot of men.
14 Ye [l]are the light of the world. A
city that is set on an hill cannot be
hid.
15 Neither do men light a candle, and
put it under a [2]bushel, but on a candlestick; and it giveth light unto all that
are in the house.
16 Let your light so shine before
men, that [m]they may see your good
works, and glorify [n]your Father which
is in heaven.
17 ¶ Think [o]not that I am come to
destroy the law, or the prophets: I am
not come to destroy, but to fulfil.
18 For verily I say unto you, Till
[p]heaven and earth pass, one jot or one
tittle shall in no wise pass from t
law, till all be fulfilled.
19 Whosoever [q]therefore shall bre
one of these least commandmen
and shall teach men so, he shall
called the least in the kingdom
heaven: but whosoever shall do a
teach *them*, the same shall be call
great in the kingdom of heaven.
20 For I say unto you, That exce
your righteousness shall exceed [r]t
righteousness of the scribes and Pha
sees, ye shall in no case enter into t
kingdom of heaven.
21 ¶ Ye have heard that it was sa
[3]by them of old time, Thou shalt [s]n
kill; and whosoever shall kill shall
in danger of the judgment:
22 But I say unto you, That whos
ever [t]is angry with his brother wit
out a cause shall be in danger of t
judgment: and whosoever shall say
his brother, [4]Rā´-că, shall be in dang
of the council: but whosoever sh
say, Thou [5]fool, shall be in danger
hell fire.
23 Therefore if thou bring thy gift
the altar, and there rememberest th
thy brother hath ought against the
24 Leave [u]there thy gift before t
altar, and go thy way; first be reco
ciled to thy brother, and then co
and offer thy gift.
25 Agree [v]with thine adversary quic
ly, whiles [w]thou art in the way w
him; lest at any time the adversa
deliver thee to the judge, and t
judge deliver thee to the officer, a
thou be cast into prison.
26 Verily I say unto thee, [x]Th
shalt by no means come out then
till thou hast paid the uttermo
farthing.
27 ¶ Ye have heard that it was sa
by them of old time, Thou shalt n
commit adultery:
28 But I say unto you, That whos
ever looketh [y]on a woman to lust af
her hath committed adultery with h
already in his heart.
29 And [z]if thy right eye [6]offend th
pluck it out, and cast *it* from thee:
it is profitable for thee that one of t
members should perish, and not *t*
thy whole body should be cast in
hell.
30 And if thy right hand offend th
cut it off, and cast *it* from thee: fo
is profitable for thee that one of t
members should perish, and not *t*
thy whole body should be cast in
hell.
31 It hath been said, [a]Whosoe

CHAP. 5
a Mark 3.13.
b Ps. 51.17. Pro. 16.19. Isa. 57.15. Luke 6.20. 1 Cor. 1.26.
c Isa. 61.2,3. John 16.20. 2 Cor. 1.7. Rev. 21.4.
d Num. 12.3. Ps. 37.11. Isa. 11.4. Gal. 5.23.
e Rom. 4.13.
f Isa. 65.13.
g Ps. 41.1. ch. 6.14. Mark 11.25. Heb. 6.10. Jas. 2.13.
h Ps. 15.2. Heb. 12.14.
i 1 Cor. 13.12. 1 John 3.2,3.
j Heb. 12.14.
k Mark 10.30. Luke 6.22, 23. John 15.20, 21. Acts 5.40, 41. 2 Cor. 4.17.
1 lying.
l Pro. 4.18. Phil. 2.15.
2 modius. It contained nearly a peck.
m 1 Pet. 2.12.
n John 15.8. 1 Cor. 14.25.
o Dan. 9.24. Rom. 10.4. Gal. 3.24.
p Luke 16.17.
q James 2.10.
r Rom. 10.3.
3 Or, to them.
s Ex. 20.13.
t 1 John 3.15.
4 That is, vain fellow.
5 Or, graceless wretch. John 8.44. Acts 13.10.
u Job 42.8. 1 Pet. 3.7.
v Job 22.21. Pro. 25.8. Heb. 3.7.
w Job 22.21. Ps. 32.6. Isa. 55.6.
x 2 Thes. 1.9.
y Gen. 34.2. Pro. 6.25. Eph. 5.5.
z Mark 9.43.
6 Or, do cause thee to offend.
a Deut. 24.1. Jer. 3.1. Mark 10.2.

all put away his wife, let him give her
writing of divorcement:
2 But I say unto you, That [b]whoso-
er shall put away his wife, saving
r the cause of fornication, causeth
r to commit adultery: and whoso-
er shall marry her that is divorced
mmitteth adultery.
3 ¶ Again, ye have heard that it
th been said [7]by them of old time,
hou shalt not forswear thyself, but
halt perform unto the Lord thine
ths:
4 But I say unto you, [e]Swear not at
l; neither by heaven; for it is [f]God's
rone:
5 Nor by the earth; for it is his foot-
ool: neither by Jerusalem; for it is
e city of the great King.
6 Neither shalt thou swear by thy
ad, because thou canst not make
e hair white or black.
7 But [g]let your communication be,
ea, yea; Nay, nay: for whatso-
er is more than these cometh of
il.
8 ¶ Ye have heard that it hath been
id, [h]An eye for an eye, and a tooth
r a tooth:
9 But I say unto you, [i]That ye rest not evil: [j]but whosoever shall
nite thee on thy right cheek, turn to
m the other also.
0 And if any man will sue thee at
e law, and take away thy coat, let
m have *thy* cloke also.
1 And whosoever [k]shall compel
ee to go a mile, go with him twain.
2 Give to him that asketh thee, and
om [l]him that would borrow of thee
rn not thou away.
3 ¶ Ye have heard that it hath been
id, [m]Thou shalt love thy neighbour,
nd hate thine enemy.
4 But I say unto you, [o]Love your
emies, bless them that curse you,
o good to them that hate you, and
ray [p]for them which despitefully
se you, and persecute you;
5 That ye may be the children of
our Father which is in heaven: for
e maketh his sun to rise on the evil
nd on the good, and sendeth rain on
e just and on the unjust.
6 For [q]if ye love them which love
ou, what reward have ye? do not
ven the publicans the same?
7 And if ye salute your brethren
nly, what do ye more *than others?* do
ot even the publicans so?
8 Be [r]ye therefore perfect, even as
our Father which is in heaven is
erfect.

b Rom. 7.3. 1 Cor. 7.10.
7 to the ancients.
c Ex. 20.7. Lev. 19.12. Num. 30.2. Deut. 5.11.
d Deut. 23. 23.
e Jas. 5.12.
f Isa. 66.1.
g Col. 4.6. Jas. 5.12.
h Lev. 24.20.
i Pro. 20.22. Rom. 12.17. 1 Cor. 6.7. 1 Thes. 5.15. 1 Pet. 3.9.
j Isa. 50.6.
k Mark 15. 21.
l Deut. 15.8.
m Lev. 19.18.
n Deut. 23.6.
o Pro. 25.21. Rom. 12.14.
p Luke 23.34. Acts 7.60. 1 Cor. 4.12. 1 Pet. 2.23.
q Luke 6.32.
r Gen. 17.1. Lev. 19.2. Col. 1.28. Jas. 1.4. 1 Pet. 1.15.
s Eph. 5.1.

CHAP. 6

1 Or, righteousness. 2 Cor. 9.9.
2 Or, with.
a Rom. 12.8.
3 Or, cause not a trumpet to be sounded. 1 Cor. 10.31.
b 2 Ki. 4.33.
c Jer. 17.10.
d Eccl. 5.2.
e 1 Ki. 18.26.
f Ps. 139.2.
g Deut. 32.6. ch. 23.9. Luke 11.2. Rom. 8.15, 16. 1 Cor. 8.6. Heb. 12.9.
h Lev. 10.3. Isa. 6.3. Rev. 4.11.
i Ps. 103.20.
j Job 23.12. Pro. 30.8.
k ch. 26.41. Luke 22.40, 46. 1 Cor. 10.13. Jas. 1.13. 2 Pet. 2.9. Rev. 3.10.
l John 17.15. Gal. 1.4.
m Mark 11. 25. Eph. 4.32. Col. 3.13.
n ch. 18.35. Jas. 2.13.
o Isa. 58.5.

CHAPTER 6

TAKE heed that ye do not your
[1]alms before men, to be seen of
them: otherwise ye have no reward [2]of
your Father which is in heaven.
2 Therefore [a]when thou doest *thine*
alms, [3]do not sound a trumpet before
thee, as the hypocrites do in the synagogues and in the streets, that they
may have glory of men. Verily I say
unto you, They have their reward.
3 But when thou doest alms, let not
thy left hand know what thy right
hand doeth:
4 That thine alms may be in secret:
and thy Father which seeth in secret
himself shall reward thee openly.
5 ¶ And when thou prayest, thou
shalt not be as the hypocrites *are:*
for they love to pray standing in the
synagogues and in the corners of the
streets, that they may be seen of men.
Verily I say unto you, They have their
reward.
6 But thou, when thou prayest, enter
[b]into thy closet, and when thou hast
shut thy door, pray to thy Father
which is in secret; and thy Father
[c]which seeth in secret shall reward
thee openly.
7 But when ye pray, [d]use not vain
repetitions, as the heathen *do:* [e]for
they think that they shall be heard for
their much speaking.
8 Be not ye therefore like unto them:
for your [f]Father knoweth what things
ye have need of, before ye ask him.
9 After this manner therefore pray
ye: [g]Our Father which art in heaven,
[h]Hallowed be thy name.
10 Thy kingdom come. Thy will be
done in earth, [i]as *it is* in heaven.
11 Give us this day our [j]daily bread.
12 And forgive us our debts, as we
forgive our debtors.
13 And [k]lead us not into temptation,
but deliver [l]us from evil: For thine is
the kingdom, and the power, and the
glory, for ever. Ā-měn.
14 For [m]if ye forgive men their trespasses, your heavenly Father will also
forgive you:
15 But [n]if ye forgive not men their
trespasses, neither will your Father
forgive your trespasses.
16 ¶ Moreover [o]when ye fast, be not,
as the hypocrites, of a sad countenance: for they disfigure their faces,
that they may appear unto men to
fast. Verily I say unto you, They have
their reward.
17 But thou, when thou fastest,
anoint thine head, and wash thy face;

18 That thou appear not unto men to fast, but unto thy Father which is in secret: and thy Father, which seeth in secret, shall reward thee openly.

19 ¶ Lay [p]not up for yourselves treasures upon earth, where moth and rust doth corrupt, and where thieves break through and steal:

20 But [q]lay up for yourselves treasures in heaven, where neither moth nor rust doth corrupt, and where thieves do not break through nor steal:

21 For where your treasure is, there will your heart be also.

22 The [r]light of the body is the eye: if therefore thine eye be single, thy whole body shall be full of light.

23 But if thine eye be evil, thy whole body shall be full of darkness. If therefore the light that is in thee be darkness, [s]how great *is* that darkness!

24 ¶ No [t]man can serve two masters: for either he will hate the one, and love the other; or else he will hold to the one, and despise the other. [u]Ye cannot serve God and mammon.

25 Therefore I say unto you, [4]Take no thought for your life, what ye shall eat, or what ye shall drink; nor yet for your body, what ye shall put on. Is not the life more than meat, and the body than raiment?

26 Behold [v]the fowls of the air: for they sow not, neither do they reap, nor gather into barns; yet your heavenly Father feedeth them. Are ye not much better than they?

27 Which of you by taking thought can add one cubit unto his stature?

28 And why take ye thought for raiment? Consider the lilies of the field, how they grow; they toil not, neither do they spin:

29 And yet I say unto you, That even Solomon in all his glory was not arrayed like one of these.

30 Wherefore, if God so clothe the grass of the field, which to day is, and to morrow is cast into the oven, *shall he* not much more *clothe* you, O ye of little faith?

31 Therefore take no thought, saying, What shall we eat? or, What shall we drink? or, Wherewithal shall we be clothed?

32 (For after all these things do the Gentiles seek:) for [w]your heavenly Father knoweth that ye have need of all these things.

33 But [x]seek ye first the kingdom of God, and his righteousness; and all these things shall be added unto you.

p Pro. 23.4. 1 Tim. 6.17. Heb. 13.5. Jas. 5.1.
q ch. 19.21. Luke 12.33, 34. 1 Tim. 6.19. 1 Pet. 1.4.
r Ps. 119.18. Luke 11.34.
s Rom. 1.21. 2 Cor. 4.4.
t Luke 16.13.
u Gal. 1.10. 1 Tim. 6. 17. Jas. 4.4. 1 John 2.15.
4 Be not anxiously careful. Ps. 55.22. Luke 12.22, 23.
v Job 38.41. Ps. 147.9.
w Ps. 23.1. Phil. 4.19.
x 1 Ki. 3.13. Ps. 34.9. Ps. 37.25. Mark 10.30. Luke 12.31.
5 anxious thought.

CHAP. 7

a Eze. 16.52. Luke 6.37. Rom. 2.1. Rom. 14.3. 1 Cor. 4.3, 5. Jas. 4.11.
b Mark 4.24. Luke 6.38.
c Luke 6.41.
d Pro. 9.7, 8. Acts 13.45.
e ch. 21.22. Mark 11.24. Luke 11.9, 10. Luke 18.1. John 14.13. John 15.7. John 16.23.
f Pro. 8.17. Jonah 2.2. Jonah 3.8. Luke 23.42, 43. Acts 9.11.
g Isa. 49.15. Rom. 8.32.
h Luke 6.31.
i Lev. 19.18. Rom. 13.8. Gal. 5.14. 1 Tim. 1.5.
j Eze. 18. 30-32. Luke 9.23. Luke 13.24. Luke 14.33.
k 1 John 5.19.
1 Or, How.
l Deut. 13.3. Jer. 23.16. Rom. 16.17. Eph. 5.6. Col. 2.8.
m Micah 3.5. 2 Tim. 3.5.
n Acts 20.29.
o Luke 6.43.
p Jer. 11.19.

34 Take therefore no [5]thought for t
morrow: for the morrow shall ta
thought for the things of itself. Su
cient unto the day *is* the evil there

CHAPTER 7

JUDGE [a]not, that ye be not judge
2 For with what judgment
judge, ye shall be judged: [b]and wi
what measure ye mete, it shall
measured to you again.
3 And [c]why beholdest thou the mo
that is in thy brother's eye, but co
siderest not the beam that is in thi
own eye?
4 Or how wilt thou say to thy b
ther, Let me pull out the mote out
thine eye; and, behold, a beam *is*
thine own eye?
5 Thou hypocrite, first cast out t
beam out of thine own eye; and th
shalt thou see clearly to cast out t
mote out of thy brother's eye.
6 ¶ Give [d]not that which is holy un
the dogs, neither cast ye your pea
before swine, lest they trample the
under their feet, and turn again a
rend you.
7 ¶ Ask, [e]and it shall be given yo
seek, and ye shall find; knock, a
it shall be opened unto you:
8 For [f]every one that asketh rece
eth; and he that seeketh findeth; a
to him that knocketh it shall
opened.
9 Or what man is there of you, wh
if his son ask bread, will he give hi
a stone?
10 Or if he ask a fish, will he give hi
a serpent?
11 If ye then, being evil, know h
to give good gifts unto your childre
how [g]much more shall your Fath
which is in heaven give good things
them that ask him?
12 Therefore all things [h]whatsoev
ye would that men should do to yo
do ye even so to them: for this [i]is t
law and the prophets.
13 ¶ Enter [j]ye in at the strait ga
[k]for wide *is* the gate, and broad *is* t
way, that leadeth to destruction, a
many there be which go in thereat:
14 [1]Because strait *is* the gate, a
narrow *is* the way, which leadeth un
life, and few there be that find it.
15 ¶ Beware of [l]false prophets, whi
[m]come to you in sheep's clothing, b
inwardly they [n]are ravening wolves.
16 Ye shall know them by th
fruits. [o]Do men gather grapes
thorns, or figs of thistles?
17 Even so [p]every good tree bringe

orth good fruit; but a corrupt tree
ringeth forth evil fruit.
18 A good tree cannot bring forth
vil fruit, neither *can* a corrupt tree
ring forth good fruit.
19 Every tree that bringeth not forth
ood fruit is hewn down, and cast into
he fire.
20 Wherefore by their fruits ye shall
now them.
21 ¶ Not every one that saith unto
ne, [q]Lord, Lord, shall enter into the
ingdom of heaven; but he that doeth
he will of my Father which is in
eaven.
22 Many will say to me in that day,
ord, Lord, have we [r]not prophesied
n thy name? and in thy name have
ast out devils? and in thy name done
nany wonderful works?
23 And then will I profess unto them,
never knew you: [s]depart from me,
e that work iniquity.
24 ¶ Therefore [t]whosoever heareth
hese sayings of mine, and doeth
hem, I will liken him unto a wise man,
vhich built his house upon a rock:
25 And [u]the rain descended, and the
loods came, and the winds blew, and
eat upon that house; and [v]it fell not:
or it was founded upon a rock.
26 And every one that heareth these
ayings of mine, and doeth them not,
hall be likened unto a foolish man,
vhich built his house upon the
and:
27 And the rain descended, and the
loods came, and the winds blew, and
eat upon that house; and it fell: [w]and
reat was the fall of it.
28 And it came to pass, when Jesus
ad ended these sayings, [x]the people
vere astonished at his doctrine:
29 For [y]he taught them as *one* having
uthority, and not as the scribes.

CHAPTER 8

WHEN he was come down from
the mountain, great multitudes
ollowed him.
2 And, [a]behold, there came a leper
nd worshipped him, saying, Lord, if
hou wilt, thou canst make me clean.
3 And Jesus put forth *his* hand, and
ouched him, saying, I will; be thou
lean. And immediately his leprosy
was cleansed.
4 And Jesus saith unto him, [b]See
thou tell no man; but go thy way,
shew thyself to the priest, and offer
the gift that [c]Moses commanded, for
a testimony unto them.
5 ¶ And [d]when Jesus was entered into Că-pĕr'-nă-ŭm, there came unto
him a centurion, beseeching him,
6 And saying, Lord, my servant lieth
at home sick of the palsy, grievously
tormented.
7 And Jesus saith unto him, I will
come and heal him.
8 The centurion answered and said,
Lord, I [e]am not worthy that thou
shouldest come under my roof: but
[f]speak the word only, and my servant
shall be healed.
9 For I am a man under authority,
having soldiers under me: and I say
to this *man*, Go, and he goeth; and to
another, Come, and he cometh; and
to my servant, Do this, and he doeth
it.
10 When Jesus heard *it*, he marvelled,
and said to them that followed, Verily
I say unto you, I have not found so
great faith, no, not in Israel.
11 And I say unto you, [g]That many
shall come from the east and west,
and shall sit down with Abraham, and
Isaac, and Jacob, in the kingdom of
heaven.
12 But [h]the children of the kingdom
[i]shall be cast out into outer darkness:
there shall be weeping and gnashing
of teeth.
13 And Jesus said unto the centurion,
Go thy way; and as thou hast believed, *so* be it done unto thee. And his
servant was healed in the selfsame
hour.
14 ¶ And [j]when Jesus was come into
Peter's house, he saw [k]his wife's
mother laid, and sick of a fever.
15 And he touched her hand, and the
fever left her: and she arose, and
ministered unto them.
16 ¶ When [l]the even was come, they
brought unto him many that were
possessed with devils: and he cast out
the spirits with *his* word, and healed
all that were sick:
17 That it might be fulfilled which
was spoken by Ē-sāi'-ăs the prophet,
saying, Himself [m]took our infirmities,
and bare *our* sicknesses.
18 ¶ Now when Jesus saw great multitudes about him, he gave commandment to depart unto the other
side.
19 And a [n]certain scribe came, and
said unto him, Master, I will follow
thee whithersoever thou goest.
20 And Jesus saith unto him, The
foxes have holes, and the birds of the
air *have* nests; but [o]the Son of man
hath not where to lay *his* head.
21 And [p]another of his disciples said

[q] Hos. 8.2. Acts 19.13. Rom. 2.13. Jas. 1.22.
[r] Num. 24.4. Luke 14.26, 27. John 11.51.
[s] Ps. 5.5. Ps. 6.8. ch. 25.41.
[t] Luke 6.47.
[u] Acts 14.22. 2 Tim. 3.12.
[v] 2 Tim. 2.19. 1 Pet. 1.5.
[w] Heb. 10.31. 2 Pet. 2.20.
[x] ch. 13.54. Mark 1.22. Mark 6.2. Luke 4.32.
[y] Isa. 50.4. John 7.46.

CHAP. 8

[a] Mark 1.40. Luke 5.12.
[b] ch. 9.30. Mark 5.43.
[c] Lev. 14.3. Luke 5.14.
[d] Luke 7.1.
[e] Luke 15.19.
[f] Ex. 15.26. Deut. 32.39. Ps. 33.9. Ps. 103.3. Ps. 107.20. Jer. 17.14.
[g] Gen. 12.3. Isa. 2.2,3. Isa. 11.10. Luke 13.29. Acts 10.45. Acts 11.18. Acts 14.27. Rom. 15.9. Eph. 3.6. Rev. 5.9. Rev. 7.9. Rev. 14.6.
[h] ch. 21.43.
[i] ch. 13.42. ch. 22.13. ch. 24.51. ch. 25.30. Luke 13.28. 2 Pet. 2.17. Jude 13.
[j] Mark 1.29. Luke 4.38.
[k] 1 Cor. 9.5.
[l] Mark 1.32. Luke 4.40.
[m] Isa. 53.4. 1 Pet. 2.24.
[n] Luke 9.57.
[o] Ps. 22.6. Ps. 40.17. Ps. 69.29. Luke 2.7,12. Luke 8.3. John 1.10, 11. 2 Cor. 8.9. Phil. 2.7,8.
[p] Luke 9.59.

unto him, Lord, [q]suffer me first to go
and bury my father.
22 But Jesus said unto him, Follow
me; and let [r]the dead bury their dead.
23 ¶ And when he was entered into
a ship, his disciples followed him.
24 And, [s]behold, there arose a great
tempest in the sea, insomuch that the
ship was covered with the waves: but
he was asleep.
25 And his disciples came to *him*,
and awoke him, saying, Lord, save
us: we perish.
26 And he saith unto them, Why [t]are
ye fearful, O ye of little faith? Then
[u]he arose, and rebuked the winds and
the sea; and there was a great calm.
27 But the men marvelled, saying,
What manner of man is this, that even
the winds and the sea obey him!
28 ¶ And [v]when he was come to the
other side into the country of the Gĕr-
gĕ-sēneṡ, there met him two possessed
with devils, coming out of the tombs,
exceeding fierce, so that no man might
pass by that way.
29 And, behold, they cried out, saying, What [w]have we to do with thee,
Jesus, thou Son of God? art thou
come hither to torment us before the
time?
30 And there was a good way off
from them an herd of many [x]swine
feeding.
31 So the devils [y]besought him, saying, If thou cast us out, suffer us to
go away into the herd of swine.
32 And he said unto them, Go. And
when they were come out, they went
into the herd of swine: and, behold,
the whole herd of swine ran violently
down a steep place into the sea, and
perished in the waters.
33 And they that kept them fled, and
went their ways into the city, and told
every thing, and what was befallen to
the possessed of the devils.
34 And, behold, the whole city came
out to meet Jesus: and when they saw
him, they [z]besought *him* that he
would depart out of their coasts.

CHAPTER 9

AND he entered into a ship, and
passed over, [a]and came into his
own city.
2 And, [b]behold, they brought to him
a man sick of the palsy, lying on a
bed: [c]and Jesus seeing their faith said
unto the sick of the palsy; Son, be
of good cheer; [d]thy sins be forgiven
thee.
3 And, behold, certain of the scribes

q 1 Ki. 19.20.
r Eph. 2.1.
s Mark 4.37. Luke 8.23.
t Phil. 4.6.
u Job 38.8-11. Ps. 65.7. Ps. 93.4. Ps. 104.3. Pro. 30.4. Nah. 1.4.
v Mark 5.1.
w 2 Sam. 16.10. 2 Sam. 19.22. Joel 3.4. Mark 1.24. Mark 5.7. Luke 4.34. Luke 8.28. 2 Pet. 2.4.
x Deut. 14.8.
y Phil. 2.10.
z Deut. 5.25. 1 Ki. 17.18. Luke 5.8. Acts 16.39.

CHAP. 9

a ch. 4.13.
b Mark 2.3. Luke 5.18.
c ch. 8.10.
d Ps. 32.1,2. Luke 5.20. Acts 13.38, 39. Rom. 4.6-8. Rom. 5.11. Eph. 1.7.
e Ps. 139.2. ch. 12.25. Mark 12.15. Luke 5.22. Luke 6.8. Luke 9.47. Luke 11.17.
f Mark 2.7, 10. Luke 5.21. Acts 5.31. 2 Cor. 2.10. Eph. 1.7.
g Mark 2.14. Luke 5.27.
h Mark 2.15. Luke 5.29.
i Isa. 64.5. ch. 18.17. Luke 5.30. Luke 15.2. Luke 19.7.
j Gal. 2.15. Eph. 2.12.
k Pro. 21.3. Hos. 6.6. Micah 6.6. ch. 12.7.
l Isa. 55.6,7. ch. 3.2,8. ch. 4.17. ch. 11.20. Luke 19.10. 1 Tim. 1.15. 1 John 3.5.
m Mark 2.18. Luke 5.33. Luke 18.12.
n John 3.29.
o Acts 13.2. Acts 14.23. 1 Cor. 7.5.
1 Or, raw, or, unwrought cloth.
p Mark 5.22. Luke 8.41.

said within themselves, This ma
blasphemeth.
4 And Jesus [e]knowing their thought
said, Wherefore think ye evil in you
hearts?
5 For whether is easier, to say, Th
sins be forgiven thee; or to say, Aris
and walk?
6 But that ye may know that th
[f]Son of man hath power on earth t
forgive sins, (then saith he to the sic
of the palsy,) Arise, take up thy bec
and go unto thine house.
7 And he arose, and departed to hi
house.
8 But when the multitudes saw i
they marvelled, and glorified Goc
which had given such power unt
men.
9 ¶ And [g]as Jesus passed forth fron
thence, he saw a man, name
Matthew, sitting at the receipt c
custom: and he saith unto him, Fo
low me. And he arose, and followe
him.
10 ¶ And [h]it came to pass, as Jesu
sat at meat in the house, behold, man
publicans and sinners came and sa
down with him and his disciples.
11 And when the Pharisees saw i
they said unto his disciples, Why eat
eth your Master [i]with publicans an
[j]sinners?
12 But when Jesus heard *that*, he sai
unto them, They that be whole nee
not a physician, but they that are sick
13 But go ye and learn what *tha*
meaneth, I [k]will have mercy, and no
sacrifice: for I am not come to call th
righteous, [l]but sinners to repentance
14 ¶ Then came to him the disciple
of John, saying, [m]Why do we and th
Pharisees fast oft, but thy disciple
fast not?
15 And Jesus said unto them, Ca
[n]the children of the bridechambe
mourn, as long as the bridegroom i
with them? but the days will come
when the bridegroom shall be take
from them, and [o]then shall they fast
16 No man putteth a piece of [1]new
cloth unto an old garment, for tha
which is put in to fill it up taketh fron
the garment, and the rent is made
worse.
17 Neither do men put new wine into
old bottles: else the bottles break, and
the wine runneth out, and the bottles
perish: but they put new wine into
new bottles, and both are preserved.
18 ¶ While [p]he spake these things unto them, behold, there came a certain
ruler, and worshipped him, saying,

Iy daughter is even now dead: but
ome and lay thy hand upon her, and
e shall live.
19 And Jesus arose, and followed
im, and *so did* his disciples.
20 ¶ And, [q]behold, a woman, which
as diseased with an issue of blood
welve years, came behind *him*, and
uched the hem of his garment:
21 For she said within herself, If I
ay but touch his garment, I shall be
hole.
22 But Jesus turned him about, and
hen he saw her, he said, Daughter,
e of good comfort; [r]thy faith hath
ade thee whole. And the woman was
ade whole from that hour.
23 And [s]when Jesus came into the
uler's house, and saw [t]the minstrels
nd the people making a noise,
24 He said unto them, [u]Give place:
or the maid is not dead, but sleepeth.
nd they laughed him to scorn.
25 But when the people were put
orth, he went in, and took her by the
and, and the maid arose.
26 And [2]the fame hereof went abroad
nto all that land.
27 ¶ And when Jesus departed thence,
wo blind men followed him, crying,
nd saying, [v]*Thou* Son of David, have
ercy on us.
28 And when he was come into the
ouse, the blind men came to him:
nd Jesus saith unto them, Believe ye
hat I am able to do this? They said
nto him, Yea, Lord.
29 Then touched he their eyes, say-
ng, According to your faith be it unto
ou.
30 And [w]their eyes were opened; and
esus straitly charged them, saying,
ee [x]*that* no man know *it*.
31 But [y]they, when they were de-
arted, spread abroad his fame in all
hat country.
32 ¶ As [z]they went out, behold, they
brought to him a dumb man possessed
with a devil.
33 And when the devil was cast out,
the dumb spake: and the multitudes
marvelled, saying, It was never so seen
in Israel.
34 But the Pharisees said, He casteth
out devils through the prince of the
devils.
35 And [a]Jesus went about all the
cities and villages, teaching in their
synagogues, and preaching the gospel
of the kingdom, and healing every
sickness and every disease among the
people.
36 ¶ But when he saw the multitudes,
he was moved with compassion on
them, because they [3]fainted, and were
scattered abroad, as sheep having no
shepherd.
37 Then saith he unto his disciples,
[b]The harvest truly *is* plenteous, but
the labourers *are* few;
38 Pray [c]ye therefore the Lord of the
harvest, that he will send forth labourers into his harvest.

CHAPTER 10

AND [a]when he had called unto *him*
his twelve disciples, he gave them
power [1]*against* unclean spirits, to cast
them out, and to heal all manner of
sickness and all manner of disease.
2 Now the names of the twelve
apostles are these; The first, Simon,
who [b]is called Peter, and Andrew his
brother; James *the son* of Zĕb-ĕ-dēē,
and John his brother;
3 Philip, and Bartholomew; Thomas,
and Matthew the publican; James *the
son* of Ăl-phæ-ŭs, and Lĕb-bæ-ŭs,
whose surname was [2]Thăd-dæ-ŭs;
4 Simon [c]the Canaanite, and Judas
[d]Iscariot, who also betrayed him.
5 These twelve Jesus sent forth, and
commanded them, saying, Go not into the way of the Gentiles, and into
any city of [e]the Să-măr-ĭ-tăns enter
ye not:
6 But [f]go rather to the [g]lost sheep of
the house of Israel.
7 And [h]as ye go, preach, saying,
The kingdom of heaven is at
hand.
8 Heal the sick, cleanse the lepers,
raise the dead, cast out devils: freely
ye have received, freely give.
9 [3]Provide neither gold, nor silver,
nor brass in your purses,
10 Nor scrip for *your* journey, neither two coats, neither shoes, nor yet
[4]staves: [i]for the workman is worthy
of his meat.
11 And into whatsoever city or town
ye shall enter, inquire who in it is
worthy; and there abide till ye go
thence.
12 And when ye come into an house,
salute it.
13 And if the house be worthy, let
your peace come upon it: but if it be
not worthy, let your peace return to
you.
14 And whosoever shall not receive
you, nor hear your words, when ye depart out of that house or city, [j]shake
off the dust of your feet.
15 Verily I say unto you, It shall be
more tolerable for the land of Sodom

q Mark 5.25. Luke 8.43.
r Mark 10.52. Luke 7.50. Luke 8.48. Luke 17.19. Luke 18.42.
s Mark 5.38. Luke 8.51.
t 2 Chr. 35.25.
u Acts 20.10.
2 Or, this fame. Isa. 52.13.
v ch. 15.22. ch. 20.30. Mark 9.22. Luke 17.13. Luke 18.38.
w Ps. 146.8. John 9.7,14, 26.
x Luke 5.14.
y Mark 7.36.
z Luke 11.14.
a Mark 6.6. Luke 13.22.
3 Or, were tired and lay down.
b Luke 10.2. John 4.35. 1 Cor. 3.9. 1 Thes. 5.12, 13.
c Acts 13.2. Acts 20.28. 1 Cor. 12.28. Eph. 4.11. 2 Thes. 3.1.

CHAP. 10

a Mark 3.13. Mark 6.7. Luke 6.13. Luke 9.1.
1 Or, over.
b ch. 4.18. ch. 16.16-18. Mark 1.16. John 1.42.
2 Or, Judas.
c Acts 1.13.
d John 13.26.
e 2 Ki. 17.24. John 4.9,20.
f ch. 15.24. Acts 3.25, 26. Acts 13.46.
g Isa. 53.6. Jer. 50. 6,17. Rom. 11.1. 1 Pet. 2.25.
h Mark 6.12. Luke 9.2. Luke 10.1, 2.
3 Or, Get. 1 Sam. 9.7. Luke 22.35.
4 a staff.
i Luke 10.7. 1 Tim. 5.18.
j Acts 13.51. Acts 18.6.

and Gō-mŏr´-rhă in the day of judgment, than for that city.

16 ¶ Behold, I send you forth as sheep in the midst of wolves: [k]be ye therefore wise as serpents, and [5]harmless as doves.

17 But beware of men: for they will deliver you up to the councils, and [l]they will scourge you in their synagogues;

18 And [m]ye shall be brought before governors and kings for my sake, for a testimony against them and the Gentiles.

19 But when they deliver you up, take no thought how or what ye shall speak: for [n]it shall be given you in that same hour what ye shall speak.

20 For [o]it is not ye that speak, but the Spirit of your Father which speaketh in you.

21 And [p]the brother shall deliver up the brother to death, and the father the child: and the children shall rise up against *their* parents, and cause them to be put to death.

22 And ye shall be hated of all *men* for my name's sake: [q]but he that endureth to the end shall be saved.

23 But [r]when they persecute you in this city, flee ye into another: for verily I say unto you, Ye shall not [6]have gone over the cities of Israel, till [s]the Son of man be come.

24 The disciple is not above *his* master, nor the servant above his lord.

25 It is enough for the disciple that he be as his master, and the servant as his lord. If they have called the master of the house [7]Bē-ĕl´-zĕ-bŭb, how much more *shall they call* them of his household?

26 Fear them not therefore: for there is nothing covered, that shall not be revealed; and hid, that shall not be known.

27 What I tell you in darkness, *that* speak ye in light: and what ye hear in the ear, *that* preach ye upon the housetops.

28 And [t]fear not them which kill the body, but are not able to kill the soul: but rather fear him which is able to destroy both soul and body in hell.

29 Are not two sparrows sold for a [8]farthing? and one of them shall not fall on the ground without your Father.

30 But the [u]very hairs of your head are all numbered.

31 Fear ye not therefore, ye are of more value than many sparrows.

32 Whosoever [v]therefore shall con-

k Rom. 16. 19. Eph. 5.15.
5 Or, simple. 1 Cor. 14.20.
l Acts 5.40.
m Acts 12.1. Acts 24.12.
n Ex. 4.12. Jer. 1.7.
o 2 Sam. 23.2. Acts 4.8. Acts 6.10.
p Micah 7.6.
q Dan. 12.12. Gal. 6.9.
r John 7.1. Acts 14.6.
6 Or, end, or, finish.
s ch. 16.28. Acts 2.1.
7 Beelzebul.
t Isa. 8.12.
8 It is in value halfpenny farthing in the original, as being the tenth part of the Roman penny. ch. 18.28.
u Acts 27.34.
v Ps. 119.46. Rom. 10.9. 1 Ti. 6.12, 13. Rev. 2.13.
w 1 Sam. 2. 30. ch. 25.34. Rev. 3.5.
x ch. 26.70-75. Mark 8.38. Luke 9.26. Luke 12.9. 2 Tim. 2.12.
y Micah 7.6. ch. 24.10. Mark 13.12.
z ch. 16.25. Luke 17.33. John 12.25. Rev. 2.10.
a 1 Ki. 17.10. 2 Ki. 4.8.
b ch. 25.40. Heb. 6.10.

CHAP. 11

a Luke 7.18.
b ch. 14.3. Mark 9.41.
c Gen. 49.10. Num. 24.17. Deut. 18.15. Dan. 9.24. Mal. 3.1-3. John 6.14.
d Isa. 29.18. Isa. 35.5. Isa. 42.7. John 5.36.
e Ps. 22.26. Isa. 61.1. Luke 4.18. Jas. 2.5.
f Isa. 8.14. ch. 13.57. ch. 24.10. ch. 26.31. Rom. 9.32. 1 Cor. 1.23. Gal. 5.11. 1 Pet. 2.8.

fess me before men, [w]him will I co
fess also before my Father which is i
heaven.

33 But [x]whosoever shall deny me b
fore men, him will I also deny befo
my Father which is in heaven.

34 Think not that I am come to sen
peace on earth: I came not to sen
peace, but a sword.

35 For I am come to set a man a
variance [y]against his father, and th
daughter against her mother, and th
daughter in law against her mother i
law.

36 And a man's foes *shall be* they c
his own household.

37 He that loveth father or mothe
more than me is not worthy of me
and he that loveth son or daughte
more than me is not worthy of me.

38 And he that taketh not his cros
and followeth after me, is not worth
of me.

39 He [z]that findeth his life shall los
it: and he that loseth his life for m
sake shall find it.

40 ¶ He that receiveth you receivet
me, and he that receiveth me receivet
him that sent me.

41 He [a]that receiveth a prophet i
the name of a prophet shall receive
prophet's reward; and he that receiv
eth a righteous man in the name of
righteous man shall receive a righ
eous man's reward.

42 And [b]whosoever shall give t
drink unto one of these little ones
cup of cold *water* only in the name c
a disciple, verily I say unto you, h
shall in no wise lose his reward.

CHAPTER 11

AND it came to pass, when Jesu
had made an end of commandin
his twelve disciples, he departe
thence to teach and to preach in thei
cities.

2 Now [a]when John had heard in [b]th
prison the works of Christ, he sen
two of his disciples,

3 And said unto him, Art thou h
[c]that should come, or do we look fo
another?

4 Jesus answered and said unt
them, Go and shew John again thos
things which ye do hear and see:

5 The [d]blind receive their sight, an
the lame walk, the lepers are cleanse
and the deaf hear, the dead are raise
up, and the [e]poor have the gosp
preached to them.

6 And blessed is *he*, whosoever sha
not be [f]offended in me.

7 ¶ And [g]as they departed, Jesus be-
an to say unto the multitudes con-
erning John, What went ye out into
he wilderness to see? A reed shaken
vith the wind?
8 But what went ye out for to see?
A man clothed in soft raiment? beold, they that wear soft *clothing* are
n kings' houses.
9 But what went ye out for to see? A
rophet? yea, I say unto you, [h]and
nore than a prophet.
10 For this is *he*, of whom it is writ-
en, [i]Behold, I send my messenger be-
ore thy face, which shall prepare thy
vay before thee.
11 Verily I say unto you, Among
hem that are born of women there
ath not risen a greater than John the
Baptist: notwithstanding he that is
east in the kingdom of heaven is
reater than he.
12 And [j]from the days of John the
Baptist until now the kingdom of
heaven [1]suffereth violence, and the
violent take it by force.
13 For [k]all the prophets and the law
prophesied until John.
14 And if ye will receive *it*, this is [l]Ē-
li-ăs, which was for to come.
15 He [m]that hath ears to hear, let him
hear.
16 ¶ But [n]whereunto shall I liken this
generation? It is like unto children
sitting in the markets, and calling unto their fellows,
17 And saying, We have piped unto
you, and ye have not danced; we have
mourned unto you, and ye have not
lamented.
18 For John came neither eating nor
drinking, and they say, He hath a
devil.
19 The Son of man came eating and
drinking, and they say, Behold a man
gluttonous, and a winebibber, [o]a
friend of publicans and sinners. [p]But
wisdom is justified of her children.
20 ¶ Then [q]began he to upbraid the
cities wherein most of his mighty
works were done, because they repented not:
21 Woe unto thee, Chō-rā-zin! woe
unto thee, Bĕth-să-i-dă! for if the
mighty works, which were done in
you, had been done in Tyre and Sī-
dŏn, they would have repented long
ago [r]in sackcloth and ashes.
22 But I say unto you, It shall be
more tolerable for Tyre and Sī-dŏn at
the day of judgment, than for you.
23 And thou, Că-pĕr-nă-ŭm, [s]which
art exalted unto heaven, shalt be

g Luke 7.24.
h Luke 1.76.
i Mal. 3.1. Mark 1.2.
j Luke 16.16.
1 Or, is gotten by force, and they that thrust men.
k Mal. 4.6.
l Mal. 4.5. ch. 17.12. Luke 1.17. John 1.23.
m ch. 13.9,43. Luke 8.8. Rev. 2.7.
n Luke 7.31.
o ch. 9.10. Luke 15.2, 3. Luke 19.7.
p Luke 7.29, 35. Phil. 2.15.
q Luke 10.13.
r Jonah 3.8.
s Isa. 14.13. Lam. 2.1.
t Ps. 8.2. 1 Cor. 1.27. 1 Cor. 2.7,8. 2 Cor. 3.14.
u ch. 28.18. Luke 10.22. John 3.35. John 17.2. 1 Cor. 15.27. Eph. 1.21.
v John 1.18. John 6.46. John 10.15.
w Phil. 2.5. 1 Pet. 2.21. 1 John 2.6.
x Zech. 9.9. ch. 2.19,20. ch. 21.5. Luke 9.45-56. 2 Cor. 10.1. Phil. 2.7,8.
y Jer. 6.16.
z 1 John 5.3.

CHAP. 12

a Deut. 23. 25. Mark 2.23.
b 1 Sam. 21.6
c Ex. 25.30. Lev. 24.5.
d Ex. 29.32. Lev. 8.31. Lev. 24.9.
e Num. 28.9. John 7.22.
f 2 Chr. 6.18. Hag. 2.7,9. Mal. 3.1.
g Hos. 6.6. Micah 6.6.
h Dan. 7.13. ch. 9.6. Mark 2.28. Luke 6.5.

brought down to hell: for if the
mighty works, which have been done
in thee, had been done in Sodom, it
would have remained until this day.
24 But I say unto you, That it shall
be more tolerable for the land of
Sodom in the day of judgment, than
for thee.
25 ¶ At that time Jesus answered
and said, I thank thee, O Father,
Lord of heaven and earth, because
thou [t]hast hid these things from the
wise and prudent, and hast revealed
them unto babes.
26 Even so, Father: for so it seemed
good in thy sight.
27 All [u]things are delivered unto me
of my Father: and no man knoweth
the Son, but the Father; neither
[v]knoweth any man the Father, save
the Son, and *he* to whomsoever the
Son will reveal *him*.
28 ¶ Come unto me, all *ye* that
labour and are heavy laden, and I
will give you rest.
29 Take my yoke upon you, [w]and
learn of me; for I am meek and lowly
[x]in heart: and [y]ye shall find rest unto
your souls.
30 For [z]my yoke *is* easy, and my
burden is light.

CHAPTER 12

AT that time [a]Jesus went on the sabbath day through the corn; and
his disciples were an hungred, and began to pluck the ears of corn, and to
eat.
2 But when the Pharisees saw *it*,
they said unto him, Behold, thy disciples do that which is not lawful to
do upon the sabbath day.
3 But he said unto them, Have ye not
read [b]what David did, when he was
an hungred, and they that were with
him;
4 How he entered into the house of
God, and did eat [c]the shewbread,
which was not lawful for him to eat,
neither for them which were with him,
[d]but only for the priests?
5 Or have ye not read in [e]the law,
how that on the sabbath days the
priests in the temple profane the sabbath, and are blameless?
6 But I say unto you, That in this
place is *one* [f]greater than the temple.
7 But if ye had known what *this*
meaneth, I [g]will have mercy, and not
sacrifice, ye would not have condemned the guiltless.
8 For the [h]Son of man is Lord even
of the sabbath day.

9 And [i]when he was departed thence, he went into their synagogue:

10 ¶ And, behold, there was a man which had *his* hand withered. And they asked him, saying, [j]Is it lawful to heal on the sabbath days? that they might accuse him.

11 And he said unto them, What man shall there be among you, that shall have one sheep, and [k]if it fall into a pit on the sabbath day, will he not lay hold on it, and lift *it* out?

12 How much then is a man better than a sheep? Wherefore it is lawful to do well on the sabbath days.

13 Then saith he to the man, Stretch forth thine hand. And he stretched *it* forth; and it was restored whole, like as the other.

14 ¶ Then [l]the Pharisees went out, and [1]held a council against him, how they might destroy him.

15 But when Jesus [m]knew *it*, [n]he withdrew himself from thence: and great multitudes followed him, and he healed them all;

16 And charged them that they should not make him known:

17 That it might be fulfilled which was spoken by Ē-sā'i-ăs the prophet, saying,

18 Behold [o]my servant, whom I have chosen; my beloved, in whom my soul is well pleased: I will put my [p]spirit upon him, and he shall shew judgment to the Gentiles.

19 He shall not strive, nor cry; neither shall any man hear his voice in the streets.

20 A [q]bruised reed shall he not break, and smoking flax shall he not quench, till he send forth judgment unto victory.

21 And in his name shall the Gentiles trust.

22 ¶ Then [r]was brought unto him one possessed with a devil, blind, and dumb: and he healed him, insomuch that the blind and dumb both spake and saw.

23 And all the people were amazed, and said, Is not this [s]the son of David?

24 But [t]when the Pharisees heard *it*, they said, This *fellow* doth not cast out devils, but by [2]Bē-ĕl'zĕ-bŭb the prince of the devils.

25 And Jesus [u]knew their thoughts, and said unto them, Every [v]kingdom divided against itself is brought to desolation; and every city or house divided against itself shall not stand:

26 And if Satan cast out Satan, he is divided against himself; how shall then his kingdom stand?

i Mark 3.1. Luke 6.6.
j Luke 13.14. Luke 14.3. John 9.16.
k Ex. 23.4. Deut. 22.4.
l Mark 3.6. Luke 6.11. John 5.18. John 10.39. John 11.53.
1 Or, took counsel.
m Ps. 139.2. Heb. 4.13.
n Mark 3.7.
o Isa. 42.1. Isa. 49.5,6. Isa. 52.13. Isa. 53.11.
p Isa. 11.2. Isa. 61.1. ch. 3.16. Luke 3.22.
q Isa. 40.11. Lam. 3.31-33. Luke 4.18.
r Mark 3.11. Luke 11.14.
s Rom. 9.5.
t Mark 3.22.
2 Beelzebul.
u ch. 9.4. John 2.25.
v Gal. 5.15. Rev. 2.23.
w Dan. 2.44. Dan. 7.14. Luke 1.33. Luke 11.20. Luke 17.20. Heb. 12.28.
x Isa. 49.24.
y Mark 3.28. Luke 12.10. Heb. 10.26. 1 John 5.16.
z Acts 7.51. Heb. 6.4.
a ch. 11.19. ch. 13.55. John 7.12.
b 1 Tim. 1.13.
c ch. 7.17. Luke 6.43.
d ch. 3.7. ch. 23.33. Luke 3.7. John 8.44. 1 John 3.10.
e Luke 6.45.
f Eph. 5.4.
g ch. 16.1. Mark 8.11. Luke 11.16. John 2.18. 1 Cor. 1.22.
h Isa. 57.3. Mark 8.38. John 4.48.
i Jonah 1.17.
j Luke 11.32.
k Jer. 3.11. Ezek. 16.51.
l Jonah 3.5.

27 And if I by Bē-ĕl'zĕ-bŭb cast out devils, by whom do your children cast *them* out? therefore they shall be your judges.

28 But if I cast out devils by the Spirit of God, then [w]the kingdom of God is come unto you.

29 Or [x]else how can one enter into a strong man's house, and spoil his goods, except he first bind the strong man? and then he will spoil his house.

30 He that is not with me is against me; and he that gathereth not with me scattereth abroad.

31 ¶ Wherefore I say unto you, [y]All manner of sin and blasphemy shall be forgiven unto men: [z]but the blasphemy *against* the *Holy* Ghost shall not be forgiven unto men.

32 And whosoever [a]speaketh a word against the Son of man, [b]it shall be forgiven him: but whosoever speaketh against the Holy Ghost, it shall not be forgiven him, neither in this world, neither in the *world* to come.

33 Either make the tree good, and his [c]fruit good; or else make the tree corrupt, and his fruit corrupt: for the tree is known by *his* fruit.

34 O [d]generation of vipers, how can ye, being evil, speak good things? [e]for out of the abundance of the heart the mouth speaketh.

35 A good man out of the good treasure of the heart bringeth forth good things: and an evil man out of the evil treasure bringeth forth evil things.

36 But I say unto you, That every [f]idle word that men shall speak, they shall give account thereof in the day of judgment.

37 For by thy words thou shalt be justified, and by thy words thou shalt be condemned.

38 ¶ Then [g]certain of the scribes and of the Pharisees answered, saying, Master, we would see a sign from thee.

39 But he answered and said unto them, An evil and [h]adulterous generation seeketh after a sign; and there shall no sign be given to it, but the sign of the prophet Jonas:

40 For [i]as Jonas was three days and three nights in the whale's belly; so shall the Son of man be three days and three nights in the heart of the earth.

41 The [j]men of Nĭn'ĕ-vĕh shall rise in judgment with this generation, and [k]shall condemn it: [l]because they repented at the preaching of Jonas; and,

:hold, [m]a greater than Jonas *is* here.
2 The [n]queen of the south shall rise
› in the judgment with this genera-
on, and shall condemn it: for she
ıme from the uttermost parts of the
ırth to hear the wisdom of Solomon;
nd, behold, a [o]greater than Solomon
here.
3 When [p]the unclean spirit is gone
ut of a man, [q]he walketh through dry
laces, seeking rest, and findeth none.
4 Then he saith, I will return into
ıy house from whence I came out;
nd when he is come, he findeth *it*
mpty, swept, and garnished.
5 Then goeth he, and taketh with
imself seven other spirits more wick-
d than himself, and they enter in and
well there: and [r]the last *state* of that
ıan is worse than the first. Even so
hall it be also unto this wicked gen-
ration.
46 ¶ While he yet talked to the peo-
le, behold, [s]*his* mother and his [t]breth-
en stood without, desiring to speak
vith him.
47 Then one said unto him, Behold,
hy mother and thy brethren stand
vithout, desiring to speak with thee.
48 But he answered and said unto
im that told him, Who is my mother?
nd who are my brethren?
49 And he stretched forth his hand
oward his disciples, and said, Be-
ıold my mother and my brethren!
50 For [u]whosoever shall do the will
of my Father which is in heaven, the
ame is my brother, and sister, and
nother.

CHAPTER 13

THE same day went Jesus out of
the house, [a]and sat by the sea
side.
2 And [b]great multitudes were gathered together unto him, so that [c]he went
into a ship, and sat; and the whole
multitude stood on the shore.
3 And he spake many things unto
them in parables, saying, Behold, a
sower went forth to sow;
4 And when he sowed, some *seeds*
fell by the way side, and the fowls
came and devoured them up:
5 Some fell upon [d]stony places,
where they had not much earth: and
forthwith they sprung up, because
they had no deepness of earth:
6 And when the sun was up, they
were scorched; and because they had
no [e]root, they withered away.
7 And some fell among thorns; and
the thorns sprung up, and choked
them:
8 But other fell into good ground,
and brought forth fruit, some [f]an
hundredfold, some sixtyfold, some
thirtyfold.
9 Who [g]hath ears to hear, let him
hear.
10 And the disciples came, and said
unto him, Why speakest thou unto
them in parables?
11 He answered and said unto them,
Because [h]it is given unto you to know
the mysteries of the kingdom of heav-
en, but to them it is not given.
12 For [i]whosoever hath, to him shall
be given, and he shall have more abundance: but whosoever hath not, from
him shall be taken away even that he
hath.
13 Therefore speak I to them in parables: because they seeing see not; and
hearing they hear not, neither do they
understand.
14 And in them is fulfilled the prophecy of Ē-ṡâi-ăs, which saith, By [j]hear-
ing ye shall hear, and shall not understand; and seeing ye shall see, and
shall not perceive:
15 For this people's heart is waxed
gross, and *their* ears [k]are dull of hearing, and their eyes they have closed;
lest at any time they should see with
their eyes, and hear with *their* ears, and
should understand with *their* heart,
and should be converted, and I should
heal them.
16 But [l]blessed *are* your eyes, for
they see: and your ears, for they
hear.
17 For verily I say unto you, That
many [m]prophets and righteous *men*
have desired to see *those things* which
ye see, and have not seen *them;* and
to hear *those things* which ye hear, and
have not heard *them.*
18 ¶ Hear [n]ye therefore the parable
of the sower.
19 When any one heareth the word
of the kingdom, and understandeth *it*
not, then cometh [o]the wicked *one*, and
catcheth away that which was sown in
his heart. This is he which received
seed by the way side.
20 But he that received the seed into
stony places, the same is he that heareth the word, and anon with [p]joy receiveth it;
21 Yet hath he not root in himself,
but dureth for a while: for when tribulation or persecution ariseth because
of the word, by and by [q]he is offended.
22 He [r]also that received seed among
[s]the thorns is he that heareth the
word; and the care of this world, and

m Isa. 9.6.
n 1 Ki. 10.1. 2 Chr. 9.1.
o Col. 2.2,3.
p Luke 11.24.
q Job 1.7. 1 Pet. 5.8.
r Heb. 6.4. Heb. 10.26. 2 Pet. 2.20.
s Mark 3.31. Luke 8.19.
t Mark 6.3. John 2.12. John 7.3,5. Acts 1.14. 1 Cor. 9.5. Gal. 1.19.
u ch. 25.40, 45. ch. 28.10. John 14.23. John 15.14. John 20.17. Rom. 8.29. Gal. 5.6. Gal. 6.15. Col. 3.11. Heb. 2.11.

CHAP. 13

a Mark 4.1.
b Gen. 49.10. ch. 4.25. ch. 15.30. Luke. 8.4.
c Luke 5.3.
d Ezek. 11.19.
e Col. 2.7.
f Gen. 26.12.
g Mark 4.9.
h ch. 11.25. ch. 16.17. Mark 4.11. 1 Cor. 2.10. Col. 1.26. 1 John 2.27.
i ch. 25.29. Mark 4.25. Luke 8.18. Luke 19.26.
j Isa. 6.9. Ezek. 12.2. Mark 4.12. Luke 8.10. John 12.40. Acts 28. 26, 27. Rom. 11.8. 2 Cor. 3.14.
k Zech. 7.11. Heb. 5.11.
l ch. 16.17. Luke 2.29, 30. Luke 10.23, 24. John 20.29. Acts 26.18. 2 Cor. 4.6.
m Heb. 11.13. 1 Pet. 1.10.
n Mark 4.14. Luke 8.11.
o 2 Cor. 2.11.
p Isa. 58.2. Ezek. 33.31. John 5.35.
q ch. 11.6. 2 Tim. 1.15.
r ch. 19.23. Mark 10.23. Luke 18.24. 1 Tim. 6.9. 2 Tim. 4.10.
s Jer. 4.3.

the deceitfulness of riches, choke the
word, and he becometh unfruitful.
23 But he that received seed into the
good ground is he that heareth the
word, and understandeth *it;* which
also beareth fruit, and bringeth forth,
some an hundredfold, some sixty,
some thirty.
24 ¶ Another parable put he forth
unto them, saying, The kingdom of
heaven is likened unto a man which
sowed good seed in his field:
25 But while men slept, [t]his enemy
came and sowed tares among the
wheat, and went his way.
26 But when the blade was sprung
up, and brought forth fruit, then appeared the tares also.
27 So the servants of the householder
came and said unto him, Sir, didst not
thou sow good seed in thy field? from
whence then hath it tares?
28 He said unto them, An enemy
hath done this. The servants said unto
him, Wilt thou then that we go and
gather them up?
29 But he said, Nay; lest while ye
gather up the tares, ye root up also
the wheat with them.
30 Let both grow together until the
harvest: and in the time of harvest I
will say to the reapers, Gather ye together first the tares, and bind them in
bundles to burn them: but [u]gather the
wheat into my barn.
31 ¶ Another parable put he forth
unto them, saying, [v]The kingdom of
heaven is like to a grain of mustard
seed, which a man took, and sowed in
his field:
32 Which indeed is the least of all
seeds: but when it is grown, it is the
greatest among herbs, and becometh
a tree, so that the birds of the air come
and lodge in the branches thereof.
33 ¶ Another [w]parable spake he unto
them; The kingdom of heaven is like
unto leaven, which a woman took, and
hid in three [1]measures of meal, till the
whole was leavened.
34 All these things spake Jesus unto
the multitude in parables; and without a parable spake he not unto
them:
35 That it might be fulfilled which
was spoken by the prophet, saying, [x]I
will open my mouth in parables; [y]I
will utter things which have been kept
secret from the foundation of the
world.
36 Then Jesus sent the multitude
away, and went into the house: and
his disciples came unto him, saying,

t Luke 10.19. 1 Pet. 5.8.

u ch. 3.12. ch. 24.31. 1 Thes. 4.17. 2 Thes. 2.1.
v Isa. 2.2,31. Micah 4.1. Mark 4.30. Luke 13.18. 2 Pet. 3.18.
w Luke 13.20.
1 The word in the Greek is a measure containing about a peck and a half, wanting a little more than a pint.
x Ps. 49.4. Ps. 78.2.
y Rom. 16.25. 1 Cor. 2.7. Eph. 3.9.
z Isa. 61.1.
a Gen. 12.3. Ps. 22.27. Isa. 49.6. Jer. 31.34. Hos. 2.23. Micah 4.2. Mal. 1.11.
b Gen. 3.15. John 8.44. Acts 13.10. 2 Pet. 2.14. 1 John 3.7,8,10.
c Joel 3.13. Rev. 14.15.
d ch. 24.31. 1 Thes. 3.16. 2 Pet. 2.1,2.
2 Or, scandals.
e ch. 3.12. ch. 8.12. Rev. 19.20. Rev. 20.10.
f Pro. 4.18. Dan. 12.3. 1 Cor. 15.42. Rev. 7.9.
g Phil. 3.7.
h Isa. 55.1. Rev. 3.18.
i Pro. 2.4. Pro. 3.14. Pro. 8.10.
j ch. 22.10.
k Song 7.13.

Declare unto us the parable of t
tares of the field.
37 He answered and said unto ther
He that [z]soweth the good seed is t
Son of man;
38 The [a]field is the world; the goo
seed are the children of the kingdon
but the tares are [b]the children of t
wicked *one;*
39 The enemy that sowed them
the devil; [c]the harvest is the end
the world; and the reapers are t
angels.
40 As therefore the tares are gathe
ed and burned in the fire; so shall
be in the end of this world.
41 The Son of man shall send fort
his angels, [d]and they shall gather ou
of his kingdom all [2]things that offen
and them which do iniquity;
42 And [e]shall cast them into a fu
nace of fire: there shall be wailing an
gnashing of teeth.
43 Then [f]shall the righteous shin
forth as the sun in the kingdom
their Father. Who hath ears to hea
let him hear.
44 ¶ Again, the kingdom of heave
is like unto treasure hid in a field; th
which when a man hath found, h
hideth, and for joy thereof goeth an
[g]selleth all that he hath, and [h]buyet
that field.
45 ¶ Again, the kingdom of heaven i
like unto a merchant man, seekin
goodly pearls:
46 Who, when he had found [i]on
pearl of great price, went and sold a
that he had, and bought it.
47 ¶ Again, the kingdom of heaven i
like unto a net, that was cast into th
sea, and gathered [j]of every kind:
48 Which, when it was full, the
drew to shore, and sat down, an
gathered the good into vessels, bu
cast the bad away.
49 So shall it be at the end of th
world: the angels shall come forth
and sever the wicked from among th
just,
50 And shall cast them into the fur
nace of fire: there shall be wailing an
gnashing of teeth.
51 Jesus saith unto them, Have ye un
derstood all these things? They sa
unto him, Yea, Lord.
52 Then said he unto them, There
fore every scribe *which is* instructe
unto the kingdom of heaven is like un
to a man *that is* an householder, whic
bringeth forth out of his treasur
[k]*things* new and old.
53 ¶ And it came to pass, *that* whe

Jesus had finished these parables, he
departed thence.
54 And [l]when he was come into his
own country, he taught them in their
synagogue, insomuch that they were
astonished, and said, Whence hath
this *man* this wisdom, and *these*
mighty works?
55 Is [m]not this the carpenter's son?
is not his mother called Mary? and
[n]his brethren, [o]James, and Jō-śĕs, and
Simon, and Judas?
56 And his sisters, are they not all
with us? Whence then hath this *man*
all these things?
57 And they [p]were offended in him.
But Jesus said unto them, [q]A prophet
is not without honour, save in his own
country, and in his own house.
58 And [r]he did not many mighty
works there because of their unbelief.

CHAPTER 14

AT that time [a]Herod the tē-trărch
heard of the fame of Jesus,
2 And said unto his servants, This is
John the Baptist; he is risen from the
dead; and therefore mighty works [1]do
shew forth themselves in him.
3 ¶ For [b]Herod had laid hold on
John, and bound him, and put *him*
in prison for Hĕ-rō-dĭ-ăs' sake, his
brother Philip's wife.
4 For John said unto him, [c]It is not
lawful for thee to have her.
5 And when he would have put him
to death, he feared the multitude, [d]be-
cause they counted him as a prophet.
6 But when Herod's [e]birthday was
kept, the daughter of Hĕ-rō-dĭ-ăs
danced [2]before them, and pleased
Herod.
7 Whereupon he promised with an
oath to give her whatsoever she would
ask.
8 And she, being before instructed
of her mother, said, Give me here
John Baptist's head in a charger.
9 And the king was sorry: [f]neverthe-
less for the oath's sake, and them
which sat with him at meat, he commanded *it* to be given *her*.
10 And he sent, and beheaded John
in the prison.
11 And his head was brought in a
charger, and given to the damsel: and
she brought *it* to her mother.
12 And his disciples came, and took
up the body, and buried it, and went
and told Jesus.
13 ¶ When [g]Jesus heard *of it*, he departed thence by ship into a desert
place apart: and when the people had
heard *thereof*, they followed him on
foot out of the cities.
14 And Jesus went forth, and saw a
great multitude, and [h]was moved
with compassion toward them, and
he healed their sick.
15 ¶ And when it was evening, his
disciples came to him, saying, This is
a desert place, and the time is now
past; send the multitude away, that
they may go into the villages, and buy
themselves victuals.
16 But Jesus said unto them, They
need not depart; [i]give ye them to eat.
17 And they say unto him, We have
here but five loaves, and two fishes.
18 He said, Bring them hither to me.
19 And he commanded the multitude
to sit down on the grass, and took the
five loaves, and the two fishes, and
looking up to heaven, he [j]blessed, and
brake, and gave the loaves to *his* disciples, and the disciples to the multitude.
20 And they did all eat, and were
filled: and they took up of the fragments that remained twelve baskets
full.
21 And they that had eaten were
about five thousand men, beside
women and children.
22 ¶ And straightway Jesus constrained his disciples to get into a ship,
and to go before him unto the other
side, while he sent the multitudes
away.
23 And [k]when he had sent the multitudes away, he went up into a mountain apart to pray: [l]and when the
evening was come, he was there alone.
24 But the ship was now in the midst
of the sea, tossed with waves: for the
wind was contrary.
25 And in the fourth watch of the
night Jesus went unto them, walking
on the sea.
26 And when the disciples [m]saw him
walking on the sea, they were troubled,
saying, It is a spirit; and they cried
out for fear.
27 But straightway Jesus spake unto
them, saying, Be of good cheer; it is
I; be not afraid.
28 And Peter answered him and
said, Lord, if it be thou, bid me come
unto thee on the water.
29 And he said, Come. And when
Peter was come down out of the ship,
he walked on the water, to go to Jesus.
30 But when he saw the wind [3]boist-
erous, he was afraid; and beginning to
sink, he cried, saying, Lord, save me.
31 And immediately Jesus stretched

l Deut. 18.15. ch. 2.23. Mark 6.1. Luke 4.16.
m Isa. 49.7. Isa. 53.2,3. Mark 6.3.
n ch. 12.46.
o Mark 15.40.
p Ps. 22.6. ch. 11.6. ch. 26.31.
q Luke 4.24. John 4.44.
r Heb. 3.19. Heb. 4.2.

CHAP. 14

a Mark 6.14. Luke 9.7.
1 Or, are wrought by him.
b Pro. 10.17. Pro. 15.10. Mark 6.17.
c Lev. 18.16. Lev. 20.21. Eph. 5.11.
d ch. 21.26. Luke 20.6.
e Gen. 40.20.
2 in the midst.
f Eccl. 5.2. Titus 1.16.
g ch. 10.23. ch. 12.15. Mark 6.32. Luke 9.10. John 6.1,2.
h Ps. 86.15. Ps. 145.8. ch. 9.36. Mark 1.41. Luke 7.13. John 11.33-35. Heb. 2.17. Heb. 4.15. Heb. 5.2.
i 2 Ki. 4.42, 43. Luke 3.11. John 13.29. 2 Cor. 8.2,3.
j ch. 15.36. ch. 26.26. Mark 8.6. Luke 22.19. John 6.11, 23. Acts 27.35.
k ch. 6.6. ch. 26.36. Mark 6.46. Luke 6.12. Acts 6.4.
l John 6.16.
m Job 9.8. Ps. 73.19. Isa. 43.16.
3 Or, strong.

forth *his* hand, and caught him, and
said unto him, O thou of little faith,
wherefore [n]didst thou doubt?
32 And when they were come into
the ship, the [o]wind ceased.
33 Then they that were in the ship
came and worshipped him, saying, Of
a truth thou [p]art the Son of God.
34 ¶ And [q]when they were gone over,
they came into the land of Gĕn-nĕś-
ă-rĕt.
35 And when the men of that place
had knowledge of him, they sent out
into all that country round about,
and brought unto him all that were
diseased;
36 And besought him that they might
only touch the hem of his garment:
and as many as touched were made
perfectly whole.

CHAPTER 15

THEN [a]came to Jesus scribes and
Pharisees, which were of Jerusalem, saying,
2 Why [b]do thy disciples transgress
[c]the tradition of the elders? for they
wash not their hands when they eat
bread.
3 But he answered and said unto
them, Why do ye also transgress the
commandment of God by your tradition?
4 For God commanded, saying,
Honour [d]thy father and mother: and,
[e]He that curseth father or mother, let
him die the death.
5 But ye say, Whosoever shall say to
his father or *his* mother, [f]*It is* a gift, by
whatsoever thou mightest be profited
by me;
6 And honour not his father or his
mother, *he shall be free*. Thus have ye
made the commandment of God of
none effect by your tradition.
7 *Ye* [g]hypocrites, well did Ē-sāi-ăs
prophesy of you, saying,
8 This [h]people draweth nigh unto me
with their mouth, and honoureth me
with *their* lips; but their heart is far
from me.
9 But in vain they do worship me,
teaching [i]*for* doctrines the commandments of men.
10 ¶ And [j]he called the multitude,
and said unto them, Hear, and understand:
11 Not [k]that which goeth into the
mouth defileth a man; but that which
cometh out of the mouth, this defileth
a man.
12 Then came his disciples, and said
unto him, Knowest thou that the
Pharisees were offended, after they
heard this saying?
13 But he answered and said, Every
[l]plant, which my heavenly Father
hath not planted, shall be rooted up.
14 Let [m]them alone: [n]they be blind
leaders of the blind. And if the blind
lead the blind, both shall fall into the
ditch.
15 Then [o]answered Peter and said un
to him, Declare unto us this parable.
16 And Jesus said, [p]Are ye also yet
without understanding?
17 Do not ye yet understand, that
whatsoever [q]entereth in at the mouth
goeth into the belly, and is cast out in
to the draught?
18 But [r]those things which procee
out of the mouth come forth from th
heart; and they defile the man.
19 For [s]out of the heart proceed evi
thoughts, murders, adulteries, forni
cations, thefts, false witness, blas
phemies:
20 These are *the things* which defil
a man: but to eat with unwashe
hands defileth not a man.
21 ¶ Then Jesus went thence, an
departed into the coasts of Tyre an
Sī-dŏn.
22 And, behold, a woman of Canaa
came out of the same coasts, an
cried unto him, saying, Have merc
on me, O Lord, *thou* Son of David
my daughter is grievously vexed wit
a devil.
23 But he answered her not a word
And his disciples came and besough
him, saying, Send her away; for sh
crieth after us.
24 But he answered and said, [t]I ar
not sent but unto the lost sheep of th
house of Israel.
25 Then came she and worshippe
him, saying, Lord, help me.
26 But he answered and said, It i
not meet to take the children's breac
and to cast *it* to [u]dogs.
27 And she said, Truth, Lord: ye
the dogs eat of the crumbs which fal
from their masters' table.
28 Then Jesus answered and said un
to her, O woman, great *is* thy faith: b
it unto thee even as thou wilt. And he
daughter was made whole from tha
very hour.
29 And [v]Jesus departed from thence
and came nigh [w]unto the sea of Gali
lee; and went up into a mountain, an
sat down there.
30 And [x]great multitudes came unt
him, having with them *those that wer*
lame, blind, dumb, maimed, an

n ch. 8.26. ch. 16.8. ch. 17.20. Mark 4.40. Mark 16.14. Luke 24.25. John 20.25, 27.
o Ps. 107.29. Mark 4.41. John 6.18, 21.
p Ps. 2.7. ch. 16.16. ch. 26.63. Mark 1.1. Luke 4.41. John 1.49. John 6.69. John 11.27. Acts 8.37. Rom. 1.4.
q Mark 6.53.

CHAP. 15

a Mark 7.1.
b Mark 7.5.
c Gal. 1.14. Col. 2.8. 1 Pet. 1.18.
d Ex. 20.12. Lev. 19.3. Deut. 5.16. Pro. 23.22. Eph. 6.2.
e Ex. 21.17. Lev. 20.9. Deut. 27.16. Pro. 20.20. Pro. 30.17.
f Mark 7.11.
g Mark 7.6.
h Isa. 29.13. Ezek. 33.31.
i Isa. 29.13. Col. 2.18. 1 Tim. 1.6,7. Titus 1.14.
j Mark 7.14.
k Mark 7.15. Acts 10.15. Rom. 14.14. 1 Tim. 4.4. Titus 1.15.
l John 15.2. 1 Cor. 3.12.
m Hos. 4.14, 17.
n Isa. 9.16. Mal. 2.8. ch. 23.16. Luke 6.39.
o Mark 7.17.
p ch. 16.9. Mark 7.18.
q 1 Cor. 6.13.
r Pro. 6.12. ch. 12.34. Jas. 3.6.
s Gen. 6.5. Gen. 8.21. Pro. 6.14. Jer. 17.9. Mark 7.21.
t Isa. 53.6. ch. 10.5,6. Acts 3.25, 26. Acts 13.46.
u Isa. 56.10, 11. ch. 7.6. Eph. 2.12. Phil. 3.2. Rev. 22.15.
v Mark 7.31.
w ch. 4.18. Mark 1.16. Luke 5.1,4. John 1.43. John 6.1,23.
x Isa. 35.5,6. ch. 11.5. Luke 7.22.

nany others, and cast them down at
esus' feet; and he healed them:
31 Insomuch that the multitude won-
lered, when they saw the dumb to
peak, the maimed to be whole, the
ame to walk, and the blind to see: and
hey glorified the God of Israel.
32 ¶ Then [y]Jesus called his disciples
nto him, and said, I [z]have compas-
ion on the multitude, because they
ontinue with me now three days, and
ave nothing to eat: and I will not
end them away fasting, lest they faint
n the way.
33 And [a]his disciples say unto him,
Vhence should we have so much
read in the wilderness, as to fill so
reat a multitude?
34 And Jesus saith unto them, How
nany loaves have ye? And they said,
even, and a few little fishes.
35 And he commanded the multitude
o sit down on the ground.
36 And [b]he took the seven loaves and
he fishes, and [c]gave thanks, and brake
hem, and gave to his disciples, and the
isciples to the multitude.
37 And they did all eat, [d]and were
lled: and they took up of the broken
neat that was left seven baskets
ull.
38 And they that did eat were four
housand men, beside women and
hildren.
39 And [e]he sent away the multitude,
nd took ship, and came into the
oasts of Măg-dă-lă.

CHAPTER 16

THE [a]Pharisees also with the Săd-
dū-çēeś came, and tempting dered him that he would shew them a
gn from heaven.
2 He answered and said unto them,
Vhen it is evening, ye say, *It will be*
ir weather: for the sky is red.
3 And in the morning, *It will be* foul
eather to day: for the sky is red and
wring. O *ye* hypocrites, ye can dis-
ern the face of the sky; but can ye not
iscern [b]the signs of the times?
4 A [c]wicked and adulterous genera-
on seeketh after a sign; and there
hall no sign be given unto it, but the
gn of the prophet Jonas. And he left
em, and departed.
5 And [d]when his disciples were come
the other side, they had forgotten
take bread.
6 ¶ Then Jesus said unto them, Take
eed and beware of the leaven of the
harisees and of the Săd-dū-çēeś.
7 And they reasoned among themselves, saying, *It is* because we have
taken no bread.
8 *Which* when Jesus perceived, he
said unto them, O ye of little faith,
why reason ye among yourselves, because ye have brought no bread?
9 Do [f]ye not yet understand, neither
remember the five loaves of the five
thousand, and how many baskets ye
took up?
10 Neither [g]the seven loaves of the
four thousand, and how many baskets
ye took up?
11 How is it that ye do not understand that I spake *it* not to you concerning bread, that ye should beware
of the leaven of the Pharisees and of
the Săd-dū-çēeś?
12 Then understood they how that
he bade *them* not beware of the leaven
of bread, but of the doctrine of the
Pharisees and of the Săd-dū-çēeś.
13 ¶ When Jesus came into the coasts
of Cǣ-să-rē-ă Philippi, he asked his
disciples, saying, [h]Whom do men say
that I the Son of man am?
14 And they said, [i]Some *say that
thou art* John the Baptist: [j]some, Ē-lī-
ăs; and others, Jeremias, or one of the
prophets.
15 He saith unto them, But whom
say ye that I am?
16 And Simon Peter answered and
said, [k]Thou art the Christ, the Son of
the living God.
17 And Jesus answered and said unto him, Blessed art thou, Simon Bär-
jō-nă: [l]for flesh and blood hath not
revealed *it* unto thee, but [m]my Father
which is in heaven.
18 And I say also unto thee, That
[n]thou art Peter, and [o]upon this rock I
will build my church; and [p]the gates
of hell shall not prevail against it.
19 And [q]I will give unto thee the keys
of the kingdom of heaven: and whatsoever thou shalt bind on earth shall
be bound in heaven: and whatsoever
thou shalt loose on earth shall be
loosed in heaven.
20 Then charged he his disciples that
they should tell no man that he was
Jesus the Christ.
21 ¶ From that time forth began
Jesus to shew unto his disciples, how
that he must go unto Jerusalem, and
suffer many things of the elders and
chief priests and scribes, and be killed,
and be raised again the third day.
22 Then Peter took him, and began
to rebuke him, saying, [1]Be it far from
thee, Lord: this shall not be unto thee.
23 But he turned, and said unto

y Mark 8.1.
z Ps. 86.15. Ps. 103.13. Ps. 111.4. Mark 1.41. Heb. 2.17. Heb. 4.15. Heb. 5.2.
a Nu. 11.21, 22. 2 Ki. 4.43.
b ch. 14.19.
c Deut. 8.10. 1 Sam. 9.13. Luke 22.19.
d Ps. 103.1,5. Ps. 104.28. Ps. 136.25. Ps. 145.15. Ps. 147.9.
e Mark 8.10.

CHAP. 16

a ch. 12.38. Mark 8.11. Luke 11.16. Luke 12.54-56. 1 Cor. 1.22.
b Gen. 49.10. Isa. 7.14. Eze. 21.27. Dan. 9.24. Micah 5.2.
c Isa. 57.3. ch. 12.39. Mark 8.38. John 4.48.
d ch. 15.37, 38. Mark 8.14.
e ch. 7.15. ch. 24.4. Luke 12.1. Rom. 16.17. Eph. 5.6. Col. 2.8.
f ch. 14.17. ch. 15.16. John 6.9.
g ch. 15.34.
h Dan. 7.13. Mark 8.27. Luke 9.18. Rom. 1.3.
i ch. 3.1. ch. 14.2. Mark 1.4.
j Mal. 4.5.
k Ps. 2.7. ch. 14.33. Mark 8.29. Luke 9.20. John 6.69.
l Eph. 2.8.
m 1 Cor. 2.10. Gal. 1.16.
n John 1.42.
o Isa. 28.16. 1 Cor. 3.11. Eph. 2.20. Rev. 21.14.
p Isa. 54.17.
q John 20.23.
1 Pity thyself.

Peter, Get thee behind me, Satan:
thou [r]art an offence unto me: for thou
savourest not the things that be of
God, but those that be of men.
24 ¶ Then [s]said Jesus unto his disciples, If any *man* will come after me,
let him deny himself, and take up his
cross, and follow me.
25 For whosoever will save his life
shall lose it: and whosoever will lose
his life for my sake shall find it.
26 For what is a man profited, if he
shall gain the whole world, and lose
his own soul? or [t]what shall a man
give in exchange for his soul?
27 For the Son of man shall come in
the glory of his Father [u]with his
angels; [v]and then he shall reward
every man according to his works.
28 Verily I say unto you, There be
some standing here, which shall not
taste of death, till they see the Son of
man coming in his [w]kingdom.

CHAPTER 17

AND [a]after six days Jesus taketh
Peter, James, and John his brother, and bringeth them up into an
high mountain apart,
2 And was transfigured before them:
and his face did shine as the sun, and
his raiment was white as the light.
3 And, behold, there appeared unto
them [b]Moses and Ē-lī-ăs talking with
him.
4 Then answered Peter, and said unto Jesus, Lord, it is good for us to be
here: if thou wilt, let us make here
three tabernacles; one for thee, and
one for Moses, and one for Ē-lī-ăs.
5 While [c]he yet spake, behold, a
bright cloud overshadowed them: and
behold a voice out of the cloud, which
said, [d]This is my beloved Son, [e]in
whom I am well pleased; [f]hear ye
him.
6 And [g]when the disciples heard *it*,
they fell on their face, and were sore
afraid.
7 And Jesus came and touched them,
and said, Arise, and be not afraid.
8 And when they had lifted up their
eyes, they saw no man, save Jesus
only.
9 And as they came down from the
mountain, Jesus charged them, saying, Tell the vision to no man, until
the Son of man be risen again from
the dead.
10 And his disciples asked him, saying, [h]Why then say the scribes that Ē-
lī-ăs must first come?
11 And Jesus answered and said unto them, Ē-lī-ăs truly shall first come
and restore [i]all things.
12 But [j]I say unto you, That Ē-lī-ă
is come already, and they knew hin
not, but have [k]done unto him whatso
ever they listed. Likewise shall also th
Son of man suffer of them.
13 Then the disciples understoo
that he spake unto them of John th
Baptist.
14 ¶ And [l]when they were come t
the multitude, there came to him
certain man, kneeling down to him
and saying,
15 Lord, have mercy on my son: fo
he is lunatick, and sore vexed: fo
ofttimes he falleth into the fire, an
oft into the water.
16 And I brought him to thy dis
ciples, and they could not cure him.
17 Then Jesus answered and said, C
faithless and perverse generatior
how long shall I be with you? hov
long shall I suffer you? bring hin
hither to me.
18 And Jesus rebuked the devil; an
he departed out of him: and the chil
was cured from that very hour.
19 Then came the disciples to Jesu
apart, and said, Why could not w
cast him out?
20 And Jesus said unto them, Be
cause of your unbelief: for verily I sa
unto you, [m]If ye have faith as a grai
of mustard seed, ye shall say unto thi
mountain, Remove hence to yor
der place; and it shall remove; an
nothing shall be impossible unto yo
21 Howbeit this kind goeth not ou
but by prayer and fasting.
22 ¶ And [n]while they abode in Gal
lee, Jesus said unto them, The Son c
man shall be betrayed into the hand
of men:
23 And they shall kill him, and th
third day he shall be raised again. An
they were exceeding sorry.
24 ¶ And [o]when they were come t
Că-pĕr-nă-ŭm, they that receive
[1]tribute *money* came to Peter, an
said, Doth not your master pay tri
ute?
25 He saith, Yes. And when he w
come into the house, Jesus prevente
him, saying, What thinkest tho
Simon? of whom do the kings of tl
earth take custom or tribute? of the
own children, or of strangers?
26 Peter saith unto him, Of stra
gers. Jesus saith unto him, Then a
the children free.
27 Notwithstanding, lest we shou
[p]offend them, go thou to the sea, a

r Gen. 3.1-6. Deut. 25.16. ch. 4.10. Mark 8.33.
s Acts 14.22. Rom. 8.17. 1 Thes. 3.3. 2 Tim. 3.12. Rev. 2.10.
t Ps. 49.7,8. Mark 8.37.
u Dan. 7.10. ch. 25.31. Zech. 14.15. Jude 14.
v Job 34.11. Ps. 62.12. Pro. 24.12. Jer. 17.10. Rom. 2.6. 2 Cor. 5.10. 1 Pet. 1.17. Rev. 2.23.
w Mark 9.1.

CHAP. 17

a Mark 9.2. Luke 9.28.
b Rom. 3.21.
c 2 Pet. 1.17.
d ch. 3.17. Mark 1.11. Luke 3.22.
e Isa. 42.1.
f Deut. 18.15. Acts 3.22. Heb. 12.25.
g 2 Pet. 1.18.
h Mal. 4.5.
i Mal. 4.6. Luke 1.16. Acts 3.21.
j Mark 9.12.
k ch. 14.3.
l Luke 9.37.
m ch. 21.21. Mark 9.23. Mark 11.23. Luke 17.6. 1 Cor. 12.9. 1 Cor. 13.2.
n ch. 16.21. ch. 20.17. Mark 8.31. Mark 9.30, 31. Mark 10.33. Luke 9.22. Luke 18.31. Luke 24.6,7.
o Mark 9. 33.
1 didrachma, in value fifteen-pence. Ex. 30.13. Ex. 38.26.
p Mark 12.17. 1 Cor. 10.32.

cast an hook, and take up the fish that
first cometh up; and when thou hast
opened his mouth, thou shalt find [2]a
piece of money: that take, and give
unto them for me and thee.

CHAPTER 18

AT the [a]same time came the disciples unto Jesus, saying, Who is
the greatest in the kingdom of heaven?
2 And Jesus called a little child unto
him, and set him in the midst of them,
3 And said, Verily I say unto you,
Except [b]ye be converted, and become
as little children, ye shall not enter into the kingdom of heaven.
4 Whosoever [c]therefore shall humble
himself as this little child, the same is
greatest in the kingdom of heaven.
5 And [d]whoso shall receive one such
little child in my name receiveth me.
6 But whoso shall offend one of these
little ones which believe in me, it were
better for him that a millstone were
hanged about his neck, and *that* he
were drowned in the depth of the
sea.
7 ¶ Woe unto the world because of
offences! for [e]it must needs be that
offences come; but [f]woe to that man
by whom the offence cometh!
8 Wherefore [g]if thy hand or thy foot
offend thee, cut them off, and cast
them from thee: it is better for thee to
enter into life halt or maimed, rather
than having two hands or two feet to
be cast into everlasting fire.
9 And if thine eye offend thee, pluck
it out, and cast *it* from thee: it is better
for thee to enter into life with one eye,
rather than having two eyes to be cast
into hell fire.
10 Take heed that ye despise not one
of these little ones; for I say unto you,
That in heaven their [h]angels do always
behold the face of my Father which
is in heaven.
11 For the Son of man is come to
save that which was lost.
12 How [i]think ye? if a man have an
hundred sheep, and one of them be
gone astray, doth he not leave the
ninety and nine, and goeth into the
mountains, and seeketh that which is
gone astray?
13 And if so be that he find it, verily
I say unto you, he rejoiceth more of
that *sheep*, than of the ninety and nine
which went not astray.
14 Even so it is not the will of your
Father which is in heaven, that one of
these little ones should perish.
15 ¶ Moreover [k]if thy brother shall

2 Or, a stater. It is half an ounce of silver, in value 2*s*. 6*d*. after 5*s*. the ounce.

CHAP. 18

a Mark 9.33. Luke 9.46. Luke 22.24.
b Ps. 131.2. ch. 19.14. Mark 10.14. Luke 18.16. 1 Cor. 14.20. 1 Pet. 2.2.
c ch. 11.29. ch. 20.27. ch. 23.11. 1 Pet. 5.5. 1 John 2.6.
d ch. 10.42. Luke 9.48.
e Mark 9.42. Luke 17.1. 1 Cor. 11.19.
f ch. 26.24.
g ch. 5.29,30. Mark 9.43.
h 2 Ki. 19.35. Ps. 34.7. Ps. 91.11. Dan. 6.22. Zech. 13.7. Luke 16.22. Acts 27.23. Heb. 1.4,7, 13,14. Rev. 5.11. Rev. 7.1,11. Rev. 15.1.
i Esther 1.14. Luke 1.19.
j Luke 15.4.
k Lev. 19.17. Luke 17.3. Jas. 5. 20. 1 Pet. 3.1.
m Num. 35. 30. Deut. 17.6. Deut. 19.15. 1 Ki. 21.13. John 8.17.
l Jas. 5.20. 2 Cor. 13.1. Heb. 10.28. 1 John 5.7-10. Rev. 11.3.
n 1 Tim. 5.20.
o Rom. 16.17. 1 Cor. 5.9. 2 John 10.
p John 20.23.
q ch. 5.24.
r Jas. 5.16. 1 John 3.22.
s Eze. 48.35. Zech. 2.5. ch. 28.20.
t Luke 17.4.
u Col. 3.13.
1 A talent is 750 ounces of silver, which after five shillings the ounce is 187*l*. 10*s*.
v Lev. 25.39. 2 Ki. 4.1. Neh. 5.8.
2 Or, besought him.
3 The Roman penny is the eighth part of an ounce, which after five shillings the ounce is sevenpence halfpenny. ch. 20.2.

trespass against thee, go and tell him
his fault between thee and him alone:
if he shall hear thee, thou [l]hast gained
thy brother.
16 But if he will not hear *thee*, *then*
take with thee one or two more, that
[m]in the mouth of two or three witnesses every word may be established.
17 And if he shall neglect to hear
them, tell *it* unto [n]the church: but if
he neglect to hear the church, let him
be unto thee as an [o]heathen man and
a publican.
18 Verily I say unto you, [p]Whatso-
ever ye shall bind on earth shall be
bound in heaven: and whatsoever ye
shall loose on earth shall be loosed in
heaven.
19 Again [q]I say unto you, That if two
of you shall agree on earth as touching
any thing that they shall ask, [r]it shall
be done for them of my Father which
is in heaven.
20 For where two or three are gathered together in my name, there [s]am
I in the midst of them,
21 ¶ Then came Peter to him, and
said, Lord, how oft shall my brother
sin against me, and I forgive him? [t]till
seven times?
22 Jesus saith unto him, I say not unto thee, Until seven times: but, [u]Until
seventy times seven.
23 ¶ Therefore is the kingdom of
heaven likened unto a certain king,
which would take account of his servants.
24 And when he had begun to reckon, one was brought unto him, which
owed him ten thousand [1]talents.
25 But forasmuch as he had not to
pay, his lord commanded him to [v]be
sold, and his wife, and children, and
all that he had, and payment to be
made.
26 The servant therefore fell down,
and [2]worshipped him, saying, Lord,
have patience with me, and I will pay
thee all.
27 Then the lord of that servant was
moved with compassion, and loosed
him, and forgave him the debt.
28 But the same servant went out,
and found one of his fellowservants,
which owed him an hundred [3]pence:
and he laid hands on him, and took
him by the throat, saying, Pay me that
thou owest.
29 And his fellowservant fell down
at his feet, and besought him, saying,
Have patience with me, and I will pay
thee all.
30 And he would not: but went and

cast him into prison, till he should
pay the debt.
31 So when his fellowservants saw
what was done, they were very sorry,
and came and told unto their lord all
that was done.
32 Then his lord, after that he had
called him, said unto him, O thou
wicked servant, I forgave thee all that
debt, because thou desiredst me:
33 Shouldest [w]not thou also have had
compassion on thy fellowservant,
even as I had pity on thee?
34 And his lord was wroth, and delivered him to the tormentors, till he
should pay all that was due unto him.
35 So [x]likewise shall my heavenly
Father do also unto you, if ye from
your hearts forgive not every one his
brother their trespasses.

CHAPTER 19

AND it came to pass, [a]*that* when
Jesus had finished these sayings,
he departed from Galilee, and came
into the coasts of Judæa beyond
Jordan;
2 And [b]great multitudes followed
him; and he healed them there.
3 ¶ The Pharisees also came unto
him, tempting him, and saying unto
him, Is it lawful for a man to put away
his wife for every cause?
4 And he answered and said unto
them, Have ye not read, [c]that he
which made *them* at the beginning
made them male and female,
5 And said, [d]For this cause shall a
man leave father and mother, and
shall cleave to his wife: [e]and they
twain shall be one flesh?
6 Wherefore they are no more twain,
but one flesh. What therefore God
hath joined together, let not man put
asunder.
7 They say unto him, [f]Why did
Moses then command to give a writing
of divorcement, and to put her away?
8 He saith unto them, Moses because of the hardness of your hearts
suffered you to put away your wives:
but [g]from the beginning it was not
so.
9 And [h]I say unto you, Whosoever
shall put away his wife, except *it be*
for fornication, and shall marry another, committeth adultery: and whoso marrieth her which is put away
doth commit adultery.
10 ¶ His disciples say unto him, If
[i]the case of the man be so with *his*
wife, it is not good to marry.
11 But he said unto them, [j]All *men*

w Eph. 4.32. Eph. 5.2. Col. 3.13.
x Pro. 21.13. ch. 6.12,14, 15. ch. 7.1,2. Mark 11.26. Luke 6.37, 38. Jas. 2.13.

CHAP. 19

a Mark 10.1. John 10.40.
b ch. 12.15.
c Gen. 1.27. Gen. 5.2. Mal. 2.15.
d Gen. 2.24. Eph. 5.31.
e 1 Cor. 6.16. 1 Cor. 7.2.
f Deut. 24.1.
g Jer. 6.16.
h ch. 5.32. Mark 10.11. Luke 16.18. 1 Cor. 7.10, 11.
i Gen. 2.18. Pro. 5.18, 19. Pro. 18.22. Pro. 21.19. 1 Tim. 4.3. 1 Tim. 5.11.
j 1 Cor. 7.2, 7,9,17.
k 1 Cor. 7.32, 34. 1 Cor. 9.5, 15.
l Mark 10.13. Luke 18.15.
m ch. 18.3. 1 Pet. 2.1,2.
n Luke 10.25.
o 1 Sam. 2.2.
p Ex. 20.13. Deut. 5.17.
q Lev. 19.3. Pro. 30.17. ch. 15.4. Eph. 6.1,2.
r Lev. 19.18. ch. 22.39. Mark 12.31. Rom. 13.9. Gal. 5.14. Jas. 2.8.
s Luke 12.33. Luke 16.9. Acts 2.45. Acts 4.34. 1 Tim. 6.18.
t Job 31.24-28. Ps. 62.10. ch. 13.22. Mark 10.24. 1 Cor. 1.26. 1 Tim. 6.9.
u Gen. 18.14. Job 42.2. Jer. 32.17. Zech. 8.6. Mark 10.27. Luke 1.37. Heb. 7.27.

cannot receive this saying, save *they*
to whom it is given.
12 For there are some eunuchs, which
were so born from *their* mother's
womb: and there are some eunuchs,
which were made eunuchs of men:
and [k]there be eunuchs, which have
made themselves eunuchs for the kingdom of heaven's sake. He that is able
to receive *it*, let him receive *it*.
13 ¶ Then [l]were there brought unto
him little children, that he should put
his hands on them, and pray: and the
disciples rebuked them.
14 But Jesus said, Suffer little children, and forbid them not, to come
unto me: for of [m]such is the kingdom
of heaven.
15 And he laid *his* hands on them,
and departed thence.
16 ¶ And, behold, one came and said
unto him, [n]Good Master, what good
thing shall I do, that I may have eternal life?
17 And he said unto him, Why callest thou me good? [o]*there is* none good
but one, *that is*, God: but if thou wilt
enter into life, keep the commandments.
18 He saith unto him, Which? Jesus
said, Thou [p]shalt do no murder, Thou
shalt not commit adultery, Thou shalt
not steal, Thou shalt not bear false
witness,
19 Honour [q]thy father and *thy*
mother: and, [r]Thou shalt love thy
neighbour as thyself.
20 The young man saith unto him,
All these things have I kept from my
youth up: what lack I yet?
21 Jesus said unto him, If thou wilt
be perfect, [s]go *and* sell that thou hast,
and give to the poor, and thou shalt
have treasure in heaven: and come
and follow me.
22 But when the young man heard
that saying, he went away sorrowful:
for he had great possessions.
23 ¶ Then said Jesus unto his disciples, Verily I say unto you, That a
[t]rich man shall hardly enter into the
kingdom of heaven.
24 And again I say unto you, It is
easier for a camel to go through the
eye of a needle, than for a rich man
to enter into the kingdom of God.
25 When his disciples heard *it*, they
were exceedingly amazed, saying,
Who then can be saved?
26 But Jesus beheld *them*, and said
unto them, With men this is impossible; but with [u]God all things are
possible.

27 ¶ Then [v]answered Peter and said
ınto him, Behold, [w]we have forsaken
.ll, and followed thee; what shall we
ıave therefore?
28 And Jesus said unto them, Verily
say unto you, That ye which have
ollowed me, in [x]the regeneration
vhen the Son of man shall sit in the
hrone of his glory, ye [y]also shall sit
ıpon twelve thrones, judging the
welve tribes of Israel.
29 And every one that hath forsaken
ıouses, or brethren, or sisters, or
ather, or mother, or wife, or children,
ɪr lands, for my name's sake, shall re-
eive an hundredfold, and shall in-
ıerit everlasting life.
30 But [z]many *that are* first shall be
ast; and the last *shall be* first.

CHAPTER 20

FOR the kingdom of heaven is like
unto a man *that is* an house-
ıolder, which went out early in the
norning to hire labourers into his
ineyard.
2 And when he had agreed with the
abourers for a [1]penny a day, he sent
hem into his vineyard.
3 And he went out about the third
ıour, and saw others standing idle
n the marketplace,
4 And said unto them; Go ye also
nto the vineyard, and whatsoever is
ight I will give you. And they went
heir way.
5 Again he went out about the sixth
nd ninth hour, and did likewise.
6 And about the eleventh hour he
vent out, and found others standing
dle, and saith unto them, Why stand
e here all the day idle?
7 They say unto him, Because no
nan hath hired us. He saith unto
hem, Go ye also into the vineyard;
nd whatsoever is right, *that* shall ye
eceive.
8 So when [a]even was come, the lord
f the vineyard saith unto his steward,
Call the labourers, and give them *their*
ire, beginning from the last unto the
irst.
9 And when they came that *were*
ired about the eleventh hour, they
eceived every man a penny.
10 But when the first came, they sup-
osed that they should have received
nore; and they likewise received every
nan a penny.
11 And when they had received *it*,
hey murmured against the goodman
f the house,
12 Saying, These last [2]have wrought
but one hour, and thou hast made
them equal unto us, which have borne
the burden and heat of the day.
13 But he answered one of them,
and said, Friend, I do thee no wrong:
didst not thou agree with me for a
penny?
14 Take *that* thine *is*, and go thy
way: I will give unto this last, even as
unto thee.
15 Is [b]it not lawful for me to do what
I will with mine own? [c]Is thine eye
evil, because I am good?
16 So [d]the last shall be first, and the
first last: [e]for many be called, but few
chosen.
17 ¶ And [f]Jesus going up to Jerusalem took the twelve disciples apart in
the way, and said unto them,
18 Behold, [g]we go up to Jerusalem;
and the Son of man shall be betrayed
unto the chief priests and unto the
scribes, and they shall condemn him
to death,
19 And [h]shall deliver him to the
Gentiles to mock, and to scourge, and
to crucify *him:* and the third day he
shall rise again.
20 ¶ Then [i]came to him [j]the mother
of Zĕb-ĕ-dēe's [k]children with her
sons, worshipping *him*, and desiring
a certain thing of him.
21 And he said unto her, What wilt
thou? She saith unto him, Grant that
these my two sons [l]may sit, the one on
thy right hand, and the other on the
left, in thy kingdom.
22 But Jesus answered and said, Ye
know not what ye ask. Are ye able to
drink of the [m]cup that I shall drink of
and to be baptized with [n]the baptism
that I am baptized with? They say unto him, We are able.
23 And he saith unto them, [o]Ye shall
drink indeed of my cup, and be baptized with the baptism that I am baptized with: but to sit on my right hand,
and on my left, is not mine to [p]give,
but *it shall be given to them* for whom
it is prepared of my Father.
24 And [q]when the ten heard *it*, they
were moved with indignation against
the two brethren.
25 But Jesus called them *unto him*,
and said, Ye know that the princes of
the Gentiles exercise dominion over
them, and they that are great exercise
authority upon them.
26 But [r]it shall not be so among you:
but whosoever [s]will be great among
you, let him be your minister;
27 And [t]whosoever will be chief
among you, let him be your servant:

v Mark 10.28.
w Deut. 33.9. ch. 4.20. ch. 9.9. Mark 1.17-20. Luke 5.11.
x 2 Cor. 5.17.
y Luke 22.28. 1 Cor. 6.2,3. Rev. 2.26.
z ch. 20.16. Mark 10.31.

CHAP. 20

1 The Roman penny is the eighth part of an ounce, which after five shillings the ounce is sevenpence halfpenny.
a Acts 17.31. 1 Thes. 4.16.
2 Or, have continued one hour only.
b Rom. 9.21.
c Deut. 15.9. Pro. 23.6. Jonah 4.1. ch. 6.23. Mark 7.22.
d ch. 8.11,12. ch. 19.30. Mark 10.31.
e ch. 7.13. ch. 22.14. Luke 14.24. 2 Thes. 2.13, 14.
f John 12.12.
g ch. 16.21.
h ch. 27.2. John 18.28. Acts 3.13.
i Mark 10.35.
j ch. 27.56. Mark 15.40.
k ch. 4.21.
l 1 Ki. 2.19. ch. 19.28. Mark 16.19. Jas. 4.3.
m Ps. 75.8. Jer. 25.15. ch. 26.39. Mark 14.36. Luke 22.42. John 18.11.
n Luke 12.50.
o Acts 12.2. Rom. 8.17. 2 Cor. 1.7.
p ch. 25.34.
q Luke 22.24.
r 1 Pet. 5.3.
s ch. 23.11. Mark 9.35. Mark 10.43.
t ch. 18.4.

28 Even [u]as the Son of man came not
to be ministered unto, but [v]to minister,
and to [w]give his life a ransom [x]for
many.
29 And [y]as they departed from Jericho, a great multitude followed him.
30 ¶ And, behold, two blind men
sitting by the way side, when they
heard that Jesus passed by, cried out,
saying, Have mercy on us, O Lord,
thou Son of David.
31 And the multitude rebuked them,
because they should hold their peace:
but they cried the more, saying, Have
mercy on us, O Lord, *thou* Son of
David.
32 And Jesus stood still, and called
them, and said, What will ye that I
shall do unto you?
33 They say unto him, Lord, that our
eyes may be opened.
34 So Jesus had compassion *on them*,
and touched their eyes: and immediately their eyes received sight, and
they followed him.

CHAPTER 21

AND [a]when they drew nigh unto
Jerusalem, and were come to
Bĕth-phă-ġē, unto [b]the mount of
Olives, then sent Jesus two disciples,
2 Saying unto them, Go into the village over against you, and straightway ye shall find an ass tied, and a
colt with her: loose *them*, and bring
them unto me.
3 And if any *man* say ought unto you,
ye shall say, [c]The Lord hath need[d] of
them; and straightway he will send
them.
4 All this was done, that it might be
fulfilled which was spoken by the
prophet, [e]saying,
5 Tell ye the daughter of Ṡī-on, Behold, thy King cometh unto thee,
meek, and sitting upon an ass, and a
colt the foal of an ass.
6 And [f]the disciples went, and did as
Jesus commanded them,
7 And brought the ass, and the colt,
and put [g]on them their clothes, and
they set *him* thereon.
8 And a very great multitude spread
their garments in the way; others [h]cut
down branches from the trees, and
strawed *them* in the way.
9 And the multitudes that went before, and that followed, cried, saying,
[i]Hō-ṡăn-nă to the Son of David:
[j]Blessed *is* he that cometh in the name
of the Lord; Hō-ṡăn-nă in the highest.
10 And [k]when he was come into Jerusalem, all the city was moved, sayin
Who is this?
11 And the multitude said, This
Jesus the [l]prophet of Nazareth
Galilee.
12 ¶ And [m]Jesus went into the temp
of God, and cast out all them th
sold and bought in the temple, an
overthrew the tables of the [n]mone
changers, and the seats of them th
sold doves,
13 And said unto them, It is writte
[o]My house shall be called the hous
of prayer; but [p]ye have made it a de
of thieves.
14 And [q]the blind and the lame cam
to him in the temple; and he heale
them.
15 And when the chief priests an
scribes saw the wonderful things th
he did, and the children crying in th
temple, and saying, Hō-ṡăn-nă to [r]th
Son of David; they were sore di
pleased,
16 And said unto him, Hearest tho
what these say? And Jesus saith unt
them, Yea; have ye never read, [s]O
of the mouth of babes and suckling
thou hast perfected praise?
17 ¶ And he left them, and we
out of the city into [t]Bethany; and h
lodged there.
18 Now in the morning as he retur
ed into the city, he hungered.
19 And when he saw [1]a fig tree in th
way, he came to it, and found nothi
thereon, but leaves only, and said un
it, Let no fruit grow on thee hencefo
ward for ever. And presently the f
tree withered away.
20 And when the disciples saw *i*
they marvelled, saying, How soon
the fig tree withered away!
21 Jesus answered and said un
them, Verily I say unto you, [u]If y
have faith, and [v]doubt not, ye sha
not only do this *which is done* to th
fig tree, [w]but also if ye shall say un
this mountain, Be thou removed, an
be thou cast into the sea; it shall b
done.
22 And [x]all things, whatsoever
shall ask in prayer, believing, ye sha
receive.
23 ¶ And [y]when he was come in
the temple, the chief priests and t
elders of the people came unto him
he was teaching, and said, [z]By wh
authority doest thou these things
and who gave thee this authority?
24 And [a]Jesus answered and said u
to them, I also will ask you one thin
which if ye tell me, I in like wise w

u John 13.4. Phil. 2.7.
v Luke 22.27. John 13.14.
w Job 33.24. Ps. 49.7. Isa. 53.10. Dan. 9.24. John 11.51. 1 Tim. 2.6.
x ch. 26.28.
y Mark 10. 46.

CHAP. 21
a Mark 11.1. Luke 19.29.
b Zech. 14.4.
c Ps. 24.1.
d 2 Cor. 8.9.
e 1 Ki. 1.33. Isa. 62.11. Zech. 9.9.
f Mark 11.4. Luke 19.29. 30.
g 2 Ki. 9.13.
h Lev. 23.40. John 12.13.
i Ps. 118.25. ch. 22.42. Mark 12.35-37. Luke 18.38. Rom. 1.3.
j ch. 23.39.
k ch. 2.3. Mark 11.15. Luke 19.45. John 12.13.
l ch. 2.23. Luke 7.16. John 6.14. John 7.40.
m Mal. 3.1,2. Mark 11.11. John 2.15.
n Deut. 14. 25.
o Isa. 56.7.
p Jer. 7.11. Mark 11.17. Luke 19.46.
q Isa. 35. 5. ch. 9.35. Acts 3.1-9.
r Isa. 11.1.
s Ps. 8.2. ch. 11.25.
t Mark 11.11. John 11.18.
1 one fig tree.
u ch. 17.20. Luke 17.6.
v Jas. 1.6.
w 1 Cor. 13.2.
x ch. 7.7. Mark 11.24. Luke 11.9. Jas. 5.16. 1 John 3.22. 1 John 5.14.
y Luke 20.1.
z Ex. 2.14. Mark 11.27. Acts 4.7. Acts 7.27.
a Job 5.13.

ll you by what authority I do these
hings.
25 The baptism of John, whence was
? from heaven, or of men? And they
easoned with themselves, saying, If
e shall say, From heaven; he will say
nto us, Why did ye not then believe
im?
26 But if we shall say, Of men; we
ear the people; [b]for all hold John as
prophet.
27 And they answered Jesus, and
aid, We cannot tell. And he said unto
hem, Neither tell I you by what
uthority I do these things.
28 ¶ But what think ye? A *certain*
nan had two sons; and he came to the
irst, and said, Son, go work to day in
my vineyard.
29 He answered and said, I will not:
but afterward he repented, and went.
30 And he came to the second, and
said likewise. And he answered and
said, I *go*, sir: and went not.
31 Whether of them twain did the
will of *his* father? They say unto him,
The first. Jesus saith unto them, [c]Veri-
ly I say unto you, That the publicans
and the harlots go into the kingdom
of God before you.
32 For [d]John came unto you in the
way of righteousness, and ye believed
him not: but [e]the publicans and the
harlots believed him: and ye, when ye
had seen *it*, repented not afterward,
that ye might believe him.
33 ¶ Hear another parable: [f]There
was a certain householder, which
planted a vineyard, and hedged it
round about, and digged a winepress
in it, and built a tower, and let it out to
husbandmen, [g]and went into a far
country:
34 And when the time of the fruit
drew near, he sent his servants to the
husbandmen, [h]that they might receive
the fruits of it.
35 And [i]the husbandmen took his
servants, and beat one, and killed
another, and stoned another.
36 Again, [j]he sent other servants
more than the first: and they did unto
them likewise.
37 But last of all he sent unto them
his son, saying, They will reverence
my son.
38 But when the husbandmen saw
the son, they said among themselves,
[k]This is the heir; [l]come, let us kill him,
and let us seize on his inheritance.
39 And [m]they caught him, and cast
him out of the vineyard, and slew *him*.
40 When the lord therefore of the

b ch. 14.5. Mark 6.20. Luke 20.6. John 5.35. John 10.41, 42.
c Luke 7.29.
d Isa. 35.8.
e Luke 3.12.
f Ps. 80.9. Song 8.11. Isa. 5.1. Jer. 2.21. Mark 12.1. Luke 20.9.
g ch. 25.14.
h Song 8.11.
i 2 Chr. 24.21. Neh. 9.26. ch. 23.34. Acts 7.52. 1 Thes. 2.15. Heb. 11.36.
j ch. 3.17. Mark 12.6. Luke 20.13. John 1.18, 34. John 3.16, 35,36. Gal. 4.4. Heb. 1.2.
k Ps. 2.8.
l Ps. 2.2. John 11.53. Acts 4.27.
m Acts 2.23.
n Luke 20.16.
o Deut. 4.26. Luke 21.24. Heb. 2.3.
p Acts 13.46. Rom. 9.1. Rom. 10.1. Rom. 11.1.
q Ps. 118.22. Isa. 28.16. Mark 12.10. Acts 4.11. Eph. 2.20. 1 Pet. 2.6,7.
r 1 Tim. 3.16.
s ch. 8.12.
t Isa. 8.14. Zech. 12.3.
u Ps. 2.9. Isa. 60.12. Dan. 2.44. ch. 26.24.
v John 7.40.

CHAP. 22

a Luke 14.16. Rev. 19.7,9.
b Pro. 9.2.
c Ps. 81.11.
d 1 Thes. 2. 14,15.
e Isa. 10.5-7. Jer. 51.20-23. Dan. 9.26. Luke 19.27.
f ch. 10.11. Luke 20.25. Acts 13.46.
g ch. 13.38.

vineyard cometh, what will he do unto
those husbandmen?
41 They [n]say unto him, [o]He will
miserably destroy those wicked men,
[p]and will let out *his* vineyard unto
other husbandmen, which shall render
him the fruits in their seasons.
42 Jesus saith unto them, [q]Did ye
never read in the scriptures, The
stone which the builders rejected, the
same is become the head of the corner:
this is the Lord's doing, and it is [r]mar-
vellous in our eyes?
43 Therefore say I unto you, [s]The
kingdom of God shall be taken from
you, and given to a nation bringing
forth the fruits thereof.
44 And whosoever [t]shall fall on this
stone shall be broken: but on whomsoever it shall fall, [u]it will grind him
to powder.
45 And when the chief priests and
Pharisees had heard his parables, they
perceived that he spake of them.
46 But when they sought to lay hands
on him, they feared the multitude, because they [v]took him for a prophet.

CHAPTER 22

AND Jesus answered [a]and spake
unto them again by parables, and
said,
2 The kingdom of heaven is like unto
a certain king, which made a marriage
for his son,
3 And sent forth his servants to call
them that were bidden to the wedding: and they would not come.
4 Again, he sent forth other servants,
saying, Tell them which are bidden,
Behold, I have prepared my dinner:
[b]my oxen and *my* fatlings *are* killed,
and all things *are* ready: come unto the
marriage.
5 But they [c]made light of *it*, and went
their ways, one to his farm, another to
his merchandise:
6 And the [d]remnant took his servants, and entreated *them* spitefully,
and slew *them*.
7 But when the king heard *thereof*,
he was wroth: and he sent forth [e]his
armies, and destroyed those murderers, and burned up their city.
8 Then saith he to his servants, The
wedding is ready, but they which were
bidden were [f]not worthy.
9 Go ye therefore into the highways,
and as many as ye shall find, bid to
the marriage.
10 So those servants went out into
the highways, and [g]gathered together
all as many as they found, both bad

and good: and the wedding was furnished with guests.
11 ¶ And when the king came in to
see the guests, he saw there a man
[h]which had not on a wedding garment:
12 And he saith unto him, Friend,
how camest thou in hither not having
a wedding garment? And he [i]was
speechless.
13 Then said the king to the servants,
Bind him hand and foot, and take him
away, and cast [j]*him* into outer darkness; there shall be weeping and
gnashing of teeth.
14 For [k]many are called, but few *are*
chosen.
15 ¶ Then [l]went the Pharisees, and
took counsel how they might entangle
him in *his* talk.
16 And they sent out unto him their
disciples with the Hĕ-rō-́dĭ-ăns, saying, Master, we know that thou art
true, and teachest the way of God in
truth, neither carest thou for any
man: for thou regardest not the person
of men.
17 Tell us therefore, What thinkest
thou? Is it lawful to give tribute unto
Cæsar, or not?
18 But Jesus perceived their wickedness, and said, Why tempt ye me, *ye*
hypocrites?
19 Shew me the tribute money. And
they brought unto him [1]a penny.
20 And he saith unto them, Whose *is*
this image and [2]superscription?
21 They say unto him, Cæsar's. Then
saith he unto them, [m]Render therefore
unto Cæsar the things which are
Cæsar's; and unto God the things that
are God's.
22 When they had heard *these words*,
they [n]marvelled, and left him, and
went their way.
23 ¶ The [o]same day came to him the
Săd-́dū-çēes̀, [p]which say that there is
no resurrection, and asked him,
24 Saying, Master, [q]Moses said, If a
man die, having no children, his
brother shall marry his wife, and raise
up seed unto his brother.
25 Now there were with us seven
brethren: and the first, when he had
married a wife, deceased, and, having
no issue, left his wife unto his brother:
26 Likewise the second also, and the
third, unto the [3]seventh.
27 And last of all the woman died
also.
28 Therefore in the resurrection
whose wife shall she be of the seven?
for they all had her.

h Zech. 3.3,4. 2 Cor. 5.3. Eph. 4.24. Col. 3.10,12. Rev. 3.4. Rev. 16.15. Rev. 19.8.
i Rom. 3.19.
j ch. 8.12.
k ch. 20.16.
l Mark 12.13. Luke 20.20.
1 In value sevenpence halfpenny. ch. 20.2.
2 Or, inscription?
m ch. 17.25. Luke 23.2. Rom. 13.7.
n Job 5.13.
o ch. 3.7. ch. 16.6. Mark 12.18. Luke 20.27. Acts 4.1.
p Acts 23.8. 1 Cor. 15.12. 2 Tim. 2.17.
q Gen. 38.8. Deut. 25.5.
3 seven.
r John 20.9.
s Ps. 103.20. Zech. 3.5. 1 Cor. 7.29. Rev. 5.11. Rev. 7.1,11.
t Ex. 3.6,16. Mark 12.26. Luke 20.37. Acts 7.32. Heb. 11.16.
u ch. 7.28.
v Luke 10.25.
w Deut. 6.5. Deut. 10.12. Deut. 30.6. Pro. 23.26. Mark 12.29, 30. Luke 10.27.
x Lev. 19.18. Mark 12.31. Rom. 13.9. Gal. 5.14. Jas. 2.8.
y ch. 7.12. 1 Tim. 1.5.
z Mark 12.35. Luke 20.41.
a 2 Sam. 23.2. Acts 2.30. 2 Pet. 1.21.
b Ps. 110.1. Acts 2.34. 1 Cor. 15.25. Heb. 1.13.
c Luke 14.6.

CHAP. 23

a Neh. 8.4,8. Mal. 2.7.

29 Jesus answered and said unto
them, Ye do err, [r]not knowing the
scriptures, nor the power of God.
30 For in the resurrection they neither marry, nor are given in marriage,
but are as [s]the angels of God in
heaven.
31 But as touching the resurrection
of the dead, have ye not read that
which was spoken unto you by God,
saying,
32 I [t]am the God of Abraham, and
the God of Isaac, and the God of
Jacob? God is not the God of the
dead, but of the living.
33 And when the multitude heard
this, they [u]were astonished at his doctrine.
34 ¶ But when the Pharisees had
heard that he had put the Săd-́dū-
çēes̀ to silence, they were gathered together.
35 Then one of them, *which was* [v]a
lawyer, asked *him a question*, tempting
him, and saying,
36 Master, which *is* the great commandment in the law?
37 Jesus said unto him, [w]Thou shalt
love the Lord thy God with all thy
heart, and with all thy soul, and with
all thy mind.
38 This is the first and great commandment.
39 And the second *is* like unto it,
[x]Thou shalt love thy neighbour as
thyself.
40 On [y]these two commandments
hang all the law and the prophets.
41 ¶ While [z]the Pharisees were gathered together, Jesus asked them,
42 Saying, What think ye of Christ?
whose son is he? They say unto him,
The Son of David.
43 He saith unto them, How then
doth David [a]in spirit call him Lord,
saying,
44 The [b]LORD said unto my Lord,
Sit thou on my right hand, till I make
thine enemies thy footstool?
45 If David then call him Lord, how
is he his son?
46 And [c]no man was able to answer
him a word, neither durst any *man*
from that day forth ask him any more
questions.

CHAPTER 23

THEN spake Jesus to the multitude, and to his disciples,
2 Saying, [a]The scribes and the Pharisees sit in Moses' seat:
3 All therefore whatsoever they bid
you observe, *that* observe and do; but

do not ye after their works: for [b]they
say, and do not.
4 For [c]they bind heavy burdens and
grievous to be borne, and lay *them* on
men's shoulders; but they *themselves*
will not move them with one of
their fingers.
5 But [d]all their works they do for to
be seen of men: [e]they make broad
their phylacteries, and enlarge the
borders of their garments,
6 And [f]love the uppermost rooms at
feasts, and the chief seats in the synagogues,
7 And greetings in the markets,
and to be called of men, Rabbi,
Rabbi.
8 But [g]be not ye called Rabbi: for one
is your Master, *even* Christ; and all
ye are brethren.
9 And call no *man* your father upon
the earth: [h]for one is your Father,
which is in heaven.
10 Neither be ye called masters: for
one is your Master, *even* Christ.
11 But [i]he that is greatest among you
shall be your servant.
12 And [j]whosoever shall exalt himself shall be abased; and he that shall
humble himself shall be exalted.
13 ¶ But [k]woe unto you, scribes and
Pharisees, hypocrites! for ye shut up
the kingdom of heaven against men:
for ye neither go in *yourselves*, neither
suffer ye them that are entering to go
in.
14 Woe unto you, scribes and Pharisees, hypocrites! [l]for ye devour
widows' houses, and for a pretence
make long prayer: therefore ye shall
receive the greater damnation.
15 Woe unto you, scribes and Pharisees, hypocrites! for ye compass sea
and land to make one proselyte, and
when he is made, ye make him twofold more the child of hell than yourselves.
16 Woe unto you, [m]*ye* blind guides,
which say, [n]Whosoever shall swear by
the temple, it is nothing; but whosoever shall swear by the gold of the
temple, he is a debtor!
17 *Ye* fools and blind: for whether is
greater, the gold, [o]or the temple that
sanctifieth the gold?
18 And, Whosoever shall swear by
the altar, it is nothing; but whosoever
sweareth by the gift that is upon it, he
is [1]guilty.
19 *Ye* fools and blind: for whether *is*
greater, the gift, or the [p]altar that
sanctifieth the gift?
20 Whoso therefore shall swear by

b Rom. 2.19.
c Luke 11.46. Acts 15.10. Gal. 6.13.
d ch. 6.1,2.
e Num. 15. 38. Deut. 22.12.
f Mark 12.38. Luke 20.46.
g Jas. 3.1.
h Mal. 1.6.
i ch. 20.26.
j Job 22.29. Pro. 15.33. Pro. 29.23. Dan. 4.37. Luke 14.11. Luke 18.14.
k Isa. 33.14. Luke 11.52.
l Eze. 22.25. Mark 12.40. Luke 20. 47. 2 Tim. 3.6. Titus 1.11.
m Isa. 56.10. ch. 15.14.
n ch. 5.33.
o Ex. 30.29.
1 Or, debtor, or, bound.
p Ex. 29.37.
q 1 Ki. 8.13. 2 Chr. 6.2. Ps. 26.8. Ps. 132.14. ch. 5.33-37. Jas. 5.12.
r Ps. 11.4. Isa. 66.1. ch. 5.34. Acts 7.49. Rev. 4.2,3.
s Luke 11.42.
2 anethon, dill.
t 1 Sam. 15. 22. Hos. 6.6. Micah 6.8. ch. 9.13. ch. 12.7.
u Mark 7.4. Luke 11.39.
v Isa. 55.7. Jer. 4.14. Jer. 13.27. Eze. 18.31. Luke 6.45. 2 Cor. 7.1. Titus 1.15. Heb. 10.22.
w Acts 23.3.
x Acts 7.51. 1 Thes. 2.15.
y Gen. 15.16. 1 Thes. 2.16.
z ch. 3.7. ch. 12.34. Luke 3.7.
a ch. 21.34. Luke 11.49.
b Acts 5.40. Acts 7.58. Acts 22.19.
c 2 Cor. 11. 24.
d Rev. 18.24.
e Gen. 4.8. 1 John 3.12.

the altar, sweareth by it, and by all
things thereon.
21 And whoso shall swear by the
temple, sweareth by it, and [q]by him
that dwelleth therein.
22 And he that shall swear by heaven,
sweareth by [r]the throne of God, and
by him that sitteth thereon.
23 Woe unto you, scribes and Pharisees, hypocrites! [s]for ye pay tithe of
mint and [2]anise and cummin, and
[t]have omitted the weightier *matters* of
the law, judgment, mercy, and faith:
these ought ye to have done, and not
to leave the other undone.
24 *Ye* blind guides, which strain at
a gnat, and swallow a camel.
25 Woe unto you, scribes and Pharisees, hypocrites! [u]for ye make clean
the outside of the cup and of the
platter, but within they are full of extortion and excess.
26 *Thou* blind Pharisee, cleanse first
that *which* [v]*is* within the cup and
platter, that the outside of them may
be clean also.
27 Woe unto you, scribes and Pharisees, hypocrites! [w]for ye are like unto
whited sepulchres, which indeed appear beautiful outward, but are within
full of dead *men's* bones, and of all uncleanness.
28 Even so ye also outwardly appear
righteous unto men, but within ye are
full of hypocrisy and iniquity.
29 Woe unto you, scribes and Pharisees, hypocrites! because ye build the
tombs of the prophets, and garnish
the sepulchres of the righteous,
30 And say, If we had been in the
days of our fathers, we would not have
been partakers with them in the blood
of the prophets.
31 Wherefore ye be witnesses unto
yourselves, that [x]ye are the children
of them which killed the prophets.
32 Fill [y]ye up then the measure of
your fathers.
33 *Ye* serpents, *ye* [z]generation of
vipers, how can ye escape the damnation of hell?
34 ¶ Wherefore, [a]behold, I send unto
you prophets, and wise men, and
scribes: and *some* [b]of them ye shall
kill and crucify; and [c]*some* of them
shall ye scourge in your synagogues,
and persecute *them* from city to city:
35 That [d]upon you may come all the
righteous blood shed upon the earth,
[e]from the blood of righteous Abel unto the blood of Zăch-ă-rī´-ăs son of
Băr-ă-chī´-ăs, whom ye slew between
the temple and the altar.

36 Verily I say unto you, All these things shall come upon this generation.

37 O Jerusalem, Jerusalem, *thou* that killest the prophets, and stonest them which are sent unto thee, how often would I [f]have gathered thy children together, even as a hen gathereth her chickens under *her* wings, and ye would not!

38 Behold, your house is left unto you desolate.

39 For I say unto you, Ye shall not see me henceforth, till ye shall say, [g]Blessed *is* he that cometh in the name of the Lord.

CHAPTER 24

AND [a]Jesus went out, and departed from the temple: and his disciples came to *him* for to shew him the buildings of the temple.

2 And Jesus said unto them, See ye not all these things? verily I say unto you, [b]There shall not be left here one stone upon another, that shall not be thrown down.

3 ¶ And as he sat upon the mount of Olives, the disciples came unto him privately, saying, [c]Tell us, when shall these things be? and what *shall be* the sign of thy coming, and of the end of the world?

4 And Jesus answered and said unto them, [d]Take heed that no man deceive you.

5 For [e]many shall come in my name, saying, I am Christ; and shall deceive many.

6 And ye shall hear of wars and rumours of wars: see that ye be not troubled: for all *these things* must come to pass, but the end is not yet.

7 For [f]nation shall rise against nation, and kingdom against kingdom: and there shall be famines, and pestilences, and earthquakes, in divers places.

8 All these *are* the beginning of sorrows.

9 Then [g]shall they deliver you up to be afflicted, and shall kill you: and ye shall be hated of all nations for my name's sake.

10 And then shall many [h]be offended, and shall betray one another, and shall hate one another.

11 And [i]many false prophets shall rise, and [j]shall deceive many.

12 And because iniquity shall abound, the love of many shall wax cold.

13 But [k]he that shall endure unto the end, the same shall be saved.

14 And this gospel of the kingdom [l]shall be preached in all the world for a witness unto all nations; and then shall the end come.

15 When ye therefore shall see the abomination of desolation, spoken of by [m]Daniel the prophet, stand in the holy place, ([n]whoso readeth, let him understand:)

16 Then let them which be in Judæa flee into the mountains:

17 Let him which is on the housetop not come down to take any thing out of his house:

18 Neither let him which is in the field return back to take his clothes.

19 And woe unto them that are with child, and to them that give suck in those days!

20 But pray ye that your flight be not in the winter, neither on the sabbath day:

21 For [o]then shall be great tribulation, such as was not since the beginning of the world to this time, no, nor ever shall be.

22 And except those days should be shortened, there should no flesh be saved: [p]but for the elect's sake those days shall be shortened.

23 Then if any man shall say unto you, Lo, here *is* Christ, or there; believe *it* not.

24 For [q]there shall arise false Christs, and false prophets, and shall shew great signs and wonders; insomuch that, [r]if *it were* possible, they shall deceive the very elect.

25 Behold, I have told you before.

26 Wherefore if they shall say unto you, Behold, he is in the desert; go not forth: behold, *he is* in the secret chambers; believe *it* not.

27 For as the lightning cometh out of the east, and shineth even unto the west; so shall also the coming of the Son of man be.

28 For [s]wheresoever the carcase is, there will the eagles be gathered together.

29 ¶ Immediately [t]after the tribulation of those days [u]shall the sun be darkened, and the moon shall not give her light, and the stars shall fall from heaven, and the powers of the heavens shall be shaken:

30 And [v]then shall appear the sign of the Son of man in heaven: and [w]then shall all the tribes of the earth mourn, [x]and they shall see the Son of man

f Deut. 32.11.

g Ps. 118.26. ch. 21.9.

CHAP. 24

a Mark 13.1. Luke 21.5.
b 1 Ki. 9.7. Jer. 5.10. Jer. 26.18. Dan. 9.26. Micah 3.12. Luke 19.44.
c 1 Thes. 5.1.
d Eph. 5.6. Col. 2.8,18. 2 Thes. 2.3. 1 John 4.1.
e Jer. 14.14. Jer. 23.21. John 5.43. Acts 5.36, 37.
f Isa. 19.2. Hag. 2.22. Zech. 14.13.
g Acts 4.2,3. Acts 7.59. Acts 12.1. 1 Pet. 4.12. Rev. 2.10, 13.
h 2 Tim. 1.15. 2 Tim. 4.10, 16.
i Acts 20.29. 2 Cor. 11.13. 2 Pet. 2.1. 1 John 2.18, 26. Jude 4.
j 1 Tim. 4.1.
k Heb. 3.6.
l Rom. 10.18. Col. 1.6,23.
m Dan. 9.27. Dan. 12.11.
n Dan. 9.23.
o Ps. 69.22-28. Isa. 65. 12-15. Isa. 66.15, 16. Dan. 9. 26. Dan. 12.1. Joel 2.2.
p Isa. 65.8,9. Zech. 14.2, 3.
q Deut. 13.1. 2 Thes. 2.9. Rev. 13.13.
r Rom. 8.28. 2 Tim. 2.19. 1 Pet. 1.5.
s Job 39.30.
t Dan. 7.11.
u Isa. 13.10. Eze. 32.7. Acts 2.20. Rev. 6.12.
v Dan. 7.13. Mark 13.4.
w Zech. 12. 12.
x Rev. 1.7.

coming in the clouds of heaven with
power and great glory.
31 And [y]he shall send his angels
with a great sound of a trumpet, and
they shall gather together his elect
from the four winds, from one end of
heaven to the other.
32 Now learn [z]a parable of the fig
tree; When his branch is yet tender,
and putteth forth leaves, ye know that
summer *is* nigh:
33 So likewise ye, when ye shall see
all these things, know that [2]it is near,
even at the doors.
34 Verily I say unto you, [a]This generation shall not pass, till all these things
be fulfilled.
35 Heaven [b]and earth shall pass
away, but my words shall not pass
away.
36 ¶ But [c]of that day and hour
knoweth no *man*, no, not the angels of
heaven, [d]but my Father only.
37 But as the days of Nō-ē *were*, so
shall also the coming of the Son of
man be.
38 For [e]as in the days that were before the flood they were eating and
drinking, marrying and giving in
marriage, until the day that Nō-ē
entered into the ark,
39 And knew not until the flood
came, and took them all away; so
shall also the coming of the Son of
man be.
40 Then shall two be in the field; the
one shall be taken, and the other left.
41 Two *women shall be* grinding at
the mill; the one shall be taken, and
the other left.
42 ¶ Watch therefore: for ye know
not what hour your Lord doth come.
43 But [f]know this, that if the goodman of the house had known in what
watch the thief would come, he would
have watched, and would not have
suffered his house to be broken up.
44 Therefore be ye also ready: for in
such an hour as ye think not the Son
of man cometh.
45 Who [g]then is a faithful and wise
servant, whom his lord hath made
ruler over his household, to give them
meat in due season?
46 Blessed [h]*is* that servant, whom his
lord when he cometh shall find so
doing.
47 Verily I say unto you, That he
shall make him ruler over all his
goods.
48 But and if that evil servant shall
say in his heart, My lord delayeth his
coming;

y 1 Cor. 15. 52. 1 Thes. 4.16.
1 Or, with a trumpet, and a great voice.
z Luke 21.29.
2 Or, he. Jas. 5.9.
a ch. 16.28. ch. 23.36.
b Ps. 102.26, 27. Isa. 34.4. Isa. 51.6. Jer. 31.35. ch. 5.18. Mark 13.31. Luke 21.33. Heb. 1.11. 2 Pet. 3.7-12. Rev. 6.14.
c Acts 1.7. 1 Thes. 5.2. 2 Pet. 3.10.
d Zech. 14.7.
e Gen. 6.3. Luke 17.26. 1 Pet. 3.20.
f 1 Thes. 5.6. Rev. 3.3. Rev. 16.15.
g 1 Cor. 4.2. Heb. 3.5.
h ch. 25.34. 1 Tim. 4.7, 8. Rev. 16.15.
3 Or, cut him off.
i Ps. 11.6. ch. 25.30. Luke 12.46.

CHAP. 25

a John 3.29. Rev. 19.7. Rev. 21.2,9.
b ch. 13.47. ch. 22.10.
c 2 Tim. 3.5.
d Song 5.2. ch. 26.40,43. Rom. 13.11. Eph. 5.14. 1 Thes. 5.6.
e Ps. 50.3-6. Luke 13.25. 1 Thes. 4.16.
f Luke 12.35.
1 Or, going out.
g Luke 13.25.
h ch. 7.21.
i Ps. 5.5. John 9.31.
j ch. 24.42. Mark 13.33. Luke 21.36. 1 Cor. 16.13. 1 Pet. 5.8. Rev. 16.15.
k Luke 19.12.
l ch. 21.33.
2 A talent is 187l 10s.
m Rom. 12.6. 1 Cor. 12.7. Eph. 4.11.
n Pro. 3.14. 1 Pet. 4.10.

49 And shall begin to smite *his* fellowservants, and to eat and drink
with the drunken;
50 The lord of that servant shall
come in a day when he looketh not for
him, and in an hour that he is not
aware of,
51 And shall [3]cut him asunder, and
appoint *him* [i]his portion with the
hypocrites: there shall be weeping and
gnashing of teeth.

CHAPTER 25

THEN shall the kingdom of heaven
be likened unto ten virgins, which
took their lamps, and went forth to
meet the [a]bridegroom.
2 And [b]five of them were wise, and
five *were* foolish.
3 They that *were* foolish took their
lamps, and took [c]no oil with
them:
4 But the wise took oil in their vessels with their lamps.
5 While the bridegroom tarried, they
[d]all slumbered and slept.
6 And at midnight [e]there was a cry
made, Behold, the bridegroom cometh; go ye out to meet him.
7 Then all those virgins arose, and
trimmed their [f]lamps.
8 And the foolish said unto the wise,
Give us of your oil; for our lamps
are [1]gone out.
9 But the wise answered, saying, *Not
so;* lest there be not enough for us and
you: but go ye rather to them that sell,
and buy for yourselves.
10 And while they went to buy, the
bridegroom came; and they that were
ready went in with him to the marriage: and the [g]door was shut.
11 Afterward came also the other
virgins, saying, [h]Lord, Lord, open to
us.
12 But he answered and said, Verily
I say unto you, [i]I know you not.
13 Watch [j]therefore, for ye know
neither the day nor the hour wherein
the Son of man cometh.
14 ¶ For [k]*the kingdom of heaven is* as
[l]a man travelling into a far country,
who called his own servants, and delivered unto them his goods.
15 And unto one he gave [2]five talents,
to another two, and to another one;
[m]to every man according to his several
ability; and straightway took his
journey.
16 Then he that had received the five
talents went and [n]traded with the
same, and made *them* other five talents.

17 And likewise he that *had received*
two, he also gained other two.
18 But he that had received one went
and digged in the earth, and hid [o]his
lord's money.
19 After a long time the lord of those
servants cometh, and reckoneth with
them.
20 And so he that had received five
talents came and brought other five
talents, saying, Lord, thou deliveredst
unto me five talents: behold, I have
gained beside them five talents more.
21 His lord said unto him, Well done,
thou good and faithful servant: thou
hast been faithful over a few things, [p]I
will make thee ruler over many things:
enter thou into the joy of thy lord.
22 He also that had received two talents came and said, Lord, thou deliveredst unto me two talents: behold,
I have gained two other talents beside
them.
23 His lord said unto him, Well done,
good and faithful servant; thou hast
been faithful over a few things, I will
make thee ruler over many things:
enter thou into [q]the joy of thy lord.
24 Then he which had received the
one talent came and said, Lord, I
knew thee that thou art an hard man,
reaping where thou hast not sown,
and gathering where thou hast not
strawed:
25 And I was afraid, and went and
hid thy talent in the earth: lo, *there*
thou hast *that is* thine.
26 His lord answered and said unto
him, *Thou* wicked and slothful servant, thou knewest that I reap where
I sowed not, and gather where I have
not strawed:
27 Thou oughtest therefore to have
put my money to the exchangers, and
then at my coming I should have received mine own with usury.
28 Take therefore the talent from
him, and give *it* unto him which hath
ten talents.
29 For [r]unto every one that hath
shall be given, and he shall have
abundance: but from him that hath
not shall be taken away even that
which he hath.
30 And cast ye the unprofitable servant into outer darkness: there shall
be weeping and gnashing of teeth.
31 ¶ When [s]the Son of man shall
come in his glory, and all the holy
angels with him, then shall he sit upon
the throne of his glory:
32 And [t]before him shall be gathered
all nations: and [u]he shall separate

o Phil. 2.21.
p ch. 24.47. Luke 12.44. Luke 22.29. Rev. 2.10, 26-28. Rev. 3.21. Rev. 21.7.
q Acts 2.28. 2 Tim. 2.12. Heb. 12.2. 1 Pet. 1.8.
r Luke 8.18. John 15.2. 1 Cor. 15.10. 2 Cor. 6.1.
s Zech. 14.5. Acts 1.11. Acts 3.21. Acts 17.31. 1 Thes. 4.16. 2 Thes. 1.7. Phil. 2.9,10. Heb. 9.28. Jude 14. Rev. 1.7.
t Rom. 14.10. 2 Cor. 5.10. Rev. 20.12.
u Ps. 1.5. Ps. 50. 3-5. Eze. 20.38. Eze. 34.17. Mal. 3.18. ch. 3.12. ch. 13.49.
v Luke 12.32. Rom. 8.17. 1 Cor. 6.9. Gal. 5.21. Eph. 5.5. 1 Pet. 1.4,9. 1 Pet. 3.9. Rev. 21.7.
w 1 Cor. 2.9. Heb. 11.16.
x Isa. 58.7. Eze. 18.7. 2 Tim. 1.16. Jas. 1.27.
y Heb. 13.2. 3 John 5.
z Jas. 2.15.
a 2 Tim. 1.16.
b Pro. 14.31. Pro. 19.17. Heb. 6.10.
c Ps. 6.8.
d ch. 13.40.
e 2 Pet. 2.4. Jude 6.
f Pro. 14.31. Pro. 17.5. Zech. 2.8. Acts 9.5.
g Dan. 12.2. John 5.29. Rom. 2.7. Rev. 14.11. Rev. 20.10, 15.
h Rev. 3.21. Rev. 7.15.

CHAP. 26
a Mark 14.1. Luke 22.1. John 13.1.
b Ps. 2.2. John 11.47. Acts 4.25.

them one from another, as a shepherd
divideth *his* sheep from the goats:
33 And he shall set the sheep on his
right hand, but the goats on the left.
34 Then shall the King say unto
them on his right hand, Come, ye
blessed of my Father, [v]inherit the
kingdom [w]prepared for you from the
foundation of the world:
35 For [x]I was an hungred, and ye
gave me meat: I was thirsty, and ye
gave me drink: [y]I was a stranger, and
ye took me in:
36 Naked, [z]and ye clothed me: I was
sick, and ye visited me: [a]I was in
prison, and ye came unto me.
37 Then shall the righteous answer
him, saying, Lord, when saw we thee
an hungred, and fed *thee?* or thirsty,
and gave *thee* drink?
38 When saw we thee a stranger, and
took *thee* in? or naked, and clothed
thee?
39 Or when saw we thee sick, or in
prison, and came unto thee?
40 And the King shall answer and
say unto them, Verily I say unto you,
[b]Inasmuch as ye have done *it* unto one
of the least of these my brethren, ye
have done *it* unto me.
41 Then shall he say also unto them
on the left hand, [c]Depart from me, ye
cursed, into [d]everlasting fire, prepared
for [e]the devil and his angels:
42 For I was an hungred, and ye gave
me no meat: I was thirsty, and ye gave
me no drink:
43 I was a stranger, and ye took me
not in: naked, and ye clothed me not:
sick, and in prison, and ye visited me
not.
44 Then shall they also answer him,
saying, Lord, when saw we thee an
hungred, or athirst, or a stranger, or
naked, or sick, or in prison, and did
not minister unto thee?
45 Then shall he answer them, saying, Verily I say unto you, [f]Inasmuch
as ye did *it* not to one of the least of
these, ye did *it* not to me.
46 And [g]these shall go away into
everlasting punishment: but the righteous into life [h]eternal.

CHAPTER 26

AND it came to pass, when Jesus
had finished all these sayings, he
said unto his disciples,
2 Ye [a]know that after two days is *the
feast of* the passover, and the Son of
man is betrayed to be crucified.
3 Then [b]assembled together the chief
priests, and the scribes, and the elders

of the people, unto the palace of the
high priest, who was called Cā̂i-ă-
phăs,
4 And consulted that they might take
Jesus by subtilty, and kill *him*.
5 But they said, Not on the feast *day*,
lest there be an uproar among the
people.
6 ¶ Now [c]when Jesus was [d]in Bethany, in the house of Simon the leper,
7 There came unto him a woman
having an alabaster box of very
precious ointment, and poured it on
his head, as he sat *at meat*.
8 But [e]when his disciples saw *it*, they
had indignation, saying, To what purpose *is* this waste?
9 For this ointment might have been
sold for much, and given to the poor.
10 When Jesus understood *it*, he
said unto them, Why trouble ye the
woman? for she hath wrought a good
work upon me.
11 For [f]ye have the poor always with
you; but [g]me ye have not always.
12 For in that she hath poured this
ointment on my body, she did *it* for
my burial.
13 Verily I say unto you, [h]Where-
soever this gospel shall be preached
in the whole world, *there* shall also
this, that this woman hath done, be
told for a memorial of her.
14 ¶ Then [i]one of the twelve, called
Judas [j]Iscariot, went unto the chief
priests,
15 And said *unto them*, [k]What will ye
give me, and I will deliver him unto
you? And they covenanted with him
for thirty pieces of silver.
16 And from that time he sought
opportunity to betray him.
17 ¶ Now [l]the first *day* of the *feast of*
unleavened bread the disciples came
to Jesus, saying unto him, Where
wilt thou that we prepare for thee to
eat the passover?
18 And he said, Go into the city to
such a man, and say unto him, The
Master saith, My time is at hand; I
will keep the passover at thy house
with my disciples.
19 And the disciples did as Jesus had
appointed them; and they made ready
the passover.
20 Now when the even was come, he
sat down with the twelve.
21 And as they did eat, he said, Verily
I say unto you, that one of you shall
betray me.
22 And they were exceeding sorrowful, and began every one of them to
say unto him, Lord, is it I?

23 And he answered and said, He
[m]that dippeth *his* hand with me in the
dish, the same shall betray me.
24 The Son of man goeth [n]as it is
written of him: but [o]woe unto that
man by whom the Son of man is betrayed! it had been good for that man
if he had not been born.
25 Then Judas, which betrayed him,
answered and said, Master, is it I?
He said unto him, Thou hast said.
26 ¶ And as they were eating, Jesus
[p]took bread, and [1]blessed *it*, and
brake *it*, and gave *it* to the disciples,
and said, Take, eat; this is [q]my body.
27 And he took the cup, and gave
thanks, and gave *it* to them, saying,
Drink ye all of it;
28 For [r]this is my blood [s]of the new
testament, which is shed [t]for many
for the remission of sins.
29 But I say unto you, I will not
drink henceforth of this fruit of the
vine, [u]until that day when I drink it
new with you in my Father's kingdom.
30 And [v]when they had sung an
[2]hymn, they went out into the mount
of Olives.
31 Then saith Jesus unto them, All
[w]ye shall [x]be offended because of me
this night: for it is written, I [y]will
smite the shepherd, and the sheep of
the flock shall be scattered abroad.
32 But after I am risen again, [z]I will
go before you into Galilee.
33 Peter answered and said unto
him, Though all *men* shall be offended
because of thee, *yet* will I never be
offended.
34 Jesus said unto him, [a]Verily I say
unto thee, That this night, before the
cock crow, thou shalt deny me thrice.
35 Peter said unto him, Though I
should die with thee, yet will I not
deny thee. Likewise also said all the
disciples.
36 ¶ Then [b]cometh Jesus with them
unto a place called Gĕth-sĕm-ă-nē,
and saith unto the disciples, Sit ye
here, while I go and pray yonder.
37 And he took with him Peter and
[c]the two sons of Zĕb-ĕ-dēe, and began
to be sorrowful and very heavy.
38 Then saith he unto them, [d]My
soul is exceeding sorrowful, even unto death: tarry ye here, and watch
[e]with me.
39 And he went a little further, and
fell on his face, and [f]prayed, saying,
[g]O my Father, if it be possible, [h]let this
cup pass from me: nevertheless [i]not
as I will, but as thou *wilt*.

c Mark 14.3. John 11.1, 2. John 12.3.
d ch. 21.17.
e John 12.4.
f Deut. 15.11. John 12.8.
g John 13.33. John 14.19. John 16.5, 28. John 17.11.
h Mark 13.10. Luke 24.47. Rom. 1.8. Rom. 10.18.
i Mark 14.10. Luke 22.3. John 13.2.
j ch. 10.4.
k Zech. 11. 12. ch. 27.3.
l Ex. 12.6. Lev. 23.5,6.
m Ps. 41.9. Luke 22.21. John 13.18.
n Gen. 3.15. Ps. 22.1. Isa. 53.1. Dan. 9.26. Acts 26.22. 1 Cor. 15.3.
o ch. 18.7. ch. 27.3-5. Mark 14.21. John 17.12.
p Luke 24.30. 1 Cor. 11.23.
1 Many Greek copies have, gave thanks.
q 1 Cor. 10.4, 16.
r Ex. 24.8. Lev. 17.11. Mark 14.24. Luke 22.20. Heb. 9.14-22.
s Jer. 31.31.
t Rom. 5.15. Heb. 9.22.
u Acts 10.41.
v Mark 14.26.
2 Or, psalm.
w John 16.32.
x ch. 11.6.
y Zech. 13.7.
z ch. 28.7. Mark 16.7.
a Luke 22.34. John 13.38.
b John 18.1.
c ch. 4.21.
d Job 6.2-4. Ps. 88.1-7, 14-16. Isa. 53.10. John 12.27.
e 1 Pet. 5.8.
f Mark 14.36. Luke 22.42. Heb. 5.7.
g John 12.27.
h ch. 20.22. John 18.11.
i 2 Sam. 15. 26. John 5.30. John 6.38. Rom. 15.3. Phil. 2.8.

40 And he cometh unto the disciples, and findeth them asleep, and saith unto Peter, What, could ye not watch with me one hour?

41 Watch [j]and pray, that ye enter not into temptation: the spirit indeed *is* willing, but the flesh *is* weak.

42 He went away again the second time, and prayed, saying, O my Father, if this cup may not pass away from me, except I drink it, thy will be done.

43 And he came and found them asleep again: for their eyes were heavy.

44 And he left them, and went away again, and prayed the third time, saying the same words.

45 Then cometh he to his disciples, and saith unto them, Sleep on now, and take *your* rest: behold, the hour is at hand, and the Son of man is betrayed into the hands of sinners.

46 Rise, let us be going: behold, he is at hand that doth betray me.

47 ¶ And [k]while he yet spake, lo, Judas, one of the twelve, came, and with him a great multitude with swords and staves, from the chief priests and elders of the people.

48 Now he that betrayed him gave them a sign, saying, Whomsoever I shall kiss, that same is he: hold him fast.

49 And forthwith he came to Jesus, and said, Hail, master; [l]and kissed him.

50 And Jesus said unto him, [3]Friend, wherefore art thou come? Then came they, and laid hands on Jesus, and took him.

51 And, behold, [m]one of them which were with Jesus stretched out *his* hand, and drew his sword, and struck a servant of the high priest's, and smote off his ear.

52 Then said Jesus unto him, Put [n]up again thy sword into his place: [o]for all they that take the sword shall perish with the sword.

53 Thinkest thou that I cannot now pray to my Father, and he shall presently give me [p]more than twelve legions of angels?

54 But how then shall [q]the scriptures be fulfilled, that thus it must be?

55 In that same hour said Jesus to the multitudes, Are ye come out as against a thief with swords and staves for to take me? I sat daily with you teaching in the temple, and ye laid no hold on me.

56 But all this was done, that the [r]scriptures of the prophets might be fulfilled. Then [s]all the disciples forsook him, and fled.

[j] Mark 13.33. Mark 14.38. Luke 22.40. 1 Cor. 16.13. Eph. 6.18. 1 Pet. 4.7. 1 Pet. 5.8. Rev. 16.15.
[k] Mark 14.43. Luke 22.47. John 18.3. Acts 1.16.
[l] 2 Sam. 20.9.
3 Companion. Ps. 41.9. Ps. 55.13.
[m] John 18.10.
[n] 1 Cor. 4.12.
[o] Gen. 9.6. Rev. 13.10.
[p] 2 Ki. 6.17. Ps. 91.11. Dan. 7.10.
[q] Isa. 53.7. Dan. 9.26.
[r] Lam. 4.20. Acts 2.23.
[s] John 18.15.
[t] Mark 14.53. Luke 22.54. John 18.13.
[u] 1 Ki. 21.10. Ps. 27.12.
[v] Deut. 19.15.
[w] ch. 27.40. John 2.19.
[x] Isa. 53.7. ch. 27.12.
[y] Lev. 5.1. 1 Sam. 14.24.
[z] Ps. 110.1. Dan. 7.13. John 1.51. Rom. 14.10. 1 Thes. 4.16. Rev. 1.7.
[a] Ps. 110.1. Acts 7.55.
[b] 2 Ki. 18.37. 2 Ki. 19.1. Job 1.20. Isa. 36.21, 22.
[c] Lev. 24.16. John 19.7. Acts 2.23. Acts 3.15. Acts 7.52. 1 Thes. 2.14, 15.
[d] Num. 12.14. Deut. 25.9. Job 30.10. Isa. 50.6. Isa. 52.14. Isa. 53.3. ch. 27.30. Mark 14.65. Mark 15.19. Luke 18.32.
[e] Micah 5.1. Luke 22.63.
4 Or, rods.
[f] Mark 14.65.

57 ¶ And [t]they that had laid hold on Jesus led *him* away to Cāi'-ă-phās the high priest, where the scribes and the elders were assembled.

58 But Peter followed him afar off unto the high priest's palace, and went in, and sat with the servants, to see the end.

59 Now the chief priests, and elders, and all the council, sought false witness against Jesus, to put him to death;

60 But found none: yea, though many [u]false witnesses came, *yet* found they none. At the last came two [v]false witnesses,

61 And said, This *fellow* said, [w]I am able to destroy the temple of God, and to build it in three days.

62 And the high priest arose, and said unto him, Answerest thou nothing? what *is it which* these witness against thee?

63 But [x]Jesus held his peace. And the high priest answered and said unto him, [y]I adjure thee by the living God, that thou tell us whether thou be the Christ, the Son of God.

64 Jesus saith unto him, Thou hast said: nevertheless I say unto you, [z]Hereafter shall ye see the Son of man [a]sitting on the right hand of power, and coming in the clouds of heaven.

65 Then the high priest rent [b]his clothes, saying, He hath spoken blasphemy; what further need have we of witnesses? behold, now ye have heard his blasphemy.

66 What think ye? They answered and said, [c]He is guilty of death.

67 Then [d]did they spit in his face, and buffeted him; [e]and others smote *him* with [4]the palms of their hands,

68 Saying, [f]Prophesy unto us, thou Christ, Who is he that smote thee?

69 ¶ Now Peter sat without in the palace: and a damsel came unto him, saying, Thou also wast with Jesus of Galilee.

70 But he denied before *them* all, saying, I know not what thou sayest.

71 And when he was gone out into the porch, another *maid* saw him, and said unto them that were there, This *fellow* was also with Jesus of Nazareth.

72 And again he denied with an oath, I do not know the man.

73 And after a while came unto *him* they that stood by, and said to Peter,

Surely thou also art *one* of them; for
thy speech bewrayeth thee.
74 Then began he to curse and to
swear, *saying*, I know not the man.
And immediately the cock crew.
75 And Peter remembered the word
of Jesus, which said unto him, Before
the cock crow, thou shalt deny me
thrice. And he went out, and [g]wept
bitterly.

CHAPTER 27

WHEN the morning was come, all
[a]the chief priests and elders of
the people took counsel against Jesus
to put him to death:
2 And when they had bound him,
they led *him* away, and [b]delivered him
to Pontius Pilate the governor.
3 ¶ Then [c]Judas, which had betrayed him, when he saw that he was
condemned, repented himself, and
brought again the thirty pieces of silver
to the chief priests and elders,
4 Saying, I have sinned in that I have
betrayed the innocent blood. And
they said, What *is that* to us? see thou
to that.
5 And he cast down the pieces of silver in the temple, [d]and departed, and
went and hanged himself.
6 And the chief priests took the silver
pieces, and said, It is not lawful for to
put them into the treasury, because it
is the price of blood.
7 And they took counsel, and bought
with them the potter's field, to bury
strangers in.
8 Wherefore that field was called,
The field of blood, unto this day.
9 Then was fulfilled that which was
spoken by Jeremy the prophet, saying, [e]And they took the thirty pieces
of silver, the price of him that was
valued, [1]whom they of the children of
Israel did value;
10 And gave them for the potter's
field, as the Lord appointed me.
11 And Jesus stood before the governor: and [f]the governor asked him,
saying, Art thou the King of the Jews?
And Jesus said unto him, [g]Thou
sayest.
12 And when he was accused of the
chief priests and elders, [h]he answered
nothing.
13 Then said Pilate unto him, Hearest [i]thou not how many things they
witness against thee?
14 And he answered him to never a
word; insomuch that the governor
marvelled greatly.
15 Now [j]at *that* feast the governor

g 2 Sam. 12. 13. Zech. 12.10. 2 Cor. 7.10. Gal. 6.1.

CHAP. 27

a Ps. 2.2. Mark 15.1. Luke 22.66. Luke 23.1. John 18.28.
b ch. 20.19. Acts 3.13. 1 Thes. 2.14.
c Job 20.5. ch. 26.14. Mark 14.10, 11,43-46. Luke 22.2-6, 47,48. 2 Cor. 7.10.
d 2 Sam. 17. 23. Acts 1.18.
e Zech. 11.12.
1 Or, whom they bought of the children of Israel.
f Mark 15.2. Luke 23.3. John 18.33.
g John 18.37. 1 Tim. 6.13.
h Isa. 53.7. ch. 26.63. John 19.9. 1 Pet. 2.23.
i ch. 26.62. John 19.10.
j Mark 15.6. Luke 23.17. John 18.39. Acts 25.9.
k Acts 7.9.
l Job 33.15.
m Mark 15. 11. Luke 23.18. John 18.40. Acts 3.14.
n Deut. 21.6.
o Num. 35. 33. Deut. 19.10. Josh. 2.19. 2 Sam. 1.16. 2 Sam. 3.28. 1 Ki. 2.32. Eze. 22.2-4. Acts 5.28.
p Isa. 53.5. Mark 15.15. John 19.1.
2 Or, governor's house.
q Luke 23.11.
r Ps. 35.15, 16. Ps. 69.19. Isa. 49.7. Isa. 53.3. Jer. 20.7. Heb. 12.2,3.
s Job 30.10. Isa. 50.6. Isa. 52.14. Mark 15.19. Luke 18.32.
t Micah 5.1. Mark 15.19. Luke 22.63.
u Isa. 53.7. ch. 20.19. ch. 21.39. Mark 15.20. Luke 23.26. John 19.16, 17.

was wont to release unto the people a
prisoner, whom they would.
16 And they had then a notable prisoner, called Bär-ăb-băs.
17 Therefore when they were gathered together, Pilate said unto them,
Whom will ye that I release unto you?
Bär-ăb-băs, or Jesus which is called
Christ?
18 For he knew that for [k]envy they
had delivered him.
19 ¶ When he was set down on the
judgment seat, his wife sent unto him,
saying, Have thou nothing to do with
that just man: for I have suffered
many things this day in [l]a dream because of him.
20 But [m]the chief priests and elders
persuaded the multitude that they
should ask Bär-ăb-băs, and destroy
Jesus.
21 The governor answered and said
unto them, Whether of the twain will
ye that I release unto you? They said,
Bär-ăb-băs.
22 Pilate saith unto them, What shall
I do then with Jesus which is called
Christ? *They* all say unto him, Let
him be crucified.
23 And the governor said, Why,
what evil hath he done? But they
cried out the more, saying, Let him be
crucified.
24 ¶ When Pilate saw that he could
prevail nothing, but *that* rather a
tumult was made, [n]he took water, and
washed *his* hands before the multitude, saying, I am innocent of the
blood of this just person: see ye *to it*.
25 Then answered all the people, and
said, [o]His blood *be* on us, and on our
children.
26 ¶ Then released he Bär-ăb-băs unto them: and when [p]he had scourged
Jesus, he delivered *him* to be crucified.
27 Then the soldiers of the governor
took Jesus into the [2]common hall, and
gathered unto him the whole band *of
soldiers*.
28 And they stripped him, and [q]put
on him a scarlet robe.
29 ¶ And [r]when they had platted a
crown of thorns, they put *it* upon his
head, and a reed in his right hand: and
they bowed the knee before him, and
mocked him, saying, Hail, King of the
Jews!
30 And they [s]spit upon him, and took
the reed, and [t]smote him on the head.
31 And after that they had mocked
him, they took the robe off from him,
and put his own raiment on him, [u]and
led him away to crucify *him*.

32 And [v]as they came out, [w]they found a man of Çȳ-rē-nē, Simon by name: him they compelled to bear his cross.

33 And when they were come unto a place called Gŏl-gŏ-thă, that is to say, a place of a skull,

34 ¶ They [x]gave him vinegar to drink mingled with gall: and when he had tasted *thereof*, he would not drink.

35 And they crucified him, and parted his garments, casting lots: that it might be fulfilled which was spoken by the prophet, [y]They parted my garments among them, and upon my vesture did they cast lots.

36 And sitting down they watched him there;

37 And set up over his head his accusation written, THIS IS JESUS THE KING OF THE JEWS.

38 Then [z]were there two thieves crucified with him, one on the right hand, and another on the left.

39 ¶ And [a]they that passed by reviled him, wagging their heads,

40 And saying, [b]Thou that destroyest the temple, and buildest *it* in three days, save thyself. If thou be the Son of God, come down from the cross.

41 Likewise also the chief priests mocking *him*, with the scribes and elders, said,

42 He saved others; himself he cannot save. If he be the King of Israel, let him now come down from the cross, and we will believe him.

43 He [c]trusted in God; let him deliver him now, if he will have him: for he said, I am the Son of God.

44 The [d]thieves also, which were crucified with him, cast the same in his teeth.

45 Now from the [e]sixth hour there was darkness over all the land unto the ninth hour.

46 And about the ninth hour Jesus [f]cried with a loud voice, saying, Ē-lī, Ē-lī, lä-mä să-băch-thă-nī? that is to say, [g]My God, my God, why hast thou forsaken me?

47 Some of them that stood there, when they heard *that*, said, This *man* calleth for Ē-lī-ăs.

48 And straightway one of them ran, and took a spunge, [h]and filled *it* with vinegar, and put *it* on a reed, and gave him to drink.

49 The rest said, Let be, let us see whether Ē-lī-ăs will come to save him.

50 ¶ Jesus, when he had cried again with a loud voice, yielded up the ghost.

v Num. 15. 35. 1 Ki. 21.13. Acts 7.58. Heb. 13.12.
w Mark 15. 21.
x Ps. 69.21.
y Ps. 22.18.
z Isa. 53.12. Mark 15.27. Luke 23.32. John 19.18.
a Ps. 22.7. Ps. 109.25.
b ch. 26.61. John 2.19.
c Ps. 22.8.
d Luke 23.39.
e Isa. 50.3. Amos 8.9.
f Heb. 5.7.
g Ps. 22.1.
h Ps. 69.21. John 19.29.
i Ex. 26.31. 2 Chr. 3.14. Mark 15.38. Luke 23.45. Eph. 2.14, 18. Heb. 6.19. Heb. 10.19, 20.
j Ex. 19.18. Ps. 18.7.
k Ps. 68.20.
l Ex. 20.18, 19. Deut. 32.31. Mark 15.39. Luke 23.47.
m Luke 8.2.
n Mark 15.40.
o Mark 15.42. Luke 23.50. John 19.38.
p Isa. 53.9.
q Ps. 2.1-6. Luke 23.2. John 7.12. Acts 4.27, 28. 2 Cor. 6.8.
r ch. 16.21. ch. 17.23. ch. 20.19. ch. 26.61. Mark 8.31.
s Dan. 6.17.

51 And, behold, [i]the veil of the temple was rent in twain from the top to the bottom; and [j]the earth did quake, and the rocks rent;

52 And the graves were opened; and [k]many bodies of the saints which slept arose,

53 And came out of the graves after his resurrection, and went into the holy city, and appeared unto many.

54 Now [l]when the centurion, and they that were with him, watching Jesus, saw the earthquake, and those things that were done, they feared greatly, saying, Truly this was the Son of God.

55 And many women were there beholding afar off, [m]which followed Jesus from Galilee, ministering unto him:

56 Among [n]which was Mary Măg-dă-lēne, and Mary the mother of James and Jō-sēs, and the mother of Zĕb-ĕ-dēe's children.

57 When [o]the even was come, there came a rich man of Ăr-ĭm-ă-thæ-ă, named Joseph, who also himself was Jesus' disciple:

58 He went to Pilate, and begged the body of Jesus. Then Pilate commanded the body to be delivered.

59 And when Joseph had taken the body, he wrapped it in a clean linen cloth,

60 And [p]laid it in his own new tomb, which he had hewn out in the rock: and he rolled a great stone to the door of the sepulchre, and departed.

61 And there was Mary Măg-dă-lēne, and the other Mary, sitting over against the sepulchre.

62 ¶ Now the next day, that followed the day of the preparation, the chief priests and Pharisees came together unto Pilate,

63 Saying, Sir, we remember that that [q]deceiver said, while he was yet alive, After [r]three days I will rise again.

64 Command therefore that the sepulchre be made sure until the third day, lest his disciples come by night, and steal him away, and say unto the people, He is risen from the dead: so the last error shall be worse than the first.

65 Pilate said unto them, Ye have a watch: go your way, make *it* as sure as ye can.

66 So they went, and made the sepulchre sure, [s]sealing the stone, and setting a watch.

CHAPTER 28

IN the [a]end of the sabbath, as it began to dawn toward the first *day* of
he week, came Mary Măǵ-dă-lēne
and the other Mary to see the
epulchre.
2 And, behold, there [1]was a great
arthquake: for [c]the angel of the Lord
lescended from heaven, and came and
olled back the stone from the door,
ınd sat upon it.
3 His [d]countenance was like light-
ıing, and his raiment white as snow:
4 And for fear of him the keepers did
hake, and became as dead *men.*
5 And the angel answered and said
ınto the women, [e]Fear not ye: for I
now that ye seek Jesus, which was
rucified.
6 He is not here: for he is risen, as [f]he
aid. Come, see the place where the
ord lay.
7 And go quickly, and tell his dis-
iples that he is risen from the dead;
nd, behold, he [g]goeth before you into
Galilee; there shall ye see him: lo, I
ave told you.
8 And they departed quickly from
he sepulchre with fear and great joy;
nd did run to bring his disciples
vord.
9 ¶ And as they went to tell his dis-
iples, behold, [h]Jesus met them, say-
ng, All hail. And they came and held
im by the feet, and worshipped
im.
10 Then said Jesus unto them, Be
not afraid: go tell [i]my brethren that
they go into Galilee, and there shall
they see me.
11 ¶ Now when they were going, behold, some of the watch came into the
city, and shewed unto the chief priests
all the things that were done.
12 And when they were assembled
with the elders, and had taken counsel, they gave large money unto the
soldiers,
13 Saying, Say ye, His disciples came
by night, and stole him *away* while we
slept.
14 And if this come to the governor's
ears, we will persuade him, and secure
you.
15 So they took the money, and did
as they were taught: and this saying is
commonly reported among the Jews
until this day.
16 ¶ Then the eleven disciples went
away into Galilee, into a mountain
[j]where Jesus had appointed them.
17 And when they saw him, they
worshipped him: but some doubted.
18 And Jesus came and spake unto
them, saying, [k]All power is given unto
me in heaven and in earth.
19 ¶ Go ye therefore, and [2]teach all
nations, baptizing them in the name
of the Father, and of the Son, and of
the Holy Ghost:
20 Teaching [l]them to observe all
things whatsoever I have commanded
you: and, lo, I am with you alway,
even unto the end of the world. Ă-mĕn.

CHAP. 28
a ch. 12.1,2, 5,8. Mark 16.1. Luke 23.54, 56.
b ch. 27.56.
1 Or, had been.
c Mark 16.5. Luke 24.4. John 20.12.
d Dan. 10.6. ch. 17.2. Rev. 10.1. Rev. 18.1.
e Rev. 1.17.
f ch. 12.40. ch. 16.21. ch. 17.23. ch. 20.19.
g ch. 26.32. Mark 16.7.
h Mark 16.9. John 20.14. Rev. 1.17, 18.
i Rom. 8.29. Heb. 2.11.
j ch. 26.32. Mark 16.7.
k Dan. 7.13. Eph. 1.21. 1 Pet. 3.22. Rev. 17.14.
2 Or, make disciples, or, Christians of all nations.
l Acts 2.42.

Unty Acts 20:29,30

THE GOSPEL ACCORDING TO

ST. MARK

CHAPTER 1

THE beginning of the gospel
of Jesus Christ, [a]the Son of
God;
2 As it is written in the prophets, Be-
ıold, [b]I send my messenger before thy
ace, which shall prepare thy way be-
ore thee.
3 The [c]voice of one crying in the wil-
lerness, Prepare ye the way of the
ord, make his paths straight.
4 John did baptize in the wilderness,
ınd preach the baptism of repentance
for the remission of sins.
5 And there went out unto him all
he land of Judæa, and they of Jeru-
alem, and were all baptized of him in
the river of Jordan, confessing their
sins.
6 And John was clothed with camel's
hair, and with a girdle of a skin about
his loins; and he did eat [d]locusts and
wild honey;
7 And preached, saying, [e]There cometh one mightier than I after me, the
latchet of whose shoes I am not
worthy to stoop down and unloose.
8 I [f]indeed have baptized you with
water: but he shall baptize you [g]with
the Holy Ghost.
9 And [h]it came to pass in those days,
that Jesus came from Nazareth of
Galilee, and was baptized of John in
Jordan.

CHAP. 1
a Ps. 2.7. Luke 1.35. John 1.34. Rom. 8.3. 1 John 4.15.
b Mal. 3.1.
c Isa. 40.3. Luke 3.4. John 1.15, 23.
1 Or, unto.
d Lev. 11.22.
e Acts 13.25.
f Acts 11.16. Acts 19.4.
g Isa. 44.3. Joel 2.28. Acts 2.4. Acts 10.45. 1 Cor. 12.13.
h Matt. 3.13. Luke 3.21.

10 And [i]straightway coming up out
of the water, he saw the heavens
[2]opened, and the Spirit like a dove
descending upon him:
11 And there came a voice from
heaven, *saying*, [j]Thou art my beloved
Son, in whom I am well pleased.
12 And [k]immediately the Spirit
driveth him into the wilderness.
13 And he was there in the wilderness forty days, tempted of Satan;
and was with the wild beasts; [l]and the
angels ministered unto him.
14 Now after that John was put in
prison, Jesus came into Galilee,
preaching [m]the gospel of the kingdom
of God,
15 And saying, [n]The time is fulfilled,
and the kingdom of God is at hand:
repent ye, and believe the gospel.
16 Now [o]as he walked by the sea of
Galilee, he saw Simon and Andrew
his brother casting a net into the sea:
for they were fishers.
17 And Jesus said unto them, Come
ye after me, and I will make you to
become fishers of men.
18 And straightway [p]they forsook
their nets, and followed him.
19 And [q]when he had gone a little
further thence, he saw James the *son*
of Zĕb´-ĕ-dē͡e, and John his brother,
who also were in the ship mending
their nets.
20 And straightway he called them:
and they left their father Zĕb´-ĕ-dē͡e in
the ship with the hired servants, and
went after him.
21 And [r]they went into Că-pĕr´-nă-
ŭm; and straightway on the sabbath
day he entered into the synagogue,
and taught.
22 And [s]they were astonished at his
doctrine: for he taught them as one
that had authority, and not as the
scribes.
23 And [t]there was in their synagogue
a man with an unclean spirit; and he
cried out,
24 Saying, Let *us* alone; [u]what have
we to do with thee, thou Jesus of
Nazareth? art thou come to destroy
us? I know thee who thou art, the
[v]Holy One of God.
25 And Jesus rebuked him, saying,
Hold thy peace, and come out of him.
26 And when the unclean spirit had
[w]torn him, and cried with a loud voice,
he came out of him.
27 And they were all amazed, insomuch that they questioned among
themselves, saying, What thing is
this? what new doctrine *is* this? for
with authority commandeth he even
the unclean spirits, and they do obey
him.
28 And immediately his fame spread
abroad throughout all the region
round about Galilee.
29 And [x]forthwith, when they were
come out of the synagogue, they entered into the house of Simon and Andrew, with James and John.
30 But Simon's wife's mother lay
sick of a fever, and anon they tell him
of her.
31 And he came and took her by the
hand, and lifted her up; [y]and immediately the fever left her, and she
ministered unto them.
32 And [z]at even, when the sun did
set, they brought unto him all that
were diseased, and them that were
possessed with devils.
33 And all the city was gathered together at the door.
34 And he healed many that were
sick of divers diseases, and cast out
many devils; and [a]suffered not the
devils [3]to speak, because they knew
him.
35 And [b]in the morning, rising up a
great while before day, he went out,
and departed into a solitary place, and
[c]there prayed.
36 And Simon and they that were
with him followed after him.
37 And when they had found him,
they said unto him, All *men* seek for
thee.
38 And he said unto them, [d]Let us go
into the next towns, that I may
preach there also: for [e]therefore came
I forth.
39 And [f]he preached in their synagogues throughout all Galilee, and
[g]cast out devils.
40 And [h]there came a leper to him,
beseeching him, and kneeling down
to him, and saying unto him, If thou
wilt, thou canst [i]make me clean.
41 And Jesus, [j]moved with compassion, put forth *his* hand, and touched
him, and saith unto him, I will; be
thou clean.
42 And as soon as he had spoken,
immediately the leprosy departed
from him, and he was cleansed.
43 And he straitly charged him, and
forthwith sent him away;
44 And saith unto him, See thou say
nothing to any man: but go thy way,
shew thyself to the priest, and offer for
thy cleansing those things [k]which
Moses commanded, for a testimony
unto them.

i John 1.32.
2 Or, cloven, or, rent.
j Ps. 2.7. Matt. 3.17. 2 Pet. 1.17.
k Matt. 4.1. Luke 4.1.
l Matt. 4.11. 1 Tim. 3.16.
m Matt. 4.23.
n Ps. 110.3. Dan. 2.44. Dan. 9.25. Gal. 4.4. Eph. 1.10.
o Matt. 4.18. Luke 5.4. John 1.35, 44.
p Matt. 19. 27. Luke 5.11.
q Matt. 4.21.
r Matt. 4.13. Luke 4.31.
s Matt. 7.28.
t Matt. 12.43. ch. 5.2. ch. 7.25. ch. 9.25. Luke 4.33.
u 2 Sam. 16. 10. 2 Sam. 19. 22. Joel 3.4. Matt. 8.29. ch. 5.7. Luke 4.34. John 2.4.
v Ps. 16.10. Luke 4.34. Acts 2.31. Jas. 2.19.
w ch. 9.20.
x Matt. 8.14. Luke 4.38.
y Ps. 103.3.
z Luke 4.40.
a ch. 3.12. Luke 4.41. Acts 16.17.
3 Or, to say that they knew him.
b Luke 4.42.
c Ps. 69.1. Matt. 26.38-44. ch. 14.32-39. Heb. 5.7.
d Luke 4.43.
e Isa. 61.1. John 16.28. John 17.4.
f Matt. 4.23. Luke 4.44. John 9.4. 2 Tim. 4.2.
g Gen. 3.15.
h Num. 12. 10-15. Deut. 24.8, 9. 2 Sam. 3.29. 2 Ki. 5.5-27. Matt. 8.2. Matt. 11.5. Luke 5.12.
i Gen. 18.14. Jer. 32.17.
j Heb. 2.17. Heb. 4.15.
k Lev. 14.3,4, 10. Luke 5.14.

45 But [l]he went out, and began to
publish *it* much, and to blaze abroad
the matter, insomuch that Jesus could
no more openly enter into the city, but
was without in desert places: [m]and
they came to him from every quarter.

CHAPTER 2

AND again [a]he entered into Că-pĕr-
nă-ŭm, after *some* days; and it was
noised that he was in the house.
2 And straightway many were gathered together, insomuch that there
was no room to receive *them*, no, not
so much as about the door: and he
[b]preached the word unto them.
3 And they come unto him, bringing
one sick of the palsy, which was borne
of four.
4 And when they could not come
nigh unto him for the press, they uncovered the roof where he was: and
when they had broken *it* up, they let
down the bed wherein the sick of the
palsy lay.
5 When Jesus [c]saw their faith, he said
unto the sick of the palsy, [d]Son, thy
sins be forgiven thee.
6 But there were certain of the
scribes sitting there, and reasoning in
their hearts,
7 Why doth this *man* thus speak
blasphemies? [e]who can forgive sins
but God only?
8 And immediately [f]when Jesus perceived in his spirit that they so reasoned within themselves, he said unto
them, Why reason ye these things in
your hearts?
9 Whether [g]is it easier to say to the
sick of the palsy, *Thy* sins be forgiven
thee; or to say, Arise, and take up thy
bed, and walk?
10 But that ye may know that the
[h]Son of man hath power on earth to
forgive sins, (he saith to the sick of
the palsy,)
11 I say unto thee, Arise, and take up
thy bed, and go thy way into thine
house.
12 And [i]immediately he arose, took
up the bed, and went forth before
them all; insomuch that they were all
amazed, and glorified God, saying,
We never saw it on this fashion.
13 And [j]he went forth again by the
sea side; and all the multitude resorted
unto him, and he taught them.
14 And [k]as he passed by, he saw Levi
the *son* of Ăl-phæ-ŭs sitting [1]at the receipt of custom, and said unto him,
Follow me. And he arose and followed
him.
15 And [l]it came to pass, that, as Jesus
sat at meat in his house, many publicans and sinners sat also together with
Jesus and his disciples: for there were
many, and they followed him.
16 And when [m]the scribes and Pharisees saw him eat with publicans and
sinners, they said unto his disciples,
How is it that he eateth and drinketh
with publicans and sinners?
17 When Jesus heard *it*, he saith unto
them, [n]They that are whole have no
need of the physician, but they that
are sick: I came not to call the righteous, but sinners to repentance.
18 And [o]the disciples of John and of
the Pharisees used to fast: and they
come and say unto him, Why do the
disciples of John and of the Pharisees
fast, but thy disciples fast not?
19 And Jesus said unto them, Can
the children of [p]the bridechamber
fast, while the bridegroom is with
them? as long as they have the [q]bride-
groom with them, they cannot fast.
20 But the days will come, when the
bridegroom shall be taken away from
them, and then shall they fast in those
days.
21 No man also seweth a piece of
[2]new cloth on an old garment: else
the new piece that filled it up taketh
away from the old, and the rent is
made worse.
22 And no man putteth new wine into old bottles: else the new wine doth
burst the bottles, and the wine is spilled, and the bottles will be marred:
but new wine must be put into new
bottles.
23 And [r]it came to pass, that he went
through the corn fields on the sabbath day; and his disciples began,
as they went, [s]to pluck the ears of
corn.
24 And the Pharisees said unto him,
Behold, why do they on the sabbath
day that which is not lawful?
25 And he said unto them, Have ye
never read [t]what David did, when he
had need, and was an hungred, he, and
they that were with him?
26 How he went into the house of
God in the days of Ă-bī-ă-thär the
high priest, and did eat the shewbread, [u]which is not lawful to eat but
for the priests, and gave also to them
which were with him?
27 And he said unto them, The sabbath was made for man, and not man
for the sabbath:
28 Therefore [v]the Son of man is Lord
also of the sabbath.

l Luke 5.15.
m ch. 2.13.
CHAP. 2
a Matt. 9.1. Luke 5.18.
b Isa. 61.1. Matt. 5.2. ch. 6.32. Luke 8.1. Eph. 2.17. Heb. 2.3.
c Gen. 22.12. Heb. 4.13.
d Ps. 103.3. Isa. 53.11.
e Job 14.4. Ps. 130.4. Isa. 43.25. Rom. 8.33.
f 1 Sam. 16.7. 1 Chr. 29.17. Ps. 7.9. Ps. 139.1. Jer. 17.10. Matt. 9.4. Heb. 4.13. Rev. 2.23.
g Matt. 9.5.
h Isa. 53.11. Dan. 7.13.
i Ps. 33.9.
j Matt. 9.9.
k Luke 5.27.
1 Or, at the place where the custom was received.
l Matt. 9.10.
m Isa. 65.5.
n Matt. 9.12, 13. Matt. 18.11. Luke 5.31, 32. Luke 15.7. Luke 19.10. 1 Tim. 1.15.
o Matt. 9.14. Luke 5.33.
p Song 1.4.
q Ps. 45. Isa. 54.5. Matt. 22.2. John 3.29. 2 Cor. 11.2. Eph. 5.25, 32. Rev. 19.7. Rev. 21.1.
2 Or, raw, or, unwrought. Matt. 9.16.
r Matt. 12.1. Luke 6.1.
s Deut. 23.25.
t 1 Sam. 21.6.
u Ex. 25.30. Ex. 29.32, 33. Lev. 24.9.
v Matt. 12.8. Eph. 1.20, 21. 1 Pet. 3. 22.

CHAPTER 3

AND [a]he entered again into the synagogue; and there was a man there which had a withered hand.

2 And they watched him, whether he would heal him on the sabbath day; that they might accuse him.

3 And he saith unto the man which had the withered hand, [1]Stand forth.

4 And he saith unto them, Is it lawful to do good on the sabbath days, or to do evil? to save life, or to kill? But they held their peace.

5 And when he had looked round about on them with [b]anger, being grieved for the [2]hardness of their hearts, he saith unto the man, Stretch forth thine hand. And he stretched *it* out: and his hand was restored whole as the other.

6 And [c]the Pharisees went forth, and straightway took counsel with [d]the Hĕ-rō´-dĭ-ăns against him, how they might destroy him.

7 But Jesus withdrew himself with his disciples to the sea: and a great multitude from Galilee followed him, [e]and from Judæa,

8 And from Jerusalem, and from Ī-dū-mæ´-ă, and *from* beyond Jordan; and they about Tyre and Sī´-dŏn, a great multitude, when they had heard what great things he did, came unto him.

9 And he spake to his disciples, that a small ship should wait on him because of the multitude, lest they should throng him.

10 For he had healed many; insomuch that they [3]pressed upon him for to touch him, as many as had plagues.

11 And [f]unclean spirits, when they saw him, fell down before him, and cried, saying, [g]Thou art the Son of God.

12 And [h]he straitly charged them that they should not make him known.

13 And [i]he goeth up into a mountain, and calleth *unto him* whom he would: and they came unto him.

14 And he ordained twelve, that they should be with him, and that he might send them forth to preach,

15 And to have power to heal sicknesses, and to cast out devils:

16 And Simon [j]he surnamed Peter;

17 And James the *son* of Zĕb´-ĕ-dēe, and John the brother of James; and he surnamed them Bō-ăn-ĕr´-gēs, which is, [k]The sons of thunder:

18 And Andrew, and Philip, and Bartholomew, and Matthew, and Thomas, and James the *son* of Ăl-phæ´-ŭs, and [l]Thăd-dæ´-ŭs, and Simon the Canaanite,

19 And Judas Iscariot, which also betrayed him: and they went [4]into an house.

20 And the multitude cometh together again, [m]so that they could not so much as eat bread.

21 And when his [5]friends heard *of it*, they went out to lay hold on him: for they said, He is beside himself.

22 ¶ And the scribes which came down from Jerusalem said, [n]He hath Bē-ĕl´-zĕ-bŭb, and by the prince of the devils casteth he out devils.

23 And [o]he called them *unto him*, and said unto them in parables, How can Satan cast out Satan?

24 And if a kingdom be divided against itself, that kingdom cannot stand.

25 And if a house be divided against itself, that house cannot stand.

26 And if Satan rise up against himself, and be divided, he cannot stand, but hath an end.

27 No [p]man can enter into a strong man's house, and spoil his goods, except he will first bind the strong man; and then he will spoil his house.

28 Verily [q]I say unto you, All sins shall be forgiven unto the sons of men, and blasphemies wherewith soever they shall blaspheme:

29 But he that shall blaspheme against the Holy Ghost hath [r]never forgiveness, but is in danger of eternal damnation:

30 Because they said, He hath an unclean spirit.

31 ¶ There [s]came then his brethren and his mother, and, standing without, sent unto him, calling him.

32 And the multitude sat about him, and they said unto him, Behold, [t]thy mother and thy brethren without seek for thee.

33 And he answered them, saying, Who is my mother, or my brethren?

34 And he looked round about on them which sat about him, and said, [u]Behold my mother and my brethren!

35 For whosoever shall do the will of God, the same is my brother, and my sister, and mother.

CHAPTER 4

AND [a]he began again to teach by the sea side: and there was gathered unto him a great multitude, so that he entered into a ship, and sat in the sea; and the whole multitude was by the sea on the land.

CHAP. 3

a Matt. 12.9. Luke 6.6.

1 Arise, stand forth in the midst. Dan. 6.10. Phil. 1.14.

b 1 Ki. 19.10. Ps. 69.9. Ps. 119. 139. ch. 11.15-17. John 2.14-17.

2 Or, blindness.

c Matt. 12. 14.

d Matt. 22. 16.

e Luke 6.17.

3 Or, rushed.

f Matt. 8.31. ch. 1.23. ch. 5.5-7. Luke 4.41.

g Matt. 4.3,6. Matt. 8.29. Matt. 14.33. ch. 1.1. Luke 8.28. Acts 16.17.

h Matt. 12.16. ch. 1.25,34. Luke 4.41.

i Matt. 10.1. Luke 6.12. Luke 9.1.

j John 1.42.

k Isa. 58.1.

l Luke 6.16. Acts 1.13. Jude 1.

4 Or, home.

m ch. 6.31.

5 Or, kinsmen. John 7.5. John 10.20.

n Matt. 9.34. Matt. 10.25. Matt. 12.24. Luke 11.15. John 8.48, 52.

o Matt. 12. 25. Luke 11.17-20.

p Isa. 49.24. Matt. 12.29.

q Matt. 12.31. Luke 12.10. Heb. 6.4-8. Heb. 10.26-31. 1 John 5.16.

r Matt. 25.46. ch. 12.40. Acts 7.51. 2 Thes. 1.9. Heb. 6.4. Jude 7.13.

s Matt.12.46. Luke 8.19.

t Matt. 13.55. ch. 6.3. John 7.3.

u Deut. 33.9. Rom. 8.29. Heb. 2.11.

CHAP. 4

a Matt. 13.1. Luke 8.4.

2 And he taught them many things by parables, [b]and said unto them in his doctrine,

3 Hearken; Behold, there went out a sower to sow:

4 And it came to pass, as he sowed, some fell by the way side, and the fowls of the air came and devoured it up.

5 And some fell on stony ground, where it had not much earth; and immediately it sprang up, because it had no depth of earth:

6 But when the sun was up, it was scorched; and because it had no root, it withered away.

7 And some fell among thorns, and the thorns grew up, and choked it, and it yielded no fruit.

8 And other fell on good ground, and [c]did yield fruit that sprang up and increased; and brought forth, some thirty, and some sixty, and some an hundred.

9 And he said unto them, He that hath ears to hear, let him hear.

10 And when he was alone, they that were about him with the twelve [d]asked of him the parable.

11 And he said unto them, Unto you it is given to know the [e]mystery of the kingdom of God: but unto [f]them that are without, all *these* things are done in parables:

12 That [g]seeing they may see, and not perceive; and hearing they may hear, and not understand; lest at any time they should be converted, and *their* sins should be forgiven them.

13 And he said unto them, Know ye not this parable? and how then will ye know all parables?

14 ¶ The [h]sower soweth the word.

15 And these are they by the way side, where the word is sown; but when they have heard, [i]Satan cometh immediately, and taketh away the word that was sown in their hearts.

16 And these are they likewise which are sown on stony ground; who, when they have heard the word, immediately receive it with gladness;

17 And have [j]no root in themselves, and so endure but for a time: afterward, when affliction or persecution ariseth for the word's sake, immediately they are offended.

18 And these are they which are sown among thorns; such as hear the word,

19 And the cares of this world, and [k]the deceitfulness of riches, and the lusts of other things entering in, choke the word, and it becometh unfruitful.

20 And these are they which are sown on good [l]ground; such as hear the word, and receive *it*, and bring forth fruit, some thirtyfold, some sixty, and some an hundred.

21 ¶ And [m]he said unto them, Is a candle brought to be put under [1]a bushel, or under a bed? and not to be set on a candlestick?

22 For [n]there is nothing hid, which shall not be manifested; neither was any thing kept secret, but that it should come abroad.

23 If [o]any man have ears to hear, let him hear.

24 And he said unto them, [p]Take heed what ye hear: [q]with what measure ye mete, it shall be measured to you: and unto you that hear shall more be given.

25 For [r]he that hath, to him shall be given: and he that hath not, from him shall be taken even that which he hath.

26 ¶ And he said, [s]So is the kingdom of God, as if a man should cast seed into the ground;

27 And should sleep, and rise night and day, and the seed should spring and grow up, he knoweth not how.

28 For the earth bringeth forth fruit of herself; first the blade, then the ear, after that the full corn in the ear.

29 But when the fruit is [2]brought forth, immediately [t]he putteth in the sickle, because the harvest is come.

30 ¶ And he said, [u]Whereunto shall we liken the kingdom of God? or with what comparison shall we compare it?

31 *It is* like a grain of mustard seed, which, when it is sown in the earth, is less than all the seeds that be in the earth:

32 But when it is sown, it [v]groweth up, and becometh greater than all herbs, and shooteth out great branches; so that the fowls of the air may lodge under the shadow of it.

33 And [w]with many such parables spake he the word unto them, as they were able to hear *it*.

34 But without a parable spake he not unto them: and when they were alone, he expounded all things to his disciples.

35 And the [x]same day, when the even was come, he saith unto them, Let us pass over unto the other side.

36 And when they had sent away the multitude, they took him even as he was in the ship. And there were also with him other little ships.

b ch. 12.38.
c John 15.5. Col. 1.6.
d Pro. 2.1. Pro. 4.7. Pro. 13.20. Matt. 13.10. Luke 8.9.
e 1 Cor. 2.10.
f 1 Cor. 1.18. 1 Cor. 5.12. Col. 4.5. 1 Thes. 4.12. 1 Tim. 3.7.
g Isa. 6.9. Isa. 44.18. Jer. 5.21. Matt. 13.14. Luke 8.10. John 12.40. Acts 28.26. Rom. 11.8.
h Matt. 13.19. Eph. 3.8. 1 Pet. 1.23, 25.
i 2 Cor. 2.11. 2 Cor. 4.4. 1 Pet. 5.8.
j Job 27.10.
k Ps. 52.7. Pro. 23.5. Eccl. 5.13. Luke 18.24. Acts 5.1. 1 Tim. 6.9, 17. Titus 1.11.
l Rom. 7.4. 2 Cor. 5.17. 2 Pet. 1.4.
m Matt. 5.15. Luke 8.16. Luke 11.33.
1 The word in the original signifieth a less measure, as at Matt. 5.15.
n Matt. 10.26. Luke 12.2. Acts 14.20. 1 John 1.2.
o Matt. 11.15.
p 1 John 4.1.
q Matt. 7.2. Luke 6.38. 2 Cor. 9.6.
r Matt. 13.12. Matt. 25.29. Luke 8.18. Luke 19.26.
s Matt. 3.2. Matt. 4.17. Matt. 13.24.
2 Or, ripe. Eph. 4.13.
t Rev. 14.15.
u Lam. 2.13. Matt. 11.16. Matt. 13.31. Luke 13.18. Acts 2.41. Acts 4.4. Acts 5.14. Acts 19.20.
v Mal. 1.11. Rev. 11.15.
w Matt. 13. 24. John 16.12.
x Isa. 42.4. Matt. 8.18, 23. Luke 8.22.

37 And there arose a great storm of wind, and the waves beat into the ship, so that it was now full.

38 And he was in the hinder part of the ship, asleep on a pillow: and they awake him, and say unto him, Master, carest thou not that we perish?

39 And he arose, and [y]rebuked the wind, and said unto the sea, Peace, be still. And the wind ceased, and there was a great calm.

40 And he said unto them, Why are ye so fearful? how is it that ye have no faith?

41 And they [z]feared exceedingly, and said one to another, What manner of man is this, that even the wind and the sea obey him?

CHAPTER 5

AND [a]they came over unto the other side of the sea, into the country of the Găd´-ă-rēneṡ.

2 And when he was come out of the ship, immediately there met him out of the tombs a man with an unclean spirit,

3 Who had *his* dwelling among the tombs; and no man could bind him, no, not with chains:

4 Because that he had been often bound with fetters and chains, and the chains had been plucked asunder by him, and the fetters broken in pieces: neither could any *man* tame him.

5 And always, night and day, he was in the mountains, and in the tombs, crying, and cutting himself with stones.

6 But when he saw Jesus afar off, he ran and [b]worshipped him,

7 And cried with a loud voice, and said, What have I to do with thee, Jesus, *thou* Son of the most high God? I adjure thee by God, that thou torment me not.

8 For he said unto him, Come out of the man, *thou* unclean spirit.

9 And he asked him, What *is* thy name? And he answered, saying, My name *is* Legion: for we are many.

10 And he besought him much that he would not send them away out of the country.

11 Now there was there nigh unto the mountains a great herd of [c]swine feeding.

12 And all the devils besought him, saying, Send us into the swine, that we may enter into them.

13 And forthwith Jesus [d]gave them leave. And the unclean spirits went out, and entered into the swine: and the herd ran violently down a steep place into the sea, (they were about two thousand;) and were choked in the sea.

14 And they that fed the swine fled, and told *it* in the city, and in the country. And they went out to see what it was that was done.

15 And they come to Jesus, and see him that was possessed with the devil, and had the legion, sitting, and clothed, and [e]in his right mind: and they were afraid.

16 And they that saw *it* told them how it befell to him that was possessed with the devil, and *also* concerning the swine.

17 And [f]they began to pray him to depart out of their coasts.

18 And when he was come into the ship, he [g]that had been possessed with the devil prayed him that he might be with him.

19 Howbeit Jesus suffered him not, but saith unto him, Go home to thy friends, and tell them how great things the Lord hath done for thee, and hath had compassion on thee.

20 And he departed, and [h]began to publish in Dĕ-căp´-ŏ-lĭs how great things Jesus had done for him: and all *men* did marvel.

21 And [i]when Jesus was passed over again by ship unto the other side, much people gathered unto him: and he was nigh unto the sea.

22 And, [j]behold, there cometh one of the rulers of the synagogue, Jā-ī´-rŭs by name; and when he saw him, he fell at his feet,

23 And besought him greatly, saying, My little daughter lieth at the point of death: *I pray thee*, come and lay thy hands on her, that she may be healed; and she shall live.

24 And *Jesus* went with him; and much people followed him, and thronged him.

25 And a certain woman, which [k]had an issue of blood twelve years,

26 And had suffered many things of many physicians, and had spent all that she had, and [l]was nothing bettered, but rather grew worse,

27 When she had heard of Jesus, came in the press behind, [m]and touched his garment.

28 For she said, If I may touch but his clothes, I shall be whole.

29 And [n]straightway the fountain of her blood was dried up; and she felt in *her* body that she was healed of that plague.

y Job 28.11. Job 38.11. Ps. 29.10. Ps. 65.5. Ps. 89.9. Ps. 93.4. Ps. 107.23-29. Ps. 135.5,6. Nah. 1.4. Matt. 8.24-27. ch. 9.25. Luke 4.39.
z Ps. 33.8,9. Ps. 46.1-3. Isa. 43.2,3. Matt. 8.26. Luke 8.25. John 6.19, 20.

CHAP. 5

a Matt. 8.28. Luke 8.26.
b Ps. 66.4. Acts 16.17. Phil. 2.10, 11.
c Lev. 11.7. Deut. 14.8. Isa. 65.4. Luke 15.15.
d 1 Ki. 22.22. Job 1.12. Job 2.6. Job 12.16. Matt. 28.18. Luke 4.36. Eph. 1.20, 23. Col. 2.10. Heb. 2.8.
e Rom. 16.20. 1 John 3.8.
f Gen. 26.16. Deut. 5.25. 1 Ki. 17.18. Job 21.14. Job 22.17. Matt. 8.34. ch. 1.24. Luke 5.8. Luke 8.37. Acts 16.39. 1 Cor. 2.14.
g Ps. 116.12. Luke 8.38. Luke 17.15, 17. Luke 23.42, 43. Phil. 1.23.
h Ex. 15.2. Ps. 116.16. Isa. 63.7. Matt. 4.25. ch. 7.31.
i Gen. 49.10. Matt. 9.1.
j Matt. 9.18. Luke 8.41.
k Lev. 15.25. Matt. 9.20. Luke 8.43.
l Ps. 108.12.
m ch. 3.10. Acts 5.15. Acts 19.12.
n Ex. 15.26. Luke 6.19. Luke 8.46, 47.

30 And Jesus, immediately knowing in himself that [o]virtue had gone out of him, turned him about in the press, and said, Who touched my clothes?

31 And his disciples said unto him, Thou seest the multitude thronging thee, and sayest thou, Who touched me?

32 And he looked round about to see her that had done this thing.

33 But the woman fearing and trembling, knowing what was done in her, came and fell down before him, and told him all the truth.

34 And he said unto her, Daughter, [p]thy faith hath made thee whole; go in peace, and be whole of thy plague.

35 While [q]he yet spake, there came from the ruler of the synagogue's *house certain* which said, Thy daughter is dead: why troublest thou the Master any further?

36 As soon as Jesus heard the word that was spoken, he saith unto the ruler of the synagogue, [r]Be not afraid, only believe.

37 And he suffered no man to follow him, save Peter, and James, and John the brother of James.

38 And he cometh to the house of the ruler of the synagogue, and seeth the tumult, and them that wept and wailed greatly.

39 And when he was come in, he saith unto them, Why make ye this ado, and weep? the damsel is not dead, but [s]sleepeth.

40 And they laughed him to scorn. But [t]when he had put them all out, he taketh the father and the mother of the damsel, and them that were with him, and entereth in where the damsel was lying.

41 And he took the damsel by the hand, and said unto her, Tăl′-ĭ-thă cū′-mī; which is, being interpreted, Damsel, I say unto thee, arise.

42 And [u]straightway the damsel arose, and walked; for she was *of the age* of twelve years. And they were astonished with a great astonishment.

43 And [v]he charged them straitly that no man should know it; and commanded that something should be given her to eat.

CHAPTER 6

AND [a]he went out from thence, and came into his own country; and his disciples follow him.

2 And when the sabbath day was come, he began to teach in the synagogue: and many hearing *him* were astonished, saying, [b]From whence hath this *man* these things? and what wisdom *is* this which is given unto him, that even such mighty works are wrought by his hands?

3 Is not [c]this the carpenter, the son of Mary, [d]the brother of James, and Jō′-sēs, and of Juda, and Simon? and are not his sisters here with us? And they [e]were offended at him.

4 But Jesus said unto them, [f]A prophet is not without honour, but in his own country, and among his own kin, and in his own house.

5 And [g]he could there do no mighty work, save that he laid his hands upon a few sick folk, and healed *them*.

6 And [h]he marvelled because of their unbelief. [i]And he went round about the villages, teaching.

7 ¶ And [j]he called *unto him* the twelve, and began to send them forth by two and two; and gave them power over unclean spirits;

8 And commanded them that they should take nothing for *their* journey, save a staff only; no scrip, no bread, no [1]money in *their* purse:

9 But [k]*be* shod with sandals; and not put on two coats.

10 And [l]he said unto them, In what place soever ye enter into an house, there abide till ye depart from that place.

11 And [m]whosoever shall not receive you, nor hear you, when ye depart thence, shake [n]off the dust under your feet for a testimony against them. [o]Verily I say unto you, It shall be more tolerable for Sodom [2]and Gō-mŏr′-rhă in the day of judgment, than for that city.

12 And they went out, and preached that men should repent.

13 And they cast out many devils, [p]and anointed with oil many that were sick, and healed *them*.

14 And [q]king Herod heard *of him;* (for his name was spread abroad:) and he said, That John the Baptist was risen from the dead, and therefore mighty works do shew forth themselves in him.

15 Others [r]said, That it is Ē-lī′-ăs. And others said, That it is a prophet, or as one of the prophets.

16 But [s]when Herod heard *thereof*, he said, It is John, whom I beheaded: he is risen from the dead.

17 For Herod himself had sent forth and laid hold upon John, and bound him in prison for Hĕ-rō′-dĭ-ăs' sake,

o Luke 6.19.
p Matt. 9.22. ch. 10.52. Luke 7.50. Luke 8.48. Luke 17.19. Luke 18.42. Acts 14.9.
q Luke 8.49.
r Ps. 103.13. John 11.25, 40.
s Dan. 12.2. John 11.11. Acts 20.9. 1 Cor. 11.30. 1 Cor. 15.20. 1 Thes. 4.14. 1 Thes. 5.10.
t Acts 9.40.
u Ps. 33.9.
v Matt. 12.16. Matt. 17.9. ch. 3.12. Luke 5.14.

CHAP. 6

a Matt. 13. 54. Luke 4.16.
b John 6.42. John 7.15.
c Isa. 53.2,3. 1 Cor. 1.23.
d Matt. 12.46. Gal. 1.19.
e Matt. 11.6.
f Jer. 11.21. Jer. 12.6. Matt. 13.57. Luke 4.24. John 4.44.
g Gen. 19.22.
h Isa. 59.1,2, 16.
i Matt. 9.35.
j Matt. 10.1. Luke 9.1.
1 The word signifieth a piece of brass money, in value somewhat less than a farthing, but here it is taken in general for money.
k Acts 12.8.
l Matt. 10.11.
m Matt. 10. 14.
n Acts 13.51. Acts 18.6.
o Heb. 10.31.
2 or.
p Jas. 5.14.
q Matt. 14.1.
r Matt. 16.14.
s Luke 3.19.

his brother Philip's wife: for he had
married her.
18 For John had said unto Herod,
It [t]is not lawful for thee to have thy
brother's wife.
19 Therefore Hĕ-rō-dĭ-ăs had [3]a
quarrel against him, and would have
killed him; but she could not:
20 For Herod [u]feared John, knowing that he was a just man and an holy,
and [4]observed him; and when he
heard him, he did many things, and
heard him gladly.
21 And [v]when a convenient day was
come, that Herod [w]on his birthday
made a supper to his lords, high captains, and chief *estates* of Galilee;
22 And when the daughter of the said
Hĕ-rō-dĭ-ăs came in, [x]and danced, and
pleased Herod and them that sat with
him, the king said unto the damsel,
Ask of me whatsoever thou wilt, and
I will give *it* thee.
23 And he sware unto her, Whatsoever [y]thou shalt ask of me, I will give
it thee, unto the half of my kingdom.
24 And she went forth, and said unto
her mother, What shall I ask? And she
said, [z]The head of John the Baptist.
25 And she came in straightway with
haste unto the king, and asked, saying,
I will that thou give me by and by in a
charger the head of John the Baptist.
26 And the king was exceeding sorry;
yet for his oath's sake, and for their
sakes which sat with him, he would
not reject her.
27 And immediately the king sent [5]an
executioner, and commanded his head
to be brought: and he went and beheaded him in the prison,
28 And brought his head in a charger, and gave it to the damsel: and the
damsel gave it to her mother.
29 And when his disciples heard *of*
it, they came and [a]took up his corpse,
and laid it in a tomb.
30 And [b]the apostles gathered themselves together unto Jesus, and told
him all things, both what they had
done, and what they had taught.
31 And [c]he said unto them, Come ye
yourselves apart into a desert place,
and rest a while; for there [d]were many
coming and going, and they had no
leisure so much as to eat.
32 And they departed into a desert
place by ship privately.
33 And the people saw them departing, and many knew him, and ran
afoot thither out of all cities, and out-
went them, and came together unto
him.

34 And Jesus, when he came out,
saw much people, and [e]was moved
with compassion toward them, because they were as sheep not having
a shepherd: and he [f]began to teach
them many things.
35 And [g]when the day was now far
spent, his disciples came unto him,
and said, This is a desert place, and
now the time *is* far passed:
36 Send them away, that they may go
into the country round about, and
into the villages, and buy themselves
bread: for they have nothing to eat.
37 He answered and said unto them,
Give ye them to eat. And they say unto
him, [h]Shall we go and buy two hundred [6]pennyworth of bread, and give
them to eat?
38 He saith unto them, How many
loaves have ye? go and see. And when
they knew, they say, Five, [i]and two
fishes.
39 And he commanded them to make
all sit down [7]by companies upon the
green grass.
40 And they sat down in ranks, by
hundreds, and by fifties.
41 And when he had taken the five
loaves and the two fishes, he looked
up to heaven, and [j]blessed, and brake
the loaves, and gave *them* to his disciples to set before them; and the two
fishes divided he among them all.
42 And they did all eat, and were
filled.
43 And they took up twelve baskets
full of the fragments, and of the fishes.
44 And they that did eat of the loaves
were about five thousand men.
45 And [k]straightway he constrained
his disciples to get into the ship, and
to go to the other side before [8]unto
Bĕth-sā-ĭ-dă, while he sent away the
people.
46 And when he had sent them away,
he departed into a mountain to pray.
47 And [l]when even was come, the
ship was in the midst of the sea, and
he alone on the land.
48 And he saw them toiling in row-
ing; for the wind was contrary unto
them: and about the fourth watch of
the night he cometh unto them, walking upon the sea, and [m]would have
passed by them.
49 But when they saw him walking
upon the sea, they supposed it had
been a spirit, and cried out:
50 For they all saw him, and were
troubled. And immediately he talked
with them, and saith unto them, Be of
good cheer: it is I; be not afraid.

t Lev. 18.16. Lev. 20.21. 2 Tim. 4.2. Heb. 13.4.
3 Or, an inward grudge.
u Matt. 21.26.
4 Or, kept him, or, saved him.
v Matt. 14.6.
w Gen. 40.20.
x Isa. 3.16.
y Esth. 5.3,6. Esth. 7.2. Eccl. 5.2. Rom. 1.28-31. Heb. 11.36-38. Jas. 2.13. Rev. 6.9-11.
z ver.16. Pro. 12.10. Matt. 3.1. Matt. 14.8. ch. 1.4.
5 Or, one of his guard.
a 1 Ki. 13.29, 30. 2 Chr. 24.15, 16. Matt. 14.12. Acts 8.2.
b Luke 9.10.
c Matt. 14.13.
d ch. 3.20.
e Ps. 86.15. Ps. 111.4. Ps. 145.8. Matt. 9.36. Matt. 14.14. Heb. 2.17. Heb. 4.15. Heb. 5.2.
f Isa. 54.13. Isa. 61.1. Luke 9.11.
g Matt. 14.15. Luke 9.12.
h Num. 11. 13,22. 2 Ki. 4.43. Matt. 15.33. John 6.7.
6 The Roman penny is sevenpence halfpenny. Matt. 18.28.
i Matt. 14.17. Matt. 15.34. ch. 8.5. Luke 9.13. John 6.9.
7 banquets, banquets. 1 Cor. 14.40.
j 1 Sam. 9.13. Matt. 14.15, 19. Matt. 26.26. ch. 8.2-9. Acts 27.35. 1 Tim. 4.4,5.
k Matt. 14. 22. John 6.17.
8 Or, over against Bethsaida.
l Matt. 14.23. John 6.16, 17.
m Luke 24. 28.

51 And he went up unto them into
the ship; and the wind ceased: and
they were sore amazed in themselves
beyond measure, and wondered.
52 For [n]they considered not *the*
miracle of the loaves: for [o]their heart
was hardened.
53 And [p]when they had passed over,
they came into the land of Gĕn-nĕś-
ă-rĕt, and drew to the shore.
54 And when they were come out of
the ship, straightway they knew him,
55 And ran through that whole region round about, and began to carry
about in beds those that were sick,
where they heard he was.
56 And whithersoever he entered, into villages, or cities, or country, they
laid the sick in the streets, and besought him that they [q]might touch if
it were but the border of his garment:
and as many as touched [9]him were
made whole.

CHAPTER 7

THEN [a]came together unto him
the Pharisees, and certain of the
scribes, which came from Jerusalem.
2 And when they saw some of his disciples eat bread with [1]defiled, that is
to say, with unwashen, hands, they
found fault.
3 For the Pharisees, and all the Jews,
except they wash *their* hands [2]oft, eat
not, holding the tradition of the
elders.
4 And *when they come* from the
market, except they wash, they eat
not. And many other things there be,
which they have received to hold, *as*
the washing of cups, and [3]pots, brasen
vessels, and of [4]tables.
5 Then [b]the Pharisees and scribes
asked him, Why walk not thy disciples according to the tradition of
the elders, but eat bread with unwash-
en hands?
6 He answered and said unto them,
Well hath Ē-ṡāí-ăs prophesied of you
hypocrites, as it is written, This [c]peo-
ple honoureth me with *their* lips, but
their heart is far from me.
7 Howbeit in vain do they worship
me, teaching *for* doctrines the commandments of men.
8 For laying aside the commandment of God, ye hold the tradition of
men, *as* the washing of pots and cups:
and many other such like things ye do.
9 And he said unto them, Full well
ye [5]reject the commandment of God,
that ye may keep your own tradition.
10 For Moses said, [d]Honour thy

n Matt. 16.9-11. ch. 7.18. ch. 8.17.
o Jer. 17.9. ch. 3.5. ch. 16.14. Rom. 8.7. Heb. 3.13.
p Matt. 14.34. Luke 5.1.
q Matt. 9.20. Luke 7.14. Luke 8.44. Acts 5.15.
9 Or, it.

CHAP. 7

a Matt. 15.1.
1 Or, common.
2 with the fist, or, diligently. Theophylact, up to the elbow.
3 Sextarius is about a pint and a half.
4 Or, beds.
b Matt. 15.2.
c Isa. 29.13. Eze. 33.31. Hos. 8.2,3. Matt. 15.8. John 5.42. Titus 1.14, 16. Jas. 2.14-17.
5 Or, frustrate. Isa. 24.5. Titus 1.14.
d Ex. 20.12. Deut. 5.16. Matt. 15.4.
e Ex. 21.17. Lev. 20.9. Pro. 20.20.
f Matt. 15.5. Matt. 23.18. 1 Tim. 5.8.
g Acts 10.14, 15. Rom. 14.17. 1 Cor. 8.8. 1 Tim. 4.4. Titus 1.15.
h Matt. 11. 15.
i Matt. 15.15.
j Gen. 6.5. Gen. 8.21. Job 14.4. Job 15.14-17. Matt. 15.19. Acts 8.22. Gal. 5.19. Titus 3.3.
6 covetousnesses, wickednesses.
k Matt. 15. 21.
7 Or, Gentile.
l Matt. 7.6. Matt. 10.5, 6. Matt. 15.23-28. Acts 13.46. Rom. 9.4. Eph. 2.12.

father and thy mother; and, Whoso
[e]curseth father or mother, let him die
the death:
11 But ye say, If a man shall say to
his father or mother, *It is* [f]Côr-băn,
that is to say, a gift, by whatsoever
thou mightest be profited by me; *he*
shall be free.
12 And ye suffer him no more to do
ought for his father or his mother;
13 Making the word of God of none
effect through your tradition, which
ye have delivered: and many such like
things do ye.
14 ¶ And when he had called all the
people *unto him*, he said unto them,
Hearken unto me every one *of you*,
and understand:
15 There is [g]nothing from without a
man, that entering into him can defile
him: but the things which come out
of him, those are they that defile the
man.
16 If [h]any man have ears to hear, let
him hear.
17 And [i]when he was entered into
the house from the people, his disciples asked him concerning the
parable.
18 And he saith unto them, Are ye
so without understanding also? Do
ye not perceive, that whatsoever thing
from without entereth into the man,
it cannot defile him;
19 Because it entereth not into his
heart, but into the belly, and goeth
out into the draught, purging all
meats?
20 And he said, That which cometh
out of the man, that defileth the man.
21 For [j]from within, out of the heart
of men, proceed evil thoughts, adulteries, fornications, murders,
22 Thefts, [6]covetousness, wickedness,
deceit, lasciviousness, an evil eye,
blasphemy, pride, foolishness:
23 All these evil things come from
within, and defile the man.
24 ¶ And [k]from thence he arose, and
went into the borders of Tyre and
Ṡī́-dŏn, and entered into an house, and
would have no man know *it:* but he
could not be hid.
25 For a *certain* woman, whose
young daughter had an unclean spirit,
heard of him, and came and fell at his
feet:
26 The woman was a [7]Greek, a Sȳ-
rō-phē-nĭḉ-ĭ-ăn by nation; and she
besought him that he would cast forth
the devil out of her daughter.
27 But Jesus said unto her, [l]Let the
children first be filled: for it is not

meet to take the children's bread, and to cast *it* unto the dogs.

28 And she answered and said unto him, Yes, Lord: yet the dogs under the table eat of the children's crumbs.

29 And he said unto her, For this saying go thy way; [m]the devil is gone out of thy daughter.

30 And when she was come to her house, she found the devil gone out, and her daughter laid upon the bed.

31 ¶ And [n]again, departing from the coasts of Tyre and Sī-dŏn, he came unto the sea of Galilee, through the midst of the coasts of Dĕ-căp-ŏ-lĭs.

32 And [o]they bring unto him one that was deaf, and had an impediment in his speech; and they beseech him to put his hand upon him.

33 And he took him aside from the multitude, and put his fingers into his ears, and he [p]spit, and touched his tongue;

34 And [q]looking up to heaven, he [r]sighed, and saith unto him, Ĕph-phă-thă, that is, Be opened.

35 And [s]straightway his ears were opened, and the string of his tongue was loosed, and he spake plain.

36 And [t]he charged them that they should tell no man: but the more he charged them, so much the more a great deal they published *it;*

37 And were beyond measure astonished, saying, He hath done all things well: he maketh both the deaf to hear, and the dumb to speak.

CHAPTER 8

IN those days [a]the multitude being very great, and having nothing to eat, Jesus called his disciples *unto him*, and saith unto them,

2 I have [b]compassion on the multitude, because they have now been with me three days, and have nothing to eat:

3 And if I send them away fasting to their own houses, they will faint by the way: for divers of them came from far.

4 And his disciples answered him, From whence [c]can a man satisfy these *men* with bread here in the wilderness?

5 And [d]he asked them, How many loaves have ye? And they said, Seven.

6 And he commanded the people to sit down on the ground: and he took the seven loaves, and [e]gave thanks, and brake, and gave to his disciples to set before *them;* and they did set *them* before the people.

m Josh. 21. 45. Matt. 9.29. ch. 9.23. 1 John 3.8.
n Matt.15.29.
o Matt. 9.32. Luke 11.14.
p ch. 8.23. John 9.6.
q ch. 6.41. John 11.41. John 17.1.
r John 11.33, 38.
s Ps. 33.9. Isa. 32.3,4. Isa. 35.5,6. Matt. 11.5.
t Isa. 42.2. ch. 5.43. ch. 8.26.

CHAP. 8

a Matt. 15. 32.
b Ps. 86.15. Ps. 111.4. Ps. 145.9. ch. 1.41. John 13.15. Heb. 2.17. Heb. 4.15. Heb. 5.2. 1 Pet. 2.21. 1 John 2.6.
c Num. 11. 21,22. 2 Ki. 4.42, 43. 2 Ki. 7.2. Matt. 15.33. ch. 6.52.
d Matt. 15. 34. ch. 6.38.
e Deut. 8.10. Matt. 15.36. ch. 6.41-44. Luke 22.19. Luke 24.30. 1 Cor. 11.23, 24. 1 Tim. 4.4,5.
f Matt. 14.19. ch. 6.41.
g Matt. 15.39.
h Matt. 12.38. Matt. 16.1. John 6.30.
i Matt. 16.5.
j Matt. 16.6. Luke 12.1. 1 Cor. 5.7.
k Matt. 16.7.
l Isa. 63.17. Matt. 15.17. Matt. 16.8. ch. 6.52.
m Matt. 14. 20. ch. 6.43. Luke 9.17. John 6.13.
n Matt. 15.37.
o ch. 6.52.
p ch. 7.33.

7 And they had a few small fishes: and he [f]blessed, and commanded to set them also before *them.*

8 So they did eat, and were filled: and they took up of the broken *meat* that was left seven baskets.

9 And they that had eaten were about four thousand: and he sent them away.

10 ¶ And [g]straightway he entered into a ship with his disciples, and came into the parts of Dăl-mă-nū-thă.

11 And [h]the Pharisees came forth, and began to question with him, seeking of him a sign from heaven, tempting him.

12 And he sighed deeply in his spirit, and saith, Why doth this generation seek after a sign? verily I say unto you, There shall no sign be given unto this generation.

13 And he left them, and entering into the ship again departed to the other side.

14 ¶ Now [i]*the disciples* had forgotten to take bread, neither had they in the ship with them more than one loaf.

15 And [j]he charged them, saying, Take heed, beware of the leaven of the Pharisees, and *of* the leaven of Herod.

16 And they reasoned among themselves, saying, *It is* [k]because we have no bread.

17 And when Jesus knew *it*, he saith unto them, Why reason ye, because ye have no bread? [l]perceive ye not yet, neither understand? have ye your heart yet hardened?

18 Having eyes, see ye not? and having ears, hear ye not? and do ye not remember?

19 When [m]I brake the five loaves among five thousand, how many baskets full of fragments took ye up? They say unto him, Twelve.

20 And [n]when the seven among four thousand, how many baskets full of fragments took ye up? And they said, Seven.

21 And he said unto them, How is it [o]that ye do not understand?

22 ¶ And he cometh to Bĕth-sā-ī-dă; and they bring a blind man unto him, and besought him to touch him.

23 And he took the blind man by the hand, and led him out of the town; and when [p]he had spit on his eyes, and put his hands upon him, he asked him if he saw ought.

24 And he looked up, and said, I see men as trees, walking.

25 After that he put *his* hands again upon his eyes, and made him look up:

and he was restored, and saw every
man clearly.
26 And he sent him away to his
house, saying, Neither go into the
town, [q]nor tell *it* to any in the town.
27 ¶ And [r]Jesus went out, and his
disciples into the towns of Çæ-să-rē-ă
Philippi: and by the way he asked his
disciples, saying unto them, Whom
do men say that I am?
28 And they answered, [s]John the
Baptist: but some *say*, Ē-lī-ăs; and
others, One of the prophets.
29 And he saith unto them, But
whom say ye that I am? And Peter
answereth and saith unto him, Thou
[t]art the Christ.
30 And he [u]charged them that they
should tell no man of him.
31 And [v]he began to teach them, that
the Son of man must suffer many
things, and be rejected of the elders,
and *of* the chief priests, and scribes,
and be killed, and after three days rise
again.
32 And he spake that saying openly.
And Peter took him, and began to rebuke him.
33 But when he had turned about and
looked on his disciples, he rebuked
Peter, saying, Get thee behind me,
Satan: [w]for thou savourest not the
things that be of God, but the things
that be of men.
34 ¶ And when he had called the people *unto him* with his disciples also, he
said unto them, [x]Whosoever will come
after me, let him deny himself, and
take up his cross, and follow me.
35 For [y]whosoever will save his life
shall lose it; but whosoever shall lose
his life for my sake and the gospel's,
the same shall save it.
36 For what shall it profit a man, if
he shall gain the whole world, and lose
his own soul?
37 Or what shall a man give in exchange for his soul?
38 Whosoever [z]therefore shall be
ashamed of me and of my words in
this adulterous and sinful generation; of him also shall the Son of man
be ashamed, when he cometh in the
glory of his Father with the holy
angels.

CHAPTER 9

AND he said unto them, [a]Verily I
say unto you, That there be some
of them that stand here, which shall
not taste of death, till they have seen
[b]the kingdom of God come with
power.
2 ¶ And [c]after six days Jesus taketh
with him Peter, and James, and John,
and leadeth them up into an high
mountain apart by themselves: and he
was transfigured before them.
3 And his raiment became shining,
exceeding [d]white as snow; so as no
fuller on earth can white them.
4 And there appeared unto them Ē-
lī-ăs with Moses: and they were talking with Jesus.
5 And Peter answered and said to
Jesus, Master, it is good for us to be
here: and let us make three tabernacles; one for thee, and one for
Moses, and one for Ē-lī-ăs.
6 For he wist not what to say; for
they were sore afraid.
7 And there was [e]a cloud that overshadowed them: and a voice came
out of the cloud, saying, This is my
beloved Son: [f]hear him.
8 And suddenly, when they had looked round about, they saw no man any
more, save Jesus only with themselves.
9 And [g]as they came down from the
mountain, he charged them that they
should tell no man what things they
had seen, till the Son of man were
risen from the dead.
10 And they kept that saying with
themselves, questioning one with another what the rising from the dead
should mean.
11 ¶ And they asked him, saying,
Why say the scribes [h]that Ē-lī-ăs must
first come?
12 And he answered and told them,
Ē-lī-ăs verily cometh first, and restoreth all things; and [i]how it is written of the Son of man, that he must
suffer many things, and [j]be set at
nought.
13 But I say unto you, [k]That Ē-lī-ăs
is indeed come, and they have done
unto him whatsoever they listed, as it
is written of him.
14 ¶ And [l]when he came to *his* disciples, he saw a great multitude about
them, and the scribes questioning
with them.
15 And straightway all the people,
when they beheld him, were greatly
amazed, and running to *him* saluted
him.
16 And he asked the scribes, What
question ye [1]with them?
17 And [m]one of the multitude answered and said, Master, I have
brought unto thee my son, which
hath a dumb spirit;
18 And wheresoever he taketh him,
he [2]teareth him: and he foameth, and

q Matt. 8.4. ch. 5.43.
r Matt. 16.13. Luke 9.18.
s Matt. 14.2.
t Matt. 16.16. John 1.41. John 4.42. John 6.69. John 11.27. Acts 8.37. Acts 9.20. 1 John 4.15. 1 John 5.1,6.
u Matt. 16.20.
v Matt. 16.21. Matt. 17.22. Luke 9.22.
w Rom. 8.7. 1 Cor. 2.14. 1 Pet. 4.2. 1 John 2.15, 16.
x Matt. 10. 38. Matt. 16.24. Luke 9.23. Luke 14.27. Gal. 5.24. Gal. 6.14.
y Matt. 10. 39. Matt. 16.25. John 12.25. Rev. 12.11.
z Matt. 10.33. Luke 9.26. Luke 12.9. Rom. 1.16. 2 Tim. 1.8. 2 Tim. 2.12. 1 John 2.23.

CHAP. 9

a Matt. 16.28. Luke 9.27.
b Matt. 24.30. Matt. 25.31. Luke 22.18. Heb. 2.8,9.
c Matt. 17.1. Luke 9.28.
d Ps. 104.1,2. Dan. 7.9. Matt. 28.3.
e Ex. 40.34. Isa. 42.1. 2 Pet. 1.17.
f Heb. 1.1,2. Heb. 2.3. Heb. 12.25, 26.
g Matt. 17.9.
h Mal. 4.5. Matt. 17.10.
i Gen. 3.15. Num. 21.9. Ps. 22.6. Isa. 50.60. Isa. 53.2. Dan. 9.26. Zech. 13.7. John 3.14.
j Luke 23.11. Phil. 2.7.
k Matt. 11. 14. Matt. 17.12. Luke 1.17.
l Matt. 17.14. Luke 9.37.
1 Or, among yourselves?
m Matt. 17. 14. Luke 9. 38.
2 Or, dasheth him.

gnasheth with his teeth, and pineth
away: and I spake to thy disciples that
they should cast him out; and they
could not.
19 He answereth him, and saith, O
faithless generation, how long shall I
be with you? how long shall I suffer
you? bring him unto me.
20 And they brought him unto him:
and when [n]he saw him, straightway
the spirit tare him; and he fell on the
ground, and wallowed foaming.
21 And he asked his father, How
long is it ago since this came unto
him? And he said, Of a child.
22 And ofttimes it hath cast him into
the fire, and into the waters, to destroy him: but if thou canst do any
thing, have compassion on us, and
help us.
23 Jesus said unto him, [o]If thou canst
believe, all things *are* possible to him
that believeth.
24 And straightway the father of the
child cried out, and said with tears,
Lord, I believe; [p]help thou mine unbelief.
25 When Jesus saw that the people
came running together, he rebuked
the [q]foul spirit, saying unto him, *Thou*
dumb and deaf spirit, I charge thee,
come out of him, and enter no more
into him.
26 And *the spirit* cried, and rent him
sore, and came out of him: and he was
as one dead; insomuch that many
said, He is dead.
27 But Jesus took him by the hand,
and lifted him up; and he arose.
28 And [r]when he was come into the
house, his disciples asked him privately, Why could not we cast him
out?
29 And he said unto them, This kind
can come forth by nothing, but by
prayer and fasting.
30 ¶ And they departed thence, and
passed through Galilee; and he would
not that any man should know *it*.
31 For [s]he taught his disciples, and
said unto them, The Son of man is delivered into the hands of men, and
they shall kill him; and after that
he is killed, he shall rise the third
day.
32 But they understood not that saying, and were afraid to ask him.
33 ¶ And [t]he came to Că-pĕr´-nă-ŭm:
and being in the house he asked them,
What was it that ye disputed among
yourselves by the way?
34 But they held their peace: [u]for by
the way they had disputed among

n ch. 1.26. Luke 9.42.
o 2 Chr. 20. 20. Matt. 17.20. ch. 11.23. Luke 17.6. John 11.40. Acts 14.9.
p Luke 17.5. Eph. 2.8. Phil. 1.29. 2 Thes. 1.3, 11. Heb. 11.1-40. Heb. 12.2.
q Zech. 3.2. Matt. 17.18. ch. 1.25. ch. 5.8. Luke 4.35. Acts 10.38. 1 John 3.8.
r Matt. 17.19.
s Matt. 16.21. Matt. 17.22. Matt. 26.1, 2. ch. 8.31. Luke 9.44.
t Matt. 18.1. Luke 9.46. Luke 22.24.
u Pro. 13.10.
v Matt. 20. 26,27. ch. 10.43. Jas. 4.6.
w Matt. 18.2. ch. 10.16.
x Matt. 10. 40. Luke 9.48. John 13.20.
y Num. 11. 28.
z 1 Cor. 12.3.
a Matt. 12. 30.
b Matt. 10. 42.
c Matt. 18.6. Luke 17.1.
3 Or, cause thee to offend. Deut. 13.6. Matt. 5.29. Matt. 18.8. Col. 3.5. Heb. 12.1.
d Isa. 66.24. 2 Thes. 1.9.
4 Or, cause thee to offend.
e Rom. 8.13. Gal. 5.24.
f Lev. 2.13. Eze. 43.24.
g Matt. 5.13. Luke 14.34.
h Eph. 4.29. Col. 4.6.
i Rom. 12.18. Rom. 14.19. 2 Cor. 13.11. 2 Tim. 2.22. Heb. 12.14.

themselves, who *should be* the greatest.
35 And he sat down, and called the
twelve, and saith unto them, If [v]any
man desire to be first, *the same* shall be
last of all, and servant of all.
36 And [w]he took a child, and set him
in the midst of them: and when he had
taken him in his arms, he said unto
them,
37 Whosoever shall receive one of
such children in my name, receiveth
me: and [x]whosoever shall receive me,
receiveth not me, but him that sent
me.
38 ¶ And [y]John answered him, saying, Master, we saw one casting out
devils in thy name, and he followeth
not us: and we forbad him, because
he followeth not us.
39 But Jesus said, Forbid him not:
[z]for there is no man which shall do a
miracle in my name, that can lightly
speak evil of me.
40 For [a]he that is not against us is on
our part.
41 For [b]whosoever shall give you a
cup of water to drink in my name,
because ye belong to Christ, verily I
say unto you, he shall not lose his reward.
42 And [c]whosoever shall offend one
of *these* little ones that believe in me,
it is better for him that a millstone
were hanged about his neck, and he
were cast into the sea.
43 And if thy hand [3]offend thee, cut
it off: it is better for thee to enter into
life maimed, than having two hands
to go into hell, into the fire that never
shall be quenched:
44 Where [d]their worm dieth not, and
the fire is not quenched.
45 And if thy foot offend thee, cut it
off: it is better for thee to enter halt
into life, than having two feet to be
cast into hell, into the fire that never
shall be quenched:
46 Where their worm dieth not, and
the fire is not quenched.
47 And if thine eye [4]offend thee,
[e]pluck it out: it is better for thee to
enter into the kingdom of God with
one eye, than having two eyes to be
cast into hell fire:
48 Where their worm dieth not, and
the fire is not quenched.
49 For every one shall be salted with
fire, and [f]every sacrifice shall be salted
with salt.
50 Salt [g]*is* good: but if the salt have
lost his saltness, wherewith will ye
season it? Have [h]salt in yourselves,
and [i]have peace one with another.

CHAPTER 10

AND [a]he arose from thence, and
cometh into the coasts of Judæa
by the farther side of Jordan: and the
people resort unto him again; and, as
he was wont, he taught them again.
2 ¶ And [b]the Pharisees came to him,
and asked him, Is it lawful for a man
to put away *his* wife? tempting him.
3 And he answered and said unto
them, What did Moses command
you?
4 And they said, [c]Moses suffered to
write a bill of divorcement, and to put
her away.
5 And Jesus answered and said unto
them, For [d]the hardness of your heart
he wrote you this precept.
6 But from the beginning of the
creation God [e]made them male and
female.
7 For [f]this cause shall a man leave
his father and mother, and cleave to
his wife;
8 And they twain shall be one flesh:
so then they are no more twain, but
one flesh.
9 What therefore God hath joined
together, let not man put asunder.
10 And in the house his disciples
asked him again of the same *matter*.
11 And he saith unto them, Whosoever [g]shall put away his wife, and
marry another, committeth adultery
against her.
12 And if a woman shall put away
her husband, and be married to another, she committeth adultery.
13 ¶ And [h]they brought young children to him, that he should touch
them: and *his* disciples rebuked those
that brought *them*.
14 But when Jesus saw *it*, he was
much displeased, and said unto them,
Suffer the little children to come unto
me, and forbid them not: for [i]of such
is the kingdom of God.
15 Verily I say unto you, [j]Whoso-
ever shall not receive the kingdom of
God as a little child, he shall not enter
therein.
16 And [k]he took them up in his arms,
put *his* hands upon them, and blessed
them.
17 ¶ And [l]when he was gone forth into the way, there came one running,
and kneeled to him, and asked him,
Good Master, what shall I do that I
may inherit eternal life?
18 And Jesus said unto him, Why
callest thou me good? *there is* none
good but one, *that is*, God.
19 Thou knowest the command-

CHAP. 10
a Matt. 19.1. John 10.40. John 11.7.
b Matt. 19.3.
c Deut. 24.1. Jer. 3.1. Matt. 5.31. Matt. 19.7.
d Deut. 9.6. Acts 13.18.
e Gen. 1.27. Gen. 2.20-23. Gen. 5.2. Matt. 19.4.
f Gen. 2.24. 1 Cor. 6.16. Eph. 5.31.
g Matt. 5.32. Matt. 19.9. Luke 16.18. Rom. 7.3.
h Matt. 19.13. Luke 18.15.
i Matt. 18.4. Matt. 19.14. Luke 18.16. 1 Cor. 14.20. 1 Pet. 2.2.
j Matt. 18.3.
k Gen. 48.14-16. Isa. 40.11. Luke 2.28-34.
l Matt. 19.16. Luke 18.18.
m Ex. 20. Rom. 13.9. Jas. 2.11.
n Acts 2.44. 1 Tim. 6.18.
o Matt. 6.19, 20. Matt. 19.21. Luke 12.33. Luke 16.9. 1 Tim. 6.17-19. 1 Pet. 1.4,5.
p Acts 14.22. 2 Tim. 3.12.
q Matt. 19.23. Luke 18.24.
r Job 31.24. Ps. 17.14. Ps. 52.7. Ps. 62.10. Jer. 9.23. Eze. 28.4-8. Zeph. 1.18. 1 Tim. 6.17. Jas. 5.1-3.
s Jer. 32.17. Matt. 19.26. Luke 1.37. Heb. 7.25.
t Matt. 19.27. Luke 18.28.
u 2 Chr. 25.9. Ps. 19.11. Luke 18.30.
v Matt. 5.11, 12. John 16.22, 23. Acts 14.22. Rom. 5.3. 1 Thes. 3.3. 2 Tim. 3.12. Heb. 12.6. Jas. 1.2-4. 1 Pet. 4.12-16.
w Matt. 19. 30. Matt. 20.16. Luke 13.30.
x Matt. 20. 17. Luke 18.31.
y ch. 8.31. ch. 9.31. Luke 9.22. Luke 18.31.

ments, [m]Do not commit adultery, Do
not kill, Do not steal, Do not bear
false witness, Defraud not, Honour
thy father and mother.
20 And he answered and said unto
him, Master, all these have I observed
from my youth.
21 Then Jesus beholding him loved
him, and said unto him, One thing
thou lackest: go thy way, sell [n]what-
soever thou hast, and give to the poor,
and thou shalt have treasure [o]in heav-
en: and come, take up [p]the cross, and
follow me.
22 And he was sad at that saying, and
went away grieved: for he had great
possessions.
23 ¶ And [q]Jesus looked round about,
and saith unto his disciples, How
hardly shall they that have riches
enter into the kingdom of God!
24 And the disciples were astonished
at his words. But Jesus answereth
again, and saith unto them, Children,
how hard is it for them [r]that trust in
riches to enter into the kingdom of
God!
25 It is easier for a camel to go
through the eye of a needle, than for a
rich man to enter into the kingdom
of God.
26 And they were astonished out of
measure, saying among themselves,
Who then can be saved?
27 And Jesus looking upon them
saith, With men *it is* impossible, but
not with God: for [s]with God all things
are possible.
28 ¶ Then [t]Peter began to say unto
him, Lo, we have left all, and have
followed thee.
29 And Jesus answered and said,
Verily I say unto you, There is no man
that hath left house, or brethren, or
sisters, or father, or mother, or wife,
or children, or lands, for my sake, and
the gospel's,
30 But [u]he shall receive an hundredfold now in this time, houses, and
brethren, and sisters, and mothers,
and children, and lands, with [v]per-
secutions; and in the world to come
eternal life.
31 But [w]many *that are* first shall be
last; and the last first.
32 ¶ And [x]they were in the way going
up to Jerusalem; and Jesus went before them: and they were amazed; and
as they followed, they were afraid.
[y]And he took again the twelve, and
began to tell them what things should
happen unto him,
33 *Saying*, Behold, we go up to Jeru-

salem; and the Son of man shall be
delivered unto the chief priests, and
unto the scribes; and they shall condemn him to death, and shall deliver
him to the Gentiles:
34 And they shall mock him, and
shall scourge him, and shall spit upon
him, and shall kill him: and the third
day he shall rise again.
35 ¶ And [z]James and John, the sons
of Zĕb'-ĕ-dēe, come unto him, saying,
Master, we would that thou shouldest
do for us whatsoever we shall desire.
36 And he said unto them, What
would ye that I should do for you?
37 They said unto him, Grant unto
us that we may sit, one on thy right
hand, and the other on thy left hand,
in thy glory.
38 But Jesus said unto them, Ye
know not what ye ask: can ye drink
of the cup that I drink of? and be baptized with the baptism that I am baptized with?
39 And they said unto him, We can.
And Jesus said unto them, [a]Ye shall
indeed drink of the cup that I drink
of; and with the baptism that I am
baptized withal shall ye be baptized:
40 But to sit on my right hand and on
my left hand is not mine to give; but
it shall be given [b]*to them* for whom it
is prepared.
41 And [c]when the ten heard *it*, they
began to be much displeased with
James and John.
42 But Jesus called them *to him*, and
saith unto them, [d]Ye know that they
which [1]are accounted to rule over the
Gentiles exercise lordship over them;
and their great ones exercise authority
upon them.
43 But [e]so shall it not be among you:
but whosoever will be great among
you, shall be your minister:
44 And whosoever of you will be the
chiefest, shall be servant of all.
45 For even [f]the Son of man came
not to be ministered unto, but to
minister, and to [g]give his life a ransom for many.
46 ¶ And [h]they came to Jericho: and
as he went out of Jericho with his disciples and a great number of people,
blind Bär-tĭ-mæ'-ŭs, the son of Tĭ-
mæ'-ŭs, sat by the highway side begging.
47 And when he heard that it was
Jesus of Nazareth, he began to cry
out, and say, Jesus, *thou* [i]Son of
David, have mercy on me.
48 And many charged him that he
should hold his peace: but he cried

z Matt. 20.20.

a Acts 12.2. Rev. 1.9.
b Jas. 4.3.
c Matt. 20. 24.
d Luke 22.25.
1 Or, think good.
e Matt. 20.26, 28. ch. 9.35. Luke 9.48.
f Matt. 20.28. Luke 22.26, 27. John 13.14. Phil. 2.7. Heb. 5.8.
g Isa. 53.10. Dan. 9.24, 26. Matt. 20.28. 2 Cor. 5.21. Gal. 3.13. 1 Tim. 2.6. Titus 2.14.
h Matt. 20.29. Luke 18.35.
i Isa. 11.1. Jer. 23.5,6. Rom. 1.3. Rev. 22.16.
2 Or, saved thee. Matt. 9.22.
j Isa. 29.18. Isa. 32.3. Isa. 35.5. Isa. 42.6,7. Isa. 43.8. ch. 8.22-26. Acts 26.18.

CHAP. 11

a Matt. 21.1. Luke 19.29. John 12.14.
b Acts 1.12.
c Acts 10.36. Heb. 1.2. Heb. 2.7-9.
d 1 Ki. 1.33. Zech. 9.9.
e Matt. 21.8.
f Ps. 118.26. Isa. 62.11. Matt. 21.9. Matt. 23.39. Luke 19.37, 38. John 12.13.
g Ps. 148.1.
h Mal. 3.1. Matt. 21.12.

the more a great deal, *Thou* Son of
David, have mercy on me.
49 And Jesus stood still, and commanded him to be called. And they
call the blind man, saying unto him,
Be of good comfort, rise; he calleth
thee.
50 And he, casting away his garment,
rose, and came to Jesus.
51 And Jesus answered and said unto him, What wilt thou that I should
do unto thee? The blind man said unto him, Lord, that I might receive my
sight.
52 And Jesus said unto him, Go thy
way; thy faith hath [2]made thee whole.
And immediately [j]he received his
sight, and followed Jesus in the way.

CHAPTER 11

AND [a]when they came nigh to Jerusalem, unto Bĕth'-phă-ġē and
Bethany, at the mount of [b]Olives, he
sendeth forth two of his disciples,
2 And saith unto them, Go your way
into the village over against you: and
as soon as ye be entered into it, ye shall
find a colt tied, whereon never man
sat; loose him, and bring *him*.
3 And if any man say unto you, Why
do ye this? say ye that [c]the Lord hath
need of him; and straightway he will
send him hither.
4 And they went their way, and found
the colt tied by the door without in a
place where the two ways met; and
they loose him.
5 And certain of them that stood
there said unto them, What do ye,
loosing the colt?
6 And they said unto them even as
Jesus had commanded: and they let
them go.
7 And they brought the colt to Jesus,
and cast their garments on him; [d]and
he sat upon him.
8 And [e]many spread their garments
in the way: and others cut down branches off the trees, and strawed *them* in
the way.
9 And they that went before, and they
that followed, cried, [f]saying, Hō-săn'-
nă; Blessed *is* he that cometh in the
name of the Lord:
10 Blessed *be* the kingdom of our
father David, that cometh in the name
of the Lord: [g]Hō-săn-nă in the highest.
11 And [h]Jesus entered into Jerusalem, and into the temple: and when
he had looked round about upon all
things, and now the eventide was
come, he went out unto Bethany with
the twelve.

12 ¶ And [i]on the morrow, when they
were come from Bethany, he was
hungry:
13 And [j]seeing a fig tree afar off having leaves, he came, if haply he might
find any thing thereon: and when he
came to it, he found nothing but
leaves; for the time of figs was not *yet*.
14 And Jesus answered and said unto
it, No man eat fruit of thee hereafter
for ever. And his disciples heard *it*.
15 ¶ And [k]they come to Jerusalem:
and Jesus went into the temple, and
began to cast out them that sold and
bought in the temple, and overthrew
the tables of the moneychangers, and
the seats of them that sold doves;
16 And would not suffer that any
man should carry *any* vessel through
the temple.
17 And he taught, saying unto them,
Is it not written, [l]My house shall be
called [1]of all nations the house of
prayer? but [m]ye have made it a den
of thieves.
18 And [n]the scribes and chief priests
heard *it*, and sought how they might
destroy him: for they feared him, because all [o]the people was astonished at
his doctrine.
19 And when even was come, he
went out of the city.
20 ¶ And [p]in the morning, as they
passed by, they saw the fig tree dried
up from the roots.
21 And Peter calling to remembrance
saith unto him, Master, behold, the
fig tree which thou cursedst is withered away.
22 And Jesus answering saith unto
them, [2]Have faith in God.
23 For [q]verily I say unto you, That
whosoever shall say unto this mountain, Be thou removed, and be thou
cast into the sea; and shall not doubt
in his heart, but shall believe that
those things which he saith shall come
to pass; he shall have whatsoever he
saith.
24 Therefore I say unto you, What
[r]things soever ye desire, when ye pray,
believe that ye receive *them*, and ye
shall have *them*.
25 And when ye stand praying, forgive, [s]if ye have ought against any:
that your Father also which is in
heaven may forgive you your trespasses.
26 But [t]if ye do not forgive, neither
will your Father which is in heaven
forgive your trespasses.
27 ¶ And they come again to Jerusalem: and [u]as he was walking in the
temple, there come to him the chief
priests, and the scribes, and the elders,
28 And say unto him, By what
authority doest thou these things? and
who gave thee this authority to do
these things?
29 And Jesus answered and said unto
them, I will also ask of you one [3]ques-
tion, and answer me, and I will tell
you by what authority I do these
things.
30 The baptism of John, was *it* from
heaven, or of men? answer me.
31 And they reasoned with themselves, saying, If we shall say, From
heaven; he will say, Why then did ye
not believe him?
32 But if we shall say, Of men; they
feared the people: for [v]all *men* counted
John, that he was a prophet indeed.
33 And they answered and said unto
Jesus, We cannot tell. And Jesus answering saith unto them, Neither [w]do
I tell you by what authority I do these
things.

CHAPTER 12

AND he began to speak unto them
by parables. A *certain* man planted [a]a vineyard, and set an hedge about
it, and digged *a place for* the winefat,
and built a tower, and let it out to
husbandmen, and went into a far
country.
2 And at the season he sent to the
husbandmen a servant, that he might
receive from the husbandmen of the
fruit of the vineyard.
3 And they caught *him*, and beat
him, and sent *him* away empty.
4 And again he sent unto them another servant; and at him they cast
stones, and wounded *him* in the head,
and sent *him* away shamefully
handled.
5 And again he sent another; and
him they killed, and many others;
beating some, and [b]killing some.
6 Having yet therefore one son, his
[c]wellbeloved, he sent him also last unto them, saying, They will reverence
my son.
7 But those husbandmen said among
themselves, This is [d]the heir; come,
let us kill him, and the inheritance
shall be ours.
8 And they took him, and [e]killed
him, and cast *him* out of the vineyard.
9 What shall therefore the lord of the
vineyard do? he will come and destroy
the husbandmen, and will [f]give the
vineyard unto others.
10 And have ye not read this scrip-

[i] Matt. 21.18.
[j] Matt. 21.19.
[k] Matt. 21. 12. Luke 19.45. John 2.14.
[l] Isa. 56.7. Isa. 60.7. Zech. 2.11.
1 Or, an house of prayer for all nations?
[m] Jer. 7.11.
[n] Matt. 21.45. Luke 19.47.
[o] Matt. 7.28. ch. 1.22. Luke 4.32.
[p] Matt. 21.19.
2 Or, Have the faith of God.
[q] Matt. 17.20. Matt.21.21. Luke 17.6.
[r] Matt. 7.7. Matt. 18.19. Matt. 21.22. Luke 11.9. John 14.13. John 15.7. John 16.24. Jas. 1.5,6.
[s] Matt. 6.14. Eph. 4.32. Col. 3.13.
[t] Matt. 18.35.
[u] Matt. 21.23. Luke 20.1.
3 Or, thing.
[v] Matt. 3.5. Matt. 14.5. ch. 6.20.
[w] Job 5.13. Ps. 9.15. Ps. 33.10. Pro. 26.4. 1 Cor. 3.19.

CHAP. 12

[a] Ps. 80.8. Song 8.11. Isa. 5.1. Jer. 2.21. Matt. 21.33. Luke 20.9.
[b] 2 Chr. 24. 21. 2 Chr. 36.16. Neh. 9.26. Matt. 5.12. Matt. 23.34, 37. Acts 7.52. 1 Thes. 2.15. Heb. 11.36.
[c] Ps. 2.7. Matt.1. 23. Rom 8.3. Gal. 4.4. 1 John 4.9. 1 John 5.11, 12.
[d] Ps. 2.8. Acts 4.27. Heb. 1.2.
[e] Acts 2.23.
[f] Acts 28.23-28.

ture; The [g]stone which the builders
rejected is become the head of the
corner:
11 This was the Lord's doing, and
[h]it is marvellous in our eyes?
12 And [i]they sought to lay hold on
him, but feared the people: for they
knew that he had spoken the parable
against them: and they left him, and
went their way.
13 ¶ And [j]they send unto him certain
of the Pharisees and of the Hĕ-rō´-dĭ-
ăns, to catch him in *his* words.
14 And when they were come, they
say unto him, Master, we know that
thou art true, and carest for no man:
for thou regardest not the person of
men, but teachest the way of God in
truth: Is it lawful to give tribute to
Cæsar, or not?
15 Shall we give, or shall we not give?
But he, knowing their hypocrisy, said
unto them, Why tempt ye me? bring
me [1]a penny, that I may see *it*.
16 And they brought *it*. And he saith
unto them, Whose *is* this image and
superscription? And they said unto
him, Cæsar's.
17 And Jesus answering said unto
them, Render to Cæsar the things that
are Cæsar's, and to God the things
that are God's. And they marvelled
at him.
18 ¶ Then [k]come unto him the Săd´-
dŭ-çēēs, which [l]say there is no resurrection; and they asked him, saying,
19 Master, [m]Moses wrote unto us, If
a man's brother die, and leave *his* wife
behind him, and leave no children,
that his brother should take his wife,
and raise up seed unto his brother.
20 Now there were seven brethren:
and the first took a wife, and dying
left no seed.
21 And the second took her, and
died, neither left he any seed: and the
third likewise.
22 And the seven had her, and left no
seed: last of all the woman died also.
23 In the resurrection therefore,
when they shall rise, whose wife shall
she be of them? for the seven had her
to wife.
24 And Jesus answering said unto
them, Do ye not therefore err, because
ye know not [n]the scriptures, neither
[o]the power of God?
25 For when they shall rise from the
dead, they neither marry, nor are giv-
en in marriage; but [p]are as the angels
which are in heaven.
26 And as touching the dead, that
they rise: have ye not read in the book

[g] Ps. 118.22. Matt. 21.42. Luke 20.17, 18. Rom. 9.33. Eph. 2.20. 1 Pet. 2.7,8.
[h] 1 Tim. 3.16.
[i] Matt. 21.45, 46. ch. 11.18. John 7.25, 30,44.
[j] Matt. 22.15. Luke 20.20.
1 In value sevenpence halfpenny.
[k] Matt. 22. 23. Luke 20.27.
[l] Acts 23.8. 1 Cor. 15.12.
[m] Gen. 38.8. Deut. 25.5.
[n] Dan. 12.2. 1 Tim. 1.7. 2 Pet. 1.19.
[o] Gen. 18.14. Jer. 32.17. Luke 1.37. Rom. 4.17. Eph. 1.19, 20.
[p] Matt. 22.30. Luke 20.35, 36. 1 Cor. 7.29. 1 Cor. 15.42, 49,52.
[q] Ex. 3.6.
[r] Matt. 22.35.
[s] Deut. 6.4. ch. 12.29. Luke 10.27. John 1.1. John 10.30.
[t] Lev. 19.18. Matt. 5.43. Rom. 13.9. 1 Cor. 13.1. Gal. 5.14. Jas. 2.8.
[u] Deut. 4.39. Isa. 45.6,14. Isa. 46.9. 1 Cor. 8.4,6.
[v] 1 Sam. 15. 22. Hos. 6.6. Micah 6.6.
[w] Matt. 22. 46.
[x] Luke 20.41.
[y] 2 Sam. 23.2. Luke 1.70. Acts 1.16. 2 Tim. 3.16. 2 Pet. 1.21.
[z] Ps. 110.1. 1 Cor. 15.25. Heb. 1.13.
[a] Rom. 1.3. Rom. 9.5. Rev. 22.16.
[b] ch. 4.2.
[c] Matt. 23.1. Luke 20.46.
[d] Luke 11.43.
[e] Matt. 23.14.
[f] Luke 21.1.

of Moses, how in the bush God spake
unto him, saying, I [q]*am* the God of
Abraham, and the God of Isaac, and
the God of Jacob?
27 He is not the God of the dead, but
the God of the living: ye therefore do
greatly err.
28 ¶ And [r]one of the scribes came,
and having heard them reasoning together, and perceiving that he had answered them well, asked him, Which
is the first commandment of all?
29 And Jesus answered him, The first
of all the commandments *is*, [s]Hear,
O Israel; The Lord our God is one
Lord:
30 And thou shalt love the Lord thy
God with all thy heart, and with all
thy soul, and with all thy mind, and
with all thy strength: this *is* the first
commandment.
31 And the second *is* like, *namely*
this, Thou [t]shalt love thy neighbour
as thyself. There is none other commandment greater than these.
32 And the scribe said unto him,
Well, Master, thou hast said the
truth: for there is one God; [u]and there
is none other but he:
33 And to love him with all the
heart, and with all the understanding,
and with all the soul, and with all the
strength, and to love *his* neighbour as
himself, [v]is more than all whole burnt
offerings and sacrifices.
34 And when Jesus saw that he answered discreetly, he said unto him,
Thou art not far from the kingdom of
God. [w]And no man after that durst
ask him *any question*.
35 ¶ And [x]Jesus answered and said,
while he taught in the temple, How
say the scribes that Christ is the Son
of David?
36 For David himself said [y]by the
Holy Ghost, [z]The Lord said to my
Lord, Sit thou on my right hand, till I
make thine enemies thy footstool.
37 David therefore himself calleth
him Lord; and [a]whence is he *then* his
son? And the common people heard
him gladly.
38 ¶ And [b]he said unto them in his
doctrine, [c]Beware of the scribes,
which love to go in long clothing, and
[d]*love* salutations in the marketplaces,
39 And the chief seats in the synagogues, and the uppermost rooms at
feasts:
40 Which [e]devour widows' houses,
and for a pretence make long prayers:
these shall receive greater damnation.
41 ¶ And [f]Jesus sat over against the

treasury, and beheld how the people
cast [2]money into the [g]treasury: and
many that were rich cast in much.
42 And there came a certain poor
widow, and she threw in [3]two mites,
which make a farthing.
43 And he called *unto him* his disciples, and saith unto them, Verily I
say unto you, That [h]this poor widow
hath cast more in, than all they which
have cast into the treasury:
44 For all *they* did cast in of their
abundance; but she of her want did
cast in all that she had, [i]*even* all her
living.

CHAPTER 13

AND [a]as he went out of the temple,
one of his disciples saith unto him,
Master, see what manner of stones
and what buildings *are here!*
2 And Jesus answering said unto
him, Seest thou these great buildings?
[b]there shall not be left one stone upon
another, that shall not be thrown
down.
3 And as he sat upon the mount of
Olives over against the temple, Peter
and James and John and Andrew asked him privately,
4 Tell [c]us, when shall these things
be? and what *shall be* the sign when
all these things shall be fulfilled?
5 And Jesus answering them began
to say, [d]Take heed lest any *man* deceive you:
6 For many shall come in my name,
saying, I am *Christ;* and shall deceive
many.
7 And when ye shall hear of wars and
rumours of wars, be ye not troubled:
for *such things* must needs be; but the
[e]end *shall* not *be* yet.
8 For nation shall rise against nation, and kingdom against kingdom:
and there shall be earthquakes in
divers places, and there shall be famines and troubles: these *are* the beginnings of [1]sorrows.
9 ¶ But [f]take heed to yourselves: for
they shall deliver you up to councils;
and in the synagogues ye shall be
beaten: and ye shall be brought before rulers and kings for my sake, for
a testimony against them.
10 And [g]the gospel must first be published among all nations.
11 But [h]when they shall lead *you*, and
deliver you up, take no thought beforehand what ye shall speak, neither
do ye premeditate: but whatsoever
shall be given you in that hour, that
speak ye: for it is not ye that speak,
[i]but the Holy Ghost.

2 A piece of brass money. Matt. 10.9.
g 2 Ki. 12.9.
3 It is the seventh part of one piece of that brass money.
h 2 Cor. 8.12.
i 1 John 3.17.
CHAP. 13
a Matt. 24.1.
b Luke 19.44.
c Luke 21.7.
d Jer. 29.8. Eph. 5.6.
e Jer. 4.27. Jer. 5.10.
1 The word in the original importeth the pains of a woman in travail.
f Matt. 10.17. Rev. 2.10.
g Matt. 24.14. Rom. 10.18.
h Ex. 24.12. Luke 12.11. Luke 21.14.
i Acts 2.4. Acts 4.8,31.
j Micah 7.6. Matt. 10.21. Matt. 24.10. Luke 21.16.
k Dan. 12.12. 2 Tim. 4.7,8. Heb. 3.6,14. Rev. 2.7,10. Rev. 3.10.
l Matt. 24.15.
m Dan. 9.27.
n Luke 21.21.
o Luke 23.29.
p Deut. 28. 15. Dan. 9.26. Dan. 12.1. Joel 2.2.
q Deut. 13.1-3. Matt. 24.5, 23-25. Luke 17.23. Luke 21.8.
r Matt. 24.24. John 10.27, 28. Rom. 8.28-39. 2 Thes. 2.8-11. 1 Pet. 1.5. 1 John 2.26.
s Matt. 7.15. Luke 21.8. 2 Pet. 3.17.
t Dan. 7.10. Zeph. 1.15. Luke 21.25.
u Dan. 7.13. Matt. 16.27. Matt. 24.30. ch. 8.38. ch. 14.62. Acts 1.11. 1 Thes. 4.16. 2 Thes. 1.7. Rev. 1.7.

12 Now [j]the brother shall betray the
brother to death, and the father the
son; and children shall rise up against
their parents, and shall cause them to
be put to death.
13 And ye shall be hated of all *men*
for my name's sake: but [k]he that shall
endure unto the end, the same shall be
saved.
14 ¶ But [l]when ye shall see the abomination of desolation, [m]spoken of by
Daniel the prophet, standing where
it ought not, (let him that readeth understand,) then let [n]them that be in
Judæa flee to the mountains:
15 And let him that is on the housetop not go down into the house, neither enter *therein*, to take any thing
out of his house:
16 And let him that is in the field not
turn back again for to take up his garment.
17 But [o]woe to them that are with
child, and to them that give suck in
those days!
18 And pray ye that your flight be
not in the winter.
19 For [p]*in* those days shall be affliction, such as was not from the beginning of the creation which God created unto this time, neither shall be.
20 And except that the Lord had
shortened those days, no flesh should
be saved: but for the elect's sake,
whom he hath chosen, he hath shortened the days.
21 And [q]then if any man shall say to
you, Lo, here *is* Christ; or, lo, *he is*
there; believe *him* not:
22 For false Christs and false prophets shall rise, and shall shew signs and
wonders, to seduce, [r]if *it were* possible,
even the elect.
23 But [s]take ye heed: behold, I have
foretold you all things.
24 ¶ But [t]in those days, after that
tribulation, the sun shall be darkened,
and the moon shall not give her light,
25 And the stars of heaven shall fall,
and the powers that are in heaven shall
be shaken.
26 And [u]then shall they see the Son
of man coming in the clouds with
great power and glory.
27 And then shall he send his angels,
and shall gather together his elect
from the four winds, from the uttermost part of the earth to the uttermost part of heaven.
28 Now learn a parable of the fig
tree; When her branch is yet tender,
and putteth forth leaves, ye know that
summer is near:

29 So ye in like manner, when ye shall
see these things come to pass, know
that it is nigh, *even* at the doors.
30 Verily I say unto you, that this
generation shall not pass, till all these
things be done.
31 Heaven and earth shall pass
away: but my [v]words shall not pass
away.
32 ¶ But of that day and *that* hour
knoweth no man, no, not the angels
which are in heaven, neither the Son,
but the Father.
33 Take [w]ye heed, watch and pray:
for ye know not when the time is.
34 *For* [x]*the Son of man is* as a man
taking a far journey, who left his
house, and gave authority to his servants, and to every man his work, and
commanded the porter to watch.
35 Watch [y]ye therefore: for ye know
not when the master of the house cometh, at even, or at midnight, or at the
cockcrowing, or in the morning:
36 Lest coming suddenly he find you
sleeping.
37 And what I say unto you I say unto all, Watch.

CHAPTER 14

AFTER [a]two days was *the feast of*
the passover, and of unleavened
bread: and the chief priests and the
scribes sought how they might take
him by craft, and put *him* to death.
2 But they said, Not on the feast *day*,
lest there be an uproar of the people.
3 ¶ And [b]being in Bethany in the
house of Simon the leper, as he sat at
meat, there came a woman having an
alabaster box of ointment of [1]spike-
nard very precious; and she brake the
box, and poured *it* on his head.
4 And there were some that had indignation within themselves, and said,
Why was this waste of the ointment
made?
5 For it might have been sold for
more than three hundred [c]pence, and
have been given to the poor. And they
murmured against her.
6 And Jesus said, Let her alone; why
trouble ye her? she hath wrought a
good work on me.
7 For [d]ye have the poor with you always, and whensoever ye will ye may
do them good: but me ye have not
always.
8 She hath done what she could:
she is come aforehand to anoint my
body to the burying.
9 Verily I say unto you, Wheresoever this gospel shall be preached
throughout the whole world, *this* also
that she hath done shall be spoken of
for a memorial of her.
10 ¶ And [e]Judas Iscariot, one of the
twelve, went unto the chief priests, to
betray him unto them.
11 And when they heard *it*, they were
glad, and promised to give him
[f]money. And he sought how he might
conveniently betray him.
12 ¶ And [g]the first day of unleavened
bread, when they [2]killed the passover,
his disciples said unto him, Where
wilt thou that we go and prepare that
thou mayest eat the passover?
13 And he sendeth forth two of his
disciples, and saith unto them, Go ye
into the city, and there shall meet you
a man bearing a pitcher of water:
follow him.
14 And wheresoever he shall go in,
say ye to the goodman of the house,
The Master saith, Where is the guestchamber, where I shall eat [h]the passover with my disciples?
15 And he will shew you a large
upper room furnished *and* prepared:
there make ready for us.
16 And his disciples went forth, and
came into the city, and found as he
had said unto them: and they made
ready the passover.
17 And [i]in the evening he cometh
with the twelve.
18 And as they sat and did eat, Jesus
said, Verily I say unto you, One of you
which eateth with me shall betray me.
19 And they began to be sorrowful,
and to say unto him one by one, *Is* it
I? and another *said*, *Is* it I?
20 And he answered and said unto
them, *It is* one of the twelve, that
dippeth with me in the dish.
21 The [j]Son of man indeed goeth, as
it is written of him: but woe to that
man by whom the Son of man is betrayed! good were it for that man if
he had never been born.
22 ¶ And [k]as they did eat, Jesus took
bread, and blessed, and brake *it*, and
gave to them, and said, Take, eat:
this is my body.
23 And he took the cup, and when he
had given thanks, he gave *it* to them:
and they all drank of it.
24 And he said unto them, This is
[l]my blood of the new testament, which
is shed for many.
25 Verily I say unto you, I will drink
no more of the fruit of the vine, until
that day that I drink it new in the kingdom of God.
26 ¶ And [m]when they had sung an

v Num. 23.19. Josh. 23.14. Ps. 102.26. Isa. 40.8. Isa. 51.6.
w Rom. 13. 11. 1 Thes. 5.6.
x Matt. 25. 14.
y 2 Pet. 3.1-18. Rev. 3.3.

CHAP. 14
a Ex. 12.6-20. Matt. 26.2.
b Matt. 26.6. Luke 7.37. John 12.1,3.
1 Or, pure nard, or, liquid nard.
c Matt. 18.28.
d Deut. 15. 11. John 12.8.
e Matt. 10.4. John 18.2,3. Acts 1.16.
f Zech. 11.12. 1 Tim. 6.10. Jude 11.
g Matt. 26. 17. Luke 22.7.
2 Or, sacrificed.
h Ex. 12.6. Lev. 23.5.
i Matt. 26.20. Luke 22.14. John 13.21.
j Gen. 23.15. Isa. 53.1,12. Dan. 9.26. Zech. 13.7.
k Matt. 26. 26. Luke 22.19. 1 Cor. 10.4, 16. 1 Cor. 11.23.
l Ex. 24.8. Zech. 9.11. 1 Cor. 11.25. Heb. 9.14.
m Matt. 26. 30.

[3]hymn, they went out into the mount
of Olives.
27 And [n]Jesus saith unto them, All
ye shall be offended because of me
this night: for it is written, [o]I will smite
the shepherd, and the sheep shall be
scattered.
28 But [p]after that I am risen, I will go
before you into Galilee.
29 But [q]Peter said unto him, Although all shall be offended, yet *will*
not I.
30 And Jesus saith unto him, Verily
I say unto thee, That this day, *even* in
this night, before the cock crow twice,
thou shalt deny me thrice.
31 But he spake the more vehemently, If I should die with thee, I will not
deny thee in any wise. Likewise also
said they all.
32 And [r]they came to a place which
was named Gĕth-sĕm'-ă-nē: and he
saith to his disciples, Sit ye here, while
[s]I shall pray.
33 And he taketh with him Peter and
James and John, and began to be
sore amazed, and to be very heavy;
34 And saith unto them, [t]My soul is
exceeding sorrowful unto death: tarry
ye here, and watch.
35 And he went forward a little, and
fell on the ground, and prayed that,
if it were possible, the hour might pass
from him.
36 And he said, [u]Abba, Father, all
[v]things *are* possible unto thee; take
away this cup from me: [w]neverthe-
less not what I will, but what thou
wilt.
37 And he cometh, and findeth them
sleeping, and saith unto Peter, Simon,
sleepest thou? couldest not thou
watch one hour?
38 Watch ye and pray, lest ye enter
into temptation. [x]The spirit truly *is*
ready, but the flesh *is* weak.
39 And again he went away, and
prayed, and spake the same words.
40 And when he returned, he found
them asleep again, (for their eyes were
heavy,) neither wist they what to answer him.
41 And he cometh the third time, and
saith unto them, Sleep on now, and
take *your* rest: it is enough, [y]the hour
is come; behold, the Son of man is betrayed into the hands of sinners.
42 Rise [z]up, let us go; lo, he that betrayeth me is at hand.
43 ¶ And [a]immediately, while he yet
spake, cometh Judas, one of the
twelve, and with him a great multitude with swords and staves, from the
chief priests and the scribes and the
elders.
44 And he that betrayed him had
given them a token, saying, Whomsoever I shall kiss, that same is he; take
him, and lead *him* away safely.
45 And as soon as he was come, he
goeth straightway to him, and saith,
[4]Master, master; and [b]kissed him.
46 ¶ And they laid their hands on
him, and took him.
47 And one of them that stood by
drew a sword, and smote a servant of
the high priest, and cut off his ear.
48 And [c]Jesus answered and said unto them, Are ye come out, as against
a thief, with swords and *with* staves to
take me?
49 I was daily with you in the temple
teaching, and ye took me not: but the
[d]scriptures must be fulfilled.
50 And [e]they all forsook him, and
fled.
51 And there followed him a certain
young man, having a linen cloth cast
about *his* naked *body;* and the young
men laid hold on him:
52 And he left the linen cloth, and
fled from them naked.
53 ¶ And [f]they led Jesus away to the
high priest: and with him were assembled all the chief priests and the elders
and the scribes.
54 And Peter followed him afar off,
even into the palace of the high
priest: and he sat with the servants,
and warmed himself at the fire.
55 And [g]the chief priests and all the
council sought for witness against
Jesus to put him to death; and [h]found
none.
56 For many bare [i]false witness
against him, but their witness agreed
not together.
57 And there arose certain, and bare
false witness against him, saying,
58 We heard him say, [j]I will destroy
this temple that is made with hands,
and within three days I will build another made without hands.
59 But neither so did their witness
agree together.
60 And [k]the high priest stood up in
the midst, and asked Jesus, saying,
Answerest thou nothing? what *is it*
which these witness against thee?
61 But [l]he held his peace, and answered nothing. [m]Again the high
priest asked him, and said unto him,
Art thou the Christ, the Son of the
Blessed?
62 And Jesus said, I am: [n]and ye
shall see the Son of man sitting on the

3 Or, psalm.
n Matt. 11.6. Matt. 26.31. John 16.32.
o Isa. 53.2-10. Dan. 9.26. Zech. 13.7.
p Matt. 16.21. ch. 16.7.
q Pro. 3.5. Jer. 9.23,24.
r Matt. 26.36. Luke 22.39. John 18.1.
s Ps. 69.1. Matt. 26.38-44. Heb. 5.7.
t Isa. 53.3,4, 12. Lam. 1.12. John 12.27.
u Luke 24.49. John 20.17. Rom. 8.15. Gal. 4.6.
v Heb. 5.7.
w John 5.30.
x Rom. 7.23. Gal. 5.17.
y John 13.1.
z Matt. 26.46. John 18.1,2.
a Matt. 26.47. Luke 22.47. John 18.3.
4 Rabbi, Rabbi. John 20.16.
b 2 Sam. 20.9.
c Matt. 26.55. Luke 22.52.
d Ps. 22.6. Isa. 53.7. Dan. 9.26. Luke 22.37.
e Job 19.13, 14. Ps. 38.11. Ps. 88.8. John 16.32. 2 Tim. 4.16.
f Matt. 26.57. Luke 22.54. John 18.13.
g Matt. 26. 59.
h Dan. 6.4. 1 Pet. 3.16.
i Ps. 35.11. Pro. 6.19. Pro. 19.5.
j ch. 15.29. John 2.19.
k Matt. 26. 62.
l Isa. 53.7. 1 Pet. 2.23.
m Matt. 26. 63.
n Zech. 14.5. Matt. 16.27. ch. 8.38. Luke 22.69. Acts 1.11. 1 Thes. 4.16. 2 Thes. 1.7. Jude 14. Rev. 1.7.

right hand of power, and coming in
the clouds of heaven.
63 Then the high priest rent his
clothes, and saith, What need we any
further witnesses?
64 Ye have heard the [o]blasphemy:
what think ye? And they all condemned him to be guilty of death.
65 And some began to [p]spit on him,
and to cover his face, and to buffet
him, and to say unto him, Prophesy:
and the servants did strike him with
the palms of their hands.
66 ¶ And [q]as Peter was beneath in
the palace, there cometh one of the
maids of the high priest:
67 And when she saw Peter warming
himself, she looked upon him, and
said, And thou also wast with Jesus
of Nazareth.
68 But he denied, saying, I know not,
neither understand I what thou sayest.
And he went out into the porch; and
the cock crew.
69 And [r]a maid saw him again, and
began to say to them that stood by,
This is *one* of them.
70 And he denied it again. [s]And a
little after, they that stood by said
again to Peter, Surely thou art *one* of
them: [t]for thou art a Galilæan, and
thy speech agreeth *thereto*.
71 But [u]he began to curse and to
swear, *saying*, I know not this man of
whom ye speak.
72 And the second time the cock
crew. And Peter called to mind the
word that Jesus said unto him, Before
the cock crow twice, thou shalt deny
me thrice. And [5]when he thought
thereon, he wept.

CHAPTER 15

AND [a]straightway in the morning
the chief priests held a consulta-
tion with the elders and scribes and
the whole council, and bound Jesus,
and carried *him* away, and delivered
him to Pilate.
2 And [b]Pilate asked him, Art thou
the King of the Jews? And he answering said unto him, [c]Thou sayest
it.
3 And the chief priests accused him
of many things: but [d]he answered
nothing.
4 And [e]Pilate asked him again, saying, Answerest thou nothing? behold
how many things they witness against
thee.
5 But [f]Jesus yet answered nothing;
so that Pilate marvelled.
6 Now [g]at *that* feast he released unto

o Lev. 24.16. 1 Ki. 21.13.
p Isa. 50.6. Isa. 53.3.
q Matt. 26. 58.
r Matt. 26.71. Luke 22.58. John 18.25.
s Matt. 26.73. Luke 22.59. John 18.26.
t Judg. 12.6. Acts 2.7.
u Pro. 29.25. 1 Cor. 10.12.
5 Or, he wept abundantly, or, he began to weep. Eze. 7.16. Zech. 12.10. Acts 3.19. Acts 17.30. 2 Cor. 7.10.

CHAP. 15

a Ps. 2.2. John 18.28. Acts 3.13. Acts 4.26.
b Matt. 2.2. John 18.33-37.
c 1 Tim. 6.13.
d 1 Pet. 2.23.
e Matt. 26.62. John 19.10.
f Isa. 53.7. John 19.9.
g Matt. 27.15. Luke 23.17. John 18.39.
h Acts 7.9,51. 1 John 3.12.
i Matt. 27.20. Acts 3.14.
j Ps. 2.6,7. Isa. 9.6,7. Jer. 23.5,6. Micah 5.2. Zech. 9.9.
k Pro. 29.25. John 19.1, 16.
l Matt. 27.32. Luke 23.26.
m Rom. 16. 13.
n John 19.17. Acts 7.58. Heb. 13.12.
o Ps. 69.21.
p Ps. 22.18. John 19.23.
q Matt. 27. 45. Luke 23.44. John 19.14.

them one prisoner, whomsoever they
desired.
7 And there was one named Bär-ăb'-
băs, *which lay* bound with them that
had made insurrection with him, who
had committed murder in the insurrection.
8 And the multitude crying aloud began to desire *him to do* as he had ever
done unto them.
9 But Pilate answered them, saying,
Will ye that I release unto you the
King of the Jews?
10 For he knew that the chief priests
had delivered him [h]for envy.
11 But [i]the chief priests moved the
people, that he should rather release
Bär-ăb'-băs unto them.
12 And Pilate answered and said
again unto them, What will ye then
that I shall do *unto him* whom ye call
[j]the King of the Jews?
13 And they cried out again, Crucify
him.
14 Then Pilate said unto them, Why,
what evil hath he done? And they
cried out the more exceedingly, Crucify him.
15 ¶ And *so* Pilate, [k]willing to content the people, released Bär-ăb'-băs
unto them, and delivered Jesus, when
he had scourged *him*, to be crucified.
16 And the soldiers led him away into
the hall, called Præ-tôr'-ĭ-ŭm; and they
call together the whole band.
17 And they clothed him with purple,
and platted a crown of thorns, and
put it about his *head*,
18 And began to salute him, Hail,
King of the Jews!
19 And they smote him on the head
with a reed, and did spit upon him, and
bowing *their* knees worshipped him.
20 And when they had mocked him,
they took off the purple from him,
and put his own clothes on him, and
led him out to crucify him.
21 And [l]they compel one Simon a
Çy̆-rē'-nĭ-ăn, who passed by, coming
out of the country, the father of Alexander [m]and Rufus, to bear his cross.
22 And [n]they bring him unto the
place Gŏl'-gŏ-thă, which is, being interpreted, The place of a skull.
23 And they gave him [o]to drink wine
mingled with myrrh: but he received
it not.
24 And when they had crucified him,
they [p]parted his garments, casting lots
upon them, what every man should
take.
25 And [q]it was the third hour, and
they crucified him.

26 And [r]the superscription of his
accusation was written over, THE
KING OF THE JEWS.
27 And with him they crucify two
thieves; the one on his right hand, and
the other on his left.
28 And the scripture was fulfilled,
which saith, [s]And he was numbered
with the transgressors.
29 And [t]they that passed by railed on
him, wagging their heads, and saying,
Ah, thou [u]that destroyest the temple,
and buildest *it* in three days,
30 Save thyself, and come down from
the cross.
31 Likewise also the chief priests
mocking said among themselves with
the scribes, He saved others; himself
he cannot save.
32 Let Christ the King of Israel descend now from the cross, that we may
see and believe. [v]And they that were
crucified with him reviled him.
33 And [w]when the sixth hour was
come, there was darkness over the
whole land until the ninth hour.
34 And at the ninth hour Jesus cried
with a loud voice, saying, [x]Ē-lō-ī,
Ē-lō-ī, lä-mä să-băch-thă-nī? which is,
being interpreted, My God, my God,
why hast thou forsaken me?
35 And some of them that stood by,
when they heard *it*, said, Behold, he
calleth Ē-lī-ăs.
36 And [y]one ran and filled a spunge
full of vinegar, and put *it* on a reed,
and [z]gave him to drink, saying, Let
alone; let us see whether Ē-lī-ăs will
come to take him down.
37 And [a]Jesus cried with a loud voice,
and gave up the ghost.
38 And [b]the veil of the temple was
rent in twain from the top to the
bottom.
39 ¶ And [c]when the centurion, which
stood over against him, saw that he so
cried out, and gave up the ghost, he
said, Truly this man was the Son of
God.
40 There [d]were also women looking
on afar [e]off: among whom was Mary
Măg-dă-lēne, and Mary the mother of
James the less and of Jō-sĕs, and Să-
lō-mē;
41 (Who also, when he was in Galilee, followed [f]him, and ministered
unto him;) and many other women
which came up with him unto Jerusalem.
42 ¶ And [g]now when the even was
come, because it was the preparation, that is, the day before the sabbath,
43 Joseph of Ăr-ĭm-ă-thæ-ă, an honourable counseller, which [h]also waited
for the kingdom of God, came, and
went in boldly unto Pilate, and craved
the body of Jesus.
44 And Pilate marvelled if he were
already dead: and calling *unto him* the
centurion, he asked him whether he
had been any while dead.
45 And when he knew *it* of the centurion, he gave the body to Joseph.
46 And he [i]bought fine linen, and
took him down, and wrapped him in
the linen, and laid him in a sepulchre
which was hewn out of a rock, and
rolled a stone unto the door of the
sepulchre.
47 And Mary Măg-dă-lēne and Mary
the mother of Jō-sĕs beheld where he
was laid.

CHAPTER 16

AND [a]when the sabbath was past,
Mary Măg-dă-lēne, and Mary the
mother of James, and Să-lō-mē, [b]had
bought sweet spices, that they might
come and anoint him.
2 And [c]very early in the morning the
first *day* of the week, they came unto
the sepulchre at the rising of the sun.
3 And they said among themselves,
Who shall roll us away the stone from
the door of the sepulchre?
4 And when they looked, they saw
that the stone was rolled away: for it
was very great.
5 And [d]entering into the sepulchre,
they saw a young man sitting on the
right side, clothed in a long white garment; and they were affrighted.
6 And [e]he saith unto them, Be not
affrighted: Ye seek Jesus of Nazareth,
which was crucified: he is [f]risen; he is
not here: behold the place where they
laid him.
7 But go your way, tell his disciples
and Peter that he goeth before you into Galilee: there shall ye see him, [g]as
he said unto you.
8 And they went out quickly, and
fled from the sepulchre; for they
trembled and were amazed: neither
[h]said they any thing to any *man;* for
they were afraid.
9 ¶ Now when *Jesus* was risen early
the first *day* of the week, [i]he appeared
first to Mary Măg-dă-lēne, out [j]of
whom he had cast seven devils.
10 *And* she went and told them that
had been with him, as they mourned
and wept.
11 And [k]they, when they had heard
that he was alive, and had been seen
of her, believed not.

r Deut. 23.5.
s Isa. 53.12. Luke 22.37.
t Ps. 22.7. Ps. 35.15, 16.
u ch. 14.58. John 2.19.
v 1 Pet. 2.23.
w Luke 23. 44.
x Ps. 22.1. Heb. 5.7.
y Matt. 27. 48. John 19.29.
z Ps. 69.21.
a Matt. 27.50. Luke 23.46. John 19.30.
b Ex. 26.31. Eph. 2.14. Heb. 4.14-16. Heb. 6.19. Heb. 9.6-8, 24. Heb. 10.19.
c Deut. 32.31.
d Luke 23.49.
e Ps. 38.11.
f Luke 8.2.
g Matt. 27.57. Luke 23.50. John 19.38.
h Ps. 25.2. Ps. 27.14. Ps. 37.7,34. Isa. 8.16. Isa. 30.18. Isa. 40.27-31. Isa. 64.4.
i Isa. 53.9.

CHAP. 16

a Matt. 28.1.
b Luke 23.56.
c John 20.1.
d Luke 24.3.
e Matt. 28.5.
f John 2.19.
g Matt. 26. 32.
h Matt. 28.8.
i John 20.14.
j Luke 8.2.
k Luke 24.11.

12 ¶ After that he appeared in another form unto two of them, as they
walked, and went into the country.
13 And they went and told *it* unto the
residue: neither believed they them.
14 ¶ Afterward [l]he appeared unto
the eleven as they sat [1]at meat, and up-
braided them with their unbelief and
hardness of heart, because they believed not them which had seen him
after he was risen.
15 And [m]he said unto them, Go ye
into all the world, [n]and preach the
gospel to every creature.
16 He [o]that believeth and is baptized
shall be saved; [p]but he that believeth
not shall be damned.

l Luke 24.36. 1 Cor. 15.5.
1 Or, together.
m John 15. 16.
n Col. 1.23.
o John 3.18, 36. Acts 2.38. Acts 16.30. Rom. 10.9. 1 Pet. 3.21.
p John 12.48.
q Matt. 8.16. Luke 4.2,13. Acts 5.16.
r Acts 2.4. Acts 10.46. Acts 19.6. 1 Cor. 12.10.
s Acts 28.5.
t Acts 9.17. Jas. 5.14.
u Ps. 110. 1. Heb. 1.3.

17 And these signs shall follow them
that believe; [q]In my name shall they
cast out devils; [r]they shall speak with
new tongues;
18 They [s]shall take up serpents; and
if they drink any deadly thing, it
shall not hurt them; they [t]shall lay
hands on the sick, and they shall
recover.
19 ¶ So then after the Lord had
spoken unto them, he was received up
into heaven, and [u]sat on the right hand
of God.
20 And they went forth, and preached every where, the Lord working with
them, and confirming the word with
signs following. Ā-mĕn.

THE GOSPEL ACCORDING TO

ST. LUKE

CHAPTER 1

FORASMUCH as many have tak-
en in hand to set forth in order a
declaration of [a]those things which are
most surely believed among us,
2 Even [b]as they delivered them unto
us, which [c]from the beginning were
eyewitnesses, and ministers of the
word;
3 It [d]seemed good to me also, having
had perfect understanding of all things
from the very first, to write unto thee
[e]in order, [f]most excellent Thē-ŏph-
ĭ-lŭs,
4 That [g]thou mightest know the certainty of those things, wherein thou
hast been instructed.
5 ¶ THERE was [h]in the days of
Herod, the king of Judæa, a
certain priest named Zăch-ă-rī-ăs, [i]of
the course of Ă-bī-ă: and his wife *was*
of the daughters of Aaron, and her
name *was* Elisabeth.
6 And they were both [j]righteous before God, walking in all the commandments and ordinances of the
Lord blameless.
7 And they had no child, because that
Elisabeth was barren, and they both
were *now* well stricken in years.
8 And it came to pass, that while he
executed the priest's office before
God [k]in the order of his course,
9 According to the custom of the
priest's office, his lot was [l]to burn incense when he went into the temple of
the Lord.

CHAP. 1

a John 20.31. Acts 1.1-3. 1 Tim. 3.16.
b Heb. 2.3. 1 Pet. 5.1. 2 Pet. 1.16. 1 John 1.1.
c John 15.27.
d 1 Cor. 7.40.
e Acts 11.4.
f Acts 1.1.
g John 20.31.
h Matt. 2.1.
i 1 Chr. 24.10, 19. Neh. 12.4.
j 1 Ki. 9.4. 2 Ki. 20.3. Ps. 119.6. Acts 24.16.
k 2 Chr. 8.14.
l Ex. 30.7,8. 1 Sam. 2.28.
m Lev. 16.17.
n Dan. 10.8. Acts 10.4. Rev. 1.17.
o Gen. 25.21. 1 Sam. 1.19.
p Gen. 12.2. Josh. 4.14.
q Num. 6.3. Judg. 13.4. ch. 7.33.
r Jer. 1.5. Gal. 1.15.
s Isa. 40.3-5. Dan. 12.3.
t Matt. 11.14.
1 Or, by.
u 1 Sam. 7.3. 1 Chr. 29.18. Ps. 10.17. Isa. 40.3. Rom. 9.5.
v Gen. 17.17.
w Dan. 8.16.

10 And [m]the whole multitude of the
people were praying without at the
time of incense.
11 And there appeared unto him an
angel of the Lord standing on the right
side of the altar of incense.
12 And when Zăch-ă-rī-ăs saw *him*,
he [n]was troubled, and fear fell upon
him.
13 But the angel said unto him, Fear
not, Zăch-ă-rī-ăs: for [o]thy prayer is
heard; and thy wife Elisabeth shall
bear thee a son, and thou shalt call his
name John.
14 And thou shalt have joy and gladness; and many shall rejoice at his
birth.
15 For he shall be [p]great in the sight
of the Lord, and [q]shall drink neither
wine nor strong drink; and he shall be
filled with the Holy Ghost, [r]even from
his mother's womb.
16 And [s]many of the children of
Israel shall he turn to the Lord their
God.
17 And [t]he shall go before him in the
spirit and power of Ē-lī-ăs, to turn the
hearts of the fathers to the children,
and the disobedient [1]to the wisdom of
the just; to make ready a people prepared for the [u]Lord.
18 And Zăch-ă-rī-ăs said unto the
angel, [v]Whereby shall I know this?
for I am an old man, and my wife well
stricken in years.
19 And the angel answering said unto
him, I am [w]Gabriel, that stand in the

presence of God; and am sent to speak
unto thee, and to shew thee these glad
tidings.
20 And, behold, [x]thou shalt be dumb,
and not able to speak, until the day
that these things shall be performed,
because thou believest not my words,
which shall be fulfilled in their season.
21 And the people [y]waited for Zăch-
ă-rī-ăs, and marvelled that he tarried
so long in the temple.
22 And when he came out, he could
not speak unto them: and they perceived that he had seen a vision in the
temple: for he beckoned unto them,
and remained speechless.
23 And it came to pass, that, as soon
as the [z]days of his ministration were
accomplished, he departed to his own
house.
24 And after those days his wife
Elisabeth conceived, and hid herself
five months, saying,
25 Thus hath the Lord dealt with me
in the days wherein he looked on *me*,
to [a]take away my reproach among
men.
26 And in the sixth month the angel
Gabriel was sent from God unto a
city of Galilee, named Nazareth,
27 To a [b]virgin espoused to a man
whose name was Joseph, of the house
of David; and the virgin's name *was*
Mary.
28 And the angel came in unto her,
and said, Hail, *thou that art* [2]highly
favoured, the Lord *is* with thee: blessed *art* thou among women.
29 And when she saw *him*, she was
troubled at his saying, and cast in her
mind what manner of salutation this
should be.
30 And the angel said unto her, Fear
not, Mary: for thou hast found favour
with God.
31 And, [c]behold, thou shalt conceive
in thy womb, and bring forth a son,
and shalt call his name JESUS.
32 He shall be [d]great, and shall be
called the Son of the Highest: and [e]the
Lord God shall give unto him the
throne of his father David:
33 And he [f]shall reign over the house
of Jacob for ever; and of his kingdom
there shall be no end.
34 Then said Mary unto the angel,
How shall this be, seeing I know not
a man?
35 And the angel answered and said
unto her, The Holy Ghost shall come
upon thee, and the power of the Highest shall overshadow thee: therefore
also that holy thing which shall be
born of thee shall be called the [g]Son of
God.
36 And, behold, thy cousin Elisabeth, she hath also conceived a son in
her old age: and this is the sixth month
with her, who was called barren.
37 For [h]with God nothing shall be
impossible.
38 And Mary said, Behold the handmaid of the Lord; be it unto me
according to thy word. And the angel
departed from her.
39 And Mary arose in those days,
and went into the hill country with
haste, [i]into a city of Juda;
40 And entered into the house of
Zăch-ă-rī-ăs, and saluted Elisabeth.
41 And it came to pass, that, when
Elisabeth heard the salutation of
Mary, the babe leaped in her womb;
and Elisabeth was filled [j]with the
Holy Ghost:
42 And she spake out with a loud
voice, and said, [k]Blessed *art* thou
among women, and blessed *is* the fruit
of thy womb.
43 And whence *is* this to me, that the
mother of my Lord should come to
me?
44 For, lo, as soon as the voice of thy
salutation sounded in mine ears, the
babe leaped in my womb for joy.
45 And blessed *is* she [3]that believed:
for there shall be a performance of
those things which were told her from
the Lord.
46 And Mary said, [l]My soul doth
magnify the Lord,
47 And my spirit hath rejoiced in
God my Saviour.
48 For [m]he hath regarded the low
estate of his handmaiden: for, behold, from henceforth [n]all generations shall call me blessed.
49 For he that is mighty hath done
to me great things; and holy *is* his
name.
50 And [o]his mercy *is* on them that
fear him from generation to generation.
51 He [p]hath shewed strength with
his arm; [q]he hath scattered the proud
in the imagination of their hearts.
52 He [r]hath put down the mighty
from *their* seats, and exalted them of
low degree.
53 He [s]hath filled the hungry with
good things; and the rich he hath sent
empty away.
54 He hath holpen his servant Israel,
[t]in remembrance of *his* mercy;
55 As [u]he spake to our fathers, to
Abraham, and to his seed for ever.

x Eze. 3.26. Eze. 24.27.
y Num. 6.23.
z 2 Ki. 11.5.
a Gen. 30.23.
b Isa. 7.14.
2 Or, graciously accepted, or, much graced.
c Gal. 4.4.
d Phil. 2.10. 1 Tim. 6.15.
e 2 Sam. 7.11. Ps. 132.11. Isa. 9.6,7. Isa. 16.5. Jer. 23.5. Jer. 33.15-17.
f Dan. 2.44. Dan. 7.14. Obad. 21. Micah 4.7. John 12.34. Heb. 1.8.
g Matt. 14. 33. John 20.31. Acts 8.37. Rom. 1.4.
h Gen. 18.14. Ps. 115.3. Jer. 32.17. Zech. 8.6. Matt. 3.9.
i Josh. 21.9.
j Acts 6.3.
k Judg. 5.24.
3 Or, which believed that there.
l 1 Sam. 2.1.
m 1 Sam. 1. 11. Ps. 138.6.
n Gen. 30.13. Mal. 3.12. ch. 11.27.
o Gen. 17.7. Ex. 20.6. Ex. 34.6,7. Ps. 85.9.
p Ps. 98.1. Ps. 118.15. Isa. 40.10.
q Ps. 33.10. 1 Pet. 5.5.
r 1 Sam. 2.6. Job 5.11. Ps. 113.6.
s 1 Sam. 2.5. Ps. 34.10. Ps. 107.8,9. Eze. 34.29.
t Ps. 98.3. Jer. 31.3,20.
u Gen. 17.19. Gal. 3.16.

56 And Mary abode with her about
three months, and returned to her
own house.
57 Now Elisabeth's full time came
that she should be delivered; and she
brought forth a son.
58 And her neighbours and her
cousins heard how the Lord had shewed great mercy upon her; and they rejoiced with her.
59 And it came to pass, that [v]on the
eighth day they came to circumcise
the child; and they called him Zăch-
ă-rī-ăs, after the name of his father.
60 And his mother answered and
said, Not *so;* but he shall be called
John.
61 And they said unto her, There is
none of thy kindred that is called by
this name.
62 And they made signs to his father,
how he would have him called.
63 And he asked for a writing table,
and wrote, saying, His name is John.
And they marvelled all.
64 And his mouth was opened immediately, and his tongue *loosed,* and
he spake, and praised God.
65 And fear came on all that dwelt
round about them: and all these [4]say-
ings were noised abroad throughout
all the hill country of Judæa.
66 And all they that heard [w]*them* laid
them up in their hearts, saying, What
manner of child shall this be! And [x]the
hand of the Lord was with him.
67 And his father Zăch-ă-rī-ăs was
[y]filled with the Holy Ghost, and prophesied, saying,
68 Blessed *be* the Lord God of Israel;
for he hath visited and redeemed his
people,
69 And hath raised up an horn of
salvation for us in the house of his
servant David;
70 As [z]he spake by the mouth of his
holy prophets, which have been since
the world began:
71 That we should be saved from our
enemies, and from the hand of all that
hate us;
72 To [a]perform the mercy *promised*
to our fathers, and to remember his
holy covenant;
73 The [b]oath which he sware to our
father Abraham,
74 That he would grant unto us, that
we being delivered out of the hand of
our enemies might [c]serve him without
fear,
75 In [d]holiness and righteousness before him, all the days of our life.
76 And thou, child, shalt be called

v Gen. 17.12. Lev. 12.3.
4 Or, things.
w ch. 2.19.
x Acts 11.21.
y 2 Chr. 20. 16. Joel 2.28.
z Jer. 23.5. Jer. 30.10. Dan. 9.24. Acts 3.21. Rom. 1.2.
a Lev. 26.42.
b Gen. 12.3. Heb. 6.13.
c Rom. 6.18. Heb. 9.14.
d Jer. 32.39. Eph. 4.24. 2 Thes. 2.13.
e Isa. 40.3.
5 Or, for.
6 Or, bowels of the mercy.
7 Or, sun-rising, or, branch. Num. 24.17. Isa. 11.1.
f Isa. 9.2.

CHAP. 2

1 Or, enrolled in order to be taxed. Acts 5.37.
a Gen. 35.19. 1 Sam. 16.1. Micah 5.2. Matt. 2.6.
b Matt. 1.16. ch. 1.27.
c Matt. 1.25. Gal. 4.4.
d Isa. 53.2. 2 Cor. 4.4.
2 Or, the night watches.
e Gen. 12.3. Ps. 72.8. Isa. 2.2. Isa. 42.6. Isa. 49.6. Isa. 60.3. Acts 13.47. Rom. 15.8. Col. 1.23.
f Isa. 7.14. Isa. 9.6. John 3.16-18.
g Phil. 2.11.
h Gen. 28.12. Ps. 103.20. Dan. 7.10. Heb. 1.14.

the prophet of the Highest: for [e]tho
shalt go before the face of the Lord t
prepare his ways;
77 To give knowledge of salvatio
unto his people [5]by the remission o
their sins,
78 Through the [6]tender mercy of ou
God; whereby the [7]dayspring from o
high hath visited us,
79 To [f]give light to them that sit i
darkness and *in* the shadow of death
to guide our feet into the way of peace
80 And the child grew, and waxe
strong in spirit, and was in the desert
till the day of his shewing unto Israel

CHAPTER 2

AND it came to pass in those days
that there went out a decree fron
Cæsar Augustus, that all the worl
should be [1]taxed.
2 (*And* this taxing was first mad
when Çȳ-rē-nĭ-ŭs was governor o
Syria.)
3 And all went to be taxed, every one
into his own city.
4 And Joseph also went up fron
Galilee, out of [a]the city of Nazareth
into Judæa, unto the city of David
which is called Bethlehem; (becaus
[b]he was of the house and lineage o
David:)
5 To be taxed with Mary his espousec
wife, being great with child.
6 And so it was, that, while they were
there, the days were accomplished tha
she should be delivered.
7 And [c]she brought forth her firstborn son, and wrapped him in swaddling clothes, and laid him in a
[d]manger; because there was no roon
for them in the inn.
8 And there were in the same country
shepherds abiding in the field, keeping
[2]watch over their flock by night.
9 And, lo, the angel of the Lord came
upon them, and the glory of the Lord
shone round about them: and they
were sore afraid.
10 And the angel said unto them,
Fear not: for, behold, I bring you
good tidings of great joy, [e]which shal
be to all people.
11 For [f]unto you is born this day in
the city of David a Saviour, which is
Christ [g]the Lord.
12 And this *shall be* a sign unto you;
Ye shall find the babe wrapped in
swaddling clothes, lying in a manger.
13 And [h]suddenly there was with the
angel a multitude of the heavenly host
praising God, and saying,
14 Glory to God in the highest, and

n earth [i]peace, [j]good will toward
ıen.
15 And it came to pass, as the angels
ʋere gone away from them into heav-
n, [3]the shepherds said one to another,
.et us now go even unto Bethlehem,
nd see this thing which is come to
ass, which the Lord hath made
nown unto us.
16 And they came with haste, and
ound Mary, and Joseph, and the
abe lying in a manger.
17 And when they had seen *it*, they
nade known abroad the saying which
vas told them concerning this child.
18 And all they that heard *it* wonder-
d at those things which were told
hem by the shepherds.
19 But Mary kept all these things,
nd pondered *them* in her heart.
20 And the shepherds returned,
lorifying and praising God for all the
hings that they had heard and seen,
s it was told unto them.
21 And [k]when eight days were ac-
omplished for the circumcising of
he child, his name was called [l]JESUS,
which was so named of the angel
efore he was conceived in the womb.
22 And when [m]the days of her puri-
ication according to the law of Moses
were accomplished, they brought him
o Jerusalem, to present *him* to the
Lord;
23 (As it is written in the law of the
Lord, Every [n]male that openeth the
womb shall be called holy to the
Lord;)
24 And to offer a sacrifice according
to that which is said in the law of the
Lord, A pair of turtledoves, or two
young pigeons.
25 And, behold, there was a man in
Jerusalem, whose name *was* Simeon;
and the same man *was* just and devout, [o]waiting for the consolation of
Israel: and the Holy Ghost was upon
him.
26 And it was revealed unto him by
the Holy Ghost, that he should not
[p]see death, before he had seen the
Lord's Christ.
27 And he came by [q]the Spirit into
the temple: and when the parents
brought in the child Jesus, to do for
him after the custom of the law,
28 Then took he him up in his arms,
and blessed God, and said,
29 Lord, [r]now lettest thou thy servant depart in peace, according to thy
word:
30 For mine eyes [s]have seen thy
salvation,
31 Which thou hast prepared before
the face of all people;
32 A [t]light to lighten the Gentiles,
and the glory of thy people Israel.
33 And Joseph and his mother marvelled at those things which were
spoken of him.
34 And Simeon blessed them, and
said unto Mary his mother, Behold,
this *child* is set for the [u]fall and rising
again of many in Israel; and for [v]a
sign which shall be spoken against;
35 (Yea, [w]a sword shall pierce
through thy own soul also,) that the
[x]thoughts of many hearts may be revealed.
36 And there was one Anna, [y]a prophetess, the daughter of Phă-nū-ĕl, of
the tribe of Ā-sĕr: she was of a great
age, and had lived with an husband
seven years from her virginity;
37 And she *was* a widow of about
fourscore and four years, which departed not from the temple, but served *God* with fastings and prayers
[z]night and day.
38 And she coming in that instant
gave thanks likewise unto the Lord,
and spake of him to all them that
[a]looked for redemption in [4]Jerusa-
lem.
39 And when they had performed all
things according to the law of the
Lord, they returned into Galilee, to
their own city Nazareth.
40 And the child grew, and waxed
strong in spirit, filled with wisdom:
and the grace of God was upon him.
41 Now his parents went to Jerusalem every [b]year at the feast of the passover.
42 And when he was twelve years
old, they went up to Jerusalem after
the custom of the feast.
43 And when they had fulfilled the
days, as they returned, the child Jesus
tarried behind in Jerusalem; and
Joseph and his mother knew not *of it*.
44 But they, supposing him to have
been in the company, went a day's
journey; and they sought him among
their kinsfolk and acquaintance.
45 And when they found him not,
they turned back again to Jerusalem,
seeking him.
46 And it came to pass, that after
three days they found him in the temple, sitting in the midst of the doctors,
[c]both hearing them, and asking them
questions.
47 And [d]all that heard him were
astonished at his understanding and
answers.

i Isa. 57.19. Col. 1.20.
j Eph. 2.4,7. 2 Thes. 2.16. 1 John 4.9.
3 the men the shepherds.
k Gen. 17.12. Lev. 12.3.
l Matt. 1.21.
m Lev. 12.2.
n Ex. 13.2. Ex. 22.29. Num. 3.13.
o Isa. 40.1.
p Ps. 89.48. Heb. 11.5.
q Acts 8.29. Rev. 1.10.
r Gen. 46.30. 1 Cor. 15.54. Phil. 1.23. Rev. 14.13.
s Gen. 49.18. 2 Sam. 23. 1-5. Isa. 52.10. Acts 4.12.
t Isa. 9.2. Acts 13.47.
u Isa. 8.14. Hos. 14.9. Rom. 9.32. 1 Cor. 1.23. 2 Cor. 2.16. 1 Pet. 2.7,8.
v Isa. 8.18. Matt. 26.65-67. Acts 24.5, 14. Acts 28.22. 1 Pet. 2.12. 1 Pet. 4.14.
w Ps. 42.10. John 19.25.
x 1 Cor. 11. 19.
y Ex. 15.20.
z Acts 26.7.
a Lam. 3.25, 26. Mark 15.43. ch. 24.21.
4 Or, Israel.
b Ex. 23.14-17. Deut. 16.1.
c Isa. 11.1-4.
d Matt. 7.28. Mark 1.22. John 7.15.

48 And when they saw him, they
were amazed: and his mother said
unto him, Son, why hast thou thus
dealt with us? behold, thy father and
I have sought thee sorrowing.
49 And he said unto them, How is it
that ye sought me? wist ye not that I
must be about [e]my Father's business?
50 ¶ And [f]they understood not the
saying which he spake unto them.
51 And he went down with them, and
came to Nazareth, and was subject
unto them: but his mother kept [g]all
these sayings in her heart.
52 And Jesus [h]increased in wisdom
and [5]stature, and in favour with God
and man.

CHAPTER 3

NOW in the fifteenth year of the
reign of Tī-bē-ʹrĭ-ŭs Cæsar, Pontius Pilate being governor of Judæa,
and Herod being tē-ʹträrch of Galilee,
and his brother Philip tē-ʹträrch of Ī-
tū-ræ-ʹă and of the region of Trăch-
ō-nī-ʹtĭs, and Lȳ-sā-ʹnĭ-ăs the tē-ʹträrch
of Ăb-ĭ-lē-ʹnē,
2 Ăn-ʹnăs and [a]Cāi-ʹă-phăs being the
high priests, the word of God came
unto John the son of Zăch-ă-rī-ʹăs in
the wilderness.
3 And [b]he came into all the country
about Jordan, preaching the baptism
of repentance [c]for the remission of
sins;
4 As it is written in the book of the
words of Ē-sāi-ʹăs the prophet, saying,
[d]The voice of one crying in the wilderness, Prepare ye the way of the Lord,
make his paths straight.
5 Every valley shall be filled, and
every mountain and hill shall be
brought low; and the crooked shall be
made straight, and the rough ways
shall be made smooth;
6 And [e]all flesh shall see the salvation
of God.
7 Then said he to the multitude that
came forth to be baptized of him, [f]O
generation of vipers, who hath warned you to flee from the wrath to come?
8 Bring [g]forth therefore fruits [1]worthy
of repentance, and begin not to say
within yourselves, We have Abraham
to *our* father: for I say unto you, That
God is able of these stones to raise
up children unto Abraham.
9 And now also the axe is laid unto
the root of the trees: [h]every tree therefore which bringeth not forth good
fruit is hewn down, and cast into the
fire.
10 And the people asked him, saying,
What [i]shall we do then?

e Ps. 40.8. Mal. 3.1,2. John 2.16. John 4.34.
f ch. 9.45. ch. 18.34.
g Gen. 37.11. Dan. 7.28.
h 1 Sam. 2.26. Pro. 3.4. Acts 2.47. Rom. 14.18.
5 Or, age.

CHAP. 3

a John 11.49. John 18.13. Acts 4.6.
b Mal. 4.6. Matt. 3.1. Mark 1.4.
c ch. 1.77.
d Isa. 40.3. Matt. 3.3.
e Ps. 98.2. Isa. 52.10.
f Matt. 3.7.
g Acts 26.20.
1 Or, meet for.
h Matt. 3.10. John 15.2,6.
i Acts 2.37.
j Mark 14.5-8. John 13.29. Acts 10.2, 31. 2 Cor. 8.14. 1 Tim. 6.18.
k Matt. 21. 32.
l Micah 6.8. ch. 19.8.
2 Or, Put no man in fear.
m Ex. 23.1. Lev. 19.11.
3 Or, allowance.
4 Or, in suspense.
5 Or, reasoned, or, debated.
n Matt. 3.11.
o Pro. 1.23. Isa. 32.15. Joel 2.28,29. John 7.39. Acts 2.4.
p Micah 4.12.
q Pro. 28.15, 16. Matt. 11.2. Mark 6.17.
r Matt. 3.13. John 1.32.
s 2 Pet. 1.17.
t Num. 4.3, 35,39,47.
u Matt. 13. 55. John 6.42.
6 son-in-law.

11 He answereth and saith unto
them, He that [j]hath two coats, let him
impart to him that hath none; and
he that hath meat, let him do likewise.
12 Then [k]came also publicans to be
baptized, and said unto him, Master,
what shall we do?
13 And he said unto them, [l]Exact no
more than that which is appointed
you.
14 And the soldiers likewise demanded of him, saying, And what
shall we do? And he said unto them,
[2]Do violence to no man, [m]neither accuse *any* falsely; and be content with
your [3]wages.
15 And as the people were [4]in expectation, and all men [5]mused in their
hearts of John, whether he were the
Christ, or not;
16 John answered, saying unto *them*
all, I [n]indeed baptize you with water;
but one mightier than I cometh, the
latchet of whose shoes I am not
worthy to unloose: he shall baptize
you with [o]the Holy Ghost and with
fire:
17 Whose fan *is* in his hand, and he
will throughly purge his floor, and
[p]will gather the wheat into his garner;
but the chaff he will burn with fire
unquenchable.
18 And many other things in his exhortation preached he unto the
people.
19 But [q]Herod the tē-ʹträrch, being
reproved by him for Hĕ-rō-ʹdĭ-ăs his
brother Philip's wife, and for all the
evils which Herod had done,
20 Added yet this above all, that he
shut up John in prison.
21 Now when all the people were
baptized, [r]it came to pass, that Jesus
also being baptized, and praying, the
heaven was opened,
22 And the Holy Ghost descended in
a bodily shape like a dove upon him,
and a voice came [s]from heaven, which
said, Thou art my beloved Son; in
thee I am well pleased.
23 And Jesus himself began to be
[t]about thirty years of age, being (as
was supposed) the [u]son of Joseph,
which was *the* [6]son of Hē-ʹlī,
24 Which was *the son* of Măt-ʹthăt,
which was *the son* of Levi, which was
the son of Mĕl-ʹchī, which was *the son*
of Jăn-ʹnă, which was *the son* of
Joseph,
25 Which was *the son* of Măt-tă-thī-ʹ
ăs, which was *the son* of Amos, which
was *the son* of Nā-ʹŭm, which was *the*

son of Ĕs´-lī, which was *the son* of
Năg´-gē,
26 Which was *the son* of Mā´-ăth,
which was *the son* of Măt-tă-thī´-ăs,
which was *the son* of Sĕm´-ĕ-ī, which
was *the son* of Joseph, which was *the*
son of Juda,
27 Which was *the son* of Jō-ăn´-nă,
which was *the son* of Rhē´-să, which
was *the son* of [7]Zŏ-rŏb´-ă-bĕl, which
was *the son* of Să-lă´-thĭ-ĕl, which was
the son of Nē´-rī,
28 Which was *the son* of Mĕl´-chī,
which was *the son* of Ăd´-dī, which was
the son of Cō´-săm, which was *the son*
of Ĕl-mō´-dăm, which was *the son* of
Ēr,
29 Which was *the son* of Jō´-sē, which
was *the son* of Ĕl-ĭ-ē´-zĕr, which was
the son of Jō´-rĭm, which was *the son*
of Măt´-thăt, which was *the son* of
Levi,
30 Which was *the son* of Simeon,
which was *the son* of Juda, which was
the son of Joseph, which was *the son*
of Jō´-năn, which was *the son* of Ē-lī´-
ă-kĭm,
31 Which was *the son* of Mĕl´-ĕ-ă,
which was *the son* of Mē´-năn, which
was *the son* of Măt´-tă-thă, which was
the son of [v]Nathan, which [w]was *the*
son of David,
32 Which [x]was *the son* of Jesse,
which was *the son* of Ō´-bĕd, which
was *the son* of Bō´-ŏz, which was *the*
son of Săl´-mŏn, which was *the son* of
Nā-ăs´-sŏn,
33 Which was *the son* of Ă-mĭn´-ă-
dăb, which was *the son* of Âr´-ăm,
which was *the son* of Ĕs´-rŏm, which
was *the son* of Phâr´-ĕs, which was *the*
son of Juda,
34 Which was *the son* of Jacob,
which was *the son* of Isaac, which was
the son of Abraham, [y]which was *the*
son of Thâr´-ă, which was *the son* of
Nā´-chôr,
35 Which was *the son* of Sâr´-ŭch,
which was *the son* of Rā´-gau, which
was *the son* of Phā´-lĕc, which was *the*
son of Hē´-bĕr, which was *the son* of
Sā´-lă,
36 Which [z]was *the son* of Cā-ī´-năn,
which was *the son* of Ăr-phăx´-ăd,
[a]which was *the son* of Sem, which was
the son of Nō´-ē, which was *the son* of
Lā´-mĕch,
37 Which was *the son* of Mă-thū´-să-
lă, which was *the son* of Ē´-nŏch, which
was *the son* of Jâr´-ĕd, which was *the*
son of Măl´-ĕ-leel, which was *the son*
of Cā-ī´-năn,
38 Which was *the son* of Ē´-nŏs, which
was *the son* of Seth, which was *the son*
of Adam, which [b]was *the son* of God.

CHAPTER 4

AND [a]Jesus being full of the Holy
Ghost returned from Jordan, and
[b]was led by the Spirit into the wilderness,
2 Being forty days [c]tempted of the
devil. And [d]in those days he did eat
nothing: and when they were ended,
he afterwards hungered.
3 And the devil said unto him, If
thou be the Son of God, command this
stone that it be made bread.
4 And Jesus answered him, saying,
[e]It is written, That man shall not live
by bread alone, but by every word of
God.
5 And the devil, taking him up into
an high mountain, shewed unto him
all the kingdoms of the world in a
moment of time.
6 And the devil said unto him, All
this power will I give thee, and the
glory of them: for [f]that is delivered
unto me; and to whomsoever I will I
give it.
7 If thou therefore wilt [1]worship me,
all shall be thine.
8 And Jesus answered and said unto
him, Get thee behind me, Satan: [g]for
it is written, Thou shalt worship the
Lord thy God, and him only shalt
thou serve.
9 And [h]he brought him to Jerusalem,
and set him on a pinnacle of the temple, and said unto him, If thou be the
Son of God, [i]cast thyself down from
hence:
10 For [j]it is written, He shall give his
angels charge over thee, to keep thee:
11 And in *their* hands they shall bear
thee up, lest at any time thou dash thy
foot against a stone.
12 And Jesus answering said unto
him, [k]It is said, Thou shalt not tempt
the Lord thy God.
13 And when the devil had ended all
the temptation, he [l]departed from him
[m]for a season.
14 ¶ And [n]Jesus returned in the
power of the Spirit into [o]Galilee: and
there went out a fame of him through
all the region round about.
15 And he taught in their synagogues, being [p]glorified of all.
16 ¶ And he came to [q]Nazareth,
where he had been brought up: and,
as his custom was, [r]he went into the
synagogue on the sabbath day, and
stood up for to read.
17 And there was delivered unto him

7 It is uncertain whether Zorobabel and Salathiel are the same as those mentioned in Matt. 1.12, 13, and 1 Chr. 3.17, 19.

v Zech. 12.12.
w 2 Sam. 5. 14. 1 Chr. 3.5.
x Ruth. 4.18. 1 Sam. 17. 58. 1 Chr. 2.10.
y Gen. 11.24, 26.
z Gen. 11.12.
a Gen. 5.6. Gen. 11.10.
b Gen. 1.26, 27. Gen. 2.7. Isa. 64.8.

CHAP. 4

a Isa. 11.2. Isa. 61.1. Matt. 4.1. Mark 1.12. John 1.33.
b 1 Ki. 18.12. Eze. 3.12. ch. 2.27. Acts 8.39.
c Gen. 3.15. Heb. 2.18.
d Ex. 34.28. 1 Ki. 19.8.
e Ex. 23.25. Deut. 8.3. Matt. 4.4. Mark 8.4. ch. 22.19. John 6.41, 48,50,51. Eph. 6.17.
f John 12.31. John 14.30. Rev. 13.2,7.
1 Or, fall down before me.
g Deut. 6.13. Deut. 10.20.
h Matt. 4.5.
i 1 Pet. 5.8.
j Ps. 91.11.
k Deut. 6.16.
l Jas. 4.7.
m John 14. 30. Heb. 4.15.
n Matt. 4.12. John 4.43.
o Acts 10.37.
p Isa. 52.13.
q Matt. 2.23.
r Acts 13.14.

the book of the prophet Ē-ṡâi´-ăs. And
when he had opened the book, he
found the place where it was written,
18 The [s]Spirit of the Lord *is* upon me,
because he hath anointed me to
preach the gospel to the poor; he hath
sent me to heal the brokenhearted, to
preach deliverance to the captives, and
recovering of sight to the blind, to set
at liberty them that are bruised,
19 To preach the [t]acceptable year of
the Lord.
20 And he closed the book, and he
gave *it* again to the minister, and sat
down. And the eyes of all them that
were in the synagogue were fastened
on him.
21 And he began to say unto them,
This day is this scripture fulfilled in
your ears.
22 And all bare him witness, and
[u]wondered at the gracious words
which proceeded out of his mouth.
And they said, [v]Is not this Joseph's
son?
23 And he said unto them, Ye will
surely say unto me this proverb,
Physician, heal thyself: whatsoever
we have heard done in [w]Că-pĕr´-nā-
ŭm, do also here in thy [x]country.
24 And he said, Verily I say unto you,
No prophet [y]is accepted in his own
country.
25 But I tell you of a truth, many
[z]widows were in Israel in the days of
Ē-lī´-ăs, when the heaven was shut up
three years and six months, when
great famine was throughout all the
land;
26 But unto none of them was Ē-lī´-ăs
sent, save unto Să-rĕp´-tă, *a city* of Ṡī´-
dŏn, unto a woman *that was* a widow.
27 And [a]many lepers were in Israel
in the time of Ĕl-ĭ-sē´-ŭs the prophet;
and none of them was cleansed, saving Nā´-ă-măn the Syrian.
28 And all they in the synagogue,
when they heard these things, were
filled with wrath,
29 And rose up, and thrust him out
of the city, and led him unto the [2]brow
of the hill whereon their city was
built, that they might cast him down
headlong.
30 But he [b]passing through the midst
of them went his way,
31 And [c]came down to Că-pĕr´-nā-
ŭm, a city of Galilee, and taught
them on the sabbath days.
32 And they were astonished at his
doctrine: [d]for his word was with
power.
33 ¶ And [e]in the synagogue there was

s Isa. 42.1. Dan. 9.24.
t Lev. 25.8. 2 Cor. 6.2.
u Ps. 45.2.
v John 6.42.
w Matt. 4.13.
x Matt. 13. 54. Mark 6.1.
y Matt. 13.57. Mark 6.4. John 4.44.
z 1 Ki. 17.9. 1 Ki. 18.1. Jas. 5.17.
a 2 Ki. 5.14.
2 Or, edge.
b John 8.59. John 10.39. Acts 12.7-11.
c Matt. 4.13. Mark 1.21.
d Matt. 7.28, 29. Titus 2.15.
e Mark 1.23.
3 Or, away.
f Ps. 16.10. Isa. 49.7. Dan. 9.24. ch. 1.35.
g Micah 5.4.
h Matt. 8.14. Mark 1.29.
i Ps. 103.3.
j Matt. 8.16. Mark 1.32.
k Mark 1.34.
l Mark 1.25, 34.
4 Or, to say that they knew him to be Christ.
m Matt. 14. 13. Mark 1.35.
n Mark 1.14, 15. John 9.4. Acts 10.38. Rom. 15.8.
o Matt. 4.53.

CHAP. 5

a Matt. 4.18. Mark 1.16.

a man, which had a spirit of an unclean devil, and cried out with a loud
voice,
34 Saying, [3]Let *us* alone; what have
we to do with thee, *thou* Jesus of Nazareth? art thou come to destroy us?
I know thee who thou art; [f]the Holy
One of God.
35 And Jesus rebuked him, saying,
Hold thy peace, and come out of him.
And when the devil had thrown him in
the midst, he came out of him, and
hurt him not.
36 And they were all amazed, and
spake among themselves, saying,
What a word *is* this! for with authority
and power he commandeth the unclean spirits, and they come out.
37 And [g]the fame of him went out into every place of the country round
about.
38 ¶ And [h]he arose out of the synagogue, and entered into Simon's
house. And Simon's wife's mother was
taken with a great fever; and they besought him for her.
39 And he stood over her, [i]and rebuked the fever; and it left her: and
immediately she arose and ministered
unto them.
40 ¶ Now [j]when the sun was setting,
all they that had any sick with divers
diseases brought them unto him; and
he laid his hands on every one of
them, and healed them.
41 And [k]devils also came out of
many, crying out, and saying, Thou
art Christ the Son of God. And [l]he
rebuking *them* suffered them not [4]to
speak: for they knew that he was
Christ.
42 And [m]when it was day, he departed and went into a desert place: and
the people sought him, and came unto
him, and stayed him, that he should
not depart from them.
43 And he said unto them, [n]I must
preach the kingdom of God to other
cities also: for therefore am I sent.
44 And [o]he preached in the synagogues of Galilee.

CHAPTER 5

AND [a]it came to pass, that, as the
people pressed upon him to hear
the word of God, he stood by the lake
of Gĕn-nĕs´-ă-rĕt,
2 And saw two ships standing by the
lake: but the fishermen were gone out
of them, and were washing *their* nets.
3 And he entered into one of the
ships, which was Simon's, and prayed
him that he would thrust out a little

from the land. And he sat down, and
taught the people out of the ship.
4 Now when he had left speaking, he
said unto Simon, [b]Launch out into the
deep, and let down your nets for a
draught.
5 And Simon answering said unto
him, Master, we have toiled all the
night, and have taken nothing: nevertheless at thy word I will let down the
net.
6 And when they had this done, they
inclosed a great multitude of fishes:
and their net brake.
7 And they beckoned unto *their* partners, which were in the other ship,
that they should come and help them.
And they came, and filled both the
ships, so that they began to sink.
8 When Simon Peter saw *it*, he fell
down at Jesus' knees, saying, Depart
[c]from me; for I am a sinful man, O
Lord.
9 For he was astonished, and all that
were with him, at the draught of the
fishes which they had taken:
10 And so *was* also James, and John,
the sons of Zĕb-ĕ-dēē, which were
partners with Simon. And Jesus said
unto Simon, Fear not; from [d]hence-
forth thou shalt catch men.
11 And when they had brought their
ships to land, [e]they forsook all, and
followed him.
12 ¶ And [f]it came to pass, when he
was in a certain city, behold a man full
of leprosy: who seeing Jesus fell on
his face, and besought him, saying,
Lord, if thou wilt, thou canst [g]make
me clean.
13 And he put forth *his* hand, and
touched him, saying, I will: be thou
clean. And immediately the leprosy
departed from him.
14 And [h]he charged him to tell no
man: but go, and shew thyself to the
priest, and offer for thy cleansing,
[i]according as Moses commanded, for
a testimony unto them.
15 But so much the more went there
a fame abroad of him: and great [j]mul-
titudes came together to hear, and to
be healed by him of their infirmities.
16 ¶ And [k]he withdrew himself into
the wilderness, and prayed.
17 And it came to pass on a certain
day, as he was teaching, that there
were Pharisees and doctors of the law
sitting by, which were come out of
every town of Galilee, and Judæa, and
Jerusalem: and the power of the Lord
was *present* to heal them.
18 ¶ And, [l]behold, men brought in a

b Matt. 17.27. John 21.6.
c Judg. 13.22. 1 Sam. 6.20. 2 Sam. 6.9. 1 Ki. 17.18. Job 42.5,6. Dan. 8.17.
d Eze. 47.9, 10. Matt. 4.19. Mark 1.17.
e Matt. 4.20. Mark 1.18. ch. 18.28. Phil. 3.7,8.
f Matt. 8.2. Mark 1.40.
g Gen. 18.14. Jer. 32.17, 27. Matt. 8.8. Mark 1.40, 41. Heb. 7.25.
h Matt. 8.4.
i Lev. 13.1. Lev. 14.4, 10,21,22.
j Matt. 4.25. ch. 12.1. John 6.2.
k Mark 14. 23.
l Matt. 9.2. Mark 2.3.
m Rev. 2.23.
n Matt. 9.2. John 5.14. Acts 5.31. 2 Cor. 2.10. Col. 3.13. Jas. 5.14, 15.
o Matt. 9.3. Mark 2.6,7.
p Ex. 34.7. Ps. 32.5. Ps. 103.3. Isa. 1.18. Isa. 43.25. Dan. 9.9.
q Acts 5.31. Col. 3.13.
r Ps. 103.1.
s Matt. 9.9. Mark 2.13, 14.
t Matt. 9.10. Mark 2.15.
u ch. 15.1.
v Matt. 9.13. 1 Tim. 1.15.
w Matt. 9.14. Mark 2.18.

bed a man which was taken with a
palsy: and they sought *means* to bring
him in, and to lay *him* before him.
19 And when they could not find by
what *way* they might bring him in because of the multitude, they went
upon the housetop, and let him down
through the tiling with *his* couch into
the midst before Jesus.
20 And when he saw their [m]faith, he
said unto him, Man, [n]thy sins are forgiven thee.
21 And [o]the scribes and the Pharisees began to reason, saying, Who is
this which speaketh blasphemies?
[p]Who can forgive sins, but God
alone?
22 But when Jesus perceived their
thoughts, he answering said unto
them, What reason ye in your hearts?
23 Whether is easier, to say, Thy sins
be forgiven thee; or to say, Rise up
and walk?
24 But that ye may know that the
[q]Son of man hath power upon earth
to forgive sins, (he said unto the sick
of the palsy,) I say unto thee, Arise,
and take up thy couch, and go into
thine house.
25 And immediately he rose up before them, and took up that whereon
he lay, and departed to his own house,
[r]glorifying God.
26 And they were all amazed, and
they glorified God, and were filled
with fear, saying, We have seen
strange things to day.
27 ¶ And [s]after these things he went
forth, and saw a publican, named
Levi, sitting at the receipt of custom:
and he said unto him, Follow me.
28 And he left all, rose up, and
followed him.
29 And [t]Levi made him a great feast
in his own house: and [u]there was a
great company of publicans and of
others that sat down with them.
30 But their scribes and Pharisees
murmured against his disciples, saying, Why do ye eat and drink with
publicans and sinners?
31 And Jesus answering said unto
them, They that are whole need not a
physician; but they that are sick.
32 I [v]came not to call the righteous,
but sinners to repentance.
33 ¶ And they said unto him, Why
[w]do the disciples of John fast often,
and make prayers, and likewise *the
disciples* of the Pharisees; but thine
eat and drink?
34 And he said unto them, Can ye
make the children of the bride-

chamber fast, while the [x]bridegroom is with them?

35 But the days will come, when the bridegroom shall [y]be taken away from them, and then shall [z]they fast in those days.

36 ¶ And [a]he spake also a parable unto them; No man putteth a piece of a new garment upon an old; if otherwise, then both the new maketh a rent, and the piece that was *taken* out of the new agreeth not with the old.

37 And no man putteth new wine into old bottles; else the new wine will burst the bottles, and be spilled, and the bottles shall perish.

38 But new wine must be put into new bottles; and both are preserved.

39 No man also having drunk old *wine* straightway desireth new: for he saith, The old is better.

CHAPTER 6

AND [a]it came to pass on the second sabbath after the first, that he went through the corn fields; and his disciples plucked the ears of corn, and did eat, rubbing *them* in *their* hands.

2 And certain of the Pharisees said unto them, [b]Why do ye that which is not lawful to do on the sabbath days?

3 And Jesus answering them said, Have ye not read so much as this, [c]what David did, when himself was an hungred, and they which were with him;

4 How he went into the house of God, and did take and eat the shewbread, and gave also to them that were with him; [d]which it is not lawful to eat but for the priests alone?

5 And he said unto them, That the Son of man is Lord also of the sabbath.

6 And [e]it came to pass also on another sabbath, that he entered into the synagogue and taught: and there was a man whose right hand was withered.

7 And the scribes and Pharisees watched him, whether he would heal on the sabbath day; that they might find an accusation against him.

8 But he [f]knew their thoughts, and said to the man which had the withered hand, Rise up, and stand forth in the midst. And he arose and stood forth.

9 Then said Jesus unto them, I will ask you one thing; [g]Is it lawful on the sabbath days to do good, or to do evil? to save life, or to destroy *it?*

10 And looking round about upon them all, he said unto the man, Stretch forth thy hand. And he did so: and his hand was restored whole as the other.

11 And they were filled with madness; and communed one with another what they might do to Jesus.

12 And [h]it came to pass in those days, that he went out into a mountain to pray, and continued all night in prayer to God.

13 ¶ And when it was day, he called *unto him* his disciples: [i]and of them he chose twelve, whom also he named apostles;

14 Simon, ([j]whom he also named Peter,) and Andrew his brother, James and John, Philip and Bartholomew,

15 Matthew and Thomas, James the *son* of Ăl-phǽ-ŭs, and Simon called Zē-lō-tēs,

16 And Judas [k]*the brother* of James, and Judas Iscariot, which also was the traitor.

17 ¶ And he came down with them, and stood in the plain, and the company of his disciples, [l]and a great multitude of people out of all Judæa and Jerusalem, and from the sea coast of Tyre and Sī-dŏn, which came to hear him, and to be healed of their diseases;

18 And they that were vexed with unclean spirits: and they were healed.

19 And the whole multitude sought [m]to touch him: for [n]there went virtue out of him, and healed *them* all.

20 ¶ And he lifted up his eyes on his disciples, and said, [o]Blessed *be ye* poor: for yours is the kingdom of God.

21 Blessed [p]*are ye* that hunger now: for ye shall be filled. [q]Blessed *are ye* that weep now: for ye shall laugh.

22 Blessed [r]are ye, when men shall hate you, and when they [s]shall separate you *from their company*, and shall reproach *you*, and cast out your name as evil, for the Son of man's sake.

23 Rejoice [t]ye in that day, and leap for joy: for, behold, your reward *is* great in heaven: for [u]in the like manner did their fathers unto the prophets.

24 But [v]woe unto you that are rich! for ye [w]have received your consolation.

25 Woe [x]unto you that are full! for ye shall hunger. [y]Woe unto you that laugh now! for ye shall mourn and weep.

26 Woe [z]unto you, when all men shall speak well of you! for so did their fathers to the false prophets.

27 ¶ But [a]I say unto you which hear,

x Matt. 22.2. ch. 14.16-23. 2 Cor. 11.2. Rev. 19.7. Rev. 21.2.
y Dan. 9.26. Zech. 13.7. John 7.33.
z Matt. 6.16, 17. Acts 13.2,3. 1 Cor. 7.5. 2 Cor. 6.4,5.
a Matt. 9.16, 17. Mark 2.21, 22.

CHAP. 6

a Matt. 12.1. Mark 2.23.
b Ex. 20.10. Matt. 12.2. Mark 2.24.
c 1 Sam. 21.6.
d Ex. 29.23, 33. Lev. 24.9.
e Matt. 12.9. Mark 3.1. ch. 13.14. ch. 14.3. John 9.16.
f 1 Sam. 16.7. ch. 5.22. John 2.24, 25. Acts 1.24. Rev. 2.23.
g Matt. 12. 12,13. Mark 3.4. ch. 14.3. John 7.23.
h Matt. 14.23.
i Matt. 10.1.
j John 1.42.
k John 14.12. Acts 1.13. Jude 1.
l Matt. 4.25.
m Matt. 14. 36.
n Mark 5.30.
o Matt. 5.3. 2 Thes. 1.5. Jas. 2.5.
p Isa. 55.1. 1 Cor. 4.11.
q Isa. 61.3. Rev. 7.14-17.
r 1 Pet. 2.19. 1 Pet. 3.14.
s John 16.2.
t Acts 5.41. Col. 1.24. Jas. 1.2.
u 2 Ki. 6.31. Acts 7.51.
v Amos 6.1. ch. 12.21.
w Matt. 6.2. ch. 16.25.
x Isa. 65.13.
y Pro. 14.13.
z John 15.19. 1 John 4.5.
a Ex. 23.4. Pro. 25.21.

Love your enemies, do good to them which hate you,

28 Bless them that curse you, and pray [b]for them which despitefully use you.

29 And [c]unto him that smiteth thee on the *one* cheek offer also the other; [d]and him that taketh away thy cloke forbid not *to take thy* coat also.

30 Give [e]to every man that asketh of thee; and of him that taketh away thy goods ask *them* not again.

31 And [f]as ye would that men should do to you, do ye also to them likewise.

32 For [g]if ye love them which love you, what thank have ye? for sinners also love those that love them.

33 And if ye do good to them which do good to you, what thank have ye? for sinners also do even the same.

34 And [h]if ye lend *to them* of whom ye hope to receive, what thank have ye? for sinners also lend to sinners, to receive as much again.

35 But love ye your enemies, and do good, and [i]lend, hoping for nothing again; and your reward shall be great, and [j]ye shall be the children of the Highest: for [k]he is kind unto the unthankful and *to* the evil.

36 Be [l]ye therefore merciful, as your Father also is merciful.

37 Judge [m]not, and ye shall not be judged: condemn not, and ye shall not be condemned: forgive, and ye shall be forgiven:

38 Give, [n]and it shall be given unto you; good measure, pressed down, and shaken together, and running over, shall men give into your [o]bosom. For [p]with the same measure that ye mete withal it shall be measured to you again.

39 And he spake a parable unto them, Can [q]the blind lead the blind? shall they not both fall into the ditch?

40 The [r]disciple is not above his master: but every one [1]that is perfect shall be as his master.

41 And [s]why beholdest thou the mote that is in thy brother's eye, but perceivest not the beam that is in thine own eye?

42 Either how canst thou say to thy brother, Brother, let me pull out the mote that is in thine eye, when thou thyself beholdest not the beam that is in thine own eye? Thou hypocrite, [t]cast out first the beam out of thine own eye, and then shalt thou see clearly to pull out the mote that is in thy brother's eye.

43 For [u]a good tree bringeth not forth corrupt fruit; neither doth a corrupt tree bring forth good fruit.

44 For every [v]tree is known by his own fruit. For of thorns men do not gather figs, nor of a bramble bush gather they [2]grapes.

45 A [w]good man out of the good treasure of his heart bringeth forth that which is good; and an evil man out of the evil treasure of his heart bringeth forth that which is evil: for of the abundance of the heart his mouth speaketh.

46 ¶ And [x]why call ye me, Lord, Lord, and do not the things which I say?

47 Whosoever [y]cometh to me, and heareth my sayings, and doeth them, I will shew you to whom he is like:

48 He is like a man which built an house, and digged deep, and laid the foundation on a rock: and when the [z]flood arose, the stream beat vehemently upon that house, and could not shake it: for it was founded upon [a]a rock.

49 But he that heareth, and doeth not, is like a man that without a foundation built an house upon the earth; against which the stream did beat vehemently, and immediately it fell; and [b]the ruin of that house was great.

b ch. 23.34. Acts 7.60.
c Matt. 5.39.
d 1 Cor. 6.7.
e Deut. 15.7. Pro. 3.27.
f Phil. 4.8.
g Matt. 5.46.
h Matt. 5.42.
i Lev. 25.35. Deut. 15.7, 8. Ps. 37.26. Pro. 14.20, 21.
j Matt. 5.45. 1 John 3.1.
k Acts 14.17.
l Matt. 5.48. Eph. 5.1,2.
m Eze. 16.52. Matt. 7.1. Rom. 2.1,2. Jas. 3.1.
n Pro. 19.17.
o Ps. 79.12.
p Deut. 19. 16-21. Judg. 1.7. Ps. 41.1,2. Matt. 7.2. Mark 4.24.
q Matt. 15.14.
r Matt. 10.24. John 13.16. John 15.20.
1 Or, shall be perfected as his master.
s Matt. 7.3.
t Pro. 18.17.
u Ps. 92.12-14. Isa. 5.4. Gal. 5.19, 23. 2 Tim. 3.1-9.
v Matt. 12.33.
2 a grape.
w Rom. 8.5-8.
x Mal. 1.6. ch. 13.25. Rom. 2.13. Jas. 1.22.
y Matt. 7.24.
z Acts 14.22. 2 Tim. 3.12.
a Ps. 125.1. 2 Tim. 2.19. 1 Pet. 1.5. Jude 1.
b Job 8.13. Heb. 10.28-31. 2 Pet. 2.20, 21.

CHAP. 7
a Matt. 8.5.

CHAPTER 7

NOW when he had ended all his sayings in the audience of the people, he entered into Că-pĕr´-nă-ŭm.

2 And [a]a certain centurion's servant, who was dear unto him, was sick, and ready to die.

3 And when he heard of Jesus, he sent unto him the elders of the Jews, beseeching him that he would come and heal his servant.

4 And when they came to Jesus, they besought him instantly, saying, That he was worthy for whom he should do this:

5 For he loveth our nation, and he hath built us a synagogue.

6 Then Jesus went with them. And when he was now not far from the house, the centurion sent friends to him, saying unto him, Lord, trouble not thyself: for I am not worthy that thou shouldest enter under my roof:

7 Wherefore neither thought I myself worthy to come unto thee: but say in a word, and my servant shall be healed.

8 For I also am a man set under authority, having under me soldiers,

and I say unto [1]one, Go, and he goeth;
and to another, Come, and he cometh;
and to my servant, Do this, and he doeth *it*.
9 When Jesus heard these things, he
marvelled at him, and turned him
about, and said unto the people that
followed him, I say unto you, I have
not found so great faith, no, not in
[b]Israel.
10 And they that were sent, returning
to the house, found the servant whole
that had been sick.
11 ¶ And it came to pass the day
after, that he went into a city called
Nā-ĭn; and many of his disciples went
with him, and much people.
12 Now when he came nigh to the
gate of the city, behold, there was a
dead man carried out, the only son of
his mother, and she was a widow: and
much people of the city was with her.
13 And when the Lord saw her, he
[c]had compassion on her, and said
unto her, Weep not.
14 And he came and touched the
[2]bier: and they that bare *him* stood
still. And he said, Young man, I say
unto thee, [d]Arise.
15 And he that was dead sat up, and
began to speak. And he delivered him
to his mother.
16 And [e]there came a fear on all: and
they glorified God, saying, That a
[f]great prophet is risen up among us;
and, [g]That God hath visited his
people.
17 And this rumour of him went
forth throughout all Judæa, and
throughout all the region round
about.
18 And the [h]disciples of John shewed
him of all these things.
19 ¶ And John calling *unto him* two
of his disciples sent *them* to Jesus,
saying, Art thou [i]he that should
come? or look we for another?
20 When the men were come unto
him, they said, John Baptist hath sent
us unto thee, saying, Art thou he
that should come? or look we for
another?
21 And in that same hour he cured
many of *their* infirmities and plagues,
and of evil spirits; and unto many *that*
were blind he gave sight.
22 Then [j]Jesus answering said unto
them, Go your way, and tell John
what things ye have seen and heard;
[k]how that the blind see, the lame
walk, the lepers are cleansed, the deaf
hear, the dead are raised, [l]to the poor
the gospel is preached.

1 this man.
b Rom. 3.1,2. Rom. 9.4.
c Lam. 3.32. John 11.33, 35. Heb. 4.15.
2 Or, coffin.
d 1 Ki. 17.21. Job 14.12, 14. ch. 8.54. John 11.43. Acts 9.40. Rom. 4.17. Eph. 5.14.
e ch. 1.65.
f ch. 24.19. John 4.19. John 6.14. John 7.40, 41. John 9.17. Acts 2.22. Acts 7.37.
g Ex. 4.31. Ps. 106.4,5. ch. 1.68.
h Matt. 11.2.
i Eze. 21.27. Eze. 34.23, 29. Dan. 9.24-26. Micah 5.2. Hag. 2.7. Zech. 9.9. Mal. 3.1-3.
j Matt. 11.4.
k Isa. 29.18. Isa. 35.5. Isa. 42.6.
l Isa. 61.1. Zeph. 3.12. ch. 4.18. Jas. 2.5.
m Matt. 11.7.
n Isa. 40.3. Mal. 3.1. ch. 1.16, 17,76. John 1.23.
o Matt. 3.5. ch. 3.12.
3 Or, frustrated.
p Acts 20.27.
4 Or, within themselves.
q Matt. 11. 16.
r Matt. 3.4. ch.1.15.
s Matt. 11.19. 1 Cor. 1.23, 24.
t Matt. 26.6. John 11.2.
u ch. 8.2.
v Zech. 12.10.

23 And blessed is *he*, whosoever shall
not be offended in me.
24 ¶ And [m]when the messengers of
John were departed, he began to speak
unto the people concerning John,
What went ye out into the wilderness
for to see? A reed shaken with the
wind?
25 But what went ye out for to see?
A man clothed in soft raiment? Behold, they which are gorgeously
apparelled, and live delicately, are in
kings' courts.
26 But what went ye out for to see?
A prophet? Yea, I say unto you, and
much more than a prophet.
27 This is *he*, of whom it is written,
[n]Behold, I send my messenger before
thy face, which shall prepare thy way
before thee.
28 For I say unto you, Among those
that are born of women there is not
a greater prophet than John the
Baptist: but he that is least in the kingdom of God is greater than he.
29 And all the people that heard *him*,
and the publicans, justified God, [o]be-
ing baptized with the baptism of John.
30 But the Pharisees and lawyers [3]re-
jected [p]the counsel of God [4]against
themselves, being not baptized of him.
31 ¶ And the Lord said, [q]Whereunto
then shall I liken the men of this generation? and to what are they like?
32 They are like unto children sitting
in the marketplace, and calling one to
another, and saying, We have piped
unto you, and ye have not danced; we
have mourned to you, and ye have not
wept.
33 For [r]John the Baptist came neither
eating bread nor drinking wine; and
ye say, He hath a devil.
34 The Son of man is come eating
and drinking; and ye say, Behold a
gluttonous man, and a winebibber, a
friend of publicans and sinners!
35 But [s]wisdom is justified of all her
children.
36 ¶ And [t]one of the Pharisees desired him that he would eat with him.
And he went into the Pharisee's house,
and sat down to meat.
37 And, behold, a [u]woman in the
city, which was a sinner, when she
knew that *Jesus* sat at meat in the
Pharisee's house, brought an alabaster box of ointment,
38 And stood at his feet behind *him*
[v]weeping, and began to wash his feet
with tears, and did wipe *them* with the
hairs of her head, and kissed his feet,
and anointed *them* with the ointment.

39 Now when the Pharisee which
had bidden him saw *it*, he spake within himself, saying, [w]This man, if he
were a prophet, would have known
who and what manner of woman *this*
is that toucheth him: for she is a
sinner.
40 And Jesus answering said unto
him, Simon, I have somewhat to say
unto thee. And he saith, Master, say
on.
41 There was a certain creditor which
had two debtors: the one owed five
hundred [x]pence, and the other fifty.
42 And when they had nothing to
pay, he frankly [y]forgave them both.
Tell me therefore, which of them will
love him most?
43 Simon answered and said, I suppose that *he*, to whom he forgave
most. And he said unto him, Thou
hast rightly judged.
44 And he turned to the woman, and
said unto Simon, Seest thou this woman? I entered into thine house, thou
gavest me no [z]water for my feet: but
she hath washed my feet with tears,
and wiped *them* with the hairs of her
head.
45 Thou gavest me no [a]kiss: but this
woman since the time I came in hath
not ceased to kiss my feet.
46 My [b]head with oil thou didst not
anoint: but this woman hath anointed
my feet with ointment.
47 Wherefore [c]I say unto thee, Her
sins, which are many, are forgiven;
for she loved much: but to whom
little is forgiven, *the same* loveth
little.
48 And he said unto her, [d]Thy sins
are forgiven.
49 And they that sat at meat with
him began to say within themselves,
[e]Who is this that forgiveth sins also?
50 And he said to the woman, Thy
[f]faith hath saved thee; go in peace.

CHAPTER 8

AND it came to pass afterward, that
he went throughout every city and
village, preaching and shewing the
glad tidings of the kingdom of God:
and the twelve *were* with him,
2 And [a]certain women, which had
been healed of evil spirits and infirmities, Mary called Măg-dă-lēne, [b]out
of whom went seven devils,
3 And Jō-ăn-nă the wife of Chû-ză
Herod's steward, and Susanna, and
many others, which ministered unto
him of their substance.
4 ¶ And [c]when much people were
gathered together, and were come to
him out of every city, he spake by a
parable:
5 A sower went out to sow his seed:
and as he sowed, some fell by the way
side; and it was trodden down, and
the fowls of the air devoured it.
6 And some fell upon a rock; and as
soon as it was sprung up, it withered
away, because it lacked moisture.
7 And some fell among thorns; and
the thorns sprang up with it, and
choked it.
8 And other fell on good ground, and
sprang up, and bare fruit an hundredfold. And when he had said these
things, he cried, He that hath ears to
hear, let him hear.
9 And [d]his disciples asked him, saying, What might this parable be?
10 And he said, Unto you it is given
to know the mysteries of the kingdom
of God: but to others in parables;
[e]that seeing they might not see, and
hearing they might not understand.
11 Now [f]the parable is this: The
[g]seed is the word of God.
12 Those by [h]the way side are they
that hear; then cometh [i]the devil, and
taketh away the word out of their
hearts, lest they should believe and be
saved.
13 They on the rock *are they*, which,
when they hear, receive the word with
joy; and these have no root, which for
a while believe, and in time of temptation fall away.
14 And that which fell among thorns
are they, which, when they have
heard, go forth, and are choked with
cares [j]and riches and pleasures of *this*
life, and bring no fruit to perfection.
15 But that on the good ground are
they, which in an honest and good
heart, having heard the word, keep *it*,
and [k]bring forth fruit with patience.
16 ¶ No [l]man, when he hath lighted
a candle, covereth it with a vessel, or
putteth *it* under a bed; but setteth *it* on
a candlestick, that they which enter in
may see the light.
17 For [m]nothing is secret, that shall
not be made manifest; neither *any*
thing hid, that shall not be known and
come abroad.
18 Take heed therefore how ye hear:
[n]for whosoever hath, to him shall be
given; and whosoever hath not, from
him shall be taken even that which he
[1]seemeth to have.
19 ¶ Then [o]came to him *his* mother
and his brethren, and could not come
at him for the press.

w ch. 15.2.
x Matt. 18. 28.
y Ps. 32.1-5. Ps. 51.1-3. Ps. 103.3. Isa. 1.18. Isa. 43.25. Isa. 44.22. Dan. 9.18, 19.
z Gen. 18.4. 1 Tim. 5.10.
a Gen. 29.11. Matt. 26.48, 49. 1 Cor. 16.20.
b Ps. 23.5. Ps. 45.7. Ps. 92.10. Eccl. 9.8.
c 1 Tim. 1.14.
d Matt. 9.2. Mark 2.5.
e Isa. 53.3. Matt. 9.3.
f Matt. 9.22. Mark 5.34. ch. 8.48. ch. 17.19. ch. 18.42.

CHAP. 8

a Matt. 27.55, 56.
b Mark 16.9.
c Matt. 13.2. Mark 4.1.
d Matt. 13. 10. Mark 4.10.
e Isa. 6.9. Mark 4.12.
f Matt. 13.18. Mark 4.14.
g Acts 20.27, 32. 1 Pet. 1.23.
h Jas. 1.23, 24.
i 2 Cor. 2.11. 2 Cor. 4.3.
j Matt. 19.23. 1 Tim. 6.9, 10. 2 Tim. 4.10.
k Eph. 2.4. 2 Pet. 1.5-10.
l Matt. 5.15. Mark 4.21. ch. 11.33. Phil. 2.15, 16.
m Eccl. 12. 14. Mark 4.22.
n Matt. 25. 29. Mark 4.25.
1 Or, thinketh that he hath.
o Matt. 12. 46. Mark 3.31. John 7.5. Acts 1.14. 1 Cor. 9.5.

20 And it was told him *by certain*
which said, Thy mother and thy
brethren stand without, desiring to
see thee.
21 And he answered and said unto
them, My mother and my brethren
are these which hear the word of God,
and do it.
22 ¶ Now [p]it came to pass on a certain day, that he went into a ship with
his disciples: and he said unto them,
Let us go over unto the other side of
the lake. And they launched forth.
23 But as they sailed he fell asleep:
and there came down a storm of wind
on the lake; and they were filled *with
water*, and were in jeopardy.
24 And they came to him, and awoke
him, saying, Master, master, we
perish. Then he [q]arose, and rebuked
the wind and the raging of the water:
and they ceased, and there was a calm.
25 And he said unto them, Where is
your faith? And they being [r]afraid
wondered, saying one to another,
What manner of man is this! for he
commandeth even the winds and
water, and they obey him.
26 ¶ And [s]they arrived at the country
of the Găd-ă-rēneṡ, which is over
against Galilee.
27 And when he went forth to land,
there met him out of the city a certain
man, which had devils long time, and
ware no clothes, neither abode in *any*
house, but in the tombs.
28 When he saw Jesus, he [t]cried out,
and fell down before him, and with a
loud voice said, What have I to do
with thee, Jesus, *thou* Son of God
most high? I beseech thee, torment
me not.
29 (For he had commanded the unclean spirit to come out of the man.
For oftentimes it had caught him: and
he was kept bound with chains and in
fetters; and he brake the bands, and
was driven of the devil into the wilderness.)
30 And Jesus asked him, saying,
What is thy name? And he said,
Legion: because many devils were
entered into him.
31 And they besought him that he
would not command them to go out
[u]into the deep.
32 And there was there an [v]herd of
many swine feeding on the mountain:
and they besought him that he would
suffer them to enter into them. And
he [w]suffered them.
33 Then went the devils out of the
man, and entered into the swine: and

p Matt. 8.23. Mark 4.35.
q Job 28.11. Job 38.11. Ps. 29.10. Ps. 46.1. Ps. 65.7.
r Ps. 33.8,9. Matt. 8.27. Mark 4.41. ch. 4.36.
s Matt. 8.28. Mark 5.1.
t Acts 16.16, 17. Phil. 2.10, 11.
u Rev. 20.3.
v Lev. 11.7. Deut. 14.8.
w Job 1.12. Job 12.16. Rev. 20.7.
x Rom. 16. 20. 1 John 3.8.
y Matt. 8.34.
z Deut. 5.25, 26. 1 Sam. 6.20. 1 Sam. 16.4. 2 Sam. 6.9. Job 21.14. Mark 1.24. ch. 4.34.
a Ps. 103.1. Ps. 116.12. Mark 5.18. ch. 18.43.
b Matt. 9.18. Mark 5.22.
c Lev. 15.25. Matt. 9.20.
d Mark 5.27, 28. Acts 5.15. Acts 19.12.
e Mark 5.30. ch. 5.17.

the herd ran violently down a steep
place into the lake, and were choked.
34 When they that fed *them* saw what
was done, they fled, and went and told
it in the city and in the country.
35 Then they went out to see what
was done; and came to Jesus, and
found the man, out of whom the devils
were departed, sitting at the feet of
Jesus, clothed, [x]and in his right mind:
and they were afraid.
36 They also which saw *it* told them
by what means he that was possessed
of the devils was healed.
37 ¶ Then [y]the whole multitude of
the country of the Găd-ă-rēneṡ round
about besought [z]him to depart from
them, for they were taken with great
fear: and he went up into the ship, and
returned back again.
38 Now [a]the man out of whom the
devils were departed besought him
that he might be with him: but Jesus
sent him away, saying,
39 Return to thine own house, and
shew how great things God hath done
unto thee. And he went his way, and
published throughout the whole city
how great things Jesus had done unto
him.
40 And it came to pass, that, when
Jesus was returned, the people *gladly*
received him: for they were all waiting
for him.
41 ¶ And, [b]behold, there came a man
named Jā-ī-rŭs, and he was a ruler of
the synagogue: and he fell down at
Jesus' feet, and besought him that he
would come into his house:
42 For he had one only daughter,
about twelve years of age, and she lay
a dying. But as he went the people
thronged him.
43 ¶ And [c]a woman having an issue
of blood twelve years, which had
spent all her living upon physicians,
neither could be healed of any,
44 Came behind *him*, and [d]touched
the border of his garment: and immediately her issue of blood stanched.
45 And Jesus said, Who touched me?
When all denied, Peter and they that
were with him said, Master, the multitude throng thee and press *thee*, and
sayest thou, Who touched me?
46 And Jesus said, Somebody hath
touched me: for I perceive that [e]virtue
is gone out of me.
47 And when the woman saw that
she was not hid, she came trembling,
and falling down before him, she declared unto him before all the people
for what cause she had touched him,

ınd how she was healed immediately.
48 And he said unto her, Daughter,
e of good comfort: thy faith hath
nade thee whole; go in peace.
49 ¶ While [f]he yet spake, there com-
th one from the ruler of the syna-
ogue's *house*, saying to him, Thy
laughter is dead; trouble not the
Master.
50 But when Jesus heard *it*, he an-
wered him, saying, Fear not: believe
only, and she shall be made whole.
51 And when he came into the house,
ıe suffered no man to go in, save
Peter, and James, and John, and the
ather and the mother of the maiden.
52 And all wept, and bewailed her:
ut he said, Weep not; she is not dead,
[h]but sleepeth.
53 And they laughed him to scorn,
nowing that she was dead.
54 And he put them all out, and took
ıer by the hand, and called, saying,
Maid, [i]arise.
55 And [j]her spirit came again, and
he arose straightway: and he com-
nanded to give her meat.
56 And her parents were astonished:
ut he [k]charged them that they should
ell no man what was done.

CHAPTER 9

THEN [a]he called his twelve disciples together, and [b]gave them
ower and authority over all devils,
nd to cure diseases.
2 And [c]he sent them to preach the
ingdom of God, and to heal the
ick.
3 And [d]he said unto them, Take
othing for *your* journey, neither
taves, nor scrip, neither bread, nei-
her money; neither have two coats
piece.
4 And [e]whatsoever house ye enter
nto, there abide, and thence depart.
5 And [f]whosoever will not receive
ou, when ye go out of that city, shake
off the very dust from your feet for a
estimony against them.
6 And [h]they departed, and went
hrough the towns, preaching the
ospel, and healing every where.
7 ¶ Now [i]Herod the tē-trärch heard
of all that was done by him: and he
vas perplexed, because that it was
aid of some, that John was risen from
he dead;
8 And of some, that Ē-lī-ăs had
ppeared; and of others, that one of
he old prophets was risen again.
9 And Herod said, John have I be-
ıeaded: but who is this, of whom I
hear such things? And he [j]desired to
see him.
10 ¶ And [k]the apostles, when they
were returned, told him all that they
had done. And [l]he took them, and
went aside privately into a desert place
belonging to the city called Běth-sā-
ĭ-dă.
11 And the people, when they knew
it, followed him: and he received
them, and spake unto them of the
kingdom of God, and healed them
that had need of healing.
12 And [m]when the day began to wear
away, then came the twelve, and said
unto him, Send the multitude away,
that they may go into the towns and
country round about, and lodge, and
get victuals: for we are here in a
desert place.
13 But he said unto them, [n]Give ye
them to eat. And they said, We [o]have
no more but five loaves and two
fishes; except we should go and buy
meat for all this people.
14 For they were about five thousand
men. And he said to his disciples,
Make them sit down by fifties in a
company.
15 And they did so, and made them
all sit down.
16 Then he took the five loaves and
the two fishes, and looking up to
heaven, he blessed them, and brake,
and gave to the disciples to set before
the multitude.
17 And they [p]did eat, and were all
filled: and there was taken up of fragments that remained to them twelve
baskets.
18 ¶ And [q]it came to pass, as he was
alone praying, his disciples were with
him: and he asked them, saying,
Whom say the people that I am?
19 They answering said, [r]John the
Baptist; but some *say*, Ē-lī-ăs; and
others *say*, that one of the old prophets is risen again.
20 He said unto them, But whom say
ye that I am? [s]Peter answering said,
The Christ of God.
21 And [t]he straitly charged them,
and commanded *them* to tell no man
that thing;
22 Saying, [u]The Son of man must
suffer many things, and be rejected
of the elders and chief priests and
scribes, and be slain, and be raised
the third day.
23 ¶ And [v]he said to *them* all, If any
man will come after me, let him deny
himself, and take up his cross daily,
and follow me.

f Mark 5.35.
g 2 Chr. 20. 20. Mark 5.36. Rom. 4.17-20.
h John 11.11, 13.
i ch. 7.14. John 11.43.
j Ps. 33.9.
k Matt. 8.4. Mark 5.43.

CHAP. 9

a Matt. 10.1. Mark 3.13.
b Matt. 10.1. Mark 16.17, 18. John 14.12. Acts 1.8. Acts 3.6.
c Matt. 10.7, 8. Mark 6.12. ch. 10.1,9.
d Ps. 37.3. Matt. 10.9. Mark 6.8. ch. 10.4.
e Matt. 10.11. Mark 6.10.
f Matt. 10.14.
g Acts 13.51.
h Matt. 9.24. Acts 9.40.
i Mark 6.14.
j ch. 23.8.
k Mark 6.30.
l Matt. 14.13.
m John 6.1, 5.
n 2 Ki. 4.42, 43.
o Num. 11. 22. Ps. 78.19,20.
p Ps. 145.15, 16.
q Matt. 16.13.
r Matt. 14.2.
s Mark 8.29. John 1.41, 49. John 6.69. Rom. 10.9. 1 John 4.14, 15.
t Matt. 16.20.
u Matt. 16. 21. Mark 8.31. ch. 18.31. ch. 24.6,7.
v Matt. 10.38. Mark 8.34. ch. 14.27.

24 For whosoever will save his life shall lose it: but whosoever will lose his life for my sake, the same shall save it.

25 For [w]what is a man advantaged, if he gain the whole world, and lose himself, or be cast away?

26 For [x]whosoever shall be ashamed of me and of my words, of him shall the Son of man be ashamed, when he shall come in his own glory, and *in his* Father's, and of the holy angels.

27 But [y]I tell you of a truth, there be some standing here, which shall not taste of death, till they see the kingdom of God.

28 ¶ And [z]it came to pass about an eight days after these [1]sayings, he took Peter and John and James, and went up into a mountain to pray.

29 And as he prayed, [a]the fashion of his countenance was altered, and his raiment *was* white *and* glistering.

30 And, behold, there talked with him two men, which were Moses and [b]Ē-lī́-ăs:

31 Who appeared in [c]glory, and spake of his decease which he should accomplish at Jerusalem.

32 But Peter and they that were with him were [d]heavy with sleep: and when they were awake, they saw his glory, and the two men that stood with him.

33 And it came to pass, as they departed from him, Peter said unto Jesus, Master, it is good for us to be here: and let us make three tabernacles; one for thee, and one for Moses, and one for Ē-lī́-ăs: not knowing what he said.

34 While he thus spake, there came a cloud, and overshadowed them: and they feared as they entered into the cloud.

35 And there came a voice out of the cloud, saying, [e]This is my beloved Son: hear [f]him.

36 And when the voice was past, Jesus was found alone. [g]And they kept *it* close, and told no man in those days any of those things which they had seen.

37 ¶ And [h]it came to pass, that on the next day, when they were come down from the hill, much people met him.

38 And, behold, a man of the company cried out, saying, Master, I beseech thee, look upon my son: for he is mine only child.

39 And, lo, a spirit taketh him, and he suddenly crieth out; and it teareth him that he foameth again, and bruising him hardly departeth from him.

40 And I besought thy disciples t cast him out; and they could not.

41 And Jesus answering said, (faithless and perverse generation how long shall I be with you, an suffer you? Bring thy son hither.

42 And as he was yet a coming, th devil threw him down, and tare *him* And Jesus rebuked the unclean spirit and healed the child, and delivere him again to his father.

43 ¶ And they were all amazed at th mighty power of God. But while the wondered every one at all thing which Jesus did, he said unto his disciples,

44 Let [i]these sayings sink down int your ears: for the Son of man shall b delivered into the hands of men.

45 But [j]they understood not this saying, and it was hid from them, tha they perceived it not: and they feare to ask him of that saying.

46 ¶ Then [k]there arose a reasonin among them, which of them shoul be greatest.

47 And Jesus, perceiving the though of their heart, took a child, and se him by him,

48 And said unto them, [l]Whosoeve shall receive this child in my nam receiveth me: and whosoever shall receive me receiveth him that sent me [m]for he that is least among you all, th same shall be great.

49 ¶ And [n]John answered and said Master, we saw one casting out devil in thy name; and we forbad him, because he followeth not with us.

50 And Jesus said unto him, Forbi *him* not: [o]for he that is not against u is for us.

51 ¶ And it came to pass, when th time was come that [p]he should be received up, he stedfastly set his face t go to Jerusalem,

52 And sent messengers before hi face: and they went, and entered int a village of the Să-măŕ-ĭ-tăns, to mak ready for him.

53 And [q]they did not receive him, because his face was as though he would go to Jerusalem.

54 And when his disciples James and John saw *this*, they said, Lord, wil thou that we command fire to com down from heaven, and consum them, even as [r]Ē-lī́-ăs did?

55 But he turned, and rebuked them, and said, Ye know not what [s]manne of spirit ye are of.

56 For the [t]Son of man is not com to destroy men's lives, but to save

w Ps. 49.6-8. Matt. 16.26. Mark 8.36. Acts 1.18, 25. Rev. 18.7,8.
x Mark 8.38. 2 Tim. 2.12.
y Matt. 16. 28.
z Matt. 17.1.
1 Or, things.
a Ex. 34.29, 35.
b 2 Ki. 2.11. Rom. 3.21.
c Ps. 17.15. Phil. 3.21. Col. 3.4. 1 John 3.2.
d Dan. 8.18. Matt. 26.40, 43. ch. 22.45.
e Matt. 3.17. John 12.28. 2 Pet. 1.16, 17.
f Ex. 23.21. Deut. 18.15, 18.
g Matt. 17.9.
h Matt. 17. 14.
i Matt. 17.22.
j Mark 9.32. ch. 2.50.
k Matt. 18.1.
l Mark 9.37. John 12.44.
m Matt. 23. 11,12.
n Num. 11. 28. Mark 9.38.
o Matt. 12. 30. ch. 11.23. 1 Cor. 12.3.
p Mark 16. 19. Acts 1.2.
q John 4.4,9.
r 1 Ki. 18.38. 2 Ki. 1.10, 12. Rev. 13.13.
s Job 2.10. Rom. 10.2.
t Matt. 9.13. John 3.17.

them. And they went to another
village.
57 ¶ And [u]it came to pass, that, as
they went in the way, a certain *man*
said unto him, Lord, I will follow thee
whithersoever thou goest.
58 And Jesus said unto him, Foxes
have holes, and birds of the air *have*
nests; but the Son of man hath not
where to lay *his* head.
59 And [v]he said unto another, Follow me. But he said, Lord, suffer me
first to go and bury my father.
60 Jesus said unto him, Let the dead
bury their dead: but go thou and
preach the kingdom of God.
61 And another also said, Lord, I
[w]will follow thee; but let me first go
bid them farewell, which are at home
at my house.
62 And Jesus said unto him, [x]No
man, having put his hand to the
plough, and looking back, is fit for the
kingdom of God.

CHAPTER 10

AFTER these things the Lord appointed other seventy also, and
sent them two and two before his face
into every city and place, whither he
himself would come.
2 Therefore said he unto them, The
harvest truly *is* great, but the labourers *are* few: [c]pray ye therefore the
Lord of the harvest, that he would
send forth labourers into his harvest.
3 Go your ways: [e]behold, I send you
forth as lambs among wolves.
4 Carry [f]neither purse, nor scrip, nor
shoes: and [g]salute no man by the way.
5 And [h]into whatsoever house ye
enter, first say, Peace *be* to this house.
6 And if the son of peace be there,
your peace shall rest upon it: if not, it
shall turn to you again.
7 And [i]in the same house remain,
eating [j]and drinking such things as
they give: for the [k]labourer is worthy
of his hire. Go not [l]from house to
house.
8 And into whatsoever city ye enter,
and they receive you, eat such things
as are set before you:
9 And [m]heal the sick that are therein,
and say unto them, [n]The kingdom of
God is come nigh unto you.
10 But into whatsoever city ye enter,
and they receive you not, go your
ways out into the streets of the same,
and say,
11 Even [o]the very dust of your city,
which cleaveth on us, we do wipe off
against you: notwithstanding be ye
sure of this, that the kingdom of God
is come nigh unto you.
12 But I say unto you, that [p]it shall
be more tolerable in that day for
Sodom, than for that city.
13 Woe [q]unto thee, Chō-rā́-zĭn! woe
unto thee, Bĕth-sā́-ĭ-dă! [r]for if the
mighty works had been done in Tyre
and Sī́-dŏn, which have been done in
you, they had a great while ago [s]re-
pented, sitting in sackcloth and ashes.
14 But it shall be more tolerable for
Tyre and Sī́-dŏn at the judgment, than
for you.
15 And [t]thou, Că-pĕŕ-nă-ŭm, which
art exalted [u]to heaven, [v]shalt be
thrust down to hell.
16 He [w]that heareth you heareth me;
and he [x]that despiseth you despiseth
me; [y]and he that despiseth me despiseth him that sent me.
17 ¶ And the seventy returned again
with joy, saying, Lord, even the devils
are subject unto us through thy name.
18 And he said unto them, [z]I beheld
Satan as lightning fall from heaven.
19 Behold, [a]I give unto you power to
tread on serpents and scorpions, and
over all the power of the enemy: and
nothing shall by any means hurt you.
20 Notwithstanding in this rejoice
not, that the spirits are subject unto
you; but rather rejoice, because your
[b]names are written in heaven.
21 ¶ In [c]that hour Jesus rejoiced in
spirit, and said, I thank thee, O
Father, Lord of heaven and earth,
that thou hast hid these things from
[d]the wise and prudent, and hast revealed them unto babes: even so,
Father; for so it seemed good in thy
sight.
22 [1]All things [e]are delivered to me of
my Father: and [f]no man knoweth
who the Son is, but the Father; and
who the Father is, but the Son, and *he*
to whom the Son will reveal *him.*
23 ¶ And he turned him unto *his* disciples, and said privately, Blessed [g]*are*
the eyes which see the things that ye
see:
24 For I tell you, [h]that many prophets and kings have desired to see those
things which ye see, and have not seen
them; and to hear those things which
ye hear, and have not heard *them.*
25 ¶ And, behold, a certain lawyer
stood up, and tempted him, saying,
[i]Master, what shall I do to inherit
eternal life?
26 He said unto him, What is written
in the law? how readest thou?
27 And he answering said, [j]Thou

u Matt. 8.19.
v Matt. 8.21.
w 1 Ki. 19.20.
x Heb. 6.4.

CHAP. 10

a Matt. 10.1.
b Matt. 9.37, 38. John 4.35. 1 Cor. 3.9.
c 2 Thes. 3.1.
d Jer. 3.15. 1 Cor. 12.28.
e Matt. 10.16.
f Matt. 10.9. ch. 9.3.
g 2 Ki. 4.29.
h Matt. 10. 12.
i Matt. 10.11.
j 1 Cor. 10. 27.
k Matt. 10. 10. 1 Cor. 9.4.
l Eph. 5.15.
m ch. 9.2.
n Isa. 2.2. Matt. 3.2. Rom. 10.8. Titus 2.11.
o Matt. 10. 14. ch. 9.5. Acts 13.51.
p Lam. 4.6. Eze. 16.48-50.
q Matt. 11. 21.
r Eze. 3.6.
s Jonah 3.5.
t Matt. 11.23.
u Gen. 11.4. Deut. 1.28. Isa. 14.13.
v Eze. 26.20.
w John 13.20.
x 1 Thes. 4.8.
y John 5.23.
z John 12.31. John 16.11. Heb. 2.14.
a Acts 28.5.
b Ex. 32.32. Ps. 69.28. Isa. 4.3. Dan. 12.1. Rev. 13.8.
c Matt. 11.25.
d 1 Cor. 1.19. 1 Cor. 2.6.
1 Many ancient copies add these words, And turning to his disciples, he said.
e Matt. 28.18. Eph. 1.21. Phil. 2.9.
f John 1.18. 2 Cor. 4.6.
g Matt. 13. 16.
h 1 Pet. 1.10.
i Matt. 22.35.
j Deut. 6.5. Mark 12.30, 31.

shalt love the Lord thy God with all
thy heart, and with all thy soul, and
with all thy strength, and with all thy
mind; and [k]thy neighbour as thyself.
28 And he said unto him, Thou hast
answered right: this do, [l]and thou
shalt live.
29 But he, willing to [m]justify himself,
said unto Jesus, And who is my
neighbour?
30 And Jesus answering said, A certain *man* went down from Jerusalem
to Jericho, and fell among thieves,
which stripped him of his raiment, and
wounded *him*, and departed, leaving
him half dead.
31 And by chance there came down
a certain priest that way: and when he
saw him, [n]he passed by on the other
side.
32 And likewise a Levite, when he
was at the place, came and looked *on
him*, and passed by on the other side.
33 But a certain [o]Să-măr′-ĭ-tăn, as he
journeyed, came where he was: and
when he saw him, he had compassion
on him,
34 And went to *him*, and bound up
his wounds, pouring in oil and wine,
and set him on his own beast, and
brought him to an inn, and took care
of him.
35 And on the morrow when he departed, he took out two pence, and
gave *them* to the host, and said unto
him, Take care of him; and whatsoever thou spendest more, when I come
again, I will repay thee.
36 Which now of these three, thinkest thou, was neighbour unto him that
fell among the thieves?
37 And he said, He that shewed
mercy on him. Then said Jesus unto
him, Go, and do thou likewise.
38 ¶ Now it came to pass, as they
went, that he entered into a certain
village: and a certain woman named
Martha received him into her house.
39 And she had a sister called Mary,
which also sat at Jesus' feet, and heard
his word.
40 But Martha was cumbered about
much serving, and came to him, and
said, Lord, dost thou not care that my
sister hath left me to serve alone? bid
her therefore that she help me.
41 And Jesus answered and said unto
her, Martha, Martha, thou art careful
and troubled about many things:
42 But one thing is needful: and
Mary hath chosen that good part,
which shall not be taken away from
her.

k Lev. 19.18. Matt. 19.19. Rom. 13.9.
l Lev. 18.5. Neh. 9.29.
m ch. 16.15.
n Ps. 38.11.
o John 4.9.

CHAP. 11
a Ps. 10.17. Ps. 19.14. Rom. 8.26, 27. 2 Cor. 3.5. Jas. 4.3. Jude 20.
b 2 Chr. 20.6. Ps. 11.4. Isa. 63.16. Matt. 5.16.
c Isa. 9.7. Dan. 7.14.
1 Or, for the day.
d Matt. 6.12, 14. Eph. 4.32.
e Matt. 6.13. ch. 22.46. 1 Cor. 10.13. Jas. 1.13. Rev. 3.10.
2 Or, out of his way.
f ch. 18.1.
g Ps. 50.15. Ps. 118.5. Jer. 33.3. Matt. 7.7. Mark 11.24. John 15.7. Jas. 1.6. 1 John 3.22. 1 John 5.14.
h Matt. 7.9.
3 give.
i Isa. 44.3. Jas. 1.15.
j Matt. 9.32.
k Matt. 9.34.
4 Beelzebul.
l Matt. 12.38.
m Mark 3.24. Rev. 2.23.

CHAPTER 11

AND it came to pass, that, as he was
praying in a certain place, when
he ceased, one of his disciples said unto him, Lord, [a]teach us to pray, as
John also taught his disciples.
2 And he said unto them, When ye
pray, say, [b]Our Father which art in
heaven, Hallowed be thy name. [c]Thy
kingdom come. Thy will be done, as
in heaven, so in earth.
3 Give us [1]day by day our daily
bread.
4 And forgive us our sins; for [d]we
also forgive every one that is indebted
to us. And [e]lead us not into temptation; but deliver us from evil.
5 And he said unto them, Which of
you shall have a friend, and shall go
unto him at midnight, and say unto
him, Friend, lend me three loaves;
6 For a friend of mine [2]in his journey
is come to me, and I have nothing to
set before him?
7 And he from within shall answer
and say, Trouble me not: the door is
now shut, and my children are with
me in bed; I cannot rise and give thee.
8 I say unto you, [f]Though he will not
rise and give him, because he is his
friend, yet because of his importunity
he will rise and give him as many as
he needeth.
9 And [g]I say unto you, Ask, and it
shall be given you; seek, and ye shall
find; knock, and it shall be opened
unto you.
10 For every one that asketh receiveth; and he that seeketh findeth; and
to him that knocketh it shall be
opened.
11 If [h]a son shall ask bread of any of
you that is a father, will he give him a
stone? or if *he ask* a fish, will he for a
fish give him a serpent?
12 Or if he shall ask an egg, will he
[3]offer him a scorpion?
13 If ye then, being evil, know how to
give good gifts unto your children:
how much more shall *your* heavenly
Father give the Holy [i]Spirit to them
that ask him? Sc Acts 5:32
14 ¶ And [j]he was casting out a devil,
and it was dumb. And it came to pass,
when the devil was gone out, the
dumb spake; and the people wondered.
15 But some of them said, [k]He casteth out devils through [4]Bē-ĕl′-zē-bŭb
the chief of the devils.
16 And others, tempting *him*, sought
[l]of him a sign from heaven.
17 But [m]he, knowing their thoughts

said unto them, Every kingdom divided against itself is brought to desolation; and a house *divided* against a
house falleth.
18 If Satan also be divided against
himself, how shall his kingdom stand?
because ye say that I cast out devils
through Bē-ĕl´-zĕ-bŭb.
19 And if I by Bē-ĕl´-zĕ-bŭb cast out
devils, by whom do [n]your sons cast
them out? therefore shall they be your
judges.
20 But if I [o]with the finger of God
cast out devils, no doubt the kingdom
of God is come upon you.
21 When [p]a strong man armed keepeth his palace, his goods are in peace:
22 But [q]when a stronger than he shall
come upon him, and overcome him,
he taketh from him all his armour
wherein he trusted, and divideth his
spoils.
23 He [r]that is not with me is against
me: and he that gathereth not with me
scattereth.
24 When [s]the unclean spirit is gone
out of a man, he walketh through dry
places, seeking rest; and finding none,
he saith, I will return unto my house
whence I came out.
25 And when he cometh, he findeth
it swept and garnished.
26 Then goeth he, and taketh *to him*
seven other spirits more wicked than
himself; and they enter in, and dwell
there: and the [t]last *state* of that man
is worse than the first.
27 ¶ And it came to pass, as he spake
these things, a certain woman of the
company lifted up her voice, and said
unto him, [u]Blessed *is* the womb that
bare thee, and the paps which thou
hast sucked.
28 But he said, Yea [v]rather, blessed
are they that hear the word of God,
and keep it.
29 ¶ And [w]when the people were
gathered thick together, he began to
say, This is an evil generation: they
seek a sign; and there shall no sign be
given it, but the sign of Jonas the
prophet.
30 For as [x]Jonas was a sign unto the
Nĭn´-ĕ-vites, so shall also the Son of
man be to this generation.
31 The [y]queen of the south shall rise
up in the judgment with the men of
this generation, and condemn them:
for she came from the utmost parts of
the earth to hear the wisdom of
Solomon; and, behold, [z]a greater than
Solomon *is* here.
32 The men of Nĭn´-ĕ-vē shall rise up
in the judgment with this generation,
and shall condemn it: [a]for they repented at the preaching of Jonas; and, behold, a greater than Jonas *is* here.
33 No [b]man, when he hath lighted a
candle, putteth *it* in a secret place,
neither under a [c]bushel, but on a
candlestick, that they which come in
may see the light.
34 The [d]light of the body is the eye:
therefore when thine eye is single, thy
whole body also is full of light; but
when *thine eye* is evil, thy body also *is*
full of darkness.
35 Take heed therefore that the light
which is in thee be not darkness.
36 If thy whole body therefore *be* full
of light, having no part dark, the
whole shall be full of light, as when
[5]the bright shining of a candle doth
give thee light.
37 ¶ And as he spake, a certain Pharisee besought him to dine with him:
and he went in, and sat down to meat.
38 And [e]when the Pharisee saw *it*, he
marvelled that he had not first washed
before dinner.
39 And [f]the Lord said unto him, Now
do ye Pharisees make clean the outside of the cup and the platter; but
[g]your inward part is full of ravening
and wickedness.
40 *Ye* fools, did not he that made
that which is without make that which
is within also?
41 But [h]rather give alms [6]of such
things as ye have; and, behold, all
things are clean unto you.
42 But [i]woe unto you, Pharisees! for
[j]ye tithe mint and rue and all manner
of herbs, and pass over judgment and
the love of God: these ought ye to
have done, and not to leave the other
undone.
43 Woe [k]unto you, Pharisees! for ye
love the uppermost seats in the synagogues, and greetings in the markets.
44 Woe [l]unto you, scribes and Pharisees, hypocrites! [m]for ye are as graves
which appear not, and the men that
walk over *them* are not aware *of them*.
45 ¶ Then answered one of the lawyers, and said unto him, Master, thus
saying thou reproachest us also.
46 And he said, Woe unto you also,
ye lawyers! [n]for ye lade men with burdens grievous to be borne, and ye
yourselves touch not the burdens with
one of your fingers.
47 Woe [o]unto you! for ye build the
sepulchres of the prophets, and your
fathers killed them.
48 Truly ye bear witness that ye allow

n Mark 9.38. ch. 9.49.
o Ex. 8.19. John 3.2. Acts 2.22.
p Matt. 12. 29. Mark 3.27. Eph. 2.2. 1 Pet. 5.8.
q Isa. 9.6. Isa. 53.12. Col. 2.15.
r Matt. 12.30.
s Matt. 12.43.
t John 5.14. Heb. 6.4.
u ch. 1.28,48.
v Ps. 1.1. Ps. 112.1. Isa. 48.17, 18. Matt. 7.21. ch. 8.21. Jas. 1.25. Rev. 22.14.
w Matt. 12. 38,39.
x Jonah 1.17.
y 1 Ki. 10.1.
z Isa. 9.6. Rom. 9.5. Phil. 2.10. Titus 2.13.
a Jonah 3.5.
b Matt. 5.15. Mark 4.21. ch. 8.16.
c Matt. 5.15.
d Ps. 119.18. Matt. 6.22. Acts 26.18. Eph. 1.18.
5 a candle by its bright shining.
e Matt. 16.2.
f Matt. 23.25.
g Gen. 6.5. Pro. 26.24. Jer. 4.14. Titus 1.15. Jas. 4.8.
h Isa. 58.7. Dan. 4.27. ch. 12.33.
6 Or, as you are able.
i Matt. 23.23.
j 1 Sam. 15. 22.
k Matt. 23.6.
l Matt. 23.27.
m Ps. 5.9. Acts 23.3.
n Matt. 23.4.
o Matt. 23.29.

the deeds of your fathers: for [p]they indeed killed them, and ye build their sepulchres.

49 Therefore also said the [q]wisdom of God, [r]I will send them prophets and apostles, and *some* of them they shall slay and persecute:

50 That the blood of all the prophets, which was shed from the foundation of the world, may be required of this generation;

51 From [s]the blood of Abel unto the blood of Zăch-ă-rī'-ăs, which perished between the altar and the temple: verily I say unto you, It shall be required of this generation.

52 Woe [t]unto you, lawyers! for ye have taken away the key of knowledge: ye entered not in yourselves, and them that were entering in ye [7]hindered.

53 And as he said these things unto them, the scribes and the Pharisees began to urge *him* vehemently, and to provoke him to speak of many things:

54 Laying wait for him, [u]and seeking to catch something out of his mouth, that they might accuse him.

CHAPTER 12

IN [a]the mean time, when there were gathered together an innumerable multitude of people, insomuch that they trode one upon another, he began to say unto his disciples first of all, [b]Beware ye of the leaven of the Pharisees, which is hypocrisy.

2 For [c]there is nothing covered, that shall not be revealed; neither hid, that shall not be known.

3 Therefore whatsoever ye have spoken in darkness shall be heard in the light; and that which ye have spoken in the ear in closets shall be proclaimed upon the housetops.

4 And [d]I say unto you my friends, Be not afraid of them that kill the body, and after that have no more that they can do.

5 But I will forewarn you whom ye shall fear: Fear him, which after he hath killed hath [e]power to cast into hell; yea, I say unto you, Fear him.

6 Are not five sparrows sold for two [f]farthings, and [g]not one of them is forgotten before God?

7 But even the very hairs of your head are all numbered. Fear not therefore: ye are of more value than many sparrows.

8 Also [h]I say unto you, Whosoever shall confess me before men, him shall the Son of man also confess before the angels of God:

9 But he that denieth me before men shall be denied before the angels of God.

10 And [i]whosoever shall speak a word against the Son of man, it shall be forgiven him: but unto him that blasphemeth against the Holy Ghost it shall not be forgiven.

11 And [j]when they bring you unto the synagogues, and *unto* magistrates, and powers, take ye no thought how or what thing ye shall answer, or what ye shall say:

12 For the [k]Holy Ghost shall teach you in the same hour what ye ought to say.

13 ¶ And one of the company said unto him, Master, speak to my brother, that he divide the inheritance with me.

14 And he said unto him, [l]Man, who made me a judge or a divider over you?

15 And he said unto them, [m]Take heed, and beware of covetousness: for a man's life consisteth not in the abundance of the things which he possesseth.

16 And he spake a parable unto them, saying, The ground of a certain rich man brought forth plentifully:

17 And he thought within himself, saying, What shall I do, because I have no room where to bestow my fruits?

18 And he said, This will I do: I will pull down my barns, and build greater; and there will I bestow all my fruits and my goods.

19 And I will say to my soul, Soul, [n]thou hast much goods laid up for many years; take thine ease, eat, drink, *and* be merry.

20 But God said unto him, *Thou* fool, this night [1]thy soul shall be required of thee: then [o]whose shall those things be, which thou hast provided?

21 So *is* he that layeth up treasure for himself, [p]and is not rich toward God.

22 ¶ And he said unto his disciples, Therefore I say unto you, Take [q]no thought for your life, what ye shall eat; neither for the body, what ye shall put on.

23 The life is more than meat, and the body *is more* than raiment.

24 Consider the ravens: for they neither sow nor reap; which neither have storehouse nor barn; and [r]God feedeth them: how much more are ye better than the fowls?

p Acts 7.51, 52.
q Pro. 1.20.
r Matt. 23.69.
s Gen. 4.8.
t Matt. 23.13.
7 Or, forbad.
u Mark 12.13.

CHAP. 12

a Matt. 16.6. Mark 8.15.
b Matt. 16. 12. 1 Cor. 5.7,8.
c Eccl. 12.14. Mark 4.22. ch. 8.17. 1 Cor. 4.5. Rev. 20.12.
d Isa. 8.12,13. Isa. 51.7,8, 12,13. Jer. 1.8. Acts 20.24.
e Ps. 9.17. Matt. 26 41, 46. 2 Pet. 2.4. Rev. 1.18.
f Matt. 10.29.
g Acts 15.18.
h 1 Sam. 2.30. Ps. 119.46. Matt. 10.32. Mark 8.38. Rom. 10.9. 2 Tim. 2.12. 1 John 2.23.
i Matt. 12.31, 32. Mark 3.28. 1 John 5.16.
j Matt. 10.19. Mark 13.11. ch. 21.14.
k Ex. 4.12. 1 Pet. 5.7.
l John 18.36.
m Pro. 28.16. 1 Tim. 6.7.
n Pro. 27.1. Eccl. 11.9. 1 Cor. 15.32.
1 Or, do they require thy soul.
o Ps. 39.6. Jer. 17.11.
p Matt. 6.20. 1 Tim. 6.18, 19. Jas. 2.5.
q Matt. 6.25. Phil. 4.6.
r Job 38.41. Ps. 147.9.

25 And which of you with taking thought can add to his stature one cubit?

26 If ye then be not able to do that thing which is least, why take ye thought for the rest?

27 Consider the lilies how they grow: they toil not, they spin not; and yet I say unto you, that Solomon in all his glory was not arrayed like one of these.

28 If then God so clothe the grass, which is to day in the field, and to morrow is cast into the oven; how much more *will he clothe* you, O ye of little faith?

29 And seek not ye what ye shall eat, or what ye shall drink, [2]neither be ye of doubtful mind.

30 For all these things do the nations of the world seek after: and your Father knoweth [s]that ye have need of these things.

31 ¶ But [t]rather seek ye the kingdom of God; and [u]all these things shall be added unto you.

32 Fear not, little flock; for [v]it is your Father's good pleasure to give you the kingdom.

33 Sell [w]that ye have, and give alms; provide [x]yourselves bags which wax not old, a treasure in the heavens that faileth not, where no thief approacheth, neither moth corrupteth.

34 For where your treasure is, there will your heart be also.

35 Let [y]your loins be girded about, [z]and *your* lights burning;

36 And ye yourselves like unto men that wait for their lord, when he will return from the wedding; that when he cometh and knocketh, they may open unto him immediately.

37 Blessed [a]*are* those servants, whom the lord when he cometh shall find watching: verily I say unto you, that he shall gird himself, and make them to sit down to meat, and will come forth and serve them.

38 And if he shall come in the second watch, or come in the third watch, and find *them* so, blessed are those servants.

39 And [b]this know, that if the goodman of the house had known what hour the thief would come, he would have watched, and not have suffered his house to be broken through.

40 Be [c]ye therefore ready also: for the Son of man cometh at an hour when ye think not.

41 ¶ Then Peter said unto him, Lord, speakest thou this parable unto us, or even to all?

42 And the Lord said, [d]Who then is that faithful and wise steward, whom *his* lord shall make ruler over his household, to give *them their* portion of meat in due season?

43 Blessed *is* that servant, whom his lord when he cometh shall find so doing.

44 Of a truth I say unto you, that [e]he will make him ruler over all that he hath.

45 But and if that servant say in his heart, My lord delayeth his coming; and shall begin to beat the menservants and maidens, and to eat and drink, and to be drunken;

46 The lord of that servant will come in a day when he looketh not for *him*, and at an hour when he is not aware, and will [3]cut him in sunder, and will appoint him his portion with the unbelievers.

47 And [f]that servant, which knew his lord's will, and prepared not *himself*, neither did according to his will, shall be beaten with many *stripes*.

48 But [g]he that knew not, and did commit things worthy of stripes, shall be beaten with few *stripes*. For unto whomsoever much is given, of him shall be much required: and to whom men have committed much, of him they will ask the more.

49 ¶ I am come to send fire on the earth; and what will I, if it be already kindled?

50 But [h]I have a baptism to be baptized with; and how am I [4]straitened till it be accomplished!

51 Suppose [i]ye that I am come to give peace on earth? I tell you, Nay; [j]but rather division:

52 For [k]from henceforth there shall be five in one house divided, three against two, and two against three.

53 The father shall be divided against the son, and the son against the father; the mother against the daughter, and the daughter against the mother; the mother in law against her daughter in law, and the daughter in law against her mother in law.

54 ¶ And he said also to the people, [l]When ye see a cloud rise out of the west, straightway ye say, There cometh a shower; and so it is.

55 And when *ye see* [m]the south wind blow, ye say, There will be heat; and it cometh to pass.

56 *Ye* [n]hypocrites, ye can discern the face of the sky and of the earth; but

---

2 Or, live not in careful suspense.
s 2 Chr. 16.9. Matt. 6.31, 32. Phil. 4.19.
t Matt. 6.33.
u Rom. 8.31. 1 Tim. 4.8.
v Matt. 11.25. 2 Thes. 1.11.
w Matt. 19. 21. Acts 2.45.
x Matt. 6.20. ch. 16.9. 1 Tim. 6.19.
y Eph. 6.14. 1 Pet. 1.13.
z Matt. 5.16. Phil. 2.15.
a Matt. 24.46. 2 Tim. 4.7,8. 1 Pet. 5.1-4. 2 Pet. 1.10, 11. Rev. 14.13.
b 1 Thes. 5.2. Rev. 16.15.
c Matt. 25.13. Mark 13.33. 1 Thes. 5.6. 2 Pet. 3.12, 14.
d Matt. 24. 45,46. ch. 19.15-19. 1 Cor. 4.2.
e 1 Pet. 5.4.
3 Or, cut him off.
f Num. 15. 30. Deut. 25.2. John 9.41. Acts 17.30. Jas. 4.17.
g Lev. 5.17. 1 Tim. 1.13.
h Matt. 20.22.
4 Or, pained.
i Matt. 10.34.
j Micah 7.6. John 7.43.
k Matt. 10. 35.
l Matt. 16.2.
m Job 37.17.
n 1 Cor. 1.19-27.

how is it that ye do not discern [o]this
time?
57 Yea, and why even of yourselves
judge ye not what is right?
58 ¶ When [p]thou goest with thine
adversary to the magistrate, *as* [q]*thou
art* in the way, give diligence that thou
mayest be delivered from him; lest he
hale thee to the judge, and the judge
deliver thee to the officer, and the
officer cast thee into prison.
59 I tell thee, thou shalt not depart
thence, till thou hast paid the very
last [r]mite.

CHAPTER 13

THERE were present at that season
some that told him [a]of the Galilæans, whose blood Pilate had mingled
with their sacrifices.
2 And Jesus answering said unto
them, Suppose [b]ye that these Galilæans were sinners above all the Galilæans, because they suffered such
things?
3 I tell you, Nay: but, except ye repent, ye shall all likewise perish.
4 Or those eighteen, upon whom the
tower in Sĭ-lō-ăm fell, and slew them,
think ye that they were [1]sinners above
all men that dwelt in Jerusalem?
5 I tell you, Nay: but, except [c]ye repent, ye shall all likewise perish.
6 ¶ He spake also this parable; [d]A
certain *man* had a fig tree planted in
his vineyard; and he came and sought
fruit thereon, and found none.
7 Then said he unto the dresser of
his vineyard, Behold, these three
[e]years I come seeking fruit on this fig
tree, and find none: cut it down; why
cumbereth it the ground?
8 And he answering said unto him,
Lord, let [f]it alone this year also, till I
shall dig about it, and dung *it:*
9 And if it bear fruit, *well:* and if not,
then after that thou shalt cut it down.
10 And he was teaching in one of the
synagogues on the sabbath.
11 ¶ And, behold, there was a woman
which had a spirit of infirmity eighteen
years, and was bowed together, and
could in no wise lift up *herself.*
12 And when Jesus saw her, he called
her to him, and said unto her, Woman,
thou art loosed from thine infirmity.
13 And [g]he laid *his* hands on her: and
immediately she was made straight,
and glorified God.
14 And the ruler of the synagogue
answered [h]with indignation, because
that Jesus had healed on the sabbath
day, and said unto the people, [i]There
are six days in which men ought to
work: in them therefore come and be
healed, and [j]not on the sabbath day.
15 The Lord then answered him, and
said, *Thou* hypocrite, [k]doth not each
one of you on the sabbath loose his ox
or *his* ass from the stall, and lead *him*
away to watering?
16 And ought not this woman, being
[l]a daughter of Abraham, whom Satan
hath bound, lo, these eighteen years,
be loosed from this bond on the sabbath day?
17 And when he had said these
things, all his adversaries were
ashamed: and all the people rejoiced
for all the glorious things that were
done by him.
18 ¶ Then [m]said he, Unto what is the
kingdom of God like? and whereunto
shall I resemble it?
19 It is like a grain of mustard seed,
which a man took, and cast into his
garden; and it grew, and waxed a
great tree; and the fowls of the air
lodged in the branches of it.
20 And again he said, Whereunto
shall I liken the kingdom of God?
21 It is like leaven, which a woman
took and hid in [n]three measures of
meal, till the whole was leavened.
22 And [o]he went through the cities
and villages, teaching, and journeying
toward Jerusalem.
23 Then said one unto him, Lord,
are there few that be saved? And he
said unto them,
24 ¶ [2]Strive to enter in at the strait
gate: for [p]many, I say unto you, will
seek to enter in, and shall not be able.
25 When [q]once the master of the
house is risen up, and [r]hath shut to
the door, and ye begin to stand without, and to knock at the door, saying,
[s]Lord, Lord, open unto us; and he
shall answer and say unto you, [t]I
know you not whence ye are:
26 Then shall ye begin to say, We
[u]have eaten and drunk in thy presence,
and thou hast taught in our streets.
27 But [v]he shall say, I tell you, I know
you not whence ye are; depart [w]from
me, all *ye* workers of iniquity.
28 There [x]shall be weeping and
gnashing of teeth, [y]when ye shall see
Abraham, and Isaac, and Jacob, and
all the prophets, in the kingdom of
God, and you *yourselves* thrust out.
29 And [z]they shall come from the
east, and *from* the west, and from the
north, and *from* the south, and shall
sit down in the kingdom of God.
30 And, [a]behold, there are last which

o ch. 19.42-44. Gal. 4.4.
p Pro. 25.8.
q Ps. 32.6. Isa. 55.6. Heb. 3.7-15.
r Matt. 18.34. Mark 12.42. 2 Thes. 1.9.
CHAP. 13
a Acts 5.37.
b Acts 28.4.
1 Or, debtors.
c Eze. 18.30.
d Isa. 5.2.
e Lev. 19.23. Rom. 2.4,5.
f Ex. 32.11. Joel 2.17.
g Ps. 103.3-5. Ps. 116.16, 17.
h John 5.15, 16. Rom. 10.2.
i Ex. 20.9.
j Matt. 12.10. ch. 14.3.
k ch. 14.5.
l ch. 19.9.
m Mark 4.30.
n Matt. 13. 33.
o Matt. 9.35. Mark 6.6.
2 Strive as in agony.
p John 7.34. Rom. 9.31.
q Ps. 32.6. Isa. 55.6.
r Matt. 25.10.
s ch. 6.46.
t Matt. 7.23.
u Titus 1.16.
v Matt. 7.23.
w Ps. 6.8.
x Matt. 8.12.
y Matt. 8.11.
z Gen. 28.14. Isa. 49.6-12. Acts 2.39. Rev. 5.9.
a Matt. 19. 30. Mark 10.31.

shall be first, and there are first which
shall be last.
31 ¶ The same day there came certain of the Pharisees, saying unto him,
Get thee out, and depart hence: for
Herod will kill thee.
32 And he said unto them, Go ye, and
tell that fox, Behold, I cast out devils,
and I do cures to day and to morrow,
and the third *day* [b]I shall be perfected.
33 Nevertheless I must walk to day,
and to morrow, and the *day* following:
for it cannot be that a prophet perish
out of Jerusalem.
34 O [c]Jerusalem, Jerusalem, which
killest the prophets, and stonest them
that are sent unto thee; how often
would I have gathered thy children
together, as a hen *doth gather* her
brood under *her* wings, and ye would
not!
35 Behold, [d]your house is left unto
you desolate: and verily I say unto
you, Ye shall [e]not see me, until *the*
time come when ye shall say, [f]Blessed
is he that cometh in the name of the
Lord.

CHAPTER 14

AND it came to pass, as he went into
the house of one of the chief Pharisees to eat bread on the sabbath day,
that they watched him.
2 And, behold, there was a certain
man before him which had the dropsy.
3 And Jesus answering spake unto
the lawyers and Pharisees, saying, [a]Is
it lawful to heal on the sabbath day?
4 And they held their peace. And he
took *him*, and healed him, and let him
go;
5 And answered them, saying, Which
[b]of you shall have an ass or an ox
fallen into a pit, and will not straightway pull him out on the sabbath day?
6 And they could not answer him
again to these things.
7 ¶ And he put forth a parable to
those which were bidden, when he
marked how they chose out the chief
rooms; saying unto them,
8 When thou art bidden of any *man*
to a wedding, sit not down in the highest room; lest a more honourable man
than thou be bidden of him;
9 And he that bade thee and him
come and say to thee, Give this man
place; and thou begin with shame to
take the lowest room.
10 But [c]when thou art bidden, go and
sit down in the lowest room; that
when he that bade thee cometh, he
may say unto thee, Friend, go up
higher: then shalt thou have worship
in the presence of them that sit at meat
with thee.
11 For [d]whosoever exalteth himself
shall be abased; and he that humbleth
himself shall be exalted.
12 ¶ Then said he also to him that
bade him, When thou makest a dinner
or a supper, call not thy friends, nor
thy brethren, neither thy kinsmen,
nor *thy* rich neighbours; lest they also
bid thee again, and a recompence be
made thee.
13 But when thou makest a feast,
call [e]the poor, the maimed, the lame,
the blind:
14 And thou shalt be blessed; for
they cannot recompense thee: for
thou shalt be recompensed [f]at the
resurrection of the just.
15 ¶ And when one of them that sat
at meat with him heard these things,
he said unto him, [g]Blessed *is* he that
shall eat bread in the kingdom of
God.
16 Then [h]said he unto him, A certain
man made a great supper, and bade
many:
17 And [i]sent his servant at supper
time to say to them that were bidden,
Come; for all things are now ready.
18 And they all with one *consent* began to make excuse. The first said unto
him, [j]I have bought a piece of ground,
and I must needs go and see it: I pray
thee have me excused.
19 And another said, I have bought
five yoke of oxen, and I go to prove
them: I pray thee have me excused.
20 And another said, I have married
a wife, and therefore I cannot come.
21 So that servant came, and shewed
his lord these things. Then the master
of the house being angry said to his
servant, Go [k]out quickly into the
streets and lanes of the city, and bring
in hither the poor, and the maimed,
and the halt, and the blind.
22 And the servant said, Lord, it is
done as thou hast commanded, and
yet there is room.
23 And the lord said unto the servant, Go out into the highways and
hedges, [l]and compel *them* to come in,
that my house may be filled.
24 For I say unto you, [m]That none of
those men which were bidden shall
taste of my supper.
25 ¶ And there went great multitudes
with him: and he turned, and said unto them,
26 If [n]any *man* come to me, [o]and hate
not his father, and mother, and wife,
and children, and brethren, and sis-

b Heb. 2.10.
c 2 Chr. 24. 21,22. Neh. 9.26, 27. Jer. 2.30.
d Ps. 69.25. Isa. 1.7. Dan. 9.27. ch. 21.24.
e Pro. 1.24-30. Hos. 3.5.
f Ps. 118.26. Isa. 62.11. Matt. 21.9. Mark 11.10. ch. 19.38. John 12.13.

CHAP. 14

a Matt. 12. 10.
b Ex. 23.5. Deut. 22.4. ch. 13.15. John 7.22, 23.
c Pro. 15.33. Pro. 18.12.
d Job 22.29. Ps. 18.27. Pro. 29.23. Matt. 23.12. ch. 18.14. Jas. 4.6. 1 Pet. 5.5.
e Neh. 8.10, 12. Job 31.14-20. Pro. 3.9,28.
f Dan. 12.2. Matt. 25.36. John 5.29. Acts 24. 15.
g Rev. 19.9.
h Matt. 22.2.
i Pro. 9.2,5.
j Matt. 6.24. ch. 8.14. John 5.40. 1 Tim. 6.9, 10. 2 Tim. 4.10.
k Matt. 28. 18,19. Acts 13.46.
l Pro. 1.20. 2 Cor. 5.20.
m Matt. 8.11, 12. Acts 13.46. Heb. 3.19.
n Deut. 13.6. Deut. 33.9. Matt. 10.37.
o Rom. 9.13.

ters, [p]yea, and his own life also, he cannot be my disciple.

27 And [q]whosoever doth not bear his cross, and come after me, cannot be my disciple.

28 For [r]which of you, intending to build a tower, sitteth not down first, and counteth the cost, whether he have *sufficient* to finish *it?*

29 Lest haply, after he hath laid the foundation, and is not able to finish *it,* all that behold *it* begin to mock him,

30 Saying, This man began to build, and was not able to finish.

31 Or what king, going to make war against another king, sitteth not down first, and consulteth whether he be able with ten thousand to meet him that cometh against him with twenty thousand?

32 Or else, while the other is yet a great way off, he sendeth an [s]ambassage, and desireth conditions of peace.

33 So likewise, whosoever [t]he be of you that forsaketh not all that he hath, he cannot be my disciple.

34 ¶ Salt [u]*is* good: but if the salt have lost his savour, wherewith shall it be seasoned?

35 It is neither fit for the land, nor yet for the dunghill; *but* men cast it out. He that hath ears to hear, let him hear.

CHAPTER 15

THEN [a]drew near unto him all the publicans and [b]sinners for to hear him.

2 And the Pharisees and scribes murmured, saying, This man receiveth sinners, and [c]eateth with them.

3 ¶ And he spake this parable unto them, saying,

4 What [d]man of you, having an hundred sheep, if he [e]lose one of them, doth not leave the ninety and nine in the wilderness, and go after that which is lost, until he find it?

5 And when he hath found *it,* he layeth *it* on his shoulders, rejoicing.

6 And when he cometh home, he calleth together *his* friends and neighbours, saying unto them, Rejoice with me; for I have found my sheep [f]which was lost.

7 I say unto you, that likewise joy shall be in heaven over one sinner that repenteth, [g]more than over ninety and nine just persons, which need no repentance.

8 ¶ Either what woman having ten [1]pieces of silver, if she lose one piece, doth not light a candle, and sweep the house, and seek diligently till she find *it?*

9 And when she hath found *it,* she calleth *her* friends and *her* neighbours together, saying, Rejoice with me; for I have found the piece which I had lost.

10 Likewise, I say unto you, there is joy in the presence of the angels of God over one sinner that repenteth.

11 ¶ And he said, A certain man had two sons:

12 And the younger of them said to *his* father, Father, give me the portion of goods that falleth *to me.* And he divided unto them [h]*his* living.

13 And not many days after the younger son gathered all together, and took his journey into a [i]far country, and there wasted his substance with riotous living.

14 And when he had spent all, there arose a mighty famine in that land; and he began to be in want.

15 And he went and joined himself to a citizen of that country; and he sent him into his fields to feed swine.

16 And he would fain have filled his belly with the husks that the swine did eat: and no man gave unto him.

17 And when he came to himself, he said, How many hired servants of my father's have bread enough and to spare, and I perish with hunger!

18 I will [j]arise and go to my father, and will say unto him, Father, [k]I have sinned against heaven, and before thee,

19 And am no more worthy to be called thy son: make me as one of thy hired servants.

20 And he arose, and came to his father. But [l]when he was yet a great way off, his father saw him, and had compassion, and ran, and fell on his neck, and kissed him.

21 And the son said unto him, Father, I have sinned against heaven, [m]and in thy sight, and am no more worthy to be called thy son.

22 But the father said to his servants, Bring forth [n]the best robe, and put *it* on him; and put a ring on his hand, and shoes on *his* feet:

23 And bring hither the fatted calf, and kill *it;* and let us eat, and be merry:

24 For [o]this my son was dead, and is alive again; he was lost, and is found. And they [p]began to be merry.

25 Now his elder son was in the field: and as he came and drew nigh to the house, he heard musick and dancing.

p Rev. 12.11.
q Matt. 16.24. Mark 8.34. ch. 9.23.
r Gen. 11.4-9. Pro. 24.27. Matt. 21.33. 1 Pet. 2.5.
s Job 22.21. ch. 12.58. 2 Cor. 6.2.
t Matt. 19.27, 28. Acts 5.1-5. 2 Tim. 4.10.
u Matt. 5.13.

CHAP. 15

a Matt. 9.10. Mark 2.15, 16. ch. 5.29.
b Eze. 18.23. 1 Tim. 1.15.
c Acts 11.3. Gal. 2.12.
d Matt. 18.12.
e 1 Pet. 2.25.
f 1 Pet. 2.10, 25.
g Pro. 30.12. ch. 5.32.
1 Drachma, here translated a piece of silver, is the eighth part of an ounce, which cometh to sevenpence halfpenny, and is equal to the Roman penny.
h Mark 12.44.
i Ps. 81.12. Jer. 2.5. Rom. 1.21.
j 2 Chr. 33. 12,13. Jer. 50.4,6. Lam. 3.40.
k Lev. 26.40. 1 Ki. 8.47, 48. Job 33.27, 28. Ps. 25.11. Pro. 28.13. ch. 18.13. 1 John 1.9.
l Isa. 49.15. Acts 2.39. Eph. 2.13, 17.
m Ps. 51.4. 1 Cor. 8.12.
n Isa. 61.10. Ps. 45.13,14. Gal. 3.27. Phil. 3.8,9. Rev. 19.8.
o Rom. 6.13. Eph. 2.1. Col. 1.13.
p Isa. 35.10.

26 And he called one of the servants, and asked what these things meant.

27 And he said unto him, Thy brother is come; and thy father hath killed the fatted calf, because he hath received him safe and sound.

28 And [q]he was angry, and would not go in: therefore came his father out, and intreated him.

29 And he answering said to *his* father, Lo, these many years do I serve thee, neither transgressed I at any time thy commandment; and [r]yet thou never gavest me a kid, that I might make merry with my friends:

30 But as soon as this thy son was come, which hath devoured thy living with harlots, thou hast killed for him the fatted calf.

31 And he said unto him, Son, thou art ever with me, and all that I have is thine.

32 It [s]was meet that we should make merry, and be glad: for this thy brother was dead, and is alive again; and was lost, and is found.

CHAPTER 16

AND he said also unto his disciples, There was a [a]certain rich man, which had a steward; and the same was accused unto him that he had wasted his goods.

2 And he called him, and said unto him, How is it that I hear this of thee? give an [b]account of thy stewardship; for thou mayest be no longer steward.

3 Then the steward said within himself, What shall I do? for my lord taketh away from me the stewardship: I cannot dig; to beg I am ashamed.

4 I am resolved what to do, that, when I am put out of the stewardship, they may receive me into their houses.

5 So he called every one of his lord's debtors *unto him*, and said unto the first, How much owest thou unto my lord?

6 And he said, An hundred [1]measures of oil. And he said unto him, Take thy bill, and sit down quickly, and write fifty.

7 Then said he to another, And how much owest thou? And he said, An hundred [2]measures of wheat. And he said unto him, Take thy bill, and write fourscore.

8 And the lord commended the unjust steward, because he had done wisely: for the children of this world are in their generation wiser than the [c]children of light.

9 And I say unto you, [d]Make to yourselves friends of the [3]mammon of unrighteousness; that, when ye fail, they may receive you into everlasting habitations.

10 He [e]that is faithful in that which is least is faithful also in much: and he that is unjust in the least is unjust also in much.

11 If therefore ye have not been faithful in the unrighteous [4]mammon, who will commit to your trust the [f]true *riches?*

12 And if ye have not been faithful in that which is another man's, who shall give you that which is your own?

13 ¶ No [g]servant can serve two masters: for either he will hate the one, and love the other; or else he will hold to the one, and despise the other. Ye cannot serve God and mammon.

14 And the Pharisees also, who [h]were covetous, heard all these things: and they derided him.

15 And he said unto them, Ye are they which [i]justify yourselves before men; but God [j]knoweth your hearts: for [k]that which is highly esteemed among men is abomination in the sight of God.

16 The [l]law and the prophets *were* until John: since that time the kingdom of God is preached, and every man presseth into it.

17 And [m]it is easier for heaven and earth to pass, than one tittle of the law to fail.

18 Whosoever [n]putteth away his wife, and marrieth another, committeth adultery: and whosoever marrieth her that is put away from *her* husband committeth adultery.

19 ¶ There was a certain rich man, which was clothed in purple and fine linen, and fared sumptuously every day:

20 And there was a certain beggar named Lăz'ă-rŭs, which was laid at his gate, [o]full of sores,

21 And desiring to be fed with the crumbs which fell from the rich man's table: moreover the dogs came and licked his sores.

22 And it came to pass, that the beggar died, and [p]was carried by the angels into Abraham's [q]bosom: the rich man also died, and was buried;

23 And in hell he lift up his eyes, being in torments, and seeth Abraham afar off, and Lăz'ă-rŭs in his bosom.

24 And he cried and said, Father Abraham, have mercy on me, and send Lăz'ă-rŭs, that he may dip the tip of his finger in water, and [r]cool my

q Acts 11.2.
r Matt. 20.11, 12.
s Rom. 15.9-12.

CHAP. 16

a Ps. 24.1.
b Eccl. 11.9, 10. Rom. 14.12. 2 Cor. 5.10. 1 Pet. 4.5.
1 The word Batus in the original containeth nine gallons three quarts. Eze. 45.10, 11,14.
2 The word here interpreted a measure, in the original containeth about fourteen bushels and a pottle.
c John 12.36. Eph. 5.8. 1 Thes. 5.5.
d Dan. 4.27. Matt. 6.19. ch. 11.41. 1 Tim. 6.17.
3 Or, riches.
e Matt. 25. 21. ch. 19.17.
4 Or, riches.
f Eph. 3.8. Rev. 3.18.
g Matt. 6.24.
h Matt. 23. 14. Titus 1.11.
i Matt. 6.2, 5,16. ch. 10.29.
j 2 Ki. 8.39. 1 Chr. 28.9. 2 Chr. 6.30. Ps. 7.9. Pro. 15.11.
k 1 Sam. 16. 7. Jas. 4.4.
l Matt. 11.12, 13.
m Ps. 102.26, 27. Isa. 40.8. 1 Pet. 1.25.
n 1 Cor. 7.10.
o Heb. 11.37.
p Ps. 34.7. Ps. 91.10,12. Heb. 1.14. Jas. 2.5.
q Matt. 8.11.
r Zech. 14.12.

tongue; for I [s]am tormented in this flame.

25 But Abraham said, Son, [t]remember that thou in thy lifetime receivedst thy good things, and likewise Lăz-ă-rŭs evil things: but now he is comforted, and thou art tormented.

26 And beside all this, between us and you there is a [u]great gulf fixed: so that they which would pass from hence to you cannot; neither can they pass to us, that *would come* from thence.

27 Then he said, I pray thee therefore, father, that thou wouldest send him to my father's house:

28 For I have five brethren; that he may testify unto them, lest they also come into this place of torment.

29 Abraham saith unto him, They have [v]Moses and the prophets; let them hear them.

30 And he said, Nay, father Abraham: but if one went unto them from the dead, they will repent.

31 And he said unto him, If they hear not Moses and the prophets, [w]neither will they be persuaded, though one rose from the dead.

CHAPTER 17

THEN said he unto the disciples, [a]It is impossible but that offences will come: but [b]woe *unto him*, through whom they come!

2 It were better for him that a millstone were hanged about his neck, and he cast into the sea, than that he should offend one of these little ones.

3 ¶ Take heed to yourselves: [c]If thy brother trespass against thee, rebuke [d]him; and if he repent, forgive [e]him.

4 And if he trespass against thee seven times in a day, and seven times in a day turn again to thee, saying, I repent; thou shalt forgive him.

5 And the apostles said unto the Lord, Increase our faith.

6 And [f]the Lord said, If ye had faith as a grain of mustard seed, ye might say unto this sycamine tree, Be thou plucked up by the root, and be thou planted in the sea; and it should obey you.

7 But which of you, having a servant plowing or feeding cattle, will say unto him by and by, when he is come from the field, Go and sit down to meat?

8 And will not rather say unto him, Make ready wherewith I may sup, and gird thyself, [g]and serve me, till I have eaten and drunken; and afterward thou shalt eat and drink?

9 Doth he thank that servant because he did the things that were commanded him? I trow not.

10 So likewise ye, when ye shall have done all those things which are commanded you, say, We are [h]unprofitable servants: we have done that which was our duty to do.

11 ¶ And it came to pass, [i]as he went to Jerusalem, that he passed through the midst of Să-mâr-ĭ-ă and Galilee.

12 And as he entered into a certain village, there met him ten men that were lepers, which [j]stood afar off:

13 And they lifted up *their* voices, and said, Jesus, Master, have mercy on us.

14 And when he saw *them*, he said unto them, [k]Go shew yourselves unto the priests. And it came to pass, that, as they went, they were cleansed.

15 And one of them, when he saw that he was healed, turned back, and with a loud voice [l]glorified God,

16 And fell down on *his* face at his feet, giving him thanks: and he was [m]a Să-măr-ĭ-tăn.

17 And Jesus answering said, Were there not ten cleansed? but where *are* the nine?

18 There are not found that returned to give glory to God, save this stranger.

19 And [n]he said unto him, Arise, go thy way: thy faith hath made thee whole.

20 ¶ And when he was demanded of the Pharisees, when the kingdom of God should come, he answered them and said, The kingdom of God cometh not [1]with observation:

21 Neither shall they say, Lo here! or, lo there! for, behold, the [o]kingdom of God is [2]within you.

22 And he said unto the disciples, [p]The days will come, when ye shall desire to see one of the days of the Son of man, and ye shall not see *it*.

23 And [q]they shall say to you, See here; or, see there: go [r]not after *them*, nor follow *them*.

24 For as the lightning, that lighteneth out of the one *part* under heaven, shineth unto the other *part* under heaven; so shall also [s]the Son of man be in his day.

25 But [t]first must he suffer many things, and be rejected of this generation.

26 And [u]as it was in the days of Nō-ĕ, so shall it be also in the days of the Son of man.

27 They did eat, they drank, they married wives, they were given in

s Isa. 66.24. Mark 9.44. Heb. 10.31.
t Job 21.13. ch. 6.24.
u 2 Thes. 1.9.
v Isa. 8.20. John 5.39, 45. Acts 15.21. 2 Tim. 3.15.
w John 12.10.

CHAP. 17
a Matt. 18.6, 7. Mark 9.42. 1 Cor. 11.19.
b Matt. 13.41, 42. 2 Thes. 1.6. Jude 11. Rev. 2.14, 15.
c Matt. 18.15.
d Lev. 19.17. Pro. 17.10. Jas. 5.19.
e 1 Cor. 13.4. Col. 3.12.
f Matt. 17.20. Mark 9.23.
g ch. 12.37.
h Job 22.3. Ps. 16.2. Matt. 25.37-40. Rom. 3.12. 1 Cor. 9.16. Phile. 11.
i ch. 9.51. John 4.4.
j Lev. 13.46. Num. 5.2.
k Lev. 13.2. Matt. 8.4.
l Ps. 103.1.
m 2 Ki. 17. 24. John 4.9. Acts 1.8.
n Matt. 9.22. Mark 5.34.
1 Or, with outward shew.
o Rom. 14.17. Col. 1.27.
2 Or, among you.
p Matt. 9.15. John 17.12.
q Matt. 24.23. ch. 21.8.
r 1 John 4.1.
s 1 Tim. 6.15.
t ch. 9.22.
u Gen. 7.1.

marriage, until the day that Nō-ē entered into the ark, and the flood came,
and destroyed them all.
28 Likewise [v]also as it was in the
days of Lot; they did eat, they drank,
they bought, they sold, they planted,
they builded;
29 But the same day that Lot went
out of Sodom it rained fire and brimstone from heaven, and destroyed *them*
all.
30 Even thus shall it be in the day
when the Son of man [w]is revealed.
31 In that day, he [x]which shall be
upon the housetop, and his stuff in the
house, let him not come down to take
it away: and he that is in the field, let
him likewise not return back.
32 Remember [y]Lot's wife.
33 Whosoever [z]shall seek to save his
life shall lose it; and whosoever shall
lose his life shall preserve it.
34 I [a]tell you, in that night there shall
be two *men* in one bed; the one shall
be taken, and the other shall be left.
35 Two *women* shall be grinding together; the one shall be taken, and the
other left.
36 [3]Two *men* shall be in the field; the
one shall be taken, and the other left.
37 And they answered and said unto
him, [b]Where, Lord? And he said unto
them, Wheresoever the body *is*,
thither will the eagles be gathered together.

CHAPTER 18

AND he spake a parable unto them
to this end, that men ought [a]al-
ways to pray, and not to faint;
2 Saying, There was [1]in a city a
judge, which feared not God, neither
regarded man:
3 And there was a widow in that city;
and she came unto him, saying,
Avenge me of mine adversary.
4 And he would not for a while: but
afterward he said within himself,
Though I fear not God, nor regard
man;
5 Yet [b]because this widow troubleth
me, I will avenge her, lest by her continual coming she weary me.
6 And the Lord said, Hear what the
unjust judge saith.
7 And [c]shall not God avenge his own
elect, which cry day and night unto
him, though he bear long with them?
8 I tell you [d]that he will avenge them
speedily. Nevertheless when the Son
of man cometh, shall he find faith on
the earth?
9 And he spake this parable unto

v Gen. 19.1.
w Matt. 24.3, 27-30. Mark 13.26. 2 Thes. 1.7. Rev. 1.7.
x Mark 13. 15.
y Gen. 19.26.
z Matt. 16.25.
a 1 Thes. 4. 17.
3 This verse is wanting in many Greek copies.
b Job 39.30.
CHAP. 18
a Gen. 32.9, 10. Ps. 55.16,17. ch. 11.5. Rom. 12.12. Eph. 6.18. Phil. 4.6. Col. 4.2.
1 in a certain city.
b Judg. 16.16. ch. 11.8.
c 1 Sam. 24. 12. Jer. 20.12. 2 Thes. 1.6.
d Heb. 10.37. 2 Pet. 3.8,9.
e Pro. 30.12. ch. 10.29. John 9.28. Phil. 3.4-6.
2 Or, as being righteous.
f Ps. 135.2.
g Isa. 1.15. Rev. 3.17.
h Ps. 40.12.
i Job 22.29. Isa. 2.11,12. Jas. 4.6. 1 Pet. 5.5,6.
j Matt. 19.13.
k Pro. 8.17.
l 1 Cor. 14.20.
m Matt. 19. 16.
n Ex. 20.12. Deut. 5.16. Rom. 13.9.
o Eph. 6.2. Col. 3.20.
p Matt. 6.19. 1 Tim. 6.19.
q Deut. 6.10-12. Ps. 10.3. Pro. 11.28. 1 Tim. 6.9. Jas. 2.5.

certain [e]which trusted in themselves
[2]that they were righteous, and despised others:
10 Two men went up into the temple
to pray; the one a Pharisee, and the
other a publican.
11 The Pharisee [f]stood and prayed
thus with himself, [g]God, I thank thee,
that I am not as other men *are*, extortioners, unjust, adulterers, or even
as this publican.
12 I fast twice in the week, I give
tithes of all that I possess.
13 And the publican, [h]standing afar
off, would not lift up so much as *his*
eyes unto heaven, but smote upon his
breast, saying, God be merciful to me
a sinner.
14 I tell you, this man went down to
his house justified *rather* than the
other: [i]for every one that exalteth
himself shall be abased; and he that
humbleth himself shall be exalted.
15 And [j]they brought unto him also
infants, that he would touch them:
but when *his* disciples saw *it*, they rebuked them.
16 But Jesus called them *unto him*,
and said, [k]Suffer little children to
come unto me, and forbid them not:
for [l]of such is the kingdom of God.
17 Verily I say unto you, Whosoever
shall not receive the kingdom of God
as a little child shall in no wise enter
therein.
18 And [m]a certain ruler asked him,
saying, Good Master, what shall I
do to inherit eternal life?
19 And Jesus said unto him, Why
callest thou me good? none *is* good,
save one, *that is*, God.
20 Thou knowest the commandments, [n]Do not commit adultery, Do
not kill, Do not steal, Do not bear
false witness, [o]Honour thy father and
thy mother.
21 And he said, All these have I kept
from my youth up.
22 Now when Jesus heard these
things, he said unto him, Yet lackest
thou one thing: sell [p]all that thou hast,
and distribute unto the poor, and thou
shalt have treasure in heaven: and
come, follow me.
23 And when he heard this, he was
very sorrowful: for he was very rich.
24 And when Jesus saw that he was
very sorrowful, he said, [q]How hardly
shall they that have riches enter into
the kingdom of God!
25 For it is easier for a camel to go
through a needle's eye, than for a rich
man to enter into the kingdom of God.

26 And they that heard *it* said, Who then can be saved?

27 And he said, [r]The things which are impossible with men are possible with God.

28 Then [s]Peter said, Lo, we have left all, and followed thee.

29 And he said unto them, Verily I say unto you, [t]There is no man that hath left house, or parents, or brethren, or wife, or children, for the kingdom of God's sake,

30 Who [u]shall not receive manifold more in this present time, and [v]in the world to come life everlasting.

31 ¶ Then [w]he took *unto him* the twelve, and said unto them, Behold, we go up to Jerusalem, and all things [x]that are written by the prophets concerning the Son of man shall be accomplished.

32 For [y]he shall be delivered unto the Gentiles, and shall be mocked, and spitefully entreated, and spitted on:

33 And they shall scourge *him*, and put him to death: and the third day he shall rise again.

34 And [z]they understood none of these things: and this saying was hid from them, neither knew they the things which were spoken.

35 ¶ And [a]it came to pass, that as he was come nigh unto Jericho, a certain blind man sat by the way side begging:

36 And hearing the multitude pass by, he asked what it meant.

37 And they told him, that Jesus of Nazareth passeth by.

38 And he cried, saying, Jesus, *thou* Son of David, have mercy on me.

39 And they which went before rebuked him, that he should hold his peace: but he cried so much the more, *Thou* Son of David, have mercy on me.

40 And Jesus [b]stood, and commanded him to be brought unto him: and when he was come near, he asked him,

41 Saying, What wilt thou that I shall do unto thee? And he said, Lord, that I may receive my sight.

42 And Jesus said unto him, Receive thy sight: [c]thy faith hath saved thee.

43 And immediately [d]he received his sight, and followed him, [e]glorifying God: and all the people, when they saw *it*, gave praise unto God.

CHAPTER 19

AND *Jesus* entered and passed through [a]Jericho.

2 And, behold, *there was* a man named Zăc-chæ'-ŭs, which was the chief among the publicans, and he was rich.

3 And he sought to see Jesus who he was; and could not for the press, because he was little of stature.

4 And he ran before, and climbed up into a sycomore tree to see him: for he was to pass that *way*.

5 And when Jesus came to the place, he looked up, and saw him, and said unto him, Zăc-chæ'-ŭs, make haste, and come down; for to day I must abide at thy house.

6 And he made haste, and came down, and received him joyfully.

7 And when they saw *it*, they all murmured, saying, [b]That he was gone to be guest with a man that is a sinner.

8 And Zăc-chæ'-ŭs stood, and said unto the Lord; Behold, Lord, the half of my goods I give to the poor; and if I have taken any thing from any man by [c]false accusation, I [d]restore *him* fourfold.

9 And Jesus said unto him, This day is salvation come to this house, forsomuch as [e]he also is a son of Abraham.

10 For [f]the Son of man is come to seek and to save that which was lost.

11 And as they heard these things, he added and spake a parable, because he was nigh to Jerusalem, and because [g]they thought that the kingdom of God should immediately appear.

12 He [h]said therefore, A certain nobleman went into a far country to receive for himself a kingdom, and to return.

13 And he called his ten servants, and delivered them ten [1]pounds, and said unto them, Occupy till I come.

14 But [i]his citizens hated him, and sent a message after him, saying, We will not have this *man* to reign over us.

15 And it came to pass, that when he was returned, having received the kingdom, then he commanded these servants to be called unto him, to whom he had given the [2]money, that he might know how much every man had gained by trading.

16 Then came the first saying, Lord, thy pound hath gained ten pounds.

17 And he said unto him, Well, thou good servant: because thou hast been [j]faithful in a very little, have thou authority over ten cities.

18 And the second came, saying, Lord, thy pound hath gained five pounds.

19 And he said likewise to him, Be thou also over five cities.

20 And another came, saying, Lord,

r Gen. 18.14. Job 42.2. Jer. 32.17. Zech. 8.6.
s Matt. 19.27.
t Deut. 33.9.
u Job 42.10.
v Rev. 2.17.
w Matt. 16. 21.
x Ps. 22. Isa. 53.
y Matt. 27.2. ch. 23.1. John 18.28. Acts 3.13.
z Mark 9.32. ch. 2.50. John 10.6.
a Matt. 20. 29.
b Heb. 2.17.
c ch. 17.19.
d Ps. 33.9. Isa. 35.5.
e Ps. 103.1. ch. 5.26. Acts 4.21. 1 Pet. 2.9.

CHAP. 19

a Josh. 6.26. 1 Ki. 16.34.
b Matt. 9.11. ch. 5.30.
c ch. 3.14.
d Ex. 22.1. Lev. 6.1-5. 1 Sam. 12.3. 2 Sam. 12.6. Pro. 6.31. 2 Cor. 7.11.
e ch. 13.16. Rom. 4.11, 12,16. Gal. 3.7.
f Matt. 9.13. Mark 2.17. ch. 5.32. Rom. 5.8.
g ch. 17.20. Acts 1.6. 2 Thes. 2.1-3.
h Matt. 25. 14.
1 Mina, here translated a Pound, is twelve ounces and a half: which, according to five shillings the ounce, is three pounds two shillings and sixpence.
i John 1.11.
2 silver.
j ch. 16.10. Rev. 2.26-28.

ehold, *here is* thy pound, which I
ave kept laid up in a napkin:
21 For [k]I feared thee, because thou
rt an austere man: thou takest up
hat thou layedst not down, and reap-
st that thou didst not sow.
22 And he saith unto him, [l]Out of
hine own mouth will I judge thee,
hou wicked servant. [m]Thou knewest
hat I was an austere man, taking up
hat I laid not down, and reaping that
did not sow;
23 Wherefore then gavest not thou
ny money into the bank, that at my
oming I might have required mine
wn with usury?
24 And he said unto them that stood
y, Take from him the pound, and
ive *it* to him that hath ten pounds.
25 (And they said unto him, Lord, he
ath ten pounds.)
26 For I say unto you, [n]That unto
very one which hath shall be given;
nd from him that hath not, even that
e hath shall be taken away from him.
27 But those mine enemies, which
vould not that I should reign over
hem, bring hither, and slay *them* be-
ore me.
28 ¶ And when he had thus spoken,
e [o]went before, ascending up to
erusalem.
29 And [p]it came to pass, when he
vas come nigh to Bĕth-phă-ġē and
3ethany, at the mount called *the*
nount of Olives, he sent two of his dis-
iples,
30 Saying, Go ye into the village over
gainst *you;* in the which at your en-
ering ye shall find a colt tied, where-
n yet never man sat: loose him, and
ring *him hither*.
31 And if any man ask you, Why do
ye loose *him?* thus shall ye say unto
im, Because [q]the Lord hath need of
im.
32 And they that were sent went
heir way, and found even as he had
aid unto them.
33 And as they were loosing the colt,
he owners thereof said unto them,
Why loose ye the colt?
34 And they said, The Lord hath
need of him.
35 And they brought him to Jesus:
nd [r]they cast their garments upon
he colt, and they set Jesus thereon.
36 And [s]as he went, they spread their
lothes in the way.
37 And when he was come nigh, even
now at the descent of the mount of
Olives, the whole multitude of the disciples began to rejoice and praise
God with a loud voice for all the
mighty works that they had seen;
38 Saying, [t]Blessed *be* the King that
cometh in the name of the Lord:
[u]peace in heaven, and glory in the
highest.
39 And some of the Pharisees from
among the multitude said unto him,
Master, rebuke thy disciples.
40 And he answered and said unto
them, I tell you that, if these should
hold their peace, [v]the stones would
immediately cry out.
41 ¶ And when he was come near, he
beheld the city, and [w]wept over it,
42 Saying, If thou hadst known, even
thou, at least in this thy day, the things
which belong unto thy peace! but now
they are hid from thine eyes.
43 For the days shall come upon
thee, that thine enemies shall [x]cast
a trench about thee, and compass
thee round, and keep thee in on every
side,
44 And [y]shall lay thee even with the
ground, and thy children within thee;
and they [z]shall not leave in thee one
stone upon another; because [a]thou
knewest not the time of thy visitation.
45 And [b]he went into the temple, and
began to cast out them that sold
therein, and them that bought;
46 Saying unto them, [c]It is written,
My house is the house of prayer: but
[d]ye have made it a den of thieves.
47 And he taught daily in the temple.
But the [e]chief priests and the scribes
and the chief of the people sought to
destroy him,
48 And could not find what they
might do: for all the people [3]were very
attentive to hear him.

CHAPTER 20

AND [a]it came to pass, *that* on one
of those days, as he taught the
people in the temple, and preached
the gospel, the chief priests and the
scribes came upon *him* with the elders,
2 And spake unto him, saying, Tell
us, by what [b]authority doest thou
these things? or who is he that gave
thee this authority?
3 And he answered and said unto
them, I will also ask you one thing;
and answer me:
4 The baptism of John, was it from
heaven, or of men?
5 And they reasoned with themselves, saying, If we shall say, From
heaven; he will say, Why then believed
ye him not?
6 But and if we say, Of men; all the

k Ex. 20.19, 20. 2 Tim. 1.7. Jas. 2.19. Rev. 21.8.
l 2 Sam. 1.16. Job 15.6. Titus 3.11.
m Matt. 25. 26.
n Matt. 13. 12. ch. 8.18.
o Mark 10. 32. ch. 9.51.
p ver. 37. Zech. 14.4. Matt. 21.1. Mark 11.1. John 8.1. Acts 1.12.
q Ps. 50.10. Acts 10.36.
r 2 Ki. 9.13. Mark 11.7. John 12.14.
s Matt. 21.8.
t Ps. 118.26. Matt. 21.9. Mark 11.9. ch. 13.35. 1 Tim. 1.17.
u ch. 2.14. Eph. 2.14.
v Hab. 2.11.
w Isa. 53.3. Hos. 11.8. John 11.35. Rom. 12.15.
x Isa. 29.3,4. Jer. 6.3,6. ch. 21.20.
y 1 Ki. 9.7.
z Mark 13.2. ch. 21.6.
a Dan. 9.24. ch. 1.68. 1 Pet. 2.12.
b Matt. 21.12. John 2.14.
c Ps. 93.5. Isa. 56.7.
d Jer. 7.11.
e Mark 11. 18. John 7.19.
3 Or, hanged on him.

CHAP. 20

a Matt. 21. 23.
b Acts. 4.7.

people will stone us: for they be persuaded that [c]John was a prophet.
7 And they answered, that [d]they
could not tell whence *it was.*
8 And Jesus said unto them, Neither
[e]tell I you by what authority I do these
things.
9 Then began he to speak to the people this parable; [f]A certain man planted a vineyard, and let it forth to
husbandmen, and went into a far
country for a long time.
10 And at the season [g]he sent a servant to the husbandmen, that they
should give him of the fruit of the
vineyard: but the husbandmen beat
him, and sent *him* away empty.
11 And again he sent another servant: and they beat him also, and entreated *him* shamefully, and sent *him*
away empty.
12 And [h]again he sent a third: and
they wounded him also, and cast *him*
out.
13 Then said the lord of the vineyard, What shall I do? I will send [i]my
beloved son: it may be they will reverence *him* when they see him.
14 But when the husbandmen saw
him, they reasoned among themselves, saying, This is [j]the heir: come,
let us kill him, that the inheritance
may be ours.
15 So they cast him out of the vineyard, and [k]killed *him.* What therefore
shall the lord of the vineyard do unto
them?
16 He shall come and destroy these
husbandmen, and shall give the vineyard to others. And when they heard
it, they said, God forbid.
17 And he beheld them, and said,
What is this then that is written, The
[l]stone which the builders rejected, the
same is become the head of the
corner?
18 Whosoever shall fall upon that
stone shall be broken; [m]but on whomsoever it shall fall, it will grind him to
powder.
19 ¶ And the chief priests and the
scribes the same hour sought to lay
hands on him; and they feared the
people: for they perceived that he had
spoken this parable against them.
20 And [n]they watched *him,* and sent
forth spies, which should feign themselves just men, that they might take
hold of his words, that so they might
deliver him unto the power and
authority of the governor.
21 And they asked him, saying,
[o]Master, we know that thou sayest

c Matt. 14.5. ch. 7.29.
d Job 24.13. Rom. 1.18, 21. 2 Cor. 4.3. 2 Thes. 2.9, 10.
e Job 5.12,13.
f Ps. 80.8. Song 8.11, 12. Isa. 5.1. Jer. 2.21.
g 2 Ki. 17.13, 14. 2 Chr. 36.15, 16. Acts 7.52. 1 Thes. 2.15. Heb. 11.36.
h Neh. 9.29, 30.
i Isa. 7.14. John 3.16. Rom. 8.3. Gal. 4.4.
j Ps. 2.6. Isa. 9.6. Phil. 2.9-11. Heb. 1.2.
k John 19. Acts 3.15. 1 Cor. 2.8.
l Ps. 118.22. 1 Pet. 2.7.
m Isa. 8.15. Dan. 2.34, 35.
n Matt. 22. 15.
o Mark 12. 14.
1 of a truth.
p Matt. 18. 28.
q Matt. 16.1, 6,12. Mark 12.18. Acts 4.1,2.
r Acts 23.6.
s Gen. 38.8. Deut. 25.5.
t 2 Thes. 1.5. Rev. 3.4.
u Matt. 22. 30. Mark 12.25. 1 Cor. 15.42, 49,52. Rev. 7.9-12.
v Rom. 8.23. 1 John 3.2.
w Ex. 3.6. Acts 7.32.
x Ps. 16.5-11. Rom. 4.17. Col. 3.3,4. Heb. 11.16.
y Rom. 6.10, 11. Rom. 14.7-9. 1 Cor. 13.4.

and teachest rightly, neither acceptest
thou the person *of any,* but teachest
the way of God [1]truly:
22 Is it lawful for us to give tribute
unto Cæsar, or no?
23 But he perceived their craftiness,
and said unto them, Why tempt ye
me?
24 Shew me a [p]penny. Whose image
and superscription hath it? They answered and said, Cæsar's.
25 And he said unto them, Render
therefore unto Cæsar the things which
be Cæsar's, and unto God the things
which be God's.
26 And they could not take hold of
his words before the people: and they
marvelled at his answer, and held their
peace.
27 ¶ Then [q]came to *him* certain of
the Săd'-dū-çēeś, [r]which deny that
there is any resurrection; and they
asked him,
28 Saying, Master, [s]Moses wrote unto us, If any man's brother die, having
a wife, and he die without children,
that his brother should take his wife,
and raise up seed unto his brother.
29 There were therefore seven brethren: and the first took a wife, and died
without children.
30 And the second took her to wife,
and he died childless.
31 And the third took her; and in like
manner the seven also: and they left
no children, and died.
32 Last of all the woman died also.
33 Therefore in the resurrection
whose wife of them is she? for seven
had her to wife.
34 And Jesus answering said unto
them, The children of this world
marry, and are given in marriage:
35 But they which shall be [t]account-
ed worthy to obtain that world,
and the resurrection from the dead,
neither marry, nor are given in
marriage:
36 Neither can they die any more:
for they [u]are equal unto the angels;
and are the children of God, [v]being
the children of the resurrection.
37 Now that the dead are raised,
even [w]Moses shewed at the bush,
when he calleth the Lord the God of
Abraham, and the God of Isaac, and
the God of Jacob.
38 For [x]he is not a God of the dead,
but of the living: for [y]all live unto
him.
39 ¶ Then certain of the scribes answering said, Master, thou hast well
said.

40 And after that they durst not ask him any *question at all.*

41 And he said unto them, How [z]say they that Christ is David's son?

42 And David himself saith in the book of Psalms, [a]The LORD said unto my Lord, Sit thou on my right hand,

43 Till I make thine enemies thy footstool.

44 David therefore calleth him Lord, how is he then his son?

45 ¶ Then [b]in the audience of all the people he said unto his disciples,

46 Beware [c]of the scribes, which desire to walk in long robes, [d]and love greetings in the markets, and the highest seats in the synagogues, and the chief rooms at feasts;

47 Which [e]devour widows' houses, and for a shew make long prayers: the same [f]shall receive greater damnation.

CHAPTER 21

AND he looked up, [a]and saw the rich men casting their gifts into the treasury.

2 And he saw also a certain poor widow casting in thither two mites.

3 And he said, Of a truth I say unto you, that [b]this poor widow hath cast in more than they all:

4 For all these have of their abundance cast in unto the offerings of God: but she of her penury hath cast in all the living that she had.

5 ¶ And [c]as some spake of the temple, how it was adorned with goodly stones and gifts, he said,

6 *As for* these things which ye behold, the days will come, in the which [d]there shall not be left one stone upon another, that shall not be thrown down.

7 And they asked him, saying, Master, but when shall these things be? and what sign *will there be* when these things shall come to pass?

8 And he said, [e]Take heed that ye be not deceived: for many shall come in my name, saying, I am *Christ;* [1]and the time draweth near: go ye not therefore after them.

9 But when ye shall hear of wars and commotions, be not terrified: for these things must first come to pass; but the end *is* not by and by.

10 Then [f]said he unto them, Nation shall rise against nation, and kingdom against kingdom:

11 And great earthquakes shall be in divers places, and famines, and pestilences; and fearful sights and great signs shall there be from heaven.

12 But [g]before all these, they shall lay their hands on you, and persecute *you*, delivering *you* up to the synagogues, and into [h]prisons, being [i]brought before kings and rulers [j]for my name's sake.

13 And [k]it shall turn to you for a testimony.

14 Settle [l]*it* therefore in your hearts, not to meditate before what ye shall answer:

15 For I will give you a mouth and wisdom, [m]which all your adversaries shall not be able to gainsay nor resist.

16 And [n]ye shall be betrayed both by parents, and brethren, and kinsfolks, and friends; [o]and *some* of you shall they cause to be put to death.

17 And [p]ye shall be hated of all *men* for my name's sake.

18 But there shall not an hair of your head perish.

19 In your patience possess ye your souls.

20 And [q]when ye shall see Jerusalem compassed with armies, then know that the desolation thereof is nigh.

21 Then let them which are in Judæa flee to the mountains; and let them which are in the midst of it depart out; and let not them that are in the countries enter thereinto.

22 For these be the days of vengeance, that [r]all things which are written may be fulfilled.

23 But woe unto them that are with child, and to them that give suck, in those days! for there shall be great distress in the land, and wrath upon this people.

24 And they shall fall by the edge of the sword, and shall be led away captive into all nations: and Jerusalem shall be trodden down of the Gentiles, [s]until the times of the Gentiles be fulfilled.

25 ¶ And [t]there shall be signs in the sun, and in the moon, and in the stars; and upon the earth distress of nations, with perplexity; the sea and the waves roaring;

26 Men's hearts failing them for fear, and for looking after those things which are coming on the earth: [u]for the powers of heaven shall be shaken.

27 And then shall they see the Son of man coming [v]in a cloud with power and great glory.

28 And when these things begin to come to pass, then look up, and lift up your heads; for your redemption draweth nigh.

29 And [w]he spake to them a parable;

z Isa. 9.6,7. Matt. 1.1. Mark 12.35. ch. 18.38.
a Ps. 110.1. Acts 2.34. 1 Cor. 15.25.
b Matt. 23.1. Mark 12.38.
c Matt. 23.5.
d ch. 11.43.
e Matt. 23. 14.
f Matt. 11.22. ch. 12.47. Jas. 4.17.

CHAP. 21

a Mark 12. 41.
b Pro. 3.9. 2 Cor. 8.12.
c Matt. 24.1. Mark 13.1.
d 1 Ki. 9.7. Isa. 64.10, 11. Jer. 5.10. Lam. 2.6-9. Micah 3.12. Matt. 24.2. Mark 13.2. ch. 19.44.
e Matt. 24.4. Mark 13.5. Eph. 5.6. 2 Thes. 2.3. 2 Tim. 3.13. 1 John 4.1. Rev. 12.9.
1 Or, and, The time.
f Matt. 24.7.
g Rev. 2.10.
h Acts 4.3. Acts 5.18.
i Acts 25.23.
j 1 Pet. 2.13.
k Phil. 1.28.
l Matt. 10.19.
m Acts 6.10.
n Micah 7.6.
o Acts 7.59.
p Matt. 10. 22.
q Matt. 24. 15.
r Dan. 9.26, 27. Zech. 11.1.
s Dan. 9.27. Rom. 11.25.
t Isa. 13.10, 13. Dan. 7.13. Joel 2.30, 31. Mark 13.24-26. Rev. 6.12-14.
u Matt. 24. 29.
v Acts 1.11. Rev. 1.7.
w Mark 13. 28.

Behold the fig tree, and all the trees;
30 When they now shoot forth, ye
see and know of your own selves that
summer is now nigh at hand.
31 So likewise ye, when ye see these
things come to pass, know ye that the
kingdom of God is nigh at hand.
32 Verily I say unto you, This generation shall not pass away, till all be fulfilled.
33 Heaven and earth shall pass
away: but my words shall not pass
away.
34 ¶ And [x]take heed to yourselves,
lest at any time your hearts be over-
charged with surfeiting, and drunkenness, and cares of this life, and *so* that
day come upon you unawares.
35 For [y]as a snare shall it come on all
them that dwell on the face of the
whole earth.
36 Watch [z]ye therefore, [a]and pray
always, that ye may be accounted
worthy to escape all these things that
shall come to pass, and [b]to stand before the Son of man.
37 And [c]in the day time he was teaching in the temple; and [d]at night he
went out, and abode in the mount that
is called *the mount* of Olives.
38 And all the people came early in
the morning to him [e]in the temple, for
to hear him.

CHAPTER 22

NOW the [a]feast of unleavened
bread drew nigh, which is called
the Passover.
2 And [b]the chief priests and scribes
sought how they might kill him; for
they feared the people.
3 ¶ Then [c]entered Satan into Judas
surnamed Iscariot, being of the number of the twelve.
4 And he went his way, and communed with the chief priests and captains, how he might betray him unto
them.
5 And they were glad, and [d]coven-
anted to give him money.
6 And he promised, and sought opportunity to betray him unto them [1]in
the absence of the multitude.
7 ¶ Then [e]came the day of unleavened bread, when the passover must be
killed.
8 And he sent Peter and John, saying, Go and prepare us the passover,
that we may eat.
9 And they said unto him, Where
wilt thou that we prepare?
10 And he said unto them, Behold,
when ye are entered into the city,

x Rom. 13. 13. 1 Pet. 4.7.
y 1 Thes. 5.2. 2 Pet. 3.10. Rev. 3.3.
z Matt. 24.42. Mark 13.33. 1 Cor. 16.13. 1 Pet. 5.8. Rev. 16.15.
a ch. 11.5. Eph. 6.18. Col. 4.2. 1 Thes. 5.17.
b Ps. 1.5. Isa. 56.4. Eph. 6.13.
c John 8.1,2.
d ch. 22.39.
e Hag. 2.7. Mal. 3.1.

CHAP. 22

a Ex. 12.3-28. Lev. 23.5,6. Matt. 26.2. Mark 14.1. 1 Cor. 5.7,8.
b Ps. 2.2. John 11.47. Acts 4.27.
c Matt. 26.14. Mark 14.10.
d Zech. 11.12. John 8.44. 1 Tim. 6.10. 1 John 3.8. Jude 11.
1 Or, without tumult.
e Matt. 26.17. Mark 14.12.
2 Or, I have heartily desired.
f Acts 10.41. Rev. 19.9.
g Matt. 26. 29. Mark 14.25.
h 1 Cor. 11. 24.
i 1 Cor. 10.16.
j Ps. 41.9. Micah 7.5, 6. Mark 14.18. John 13.21, 26.
k Gen. 3.15. Isa. 53.1-12. Dan. 9.24. Zech. 13.7. Acts 2.23.
l Mark 9.34. ch. 9.46.
m Matt. 20. 25.
n 1 Pet. 5.3.
o ch. 9.48.
p Matt. 20. 28. Phil. 2.7.

there shall a man meet you, bearing a
pitcher of water; follow him into the
house where he entereth in.
11 And ye shall say unto the goodman of the house, The Master saith
unto thee, Where is the guestchamber,
where I shall eat the passover with my
disciples?
12 And he shall shew you a large
upper room furnished: there make
ready.
13 And they went, and found as he
had said unto them: and they made
ready the passover.
14 And when the hour was come, he
sat down, and the twelve apostles
with him.
15 And he said unto them, [2]With desire I have desired to eat this passover
with you before I suffer:
16 For I say unto you, I will not any
more eat thereof, [f]until it be fulfilled
in the kingdom of God.
17 And he took the cup, and gave
thanks, and said, Take this, and divide
it among yourselves:
18 For [g]I say unto you, I will not
drink of the fruit of the vine, until the
kingdom of God shall come.
19 ¶ And he took bread, and gave
thanks, and brake *it*, and gave unto
them, saying, This is my body which
is given for you: this [h]do in remembrance of me.
20 Likewise also the cup after supper, saying, [i]This cup *is* the new testament in my blood, which is shed for
you.
21 ¶ But, [j]behold, the hand of him
that betrayeth me *is* with me on the
table.
22 And truly the Son of man goeth,
as [k]it was determined: but woe unto
that man by whom he is betrayed!
23 And they began to inquire among
themselves, which of them it was that
should do this thing.
24 ¶ And [l]there was also a strife
among them, which of them should
be accounted the greatest.
25 And [m]he said unto them, The
kings of the Gentiles exercise lordship
over them; and they that exercise
authority upon them are called
benefactors.
26 But [n]ye *shall* not *be* so: [o]but he
that is greatest among you, let him be
as the younger; and he that is chief,
as he that doth serve.
27 For whether *is* greater, he that
sitteth at meat, or he that serveth? *is*
not he that sitteth at meat? but [p]I am
among you as he that serveth.

28 Ye are they which have continued with me in [q]my temptations.

29 And [r]I appoint unto you a kingdom, as my Father hath appointed unto me;

30 That [s]ye may eat and drink at my table in my kingdom, [t]and sit on thrones judging the twelve tribes of Israel.

31 ¶ And the Lord said, Simon, Simon, behold, [u]Satan hath desired *to have* you, that he may [v]sift *you* as wheat:

32 But [w]I have prayed for thee, that thy faith fail not: [x]and when thou art converted, strengthen thy brethren.

33 And he said unto him, Lord, I am ready to go with thee, both into prison, and to death.

34 And [y]he said, I tell thee, Peter, the cock shall not crow this day, before that thou shalt thrice deny that thou knowest me.

35 And [z]he said unto them, When I sent you without purse, and scrip, and shoes, lacked ye any thing? And they said, Nothing.

36 Then said he unto them, But now, he that hath a purse, let him take *it*, and likewise *his* scrip: and he that hath no sword, let him sell his garment, and buy one.

37 For I say unto you, that this that is written must yet be accomplished in me, [a]And he was reckoned among the transgressors: for the things concerning me have an end.

38 And they said, Lord, behold, here *are* two swords. And he said unto them, It is enough.

39 ¶ And he came out, and went, as he was wont, to the mount of Olives; and his disciples also followed him.

40 And [b]when he was at the place, he said unto them, Pray that ye enter not into temptation.

41 And he was withdrawn from them about a stone's cast, and kneeled down, and prayed,

42 Saying, Father, if thou be [3]willing, remove this cup from me: nevertheless [c]not my will, but thine, be done.

43 And there appeared [d]an angel unto him from heaven, strengthening him.

44 And [e]being in an agony he prayed more earnestly: and his sweat was as it were great drops of blood falling down to the ground.

45 And when he rose up from prayer, and was come to his disciples, he found them sleeping for sorrow,

46 And said unto them, Why sleep ye? rise and pray, lest ye enter into temptation.

47 ¶ And while he yet spake, behold a multitude, and he that was called Judas, one of the twelve, went before them, and drew near unto Jesus [f]to kiss him.

48 But Jesus said unto him, Judas, betrayest thou the Son of man with a kiss?

49 When they which were about him saw what would follow, they said unto him, Lord, shall we smite with the sword?

50 ¶ And [g]one of them smote the servant of the high priest, and cut off his right ear.

51 And Jesus answered and said, Suffer ye thus far. And he touched his ear, and healed him.

52 Then Jesus said unto the chief priests, and captains of the temple, and the elders, which were come to him, Be ye come out, as against a thief, with swords and staves?

53 When I was daily with you in the temple, ye stretched forth no hands against me: [h]but this is your hour, and the power of darkness.

54 ¶ Then [i]took they him, and led *him*, and brought him into the high priest's house. [j]And Peter followed afar off.

55 And [k]when they had kindled a fire in the midst of the hall, and were set down together, Peter sat down among them.

56 But a certain maid beheld him as he sat by the fire, and earnestly looked upon him, and said, This man was also with him.

57 And he denied him, saying, Woman, I know him not.

58 And [l]after a little while another saw him, and said, Thou art also of them. And Peter said, Man, I am not.

59 And about the space of one hour after another confidently affirmed, saying, Of a truth this *fellow* also was with him: for he is a Galilæan.

60 And Peter said, Man, I know not what thou sayest. And immediately, while he yet spake, the cock crew.

61 And the Lord turned, and looked upon Peter. [m]And Peter remembered the word of the Lord, how he had said unto him, Before the [n]cock crow, thou shalt deny me thrice.

62 And Peter went out, and wept [o]bitterly.

63 ¶ And [p]the men that held Jesus mocked him, and smote *him*.

q Heb. 4.15.
r Matt. 24.47. ch. 12.32. 2 Cor. 1.7. 2 Tim. 2.12. Jas. 2.5.
s 2 Sam. 9.9, 10. 2 Sam. 19. 28. Matt. 8.11. ch. 12.37. Rev. 19.9.
t Ps. 49.14. Matt. 19.28. 1 Cor. 6.2. Rev. 2.26.
u 1 Pet. 5.8.
v Amos 9.9.
w John 17.9, 11,15.
x Ps. 51.13. John 21.15.
y Matt. 26. 34.
z Matt. 10.9. ch. 9.3.
a Isa. 53.12. Mark 15.28.
b Matt. 6.13. Mark 14.38.
3 willing to remove.
c John 6.38.
d Matt. 4.11.
e John 12.27.
f 2 Sam. 20. 9.
g Matt. 26. 51. Mark 14.47.
h Gen. 3.15. John 12.27. Acts 2.23.
i Matt. 26.57. Acts 8.32.
j John 18.15.
k Matt. 26. 69. Mark 14.66.
l Matt. 26.71. Mark 14.69. John 18.25.
m Eze. 16.63. Matt. 26.75. Mark 14.72. Rev. 2.5.
n John 13.38.
o Isa. 66.2. Eze. 7.16. 2 Cor. 7.10.
p Ps. 69.1-21. Isa. 50.6. Matt. 26.67. Mark 14.65.

64 And when they had blindfolded
him, they struck him on the face, and
asked him, saying, Prophesy, who is
it that smote thee?
65 And many other things blasphe-
mously spake they against him.
66 ¶ And [q]as soon as it was day, the
[r]elders of the people and the chief
priests and the scribes came together,
and led him into their council, saying,
67 Art [s]thou the Christ? tell us. And
he said unto them, If I tell you, ye will
not believe:
68 And if I also ask *you*, ye will not
answer me, nor let *me* go.
69 Hereafter [t]shall the Son of man
sit on the right hand of the power of
God.
70 Then said they all, Art thou then
the Son of God? And he said unto
them, Ye say that I am.
71 And they said, What need we any
further witness? for we ourselves have
heard of his own mouth.

CHAPTER 23

AND [a]the whole multitude of
them arose, and led him unto
Pilate.
2 And they began to accuse him, saying, We found this *fellow* [b]perverting
the nation, and [c]forbidding to give
tribute to Cæsar, saying [d]that he himself is Christ a King.
3 And [e]Pilate asked him, saying, Art
thou the King of the Jews? And he
answered him and said, Thou sayest
it.
4 Then said Pilate to the chief priests
and *to* the people, [f]I find no fault in
this man.
5 And they were the more fierce, saying, He stirreth up the people, teaching throughout all Jewry, beginning
from Galilee to this place.
6 When Pilate heard of Galilee, he
asked whether the man were a Galilæan.
7 And as soon as he knew that he belonged unto [g]Herod's jurisdiction,
he sent him to Herod, who himself also was at Jerusalem at that
time.
8 ¶ And when Herod saw Jesus, he
was exceeding glad: for [h]he was desirous to see him of a long *season*, because [i]he had heard many things of
him; and he hoped to have seen some
miracle done by him.
9 Then he questioned with him in
many words; but he answered him
nothing.

q Matt. 27.1.
r Ps. 2.1. Acts 4.26.
s Matt. 26.63. Mark 14.61. John 10.24.
t Ps. 110.1. Dan. 7.13, 14. Acts 1.11. 1 Thes. 4.16. Heb. 1.3. Rev. 1.7.

CHAP. 23

a Matt. 27.2. Mark 15.1. John 18.28.
b 1 Ki. 21.10-13. Ps. 35.11. Jer. 20.10. Dan. 3.12. Acts 17.7. 1 Pet. 3.16-18.
c Matt. 17.27. Mark 12.17.
d Mark 14.61, 62. John 19.12.
e 1 Tim. 6.13.
f Matt. 27.19. Mark 15.14. 2 Cor. 5.21. 1 Pet. 2.22.
g ch. 3.1.
h ch. 9.9.
i Matt. 14.1. Mark 6.14.
j Isa. 53.3.
k Acts 4.27. Jas. 4.4.
l Matt. 27.23. John 18.38.
m Dan. 6.4.
n Matt. 27. 26. Mark 15.15. John 19.1. Acts 5.40, 41.
o Matt.27.15. Mark 15.6. John 18.39.
p Acts 3.14.
1 Or, assented.
q Pro. 17.15. Matt. 27.32. Mark 15.21. John 19.17.

10 And the chief priests and scribes
stood and vehemently accused him.
11 And [j]Herod with his men of war
set him at nought, and mocked *him*,
and arrayed him in a gorgeous robe,
and sent him again to Pilate.
12 ¶ And the same day [k]Pilate and
Herod were made friends together:
for before they were at enmity between themselves.
13 ¶ And [l]Pilate, when he had called
together the chief priests and the rulers
and the people,
14 Said unto them, Ye have brought
this man unto me, as one that perverteth the people: and, behold, I, having
examined *him* before you, have
[m]found no fault in this man touching those things whereof ye accuse
him:
15 No, nor yet Herod: for I sent you
to him; and, lo, nothing worthy of
death is done unto him.
16 I [n]will therefore chastise him, and
release *him*.
17 (For [o]of necessity he must release
one unto them at the feast.)
18 And [p]they cried out all at once,
saying, Away with this *man*, and release unto us Bär-ăb-bās:
19 (Who for a certain sedition made
in the city, and for murder, was cast
into prison.)
20 Pilate therefore, willing to release
Jesus, spake again to them.
21 But they cried, saying, Crucify
him, crucify him.
22 And he said unto them the third
time, Why, what evil hath he done?
I have found no cause of death in him:
I will therefore chastise him, and let
him go.
23 And they were instant with loud
voices, requiring that he might be
crucified. And the voices of them and
of the chief priests prevailed.
24 And Pilate [1]gave sentence that it
should be as they required.
25 And [q]he released unto them him
that for sedition and murder was cast
into prison, whom they had desired;
but he delivered Jesus to their
will.
26 And [r]as they led him away, they
laid hold upon one Simon, a Çȳ-rē-
nĭ-ăn, coming out of the country, and
on him they laid the cross, that he
might bear *it* after Jesus.
27 ¶ And there followed him a great
company of people, and of women,
which also bewailed and lamented
him.
28 But Jesus turning unto them said,

Daughters of Jerusalem, weep not for
me, but weep for yourselves, and for
your children.
29 For, [s]behold, the days are coming,
in the which they shall say, Blessed
are the barren, and the wombs that
never bare, and the paps which never
gave suck.
30 Then [t]shall they begin to say to
the mountains, Fall on us; and to the
hills, Cover us.
31 For [u]if they do these things in a
green tree, what shall be done in the
dry?
32 And [v]there were also two other,
malefactors, led with him to be put
to death.
33 And [w]when they were come to the
place, which is called [2]Calvary, there
they crucified him, and the malefactors, one on the right hand, and the
other on the left.
34 ¶ Then said Jesus, Father, [x]for-
give them; for [y]they know not what
they do. And [z]they parted his raiment,
and cast lots.
35 And [a]the people stood beholding.
And the rulers also with them derided
him, saying, He saved others; let him
save himself, if he be Christ, the
chosen of God.
36 And the soldiers also mocked
him, coming to him, and offering him
vinegar,
37 And saying, If thou be the king of
the Jews, save thyself.
38 And [b]a superscription also was
written over him in letters of Greek,
and Latin, and Hebrew, THIS IS THE
KING OF THE JEWS.
39 ¶ And [c]one of the malefactors
which were hanged railed on him, saying, If thou be Christ, save thyself and
us.
40 But the other answering [d]rebuked
him, saying, Dost not thou fear God,
seeing thou art in the same condemnation?
41 And we indeed justly; for we receive the due reward of our deeds:
but this man hath done nothing
amiss.
42 And he said unto Jesus, Lord, remember me when thou comest into
[e]thy kingdom.
43 And Jesus said unto him, Verily
I say unto thee, To day shalt thou be
with me in [f]paradise.
44 And [g]it was about the sixth
hour, and there was a darkness
over all the [3]earth until the ninth
hour.
45 And the sun was darkened, and
[h]the veil of the temple was rent in the
midst.
46 ¶ And when Jesus had cried with
a loud voice, he said, [i]Father, into thy
hands I commend my spirit: [j]and having said thus, he gave up the ghost.
47 Now [k]when the centurion saw
what was done, he glorified God, saying, Certainly this was a righteous
man.
48 And [l]all the people that came together to that sight, beholding the
things which were done, smote their
breasts, and returned.
49 And all his acquaintance, and the
women that followed him from Galilee, stood afar off, beholding these
things.
50 ¶ And, [m]behold, *there was* a man
named Joseph, a counsellor; *and he*
was a good man, and a just:
51 (The same [n]had not consented to
the counsel and deed of them;) *he was*
of Ăr-ĭm-ă-thǣ-ă, a city of the Jews:
[o]who also himself waited for the kingdom of God.
52 This *man* went unto Pilate, and
begged the body of Jesus.
53 And [p]he took it down, and wrapped it in linen, and laid it in [q]a sepulchre that was hewn in stone, wherein
never man before was laid.
54 And that day was the preparation,
and the sabbath drew on.
55 And the women also, [r]which came
with him from Galilee, followed after,
and beheld [s]the sepulchre, and how
his body was laid.
56 And they returned, and [t]prepared
spices and ointments; and rested the
sabbath day [u]according to the commandment.

CHAPTER 24

NOW [a]upon the first *day* of the
week, very early in the morning,
they came unto the sepulchre, bringing the [b]spices which they had prepared, and certain *others* with
them.
2 And they found the stone rolled
away from the sepulchre.
3 And [c]they entered in, and found
not the body of the Lord Jesus.
4 And it came to pass, as they were
much perplexed thereabout, behold,
[d]two men stood by them in shining
garments:
5 And as they were afraid, and bowed
down *their* faces to the earth, they said
unto them, Why seek ye [1]the living
among the dead?
6 He is not here, but is risen: remem-

s ch. 21.23.
t Isa. 2.19. Hos. 10.8. Rev. 6.16. Rev. 9.6.
u Pro. 11.31. Jer. 25.29. Eze. 20.47. 1 Pet. 4.17.
v Isa. 53.12. Matt. 27.38.
w Matt. 27. 33. Mark 15.22. John 19.17.
2 Or, the place of a skull.
x Matt. 5.44. Acts 7.60. Rom. 12.14. 1 Cor. 4.12. 1 Pet. 2.20-23.
y Acts 3.17. 1 Cor. 2.8. 1 Tim. 1.13.
z Ps. 22.18. Matt. 27.35. Mark 15.24. John 19.24.
a Ps. 22.17. Zech. 12.10.
b John 19.19.
c Matt. 27. 44. Mark 15.32.
d Eph. 5.11.
e Heb. 1.3.
f Rev. 2.7.
g Matt. 27. 45. Mark 15.33.
3 Or, land.
h Matt. 27. 51. Mark 15.38. 2 Cor. 3.14. Eph. 2.14. Heb. 6.19.
i Ps. 31.5. 1 Pet. 2.23.
j Phil. 2.8.
k Matt. 27. 54.
l Ps. 38.11.
m Matt. 27. 57. Mark 15.42. John 19.38.
n Gen. 37.21, 22. Gen. 42.21, 22. Pro. 1.10. 1 Tim. 5.22.
o Gen. 49.18. Mark 15.43.
p Matt. 27. 59.
q Isa. 53.9.
r ch. 8.2.
s Mark 15.47.
t Mark 16.1.
u Gen. 2.3. Ex. 16.29. Lev. 23.3. Deut. 5.14. Neh. 9.14. Isa. 56.2,6. Isa. 58.13. Rev. 1.10.

CHAP. 24

a Matt. 28.1. Mark 16.1. John 20.1.
b ch. 23.56.
c Mark 16.5.
d Gen. 18.2. Matt. 28.2-6. Mark 16.5, 6. John 20.12. Acts 1.10.
1 Or, him that liveth.

ber [e]how he spake unto you when he was yet in Galilee,

7 Saying, The Son of man must be delivered into the hands of sinful men, and be crucified, and the third day rise again.

8 And [f]they remembered his words,

9 And [g]returned from the sepulchre, and told all these things unto the eleven, and to all the rest.

10 It was Mary Măg-dă-lēne, and [h]Jō-ăn-nă, and Mary *the mother* of James, and other *women that were* with them, which told these things unto the apostles.

11 And their words seemed to them as idle tales, and they believed them not.

12 Then [i]arose Peter, and ran unto the sepulchre; and stooping down, he beheld the linen clothes laid by themselves, and departed, wondering in himself at that which was come to pass.

13 ¶ And, behold, two of them went that same day to a village called Ĕm-mā-ŭs, which was from Jerusalem *about* threescore furlongs.

14 And they [j]talked together of all these things which had happened.

15 And it came to pass, that, while they communed *together* and reasoned, [k]Jesus himself drew near, and went with them.

16 But [l]their eyes were holden that they should not know him.

17 And he said unto them, What manner of communications *are* these that ye have one to another, as ye walk, and are sad?

18 And the one of them, [m]whose name was Clē-ō-păs, answering said unto him, Art thou only a stranger in Jerusalem, and hast not known the things which are come to pass there in these days?

19 And he said unto them, What things? And they said unto him, Concerning Jesus of Nazareth, which [n]was a prophet [o]mighty in deed and word before God and all the people:

20 And [p]how the chief priests and our rulers delivered him to be condemned to death, and have crucified him.

21 But we trusted [q]that it had been he which should have redeemed Israel: and beside all this, to day is the third day since these things were done.

22 Yea, and certain women also of our company made us astonished, which were early at the sepulchre;

23 And when they found not his body, they came, saying, that they had also seen a vision of angels, which said that he was alive.

24 And certain of them which were with us went to the sepulchre, and found *it* even so as the women had said: but him they saw not.

25 Then he said unto them, O fools, and slow of heart to believe all that the prophets have spoken:

26 Ought [r]not Christ to have suffered these things, and to enter into his glory?

27 And beginning at [s]Moses and all the [t]prophets, he expounded unto them in all the scriptures the things concerning himself. Sc Luke 24:44,45

28 And they drew nigh unto the village, whither they went: and [u]he made as though he would have gone further.

29 But they constrained him, saying, Abide with us: for it is toward evening, and the day is far spent. And he went in to tarry with them.

30 And it came to pass, as he sat at meat with them, he took bread, and blessed *it*, and brake, and gave to them.

31 And their eyes were opened, and they knew him; and he [2]vanished out of their sight.

32 And they said one to another, Did not our heart burn within us, while he talked with us by the way, and while he opened to us the scriptures?

33 And they rose up the same hour, and returned to Jerusalem, and found the eleven gathered together, and them that were with them,

34 Saying, The Lord is risen indeed, and hath [v]appeared to Simon.

35 And they told what things *were done* in the way, and how he was known of them in breaking of bread.

36 ¶ And as they thus spake, Jesus himself stood in the midst of them, and saith unto them, Peace *be* unto you.

37 But they were terrified and affrighted, and supposed that they had seen a spirit.

38 And he said unto them, Why are ye troubled? and why do thoughts arise in your hearts?

39 Behold my hands and my feet, that it is I myself: handle me, and see; for a spirit hath not flesh and bones, as ye see me have.

40 And when he had thus spoken, he shewed them *his* hands, and *his* feet.

41 And while they yet believed not

e Matt. 16. 21. Mark 8.31. ch. 9.22.
f John 2.22.
g Matt. 28.8. Mark 16.10.
h ch. 8.3.
i John 20.3.
j Deut. 6.7. Mal. 3.16.
k Matt. 18. 20.
l John 20.14. John 21.4.
m John 19. 25.
n John 3.2. John 6.14. Acts 2.22.
o Acts 7.22.
p Acts 13.27.
q Acts 1.6.
r Ps. 22.1-31. Isa. 53.1-12. Acts 17.3. 1 Cor. 15.3, 4. Phil. 2.6-11. Heb. 2.8-10. 1 Pet. 1.11.
s Gen. 3.15. Gen. 22.18. Gen. 26.4. Gen. 49.10. Num. 21.9. Deut. 18.15.
t Ps. 16.9. Ps. 22. Ps. 132.11. Isa. 7.14. Isa. 9.6. Isa. 40.10. Isa. 50.6. Isa. 53. Jer. 23.5. Jer. 33.14. Eze. 34.23. Eze. 37.25. Dan. 9.24. Micah 7.20. Mal. 3.1. Mal. 4.2. John 1.45.
u Gen. 19.2. Gen. 32.26.
2 Or, ceased to be seen of them.
v 1 Cor. 15.5.

for joy, and wondered, he said unto
them, Have ye here any meat?
42 And they gave him a piece of a
broiled fish, and of an honeycomb.
43 And [w]he took *it*, and did eat before them.
44 And he said unto them, [x]These
are the words which I spake unto you,
while I was yet with you, that all things
must be fulfilled, which were written
in the law of Moses, and *in* the prophets, and *in* the psalms, concerning me.
45 Then [y]opened he their understanding, that they might understand
the scriptures,
46 And said unto them, Thus it is
written, and thus it behoved Christ to
suffer, and to rise from the dead the
third day:
47 And that repentance and [z]re-
mission of sins should be preached in
his name among [a]all nations, beginning at Jerusalem.
48 And [b]ye are witnesses of these
things.
49 ¶ And, [c]behold, I send the promise of my Father upon you: but tarry
ye in the city of Jerusalem, until ye be
endued with power from on high.
50 ¶ And he led them out as far as to
Bethany, and he lifted up his hands,
and blessed them.
51 And [d]it came to pass, while he
blessed them, he was parted from
them, and carried up into heaven.
52 And they worshipped him, and
returned to Jerusalem with great joy:
53 And were continually [e]in the
temple, praising and blessing God.
Ä-mĕn.

w Acts 10.41.
x Matt. 16. 21.
y Mark 9.31. Acts 16.14. 2 Cor. 4.6.
z Dan. 9.24.
a Gen. 12.3. Ps. 22.27. Isa. 49.6. Jer. 31.34. Hos. 2.23. Micah 4.2. Mal. 1.11. Gal. 3.14.
b John 15.27. Acts 1.22.
c Isa. 44.3. Joel 2.28. Acts 2.1.
d Eph. 1.20.
e Acts 2.46.

THE GOSPEL ACCORDING TO

ST. JOHN

CHAPTER 1

IN the beginning was [a]the Word,
and the Word was [b]with God, and
the [c]Word was God.
2 The same was in the beginning
with God.
3 All things were made by him; and
without him was not any thing made
that was made.
4 In him was life; and the life was the
light of men.
5 And [d]the light shineth in darkness;
and the darkness comprehended it
not.
6 ¶ There [e]was a man sent from God,
whose name *was* John.
7 The same came for a witness, to
bear witness of the Light, that all
men through him might believe.
8 He [f]was not that Light, but *was*
sent to bear witness of that Light.
9 *That* [g]was the true Light, which
lighteth every man that cometh into
the world.
10 He was in the world, and [h]the
world was made by him, and the
world knew him not.
11 He [i]came unto his own, and his
own received him not.
12 But [j]as many as received him, to
them gave he [1]power to become the
sons of God, *even* to them that believe on his name:
13 Which were born, not of blood,
nor of the will of the flesh, nor of the
will of man, [k]but of God.
14 And the [l]Word [m]was made [n]flesh,
and dwelt among us, (and we [o]beheld
his glory, the glory as of the only begotten of the Father,) full [p]of grace
and truth.
15 ¶ John bare witness of him, and
cried, saying, This was he of whom I
spake, He that cometh after me is preferred before me: for [q]he was before
me.
16 And of his [r]fulness have all we received, and grace for grace.
17 For the [s]law was given by Moses,
[t]*but* grace and [u]truth came by Jesus
Christ.
18 No [v]man hath seen God at any
time; the [w]only begotten Son, which
is in [x]the bosom of the Father, he hath
declared *him*.
19 ¶ And this is the record of John,
when the Jews sent priests and Levites from Jerusalem to ask him, Who
art thou?
20 And he confessed, and denied
not; but confessed, I am not the
Christ.
21 And they asked him, What then?
Art thou [y]Ē-lī-ăs? And he saith, [z]I am
not. Art thou [2]that prophet? And he
answered, No.
22 Then said they unto him, Who art
thou? that we may give an answer to

CHAP. 1
a Rev. 19.13.
b Zech. 13.7.
c Isa. 9.6. Phil. 2.6.
d ch. 3.19.
e Mal. 3.1.
f Acts 13.25.
g Isa. 49.6.
h Ps. 33.6. 1 Cor. 8.6.
i Luke 19.14.
j Isa. 56.5. Rom. 8.15. 2 Pet. 1.4.
1 Or, the right, or, privilege.
k Deut. 30.6. Jas. 1.18.
l Matt. 1.20. 1 Tim. 3.16.
m Rom. 1.3.
n Heb. 2.14.
o Isa. 40.5. Matt. 17.2.
p Col. 2.3.
q Col. 1.17.
r Eph. 1.6.
s Ex. 20.1.
t Rom. 5.21.
u ch. 14.6.
v Ex. 33.20.
w 1 John 4.9.
x Pro. 8.30.
y Mal. 4.5.
z Luke 1.17.
2 Or, a prophet?

them that sent us. What sayest thou
of thyself?
23 He said, I *am* the voice of one crying in the wilderness, Make straight
the way of the Lord, as said [a]the
prophet Ē-sâi-ăs.
24 And they which were sent were
of the Pharisees.
25 And they asked him, and said unto him, Why baptizest thou then, if
thou be not that Christ, nor Ē-lī-ăs,
neither that prophet?
26 John answered them, saying, I
baptize with water: [b]but there standeth one among you, whom ye know
not;
27 He it is, who coming after me is
preferred before me, whose shoe's
latchet I am not worthy to unloose.
28 These things were done in Bĕth-
ăb-ă-ră beyond Jordan, where John
was baptizing.
29 ¶ The next day John seeth Jesus
coming unto him, and saith, Behold
[c]the Lamb of God, [d]which [3]taketh
away the sin of the world.
30 This is he of whom I said, After
me cometh a man which is preferred
before me: for he was before me.
31 And I knew him not: but that he
should be made manifest to Israel,
therefore am I come baptizing with
water.
32 And John bare record, saying, I
saw the Spirit descending from heaven
like a dove, and it abode upon him.
33 And I knew him not: but he that
sent me to baptize with water, the
same said unto me, Upon whom thou
shalt see the Spirit descending, and
remaining on him, [e]the same is he
which baptizeth with the Holy Ghost.
34 And I saw, and bare record that
this is the Son of God.
35 ¶ Again the next day after John
stood, and two of his disciples;
36 And looking upon Jesus as he
walked, he saith, Behold the Lamb of
God!
37 And the two disciples heard him
speak, and they followed Jesus.
38 Then Jesus turned, and saw them
following, and saith unto them, What
seek ye? They said unto him, Rabbi,
(which is to say, being interpreted,
Master,) where [4]dwellest thou?
39 He saith unto them, Come and
see. They came and saw where he
dwelt, and abode with him that day:
for it was [5]about the tenth hour.
40 One of the two which heard John
speak, and followed him, was Andrew,
[f]Simon Peter's brother.
41 He first findeth his own brother
Simon, and saith unto him, We have
found the Mĕs-sī-ăs, which is, being
interpreted, [6]the Christ.
42 And he brought him to Jesus.
And when Jesus beheld him, he said,
Thou art Simon the son of Jona: thou
shalt be called Cē-phăs, which is by
interpretation, [7]A stone.
43 ¶ The day following Jesus would
go forth into Galilee, and findeth
Philip, and saith unto him, Follow
me.
44 Now [g]Philip was of Bĕth-sā-ĭ-dă,
the city of Andrew and Peter.
45 Philip findeth [h]Nă-thăn-ă-ĕl, and
saith unto him, We have found him,
of whom Moses [i]in the law, and the
[j]prophets, did write, Jesus of Nazareth, the son of Joseph.
46 And Nă-thăn-ă-ĕl said unto him,
Can there any good thing come out of
Nazareth? Philip saith unto him,
Come and see.
47 Jesus saw Nă-thăn-ă-ĕl coming to
him, and saith of him, Behold an Israelite indeed, in whom is no guile!
48 Nă-thăn-ă-ĕl saith unto him,
Whence knowest thou me? Jesus answered and said unto him, Before that
Philip called thee, when thou wast under the fig tree, I saw thee.
49 Nă-thăn-ă-ĕl answered and saith
unto him, Rabbi, thou art the Son of
God; thou art the [k]King of Israel.
50 Jesus answered and said unto him,
Because I said unto thee, I saw thee
under the fig tree, believest thou?
thou shalt see greater things than these.
51 And he saith unto him, Verily,
verily, I say unto you, [l]Hereafter ye
shall see heaven open, and the angels
of God ascending and descending upon [m]the Son of man.

CHAPTER 2

AND the third day there was a
marriage in Cana of Galilee; and
the mother of Jesus was there:
2 And both Jesus was called, and his
disciples, to the marriage.
3 And when they wanted wine, the
mother of Jesus saith unto him, They
have no wine.
4 Jesus saith unto her, [a]Woman,
what [b]have I to do with thee? mine
[c]hour is not yet come.
5 His mother saith unto the servants,
Whatsoever he saith unto you, do *it*.
6 And there were set there six water-
pots of stone, [d]after the manner of
the purifying of the Jews, containing
two or three firkins apiece.

a Isa. 40.3.
b Mal. 3.1.
c Ex. 12.3. Isa. 53.7. 1 Pet. 1.19. Rev. 5.6.
d 1 Cor. 15.3. Gal. 1.4. Heb. 1.3. Heb. 2.17. Heb. 9.28. 1 John 2.2. Rev. 1.5.
3 Or, beareth.
e ch. 14.26. ch. 20.22. Acts 1.5. Acts 2.4. Acts 4.8,31. Acts 6.3,5,8. Acts 7.55.
4 Or, abidest.
5 That was two hours before night.
f Matt. 4.18.
6 Or, the Anointed.
7 Or, Peter.
g ch. 12.21.
h ch. 21.2.
i Gen. 3.15. Gen. 22.18. Gen. 26.4. Gen. 49.10. Num. 21.9. Deut. 18.18.
j Ps. 16.9. Ps. 22. Ps. 132.11. Isa. 7.14. Isa. 9.6. Isa. 40.10. Isa. 50.6. Isa. 53. Jer. 23.5. Jer. 33.14, 15. Eze. 34.23. Eze. 37.25. Micah 5.2. Micah 7.20. Zech. 6.12. Zech. 9.9. Mal. 3.1.
k Matt. 21.5. Matt. 27.11. Mark 15.2. Luke 23.3. ch. 18.33. ch. 19.14-19.
l Gen. 28.12.
m Dan. 7.13.

CHAP. 2

a ch. 19.26.
b 2 Sam. 16. 10. Luke 2.49. Gal. 2.5,6.
c Eccl. 3.1. ch. 7.6. ch. 12.23.
d Mark 7.3. Heb. 10.22.

7 Jesus saith unto them, Fill the
vaterpots with water. And they filled
hem up to the brim.
8 And he saith unto them, Draw out
ıow, and bear unto the governor of
he feast. And they bare *it*.
9 When the ruler of the feast had
asted [e]the water that was made wine,
ınd knew not whence it was: (but the
ervants which drew the water knew;)
he governor of the feast called the
oridegroom,
10 And saith unto him, Every man
t the beginning doth set forth good
vine; and when men have well drunk,
hen that which is worse: *but* thou
ıast kept the good wine until now.
11 This beginning of miracles did
'esus in [f]Cana of Galilee, [g]and mani-
ested forth his glory; and his dis-
iples believed on him.
12 ¶ After this he went down to Că-
ěr-nā-ŭm, he, and his mother, and
his brethren, and his disciples: and
hey continued there not many days.
13 ¶ And [i]the Jews' passover was at
ıand, and Jesus went up to Jerusa-
em,
14 And [j]found in the temple those
hat sold oxen and sheep and doves,
ınd the changers of money sitting:
15 And when he had made a scourge
f small cords, he drove them all out
f the temple, and the sheep, and the
xen; and poured out the changers'
noney, and overthrew the tables;
16 And said unto them that sold
loves, Take these things hence; make
not my Father's house an house of
nerchandise.
17 And his disciples remembered
hat it was written, [l]The zeal of thine
ıouse hath eaten me up.
18 ¶ Then answered the Jews and
aid unto him, What sign shewest thou
ınto us, seeing that thou doest these
hings?
19 Jesus answered and said unto
hem, [m]Destroy this temple, and in
hree days I will raise it up.
20 Then said the Jews, Forty and six
ears was this temple in building,
nd wilt thou rear it up in three
lays?
21 But he spake [n]of the temple of his
ody.
22 When therefore he was risen from
he dead, [o]his disciples remembered
hat he had said this unto them; and
hey believed the scripture, and the
vord which Jesus had said.
23 ¶ Now when he was in Jerusalem
t the passover, in the feast *day*, many

e ch. 4.46.
f Josh. 19.28.
g Deut. 5.24. Ps. 72.19. ch. 1.14.
h Matt. 12. 46.
i Ex. 12.14. Num. 28.16. Deut. 16.1. ch. 5.1. ch. 6.4.
j Matt. 21.12. Mark 11.15. Luke 19.45.
k Ps. 93.5. 1 Tim. 6.9.
l Ps. 69.9.
m Matt. 26. 61. Matt. 27.40. Mark 14.58.
n Matt. 26. 61. 1 Cor. 3.16. 2 Cor. 6.16. Eph. 2.20, 22. Col. 2.9. Heb. 8.2.
o Luke 24.8, 25,45. ch. 14.26.
p 1 Sam. 16.7. 1 Chr. 28.9. Matt. 9.4. Mark 2.8. ch. 6.64. Acts 1.24. Rev. 2.23.

CHAP. 3

a ch. 5.36. ch. 7.31. Acts 2.22.
b Acts 10.38.
c ch. 1.13. 2 Cor. 5.17. Gal. 6.15. Eph. 2.5,10. Titus 3.5. Jas. 1.18. 1 Pet. 1.23. 1 John 2.29.
1 Or, from above.
d Isa. 44.3,4. Matt. 3.11. Mark 16.16. Acts 2.38. Titus 3.5. 1 Pet. 3.21.
2 Or, from above.
e Eccl. 11.5. 1 Cor. 2.11.
f ch. 6.52.
g Pro. 30.4. ch. 6.33. Acts 2.34. 1 Cor. 15.47. Eph. 4.9.
h Num. 21.9. ch. 8.28.
i Luke 2.14. Rom. 5.8. Titus 3.4.

believed in his name, when they saw
the miracles which he did.
24 But Jesus did not commit himself
unto them, because he knew all *men*,
25 And needed not that any should
testify of man: for [p]he knew what was
in man.

CHAPTER 3

THERE was a man of the Pharisees named Nĭc-ŏ-dḗ-mŭs, a ruler
of the Jews:
2 The same came to Jesus by night,
and said unto him, Rabbi, we know
that thou art a teacher come from
God: for [a]no man can do these
miracles that thou doest, except [b]God
be with him.
3 Jesus answered and said unto him,
Verily, verily, I say unto thee, [c]Except
a man be born [1]again, he cannot see
the kingdom of God.
4 Nĭc-ŏ-dḗ-mŭs saith unto him, How
can a man be born when he is old? can
he enter the second time into his
mother's womb, and be born?
5 Jesus answered, Verily, verily, I
say unto thee, [d]Except a man be born
of water and *of* the Spirit, he cannot
enter into the kingdom of God.
6 That which is born of the flesh is
flesh; and that which is born of the
Spirit is spirit.
7 Marvel not that I said unto thee,
Ye must be born [2]again.
8 The [e]wind bloweth where it listeth,
and thou hearest the sound thereof,
but canst not tell whence it cometh,
and whither it goeth: so is every one
that is born of the Spirit.
9 Nĭc-ŏ-dḗ-mŭs answered and said
unto him, [f]How can these things be?
10 Jesus answered and said unto
him, Art thou a master of Israel, and
knowest not these things?
11 Verily, verily, I say unto thee, We
speak that we do know, and testify
that we have seen; and ye receive not
our witness.
12 If I have told you earthly things,
and ye believe not, how shall ye believe, if I tell you *of* heavenly things?
13 And [g]no man hath ascended up to
heaven, but he that came down from
heaven, *even* the Son of man which is
in heaven.
14 ¶ And [h]as Moses lifted up the
serpent in the wilderness, even so
must the Son of man be lifted up:
15 That whosoever believeth in him
should not perish, but have eternal
life.
16 ¶ For [i]God so loved the world,
that he gave his only begotten Son,

that whosoever believeth in him should not perish, but have everlasting life.

17 For [j]God sent not his Son into the world to condemn the world; but that the world through him might be saved.

18 ¶ He that believeth on him [k]is not condemned: but he that believeth not is condemned already, because he hath not believed in the name of the only begotten Son of God.

19 And this is the condemnation, that [l]light is come into the world, and men loved darkness rather than light, because their deeds were evil.

20 For every one that doeth evil hateth the light, neither cometh to the light, lest his deeds should be [3]reproved.

21 But he that doeth truth cometh to the light, that his deeds may be made manifest, that they are wrought in God.

22 ¶ After these things came Jesus and his disciples into the land of Judæa; and there he tarried with them, [m]and baptized.

23 ¶ And John also was baptizing in Æ-nŏn near to [n]Sā-lĭm, because there was much water there: and they came, and were baptized.

24 For [o]John was not yet cast into prison.

25 ¶ Then there arose a question between *some* of John's disciples and the Jews about purifying.

26 And they came unto John, and said unto him, Rabbi, he that was with thee beyond Jordan, [p]to whom thou barest witness, behold, the same baptizeth, and all *men* come to him.

27 John answered and said, [q]A man can [4]receive nothing, except it be given him from heaven.

28 Ye yourselves bear me witness, that I said, I am not the Christ, but [r]that I am sent before him.

29 He [s]that hath the bride is the bridegroom: but [t]the friend of the bridegroom, which standeth and heareth him, rejoiceth greatly because of the bridegroom's voice: this my joy therefore is fulfilled.

30 He [u]must increase, but [v]I *must* decrease.

31 He [w]that cometh from above is [x]above all: [y]he that is of the earth is earthly, and speaketh of the earth: [z]he that cometh from heaven is above all.

32 And [a]what he hath seen and heard, that he testifieth; and no man receiveth his testimony.

33 He that hath received his testimony hath [b]set to his seal that God is true.

34 For [c]he whom God hath sent speaketh the words of God: for God giveth not the Spirit [d]by measure *unto him*.

35 The [e]Father loveth the Son, and hath given all things into his hand.

36 He [f]that believeth on the Son hath everlasting life: and he that believeth not the Son shall not see life; but [g]the wrath of God abideth on him.

CHAPTER 4

WHEN therefore the Lord knew how the Pharisees had heard that Jesus made and baptized more disciples than John,

2 (Though Jesus himself baptized not, but his disciples,)

3 He left Judæa, and departed again into Galilee.

4 And he must needs go through Să-mâr-ĭ-ă.

5 Then cometh he to a city of Să-mâr-ĭ-ă, which is called Sȳ-chär, near to the parcel of ground [a]that Jacob gave to his son Joseph.

6 Now Jacob's well was there. Jesus therefore, being wearied with *his* journey, sat thus on the well: *and* it was about the sixth hour.

7 There cometh a woman of Să-mâr-ĭ-ă to draw water: Jesus saith unto her, Give me to drink.

8 (For his disciples were gone away unto the city to buy meat.)

9 Then saith the woman of Să-mâr-ĭ-ă unto him, How is it that thou, being a Jew, askest drink of me, which am a woman of Să-mâr-ĭ-ă? for [b]the Jews have no dealings with the Să-măr-ĭ-tăns.

10 Jesus answered and said unto her, If thou knewest [c]the gift of God, and who it is that saith to thee, Give me to drink; thou wouldest have asked of him, and he would have given thee [d]living water.

11 The woman saith unto him, Sir, thou hast nothing to draw with, and the well is deep: from whence then hast thou that living water?

12 Art thou greater than our father Jacob, which gave us the well, and drank thereof himself, and his children, and his cattle?

13 Jesus answered and said unto her, Whosoever drinketh of this water shall thirst again:

14 But [e]whosoever drinketh of the water that I shall give him shall never

---

j Luke 9.56. 1 John 4.14.
k Rom. 8.1.
l Isa. 5.20. ch. 1.4.
3 Or, discovered.
m ch. 4.2.
n Gen. 14.18. 1 Sam. 9.4.
o Matt. 14.3. Luke 3.19, 20.
p ch. 1.34.
q Heb. 5.4. Jas. 1.17.
4 Or, take unto himself.
r Mal. 3.1. Matt. 3.3, 11,12. Mark 1.2,3. Luke 3.4-6.
s Matt. 22.2. 2 Cor. 11.2. Eph. 5.25. Rev. 21.9.
t Song 5.1.
u Isa. 9.7.
v Phil. 3.8,9.
w ch. 8.23.
x Matt. 28. 18. Rom. 9.5.
y 1 Cor. 15. 47.
z Eph. 1.21.
a ch. 15.15.
b 2 Cor. 1.22.
c ch. 7.16.
d ch. 1.16. Col. 1.19.
e Dan. 7.14.
f Hab. 2.4. Rom. 1.17.
g Gal. 3.10.

CHAP. 4

a Gen. 33.19. Josh. 24.32.
b 2 Ki. 17.24. Ezra 4.3. Acts 10.28.
c Isa. 9.6. Isa. 42.6. Rom. 8.32. 1 Cor. 1.30. 2 Cor. 9.15.
d Ex. 17.6. Isa. 12.3. Isa. 44.3. Jer. 2.13. Zech. 13.1. Rev. 7.17.
e ch. 6.35.

thirst; but the water that I shall give
him [f]shall be in him a well of water
springing up into everlasting life.
15 The [g]woman saith unto him, Sir,
give me this water, that I thirst not,
neither come hither to draw.
16 Jesus saith unto her, Go, call thy
husband, and come hither.
17 The woman answered and said,
I have no husband. Jesus said unto
her, Thou hast well said, I have no
husband:
18 For thou hast had five husbands;
and he whom thou now hast is not thy
husband: in that saidst thou truly.
19 The woman saith unto him, Sir,
[h]I perceive that thou art a prophet.
20 Our fathers worshipped [i]in this
mountain; and ye say, that in [j]Jeru-
salem is the place where men ought
to worship.
21 Jesus saith unto her, Woman, believe me, the hour cometh, when [k]ye
shall neither in this mountain, nor yet
at Jerusalem, worship the Father.
22 Ye worship [l]ye know not what:
we know what we worship: for [m]sal-
vation is of the Jews.
23 But the hour cometh, and now is,
when the true worshippers shall worship the Father in [n]spirit and in [o]truth:
for the Father seeketh such to worship
him.
24 God [p]*is* a Spirit: and they that
worship him must worship *him* in
spirit and in truth.
25 The woman saith unto him, I
know that [q]Mĕs-sī-ăs cometh, which
is called Christ: when he is come, he
will tell us all things.
26 Jesus saith unto her, [r]I that speak
unto thee am *he*.
27 ¶ And upon this came his disciples, and marvelled that he talked
with the woman: yet no man said,
What seekest thou? or, Why talkest
thou with her?
28 The woman then left her water-
pot, and went her way into the city,
and saith to the men,
29 Come, see a man, which told me
all things that ever I did: is not this
the Christ?
30 Then they went out of the city,
and came unto him.
31 ¶ In the mean while his disciples
prayed him, saying, Master, eat.
32 But he said unto them, I have
meat to eat that ye know not of.
33 Therefore said the disciples one
to another, Hath any man brought
him *ought* to eat?
34 Jesus saith unto them, [s]My meat
is to do the will of him that sent me,
and to finish his work.
35 Say not ye, There are yet four
months, and *then* cometh harvest?
behold, I say unto you, Lift up your
eyes, and look on the fields; [t]for they
are white already to harvest.
36 And he that reapeth [u]receiveth
wages, and gathereth fruit unto life
eternal: that both he that soweth and
he that reapeth may rejoice together.
37 And herein is that saying true,
One soweth, and another reapeth.
38 I sent you to reap that whereon
ye bestowed no labour: [v]other men
laboured, and ye are entered into their
labours.
39 ¶ And [w]many of the Să-măr-ĭ-tăns
of that city believed on him for the
saying of the woman, which testified,
He told me all that ever I did.
40 So [x]when the Să-măr-ĭ-tăns were
come unto him, they besought him
that he would tarry with them: and
he abode there two days.
41 And [y]many more believed because of his own word;
42 And said unto the woman, Now
we believe, not because of thy saying:
for [z]we have heard *him* ourselves, and
know that this is indeed the Christ,
[a]the Saviour of the world.
43 ¶ Now after two days he departed
thence, and went into Galilee.
44 For [b]Jesus himself testified, that
a prophet hath no honour in his own
country.
45 Then when he was come into Galilee, the Galilæans received him, [c]hav-
ing seen all the things that he did at
Jerusalem at the feast: [d]for they also
went unto the feast.
46 So Jesus came again into Cana of
Galilee, [e]where he made the water
wine. And there was a certain [1]noble-
man, whose son was sick at Că-pĕr-
nă-ŭm.
47 When he heard that Jesus was
come out of Judæa into Galilee, he
went unto him, and besought him that
he would come down, and heal
his son: for he was at the point of
death.
48 Then said Jesus unto him, Except
[f]ye see signs and wonders, ye will not
believe.
49 The nobleman saith unto him, Sir,
come down ere my child die.
50 Jesus saith unto him, [g]Go thy
way; thy son liveth. And the man believed the word that Jesus had spoken
unto him, and he went his way.
51 And as he was now going down,

f ch. 7.38.
g Rom. 6.23. 1 John 5.20.
h Luke 7.16.
i Gen. 12.6. Judg. 9.7.
j Deut. 12.5. 2 Chr. 7.12.
k Mal. 1.11. 1 Tim. 2.8.
l 2 Ki. 17.29.
m Isa. 2.3. Luke 24.47. Rom. 9.4,5.
n ch. 14.17. Rom. 8.4. 1 Cor. 3.16. Gal. 5.25. Phil. 3.3.
o ch. 1.17.
p Acts 17.24-29. 2 Cor. 3.17.
q Deut. 18. 15. Dan. 9.24.
r Matt. 16.20. Mark 14.61. ch. 9.37. Rom. 10.20, 21.
s Job 23.12. ch. 6.38.
t Matt. 9.37. Luke 10.2.
u Gen. 17.1. Ps. 19.11. Pro. 11.18. Dan. 12.3. 1 Cor. 3.8. 2 John 8. Jas. 5.20.
v Acts 10.43. 1 Pet. 1.12.
w Gen. 49.10.
x Gen. 32.26.
y Gen. 49.10. Isa. 42.1. Acts 1.8. Rom. 15.8.
z ch. 17.8. 1 John 4.14.
a Isa. 49.6. Matt. 1.21. Luke 2.30. ch. 1.29. Acts 13.23. Eph. 2.13. Phil. 3.20. 1 Tim. 1.15.
b Matt. 13. 57. Mark 6.4. Luke 4.24.
c ch. 2.23.
d Deut. 16. 16.
e ch. 2.1,11.
1 Or, courtier, or, ruler.
f Num. 14. 11. Matt. 16.1. Matt. 27.42. Luke 16.31. ch. 2.18. 1 Cor. 1.22.
g Matt. 8.13.

his servants met him, and told *him*, saying, Thy son liveth.

52 Then inquired he of them the hour when he began to amend. And they said unto him, Yesterday at the seventh hour the fever left him.

53 So the father knew that *it was* at the same hour, in the which Jesus said unto him, Thy son liveth: and [h]himself believed, and his whole house.

54 This *is* again the second miracle *that* Jesus did, when he was come out of Judæa into Galilee.

CHAPTER 5

AFTER [a]this there was a feast of the Jews; and Jesus went up to Jerusalem.

2 Now there is at Jerusalem [b]by the sheep [1]*market* a pool, which is called in the Hebrew tongue [2]Bĕth-ĕṣ'-dă, having five porches.

3 In these lay a great multitude of impotent folk, of blind, halt, withered, waiting for the moving of the water.

4 For an angel went down at a certain season into the pool, and troubled the water: whosoever then first after the troubling of the water stepped in was made whole of whatsoever disease he had.

5 And a certain man was there, which had an infirmity thirty and eight years.

6 When Jesus saw him lie, [c]and knew that he had been now a long time *in that case*, he saith unto him, [d]Wilt thou be made whole?

7 The impotent man answered him, Sir, I have no man, when the water is troubled, to put me into the pool: but while I am coming, another steppeth down before me.

8 Jesus saith unto him, [e]Rise, take up thy bed, and walk.

9 And immediately the man was made whole, and took up his bed, and walked: and on the [f]same day was the sabbath.

10 ¶ The Jews therefore said unto him that was cured, It is the sabbath day: [g]it is not lawful for thee to carry *thy* bed.

11 He answered them, He that made me whole, the same said unto me, Take up thy bed, and walk.

12 Then asked they him, What man is that which said unto thee, Take up thy bed, and walk?

13 And he that was healed wist not who it was: for Jesus had conveyed himself away, [3]a multitude being in *that* place.

h Acts 16.34.

CHAP. 5

a Lev. 23.2. Deut. 16.1. ch. 2.13.
b Neh. 3.1.
1 Or, gate.
2 That is, House of mercy.
c Heb. 4.13.
d Ps. 72.13. Isa. 55.1.
e Matt. 9.6. Mark 2.11. Luke 5.24.
f ch. 9.14.
g Ex. 20.10. Neh. 13.19. Matt. 12.2. Mark 2.24. Luke 6.2.
3 Or, from the multitude that was.
h Ps. 103.2.
i Matt. 12.45. ch. 8.11.
j Gen. 2.1,2. Isa. 40.26. ch. 9.4. Acts 14.17.
k ch. 7.19.
l Zech. 13.7. ch. 10.30. Phil. 2.6.
m ch. 8.28. ch. 9.4. Eph. 3.9.
n Matt. 3.17. ch. 3.35. 2 Pet. 1.17.
o Luke 7.14. ch. 11.25.
p Matt. 11. 27. ch. 3.35. Acts 17.31. 1 Pet. 4.5.
q Matt. 28. 19. 1 John 2.23. Rev. 5.8.
r 1 John 3.14.
s Gal. 2.20. Eph. 2.1,5. Col. 2.13. Rev. 3.1.
t Acts 17.31.
u Dan. 7.13.
v 1 Cor. 15. 52.
w Dan. 12.2. Luke 14.14. 1 Tim. 6.18. 1 Pet. 3.11.

14 Afterward Jesus findeth him in [h]the temple, and said unto him, Behold, thou art made whole: [i]sin no more, lest a worse thing come unto thee.

15 The man departed, and told the Jews that it was Jesus, which had made him whole.

16 And therefore did the Jews persecute Jesus, and sought to slay him, because he had done these things on the sabbath day.

17 ¶ But Jesus answered them, My [j]Father worketh hitherto, and I work.

18 Therefore the Jews [k]sought the more to kill him, because he not only had broken the sabbath, but said also that God was his Father, [l]making himself equal with God.

19 Then answered Jesus and said unto them, Verily, verily, I say unto you, [m]The Son can do nothing of himself, but what he seeth the Father do: for what things soever he doeth, these also doeth the Son likewise.

20 For [n]the Father loveth the Son, and sheweth him all things that himself doeth: and he will shew him greater works than these, that ye may marvel.

21 For as the Father raiseth up the dead, and quickeneth *them;* even [o]so the Son quickeneth whom he will.

22 For the Father judgeth no man, but hath [p]committed all judgment unto the Son:

23 That all *men* should [q]honour the Son, even as they honour the Father. He that honoureth not the Son honoureth not the Father which hath sent him.

24 Verily, verily, I say unto you, He that heareth my word, and believeth on him that sent me, hath everlasting life, and shall not come into condemnation; [r]but is passed from death unto life.

25 Verily, verily, I say unto you, The hour is coming, and now is, when [s]the dead shall hear the voice of the Son of God: and they that hear shall live.

26 For as the Father hath [t]life in himself; so hath he given to the Son to have life in himself;

27 And hath given him authority to execute judgment also, [u]because he is the Son of man.

28 Marvel not at this: for the hour is coming, in the which all that are in the graves shall hear his voice,

29 And [v]shall come forth; [w]they that have done good, unto the resurrection of life; and they that have done evil,

Mil 1 Thes 4:16-18

unto the resurrection of damnation.
30 I can of mine own self do nothing:
as I hear, I judge: and my judgment
is just; because [x]I seek not mine own
will, but the will of the Father which
hath sent me.
31 If [y]I bear witness of myself, my
witness is not true.
32 ¶ There is another that beareth
witness of me; and I know that the
witness which he witnesseth of me is
true.
33 Ye sent unto John, and [z]he bare
witness unto the truth.
34 But I receive not testimony from
man: but these things I say, that ye
might be saved.
35 He was a burning and [a]a shining
light: and [b]ye were willing for a season
to rejoice in his light.
36 ¶ But [c]I have greater witness than
that of John: for [d]the works which the
Father hath given me to finish, the
same works that I do, bear witness of
me, that the Father hath sent me.
37 And the Father himself, which
hath sent me, [e]hath borne witness of
me. Ye have neither heard his voice
at any time, nor [f]seen his shape.
38 And ye have not his word abiding
in you: for whom he hath sent, him
ye believe not.
39 ¶ Search [g]the scriptures; for in
them ye think ye have eternal life: and
they are [h]they which testify of me.
40 And ye will not come to me, that
ye might have life.
41 I [i]receive not honour from men.
42 But I know you, that ye have not
the love of God in you.
43 I am come in my Father's name,
and ye receive me not: if another shall
come in his own name, him ye will
receive.
44 How can ye believe, which receive
honour one of another, and seek not
[j]the honour that *cometh* from God
only?
45 Do not think that I will accuse
you to the Father: [k]there is *one* that
accuseth you, *even* Moses, in whom
ye trust.
46 For had ye believed Moses, ye
would have believed me: [l]for he
wrote of me.
47 But if [m]ye believe not his writings,
how shall ye believe my words?

CHAPTER 6

AFTER [a]these things Jesus went
over the sea of Galilee, which is
the sea of Tī-bē'-rĭ-ăs.
2 And a great multitude followed
him, because they saw his miracles
which he did on them that were
diseased.
3 And Jesus went up into a mountain, and there he sat with his disciples.
4 And [b]the passover, a feast of the
Jews, was nigh.
5 ¶ When [c]Jesus then lifted up *his*
eyes, and saw a great company come
unto him, he saith unto Philip, Whence
shall we buy bread, that these may
eat?
6 And this he said to prove him: for
he himself knew what he would do.
7 Philip answered him, [d]Two hundred pennyworth of bread is not sufficient for them, that every one of them
may take a little.
8 One of his disciples, Andrew,
Simon Peter's brother, saith unto him,
9 There is a lad here, which hath five
barley loaves, and two small fishes:
[e]but what are they among so many?
10 And Jesus said, Make the men
sit down. Now there was much grass
in the place. So the men sat down, in
number about five thousand.
11 And Jesus took the loaves; and
when he had [f]given thanks, he distributed to the disciples, and the disciples to them that were set down;
and likewise of the fishes as much as
they would.
12 When they were filled, he said unto his disciples, Gather up the fragments that remain, that nothing be
lost.
13 Therefore they gathered *them* together, and filled twelve baskets with
the fragments of the five barley loaves,
which remained over and above unto
them that had eaten.
14 Then those men, when they had
seen the miracle that Jesus did, said,
This is of a truth [g]that prophet that
should come into the world.
15 ¶ When Jesus therefore perceived
that they would come and take him
by force, to make him a king, he departed again into a mountain himself
alone.
16 And [h]when even was *now* come,
his disciples went down unto the sea,
17 And entered into a ship, and went
over the sea toward Că-pĕr'-nă-ŭm.
And it was now dark, and Jesus was
not come to them.
18 And the sea arose by reason of a
great wind that blew.
19 So when they had rowed about
five and twenty or thirty furlongs, they
see Jesus walking on the sea, and

x Matt. 26. 39.
y Isa. 55.4. 1 John 5.6. Rev. 3.14.
z ch. 1.15.
a 2 Pet. 1.19.
b Matt. 13. 20. Mark 6.20.
c 1 John 5.9.
d Matt. 11.4, 5. ch. 3.2.
e Matt. 3.17. ch. 6.27. 2 Pet. 1.17. 1 John 5.6.
f Deut. 4.12. ch. 1.18. 1 Tim. 1. 17. 1 John 4.12.
g Isa. 8.20. Luke 16.29. Acts 17.11.
h Deut. 18. 15. Luke 24.27.
i 1 Thes. 2.6.
j 1 Sam. 2.39. Matt. 25.21-23. Luke 19.17. Rom. 2.29.
k Rom. 2.12.
l Gen. 3.15. Gen. 12.3. Deut. 18.15. Acts 26.22.
m Luke 16. 29,31.

CHAP. 6

a Matt. 14. 15. Mark 6.35. Luke 9.10.
b Ex. 12.21. Lev. 23.5,7. Num. 28.16. Deut. 16.1. ch. 2.13. ch. 5.1. ch. 11.55.
c Matt. 14. 14. Mark 6.35. Luke 9.12.
d Num. 11. 21,22. 2 Ki. 7.2. Matt. 15.32, 33. Mark 6.37. Mark 8.4.
e 2 Ki. 4.43.
f Ex. 23.25. 1 Tim. 4.5.
g Gen. 49.10. Deut. 18.15, 18. Isa. 7.14. Isa. 9.6. Matt. 11.3. ch. 1.21. ch. 4.19.
h Matt. 14. 23. Mark 6.47.

drawing nigh unto the ship: and they
were afraid.
20 But he saith unto them, It is I; be
not afraid.
21 Then they willingly received him
into the ship: and immediately the
ship was at the land whither they went.
22 ¶ The day following, when the
people which stood on the other side
of the sea saw that there was none
other boat there, save that one whereinto his disciples were entered, and
that Jesus went not with his disciples
into the boat, but *that* his disciples
were gone away alone;
23 (Howbeit there came other boats
from Tī-bē-ri-ăs nigh unto the place
where they did eat bread, after that
the Lord had given thanks:)
24 When the people therefore saw
that Jesus was not there, neither his
disciples, they also took shipping, and
came to Că-pĕr-nă-ŭm, seeking for
Jesus.
25 And when they had found him
on the other side of the sea, they said
unto him, Rabbi, when camest thou
hither?
26 Jesus answered them and said,
Verily, verily, I say unto you, Ye seek
me, not because ye saw the miracles,
but because ye did eat of the loaves,
and were filled.
27 [1]Labour not for the meat which
perisheth, but [i]for that meat which endureth unto everlasting life, which the
Son of man shall give unto you: [j]for
him hath God the Father sealed.
28 Then said they unto him, What
shall we do, that we might work the
works of God?
29 Jesus answered and said unto
them, This [k]is the work of God, that
ye believe on him whom he hath sent.
30 They said therefore unto him,
What [l]sign shewest thou then, that
we may see, and believe thee? what
dost thou work?
31 Our [m]fathers did eat măn-nă in
the desert; as it is written, [n]He gave
them bread from heaven to eat.
32 Then Jesus said unto them, Verily, verily, I say unto you, Moses gave
you not that bread from heaven; but
my Father giveth you the true bread
from heaven.
33 For the bread of God is he which
cometh down from heaven, and giveth life unto the world.
34 Then said they unto him, Lord,
evermore give us this bread.
35 And Jesus said unto them, I am
the bread of life: [o]he that cometh to

1 Or, Work not.
i ch. 4.14. Rom. 6.23.
j Matt. 3.17. Matt. 17.5. Mark 1.11. Luke 3.22. ch. 1.33. ch. 5.37. Acts 2.22. 2 Pet. 1.17.
k 1 John 3.23.
l Matt. 12.38. Mark 8.12. Luke 11.16. ch. 2.18. 1 Cor. 1.22.
m Ex. 16.15. Num. 11.7. Neh. 9.15. 1 Cor. 10.3.
n Neh. 9.15. Ps. 78.24. 1 Cor. 10.3. Rev. 2.17.
o ch. 4.14. ch. 7.37. Rev. 22.17.
p Job 8.20. Isa. 1.18,19. Jer. 31.35. Jer. 33.25, 26. Matt. 24.24. ch. 10.28,29. 2 Tim. 2.19. 1 John 2.19.
q Matt. 26. 39. ch. 5.30.
r Luke 22.42. ch. 4.34. ch. 5.30.
s ch. 5.24. ch. 10.28. ch. 17.12. ch. 18.9. Col. 3.3. Jude 1.
t ch. 4.14.
u Isa. 54.13. Jer. 31.34. Micah 4.2. Heb. 8.10.
v ch. 1.18. ch. 5.37.
w Matt. 11. 27. Luke 10.22. ch. 1.18. ch. 7.29. 2 Cor. 4.6.
x ch. 3.16.
y Heb. 10.5, 10.
z ch. 7.43. ch. 9.16.
a ch. 3.9.
b Matt. 26. 26.

me shall never hunger; and he that believeth on me shall never thirst.
36 But I said unto you, That ye also
have seen me, and believe not.
37 All that the Father giveth me shall
come to me; and [p]him that cometh to
me I will in no wise cast out.
38 For I came down from heaven,
[q]not to do mine own will, but [r]the will
of him that sent me.
39 And this is the Father's will which
hath sent me, [s]that of all which he
hath given me I should lose nothing,
but should raise it up again at the
last day.
40 And this is the will of him that
sent me, that [t]every one which seeth
the Son, and believeth on him, may
have everlasting life: and I will raise
him up at the last day.
41 The Jews then murmured at him,
because he said, I am the bread which
came down from heaven.
42 And they said, Is not this Jesus,
the son of Joseph, whose father and
mother we know? how is it then that
he saith, I came down from heaven?
43 Jesus therefore answered and said
unto them, Murmur not among yourselves.
44 No man can come to me, except
the Father which hath sent me draw
him: and I will raise him up at the
last day.
45 It [u]is written in the prophets, And
they shall be all taught of God. Every
man therefore that hath heard, and
hath learned of the Father, cometh
unto me.
46 Not [v]that any man hath seen the
Father, save [w]he which is of God, he
hath seen the Father.
47 Verily, verily, I say unto you, He
[x]that believeth on me hath everlasting
life.
48 I am that bread of life.
49 Your fathers did eat măn-nă in
the wilderness, and are dead.
50 This is the bread which cometh
down from heaven, that a man may
eat thereof, and not die.
51 I am the living bread which came
down from heaven: if any man eat of
this bread, he shall live for ever: and
[y]the bread that I will give is my flesh,
which I will give for the life of the
world.
52 The Jews therefore [z]strove among
themselves, saying, [a]How can this
man give us *his* flesh to eat?
53 Then Jesus said unto them, Verily,
verily, I say unto you, Except [b]ye eat
the flesh of the Son of man, and

drink his blood, ye have no life in you.
54 Whoso eateth my flesh, and drinketh my blood, hath eternal life; and I will raise him up at the last day.
55 For my flesh is meat indeed, and my blood is drink indeed.
56 He that eateth my flesh, and drinketh my blood, [c]dwelleth in me, and I in him.
57 As the living Father hath sent me, and I live by the Father: so he that eateth me, even he shall live by me.
58 This is that bread which came down from heaven: not as your fathers did eat măn´-nă, and are dead: he that eateth of this bread shall live for ever.
59 These things said he in the synagogue, as he taught in Că-pĕr´-nă-ŭm.
60 Many [d]therefore of his disciples, when they had heard *this*, said, This is an hard saying; who can hear it?
61 When Jesus knew in himself that his disciples murmured at it, he said unto them, Doth this offend you?
62 *What* and [e]if ye shall see the Son of man ascend up where he was before?
63 It [f]is the spirit that quickeneth; the flesh profiteth nothing: the words that I speak unto you, *they* [g]are spirit, and *they* are life.
64 But there are some of you that believe not. For [h]Jesus knew from the beginning who they were that believed not, and who should betray him.
65 And he said, Therefore said I unto you, that no man can come unto me, except it were given unto him of my Father.
66 ¶ From that *time* many of his disciples went [i]back, and walked no more with him.
67 Then said Jesus unto the twelve, Will ye also go away?
68 Then Simon Peter answered him, Lord, to whom shall we go? thou hast the words of eternal life.
69 And we believe and are sure that thou art that Christ, the Son of the living God.
70 Jesus answered them, Have not I chosen you twelve, and one of you is a devil?
71 He spake of Judas Iscariot *the son* of Simon: for he it was that should betray him, being one of the twelve.

CHAPTER 7

AFTER these things Jesus walked in Galilee: for he would not walk in Jewry, [a]because the Jews sought to kill him.
2 Now [b]the Jews' feast of tabernacles was at hand.
3 His [c]brethren therefore said unto him, Depart hence, and go into Judæa, that thy disciples also may see the works that thou doest.
4 For *there is* no man *that* doeth any thing in secret, and he himself seeketh to be known openly. If thou do these things, shew thyself to the world.
5 For [d]neither did his brethren believe in him.
6 Then Jesus said unto them, [e]My time is not yet come: but your time is alway ready.
7 The [f]world cannot hate you; but me it hateth, [g]because I testify of it, that the works thereof are evil.
8 Go ye up unto this feast: I go not up yet unto this feast; [h]for my time is not yet full come.
9 When he had said these words unto them, he abode *still* in Galilee.
10 ¶ But when his brethren were gone up, then went he also up unto the feast, not openly, but as it were in secret.
11 Then [i]the Jews sought him at the feast, and said, Where is he?
12 And [j]there was much murmuring among the people concerning him: for some [k]said, He is a good man: others said, Nay; but he deceiveth the people.
13 Howbeit no man spake openly of him for fear of the Jews.
14 ¶ Now about the midst of the feast Jesus went up into the temple, and taught.
15 And [l]the Jews marvelled, saying, How knoweth this man [1]letters, having never learned?
16 Jesus answered them, and said, [m]My doctrine is not mine, but his that sent me.
17 If [n]any man will do his will, he shall know of the doctrine, whether it be of God, or *whether* I speak of myself.
18 He [o]that speaketh of himself seeketh his own glory: but he that seeketh his glory that sent him, the same is true, and no unrighteousness is in him.
19 Did [p]not Moses give you the law, and *yet* none of you keepeth the law? [q]Why go ye about to kill me?
20 The people answered and said, Thou [r]hast a devil: who goeth about to kill thee?
21 Jesus answered and said unto them, I have done one work, and ye all marvel.

c Isa. 57.15. ch. 14.23. Rom. 8.9. 1 Cor. 3.16. 1 Cor. 6.17. 2 Cor. 6.16. Eph. 3.17. Eph. 5.30. 2 Tim. 1.14. 1 John 3.24. Rev. 3.20.
d Matt. 11.6.
e Mark 16.19. ch. 3.13. Acts 1.9. Eph. 4.8.
f Rom. 8.2. 1 Cor. 15.45. 2 Cor. 3.6.
g Ps. 119.50. Eph. 1.17. 1 Thes. 2.13. Heb. 4.12.
h Matt. 9.4. ch. 2.24. ch. 13.11. Acts 15.18. Rev. 2.23.
i Luke 9.62. Heb. 6.4-6. 1 John 2.19.

CHAP. 7

a ch. 5.16. ch. 13.1. ch. 17.1.
b Lev. 23.34.
c Matt. 12.46. Mark 3.31. Mark 6.3. Luke 8.19. ch. 2.12. Acts 1.14. 1 Cor. 10.5. Gal. 1.19.
d Mark 3.21.
e Eccl. 3.1,2. ch. 2.4. Acts 1.7.
f ch. 15.19.
g ch. 3.19.
h ch. 8.20.
i ch. 11.56.
j ch. 9.16.
k Matt. 21.46. Luke 7.16. ch. 6.14.
l Matt. 13.54. Mark 6.2,3. Luke 4.22. Acts 2.7.
1 Or, learning.
m ch. 3.31-34. ch. 8.28. ch. 12.49. Rev. 1.1.
n Ps. 25.8,9, 12. Hos. 6.2,3. Micah 4.2. Luke 8.15. ch. 8.43.
o ch. 5.41.
p Acts 7.38.
q Matt. 12.14. Mark 3.6. ch. 5.16.
r ch. 8.48.

22 Moses [s]therefore gave unto you circumcision; (not because it is of Moses, but [t]of the fathers;) and ye on the sabbath day circumcise a man.

23 If a man on the sabbath day receive circumcision, [2]that the law of Moses should not be broken; are ye angry at me, because I [u]have made a man every whit whole on the sabbath day?

24 Judge [v]not according to the appearance, but judge righteous judgment.

25 Then said some of them of Jerusalem, Is not this he, whom they seek to kill?

26 But, lo, he speaketh boldly, and they say nothing unto him. Do the rulers know indeed that this is the very Christ?

27 Howbeit we know this man whence he is: but when Christ cometh, no man knoweth whence he is.

28 Then cried Jesus in the temple as he taught, saying, [w]Ye both know me, and ye know whence I am: and [x]I am not come of myself, but he that sent me [y]is true, whom ye [z]know not.

29 But [a]I know him: for I am from him, and he hath sent me.

30 Then they sought to take him: but no man laid hands on him, because his hour was not yet come.

31 And many of the people believed on him, and said, When Christ cometh, will he do more miracles than these which this *man* hath done?

32 ¶ The Pharisees heard that the people murmured such things concerning him; and the Pharisees and the chief priests sent officers to take him.

33 Then said Jesus unto them, [b]Yet a little while am I with you, and *then* I go unto him that sent me.

34 Ye [c]shall seek me, and shall not find *me:* and where I am, *thither* ye cannot come.

35 Then said the Jews among themselves, Whither will he go, that we shall not find him? will he go unto [d]the dispersed among the [3]Gentiles, and teach the Gentiles?

36 What *manner of* saying is this that he said, Ye shall seek me, and shall not find *me:* and where I am, *thither* ye cannot come?

37 In the last day, that great *day* of the feast, Jesus stood and cried, saying, [e]If any man thirst, let him come unto me, and drink.

38 He [f]that believeth on me, as the scripture hath said, [g]out of his belly shall flow rivers of living water.

s Gen. 17.12. Lev. 12.3. Luke 1.59. Rom. 4.11, 12. Phil. 3.5.
t Gen. 17.10.
2 Or, without breaking the law of Moses.
u ch. 5.8.
v Deut. 1.16. Pro. 24.23. ch. 8.15. Jas. 2.1.
w ch. 8.14.
x ch. 5.43.
y ch. 5.32. Rom. 3.4.
z ch. 1.18.
a Matt. 11. 27. ch. 10.15.
b ch. 13.33.
c Hos. 5.6. ch. 8.21.
d Isa. 11.12. Jas. 1.1. 1 Pet. 1.1.
3 Or, Greeks.
e Isa. 55.1. Rev. 22.17.
f Deut. 18.15.
g Isa. 12.3.
h Isa. 44.3. Joel 2.28. ch. 16.7. Acts 2.17.
i ch. 12.16.
j Deut. 18.15. ch. 1.21.
k ch. 4.42.
l Ps. 132.11. Luke 2.4.
m 1 Sam. 16. 1.
n 1 Cor. 1.20.
o ch. 3.2.
4 to him.
p Deut. 1.17. Deut. 17.8. ch. 3.2.
q 1 Ki. 17.1. 2 Ki. 14.25. Isa. 9.1,2. Matt. 4.15. ch. 1.46.

CHAP. 8

a Ex. 20.14. Lev. 18.20. Lev. 20.10. Deut. 5.18. Job 31.9. Pro. 6.29,32. Mal. 3.5. Matt. 5.27, 28.

39 (But [h]this spake he of the Spirit, which they that believe on him should receive: for the Holy Ghost was not yet *given;* because that Jesus was not yet [i]glorified.)

40 ¶ Many of the people therefore, when they heard this saying, said, Of a truth this is [j]the Prophet.

41 Others said, [k]This is the Christ. But some said, Shall Christ come out of Galilee?

42 Hath [l]not the scripture said, That Christ cometh of the seed of David, and out of the town of Bethlehem, [m]where David was?

43 So there was a division among the people because of him.

44 And some of them would have taken him; but no man laid hands on him.

45 ¶ Then came the officers to the chief priests and Pharisees; and they said unto them, Why have ye not brought him?

46 The officers answered, Never man spake like this man.

47 Then answered them the Pharisees, Are ye also deceived?

48 Have [n]any of the rulers or of the Pharisees believed on him?

49 But this people who knoweth not the law are cursed.

50 Nĭc-ŏ-dē′-mŭs saith unto them, (he [o]that came [4]to Jesus by night, being one of them,)

51 Doth [p]our law judge *any* man, before it hear him, and know what he doeth?

52 They answered and said unto him, Art thou also of Galilee? Search, and look: for out [q]of Galilee ariseth no prophet.

53 And every man went unto his own house.

CHAPTER 8

JESUS went unto the mount of Olives.

2 And early in the morning he came again into the temple, and all the people came unto him; and he sat down, and taught them.

3 And the scribes and Pharisees brought unto him a woman taken in adultery; and when they had set her in the midst,

4 They say unto him, Master, this woman was taken in adultery, in the very act.

5 Now [a]Moses in the law commanded us, that such should be stoned: but what sayest thou?

6 This they said, tempting him, that they might have to accuse him. But

Jesus stooped down, and with *his*
finger wrote on the ground, *as though*
he heard them not.
7 So when they continued asking
him, he lifted up himself, and said unto them, [b]He that is without sin among
you, let him first cast a stone at her.
8 And again he stooped down, and
wrote on the ground.
9 And they which heard *it*, [c]being
convicted by *their own* conscience,
went out one by one, beginning at the
eldest, *even* unto the last: and Jesus
was left alone, and the woman standing in the midst.
10 When Jesus had lifted up himself, and saw none but the woman, he
said unto her, Woman, where are
those thine accusers? hath no man
condemned thee?
11 She said, No man, Lord. And
Jesus said unto her, [d]Neither do I condemn thee: go, and sin no more.
12 ¶ Then spake Jesus again unto
them, saying, I am the light of the
world: he that followeth me shall not
walk in darkness, but shall have the
light of life.
13 The Pharisees therefore said unto
him, [e]Thou bearest record of thyself;
thy record is not true.
14 Jesus answered and said unto
them, Though I bear record of myself, *yet* my record is true: for I know
whence I came, and whither I go; but
[f]ye cannot tell whence I come, and
whither I go.
15 Ye [g]judge after the flesh; [h]I judge
no man.
16 And yet if I judge, my judgment is
true: for [i]I am not alone, but I and
the Father that sent me.
17 It [j]is also written in your law, that
the testimony of two men is true.
18 I am one that bear witness of myself, and [k]the Father that sent me
beareth witness of me.
19 Then said they unto him, Where
is thy Father? Jesus answered, [l]Ye
neither know me, nor my Father: [m]if
ye had known me, ye should have
known my Father also.
20 These words spake Jesus in [n]the
treasury, as he taught in the temple:
and [o]no man laid hands on him; for
[p]his hour was not yet come.
21 Then said Jesus again unto them,
I go my way, and [q]ye shall seek me,
and shall die in your sins: whither I
go, ye cannot come.
22 Then said the Jews, Will he kill
himself? because he saith, Whither I
go, ye cannot come.
23 And he said unto them, [r]Ye are
from beneath; I am from above: y
[s]are of this world; I am not of this
world.
24 I said therefore unto you, that ye
shall die in your sins: [t]for if ye believe
not that I am *he*, ye shall die in your
sins.
25 Then said they unto him, Who
art thou? And Jesus saith unto them,
Even *the same* that I said unto you
from the beginning.
26 I have many things to say and to
judge of you: but [u]he that sent me is
true; and [v]I speak to the world those
things which I have heard of him.
27 They understood not that he
spake to them of the Father.
28 Then said Jesus unto them, When
ye have [w]lifted up the Son of man,
[x]then shall ye know that I am *he*, and
[y]*that* I do nothing of myself; but [z]as
my Father hath taught me, I speak
these things.
29 And [a]he that sent me is with me:
the Father hath not left me alone; [b]for
I do always those things that please
him.
30 As he spake these words, many
believed on him.
31 Then said Jesus to those Jews
which believed on him, If ye continue
in my word, *then* are ye my disciples
indeed;
32 And ye shall know the truth, and
[c]the truth shall make you free.
33 ¶ They answered him, [d]We be
Abraham's seed, and were never in
bondage to any man: how sayest
thou, Ye shall be made free?
34 Jesus answered them, Verily, verily, I say unto you, [e]Whosoever committeth sin is the servant of sin.
35 And [f]the servant abideth not in
the house for ever: *but* the Son abideth ever.
36 If [g]the Son therefore shall make
you free, ye shall be free indeed.
37 I know that ye are Abraham's
seed; but ye [h]seek to kill me, because
my word hath no place in you.
38 I speak that which I have seen
with my Father: and ye do that which
ye have seen with your father.
39 They answered and said unto him,
Abraham [i]is our father. Jesus saith unto them, [j]If ye were Abraham's children, ye would do the works of Abraham.
40 But now ye seek to kill me, a man
that hath told you the truth, which I
have heard of God: this did not
Abraham.

b Deut. 17.7. Job 5.12. Matt. 7.1-5. Matt. 23.25-28. Rom. 2.1.
c 1 Ki. 2.44. 1 Ki. 17.18. Ps. 50.21. Eccl. 7.22. Rom. 2.22. 1 John 3.20.
d Luke 9.56. Luke 12.14. ch. 3.17. Rom. 13.4.
e ch. 5.31.
f ch. 7.28.
g 1 Sam. 16.7. ch. 7.24.
h Luke 12.14. ch. 3.17.
i ch. 14.10, 11. ch. 16.32.
j Deut. 17.6. Matt. 18.16. 2 Cor. 13.1. Heb. 10.28. Rev. 11.3.
k ch. 5.37. 2 Pet. 1.17. 1 John 5.6-12.
l ch. 16.3.
m ch. 14.7.
n Mark 12. 41.
o ch. 7.30.
p ch. 7.8.
q ch. 13.33.
r ch. 3.31.
s ch. 15.19. 1 John 4.5.
t Mark 16.16.
u ch. 7.28.
v ch. 3.32.
w ch. 3.14.
x Rom. 1.4.
y ch. 5.19,30.
z ch. 3.11.
a Isa. 49.1. ch. 14.10. 2 Tim. 4.17.
b ch. 4.34.
c Ps. 119.45. Isa. 61.1. Rom. 6.14. 2 Cor. 3.17, 18.
d Lev. 25.42. Matt. 3.9.
e 1 Ki. 21.25. Pro. 5.22. Acts 8.22. Rom. 6.6, 12,16,19,20. 2 Pet. 2.19.
f Gal. 4.30.
g Isa. 49.24. Rom. 8.2. 2 Cor. 3.17. Gal. 5.1. Rev. 1.5.
h ch. 7.19.
i Matt. 3.9.
j Rom. 2.28. Gal. 3.7,29.

41 Ye do the deeds of your father.
Then said they to him, We be not
born of fornication; [k]we have one
Father, *even* God.
42 Jesus said unto them, [l]If God
were your Father, ye would love me:
[m]for I proceeded forth and came from
God; [n]neither came I of myself, but
he sent me.
43 Why [o]do ye not understand my
speech? *even* because ye cannot hear
my word.
44 Ye [p]are of *your* father the devil,
and the lusts of your father ye will do.
He was a murderer from the beginning, and [q]abode not in the truth, because there is no truth in him. When he
speaketh a lie, he speaketh of his own:
for he is a liar, and the father of it.
45 And because I tell *you* the truth,
ye believe me not.
46 Which of you convinceth me of
sin? And if I say the truth, why do ye
not believe me?
47 He [r]that is of God heareth God's
words: ye therefore hear *them* not, because ye are not of God.
48 Then answered the Jews, and said
unto him, Say we not well that thou
art a Să-măr'-ĭ-tăn, and hast a devil?
49 Jesus answered, I have not a
devil; but I honour my Father, and ye
do dishonour me.
50 And [s]I seek not mine own glory:
there is one that seeketh and judgeth.
51 Verily, verily, I say unto you, If
[t]a man keep my saying, he shall never
see death.
52 Then said the Jews unto him,
Now we know that thou hast a devil.
[u]Abraham is dead, and the prophets;
and thou sayest, If a man keep my saying, he shall never taste of death.
53 Art thou greater than our father
Abraham, which is dead? and the
prophets are dead: whom makest
thou thyself?
54 Jesus answered, If I honour myself, my honour is nothing: [v]it is my
Father that honoureth me; of whom
ye say, that he is your God:
55 Yet [w]ye have not known him; but
I know him: and if I should say, I
know him not, I shall be a liar like unto you: but I know him, and keep his
saying.
56 Your father Abraham [x]rejoiced to
see my day: [y]and he saw *it*, and was
glad.
57 Then said the Jews unto him,
Thou art not yet fifty years old, and
hast thou seen Abraham?
58 Jesus said unto them, Verily, verily, I say unto you, Before Abraham
was, [z]I am.
59 Then took they up stones to cast
at him: but Jesus hid himself, and
went out of the temple, going through
the midst of them, and so passed by.

CHAPTER 9

AND as *Jesus* passed by, he saw a
man which was blind from *his*
birth.
2 And his disciples asked him, saying, Master, who did [a]sin, this man,
or his parents, that he was born blind?
3 Jesus answered, Neither hath this
man sinned, nor his parents: but [b]that
the works of God should be made
manifest in him.
4 I [c]must work the works of him that
sent me, while it is day: the night cometh, when no man can work.
5 As long as I am in the world, I [d]am
the light of the world.
6 When he had thus spoken, [e]he spat
on the ground, and made clay of the
spittle, and he [1]anointed the eyes of
the blind man with the clay,
7 And said unto him, Go, [f]wash in
the pool of Sī-lō'-ăm, (which is by interpretation, Sent.) [g]He went his way
therefore, and washed, and came
seeing.
8 ¶ The neighbours therefore, and
they which before had seen him that
he was blind, said, Is not this he that
sat and begged?
9 Some said, This is he: others *said*,
He is like him: *but* he said, I am *he*.
10 Therefore said they unto him,
How were thine eyes opened?
11 He answered and said, A man
that is called Jesus made clay, and
anointed mine eyes, and said unto me,
Go to the pool of Sī-lō'-ăm, and wash:
and I went and washed, and I received
sight.
12 Then said they unto him, Where
is he? He said, I know not.
13 ¶ They brought to the Pharisees
him that aforetime was blind.
14 And it was the sabbath day when
Jesus made the clay, and opened his
eyes.
15 Then again the Pharisees also asked him how he had received his sight.
He said unto them, He put clay upon
mine eyes, and I washed, and do see.
16 Therefore said some of the Pharisees, This man is not of God, because
he keepeth not the sabbath day.
Others said, [h]How can a man that is a
sinner do such miracles? And [i]there
was a division among them.

k Isa. 63.16. Mal. 1.6.
l 1 John 4.19.
m ch. 1.14. ch. 3.16. Gal. 4.4.
n ch. 5.43.
o ch. 7.17.
p Matt. 13. 38.
q Gen. 3.1. 2 Cor. 11.3. Jude 6.
r 1 John 4.6.
s ch. 5.41.
t ch. 5.24.
u Zech. 1.5.
v ch. 16.14. Acts 3.13.
w ch. 7.28.
x Gen. 22.18. Luke 10.24. Gal. 3.8,16.
y Heb. 11.13.
z Ex. 3.14. Isa. 9.6. Micah 5.2. Col. 1.17. Heb. 13.8. Rev. 1.8.

CHAP. 9

a Acts 28.4.
b Matt. 11.5. ch. 11.4. Acts 4.21, 22.
c ch. 4.34. ch. 5.19,36. ch. 11.9. ch. 12.35. ch. 17.4.
d Isa. 42.6. Isa. 49.6. Luke 2.32. ch. 1.5,9. ch. 3.19. ch. 8.12. Acts 13.47. 1 John 2.8.
e Mark 7.33.
1 Or, spread the clay upon the eyes of the blind man.
f Neh. 3.15. Isa. 8.6.
g Ex. 4.11. 2 Ki. 5.14. Ps. 146.8. Isa. 29.18. Isa. 35.5. Isa. 42.7.
h ch. 3.2.
i Luke 12.51-53. ch. 7.12,43.

17 They say unto the blind man
again, What sayest thou of him, that
he hath opened thine eyes? He said,
[j]He is a prophet.
18 But the Jews did not believe concerning him, that he had been blind,
and received his sight, until they called
the parents of him that had received
his sight.
19 And they asked them, saying, Is
this your son, who ye say was born
blind? how then doth he now see?
20 His parents answered them and
said, We know that this is our son,
and that he was born blind:
21 But by what means he now seeth,
we know not; or who hath opened his
eyes, we know not: he is of age; ask
him: he shall speak for himself.
22 These *words* spake his parents,
because they [k]feared the Jews: for the
Jews had agreed already, that if any
man did confess that he was Christ,
[l]he should be put out of the synagogue.
23 Therefore said his parents, He is
of age; ask him.
24 Then again called they the man
that was blind, and said unto him,
[m]Give God the praise: we know that
this man is a sinner.
25 He answered and said, Whether
he be a sinner *or no*, I know not: one
thing I know, that, whereas I was
blind, now I see.
26 Then said they to him again,
What did he to thee? how opened he
thine eyes?
27 He answered them, I have told
you already, and ye did not hear:
wherefore would ye hear *it* again? will
ye also be his disciples?
28 Then they reviled him, and said,
Thou art his disciple; but we are
Moses' disciples.
29 We know that God spake unto
Moses: *as for* this *fellow*, [n]we know
not from whence he is.
30 The man answered and said unto
them, [o]Why herein is a marvellous
thing, that ye know not from whence
he is, and *yet* he hath opened mine
eyes.
31 Now we know [p]that God heareth
not sinners: but if any man be a worshipper of God, and doeth his will,
him he heareth.
32 Since the world began was it not
heard that any man opened the eyes
of one that was born blind.
33 If this man were not of God, he
could do nothing.
34 They answered and said unto him,
Thou wast altogether born in sins,
and dost thou teach us? And they
[2]cast him out.
35 Jesus heard that they had cast him
out; and when he had found him, he
said unto him, Dost thou believe on
[q]the Son of God?
36 He answered and said, Who is he,
Lord, that I might believe on him?
37 And Jesus said unto him, Thou
hast both seen him, and [r]it is he that
talketh with thee.
38 And he said, Lord, I believe. And
he worshipped him.
39 ¶ And Jesus said, [s]For judgment
I am come into this world, that [t]they
which see not might see; and that
they which see might be made blind.
40 And *some* of the Pharisees which
were with him heard these words,
[u]and said unto him, Are we blind
also?
41 Jesus said unto them, [v]If ye were
blind, ye should have no sin: but now
ye say, We see; therefore your sin remaineth.

CHAPTER 10

VERILY, verily, I say unto you, He
[a]that entereth not by the door into
the sheepfold, but climbeth up some
other way, the same is a thief and a
robber.
2 But he that entereth in by the [b]door
is the shepherd of the sheep.
3 To him [c]the porter openeth; and
the sheep hear his voice: and he calleth his own sheep by name, and leadeth them out.
4 And when he putteth forth his own
sheep, he goeth before them, and the
sheep follow him: for they know his
voice.
5 And [d]a stranger will they not follow, but will flee from him: for they
know not the voice of strangers.
6 This parable spake Jesus unto
them: but they understood not what
things they were which he spake unto
them.
7 Then said Jesus unto them again,
Verily, verily, I say unto you, I am
[e]the door of the sheep.
8 All [f]that ever came before me are
thieves and robbers: but the sheep did
not hear them.
9 I am the door: by me if any man
enter in, he shall be saved, and shall
go in and out, and find pasture.
10 The [g]thief cometh not, but for to
steal, and to kill, and to destroy: I am
come that they might have life, and
that they might have *it* more abundantly.

j Deut. 18.15. ch. 4.19.
k ch. 7.13. Acts 5.13.
l ch. 12.42.
m Josh. 7.19. 1 Sam. 6.5. Isa. 66.5. ch. 5.23.
n ch. 1.10. ch 7.8.
o ch. 3.10.
p Job 27.9. Ps. 18.41. Ps. 34.15. Pro. 1.28. Pro. 15.29. Isa. 1.15. Jer. 11.11. Eze. 8.18. Micah 3.4. Zech. 7.13.
2 Or, excommunicated him.
q Matt. 14. 33. Mark 1.1. ch. 10.36. 1 John 5.13.
r Matt. 13.11. ch. 4.26.
s ch. 5.22. ch. 3.17.
t Matt. 13.13. Luke 2.34. Acts 28.26, 27. 2 Cor. 2.16.
u Rom. 2.19.
v ch. 15.22.

CHAP. 10

a Isa. 56.10. Heb. 5.4.
b Acts 20.28. 1 Cor. 12.28.
c 1 Cor. 16.9. 1 Pet. 1.12.
d Pro. 19.27. Gal. 1.8. Col. 2.8.
e Eph. 2.18. Heb. 10.19.
f Jer. 23.1. Jer. 50.6. Eze. 22.25. Micah 2.12. Zech. 11.4, 5. Acts 5.36, 37.
g Matt. 7.15. Acts 20.29. 2 Pet. 2.1.

11 I [h]am the good shepherd: the good shepherd giveth his life for the sheep.
12 But he that is an hireling, and not the shepherd, whose own the sheep are not, seeth the wolf coming, [i]and leaveth the sheep, and fleeth: and the wolf catcheth them, and scattereth the sheep.
13 The hireling fleeth, because he is an hireling, and careth not for the sheep.
14 I am the good shepherd, [j]and know my *sheep*, and [k]am known of mine.
15 As the Father knoweth me, even so know I the Father: and I lay down my life for the sheep.
16 And [l]other sheep I have, which are not of this fold: them also I must bring, and they shall hear my voice; [m]and there shall be one fold, *and* one shepherd. Unty 2 Jn Vv 9-11
17 Therefore doth my Father love me, [n]because I lay down my life, that I might take it again.
18 No man taketh it from me, but I lay it down of myself. I have power to lay it down, and I have power to take it again. This commandment [o]have I received of my Father.
19 ¶ There was a division therefore again among the Jews for these sayings.
20 And many of them said, He hath a devil, and is mad; why hear ye him?
21 Others said, These are not the words of him that hath a devil. Can [p]a devil open the eyes of the blind?
22 ¶ And it was at Jerusalem the feast of the dedication, and it was winter.
23 And Jesus walked in the temple [q]in Solomon's porch.
24 Then came the Jews round about him, and said unto him, How long dost thou [1]make us to doubt? If thou be the Christ, tell us plainly.
25 Jesus answered them, I told you, and ye believed not: the works that I do in my Father's name, they bear witness of me.
26 But [r]ye believe not, because ye are not of my sheep, as I said unto you.
27 My sheep hear my voice, and I know them, and they follow me:
28 And I give unto them eternal life; and they shall never perish, neither shall any *man* pluck them out of my hand.
29 My [s]Father, [t]which gave *them* me, is greater than all; and no *man* is able to pluck *them* out of my Father's hand.
30 I [u]and *my* Father are one.
31 Then the Jews took up stones again to stone him.
32 Jesus answered them, Many good works have I shewed you from my Father; for which of those works do ye stone me?
33 The Jews answered him, saying, For a good work we stone thee not; but for blasphemy; and because that thou, being a man, makest [v]thyself God.
34 Jesus answered them, [w]Is it not written in your law, I said, Ye are gods?
35 If he called them gods, [x]unto whom the word of God came, and the scripture cannot be broken;
36 Say ye of him, [y]whom the Father hath sanctified, and [z]sent into the world, Thou blasphemest; because I said, I am [a]the Son of God?
37 If [b]I do not the works of my Father, believe me not.
38 But if I do, though ye believe not me, believe the works: that ye may know, and believe, [c]that the Father *is* in me, and I in him.
39 Therefore they sought again to take him: but he escaped out of their hand,
40 And went away again beyond Jordan into the place [d]where John at first baptized; and there he abode.
41 And many resorted unto him, and said, John did no miracle: but [e]all things that John spake of this man were true.
42 And [f]many believed on him there.

CHAPTER 11

NOW a certain *man* was sick, *named* Lăz'ă-rŭs, of Bethany, the town [a]of Mary and her sister Martha.
2 (It [b]was *that* Mary which anointed the Lord with ointment, and wiped his feet with her hair, whose brother Lăz'ă-rŭs was sick.)
3 Therefore his sisters sent unto him, saying, Lord, behold, he whom thou lovest is sick.
4 When Jesus heard *that*, he said, This sickness is not unto death, but [c]for the glory of God, that the Son of God might be glorified thereby.
5 Now Jesus loved Martha, and her sister, and Lăz'ă-rŭs.
6 When he had heard therefore that he was sick, [d]he abode two days still in the same place where he was.

h Isa. 40.11. Heb. 13.20. 1 Pet. 2.25.
i Zech. 11.16.
j 2 Tim. 2.19.
k Isa. 53.6,7. Phil. 3.10. 1 John 5.20.
l Isa. 56.8.
m Eph. 2.14.
n Isa. 53.7. 2 Cor. 5.15. Heb. 2.9.
o Acts 2.24.
p Ex. 4.11. Ps. 94.9. Pro. 20.12. Isa. 35.5.
q Acts 3.11.
1 Or, hold us in suspense?
r ch. 8.47. 1 John 4.6.
s ch. 14.28.
t Ps. 145.3. Dan. 4.3. Mal. 1.14. ch. 17.2,6.
u Deut. 6.4. Zech. 13.7. ch. 1.1,14. 1 Cor. 8.4,6. Eph. 3.9. Col. 1.15,16. 1 Tim. 3.16. 1 John 1.3.
v ch. 5.18. Phil. 2.6.
w Ps. 82.6.
x Rom. 13.1.
y ch. 6.27.
z ch. 3.17.
a Luke 1.35. ch. 9.35.
b ch. 15.24.
c ch. 14.10.
d ch. 1.28.
e ch. 1.29.
f ch. 8.30.

CHAP. 11

a Luke 10.38.
b Matt. 26.7. Mark 14.3. Luke 7.37. ch. 12.3.
c ch. 9.3. Phil. 1.11. 1 Pet. 4.11, 14.
d ch. 10.40.

7 Then after that saith he to *his* disciples, Let us go into Judæa again.
8 *His* disciples say unto him, Master, [e]the Jews of late sought to stone
thee; and goest thou thither again?
9 Jesus answered, Are there not
twelve hours in the day? [f]If any man
walk in the day, he stumbleth not, because he seeth the light of this world.
10 But [g]if a man walk in the night, he
stumbleth, because there is no light
in him.
11 These things said he: and after
that he saith unto them, Our friend
Lăz'-ă-rŭs [h]sleepeth; but I go, that I
may awake him out of sleep.
12 Then said his disciples, Lord, if he
sleep, he shall do well.
13 Howbeit Jesus spake of his death:
but they thought that he had spoken
of taking of rest in sleep.
14 Then said Jesus unto them plainly, Lăz'-ă-rŭs is dead.
15 And I am glad for your sakes that
I was not there, to the intent ye may
believe; nevertheless let us go unto
him.
16 Then said Thomas, which is called
Dĭd'-ў-mŭs, unto his fellowdisciples,
Let us also go, that we may die with
him.
17 Then when Jesus came, he found
that he had *lain* in the grave four days
already.
18 Now Bethany was nigh unto Jerusalem, [1]about fifteen furlongs off:
19 And many of the Jews came to
Martha and Mary, to comfort them
concerning their brother.
20 Then Martha, as soon as she
heard that Jesus was coming, went
and met him: but Mary sat *still* in the
house.
21 Then said Martha unto Jesus,
Lord, if thou hadst been here, my
brother had not died.
22 But I know, that even now, whatsoever [i]thou wilt ask of God, God will
give *it* thee.
23 Jesus saith unto her, Thy brother
shall [j]rise again.
24 Martha saith unto him, [k]I know
that he shall rise again in the resurrection at the last day.
25 Jesus said unto her, I am [l]the
resurrection, and [m]the life: he [n]that
believeth in me, though he were dead,
yet shall he live:
26 And whosoever liveth and believeth in me shall never die. Believest
thou this?
27 She saith unto him, Yea, Lord:
[o]I believe that thou art the Christ, the
Son of God, which should come into
the world.
28 And when she had so said, she
went her way, and called Mary her
sister secretly, saying, The Master is
come, and calleth for thee.
29 As soon as she heard *that*, she
arose quickly, and came unto him.
30 Now Jesus was not yet come into
the town, but was in that place where
Martha met him.
31 The Jews then which were with
her in the house, and comforted her,
when they saw Mary, that she rose up
hastily and went out, followed her,
saying, She goeth unto the grave to
weep there.
32 Then when Mary was come where
Jesus was, and saw him, she fell down
at his feet, saying unto him, Lord, if
thou hadst been here, my brother had
not died.
33 When Jesus therefore saw her
weeping, and the Jews also weeping
which came with her, he groaned in
the spirit, and [2]was troubled,
34 And said, Where have ye laid
him? They said unto him, Lord, come
and see.
35 Jesus [p]wept.
36 Then said the Jews, Behold how
he loved him!
37 And some of them said, Could
not this man, [q]which opened the eyes
of the blind, have caused that even
this man should not have died?
38 Jesus therefore again groaning in
himself cometh to the grave. It was
a cave, and a stone lay upon it.
39 Jesus said, Take ye away the
stone. Martha, the sister of him that
was dead, saith unto him, Lord, by
this time he stinketh: for he hath been
dead four days.
40 Jesus saith unto her, Said I not
unto thee, that, if thou wouldest believe, thou shouldest see the glory of
God?
41 Then they took away the stone
from the place where the dead was
laid. And Jesus lifted up *his* eyes, and
said, Father, I thank thee that thou
hast heard me.
42 And I knew that thou hearest me
always: but [r]because of the people
which stand by I said *it*, that they may
believe that thou hast sent me.
43 And when he thus had spoken, he
cried with a loud voice, Lăz'-ă-rŭs,
[s]come forth.
44 And he that was dead came forth,
bound hand and foot with grave-
clothes: and [t]his face was bound about

[e] ch. 10.31.
[f] Ps. 97.11. Pro. 4.18. ch. 9.4.
[g] Job 38.15. Ps. 27.2. Pro. 4.18,19. Jer. 13.16. ch. 12.35. 1 John 2.11.
[h] Deut. 31.16. Dan. 12.2. Matt. 9.24. Mark 5.39. Acts 7.60.
1 That is, about two miles.
[i] Mark 9.23, 24. ch. 9.31. Heb. 11.17-19.
[j] Dan. 12.2. Phil. 3.21. 1 Thes. 4.14.
[k] Luke 14.14. ch. 5.29.
[l] ch. 5.21. Rom. 5.17-19. 1 Cor. 15. 20-26.
[m] Ps. 36.9. ch. 1.4. ch. 6.35. Acts 3.15. Rom. 8.2. Col. 3.4. 1 John 1.1, 2.
[n] ch. 3.36. 1 John 5.10.
[o] Mal. 3.1. Matt. 11.3. Luke 7.19, 20. ch. 4.42. 1 Tim. 1.15, 16.
2 he troubled himself.
[p] Isa. 53.3. Luke 19.41. Rom. 12.15. Heb. 4.15.
[q] ch. 9.6.
[r] ch. 12.30.
[s] Deut. 32.39. 1 Sam. 2.6. Ps. 33.9. Luke 7.14. Acts 3.15. Rom. 4.17.
[t] ch. 20.7.

with a napkin. Jesus saith unto them,
Loose him, and let him go.
45 Then many of the Jews which
came to Mary, [u]and had seen the
things which Jesus did, believed on
him.
46 But some of them went their ways
to the Pharisees, and told them what
things Jesus had done.
47 ¶ Then [v]gathered the chief priests
and the Pharisees a council, and said,
[w]What do we? for this man doeth
many miracles.
48 If we let him thus alone, all *men*
will believe on him: and [x]the Romans
shall come and take away both our
place and nation.
49 And one of them, *named* [y]Căi'-ā-
phăs, being the high priest that
same year, said unto them, Ye know
nothing at all.
50 Nor [z]consider that it is expedient
for us, that one man should die for
the people, and that the whole nation
perish not.
51 And this spake he not of himself:
but being high priest that year, he
prophesied that Jesus should die for
that nation;
52 And [a]not for that nation only,
[b]but that also he should gather together in one the children of God that
were scattered abroad.
53 Then from that day forth they
took counsel together for to put him
to death.
54 Jesus [c]therefore walked no more
openly among the Jews; but went
thence unto a country near to the wilderness, into a city called [d]Ē'-phră-ĭm,
and there continued with his disciples.
55 ¶ And [e]the Jews' passover was
nigh at hand: and many went out of
the country up to Jerusalem before
the passover, to [f]purify themselves.
56 Then [g]sought they for Jesus, and
spake among themselves, as they
stood in the temple, [h]What think ye,
that he will not come to the feast?
57 Now both the chief priests and the
Pharisees had given a commandment,
that, if any man knew where he were,
he should shew *it*, that they might take
him.

CHAPTER 12

THEN Jesus six days before the
passover came to Bethany, where
[a]Lăz'-ā-rŭs was which had been dead,
whom he raised from the dead.
2 There [b]they made him a supper;
and Martha served: but Lăz'-ā-rŭs
was one of them that sat at the table
with him.

u ch. 2.23.
v Ps. 2.2. Matt. 26.3. Mark 14.1. Luke 22.2.
w ch. 12.19. Acts 4.16.
x Dan. 9.26. Zech. 13.7, 8. Matt. 21.40, 41.
y Luke 3.2. ch. 18.14. Acts 4.6.
z ch. 18.14.
a Isa. 49.6. 1 John 2.2.
b ch. 10.16. Acts 13.47. Gal. 3.28. Eph. 3.6. 1 Pet. 5.9.
c ch. 4.1,3.
d 2 Chr. 13. 19.
e ch. 2.13.
f Ex. 19.10. Num. 9.6. 1 Sam. 16.5. Job 1.5. Acts 24.18.
g ch. 7.11.
h Ps. 2.1.

CHAP. 12

a 1 Sam. 2.6. Ps. 33.9. Luke 7.14. ch. 11.1,43. Acts 3.15. Rom. 4.17.
b Matt. 26.6. Mark 14.3.
c Song 1.12. Luke 10.38, 39. ch. 11.2.
d Pro. 26.25. ch. 13.29. 1 Cor. 6.10. Eph. 5.5. Col. 3.5.
e Deut. 15. 11. Matt. 26.11. Mark 14.7.
f Pro. 1.16. Luke 16.31.
g Mark 15.10. ch. 11.45.
h Luke 19.35.
i Ps. 72.17-19. 1 Tim. 1.17.
j Isa. 62.11. Zech. 9.9.
k Luke 18.34.
l ch. 7.39.
m ch. 14.26.

3 Then took [c]Mary a pound of ointment of spikenard, very costly, and
anointed the feet of Jesus, and wiped
his feet with her hair: and the house
was filled with the odour of the ointment.
4 Then saith one of his disciples,
Judas Iscariot, Simon's *son*, which
should betray him,
5 Why was not this ointment sold for
three hundred pence, and given to
the poor?
6 This he said, not that he cared for
the poor; but because he was a thief,
and [d]had the bag, and bare what was
put therein.
7 Then said Jesus, Let her alone:
against the day of my burying hath
she kept this.
8 For [e]the poor always ye have
with you; but me ye have not always.
9 Much people of the Jews therefore
knew that he was there: and they came
not for Jesus' sake only, but that they
might see Lăz'-ā-rŭs also, whom he
had raised from the dead.
10 ¶ But [f]the chief priests consulted
that they might put Lăz'-ā-rŭs also to
death;
11 Because [g]that by reason of him
many of the Jews went away, and believed on Jesus.
12 ¶ On [h]the next day much people
that were come to the feast, when
they heard that Jesus was coming to
Jerusalem,
13 Took branches of palm trees, and
went forth to meet him, and cried,
[i]Hō-săn'-nă: Blessed *is* the King of
Israel that cometh in the name of the
Lord.
14 And Jesus, when he had found
a young ass, sat thereon; as it is
written,
15 Fear [j]not, daughter of Sī'-on: behold, thy King cometh, sitting on an
ass's colt.
16 These things [k]understood not his
disciples at the first: [l]but when Jesus
was glorified, [m]then remembered they
that these things were written of him,
and *that* they had done these things
unto him.
17 The people therefore that was
with him when he called Lăz'-ā-rŭs out
of his grave, and raised him from the
dead, bare record.
18 For this cause the people also met
him, for that they heard that he had
done this miracle.
19 The Pharisees therefore said
among themselves, Perceive ye how

ye prevail nothing? behold, the world
is gone after him.
20 ¶ And there [n]were certain Greeks
among them [o]that came up to worship
at the feast:
21 The same came therefore to
Philip, which was of Bĕth-să'-ĭ-dă of
Galilee, and desired him, saying, Sir,
we would see Jesus.
22 Philip cometh and telleth Andrew: and again Andrew and Philip
tell Jesus.
23 ¶ And Jesus answered them, saying, The [p]hour is come, that the Son
of man should be glorified.
24 Verily, verily, I say unto you, Except [q]a corn of wheat fall into the
ground and die, it abideth alone: but
if it die, it bringeth forth much fruit.
25 He [r]that loveth his life shall lose
it; and he that hateth his life in this
world shall keep it unto life eternal.
26 If any man serve me, let him
follow me; and [s]where I am, there
shall also my servant be: if any man
serve me, him will *my* Father honour.
27 Now [t]is my soul troubled; and
what shall I say? Father, save me from
this hour: [u]but for this cause came I
unto this hour.
28 Father, glorify thy name. Then
[v]came there a voice from heaven, *saying*, I have both glorified *it*, and will
glorify *it* again.
29 The people therefore, that stood
by, and heard *it*, said that it thundered: others said, An angel spake to him.
30 Jesus answered and said, [w]This
voice came not because of me, but for
your sakes.
31 Now is the judgment of this
world: now shall [x]the prince of this
world be cast out.
32 And I, if I be lifted up from the
earth, will draw [y]all *men* unto me.
33 This he said, signifying what death
he should die.
34 The people answered him, We
[z]have heard out of the law that Christ
abideth for ever: and how sayest thou,
The Son of man must be lifted up?
who is this Son of man?
35 Then Jesus said unto them, Yet a
little while [a]is the light with you.
[b]Walk while ye have the light, lest
darkness come upon you: for [c]he that
walketh in darkness knoweth not
whither he goeth.
36 While ye have light, believe in the
light, that ye may be the [d]children of
light. These things spake Jesus, and
departed, and did hide himself from
them.

n Acts 17.4.
o 1 Ki. 8.41.
p ch. 13.32.
q 1 Cor. 15. 36. Heb. 2.10. 1 John 4.14. Rev. 5.9.
r Luke 9.24.
s 1 Thes. 4.17.
t Luke 12.50. ch. 13.21.
u Luke 22.53.
v 2 Pet. 1.17.
w ch. 11.42.
x Luke 10.18. ch. 14.30. Acts 26.18. 2 Cor. 4.4. Eph. 2.2. 1 John 3.8.
y Rom. 5.18. Heb. 2.9.
z 2 Sam. 7.13. Ps. 89.36. Isa. 9.7. Dan. 2.44. Micah 4.7.
a Isa. 42.6. ch. 1.9.
b Isa. 2.5. Jer. 13.16. ch. 1.5-9. Eph. 5.8.
c ch. 11.10. 1 John 2.11.
d Luke 16. 8. Eph. 5.8. 1 Thes. 5.5.
e Isa. 53.1. Rom. 10.16.
f Isa. 6.9. Matt. 13.14.
g Isa. 6.1. Heb. 11.13.
h Matt. 6.2. Luke 16.15. ch. 5.44. Rom. 2.29.
i Matt. 10.40. Mark 9.37. ch. 13.20.
j ch. 14.9. Heb. 1.3.
k ch. 3.19.
l ch. 5.45.
m ch. 3.17.
n Luke 10.16.
o Deut. 18.19. Mark 16.16.
p ch. 8.38.

CHAP. 13

a Luke 22.3.
b ch. 3.35. Acts 2.36. 1 Cor. 15.27. Heb. 2.8.

37 ¶ But though he had done so many
miracles before them, yet they believed not on him:
38 That the saying of Ē-ṡâi'-ăs the
prophet might be fulfilled, which he
spake, [e]Lord, who hath believed our
report? and to whom hath the arm of
the Lord been revealed?
39 Therefore they could not believe,
because that Ē-ṡâi'-ăs said again,
40 He [f]hath blinded their eyes, and
hardened their heart; that they should
not see with *their* eyes, nor understand
with *their* heart, and be converted, and
I should heal them.
41 These things said Ē-ṡâi'-ăs, when
he [g]saw his glory, and spake of him.
42 ¶ Nevertheless among the chief
rulers also many believed on him; but
because of the Pharisees they did not
confess *him*, lest they should be put
out of the synagogue:
43 For [h]they loved the praise of men
more than the praise of God.
44 ¶ Jesus cried and said, [i]He that
believeth on me, believeth not on me,
but on him that sent me.
45 And [j]he that seeth me seeth him
that sent me.
46 I [k]am come a light into the world,
that whosoever believeth on me
should not abide in darkness.
47 And if any man hear my words,
and believe not, I [l]judge him not: for
I [m]came not to judge the world, but to
save the world.
48 He [n]that rejecteth me, and receiveth not my words, hath one that
judgeth him: the [o]word that I have
spoken, the same shall judge him in
the last day.
49 For [p]I have not spoken of myself;
but the Father which sent me, he gave
me a commandment, what I should
say, and what I should speak.
50 And I know that his commandment is life everlasting: whatsoever I
speak therefore, even as the Father
said unto me, so I speak.

CHAPTER 13

NOW before the feast of the passover, when Jesus knew that his
hour was come that he should depart
out of this world unto the Father,
having loved his own which were in
the world, he loved them unto the
end.
2 And supper being ended, [a]the devil
having now put into the heart of Judas
Iscariot, Simon's *son*, to betray him;
3 Jesus knowing [b]that the Father had
given all things into his hands, and

that he was come from God, and went
to God;
4 He [c]riseth from supper, and laid
aside his garments; and took a towel,
and girded himself.
5 After that he poureth water into a
bason, and began to wash the disciples' feet, and to wipe *them* with the
towel wherewith he was girded.
6 Then cometh he to Simon Peter:
and [1]Peter saith unto him, Lord, [d]dost
thou wash my feet?
7 Jesus answered and said unto him,
What I do thou knowest not now; but
thou shalt know hereafter.
8 Peter saith unto him, Thou shalt
never wash my feet. Jesus answered
him, [e]If I wash thee not, thou hast no
part with me.
9 Simon Peter saith unto him, Lord,
not my feet only, but also *my* hands
and *my* head.
10 Jesus saith to him, [f]He that is
washed needeth not save to wash *his*
feet, but is clean every whit: and [g]ye
are clean, but not all.
11 For he knew who should betray
him; therefore said he, Ye are not all
clean.
12 So after he had washed their feet,
and had taken his garments, and was
set down again, he said unto them,
Know ye what I have done to you?
13 Ye [h]call me Master and Lord: and
ye say well; for *so* I am.
14 If [i]I then, *your* Lord and Master,
have washed your feet; [j]ye also ought
to wash one another's feet.
15 For [k]I have given you an example,
that ye should do as I have done to
you.
16 Verily, [l]verily, I say unto you,
The servant is not greater than his
lord; neither he that is sent greater
than he that sent him.
17 If [m]ye know these things, happy
are ye if ye do them.
18 ¶ I speak not of you all: [n]I know
whom I have chosen: but that the
scripture may be fulfilled, He [o]that
eateth bread with me hath lifted up
his heel against me.
19 [2]Now I tell you before it come,
that, when it is come to pass, ye may
believe that I am *he*.
20 Verily, [p]verily, I say unto you, He
that receiveth whomsoever I send receiveth me; and he that receiveth me
receiveth him that sent me.
21 When [q]Jesus had thus said, he
[r]was troubled in spirit, and testified,
and said, Verily, verily, I say unto you,
that [s]one of you shall betray me.

c Luke 22.27.
1 he.
d Matt. 3.14.
e Ps. 51.2,7. Isa. 52.15. Mark 16.16. ch. 3.5. Acts 2.38. 1 Cor. 6.11. Eph. 5.26. Titus 3.5.
f 2 Cor. 7.1. Eph. 4.22-24. 1 Thes. 5.23.
g ch. 15.3.
h Luke 6.46. 1 Cor. 8.6. Phil. 2.11.
i Luke 22.27.
j Rom. 12.10. Gal. 6.1. Phil. 2.2-5. 1 Pet. 5.5.
k Phil. 2.5. 1 Pet. 2.21.
l Luke 6.40. ch. 15.20.
m Jas. 1.25.
n ch. 17.12. 2 Tim. 2.19. Rev. 2.23.
o Ps. 41.9.
2 From henceforth.
p Luke 10.16. Gal. 4.14.
q Luke 22.21.
r Matt. 26.38. Mark 3.5. ch. 12.27. Acts 17.16.
s Acts 1.17. 1 John 2.19.
t ch. 19.26. ch. 20.2.
3 Or, morsel.
u Ps. 109.6. Luke 22.3. ch. 6.70.
v ch. 12.6.
w ch. 14.13. 1 Pet. 4.11.
x ch. 17.1.
y Lev. 19.18. Eph. 5.2. 1 Thes. 4.9. Jas. 2.8. 1 Pet. 1.22. 1 John 2.7.
z Acts 2.46.
a ch. 21.18. 2 Pet. 1.14.
b Luke 22.33.

22 Then the disciples looked one
on another, doubting of whom he
spake.
23 Now [t]there was leaning on Jesus'
bosom one of his disciples, whom
Jesus loved.
24 Simon Peter therefore beckoned
to him, that he should ask who it
should be of whom he spake.
25 He then lying on Jesus' breast
saith unto him, Lord, who is it?
26 Jesus answered, He it is, to whom
I shall give a [3]sop, when I have dipped
it. And when he had dipped the sop,
he gave *it* to Judas Iscariot, *the son* of
Simon.
27 And [u]after the sop Satan entered
into him. Then said Jesus unto him,
That thou doest, do quickly.
28 Now no man at the table knew
for what intent he spake this unto
him.
29 For some *of them* thought, [v]be-
cause Judas had the bag, that Jesus
had said unto him, Buy *those things*
that we have need of against the feast;
or, that he should give something to
the poor.
30 He then having received the sop
went immediately out: and it was
night.
31 ¶ Therefore, when he was gone
out, Jesus said, Now is the Son of man
glorified, and [w]God is glorified in
him.
32 If [x]God be glorified in him, God
shall also glorify him in himself, and
shall straightway glorify him.
33 Little children, yet a little while I
am with you. Ye shall seek me: and
as I said unto the Jews, Whither I go,
ye cannot come; so now I say to
you.
34 A [y]new commandment I give unto
you, That ye love one another; as I
have loved you, that ye also love one
another.
35 By this shall all *men* know that ye
are my disciples, if ye have love [z]one
to another.
36 ¶ Simon Peter said unto him,
Lord, whither goest thou? Jesus answered him, Whither I go, thou canst
not follow me now; [a]but thou shalt
follow me afterwards.
37 Peter said unto him, Lord, why
cannot I follow thee now? I will [b]lay
down my life for thy sake.
38 Jesus answered him, Wilt thou
lay down thy life for my sake? Verily,
verily, I say unto thee, The cock shall
not crow, till thou hast denied me
thrice.

CHAPTER 14

LET not your heart be troubled: ye believe in God, believe also in me.

2 In [a]my Father's house are many mansions: if *it were* not *so*, I would have told you. [b]I go to prepare a place for you.

3 And if I go and prepare a place for you, [c]I will come again, and receive you unto myself; [d]that where I am, *there* ye may be also.

4 And whither I go ye know, and the way ye know.

5 Thomas saith unto him, Lord, we know not whither thou goest; and how can we know the way?

6 Jesus saith unto him, I am [e]the way, [f]the truth, and [g]the life: [h]no man cometh unto the Father, but by me.

7 If [i]ye had known me, ye should have known my Father also: and from henceforth ye know him, and have seen him.

8 Philip saith unto him, Lord, shew us the Father, and it sufficeth us.

9 Jesus saith unto him, Have I been so long time with you, and yet hast thou not known me, Philip? he [j]that hath seen me hath seen the Father; and how sayest thou *then*, Shew us the Father?

10 Believest thou not that [k]I am in the Father, and the Father in me? the words that I speak unto you [l]I speak not of myself: but the Father that dwelleth in me, he doeth the works.

11 Believe me that I *am* in the Father, and the Father in me: or else believe me for the very works' sake.

12 Verily, verily, I say unto you, He that believeth on me, the works that I do shall he do also; and greater *works* than these shall he do; because I go unto my Father.

13 And whatsoever ye shall ask in [m]my name, that will I do, that the Father may be glorified in the Son.

14 If ye shall ask any thing in my name, I will do *it*.

15 ¶ If [n]ye love me, keep my commandments.

16 And I will pray the Father, and [o]he shall give you another Comforter, that he may abide with you for ever;

17 *Even* [p]the Spirit of truth; whom [q]the world cannot receive, because it seeth him not, neither knoweth him: but ye know him; for he dwelleth with you, and [r]shall be in you.

18 I will not leave you [1]comfortless: I will come to you.

19 Yet a little while, and the world seeth me no more; but [s]ye see me: [t]because I live, ye shall live also.

20 At that day ye shall know that [u]I *am* in my Father, and ye in me, and I in you.

21 He [v]that hath my commandments, and keepeth them, he it is that loveth me: and he that loveth me shall be loved of my Father, and I will love him, and will manifest myself to him.

22 Judas saith unto him, not Iscariot, Lord, how is it that thou wilt manifest thyself unto us, and not unto the world?

23 Jesus answered and said unto him, If a man love me, he will keep my words: and my Father will love him, and [w]we will come unto him, and make our abode with him.

24 He that loveth me not keepeth not my sayings: and [x]the word which ye hear is not mine, but the Father's which sent me.

25 These things have I spoken unto you, being *yet* present with you.

26 But [y]the Comforter, *which is* the Holy Ghost, whom the Father will send in my name, [z]he shall teach you all things, and bring all things to your remembrance, whatsoever I have said unto you.

27 Peace [a]I leave with you, my peace I give unto you: not as the world giveth, give I unto you. Let not your heart be troubled, neither let it be afraid.

28 Ye have heard how I said unto you, I go away, and come *again* unto you. If ye loved me, ye would rejoice, because I said, I go unto the Father: for [b]my Father is greater than I.

29 And now I have told you before it come to pass, that, when it is come to pass, ye might believe.

30 Hereafter I will not talk much with you: [c]for the prince of this world cometh, and [d]hath nothing in me.

31 But that the world may know that I love the Father; and [e]as the Father gave me commandment, even so I do. Arise, let us go hence.

CHAP. 14

a 2 Cor. 5.1. Rev. 3.12, 21.
b ch. 13.33.
c Matt. 25. 32-34. Acts 1.11. 2 Cor. 5.6-8.
d ch. 12.26. ch. 17.24. 1 Thes. 4.17.
e Matt. 11.27. Heb. 9.8. Rom. 5.2.
f ch. 1.17.
g ch. 1.4.
h ch. 10.9. 2 John 9. Rev. 5.8,9.
i ch. 8.19.
j Col. 1.15. Heb. 1.3.
k ch. 10.38. 1 John 5.7.
l ch. 5.19.
m Matt. 7.7, 8. Mark 11.24. Luke 11.9. ch. 15.7,16. Jas. 1.5.
n Matt. 10. 37. 1 Cor. 16.22. 1 John 5.3.
o Rom. 8.15.
p 1 John 2.7.
q Rom. 8.7. 1 Cor. 2.14.
r 1 John 2.27.
1 Or, orphans.
s ch. 16.16.
t 1 Cor. 15.20.
u ch. 10.38.
v 1 John 2.5.
w Ps. 91.1. 1 John 2.24. Rev. 3.20.
x ch. 7.16.
y Luke 24.49.
z 1 John 2.27.
a Phil. 4.7. Col. 3.15.
b Isa. 9.6. 1 Cor. 11.3. Gal. 4.4. Phil. 2.6-8.
c ch. 12.31.
d 2 Cor. 5.21. 1 John 3.5.
e Phil. 2.8. Heb. 5.8.

CHAPTER 15

I AM the true vine, and my Father is the husbandman.

2 Every [a]branch in me that beareth not fruit he taketh away: and every *branch* that beareth fruit, he purgeth it, that it may bring forth more fruit.

3 Now [b]ye are clean through the word which I have spoken unto you.

4 Abide [c]in me, and I in you. As the branch cannot bear fruit of itself, ex-

CHAP. 15

a Matt. 15.13. Heb. 6.8.
b ch. 13.10. Eph. 5.26. 1 Pet. 1.22.
c Eph. 2.21, 22. Col. 1.23. 1 John 2.6.

cept it abide in the vine; no more can
ye, except ye abide in me.
5 I am the vine, ye *are* the branches:
He that abideth in me, and I in him,
the same bringeth forth much [d]fruit:
for [1]without me ye can do nothing.
6 If a [e]man abide not in me, he is
cast forth as a branch, and is withered; and men gather them, and cast
them into the fire, and they are burned.
7 If ye abide in me, and my words
abide in you, ye shall ask what ye will
and it shall be done unto you.
8 Herein [f]is my Father glorified, that
ye bear much fruit; so shall ye be my
disciples.
9 As the Father hath loved me, so
have I loved you: continue ye in my
love.
10 If ye keep my commandments, ye
shall abide in my love; even as I have
kept my Father's commandments,
and abide in his love.
11 These things have I spoken unto
you, that my joy might remain in you,
and [g]*that* your joy might be full.
12 This [h]is my commandment, That
ye love one another, as I have loved
you.
13 Greater [i]love hath no man than
this, that a man lay down his life for
his friends.
14 Ye are my friends, if ye do whatsoever I command you.
15 Henceforth I call you not servants; for the servant knoweth not
what his lord doeth: but I have called
you friends; [j]for all things that I have
heard of my Father I have made
known unto you.
16 Ye [k]have not chosen me, but I
have chosen you, and [l]ordained you,
that ye should go and bring forth
fruit, and *that* your fruit should remain: that whatsoever ye shall ask of
the Father in my name, he may give it
you.
17 These things I command you, that
ye love one another.
18 If [m]the world hate you, ye know
that it hated me before *it hated* you.
19 If [n]ye were of the world, the world
would love his own: [o]but because ye
are not of the world, but I have chosen
you out of the world, therefore the
world hateth you.
20 Remember the word that I said
unto you, The servant is not greater
than his lord. If they have persecuted
me, they will also persecute you; [p]if
they have kept my saying, they will
keep yours also.
21 But all these things will they do
unto you for my name's sake, because
they know not him that sent me.
22 If [q]I had not come and spoken unto them, they had not had sin: but
[r]now they have no [2]cloke for their sin.
23 He [s]that hateth me hateth my
Father also.
24 If I had not done among them the
works which none other man did,
they had not had sin: but now have
they both seen and hated both me and
my Father.
25 But *this cometh to pass*, that the
word might be fulfilled that is written
in their law, [t]They hated me without a
cause.
26 But [u]when the Comforter is come,
whom I will send unto you from the
Father, *even* the Spirit of truth, which
proceedeth from the Father, [v]he shall
testify of me:
27 And [w]ye also shall bear witness,
because [x]ye have been with me from
the beginning.

CHAPTER 16

THESE things have I spoken unto
you, that ye should not be
offended.
2 They shall put you out of the synagogues: yea, the time cometh, that
[a]whosoever killeth you will think that
he doeth God service.
3 And [b]these things will they do unto
you, because they have not known the
Father, nor me.
4 But these things have I told you,
that when the time shall come, ye may
remember that I told you of them.
And these things I said not unto you
at the beginning, because I was with
you.
5 But now I go my way to him that
sent me; and none of you asketh me,
Whither goest thou?
6 But because I have said these things
unto you, sorrow hath filled your
heart.
7 Nevertheless I tell you the truth;
It is expedient for you that I go away:
for if I go not away, the Comforter
will not come unto you; but [c]if I depart, I will send him unto you.
8 And when he is come, he will [1]re-
prove the world of sin, and of righteousness, and of judgment:
9 Of [d]sin, because they believe not
on me;
10 Of [e]righteousness, because I go
to my Father, and ye see me no
more;
11 Of [f]judgment, because [g]the prince
of this world is judged.

d Pro. 11.30. Hosea 14.8. Luke 13.6-9. Gal. 5.22. Phil. 4.13.
1 Or, severed from me.
e Matt. 3.10. Heb. 6.4-6.
f Matt. 5.16. Phil. 1.11.
g ch. 16.24. 1 John 1.4.
h 1 Thes. 4.9. 1 Pet. 4.8.
i Rom. 5.7. Eph. 5.2.
j Gen. 18.17-19. Matt. 13.11. Acts 20.27. Rom. 16.25, 26.
k 1 John 4.10.
l Mark 16.15.
m 1 John 3. 13.
n 1 John 4.5.
o ch. 17.14.
p Eze. 3.7.
q ch. 9.41.
r Rom. 1.20.
2 Or, excuse.
s 1 John 2.23.
t Ps. 35.19. Ps. 69.4.
u ch. 14.26. Acts 1.4.
v 1 John 5.6.
w Acts 1.8. 1 Pet. 5.1. 2 Pet. 1.16.
x Luke 1.2.

CHAP. 16

a Acts 8.1.
b Rom. 10.2. 1 Cor. 2.8. 1 Tim. 1.13.
c Acts 2.33. Eph. 4.8.
1 Or, convince.
d Acts 2.22. Rom. 3.9. Gal. 3.22.
e Isa. 42.6,21. Dan. 9.24. Acts 2.32. 1 Cor. 1.30. Gal. 5.5.
f Matt. 12.18, 36. Acts 10.42. 1 Cor. 4.5. Heb. 6.2. Rev. 1.7.
g Luke 10.18. ch. 12.31. Eph. 2.2.

12 I have yet many things to say unto
you, but ye cannot bear them now.
13 Howbeit when he, the Spirit of
truth, is come, [h]he will guide you into
all truth: for he shall not speak of
himself; but whatsoever he shall hear,
that shall he speak: and he will [i]shew
you things to come.
14 He shall glorify me: for he shall
receive of mine, and shall shew *it* unto
you.
15 All [j]things that the Father hath
are mine: therefore said I, that he
shall take of mine, and shall shew *it*
unto you.
16 A little while, and ye shall not see
me: and again, a little while, and ye
shall see me, because I go to the
Father.
17 Then said *some* of his disciples
among themselves, What is this that
he saith unto us, A little while, and ye
shall not see me: and again, a little
while, and ye shall see me: and, Because I go to the Father?
18 They said therefore, What is this
that he saith, A little while? we cannot tell what he saith.
19 Now Jesus knew that they were
desirous to ask him, and said unto
them, Do ye inquire among yourselves of that I said, A little while, and
ye shall not see me: and again, a little
while, and ye shall see me?
20 Verily, verily, I say unto you, That
ye shall weep and lament, but the
world shall rejoice: and ye shall be
sorrowful, but your sorrow shall be
turned into joy.
21 A woman when she is in travail
hath sorrow, because her hour is
come: but as soon as she is delivered
of the child, she remembereth no
more the anguish, for joy that a man
is born into the world.
22 And ye now therefore have sorrow:
but I will see you again, and [k]your
heart shall rejoice, and your joy no
man taketh from you.
23 And in that day ye shall ask me
nothing. [l]Verily, verily, I say unto
you, Whatsoever ye shall ask the
Father in my name, he will give *it*
you.
24 Hitherto have ye asked nothing
in my name: ask, and ye shall receive,
that your joy may be full.
25 These things have I spoken unto
you in [2]proverbs: but the time cometh,
when I shall no more speak unto you
in [3]proverbs, but I shall shew you
plainly of the Father.
26 At that day ye shall ask in my
name: and I say not unto you, that I
will pray the Father for you:
27 For [m]the Father himself loveth
you, because ye have loved me, and
[n]have believed that I came out from
God.
28 I [o]came forth from the Father,
and am come into the world: again,
I leave the world, and go to the
Father.
29 His disciples said unto him, Lo,
now speakest thou plainly, and speakest no [4]proverb.
30 Now are we sure that [p]thou knowest all things, and needest not that any
man should ask thee: by this [q]we believe that thou camest forth from God.
31 Jesus answered them, Do ye now
believe?
32 Behold, the hour cometh, yea, is
now come, that ye shall be scattered,
every man to [5]his own, and shall leave
me alone: and yet I am not alone, because the Father is with me.
33 These things I have spoken unto
you, that [r]in me ye might have peace.
[s]In the world ye shall have tribulation: but be of good cheer; [t]I have
overcome the world.

CHAPTER 17

THESE words spake Jesus, and
lifted up his eyes to heaven, and
said, Father, the hour is come; glorify
thy Son, that thy Son also may glorify
thee:
2 As [a]thou hast given him power over
all flesh, that he should give eternal
life to as many [b]as thou hast given
him.
3 And [c]this is life eternal, that they
might know thee [d]the only true God,
and Jesus Christ, whom thou hast
sent.
4 I have glorified thee on the earth:
I have finished the work which thou
gavest me to do.
5 And now, O Father, glorify thou
me with thine own self with the glory
[e]which I had with thee before the
world was.
6 I [f]have manifested thy name unto
the men which thou gavest me out of
the world: thine they were, and thou
gavest them me; and they have kept
thy word.
7 Now they have known that all
things whatsoever thou hast given me
are of thee.
8 For I have given unto them the
words which thou gavest me; and they
have received *them*, and have known
surely that I came out from thee, and

h ch. 14.26.
i 1 Tim. 4.1.
j Matt. 11.27. ch. 17.10. Col. 1.19.
k Luke 24.41. ch. 14.1,27. ch. 20.20. Acts 2.46. 1 Pet. 1.8.
l ch. 14.13.
2 Or, parables.
3 Or, parables.
m Heb. 12.6. Jude 20,21.
n ch. 3.13.
o ch. 13.3.
4 Or, parable.
p ch. 21.17.
q ch. 17.8.
5 Or, his own home.
r Isa. 9.6. ch. 14.27. Eph. 2.14. Col. 1.20.
s Matt. 10.38. Acts 14.22. Rom. 8.17. Heb. 12.6. Rev. 3.19.
t Isa. 49.24, 25. Rom. 8.37. Eph. 6.12. 1 Cor. 15.27. Gal. 6.14. 1 John 4.4.

CHAP. 17

a Ps. 2.6. Dan. 7.14. Matt. 11.27. 1 Cor. 15.25. Phil. 2.10. Heb. 2.8.
b ch. 6.37.
c Isa. 53.11.
d 1 Cor. 8.4. 1 Thes. 1.9.
e ch. 1.1. Phil. 2.6. Col. 1.15. Heb. 1.3-10.
f Ps. 22.22.

they have believed that thou didst send me.

9 I pray for them: [g]I pray not for the world, but for them which thou hast given me; for they are thine.

10 And [h]all mine are thine, and thine are mine; and I am glorified in them.

11 And now I am no more in the world, but these are in the world, and I come to thee. Holy Father, [i]keep through thine own name those whom thou hast given me, that they may be one, [j]as we *are*.

12 While I was with them in the world, [k]I kept them in thy name: those that thou gavest me I have kept, and [l]none of them is lost, [m]but the son of perdition; that [n]the scripture might be fulfilled.

13 And now come I to thee; and these things I speak in the world, that they might have my joy fulfilled in themselves.

14 I have given them thy word; and [o]the world hath hated them, because they are not of the world, even as I am not of the world.

15 I pray not that thou shouldest take them out of the world, but that [p]thou shouldest keep them from the evil.

16 They are not of the world, even as I am not of the world.

17 Sanctify them through thy truth: thy word is truth.

18 As thou hast sent me into the world, even so have I also sent them into the world.

19 And [q]for their sakes I sanctify myself, that they also might be [1]sanctified through the truth.

20 Neither pray I for these alone, but for them also which shall believe on me through their word;

21 That they all may be one; as [r]thou, Father, *art* in me, and I in thee, that they also may be one in us: that the world may believe that thou hast sent me.

22 And the glory which thou gavest me I have given them; that [s]they may be one, even as we are one:

23 I in them, and thou in me, that [t]they may be made [u]perfect in one; and that the world may know that thou hast sent me, and hast loved them, as thou hast loved me.

24 Father, [v]I will that they also, whom thou hast given me, be with me where I am; that they may behold [w]my glory, which thou hast given me: for thou lovedst me before the foundation of the world.

g 1 John 5.19.
h Rom. 8.30.
i 1 Pet. 1.5.
j ch. 10.30.
k ch. 6.39. ch. 10.28. Heb. 2.13.
l ch. 18.9. 1 John 2.19.
m Ps. 41.9. ch. 13.18.
n Ps. 109.8. Acts 1.20.
o 1 John 3.13.
p Gal. 1.4. 2 Thes. 3.3.
q 1 Cor. 1.30. 1 Thes. 4.7. Heb. 10.10.
1 Or, truly sanctified.
r ch. 10.38. Phil. 2.6. 1 John 5.7.
s 1 John 1.3.
t Rom. 12.5. Gal. 3.28. Col. 3.14.
u ch. 10.38. Heb. 12.23.
v 1 Thes. 4. 17.
w 2 Cor. 3.18. 1 John 3.2.
x Eph. 3.17.

CHAP. 18

a Luke 22.39.
b 2 Sam. 15. 23.
c Luke 21.37.
d Matt. 26. 47. Mark 14.43. Luke 22.47. Acts 1.16.
e 1 Pet. 5.7.
f ch. 6.39. 2 Tim. 4.18. 1 Pet. 1.5. Jude 1.
g Matt. 26. 51. Mark 14.47. Luke 22.49.
h Matt. 20. 22.
i Matt. 26.57.
j Luke 3.2. Acts 4.6.
1 And Annas sent Christ bound unto Caiaphas, the high priest.
k Luke 3.2. ch. 11.50. Acts 4.6.

25 O righteous Father, the world hath not known thee: but I have known thee, and these have known that thou hast sent me.

26 And I have declared unto them thy name, and will declare *it*: that the love wherewith thou hast loved me may be in them, and [x]I in them.

CHAPTER 18

WHEN Jesus had spoken these words, he [a]went forth with his disciples over the [b]brook Çē-drŏn, where was a garden, into the which he entered, and his disciples.

2 And Judas also, which betrayed him, knew the place: [c]for Jesus ofttimes resorted thither with his disciples.

3 Judas [d]then, having received a band *of men* and officers from the chief priests and Pharisees, cometh thither with lanterns and torches and weapons.

4 Jesus therefore, knowing all things that should come upon him, went forth, and said unto them, Whom seek ye?

5 They answered him, Jesus of Nazareth. Jesus saith unto them, I am *he*. And Judas also, which betrayed him, stood with them.

6 As soon then as he had said unto them, I am *he*, they went backward, and fell to the ground.

7 Then asked he them again, Whom seek ye? And they said, Jesus of Nazareth.

8 Jesus answered, I have told you that I am *he*: if therefore ye seek me, [e]let these go their way:

9 That the saying might be fulfilled, which he spake, [f]Of them which thou gavest me have I lost none.

10 Then [g]Simon Peter having a sword drew it, and smote the high priest's servant, and cut off his right ear. The servant's name was Măl-chŭs.

11 Then said Jesus unto Peter, Put up thy sword into the sheath: the [h]cup which my Father hath given me, shall I not drink it?

12 Then the band and the captain and officers of the Jews took Jesus, and bound him,

13 And [i]led him away to [j]Annas first; for he was father in law to Cāi-ă-phās, which was the high priest that same year.[1]

14 Now [k]Cāi-ă-phās was he, which gave counsel to the Jews, that it was

expedient that one man should die for
the people.
15 ¶ And Simon Peter followed Jesus,
and *so did* another disciple: that disciple was known unto the high priest,
and went in with Jesus into the palace
of the high priest.
16 But Peter stood at the door without. Then went out that other disciple, which was known unto the
high priest, and spake unto her that
kept the door, and brought in Peter.
17 Then saith the damsel that kept
the door unto Peter, Art not thou also
one of this man's disciples? He saith,
I am not.
18 And the servants and officers
stood there, who had made a fire of
coals; for it was cold: and they warmed themselves: and Peter stood with
them, and warmed himself.
19 ¶ The high priest then asked Jesus
of his disciples, and of his doctrine.
20 Jesus answered him, I [l]spake
openly to the world; I ever taught in
the synagogue, and in the temple,
whither the Jews always resort; and
in secret have I said nothing.
21 Why askest thou me? ask them
which heard me, what I have said unto them: behold, they know what I
said.
22 And when he had thus spoken,
one of the officers which stood by
[m]struck Jesus [2]with the palm of his
hand, saying, Answerest thou the
high priest so?
23 Jesus answered him, [n]If I have
spoken evil, bear witness of the evil:
but if well, why smitest thou me?
24 Now Annas had sent him bound
unto Cāi-ă-phăs the high priest.
25 And Simon Peter stood and
warmed himself. [o]They said therefore
unto him, Art not thou also *one* of his
disciples? He denied *it*, and said, I
am not.
26 One of the servants of the high
priest, being *his* kinsman whose ear
Peter cut off, saith, Did not I see thee
in the garden with him?
27 Peter then denied again: and immediately the [p]cock crew.
28 ¶ Then [q]led they Jesus from Cāi-
ă-phăs unto [3]the hall of judgment:
and it was early; and [r]they themselves went not into the judgment
hall, lest they should be defiled; but
that they might eat [s]the passover.
29 Pilate then went out unto them,
and said, What accusation bring ye
against this man?
30 They answered and said unto
him, If he were not a malefactor, we
would not have delivered him up unto
thee.
31 Then said Pilate unto them, Take
ye him, and judge him according to
your law. The Jews therefore said unto him, [t]It is not lawful for us to put
any man to death:
32 That [u]the saying of Jesus might
be fulfilled, which he spake, signifying what death he should die.
33 Then Pilate entered into the judgment hall again, and called Jesus, and
said unto him, Art thou the King of
the Jews?
34 Jesus answered him, Sayest thou
this thing of thyself, or did others tell
it thee of me?
35 Pilate answered, Am I a Jew?
Thine own nation and the chief priests
have delivered thee unto me: what
hast thou done?
36 Jesus [v]answered, [w]My kingdom is
not of this world: if my kingdom were
of this world, then would my servants
fight, that I should not be delivered
to the Jews: but now is my kingdom
not from hence.
37 Pilate therefore said unto him,
Art thou a king then? Jesus answered,
Thou sayest that I am a king. To this
end was I born, and for this cause
came I into the world, that I should
[x]bear witness unto the truth. Every
one that [y]is of the truth heareth my
voice.
38 Pilate saith unto him, What is
truth? And when he had said this, he
went out again unto the Jews, and
saith unto them, I [z]find in him no
fault *at all*.
39 But ye have a custom, that I
should release unto you one at the
passover: will ye therefore that I release unto you the King of the Jews?
40 Then [a]cried they all again, saying, Not this man, but Băr-ăb-băs.
[b]Now Băr-ăb-băs was a robber.

CHAPTER 19

THEN [a]Pilate therefore took Jesus,
and scourged *him*.
2 And the soldiers platted a crown of
thorns, and put *it* on his head, and
they put on him a purple robe,
3 And said, Hail, King of the Jews!
and they smote him with their hands.
4 Pilate therefore went forth again,
and saith unto them, Behold, I bring
him forth to you, that [b]ye may know
that I find no fault in him.
5 Then came Jesus forth, wearing
the crown of thorns, and the purple

l Matt. 26.55. ch. 3.21.
m Job 16.10. Isa. 50.6. Jer. 20.2. Micah 5.1. Acts 23.2.
2 Or, with a rod.
n Heb. 12.3.
o Mark 14.69. Luke 22.58.
p Matt. 26. 74. Luke 22.60. ch. 13.38.
q Matt. 27.2. Mark 15.1. Acts 3.13.
3 Or, Pilate's house.
r Matt. 26.69. Mark 14.69. Acts 11.3.
s Deut. 16.2.
t Gen. 49.10.
u Matt. 20. 19. ch. 12.32, 33.
v 1 Tim. 6.13. Rev. 1.3. Rev. 3.14.
w Isa. 9.6. Dan. 2.44. Luke 12.14. ch. 6.15. 2 Cor. 10.4.
x Isa. 55.4. Rev. 1.5.
y ch. 8.47. 1 Pet. 1.23. 1 John 3.19.
z Matt. 27.18, 19-24. Mark 15.14. Luke 23.4, 14-16. ch. 19.4,6.
a Acts 3.14.
b Luke 23.19.

CHAP. 19

a Isa. 50.6. Matt. 20.19. Mark 15.15. Luke 18.33.
b ch. 18.38. 2 Cor. 5.21.

robe. And *Pilate* saith unto them, Behold the man!
6 When [c]the chief priests therefore
and officers saw him, they cried out,
saying, Crucify *him*, crucify *him*.
Pilate saith unto them, Take ye him,
and crucify *him:* for I find no fault in
him.
7 The Jews answered him, [d]We have
a law, and by our law he ought to die,
because he [e]made himself the Son of
God.
8 ¶ When Pilate therefore heard that
saying, he was the more afraid;
9 And went again into the judgment
hall, and saith unto Jesus, Whence
art thou? [f]But Jesus gave him no
answer.
10 Then saith Pilate unto him,
Speakest thou not unto me? knowest
thou not that I have power to crucify
thee, and have power to release thee?
11 Jesus answered, [g]Thou couldest
have no power *at all* against me, except it were given thee from above:
therefore he that delivered me unto
thee hath the greater sin.
12 And from thenceforth Pilate
sought to release him: but the Jews
cried out, saying, [h]If thou let this man
go, thou art not Cæsar's friend: whosoever [i]maketh himself a king speaketh against Cæsar.
13 ¶ When Pilate therefore heard
that saying, he brought Jesus forth,
and sat down in the judgment seat in
a place that is called the Pavement,
but in the Hebrew, [1]Găb´-bă-thă.
14 And [j]it was the preparation of the
passover, and about the sixth hour:
and he saith unto the Jews, Behold
your king!
15 But they cried out, Away with
him, away with *him*, crucify him.
Pilate saith unto them, Shall I crucify
your King? The chief priests answered, [k]We have no king but Cæsar.
16 Then [l]delivered he him therefore
unto them to be crucified. And they
took Jesus, and led *him* away.
17 And he bearing his cross [m]went
forth into a place called *the place* of a
skull, which is called in the Hebrew
Gŏl´-gŏ-thă:
18 Where they [n]crucified him, and
two other with him, on either side
one, and Jesus in the midst.
19 ¶ And Pilate wrote a title, and put
it on the cross. And the writing was,
JESUS OF NAZARETH THE KING OF THE
JEWS.
20 This title then read many of the
Jews: for the place where Jesus was

c Acts 3.13.
d Lev. 24.16.
e Matt. 26. 65. ch. 5.18.
f Isa. 53.7. Matt. 27.12-14. Acts 8.32.
g Gen. 45.7, 8. Ps. 62.11. Dan. 4.17, 25. Luke 22.53. ch. 7.30. Acts 2.23.
h Luke 23.2.
i Acts 17.7.
1 That is, elevated.
j Matt. 27.62.
k Gen. 49.10.
l Matt. 27.26, 31. Mark 15.15. Luke 23.24.
m Num. 15. 36. 1 Ki. 21.13. Luke 23.33. Heb. 13.12.
n Isa. 53.12. Dan. 9.26. Gal. 3.13.
2 Or, wrought.
o Ps. 22.18. Matt. 27.35. Mark 15.24.
3 Or, Clopas.
p ch. 13.23.
q ch. 2.4.
r Gen. 47.12. ch. 1.11.
s Gen. 3.15. Ps. 2.1-3. Isa. 50.6.
t Ps. 69.21.
u Isa. 42.21. Dan. 9.24. ch. 17.4. Rom. 10.4. Heb. 10.1-14.
v Matt. 20. 28. Acts 7.60. Phil. 2.8. 1 Thes. 5.10.
w Mark 15. 42.
x Deut. 21. 23.
y Ex. 12.18.
z Zech. 13.1.

crucified was nigh to the city: and it
was written in Hebrew, *and* Greek,
and Latin.
21 Then said the chief priests of the
Jews to Pilate, Write not, The King of
the Jews; but that he said, I am King
of the Jews.
22 Pilate answered, What I have
written I have written.
23 ¶ Then the soldiers, when they
had crucified Jesus, took his garments,
and made four parts, to every soldier
a part; and also *his* coat: now the coat
was without seam, [2]woven from the
top throughout.
24 They said therefore among themselves, Let us not rend it, but cast lots
for it, whose it shall be: that the scripture might be fulfilled, which saith,
[o]They parted my raiment among
them, and for my vesture they did
cast lots. These things therefore the
soldiers did.
25 ¶ Now there stood by the cross of
Jesus his mother, and his mother's
sister, Mary the *wife* of [3]Clĕ´-ō-phăs,
and Mary Măg´-dă-lēne.
26 When Jesus therefore saw his
mother, and [p]the disciple standing
by, whom he loved, he saith unto his
mother, Woman, [q]behold thy son!
27 Then saith he to the disciple, Behold thy mother! And from that hour
that disciple took her unto [r]his own
home.
28 ¶ After this, Jesus knowing that
[s]all things were now accomplished,
[t]that the scripture might be fulfilled,
saith, I thirst.
29 Now there was set a vessel full of
vinegar: and they filled a spunge with
vinegar, and put *it* upon hyssop, and
put *it* to his mouth.
30 When Jesus therefore had received the vinegar, he said, [u]It is finished:
and he bowed his head, and [v]gave up
the ghost.
31 The Jews therefore, [w]because it
was the preparation, [x]that the bodies
should not remain upon the cross on
the sabbath day, (for that sabbath day
was [y]an high day,) besought Pilate
that their legs might be broken, and
that they might be taken away.
32 Then came the soldiers, and brake
the legs of the first, and of the other
which was crucified with him.
33 But when they came to Jesus, and
saw that he was dead already, they
brake not his legs:
34 But one of the soldiers with a
spear pierced his side, and forthwith
[z]came there out blood and water.

35 And [a]he that saw *it* bare record, and his record is true: and he knoweth that he saith true, that ye might believe.

36 For these things were done, that [b]the scripture should be fulfilled, A bone of him shall not be broken.

37 And again another scripture saith, They [c]shall look on him whom they pierced.

38 ¶ And [d]after this Joseph of Ăr-ĭm-ă-thǣ'-ă, being a disciple of Jesus, but secretly [e]for fear of the Jews, besought Pilate that he might take away the body of Jesus: and Pilate gave *him* leave. He came therefore, and took the body of Jesus.

39 And there came also [f]Nĭc-ŏ-dē'-mŭs, which at the first came to Jesus by night, and brought [g]a mixture of myrrh and aloes, about an hundred pound *weight*.

40 Then took they the body of Jesus, and wound [h]it in linen clothes with the spices, as the manner of the Jews is to bury.

41 Now in the place where he was crucified there was a garden; and in the garden a [i]new sepulchre, wherein was never man yet laid.

42 There [j]laid they Jesus therefore because of the Jews' preparation *day;* for the sepulchre was nigh at hand.

CHAPTER 20

THE [a]first *day* of the week cometh Mary Măg'-dă-lēne early, when it was yet dark, unto the sepulchre, and seeth the stone taken away from the sepulchre.

2 Then she runneth, and cometh to Simon Peter, and to the [b]other disciple, whom Jesus loved, and saith unto them, They have taken away the Lord out of the sepulchre, and we know not where they have laid him.

3 Peter [c]therefore went forth, and that other disciple, and came to the sepulchre.

4 So they ran both together: and the other disciple did outrun Peter, and came first to the sepulchre.

5 And he stooping down, *and looking in*, saw the [d]linen clothes lying; yet went he not in.

6 Then cometh Simon Peter following him, and went into the sepulchre, and seeth the linen clothes lie,

7 And the [e]napkin, that was about his head, not lying with the linen clothes, but wrapped together in a place by itself.

8 Then went in also that other disciple, which came first to the sepulchre, and he saw, and believed.

9 For as yet they knew not [f]the scripture, that he must rise again from the dead.

10 Then the disciples went away again unto their own home.

11 ¶ But [g]Mary stood without at the sepulchre weeping: and as she wept, she stooped down, *and looked* into the sepulchre,

12 And seeth two angels in white sitting, the one at the head, and the other at the feet, where the body of Jesus had lain.

13 And they say unto her, Woman, why weepest thou? She saith unto them, Because they have taken away my Lord, and I know not where they have laid him.

14 And [h]when she had thus said, she turned herself back, and saw Jesus standing, and [i]knew not that it was Jesus.

15 Jesus saith unto her, Woman, why weepest thou? whom seekest thou? She, supposing him to be the gardener, saith unto him, Sir, if thou have borne him hence, tell me where thou hast laid him, and I will take him away.

16 Jesus saith unto her, Mary. She turned herself, and saith unto him, [j]Răb-bō'-nī; which is to say, Master.

17 Jesus saith unto her, Touch me not; for I am not yet ascended to my Father: but go to [k]my brethren, and say unto them, [l]I ascend unto my Father, and your Father; and *to* [m]my God, and your God.

18 Mary [n]Măg'-dă-lēne came and told the disciples that she had seen the Lord, and *that* he had spoken these things unto her.

19 ¶ Then [o]the same day at evening, being the first *day* of the week, when the doors were shut where the disciples were assembled for fear of the Jews, came Jesus and stood in the midst, and saith unto them, Peace *be* unto you.

20 And when he had so said, he [p]shewed unto them *his* hands and his side. [q]Then were the disciples glad, when they saw the Lord.

21 Then said Jesus to them again, Peace *be* unto you: [r]as *my* Father hath sent me, even so send I you.

22 And when he had said this, he breathed on *them*, and saith unto them, Receive ye the Holy Ghost:

23 Whose [s]soever sins ye remit, they are remitted unto them; *and* whose

a ch. 17.21, 23. ch. 20.31. 1 John 1.1.
b Ex. 12.46. Num. 9.12. Ps. 34.20.
c Ps. 22.16. Zech. 12.10. Rev. 1.7.
d Matt. 27. 57. Mark 15.42. Luke 23.50.
e Pro. 29.25. ch. 9.22.
f ch. 3.1,2.
g 2 Chr. 16. 14. Luke 23.56.
h Acts 5.6.
i 2 Ki. 23.30. Isa. 22.16. Matt. 27.60. Luke 23.53.
j Isa. 53.9.

CHAP. 20

a Matt. 28.1. Mark 16.1. Luke 24.1.
b ch. 13.23.
c Luke 24.12.
d ch. 19.40.
e ch. 11.44.
f Ps. 16.10. Isa. 26.19. Matt. 16.21. Acts 2.25-32. 1 Cor. 15.4.
g Mark 16.5.
h Song 3.3,4. Matt. 28.9.
i Luke 24.16, 31. ch. 21.4.
j Song 2.8. Matt. 23.8-10. ch. 1.38-49.
k Ps. 22.22. Matt. 28.10. Rom. 8.29. Heb. 2.11.
l ch. 16.28. 1 Pet. 1.3.
m Eph. 1.17.
n Matt. 28. 10. Luke 24.10.
o Mark 16. 14. Luke 24.36.
p 1 John 1.1.
q ch. 16.22.
r Isa. 61.1. Matt. 28.18. ch. 17.18, 19. 2 Tim. 2.2. Heb. 3.1.
s Matt. 16.19. Mark 2.5-10. Acts 2.38.

soever *sins* ye retain, they are retained.

24 ¶ But Thomas, one of the twelve, [t]called Dĭd'ŷ-mŭs, was not with them when Jesus came.

25 The other disciples therefore said unto him, We have seen the Lord. But he said unto them, Except I shall see in his hands the print of the nails, and put my finger into the print of the nails, and thrust my hand into his side, I will not believe.

26 ¶ And after eight days again his disciples were within, and Thomas with them: *then* came Jesus, the doors being shut, and stood in the midst, and said, Peace [u]*be* unto you.

27 Then saith he to Thomas, Reach hither thy finger, and behold my hands; [v]and reach hither thy hand, and thrust *it* into my side: and be not faithless, but believing.

28 And Thomas answered and said unto him, [w]My Lord and my God.

29 Jesus saith unto him, Thomas, because thou hast seen me, thou hast believed: blessed [x]*are* they that have not seen, and *yet* have believed.

30 ¶ And [y]many other signs truly did Jesus in the presence of his disciples, which are not written in this book:

31 But [z]these are written, that ye might believe that Jesus is the Christ, the Son of God; and [a]that believing ye might have life through his name.

CHAPTER 21

AFTER these things Jesus shewed himself again to the disciples at the sea of Tī-bē'-rĭ-ăs; and on this wise shewed he *himself*.

2 There were together Simon Peter, and Thomas called Dĭd'ŷ-mŭs, and [a]Nă-thăn'-ā-ĕl of Cana in Galilee, and [b]the *sons* of Zĕb'-ĕ-dēe, and two other of his disciples.

3 Simon Peter saith unto them, I go a fishing. They say unto him, We also go with thee. They went forth, and entered into a ship immediately; and that night they caught nothing.

4 But when the morning was now come, Jesus stood on the shore: but the disciples knew [c]not that it was Jesus.

5 Then [d]Jesus saith unto them, [1]Children, have ye any meat? They answered him, No.

6 And he said unto them, [e]Cast the net on the right side of the ship, and ye shall find. They cast therefore, and now they were not able to draw it for the multitude of fishes.

7 Therefore [f]that disciple whom Jesus loved saith unto Peter, It is the Lord. Now when Simon Peter heard that it was the Lord, he girt *his* fisher's coat *unto him*, (for he was naked,) and [g]did cast himself into the sea.

8 And the other disciples came in a little ship; (for they were not far from land, but as it were two hundred cubits,) dragging the net with fishes.

9 As soon then as they were come to land, they [h]saw a fire of coals there, and fish laid thereon, and bread.

10 Jesus saith unto them, Bring of the fish which ye have now caught.

11 Simon Peter went up, and drew the net to land full of great fishes, an hundred and fifty and three: and for all there were so many, yet was not the net broken.

12 Jesus saith unto them, [i]Come *and* dine. And none of the disciples durst ask him, Who art thou? knowing that it was the Lord.

13 Jesus then cometh, and taketh bread, and giveth them, and fish likewise.

14 This is now the [j]third time that Jesus shewed himself to his disciples, after that he was risen from the dead.

15 ¶ So when they had dined, Jesus saith to Simon Peter, Simon, *son* of Jonas, lovest thou me [k]more than these? He saith unto him, Yea, Lord; [l]thou knowest that I love thee. He saith unto him, Feed [m]my lambs.

16 He saith to him again the second time, Simon, *son* of Jonas, lovest thou me? He saith unto him, Yea, Lord; thou knowest that I love thee. He [n]saith unto him, Feed my sheep.

17 He saith unto him the [o]third time, Simon, *son* of Jonas, lovest thou me? Peter was grieved because he said unto him the third time, Lovest thou me? And he said unto him, Lord, thou knowest all things; [p]thou knowest that I love thee. Jesus saith unto him, Feed my sheep.

18 Verily, [q]verily, I say unto thee, When thou wast young, thou girdedst thyself, and walkedst whither thou wouldest: but when thou shalt be old, thou shalt stretch forth thy hands, and another shall gird thee, and carry *thee* whither thou wouldest not.

19 This spake he, signifying [r]by what death he should glorify God. And when he had spoken this, he saith unto him, Follow me.

20 Then Peter, turning about, seeth the disciple [s]whom Jesus loved following; which also leaned on his breast

t ch. 11.16.
u Isa. 9.7. Micah 5.5. Col. 1.20.
v Ps. 103.13, 14. 1 John 1.1.
w Ps. 73.25, 26. Luke 1.46, 47. 1 Tim. 1.17.
x 2 Cor. 5.7. 1 Pet. 1.8.
y ch. 21.25.
z Luke 1.4. Rom. 15.4.
a ch. 3.15, 16. 1 Pet. 1.9.

CHAP. 21

a ch. 1.45.
b Matt. 4.21.
c ch. 20.14.
d Ps. 37.3. Luke 24.41. Heb. 13.5.
1 Or, Sirs.
e Luke 5.4, 6, 7.
f ch. 13.23.
g Song 8.7.
h 1 Ki. 19.6. Mark 8.3-9. Luke 12.29-31.
i Acts 10.41.
j ch. 20.19, 26.
k Matt. 26. 33.
l 2 Ki. 20.3.
m Acts 20.28. Eph. 4.11. 1 Tim. 4.16. 1 Pet. 5.2.
n Heb. 13.20. 1 Pet. 2.25.
o ch. 13.38.
p 1 Sam. 16.7. 1 Chr. 28.9. 2 Chr. 6.30. Ps. 7.8. Jer. 11.20. Matt. 9.4. Mark 2.8. ch. 2.24,25. ch. 6.64. Acts 1.24. Rom. 8.27. 1 Thes. 2.4. Rev. 2.23.
q ch. 13.36. Acts 12.3,4.
r Deut. 4.21. Phil. 1.20. 2 Pet. 1.14.
s ch. 13.23, 25. ch. 19.26.

at supper, and said, Lord, which is he
that betrayeth thee?
21 Peter seeing him saith to Jesus,
Lord, and [t]what *shall* this man
do?
22 Jesus saith unto him, If I will that
he tarry [u]till I come, what *is* [v]*that* to
thee? follow thou me.
23 Then went this saying abroad
among the brethren, that that disciple
should not die: yet Jesus said not unto
him, He shall not die; but, If I will
that he tarry till I come, what *is that*
to thee?
24 This is the disciple which testifieth of these things, and wrote these
things: [w]and we know that his testimony is true.
25 And there are also many other
things which Jesus did, the which, if
they should be written every one, [x]I
suppose that even the world itself
could not contain the books that
should be written. Ā-mĕn.

t Acts 1.6.
u Matt. 16. 27. 1 Cor. 4.5. Rev. 2.25.
v Deut. 29. 29.
w ch. 7.17. 3 John 12.
x Amos 7.10.

THE

ACTS OF THE APOSTLES

CHAPTER 1

THE former treatise have I made,
[a]O Thē-ŏph-ĭ-lŭs, of all that Jesus
began both to do and teach,
2 Until [b]the day in which he was
taken up, after that he through the
Holy Ghost had given commandments unto the apostles whom he had
chosen:
3 To [c]whom also he shewed himself
alive after his passion by many in-
fallible proofs, being seen of them
forty days, and speaking of the things
pertaining to the kingdom of God:
4 And, [1]being assembled together
with *them*, commanded them that
they should not depart from Jerusalem, but wait for the promise of the
Father, [d]which, *saith he*, ye have heard
of me.
5 For [e]John truly baptized with
water; but [f]ye shall be baptized with
the Holy Ghost not many days hence.
6 When they therefore were come together, they asked of him, saying,
Lord, wilt thou at this time restore
[g]again the kingdom to Israel?
7 And he said unto them, [h]It is not
for you to know the times or the
seasons, which the Father hath put in
his own power.
8 But ye shall receive [2]power, after
that the Holy Ghost is come upon
you: and ye shall be witnesses unto
me both in Jerusalem, and in all
Judæa, and in Să-mâr-ĭ-ă, and unto
the uttermost part of the earth.
9 And [i]when he had spoken these
things, while they beheld, he was
taken up; and a cloud received him
out of their sight.
10 And while they looked stedfastly
toward heaven as he went up, behold,
two men stood by them in [j]white
apparel;
11 Which also said, Ye men of Galilee, why stand ye gazing up into heav-
en? this same Jesus, which is taken up
from you into heaven, [k]shall so come
in like manner as ye have seen him go
into heaven.
12 Then returned they unto Jerusalem from the mount [l]called Olivet,
which is from Jerusalem a [m]sabbath
day's journey.
13 And when they were come in, they
went up [n]into an upper room, where
abode both Peter, and James, and
John, and Andrew, Philip, and
Thomas, Bartholomew, and Matthew,
James *the son* of Ăl-phæ-ŭs, and
[o]Simon Zē-lō-tēs, and [p]Judas *the bro-*
ther of James.
14 These all continued with one
accord in prayer and supplication,
with [q]the women, and Mary the
mother of Jesus, and with [r]his brethren.
15 ¶ And in those days Peter stood
up in the midst [s]of the disciples, and
said, (the number of names together
were about an hundred and twenty,)
16 Men *and* brethren, this scripture
must needs have been fulfilled, [t]which
the Holy Ghost by the mouth of
David spake before concerning Judas,
[u]which was guide to them that took
Jesus.
17 For [v]he was numbered with us,
and had obtained part of [w]this ministry.
18 Now [x]this man purchased a field
with the [y]reward of iniquity; and
[z]falling headlong, he burst asunder in

CHAP. 1
a Luke 1.3.
b 1 Tim. 3.16. Heb. 1.3.
c Matt. 28.9, 16,17. 1 Cor. 15.5.
1 Or, eating together with them.
d John 14.16.
e ch. 11.16.
f Joel 2.28, 29. Matt. 3.11. John 7.3,9. ch. 2.4.
g Isa. 1.26. Dan. 7.27. Amos 9.11.
h Deut. 29. 29. 1 Thes. 5.1.
2 Or, the power of the Holy Ghost coming upon you.
i John 6.62.
j ch. 10.3.
k Dan. 7.13. John 14.3. 1 Thes. 1.10. 2 Thes. 1.10. Rev. 1.7.
l Zech. 14.4.
m John 11. 18.
n ch. 9.37.
o Luke 6.15.
p Jude 1.
q Luke 23.49.
r Matt. 13.55.
s Rev. 3.4.
t Ps. 41.9. Mark 12.36. Heb. 3.7,8.
u John 18.3.
v Luke 6.16.
w ch. 12.25.
x Matt. 27.5.
y 2 Pet. 2.15.
z Ps. 55.23.

the midst, and all his bowels gushed
out.
19 And it was known unto all the
dwellers at Jerusalem; insomuch as
that field is called in their proper
tongue, Ă-çĕl´-dă-mă, that is to say,
The field of blood.
20 For it is written in the book of
Psalms, [a]Let his habitation be desolate, and let no man dwell therein: and
his [3]bishoprick let another take.
21 Wherefore of these men which
have companied with us all the time
that the Lord Jesus went in and out
among us,
22 Beginning from the baptism of
John, unto that same day that he was
taken up from us, must one be ordained [b]to be a witness with us of his
resurrection.
23 And they appointed two, Joseph
called Bär´-să-băs, who was surnamed
Justus, and Mătth-ī´-ăs.
24 And they prayed, and said, Thou,
Lord, which [c]knowest the hearts of all
men, shew whether of these two thou
hast chosen,
25 That he may take part of this
ministry and apostleship, from which
Judas by transgression fell, that he
might go to his own place.
26 And they gave forth their [d]lots;
and the lot fell upon Mătth-ī´-ăs; and
he was numbered with the eleven
apostles.

CHAPTER 2

AND when [a]the day of Pentecost
was fully come, [b]they were all with
one accord in one place.
2 And suddenly there came a sound
from heaven as of a rushing mighty
wind, and it [c]filled all the house where
they were sitting.
3 And there appeared unto them
cloven tongues like as of fire, and it
sat upon each of them.
4 And [d]they were all filled with the
Holy Ghost, and [e]began to speak with
other tongues, as the Spirit gave them
utterance.
5 And there were dwelling [f]at Jerusalem Jews, devout men, out of every
nation under heaven.
6 Now [1]when this was noised abroad,
the multitude came together, and
were [2]confounded, because that every
man heard them speak in his own
language.
7 And they were all amazed and marvelled, saying one to another, Behold,
are not all these which speak Galilæans?
8 And how hear we every man in our

a Ps. 69.25.
3 Or, office, or, charge.
b Heb. 2.3.
c John 2.24. Heb. 4.13. Rev. 2.23.
d Lev. 16.8.

CHAP. 2

a Lev. 23.15. Deut. 16.9.
b ch. 1.14.
c ch. 4.31.
d Luke 4.1. John 14.26. ch. 1.5. ch. 6.3.
e Mark 16.17. 1 Cor. 12.10.
f Ex. 23.17.
1 when this voice was made.
2 Or, troubled in mind.
g 1 Pet. 1.1.
h Ex. 12.48. Isa. 56.6.
i 1 Sam. 1.14. 1 Cor. 2.14. Eph. 6.18.
j Isa. 44.3. Eze. 11.19. Joel 2.28. Zech. 12.10. John 7.38.
k ch. 10.45.
l ch. 21.9.
m ch. 21.4. 1 Cor. 12.10.
n Joel 2.30.
o Isa. 13.10. Eze. 32.7. Matt. 24.29. Rev. 6.12.
p Rom. 10. 13.
q Heb. 2.4.
r Luke 24.44. ch. 4.28.
s ch. 3.15. ch. 4.10. Rom. 4.24. 1 Cor. 6.14. 2 Cor. 4.14. Gal. 1.1. Eph. 1.20. Col. 2.12. 1 Thes. 1.10. Heb. 13.20. 1 Pet. 1.21.

own tongue, wherein we were born?
9 Pär´-thĭ-ăns, and Mēdeṡ, and Ē´-
lăm-ītes, and the dwellers in Mĕs-ō-
pŏ-tā´-mĭ-ă, and in Judæa, and [g]Căp-
pă-dō´-çĭ-ă, in Pontus, and Asia,
10 Phrȳġ´-ĭ-ă, and Păm-phȳl´-ĭ-ă, in
Egypt, and in the parts of Lĭb´-ȳ-ă
about Çȳ-rē´-nē, and strangers of
Rome, Jews and [h]proselytes,
11 Cretes and Arabians, we do hear
them speak in our tongues the wonderful works of God.
12 And they were all amazed, and
were in doubt, saying one to another,
What meaneth this?
13 Others [i]mocking said, These men
are full of new wine.
14 ¶ But Peter, standing up with the
eleven, lifted up his voice, and said
unto them, Ye men of Judæa, and all
ye that dwell at Jerusalem, be this
known unto you, and hearken to my
words:
15 For these are not drunken, as ye
suppose, seeing it is *but* the third hour
of the day.
16 But this is that which was spoken
by the prophet Jō´-ĕl;
17 And [j]it shall come to pass in the
last days, saith God, [k]I will pour out
of my Spirit upon all flesh: and your
sons and your [l]daughters shall prophesy and your young men shall see
visions, and your old men shall dream
dreams:
18 And on my servants and on my
handmaidens I will pour out in those
days of my Spirit; [m]and they shall
prophesy:
19 And [n]I will shew wonders in heav-
en above, and signs in the earth beneath; blood, and fire, and vapour of
smoke:
20 The [o]sun shall be turned into
darkness, and the moon into blood,
before that great and notable day of
the Lord come:
21 And it shall come to pass, [p]*that*
whosoever shall call on the name of
the Lord shall be saved.
22 Ye men of Israel, hear these
words; Jesus of Nazareth, a man approved of God among you [q]by miracles and wonders and signs, which
God did by him in the midst of you, as
ye yourselves also know:
23 Him, [r]being delivered by the de-
terminate counsel and foreknow-
ledge of God, ye have taken, and by
wicked hands have crucified and
slain:
24 Whom [s]God hath raised up, having loosed the pains of death: because

it was not possible that he should be holden of it.

25 For David speaketh concerning him, [t]I foresaw the Lord always before my face, for he is on my right hand, that I should not be moved:

26 Therefore did my heart rejoice, and my tongue was glad; moreover also my flesh shall rest in hope:

27 Because thou wilt not leave my soul in hell, neither wilt thou suffer thine [u]Holy One to see corruption.

28 Thou hast made known to me the ways of life; thou shalt make me full of joy with thy countenance.

29 Men *and* brethren, [3]let me freely speak unto you [v]of the patriarch David, that he is both dead and buried, and his sepulchre is with us unto this day.

30 Therefore being a prophet, and knowing that God had sworn with an oath to him, that of [w]the fruit of his loins, according to the flesh, he would raise up Christ to sit on his throne;

31 He seeing this before spake of the resurrection of Christ, [x]that his soul was not left in hell, neither his flesh did see corruption.

32 This Jesus hath God raised up, whereof [y]we all are witnesses.

33 Therefore [z]being by the right hand of God exalted, and [a]having received of the Father the promise of the Holy Ghost, he hath [b]shed forth this, which ye now see and hear.

34 For David is not ascended into the heavens: but he saith himself, The [c]LORD said unto my Lord, Sit thou on my right hand,

35 Until I make thy foes thy footstool.

36 Therefore let all the house of Israel know assuredly, that God hath [d]made that same Jesus, whom ye have crucified, both Lord and Christ.

37 ¶ Now when they heard *this*, they [e]were pricked in their heart, and said unto Peter and to the rest of the apostles, Men *and* brethren, what shall we do?

38 Then Peter said unto them, Repent, [f]and be baptized every one of you in the name of Jesus Christ for the remission of sins, and ye shall receive the gift of the Holy Ghost.

39 For the [g]promise is unto you, and [h]to your children, and [i]to all that are afar off, *even* as many as the Lord our God shall call.

40 And with many other words did he testify and exhort, saying, Save yourselves from this untoward generation.

41 ¶ Then they that gladly received his word were baptized: and the same day there were added *unto them* about three thousand souls.

42 And [j]they continued stedfastly in the apostles' doctrine and fellowship, and in breaking of bread, and in prayers.

43 And fear came upon every soul: [k]and many wonders and signs were done by the apostles.

44 And all that believed were together, and had [l]all things common;

45 And sold their possessions and goods, and [m]parted them to all *men*, as every man had need.

46 And they, continuing daily with one accord [n]in the temple, and [o]breaking bread [4]from house to house, did eat their meat with gladness and singleness of heart,

47 Praising God, and [p]having favour with all the people. And [q]the Lord added to the church daily such as should be saved.

t Ps. 16.8.
u Dan. 9.24. Luke 1.35.
3 Or, I may.
v ch. 13.36.
w 2 Sam. 7.13. Ps. 132.11. Luke 1.32. Rom. 1.3.
x Ps. 16.10.
y Luke 24.46-48. ch. 1.8. ch. 3.15.
z ch. 5.31. Phil. 2.9. Heb. 10.12.
a John 14.26. ch. 1.4.
b ch. 10.45. Eph. 4.8.
c Ps. 110.1. Matt. 22.44. Eph. 1.20. Heb. 1.13.
d Ps. 2.1,6. ch. 5.31. 2 Thes. 1.7-10.
e Zech. 12.10. Luke 3.10.
f Matt. 3.2,8. Luke 24.47. ch. 3.19. 2 Cor. 7.10.
g Rom. 9.8.
h Joel 2.28.
i Eph. 2.13.
j Heb. 10.25.
k Esther 8.17. Mark 16.17. Luke 7.16.
l ch. 4.32.
m Isa. 58.7.
n Luke 24.53.
o ch. 20.7.
4 Or, at home.
p Rom. 14.18.
q Rom. 8.30.

CHAPTER 3

NOW Peter and John went up together into the temple at the hour of prayer, *being* the ninth *hour*.

2 And a certain man lame from his mother's womb was carried, whom they laid daily at the gate of the temple which is called Beautiful, [a]to ask alms of them that entered into the temple;

3 Who seeing Peter and John about to go into the temple asked an alms.

4 And Peter, fastening his eyes upon him with John, said, Look on us.

5 And he gave heed unto them, expecting to receive something of them.

6 Then Peter said, [b]Silver and gold have I none; but such as I have give I thee: [c]In the name of Jesus Christ of Nazareth rise up and walk.

7 And he took him by the right hand, and lifted *him* up: and immediately his feet and ancle bones received strength.

8 And he [d]leaping up stood, and walked, and entered with them into the temple, walking, and leaping, and praising God.

9 And [e]all the people saw him walking and praising God:

10 And they knew that it was he which sat for alms at the Beautiful gate of the temple: and they were filled with wonder and amazement at that which had happened unto him.

CHAP. 3
a John 9.8.
b 1 Pet. 4.10.
c ch. 4.10.
d Isa. 35.6.
e ch. 4.21.

11 And as the lame man which was
healed held Peter and John, all the
people ran together unto them in the
porch [f]that is called Solomon's,
greatly wondering.
12 ¶ And when Peter saw *it*, he answered unto the people, Ye men of
Israel, why marvel ye at this? or why
look ye so earnestly on us, as though
by our own [g]power or holiness we had
made this man to walk?
13 The [h]God of Abraham, and of
Isaac, and of Jacob, the God of our
fathers, [i]hath glorified his Son Jesus;
whom ye delivered up, and denied him
in the presence of Pilate, when he was
determined to let *him* go.
14 But ye denied [j]the Holy One and
[k]the Just, and desired a murderer to
be granted unto you;
15 And killed the [1]Prince of life,
whom God hath raised from the
dead; whereof we are witnesses.
16 And [l]his name through faith in his
name hath made this man strong,
whom ye see and know: yea, the faith
which is by him hath given him this
perfect soundness in the presence of
you all.
17 And now, brethren, I wot that
through ignorance [m]ye did *it*, as *did*
also your rulers.
18 But those things, which God before had shewed [n]by the mouth of all
his prophets, that Christ should suffer,
he hath so fulfilled.
19 ¶ Repent ye therefore, and be
converted, that your sins may be
blotted out, when the times of refreshing shall come from the presence of
the Lord;
20 And he shall send Jesus Christ,
which before was preached unto you:
21 Whom [o]the heaven must receive
until the times of [p]restitution of all
things, which God hath spoken by the
mouth of all his holy prophets since
the world began.
22 For Moses truly said unto the
fathers, A [q]prophet shall the Lord
your God raise up unto you of your
brethren, [r]like unto me; him shall ye
hear in all things whatsoever he shall
say unto you.
23 And it shall come to pass, *that*
every [s]soul, which will not hear that
prophet, shall be destroyed from
among the people.
24 Yea, and all the prophets from
Samuel and those that follow after, as
many as have spoken, have likewise
foretold of these days.
25 Ye [t]are the children of the proph-

f John 10.23. ch. 5.12.
g 2 Cor. 3.5.
h ch. 5.30.
i John 7.39. Phil. 2.9.
j Ps. 16.10. Mark 1.24. Luke 1.35. ch. 2.27.
k ch. 7.52. ch. 22.14.
1 Or, Author.
l Matt. 9.22. 1 Pet. 1.21.
m Luke 23. 34. 1 Cor. 2.8. 1 Tim. 1.13.
n Ps. 22. Isa. 50.6. Dan. 9.26. 1 Pet. 1.10.
o ch. 1.11. Heb. 8.1.
p Matt. 17. 11.
q Deut. 18. 15. Luke 13.33. Luke 24.19.
r Heb. 3.2-5.
s Mark 16.16. John 3.18. ch. 13.38-41. Heb. 2.2,3.
t Rom. 9.4,8. Gal. 3.26.
u Gen. 12.3. Gal. 3.8.

CHAP. 4

1 Or, ruler.
a Neh. 2.10. Matt. 22.23. ch. 23.8.
b Luke 3.2. John 11.49.
c Ex. 2.14. Matt. 21.23. Mark 11.28. ch. 7.27.
d Luke 12.11.
e ch. 3.6.
f Ps. 118.22. Isa. 28.16. Matt. 21.42.
g Matt. 1.21. ch. 10.43. Rom. 3.24.
h Matt. 11. 25. 1 Cor. 1.27.

ets, and of the covenant which God
made with our fathers, saying unto
Abraham, [u]And in thy seed shall all
the kindreds of the earth be blessed.
26 Unto you first God, having raised
up his Son Jesus, sent him to bless you,
in turning away every one of you from
his iniquities.

CHAPTER 4

AND as they spake unto the people,
the priests, and the [1]captain of
the temple, and the Săd-dū-çēes,
came upon them,
2 Being [a]grieved that they taught the
people, and preached through Jesus
the resurrection from the dead.
3 And they laid hands on them, and
put *them* in hold unto the next day:
for it was now eventide.
4 Howbeit many of them which
heard the word believed; and the
number of the men was about five
thousand.
5 ¶ And it came to pass on the
morrow, that their rulers, and elders,
and scribes,
6 And [b]Annas the high priest, and
Cāi-ă-phăs, and John, and Alexander,
and as many as were of the kindred
of the high priest, were gathered together at Jerusalem.
7 And when they had set them in the
midst, they asked, [c]By what power, or
by what name, have ye done this?
8 Then [d]Peter, filled with the Holy
Ghost, said unto them, Ye rulers of
the people, and elders of Israel,
9 If we this day be examined of the
good deed done to the impotent man,
by what means he is made whole;
10 Be it known unto you all, and to
all the people of Israel, [e]that by the
name of Jesus Christ of Nazareth,
whom ye crucified, whom God raised
from the dead, *even* by him doth this
man stand here before you whole.
11 This [f]is the stone which was set at
nought of you builders, which is become the head of the corner.
12 Neither [g]is there salvation in any
other: for there is none other name
under heaven given among men,
whereby we must be saved.
13 ¶ Now when they saw the boldness of Peter and John, [h]and perceived
that they were unlearned and ignorant men, they marvelled; and they
took knowledge of them, that they had
been with Jesus.
14 And beholding the man which
was healed standing with them, they
could say nothing against it.

15 But when they had commanded
them to go aside out of the council,
they conferred among themselves,
16 Saying, [i]What shall we do to these
men? for that indeed a notable
miracle hath been done by them *is*
manifest [j]to all them that dwell in
Jerusalem; and we cannot deny *it*.
17 But that it spread no further
among the people, let us straitly
threaten them, that they speak henceforth to no man in this name.
18 And they called them, and commanded them not to speak at all nor
teach in the name of Jesus.
19 But Peter and John answered and
said unto them, [k]Whether it be right
in the sight of God to hearken unto
you more than unto God, judge ye.
20 For [l]we cannot but speak the
things which [m]we have seen and heard.
21 So when they had further threatened them, they let them go, finding
nothing how they might punish them,
because [n]of the people: for all *men*
glorified God for that [o]which was
done.
22 For the man was above forty
years old, on whom this miracle of
healing was shewed.
23 ¶ And being let go, [p]they went to
their own company, and reported all
that the chief priests and elders had
said unto them.
24 And when they heard that, they
[q]lifted up their voice to God with one
accord, and said, Lord, thou [r]*art* God,
which hast made heaven, and earth,
and the sea, and all that in them is:
25 Who by the mouth of thy servant
David hast said, [s]Why did the heathen
rage, and the people imagine vain
things?
26 The kings of the earth stood up,
and the rulers were gathered together
against the Lord, and against his
Christ.
27 For of a truth against [t]thy holy
child Jesus, [u]whom thou hast anointed, both Herod, and Pontius Pilate,
with the Gentiles, and the people of
Israel, were gathered together,
28 For [v]to do whatsoever thy hand
and thy counsel determined before to
be done.
29 And now, Lord, behold their
threatenings: and grant unto thy servants, [w]that with all boldness they
may speak thy word,
30 By stretching forth thine hand to
heal; and [x]that signs and wonders
may be done by [y]the name of thy holy
child Jesus.

i John 11.47. ch. 12.19.
j ch. 3.9.
k ch. 5.29. Gal. 1.10.
l ch. 1.8.
m ch. 22.15. 1 John 1.1.
n Matt. 9.33. Matt. 21.26. Luke 5.26. Luke 20.6.
o ch. 3.7,8.
p ch. 12.12.
q Ps. 55.16, 17. Ps. 103.1. Jer. 20.13.
r Ex. 20.11. Jer. 32.17.
s Ps. 2.1.
t Heb. 7.26.
u Isa. 61.1. John 10.36.
v ch. 2.23.
w Isa. 58.1. Eze. 2.6. ch. 19.8. Eph. 6.19.
x ch. 5.12.
y ch. 3.6,16.
z ch. 2.2,4.
a Rom. 15.5. Phil. 1.27. 1 Pet. 3.8.
b ch. 2.44.
c Mark 16. 20. 1 Thes. 1.5. Heb. 2.4.
d ch. 1.22.
e ch. 2.47.
f 1 John 3.17.
g ch. 2.45.
h ch. 6.1.
i Pro. 3.9. Matt. 19.29. Luke 12.33. 1 Tim. 6.19.

CHAP. 5

a Josh. 7.1. 1 Tim. 6.10.
b Num. 30.2. Deut. 23.21. Eccl. 5.4.
c 1 Ki. 22.21, 22. Luke 22.3. Jas. 4.7.
1 Or, to deceive.
d Num. 14. 36.
e John 19.40.

31 ¶ And when they had prayed, the
[z]place was shaken where they were
assembled together; and they were
all filled with the Holy Ghost, and they
spake the word of God with boldness.
32 And the multitude of them that
believed [a]were of one heart and of one
soul: neither [b]said any *of them* that
ought of the things which he possessed
was his own; but they had all things
common.
33 And with [c]great power gave the
apostles [d]witness of the resurrection
of the Lord Jesus: and great [e]grace
was upon them all.
34 Neither [f]was there any among
them that lacked: [g]for as many as
were possessors of lands or houses
sold them, and brought the prices of
the things that were sold,
35 And laid *them* down at the
apostles' feet: [h]and distribution was
made unto every man according as he
had need.
36 And Jō-ŝēs, who by the apostles
was surnamed Barnabas, (which is,
being interpreted, The son of consolation,) a Levite, *and* of the country
of Cyprus,
37 Having land, [i]sold *it*, and brought
the money, and laid *it* at the apostles'
feet.

CHAPTER 5

BUT a certain man named Ăn-ă-nī-
ăs, with Săpph-ī-ră his wife, sold
a possession,
2 And [a]kept back *part* of the price,
his wife also being privy *to it*, and
brought a certain part, and laid *it* at
the apostles' feet.
3 But [b]Peter said, Ăn-ă-nī-ăs, why
hath Satan [c]filled thine heart [1]to lie to
the Holy Ghost, and to keep back *part*
of the price of the land?
4 Whiles it remained, was it not
thine own? and after it was sold, was
it not in thine own power? why hast
thou conceived this thing in thine
heart? thou hast not lied unto men,
but unto God.
5 And Ăn-ă-nī-ăs hearing these
words [d]fell down, and gave up the
ghost: and great fear came on all them
that heard these things.
6 And the young men arose, wound
[e]him up, and carried *him* out, and
buried *him*.
7 And it was about the space of three
hours after, when his wife, not knowing what was done, came in.
8 And Peter answered unto her, Tell
me whether ye sold the land for so

much? And she said, Yea, for so much.

9 Then Peter said unto her, How is it that ye have agreed together to [f]tempt the Spirit of the Lord? behold, the feet of them which have buried thy husband *are* at the door, and shall carry thee out.

10 Then fell she down straightway at his feet, and yielded up the ghost: and the young men came in, and found her dead, and, carrying *her* forth, buried *her* by her husband.

11 And great fear came upon all the church, and upon as many as heard these things.

12 ¶ And [g]by the hands of the apostles were many signs and wonders wrought among the people; (and [h]they were all with one accord in Solomon's porch.

13 And [i]of the rest durst no man join himself to them: [j]but the people magnified them.

14 And believers were the more added to the Lord, multitudes both of men and women.)

15 Insomuch that they brought forth the sick [2]into the streets, and laid *them* on beds and couches, that [k]at the least the shadow of Peter passing by might overshadow some of them.

16 There came also a multitude *out* of the cities round about unto Jerusalem, bringing [l]sick folks, and them which were vexed with unclean spirits: and they were healed every one.

17 ¶ Then [m]the high priest rose up, and all they that were with him, (which is the sect of the Săd-dū-çēes,) and were filled with [3]indignation,

18 And [n]laid their hands on the apostles, and put them in the common prison.

19 But [o]the angel of the Lord by night opened the prison doors, and brought them forth, and said,

20 Go, stand and speak in the temple to the people [p]all the words of this life.

21 And when they heard *that*, they entered into the temple early in the morning, and taught. [q]But the high priest came, and they that were with him, and called the council together, and all the senate of the children of Israel, and sent to the prison to have them brought.

22 But when the officers came, and found them not in the prison, they returned, and told,

23 Saying, The prison truly found we shut with all safety, and the keepers standing without before the doors: but when we had opened, we found no man within.

24 Now when the high priest [r]and the captain of the temple and the chief priests heard these things, they doubted of them whereunto this would grow.

25 Then came one and told them, saying, Behold, the men whom ye put in prison are standing in the temple, and teaching the people.

26 Then went the captain with the officers, and brought them without violence: [s]for they feared the people, lest they should have been stoned.

27 And when they had brought them, they set *them* before the council: and the high priest asked them,

28 Saying, [t]Did not we straitly command you that ye should not teach in this name? and, behold, ye have filled Jerusalem with your doctrine, and [u]intend to bring this man's blood [v]upon us.

29 ¶ Then Peter and the *other* apostles answered and said, [w]We ought to obey God rather than men.

30 The God of our fathers raised up Jesus, whom ye slew and hanged [x]on a tree.

31 Him [y]hath God exalted with his right hand *to be* [z]a Prince and a [a]Saviour, [b]for to give repentance to Israel, and forgiveness of sins.

32 And [c]we are his witnesses of these things; and *so is* also the Holy Ghost, whom God hath given to them that obey him. Sc John 7:17

33 ¶ When they heard *that*, they were cut *to the heart*, and took counsel to slay them.

34 Then stood there up one in the council, a Pharisee, named [d]Gă-mā-lĭ-ĕl, a doctor of the law, had in reputation among all the people, and commanded to put the apostles forth a little space;

35 And said unto them, Ye men of Israel, take heed to yourselves what ye intend to do as touching these men.

36 For before these days rose up Theū-dăs, boasting himself to be somebody; to whom a number of men, about four hundred, joined themselves: who was slain; and all, as many as [4]obeyed him, were scattered, and brought to nought.

37 After this man rose up Judas of Galilee in the days [e]of the taxing, and drew away much people after him: he also perished; and all, *even* as many as obeyed him, were dispersed.

f Deut. 6.16. Ps. 95.9. Matt. 4.7. Luke 4.12. 1 Cor. 10.9. Heb. 3.8,9.
g Mark 16. 15-20. ch. 14.3. Rom. 15.18. 1 Cor. 2.4,5. Heb. 2.4.
h ch. 3.11.
i John 9.22.
j ch. 2.47.
2 Or, in every street.
k Matt. 9.21. Matt. 14.36.
l Mark 16.17.
m John 11. 47-49. John 12.10, 11,19. ch. 4.1,2.
3 Or, envy.
n Luke 21.12.
o Ps. 34.7. Isa. 61.1. ch. 12.7. ch. 16.26. Heb. 1.14.
p Jer. 7.2. Matt. 21.23. John 6.68.
q ch. 4.5,6.
r Luke 22.4. ch. 4.1.
s Matt. 14.5. Luke 20.6.
t ch. 4.18.
u ch. 2.23. ch. 3.15.
v Matt. 23. 35.
w Gal. 1.10.
x ch. 10.39. Gal. 3.13. 1 Pet. 2.24.
y ch. 2.33. Phil. 2.9. Heb. 2.10.
z Isa. 9.6. Dan. 9.25. ch. 3.15. Rev. 1.5.
a Matt. 1.21.
b Eph. 1.7. Col. 1.14.
c John 15.26.
d ch. 22.3.
4 Or, believed.
e Luke 2.1.

38 And now I say unto you, Refrain
from these men, and let them
alone: for [f]if this counsel or this
work be of men, it will come to
nought:
39 But [g]if it be of God, ye cannot
overthrow it; lest haply ye be found
even [h]to fight against God.
40 And to him they agreed: and when
they had called the apostles, and [i]beat-
en *them*, they commanded that they
should not speak in the name of Jesus,
and let them go.
41 ¶ And they departed from the presence of the council, [j]rejoicing that
they were counted worthy to suffer
shame for his name.
42 And daily in the temple, and in
every house, they ceased not to teach
and preach Jesus Christ.

CHAPTER 6

AND in those days, [a]when the number of the disciples was multiplied,
there arose a murmuring of the [b]Gre-
cians against the Hebrews, because
their widows were neglected [c]in the
daily ministration.
2 Then the twelve called the multitude of the disciples *unto them*, and
said, [d]It is not reason that we should
leave the word of God, and serve
tables.
3 Wherefore, brethren, [e]look ye out
among you seven men of honest report, full of the Holy Ghost and wisdom, whom we may appoint over this
business.
4 But we [f]will give ourselves continually to prayer, and to the ministry
of the word.
5 ¶ And the saying pleased the whole
multitude: and they chose Stephen,
a [g]man full of faith and of the Holy
Ghost, [h]and Philip, and Prŏch-ŏ-rŭs,
and Nī-cā-nôr, and Tī-mŏn, and Pär-
mĕ-năs, and Nicolas a proselyte of
Ăn-tī-ŏch:
6 Whom they set before the apostles:
and when [i]they had prayed, [j]they laid
their hands on them.
7 And [k]the word of God increased;
and the number of the disciples multiplied in Jerusalem greatly; and a great
company [l]of the priests were obedient
to the faith.
8 And Stephen, full of faith and
power, did great wonders and miracles
among the people.
9 ¶ Then there arose certain of the
synagogue, which is called *the synagogue* of the Lī-bĕr-tīnes, and Çȳ-rē-
nī-ăns, and Ăl-ĕx-ăn-drĭ-ăns, and of
them of Çĭ-lĭç-ĭ-ă and of Asia, disputing with Stephen.
10 And [m]they were not able to resist
the wisdom and the spirit by which he
spake.
11 Then [n]they suborned men, which
said, We have heard him speak blasphemous words against Moses, and
against God.
12 And they stirred up the people,
and the elders, and the scribes, and
came upon *him*, and caught him, and
brought *him* to the council,
13 And set up false witnesses, which
said, This man ceaseth not to speak
blasphemous words against this holy
place, and the law:
14 For [o]we have heard him say, that
this Jesus of Nazareth [p]shall destroy
this place, and shall change the [1]cus-
toms which Moses delivered us.
15 And all that sat in the council,
looking stedfastly on him, saw his face
as it had been the face of [q]an angel.

CHAPTER 7

THEN said the high priest, Are
these things so?
2 And he said, Men, brethren, and
fathers, hearken; The God of glory
appeared unto our father Abraham,
when he was in Mĕs-ŏ-pŏ-tā-mĭ-ă, before he dwelt in Chăr-răn,
3 And said unto him, Get thee out of
thy country, and from thy kindred,
and come into the land which [a]I shall
shew thee.
4 Then [b]came he out of the land of
the Chăl-dæ-ăns, and dwelt in Chăr-
răn: and from thence, when his father
was dead, he removed him into this
land, wherein ye now dwell.
5 And he gave him none inheritance
in it, no, not *so much as* to set his foot
on: yet he [c]promised that he would
give it to him for a possession, and to
his seed after him, when *as yet* he had
no child.
6 And God spake on this wise, That
[d]his seed should sojourn in a strange
land; and that they should bring them
into bondage, and entreat *them* [e]evil
four hundred years.
7 And the nation to whom they shall
be in bondage will I judge, said God:
and after that shall they come forth,
and [f]serve me in this place.
8 And [g]he gave him the covenant of
circumcision: [h]and so *Abraham* begat
Isaac, and circumcised him the eighth
day; [i]and Isaac *begat* Jacob; and
Jacob [j]*begat* the twelve patriarchs.
9 And [k]the patriarchs, moved with

f Ps. 127.1. Pro. 21.30. Matt. 15.13.
g Gen. 24.50. Matt. 16.18. 1 Cor. 1.25. Rev. 17.14.
h ch. 9.5.
i Matt. 10.17. Mark 13.9. Luke 20.10.
j Matt. 5.12. Rom. 5.3. 2 Cor. 12.10. Phil. 1.29. Heb. 10.34. 1 Pet. 4.13.

CHAP. 6
a Ps. 72.16. Matt. 13.31.
b ch. 9.29.
c ch. 4.35.
d Ex. 18.17. 2 Tim. 2.4.
e Deut. 1.13. 1 Tim. 3.7.
f ch. 2.42.
g ch. 9.31.
h ch. 8.5.
i Ps. 37.5. Pro. 16.3. ch. 1.24. Phil. 4.6.
j ch. 8.17. 1 Tim. 4.14. 2 Tim. 1.6. Heb. 6.2.
k Col. 1.6. 2 Thes. 3.1.
l John 12.42.
m Isa. 54.17. Luke 21.15.
n Matt. 26. 15.
o ch. 25.8.
p Dan. 9.26. Matt. 24.2.
1 Or, rites.
q Dan. 10.6. Matt. 17.2. Rev. 10.1.

CHAP. 7
a Gen. 12.1.
b Gen. 11.31. Heb. 11.8.
c Gen. 12.7. Ex. 6.7,8. Deut. 6.10. Neh. 9.8,24. Ps. 105.8-11.
d Gen. 15.13. 1 Pet. 2.11.
e Ex. 12.40. Gal. 3.17.
f Ex. 3.12.
g Gen. 17.9. Gal. 3.15-17.
h Gen. 21.2. 1 Chr. 1.34. Matt. 1.2.
i Gen. 25.26.
j Gen. 29.31.
k Gen. 37.4. Ps. 105.17.

envy, sold Joseph into Egypt: but
[l]God was with him,
10 And delivered him out of all his
afflictions, [m]and gave him favour and
wisdom in the sight of Pharaoh king
of Egypt; and he made him governor
over Egypt and all his house.
11 Now there came a dearth over all
the land of Egypt and Chā-nă-ăn, and
great affliction: and our fathers found
no sustenance.
12 But when Jacob heard that there
was corn in Egypt, he sent out our
fathers first.
13 And at the second *time* Joseph was
made known to his brethren; and
Joseph's kindred was made known
unto Pharaoh.
14 Then [n]sent Joseph, and called his
father Jacob to *him*, and all his kindred, [o]threescore and fifteen souls.
15 So Jacob went down into Egypt,
[p]and died, he, and our fathers,
16 And [q]were carried over into Sȳ-
chĕm, and laid in [r]the sepulchre that
Abraham bought for a sum of money
of the sons of Ĕm-môr *the father* of
Sȳ-chĕm.
17 But when [s]the time of the promise
drew nigh, which God had sworn to
Abraham, the people grew and multiplied in Egypt,
18 Till another king arose, which
knew not Joseph.
19 The same dealt subtilly with our
kindred, and evil entreated our fathers, so that they cast out their young
children, to the end they might not
live.
20 In [t]which time Moses was born,
and was [1]exceeding fair, and nourished up in his father's house three
months:
21 And when he was cast out,
Pharaoh's daughter took him up, and
nourished him for her own son.
22 And Moses was learned in all the
wisdom of the Egyptians, and was
[u]mighty in words and in deeds.
23 And [v]when he was full forty years
old, it came into his heart to visit his
brethren the children of Israel.
24 And seeing one *of them* suffer
wrong, he defended *him*, and avenged
him that was oppressed, and smote
the Egyptian:
25 [2]For he supposed his brethren
would have understood how that God
by his hand would deliver them: but
they understood not.
26 And the next day he shewed himself unto them as they strove, and
would have set them at one again,

l Gen. 39.2.
m Gen. 42.6. Gen. 45.8,9. 1 Sam. 2.30. Ps. 37.23. Pro. 8.15.
n Gen. 45.9.
o Gen. 46.27. Deut. 10.22. Including the wives of his brethren.
p Gen. 49.33. Ex. 1.6.
q Gen. 50.25. Ex. 13.19.
r Gen. 23.16.
s Gen. 15.13.
t Ex. 2.2.
1 Or, fair to God. Heb. 11.23.
u Luke 24.19.
v Ex. 2.11.
2 Or, Now.
w Luke 12. 14.
x Ex. 2.15.
y Num. 12.1.
z Gen. 48.16. Ex. 3.2. Deut. 33.16. Isa. 63.9. Zech. 13.7. John 1.14. Titus 2.13.
a Gen. 50.24. Ex. 3.6,15. Matt. 22.32. Heb. 11.16.
b Josh. 5.15.
c Ex. 14.19. Num. 20.16.
d Ex. 12.41. Deut. 6.21, 22. Ps. 78.12, 13.
e Ex. 16.1.
f Deut. 18.15.
3 Or, as myself.
g Matt. 17.5. Mark 9.7. John 18.37. ch. 3.23.
h Ex. 19.3.
i Isa. 63.9. Gal. 3.19. Heb. 2.2.
j Ex. 21.1. John 1.17.
k Rom. 3.2.
l Ex. 32.1.

saying, Sirs, ye are brethren; why do
ye wrong one to another?
27 But he that did his neighbour
wrong thrust him away, saying, Who
[w]made thee a ruler and a judge over
us?
28 Wilt thou kill me, as thou diddest
the Egyptian yesterday?
29 Then [x]fled Moses at this saying,
and was a stranger in the land of Mā-
dĭ-ăn, where he [y]begat two sons.
30 And when forty years were expired, there appeared to him in the
wilderness of mount Sī-nă [z]an angel
of the Lord in a flame of fire in a bush.
31 When Moses saw *it*, he wondered
at the sight: and as he drew near to
behold *it*, the voice of the Lord came
unto him,
32 *Saying*, [a]I *am* the God of thy
fathers, the God of Abraham, and the
God of Isaac, and the God of Jacob.
Then Moses trembled, and durst not
behold.
33 Then [b]said the Lord to him, Put
off thy shoes from thy feet: for the
place where thou standest is holy
ground.
34 I have seen, I have seen the affliction of my people which is in Egypt,
and I have heard their groaning, and
am come down to deliver them. And
now come, I will send thee into Egypt.
35 This Moses whom they refused,
saying, Who made thee a ruler and
a judge? the same did God send *to be*
a ruler and a deliverer [c]by the hand of
the angel which appeared to him in
the bush.
36 He [d]brought them out, after that
he had shewed wonders and signs in
the land of Egypt, and in the Red sea,
[e]and in the wilderness forty years.
37 ¶ This is that Moses, which said
unto the children of Israel, [f]A prophet
shall the Lord your God raise up unto
you of your brethren, [3]like unto me;
him [g]shall ye hear.
38 This [h]is he, that was in the church
in the wilderness with [i]the angel which
spake to him in the mount Sī-nă, and
with our fathers: who [j]received the
[k]lively oracles to give unto us:
39 To whom our fathers would not
obey, but thrust *him* from them, and
in their hearts turned back again into
Egypt,
40 Saying [l]unto Aaron, Make us
gods to go before us: for *as for* this
Moses, which brought us out of the
land of Egypt, we wot not what is become of him.
41 And they made a calf in those

days, and offered sacrifice unto the idol, and rejoiced in the works of their own hands.

42 Then God [m]turned, and gave them up to worship [n]the host of heaven; as it is written in the book of the prophets, [o]O ye house of Israel, have ye offered to me slain beasts and sacrifices *by the space of* forty years in the wilderness?

43 Yea, ye took up the tabernacle of Moloch, and the star of your god Rĕm′-phăn, figures which ye made to worship them: and I will carry you away beyond Babylon.

44 Our fathers had the tabernacle of witness in the wilderness, as he had appointed, [4]speaking unto Moses, that [p]he should make it according to the fashion that he had seen.

45 Which [q]also our fathers [5]that came after brought in with [6]Jesus into the possession of the Gentiles, whom God drave out before the face of our fathers, unto the days of David;

46 Who [r]found favour before God, and desired [s]to find a tabernacle for the God of Jacob.

47 But Solomon built him an house.

48 Howbeit [t]the most High dwelleth not in temples made with hands; as saith the prophet,

49 Heaven [u]*is* my throne, and earth *is* my footstool: what house will ye build me? saith the Lord: or what *is* the place of my rest?

50 Hath not my hand made all these things?

51 ¶ Ye [v]stiffnecked and [w]uncircumcised in heart and ears, ye do always resist the Holy Ghost: as your fathers *did*, so *do* ye.

52 Which [x]of the prophets have not your fathers persecuted? and they have slain them which shewed before of the coming of [y]the Just One; of whom ye have been now the betrayers and murderers:

53 Who [z]have received the law by the disposition of angels, and have not kept *it*.

54 ¶ When they heard these things, they were cut to the heart, and they gnashed on him with *their* teeth.

55 But he, being full of the Holy Ghost, looked up stedfastly into heaven, and saw the glory of God, and Jesus standing on the right hand of God,

56 And said, Behold, [a]I see the heavens opened, and the [b]Son of man standing on the right hand of God.

57 Then they cried out with a loud voice, and stopped their ears, and ran upon him with one accord,

58 And [c]cast *him* out of the city, and [d]stoned *him:* and [e]the witnesses laid down their clothes at a young man's feet, whose name was Saul.

59 And they stoned Stephen, calling upon *God*, and saying, Lord Jesus, receive [f]my spirit.

60 And he kneeled down, and cried with a loud voice, [g]Lord, lay not this sin to their charge. And when he had said this, he [h]fell asleep.

CHAPTER 8

AND [a]Saul was consenting unto his death. And at that time there was a great persecution against the church which was at Jerusalem; and they [b]were all scattered abroad throughout the regions of Judæa and Să-mâr′-ĭ-ă, except the apostles.

2 And devout men carried Stephen *to his burial*, and [c]made great lamentation over him.

3 As for Saul, [d]he made havock of the church, entering into every house, and haling men and women committed *them* to prison.

4 Therefore [e]they that were scattered abroad went every where preaching the word.

5 Then [f]Philip went down to the city of Să-mâr′-ĭ-ă, and preached Christ unto them.

6 And the people with one accord gave heed unto those things which Philip spake, hearing and seeing the miracles which he did.

7 For [g]unclean spirits, crying with loud voice, came out of many that were possessed *with them:* and many taken with palsies, and that were lame, were healed.

8 And there was great joy in that city.

9 But there was a certain man, called Simon, which beforetime in the same city used [h]sorcery, and bewitched the people of Să-mâr′-ĭ-ă, giving [i]out that himself was some great one:

10 To whom [j]they all gave heed, from the least to the greatest, saying, This man is the great power of God.

11 And to him they had regard, because that of long time he had bewitched them with sorceries.

12 But when they believed Philip preaching the things [k]concerning the kingdom of God, and the name of Jesus Christ, they were baptized, both men and women.

13 Then Simon himself [l]believed

m Eze. 20.25. Rom. 1.24. 2 Thes. 2.11.
n Deut. 17.3. 2 Ki. 17.16. Jer. 19.13.
o Amos 5.25.
4 Or, who spake. Ex. 25.40. Heb. 8.5.
q Josh 3.14.
5 Or, having received.
6 That is, Joshua.
r 1 Sam. 15. 28. Ps. 78.68-72.
s 1 Ki. 8.17.
t 2 Chr. 2.6. ch. 17.24,25.
u Ps. 11.4. Isa. 66.1,2. Matt. 5.34. Rev. 3.21.
v Isa. 48.4.
w Eze. 44.9.
x 2 Chr. 36. 16. Jer. 26. 15, 23. Matt. 23.34. 1 Thes. 2.15.
y ch. 3.14.
z Ex. 20.1. Gal. 3.19. Heb. 2.2.
a Matt. 3.16.
b Dan. 7.13.
c Heb. 13.12.
d Lev. 24.16.
e Deut. 13.9.
f Ps. 31.5.
g Matt. 5.44. Luke 6.28.
h 1 Thes. 4. 13. Rev. 14.13.

CHAP. 8

a ch. 7.58.
b ch. 11.19.
c 2 Sam. 3.31.
d 1 Cor. 15.9. Gal. 1.13. Phil. 3.6. 1 Tim. 1.13.
e Matt. 10. 23. ch. 11.19. 1 Cor. 14.31. 1 Thes. 2.2.
f ch. 6.5.
g Matt. 10.1. Mark 16.17. Luke 10.17.
h ch. 13.6.
i ch. 5.36.
j Eph. 4.14. Rev. 13.3.
k ch. 1.3.
l Luke 8.13.

also: and when he was baptized, he
continued with Philip, and wondered,
beholding the [1]miracles and signs
which were done.
14 Now when the apostles which
were at Jerusalem heard that Să-mâr′-
ĭ-ă had received the word of God,
they sent unto them Peter and
John:
15 Who, when they were come down,
prayed for them, [m]that they might receive the Holy Ghost:
16 (For [n]as yet he was fallen upon
none of them: only [o]they were baptized in [p]the name of the Lord Jesus.)
17 Then [q]laid they *their* hands on
them, and they received the Holy
Ghost.
18 And when Simon saw that through
laying on of the apostles' hands the
Holy Ghost was given, he offered
them money,
19 Saying, Give me also this power,
that on whomsoever I lay hands, he
may receive the Holy Ghost.
20 But Peter said unto him, Thy
money perish with thee, because thou
[r]hast thought that [s]the gift of God
may be purchased with money.
21 Thou hast neither part nor lot in
this matter: for thy [t]heart is not right
in the sight of God.
22 Repent therefore of this thy wickedness, and pray God, [u]if perhaps the
thought of thine heart may be forgiven
thee.
23 For I perceive that thou art in the
gall [v]of bitterness, and *in* the bond of
iniquity.
24 Then answered Simon, and said,
Pray ye [w]to the Lord for me, that none
of these things which ye have spoken
come upon me.
25 And they, when they had testified
and preached the word of the Lord,
returned to Jerusalem, and preached
the gospel in many villages of the Să-
măr′-ĭ-tăns.
26 And [x]the angel of the Lord spake
unto Philip, saying, Arise, and go
toward the south unto the way that
goeth down from Jerusalem unto Gā′-
ză, which is desert.
27 And he arose and went: and, behold a [y]man of Ē-thĭ-ō′-pĭ-ă, an
eunuch of great authority under Căn′-
dă-çē queen of the Ē-thĭ-ō′-pĭ-ăns,
who had the charge of all her treasure,
and [z]had come to Jerusalem for to
worship,
28 Was returning, and sitting in his
chariot read Ē-ṣāi′-ăs the prophet.
29 Then the Spirit said unto Philip,

1 signs and great miracles.
m Matt. 18. 19. John 14.13, 14.
n ch. 19.2.
o Matt. 28. 19. ch. 2.38.
p ch. 10.48.
q ch. 6.6. Heb. 6.2.
r 2 Ki. 5.16. Matt. 10.8.
s ch. 2.38.
t Pro. 6.16, 18. Pro. 11.20. Isa. 44.20. Jer. 17.9. Rom. 8.7. 2 Tim. 3.5.
u Isa. 55.7. Dan. 4.27. 2 Tim. 2.25.
v Job 20.14. Heb. 12.15.
w Gen. 20.7. Ex. 8.8. Num. 21.7. 1 Ki. 13.6. Jas. 5.16.
x Ps. 91.11. Heb. 1.14.
y Ps. 68.31. Isa. 43.6. Jer. 13.23. Zeph. 3.10.
z 1 Ki. 8.41. Ps. 68.29. Isa. 56.3-8. John 12.20.
a Isa. 53.7. Phil. 2.7.8. 1 Pet. 1.19.
b Luke 24.27. ch. 18.28. 2 Cor. 1.20. Col. 2.17. 1 Pet. 1.11.
c ch. 10.47.
d Matt. 28. 19. Mark 16.16.
e Matt. 14. 33. Mark 8.29. John 6.69. Rom. 10.10.
f 1 Ki. 18.12. 2 Ki. 2.16. Eze. 3.12. 2 Cor. 12.2-4.
g Zech. 9.6.

CHAP. 9

a ch. 8.3. Gal. 1.13. 1 Tim. 1.13.
1 of the way.
b ch. 22.6. 1 Cor. 15.8.
c Matt. 25. 40. 1 Cor. 12.12. Eph. 5.30.

Go near, and join thyself to this
chariot.
30 And Philip ran thither to *him*, and
heard him read the prophet Ē-ṣāi′-ăs,
and said, Understandest thou what
thou readest?
31 And he said, How can I, except
some man should guide me? And he
desired Philip that he would come up
and sit with him. Sc Isa 8:20
32 The place of the scripture which
he read was this, [a]He was led as a
sheep to the slaughter; and like a
lamb dumb before his shearer, so
opened he not his mouth:
33 In his humiliation his judgment
was taken away: and who shall declare his generation? for his life is
taken from the earth.
34 And the eunuch answered Philip,
and said, I pray thee, of whom speaketh the prophet this? of himself, or of
some other man?
35 Then Philip opened his mouth,
and began [b]at the same scripture, and
preached unto him Jesus.
36 And as they went on *their* way,
they came unto a certain water: and
the eunuch said, See, *here is* water;
what [c]doth hinder me to be baptized?
37 And Philip said, [d]If thou believest
with all thine heart, thou mayest. And
he answered and said, I [e]believe that
Jesus Christ is the Son of God.
38 And he commanded the chariot to
stand still: and they went down both
into the water, both Philip and the
eunuch; and he baptized him.
39 And when they were come up out
of the water, [f]the Spirit of the Lord
caught away Philip, that the eunuch
saw him no more: and he went on his
way rejoicing.
40 But Philip was found [g]at Ă-zō′-tŭs:
and passing through he preached in all
the cities, till he came to Çæ-să-rē′-ă.

CHAPTER 9

AND [a]Saul, yet breathing out threatenings and slaughter against the
disciples of the Lord, went unto the
high priest,
2 And desired of him letters to
Damascus to the synagogues, that if
he found any [1]of this way, whether
they were men or women, he might
bring them bound unto Jerusalem.
3 And [b]as he journeyed, he came near
Damascus: and suddenly there shined
round about him a light from heaven:
4 And he fell to the earth, and heard
a voice saying unto him, Saul, Saul,
why persecutest [c]thou me?

5 And he said, [d]Who art thou, Lord?
And the Lord said, I am Jesus whom
thou persecutest: [e]*it is* hard for thee to
kick against the pricks.
6 And he trembling and astonished
said, Lord, [f]what wilt thou have me to
do? And the Lord *said* unto him,
Arise, and go into the city, and it shall
be told thee what thou must do.
7 And [g]the men which journeyed with
him stood speechless, hearing a voice,
but seeing no man.
8 And Saul arose from the earth; and
when his eyes were opened, he saw no
man: but they led him by the hand,
and brought *him* into Damascus.
9 And he was three days without
sight, and neither did eat nor drink.
10 ¶ And there was a certain disciple
at Damascus, named Ăn-ă-nī-ăs; and
to him said the Lord in a vision, Ăn-
ă-nī-ăs. And he said, Behold, I *am*
here, Lord.
11 And the Lord *said* unto him,
Arise, and go into the street which is
called Straight, and inquire in the
house of Judas for *one* called Saul, of
[h]Tarsus: for, behold, he prayeth,
12 And hath seen in a vision a man
named Ăn-ă-nī-ăs coming in, and
putting *his* hand on him, that he might
receive his sight.
13 Then Ăn-ă-nī-ăs answered, Lord,
I have heard by many of this man,
how much evil he hath done to thy
saints at Jerusalem:
14 And here he hath authority from
the chief priests to bind all that [i]call
on thy name.
15 But the Lord said unto him, Go
thy way: for [j]he is a chosen vessel unto
me, to bear my name before [k]the Gentiles, and [l]kings, and the children of
Israel:
16 For [m]I will shew him how great
things he must suffer for my name's
sake.
17 And Ăn-ă-nī-ăs went his way, and
entered into the house; and putting
his hands on him said, Brother Saul,
the Lord, *even* Jesus, that appeared
unto thee in the way as thou camest,
hath sent me, that thou mightest receive thy sight, and [o]be filled with the
Holy Ghost.
18 And immediately there fell from
his eyes as it had been scales: and he
received sight forthwith, and arose,
and was baptized.
19 And when he had received meat,
he was strengthened. [p]Then was Saul
certain days with the disciples which
were at Damascus.

d 1 Tim. 1.13.
e ch. 5.39.
f Luke 3.10. ch. 2.37.
g Dan. 10.7. ch. 22.9.
h ch. 21.39.
i ch. 7.59. ch. 22.16. 1 Cor. 1.2. 2 Tim. 2.22.
j ch. 13.2. ch. 22.21. Rom. 1.1. 1 Cor. 15.10. Gal. 1.15. Eph. 3.7. 1 Tim. 2.7. 2 Tim. 1.11.
k Rom. 1.5. Gal. 2.7,8. Eph. 3.7. Col. 1.25-27. 1 Tim. 2.7.
l ch. 25.22.
m Matt. 10. 21-25. John 15.20. ch. 20.23. 2 Cor. 4.9-13. 2 Cor. 11.23. 2 Tim. 1.12.
n ch. 22.12.
o ch. 2.4.
p ch. 26.20.
q ch. 8.37.
r Matt. 13. 54-57. ch. 3.10. Gal. 1.13.
s ch. 18.28.
t ch. 23.12.
u Josh. 2.15. 1 Sam. 19. 12.
v ch. 22.17. Gal. 1.17.
w ch. 4.36.
x Eph. 6.19.
y ch. 6.1.
z 2 Cor. 11. 26.
a Ps. 119.165.
b ch. 8.14.
c Matt. 8.3. John 2.11. ch. 3.6.

20 And straightway he preached
Christ in the synagogues, [q]that he is
the Son of God.
21 But all that heard *him* were amazed, and said; [r]Is not this he that
destroyed them which called on
this name in Jerusalem, and came
hither for that intent, that he might
bring them bound unto the chief
priests?
22 But Saul increased the more in
strength, and [s]confounded the Jews
which dwelt at Damascus, proving
that this is very Christ.
23 ¶ And after that many days were
fulfilled, [t]the Jews took counsel to
kill him:
24 But their laying await was known
of Saul. And they watched the gates
day and night to kill him.
25 Then the disciples took him by
night, and [u]let *him* down by the wall
in a basket.
26 And [v]when Saul was come to Jerusalem, he assayed to join himself to
the disciples: but they were all afraid
of him, and believed not that he was
a disciple.
27 But [w]Barnabas took him, and
brought *him* to the apostles, and declared unto them how he had seen the
Lord in the way, and that he had
spoken to him, and how he had
preached boldly at Damascus in the
name of Jesus.
28 And he was with them coming in
and going out at Jerusalem.
29 And he spake [x]boldly in the name
of the Lord Jesus, and disputed
against the [y]Grecians: [z]but they went
about to slay him.
30 *Which* when the brethren knew,
they brought him down to Çæ-să-rē-ă,
and sent him forth to Tarsus.
31 Then [a]had the churches rest
throughout all Judæa and Galilee and
Să-mâr-ĭ-ă, and were edified; and
walking in the fear of the Lord, and
in the comfort of the Holy Ghost,
were multiplied.
32 ¶ And it came to pass, as Peter
passed throughout [b]all *quarters*, he
came down also to the saints which
dwelt at Lўd-dă.
33 And there he found a certain man
named Æ-nē-ăs, which had kept his
bed eight years, and was sick of the
palsy.
34 And Peter said unto him, Æ-nē-
ăs, [c]Jesus Christ maketh thee whole:
arise, and make thy bed. And he arose
immediately.
35 And all that dwelt at Lўd-dă and

[d]Sâr'-ŏn saw him, and [e]turned to the
Lord.
36 ¶ Now there was at Joppa a certain disciple named Tabitha, which by
interpretation is called [2]Dorcas: this
woman was full [f]of good works and
almsdeeds which she did.
37 And it came to pass in those days,
that she was sick, and died: whom
when they had washed, they laid *her*
in [g]an upper chamber.
38 And forasmuch as Lўd'-dă was
nigh to Joppa, and the disciples had
heard that Peter was there, they sent
unto him two men, desiring *him* that
he would not [3]delay to come to them.
39 Then Peter arose and went with
them. When he was come, they
brought him into the upper chamber:
and all the widows stood by him weeping, and shewing the coats and garments which Dorcas made, while she
was with them.
40 But Peter [h]put them all forth, and
kneeled [i]down, and prayed; and
turning *him* to the body [j]said, Tabitha, arise. And she opened her eyes:
and when she saw Peter, she sat
up.
41 And he gave her *his* hand, and
lifted her up, and when he had called
the saints and widows, presented her
alive.
42 And it was known throughout all
Joppa; [k]and many believed in the
Lord.
43 And it came to pass, that he tarried many days in [l]Joppa with one
Simon [m]a tanner.

CHAPTER 10

THERE was a certain man in Çæ-
să-rē'-ă called Cornelius, a centurion of the band called the Italian
band,
2 *A* [a]devout *man*, and one that feared
God with all his house, which gave
much alms to the people, and prayed
to God alway.
3 He [b]saw in a vision evidently about
the ninth hour of the day an [c]angel of
God coming in to him, and saying
unto him, Cornelius.
4 And when he looked on him, he
was afraid, and said, What is it, Lord?
And he said unto him, Thy prayers
and thine alms are come up for [d]a
memorial before God.
5 And now send men to Joppa, and
call for *one* Simon, whose surname is
Peter:
6 He lodgeth with one [e]Simon a
tanner, whose house is by the sea side:
he [f]shall tell thee what thou oughtest
to do.
7 And when the angel which spake
unto Cornelius was departed, he called two of his household servants, and
a devout soldier of them that waited
on him continually;
8 And when he had declared all *these*
things unto them, he sent them to
Joppa.
9 ¶ On the morrow, as they went on
their journey, and drew nigh unto the
city, Peter went up upon the housetop
to pray about [g]the sixth hour:
10 And he became very hungry, and
would have eaten: but while they
made ready, he fell into a trance,
11 And [h]saw heaven opened, and a
certain vessel descending unto him,
as it had been a great sheet knit at the
four corners, and let down to the
earth:
12 Wherein were all manner of four-
footed beasts of the earth, and wild
beasts, and creeping things, and fowls
of the air.
13 And there came a voice to him,
Rise, Peter; kill, and eat.
14 But Peter said, Not so, Lord; for
[i]I have never eaten any thing that is
common or unclean.
15 And the voice *spake* unto him
again the second time, [j]What God
hath cleansed, *that* call not thou common.
16 This was done thrice: and the
vessel was received up again into
heaven.
17 Now while Peter doubted in himself what this vision which he had seen
should mean, behold, the men which
were sent from Cornelius had made
inquiry for Simon's house, and stood
before the gate,
18 And called, and asked whether
Simon, which was surnamed Peter,
were lodged there.
19 ¶ While Peter thought on the
vision, the Spirit [k]said unto him, Behold, three men seek thee.
20 Arise [l]therefore, and get thee
down, and go with them, doubting
nothing: for I have sent them.
21 Then Peter went down to the men
which were sent unto him from
Cornelius; and said, Behold, I am he
whom ye seek: what *is* the cause
wherefore ye are come?
22 And they said, Cornelius the centurion, a just man, and one that feareth God, and of [m]good report among
all the nation of the Jews, was warned from God by an holy angel to send

d 1 Chr. 5.16.
e ch. 11.21.
2 Or, Doe, or, Roe.
f Pro. 31.31. John 15.5,8. 1 Tim. 2.10. Titus 3.8. Heb. 13.21. Jas. 1.27.
g ch. 1.13.
3 Or, be grieved.
h Matt. 9.25.
i 1 Ki. 17.19-23. 2 Ki. 4.32-36. ch. 7.60.
j Mark 5.41. John 11.43.
k John 11.45.
l Josh. 19.46. 2 Chr. 2.16. Ezra 3.7. Jonah 1.3.
m ch. 10.6.

CHAP. 10
a Gen. 18.19. Josh. 24.15. ch. 8.2. 1 Thes. 5.17.
b ch. 11.13.
c Ps. 34.7. ch. 5.19. ch. 11.13. Heb. 1.14.
d 2 Chr. 7.15. Ps. 65.2. Ps. 102.17. Pro. 15.8,29. Phil. 4.18. Heb. 13.16. Jas. 5.16. 1 Pet. 3.12. Rev. 5.8.
e ch. 9.43.
f John 7.17. ch. 9.6.
g Ps. 55.17. Dan. 6.10. Luke 18.1. ch. 3.1. 1 Thes. 5.17.
h Eze. 1.1. Matt. 3.16. ch. 7.56. Rev. 19.11.
i Lev. 11.4. Deut. 14.3, 7. Eze. 4.14. Rom. 10.2.
j Matt. 15.11. 1 Cor. 10.25. 1 Tim. 4.4. Titus 1.15.
k John 16.13. ch. 8.29. Rev. 22.17.
l Matt. 28.19. Mark 16.15. ch. 15.7.
m ch. 22.12.

for thee into his house, and to hear
words of thee.
23 Then called he them in, and
lodged *them*. And on the morrow
Peter went away with them, and
certain brethren from Joppa accompanied him.
24 And the morrow after they entered into Çǣ-să-rē-ă. And Cornelius
waited for them, and had called together his kinsmen and near friends.
25 And as Peter was coming in,
Cornelius met him, and fell down at
his feet, and worshipped *him*.
26 But Peter took him up, saying,
Stand [n]up; I myself also am a man.
27 And as he talked with him, he
went in, and found many that were
come together.
28 And he said unto them, Ye know
how that [o]it is an unlawful thing for a
man that is a Jew to keep company, or
come unto one of another nation; but
[p]God hath shewed me that I should
not call any man common or unclean.
29 Therefore came I *unto you* without gainsaying, as [q]soon as I was sent
for: I ask therefore for what intent ye
have sent for me?
30 And Cornelius said, Four days
ago I was fasting until this hour; and
at the ninth hour I prayed in my
house, and, behold, [r]a man stood before [s]me in bright clothing,
31 And said, Cornelius, [t]thy prayer
is heard, [u]and thine alms are had in
remembrance in the sight of God.
32 Send therefore to Joppa, and call
hither Simon, whose surname is Peter;
he is lodged in the house of *one* Simon
a tanner by the sea side: who, when
he cometh, shall speak unto thee.
33 Immediately therefore I sent to
thee; and thou hast well done that
thou art come. Now therefore are we
all here present before God, to hear
all things that are commanded thee of
God.
34 ¶ Then Peter opened *his* mouth,
and said, [v]Of a truth I perceive that
God is no respecter of persons:
35 But [w]in every nation he that feareth him, and worketh righteousness,
is accepted with him.
36 The word which *God* sent unto the
children of Israel, preaching [x]peace
by Jesus Christ: ([y]he is Lord of all:)
37 That word, *I say*, ye know, which
was published throughout all Judæa,
and began from Galilee, after the baptism which John preached;
38 How [z]God anointed Jesus of
Nazareth with the Holy Ghost and
with power: who went about doing
good, and healing all that were oppressed of the devil; for [a]God was
with him.
39 And we are witnesses of all things
which he did both in the land of the
Jews, and in Jerusalem; whom they
slew and hanged on a tree:
40 Him God raised up the third day,
and shewed him openly;
41 Not [b]to all the people, but unto
witnesses chosen before of God, *even*
to us, who [c]did eat and drink with him
after he rose from the dead.
42 And [d]he commanded us to preach
unto the people, and to testify [e]that
it is he which was ordained of God *to
be* the Judge of [f]quick and dead.
43 To [g]him give all the prophets
witness, that through his name whosoever believeth in him shall receive
remission of sins.
44 ¶ While Peter yet spake these
words, the Holy Ghost fell on all them
which heard the word.
45 And they of the circumcision
which believed were astonished, as
many as came with Peter, because that
on the Gentiles also was poured out
the gift of the Holy Ghost.
46 For they heard them speak with
tongues, and magnify God. Then answered Peter,
47 Can any man forbid water, that
these should not be baptized, which
have received the Holy Ghost as well
as we?
48 And he commanded them to be
baptized in the name of the Lord.
Then prayed they him to tarry certain
days.

CHAPTER 11

AND the apostles and brethren that
were in Judæa heard that the Gentiles [a]had also received the word of
God.
2 And when Peter was come up to
Jerusalem, [b]they that were of the circumcision contended with him,
3 Saying, [c]Thou wentest in to men
uncircumcised, and didst eat with
them.
4 But Peter rehearsed *the matter* from
the beginning, and expounded *it* [d]by
order unto them, saying,
5 I [e]was in the city of Joppa praying:
and in a trance I saw a vision, A certain vessel descend, as it had been a
great sheet, let down from heaven by
four corners; and it came even to me:
6 Upon the which when I had fastened mine eyes, I considered, and saw
fourfooted beasts of the earth, and

n Ex. 34.14. Deut. 11.16. Ps. 81.9. Matt. 4.10. Luke 4.8. ch. 14.14. Col. 2.18. Rev. 14.7.
o John 4.9. Gal. 2.12.
p ch. 15.8. Eph. 3.6.
q Gal. 1.16.
r ch. 1.10.
s Gen. 18.2. Matt. 28.2-6. Mark 16.5, 6. Luke 24.4.
t Dan. 10.12.
u Pro. 14.31. Matt. 6.4. Heb. 6.10.
v Deut. 10. 17. 2 Chr. 19.7. Rom. 2.11. Gal. 2.6. Eph. 6.9. 1 Pet. 1.17.
w ch. 15.9. Rom. 2.13. 1 Cor. 12.13. Gal. 3.28. Eph. 2.13.
x Isa. 57.19. Eph. 2.17. Col. 1.20.
y Dan. 7.14. Matt. 28.18. ch. 2.22. Rom. 10.12. Eph. 1.20. 1 Pet. 3.22. Rev. 17.14.
z Luke 4.18. Heb. 1.9.
a John 3.2. Col. 2.9.
b John 14.17.
c John 21.13.
d Matt. 28. 19. Mark 16.15, 16. ch. 1.8. ch. 4.19,20.
e John 5.22. ch. 17.31. Rev. 1.7.
f Rom. 14.9. 2 Cor. 5.10. 2 Tim. 4.1. 1 Pet. 4.5.
g Isa. 53.11. Jer. 31.34. Dan. 9.24. Micah 7.18. Zech. 13.1. Mal. 4.2.

CHAP. 11

a Gen. 49.10. Zech. 2.11. Mal. 1.11. Mark 16.15. Luke 2.32. ch. 14.27. ch. 15.3.
b Gal. 2.12.
c ch. 10.28.
d Luke 1.3.
e ch. 10.9.

wild beasts, and creeping things, and
fowls of the air.
7 And I heard a voice saying unto
me, Arise, Peter; slay and eat.
8 But I said, [f]Not so, Lord: for
nothing common or unclean hath
at any time entered into my mouth.
9 But the voice answered me again
from heaven, What God hath cleansed, *that* call not thou common.
10 And this was done three times:
and all were drawn up again into
heaven.
11 And, behold, immediately there
were three men already come unto the
house where I was, sent from Çæ-să-
rē´-ă unto me.
12 And [g]the spirit bade me go with
them, nothing doubting. Moreover
these [h]six brethren accompanied me,
and we entered into the man's house:
13 And [i]he shewed us how he had
seen an angel in his house, which
stood and said unto him, Send men to
Joppa, and call for Simon, whose
surname is Peter;
14 Who shall tell thee words, whereby thou and all thy house shall be
saved.
15 And as I began to speak, the Holy
Ghost fell on them, [j]as on us at the
beginning.
16 Then remembered I the word of
the Lord, how that he said, John [k]in-
deed baptized with water; but [l]ye shall
be baptized with the Holy Ghost.
17 Forasmuch [m]then as God gave
them the like gift as *he did* unto us,
who believed on the Lord Jesus
Christ; what [n]was I, that I could
withstand God?
18 When they heard these things,
they held their peace, and glorified
God, saying, Then [o]hath God also to
the Gentiles granted repentance unto
life.
19 ¶ Now [p]they which were scattered
abroad upon the persecution that
arose about Stephen travelled as far
as Phē-nī´-çē, and Cyprus, and Ăn´-tĭ-
ŏch, preaching the word to none but
unto the Jews only.
20 And some of them were men of
Cyprus and Çȳ-rē´-nē, which, when
they were come to Ăn´-tĭ-ŏch, spake
[q]unto the Grecians, preaching [r]the
Lord Jesus.
21 And [s]the hand of the Lord was
with them: and a great number believed, and turned [t]unto the Lord.
22 ¶ Then tidings of these things
came unto the ears of the church
which was in Jerusalem: and they sent
forth [u]Barnabas, that he should go as
far as Ăn´-tĭ-ŏch.
23 Who, when he came, and had seen
the grace of God, was glad, and [v]ex-
horted them all, that with purpose of
heart they would cleave unto [w]the
Lord.
24 For he was a good man, and full of
the Holy Ghost and of faith: and
[x]much people was added unto the
Lord.
25 Then departed Barnabas to Tarsus, [y]for to seek Saul:
26 And when he had found him, he
brought him unto Ăn´-tĭ-ŏch. And it
came to pass, that a whole year they
assembled themselves [1]with the
church, and taught much people. And
the disciples were called Christians
first in Ăn´-tĭ-ŏch.
27 ¶ And in these days [z]came prophets from Jerusalem unto Ăn´-tĭ-ŏch.
28 And there stood up one of them
named Ăg´-ă-bŭs, [a]and signified by the
spirit that there should be great dearth
throughout all the world: which came
to pass in the days of Claudius Cæsar.
29 Then the disciples, every man
according to his ability, determined to
send [b]relief unto the brethren which
dwelt in Judæa:
30 Which also they did, and sent it to
the [c]elders by the hands of Barnabas
and Saul.

CHAPTER 12

NOW about that time Herod the
king [1]stretched forth *his* hands [a]to
vex certain of the church.
2 And he killed James [b]the brother
of John with the sword.
3 And because he saw it pleased the
Jews, he proceeded further to take
Peter also. (Then were [c]the days of unleavened bread.)
4 And [d]when he had apprehended
him, he put *him* in prison, and delivered *him* to four quaternions of soldiers
to keep him; intending after Easter to
bring him forth to the people.
5 Peter therefore was kept in prison:
but [2]prayer was made without ceasing
of the church unto God for him.
6 And when Herod would have
brought him forth, the same night
Peter was sleeping between two
soldiers, bound with two chains: and
the keepers before the door kept the
prison.
7 And, behold, [e]the angel of the Lord
came upon *him*, and a light shined in
the prison: and he smote Peter on the
side, and raised him up, saying, Arise

f Eze. 4.14.
g John 16.13. ch. 15.7.
h ch. 10.23.
i ch. 10.30.
j ch. 2.4.
k Matt. 3.11. Mark 1.8. Luke 3.16. John 1.26. ch. 1.5.
l Isa. 44.3. Joel. 2.28.
m Matt. 20. 14,15. ch. 15.8,9.
n Job 9.12-14. Dan. 4.35. ch. 10.47.
o Rom. 10. 12.
p ch. 8.1.
q ch. 6.1.
r ch. 8.5,35. Eph. 3.8.
s Luke 1.66.
t ch. 9.35.
u ch. 9.27.
v ch. 13.43. Jude 3.
w Deut. 10. 20. 1 Cor. 15.58. Gal. 2.20. Col. 2.6.
x ch. 2.41,47. ch.4.4. ch. 5.14. ch. 9.31.
y ch. 9.30.
1 Or, in the church.
z ch. 2.17. 1 Cor. 12.28. Eph. 4.11.
a ch. 21.10.
b Rom. 15.26. 1 Cor. 16.1. 2 Cor. 9.1. Gal. 2.10. 1 Pet. 4.11.
c 1 Pet. 5.1.

CHAP. 12

1 Or, began.
a Matt. 10. 17. John 15.20, 21.
b Matt. 4.21.
c Ex. 12.14.
d John 21.18.
2 Or, instant and earnest prayer was made.
e Ps. 34.7. Isa. 37.36. ch. 5.19. Heb. 1.14.

up quickly. And his chains fell off
from *his* hands.
8 And the angel said unto him, Gird
thyself, and bind on thy sandals. And
so he did. And he saith unto him,
Cast thy garment about thee, and
follow me.
9 And he went out, and followed
him; and [f]wist not that it was true
which was done by the angel; but
thought he [g]saw a vision.
10 When they were past the first and
the second ward, they came unto the
iron gate that leadeth unto the city;
which [h]opened to them of his own
accord: and they went out, and passed
on through one street; and forthwith
the angel departed from him.
11 And when Peter was come to himself, he said, Now I know of a surety,
that [i]the Lord hath sent his angel, and
[j]hath delivered me out of the hand of
Herod, and *from* all the expectation of
the people of the Jews.
12 And when he had considered *the*
thing, he [k]came to the house of Mary
the mother of [l]John, whose surname
was Mark; where many were gathered
together praying.
13 And as Peter knocked at the door
of the gate, a damsel came [3]to hearken,
named Rhoda.
14 And when she knew Peter's voice,
she opened not the gate for gladness,
but ran in, and told how Peter stood
before the gate.
15 And they said unto her, Thou art
mad. But she constantly affirmed that
it was even so. Then said they, It [m]is
his angel.
16 But Peter continued knocking:
and when they had opened *the door*,
and saw him, they were astonished.
17 But he, beckoning unto them with
the hand to hold their peace, declared
unto them how the Lord had brought
him out of the prison. And he said,
Go shew these things unto James, and
to the brethren. And he departed, and
went into another place.
18 Now as soon as it was day, there
was no small stir among the soldiers,
what was become of Peter.
19 And when Herod had sought for
him, and found him not, he examined
the keepers, and commanded that *they*
should be put to death. And he went
down from Judæa to Çæ-ṡă-rē´-ă, and
there abode.
20 ¶ And Herod [4]was highly displeased with them of Tyre and Ṡī´-dŏn:
but they came with one accord to him,
and, having made Blăs´-tŭs [5]the king's
chamberlain their friend, desired
peace; because their [n]country was
nourished by the king's *country*.
21 And upon a set day Herod, arrayed in royal apparel, sat upon his
throne, and made an oration unto
them.
22 And the people gave a shout, *say-*
ing, [o]*It is* the voice of a god, and not of
a man.
23 And immediately the angel of the
Lord [p]smote him, because [q]he gave
not God the glory: and he was eaten
of worms, and gave up the ghost.
24 ¶ But [r]the word of God grew and
multiplied.
25 And Barnabas and Saul returned
from Jerusalem, when they had fulfilled *their* [6]ministry, [s]and took with
them John, whose surname was Mark.

CHAPTER 13

NOW there were [a]in the church
that was at Ăn´-tĭ-ŏch certain prophets and teachers; as [b]Barnabas, and
Simeon that was called Nī´-ġĕr, and
Lû´-cĭ-ŭs [c]of Çȳ-rē´-nē, and Măn´-ā-ĕn,
[1]which had been brought up with
Herod the tē´-trärch, and Saul.
2 As they ministered to the Lord, and
fasted, the Holy Ghost said, Separate
[d]me Barnabas and Saul for the work
[e]whereunto I have called them.
3 And when they had fasted and
prayed, and laid *their* hands on them,
they sent *them* away.
4 ¶ So they, being sent forth by the
Holy Ghost, departed unto Sĕ-leû´-
çĭ-ă; and from thence they sailed to
[f]Cyprus.
5 And when they were at Săl´-ă-mĭs,
they preached the word of God in the
synagogues of the Jews: and they had
also [g]John to *their* minister.
6 And when they had gone through
the isle unto Pā´-phŏs, they found a
certain sorcerer, a false prophet, a
Jew, whose name *was* Bär–jē´-sŭs:
7 Which was with the deputy of the
country, Sĕr´-ġĭ-ŭs Paulus, a prudent
man; who called for Barnabas and
Saul, and desired to hear the word of
God.
8 But [h]Ĕl´-ȳ-măs the sorcerer (for so
is his name by interpretation) withstood them, seeking to turn away the
deputy from the faith.
9 Then [2]Saul, (who also *is called*
[3]Paul,) filled with the Holy Ghost, set
his eyes on him,
10 And said, O full of all subtilty and
all mischief, [i]*thou* child of the devil,
thou enemy of all righteousness, wilt

f Ps. 126.1.
g ch. 10.3.
h ch. 16.26.
i Ps. 34.7. Dan. 6.22.
j Job 5.19. Ps. 33.18. 2 Pet. 2.9.
k ch. 4.23.
l ch. 13.5. 2 Tim. 4.11.
3 Or, to ask who was there.
m Gen. 48.16. Matt. 18.10. Luke 24.37, 38.
4 Or, bare an hostile mind, intending war.
5 that was over the king's bedchamber.
n 1 Ki. 5.9. Eze. 27.17.
o Jude 16.
p Ex. 12.12, 23,29. 1 Sam. 25. 38. 2 Sam. 24. 17. 2 Chr. 32.21. Dan. 4.30-37.
q Lev. 10.3. Deut. 28.58, 59. Ps. 115.1. Isa. 42.8. 1 Cor. 1.29. Rev. 15.4.
r Isa. 55.11. Dan. 2.34. ch. 6.7.
6 Or, charge.
s ch. 15.37.

CHAP. 13

a ch. 14.26.
b ch. 9.27.
c Rom. 16. 21.
1 Or, Herod's foster-brother.
d Num. 8.14. Gal. 1.15.
e Matt. 9.38. Rom. 10.15. Eph. 3.7,8. 1 Tim. 2.7. Heb. 5.4.
f ch. 4.36.
g ch. 12.25.
h Ex. 7.11. 2 Tim. 3.8.
2 That is, Destroyer.
3 That is, Worker.
i Matt. 13.38. John 8.44. 1 John 3.8.

thou not cease to pervert the right
ways of the Lord?
11 And now, behold, [j]the hand of
the Lord *is* upon thee, and thou shalt
be blind, not seeing the sun for a
season. And immediately there fell on
him a mist and a darkness; and he
went about seeking some to lead him
by the hand.
12 Then the deputy, when he saw
what was done, believed, being astonished at the doctrine of the Lord.
13 Now when Paul and his company
loosed from Pā-phŏs, they came to
Pĕr-gă in Păm-phy̆l-ĭ-ă: and John [k]de-
parting from them returned to Jerusalem.
14 ¶ But when they departed from
Pĕr-gă, they came to Ăn-tĭ-ŏch in Pi-
sĭd-ĭ-ă, and went into the synagogue
on the sabbath day, and sat down.
15 And [l]after the reading of the law
and the prophets the rulers of the
synagogue sent unto them, saying,
Ye men *and* brethren, if ye [m]have any
word of exhortation for the people,
say on.
16 Then Paul stood up, and beckoning with *his* hand said, Men of Israel,
and ye that fear God, give audience.
17 The God of this people of Israel
chose our fathers, and exalted the
people when they dwelt as strangers
in the land of Egypt, and with an high
arm brought he them out of it.
18 And about the time of forty years
[4]suffered he their manners in the
wilderness.
19 And when he had destroyed seven
nations in the land of Chā-nă-ăn, he
divided their land to them by lot.
20 And after that he gave *unto them*
judges about the space of four hundred and fifty years, until Samuel the
prophet.
21 And afterward they desired a
king: and God gave unto them Saul
the son of Çĭs, a man of the tribe of
Benjamin, by the space of forty years.
22 And [n]when he had removed him,
he raised up unto them David to be
their king; to whom also he gave testimony, and said, I have found David
the *son* of Jesse, a man after mine own
heart, which shall fulfil all my will.
23 Of [o]this man's seed hath God
according to [p]*his* promise raised unto
Israel [q]a Saviour, Jesus:
24 When John had first preached before his coming the baptism of repentance to all the people of Israel.
25 And as John fulfilled his course,
he said, Whom think ye that I am? I

j Ex. 9.3. 2 Ki. 6.18. Ps. 32.4.
k ch. 15.38.
l Luke 4.16.
m Heb. 13. 22.
4 etropophoresen, perhaps for etrophophoresen, bore, or, fed them, as a nurse beareth, or, feedeth her child. (Ex. 19.4. Deut. 1.31. Deut. 32.11, 12. Isa. 46.3,4. Isa. 63.9. Hos. 11.3.) according to the LXX. and so Chrysostom.
n Hosea 13. 11.
o Ps. 132.11. Isa. 11.1. Luke 1.32. Rom. 1.3.
p 2 Sam. 7.12.
q Rom. 11. 26.
r 1 Cor. 2.8.
s Matt. 28.6. ch. 2.24,32. Heb. 13.20.
t 1 Cor. 15.5.
u Gen. 3.15. Gen. 12.3. Rom. 4.13. Gal. 3.16.
v Ps. 2.7. Heb. 5.5.
5 ta osia, holy, or, just things: which word the LXX., both in the place of Isa. 55.3, and in many others, use for that which is in the Hebrew, mercies.
w Ps. 16.10.
6 Or, after he had in his own age served the will of God.
x Dan. 9.24. Zech. 13.1. Luke 24.47. John 1.29. Col. 1.14.
y Isa. 53.11. 1 Cor. 6.11. Gal. 2.16. Eph. 5.26. Heb. 10.22.
z Hab. 1.5.

am not *he*. But, behold, there cometh
one after me, whose shoes of *his* feet
am not worthy to loose.
26 Men *and* brethren, children of the
stock of Abraham, and whosoever
among you feareth God, to you is the
word of this salvation sent.
27 For they that dwell at Jerusalem
and their rulers, [r]because they knew
him not, nor yet the voices of the
prophets which are read every sabbath day, they have fulfilled *them* in
condemning *him*.
28 And though they found no cause
of death *in him*, yet desired they Pilate
that he should be slain.
29 And when they had fulfilled all
that was written of him, they took *him*
down from the tree, and laid *him* in a
sepulchre.
30 But [s]God raised him from the
dead:
31 And [t]he was seen many days of
them which came up with him from
Galilee to Jerusalem, who are his
witnesses unto the people.
32 And we declare unto you glad
tidings, how that the [u]promise which
was made unto the fathers,
33 God hath fulfilled the same unto
us their children, in that he hath raised
up Jesus again; as it is also written
in the second psalm, Thou [v]art
my Son, this day have I begotten
thee.
34 And as concerning that he raised
him up from the dead, *now* no more to
return to corruption, he said on this
wise, I will give you the sure [5]mercies
of David.
35 Wherefore he saith also in another
psalm, [w]Thou shalt not suffer thine
Holy One to see corruption.
36 For David, [6]after he had served
his own generation by the will of God,
fell on sleep, and was laid unto his
fathers, and saw corruption:
37 But he, whom God raised again,
saw no corruption.
38 ¶ Be it known unto you therefore,
men *and* brethren, [x]that through this
man is preached unto you the forgiveness of sins:
39 And [y]by him all that believe are
justified from all things, from which
ye could not be justified by the law of
Moses.
40 Beware therefore, lest that come
upon you, which is spoken of in the
[z]prophets;
41 Behold, ye despisers, and wonder,
and perish: for I work a work in your
days, a work which ye shall in no wise

believe, though a man declare it unto
you.
42 And when the Jews were gone out
of the synagogue, the Gentiles besought that these words might be
preached to them [7]the next sabbath.
43 Now when the congregation was
broken up, many of the Jews and religious proselytes followed Paul and
Barnabas: who, speaking to them,
persuaded them to continue in [a]the
grace of God.
44 ¶ And the next sabbath day came
almost the whole city together to hear
the word of God.
45 But when the Jews saw the multitudes, they were filled with envy, and
[b]spake against those things which
were spoken by Paul, contradicting
and blaspheming.
46 Then Paul and Barnabas waxed
bold, and said, [c]It was necessary that
the word of God should first have
been spoken to you: but [d]seeing ye put
it from you, and judge yourselves un-
worthy of everlasting life, lo, we turn
to the Gentiles.
47 For so hath the Lord commanded
us, *saying*, [e]I have set thee to be a light
of the Gentiles, that thou shouldest be
for salvation unto the ends of the
earth.
48 And when the Gentiles heard this,
they were glad, and glorified the word
of the Lord: [f]and as many as were ordained to eternal life believed.
49 And the word of the Lord was
published throughout all the region.
50 But the Jews stirred up the devout
and honourable women, and the chief
men of the city, and raised [g]persecu-
tion against Paul and Barnabas, and
expelled them out of their coasts.
51 But [h]they shook off the dust of
their feet against them, and came unto
Ī-cō-́nĭ-ŭm.
52 And the disciples [i]were filled with
joy, and with the Holy Ghost.

CHAPTER 14

AND it came to pass in Ī-cō-́nĭ-ŭm,
that they went both together into
the synagogue of the Jews, and so
spake, that a great [a]multitude both of
the Jews and also of the Greeks believed.
2 But the unbelieving Jews stirred
up the Gentiles, and made their
minds evil affected against the
brethren.
3 Long time therefore abode they
speaking boldly in the Lord, which
[b]gave testimony unto the word of his
grace, and granted signs and wonders
to be done by their hands.
4 But the multitude of the city was
divided: and part held with the Jews,
and part with the apostles.
5 And when there was an assault
made both of the Gentiles, and also of
the Jews with their rulers, to [c]use *them*
despitefully, and to stone them,
6 They were ware of *it*, and [d]fled unto
Lȳs-́tră and Dĕr-́bē, cities of Lȳ-că-
ō-́nĭ-ă, and unto the region that lieth
round about:
7 And there they preached the gospel.
8 ¶ And [e]there sat a certain man at
Lȳs-́tră, impotent in his feet, being a
cripple from his mother's womb, who
never had walked:
9 The same heard Paul speak: who
stedfastly beholding him, and perceiving [f]that he had faith to be healed,
10 Said with a loud voice, [g]Stand upright on thy feet. And he leaped and
walked.
11 And when the people saw what
Paul had done, they lifted up their
voices, saying in the speech of Lȳ-că-
ō-́nĭ-ă, [h]The gods are come down to
us in the likeness of men.
12 And they called Barnabas, Jupiter; and Paul, Mĕr-cū-́rĭ-ŭs, because
he was the chief speaker.
13 Then the priest of Jupiter, which
was before their city, brought oxen
and garlands unto the gates, and
[i]would have done sacrifice with the
people.
14 *Which* when the apostles, Barnabas and Paul, heard *of*, [j]they rent their
clothes, and ran in among the people,
crying out,
15 And saying, Sirs, why do ye these
things? [k]We also are men of like
passions with you, and preach unto
you that ye should turn from [l]these
vanities [m]unto the living God, [n]which
made heaven, and earth, and the sea,
and all things that are therein:
16 Who [o]in times past suffered all
nations to walk in their own ways.
17 Nevertheless [p]he left not himself
without witness, in that he did good,
and [q]gave us rain from heaven, and
fruitful seasons, filling our hearts with
food and gladness.
18 And with these sayings scarce restrained they the people, that they had
not done sacrifice unto them.
19 ¶ And [r]there came thither *certain*
Jews from Ăn-́tĭ-ŏch and Ī-cō-́nĭ-ŭm,
who persuaded the people, [s]and, having stoned Paul, drew *him* out of the
city, supposing he [t]had been dead.

7 in the week between, or, in the sabbath between.
a Luke 1.32. ch. 11.23. Titus 2.11. 1 Pet. 5.12.
b ch. 18.6. 1 Pet. 4.4. Jude 10.
c Matt. 10.6. ch. 3.26. Rom. 1.16.
d Ex. 32.10. Deut. 32.21. Isa. 52.15. Matt. 21.43. Rom. 10.19.
e Isa. 42.6. Luke 2.32.
f ch. 2.47. Rom. 8.30. 2 Tim. 2.19.
g Matt. 5.12. ch. 7.52. 2 Tim. 3.11.
h Luke 9.5.
i Matt. 5.12. ch. 2.46. 1 Pet. 1.8.

CHAP. 14

a Isa. 11.11. ch. 17.4.
b Mark 16. 20. Rom. 15.19. 1 Cor. 2.4. Heb. 2.4.
c 1 Thes. 2. 14-16. 2 Tim. 3.11.
d Matt. 10. 23. ch. 16.1,2. 2 Tim. 3.11.
e John 5.5. ch. 3.2.
f Matt. 8.10. Matt. 9.28. Mark 1.40, 41.
g Isa. 35.6.
h ch. 28.6.
i Dan. 2.46.
j Matt. 26.65.
k Jas. 5.17. Rev. 19.10.
l Jer. 14.22. Amos 2.4. 1 Cor. 8.4.
m 1 Thes. 1.9.
n Rev. 14.7.
o Ps. 81.12. 1 Pet. 4.3.
p ch. 17.27. Rom. 1.20.
q Lev. 26.4. Deut. 11.14. Job. 5.10. Ps. 65.10. Matt. 5.45.
r ch. 13.45.
s 2 Cor. 11. 25.
t 2 Cor. 1.8.

20 Howbeit, as the disciples stood
round about him, he rose up, and
came into the city: and the next day
he departed with Barnabas to Dĕr'-bē.
21 And when they had preached the
gospel to that city, and [1]had taught
many, they returned again to Lȳs'-tră,
and *to* Ī-cō'-nĭ-ŭm, and Ăn'-tĭ-ŏch,
22 Confirming the souls of the disciples, *and* exhorting them to continue in the faith, and that we must
[u]through much tribulation enter into
the kingdom of God.
23 And when they had [v]ordained
them elders in every church, and had
prayed with fasting, they commended
them to the Lord, on whom they believed.
24 And after they had passed
throughout Pī-sĭd'-ĭ-ă, they came to
Păm-phȳl'-ĭ-ă.
25 And when they had preached the
word in Pĕr'-gă, they went down into
Ăt-tā'-lĭ-ă:
26 And thence sailed to Ăn'-tĭ-ŏch,
from whence [w]they had been recommended to the grace of God for the
work which they fulfilled.
27 And when they were come, and
had gathered the church together,
they rehearsed all that God had done
with them, and how he had [x]opened
the door of faith unto the Gentiles.
28 And there they abode long time
with the disciples.

CHAPTER 15

AND [a]certain men which came
down from Judæa taught the
brethren, *and said*, [b]Except ye be circumcised [c]after the manner of Moses,
ye cannot be saved.
2 When therefore Paul and Barnabas
had no small dissension and disputa-
tion with them, they determined that
[d]Paul and Barnabas, and certain other
of them, should go up to Jerusalem
unto the apostles and elders about
this question.
3 And [e]being brought on their way by
the church, they passed through Phē-
nī'-çē and Să-mâr'-ĭ-ă, declaring [f]the
conversion of the Gentiles: and they
caused great joy unto all the brethren.
4 And when they were come to Jerusalem, they were received of the
church, and *of* the apostles and elders,
and they declared all things that God
had done with them.
5 But there [1]rose up certain of the
sect of the Pharisees which believed,
saying, That it was needful to circumcise them, and to command *them* to
keep the law of Moses.
6 ¶ And the apostles and elders came
together for to consider of this matter.
7 And when there had been much
disputing, Peter rose up, and said unto
them, Men *and* brethren, ye know how
that a good while ago God made
choice among us, that the Gentiles by
my mouth should hear the word of the
gospel, and believe.
8 And God, [g]which knoweth the
hearts, bare them witness, [h]giving
them the Holy Ghost, even as *he did*
unto us;
9 And [i]put no difference between us
and them, [j]purifying their hearts by
faith.
10 Now therefore why tempt ye God,
to [k]put a yoke upon the neck of the
disciples, which neither our fathers
nor we were able to bear?
11 But [l]we believe that through the
grace of the Lord Jesus Christ we shall
be saved, even as they.
12 ¶ Then all the multitude kept
silence, and gave audience to Barnabas and Paul, declaring what miracles
and wonders God had wrought among
the Gentiles by them.
13 ¶ And after they had held their
peace, James [m]answered, saying, Men
and brethren, hearken unto me:
14 Simeon hath declared how God
at the first did visit the Gentiles, to
take out of them a people for his
name.
15 And to this agree the [n]words of
the prophets; as it is written,
16 After [o]this I will return, and will
build again the tabernacle of David,
which is fallen down; and I will build
again the ruins thereof, and I will set
it up:
17 That the residue of men might
seek after the Lord, and all the Gentiles, upon whom my name is called,
saith the Lord, who doeth all these
things.
18 Known unto God are all his works
from the beginning of the world.
19 Wherefore my sentence is, that
we trouble not them, which from
among the Gentiles [p]are turned to
God:
20 But that we write unto them, that
they abstain [q]from pollutions of idols,
and *from* [r]fornication, and *from* things
strangled, [s]and *from* blood.
21 For Moses of old time hath in
every city them that preach him, being [t]read in the synagogues every sabbath day.

1 had made many disciples.
u Matt. 10. 38. John 15.18. Rom. 8.17. 2 Tim. 2.11.
v Mark 3.12. Titus 1.5.
w ch. 13.1,3.
x 1 Cor. 16.9. 2 Cor. 2.12. Col. 4.3. Rev. 3.8.

CHAP. 15

a Gal. 2.12.
b John 7.22. Gal. 5.2. Phil. 3.2.
c Gen. 17.10.
d Gal. 2.1.
e Rom. 15. 24. 1 Cor. 16.6.
f ch. 14.27.
1 Or, rose up, said they, certain.
g 1 Chr. 28.9. 1 Chr. 29.17. Jer. 11.20. ch. 1.24. Heb. 4.13. Rev. 2.23.
h Luke 4.18. ch. 10.44. Heb. 1.9.
i Rom. 10.11.
j ch. 10.43. Rom. 8.1. 1 Cor. 1.2. Col. 1.14. 1 Pet. 1.22.
k Matt. 23.4. Gal. 5.1.
l Isa. 53.11. Matt. 20.28. Rom. 3.24. Eph. 1.7.
m ch. 12.17.
n Isa. 11.10.
o Isa. 54.1-5. Hosea 3.5. Amos 9.11. Micah 5.2.
p 1 Thes. 1.9.
q Gen. 35.2. Ex. 20.3. Eze. 20.30. 1 Cor. 8.1. Rev. 2.20.
r 1 Cor. 6.9. Col. 3.5. 1 Thes. 4.3. 1 Pet. 4.3.
s Gen. 9.4. Lev. 3.17. 1 Sam. 14. 32.
t ch. 13.15.

22 Then pleased it the apostles and
elders, with the whole church, to send
chosen men of their own company to
Ăn-ʹtĭ-ŏch with Paul and Barnabas;
namely, Judas surnamed [u]Bär-ʹsă-băs,
and Silas, chief men among the brethren:
23 And they wrote *letters* by them
after this manner; The apostles and
elders and brethren *send* greeting unto
the brethren which are of the Gentiles
in Ăn-ʹtĭ-ŏch and Syria and Çĭ-lĭç-ʹĭ-ă:
24 Forasmuch as we have heard, that
certain [v]which went out from us have
troubled you with words, subverting
your souls, saying, *Ye must* be circumcised,
and keep the law: to whom we
gave no *such* commandment:
25 It seemed good unto us, being
assembled with one accord, to send
chosen men unto you with our beloved
Barnabas and Paul,
26 Men [w]that have hazarded their
lives for the name of our Lord Jesus
Christ.
27 We have sent therefore Judas and
Silas, who shall also tell *you* the same
things by [2]mouth.
28 For it seemed good to [x]the Holy
Ghost, and to us, to lay upon you no
greater burden than these necessary
things;
29 That [y]ye abstain from meats offered
to idols, and [z]from blood, and from
things strangled, and from fornication:
from which if ye keep yourselves, ye
shall do well. Fare ye well.
30 So when they were dismissed, they
came to Ăn-ʹtĭ-ŏch: and when they had
gathered the multitude together, they
delivered the epistle:
31 *Which* when they had read, they
rejoiced for the [3]consolation.
32 And Judas and Silas, being [a]prophets
also themselves, [b]exhorted the
brethren with many words, and confirmed
them.
33 And after they had tarried *there*
a space, they were let [c]go in peace
from the brethren unto the apostles.
34 Notwithstanding it pleased Silas
to abide there still.
35 Paul [d]also and Barnabas continued
in Ăn-ʹtĭ-ŏch, teaching and
preaching the word of the Lord, with
many others also.
36 ¶ And some days after Paul said
unto Barnabas, Let us go again and
visit our brethren [e]in every city where
we have preached the word of the
Lord, *and see* how they do.
37 And Barnabas determined to take

u ch. 1.23.
v Jer. 23.16. Gal. 2.4. Titus 1.10. 1 John 2.19.
w Judg. 5.18. ch. 13.50. 1 Cor. 15.30. 2 Cor. 11.23, 26. Phil. 2.29, 30.
2 word.
x John 16.13. 1 Cor. 7.25, 40.
y ch. 21.25. Rev. 2.14.
z Lev. 17.14.
3 Or, exhortation.
a ch. 13.1. 1 Cor. 12.28.
b ch. 14.22.
c 1 Cor. 16. 11. Heb. 11.31.
d ch. 13.1.
e ch. 14.1.
f ch. 12.12. Col. 4.10. 2 Tim. 4.11. Philem. 24.
g ch. 13.13.

CHAP. 16

a Matt. 10. 23. ch. 14.6. 2 Tim. 3.11.
b ch. 19.22. Rom. 16.21. 1 Cor. 4.17. Phil. 2.19. 1 Thes. 3.2. 1 Tim. 1.2. 2 Tim. 1.2.
c ch. 6.3. 2 Tim. 3.15.
d 1 Cor. 9.20. Gal. 2.3.
e ch. 15.28.
f ch. 15.41. Col. 1.23. Jude 20,21.
g 2 Cor. 2.12. 2 Tim. 4.13.
h Num. 12.6. ch. 9.10-12. ch. 10.30. 2 Cor. 12.1-4.
i Ps. 119.60. Eccl. 9.10. Rom. 12.11. 2 Cor. 2.13.

with them [f]John, whose surname was
Mark.
38 But Paul thought not good to take
him with them, [g]who departed from
them from Păm-phỹl-ʹĭ-ă, and went
not with them to the work.
39 And the contention was so sharp
between them, that they departed
asunder one from the other: and so
Barnabas took Mark, and sailed unto
Cyprus;
40 And Paul chose Silas, and departed,
being recommended by the brethren
unto the grace of God.
41 And he went through Syria and
Çĭ-lĭç-ʹĭ-ă, confirming the churches.

CHAPTER 16

THEN came he to [a]Dĕr-ʹbē and
Lỹs-ʹtră: and, behold, a certain
disciple was there, [b]named Timotheus,
the son of a certain woman, which was
a Jewess, and believed; but his father
was a Greek:
2 Which [c]was well reported of by the
brethren that were at Lỹs-ʹtră and Ī-cō-ʹnĭ-ŭm.
3 Him would Paul have to go forth
with him; and [d]took and circumcised
him because of the Jews which were
in those quarters: for they knew all
that his father was a Greek.
4 And as they went through the cities,
they delivered them the decrees
for to keep, that [e]were ordained of the
apostles and elders which were at
Jerusalem.
5 And [f]so were the churches established
in the faith, and increased in
number daily.
6 Now when they had gone throughout
Phrỹg-ʹĭ-ă and the region of Galatia,
and were forbidden of the Holy
Ghost to preach the word in Asia,
7 After they were come to Mỹs-ʹĭ-ă,
they assayed to go into Bĭ-thỹn-ʹĭ-ă: but
the Spirit suffered them not.
8 And they passing by Mỹs-ʹĭ-ă came
down to [g]Trō-ʹăs.
9 And a [h]vision appeared to Paul in
the night; There stood a man of Măç-ē-dō-ʹnĭ-ă,
and prayed him, saying,
Come over into Măç-ē-dō-ʹnĭ-ă, and
help us.
10 And after he had seen the vision,
immediately we endeavoured to [i]go
into Măç-ē-dō-ʹnĭ-ă, assuredly gathering
that the Lord had called us for to
preach the gospel unto them.
11 Therefore loosing from Trō-ʹăs, we
came with a straight course to Săm-ō-thrā-ʹçĭ-ă,
and the next *day* to Nē-ă-ʹpō-lĭs;

12 And from thence to [j]Philippi,
which is [1]the chief city of that part of
Măç-ē-dō-nĭ-ă, *and* a colony: and we
were in that city abiding certain days.
13 And on the [2]sabbath we went out
of the city by a river side, where prayer
was wont to be made; and we sat
down, and spake unto the women
which resorted *thither*.
14 ¶ And a certain woman named
Lydia, a seller of purple, of the city of
[k]Thȳ-ă-tī-ră, which worshipped God,
heard *us:* whose heart [l]the Lord opened,
that she attended unto the things
which were spoken of Paul.
15 And when she was baptized, and
her household, she besought *us*, saying,
If ye have judged me to be faithful
[m]to the Lord, come into my house,
and abide *there*. And she [n]constrained
us.
16 ¶ And it came to pass, as we went
to prayer, a certain [o]damsel possessed
with a spirit [3]of divination met us,
which brought her masters [p]much
gain by soothsaying:
17 The same followed Paul and us,
and cried, saying, These men are the
servants of the most high God, which
shew unto us the way of salvation.
18 And this did she many days. But
Paul, being [q]grieved, turned and said
to the spirit, I command thee in the
name of Jesus Christ to come out of
her; [r]And he came out the same hour.
19 ¶ And [s]when her masters saw that
the hope of their gains was gone, [t]they
caught Paul and Silas, and [u]drew
them into the [4]marketplace unto the
rulers,
20 And brought them to the magistrates,
saying, These men, being Jews,
do [v]exceedingly trouble our city,
21 And teach customs, which are not
lawful for us to receive, neither to observe,
being Romans.
22 And the multitude rose up together
against them: and the magistrates
rent off their clothes, and
[w]commanded to beat *them*.
23 And [x]when they had laid many
stripes upon them, they cast *them* into
prison, charging the jailor to keep
them safely:
24 Who, having received such a
charge, thrust them into the inner
prison, and made their feet fast in the
[y]stocks.
25 ¶ And at midnight Paul and Silas
prayed, and [z]sang praises unto God:
and the prisoners heard them.
26 And [a]suddenly there was a great
earthquake, so that the foundations

[j] Phil. 1.1.
1 Or, the first.
2 sabbath day.
[k] Rev. 2.18.
[l] Ps. 110.3. Isa. 50.5. Luke 24.45. Eph. 1.17.
[m] Gal. 6.10.
[n] Gen. 19.3. Judg. 19.21. Luke 24.29.
[o] 1 Sam. 28.7.
3 Or, of Python.
[p] ch. 19.24.
[q] Mark 1.25, 34.
[r] Mark 16.17.
[s] ch. 19.25. Phil. 3.19.
[t] 2 Cor. 6.5.
[u] Matt. 10. 18.
4 Or, court.
[v] 1 Ki. 18.17. ch. 17.6.
[w] 2 Cor. 6.5.
[x] Luke 21.12. Eph. 3.1,13.
[y] Ps. 105.18. Jer. 20.2.
[z] ch. 5.41. Col. 1.24. 2 Tim. 1.8.
[a] Matt. 28.2. ch. 4.31.
[b] ch. 5.19.
[c] Ex. 20.13.
[d] Luke 3.10. ch. 2.37.
[e] Isa. 45.22. John 6.47. 1 John 5.10.
[f] Luke 5.29.
[g] 1 Sam. 2.1. 1 Chr. 16.10. Ps. 5.11. Ps. 9.14. Ps. 13.5. Ps. 20.5. Rom. 5.2. Heb. 3.6. 1 Pet. 1.6,8.
[h] ch. 22.25.
[i] Ps. 37.6. Matt. 10.16.
[j] Matt. 8.34. Luke 5.8.
[k] Ps. 51.12, 13. Luke 22.32. 2 Cor. 1.4. 1 Thes. 3.2, 3.

of the prison were shaken: and immediately
[b]all the doors were opened,
and every one's bands were loosed.
27 And the keeper of the prison
awaking out of his sleep, and seeing
the prison doors open, he drew out his
sword, and would have killed himself,
supposing that the prisoners had been
fled.
28 But Paul cried with a loud voice,
saying, [c]Do thyself no harm: for we
are all here.
29 Then he called for a light, and
sprang in, and came trembling, and
fell down before Paul and Silas,
30 And brought them out, and said,
Sirs, what [d]must I do to be saved?
31 And they said, [e]Believe on the
Lord Jesus Christ, and thou shalt be
saved, and thy house.
32 And they spake unto him the word
of the Lord, and to all that were in his
house.
33 And he took them the same hour
of the night, and washed *their* stripes;
and was baptized, he and all his,
straightway.
34 And when he had brought them
into his house, [f]he set meat before
them, [g]and rejoiced, believing in God
with all his house.
35 And when it was day, the magistrates
sent the serjeants, saying, Let
those men go.
36 And the keeper of the prison told
this saying to Paul, The magistrates
have sent to let you go: now therefore
depart, and go in peace.
37 But Paul said unto them, They
have beaten us openly uncondemned,
[h]being Romans, and have cast *us* into
prison; and now do they thrust us out
privily? nay verily; [i]but let them come
themselves and fetch us out.
38 And the serjeants told these
words unto the magistrates: and they
feared, when they heard that they
were Romans.
39 And they came and besought
them, and brought *them* out, [j]and desired
them to depart out of the city.
40 And they went out of the prison,
and entered into *the house of* Lydia:
and when they had seen the brethren,
they [k]comforted them, and departed.

CHAPTER 17

NOW when they had passed
through Ăm-phĭp-ŏ-lĭs and Ăp-
ŏl-lō-nĭ-ă, they came to Thĕss-ă-lō-
nĭ-că, where was a synagogue of the
Jews:
2 And Paul, as his manner was, went

[a]in unto them, and three sabbath days reasoned with them out of the scriptures,

3 Opening and alleging, [b]that Christ must needs have suffered, and risen again from the dead; and that this Jesus, [1]whom I preach unto you, is Christ.

4 And [c]some of them believed, and consorted with Paul [d]and Silas; and of the devout Greeks a great multitude, and of the chief women not a few.

5 ¶ But the Jews which believed not, moved with envy, took unto them certain lewd fellows of the baser sort, and gathered a company, and set all the city on an uproar, and assaulted the house [e]of Jā-ṣọn, and sought to bring them out to the people.

6 And when they found them not, they drew Jā-ṣọn and certain brethren unto the rulers of the city, crying, These [f]that have turned the world upside down are come hither also;

7 Whom Jā-ṣọn hath received: and these all [g]do contrary to the decrees of Cæsar, saying [h]that there is another king, *one* Jesus.

8 And they troubled the people and the rulers of the city, when they heard these things.

9 And when they had taken security of Jā-ṣọn, and of the other, they let them go.

10 ¶ And [i]the brethren immediately sent away Paul and Silas by night unto Bĕ-rē-ă: who coming *thither* went into the synagogue of the Jews.

11 These were more noble than those in Thĕss-ă-lō-nī-că, in that they received the word with all readiness of mind, and searched [j]the scriptures daily, whether those things were so.

12 Therefore many of them believed; also of honourable women which were Greeks, and of men, not a few.

13 But when the Jews of Thĕss-ă-lō-nī-că had knowledge that the word of God was preached of Paul at Bĕ-rē-ă, [k]they came thither also, and stirred up the people.

14 And [l]then immediately the brethren sent away Paul to go as it were to the sea: but Silas and Timotheus abode there still.

15 And they that conducted Paul brought him unto Athens: and receiving [m]a commandment unto Silas and Timotheus for to come to him with all speed, they departed.

16 ¶ Now while Paul waited for them at Athens, [n]his spirit was stirred in him, when he saw the city [2]wholly given to idolatry.

17 Therefore disputed he in the synagogue with the Jews, and with the devout persons, and in the market daily with them that met with him.

18 Then certain philosophers of the Ĕp-ĭ-cū-rē-ăns, and of the Stō-ĭcks, encountered him. And some said, What will this [3]babbler say? other some, He seemeth to be a setter forth of strange gods: because he preached unto them Jesus, and the resurrection.

19 And they took him, and brought him unto [4]Ăr-ĕ-ŏp-ă-gŭs, saying, May we know what this new doctrine, whereof thou speakest, *is?*

20 For thou bringest certain strange things to our ears: we would know therefore what these things mean.

21 (For all the Athenians and strangers which were there spent their time in nothing else, but either to tell, or to hear some new thing.)

22 ¶ Then Paul stood in the midst of [5]Mars' hill, and said, *Ye* men of Athens, I perceive that in all things ye are [o]too superstitious.

23 For as I passed by, and beheld your [6]devotions, I found an altar with this inscription, [p]TO THE UNKNOWN GOD. Whom therefore ye ignorantly worship, him declare I unto you.

24 God [q]that made the world and all things therein, seeing that he is [r]Lord of heaven and earth, dwelleth [s]not in temples made with hands;

25 Neither is worshipped with men's hands, [t]as though he needed any thing, seeing [u]he giveth to all life, and breath, and all things;

26 And hath made of one blood all nations of men for to dwell on all the face of the earth, and [v]hath determined the times before appointed, and [w]the bounds of their habitation;

27 That [x]they should seek the Lord, if haply they might feel after him, and find him, [y]though he be not far from every one of us:

28 For [z]in him we live, and move, and have our being; [a]as certain also of your own poets have said, For we are also his offspring.

29 Forasmuch then as we are the offspring of God, [b]we ought not to think that the Godhead is like unto gold, or silver, or stone, graven by art and man's device.

30 And [c]the times of this ignorance God winked at; but [d]now commandeth all men every where to repent:

31 Because he hath appointed a day,

CHAP. 17

a Luke 4.16. ch. 8.37. ch. 9.20. ch. 14.1. ch. 16.13.
b Ps. 22. Isa. 53. Zech. 13.7. ch. 18.28. Gal. 3.1. Heb. 2.8-10.
1 Or, whom, said he, I preach.
c ch. 28.24.
d ch. 15.22, 27,32,40.
e Rom. 16. 21.
f 1 Ki. 18.17.
g Ezra 4.12.
h Luke 23.2. 1 Pet. 2.13.
i ch. 9.25.
j Isa. 34.16. Luke 16.29.
k Luke 11.52. 1 Thes. 2.15.
l Matt. 10.23.
m ch. 18.5.
n Ex. 32.19, 20. Ps. 119.158. Mark 3.5. 2 Pet. 2.8.
2 Or, full of idols.
3 Or, base fellow.
4 Or, Mars' hill. It was the highest court in Athens.
5 Or, the court of the Areopagites.
o Jer. 50.38.
6 Or, gods that ye worship.
p Ps. 147.20. Eph. 2.12.
q Ps. 146. 5,6. Isa. 40.12, 28. ch. 14.15. Heb. 1.1,2.
r Matt. 11.25.
s ch. 7.48.
t Ps. 50.8.
u Num. 16. 22. Isa. 42.5. Dan. 4.35.
v Deut. 30. 20.
w Deut. 32.8.
x Rom. 1.20.
y 1 Ki. 8.27. Jer. 23.24.
z 1 Sam. 25. 29. Col. 1.17. Heb. 1.3.
a Titus 1.12.
b Isa. 40.18.
c Rom. 3.25.
d Luke 24.47.

in the which [e]he will judge the world in righteousness by *that* man whom he hath ordained; *whereof* he hath [7]given assurance unto all *men*, in that he hath raised him from the dead.

32 ¶ And when they heard of the resurrection of the dead, some mocked: and others said, We will hear thee again of this *matter*.

33 So Paul departed from among them.

34 Howbeit [f]certain men clave unto him, and believed: among the which *was* Dī-ō-nȳsʹĭ-ŭs the Ăr-ē-ŏpʹă-gīte, and a woman named Dămʹă-rĭs, and others with them.

e Rom. 2.16.
7 Or, offered faith.
f Rom. 11.5.

CHAPTER 18

AFTER these things Paul departed from Athens, and came to Corinth;

2 And found a certain [a]Jew named Ă-quĭlʹă, born in Pontus, lately come from Italy, with his wife Priscilla; (because that Claudius had commanded all Jews to depart from Rome:) and came unto them.

3 And because he was of the same craft, he abode with them, and [b]wrought: for by their occupation they were tentmakers.

4 And he reasoned in the synagogue every sabbath, and persuaded the Jews and the Greeks.

5 And [c]when Silas and Timotheus were come from Măç-ē-dōʹnĭ-ă, Paul was pressed in the spirit, [d]and testified to the Jews *that* Jesus [1]*was* Christ.

6 And [e]when they opposed themselves, and blasphemed, [f]he shook *his* raiment, and said unto them, Your [g]blood *be* upon your own heads; I [h]*am* clean: [i]from henceforth I will go unto the Gentiles.

7 ¶ And he departed thence, and entered into a certain *man's* house, named Justus, *one* that worshipped God, whose house joined hard to the synagogue.

8 And [j]Crĭsʹpŭs, the chief ruler of the synagogue, believed on the Lord with all his house; and many of the Corinthians hearing believed, and were baptized.

9 Then [k]spake the Lord to Paul in the night by a vision, Be not afraid, but speak, and hold not thy peace:

10 For [l]I am with thee, and no man shall set on thee to hurt thee: [m]for I have much people in this city.

11 And he [2]continued *there* a year and six months, teaching the word of God among them.

12 ¶ And when Gălʹlĭ-ō was the deputy of Ă-chāiʹă, the Jews made insurrection with one accord against Paul, and brought him to the judgment seat,

13 Saying, This *fellow* persuadeth men to worship God contrary to the law.

14 And when Paul was now about to open *his* mouth, Gălʹlĭ-ō said unto the Jews, [n]If it were a matter of wrong or wicked lewdness, O *ye* Jews, reason would that I should bear with you:

15 But if it be a question of words and names, and *of* your law, look ye *to it;* for I will be no judge of such *matters*.

16 And he drave them from the judgment seat.

17 Then all the Greeks [o]took Sŏsʹthĕ-nēs, the chief ruler of the synagogue, and beat *him* before the judgment seat. And Gălʹlĭ-ō cared for none of those things.

18 ¶ And Paul *after this* tarried *there* yet a good while, and then took his leave of the brethren, and sailed thence into Syria, and with him Priscilla and Ă-quĭlʹă; having shorn [p]*his* head in [q]Çĕn-chrēʹă: for he had a vow.

19 And he came to Ĕphʹē-sŭs, and left them there: but he himself entered into the synagogue, and reasoned with the Jews.

20 When they desired *him* to tarry longer time with them, he consented not;

21 But bade them farewell, saying, [r]I must by all means keep this feast that cometh in Jerusalem: but I will return again unto you, if [s]God will. And he sailed from Ĕphʹē-sŭs.

22 And when he had landed at Çē-săʹrē-ă, and gone up, and saluted the church, he went down to Ănʹtĭ-ŏch.

23 And after he had spent some time *there*, he departed, and went over *all* the country of [t]Galatia and Phrȳġʹĭ-ă in order, strengthening [u]all the disciples.

24 ¶ And [v]a certain Jew named Ă-pŏlʹlŏs, born at Alexandria, an eloquent man, *and* mighty in the scriptures, came to Ĕphʹē-sŭs.

25 This man was instructed in the way of the Lord; and being fervent [w]in the spirit, he spake and taught diligently the things of the Lord, knowing [x]only the baptism of John.

26 And he began to speak boldly in the synagogue: whom when Ă-quĭlʹă and Priscilla had heard, they took him

CHAP. 18
a 1 Cor. 16. 19. 2 Tim. 4.19.
b 1 Cor. 4.12. 1 Thes. 2.9.
c ch. 17.14.
d Job 32.18. Matt. 3.2. Mark 6.12. Luke 13.5. ch. 3.19. 2 Cor. 7.10.
1 Or, is the Christ.
e 1 Pet. 4.4.
f Matt. 10.14.
g Eze. 33.4.
h Eze. 3.18.
i ch. 28.28.
j 1 Cor. 1.14.
k Isa. 58.21.
l Isa. 41.10. Jer. 1.18. Matt. 28.20. Rom. 8.31.
m 2 Tim. 2. 19.
2 sat there.
n ch. 23.29. ch. 25.11,19.
o 1 Cor. 1.1.
p Num. 6.18. ch. 21.24. 1 Cor. 9.20.
q Rom. 16.1.
r ch. 19.21.
s Matt. 26.39. ch. 19.21. 1 Cor. 4.19. Heb. 6.3.
t Gal. 1.2.
u Isa. 35.3. Dan. 11.1. 1 Thes. 3.2.
v 1 Cor. 1.12. Titus 3.13.
w Rom. 12. 11.
x ch. 19.3.

unto *them*, and expounded unto him
the way of God more perfectly.
27 And when he was disposed to pass
into Ă-chā-ĭ-ă, the brethren wrote, exhorting the disciples to receive him:
who, when he was come, [y]helped them
much which had believed through
grace:
28 For he mightily convinced the
Jews, *and that* publickly, [z]shewing by
the scriptures that Jesus [3]was Christ.

CHAPTER 19

AND it came to pass, that, while
Ă-pŏl-lŏs was [a]at Corinth, Paul
having passed through the upper
coasts came to Ĕph-ĕ-sŭs: and finding
certain disciples,
2 He said unto them, Have ye received the Holy Ghost since ye believed?
And they said unto him, [b]We have not
so much as heard whether there be any
Holy Ghost.
3 And he said unto them, Unto what
then were ye baptized? And they said,
Unto [c]John's baptism.
4 Then said Paul, [d]John verily baptized with the baptism of repentance,
saying unto the people, that they
should believe on him which should
come after him, that is, on Christ
Jesus.
5 When they heard *this*, they were
baptized [e]in the name of the Lord
Jesus.
6 And when Paul had [f]laid *his* hands
upon them, the Holy Ghost came on
them; and they [g]spake with tongues,
and prophesied.
7 And all the men were about
twelve.
8 And [h]he went into the synagogue,
and spake boldly for the space of three
months, disputing and persuading the
things [i]concerning the kingdom of
God.
9 But [j]when divers were hardened,
and believed not, but spake evil [k]of
that way before the multitude, he departed from them, and separated the
disciples, disputing daily in the school
of one Tȳ-răn-nŭs.
10 And [l]this continued by the space
of two years; so that all they which
dwelt in Asia heard the word of the
Lord Jesus, both Jews and Greeks.
11 And [m]God wrought special miracles by the hands of Paul:
12 So [n]that from his body were
brought unto the sick handkerchiefs
or aprons, and the diseases departed
from them, and the evil spirits went
out of them.
13 ¶ Then [o]certain of the vagabond
Jews, exorcists, [p]took upon them to
call over them which had evil spirits
the name of the Lord Jesus, saying,
We adjure you by Jesus whom Paul
preacheth.
14 And there were seven sons of *one*
Sçē-vă, a Jew, *and* chief of the priests,
which did so.
15 And the evil spirit answered and
said, Jesus [q]I know, and Paul I know;
but who are ye?
16 And the man in whom the evil
spirit was leaped on them, and overcame them, and prevailed against
them, so that they fled out of that
house naked and wounded.
17 And this was known to all the
Jews and Greeks also dwelling at Ĕph-
ĕ-sŭs; and fear [r]fell on them all, and
the name of the Lord Jesus was magnified.
18 And many that believed came,
and [s]confessed, and shewed their
deeds.
19 Many of them also which [t]used
curious arts brought their books together, and burned them before all
men: and they counted the price of
them, and found *it* fifty thousand
pieces of silver.
20 So [u]mightily grew the word of
God and prevailed.
21 ¶ After [v]these things were ended,
Paul purposed [w]in the spirit, when he
had passed through Măç-ē-dō-nĭ-ă
and Ă-chā-ĭ-ă, to go to Jerusalem, saying, After I have been there, [x]I must
also see Rome.
22 So he sent into Măç-ē-dō-nĭ-ă
two of them [y]that ministered unto
him, Timotheus and [z]Ē-răs-tŭs; but
he himself stayed in Asia for a
season.
23 And [a]the same time there arose
no small stir about [b]that way.
24 For a certain *man* named Dē-mē-
trĭ-ŭs, a silversmith, which made silver shrines for Diana, brought no
[c]small gain unto the craftsmen;
25 Whom he called together with the
workmen of like occupation, and said,
Sirs, ye know that by this craft [d]we
have our wealth.
26 Moreover ye see and hear, that
not alone at Ĕph-ĕ-sŭs, but almost
throughout all Asia, this Paul hath
persuaded and turned away much
people, saying that they [e]be no gods,
which are made with hands:
27 So that not only this our craft is in
danger to be set at nought; but also
that the temple of the great goddess

y John 1.12. 1 Cor. 3.6.
z Luke 24.26, 46. ch. 9.22. 1 Cor. 15.3, 4. Gal. 3.1.
3 Or, is the Christ. Gen. 49.10. Num. 21.9. Deut. 18.15. Ps. 16.9,10. Isa. 7.14. Micah 5.2. Mal. 3.1.

CHAP. 19

a 1 Cor. 1.12.
b 1 Sam. 3.7. ch. 8.16. 1 Cor. 6.19.
c ch. 18.25.
d Matt. 3.11. Mark 1.4-12. ch. 1.5.
e ch. 8.12,16. Rom. 6.3. Gal. 3.27.
f ch. 6.6. 2 Tim. 1.6.
g ch. 2.4.
h Luke 4.16.
i ch. 1.3.
j 2 Tim. 1.15. 2 Pet. 2.2.
k ch. 9.2.
l ch. 20.31.
m Mark 16.20.
n 2 Ki. 4.29.
o Matt. 12.27.
p Mark 9.38.
q Matt. 8.29. Mark 1.24. Luke 4.34. ch. 16.17.
r Luke 1.65. ch. 2.43.
s Lev. 16.21, 22. Matt. 3.6.
t 1 Sam. 28.7-9. 1 Chr. 10.13. Isa. 8.19. Dan. 2.2. ch. 8.9-11.
u Isa. 55.11. ch. 6.7. Col. 1.6. 2 Thes. 3.1.
v Rom. 15.25. Gal. 2.1.
w ch. 20.22.
x ch. 23.11. Rom. 15.24.
y ch. 13.5.
z Rom. 16.23. 2 Tim. 4.20.
a 2 Cor. 1.8.
b ch. 9.2.
c ch. 16.16, 19.
d Pro. 15.27. 1 Tim. 6.10. Rev. 18.16.
e 1 Chr. 16.26. Ps. 115.4. Isa. 41.24. Isa. 44.10-20. Jer. 10.3. ch. 17.29. 1 Cor. 8.4.

Diana should be despised, and her
magnificence should be destroyed,
whom all Asia and the world worshippeth.
28 And when they heard *these sayings*, they were full of wrath, and cried
out, saying, [f]Great *is* Diana of the
Ĕph-ē-'sĭăns.
29 And the whole city was filled with
confusion: and having [g]caught Gā̆i-'ŭs
and [h]Ăr-ĭs-tär-'chŭs, men of Măç-ē-
dō-'nĭ-ă, Paul's companions in travel,
they rushed with one accord into the
theatre.
30 And when Paul would have entered in unto the people, the disciples
suffered him not.
31 And certain of the chief [i]of Asia,
which were his friends, sent unto him,
desiring *him* that he would not adven-
ture himself into the theatre.
32 Some therefore cried one thing,
and some another: for the assembly
was confused; and the more part
knew not wherefore they were come
together.
33 And they drew Alexander out of
the multitude, the Jews putting him
orward. And [j]Alexander beckoned
with the hand, and would have made
his defence unto the people.
34 But when they knew that he was
a Jew, all with one voice about the
space of two hours cried out, Great *is*
Diana of the Ĕph-ē-'sĭăns.
35 And when the townclerk had
appeased the people, he said, *Ye* men
of Ĕph-'ē-sŭs, what man is there that
knoweth not how that the city of the
Ĕph-ē-'sĭăns is [1]a worshipper of the
great goddess Diana, and of the *image*
which fell down from Jupiter?
36 Seeing then that these things cannot be spoken against, ye ought to be
quiet, and to do nothing rashly.
37 For ye have brought hither these
men, which are neither robbers of
churches, nor yet blasphemers of your
goddess.
38 Wherefore if Dē-mē-'trĭ-ŭs, and
the craftsmen which are with him,
have a matter against any man, [2]the
law is open, and there are deputies:
let them implead one another.
39 But if ye inquire any thing concerning other matters, it shall be determined in a [3]lawful assembly.
40 For we are in danger to be called
in question for this day's uproar,
there being no cause whereby we may
give an account of this concourse.
41 And [k]when he had thus spoken,
he dismissed the assembly.

f Hab. 2.18, 19. Rev. 13.4.
g Rom. 16. 23. 1 Cor. 1.14.
h ch. 20.4. Col. 4.10. Philem. 24.
i ch. 16.6. 1 Pet. 1.1. Rev. 1.11.
j ch. 12.17. 1 Tim. 1.20. 2 Tim. 4.14.
1 the temple keeper.
2 Or, the court days are kept.
3 Or, ordinary.
k Pro. 15.1. Eccl. 9.17.

CHAP. 20

a 1 Cor. 16.5. 2 Cor. 7.5. 1 Tim. 1.3.
b ch. 9.23. 2 Cor. 11.26.
c ch. 27.2. Col. 4.10.
d ch. 19.29.
e ch. 16.1.
f Eph. 6.21. Col. 4.7. 2 Tim. 4.12. Titus 3.12.
g ch. 21.29. 2 Tim. 4.20.
h Ex. 12.14. Ex. 23.15. 1 Cor. 5.7,8.
i ch. 16.8. 2 Cor. 2.12. 2 Tim. 4.13.
j John 20.1. 1 Cor. 16.2. Rev. 1.10.
k Luke 22.19. ch. 2.42. 1 Cor. 10.16.
l ch. 1.13.
m 1 Ki. 17.21. 2 Ki. 4.34.
n Matt. 9.24. John 11.40. ch. 9.40.

CHAPTER 20

AND after the uproar was ceased,
Paul called unto *him* the disciples,
and embraced *them*, and [a]departed
for to go into Măç-ē-dō-'nĭ-ă.
2 And when he had gone over those
parts, and had given them much exhortation, he came into Greece,
3 And *there* abode three months.
And when [b]the Jews laid wait for him,
as he was about to sail into Syria, he
purposed to return through Măç-ē-
dō-'nĭ-ă.
4 And there accompanied him into
Asia Sō-'pă-tĕr of Bĕ-rē-'ă; and of the
Thĕss-ă-lō-'nĭ-ăns, [c]Ăr-ĭs-tär-'chŭs and
Sĕ-cŭn-'dŭs; [d]and Gā̆i-'ŭs of Dĕr-'bē,
and [e]Timotheus; and of Asia, [f]Tȳch-'
ĭ-cŭs and [g]Trŏph-'ĭ-mŭs.
5 These going before tarried for us at
Trō-'ăs.
6 And we sailed away from Philippi
after the days [h]of unleavened bread,
and came unto them [i]to Trō-'ăs in five
days; where we abode seven days.
7 And upon [j]the first *day* of the week,
when the disciples came together [k]to
break bread, Paul preached unto
them, ready to depart on the morrow;
and continued his speech until midnight.
8 And there were many lights [l]in the
upper chamber, where they were gathered together.
9 And there sat in a window a certain
young man named Eū-'tȳ-chŭs, being
fallen into a deep sleep: and as Paul
was long preaching, he sunk down
with sleep, and fell down from the
third loft, and was taken up dead.
10 And Paul went down, [m]and fell on
him, and embracing *him* said, [n]Trouble
not yourselves; for his life is in him.
11 When he therefore was come up
again, and had broken bread, and
eaten, and talked a long while, even
till break of day, so he departed.
12 And they brought the young man
alive, and were not a little comforted.
13 ¶ And we went before to ship, and
sailed unto Ăs-'sŏs, there intending to
take in Paul: for so had he appointed,
minding himself to go afoot.
14 And when he met with us at Ăs-'
sŏs, we took him in, and came to Mĭt-
ȳ-lē-'nē.
15 And we sailed thence, and came
the next *day* over against Chī-'ŏs; and
the next *day* we arrived at Sā-'mŏs, and
tarried at Trō-gȳl-'lĭ-ŭm; and the next
day we came to Mī-lē-'tŭs.
16 For Paul had determined to sail
by Ĕph-'ē-sŭs, because he would not

spend the time in Asia: [o]for he hasted,
if it were possible for him, [p]to be at
Jerusalem [q]the day of Pentecost.
17 ¶ And from Mi-lē'-tŭs he sent to
Ĕph'-ĕ-sŭs, and called [r]the elders of
the church.
18 And when they were come to him,
he said unto them, Ye know, from
[s]the first day that I came into Asia,
after what manner I have been with
you at all seasons,
19 Serving the Lord with all humility
of mind, and with many tears, and
temptations, which befell me by the
lying in wait of the Jews:
20 *And* how I kept back nothing that
was profitable *unto you*, but have
shewed you, and have taught you
publickly, and from house to house,
21 Testifying [t]both to the Jews, and
also to the Greeks, [u]repentance toward God, and faith toward our Lord
Jesus Christ.
22 And now, behold, [v]I go bound in
the spirit unto Jerusalem, not knowing the things that shall befall me
there:
23 Save that [w]the Holy Ghost witnesseth in every city, saying that bonds
and afflictions [1]abide me.
24 But [x]none of these things move
me, neither count I my life dear unto
myself, so [y]that I might finish my
course with joy, and [z]the ministry,
which [a]I have received of the Lord
Jesus, to testify the gospel of the grace
of God.
25 And now, behold, [b]I know that ye
all, among whom I have gone preaching the kingdom of God, shall see my
face no more.
26 Wherefore I take you to record
this day, that I *am* [c]pure from the
blood of all *men*.
27 For I have not shunned to declare
unto you all [d]the counsel of God.
28 ¶ Take [e]heed therefore unto yourselves, and to all the flock, over the
which the [f]Holy Ghost hath made you
overseers, to feed the church of God,
[g]which he hath purchased [h]with his
own blood.
29 For I know this, that after my departing [i]shall grievous wolves enter in
among you, not sparing the flock.
30 Also [j]of your own selves shall
men arise, speaking perverse things,
to draw away disciples after them.
31 Therefore watch, and remember,
that by [k]the space of three years I
ceased not to warn every one night and
day with tears.
32 And now, brethren, I commend

o ch. 21.4,12.
p ch. 24.17.
q ch. 2.1. 1 Cor. 16.8.
r 1 Tim. 4.14.
s ch. 18.19.
t ch. 18.5.
u Mark 1.15. Luke 24.47. ch. 2.38. Rom. 2.4.
v ch. 19.21.
w ch. 9.16. 1 Thes. 3.3. 2 Tim. 2.12.
1 Or, wait for me.
x Rom. 8.35. 2 Cor. 4.16.
y 1 Cor. 9.24-27. 2 Tim. 4.7.
z ch. 1.17. 2 Cor. 4.1. Titus 1.3.
a Gal. 1.1.
b Rom. 15. 23.
c 2 Cor. 7.2. 1 Thes. 2.10.
d Matt. 28. 20. Luke 7.30. John 15.15. Eph. 1.11.
e 1 Tim. 4.16. 1 Pet. 5.2.
f ch. 13.2. 1 Cor. 12.28. 1 Tim. 4.14.
g Eph. 1.7. Col. 1.14. 1 Pet. 1.19. Rev. 5.9.
h Heb. 9.14.
i Matt. 7.15. 2 Pet. 2.1.
j 1 John 2.19.
k ch. 19.10.
l Heb. 13.9.
m John 17. 17. ch. 9.31.
n ch. 26.18. Eph. 1.18. Col. 3.24. Heb. 9.15.
o 1 Sam. 12.3. 1 Cor. 9.12. 2 Cor. 7.2.
p ch. 18.3. 1 Cor. 4.12. 1 Thes. 2.9. 2 Thes. 3.8.
q Rom. 15.1. Eph. 4.28. 1 Thes. 4.11. 2 Thes. 3.8.
r Ps. 41.1. Pro. 19.17. Matt. 10.8. 1 Cor. 9.12. 2 Cor. 11.9. Heb. 13.1,3.
s Gen. 45.14.

Unty 2 Thes 2:3

a ch. 20.23.
b ch. 9.40.
c John 1.11.
d Eph. 4.11. 2 Tim. 4.5.
e ch. 6.5.

you to God, and [l]to the word of his
grace, which is able [m]to build you up,
and to give you an [n]inheritance among
all them which are sanctified.
33 I [o]have coveted no man's silver,
or gold, or apparel.
34 Yea, ye yourselves know, [p]that
these hands have ministered unto my
necessities, and to them that were
with me.
35 I have shewed you all things, how
that [q]so labouring ye ought to support
the weak, and to remember the words
of the Lord Jesus, how he said, [r]It is
more blessed to give than to receive.
36 ¶ And when he had thus spoken,
he kneeled down, and prayed with
them all.
37 And they all wept sore, [s]and fell
on Paul's neck, and kissed him,
38 Sorrowing most of all for the
words which he spake, that they
should see his face no more. And they
accompanied him unto the ship.

CHAPTER 21

AND it came to pass, that after we
were gotten from them, and had
launched, we came with a straight
course unto Cō'-ŏs, and the *day* following unto Rhodes, and from thence
unto Păt'-ă-ră:
2 And finding a ship sailing over unto
Phē-niç'-ĭă, we went aboard, and set
forth.
3 Now when we had discovered
Cyprus, we left it on the left hand, and
sailed into Syria, and landed at Tyre:
for there the ship was to unlade her
burden.
4 And finding disciples, we tarried
there seven days: [a]who said to Paul
through the Spirit, that he should not
go up to Jerusalem.
5 And when we had accomplished
those days, we departed and went our
way; and they all brought us on our
way, with wives and children, till *we*
were out of the city: and we [b]kneeled
down on the shore, and prayed.
6 And when we had taken our leave
one of another, we took ship; and
they returned [c]home again.
7 And when we had finished *our*
course from Tyre, we came to Ptŏl-ĕ-
mā'-ĭs, and saluted the brethren, and
abode with them one day.
8 And the next *day* we that were of
Paul's company departed, and came
unto Çæ-să-rē'-ă: and we entered into
the house of Philip [d]the evangelist,
which was [e]*one* of the seven; and
abode with him.

9 And the same man had four
daughters, virgins, [f]which did prophesy.
10 And as we tarried *there* many
days, there came down from Judæa
a certain prophet, named [g]Ăg-ă-bŭs.
11 And when he was come unto us,
he took Paul's girdle, and bound his
own hands and feet, and said, Thus
saith the Holy Ghost, [h]So shall the
Jews at Jerusalem bind the man that
owneth this girdle, and shall deliver
him into the hands of the Gentiles.
12 And when we heard these things,
both we, and they of that place, besought him not to go up to Jerusalem.
13 Then Paul answered, [i]What mean
ye to weep and to break mine heart?
for [j]I am ready not to be bound only,
but also to die at Jerusalem for the
name of the Lord Jesus.
14 And when he would not be persuaded, we ceased, saying, [k]The will
of the Lord be done.
15 And after those days we took up
our carriages, and went up to Jerusalem.
16 There went with us also *certain*
of the disciples of Çæ-să-rē-ă, and
brought with them one Mnā-sŏn of
Cyprus, an old disciple, with whom
we should lodge.
17 And [l]when we were come to Jerusalem, the brethren received us gladly.
18 And the *day* following Paul went
in with us unto [m]James; and all the
elders were present.
19 And when he had saluted them,
he declared [n]particularly what things
God had wrought among the Gentiles
by [o]his ministry.
20 And when they heard *it*, they
glorified the Lord, and said unto him,
Thou seest, brother, how many thousands of Jews there are which believe;
and they are all [p]zealous of the law:
21 And they are informed of thee,
that thou [q]teachest all the Jews which
are among the Gentiles to forsake
Moses, saying that they ought not to
circumcise *their* children, neither to
walk after the customs.
22 What is it therefore? the multitude must needs come together: for
they will hear that thou art come.
23 Do therefore this that we say to
thee: We have four men which have a
vow on them;
24 Them take, and purify thyself
with them, and be at charges with
them, that they may [r]shave *their*
heads: and all may know that those
things, whereof they were informed

f Joel 2.28. ch. 2.17.
g ch. 11.28.
h Eph. 3.1.
i Isa. 3.15. ch. 20.24.
j Rom. 8.35. 2 Cor. 4.10. Col. 1.24. 2 Tim. 4.6.
k Gen. 43.14. 1 Sam. 3.18. Matt. 26.42.
l ch. 15.4.
m ch. 15.13. Gal. 1.19. Jas. 1.1.
n ch. 11.4. ch. 14.27. Rom. 15.18. 1 Cor. 3.5-9. Col. 1.28,29.
o ch. 1.17.
p ch. 22.3. Rom. 10.2. Gal. 1.14.
q ch. 6.14. Gal. 5.1.
r Num. 6.2, 13. ch. 18.18.
s 1 Cor. 9.20.
t Gen. 9.4. Lev. 17.14. 1 Cor. 5.1,9. 1 Thes. 4.3. Heb. 13.4.
u ch. 24. 18.
v Num. 6.13.
w Mark 10. 30. Luke 21.12. ch. 4.3. ch. 5.18. Rom. 8.35. 2 Cor. 4.9. 1 Thes. 2.14, 16. 2 Tim. 3.12.
x Matt. 5.11. Luke 6.22. Luke 11.49. Luke 21.12. John 15.20. ch. 6.13. ch. 16.20. ch. 17.6. 1 Cor. 4.12. 1 Pet. 2.12.
y ch. 20.4. 2 Tim. 4.20.
z ch. 12.6. ch. 22.25-29. ch. 23.27.
a ch. 20.23. ch. 28.20.
b Luke 23.18. John 19.15. ch. 22.22.

concerning thee, are nothing; but *that*
thou thyself also walkest orderly, and
[s]keepest the law.
25 As touching the Gentiles which
believe, we [t]have written *and* concluded that they observe no such
thing, save only that they keep themselves from *things* offered to idols, and
from blood, and from strangled, and
from fornication.
26 Then Paul took the men, and the
next day purifying himself with them
entered into [u]the temple, [v]to signify
the accomplishment of the days of
purification, until that an offering
should be offered for every one of
them.
27 And when the seven days were
almost ended, the Jews which were
of Asia, when they saw him in the
temple, stirred up all the people, and
laid [w]hands on him,
28 Crying out, Men of Israel, help:
This is the man, [x]that teacheth all *men*
every where against the people, and
the law, and this place: and further
brought Greeks also into the temple,
and hath polluted this holy place.
29 (For they had seen before with
him in the city [y]Trŏph-ĭ-mŭs an Ĕph-
ē-sĭăn, whom they supposed that Paul
had brought into the temple.)
30 And all the city was moved, and
the people ran together: and they took
Paul, and drew him out of the temple:
and forthwith the doors were shut.
31 And as they went about to kill
him, tidings came unto the chief
captain of the band, that all Jerusalem
was in an uproar.
32 Who [z]immediately took soldiers
and centurions, and ran down unto
them: and when they saw the chief
captain and the soldiers, they left
beating of Paul.
33 Then the chief captain came near,
and took him, and [a]commanded *him*
to be bound with two chains; and demanded who he was, and what he had
done.
34 And some cried one thing, some
another, among the multitude: and
when he could not know the certainty
for the tumult, he commanded him to
be carried into the castle.
35 And when he came upon the
stairs, so it was, that he was borne of
the soldiers for the violence of the
people.
36 For the multitude of the people
followed after, crying, [b]Away with
him.
37 And as Paul was to be led into the

castle, he said unto the chief captain, May I speak unto thee? Who said, Canst thou speak Greek?

38 Art not thou that [1]Egyptian, which before these days madest an uproar, and leddest out into the wilderness four thousand men that were murderers?

39 But Paul said, [c]I am a man *which am* a Jew of Tarsus, *a city* in Çi-lĭç-ĭ-ă, a citizen of no mean city: and, I beseech thee, [d]suffer me to speak unto the people.

40 And when he had given him licence, Paul stood on the stairs, and beckoned with the hand unto the people. And when there was made a great silence, he spake unto *them* in the Hebrew tongue, saying,

CHAPTER 22

MEN, [a]brethren, and fathers, hear ye my defence *which I make* now unto you.

2 (And when they heard that he spake in the Hebrew tongue to them, they kept the more silence: and he saith,)

3 I [b]am verily a man *which am* a Jew, born in Tarsus, *a city* in Çi-lĭç-ĭ-ă, yet brought up in this city at [c]the feet of [d]Gă-mā-lĭ-ĕl, *and* taught [e]according to the perfect manner of the law of the fathers, and [f]was zealous toward God, [g]as ye all are this day.

4 And [h]I persecuted this way unto the death, binding and delivering into prisons both men and women.

5 As also the high priest doth bear me witness, and [i]all the estate of the elders: from [j]whom also I received letters unto [k]the brethren, and went to Damascus, to bring them which were there bound unto Jerusalem, for to be punished.

6 And [l]it came to pass, that, as I made my journey, and was come nigh unto Damascus about noon, suddenly there shone from heaven a great light round about me.

7 And I fell unto the ground, and heard a voice saying unto me, Saul, Saul, why persecutest thou me?

8 And I answered, Who art thou, Lord? And he said unto me, I am Jesus of Nazareth, whom thou persecutest.

9 And [m]they that were with me saw indeed the light, and were afraid; but they heard not the voice of him that spake to me.

10 And I said, What shall I do, Lord? And the Lord said unto me, Arise, and go into Damascus; and there it shall be told thee of all things which are appointed for thee to do.

11 And when I could not see for the glory of that light, being led by the hand of them that were with me, I came into Damascus.

12 And [n]one Ăn-ă-nī-ăs, a devout man according to the law, [o]having a good report of all the [p]Jews which dwelt *there*,

13 Came unto me, and stood, and said unto me, Brother Saul, receive thy sight. And the same hour I looked up upon him.

14 And he said, [q]The God of our fathers hath [r]chosen thee, that thou shouldest know his will, [s]and see that [t]Just One, and [u]shouldest hear the voice of his mouth.

15 For [v]thou shalt be his witness unto all men of [w]what thou hast seen and heard.

16 And now why tarriest thou? arise, and be baptized, and [x]wash away thy sins, [y]calling on the name of the Lord.

17 And [z]it came to pass, that, when I was come again to Jerusalem, even while I prayed in the temple, I was in a trance;

18 And saw him saying unto me, Make haste, and [a]get thee quickly out of Jerusalem: for they will not receive thy testimony concerning me.

19 And I said, Lord, [b]they know that I imprisoned and [c]beat in every synagogue them that believed on thee:

20 And [d]when the blood of thy martyr Stephen was shed, I also was standing by, and [e]consenting unto his death, and kept the raiment of them that slew him.

21 And he said unto me, Depart: for [f]I will send thee far hence unto the Gentiles.

22 And they gave him audience unto this word, and *then* lifted up their voices, and said, [g]Away with such a *fellow* from the earth: for it is not fit that [h]he should live.

23 And as they cried out, and cast off *their* clothes, and threw dust into the air,

24 The chief captain commanded him to be brought into the castle, and bade that he should be examined by scourging; that he might know wherefore they cried so against him.

25 And as they bound him with thongs, Paul said unto the centurion that stood by, [i]Is it lawful for you to scourge a man that is a Roman, and uncondemned?

26 When the centurion heard *that*, he

1 This Egyptian rose A.D. 55.

c ch. 9.11. Phil. 3.5. Col. 4.3. 2 Tim. 2.9.
d 1 Pet. 3.15.

CHAP. 22
a ch. 7.2.
b ch. 9.30. Rom. 11.1. 2 Cor. 11.22. Phil. 3.5.
c Deut. 33.3. 2 Ki. 4.38. Luke 8.35.
d ch. 5.34.
e ch. 26.5.
f 2 Sam. 21.2. ch. 21.20. Gal. 1.14. Phil. 3.6.
g Rom. 10.2.
h ch. 8.3. 1 Tim. 1.13.
i Luke 22.66. ch. 4.5.
j ch. 9.2.
k Rom. 9.3.
l ch. 26.12.
m Dan. 10.7.
n ch. 9.17.
o ch. 10.22.
p 1 Tim. 3.7.
q ch. 3.13. ch. 5.30.
r John 15.16. ch. 9.15. Rom. 1.1. Titus 1.1. Gal. 1.1.
s 1 Cor. 9.1.
t ch. 3.14. Heb. 7.26. 1 John 1.1.
u 1 Cor. 11. 23. Gal. 1.12.
v ch. 23.11.
w ch. 26.16.
x ch. 2.38. Heb. 10.22.
y ch. 2.21. Rom. 10.13.
z 2 Cor. 12.2
a Matt. 10. 14.
b ch. 8.3.
c Matt. 10. 17.
d ch. 7.58.
e Luke 11.48. Rom. 1.32.
f ch. 13.2. ch. 18.6. Rom. 1.5. Rom. 11.13. Gal. 2.7,8. 1 Tim. 2.7. 2 Tim. 1.11.
g ch. 21.36.
h ch. 25.24.
i ch. 16.37.

went and told the chief captain, saying, Take heed what thou doest: for this man is a Roman.

27 Then the chief captain came, and said unto him, Tell me, art thou a Roman? He said, Yea.

28 And the chief captain answered, With a great sum obtained I this freedom. And Paul said, But I was *free* born.

29 Then straightway they departed from him which should have [1]examined him: and the chief captain also was afraid, after he knew that he was a Roman, and because he had bound him.

30 On the morrow, because he would have known the certainty wherefore he was accused of the Jews, he loosed him from *his* bands, and [j]commanded the chief priests and all their council to appear, and brought Paul down, and set him before them.

CHAPTER 23

AND Paul, earnestly beholding the council, said, Men *and* brethren, I [a]have lived in all good conscience before God until this day.

2 And the high priest Ăn-ă-nī'-ăs commanded them that stood by him [b]to smite him on the mouth.

3 Then said Paul unto him, God shall smite thee, *thou* whited wall: for sittest thou to judge me after the law, and [c]commandest me to be smitten contrary to the law?

4 And they that stood by said, Revilest thou God's high priest?

5 Then said Paul, [d]I wist not, brethren, that he was the high priest: for it is written, [e]Thou shalt not speak evil of the ruler of thy people.

6 But when Paul perceived that the one part were Săd'-dū-çēes, and the other Pharisees, he cried out in the council, Men *and* brethren, I [f]am a Pharisee, the son of a Pharisee: [g]of the hope and resurrection of the dead I am called in question.

7 And when he had so said, there arose a dissension between the Pharisees and the Săd'-dū-çēes: and the multitude was divided.

8 For [h]the Săd'-dū-çēes say that there is no resurrection, neither angel, nor spirit: but the Pharisees confess both.

9 And there arose a great cry: and the scribes *that were* of the Pharisees' part arose, and strove, saying, [i]We find no evil in this man: but [j]if a spirit or an angel hath spoken to him, let [k]us not fight against God.

10 And when there arose a great dissension, the chief captain, fearing lest Paul should have been pulled in pieces of them, commanded the soldiers to go down, and to take him by force from among them, and to bring *him* into the castle.

11 And [l]the night following the Lord stood by him, and said, Be of good cheer, Paul: for as thou hast testified of me in Jerusalem, so must thou bear witness also at Rome.

12 And when it was day, [m]certain of the Jews banded together, and bound themselves [1]under a curse, saying that they would neither eat nor drink till they had killed Paul.

13 And they were more than forty which had made this conspiracy.

14 And they came to the chief priests and elders, and said, We have bound ourselves under a great curse, that we will eat nothing until we have slain Paul.

15 Now therefore ye with the council signify to the chief captain that he bring him down unto you to morrow, as though ye would inquire something more perfectly concerning him: and we, or ever he come near, are ready to kill him.

16 And [n]when Paul's sister's son heard of their lying in wait, he went and entered into the castle, and told Paul.

17 Then [o]Paul called one of the centurions unto *him*, and said, Bring this young man unto the chief captain: for he hath a certain thing to tell him.

18 So he took him, and brought *him* to the chief captain, and said, Paul the prisoner called me unto *him*, and prayed me to bring this young man unto thee, who hath something to say unto thee.

19 Then the chief captain took him by the hand, and went *with him* aside privately, and asked *him*, What is that thou hast to tell me?

20 And he said, [p]The Jews have agreed to desire thee that thou wouldest bring down Paul to morrow into the council, as though they would inquire somewhat of him more perfectly.

21 But do not thou yield unto them: for there [q]lie in wait for him of them more than forty men, which have bound themselves with an oath, that they will neither eat nor drink till they have killed him: and now are they ready, looking for a promise from thee.

1 Or, tortured him.
j Matt. 10.17. Luke 21.12.

CHAP. 23

a ch. 24.16. 1 Cor. 4.4. 2 Cor. 1.12. 2 Tim. 1.3. Heb. 13.18. 1 Pet. 3.16.
b 1 Ki. 22.24. John 18.22.
c Lev. 19.35.
d ch. 24.17.
e Ex. 22.28. Eccl. 10.20. 2 Pet. 2.10, 11. Jude 8.
f Phil. 3.5.
g ch. 24.15, 21. ch. 28.20.
h Matt. 22. 23. Mark 12.18. Luke 20.27.
i Pro. 16.7. Luke 23.4.
j ch. 22.7.
k ch. 5.39. ch. 11.17.
l Ps. 46.1. Isa. 41.10. ch. 2.25. ch. 18.9.
m Isa. 8.9, 10. ch. 25.3. Rom. 8.31.
1 Or, with an oath of execration. 1 Sam. 3.17. 2 Sam. 3.9. 1 Ki. 2.23. Matt. 26.74.
n Job 5.13. Pro. 21.30.
o Matt. 8.8,9. ch. 22.26. Eph. 5.15.
p ch. 20.3.
q Ps. 10.9. Pro. 1.16. Isa. 59.7. Micah 7.2. ch. 9.23,24. ch. 14.5,6. 2 Cor. 11.26, 32,33.

22 So the chief captain *then* let the young man depart, and charged *him*, *See thou* tell no man that thou hast shewed these things to me.

23 And he called unto *him* two centurions, saying, Make ready two hundred soldiers to go to Çæ-ṡă-rēʹă, and horsemen threescore and ten, and [2]spearmen two hundred, at the third hour of the night;

24 And provide *them* beasts, that they may set Paul on, and bring *him* safe unto Felix the governor.

25 And he wrote a letter after this manner:

26 Claudius Lȳsʹĭ-ăs unto the most excellent governor Felix *sendeth* greeting.

27 This [r]man was taken of the Jews, and should have been killed of them: then came I with an army, and rescued him, having understood that he was a Roman.

28 And [s]when I would have known the cause wherefore they accused him, I brought him forth into their council:

29 Whom I perceived to be accused of questions [t]of their law, but [u]to have nothing laid to his charge worthy of death or of bonds.

30 And when it was told me how that the Jews laid wait for the man, I sent straightway to thee, and [v]gave commandment to his accusers also to say before thee what *they had* against him. Farewell.

31 Then the soldiers, as it was commanded them, took Paul, and brought *him* by night to Ăn-tĭpʹă-trĭs.

32 On the morrow they left the horsemen to go with him, and returned to the castle:

33 Who, when they came [w]to Çæ-ṡă-rēʹă, and delivered the epistle to the governor, presented Paul also before him.

34 And when the governor had read *the letter*, he asked of what province he was. And when he understood that *he was* [x]of Çĭ-lĭçʹĭ-ă;

35 I [y]will hear thee, said he, when thine accusers are also come. And he commanded him to be kept [z]in Hĕrʹọd's judgment hall.

CHAPTER 24

AND after [a]five days [b]Ăn-ă-nīʹăs the high priest descended with the elders, and *with* a certain orator *named* Tĕr-tŭlʹlŭs, who informed the governor against Paul.

2 And when he was called forth, Tĕr-tŭlʹlŭs began to accuse *him*, saying, Seeing [c]that by thee we enjoy great quietness, and that very worthy deeds are done unto this nation by thy providence,

3 We accept *it* always, and in all places, most noble Felix, with all thankfulness.

4 Notwithstanding, that I be not further tedious unto thee, I pray thee that thou wouldest hear us of thy clemency a few words.

5 For [d]we have found this man [1]*a* pestilent *fellow*, and a mover of sedition among all the Jews throughout the world, and a ringleader of the sect of the Nazarenes:

6 Who [e]also hath gone about to profane the temple: whom we took, and would have [f]judged according to our law.

7 But [g]the chief captain Lȳsʹĭ-ăs came *upon us*, and with great violence took *him* away out of our hands,

8 Commanding [h]his accusers to come unto thee: by examining of whom thyself mayest take knowledge of all these things, whereof we accuse him.

9 And the Jews also assented, saying that these things were so.

10 Then Paul, after that the governor had beckoned unto him to speak, answered, Forasmuch as I know that thou hast been of many years [2]a judge unto this nation, I do the more cheerfully answer for myself:

11 Because that thou mayest understand, that there are yet but twelve days since I went up to Jerusalem for [i]to worship.

12 And [j]they neither found me in the temple disputing with any man, neither raising up the people, neither in the synagogues, nor in the city:

13 Neither can they prove the things whereof they now accuse me.

14 But this I confess unto thee, that after the [k]way which they call heresy, so worship I the [l]God of my fathers, believing all things which are written in [m]the law and in the prophets:

15 And [n]have hope toward God, which they themselves also allow, that [o]there shall be a resurrection of the dead, both of the just and unjust.

16 And [p]herein do I exercise myself, to have always a conscience void of offence toward God, and *toward* men.

17 Now after many years [q]I came to bring alms to my nation, and offerings.

18 Whereupon [r]certain Jews from Asia found me purified in the temple,

2 Or, archers, or, javelin casters.

r ch. 20.23. ch. 21.33. ch. 24.7.
s ch. 22.30.
t ch. 18.15. ch. 24.5,6.
u Ps. 27.12. Matt. 5.11, 12. ch. 26.31.
v ch. 24.8.
w ch. 8.40. A city on the north-west of Canaan.
x ch. 6.9.
y ch. 24.1.
z Matt. 27. 27.

CHAP. 24

a ch. 21.27.
b ch. 23.2,30, 35.
c Ps. 12.2. Ps. 55.21.
d Matt. 5.11. Mark 10.30. Luke 11.49. John 15.20. ch. 6.13. ch. 16.20. ch. 17.6. Rom. 8.35. 1 Cor. 4.12, 13. 2 Tim. 3.12. 1 Pet. 2.12.
1 a plague.
e ch. 21.28.
f John 18.31.
g ch. 21.33.
h ch. 23.30.
2 Felix was made procurator over Judæa A.D. 53.
i ch. 21.26.
j ch. 25.8.
k Ps. 119.46. Amos 8.14. ch. 9.2.
l Ex. 3.15. ch. 3.13. 2 Tim. 1.3.
m Luke 16. 16. ch. 13.15. Rom. 3.21.
2 Cor. 1.20.
n ch. 23.6.
o Dan. 12.2. Matt. 22.31. John 5.28. 1 Thes. 4.14. Rev. 20.12.
p ch. 23.1.
q ch. 11.29. Rom. 15.25. 2 Cor. 8.4. Gal. 2.10.
r ch. 21.26.

neither with multitude, nor with
tumult.
19 Who [s]ought to have been here before thee, and object, if they had ought
against me.
20 Or else let these same *here* say, if
they have found any evil doing in me,
while I stood before the council,
21 Except it be for this one voice,
that I cried standing among them,
Touching [t]the resurrection of the dead
I am called in question by you this
day.
22 And when Felix heard these
things, having more perfect knowledge of *that* way, he deferred them,
and said, When Lȳs-ĭ-ăs the chief
captain shall come down, I will know
the uttermost of your matter.
23 And he commanded a centurion
to keep Paul, and to let *him* have
liberty, and [u]that he should forbid
none of his acquaintance to minister
or come unto him.
24 And after certain days, when
Felix came with his wife Drû-sĭl-lă,
which was a Jewess, he sent for Paul,
and heard him concerning the faith in
Christ.
25 And as he reasoned of righteousness, temperance, and judgment to
come, Felix trembled, and answered,
Go thy way for this time; when I have
a convenient season, I will call for
thee.
26 He hoped also that [v]money
should have been given him of Paul,
that he might loose him: wherefore he
sent for him the oftener, and communed with him.
27 But after two years Pôr-çĭ-ŭs
Festus came into Felix' room: and
Felix, [w]willing to shew the Jews a
pleasure, left Paul bound.

CHAPTER 25

NOW when Festus was come into
the province, after three days he
ascended from Çǣ-să-rē-ă to Jerusalem.
2 Then [a]the high priest and the chief
of the Jews informed him against
Paul, and besought him,
3 And desired favour against him,
that he would send for him to Jerusalem, laying wait [b]in the way to kill
him.
4 But Festus answered, that Paul
should be kept at Çǣ-să-rē-ă, and
that he himself would depart shortly
thither.
5 Let them therefore, said he, which
among you are able, go down with *me*,

s ch. 23.30.
t ch. 23.6.
u ch. 27.3.
v Ex. 23.8. Ps. 26.10. 1 Tim. 6.10.
w Ex. 23.2. Pro. 29.25. ch. 25.9.

CHAP. 25

a ch. 24.1.
b Ps. 37.32, 33. Ps. 64.2-6. ch. 23.12.
c 1 Sam. 24. 11,12. Ps. 7.3-5. ch. 18.14.
1 Or, as some copies read, no more than eight or ten days.
d Esth. 3.8. Ps. 27.12. Ps. 35.1. Matt. 5.11, 12. Mark 15.3. Luke 23.2. 1 Thes. 2.15. 1 Pet. 4.14-16.
e ch. 6.13.
f Deut. 27.19. 2 Chr. 19.6. Pro. 29.25. ch. 12.3. ch. 24.27. Gal. 1.10. Jas. 2.6,9.
g ch. 18.14.
h Pro. 14.8. Pro. 21.22. Eccl. 9.18. Matt. 10.16. ch. 26.32. Eph. 5.15.
i ch. 24.27.
j ch. 18.15. ch. 23.29. 1 Cor. 1.18. 1 Cor. 2.14.

and accuse this man, [c]if there be any
wickedness in him.
6 And when he had tarried among
them [1]more than ten days, he went
down unto Çǣ-să-rē-ă; and the next
day sitting on the judgment seat commanded Paul to be brought.
7 And when he was come, the Jews
which came down from Jerusalem
stood round about, [d]and laid many
and grievous complaints against Paul,
which they could not prove.
8 While he answered for himself,
Neither against [e]the law of the Jews,
neither against the temple, nor yet
against Cæsar, have I offended any
thing at all.
9 But Festus, [f]willing to do the Jews
a pleasure, answered Paul, and said,
Wilt thou go up to Jerusalem, and
there be judged of these things before
me?
10 Then said Paul, I stand at Cæsar's
judgment seat, where I ought to be
judged: to the Jews have I done no
wrong, as thou very well knowest.
11 For [g]if I be an offender, or have
committed any thing worthy of death,
I refuse not to die: but if there be none
of these things whereof these accuse
me, no man may deliver me unto
them. [h]I appeal unto Cæsar.
12 Then Festus, when he had conferred with the council, answered,
Hast thou appealed unto Cæsar? unto
Cæsar shalt thou go.
13 And after certain days king
Agrippa and Bĕr-nī-çē came unto Çǣ-
să-rē-ă to salute Festus.
14 And when they had been there
many days, Festus declared Paul's
cause unto the king, saying, [i]There is
a certain man left in bonds by Felix:
15 About whom, when I was at Jerusalem, the chief priests and the elders
of the Jews informed *me*, desiring *to
have* judgment against him.
16 To whom I answered, It is not the
manner of the Romans to deliver any
man to die, before that he which is
accused have the accusers face to face,
and have licence to answer for himself concerning the crime laid against
him.
17 Therefore, when they were come
hither, without any delay on the
morrow I sat on the judgment seat,
and commanded the man to be
brought forth.
18 Against whom when the accusers
stood up, they brought none accusation of such things as I supposed:
19 But [j]had certain questions against

him of their own superstition, and
of one Jesus, which was dead, whom
Paul affirmed to be alive.
20 And because [2]I doubted of such
manner of questions, I asked *him*
whether he would go to Jerusalem,
and there be judged of these matters.
21 But when Paul had appealed to
be reserved unto the [3]hearing of
Augustus, I commanded him to be
kept till I might send him to Cæsar.
22 Then [k]Agrippa said unto Festus,
I would also hear the man myself. To
morrow, said he, thou shalt hear him.
23 And on the morrow, when Agrippa was come, and Bĕr-nī-çē, with
[l]great pomp, and was entered into the
place of hearing, with the chief captains, and principal men of the city, at
Festus' commandment Paul was
brought forth.
24 And Festus said, King Agrippa,
and all men which are here present
with us, ye see this man, about whom
all the multitude of the Jews have
dealt with me, both at Jerusalem, and
also here, crying that he ought not [m]to
live any longer.
25 But when I found that [n]he had
committed nothing worthy of death,
and that he himself hath appealed to
Augustus, I have determined to send
him.
26 Of whom I have no certain thing
to write unto my lord. Wherefore I
have brought him forth before you,
and specially before thee, O king
Agrippa, that, after examination had,
I might have somewhat to write.
27 For it seemeth to me unreason-
able to send a prisoner, and not withal
to signify the crimes *laid* against him.

CHAPTER 26

THEN Agrippa said unto Paul,
Thou art permitted to speak for
thyself. Then Paul stretched forth the
hand, and answered for himself:
2 I think myself happy, king Agrippa,
because I shall answer for myself
this day before thee touching all the
things whereof I am accused of the
Jews:
3 Especially *because I know* thee to
be [1]expert in all customs and questions
which are among the Jews: wherefore
I beseech thee to hear me patiently.
4 My manner of life from my youth,
which was at the first among mine
own nation at Jerusalem, know all the
Jews;
5 Which knew me from the beginning, if they would testify, that after
[a]the most straitest sect of our religion
I lived a Pharisee.
6 And now I stand and am judged for
the hope of [b]the promise made of God
unto our fathers:
7 Unto which *promise* [c]our twelve
tribes, instantly serving *God* [2]day and
night, hope [d]to come. For which
hope's sake, king Agrippa, I am accused of the Jews.
8 Why should it be thought a thing
incredible with you, that God should
raise [e]the dead?
9 I [f]verily thought with myself, that
I ought to do many things contrary to
the name of Jesus of Nazareth.
10 Which [g]thing I also did in Jerusalem: and many of the saints did I
shut up in prison, having received
authority [h]from the chief priests;
and when they were put to death, I
gave my voice against *them*.
11 And [i]I punished them oft in every
synagogue, and compelled *them* to
blaspheme; and being exceedingly
mad against them, I persecuted *them*
even unto strange cities.
12 Whereupon [j]as I went to Damascus with authority and commission
from the chief priests,
13 At midday, O king, I saw in the
way a light from heaven, above the
brightness of the sun, shining round
about me and them which journeyed
with me.
14 And when we were all fallen to the
earth, I heard a voice speaking unto
me, and saying in the Hebrew tongue,
Saul, Saul, why persecutest thou me?
it is hard for thee to kick against the
pricks.
15 And I said, Who art thou, Lord?
And he said, I am Jesus whom thou
persecutest.
16 But rise, and stand upon thy feet:
for I have appeared unto thee for this
purpose, to [k]make thee a minister and
a witness both of these things which
thou hast seen, and of those things in
the which I will appear unto thee;
17 Delivering thee from the people,
and *from* the Gentiles, [l]unto whom
now I send thee,
18 To [m]open their eyes, *and* [n]to turn
them from darkness to light, and [o]*from*
the power of Satan unto God, that
[p]they may receive forgiveness of sins,
and [q]inheritance among them which
are [r]sanctified by faith that is in me.
19 Whereupon, O king Agrippa, I
was not disobedient unto the heavenly
vision:
20 But [s]shewed first unto them of

2 Or, I was doubtful how to inquire hereof.
3 Or, judgment.
k ch. 9.15. ch. 26.1.
l Eccl. 1.2. Jas. 1.11. 1 Pet. 1.24.
m ch. 22.22.
n Matt. 27. 19,24. Mark 15.14. Luke 23.4. John 18.38. 2 Cor. 5.21. 1 Pet. 2.22.

CHAP. 26

1 a knower. Deut. 17.14-20. ch. 25.26.
a ch. 22.3. Gal. 1.13. Phil. 3.5.
b Gen. 3.15. Deut. 18.15. 2 Sam. 7.12. Ps. 132.11. Isa. 4.2. Eze. 21.7. Dan. 9.24. Mal. 3.1. ch. 13.32. Rom. 15.8.
c Jas. 1.1.
2 night and day.
d Phil. 3.11.
e Dan. 12.2.
f John 16.2. 1 Tim. 1.13.
g ch. 8.3.
h ch. 22.5.
i ch. 22.19.
j ch. 9.3.
k ch. 22.15. 2 Cor. 3.5,6. Gal. 1.12. Col. 1.25. 1 Tim. 1.12.
l ch. 9.15. ch. 18.6. Rom. 1.5. Gal. 1.15, 16. 1 Tim. 2.7. 2 Tim. 1.11.
m Isa. 35.5. Luke 1.79.
n 2 Cor. 6.14. Eph. 4.18. Col. 1.13. 1 Pet. 2.9.
o 1 John 3.5.
p Luke 1.77.
q Eph. 1.11.
r ch. 20.32.
s ch. 9.20.

Damascus, and at Jerusalem, and throughout all the coasts of Judæa, and *then* to the Gentiles, that they should repent and turn to God, and do [t]works meet for repentance.

21 For these causes [u]the Jews caught me in the temple, and went about to kill *me*.

22 Having therefore obtained help of God, I continue unto this day, witnessing both to small and great, saying none other things than those which [v]the prophets and [w]Moses did say should come:

23 That [x]Christ should suffer, *and* that he [y]should be the first that should rise from the dead, and should [z]shew light unto the people, and to the Gentiles.

24 And as he thus spake for himself, Festus said with a loud voice, Paul, [a]thou art beside thyself; much learning doth make thee mad.

25 But he said, I am not mad, most noble Festus; but speak forth the words of truth and soberness.

26 For the king knoweth of these things, before whom also I speak freely: for I am persuaded that none of these things are hidden from him; for this thing was not done in a corner.

27 King Agrippa, believest thou the prophets? I know that thou believest.

28 Then Agrippa said unto Paul, Almost [b]thou persuadest me to be a Christian.

29 And Paul said, [c]I would to God, that not only thou, but also all that hear me this day, were both almost, and altogether such as I am, except these bonds.

30 And when he had thus spoken, the king rose up, and the governor, and Bĕr-nī-çē, and they that sat with them:

31 And when they were gone aside, they talked between themselves, saying, [d]This man doeth nothing worthy of death or of bonds.

32 Then said Agrippa unto Festus, This man might have been set at liberty, [e]if he had not appealed unto Cæsar.

CHAPTER 27

AND when [a]it was determined that we should sail into Italy, they delivered Paul and certain other prisoners unto *one* named Julius, a centurion of Augustus' band.

2 And entering into a ship of Ăd-ră-mўt-tĭ-ŭm, we launched, meaning to sail by the coasts of Asia; *one* [b]Âr-ĭs-tär-chŭs, a Măç-ē-dō-nĭ-ăn of Thĕss-ă-lō-nī-că, being with us.

3 And the next *day* we touched at Sī-dŏn. And Julius [c]courteously entreated Paul, and gave *him* liberty to go unto his friends to refresh himself.

4 And when we had launched from thence, we sailed under Cyprus, because the winds were contrary.

5 And when we had sailed over the sea of Çĭ-lĭç-ĭ-ă and Păm-phўl-ĭ-ă, we came to Mȳ-ră, *a city* of Lўç-ĭ-ă.

6 And there the centurion found a ship of Alexandria sailing into Italy; and he put us therein.

7 And when we had sailed slowly many days, and scarce were come over against Cnī-dŭs, the wind not suffering us, we sailed under [1]Crete, over against Săl-mō-nē;

8 And, hardly passing it, came unto a place which is called The fair havens; nigh whereunto was the city *of* Lă-sē-ă.

9 Now when much time was spent, and when sailing was now dangerous, because [2]the fast was now already past, Paul admonished *them*,

10 And said unto them, Sirs, I perceive that this voyage will be with [3]hurt and much damage, not only of the lading and ship, but also of our lives.

11 Nevertheless the centurion believed the master and the owner of the ship, more than those things which were spoken by Paul.

12 And because the haven was not commodious to winter in, the more part advised to depart thence also, if by any means they might attain [d]to Phē-nī-çē, *and there* to winter; *which is* an haven of Crete, and lieth toward the south west and north west.

13 And when the south wind blew softly, supposing that they had obtained *their* purpose, loosing *thence*, they sailed close by Crete.

14 But not long after there [4]arose against it a tempestuous wind, called [5]Eû-rŏç-lў-dŏn.

15 And when the ship was caught, and could not bear up into the wind, we let *her* drive.

16 And running under a certain island which is called Clauda, we had much work to come by the boat:

17 Which when they had taken up, they used helps, undergirding the ship; and, fearing lest they should fall into the quicksands, strake sail, and so were driven.

18 And we being exceedingly tossed

---

t Isa. 55.7. Matt. 3.8.
u ch. 21.30.
v Rom. 3.21.
w John 5.46.
x Ps. 22. Isa. 53.
y Ps. 16.8-11. 1 Cor. 15.20. Col. 1.18. Rev. 1.5.
z Isa. 42.6.
a 2 Ki. 9.11. 1 Cor. 1.23.
b Mark 6.20.
c 1 Cor. 7.7.
d ch. 23.9. ch. 25.25.
e ch. 25.11.

CHAP. 27

a ch. 25.12, 25.
b ch. 19.29. ch. 20.4. Col. 4.10.
c ch. 28.16.
1 Or, Candy, a large island in the Mediterranean.
2 The Fast was on the tenth day of the seventh month.
3 Or, injury.
d Not Phenicia, the country on the north-west of Canaan. ch. 11.19. ch. 21.2.
4 Or, beat.
5 A north-east wind.

with a tempest, the next *day* they
lightened the ship;
19 And the third *day* [e]we cast out
with our own hands the tackling of the
ship.
20 And when neither sun nor stars in
many days appeared, and no small
tempest lay on *us*, all hope that we
should be saved was then taken away.
21 But after long abstinence Paul
stood forth in the midst of them, and
said, Sirs, ye should have hearkened
unto me, and not have loosed from
Crete, and to have gained this harm
and loss.
22 And now I exhort you to be of
good cheer: for there shall be no loss
of *any man's* life among you, but of
the ship.
23 For [f]there stood by me this
night the angel of God, whose I am,
and whom [g]I serve,
24 Saying, [h]Fear not, Paul; thou
must be brought [i]before Cæsar: and,
lo, God hath given [j]thee all them that
sail with thee.
25 Wherefore, sirs, be of good cheer:
for I [k]believe God, that it shall be even
as it was told me.
26 Howbeit [l]we must be cast upon a
certain island.
27 But when the fourteenth night
was come, as we were driven up and
down in Ā-drĭ-ă, about midnight the
shipmen deemed that they drew near
to some country;
28 And sounded, and found *it* twenty
fathoms: and when they had gone a
little further, they sounded again, and
found *it* fifteen fathoms.
29 Then fearing lest we should have
fallen upon rocks, they cast four
anchors out of the stern, and wished
for the day.
30 And as the shipmen were about to
flee out of the ship, when they had let
down the boat into the sea, under
colour as though they would have cast
anchors out of the foreship,
31 Paul said to the centurion and to
the soldiers, [m]Except these abide in
the ship, ye cannot be saved.
32 Then the soldiers cut off the ropes
of the boat, and let her fall off.
33 And while the day was coming on,
Paul besought *them* all to take meat,
saying, This day is the fourteenth day
that ye have tarried and continued
fasting, having taken nothing.
34 Wherefore I pray you to take
some meat: for this is for your health:
for [n]there shall not an hair fall from
the head of any of you.

e Jonah 1.5.
f Ps. 25.14. Amos 3.7. ch. 5.19. ch. 23.11. Heb. 1.13, 14.
g Ps. 143.12. Dan. 3.28. John 12.26. Rom. 1.9. Rom. 6.22. 2 Tim. 1.3.
h Isa. 41.10, 14. Isa. 43.1.
i ch. 19.21. ch. 23.11. ch. 25.11.
j Gen. 18.23-32. Gen. 19.29. Job 42.8. Isa. 6.13. Jas. 1.16.
k Num. 23. 19. 2 Chr. 20.20. Luke 1.45. 2 Tim. 1.12. Titus 1.2.
l ch. 28.1.
m Isa. 38.21. Matt. 4.7.
n 1 Ki. 1.52. Matt. 10.30. Luke 12.7.
o 1 Sam. 9.13. Matt. 15.36. Mark 8.6. John 6.11. Rom. 14.6.
p ch. 2.41. Rom. 13.1. 1 Pet. 3.20.
q Job 2.4. Matt. 6.25.
6 Or, cut the anchors, they left them in the sea, etc.
r 2 Cor. 11. 25.
s Pro. 1.16. Eccl. 9.3. Isa. 59.7. Mark 15.15-20. Rom. 3.15.
t Ps. 34.17, 19. Pro. 16.7. ch. 23.10. 2 Pet. 2.9.
u Ps. 107.30.

CHAP. 28

a Or, Malta. ch. 27.26.
b Lev. 19.18, 34. ch. 27.3. Rom. 1.14. 1 Cor. 14.11. Col. 3.11. Heb. 13.1,2.
c Luke 13.2. John 9.2.
d Num. 21.9. Ps. 91.13. Mark 16.18. Luke 10.19. Rev. 9.3,4.

35 And when he had thus spoken, he
took bread, and [o]gave thanks to God
in presence of them all: and when he
had broken *it*, he began to eat.
36 Then were they all of good cheer,
and they also took *some* meat.
37 And we were in all in the ship
two hundred threescore and sixteen
[p]souls.
38 And when they had eaten enough,
they lightened the ship, and [q]cast out
the wheat into the sea.
39 And when it was day, they knew
not the land: but they discovered a
certain creek with a shore, into the
which they were minded, if it were
possible, to thrust in the ship,
40 And when they had [6]taken up the
anchors, they committed *themselves*
unto the sea, and loosed the rudder
bands, and hoised up the mainsail to
the wind, and made toward shore.
41 And falling into a place where two
seas met, [r]they ran the ship aground;
and the forepart stuck fast, and remained unmoveable, but the hinder
part was broken with the violence of
the waves.
42 And the soldiers' counsel [s]was to
kill the prisoners, lest any of them
should swim out, and escape.
43 But the centurion, [t]willing to save
Paul, kept them from *their* purpose;
and commanded that they which
could swim should cast *themselves*
first *into the sea*, and get to land:
44 And the rest, some on boards, and
some on *broken pieces* of the ship. And
so it came to pass, that they escaped
[u]all safe to land.

CHAPTER 28

AND when they were escaped, then
they knew that the island was called [a]Mĕl-ĭ-tă.
2 And the barbarous people shewed
[b]us no little kindness: for they kindled
a fire, and received us every one, because of the present rain, and because
of the cold.
3 And when Paul had gathered a
bundle of sticks, and laid *them* on the
fire, there came a viper out of the heat,
and fastened on his hand.
4 And when the barbarians saw the
venomous beast hang on his hand,
they said among themselves, No
[c]doubt this man is a murderer, whom,
though he hath escaped the sea, yet
vengeance suffereth not to live.
5 And he shook off the beast into the
fire, and [d]felt no harm.
6 Howbeit they looked when he

should have swollen, or fallen down
dead suddenly: but after they had
looked a great while, and saw no harm
come to him, they changed their
minds, and [e]said that he was a god.
7 In the same quarters were possessions of the chief man of the island,
whose name was Publius; who received us, and lodged us three days court-
eously.
8 And it came to pass, that the father
of Publius lay sick of a fever and of a
bloody flux: to whom Paul entered in,
and [f]prayed, and laid [g]his hands on
him, and healed him.
9 So when this was done, others also,
which had diseases in the island,
came, and were healed:
10 Who also honoured us with many
[h]honours; and when we departed,
they laded *us* with such things as were
necessary.
11 And after three months we departed in a ship of Alexandria, which
had wintered in the isle, whose sign
was Castor and Pollux.
12 And landing at Sўr-ā-cūse, we
tarried *there* three days.
13 And from thence we fetched a
compass, and came to Rhē-ġĭ-ŭm: and
after one day the south wind blew, and
we came the next day to Pū-tē-ŏ-lī:
14 Where we found brethren, and
were desired to tarry with them seven
days: and so we went toward Rome.
15 And from thence, when the brethren heard of us, they came to meet us
as far as Ăp-pĭ-ī fôr-ŭm, and The
three taverns: whom when Paul saw,
he thanked God, and took courage.
16 And when we came to Rome, the
centurion delivered the prisoners to
the captain of the guard: but [i]Paul
was suffered to dwell by himself with
a soldier that kept him.
17 And it came to pass, that after
three days Paul called the chief of the
Jews together: and when they were
come together, he said unto them,
Men *and* brethren, though I [j]have
committed nothing against the people,
or customs of our fathers, yet was I
[k]delivered prisoner from Jerusalem
into the hands of the Romans.
18 Who, [l]when they had examined
me, would have let *me* go, because
there was no cause of death in me.
19 But when the Jews spake against

e ch. 8.10. ch. 10.25. ch. 12.22. Rev. 22.8,9.
f 1 Ki. 17.20-22. ch. 9.40.
g Matt. 8.8. Mark 6.5. Mark 7.32. Luke 4.40. ch. 19.11. 1 Cor. 12.9, 28.
h Matt. 15.6. 1 Tim. 5.17.
i Gen. 39.21. ch. 24.23.
j ch. 24.12. ch. 25.8.
k Judg. 15. 13. ch. 21.33.
l ch. 22.24. ch. 24.10. ch. 25.8.
m ch. 25.11. ch. 26.32.
n ch. 26.6,7.
o ch. 26.29. Eph. 3.1. Eph. 4.1. Eph. 6.20. 2 Tim. 1.16. Philem. 10, 13.
p Luke 2.34. ch. 24.5. 1 Pet. 2.12.
q Luke 24.27. ch. 17.2.3. ch. 26.22,23.
r ch. 26.6.
s ch. 13.48-50. ch. 14.4. ch. 18.6-8. Rom. 3.3.
t Isa. 6.9. Jer. 5.21. Eze. 12.2. Matt. 13.14. Mark 4.12. Luke 8.10.
u Isa. 44.18.
v Matt. 21. 41. Rom. 11.11.
w Eph. 6.19. Phil. 1.13.

it, I [m]was constrained to appeal unto
Cæsar; not that I had ought to accuse
my nation of.
20 For this cause therefore have I
called for you, to see *you*, and to
speak with *you*: because that [n]for the
hope of Israel I am bound with this
[o]chain.
21 And they said unto him, We
neither received letters out of Judæa
concerning thee, neither any of the
brethren that came shewed or speak
any harm of thee.
22 But we desire to hear of thee what
thou thinkest: for as concerning this
sect, we know that every where [p]it is
spoken against.
23 And when they had appointed
him a day, there came many to him
into *his* lodging; [q]to whom he expounded and testified the kingdom of
God, persuading them concerning
Jesus, [r]both out of the law of Moses,
and *out of* the prophets, from morning
till evening.
24 And [s]some believed the things
which were spoken, and some believed
not.
25 And when they agreed not among
themselves, they departed, after that
Paul had spoken one word, Well spake
the Holy Ghost by Ē-sāi-ăs the prophet unto our fathers,
26 Saying, [t]Go unto this people, and
say, Hearing ye shall hear, and shall
not understand; and seeing ye shall
see, and not perceive:
27 For [u]the heart of this people is
waxed gross, and their ears are dull
of hearing, and their eyes have they
closed; lest they should see with *their*
eyes, and hear with *their* ears, and understand with *their* heart, and should
be converted, and I should heal them.
28 Be it known therefore unto you
that the salvation of God is sent
[v]unto the Gentiles, and *that* they will
hear it.
29 And when he had said these
words, the Jews departed, and had
great reasoning among themselves.
30 And Paul dwelt two whole years
in his own hired house, and received
all that came in unto him,
31 Preaching [w]the kingdom of God,
and teaching those things which concern the Lord Jesus Christ, with all
confidence, no man forbidding him.

THE EPISTLE OF PAUL THE APOSTLE TO THE

ROMANS

CHAPTER 1

PAUL, a servant of Jesus Christ, called *to* [a]*be* an apostle, [b]separated unto the gospel of God,

2 (Which [c]he had promised afore by his prophets in the holy scriptures,)

3 Concerning his Son Jesus Christ our Lord, which was made of the seed of David according to the flesh;

4 And [1]declared *to be* the Son of God with power, according [d]to the spirit of holiness, by the resurrection from the dead:

5 By whom [e]we have received grace and apostleship, [2]for obedience to the faith among all nations, [f]for his name:

6 Among whom are ye also the called of Jesus Christ:

7 To all that be in Rome, beloved of God, called *to be* saints: Grace to you and peace from God our Father, and the Lord Jesus Christ.

8 First, [g]I thank my God through Jesus Christ for you all, that [h]your faith is spoken of throughout the whole world.

9 For God is my witness, whom I serve [3]with my spirit in the gospel of his Son, that without ceasing I make mention of you always in my prayers;

10 Making request, if by any means now at length I might have a prosperous journey [i]by the will of God to come unto you.

11 For I long to see you, that [j]I may impart unto you some spiritual gift, to the end ye may be established;

12 That is, that I may be comforted together [4]with you by the mutual faith both of you and me.

13 Now I would not have you ignorant, brethren, that [k]oftentimes I purposed to come unto you, (but [l]was let hitherto,) that I might have some fruit [5]among you also, even as among other Gentiles.

14 I [m]am debtor both to the Greeks, and to the Barbarians; both to the wise, and to the unwise.

15 So, as much as in me is, I am ready to preach the gospel to you that are at Rome also.

16 For [n]I am not ashamed of the gospel of Christ: for [o]it is the power of God unto salvation to every one that believeth; to the Jew first, and also to the Greek.

17 For [p]therein is the righteousness of God revealed from faith to faith: as it is written, [q]The just shall live by faith.

18 For [r]the wrath of God is revealed from heaven against all ungodliness and unrighteousness of men, [s]who hold the truth in unrighteousness;

19 Because [t]that which may be known of God is manifest [6]in them; for [u]God hath shewed *it* unto them.

20 For [v]the invisible things of him from the creation of the world are clearly seen, being understood by the things that are made, *even* his eternal power and Godhead; [7]so that they are without excuse:

21 Because that, when they knew God, they glorified *him* not as God, [w]neither were thankful; but [x]became vain in their imaginations, and their foolish heart was darkened.

22 Professing [y]themselves to be wise, they became fools,

23 And changed the glory of the uncorruptible [z]God into an image made like to corruptible man, and to birds, and fourfooted beasts, and creeping things.

24 Wherefore [a]God also gave them up to uncleanness through the lusts of their own hearts, [b]to dishonour their own bodies between [c]themselves:

25 Who [d]changed the truth of God into a [e]lie, and worshipped and served the creature [8]more than the Creator, who is blessed for ever. Ä-mĕn.

26 For this cause God gave them up unto vile [f]affections: for even their women did change the natural use into that which is against nature:

27 And likewise also the men, leaving the natural use of the woman, burned in their lust one toward another; men with men working that which is unseemly, and receiving in themselves that recompence of their error which was meet.

28 And even as they did not like [9]to retain God in *their* knowledge, God gave them over to [10]a reprobate mind,

CHAP. 1

a Acts 22.21. 2 Cor. 1.1. Col. 1.1,25.
b Acts 9.15.
c Titus 1.2.
1 determined.
d Heb. 9.14. 1 Pet. 3.18.
e Eph. 3.8.
2 Or, to the obedience of faith.
f Acts 9.15. ch. 11.13.
g Phil. 1.3.
h 1 Thes. 1.8.
3 Or, in my spirit.
i Jas. 4.15.
j ch. 15.29.
4 Or, in you.
k ch. 15.23.
l Acts 16.7. 1 Thes. 2.18.
5 Or, in you.
m Ps. 40.9. Mark 8.38.
n Ps. 40.9,10. 2 Tim. 1.8.
o ch. 10.17. 1 Cor. 1.18. 2 Cor. 10.4.
p ch. 3.21.
q Hab. 2.4. Gal. 3.11. Phil. 3.9. Heb. 10.38.
r Acts 17.30. ch. 2.5,6.
s Job 24.13.
t Acts 14.17.
6 Or, to them.
u John 1.9.
v Ps. 19.1.
7 Or, that they may be.
w Ps. 106.13.
x Gen. 5.6.
y Jer. 10.14.
z Isa. 40.18.
a Ps. 81.12. Acts 7.42.
b 1 Cor. 6.18. 1 Pet. 4.3.
c Lev. 18.22.
d 1 Thes. 1.9.
e Isa. 44.20. Amos 2.4.
8 Or, rather.
f Jude 10.
9 Or, to acknowledge.
10 Or, a mind void of judgment.

to do those things[g] which are not convenient;

29 Being filled with all unrighteousness, fornication, wickedness, covetousness, maliciousness; full of envy, murder, debate, deceit, malignity; whisperers,

30 Backbiters, haters of God, despiteful, proud, boasters, inventors of evil things, disobedient to parents,

31 Without understanding, covenantbreakers, [11]without natural affection, implacable, unmerciful:

32 Who knowing the judgment of God, that they which commit such things are worthy of death, not only do the same, but [12]have pleasure in them that do them.

CHAPTER 2

THEREFORE thou art inexcusable, O man, whosoever thou art that judgest: for wherein thou judgest another, thou condemnest thyself; for thou that judgest doest the same things.

2 But we are sure that the judgment of God is according [a]to truth against them which commit such things.

3 And [b]thinkest thou this, O man, that judgest them which do such things, and doest the same, that thou shalt escape the judgment of God?

4 Or despisest thou [c]the riches of his goodness and forbearance [d]and longsuffering; [e]not knowing that the goodness of God leadeth thee to repentance?

5 But after thy hardness and impenitent heart [f]treasurest up unto thyself wrath against the day of wrath and revelation of the righteous judgment of God;

6 Who [g]will render to every man according to his deeds:

7 To [h]them who by patient continuance in well doing seek for glory and honour and immortality, eternal life:

8 But [i]unto them that are contentious, and do not obey the truth, but obey unrighteousness, indignation and wrath,

9 Tribulation and anguish, upon every soul of man that doeth evil, of the [j]Jew first, and also of the [1]Gentile;

10 But [k]glory, honour, and peace, to every man that worketh good, to the Jew first, and also to the [2]Gentile:

11 For there is [l]no respect of persons with God.

12 For as many as have sinned without law shall also perish without law: and as many as have sinned in the law shall be judged by the law;

13 (For [m]not the hearers of the law *are* just before God, but the doers of the law shall be justified.

14 For when the Gentiles, which have not the law, do by nature the things contained in the law, these, having not the law, are a law unto themselves:

15 Which shew the work of the law written in their hearts, [3]their conscience also bearing witness, and *their* thoughts [4]the mean while accusing or else excusing one another;)

16 In [n]the day when God shall judge the secrets of men [o]by Jesus Christ according to my gospel.

17 Behold, [p]thou art called a Jew, and restest [q]in the law, [r]and makest thy boast of God,

18 And [s]knowest *his* will, and [5]approvest the things that are more excellent, being instructed out of the law;

19 And art confident that thou thyself art a guide of the blind, a light of them which are in darkness,

20 An instructor of the foolish, a teacher of babes, [t]which hast the form of knowledge and of the truth in the law.

21 Thou [u]therefore which teachest another, teachest thou not thyself? thou that preachest a man should not steal, dost thou steal?

22 Thou that sayest a man should not commit adultery, dost thou commit adultery? thou that abhorrest idols, [v]dost thou commit sacrilege?

23 Thou that makest thy boast of the law, through breaking the law dishonourest thou God?

24 For the name of God is blasphemed among the Gentiles through you, as it [w]is written.

25 For [x]circumcision verily profiteth, if thou keep the law: but if thou be a breaker of the law, thy circumcision is made uncircumcision.

26 Therefore [y]if the uncircumcision keep the righteousness of the law, shall not his uncircumcision be counted for circumcision?

27 And shall not uncircumcision which is by nature, if it fulfil the law, judge [z]thee, who by the letter and circumcision dost transgress the law?

28 For [a]he is not a Jew, which is one outwardly; neither *is that* circumcision, which is outward in the flesh:

29 But he *is* a Jew, [b]which is one inwardly; and [c]circumcision *is that* of

g Eph. 5.4.
11 Or, unsociable.
12 Or, consent with them.

CHAP. 2

a Gen. 18.25. 2 Thes. 1.6.
b Pro. 11.21.
c Ps. 86.5. Eph. 1.7.
d Ex. 34.6.
e 2 Pet. 3.9.
f Jas. 5.3.
g Ps. 62.12. Isa. 3.10,11. Matt. 16.27.
h 2 Cor. 4.17. Jude 21. Rev. 2.7.
i Isa. 3.11. 2 Thes. 2.12.
j 1 Pet. 4.17.
1 Greek.
k Ps. 112.6-9. Pro. 3.16, 17. 1 Pet. 1.7.
2 Greek.
l Deut. 10.17. Deut. 16.19. Luke 20.21.
m Deut. 30. 12-14. Eze. 20.11. Luke 8.21.
3 Or, the conscience witnessing with them.
4 Or, between themselves.
n Rev. 20.12.
o John 5.22.
p ch. 9.6.
q Micah 3.11.
r John 8.41.
s Deut. 4.8.
5 Or, triest the things that differ.
t 2 Tim. 3.5.
u Matt. 23.3.
v Mal. 3.8.
w 2 Sam. 12. 14. Isa. 52.5.
x Gal. 5.3.
y Acts 10.34.
z Matt. 12.41.
a Matt. 3.9. John 8.33. Acts 13.26. Gal. 6.15. Rev. 2.9.
b 1 Pet. 3.4.
c Col. 2.11. Phil. 3.3.

the heart, [d]in the spirit, *and* not in the letter; whose praise *is* not of men, but of God.

CHAPTER 3

WHAT advantage then hath the Jew? or what profit *is there* of circumcision?

2 Much every way: chiefly, because that unto [a]them were committed the oracles of God.

3 For what if [b]some did not believe? shall their [c]unbelief make the faith of God without effect?

4 God [d]forbid: yea, let [e]God be true, but every [f]man a liar; as it is written, [g]That thou mightest be justified in thy sayings, and mightest overcome when thou art judged.

5 But if our unrighteousness commend the righteousness of God, what shall we say? *Is* God unrighteous who taketh vengeance? (I [h]speak as a man)

6 God forbid: for then [i]how shall God judge the world?

7 For if the truth of God hath more abounded through my lie unto his glory; why yet am I also judged as a sinner?

8 And not *rather*, (as we be slanderously reported, and as some affirm that we say,) Let [j]us do evil, that good may come? whose damnation is just.

9 What then? are we better *than they?* No, in no wise: for we have before [1]proved both Jews and Gentiles, that [k]they are all under sin;

10 As it is written, [l]There is none righteous, no, not one:

11 There is none that understandeth, there is none that seeketh after God.

12 They are all gone out of the way, they are together become unprofitable; there is none that doeth good, no, not one.

13 Their [m]throat *is* an open sepulchre; with their tongues they have used deceit; the [n]poison of asps *is* under their lips:

14 Whose [o]mouth *is* full of cursing and bitterness:

15 Their [p]feet *are* swift to shed blood:

16 Destruction and misery *are* in their ways:

17 And the way of peace have they not known:

18 There [q]is no fear of God before their eyes.

19 Now we know that what things soever the law saith, it saith to them who are under the law: that [r]every mouth may be stopped, and [s]all the world may become [2]guilty before God.

20 Therefore [t]by the deeds of the law there shall no flesh be justified in his sight: for [u]by the law *is* the knowledge of sin.

21 But now [v]the righteousness of God without the law is manifested, being witnessed by the law [w]and the prophets;

22 Even the righteousness of God *which is* by [x]faith of Jesus Christ unto all and upon all them that believe: for [y]there is no difference:

23 For [z]all have sinned, and come short of the glory of God;

24 Being justified freely [a]by his grace through the redemption that is in Christ Jesus:

25 Whom God hath [3]set forth *to* [b]*be* a propitiation through faith in his blood, to declare his righteousness for the [4]remission of sins that are past, through the forbearance of God;

26 To declare, *I say*, at this time his righteousness: that he might be just, and the justifier of him which believeth in Jesus.

27 Where [c]*is* boasting then? It is excluded. By what law? of works? Nay: but by the law of faith.

28 Therefore we conclude [d]that a man is justified by faith without the deeds of the law.

29 *Is he* the God of the Jews only? *is he* not also of the Gentiles? Yes, of the Gentiles also:

30 Seeing *it is* one God, which shall justify the circumcision by faith, and uncircumcision through faith.

31 Do we then make void the law through faith? God forbid: yea, we establish the law.

CHAPTER 4

WHAT shall we say then that Abraham our father, as pertaining to the flesh, hath found?

2 For if Abraham were justified by works, he hath *whereof* to glory; but not before God.

3 For what saith the scripture? Abraham believed [a]God, and it was counted unto him for righteousness.

4 Now to [b]him that worketh is the reward not reckoned of grace, but of debt.

5 But to him that worketh not, but believeth on him that justifieth the [c]ungodly, his faith is counted for righteousness.

6 Even as David also describeth the blessedness of the man, unto whom God [d]imputeth righteousness without works,

d ch. 7.6. 2 Cor. 3.6.

CHAP. 3

a Deut. 4.7.
b Heb. 4.2.
c Num. 23.19.
d Job 40.8.
e John 3.33.
f Ps. 62.9.
g Ps. 51.4.
h Gal. 3.15.
i Gen. 18.25. Ps. 9.8.
j ch. 5.20.
1 charged. ch. 1.28.
k Gal. 3.22.
l Ps. 14.1.
m Ps. 5.9.
n Ps. 140.3.
o Ps. 10.7.
p Pro. 1.16.
q Ps. 36.1. Luke 23.40.
r Eze. 16.63.
s ch. 2.2.
2 Or, subject to the judgment of God.
t Ps. 143.2. Gal. 2.16. Eph. 2.8,9. Titus 3.5.
u ch. 7.7.
v Isa. 45.24. ch. 1.17. Heb. 11.4. 2 Pet. 1.1.
w 1 Pet. 1.10.
x ch. 4.
y Col. 3.11.
z Gal. 3.22.
a Matt. 20. 28. Eph. 1.7. Col. 1.14. 1 Tim. 2.6. Heb. 9.12. 1 Pet. 1.18, 19.
3 Or, fore-ordained.
b Lev. 16.15. Isa. 53.11. 1 John 4.10.
4 Or, passing over.
c 1 Cor. 1.29. Eph. 2.9.
d Gal. 2.16. Titus 3.5.

CHAP. 4

a Gen. 15.6. Gal. 3.6. Jas. 2.23.
b ch. 9.32. ch. 11.6.
c Josh. 24.2. Acts 13.39. Gal. 2.16.
d Jer. 23.6. Dan. 9.24. 1 Cor. 1.30. 2 Cor. 5.19. 2 Pet. 1.1. Rev. 5.9.

7 *Saying*, [e]Blessed *are* they whose iniquities are forgiven, and whose sins are covered.

8 Blessed *is* the man to whom the Lord will not impute sin.

9 *Cometh* this blessedness then upon the circumcision *only*, or upon the uncircumcision also? for we say that faith was reckoned to Abraham for righteousness.

10 How was it then reckoned? when he was in circumcision, or in uncircumcision? Not in circumcision, but in uncircumcision.

11 And [f]he received the sign of circumcision, a seal of the righteousness of the faith which *he had yet* being uncircumcised: that [g]he might be the father of all them that believe, though they be not circumcised; that righteousness might be imputed unto them also:

12 And the father of circumcision to them who are not of the circumcision only, but who also walk in the steps of that faith of our father Abraham, which *he had* being *yet* uncircumcised.

13 For the promise, that he should be the [h]heir of the world, *was* not to Abraham, or to his seed, through the law, but through the righteousness of faith.

14 For [i]if they which are of the law *be* heirs, faith is made void, and the promise made of none effect:

15 Because the law worketh wrath: for where no law is, *there is* no transgression.

16 Therefore *it is* of faith, that *it might be* [j]by grace; to the end the promise might be sure to all the seed; not to that only which is of the law, but to that also which is of the faith of Abraham; [k]who is the father of us all,

17 (As it is written, I have made thee a father of many nations,) [1]before him whom he believed, *even* God, who [l]quickeneth the dead, and calleth those [m]things which be not as though they were.

18 Who against hope believed in hope, that he might become the father of many nations; according to that which was spoken, [n]So shall thy seed be.

19 And being not weak in faith, [o]he considered not his own body now dead, when he was about an hundred years old, neither yet the deadness of Sarah's womb:

20 He staggered not at the promise of God through unbelief; but was strong in faith, giving glory to God;

21 And being fully persuaded that, what he had promised, he was able also to perform.

22 And therefore it was imputed to him for righteousness.

23 Now [p]it was not written for his sake alone, that it was imputed to him;

24 But for us also, to whom it shall be imputed, if we believe [q]on him that raised up Jesus our Lord from the dead;

25 Who [r]was delivered for our offences, and was raised again for our justification.

CHAPTER 5

THEREFORE being justified by faith, we have [a]peace with God through our Lord Jesus Christ:

2 By [b]whom also we have access by faith into this grace [c]wherein we stand, [d]and rejoice in hope of the glory of God.

3 And not only *so*, but [e]we glory in tribulations also: knowing that tribulation worketh patience;

4 And patience, experience; and experience, hope:

5 And [f]hope maketh not ashamed; because [g]the love of God is shed abroad in our hearts by the Holy Ghost which is given unto us.

6 For when we were yet without strength, [1]in due time Christ died for the ungodly.

7 For scarcely for a righteous man will one die: yet peradventure for a good man some would even dare to die.

8 But [h]God commendeth his love toward us, in that, while we were yet sinners, Christ died for us.

9 Much more then, being now justified by [i]his blood, we shall be saved [j]from wrath through him.

10 For if, when we were enemies, [k]we were reconciled to God by the death of his Son, much more, being reconciled, we shall be saved [l]by his life.

11 And not only *so*, but we also joy in God through our Lord Jesus Christ, by whom we have now received the [2]atonement.

12 Wherefore, as [m]by one man sin entered into the world, and death by sin; and so death passed upon all men, [3]for that all have sinned:

13 (For until the law sin was in the world: but [n]sin is not imputed when there is no law.

e Ps. 32.1.2.
f Gen. 17.10.
g Luke 19.9. John 8.39.
h Gen. 12.3. Gal. 3.29.
i Gal. 3.18.
j ch.3.24. Col. 3.11.
k ch. 9.8.
1 Or, like unto him.
l ch. 8.11. Eph. 2.1. 1 Tim. 6.13.
m 1 Cor. 1. 28. 1 Pet. 2.10.
n Gen. 15.5.
o Heb. 11.11.
p 2 Tim. 3.16. Acts 13.30. 1 Pet. 1.21.
r Isa. 53.5. Heb. 9.28. 1 Pet. 3.18. 1 John 1.7.

CHAP. 5

a Isa. 32.17. John 16.33. Eph. 2.14. Col. 1.20.
b John 10.9. Eph. 3.12. Heb. 10.19.
c 1 Cor. 15.1.
d Ps. 16.9-11. ch. 15.13. Heb. 3.6.
e Matt. 5.11. ch. 8.35-37. Phil. 2.17.
f Phil. 1.20.
g Matt. 22. 36,37. 2 Cor. 1.22. Gal. 4.6. Eph. 1.13. Heb. 8.10.
1 Or, according to the time.
h John 15.13. 1 Pet. 3.18.
i 1 John 1.7.
j 1 Thes. 1.10.
k 2 Cor. 5.18.
l John 14.19.
2 Or, reconciliation.
m Eze. 18.4.
3 Or, in whom.
n 1 John 3.4.

14 Nevertheless death reigned from
Adam to Moses, even over them that
had not sinned after the similitude of
Adam's transgression, who is the
figure of him that was to come.
15 But not as the offence, so also *is*
the free gift. For if through the offence
of one many be dead, much more the
grace of God, and the gift by grace,
which is by one man, Jesus Christ,
hath abounded [o]unto many.
16 And not as *it was* by one that
sinned, *so is* the gift: for the judgment
was by one to condemnation, but the
free gift *is* of many offences unto
justification.
17 For if [4]by one man's offence death
reigned by one; much more they
which receive abundance of grace and
of the gift of righteousness shall reign
in life by one, Jesus Christ.)
18 Therefore as [5]by the offence of one
judgment came upon all men to condemnation; even so [6]by the righteousness of one *the free gift came*
upon [p]all men unto justification of
life.
19 For as by one man's disobedience
many were made sinners, so by the
obedience of one shall many be made
righteous.
20 Moreover [q]the law entered, that
the offence might abound. But where
sin abounded, grace did [r]much more
abound:
21 That as sin hath reigned unto
death, even so might grace reign
through righteousness unto eternal
life by Jesus Christ our Lord.

CHAPTER 6

WHAT shall we say then? Shall
we continue in sin, that grace
may abound?
2 God forbid. How shall we, that are
dead [a]to sin, live any longer therein?
3 Know ye not, that [b]so many of us
as [1]were baptized into Jesus [c]Christ
were baptized into his death?
4 Therefore we are [d]buried with him
by baptism into death: that [e]like as
Christ was raised up from the dead
by the glory of the Father, [f]even so
we also should walk in newness of
life.
5 For [g]if we have been planted together in the likeness of his death, we
shall be also *in the likeness* of *his*
resurrection:
6 Knowing this, that [h]our old man is
crucified with *him*, that [i]the body of
sin might be destroyed, that henceforth we should not serve sin.

o Isa. 53.11. Matt. 20.28. Heb. 9.28.
4 Or, by one offence.
5 Or, by one offence.
6 Or, by one righteousness.
p John 12.32. Heb. 2.9.
q John 15.22. ch. 3.20. Gal. 3.19.
r Luke 7.47. 1 Tim. 1.14.

CHAP. 6

a ch. 3.19,20. Gal. 2.19. 1 Pet. 2.24.
b Col. 3.3. 1 Pet. 2.24.
1 Or, are.
c 1 Cor. 15. 29.
d Col. 2.12.
e 1 Cor. 6.14.
f 2 Cor. 5.17. Gal. 6.15. Eph. 4.22. Heb. 12.1,2. 1 Pet. 4.1.
g Eph. 2.5,6. Phil. 3.10.
h Gal. 2.20.
i Col. 2.11.
2 justified.
j 2 Cor. 5.1. 2 Tim. 2.11.
k Rev. 1.18.
l Gal. 2.19.
m Eph. 4.22.
3 arms, or, weapons.
n Ps. 130.7,8. Micah 7.19. John 8.36. Gal. 5.18. Titus 2.14. Heb. 8.10.
o 1 Cor. 9.21.
4 whereto ye were delivered.
p Luke 1.74, 75. Gal. 5.1. 1 Pet. 2.16.
5 to righteousness.
q Gen. 2.17. ch. 5.12. Jas. 1.15. Rev. 21.8.
r John 3.14. ch. 2.7.

7 For he that is dead is [2]freed from
sin.
8 Now [j]if we be dead with Christ, we
believe that we shall also live with
him:
9 Knowing that [k]Christ being raised
from the dead dieth no more; death
hath no more dominion over
him.
10 For in that he died, he died unto
sin once: but in that he liveth, he liveth
unto God.
11 Likewise reckon ye also yourselves to be dead indeed unto sin, but
[l]alive unto God through Jesus Christ
our Lord.
12 Let [m]not sin therefore reign in
your mortal body, that ye should obey
it in the lusts thereof.
13 Neither yield ye your members *as*
[3]instruments of unrighteousness unto
sin: but yield yourselves unto God, as
those that are alive from the dead, and
your members *as* instruments of righteousness unto God.
14 For [n]sin shall not have dominion
over you: for ye are not under the
law, but under grace.
15 What then? shall we sin, [o]because
we are not under the law, but under
grace? God forbid.
16 Know ye not, that to whom ye
yield yourselves servants to obey, his
servants ye are to whom ye obey;
whether of sin unto death, or of
obedience unto righteousness?
17 But God be thanked, that ye were
the servants of sin, but ye have obeyed
from the heart that form of doctrine
[4]which was delivered you.
18 Being then [p]made free from sin,
ye became the servants of righteousness.
19 I speak after the manner of men
because of the infirmity of your flesh:
for as ye have yielded your members
servants to uncleanness and to iniquity unto iniquity; even so now yield
your members servants to righteousness unto holiness.
20 For when ye were the servants of
sin, ye were free [5]from righteousness.
21 What fruit had ye then in those
things whereof ye are now ashamed?
for the end of those things *is* death.
22 But now being made free from
sin, and become servants to God, ye
have your fruit unto holiness, and the
end everlasting life.
23 For [q]the wages of sin *is* death; but
[r]the gift of God *is* eternal life through
Jesus Christ our Lord.

CHAPTER 7

KNOW ye not, brethren, (for I
speak to them that know the law,)
how that the law hath dominion over
a man as long as he liveth?
2 For [a]the woman which hath an
husband is bound by the law to *her*
husband so long as he liveth; but if the
husband be dead, she is loosed from
the law of *her* husband.
3 So then [b]if, while *her* husband liveth, she be married to another man,
she shall be called an adulteress: but
if her husband be dead, she is free
from that law; so that she is no adulteress, though she be married to
another man.
4 Wherefore, my brethren, ye also
are become [c]dead to the law by the
body of Christ; that ye should [d]be
married to another, *even* to him who
is raised from the dead, that we
should bring forth fruit unto God.
5 For when we were in the flesh, the
[1]motions of sins, which were by the
law, did work in our members [e]to
bring forth fruit unto death.
6 But now we are delivered from the
law, [2]that being dead wherein we
were held; that we should serve [f]in
newness of spirit, and not *in* the old-
ness of the letter.
7 What shall we say then? *Is* the law
sin? God forbid. Nay, [g]I had not
known sin, but by the law: for I had
not known [3]lust, except the law had
said, [h]Thou shalt not covet.
8 But [i]sin, taking occasion by the
commandment, wrought in me all
manner of concupiscence. For [j]with-
out the law sin *was* dead.
9 For I was alive without the law
once: but when the commandment
came, sin revived, and I died.
10 And the commandment, [k]which
was ordained to life, I found *to be* unto
death.
11 For sin, taking occasion by the
commandment, deceived me, and by
it slew *me*.
12 Wherefore [l]the law *is* holy, and
the commandment holy, and just, and
good.
13 Was then that which is good made
death unto me? God forbid. But sin,
that it might appear sin, working
death in me by that which is good;
that sin by the commandment might
become exceeding sinful.
14 For we know that the law is
spiritual: but I am carnal, [m]sold under
sin.
15 For that which I do I [4]allow not:
for what [n]I would, that do I not; but
what I hate, that do I.
16 If then I do that which I would
not, I consent unto the law that *it is*
good.
17 Now then it is no more I that do
it, but sin that dwelleth in me.
18 For I know that [o]in me (that is, in
my flesh,) dwelleth no good thing: for
to will is present with me; but *how* to
perform that which is good I find not.
19 For the good that I would I do
not: but the evil which I would not,
that I do.
20 Now if I do that I would not, it is
no more I that do it, but sin that dwelleth in me.
21 I find then a law, that, when I
would do good, evil is present with
me.
22 For I [p]delight in the law of God
after the [q]inward man:
23 But I see another law in my members, warring against the law of my
mind, and bringing me into captivity
to the law of sin which is in my members.
24 O wretched man that I am! who
shall deliver me from [5]the body of this
death?
25 I thank God through Jesus Christ
our Lord. So then with the mind I myself serve the law of God; but with the
flesh the law of sin.

CHAPTER 8

THERE is therefore now no condemnation to them which are in
Christ Jesus, who [a]walk not after the
flesh, but after the Spirit.
2 For [b]the law of the [c]Spirit of life
in Christ Jesus hath made me free
from the law of sin and death.
3 For [d]what the law could not do, in
that it was weak through the flesh,
God sending his own Son in the likeness of sinful flesh, and [1]for sin, condemned sin in the flesh:
4 That the righteousness of the law
might be fulfilled in us, who walk not
after the flesh, but after the Spirit.
5 For they that are after the flesh do
mind the things of the flesh; but they
that are after the Spirit [e]the things of
the Spirit.
6 For [2]to be carnally minded *is* death;
but [3]to be spiritually minded *is* life and
peace.
7 Because [4]the carnal mind *is* enmity
against God: for it is not subject to
the law of God, neither indeed can be.
8 So then they that are in the flesh
cannot please God.

CHAP. 7

a Matt. 19.6. 1 Cor. 7.39.
b Matt. 5.32. Mark 10.12. Luke 16.18. 1 Cor. 6.9. Gal. 5.19, 21. Heb. 13.4.
c ch. 6.14. Gal. 2.19. Eph. 2.15. Col. 2.14. 1 Pet. 2.24.
d Hosea 2.19. 2 Cor. 11.2.
1 passions.
e ch. 6.21. Gal. 5.19, 21. Jas. 1.15.
2 Or, being dead to that.
f Eze. 11.19. John 4.23. ch. 2.29. 2 Cor. 3.6. Gal. 2.19, 20.
g ch. 3.20.
3 Or, concupiscence.
h Ex. 20.17. Micah 2.2. Eph. 5.3.
i ch. 4.15.
j 1 Cor. 15. 56.
k Lev. 18.5. Eze. 20.13. 2 Cor. 3.7.
l Ps. 19.8. 1 Tim. 1.8.
m 1 Ki. 21.20, 25.
4 know.
n Gal. 5.17.
o Gen. 8.21.
p Job 23.12. Ps. 1.2. Heb. 8.10.
q 2 Cor. 4.16.
5 Or, this body of death.

CHAP. 8

a Gal. 5.16.
b John 8.36. ch. 3.27. Gal. 2.19.
c 1 Cor. 15. 45. 2 Cor. 3.6.
d Heb. 7.18.
1 Or, by a sacrifice for sin.
e 1 Cor. 2.15. Gal. 5.22.
2 the minding of the flesh.
3 the minding of the Spirit.
4 the minding of the flesh.

9 But ye are not in the flesh, but in
the Spirit, if so be that [f]the Spirit of
God dwell in you. Now if any man
have not the [g]Spirit of Christ, he is
none of his.
10 And if Christ *be* in you, the body
is dead because of sin; but the Spirit *is*
life because of righteousness.
11 But if the Spirit of him that raised
up Jesus from the dead dwell in you,
[h]he that raised up Christ from the
dead shall also quicken your mortal
bodies [5]by his Spirit that dwelleth in
you.
12 Therefore, brethren, we are debtors, not to the flesh, to live after the
flesh.
13 For [i]if ye live after the flesh, ye
shall die: but if ye through the Spirit
do mortify the deeds of the body, ye
shall live.
14 For as many as are led by the
Spirit of God, they are the sons of
God.
15 For [j]ye have not received the
spirit of bondage again [k]to fear; but
ye have received the Spirit [l]of adoption, whereby we cry, Abba, Father.
16 The [m]Spirit itself beareth witness
with our spirit, that we are the children
of God:
17 And if children, then heirs; [n]heirs
of God, and joint-heirs with Christ;
if so be that we suffer with *him*, that
we may be also glorified together.
18 For I reckon that [o]the sufferings
of this present time *are* not worthy *to
be compared* with the glory which shall
be revealed in us.
19 For [p]the earnest expectation of
the creature waiteth for the [q]mani-
festation of the sons of God.
20 For [r]the creature was made subject to vanity, not willingly, but by
reason of him who hath subjected *the
same* in hope,
21 Because the creature itself also
shall be delivered from the bondage
of corruption into the glorious liberty
of the children of God.
22 For we know that [6]the whole creation groaneth [s]and travaileth in pain
together until now.
23 And not only *they*, but ourselves
also, which have [t]the firstfruits of the
Spirit, even we ourselves groan within
ourselves, waiting [u]for the adoption,
to wit, the redemption of our body.
24 For we are saved by hope: but hope
that [v]is seen is not hope: for what a
man seeth, why doth he yet hope for?
25 But if we hope for that we see not,
then do we with patience wait for *it*.

[f] 1 Cor. 3.16.
[g] John 3.34. 1 Pet. 1.11.
[h] Isa. 26.19. ch. 6.4,5. 1 Cor. 6.14. 2 Cor. 4.14. Eph. 2.5.
5 Or, because of his Spirit.
[i] ch. 6.21,22. Gal. 6.8.
[j] Heb. 2.15.
[k] 2 Tim. 1.7. 1 John 4.18.
[l] Isa. 56.5. Mark 14.36. Gal. 4.5,6.
[m] 2 Cor. 1.22. Eph. 1.13.
[n] Matt. 25. 21. John 17.24. Acts 26.18. Gal. 4.7.
[o] 2 Cor. 4.17. 1 Pet. 1.6,7.
[p] 2 Pet. 3.13.
[q] 1 John 3.2.
[r] Gen. 3.19.
6 Or, every creature.
[s] Jer. 12.11.
[t] 2 Cor. 5.5.
[u] Luke 20.36.
[v] Heb. 11.1.
[w] Matt. 20. 22.
[x] Zech. 12. 10. Matt. 10.20. Eph. 6.18.
[y] 1 Thes. 2.4. Rev. 2.23.
7 Or, that.
[z] 1 John 5.14.
[a] Gen. 50.20. Pro. 12.21. 2 Cor. 4.17.
[b] 2 Tim. 1.9.
[c] Ps. 1.6. Jer. 1.5. Matt. 7.23. 2 Tim. 2.19.
[d] Eph. 1.5.
[e] John 17.22.
[f] Col. 1.18.
[g] Eph. 4.4. Heb. 9.15.
[h] 1 Cor. 6.11.
[i] Isa. 50.8. Gal. 3.8.
[j] Isa. 53.12. Heb. 7.25.
[k] Ps. 44.22.
[l] 1 John 5.4.
[m] Col. 1.16. 1 Pet. 3.22.
[n] John 10.28.

26 Likewise the Spirit also helpeth
our infirmities: for [w]we know not
what we should pray for as we ought:
but [x]the Spirit itself maketh intercession for us with groanings which cannot be uttered.
27 And [y]he that searcheth the hearts
knoweth what *is* the mind of the
Spirit, [7]because he maketh intercession for the saints [z]according to *the
will of* God.
28 And we know that [a]all things
work together for good to them that
love God, to them [b]who are the called
according to *his* purpose.
29 For whom [c]he did foreknow, [d]he
also did predestinate [e]*to be* conformed to the image of his Son, [f]that he
might be the firstborn among many
brethren.
30 Moreover whom he did predestinate, them he also [g]called: and whom
he called, them he also [h]justified: and
whom he justified, them he also glorified.
31 What shall we then say to these
things? If God *be* for us, who *can be*
against us?
32 He that spared not his own Son,
but delivered him up for us all, how
shall he not with him also freely give
us all things?
33 Who shall lay any thing to the
charge of God's elect? [i]*It is* God that
justifieth.
34 Who *is* he that condemneth? *It is*
Christ that died, yea rather, that is
risen again, who is even at the right
hand of God, [j]who also maketh intercession for us.
35 Who shall separate us from the
love of Christ? *shall* tribulation, or
distress, or persecution, or famine, or
nakedness, or peril, or sword?
36 As it is written, [k]For thy sake we
are killed all the day long; we are
accounted as sheep for the slaughter.
37 Nay, [l]in all these things we are
more than conquerors through him
that loved us.
38 For I am persuaded, that neither
death, nor life, nor angels, nor [m]prin-
cipalities, nor powers, nor things present, nor things to come,
39 Nor height, nor depth, nor any
other creature, shall [n]be able to separate us from the love of God, which is
in Christ Jesus our Lord.

CHAPTER 9

I SAY the truth in Christ, I lie not,
my conscience also bearing me
witness in the Holy Ghost,

2 That I have great heaviness and
continual sorrow in my heart.
3 For [a]I could wish that myself were
[1]accursed from Christ for my brethren, my kinsmen according to the flesh:
4 Who [b]are Israelites; [c]to whom *pertaineth* the adoption, and [d]the glory,
and the [2]covenants, and the giving of
the law, and the service *of God*, and
[e]the promises;
5 Whose *are* the fathers, and of
whom as concerning the flesh Christ
came, [f]who is over all, God blessed
for ever. Ä-mĕn.
6 Not as though the word of God
hath taken none effect. For [g]they *are*
not all Israel, which are of Israel:
7 Neither, [h]because they are the seed
of Abraham, *are they* all children:
but, In Isaac [i]shall thy seed be called.
8 That is, They which are the children
of the flesh, these *are* not the children
of God: but the children of the promise are counted for the seed.
9 For this *is* the word of promise, [j]At
this time will I come, and Sara shall
have a son.
10 And not only *this;* but when [k]Re-
becca also had conceived by one, *even*
by our father Isaac;
11 (For *the children* being [l]not yet
born, neither having done any good
or evil, that the purpose of God according to election might stand, not of
works, but of him that calleth;)
12 It was said unto her, The [3]elder
shall serve the [4]younger.
13 As it is written, [m]Jacob have I
loved, but Esau have I hated.
14 What shall we say then? [n]*Is there*
unrighteousness with God? God forbid.
15 For he saith to Moses, [o]I will have
mercy on whom I will have mercy, and
I will have compassion on whom I will
have compassion.
16 So [p]then *it is* not of him that will-
eth, nor of him that runneth, but of
God that sheweth mercy.
17 For the scripture saith unto Pharaoh, Even [q]for this same purpose
have I raised thee up, that I might
shew my power in thee, and that my
name might be declared throughout
all the earth.
18 Therefore hath he mercy on
whom he will *have mercy*, and whom
he will he hardeneth.
19 Thou wilt say then unto me, Why
doth he yet find fault? For [r]who hath
resisted his will?
20 Nay but, O man, who art thou
that [5]repliest against God? [s]Shall the
thing formed say to him that formed
it, Why hast thou made me thus?
21 Hath not the [t]potter power over
the clay, of the same lump to make
[u]one vessel unto honour, and another
unto dishonour?
22 *What* if God, willing to shew *his*
wrath, and to make his power known,
endured with much longsuffering the
[v]vessels of wrath [6]fitted to destruction:
23 And that he might make known
the riches of his glory on the vessels of
mercy, which he had afore prepared
unto glory,
24 Even us, whom he hath called,
not of the Jews only, but also of the
Gentiles?
25 As he saith also in Ō-sēē, [w]I will
call them my people, which were not
my people; and her beloved, which
was not beloved.
26 And [x]it shall come to pass, *that* in
the place where it was said unto them,
Ye *are* not my people; there shall they
be called the children of the living
God.
27 Ē-sâi-ăs also crieth concerning
Israel, Though [y]the number of the
children of Israel be as the sand of the
sea, a remnant shall be saved:
28 For he will finish [7]the work, and
cut *it* short in righteousness: [z]because
a short work will the Lord make upon
the earth.
29 And as Ē-sâi-ăs said before, [a]Ex-
cept the Lord of Să-bā-ōth had left us
a seed, we [b]had been as Sŏd-ŏ-mă, and
been made like unto Gō-mŏr-rhă.
30 What shall we say then? That the
Gentiles, which followed not after
righteousness, have attained to righteousness, even the righteousness
which is of faith.
31 But Israel, which followed after
the law of righteousness, [c]hath not
attained to the law of righteousness.
32 Wherefore? Because *they sought
it* not by faith, but as it were by the
works of the law. For [d]they stumbled
at that stumblingstone;
33 As it is written, [e]Behold, I lay in
Sī-ǫn a stumblingstone and rock of
offence: and whosoever believeth on
him shall not be [8]ashamed.

CHAPTER 10

BRETHREN, my heart's desire
and prayer to God for Israel is,
that they might be saved.
2 For I bear them record [a]that they
have a zeal of God, but not according
to knowledge.

CHAP. 9
a Ex. 32.32.
1 Or, separated.
b Deut. 7.6. Ps. 50.5.
c Deut. 14.1.
d Ps. 63.2.
2 Or, testaments.
e Acts 13.32. ch. 4.13. Gal. 3.16. Eph. 2.12.
f Ps. 45.6. Jer. 23.6. Micah 5.2. John 1.1. Acts 20.28. Heb. 1.8. 1 John 5.20.
g Gal. 6.16.
h Gal. 4.23.
i Gen. 21.12. Heb. 11.18.
j Gen. 17.21.
k Gen. 25.21.
l Eph. 1.4.
3 Or, greater.
4 Or, lesser.
m Deut. 21.15. Luke 14.26.
n Gen. 18.25. Deut. 32.4. 2 Chr. 19.7. ch. 2.2.
o Ex. 33.19.
p Ps. 115.3.
q Ex. 9.16. Pro. 16.4.
r Job 9.12.
5 Or, answerest again, or, disputest with God? Job 33.13.
s Isa. 29.16. Isa. 45.9.
t Jer. 18.6.
u 2 Tim. 2.20.
v 1 Thes. 5.9.
6 Or, made up.
w Hosea 2.23.
x Hosea 1.10.
y Isa. 10.22.
7 Or, the account.
z Isa. 28.22.
a Isa. 1.9. Lam. 3.22.
b Isa. 13.19.
c Gal. 5.4.
d Luke 2.34. 1 Cor. 1.23.
e Ps. 118.22. Isa. 8.14. Matt. 21.42. 1 Pet. 2.6,8.
8 Or, confounded.

CHAP. 10
a 2 Ki. 10.16. Phil. 3.9. John 16.2.

3 For they being ignorant [b]of God's righteousness, and going about to establish their own [c]righteousness, have [d]not submitted themselves unto the righteousness of God.
4 For [e]Christ *is* the end of the law for righteousness to every one that believeth.
5 For Moses describeth the righteousness which is of the law, [f]That the man which doeth those things shall live by them.
6 But the righteousness which is of faith speaketh on this wise, [g]Say not in thine heart, Who shall ascend into heaven? (that is, to [h]bring Christ down *from above:*)
7 Or, Who shall descend into the deep? (that is, to [i]bring up Christ again from the dead.)
8 But what saith it? The word is nigh thee, *even* in thy mouth, and in thy heart: that is, the word of faith, which we preach;
9 That if thou shalt confess with thy mouth the Lord Jesus, and shalt believe in thine heart that God hath raised him from the dead, thou shalt be saved.
10 For with the heart man believeth unto righteousness; and with the mouth confession is made unto salvation.
11 For the scripture saith, [j]Whosoever believeth on him shall not be ashamed.
12 For [k]there is no difference between the Jew and the Greek: for the [l]same Lord over all [m]is rich unto all that call upon him.
13 For [n]whosoever shall call upon the name of the Lord shall be saved.
14 How then shall they call on him in whom they have not believed? and how shall they believe in him of whom they have not heard? and how shall they hear without [o]a preacher?
15 And how shall they preach, except they be sent? as it is written, [p]How beautiful are the feet of them that preach the gospel of peace, and bring glad tidings of good things!
16 But [q]they have not all obeyed the gospel. For Ē-ṡâi-ăs saith, [r]Lord, who hath believed [1]our [2]report?
17 So then faith *cometh* by hearing, and hearing by the word of God.
18 But I say, Have they not heard? Yes verily, [s]their sound went into all the earth, and their words unto the ends of the world.
19 But I say, Did not Israel know? First Moses saith, [t]I will provoke you to jealousy by *them that are* no people, *and* by a [u]foolish nation I will anger you.
20 But Ē-ṡâi-ăs is very bold, and saith, [v]I was found of them that sought me not; I was made manifest unto them that asked not after me.
21 But to Israel he saith, All day long I have stretched forth my hands unto a disobedient and gainsaying people.

CHAPTER 11

I SAY then, [a]Hath God cast away his people? God forbid. For [b]I also am an Israelite, of the seed of Abraham, *of* the tribe of Benjamin.
2 God hath not cast away his people which he [c]foreknew. Wot ye not what the scripture saith [1]of Ē-lī-ăs? how he maketh intercession to God against Israel, saying,
3 Lord, [d]they have killed thy prophets, and digged down thine altars; and I am left alone, and they seek my life.
4 But what saith the answer of God unto him? I have reserved to myself seven thousand men, who have not bowed the knee to *the image of* Bā-ăl.
5 Even [e]so then at this present time also there is a remnant according to the election of grace.
6 And [f]if by grace, then *is it* no more of works: otherwise grace is no more grace. But if *it be* of works, then is it no more grace: otherwise work is no more work.
7 What then? [g]Israel hath not obtained that which he seeketh for; but the [h]election hath obtained it, and the rest were [2]blinded
8 (According as it is written, [i]God hath given them the spirit of [3]slumber, [j]eyes that they should not see, and ears that they should not hear;) unto this day.
9 And David saith, [k]Let their table be made a snare, and a trap, and a stumblingblock, and a recompence unto them:
10 Let their eyes be darkened, that they may not see, and bow down their back alway.
11 I say then, Have they stumbled that they [l]should fall? God forbid: but *rather* through [m]their fall salvation *is come* unto the Gentiles, for to provoke them to jealousy.
12 Now if the fall of them *be* the riches of the world, and the [4]diminishing of them the riches of the Gentiles; how much more their [n]fulness?
13 For I speak to you Gentiles, inas-

b Ps. 71.15, 16,19. John 16.8, 9,10. ch. 1.17. 2 Pet. 1.1.
c Phil. 3.9.
d Heb. 10.29.
e Matt. 5.17. Gal. 3.24.
f Lev. 18.5.
g Deut. 30. 12.
h Heb. 8.1.
i ch. 4.25. 1 Cor. 15.3, 4. Rev. 1.18.
j Isa. 28.16. Jer. 17.7. ch. 9.33.
k Acts 15.9.
l Acts 10.36.
m Eph. 1.7.
n Joel 2.32. Acts 2.21.
o Titus 1.3.
p Isa. 52.7.
q Heb. 4.2.
r John 12.38.
1 the hearing of us?
2 Or, preaching?
s Ps. 19.4. Matt. 24.14.
t Deut. 32.21.
u Titus 3.3.
v Isa. 65.1.

CHAP. 11

a 1 Sam. 12. 22. Ps. 94.14. Amos 9.8,9.
b Acts 22.3. Phil. 3.5.
c ch. 8.29.
1 in Elias?
d 1 Ki. 19.10.
e ch. 9.27.
f Deut. 9.4,5.
g ch. 10.3.
h John 10.28. 2 Tim. 2.19.
2 Or, hardened. 2 Cor. 3.14.
i Isa. 29.10. Matt. 13.14. John 12.40. Acts 28.26, 27.
3 Or, remorse.
j Deut. 29.4. Isa. 6.9. Jer. 5.21. Eze. 12.2.
k Ps. 69.22.
l Eze. 18.23.
m Acts 13.46. Acts 18.6.
4 Or, decay, or, loss.
n Isa. 11.11, 12,16. Jer. 30.4. Micah 4.1,2. Zech. 2.11.

much as [o]I am the apostle of the Gentiles, I magnify mine office:
14 If by any means I may provoke to
emulation *them which are* my flesh,
and [p]might save some of them.
15 For if the casting away of them *be*
the reconciling of the world, what
shall the receiving *of them be*, but life
from the dead?
16 For [q]if the firstfruit *be* holy, the
lump *is* also *holy:* and if the root *be*
holy, so *are* the branches.
17 And if [r]some of the branches be
broken off, [s]and thou, being a wild
olive tree, wert graffed in [5]among
them, and with them partakest of the
root and fatness of the olive tree;
18 Boast [t]not against the branches.
But if thou boast, thou bearest not the
root, but the root thee.
19 Thou wilt say then, The branches
were broken off, that I might be graffed in.
20 Well; because of unbelief they
were broken off, and thou standest by
faith. Be [u]not highminded, [v]but fear:
21 For if God spared not the natural
branches, *take heed* lest he also spare
not thee.
22 Behold therefore the goodness
and severity of God: on them which
fell, severity; but toward thee, goodness, if [w]thou continue in *his* goodness: otherwise [x]thou also shalt be cut
off.
23 And they also, [y]if they abide not
still in unbelief, shall be graffed in:
for God is able to graff them in again.
24 For if thou wert cut out of the
olive tree which is wild by nature, and
wert graffed contrary to nature into a
good olive tree: how much more shall
these, which be the natural *branches*,
be graffed into their own olive tree?
25 For I would not, brethren, that ye
should be ignorant of this mystery,
lest ye should be wise in your own
conceits; that [6]blindness in part is
happened to Israel, until [z]the fulness
of the Gentiles be come in.
26 And so [a]all Israel shall be saved:
as it is written, [b]There shall come out
of Sī-ŏn the Deliverer, and shall turn
away ungodliness from Jacob:
27 For [c]this *is* my covenant unto
them, when I shall take away their
sins.
28 As concerning the gospel, *they*
are enemies for your sakes: but as
touching the election, *they are* [d]be-
loved for the fathers' sakes.
29 For the gifts and calling of God
are without [e]repentance.

o Acts 9.15. Acts 22.21. Gal. 1.16. Eph. 3.8.
p 1 Cor. 7.16. Jas. 5.20.
q Lev. 23.10.
r Jer. 11.16.
s Eph. 2.12.
5 Or, for them.
t 1 Cor. 10.12.
u ch. 12.16.
v Phil. 2.12.
w 1 Cor. 15.2. Heb. 3.6.
x John 15.2.
y 2 Cor. 3.16.
6 hardness.
z Luke 21.24. Rev. 7.9.
a Isa. 60.15. Jer. 3.18.
b Ps. 14.7. Isa. 59.20.
c Jer. 31.31. Heb. 8.8.
d Deut. 9.5.
e Num. 23. 19.
7 Or, obeyed.
8 Or, obeyed.
9 Or, shut them all up together.
f Isa. 40.13.
g Job 35.7.
h John 1.3. 1 Cor. 8.6.
10 him. Rev. 1.6.

CHAP. 12

a 1 Cor. 6.13.
b Heb. 10.20.
c John 7.7. Gal. 1.4. Eph. 2.2. 1 Pet. 1.14.
d Eph. 1.18. Col. 1.21, 22.
e Eph. 5.10, 17. 1 Thes. 4.3.
1 to sobriety.
f 1 Cor. 12.7. Eph. 4.7.
g Eph. 1.23.
h 1 Cor. 12.4-11. 1 Pet. 4.10.
i 1 Cor. 12.10.
j Gal. 6.6.
k Acts 15.32. 1 Cor. 14.3.
2 Or, imparteth.
3 liberally.
l Acts 20.28. 1 Pet. 5.2.
m Amos 5.15.

30 For as ye in times past have not
[7]believed God, yet have now obtained
mercy through their unbelief:
31 Even so have these also now not
[8]believed, that through your mercy
they also may obtain mercy.
32 For God hath [9]concluded them all
in unbelief, that he might have mercy
upon all.
33 O the depth of the riches both of
the wisdom and knowledge of God!
how unsearchable *are* his judgments,
and his ways past finding out!
34 For [f]who hath known the mind
of the Lord? or who hath been his
counseller?
35 Or [g]who hath first given to him,
and it shall be recompensed unto him
again?
36 For [h]of him, and through him,
and to him, *are* all things: to [10]whom
be glory for ever. Ā-mĕn.

CHAPTER 12

I BESEECH you therefore, brethren, by the mercies of God, that [a]ye
present your bodies [b]a living sacrifice,
holy, acceptable unto God, *which is*
your reasonable service.
2 And [c]be not conformed to this
world: but [d]be ye transformed by the
renewing of your mind, that ye may
prove [e]what *is* that good, and acceptable, and perfect, will of God.
3 For I say, through the grace given
unto me, to every man that is among
you, not to think *of himself* more
highly than he ought to think; but to
think [1]soberly, according as God hath
dealt [f]to every man the measure of
faith.
4 For as we have many members in
one body, and all members have not
the same office:
5 So [g]we, *being* many, are one body
in Christ, and every one members one
of another.
6 Having [h]then gifts differing according to the grace that is given to us,
whether prophecy, [i]*let us prophesy*
according to the proportion of faith;
7 Or ministry, *let us wait* on *our* ministering: or [j]he that teacheth, on
teaching;
8 Or [k]he that exhorteth, on exhortation: he that [2]giveth, *let him do it* [3]with
simplicity; [l]he that ruleth, with diligence; he that sheweth mercy, with
cheerfulness.
9 *Let* love be without dissimulation.
Abhor that [m]which is evil; cleave to
that which is good.
10 *Be* kindly affectioned one to an-

other [4]with brotherly love; in honour
preferring one another;
11 Not slothful in business; [n]fervent
in spirit; serving the Lord;
12 Rejoicing [o]in hope; [p]patient in
tribulation; continuing instant in
prayer;
13 Distributing [q]to the necessity of
saints; given [r]to hospitality.
14 Bless [s]them which persecute you:
bless, and curse not.
15 Rejoice with them that do rejoice,
and weep with them that weep.
16 *Be* of the same mind one toward
another. Mind not high things, but
[5]condescend to men of low estate. Be
not wise in your own conceits.
17 Recompense to no man evil for
evil. Provide things honest in the
sight of all men.
18 If it be possible, as much as lieth
in you, live peaceably with all men.
19 Dearly beloved, avenge not yourselves, but *rather* give place unto
wrath: for it is written, [t]Vengeance *is*
mine; I will repay, saith the Lord.
20 Therefore [u]if thine enemy hunger,
feed him; if he thirst, give him drink:
for in so doing thou shalt heap coals
of fire on his head.
21 Be [v]not overcome of evil, but
overcome evil with good.

CHAPTER 13

LET every soul [a]be subject unto the
higher powers. For [b]there is no
power but of God: the powers that be
are [1]ordained of God.
2 Whosoever therefore resisteth the
power, resisteth the ordinance of
God: and they that resist shall receive
to themselves damnation.
3 For [c]rulers are not a terror to good
works, but to the evil. Wilt thou then
not be afraid of the power? do [d]that
which is good, and thou shalt have
praise of the same:
4 For he is the minister of God to
thee for good. But if thou do that
which is evil, be afraid; for he beareth
not the sword in vain: for he is
the minister of God, a revenger to
execute wrath upon him that doeth
evil.
5 Wherefore [e]*ye* must needs be subject, not only for wrath, but also for
conscience sake.
6 For for this cause pay ye tribute
also: for they are God's ministers,
attending continually upon this very
thing.
7 Render [f]therefore to all their dues:
tribute to whom tribute *is due;* custom

4 Or, in the love of the brethren.
n Rev. 3.15.
o Heb. 3.6.
p Heb. 10.36.
q Heb. 6.10.
r Heb. 13.2.
s 1 Pet. 3.9.
5 Or, be contented with mean things.
t Deut. 32.35.
u Pro. 25.21.
v 1 Pet. 2.21.

CHAP. 13

a 1 Cor. 7.21. Titus 3.1.
b Pro. 8.15. Dan. 2.21. John 19.11.
1 Or, ordered.
c 2 Sam. 23.3. Ps. 94.20.
d 1 Pet. 3.13.
e Eccl. 8.2.
f Luke 20.25.
g Lev. 19.3. 1 Sam. 12. 18. Pro. 24.21. Eph. 6.5.
h Matt. 7.12.
i Lev. 19.18. Matt. 22.39. Luke 10.27. Gal. 5.14.
j 1 Cor. 15. 34.
k Eph. 6.13.
l Phil. 4.8.
2 Or, decently.
m Phil. 2.3. Jas. 3.14. 1 Pet. 2.1,2.
n Gal. 3.27.
o Gal. 5.16.

CHAP. 14

a Job 4.3. Isa. 35.3,4. Matt. 12.20.
1 Or, not to judge his doubtful thoughts.
b 1 Cor. 10. 25.
c Col. 2.16.
d 1 Cor. 4.4, 5. Jas. 4.12.
e Gal. 4.10.
2 Or, fully assured.
3 Or, observeth.
f 1 Cor. 10. 31. 1 Tim. 4.3.
g 1 Cor. 6.19. Gal. 2.20.

to whom custom; [g]fear to whom fear;
honour to whom honour.
8 Owe no man any thing, but to love
one another: [h]for he that loveth
another hath fulfilled the law.
9 For this, Thou shalt not commit
adultery, Thou shalt not kill, Thou
shalt not steal, Thou shalt not bear
false witness, Thou shalt not covet;
and if *there be* any other commandment, it is briefly comprehended in
this saying, namely, [i]Thou shalt love
thy neighbour as thyself.
10 Love worketh no ill to his neighbour: therefore love *is* the fulfilling of
the law.
11 And that, knowing the time, that
now *it is* high time [j]to awake out of
sleep: for now *is* our salvation nearer
than when we believed.
12 The night is far spent, the day is
at hand: let us therefore cast off the
works of darkness, and [k]let us put on
the armour of light.
13 Let [l]us walk [2]honestly, as in the
day; not in rioting and drunkenness,
not in chambering and wantonness,
not [m]in strife and envying.
14 But [n]put ye on the Lord Jesus
Christ, and [o]make not provision for
the flesh, to *fulfil* the lusts *thereof.*

CHAPTER 14

HIM that is [a]weak in the faith receive ye, *but* [1]not to doubtful dis-
putations.
2 For one believeth that he [b]may eat
all things: another, who is weak, eateth herbs.
3 Let not him that eateth despise him
that eateth not; and [c]let not him
which eateth not judge him that eateth: for God hath received him.
4 Who [d]art thou that judgest another
man's servant? to his own master he
standeth or falleth. Yea, he shall be
holden up: for God is able to make
him stand.
5 One [e]man esteemeth one day above
another: another esteemeth every day
alike. Let every man be [2]fully persuaded in his own mind.
6 He that [3]regardeth the day, regardeth *it* unto the Lord; and he that
regardeth not the day, to the Lord he
doth not regard *it.* He that eateth,
eateth to the Lord, for [f]he giveth God
thanks; and he that eateth not, to the
Lord he eateth not, and giveth God
thanks.
7 For [g]none of us liveth to himself,
and no man dieth to himself.
8 For whether we live, we live unto

the Lord; and whether we die, we die unto the Lord: whether we live therefore, or die, we are the Lord's.
9 For [h]to this end Christ both died, and rose, and revived, that he might be [i]Lord both of the dead and living.
10 But why dost thou judge thy brother? or why dost thou set at nought thy brother? for [j]we shall all stand before the judgment seat of Christ.
11 For it is written, [k]*As* I live, saith the Lord, every knee shall bow to me, and every tongue shall confess to God.
12 So then [l]every one of us shall give account of himself to God.
13 Let us not therefore judge one another any more: but judge this rather, that [m]no man put a stumblingblock or an occasion to fall in *his* brother's way.
14 I know, and am persuaded by the Lord Jesus, that [n]*there is* nothing [4]unclean of itself: but [o]to him that esteemeth any thing to be [5]unclean, to him *it is* unclean.
15 But if thy brother be grieved with *thy* meat, now walkest thou not [6]charitably. Destroy not him with thy meat, for whom Christ died.
16 Let [p]not then your good be evil spoken of:
17 For [q]the kingdom of God is not meat and drink; but righteousness, and peace, and joy in the Holy Ghost.
18 For he that in these things serveth Christ [r]*is* acceptable to God, and approved of men.
19 Let [s]us therefore follow after the things which make for peace, and things wherewith [t]one may edify another.
20 For meat destroy not the work of God. All [u]things indeed *are* pure; but *it is* evil for that man who eateth with offence.
21 *It is* good neither to eat flesh, nor to drink wine, nor *any thing* whereby thy brother stumbleth, or is offended, or is made weak.
22 Hast thou faith? have *it* to thyself before God. Happy *is* he that condemneth not himself in that thing which he alloweth.
23 And he that [7]doubteth is damned if he eat, because *he eateth* not of faith: for whatsoever [v]*is* not of faith is sin.

CHAPTER 15

WE [a]then that are strong ought to bear the [b]infirmities of the weak, and not to please ourselves.
2 Let [c]every one of us please *his* neighbour for *his* good [d]to edification.
3 For even Christ pleased not himself; but, as it is written, The [e]reproaches of them that reproached thee fell on me.
4 For [f]whatsoever things were written aforetime were written for our learning, that we through patience and comfort of the scriptures might have hope.
5 Now [g]the God of patience and consolation grant you to be likeminded one toward another [1]according to Christ Jesus:
6 That ye may with one mind *and* one mouth glorify God, even the Father of our Lord Jesus Christ.
7 Wherefore receive ye one another, [h]as Christ also received us to the glory of God.
8 Now I say that [i]Jesus Christ was a minister of the circumcision for the truth of God, [j]to confirm the promises *made* unto the fathers:
9 And [k]that the Gentiles might glorify God for *his* mercy; as it is written, [l]For this cause I will confess to thee among the Gentiles, and sing unto thy name.
10 And again he saith, [m]Rejoice, ye Gentiles, with his people.
11 And again, [n]Praise the Lord, all ye Gentiles; and laud him, all ye people.
12 And again, Ē-sâi-âs saith, [o]There shall be a root of Jesse, and he that shall rise to reign over the Gentiles; in him shall the Gentiles trust.
13 Now the God of hope fill you with all joy and peace in believing, that ye may abound in hope, through the power of the Holy Ghost.
14 And [p]I myself also am persuaded of you, my brethren, that ye also are full of goodness, [q]filled with all knowledge, able also to admonish one another.
15 Nevertheless, brethren, I have written the more boldly unto you in some sort, as putting you in mind, because [r]of the grace that is given to me of God,
16 That [s]I should be the minister of Jesus Christ to the Gentiles, ministering the gospel of God, that the [2]offering up of the Gentiles might be acceptable, being sanctified by the Holy Ghost.
17 I have therefore whereof I may glory through Jesus Christ [t]in those things which pertain to God.
18 For I will not dare to speak of any of those things [u]which Christ hath not

h 2 Cor. 5.15.
i Acts 10.36.
j Matt. 25.31. Jude 14.15.
k Isa. 45.23. Luke 24.26. 2 Cor. 5.15. 1 Pet. 1.21.
l Matt. 12.36.
m 1 Cor. 8.9.
n Titus 1.15.
4 common.
o 1 Cor. 8.7.
5 common.
6 according to charity.
p ch. 12.17.
q 1 Cor. 8.8.
r 2 Cor. 8.21.
s Ps. 34.14.
t 1 Cor. 14.12.
u Acts 10.15.
7 Or, discerneth and putteth a difference between meats, or, staggers.
v Titus 1.15.

CHAP. 15

a Gal. 6.1.
b ch. 14.1.
c Phil. 2.4,5.
d ch. 14.19.
e Ps. 69.9.
f 2 Tim. 3.16.
g Ex. 34.6. Ps. 86.15.
1 Or, after the example of.
h ch. 5.2.
i Matt. 15.24. John 1.11. Acts 3.25, 26.
j ch. 3.3. 2 Cor. 1.20.
k John 10.16. ch. 9.23.
l Ps. 18.49.
m Deut. 32.43.
n Ps. 117.1.
o Isa. 9.6,7. Rev. 5.5.
p 2 Pet. 1.12. 1 John 2.21.
q 1 Cor. 8.1.
r Isa. 49.1,5. Acts 9.15. Gal. 1.15.
s Gal. 2.7,9. 1 Tim. 2.7.
2 Or, sacrificing.
t Heb. 5.1.
u Acts 14.27. 1 Cor. 3.6-9. 2 Cor. 1.1-3.

wrought by me, [v]to make the Gentiles obedient, by word and deed,

19 Through [w]mighty signs and wonders, by the power of the Spirit of God; so that from Jerusalem, and round about unto Ĭl-lỹr'-ĭ-cŭm, I have fully preached the gospel of Christ.

20 Yea, so have I strived to preach the gospel, not where Christ was named, [x]lest I should build upon another man's foundation:

21 But as it is written, [y]To whom he was not spoken of, they shall see: and they that have not heard shall understand.

22 For which cause also [z]I have been [3]much hindered from coming to you.

23 But now having no more place in these parts, and [a]having a great desire these many years to come unto you;

24 Whensoever I take my journey into Spain, I will come to you: for I trust to see you in my journey, [b]and to be brought on my way thitherward by you, if first I be somewhat filled [4]with your *company*.

25 But now [c]I go unto Jerusalem to minister unto the saints.

26 For [d]it hath pleased them of Măç-ē-dō'-nĭ-ă and Ă-chāi'-ă to make a certain contribution for the poor saints which are at Jerusalem.

27 It hath pleased them verily; and their debtors they are. For if the Gentiles have been made partakers of their spiritual things, [e]their duty is also to minister unto them in carnal things.

28 When therefore I have performed this, and have sealed to them [f]this fruit, I will come by you into Spain.

29 And [g]I am sure that, when I come unto you, I shall come in [h]the fulness of the blessing of the gospel of Christ.

30 Now I beseech you, brethren, for the Lord Jesus Christ's sake, and [i]for the love of the Spirit, [j]that ye strive together with me in *your* prayers to God for me;

31 That [k]I may be delivered from them that [5]do not believe in Judæa; and that my service which *I have* for Jerusalem may be accepted of the saints;

32 That I may come unto you with joy by [l]the will of God, and may with you [m]be refreshed.

33 Now the God of peace *be* with you all. Ā'-mĕn.

CHAPTER 16

I COMMEND unto you Phē'-bē our sister, which is a servant of the church which is at [a]Çĕn-chrē'-ă:

2 That [b]ye receive her in the Lord, as becometh saints, and that ye assist her in whatsoever business she hath need of you: for she hath been a succourer of many, and of myself also.

3 Greet [c]Priscilla and Ă-quĭl'-ă my helpers in Christ Jesus:

4 Who have for my life laid down their own necks: unto whom not only I give thanks, but also all the churches of the Gentiles.

5 Likewise *greet* [d]the church that is in their house. Salute my wellbeloved Ĕp-æ'-nĕ-tŭs, who is [e]the firstfruits of Ă-chāi'-ă unto Christ.

6 Greet Mary, who [f]bestowed much labour on us.

7 Salute Ăn-drō-nī'-cŭs and Junia, my kinsmen, and my fellowprisoners, who are of note among the apostles, who also [g]were in Christ before me.

8 Greet Ăm'-plĭ-ăs my beloved in the Lord.

9 Salute Ŭr'-bāne, our helper in Christ, and Stăch'-ỹs my beloved.

10 Salute Ă-pĕl'-lēs approved in Christ. Salute them which are of Ă-rĭs-tō-bū'-lŭs' [1]*household*.

11 Salute Hē-rō'-dĭ-on my kinsman. Greet them that be of the [2]*household* of Năr-çĭs'-sŭs, which are in the Lord.

12 Salute Trỹ-phē'-nă and Trỹ-phō'-să, who labour in the Lord. Salute the beloved Persis, which laboured much in the Lord.

13 Salute Rufus [h]chosen in the Lord, and his mother and mine.

14 Salute Ă-sỹn'-crĭ-tŭs, Phlĕg'-ŏn, Hĕr'-măs, Păt'-rō-băs, Hĕr'-mēs, and the brethren which are with them.

15 Salute Phĭ-lŏl'-ō-gŭs, and Julia, Nē'-reūs, and his sister, and Ō-lỹm'-păs, and all the saints which are with them.

16 Salute [i]one another with an holy kiss. The churches of Christ salute you.

17 Now I beseech you, brethren, mark them [j]which cause divisions and offences contrary to the doctrine which ye have learned; and [k]avoid them.

18 For they that are such serve not our Lord Jesus Christ, but [l]their own belly; and [m]by good words and fair speeches deceive the hearts of the simple.

19 For your obedience is come abroad unto all *men*. I am glad therefore on your behalf: but yet I would have you wise [n]unto that which is good, and [3]simple concerning evil.

20 And the God of peace shall [4]bruise

v Mark 16. 20. ch. 1.5.
w Acts 1.8. 1 Cor. 12.4-11.
x 2 Cor. 10. 13.
y Isa. 52.15.
z ch. 1.13.
3 Or, many ways, or, oftentimes.
a Acts 19.21.
b Acts 15.3.
4 with you.
c Acts 24.17.
d 1 Cor. 16.1. 2 Cor. 8.1.
e 1 Cor. 9.11. Gal. 6.6.
f Phil. 4.17.
g ch. 1.11.
h Eph. 3.8.
i Phil. 2.1.
j 2 Cor. 1.11.
k 2 Thes. 3.2.
5 Or, are disobedient.
l Jas. 4.15.
m 2 Cor. 7. 13. 2 Tim. 1.16.

CHAP. 16

a Acts 18.18.
b Matt. 25. 40. Phil. 2.29. Col. 4.10. 3 John 5,6.
c Acts 18.2. 2 Tim. 4.19.
d 1 Cor. 16. 19. Col. 4.15. Philem. 2.
e 1 Cor. 16. 15.
f 1 Tim. 5.10.
g Gal. 1.22.
1 Or, friends.
2 Or, friends.
h Eph. 1.4.
i 1 Thes. 5.26. 1 Pet. 5.14.
j Acts 15. Phil. 3.2. Col. 2.8. 1 Tim. 6.3.
k 1 Cor. 5.9. 2 Thes. 3.6. 2 Tim. 3.5. Titus 3.10. 2 John 10.
l Isa. 56.10-12. Hos. 4.8-11. Phil. 3.19. 1 Tim. 6.3.
m Col. 2.4. 2 Pet. 2.3.
n Matt. 10. 16.
3 Or, harmless.
4 Or, tread.

Satan under your feet shortly. The
grace of our Lord Jesus Christ *be*
with you. Ä-mĕn.
21 Timotheus [o]my workfellow, and
[p]Lû-çĭ-ŭs, and [q]Jā-sọn, and [r]Sō-sĭp-ă-
tĕr, my kinsmen, salute you.
22 I Tĕr-tĭŭs, who wrote *this* epistle,
salute you in the Lord.
23 Gâi-ŭs [s]mine host, and of the
whole church, saluteth you. [t]Ē-răs-
tŭs the chamberlain of the city saluteth you, and Quartus a brother.
24 The [u]grace of our Lord Jesus
Christ *be* with you all. Ä-mĕn.
25 Now to him that is of power to
stablish you [v]according to my gospel,
and the preaching of Jesus Christ, according [w]to the revelation of the
mystery, [x]which was kept secret since
the world began,
26 But [y]now is made manifest, and
by the scriptures of the prophets, according to the commandment of
the everlasting God, made known
to all nations for the obedience of
faith:
27 To God only wise, *be* glory
through Jesus Christ for ever. Ä-mĕn.

¶ Written to the Romans from Corinthus, *and sent* by Phebe servant of the church at Cenchrea.

o Acts 16.1. 1 Tim. 1.2.
p Acts 13.1.
q Acts 17.5.
r Acts 20.4.
s 1 Cor. 1.14.
t Acts 19.22. 2 Tim. 4.20.
u 1 Thes. 5. 28.
v ch. 2.16.
w Eph. 3.3,5. Col. 1.27. 1 Pet. 1.20.
x 1 Cor. 2.7.
y 2 Tim. 1.10.

THE FIRST EPISTLE OF PAUL THE APOSTLE TO THE

CORINTHIANS

CHAPTER 1

PAUL, called *to be* an apostle of
Jesus Christ through the will of
God, [a]and Sŏs-thĕ-nēs *our* brother,
2 Unto the church of God which is at
Corinth, to them that [b]are sanctified
in Christ Jesus, [c]called *to be* saints,
with all that in every place call upon
the name of Jesus Christ our [d]Lord,
[e]both theirs and ours:
3 Grace *be* unto you, and peace,
from God our Father, and *from* the
Lord Jesus Christ.
4 I thank my God always on your
behalf, for the grace of God which is
given you by Jesus Christ;
5 That in every thing ye are enriched
by him, [f]in all utterance, and *in* all
knowledge;
6 Even as [g]the testimony of Christ
was confirmed in you:
7 So that ye come behind in no gift;
waiting for the [1]coming of our Lord
Jesus Christ:
8 Who [h]shall also confirm you unto
the end, [i]*that ye may be* blameless in
the day of our Lord Jesus Christ.
9 God *is* [j]faithful, by whom ye were
called unto [k]the fellowship of his Son
Jesus Christ our Lord.
10 Now I beseech you, brethren, by
the name of our Lord Jesus Christ,
that ye all speak the same thing, and
that there be no [2]divisions among
you; but *that* ye be perfectly joined
together in the same mind and in the
same judgment.
11 For it hath been declared unto me
of you, my brethren, by them *which*
are of the house of Chlō-ĕ, that there
are contentions among you.
12 Now this I say, [l]that every one of
you saith, I am of Paul; and I of [m]Ä-
pŏl-lŏs; and I of [n]Çē-phăs; and I of
Christ.
13 Is [o]Christ divided? was Paul crucified for you? or were ye baptized in
the name of Paul?
14 I thank God that I baptized none
of you, but [p]Crĭs-pŭs and [q]Gâi-ŭs;
15 Lest any should say that I had
baptized in mine own name.
16 And I baptized also the household [r]of Stĕph-ă-năs: besides, I know
not whether I baptized any other.
17 For [s]Christ sent me not to baptize, but to preach the gospel: not with
wisdom of [3]words, lest the cross of
Christ should be made of none effect.
18 For the preaching of the cross is
to them [t]that perish [u]foolishness; but
unto us which are saved it is [v]the
power of God.
19 For it is written, [w]I will destroy
the wisdom of the wise, and will bring
to nothing the understanding of the
prudent.
20 Where [x]*is* the wise? where *is* the
scribe? where *is* the disputer of this
world? hath [y]not God made foolish
the wisdom of this world?
21 For [z]after that in the wisdom of
God the world by wisdom knew not
God, it pleased God by the foolishness of preaching to save them that
believe.
22 For the [a]Jews require a sign, and
the Greeks seek after wisdom:

CHAP. 1
a Acts 18.17.
b John 17.19. ch. 6.9-11. Heb. 2.11.
c Rom. 1.7. 1 Thes. 4.7. 2 Tim. 1.9.
d ch. 8.6.
e Rom. 3.22.
f 2 Cor. 8.7.
g Acts 18.5. ch. 2.1,2.
1 revelation.
h 2 Thes. 3.3.
i 1 Thes. 5.23.
j Num. 23.10. Deut. 7.9. Ps. 100.5. Isa. 49.7. Matt. 24.35. Heb. 10.23.
k John 15.4.
2 schisms.
l ch. 3.4.
m Acts 18.24.
n John 1.42.
o 2 Cor. 11.4.
p Acts 18.8.
q Rom. 16. 23.
r ch. 16.15.
s Acts 26.17.
3 Or, speech.
t 2 Cor. 2.15.
u Acts 17.18.
v Rom. 1.16.
w Isa. 29.14.
x Isa. 33.18.
y 2 Sam. 15. 31. Isa. 44.25. Rom. 1.22.
z Luke 10.21.
a Luke 11.16.

23 But we preach Christ crucified,
unto the [b]Jews a stumblingblock, and
unto the Greeks foolishness;
24 But unto them which are called,
both Jews and Greeks, Christ [c]the
power of God, and the [d]wisdom of
God.
25 Because the [e]foolishness of God
is wiser than men; and the weakness
of God is stronger than men.
26 For ye see your calling, brethren,
how that [f]not many wise men after
the flesh, not many mighty, not many
noble, *are called:*
27 But [g]God hath chosen the foolish
things of the world to confound the
wise; and God hath chosen the weak
things of the world to confound the
things which are mighty;
28 And base things of the world, and
things which are despised, hath God
chosen, *yea,* and [h]things which are
not, [i]to bring to nought things that
are:
29 That no flesh should glory in his
presence.
30 But of him are ye in Christ Jesus,
who of God is made unto us wisdom,
and righteousness, and sanctification,
and redemption:
31 That, according as it is written,
[j]He that glorieth, let him glory in the
Lord.

CHAPTER 2

AND I, brethren, when I came to
you, came [a]not with excellency of
speech or of wisdom, declaring unto
you the testimony of God.
2 For I determined not to know any
thing among you, [b]save Jesus Christ,
and him crucified.
3 And [c]I was with you [d]in weakness,
and in fear, and in much trembling.
4 And my speech and my preaching
[e]*was* not with [1]enticing words of man's
wisdom, but in demonstration of the
Spirit and of power:
5 That your faith should not [2]stand
in the wisdom of men, but [f]in the
power of God.
6 Howbeit we speak wisdom among
them that [g]are perfect: yet not the
wisdom of this world, nor of the
princes of this world, that come to
nought:
7 But we speak the wisdom of God in
a mystery, *even* the hidden *wisdom,*
[h]which God ordained before the
world unto our glory:
8 Which [i]none of the princes of this
world knew: for had they known *it,*
they would not have crucified the
Lord of glory.

b Isa. 8.14. Matt. 11.6.
c Rom. 1.4.
d Col. 2.3.
e 2 Cor. 4.7.
f John 7.48.
g Ps. 8.2. Matt. 11.25.
h Rom. 4.17.
i ch. 2.6.
j Jer. 9.23.

CHAP. 2

a ch. 1.17.
b Gal. 6.14. Phil. 3.8.
c Acts 18.1.
d 2 Cor. 10.1. Gal. 4.13.
e 2 Pet. 1.16.
1 Or, persuasible.
2 be.
f Acts 16.14. 2 Cor. 4.7. 1 Pet. 1.5.
g Eph. 4.13. Phil. 3.15.
h Rom. 16. 25. 2 Tim. 1.9.
i Acts 13.27.
j Isa. 64.4.
k Matt. 16. 17. Luke 2.26. Eph. 3.3,5. 1 Pet. 1.12. Rev. 1.1.
l Jer. 17.9.
m Rom. 11. 33.
n Rom. 8.15.
o 2 Pet. 1.16.
p Matt. 16. 23.
q Rom. 8.5. Jude 19.
r Pro. 28.5. Gal. 6.1. Col. 1.9.
3 Or, discerneth.
4 Or, discerned.
s Job 15.8. Isa. 40.13. Rom. 11.34.
5 shall.
t Ps. 25.14. John 15.15.

CHAP. 3

a Heb. 5.13. 1 Pet. 2.2.
1 Or, factions.
2 according to man?
b Rom. 12.3.
c Acts 18.4.
d Acts 19.1.
e Isa. 55.10.
f Ps. 62.12. Rom. 2.6. Rev. 2.23.

9 But as it is written, [j]Eye hath not
seen, nor ear heard, neither have entered into the heart of man, the things
which God hath prepared for them
that love him.
10 But [k]God hath revealed *them* unto
us by his Spirit: for the Spirit searcheth all things, yea, the deep things of
God.
11 For what man knoweth the things
of a man, [l]save the spirit of man
which is in him? [m]even so the things
of God knoweth no man, but the
Spirit of God.
12 Now we have received, not the
spirit of the world, but [n]the spirit
which is of God; that we might know
the things that are freely given to us of
God.
13 Which [o]things also we speak, not
in the words which man's wisdom
teacheth, but which the Holy Ghost
teacheth; comparing spiritual things
with spiritual.
14 But [p]the natural man receiveth
not the things of the Spirit of God:
for they are foolishness unto him:
neither [q]can he know *them,* because
they are spiritually discerned.
15 But [r]he that is spiritual [3]judgeth
all things, yet he himself is [4]judged of
no man.
16 For [s]who hath known the mind of
the Lord, that he [5]may instruct him?
But [t]we have the mind of Christ.

CHAPTER 3

AND I, brethren, could not speak
unto you as unto spiritual, but as
unto carnal, *even* as unto babes in
Christ.
2 I have fed you with [a]milk, and not
with meat: for hitherto ye were not
able *to bear it,* neither yet now are ye
able.
3 For ye are yet carnal: for whereas
there is among you envying, and
strife, and [1]divisions, are ye not carnal,
and walk [2]as men?
4 For while one saith, I am of Paul;
and another, I *am* of Ă-pŏl-lŏs; are ye
not carnal?
5 Who then is Paul, and who *is* Ă-
pŏl-lŏs, but ministers by whom ye believed, even [b]as the Lord gave to every
man?
6 I [c]have planted, [d]Ă-pŏl-lŏs watered; but God [e]gave the increase.
7 So then neither is he that planteth
any thing, neither he that watereth;
but God that giveth the increase.
8 Now he that planteth and he that
watereth are one: [f]and every man

shall receive his own reward according to his own labour.

9 For [g]we are labourers together with God: ye are God's [3]husbandry, *ye are* God's [h]building.

10 According to the grace of God which is given unto me, as a wise masterbuilder, I have laid [i]the foundation, and another buildeth thereon. But [j]let every man take heed how he buildeth thereupon.

11 For other foundation can no man lay than [k]that is laid, which is Jesus Christ.

12 Now if any man build upon this foundation gold, silver, precious stones, wood, hay, stubble;

13 Every man's work shall be made manifest: for the day [l]shall declare it, because it [4]shall be revealed by fire; and the fire shall try every man's work of what sort it is.

14 If any man's work abide which he hath built thereupon, he shall receive a reward.

15 If any man's work shall be burned, he shall suffer loss: but he himself shall be saved; [m]yet so as by fire.

16 Know ye not that ye are the temple of God, and *that* the Spirit of God dwelleth in you?

17 If any man [5]defile the temple of God, him shall God destroy; for the [n]temple of God is holy, which *temple* ye are.

18 Let no man deceive himself. If any man among you seemeth to be wise in this world, let him become a fool, that he may be wise.

19 For the wisdom of this world is foolishness with God. For it is written, [o]He taketh the wise in their own craftiness.

20 And again, [p]The Lord knoweth the thoughts of the wise, that they are vain.

21 Therefore let no man glory in men. For [q]all things are yours;

22 Whether Paul, or Ă-pŏl-lŏs, or Çē-phăs, or the world, or life, or death, or things present, or things to come; all are yours;

23 And [r]ye are Christ's; and [s]Christ *is* God's.

CHAPTER 4

LET a man so account of us, as of the ministers of Christ, [a]and stewards of the mysteries of God.

2 Moreover it is required in stewards, that a man be found faithful.

3 But with me it is a very small thing that I should be judged of you, or of man's [1]judgment: yea, I judge not mine own self.

4 For I know nothing by myself; yet am I not hereby justified: but he that judgeth me is the Lord.

5 Therefore [b]judge nothing before the time, until the Lord come, who both will bring to light the hidden things of darkness, and will make manifest the counsels of the hearts: and [c]then shall every man have praise of God.

6 And these things, brethren, I have in a figure transferred to myself and *to* Ă-pŏl-lŏs for your sakes; [d]that ye might learn in us not to think *of men* above that which is written, that no one of you be puffed up for one against another.

7 For who [2]maketh thee to differ *from another*? and [e]what hast thou that thou didst not receive? now if thou didst receive *it*, why dost thou glory, as if thou hadst not received *it*?

8 Now ye are full, [f]now ye are rich, ye have reigned as kings without us: and I would to God ye did reign, that we also might reign with you.

9 For I think that God hath set forth [3]us the apostles last, [g]as it were appointed to death: for [h]we are made a [4]spectacle unto the world, and to angels, and to men.

10 We *are* [i]fools for Christ's sake, but ye *are* wise in Christ; [j]we *are* weak, but ye *are* strong; ye *are* honourable, but we *are* despised.

11 Even unto this present hour we both hunger, and thirst, and are naked, and are [k]buffeted, and have no certain dwellingplace;

12 And [l]labour, working with our own hands: [m]being reviled, we bless; being persecuted, we suffer it:

13 Being defamed, we intreat: we are made as the filth of the world, *and are* the offscouring of all things unto this day.

14 I write not these things to shame you, but as my beloved sons I warn *you*.

15 For though ye have ten thousand instructors in Christ, yet *have ye* not many fathers: for [n]in Christ Jesus I have begotten you through the gospel.

16 Wherefore I beseech you, [o]be ye followers of me.

17 For this cause have I sent unto you Timotheus, [p]who is my beloved son, and faithful in the Lord, who shall bring you into remembrance of my ways which be in Christ, as I teach every where in every church.

g Acts 15.4.
3 Or, tillage.
h Zech. 6.12, 13. Matt. 16.18. ch. 6.19. Eph. 2.20. Col. 2.7.
i Rom. 15.20.
j 1 Pet. 4.11.
k Isa. 28.16. Matt. 16.18.
l 1 Pet. 1.7.
4 is revealed.
m Jude 23.
5 Or, destroy.
n Heb. 3.1.
o Job 5.13.
p Ps. 94.11.
q 2 Cor. 4.5.
r John 17.9, 10. Rom. 14.8. Gal. 3.29.
s ch. 8.6. ch. 11.3. Heb. 1.3.

CHAP. 4

a Matt. 13. 11. Luke 12.42. Rom. 16.25. Eph. 1.9. Col. 1.26,27. 1 Tim. 3.9, 16.
1 day.
b Matt. 7.1. Rev. 20.12.
c Rom. 2.29.
d Rom. 12.3.
2 distinguisheth thee.
e John 3.27. 1 Pet. 4.10.
f Rev. 3.17.
3 Or, us the last apostles, as.
g Ps. 44.22. 2 Cor. 4.11.
h Eph. 6.12. Heb. 10.33.
4 theatre.
i Matt. 5.11. Luke 6.22. Acts 26.24.
j 2 Cor. 13.9.
k Acts 23.2.
l Acts 18.3. 1 Tim. 4.10.
m Matt. 5.44. 1 Pet. 2.23.
n Rom. 15. 20. Jas. 1.18.
o ch. 11.1.
p Acts 19.22. 1 Tim. 1.2.

18 Now some are puffed up, as
though I would not come to you.
19 But [q]I will come to you shortly, if
the Lord will, and will know, not the
speech of them which are puffed up,
but the power.
20 For [r]the kingdom of God *is* not
in word, but in power.
21 What will ye? shall I come unto
you with a rod, or in love, and *in* the
spirit of meekness?

CHAPTER 5

IT is reported commonly *that there*
is fornication among you, and such
fornication as is not so much as named [a]among the Gentiles, [b]that one
should have his father's [c]wife.
2 And ye are puffed up, and have not
rather mourned, that he that hath
done this deed might be taken away
from among you.
3 For [d]I verily, as absent in body, but
present in spirit, have [1]judged already,
as though I were present, *concerning*
him that hath so done this deed,
4 In the name of our Lord Jesus
Christ, when ye are gathered together,
and my spirit, [e]with the power of our
Lord Jesus Christ,
5 To [f]deliver such an one unto Satan
for the destruction of the flesh, that
the spirit may be saved in the day of
the Lord Jesus.
6 Your glorying *is* not good. Know
ye not that [g]a little leaven leaveneth
the whole lump?
7 Purge out therefore the old leaven,
that ye may be a new lump, as ye are
unleavened. For [h]even Christ [i]our
passover [2]is sacrificed for us:
8 Therefore [j]let us keep [3]the feast,
not with [k]old leaven, neither with the
leaven of malice and wickedness; but
with the unleavened *bread* of sincerity
and truth.
9 I wrote unto you in an epistle [l]not
to company with fornicators:
10 Yet not altogether with the fornicators of this world, or with the
covetous, or extortioners, or with
idolaters; for then must ye needs go
out [m]of the world.
11 But now I have written unto you
not to keep company, [n]if any man that
is called a brother be a fornicator, or
covetous, or an idolater, or a railer, or
a drunkard, or an extortioner; with
such an one no [o]not to eat.
12 For what have I to do to judge
them also [p]that are without? do not ye
judge them that are within?
13 But them that are without [q]God
judgeth. Therefore put away from
among yourselves that wicked person.

CHAPTER 6

DARE any of you, having a matter
against another, go to law before
the unjust, and not before the saints?
2 Do ye not know that [a]the saints
shall judge the world? and if the world
shall be judged by you, are ye un-
worthy to judge the smallest matters?
3 Know ye not that we shall [b]judge
angels? how much more things that
pertain to this life? Mil Rom 6:23
4 If then ye have judgments of things
pertaining to this life, set them to
judge who are least esteemed in the
church.
5 I speak to your shame. Is it so, that
there is not a wise man among you?
no, not one that shall be able to judge
between his brethren?
6 But brother goeth to law with
brother, and that before the unbelievers.
7 Now therefore there is utterly a
fault among you, because ye go to law
one with another. [c]Why do ye not
rather take wrong? why do ye not
rather *suffer yourselves to* be defrauded?
8 Nay, ye do wrong, and defraud,
and that [d]*your* brethren.
9 Know ye not that [e]the unrighteous
shall not inherit the kingdom of God?
Be not deceived: neither fornicators,
nor idolaters, nor adulterers, nor
effeminate, nor abusers of themselves
with mankind,
10 Nor thieves, nor covetous, nor
drunkards, nor revilers, nor extortioners, shall inherit the kingdom of
God.
11 And such were some of you: [f]but
ye are washed, but ye are sanctified,
but ye are justified in the name of the
Lord Jesus, and by the Spirit of our
God.
12 All [g]things are lawful unto me,
but all things are not [1]expedient: all
things are lawful for me, but I will not
be brought under the power of any.
13 Meats for the belly, and the belly
for meats: but God shall destroy both
it and them. Now the body *is* not for
fornication, [h]but for the Lord; and
[i]the Lord for the body.
14 And [j]God hath both raised up the
Lord, and will also raise up us [k]by his
own power.
15 Know ye not that your bodies are
the members of Christ? shall I then
take the members of Christ, and make

q Acts 19.21.
r 1 Thes. 1.5.

CHAP. 5

a Eph. 5.3.
b Deut. 27. 20.
c 2 Cor. 7.12.
d Col. 2.5.
1 Or, determined.
e Matt. 18.18. John 20.23. 2 Cor. 2.10.
f Ps. 109.6. Acts 26.18. 1 Tim. 1.20.
g Gal. 5.9.
h Isa. 53.7. 1 Pet. 1.19. Rev. 5.6.
i Ex. 12.5,6. John 19.14. Rev. 5.6-9.
2 Or, is slain.
j Ex. 12.15.
3 Or, holyday.
k Deut. 16.3.
l 2 Cor. 6.14.
m John 17. 15.
n Matt. 18. 17. Rom. 16.17. 2 John 10.
o Gal. 2.12.
p Mark 4.11. 1 Tim. 3.7.
q Eccl. 12.14. Heb. 13.4.

CHAP. 6

a Ps. 49.14. Dan. 7.22. Luke 22.30. Rev. 2.26.
b 2 Pet. 2.4. Jude 6.
c Pro. 20.22. Matt. 5.39. Rom. 12.17.
d 1 Thes. 4.6.
e Isa. 3.11. Acts 24.25.
f John 13.10. Acts 22.16. Eph. 5.26. Heb. 10.22. 1 Pet. 3.21.
g ch. 10.23.
1 Or, profitable.
h 1 Thes. 4.3.
i Eph. 5.23.
j Acts 2.24. Rom. 6.5. 2 Cor. 4.14.
k Eph. 1.19.

them the members of an harlot? God forbid.

16 What? know ye not that he which is joined to an harlot is one body? [l]for two, saith he, shall be one flesh.

17 But [m]he that is joined unto the Lord is one spirit.

18 Flee fornication. Every sin that a man doeth is without the body; but he that committeth fornication sinneth [n]against his own body.

19 What? [o]know ye not that your body is the temple of the Holy Ghost *which is* in you, which ye have of God, and [p]ye are not your own?

20 For [q]ye are bought with a price: therefore [r]glorify God in your body, and in your spirit, which are God's.

CHAPTER 7

NOW concerning the things whereof ye wrote unto me: *It is* good for a man not to touch a woman.

2 Nevertheless, [a]*to avoid* fornication, let every man have his own wife, and let every woman have her own husband.

3 Let [b]the husband render unto the wife due benevolence: and likewise also the wife unto the husband.

4 The wife hath not power of her own body, but the husband: and likewise also the husband hath not power of his own body, but the wife.

5 Defraud ye not one the other, except *it be* with consent for a time, that ye may give yourselves to fasting and prayer; and come together again, that [c]Satan tempt you not for your incontinency.

6 But I speak this by permission, [d]*and* not of commandment.

7 For [e]I would that all men were even [f]as I myself. But [g]every man hath his proper gift of God, one after this manner, and another after that.

8 I say therefore to the unmarried and widows, [h]It is good for them if they abide even as I.

9 But [i]if they cannot contain, let them marry: for it is better to marry than to burn.

10 And unto the married I command, *yet* not I, but the Lord, [j]Let not the wife depart from *her* husband:

11 But and if she depart, let her remain unmarried, or be reconciled to *her* husband: and let not the husband put away *his* wife.

12 But to the rest speak I, not the Lord: If any brother hath a wife that believeth not, and she be pleased to dwell with him, let him not put her away.

13 And the woman which hath an husband that believeth not, and if he be pleased to dwell with her, let her not leave him.

14 For the unbelieving husband is sanctified by the wife, and the unbelieving wife is sanctified by the husband: else [k]were your children unclean; but now are they holy.

15 But if the unbelieving depart, let him depart. A brother or a sister is not under bondage in such *cases:* but God hath called us [1]to peace.

16 For what knowest thou, O wife, whether thou shalt save [l]*thy* husband? or [2]how knowest thou, O man, whether thou shalt save *thy* wife?

17 But as God hath distributed to every man, as the Lord hath called every one, so let him walk. And [m]so ordain I in all churches.

18 Is any man called being circumcised? let him not become uncircumcised. Is any called in uncircumcision? let [n]him not be circumcised.

19 Circumcision [o]is nothing, and uncircumcision is nothing, but [p]the keeping of the commandments of God.

20 Let [q]every man abide in the same calling wherein he was called.

21 Art [r]thou called *being* a servant? care not for it: but if thou mayest be [s]made free, use *it* rather.

22 For he that is called in the Lord, *being* a servant, is the Lord's [3]freeman: likewise also he that is called, *being* free, is [t]Christ's servant.

23 Ye [u]are bought with a price; be not ye the servants of men.

24 Brethren, let every man, wherein he is called, therein abide with God.

25 Now concerning virgins [v]I have no commandment of the Lord: yet I give my judgment, as one [w]that hath obtained mercy of the Lord [x]to be faithful.

26 I suppose therefore that this is good for the present [4]distress, *I say,* that *it is* good for a man so to be.

27 Art thou bound unto a wife? seek not to be loosed. Art thou loosed from a wife? seek not a wife.

28 But and if thou marry, thou hast not sinned; and if a virgin marry, she hath not sinned. Nevertheless such shall have trouble in the flesh: but I spare you.

29 But [y]this I say, brethren, the time *is* short: it remaineth, that both they that have wives be as though they had none;

l Gen. 2.24. Matt. 19.5.
m John 17. 21. Eph. 4.4.
n Rom. 1.24. 1 Thes. 4.4.
o 2 Cor. 6.16.
p Rom. 14.7.
q Gal. 3.13. Heb. 9.12. 1 Pet. 1.18. Rev. 5.9.
r Matt. 5.16.

CHAP. 7

a Pro. 5.19.
b Ex. 21.10. 1 Pet. 3.7.
c 2 Cor. 11.3.
d 2 Cor. 8.8.
e Acts 26.29.
f ch. 9.5.
g Matt. 19. 12. ch. 12.11.
h ver. 26.
i 1 Tim. 5.14.
j Jer. 3.20. Mal. 2.14, 16. Matt. 5.32. Matt. 19.6. Mark 10.11, 12. Luke 16.18.
k Mal. 2.15.
1 in peace.
l Jas. 5.19,20. 1 Pet. 3.1.
2 what.
m 2 Cor. 11. 28.
n Acts 15. Gal. 5.2.
o Gal. 6.15. Col. 3.11.
p 1 Sam. 15. 22. Jer. 7.22,23. Matt. 5.19. John 15.14. 1 John 2.3. Rev. 22.14.
q Eph. 4.1. 2 Thes. 3.11.
r Gal. 3.28.
s Isa. 58.6.
3 made free.
t Gal. 5.13. Eph. 6.6. 1 Pet. 2.16.
u Lev. 25.42. 1 Pet. 1.18.
v 2 Cor. 8.8, 10.
w 1 Tim. 1. 16.
x ch. 4.2.
4 Or, necessity.
y Matt. 24. 13. Rom. 13.12. Phil. 4.5. Heb. 10.25. 1 Pet. 4.7.

30 And they that weep, as though
they wept not; and they that rejoice,
as though they rejoiced not; and they
that buy, as though they possessed
not;
31 And they that use this world, as
not abusing *it:* for [a]the fashion of this
world passeth away.
32 But I would have you without
carefulness. [b]He that is unmarried
careth for the things [5]that belong to
the Lord, how he may please the Lord:
33 But he that is married careth for
the things that are of the world, how
he may please *his* wife.
34 There is difference *also* between a
wife and a virgin. The [c]unmarried
woman careth for the things of the
Lord, that she may be holy both in
body and in spirit: but she that is
married careth for the things of the
world, how she may please *her* husband.
35 And this I speak for your own
profit; not that I may cast a snare upon you, but for that which is comely,
and that ye may attend upon the Lord
without distraction.
36 But if any man think that he be-
haveth himself uncomely toward his
virgin, if she pass the flower of *her* age,
and need so require, let him do what
he will, he sinneth not: let them marry.
37 Nevertheless he that standeth
stedfast in his heart, having no necessity, but hath power over his own will,
and hath so decreed in his heart that
he will keep his virgin, doeth well.
38 So [d]then he that giveth *her* in
marriage doeth well; but he that giveth *her* not in marriage doeth better.
39 The [e]wife is bound by the law as
long as her husband liveth; but if her
husband be dead, she is at liberty to
be married to whom she will; [f]only in
the Lord.
40 But she is happier if she so abide,
after my judgment: and I think also
that I have the Spirit of God.

CHAPTER 8

NOW [a]as touching things offered
unto idols, we know that we all
have [b]knowledge. Knowledge puffeth
up, but charity edifieth.
2 And [c]if any man think that he
knoweth any thing, he knoweth nothing yet as he ought to know.
3 But if any man love God, [d]the same
is known of him.
4 As concerning therefore the eating
of those things that are offered in
sacrifice unto idols, we know that [e]an
idol *is* nothing in the world, [f]and that
there is none other God but one.
5 For though there be that [g]are called
gods, whether in heaven or in earth,
(as there be gods many, and lords
many,)
6 But [h]to us *there is but* one God, the
Father, [i]of whom *are* all things, and
we [1]in him; and [j]one Lord Jesus
Christ, [k]by whom *are* all things, and
we by him.
7 Howbeit *there is* not in every
man that knowledge: for some with
conscience of the idol unto this hour
eat *it* as a thing offered unto an idol;
and their conscience being weak is
defiled.
8 But meat commendeth us not to
God: for neither, if we eat, [2]are we
the better; neither, if we eat not, [3]are
we the worse.
9 But take heed lest by any means
this [4]liberty of yours become a stumblingblock to them that are weak.
10 For if any man see thee which
hast knowledge sit at meat in the
idol's temple, shall not the conscience
of him which is weak be [5]emboldened
to eat those things which are offered
to idols;
11 And through thy knowledge shall
the weak brother perish, for whom
Christ died?
12 But [l]when ye sin so against the
brethren, and wound their weak
conscience, ye sin against Christ.
13 Wherefore, if meat make my
brother to offend, I will eat no flesh
while the world standeth, lest I make
my brother to offend.

CHAPTER 9

AM [a]I not an apostle? am I not free?
have [b]I not seen Jesus Christ our
Lord? are not ye my work in the
Lord?
2 If I be not an apostle unto others,
yet doubtless I am to you: for [c]the
seal of mine apostleship are ye in the
Lord.
3 Mine answer to them that do
examine me is this,
4 Have [d]we not power to eat and to
drink?
5 Have we not power to lead about
a sister, a [1]wife, as well as other
apostles, and *as* [e]the brethren of the
Lord, and [f]Çē-phăs?
6 Or I only and Barnabas, [g]have not
we power to forbear working?
7 Who [h]goeth a warfare any time at
his own charges? who [i]planteth a
vineyard, and eateth not of the fruit

z ch. 9.18.
a Ps. 39.6. Jas. 4.14.
b 1 Tim. 5.5.
5 of the Lord.
c Luke 10.40.
d Heb. 13.4.
e Rom. 7.2.
f Deut. 17.3.

CHAP. 8

a Acts 15.20.
b Rom. 14. 14.
c Gal. 6.3. 1 Tim. 6.4.
d Ex. 33.12. Nah. 1.7. Matt. 7.23. Gal. 4.9.
e Isa. 41.24.
f Deut. 3.24. Deut. 4.39. Isa. 37.16. Mark 12.29.
g John 10.34.
h Mal. 2.10. Eph. 4.6.
i Acts 17.28. Rom. 11.36.
1 Or, for him.
j Matt. 11.27. John 5.20-29. Acts 2.36. Eph. 1.20-23. Phil. 2.11.
k John 1.3. Heb. 1.2.
2 Or, have we the more.
3 Or, have we the less.
4 Or, power.
5 edified.
l Matt. 25.40. Acts 9.4.

CHAP. 9

a 1 Tim. 2.7.
b Acts 9.3.
c 2 Cor. 3.2.
d 2 Thes. 3.9.
1 Or, woman.
e Matt. 13. 55. Mark 6.3. Luke 6.15. Gal. 1.19.
f Matt. 8.14.
g Acts 18.3.
h 2 Cor. 10.4.
i Deut. 20.6. Pro. 27.18.

thereof? or who feedeth a [j]flock, and
eateth not of the milk of the flock?
8 Say I these things as a man? or
saith not the law the same also?
9 For it is written in the law of
Moses, Thou [k]shalt not muzzle the
mouth of the ox that treadeth out the
corn. Doth God take care for oxen?
10 Or saith he *it* altogether for our
sakes? For our sakes, no doubt, *this* is
written: that [l]he that ploweth should
plow in hope; and that he that thresheth in hope should be partaker of his
hope.
11 If [m]we have sown unto you spiritual things, *is it* a great thing if we shall
reap your carnal things?
12 If others be partakers of *this*
power over you, *are* not we rather?
Nevertheless we [n]have not used this
power; but suffer all things, lest we
should hinder the gospel of Christ.
13 Do [o]ye not know that they which
minister about holy things [2]live *of the*
things of the temple? and they which
wait at the altar are partakers with the
altar?
14 Even so [p]hath the Lord ordained
that they [q]which preach the gospel
should live of the gospel.
15 But I have used none of these
things: neither have I written these
things, that it should be so done unto
me: for *it were* better for me to die,
than that any man should make my
glorying void.
16 For though I preach the gospel, I
have nothing to glory of: for necessity
is laid upon me; yea, woe is unto me,
if I preach not the gospel!
17 For if I do this thing willingly, I
have a reward: but if against my will,
a [r]dispensation *of the gospel* is committed unto me.
18 What is my reward then? *Verily*
that, when I preach the gospel, I may
make the gospel of Christ without
charge, that I abuse not my power in
the gospel.
19 For though I be free from all *men*,
yet have [s]I made myself servant unto
all, [t]that I might gain the more.
20 And [u]unto the Jews I became as
a Jew, that I might gain the Jews; to
them that are under the law, as under
the law, that I might gain them that
are under the law;
21 To [v]them that are without law, as
without law, ([w]being not without law
to God, but under the law to Christ,)
that I might gain them that are without law.
22 To [x]the weak became I as weak,
that I might gain the weak: I am made
all things to all *men*, that I might by
all means save some.
23 And this I do for the gospel's sake,
that I might be partaker thereof with
you.
24 Know ye not that they which run
in a race run all, but one receiveth the
prize? So [y]run, that ye may obtain.
25 And every man that [z]striveth for
the mastery is temperate in all things.
Now they *do it* to obtain a corruptible
crown; but we [a]an incorruptible.
26 I therefore so run, not as [b]un-
certainly; so fight I, not as one that
beateth the air:
27 But I keep under my body, and
bring *it* into subjection: lest that by
any means, when I have preached to
others, I myself should be [c]a cast-
away.

CHAPTER 10

MOREOVER, brethren, I would
not that ye should be ignorant,
how that all our fathers were under
the [a]cloud, and all passed through
the [b]sea;
2 And were all baptized unto Moses
in the cloud and in the sea;
3 And did all eat the [c]same spiritual
meat;
4 And did all drink the same [d]spiri-
tual drink: for they drank of that
spiritual Rock that [1]followed them:
and that Rock was Christ.
5 But with many of them God was
not well pleased: for they were overthrown in the wilderness.
6 Now these things were [2]our examples, to the intent we should not lust
after evil things, as they also lusted.
7 Neither be ye idolaters, as *were*
some of them; as it is written, [e]The
people sat down to eat and drink, and
rose up to play.
8 Neither let us commit fornication,
as some of them committed, and [f]fell
in one day three and twenty thousand.
9 Neither let us tempt Christ, as
some [g]of them also tempted, and were
destroyed of serpents.
10 Neither murmur ye, as some of
them also murmured, and were destroyed of the destroyer.
11 Now all these things happened
unto them for [3]ensamples: and [h]they
are written for our admonition, [i]upon
whom the ends of the world are come.
12 Wherefore let him that thinketh
he standeth take heed lest he fall.
13 There hath no temptation taken
you but such as is [4]common to man:
but God *is* faithful, [j]who will not

j John 21.15. 1 Pet. 5.2.
k Deut. 25.4.
l 2 Tim. 2.6.
m Matt. 10. 10. Rom. 15.27.
n 2 Cor. 11.7.
o Lev. 6.16.
2 Or, feed.
p Luke 10.7.
q Gal. 6.6. 1 Tim. 5.17.
r Gal. 2.7. Phil. 1.17.
s Gal. 5.13.
t Matt. 18.15. 1 Pet. 3.1.
u Acts 16.3.
v Rom. 2.12. Gal. 3.2.
w Matt. 5.17-20. Rom. 7.22, 25. ch. 7.22. Gal. 5.13, 14,22,23.
x Rom. 15.1.
y Matt. 10. 22. Matt. 24.13. Gal. 2.2. Heb. 6.15.
z 1 Tim. 6.12.
a Jas. 1.12. Rev. 2.10.
b 2 Cor. 5.1.
c Jer. 6.30.

CHAP. 10

a Ex. 13.21. Isa. 63.11.
b Ex. 14.22.
c Ex. 16.15. Deut. 8.3.
d Ex. 17.6. Num. 20.11. Ps. 78.15. John 4.10. Rev. 22.17.
1 Or, went with them.
2 our figures.
e Ex. 32.6.
f Num. 25.1.
g Ex. 17.2,7. Num. 21.5. Deut. 6.16. Ps. 78.18, 56.
3 Or, types.
h Rom. 15.4.
i Heb. 10.25.
4 Or, moderate.
j Ex. 13.17. Ps. 125.3. Luke 22.32. 2 Pet. 2.9.

suffer you to be tempted above that
ye are able; but will with the temptation also [k]make a way to escape, that
ye may be able to bear *it*.
14 Wherefore, my dearly beloved,
flee from idolatry.
15 I speak as to wise men; judge ye
what I say.
16 The [l]cup of blessing which we
bless, is it not the communion of the
blood of Christ? [m]The bread which
we break, is it not the communion of
the body of Christ?
17 For [n]we *being* many are one bread,
and one body: for we are all partakers
of that one bread.
18 Behold [o]Israel after the flesh: [p]are
not they which eat of the sacrifices
partakers of the altar?
19 What say I then? that the idol is
any thing, or that which is offered in
sacrifice to idols is any thing?
20 But *I say*, that the things which
the Gentiles [q]sacrifice, they sacrifice
to devils, and not to God: and I would
not that ye should have fellowship
with devils.
21 Ye [r]cannot drink the cup of the
Lord, and [s]the cup of devils: ye cannot be partakers of the Lord's table,
and of the table of devils.
22 Do we provoke the Lord to
jealousy? are [t]we stronger than he?
23 All things are lawful for me, but
all things are not expedient: all things
are lawful for me, but all things edify
not.
24 Let [u]no man seek his own, but
every man another's *wealth*.
25 Whatsoever [v]is sold in the sham-
bles, *that* eat, asking no question for
conscience sake:
26 For the earth *is* the Lord's, and
the fulness thereof.
27 If any of them that believe not bid
you *to a feast*, and ye be disposed to
go; [w]whatsoever is set before you, eat,
asking no question for conscience
sake.
28 But if any man say unto you, This
is offered in sacrifice unto idols, eat
not [x]for his sake that shewed it, and
for conscience sake: for [y]the earth *is*
the Lord's, and the fulness thereof:
29 Conscience, I say, not thine own,
but of the other: for [z]why is my liberty
judged of another *man's* conscience?
30 For if I by [5]grace be a partaker,
why am I evil spoken of for that for
which I give thanks?
31 Whether [a]therefore ye eat, or
drink, or whatsoever ye do, do all to
the glory of God.

k Gen. 19.20, 21. Ps. 124.7. Jer. 29.11. Acts 27.44.
l Matt. 26.26.
m Acts 2.42.
n Rom. 12.5.
o Rom. 4.12.
p Lev. 3.3.
q Deut. 32. 17.
r 2 Cor. 6.15.
s Deut. 32.38.
t Job 9.4. Eze. 22.14.
u Rom. 15.1.
v 1 Tim. 4.4.
w Luke 10.7.
x ch. 8.10.
y Deut. 10. 14.
z Rom. 14. 16.
5 Or, thanksgiving.
a Zech. 7.6. Matt. 5.16. John 15.8. Phil. 1.11.
6 Greeks.

CHAP. 11

a Eph. 5.1,2. Phil. 2.4,5. 2 Thes. 3.9.
b ch. 7.17.
1 Or, traditions.
c Rom. 14.9. Eph. 5.23.
d Gen. 3.16.
e John 4.34. Gal. 4.4. Phil. 2.7.
f Acts 21.9.
g Deut. 21. 12.
h Num. 5.18.
i Gen. 1.26.
j Gen. 2.21. Pro. 18.22.
k Gen. 24.65.
2 That is, a covering, in sign that she is under the power of her husband.
l Eccl. 5.6.
m Gal. 3.28.
n Pro. 16.4. Rom. 11.36. ch. 8.6.
3 Or, veil.
o 1 Tim. 6.4.

32 Give none offence, neither to the
Jews, nor to the [6]Gentiles, nor to the
church of God:
33 Even as I please all *men* in all
things, not seeking mine own profit,
but the *profit* of many, that they may
be saved.

CHAPTER 11

BE ye [a]followers of me, even as I
also *am* of Christ.
2 Now I praise you, brethren, that
ye remember me in all things, [b]and
keep the [1]ordinances, as I delivered
them to you.
3 But I would have you know, that
[c]the head of every man is Christ; and
the [d]head of the woman *is* the man;
and [e]the head of Christ *is* God.
4 Every man praying or prophesying, having *his* head covered, dishonoureth his head.
5 But [f]every woman that prayeth or
prophesieth with *her* head uncovered
dishonoureth her head: for that is
even all one as if she were [g]shaven.
6 For if the woman be not covered,
let her also be shorn: but if it be [h]a
shame for a woman to be shorn or
shaven, let her be covered.
7 For a man indeed ought not to
cover *his* head, forasmuch as [i]he is the
image and glory of God: but the
woman is the glory of the man.
8 For [j]the man is not of the woman;
but the woman of the man.
9 Neither was the man created for
the woman; but the woman for the
man.
10 For this cause ought the woman
[k]to have [2]power on *her* head [l]because
of the angels.
11 Nevertheless [m]neither is the man
without the woman, neither the woman without the man, in the Lord.
12 For as the woman *is* of the man,
even so *is* the man also by the woman;
but [n]all things of God.
13 Judge in yourselves: is it comely
that a woman pray unto God uncovered?
14 Doth not even nature itself teach
you, that, if a man have long hair, it is
a shame unto him?
15 But if a woman have long hair, it
is a glory to her: for *her* hair is given
her for a [3]covering.
16 But [o]if any man seem to be contentious, we have no such custom,
neither the churches of God.
17 Now in this that I declare *unto
you* I praise *you* not, that ye come
together not for the better, but for
the worse.

18 For first of all, when ye come together in the church, [p]I hear that there be [4]divisions among you; and I partly believe it.

19 For [q]there must be also [5]heresies among you, [r]that they which are approved may be made manifest among you.

20 When ye come together therefore into one place, [6]*this* is not to eat the Lord's supper.

21 For in eating every one taketh before *other* his own supper: and one is hungry, and [s]another is drunken.

22 What? have ye not houses to eat and to drink in? or [t]despise ye the church of God, and shame [7]them that have not? What shall I say to you? shall I praise you in this? I praise *you* not.

23 For [u]I have received of the Lord that which also I delivered unto you, That the Lord Jesus the *same* night in which he was betrayed took bread:

24 And when he had given thanks, he brake *it*, and said, Take, eat: this is my body, which is broken for you: this do [8]in remembrance of me.

25 After the same manner also *he took* the cup, when he had supped, saying, This cup is the [v]new testament in my blood: this do ye, as oft as ye drink *it*, in remembrance of me.

26 For as often as ye eat this bread, and drink this cup, [9]ye do shew the Lord's death [w]till he come.

27 Wherefore [x]whosoever shall eat this bread, and drink *this* cup of the Lord, unworthily, shall be guilty of the body and blood of the Lord.

28 But [y]let a man examine himself, and so let him eat of *that* bread, and drink of *that* cup.

29 For he that eateth and drinketh unworthily, eateth and drinketh [10]damnation to himself, not discerning the Lord's body.

30 For this cause many *are* weak and sickly among you, and many sleep.

31 For [z]if we would judge ourselves, we should not be judged.

32 But when we are judged, [a]we are chastened of the Lord, that we should not be condemned with the world.

33 Wherefore, my brethren, when ye come together to eat, tarry one for another.

34 And if any man hunger, let him eat at home; that ye come not together unto [11]condemnation. And the rest [b]will I set in order when I [c]come.

p ch. 1.10.
4 Or, schisms.
q Luke 17.1.
5 Or, sects.
r Luke 2.35.
6 Or, ye cannot eat.
s Jude 12.
t Lev. 19.30. Ps. 89.7.
7 Or, them that are poor?
u Gal. 1.1.
8 Or, for a remembrance.
v Heb. 9.15.
9 Or, shew ye.
w Acts 1.11. ch. 4.5. Heb. 9.28.
x Num. 9.10. Matt. 22.11.
y 2 Cor. 13.5. Gal. 6.4.
10 Or, judgment.
z 1 John 1.9.
a Heb. 12.5.
11 Or, judgment.
b Titus 1.5.
c ch. 4.19.

CHAP. 12

a ch. 14.1.
b Eph. 2.11.
c Mark 9.39.
1 Or, anathema.
d Matt. 16. 17.
e Heb. 2.4.
f Eph. 4.4.
2 Or, ministeries.
g Eph. 1.23.
h Rom. 12.6.
i Gen. 41.38, 39. Matt. 13.11. Acts 6.3. ch. 2.6. Eph. 1.17, 18.
j 2 Cor. 8.7.
k Matt. 17. 19.
l Mark 16.18.
m Gal. 3.5.
n Rom. 12.6.
o 1 John 4.1.
p Acts 2.4.
q Rom. 12.6-8. ch. 7.7. Eph. 4.7.
r John 3.8. Heb. 2.4.
s Gal. 3.16.
t Isa. 44.3-5. Eze. 36.25-27. Matt. 3.11. John 1.33. Rom. 6.5.
u Gal. 3.28. Eph. 2.13, 14,16. Col. 3.11.
3 Greeks.
v John 6.63.

CHAPTER 12

NOW [a]concerning spiritual *gifts*, brethren, I would not have you ignorant.

2 Ye know [b]that ye were Gentiles, carried away unto these dumb idols, even as ye were led.

3 Wherefore I give you to understand, that [c]no man speaking by the Spirit of God calleth Jesus [1]accursed: and [d]*that* no man can say that Jesus is the Lord, but by the Holy Ghost.

4 Now [e]there are diversities of gifts, but the [f]same Spirit.

5 And there are differences of [2]administrations, but the same Lord.

6 And there are diversities of operations, but it is the same God [g]which worketh all in all.

7 But [h]the manifestation of the Spirit is given to every man to profit withal.

8 For to one is given by the Spirit the word [i]of wisdom; to another the [j]word of knowledge by the same Spirit;

9 To [k]another faith by the same Spirit; to another [l]the gifts of healing by the same Spirit;

10 To [m]another the working of miracles; to another [n]prophecy; [o]to another discerning of spirits; to another [p]*divers* kinds of tongues; to another the interpretation of tongues:

11 But all these worketh that one and the selfsame Spirit, [q]dividing to every man severally [r]as he will.

12 For as the body is one, and hath many members, and all the members of that one body, being many, are one body: [s]so also *is* Christ.

13 For [t]by one Spirit are we all baptized into one body, [u]whether *we be* Jews or [3]Gentiles, whether *we be* bond or free; and [v]have been all made to drink into one Spirit.

14 For the body is not one member, but many.

15 If the foot shall say, Because I am not the hand, I am not of the body; is it therefore not of the body?

16 And if the ear shall say, Because I am not the eye, I am not of the body; is it therefore not of the body?

17 If the whole body *were* an eye, where *were* the hearing? If the whole *were* hearing, where *were* the smelling?

18 But now hath God set the members every one of them in the body, as it hath pleased him.

19 And if they were all one member, where *were* the body?

20 But now *are they* many members,
yet but one body.
21 And the eye cannot say unto the
hand, I have no need of thee: nor
again the head to the feet, I have no
need of you.
22 Nay, much more those members
of the body, which seem to be more
feeble, are necessary:
23 And those *members* of the body,
which we think to be less honourable,
upon these we [4]bestow more abundant
honour; and our uncomely *parts* have
more abundant comeliness.
24 For our comely *parts* have no
need: but God hath tempered the
body together, having given more
abundant honour to that *part* which
lacked:
25 That there should be no [5]schism
in the body; but *that* the members
should have the same care one for
another.
26 And whether one member suffer,
all the members suffer with it; or one
member be honoured, all the members rejoice with it.
27 Now [w]ye are the body of Christ,
and members in particular.
28 And [x]God hath set some in the
church, first [y]apostles, secondarily
[z]prophets, thirdly teachers, after that
miracles, then gifts of healings, [a]helps,
[b]governments, [6]diversities of tongues.
29 *Are* all apostles? *are* all prophets?
are all teachers? *are* all [7]workers of
miracles?
30 Have all the gifts of healing? do
all speak with tongues? do all interpret?
31 But [c]covet earnestly the best gifts:
and yet shew I unto you a more excellent way.

CHAPTER 13

THOUGH I speak with the tongues
of men and of angels, and have
not [a]charity, I am become *as* sounding brass, or a tinkling cymbal.
2 And though I have *the gift of* [b]prophecy, and understand all mysteries,
and all knowledge; and though I have
all faith, [c]so that I could remove
mountains, and have not charity, I am
nothing.
3 And [d]though I bestow all my goods
to feed *the poor*, and though I give my
body to be burned, and have not
charity, it profiteth me nothing.
4 Charity [e]suffereth long, *and* is
kind; charity envieth not; charity
[1]vaunteth not itself, is not puffed
up,
5 Doth not behave itself [f]unseemly,
seeketh [g]not her own, is not easily
provoked, thinketh no evil;
6 Rejoiceth [h]not in iniquity, [i]but rejoiceth [2]in the truth;
7 Beareth [j]all things, believeth all
things, hopeth all things, endureth
all things.
8 Charity never faileth: but whether
there be prophecies, they shall fail;
whether *there be* tongues, they shall
cease; whether *there be* knowledge, it
shall vanish away.
9 For [k]we know in part, and we prophesy in part.
10 But [l]when that which is perfect is
come, then that which is in part shall
be done away.
11 When I was a child, I spake as a
child, I understood as a child, I
[3]thought as a child: but when I became a man, I put away childish
things.
12 For [m]now we see through a glass,
[4]darkly; but then [n]face to face: now
I know in part; but then shall I know
even as also I am known.
13 And now abideth faith, hope,
charity, these three; but [o]the greatest
of these *is* charity.

CHAPTER 14

FOLLOW after [a]charity, and [b]desire spiritual *gifts*, [c]but rather that
ye may prophesy.
2 For he that [d]speaketh in an *unknown* tongue speaketh not unto men,
but unto God: for no man [1]understandeth *him;* howbeit in the spirit he
speaketh [e]mysteries.
3 But he that prophesieth [f]speaketh
unto men *to* edification, and exhortation, and comfort.
4 He that speaketh in an *unknown*
tongue edifieth himself; but he that
prophesieth edifieth the church.
5 I would that ye all spake with
tongues, but rather that ye prophesied: for greater *is* he that prophesieth
than he that speaketh with tongues,
except he interpret, that the church
may receive edifying.
6 Now, brethren, if I come unto you
speaking with tongues, what shall I
profit you, except I shall speak to you
either by revelation, or by knowledge,
or by prophesying, or by doctrine?
7 And even things without life giving
sound, whether [g]pipe or harp, except
they give a distinction in the [2]sounds,
how shall it be known what is piped
or harped?
8 For if the trumpet give an uncertain

4 Or, put on.
5 Or, division.
w Rom. 12.5. Eph. 1.23. Eph. 4.12.
x Eph. 4.11.
y Eph. 2.20.
z Acts 13.1. Rom. 12.6.
a Num. 11. 17.
b Rom. 12.8. Heb. 13.17.
6 Or, kinds.
7 Or, powers.
c ch. 14.1.

CHAP. 13

a Matt. 25. 45. Rom. 14.
b Matt. 7.22.
c Luke 17.6.
d Matt. 6.1,2.
e 1 Pet. 4.8.
1 Or, is not rash.
f Phil. 4.8.
g Rom. 14. 12-15. Phil. 2.4.
h Ps. 10.3. Rom. 1.32.
i 2 John 4.
2 Or, with the truth.
j Gal. 6.2.
k ch. 8.2. 1 Tim. 6.4.
l Isa. 54.13. John 6.45.
3 Or, reasoned.
m 2 Cor. 3. 18. Phil. 3.12.
4 in a riddle.
n Esther 1.14. Matt. 18.10.
o Matt. 22.38, 39.

CHAP. 14

a Lev. 19.18. Matt. 22.39. Mark 12.31. Rom. 13.8-10. Gal. 5.14. Eph. 5.2.
b ch. 12.30, 31.
c Num. 11. 25. Rom. 12.6.
d Acts 2.4. Acts 10.46.
1 heareth.
e Matt. 13. 11. Matt. 16.17. Mark 4.11. Col. 1.26.
f Rom. 15.4.
g Job 21.11, 12.
2 Or, tunes.

sound, who shall prepare himself to the battle?

9 So likewise ye, except ye utter by the tongue words [3]easy to be understood, how shall it be known what is spoken? for ye shall speak [h]into the air.

10 There are, it may be, so many kinds of voices in the world, and none of them *is* without signification.

11 Therefore if I know not the meaning of the voice, I shall be unto him that speaketh a barbarian, and he that speaketh *shall be* a barbarian unto me.

12 Even so ye, forasmuch as ye are zealous [4]of spiritual *gifts*, seek that ye may excel to the edifying of the church.

13 Wherefore let him that speaketh in an *unknown* tongue pray that [i]he may interpret.

14 For if I pray in an *unknown* tongue, my spirit prayeth, but my understanding is unfruitful.

15 What is it then? I will pray with the spirit, and I will pray with the understanding also: [j]I will sing with the spirit, and I will sing [k]with the understanding also.

16 Else when thou shalt bless with the spirit, how shall he that occupieth the room of the unlearned say [l]Ä-měn at thy giving of thanks, seeing he understandeth not what thou sayest?

17 For thou verily givest thanks well, but the other is not edified.

18 I thank my God, I speak with tongues more than ye all:

19 Yet in the church I had rather speak five words with my understanding, that *by my voice* I might teach others also, than ten thousand words in an *unknown* tongue.

20 Brethren, [m]be not children in understanding: howbeit in malice [n]be ye children, but in understanding be [5]men.

21 In [o]the law it is written, [p]With *men of* other tongues and other lips will I speak unto this people; and yet for all that will they not hear me, saith the Lord.

22 Wherefore tongues are for a sign, not to them that believe, but to them that believe not: but prophesying *serveth* not for them that believe not, but for them which believe.

23 If therefore the whole church be come together into one place, and all speak with tongues, and there come in *those that are* unlearned, or unbelievers, [q]will they not say that ye are mad?

24 But if all prophesy, and there come in one that believeth not, or *one*

3 significant.
h ch. 9.26.
4 of spirits.
i ch. 12.10.
j Eph. 5.19.
k Ps. 47.7.
l ch. 11.24.
m Ps. 119.99. Matt. 11.25. Rom. 16.19. Heb. 5.12.
n Matt. 18.3. 1 Pet. 2.2.
5 perfect, or, of a ripe age.
o John 10.34.
p Isa. 28.11.
q Hosea 9.7. Acts 2.13.
r Isa. 45.14. Zech. 8.23.
s ch. 12.8,9.
t Rom. 14.19. Eph. 4.12.
u 1 Thes. 5. 19.
v Deut. 33. 10. Eccl. 12.9. Rom. 12.7.
w 1 John 4.1.
6 tumult, or, unquietness.
x ch. 11.16.
y 1 Tim. 2.11.
z ch. 11.3. Eph. 5.22. 1 Pet. 3.1.
a Gen. 3.16.
b Isa. 2.3.
c Luke 10.16.
d ch. 12.31.
CHAP. 15
a Rom. 5.2.
b Rom. 1.16.

unlearned, he is convinced of all, he is judged of all:

25 And thus are the secrets of his heart made manifest; and so falling down on *his* face he will worship God, and report [r]that God is in you of a truth.

26 How is it then, brethren? when ye come together, every one of you hath a psalm, [s]hath a doctrine, hath a tongue, hath a revelation, hath an interpretation. Let [t]all things be done unto edifying.

27 If any man speak in an *unknown* tongue, *let it be* by two, or at the most *by* three, and *that* by course; and let one interpret.

28 But if there be no interpreter, let him keep silence in the church; and let him speak to himself, and to God.

29 Let the prophets speak two or three, and let the other judge.

30 If *any thing* be revealed to another that sitteth by, [u]let the first hold his peace.

31 For [v]ye may all prophesy one by one, that all may learn, and all may be comforted.

32 And [w]the spirits of the prophets are subject to the prophets.

33 For God is not *the author* of [6]confusion, but of peace, [x]as in all churches of the saints.

34 Let [y]your women keep silence in the churches: for it is not permitted unto them to speak; but [z]*they are commanded* to be under obedience, as also saith the [a]law.

35 And if they will learn any thing, let them ask their husbands at home: for it is a shame for women to speak in the church.

36 What? came the word of [b]God out from you? or came it unto you only?

37 If [c]any man think himself to be a prophet, or spiritual, let him acknowledge that the things that I write unto you are the commandments of the Lord.

38 But if any man be ignorant, let him be ignorant.

39 Wherefore, brethren, [d]covet to prophesy, and forbid not to speak with tongues.

40 Let all things be done decently and in order.

CHAPTER 15

MOREOVER, brethren, I declare unto you the gospel which I preached unto you, which also ye have received, and [a]wherein ye stand;

2 By [b]which also ye are saved, if ye

[1]keep in memory [2]what I preached unto you, unless [c]ye have believed in
vain.
3 For I delivered unto you first of all
that which I also received, how that
Christ died for our sins [d]according to
the scriptures;
4 And that he was buried, and that
he rose again the third day [e]according
to the scriptures:
5 And [f]that he was seen of Çē-phăs,
then of [g]the twelve:
6 After that, he was seen of above
five hundred brethren at once; of
whom the greater part remain unto
this present, but some are fallen
asleep.
7 After that, he was seen of James;
then [h]of all the apostles.
8 And [i]last of all he was seen of me
also, as of [3]one born out of due time.
9 For I am the least of the apostles,
that am not meet to be called an
apostle, because [j]I persecuted the
church of God.
10 But [k]by the grace of God I am
what I am: and his grace which *was
bestowed* upon me was not in vain;
but [l]I laboured more abundantly than
they all: [m]yet not I, but the grace of
God which was with me.
11 Therefore whether *it were* I or
they, so we preach, and so ye believed.
12 Now if Christ be preached that he
rose from the dead, how say some
among you that [n]there is no resurrection of the dead?
13 But if there be no resurrection of
the dead, [o]then is Christ not risen:
14 And if Christ be not risen, then *is*
our preaching vain, and your faith *is*
also vain.
15 Yea, and we are found false
witnesses of God; because we have
testified of God that he raised up
Christ: whom he raised not up, if so
be that the dead rise not.
16 For if the dead rise not, then is not
Christ raised:
17 And if Christ be not raised, your
faith *is* vain; [p]ye are yet in your sins.
18 Then they also which are fallen
asleep in Christ are perished.
19 If [q]in this life only we have hope
in Christ, we are of all men most
miserable.
20 But now [r]is Christ risen from the
dead, *and* become [s]the firstfruits of
them that slept.
21 For [t]since by man *came* death, [u]by
man *came* also the resurrection of the
dead.

1 Or, hold fast.
2 by what speech.
c Gal. 3.4.
d Gen. 3.15. Ps. 22.15. Isa. 53.5. Dan. 9.26. 1 Pet. 2.24.
e Ps. 2.7. Isa. 53.10. Hosea 6.2.
f Luke 24.34.
g John 20.19.
h Acts 1.3.
i Acts 9.4.
3 Or, an abortive.
j Acts 8.3.
k Eph. 3.7.
l 2 Cor. 11. 23.
m Gal. 2.8.
n 2 Tim. 2.17.
o 1 Thes. 4. 14.
p Rom. 4.25.
q 2 Tim. 3.12.
r 1 Pet. 1.3.
s Acts 26.23.
t Rom. 5.12.
u John 11.25.
v 1 Thes. 4. 15.
w Dan. 7.14. Eph. 5.27.
x Ps. 110.1. Matt. 22.44. Mark 12.36. Luke 20.42, 43. Eph. 1.22. Heb. 1.13.
y Heb. 2.14.
z Matt. 28. 18. 1 Pet. 3.22.
a Matt. 13. 41. Eph. 1.10.
b John 14.28. ch. 3.23. ch. 11.3.
c 2 Cor. 11. 26.
4 Some read, our.
d Acts 20.23. Rom. 8.36.
5 Or, to speak after the manner of men.
e 2 Cor. 1.8.
f Isa. 22.13. Luke 12.19.
g Eph. 5.14.
h 1 Thes. 4.5.
i Eze. 37.3.
j John 12.24.
k Ps. 104.14.

22 For as in Adam all die, even so in
Christ shall all be made alive.
23 But [v]every man in his own order:
Christ the firstfruits; afterward they
that are Christ's at his coming.
24 Then *cometh* the end, when he
shall have delivered up [w]the kingdom
to God, even the Father; when he shall
have put down all rule and all authority and power.
25 For he must reign, [x]till he hath
put all enemies under his feet.
26 The [y]last enemy *that* shall be destroyed *is* death.
27 For he [z]hath put all things under
his feet. But when he saith, all things
are put under *him*, *it is* manifest that
he is excepted, which did put all
things under him.
28 And [a]when all things shall be subdued unto him, then [b]shall the Son
also himself be subject unto him that
put all things under him, that God
may be all in all.
29 Else what shall they do which are
baptized for the dead, if the dead rise
not at all? why are they then baptized
for the dead?
30 And [c]why stand we in jeopardy
every hour?
31 I protest by [4]your rejoicing which
I have in Christ Jesus our Lord, [d]I die
daily.
32 If [5]after the manner of men [e]I
have fought with beasts at Ĕph-ĕ-sŭs,
what advantageth it me, if the dead
rise not? [f]let us eat and drink; for to
morrow we die.
33 Be not deceived: evil communications corrupt good manners.
34 Awake [g]to righteousness, and sin
not; for [h]some have not the knowledge of God: I speak *this* to your
shame.
35 But some *man* will say, [i]How are
the dead raised up? and with what
body do they come?
36 *Thou* fool, [j]that which thou
sowest is not quickened, except it
die:
37 And that which thou sowest, thou
sowest not that body that shall be, but
bare grain, it may chance of wheat, or
of some other *grain:*
38 But [k]God giveth it a body as it
hath pleased him, and to every seed
his own body.
39 All flesh *is* not the same flesh:
but *there is* one *kind of* flesh of men,
another flesh of beasts, another of
fishes, *and* another of birds.
40 *There are* also celestial bodies, and
bodies terrestrial: but the glory of the

celestial *is* one, and the *glory* of the
terrestrial *is* another.
41 *There is* one glory of the sun,
and another glory of the moon, and
another glory of the stars: for *one* star
differeth from *another* star in glory.
42 So [l]also *is* the resurrection of the
dead. It is sown in corruption; it is
raised in incorruption:
43 It [m]is sown in dishonour; it is
raised in glory: it is sown in weakness;
it is raised in power:
44 It is sown a natural body; it is
raised a spiritual body. There is a
natural body, and there is a spiritual
body.
45 And so it is written, The first man
Adam [n]was made a living soul; the
[o]last Adam *was made* [p]a quickening
spirit.
46 Howbeit that *was* not first which
is spiritual, but that which is natural;
and afterward that which is spiritual.
47 The [q]first man *is* of the earth,
[r]earthy: the second man *is* the Lord
from [s]heaven.
48 As *is* the earthy, such *are* they
also that are earthy: [t]and as *is* the
heavenly, such *are* they also that are
heavenly.
49 And [u]as we have borne the image
of the earthy, [v]we shall also bear the
image of the heavenly.
50 Now this I say, brethren, that
[w]flesh and blood cannot inherit the
kingdom of God; neither doth corruption inherit incorruption.
51 Behold, I shew you a mystery;
[x]We shall not all sleep, [y]but we shall
all be changed,
52 In a moment, in the twinkling of
an eye, at the last trump: for [z]the
trumpet shall sound, and the dead
shall be raised incorruptible, and we
shall be changed.
53 For this corruptible must put on
incorruption, and [a]this mortal *must*
put on immortality.
54 So when this corruptible shall
have put on incorruption, and this
mortal shall have put on immortality,
then shall be brought to pass the saying that is written, Death is [b]swallow-
ed up in victory.
55 O [c]death, where *is* thy sting? O
[6]grave, where *is* thy victory?
56 The sting of death *is* sin; and [d]the
strength of sin *is* the law.
57 But [e]thanks *be* to God, which giveth us [f]the victory through our Lord
Jesus Christ.
58 Therefore, my beloved brethren,

l Dan. 12.3. Matt. 13.43.
m Phil. 3.21.
n Gen. 2.7.
o Rom. 5.14.
p John 5.21.
q Gen. 2.7.
r Gen. 3.19.
s Isa. 9.6. Luke 2.11.
t Phil. 3.20.
u Gen. 5.3.
v Rom. 8.29. Phil. 3.21.
w Matt. 16. 17.
x 1 Thes. 4. 15.
y Phil. 3.21.
z Matt. 24. 31.
a 2 Cor. 5.4.
b Rev. 20.14.
c Hos. 13.14.
6 Or, hell.
d Rom. 3.19.
e Rom. 7.25.
f Ps. 98.1.
g 2 Chr. 15.7.
h Ps. 19.11. Isa. 3.10.

CHAP. 16

a Acts 11.29. Rom. 15.26. Gal. 2.10.
b Luke 24.1. Acts 20.7. Rev. 1.10.
c 2 Cor. 8.19.
1 gift.
d Acts 19.21.
e Acts 15.3.
f Acts 14.27. Rev. 3.8.
g Acts 19.9.
h Rom. 16. 21. Phil. 2.19-22.
i Luke 10.16.
j Acts 18.24. ch. 1.12.

[g]be ye stedfast, unmoveable, always
abounding in the work of the Lord,
forasmuch as ye know [h]that your
labour is not in vain in the Lord.

CHAPTER 16

NOW concerning [a]the collection
for the saints, as I have given
order to the churches of Galatia, even
so do ye.
2 Upon [b]the first *day* of the week let
every one of you lay by him in store,
as *God* hath prospered him, that there
be no gatherings when I come.
3 And when I come, [c]whomsoever
ye shall approve by *your* letters, them
will I send to bring your [1]liberality unto Jerusalem.
4 And if it be meet that I go also, they
shall go with me.
5 Now I will come unto you, [d]when
I shall pass through Măç-ē-dō-nĭ-ă:
for I do pass through Măç-ē-dō-
nĭ-ă.
6 And it may be that I will abide, yea,
and winter with you, that ye may
[e]bring me on my journey whithersoever I go.
7 For I will not see you now by the
way; but I trust to tarry a while with
you, if the Lord permit.
8 But I will tarry at Ĕph-ĕ-sŭs until
Pentecost.
9 For [f]a great door and effectual is
opened unto me, and [g]*there are* many
adversaries.
10 Now if Timotheus come, see that
he may be with you without fear: for
[h]he worketh the work of the Lord, as I
also *do*.
11 Let [i]no man therefore despise
him: but conduct him forth in peace,
that he may come unto me: for I look
for him with the brethren.
12 As touching *our* brother [j]Ă-pŏl-
lŏs, I greatly desired him to come unto
you with the brethren: but his will was
not at all to come at this time; but he
will come when he shall have convenient time.
13 Watch ye, stand fast in the faith,
quit you like men, be strong.
14 Let all your things be done with
charity.
15 I beseech you, brethren, (ye know
the house of Stĕph-ă-năs, that it is the
firstfruits of Ă-chāi-ă, and *that* they
have addicted themselves to the ministry of the saints,)
16 That ye submit yourselves unto
such, and to every one that helpeth
with *us*, and laboureth.
17 I am glad of the coming of Stĕph-

ă-năs and Fôr-tū-nā′-tŭs and Ă-chā′-
ĭ-cŭs: for [k]that which was lacking on
your part they have supplied.
18 For [l]they have refreshed my
spirit and yours: therefore acknowledge ye them that are such.
19 The [m]churches of Asia salute you.
Ă-quĭl′-ă and Priscilla salute you much
in the Lord, [n]with the church that is
in their house.
20 All the brethren greet you. Greet
ye one another with an holy kiss.

k 2 Cor. 11.9.
l Col. 4.8.
m Acts 16.6. Acts 19.10. Rev. 1.4, 11.
n Rom. 16.5. Philem. 2.
o Gal. 1.8,9. Heb. 10.26.
p Jude 14,15.

21 The salutation of *me* Paul with
mine own hand.
22 If any man love not the Lord
Jesus Christ, [o]let him be Ă-năth′-ĕ-mă
[p]Măr′-ăn-ā′-thă.
23 The grace of our Lord Jesus
Christ *be* with you.
24 My love *be* with you all in Christ
Jesus. Ā′-mĕn.

¶ The first *epistle* to the Corinthians was written from Philippi by Stephanas, and Fortunatus, and Achaicus, and Timotheus.

THE SECOND EPISTLE OF PAUL THE APOSTLE TO THE

CORINTHIANS

CHAPTER 1

PAUL, an apostle of Jesus Christ
by the will of God, and Timothy
our brother, unto the church of God
which is at Corinth, with [a]all the
saints which are in all Ă-chā′-ĭ-ă:
2 Grace [b]*be* to you and peace from
God our Father, and *from* the Lord
Jesus Christ.
3 Blessed [c]*be* God, even the Father of
our Lord Jesus Christ, [d]the Father of
mercies, and the God of all comfort;
4 Who [e]comforteth us in all our tribulation, that we may be able to comfort them which are in any trouble, by
the comfort wherewith we ourselves
are comforted of God.
5 For as [f]the sufferings of Christ
abound in us, so our consolation also
aboundeth by Christ.
6 And whether we be afflicted, [g]*it is*
for your consolation and salvation,
which [1]is effectual in the enduring of
the same sufferings which we also
suffer: or whether we be comforted,
it is for your consolation and salvation.
7 And our hope of you *is* stedfast,
knowing, that [h]as ye are partakers of
the sufferings, so *shall ye be* also of
the consolation.
8 For we would not, brethren, have
you ignorant of [i]our trouble which
came to us in Asia, that we were pressed out of measure, above strength, insomuch that we despaired even of
life:
9 But we had the [2]sentence of death
in ourselves, that we should [j]not trust
in ourselves, but in God which raiseth
the dead:
10 Who [k]delivered us from so great

CHAP. 1
a Col. 1.2.
b Phil. 1.2.
c Eph. 1.3.
d Ex. 34.6.
e 2 Thes. 2. 16.
f Acts 9.4. ch. 4.10-14. Phil. 1.20.
g ch. 4.15.
1 Or, is wrought.
h Rom. 8.17.
i Acts 19.23.
2 Or, answer.
j Jer. 17.5,7. Rom. 4.17. Heb. 11.19.
k 1 Sam. 7.12. Job. 5.17-22. Ps. 34.19. 2 Pet. 2.9.
l Rom. 15.30. Phil. 1.19. Philem. 22.
m ch. 4.15.
n ch. 2.17.
o 1 Cor. 2.4.
p ch. 5.12.
q Phil. 2.16.
r 1 Cor. 4.19.
s Rom. 1.11.
3 Or, grace.
t 1 Cor. 16.5.
u ch. 10.2.
4 Or, preaching.
v Ex. 3.14. Mark 1.1. Luke 1.35. Acts 9.20. Heb. 13.8.
w Acts 18.5.

a death, and doth deliver: in whom
we trust that he will yet deliver *us;*
11 Ye also [l]helping together by
prayer for us, that [m]for the gift *bestowed* upon us by the means of many
persons thanks may be given by many
on our behalf.
12 For our rejoicing is this, the testimony of our conscience, that in simplicity [n]and godly sincerity, [o]not with
fleshly wisdom, but by the grace of
God, we have had our conversation
in the world, and more abundantly to
you-ward.
13 For we write none other things
unto you, than what ye read or
acknowledge; and I trust ye shall
acknowledge even to the end;
14 As also ye have acknowledged us
in part, [p]that we are your rejoicing,
even as ye [q]also *are* ours in the day of
the Lord Jesus.
15 And in this confidence [r]I was
minded to come unto you before, that
ye might have [s]a second [3]benefit;
16 And to pass by you into Măç-ē-
dō′-nĭ-ă, and [t]to come again out of
Măç-ē-dō′-nĭ-ă unto you, and of you
to be brought on my way toward
Judæa.
17 When I therefore was thus minded, did I use lightness? or the things
that I purpose, do I purpose [u]accord-
ing to the flesh, that with me there
should be yea yea, and nay nay?
18 But *as* God *is* true, our [4]word toward you was not yea and nay.
19 For the [v]Son of God, Jesus Christ,
who was preached among you by us,
even by me and [w]Sĭl-vā′-nŭs and
Timotheus, was not yea and nay, but
in him was yea.

20 For [x]all the promises of God in
him *are* yea, and in him Ā-měn, unto
the glory of God by us.
21 Now he which stablisheth us with
you in Christ, and [y]hath anointed us,
is God;
22 Who [z]hath also sealed us, [a]and
given the earnest of the Spirit in our
hearts.
23 Moreover I call God for a record
upon my soul, [b]that to spare you I
came not as yet unto Corinth.
24 Not for that we have dominion
over your faith, but are helpers of your
joy: for by [c]faith ye stand.

CHAPTER 2

BUT I determined this with myself,
that I [a]would not come again to
you in heaviness.
2 For if I make you sorry, who is he
then that maketh me glad, but the
same which is made sorry by me?
3 And I wrote this same unto you,
lest, when I came, I should have sorrow from them of whom I ought to rejoice; [b]having confidence in you all,
that my joy is *the joy* of you all.
4 For out of much affliction and
anguish of heart I wrote unto you with
many tears; not [c]that ye should be
grieved, but that ye might know the
love which I have more abundantly
unto you.
5 But [d]if any have caused grief, he
hath not [e]grieved me, but in part: that
I may not overcharge you all.
6 Sufficient to such a man *is* this
[1]punishment, which *was inflicted* [f]of
many.
7 So [g]that contrariwise ye *ought*
rather to forgive *him*, and comfort
him, lest perhaps such a one should be
swallowed up with overmuch sorrow.
8 Wherefore I beseech you that ye
would confirm *your* love toward him.
9 For to this end also did I write,
that I might know the proof of you,
whether ye be obedient in all things.
10 To whom ye forgive any thing, I
forgive also: for if I forgave any
thing, to whom I forgave *it*, for your
sakes *forgave I it* [2]in the person of
Christ;
11 Lest [h]Satan should get an advantage of us: for we are not ignorant of
his devices.
12 Furthermore, [i]when I came to
Trō-ăs to *preach* Christ's gospel, and
a door was opened unto me of the
Lord,
13 I had no rest in my spirit, because
I found not Titus my brother: but taking my leave of them, I went from
thence into Măç-ē-dō-nĭ-ă.
14 Now thanks *be* unto God, which
always causeth us to triumph in
Christ, and maketh manifest the savour of his knowledge by us in every
place.
15 For we are unto God a sweet savour of Christ, in them that are saved,
and in them that perish:
16 To the one *we are* the savour of
death unto death; and to the other the
savour of life unto life. And who *is*
sufficient for these things?
17 For we are not as many, which
[3]corrupt the word of God: but as of
sincerity, but as of God, in the sight
of God speak we [4]in Christ.

CHAPTER 3

DO [a]we begin again to commend
ourselves? or need we, as some
others, epistles [b]of commendation to
you, or *letters* of commendation from
you?
2 Ye [c]are our epistle written in our
hearts, known and read of all men:
3 *Forasmuch as ye are* manifestly declared to be the epistle of Christ ministered by [d]us, written not with ink,
but with the Spirit of the living God;
not [e]in tables of stone, but [f]in fleshy
tables of the heart.
4 And such trust have we through
Christ to God-ward:
5 Not [g]that we are sufficient of ourselves to think any thing as of ourselves; but our [h]sufficiency *is* of God;
6 Who also hath made us able ministers of [i]the new testament; not [j]of
the letter, but of the spirit: for the
[k]letter killeth, but [l]the spirit [1]giveth
life.
7 But if the ministration of death,
written *and* engraven in stones, was
glorious, so that the children of Israel
could not stedfastly behold the face
of Moses for the glory of his countenance; which *glory* was to be done
away:
8 How shall not [m]the ministration of
the spirit be rather glorious?
9 For if the ministration of condemnation *be* glory, much more doth the
ministration of [n]righteousness exceed
in glory.
10 For even that which was made
glorious had no glory in this respect,
by reason of the glory that excelleth.
11 For if that which is done away
was glorious, much more that which
remaineth *is* glorious.
12 Seeing then that we have such

x Gen. 3.15. Ps. 72.17. Isa. 7.14. Rom. 15.8, 9.
y 1 John 2. 20,27.
z Eph. 4.30. 2 Tim. 2.19. Rev. 2.17.
a Eph. 1.14.
b 1 Cor. 4.21.
c Rom. 11. 20.

CHAP. 2
a ch. 12.20.
b Gal. 5.10.
c ch. 7.8,9.
d 1 Cor. 5.1.
e Gal. 4.12.
1 Or, censure.
f 1 Tim. 5.20.
g Gal. 6.1. Heb. 12.12.
2 Or, in the sight.
h Eph. 6.11, 12. 1 Pet. 5.8.
i Acts 16.8. Acts 20.6.
3 Or, deal deceitfully with.
4 Or, of.

CHAP. 3
a ch. 5.12.
b Acts 18.27.
c 1 Cor. 9.2.
d 1 Cor. 3.5.
e Ex. 24.12.
f Ps. 40.8. Eze. 11.19.
g John 15.5.
h 1 Cor. 15. 10.
i Matt. 26.28. Heb. 8.6,8.
j Rom. 2.27.
k Rom. 3.20. Gal. 3.10.
l Rom. 8.2.
1 Or, quickeneth.
m Gal. 3.5.
n Rom. 1.17.

hope, we use great [2]plainness of
speech:
13 And not as Moses, [o]*which* put a
vail over his face, that the children of
Israel could not stedfastly look to the
[p]end of that which is abolished:
14 But [q]their minds were blinded:
for until this day remaineth the same
vail untaken away in the reading of
the old testament; which *vail* is done
away in Christ.
15 But even unto this day, when
Moses is read, the vail is upon their
heart.
16 Nevertheless [r]when it shall turn to
the Lord, [s]the vail shall be taken
away.
17 Now the Lord is that Spirit: and
where the Spirit of the Lord *is*, there
is liberty.
18 But we all, with open face beholding as [t]in a glass the glory of the Lord,
[u]are changed into the same image
from glory to glory, *even* as [3]by the
Spirit of the Lord.

CHAPTER 4

THEREFORE seeing we have this
ministry, as we have received
mercy, we faint not;
2 But have renounced the hidden
things of [1]dishonesty, not walking in
craftiness, nor [a]handling the word of
God deceitfully; but by manifestation
of the truth commending ourselves to
every man's conscience in the sight of
God.
3 But if our gospel be hid, [b]it is hid to
them that are lost:
4 In whom [c]the god of this world
[d]hath blinded the minds of them
which believe not, lest the light of the
glorious gospel of Christ, [e]who is the
image of God, should shine unto
them.
5 For we preach not ourselves, but
Christ Jesus the Lord; and [f]ourselves
your servants for Jesus' sake.
6 For God, [g]who commanded the
light to shine out of darkness, [2]hath
shined [h]in our hearts, to *give* [i]the light
of the knowledge of the glory of
God in the face of Jesus Christ.
7 But we have this treasure [j]in earth-
en vessels, [k]that the excellency of the
power may be of God, and not of us.
8 *We are* troubled on every side, yet
not distressed; *we are* perplexed, but
[3]not in despair;
9 Persecuted, but not forsaken; cast
down, but not destroyed;
10 Always [l]bearing about in the body
the dying of the Lord Jesus, [m]that the
life also of Jesus might be made manifest in our body.
11 For we which live are alway delivered unto death for Jesus' sake,
that the life also of Jesus might be
made manifest in our mortal flesh.
12 So then death worketh in us, but
life in you.
13 We having the same spirit of
faith, according as it is written, [n]I believed, and therefore have I spoken;
we also believe, and therefore speak;
14 Knowing that he which raised up
the Lord Jesus shall raise up us also
by Jesus, and shall present *us* with
you.
15 For all things *are* for your sakes,
that the abundant grace might
through the thanksgiving of many re-
dound to the glory of God.
16 For which cause we faint not; but
though our outward man perish, yet
the inward *man* is renewed day by day.
17 For our light affliction, which is
but for a moment, worketh for us a far
more exceeding *and* eternal weight of
glory;
18 While we look not at the things
which are seen, but at the things which
are not seen: for the things which are
seen *are* temporal; but the things
which are not seen *are* eternal.

CHAPTER 5

FOR we know that if [a]our earthly
house of *this* tabernacle were dissolved, we have [b]a building of God,
an house not made with hands,
eternal in the heavens.
2 For in this [c]we groan, earnestly
desiring to be clothed upon with our
house which is from heaven:
3 If so be that [d]being clothed we shall
not be found naked.
4 For we that are in *this* tabernacle
do groan, being burdened: not for
that we would be unclothed, [e]but
clothed upon, that mortality might be
swallowed up of life.
5 Now [f]he that hath wrought us for
the selfsame thing *is* God, who [g]also
hath given unto us the earnest of the
Spirit.
6 Therefore *we are* always confident,
knowing that, whilst we are at home
in the body, we are absent from the
Lord:
7 (For [h]we walk by faith, not by
sight:)
8 We are confident, *I say*, and [i]willing
rather to be absent from the body, and
to be present with the Lord.
9 Wherefore we [1]labour, that, wheth-

2 Or, boldness.
o Ex. 34.33.
p Rom. 10.4. Gal. 3.23.
q Isa. 6.10.
r Rom. 11.23.
s Isa. 25.7.
t ch. 4.4,6.
u John 17.17. Rom. 8.29. 2 Pet. 1.5.
3 Or, of the Lord the Spirit.

CHAP. 4

1 shame.
a 1 Thes. 2.3, 5.
b Isa. 6.9.
c John 12.31. Eph. 6.12.
d Isa. 6.10. Matt. 13.4.
e Zech. 13.7. John 1.18. Phil. 2.6.
f 1 Cor. 9.19.
g Gen. 1.3.
2 is he who hath.
h 2 Pet. 1.19.
i Ps. 27.1. Isa. 2.5. Eph. 5.8,14.
j ch. 5.1.
k 1 Cor. 2.5. Eph. 1.19, 20.
3 Or, not altogether without help, or, means.
l Gal. 6.17. Phil. 3.10.
m Rom. 8.17. 1 Pet. 4.13.
n Ps. 116.10.

CHAP. 5

a 2 Pet. 1.13.
b Phil. 3.21. Heb. 11.10.
c Rom. 8.23.
d Rev. 3.18.
e 1 Cor. 15. 53.
f Isa. 29.23.
g Rom. 8.23. Eph. 1.14.
h Deut. 12.9. Rom. 8.24, 25. 1 Cor. 13.12. 1 Pet. 1.8,9.
i Phil. 1.23.
1 Or, endeavour.

er present or absent, we may be accepted of him.

10 For we must all appear before the judgment seat of Christ; [j]that every one may receive the things *done* in *his* body, according to that he hath done. whether *it be* good or bad. Mil 1 Cor 6:2,3

11 Knowing therefore the terror of the Lord, we persuade men; but we are made manifest unto God; and I trust also are made manifest in your consciences.

12 For we commend not ourselves again unto you, but give you occasion to glory on our behalf, that ye may have somewhat to *answer* them which glory [2]in appearance, and not in heart.

13 For [k]whether we be beside ourselves, *it is* to God: or whether we be sober, *it is* for your cause.

14 For the love of Christ constraineth us; because we thus judge, that if [l]one died for all, then were all dead:

15 And *that* he died for all, [m]that they which live should not henceforth live unto themselves, but unto him which died for them, and rose again.

16 Wherefore [n]henceforth know we no man after the flesh: yea, though we have known Christ after the flesh, yet [o]now henceforth know we *him* no more.

17 Therefore if any man *be* in Christ, [3]*he is* a new creature: [p]old things are passed away; behold, all things are become new.

18 And all things *are* of God, who hath reconciled us to himself by Jesus Christ, and hath given to us the ministry of reconciliation;

19 To wit, that [q]God was in Christ, reconciling the world unto himself, not imputing their trespasses unto them; and hath [4]committed unto us the word of reconciliation.

20 Now then we are [r]ambassadors for Christ, as though God did beseech *you* by us: we pray *you* in Christ's stead, be ye reconciled to God.

21 For [s]he hath made him *to be* sin for us, who [t]knew no sin; that we might be made [u]the righteousness of God in him.

CHAPTER 6

WE then, *as* [a]workers together *with him*, beseech *you* also [b]that ye receive not the grace of God in vain.

2 (For he saith, [c]I have heard thee in a time accepted, and in the day of salvation have I succoured thee: behold, now *is* the accepted time; behold, now *is* the day of salvation.)

j Rev. 22.12.

2 in the face.
k ch. 11.1.
l Isa. 53.6. Matt. 20.28. Rom. 5.15. 1 John 2.1, 2.
m 1 Pet. 4.2.
n Matt. 12. 50.
o John 6.63.
3 Or, let him be.
p Isa. 65.17. Rev. 21.5.
q Isa. 43.25. Rom. 3.24. Rom. 11.15. 1 John 2.1,2.
4 put in us.
r Job 33.23. Pro. 13.17. Mal. 2.7. Acts 26.17, 18. Eph. 6.20.
s Isa. 53.6.9. Gal. 3.13. 1 Pet. 2.22.
t Isa. 53.9. Luke 1.35. Heb. 7.26.
u Jer. 23.6. Dan. 9.24. Rom. 1.17. Phil. 3.9.

CHAP. 6

a 1 Cor. 3.9. ch. 5.20.
b Heb. 12.15.
c Isa. 49.8.
d 1 Cor. 9.12.
1 commending.
e 1 Cor. 4.1.
2 Or, in tossings to and fro.
f Acts 11.21. Eph. 1.19, 20. Heb. 2.4.
g 2 Tim. 4.7.
h ch. 5.11.
i 1 Cor. 4.9.
j Ps. 118.18.
k ch. 12.15.
l Ex. 34.16. Deut. 7.2,3.
m 1 Sam. 5.2. Eph. 5.7.
n 1 Pet. 2.5.
o Lev. 26.12. Jer. 31.33. Eze. 37.26. Zech. 8.8.
p Isa. 52.11. Rev. 18.4.
q Jer. 31.1.9. Rev. 21.7.

CHAP. 7

a 1 John 3.3.

3 Giving [d]no offence in any thing, that the ministry be not blamed:

4 But in all *things* [1]approving ourselves as [e]the ministers of God, in much patience, in afflictions, in necessities, in distresses,

5 In stripes, in imprisonments, [2]in tumults, in labours, in watchings, in fastings;

6 By pureness, by knowledge, by longsuffering, by kindness, by the Holy Ghost, by love unfeigned,

7 By the word of truth, by [f]the power of God, by [g]the armour of righteousness on the right hand and on the left,

8 By honour and dishonour, by evil report and good report: as deceivers, and *yet* true;

9 As unknown, and [h]*yet* well known; [i]as dying, and, behold, we live; [j]as chastened, and not killed;

10 As sorrowful, yet alway rejoicing; as poor, yet making many rich; as having nothing, and *yet* possessing all things.

11 O *ye* Corinthians, our mouth is open unto you, our heart is enlarged.

12 Ye are not straitened in us, [k]but ye are straitened in your own bowels.

13 Now for a recompence in the same, (I speak as unto *my* children,) be ye also enlarged.

14 Be [l]ye not unequally yoked together with unbelievers: for [m]what fellowship hath righteousness with unrighteousness? and what communion hath light with darkness?

15 And what concord hath Christ with Bē-lĭ-ăl? or what part hath he that believeth with an infidel?

16 And what agreement hath the temple of God with idols? for [n]ye are the temple of the living God; as God hath said, [o]I will dwell in them, and walk in *them;* and I will be their God, and they shall be my people.

17 Wherefore [p]come out from among them, and be ye separate, saith the Lord, and touch not the unclean *thing;* and I will receive you,

18 And [q]will be a Father unto you, and ye shall be my sons and daughters, saith the Lord Almighty.

CHAPTER 7

HAVING [a]therefore these promises, dearly beloved, let us cleanse ourselves from all filthiness of the flesh and spirit, perfecting holiness in the fear of God.

2 Receive us; we have wronged no man, we have corrupted no man, we have defrauded no man.

3 I speak not *this* to condemn *you:*
for I have said before, that ye are in
our hearts to die and live with *you.*
4 Great *is* my boldness of speech toward you, great [b]*is* my glorying of
you: [c]I am filled with comfort, I am
exceeding joyful in all our tribulation.
5 For, [d]when we were come into
Măç-ē-dō-ni-ă, our flesh had no rest,
but we [e]were troubled on every side;
without [f]*were* fightings, within *were*
fears.
6 Nevertheless [g]God, that comforteth those that are cast down, comforted us by the coming of Titus;
7 And not by his coming only, but by
the consolation wherewith he was
comforted in you, when he told us
your earnest desire, your mourning,
your fervent mind toward me; so that
I rejoiced the more.
8 For though I made you sorry with
a letter, I do not repent, [h]though I did
repent: for I perceive that the same
epistle hath made you sorry, though *it*
were but for a season.
9 Now I rejoice, not that ye were
made sorry, but that ye sorrowed to
repentance: for ye were made sorry
[1]after a godly manner, that ye might
receive damage by us in nothing.
10 For [i]godly sorrow worketh repentance to salvation not to be repented of: [j]but the sorrow of the
world worketh death.
11 For behold this selfsame thing,
that ye [k]sorrowed after a godly sort,
what carefulness it wrought in you,
yea, *what* clearing of yourselves, yea,
what indignation, yea, *what* fear, yea,
what vehement desire, yea, *what* zeal,
yea, *what* revenge! In all *things* ye
have approved yourselves to be clear
in this matter.
12 Wherefore, though I wrote unto
you, *I did it* not for his cause that had
done the wrong, nor for his cause that
suffered wrong, but that our care for
you in the sight of God might appear
unto you.
13 Therefore we were comforted in
your comfort: yea, and exceedingly
the more joyed we for the joy of Titus,
because his spirit [l]was refreshed by you
all.
14 For if I have boasted any thing
to him of you, I am not ashamed; but
as we spake all things to you in truth,
even so our boasting, which *I made*
before Titus, is found a truth.
15 And his [2]inward affection is more
abundant toward you, whilst he remembereth [m]the obedience of you all,
how with fear and trembling ye received him.
16 I rejoice therefore that [n]I have
confidence in you in all *things.*

CHAPTER 8

MOREOVER, brethren, [1]we do
you to wit of the grace of God bestowed on the churches of Măç-ē-dō-
ni-ă;
2 How that in a great trial of affliction the abundance of their joy [a]and
their deep poverty abounded unto the
riches of their [2]liberality.
3 For to *their* power, I bear record,
yea, and beyond *their* power *they were*
willing of themselves;
4 Praying us with much intreaty that
we would receive the gift, and *take up-*
on us [b]the fellowship of the ministering to the saints.
5 And *this they did,* not as we hoped,
but first [c]gave their own selves to the
Lord, and unto us by the will of God.
6 Insomuch that [d]we desired Titus,
that as he had begun, so he would also
finish in you the same [3]grace also.
7 Therefore, as [e]ye abound in every
thing, in faith, and utterance, and
knowledge, and *in* all diligence, and *in*
your love to us, *see* [f]that ye abound in
this grace also.
8 I [g]speak not by commandment, but
by occasion of the forwardness of
others, and to prove the sincerity of
your love.
9 For ye know the grace of our Lord
Jesus Christ, [h]that, though he was
rich, yet for your sakes he became
poor, that ye through his poverty
might be rich.
10 And herein [i]I give *my* advice: for
this is [j]expedient for you, who have
begun before, not only to do, but also
to be [4]forward a year ago.
11 Now therefore perform the doing
of it; that as *there was* a readiness to
will, so *there may be* a performance
also out of that which ye have.
12 For [k]if there be first a willing
mind, *it is* accepted according to that
a man hath, *and* not according to that
he hath not.
13 For *I mean* not that other men be
eased, and ye burdened:
14 But by an equality, *that* now at
this time your abundance *may be a*
supply for their want, that their abundance also may be *a supply* for your
want: that there may be equality:
15 As it is written, [l]He that *had*
gathered much had nothing over; and
he that *had gathered* little had no lack.

b 1 Cor. 1.4.
c Phil. 2.17.
d ch. 2.13.
e ch. 4.8.
f Deut. 32.25.
g 2 Thes. 2. 16.
h ch. 2.4.
1 Or, according to God.
i 2 Sam. 12. 13. Jer. 31.18-20. Matt. 26.75.
j Gen. 4.13. Matt. 27.4, 5.
k Jer. 50.4,5. Zech. 12.10.
l Rom. 15.32. 1 Cor. 16.18.
2 bowels.
m ch. 2.9. Phil. 2.12.
n Philem. 8, 21.

CHAP. 8

1 we must inform you.
a Mark 12. 44.
2 simplicity.
b Acts 11.29. Rom. 15.25. ch. 9.1.
c 1 Sam. 1.28. Jer. 31.33. Zech. 13.9. Matt. 25.40. Rom. 6.13. Phil. 4.18. Heb. 13.16.
d ch. 12.18.
3 Or, gift.
e 1 Cor. 1.5.
f Ps. 112.9. Pro. 22.9. Matt. 19.21. Mark 10.21. Luke 18.22. ch. 9.8.
g 1 Cor. 7.6.
h Matt. 8.20. Luke 9.58. Phil. 2.6,7.
i 1 Cor. 7.25.
j Pro. 19.17. Matt. 10.42.
4 willing.
k Mark 12. 43,44. Luke 21.3.
l Ex. 16.18.

16 But thanks *be* to God, which put the same earnest care into the heart of Titus for you.

17 For indeed he accepted the exhortation; but being more forward, of his own accord he went unto you.

18 And we have sent with him [m]the brother, whose praise *is* in the gospel throughout all the churches;

19 And not *that* only, but who was also chosen [n]of the churches to travel with us with this [5]grace, which is administered by us [o]to the glory of the same Lord, and *declaration of* your ready mind:

20 Avoiding [p]this, that no man should blame us in this abundance which is administered by us:

21 Providing [q]for honest things, not only in the sight of the Lord, but also in the sight of men.

22 And we have sent with them our brother, whom we have oftentimes proved diligent in many things, but now much more diligent, upon the great confidence which [6]*I have* in you.

23 Whether *any do inquire* of Titus, *he is* my partner and fellowhelper concerning you: or our brethren *be inquired of, they are* the [r]messengers of the churches, *and* the glory of Christ.

24 Wherefore shew ye to them, and before the churches, the proof of your love, and of our boasting on your behalf.

CHAPTER 9

FOR as touching [a]the ministering to the saints, it is superfluous for me to write to you:

2 For I know the [b]forwardness of your mind, [c]for which I boast of you to them of Măç-ē-dō-'nĭ-ă, that [d]Ā-châi-'ă was ready a year ago; and your zeal hath provoked very many.

3 Yet [e]have I sent the brethren, lest our boasting of you should be in vain in this behalf; that, as I said, ye may be ready:

4 Lest haply if they of Măç-ē-dō-'nĭ-ă come with me, and find you unprepared, we (that we say not, ye) should be ashamed in this same confident boasting.

5 Therefore I thought it necessary to exhort the brethren, that they would go before unto you, and make up beforehand your [1]bounty, [2]whereof ye had notice before, that the same might be ready, as *a matter of* bounty, and not as *of* covetousness.

6 But [f]this *I say*, He which soweth sparingly shall reap also sparingly; and he which soweth bountifully shall reap also bountifully.

7 Every man according as he purposeth in his heart, *so let him give;* [g]not grudgingly, or of necessity: for [h]God loveth a cheerful giver.

8 And [i]God *is* able to make all grace abound toward you; that ye, always having all sufficiency in all *things*, may abound to every good work:

9 (As it is written, [j]He hath dispersed abroad; he hath given to the poor: his righteousness remaineth for ever.

10 Now he that [k]ministereth seed to the sower both minister bread for *your* food, and multiply your seed sown, and increase the fruits of [l]your righteousness;)

11 Being enriched in every thing to all [3]bountifulness, [m]which causeth through us thanksgiving to God.

12 For the administration of this service not only supplieth the want of the saints, but is abundant also by many thanksgivings unto God;

13 Whiles by the experiment of this ministration they [n]glorify God for your professed subjection unto the gospel of Christ, and for *your* liberal distribution [o]unto them, and unto all *men;*

14 And by their prayer for you, which long after you for the exceeding grace of God in you.

15 Thanks *be* unto God [p]for his unspeakable gift.

CHAPTER 10

NOW [a]I Paul myself beseech you by the meekness and gentleness of Christ, who [1]in presence *am* base among you, but being absent am bold toward you:

2 But I beseech *you*, [b]that I may not be bold when I am present with that confidence, wherewith I think to be bold against some, which [2]think of us as if we walked according to the flesh.

3 For though we walk in the flesh, we do not war after the flesh:

4 (For [c]the weapons of our warfare *are* not carnal, but mighty [3]through God [d]to the pulling down of strong holds;)

5 Casting [e]down [4]imaginations, and every high thing that exalteth itself against the knowledge of God, and bringing into captivity every thought to the obedience of Christ;

6 And [f]having in a readiness to revenge all disobedience, when [g]your obedience is fulfilled.

7 Do ye look on things after the out-

m ch. 12.18.
n 1 Cor. 16.3.
5 Or, gift.
o ch. 4.15.
p Eph. 5.15.
q Pro. 3.4. Matt. 5.16. Phil. 4.8.
6 Or, he hath.
r Phil. 2.25.

CHAP. 9

a Acts 11.29. Rom. 15.26. 1 Cor. 16.1.
b ch. 8.19.
c ch. 8.24.
d ch. 8.10.
e ch. 8.6,17.
1 blessing.
2 Or, which hath been so much spoken of before.
f Pro. 11.24. Pro. 19.17. Eccl. 11.1,6. Luke 6.38. Gal. 6.7,9. Heb. 6.10.
g Deut. 15.7.
h Ex. 25.2. 1 Chr. 29.17. Acts 20.35. Rom. 12.8.
i Ps. 84.11. Pro. 10.22. Mal. 3.10. Phil. 4.19.
j Ps. 112.9.
k Gen. 1.11, 12. Isa. 55.10.
l Hos. 10.12. Matt. 6.1.
3 simplicity, or, liberality.
m ch. 4.15.
n Matt. 5.16.
o Heb. 13.16.
p Jas. 1.17.

CHAP. 10

a Isa. 42.2.
1 Or, in outward appearance.
b 1 Cor. 4.21.
2 Or, reckon.
c Eph. 6.13.
3 Or, to God.
d Jer. 1.10.
e 1 Cor. 1.19.
4 Or, reasonings.
f ch. 13.2.
g ch. 7.15.

ward appearance? [h]If any man trust
to himself that he is Christ's, let him
of himself think this again, that, as he
is Christ's, even so *are* [i]we Christ's.
8 For though I should boast somewhat more of our authority, which the
Lord hath given us for edification, and
not for your destruction, I should not
be ashamed:
9 That I may not seem as if I would
terrify you by letters.
10 For *his* letters, [5]say they, *are*
weighty and powerful; but [j]*his* bodily
presence *is* weak, and *his* [k]speech contemptible.
11 Let such an one think this, that,
such as we are in word by letters
when we are absent, such *will we be*
also in deed when we are present.
12 For [l]we dare not make ourselves
of the number, or compare ourselves
with some that commend themselves:
but they measuring themselves by
themselves, and comparing themselves among themselves, [6]are not
wise.
13 But we will not boast of things
without *our* measure, but according to
the measure of the [7]rule which God
hath distributed to us, a measure to
reach even unto you.
14 For we stretch not ourselves beyond *our measure*, as though we
reached not unto you: [m]for we are
come as far as to you also in *preaching* the gospel of Christ:
15 Not boasting of things without *our*
measure, *that is*, [n]of other men's
labours; but having hope, when your
faith is increased, that we shall be [8]en-
larged by you according to our rule
abundantly,
16 To preach the gospel in the
regions beyond you, *and* not to boast
in another man's [9]line of things made
ready to our hand.
17 But [o]he that glorieth, let him glory
in the Lord.
18 For [p]not he that commendeth
himself is approved, but [q]whom the
Lord commendeth.

CHAPTER 11

WOULD to God ye could bear
with me a little in [a]*my* folly: and
indeed [1]bear with me.
2 For I am [b]jealous over you with
godly jealousy: for [c]I have espoused
you to one husband, [d]that I may present *you* [e]*as* a chaste virgin to Christ.
3 But I fear, lest by any means, as
[f]the serpent beguiled Eve through his
subtilty, so your minds [g]should be
corrupted from the simplicity that is
in Christ.
4 For if he that cometh preacheth
another Jesus, whom we have not
preached, or *if* ye receive another
spirit, which ye have not received, or
[h]another gospel, which ye have not
accepted, ye might well bear [2]with
him.
5 For I suppose I was not a whit behind the very chiefest apostles.
6 But though *I be* rude in speech, yet
not in [i]knowledge; but we have been
throughly made manifest among you
in all things.
7 Have I committed an offence [j]in
abasing myself that ye might be exalted, because I have preached to you
the gospel of God freely?
8 I robbed other churches, taking
wages *of them*, to do you service.
9 And when I was present with you,
and wanted, [k]I was chargeable to no
man: for that which was lacking to
me [l]the brethren which came from
Măç-ē-dō'-nĭ-ă supplied: and in all
things I have kept myself [m]from being
burdensome unto you, and *so* will I
keep *myself*.
10 As [n]the truth of Christ is in me,
[3]no man shall stop me of this boasting
in the regions of Ă-chā̤i'-ă.
11 Wherefore? [o]because I love you
not? God knoweth.
12 But what I do, that I will do, that
I [p]may cut off occasion from them
which desire occasion; that wherein
they glory, they may be found even as
we.
13 For such *are* false apostles, deceitful workers, transforming themselves into the apostles of Christ.
14 And no marvel; for Satan himself
is transformed into [q]an angel of light.
15 Therefore *it is* no great thing if his
ministers also be transformed as the
ministers of righteousness; whose
[r]end shall be according to their works.
16 I say again, Let no man think me
a fool; if otherwise, yet as a fool [4]re-
ceive me, that I may boast myself a
little.
17 That which I speak, [s]I speak *it* not
after the Lord, but as it were foolishly, [t]in this confidence of boasting.
18 Seeing [u]that many glory after the
flesh, I will glory also.
19 For ye suffer fools gladly, seeing
ye *yourselves* are wise.
20 For ye suffer, [v]if a man bring you
into bondage, if a man devour *you*, if
a man take *of you*, if a man exalt himself, if a man smite you on the face.

h 1 Cor. 14. 37.
i ch. 11.23.
5 saith he.
j Gal. 4.13.
k 1 Cor. 1.17.
l ch. 5.12.
6 Or, understand it not.
7 Or, line.
m 1 Cor. 9.1.
n Rom. 15. 20.
8 Or, magnified in you.
9 Or, rule.
o Isa. 65.16. Jer. 9.24.
p Luke 18.10.
q Rom. 2.29.

CHAP. 11
a ch. 5.13.
1 Or, ye do bear with me.
b Gal. 4.17.
c Hosea 2.19.
d Col. 1.28.
e Lev. 21.13.
f Gen. 3.4. John 8.44.
g 1 Tim. 1.3. Heb. 13.9.
h Gal. 1.7,8.
2 Or, with me.
i Eph. 3.4.
j Acts 18.3.
k Acts 20.33.
l Phil. 4.10.
m ch. 12.14.
n Rom. 9.1.
3 this boasting shall not be stopped in me.
o ch. 7.3.
p 1 Cor. 9.12.
q Rev. 12.9.
r Jer. 29.32. Phil. 3.19.
4 Or, suffer.
s 1 Cor. 7.6.
t ch. 9.4.
u Jer. 9.23, 24. Phil. 3.3.
v Gal. 2.4.

21 I speak as concerning reproach, [w]as though we had been weak. Howbeit whereinsoever any is bold, (I speak foolishly,) I am bold also.

22 Are they Hebrews? [x]so *am* I. Are they Israelites? so *am* I. Are they the seed of Abraham? so *am* I.

23 Are they ministers of Christ? (I speak as a fool) I *am* more; [y]in labours more abundant, [z]in stripes above measure, in prisons more frequent, in deaths oft.

24 Of the Jews five times received I [a]forty *stripes* save one.

25 Thrice was I [b]beaten with rods, once was I [c]stoned, thrice I [d]suffered shipwreck, a night and a day I have been in the deep;

26 *In* journeyings often, *in* perils of waters, *in* perils of robbers, [e]*in* perils by *mine own* countrymen, [f]*in* perils by the heathen, *in* perils in the city, *in* perils in the wilderness, *in* perils in the sea, *in* perils among false brethren;

27 In weariness and painfulness, in watchings often, [g]in hunger and thirst, in fastings often, in cold and nakedness.

28 Beside those things that are without, that which cometh upon me daily, [h]the care of all the churches.

29 Who is weak, and I am not weak? who is offended, and I burn not?

30 If I must needs glory, I will glory of the things which concern mine infirmities.

31 The God and Father of our Lord Jesus Christ, [i]which is blessed for evermore, knoweth that I lie not.

32 In [j]Damascus the governor under Ăr-ĕ-tăs the king kept the city of the Dăm-ăs-çēnes with a garrison, desirous to apprehend me:

33 And through a window in a basket was I let down by the wall, and escaped his hands.

CHAPTER 12

It is not expedient for me doubtless to glory. [1]I will come to visions and revelations of the Lord.

2 I knew a man [a]in Christ above fourteen years ago, (whether in the body, I cannot tell; or whether out of the body, I cannot tell: God knoweth;) such an one [b]caught up to the third heaven.

3 And I knew such a man, (whether in the body, or out of the body, I cannot tell: God knoweth;)

4 How that he was caught up [c]into paradise, and heard unspeakable words, which it is not [2]lawful for a man to utter.

w 1 Cor. 1.17. ch. 10.10. Gal. 4.13.
x Acts 9.30. Rom. 11.1.
y 1 Cor. 15. 10.
z Acts 9.16.
a Deut. 25.3.
b Acts 16.22. ch. 6.5.
c Acts 14.19.
d Acts 27.41.
e Acts 9.23. Acts 13.50. Acts 17.5. Acts 21.31.
f Acts 19.23.
g 1 Cor. 4.11.
h Acts 20.18. Rom. 1.14.
i Rom. 9.5.
j Acts 9.24.
CHAP. 12
1 For I will come.
a Rom. 16.7. ch. 5.17. Gal. 1.22.
b Acts 22.17.
c Luke 23.43.
2 Or, possible.
d ch. 11.30.
e ch. 10.8.
f Eze. 28.24. Gal. 4.13.
g Luke 13.16.
h Deut. 3.23. Matt. 26.44.
i Eccl. 7.18. Isa. 40.29. 1 Cor. 3.5. Heb. 2.18. 2 Pet. 2.9.
j Matt. 28. 18-20. 1 Pet. 4.14.
k Rom. 5.3. ch. 7.4.
l ch. 13.4.
m 1 Cor. 3.4-7. Gal. 2.6.
n Rom. 15. 18.
o 1 Cor. 1.7.
p 1 Cor. 9.12.
q ch. 13.1.
r Acts 20.33.
s 1 Cor. 4.14.
t Phil. 2.17. 1 Thes. 2.8.
3 your souls.
u ch. 6.12.
v ch. 11.9.
w ch. 7.2.
x ch. 8.6.

5 Of such an one will I glory: [d]yet of myself I will not glory, but in mine infirmities.

6 For [e]though I would desire to glory, I shall not be a fool; for I will say the truth: but *now* I forbear, lest any man should think of me above that which he seeth me *to be*, or *that* he heareth of me.

7 And lest I should be exalted above measure through the abundance of the revelations, there was given to me a [f]thorn in the flesh, [g]the messenger of Satan to buffet me, lest I should be exalted above measure.

8 For [h]this thing I besought the Lord thrice, that it might depart from me.

9 And he said unto me, [i]My grace is sufficient for thee: for my strength is made perfect in weakness. Most gladly therefore will I rather glory in my infirmities, that [j]the power of Christ may rest upon me.

10 Therefore [k]I take pleasure in infirmities, in reproaches, in necessities, in persecutions, in distresses for Christ's sake: for [l]when I am weak, then am I strong.

11 I am become a fool in glorying; ye have compelled me: for I ought to have been commended of you: for [m]in nothing am I behind the very chiefest apostles, though I be nothing.

12 Truly [n]the signs of an apostle were wrought among you in all patience, in signs, and wonders, and mighty deeds.

13 For [o]what is it wherein ye were inferior to other churches, except *it be* that I [p]myself was not burdensome to you? forgive me this wrong.

14 Behold, [q]the third time I am ready to come to you; and I will not be burdensome to you: for [r]I seek not yours, but you: [s]for the children ought not to lay up for the parents, but the parents for the children.

15 And [t]I will very gladly spend and be spent for [3]you; though [u]the more abundantly I love you, the less I be loved.

16 But be it so, [v]I did not burden you: nevertheless, being crafty, I caught you with guile.

17 Did [w]I make a gain of you by any of them whom I sent unto you?

18 I [x]desired Titus, and with *him* I sent a brother. Did Titus make a gain of you? walked we not in the same spirit? *walked we* not in the same steps?

19 Again, [y]think ye that we excuse ourselves unto you? [z]we speak before God in Christ: [a]but *we do* all things, dearly beloved, for your edifying.

20 For I fear, lest, when I come, I shall not find you such as I would, and *that* [b]I shall be found unto you such as ye would not: lest *there be* debates, envyings, wraths, strifes, backbitings, whisperings, swellings, tumults:

21 *And* lest, when I come again, my God will [c]humble me among you, and *that* I shall bewail many which have sinned already, and have not repented of the uncleanness and [d]fornication and lasciviousness which they have committed.

y ch. 5.12.
z Rom. 9.1.
a 1 Cor. 10. 33.
b 1 Cor. 4.21.
c ch. 2.1,4.
d 1 Cor. 5.1.

CHAPTER 13

THIS *is* [a]the third *time* I am coming to you. [b]In the mouth of two or three witnesses shall every word be established.

2 I [c]told you before, and foretell you, as if I were present, the second time; and being absent now I write to them [d]which heretofore have sinned, and to all other, that, if I come again, I will not spare:

3 Since ye seek a proof of Christ speaking in [e]me, which to you-ward is not weak, but is mighty [f]in you.

4 For [g]though he was crucified through weakness, yet [h]he liveth by the power of God. For [i]we also are weak [1]in him, but we shall live with him by the power of God toward you.

5 Examine [j]yourselves, whether ye be in the faith; prove your own selves. Know ye not your own selves, [k]how that Jesus Christ is in you, except ye be [l]reprobates?

6 But I trust that ye shall know that we are not reprobates.

7 Now I pray to God that ye do no evil; not that we should appear approved, but that ye should do that which is honest, though [m]we be as reprobates.

8 For we can do nothing against the truth, but for the truth.

9 For we are glad, [n]when we are weak, and ye are strong: and this also we wish, *even* [o]your perfection.

10 Therefore I write these things being absent, lest being present [p]I should use sharpness, according to the power which the Lord hath given me to edification, and not to destruction.

11 Finally, brethren, farewell. Be perfect, be of good comfort, [q]be of one mind, live in peace; and the God of love [r]and peace shall be with you.

12 Greet one another with an holy kiss.

13 All the saints salute you.

14 The grace of the Lord Jesus Christ, and the love of God, and the communion of the Holy Ghost, *be* with you all. Ā-mĕn.

¶ The second *epistle* to the Corinthians was written from Philippi, *a city* of Macedonia, by Titus and Lucas.

CHAP. 13
a ch. 12.14.
b Num. 35. 30.
c ch. 10.2.
d ch. 12.21.
e Matt. 10. 20.
f 1 Cor. 9.2.
g Phil. 2.7,8.
h Rom. 6.4.
i ch. 10.3.
1 Or, with him.
j 1 Cor. 11. 28.
k John 17.23. Rom. 8.10.
l 1 Cor. 9.27.
m ch. 6.9.
n 1 Cor. 4.10.
o 1 Thes. 3. 10.
p Titus 1.13.
q Rom. 12. 16. 1 Pet. 3.8.
r Rom. 15.33. Heb. 13.20, 21.

THE EPISTLE OF PAUL THE APOSTLE TO THE

GALATIANS

CHAPTER 1

PAUL, an apostle, (not of men, neither by man, but [a]by Jesus Christ, and God the Father, who raised him from the dead;)

2 And all the brethren [b]which are with me, [c]unto the churches of Galatia:

3 Grace [d]*be* to you and peace from God the Father, and *from* our Lord Jesus Christ,

4 Who [e]gave himself for our sins, that he might deliver us [f]from this present evil world, according to the will of God and our Father:

5 To whom *be* glory for ever and ever. Ā-mĕn.

6 I marvel that ye are so soon removed from him that called you into the grace of Christ unto another gospel:

7 Which [g]is not another; but there be some [h]that trouble you, and would pervert the gospel of Christ.

8 But though [i]we, or an angel from heaven, preach any other gospel unto you than that which we have preached unto you, let him be accursed.

9 As we said before, so say I now again, If any *man* preach any other gospel unto you [j]than that ye have received, let him be accursed.

10 For [k]do I now [l]persuade men, or God? or [m]do I seek to please men? for

CHAP. 1
a Acts 9.6.
b Phil. 2.22.
c 1 Cor. 16.1.
d 1 Cor. 1.3.
e 1 John 2.2.
f Isa. 65.17. Matt. 26.42. Luke 22.42. John 15.19.
g 2 Cor. 11.4.
h Acts 15.1.
i 1 Cor. 16. 22.
j Deut. 4.2. Deut. 12.32. Pro. 30.6. Rev. 22.18.
k 1 Thes. 2.4.
l 1 John 3.19.
m Jas. 4.4.

if I yet pleased men, I should not be
the servant of Christ.
11 But [n]I certify you, brethren, that
the gospel which was preached of me
is not after man.
12 For I neither received it of man,
neither was I taught *it*, but [o]by the
revelation of Jesus Christ.
13 For ye have heard of my conversation in time past in the Jews' religion, how that [p]beyond measure I
persecuted the church of God, and
[q]wasted it:
14 And profited in the Jews' religion
above many my [1]equals in mine own
nation, [r]being more exceedingly
zealous [s]of the traditions of my
fathers.
15 But when it pleased God, [t]who
separated me from my mother's
womb, and called *me* by his grace,
16 To [u]reveal his Son in me, that I
might preach him among the heathen;
immediately I conferred not [v]with
flesh and blood:
17 Neither went I up to Jerusalem
to them which were apostles before
me; but I went into Arabia, and returned again unto Damascus.
18 Then after three years I [2]went up
to Jerusalem to see Peter, and abode
with him fifteen days.
19 But [w]other of the apostles saw I
none, save [x]James the Lord's brother.
20 Now the things which I write unto
you, behold, before God, I lie not.
21 Afterwards [y]I came into the regions of Syria and Çi-lĭç-ĭ-ă;
22 And was unknown by face unto
the churches of Judæa which were in
Christ:
23 But they had heard only, That he
which persecuted us in times past now
preacheth the faith which once he destroyed.
24 And they glorified God in me.

CHAPTER 2

THEN fourteen years after [a]I went
up again to Jerusalem with Barnabas, and took Titus with *me* also.
2 And I went up by [b]revelation, and
communicated unto them that gospel
which I preach among the Gentiles,
but [1]privately to them which were of
reputation, lest by any means [c]I should
run, or had run, in vain.
3 But neither Titus, who was with
me, being a Greek, was compelled
to be circumcised:
4 And that because of false brethren
unawares brought in, who came in
privily to spy out our [d]liberty which
we have in Christ Jesus, [e]that they
might bring us into bondage:
5 To whom we gave place by subjection, no, not for an hour; that the
truth of the gospel might continue
with you.
6 But of these [f]who seemed to be
somewhat, (whatsoever they were, it
maketh no matter to me: [g]God accepteth no man's person:) for they
who seemed *to be somewhat* [h]in conference added nothing to me:
7 But contrariwise, [i]when they saw
that the gospel of the uncircumcision
was [j]committed unto me, as *the gospel*
of the circumcision *was* unto Peter;
8 (For he that wrought effectually in
Peter to the apostleship of the circumcision, [k]the same was mighty in
me toward the Gentiles:)
9 And when James, Çē-phăs, and
John, who seemed to be [l]pillars, perceived [m]the grace that was given unto
me, they gave to me and Barnabas the
right hands of fellowship; that we
should go unto the heathen, and they
unto the circumcision.
10 Only *they would* that we should
remember the poor; [n]the same which
I also was forward to do.
11 But [o]when Peter was come to Ăn-
tĭ-ŏch, I withstood him to the face, because he was to be blamed.
12 For before that certain came from
James, [p]he did eat with the Gentiles:
but when they were come, he withdrew and separated himself, fearing
them which were of the circumcision.
13 And the other Jews dissembled
likewise with him; insomuch that
Barnabas also was carried away with
their dissimulation.
14 But when I saw that they walked
not uprightly [q]according to the truth
of the gospel, I said unto Peter before
them all, If [r]thou, being a Jew, livest
after the manner of Gentiles, and not
as do the Jews, why compellest thou
the Gentiles to live as do the Jews?
15 We [s]*who are* Jews by nature, and
not [t]sinners of the Gentiles,
16 Knowing [u]that a man is not justified by the works of the law, but by
[v]the faith of Jesus Christ, even we have
believed in Jesus Christ, that we
might be justified by the faith of
Christ, and not by the works of the
law: for [w]by the works of the law
shall no flesh be justified.
17 But if, while we seek to be justified by Christ, we ourselves also are
found sinners, [x]*is* therefore Christ the
minister of sin? God forbid.

n 1 Cor. 15.1.
o Rom. 16. 25. Eph. 3.3. 1 Pet. 1.20.
p 1 Tim. 1.13.
q Acts 8.3.
1 equals in years.
r Phil. 3.6.
s Jer. 9.14. Mark 7.5.
t Isa. 49.1,5. Jer. 1.5. Acts 9.15.
u 2 Cor. 4.6.
v Matt. 16. 17.
2 Or, returned.
w 1 Cor. 9.5.
x Matt. 13. 55. Mark 6.3.
y Acts 9.30.

CHAP. 2
a Acts 15.2.
b Acts 19.21.
1 Or, severally.
c 1 Cor. 9.26. Phil. 2.16.
d John 8.31, 36. ch. 3.25. 1 Pet. 2.16.
e ch. 4.3,9.
f ch. 6.3.
g Acts 10.34. Rom. 2.11.
h 2 Cor. 12. 11.
i Acts 13.46.
j 1 Thes. 2.4.
k Acts 9.15. Acts 13.2. Acts 22.21. Col. 1.29.
l Matt. 16.18. Rev. 21.14.
m Rom. 1.5.
n Acts 11.30.
o Acts 15.35.
p Acts 10.28.
q Eccl. 7.20.
r Acts 11.3. 1 Tim. 5.20.
s Acts 15.10.
t Matt. 9.11. Eph. 2.3.
u Acts 13.38.
v Rom. 1.17. Rom. 8.3. 1 Cor. 6.11. Heb. 7.18.
w Ps. 143.2.
x Rom. 15.8. 1 John 3.8.

18 For if I build again the things which I destroyed, I make myself a transgressor.

19 For I [y]through the law [z]am dead to the law, that I might [a]live unto God.

20 I am [b]crucified with Christ: nevertheless I live; yet not I, but Christ liveth in me: and the life which I now live in the flesh [c]I live by the faith of the Son of God, who loved me, and gave himself for me.

21 I do not frustrate the grace of God: for [d]if righteousness *come* by the law, then Christ is dead in vain.

CHAPTER 3

O FOOLISH Galatians, [a]who hath bewitched you, that ye should not obey the truth, [b]before whose eyes Jesus Christ hath been evidently set forth, crucified among you?

2 This only would I learn of you, Received ye [c]the Spirit by the works of the law, [d]or by the hearing of faith?

3 Are ye so foolish? [e]having begun in the Spirit, are ye now made perfect by [f]the flesh?

4 Have [g]ye suffered [1]so many things in vain? if *it be* yet in vain.

5 He therefore [h]that ministereth to you the Spirit, and worketh miracles among you, *doeth he it* by the works of the law, or by the hearing of faith?

6 Even as Abraham believed God, and it was [2]accounted to him for righteousness.

7 Know ye therefore that [i]they which are of faith, the same are the children of Abraham.

8 And the scripture, foreseeing that God would justify the heathen through faith, preached before the gospel unto Abraham, *saying*, [j]In thee shall all nations be blessed.

9 So then they which be of faith are blessed with faithful Abraham.

10 For as many as are of the works of the law are under the curse: for it is written, [k]Cursed *is* every one that continueth not in all things which are written in the book of the law to do them.

11 But that no man is justified by the law in the sight of God, *it is* evident: for, The [l]just shall live by faith.

12 And [m]the law is not of faith: but, The man [n]that doeth them shall live in them.

13 Christ hath redeemed us from the curse of the law, being made a curse for us: for it is written, [o]Cursed *is* every one that hangeth on a tree:

14 That [p]the blessing of Abraham might come on the Gentiles through Jesus Christ; that we might receive the [q]promise of the Spirit through faith.

15 Brethren, I speak after the manner of men; [r]Though *it be* but a man's [3]covenant, yet *if it be* confirmed, no man disannulleth, or addeth thereto.

16 Now to Abraham and his seed were the promises made. He saith not, And to seeds, as of many; but as of one, And to thy seed, which [s]is Christ.

17 And this I say, *that* the covenant, that was confirmed before of God in Christ, the law, [t]which was four hundred and thirty years after, cannot disannul, [u]that it should make the promise of none effect.

18 For if [v]the inheritance *be* of the law, [w]*it is* no more of promise: but God gave *it* to Abraham by promise.

19 Wherefore then *serveth* the law? [x]It was added because of transgressions, till the seed should come to whom the promise was made; *and it was* [y]ordained by angels in the hand of [z]a mediator.

20 Now a mediator is not *a mediator* of one, [a]but God is one.

21 *Is* the law then against the promises of God? God forbid: for if there had been a law given which could have given life, verily righteousness should have been by the law.

22 But the scripture hath concluded all under sin, that the promise by faith of Jesus Christ might be given to them that believe.

23 But before faith came, we were kept under the law, shut up unto the faith which should afterwards be revealed.

24 Wherefore [b]the law was our schoolmaster *to bring us* unto Christ, that [c]we might be justified by faith.

25 But after that faith is come, we are no longer under a schoolmaster.

26 For ye [d]are all the children of God by faith in Christ Jesus.

27 For as many of you as have been baptized into Christ have put on Christ.

28 There [e]is neither Jew nor Greek, there is neither bond nor free, there is neither male nor female: for ye are all [f]one in Christ Jesus.

29 And [g]if ye *be* Christ's, then are ye Abraham's seed, and [h]heirs according to the promise.

---

y Rom. 3.19, 20. Rom. 8.2.
z Rom. 6.14.
a Rom. 14.7, 8. 1 Cor. 10.31. 1 Thes. 5.10. Heb. 9.14. 1 Pet. 4.1,2, 6.
b Rom. 6.6.
c 2 Cor. 5.15.
d Heb. 7.11.

CHAP. 3
a ch. 5.7.
b 1 Cor. 1.23.
c Acts 2.38. Heb. 6.4.
d Rom. 10. 16.
e ch. 4.9.
f Heb. 7.16.
g 2 John 8.
1 Or, so great.
h 2 Cor. 3.8.
2 Or, imputed.
i John 8.39.
j Gen. 12.3.
k Deut. 27. 26. Jer. 11.3.
l Hab. 2.4. Heb. 10.38.
m Rom. 4.4.
n Lev. 18.5.
o Deut. 21. 23. Josh. 10.26, 27.
p Rom. 4.9.
q Isa. 32.15. Eze. 11.19. Joel 2.28.
r Heb. 9.17.
3 Or, testament.
s 1 Cor. 12. 12.
t Ex. 12.40.
u Rom. 4.13, 14.
v Rom. 8.17.
w Rom. 4.14.
x John 15.22. 1 Tim. 1.9.
y Acts 7.53. Heb. 2.2.
z Ex. 20.19. Deut. 5.5.
a Rom. 3.29.
b Matt. 5.17.
c Acts 13.39.
d John 1.12. Rom. 8.14-17. Phil. 2.15. Heb. 2.10.
e Rom. 10. 12.
f John 10.16.
g Gen. 21.10. Rom. 9.7. Heb. 11.18.
h Rom. 8.17.

CHAPTER 4

NOW I say, *That* the heir, as long
as he is a child, differeth nothing
from a servant, though he be lord of
all;
2 But is under tutors and governors
until the time appointed of the
father.
3 Even so we, when we were children,
were [a]in bondage under the [1]elements
of the world:
4 But [b]when the fulness of the time
was come, God sent forth his Son,
made [c]of a woman, [d]made under the
law,
5 To [e]redeem them that were under
the law, [f]that we might receive the
adoption of sons.
6 And because ye are sons, God hath
sent forth the Spirit of his Son into
your hearts, crying, Abba, Father.
7 Wherefore thou art no more a servant, but a son; [g]and if a son, then an
heir of God through Christ.
8 Howbeit then, [h]when ye knew not
God, ye [i]did service unto them which
by nature are no gods.
9 But now, [j]after that ye have known
God, or rather are known of God,
[k]how turn ye [2]again to the [l]weak and
beggarly [3]elements, whereunto ye desire again to be in bondage?
10 Ye [m]observe days, and months,
and times, and years.
11 I am afraid of you, lest I have bestowed upon you labour in vain.
12 Brethren, I beseech you, be as [n]I
am; for I *am* as ye *are:* ye have not in-
jured me at all.
13 Ye know how [o]through infirmity
of the flesh I preached the gospel unto
you [p]at the first.
14 And my temptation which was in
my flesh ye despised not, nor rejected;
but received me [q]as an angel of God,
even [r]as Christ Jesus.
15 [4]Where is then the blessedness ye
spake of? for I bear you record, that,
if *it had been* possible, ye would have
plucked out your own eyes, and have
given them to me.
16 Am I therefore become your
enemy, because I tell you the truth?
17 They [s]zealously affect you, *but* not
well; yea, they would exclude [5]you,
that ye might affect them.
18 But *it is* good to be zealously
affected always in *a* good *thing*, and
not only when I am present with
you.
19 My [t]little children, of whom I
travail in birth again until Christ be
formed in you,
20 I desire to be present with you
now, and to change my voice; for [6]I
stand in doubt of you.
21 Tell me, ye that desire to be under
the law, do ye not hear the law?
22 For it is written, that Abraham
had two sons, [u]the one by a bondmaid, [v]the other by a freewoman.
23 But he *who was* of the bondwoman was [w]born after the flesh; but
[x]he of the freewoman *was* by promise.
24 Which things are an allegory: for
these are the two [7]covenants; the one
from the mount [8]Sī'-nâi, which gendereth to bondage, which is Agar.
25 For this Agar is mount Sī'-nâi in
Arabia, and [9]answereth to Jerusalem
which now is, and is in bondage with
her children.
26 But [y]Jerusalem which is above is
free, which is the mother of us all.
27 For it is written, [z]Rejoice, *thou*
barren that bearest not; break forth
and cry, thou that travailest not: for
the desolate hath many more children
than she which hath an husband.
28 Now we, brethren, as Isaac was,
are the [a]children of promise.
29 But as then [b]he that was born
after the flesh persecuted him *that*
was born after the Spirit, even so *it is*
now.
30 Nevertheless what saith [c]the scripture? Cast out the bondwoman and
her son: for [d]the son of the bondwoman shall not be heir with the son
of the freewoman.
31 So then, brethren, we are not children of the bondwoman, but of the
free.

CHAPTER 5

STAND fast therefore in [a]the
liberty wherewith Christ hath made
us free, and be not entangled again
with [b]the yoke of bondage.
2 Behold, I Paul say unto you, that
if [c]ye be circumcised, Christ shall
profit you nothing.
3 For I testify again to every man
that is circumcised, [d]that he is a debtor
to do the whole law.
4 Christ [e]is become of no effect unto
you, whosoever of you are justified by the law; ye [f]are fallen from
grace.
5 For we through the Spirit [g]wait for
the hope of righteousness by faith.
6 For [h]in Jesus Christ neither circumcision availeth any thing, nor uncircumcision; but [i]faith which worketh by love.
7 Ye [j]did run well; [1]who did hinder

CHAP. 4

a Col. 2.8. Heb. 9.10.
1 Or, rudiments.
b Gen. 49.10. Dan. 9.24. Mark 1.15. Eph. 1.10.
c Gen. 3.15. John 1.14. Heb. 2.14.
d Matt. 5.17.
e Matt. 20. 28. 1 Pet. 1.18.
f John 1.12.
g Rom. 8.16.
h Eph. 2.12.
i Rom. 1.25.
j 1 Cor. 8.3.
k Col. 2.20.
2 Or, back.
l Heb. 7.18.
3 Or, rudiments.
m Rom. 14.5.
n ch. 6.14.
o 1 Cor. 2.3.
p ch. 1.6.
q 2 Sam. 19. 27.
r Matt. 10.40.
4 Or, What was then.
s Rom. 10.2.
5 Or, us.
t 1 Cor. 4.15.
6 Or, I am perplexed for you.
u Gen. 16.15.
v Gen. 21.2.
w Rom. 9.7, 8.
x Gen. 18.10.
7 Or, testaments.
8 Sina.
9 Or, is in the same rank with.
y Isa. 2.2. Heb. 12.22. Rev. 3.12.
z Isa. 54.1.
a Rom. 4.16.
b Gen. 21.9.
c ch. 3.8.
d John 8.35.

CHAP. 5

a John 8.32. 1 Cor. 7.22.
b Acts 15.10.
c Acts 15.1.
d ch. 3.10.
e Rom. 9.31.
f Heb. 12.15.
g Rom. 8.24.
h Col. 3.11.
i 1 Thes. 1.3.
j 1 Cor. 9.24.
1 Or, who did drive you back.

you that ye should not obey the
truth?
8 This persuasion *cometh* not of him
that calleth you.
9 A little leaven leaveneth the whole
lump.
10 I [k]have confidence in you through
the Lord, that ye will be none otherwise minded: but [l]he that troubleth
you shall [m]bear his judgment, whosoever he be.
11 And [n]I, brethren, if I yet preach
circumcision, [o]why do I yet suffer persecution? then is the [p]offence of the
cross ceased.
12 I [q]would they were even [r]cut off
which trouble you.
13 For, brethren, ye have been called
unto liberty; only [s]*use* not liberty for
an occasion to the flesh, but by love
serve one another.
14 For all the law is fulfilled in one
word, *even* in this; [t]Thou shalt love
thy neighbour as thyself.
15 But if ye bite and devour one another, take heed that ye be not consumed one of another.
16 *This* I say then, [u]Walk in the
Spirit, and [2]ye shall not fulfil the lust
of the flesh.
17 For [v]the flesh lusteth against the
Spirit, and the Spirit against the flesh:
and these are contrary the one to the
other: so [w]that ye cannot do the
things that ye would.
18 But [x]if ye be led of the Spirit, ye
are not under the law.
19 Now [y]the works of the flesh are
manifest, which are *these;* Adultery,
fornication, uncleanness, lasciviousness,
20 Idolatry, witchcraft, hatred, variance, emulations, wrath, strife, sedi-
tions, heresies,
21 Envyings, murders, drunkenness,
revellings, and such like: of the which
I tell you before, as I have also told
you in time past, that [z]they which do
such things shall not inherit the kingdom of God.
22 But [a]the fruit of the Spirit is love,
joy, peace, longsuffering, [b]gentleness,
goodness, [c]faith,
23 Meekness, temperance: against
such there is no law.
24 And they that are Christ's [d]have
crucified the flesh with the [3]affections
and lusts.
25 If we live in the Spirit, let us also
walk in the Spirit.
26 Let us not be desirous of vain
glory, provoking one another, envying one another.

k 2 Cor. 8.22.
l ch. 1.7.
m 2 Cor. 10.6.
n ch. 6.12.
o 1 Cor. 15. 30.
p 1 Cor. 1.23.
q 1 Cor. 5.13.
r Acts 15.1.
s 1 Pet. 2.16.
t Lev. 19.18.
u Rom. 6.12.
2 Or, fulfil not.
v Rom. 7.23.
w Rom. 7.15.
x Rom. 6.14.
y Eph. 5.3. Jas. 3.14.
z Rev. 22.15.
a John 15.2.
b Jas. 3.17.
c 1 Cor. 13.7.
d Col. 3.9.
3 Or, passions.

CHAP. 6

1 Or, although.
a 1 Cor. 2.15.
b 2 Thes. 3. 15.
c 1 Cor. 7.5.
d Rom. 15.1.
e John 13.14.
f Rom. 12.3.
g 2 Cor. 3.5.
h 2 Cor. 13.5.
i Luke 18.11.
j Rom. 2.6.
k Rom. 15. 27.
l 1 Cor. 6.9.
m Job 13.9.
n Luke 16.25.
o Jas. 3.18.
p 2 Thes. 3. 13.
q Matt. 24. 13.
r John 9.4.
s 1 Tim. 6.18.
t Eph. 2.19.
u Phil. 3.18.
2 Or, whereby.
v 2 Cor. 5.17. Eph. 2.10.
w Ps. 73.1. Ps. 125.5. ch. 3.7-9.
x Col. 1.24.

CHAPTER 6

BRETHREN, [1]if a man be overtaken in a fault, ye [a]which are
spiritual, restore such an one [b]in the
spirit of meekness; considering thyself, [c]lest thou also be tempted.
2 Bear [d]ye one another's burdens,
and so fulfil [e]the law of Christ.
3 For [f]if a man think himself to be
something, when he [g]is nothing, he
deceiveth himself.
4 But [h]let every man prove his own
work, and then shall he have rejoicing
in himself alone, and [i]not in another.
5 For [j]every man shall bear his own
burden.
6 Let [k]him that is taught in the word
communicate unto him that teacheth
in all good things.
7 Be [l]not deceived; [m]God is not
mocked: for [n]whatsoever a man soweth, that shall he also reap.
8 For he that soweth to his flesh
shall of the flesh reap corruption; but
he that soweth to the [o]Spirit shall of
the Spirit reap life everlasting.
9 And [p]let us not be weary in well
doing: for in due season we shall
reap, [q]if we faint not.
10 As [r]we have therefore opportunity, let [s]us do good unto all *men*,
especially unto them who are of [t]the
household of faith.
11 Ye see how large a letter I have
written unto you with mine own hand.
12 As many as desire to make a fair
shew in the flesh, they constrain you
to be circumcised; [u]only lest they
should suffer persecution for the cross
of Christ.
13 For neither they themselves who
are circumcised keep the law; but desire to have you circumcised, that they
may glory in your flesh.
14 But God forbid that I should
glory, save in the cross of our Lord
Jesus Christ, [2]by whom the world is
crucified unto me, and I unto the
world.
15 For in Christ Jesus neither circumcision availeth any thing, nor uncircumcision, but [v]a new creature.
16 And [w]as many as walk according
to this rule, peace *be* on them, and
mercy, and upon the Israel of God.
17 From henceforth let no man
trouble me: for [x]I bear in my body the
marks of the Lord Jesus.
18 Brethren, the grace of our Lord
Jesus Christ *be* with your spirit.
Ā-měn.

¶ Unto the Galatians written from Rome.

THE EPISTLE OF PAUL THE APOSTLE TO THE

EPHESIANS

CHAPTER 1

PAUL, an apostle of Jesus Christ by the will of God, to the saints which are at Ĕph′-ĕ-sŭs, [a]and to the faithful in Christ Jesus:

2 Grace [b]*be* to you, and peace, from God our Father, and *from* the Lord Jesus Christ.

3 Blessed [c]*be* the God and Father of our Lord Jesus Christ, who hath blessed us with all spiritual blessings in heavenly [1]*places* in Christ:

4 According as [d]he hath chosen us in him [e]before the foundation of the world, that we should [f]be holy and without blame before him in love:

5 Having [g]predestinated us unto [h]the adoption of children by Jesus Christ to himself, [i]according to the good pleasure of his will,

6 To [j]the praise of the glory of his grace, wherein [k]he hath made us accepted in the [l]beloved.

7 In [m]whom we have redemption through his blood, the forgiveness of sins, according to the [n]riches of his grace;

8 Wherein he hath abounded toward us in all wisdom and prudence;

9 Having [o]made known unto us the mystery of his will, according to his good pleasure [p]which he hath purposed in himself:

10 That in the dispensation of [q]the fulness of times [r]he might gather together in one [s]all things in Christ, both which are in [2]heaven, and which are on earth; *even* in him:

11 In [t]whom also we have obtained an inheritance, being predestinated according to [u]the purpose of him who worketh all things after the counsel of his own will:

12 That [v]we should be to the praise of his glory, [w]who first [3]trusted in Christ.

13 In whom ye also *trusted*, after that ye heard the word of truth, the gospel of your salvation: in whom also after that ye believed, ye [x]were sealed with that holy Spirit of promise,

14 Which [y]is the earnest of our inheritance until [z]the redemption [a]of the purchased possession, unto the praise of his glory.

15 Wherefore I also, after I heard of your faith in the Lord Jesus, and love unto all the saints,

16 Cease not to give thanks for you, making mention of you in my prayers;

17 That the God of our Lord Jesus Christ, the Father of glory, [b]may give unto you the spirit of wisdom and revelation [4]in the knowledge of him:

18 The [c]eyes of your understanding being enlightened; that ye may know what is the hope of his calling, and what the riches of the glory of his inheritance in the saints,

19 And what *is* the exceeding greatness of his power to us-ward who believe, [d]according to the working [5]of his mighty power,

20 Which he wrought in Christ, when he raised him from the dead, and set *him* at his own right hand in the heavenly *places*,

21 Far [e]above all principality, and power, and might, and dominion, and every name that is named, not only in this world, but also in that which is to come:

22 And [f]hath put all *things* under his feet, and gave him [g]*to be* the head over all *things* to the church,

23 Which [h]is his body, the fulness of him that [i]filleth all in all.

CHAPTER 2

AND [a]you *hath he quickened*, who were dead in trespasses and sins;

2 Wherein [b]in time past ye walked according to the course of this world, according to the prince of the power of the air, the spirit that now worketh in the [c]children of disobedience:

3 Among [d]whom also we all had our conversation in times past in [e]the lusts of our flesh, fulfilling [1]the desires of the flesh and of the mind; [f]and were by nature the children of wrath, even as others.

4 But God, [g]who is rich in mercy, for his great love wherewith he loved us,

5 Even [h]when we were dead in sins, hath [i]quickened us together with Christ, ([2]by grace ye are saved;)

CHAP. 1

a Col. 1.2.
b Titus 1.4.
c Ps. 72.17.
1 Or, things.
d 1 Pet. 1.2.
e 1 Pet. 1.20.
f Luke 1.75.
g Rom. 8.29.
h John 1.12.
i Luke 12.32.
j Isa. 43.21.
k Rom. 3.24.
l Matt. 17.5.
m Heb. 9.12.
n Rom. 3.24.
o Col. 1.26.
p 2 Tim. 1.9.
q Zech. 13.1. Heb. 9.10.
r 1 Cor. 3.22.
s Phil. 2.9.
2 the heavens.
t Rom. 8.17.
u Isa. 46.10.
v 2 Thes. 2. 13.
w Jas. 1.18.
3 Or, hoped.
x 2 Cor. 1.22.
y 2 Cor. 5.5.
z Rom. 8.23.
a Acts 20.28.
b Col. 1.9.
4 Or, for the acknowledgment.
c Acts 26.18.
d Col. 1.29.
5 of the might of his power.
e Phil. 2.9. Heb. 1.4.
f Matt.28.18.
g Heb. 2.7.
h Rom. 12.5.
i John 1.14, 16. Col. 3.11.

CHAP. 2

a John 5.24.
b 1 John 5.19.
c Col. 3.6.
d Titus 3.3.
e Gal. 5.16.
1 the wills.
f Ps. 51.5. Luke 15.21.
g Rom. 10. 12.
h Rom. 5.6.
i Rom. 6.4.
2 Or, by whose grace.

6 And hath raised *us* up together,
and made *us* sit together in heavenly
places in Christ Jesus:
7 That in the ages to come he might
shew the exceeding riches of his grace
in *his* kindness toward us through
Christ Jesus.
8 For by grace are ye saved [j]through
faith; and that not of yourselves: [k]*it*
is the gift of God:
9 Not [l]of works, lest any man should
boast.
10 For we are his workmanship,
created in Christ Jesus unto good
works, [m]which God hath before
[3]ordained that we should walk in
them.
11 Wherefore remember, that ye *be-*
ing in time past Gentiles in the flesh,
who are called Uncircumcision by
that which is called [n]the Circumcision in the flesh made by hands;
12 That [o]at that time ye were without
Christ, [p]being aliens from the commonwealth of Israel, and strangers
from [q]the covenants of promise, having [r]no hope, and [s]without God in the
world:
13 But [t]now in Christ Jesus ye who
sometimes were far off are made nigh
by the blood of Christ.
14 For [u]he is our peace, who hath
made both one, and hath broken
down the middle wall of partition *be-*
tween us;
15 Having abolished in [v]his flesh the
enmity, *even* the law of commandments *contained* in ordinances; for to
make in himself of twain one [w]new
man, *so* making peace;
16 And that he might reconcile
both unto God in one body by the
cross, having [x]slain the enmity [4]there-
by:
17 And came [y]and preached peace to
you which were afar off, and to them
that were nigh.
18 For through him we both have
access by one Spirit unto the Father.
19 Now therefore ye are no more
strangers and foreigners, but fellow-
citizens with the saints, and of the
household of God;
20 And are built [z]upon the foundation of the [a]apostles and prophets,
Jesus Christ himself being [b]the chief
corner *stone;*
21 In whom all the building fitly
framed together groweth unto an
holy temple in the Lord:
22 In whom ye also are builded together for [c]an habitation of God
through the Spirit.

j Rom. 4.16. Phil. 1.29.
k John 6.44.
l Rom. 3.20.
m ch. 1.4.
3 Or, prepared.
n Rom. 2.28.
o Col. 1.21.
p John 10.16.
q Rom. 9.4,8.
r 1 Thes. 4. 13.
s Gal. 4.8.
t John 10.16. Gal. 3.28.
u Micah 5.5.
v Col. 1.22.
w 2 Cor. 5.17.
x Rom. 6.6. Gal. 2.20.
4 Or, in himself.
y Isa. 57.19.
z Matt. 16. 18.
a 1 Cor. 12. 28.
b Ps. 118.22. Matt. 21.42.
c John 17.23.

CHAP. 3

a Acts 21.33.
b 2 Tim. 2.10.
c Rom. 1.5.
d Acts 9.15. Acts 13.46.
e Rom. 16. 25.
1 Or, a little before.
f 1 Cor. 4.1.
g Acts 10.28.
h Gal. 3.14.
i Rom. 15.18.
j John 1.16. Phil. 4.19.
k Rom. 16. 25.
l Ps. 33.6. John 1.3.
m 1 Pet. 1.12.
n 1 Pet. 3.22.
o 1 Cor. 2.7.
p Phil. 2.9.
q Phil. 4.19.
r Job 23.6. Ps. 28.8.
s Rom. 7.22.
t John 14.23.
u Rom. 10.3.

CHAPTER 3

FOR this cause I Paul, [a]the prisoner
of Jesus Christ [b]for you Gentiles,
2 If ye have heard of [c]the dispensation of the grace of God [d]which is giv-
en me to you-ward:
3 How that by revelation [e]he made
known unto me the mystery; (as I
wrote [1]afore in few words,
4 Whereby, when ye read, ye may
understand my knowledge [f]in the
mystery of Christ)
5 Which [g]in other ages was not made
known unto the sons of men, as it is
now revealed unto his holy apostles
and prophets by the Spirit;
6 That the Gentiles should be fellow-
heirs, and of the same body, [h]and
partakers of his promise in Christ by
the gospel:
7 Whereof I was made a minister,
according to the gift of the grace of
God given unto me by the [i]effectual
working of his power.
8 Unto me, who am less than the
least of all saints, is this grace given,
that I should preach among the Gentiles [j]the unsearchable riches of
Christ;
9 And to make all *men* see what *is* the
fellowship of the mystery, [k]which
from the beginning of the world hath
been hid in God, [l]who created all
things by Jesus Christ:
10 To [m]the intent that now [n]unto the
principalities and powers in heavenly
places [o]might be known by the church
the manifold wisdom of God,
11 According to the eternal purpose
which he purposed in Christ Jesus our
Lord:
12 In whom we have boldness and
access with confidence by the faith of
him.
13 Wherefore I desire that ye faint
not at my tribulations for you, which
is your glory.
14 For this cause I bow my knees
unto the Father of our Lord Jesus
Christ,
15 Of whom [p]the whole family in
heaven and earth is named,
16 That he would grant you, [q]accord-
ing to the riches of his glory, [r]to be
strengthened with might by his
Spirit in [s]the inner man;
17 That [t]Christ may dwell in your
hearts by faith; that ye, being rooted
and grounded in love,
18 May be able to comprehend with
all saints [u]what *is* the breadth, and
length, and depth, and height;
19 And to know the love of Christ,

which passeth knowledge, that ye might be filled [v]with all the fulness of God.

20 Now unto him that is able to do exceeding abundantly above all that we ask or think, according to the power that worketh in us,

21 Unto him *be* [w]glory in the church by Christ Jesus throughout all ages, world without end. Ā-mĕn.

CHAPTER 4

I THEREFORE, the prisoner [1]of the Lord, beseech you that [a]ye walk worthy of the vocation wherewith ye are called,

2 With [b]all lowliness and meekness, with longsuffering, forbearing one another in love;

3 Endeavouring to keep the unity of the Spirit [c]in the bond of peace.

4 *There* [d]*is* one body, and one Spirit, even as ye are called in one hope of your calling;

5 One [e]Lord, one faith, [f]one baptism,

6 One [g]God and Father of all, who *is* above all, and [h]through all, and in you all.

7 But unto every one of us is given grace according to the measure of the gift of Christ.

8 Wherefore he saith, [i]When he ascended up on high, [j]he led [2]captivity captive, and gave gifts unto men.

9 (Now [k]that he ascended, what is it but that he also descended first into the lower parts of the earth?

10 He that descended is the same also that [l]ascended up far above all heavens, that he might [3]fill all things.)

11 And [m]he gave some, apostles; and some, prophets; and some, evangelists; and some, pastors and teachers;

12 For the perfecting of the saints, for the work of the ministry, for [n]the edifying of the [o]body of Christ:

13 Till we all come [4]in the unity of the faith, [p]and of the knowledge of the Son of God, unto a perfect man, unto the measure of the [5]stature of the fulness of Christ:

14 That we *henceforth* be no more children, tossed to and fro, and carried about with every [q]wind of doctrine, by the sleight of men, *and* cunning craftiness, whereby they lie in wait to deceive;

15 But [6]speaking the truth in love, may grow up into him in all things, which is the head, *even* Christ:

v John 1.16.
w 1 Tim. 1.17.
CHAP. 4
1 Or, in the Lord.
a Col. 1.10.
b Gal. 5.22.
c John 13.34.
d Rom. 12.5.
e 1 Cor. 8.6.
f Heb. 6.6.
g Ps. 83.18. Mal. 2.10.
h Rom. 11. 36.
i Ps. 68.18.
j Col. 2.15.
2 Or, a multitude of captives.
k John 3.13.
l Acts 1.9. Heb. 4.14. Heb. 7.26. Heb. 8.1.
3 Or, fulfil.
m ch. 2.20.
n Rom. 14. 19.
o ch. 1.23.
4 Or, into the unity.
p Col. 2.2.
5 Or, age.
q Matt. 11.7.
6 Or, being sincere.
r Col. 2.19.
s Acts 26.18. Gal. 4.8. ch. 2.12. 1 Thes. 4.5.
7 Or, hardness.
t Rom. 1.24.
u Rom. 8.6. 1 Pet. 1.22, 23.
8 Or, holiness of truth.
v Acts 5.3. ch. 6.11,16. Jas. 4.7.
9 Or, to distribute.
10 Or, to edify profitably.
w Ps. 78.40. Isa. 63.10. Rom. 8.23.

16 From [r]whom the whole body fitly joined together and compacted by that which every joint supplieth, according to the effectual working in the measure of every part, maketh increase of the body unto the edifying of itself in love.

17 This I say therefore, and testify in the Lord, that ye henceforth walk not as other Gentiles walk, in the vanity of their mind,

18 Having the understanding darkened, [s]being alienated from the life of God through the ignorance that is in them, because of the [7]blindness of their heart:

19 Who [t]being past feeling have given themselves over unto lasciviousness, to work all uncleanness with greediness.

20 But ye have not so learned Christ;

21 If so be that ye have heard him, and have been taught by him, as the truth is in Jesus:

22 That ye put off concerning the former conversation the old man, which is corrupt according to the deceitful lusts;

23 And [u]be renewed in the spirit of your mind;

24 And that ye put on the new man, which after God is created in righteousness and [8]true holiness.

25 Wherefore putting away lying, speak every man truth with his neighbour: for we are members one of another.

26 Be ye angry, and sin not: let not the sun go down upon your wrath:

27 Neither [v]give place to the devil.

28 Let him that stole steal no more: but rather let him labour, working with *his* hands the thing which is good, that he may have [9]to give to him that needeth.

29 Let no corrupt communication proceed out of your mouth, but that which is good [10]to the use of edifying, that it may minister grace unto the hearers.

30 And [w]grieve not the holy Spirit of God, whereby ye are sealed unto the day of redemption.

31 Let all bitterness, and wrath, and anger, and clamour, and evil speaking, be put away from you, with all malice:

32 And be ye kind one to another, tenderhearted, forgiving one another, even as God for Christ's sake hath forgiven you.

CHAPTER 5

BE [a]ye therefore followers of God,
as dear children;
2 And [b]walk in love, as Christ also
hath loved us, and hath given himself
for us an offering and a sacrifice to
God [c]for a sweetsmelling savour.
3 But fornication, and all uncleanness, or covetousness, let it not be
once named among you, as becometh
saints;
4 Neither filthiness, nor foolish talking, nor jesting, [d]which are not convenient: but rather giving of thanks.
5 For this ye know, that no whore-
monger, nor unclean person, nor
covetous man, who is an idolater, hath
[e]any inheritance in the kingdom of
Christ and of God.
6 Let [f]no man deceive you with vain
words: for because of these things
cometh the wrath of God upon the
children of [1]disobedience.
7 Be not ye therefore partakers with
them.
8 For [g]ye were sometimes darkness,
but now [h]*are ye* light in the Lord:
walk as children [i]of light:
9 (For the fruit of the Spirit *is* in all
goodness and righteousness and
truth;)
10 Proving [j]what is acceptable unto
the Lord.
11 And [k]have no fellowship with the
unfruitful works of darkness, but
rather [l]reprove *them.*
12 For it is a shame even to speak of
those things which are done of them
in secret.
13 But [m]all things that are [2]reproved
are made manifest by the light: for
whatsoever doth make manifest is
light.
14 Wherefore [3]he saith, [n]Awake thou
that sleepest, and [o]arise from the dead,
and Christ shall give thee light.
15 See then that ye walk circum-
spectly, not as fools, but as wise,
16 Redeeming the time, because the
days are evil.
17 Wherefore [p]be ye not unwise,
[q]but understanding what [r]the will of
the Lord *is.*
18 And be not drunk with wine,
wherein is excess; but be filled with
the Spirit;
19 Speaking to yourselves [s]in psalms
and hymns and spiritual songs, singing and making melody in your heart
to the Lord;
20 Giving [t]thanks always for all
things unto God and the Father in the
name of our Lord Jesus Christ;
21 Submitting [u]yourselves one to
another in the fear of God.
22 Wives, [v]submit yourselves unto
your own husbands, as unto the
Lord.
23 For the husband is the head of
the wife, even as Christ is the head of
the church: and he is the saviour of
the body.
24 Therefore as the church is subject
unto Christ, so *let* the wives *be* to their
own husbands in every thing.
25 Husbands, love your wives, even
as Christ also loved the church, and
gave himself for it;
26 That he might sanctify and
cleanse [w]it with the washing of water
[x]by the word,
27 That he might present it to himself a glorious church, not having
spot, or wrinkle, or any such thing;
but that it should be holy and without
blemish Unty Matt 28:19, 20
28 So ought men to love their wives
as their own bodies. He that loveth
his wife loveth himself.
29 For no man ever yet hated his
own flesh; but nourisheth and cherisheth it, even as the Lord the church:
30 For we are members of his body,
of his flesh, and of his bones.
31 For this cause shall a man leave
his father and mother, and shall be
joined unto his wife, and they two
shall be one flesh.
32 This is a great mystery: but I
speak concerning Christ and the
church.
33 Nevertheless let every one of you
in particular so love his wife even as
himself; and the wife *see* that she
reverence *her* husband.

CHAPTER 6

CHILDREN, [a]obey your parents
in the Lord: for this is right.
2 Honour [b]thy father and mother;
(which is the first commandment with
promise;)
3 That it may be well with thee, and
thou mayest live long on the earth.
4 And, [c]ye fathers, provoke not your
children to wrath: but [d]bring them up
in the nurture and admonition of the
Lord.
5 Servants, be obedient to them that
are *your* masters according to the
flesh, with fear and trembling, in
singleness of your heart, as unto
Christ;
6 Not with eyeservice, as menpleasers; but as the servants of Christ,
doing the will of God from the heart;

CHAP. 5
a Lev. 11.45. Matt. 5.45. Luke 6.36. ch. 4.32.
b John 13.34.
c Gen. 8.21. Lev. 1.9.
d Rom. 1.28.
e Rev. 22.15.
f Jer. 29.8. Matt. 24.4.
1 Or, unbelief.
g Isa. 9.2.
h John 8.12. 1 John 2.9.
i Luke 16.8.
j Ps. 19.7,11. Rom. 14.18. Phil. 1.10. Heb. 12.28.
k Job 24.13-17.
l Lev. 19.17.
m Heb. 4.13.
2 Or, discovered.
3 Or, it.
n Isa. 60.1.
o Eze. 37.4-10. John 5.25. Rom. 6.4,5. ch. 2.5.
p Col. 4.5.
q Rom. 12.2.
r 1 Thes. 4.3.
s Jas. 5.13.
t Job 1.21.
u Phil. 2.3.
v Gen. 3.16.
w John 3.5. Heb. 10.22.
x John 15.3.

CHAP. 6
a Pro. 23.22. Luke 2.51.
b Ex. 20.12. Deut. 5.16. Matt. 15.4.
c Col. 3.21.
d Gen. 18.19.

7 With good will doing service, as to
the Lord, and not to men:
8 Knowing [e]that whatsoever good
thing any man doeth, the same shall
he receive of the Lord, whether *he*
be bond or free.
9 And, ye [f]masters, do the same
things unto them, [1]forbearing threat-
ening: knowing that [2]your Master
also is in heaven; neither [g]is there respect of persons with him.
10 Finally, my brethren, be strong in
the Lord, and in the power of his
might.
11 Put [h]on the whole armour of God,
that ye may be able to stand against
the wiles of the devil.
12 For we wrestle not against [3]flesh
and blood, but against [i]principalities,
against powers, against [j]the rulers of
the darkness of this world, against
[4]spiritual wickedness in [5]high *places*.
13 Wherefore take unto you the
whole armour of God, that ye may be
able to withstand in the evil day, and
[6]having done all, to stand.
14 Stand therefore, having your loins
girt about with truth, and [k]having on
the breastplate of righteousness;
15 And [l]your feet shod with the preparation of the gospel of peace;
16 Above all, taking [m]the shield of
faith, wherewith ye shall be able to
quench all the fiery darts of the
wicked.
17 And take the helmet of salvation,
and [n]the sword of the Spirit, which is
the word of God:
18 Praying always with all prayer and
supplication in the Spirit, and watching thereunto with all perseverance
and [o]supplication for all saints;
19 And for me, that utterance may be
given unto me, that I may open my
mouth boldly, to make known the
mystery of the gospel,
20 For which I am an ambassador
[7]in bonds: that [8]therein [p]I may speak
boldly, as I ought to speak.
21 But that ye also may know my
affairs, *and* how I do, [q]Tȳch-ĭ-cŭs, a
beloved brother and faithful minister
in the Lord, shall make known to you
all things:
22 Whom I have sent unto you for
the same purpose, that ye might
know our affairs, and *that* he might
comfort your hearts.
23 Peace *be* to the brethren, and love
with faith, from God the Father and
the Lord Jesus Christ.
24 Grace *be* with all them that love
our Lord Jesus Christ [9]in sincerity.
Ä-mĕn.

¶ Written from Rome unto the Ephesians by Tychicus.

e Rom. 2.6.
f Col. 4.1.
1 Or, moderating.
2 Some read, both your and their Master.
g 1 Pet. 1.17.
h Rom. 13. 12.
3 blood and flesh.
i Rom. 8.38.
j John 12.31.
4 Or, wicked spirits.
5 Or, heavenly, as ch. 1.3.
6 Or, having overcome all.
k Isa. 59.17.
l Isa. 52.7.
m 1 John 5.4.
n Heb. 4.12. Rev. 1.16.
o Phil. 1.4.
7 Or, in a chain.
8 Or, thereof.
p 1 Thes. 2.2.
q Acts 20.4.
9 Or, without corruption.

THE EPISTLE OF PAUL THE APOSTLE TO THE

PHILIPPIANS

CHAPTER 1

PAUL and Timotheus, the servants
of Jesus Christ, to all the saints in
Christ Jesus which are at Philippi,
with the [1]bishops and deacons:
2 Grace *be* unto you, and peace, from
God our Father, and *from* the Lord
Jesus Christ.
3 I [a]thank my God upon every [2]re-
membrance of you,
4 Always in every prayer of mine
for you all making request with
joy,
5 For [b]your fellowship in the gospel
from the first day until now;
6 Being confident of this very thing,
that he which hath begun [c]a good
work in you [3]will perform *it* until the
day of Jesus Christ:
7 Even as it is meet for me to think
this of you all, because [4]I have you in
my heart; inasmuch as both in [d]my
bonds, and in the defence and confirmation of the gospel, [e]ye all are
[5]partakers of my grace.
8 For God is my record, how greatly
I long after you all in the bowels of
Jesus Christ.
9 And this I pray, that [f]your love may
abound yet more and more in knowledge and *in* all [6]judgment;
10 That [g]ye may [7]approve things
that [8]are excellent; [h]that ye may be
sincere and without offence till the
day of Christ;
11 Being filled with the fruits of
righteousness, [i]which are by Jesus
Christ, unto the glory and praise of
God.
12 But I would ye should understand, brethren, that the things *which*
happened unto me have fallen out

CHAP. 1
1 Or, overseers.
a Col. 1.3.
2 Or, mention.
b 2 Cor. 8.1.
c John 6.29.
3 Or, will finish it.
4 Or, ye have me in your heart.
d Eph. 3.1.
e ch. 4.14.
5 Or, partakers with me of grace.
f Philem. 6.
6 Or, sense.
g Rom. 12.2.
7 Or, try.
8 Or, differ.
h Acts 24.16.
i John 15.4.

rather unto the furtherance of the
gospel;
13 So that my bonds [9]in Christ are
manifest [j]in all [10]the palace, and [11]in
all other *places;*
14 And many of the brethren in the
Lord, waxing confident by my bonds,
are much more bold to speak the word
without fear.
15 Some indeed preach Christ even
of envy and [k]strife; and some also of
good will:
16 The one preach Christ of contention, not sincerely, supposing to add
affliction to my bonds:
17 But the other of love, knowing
that I am set for the defence of the
gospel.
18 What then? notwithstanding,
every way, whether in pretence, or in
truth, Christ is preached; and I therein
do rejoice, yea, and will rejoice.
19 For I know that this shall turn to
my salvation [l]through your prayer,
and the supply of [m]the Spirit of Jesus
Christ,
20 According to my earnest expectation and *my* hope, that [n]in nothing I
shall be ashamed, but *that* with all
boldness, as always, *so* now also
Christ shall be magnified in my body,
whether *it be* by life, or by death.
21 For to me to live *is* Christ, and to
die *is* gain.
22 But if I live in the flesh, this *is* the
fruit of my labour: yet what I shall
choose I wot not.
23 For [o]I am in a strait betwixt two,
having a desire to [p]depart, and to be
with Christ; which is far better:
24 Nevertheless to abide in the flesh
is more needful for you.
25 And having this confidence, I
know that I shall abide and continue
with you all for your furtherance and
joy of faith;
26 That your rejoicing may be more
abundant in Jesus Christ for me by
my coming to you again.
27 Only let your conversation be as
it becometh the gospel of Christ: that
whether I come and see you, or else
be absent, I may hear of your affairs,
that ye stand fast in one spirit, with
one mind striving together for the
faith of the gospel;
28 And in nothing [q]terrified by your
adversaries: which is to them an
evident token of perdition, but to [r]you
of salvation, and that of God.
29 For unto you it is given in the behalf of Christ, [s]not only to believe on
him, but also to suffer for his sake;

9 Or, for Christ.
j ch. 4.22.
10 Or, Cæsar's court.
11 Or, to all others.
k ch. 2.3.
l 2 Cor. 1.11.
m Rom. 8.9. 1 Pet. 1.11.
n Rom. 5.5.
o 2 Cor. 5.8.
p Luke 2.29, 30.
q Isa. 41.10. Matt. 10.28. Heb. 13.5.
r Matt. 5.10-12.
s Acts 5.41. Eph. 2.8.
t Col. 2.1.
u Acts 16.19.

CHAP. 2

a 2 Cor. 13.1.4
b John 3.29.
c 1 Pet. 3.8.
d Rom. 13. 13. Jas. 3.14.
e Isa. 66.2. Eph. 5.21.
f 1 Cor. 10. 24.
g John 13.15.
h Isa. 9.6. Zech. 13.7. John 1.1,2. Heb. 1.3.
i Zech. 13.7. John 5.18.
j Ps. 22.6. Isa. 53.3. Dan. 9.26.
k Isa. 42.1. Eze. 34.23. Zech. 3.8. Matt. 12.18.
l John 1.14. Gal. 4.4.
1 Or, habit.
m Heb. 12.2.
n Ps. 2.6-12. Luke 10.22.
o Heb. 1.4.
p Isa. 45.23.
q John 13.13.
r Heb. 13.21.
2 Or, sincere.
3 Or, shine ye.
4 poured forth.

30 Having [t]the same conflict which
[u]ye saw in me, and now hear *to be* in
me.

CHAPTER 2

IF *there be* therefore any consolation
in Christ, if any comfort of love, if
[a]any fellowship of the Spirit, if any
bowels and mercies,
2 Fulfil [b]ye my joy, [c]that ye be likeminded, having the same love, *being* of
one accord, of one mind.
3 *Let* [d]nothing *be done* through strife
or vainglory; but [e]in lowliness of mind
let each esteem other better than
themselves.
4 Look [f]not every man on his own
things, but every man also on the
things of others.
5 Let [g]this mind be in you, which
was also in Christ Jesus:
6 Who, [h]being in the form of God,
thought it [i]not robbery to be equal
with God:
7 But [j] made himself of no reputation, and took upon him the form [k]of
a servant, and [l]was made in the likeness of men:
8 And being found in [1]fashion as a
man, he humbled himself, and [m]be-
came obedient unto death, even the
death of the cross.
9 Wherefore God also [n]hath highly
exalted him, and [o]given him a name
which is above every name:
10 That [p]at the name of Jesus every
knee should bow, of *things* in heaven,
and *things* in earth, and *things* under
the earth;
11 And [q]*that* every tongue should
confess that Jesus Christ *is* Lord, to
the glory of God the Father.
12 Wherefore, my beloved, as ye
have always obeyed, not as in my
presence only, but now much more
in my absence, work out your own
salvation with fear and trembling.
13 For [r]it is God which worketh in
you both to will and to do of *his* good
pleasure.
14 Do all things without murmurings
and disputings:
15 That ye may be blameless and
[2]harmless, the sons of God, without
rebuke, in the midst of a crooked and
perverse nation, among whom [3]ye
shine as lights in the world;
16 Holding forth the word of life;
that I may rejoice in the day of Christ,
that I have not run in vain, neither
laboured in vain.
17 Yea, and if I be [4]offered upon the
sacrifice and service of your faith, I
joy, and rejoice with you all.

18 For the same cause also do ye joy,
and rejoice with me.
19 [5]But I trust in the Lord Jesus to
send Timotheus shortly unto you, that
I also may be of good comfort, when
I know your state.
20 For I have no man [6]likeminded,
who will naturally care for your state.
21 For all seek their own, not the
things which are Jesus Christ's.
22 But ye know the proof of him,
that, as a son with the father, he hath
served with me in the gospel.
23 Him therefore I hope to send
presently, so soon as I shall see how
it will go with me.
24 But I trust in the Lord that I also
myself shall come shortly.
25 Yet I supposed it necessary to
send to you [s]Ĕp-ăph-rō-dī'-tŭs, my
brother, and companion in labour,
and fellowsoldier, but your [t]messen-
ger, and he [u]that ministered to my
wants.
26 For he longed after you all, and
was full of heaviness, because that ye
had heard that he had been sick.
27 For indeed he was sick nigh unto
death: but God had mercy on him;
and not on him only, but on me also,
lest I should have sorrow upon
sorrow.
28 I sent him therefore the more
carefully, that, when ye see him again,
ye may rejoice, and that I may be the
less sorrowful.
29 Receive him therefore in the Lord
with all gladness; and [7]hold such in
reputation:
30 Because for the work of Christ he
was nigh unto death, not regarding
his life, [v]to supply your lack of service
toward me.

CHAPTER 3

FINALLY, my brethren, rejoice in
the Lord. To write the same things
to you, to me indeed *is* not grievous,
but for you *it is* safe.
2 Beware [a]of dogs, beware of evil
workers, beware [b]of the concision.
3 For we are [c]the circumcision, which
worship [d]God in the spirit, and rejoice
in Christ Jesus, and have no confidence in the flesh.
4 Though I might also have confidence in the flesh. If any other man
thinketh that he hath whereof he
might trust in the flesh, I more:
5 Circumcised the eighth day, of the
stock of Israel, *of* the tribe of Benjamin, an Hebrew of the Hebrews; as
touching the law, [e]a Pharisee;
6 Concerning [f]zeal, [g]persecuting the
church; touching the righteousness
which is in the law, blameless.
7 But what things were gain to me,
those I counted loss for Christ.
8 Yea doubtless, and I count all
things *but* loss [h]for the excellency of
the knowledge of Christ Jesus my
Lord: for whom I have suffered the
loss of all things, and do count them
but dung, that I may win Christ,
9 And be found in him, [i]not having
mine own righteousness, which is of
the law, but [j]that which is through the
faith of Christ, the righteousness
which is of God by faith:
10 That I may know him, and the
power of his resurrection, and the
[k]fellowship of his sufferings, being
made conformable unto his death;
11 If by any means I might [l]attain
unto the resurrection of the dead.
12 Not as though I had already
[m]attained, either were already [n]per-
fect: but I follow after, if that I may
apprehend that for which also I am
apprehended of Christ Jesus.
13 Brethren, I count not myself to
have apprehended: but *this* one thing
I do, forgetting those things which
are behind, and reaching [o]forth unto
those things which are before,
14 I [p]press toward the mark for the
prize [q]of the high calling of God in
Christ Jesus.
15 Let us therefore, as many as be
[r]perfect, [s]be thus minded: and if in
anything ye be otherwise minded,
God shall reveal even this unto
you.
16 Nevertheless, whereto we have
already attained, let us walk by
the same rule, let us mind the same
thing.
17 Brethren, be followers together of
me, and mark them which walk so as
ye [t]have us for an ensample.
18 (For many walk, of whom I have
told you often, and now tell you even
weeping, *that they are* the enemies of
the cross of Christ:
19 Whose end *is* destruction, whose
God *is their* belly, and *whose* glory *is*
in their shame, who mind earthly
things.)
20 For [u]our conversation is in heaven; from whence also we [v]look for
the Saviour, the Lord Jesus Christ:
21 Who [w]shall change our vile body,
that it may be fashioned like unto his
glorious body, [x]according to the
working whereby he is able even to
subdue all things unto himself.

5 Or, Moreover.
6 Or, so dear unto me.
s ch. 4.18.
t 2 Cor. 8.23.
u ch. 4.18.
7 Or, honour such.
v 1 Cor. 16.17. ch. 4.10.

CHAP. 3

a Gal. 5.15. Rev. 22.15.
b Rom. 2.28. Gal. 5.2.
c Deut. 10.16. Jer. 4.4. Rom. 2.29.
d Mal. 1.11. John 4.23. Eph. 6.18. Jude 20.
e Acts 23.6.
f Acts 22.3. Gal. 1.13.
g Acts 8.3.
h Isa. 53.11. John 17.3.
i Ps. 143.2. Isa. 64.6.
j Gal. 2.16. 2 Pet. 1.1.
k 1 Pet. 4.13.
l Luke 20.35. Acts 26.7.
m 1 Tim. 6.12.
n Heb. 12.23.
o Heb. 6.1.
p Heb. 12.1.
q Rom. 9.23, 24. Heb. 3.1.
r 1 Cor. 2.6.
s Gal. 5.10.
t Ps. 37.37. 1 Pet. 5.3.
u Col. 3.1,3.
v 1 Cor. 1.7. 1 Thes. 1.10.
w Ps. 17.15. 1 John 3.2.
x Isa. 63.1. Matt. 28.18. Eph. 1.19. Heb. 7.25.

15 IH Rev 21:4

CHAPTER 4

THEREFORE, my brethren dearly beloved and longed for, [a]my joy
and crown, so stand fast in the Lord,
my dearly beloved.
2 I beseech Eû-ō-́dĭ-ăs, and beseech
Sȳn-́tȳ-chē, that they be of the same
mind in the Lord.
3 And I intreat thee also, true yoke-
fellow, help those women which
laboured with [b]me in the gospel, with
Clement also, and *with* other my
fellowlabourers, whose names *are* in
the [c]book of life.
4 Rejoice in the Lord alway: *and*
again I say, Rejoice.
5 Let your moderation be known unto all men. [d]The Lord *is* at hand.
6 Be [e]careful for nothing; but in every
thing by prayer and supplication with
thanksgiving let your requests be
made known unto God.
7 And [f]the peace of God, which
passeth all understanding, shall keep
your hearts and minds through
Christ Jesus.
8 Finally, brethren, whatsoever
things are true, whatsoever things *are*
[1]honest, whatsoever things *are* just,
whatsoever things *are* pure, whatsoever things *are* lovely, whatsoever
things *are* of good report; if *there be*
any virtue, and if *there be* any praise,
think on these things.
9 Those things, which ye have both
learned, and received, and heard, and
seen in me, do: and the God of peace
shall be with you.
10 But I rejoiced in the Lord greatly,
that now at the last [g]your care of me
[2]hath flourished again; wherein ye
were also careful, but ye lacked
opportunity.
11 Not that I speak in respect of
want: for I have learned, in whatsoever state I am, [h]*therewith* to be content.
12 I [i]know both how to be ab ased
and I know how to abound: every,
where and in all things I am instructed
both to be full and to be hungry, both
to abound and to suffer need.
13 I can do all things [j]through Christ
which strengtheneth me.
14 Notwithstanding ye have well
done, that [k]ye did communicate with
my affliction.
15 Now ye Philippians know also,
[l]that in the beginning of the gospel,
when I departed from Măç-ē-dō-́nĭ-ă,
[m]no church communicated with me as
concerning giving and receiving, but
ye only.
16 For even [n]in Thĕss-ă-lō-nī-́că ye
sent once and again unto my necessity.
17 Not because I desire a gift: but I
desire fruit [o]that may abound to your
account.
18 But [3]I have all, and abound: I am
full, having received [p]of Ĕp-ăph-rō-
dī-́tŭs the things *which were sent* from
you, an odour of a sweet smell, [q]a
sacrifice acceptable, wellpleasing to
God.
19 But my God [r]shall supply all your
need according to his riches in glory
by Christ Jesus.
20 Now unto God and our Father *be*
glory for ever and ever. Ä-́mĕn.
21 Salute every saint in Christ Jesus.
The brethren which are with me greet
you.
22 All the saints salute you, chiefly
[s]they that are of Cæsar's household.
23 The grace of our Lord Jesus
Christ *be* with you all. Ä-́mĕn.

¶ It was written to the Philippians from Rome by Epaphroditus.

CHAP. 4

a 2 Cor. 1.14. ch. 1.26.
b Acts 18.2. Rom. 16.3. ch. 1.27.
c Ex. 32.32. Ps. 69.28. Dan. 12.1. Luke 10.20. Rev. 3.5. Rev. 13.8. Rev. 20.12.
d Matt. 24. 48-50. Heb. 10.25. Jas. 5.8,9. 1 Pet. 4.7. 2 Pet. 3.8.
e Ps. 55.22. Pro. 16.3. Matt. 6.25. Luke 12.22. 1 Pet. 5.7.
f Num. 6.26. Isa. 26.3. John 14.27. Rom. 5.1.
1 Or, venerable.
g 2 Cor. 11.9.
2 Or, is revived.
h 1 Tim. 6.6.
i 1 Cor. 4.11.
j John 15.5.
k ch. 1.7.
l Acts 11.15.
m 2 Cor.11.8.
n 2 Thes. 3.8.
o Rom. 15. 28.
3 Or, I have received all.
p ch. 2.25.
q Heb. 13.16.
r Ps. 23.1. Pro. 8.21.
s ch. 1.13.

THE EPISTLE OF PAUL THE APOSTLE TO THE

COLOSSIANS

CHAPTER 1

PAUL, an apostle of Jesus Christ
by the will of God, and Timotheus
our brother,
2 To the saints [a]and faithful brethren
in Christ which are at Cŏ-lŏs-́sē:
Grace *be* unto you, and peace, from
God our Father and the Lord Jesus
Christ.
3 We give thanks to God and the
Father of our Lord Jesus Christ, praying always for you,
4 Since [b]we heard of your faith in
Christ Jesus, and of [c]the love *which*
ye have to all the saints,
5 For the hope [d]which is laid up for
you in heaven, whereof ye heard before in the word of the truth of the
gospel;
6 Which is come unto you, [e]as *it is*

CHAP. 1

a Eph. 6.21.
b Eph. 1.15.
c Heb. 6.10.
d Matt. 5.12. 1 Pet. 1.4.
e Matt. 24.

in all the world; and [f]bringeth forth
fruit, as *it doth* also in you, since the
day ye heard *of it*, and knew [g]the
grace of God in truth:
7 As ye also learned of [h]Ĕp´-ă-phrăs
our dear fellowservant, who is for
you a faithful minister of Christ;
8 Who also declared unto us your
love in the Spirit.
9 For [i]this cause we also, since the
day we heard *it*, do not cease to pray
for you, and to desire that ye might
be filled with the [j]knowledge of his
will in all wisdom and spiritual understanding;
10 That [k]ye might walk worthy of the
Lord [l]unto all pleasing, [m]being fruitful
in every good work, and increasing in
the knowledge of God;
11 Strengthened with all might, according to his glorious power, unto
all patience and longsuffering [n]with
joyfulness;
12 Giving [o]thanks unto the Father,
which hath made us meet to be partakers of the [p]inheritance of the saints
in light:
13 Who hath delivered us from [q]the
power of darkness, [r]and hath translated *us* into the kingdom of [1]his dear
Son:
14 In whom we have redemption
through his blood, *even* the forgiveness of sins:
15 Who is [s]the image of the invisible
God, the [t]firstborn of every creature:
16 For [u]by him were all things
created, that are in heaven, and that
are in earth, visible and invisible,
whether *they be* thrones, or dominions, or principalities, or powers: all
things were created by [v]him, and for
him:
17 And [w]he is before all things, and
by him all things consist.
18 And he is the head of the body,
the church: who is the beginning, [x]the
firstborn from the dead; that [2]in all
things he might have the preeminence. Unty John 10:16
19 For it pleased *the Father* that [y]in
him should all fulness dwell;
20 And, [3]having made peace through
the blood of his cross, by him to reconcile all things unto himself; by him, *I
say*, whether *they be* things in earth,
or things in heaven.
21 And you, that were sometime
alienated and enemies [4]in *your* mind
by wicked works, yet now hath he
reconciled
22 In the body of his flesh through
death, to present you holy and un-

f John 15.16.
g Ps. 110.3. Eph. 3.2. Titus 2.11. 1 Pet. 5.12.
h Philem. 23.
i Eph. 1.15.
j Rom. 12.2.
k 1 Thes. 2. 12.
l 1 Thes. 4.1.
m John 15. 16.
n Acts 5.41.
o Eph. 5.20.
p Rom. 8.17. Gal. 4.7. Eph. 1.11.
q Heb. 2.14.
r 2 Pet. 1.11.
1 the Son of his love.
s John 14.9. Phil. 2.6. ch. 2.9. Heb. 1.3.
t Ps. 89.27. Rev. 3.14.
u John 1.3. 1 Pet. 3.22.
v Rom. 11. 36.
w John 17.5. Heb. 13.8.
x John 11.25. Rev. 1.5.
2 Or, among all.
y Matt. 28. 18. John 1.16. Eph. 1.23.
3 Or, making peace.
4 Or, by your mind in wicked works.
z Phil. 3.10.
a Eph. 1.23.
5 Or, fully to preach the word of God.
b Rom. 16. 25.
6 Or, among you.

CHAP. 2

1 Or, fear, or, care.
a 2 Cor. 1.6.
b 2 Pet. 3.18.
2 Or, Wherein.
c Jer. 29.8. Rom. 16.17. Heb. 13.9.

blameable and unreproveable in his
sight:
23 If ye continue in the faith grounded and settled, and *be* not moved away
from the hope of the gospel, which ye
have heard, *and* which was preached
to every creature which is under
heaven; whereof I Paul am made a
minister;
24 Who now rejoice in my sufferings
for you, and fill up [z]that which is behind of the afflictions of Christ in my
flesh for [a]his body's sake, which is the
church:
25 Whereof I am made a minister,
according to the dispensation of God
which is given to me for you, [5]to fulfil
the word of God;
26 *Even* [b]the mystery which hath
been hid from ages and from generations, but now is made manifest to his
saints:
27 To whom God would make known
what *is* the riches of the glory of this
mystery among the Gentiles; which is
Christ [6]in you, the hope of glory:
28 Whom we preach, warning every
man, and teaching every man in all
wisdom; that we may present every
man perfect in Christ Jesus:
29 Whereunto I also labour, striving
according to his working, which
worketh in me mightily.

CHAPTER 2

FOR I would that ye knew what
great [1]conflict I have for you, and
for them at Lā-ŏd-ĭ-çē´-ă, and *for* as
many as have not seen my face in the
flesh;
2 That [a]their hearts might be comforted, being knit together in love, and
unto all [b]riches of the full assurance
of understanding, to the acknowledge-
ment of the mystery of God, and of
the Father, and of Christ;
3 [2]In whom are hid all the treasures
of wisdom and knowledge.
4 And this I say, lest any man should
beguile you with enticing words.
5 For though I be absent in the flesh,
yet am I with you in the spirit, joying
and beholding your order, and the
stedfastness of your faith in Christ.
6 As ye have therefore received
Christ Jesus the Lord, *so* walk ye in
him:
7 Rooted and built up in him, and
stablished in the faith, as ye have
been taught, abounding therein with
thanksgiving.
8 Beware [c]lest any man spoil you
through philosophy and vain deceit,

after [d]the tradition of men, after the
[3]rudiments of the world, and not after
Christ.
9 For [e]in him dwelleth all the fulness
of the Godhead bodily.
10 And [f]ye are complete in him,
which [g]is the head of all principality
and power:
11 In whom also ye are [h]circumcised
with the circumcision made without
hands, in putting off the body of the
sins of the flesh by the circumcision
of Christ:
12 Buried [i]with him in baptism,
wherein also ye are risen with *him*
through [j]the faith of the operation of
God, who hath raised him from the
dead.
13 And you, being dead in your sins
and the uncircumcision of your flesh,
hath he quickened together with him,
having forgiven you all trespasses;
14 Blotting out the handwriting of
ordinances that was against us, which
was contrary to us, and took it out of
the way, nailing it to his cross;
15 *And* [k]having spoiled principalities
and powers, he made a shew of them
openly, triumphing over them [4]in it.
16 Let no man therefore [l]judge you
[5]in meat, or in drink, or [6]in respect of
[m]an holyday, or of the new moon, or
of the sabbath *days:*
17 Which [n]are a shadow of things to
come; but the body *is* of Christ.
18 Let no man [7]beguile you of your
reward [8]in a voluntary humility and
worshipping of angels, intruding into
those things which he hath not seen,
vainly puffed up by his fleshly mind,
19 And not holding the Head, from
which all the body by joints and
bands having nourishment ministered, and knit together, increaseth
with the increase of God.
20 Wherefore if ye be dead with
Christ from the [9]rudiments of the
world, why, as though living in the
world, are ye subject to ordinances,
21 (Touch not; taste not; handle not;
22 Which all are to perish with the
using;) after the commandments and
doctrines of men?
23 Which things have indeed a shew
of wisdom in will worship, and humility, and [10]neglecting of the body; not
in any honour to the satisfying of the
flesh.

CHAPTER 3

IF ye then [a]be risen with Christ, seek
those [b]things which are above,
where Christ sitteth on the right hand
of God.
2 Set your [1]affection on things above,
not on things on the earth.
3 For [c]ye are dead, [d]and your life is
hid with Christ in God.
4 When [e]Christ, *who is* [f]our life,
shall appear, then shall ye also appear
with him in [g]glory.
5 Mortify therefore your members
which are upon the earth; fornication,
uncleanness, inordinate affection, evil
concupiscence, and covetousness,
which is idolatry:
6 For which things' sake the wrath of
God cometh on the children of
disobedience:
7 In the which ye also walked some
time, when ye lived in them.
8 But [h]now ye also put off all these;
anger, wrath, malice, blasphemy,
filthy communication out of your
mouth.
9 Lie [i]not one to another, seeing that
ye have put off the old man with his
deeds;
10 And have put on the new *man*,
which is [j]renewed in knowledge after
the image of him that [k]created him:
11 Where there is neither [l]Greek nor
Jew, circumcision nor uncircumcision, Barbarian, Sçy̆th-ĭ-ăn, bond
nor free: [m]but Christ *is* all, and in
all.
12 Put on therefore, [n]as the elect of
God, holy and beloved, [o]bowels of
mercies, kindness, humbleness of
mind, meekness, longsuffering;
13 Forbearing one another, and forgiving one another, if any man have a
[2]quarrel against any: even as Christ
forgave you, so also *do* ye.
14 And above all these things [p]*put on*
charity, which is the bond of perfect-
ness.
15 And let [q]the peace of God rule in
your hearts, [r]to the which also ye are
called in [s]one body; and be ye thankful.
16 Let [t]the word of Christ dwell in
you richly in all wisdom; teaching and
admonishing one another in psalms
and hymns and spiritual songs, [u]sing-
ing with grace [v]in your hearts to the
Lord.
17 And [w]whatsoever ye do in word
or deed, *do* all in the name of the Lord
Jesus, giving [x]thanks to God and the
Father by him.
18 Wives, submit yourselves unto
your own husbands, as it is fit in the
Lord.
19 Husbands, love *your* wives, and
be not bitter against them.
20 Children, obey *your* [y]parents in all

d Matt. 15.2. Gal. 1.14.
3 Or, elements.
e Isa. 7.14. Matt. 1.23. John 1.14. Rom. 9.5. ch. 1.19. 1 Tim. 3.16.
f John 1.16.
g 1 Pet. 3.22.
h Jer. 4.4.
i Rom. 6.4.
j Eph. 3.7.
k Gen. 3.15. Ps. 68.18. Isa. 53.12. Matt. 12.29. Luke 10.18. Eph. 4.8.
4 Or, in himself.
l Rom. 14.3.
5 Or, for eating and drinking.
6 Or, in part.
m Rom. 14.5. Gal. 4.10.
n Heb. 8.5.
7 Or, judge against you.
8 being a voluntary in humility.
9 Or, elements.
10 Or, punishing, or, not sparing.

CHAP. 3

a Eph. 2.6.
b Matt. 6.33.
1 Or, mind.
c Gal. 2.20.
d John 3.16.
e 1 John 3.2.
f John 11.25.
g 1 Cor. 15. 43.
h Jas. 1.21.
i Lev. 19.11.
j Rom. 12.2.
k Eph. 2.10.
l Gal. 3.28.
m Eph. 1.23.
n 1 Pet. 1.2.
o Gal. 5.22. Phil. 2.1.
2 Or, complaint.
p Rom. 13.8.
q Ps. 29.11. Isa. 26.3. Phil. 4.7.
r 1 Cor. 7.15.
s Eph. 2.16.
t Jer. 15.16. 2 Tim. 3.15-17.
u Eph. 5.19.
v ch. 4.6.
w 1 Cor. 10. 31.
x Eph. 5.20. ch. 2.7.
y Pro. 23.22. Luke 2.51. Eph. 6.1.

things: for this is well pleasing unto
the Lord.
21 Fathers, [z]provoke not your children *to anger*, lest they be discouraged.
22 Servants, obey in all things *your*
masters according to the flesh; not
with eyeservice, as menpleasers; but
in singleness of heart, fearing God:
23 And whatsoever ye do, do *it*
heartily, as to the Lord, and not unto
men;
24 Knowing that of the Lord ye shall
receive the reward of the inheritance:
for ye serve the Lord Christ.
25 But he that doeth wrong shall receive for the wrong which he hath
done: and there is no respect of
persons.

CHAPTER 4

MASTERS, [a]give unto *your* servants that which is just and
equal; knowing that ye also have a
Master in heaven.
2 Continue [b]in prayer, and watch in
the same with thanksgiving;
3 Withal [c]praying also for us, that
God would [d]open unto us a door of
utterance, to speak the [e]mystery of
Christ, [f]for which I am also in bonds:
4 That I may make it manifest, as I
ought to speak.
5 Walk [g]in wisdom toward them that
are without, redeeming the time.
6 Let your speech *be* alway [h]with
grace, seasoned [i]with salt, [j]that ye
may know how ye ought to answer
every man.
7 All my state shall Tȳch-ĭ-cŭs declare unto you, *who is* a beloved
brother, and a faithful minister and
fellowservant in the Lord:
8 Whom I have sent unto you for the
same purpose, that he might know
your estate, and comfort your hearts;
9 With [k]Ō-nĕs-ĭ-mŭs, a faithful and
beloved brother, who is *one* of you.
They shall make known unto you all
things which *are done* here.
10 Ăr-ĭs-tär-chŭs [l]my fellowprisoner
saluteth you, and [m]Marcus, sister's
son to Barnabas, (touching whom ye
received commandments: if he come
unto you, receive him;)
11 And Jesus, which is called Justus,
who are of the circumcision. These
only *are my* fellowworkers unto the
kingdom of God, which have been a
comfort unto me.
12 Ĕp-ă-phrăs, [n]who is *one* of you, a
servant of Christ, saluteth you, always [1]labouring fervently for you in
prayers, that ye may stand [o]perfect
and [2]complete in all the will of God.
13 For I bear him record, that he
hath a great zeal for you, and them
that are in Lā-ŏd-ĭ-çē-ă, and them in
Hī-ĕr-ă-pŏ-lĭs.
14 Luke, [p]the beloved physician, and
[q]Dē-măs, greet you.
15 Salute the brethren which are in
Lā-ŏd-ĭ-çē-ă, and Nȳm-phăs, and the
church which is in his house.
16 And when [r]this epistle is read
among you, cause that it be read also
in the church of the Lā-ŏd-ĭ-çē-ăns;
and that ye likewise read the *epistle*
from Lā-ŏd-ĭ-çē-ă.
17 And say to [s]Är-chĭp-pŭs, Take
heed to the [t]ministry which thou hast
received in the Lord, that thou fulfil
it.
18 The salutation by the hand of me
Paul. Remember [u]my bonds. Grace
be with you. Ā-mĕn.

¶ Written from Rome to the Colossians by Tychicus and Onesimus.

z Eph. 6.4.

CHAP. 4
a Lev. 19.13. Mal. 3.5. Eph. 6.9.
b Luke 18.1. Eph. 6.18.
c 2 Thes. 3.1.
d 1 Cor. 16.9.
e Matt. 13. 11.
f Phil. 1.7.
g Eph. 5.15.
h Eccl. 10.12.
i Mark 9.50.
j 1 Pet. 3.15.
k Philem. 10.
l Acts 19.29. Acts 20.4. Philem. 24.
m Acts 15.37.
n ch. 1.7.
1 Or, striving.
o Matt. 5.48.
2 Or, filled.
p Luke 1.3. Acts 1.1.
q Philem. 24.
r 1 Thes. 5. 27.
s Philem. 2.
t 1 Tim. 4.6.
u Heb. 13.3.

THE FIRST EPISTLE OF PAUL THE APOSTLE TO THE

THESSALONIANS

CHAPTER 1

PAUL, and [a]Sĭl-vā-nŭs, and Timotheus, unto the church of the
Thĕss-ă-lō-nĭ-ăns *which is* [b]in God
the Father and *in* the Lord Jesus
Christ: Grace *be* unto you, and peace,
from God our Father, and the Lord
Jesus Christ.
2 We give thanks to God always for
you all, making mention of you in our
prayers;
3 Remembering without ceasing your
work of [c]faith, [d]and labour of love,
and patience of hope in our Lord Jesus
Christ, in the sight of God and our
Father;
4 Knowing, brethren [1]beloved, [e]your
election of God.
5 For [f]our gospel came not unto you
in word only, but also in power, and in
[g]the Holy Ghost, [h]and in much assurance; as ye [i]know what manner of

CHAP. 1
a 2 Thes. 1.1. 1 Pet. 5.12.
b John 14.23.
c John 6.29. Gal. 5.6. ch. 3.6.
d Heb. 6.10.
1 Or, beloved of God, your election.
e Col. 3.12.
f 1 Cor. 2.4.
g 2 Cor. 6.6.
h Heb. 2.3.
i 2 Thes. 3.7.

men we were among you for your
sake.
6 And ye became followers of us, and
of the Lord, having received the word
in much affliction, with joy of the
Holy Ghost:
7 So that ye were ensamples to all
that believe in Măç-ē-dō´-nĭ-ă and
Ă-chā̂i´-ă.
8 For from you [j]sounded out the
word of the Lord not only in Măç-ē-
dō´-nĭ-ă and Ă-chā̂i´-ă, but also in every
place your faith to God-ward is spread
abroad; so that we need not to speak
any thing.
9 For they themselves shew of us
what manner of entering in we had
unto you, and how ye turned to God
from idols to serve the living and true
God;
10 And to wait [k]for his Son [l]from
heaven, whom he raised from the
dead, *even* Jesus, which delivered us
from [m]the wrath to come.

CHAPTER 2

FOR yourselves, brethren, know
our entrance in unto you, that it
was not in vain:
2 But even after that we had suffered
before, and were shamefully entreated, as ye know, [a]at Philippi, we were
bold in our God [b]to speak unto you
the gospel of God with much contention.
3 For our exhortation *was* not of deceit, nor of uncleanness, nor in guile:
4 But as [c]we were allowed of God to
[d]be put in trust with the gospel, even
so we speak; not as pleasing men, but
God, which [e]trieth our hearts.
5 For neither at any time used we
flattering words, as ye know, nor a
cloke of covetousness; God *is* witness:
6 Nor [f]of men sought we glory,
neither of you, nor *yet* of others, when
we might have [1]been burdensome, as
the apostles of Christ.
7 But we were gentle among you,
even as a nurse cherisheth her children:
8 So being affectionately desirous of
you, we were willing [g]to have imparted unto you, not the gospel of
God only, but also our [h]own souls,
because ye were dear unto us.
9 For ye remember, brethren, our
labour and travail: for labouring
night and day, because [i]we would not
be chargeable unto any of you, we
preached unto you the gospel of God.
10 Ye *are* witnesses, and God *also*,
how holily and justly and unblame-

j Rom. 10.18.
k Rom. 2.7. Phil. 3.20. Heb. 9.28. 2 Pet. 3.12. Rev. 1.7.
l Acts 1.11.
m ch. 5.9.

CHAP. 2

a Acts 16.22.
b Acts 17.2.
c 1 Cor. 4.15, 16.
d Titus 1.3.
e Pro. 17.3.
f John 5.41.
1 Or, used authority.
g Rom. 1.11.
h 2 Cor. 12. 15.
i 2 Cor. 11.9.
j Gal. 5.16. Eph. 4.1. ch. 4.12. 1 Pet. 1.15.
k Matt. 10. 40. Luke 5.1. Rom. 10.17. Heb. 4.12.
l Gal. 1.22.
m Acts 17.5.
n Heb. 10.33.
o Matt. 5.12. Acts 7.52.
2 Or, chased us out.
p Luke 11.52. Acts 13.50. Acts 14.19. Acts 17.5.
q Gen. 15.16.
r Matt. 24.6.
s Rom. 1.13.
3 Or, glorying?
t ch. 3.13. Rev. 1.7.

CHAP. 3

a Acts 17.15.
b Rom. 16. 21.
c Ps. 112.6. Acts 20.24. Eph. 3.13.
d Acts 14.22. Acts 20.23.
e Acts 20.24.
f 1 Cor. 7.5.

ably we behaved ourselves among you
that believe:
11 As ye know how we exhorted and
comforted and charged every one of
you, as a father *doth* his children,
12 That [j]ye would walk worthy of
God, who hath called you unto his
kingdom and glory.
13 For this cause also thank we God
without ceasing, because, when ye received the word of God which ye
heard of us, ye received *it* [k]not *as* the
word of men, but as it is in truth, the
word of God, which effectually worketh also in you that believe.
14 For ye, brethren, became followers of the [l]churches of God which in
Judæa are in Christ Jesus: for [m]ye also
have suffered like things of your own
countrymen, [n]even as they *have* of the
Jews:
15 Who both killed the Lord Jesus,
[o]and their own prophets, and have
[2]persecuted us; and they please not
God, and are contrary to all men:
16 Forbidding [p]us to speak to the
Gentiles that they might be saved, [q]to
fill up their sins alway: [r]for the wrath
is come upon them to the uttermost.
17 But we, brethren, being taken
from you for a short time in presence,
not in heart, endeavoured the more
abundantly to see your face with
great desire.
18 Wherefore we would have come
unto you, even I Paul, once and
again; but [s]Satan hindered us.
19 For what *is* our hope, or joy, or
crown of [3]rejoicing? *Are* not even ye
in the presence of our Lord Jesus
Christ [t]at his coming?
20 For ye are our glory and joy.

CHAPTER 3

WHEREFORE when we could
no longer forbear, [a]we thought
it good to be left at Athens alone;
2 And sent [b]Timotheus, our brother,
and minister of God, and our fellowlabourer in the gospel of Christ, to
establish you, and to comfort you concerning your faith:
3 That [c]no man should be moved by
these afflictions: for yourselves know
that [d]we are appointed thereunto.
4 For [e]verily, when we were with
you, we told you before that we should
suffer tribulation; even as it came to
pass, and ye know.
5 For this cause, when I could no
longer forbear, I sent to know your
faith, [f]lest by some means the tempter

have tempted you, and [g]our labour be
in vain.
6 But [h]now when Timotheus came
from you unto us, and brought us
good tidings of your faith and charity,
and that ye have good remembrance
of us always, desiring greatly to see us,
[i]as we also *to see* you:
7 Therefore, brethren, we were comforted over you in all our affliction and
distress by your faith:
8 For now we live, if ye [j]stand fast in
the Lord.
9 For what thanks can we render to
God again for you, for all the joy
wherewith we joy for your sakes before our God;
10 Night [k]and day praying exceedingly that we might see your face, and
might perfect that which is lacking in
your faith?
11 Now God himself and our Father,
and our Lord Jesus Christ, [1]direct our
way unto you.
12 And the Lord make you to increase and abound in love one toward
another, and toward all *men*, even as
we *do* toward you:
13 To the end he may stablish your
hearts unblameable in holiness before
God, even our Father, at the coming
of our Lord Jesus Christ [l]with all his
saints.

CHAPTER 4

FURTHERMORE then we [1]be-
seech you, brethren, and [2]exhort
you by the Lord Jesus, that as ye have
received of us how ye ought to walk
and [a]to please God, *so* ye would
abound more and more.
2 For ye know what commandments
we gave you by the Lord Jesus.
3 For this is [b]the will of God, *even*
your sanctification, that ye should
abstain from fornication:
4 That [c]every one of you should
know how to possess his vessel in
sanctification and honour;
5 Not in the lust of concupiscence,
even as the Gentiles [d]which know not
God:
6 That [e]no *man* go beyond and [3]de-
fraud his brother [4]in *any* matter: because that the Lord *is* the avenger of
all such, as we also have forewarned
you and testified.
7 For God hath not called us unto
uncleanness, [f]but unto holiness.
8 He [g]therefore that [5]despiseth, despiseth not man, but God, [h]who hath
also given unto us his holy Spirit.
9 But as touching brotherly love ye
need not that I write unto you: for ye
[i]yourselves are taught of God [j]to love
one another.
10 And indeed ye do it toward all the
brethren which are in all Măç-ē-dō-
nĭ-ă: but we beseech you, brethren,
that ye increase more and more;
11 And that ye study to be quiet, and
to do your own business, and to work
with your own hands, as we commanded you;
12 That ye may walk honestly toward them that are without, and *that*
ye may have lack [6]of nothing.
13 But I would not have you to be
ignorant, brethren, concerning them
which are asleep, that ye sorrow not,
even [k]as others which have no hope.
14 For [l]if we believe that Jesus died
and rose again, even so them also
which sleep in Jesus will God bring
with him.
15 For this we say unto you [m]by the
word of the Lord, that we which are
alive *and* remain unto the coming of
the Lord shall not prevent them which
are asleep.
16 For [n]the Lord himself shall descend from heaven with a shout, with
the voice of the archangel, and with
the trump of God: and the dead in
Christ shall rise first:
17 Then we which are alive *and* remain shall be caught up together with
them [o]in the clouds, to meet the Lord
in the air: and so [p]shall we ever be
with the Lord.
18 Wherefore [7]comfort one another
with these words.

CHAPTER 5

BUT of [a]the times and the seasons,
brethren, ye have no need that I
write unto you.
2 For yourselves know perfectly
[b]that the day of the Lord so cometh as
a thief in the night.
3 For when they shall say, Peace and
safety; then [c]sudden destruction cometh upon them, as travail upon a
woman with child; and they shall not
escape.
4 But [d]ye, brethren, are not in darkness, that that day should overtake
you as a thief.
5 Ye are all [e]the children of light, and
the children of the day: we are not of
the night, nor of darkness.
6 Therefore let us not sleep, as
do others; but let us watch and be
sober.
7 For [f]they that sleep sleep in the
night; and they that be drunken [g]are
drunken in the night.

g Gal. 2.2.
h Acts 18.1.
i Phil. 1.8.
j Phil. 4.1.
k Acts 26.7.
1 Or, guide.
l Zech. 14.5. Rev. 20.11.

CHAP. 4

1 Or, request.
2 Or, beseech.
a Col. 1.10.
b Rom. 12.2. Eph. 5.17.
c Rom. 6.19.
d Gal. 4.8. Eph. 2.12.
e Lev. 19.11.
3 Or, oppress, or, overreach.
4 Or, in the matter.
f Lev. 11.44.
g Luke 10.16.
5 Or, rejecteth.
h 1 John 3.24.
i Jer. 31.34. John 6.45.
j John 13.34.
6 Or, of no man.
k Lev. 19.28. Deut. 14.1, 2. 2 Sam. 12. 20.
l 1 Cor. 15. 13.
m 1 Ki. 13.17.
n Matt. 24. 30. Acts 1.11.
o Acts 1.9. Rev. 11.12.
p John 12.26. Rev. 21.3,4.
7 Or, exhort.

CHAP. 5

a Matt. 24.3. Acts 1.7.
b Matt. 25. 13. 2 Pet. 3.10. Rev. 3.3.
c Ex. 15.9,10. Ps. 73. 18-20. Isa. 13.6. Acts 13.41.
d 1 John 2.8.
e Eph. 5.8.
f Luke 21.34.
g Acts 2.15.

8 But let us, who are of the day, be
sober, putting [h]on the breastplate of
faith and love; and for an helmet, the
hope of salvation.
9 For [i]God hath not appointed us to
wrath, but to obtain salvation by our
Lord Jesus Christ,
10 Who died for us, that, whether
we wake or sleep, we should live together with him.
11 Wherefore [1]comfort yourselves
together, and edify one another, even
as also ye do.
12 And we beseech you, brethren,
[j]to know them which labour among
you, and are over you in the Lord, and
admonish you;
13 And to esteem them very highly
in love for their work's sake. *And* be
at peace among yourselves.
14 Now we [2]exhort you, brethren,
warn them that are [3]unruly, comfort
the feebleminded, support the weak,
be patient toward all *men*.
15 See [k]that none render evil for
evil unto any *man;* but ever [l]follow
that which is good, both among yourselves, and to all *men*.

h Isa. 59.17. Rom. 13.12. Eph. 6.14.
i Rom. 9.22. 1 Pet. 2.8.
1 Or, exhort.
j Phil. 2.29.
2 Or, beseech.
3 Or, disorderly.
k Lev. 19.18. Pro. 20.22.
l Gal. 6.10.
m Luke 18.1.
n Ps. 78.40. Isa. 63.10. Eph. 4.30.
o 1 Cor. 14.1.
p 1 John 4.1.
q Ex. 23.7.
r Phil. 4.9.
s 1 Cor. 1.8.
t 1 Cor. 10. 13.
4 Or, adjure.

16 Rejoice evermore.
17 Pray [m]without ceasing.
18 In every thing give thanks: for
this is the will of God in Christ Jesus
concerning you.
19 Quench [n]not the Spirit.
20 Despise [o]not prophesyings.
21 Prove [p]all things; hold fast that
which is good.
22 Abstain [q]from all appearance of
evil.
23 And [r]the very God of peace sanctify you wholly; and *I pray God* your
whole spirit and soul and body be
[s]preserved blameless unto the coming
of our Lord Jesus Christ.
24 Faithful [t]*is* he that calleth you,
who also will do *it*.
25 Brethren, pray for us.
26 Greet all the brethren with an
holy kiss.
27 I [4]charge you by the Lord that this
epistle be read unto all the holy brethren.
28 The grace of our Lord Jesus
Christ *be* with you. Ā-měn.

¶ The first *epistle* unto the Thessalonians was written from Athens.

THE SECOND EPISTLE OF PAUL THE APOSTLE TO THE

THESSALONIANS

CHAPTER 1

PAUL, [a]and Sĭl-vā-nŭs, and Timotheus, unto the church of the
[b]Thĕss-ă-lō-nĭ-ăns in God our Father
and the Lord Jesus Christ:
2 Grace unto you, and peace, from
God our Father and the Lord Jesus
Christ.
3 We are bound to thank God always
for you, brethren, as it is meet, because that your faith [c]groweth exceedingly, and the charity of every one of
you all toward each other aboundeth;
4 So that [d]we ourselves glory in you
in the churches of God [e]for your
patience and faith [f]in all your persecutions and tribulations that ye
endure:
5 *Which is* [g]a manifest token of the
righteous judgment of God, that ye
may be counted [h]worthy of the kingdom of God, for which ye also suffer:
6 Seeing [i]*it is* a righteous thing with
God to recompense tribulation to
them that trouble you;

CHAP. 1
a 2 Cor. 1.19.
b 1 Thes. 1.1.
c Job 17.9. Ps. 84.7.
d 2 Cor. 7.14.
e 1 Thes. 1.3.
f 1 Thes. 2. 14.
g Ps. 9.7,8. Ps. 33.5.
h Luke 20.35, 36. Rev. 3.4.
i Rev. 6.10.
j Rev. 14.13.
1 the angels of his power.
k Heb. 10.27. 2 Pet. 3.7. Rev. 21.8.
2 Or, yielding.
l Ps. 79.6.
m Deut. 33.2. Isa. 2.19.
3 Or, vouchsafe.
n 1 Pet. 1.7.

7 And to you who are troubled [j]rest
with us, when the Lord Jesus shall be
revealed from heaven with [1]his mighty
angels,
8 In [k]flaming fire [2]taking vengeance
on them [l]that know not God, and that
obey not the gospel of our Lord Jesus
Christ:
9 Who shall be punished with everlasting destruction from the presence
of the Lord, and [m]from the glory of
his power;
10 When he shall come to be glorified
in his saints, and to be admired in all
them that believe (because our testimony among you was believed) in that
day.
11 Wherefore also we pray always for
you, that our God would [3]count you
worthy of *this* calling, and fulfil all
the good pleasure of *his* goodness, and
the work of faith with power:
12 That [n]the name of our Lord Jesus
Christ may be glorified in you, and ye
in him, according to the grace of our
God and the Lord Jesus Christ.

CHAPTER 2

NOW we beseech you, brethren, by
the coming of our Lord Jesus
Christ, [a]and *by* our gathering together
unto him,
2 That ye be not soon shaken in
mind, or be troubled, neither by spirit,
nor by word, nor by letter as from
us, as that the day of Christ is at
hand.
3 Let no man deceive you by any
means: for *that day shall not come*,
except [b]there come a falling away first,
and [c]that man of sin be revealed, the
[d]son of perdition;
4 Who opposeth and [e]exalteth himself above [f]all that is called God, or
that is worshipped; so that he as God
sitteth in the temple of God, shewing
himself that he is God.
5 Remember ye not, that, when I
was yet with you, I told you these
things?
6 And now ye know what [1]with-
holdeth that he might be revealed in
his time.
7 For [g]the mystery of iniquity doth
already work: only he who now letteth
will let, until he be taken out of the
way.
8 And then shall that Wicked be revealed, whom [h]the Lord shall consume [i]with the spirit of his mouth, and
shall destroy [j]with the brightness of
his coming:
9 *Even him*, whose coming is [k]after
the working of Satan with all power
[l]and signs and lying wonders,
10 And with all deceivableness of
unrighteousness in [m]them that
perish; because they received not the
love of the truth, that they might be
saved.
11 And [n]for this cause God shall
send them strong delusion, [o]that they
should believe a lie:
12 That they all might be damned
who believed not the truth, but had
pleasure in unrighteousness.
13 But we are bound to give thanks
alway to God for you, brethren
beloved of the Lord, because God
hath from the beginning chosen
you to salvation through sanctification of the Spirit and belief of the
truth:
14 Whereunto he called you by our
gospel, to the obtaining of the glory of
our Lord Jesus Christ.
15 Therefore, brethren, stand fast,
and hold [p]the traditions which ye have
been taught, whether by word, or our
epistle.
16 Now our Lord Jesus Christ himself, and God, even our Father, which
[q]hath loved us, and hath given *us* everlasting consolation and good hope
through grace,
17 Comfort your hearts, and stablish you in every good word and
work.

CHAPTER 3

FINALLY, brethren, pray for us,
that the word of the Lord [1]may
have *free* course, and be glorified,
even as *it is* with you:
2 And that we may be delivered from
[2]unreasonable and wicked men: for
all *men* have not faith.
3 But the Lord is faithful, who shall
stablish you, and [a]keep *you* from
evil.
4 And we have confidence in the
Lord touching you, that ye both do
and will do the things which we command you.
5 And [b]the Lord direct your hearts
into the love of God, and into [3]the
patient waiting for Christ.
6 Now we command you, brethren,
in the name of our Lord Jesus Christ,
that [c]ye withdraw yourselves [d]from
every brother that walketh disorderly,
and not after the tradition which he
received of us.
7 For yourselves know how ye
ought to follow us: for we behaved
not ourselves disorderly among
you;
8 Neither did we eat any man's
bread for nought; but [e]wrought with
labour and travail night and day, that
we might not be chargeable to any of
you:
9 Not [f]because we have not power,
but to make ourselves an ensample
[g]unto you to follow us.
10 For even when we were with you,
this we commanded you, that [h]if any
would not work, neither should he
eat.
11 For we hear that there are some
which walk among you [i]disorderly,
working not at all, but are busybodies.
12 Now them that are such we command and exhort by our Lord Jesus
Christ, [j]that with quietness they
work, and eat their own bread.
13 But ye, brethren, [4]be not weary in
well doing.
14 And if any man obey not our word
[5]by this epistle, note that man, and
have no company with him, that he
may be ashamed.

CHAP. 2

a Matt. 24. 31.
b 2 Pet. 2.1. Rev. 9.20.
c Isa. 37.23. Dan. 7.25. Rev. 13.11.
d John 17.12.
e Isa. 14.13. Rev. 13.6.
f John 10.34.
1 Or, holdeth.
g 1 John 4.3.
h Dan. 7.10.
i Job. 4.9. Isa. 11.4. Rev. 2.16.
j Heb. 10.27.
k John 8.41. Eph. 2.2. Rev. 18.23.
l Deut. 13.1. Matt. 24.24. Rev. 13.13.
m 2 Cor. 2. 15.
n 1 Ki. 22.22. Eze. 14.9. Rom. 1.24.
o Matt. 24.5.
p ch. 3.6.
q 1 John 4.10. Rev. 1.5.

CHAP. 3

1 may run.
2 absurd.
a Matt. 6.13. Luke 11.4.
b 1 Ki. 8.58. Pro. 3.6. Matt. 22.37.
3 Or, the patience of Christ.
c Rom. 16. 17.
d 1 Tim. 6.5. 2 John 10.
e Acts 18.3. Acts 20.34. 1 Cor. 4.12.
f Matt. 10.10.
g 1 Pet. 5.3.
h Gen. 3.19.
i Isa. 56.10.
j Rom. 12.11.
4 Or, faint not.
5 Or, signify that man by an epistle.

15 Yet [k]count *him* not as an enemy,
but admonish *him* as a brother.
16 Now the Lord of peace himself
give you peace always by all means.
The Lord *be* with you all.
17 The salutation of Paul with mine

k Lev. 19.17.

own hand, which is the token in every
epistle: so I write.
18 The grace of our Lord Jesus
Christ *be* with you all. Ä-mĕn.

¶ The second *epistle* to the Thessalonians was written from Athens.

THE FIRST EPISTLE OF PAUL THE APOSTLE TO

TIMOTHY

CHAPTER 1

PAUL, an apostle of Jesus Christ by
[a]the commandment [b]of God our
Saviour, and Lord Jesus Christ, *which*
[c]*is* our hope;
2 Unto [d]Timothy, *my* own son in the
faith: Grace, mercy, *and* peace, from
God our Father and Jesus Christ our
Lord.
3 As I besought thee to abide still at
Ĕph-ĕ-sŭs, [e]when I went into Măç-
ē-dō-nĭ-ă, that thou mightest charge
some that [f]they teach no other doctrine,
4 Neither give heed to fables and
endless genealogies, which minister
questions, rather than godly edifying
which is in faith: *so do.*
5 Now [g]the end of the commandment
is charity [h]out of a pure heart, and *of*
a good conscience, and *of* faith unfeigned:
6 From which some [1]having swerved
have turned aside unto vain jangl-
ing;
7 Desiring to be teachers of the law;
understanding neither what they say,
nor whereof they affirm.
8 But we know that [i]the law *is* good,
if a man use it lawfully;
9 Knowing [j]this, that the law is not
made for a righteous man, but for
[k]the lawless and disobedient, for the
ungodly and for sinners, for unholy
and profane, for murderers of fathers
and murderers of mothers, for man-
slayers,
10 For whoremongers, for them that
defile themselves with mankind, for
menstealers, for liars, for perjured
persons, and if there be any other
thing that is contrary to sound doctrine;
11 According to the glorious gospel
of the blessed God, which was committed to my trust.
12 And I thank Christ Jesus our
Lord, who hath enabled me, [l]for that

CHAP. 1

a Gal. 1.1.
b ch. 2.3.
ch. 4.10.
Titus. 1.3.
Jude 25.
c Col. 1.27.
d Acts 16.1.
e Acts 20.1,3.
Phil. 2.24.
f Gal. 1.6,7.
g Rom. 13.8.
Gal. 5.14.
h 2 Tim. 2.22.
1 Or, not aiming at.
i Rom. 7.12.
j Gal. 3.19.
k Rev. 21.8.
l 1 Cor. 7.25.
m 2 Cor. 3.5, 6.
n Acts 8.3.
Acts 9.1.
Phil. 3.6.
o Luke 23.34.
Acts 26.9.
p Luke 7.47.
q Matt. 9.13.
Luke 19.10.
Rom. 5.8.
r Ps. 10.16.
Ps. 45.6.
Dan. 7.14.
Matt. 6.13.
s Rom. 1.23.
t ch. 4.14.
u 2 Tim. 2.17.
v 2 Tim. 4.14.
w Ps. 109.6.
Matt. 18.17.
Acts 26.18.

CHAP. 2

1 Or, desire.
a Jer. 29.7.
b Rom. 13.1.
2 Or, eminent place.
c Rom. 12.2.
d Isa. 55.1,7.
Eze. 18.23.
Luke 14.23.
2 Pet. 3.9.

he counted me faithful, [m]putting me
into the ministry;
13 Who [n]was before a blasphemer,
and a persecutor, and injurious: but I
obtained mercy, because [o]I did *it*
ignorantly in unbelief.
14 And the grace of our Lord was
exceeding abundant with faith and
[p]love which is in Christ Jesus.
15 This *is* a faithful saying, and
worthy of all acceptation, [q]that Christ
Jesus came into the world to save
sinners; of whom I am chief.
16 Howbeit for this cause I obtained
mercy, that in me first Jesus Christ
might shew forth all longsuffering, for
a pattern to them which should hereafter believe on him to life everlasting.
17 Now unto [r]the King eternal, immortal, [s]invisible, the only wise God,
be honour and glory for ever and ever.
Ä-mĕn.
18 This charge I commit unto thee,
son Timothy, [t]according to the prophecies which went before on thee,
that thou by them mightest war a
good warfare;
19 Holding faith, and a good conscience; which some having put away
concerning faith have made shipwreck:
20 Of whom is [u]Hȳ-mĕ-næ-ŭs [v]and
Alexander; whom I have [w]delivered
unto Satan, that they may learn not
to blaspheme.

CHAPTER 2

I [1]EXHORT therefore, that, first of
all, supplications, prayers, inter-
cessions, *and* giving of thanks, be
made for all men;
2 For [a]kings, and [b]*for* all that are in
[2]authority; that we may lead a quiet
and peaceable life in all godliness and
honesty.
3 For this *is* [c]good and acceptable in
the sight of God our Saviour;
4 Who [d]will have all men to be saved

and to [e]come unto the knowledge of the truth.

5 For *there is* one God, and one mediator between God and men, the man Christ Jesus;

6 Who gave himself a ransom for all, [3]to be testified [f]in due time.

7 Whereunto I am ordained a preacher, and an apostle, (I speak the truth in Christ, *and* lie not;) a teacher of the Gentiles in faith and verity.

8 I will therefore that men pray every [g]where, lifting up holy hands, without wrath and doubting.

9 In like manner also, that women adorn themselves in modest apparel, with shamefacedness and sobriety; not with [4]broided hair, or gold, or pearls, or costly array;

10 But (which becometh women professing godliness) with good works.

11 Let the woman learn in silence with all subjection.

12 But I suffer not a woman to teach, nor to usurp authority over the man, but to be in silence.

13 For Adam was first formed, then Eve.

14 And Adam was not deceived, but the woman being deceived was in the transgression.

15 Notwithstanding she shall be saved [h]in childbearing, if they continue in faith and charity and holiness with sobriety.

CHAPTER 3

THIS *is* a true saying, If a man desire the office of a [a]bishop, he desireth a good work.

2 A bishop then must be blameless, the husband of one wife, vigilant, sober, [1]of good behaviour, given to hospitality, apt to teach;

3 [2]Not given to wine, no striker, not greedy of filthy lucre; but patient, not a brawler, not covetous;

4 One [b]that ruleth well his own house, having his children in subjection with all gravity;

5 (For if a man know not how to rule his own house, how shall he take care of the church of God?)

6 Not [3]a novice, lest being lifted up with pride he fall into the condemnation of the devil.

7 Moreover he must have a good report of them which are without; lest he fall into reproach and the snare of the devil.

8 Likewise *must* the deacons *be* grave, not doubletongued, not given to much wine, not greedy of filthy lucre;

e John 17.3.
3 Or, a testimony.
f Gal. 4.4.
g Mal. 1.11.
4 Or, plaited.
h Gen. 3.15, 16. Isa. 7.14.

CHAP. 3
a Acts 20.28. Phil. 1.1.
1 Or, modest.
2 Or, Not ready to quarrel, and offer wrong, as one in wine.
b Josh. 24.15.
3 Or, one newly come to the faith.
4 Or, ministered.
5 Or, stay.
c Isa. 7.14. Micah 5.2. Matt. 1.23. Phil. 2.6-8. 1 John 1.2.
6 manifested.
d Matt. 3.16. John 1.32. 1 Pet. 3.18. 1 John 5.6.
e Matt. 28.2. Luke 2.13. Eph. 3.10. 1 Pet. 1.12.

CHAP. 4
a John 16.13.
b 1 Pet. 1.20.
c 2 Pet. 2.1.
d Dan. 11.35.
e Eph. 4.19.
f Pro. 18.22.
g 1 Cor. 6.13.
h Gen. 9.3.
i Titus 1.15.
j Jer. 15.16.
1 Or, for a little time.
k Ps. 37.4. Pro. 3.16-18. Matt. 6.33.

9 Holding the mystery of the faith in a pure conscience.

10 And let these also first be proved; then let them use the office of a deacon, being *found* blameless.

11 Even so *must their* wives *be* grave, not slanderers, sober, faithful in all things.

12 Let the deacons be the husbands of one wife, ruling their children and their own houses well.

13 For they that have [4]used the office of a deacon well purchase to themselves a good degree, and great boldness in the faith which is in Christ Jesus.

14 These things write I unto thee, hoping to come unto thee shortly:

15 But if I tarry long, that thou mayest know how thou oughtest to behave thyself in the house of God, which is the church of the living God, the pillar and [5]ground of the truth.

16 And without controversy great is the mystery of godliness: [c]God was [6]manifest in the flesh, [d]justified in the Spirit, [e]seen of angels, preached unto the Gentiles, believed on in the world, received up into glory.

CHAPTER 4

NOW the Spirit [a]speaketh expressly, that [b]in the latter times some shall depart from the faith, giving heed to [c]seducing spirits, [d]and doctrines of devils;

2 Speaking lies in hypocrisy; having [e]their conscience seared with a hot iron;

3 Forbidding [f]to marry, [g]*and commanding* to abstain from meats, which God hath created [h]to be received with thanksgiving of them which believe and know the truth.

4 For [i]every creature of God *is* good, and nothing to be refused, if it be received with thanksgiving:

5 For it is sanctified by the word of God and prayer.

6 If thou put the brethren in remembrance of these things, thou shalt be a good minister of Jesus Christ, nourished up [j]in the words of faith and of good doctrine, whereunto thou hast attained.

7 But refuse profane and old wives' fables, and exercise thyself *rather* unto godliness.

8 For bodily exercise profiteth [1]little: but godliness is profitable unto all things, having [k]promise of the life that now is, and of that which is to come.

9 This *is* a faithful saying and worthy of all acceptation.

10 For therefore we both labour and suffer reproach, because we trust in the living God, [l]who is the Saviour of all men, specially of those that believe.

11 These things command and teach.

12 Let [m]no man despise thy youth; but be thou an example of the believers, in word, in conversation, in charity, in spirit, in faith, in purity.

13 Till I come, give attendance to reading, to exhortation, to doctrine.

14 Neglect [n]not the gift that is in thee, which was given thee [o]by prophecy, [p]with the laying on of the hands of the presbytery.

15 Meditate upon these things; give thyself wholly to them; that thy profiting may appear [2]to all.

16 Take heed unto thyself, and unto the doctrine; continue in them: for in doing this thou shalt both [q]save thyself, and them that hear thee.

CHAPTER 5

REBUKE [a]not an elder, but intreat *him* as a father; *and* the younger men as brethren;

2 The elder women as mothers; the younger as sisters, with all purity.

3 Honour widows that are widows indeed.

4 But if any widow have children or nephews, let them learn first to shew [1]piety at home, and [b]to requite their parents: for that is good and acceptable before God.

5 Now she that is a widow indeed, and desolate, trusteth in God, and continueth in supplications and prayers night and day.

6 But she that liveth [2]in pleasure is dead while she liveth.

7 And these things give in charge, that they may be blameless.

8 But if any provide not for his own, and specially for those of his own [3]house, he hath denied the faith, and is worse than an infidel.

9 Let not a widow be [4]taken into the number under threescore years old, having been the wife of one man,

10 Well reported of for good works; if she have brought up children, if she have lodged [c]strangers, if she [d]have washed the saints' feet, if she have relieved the afflicted, if she have diligently followed every good work.

11 But the younger widows refuse: for when they have begun to wax wanton against Christ, they will marry;

12 Having [e]damnation, because they have cast off their first faith.

13 And [f]withal they learn *to be* idle, wandering about from house to house; and not only idle, but tattlers also and busybodies, speaking things which they ought not.

14 I [g]will therefore that the younger women marry, bear children, guide the house, give [h]none occasion to the adversary [5]to speak reproachfully.

15 For some are already turned aside after Satan.

16 If [i]any man or woman that believeth have widows, let them relieve them, and let not the church be charged; that it may relieve them that are widows indeed.

17 Let [j]the elders that rule well be counted worthy of double honour, especially they who labour in the word and doctrine.

18 For the scripture saith, [k]Thou shalt not muzzle the ox that treadeth out the corn. And, [l]The labourer *is* worthy of his reward.

19 Against an elder receive not an accusation, but [6]before two or three witnesses.

20 Them [m]that sin rebuke before all, that others [n]also may fear.

21 I charge *thee* before God, and the Lord Jesus Christ, and the elect angels, that thou observe these things [7]without preferring one before another, doing nothing by partiality.

22 Lay [o]hands suddenly on no man, neither [p]be partaker of other men's sins: keep thyself pure.

23 Drink no longer water, but use a little wine for thy stomach's sake and thine often infirmities.

24 Some men's sins are open beforehand, going before to judgment; and some *men* they follow after.

25 Likewise also [q]the good works *of some* are manifest beforehand; and they that are otherwise cannot be hid.

CHAPTER 6

LET as many [a]servants as are under the yoke count their own masters worthy of all honour, that the [b]name of God and *his* doctrine be not blasphemed.

2 And they that have believing masters, let them not despise *them*, because [c]they are brethren; but rather do *them* service, because they are [1]faithful and beloved, partakers of the benefit. These things teach and exhort.

3 If any man teach otherwise, and consent not to wholesome words, *even*

---

l Ps. 36.6. Acts 14.17.
m Titus 2.15.
n 2 Tim. 1.6.
o ch. 1.18.
p Acts 6.6. Acts 19.6. ch. 5.22.
2 Or, in all things.
q Eze. 33.9.

CHAP. 5
a Lev. 19.32.
1 Or, kindness.
b Matt. 15.4. Eph. 6.1,2.
2 Or, delicately.
3 Or, kindred.
4 Or, chosen.
c Acts 16.15.
d Gen. 18.4. Luke 7.38.
e Heb. 6.4,6.
f 2 Thes. 3.11.
g 1 Cor. 7.9.
h 2 Sam. 12. 13. Dan. 6.4. ch. 6.1.
5 for their railing.
i Gen. 47.12. Matt. 15.4.
j Rom. 12.8. Gal. 6.6. Phil. 2.29.
k Deut. 25.4.
l Deut. 24.14. Luke 10.7.
6 Or, under.
m Titus 1.13.
n Deut. 13. 11.
7 Or, without prejudice.
o ch. 4.14.
p 2 John 11.
q 1 Pet. 3.8-16.

CHAP. 6
a Titus 2.9.
b 2 Sam. 12. 14. Isa. 52.5.
c Col. 4.1.
1 Or, believing.

the words of our Lord Jesus Christ, and to the doctrine which is according to godliness;

4 He is [2]proud, [d]knowing nothing, but [3]doting about questions and strifes of words, whereof cometh envy, strife, railings, evil surmisings,

5 [4]Perverse disputings of [e]men of corrupt minds, and destitute of the truth, [f]supposing that gain is godliness: [g]from such withdraw thyself.

6 But [h]godliness with contentment is great gain.

7 For [i]we brought nothing into *this* world, *and it is* certain we can carry nothing out.

8 And [j]having food and raiment let us be therewith content.

9 But [k]they that will be rich fall into temptation and a snare, and *into* many foolish and hurtful lusts, which drown men in destruction and perdition.

10 For [l]the love of money is the root of all evil: which while some coveted after, they have [5]erred from the faith, and pierced themselves through with many sorrows.

11 But thou, [m]O man of God, flee these things; and follow after righteousness, godliness, faith, love, patience, meekness.

12 Fight [n]the good fight of faith, lay hold on [o]eternal life, whereunto thou art also called, [p]and hast professed a good profession before many witnesses.

13 I give thee charge in the sight of God, who [q]quickeneth all things, and *before* Christ Jesus, [r]who before Pontius Pilate witnessed a good [6]confession;

14 That thou keep *this* commandment without spot, unrebukeable, until [s]the appearing of our Lord Jesus Christ:

15 Which in his times he shall shew, *who is* [t]the blessed and only Potentate, [u]the King of kings, and Lord of lords;

16 Who [v]only hath immortality, dwelling in [w]the light which no man can approach unto; [x]whom no man hath seen, nor can see: [y]to whom *be* honour and power everlasting. Ā-mĕn.

17 Charge them that are rich in this world, that they be not highminded, nor trust in [7]uncertain riches, but in the living God, who giveth us richly all things to enjoy;

18 That they do good, that they be rich in good works, ready to distribute, [8]willing to communicate;

19 Laying up in store for themselves a good foundation against the time to come, that they may lay hold on eternal life.

20 O Timothy, keep that which is committed to thy trust, avoiding profane *and* vain babblings, and oppositions of science falsely so called:

21 Which some professing have erred concerning the faith. Grace *be* with thee. Ā-mĕn.

¶ The first to Timothy was written from Laodicea which is the chiefest city of Phrygia Pacatiana.

2 Or, a fool.
d 1 Cor. 8.2.
3 Or, sick.
4 Or, Gallings one of another.
e 2 Tim. 3.8.
f Titus 1.11.
g Rom. 16. 17.
h Ps. 37.16. Luke 12.31, 32.
i Eccl. 5.15.
j Gen. 28.20.
k Matt. 13. 22.
l Ex. 23.8.
5 Or, been seduced.
m Deut. 33.1.
n Zech. 10.5. Eph. 6.10-18.
o Phil. 3.12.
p Heb. 13.23.
q John 5.21.
r Rev. 1.5.
6 Or, profession.
s 1 Thes. 3. 13.
t ch. 1.11.
u Rev. 17.14.
v John 5.26.
w 2 Chr. 5.14.
x Ex. 33.20. Deut. 4.12. John 6.46.
y Eph. 3.21. Phil. 4.20.
7 uncertainty of riches.
8 Or, sociable.

THE SECOND EPISTLE OF PAUL THE APOSTLE TO

TIMOTHY

CHAPTER 1

PAUL, an apostle of Jesus Christ by the will of God, according to [a]the promise of life which is in Christ Jesus,

2 To Timothy, *my* dearly beloved son: Grace, mercy, *and* peace, from God the Father and Christ Jesus our Lord.

3 I thank God, whom I serve from *my* forefathers with pure conscience, that without ceasing I have remembrance of thee in my prayers night and day;

4 Greatly desiring to see thee, being mindful of thy tears, that I may be filled with joy;

5 When I call to remembrance the unfeigned faith that is in thee, which dwelt first in thy grandmother Lō-ĭs, and [b]thy mother Eû-nī-çē; and I am persuaded that in thee also.

6 Wherefore I put thee in remembrance that [c]thou stir up the gift of God, which is in thee by the putting on of my hands.

7 For [d]God hath not given us the spirit of fear; [e]but of power, and of love, and of a sound mind.

8 Be [f]not thou therefore ashamed of the testimony of our Lord, nor of me his prisoner: but be thou partaker of

CHAP. 1
a John 5.24, 39,40. Eph. 3.6. Heb. 9.15.
b Acts 16.1.
c 1 Tim. 4.14.
d Rom. 8.15.
e Micah 3.8. Luke 24.49.
f Mark 8.38. Rom. 1.16.

the afflictions of the gospel according
to the power of God;
9 Who hath saved us, and [g]called *us*
with an holy calling, [h]not according
to our works, but according [i]to his
own purpose and grace, which was
given us in Christ Jesus before [j]the
world began,
10 But [k]is now made manifest by the
appearing of our Saviour Jesus Christ,
who [l]hath abolished death, and hath
brought life and immortality to light
through the gospel:
11 Whereunto I am appointed a
preacher, and an apostle, and a teacher of the Gentiles.
12 For the which cause I also suffer
these things: nevertheless I am not
ashamed: for I know whom I have
[1]believed, and am persuaded that he
is able to keep that which I have committed [m]unto him against that day.
13 Hold [n]fast the [o]form of sound
words, which [p]thou hast heard of me,
in faith and love which is in Christ
Jesus.
14 That good thing which was committed unto thee keep by the Holy
Ghost which dwelleth in us.
15 This thou knowest, that all they
which are in Asia be turned away
from me; of whom are Phȳ-ġĕl'-lŭs
and Hĕr-mŏġ'-ĕ-nēs.
16 The Lord [q]give mercy unto the
house of Ō-nĕs-ĭph'-ŏ-rŭs; [r]for he oft
refreshed me, and was not ashamed
of my chain:
17 But, when he was in Rome, he
sought me out very diligently, and
found *me*.
18 The Lord grant unto [s]him that he
may find mercy of the Lord [t]in that
day: and in how many things he
[u]ministered unto me at Ĕph'-ĕ-sŭs,
thou knowest very well.

CHAPTER 2

THOU therefore, my son, [a]be
strong in the grace that is in Christ
Jesus.
2 And the things that thou hast heard
of me [1]among many witnesses, [b]the
same commit thou to faithful men,
who shall be able to teach others also.
3 Thou therefore endure hardness,
as a good soldier of Jesus Christ.
4 No [c]man that warreth entangleth
himself with the affairs of *this* life;
that he may please him who hath
chosen him to be a soldier.
5 And if a man also strive for mas-
teries, *yet* is he not crowned, except he
strive lawfully.

g Rom. 8.30. 1 Thes. 4.7. Heb. 3.1.
h Titus 3.5.
i Rom. 8.28.
j Eph. 1.4. 1 Pet. 1.20.
k Eph. 1.9. 1 Pet. 1.20.
l John 14.6. Heb. 2.14.
1 Or, trusted.
m Ps. 31.5. Luke 23.46. 1 Pet. 4.19.
n Heb. 10.23.
o Rom. 2.20. 1 Tim. 1.10.
p ch. 2.2.
q Matt. 5.7.
r 2 Cor. 7.13. Philem. 7.
s Matt. 25.34.
t 2 Thes. 1.10.
u Heb. 6.10.

CHAP. 2

a Ps. 68.35. Eph. 1.19. Col. 1.11. 1 Tim. 1.2. ch. 1.2.
1 Or, by.
b 1 Tim. 1.18.
c 1 Cor. 9.25.
2 Or, The husbandman, labouring first, must be partaker of the fruits.
d Luke 1.32. Acts 2.30.
e 1 Cor. 15.3, 4.
f Rom. 2.16.
g 2 Cor. 1.6.
h 1 Tim. 1.15.
i Rom. 6.5,8.
j 1 Pet. 4.13.
k Matt. 10. 33. Mark 8.38. Luke 12.9.
l Isa. 25.1. Matt. 24.35. Rom. 3.3.
m Num. 23. 19.
n 1 Tim. 5.21. ch. 4.1.
o 1 Tim. 1.4. Titus 3.9.
p 1 Tim. 4.7. Titus 1.14.
3 Or, gangrene.
q 1 Tim. 1.20.
r 1 Cor. 15.12.
s Pro. 10. 25. Matt. 7.25. Eph. 2.20. 1 John 2.19.
4 Or, steady.
t Nah. 1.7.

6 [2]The husbandman that laboureth
must be first partaker of the fruits.
7 Consider what I say; and the Lord
give thee understanding in all things.
8 Remember that Jesus Christ of the
[d]seed of David [e]was raised from the
dead according [f]to my gospel:
9 Wherein I suffer trouble, as an evil
doer, *even* unto bonds; but the word
of God is not bound.
10 Therefore I endure all things for
the elect's sakes, [g]that they may also
obtain the salvation which is in Christ
Jesus with eternal glory.
11 *It* [h]*is* a faithful saying: For [i]if we
be dead with *him*, we shall also live
with *him:*
12 If [j]we suffer, we shall also reign
with *him:* [k]if we deny *him*, he also will
deny us:
13 If [l]we believe not, *yet* he abideth
faithful: [m]he cannot deny himself.
14 Of these things put *them* in remembrance, [n]charging *them* before
the Lord that [o]they strive not about
words to no profit, *but* to the subverting of the hearers.
15 Study to shew thyself approved
unto God, a workman that needeth
not to be ashamed, rightly dividing
the word of truth.
16 But [p]shun profane *and* vain babblings: for they will increase unto
more ungodliness.
17 And their word will eat as doth
a [3]canker: of whom is Hȳ-mĕ-næ'-ŭs
[q]and Phī-lē'-tŭs;
18 Who concerning the truth have
erred, saying [r]that the resurrection is
past already; and overthrow the faith
of some.
19 Nevertheless [s]the foundation of
God standeth [4]sure, having this seal,
[t]The Lord knoweth them that are his.
And, Let every one that nameth the
name of Christ depart from iniquity.
20 But in a great house there are not
only vessels of gold and of silver, but
also of wood and of earth; and some
to honour, and some to dishonour.
21 If a man therefore purge himself
from these, he shall be a vessel unto
honour, sanctified, and meet for the
master's use, *and* prepared unto every
good work.
22 Flee also youthful lusts: but
follow righteousness, faith, charity,
peace, with them that call on the Lord
out of a pure heart.
23 But foolish and unlearned questions avoid, knowing that they do
gender strifes.
24 And the servant of the Lord must

not strive; but be gentle unto all *men*,
apt to teach, [5]patient,
25 In meekness instructing those that
oppose themselves; if God peradventure will give them repentance to the
acknowledging of the truth;
26 And *that* they may [6]recover themselves out of the snare of the devil,
who are [7]taken captive by him at his
will.

CHAPTER 3

THIS know also, that [a]in the last
days perilous times shall come.
2 For men shall be lovers of their
own selves, covetous, boasters, proud,
blasphemers, [b]disobedient to parents,
unthankful, unholy,
3 Without natural affection, truce-
breakers, [1]false accusers, incontinent,
fierce, despisers of those that are good.
4 Traitors, heady, highminded, lovers of pleasures more than lovers of
God;
5 Having a form of godliness, but
denying the [c]power thereof: from such
turn away.
6 For [d]of this sort are they which
creep into houses, and lead captive
silly women laden with sins, led away
with divers lusts,
7 Ever learning, and never able to
[e]come to the knowledge of the truth.
8 Now [f]as Jăn'-nēš and Jăm'-brēš
withstood Moses, so do these also
resist the truth: men of corrupt minds,
[2]reprobate concerning the faith.
9 But they shall proceed no further:
for their folly shall be manifest unto
all *men*, as [g]theirs also was.
10 But [3]thou hast fully known my
doctrine, manner of life, purpose,
faith, longsuffering, charity, patience,
11 Persecutions, afflictions, which
came unto me [h]at Ăn'-tĭ-ŏch, [i]at Ī-cō'-
nĭ-ŭm, at Lȳs'-tră; what persecutions I
endured: [j]but out of *them* all the
Lord delivered me.
12 Yea, and [k]all that will live godly
in Christ Jesus shall suffer persecution.
13 But evil men and seducers shall
wax worse and worse, deceiving, and
being deceived.
14 But continue thou in the things
which thou hast learned and hast
been assured of, knowing of whom
thou hast learned *them;*
15 And that from a child thou hast
known the holy scriptures, which [l]are
able to make thee wise unto salvation through faith which is in Christ
Jesus.
16 All [m]scripture *is* given by inspiration of God, and *is* profitable for doctrine, for reproof, for correction, for
instruction in righteousness:
17 That [n]the man of God may be
perfect, [4]throughly furnished unto all
good works.

CHAPTER 4

I CHARGE *thee* therefore before
God, and the Lord Jesus Christ, who
shall judge the quick and the dead at
his appearing and his kingdom;
2 Preach the word; be instant in
season, out of season; reprove, [a]re-
buke, exhort with [b]all longsuffering
and doctrine.
3 For the time will come when they
will not endure [c]sound doctrine; but
after their own lusts shall they heap
to themselves teachers, having itching
ears;
4 And they shall turn away *their* ears
from the truth, and [d]shall be turned
unto fables.
5 But watch thou in all things, endure afflictions, do the work of an
[e]evangelist, [1]make full proof of thy
ministry.
6 For I am now ready to be offered,
and the time of my departure is at
hand.
7 I have fought a good fight, I have
finished *my* course, I have kept the
faith:
8 Henceforth there is laid up for me
[f]a crown of righteousness, which the
Lord, the righteous judge, shall give
me at that day: and not to me only,
but unto all them also that love his
appearing.
9 Do thy diligence to come shortly
unto me:
10 For [g]Dē'-măs hath forsaken me,
having loved [h]this present world, and
is departed unto Thĕss-ă-lō-nī'-că;
Crēs'-çēns to Galatia, Titus unto Dal-
matia.
11 Only Luke is with me. [i]Take
Mark, and bring him with thee: for he
is profitable to me for the ministry.
12 And [j]Tȳch'-ĭ-cŭs have I sent to
Ĕph'-ĕ-sŭs.
13 The cloke that I left at Trō'-ăs
with Carpus, when thou comest, bring
with thee, and the books, *but* especially the parchments.
14 Alexander [k]the coppersmith did
me much evil: the [l]Lord reward him
according to his works:
15 Of whom be thou ware also;
for he hath greatly withstood [2]our
words.
16 At my first answer no man stood

5 Or, forbearing.
6 awake.
7 taken alive.

CHAP. 3
a Jude 18.
b Rom. 1.30.
1 Or, makebates.
c Isa. 29.13. Eze. 33. 30-32.
d Matt. 23. 14.
e 1 Tim. 2.4.
f Ex. 7.11.
2 Or, of no judgment.
g Ex. 8.13. Ex. 9.11.
3 Or, thou hast been a diligent follower of.
h Acts 13.45.
i Acts 14.2.
j Gen. 48.16. Job 5.19. Ps. 34.19. Jer. 1.19. Dan. 6.27.
k Matt. 16. 24. John 17.14. Acts 14.22.
l Ps. 119.11. John 5.39, 40. John 20.31. Acts 10.43.
m 2 Sam. 23. 2. Mark 12.24. Luke 1.70. Acts 1.16. Heb. 3.7. 2 Pet. 1.20.
n 1 Tim. 6.11.
4 Or, perfected.

CHAP. 4
a Titus 1.13.
b 1 Tim. 4.13.
c 1 Tim. 1.10.
d 1 Tim. 1.4.
e Acts 21.8.
1 Or, fulfil.
f Rev. 2.10.
g Col. 4.14. Philem. 24.
h 1 John 2.15.
i Acts 12.25.
j Acts 20.4.
k Acts 19.33.
l 2 Sam. 3.39. Ps. 28.4.
2 Or, our preachings.

with me, but all *men* forsook me: [m]*I*
pray God that it may not be laid to
their charge.
17 Notwithstanding [n]the Lord stood
with me, and strengthened me; that
by me the preaching might be fully
known, and *that* all the Gentiles might
hear: and I was delivered [o]out of the
mouth of the lion.
18 And [p]the Lord shall deliver me
from every evil work, and will preserve
me unto his heavenly kingdom: to
whom *be* glory for ever and ever.
Ä-mĕn.

m Acts 7.60.
n Ps. 37.39, 40. Matt. 10.19.
o 2 Pet. 2.9.
p Ps. 121.7.
q Acts 18.2.
r ch. 1.16.
s Acts 19.22.
t Acts 20.4.
3 Cæsar Nero, or, the emperor Nero.

19 Salute [q]Prisca and Ă-quĭl-ă, and
the household [r]of Ō-nĕs-ĭph-ŏ-rŭs.
20 Ē-răs-tŭs [s]abode at Corinth: but
Trŏph-ĭ-mŭs [t]have I left at Mĭ-lē-tŭm
sick.
21 Do thy diligence to come before
winter. Eû-bū-lŭs greeteth thee, and
Pū-dĕns, and Lī-nŭs, and Claudia,
and all the brethren.
22 The Lord Jesus Christ *be* with
thy spirit. Grace *be* with you. Ä-mĕn.

¶ The second *epistle* unto Timotheus, ordained the first bishop of the church of the Ephesians, was written from Rome, when Paul was brought before [3]Nero the second time.

THE EPISTLE OF PAUL TO

TITUS

CHAPTER 1

PAUL, a servant of God, and an
apostle of Jesus Christ, according
to the faith of God's elect, [a]and the
acknowledging of the truth which [b]is
after godliness;
2 [1]In hope of eternal life, which God,
that cannot lie, promised before [c]the
world began;
3 But hath in due times manifested
his word through preaching, which is
committed unto me [d]according to the
commandment of God our Saviour;
4 To [e]Titus, *mine* own son after the
common faith: Grace, mercy, *and*
peace, from God the Father and the
Lord Jesus Christ our Saviour.
5 For this cause left I thee in Crete,
that thou shouldest [f]set in order the
things that are [2]wanting, and [g]ordain
elders in every city, as I had appointed
thee:
6 If any be blameless, the husband of
one wife, having faithful children not
accused of riot or unruly.
7 For a bishop must be blameless, as
[h]the steward of God; not selfwilled,
not soon angry, [i]not given to wine, no
striker, not given to filthy lucre;
8 But a lover of hospitality, a lover
of [3]good men, sober, just, holy, temperate;
9 Holding fast the faithful word [4]as
he hath been taught, that he may be
able [j]by sound doctrine both to exhort
and to convince the gainsayers.
10 For there are many unruly and
vain talkers and deceivers, specially
[k]they of the circumcision:

CHAP. 1
a 2 Tim. 2.25.
b 1 Tim. 6.3.
1 Or, For.
c 2 Tim. 1.9. 1 Pet. 1.20.
d Isa. 12.2. Acts 9.15. ch. 2.10,13.
e 2 Cor. 2.13. Gal. 2.3.
f 1 Cor. 11. 34.
2 Or, left undone.
g Acts 14.23.
h Matt. 24. 45.
i Lev. 10.9.
3 Or, good things.
4 Or, in teaching.
j 1 Tim. 1.10.
k Acts 15.1.
Matt. 23.14.
m Acts 17.28.
n Isa. 29.13. Matt. 15.9.
o Luke 11.39. Acts 10.15. Rom. 14.14.
p Eze. 33.31.
5 Or, void of judgment.
CHAP. 2
a 1 Tim. 6.3.
1 Or, vigilant.
b 1 Pet. 3.3,4.
2 Or, holy women.
3 Or, makebates.
4 Or, wise.
c Col. 3.18. 1 Pet. 3.1,5.

11 Whose mouths must be stopped,
who subvert [l]whole houses, teaching
things which they ought not, for filthy
lucre's sake.
12 One [m]of themselves, *even* a prophet of their own, said, The Cretians
are alway liars, evil beasts, slow
bellies.
13 This witness is true. Wherefore
rebuke them sharply, that they may
be sound in the faith;
14 Not giving heed to Jew-ĭsh fables,
and commandments [n]of men, that
turn from the truth.
15 Unto [o]the pure all things *are* pure:
but unto them that are defiled and unbelieving *is* nothing pure; but even
their mind and conscience is defiled.
16 They [p]profess that they know
God; but in works they deny *him*, being abominable, and disobedient, and
unto every good work [5]reprobate.

CHAPTER 2

BUT speak thou the things which
become [a]sound doctrine:
2 That the aged men be [1]sober,
grave, temperate, sound in faith, in
charity, in patience.
3 The [b]aged women likewise, that
they be in behaviour as becometh
[2]holiness, not [3]false accusers, not
given to much wine, teachers of good
things;
4 That they may teach the young
women to be [4]sober, to love their husbands, to love their children,
5 *To be* discreet, chaste, keepers at
home, good, [c]obedient to their own

husbands, that the word of God be
not blasphemed.
6 Young men likewise exhort to be
[5]sober minded.
7 In [d]all things shewing thyself a
pattern of good works: in doctrine
shewing uncorruptness, gravity, [e]sin-
cerity,
8 Sound [f]speech, that cannot be condemned; [g]that he that is of the contrary part may be ashamed, having no
evil thing to say of you.
9 *Exhort* servants to be obedient unto
their own masters, *and* to please *them*
well in all *things;* not [6]answering
again;
10 Not purloining, but shewing all
good fidelity; that they may adorn the
doctrine of God our Saviour in all
things.
11 For the grace of God that [7]bring-
eth salvation [h]hath appeared to all
men,
12 Teaching us that, [i]denying ungodliness and worldly lusts, we should
live soberly, righteously, and godly,
in this present world;
13 Looking for that blessed [j]hope,
and the glorious appearing of the
great God and our Saviour Jesus
Christ;
14 Who gave himself for us, that he
might redeem us from all iniquity,
[k]and purify unto himself [l]a peculiar
people, zealous of good works.
15 These things speak, and exhort,
and rebuke with all authority. Let no
man despise thee.

CHAPTER 3

PUT them in mind to be subject to
principalities and powers, to obey
magistrates, [a]to be ready to every
good work,
2 To [b]speak evil of no man, to be no
brawlers, *but* gentle, shewing all
meekness unto all men.
3 For we ourselves also were sometimes foolish, disobedient, deceived,

- 5 Or, discreet.
- *d* Ps. 74.2. 1 Pet. 5.3.
- *e* Eph. 6.24.
- *f* 1 Tim. 6.3.
- *g* Neh. 5.9.
- 6 Or, gainsaying.
- 7 Or, that bringeth salvation to all men, hath appeared.
- *h* Isa. 49.6. John 1.9.
- *i* Luke 1.75.
- *j* Acts 24.15.
- *k* Mal. 3.3. Matt. 3.12. Acts 15.9. Heb. 9.14.
- *l* Ex. 15.16. Deut. 7.6.

CHAP. 3

- *a* Heb. 13.21.
- *b* Ex. 20.16. Eph. 4.31.
- 1 Or, pity.
- *c* Rom. 3.20. Gal. 2.16.
- *d* Matt. 3.11. John 3.3,5. 1 Pet. 3.21.
- *e* Eze. 36.25. Joel 2.28.
- 2 richly.
- *f* 1 Tim. 1.4.
- *g* 2 Cor. 13.2.
- *h* Matt. 18. 17. 2 John 10.
- *i* Matt. 25.26-28. Acts 13.46.
- *j* Acts 20.4.
- *k* Acts 18.24.
- 3 Or, profess honest trades.
- *l* Col. 1.10.

serving divers lusts and pleasures,
living in malice and envy, hateful, *and*
hating one another.
4 But after that the kindness and
[1]love of God our Saviour toward man
appeared,
5 Not [c]by works of righteousness
which we have done, but according to
his mercy he saved us, [d]by the washing
of regeneration, and renewing of the
Holy Ghost;
6 Which [e]he shed on us [2]abundantly
through Jesus Christ our Saviour;
7 That being justified by his grace,
we should be made heirs according to
the hope of eternal life.
8 *This is* a faithful saying, and these
things I will that thou affirm constantly, that they which have believed in
God might be careful to maintain
good works. These things are good
and profitable unto men.
9 But [f]avoid foolish questions, and
genealogies, and contentions, and
strivings about the law; for they are
unprofitable and vain.
10 A man that is an heretick [g]after
the first and second [h]admonition
reject;
11 Knowing that he that is such is
subverted, and sinneth, [i]being condemned of himself.
12 When I shall send Artemas unto
thee, or [j]Tȳch´-ĭ-cŭs, be diligent to
come unto me to Nĭ-cŏp´-ŏ-lĭs: for I
have determined there to winter.
13 Bring Zē´-năs the lawyer [k]and
Ă-pŏl´-lŏs on their journey diligently, that nothing be wanting unto
them.
14 And let ours also learn to [3]main-
tain good works for necessary uses,
that they be [l]not unfruitful.
15 All that are with me salute thee.
Greet them that love us in the faith.
Grace *be* with you all. Ā´-mĕn.

¶ It was written to Titus, ordained the first bishop of the church of the Cretians, from Nicopolis of Macedonia.

THE EPISTLE OF PAUL TO

PHILEMON

PAUL, [a]a prisoner of Jesus Christ,
and Timothy *our* brother, unto
Phī-lē-mon our dearly beloved, [b]and
fellowlabourer,
2 And to *our* beloved Ăpph-ĭ-ă, and
Är-chĭp-pŭs [c]our fellowsoldier, and to
the [d]church in thy house:
3 Grace [e]to you, and peace, from
God our Father and the Lord Jesus
Christ.
4 I [f]thank my God, making mention
of thee always in my prayers,
5 Hearing [g]of thy love and faith,
which thou hast toward the Lord
Jesus, and toward all saints;
6 That the communication of thy
faith may become effectual [h]by the
acknowledging of every good thing
which is in you in Christ Jesus.
7 For we have great joy and consolation in thy love, because the bowels of
the saints [i]are refreshed by thee,
brother.
8 Wherefore, [j]though I might be
much bold in Christ to enjoin thee
that which is convenient,
9 Yet for love's sake I rather beseech
thee, being such an one as Paul the
aged, and now also a prisoner of Jesus
Christ.
10 I beseech thee for my [k]son Ō-nĕs-
ĭ-mŭs, whom [l]I have begotten in my
bonds:
11 Which in time past was to thee
unprofitable, but now profitable to
thee and to me:
12 Whom I have sent again: thou
therefore receive him, that is, mine
own bowels:

a Eph. 4.1.
b Phil. 2.25.
c Col. 4.17.
d Rom. 16.5.
e Eph. 1.2.
f Phil. 1.3. 1 Thes. 1.2.
g Eph. 1.15. 1 John 3.23.
h Phil. 1.9.
i 2 Tim. 1.16.
j 2 Cor. 3.12.
k Col. 4.9.
l 1 Cor. 4.15. Gal. 4.19.
m Phil. 2.30.
n 2 Cor. 9.7.
o Gen. 45.5, 8.
p Matt. 23.8. 1 Tim. 6.2.
q Eph. 6.5-7. Col. 3.22.
r 2 Cor. 8.23.
s 2 Cor. 7.16.
t Phil. 1.25.
u Rom. 15. 30-32. Jas. 5.16.
v Col. 1.7.
w Acts 12.12.
x Acts 19.29. Acts 20.4.
y Col. 4.14. 2 Tim. 4.11.

13 Whom I would have retained with
me, that [m]in thy stead he might have
ministered unto me in the bonds of
the gospel:
14 But without thy mind would I do
nothing; [n]that thy benefit should not
be as it were of necessity, but willingly.
15 For [o]perhaps he therefore departed for a season, that thou shouldest
receive him for ever;
16 Not now as a servant, but above
a servant, [p]a brother beloved, specially
to me, but how much more unto thee,
both [q]in the flesh, and in the Lord?
17 If thou count me therefore [r]a
partner, receive him as myself.
18 If he hath wronged thee, or oweth
thee ought, put that on mine account;
19 I Paul have written *it* with mine
own hand, I will repay *it:* albeit I do
not say to thee how thou owest unto
me even thine own self besides.
20 Yea, brother, let me have joy of
thee in the Lord: refresh my bowels
in the Lord.
21 Having [s]confidence in thy obedience I wrote unto thee, knowing that
thou wilt also do more than I say.
22 But withal prepare me also a
lodging: for [t]I trust that [u]through
your prayers I shall be given unto you.
23 There salute thee [v]Ĕp-ă-phrăs, my
fellowprisoner in Christ Jesus;
24 [w]Marcus, [x]Ăr-ĭs-tär-chŭs, Dē-
măs, Lucas, [y]my fellowlabourers.
25 The grace of our Lord Jesus
Christ *be* with your spirit. Ā-mĕn.

¶ Written from Rome to Philemon, by Onesimus a servant.

THE EPISTLE OF PAUL THE APOSTLE TO THE

HEBREWS

CHAPTER 1

GOD, who at sundry times and in
[a]divers manners spake in time
past unto the fathers by the prophets,
2 Hath [b]in these last days spoken unto [c]us by *his* Son, [d]whom he hath
appointed heir of all things, by [e]whom
also he made the worlds;
3 Who [f]being the brightness of *his*
glory, and the express image of his
person, [g]and upholding all things by
the word of his power, when he had
by himself purged our sins, [h]sat down
on the right hand of the Majesty on
high;
4 Being made so much better than
the angels, as [i]he hath by inheritance
obtained a more excellent name than
they.
5 For unto which of the angels said
he at any time, [j]Thou art my Son, this
day have I begotten thee? And again,
[k]I will be to him a Father, and he shall
be to me a Son?
6 [1]And again, when he bringeth in
[l]the firstbegotten into the world, he
saith, And [m]let all the angels of God
worship him.
7 And [2]of the angels he saith, Who
[n]maketh his angels spirits, and his
ministers a flame of fire.
8 But unto the Son *he saith*, [o]Thy
throne, O God, *is* for ever and ever:
a sceptre of [3]righteousness *is* the
sceptre of thy kingdom.
9 Thou hast loved righteousness, and
hated iniquity; therefore God, *even*
thy God, [p]hath anointed thee with the
oil of gladness above thy fellows.
10 And, [q]Thou, Lord, in the beginning hast laid the foundation of the
earth; and the heavens are the works
of thine hands:
11 They [r]shall perish; but thou remainest; and they all shall wax old
as doth a garment;
12 And as a vesture shalt thou fold
them up, and they shall be changed:
but thou art the same, and thy years
shall not fail.
13 But to which of the angels said he
at any time, [s]Sit on my right hand, until I make thine enemies thy footstool?
14 Are they not all ministering

CHAP. 1

a Num. 12.6, 8.
b Gal. 4.4.
c Matt. 13. 11. Luke 10.23, 24. John 1.17.
d Ps. 2.8. Ps. 33.6. Matt. 21.38.
e John 1.3.
f Zech. 13.7. John 14.9. 2 Cor. 4.4.
g Rev. 4.11.
h Ps. 45.6. Matt. 22.44. Mark 12.36. Luke 20.42. Acts 2.34.
i Phil. 2.9.
j Ps. 2.7.
k Ps. 89.26.
1 Or, When he bringeth again.
l Rom. 8.29.
m Ps. 97.7. 1 Pet. 3.22.
2 unto.
n Ps. 104.4.
o Ps. 45.6,7.
3 rightness, or, straightness.
p Isa. 61.1.
q Ps. 102.25.
r Isa. 34.4.
s Ps. 110.1.

CHAP. 2

1 run out as leaking vessels.
a Isa. 45.17.
2 Or, distributions.
b Ps. 8.4.
3 Or, a little while inferior to.
4 Or, by.
c Pro. 16.4. Isa. 43.21. Luke 24.46.
d Matt. 3.15. ch. 6.20.
e Matt. 28. 10. John 20.17.
f Ps. 22.22.

spirits, sent forth to minister for them
who shall be heirs of salvation?

CHAPTER 2

THEREFORE we ought to give
the more earnest heed to the things
which we have heard, lest at any time
we should [1]let *them* slip.
2 For if the word spoken by angels
was stedfast, and every transgression
and disobedience received a just recompence of reward;
3 How shall we escape, if we neglect
so great [a]salvation; which at the first
began to be spoken by the Lord, and
was confirmed unto us by them that
heard *him;*
4 God also bearing *them* witness,
both with signs and wonders, and
with divers miracles, and [2]gifts of the
Holy Ghost, according to his own
will?
5 For unto the angels hath he not
put in subjection the world to come,
whereof we speak.
6 But one in a certain place testified,
saying, [b]What is man, that thou art
mindful of him? or the son of man,
that thou visitest him?
7 Thou madest him [3]a little lower
than the angels; thou crownedst him
with glory and honour, and didst set
him over the works of thy hands:
8 Thou hast put all things in subjection under his feet. For in that he put
all in subjection under him, he left
nothing *that is* not put under him. But
now we see not yet all things put under
him.
9 But we see Jesus, who was made
a little lower than the angels [4]for the
suffering of death, crowned with glory
and honour; that he by the grace of
God should taste death for every man.
10 For [c]it became him, for whom *are*
all things, and by whom *are* all things,
in bringing many sons unto glory, to
make the captain of their salvation
[d]perfect through sufferings.
11 For both he that sanctifieth and
they who are sanctified *are* all of one:
for which cause [e]he is not ashamed to
call them brethren,
12 Saying, [f]I will declare thy name

unto my brethren, in the midst of the
church will I sing praise unto thee.
13 And again, [g]I will put my trust in
him. And again, [h]Behold I and the
children which God hath given me.
14 Forasmuch then as the children
are partakers of flesh and blood, [i]he
also himself likewise took part of the
same; [j]that through death he might
destroy him that had the power of
death, that is, the devil;
15 And deliver them who through
[k]fear of death were all their lifetime
subject to bondage.
16 For verily [5]he took not on *him the*
nature of angels; but he took on *him*
the seed of Abraham.
17 Wherefore in all things it behoved
him to be made [l]like unto *his* brethren,
that he might be a merciful and faithful high priest in things *pertaining* to
God, to make reconciliation for the
sins of the people.
18 For [m]in that he himself hath
suffered being tempted, he is able to
succour them that are tempted.

CHAPTER 3

WHEREFORE, holy brethren,
partakers of the heavenly calling, consider the [a]Apostle and High
Priest of our profession, Christ Jesus;
2 Who was faithful to him that
[1]appointed him, as also [b]Moses *was*
faithful in all his house.
3 For this *man* was counted worthy
of more glory than Moses, inasmuch
as [c]he who hath builded the house
hath more honour than the house.
4 For every house is builded by some
man; but [d]he that built all things *is*
God.
5 And Moses verily *was* faithful in
all his house, as a servant, [e]for a testimony of those things which were to
be spoken after;
6 But Christ as a son over his own
house; whose [f]house are we, if [g]we
hold fast the confidence and the rejoicing of the hope firm unto the
end.
7 Wherefore (as [h]the Holy Ghost
saith, [i]To day if ye will hear his voice,
8 Harden not your hearts, as in the
provocation, in the day of temptation
in the wilderness:
9 When your fathers tempted me,
proved me, and saw my works forty
years.
10 Wherefore I was grieved with that
generation, and said, They do alway
err in *their* heart; and they have not
known my ways.

g Ps. 18.2. Isa. 12.2.
h Isa. 8.18. John 10.29.
i John 1.14. Rom. 8.3.
j Col. 2.15. 2 Tim. 1.10.
k Job 33.24, 28. Ps. 33.19. Luke 1.74.
5 he taketh not hold of angels, but of the seed of Abraham he taketh hold.
l Phil. 2.7.
m ch. 4.15. ch. 5.2.

CHAP. 3

a Matt. 15. 24. 1 Tim. 3.15.
1 made, 1 Sam. 12.6.
b Num. 12.7.
c Zech. 6.12. Matt. 16.18.
d Eph. 2.10.
e Deut. 18. 15,18,19.
f Eph. 4.12. 1 Pet. 2.5.
g Matt. 10. 22.
h 2 Sam. 23. 2. Acts 1.16.
i Ps. 81.11. Isa. 55.3. Matt. 17.5.
2 If they shall enter.
j Num. 14.2. Deut. 1.34.
k Num. 14. 22,29. Num. 26.65. Ps. 106.26.

CHAP. 4

1 the word of hearing.
2 Or, because they were not united by faith to.
a Ps. 95.11.
b Gen. 2.2. Ex. 20.11.
c ch. 3.19.
3 Or, the gospel was first preached.
d Ps. 95.7.
4 That is, Joshua.

11 So I sware in my wrath, [2]They
shall not enter into my rest.)
12 Take heed, brethren, lest there be
in any of you an evil heart of unbelief,
in departing from the living God.
13 But exhort one another daily,
while it is called To day; lest any of
you be hardened through the deceitfulness of sin.
14 For we are made partakers of
Christ, if we hold the beginning of
our confidence stedfast unto the
end;
15 While it is said, To day if ye will
hear his voice, harden not your hearts,
as in the provocation.
16 For [j]some, when they had heard,
did provoke: howbeit not all that
came out of Egypt by Moses.
17 But with whom was he grieved
forty years? *was it* not with them that
had sinned, [k]whose carcases fell in the
wilderness?
18 And to whom sware he that they
should not enter into his rest, but to
them that believed not?
19 So we see that they could not enter
in because of unbelief.

CHAPTER 4

LET us therefore fear, lest, a promise
being left *us* of entering into his
rest, any of you should seem to come
short of it.
2 For unto us was the gospel
preached, as well as unto them: but
[1]the word preached did not profit
them, [2]not being mixed with faith in
them that heard *it*.
3 For we which have believed do enter into rest, as he said, [a]As I have
sworn in my wrath, if they shall enter
into my rest: although the works were
finished from the foundation of the
world.
4 For he spake in a certain place of
the seventh *day* on this wise, And
[b]God did rest the seventh day from
all his works.
5 And in this *place* again, If they
shall enter into my rest.
6 Seeing therefore it remaineth that
some must enter therein, and [c]they to
whom [3]it was first preached entered
not in because of unbelief:
7 Again, he limiteth a certain day,
saying in David, To day, after so long
a time; as it is said, [d]To day if ye will
hear his voice, harden not your
hearts.
8 For if [4]Jesus had given them rest,
then would he not afterward have
spoken of another day.

9 There remaineth therefore a [5]rest to
the people of God.
10 For he that is entered into his
rest, he also hath ceased from his own
works, as God *did* from his.
11 Let us labour therefore to enter
into that rest, lest any man fall after
the same example of [6]unbelief.
12 For the word of God *is* [e]quick, and
powerful, and sharper than any [f]two-
edged sword, piercing even to the
dividing asunder of soul and spirit,
and of the joints and marrow, and *is* a
[g]discerner of the thoughts and intents
of the heart.
13 Neither is there any creature that
is not manifest in his sight: but all
things *are* naked and opened unto the
eyes of him with whom we have to do.
14 Seeing then that we have a great
high priest, that is passed into the
heavens, Jesus the Son of God, let us
hold fast *our* profession.
15 For [h]we have not an high priest
which cannot be touched with the
feeling of our infirmities; but [i]was in
all points tempted like as *we are*, [j]*yet*
without sin.
16 Let us therefore come boldly unto
the throne of grace, that we may obtain mercy, and find grace to help in
time of need.

CHAPTER 5

FOR every high priest taken from
among men is ordained for men in
things *pertaining* to God, [a]that he
may offer both gifts and sacrifices for
sins:
2 Who [1]can have compassion on the
ignorant, and on them that are out of
the way; for that he himself also is
compassed with infirmity.
3 And [b]by reason hereof he ought, as
for the people, so also for himself, to
offer for sins.
4 And [c]no man taketh this honour
unto himself, but he that is called of
God, as *was* [d]Aaron.
5 So [e]also Christ glorified not himself to be made an high priest; but he
that said unto him, [f]Thou art my Son,
to day have I begotten thee.
6 As he saith also in another *place*,
[g]Thou *art* a priest for ever after the
order of Měl-c͟hĭs'-ĕd-ĕc.
7 Who in the days of his flesh, when
he had [h]offered up prayers and supplications with [i]strong crying and
tears unto [j]him that was able to save
him from death, and was heard [2]in
that he feared;
8 Though he were a Son, yet learned

5 Or, keeping of a sabbath.
6 Or, disobedience.
e Isa. 49.2. Jer. 23.29.
f Rev. 1.16.
g 1 Cor. 14. 24,25.
h Isa. 53.3.
i Luke 22.28.
j Dan. 9.24. 2 Cor. 5.21. 1 Pet. 2.22. 1 John 3.5.

CHAP. 5

a ch. 8.3,4.
1 Or, can reasonably bear with.
b Lev. 4.3.
c 1 Sam. 13.9. 2 Sam. 6.6.
d Ex. 28.1. Num. 16.5, 40.
e John 8.54. Acts 13.33.
f Ps. 2.7.
g Ps. 110.4.
h John 17.1.
i Ps. 22.1.
j Matt. 26.53.
2 Or, for his piety.
k Phil. 2.8.
l ch. 6.20.
3 hath no experience.
m Eph. 4.13.
4 Or, perfect.
5 Or, of an habit, or, perfection.
n 1 Cor. 2.14, 15.

CHAP. 6

1 Or, the word of the beginning of Christ.
a Acts 19.4.
b Acts 8.14.
c Acts 17.31.
d Acts 24.25.
e 1 Cor. 4.19.
f Matt. 12.32. ch. 10.26. 2 Pet. 2.20. 1 John 5.16.
g Matt. 7.22. ch. 10.32.
h John 4.10. Eph. 2.8.
i ch. 10.29.
2 Or, for.
j Matt. 10.42. John 13.20.

he obedience [k]by the things which he
suffered;
9 And being made perfect, he became the author of eternal salvation
unto all them that obey him;
10 Called of God an high priest after
[l]the order of Měl-c͟hĭs'-ĕd-ĕc.
11 Of whom we have many things to
say, and hard to be uttered, seeing ye
are dull of hearing.
12 For when for the time ye ought
to be teachers, ye have need that one
teach you again which *be* the first
principles of the oracles of God; and
are become such as have need of milk,
and not of strong meat.
13 For every one that useth milk [3]*is*
unskilful in the word of righteousness:
for he is [m]a babe.
14 But strong meat belongeth to
them that are [4]of full age, *even* those
who by reason [5]of use have their
senses exercised [n]to discern both good
and evil.

CHAPTER 6

THEREFORE leaving [1]the principles of the doctrine of Christ, let
us go on unto perfection; not laying
again the foundation of repentance
from dead works, and of faith toward
God,
2 Of [a]the doctrine of baptisms, and
[b]of laying on of hands, [c]and of resurrection of the dead, [d]and of eternal
judgment.
3 And this will we do, [e]if God permit.
4 For [f]*it is* impossible for [g]those who
were once enlightened, and have
tasted of [h]the heavenly gift, and were
made partakers of the Holy Ghost,
5 And have tasted the good word
of God, and the powers of the world
to come,
6 If they shall fall away, to renew
them again unto repentance; [i]seeing
they crucify to themselves the Son of
God afresh, and put *him* to an open
shame.
7 For the earth which drinketh in the
rain that cometh oft upon it, and
bringeth forth herbs meet for them
[2]by whom it is dressed, receiveth blessing from God:
8 But that which beareth thorns and
briers *is* rejected, and *is* nigh unto
cursing; whose end *is* to be burned.
9 But, beloved, we are persuaded
better things of you, and things that
accompany salvation, though we thus
speak.
10 For [j]God *is* not unrighteous to
forget your work and labour of love,
which ye have shewed toward his

name, in that ye have ministered to the saints, and do minister.

11 And we desire that every one of you do shew the same diligence to [k]the full assurance of hope unto the end:

12 That ye be not slothful, but followers of them who through faith and patience inherit [l]the promises.

13 For when God made promise to Abraham, because he could swear by no greater, he [m]sware by himself,

14 Saying, Surely blessing I will bless thee, and multiplying I will multiply thee.

15 And so, after he had patiently endured, he obtained the promise.

16 For men verily swear by the greater: and [n]an oath for confirmation *is* to them an end of all strife.

17 Wherein God, willing more abundantly to shew unto [o]the heirs of promise [p]the immutability of his counsel, [3]confirmed *it* by an oath:

18 That by two immutable things, in which *it was* impossible for God to lie, we might have a strong consolation, who have fled for refuge to lay hold upon the hope [q]set before us:

19 Which [r]*hope* we have as an anchor of the soul, both sure and stedfast, [s]and which entereth into that within the veil;

20 Whither [t]the forerunner is for us entered, *even* Jesus, made an high priest for ever after the order of Mĕl-chĭs´-ĕd-ĕc.

CHAPTER 7

FOR this [a]Mĕl-chĭs´-ĕd-ĕc, king of Sā´-lĕm, priest of the most high God, who met Abraham returning from the slaughter of the kings, and blessed him;

2 To whom also Abraham gave a tenth part of all; first being by interpretation King of righteousness, and after that also King of Sā´-lĕm, which is, King of peace;

3 Without father, without mother, [1]without descent, having neither beginning of days, nor end of life; but made like unto the Son of God; abideth a priest continually.

4 Now consider how great this man *was*, [b]unto whom even the patriarch Abraham gave the tenth of the spoils.

5 And verily [c]they that are of the sons of Levi, who receive the office of the priesthood, have a commandment to take tithes of the people according to the law, that is, of their brethren, though they come out of the loins of Abraham:

6 But he whose [2]descent is not counted from them received tithes of Abraham, and blessed [d]him that had the promises.

7 And without all contradiction the less is blessed of the better.

8 And here men that die receive tithes; but there he *receiveth them*, of [e]whom it is witnessed that he liveth.

9 And as I may so say, Levi also, who receiveth tithes, payed tithes in Abraham.

10 For he was yet in the loins of his father, when Mĕl-chĭs´-ĕd-ĕc met him.

11 If [f]therefore perfection were by the Lē-vĭt´-ĭ-căl priesthood, (for under it the people received the law,) what further need *was there* that another priest should rise after the order of Mĕl-chĭs´-ĕd-ĕc, and not be called after the order of Aaron?

12 For the priesthood being changed, there is made of necessity a change also of the law.

13 For he of whom these things are spoken pertaineth to another tribe, of which no man gave attendance at the altar.

14 For *it is* evident that [g]our Lord sprang out of Juda; of which tribe Moses spake nothing concerning priesthood.

15 And it is yet far more evident: for that after the similitude of Mĕl-chĭs´-ĕd-ĕc there ariseth another priest,

16 Who is made, not after the law of a carnal commandment, but after the power of an endless life.

17 For he testifieth, [h]Thou *art* a priest for ever after the order of Mĕl-chĭs´-ĕd-ĕc.

18 For there is verily a disannulling of the commandment going before for [i]the weakness and unprofitableness thereof.

19 For [j]the law made nothing perfect, [3]but the bringing in of [k]a better hope *did;* by the which [l]we draw nigh unto God.

20 And inasmuch as not without an oath *he was made priest:*

21 (For those priests were made [4]without an oath; but this with an oath by him that said unto him, The [m]Lord sware and will not repent, Thou *art* a priest for ever after the order of Mĕl-chĭs´-ĕd-ĕc:)

22 By so much was Jesus made a surety of a better testament.

23 And they truly were many priests,

k Col. 2.2.
l ch. 10.36.
m Gen. 22.16.
n Ex. 22.11.
o ch. 11.9.
p Job 23.13. Isa. 14.24. Rom. 11.29. Jas. 1.17.
3 interposed himself by an oath.
q Isa. 27.5. ch. 12.1.
r Ps. 130.7.
s Lev. 16.15. ch. 9.7.
t John 14.2,3. ch. 4.14. ch. 8.1.

CHAP. 7
a Gen. 14.18. Ps. 110.4. ch. 5.6,10.
1 without pedigree.
b Gen. 14.20.
c Num. 18.21.
2 Or, pedigree.
d Gen. 12.2. Acts 3.25. Gal. 3.16.
e ch. 5.6.
f Gal. 2.21. ch. 8.7.
g Gen. 49.10. Isa. 11.1. Matt. 1.3. Luke 3.33. Rom. 1.3.
h Ps. 110.4. ch. 5.6,10.
i Rom. 8.3.
j Acts 13.39. Rom. 3.20. Gal. 2.16. ch. 9.9.
3 Or, but it was the bringing in.
k ch. 6.18.
l Rom. 5.2.
4 Or, without swearing of an oath.
m Ps. 110.4.

because they were not suffered to continue by reason of death:
24 But this *man*, because he [n]con-
tinueth ever, hath [5]an unchangeable
priesthood.
25 Wherefore he is able also to save
them [6]to the uttermost that come unto
God by him, seeing he ever liveth [o]to
make intercession for them.
26 For such an high priest became
us, *who is* holy, harmless, undefiled,
separate from sinners, [p]and made
higher than the heavens;
27 Who needeth not daily, as those
high priests, to offer up sacrifice, [q]first
for his own sins, [r]and then for the
people's: for this [s]he did once, when
he offered up himself.
28 For the law maketh [t]men high
priests which have infirmity; but the
word of the oath, which was since the
law, *maketh* the Son, who [u]is [7]con-
secrated for evermore.

CHAPTER 8

NOW of the things which we have
spoken *this is* the sum: We have
such an high priest, who [a]is set on the
right hand of the throne of the
Majesty in the heavens;
2 A minister [1]of the sanctuary, and
of the [b]true tabernacle, which the
Lord pitched, and not man.
3 For every high priest is ordained to
offer gifts and sacrifices: wherefore *it*
[c]*is* of necessity that this man have
somewhat also to offer.
4 For if he were on earth, he should
not be a priest, seeing that [2]there are
priests that offer gifts according to the
law:
5 Who serve unto the example and
[d]shadow of heavenly things, as Moses
was admonished of God when he was
about to make the tabernacle: [e]for,
See, saith he, *that* thou make all things
according to the pattern shewed to
thee in the mount.
6 But now [f]hath he obtained a more
excellent ministry, by how much also
he is the mediator of a better [3]cov-
enant, which was established upon
better promises.
7 For if that first *covenant* had been
faultless, then should no place have
been sought for the second.
8 For finding fault with them, he
saith, [g]Behold, the days come, saith
the Lord, when I will make a new
covenant with the house of Israel and
with the house of Judah:
9 Not according to the covenant that
I made with their fathers in the day

n Isa. 9.6,7. John 12.34. ch. 13.8.
5 Or, which passeth not from one to another.
6 Or, evermore.
o Isa. 53.12. Rom. 8.34. 1 John 2.1.
p Eph. 1.20.
q Lev. 9.7. Lev. 16.6, 11. ch. 5.3.
r Lev. 16.15.
s Rom. 6.10.
t ch. 5.1,2.
u ch. 2.10.
7 perfected.

CHAP. 8
a Col. 3.1.
1 Or, of holy things.
b ch. 9.11.
c Eph. 5.2.
2 Or, they are priests.
d Col. 2.17.
e Ex. 25.40. Num. 8.4.
f ch. 7.22.
3 Or, testament.
g Jer. 31.31.
4 give.
5 Or, upon.
h Gen. 17.7, 8. Jer. 24.7. Eze. 37.27. Zech. 8.8.
i Isa. 54.13. 1 John 2.27.

CHAP. 9
1 Or, ceremonies.
a Ex. 25.8. Lev. 4.6.
b Ex. 26.1.
c Lev. 24.5.
2 Or, holy.
d Ex. 40.3.
e Ex. 16.33.
f Num. 17. 10.
g Ex. 25.16. Deut. 10.2, 5.
h Lev. 16.2.
i Num. 28.3. Dan. 8.11.
j Ex. 30.10.
k ch. 10.19.
l John 14.6.
m Gal. 3.21.

when I took them by the hand to lead
them out of the land of Egypt; because
they continued not in my covenant,
and I regarded them not, saith the
Lord.
10 For this *is* the covenant that I will
make with the house of Israel after
those days, saith the Lord; I will [4]put
my laws into their mind, and write
them [5]in their hearts: and [h]I will be to
them a God, and they shall be to me a
people:
11 And [i]they shall not teach every
man his neighbour, and every man his
brother, saying, Know the Lord: for
all shall know me, from the least to
the greatest.
12 For I will be merciful to their unrighteousness, and their sins and their
iniquities will I remember no more.
13 In that he saith, A new *covenant*,
he hath made the first old. Now that
which decayeth and waxeth old *is*
ready to vanish away.

CHAPTER 9

THEN verily the first *covenant* had
also [1]ordinances of divine service,
and [a]a worldly sanctuary.
2 For [b]there was a tabernacle made;
the first, wherein *was* the candlestick,
and the [c]table, and the shewbread;
which is called [2]the sanctuary.
3 And [d]after the second veil, the
tabernacle which is called the Holiest
of all;
4 Which had the golden censer, and
the ark of the covenant overlaid round
about with gold, wherein *was* the
[e]golden pot that had măn′-nă, [f]and
Aaron's rod that budded, and [g]the
tables of the covenant;
5 And [h]over it the chĕr′-ū-bĭms of
glory shadowing the mercyseat; of
which we cannot now speak particu-
larly.
6 Now when these things were thus
ordained, [i]the priests went always into
the first tabernacle, accomplishing the
service *of God*.
7 But into the second *went* the high
priest alone [j]once every year, not without blood, which he offered for himself, and *for* the errors of the people:
8 The [k]Holy Ghost this signifying,
that the [l]way into the holiest of all was
not yet made manifest, while as the
first tabernacle was yet standing:
9 Which *was* a figure for the time
then present, in which were offered
both gifts and sacrifices, [m]that could
not make him that did the service perfect, as pertaining to the conscience;

10 *Which stood* only in [n]meats and
drinks, and [o]divers washings, [p]and
carnal [3]ordinances, imposed *on them*
until the time of reformation.
11 But Christ being come an high
priest of [q]good things to come, [r]by a
greater and more perfect tabernacle,
not made with hands, that is to say,
not of this building;
12 Neither by the blood of goats and
calves, but [s]by his own blood he entered in [t]once into the holy place,
having [u]obtained eternal redemption
for us.
13 For [v]if the blood of bulls and of
goats, and [w]the ashes of an heifer
sprinkling the unclean, sanctifieth to
the purifying of the flesh:
14 How much more [x]shall the blood
of Christ, [y]who through the eternal
Spirit offered [z]himself without [4]spot
to God, purge [a]your conscience from
dead [b]works [c]to serve the living God?
15 And [d]for this cause he is the mediator of the new testament, that [e]by
means of death, for the redemption of
the transgressions *that were* under
the first testament, they [f]which are
called might receive the promise of
eternal inheritance.
16 For where a testament *is*, there
must also of necessity [5]be the death of
the testator.
17 For [g]a testament *is* of force after
men are dead: otherwise it is of no
strength at all while the testator liveth.
18 Whereupon [h]neither the first
testament was [6]dedicated without
blood.
19 For when Moses had spoken
every precept to all the people according to the law, he took the blood of
calves and of goats, [i]with water, and
[7]scarlet wool, and hyssop, and
sprinkled both the book, and all the
people,
20 Saying, [j]This *is* the blood of the
testament which God hath enjoined
unto you.
21 Moreover [k]he sprinkled with
blood both the tabernacle, and all the
vessels of the ministry.
22 And almost all things are by the
law purged with blood; and without
[l]shedding of blood is no remission.
23 *It was* therefore necessary that
the [m]patterns of things in the heavens
should be purified with these; but the
heavenly things themselves with better
sacrifices than these.
24 For [n]Christ is not entered into the
holy places made with hands, *which
are* the figures of the true; but into
heaven itself, now [o]to appear in the
presence of God for us:
25 Nor yet that he should offer himself often, as the high priest entereth
into the holy place every year with
blood of others;
26 For then must he often have
suffered since the foundation of the
world: but now once [p]in the end of
the world hath he appeared to put
away sin by the sacrifice of himself.
27 And [q]as it is appointed unto men
once to die, but after this the judgment:
28 So [r]Christ was once [s]offered to
bear the sins of many; and unto them
that look for him shall he appear [t]the
second time without sin unto salvation. 45c Rev 22:20

CHAPTER 10

FOR the law having [a]a shadow of
good things to come, *and* not the
very image of the things, can never
with those sacrifices which they offered year by year continually make the
comers thereunto perfect.
2 For then [1]would they not have
ceased to be offered? because that the
worshippers once purged should have
had no more conscience of sins.
3 But [b]in those *sacrifices there is* a
remembrance again *made* of sins
every year.
4 For [c]*it is* not possible that the blood
of bulls and of goats should take away
sins.
5 Wherefore when he cometh into
the world, he saith, [d]Sacrifice and
offering thou wouldest not, but a body
[2]hast thou prepared me:
6 In burnt offerings and *sacrifices* for
sin thou hast had no pleasure.
7 Then said I, Lo, I come (in the
volume of the book it is written of me,)
to do thy will, O God.
8 Above when he said, Sacrifice and
offering and burnt offerings and *offering* for sin thou wouldest not, neither
hadst pleasure *therein;* which are
offered by the law;
9 Then said he, Lo, I come to do thy
will, O God. He taketh away the first,
that he may establish the second.
10 By [e]the which will we are sanctified through the offering of the body
of Jesus Christ once *for all.*
11 And every priest standeth [f]daily
ministering and offering oftentimes
the same sacrifices, which can never
take away sins:
12 But [g]this man, after he had offered
one sacrifice for sins for ever, sat
down on the right hand of God;

n Rom. 14. 17.
o Lev. 11.25. Num. 19.7.
p Eph. 2.15.
3 Or, rites, or, ceremonies.
q ch. 10.1.
r ch. 8.2.
s Rev. 1.5.
t Zech. 3.9.
u Dan. 9.24.
v Lev. 8.11. Rom. 3.24-26.
w Num. 19.2.
x 1 John 1.7.
y Rom. 1.4. 1 Pet. 3.18.
z Eph. 2.5.
4 Or, fault.
a ch. 1.3.
b ch. 6.1.
c Luke 1.74.
d 1 Tim. 2.5.
e 1 Pet. 3.18.
f ch. 3.1.
5 Or, be brought in.
g Gal. 3.15.
h Ex. 24.6.
6 Or, purified.
i Ex. 24.5-8. Lev. 14.4.
7 Or, purple.
j Ex. 24.8. Matt. 26.28. ch. 13.20. 1 Pet. 1.2.
k Ex. 29.12. Lev. 8.15.
l Lev. 17.11.
m ch. 8.5.
n ch. 6.20.
o ch. 7.25. 1 John 2.1.
p 1 Cor. 10. 11. Gal. 4.4. Eph. 1.10. ch. 7.27.
q Gen. 3.19. Eccl. 3.20.
r Rom. 6.10.
s Matt. 26.28. 1 Pet. 2.24. 1 John 3.5.
t Matt. 25.34. John 14.3.

CHAP. 10

a Col. 2.17. ch. 8.5.
1 Or, they would have ceased to be offered, because, etc.
b Lev. 16.21. ch. 9.7.
c Micah 6.6. ch. 9.13.
d Ps. 40.6. Isa. 1.11. Jer. 6.20. Amos. 5.21.
2 Or, thou hast fitted me.
e John 17.19. ch. 13.12.
f Num. 28.3. ch. 7.27.
g Col. 3.1. ch. 1.3.

13 From henceforth expecting till
[h]his enemies be made his footstool.
14 For by one offering he hath perfected for ever them that are sanctified.
15 *Whereof* [i]the Holy Ghost also is a
witness to us: for after that he had
said before,
16 This [j]*is* the covenant that I will
make with them after those days,
saith the Lord, I will put my laws into
their hearts, and in their minds will I
write them;
17 [3]And their sins and iniquities will
I remember no more.
18 Now where remission of these
is, there is no more offering for
sin.
19 Having therefore, brethren, [4]bold-
ness to enter into the holiest by the
blood of Jesus,
20 By [k]a new and living way, which
he hath [5]consecrated for us, through
the veil, that is to say, his flesh;
21 And *having* an high priest over
[l]the house of God;
22 Let us draw near with a true
heart [m]in full assurance of faith, having our hearts sprinkled from an evil
conscience, and our [n]bodies washed
with pure water.
23 Let us hold fast the profession of
our faith without wavering; (for he [o]*is*
faithful that promised;)
24 And let us consider one another
to provoke unto love and to good
works:
25 Not [p]forsaking the assembling of
ourselves together, as the manner of
some *is;* but exhorting *one another:*
and [q]so much the more, as ye see [r]the
day approaching.
26 For [s]if we sin wilfully [t]after that
we have received the knowledge of the
the truth, there remaineth no more
sacrifice for sins,
27 But a certain fearful looking for
of judgment and [u]fiery indignation,
which shall devour the adversaries.
28 He that despised Moses' law died
without mercy under two or three
witnesses:
29 Of how much sorer punishment,
suppose ye, shall he be thought
worthy, who hath trodden under foot
the Son of God, and hath [v]counted
the blood of the covenant, wherewith
he was sanctified, an unholy thing,
[w]and hath done despite unto the Spirit
of grace?
30 For we know him that hath said,
Vengeance [x]*belongeth* unto me, I will
recompense, saith the Lord. And

h Ps. 110.1. Acts 2.34, 35. ch. 1.13.
i 2 Pet. 1.21.
j Jer. 31.33.
3 Some copies have, Then he said, And their.
4 Or, liberty.
k Matt. 11. 27. John 10.9. ch. 9.8.
5 Or, new made.
l 1 Tim. 3.15.
m Eph. 3.12. 1 John 3.21.
n Num. 19. 13. Isa. 52.15. Eze. 36.25.
o 1 Cor. 1.9. 1 Thes. 5.24. 2 Thes. 3.3.
p Acts 2.42.
q Rom. 13. 11.
r 2 Pet. 3.9.
s Num. 15. 30. 1 John 5.16.
t 2 Pet. 2.20.
u Eze. 36.5.
v 1 Cor. 11. 29.
w Matt. 12. 31.
x Deut. 32. 35.
y Ps. 50.4.
z Isa. 33.14.
a Gal. 3.4.
b Phil. 1.29, 30.
c Phil. 1.7. 1 Thes. 2.14.
d Matt. 5.12.
6 Or, that ye have in yourselves, or, for yourselves.
e Luke 21.19. ch. 12.1.
f Col. 3.24.
g Luke 18.8.
h Hab. 2.3,4.

CHAP. 11
1 Or, ground, or, confidence.
a Rom. 8.24.
b John 1.3.
c Gen. 4.4.
2 Or, is yet spoken of.
d Gen. 5.22.
e John 3.18, 36.
f Gen. 6.13.
3 Or, being wary.

again, [y]The Lord shall judge his
people.
31 *It* [z]*is* a fearful thing to fall into the
hands of the living God.
32 But [a]call to remembrance the
former days, in which, after ye were
illuminated, ye endured [b]a great fight
of afflictions;
33 Partly, whilst ye were made a
gazingstock both by reproaches and
afflictions; and partly, whilst ye [c]be-
came companions of them that were
so used.
34 For ye had compassion of me in
my bonds, and [d]took joyfully the
spoiling of your goods, knowing [6]in
yourselves that ye have in heaven a
better and an enduring substance.
35 Cast not away therefore your confidence, which hath great recompence
of reward.
36 For [e]ye have need of patience,
that, after ye have done the will of
God, [f]ye might receive the promise.
37 For [g]yet a little while, and he [h]that
shall come will come, and will not
tarry.
38 Now the just shall live by faith:
but if *any man* draw back, my soul
shall have no pleasure in him.
39 But we are not of them who draw
back unto perdition; but of them that
believe to the saving of the soul.

CHAPTER 11

NOW faith is the [1]substance of
things hoped for, the evidence [a]of
things not seen.
2 For by it the elders obtained a good
report.
3 Through faith we understand that
the worlds [b]were framed by the word
of God, so that things which are seen
were not made of things which do
appear.
4 By faith [c]Abel offered unto God a
more excellent sacrifice than Cain, by
which he obtained witness that he was
righteous, God testifying of his gifts:
and by it he being dead [2]yet speaketh.
5 By faith [d]Ē′-nŏch was translated
that he should not see death; and was
not found, because God had translated him: for before his translation
he had this testimony, that he pleased
God.
6 But [e]without faith *it is* impossible
to please *him:* for he that cometh to
God must believe that he is, and *that*
he is a rewarder of them that diligently seek him.
7 By faith [f]Noah, being warned of
God of things not seen as yet, [3]moved

with fear, prepared an ark to the saving of his house; by the which he
condemned the world, and became
heir of [g]the righteousness which is by
faith.
8 By faith Abraham, when he was
called to go out into a place which he
should after receive for an inheritance,
obeyed; and he went out, not knowing
whither he went.
9 By faith he sojourned in the land
of promise, as *in* a strange country,
dwelling in [h]tabernacles with Isaac
and Jacob, the heirs with him of the
same promise:
10 For he looked for a city which
hath foundations, [i]whose builder and
maker *is* God.
11 Through faith also [j]Sara herself
received strength to conceive seed, and
[k]was delivered of a child when she was
past age, because she judged him faithful who had promised.
12 Therefore sprang there even of
one, and [l]him as good as dead, *so
many* as the stars of the sky in multitude, and as the sand which is by the
sea shore innumerable.
13 These all died [4]in faith, not having
received the promises, but having
[m]seen them afar off, and were persuaded of *them*, and embraced *them*,
and [n]confessed that they were strangers and pilgrims on the earth.
14 For they that say such things declare [o]plainly that they seek a country.
15 And truly, if they had been mindful of that *country* from whence they
came out, they might have had opportunity to have returned.
16 But now they desire a better
country, that is, an heavenly: wherefore God is not ashamed [p]to be called
their God: for [q]he hath prepared for
them a city.
17 By faith [r]Abraham, when he was
tried, offered up Isaac: and he that
had received the promises offered [s]up
his only begotten *son*,
18 [5]Of whom it was said, [t]That in
Isaac shall thy seed be called:
19 Accounting that God *was* able to
raise *him* up, even from the dead;
from whence also he received him in
a figure.
20 By faith [u]Isaac blessed Jacob and
Esau concerning things to come.
21 By faith Jacob, when he was a
dying, blessed [v]both the sons of
Joseph; and worshipped, [w]*leaning*
upon the top of his staff.
22 By faith [x]Joseph, when he died,
[6]made mention of the departing of
the children of Israel; and gave commandment concerning his bones.
23 By faith [y]Moses, when he was
born, was hid three months of his
parents, because they saw *he was* a
proper child; and they were not afraid
of the king's [z]commandment.
24 By faith Moses, when he was come
to years, refused to be called the son
of Pharaoh's daughter;
25 Choosing [a]rather to suffer affliction with the people of God, than to
enjoy the pleasures of sin for a season;
26 Esteeming the reproach [7]of Christ
greater riches than the treasures in
Egypt: for he had respect unto the
recompence of the reward.
27 By faith [b]he forsook Egypt, not
fearing the wrath of the king: for he
endured, as seeing him who is invisible.
28 Through faith [c]he kept the passover, and the sprinkling of blood, lest
he that destroyed the firstborn should
touch them.
29 By faith they passed through the
Red sea as by dry *land:* which the
Egyptians assaying to do were
drowned.
30 By faith [d]the walls of Jericho fell
down, after they were compassed
about seven days.
31 By faith [e]the harlot Rahab perished not with them [8]that believed not,
when she had received the spies with
peace.
32 And what shall I more say? for
the time would fail me to tell of [f]Gĕd-
ĕ-o̱n, and *of* [g]Bâr-ăk, and *of* [h]Samson,
and *of* [i]Jĕph-thāē; *of* [j]David also, and
[k]Samuel, and *of* the prophets:
33 Who through faith subdued kingdoms, wrought righteousness, obtained promises, stopped [l]the mouths
of lions,
34 Quenched [m]the violence of fire,
escaped the [n]edge of the sword, [o]out
of weakness were made strong, waxed
valiant in fight, turned [p]to flight the
armies of the aliens.
35 Women [q]received their dead raised to life again: and others were
[r]tortured, not accepting deliverance;
that they might obtain a better resurrection:
36 And others had trial of *cruel*
mockings and scourgings, yea, moreover [s]of bonds and imprisonment:
37 They [t]were stoned, they were sawn
asunder, were tempted, were slain
with the sword: [u]they wandered about
in sheepskins and goatskins; being
destitute, afflicted, tormented;

g Rom. 3.22. Phil. 3.9.
h Gen. 12.8.
i Isa. 14.32.
j Gen. 17.19.
k Luke 1.36.
l Rom. 4.19.
4 according to faith.
m Gen. 49. 10. Num. 24.17.
n Gen. 47.9.
o ch. 13.14.
p Ex. 3.6,15.
q Phil. 3.20.
r Gen. 22.1.
s Jas. 2.21.
5 Or, To.
t Gen. 21.12.
u Gen. 27.27.
v Gen. 48.5.
w Gen. 47.31.
x Gen. 50.24. Ex. 13.19.
6 Or, remembered.
y Ex. 2.2.
z Ex. 1.16.
a Ps. 84.10. Matt. 5.10-12.
7 Or, for Christ.
b Ex. 10.29.
c Ex. 12.21.
d Josh. 6.20.
e Jas. 2.25.
8 Or, that were disobedient.
f Judg. 6.11.
g Judg. 4.6.
h Judg. 13. 24.
i Judg. 11.1.
j 1 Sam.16.1.
k 1 Sam. 1. 20.
l 1 Sam. 17. 34. Dan. 6.22.
m Dan. 3.25.
n 1 Sam. 20.1. 1 Ki. 19.3. 2 Ki. 6.16.
o 2 Ki. 20.7. Ps. 6.8.
p 1 Sam. 14. 13.
q 1 Ki. 17.22. 2 Ki. 4.35.
r Acts 22.25.
s Gen. 39.20. Jer. 20.2.
t 1 Ki. 21.13. 2 Chr. 24.21. Acts 7.58.
u 2 Ki. 1.8.

38 (Of whom the world was not
worthy:) they wandered in deserts,
and *in* mountains, and [v]*in* dens and
caves of the earth.
39 And these all, having obtained a
good report through faith, received
not the promise:
40 God having [9]provided some better
thing for us, that they without us
should not be [w]made perfect.

CHAPTER 12

WHEREFORE seeing we also
are compassed about with so
great a cloud of witnesses, let us lay
aside every weight, and the sin which
doth so easily beset *us*, and let us run
with patience the race that is set before us,
2 Looking [a]unto Jesus the [1]author
and finisher of *our* faith; [b]who for the
joy that was set before him endured
the cross, despising the shame, [c]and
is set down at the right hand of the
throne of God.
3 For [d]consider him that endured
such contradiction of sinners against
himself, lest [e]ye be wearied and faint
in your minds.
4 Ye have not yet resisted unto
blood, striving against sin.
5 And ye have forgotten the exhortation which speaketh unto you as unto
children, [f]My son, despise not thou
the chastening of the Lord, nor faint
when thou art rebuked of him:
6 For [g]whom the Lord loveth he
chasteneth, and scourgeth every son
whom he receiveth.
7 If ye endure chastening, God
dealeth with you as with sons; for
what son is he whom the father
chasteneth not?
8 But if ye be without chastisement,
whereof [h]all are partakers, then are
ye bastards, and not sons.
9 Furthermore we have had fathers
of our flesh which corrected *us*, and
we gave *them* reverence: shall we not
much rather be in subjection unto the
Father of spirits, and live?
10 For they verily for a few days
chastened *us* [2]after their own pleasure; but he for *our* profit, that [i]*we*
might be partakers of his holiness.
11 Now no chastening for the present
seemeth to be joyous, but grievous:
nevertheless afterward it yieldeth [j]the
peaceable fruit of righteousness unto
them which are exercised thereby.
12 Wherefore [k]lift up the hands
which hang down, and the feeble
knees;
13 And make [3]straight paths for your
feet, lest that which is lame be turned
out of the way; [l]but let it rather be
healed.
14 Follow peace with all *men*, and
holiness, [m]without which no man shall
see the Lord:
15 Looking diligently lest any man
[4]fail of the grace of God; lest [n]any root
of bitterness springing up trouble *you*,
and thereby many be defiled;
16 Lest there *be* any fornicator, or
profane person, as Esau, [o]who for one
morsel of meat sold his birthright.
17 For ye know how that afterward,
when he [p]would have inherited the
blessing, he was rejected: for he found
no [5]place of repentance, though he
sought it carefully with tears.
18 For ye are not come unto [q]the
mount that might be touched, and
that burned with fire, nor unto blackness, and darkness, and tempest,
19 And the sound of a trumpet, and
the voice of words; which *voice* they
that heard intreated that [r]the word
should not be spoken to them any
more:
20 (For they could not endure that
which was commanded, And if so
much as a beast touch the mountain,
it shall be stoned, or thrust through
with a dart:
21 And so terrible was the sight, *that*
Moses said, I exceedingly fear and
quake:)
22 But ye are come [s]unto mount
Sī-on, and [t]unto the city of the
living God, the heavenly Jerusalem,
[u]and to an innumerable company of
angels,
23 To the general assembly and
church of the firstborn, which are
[6]written in heaven, and to God the
Judge of all, and to the spirits of just
men [v]made perfect,
24 And to Jesus the mediator of the
new [7]covenant, and to [w]the blood of
sprinkling, that speaketh better things
than [x]*that of* Abel.
25 See that ye refuse not him that
speaketh. For if they escaped not who
refused him [y]that spake on earth,
much more *shall not* we *escape*, if we
turn away from him that *speaketh*
from heaven:
26 Whose [z]voice then shook the
earth: but now he hath promised,
saying, [a]Yet once more I shake not
the earth only, but also heaven.
27 And this *word*, Yet once more,
signifieth [b]the removing of those
things that [8]are shaken, as of things

v 1 Ki. 18.4.
9 Or, foreseen.
w Rom. 11. 26.

CHAP. 12

a 2 Cor. 3.18.
1 Or, beginner.
b 1 Pet. 1.11.
c Ps. 110.1.
d John 15.20.
e Gal. 6.9.
f Job 5.17.
g Ps. 94.12. Jas. 1.12. Rev. 3.19.
h Ps. 73.14.
2 Or, as seemed good, or, meet to them.
i Lev. 19.2.
j Jas. 3.18.
k Job 4.3,4. Isa. 35.3.
3 Or, even.
l Gal. 6.1.
m Matt. 5.8.
4 Or, fall from.
n Deut. 29. 18.
o Gen. 25.33.
p Gen. 27.34.
5 Or, way to change his mind.
q Ex. 19.12. Deut. 4.11. 2 Tim. 1.7.
r Ex. 20.19.
s Gal. 4.26. Rev. 3.12.
t Phil. 3.20.
u Ps. 68.17. Dan. 7.10. Jude 14.
6 Or, enrolled.
v Phil. 3.12.
7 Or, testament.
w Ex. 24.8. 1 Pet. 1.2.
x Gen. 4.10.
y Num. 16.
z Ex. 19.18.
a Hag. 2.6.
b Ps. 102.26. Matt. 24.35. 2 Pet. 3.10.
8 Or, may be shaken.

that are made, that those things which
cannot be shaken may remain.
28 Wherefore we receiving a kingdom which cannot be moved, [9]let us
have grace, whereby we may serve
God acceptably with reverence and
godly fear:
29 For [c]our God *is* a consuming fire.

CHAPTER 13

LET brotherly love continue.
2 Be [a]not forgetful to entertain
strangers: for thereby [b]some have en-
tertained angels unawares.
3 Remember [c]them that are in bonds,
as bound with them; *and* them which
suffer adversity, as being yourselves
also in the body.
4 Marriage *is* honourable in all, and
the bed undefiled: but whoremongers
and adulterers God will judge.
5 *Let your* conversation *be* without
covetousness; *and be* content with
such things as ye have: for he hath
said, [d]I will never leave thee, nor forsake thee.
6 So that we may boldly say, The
Lord [e]*is* my helper, and I will not fear
what man shall do unto me.
7 Remember them which [1]have the
rule over you, who have spoken unto
you the word of God: whose faith
follow, considering the end of *their*
conversation.
8 Jesus Christ [f]the same yesterday,
and to day, and for ever.
9 Be not carried about with divers
and strange doctrines. For *it is* a good
thing that the heart be established
with grace; not with meats, which
have not profited them that have been
occupied therein.
10 We [g]have an altar, whereof they
have no right to eat which serve the
tabernacle.
11 For [h]the bodies of those beasts,
whose blood is brought into the sanctuary by the high priest for sin, are
burned without the camp.
12 Wherefore Jesus also, that he
might sanctify the people with his
own blood, suffered [i]without the
gate.
13 Let us go forth therefore unto him
without the camp, bearing his [j]re-
proach.
14 For [k]here have we no continuing
city, but we seek one to come.
15 By him therefore let us [l]offer the
sacrifice of praise to God continually,
that is, the fruit of *our* lips [2]giving
thanks to his name.
16 But to do good and to communicate forget not: for with such sacrifices God is well pleased.
17 Obey them that [3]have the rule
over you, and submit yourselves: [m]for
they watch for your souls, as they that
must give account, that they may do it
with joy, and not with grief: for that *is*
unprofitable for you.
18 Pray for us: for we trust we have
a good conscience, in all things willing
to live honestly.
19 But I beseech *you* the rather to do
this, that I may be restored to you the
sooner.
20 Now the God of peace, that
brought again from the dead our Lord
Jesus, [n]that great shepherd of the
sheep, [o]through the blood of the everlasting [4]covenant,
21 Make you perfect in every good
work to do his will, [5]working in you
that which is wellpleasing in his sight,
through Jesus Christ; [p]to whom *be*
glory for ever and ever. Ă-mĕn.
22 And I beseech you, brethren,
suffer the word of exhortation: for I
have written a letter unto you in few
words.
23 Know ye that [q]*our* brother
Timothy is [r]set at liberty; with whom,
if he come shortly, I will see you.
24 Salute all them that have the rule
over you, and all the saints. They of
Italy salute you.
25 Grace *be* with you all. Ă-mĕn.

¶ Written to the Hebrews from Italy by Timothy.

9 Or, let us hold fast.
c Ex. 24.17. Deut. 4.24. Ps. 50.3. Isa. 66.15. ch. 10.27.

CHAP. 13
a Gen. 19.2. Matt. 25.35.
b Gen. 18.3.
c Matt. 25. 36. Rom. 12.15.
d Gen. 28.15. Deut. 31.6, 8. Josh. 1.5. Ps. 37.25. Isa. 41.10, 17.
e Ps. 27.1.
1 Or, are the guides.
f John 8.58. Eph. 4.5. ch. 1.12. Rev. 1.4.
g 1 Cor. 9.13.
h Lev. 4.11.
i John 19.17. Acts 7.58.
j 1 Pet. 4.14.
k Micah 2.10.
l Lev. 7.12. Ps. 50.14.
2 confessing to.
3 Or, guide.
m Eze. 3.17.
n Isa. 40.11. Eze. 34.23. John 10.11.
o Zech. 9.11. Matt. 26.28. Luke 22.20.
4 Or, testament.
5 Or, doing.
p Gal. 1.5.
q 1 Thes. 3.2.
r 1 Tim. 6.12.

THE GENERAL EPISTLE OF

JAMES

CHAPTER 1

JAMES, [a]a servant of God and of
the Lord Jesus Christ, [b]to the twelve
tribes which [c]are scattered abroad,
greeting.
2 My brethren, count it all joy when
ye fall into divers temptations;
3 Knowing *this*, that the trying of
your faith worketh patience.
4 But let patience have *her* perfect
work, that ye may be perfect and entire, wanting nothing.
5 If [d]any of you lack wisdom, let
[e]him ask of God, that giveth to all
men liberally, and upbraideth not;
and [f]it shall be given him.
6 But [g]let him ask in faith, nothing
wavering. For he that wavereth is like
a wave of the sea driven with the wind
and tossed.
7 For let not that man think that he
shall receive any thing of the Lord.
8 A double minded man *is* unstable
in all his ways.
9 Let the brother of low degree [1]re-
joice in that he is exalted:
10 But the rich, in that he is made
low: because as the flower of the grass
he shall pass away.
11 For the sun is no sooner risen
with a burning heat, but it withereth
the grass, and the flower thereof falleth, and the grace of the fashion of it
perisheth: so also shall the rich man
fade away in his ways.
12 Blessed [h]*is* the man that endureth
temptation: for when he is tried, he
shall receive the [i]crown of life, which
the Lord hath promised to them that
love him.
13 Let no man say when he is tempted, I am tempted of God: for God
cannot be tempted with [2]evil, neither
tempteth he any man:
14 But every man is tempted, when
he is drawn away of his own lust, and
enticed.
15 Then when lust hath conceived, it
bringeth forth sin: and sin, when it is
finished, bringeth forth death.
16 Do not err, my beloved brethren.
17 Every good gift and every perfect
gift is from above, and cometh down
from the Father of lights, with [j]whom
is no variableness, neither shadow of
turning.
18 Of [k]his own will begat he us with
the word of truth, that we should be
a kind of firstfruits [l]of his creatures.
19 Wherefore, my beloved brethren,
let every man be swift to hear, slow to
speak, slow to wrath:
20 For the wrath of man worketh
not the righteousness of God.
21 Wherefore lay apart all filthiness
and superfluity of naughtiness, and
receive with meekness the engrafted
word, [m]which is able to save your
souls.
22 But be ye doers of the word, and
not hearers only, deceiving your own
selves.
23 For [n]if any be a hearer of the
word, and not a doer, he is like unto a
man beholding his natural face in a
glass:
24 For he beholdeth himself, and goeth his way, and straightway forgetteth what manner of man he was.
25 But [o]whoso looketh into the perfect law of liberty, and continueth
therein, he being not a forgetful
hearer, but a doer of the work, this
[p]man shall be blessed in his [3]deed.
26 If any man among you seem to be
religious, and bridleth not his tongue,
but deceiveth his own heart, this
man's religion *is* vain.
27 Pure religion and undefiled before
God and the Father is this, [q]To visit
the fatherless and widows in their
affliction, [r]*and* to keep himself un-
spotted from the world.

CHAP. 1
[a] Matt. 10.3.
[b] Acts 26.7.
[c] John 7.35. Acts 2.5.
[d] 1 Ki. 3.9. Job 28.12, 28. Pro. 2.3. Pro. 3.5-7.
[e] Matt. 7.7. Mark 11.24. John 14.13.
[f] Jer. 29.12.
[g] Matt. 21. 22. Mark 11.22-24. 1 John 5.14, 15. 1 Tim. 2.8.
1 Or, glory.
[h] Heb. 12.5. Rev. 3.19.
[i] Matt. 25.34. Luke 22.28-30. 1 Pet. 5.4.
2 Or, evils.
[j] Num. 23.19. Mal. 3.6.
[k] John 1.13. 1 Cor. 4.15. 1 Pet. 1.23.
[l] Jer. 2.3. Rev. 14.4.
[m] Acts 13. 26. Rom. 1.16. 1 Cor. 15.2. Eph. 1.13. Heb. 2.3. 1 Pet. 1.9.
[n] Luke 6.47.
[o] 2 Cor. 3.18.
[p] John 13.17.
3 Or, doing.
[q] Isa. 1.16. 1 Tim. 1.5.
[r] Ex. 23.2. Lev. 18.29, 30. Gal. 1.4. Eph. 2.2.

CHAPTER 2

MY brethren, have not the faith of
our Lord Jesus Christ, [a]*the Lord*
of glory, with [b]respect of persons.
2 For if there come unto your [1]assem-
bly a man with a gold ring, in goodly
apparel, and there come in also a poor
man in vile raiment;
3 And ye have respect to him that
weareth the gay clothing, and say unto
him, Sit thou here [2]in a good place;
and say to the poor, Stand thou there,
or sit here under my footstool:
4 Are ye not then partial in your-

CHAP. 2
[a] Acts 7.2. 1 Cor. 2.8. Phil. 2.9.
[b] Lev. 19.15. Deut. 1.17. Pro. 24.23. Matt. 22.16. Jude 16.
1 synagogue.
2 Or, well, or, seemly.

selves, and are become judges of evil
thoughts?
5 Hearken, my beloved brethren,
Hath [c]not God chosen the poor of this
world rich in faith, and heirs of [3]the
kingdom [d]which he hath promised to
them that love him?
6 But ye have despised the poor. Do
not rich men oppress you, and draw
you before the judgment seats?
7 Do not they blaspheme that worthy
name by the which ye are called?
8 If ye fulfil the royal law according
to the scripture, [e]Thou shalt love thy
neighbour as thyself, ye do well:
9 But if ye have respect to persons,
ye commit sin, and are convinced of
the law as transgressors.
10 For whosoever shall keep the
whole law, and yet offend in one *point*,
he [f]is guilty of all.
11 For [4]he that said, [g]Do not commit
adultery, said also, Do not kill. Now
if thou commit no adultery, yet if thou
kill, thou art become a transgressor of
the law.
12 So speak ye, and so do, as they
that shall be judged by the law of
liberty.
13 For he shall have judgment without mercy, that hath shewed no
mercy; and mercy [5]rejoiceth against
judgment.
14 What *doth it* profit, my brethren,
though a man say he hath faith, and
have not works? can faith save him?
15 If a brother or sister be naked, and
destitute of daily food,
16 And one of you say unto them,
Depart in peace, be *ye* warmed and
filled; notwithstanding ye give them
not those things which are needful to
the body; what *doth it* profit?
17 Even so faith, if it hath not works,
is dead, being [6]alone.
18 Yea, a man may say, Thou hast
faith, and I have works: shew me thy
faith [7]without thy works, and I will
shew thee my faith by my works.
19 Thou believest that there is one
God; thou doest well: the [h]devils also
believe, and tremble.
20 But wilt thou know, O vain man,
that faith [i]without works is dead?
21 Was not Abraham our father
justified by works, [j]when he had offered Isaac his son upon the altar?
22 [8]Seest thou how faith wrought
with his works, and by works was faith
made perfect?
23 And the scripture was fulfilled
which saith, [k]Abraham believed God,
and it was imputed unto him for

c John 7.48.
3 Or, that.
d Ex. 20.6. 1 Sam. 2.30. Pro. 8.17. Matt. 5.3. Luke 6.20.
e Lev. 19.18. Matt. 22.39.
f Deut. 27.26. Matt. 5.19. Gal. 3.10.
4 Or, that law which said.
g Ex. 20.13. Deut. 5.18. Matt. 19.18. Mark 10.19.
5 Or, glorieth.
6 by itself.
7 Some copies read, by thy works.
h Matt. 8.29. Mark 1.24. Luke 4.34. Acts 16.17.
i Gal. 5.6.
j Gen. 22.9.
8 Or, Thou seest.
k Gen. 15.6. Rom. 4.3.
l 2 Chr. 20.7. Isa. 41.8.
m Heb. 11. 31.
9 Or, breath.

CHAP. 3

a Matt. 23.8. 1 Pet. 5.3.
b Luke 6.37.
1 Or, judgment.
c 1 Ki. 8.46. Pro. 20.9. Eccl. 7.20. 1 John 1.8.
d Ps. 34.13. 1 Pet. 3.10.
e Matt. 12. 37.
2 Or, wood.
f Matt. 15.11, 18,19,20. Mark 7.15, 20,23.
3 wheel.
4 nature.
5 nature of man.
g Gen. 1.26. 1 Cor. 11.7.
6 Or, hole.
h Gal. 6.4.
i Rom. 13.13.

righteousness: and he was called [l]the
Friend of God.
24 Ye see then how that by works
a man is justified, and not by faith
only.
25 Likewise also [m]was not Rahab the
harlot justified by works, when she
had received the messengers, and had
sent *them* out another way?
26 For as the body without the
[9]spirit is dead, so faith without works
is dead also.

CHAPTER 3

MY brethren, [a]be not many masters, knowing [b]that we shall receive the greater [1]condemnation.
2 For [c]in many things we offend all.
[d]If any man offend not in word, [e]the
same *is* a perfect man, *and* able also to
bridle the whole body.
3 Behold, we put bits in the horses'
mouths, that they may obey us; and
we turn about their whole body.
4 Behold also the ships, which though
they be so great, and *are* driven of
fierce winds, yet are they turned about
with a very small helm, whithersoever
the governor listeth.
5 Even so the tongue is a little member, and boasteth great things. Behold,
how great [2]a matter a little fire
kindleth!
6 And the tongue *is* a fire, a world of
iniquity: so is the tongue among our
members, that [f]it defileth the whole
body, and setteth on fire the [3]course
of nature; and it is set on fire of hell.
7 For every [4]kind of beasts, and of
birds, and of serpents, and of things
in the sea, is tamed, and hath been
tamed of [5]mankind:
8 But the tongue can no man tame;
it is an unruly evil, full of deadly
poison.
9 Therewith bless we God, even the
Father; and therewith curse we men,
which are [g]made after the similitude
of God.
10 Out of the same mouth proceedeth blessing and cursing. My brethren,
these things ought not so to be.
11 Doth a fountain send forth at the
same [6]place sweet *water* and bitter?
12 Can the fig tree, my brethren,
bear olive berries? either a vine, figs?
so *can* no fountain both yield salt
water and fresh.
13 Who [h]*is* a wise man and endued
with knowledge among you? let him
shew out of a good conversation his
works with meekness of wisdom.
14 But if ye have [i]bitter envying and

strife in your hearts, glory not, and lie not against the truth.

15 This [j]wisdom descendeth not from above, but *is* earthly, [7]sensual, devilish.

16 For [k]where envying and strife *is*, there *is* [8]confusion and every evil work.

17 But [l]the wisdom that is from above is first pure, then peaceable, gentle, *and* easy to be intreated, full of mercy and good fruits, [9]without partiality, [m]and without hypocrisy.

18 And [n]the fruit of righteousness is sown in peace of them that make peace.

CHAPTER 4

FROM whence *come* wars and [1]fightings among you? *come they* not hence, *even* of your [2]lusts that war in your members?

2 Ye lust, and have not: ye [3]kill, and desire to have, and cannot obtain: ye fight and war, yet ye have not, because ye [a]ask not.

3 Ye [b]ask, and receive not, [c]because ye ask amiss, that ye may consume *it* upon your [4]lusts.

4 Ye adulterers and adulteresses, know ye not that [d]the friendship of the world is enmity with God? whosoever [e]therefore will be a friend of the world is the enemy of God.

5 Do ye think that the scripture saith in vain, [f]The spirit that dwelleth in us lusteth [5]to envy?

6 But he giveth more grace. Wherefore he saith, [g]God resisteth the proud, but giveth grace unto the humble.

7 Submit yourselves therefore to God. [h]Resist the devil, and he will flee from you.

8 Draw [i]nigh to God, and he will draw nigh to you. Cleanse *your* hands, *ye* sinners; and purify *your* hearts, *ye* double minded.

9 Be afflicted, and mourn, and weep: let your laughter be turned to mourning, and *your* joy to heaviness.

10 Humble yourselves in the sight of the Lord, and he shall lift you up.

11 Speak not evil one of another, brethren. He that speaketh evil of *his* brother, and judgeth his brother, speaketh evil of the law, and judgeth the law: but if thou judge the law, thou art not a doer of the law, but a judge.

12 There is one lawgiver, [j]who is able to save and to destroy: who art thou that judgest another?

13 Go to now, ye that say, To day or to morrow we will go into such a city,

j Phil. 3.19.
7 Or, natural.
k 1 Cor. 3.3.
8 tumult, or, unquietness.
l 1 Cor. 2.6.
9 without wrangling.
m 1 Pet. 1.22.
n Matt. 5.9.

CHAP. 4

1 Or, brawlings.
2 Or, pleasures.
3 Or, envy.
a Ps. 10.4.
b Job 27.9. Pro. 1.28.
c Ps. 66.18.
4 Or, pleasures.
d 1 John 2.15.
e John 15.19. Gal. 1.10.
f Gen. 8.21.
5 Or, enviously?
g Ps. 138.6. Pro. 3.34. Matt. 23.12. Luke 18.14.
h Eph. 4.27. 1 Pet. 5.9.
i Gen. 18.23. Isa. 55.6,7. Hos. 6.1,2.
j Matt. 10.28.
6 Or, For it is.
k Luke 12.47. John 9.41. Rom. 1.20.

CHAP. 5

a Rom. 2.5.
b Lev. 19.13. Jer. 22.13. Mal. 3.5.
c Gen. 4.10. Ex. 2.23,24. Ex. 3.9. Deut. 24.15.
1 Or, Be long patient, or, Suffer with long patience.
d Deut. 11. 14.
e Phil. 4.5.
2 Or, Groan, or, Grieve not.
f Matt. 24.33.
g Matt. 5.12.
h Job 1.21.
i Job 42.10.
j Ex. 34.6. Num. 14.18. Ps. 25.6,7. Dan. 9.9. Luke 6.36. Rom. 2.4.
k Matt. 5.34.

and continue there a year, and buy and sell, and get gain:

14 Whereas ye know not what *shall be* on the morrow. For what *is* your life? [6]It is even a vapour, that appeareth for a little time, and then vanisheth away.

15 For that ye *ought* to say, If the Lord will, we shall live, and do this, or that.

16 But now ye rejoice in your boastings: all such rejoicing is evil.

17 Therefore [k]to him that knoweth to do good, and doeth *it* not, to him it is sin.

CHAPTER 5

GO to now, *ye* rich men, weep and howl for your miseries that shall come upon *you*.

2 Your riches are corrupted, and your garments are motheaten.

3 Your gold and silver is cankered; and the rust of them shall be a witness against you, and shall eat your flesh as it were fire. [a]Ye have heaped treasure together for the last days.

4 Behold, [b]the hire of the labourers who have reaped down your fields, which is of you kept back by fraud, crieth: and [c]the cries of them which have reaped are entered into the ears of the Lord of sabaoth.

5 Ye have lived in pleasure on the earth, and been wanton; ye have nourished your hearts, as in a day of slaughter.

6 Ye have condemned *and* killed the just; *and* he doth not resist you.

7 [1]Be patient therefore, brethren, unto the coming of the Lord. Behold, the husbandman waiteth for the precious fruit of the earth, and hath long patience for it, until he receive [d]the early and latter rain.

8 Be ye also patient; stablish your hearts: for [e]the coming of the Lord draweth nigh.

9 [2]Grudge not one against another, brethren, lest ye be condemned: behold, the judge [f]standeth before the door.

10 Take, [g]my brethren, the prophets, who have spoken in the name of the Lord, for an example of suffering affliction, and of patience.

11 Behold, we count them happy which endure. Ye have heard of [h]the patience of Job, and have seen [i]the end of the Lord; [j]that the Lord is very pitiful, and of tender mercy.

12 But above all things, my brethren, swear [k]not, neither by heaven, neither by the earth, neither by any other

oath: but let your yea be yea; and
your nay, nay; lest ye fall into condemnation.
13 Is any among you afflicted? let
him pray. Is any merry? let him sing
psalms.
14 Is any sick among you? let him
call for [l]the elders of the church; and
let them pray over him, [m]anointing
him with oil in the name of the
Lord:
15 And the prayer of faith shall save
the sick, and the Lord shall raise him
up; [n]and if he have committed sins,
they shall be forgiven him.
16 Confess *your* faults one to another, and pray one for another, that
ye may be healed. The effectual [o]fer-
vent prayer of a righteous man availeth much.
17 Ē-lī'-ăs was a man subject to like
passions as we are, and [p]he prayed
[3]earnestly that it might not rain: and
it rained not on the earth by the space
of three years and six months.
18 And he prayed again, and the
heaven gave rain, and the earth
brought forth her fruit.
19 Brethren, if any of you do err from
the truth, and one convert him;
20 Let him know, that he which con-
verteth the sinner from the error of
his way shall [q]save a soul from death,
and [r]shall hide a multitude of sins.

l 1 Tim. 5.17. 1 Pet. 5.1.
m Mark 6.13.
n Isa. 33.24. Matt. 9.2.
o Gen. 20.17. Num. 11.2. Deut. 9.18.
p 1 Ki. 17.1.
3 Or, in his prayer.
q 1 Tim. 4.16.
r Ps. 32.1.

THE FIRST EPISTLE GENERAL OF

PETER

CHAPTER 1

PETER, an apostle of Jesus Christ,
to the strangers [a]scattered throughout Pontus, Galatia, Căp-pă-dō'-çĭ-ă,
Asia, and Bī-thy̆n'-ĭ-ă,
2 Elect [b]according to the foreknow-
ledge of God the Father, through
[c]sanctification of the Spirit, unto
obedience and sprinkling [d]of the blood
of Jesus Christ: Grace unto you, and
peace, be multiplied.
3 Blessed *be* the God and Father of
our Lord Jesus Christ, which according to his [1]abundant mercy hath [e]be-
gotten us again unto a lively hope by
[f]the resurrection of Jesus Christ from
the dead,
4 To an inheritance incorruptible,
and undefiled, and that fadeth not
away, reserved in heaven [2]for you,
5 Who [g]are kept by the power of God
through faith unto salvation ready
to be revealed in the last time.
6 Wherein [h]ye greatly rejoice, though
now for a season, if need be, ye are in
heaviness through manifold temptations:
7 That the trial of your faith, being
much more precious than of gold that
perisheth, though [i]it be tried with fire,
might be found unto praise and
honour and glory at the appearing of
Jesus Christ:
8 Whom [j]having not seen, ye love;
[k]in whom, though now ye see *him* not,
yet believing, ye rejoice with joy unspeakable and full of glory:
9 Receiving the end of your faith,
even the salvation of *your* souls.
10 Of [l]which salvation the prophets
have inquired and searched diligently,
who prophesied of the grace *that*
should come unto you:
11 Searching what, or what manner
of time [m]the Spirit of Christ which was
in them did signify, when it testified
beforehand [n]the sufferings of Christ,
and the glory that should follow.
12 Unto [o]whom it was revealed, that
not unto [p]themselves, but unto us
they did minister the things, which
are now reported unto you by them
that have preached the gospel unto
you with [q]the Holy Ghost sent down
from heaven; which [r]things the angels
desire to look into.
13 Wherefore gird up the loins of
your mind, be sober, and hope [3]to the
end for the grace that is to be brought
unto you at [s]the revelation of Jesus
Christ;
14 As obedient children, not fashion-
ing yourselves according to the former
lusts in your ignorance:
15 But as he which hath called you is
holy, so be ye holy in all manner of
conversation;
16 Because it is written, [t]Be ye holy;
for I am holy.
17 And if ye call on the Father, who
without respect of persons judgeth
according to every man's work, pass
the time of your [u]sojourning *here* in
fear:

CHAP. 1
a John 7.35. Acts 2.5,9.
b Rom. 8.29.
c 2 Thes. 2.13.
d Heb. 10.22.
1 much.
e Jas. 1.18.
f 1 Thes. 4. 14.
2 Or, for us.
g John 10.28.
h Matt. 5.12. Rom. 12.12.
i Ps. 66.10. Pro. 17.3. Isa. 48.10.
j 1 John 4.20.
k John 20.29.
l Dan. 2.44. Haggai 2.7. Zech. 6.12.
m Gal. 4.6. ch. 3.19. 2 Pet. 1.21.
n Ps. 22.6. Isa. 53.3.
o Dan. 12.9.
p Heb. 11.39.
q Acts 2.4.
r Ex. 25.20. Dan. 8.13. Eph. 3.10.
3 perfectly.
s Luke 17.30.
t Ex. 19.6. Lev. 11.44.
u Gen. 47.9. 2 Cor. 5.6. Heb. 11.13.

18 Forasmuch as ye know that ye
were not redeemed with corruptible
things, *as* silver and gold, from your
vain conversation *received* [v]by tradition from your fathers;
19 But with the [w]precious blood of
Christ, [x]as of a lamb without blemish
and without spot:
20 Who [y]verily was foreordained
before the foundation of the world,
but was manifest in [z]these last times
for you,
21 Who by him do believe in God,
that raised him up from the dead, and
[a]gave him glory; that your faith and
hope might be in God.
22 Seeing ye have purified your souls
in obeying the truth through the
Spirit unto unfeigned love of the
brethren, *see that ye* love one another
with a pure heart fervently:
23 Being [b]born again, not of corruptible seed, but of incorruptible, by
[c]the word of God, which liveth and
abideth for ever.
24 [4]For all flesh *is* as grass, and all
the glory of man as the flower of grass.
The grass withereth, and the flower
thereof falleth away:
25 But [d]the word of the Lord endureth for ever. And this is the word
which by the gospel is preached unto
you.

CHAPTER 2

WHEREFORE laying aside all
malice, and all guile, and hypo-
crisies and envies, and all evil speak-
ings,
2 As [a]newborn babes, desire the
sincere [b]milk of the word, that ye may
grow thereby:
3 If so be ye have [c]tasted that the
Lord *is* gracious.
4 To whom coming, *as unto* a living
stone, disallowed indeed of men, but
chosen of God, *and* precious,
5 Ye [d]also, as lively stones, [1]are
built up a spiritual house, [e]an holy
priesthood, to offer up [f]spiritual sacrifices, [g]acceptable to God by Jesus
Christ.
6 Wherefore also it is contained in
the scripture, [h]Behold, I lay in Sī-ọn a
chief corner stone, elect, precious: and
he that believeth on him shall not be
confounded.
7 Unto you therefore which believe
he is [2]precious: but unto them which
be disobedient, [i]the stone which the
builders disallowed, the same is made
the head of the corner,
8 And [j]a stone of stumbling, and a
rock of offence, *even to them* which
stumble at the word, being disobedient: [k]whereunto also they were
appointed.
9 But ye *are* a [l]chosen generation, a
[m]royal priesthood, [n]an holy nation, [3]a
peculiar people; that ye should shew
forth the [4]praises of him who hath
called you out of darkness into his
marvellous light:
10 Which [o]in time past *were* not a
people, but *are* now the people of
God: which had not obtained mercy,
but now have obtained mercy.
11 Dearly beloved, I beseech *you* as
strangers and pilgrims, abstain from
fleshly lusts, which war against the
soul;
12 Having your conversation honest
among the Gentiles: that, [5]whereas
they speak against you as evildoers,
they may by *your* good works, which
they shall behold, glorify God [p]in the
day of visitation.
13 Submit yourselves to every ordinance of man for the Lord's sake:
whether it be to the king, as supreme;
14 Or unto governors, as unto them
that are sent by him for the punishment of evildoers, and for the praise
of them that do well.
15 For so is the will of God, that with
well doing ye may put to silence the
ignorance of foolish men:
16 As free, and not [6]using *your*
liberty for a cloke of maliciousness,
but as the servants of God.
17 [7]Honour all *men*. Love the brotherhood. Fear God. Honour the
king.
18 Servants, *be* subject to *your*
masters with all fear; not only to the
good and gentle, but also to the froward.
19 For this *is* [8]thankworthy, if a man
for conscience toward God endure
grief, suffering wrongfully.
20 For what glory *is it*, if, when ye be
buffeted for your faults, ye shall take
it patiently? but if, when ye do well,
and suffer *for it*, ye take it patiently,
this *is* [9]acceptable with God.
21 For even hereunto were ye called:
because Christ also suffered [10]for us,
leaving us an example, that ye should
follow his steps:
22 Who [q]did no sin, neither was
guile found in his mouth:
23 Who, [r]when he was reviled, reviled not again; when he suffered, he
threatened not; but [11]committed *himself* to him that judgeth righteously:
24 Who his own self bare our sins in
his own body [12]on the tree, that we,

v Eze. 20.18. ch. 4.3.
w Matt. 26. 28. Acts 20.28. Rev. 5.9.
x Ex. 12.5. John 1.29.
y Titus 1.2,3. Rev. 13.8.
z Gal. 4.4.
a Phil. 2.9.
b John 1.13. 1 John 3.9.
c John 1.13.
4 Or, For that.
d Isa. 40.8. Luke 16.17.

CHAP. 2

a Matt. 18.3.
b 1 Cor. 3.2.
c Heb. 6.5.
d Eph. 2.21.
1 Or, be ye built.
e Isa. 66.21.
f Hosea 14.2. Mal. 1.11.
g Phil. 4.18.
h Isa. 28.16.
2 Or, an honour.
i Ps. 118.22. Isa. 28.16. Matt. 21.42. Mark 12.10. Luke 20.16-18.
j Isa. 8.14. Luke 2.34.
k Rom. 9.22.
l Deut. 10.15.
m Ex. 19.5,6. Rev. 5.10.
n John 17.19.
3 Or, a purchased people.
4 Or, virtues.
o Hosea 2.23.
5 Or, wherein.
p Luke 19.44.
6 having.
7 Or, Esteem.
8 Or, thank.
9 Or, thank.
10 Some read, for you.
q Isa. 53.9. Luke 23.41.
r Isa. 53.7.
11 Or, committed his cause.
12 Or, to.

being dead to sins, should live unto
righteousness: [s]by whose stripes ye
were healed.
25 For [t]ye were as sheep going
astray; but are now returned [u]unto
the Shepherd and Bishop of your
souls.

CHAPTER 3

LIKEWISE, ye wives, *be* in subjection to your own husbands; that,
if any obey not the word, they [a]also
may without the word be [b]won by the
conversation of the wives;
2 While they behold your chaste
conversation *coupled* with fear.
3 Whose [c]adorning let it not be that
outward *adorning* of plaiting the hair,
and of wearing of gold, or of putting
on of apparel;
4 But *let it be* [d]the hidden man of the
heart, in that which is not corruptible,
even the ornament of a meek and quiet
spirit, which is in the sight of God of
great price.
5 For after this manner in the old
time the holy women also, who trusted
in God, adorned themselves, being in
subjection unto their own husbands:
6 Even as Sara obeyed Abraham,
calling him [e]lord: whose [1]daughters
ye are, as long as ye do well, and are
not afraid with any amazement.
7 Likewise, ye husbands, dwell with
them according to knowledge, giving
honour unto the wife, as unto the
weaker vessel, and as being heirs together of the grace of life; [f]that your
prayers be not hindered.
8 Finally, *be ye* all of one mind, having compassion one of another, [2]love
as brethren, *be* pitiful, *be* courteous:
9 Not rendering evil for evil, or railing for railing: but contrariwise blessing; knowing that ye are thereunto
called, [g]that ye should inherit a
blessing.
10 For [h]he that will love life, and see
good days, let him refrain his tongue
from evil, and his lips that they speak
no guile:
11 Let him eschew evil, and do
good; let him seek peace, and ensue it.
12 For the eyes of the Lord *are* over
the righteous, [i]and his ears *are open*
unto their prayers: but the face of the
Lord *is* [3]against them that do evil.
13 And [j]who *is* he that will harm you,
if ye be followers of that which is
good?
14 But [k]and if ye suffer for righteousness' sake, happy *are ye:* and be [l]not
afraid of their terror, neither be
troubled;

s Isa. 53.5.
t Isa. 53.6. Ps. 119.176. Matt. 10.6. Luke 15.4.
u Eze. 34.23. John 10.11. Heb. 13.20.

CHAP. 3

a 1 Cor. 7.16.
b Matt. 18. 15.
c Isa. 3.16-24.
d Ps. 45.13.
e Gen. 18.12.
1 children.
f Job 42.8. Matt. 5.23.
2 Or, loving to the brethren.
g Matt. 25. 34. Luke 12.32. Rev. 21.7.
h Ps. 34.12.
i John 9.31.
3 upon.
j Pro. 16.7.
k Matt. 5.10.
l Isa. 8.12.
m Ps. 119.46. Acts 4.8-12.
4 Or, reverence.
n 2 Tim. 3.12.
o Col. 1.21.
p Rom. 1.4.
q Gen. 6.3. ch. 1.11,12. 2 Pet. 1.21
r Isa. 42.7.
s Heb. 11.7.
t 2 Pet. 2.5.
u Eph. 5.26.
v Ps. 110.1. Acts 1.11. Rom. 3.34. Eph. 1.20. Heb. 1.3.

CHAP. 4

a Rom. 6.2,7. Gal. 5.24.
b Acts 10.42. Rom. 14.10. 2 Tim. 4.1.
c ch. 3.19.

15 But sanctify the Lord God in your
hearts: and [m]*be* ready always to *give*
an answer to every man that asketh
you a reason of the hope that is in you
with meekness and [4]fear:
16 Having a good conscience; that,
whereas they speak evil of you, as of
evildoers, they may be ashamed that
falsely accuse your good conversation
in Christ.
17 For *it is* better, if the will of God
be so, that ye [n]suffer for well doing,
than for evil doing.
18 For Christ also hath once suffered
for sins, the just for the unjust, that he
might bring us to God, being put to
death [o]in the flesh, but [p]quickened by
the Spirit:
19 By [q]which also he went and
preached unto the spirits [r]in prison;
20 Which sometime were disobedient, when once the longsuffering of
God waited in the days of Noah, while
the ark [s]was a preparing, [t]wherein
few, that is, eight souls were saved by
water.
21 The [u]like figure whereunto *even*
baptism doth also now save us (not
the putting away of the filth of the
flesh, but the answer of a good
conscience toward God,) by the resurrection of Jesus Christ:
22 Who is gone into heaven, and is
[v]on the right hand of God; angels and
authorities and powers being made
subject unto him.

CHAPTER 4

FORASMUCH then as Christ hath
suffered for us in the flesh, arm
yourselves likewise with the same
mind: for he [a]that hath suffered in the
flesh hath ceased from sin;
2 That he no longer should live the
rest of *his* time in the flesh to the lusts
of men, but to the will of God.
3 For the time past of *our* life may
suffice us to have wrought the will of
the Gentiles, when we walked in lasciviousness, lusts, excess of wine, revellings, banquetings, and abominable
idolatries:
4 Wherein they think it strange that
ye run not with *them* to the same excess of riot, speaking evil of *you:*
5 Who shall give account to him that
is ready [b]to judge the quick and the
dead.
6 For for this cause [c]was the gospel
preached also to them that are dead,
that they might be judged according
to men in the flesh, but live according
to God in the spirit.

7 But [d]the end of all things is at hand:
be ye therefore sober, and watch unto
prayer.
8 And above all things have fervent charity among yourselves: for
[e]charity [1]shall cover the multitude of
sins.
9 Use hospitality one to another
without [f]grudging.
10 As [g]every man hath received the
gift, *even so* minister the same one
to another, as good stewards of the
manifold grace of God.
11 If [h]any man speak, *let him speak*
as the oracles of God; if any man
minister, *let him do it* as of the ability
which God giveth: that [i]God in
all things may be glorified through
Jesus Christ, [j]to whom be praise
and dominion for ever and ever.
Ä-mĕn.
12 Beloved, think it not strange concerning the fiery trial which is to try
you, as though some strange thing
happened unto you:
13 But rejoice, inasmuch as [k]ye are
partakers of Christ's sufferings; that,
when his glory shall be revealed, ye
may be glad also with exceeding
joy.
14 If [l]ye be reproached for the name
of Christ, happy *are ye;* for the [m]spirit
of glory and of God resteth upon you:
on their part he is evil spoken of, but
on your part he is glorified.
15 But let none of you suffer as a
murderer, or *as* a thief, or *as* an evildoer, or as a busybody in other men's
matters.
16 Yet if *any man suffer* as a Christian, let him not be ashamed; but
[n]let him glorify God on this behalf.
17 For the time *is come* [o]that judgment must begin at the house of God:
and [p]if *it* first *begin* at us, what [q]shall
the end *be* of them that obey not the
gospel of God?
18 And [r]if the righteous scarcely be
saved, where shall the ungodly and
the sinner appear?
19 Wherefore let them that suffer
according to the will of God [s]commit
the keeping of their souls *to him* in
well doing, as unto a faithful Creator.

CHAPTER 5

THE elders which are among you
I exhort, who am [a]also an elder,
and [b]a witness of the sufferings of
Christ, and also [c]a partaker of the
glory that shall be revealed:
2 Feed [d]the flock of God [1]which is
among you, taking the oversight
thereof, not by constraint, but willingly; not for filthy lucre, but of a
ready mind;
3 Neither as [2]being lords [e]over *God's*
heritage, but being ensamples to the
flock.
4 And when [f]the chief Shepherd
shall appear, ye shall receive a crown
of glory that fadeth not away.
5 Likewise, ye younger, submit yourselves unto the elder. Yea, all [g]*of you*
be subject one to another, and be
clothed with humility: for God resisteth the proud, and giveth [h]grace
to the humble.
6 Humble yourselves therefore under
the mighty hand of God, that he may
exalt you in due time:
7 Casting [i]all your care upon him;
for he careth for you.
8 Be sober, be vigilant; because your
adversary the devil, as a roaring lion,
walketh about, seeking whom he may
devour:
9 Whom resist stedfast in the faith,
knowing that the same afflictions are
accomplished in your brethren that
are in the world.
10 But the God of all grace, who hath
called us unto his eternal glory by
Christ Jesus, after that ye have suffered a while, make you perfect, stablish,
strengthen, settle *you*.
11 To him *be* glory and dominion for
ever and ever. Ä-mĕn.
12 By [j]Sĭl-vā-nŭs, a faithful brother
unto you, as I suppose, I have written
[k]briefly, exhorting, and testifying that
this is the true grace of God wherein
ye stand.
13 The *church that is* at [l]Babylon,
elected together with *you*, saluteth
you; and *so doth* [m]Marcus my son.
14 Greet ye one another with a kiss
of charity. Peace *be* with you all that
are in Christ Jesus. Ä-mĕn.

d Matt. 24. 13. Phil. 4.5. Heb. 10.25.
e Pro. 10.12. Jas. 5.20.
1 Or, will.
f Deut. 15.7.
g 1 Cor. 4.7.
h Jer. 23.22.
i Eph. 5.20. ch. 2.5.
j ch. 5.11. Rev. 1.6.
k Rom. 8.17. 2 Cor. 1.7. Phil. 3.10. Col. 1.24. Rev. 1.9.
l Matt. 5.11.
m Matt. 10. 20. 2 Cor. 12.9.
n Acts 5.41.
o Isa. 10.12. Jer. 25.29. Mal. 3.5.
p Luke 23.31.
q Luke 10.12.
r Pro. 11.31.
s Ps. 31.5. Luke 23.46.

CHAP. 5

a Philem. 9.
b Luke 24.48. Acts 1.8.
c Rom. 8.17. Rev. 1.9.
d John 21.15.
1 Or, as much as in you is.
2 Or, over-ruling.
e Ps. 74.2.
f Heb. 13.20.
g Eph. 5.21. Phil. 2.3.
h Ps. 34.18. Isa. 57.16.
i Ps. 37.5. Matt. 6.25. Luke 12.11. Phil. 4.6.
j 2 Cor. 1.19.
k Heb. 13.22.
l Gen. 10.10. Rev. 17.5, 18.
m Acts 12.12.

THE SECOND EPISTLE GENERAL OF

PETER

CHAPTER 1

SIMON Peter, a servant and an apostle of Jesus Christ, to them that have obtained [a]like precious faith with us through the righteousness [1]of God and our Saviour Jesus Christ:

2 Grace and peace be multiplied unto you through the knowledge of God, and of Jesus our Lord,

3 According as his divine power hath given unto us all things that *pertain* unto life and godliness, through [b]the knowledge of him that [c]hath called us [2]to glory and virtue:

4 Whereby [d]are given unto us exceeding great and precious promises: that by these ye might [e]be partakers of the divine nature, having escaped the corruption that is in the world through lust.

5 And beside this, giving all diligence, add to your faith virtue; and [f]to virtue knowledge;

6 And to knowledge temperance; and to temperance patience; and to patience godliness;

7 And to godliness brotherly kindness; and [g]to brotherly kindness charity.

8 For if these things be in you, and abound, they make *you that ye shall* neither *be* [3]barren nor unfruitful in the knowledge of our Lord Jesus Christ.

9 But he that lacketh these things [h]is blind, and cannot see afar off, and hath forgotten that he was [i]purged from his old sins.

10 Wherefore the rather, brethren, give diligence [j]to make your calling and election sure: for if ye do these things, ye shall never fall:

11 For [k]so an entrance shall be ministered unto you abundantly into the everlasting kingdom of our Lord and Saviour Jesus Christ.

12 Wherefore I will not be negligent to put you always in remembrance of these things, though ye know *them*, and be established in the present truth.

13 Yea, I think it meet, as long as I am in this tabernacle, to stir you up by putting *you* in remembrance;

14 Knowing [l]that shortly I must put off *this* my tabernacle, even as our [m]Lord Jesus Christ hath shewed me.

15 Moreover I will endeavour that ye may be able after my decease to have these things always in remembrance.

16 For we have not followed cunningly devised fables, when we made known unto you the power and coming of our Lord Jesus Christ, but were eyewitnesses of his majesty.

17 For he received from God the Father honour and glory, when there came such a voice to him from the excellent glory, This [n]is my beloved Son, in whom I am well pleased.

18 And this voice which came from heaven we heard, when we were with him in [o]the holy mount.

19 We have also a more [p]sure word of prophecy; whereunto ye do well that ye take heed, as unto a light that shineth in a dark place, until the day dawn, and the [q]day star arise in your hearts:

20 Knowing this first, that [r]no prophecy of the scripture is of any private interpretation.

21 For [s]the prophecy came not [4]in old time by the will of man: but [t]holy men of God spake *as they were* moved by the Holy Ghost.

CHAPTER 2

BUT [a]there were false prophets also among the people, even as [b]there shall be false teachers among you, who privily shall bring in damnable heresies, even denying the Lord [c]that bought them, and bring upon themselves swift destruction.

2 And many shall follow their [1]pernicious ways; by reason of whom the way of truth shall be evil spoken of.

3 And through covetousness shall they with feigned words make merchandise of you: whose judgment now of a long time lingereth not, and their damnation slumbereth not.

4 For if God spared not [d]the angels [e]that sinned, but [f]cast *them* down to hell, and delivered *them* into chains of darkness, to be reserved unto judgment;

5 And spared not the old world, but

CHAP. 1

a Acts 11.17. Eph. 4.5.
1 of our God and Saviour.
b John 17.3.
c 1 Thes. 2. 12. 2 Tim. 1.9. 1 Pet. 2.9.
2 Or, by.
d 2 Cor. 7.1.
e Eph. 4.24. Heb. 12.10. 1 John 3.2.
f Pro. 1.7. Hosea 4.6. 2 Cor. 6.4,6. 1 Pet. 3.7. ch. 3.18.
g Gal. 6.10. 1 Thes. 3.12. 1 John 4.21.
3 idle.
h 1 John 2.9.
i Eph. 5.26. Heb. 9.14. 1 John 1.7.
j 1 John 3.19.
k 2 Tim. 4.8.
l Deut. 4.21.
m John 21. 18.
n Matt. 3.17. Mark 1.11. Luke 3.22.
o Gen. 28.16, 17. Ex. 3.5. Acts 7.33.
p Isa. 8.20.
q 2 Cor. 4.4, 6. Rev. 2.28.
r Rom. 12.6.
s 2 Tim. 3.16. 1 Pet. 1.11.
4 Or, at any time.
t 2 Sam. 23.2. Luke 1.70. Acts 1.16.

CHAP. 2

a Deut. 13.1.
b Matt. 24. 11.
c 1 Cor. 6.20. Gal. 3.13. Eph. 1.7. Heb. 10.29.
1 Or, lascivious ways, as some copies read.
d Job 4.18.
e John 8.44.
f Luke 8.31.

saved Noah [g]the eighth *person*, a
preacher of righteousness, bringing
in the flood upon the world of the ungodly;
6 And [h]turning the cities of Sodom
and Gō-mŏr′-rhă into ashes condemned *them* with an overthrow, making
them an ensample unto those that
after should live ungodly;
7 And delivered just Lot, vexed with
the filthy conversation of the wicked:
8 (For that righteous man dwelling
among them, in seeing and hearing,
vexed *his* righteous soul from day to
day with *their* unlawful deeds;)
9 The [i]Lord knoweth how to deliver
the godly out of temptations, and to
reserve the unjust unto the day of
judgment to be punished:
10 But chiefly them that walk after
the flesh in the lust of uncleanness, and
despise [2]government. Presumptuous
are they, selfwilled, they are not afraid
to speak evil of dignities.
11 Whereas [j]angels, which are greater in power and might, bring not
railing accusation [3]against them before the Lord.
12 But these, [k]as natural brute
beasts, made to be taken and destroyed, speak evil of the things that they
understand not; and shall utterly
perish in their own corruption;
13 And [l]shall receive the reward of
unrighteousness, *as* they that count it
pleasure [m]to riot in the day time.
Spots *they are* and blemishes, sporting themselves with their own deceiv-
ings while they [n]feast with you;
14 Having eyes full of [4]adultery, and
that cannot cease from sin; beguiling
unstable souls: an heart they have
exercised with covetous practices;
cursed children:
15 Which have forsaken the right
way, and are gone astray, following
the way of [o]Bā′-lāam *the son* of Bō′-sŏr,
who loved the wages of unrighteousness;
16 But was rebuked for his iniquity:
the dumb ass speaking with man's
voice forbad the madness of the
prophet.
17 These are wells without water,
clouds that are carried with a tempest;
to whom the mist of darkness is reserved for ever.
18 For when they speak great swelling *words* of vanity, they allure
through the lusts of the flesh, *through
much* wantonness, those that [p]were
[5]clean escaped from them who live in
error.
19 While they promise [q]them liberty,
they themselves are [r]the servants of
corruption: for of whom a man is
overcome, of the same is he brought
in bondage.
20 For [s]if after they have [t]escaped
the pollutions of the world through
the knowledge of the Lord and
Saviour Jesus Christ, they are again
entangled therein, and overcome, the
latter end is worse with them than the
beginning.
21 For [u]it had been better for them
not to have known the way of righteousness, than, after they have known
it, to turn from the holy commandment delivered unto them.
22 But it is happened unto them
according to the true proverb, [v]The
dog *is* turned to his own vomit again;
and the sow that was washed to her
wallowing in the mire.

CHAPTER 3

THIS second epistle, beloved, I
now write unto you; in *both* which
[a]I stir up your pure minds by way of
remembrance:
2 That ye may be mindful of the
words which were spoken before by
the holy prophets, [b]and of the commandment of us the apostles of the
Lord and Saviour:
3 Knowing [c]this first, that there shall
come in the last days scoffers, walking
[d]after their own lusts,
4 And saying, [e]Where is the promise
of his coming? for since the fathers
fell asleep, all things continue as *they
were* from the beginning of the
creation.
5 For this they willingly are ignorant
of, that [f]by the word of God the heavens were of old, and the earth [1]stand-
ing out of the water and in the water:
6 Whereby [g]the world that then
was, being overflowed with water,
perished:
7 But the heavens and the earth,
which are now, by the same word are
kept in store, reserved unto [h]fire
against the day of judgment and perdition of ungodly men.
8 But, beloved, be not ignorant of
this one thing, that one day *is* with the
Lord as [i]a thousand years, and a thousand years as one day.
9 The [j]Lord is not slack concerning
his promise, as some men count
slackness; but is [k]longsuffering to
us-ward, not [l]willing that any should
perish, but [m]that all should come to
repentance.

g Gen. 7.1. Heb. 11.7.
h Gen. 19.24.
i Ps. 34.17.
2 Or, dominion.
j Jude 9.
3 Some read, against themselves.
k Jer. 12.3.
l Isa. 3.11. Phil. 3.19.
m Rom. 13. 13.
n 1 Cor. 11. 20,21.
4 an adulteress.
o Num. 22.
p Acts 2.40. ch. 1.4.
5 Or, for a little, or, a while, as some read.
q Gal. 5.13. 1 Pet. 2.16.
r John 8.34.
s Matt. 12.45. Luke 11.26. Heb. 6.4.
t ch. 1.4.
u Luke 12.47. John 9.41.
v Pro. 26.11.

CHAP. 3

a 2 Tim. 1.6. ch. 1.13.
b Jude 17.
c 1 Tim. 4.1. 2 Tim. 3.1.
d ch. 2.10.
e Isa. 5.19. Matt. 24.48. Luke 12.45.
f Gen. 1.6. Ps. 33.6. Heb. 11.3.
1 consisting.
g Gen. 7.11. ch. 2.5.
h Matt. 25. 41. Heb. 1.11.
i Ps. 90.4.
j Hab. 2.3.
k Isa. 30.18. 1 Pet. 3.20.
l Eze. 18.23.
m Rom. 2.4.

10 But [n]the day of the Lord will come
as a thief in the night; in the which
[o]the heavens shall pass away with a
great noise, and the elements shall
melt with fervent heat, the earth also
and the works that are therein shall
be burned up.
11 *Seeing* then *that* all these things
shall be dissolved, what manner *of*
persons ought ye to be in *all* holy conversation and godliness,
12 Looking for and [2]hasting unto the
coming of the day of God, wherein
the heavens being on fire shall [p]be
dissolved, and the elements shall [q]melt
with fervent heat?
13 Nevertheless we, according to his
promise, look for [r]new heavens and a
new earth, wherein dwelleth righteousness. 10 IH Isa. 35:1,2
14 Wherefore, beloved, seeing that
ye look for such things, be diligent
that ye may be found of him in peace,
without spot, and blameless.
15 And account *that* [s]the longsuffering of our Lord *is* salvation; even as
our beloved brother Paul also according to the wisdom given unto him hath
written unto you;
16 As also in all *his* epistles, speaking
[t]in them of these things; in which are
some things hard to be understood,
which they that are unlearned and unstable wrest, as *they do* also the other
scriptures, unto their own destruction. Sc Rev 1:1
17 Ye therefore, beloved, seeing ye
know *these things* before, [u]beware lest
ye also, being led away with the error
of the wicked, fall from your own
stedfastness.
18 But grow in grace, and *in* the
knowledge of our Lord and Saviour
Jesus Christ. To him *be* glory both
now and for ever. Ā-mĕn.

n Matt. 24. 43. Luke 12.39. *o* Matt. 24. 35. Rev. 20.11. 2 Or, hasting the coming. *p* Ps. 50.3. Isa. 34.4. *q* Micah 1.4. *r* Isa. 65.17. Rev. 21. *s* Rom. 2.4. Eph. 1.7. Col. 1.27. 1 Pet. 3.20. *t* Rom. 8.19. 1 Cor. 15.24. 1 Thes. 4.15. *u* Eph. 4.14.

THE FIRST EPISTLE GENERAL OF
JOHN

CHAPTER 1

THAT [a]which was from the beginning, which we have heard,
[b]which we have seen with our eyes,
which we have looked upon, and our
[c]hands have handled, of the [d]Word
of life;
2 (For the life was manifested, and
we have seen *it*, and bear witness, and
shew unto you that eternal life, which
was with the Father, [e]and was manifested unto us;)
3 That which we have seen and heard
declare we unto you, that ye also may
have fellowship with us: and [f]truly
our fellowship *is* with the Father, and
with his Son Jesus Christ.
4 And these things write we unto you,
that your joy may be full.
5 This then is the message which we
have heard of him, and declare unto
you, that God [g]is light, and in him is
no darkness at all.
6 If we say that we have fellowship
with him, and walk in darkness, we
lie, and do not the truth:
7 But if we walk in the light, as he is
in the light, we have fellowship one
with another, and the blood of Jesus
Christ his Son cleanseth us from all
sin.
8 If [h]we say that we have no sin, we
deceive ourselves, and the truth is not
in us.
9 If [i]we confess our sins, he is faithful and just to forgive us *our* sins, and
to cleanse us from all unrighteousness.
10 If we say that we have not sinned,
we make him a liar, and his word is
not in us.

CHAPTER 2

MY little children, these things
write I unto you, that ye sin not.
And if any man sin, [a]we have an advocate with the Father, Jesus Christ the
righteous:
2 And [b]he is the propitiation for our
sins: and not for ours only, but [c]also
for *the sins of* the whole world.
3 And hereby we do know that we
know him, if we keep his commandments.
4 He that saith, I know him, and
keepeth not his commandments, is a
liar, and the truth is not in him. 14LG Hebs:10
5 But whoso [d]keepeth his word, in
him verily is the love of God perfected: hereby know we that we are in
him.
6 He [e]that saith he abideth in him
ought himself [f]also so to walk, even as
he walked.
7 Brethren, [g]I write no new commandment unto you, but an old com-

CHAP. 1 *a* Micah 5.2. *b* 2 Pet. 1.16. *c* Luke 24.39. *d* Rev. 19.13. *e* John 1.1,2. *f* John 15.4. 1 Cor. 1.9. *g* John 1.9. John 8.12. Rev. 1.5. *h* 1 Ki. 8.46. Eccl. 7.20. Jas. 3.2. *i* Lev. 26.40-42. Ps. 32.5. Pro. 28.13.

CHAP. 2 *a* Rom. 8.34. 1 Tim. 2.5. Heb. 9.24. *b* Rom. 3.25. ch. 4.10. *c* John 1.29. John 4.42. 2 Cor. 5.18-21. *d* Titus 2.11. *e* John 15.4. *f* Matt. 11.29. *g* 2 John 5.

mandment which [h]ye had from the
beginning. The old commandment is
the word which ye have heard from
the beginning.
8 Again, [i]a new commandment I
write unto you, which thing is true in
him and in you: [j]because the darkness
is past, and the [k]true light now shineth.
9 He that saith he is in the light, and
hateth his brother, is in darkness even
until now.
10 He that loveth his brother abideth
in the light, and [l]there is none [1]oc-
casion of stumbling in him.
11 But he that hateth his brother is in
darkness, [m]and walketh in darkness,
and knoweth not whither he goeth, because that darkness hath blinded his
eyes.
12 I write unto you, little children,
because [n]your sins are forgiven you
for his name's sake.
13 I write unto you, fathers, because
ye have known him [o]*that is* from the
beginning. I write unto you, young
men, because ye have overcome the
wicked one. I write unto you, little
children, because ye have known the
Father.
14 I have written unto you, fathers,
because ye have known him *that is*
from the beginning. I have written unto you, young men, because [p]ye are
strong, and [q]the word of God abideth
in you, and ye have overcome the
wicked one.
15 Love not the world, neither the
things *that are* in the world. If [r]any
man love the world, the love of the
Father is not in him.
16 For all that *is* in the world, the lust
of the flesh, [s]and the lust of the eyes,
and the pride of life, is not of the
Father, but is of the world.
17 And the world passeth away, and
the lust thereof: but he that doeth the
will of God [t]abideth for ever.
18 Little children, [u]it is the last time:
and as ye have heard [v]that ăn-tī-chrīst
shall come, [w]even now are there many
ăn-tī-christs; whereby we know that
it is the last time.
19 They went out from us, but they
were not of us; for [x]if they had been
of us, they would *no doubt* have continued with us: but *they went out*, that
[y]they might be made manifest that
they were not all of us.
20 But [z]ye have an unction [a]from the
Holy One, and [b]ye know all things.
21 I have not written unto you because ye know not the truth, but because ye know it, and that no lie is of
the truth.
22 Who is a liar but he that denieth
that Jesus is the Christ? He is ăn-tī-
chrīst, that denieth the Father and the
Son.
23 Whosoever denieth the Son, the
same hath not the Father: [*but*] [c]*he
that acknowledgeth the Son hath the
Father also.*
24 Let that therefore abide in you,
which ye [d]have heard from the beginning. If that which ye have heard from
the beginning shall remain in you, [e]ye
also shall continue in the Son, and in
the Father.
25 And [f]this is the promise that he
hath promised us, *even* eternal life.
26 These *things* have I written unto
you concerning them that seduce you.
27 But the anointing which ye have
received of him abideth in you, and
[g]ye need not that any man teach you:
but as the same anointing [h]teacheth
you of all things, and is truth, and is no
lie, and even as it hath taught you, ye
shall abide in [2]him.
28 And now, little children, abide in
him; that, when he shall appear, we
may have confidence, and not be
ashamed before him at his coming.
29 If [i]ye know that he is righteous,
[3]ye know that every one that doeth
righteousness is born of him.

CHAPTER 3

BEHOLD, what manner of love the
Father hath bestowed upon us,
that [a]we should be called the sons of
God: therefore the world knoweth us
not, [b]because it knew him not.
2 Beloved, now are we the sons of
God, and [c]it doth not yet appear what
we shall be: but we know that, when
he shall appear, we [d]shall be like him;
for [e]we shall see him as he is.
3 And every man that hath this hope
in him purifieth himself, even as he is
pure.
4 Whosoever committeth sin transgresseth also the law: for sin is the
transgression of the law.
5 And ye know that he was manifested to [f]take away our sins; and [g]in
him is no sin.
6 Whosoever abideth in him sinneth
not: whosoever sinneth hath not seen
him, neither known him.
7 Little children, let no man deceive
you: he [h]that doeth righteousness is
righteous, even as he is righteous.
8 He [i]that committeth sin is of the
devil; for the devil sinneth from the

h ch. 3.11.
i John 13.34.
j Rom. 13.12. Eph. 5.8.
k John 1.9. John 8.12.
l 2 Pet. 1.10.
1 scandal.
m John 12. 35.
n Luke 24.47. Acts 4.12.
o ch. 1.1.
p Eph. 6.10.
q Jer. 31.33.
r Matt. 6.24. Gal. 1.10.
s Eccl. 5.11.
t Ps. 125.1. Pro. 10.25.
u Heb. 1.2.
v 2 Thes. 2.3.
w Matt. 24.5.
x Matt. 24. 24. John 6.37.
y 1 Cor. 11. 19.
z Ps. 23.5. Isa. 44.3. Luke 4.18. Acts 10.38. Heb. 1.9.
a Mark 1.24. Acts 3.14.
b John 10.4, 5.
c John 14.7.
d 2 John 6.
e John 15.9, 10. ch. 1.3.
f John 17.3.
g John 14.26. Heb. 8.10.
h John 16.13.
2 Or, it.
i Acts 22.14.
3 Or, know ye.

CHAP. 3

a John 1.12.
b John 15.18.
c 1 Cor. 2.9. 2 Cor. 4.17.
d Ps. 17.15. Rom. 8.29.
e Ps. 16.11. Matt. 5.8. 1 Cor. 13.12. 2 Cor. 5.7.
f Isa. 53. Heb. 1.3.
g Isa. 53.9. Gal. 3.13. 1 Pet. 2.22.
h Eze. 18.5.
i Matt. 13.38.

beginning. For this purpose the Son
of God was manifested, [j]that he
might destroy the works of the devil.
9 Whosoever [k]is born of God doth
not commit sin; for [l]his seed remaineth in him: and he cannot sin, because
he is born of God.
10 In this the children of God are
manifest, and the children of the
devil: whosoever doeth not righteousness is not of God, neither he that
loveth not his brother.
11 For this is the [1]message that ye
heard from the beginning, [m]that we
should love one another.
12 Not as [n]Cain, *who* was of that
wicked one, and slew his brother. And
wherefore slew he him? Because his
own works were evil, and his brother's
righteous.
13 Marvel not, my brethren, if the
world hate you.
14 We know that we have passed
from death unto life, because we love
the brethren. He that loveth not *his*
brother abideth in death.
15 Whosoever [o]hateth his brother is
a murderer: and ye know that no
[p]murderer hath eternal life abiding in
him.
16 Hereby [q]perceive we the love *of
God*, because he laid down his life for
us: and we ought to lay down *our*
lives for the brethren.
17 But [r]whoso hath this world's
good, and seeth his brother have need,
and shutteth up his bowels *of compassion* from him, how dwelleth the
love of God in him?
18 My little children, let us not love
in word, neither in tongue; but in deed
and in truth.
19 And hereby we know [s]that we are
of the truth, and shall [2]assure our
hearts before him.
20 For if our heart condemn us, God
is greater than our heart, and knoweth
all things.
21 Beloved, [t]if our heart condemn us
not, [u]*then* have we confidence toward
God.
22 And [v]whatsoever we ask, we receive of him, because we keep his
commandments, [w]and do those things
that are pleasing in his sight.
23 And this is his commandment,
That we should believe on the name
of his Son Jesus Christ, and love one
another, as he gave us commandment.
24 And he that keepeth his commandments [x]dwelleth in him, and he
in him. And [y]hereby we know that he
abideth in us, by the Spirit which he
hath given us.

CHAPTER 4

BELOVED, [a]believe not every
spirit, but try the spirits whether
they are of God: because many [b]false
prophets are gone out into the world.
2 Hereby know ye the Spirit of God:
Every [c]spirit that confesseth that Jesus
Christ is come in the flesh is of God:
3 And [d]every spirit that confesseth
not that Jesus Christ is come in the
flesh is not of God: and this is that
spirit of ăn-tī-christ, whereof ye have
heard that it should come; and even
now already is it in the world.
4 Ye are of God, little children, and
have overcome them: because greater
is he that is in you, than he [e]that is in
the world.
5 They [f]are of the world: therefore
speak they of the world, [g]and the
world heareth them.
6 We are of God: [h]he that knoweth
God heareth us; he that is not of God
heareth not us. Hereby know we [i]the
spirit of truth, and the spirit of error.
7 Beloved, let us love one another:
for love is of God; and every one that
loveth is born of God, and knoweth
God.
8 He that loveth not knoweth not
God; for [j]God is love.
9 In this was manifested the love of
God toward us, because that God sent
his only begotten Son into the world,
that we might live through him.
10 Herein is love, [k]not that we loved
God, but that he loved us, and sent
his Son *to be* the propitiation for our
sins.
11 Beloved, if God so loved us, we
ought also to love one another.
12 No [l]man hath seen God at any
time. If we love one another, God
dwelleth in us, and his love is perfected in us.
13 Hereby [m]know we that we dwell
in him, and he in us, because he hath
given us of his Spirit.
14 And [n]we have seen and do testify
that the [o]Father sent the Son *to be* the
Saviour of the world.
15 Whosoever [p]shall confess that
Jesus is the Son of God, God dwelleth
in him, and he in God.
16 And we have known and believed
the love that God hath to us. God is
love; and he that dwelleth in love
dwelleth in God, and God in him.
17 Herein is [1]our love made perfect,
that we [q]may have boldness in the

j Gen. 3.15. Luke 10.18.
k ch. 5.18.
l 1 Pet. 1.23.
1 Or, commandment.
m John 15. 12.
n Gen. 4.4.
o Matt. 5.21. ch. 4.20.
p 1 Cor. 6.9, 10. Gal. 5.21. Eph. 5.5. 1 Tim. 1.9. Heb. 12.14. Rev. 21.8.
q Rom. 5.8. Eph. 5.2,25.
r Deut. 15.7. Luke 3.11.
s John 18.37.
2 persuade.
t Job 22.26.
u Heb. 10.22.
v Ps. 34.15. Matt. 21.22. Mark 11.24.
w John 8.29.
x John 17.21.
y Eze. 37.27.

CHAP. 4

a Jer. 14.14. Jer. 23.21.
b Matt. 24.5.
c 1 Cor. 12.3. ch. 5.1.
d ch. 2.22. 2 John 7.
e John 12.31. Eph. 2.2.
f John 3.31.
g John 15.19.
h John 8.47. John 10.27. 1 Cor. 14.37. 2 Cor. 10.7. 2 Thes. 1.8.
i Isa. 8.20.
j Ex. 34.6,7. Micah 7.18.
k John 15.16. Titus 3.4.
l Ex. 33.20. 1 Tim. 6.16.
m John 10. 38.
n John 1.14.
o John 3.17.
p Rom. 10.9.
1 love with us.
q Jas. 2.13. ch. 2.28.

day of judgment: [r]because as he is, so
are we in this world.
18 There is no fear in love; but perfect love casteth out fear: because fear
hath torment. He that feareth is not
made perfect in love.
19 We love him, because he first
loved us.
20 If a man say, I love God, and
hateth his brother, he is a liar: for he
that loveth not his brother whom he
hath seen, how can he love God whom
he hath not seen?
21 And [s]this commandment have we
from him, That he who loveth God
love his brother also.

CHAPTER 5

WHOSOEVER [a]believeth that
Jesus [b]is the Christ is born of
God: [c]and every one that loveth him
that begat loveth him also that is begotten of him.
2 By this we know that we love the
children of God, when we love God,
and keep his commandments.
3 For [d]this is the love of God, that we
keep his commandments: and [e]his
commandments are not grievous.
4 For [f]whatsoever is born of God
overcometh the world: and this is the
victory that overcometh the world,
even our faith.
5 Who is he that overcometh the
world, but [g]he that believeth that
Jesus is the Son of God?
6 This is he that came [h]by water and
blood, *even* Jesus Christ; not by water
only, but by water and blood. And
[i]it is the Spirit that beareth witness,
because the Spirit is truth.
7 For there [j]are three that bear
record in heaven, the Father, [k]the
Word, and the Holy Ghost: [l]and these
three are one.
8 And there are three that bear witness in earth, the spirit, and the water,
and the blood: and these three agree
in one.
9 If we receive [m]the witness of men,
the witness of God is greater: for [n]this
is the witness of God which he hath
testified of his Son.
10 He that believeth on the Son of
God hath [o]the witness in himself: he
that believeth not God hath [p]made
him a liar; because he believeth not
the record that God gave of his
Son.
11 And this is the record, that God
hath given to us eternal life, and [q]this
life is in his Son.
12 He [r]that hath the Son hath life;
and he that hath not the Son of God
hath not life.
13 These [s]things have I written unto
you that believe on the name of the
Son of God; [t]that ye may know that
ye have eternal life, and that ye may
believe on the name of the Son of God.
14 And this is the confidence that we
have [1]in him, that, if we ask any thing
according to his will, he heareth us:
15 And if we know that he hear us,
whatsoever we ask, we know that we
have the petitions that we desired of
him.
16 If any man see his brother sin a
sin *which is* not unto death, he shall
ask, and he [u]shall give him life for
them that sin not unto death. [v]There
is a sin unto death: I [w]do not say that
he shall pray for it.
17 All unrighteousness is sin: and
there is a sin not unto death.
18 We know that whosoever is born
of God sinneth not; but he that is begotten of God keepeth himself, and
that wicked one toucheth him not.
19 *And* we know that we are of God,
and the whole world lieth in wickedness.
20 And we know that the Son of God
is come, and hath given us an understanding, that we may know him that
is true, and we are in him that is true,
even in his Son Jesus Christ. This [x]is
the true God, and eternal life.
21 Little children, keep yourselves
from idols. Ä-mĕn.

r ch. 3.3.
s Lev. 19.18. Eph. 5.2. 1 Thes. 4.9.

CHAP. 5
a John 1.12.
b ch. 2.22.
c John 15.23.
d John 14.15.
e Micah 6.8. Matt. 11.30.
f John 16.33.
g Rom. 7.25. 1 Cor. 15.57.
h John 19.34.
i John 15.26.
j Isa. 48.16. Hag. 2.5,7.
k John 1.1.
l Deut. 6.4.
m John 8.17.
n Matt. 3.16.
o Rom. 8.16. Gal. 4.6.
p John 3.33.
q John 1.4.
r Heb. 3.14. ch. 2.23,24.
s John 20.31.
t ch. 1.1,2.
1 Or, concerning him.
u Job 42.8.
v Num. 15. 30. 1 Sam. 2.25. Matt. 12.31, 32. Mark 3.29. Luke 12.10. Heb. 6.4,6.
w Jer. 7.16.
x Isa. 9.6. Acts 20.28. Rom. 9.5.

THE SECOND EPISTLE OF

JOHN

THE [a]elder unto the elect lady and
her children, [b]whom I love in the
truth; and not I only, but also all they
that have known the [c]truth;
2 For the truth's sake, which dwelleth in us, and shall be with us for ever.
3 Grace [1]be with you, mercy, *and*
peace, from God the Father, and from
the Lord Jesus Christ, the Son of the
Father, in truth and love.
4 I rejoiced greatly that I found of
thy children [d]walking in truth, as we
have received a commandment from
the Father.
5 And now I beseech thee, lady, not
[e]as though I wrote a new commandment unto thee, but that which we had
from the beginning, that [f]we love one
another.
6 And [g]this is love, that we walk after
his commandments. This is the commandment, That, [h]as ye have heard
from the beginning, ye should walk
in it.
7 For many deceivers are entered into the world, who confess not that
Jesus Christ is come in the flesh. This
is a deceiver and an ăn-tĭ-chrīst.
8 Look to yourselves, that we lose
not those things which we have
[2]wrought, but that we receive a full
reward.
9 Whosoever transgresseth, and
abideth not in the doctrine of Christ,
hath not God. He that abideth in the
doctrine of Christ, he hath both the
Father and the Son.
10 If there come any unto you, and
bring not this doctrine, receive him
not into *your* house, [i]neither bid him
God speed:
11 For he that biddeth him God
speed is partaker of his evil deeds.
12 Having many things to write unto you, I would not *write* with paper
and ink: but I trust to come unto you,
and speak [3]face to face, that [4]our joy
may be full.
13 The children of thy elect sister
greet thee. Ā-mĕn.

a 1 Pet. 5.1. *b* 1 John 3.18. *c* John 8.32. 2 Thes. 2.13. 1 Tim. 2.4. Heb. 10.26. 1 shall be. *d* 3 John 3. *e* 1 John 2.7. *f* John 15.12. *g* Rom. 13.8, 9. 1 John 5.3. *h* 1 John 1.3. 2 Or, gained: Some copies read, which ye have gained, but that ye receive, etc. *i* Rom. 16.17. 1 Cor. 5.11. 2 Tim. 3.5. 3 mouth to mouth. 4 Or, your.

THE THIRD EPISTLE OF

JOHN

THE elder unto the [a]wellbeloved
Gāi-ŭs, whom I love [1]in the truth.
2 Beloved, I [2]wish above all things
that thou mayest prosper and be
in health, even as thy soul prospereth.
3 For I rejoiced greatly, when the
brethren came and testified of the
truth that is in thee, even as [b]thou
walkest in the truth.
4 I have no greater joy than to hear
that my [c]children walk in truth.
5 Beloved, thou [d]doest faithfully
whatsoever thou doest to the brethren,
and to strangers;
6 Which have borne witness of thy
charity before the church: whom if
thou bring forward on their journey
[3]after a godly sort, thou shalt do
well:
7 Because that for his name's sake
they went forth, [e]taking nothing of
the Gentiles.
8 We therefore ought to receive such,
that we might be fellowhelpers to the
truth.
9 I wrote unto the church: but Dĭ-
ŏt-rĕ-phēs, who loveth to have the
preeminence among them, receiveth
us not.
10 Wherefore, if I come, I will remember his deeds which he doeth,
prating against us with malicious
words: and not content therewith,
neither doth he himself receive the
brethren, and forbiddeth them that
would, and casteth *them* out of the
church.
11 Beloved, [f]follow not that which is
evil, but that which is good. He [g]that

a Acts 19.29. Rom. 16.23. 1 Or, truly. 2 Or, pray. *b* 2 John 4. *c* 1 Cor. 4.15. *d* Luke 12.42. 3 worthy of God. *e* 1 Cor. 9.12, 15. 2 Cor. 11.7. *f* Ps. 37.27. Isa. 1.16. John 10.27. 1 Cor. 4.16. Eph. 5.1. Phil. 3.17. Heb. 6.12. *g* 1 John 2.29.

doeth good is of God: but he that doeth evil hath not seen God.
12 Dē-mē´-trĭ-ŭs [h]hath good report
of all *men*, and of the truth itself: yea,
and we *also* bear record; [i]and ye know
that our record is true.
13 I had many things to write, but I
will not with ink and pen write unto
thee:
14 But I trust I shall shortly see
thee, and we shall speak [4]face to
face. Peace *be* to thee. *Our* friends
salute thee. Greet the friends by
name.

h 1 Thes. 4. 12.
i John 21.24.
4 mouth to mouth.

THE GENERAL EPISTLE OF

JUDE

JUDE, the servant of Jesus Christ,
and [a]brother of James, to them
that are sanctified by God the
Father, and [b]preserved in Jesus
Christ, [c]*and* called:
2 Mercy unto you, and peace, and
love, be multiplied.
3 Beloved, when I gave all diligence
to write unto you [d]of the common
salvation, it was needful for me to
write unto you, and exhort *you* that
ye should earnestly contend for the
faith which was once delivered unto
the saints.
4 For there are certain men crept in
unawares, [e]who were before of old ordained to this condemnation, ungodly
men, turning [f]the grace of our God
into lasciviousness, and [g]denying the
only Lord God, and our Lord Jesus
Christ.
5 I will therefore put you in remembrance, though ye once knew this,
how that the Lord, having saved the
people out of the land of Egypt, afterward [h]destroyed them that believed
not.
6 And [i]the angels which kept not
their [1]first estate, but left their own
habitation, he hath reserved in everlasting chains under darkness unto
[j]the judgment of the great day. Mil Jer 4:23-28
7 Even as [k]Sodom and Gō-mŏr´-rhă,
and the cities about them in like manner, giving themselves over to fornication, and going after [2]strange flesh,
are set forth for an example, suffering
the vengeance of eternal fire.
8 Likewise also these *filthy* dreamers
defile the flesh, despise dominion, and
[l]speak evil of dignities.
9 Yet [m]Michael the archangel, when
contending with the devil he disputed
about [n]the body of Moses, [o]durst not
bring against him a railing accusation,
but said, [p]The Lord rebuke thee.
10 But these speak evil of those
things which they know not: but what
they know naturally, as brute beasts,
in those things they corrupt themselves.
11 Woe unto them! for they have
gone in the way [q]of Cain, and ran
[r]greedily after the error of Bā´-lāam
for reward, and [s]perished in the gainsaying of Côr´-ē.
12 These are spots in your [t]feasts of
charity, when they feast with you,
feeding themselves without fear:
clouds *they are* without water, carried
about [u]of winds; trees whose fruit
withereth, without fruit, twice dead,
plucked up by the roots;
13 Raging [v]waves of the sea, foaming
out their own shame; wandering
stars, to whom is reserved the blackness of darkness for ever.
14 And Ē´-nŏch also, [w]the seventh
from Adam, prophesied of these, saying, Behold, the [x]Lord cometh with
ten thousands of his saints,
15 To execute judgment upon all,
and to convince all that are ungodly
among them of all their ungodly deeds
which they have ungodly committed,
and of all their hard *speeches* which
ungodly sinners have spoken against
him.
16 These are murmurers, complainers, walking after their own lusts; and
their mouth speaketh great swelling
words, having [y]men's persons in
admiration because of advantage.
17 But, beloved, remember ye the
words which were spoken before of
the apostles of our Lord Jesus Christ;
18 How that they told you there
should be mockers in the last time,
who should walk after their own ungodly lusts.
19 These be they [z]who separate
themselves, sensual, having not the
Spirit.
20 But ye, beloved, [a]building up

a Luke 6.16. Acts 1.13.
b John 17.11.
c Rom. 1.7.
d Titus 1.4.
e Rom. 9.21. 1 Pet. 2.8.
f Titus 2.11. Heb. 12.15.
g 2 Pet. 2.1. 1 John 2.22.
h Num. 14. 29. Heb. 3.17. 19.
i Matt. 8.29. 2 Pet. 2.4.
1 Or, principality.
j Rev. 20.10.
k Deut. 29. 23. [illegible] Pet. 2.6.
[illegible]er.
l Ex. 22.28.
m Dan. 10. 13. Rev. 12.7.
n Deut. 34.6.
o 2 Pet. 2.11.
p Zech. 3.2.
q 1 John 3.12.
r Num. 22.7.
s Num. 16.1.
t 1 Cor. 11. 21.
u Eph. 4.14.
v Isa. 57.20.
w Gen. 5.18.
x Dan. 7.10. Heb. 11.5.
y Pro. 28.21.
z Pro. 18.1. Eze. 14.7. Hosea 4.14. Heb. 10.25.
a Col. 2.7. 1 Tim. 1.4.

yourselves on your most holy faith,
praying in [b]the Holy Ghost,
21 Keep yourselves in the love
of God, looking for the mercy of
our Lord Jesus Christ unto eternal
life.
22 And of some have compassion,
making a difference:
23 And others [c]save with fear, pulling [d]*them* out of the fire; hating
even the [e]garment spotted by the
flesh.
24 Now [f]unto him that is able to
keep you from falling, and [g]to present
you faultless before the presence of his
glory with exceeding joy,
25 To [h]the only wise God our
Saviour, *be* glory and majesty, dominion and power, both now and ever.
Ä-mĕn.

b Zech. 12. 10. Matt. 10.20. Rom. 8.26. Gal. 4.6.
c Rom. 11.14. 1 Tim. 4.16.
d Amos 4.11.
e Zech. 3.4,5.
f Eph. 3.20.
g Col. 1.22.
h 1 Tim. 1.17.

THE REVELATION

OF ST. JOHN THE DIVINE

CHAPTER 1

THE Revelation of Jesus Christ,
which [a]God gave unto him, to
shew unto his servants things which
must shortly come to pass; and [b]he
sent and signified *it* by his angel unto
his servant John:
2 Who bare record of the word of
God, and of the testimony of Jesus
Christ, and of all things [c]that he saw.
3 Blessed [d]*is* he that readeth, and
they that hear the words of this prophecy, and keep those things which
are written therein: for the time *is* at
hand.
4 JOHN to the seven churches
which are in Asia: Grace *be* unto
you, and peace, [e]from him which
is, and [f]which was, and which is to
come; and [g]from the seven Spirits
which are before his throne;
5 And from Jesus Christ, [h]*who is* the
faithful witness, *and* the [i]first begotten of the dead, and [j]the prince of the
kings of the earth. Unto [k]him that
loved us, [l]and washed us from our
sins in his own blood,
6 And hath made us kings and
priests unto God and his Father; to
[m]him *be* glory and dominion for ever
and ever. Ä-mĕn.
7 Behold, he [n]cometh with clouds;
and every eye shall see him, [o]and they
also which pierced him: and all kindreds of the earth shall wail because of
him. Even so, Ä-mĕn.
8 I [p]am Alpha and Omega, the beginning and the ending, saith the
Lord, which is, and which was, and
which is to come, the Almighty.
9 I John, who also am your brother,
and companion in tribulation, and [q]in
the kingdom and patience of Jesus
Christ, was in the isle that is called
Patmos, for the word of God, and for
the testimony of Jesus Christ.
10 I [r]was in the Spirit on the [s]Lord's
day, and heard behind me a great
voice, as of a trumpet,
11 Saying, I am Alpha and Omega,
the first and the last: and, What thou
seest, write in a book, and send *it* unto
the seven churches which are in Asia;
unto Ĕph-ĕ-sŭs, and unto Smyrna,
and unto Pĕr-gă-mŏs, and unto Thȳ-
ă-tī-ră, and unto Săr-dĭs, and unto
Philadelphia, and unto Lā-ŏd-ĭ-çē-ă.
12 And I turned to see the voice that
spake with me. And being turned, [t]I
saw seven golden candlesticks;
13 And in the midst of the seven
candlesticks [u]*one* like unto the Son of
man, clothed [v]with a garment down to
the foot, and girt about the paps with
a golden girdle.
14 His head and [w]*his* hairs *were*
white like wool, as white as snow; and
[x]his eyes *were* as a flame of fire;
15 And [y]his feet like unto fine brass,
as if they burned in a furnace; [z]and his
voice as the sound of many waters.
16 And he had in his right hand
seven stars: and [a]out of his mouth
went a sharp twoedged sword: and
his countenance *was* as the sun shineth
in his strength.
17 And [c]when I saw him, I fell at his
feet as dead. And [d]he laid his right
hand upon me, saying unto me, Fear
not; [e]I am the first and the last:
18 *I* [f]*am* he that liveth, and was dead;
and, behold, I am alive for evermore,
Ä-mĕn; and [g]have the keys of hell and
of death.
19 Write the things which thou hast
seen, and the things which are, and
the things which shall be hereafter;
20 The mystery of the seven stars

CHAP. 1
a John 12.49.
b ch. 22.16.
c 1 John 1.1.
d Luke 11.28. ch. 22.7.
e Ex. 3.14. John 8.58. Col. 1.17. Jas. 1.17.
f John 1.1.
g Zech. 3.9.
h John 8.14.
i Col. 1.18.
j Eph. 1.20.
k John 13.34.
l Heb. 9.14.
m 1 Tim. 6. 16.
n Dan. 7.13.
o Zech. 12. 10.
p Isa. 41.4.
q Rom. 8.17.
r 2 Cor. 12.2.
s Acts 20.7. 1 Cor. 16.2.
t Ex. 25.37. Zech. 4.2.
u Dan. 7.13.
v Dan. 10.5.
w Dan. 7.9.
x ch. 2.18.
y Eze. 1.7.
z Eze. 43.2.
a Eph. 6.17. Heb. 4.12.
b Acts 26.13.
c Eze. 1.28.
d Dan. 8.18.
e Isa. 41.4. Isa. 44.6.
f Rom. 6.9.
g Ps. 68.20. Isa. 22.22. Matt. 16.19. ch. 3.7. ch. 20.1.

which thou sawest in my right hand,
and the seven golden candlesticks.
The seven stars are [h]the angels of the
seven churches: and the [i]seven candlesticks which thou sawest are the
seven churches.

CHAPTER 2

UNTO the angel of the church of
[a]Ĕph'-ĕ-sŭs write; These things
saith [b]he that holdeth the seven stars
in his right hand, who walketh in the
midst of the seven golden candlesticks;
2 I [c]know thy works, and thy labour,
and thy patience, and how thou canst
not bear them which are evil: and
thou [d]hast tried them [e]which say they
are apostles, and are not, and hast
found them liars:
3 And hast borne, and hast patience,
and for my name's sake hast laboured,
and hast [f]not fainted.
4 Nevertheless I have *somewhat*
against thee, because thou hast left
thy first love.
5 Remember therefore from whence
thou art fallen, and repent, and do the
first works; [g]or else I will come unto
thee quickly, and will remove thy
candlestick out of his place, except
thou repent.
6 But this thou hast, that thou hatest
the deeds of the Nĭc-ō-lā-ĭ'-tāns, which
I also hate.
7 He [h]that hath an ear, let him
hear what the Spirit saith unto the
churches; To him that overcometh
will I give [i]to eat of [j]the tree of life,
which is in the midst of the paradise
of God.
8 And unto the angel of the church
in Smyrna write; These things saith
[k]the first and the last, which was dead,
and is alive;
9 I know thy works, and tribulation,
and poverty, (but thou [l]art rich) and
I know the blasphemy of [m]them which
say they are Jews, and are not, but *are*
the synagogue of Satan.
10 Fear [n]none of those things which
thou shalt suffer: behold, the devil
shall cast *some* of you into prison, that
ye may be tried; and ye shall have
tribulation ten days: be [o]thou faithful unto death, and I will give thee [p]a
crown of life.
11 He [q]that hath an ear, let him
hear what the Spirit saith unto the
churches; He that overcometh shall
not be hurt of the [r]second death.
12 And to the angel of the church in
Pĕr'-gă-mŏs write; These things saith
he [s]which hath [t]the sharp sword with
two edges;
13 I know thy works, and where thou
dwellest, *even* where Satan's seat *is*:
and thou holdest fast my name, and
hast not denied my faith, even in those
days wherein Ăn'-tĭ-păs *was* my faithful martyr, who was slain among you,
[u]where Satan dwelleth.
14 But I have a few things against
thee, because thou hast there them
that hold the doctrine of [v]Bā-lāam,
who taught Balac to cast a stumblingblock before the children of Israel,
[w]to eat things sacrificed unto idols,
[x]and to commit fornication.
15 So hast thou also them that hold
the doctrine of the Nĭc-ō-lā-ĭ'-tāns,
which thing I hate.
16 Repent; or else I will come unto
thee quickly, and [y]will fight against
them with the sword of my mouth.
17 He that hath an ear, let him
hear what the Spirit saith unto the
churches; To him that overcometh
will I give to eat of the hidden măn'-nă,
and will give him a white stone, and
in the stone [z]a new name written,
which no man knoweth saving he that
receiveth *it*.
18 And unto the angel of the church
in Thȳ-ă-tī'-ră write; These things
saith the Son of God, who [a]hath his
eyes like unto a flame of fire, and his
feet *are* like fine brass;
19 I know thy works, and charity,
and service, and faith, and thy
patience, and thy works; and the last
to be more than the first.
20 Notwithstanding I have a few
things against thee because thou
sufferest that woman [b]Jĕz'-ĕ-bĕl, which
calleth herself a prophetess, to teach
and to seduce my servants to commit
fornication, and to eat things sacrificed unto idols.
21 And I gave her space [c]to repent
of her fornication; and she repented
not.
22 Behold, I will cast her into a bed,
and them that commit adultery with
her into great tribulation, except they
repent of their deeds.
23 And I will kill her children with
death; and all the churches shall know
that [d]I am he which searcheth the
reins and hearts: and [e]I will give unto
every one of you according to your
works.
24 But unto you I say, and unto the
rest in Thȳ-ă-tī-ră, as many as have
not this doctrine, and which have not
known [f]the depths of Satan, as they

h Mal. 2.7.
i Matt. 5.15. Phil. 2.15.
CHAP. 2
a Acts 19.
b ch. 1.16.
c Ps. 1.6. 1 Thes. 1.3. ch. 3.1,8, 15.
d 1 John 4.1.
e 2 Cor. 11. 13.
f Gal. 6.9. Heb. 12.3,5.
g Matt. 21. 41. Mark 12.9. ch. 3.3.
h Matt. 11. 15. ch. 13.9.
i ch. 22.
j Gen. 2.9.
k ch. 1.8.
l Luke 12.21. Jas. 2.5.
m Rom. 2.17.
n Matt.10.22.
o Matt. 24. 13. Mark 13.13.
p Jas. 1.12.
q ch. 13.9.
r ch. 20.14.
s ch. 1.16.
t Josh. 5.13.
u Lev. 17.7. Deut. 32.16, 17.
v Num. 25.1. 2 Pet. 2.15.
w Acts 15.29.
x 1 Cor. 6.13.
y Isa. 11.4.
z ch. 3.12.
a ch. 1.14.
b 1 Ki. 16.31.
c Rom. 2.4.
d 1 Sam. 16.7. 1 Chr. 28.9. Ps. 7.9. Acts 1.24.
e Ps. 62.12. Matt. 16.27. ch. 20.12.
f 2 Cor. 2.11. ch. 12.9.

speak; [g]I will put upon you none other burden.

25 But that which ye have *already* hold fast till I come.

26 And he that overcometh, and keepeth my [h]works unto the end, to [i]him will I give power over the nations:

27 And [j]he shall rule them with a rod of iron; as the vessels of a potter shall they be broken to shivers: even as I received of my Father.

28 And I will give him [k]the morning star.

29 He that hath an ear, let him hear what the Spirit saith unto the churches.

CHAPTER 3

AND unto the angel of the church in Sär′dĭs write; These things saith he that hath the seven Spirits of God, and the seven stars; I know thy works, that thou hast a name that thou livest, [a]and art dead.

2 Be watchful, and strengthen the things which remain, that are ready to die: for I have not found thy works perfect before God.

3 Remember therefore how thou hast received and heard, and hold fast, and repent. [b]If therefore thou shalt not watch, I will come on thee as a thief, and thou shalt not know what hour I will come upon thee.

4 Thou hast [c]a few names even in Sär′dĭs which have not [d]defiled their garments; and they shall walk with me [e]in white: for they are worthy.

5 He that overcometh, the same shall be clothed in white raiment; and I will [f]not blot out his name out of the book [g]of life, but [h]I will confess his name before my Father, and before his angels.

6 He that hath an ear, let him hear what the Spirit saith unto the churches.

7 And to the angel of the church in Philadelphia write; These things saith he [i]that is holy, [j]he that is true, he that hath [k]the key of David, [l]he that openeth, and no man shutteth; [m]and shutteth, and no man openeth;

8 I know thy works: behold, I have set before thee [n]an open door, and no man can shut it: for thou hast a little strength, and hast kept my word, and hast not denied my name.

9 Behold, I will make them of the synagogue of Satan, which say they are Jews, and are not, but do lie; behold, [o]I will make them to come and worship before thy feet, and to know that I have loved thee.

10 Because thou hast kept the word of my patience, [p]I also will keep thee from the hour of temptation, which shall come upon all the world, to try them that dwell upon the earth.

11 Behold, I come quickly: hold that fast which thou hast, that no man take thy crown.

12 Him that overcometh will I make [q]a pillar in the temple of my God, and he shall go no more out: and [r]I will write upon him the name of my God, and the name of the city of my God, *which is* new [s]Jerusalem, which cometh down out of heaven from my God: [t]and *I will write upon him* my new name.

13 He that hath an ear, let him hear what the Spirit saith unto the churches.

14 And unto the angel of the church [1]of the Lā-ŏd-ĭ-çē′ăns write; These things saith the [u]A′mĕn, the faithful and true [v]witness, the [w]beginning of the creation of God;

15 I know thy works, that thou art neither cold nor hot: I would thou wert cold or hot.

16 So then because thou art lukewarm, and neither cold nor hot, I will spue thee out of my mouth.

17 Because thou sayest, [x]I am rich, and increased with goods, and have need of nothing; and knowest not that thou art wretched, and miserable, and poor, and blind, and naked:

18 I counsel thee [y]to buy of me gold tried in the fire, that thou mayest be rich; [z]and white raiment, that thou mayest be clothed, and *that* the shame of thy nakedness do not appear; and anoint thine eyes with eyesalve, that thou mayest see.

19 As [a]many as I love, I rebuke and chasten: be zealous therefore, and repent.

20 Behold, [b]I stand at the door, and knock: if [c]any man hear my voice, and open the door, [d]I will come in to him, and will sup with him, and he with me.

21 To him that overcometh [e]will I grant to sit with me in my throne, even as I also overcame, and am set down with my Father in his throne.

22 He that hath an ear, let him hear what the Spirit saith unto the churches.

CHAPTER 4

AFTER this I looked, and, behold, a door *was* opened in heaven: and the first voice which I heard *was* as it

g Acts 15.28.
h John 6.29.
i Matt. 19.28. Luke 22.29. 1 Cor. 6.3. ch. 3.21.
j Ps. 2.8,9. Dan. 7.22. ch. 19.15.
k 2 Pet. 1.19. ch. 22.16.

CHAP. 3

a Luke 15.24, 32. Eph. 2.1. Col. 2.13.
b Luke 12.39.
c Acts 1.15.
d Jude 23.
e ch. 7.9,13.
f Ex. 32.32. Ps. 69.28.
g Phil. 4.3. ch. 21.27.
h Matt. 10. 32.
i Acts 3.14.
j 1 John 5.20.
k Isa. 22.22. Luke 1.32. ch. 1.18.
l Matt. 16.19.
m Job 12.14.
n 2 Cor. 2.12.
o Isa. 49.23.
p 2 Pet. 2.9.
q Gal. 2.9.
r ch. 14.1.
s Gal. 4.26. Heb. 12.22. ch. 21.
t Isa. 65.15. ch. 22.4.
1 Or, in Laodicea.
u 2 Cor. 1.20.
v Isa. 55.4. ch. 22.6.
w Pro. 8.22. John 1. Col. 1.15.
x Pro. 13.7. Hosea 12.8. Zech. 11.5. Luke 1.53.
y Isa. 55.1. Matt. 13.44.
z 2 Cor. 5.3.
a Deut. 8.5. Pro. 3.11. Isa. 26.16. Heb. 12.5,6.
b Song 5.2. Isa. 1.18.
c Luke 12.37.
d John 14.23.
e Matt. 19. 28. 1 Cor. 6.2. ch. 2.26.

were of a trumpet talking with me;
which said, Come up hither, and I
will shew thee things which must be
hereafter.
2 And immediately I [a]was in the
spirit: and, behold, [b]a throne was
set in heaven, and *one* sat on the
throne.
3 And he that sat was to look upon
like a jasper and a sardine stone: [c]and
there was a rainbow round about
the throne, in sight like unto an
emerald.
4 And round about the throne *were*
four and twenty seats: and upon the
seats I saw four and twenty elders
sitting, clothed in white raiment; and
they had on their heads crowns of
gold.
5 And out of the throne proceeded
lightnings and thunderings and
voices: [d]and *there were* seven lamps
of fire burning before the throne,
which are the seven Spirits of God.
6 And before the throne *there was*
[e]a sea of glass like unto crystal: and
[f]in the midst of the throne, and round
about the throne, *were* four beasts
full of eyes before and behind.
7 And the [g]first beast *was* like a lion,
and the second beast like a calf, and
the third beast had a face as a man,
and the fourth beast *was* like a flying
eagle.
8 And the four beasts had each of
them six [h]wings about *him;* and *they*
were full of eyes within: and [1]they
rest not day and night, saying, Holy,
holy, holy, Lord God Almighty, which
was, and is, and is to come.
9 And when those beasts give glory
and honour and thanks to him that sat
on the throne, who liveth for ever and
ever,
10 The four and twenty elders fall
down before him that sat on the
throne, and worship him that liveth
for ever and ever, and cast their
crowns before the throne, saying,
11 Thou art worthy, O Lord, to receive glory and honour and power:
for thou hast created all things, and
for thy pleasure they are and were
created.

CHAPTER 5

AND I saw in the right hand of him
that sat on the throne [a]a book
written within and on the backside,
sealed with [b]seven seals.
2 And I saw a strong angel proclaiming with a loud voice, Who is worthy
to open the book, and to loose the
seals thereof?
3 And [c]no man in heaven, nor in
earth, neither under the earth, was
able to open the book, neither to look
thereon.
4 And I wept much, because no
man was found worthy to open and
to read the book, neither to look
thereon.
5 And one of the elders saith unto
me, Weep not: behold, [d]the Lion
of the tribe of Juda, [e]the Root of
David, hath [f]prevailed to open the
book, and to loose the seven seals
thereof.
6 And I beheld, and, lo, in the midst
of the throne and of the four beasts,
and in the midst of the elders, stood a
[g]Lamb as it had been slain, having
seven horns and seven [h]eyes, which
are [i]the seven Spirits of God sent
forth into all the earth.
7 And he came and took the book out
of the right hand of him that sat upon
the throne.
8 And when he had taken the book,
the four beasts and four *and* twenty
elders fell down before the Lamb, having every one of [j]them harps, and
golden vials full of [1]odours, [k]which
are the prayers of saints.
9 And [l]they sung a new song, saying,
[m]Thou art worthy to take the book,
and to open the seals thereof: for thou
wast slain, and hast [n]redeemed us to
God by thy blood [o]out of every kindred, and tongue, and people, and
nation;
10 And [p]hast made us unto our God
kings and priests: and we shall reign
on the earth.
11 And I beheld, and I heard the
voice of many angels round about the
throne and the beasts and the elders:
and the number of them was [q]ten
thousand times ten thousand, and
thousands of thousands;
12 Saying with a loud voice, Worthy
is the Lamb that was slain to receive
power, and riches, and wisdom, and
strength, and honour, and glory, and
blessing.
13 And [r]every creature which is in
heaven, and on the earth, and under
the earth, and such as are in the sea,
and all that are in them, heard I saying, [s]Blessing, and honour, and glory,
and power, *be* unto him that sitteth
upon the throne, [t]and unto the Lamb
for ever and ever.
14 And the four beasts said, Ā-mĕn.
And the four *and* twenty elders fell
down and worshipped him that liveth
for ever and ever.

CHAP. 4
a ch. 1.10.
b Isa. 6.1. Dan. 7.9.
c Eze. 1.28.
d Ex. 37.23. Eze. 1.13. Zech. 4.2. Rev. 5.6.
e Ex. 38.8.
f Eze. 1.5.
g Num. 2.2.
h Isa. 6.2.
1 they have no rest.

CHAP. 5
a Eze. 2.9.
b Isa. 29.11. Dan. 12.4. ch. 6.1.
c John 1.18.
d Gen. 49.9, 10. Heb. 7.14.
e Isa. 11. Rom. 15.12. ch. 22.16.
f Heb. 2.10.
g Isa. 53.7. John 1.29. 1 Pet. 1.19. ch. 6.16.
h Zech. 3.9.
i ch. 4.5.
j ch. 14.2.
1 Or, incense.
k Ps. 141.2. ch. 8.3,4.
l Ps. 33.3. Isa. 42.10. ch. 14.3.
m ch. 4.11.
n Matt. 26. 28. Acts 20.28. Eph. 1.7. Heb. 9.12. 2 Pet. 2.1.
o Dan. 4.1.
p Ex. 19.6.
q Ps. 68.17. Dan. 7.10. Heb. 12.22.
r Phil. 2.10.
s Eph. 3.21. 1 Tim. 1.17.
t John 5.23.

CHAPTER 6

AND I saw when the Lamb opened
one of the seals, and I heard, as it
were the noise of thunder, one of the
four beasts saying, Come and see.
2 And I saw, and behold [a]a white
horse: and [b]he that sat on him had a
bow; [c]and a crown was given unto
him: and he went forth conquering,
and to conquer.
3 And when he had opened the
second seal, I heard the second beast
say, Come and see.
4 And [d]there went out another horse
that was red: and *power* was given to
him that sat thereon to take peace
from the earth, and that they should
kill one another: and there was given
unto him a great sword.
5 And when he had opened the third
seal, I heard the third beast say,
Come and see. And I beheld, and lo
a [e]black horse; and he that sat on
him had a pair of balances in his hand.
6 And I heard a voice in the midst of
the four beasts say, [1]A measure of
wheat for a penny, and three measures of barley for a penny; and [f]*see*
thou hurt not the oil and the wine.
7 And when he had opened the fourth
seal, I heard the voice of the fourth
beast say, Come and see.
8 And I looked, and behold a pale
horse: and his name that sat on him
was Death, and Hell followed with
him. And power was given [2]unto them
over the fourth part of the earth, [g] to
kill with sword, and with hunger, and
with death, [h]and with the beasts of the
earth.
9 And when he had opened the fifth
seal, I saw under [i]the altar the [j]souls
of them that were slain for the word
of God, and for [k]the testimony which
they held:
10 And they cried with a loud voice,
saying, [l]How long, O Lord, holy and
true, dost thou not judge and avenge
our blood on them that dwell on the
earth?
11 And white robes were given unto
every one of them; and it was said
unto them, that [m]they should rest yet
for a little season, until their fellowservants also and their brethren, that
should be killed as they *were*, should
be fulfilled.
12 And I beheld when he had opened
the sixth seal, [n]and, lo, there was a
great earthquake; and [o]the sun became black as sackcloth of hair, and
the moon became as blood;
13 And the stars of heaven fell unto

CHAP. 6

a Zech. 6.3. ch. 19.11.
b Ps. 45.4,5. LXX.
c ch. 14.14.
d Zech. 6.2.
e Zech. 6.2.
1 The word Chœnix signifieth a measure containing one wine quart, and the twelfth part of a quart.
f ch. 9.4.
2 Or, to him.
g Jer. 15.2,3. Eze. 5.17. Amos 4.10-12.
h Lev. 26.22.
i ch. 8.3.
j ch. 20.4.
k 2 Tim. 1.8.
l Gen. 4.10. Zech. 1.12.
m Heb. 11. 40.
n ch. 16.18.
o Joel 2.10. Matt. 24.29. Acts 2.20.
3 Or, green figs.
p Isa. 34.4. Heb. 1.12.
q Jer. 3.23.
r Isa. 2.19.
s Isa. 13.6. Zeph. 1.14.
t Ps. 76.7.

CHAP. 7

a Ps. 34.7. Dan. 6.22. Heb. 1.14.
b Dan. 7.2.
c ch. 9.4.
d ch. 6.6. ch. 9.4.
e Eph. 4.30. 2 Tim. 2.19. ch. 14.1.
f ch. 22.4.
g ch. 9.16.
h Isa. 4.2,3. ch. 14.1.
i Gen. 12.3. Gen. 22.17. Ps. 22.27. Isa. 2.2,3. Zech. 2.11. Rom. 11.25.

the earth, even as a fig tree casteth her
[3]untimely figs, when she is shaken of
a mighty wind.
14 And [p]the heaven departed as a
scroll when it is rolled together; and
every mountain [q]and island were
moved out of their places.
15 And the kings of the earth, and
the great men, and the rich men, and
the chief captains, and the mighty
men, and every bondman, and every
free man, [r]hid themselves in the dens
and in the rocks of the mountains;
16 And said to the mountains and
rocks, Fall on us, and hide us from the
face of him that sitteth on the throne,
and from the wrath of the Lamb:
17 For [s]the great day of his wrath is
come; and [t]who shall be able to
stand?

CHAPTER 7

AND after these things I saw four
angels [a]standing on the four
corners of the earth, [b]holding the four
winds of the earth, that the [c]wind
should not blow on the earth, nor on
the sea, nor on any tree.
2 And I saw another angel ascending
from the east, having the seal of the
living God: and he cried with a loud
voice to the four angels, to whom it
was given to hurt the earth and the sea,
3 Saying, [d]Hurt not the earth, neither
the sea, nor the trees, till we have
sealed [e]the servants of our God in
[f]their foreheads.
4 And [g]I heard the number of them
which were sealed: *and there were*
sealed an [h]hundred *and* forty *and* four
thousand of all the tribes of the children of Israel.
5 Of the tribe of Juda *were* sealed
twelve thousand. Of the tribe of Reuben *were* sealed twelve thousand. Of
the tribe of Gad *were* sealed twelve
thousand.
6 Of the tribe of Ā-sĕr *were* sealed
twelve thousand. Of the tribe of Nĕph-
thă-lĭm *were* sealed twelve thousand.
Of the tribe of Mă-năs-sēs *were* sealed
twelve thousand.
7 Of the tribe of Simeon *were* sealed
twelve thousand. Of the tribe of Levi
were sealed twelve thousand. Of the
tribe of Ĭs-să-chăr *were* sealed twelve
thousand.
8 Of the tribe of Ză-bū-lon *were* sealed twelve thousand. Of the tribe of
Joseph *were* sealed twelve thousand.
Of the tribe of Benjamin *were* sealed
twelve thousand.
9 After this I beheld, and, lo, [i] a great
multitude, which no man could num-

ber, [j]of all nations, and kindreds, and
people, and tongues, stood before the
throne, and before the Lamb, [k]clothed
with white robes, and palms in their
hands;
10 And cried with a loud voice, saying, Salvation [l]to our God [m]which
sitteth upon the throne, and unto the
Lamb.
11 And [n]all the angels stood round
about the throne, and *about* the elders
and the four beasts, and fell before
the throne on their faces, and worshipped God,
12 Saying, [o]Ā-mĕn: Blessing, and
glory, and wisdom, and thanksgiving,
and honour, and power, and might,
be unto our God for ever and ever.
Ā-mĕn.
13 And one of the elders answered,
saying unto me, What are these which
are arrayed in white robes? and
whence came they?
14 And I said unto him, Sir, thou
knowest. And he said to me, These
[p]are they which came out of great
tribulation, and have washed [q]their
robes, and made them white in the
blood of the Lamb.
15 Therefore are they before the
throne of God, and serve him day and
night in his temple: and he that sitteth
on the throne shall dwell [r]among
them.
16 They [s]shall hunger no more,
neither thirst any more; [t]neither shall
the sun light on them, nor any heat.
17 For the Lamb which is in the
midst of the throne [u]shall feed them,
and shall lead them unto living fountains of waters: and God [v]shall wipe
away all tears from their eyes.

CHAPTER 8

AND when he had opened the
seventh seal, there was silence in
heaven about the space of half an
hour.
2 And I [a]saw the seven angels which
stood before God; [b]and to them were
given seven trumpets.
3 And another [c]angel came and stood
at the altar, having a golden censer;
and there was given unto him much
[d]incense, that he should [1]offer *it* with
[e]the prayers of all saints upon the
[f]golden altar which was before the
throne.
4 And [g]the smoke of the incense,
which came with the prayers of the
saints, ascended up before God out of
the angel's hand.
5 And the angel took the censer, and
filled it with fire of the altar, and cast
it [2]into the earth: [h]and there were
voices, and thunderings, and lightnings, [i]and an earthquake.
6 And the seven angels which had
the seven trumpets prepared themselves to sound.
7 The first angel sounded, [j]and there
followed hail and fire mingled with
blood, and they were cast [k]upon the
earth: and the third part [l]of trees was
burnt up, and all green grass was
burnt up.
8 And the second angel sounded, and
as it were a great mountain burning
with fire was cast into the sea: and the
third part of the sea became [m]blood;
9 And the third part of the creatures
which were in the sea, and had life,
died; and the third part of the ships
were destroyed.
10 And the third angel sounded, and
there fell a great star from heaven,
burning as it were a lamp, and it fell
upon the third part of the rivers, and
upon the fountains of waters;
11 And the name of the star is called
Wormwood: [n]and the third part of
the waters became wormwood; and
many men died of the waters, because
they were made bitter.
12 And [o]the fourth angel sounded,
and the third part of the sun was smitten, and the third part of the moon,
and the third part of the stars; so as
the third part of them was darkened,
and the day shone not for a third part
of it, and the night likewise.
13 And I beheld, and [p]heard an
angel flying through the midst of heaven, saying with a loud voice, [q]Woe,
woe, woe, to the inhabiters of the
earth by reason of the other voices of
the trumpet of the three angels, which
are yet to sound!

CHAPTER 9

AND the fifth angel sounded, and
[a]I saw a star fall from heaven unto the earth: and to him was given the
key of [b]the bottomless pit.
2 And he opened the bottomless pit;
and there arose [c]a smoke out of the
pit, as the smoke of a great furnace;
and the sun and the air were darkened
by reason of the smoke of the pit.
3 And there came out of the smoke
[d]locusts upon the earth: and unto
them was given power, as the scorpions of the earth have power.
4 And it was commanded them that
[e]they should not hurt [f]the grass of the
earth, neither any green thing, neither

j ch. 5.9.
k ch. 3.5.
l Ps. 3.8. Isa. 43.11. Jer. 3.23. Hosea 13.4. Zech. 9.9. Luke 3.6.
m ch. 5.13.
n ch. 4.6.
o ch. 5.13.
p Acts 14.22.
q Isa. 1.18. Heb. 9.14. 1 John 1.7. ch. 1.5.
r Isa. 4.5,6.
s Isa. 49.10.
t Ps. 121.6.
u Ps. 23.1. John 10.11.
v Isa. 25.8.

CHAP. 8

a Matt. 18. 10. Luke 1.19. ch. 15.1.
b 2 Chr. 29. 25-28.
c Acts 7.30.
d Eph. 5.2.
1 Or, add it to the prayers.
e Luke 1.10. ch. 5.8.
f Ex. 30.1.
g Ps. 141.2.
2 Or, upon.
h ch. 16.18.
i 2 Sam. 22.8.
j Eze. 38.22.
k ch. 16.2.
l Isa. 2.13.
m Eze. 14.19.
n Ex. 15.23. Jer. 9.15. Lam. 3.15.
o Isa. 13.10. Amos 8.9.
p ch. 14.6.
q ch. 9.12.

CHAP. 9

a Isa. 14.12. Luke 10.18. ch. 8.10.
b Luke 8.31. ch. 17.8.
c Joel 2.2,10.
d Ex. 10.4.
e ch. 6.6.
f ch. 8.7.

any tree; but only those men which
have not [g]the seal of God in their foreheads.
5 And to them it was given that they
should not kill them, [h]but that they
should be tormented five months: and
their torment *was* as the torment of
a scorpion, when he striketh a man.
6 And in those days [i]shall men seek
death, and shall not find it; and shall
desire to die, and death shall flee from
them.
7 And [j]the shapes of the locusts *were*
like unto horses prepared unto battle;
and [k]on their heads *were* as it were
crowns like gold, [l]and their faces *were*
as the faces of men.
8 And they had hair as the hair of
women, and [m]their teeth were as *the*
teeth of lions.
9 And they had breastplates, as it
were breastplates of iron; and the
sound of their wings *was* as the sound
of chariots of many horses running to
battle.
10 And they had tails like unto scorpions, and there were stings in their
tails: and their power *was* to hurt men
five months.
11 And [n]they had a king over them,
which is the angel of the bottomless
pit, whose name in the Hebrew tongue
is Ă-băd́-dŏn, but in the Greek
tongue hath *his* name [1]Ă-pŏĺ-lȳ-on.
12 One [o]woe is past; *and*, behold,
there come two woes more hereafter.
13 And the sixth angel sounded, and
I heard a voice from the four horns of
the golden altar which is before God,
14 Saying to the sixth angel which
had the trumpet, Loose the four angels
which are bound [p]in the great river
Eû-phrā́-tēs.
15 And the four angels were loosed,
which were prepared [2]for an hour, and
a day, and a month, and a year, for to
slay the third part of men.
16 And [q]the number of the army of
[r]the horsemen *were* two hundred
thousand thousand: [s]and I heard the
number of them.
17 And thus I saw the horses in the
vision, and them that sat on them,
having breastplates of fire, and of
jacinth, and brimstone: and [t]the
heads of the horses *were* as the heads
of lions; and out of their mouths
issued fire and smoke and brimstone.
18 By these three was the third part
of men killed, by the fire, and by the
smoke, and by the brimstone, which
issued out of their mouths.
19 For their power is in their mouth,
and in their tails: [u]for their tails *were*
like unto serpents, and had heads, and
with them they do hurt.
20 And the rest of the men which
were not killed by these plagues yet
[v]repented not of the works of their
hands, that they should not worship
[w]devils, [x]and idols of gold, and silver,
and brass, and stone, and of wood:
which neither can see, nor hear, nor
walk:
21 Neither repented they of their
murders, nor of their sorceries, nor of
their fornication, nor of their thefts.

CHAPTER 10

AND I saw another mighty angel
come down from heaven, clothed
with a cloud: [a]and a rainbow *was*
upon his head, and [b]his face *was* as it
were the sun, and his feet as [c]pillars
of fire:
2 And he had in his hand a little book
open: [d]and he set his right foot upon
the sea, and *his* left *foot* on the earth,
3 And cried with a loud voice, as
when a lion roareth: and when he had
cried, seven [e]thunders uttered their
voices.
4 And when the seven thunders had
uttered their voices, I was about to
write: and I heard a voice from heaven
saying unto me, [f]Seal up those things
which the seven thunders uttered, and
write them not.
5 And the angel which I saw stand
upon the sea and upon the earth lifted
up his hand to heaven,
6 And sware by him that [g]liveth for
ever and ever, who created heaven,
and the things that therein are, and
the earth, and the things that therein
are, and the sea, and the things which
are therein, [h]that there should be time
no longer:
7 But [i]in the days of the voice of the
seventh angel, when he shall begin to
sound, the mystery of God should be
finished, as he hath declared to his
servants the prophets.
8 And the voice which I heard from
heaven spake unto me again, and
said, Go *and* take the little book which
is open in the hand of the angel which
standeth upon the sea and upon the
earth.
9 And I went unto the angel, and
said unto him, Give me the little book.
And he said unto me, Take [j]*it*, and
eat it up; and it shall make thy belly
bitter, but it shall be in thy mouth
sweet as honey.
10 And I took the little book out of

g Ex. 12.23. Eze. 9.4. Eph. 4.30. ch. 7.3.
h ch. 11.7.
i Job 3.21. Isa. 2.19. Jer. 8.3. Hosea 10.8. Jonah 4.8. ch. 6.16.
j Joel 2.4.
k Nah. 3.17.
l Dan. 7.8.
m Joel 1.6.
n John 12.31. Eph. 2.2. 2 Thes. 2.3, 10.
1 That is to say, a destroyer.
o ch. 8.13.
p ch. 16.12.
2 Or, at.
q Ps. 68.17. Dan. 7.10.
r Eze. 38.4.
s ch. 7.4.
t 1 Chr. 12.8. Isa. 5.28.
u Isa. 9.15.
v Deut. 31. 29. 2 Chr. 28.22. Jer. 5.3. Matt. 21.32. ch. 2.21.
w Lev. 17.7. Deut. 32.17. Ps. 106.37. 1 Cor. 10.20.
x Ps. 115.4. Dan. 5.23.

CHAP. 10

a Eze. 1.28.
b Matt. 17.2. ch. 1.16.
c ch. 1.15.
d Matt. 28. 18.
e ch. 8.5.
f Dan. 8.26
g Jer. 10.10. ch. 4.9.
h Dan. 12.7. ch. 16.17.
i ch. 11.15.
j Jer. 15.16. Eze. 2.8.

the angel's hand, and ate it up; and it
was in my mouth sweet as honey: and
as soon as I had eaten it, my belly was
bitter.
11 And he said unto me, Thou must
prophesy again before many peoples,
and nations, and tongues, and kings.

CHAPTER 11

AND there was given me [a]a reed like
unto a rod: and the angel stood,
saying, Rise, [b]and measure the temple
of God, and the altar, and them that
worship therein.
2 But [c]the court which is without the
temple [1]leave out, and measure it not;
for [d]it is given unto the Gentiles: and
the holy city shall they [e]tread under
foot [f]forty *and* two months.
3 And [2]I will give *power* unto my [g]two
witnesses, [h]and they shall prophesy
[i]a thousand two hundred *and* threescore days, clothed in sackcloth.
4 These are the [j]two olive trees, and
the two candlesticks standing before
the God of the earth.
5 And if any man will hurt them, fire
[k]proceedeth out of their mouth, and
devoureth their enemies: [l]and if any
man will hurt them, he must in this
manner be killed.
6 These [m]have power to shut heaven,
that it rain not in the days of their
prophecy: and [n]have power over
waters to turn them to blood, and to
smite the earth with all plagues, as
often as they will.
7 And when they [o]shall have finished
their testimony, [p]the beast that
ascendeth out of the bottomless [q]pit
shall make war against them, and
shall overcome them, and kill them.
8 And their dead bodies *shall lie* in
the street of [r]the great city, which
spiritually is called Sodom and Egypt,
where [s]also our Lord was crucified.
9 And [t]they of the people and kindreds and tongues and nations shall
see their dead bodies three days and
an half, [u]and shall not suffer their
dead bodies to be put in graves.
10 And [v]they that dwell upon the
earth shall rejoice over them, and
make merry, and shall send gifts one
to another; because these two prophets tormented them that dwelt on
the earth.
11 And after three days and an half
[w]the Spirit of life from God entered
into them, and they stood upon their
feet; and great fear fell upon them
which saw them.
12 And they heard a great voice from

CHAP. 11
a Eze. 40.3. Zech. 2.1.
b Num. 23. 18.
c Eze. 40.17.
1 cast out.
d 2 Ki. 25.9. Ps. 79.1. Luke 21.24.
e Dan. 8.10.
f ch. 13.5.
2 Or, I will give unto my two witnesses that they may prophesy.
g ch. 6.9.
h ch. 19.10.
i ch. 12.6.
j Ps. 52.8. Jer. 11.16. Zech. 4.3. Rom. 11.17.
k 2 Ki. 1.10. Jer. 1.10. Hosea 6.5.
l Num. 16.29.
m 1 Ki. 17.1. Jas. 5.16.
n Ex. 7.19.
o Luke 13.32.
p ch. 13.1.
q Dan. 7.21. Zech. 14.2.
r ch. 14.8.
s Heb. 13.12. ch. 18.24.
t ch. 17.15.
u Ps. 79.2,3.
v ch. 12.12.
w Eze. 37.
x Isa. 14.13.
y Isa. 60.8. Acts 1.9.
z ch. 14.8.
3 names of men.
a Isa. 27.13.
b Ps. 145.13. Dan. 2.44. Dan. 4.3,34. Micah 4.7. Luke 1.33. John 12.34. Heb. 1.8.
c Dan. 7.9. Eccl. 3.17. Acts 10.42. 1 Pet. 4.5.
4 Or, corrupt.
d Num. 4.5. Heb. 9.4.

CHAP. 12
1 Or, sign.
a Isa. 60.19. Rom. 13.14. 2 Cor. 11.2. Gal. 4.26.
b Isa. 53.11. Micah 5.3. Gal. 4.19.
2 Or, sign.
c ch. 17.3.
d ch. 17.9.
e ch. 13.1.
f ch. 9.10.
g ch. 17.18.
h Dan. 8.10.
i Ex. 1.16. 1 Pet. 5.8.

heaven saying unto them, Come up
hither. And [x]they ascended up to
heaven [y]in a cloud; and their enemies
beheld them.
13 And the same hour was there a
great earthquake, [z]and the tenth part
of the city fell, and in the earthquake
were slain [3]of men seven thousand:
and the remnant were affrighted, and
gave glory to the God of heaven.
14 The second woe is past; *and*,
behold, the third woe cometh quickly.
15 And the seventh angel sounded;
and there [a]were great voices in heaven, saying, The kingdoms of this
world are become *the kingdoms* of our
Lord, and of his Christ; and [b]he shall
reign for ever and ever.
16 And the four and twenty elders,
which sat before God on their seats,
fell upon their faces, and worshipped
God,
17 Saying, We give thee thanks, O
Lord God Almighty, which art, and
wast, and art to come; because thou
hast taken to thee thy great power,
and hast reigned.
18 And the nations were angry, and
thy wrath is come, [c]and the time of
the dead, that they should be judged,
and that thou shouldest give reward
unto thy servants the prophets and to
the saints, and them that fear thy
name, small and great; and shouldest
[4]destroy them which destroy the
earth.
19 And the temple of God was opened in heaven, and there was seen [d]in
his temple the ark of his testament:
and there were lightnings, and voices,
and thunderings, and an earthquake,
and great hail.

CHAPTER 12

AND there appeared a great [1]won-
der in heaven; [a]a woman clothed
with the sun, and the moon under her
feet, and upon her head a crown of
twelve stars:
2 And she being with child cried,
travailing [b]in birth, and pained to be
delivered.
3 And there appeared another [2]won-
der in heaven; and behold a [c]great red
dragon, having [d]seven heads and ten
horns, [e]and seven crowns upon his
heads.
4 And [f]his tail drew the third part of
the [g]stars of heaven, [h]and did cast
them to the earth: and the dragon
stood before the woman which was
ready to be delivered, for [i]to devour
her child as soon as it was born.

5 And she brought forth a man child,
who [j]was to rule all nations with a rod
of iron: and her child was caught up
unto God, and *to* his throne.
6 And the woman fled into the wilderness, where she hath a place
prepared of God, that they should
feed her there [k]a thousand two hundred *and* threescore days.
7 And there was war in heaven:
Michael [l]and his angels fought against
the [m]dragon; and the dragon fought
and his angels,
8 And prevailed not; neither was
their place found any more in heaven.
9 And [n]the great dragon was cast
out, that [o]old serpent, called the
Devil, and Satan, which deceiveth the
whole world: he [p]was cast out into
the earth, and his angels were cast out
with him.
10 And I heard a loud voice saying in
heaven, [q]Now is come salvation, and
strength, and the kingdom of our
God, and the power of his Christ: for
the accuser of our brethren is cast
down, [r]which accused them before
our God day and night.
11 And [s]they overcame him by the
blood of the Lamb, and by the word
of their testimony; and [t]they loved
not their lives unto the death.
12 Therefore rejoice, *ye* heavens, and
ye that dwell in them. [u]Woe to the inhabiters of the earth and of the sea!
for the devil is come down unto you,
having great wrath, because [v]he
knoweth that he hath but a short
time.
13 And when the dragon saw that he
was cast unto the earth, he persecuted
the woman which brought forth the
man *child*.
14 And [w]to the woman were given
two wings of a great eagle, that she
might fly into [x]the wilderness, into her
place, where she is nourished for [y]a
time, and times, and half a time, from
the face of the serpent.
15 And the serpent [z]cast out of his
mouth water as a flood after the woman, that he might cause her to be
carried away of the flood.
16 And the earth helped the woman,
and the earth opened her mouth, and
swallowed up the flood which the
dragon cast out of his mouth.
17 And the dragon was wroth with
the woman, [a]and went to make war
with the remnant of her seed, which
keep the commandments of God,
and have [b]the testimony of Jesus
Christ.

j Ps. 2.9. ch. 2.27.
k ch. 11.3.
l Dan. 10.13.
m ch. 20.2.
n Luke 10.18.
o Gen. 3.1. 2 Pet. 2.4. Jude 6. ch. 20.2.
p John 12.31. ch. 9.1.
q ch. 11.15.
r Job 1.9. Zech. 3.1.
s Rom. 8.37.
t Luke 14.26.
u ch. 8.13.
v ch. 10.6.
w Ex. 19.4.
x ch. 17.3.
y Dan. 7.25.
z Isa. 59.19.
a Gen. 3.15.
b ch. 1.2,9.

CHAP. 13

a Dan. 7.2,7.
1 Or, names.
b Dan. 7.6.
c ch. 12.9.
2 slain.
d 2 Thes. 2.3.
e ch. 18.18.
f Dan. 7.8-25.
3 Or, to make war.
g ch. 11.2.
h John 1.14. Col. 2.9.
i Dan. 7.21. ch. 11.7.
j Ex. 32.32. Dan. 12.1. Luke 10.20. Phil. 4.3. ch. 3.5. ch. 21.27.
k Eph. 1.4. 1 Pet. 1.19, 20. ch. 5.6-13.
l Isa. 14.2. Matt. 7.2.
m Gen. 9.6. Matt. 26. 52.
n Lam. 3.26. Heb. 12.3,4. ch. 14.12.
o Deut. 13.1. Matt. 24.24. 2 Thes. 2.9. ch. 16.14.
p 1 Ki. 18.38. 2 Ki. 1.10.

CHAPTER 13

AND I stood upon the sand of the
sea, and saw [a]a beast rise up out
of the sea, having seven heads and ten
horns, and upon his horns ten crowns,
and upon his heads [1]the name of
blasphemy.
2 And [b]the beast which I saw was
like unto a leopard, and his feet were
as *the feet* of a bear, and his mouth as
the mouth of a lion: and the [c]dragon
gave him his power, and his seat, and
great authority.
3 And I saw one of his heads as it
were [2]wounded to death; and his
deadly wound was healed: and all [d]the
world wondered after the beast.
4 And they worshipped the dragon
which gave power unto the beast: and
they worshipped the beast, saying,
[e]Who *is* like unto the beast? who is
able to make war with him?
5 And there was given unto him [f]a
mouth speaking great things and blasphemies; and power was given unto
him [3]to continue [g]forty *and* two
months.
6 And he opened his mouth in blasphemy against God, to blaspheme
his name, [h]and his tabernacle, and
them that dwell in heaven.
7 And it was given unto him [i]to make
war with the saints, and to overcome
them: and power was given him over
all kindreds, and tongues, and nations.
8 And all that dwell upon the earth
shall worship him, [j]whose names are
not written in the book of life of the
Lamb [k]slain from the foundation of
the world.
9 If any man have an ear, let him
hear.
10 He [l]that leadeth into captivity
shall go into captivity: [m]he that killeth
with the sword must be killed with the
sword. Here [n]is the patience and the
faith of the saints.
11 And I beheld another beast coming up out of the earth; and he had two
horns like a lamb, and he spake as a
dragon.
12 And he exerciseth all the power
of the first beast before him, and causeth the earth and them which dwell
therein to worship the first beast,
whose deadly wound was healed.
13 And [o]he doeth great wonders, so
[p]that he maketh fire come down from
heaven on the earth in the sight of
men,
14 And deceiveth them that dwell on
the earth by *the means of* those

miracles which he had power to do in the sight of the beast; saying to them that dwell on the earth, that they should make an image to the beast, which had the wound by a sword, and [q]did live.

15 And he had power to give [4]life unto the image of the beast, that the image of the beast should both speak, and [r]cause that as many as would not worship the image of the beast should be killed.

16 And he causeth all, both small and great, rich and poor, free and bond, [5]to receive a mark in their right hand, or in their foreheads:

17 And that no man might buy or sell, save he that had the mark, or [s]the name of the beast, [t]or the number of his name.

18 Here [u]is wisdom. Let him that hath understanding count the number of the beast: for it is the number of a man; and his number *is* Six hundred threescore *and* six.

q 2 Ki. 20.7.
4 breath.
r ch. 20.4.
5 to give them.
s ch. 14.11.
t ch. 15.2.
u Ps. 107.43. Hosea 14.9. ch. 2.17.

CHAPTER 14

AND I looked, and, lo, [a]a Lamb stood on the mount Sī-ŏn, and with him an hundred forty *and* four thousand, [b]having his Father's name written in their foreheads.

2 And I heard a voice from heaven, as the voice of many waters, and as the voice of a great thunder: and I heard the voice of harpers harping with their harps:

3 And they sung as it were a new song before the throne, and before the four beasts, and the elders: and no man could learn that song but the hundred *and* forty *and* four thousand, which were redeemed from the earth.

4 These are they which were not defiled with women; [c]for they are virgins. These are they which follow the Lamb whithersoever he goeth. These [1]were redeemed from among men, [d]*being* the firstfruits unto God and to the Lamb.

5 And [e]in their mouth was found no guile: for [f]they are without fault before the throne of God.

6 And I saw another angel fly in the midst of heaven, [g]having the everlasting gospel to preach unto them that dwell on the earth, and to every nation, and kindred, and tongue, and people,

7 Saying with a loud voice, Fear God, and give glory to him; for the hour of his judgment is come: and [h]worship him that made heaven, and earth, and the sea, and the fountains of waters.

8 And there followed another angel, saying, [i]Babylon is fallen, is fallen, that great city, because she made all nations drink of the wine of the wrath of her fornication.

9 And the third angel followed them, saying with a loud voice, If any man worship the beast and his image, and receive *his* mark in his forehead, or in his hand,

10 The same [j]shall drink of the wine of the wrath of God, which is poured out without mixture into the cup of his indignation; and he shall be tormented with fire and brimstone in the presence of the holy angels, and in the presence of the Lamb:

11 And [k]the smoke of their torment ascendeth up for ever and ever: and they have no rest day nor night, who worship the beast and his image, and whosoever receiveth the mark of his name.

12 Here [l]is the patience of the saints: here *are* [m]they that keep the commandments of God, and the faith of Jesus.

13 And I heard a voice from heaven saying unto me, Write, Blessed [n]*are* the dead [o]which die in the Lord [2]from henceforth: Yea, saith the Spirit, that [p]they may rest from their labours; and their works do follow them.

14 And I looked, and behold a white cloud, and upon the cloud *one* sat like unto [q]the Son of man, having on his head a golden crown, and in his hand a sharp sickle.

15 And another angel came out of the temple, crying with a loud voice to him that sat on the cloud, Thrust [r]in thy sickle, and reap: for the time is come for thee to reap; for the harvest [s]of the earth is [3]ripe.

16 And he that sat on the cloud thrust in his sickle on the earth; and the earth was reaped.

17 And another angel came out of the temple which is in heaven, he also having a sharp sickle.

18 And another angel came out from the altar, [t]which had power over fire; and cried with a loud cry to him that had the sharp sickle, saying, [u]Thrust in thy sharp sickle, and gather the clusters of the vine of the earth; for her grapes are fully ripe.

19 And the angel thrust in his sickle into the earth, and gathered the vine of the earth, and cast *it* into the [v]great winepress of the wrath of God.

CHAP. 14
a Ex. 12.3. Isa. 53.7. 1 Pet. 1.19. ch. 5.6.
b ch. 7.3.
c 2 Cor. 11.2.
1 were bought.
d Jas. 1.18.
e Ps. 32.2. Zeph. 3.13.
f Eph. 5.27.
g Matt. 28. 19. Eph. 3.9. Titus 1.2.
h Ps. 33.6. Ps. 95.5. Ps. 124.8. Acts 14.15.
i Isa. 21.9. ch. 16.19. ch. 17.5.
j Ps. 75.8.
k Isa. 34.10.
l ch. 13.10.
m ch. 12.17.
n Eccl. 4.1,2.
o 1 Cor. 15. 18. 1 Thes. 4.16.
2 Or, from henceforth saith the Spirit, Yea.
p Isa. 57.1,2. Heb. 4.9. ch. 6.11.
q Dan. 7.13. ch. 1.13.
r Matt. 13.39.
s ch. 13.12.
3 Or, dried.
t ch. 16.8.
u Joel 3.13.
v ch. 19.15.

20 And [w]the winepress was trodden without [x]the city, and blood came out of the winepress, even unto the horse bridles, by the space of a thousand *and* six hundred furlongs.

CHAPTER 15

AND I saw another sign in heaven, great and marvellous, seven [a]angels having the seven last plagues; for [b]in them is filled up the wrath of God.

2 And I saw as it were [c]a sea of [d]glass mingled with fire: and them that had gotten the victory over the beast, [e]and over his image, and over his mark, *and* over the number of his name, stand on the sea of glass, having the harps of God.

3 And they sing [f]the song of Moses the servant of God, and the song of the Lamb, saying, [g]Great and marvellous *are* thy works, Lord God Almighty; just [h]and true *are* thy ways, thou King of [1]saints.

4 Who [i]shall not fear thee, O Lord, and glorify thy name? for *thou* only *art* holy: for [j]all nations shall come and worship before thee; for thy judgments are made manifest.

5 And after that I looked, and, behold, [k]the temple of the tabernacle of the testimony in heaven was opened:

6 And the seven angels came out of the temple, having the seven plagues, clothed in [l]pure and white linen, and having their breasts girded with golden girdles.

7 And [m]one of the four beasts gave unto the seven angels seven golden vials full of the wrath of God, who liveth for ever and ever.

8 And [n]the temple was filled with smoke from the [o]glory of God, and from his power; and no man was able to enter into the temple, till the seven plagues of the seven angels were fulfilled.

CHAPTER 16

AND I heard a great voice out of the temple saying to the seven angels, Go your ways, and pour out the vials of the wrath of God upon the earth.

2 And the first went, and poured out his vial [a]upon the earth; [b]and there fell a noisome and grievous sore upon the men which [c]had the mark of the beast, and *upon* them which worshipped his image.

3 And the second angel poured out his vial upon the sea; and [d]it became as the blood of a dead *man:* [e]and every living soul died in the sea.

4 And the third angel poured out his vial upon the rivers and fountains of waters; and they became blood.

5 And I heard the angel of the waters say, Thou [f]art righteous, O Lord, which [g]art, and wast, and shalt be, because thou hast judged thus.

6 For [h]they have shed the blood of saints and prophets, [i]and thou hast given them blood to drink; for they are worthy.

7 And I heard another out of the altar say, Even so, Lord God Almighty, [j]true and righteous *are* thy judgments.

8 And the fourth angel poured out his vial upon the sun; and power was given unto him to scorch men with fire.

9 And men were [1]scorched with great heat, and blasphemed the name of God, which hath power over these plagues: and [k]they repented not to give him glory.

10 And the fifth angel poured out his vial upon [l]the seat of the beast; and his kingdom was full of darkness; and they gnawed their tongues for pain,

11 And blasphemed the God of heaven because of their pains and their sores, and repented not of their deeds.

12 And the sixth angel poured out his vial [m]upon the great river Eû-phrā'-tēs; and [n]the water thereof was dried up, that [o]the way of the kings of the east might be prepared.

13 And I saw three [p]unclean spirits like frogs *come* out of the mouth of the [q]dragon, and out of the mouth of the beast, and out of the mouth of the false prophet.

14 For [r]they are the spirits of devils, working [s]miracles, *which* go forth unto the kings of the earth [t]and of the whole world, to gather them to the [u]battle of that great day of God Almighty.

15 Behold, [v]I come as a thief. Blessed *is* he that watcheth, and keepeth his garments, [w]lest he walk naked, and they see his shame.

16 And he gathered them together into a place called in the Hebrew tongue Ăr-mă-gĕd'-dŏn.

17 And the seventh angel poured out his vial into the air; and there came a great voice out of the temple of heaven, from the throne, saying, [x]It is done.

18 And there were voices, and thunders, and lightnings; and there was a great earthquake, such [y]as was not

w Isa. 63.3. Lam. 1.15.
x Heb. 13.12. ch. 11.8.

CHAP. 15

a ch. 16.1.
b ch. 14.10.
c ch. 4.6.
d Matt. 3.11.
e ch. 13.15.
f Ex. 15.1.
g Deut. 32.4.
h Hosea 14.9.
1 Or, nations, or, ages.
i Ex. 15.14. Ps. 8.9,7. Jer. 10.7.
j Isa. 66.23.
k ch. 11.19. Num. 1.50.
l Ex. 28.6.
m ch. 4.6.
n Ex. 40.34. 1 Ki. 8.10. 2 Chr. 5.14.
o Deut. 33.2. Isa. 2.19.

CHAP. 16

a ch. 8.7.
b Ex. 9.9.
c ch. 13.16.
d Ex. 7.17.
e ch. 8.9.
f Gen. 18.25. Ps. 97.2. Lam. 1.18. ch. 15.3.
g ch. 1.4,8. ch. 4.8.
h Matt. 23. 34.
i Isa. 49.26.
j ch. 13.10. ch. 14.10.
1 Or, burned.
k 2 Chr. 28. 22. Isa. 8.21. Dan. 5.22.
l ch. 13.2.
m ch. 9.14.
n Jer. 50.38.
o Isa. 41.2.
p 1 John 4.1.
q ch. 12.3.
r 1 Tim. 4.1.
s 2 Thes. 2.9.
t Luke 2.1.
u ch. 20.8.
v Matt. 24. 43. 1 Thes. 5.2.
w 2 Cor. 5.3.
x ch. 21.6.
y Dan. 12.1.

since men were upon the earth,
so mighty an earthquake, *and* so
great.
19 And [z]the great city was divided
into three parts, and the cities of the
nations fell: and great Babylon [a]came
in remembrance before God, to [b]give
unto her the cup of the wine of the
fierceness of his wrath.
20 And [c]every island fled away, and
the mountains were not found.
21 And [d]there fell upon men a great
hail out of heaven, *every stone* about
the weight of a talent: and men blasphemed God because of the plague of
the hail; for the plague thereof was
exceeding great.

CHAPTER 17

AND there came [a]one of the seven
angels which had the seven vials,
and talked with me, saying unto me,
Come hither; I will shew unto thee
the judgment of [b]the great whore that
[c]sitteth upon many waters:
2 With whom the kings of the earth
have committed fornication, and [d]the
inhabitants of the earth have been
made drunk with the wine of her fornication.
3 So he carried me away in the spirit
into the [e]wilderness: and I saw a woman sit upon a [f]scarlet coloured
beast, full [g]of names of blasphemy,
having seven heads and ten horns.
4 And the woman was arrayed in
purple [h]and scarlet colour, and [1]deck-
ed with gold and precious stones and
pearls, [i]having a golden cup in her
hand full of abominations and filthiness of her fornication:
5 And upon her forehead *was* a name
written, [j]MYSTERY, BABYLON [k]THE
GREAT, [l]THE MOTHER OF [2]HARLOTS AND
ABOMINATIONS OF THE EARTH.
6 And I saw the woman drunken
with the blood of the saints, and with
the blood of [m]the martyrs of Jesus:
and when I saw her, I wondered with
great admiration.
7 And the angel said unto me,
Wherefore didst thou marvel? I will
tell thee the mystery of the woman,
and of the beast that carrieth her,
which hath the seven heads and ten
horns.
8 The beast that thou sawest was,
and is not; and [n]shall ascend out of
the bottomless pit, and go into perdition: and they that dwell on the earth
shall wonder, whose names were not
written in the book of life from the
foundation of the world, when they

z ch. 14.8.
a ch. 18.5.
b Isa. 51.17. ch. 14.10.
c ch. 6.14.
d ch. 11.19.

CHAP. 17
a ch. 15.1.6. ch. 16.1-17. ch. 21.9.
b Nah. 3.4. 2 Tim. 3.1-6. ch. 19.2.
c Jer. 51.13.
d Jer. 51.7.
e ch. 12.6.
f ch. 12.3.
g ch. 13.1.
h ch. 18.12.
1 gilded.
i Jer. 51.7.
j 2 Thes. 2.7.
k ch. 11.8.
l ch. 18.9.
2 Or, fornications.
m Acts 22.20. ch. 6.9.
n ch. 11.7.
o Ps. 107.43. Hosea 14.9. ch. 13.18.
p ch. 13.1.
q Dan. 7.20. Zech. 1.18.
r Rom. 8.7.
s Ps. 136.2,3. ch. 16.14.
t 1 Tim. 6.15.
u 1 Pet. 2.9. ch. 14.4.
v Isa. 8.7.
w ch. 13.7.
x Jer. 50.41.
y Eze. 16.37.
z ch. 18.8.
a Rom. 1.26.
b ch. 10.7.
c ch. 16.19.
d ch. 12.4.

CHAP. 18
a 2 Thes. 2.3.
b Isa. 13.19. ch. 14.8. ch. 16.19.
c Isa. 34.14.
d Isa. 14.23. Mark 5.2,3.
1 Or, power.

behold the beast that was, and is not,
and yet is.
9 And [o]here *is* the mind which hath
wisdom. [p]The seven heads are seven
mountains, on which the woman
sitteth.
10 And there are seven kings: five
are fallen, and one is, *and* the other is
not yet come; and when he cometh,
he must continue a short space.
11 And the beast that was, and is not,
even he is the eighth, and is of the
seven, and goeth into perdition.
12 And [q]the ten horns which thou
sawest are ten kings, which have received no kingdom as yet; but receive
power as kings one hour with the
beast.
13 These have [r]one mind, and shall
give their power and strength unto
the beast.
14 These [s]shall make war with the
Lamb, and the Lamb shall overcome
them: [t]for he is Lord of lords, and
King of kings: and they [u]that are
with him *are* called, and chosen, and
faithful.
15 And he saith unto me, [v]The
waters which thou sawest, where the
whore sitteth, [w]are peoples, and multitudes, and nations, and tongues.
16 And the ten horns which thou
sawest upon the beast, [x]these shall
hate the whore, and shall make her
desolate [y]and naked, [z]and shall eat
her flesh, and burn her with fire.
17 For [a]God hath put in their hearts
to fulfil his will, and to agree, and give
their kingdom unto the beast, [b]until
the words of God shall be fulfilled.
18 And the woman which thou saw-
est [c]is that great city, [d]which reigneth
over the kings of the earth.

CHAPTER 18

AND after these things I saw another angel come down from
heaven, having great power; [a]and the
earth was lightened with his glory.
2 And he cried mightily with a strong
voice, saying, [b]Babylon the great is
fallen, is fallen, and [c]is become the
habitation of devils, and the hold of
every foul spirit, and [d] a cage of every
unclean and hateful bird.
3 For all nations have drunk of the
wine of the wrath of her fornication,
and the kings of the earth have committed fornication with her, and the
merchants of the earth are waxed
rich through the [1]abundance of her
delicacies.
4 And I heard another voice from

heaven, saying, [e]Come out of her, my
people, that ye be not partakers of her
sins, and that ye receive not of her
plagues.
5 For [f]her sins have reached unto
heaven, and God hath remembered
her iniquities.
6 Reward [g]her even as she rewarded
you, and double unto her double according to her works: in the cup which
she hath filled fill to her double.
7 How [h]much she hath glorified herself, and lived deliciously, so much
torment and sorrow give her: for she
saith in her heart, I sit a [i]queen, and
am no widow, and shall see no sorrow.
8 Therefore shall her plagues come
in one day, death, and mourning, and
famine; and she shall be utterly burned with fire: [j]for strong *is* the Lord
God who judgeth her.
9 And [k]the kings of the earth, who
have committed fornication and lived
deliciously with her, shall [l]bewail her,
and lament for her, when they shall
see the smoke of her burning,
10 Standing afar off for the fear of
her torment, saying, [m]Alas, alas, that
great city Babylon, that mighty city!
for in one hour is thy judgment come.
11 And [n]the merchants of the earth
shall weep and mourn over her; for no
man buyeth their merchandise any
more:
12 The merchandise of gold, and silver, and precious stones, and of pearls,
and fine linen, and purple, and silk,
and scarlet, and all [2]thyine wood, and
all manner vessels of ivory, and all
manner vessels of most precious
wood, and of brass, and iron, and
marble,
13 And cinnamon, and odours, and
ointments, and frankincense, and
wine, and oil, and fine flour, and
wheat, and beasts, and sheep, and
horses, and chariots, and [3]slaves, and
[o]souls of men.
14 And the fruits that thy soul lusted
after are departed from thee, and all
things which were dainty and goodly
are departed from thee, and thou
shalt find them no more at all.
15 The merchants of these things,
which were made rich by her, shall
stand afar off for the fear of her torment, weeping and wailing,
16 And saying, Alas, alas, that great
city, that was clothed in fine linen, and
purple, and scarlet, and decked with
gold, and precious stones, and pearls!
17 For in one hour so great riches is
come to nought. And [p]every shipmaster, and all the company in ships,
and sailors, and as many as trade by
sea, stood afar off,
18 And [q]cried when they saw the
smoke of her burning, saying, What
city is like unto this great city!
19 And [r]they cast dust on their
heads, and cried, weeping and wailing, saying, Alas, alas, that great city,
wherein were made rich all that had
ships in the sea by reason of her cost-
liness! for in one hour is she made
desolate.
20 Rejoice [s]over her, *thou* heaven,
and *ye* holy apostles and prophets;
for [t]God hath avenged you on her.
21 And a mighty angel took up a
stone like a great millstone, and cast
it into the sea, saying, [u]Thus with
violence shall that great city Babylon
be thrown down, and shall be found
no more at all.
22 And [v]the voice of harpers, and
musicians, and of pipers, and trumpeters, shall be heard no more at all
in thee; and no craftsman, of whatsoever craft *he be*, shall be found any
more in thee; and the sound of a millstone shall be heard no more at all in
thee;
23 And the light of a candle shall
shine no more at all in thee; [w]and the
voice of the bridegroom and of the
bride shall be heard no more at all in
thee: [x]for thy merchants were the
great men of the earth; for [y]by thy
sorceries were all nations deceived.
24 And in her was found the blood of
prophets, and of saints, and of all that
[z]were slain upon the earth.

CHAPTER 19

AND after these things I heard a
great voice of much people in
heaven, saying, Alleluia; [a]Salvation,
and glory, and honour, and power,
unto the Lord our God:
2 For true and righteous *are* his
judgments: for he hath judged the
great whore, which did corrupt the
earth with her fornication, and hath
avenged [b]the blood of his servants at
her hand.
3 And again they said, Alleluia. And
[c]her smoke rose up for ever and ever.
4 And [d]the four and twenty elders
and the four beasts fell down and worshipped God that sat on the throne,
saying, [e]Ā-mĕn; Alleluia.
5 And a voice came out of the throne,
saying, [f]Praise our God, all ye his
servants, and ye that fear him, both
small and great.

Gen. 19.12. Isa. 48.20. Jer. 50.8. 2 Cor. 6.17.
f Gen. 4.10. Gen. 18.20. Jonah 1.2.
g Ps. 137.8. Jer. 50.15. 2 Tim. 4.14. ch. 13.10.
h Eze. 28.2.
i Isa. 47.7,8. Zeph. 2.15.
j Jer. 50.34.
k ch. 17.2.
l Jer. 50.46.
m Isa. 21.9. ch. 14.8.
n Eze. 27.27.
2 Or, sweet.
3 Or, bodies.
o 2 Pet. 2.3.
Isa. 23.14
q Eze. 27.30.
r 1 Sam. 4.12. Job 2.12.
s Judg. 5.31. Ps. 48.11. Ps. 58.10. Pro. 11.10. Isa. 44.23. Jer. 51.48. ch. 19.1-3.
t Ps. 18.47. Isa. 26.21. Luke 11.49.
u Jer. 51.64.
v Isa. 24.8. Jer. 7.34.
w Jer. 33.11.
x Isa. 23.8.
y 2 Ki. 9.22. Nah. 3.4. ch. 17.2.
z Jer. 51.49.

CHAP. 19

a Ps. 3.8. Matt. 6.13. ch. 4.11. ch. 7.10.
b Deut. 32. 43. ch. 6.10.
c Isa. 34.10. ch. 14.11.
d ch. 4.4.
e Neh. 5.13.
f Ps. 134.1.

6 And [g]I heard as it were the voice of
a great multitude, and as the voice of
many waters, and as the voice of
mighty thunderings, saying, Alleluia:
for the Lord God omnipotent reigneth.
7 Let us be [h]glad and rejoice, and
give honour to him: for [i]the marriage
of the Lamb is come, and his wife hath
made herself ready.
8 And [j]to her was granted that she
should be arrayed in fine linen, clean
and [1]white: for [k]the fine linen is the
righteousness of saints.
9 And he saith unto me, Write,
Blessed [l]*are* they which are called unto
the marriage supper of the Lamb.
And he saith unto me, These are the
true sayings of God.
10 And [m]I fell at his feet to worship
him. And he said unto me, See [n]*thou
do it* not: I am thy fellowservant, and
of thy brethren [o]that have the testimony of Jesus: worship God: for the
testimony of Jesus is the spirit of
prophecy.
11 And I saw heaven opened, and
behold a white horse; and he that sat
upon him *was* [p]called Faithful and
True, and [q]in righteousness he doth
judge and make war.
12 His eyes *were* as a flame of fire,
and on his head *were* many crowns;
and he had a [r]name written, that no
man knew, but he himself.
13 And [s]he *was* clothed with a vesture
dipped in blood: and his name is called [t]The Word of God.
14 And the armies *which were* in
heaven followed him upon white
horses, [u]clothed in fine linen, white
and clean.
15 And [v]out of his mouth goeth a
sharp sword, that with it he should
smite the nations: and [w]he shall rule
them with a rod of iron: and [x]he
treadeth the winepress of the fierceness and wrath of Almighty God.
16 And he hath on *his* vesture and on
his thigh a name written, [y]KING OF
KINGS, AND LORD OF LORDS.
17 And I saw an angel standing in
the sun; and he cried with a loud voice,
saying to all the fowls that fly in the
midst of heaven, [z]Come and gather
yourselves together unto the supper
of the great God; 3rd Gen 1:14-17
18 That ye may eat the flesh of kings,
and the flesh of captains, and the flesh
of mighty men, and the flesh of horses,
and of them that sit on them, and the
flesh of all *men*, *both* free and bond,
both small and great.

g Eze. 1.24.
h Isa. 44.23.
i Matt. 22.2. 2 Cor. 11.2. Eph. 5.32.
j Ps. 45.13.
1 Or, bright.
k Ps. 132.9.
l Luke 14.15.
m ch. 22.8.
n Acts 10.26.
o 1 John 5.10.
p John 14.6. ch. 3.14.
q Isa. 11.4.
r Isa. 9.6.
s Isa. 63.2,3.
t John 1.1.
u Dan. 10.6. Matt. 17.2. ch. 4.4. ch. 7.9.
v Isa. 11.4. 2 Thes. 2.8. ch. 1.16.
w Ps. 2.9. ch. 2.27.
x Isa. 63.3. ch. 14.19,20.
y Ps. 72. Dan. 2.47. ch. 17.14.
z Eze. 39.17.
a ch. 16.16.
b Dan. 7.11. ch. 20.10.

CHAP. 20

a ch. 1.18.
b 2 Pet. 2.4. ch. 12.9.
c Dan. 6.17.
d Matt. 24. 24. ch. 16.14.
e Dan. 7.9. Matt. 19.28. Luke 22.30.
f 1 Cor. 6.2,3.
g ch. 6.9.
h ch. 13.12.
i Rom. 8.17.
j ch. 21.8.
k Isa. 61.6. 1 Pet. 2.9. ch. 5.10.
l 1 Pet. 5.8.
m Eze. 38.2.
n ch. 16.14

19 And [a]I saw the beast, and the
kings of the earth, and their armies,
gathered together to make war against
him that sat on the horse, and against
his army.
20 And the beast was taken, and with
him the false prophet that wrought
miracles before him, with which he
deceived them that had received the
mark of the beast, and them that worshipped his image. These [b]both were
cast alive into a lake of fire burning
with brimstone.
21 And the remnant were slain with
the sword of him that sat upon the
horse, which *sword* proceeded out of
his mouth: and all the fowls were filled
with their flesh.

CHAPTER 20

AND I saw an angel come down
from heaven, [a]having the key of
the bottomless pit and a great chain in
his hand.
2 And he laid hold on [b]the dragon,
that old serpent, which is the Devil,
and Satan, and bound him a thousand
years,
3 And cast him into the bottomless
pit, and shut him up, and [c]set a seal
upon him, that [d]he should deceive the
nations no more, till the thousand
years should be fulfilled: and after
that he must be loosed a little season.
4 And I saw [e]thrones, and they sat
upon them, and [f]judgment was given
unto them: and *I saw* the [g]souls of
them that were beheaded for the
witness of Jesus, and for the word of
God, [h]and which had not worshipped
the beast, neither his image, neither
had received *his* mark upon their foreheads, or in their hands; and they
lived and [i]reigned with Christ a thousand years.
5 But the rest of the dead lived not
again until the thousand years were
finished. This *is* the first resurrection.
6 Blessed and holy *is* he that hath
part in the first resurrection: on such
the [j]second death hath no power, but
they shall be priests of [k]God and of
Christ, and shall reign with him a
thousand years Mil John 5:28,29
7 And when the thousand years are
expired, Satan shall be loosed out of
his prison,
8 And shall [l]go out to deceive the
nations which are in the four quarters
of the earth, [m]Gog and Mā-gŏg, to
[n]gather them together to battle: the
number of whom *is* as the sand of
the sea.

9 And [o]they went up on the breadth
of the earth, and compassed the camp
of the saints about, and the beloved
city: and fire came down from
God out of heaven, and devoured
them.
10 And the devil that deceived them
was cast into the lake of fire and brimstone, where the beast and the false
prophet *are*, and shall be tormented
day and night for ever and ever. Mil ch 21:10
11 And I saw a great white throne,
and him that sat on it, from whose
face [p]the earth and the heaven fled
away; [q]and there was found no place
for them.
12 And [r]I saw the dead, small and
great, stand before God; [s]and the
books were opened: and [t]another
book was opened, which is *the book* of
life: and the dead were judged out of
those things which were written in the
books, [u]according to their works.
13 And the sea gave up the dead
which were in it; and death and [1]hell
delivered up the dead which were in
them: and they were judged every
man according to their works.
14 And [v]death and hell were cast
into the lake of fire. This is the second
death.
15 And whosoever was not found
written in the book of life was cast into
the lake of fire. Mil 2 Cor 5:10

CHAPTER 21

AND [a]I saw a new heaven and a new
earth: for the first heaven and the
first earth were passed away; and
there was no more [b]sea.
2 And I John saw the [c]holy city, new
Jerusalem, coming down from God
out of heaven, prepared [d]as a bride
adorned for her husband. 9IH 2 Peter 3:10-13
3 And I heard a great voice out of
heaven saying, Behold, the [e]taber-
nacle of God *is* with men, and he will
dwell with them, and they shall be his
people, and God himself shall be with
them, *and be* their God.
4 And [f]God shall wipe away all tears
from their eyes; and [g]there shall be no
more death, [h]neither sorrow, nor crying, neither shall there be any more
pain: for the former things are passed
away. 16 IH Rev 22:14
5 And [i]he that sat upon the throne
said, Behold, [j]I make all things new.
And he said unto me, Write: for these
words are true and faithful.
6 And he said unto me, It is done. I
am Alpha and Omega, the beginning
and the end. [k]I will give unto him that
is athirst of the fountain of the water
of life freely.
7 He that [l]overcometh shall inherit
[1]all things; and [m]I will be his God, and
he shall be my son.
8 But [n]the fearful, and unbelieving,
and the abominable, and murderers,
and whoremongers, and sorcerers,
and idolaters, and all liars, shall have
their part in the lake which burneth
with fire and brimstone: which is the
second death.
9 And there came unto me one of the
seven angels which had the seven vials
full of the seven last plagues, and
talked with me, saying, Come hither,
I will shew thee the bride, the Lamb's
wife.
10 And he carried me away in the
spirit to a great and high mountain,
and shewed me [o]that great city, the
holy Jerusalem, descending out of
heaven from God, Mil Vv 1,2
11 Having the glory of God: and her
light *was* like unto a stone most precious, even like a jasper stone, clear
as crystal;
12 And had a wall great and high,
and had twelve gates, and at the gates
twelve angels, and names written
thereon, which are *the names* of the
twelve tribes of the children of Israel:
13 On the east three gates; on the
north three gates; on the south three
gates; and on the west three gates.
14 And the wall of the city had
twelve foundations, and [p]in them the
names of the twelve apostles of the
Lamb.
15 And he that talked with me had a
[q]golden reed to measure the city, and
the gates thereof, and the wall thereof.
16 And the city lieth foursquare, and
the length is as large as the breadth:
and he measured the city with the
reed, twelve thousand furlongs. The
length and the breadth and the height
of it are equal. 8 IH Rev 21:2
17 And he measured the wall thereof, an hundred *and* forty *and* four
cubits, *according to* the measure of a
man, that is, of the angel.
18 And the building of the wall of it
was *of* jasper: and the city *was* pure
gold, like unto clear glass.
19 And [r]the foundations of the wall
of the city *were* garnished with all
manner of precious stones. The first
foundation *was* jasper; the second,
sapphire; the third, a chalcedony; the
fourth, an emerald;
20 The fifth, sardonyx; the sixth,
sardius; the seventh, chrysolite; the

[o] Isa. 8.8.
[p] 2 Pet. 3.7.
[q] Dan. 2.35.
[r] 2 Cor. 5.10. 1 Thes. 4.15, 17.
[s] Dan. 7.10.
[t] Ps. 69.28. Dan. 12.1. Phil. 4.3.
[u] Matt. 16. 27. Rom. 2.6.
[1] Or, the grave.
[v] 1 Cor. 15. 26.

CHAP. 21

[a] Isa. 65.17. 2 Pet. 3.13.
[b] Isa. 57.20.
[c] Isa. 52.1. Gal. 4.26. Heb. 11.10.
[d] Isa. 54.5. 2 Cor. 11.2.
[e] Lev. 26.11. 2 Cor. 6.16. ch. 7.15.
[f] Isa. 25.8.
[g] 1 Cor. 15. 26,54.
[h] Isa. 35.10.
[i] ch. 4.2.
[j] Isa. 43.19. 2 Cor. 5.17.
[k] Isa. 12.3. John 7.37. ch. 22.17.
[l] Rom. 8.17, 32. ch. 2.7,11.
[1] Or, these things.
[m] Zech. 8.8. Rom. 8.15-17. Heb. 8.10.
[n] 1 Cor. 6.9. Eph. 5.5. 1 Tim. 1.9. Heb. 12.14. ch. 22.15.
[o] Eze. 48.
[p] Matt. 10.2. Gal. 2.9. Eph. 2.20. ch. 18.20.
[q] Zech. 2.1. ch. 11.1.
[r] Isa. 54.11.

eighth, beryl; the ninth, a topaz; the tenth, a chrysoprasus; the eleventh, a jacinth; the twelfth, an amethyst.

21 And the twelve gates *were* twelve pearls; every several gate was of one pearl: [s]and the street of the city *was* pure gold, as it were transparent glass.

22 And [t]I saw no temple therein: for the Lord God Almighty and the Lamb are the temple of it.

23 And [u]the city had no need of the sun, neither of the moon, to shine in it: for the glory of God did lighten it, and the Lamb *is* the light thereof.

24 And [v]the nations of them which are saved shall walk in the light of it: and the kings of the earth do bring their glory and honour into it.

25 And the gates of it shall not be shut at all by day: for [w]there shall be no night there.

26 And they shall bring the glory and honour of the nations into it.

27 And [x]there shall in no wise enter into it any thing that defileth, neither *whatsoever* worketh abomination, or *maketh* a lie: but they which are written in the Lamb's book [y]of life.

CHAPTER 22

AND he shewed me [a]a pure river of water of life, clear as crystal, proceeding out of the throne of God and of the Lamb.

2 In the midst of the street of it, and on either side of the river, *was there* the [b]tree of life, which bare twelve *manner of* fruits, *and* yielded her fruit every month: and the leaves of the tree *were* [c]for the healing of the nations.

3 And [d]there shall be no more curse: but the [e]throne of God and of the Lamb shall be in it; and his servants shall serve him:

4 And [f]they shall see his face; and his name *shall be* in their foreheads.

5 And there shall be no night there; and they need no candle, neither light of the sun; for [g]the Lord God giveth them light: and they [h]shall reign for ever and ever.

6 And he said unto me, These sayings *are* faithful and true: and the [i]Lord God of the holy prophets sent his angel to shew unto his servants the things which must shortly be done.

7 Behold, I come quickly: blessed *is* he that keepeth the sayings of the prophecy of this book.

8 And I John saw these things, and heard *them*. And when I had heard and seen, I fell down to worship before the feet of the angel which shewed me these things.

9 Then saith he unto me, See *thou do it* not: for I am thy fellowservant, and of thy brethren the prophets, and of them which keep the sayings of this book: worship God.

10 And he [j]saith unto me, Seal not the sayings of the prophecy of this book: for the time is at hand.

11 He [k]that is unjust, let him be unjust still: and he which is filthy, let him be filthy still: and he that is righteous, let him be righteous still: and he that is holy, let him be holy still.

12 And, behold, I come quickly; and my reward [l]*is* with me, to give every man according as his work shall be.

13 I [m]am Alpha and Omega, the beginning and the end, the first and the last.

14 Blessed [n]*are* they that do his commandments, that they may have right to the tree of life, and may enter in through the gates into the city.

15 For without *are* dogs, and sorcerers, and whoremongers, and murderers, and idolaters, and whosoever loveth and maketh a lie.

16 I [o]Jesus have sent mine angel to testify unto you these things in the churches. I am [p]the root and the offspring of David, *and* [q]the bright and morning star.

17 And the Spirit and the bride say, Come. And let him that heareth say, Come. [r]And let him that is athirst come. And whosoever will, let him take the water of life freely.

18 For I testify unto every man that heareth the words of the prophecy of this book, If [s]any man shall add unto these things, God shall add unto him the plagues that are written in this book:

19 And if any man shall take away from the words of the book of this prophecy, God [t]shall take away his part [1]out of the book of life, and out of the holy city, and *from* the things which are written in this book.

20 He which testifieth these things saith, Surely [u]I come quickly. Ă-mĕn. Even so, come, Lord Jesus.

21 The grace of our Lord Jesus Christ *be* with you all. Ă-mĕn.

s ch. 22.2.
t 1 Ki. 8.27. Isa. 66.1. John 4.23. 1 Cor. 13.12.
u Isa. 24.23.
v Isa. 60.3. Isa. 66.12.
w Isa. 60.20.
x Isa. 35.8.
y Ps. 69.28. Dan. 12.1. Phil. 4.3. ch. 3.5. ch. 13.8. ch. 20.12.

CHAP. 22

a Ps. 36.8. Eze. 47.1. Zech. 14.8. John 7.38, 39.
b Gen. 2.9. Gen. 3.22. ch. 2.7.
c ch. 21.24.
d Zech. 14. 11. Matt. 25.41. ch. 21.4.
e Ps. 16.11. Eze. 48.35. ch. 7.15-17.
f Matt. 5.8. 1 Cor. 13.12. 1 John 3.2.
g Ps. 36.9. Ps. 84.11.
h Dan. 7.27. Rom. 5.17. 2 Tim. 2.12. 1 Pet. 1.3,4. ch. 3.21.
i Heb. 1.1.
j Dan. 8.26. Dan. 12.4,9.
k Eze. 3.27. 2 Tim. 3.13.
l Isa. 40.10. Matt. 16.27. Rom. 2.6-11. Rom. 14.12.
m Isa. 44.6.
n Dan. 12.12.
o 1 Pet. 3.22.
p Isa. 11.1. Jer. 23.5,6.
q Num. 24. 17. Zech. 6.12.
r Isa. 55.1. John 4.14. John 7.37. ch. 21.6.
s Deut. 4.2. Deut. 12.32. Pro. 30.6.
t Ex. 32.33.
1 Or, from the tree of life.
u Heb. 9.28.

THE END OF THE NEW TESTAMENT

SPECIAL
BIBLE SUBJECT HELPS

A Guide to Bible Truth
and
Exposition of Bible Prophecy

EIGHTY-ONE DIVISIONS
FOUR HUNDRED AND EIGHTY BIBLE SUBJECT OUTLINES
THOUSANDS OF SCRIPTURE REFERENCES

By
H. M. S. RICHARDS
RADIO EVANGEL
LOS ANGELES, CALIFORNIA

"THY WORD IS TRUTH"
John 17 : 17

LONDON AND NEW YORK
COLLINS' CLEAR-TYPE PRESS
GLASGOW · TORONTO · SYDNEY
AND AUCKLAND

SPECIAL INDEX FOR THE

ORDERLY STUDY

OF

THE WORD OF GOD

CONTENTS

INTRODUCTORY

CONNECTED STUDIES ON GREAT BIBLE PROPHECIES

CONNECTED STUDIES ON THE MESSAGE OF CHRIST IN THE LAW AND PROPHECY

CONTENTS

PAGE

CONNECTED STUDIES ON MAN—HERE AND HEREAFTER

OTHER VITAL TRUTH

THE AUTHOR OF THE BIBLE

"For the prophecy came not in old time by the will of man: but holy men of God spake as they were moved by the Holy Ghost." 2 Pet. 1 : 21.

"Of which salvation the prophets have inquired and searched diligently, who prophesied of the grace that should come unto you:

"Searching what, or what manner of time the Spirit of Christ which was in them did signify, when it testified beforehand the sufferings of Christ, and the glory that should follow.

"Unto whom it was revealed, that not unto themselves, but unto us they did minister the things, which are now reported unto you by them that have preached the gospel unto you with the Holy Ghost sent down from heaven; which things the angels desire to look into." 1 Pet. 1 : 10-12.

"But shun profane and vain babblings: for they will increase unto more ungodliness." 2 Tim. 2 : 16.

JESUS PLACED HIS APPROVAL ON THE SCRIPTURES

Luke 24 : 27, 44, 45; John 5 : 44-47; John 17 : 17.

PAUL BELIEVED ALL THE SCRIPTURES

Acts 24 : 14; Rom. 15 : 4; Heb. 4 : 12; Jer. 23 : 29.

THE PURPOSE OF THE SCRIPTURES

"And many other signs truly did Jesus in the presence of His disciples, which are not written in this book:

"But these are written, that ye might believe that Jesus is the Christ, the Son of God; and that believing ye might have life through His name." John 20 : 30, 31.

"Thy word have I hid in mine heart, that I might not sin against thee." Ps. 119 : 11.

"Thy word is a lamp unto my feet, and a light unto my path." Ps. 119 : 105.

"For whatsoever things were written aforetime were written for our learning, that we through patience and comfort of the scriptures might have hope." Rom. 15 : 4.

John 5 : 39; 1 Pet. 3 : 15; Isa. 8 : 20; 1 Pet. 1 : 22-25; John 8 : 31, 32; Acts 20 : 32.

MAN IS NOT TO ADD OR TO TAKE AWAY FROM THE SCRIPTURES

The First Part

"Ye shall not add unto the word which I command you, neither shall ye diminish ought from it, that ye may keep the commandments of the Lord your God which I command you." Deut. 4 : 2.

The Middle

Prov. 30 : 5, 6.

The Last Part

Rev. 22 : 18, 19; John 10 : 35; Isa. 55 : 11; Jer. 23 : 28; Isa. 40 : 7, 8.

BEATITUDES

"And seeing the multitudes, He went up into a mountain: and when He was set, His disciples came unto Him:
And He opened His mouth, and taught them, saying,
Blessed are the poor in spirit: for theirs is the kingdom of heaven.
Blessed are they that mourn: for they shall be comforted.
Blessed are the meek: for they shall inherit the earth.
Blessed are they which do hunger and thirst after righteousness: for they shall be filled.
Blessed are the merciful: for they shall obtain mercy.
Blessed are the pure in heart: for they shall see God.
Blessed are the peacemakers: for they shall be called the children of God.
Blessed are they which are persecuted for righteousness' sake: for theirs is the kingdom of heaven.
Blessed are ye, when men shall revile you, and persecute you, and shall say all manner of evil against you falsely, for my sake.
Rejoice, and be exceeding glad: for great is your reward in heaven: for so persecuted they the prophets which were before you." Matthew 5 : 1-12.

BIBLE STORIES

WHERE TO FIND THEM

1. Creation of the World—Genesis 1, 2.
2. Adam and Eve Cast Out of the Garden—Genesis 3.
3. Cain and Abel—Genesis 4.
4. Noah's Ark and the Flood—Genesis 6-8.
5. The Tower of Babel—Genesis 11 : 1-9.
6. God Calls Abraham—Genesis 12.
7. Abraham Saves Lot—Genesis 14.
8. Hagar Flees into the Desert—Genesis 16 : 6-13.
9. Angels Visit Abraham—Genesis 18; also 19 : 1.
10. God Destroys Sodom and Gomorrah—Genesis 19 : 24-29.
11. Abraham Offering Up Isaac—Genesis 22 : 1-19.
12. Abraham's Servant Seeks a Wife for Isaac—Genesis 24.
13. Esau Sells His Birthright—Genesis 25 : 29-34.
14. Jacob and Esau—Genesis 27.

15. The Dream of Jacob's Ladder—Genesis 28 : 10-15.
16. Jacob and Laban—Genesis 29.
17. Rachel Hides the Images—Genesis 31.
18. Jacob Wrestles with an Angel—Genesis 32.
19. Joseph and His Brothers—Genesis 37-48.
20. Pharaoh's Dream—Genesis 41.
21. Moses in an Ark of Bulrushes—Exodus 2 : 1-10.
22. Moses at the Burning Bush—Exodus 3.
23. Moses' Rod Turns into a Serpent—Exodus 4 : 1-5.
24. The Ten Plagues of Egypt—Exodus 7-12.
25. Israelites Cross the Red Sea—Exodus 14.
26. Manna Sent—Exodus 16.
27. Ten Commandments Given—Exodus 20.
28. The Golden Calf—Exodus 32.
29. Nadab and Abihu—Leviticus 10 : 1-11.
30. The Quails Come—Numbers 11 : 4-35.
31. Miriam Becomes a Leper—Numbers 12.
32. The Twelve Spies—Numbers 13, 14.
33. Korah, Dathan, and Abiram—Numbers 16.
34. Moses Smites the Rock—Numbers 20 : 1-13.
35. Fiery Serpents—Numbers 21 : 4-9.
36. Balaam—Numbers 22-24.
37. Moses' Death—Deuteronomy 34.
38. Rahab Hides the Spies—Joshua 2.
39. The Fall of Jericho—Joshua 6.
40. Achan—Joshua 7.
41. Ai Captured—Joshua 8 : 1-29.
42. Sun and Moon Stand Still—Joshua 10 : 1-14.
43. Gideon and His Army—Judges 6, 7.
44. Parable of Talking Trees—Judges 9 : 7-15.
45. Samson—Judges 13-16.
46. Story of Ruth—Book of Ruth.
47. Samuel Hears a Voice—1 Samuel 3.
48. The Philistines Capture the Ark—1 Samuel, 5, 6.
49. Israel Asks a King—1 Samuel 8.
50. Jonathan and His Armor-Bearer—1 Samuel 14 : 1-23.
51. Saul Disobeys—1 Samuel 15.
52. David Anointed—1 Samuel 16.
53. David and Goliath—1 Samuel 17.
54. David and Jonathan—1 Samuel 18 : 1-4.
55. David in the Cave—1 Samuel 24.
56. David in Saul's Camp—1 Samuel 26.
57. Saul and the Witch of Endor—1 Samuel 28.
58. Uzza Slain—2 Samuel 6 : 1-7.
59. David's Great Sin—2 Samuel 11, 12
60. Absalom—2 Samuel 15-18.
61. The Six Giants Killed—2 Samuel 21 : 15-22.
62. Solomon's Dream—1 Kings 3 : 5-15.
63. The Judgment of Solomon—1 Kings 3 : 16-28.
64. The Queen of Sheba—1 Kings 10.
65. Solomon's Wives—1 Kings 11 : 1-13.
66. The Prophet and the Lion—1 Kings 13.
67. Elijah and the Ravens—1 Kings 17.
68. Elijah and the Prophets of Baal—1 Kings 18.
69. Elijah in the Cave—I Kings 19 : 1-14.
70. Jezebel and Naboth's Vineyard—1 Kings 21.
71. Ahab's Death—1 Kings 22 : 1-40.
72. Elijah Brings Down Fire from Heaven—2 Kings 1 : 5-16.
73. Elijah Translated—2 Kings 2 : 1-18.
74. Elisha and the Bears—2 Kings 2 : 23-25.
75. The Widow's Oil Multiplied—2 Kings 4 : 1-15.
76. The Shunammite's Son—2 Kings 4 : 16-37.
77. Naaman's Leprosy—2 Kings 5.
78. The Floating Ax Head—2 Kings 6 : 1-7.
79. The Great Famine in Samaria—2 Kings 7.
80. Baal Worshippers Slain—2 Kings 10 : 18-28.
81. Hezekiah's Life Lengthened Fifteen Years—2 Kings 20 : 1-11.
82. Good Queen Esther—Book of Esther
83. The Virtuous Woman—Proverbs 31 : 10-30.
84. The New Earth—Isaiah 35; 65 : 17-25; 66 : 22, 23.
85. History of Satan—Isaiah 14 : 6-20; Ezekiel 28 : 11-19; Revelation 12 : 1-9.
86. Jeremiah in the Dungeon—Jeremiah 38 : 1-13.
87. Daniel Refuses the King's Meat—Daniel 1.
88. The Great Image—Daniel 2.
89. The Hebrew Children in the Fiery Furnace—Daniel 3.
90. Nebuchadnezzar Eats Grass—Daniel 4.
91. Belshazzar's Feast—Daniel 5.
92. Daniel in the Lion's Den—Daniel 6.
93. Jonah and the Whale—Book of Jonah.
94. Jesus Born in Bethlehem—Matthew 2.
95. Jesus and the Doctors of the Law—Luke 2 : 39-52.
96. John Baptizes Jesus—Matthew 3.
97. The Temptation—Matthew 4 : 1-11.
98. Christ Stills the Storm—Matthew 8 : 23-27.
99. Walking on the Water—Matthew 14 : 22-23.
100. The Ten Virgins—Matthew 25 : 1-13.
101. The Prodigal Son—Luke 15 : 11-32.
102. The Resurrection of Lazarus—John 11.

103. Christ's Death and Resurrection—Matthew 27, 28.
104. Christ's Ascension to Heaven—Acts 1 : 1-12.
105. The Stoning of Stephen—Acts 6 : 9-15; 7 : 54-60.
106. Saul Converted—Acts 9 : 1-30.
107. Peter Delivered from Prison by an Angel—Acts 12.
108. The New Jerusalem—Revelation 21, 22.

CURIOUS BIBLE FACTS

The Bible was the first book printed (about A.D. 1450). The King James or Authorised Version of the Bible was first printed in A.D. 1611 and is the greatest monument of classical English in the world.

Books in the Old Testament, 39; in the New Testament, 27; Total, 66. Chapters in the Old Testament, 929; in the New Testament, 260; Total 1189. Verses in the Old Testament, 23,214; in New Testament, 7959; Total 31,173. Words in the Old Testament, 592,493; in New Testament, 181,253; Total, 773,742. Letters in the Old Testament, 2,728,100; in New Testament, 838,380; Total, 3,566,480. Middle Chapter and the shortest, Psalm 117. Middle Verse, Psalm 118 : 8. The word " and " in Old Testament, 35,535; in the New Testament, 10,684; Total 46,219. Word "Jehovah," 6855 times. Of the Old Testament, Proverbs is the middle book; Job 29 is the middle chapter; 2 Chronicles 20 : 18 middle verse, and 1 Chronicles 1 : 1 the shortest verse. Of the New Testament, 2 Thessalonians is the middle book; between Romans 13 and 14 the middle chapter; Acts 17 : 17 middle verse, and John 11 : 35 shortest verse, both in the New Testament and in the whole Bible. All the letters in the alphabet except "J" are in Ezra 7: 21. Two chapters nearly alike are 2 Kings 19 and Isaiah 37; neither the word " God " nor " Lord " occurs in Esther.

The word " and " occurs 46,219 times and the word " reverend " but once (Ps. 111 : 9), and that applies to God. The longest word is in the eighth chapter of Isaiah, verse one.

THE LORD'S PRAYER

"Our Father which art in heaven, Hallowed be Thy name.
Thy kingdom come. Thy will be done in earth, as it is in heaven.
Give us this day our daily bread.
And forgive us our debts, as we forgive our debtors.
And lead us not into temptation, but deliver us from evil:
For thine is the kingdom, and the power, and the glory, for ever. A-men."
Matt. 6: 9-13.

PSALM 23

"The Lord is my shepherd; I shall not want.
He maketh me to lie down in green pastures: He leadeth me beside the still waters.
He restoreth my soul: He leadeth me in the paths of righteousness for His name's sake.
Yea, though I walk through the valley of the shadow of death, I will fear no evil: for Thou art with me; Thy rod and Thy staff they comfort me.
Thou preparest a table before me in the presence of mine enemies: Thou anointest my head with oil; my cup runneth over.
Surely goodness and mercy shall follow me all the days of my life: and I will dwell in the house of the Lord for ever."

A PURPORTED DESCRIPTION OF JESUS CHRIST

This is a purported word picture of our Blessed Lord, written of Him while He was yet on earth, and is on the Civic Records of the Romans, who were in power in the Holy Land at that time, hence quite authentic as a matter of history. This remarkable letter is supposed to have been written to the Roman Senate by Publius Lentulus, then President in Judea, about A.D. 33, and was published in the Meadville, Pennsylvania, Republican in 1873.

"There lives at this time in Judea, Jesus Christ, whom the barbarians esteem as a prophet, but His followers love and adore Him as the offspring of the immortal God. He calls the dead from their graves, and heals all sorts of diseases with a word or a touch. He is a tall man and well shaped, of an amiable and reverend aspect, His hair of a color that can hardly be matched, falling into graceful curls, waving about and very agreeably crouching upon His shoulders, parted on the crown of the head, running as a stream to the front after the manner of the Nazarites. His forehead high, large and imposing; His cheeks a lovely red; nose and mouth formed with exquisite symmetry; His beard thick and of a color suitable to the hair and parting in the middle like a fork; His eyes bright blue, clear and serene; look innocent, dignified, manly and mature; His hands and arms most delectable to behold.

"He rebukes with majesty, counsels with mildness; His whole address, whether in word or deed, being eloquent and grave. No man has seen Him laugh, yet His manners are exceedingly pleasant, but He has wept frequently in the presence of men.

"He is temperate, modest and wise—a man, for His extraordinary beauty and divine perfections—surpassing the children of men in every sense."

HOW TO STUDY THE BIBLE

DAILY STUDY

" These were more noble than those in Thessalonica, in that they received the word with all readiness of mind, and searched the scriptures daily, whether those things were so." Acts 17 : 11.

2 Tim. 3 : 15.

UNCONVERTED AND UNSPIRITUAL CANNOT FULLY UNDERSTAND IT

" At that time Jesus answered and said, I thank thee, O Father, Lord of heaven and earth, because thou hast hid these things from the wise and prudent, and hast revealed them unto babes." Matt. 11 : 25.

2 Pet. 3 : 15, 16—Such people " wrest " or twist the Bible, out of its true meaning.

1 Cor. 2 : 13, 14.

THE BIBLE MUST INTERPRET ITSELF

" For precept must be upon precept, precept upon precept; line upon line, line upon line; here a little, and there a little." Isa. 28 : 10.

" But the word of the Lord was unto them precept upon precent, precept upon precept; line upon line, line upon line; here a little, and there a little; that they might go, and fall backward, and be broken, and snared, and taken." Isa. 28 : 13.

" Study to shew thyself approved unto God, a workman that needeth not to be ashamed, rightly dividing the word of truth." 2 Tim. 2 : 15.

Lu. 24 : 27, 32—Jesus rightly divided it by subjects. Took subject of His First Advent through whole Old Testament.

Luke 4 : 16-20.

WE MUST STUDY PRAYERFULLY

" And I set my face unto the Lord God, to seek by prayer and supplications, with fasting, and sackcloth, and ashes :

" And he informed me, and talked with me, and said, O Daniel, I am now come forth to give thee skill and understanding." Dan. 9 : 3, 22.

Ps. 119 : 99, 100; Prov. 2 : 3-5.

WE ARE TO RECEIVE THE BIBLE AS THE VOICE OF GOD TO US PERSONALLY

" My sheep hear My voice, and I know them, and they follow Me." John 10 : 27.

" Search the scriptures; for in them ye think ye have eternal life : and they are they which testify of me." John 5 : 39.

" For this cause also thank we God without ceasing, because, when ye received the word of God which ye heard of us, ye received it not as the word of men, but as it is in truth, the word of God, which effectually worketh also in you that believe." 1 Thess. 2 : 13.

Ps. 119 : 105; John 7 : 17; 1 Tim. 4 : 16; 1 Pet. 1 : 22-25; Job 22 : 21, 22.

WONDERS OF PROPHECY

WHY WAS BIBLE PROPHECY GIVEN ?

" For whatsoever things were written aforetime were written for our learning, that we through patience and comfort of the scriptures might have hope." Rom. 15 : 4.

" Surely the Lord God will do nothing, but He revealeth His secret unto His servants the prophets." Amos 3 : 7.

2 Pet. 1 : 21—Prophecy came by Inspiration.

Deut. 29 : 29; 2 Pet. 1 : 16-19.

1 Pet. 1 : 9-11—Our Salvation the object.

Matt. 24 : 15—Daniel recognised as a Prophet by Christ.

Rev. 1 : 1—Book of Revelation given by Christ.

PROPHECY, GOD'S CHALLENGE TO UNBELIEF

" Remember the former things of old : for I am God, and there is none else; I am God, and there is none like me.

" Declaring the end from the beginning, and from ancient times the things that are not yet done, saying, My counsel shall stand, and I will do all my pleasure." Isa. 46 : 9, 10.

" Behold, the former things are come to pass, and new things do I declare : before they spring forth I tell you of them." Isa. 42 : 9.

" Produce your cause, saith the Lord; bring forth your strong reasons, saith the King of Jacob.

" Let them bring them forth, and shew us what shall happen : let them shew the former things, what they be, that we may consider them, and know the latter end of them; or declare us things for to come.

" Shew the things that are to come hereafter, that we may know that ye are gods : yea, do good, or do evil, that we may be dismayed, and behold it together." Isa. 41 : 21-23.

John 13 : 19—Christ was a Prophet.

Isa. 44 : 8.

SOME DEFINITE BIBLE PROPHECIES FULFILLED IN DETAIL

Isa. 13 : 19-22—Babylon destroyed, Arabian will not pitch his tent there, even to-day.

Jer. 51 : 24-26.

Zeph. 2 : 13—Assyria.

Eze. 26—Tyre. To be destroyed. It is.

Eze. 28 : 20-23—Sidon. Prophecy said Sidon would receive terrible punishment but would not be destroyed. It is still there after thousands of years.

Eze. 29 : 15; 30 : 13—Egypt to be " there." Not destroyed like Babylon and

Assyria. Egypt is still here, but a base or weak kingdom. It has been ruled by the Persians; Greeks; Romans; Byzantines; Saracens; Turks; French; British.

Deut. 28 : 25, 37—The Jews. This prophecy made before there were a kingdom, 1500 years B.C. and has continued to be true of the Jews over 1900 years this side the cross, a total of 3400 years. They are not destroyed but scattered in all nations.

THE GREAT PROPHECIES OF DANIEL

"When ye therefore shall see the abomination of desolation, spoken of by Daniel the prophet, stand in the holy place (whoso readeth, let him understand). Matt. 24 : 15. Christ recognised Daniel as a Prophet.

THE VISION OF THE GREAT IMAGE

"But there is a God in heaven that revealeth secrets, and maketh known to the King Nebuchadnezzar what shall be in the latter days. Thy dream, and the visions of thy head upon thy bed, are these." Dan. 2 : 28.

THE FOUR GREAT KINGDOMS OF THIS WORLD

(Read the entire second chapter of Daniel)

BABYLON : Dan. 2 : 38 (Golden Kingdom) 603 to 538 B.C.

Isa. 14 : 4—" Golden City."

Isa. 13 : 19—To be like Sodom and Gomorrah.

Isa. 44 : 27—Waters to be dried up in its capture.

Jer. 50 : 38; 51 : 32, 36—Dry up rivers.

Note.—In order to capture Babylon, Cyrus and Darius, with the Medes and Persians, drained the Euphrates River into a great depression north of the city and marched into Babylon along the bed of the river. The city fell in 538 B.C. Read Daniel, chapter 5.

MEDO-PERSIA : Dan. 2 : 39 (Silver Kingdom) 538 B.C. to 331 B.C.

Note.—In 331 B.C. the Persian Empire was overthrown by Alexander the Great at the Battle of Arbela.

GRECIA : Dan. 2 : 39 (Brass Kingdom) 331 to 168 B.C.

Note.—In 168 B.C., the Greeks were overthrown by the Romans in the Battle of Pydna.

ROME : Dan. 2 : 40 (Iron Kingdom) 168 B.C. to A.D. 476.

"And it came to pass in those days, that there went out a decree from Caesar Augustus, that all the world should be taxed." Lu. 2 : 1.

A ruler who can tax the world rules the world.

Note. — Describing the Roman conquests, Gibbon uses the very imagery employed in the vision of Daniel 2. He says : "The arms of the republic, sometimes vanquished in battle, always victorious in war, advanced with rapid steps to the Euphrates, the Danube, the Rhine, and the ocean ; and the images of gold, or silver, or brass, that might serve to represent the nations and their kings, were successively broken by the iron monarchy of Rome."—*Decline and Fall of the Roman Empire*, chap. 38, par. 1, under "General Observations," at the close of the chapter.

THE BREAK UP OF ROME AND THE GREAT NATIONS OF TO-DAY

"And whereas thou sawest the feet and toes, part of potters' clay and part of iron, the kingdom shall be divided; but there shall be in it of the strength of the iron, forasmuch as thou sawest the iron mixed with miry clay.

"And as the toes of the feet were part of iron and part of clay, so the kingdom shall be partly strong, and partly broken.

"And whereas thou sawest iron mixed with miry clay, they shall mingle themselves with the seed of men : but they shall not cleave one to another, even as iron is not mixed with clay." Dan. 2 : 41-43. (Feet and toes of Image.)

A.D. 476 to the Coming of Christ.

NOTE.—Between A.D. 351 and A.D. 476, the great empire of Rome was broken up and divided by ten tribes or nations, as follows : the Lombards; Franks; Ostrogoths; Visigoths; Burgundians; Suevi; Heruli; Vandals; Alemanni and Saxons. These kingdoms are represented in the nations of Europe to-day : Italy; France; England; Austria; Belgium; Holland; Spain; Portugal; Germany; Switzerland.

THE UNIVERSAL KINGDOM OF THE GOD OF HEAVEN

"And in the days of these kings shall the God of heaven set up a kingdom, which shall never be destroyed : and the kingdom shall not be left to other people, but it shall break in pieces and consume all these kingdoms, and it shall stand for ever." Dan. 2 : 44.

TIME.—The Second Coming of Christ to Eternity.

CHRIST REPRESENTED BY A STONE

Gen. 49 : 24; Acts 4 : 11; 1 Pet. 2 : 7, 8; Eph. 2 : 20.

HIS KINGDOM FUTURE AT HIS FIRST ADVENT

Matt. 26 : 2; Acts 1 : 6; 2 Tim. 4 : 1; Matt. 25 : 31.

Note.—This universal kingdom of God is founded "in the days of these kings" (kingdoms) which arose out of the ruins of the Roman Empire. These kingdoms were not yet in existence at the first advent of Christ. Therefore this predicted kingdom of God is the Kingdom of Glory to be set up at the Second Coming of Christ.

Matt. 6 : 10; Rev. 11 : 15; 2 Tim. 4 : 1; Rev. 22 : 20.

LOOK FOR THE WAY-MARKS

" Look for the way-marks as you journey on,
Look for the way-marks, passing one by one;
Down thro' the ages, past the kingdoms four,
Where are we standing ? Look the way-marks o'er.

" First, the Assyrian kingdom ruled the world,
Then Medo-Persia's banners were unfurled;
And after Greece held universal sway
Rome seized the scepter,—
Where are we to-day ?

" Down in the feet of iron and of clay,
Weak and divided, soon to pass away;
What will the next great, glorious drama be ?
Christ and His coming, and eternity.

" Look for the way-marks, the great prophetic way-marks,
Down thro' the ages, past the kingdoms four,
Look for the way-marks, the great prophetic way-marks;
The journey's almost o'er."

By F. E. Belden.

Daniel 7

THE VISION OF THE FOUR GREAT BEASTS

Read the entire seventh chapter of Daniel.

Note.—The vision of Daniel 2 was given to a heathen King who would naturally show interest in an image, but this vision of Daniel 7 was given to Daniel himself, the true servant of God, and the nature of worldly kingdoms is more clearly portrayed under the symbols of beasts.

SYMBOLS IN THE VISION

BEASTS: Represent kingdoms. Dan. 7 : 23.
SEA OR WATERS: Represent peoples, multitudes. Rev. 17 : 15; Isa. 8 : 6, 8.
WINDS: Represent Strife, commotion, war. Jer. 25 : 31-33; 49 : 36, 37.
HORNS: Represent Kings or Powers. Dan. 7 : 24.

THE FOUR GREAT KINGDOMS

BABYLON (Lion with Eagle's wings):

"The first was like a lion, and had eagle's wings: I beheld till the wings thereof were plucked, and it was lifted up from the earth, and made stand upon the feet as a man, and a man's heart was given to it." Dan. 7 : 4.

603 to 538 B.C.

MEDO-PERSIA (Bear):

" And behold another beast, a second, like to a bear, and it raised up itself on one side, and it had three ribs in the mouth of it between the teeth of it: and they said thus unto it, Arise, devour much flesh." Dan. 7 : 5.

538 to 331 B.C.

GRECIA (Leopard):

" After this I beheld, and lo another, like a leopard, which had upon the back of it four wings of a fowl; the beast had also four heads; and dominion was given to it." Dan. 7 : 6.

331 to 168 B.C.

ROME (Unnamed Beast):

"After this I saw in the night visions, and behold a fourth beast, dreadful and terrible, and strong exceedingly; and it had great iron teeth: it devoured and brake in pieces, and stamped the residue with the feet of it: and it was diverse from all the beasts that were before it; and it had ten horns." Dan. 7 : 7.

Note.—For list of the ten kingdoms 168 B.C. to A.D. 476, which arose on the ruins of Rome, denoted by the ten horns (Dan. 7 : 24), see the Vision of the Great Image.

THE LITTLE HORN

" I considered the horns, and, behold, there came up among them another little horn, before whom there were three of the first horns plucked up by the roots: and, behold, in this horn were eyes like the eyes of man, and a mouth speaking great things." Dan. 7 : 8.

" And of the ten horns that were in his head, and of the other which came up, and before whom three fell; even of that horn that had eyes, and a mouth that spake very great things, whose look was more stout than his fellows.

" I beheld, and the same horn made war with the saints, and prevailed against them;

"Until the Ancient of days came, and judgment was given to the saints of the most High; and the time came that the saints possessed the kingdom." Dan. 7 : 20-22.

Note.—Papal Rome succeeded Pagan Rome. It was a religious power as well as a political power. It arose among the ten divisions of Rome and overthrew three of these kingdoms which were Arian in religion and opposed the spiritual supremacy of the Papacy; the Heruli (A.D. 493), the Vandals (A.D. 534) and the Ostrogoths (A.D. 538).

FOUR MARKS OF IDENTIFICATION

" And the ten horns out of this kingdom are ten kings that shall arise: and another shall rise after them; and he shall be diverse from the first, and he shall subdue three kings.

"And he shall speak great words against the most High, and shall wear out the saints of the most High, and think to change times and laws: and they shall be given into his hand until a time and times and the dividing of time.

"But the judgment shall sit, and they shall take away his dominion, to consume and to destroy it unto the end." Dan. 7:24-26.

1. SPEAK GREAT WORDS against the most High.

Note.—The title "Father" in a spiritual sense is employed. This is contrary to scripture.

"And call no man your father upon the earth: for one is your Father, which is in heaven." Matt. 23:9.

HISTORICAL QUOTATION

"For thou art the Shepherd, thou art the physician, thou art the director, thou art the husbandman, finally thou art another God on earth."—From oration of Christopher Marcellus in fourth session of Fifth Lateran Council, Labbe & Cossart's *History of the Councils*: published in 1672, Vol. XIV., col. 109.

Read 1 Thess. 2:3, 4: "For our exhortation was not of deceit, nor of uncleanness, nor in guile:

"But as we were allowed of God to be put in trust with the gospel, even so we speak; not as pleasing men, but God, which trieth our hearts."

2. HE SHALL WEAR OUT THE SAINTS OF THE MOST HIGH

Note.—During the Dark Ages thousands were put to death. According to Llorente, formerly Secretary of the Inquisition, 31,912 were burned to death in Spain. See *The History of the Inquisition in Spain*, p. 206.

"The church has persecuted. Only a tyro in church history will deny that. . . . One hundred and fifty years after Constantine the Donatists were persecuted, and sometimes put to death. . . . Protestants were persecuted in France and Spain with the full approval of the church authorities. We have always defended the persecution of the Huguenots, and the Spanish Inquisition. Wherever and whenever there is honest Catholicity, there will be a clear distinction drawn between truth and error, and Catholicity and all forms of error. When she thinks it good to use physical force, she will use it."—*The Western Watchman* (Roman Catholic), St. Louis, Dec. 24, 1908.

3. HE SHALL THINK TO CHANGE TIMES AND LAWS

Note. — By expunging the second commandment and dividing the tenth in order to make the number ten. Also by the attempted change of the Sabbath from the seventh to the first day of the week.

QUOTATION

"*Question:* Have you any other way of proving that the Church has power to institute festivals of precept?

"*Answer:* Had she not such power, she could not have done that in which all modern religionists agree with her; she could not have substituted the observance of Sunday the first day of the week, for the observance of Saturday the seventh day, a change for which there is no Scriptural authority." From *A Doctrinal Catechism*, by Rev. Stephen Keenan, p. 174.

4. THE "TIME, TIMES AND DIVIDING OF TIME" OF THE LITTLE HORN'S SUPREMACY

". . . And they shall be given into his hand until a time and times and the dividing of time." Dan. 7:25, last clause.

See Rev. 12:14; Rev. 13:5; Rev. 11:2; Rev. 12:6.

IN SYMBOLIC PROPHECY, A DAY STANDS FOR A YEAR

Num. 14:34; Eze. 4:6.

Note.—The calendar year of 360 days, or twelve months of 30 days each, is used in prophetic chronology.

The Papal supremacy would then last 1260 years, from A.D. 538, when the last of the three opposing "horns" was uprooted, to 1798. Then Berthier, with the French Army, took Pope Pius VI. prisoner, abolished the Papacy and set up a Republic in Rome.

THE FINAL VICTORY OF GOD'S PEOPLE

Dan. 7:26, 27.

THE SECOND COMING OF CHRIST

CHRIST PROMISED TO RETURN AGAIN

"Let not your heart be troubled: ye believe in God, believe also in me.

"In my Father's house are many mansions: if it were not so, I would have told you. I go to prepare a place for you.

"And if I go and prepare a place for you, I will come again, and receive you unto myself; that where I am, there ye may be also." John 14:1-3.

"And then shall appear the sign of the Son of man in heaven: and then shall all the tribes of the earth mourn, and they shall see the Son of man coming in the clouds of heaven with power and great glory." Matt. 24:30.

Luke 21:27-30; Rev. 22:7, 12, 20.

THE APOSTLES BELIEVED IN CHRIST'S SECOND COMING

PAUL:

"For the Lord himself shall descend from heaven with a shout, with the voice of the archangel, and with the trump of God: and the dead in Christ shall rise first." 1 Thess. 4 : 16.

PETER:

"Repent ye therefore, and be converted, that your sins may be blotted out, when the times of refreshing shall come from the presence of the Lord." Acts 3 : 19.

JOHN:

"Behold, he cometh with clouds; and every eye shall see him, and they also which pierced him: and all kindreds of the earth shall wail because of him. Even so, Amen." Rev. 1 : 7.

JAMES (Brother of Jesus) Jas. 5 : 7, 8.

THE ANGELS BELIEVE IN THE SECOND COMING OF CHRIST

"And when he had spoken these things, while they beheld, he was taken up; and a cloud received him out of their sight.

"And while they looked stedfastly toward heaven as he went up, behold, two men stood by them in white apparel;

"Which also said, Ye men of Galilee, why stand ye gazing up into heaven? this same Jesus, which is taken up from you into heaven, shall so come in like manner as ye have seen him go into heaven." Acts 1 : 9-11.

Matt. 25 : 31. 2 Thess. 1 : 7.

THE SECOND COMING OF CHRIST IS NOT CONVERSION

For in Conversion, the sinner comes to Christ, but in the Second Advent, Christ comes for the Saint.

"Come unto me, all ye that labour and are heavy laden, and I will give you rest." Matt. 11 : 28.

"Come now, and let us reason together, saith the Lord: though your sins be as scarlet, they shall be as white as snow; though they be red like crimson, they shall be as wool." Isa. 1 : 18.

IT IS NOT DEATH

It is just the opposite for it brings the resurrection.

"Behold, I shew you a mystery: We shall not all sleep, but we shall all be changed,

"In a moment, in the twinkling of an eye, at the last trump: for the trumpet shall sound, and the dead shall be raised incorruptible, and we shall be changed.

"For this corruptible must put on incorruption, and this mortal must put on immortality.

"So when this corruptible shall have put on incorruption, and this mortal shall have put on immortality, then shall be brought to pass the saying that is written, Death is swallowed up in victory." 1 Cor. 15 : 51-54.

"For the Lord himself shall descend from heaven with a shout, with the voice of the archangel, and with the trump of God: and the dead in Christ shall rise first:

"Then we which are alive and remain shall be caught up together with them in the clouds, to meet the Lord in the air: and so shall we ever be with the Lord." 1 Thess. 4 : 16, 17.

Matt. 24 : 30, 31; Job 19 : 23-26; John 21 : 21-23.

IT IS NOT THE DAY OF PENTECOST

On that day "Another Comforter" the Holy Ghost came, and not Jesus Himself.

"And I will pray the Father, and he shall give you another Comforter, that he may abide with you for ever;

"Even the Spirit of truth; whom the world cannot receive, because it seeth him not, neither knoweth him: but ye know him: for he dwelleth with you, and shall be in you." John 14 : 16, 17.

"But ye shall receive power, after that the Holy Ghost is come upon you: and ye shall be witnesses unto me both in Jerusalem, and in all Judea, and in Samaria, and unto the uttermost part of the earth." Acts 1 : 8.

Acts 2 : 1-6.

Over fifty times after the Day of Pentecost, the promise of the second coming of Christ is repeated.

IT WAS NOT THE DESTRUCTION OF JERUSALEM

That was a scattering. The second coming is a gathering of God's people.

"Now we beseech you, brethren, by the coming of our Lord Jesus Christ, and by our gathering together unto him." 2 Thess. 2 : 1.

"And He shall send his angels with a great sound of a trumpet, and they shall gather together his elect from the four winds, from one end of heaven to the other." Matt. 24 : 31.

The Book of Revelation which contains His promise to return was written 20 or 30 years after the destruction of Jerusalem.

IT WAS NOT THE SPREAD OF CHRISTIANITY

That has been a process—the second coming is a stupendous event.

"For the Lord himself shall descend from heaven with a shout, with the voice of the archangel, and with the trump of God: and the dead in Christ shall rise first." 1 Thess. 4 : 16.

Rev. 6 : 14-17; Rev. 1 : 7.

THE PROPHETS OF THE OLD TESTAMENT FORETOLD THE SECOND COMING OF CHRIST

"For I know that my redeemer liveth, and that he shall stand at the latter day upon the earth." Job. 19 : 25.

"Our God shall come, and shall not keep silence: a fire shall devour before him, and it shall be very tempestuous round about him." Ps. 50 : 3.

"And Enoch also, the seventh from Adam, prophesied of these, saying,

Behold, the Lord cometh with ten thousands of his saints,

"To execute judgment upon all, and to convince all that are ungodly among them of all their ungodly deeds which they have ungodly committed, and of all their hard speeches, which ungodly sinners have spoken against him." Jude 14, 15.

Ps. 96 : 13.

THE COMING OF OUR LORD WILL BE LITERAL AND VISIBLE. ALL THE WORLD WILL KNOW ABOUT IT.

"And when he had spoken these things, while they beheld, he was taken up; and a cloud received him out of their sight.

"And while they looked stedfastly toward heaven as he went up, behold, two men stood by them in white apparel;

"Which also said, 'Ye men of Galilee, why stand ye gazing up into heaven? this same Jesus which is taken up from you into heaven, shall so come in like manner as ye have seen him go into heaven." Acts 1 : 9-11.

"Behold, he cometh with clouds, and every eye shall see him, and they also which pierced him: and all kindreds of the earth shall wail because of him. Even so, Amen." Rev. 1 : 7.

Matt. 24 : 23-26; Matt. 16 : 27; Luke 9 : 26; Matt. 24 : 30; 1 Thess. 4 : 16; Matt. 24 : 27; Heb. 9 : 28; Matt. 26 : 64; Isa. 25 : 9.

Note.—Some have contended that the Greek word "Parousia" translated "coming" means secret presence. That this is not the necessary meaning of the word, the following texts make clear, for the word "coming" or "come" in each one, comes from "Parousia."

1 Cor. 16 : 17; 2 Cor. 7 : 6, 7; Phil. 1 : 26; 1 Jno. 2 : 28.

THE COMING OF CHRIST WILL BE AN "APPEARING," A REAL COMING

"When Christ, who is our life, shall appear, then shall ye also appear with him in glory." Col. 3 : 4.

"And when the chief Shepherd shall appear, ye shall receive a crown of glory that fadeth not away." 1 Pet. 5 : 4.

See 1 Jno. 2 : 28; 3 : 2; 1 Pet. 1 : 7; 1 Tim. 6 : 14; 2 Tim. 4 : 1.

THE TRANSFIGURATION OF CHRIST WAS AN ACTUAL PROPHECY OF HIS SECOND COMING

Matt. 16 : 28.

"And after six days Jesus taketh Peter, James, and John his brother, and bringeth them up into an high mountain apart,

"And was transfigured before them: and his face did shine as the sun, and his raiment was white as the light.

"And, behold, there appeared unto them Moses and Elias talking with him.

"Then answered Peter, and said unto Jesus, Lord, it is good for us to be here: if thou wilt, let us make here three tabernacles; one for thee, and one for Moses, and one for Elias.

"While he yet spake, behold, a bright cloud overshadowed them: and behold a voice out of the cloud, which said, This is my beloved Son, in whom I am well pleased; hear ye him.

"And when the disciples heard it, they fell on their face, and were sore afraid." Matt. 17 : 1-6.

"For we have not followed cunningly devised fables, when we made known unto you the power and coming of our Lord Jesus Christ, but were eye-witnesses of his majesty.

"For he received from God the Father honour and glory, when there came such a voice to him from the excellent glory, This is my beloved Son, in whom I am well pleased.

"And this voice which came from heaven we heard, when we were with him in the holy mount." 2 Peter 1 : 16-18.

Christ appeared as He will when He comes in glory (Matt. 25 : 31); Moses represented the resurrected saints, as he was raised from the dead (Jude 9; Rom. 5 : 14; Deut. 18 : 15; 1 Thess. 4 : 13-18); Elijah represented the translated saints, for he never died (2 Kings 2 : 11; 1 Thess. 4 : 17; 1 Cor. 15 : 54).

WHY IS CHRIST COMING?

He is coming to raise the righteous dead, translate the living righteous.

"Marvel not at this: for the hour is coming, in the which all that are in the graves shall hear his voice.

"And shall come forth; they that have done good, unto the resurrection of life; and they that have done evil, unto the resurrection of damnation." John 5 : 28, 29.

"For as in Adam all die, even so in Christ shall all be made alive.

"But every man in his own order: Christ the firstfruits; afterward they that are Christ's at his coming." 1 Cor. 15 : 22, 23.

1 Thess. 4 : 16, 17; Dan. 12 : 1, 2; 1 Cor. 15 : 51-53; 1 John 3 : 2: Matt. 24 : 31; John 14 : 1-3.

HE IS COMING TO REWARD HIS PEOPLE AND TO JUDGE THE WORLD

"And, behold, I come quickly; and my reward is with me, to give every man according as his work shall be." Rev. 22 : 12.

"Henceforth there is laid up for me a crown of righteousness, which the Lord, the righteous judge, shall give me at that day: and not to me only, but unto all them also that love his appearing." 2 Tim. 4 : 8.

Heb. 9 : 28; Isa. 25 : 8, 9; Rev. 5 : 10; Dan. 7 : 27; Matt. 25 : 34; 2 Pet. 2 : 9; Eccl. 3 : 17; Deut. 32 : 36; Eccl. 12 : 14;

Ps. 96 : 13; 2 Tim. 4 : 1; Matt. 25 : 31, 32; Acts 3 : 20, 21; Ps. 37 : 11, 29; 2 Pet. 3 : 13.

HE IS COMING TO DESTROY THE WICKED AND BEGIN HIS REIGN IN GLORY

"For the mystery of iniquity doth already work: only he who now letteth will let, until he be taken out of the way.

"And then shall that Wicked be revealed, when the Lord shall consume with the spirit of his mouth, and shall destroy with the brightness of his coming." 2 Thess. 2 : 7, 8.

"And the nations were angry, and thy wrath is come, and the time of the dead, that they should be judged, and that thou shouldest give reward unto thy servants the prophets, and to the saints, and them that fear thy name, small and great; and shouldest destroy them which destroy the earth." Rev. 11 : 18.

Isa. 11 : 4; Rev. 19 : 11, 16; Matt. 25 : 31; Dan. 2 : 44; Dan. 7 : 14; Micah 4 : 7; Luke 1 : 33; 2 Pet. 3 : 13, 14.

SIGNS OF THE TIMES

"And in the morning, It will be foul weather to-day: for the sky is red and lowring. O ye hypocrites, ye can discern the face of the sky; but can ye not discern the signs of the times?" Matt. 16 : 3.

See Matt. 24 : 1-51.

Note.—These signs are to indicate the soon Coming of Christ.

1. DARKENED SUN AND MOON LIKE BLOOD

Matt. 24 : 29; Rev. 6 : 12.

Fulfilled May 19, 1780, in the great Dark Day. See encyclopedias.

2. FALLING STARS

Matt. 24 : 29; Rev. 6 : 13.

Fulfilled Nov. 13, 1833, in the great star shower.

3. INCREASE OF KNOWLEDGE

Dan. 12 : 4.

Fulfilled in this last generation. See *Scientific American.*

4. RUNNING TO AND FRO

Dan. 12 : 4.

Modern trains, automobiles, airplanes, steamships, etc. Nahum 2; Isa. 2 : 7.

5. WARS AND RUMOURS OF WAR

Matt. 24 : 6, 7; Joel 3 : 9-14; Rev. 11 : 18.

6. EARTHQUAKES, PESTILENCES AND STORMS

Matt. 24 : 7; Joel 2 : 30; Luke 21 : 11; Ps. 148 : 8; Eze. 38 : 20-22.

7. CAPITAL AND LABOUR TROUBLE

Jas. 5 : 1-6; Isa. 8 : 12, 13; Jas. 5 : 7, 8.

8. LAWLESSNESS AND SIN

Lu. 17 : 26-30; Matt. 24 : 12; Gen. 6 : 5, 11; 2 Tim. 3 : 1-5.

9. DOUBT AND EVOLUTIONARY PHILOSOPHY

2 Pet. 3 : 3-7.

10. DISTRESS OF NATIONS

Luke 21 : 25-28; Rev. 11 : 18.

11. SPIRITUALISM

1 Tim. 4 : 1, 2; Lev. 19 : 31; Matt. 24 : 14; Rev. 22 : 15; Gal. 5 : 19-21.

12. DOUBT AND APOSTASY IN THE CHURCH

2 Tim. 4 : 1-4; Luke 18 : 8; 1 Tim. 4 : 3, 4; Matt. 24 : 12.

13. THE GOSPEL OF THE KINGDOM TO ALL NATIONS—THE GREATEST SIGN OF ALL

Matt. 24 : 14.

Note.—It is going now in over 500 languages.

Rev. 14 : 14, 15; Rev. 14 : 6.

MODERN INVENTIONS IN THE BIBLE

ARE AUTOMOBILES, RAILROADS, AIRPLANES AND GREAT MODERN INVENTIONS IN BIBLE PROPHECY AS SIGNS OF THE TIMES?

"But thou, O Daniel, shut up the words, and seal the book, even to the time of the end: many shall run to and fro, and knowledge shall be increased." Dan. 12 : 4.

Note.—A great increase of knowledge, inventions and travel has come in the last generation.

Isa. 2 : 6, 7. Chariots—wheeled vehicles.

"The shield of his mighty men is made red, the valiant men are in scarlet: the chariots shall be with flaming torches in the day of his preparation, and the fir trees shall be terribly shaken.

"The chariots shall rage in the streets, they shall justle one against another in the broad ways: they shall seem like torches, they shall run like the lightnings.

"He shall recount his worthies: they shall stumble in their walk; they shall make haste to the wall thereof, and the defence shall be prepared." Nahum 2 : 3-5. Chariots (wheeled vehicles—autos, railroad trains, etc.) will be with flaming torches (headlights). Run like the lightnings. Great speed trials for motor cars and streamline trains.

Isa. 60 : 8. Air ships and airplanes.

Job 38 : 35. Electric messages.

Rom. 9 : 28. These things to help carry God's work to the world quickly.

THE SEVEN SEALS

Revelation, chapters 5 and 6. Also Rev. 8 : 1.

1. WHITE HORSE

Rev. 6 : 1, 2 (to A.D. 100).

White represents purity of the Church as it went forth with conquering power in the first century. Zech. 4 : 6; Col. 1 : 23. See Rev. 19 : 11-16.

2. RED HORSE

Rev. 6 : 3, 4 (A.D. 100 to 323).

Corruption was creeping in and persecution resulted. Bloodshed was common. 2 Cor. 12 : 10. Persecution; Rev. 2 : 10. Ten days of tribulation; Acts 20 : 29. Apostasy; 2 Thess. 2 : 7.

3. BLACK HORSE

Rev. 6 : 5, 6 (A.D. 323 to 538).

Apostasy Rampant—Spiritual darkness.

4. PALE HORSE

Rev. 6 : 7, 8 (A.D. 538-1517).

Time of deadly persecution to people of God under Papal supremacy, until the dawn of the Reformation put a check on its work of death. Dark Ages Inquisition.

5. SOULS UNDER THE ALTAR

Rev. 6 : 9-11 (A.D. 1517-1755).

From the Reformation to the great Lisbon Earthquake, Nov. 1, 1755, these had been killed under the preceding Seal. If, as is sometimes taught, these martyrs were already in Heaven and persecutors in Hell, what more vengeance could they desire? But here the figure of personification is used. See examples where inanimate things are represented as being alive. Hab. 2 : 11; Gen. 4 : 10; Judges 9 : 8-15; Rom. 4 : 17. These martyrs had gone down as the worst of evil men, but the Reformation threw a new light on their work and character. White robes were given to them (Rev. 19 : 8) and they were to rest a little longer until the Resurrection. 1 Thess. 4 : 16-18. The "altar" is the altar of sacrifice or this earth where their lives were offered. God does not confine His people in an altar or other receptacle in heaven!

6. GREAT EARTHQUAKE

Rev. 6 : 12-17 (1755 to the end).

The great Lisbon earthquake of Nov. 1, 1755, shook an area of 4,000,000 miles. In the city of Lisbon, nearly 100,000 people were killed.

Great Dark Day : May 19, 1780.

Moon as Blood : May 19, 1780 (night following).

(See Amos 5 : 8; Isa. 13 : 10; Eze. 32 : 7).

Verse 13—Stars Fell from Heaven : Nov. 13, 1833.

Matt. 24 : 29; Mk. 13 : 25.

Verse 14—Heavens Roll Back as a Scroll—Occurs at the Second Coming of Christ : Isa. 34 : 4; 2 Pet. 3 : 10.

We are now living between verses 13 and 14 of Rev. 6.

7. SILENCE IN HEAVEN FOR HALF AN HOUR

"And when he had opened the seventh seal, there was silence in heaven about the space of half an hour." Rev. 8 : 1.

Christ will come for His people with all the holy angels. Heaven will be empty. Matt. 25 : 31; Rev. 5 : 11-13.

THE SEVEN CHURCHES

Revelation, chapters 2 and 3.

1. EPHESUS

Rev. 2 : 1-7 (to A.D. 100). Means "Desirable."

Represents the condition of the Church in the Apostolic Age.

Verse 2 : "found them liars." See Acts 13 : 8.

Verse 3 : "hast laboured." Gospel went to whole world. See Col. 1 : 23; Acts 8 : 4.

Verse 7 : "Paradise" is where God's throne is located, or Heaven. 2 Cor. 12 : 2, 4; Rev. 22 : 2.

2. SMYRNA

Rev. 2 : 8-11 (A.D. 100 to 323). Means "Myrrh."

Describes Church to conversion of Constantine when the Empire became Christian and Pagan persecution largely ceased.

Verse 9 : "say they are Jews, and are not." See Rom. 2 : 28, 29; Rom. 9 : 6, 7; Gal. 3 : 26-28.

Verse 10 : "tribulation ten days." Ten years of Pagan persecution under Diocletian, A.D. 303 to 313. See Luke 21 : 12; "crown of life," see 2 Tim. 4 : 8; 1 Pet. 5 : 4.

Verse 11 : "not be hurt of the second death." Matt. 10 : 28.

3. PERGAMOS

Rev. 2 : 12-17 (A.D. 323 to 538). Means "Height" or "Elevation."

Portraying the condition of the Church from the time of Constantine to the beginning of the 1260 years of Papal supremacy.

Verse 13 : "Antipas"—Anti-Papal. See 2 Thess. 2 : 3.

Verse 14 : "Balaam." See Numbers 24 and 25; 2 Pet. 2 : 15; Jude 11.

4 THYATIRA

Rev. 2 : 18-29 (538 to 1798) means "Contrition" or "Song of Labor."

Illustrates suffering of God's true people during 1260 years of Papal supremacy. See Matt. 24 : 21, 22.

5. SARDIS

Rev. 3 : 1-6 (1798-1833). Means, "That which Remains."

Symbolises the people of God remaining as a result of the Reformation from Papal error.

6. PHILADELPHIA

Rev. 3 : 7-13 (1833-44).

Means "Brotherly Love." Fittingly represents the Church during the great Advent Movement under the Judgment Hour Message.

Key words "open door" (work in Most Holy Place in Heavenly Sanctuary started 1844 when Christ went into Second Apartment). "Word of Patience" (see Rev. 14 : 12). "Come quickly" (Heb. 10 : 25).

7. LAODICEA

Rev. 3 : 14-22 (1844 to the end).

Means "Judging the People." The Judgment of God's people began in 1844 (Dan. 8 : 14).

Verse 18: "buy." See Isa. 55 : 1; "white raiment"; Isa. 64 : 6; "eye salve"; Acts 10 : 38; "Holy Spirit"; 1 Jno. 2 : 20, 27; John 14 : 26.

THE LAST CHURCH

See Rev. 12 : 17. A commandment keeping church.

The message to the seven churches are for God's people to-day and the seven great promises should be studied. (See Rev. 2 : 7, 11, 17, 26-28; Rev. 3 : 5, 12, 21.)

THE SEVEN TRUMPETS

Read Rev. 8 : 2-13; Rev. 9 : 1-21; Rev. 10 : 7; Rev. 11 : 15-19.

THE TRUMPET IS A SYMBOL OF WAR

Jer. 4 : 19, 20; Joel 2 : 1-11.

The first four trumpets deal with the downfall of the Roman Empire. The fifth and sixth with the downfall of the Eastern division of Rome, and the seventh with the downfall of all the kingdoms of the world.

1. FIRST TRUMPET

"The first angel sounded, and there followed hail and fire mingled with blood, and they were cast upon the earth : and the third part of trees was burnt up, and all green grass was burnt up." Rev. 8 : 7. (Invasion from the North by the Goths under Alaric; A.D. 395 to 410.)

2. SECOND TRUMPET

"And the second angel sounded, and as it were a great mountain burning with fire was cast into the sea : and the third part of the sea became blood;

"And the third part of the creatures which were in the sea, and had life, died; and the third part of the ships were destroyed." Rev. 8 : 8, 9.

Terrible invasion of the Vandals under Genseric of both the African provinces, and of Italy itself, A.D. 428 to 476. His power was largely on the sea. In one night battle, he completely destroyed the Roman fleet of 1113 ships and over 100,000 men. See Gibbon, *Decline and Fall of the Roman Empire*, chap. 36.

3. THIRD TRUMPET

"And the third angel sounded, and there fell a great star from heaven, burning as it were a lamp, and it fell upon the third part of the rivers, and upon the fountains of waters;

"And the name of the star is called Wormwood : and the third part of the waters became wormwood; and many men died of the waters, because they were made bitter." Rev. 8 : 10, 11.

Invasion of Western Empire of Rome by the Huns under Attila, A.D. 451. In the great Battle of Chalons in Gaul, 300,000 men were slain. He was called the "Scourge of God," and boasted that the grass never grew again where his horse had trod.

4. FOURTH TRUMPET

"And the fourth angel sounded, and the third part of the sun was smitten, and the third part of the moon, and the third part of the stars; so as the third part of them was darkened, and the day shone not for a third part of it, and the night likewise." Rev. 8 : 12.

Fall of Western Rome in A.D. 476, at hands of the Heruli under Odoacer. Italy now became a province of the Emperor of Eastern Rome ruling from Constantinople.

5. FIFTH TRUMPET

"And I beheld, and heard an angel flying through the midst of heaven, saying with a loud voice, Woe, woe, woe, to the inhabiters of the earth by reason of the other voices of the trumpet of the three angels, which are yet to sound." Rev. 8 : 13.

The last three trumpets are "woe" trumpets because of their devastating character.

"And the fifth angel sounded, and I saw a star fall from heaven unto the earth : and to him was given the key of the bottomless pit.

"And he opened the bottomless pit; and there arose a smoke out of the pit, as the smoke of a great furnace; and the sun and the air were darkened by reason of the smoke of the pit.

"And there came out of the smoke locusts upon the earth : and unto them was given power, as the scorpions of the earth have power." Rev. 9 : 1-3.

Mohammed, the star of the bottomless pit, or desolate wastes of Arabia. Smoke represents the dark and delusive doctrines of Islam. Conquests of the Mohammedans against Eastern Rome by Mohammed and Othman. Like the locusts (Prov. 30 : 27) they had no Central government for centuries, but in 1299 Othman assumed control, issued his own money, and on July 27 invaded the territory of Eastern Rome. *Decline and Fall of Rome*, chap. 64, par. 14.

" And they had tails like unto scorpions, and there were stings in their tails: and their power was to hurt men five months." Rev. 9 : 10.

Five months—thirty days to a month—150 days or years (Num. 14 : 34, Eze. 4 : 6), from July 27, 1299, bring us to July 27, 1449. During this time, the Turks carried on war with the Greek or Eastern Roman Empire, but did not " kill " it politically.

6. SIXTH TRUMPET

Rev. 9 : 12-21.

The four angels or messengers are understood to refer to the four Sultanies of Bagdad, Iconium, Aleppo and Damascus situated in the Valley of the Euphrates. See Rev. 16 : 12-16 and 7 : 1-3.

Note.—In 1453, the Turks took Constantinople and the last remnant of the Roman power was gone.

Verses 16 and 17 seem to refer to the use of gunpowder which was used in the siege.

" And the four angels were loosed, which were prepared for an hour, and a day, and a month, and a year, for to slay the third part of men." Rev. 9 : 15.

An hour (15 days), a day (one year), month (30 years), a year (360 years), total 391 years and 15 days, added to July 27, 1449, bring us to Aug. 11, 1840.

Note.—In 1449, the Emperor at Constantinople died and before his brother, Constantine XIII. dared take the throne, he asked permission of Amurath, the Turkish Sultan who had his capital at Adrianople. Thus the independence of the Eastern Empire was gone, voluntarily surrendered to the Turks. 391 years and 15 days later, on Aug. 11, 1840, the Turks voluntarily surrendered their independence into the hands of the great powers of Europe. Almost overcome by Mehemet Ali, Pasha of Egypt, the Sultan of Turkey put his affairs in the hands of the great powers—England, Russia, Austria and Prussia, and on Aug. 11, 1840, placed in the hands of Mehemet Ali the ultimatum of these powers. Where was his independence? Gone! And prophecy was fulfilled.

7. THE SEVENTH TRUMPET

" But in the days of the voice of the seventh angel, when he shall begin to sound, the mystery of God should be finished, as He hath declared to his servants the prophets." Rev. 10 : 7.

" And the seventh angel sounded; and there were great voices in heaven, saying, The kingdoms of this world are become the kingdoms of our Lord, and of His Christ; and He shall reign for ever and ever.

" And the four and twenty elders, which sat before God on their seats, fell upon their faces, and worshipped God.

" Saying, We give thee thanks, O Lord God Almighty, which art, and wast, and art to come; because thou hast taken to thee thy great power, and hast reigned." Rev. 11 : 15-17.

THE MYSTERY OF GOD IN THE GOSPEL

Eph. 3 : 3-6; Gal. 1 : 11, 12.

THE NATIONS ARE ANGRY AND PREPARING FOR WAR, EVEN WHILE PROCLAIMING PEACE

" And the nations were angry, and thy wrath is come, and the time of the dead, that they should be judged, and that thou shouldest give reward unto thy servants the prophets, and to the saints, and them that fear thy name, small and great; and shouldest destroy them which destroy the earth." Rev. 11 : 18.

" And at that time shall Michael stand up, the great Prince which standeth for the children of thy people: and there shall be a time of trouble, such as never was since there was a nation even to that same time: and at that time thy people shall be delivered, every one that shall be found written in the book." Dan. 12 : 1.

The Judgment began in 1844 and will soon be completed. Christ will then come. Rev. 22 : 10-12. His people will sit in Judgment during the 1000 years. 1 Cor. 6 : 1-3; Rev. 20 : 4.

" And the temple of God was opened in heaven, and there was seen in His temple the ark of His testament: and there were lightnings, and voices, and thunderings, and an earthquake, and great hail." Rev. 11 : 19.

The seventh trumpet covers the last days and events to the end of the seven last plagues. See Rev. 16 : 17, 18.

SEVEN LAST PLAGUES

" And I saw another sign in heaven, great and marvellous, seven angels having the seven last plagues; for in them is filled up the wrath of God." Rev. 15 : 1.

Read all of Revelation, chap. 16.

Rev. 14 : 9, 10. Beast worshippers drink of the wrath of God unmixed with mercy.

Gen. 7 : 16. Just before the flood ark closed. Then probation of world before flood ended.

Luke 17 : 26. A type of last days.

Rev. 22 : 11-13. Probation of world ceases. Door of mercy closes just before Jesus comes back to this world.

See Heb. 4 : 16. Access to mercy seat.

Lev. 23 : 28, 29. Those unrepentant " cut off."

PLAGUES ON EGYPT A TYPE

" Now all these things happened unto them for ensamples: and they are written for our admonition, upon whom the ends of the world are come." 1 Cor. 10 : 11.

Read Exodus, chapters 8 to 11.

Notice Ex. 8 : 22-24. There were ten plagues in Egypt, and after the third plague God said to Pharaoh, " I will put a division between my people and thy people." From that time on no plague came nigh the dwellings of God's people, Israel. The Seven LAST Plagues of Egypt fell on the Egyptians alone. Then the Lord took His people out. These things are a type for God's people in the last days. In Rev. 16 we read of the seven LAST Plagues. They fall after God has put a " division " between His people and the world. Probation will then be closed.

FIRST PLAGUE

Rev. 16 : 2. A sore or cancer. Here, at last, God marks outwardly those who, inwardly have the mark of the Beast.

SECOND PLAGUE

Rev. 16 : 3. The sea as blood. See Rev. 18 : 17, ships. Small parts of the sea have already become red and putrid. How terrible when large sections are affected.

THIRD PLAGUE

Rev. 16 : 4-7. Rivers and sources of water supply become bloody. Matt. 23 : 35; 1 John 3 : 15.

FOURTH PLAGUE

Rev. 16 : 8, 9. The sun scorching men. They blaspheme God, but do not seek His forgiveness. Characters unmarked. Isa. 26 : 9, normally God's judgments lead to repentance.

Rev. 14 : 18. The harvest of the vine of the earth (the wicked) is fully ripe for judgment. They honor the day of the sun. Now the sun is a plague to them. They call down fire from heaven. Now they taste it. Rev. 13 : 13.

FIFTH PLAGUE

Rev. 16 : 10, 11. Darkness in the kingdom of the Beast.

Ex. 10 : 21. Darkness that was palpable—it could be felt.

Amos 8 : 9; Zeph. 1 : 15-18.

They scoffed at God's sign of the dark day (Matt. 24 : 29; Joel 2 : 10; Amos 5 : 20).

Now they are in darkness.

SIXTH PLAGUE

Rev. 16 : 12-16. River Euphrates (Great power located in Euphrates region —Turkish power—Isa. 8 : 7) dried up, preparing the way of the Kings (kingdoms) of the East (sunrise).

The Battle of Armageddon, earth's last battle, begins.

SEVENTH PLAGUE

Rev. 16 : 17-21. Plague of Hail.

Ver. 17: " It is done." See Jer. 25 : 30, Lord's voice.

Isa. 28 : 17, Hail sweeps away refuge of lies.

Job. 38 : 22, treasures of hail for day of battle and war (Armageddon).

GOD WILL PROTECT HIS CHILDREN IN THE TIME OF THE PLAGUES

" Surely he shall deliver thee from the snare of the fowler, and from the noisome pestilence.

" He shall cover thee with his feathers, and under his wings shalt thou trust: his truth shall be thy shield and buckler.

" Thou shalt not be afraid for the terror by night; nor for the arrow that flieth by day;

" Nor for the pestilence that walketh in darkness; not for the destruction that wasteth at noonday.

" A thousand shall fall at thy side, and ten thousand at thy right hand; but it shall not come nigh thee.

" Only with thine eyes shalt thou behold and see the reward of the wicked.

" Because thou hast made the Lord, which is my refuge, even the most High, thy habitation;

" There shall no evil befall thee, neither shall any plague come nigh thy dwelling." Ps. 91 : 3-10.

Pestilence (sore); terror by night (darkness); destruction at noonday (sun scorching); no plague near thy dwelling. See Ex. 8 : 22-24; Ps. 27 : 5; Job. 22 : 30; Joel 3 : 16; Isa. 26 : 20; Prov. 29 : 1.

GOD'S PEOPLE DELIVERED AT MIDNIGHT

Ex. 11 : 4-8 (1 Cor. 10 : 11).

Job. 34 : 20; Isa. 30 : 29, 30.

Read all of Ps. 46, the Song of God's people during the time of trouble.

THE TWO WITNESSES OF REVELATION XI.

Read Rev. 11 : 3-13.

WRITTEN TESTIMONY STRONGER THAN ORAL

John 5 : 39. Old Testament testifies (bears witness) of Christ. See Luke 24 : 27; Deut. 18 : 15, 18; John 1 : 45.

CHRIST'S WORKS AND WORDS IN THIS DISPENSATION BEAR WITNESS TO HIM. THEY ARE RECORDED ONLY IN THE NEW TESTAMENT

John 5 : 36; 14 : 11; 15 : 24.

GOD'S TWO WITNESSES ARE THESE THE OLD AND NEW TESTAMENTS

The Bible often uses the figure of personification.

Judges 9 : 7-15; Gen. 4 : 10; so here in Rev. 11.

See Zech. 4 : 11-14; compare Ps. 119: 130, 105.

God's two witnesses bring light.

"Fire out of their mouth." See Mal. 4 : 1; Rev. 20 : 15; 22 : 18.

"Spiritually Egypt." Ex. 5 : 2. "Know not the Lord."

"Sodom." Jude 7. "Uncleanness."

"Ascended to heaven in cloud." See Dan. 4 : 22. Great Exaltation.

Note.—When end of dark ages came and days of papal supremacy, a great earthquake (French Revolution) shook one tenth of the city (France was one of the ten divisions of Rome). In 1793 a decree to abolish the Bible was passed; exactly three and one-half years later the law was rescinded. See Rev. 11 : 11, 13. Also exactly 7000 "names" or titles of nobility were destroyed in the French Revolution.

TURKEY IN BIBLE PROPHECY

WHEN THE TURK COMES TO HIS END. IS THE END OF THE WORLD AT HAND? THE WHOLE ELEVENTH CHAPTER OF DANIEL IS A DETAILED HISTORICAL PROPHECY OF EVENTS CONNECTED WITH THE NEAR EAST FROM THE TIME OF THE PROPHET DANIEL TO THE END OF THE WORLD

PERSIA

"And now will I shew thee the truth. Behold, there shall stand up yet three kings in Persia; and the fourth shall be far richer than they all: and by his strength through his riches he shall stir up all against the realm of Grecia." Dan. 11 : 2.

The four Persian kings were: (1) Cambyses; (2) Smerdis; (3) Darius; (4) Xerxes, who was far richer than they all, and led a great army against Greece.

GRECIA

"And a mighty king shall stand up, that shall rule with great dominion, and do according to his will.

"And when he shall stand up, his kingdom shall be broken, and shall be divided toward the four winds of heaven; and not to his posterity, nor according to his dominion which he ruled: for his kingdom shall be plucked up, even for others beside those." Dan. 11 : 3, 4.

Alexander the Great ruled from Grecia to India. At the height of his career, he died suddenly at the age of 32 in the year 323 B.C. His Empire was divided into just FOUR parts and ruled by his four leading generals; Macedonia (West) by Cassander; Asia Minor (North), Lysinmachus; Syria (East to Euphrates); Seleucus and Egypt (South) by Ptolemy. The kingdom of the north largely absorbed the west and east, and in the end of Dan. 11, we find the King of the North and the King of the South in evidence.

The King of the North in the time of the end is the power which rules the territory once the northern part of Alexander's Empire and is of course the Turkish power to-day.

Dan. 11 : 40—The King of the North a chief actor in the time of the end.

Note.—Time after time the great nations have helped Turkey, otherwise that power would have come to his end long ago. Since April, 1920, his capital has been removed to Angora, a city of Asia Minor, the old homeland of the King of the North. Every Mohammedan looks to Jerusalem in the Holy Land as a sacred place.

"But tidings out of the east and out of the north shall trouble him: therefore he shall go forth with great fury to destroy, and utterly to make away many.

"And he shall plant the tabernacles of his palace between the seas in the glorious holy mountain; yet he shall come to his end, and none shall help him." Dan. 11 : 44, 45.

"And at that time shall Michael stand up, the great prince which standeth for the children of thy people: and there shall be a time of trouble, such as never was since there was a nation even to that same time; and at that time thy people shall be delivered, every one that shall be found written in the book." Dan. 12 : 1.

Zech. 8 : 3—Jerusalem is the "holy mountain." When Turkey "comes to his end" as King of the North, Michael will stand up (begin to reign—see Dan. 11 : 2). Michael is Christ—Jude 9; 1 Thess. 4:16; John 5 : 25 28; and His "standing up" is the closing of His ministry as our High Priest in the heavenly Sanctuary and the close of human probation, followed "quickly" (Rev. 22 : 12) by His Second Coming.

THE MILLENNIUM

Read Rev. 20 : 1-9.

THE LAST DAYS A TIME OF GREAT WICKEDNESS

"And as it was in the days of Noe, so shall it be also in the days of the Son of man." Luke 17 : 26.

"And God saw that the wickedness of man was great in the earth, and that every imagination of the thoughts of his heart was only evil continually." Gen. 6 : 5.

2 Tim. 3 : 1-5, 13; Matt. 13 : 38, 30; 2 Thess. 2 : 8; 2 Pet. 3 : 3, 4.

Micah 4 : 1-3. The nations will join in great peace movements, yet prepare for war. See Joel 3 : 9, 10.

We are to look, not for world conversion, but for the coming of Christ.

Titus 2 : 13; 1 Thess. 4 : 14-18; 1 Pet. 5 : 4; 2 Tim. 4 : 6-8.

THE BEGINNING OF THE MILLENNIUM

Note.—The word "millennium" simply means 1000 years.

"Bottomless pit" (Greek—abyss). The word used in Greek version of Gen. 1 : 2 for condition of this earth before man was created.

Satan's work to tempt saints and deceive sinners.

When Christ comes, Saints taken from the earth (John 14 : 1-3; 1 Thess. 4 : 16-18) and sinners slain (2 Thess. 1 : 7-9; 2 Thess. 2 : 8), thus no man will be left on the earth (Jer. 4 : 23-26). The earth will be chaotic and in ruins (Jer. 4 : 23) "without form and void" as it was when called "abyss" or bottomless pit at the beginning (Gen. 1 : 2).

Isa. 24 : 19-22.

THE ENDING OF THE MILLENNIUM

Satan will be bound under chains of darkness for one thousand years in this desolated earth. At the end of one thousand years the second resurrection (the resurrection of the wicked) unbinds him.

Jude 14, 15.

Rev. 20 : 5, 3, 7, 8.

Rev. 21 : 2. The Holy City Descends. (See Zech. 14 : 4-9.)

The resurrection wicked, led by Satan, attempt to take the city. Here the whole human race meet for the first and last time (Luke 13 : 28). Fire comes down from God out of heaven and devours the wicked. This is the end of Satan and sinners and sin (2 Pet. 3; Mal. 4). Before the eyes of God's people there will be brought forth a new heaven and a new earth. Rev. 21 : 5; Isa. 43 : 19; 65 : 17-25.

DESTINY OF THE WICKED

WHAT HAPPENS TO THE WICKED

"For the time is come that judgment must begin at the house of God : and if it first begin at us, what shall the end be of them that obey not the gospel of God?" 1 Pet. 4 : 17.

"For God so loved the world, that He gave His only begotten Son, that whosoever believeth in Him should not perish, but have everlasting life." John 3 : 16.

"THE WAGES OF SIN IS DEATH"

"For the wages of sin is death; but the gift of God is eternal life through Jesus Christ our Lord." Rom. 6 : 23.

"But of the tree of the knowledge of good and evil, thou shalt not eat of it : for in the day that thou eatest thereof thou shalt surely die." Gen. 2 : 17.

"Behold, all souls are mine; as the soul of the father, so also the soul of the son is mine : the soul that sinneth, it shall die." Eze. 18 : 4.

Rom. 5 : 12; Deut. 30 : 15, 19; John 6 : 50; 8 : 51; 11 : 26; Matt. 10 : 39; Rom. 6 : 21; 8 : 13; Jas. 1 : 15; Rev. 20 : 6, 14; Rev. 21 : 8; 2 Chron. 25 : 4; Prov. 2 : 18; Prov. 8 : 36.

"ALL THE WICKED WILL BE DESTROYED"

"The Lord preserveth all them that love him : but all the wicked will He destroy." Ps. 145 : 20.

"Who shall be punished with everlasting destruction from the presence of the Lord, and from the glory of His power; 2 Thess. 1 : 9.

"But these, as natural brute beasts, made to be taken and destroyed, speak evil of the things that they understand not; and shall utterly perish in their own corruption." 2 Pet. 2 : 12.

Ps. 5 : 6; Ps. 37 : 38; Ps. 92 : 7; Prov. 1 : 32; 13 : 13; Isa. 1 : 28; Matt. 7 : 13; 10 : 28; Rom. 9 : 22; Phil. 3 : 19; 1 Cor. 3 : 17.

"THE WICKED SHALL PERISH"

"But the wicked shall perish, and the enemies of the Lord shall be as the fat of lambs : they shall consume; into smoke shall they consume away." Ps. 37 : 20.

Ps. 2 : 12; Job 20 : 4-9; John 3 : 15, 16; 2 Thess. 2 : 10; 2 Pet. 2 : 12; Ps. 68 : 2; Prov. 19 : 9; Isa. 41 : 11.

"SHALL GO INTO PERDITION"

"The beast that thou sawest was, and is not; and shall ascend out of the bottomless pit, and go into perdition : and they that dwell on the earth shall wonder, whose names were not written in the book of life from the foundation of the world, when they behold the beast that was, and is not, and yet is." Rev. 17 : 8.

"And the beast that was, and is not even he is the eighth, and is of the seven, and goeth into perdition." Rev. 17 : 11.

"But the heavens and the earth, which are now, by the same word are kept in store, reserved unto fire against the day of judgment and perdition of ungodly men." 2 Pet. 3 : 7.

John 17 : 12; Phil. 1 : 28; 2 Thess. 2 : 3; 1 Tim. 6 : 9; Heb. 10 : 39.

"SHALL CONSUME INTO SMOKE"

"But the wicked shall perish, and the enemies of the Lord shall be as the fat of lambs : they shall consume; into smoke shall they consume away." Ps. 37 : 20.

"And then shall that Wicked be revealed, whom the Lord shall consume with the spirit of His mouth, and shall destroy with the brightness of His coming." 2 Thess. 2 : 8.

Isa. 1 : 28; 66 : 17; Ps. 59 : 13; 104 : 35; Zeph. 1 : 2, 3.

"THEY SHALL BE DEVOURED AS STUBBLE"

"For while they be folden together as thorns, and while they are drunken as drunkards, they shall be devoured as stubble fully dry." Nahum 1 : 10.

"And they went up on the breadth of the earth, and compassed the camp of the saints about, and the beloved city: and fire came down from God out of heaven, and devoured them." Rev. 20 : 9.

Ps. 21 : 9; Heb. 10 : 27.

THE LORD WILL "SLAY THE WICKED"

"Surely thou wilt slay the wicked, O God: depart from me therefore, ye bloody men." Ps. 139 : 19.

"But those mine enemies, which would not that I should reign over them, bring hither, and slay them before me." Luke 19 : 27.

Ps. 62 : 3; Isa. 11 : 4.

THE WICKED SHALL COME TO AN END AND BE CUT OFF

"Behold, all they that were incensed against thee shall be ashamed and confounded: they shall be as nothing; and they that strive with thee shall perish." Isa. 41 : 11.

"Thou shalt seek them, and shalt not find them, even them that contended with thee: they that war against thee shall be as nothing, and as a thing of nought." Isa. 41 : 12.

"For as ye have drunk upon my holy mountain, so shall all the heathen drink continually, yea, they shall drink, and they shall swallow down, and they shall be as though they had not been." Obadiah 16.

Ps. 37 : 10-38; Jer. 10 : 24; Prov. 2 : 22; Job 18 : 18; Ps. 94 : 23; Hosea 13 : 3.

"THE DAY THAT COMETH SHALL BURN THEM UP"

"For, behold, the day cometh, that shall burn as an oven; and all the proud, yea, and all that do wickedly, shall be stubble: and the day that cometh shall burn them up, saith the Lord of hosts, that it shall leave them neither root nor branch." Mal. 4 : 1.

"Therefore shall her plagues come in one day, death, and mourning, and famine; and she shall be utterly burned with fire: for strong is the Lord God who judgeth her." Rev. 18 : 8.

Ps. 97 : 3; Heb. 6 : 8; Ps. 21 : 9; Matt. 3 : 12; 7 : 19; 13 : 30, 40; John 15 : 6.

WHAT AND WHERE IS HEAVEN?

"For since the beginning of the world men have not heard, nor perceived by the ear, neither hath the eye seen, O God, beside thee, what He hath prepared for him that waiteth for Him." Isa. 64 : 4.

(1 Cor. 2 : 9.)

SINCE THE BEGINNING OF THE WORLD, MEN HAVE NOT SEEN WHAT GOD HAS PREPARED FOR HIS PEOPLE. AT THE BEGINNING, MAN DID SEE THE GARDEN OF EDEN, WHICH WAS A PICTURE OF GOD'S PLAN FOR THIS WORLD

"For thus saith the Lord that created the heavens; God Himself that formed the earth and made it; He hath established it, He created it not in vain, He formed it to be inhabited: I am the Lord; and there is none else." Isa. 45 : 18.

GOD CREATED THIS EARTH TO BE INHABITED

"The heaven, even the heavens, are the Lord's: but the earth hath He given to the children of men." Ps. 115 : 16.

Gen. 1 : 26—Gave him dominion.

MAN LOST THIS FIRST DOMINION THROUGH SIN. IT IS TO BE RESTORED THROUGH CHRIST

"While they promise them liberty, they themselves are the servants of corruption: for of whom a man is overcome, of the same is he brought in bondage." 2 Pet. 2 : 19.

"For the Son of man is come to seek and to save that which was lost." Luke 19 : 10.

Note.—Christ was to save "that" which was lost, as well as "them" that were lost.

"And thou, O tower of the flock, the stronghold of the daughter of Zion, unto thee shall it come, even the first dominion; the kingdom shall come to the daughter of Jerusalem." Micah 4 : 8.

Gen. 13 : 14, 15—Promised to Abraham.

Rom. 4 : 13—The promise included not only Palestine but the entire world.

Heb. 11 : 8-18—Abraham did not receive the fulfilment of the promise in his life-time.

"And the scripture, foreseeing that God would justify the heathen through faith, preached before the gospel unto Abraham, saying, In thee shall all nations be blessed."

"And if ye be Christ's, then are ye Abraham's seed, and heirs according to the promise." Gal. 3 : 8, 29.

THE NEW EARTH WILL BE THE HOME OF THE REDEEMED FOREVER

"Blessed are the meek: for they shall inherit the earth." Matt. 5 : 5.

"But the meek shall inherit the earth; and shall delight themselves in the abundance of peace." Ps. 37 : 11.

Luke 20 : 34, 35—This world—that world.

Heb. 2 : 5—The world to come.

2 Pet. 3 : 6, 7—Three worlds: (1) "That then was"; (2) "Which are now"; (3) "New heavens and a new earth."

Isa. 65 : 21—A real place. Build houses. Plant vineyards.

Isa. 66 : 22—A permanent home.

Rev. 2 : 7—Tree of Life restored to man.

Mal. 4 : 2, 3—Grow up.

Matt. 6 : 10—God's will to be done.

AT THE SECOND COMING OF CHRIST, THE REDEEMED WILL BE TAKEN TO HEAVEN FOR ONE THOUSAND YEARS

"Let not your heart be troubled: ye believe in God, believe also in me. In my Father's house are many mansions: if it were not so, I would have told you. I go to prepare a place for you.

"And if I go and prepare a place for you, I will come again, and receive you unto myself; that where I am, there ye may be also." John 14 : 1-3.

Rev. 20 : 4-6.

THERE ARE THREE HEAVENS

"I knew a man in Christ above fourteen years ago (whether in the body, I cannot tell; or whether out of the body, I cannot tell: God knoweth); such an one caught up to the third heaven." 2 Cor. 12 : 2.

1. FIRST, OR ATMOSPHERIC HEAVEN OR HEAVENS (Heb. "Rakia")

Gen. 1 : 6-8—Made on second day of creation.

Jer. 8 : 7—Where birds fly.

Jer. 10 : 13—Where clouds float.

Isa. 55 : 10—Where rain and snow originate.

Matt. 5 : 18—Pass away some day.

Job 14 : 12; 2 Pet. 3 : 10; Rev. 6 : 14; Matt. 24 : 35.

Rev. 21 : 1—To be made new again.

2. SECOND, OR STARRY HEAVEN OR HEAVENS (Heb. "Shamayim")

"The heavens declare the glory of God; and the firmament sheweth His handywork.

"Day unto day uttereth speech, and night unto night sheweth knowledge.

"There is no speech nor language, where their voice is not heard.

"Their line is gone out through all the earth, and their words to the end of the world. In them hath He set a tabernacle for the sun.

"Which is as a bridegroom coming out of his chamber, and rejoiceth as a strong man to run a race.

"His going forth is from the end of the heaven, and his circuit unto the ends of it: and there is nothing hid from the heat thereof." Ps. 19 : 1-6.

Jer. 44 : 17, 25—Moon queen of heaven.

Ps. 8 : 3—Subject of study.

Job. 26 : 13, 14—Garnished by the Spirit of the Lord.

Matt. 24 : 29.

3. THIRD HEAVEN WHERE GOD DWELLS (Heb. "Shemi Hashamayim")

"After this manner therefore pray ye: Our Father which art in heaven, Hallowed be thy name." Matt. 6 : 9.

1 Kings 8 : 27—"The Heaven of Heavens."

Deut. 26 : 15—"The Holy Habitation."

2 Chron. 6 : 33—"Thy Dwelling Place."

Eccl. 5 : 2—"God is in Heaven."

PARADISE IS THE THIRD HEAVEN WHERE GOD DWELLS

Rev. 2 : 7—Tree of Life is in the midst of Paradise.

Rev. 22 : 2—The Tree of Life is by the River of Life. The River of Life is by the Throne of God. Therefore Paradise is where the Throne of God is located.

John 14 : 1-3—Heaven is a Place.

Heb. 6 : 20—Christ is there now (Eph. 4 : 10).

John 17 : 24—Wants us there.

Ps. 73 : 25; Eph. 3 : 15; 1 Pet. 1 : 4.

Ps. 119 : 89—God's Word settled there.

WE SHALL KNOW EACH OTHER THERE

"For now we see through a glass, darkly; but then face to face: now I know in part; but then shall I know even as also I am known." 1 Cor. 13 : 12.

Heb. 12 : 23—Names written there.

1 Jno. 3 : 1, 2—Be like Jesus.

Phil. 3 : 20, 21—Our bodies like His.

Luke 24 : 1-35—He was REAL and was KNOWN after His Resurrection.

Luke 24 : 36-43—They SAW Jesus. They HEARD Jesus. He also ATE before them. We will be like Him.

Acts 7 : 55—Stephen knew Jesus.

Job 19 : 23-27; Luke 10 : 20.

TWELVES STONES IN THE FOUNDATIONS OF THE NEW JERUSALEM

"And the foundations of the wall of the city were garnished with all manner of precious stones." Rev. 21 : 19. These twelve foundations have been described as follows:

"First, Jasper. Jasper is a stone, of a beautiful sea-green; sometimes, however, of various colors, as purple, with red veins. There are many varieties.

"Second, Sapphire. A stone of a very fine sky-blue color, next in hardness to the diamond, and transparent.

"Third, Chalcedony. A species of agate or onyx of different colors, the yellow and red being the most beautiful and valuable of its species. It is seldom discovered.

"Fourth, Emerald. A stone of a very bright green color without any mixture, and is one of the most beautiful gems known. It is also rare.

" Fifth, Sardonyx. A species of agate, and in color sometimes red, and sometimes of a flesh color.

" Sixth, Sardius or sardine stone. A precious stone of a blood-red color.

" Seventh, Chrysolite. A transparent precious stone, having the color of gold, with a mixture of green, possessing a fine luster. It is sometimes termed the " gold stone." It is a species of the topaz.

" Eighth, Beryl. A very hard, transparent gem of great luster and beauty, in color bluish-green.

" Ninth, Topaz. A highly colored gem of wine-yellow color, with occasional pale tinges of green or red. It was one of the twelve gems of the high priests' breastplate." Ex. 39 : 10.

" Tenth, Chrysoprasus. Its color is green, inclining to gold. It differs from the chrysolite only in having a bluish hue.

" Eleventh, Jacinth. A precious stone of dead red color, with a mixture of yellow. It is the same as the cinnamon stone.

" Twelfth, Amethyst. A very beautiful gem, generally of a purple of violet color, composed of a strong blue and deep red. It is seldom uniform in color, and is generally cloudy, and spotted with zig-zag stripes."

One writer speaking of the blending of the colors in the arrangement of these stones in the walls says:

" In looking over these various classes, we find the first four to be of a green or bluish cast, the fifth and sixth of a red or scarlet: the seventh, yellow: the eighth, ninth, and tenth of different shades of the lighter green; the eleventh and twelfth of a scarlet or splendid red. There is classification, therefore, in this arrangement in the rainbow, with the exception that it is more complex."

THE RETURN OF THE JEWS

ALL OF THE TRUE ISRAEL WILL BE SAVED

" And so all Israel shall be saved: as it is written, There shall come out of Sion the Deliverer, and shall turn away ungodliness from Jacob." Rom. 11 : 26.

Gal. 6 : 15, 16—True Israel are true Christians.

Gen. 32 : 28—The term " Israel " means an " overcomer."

GOD'S COVENANTS ARE ALL WITH ISRAEL

" Who are Israelites; to whom pertaineth the adoption, and the glory, and the covenants, and the giving of the law, and the service of God, and the promises." Rom. 9 : 4.

Exodus 19 : The Old Covenant.

Jer. 31 : 31—The New Covenant. See Heb. 8.

Heb. 8 : 13—The Old Covenant " vanished away."

Heb. 9 : 15—Christ the Mediator of the New Covenant.

THEREFORE ALL PROMISES FULFILLED TO ISRAEL MUST BE RECEIVED THROUGH CHRIST AS THE MEDIATOR OF THE NEW COVENANT

PARABLE OF THE OLIVE TREE

Jer. 11 : 16—Israel symbolized by an olive tree.

Rom. 11 : 17—Unbelievers broken off and believers graffed in " contrary to nature."

Rom. 11 : 26—" And so (in this way—grafting Gentiles into the true Israel) all Israel shall be saved."

ALL WHO PARTAKE OF THE PROMISES MUST BE ISRAELITES (CHRISTIANS) BY BEING " GRAFFED " INTO THE PARENT STOCK

" Having abolished in His flesh the enmity, even the law of commandments contained in ordinances; for to make in Himself of twain one new man, so making peace." Eph. 2 : 15. (All national distinction abolished.)

Rom. 9 : 6—To be of Israel according to the flesh, that is, to simply be a Jew by nationality, does not make one a true Israelite in God's sight.

Eph. 2 : 19, 20—Gentiles must be naturalized and become " fellow citizens with the saints."

" For he is not a Jew, which is one outwardly; neither is that circumcision, which is outward in the flesh:

" But he is a Jew, which is one inwardly; and circumcision is that of the heart, in the spirit, and not in the letter; whose praise is not of men, but of God." Rom. 2 : 28, 29.

" And if ye be Christ's, then are ye Abraham's seed, and heirs according to the promise." Gal. 3 : 29.

ALL OLD TESTAMENT PROPHECIES REFERRING TO THE RETURN OF THE JEWS TO JERUSALEM AND THE HOLY LAND WERE WRITTEN BEFORE 486 B.C.

(See margin of Zechariah)

IN THE RETURN FROM BABYLONIAN CAPTIVITY THESE PROPHECIES WERE FULFILLED AS FAR AS THEY WILL EVER BE TO THE NATURAL ISRAEL

Ezra 7 : 11-26—The Restoration Decree of 457 B.C.

Verse 13—All could return.

Ezra 6 : 16—All the tribes were represented.

Neh. 7 : 73—In their cities.

(See Josephus, Book 12, chapter 2, Sec. 4-7.)

Jer. 18 : 7, 8—God's promises to nations based on conditions.

Jer. 19 : 1-11—Ancient Israel like earthen bottle broken.

THE TRUE ISRAEL WILL BE GATHERED ONE BY ONE AT THE COMING OF CHRIST

Isa. 27 : 12, 13—When the great trumpet is blown.

Matt. 24 : 30, 31—Christ comes with "a great sound of a trumpet."

Eze. 34 : 11-13, 23—David to rule over them.

Eze. 37 : 24, 26, 27.

Acts 2 : 29-34—David dead yet.

Heb. 11 : 32—David a hero of faith.

Jer. 30 : 9—David to be "raised up."

Note.—The word here for "raised up" is "Cumi" (Hebrew). See Mark 5 : 41, where the same word is used by Jews.

Eze. 37 : 11-14; 1 Thess. 4 : 16, 17; Matt. 22 : 23—proves the Resurrection necessary.

PRE-EXISTENCE OF CHRIST

CHRIST WAS WITH GOD IN CREATION

"In the beginning was the Word, and the Word was with God, and the Word was God.

"The same was in the beginning with God.

"All things were made by Him; and without Him was not any thing made that was made." John 1 : 1-3.

"And the Word was made flesh, and dwelt among us (and we beheld His glory, the glory as of the only begotten of the Father,) full of grace and truth." John 1 : 14.

"God, who at sundry times and in divers manners spake in time past unto the fathers by the prophets,

"Hath in these last days spoken unto us by His Son, whom He hath appointed heir of all things, by whom also He made the worlds;

"Who being the brightness of His glory, and the express image of His person, and upholding all things by the word of His power, when He had by Himself purged our sins, sat down on the right hand of the Majesty on high." Heb. 1 : 1-3.

"But unto the Son He saith, Thy throne, O God, is for ever and ever: a sceptre of righteousness is the sceptre of thy kingdom.

"Thou hast loved righteousness, and hated iniquity; therefore God, even thy God, hath anointed thee with the oil of gladness above thy fellows.

"And, Thou, Lord, in the beginning hast laid the foundation of the earth; and the heavens are the works of thine hands". Heb. 1 : 8-10.

"In whom we have redemption through His blood, even the forgiveness of sins:

"Who is the image of the invisible God, the firstborn of every creature:

"For by Him were all things created, that are in heaven, and that are in earth, visible and invisible, whether they be thrones, or dominions, or principalities, or powers: all things were created by Him, and for Him:

"And He is before all things, and by Him all things consist." Col. 1 : 14-17. See Rev. 22 : 13 and Gen. 1 : 1.

CHRIST CLAIMED PRE-EXISTENCE

"Jesus said unto them, Verily, verily, I say unto you, Before Abraham was, I am." John 8 : 58.

"Jesus said unto them, If God were your Father, ye would love me; for I proceeded forth and came from God; neither came I of myself, but He sent me." John 8 : 42.

"And now, O Father, glorify thou me with thine own self with the glory which I had with thee before the world was." John 17 : 5.

See Exodus 3 : 14; Micah 5 : 2.

THE PLAN OF REDEMPTION

ALL THINGS, INCLUDING MAN, WERE CREATED PERFECT IN THE BEGINNING

"In the beginning God created the heaven and the earth." Gen 1 : 1.

"And God saw every thing that He had made, and, behold, it was very good. And the evening and the morning were the sixth day." Gen. 1 : 31.

"So God created man in His own image, in the image of God created He him; male and female created He them." Gen. 1 : 27.

Eccl. 7 : 29; Gen. 2 : 8-15.

Isa. 45 : 18.

THE ORIGIN OF EVIL

"He that committeth sin is of the devil; for the devil sinneth from the beginning. For this purpose the Son of God was manifested, that He might destroy the works of the devil." 1 John 3 : 8.

"Thou wast perfect in thy ways from the day that thou wast created. till iniquity was found in thee." Ezekiel 28 : 15.

John 8 : 44; Jude 6; 2 Pet. 2 : 4; Rev. 12 : 9; Matt. 25 : 41; Isa. 14 : 12-15.

SATAN BROUGHT SIN AND DEATH INTO THIS WORLD BY DECEPTION

"Now the serpent was more subtil than any beast of the field which the Lord God had made. And he said unto the woman, Yea, hath God said, Ye shall not eat of every tree of the garden,

"And the woman said unto the serpent, We may eat of the fruit of the trees of the garden.

"But of the fruit of the tree which is

in the midst of the garden, God hath said, Ye shall not eat of it, neither shall ye touch it, lest ye die.

" And the serpent said unto the woman. Ye shall not surely die:

" For God doth know that in the day ye eat thereof, then your eyes shall be opened, and ye shall be as gods, knowing good and evil.

" And when the woman saw that the tree was good for food, and that it was pleasant to the eyes, and a tree to be desired to make one wise, she took of the fruit thereof, and did eat, and gave also unto her husband with her; and he did eat." Gen. 3 : 1-6. See Gen. 3 : 7-24.

" Wherefore, as by one man sin entered into the world, and death by sin; and so death passed upon all men, for that all have sinned." Rom 5 : 12.

1 Cor. 15 : 22; Rom. 8 : 22; 1 John 3 : 5-8.

MAN CANNOT SAVE HIMSELF

" Can the Ethiopian change his skin, or the leopard his spots ? then may ye also do good, that are accustomed to do evil." Jer. 13 : 23.

" Neither is there salvation in any other, for there is none other name under heaven given among men, whereby we must be saved." Acts 4 : 12.

John 15 : 5.

GOD SENT HIS ONLY BEGOTTEN SON INTO THE WORLD TO SAVE THAT WHICH WAS LOST

Luke 19 : 10.

" For God so loved the world, that He gave His only begotten Son, that whosoever believeth in Him should not perish, but have everlasting life." John 3 : 16.

" And ye know that He was manifested to take away our sins; and in Him is no sin." 1 John 3 : 5.

Heb. 2 : 14; Matt. 18 : 11; Eze. 18 : 32; Rev. 22 : 17; Rom. 5 : 8, 9; Isa. 53.

THE PLAN OF REDEMPTION INCLUDES THE RESTORATION OF MAN'S HOME, THE EARTH, TO ITS ORIGINAL CONDITION

" And thou, O tower of the flock, the strong hold of the daughter of Zion, unto thee shall it come, even the first dominion; the kingdom shall come to the daughter of Jerusalem." Micah 4 : 8. See Gen. 1 : 26.

" Behold, the righteous shall be recompensed in the earth: much more the wicked and the sinner." Prov. 11 : 31.

" Blessed are the meek: for they shall inherit the earth." Matt. 5 : 5.

Isa. 35 : 5, 6; Isa. 45 : 18.

2 Pet. 3 : 10, 13—" But the day of the Lord will come as a thief in the night; in the which the heavens shall pass away with a great noise, and the elements shall melt with fervent heat, the earth also and the works that are therein shall be burned up." 2 Pet. 3 : 10.

" Nevertheless we, according to His promise, look for new heavens and a new earth, wherein dwelleth righteousness." 2 Peter 3 : 13.

Rev. 21 : 1, 5; Isa. 65 : 17-25.

THE VISION OF THE TWENTY-THREE HUNDRED DAYS

READ THE ENTIRE EIGHTH CHAPTER OF DANIEL. SYMBOLS EXPLAINED

" The Ram"—represents Medo-Persia. Dan. 8 : 20.

" The Goat "—represents Grecia. Dan. 8 : 21.

" The Four Horns "—represent the four divisions of Alexander's kingdom, Macedonia—Asia Minor—Syria—Egypt.

THE EXCEEDING GREAT HORN

The Roman Power, which succeeded Greece, when the Macedonian Horn was broken by Rome at the Battle of Pydna, 168 B.C.

THE 2300 DAYS REPRESENT 2300 YEARS

Num. 14 : 34; Eze. 4 : 6.

THE ANGEL GABRIEL WAS COMMANDED TO MAKE DANIEL UNDERSTAND THE VISION

" And I heard a man's voice between the banks of Ulai, which called, and said, Gabriel, make this man to understand the vision." Dan. 8 : 16.

Dan. 8 : 17—The vision reaches to the time of the end.

Verses 18-25—The angel explains the vision.

Verse 26—The angel declares the vision of the 2300 days (evening, morning—see verse 14, margin), was to be shut up for a time, and would not be fulfilled for " many days." The first part of the vision Daniel understood, but not the part about the 2300 days.

As Daniel saw the persecuting power of the " little horn " over the people of God, he fainted and was sick for a time. After searching the prophetic writings and seeking divine guidance in prayer, Daniel is again visited by the angel Gabriel who comes to finish the work of making known to Daniel the vision of chapter 8. See Dan. 8 : 27 to 9 : 23.

THE SEVENTY WEEKS DETERMINED OR CUT OFF UPON THE JEWS

" Seventy weeks are determined upon thy people and upon thy holy city, to finish the transgression, and to make an end of sins, and to make reconciliation for iniquity, and to bring in everlasting righteousness, and to seal up the vision and prophecy, and to anoint the most Holy.

"Know therefore and understand, that from the going forth of the commandment to restore and to build Jerusalem unto the Messiah the Prince shall be seven weeks, and threescore and two weeks: the street shall be built again, and the wall, even in troublous times.

"And after threescore and two weeks shall Messiah be cut off, but not for Himself: and the people of the prince that shall come shall destroy the city and the sanctuary; and the end thereof shall be with a flood, and unto the end of the war desolations are determined.

And He shall confirm the covenant with many for one week: and in the midst of the week He shall cause the sacrifice and the oblation to cease, and for the overspreading of abominations He shall make it desolate, even until the consummation, and that determined shall be poured upon the desolate." Dan. 9 : 24-27.

70 weeks, each day standing for a year, equals 490 years (70 × 7).

Starting in 457 B.C. when the decree to restore and build Jerusalem was given (see Ezra 7 : 11-26; Dan. 7 : 25) seven prophetic weeks or 49 years, reach 408 B.C. when the city and temple were completed. Sixty-two weeks more (434 years) reach to the Messiah. This is a total of 69 weeks (483 years) from the autumn of 457 B.C. to the autumn of A.D. 27. In that very year, Christ was anointed at His Baptism.

(Acts 10 : 38; Matt. 3 : 13-17.)

In the midst of the 70th week (seven years following A.D. 27), Messiah (Christ) was "cut off" (Isa. 53 : 8), crucified (A.D. 31), which marked the time for the sacrifices and oblations of the earthly sanctuary to cease. (Dan. 9 : 27; Col. 2 : 14-17; Matt. 27 : 50, 51.) Three and one half years later Stephen was stoned, the first Christian martyr and the first great persecution of the church broke out. Acts 7 : 59; 8 : 1. Saul was converted and became Paul the great Apostle to the Gentiles. This year (A.D. 34) of the rejection of the Jews, marked the end of the 70 weeks or 490 years which were "cut off" of the 2300 days (years). There remain 1810 years, added to A.D. 34 take us to A.D. 1844.

Read Dan. 8 : 14—"And he said unto me, Unto two thousand and three hundred days; then shall the sanctuary be cleansed."

THE CLEANSING OF THE HEAVENLY SANCTUARY

"And he said unto me, Unto two thousand and three hundred days; then shall the sanctuary be cleansed." Dan. 8 : 14.

THE ANCIENT SANCTUARY OR TABERNACLE WITH ITS SERVICE WAS TYPE OF HEAVENLY THINGS

"Who serve unto the example and shadow of heavenly things, as Moses was admonished of God when he was about to make the tabernacle: for, See, saith He, that thou make all things according to the pattern shewed to thee in the mount." Heb. 8 : 5.

"Now of the things which we have spoken this is the sum: We have such an high priest, who is set on the right hand of the throne of the Majesty in the heavens;

"A minister of the sanctuary, and of the true tabernacle, which the Lord pitched, and not man." Heb. 8 : 1, 2.

Heb. 9 : 11.

Ex. 25 : 8; Heb. 9 : 1-9; Ex. 30 : 1-6.

THE DAY OF ATONEMENT IN THE EARTHLY SANCTUARY A SYMBOL OF THE JUDGMENT

The sanctuary cleansed of all sins of the people. Those whose sins not transferred by a sacrifice to the Sanctuary, "cut off" from Israel.

Lev. 16 : 5-34; Lev. 23 : 27-32.

Lev. 4 : 27-30—Sinner in type transfers his sin to the substitute. Sin, the transgression of God's law, inscribed on the Tables of Stone in the Most Holy Place of the sanctuary or temple. 1 John, 3 : 4; Rom. 6 : 23; Heb. 9 : 3, 4; Ex. 40 : 20, 21; Ex. 25 : 21, 22; Deut. 10 : 4, 5.

Heb. 9 : 6—The Priests carried on the service of the sanctuary every day in the First Apartment.

Heb. 9 : 7—Into the Second Apartment or Most Holy Place, the High Priest alone went once each year (the Day of Atonement).

Lev. 16 : 29, 30—This was the Day of Atonement or cleansing.

THE TWO GOATS

Lev. 16 : 5, 8, 15, 16, 20-22.

THE LORD'S GOAT

Represented Jesus, whose blood cleanses from sin (Acts 8 : 32; 1 Pet. 1 : 19; Rev. 6 : 16).

This offering cleansed the sanctuary. The sins of the people were atoned for but they were not by it finally disposed of. This was done in the last part of the service on the Day of Atonement.

THE SCAPE GOAT

Symbolizing Satan, the great tempter and originator of all sin, was brought to the door of the sanctuary and on his head were placed all the sins he had tempted God's people to commit. He was then led away into a land "not inhabited." Lev. 16 : 22.

THE HEAVENLY SANCTUARY MUST ALSO BE CLEANSED BY CHRIST, OUR GREAT HIGH PRIEST. THIS CLEANSING IS NOT FROM ANY PHYSICAL UNCLEANNESS, BUT FROM THE RECORD OF OUR SINS

"It was therefore necessary that the patterns of things in the heavens should be purified with these; but the heavenly things themselves with better sacrifices than these." Heb. 9 : 23.

Heb. 9 : 9—The earthly sanctuary a figure of that time.

Heb. 8 : 2—Christ a Minister of the heavenly sanctuary.

Heb. 9 : 12 (Eph. 5 : 2) Offers His own Blood.

Note.—The work in the heavenly sanctuary could not start until after Christ's offering for sin on the Cross (Heb. 9 : 25, 26). He is now our Mediator or High Priest in the heavenly sanctuary. The cleansing of the heavenly sanctuary started in 1844 (see Dan. 8 : 14). When that is finished, all the people of God will be ready for His Appearing. The great anti-typical scape goat, Satan, will bear his responsibility for their sins into "a land not inhabited"; this earth desolated at the Second Coming of the Lord, for 1000 years.

"So Christ was once offered to bear the sins of many; and unto them that look for Him shall He appear the second time without sin unto salvation." Heb. 9 : 28; Acts 3 : 19-21.

SATAN, WITH ALL THE WICKED, WILL THEN BE DESTROYED

Ps. 7 : 16; Rev. 20 : 1-3, 7-9; Eze. 28 : 18, 19; 2 Pet. 3 : 10-13; Nahum 1 : 9.

THE JUDGMENT HOUR MESSAGE

"And I saw another angel fly in the midst of heaven, having the everlasting gospel to preach unto them that dwell on the earth, and to every nation, and kindred, and tongue, and people,

"Saying with a loud voice, Fear God, and give glory to Him; for the hour of His judgment is come: and worship Him that made heaven, and earth, and the sea, and the fountains of water." Rev. 14 : 6, 7.

Before an earthly court opens public announcement is made. Here an angel representing a world-wide message announces the judgment hour.

"And he said unto me, Unto two thousand and three hundred days; then shall the sanctuary be cleansed." Dan. 8 : 14.

The cleansing of the ancient sanctuary, a typical day of judgment. See Lev. 16 and 23; Heb. 10 : 4. Only a type—could not take away sins.

Sins forgiven but still on the record in the heavenly sanctuary till the judgment or cleansing of the heavenly sanctuary where the record of sin will be blotted out, through the merits and mediation of Jesus Christ, our Great High Priest.

Matt. 18 : 23-35, after forgiven "pay all," because he was unmerciful.

Dan. 7 : 9, 10—Judged according to books—our record there.

Jer. 50 : 20—Sin sought for and not found.

Acts 3 : 19—Sins blotted out for righteous.

Ex. 32 : 33—Names blotted out for wicked.

Rev. 20 : 15; Rev. 3 : 5; Luke 12 : 8, 9.

Rev. 22 : 11, 12—All decided for eternity.

THE SECOND ANGEL'S MESSAGE

Rev. 14 : 8—Great moral fall. Popular religion called Babylon.

Rev. 18 : 1-5—God calls His people out of Babylon.

THIRD ANGEL'S MESSAGE

Rev. 14 : 9-14 (See study on Mark of the Beast)—This three-fold message (Rev. 14 : 6-14) develops a people who keep the commandments of God (ver. 12) and look for the coming of Christ (ver. 14).

THE LAW OF GOD

THE TEN COMMANDMENTS

"Thou shalt have no other gods before me.

"Thou shalt not make unto thee any graven image, or any likeness of any thing that is in heaven above, or that is in the earth beneath, or that is in the water under the earth:

"Thou shalt not bow down thyself to them, nor serve them: for I the Lord thy God am a jealous God, visiting the iniquity of the fathers upon the children unto the third and fourth generation of them that hate me;

"And shewing mercy unto thousands of them that love me, and keep my commandments.

"Thou shalt not take the name of the Lord thy God in vain; for the Lord will not hold him guiltless that taketh His name in vain.

"Remember the sabbath day, to keep it holy.

"Six days shalt thou labour, and do all thy work:

"But the seventh day is the sabbath of the Lord thy God: in it thou shalt not do any work, thou, nor thy son, nor thy daughter, thy manservant, nor thy maidservant, nor thy cattle, nor thy stranger that is within thy gates:

"For in six days the Lord made heaven and earth, the sea, and all that in them is, and rested the seventh day: wherefore the Lord blessed the sabbath day, and hallowed it.

"Honour thy father and thy mother:

that thy days may be long upon the land which the Lord thy God giveth thee.

"Thou shalt not kill.

"Thou shalt not commit adultery.

"Thou shalt not steal.

"Thou shalt not bear false witness against thy neighbour.

"Thou shalt not covet thy neighbour's house, thou shalt not covet thy neighbour's wife, nor his manservant, nor his maidservant, nor his ox, nor his ass, nor any thing that is thy neighbour's." Exodus 20 : 3-17.

GOD SPOKE HIS LAW ON MT. SINAI

"And the Lord spake unto you out of the midst of the fire: ye heard the voice of the words, but saw no similitude; only ye heard a voice.

"And He declared unto you His covenant, which He commanded you to perform, even ten commandments; and He wrote them upon two tables of stone." Deut. 4 : 12, 13.

Ex. 20 : 1-17; Neh. 9 : 13, 14.

The first four commandments reveal our duty to God.

The last six commandments reveal our duty to man.

CHRIST TAUGHT THE PERPETUITY OF THE LAW

"If ye keep my commandments, ye shall abide in my love; even as I have kept my Father's commandments, and abide in His love." John 15 : 10.

"Think not that I am come to destroy the law, or the prophets: I am not come to destroy, but to fulfil." Matt. 5 : 17.

"For verily I say unto you, Till heaven and earth pass, one jot or one tittle shall in no wise pass from the law, till all be fulfilled.

"Whosoever therefore shall break one of these least commandments, and shall teach men so, he shall be called the least in the kingdom of heaven: but whosoever shall do and teach them, the same shall be called great in the kingdom of heaven." Matt. 5 : 18, 19.

Ps. 40 : 7, 9 (See Heb. 10 : 5, 7).
Matt. 15 : 3; Matt. 19 : 16-19.

THE APOSTLES UPHELD THE LAW

"Wherefore the law is holy, and the commandment holy, and just, and good." Rom. 7 : 12.

"There is therefore now no condemnation to them which are in Christ Jesus, who walk not after the flesh, but after the Spirit." Rom. 8 : 1.

"For the law of the Spirit of life in Christ Jesus hath made me free from the law of sin and death.

"For what the law could not do, in that it was weak through the flesh, God sending His own Son in the likeness of sinful flesh, and for sin, condemned sin in the flesh. That the righteousness of the law might be fulfilled in us, who walk not after the flesh, but after the Spirit." Rom. 8 : 2-4.

Rom. 3 : 20; Rom. 7 : 7; James 2 : 10, 11; 1 John 3 : 4; Rev. 22 : 14; Rev. 12 : 17.

THE PRINCIPLES OF THE TEN COMMANDMENTS WERE KNOWN BEFORE THEY WERE GIVEN IN WRITTEN FORM ON MT. SINAI.

1. Gen. 35 : 1-4.
2. Gen. 31 : 19, 34, 35; Gen. 35 : 2-4.
3. Lev. 18 : 3, 21, 24, 27.
4. Gen. 2 : 1-4; Mk. 2 : 27; Gen. 8 : 10, 12; 29 : 27, 28; Ex. 16 : 4, 22, 23, 25-30.
5. Gen. 9 : 22-25.
6. Gen. 4 : 8-11, 23, 24; Gen. 9 : 5, 6.
7. Gen. 20 : 5-9; 38 : 24; 39 : 7-9.
8. Gen. 30 : 33; 31 : 19, 30, 32, 39; 44 : 8.
9. Gen. 39 : 7-20.
10. Had to be broken before the eighth was broken.

THE LAW OF GOD

TEN COMMANDMENTS IN NEW TESTAMENT

In the following scriptures it will be seen that each of the ten commandments was taught by the apostles:

FIRST COMMANDMENT

Acts 14 : 11-15—"Living and True God."

1 Cor. 8 : 4-6—"Idol nothing—One God."

SECOND COMMANDMENT

1 Cor. 12 : 2—"Gentiles—These Dumb Idols."

1 Cor. 10 : 14—"Flee from Idolatry."

Acts 17 : 29—"Ought Not Think God Like Gold, Silver, etc."

1 John 5 : 21—"Keep Yourselves From Idols."

THIRD COMMANDMENT

James 5 : 12—"Swear Not—Yea Be Yea."

FOURTH COMMANDMENT

Heb. 4 : 9—"There Remaineth—"

Acts 16 : 13—"Sabbath Day—River Side."

Acts 17 : 2—"His Manner—Three Sabbath Days."

FIFTH COMMANDMENT

Eph. 6 : 2—"Honor Thy Father and Mother."

SIXTH COMMANDMENT

Rom. 13 : 9—"Shalt Not Kill—"

SEVENTH COMMANDMENT

Rom. 13 : 9—" Shalt Not Commit Adultery—"
James 2 : 11.

EIGHTH COMMANDMENT

Rom. 13 : 9—" Steal—"
James 2 : 11.

NINTH COMMANDMENT

Rom. 13 : 9—" Not Bear False Witness—"

TENTH COMMANDMENT

Rom. 13 : 9—" Not Covet—"

THE LAW OF GOD A RULE OF RIGHTEOUSNESS

" And, behold, one came and said unto Him, Good Master, what good thing shall I do, that I may have eternal life ?

" And He said unto him, Why callest thou me good ? there is none good but one, that is, God: but if thou wilt enter into life, keep the commandments." Matt. 19 : 16, 17.

" Let us hear the conclusion of the whole matter: Fear God, and keep His commandments: for this is the whole duty of man." Eccl. 12 : 13.

Deut. 11 : 18, 19; 30 : 15, 16.

Rom. 2 : 13; 3 : 19, 20; Jas. 1 : 25; Rom. 7 : 7; 1 John 3 : 4; Rev. 22 : 14; Jas. 2 : 8-12; Ps. 37 : 30, 31.

THE LAW OF GOD CAN NEVER PASS AWAY

" For verily I say unto you, Till heaven and earth pass, one jot or one tittle shall in no wise pass from the law till all be fulfilled." Matt. 5 : 18.

" He hath remembered His covenant for ever, the word which He commanded to a thousand generations." Ps. 105 : 8.

Ps. 119 : 144, 152, 160; 1 Chron. 16 : 15-17; Ps. 111 : 7, 8.

THE LAW OF GOD IS PERFECT AND CANNOT BE IMPROVED UPON

" The law of the Lord is perfect, converting the soul: the testimony of the Lord is sure, making wise the simple.

" The statutes of the Lord are right, rejoicing the heart: the commandment of the Lord is pure, enlightening the eyes.

" The fear of the Lord is clean, enduring for ever: the judgments of the Lord are true and righteous altogether." Ps. 19 : 7-9.

" Wherefore the law is holy, and the commandment holy, and just, and good.

" For we know that the law is spiritual: but I am carnal, sold under sin." Rom. 7 : 12, 14.

Ps. 119 : 138, 142, 151; Rom. 7 : 22, 25; Isa. 48 : 18.

THE SABBATH OF THE LORD

THE SABBATH COMMANDMENT

" Remember the sabbath day, to keep it holy. Six days shalt thou labor, and do all thy work: but the seventh day is the sabbath of the Lord thy God: in it thou shalt not do any work, thou, nor thy son, nor thy daughter, thy manservant, nor thy maidservant, nor thy cattle, nor thy stranger that is within thy gates." Ex. 20 : 8-10.

THE SABBATH A SIGN FOREVER

" Wherefore the children of Israel shall keep the sabbath, to observe the sabbath throughout their generations, for a perpetual covenant. It is a sign between me and the children of Israel forever: for in six days the Lord made heaven and earth, and on the seventh day He rested, and was refreshed." Ex. 31 : 16, 17.

THE SABBATH A SIGN OF GOD AS THE SANCTIFIER

" Moreover also I gave them my sabbaths, to be a sign between me and them, that they might know that I am the Lord that sanctify them. And hallow my sabbaths; and they shall be a sign between me and you, that ye may know that I am the Lord your God." Eze. 20 : 12, 20.

THE BLESSING UPON SABBATH-KEEPERS

" Thus saith the Lord, Keep ye judgment, and do justice: for my salvation is near to come, and my righteousness to be revealed. Blessed is the man that doeth this, and the son of man that layeth hold on it; that keepeth the sabbath from polluting it, and keepeth his hand from doing any evil." Isa. 56 : 1, 2.

A SABBATH REFORM

" And they that shall be of thee shall build the old waste places: thou shalt raise up the foundations of many generations: and thou shalt be called, The repairer of the breach, The restorer of paths to dwell in. If thou turn away thy foot from the sabbath, from doing thy pleasure on my holy day; and call the sabbath a delight, the holy of the Lord, honorable; and shalt honor Him, not doing thine own ways, nor finding thine own pleasure, nor speaking thine own words: then shalt thou delight thyself in the Lord; and I will cause thee to ride upon the high places of the earth, and feed thee with the heritage of Jacob thy father: for the mouth of the Lord hath spoken it." Isa. 58 : 12-14.

THE SABBATH IN THE NEW EARTH

" For as the new heavens and the new earth, which I will make, shall remain before me, saith the Lord, so shall your seed and your name remain. And it shall come to pass, that from one new moon to another, and from one sabbath to another, shall all flesh come to worship before me, saith the Lord." Isa. 66 : 22, 23.

THE SABBATH IN THE NEW TESTAMENT

"And He came to Nazareth, where He had been brought up: and, as His custom was, He went into the synagogue on the sabbath day, and stood up for to read." Luke 4 : 16.

"And Paul, as his manner was, went in unto them, and three sabbath days reasoned with them out of the scriptures." Acts 17 : 2.

Mark 2 : 27, 28; Luke 23 : 54-56; Matt. 24 : 20; Luke 21 : 20.

Matt. 28 : 1; Mark 15 : 42; 16 : 1; Acts 1 : 12.

Acts 13 : 42, 44; Acts 16 : 13; Acts 18 : 4; Heb. 4 : 9.

IS SUNDAY IN THE BIBLE?

The word "Sunday" is not found in the Bible, but the term "First Day of the Week" is found eight times, as follows:

Matt. 28 : 1; Mark 16 : 1, 2, 9; Luke 24 : 1; John 20 : 1, 19; Acts 20 : 7; 1 Cor. 16 : 1, 2.

The first six texts all refer to the fact of Christ's Resurrection.

Acts 20 : 7—Speaks of a special meeting held by Paul at Troas, and was a night meeting (see verse 8) as the day begins at sunset, according to the Bible (Lev. 23 : 32, Mark 1 : 32). This meeting was on, what we call, Saturday night. Paul walked 19 miles to Assos the next day (Sunday).

1 Cor. 16 : 2—Refers to a collection for the poor saints, and was to be "laid by in store" at home and has no reference to any public meeting.

Thus, no Bible text attributes holiness or sacredness to any day, except the seventh day Sabbath of the Lord.

Rev. 1 : 10; Mark 2 : 28; Isa. 58 : 13; Ex. 20 : 8-10; Luke 4 : 16; Matt. 24 : 20.

HAS TIME BEEN LOST?

ORIGIN OF THE WEEK

Genesis, chapters 1 and 2. Also Gen. 7 : 4; 8 : 10, 12.

Gen. 29 : 27, 28.

FROM EDEN TO ABRAHAM

Adam and Methuselah—Lives overlap 243 years.

Methuselah and Shem—100 years.

Shem and Abraham—150 years.

No chance to forget the facts of creation and Institution of the Sabbath (Gen. 1 and 2).

SABBATH NOT LOST IN EGYPT

Ex. 16 : 4, 5, 21-30, 35—People knew when Sabbath came before the law was given on Mt. Sinai.

Ex. 20 : 8-12—This was the creation Sabbath.

SABBATH NOT LOST IN PROMISED LAND

Strict Laws regarding the Sabbath. God called attention to the Sabbath by His prophets.

2 Kings 4 : 23; 1 Chron. 9 : 32; Isa. 56 : 2-6; Isa. 58 : 13, 14; Jer. 17 : 24-27; Eze. 20 : 10-24; Amos 8 : 4-6.

SABBATH NOT LOST DURING SEVENTY YEARS' CAPTIVITY

Jer. 17—Were sent into captivity for breaking the Sabbath.

Neh. 13 : 15—Knew Sabbath when returned from captivity.

Dan. 6 : 5.

70 years too short a time in which to lose track of calendar. Genealogies were kept. See Ezra. They returned to the Holy Land keeping the Sabbath.

THEY DID NOT LOSE IT UP TO THE TIME OF CHRIST

Matt. 12 : 1-12—Christ found them keeping it very strictly.

Mark 2 : 27—Christ said it was made for man. (At creation. See Gen. 2 : 1-3; Ex. 20 : 8-12.)

Luke 23 : 54—It was the Sabbath according to the commandment and therefore the creation Sabbath, for the fourth commandment refers back to creation.

Acts 13 : 14; 15 : 21; 16 : 13; 17 : 2; 18 : 4; Rev. 1 : 10.

(Mark 2 : 27, 28.)

This brings us to about A.D. 96, over 4000 years without a break. Since the time of Christ no time has been lost. The calendar we use to-day, with some modifications regarding the months that did not affect the week at all, was in use over 40 years before Christ.

Astronomy says there is no lost time. Almanacs, histories, encyclopedias, dictionaries, old family Bibles, all the laws of Christendom, the customs of Islam, the Greek Catholic Church, the Roman Catholic Church, the Protestant Church, the Jews, and all modern science—testify that we have not lost track of the days of the week.

THE CHRISTIAN SABBATH

GOD HAS A DAY

"I was in the Spirit on the Lord's day, and heard behind me a great voice, as of a trumpet." Rev. 1 : 10.

Isa. 58 : 13—"My Holy Day."

THAT DAY IS THE SABBATH OR REST DAY

"And He said unto them, The sabbath was made for man, and not man for the sabbath:

"Therefore the Son of man is Lord also of the sabbath." Mark 2 : 27, 28.

SINCE JESUS DECLARES HE IS LORD OF THE SABBATH, THE SABBATH MUST THEREFORE BE THE LORD'S DAY

In Isa. 58 : 12-14, God calls the Sabbath "My Holy Day."

THE SABBATH IS THE SEVENTH DAY

"Thus the heavens and the earth were finished, and all the host of them.

"And on the seventh day God ended His work which He had made; and He rested on the seventh day from all His work which He had made.

"And God blessed the seventh day, and sanctified it: because that in it He had rested from all His work which God created and made." Gen. 2 : 1-3.

"Remember the sabbath day, to keep it holy.

"Six days shalt thou labour, and do all thy work:

"But the seventh day is the sabbath of the Lord thy God: in it thou shalt not do any work, thou, nor thy son, nor thy daughter, thy manservant, nor thy maidservant, nor thy cattle, nor thy stranger that is within thy gates." Ex. 20 : 8-10.

"For He spake in a certain place of the seventh day on this wise, And God did rest the seventh day from all His works." Heb. 4 : 4.

THE SEVENTH DAY IS THE CHRISTIAN SABBATH

"In the beginning was the Word, and the Word was with God.

"The same was in the beginning with God.

"All things were made by Him; and without Him was not any thing made that was made." John 1 : 1-3.

"And the Word was made flesh, and dwelt among us (and we beheld His glory, the glory as of the only begotten of the Father), full of grace and truth." John 1 : 14. See also Heb. 1 : 1-3, 9, 10.

"And He said unto them, The sabbath was made for man, and not man for the sabbath:

"Therefore the Son of man is Lord also of the sabbath." Mark 2 : 27, 28. Notice, it was made for man (Mankind).

Col. 1 : 14-17—Christ made all things at Creation. The Sabbath was made then therefore, Christ made the Sabbath (Gen. 2 : 1-3; Ex. 20 : 8-10) and it is the Christian Sabbath.

CHRIST KEPT THE SABBATH

"And He came to Nazareth, where He had been brought up: and, as His custom was, He went into the synagogue on the sabbath day, and stood up for to read." Luke 4 : 16.

John 15 : 10; Heb. 10 : 7; (Ps. 40 : 8); Heb. 5 : 8; 1 Cor. 2 : 1, 2.

CHRIST AS A SABBATH KEEPER IS OUR EXAMPLE

"For even hereunto were ye called: because Christ also suffered for us, leaving us an example, that ye should follow His steps." 1 Pet. 2 : 21.

Col. 1 : 22; 1 Cor. 10 : 4; 1 John 4 : 17; 1 John 2 : 6.

THE SABBATH BEGINS AT SUNSET AND CLOSES AT SUNSET

"It shall be unto you a sabbath of rest, and ye shall afflict your souls: in the ninth day of the month at even, from even unto even, shall ye celebrate your sabbath." Lev. 23 : 32.

"And at even, when the sun did set, they brought unto Him all that were diseased, and them that were possessed with devils." Mark 1 : 32.

Luke 23 : 50-56; Luke 24 : 1—See also Gen. 1 : 5, 8, 13, 19, 23, 31; Gen. 2 : 1-3.

THE CHANGE OF THE SABBATH

THE SEVENTH DAY IS THE TRUE SABBATH MADE BY CHRIST AT CREATION BUT THE FIRST DAY IS OBSERVED BY MANY NOW. HOW DID THIS CHANGE COME ABOUT?

CHRIST DID NOT CHANGE THE SABBATH

"Think not that I am come to destroy the law, or the prophets: I am not come to destroy, but to fulfil.

"For verily I say unto you, Till heaven and earth pass, one jot or one tittle shall in no wise pass from the law, till all be fulfilled.

"Whosoever therefore shall break one of these least commandments, and shall teach men so, he shall be called the least in the kingdom of heaven: but whosoever shall do and teach them, the same shall be called great in the kingdom of heaven." Matt. 5 : 17-19.

"And He said unto them, The sabbath was made for man, and not man for the sabbath." Mark 2 : 27.

"Therefore the Son of man is Lord also of the sabbath." Mark 2 : 28.

"On these two commandments hang all the law and the prophets." Matt. 22 : 40.

"And He came to Nazareth, where He had been brought up: and, as His custom was, He went into the synagogue on the sabbath day, and stood up for to read." Luke 4 : 16.

John 15 : 10; Matt. 24 : 20; Isa. 42 : 21; Heb. 13 : 8; Matt. 15 : 19.

THE APOSTLES DID NOT CHANGE THE SABBATH

PAUL

"What shall we say then? Is the law sin? God forbid. Nay, I had not known sin, but by the law: for I had not known lust, except the law had said, Thou shalt not covet." Rom. 7 : 7.

"Wherefore the law is holy, and the commandment holy, and just and good." Rom. 7 : 12.

"For we know that the law is spiritual: but I am carnal, sold under sin." Rom. 7 : 14.

"And Paul, as his manner was, went in unto them, and three sabbath days reasoned with them out of the scriptures." Acts 17 : 2.

Acts 13 : 14; Acts 13 : 42, 44; Acts 16 : 13.

"For I have not shunned to declare unto you all the counsel of God." Acts 20 : 27.

He declared all God's counsel, but never mentioned any change of the Sabbath, therefore such a change is not a part of God's counsel and must be man's counsel.

"And it came to pass, that after three days Paul called the chief of the Jews together: and when they were come together, he said unto them, Men and brethren, though I have committed nothing against the people, or customs of our fathers, yet was I delivered prisoner from Jerusalem into the hands of the Romans." Acts 28 : 17.

PETER

"For even hereunto were ye called: because Christ also suffered for us, leaving us an example, that ye should follow His steps." 1 Peter 2 : 21.

We are to follow Christ's steps and He was a Sabbath keeper.

JOHN

Rev. 1 : 10 (See Mark 2 : 27, 28; Isa. 58 : 12-14); Rev. 12 : 17; Rev. 22 : 14; John 15 : 10; 1 John 2 : 4.

GOD'S WORD DECLARED THAT MAN WOULD ATTEMPT TO CHANGE GOD'S TIMES AND LAWS.

"And he shall speak great words against the Most High, and shall wear out the saints of the Most High, and think to change times and laws: and they shall be given into his hand until a time and times and the dividing of time." Dan. 7 : 25.

"Let no man deceive you by any means: for that day shall not come, except there come a falling away first, and that man of sin be revealed, the son of perdition. Who opposeth and exalteth himself above all that is called God, or that is worshipped; so that he as God sitteth in the temple of God, shewing himself that he is God." 2 Thess. 2 : 3, 4.

Note.—The only way a human power could exalt itself above God would be to change the law of God.

THE PAPACY CLAIMS TO HAVE DONE THIS

"*Question:* Have you any other way of proving that the Church has power to institute festivals of precept?

"*Answer:* Had she not such power, she could not have done that in which all modern religionists agree with her; she could not have substituted the observance of Sunday the first day of the week, for the observance of Saturday the seventh day, a change for which there is no Scriptural authority."—*A Doctrinal Catechism*, by Rev. Stephen Keenan, p. 174.

"*Question:* What day was the Sabbath?

"*Answer:* Saturday."

"*Question:* Who changed it?

"*Answer:* The Catholic Church."—From Rev. Dr. Butler's *Catechism*, Revised, p. 57.

"It was the Catholic Church which, by the authority of Jesus Christ, has transferred this rest to the Sunday in remembrance of the resurrection of our Lord. Thus the observance of Sunday by the Protestants is an homage they pay, in spite of themselves, to the authority of the (Catholic) Church."—*Plain Talk About the Protestantism of Today*," by Mgr. Segur, p. 213.

The first Sunday law ever made was that issued by the Emperor Constantine —March 7, A.D. 321, and reads as follows:

"Let all the judges and town people, and the occupation of all trades rest on the venerable day of the sun; but let those who are situated in the country, freely and at full liberty, attend to the business of agriculture; because it often happens that no other day is so fit for sowing corn and planting vines; lest the critical moment being let slip, men should lose the commodities granted by heaven." *Corpus Juris Civilis Cod.*: lib. 3, tit. 12, 3.

The Catholic Council of Laodicea (A.D. 364) forbade the observance of the true Bible Sabbath.

"Sabbath, Change of, Action of Council of Laodicea on (about A.D. 364).—Christians shall not Judaize and be idle on Saturday (Sabbath, original), but shall work on that day; but the Lord's day they shall especially honor, and, as being Christians, shall, if possible, do no work on that day. If, however, they are found Judaizing, they shall be shut out from Christ." *A History of the Councils of the Church*: *from the Original Documents*, Rt. Rev. Charles Joseph Hefele, D.D., Bishop of Rottenburg, book 6, sec. 93, canon 29 (vol. II., p. 316). Edinburgh: T. & T. Clark, 1896.

The Bishop Eusebius (A.D. 270-338) who worked with the Emperor Constantine says: " All things whatsoever that it was duty to do on the Sabbath, these we have transferred to the Lord's day." *Commentary on the Psalms*, Eusebius; cited in the *Commentary on the Apocalypse*, Moses Stuart, vol. II., 9. 40. Andover: Allen, Morrill, and Wardwell, 1845.

WHAT DO PROTESTANTS SAY?

LUTHER

" They (the Catholics) allege the Sabbath changed into Sunday, the Lord's day, contrary to the decalogue, as it appears; neither is there any example more boasted of than the changing of the Sabbath day. Great, say they, is the power and authority of the church, since it dispensed with one of the ten commandments." *Auxsburg Confession*, art. XXVIII.

METHODIST

" It is true there is no positive command for infant baptism, nor is there any against it, as there should have been if Christ intended to abridge the rights of Jewish parents under the Abrahamic covenant. Nor is there any for keeping holy the first day of the week, or for family devotion, or for women to receive the Lord's Supper. The reasons are obvious; there was no controversy in either case that called for it." *Theological Compend.*, Rev. Amos Binney, pp. 180, 181. New York: Methodist Book Concern, 1902.

CHRISTIAN

"I do not believe that the Lord's day came in the room of the Jewish Sabbath, or that the Sabbath was changed from the seventh to the first day, for this plain reason, that where there is no testimony, there can be no faith. Now there is no testimony in all the oracles of heaven that the Sabbath was changed, or that the Lord's day came in the room of it. . . . There is no divine testimony that the Sabbath was changed, or that the Lord's day came in the room of it; therefore there can be no divine faith that the Sabbath was changed or that the Lord's day came in the room of it." Alexander Campbell (Candidus), in *Washington (Pa.) Reporter*, Oct. 8, 1821.

CONGREGATIONALIST

" Much has been made of the attitude of Christ in speech and deed toward the Sabbath. Some have imagined that by words He uttered and by deeds He did He relaxed the binding nature of the old command. This view, however, is to absolutely misunderstand and misinterpret the doing and the teaching of Jesus." *The Ten Commandments*, G. Campbell Morgan (Congregationalist), p. 50. New York: Fleming H. Revell.

" It is quite clear that, however rigidly or devoutly we may spend Sunday, we are not keeping the Sabbath. . . . The Sabbath was founded on a specific, divine command. We can plead no such command for the observance of Sunday. . . . There is not a single sentence in the New Testament to suggest that we incur any penalty by violating the supposed sanctity of Sunday." *The Ten Commandments*, R. W. Dale, D.D. (Congregationalist), pp. 106, 107. London: Hodder and Stoughton.

PRESBYTERIAN

" The moral law doth for ever bind all, as well justified persons as others, to the obedience thereof, and that not only in regard of the matter contained in it, but also in respect of the authority of God the Creator who gave it. Neither doth Christ in the gospel any way dissolve, but much strengthen, this obligation." From *The Constitution of the Presbyterian Church in the U.S.A.*

CHURCH OF ENGLAND

" There is no word, no hint, in the New Testament about abstaining from work on Sunday. . . . The observance of Ash Wednesday or Lent stands on exactly the same footing as the observance of Sunday. . . . Into the rest of Sunday no divine law enters. *The Ten Commandments*, Canon Eyton (Church of England). London: Trubner.

BAPTIST

Dr. Hiscox's Solemn Question and Declaration: " There was and is a commandment to keep holy the Sabbath day, but that Sabbath day was not Sunday. It will be said, however, and with some show of triumph, that the Sabbath was transferred from the seventh to the first day of the week, with all its duties, privileges, and sanctions. Earnestly desiring information on this subject, which I have studied for many years, I ask, Where can the record of such a transaction be found? Not in the New Testament, absolutely not. There is no Scriptural evidence of the change of the Sabbath institution from the seventh to the first day of the week. . . . Of course, I quite well know that Sunday did come into use in early Christian history as a religious day, as we learn from the Christian Fathers and other sources. But what a pity that it comes branded with the mark of paganism, and christened with the name of the sun god, when adopted and sanctioned by the papal apostasy, and bequeathed as a sacred legacy to Protestantism! " Dr. Edward T. Hiscox, author of *The Baptist Manual*, in a paper read before a New York Ministers' Conference, held Nov. 13, 1893.

WHAT ENCYCLOPEDIAS SAY

"The earliest recognition of the observance of Sunday as a legal duty is a constitution of Constantine in A.D. 321, enacting that all courts of justice, inhabitants of towns, and workshops were to be at rest on Sunday (*venerabili die solis*), with an exception in favor of those engaged in agricultural labor." *Encyclopedia Britannica*: vol. XXVI., 11th edition, art. "Sunday," p. 95.

"Unquestionably the first law, either ecclesiastical or civil, by which the Sabbatical observance of that day is known to have been ordained, is the edict of Constantine, A.D. 321." *Chambers' Encyclopedia*: art. "Sabbath."

WHAT DOES GOD SAY?

"Know ye not, that to whom ye yield yourself servants to obey, his servants ye are to whom ye obey; whether of sin unto death, or of obedience unto righteousness?" Rom. 6 : 16.

"I know that, whatsoever God doeth, it shall be for ever: nothing can be put to it, nor any thing taken from it: and God doeth it, that men should fear before Him." Eccl. 3 : 14.

"But in vain they do worship me, teaching for doctrines the commandments of men.

"But He answered and said, Every plant, which my heavenly Father hath not planted, shall be rooted up." Matt. 15 : 9, 13.

Acts 5 : 29; Matt. 4 : 10, 11.

"And Elijah came unto all the people, and said, "How long halt ye between two opinions? If the Lord be God, follow Him: but if Baal, then follow him. And the people answered him not a word." 1 Kings 18 : 21.

THE LAW OF GOD

AS GIVEN BY GOD	AS CHANGED BY MAN
"I will not alter the thing that is gone out of my lips." Ps. 89 : 34.	"He shall think himself able to change times and laws." Dan. 7 : 25.
I Thou shalt have no other gods before me.	I I am the Lord thy God: thou shalt not have strange gods before me.
II Thou shalt not make unto thee any graven image, or any likeness of any thing that is in heaven above, or that is in the earth beneath, or that is in the water under the earth; thou shalt not bow down thyself to them, nor serve them; for I the Lord thy God am a jealous God, visiting the iniquity of the fathers upon the children unto the third and fourth generation of them that hate me, and showing mercy unto thousands of them that love me, and keep my commandments.	
III Thou shalt not take the name of the Lord thy God in vain; for the Lord will not hold him guiltless that taketh His name in vain.	II Thou shalt not take the name of the Lord thy God in vain.
IV Remember the Sabbath day to keep it holy. Six days shalt thou labor, and do all thy work; but the seventh day is the Sabbath of the Lord thy God: in it thou shalt not do any work, thou, nor thy son, nor thy daughter, thy manservant, nor thy maidservant, nor thy cattle, nor thy stranger that is within thy gates; for in six days the Lord made heaven and earth, the sea, and all that in them is, and rested the seventh day; wherefore the Lord blessed the Sabbath day, and hallowed it.	III Remember that thou keep holy the Sabbath day.
V Honor thy father and thy mother, that thy days may be long upon the land which the Lord thy God giveth thee.	IV Honor thy father and thy mother.
VI Thou shalt not kill.	V Thou shalt not kill.

AS GIVEN BY GOD	AS CHANGED BY MAN
VII Thou shalt not commit adultery.	VI Thou shalt not commit adultery.
VIII Thou shalt not steal.	VII Thou shalt not steal.
IX Thou shalt not bear false witness against thy neighbor.	VIII Thou shalt not bear false witness against thy neighbor.
X Thou shalt not covet thy neighbor's house, thou shalt not covet thy neighbor's wife, nor his manservant, nor his maid-servant, nor his ox, nor his ass, nor any thing that is thy neighbor's.	IX Thou shalt not covet thy neighbor's wife.
	X Thou shalt not covet thy neighbor's goods.
(See Ex. 20 : 3-17).	(See Convert's *Catechism of Catholic Doctrine*: p. 37, edition 1921, published by B. Herder Book Co., 17 So. Broadway, St. Louis, Mo.)

SIX HUNDRED SIXTY-SIX

"Here is wisdom. Let him that hath understanding count the number of the beast : for it is the number of a man; and his number is six hundred threescore and six." Rev. 13 : 18.

People often take this out of context and speculate. Some try Napoleon, some the Kaiser, some Mussolini or other well-known characters.

BUT IT IS THE NUMBER OF THE BEAST

No need to speculate.

Rev. 13 : 13, 14—The Beast had image and a wound.

Thus the Beast of Rev. 13 : 1-10 is the Beast of verses 17, 18. See Rev. 15 : 2. Has image, mark and number.

BEAST SUCCEEDS THE DRAGON—HAS DRAGON'S CAPITAL CITY

See Rev. 13 : 2.

The Dragon is primarily Satan, but secondarily the Roman Empire through which Satan worked in an attempt to destroy Christ. See Rev. 12 : 1-6.

"Dragon"—Rome (Dan. 7, "Beasts"); "Woman"—The Church (2 Cor. 11 : 2); "Man-child"—Christ (Rev. 19 : 15).

Papal Rome succeeded Pagan Rome and received control of the city of Rome as its capitol. It is a religious power. (See Rev. 13 : 1). "Blasphemy" shows we are dealing with a religious power. (See John 10 : 33 and Luke 5 : 21.) Claiming power to forgive sins and man receiving honor due to God alone, are blasphemy. The papacy does both.

THE NUMBER 666 IS THE NUMBER OF A MAN AND IT IS IN HIS NAME

The letters of the Latin or Roman phrase Vicarius Filii Dei (Vicar of the Son of God) have the numerical value 666.

V	=	5
I	=	1
C	=	100
A	=	0
R	=	0
I	=	1
U	=	5
S	=	0
F	=	0
I	=	1
L	=	50
I	=	1
I	=	1
D	=	500
E	=	0
I	=	1
Total		666

"Verse 18—Six hundred sixty-six. The numeral letters of his name shall make up this number." Douay (Catholic) Bible, note on Rev. 13 : 18.

"The Pope is the vicar of Christ, the successor of St. Peter, and the visible head of the Church."—*Manual of Christian Doctrine*, John Joseph McVey, 1914, p. 123.

"Beatus Petrus in terris Vicarius Filii Dei Videtur esse constitutus (Blessed Peter seems to have been appointed the vicar of the Son of God on earth)." Decretum Gratiani.

"The letters inscribed in the Pope's miter are these : Vicarius Filii Dei, which is the Latin for 'Vicar of the Son of God.' Catholics hold that the church, which is a visible society, must have a visible head. Christ, before His ascension into heaven, appointed St. Peter to act as His representative. Upon the death of Peter the man who succeeded to the office of Peter as Bishop of Rome was recognised as head of the church. Hence to the Bishop of Rome, as head of the church, was given the title 'Vicar of Christ.'" *Our Sunday Visitor*: April 18, 1915 (Catholic).

THE MARK OF THE BEAST

"And the third angel followed them, saying with a loud voice, If any man worship the beast and his image, and receive his mark in his forehead, or in his hand.

"The same shall drink of the wine of the wrath of God, which is poured out without mixture into the cup of his indignation; and he shall be tormented with fire and brimstone in the presence of the holy angels, and in the presence of the Lamb.

"And the smoke of their torment ascendeth up for ever and ever: and they have no rest day nor night, who worship the beast and his image, and whosoever receiveth the mark of his name.

"Here is the patience of the saints: here are they that keep the commandments of God, and the faith of Jesus." Rev. 14 : 9-12.

Most terrible warning in the Bible and applies just before the Lord returns. "Mark" not an outward symbol. If so, none could resist it. It is a religious symbol because acceptance of it is worship of the "beast." The "beast" is a symbol of Papal apostasy. See Bible study on "The Beast of Rev. 13."

GOD'S SEAL—SIGN OR MARK IS HIS SABBATH

"Speak thou also unto the children of Israel, saying, Verily my sabbaths ye shall keep: for it is a sign between me and you throughout your generations; that ye may know that I am the Lord that doth sanctify you." Ex. 31 : 13.

"It is a sign between me and the children of Israel for ever: for in six days the Lord made heaven and earth, and on the seventh day He rested, and was refreshed." Ex. 31 : 17.

"Moreover also I gave them my sabbaths, to be a sign between me and them, that they might know that I am the Lord that sanctify them." Ezek, 20 : 12.

THOSE WHO REFUSE THE MARK KEEP THE COMMANDMENTS, THEREFORE THOSE WHO HAVE THE MARK DO NOT KEEP THEM

"The same shall drink of the wine of the wrath of God, which is poured out without mixture into the cup of His indignation; and He shall be tormented with fire and brimstone in the presence of the holy angels, and in the presence of the Lamb." Rev. 14 : 10.

THOSE WHO RECEIVE THE SEAL OF GOD ARE VICTORIOUS OVER THE MARK OF THE BEAST, THUS THE MARK INVOLVES A VIOLATION OF THE FOURTH COMMANDMENT BECAUSE THE SEAL OF GOD CONCERNS THE SABBATH

"Saying, Hurt not the earth, neither the sea, nor the trees, till we have sealed the servants of our God in their foreheads.

"And I heard the number of them which were sealed: and there were sealed an hundred and forty and four thousand of all the tribes of the children of Israel." Rev. 7 : 3, 4.

"And I looked, and, lo, a Lamb stood on the mount Sion, and with Him an hundred forty and four thousand, having His Father's name written in their foreheads.

"And I heard a voice from heaven, as the voice of many waters, and as the voice of a great thunder: and I heard the voice of harpers harping with their harps:

"And they sung as it were a new song before the throne, and before the four beasts, and the elders: and no man could learn that song but the hundred and forty and four thousand, which were redeemed from the earth." Rev. 14 : 1-3. See Rev. 15 : 1-3.

THE PAPACY CLAIMS THE CHANGE OF THE SABBATH FROM THE SEVENTH TO THE FIRST DAY WAS HER ACT AND IS THE MARK OF HER AUTHORITY IN RELIGIOUS THINGS

"*Question:* Have you any other way of proving that the Church has power to institute festivals of precept?

"*Answer:* Had she not such power, she could not have done that in which all modern religionists agree with her; she could not have substituted the observance of Sunday the first day of the week, for the observance of Saturday the seventh day, a change for which there is no Scriptural authority." *Doctrinal Catechism* by The Rev. Stephen Keenan, page 174.

"Of course the Catholic Church claims that the change was her act . . . and the act is a mark of her ecclesiastical authority in religious things."

(This is a quotation from a letter written in November, 1895, Mr. H. F. Thomas, chancellor to Cardinal Gibbons, replying to an inquiry as to whether the Catholic Church claims to have changed the Sabbath.)

"And he shall speak great words against the most High, and shall wear out the saints of the most High, and think to change times and laws: and they shall be given into his hand until a time and times and the dividing of time." Dan. 7 : 25.

A CALL TO OBEY GOD RATHER THAN MAN

"And Samuel said, Hath the Lord as great delight in burnt offerings and sacrifices, as in obeying the voice of the Lord? Behold, to obey is better than sacrifice, and to hearken than the fat of rams." 1 Sam. 15 : 22.

"And I saw as it were a sea of glass mingled with fire: and them that had gotten the victory over the beast, and over his image, and over his mark, and over the number of his name, stand on the sea of glass, having the harps of God." Rev. 15 : 2.

Phil. 2 : 8; Heb. 5 : 8; Rom. 15 : 18; 16 : 26; Mark. 7 : 9; Isa. 1 : 19.

THE SEAL OF GOD

THE SERVANTS OF GOD TO BE SEALED IN THE LAST DAYS

"And after these things I saw four angels standing on the four corners of the earth, holding the four winds of the earth, that the wind should not blow on the earth, nor on the sea, nor on any tree.

"And I saw another angel ascending from the east, having the seal of the living God: and he cried with a loud voice to the four angels, to whom it was given to hurt the earth and the sea,

"Saying, Hurt not the earth, neither the sea, nor the trees, till we have sealed the servants of our God in their foreheads.

"And I heard the number of them which were sealed: and there were sealed an hundred and forty and four thousand of all the tribes of the children of Israel." Rev. 7 : 1-4.

Read Eze. 9 : 1-6; Rev. 14 : 1.

A SIGN OR SEAL USED WITH SAME MEANING IN THE BIBLE AND ALWAYS USED IN CONNECTION WITH SOME LAW OR LEGAL DOCUMENT

"And he received the sign of circumcision, a seal of the righteousness of the faith which he had yet being uncircumcised: that he might be the father of all them that believe, though they be not circumcised; that righteousness might be imputed unto them also." Rom. 4 : 11.

"Now, O king, establish the decree, and sign the writing, that it be not changed, according to the law of the Medes and Persians, which altereth not." Daniel 6 : 8.

"So she wrote letters in Ahab's name, and sealed them with his seal, and sent the letters unto the elders and to the nobles that were in his city, dwelling with Naboth." 1 Kings 21 : 8.

"Then were the king's scribes called on the thirteenth day of the first month, and there was written according to all that Haman had commanded unto the king's lieutenants, and to the governors that were over every province, and to the rulers of every people of every province according to the writing thereof, and to every people after their language; in the name of king Ahasuerus was it written, and sealed with the king's ring." Esther 3 : 12.

Note.—An official seal must show three things: (1) The name of the law-giver; (2) His official position or title or right to rule; (3) His kingdom or the territory over which he rules. For instance—

George Washington (Name)
President (Official Position)
United States (Extent of Jurisdiction).

GOD'S SEAL IS CONNECTED WITH HIS LAW AND IS FOUND IN THE FOURTH COMMANDMENT

"Bind up the testimony, seal the law among my disciples." Isa. 8 : 16.

Verse 17 shows this message due while people are looking for the Lord to come.

"Remember the sabbath day, to keep it holy.

"Six days shalt thou labour, and do all thy work:

"But the seventh day is the sabbath of the Lord thy God: in it thou shalt not do any work, thou, nor thy son, nor thy daughter, thy manservant, nor thy maidservant, nor thy cattle, nor thy stranger that is within thy gates:

"For in six days the Lord made heaven and earth, the sea, and all that in them is, and rested the seventh day: wherefore the Lord blessed the sabbath day, and hallowed it." Ex. 20 : 8-11.

Read all the Ten Commandments.

Only in the *Fourth* do we find: (1) God's name, "Lord Thy God"; (2) His official position, "Creator" (God created heaven and earth); (3) The extent of His domain (heaven and earth).

THE BIBLE SAYS THE SABBATH IS GOD'S SIGN (SEAL)

"Moreover also I gave them my sabbaths, to be a sign between me and them, that they might know that I am the Lord that sanctify them.

"And hallow my sabbaths; and they shall be a sign between me and you, that ye may know that I am the Lord your God." Eze. 20 : 12, 20.

"Speak thou also unto the children of Israel, saying, Verily my sabbaths ye shall keep: for it is a sign between me and you throughout your generations; that ye may know that I am the Lord that doth sanctify you.

"It is a sign between me and the children of Israel for ever: for in six days the Lord made heaven and earth, and on the seventh day He rested, and was refreshed." Ex. 31 : 13, 17.

THE SABBATH SIGN OR SEAL DISTINGUISHES THE TRUE GOD AS THE CREATOR FROM ALL FALSE GODS

"For all the gods of the nations are idols: but the Lord made the heavens." Ps. 96 : 5.

"God that made the world and all things therein, seeing that he is Lord of heaven and earth, dwelleth not in temples made with hands." Acts 17 : 24.

Jeremiah 10 : 10-12.

IT TAKES THE SAME CREATIVE POWER OF CHRIST TO GIVE A SINNER A NEW HEART THAT IT TAKES TO CREATE A WORLD

"Therefore if any man be in Christ, he is a new creature: old things are passed away; behold, all things are become new." 2 Cor. 5 : 17 (New creation).

"Create in me a clean heart, O God; and renew a right spirit within me." Ps. 51 : 10.

1 Cor. 6 : 11; 2 Thess. 2 : 13; Eph.

2 : 10; Eph. 4 : 24; Isa. 43 : 1; Col. 1 : 13-16.

THE SABBATH IS THUS THE SEAL OF GOD'S CREATIVE AND SANCTIFYING POWER WHICH IS EXERCISED THROUGH THE HOLY SPIRIT

"In the beginning God created the heaven and the earth.

"And the earth was without form, and void; and darkness was upon the face of the deep. And the Spirit of God moved upon the face of the waters." Gen. 1 : 1, 2.

"And grieve not the holy Spirit of God, whereby ye are sealed unto the day of redemption." Eph. 4 : 30.

Note.—In ancient times the Passover, which was a day of special religious services in memory of Israel's deliverance from Egypt, was called a sign (or seal) in the forehead.

"And Moses said unto the people, Remember this day, in which ye came out from Egypt, out of the house of bondage; for by strength of hand the Lord brought you out from this place: there shall no leavened bread be eaten.

"And it shall be for a sign unto thee upon thine hand, and for a memorial between thine eyes, that the Lord's law may be in thy mouth: for with a strong hand hath the Lord brought thee out of Egypt.

"Thou shalt therefore keep this ordinance in his season from year to year." Ex. 13 : 3, 9, 10. See Ex. 12 : 14.

GOD'S SABBATH SEAL TO BE PLACED UPON THE FOREHEADS OF HIS SERVANTS BEFORE THE SECOND COMING OF CHRIST

"Saying, Hurt not the earth, neither the sea, nor the trees, till we have sealed the servants of our God in their foreheads." Rev. 7 : 3.

Compare verses 1-4 with Rev. 14 : 1 and Rev. 15 : 2, 3.

These Scriptures show the 144,000, who have the seal of God, also have the victory over the Mark of the Beast.

"Here is the patience of the saints: here are they that keep the commandments of God, and the faith of Jesus." Rev. 14 : 12.

"And the dragon was wroth with the woman, and went to make war with the remnant of her seed, which keep the commandments of God, and have the testimony of Jesus Christ." Rev. 12 : 17.

WALKING IN THE LIGHT

"The same came for a witness, to bear witness of the Light, that all men through Him might believe." John 1 : 7.

"O house of Jacob, come ye, and let us walk in the light of the Lord." Isa. 2 : 5.

WHAT IS THE LIGHT?

"This then is the message which we have heard of Him, and declare unto you, that God is light, and in Him is no darkness at all." 1 John 1 : 5.

Ps. 119 : 105—"Thy Word is a lamp unto my feet, and a light unto my path."

Eph. 5 : 13; Prov. 6 : 23; Ps. 119 : 130.

GOD CALLS US TO WALK IN THE LIGHT

"But ye are a chosen generation, a royal priesthood, an holy nation, a peculiar people; that ye should shew forth the praises of Him who hath called you out of darkness into His marvellous light." 1 Peter 2 : 9.

"But the path of the just is as the shining light, that shineth more and more unto the perfect day." Prov. 4 : 18.

"But he that doeth truth cometh to the light, that his deeds may be made manifest that they were wrought in God." John 3 : 21.

Ps. 43 : 3; Eph. 5 : 8; 1 Thess. 5 : 4, 5; 1 John 1 : 7.

MORAL AND CEREMONIAL LAW

MORAL LAW OF GOD THE TEN COMMANDMENTS	CEREMONIAL LAW OF MOSES LAW OF ORDINANCES
Spoken by God—Deut. 4 : 12, 13.	Spoken by Moses—Lev. 1 : 1, 2; Neh. 9 : 14.
Called the "Royal Law"—Jas. 2 : 8.	Called "Law . . . contained in ordinances"—Eph. 2 : 15.
Written by God—Ex. 24 : 12.	Written by Moses—Deut. 31 : 9.
Written on Tables of Stone—Deut. 10 : 1-4	Written in a book—Deut. 31 : 24; 2 Chron. 35 : 12.
Written "with the finger of God"—Ex. 31 : 18.	Was the "handwriting of ordinances"—Col. 2 : 14.
Placed in the Ark—Deut. 10 : 5; Heb. 9 : 4; 1 Kings 8 : 9.	Placed at side of ark—Deut. 31 : 26.
Called "The Testimony"—Ex. 40 : 20; Ex. 31 : 18.	Called "Book of Law"—Deut. 31 : 26.
Called Law of God—Ps. 1 : 2; Ps. 119 : 1.	Called Law of Moses—Mal. 4 : 4; Acts 15 : 5.
Lasts Forever—Ps. 111 : 7, 8.	Came to an end at the Cross—Col. 2 : 14; Heb. 9 : 10, 11.
A Perfect Law—Ps. 19 : 7.	"Made nothing perfect"—Heb. 7 : 19.

MORAL LAW OF GOD THE TEN COMMANDMENTS	CEREMONIAL LAW OF MOSES LAW OF ORDINANCES
Points out sin—1 Jno. 3 : 4.	Pointed to Sacrifice of Christ—Col. 2 : 14-17.
Gives recognition of Sin—Rom. 3 : 20; 7 : 7.	Given in consequence of Sin—Lev. chap. 3-7.
Not abolished by Christ—Matt. 5 : 17.	Was abolished by Christ—Eph. 2 : 15.
Magnified by Christ—Isa. 42 : 21.	Nailed to the Cross—by Christ—Col. 2 : 14
Is *Holy, Just* and *Good*—Rom. 7 : 12.	Only shadow of good things to come—Heb. 10 : 1.
Faith establishes this Law—Rom. 3 : 31.	If kept now, shows lack of faith in Christ as Saviour—Gal. 5 : 2-5.
A Spiritual Law—Rom. 7 : 14.	Concerns material things—meats, drinks, washings—Heb. 9 : 10.

WHAT WAS NAILED TO THE CROSS?

"Blotting out the handwriting of ordinances that was against us, which was contrary to us, and took it out of the way, nailing it to His cross;

"And having spoiled principalities and powers, He made a shew of them openly, triumphing over them in it.

"Let no man therefore judge you in meat, or in drink, or in respect of an holy day, or of the new moon, or of the sabbath days." Col. 2 : 14-17.

Deut. 4 : 13 — Ten commandments written on stone tables. Could not be blotted out.

Ex. 32 : 16—Written by God's finger.

Note.—Paul speaks in Col. 2 : 14-17 not of the ten commandment law, but of the handwriting of ordinances, written by Moses in a book, giving rules for the yearly shadowy feasts, and Sabbaths, and the appropiate meat and drink offerings which went with them. There is nothing about meats and drinks in the Ten Commandments.

Lev. 23 : 24, 27-32, 37—Yearly Sabbaths.

Lev. 23 : 38—These Sabbaths were "beside the sabbaths of the Lord."

See Matt. 23 : 4; Heb. 9 : 10; 1 Cor. 7 : 19.

See also Mark 2 : 27, 28—"And He said unto them, The sabbath was made for man, and not man for the sabbath:

"Therefore the Son of man is Lord also of the sabbath."

Note.—The Sabbath was made FOR man and is not against him.

THE NAMES OF THE DAYS OF THE WEEK

NAMES WHICH GOD GAVE	LATIN NAMES
First Day—Gen. 1 : 5	1. Dies Solis.
Second Day—Gen. 1 : 8	2. Dies Lunae
Third Day—Gen. 1 : 13	3. Dies Martis
Fourth Day—Gen. 1 : 19	4. Dies Mercurii
Fifth Day—Gen. 1 : 23	5. Dies Jovis
Sixth Day—Gen. 1 : 31	6. Dies Veneris
Seventh Day or Sabbath, which means Rest Gen. 2 : 1-3	7. Dies Saturni

SAXON NAMES	ENGLISH
1. Sun's Day	1
2. Moon's Day	2
3. Tiw's Day	3
4. Woden's Day	4
5. Thor's Day	5
6. Friga's Day	6
7. Satern's Day	7

Exodus 20 : 8-10.

"The week is a period of seven days, having no reference to the celestial motions, a circumstance to which it owes its unalterable uniformity. . . . The English names of the days of the week are derived from the Saxons. The ancient Saxons had borrowed the week from some Eastern nation, and substituted the names of their own divinities for the gods of Greece. In legislative and judiciary acts, the Latin names are still retained."—*Encyclopedia Brittanica,* Article Calendar.

THE TWO COVENANTS

WAS THE OLD COVENANT MADE WITH THE JEWS AND THE NEW COVENANT WITH THE GENTILES?

The Old Covenant was made at Sinai and was an agreement between God and Israel.

"Ye have seen what I did unto the Egyptians, and how I bare you on eagles' wings, and brought you unto myself.

"Now, therefore, if ye will obey my voice indeed, and keep my covenant, then ye shall be a peculiar treasure unto me above all people: for all the earth is mine:

"And ye shall be unto me a kingdom of priests, and an holy nation. These are the words which thou shalt speak unto the children of Israel.

"And Moses came and called for the elders of the people, and laid before their faces all these words which the Lord commanded him.

"And all the people answered together, and said, All that the Lord hath spoken we will do. And Moses returned the words of the people unto the Lord." Ex. 19 : 4-8.

The people promised to keep "all these words," that is, the Ten Commandments—also called "my voice" and "my Covenant."

"And Moses took the blood, and

sprinkled it on the people, and said, Behold the blood of the covenant, which the Lord hath made with you concerning all these words." Ex. 24 : 8.

"Now therefore, if ye will obey my voice indeed, and keep my covenant." Ex. 19 : 5.

"And the Lord spake unto you out of the midst of the fire: ye heard the voice of the words, but saw no similitude; only ye heard a voice.

"And he declared unto you His covenant, which He commanded you to perform, even ten commandments; and He wrote them upon two tables of stone." Deut. 4 : 12, 13.

GOD THEN SPOKE THE TEN COMMANDMENTS AND "HE ADDED NO MORE"

"These words the Lord spake unto all your assembly in the mount out of the midst of the fire, of the cloud, and of the thick darkness, with a great voice: and He added no more. And He wrote them in two tables of stone, and delivered them unto me." Deut. 5 : 22.

Ex. 20 : 3-17.

Ex. 20 : 22.

To the end of Exodus 23 is an explanation of the Ten Commandments, so that the people might better understand how to keep them.

AFTER HEARING THE WORDS OF THE LORD REPEATED BY MOSES AND THEN READ BY MOSES, THE PEOPLE PROMISED TWICE TO OBEY

"And Moses came and told the people all the words of the Lord, and all the judgments: and all the people answered with one voice, and said, All the words which the Lord hath said will we do.

"And he took the book of the covenant and read in the audience of the people: and they said, All that the Lord hath said will we do, and be obedient." Ex. 24 : 3, 7.

THE COVENANT WAS THEN SEALED WITH THE BLOOD OF A SACRIFICE

"And Moses took the blood, and sprinkled it on the people, and said, Behold the blood of the covenant, which the Lord hath made with you concerning all these words." Ex. 24 : 8.

Heb. 9 : 19, 20.

THE PEOPLE OF ISRAEL HAD VOLUNTARILY PROMISED TO MAKE THEMSELVES RIGHTEOUS, FOR IN THIS COVENANT (AGREEMENT) BETWEEN GOD AND ISRAEL AT SINAI GOD MADE NO PROMISE TO HELP THEM AND THEY FAILED TO ASK DIVINE AID

Therefore, their promises to keep the Ten Commandments were just as impossible for them to fulfil as it is impossible for us to keep these same commandments without the grace of our Lord Jesus Christ. In the New Covenant its "better promises" are that God Himself will forgive our past sins and write these holy commandments in our hearts by His gracious Spirit.

"I am the vine, ye are the branches: He that abideth in me, and I in Him, the same bringeth forth much fruit: for without me ye can do nothing." John 15 : 5.

"And be found in Him, not having mine own righteousness, which is of the law, but that which is through the faith of Christ, the righteousness which is of God by faith." Phil. 3 : 9.

"Forasmuch as ye are manifestly declared to be the epistle of Christ ministered by us, written not with ink, but with the Spirit of the living God; not in tables of stone, but in fleshy tables of the heart." 2 Cor. 3 : 3.

"By this we know that we love the children of God, when we love God, and keep His commandments.

"For this is the love of God, that we keep His commandments: and His commandments are not grievous." 1 John 5 : 2, 3.

Isa. 64 : 6; Jer. 23 : 6; Isa. 54 : 17.

WHILE THE OLD COVENANT WAS BASED UPON THE PROMISES OF THE PEOPLE TO MAKE THEMSELVES RIGHTEOUS, THE NEW COVENANT IS BASED UPON "BETTER PROMISES"

"But now hath He obtained a more excellent ministry, by how much also He is the mediator of a better covenant, which was established upon better promises.

"For if that first covenant had been faultless, then should no place have been sought for the second.

"For finding fault with them, He saith, Behold, the days come, saith the Lord, when I will make a new covenant with the house of Israel and with the house of Judah." Heb. 8 : 6-8.

Heb. 8 : 10, 11.

THE NEW COVENANT IS ALSO MADE WITH ISRAEL BUT IT IS THE SPIRITUAL ISRAEL. GENTILES, AS SUCH, DO NOT SHARE ITS BENEFITS

"Behold, the days come, saith the Lord, that I will make a new covenant with the house of Israel, and with the house of Judah." Jer. 31 : 31.

"Not according to the covenant that I made with their fathers in the day that I took them by the hand to bring them out of the land of Egypt; which my covenant they brake, although I was an husband unto them, saith the Lord." Jer. 31 : 31, 32 (Rom. 9 : 4).

"Wherefore remember, that ye being in time past Gentiles in the flesh, who are called Uncircumcision by that which is called the Circumcision in the flesh made by hands;

"That at that time ye were without Christ, being aliens from the commonwealth of Israel, and strangers from the covenants of promise, having no hope, and without God in the world:

"But now in Christ Jesus ye who sometimes were far off are made nigh by the blood of Christ." Eph. 2 : 11-13.

Rom. 2 : 28, 29; Gal. 3 : 28, 29.

IT IS CALLED THE NEW OR SECOND COVENANT BECAUSE IT WAS NOT DEDICATED WITH BLOOD TILL AFTER THE FIRST OR OLD COVENANT WAS

"For where a testament is, there must also of necessity be the death of the testator.

"For a testament is of force after men are dead: otherwise it is of no strength at all while the testator liveth.

"Whereupon neither the first testament was dedicated without blood." Heb. 9 : 16-18.

Luke 22 : 20; Dan. 9 : 27.

IT IS REALLY THE GOSPEL IN PROMISE AND IS CALLED THE EVERLASTING COVENANT. ITS PROMISES EXTEND BACK TO THE ENTRANCE OF SIN INTO THIS WORLD, AND FORWARD TO THE FINAL REWARD OF THE RIGHTEOUS

"But this shall be the covenant that I will make with the house of Israel; After those days, saith the Lord, I will put my law in their inward parts, and write it in their hearts; and will be their God, and they shall be my people.

"And they shall teach no more every man his neighbor, and every man his brother, saying, Know the Lord: for they shall all know me, from the least of them unto the greatest of them, saith the Lord: for I will forgive their iniquity, and I will remember their sin no more." Jer. 31 : 33, 34.

ORDER OF REALIZATION

(1) Forgiveness of Sin; (2) God writing His law in our hearts; (3) Remembering our sins no more, or blotting out sin in Investigative Judgment; (4) Translating of God's people to the New Jerusalem where they shall all know God. Isa. 54 : 11-13; Rev. 21 : 2-4.

THE OLD COVENANT REVEALED THE NEED OF THE NEW OR EVERLASTING COVENANT THROUGH THE PROVISION OF WHICH THERE IS FORGIVENESS AND SALVATION

"How much more shall the blood of Christ, who through the eternal Spirit offered Himself without spot to God, purge your conscience from dead works to serve the living God?

"And for this cause He is the mediator of the New Testament, that by means of death, for the redemption of the transgressions that were under the first testament, they which are called might receive the promise of eternal inheritance." Heb. 9 : 14, 15.

Heb. 6 : 13, 16-20; Rom. 4 : 17; Gal. 3 : 17.

THE WORKS OF RIGHTEOUSNESS REQUIRED BY THE LAW APPEAR IN OUR LIVES ONLY AS GOD, UNDER THE NEW COVENANT OF GRACE, WRITES THE LAW IN OUR HEARTS

"For this is the covenant that I will make with the house of Israel after those days, saith the Lord; I will put my laws into their mind, and write them in their hearts: and I will be to them a God, and they shall be to me a people.

"And they shall not teach every man his neighbor, and every man his brother, saying, Know the Lord: for all shall know me, from the least to the greatest." Heb. 8 : 10, 11.

John 15 : 4, 5; Eph. 2 : 10; Heb. 13 : 21; Gal 2 : 20; Phil. 2 : 13.

SAVED BY GRACE

"Neither is there salvation in any other: for there is none other name under heaven given among men, whereby we must be saved." Acts 4 : 12.

SINNERS SAVED BY GRACE IN ALL AGES

Titus 2 : 11; Ex. 34 : 6 ("gracious"); Gen. 6 : 8 ("found grace").

Some say men saved by keeping law in Old Dispensation and by Grace in New Dispensation. This is a false view. Would make a divided Heaven. Some extolling their own works and others the merits of Christ.

Acts 4 : 12—All saved through Christ alone.

Rom 4-6—God imparted righteousness that the law requires.

Note.—Law and Grace not antagonistic. It is because God's Law is Eternal and unchangeable, and demands the life of the Lawbreaker, that Grace becomes necessary if sinners are to be saved. God's Grace (unmerited favour) was taught in the Sacrificial System of the Jews, where an innocent victim died in the place of the sinner.

Ps. 19 : 7—Perfect.

Rom 7 : 12, 14, 16—"holy—good—spiritual."

Matt. 5 : 18.

CHRIST DIED FOR OUR SINS, BECAUSE THE LAW DEMANDED DEATH FOR TRANSGRESSORS

Rom. 6 : 23—"wages of sin is death."

1 John 3 : 4—"Sin is the transgression of the law."

Rom. 5 : 6—He died for ungodly.
2 Cor. 5 : 14, 15—He died for all.
Rom. 4 : 15—No law, no transgression.
Rom. 3 : 23—Died for all, therefore all under death sentence.
Verse 20.
Rom. 6 : 15, 1, 2—Grace does not destroy our obligation to keep God's commandments but puts a double obligation upon us to do so. Not only our duty as human beings to obey God, but our gratitude to God for freeing us from the death penalty.

CAN'T KEEP LAW IN OUR OWN STRENGTH BUT CHRIST KEEPS IT IN OUR HEARTS BY HIS SPIRIT

1 John 2 : 6; Ps. 40 : 8; Prov. 4 : 23; 23 : 7; Ps. 1 : 2; Rom. 7 : 25, 16, 22, 18; 1 Jno. 2 : 4; Rom. 8 : 1-9.

MAN, BY NATURE, IS MORTAL, THAT IS, SUBJECT TO DEATH

"Shall mortal man be more just than God? shall a man be more pure than his maker?" Job. 4 : 17.

"And changed the glory of the uncorruptible God into an image made like to corruptible man, and to birds, and four-footed beasts, and creeping things." Rom. 1 : 23.

Isa. 40 : 6, 7; Rom. 6 : 23; Ps. 90 : 5, 6; 1 Cor. 15 : 53, 54.

GOD ALONE IS NATURALLY IMMORTAL

"Which in His times He shall shew, who is the blessed and only Potentate, the King of kings, and Lord of lords;

"Who only hath immortality, dwelling in the light which no man can approach unto; whom no man hath seen, nor can see: to whom be honour and power everlasting. Amen." 1 Tim. 6 : 15, 16.

"But is now made manifest by the appearing of our Saviour Jesus Christ, who hath abolished death, and hath brought life and immortality to light through the gospel." 2 Tim. 1 : 10.

IMMORTALITY OR ETERNAL LIFE COMES TO MAN AS A GIFT FROM GOD THROUGH CHRIST AND MAN IS TO SEEK FOR IT.

"Who will render to every man according to his deeds:

"To them who by patient continuance in well doing seek for glory and honour and immortality, eternal life." Rom. 2 : 6, 7.

"For the wages of sin is death; but the gift of God is eternal life through Jesus Christ our Lord." Rom. 6 : 23.

Matt. 7 : 13, 14; Matt. 19 : 16, 17; John 5 : 39, 40; 6 : 40, 47, 54, 68; Rom. 5 : 21; 8 : 13; 2 Cor. 2 : 16; 2 Tim. 1 : 1; Titus 1 : 2; 1 John 4 : 9; Jude 21.

IMMORTALITY IS THE BLESSED HOPE OF THE CHRISTIAN NOW AND WILL BE ACTUALLY RESTORED AT THE RESURRECTION

"For this corruptible must put on incorruption, and this mortal must put on immortality." 1 Cor. 15 : 53.

"So when this corruptible shall have put on incorruption, and this mortal shall have put on immortality, then shall be brought to pass the saying that is written, Death is swallowed up in victory." 1 Cor. 15 : 54.

"That being justified by His grace, we should be made heirs according to the hope of eternal life." Titus 3 : 7.

Luke 14 : 14; John 5 : 28, 29; John 6 : 40, 54; John 14 : 1-3; Col. 3 : 4; 1 Pet. 5 : 4; Jer. 31 : 17; Acts 23 : 6; Acts 26 : 6-8; Titus 1 : 2; 1 John 2 : 25.

THE SPIRIT

The word "spirit" in the Old Testament occurs 234 times and is always translated from the Hebrew word "Ruahh" (except Job 26 : 4 and Prov. 20 : 27). "Ruahh" occurs 442 times and is translated 16 different ways. It is rendered "Spirit," 232 times; "wind," 97 times; "breath," 28 times; "smell," 8 times; "mind," 6 times; "blast," 4 times, etc.

Examples:

Breath: Gen. 6 : 17; 2 Sam. 22 : 16; Job. 4 : 9; Ps. 18 : 15, Eccl. 3 : 19; Isa. 11 : 4; Jer. 10 : 14; Lam. 4 : 20; Eze. 37 : 5, 6; Hab. 2 : 19.

Wind: Gen 8 : 1; Ex. 10 : 13; Num. 11 : 31; 2 Sam. 22 : 11; I Kings 18 : 45; 2 Kings 3 : 17; Job 1 : 19; Ps. 1 : 4; Prov. 11 : 29; Eccl. 1 : 6; Isa. 7 : 2; Jer. 2 : 24; Eze. 1 : 4; Dan. 8 : 8; Hos. 4 : 19; Amos 4 : 13; Jonah 1 : 4; Zech. 2 : 6.

Smell: Gen. 8 : 21; Ex. 30 : 38; Lev. 26 : 31; Deut. 4 : 28; Job 39 : 25; Ps. 115 : 6; Amos 5 : 21.

Mind: Gen. 26 : 35; Prov. 29 : 11; Eze. 11 : 5; Hab. 1 : 11.

Blast: Ex. 15 : 8; 2 Kings 19 : 7; Isa. 25 : 4.

Also "tempest" (Ps. 11 : 6); "air" (Job 41 : 16); "courage" (Josh. 2 : 11); "anger" (Judges 8 : 3); "toucheth" (Judges 16 : 9); "understanding" (Isa. 11 : 3); "accept" (1 Sam. 26 : 19).

Note.—"Ruahh" (spirit) is never said to be immortal.

ANOTHER WORD TRANSLATED "SPIRIT" IN OLD TESTAMENT

"N'shahmah," occurs 24 times. Translated "breath," 17 times; "blast," 3 times; "spirit," twice; "soul," once; "inspiration," once.

Examples:

Breath: Gen. 2 : 7; Deut. 20 : 16; 1 Kings 15 : 29; Job 27 : 3; Ps. 150 : 6; Isa. 2 : 22; Dan. 10 : 17.

Blast: 2 Sam. 22 : 16; Job 4 : 9; Ps. 18 : 15.

Spirit: Job 26 : 4; Prov. 20 : 27.

Soul: Isa. 57 : 16.

Inspiration: Job 32 : 8.

The word " Spirit " in the New Testament is translated from the Greek word " Pneuma " which occurs 385 times.

" Pneuma " is translated " Spirit " 291 times. It is also rendered " ghost " 92 times; " wind," once, and " life," once, four different ways.

Examples :

Ghost: Matt. 1 : 18; Mark 1 : 8; Luke 1 : 15; John 1 : 33; Acts 1 : 2; Rom. 5 : 5; 1 Cor. 2 : 13; 2 Cor. 6 : 6; 1 Thess. 1 : 5, 6; 2 Tim. 1 : 14; Titus 3 : 5; Heb. 2 : 4; 1 Pet. 1 : 12; 2 Pet. 1 : 21; 1 John 5 : 7; Jude 20.

Wind: John 3 : 8.

Life: Rev. 13 : 15.

Note.—Thus, we see the Hebrew and Greek words from which " soul " is translated in our English Bible occur 768 times in the Old Testament and 155 times in the New Testament. The word " Spirit " occurs 442 times in the Old Testament and translated 385 times in the New Testament. Thus, the words from which " soul " and " spirit " are translated occur about 1700 times in the Bible, but they are never modified by such expressions as " deathless," " never dying," or " immortal."

THE SOUL

In the Old Testament, the word " soul " is translated from the Hebrew, " Nehphesh," with two exceptions: Job. 30 : 16, where " soul " comes from " N'deevah," and Isa. 57 : 16, where it is from " N'shahmah." " Nehphesh " occurs 745 times in the original Hebrew and is translated " soul " 473 times in our English Bible. It is translated " life " or " lives " 120 times.

Examples :

Gen. 1 : 20, 30; Ex. 4 : 19; Lev. 17 : 11; Num. 35 : 31; Deut. 12 : 23; Joshua 2 : 13; Judges 5 : 18; Ruth 4 : 15; 1 Sam. 19 : 5; 2 Sam. 1 : 9; I. Kings 1 : 12; 2 Kings 1 : 13; 1 Chron. 11 : 19; 2 Chron. 1 : 11; Esther 7 : 3; Job 2 : 4; Ps. 31 : 13; Prov. 1 : 18; Isa. 15 : 4; Lam. 2 : 19; Eze. 32 : 10; Jonah 1 : 14.

" Nephesh " is translated " person " 30 times.

Examples :

Gen. 14 : 21; Ex. 16 : 16; Lev. 27 : 2; Num. 5 : 6; Deut. 10 : 22; Joshua 20 : 3; 1 Sam. 22 : 22; 2 Sam. 14: 14; Prov. 28 : 17; Jer. 43 : 6; Eze. 16 : 5.

"Nehphesh " translated " mind " 16 times.

Examples :

Gen. 23 : 8; Deut. 18 : 6; 1 Sam. 2 : 35; 2 Sam. 17 : 8; 2 Kings 9 : 15; 1 Chron. 28 : 9; Jer. 15 : 1; Eze. 23 : 17.

" Nehphesh " translated " heart " 15 times.

Examples :

Ex. 23 : 9; Lev. 26 : 16; Deut. 24 : 15; 1 Sam. 2 : 33; 2 Sam. 3 : 21; Ps. 10 : 3; Prov. 23 : 7; Jer. 42 : 20; Lam. 3 : 51; Eze. 25 : 6; Hos. 4 : 8.

" Nehphesh " translated " the dead " and " dead body " 13 times.

Examples :

Lev. 19 : 28; Num. 5 : 2; Hag. 2 : 13.

" Nehphesh " translated " creature " 9 times.

Examples :

Gen. 1 : 21; Gen. 9 : 10; Lev. 11 : 46.

" Nehphesh " also translated:

" Will " : Deut. 21 : 14; Ps. 27 : 12; 41 : 2; Eze. 16 : 27 (4 times).

" Appetite " : Prov. 23 : 2; Eccl. 6 : 7 (2 times).

" Lust " : Ex. 15 : 9; Ps. 78 : 18 (2 times).

" Thing " : Lev. 11 : 10; Eze. 47 : 9 (2 times).

" Nehphesh " is translated in 43 different ways. Besides the words already given it is rendered " breath," " beast," " fish," " desire," " ghost," " pleasure," etc. It is never translated " spirit " and it is never said to be " immortal."

" NEHPHESH " (SOUL) IS MORTAL (SUBJECT TO DEATH)

" Like sheep they are laid in the grave; death shall feed on them; and the upright shall have dominion over them in the morning; and their beauty shall consume in the grave from their dwelling.

" But God will redeem my soul from the power of the grave: for he shall receive me. Ps. 49 : 14, 15.

" Behold, for peace I had great bitterness: but thou hast in love to my soul delivered it from the pit of corruption: for thou hast cast all my sins behind thy back. Isa. 38 : 17.

Ps. 89 : 48; Job 33 : 18, 20, 22.

" NEHPHESH " (SOUL) MAY BE " KILLED," " DESTROYED," ETC.

Gen. 17 : 14; Ex. 31 : 14; Joshua 10 : 30, 32, 35, 37, 39.

The word " soul " in the New Testament comes from the Greek word, " psuchee." This word " psuchee," occurs 105 times. It is translated " soul " 58 times.

Examples :

Matt. 10 : 28; Mark 8 : 36, 37; Luke 1 : 46; John 12 : 27; Acts 2 : 27; Rom. 2 : 9; 1 Cor. 15 : 45; 2 Cor. 1 : 23; 1 Thess. 2 : 8; Heb. 4 : 12; Jas. 1 : 21; I Pet. 1 : 9; 2 Pet. 2 : 8; 3 John 2; Rev. 6 : 9.

It is translated " life " or " lives " 40 times.

Examples :

Matt. 2 : 20; Mark 3 : 4; Luke 6 : 9; John 10 : 11; Acts 15 : 26; Rom. 11 : 3; Phil. 2 : 30; 1 John 3 : 16; Rev. 8 : 9.

It is also translated "mind," Acts 14 : 2; Phil. 1 : 27; Heb. 12 : 3.
"Heart" : Eph. 6 : 6; Col. 3 : 23.
"Us" : John 10 : 24.
"You" : 2 Cor. 12 : 15.
Note.—Nowhere in the Bible is the soul (psuchee) said to be immortal, nor is it called a never-dying soul.

SPIRIT, SOUL AND BODY

THE QUESTION

"What is man, that thou art mindful of him? and the son of man that thou visitest him?" Ps. 8 : 4.

THE ANSWER

"And the very God of peace sanctify you wholly; and I pray God your whole spirit and soul and body be preserved blameless unto the coming of our Lord Jesus Christ." 1 Thess. 5 : 23.

THE BIBLE ALONE TELLS THE DIFFERENCE BETWEEN SOUL AND SPIRIT

"For the word of God is quick, and powerful, and sharper than any two-edged sword, piercing even to the dividing asunder of soul and spirit, and of the joints and marrow, and is a discerner of the thoughts and intents of the heart." Heb. 4 : 12.

IN THE SENSE OF MAN'S NATURE, THE SPIRIT IS WHAT GOD GIVES AND TAKES

"Thou hidest thy face, they are troubled; thou takest away their breath, they die, and return to their dust." Ps. 104 : 29.
"If He set his heart upon man, if He gather unto Himself His spirit and His breath;
"All flesh shall perish together, and man shall turn again unto dust." Job 34 : 14, 15.
Note.—Therefore, the Spirit is the Breath of Life.

THE CREATION OF MAN

"And the Lord God formed man of the dust of the ground, and breathed into his nostrils the breath of life; and man became a living soul.
"And the Lord God planted a garden eastward in Eden; and there He put the man whom He had formed.
"And out of the ground made the Lord God to grow every tree that is pleasant to the sight, and good for food; the tree of life also in the midst of the garden, and the tree of knowledge of good and evil." Gen. 2 : 7-9.
Jas. 2 : 26; Eccl. 3 : 19-21.
(Here the entire man is called a "living soul.")

DO BEASTS, AS WELL AS MAN, HAVE THE BREATH OF LIFE IN THEIR NOSTRILS?

"And all flesh died that moved upon the earth, both of fowl, and of cattle, and of beast, and of every creeping thing that creepeth upon the earth, and every man:
"All in whose nostrils was the breath of life, of all that was in the dry land, died." Gen. 7 : 21, 22.
"For that which befalleth the sons of men befalleth beasts; even one thing befalleth them: as the one dieth, so dieth the other; yea, they have all one breath; so that a man hath no pre-eminence above a beast: for all is vanity.
"All go unto one place; all are of the dust, and all turn to dust again.
"Who knoweth the spirit of man that goeth upward, and the spirit of the beast that goeth downward to the earth?" Eccl. 3 : 19-21.
Gen. 1 : 30; Rev. 16 : 3—Also called "living souls."
Eze. 37 : 1-15.

THE SOUL IS THE PART OF MAN THAT SINS AND DIES FOR ITS SIN. IT IS NOT THE SPIRIT AND SHOULD NOT BE CONFUSED WITH THE BREATH OF LIFE FROM GOD

1 Thess. 5 : 23.
"Behold, all souls are mine; as the soul of the father, so also the soul of the son is mine: the soul that sinneth, it shall die." Eze. 18 : 4.
Matt. 5 : 21, 22—Hate is sin. (1 John 3 : 14.)
Matt. 5 : 27, 28—The lustful look—is sin—in the heart.
Prov. 23 : 7—We think in the "heart." We think with the mind.
Jas. 4 : 17—We SIN when we fail to do what we know is right. The knowing part of man—the heart—the mind is the part here called the "soul," therefore the soul is the intelligent part of man.

WHAT HAPPENS AT DEATH?

"Then shall the dust return to the earth as it was: and the spirit shall return unto God who gave it." Eccl. 12 : 7.

THE DUST RETURNS TO THE EARTH AS IT WAS—THE SPIRIT, OR BREATH OF LIFE, RETURNS TO GOD WHO GAVE IT

"For the living know that they shall die: but the dead know not any thing, neither have they any more a reward; for the memory of them is forgotten." Eccl. 9 : 5.
"Also their love, and their hatred, and their envy, is now perished; neither have they any more a portion for ever in any thing that is done under the sun." Eccl. 9 : 6.
"Whatsoever thy hand findeth to do, do it with thy might; for there is no work, nor device, nor knowledge, nor wisdom,

in the grave, whither thou goest." Eccl. 9 : 10.

THE INTELLIGENT PART OF MAN CEASES TO OPERATE. INTELLIGENCE, EMOTION, WILL, ALL FUNCTIONS OF THE MIND, CEASE.

"Put not your trust in princes, nor in the son of man, in whom there is no help.

"His breath goeth forth, he returneth to his earth; in that very day his thoughts perish." Ps. 146 : 3, 4.

The part of man that once had knowledge, that loved, hated and envied, in death does not know love, hate or envy.

THE RESURRECTION THE SOUL'S HOPE

"What man is he that liveth, and shall not see death? shall he deliver his soul from the hand of the grave?" Ps. 89 : 48.

"For thou wilt not leave my soul in hell; neither wilt thou suffer thine Holy One to see corruption." Ps. 16 : 10.

Quoting this last text (Ps. 16 : 10), and applying it to Christ in Acts 2 : 31, Peter declares that it cannot apply to David himself because "he is both dead and buried and his sepulchre is with us unto this day" (verse 29). "For David is not ascended into the heavens." Acts 2 : 34. This proves that unless a man is resurrected from the dead, his soul will be left in hell (Hades—the grave).

Verse 34 declares that David had not yet ascended to heaven, nearly a thousand years after he died.

Luke 23 : 46—When Jesus died, He commended His Spirit into the hands of God.

Isa. 53 : 12—He poured out His soul unto death.

Matt. 10 : 28—The soul can be destroyed.

CAN THE SOUL BE KILLED?

"And fear not them which kill the body, but are not able to kill the soul: but rather fear him which is able to destroy both soul and body in hell." Matt. 10 : 28.

STATE OF THE DEAD

THE DEAD ARE ASLEEP AND UNCONSCIOUS

"For the living know that they shall die: but the dead know not any thing, neither have they any more a reward; for the memory of them is forgotten.

"Also their love, and their hatred, and their envy, is now perished; neither have they any more a portion for ever in any thing that is done under the sun." Eccl. 9 : 5, 6.

"Whatsoever thy hand findeth to do, do it with thy might; for there is no work, nor device, ncr knowledge, nor wisdom, in the grave, whither thou goest." Eccl. 9: 10.

"Put not your trust in princes, nor in the son of man, in whom there is no help.

"His breath goeth forth, he returneth to his earth; in that very day his thoughts perish." Ps. 146 : 3, 4.

"These things said He: and after that He saith unto them, Our friend Lazarus sleepeth; but I go, that I may awake him out of sleep." John 11 : 11.

1 Thess. 4 : 13; Acts 7 : 60; 1 Cor. 15 : 6, 18, 20.

Ps. 6 : 5; Job 14 : 12, 21; 2 Chron. 26 : 23.

ALL MEN, GOOD AND BAD, REST IN THE GRAVE

"Marvel not at this: for the hour is coming, in the which all that are in the graves shall hear His voice,

"And shall come forth; they that have done good, unto the resurrection of life; and they that have done evil, unto the resurrection of damnation." John 5 : 28, 29.

"Men and brethren, let me freely speak unto you of the patriarch David, that he is both dead and buried, and his sepulchre is with us unto this day." Acts 2 : 29.

"He seeing this before spake of the resurrection of Christ, that His soul was not left in hell, neither His flesh did see corruption." Acts 2 : 31.

"All go on unto one place; all are of the dust, and all turn to dust again." Eccl. 3 : 20.

Eccl. 9 : 10; 12 : 7; Job 5 : 26; 14 : 10-14; 17 : 13, 16.

Job 21 : 13, 23-26; Ps. 31 : 17; Hos. 13 : 14.

Eze. 37 : 12; Matt. 27 : 52, 53.

THE RIGHTEOUS WILL ASCEND TO HEAVEN AT THE FIRST RESURRECTION

"Blessed and holy is he that hath part in the first resurrection: on such the second death hath no power, but they shall be priests of God and of Christ, and shall reign with Him a thousand years." Rev. 20 : 6.

"Marvel not at this: for the hour is coming, in the which all that are in the graves shall hear His voice,

"And shall come forth; they that have done good, unto the resurrection of life; and they that have done evil, unto the resurrection of damnation." John 5 : 28, 29.

"And have hope toward God, which they themselves also allow, that there shall be a resurrection of the dead, both of the just and unjust." Acts 24 : 15.

THE SECOND RESURRECTION, THE RESURRECTION TO DAMNATION, ALSO CALLED THE RESURRECTION OF THE UNJUST, OCCURS ONE THOUSAND YEARS LATER

See Rev. 20 : 4, 5.

1 Thess. 4 : 13-18; 1 Cor. 15 : 22, 23; 1 Cor. 15 : 50-55; Luke 14 : 14; Phil. 3 : 10, 11; Heb. 11 : 35; John 6 : 40, 44, 54.

GOD'S PEOPLE DEPEND FOR THEIR REWARD UPON THE SECOND COMING OF CHRIST AND THE RESURRECTION

"And thou shalt be blessed; for they cannot recompense thee: for thou shalt be recompensed at the resurrection of the just." Luke 14 : 14.

"Behold, I shew you a mystery; We shall not all sleep, but we shall all be changed.

"In a moment, in the twinkling of an eye, at the last trump: for the trumpet shall sound, and the dead shall be raised incorruptible, and we shall be changed.

"For this corruptible must put on incorruption, and this mortal must put on immortality.

"So when this corruptible shall have put on incorruption, and this mortal shall have put on immortality, then shall be brought to pass the saying that is written, Death is swallowed up in victory.

"O death, where is thy sting? O grave, where is thy victory." 1 Cor. 15 : 51-55.

Jer. 31 : 15-17; Matt. 16 : 27; Acts 23 : 6; Acts 26 : 6-8; Titus 2 : 13; Jas. 5 : 7, 8; 1 Pet. 5 : 4; 2 Pet. 3 : 3, 4, 11-13; 1 John 3 : 3; Rev. 11 : 17, 18, 22 : 12.

THE WICKED ARE MORTAL AND HAVE NO PROMISE OF ETERNAL LIFE

"For God so loved the world, that He gave His only begotten Son, that whosoever believeth in Him should not perish, but have everlasting life." John 3 : 16.

"He that believeth on the Son hath everlasting life: and he that believeth not the Son shall not see life; but the wrath of God abideth on him." John 3 : 36.

"And to you who are troubled rest with us, when the Lord Jesus shall be revealed from heaven with His mighty angels.

"In flaming fire taking vengeance on them that know not God, and that obey not the gospel of our Lord Jesus Christ:

"Who shall be punished with everlasting destruction from the presence of the Lord, and from the glory of His power;" 2 Thess. 1 : 7-9.

Ps. 37 : 1, 2, 10, 20, 38; Deut. 30 : 17-19; Prov. 13 : 13; Ezek. 18 : 4, 26; Rom. 8 : 6; Rev. 21 : 8.

WHAT AND WHERE IS HELL?

"The wicked shall be turned into hell, and all the nations that forget God." Ps. 9 : 17.

"For the time is come that judgment must begin at the house of God: and if it first begin at us, what shall the end be of them that obey not the gospel of God?" 1 Pet. 4 : 17.

1 Jno. 3 : 8; Eccl. 3 : 17.

THE WICKED DO NOT HAVE LIFE

"He that believeth on the Son hath everlasting life: and he that believeth not the Son shall not see life; but the wrath of God abideth on him." John 3 : 36.

"The thief cometh not, but for to steal, and to kill, and to destroy: I am come that they might have life, and that they might have it more abundantly." John 10 : 10.

John 10 : 27, 28; Rom. 6 : 23; Eph. 2 : 12; 1 John 5 : 12; 2 Tim. 1 : 10; Rom. 2 : 7.

EVERLASTING PUNISHMENT FOR LAW BREAKERS

"Who shall be punished with everlasting destruction from the presence of the Lord, and from the glory of His power." 2 Thess. 1 : 9.

Note.—The punishment is everlasting *destruction*.

2 Pet. 2 : 12; Luke 13 : 3.

THE DESTRUCTION OF THE WICKED WILL BE COMPLETE

"And fear not them which kill the body, but are not able to kill the soul; but rather fear him which is able to destroy both soul and body in hell." Matt. 10 : 28.

"Behold, all souls are mine; as the soul of the father, so also the soul of the son is mine: the soul that sinneth, it shall die." Eze. 18 : 4.

"But the wicked shall perish, and the enemies of the Lord shall be as the fat of lambs: they shall consume; into smoke shall they consume away." Ps. 37 : 20.

"For while they be folden together as thorns, and while they are drunken as drunkards, they shall be devoured as stubble fully dry." Nahum 1 : 10.

THE FIRE IS CALLED EVERLASTING FIRE AND ITS EFFECTS ARE ETERNAL

"Then shall He say also unto them on the left hand, Depart from me, ye cursed, into everlasting fire, prepared for the devil and his angels." Matt. 25 : 41.

Jude 7—Sodom and Gomorrha were destroyed by eternal or everlasting fire. Note:—See page 63.

2 Pet. 2 : 6—They were reduced to ashes, as an example to the ungodly, and are not burning now. The fire was "everlasting" but the cities were not.

Rev. 14 : 11—The smoke goes up "forever and ever."

Isa. 34 : 10—The same phrase "forever and ever" used of the Land of Idumea which is not burning now.

Note.—"Forever" often refers to a limited period, for instance, a man's lifetime. (Exodus 21 : 5, 6.) "Three days and nights." (Jonah 1 : 17; 2 : 6.)

THE FIRE THAT DESTROYS THE WICKED IS SAID TO BE UNQUENCHABLE, THAT IS, IT CANNOT BE QUENCHED, OR PUT OUT

"I indeed baptize you with water unto repentance: but He that cometh after me is mightier than I, whose shoes I am not worthy to bear: He shall baptize you with the Holy Ghost and with fire:

"Whose fan is in His hand, and He will thoroughly purge His floor, and gather His wheat into the garner; but He will burn up the chaff with unquenchable fire." Matt. 3 : 11, 12.

Jer. 17 : 19-27—Because of the disobedience of Israel, God threatened to kindle a fire in the gates of Jerusalem that "shall not be quenched." This fire was kindled when the Babylonians captured Jerusalem. See 2 Chron. 36 : 14-19. This was unquenchable fire, but it did its work, according to God's word, and is not burning in the gates of Jerusalem now.

Prov. 10 : 25; Mal. 4 : 1-3; Ps. 68 : 2; Obadiah 16.

WHEN WILL THE WICKED BE CAST INTO HELL FIRE?

"Let both grow together until the harvest: and in the time of harvest I will say to the reapers, Gather ye together first the tares, and bind them in bundles to burn them: but gather the wheat into my barn." Matt. 13 : 30.

"If a man abide not in me, he is cast forth as a branch, and is withered; and men gather them, and cast them into the fire, and they are burned." John 15 : 6.

Matt. 13 : 39—The "harvest" is the end of the world, therefore the wicked are not being punished now.

"For if God spared not the angels that sinned, but cast them down to hell, and delivered them into chains of darkness, to be reserved unto judgment;

"The Lord knoweth how to deliver the godly out of temptations, and to reserve the unjust unto the day of judgment to be punished." 2 Pet. 2 : 4, 9.

Matt. 16 : 27—Notice the word "then."

Jer. 32 : 19—The "fruit" of man's life will not be known till the end of the world.

WHERE WILL HELL BE LOCATED?

"Behold, the righteous shall be recompensed in the earth: much more the wicked and the sinner." Prov. 11 : 31.

"But the heavens and the earth, which are now, by the same word are kept in store, reserved unto fire against the day of judgment and perdition of ungodly men.

"But the day of the Lord will come as a thief in the night; in the which the heavens shall pass away with a great noise, and the elements shall melt with fervent heat, the earth also and the works that are therein shall be burned up.

"Looking for and hasting unto the coming of the day of God, wherein the heavens being on fire shall be dissolved, and the elements shall melt with fervent heat?" 2 Pet. 3 : 7, 10, 12.

Isa. 34 : 8, 9; Rev. 20 : 9, 10; Nah. 1 : 5-9; Mal. 4 : 1-3.

Job 21 : 21—The wicked will be brought forth in the second resurrection and cast into the lake of fire.

Rev. 20 : 5, 12-15; Ps. 9 : 3, 5, 6; Eze. 18 : 26; Isa. 24 : 21; Jude 6—Evil angels will be destroyed. Isa. 14 : 4-7.

GOD WILL HAVE A STAINLESS WORLD

"And every creature which is in heaven, and on the earth, and under the earth, and such as are in the sea, and all that are in them, heard I saying, Blessing, and honour and glory, and power, be unto Him that sitteth upon the throne, and unto the Lamb for ever and ever." Rev. 5 : 13.

"For yet a little while, and the wicked shall not be: yea, thou shalt diligently consider his place, and it shall not be." Ps. 37 : 10.

Even the "place" of the wicked (the lake of fire) will not be.

Isa. 47 : 14—Not a coal to warm at.

Rev. 21 : 1-4—There will be no pain.

Rev. 22 : 3—No more curse.

THERE ARE FOUR WORDS TRANSLATED "HELL" IN THE BIBLE

"Sheol"—Hebrew word. In the Old Testament translated "Hell," 31 times and "pit" 3 times. It is also translated "grave" 31 times. It refers to the place or state of the dead.

Examples:

Translated "Hell": Ps. 9 : 17; 16 : 10; Prov. 15 : 11; 23 : 14; Isa. 5 : 14; Deut. 32 : 22; 2 Sam. 22 : 6; Job 11 : 8; Job 26 : 6; Ps. 18 : 5; 55 : 15; Ps. 86 : 13; Ps. 116 : 3; Ps. 139 : 8; Prov. 5 : 5; Prov. 7 : 27; Prov. 9 : 18; Prov. 27 : 20; Isa. 14 : 9, 15; Isa. 28 : 15, 18; Isa. 57 : 9; Eze. 31 : 16, 17; Eze. 32 : 21, 27; Amos 9 : 2; Jonah 2 : 2; Hab. 2 : 5.

Translated "Grave": Gen. 37 : 35; 42 : 38; Gen. 44 : 29, 31; 1 Sam. 2 : 6; 1 Kings 2 : 6, 9; Job 7 : 9; Job 14 : 13; Job 17 : 13; Job 21 : 13; Job 24 : 19; Ps. 6 : 5; Ps. 30 : 3; Ps. 31 : 17; Ps. 49 : 14, 15; Ps. 88 : 3; Ps. 89 : 48; Ps. 141 : 7; Prov. 1 : 12; Prov. 30 : 16; Eccl. 9 : 10; Cant. 8 : 6; Isa. 14 : 11; Isa. 38 : 10, 18; Eze. 31 : 15; Hos. 13 : 14.

Translated "Pit": Num. 16 : 30, 33; Job 17 : 16.

From these texts, it is clear that "Sheol" is a place of rest, silence, secrecy, darkness, sleep and corruption.

BOTH RIGHTEOUS AND WICKED GO TO SHEOL

(The Grave or state of the dead)

Gen. 37 : 35—Jacob, a man of God went to "Sheol."

Num. 16 : 30, 33—Wicked men went there.

Ps. 89 : 48—All men go to "Sheol."

"Sheol" is the same as "Hades" in the New Testament. See Ps. 16 : 10 compared with Acts 2 : 27.

"Hades," a Greek word in the New Testament translated "Hell."

It never means the place of punishment. Its meaning is "an unseen place, the grave, pit, region of the dead."

Examples:

Matt. 11 : 23; 16 : 18; Luke 10 : 15; 16 : 23; Acts 2 : 27, 31; 1 Cor. 15 : 55; Rev. 1 : 18; 6 : 8; Rev. 20 : 13, 14.

Note.—These texts include every instance of the use of the word "Hades" in the Bible. The reader may decide whether it refers to a place of torment or the grave or state of the dead in general.

"Gehenna": In New Testament translated "Hell." Comes from Greek mode of spelling Hebrew words which are translated "Valley of Hinnom." This valley was a place where the refuse of Jerusalem, together with the bodies of animals, was consumed. It is used as a symbol or type of slaughter and destruction. It is not a place where the wicked are now being punished or where they will be kept alive in endless torments. See Joshua 15 : 8; 18 : 16; 2 Kings 23 : 10; 2 Chron. 28 : 3; 33 : 6; Jer. 7 : 31, 32; 19 : 2, 6; 32 : 35.

Examples:

Matt. 5 : 22, 29, 30; 10 : 28; 18 : 9; 23 : 15, 33; Mark 9 : 43, 45, 47; Luke 12 : 5; James 3 : 6.

Note.—It is clear from the use of this word that it refers to the lake of fire where the wicked will be destroyed.

"Tartaroo": A Greek word found only once in the New Testament and referring to the darkness that surrounds the material universe. See Greek Lexicon, by Parkhurst.

Example:

2 Pet. 2 : 4—"For if God spared not the angels that sinned, but cast them down to hell, and delivered them into chains of darkness, to be reserved unto judgment;" Compare verse 6.

Note.—It will be seen that "Hades" is the place of the dead, both righteous and wicked, from which they are brought only by a resurrection. Rev. 20 : 13. On the other hand, "Gehenna" is the lake of fire into which the wicked will be cast alive, and destroyed body and soul. (Matt. 10 : 28.)

PARABLE OF RICH MAN IN HELL

Read Luke 16 : 19-31.

This parable comes as last of a series of parables.

Mustard seed—leaven (Luke 13). Great supper.

Salt with no savour (Luke 14). Lost sheep.

Piece of silver, prodigal son (Luke 15).

Unjust steward, rich man and Lazarus (Luke 16).

IT CANNOT BE A LITERAL DESCRIPTION OF THE CONDITION OF MAN AFTER DEATH

"Abraham's Bosom" figurative—not literal.

"One drop of water"—not enough to cool man in Hell.

Heaven and hell not so near, people talk back and forth.

BIBLE TEACHES SINNERS NOT PUNISHED TILL DAY OF JUDGMENT

"The Lord knoweth how to deliver the godly out of temptations, and to reserve the unjust unto the day of judgment to be punished." 2 Peter 2 : 9; Rev. 20 : 15.

RIGHTEOUS NOT REWARDED TILL RESURRECTION AT SECOND COMING OF CHRIST

"Marvel not at this: for the hour is coming, in the which all that are in the graves shall hear his voice,

"And shall come forth; they that have done good, unto the resurrection of life; and they that have done evil, unto the resurrection of damnation." John 5 : 28, 29.

John 6 : 39, 40; John 14 : 1-3; 2 Tim. 4 : 6-8; 1 Thess. 4 : 13-18; 1 Cor. 15 : 51-54.

THE DEAD ARE NOT CONSCIOUS

"Put not your trust in princes, nor in the son of man, in whom there is no help.

"His breath goeth forth, he returneth to his earth; in that very day his thoughts perish." Ps. 146 : 3, 4.

Eccl. 9 : 5, 6, 10.

In this parable Jesus taught no man was valued for his possessions. In this life we settle our eternal destiny. After death a great gulf is fixed.

"They have Moses and the Prophets." (Luke 16 : 29-31.) This shows the writings of the Old Testament give the true teaching on the state of man after death, for the brothers of the rich man were referred to them. They teach the sleep of the dead.

ABSENT FROM THE BODY AND PRESENT WITH THE LORD

"For we know that if our earthly house of this tabernacle were dissolved, we have a building of God, an house not made with hands, eternal in the heavens.

"For in this we groan, earnestly desiring to be clothed upon with our house which is from heaven:

"If so be that being clothed we shall not be found naked.

"For we that are in this tabernacle do groan, being burdened: not for that we would be unclothed, but clothed upon, that mortality might be swallowed up of life.

"Now He that hath wrought us for the

self-same thing is God, who also hath given unto us the earnest of the Spirit.

"Therefore we are always confident, knowing that, whilst we are at home in the body, we are absent from the Lord." 2 Cor. 5 : 1-6.

Note.—The part that is mortal is to lose its mortality, be "swallowed up of life" at the Resurrection. See Paul's statement in 1 Cor. 15 : 51-54 and 1 Thess. 4 : 13-18. To be present with the Lord, we must look to the Resurrection or Translation at the Coming of the Lord. (1 Thess. 4 : 17).

See Rom. 8 : 11, 22, 23.

DEPARTING AND BEING WITH CHRIST

"According to my earnest expectation and my hope, that in nothing I shall be ashamed, but that with all boldness, as always, so now also Christ shall be magnified in my body, whether it be by life, or by death.

"For me to live is Christ, and to die is gain.

"But if I live in the flesh, this is the fruit of my labour : yet what I shall choose I wot not.

"For I am in a strait betwixt two, having a desire to depart, and to be with Christ; which is far better :

"Nevertheless to abide in the flesh is more needful for you.

"And having this confidence, I know that I shall abide and continue with you all for your furtherance and joy of faith;" Phil. 1 : 20-25.

These texts must be interpreted by other scriptures. Paul wrote much on subject of being with Christ.

"But I would not have you to be ignorant, brethren, concerning them which are asleep, that ye sorrow not, even as others which have no hope.

"For if we believe that Jesus died and rose again, even so them also which sleep in Jesus will God bring with Him.

"For this we say unto you by the word of the Lord, that we which are alive and remain unto the coming of the Lord shall not prevent them which are asleep.

"For the Lord Himself shall descend from heaven with a shout, with the voice of the archangel, and with the trump of God : and the death in Christ shall rise first :

"Then we which are alive and remain shall be caught up together with them in the clouds, to meet the Lord in the air : and so shall we ever be with the Lord.

"Wherefore comfort one another with these words." 1 Thess. 4 : 13-18.

This says plainly that the Righteous go to be with Christ at the Second Coming of Christ, by Resurrection or Translation.

1 Cor. 15 : 51-54—Paul says we get Immortality at the Resurrection.

Col. 3 : 4—"Then" shall we appear with Him (when He comes).

2 Tim. 4 : 8—"crown of righteousness" given me "at that day."

THIEF ON THE CROSS

Read Luke 23 : 39-45.

Remember the comma is not inspired. Put it where it belongs, after "today," and this text is in harmony with all the rest of Scripture.

See use of word "today" in Heb. 3 : 7, 15; 4 : 7; 5 : 5; Zech. 9 : 12.

JESUS NOT IN PARADISE THAT DAY

Rev. 2 : 7—Tree of life in midst of Paradise.

Rev. 22 : 1, 2—Tree of Life by throne.

Paradise is therefore third heaven where God is. 2 Cor. 12 : 1-4.

John 20 : 17—Three days later Jesus said he had not ascended to the Father.

John 19 : 31-37—The thief did not die that day. Day ends at sunset in Bible (Lev. 23 : 32); two thieves still alive when soldiers came to break bones.

SPIRITUALISM

THE FOUNDATION DOCTRINE OF SPIRITUALISM IS THAT THE DEAD RETURN TO COMMUNICATE WITH THE LIVING. THE BIBLE SAYS THIS IS IMPOSSIBLE

"Also their love, and their hatred, and their envy, is now perished; neither have they any more a portion for ever in any thing that is done under the sun." Eccl. 9 : 6.

"He shall return no more to his house, neither shall his place know him any more." Job 7 : 10.

GOD'S WORD CONDEMNS SPIRITUALISM AS SINFUL AND DANGEROUS

"Regard not them that have familiar spirits, neither seek after wizards, to be defiled by them : I am the Lord your God." Lev. 19 : 31.

Deut. 13 : 1-5.

"When thou art come into the land which the Lord thy God giveth thee, thou shalt not learn to do after the abominations of those nations.

"There shall not be found among you any one that maketh his son or his daughter to pass through the fire, or that useth divination, or an observer of times, or an enchanter, or a witch.

"Or a charmer, or a consulter with familiar spirits, or a wizard, or a necromancer.

"For all that do these things are an abomination unto the Lord : and because of these abominations the Lord thy God doth drive them out from before thee.

"Thou shalt be perfect with the Lord thy God." Deut. 18 : 9-13.

Isa. 8 : 19; Acts 16 : 16.

SATAN AND HIS FALLEN ANGELS ARE THE SPIRITS OF SPIRITUALISM WHICH MASQUERADE AS THE SPIRITS OF THE DEAD

"And there was war in heaven: Michael and his angels fought against the dragon; and the dragon fought and his angels.

"And prevailed not; neither was their place found any more in heaven.

"And the great dragon was cast out, that old serpent, called the Devil, and Satan, which deceiveth the whole world: he was cast out into the earth, and his angels were cast out with him." Rev. 12 : 7-9.

"For if God spared not the angels that sinned, but cast them down to hell, and delivered them into chains of darkness, to be reserved unto judgment;" 2 Pet. 2 : 4.

Jude 6 (1 Sam. 28, compare with 1 Chron. 10 : 13, 14).

Beware of these spirits which become very "familiar."

See Gen. 3 : 1-6—Satan's first lie was told through a medium (the serpent). He denied the Word of God and declared that those who disobey God (and die as a result) will know more than they knew before. Spiritualism continues to propagate this falsehood.

THESE EVIL SPIRITS ARE CALLED DEMONS OR DEVILS IN THE BIBLE. OPPOSED THE WORK OF CHRIST ON EARTH

"And he asked him, What is thy name? And he answered, saying, My name is Legion: for we are many." Mark 5 : 9.

"And, behold, they cried out, saying, What have we to do with thee, Jesus, thou Son of God? art thou come hither to torment us before the time?" Matt. 8 : 29.

Acts 13 : 8—Elymas the sorcerer (medium).

Acts 16 : 16-18—(Damsel at Philippi—medium.)

THERE IS TO BE A GREAT REVIVAL OF SPIRITUALISM IN THE LAST DAYS

"Now the spirit speaketh expressly, that in the latter times some shall depart from the faith, giving heed to seducing spirits, and doctrines of devils;" 1 Tim. 4 : 1.

"Then if any man shall say unto you, Lo, here is Christ, or there; believe it not.

"For there shall arise false Christs, and false prophets, and shall shew great signs and wonders; insomuch that, if it were possible, they shall deceive the very elect." Matt. 24 : 23, 24.

"And he doeth great wonders, so that he maketh fire come down from heaven on the earth in the sight of men." Rev. 13 : 13.

"Even him, whose coming is after the working of Satan with all power and signs and lying wonders,

"And with all deceivableness of unrighteousness in them that perish; because they received not the love of the truth, that they might be saved." 2 Thess. 2 : 9, 10.

Gal. 5 : 19—One of the works of the flesh.

Eph. 6 : 12.

ORIGIN AND DESTINY OF SATAN

SATAN WAS A HIGH ANGEL IN HEAVEN, BUT FELL THROUGH PRIDE

"And the great dragon was cast out, that old serpent, called the Devil, and Satan, which deceiveth the whole world: he was cast out into the earth, and his angels were cast out with him." Rev. 12 : 9.

"And he said unto them, I beheld Satan as lightning fall from heaven." Luke 10 : 18.

SATAN WAS CREATED A PERFECT BEING, WITH FREE MORAL AGENCY AND IS WHOLLY RESPONSIBLE FOR HIS SIN

"How art thou fallen from heaven, O Lucifer, son of the morning? how art thou cut down to the ground, which didst weaken the nations." Isa. 14 : 12.

"For thou hast said in thine heart, I will ascend into heaven, I will exalt my throne above the stars of God: I will sit also upon the mount of the congregation, in the sides of the north: I will ascend above the heights of the clouds; I will be like the most High. Yet thou shalt be brought down to hell, to the sides of the pit." Isa. 14 : 13-15.

"Son of man, take up a lamentation upon the king of Tyrus, and say unto him, Thus saith the Lord God; Thou sealest up the sum, full of wisdom, and perfect in beauty.

"Thou hast been in Eden the garden of God; every precious stone was thy covering, the sardius, topaz, and the diamond, the veryl, the onyx, and the jasper, the sapphire, the emerald, and the carbuncle, and gold: the workmanship of thy tabrets and of thy pipes was prepared in thee in the day that thou wast created.

"Thou art the anointed cherub that covereth; and I have set thee so: thou wast upon the holy mountain of God; thou hast walked up and down in the midst of the stones of fire.

"Thou wast perfect in thy ways from the day that thou wast created, till iniquity was found in thee.

"By the multitude of thy merchandise they have filled the midst of thee with violence, and thou hast sinned: therefore I will cast thee as profane out of the mountain of God: and I will destroy thee,

O covering cherub, from the midst of the stones of fire.

"Thine heart was lifted up because of thy beauty, thou hast corrupted thy wisdom by reason of thy brightness: I will cast thee to the ground, I will lay thee before kings, that they may behold thee.

"Thou hast defiled thy sanctuaries by the multitude of thine iniquities, by the iniquity of thy traffick; therefore will I bring forth a fire from the midst of thee, it shall devour thee, and I will bring thee to ashes upon the earth in the sight of all them that behold thee.

"All they that know thee among the people shall be astonished at thee: thou shalt be a terror, and never shalt thou be any more." Eze. 28 : 12-19.

SATAN'S CHARACTER SINCE THE FALL HAS BEEN EVIL

"Ye are of your father the devil, and the lusts of your father ye will do. He was a murderer from the beginning, and abode not in the truth, because there is no truth in him. When he speaketh a lie, he speaketh of his own: for he is a liar, and the father of it." John 8 : 44.

"He that committeth sin is of the devil; for the devil sinneth from the beginning. For this purpose the Son of God was manifested, that he might destroy the works of the devil." 1 John 3 : 8.

Gen. 3 : 1-6; 2 Cor. 11 : 3, 14.

John 12 : 31—See Job 1 : 6; 2 : 1; Rev. 12 : 13, 17.

SATAN OPPOSED CHRIST DURING HIS EARTHLY MINISTRY

Matt. 2 : 13-21—Tried to kill.

Matt. 4 : 1-11—Temptation to sin.

Matt. 22 : 15-46—Tried to lead Jesus to mistake.

Matt. 8 : 29—Before the time

Heb. 2 : 14—"Destroy Him."

John 12 : 31—"Now . . . cast out."

HOW TO RESIST SATAN

"Humble yourselves therefore under the mighty hand of God, that He may exalt you in due time:

"Casting all your care upon Him; for He careth for you.

"Be sober, be vigilant; because your adversary the devil, as a roaring lion, walketh about, seeking whom he may devour:

"Whom resist stedfast in the faith, knowing that the same afflictions are accomplished in your brethren that are in the world." 1 Pet. 5 : 6-9.

Matt. 4 : 4-10—"It is written."

"Submit yourselves therefore to God. Resist the devil, and he will flee from you.

"Draw nigh to God, and He will draw nigh to you. Cleanse your hands, ye sinners; and purify your hearts, ye double minded." James 4 : 7, 8; Eph. 6 : 16; Eph. 4 : 27.

SATAN WILL BE DESTROYED IN THE LAKE OF FIRE

"And when the thousand years are expired, Satan shall be loosed out of his prison.

"And shall go out to deceive the nations which are in the four quarters of the earth, Gog and Magog, to gather them together to battle: the number of whom is as the sand of the sea.

"And they went up on the breadth of the earth, and compassed the camp of the saints about, and the beloved city: and fire came down from God out of heaven and devoured them." Rev. 20 : 7-9.

"Thou hast defiled thy sanctuaries by the multitude of thine iniquities, by the iniquity of thy traffick; therefore will I bring forth a fire from the midst of thee, it shall devour thee, and I will bring thee to ashes upon the earth in the sight of all them that behold thee.

"All they that know thee among the people shall be astonished at thee; thou shalt be a terror, and never shalt thou be any more." Eze. 28 : 18, 19.

Heb. 2 : 14; Matt. 25 : 41; Mal. 4 : 1.

SATAN'S WORK IN THE LAST DAYS

"And with all deceivableness of unrighteousness in them that perish; because they received not the love of the truth, that they might be saved.

"And for this cause God shall send them strong delusion, that they should believe a lie:

"That they all might be damned who believed not the truth, but had pleasure in unrighteousness." 2 Thess. 2 : 10-12.

"And the dragon was wroth with the woman, and went to make war with the remnant of her seed, which keep the commandments of God, and have the testimony of Jesus Christ." Rev. 12 : 17.

"For they are the spirits of devils, working miracles, which go forth unto the kings of the earth, and of the whole world, to gather them to the battle of that great day of God Almighty." Rev. 16 : 14.

Rev. 13 : 14.

Rev. 20 : 1, 2, 7, 8, 9.

SATAN'S DIFFERENT NAMES—SHOWING HE HAS PERSONALITY

"Accuser of Brethren" (Rev. 12 : 10). See Gen. 3 : 2-5; Job 1 : 6, 12; Zech. 3 : 1; Acts 24 : 8.

"Adversary" (1 Pet. 5 : 8); Luke 12 : 58.

"Anointed Cherub" (Eze. 28 : 14).

"Angel of Light" (2 Cor. 11 : 14); Matt. 4 : 1-11.

"Belial" (2 Cor. 6 : 15; Deut. 13 : 13).

"Beelzebub" (Matt. 12 : 24); 9 : 34; Mark 3 : 22-30; Luke 11 : 14.

"Crooked Serpent" (Isa. 27 : 1).

"Devil" (Matt. 4 : 1), 35 times in New Testament. 100 times in Bible.

" Deceiver of Whole World " (Rev. 12 : 9).
" Dragon " (Rev. 20 : 2; Rev. 12 : 1-9).
" Enemy " (Matt. 13 : 39).
" Father of Lies " (John 8 : 44).
" God of This World " (2 Cor. 4 : 4).
" King of Tyre " (Eze. 28 : 12).
" Leviathan " (Isa. 27 : 1).
" Liar " (John 8 : 44).
" Lucifer " (Isa. 14 : 12).
" Murderer " (John 8 : 44); 1 John 3 : 12-15.
" Old Serpent " (Rev. 12 : 9).
" Piercing Serpent " (Isa. 27 : 1).
" Prince of Demons " (Matt. 9 : 34).
" Prince of Power of Air " (Eph. 2 : 2).
" Prince of This World " (John 14 : 30). See John 12 : 31; 16 : 11; Luke 4 : 5-7.
" Roaring Lion " (1 Pet. 5 : 8; Ps. 22 : 20).
" Ruler of Darkness " (Eph. 6 : 12).
" Satan " (1 Chron. 21 : 1) 35 times in New Testament and 15 times in Old Testament.
" Serpent " (Gen. 3 : 1).
" Son of Morning " (Isa. 14 : 12).
" Tempter " (Matt. 4 : 3) 6 times in Bible.
" Unclean Spirit " (Matt. 12 : 43).
" Wicked One " (1 John 3 : 12) 6 times in Bible.

SATAN

WHO CARRIES HIS BUSINESS ON?

Men don't believe in a devil now,
As their fathers used to do;
They've forced the door of the broadest creed,
To let his majesty through
There isn't a print of his cloven foot
Or a fiery dart from his bow
To be found in the earth or the air to-day.
For the world has voted so.
They say he doesn't go round about
As a roaring lion now;
But whom shall we hold responsible
For the everlasting row
To be heard in home and church and state
To the earth's remotest bound,
If the devil, by a unanimous vote,
Is nowhere to be found?
Who is it mixing the fatal draught
That palsies heart and brain,
And loads the bier of each passing year
With ten hundred thousand slain?
Who blights the bloom of the land to-day
With the fiery breath of hell,
If the devil isn't and never was?
Won't somebody rise and tell?
Who dogs the steps of the toiling saint,
And digs the pits for his feet?
Who sows the tares in the fields of time
Wherever God sows His wheat?
The devil was voted not to be,
And of course the thing is true;
But who is doing the kind of work
The devil used to do?
Won't somebody step to the front forthwith,
And make his bow, and show
How the frauds and the crimes of a single day spring up?
We want to know.
The devil was fairly voted out,
And of course the devil's gone;
But simple people want to know
Who carries his business on.

Selected.

THE ANGELS OF GOD

ARE THEY GOOD THOUGHTS? ARE THEY THE SPIRITS OF THE DEAD? ANGELS LIVED BEFORE MAN EVER DIED AND ARE THEREFORE NOT THE SPIRITS OF THE DEAD

" So He drove out the man; and He placed at the east of the garden of Eden Cherubims, and a flaming sword which turned every way, to keep the way of the tree of life." Gen. 3 : 24.

Cherubims are angels (Ex. 25 : 18-20; 37 : 7-9; Num. 7 : 89; Ps. 80 : 1); Job 38 : 4-7.

THE ANGELS ARE CREATED BEINGS AND ARE OF A HIGHER ORDER THAN MAN

" What is man, that thou art mindful of him? and the son of man, that thou visitest him?

" For thou hast made him a little lower than the angels, and has crowned him with glory and honour." Ps. 8 : 4, 5.

Heb. 2 : 16—Nature of angels not the same as man's nature.

Luke 20 : 36—Will be equal at the Resurrection.

ANGELS ARE REAL BEINGS AND NOT SIMPLY GOOD THOUGHTS

" And he took butter, and milk, and the calf which he had dressed, and set it before them; and he stood by them under the tree, and they did eat." Gen. 18 : 8. See also verses 1 to 7. Also Gen. 19 : 1-3.

Ps. 78 : 23-25—They were visible, they talked, they could be touched, they ate food.

Heb. 13 : 2.

THE NUMBER AND ORDER OF THE ANGELS

" And I beheld, and I heard the voice of many angels round about the throne and the beasts and the elders: and the number of them was ten thousand times ten thousand, and thousands of thousands;" Rev. 5 : 11.

Note.—10,000times10,000is100,000,000 and this was only part of the heavenly host.

Dan. 7 : 10; Heb. 12 : 22.

Matt. 26 : 53—A " legion " in Roman times was from 5000 to 6000 men. The order of the angels, as well as number, is seen in this verse.

Rom. 8 : 38; Eph. 1 : 21; 3 : 10; Col. 1 : 16; 2 : 10; Jude 6 (margin).

THE STRENGTH AND SURPASSING GLORY OF THE ANGELS

"Then I lifted up mine eyes, and looked, and behold a certain man clothed in linen, whose loins were girded with fine gold of Uphaz:

"His body also was like the beryl, and his face as the appearance of lightning, and his eyes as lamps of fire, and his arms and his feet like in colour to polished brass, and the voice of his words like the voice of a multitude." Dan. 10 : 5, 6.

Matt. 28 : 3—One angel caused the earth to quake and the guards to fall as dead men.

Rev. 18 : 1—One angel fills the earth with glory.

Ps. 103 : 20—They excel in strength.

Acts 12 : 7—Free prisoners.

Eze. 1 : 14—Lightning speed (Dan. 9 : 21).

MINISTERING SPIRITS TO GOD'S PEOPLE

"But to which of the angels said He at any time, Sit on my right hand, until I make thine enemies thy footstool?" Heb. 1 : 13.

"Are they not all ministering spirits, sent forth to minister for them who shall be heirs of salvation?" Heb. 1 : 14.

Ps. 34 : 7; Gen. 28 : 12; Acts 12 : 1-11; Gen. 24 : 7; Gen. 48 : 16; Ex. 23 : 20; 1 Kings 19 : 5, 6; Dan. 6 : 22; Acts 27 : 23.

EVERY CHILD OF GOD HAS A GUARDIAN ANGEL

"Take heed that ye despise not one of these little ones; for I say unto you, That in heaven their angels do always behold the face of My Father which is in heaven." Matt. 18 : 10.

"The angel of the Lord encampeth round about them that fear Him, and delivereth them." Ps. 34 : 7.

Acts 12 : 15; Ps. 91 : 11, 12.

THE ANGELS ARE INTERESTED IN MAN'S SALVATION

"Of which salvation the prophets have inquired and searched diligently, who prophesied of the grace that should come unto you:

"Searching what, or what manner of time the Spirit of Christ which was in them did signify, when it testified beforehand the sufferings of Christ, and the glory that should follow.

"Unto whom it was revealed, that not unto themselves, but unto us they did minister the things, which are now reported unto you by them that have preached the gospel unto you with the Holy Ghost sent down from heaven; which things the angels desire to look into." 1 Pet. 1 : 10-12.

Luke 2 : 9-14—Rejoiced at Jesus' birth.

Rev. 8 : 3—Assist in the Heavenly Sanctuary.

Luke 15 : 10—Rejoice over sinners that repent.

THE ANGELS EXECUTE GOD'S JUDGMENTS

"And I saw another sign in heaven, great and marvellous, seven angels having the seven last plagues; for in them is filled up the wrath of God." Rev. 15 : 1.

"And I heard a great voice out of the temple saying to the seven angels, Go your ways, and pour out the vials of the wrath of God upon the earth." Rev. 16 : 1.

Gen. 19 : 13; Num. 22 : 22; 1 Chron. 21 : 14-30; 2 Chron. 32 : 21; Acts 12 : 23; Matt. 13 : 39-42; Mal. 3 : 16; Rev. 20 : 11, 12—Keep the records.

THE ANGELS WILL COME TO GATHER THE REDEEMED AT THE COMING OF THE LORD

"For the Lord Himself shall descend from heaven with a shout, with the voice of the archangel, and with the trump of God: and the dead in Christ shall rise first:

"Then we which are alive and remain shall be caught up together with them in the clouds, to meet the Lord in the air: and so shall we ever be with the Lord.

"Wherefore comfort one another with these words." 1 Thess. 4 : 16-18.

"And then shall appear the sign of the Son of man in heaven: and then shall all the tribes of the earth mourn, and they shall see the Son of man coming in the clouds of heaven with power and great glory.

"And he shall send His angels with a great sound of a trumpet, and they shall gather together His elect from the four winds, from one end of heaven to the other." Matt. 24 : 30, 31.

THE SPIRITS IN PRISON

"For Christ also hath once suffered for sins, the just for the unjust, that he might bring us to God, being put to death in the flesh, but quickened by the Spirit:

"By which also he went and preached unto the spirits in prison;

"Which sometime were disobedient, when once the longsuffering of God waited in the days of Noah, while the ark was a preparing, wherein few, that is, eight souls were saved by water." 1 Pet. 3 : 18-20.

Verse 18—"He" is Christ. "Which" is the Spirit. See 1 Pet. 1 : 10-12; Rom. 8 : 11; Rom. 1 : 4.

THE PRISON HOUSE OF SIN

Rom. 7 : 14; 2 Pet. 2 : 19; Gal. 3 : 22; Gal. 5 : 16, 17 (Verse 1—"Liberty").

JESUS LIBERATED PRISONERS FROM THE PRISON OF SIN BY HIS PERSONAL PREACHING WHILE HE WAS ON EARTH

"And he came to Nazareth, where he had been brought up: and, as his custom was, he went into the synagogue on the sabbath day, and stood up for to read." Luke 4 : 16. See Isa. 61 : 1.

"That very sabbath day the Scripture was fulfilled—that is, the prison was opened and the prisoners loosed from the fetters of sin and condemnation." John 8 : 32, 36.

BY HIS SPIRIT, CHRIST PREACHED THROUGH NOAH TO THE PEOPLE IN THE PRISON HOUSE OF SIN IN THE DAYS BEFORE THE FLOOD

"And spared not the old world, but saved Noah the eighth person, a preacher of righteousness, bringing in the flood upon the world of the ungodly." 2 Pet. 2 : 5.

Heb. 11 : 7; Rom. 8 : 1, 2.

"And the Lord said, My spirit shall not always strive with man, for that he also is flesh: yet his days shall be an hundred and twenty years." Gen. 6 : 3.

"SPIRITS IN PRISON" ARE NOT DISEMBODIED SPIRITS

"To the general assembly and church of the firstborn, which are written in heaven, and to God the Judge of all, and to the spirits of just men made perfect.

"Furthermore we have had fathers of our flesh which corrected us, and we gave them reverence: shall we not much rather be in subjection unto the Father of spirits, and live?" Heb. 12 : 23, 9.

Num. 16 : 22; 27 : 16.

All must agree that in these texts the reference is to people alive on this earth.

IN THIS LIFE ALONE MAN HEARS THE GOSPEL AND ACCEPTS SALVATION

"And as it is appointed unto men once to die, but after this the judgment." Heb. 9 : 27.

Eccl. 11 : 3; Eccl. 9 : 10, 5.

ASTRONOMY AND THE BIBLE

Isa. 40 : 26—God's invitation to study Astronomy.

Heb. 1 : 2—Christ made the worlds.

Heb. 11 : 3—Worlds framed by Word (John 1 : 1, 14).

See Prov. 8; Micah 5 : 2; 1 Cor. 1 : 30; Col. 1 : 16-19; Eph. 3 : 9.

OUR WORLD NOT THE FIRST CREATED

Job 38 : 4-7—Sons of God rejoice at creation of this earth.

Luke 3 : 38—Adam a Son of God (by creation).

Note.—Other Sons of God at creation of this earth indicate other worlds in existence.

VAST NUMBER OF THE STARS

Gen. 15 : 5; Ps. 147 : 4.

OTHER WORLDS INHABITED

Rev. 12 : 12; Isa. 40 : 15—Nations of this earth only a "drop" of a bucket.

Isa. 40 : 22—Heavens a tent to dwell in.

Job 26 : 7—Earth hangs on nothing.

Job 38 : 14—The earth turns.

Ps. 19 : 4-6—Sun moves also.

Job 38 : 31—Stars in cluster (bands).

Verse 32—"Arcturus" fast traveller—257 miles a second, 15,420 miles a minute. One thousand times bigger than the sun. Only the power of God can guide such speed and mass.

1 Cor. 15 : 41—Stars differ in glory.

Job. 38 : 24—Light is parted—the Spectrum.

Isa. 40 : 22—World is round.

Other texts—Jer. 33 : 20, 21; Ps. 89 : 34-37; Isa. 40 : 26; Isa. 30 : 26.

CHRIST IN ALL THE BIBLE

"In the beginning was the Word, and the Word was with God, and the Word was God." John 1 : 1.

"In the beginning God created the heaven and the earth." Gen 1 : 1.

"The grace of our Lord Jesus Christ be with you all. Amen." Rev. 22 : 21.

CHRIST FIRST AND LAST

"I am Alpha and Omega, the beginning and the end, the first and the last." Rev. 22 : 13.

Acts. 4 : 12.

CHRIST THE THEME OF THE OLD TESTAMENT

Luke 24 : 27, 44; 2 Pet 3 : 2—Both Testaments needed for full revelation; Acts 26 : 22, Paul preached from Old Testament.

Gen. 3 : 15—"Promised Seed."

Gen. 49 : 10—"Shiloh," "Prince of Life."

Ex. 3 : 14 (John 8 : 58) great "I Am."

Lev. Sacrifices—"Lamb of God"—John 1 : 29.

Heb. 4 : 2—Gospel to Them.

Num. 24 : 17—"Star of Jacob."

Deut. 18 : 15—"Great Prophet."

Joshua 5 : 13-15—"Cap. of Lord's Host."

Isa. 9 : 6—"Wonderful."

Lev. 25 and Ruth 3—the "Kinsman."

2 Sam. 7—"Seed of David"—on his Throne—Luke 1 : 32.

Ps. 110—"High Priest."

Isa. 53—"Suffering Servant."

Jer. 23 : 6—"Lord our Righteousness."

Eze. 21 : 27—"Coming King."

Dan. 7 : 13—"Son of Man."

Zech. 6 : 12—"The Branch."

Mal. 3 : 1—"Messenger of God's Covenant."

TWO DIFFERENT WORDS

Mk. 7 : 13; Rev. 19 : 13.

Phil. 2 : 16—"Word of Life"—1 Jno. 1 : 1.

CHRIST IS	WORDS OF BIBLE ARE
Holy—Heb. 7 : 26	Holy—2 Tim. 3 : 15
Pure—1 Jno. 3 : 3	Pure—Ps. 119 : 140
Powerful—1 Cor. 1 : 24	Powerful—Heb. 4 : 12
Faithful—Heb. 3 : 1, 2	Faithful—Rev. 21 : 5
Righteous—1 Jno. 2 : 29	Righteous—Ps. 33 : 4
True—Jno. 14 : 6	True—Jno. 17 : 17
Life—Jno. 14 : 6	Life—Jno. 6 : 63
Sure—Isa. 28 : 16	Sure—Ps. 19 : 7; 18 : 30
Food—Jno. 6 : 35	Food—Matt. 4 : 4; 1 Pet. 2 : 2
Light—Jno. 1 : 8, 9	Light—Ps. 119 : 105, 130
Spiritual—Jno. 4 : 24	Spiritual—Jno. 6 : 63

CHRIST IS THE ROCK

" And did all drink the same spiritual drink : for they drank of that spiritual Rock that followed them : and that Rock was Christ." 1 Cor. 10 : 4.

" For other foundation can no man lay than that is laid, which is Jesus Christ." 1 Cor. 3 : 11.

Deut. 32 : 4; 2 Sam. 22 : 3; 23 : 3; Ps. 18 : 2, 31, 46; Eph. 2 : 20; Isa. 28 : 16; Rom. 15 : 20; Isa. 17 : 10.

WORDS OF PETER HIMSELF ABOUT THE ROCK

" This is the stone which was set at nought of you builders, which is become the head of the corner.

" Neither is there salvation in any other : for there is none other name under heaven given among men, whereby we must be saved." Acts 4 : 11, 12.

1 Pet. 2 : 4-8.

PETER DID NOT EXERCISE AUTHORITY OVER THE OTHER APOSTLES

" And when there had been much disputing, Peter rose up, and said unto them, Men and brethren, ye know how that a good while ago God made choice among us, that the Gentiles by my mouth should hear the word of the gospel, and believe.

" And after they had held their peace, James answered, saying, Men and brethren, hearken unto me :" Acts 15 : 7, 13.

James was chairman, not Peter.

" And as they went through the cities, they delivered them the decrees for to keep, that were ordained of the apostles and elders which were at Jerusalem." Acts 16 : 4. Decrees of the elders, not of " Pope " Peter.

Acts 8 (Peter sent out by others).

WAS PETER THE FIRST POPE?

" He saith unto them, But whom say ye that I am ?

" And Simon Peter answered and said, Thou art the Christ, the Son of the living God.

" And Jesus answered and said unto him, Blessed art thou, Simon Bar-jona : for flesh and blood hath not revealed it unto thee, but my Father which is in heaven.

" And I say also unto thee, That thou art Peter, and upon this rock I will build my church ; and the gates of hell shall not prevail against it.

" And I will give unto thee the keys of the kingdom of heaven : and whatsoever thou shalt bind on earth shall be bound in heaven : and whatsoever thou shalt loose on earth shall be loosed in heaven.

" Then charged he his disciples that they should tell no man that he was Jesus the Christ.

" From that time forth began Jesus to shew unto his disciples how that he must go unto Jerusalem, and suffer many things of the elders and chief priests and scribes, and be killed, and be raised again the third day.

" Then Peter took him, and began to rebuke him, saying, Be it far from thee, Lord : this shall not be unto thee.

" But he turned, and said unto Peter, Get thee behind me, Satan : thou art an offence unto me : for thou savourest not the things that be of God, but those that be of men." Matt. 16 : 15-23.

Upon this text some have built the doctrine of the Primacy of Peter and teach that Peter and his successors as Bishops of Rome are the Popes or Rulers of the Church. But Jesus refers to Peter's confession of faith in Jesus as the Christ, the Son of the living God, and not to Peter himself, as the Rock.

2 Pet. 3 : 2—" Us the apostles."
1 Pet. 5 : 1-3—" An elder."
1 Pet. 1 : 1—" An apostle."
Matt. 23 : 8-10 — " One Master, Christ."

PAUL MET PETER AS AN EQUAL

" For I suppose I was not a whit behind the very chiefest apostles." 2 Cor. 11 : 5.

" I am become a fool in glorying ; ye have compelled me : for I ought to have been commended of you : for in nothing am I behind the very chiefest apostles, though I be nothing." 2 Cor. 12 : 11.

Gal. 2 : 6-14.

PETER NOT ALWAYS NAMED FIRST

" And these signs shall follow them that believe ; In my name shall they cast out devils ; they shall speak with new tongues." Mark 16 : 17.

" Now Philip was of Bethsaida, the city of Andrew and Peter." John 1 : 44.

Gal. 2 : 9—Shared government of church with others.

DREAMS

ORDINARY DREAMS OF NATURAL ORIGIN

"For a dream cometh through the multitude of business; and a fool's voice is known by multitude of words." Eccl. 5 : 3.

"For in the multitude of dreams and many words there are also divers vanities: but fear thou God." Eccl. 5 : 7.

Jer. 29 : 8; Jer. 23 : 28; Job 7 : 13-15; Ps. 126 : 1, 2.

GOD SOMETIMES INSTRUCTS MEN BY DREAMS

"And He said, hear now my words: If there be a prophet among you, I the Lord will make myself known unto him in a vision, and will speak unto him in a dream." Num. 12 : 6.

Job 33 : 14-17; Gen. 20 : 3—First dream mentioned in Bible.

Deut. 13 : 1-5—Dreams of TRUE prophet always come to pass.

Deut. 18 : 22; Gen. 37 : 5-10—Joseph's dream (fulfilled Gen. 42 : 6, 9; 43 : 26; 44 : 14).

Gen. 40 : 9-13, 16-19—Dream of Butler and Baker (fulfilled verses 20-22).

Gen. 41 : 1-7—Pharaoh's Dream (fulfilled Gen. 41 : 53, 54—read all chap. 41).

Joel 2 : 28; Acts 2 : 16, 47—Dreams promised for Last Days.

OTHER IMPORTANT DREAMS

Dan. 2 : 1, 31-35—Nebuchadnezzar's dream of a great Image.

Dan. 4 : 5, 9-18—Nebuchadnezzar's dream of a great Tree.

Matt. 2 : 12—Dream of the Wise Men.

Matt. 1 : 20; 2 : 13, 19-22—Dream of Joseph.

Matt. 27 : 19—Dream of Pilate's Wife.

THE SPIRIT OF PROPHECY IN THE REMNANT CHURCH

A PROPHET IS A SPOKESMAN FOR GOD

Ex. 7 : 1—Moses as God—Aaron his Prophet (Ex. 4 : 15).

1 Pet. 1 : 10, 11—The Spirit of Christ speaks through them.

2 Pet. 1 : 20, 21—They were moved by the Holy Ghost in writing the prophecies of Scripture.

2 Sam. 23 : 2; Rev. 1 : 1; Jer. 36 : 1-4; Eze. 3 : 17.

IN THE PAST, LEADING PROPHETS HAVE APPEARED TO GUIDE GOD'S PEOPLE AND WORK IN TIMES OF NEED

Isa. 63 : 12—Israel led by Moses.

Deut. 34 : 10—No other Prophet like him.

Other Leading Prophets were:

Samuel (1 Sam. 7 : 5, 6); Elijah; Elisha; Isaiah; Jeremiah; John the Baptist (Luke 7 : 24-30), and Paul (2 Cor. 11 : 28).

A PROPHET (MOSES) LED ISRAEL OUT OF EGYPT TO THE BORDERS OF CANAAN, SO GOD'S PEOPLE IN THE LAST DAYS WILL HAVE THE SPIRIT OF PROPHECY

"And by a prophet the Lord brought Israel out of Egypt, and by a prophet was he preserved." Hos 12 : 13.

1 Cor. 10 : 1-6, 11—Their experience an example to God's people in the last days.

1 Cor. 1 : 4-8—The people of God waiting for the coming of the Lord will come behind in no gift.

(1 Cor. 12 : 8-10; 1 Cor. 12 : 28; Eph. 4 : 8-14; Acts 2 : 16-18.)

"And the dragon was wroth with the woman, and went to make war with the remnant of her seed, which keep the commandments of God, and have the testimony of Jesus Christ." Rev. 12 : 17.

Rev. 19 : 10—"The testimony of Jesus is the spirit of prophecy." As the gift of tongues was the leading gift at the beginning of the Church, so the Spirit of Prophecy is the leading gift in the Remnant Church.

"And they rose early in the morning, and went forth into the wilderness of Tekoa: and as they went forth, Jehoshaphat stood and said, Hear me, O Judah, and ye inhabitants of Jerusalem; Believe in the Lord your God, so shall ye be established; believe his prophets, so shall ye prosper." 2 Chron. 20 : 20.

HOW TO BE SAVED

BELIEVE

"And brought them out, and said, Sirs, what must I do to be saved?

"And they said, Believe on the Lord Jesus Christ, and thou shalt be saved, and thy house." Acts. 16 : 30-31. See Matt. 26 : 28.

REPENT

"Now when they heard this, they were pricked in their heart, and said unto Peter and to the rest of the apostles, Men and brethren, what shall we do?

"Then Peter said unto them, Repent, and be baptized every one of you in the name of Jesus Christ for the remission of sins, and ye shall receive the gift of the Holy Ghost." Acts. 2 : 37, 38.

See also Acts 26 : 19, 20; Acts 5 : 31; 1 John 1 : 6-10; 2 : 1-6.

SALVATION'S THREE SIDES

Past Tense

"Who hath saved us, and called us with an holy calling, not according to our works, but according to his own purpose and grace, which was given us in Christ Jesus before the world began." 2 Tim. 1 : 9.

1 John 5 : 13; Rom. 5 : 1.

This is Justification—We are saved.

Present Tense

"For if, when we were enemies, we were reconciled to God by the death of His

Son, much more, being reconciled, we shall be saved by His life." Rom 5 : 10.

Rom. 8 : 29; 2 Cor. 3 : 18; Phil. 2 : 12, 13.

This is Sanctification—We are being saved.

Future Tense

" Beloved, now are we the sons of God, and it doth not yet appear what we shall be: but we know that, when He shall appear, we shall be like Him; for we shall see Him as He is." 1 John 3 : 2.

Heb. 9 : 28; Rom. 8 : 11; 1 Pet. 1 : 5.

This is glorification. We will be saved.

See 1 Thess. 1 : 9, 10; 2 Cor. 1 : 10; Heb. 10 : 35.

THE PROTESTANT PURGATORY

ONLY THE PURE CAN SEE GOD

" Blessed are the pure in heart: for they shall see God." Matt. 5 : 8.

John 1 : 18—Sinful men have never seen God.

1 John 3 : 2—The saved will see Christ in glory.

Ex. 33 : 20—Even Moses unable to see God's face.

Isa. 59 : 2—Sins to blame.

Heb. 12 : 29—God a consuming fire.

IN ORDER TO MEET THE LORD, WE MUST BE PURIFIED FOR ALL HAVE SINNED

" Who gave Himself for us, that He might redeem us from all iniquity, and purify unto Himself a peculiar people, zealous of good works." Titus 2 : 14.

" Purge me with hyssop, and I shall be clean: wash me, and I shall be whiter than snow." Ps. 51 : 7.

Ex. 12 : 22; John 15 : 2; 1 Cor. 5 : 7; Rom. 5 : 12.

THIS PURGING MUST BE DONE IN THIS LIFE

" So Christ was once offered to bear the sins of many; and unto them that look for Him shall He appear the second time without sin unto salvation." Heb. 9 : 28.

There is no opportunity to purge the life after death.

Jas. 4 : 8—Hearts must be pure.

Acts 15 : 9—Purify hearts by faith.

1 Pet. 1 : 21—By obeying the Truth.

1 Jno. 3 : 3—By hope of Lord's Coming.

Heb. 9 : 14; 2 Pet. 1 : 9; Eze. 24 : 13; Heb. 1 : 3; 9 : 22.

THIS PURGING IS GOD'S WORK ALONE

Mal. 3 : 2, 3—God is the Refiner.

1 Pet. 4 : 12—Fiery trials try or test us.

1 Cor. 3 : 12-15—Wood, hay, stubble burned.

Mal. 4 : 1—What happens to the dross.

Mal. 3 : 3—Silver and gold stand the fire.

Jude 24.

BAPTISM

IS IT AN INWARD EXPERIENCE OR AN OUTWARD ORDINANCE ? IS IT SPRINKLING ? IS IT POURING ? IS IT IMMERSION ?

BAPTISM WAS COMMANDED BY CHRIST AS A MEMORIAL OF THE GREAT FACTS OF THE GOSPEL

" Go ye therefore, and teach all nations, baptizing them in the name of the Father, and of the Son, and of the Holy Ghost :" Matt. 28 : 19. 1 Cor. 15 : 3, 4—Christ's Death, Burial and Resurrection, the great facts of gospel truth.

BAPTISM IS AN OUTWARD SYMBOL OF AN INWARD EXPERIENCE. IT IS FOR THOSE WHO HEAR THE GOSPEL, BELIEVE AND REPENT

" And He said unto them, Go ye into all the world, and preach the gospel to every creature.

" He that believeth and is baptized shall be saved; but he that believeth not shall be damned." Mark 16 : 15, 16.

" Then Peter said unto them, Repent, and be baptized every one of you in the name of Jesus Christ for the remission of sins, and ye shall receive the gift of the Holy Ghost." Acts. 2 : 38.

" And as they went on their way, they came unto a certain water: and the eunuch said, See, here is water; what doth hinder me to be baptized ?

" And Philip said, If thou believest with all thine heart, thou mayest. And he answered and said, I believe that Jesus Christ is the Son of God." Acts 8 : 36, 37.

Acts 16 : 30-34; Acts 8 : 12; 10 : 47, 48; 1 Cor. 12 : 12, 13.

THE EXPERIENCE SIGNIFIED BY BAPTISM

" Know ye not, that so many of us as were baptized into Jesus Christ were baptized into His death ?

" Therefore we are buried with Him by baptism into death: that like as Christ was raised up from the dead by the glory of the Father, even so we also should walk in newness of life.

" For if we have been planted together in the likeness of His death, we shall be also in the likeness of His resurrection:" Rom. 6 : 3-5.

" For as many of you as have been baptized into Christ have put on Christ." Gal. 3 : 27.

1 Cor. 15 : 29—Represents death.

BAPTISM IS A SYMBOLIC BURIAL AND IS IMMERSION

" Buried with Him in baptism, wherein also ye are risen with Him through the faith of the operation of God, who hath raised Him from the dead." Col. 2 : 12.

" One Lord, one faith, one baptism." Eph. 4 : 5.

Matt. 3 : 16—Came up out of water.

Acts. 8 : 38—Went down into water.
Rom. 6 : 4, 5—A burial.
John 3 : 23—" much water " needed.
Heb. 10 : 22—Hearts sprinkled, but bodies washed.

1 Pet. 2 : 21—We are to follow His steps and He went down into water of Baptism. See John 15 : 10.

Acts 22 : 16 — Why tarriest thou, reader ?

HOW TO PAY THE PREACHER

GOD OWNS ALL BY CREATION AND REDEMPTION

" The earth is the Lord's, and the fullness thereof; the world, and they that dwell therein." Ps. 24 : 1.

" Forasmuch as ye know that ye were not redeemed with corruptible things, as silver and gold, from your vain conversation received by tradition from your fathers;

" But with the precious blood of Christ, as of a lamb without blemish and without spot." 1 Pet. 1 : 18, 19.

Gen. 14 : 19, 22; 1 Cor. 10 : 26, 28; Ex. 9 : 29.

WHAT IT MEANS TO BE REDEEMED

" For ye are bought with a price: therefore glorify God in your body, and in your spirit, which are God's." 1 Cor. 6 : 20.

" Take heed therefore unto yourselves, and to all the flock, over the which the Holy Ghost hath made you overseers, to feed the church of God, which He hath purchased with His own blood." Acts 20 : 28.

Matt. 22 : 36, 37.

GOD WANTS THE WORLD TO KNOW ABOUT THIS GREAT REDEMPTION

Matt. 20 : 4—He says to His servants " go ye " and promises to pay them.

" And all the tithe of the land, whether of the seed of the land, or of the fruit of the tree, is the Lord's: it is holy unto the Lord.

" And if a man will at all redeem ought of his tithes, he shall add thereto the fifth part thereof.

" And concerning the tithe of the herd, or of the flock, even of whatsoever passeth under the rod, the tenth shall be holy unto the Lord.

" He shall not search whether it be good or bad, neither shall he change it: and if he change it at all, then both it and the change thereof shall be holy; it shall not be redeemed." Lev. 27 : 30-33.

1 Cor. 9 : 14—" Even so," that is, in the same way the Lord's Ministers now are to be supported.

JESUS TAUGHT TITHE PAYING WHICH MEANS RETURNING ONE-TENTH OF OUR INCREASE TO GOD

" Woe unto you, scribes and Pharisees, hypocrites! for ye pay tithe of mint and anise and cummin, and have omitted the weightier matters of the law, judgment, mercy, and faith: these ought ye to have done, and not to leave the other undone." Matt. 23 : 23.

Heb. 7 : 1-2—Compared with Heb. 6 : 20.

CHRIST IS A PRIEST AFTER THE ORDER OF MELCHISEDEC WHO RECEIVED TITHES FROM ABRAHAM

" And blessed be the most high God, which hath delivered thine enemies into thy hand. And he gave him tithes of all." Gen. 14 : 20.

MELCHISEDEC BROUGHT FORTH BREAD AND WINE FOR ABRAHAM. THE CHRISTIAN WHO PARTAKES OF THE BREAD AND WINE OF THE LORD'S SUPPER OUGHT TO RETURN THE TENTH OR TITHE TO THE LORD

" And this stone, which I have set for a pillar, shall be God's house: and of all that thou shalt give me I will surely give the tenth unto thee." Gen. 28 : 22.

RESULTS OF WITHHOLDING THE TITHE

" There is that scattereth, and yet increaseth; and there is that withholdeth more than is meet, but it tendeth to poverty." Prov. 11 : 24.

Hab. 1 : 2-6, 9; Hag. 2 : 10-19; Neh. 13 : 10; Prov. 26 : 2; Deut. 8 : 18.

WILL A MAN ROB GOD ?

" Will a man rob God ? Yet ye have robbed me. But ye say, Wherein have we robbed thee ? In tithes and offerings.

" Ye are cursed with a curse: for ye have robbed me, even this whole nation.

" Bring ye all the tithes into the storehouse, that there may be meat in mine house, and prove me now herewith, saith the Lord of hosts, if I will not open you the windows of heaven, and pour you out a blessing, that there shall not be room enough to receive it.

" And I will rebuke the devourer for your sakes, and he shall not destroy the fruits of your ground; neither shall your vine cast her fruit before the time in the field, saith the Lord of hosts.

" And all nations shall call you blessed: for ye shall be a delightsome land, saith the Lord of hosts." Mal. 3 : 8-12.

Num. 23 : 19; Prov. 10 : 22; 2 Cor. 9 : 6.

TALKING IN TONGUES

THE GIFT OF TONGUES ON THE DAY OF PENTECOST WAS MANIFESTED IN REAL LANGUAGES UNDERSTOOD BY PEOPLE WHO HEARD THEM

"And there were dwelling at Jerusalem Jews, devout men, out of every nation under heaven.

"Now when this was noised abroad, the multitude came together, and were confounded, because that every man heard them speak in his own language." Acts 2 : 5, 6. (See verses 7 to 11.)

THE APOSTLES WERE TO PREACH THE GOSPEL TO ALL THE WORLD, AND THE GIFTS OF THE SPIRIT WERE GIVEN FOR THAT PURPOSE

"And that repentance and remission of sins should be preached in His name among all nations, beginning at Jerusalem.

"And ye are witnesses of these things.

"And, behold, I send the promise of my Father upon you: but tarry ye in the city of Jerusalem, until ye be endued with power from on high." Luke 24 : 47-49.

Matt. 3 : 11; 1 Pet. 1 : 12; Acts 2 : 32-36; Heb. 2 : 3.

IT IS NOT SCRIPTURAL TO "TARRY FOR THE HOLY SPIRIT" AFTER THE COMING OF THE SPIRIT ON THE DAY OF PENTECOST

Lev. 23 : 16—Pentecost came 50 days after Feast of Firstfruits.

1 Cor. 15 : 23—Firstfruits typified Resurrection of Christ.

Pentecost Typified the Coming of the Spirit

Acts 1 : 3—Christ was with the disciples forty days after His Resurrection. Ten days after His Ascension, the full fifty days were complete and Pentecost came.

Acts 2 : 1—"When the day of Pentecost was fully come," the Spirit was poured out because God's time had arrived.

As the Incarnation—Crucifixion and Resurrection of Christ are not repeated, so Pentecost is not repeated. The Holy Spirit is already here.

IF WE ARE CONVERTED CHRISTIANS THE HOLY SPIRIT IS IN OUR HEARTS

"But ye are not in the flesh, but in the Spirit, if so be that the Spirit of God dwell in you. Now if any man have not the Spirit of Christ, he is none of His." Rom. 8 : 9.

"Then Peter said unto them, Repent, and be baptized every one of you in the name of Jesus Christ for the remission of sins, and ye shall receive the gift of the Holy Ghost." Acts 2 : 38.

Acts 5 : 32; Gal. 3 : 1-3; John 7 : 39.

THE SCRIPTURES TEACH THAT ALL (NOT SOME) CHRISTIANS ARE BORN OF THE SPIRIT INTO CHRIST'S BODY, AND NEVER SPEAK OF CERTAIN ONES AS HAVING "RECEIVED THEIR PENTECOST" OR "RECEIVED THEIR BAPTISM"

"For by one Spirit are we all baptized into one body, whether we be Jews or Gentiles, whether we be bond or free; and have been all made to drink into one Spirit." 1 Cor. 12 : 13.

Eph. 1 : 13, 14; 1 Cor. 6 : 19; Eph. 5 : 18; Isa. 8 : 20; 1 John 4 : 1.

IT IS NOT SCRIPTURAL TO MAKE SPEAKING IN TONGUES THE EVIDENCE OF THE BAPTISM OF THE HOLY SPIRIT

"Have all the gifts of healing? do all speak with tongues? do all interpret?" 1 Cor. 12 : 30.

The plain inference is that all do not speak in tongues. He is speaking of Christians who are baptized by the Spirit. See verse 13.

TONGUES AFTER PENTECOST

Acts 10 : 45, 46—Experience of Cornelius, the Gentile. This convinced Peter, the six witnesses, and the Church Council at Jerusalem that the Gentiles could receive the gospel. See Acts 11 : 15—"At the beginning"—shows such a demonstration unknown since Pentecost.

Acts 19 : 1-7—A special miracle in the stronghold of Pagan Black Art (verse 19). See verses 11, 12.

Note.—In none of these cases was the Holy Spirit "sought" nor was the gift of tongues "sought," as by some today.

1 Cor. 12 and 14—In the Church.

1 Cor. 12 : 7-11—"As He will"—It is not a matter for our decision.

Verse 30—Indicates all will not speak with tongues.

Verse 17—Not every member a "tongue."

Chapter 14 shows Prophecy edifies. It is therefore a work of Love (1 Cor. 8 : 1).

Tongues apt to lead to vain display (verses 18, 19). It is two thousand times better to speak in a language that all can understand.

Verses 20-22—A sign to unbelieving Jews.

See Isa 28 : 11, 12 with John 4 : 48; 6 : 30.

THE EVIDENCE OF THE PRESENCE OF THE HOLY SPIRIT IN THE LIFE OF THE CHRISTIAN IS FRUIT RATHER THAN SIGNS

"Wherefore by their fruits ye shall know them." Matt. 7 : 20.

"But the fruit of the Spirit is love, joy, peace, longsuffering, gentleness, goodness, faith,

"Meekness, temperance: against such there is no law." Gal. 5 : 22, 23.

John 13 : 35.

Mk. 16 : 17, 18—Not only tongues but serpents and devils too. This text already fulfilled (verse 20). Notice the promise is to "them that believe," not "receive" which some teach is a separate experience.

1 Cor. 13 : 8—"Tongues shall cease."

THREE DAYS AND THREE NIGHTS IN THE HEART OF THE EARTH

"For as Jonas was three days and three nights in the whale's belly; so shall the Son of man be three days and three nights in the heart of the earth." Matt. 12 : 40.

This either means three full days or is an idiom for parts of three days. It must be the latter, for if it means 72 full hours (3 days and 3 nights) Christ could not rise till after the third day was over and would then have risen on the second day of the week. But we read (Mark 16 : 9) that he rose on the first day of the week.

See also Matt. 16 : 21; 20 : 19; Mark 9 : 31; 10 : 34; Luke 9 : 22; 18 : 33; 24 : 6, 7. The phrase therefore does not mean 72 full hours.

It was a Jewish maxim that a part stood for the whole, and as Jesus was in the tomb part of the sixth day, all the 7th day and part of the 1st day, the phrase "three days and three nights" is used to express this time.

1 Kings 12 : 5—Compare 2 Chron. 10 : 5

1 Kings 12 : 12—Compare 2 Chron. 10 : 12.

Esther 4 : 16—Compare Esther 5 : 1.

See Gen. 42 : 17, 18.

Matt. 27 : 62-64—The Jews understood Jesus to mean that He would rise on the third day from His crucifixion.

Luke 23 : 54-56; 24 : 1—Christ was crucified on the day before the Sabbath and rose on the day after the Sabbath. See Luke 24 : 21.

Matt. 28 : 1—See 2 Pet. 1 : 19; Joshua 6 : 15; Judges 19 : 26; Job 3 : 9; 7 : 4; Ps. 119 : 147. Dawn always means morning in the Bible.

WHAT WILL HAPPEN TO THE MILLIONS OF HEATHEN?

Gen. 18 : 23-25.

"That be far from thee to do after this manner, to slay the righteous with the wicked: and that the righteous should be as the wicked, that be far from thee: Shall not the Judge of all the earth do right?" Gen. 18 : 25.

"And they sung a new song, saying, Thou art worthy to take the book, and to open the seals thereof: for thou wast slain, and hast redeemed us to God by thy blood out of every kindred, and tongue, and people, and nation." Rev. 5 : 9.

"But in every nation he that feareth Him, and worketh righteousness, is accepted with Him." Acts 10 : 35.

CANNOT SAY HEATHEN KNOW NOTHING OF GOD AND CHRIST

Rom. 10 : 13-21—"But I say, Have they not heard, Yes verily, their sound went unto all the earth, and their words unto the ends of the world." Rom. 10 : 18.

How?—Ps. 19 : 1-6.

GOD GAVE SOME KNOWLEDGE OF HIMSELF IN HIS WORKS

"For the wrath of God is revealed from heaven against all ungodliness and unrighteousness of men, who hold the truth in unrighteousness,

"Because that which may be known of God is manifest in them; for God hath shewed it unto them. For the invisible things of Him from the creation of the world are clearly seen, being understood by the things that are made, even His eternal power and Godhead: so that they are without excuse." Rom. 1 : 18-20.

Acts 17 : 23-30—Some worship ignorantly.

2 Chron. 16 : 9—Lord looks for perfect hearts.

Ps. 112 : 4—Upright or honest in heart.

LIGHT FROM GOD TO ALL HEARTS

"For the grace of God that bringeth salvation hath appeared to all men." Titus 2 : 11.

"That was the true Light, which lighteth every man that cometh into the world." John 1 : 9.

Isa. 49 : 6.

Zech. 13 : 6—Never heard story of Salvation.

Rom. 2 : 10-15—Not complete knowledge but complete principle.

Heb. 2 : 1-3—Tested by light revealed.

HOW READEST THOU?

"It is one thing to read the Bible through,
Another thing to read to learn and do.
Some read it with design to learn to read,
But to the subject pay but little heed.
Some read it as their duty once a week,
But no instruction from the Bible seek;
While others read it with but little care,
With no regard to how they read, nor where.
Some read it as a history, to know
How people lived three thousand years ago.
Some read to bring themselves into repute,
By showing others how they can dispute;
While others read because their neighbors do,
To see how long 'twill take to read it through.
Some read it for the wonders that are there,—
How David killed a lion and a bear;
While others read it with uncommon care,
Hoping to find some contradictions there!
Some read as though it did not speak to them,
But to the people at Jerusalem.
One reads it as a book of mysteries,
And won't believe the very thing he sees.
One reads with father's specs upon his head,
And sees the thing just as his father said.

Some read to prove a pre-adopted creed,
Hence understand but little that they read;
For every passage in the book they bend,
To make it suit that all-important end!
Some people read, as I have often thought,
To teach the book instead of being taught,
And some there are who read it out of spite—
I fear there are but few who read it right.
So, many people in these latter days,
Have read the Bible in so many ways
That few can tell which system is the best,
For every party contradicts the rest!
But read it prayerfully, and you will see,
Although men contradict, God's words agree.

How Readest Thou?

For what the early Bible prophets wrote
We find that Christ and His apostles quote:
So trust no creed that trembles to recall
What has been penned by one and verified by all."

USE OF WORDS "ETERNAL AND EVERLASTING"

Dr. Adam Clarke places in our hands a key to the interpretation to the words "forever" and "forever and ever," which is adapted to every instance of their use. According to his rule they are to be taken to mean as long as a thing, considering the surrounding circumstances, can exist.

A - The Lord's Sabbath - Exodus 20: 8-11

ATTRIBUTES OF CHRISTIANITY

1. MEEKNESS
2. GENTLENESS
3. YIELDEDNESS negative active
4. TAMENESS
5. FOREBEARANCE
6. PATIENCE
7. MERCY

DANGERS

a) self-sufficiency
b) secret sin
c) cares of life

Alphabetical Index to List of Subjects

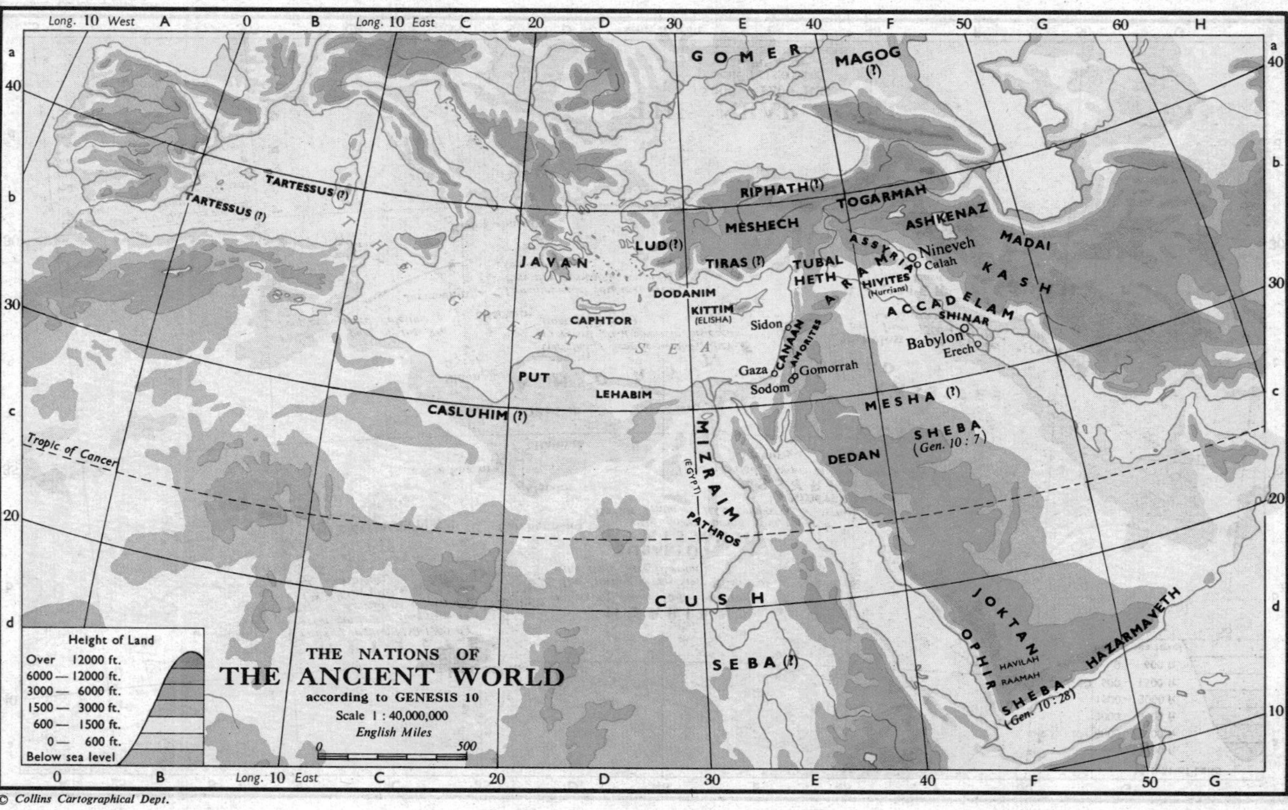
THE NATIONS OF
THE ANCIENT WORLD
according to GENESIS 10
Scale 1 : 40,000,000
English Miles
0
500
Height of Land
Over 12000 ft.
6000 — 12000 ft.
3000 — 6000 ft.
1500 — 3000 ft.
600 — 1500 ft.
0 — 600 ft.
Below sea level
Long. 10 West
Long. 10 East
Tropic of Cancer
THE GREAT SEA
GOMER
MAGOG (?)
TARTESSUS (?)
TARTESSUS (?)
RIPHATH (?)
TOGARMAH
ASHKENAZ
MADAI
MESHECH
LUD (?)
JAVAN
TIRAS (?)
TUBAL
HETH
ASSYRIA
ARAM
HIVITES
(Hurrians)
Nineveh
Calah
KASH
DODANIM
KITTIM
(ELISHA)
CAPHTOR
ACCAD
ELAM
SHINAR
Sidon
CANAAN
AMORITES
Babylon
Erech
Gaza
Gomorrah
Sodom
PUT
LEHABIM
CASLUHIM (?)
MESHA (?)
SHEBA
(Gen. 10 : 7)
DEDAN
MIZRAIM
(EGYPT)
PATHROS
CUSH
JOKTAN
OPHIR
HAVILAH
RAAMAH
SHEBA
(Gen. 10 : 28)
HAZARMAVETH
SEBA (?)

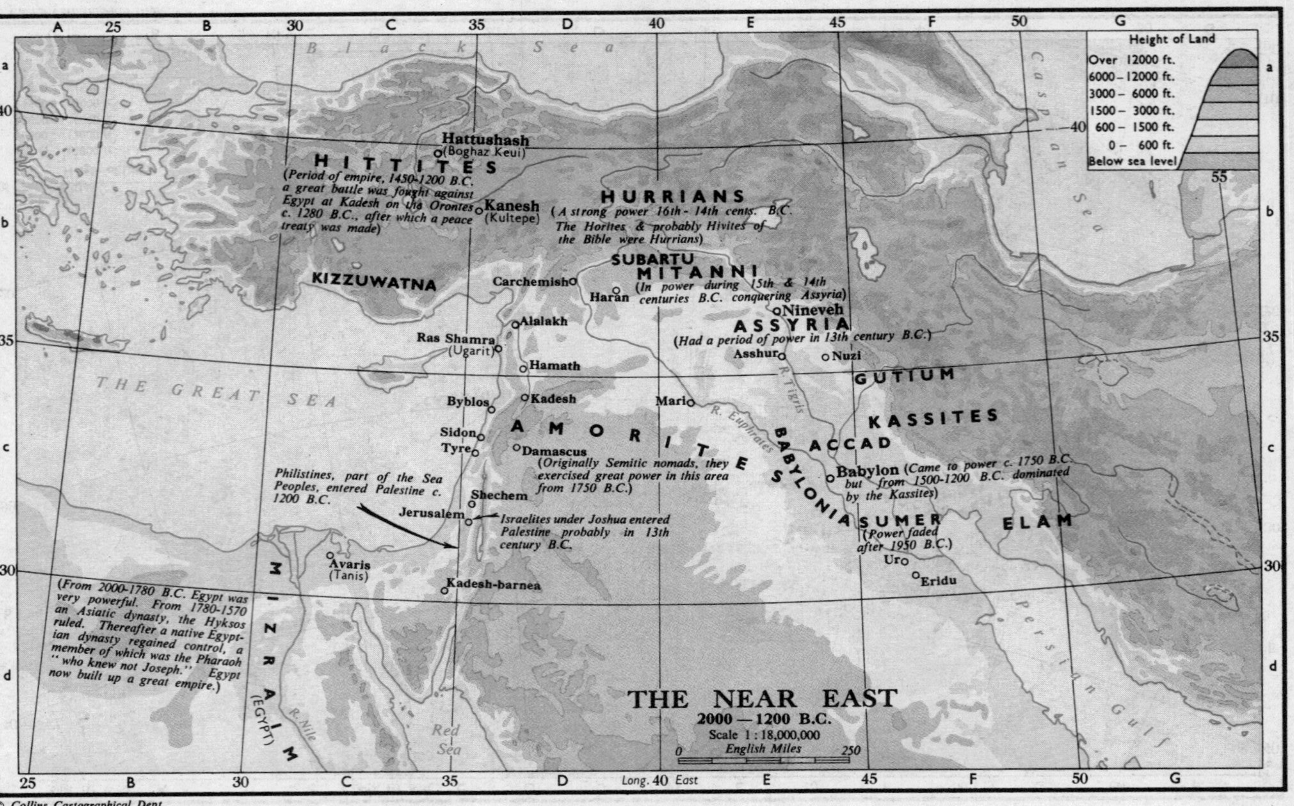
THE NEAR EAST
2000 — 1200 B.C.
Scale 1 : 18,000,000
English Miles
0
250
Height of Land
Over 12000 ft.
6000 – 12000 ft.
3000 – 6000 ft.
1500 – 3000 ft.
600 – 1500 ft.
0 – 600 ft.
Below sea level
Black Sea
Caspian Sea
THE GREAT SEA
Red Sea
Persian Gulf
R. Nile
R. Euphrates
R. Tigris
Long. 40 East
HITTITES
(Period of empire, 1450-1200 B.C. a great battle was fought against Egypt at Kadesh on the Orontes c. 1280 B.C., after which a peace treaty was made)
Hattushash
(Boghaz Keui)
Kanesh
(Kultepe)
HURRIANS
(A strong power 16th - 14th cents. B.C. The Horites & probably Hivites of the Bible were Hurrians)
SUBARTU
MITANNI
(In power during 15th & 14th centuries B.C. conquering Assyria)
KIZZUWATNA
Carchemish
Haran
Nineveh
ASSYRIA
(Had a period of power in 13th century B.C.)
Asshur
Nuzi
Alalakh
Ras Shamra
(Ugarit)
Hamath
Kadesh
Byblos
Sidon
Tyre
Damascus
Mari
AMORITES
(Originally Semitic nomads, they exercised great power in this area from 1750 B.C.)
GUTIUM
KASSITES
ACCAD
BABYLONIA
Babylon
(Came to power c. 1750 B.C. but from 1500-1200 B.C. dominated by the Kassites)
SUMER
(Power faded after 1950 B.C.)
ELAM
Ur
Eridu
Philistines, part of the Sea Peoples, entered Palestine c. 1200 B.C.
Shechem
Jerusalem
Israelites under Joshua entered Palestine probably in 13th century B.C.
Avaris
(Tanis)
Kadesh-barnea
MIZRAIM
(EGYPT)
(From 2000-1780 B.C. Egypt was very powerful. From 1780-1570 an Asiatic dynasty, the Hyksos ruled. Thereafter a native Egyptian dynasty regained control, a member of which was the Pharaoh "who knew not Joseph." Egypt now built up a great empire.)

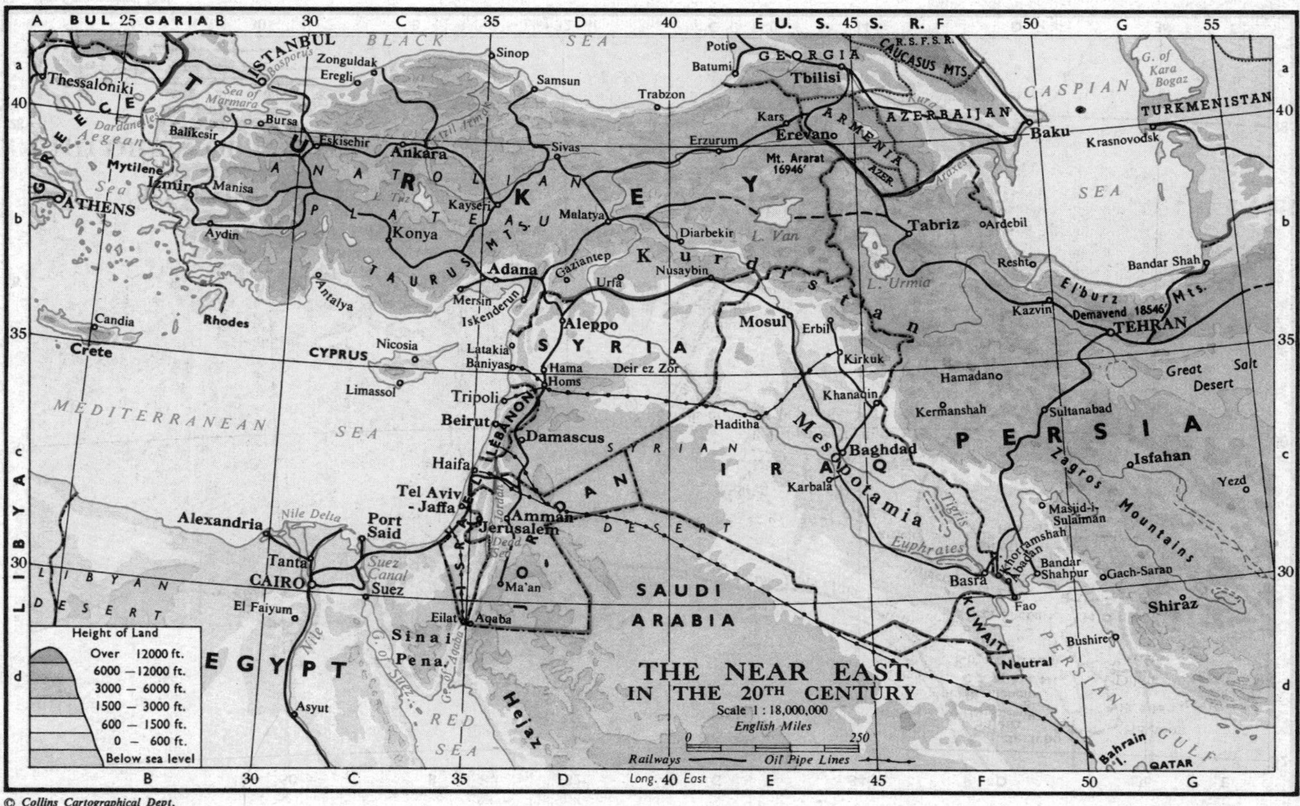
THE NEAR EAST
IN THE 20TH CENTURY
Scale 1 : 18,000,000
English Miles
0
250
Railways
Oil Pipe Lines
Long. 40 East
Height of Land
Over 12000 ft.
6000 – 12000 ft.
3000 – 6000 ft.
1500 – 3000 ft.
600 – 1500 ft.
0 – 600 ft.
Below sea level
U. S. S. R.
R. S. F. S. R.
TURKMENISTAN
GEORGIA
ARMENIA
AZERBAIJAN
AZER.
CAUCASUS MTS.
TURKEY
ANATOLIAN PLATEAU
TAURUS MTS.
Kurdistan
SYRIA
LEBANON
ISRAEL
JORDAN
IRAQ
PERSIA
KUWAIT
Neutral
SAUDI ARABIA
Hejaz
EGYPT
Sinai Pena.
LIBYA
LIBYAN DESERT
SYRIAN DESERT
Mesopotamia
GREECE
BULGARIA
CYPRUS
Crete
Rhodes
BLACK SEA
CASPIAN SEA
MEDITERRANEAN SEA
Aegean Sea
Sea of Marmara
RED SEA
PERSIAN GULF
G. of Suez
G. of Aqaba
G. of Kara Bogaz
Suez Canal
Nile Delta
Nile
Tigris
Euphrates
Kizil Irmak
Kura
Araxes
Jordan
L. Tuz
L. Van
L. Urmia
Dead Sea
El'burz Mts.
Zagros Mountains
Great Salt Desert
Demavend 18546'
Mt. Ararat 16946'
Dardanelles
Bosporus
ISTANBUL
Thessaloniki
ATHENS
Mytilene
Candia
Izmir
Balikesir
Manisa
Aydin
Bursa
Eskisehir
Zonguldak
Eregli
Ankara
Konya
Antalya
Kayseri
Sinop
Samsun
Sivas
Malatya
Trabzon
Erzurum
Batumi
Poti
Tbilisi
Kars
Erevano
Baku
Krasnovodsk
Diarbekir
Adana
Mersin
Iskenderun
Gaziantep
Urfa
Aleppo
Nusaybin
Deir ez Zor
Latakia
Baniyas
Hama
Homs
Tripoli
Beirut
Damascus
Haifa
Tel Aviv - Jaffa
Jerusalem
Amman
Ma'an
Aqaba
Eilat
Nicosia
Limassol
Port Said
Suez
Alexandria
Tanta
CAIRO
El Faiyum
Asyut
Mosul
Erbil
Kirkuk
Haditha
Baghdad
Khanaqin
Karbala
Basra
Fao
Tabriz
Ardebil
Resht
Kazvin
TEHRAN
Bandar Shah
Hamadano
Kermanshah
Sultanabad
Isfahan
Yezd
Shiraz
Masjid-i-Sulaiman
Abadan
Khorramshah
Bandar Shahpur
Gach-Saran
Bushire
Bahrain I.
QATAR

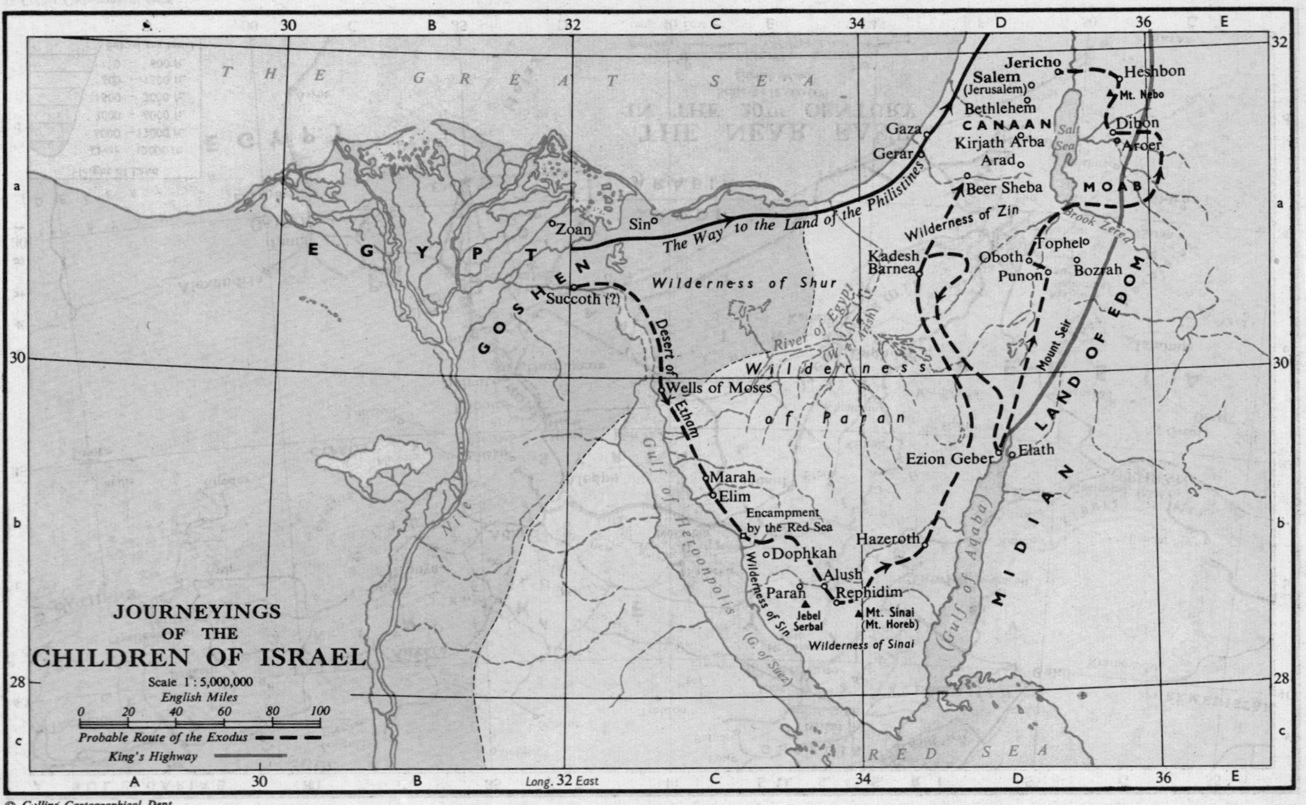

JOURNEYINGS
OF THE
CHILDREN OF ISRAEL
Scale 1 : 5,000,000
English Miles
0 20 40 60 80 100
Probable Route of the Exodus
King's Highway
© Collins Cartographical Dept.
THE GREAT SEA
EGYPT
GOSHEN
CANAAN
MOAB
LAND OF EDOM
MIDIAN
Jericho
Heshbon
Mt. Nebo
Salem (Jerusalem)
Bethlehem
Gaza
Gerar
Kirjath Arba
Arad
Beer Sheba
Salt Sea
Dibon
Aroer
Zoan
Sin
The Way to the Land of the Philistines
Wilderness of Zin
Brook Zered
Kadesh Barnea
Oboth
Tophel
Punon
Bozrah
Succoth (?)
Wilderness of Shur
River of Egypt
(W. el Arish)
Mount Seir
Desert of Etham
Wilderness of Paran
Wells of Moses
Ezion Geber
Elath
Marah
Elim
Nile
Gulf of Heroonpolis
Encampment by the Red Sea
Hazeroth
Dophkah
Alush
Paran
Rephidim
Wilderness of Sin
Jebel Serbal
Mt. Sinai (Mt. Horeb)
Wilderness of Sinai
(G. of Suez)
Gulf of Aqaba
RED SEA
Long. 32 East

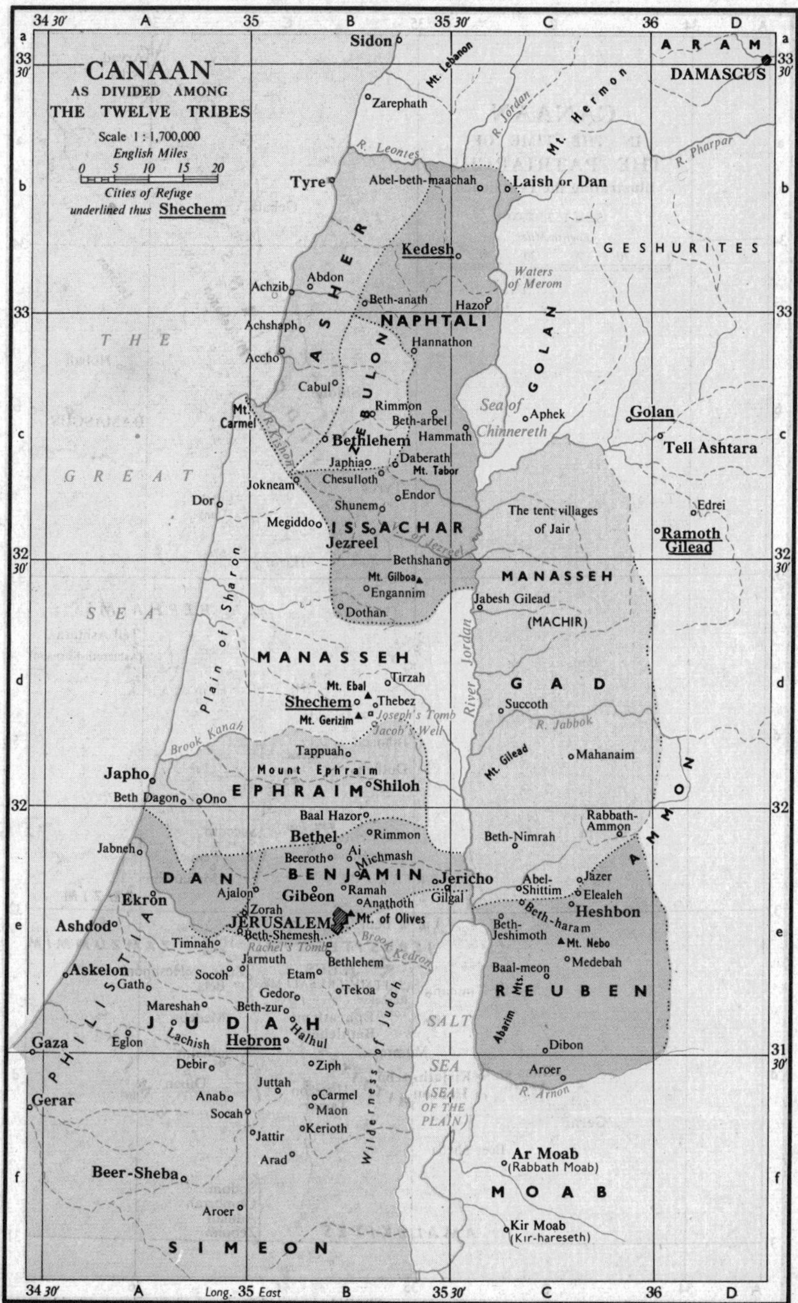

© Collins Cartographical Dept.

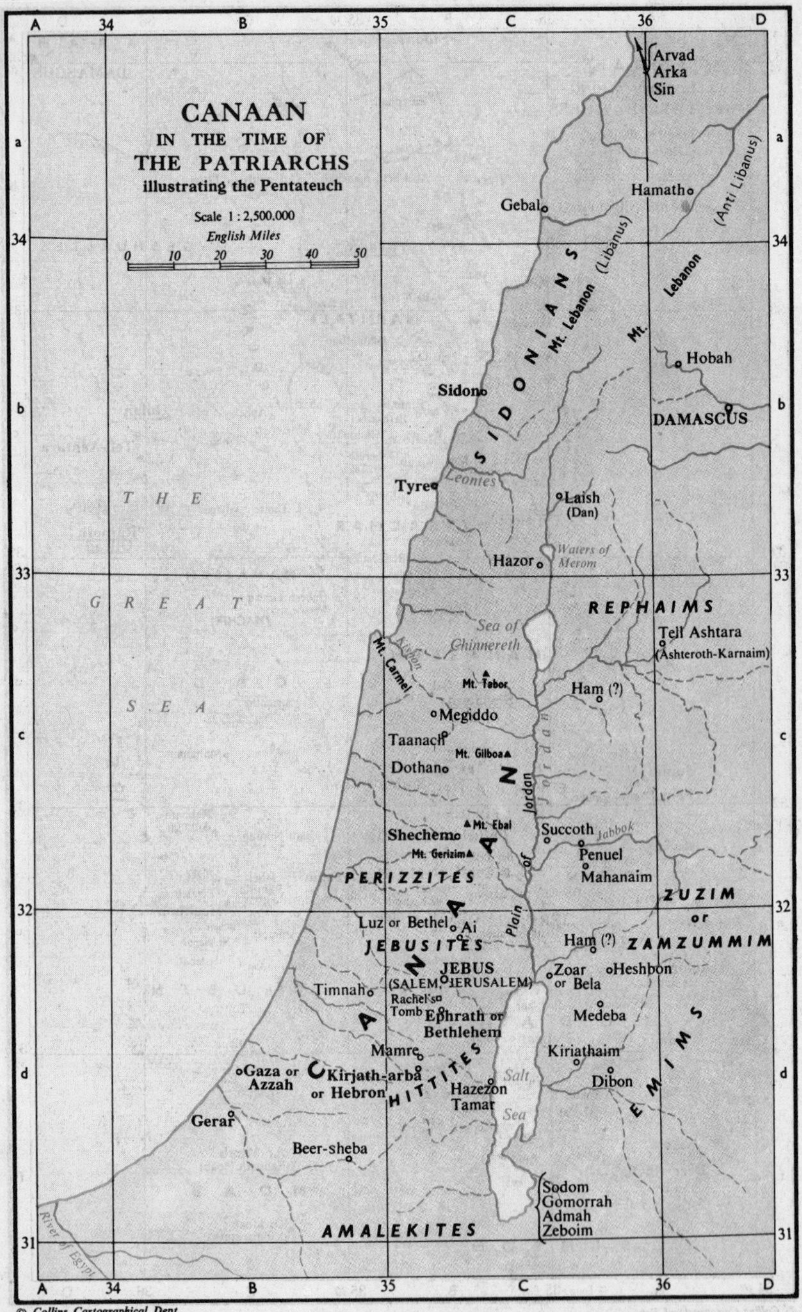

CANAAN
IN THE TIME OF
THE PATRIARCHS
illustrating the Pentateuch
Scale 1 : 2,500,000
English Miles
0 10 20 30 40 50
Arvad
Arka
Sin
Hamath
Gebal
(Anti Libanus)
Mt. Lebanon (Libanus)
Mt. Lebanon
SIDONIANS
Hobah
Sidon
DAMASCUS
Tyre
Leontes
Laish (Dan)
THE
Waters of Merom
Hazor
GREAT
SEA
REPHAIMS
Sea of Chinnereth
Tell Ashtara (Ashteroth-Karnaim)
Kishon
Mt. Carmel
Mt. Tabor
Ham (?)
Megiddo
Taanach
Mt. Gilboa
Dothan
Jordan
Plain of Jordan
Mt. Ebal
Succoth
Jabbok
Shechem
Mt. Gerizim
Penuel
Mahanaim
PERIZZITES
ZUZIM or ZAMZUMMIM
Luz or Bethel
Ai
Ham (?)
JEBUSITES
JEBUS (SALEM, JERUSALEM)
Zoar or Bela
Heshbon
Timnah
Rachel's Tomb
Ephrath or Bethlehem
Medeba
CANAAN
EMIMS
Mamre
Kiriathaim
Gaza or Azzah
Kirjath-arba or Hebron
HITTITES
Hazezon Tamar
Salt Sea
Dibon
Gerar
Beer-sheba
Sodom
Gomorrah
Admah
Zeboim
AMALEKITES
River of Egypt

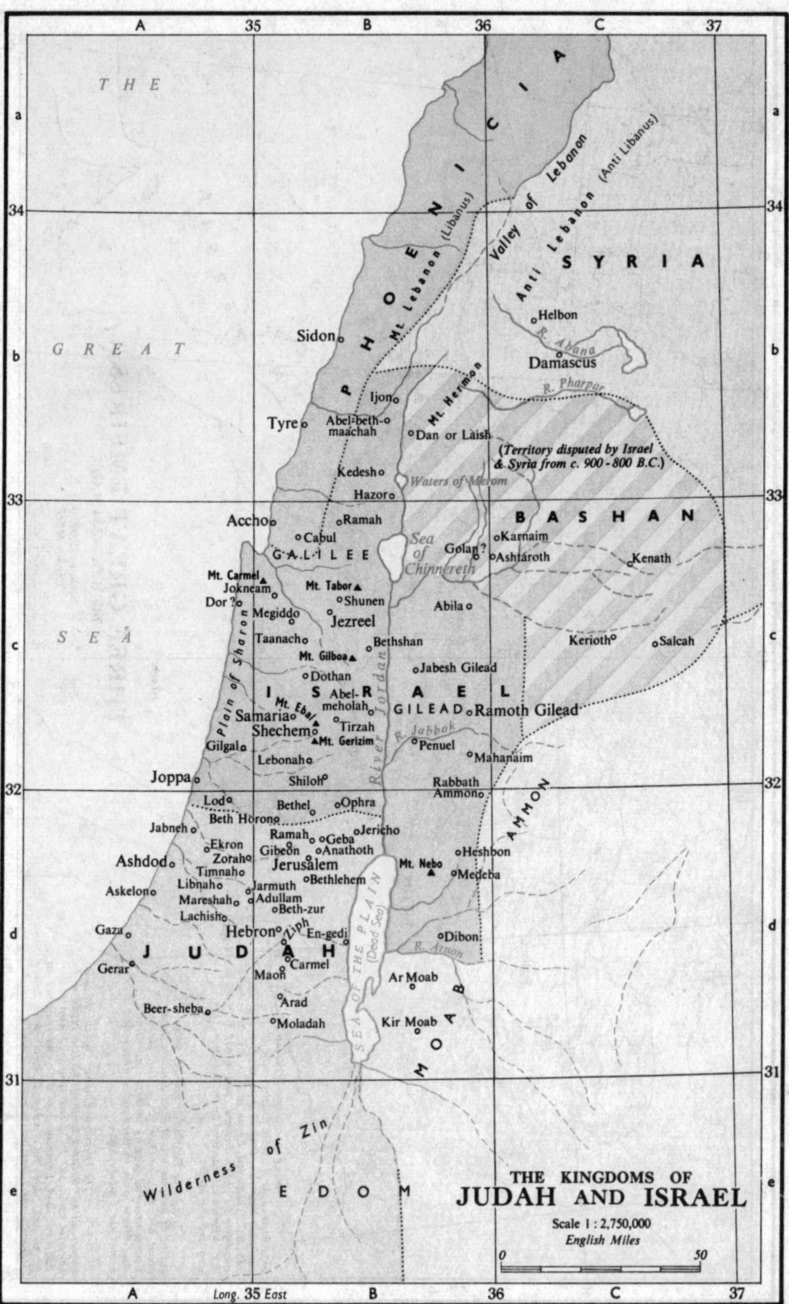
THE KINGDOMS OF
JUDAH AND ISRAEL
Scale 1 : 2,750,000
English Miles
0
50
Long. 35 East
THE GREAT SEA
PHOENICIA
SYRIA
BASHAN
GALILEE
ISRAEL
JUDAH
EDOM
MOAB
AMMON
GILEAD
Mt. Lebanon (Libanus)
Valley of Lebanon
Anti Lebanon (Anti Libanus)
Mt. Hermon
(Territory disputed by Israel & Syria from c. 900 - 800 B.C.)
Sidon
Tyre
Ijon
Abel-beth-maachah
Dan or Laish
Helbon
Damascus
R. Abana
R. Pharpar
Kedesh
Waters of Merom
Hazor
Accho
Ramah
Cabul
Sea of Chinnereth
Golan ?
Karnaim
Ashtaroth
Kenath
Mt. Carmel
Jokneam
Dor ?
Mt. Tabor
Shunen
Megiddo
Jezreel
Abila
Taanach
Bethshan
Mt. Gilboa
Kerioth
Salcah
Jabesh Gilead
Dothan
Plain of Sharon
Mt. Ebal
Abel-meholah
Samaria
Shechem
Tirzah
Ramoth Gilead
Mt. Gerizim
R. Jabbok
Penuel
Mahanaim
Gilgal
Lebonah
River Jordan
Joppa
Shiloh
Rabbath Ammon
Lod
Bethel
Ophra
Beth Horon
Jabneh
Ramah
Geba
Jericho
Ekron
Gibeon
Anathoth
Ashdod
Zorah
Jerusalem
Mt. Nebo
Heshbon
Medeba
Timnah
Bethlehem
Askelon
Libnah
Jarmuth
Mareshah
Adullam
Beth-zur
Lachish
SEA OF THE PLAIN (Dead Sea)
Gaza
Hebron
Ziph
En-gedi
Dibon
R. Arnon
Gerar
Carmel
Maon
Ar Moab
Arad
Beer-sheba
Kir Moab
Moladah
Wilderness of Zin

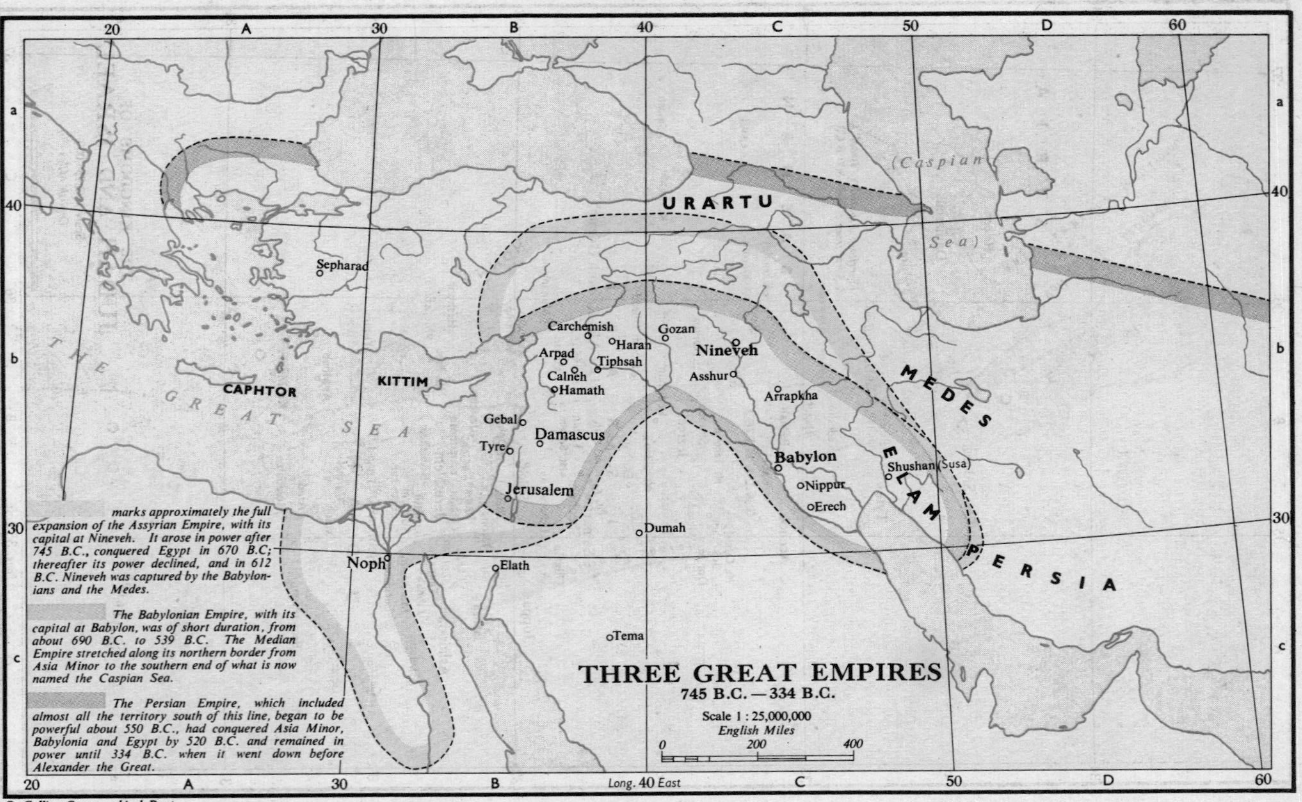

THREE GREAT EMPIRES
745 B.C. — 334 B.C.
Scale 1 : 25,000,000
English Miles
0
200
400
marks approximately the full expansion of the Assyrian Empire, with its capital at Nineveh. It arose in power after 745 B.C., conquered Egypt in 670 B.C; thereafter its power declined, and in 612 B.C. Nineveh was captured by the Babylonians and the Medes.
The Babylonian Empire, with its capital at Babylon, was of short duration, from about 690 B.C. to 539 B.C. The Median Empire stretched along its northern border from Asia Minor to the southern end of what is now named the Caspian Sea.
The Persian Empire, which included almost all the territory south of this line, began to be powerful about 550 B.C., had conquered Asia Minor, Babylonia and Egypt by 520 B.C. and remained in power until 334 B.C. when it went down before Alexander the Great.
URARTU
MEDES
ELAM
PERSIA
(Caspian Sea)
THE GREAT SEA
CAPHTOR
KITTIM
Sepharad
Carchemish
Haran
Gozan
Nineveh
Asshur
Arrapkha
Arpad
Tiphsah
Calneh
Hamath
Gebal
Damascus
Tyre
Jerusalem
Babylon
Shushan (Susa)
Nippur
Erech
Dumah
Noph
Elath
Tema
Long. 40 East
20
A
30
B
40
C
50
D
60
a
b
c

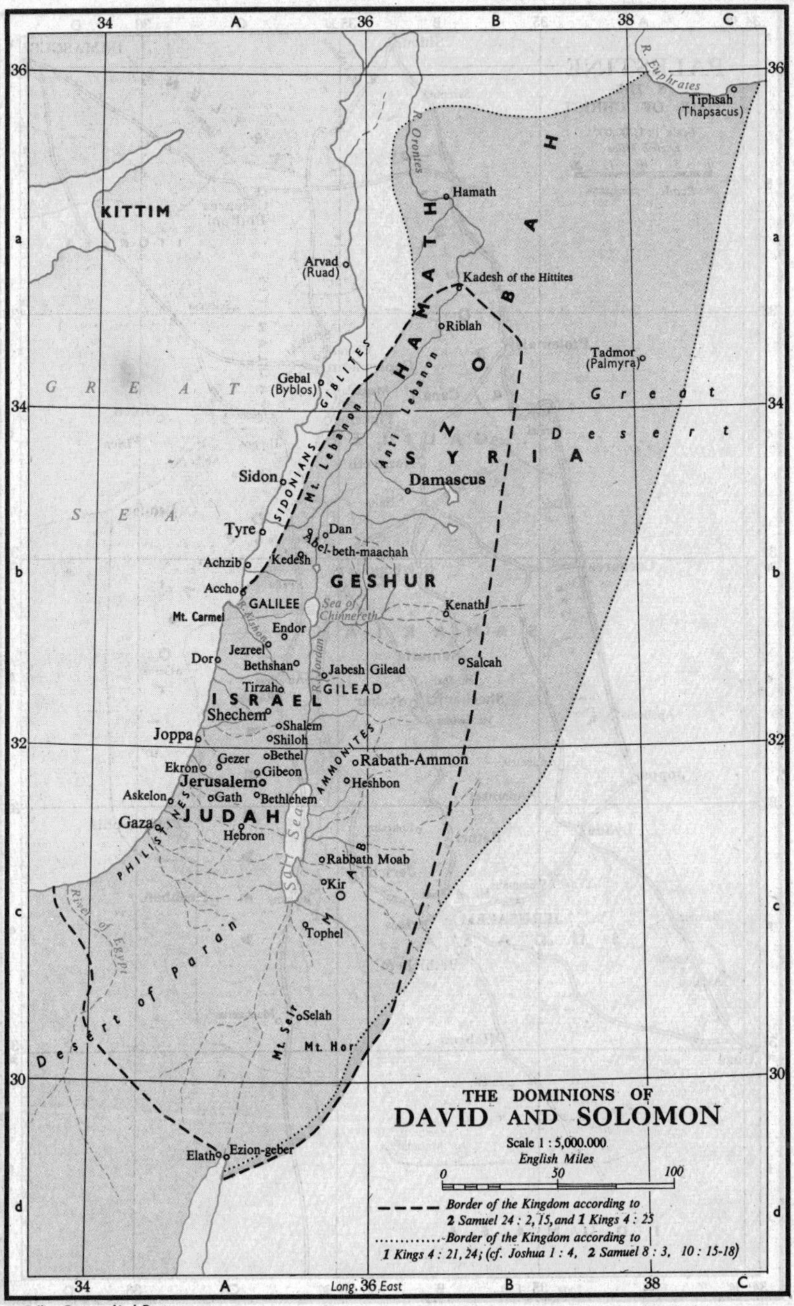
THE DOMINIONS OF
DAVID AND SOLOMON
Scale 1 : 5,000.000
English Miles
0 50 100
Border of the Kingdom according to 2 Samuel 24 : 2, 15, and 1 Kings 4 : 25
Border of the Kingdom according to 1 Kings 4 : 21, 24; (cf. Joshua 1 : 4, 2 Samuel 8 : 3, 10 : 15-18)
KITTIM
GREAT SEA
HAMATH
ZOBAH
SYRIA
Great Desert
GESHUR
GALILEE
ISRAEL
GILEAD
JUDAH
MOAB
AMMONITES
PHILISTINES
SIDONIANS
GIBLITES
Desert of Paran
R. Euphrates
Tiphsah
(Thapsacus)
R. Orontes
Hamath
Arvad
(Ruad)
Kadesh of the Hittites
Riblah
Tadmor
(Palmyra)
Gebal
(Byblos)
Mt. Lebanon
Anti Lebanon
Sidon
Damascus
Tyre
Dan
Abel-beth-maachah
Achzib
Kedesh
Accho
Kenath
Mt. Carmel
R. Kishon
Sea of Chinnereth
Endor
Jezreel
Dor
Bethshan
R. Jordan
Jabesh Gilead
Salcah
Tirzah
Shechem
Shalem
Joppa
Shiloh
Gezer
Bethel
Ekron
Gibeon
Rabath-Ammon
Jerusalem
Heshbon
Askelon
Gath
Bethlehem
Gaza
Hebron
Salt Sea
Rabbath Moab
Kir
Tophel
River of Egypt
Selah
Mt. Seir
Mt. Hor
Elath
Ezion-geber
Long. 36 East
34
36
38
A
B
C
a
b
c
d
30
32

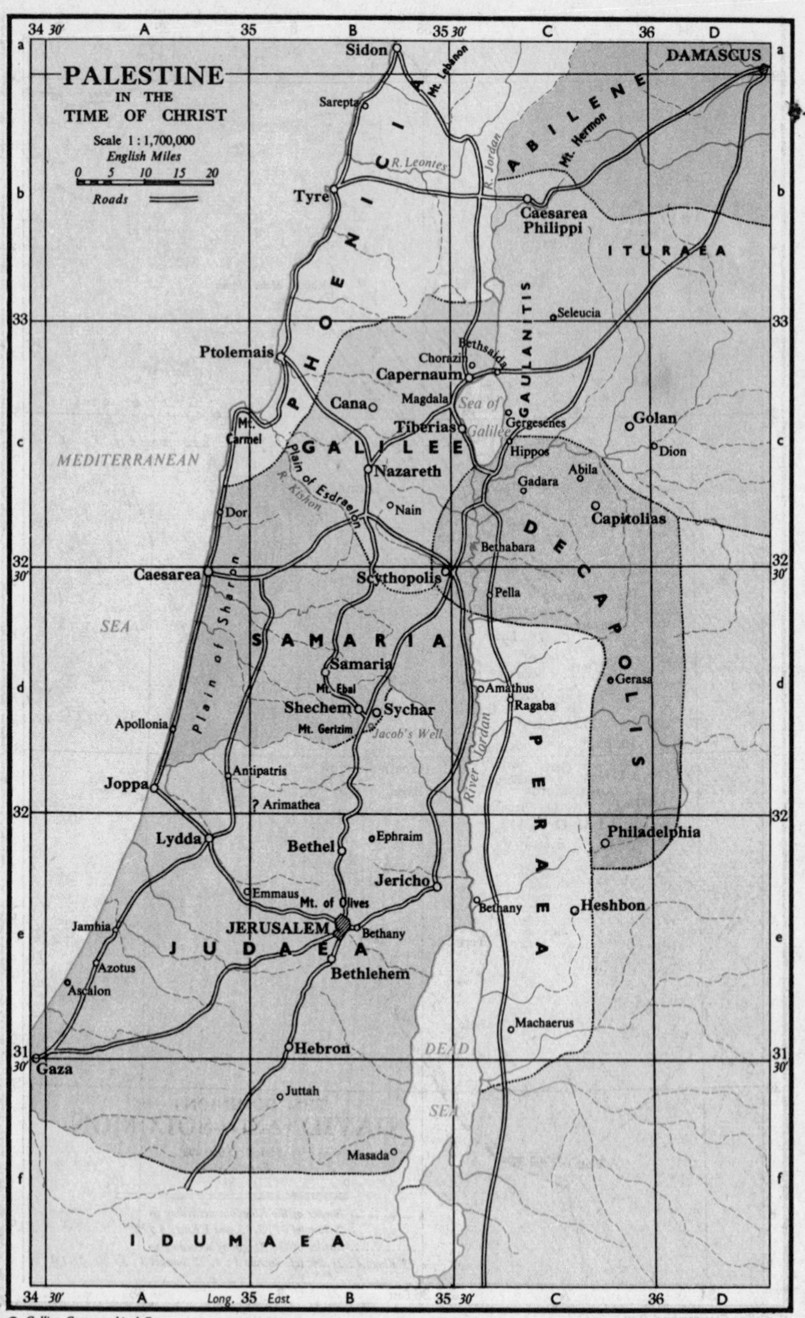
PALESTINE
IN THE
TIME OF CHRIST
Scale 1 : 1,700,000
English Miles
0 5 10 15 20
Roads
MEDITERRANEAN
SEA
Sidon
Sarepta
Mt. Lebanon
PHOENICIA
R. Leontes
Tyre
R. Jordan
ABILENE
Mt. Hermon
DAMASCUS
Caesarea Philippi
ITURAEA
Seleucia
GAULANITIS
Ptolemais
Chorazin
Bethsaida
Capernaum
Cana
Magdala
Sea of Galilee
Gergesenes
Mt. Carmel
Tiberias
GALILEE
Plain of Esdraelon
R. Kishon
Hippos
Golan
Dion
Nazareth
Abila
Gadara
Dor
Nain
Capitolias
DECAPOLIS
Bethabara
Caesarea
Scythopolis
Pella
Plain of Sharon
SAMARIA
Samaria
Mt. Ebal
Gerasa
Amathus
Shechem
Sychar
Ragaba
Mt. Gerizim
Jacob's Well
Apollonia
River Jordan
PERAEA
Antipatris
Joppa
? Arimathea
Lydda
Bethel
Ephraim
Philadelphia
Jericho
Emmaus
Mt. of Olives
Bethany
Heshbon
Jamnia
JERUSALEM
Bethany
JUDAEA
Azotus
Bethlehem
Ascalon
Machaerus
Hebron
DEAD SEA
Gaza
Juttah
Masada
IDUMAEA
34 30′
A
35
B
35 30′
C
36
D
a
b
c
d
e
f
33
32 30′
32
31 30′
Long. 35 East

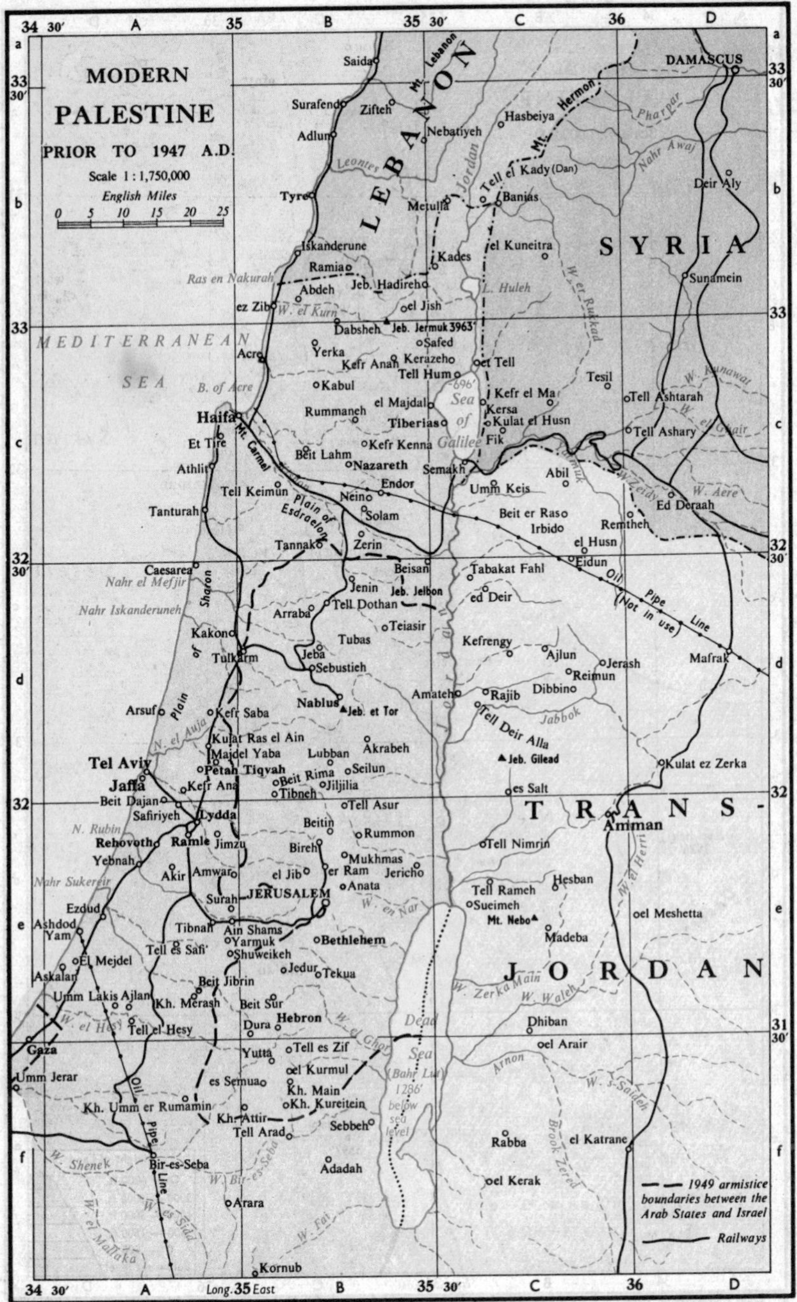
MODERN
PALESTINE
PRIOR TO 1947 A.D.
Scale 1 : 1,750,000
English Miles
0 5 10 15 20 25
34 30′
A
35
B
35 30′
C
36
D
a
b
c
d
e
f
33
30′
33
32
30′
32
31
30′
Long. 35 East
LEBANON
SYRIA
TRANS-JORDAN
MEDITERRANEAN SEA
Mt. Lebanon
Mt. Hermon
DAMASCUS
Saida
Surafend
Zifteh
Adlun
Nebatiyeh
Hasbeiya
Pharpar
Nahr Awaj
Leontes
Jordan
Tell el Kady (Dan)
Banias
Deir Aly
Tyre
Metulla
Iskanderune
Kades
el Kuneitra
Ramia
Sunamein
Ras en Nakurah
Jeb. Hadireh
L. Huleh
W. er Rukkad
Abdeh
ez Zib
W. el Kurn
el Jish
Dabsheh
Jeb. Jermuk 3963′
Safed
Yerka
Acre
Kefr Anan
Kerazeh
et Tell
Tell Hum
Tesil
Kabul
B. of Acre
696′
Sea of Galilee
Kefr el Ma
Tell Ashtarah
el Majdal
Kersa
Rummaneh
Tiberias
Kulat el Husn
Haifa
Mt. Carmel
Tell Ashary
Et Tire
Kefr Kenna
Fik
Beit Lahm
Nazareth
Semakh
Athlit
Abil
Endor
Umm Keis
Tell Keimun
Neino
W. Zeidy
W. Aere
Ed Deraah
Plain of Esdraelon
Tanturah
Solam
Beit er Raso
Irbid
Remtheh
Tannak
Zerin
el Husn
Eidun
Caesarea
Beisan
Tabakat Fahl
Nahr el Mefjir
Jenin
Jeb. Jelbon
ed Deir
Oil Pipe Line (Not in use)
Nahr Iskanderuneh
Tell Dothan
Arraba
Teiasir
Kakon
Tubas
Kefrengy
Ajlun
Jerash
Mafrak
Tulkarm
Jeba
Sebustieh
Reimun
Plain of Sharon
Dibbino
Amateh
Rajib
Nablus
Jeb. et Tor
Arsuf
Kefr Saba
Tell Deir Alla
Jabbok
N. el Auja
Kulat Ras el Ain
Akrabeh
Majdel Yaba
Lubban
Jeb. Gilead
Kulat ez Zerka
Tel Aviv
Petah Tiqvah
Seilun
Jaffa
Kefr Ana
Beit Rima
Jiljilia
Tibneh
es Salt
Beit Dajan
Tell Asur
Safiriyeh
Lydda
Beitin
Amman
N. Rubin
Rummon
Rehovoth
Ramle
Jimzu
Bireh
Tell Nimrin
Yebnah
Mukhmas
Akir
Amwas
el Jib
er Ram
Jericho
Nahr Sukereir
Anata
Hesban
Surah
JERUSALEM
Tell Rameh
Ezdud
Suelmeh
W. en Nar
el Meshetta
Ashdod Yam
Tibnah
Ain Shams
Mt. Nebo
Yarmuk
Bethlehem
Madeba
Tell es Safi
Shuweikeh
El Mejdel
Jedur
Tekua
Askalan
Beit Jibrin
W. Zerka Main
W. Waleh
Umm Lakis
Ajlan
Kh. Merash
Beit Sur
Dead Sea
W. el Hesy
Dura
Hebron
Dhiban
Tell el Hesy
W. el Ghor
Gaza
Yutta
Tell es Zif
el Arair
el Kurmul
Arnon
Umm Jerar
es Semua
Kh. Main
(Bahr Lut)
1286′ below sea level
Kh. Umm er Rumamin
Kh. Kureitein
Kh. Attir
Tell Arad
Sebbeh
Rabba
el Katrane
Brook Zered
Oil Pipe Line
Bir-es-Seba
W. Shenek
Adadah
W. Bir-es-Seba
el Kerak
Arara
W. es Sidd
W. el Mallaka
W. Fai
Kornub
1949 armistice boundaries between the Arab States and Israel
Railways

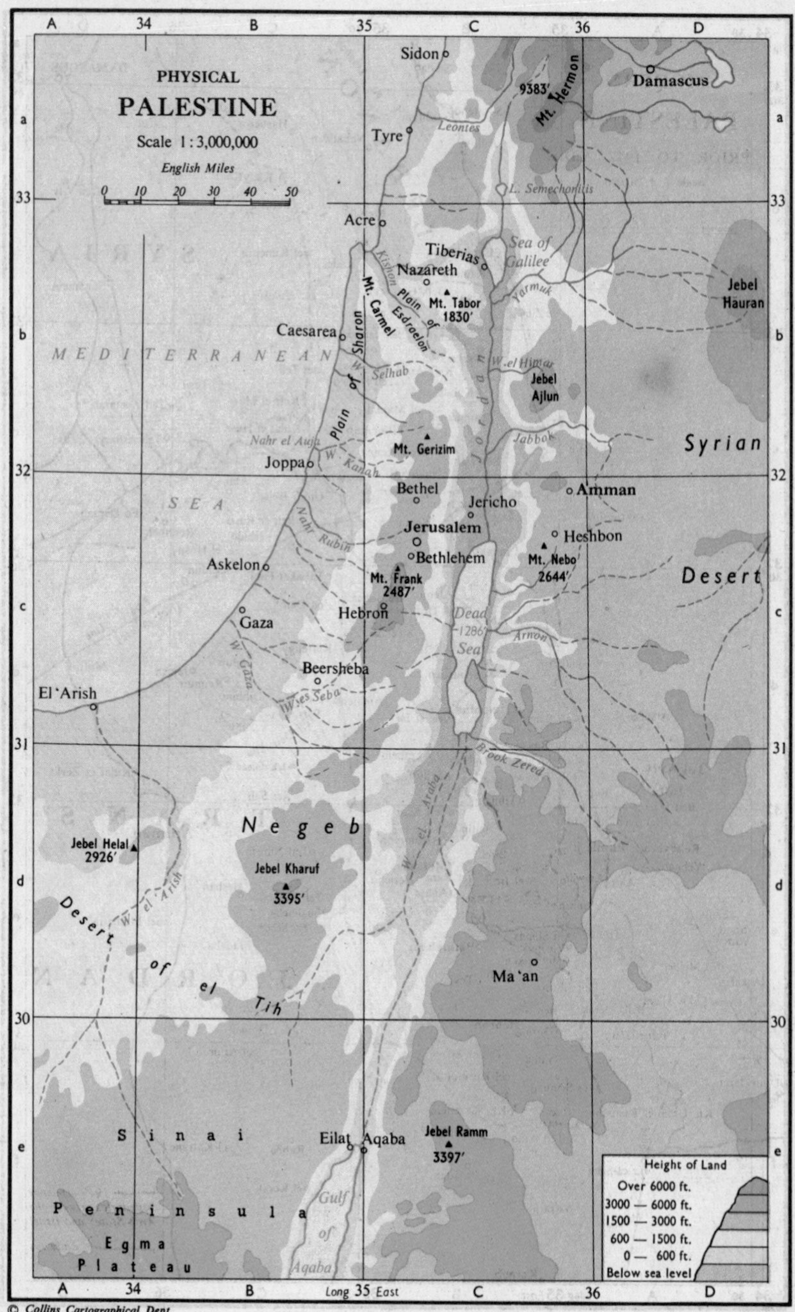
PHYSICAL
PALESTINE
Scale 1 : 3,000,000
English Miles
0 10 20 30 40 50
A
34
B
35
C
36
D
a
b
c
d
e
33
32
31
30
Sidon
Damascus
9383′
Mt. Hermon
Tyre
Leontes
L. Semechonitis
Acre
Tiberias
Sea of Galilee
Nazareth
Kishon
Mt. Carmel
Plain of Esdraelon
Mt. Tabor 1830′
Yarmuk
Jebel Hauran
Caesarea
Plain of Sharon
MEDITERRANEAN
SEA
W. Selhab
W. el Himar
Jebel Ajlun
Jordan
Nahr el Auja
Mt. Gerizim
Jabbok
Syrian
Desert
Joppa
W. Kanah
Bethel
Jericho
Amman
Jerusalem
Heshbon
Nahr Rubin
Bethlehem
Mt. Nebo 2644′
Askelon
Mt. Frank 2487′
Hebron
Dead Sea
-1286′
Gaza
Arnon
W. Gaza
Beersheba
W. es Seba
El 'Arish
Brook Zered
W. el Araba
Negeb
Jebel Helal 2926′
Jebel Kharuf 3395′
W. el 'Arish
Desert of el Tih
Ma 'an
Sinai Peninsula
Eilat
Aqaba
Jebel Ramm 3397′
Gulf of Aqaba
Egma Plateau
Long 35 East
Height of Land
Over 6000 ft.
3000 — 6000 ft.
1500 — 3000 ft.
600 — 1500 ft.
0 — 600 ft.
Below sea level

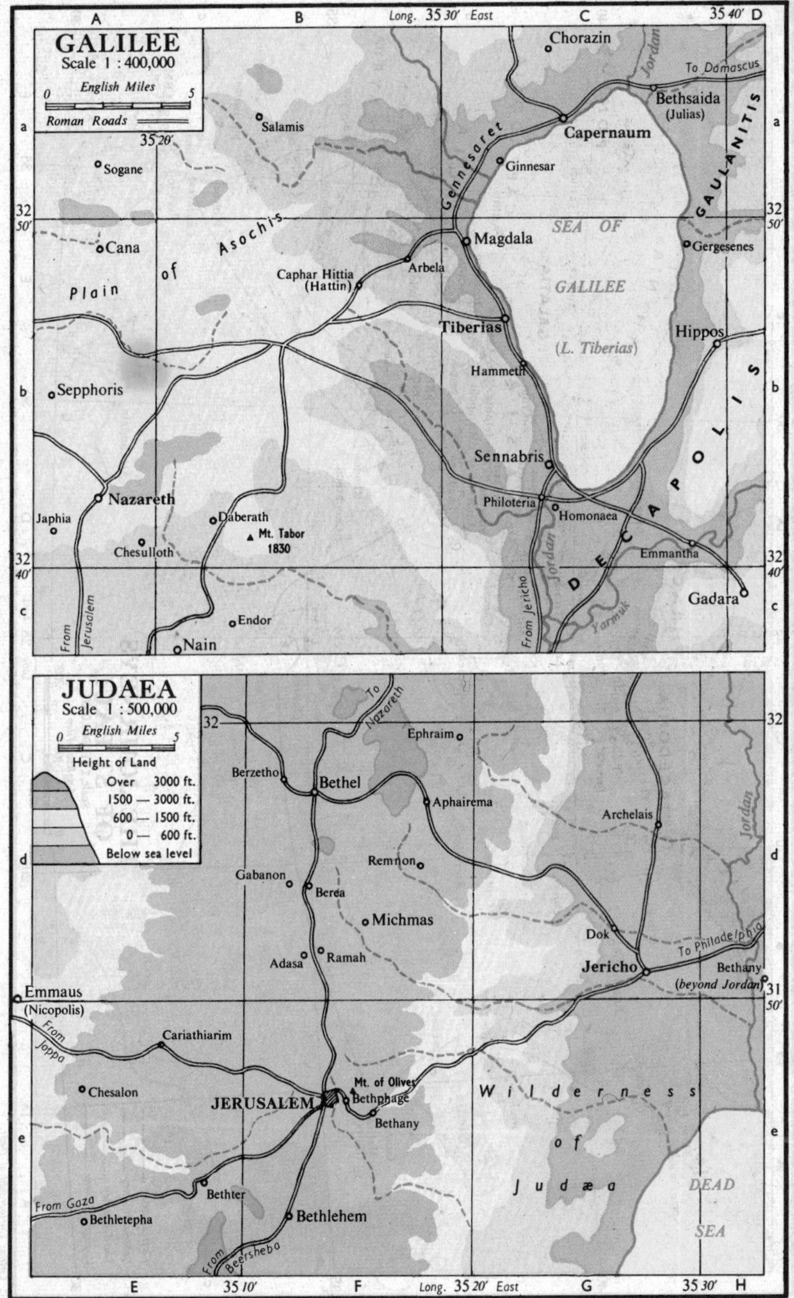
GALILEE
Scale 1 : 400,000
English Miles
0
5
Roman Roads
A
B
C
D
Long. 35 30′ East
35 40′
35 20′
32 50′
32 40′
a
b
c
Chorazin
Jordan
To Damascus
Bethsaida
(Julias)
Capernaum
GAULANITIS
Salamis
Sogane
Gennesaret
Ginnesar
SEA OF
GALILEE
(L. Tiberias)
Magdala
Gergesenes
Cana
Asochis
of
Plain
Arbela
Caphar Hittia
(Hattin)
Tiberias
Hippos
Hammeth
Sepphoris
DECAPOLIS
Sennabris
Nazareth
Philoteria
Homonaea
Japhia
Daberath
Mt. Tabor
1830
Chesulloth
Emmantha
Gadara
Endor
Nain
From Jerusalem
From Jericho
Yarmuk
JUDAEA
Scale 1 : 500,000
English Miles
0
5
Height of Land
Over 3000 ft.
1500 — 3000 ft.
600 — 1500 ft.
0 — 600 ft.
Below sea level
E
F
G
H
35 10′
Long. 35 20′ East
35 30′
32
31 50′
d
e
To Nazareth
Ephraim
Berzetho
Bethel
Aphairema
Archelais
Jordan
Remmon
Gabanon
Berea
Michmas
Dok
To Philadelphia
Adasa
Ramah
Jericho
Bethany
(beyond Jordan)
Emmaus
(Nicopolis)
From Joppa
Cariathiarim
Chesalon
Mt. of Olives
JERUSALEM
Bethphage
Bethany
Wilderness
of
Judæa
DEAD
SEA
Bethter
From Gaza
Bethletepha
Bethlehem
From Beersheba

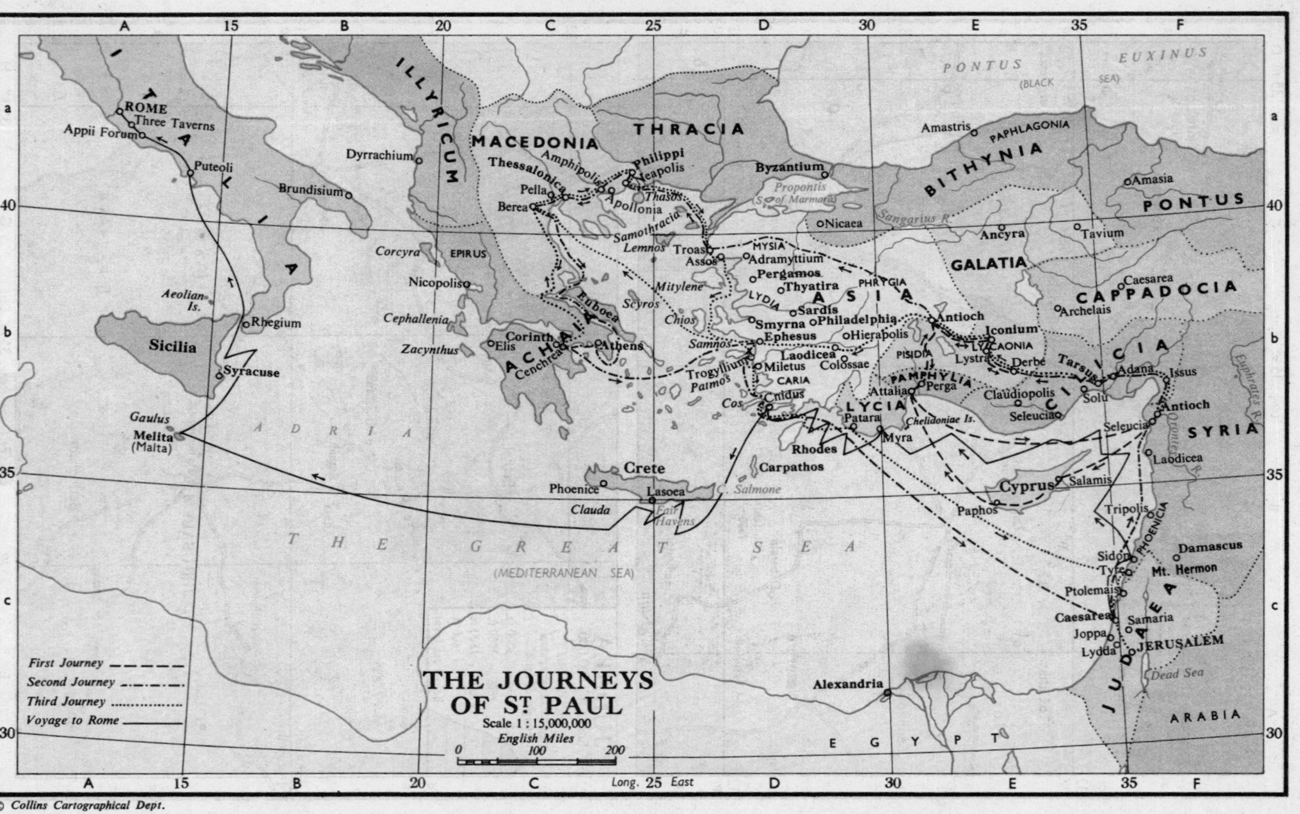

THE JOURNEYS OF ST PAUL
Scale 1 : 15,000,000
English Miles
0 100 200
First Journey
Second Journey
Third Journey
Voyage to Rome
Long. 25 East
ITALIA
ILLYRICUM
MACEDONIA
THRACIA
BITHYNIA
PAPHLAGONIA
PONTUS
GALATIA
CAPPADOCIA
ASIA
MYSIA
LYDIA
PHRYGIA
CARIA
PISIDIA
LYCAONIA
PAMPHYLIA
LYCIA
CILICIA
SYRIA
PHOENICIA
JUDAEA
ARABIA
EGYPT
ACHAIA
EPIRUS
PONTUS EUXINUS
(BLACK SEA)
THE GREAT SEA
(MEDITERRANEAN SEA)
ADRIA
ROME
Three Taverns
Appii Forum
Puteoli
Brundisium
Rhegium
Syracuse
Sicilia
Aeolian Is.
Gaulus
Melita
(Malta)
Dyrrachium
Corcyra
Nicopolis
Cephallenia
Zacynthus
Thessalonica
Amphipolis
Pella
Berea
Apollonia
Philippi
Neapolis
Thasos
Samothracia
Lemnos
Byzantium
Propontis
(S. of Marmara)
Nicaea
Sangarius R.
Troas
Assos
Adramyttium
Pergamos
Thyatira
Mitylene
Scyros
Chios
Sardis
Smyrna
Philadelphia
Ephesus
Hierapolis
Samos
Laodicea
Colossae
Miletus
Trogyllium
Patmos
Cos
Cnidus
Euboea
Athens
Corinth
Elis
Cenchreae
Crete
Phoenice
Lasoea
Clauda
Fair Havens
C. Salmone
Rhodes
Carpathos
Patara
Myra
Chelidoniae Is.
Attalia
Perga
Antioch
Iconium
Lystra
Derbe
Claudiopolis
Seleucia
Tarsus
Solu
Adana
Issus
Antioch
Orontes R.
Euphrates R.
Seleucia
Laodicea
Cyprus
Salamis
Paphos
Tripolis
Sidon
Tyre
Ptolemais
Caesarea
Samaria
Joppa
Lydda
JERUSALEM
Dead Sea
Damascus
Mt. Hermon
Alexandria
Amastris
Amasia
Ancyra
Tavium
Caesarea
Archelais
© Collins Cartographical Dept.

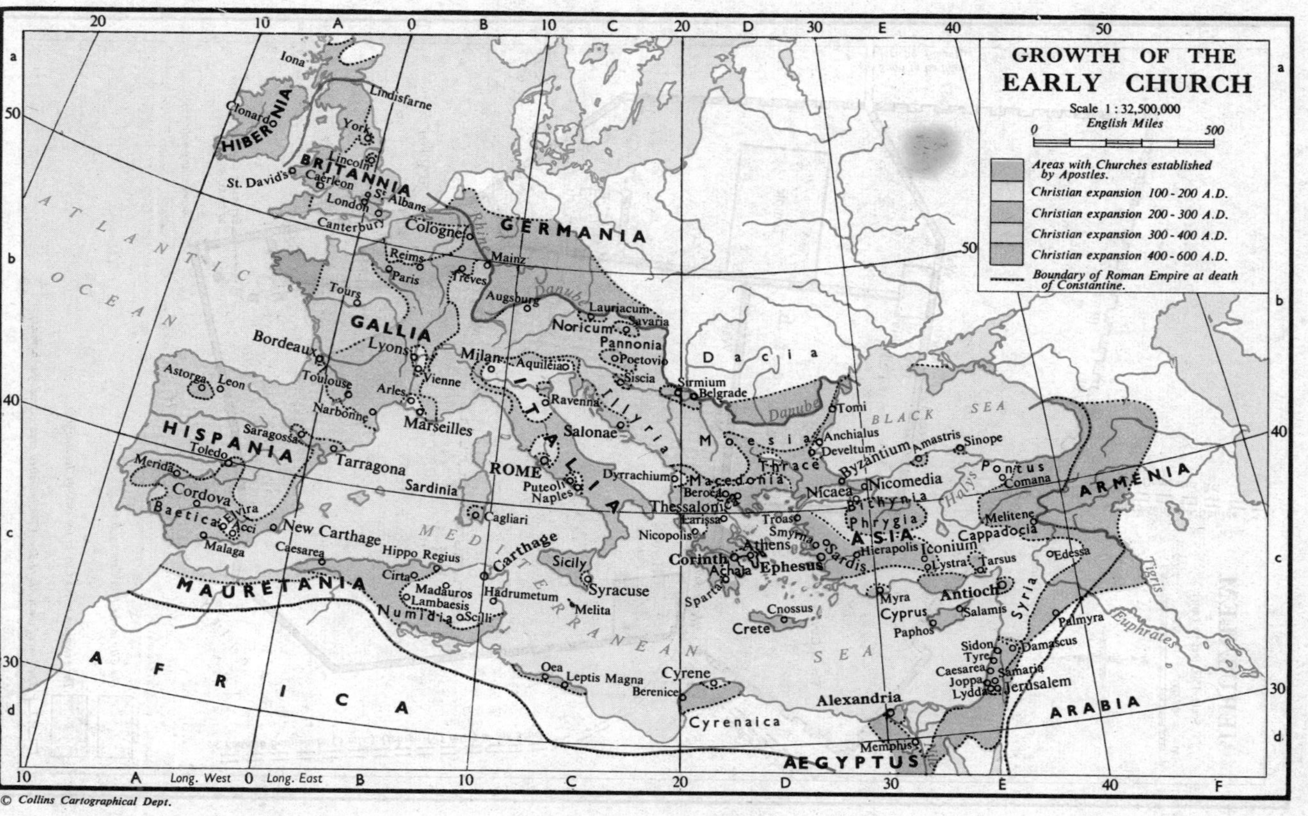
GROWTH OF THE EARLY CHURCH
Scale 1 : 32,500,000
English Miles
0
500
Areas with Churches established by Apostles.
Christian expansion 100 - 200 A.D.
Christian expansion 200 - 300 A.D.
Christian expansion 300 - 400 A.D.
Christian expansion 400 - 600 A.D.
Boundary of Roman Empire at death of Constantine.
ATLANTIC OCEAN
HIBERNIA
Clonard
Iona
Lindisfarne
York
Lincoln
BRITANNIA
St. David's
Caerleon
St Albans
London
Canterbury
GERMANIA
Cologne
Rhine
Mainz
Reims
Paris
Treves
Tours
GALLIA
Augsburg
Danube
Lauriacum
Savaria
Noricum
Pannonia
Poetovio
Siscia
Bordeaux
Lyons
Milan
Aquileia
Toulouse
Vienne
Arles
Narbonne
Marseilles
Astorga
Leon
HISPANIA
Saragossa
Toledo
Tarragona
Merida
Cordova
Baetica
Elvira
Acci
Malaga
New Carthage
Caesarea
Sardinia
Cagliari
ROME
Puteoli
Naples
ITALIA
Ravenna
Illyria
Salonae
Dyrrachium
MEDITERRANEAN SEA
Hippo Regius
Carthage
Sicily
Syracuse
Cirta
Madauros
Lambaesis
Numidia
Scilli
Hadrumetum
Melita
MAURETANIA
AFRICA
Oea
Leptis Magna
Cyrene
Berenice
Cyrenaica
Dacia
Sirmium
Belgrade
Danube
Tomi
BLACK SEA
Moesia
Anchialus
Develtum
Thrace
Byzantium
Amastris
Sinope
Macedonia
Beroea
Thessalonica
Nicaea
Nicomedia
Bithynia
Pontus
Comana
Halys
ARMENIA
Larissa
Nicopolis
Troas
Smyrna
Phrygia
ASIA
Athens
Corinth
Achaia
Sparta
Ephesus
Sardis
Hierapolis
Iconium
Lystra
Tarsus
Cappadocia
Melitene
Edessa
Tigris
Euphrates
Cnossus
Crete
Myra
Cyprus
Paphos
Antioch
Salamis
Syria
Palmyra
Damascus
Sidon
Tyre
Caesarea
Samaria
Joppa
Lydda
Jerusalem
Alexandria
Memphis
AEGYPTUS
ARABIA
Long. West
Long. East
© Collins Cartographical Dept.

MARCIA CORRIGAN

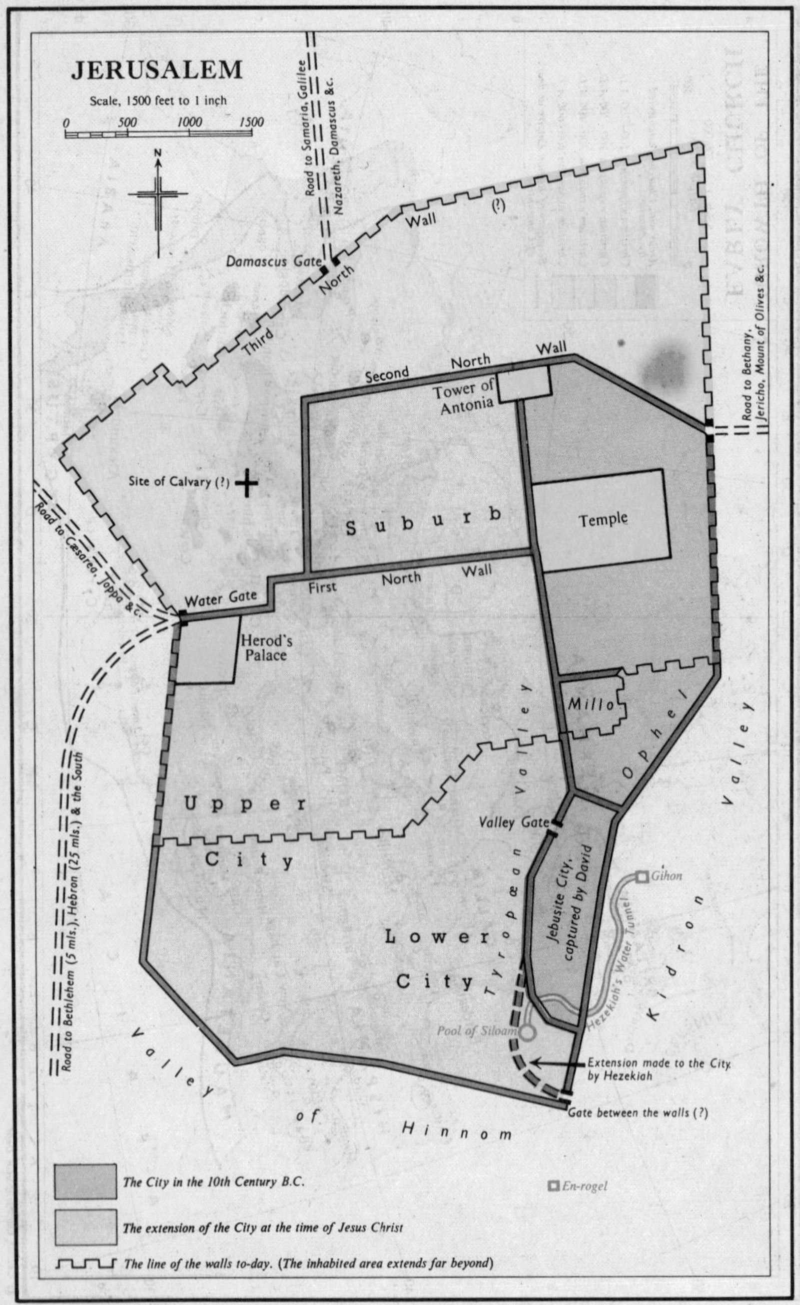

JERUSALEM
Scale, 1500 feet to 1 inch
0 500 1000 1500
N
Road to Samaria, Galilee
Nazareth, Damascus &c.
Damascus Gate
Third North Wall (?)
Second North Wall
Tower of Antonia
Road to Bethany, Jericho, Mount of Olives &c.
Site of Calvary (?)
Suburb
Temple
Road to Cæsarea, Joppa &c.
Water Gate
First North Wall
Herod's Palace
Millo
Ophel
Upper City
Valley Gate
Tyropœan Valley
Jebusite City, captured by David
Gihon
Hezekiah's Water Tunnel
Kidron Valley
Lower City
Pool of Siloam
Extension made to the City by Hezekiah
Gate between the walls (?)
Road to Bethlehem (5 mls.), Hebron (25 mls.) & the South
Valley of Hinnom
En-rogel
The City in the 10th Century B.C.
The extension of the City at the time of Jesus Christ
The line of the walls to-day. (The inhabited area extends far beyond)

1. Spiritualism
2. Apostate Protestantism
3. Catholicism

PAUL JAMA
VELLA LA VELLA
B. S. I. P.

Gail Houghton
Julie Speck
Lesley Imrloom
Ken Roberts

BIBLE MARKING

(1) GOD'S WONDERFUL BOOK
KEYE = 1GB 2 Peter 1:20, 21
(2) SECOND COMING OF CHRIST
KEYE = 1SC John 14:1-3
(3) HEAVEN KEYE = 1H 2 Corinthians 12:2
(4) STATE OF THE DEAD KEYE = 1SD Genesis 2:7
(5) BIBLE SABBATH KEYE = 1BS Genesis 2:1-3
(6) SUNDAY TEXTS
(7) LAW OF GOD KEYE = 1LG Exodus 20:1-17
(8) CHRISTIAN BAPTISM KEYE 1CB Matthew 3:1-6

GRAEME – SDA
DAVID – SDA
DAVID –
GEOFF – SDA
PAUL – SDA
ALLAN – SDA
PETER – Christian

1 MARTIN – SDA